THE SPORTS ILLU

1996

DATE DUE

SPORTS ALMANAC

By the Editors of Sports Illustrated

LITTLE, BROWN AND COMPANY

Boston   New York   Toronto   London

Sports Illustrated

1996
SPORTS
ALMANAC

First Edition

ISBN 0-316-80883-0

Sports Illustrated 1996 Sports Almanac was produced by Bishop Books of New York City.

Sports Illustrated Editorial Director for Books: Joe Marshall

Front cover photography credits:
Grant Hill (top left): John Biever
Steve Young (bottom): John Biever
Back cover photography credits:
Jim Brown (top): Neil Leifer
Ben Crenshaw (middle): John Biever
Rebecca Lobo (bottom): *The Hartford Courant*
Title page photography credit: David Liam Kyle

10   9   8   7   6   5   4   3   2   1

COM

Published simultaneously in Canada by
Little, Brown & Company (Canada) Limited

PRINTED IN THE UNITED STATES OF AMERICA

CONTENTS

Expanded Contents

Expanded Contents *(Cont.)*

Expanded Contents (Cont.)

Expanded Contents *(Cont.)*

SOURCES

In compiling the *Sports Illustrated 1996 Sports Almanac*, the editors would again like to thank Natasha Simon and Linda Wachtel of the Sports Illustrated library for their invaluable assistance. They would also like to extend their gratitude to the media relations offices of the following organizations for their help in providing information and materials relating to their sports: Major League Baseball; the Canadian Football League; the National Football League; the National Collegiate Athletic Association; the National Basketball Association; the National Hockey League; the Association of Tennis Professionals; the World Tennis Association; the U.S. Tennis Association; the U.S. Golf Association; the Ladies Professional Golf Association; the Professional Golfers Association; Thoroughbred Racing Communications, Inc.; the U.S. Trotting Association; the Breeders' Cup; Churchill Downs; the New York Racing Association Inc.; the Maryland Jockey Club; Championship Auto Racing Teams; the National Hot Rod Association; the International Motor Sports Association; the National Association for Stock Car Auto Racing; the Professional Bowlers Association; the Ladies Professional Bowlers Tour; the American Professional Soccer League; the National Professional Soccer League; the *Fédération Internationale De Football* Association; the U.S. Soccer Federation; the U.S. Olympic Committee; USA Track & Field; U.S. Swimming; U.S. Diving; U.S. Skiing; U.S. Skating; the U.S. Chess Federation; U.S. Curling; the Iditarod Trail Committee; the International Game Fish Association; the U.S. Gymnastics Federation; the Lacrosse Foundation; the American Power Boat Association; the Professional Rodeo Cowboys Association; U.S. Rowing; the American Softball Association; the Triathlon Federation USA; the National Archery Association; USA Wrestling; the U.S. Squash Racquets Association; the U.S. Polo Association; ABC Sports and the U.S. Volleyball Association.

The following sources were consulted in gathering information:

Baseball   *The Baseball Encyclopedia*, Macmillan Publishing Co., 1990; *Total Baseball*, Warner Books, 1995; *Baseballistics*, St. Martin's Press, 1990; *The Book of Baseball Records*, Seymour Siwoff, publisher, 1991; *The Complete Baseball Record Book*, The Sporting News Publishing Co., 1992; *The Sporting News Baseball Guide*, The Sporting News Publishing Co., 1993; *The Sporting News Baseball Register*, The Sporting News Publishing Co., 1993; *National League Green Book—1994*, The Sporting News Publishing Co., 1993; *American League Red Book—1994*, The Sporting News Publishing Co., 1993; *The Scouting Report: 1995*, Stats, Inc., Harper Perennial, 1995.

Pro Football   *The Official 1994 National Football League Record & Fact Book*, The National Football League, 1994; *The Official National Football League Encyclopedia*, New American Library, 1990; *The Sporting News Football Guide*, The Sporting News Publishing Co., 1993; *The Sporting News Football Register*, The Sporting News Publishing Co., 1993; *The 1993 National Football League Record & Fact Book*, Workman Publishing, 1993; *The Football Encyclopedia*, David Neft and Richard Cohen, St. Martin's Press, 1991.

College Football   *1994 NCAA Football*, The National Collegiate Athletic Association, 1993.

Pro Basketball   *The Official NBA Basketball Encyclopedia*, Villard Books, 1989; *The Sporting News Official 1993–94 NBA Guide*, The Sporting News Publishing Co., 1993.

College Basketball   *1994 NCAA Basketball*, The National Collegiate Athletic Association, 1993.

Hockey   *The National Hockey League Official Guide & Record Book 1994-95*, The National Hockey League, 1994; *The Sporting News Complete Hockey Book*, The Sporting News Publishing Co., 1993; *The Complete Encyclopedia of Hockey*, Visible Ink Press, 1993.

Tennis   *1993 Official USTA Tennis Yearbook*, H. O. Zimman, Inc., 1993; *IBM/ATP Tour 1995 Player Guide*, Association of Tennis Professionals, 1995; *WTA Official 1995 Media Guide*, Women's Tennis Association, 1995.

Golf   *PGA Tour Book 1994*, PGA Tour Creative Services, 1994; *LPGA 1994 Player Guide*, LPGA Communications Department, 1994; *Senior PGA Tour Book 1994*, PGA Tour Creative Services, 1994; *USGA Yearbook 1994*, U.S. Golf Association, 1994.

Boxing   *The Ring 1986–87 Record Book and Boxing Encyclopedia*, The Ring Publishing Corp., 1987. (To subscribe to *The Ring* magazine, write to P.O. Box 768, Rockville Centre, New York 11571-9905; or call (516) 678-7464); *Computer Boxing Update*, Ralph Citro, Inc., 1992; Bob Yalen, boxing statistician at ESPN.

Horse Racing   *The American Racing Manual 1994*, Daily Racing Form, Inc., 1994; *1994 Directory and Record Book*, The Thoroughbred Racing Association, 1994; *The Trotting and Pacing Guide, 1994*, United States Trotting Association, 1994; *Breeders' Cup 1993 Statistics*, Breeders' Cup Limited, 1993; *NYRA Media Guide 1993*, The New York Racing Association, 1994; *The 120th Kentucky Derby Media Guide, 1994*, Churchill Downs Public Relations Dept., 1994; *The 120th Preakness Press Guide, 1994*, Maryland Jockey Club, 1994; *Harness Racing News,* Harness Racing Communications.

Motor Sports   *The Official NASCAR Yearbook and Press Guide 1994*, UMI Publications, Inc., 1994; *1994 Indianapolis 500 Media Fact Book*, Indy 500 Publications, 1994; *IMSA 1994 Yearbook*, International Motor Sports Association, 1994; *1994 Winston Drag Racing Series Media Guide*, Sports Marketing Enterprises, 1994.

Bowling   *1994 Professional Bowlers Association Press, Radio and Television Guide*, Professional Bowlers Association, Inc., 1994; *The Ladies Pro Bowlers Tour 1994 Souvenir Tour Guide*, Ladies Pro Bowlers Tour, 1994.

Soccer   *Major Soccer League Official Guide 1991–92*, Major Soccer League, Inc., 1991; *Rothmans Football Yearbook 1993–94*, Headline Book Publishing, 1993; *American Professional Soccer League 1992 Media Guide*, APSL Media Relations Department, 1992; *The European Football Yearbook*, Facer Publications Limited, 1988; *Soccer America*, Burling Communications.

NCAA Sports   *1993–94 National Collegiate Championships*, The National Collegiate Athletic Association, 1994; *1993-94 National Directory of College Athletics,* Collegiate Directories Inc., 1993.

Olympics   *The Complete Book of the Olympics*, Little, Brown and Co., 1991.

Track and Field   *American Athletics Annual 1993*, The Athletics Congress/USA, 1993.

Swimming   *6th World Swimming Championships Media Guide*, The World Swimming Championships Organizing Committee, 1991.

Skiing   *U.S. Ski Team 1994 Media Guide / USSA Directory*, U.S. Ski Association, 1993; *Ski Racing Annual Competition Guide 1993–94*, Ski Racing International, 1993; *Ski Magazine's Encyclopedia of Skiing*, Harper & Row, 1974; *Caffä Lavazza Ski World Cup Press Kit*, Biorama, 1991.

Scorecard

Why the Patriots don't win Why Steve Spurrier doesn't lose

OCTOBER 23, 1995
$2.95 (CAN. $3.95)

Sports Illustrated

AIR & SPACE

Can Michael Jordan tame the NBA's weirdest player?
A report from inside the Bulls' camp

JOHN W. McDONOUGH

A summary of Fall 1995 events

PASCAL RONDEAU/ALLSPORT

After locking up his second straight F1 title, Schumacher popped off at his rival Hill.

AUTO RACING

Michael Schumacher clinched his second straight Formula One championship when he won the Pacific Grand Prix on Oct. 22 in Aida, Japan, but the win did not come without controversy. Schumacher was incensed by the blocking tactics of Damon Hill, with whom he had crashed twice earlier in the season. "He pushed me to the outside, but in doing that he spoiled his race as well," said the German, who at 26 became the youngest man to win back-to-back F1 driving titles. Hostilities continued on the victory podium when Hill refused to shake Schumacher's hand. "This is something between me and Damon," said Schumacher. "We should sort it out ourselves."

PRO BASKETBALL

The bull staring so menacingly from the back of Dennis Rodman's head was charcoal black, while the rest of his head was a volatile mixture of Halloween pumpkin orange and fiery red. How did you think the flamboyant Rodman was going to tell the world that he had become a Chicago Bull? On Oct. 2 Chicago traded its 7-foot center Will Perdue to the San Antonio Spurs in exchange for Rodman, the 6'8" forward who, depending on what you think of his antics, is a rebounding fool, a just-plain-fool or both. "Why run off to the circus when the circus comes to you?" asked Bull coach Phil Jackson. "We're going to see a lot of unusual behavior in Chicago."

But make no mistake. This is one circus that should do a lot more than just entertain. Rodman, after all, has led the NBA in rebounding by a wide margin each of the last four years, averaging 17.8 per game over that stretch. He was also named the NBA's top defensive player in 1990 and '91. So forgive his new teammates if, in spite of his dabbling in black and red, everything was looking just rosy to them. "He's here because he wants to win," said Michael Jordan. "I expect him to give his heart on the basketball floor, and that's what counts. He's a grown man. We cannot control him or dictate what he should do off the court."

Certainly the addition of Rodman meant that the Bulls would pose a considerable obstacle to the title hopes of both the Houston Rockets, who were aiming to emulate the three-peat success of the 1991–93 Bulls, and the young and talented Orlando Magic. Indeed, Orlando's chances of getting off to a quick start were dampened considerably when center Shaquille O'Neal fractured a bone in the base of his right thumb on Oct. 24. O'Neal, who underwent surgery two days later, was expected to miss at least six weeks of the regular season. Also missing opening day was Chris Webber of the Washington Bullets, who was expected to sit out at least four weeks with a dislocated left shoulder.

In other major trades, the Bullets acquired four-time All-Star guard Mark Price from the

Cleveland Cavaliers in exchange for a No. 1 pick in the 1996 draft, and the Phoenix Suns, shopping for size, traded 6'6" guard Dan Majerle to the Cleveland Cavaliers for 6' 11" forward John Williams.

BOXING

For years now, boxing has been its own most fearsome opponent. In October the sport absorbed blows heavy enough to stop—or at least slow down—any sport ruled by common sense, decency or law, but that, of course, rarely seems to include the sweet science.

Quite simply, there continue to be far too many reminders of the sport's inherent brutality. On Oct. 15, two days after he was knocked out by Drew Docherty in the 12th round of their fight for the British bantamweight title, James Murray of Scotland was taken off a life-support machine and died. Later that day Filipino flyweight Restituto Espineli died from a brain hemorrhage sustained during a fight against Marlon Carillo near Manila. A week later flyweight Marvin Corpuz died of head injuries sustained in his Oct. 21 bout against Allan Llaneta. Coming as they did in a year that had already borne tragic witness to Gerald McClellan's descent into an 11-day coma in February and

What, me worry? King spent most of the fall in court, battling mail fraud charges.

JOHN IACONO

the deaths of super featherweight Jimmy Garcia of Colombia on May 19 and South Korean Lee Tong-choon on Sept. 9, these three deaths again raised questions about the brutal business of boxing.

If boxing doesn't succeed in pummelling itself into oblivion, it may yet manage to be litigated to death. Don King spent much of the fall in a federal court in Manhattan, facing nine counts of mail fraud. The charges stemmed from a fight between Julio César Chávez and Harold Brazier that was scheduled for June 28, 1991, but was canceled when Chávez cut his nose. King, 63, was alleged to have submitted to Lloyds of London a bogus insurance claim for $350,000 in unrefundable training expenses. On Oct. 17 Chávez testified that the contract King submitted to Lloyds was not the one he'd signed and that the first time he'd seen the part of the contract mentioning training expenses was when prosecutors showed it to him in court. Chávez also said he'd only spent $50,000 to $60,000 training for the fight. However, on Oct. 26 Richard Hummers, an accountant who worked for King, testified that King was entitled to the settlement, citing paperwork that he'd submitted to Lloyds in January 1992. If convicted King faced up to five years in prison and a $250,000 fine on each of the nine charges.

CHESS

The Intel World Chess Championship was held, appropriately enough, high above the heads of ordinary folk, in a soundproof glass cage on the 107th floor of New York City's World Trade Center. Though it was expected to be a one-sided match, with 32-year-old Russian Gary Kasparov the overwhelming favorite to beat Viswanathan Anand, a 25-year-old from India, the best-of-20 series actually looked like a battle—for nine games. Upon winning Game 9 after eight straight draws, Anand said prophetically, "You catch a tiger by the whiskers, next day he's going to be ferocious."

Sure enough, Kasparov came roaring back in the next match. He captured Games 10, 11, 13 and 14. He drew Game 17 on Oct. 9 to secure his fifth title defense since 1985 and claim the winner's purse of $900,000. Chess

If the view wasn't enough to dizzy him, Anand had to cope with Kasparov's play.

mavens were left wondering how well Anand, the constitutionally jokey son of a Madras railroad executive, would cope with the intellectual battering he had absorbed.

COLLEGE FOOTBALL

Along with the most wide-open Heisman race in years, the 1995 season had more than its share of surprises. Who would have guessed that at the beginning of November the University of Miami would have fallen far out of the Top 25—a week earlier *The New York Times*'s computer poll had actually placed the 'Canes 41st, one spot behind Miami of Ohio!—and that Northwestern would be in the Top 10? But for all its surprises, 1995 also had something in common with its 52 predecessors. Nineteen-ninety-five marks Eddie Robinson's 53rd year as football coach at Grambling. To appreciate how long that really is, one need only remember that when Robinson took over the program in 1941, the president of the United States was Franklin Delano Roosevelt. On Oct. 7 Robinson beat the rest of the coaching fraternity to yet another milestone, notching his 400th win in the Tigers' 42–6 drubbing of Mississippi Valley State.

The great surprise of the 1995 season was the success of Northwestern. It was not so long ago that the Wildcats were the unrivaled patsies of the Big Ten, bad enough to have lost 34 straight games from 1979–82. In 1994 Northwestern

failed to win a single Big Ten game and finished the season 2–9. But when November arrived, the Wildcats were tied with Ohio State atop the Big Ten with a 5–0 conference record. One reason for their improvement was Darnell Autry, who had rushed for at least 100 yards every game and was averaging 131 per game.

The Big Ten's other great running back was Ohio State's Eddie George, who through eight games had rushed for 1,100 yards and 15 touchdowns. But in winning their first eight games, the Buckeyes relied not just on George but also on quarterback Bob Hoying, who was leading the nation in passing efficiency.

Indeed, as the season entered its final month, the Buckeyes were only one of four major programs that still boasted perfect records. Florida State, led by another pair of Heisman candidates—tailback Warrick Dunn (9.4 yards per carry) and quarterback Danny Kanell (168 for 230 with 25 TDs)—was 7–0 and ranked first in many polls. The Gators had their own Heisman candidate in quarterback Danny Wuerffel, who had completed 65.2% of his passes and thrown 22 touchdown passes.

There was no shortage of worthy Heisman candidates. Among them were Iowa State's Troy Davis, who led the nation in rushing with 190.8 yards per game; Karim Abdul-Jabbar of UCLA, who was averaging 151.5 rushing yards a game; and Tennessee quarterback Peyton Manning, who had completed 67.8% of his passes for the 7–1 Volunteers.

Still, many were of the opinion that the most valuable player in the college game was Nebraska quarterback Tommie Frazier. Frazier's numbers might not have been as gaudy as some of his rivals', but his performance in key games made him a strong contender, especially if the Huskers end up going undefeated for the regular season. That became more likely on Oct. 28, when Nebraska passed what was probably its final big test, whipping Big Eight rival Colorado 44–21 on the road. The Huskers ran their winning streak to 21 games, best among major colleges. Frazier completed 14 of 23 passes for 241 yards and two touchdowns, and by the end of the game their fans were chanting, perhaps prophetically, *Tommie Heisman, Tommie Heisman, Tommie Heisman.*

AL MESSERSCHMIDT

1999, the uncapped year of the collective bargaining agreement.

The league struck back quickly. On Sept. 18 it filed a $300 million lawsuit challenging Jones's deals with Pepsi and Nike. That hardly deterred Jones, who went right back out and negotiated a deal with American Express.

The Cowboy players did not seem to be troubled by all the legal maneuvering going on around them. They jumped out to a 7–1 start, tying the Kansas City Chiefs for the best record midway through the season. Cowboy running back Emmitt Smith seemed to be well on his way to threatening John Riggins's record for touchdowns in a season, scoring 14 in the Cowboys' first eight games.

Injuries sidelined an alarming number of the game's top players, quarterbacks especially. San Francisco's Steve Young, the NFL's top-rated passer in each of the last four years, bruised his throwing shoulder in the Niners' 18–17 loss to the Indianapolis Colts on Oct. 15 and was expected to miss at least a month. Also spending time on the DL were Boomer Esiason of the New York Jets and Dan Marino of the Miami Dolphins, both of whom got hurt on Oct. 8. Marino injured his right knee and left hip, underwent surgery on Oct. 9 and missed two games. Esiason sustained a concussion after getting hit by the Buffalo Bills' Bruce Smith and still had not returned as of Oct. 29.

Two of the game's alltime greats set NFL career records. On Oct. 8, in the Miami Dolphins' 27–24 loss to the Colts, Dan Marino completed 19 passes to surpass by 16 Fran Tarkenton's NFL record of 3,686 completions. Three weeks later, Jerry Rice of the 49ers became the NFL career leader in receiving yardage. Though the Niners lost 11–7 to the lowly New Orleans Saints, Rice's 108 yards gave him 14,040 yards, 36 more than James Lofton.

Elsewhere, in October the Carolina Pan-

PRO FOOTBALL

The fiercest battling in the first half of the 1995 NFL season came not on the playing field, but in boardrooms around the league and in the NFL's head office. Most of it focused on Cowboy owner Jerry Jones, who seemed determined to challenge the way the NFL does business on every possible front, flaunting the concepts of revenue sharing and the salary cap. First Jones defied the league by signing a $25 million deal to sell Pepsi at Texas Stadium when the league has a contract with Coca Cola. Then on Sept. 4 he announced—with a press release headlined COWBOY OWNER BUCKS NFL AGAIN—that he had signed a seven-year, $2.5 million sponsorship deal with Nike. Less than a week later, Jones announced that he had signed cornerback Deion Sanders to a seven-year, $35 million contract, the specific terms of which were creative, to say the least, loading the bulk of the Cowboys' payment to Sanders up front, as a $13 million signing bonus, and paying the bulk of the difference after

thers set a record for expansion teams by winning three straight games. After beating the New York Jets 26–15 on Oct. 15—the first win in franchise history—the Panthers went on to defeat New Orleans 20–3 and New England 20–17 in overtime.

GOLF

In the wake—and boy, is *that* the right word— of the U.S. team's collapse at the Ryder Cup, a number of U.S. players traveled to Europe in hopes of reestablishing the nation's golfing supremacy. "Maybe if I can win this, the Americans will forget for a while that we lost the Ryder Cup," said Lee Janzen, on the eve of the World Match Play Championship, held Oct. 12–15 in Surrey, England. Janzen started beautifully, beating match play champion Katsuyoshi Tomori of Japan 7 and 6 in their scheduled 36-hole match. On the following day, however, Janzen ran into Ernie Els, the man who succeeded him as U.S. Open champion. After dispatching Janzen 4 and 3, Els proceeded to edge Bernhard Langer 1-up in the semis and then to defend his title successfully by beating Steve Elkington 2 and 1 in the final.

Host team Scotland won the Dunhill Cup for the first time in 11 years, beating Zimbabwe 2–1 in the final, which was held Oct. 22 at St. Andrews. To do so, the Scottish team of Colin Montgomerie, Sam Torrance and Andrew Coltart had to offset the sterling play of Nick Price, who shot five straight sub-70 rounds and finished 20-under-par, a St. Andrews record. The U.S. team of Ben Crenshaw, Lee Janzen and Peter Jacobsen finished last in its group, losing to both Canada and Ireland.

The 1995 PGA tour concluded on Oct. 29 with the TOUR Championship at Southern Hills Country Club in Tulsa. For the first time in 15 years, a 72-hole score of even-par was enough to win a PGA tournament. Indeed, on the final day Billy Mayfair shot a three-over-par 73 and still beat Corey Pavin and Steve Elkington by three strokes. "When I was adding up my score and saw it was 73 I thought, 'Boy, you're not supposed to win on this tour shooting 73 on the last day,' " said the 29-year-old Mayfair. His winner's share of $540,000 gave him $1,543,192 for the season, second on the annual money list to Greg Norman, who won $1,654,959.

Norman also finished the season with the lowest scoring average on the tour, 69.06, but was miffed at being locked out of the Vardon Trophy (won by Steve Elkington with 69.62) because he withdrew from the second round of the MCI Heritage Classic.

ICE HOCKEY

On Oct. 18 a group of investors from Minnesota bought the Winnipeg Jets for $68 million, despite the fact that they had not yet secured a home arena for the team. New owners Steven Gluckstern and Richard Burke hoped to place the team in Minneapolis's Target Center, but insisted that they couldn't do so unless the Center and its principal current residents, the Minnesota Timberwolves, gave them favorable terms.

Pittsburgh Penguin wing Mario Lemieux returned to the ice after a 17-month absence while fighting Hodgkin's disease and back problems. On Oct. 26, in the Penguins' 7–5 defeat of the New York Islanders, Lemieux scored the 500th goal of his career, making him the 20th player to reach that plateau but the second fastest. Lemieux's historic goal came in his 605th NHL game; only Wayne Gretzky reached that plateau more quickly (in 575 games).

Els won his second consecutive world match play title.

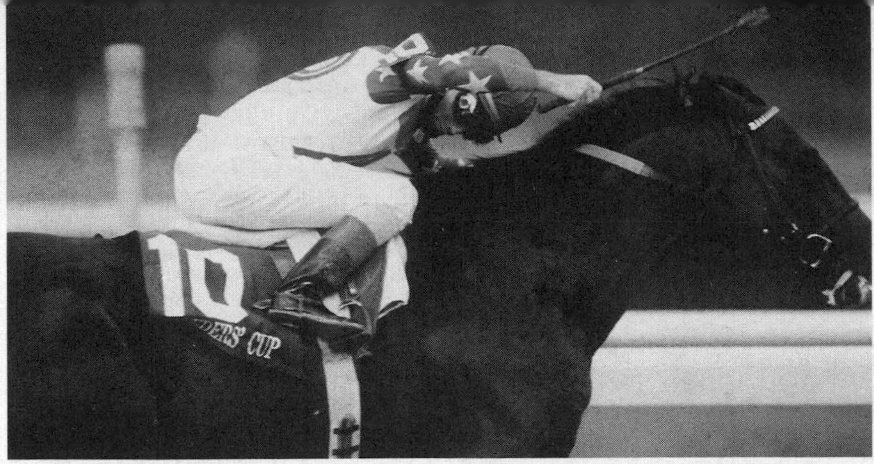

LOU CAPOZZOLA

Cigar won his 12th straight race at the Breeders' Cup, four short of the record.

HORSE RACING

If any questions lingered over just how great a horse Cigar is, they were put to rest once and for all at the 12th running of the Breeders' Cup Classic, held Oct. 28 at New York's Belmont Park. Starting from the No. 10 slot, Cigar, with Jerry Bailey up, bided his time in the race's early stages, running just off the pace. Then, when the field turned for home, he made a strong move and pulled away to score a two-and-a-half length victory over runnerup L'Carriere. Despite running on a Belmont track rated "muddy," Cigar ran the mile-and-a-quarter in 1:59⅖, making him the first horse to break two minutes in the Breeders' Cup Classic.

"We overcame today," said Bailey, who has ridden four of the last five winners of the Classic. "Tenth hole, wet track, delays. We overcame it all."

And Cigar set other records too. With the $1.5 million first prize, he raised his 1995 earnings to $4,819,800—a record for one year—and guaranteed himself Horse of the Year honors. He also became the first colt or stallion since Spectacular Bid in 1980 to go through an entire year undefeated.

It was a remarkable year for a horse whose early career did not produce such lofty expectations. Bred to run on grass, Cigar won his first race on a dirt track in 1993 and then was switched to the grass, where he performed disappointingly for 17 months. Trainer Bill Mott decided to give him one more chance on dirt, at Aqueduct on Oct. 28, 1994. He won by eight lengths and the following month won again at Aqueduct, by seven lengths. The rest, as they say, is history. Though Cigar's win in the Breeders' Cup Classic was his 12th straight, leaving him four shy of Citation's record string of 16 wins from 1948 to '50, his owner, Allen Paulson, was noncommital about his future, offering only that "We'll have to see."

Here are the results of other Breeders' Cup races:

- In the Distaff, Inside Information, with Mike Smith up, beat her stablemate Heavenly Prize by 13½ lengths, easily the largest margin of victory in Breeders' Cup history. Inside Information ran the 1⅛ miles in 1:46.
- Jerry Bailey, atop My Flag, took the 1¹⁄₁₆-mile race for Juvenile Filies in a stakes-record 1:42⅕, edging runnerup Cara Rafaela by half-a-length.
- In the Sprint, Desert Stormer, with Kent Desormeaux in the saddle, held off Mr. Greeley to win by a neck. Starting at 14–1, the filly ran the six furlongs in 1:09 to become just the second field horse to win a Breeders' Cup race.
- European horses swept the Mile, with Ridgewood Pearl, from Ireland, pulling steadily away in the home straight to beat Fastness by two lengths. With John Murtagh up, Ridgewood Pearl ran the mile in 1:43⅗.
- Unbridled's Song, with Mike Smith up, barrelled from off the pace and beat Hennessy by a neck to win the Juvenile. Unbridled's Song ran the 1¹⁄₁₆-mile course in 1:41⅗ to make himself an early favorite for next year's Triple Crown.

DAVID LEAH/ALLSPORT

• In the Turf race, Northern Spur, with Chris McCarron in the saddle, beat Freedom Cry by a neck, finishing the 1½ miles in a slow 2:42.

TENNIS

With Andre Agassi sidelined for several weeks with a pulled chest muscle, Pete Sampras headed to the Paris Open assured that no matter how he played he would regain the world No. 1 ranking which Andre Agassi had held since wresting it from Sampras on April 10.

The world's top-ranked female player could also have used a little bit of luck. Steffi Graf's father, Peter, had been in jail since early August, suspected of failing to report $35.3 million of her income. Graf herself was questioned as part of

Smyers won her first Ironman when Newby-Fraser collapsed near the finish.

an ongoing investigation. Despite the fact that charges had not been filed against her, on Oct. 16 Opel, the German subsidiary of General Motors, announced it would not renew its $1.2 million annual sponsorship deal with her. On Oct. 28 Graf's lawyer said that, after locating some overseas accounts, Graf had deposited $14.3 million with German authorities to cover back taxes she and her father might not have paid.

TRIATHLON

Is there a more punishing route than the 140.6 miles of road and rough water that comprise the course for the Ironman Triathlon in Kailua-Kona, Hawaii? Over the years they've offered athletes an extreme test, separating the men from the boys, the women from the girls. This year they succeeded in temporarily separating the race's most decorated champion from her mind.

Having announced before the race that it would be her last, seven-time women's champion Paula Newby-Fraser was determined to go out with a bang. Setting off at an ambitious pace, she looked the sure winner until, just 500 feet from the finish, she began weaving, waving her arms and crying, "Where's Karen [Smyers, who at the time was her closest pursuer]?" Two hundred feet from the finish Newby-Fraser sat on the curb and wept. Smyers raced past the weeping Newby-Fraser, who sat for 22 minutes before pulling herself together and walking barefoot across the finish line in fourth place. "I thought I was going to die," she said. "I was delusional. I felt like I was going into a seizure." Smyers's winning time was 9:16:46.

For Mark Allen, who had won the Ironman five straight years from 1989 through '93 before choosing not to enter last year's race, the 1995 race marked a return to business as normal. At the end of the bike leg, Allen trailed the leader, Thomas Hellriegel of Germany, by 13 minutes. Allen picked Hellriegel off just two miles from the finish, sweeping past the exhausted German to win his sixth title in 8:20:34.

"A lot of people go too hard on the bike, forgetting they have to run 26.2 miles," said Allen. "There's a finite equation to the amount of energy anybody has."

Year in Sport

Sports Illustrated
The Real
Super Bowl

NFL PLAYOFFS
NFC CHAMPIONSHIP
SAN FRANCISCO 49ERS vs. DALLAS COWBOYS
SUNDAY 1:00
MEZZANINE
JAN. 15

JOHN BIEVER (TOP), RICHARD MACKSON

Sports Illustrated
Return to Glory
Ed O'Bannon Celebrates UCLA's NCAA Title

UCONN'S PERFECT SEASON

JOHN BIEVER

NCAAs: Best Sweet 16 Ever
Sports Illustrated
'I'm Back'

DAVID E. KLUTHO

NFL Takes Off • Notre Dame Crashes • Nomo, Wakefield Wake Up
Sports Illustrated
IRON MAN

ILLUSTRATION BY C.F. PAYNE

Hails and Farewells

In a weird year, full of long-awaited returns and sudden departures, sports fans were lucky just to have games to root for

by Alexander Wolff

NINETEEN NINETY-FIVE had no Olympics, no World Cup and very nearly no baseball or hockey. The year was a sort of caesura—in short, shortened; on the whole, humdrum; in essence, a time of interruption and change, marked by events postponed or canceled or otherwise rendered not as we knew them. The grandiose yielded to the novel, the quirky, the black-and-white. If the year were to be recorded on film, Cecil B. DeMille wouldn't get the call to shoot it; Jim Jarmusch would.

Work stoppages bedeviled the majors and the NHL. Pro basketball's big story was its greatest player's transit from retirement to reactivity. Hockey conjurer Mario Lemieux and college basketball maestro Mike Krzyzewski sat the entire year out, albeit not by choice, while one of college football's leading coaches, Bill McCartney of Colorado, chucked it all to devote himself full time to Promise Keepers, the Christian men's group he had founded. Major League Soccer, conceived to exploit the footie-frenzy whipped up by the World Cup of the previous summer, dawdled, thus missing a spring start-up that would have been welcomed by fans fed up with baseball.

But it was also a year of getting back on the beam, of restoration—of absences ended, as sport welcomed back not only Michael Jordan but also Evander Holyfield, Monica Seles, Mike Tyson and Jerry Tarkanian, plus boxing to Madison Square Garden after an absence of almost three years.

In short, if only to keep up with Deion Sanders (who went from the 49ers to the baseball Giants to the Cowboys), it was a good year for sports fans to turn first to the TRANSACTIONS section of the agate page.

ALTERED: The gender of *America³*, the yacht originally featuring an all-female crew, with the addition of a y-chromosome-carrying tactician midway through the Defender's Series of the America's Cup.

LEFT TO TWIST SLOWLY, SLOWLY: Interim U.S. national soccer coach Steve Sampson, despite guiding the Americans to a U.S. Cup title and into the semifinals of the Copa America. (He was eventually hired permanently.)

HOSED: Steve McNair, the quarterback who put up Heisman-worthy numbers at Alcorn State but placed third in the ballot-

CHUCK SOLOMON/USA NETWORK

Seles gathered up her courage and made a brilliant return to tennis.

ing because voters were loath to honor someone who plays at a Division I-AA school—even if he did set an NCAA record for total offense, racking up more than 500 yards each time out.

FREQUENTLY MISPRONOUNCED: The name of Haile Gebrselassie, the Ethiopian who set world records in the 10,000 meters and the two-mile, and lowered the standard in the 5,000 meters by almost 11 jaw-dropping seconds.

The year wasn't rendered in broad strokes so much as niggling details. A technicality in Hideo Nomo's Japanese contract allowed him to sign with the Los Angeles Dodgers and bring his Tiantesque delivery to Ameri-

can mounds. Olympic negotiators granted NBC a chance to bid preemptively for the Sydney and Salt Lake Games, both of which the Peacock strutted off with for $1.27 billion in rights fees. We thought we knew the rules of the America's Cup, but when it became clear that the existing bylaws weren't going to permit Dennis Conner to sail into the finals on merit, we got to see the rules rewritten to accommodate him and his corporate sponsors. Conner was outchutzpah-ed only by the Lord of the Olympic Rings, Juan Antonio Samaranch. The president of the International Olympic Committee somehow engineered a rules change that pushed the mandatory retirement age for his position back five years, from 75—the age he happened to be—to 80.

There was a brace of almosts and not

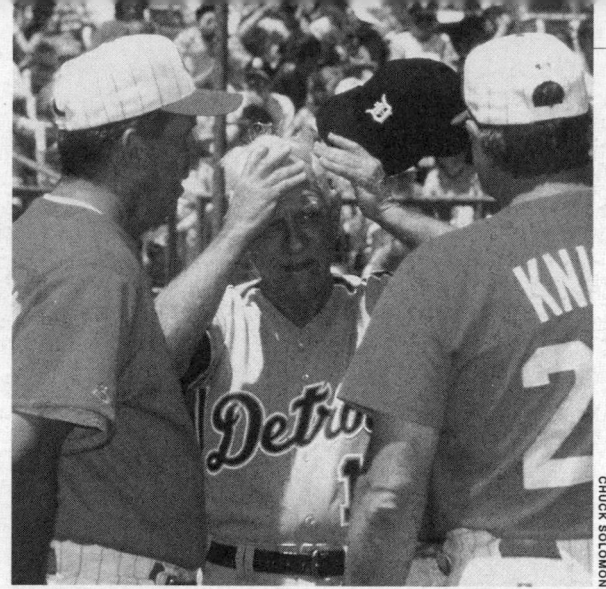

40-year-old golfer named Brad (Dr. Dirt) Bryant, after 18 years and 460 events, finally won a Tour title. The New York Yankees' Don Mattingly suited up for a playoff game for the first time in his 14-year career. And Nebraska coach Tom Osborne's Cornhuskers, who had been to college football's base camp many times during his 22 years in Lincoln, finally reached the summit of a national championship.

quites: Seven-time Ironman Triathlon winner Paula Newby-Fraser had a physical and mental breakdown 500 feet from the finish of this year's event; the California Angels pulled an *el foldo* in the American League West worthy of the '64 Phillies and the '69 Cubs; and Cuba's Ivan Pedroso seemed to have broken Mike Powell's world record in the long jump, only to have the leap disallowed because a factotum in a raincoat had blocked the wind gauge. All the aforementioned were close, but no . . . Cigar, the 5-year-old Horse of the Year who ripped off 11 stakes race wins in a row.

Those absent made news as often as those who cried "here": In 1995 we witnessed an Indy 500 without Team Penske, an entire PGA calendar without Nick Price atop the leader board at the end of a Sunday afternoon, and an America's Cup that ended without *oneAustralia 95*, the Aussie boat that broke in two and sank during the Challenger's Series. Those announcing their retirement included Jud Heathcote, Vreni Schneider, Sparky Anderson and John Kruk, the man who once said, "I'm not an athlete, I'm a baseball player."

And longstanding droughts came to noteworthy ends. The Cleveland Indians won a pennant for the first time in 41 years. A

UCLA's basketball title, which came 20 years after the Bruins won the last of their 10 NCAA crowns, was just one of many harkenings back. In flashes Jordan resurrected his form of 21 months earlier, before he had become a banjo-hitting rightfielder and still played the NBA's big rooms with his gutbucket style; the Baltimore Orioles' Cal Ripken Jr. evoked 1982, when he trotted out to short for the first of those 2,130 consecutive games.

Despite the work stoppages there was a businesslike, get-it-done style pervading much of what happened in sport. By breaking Lou Gehrig's consecutive-game streak Ripken served baseball's desperate need, in the aftermath of a labor dispute soiling parts of two seasons, to showcase someone who worked hard for his money. Steve Young merely led the NFL in passing for the fourth straight season without harvesting any of the accolades accorded his more swashbuckling predecessor, Joe Montana. (The name of the 49er president—Carmen Policy—seemed to get just right the team that easily throttled the San Diego Chargers in the Super Bowl: operatic drama, routinely supplied.)

Others who abided by this workaday spirit included Peter Blake and the New Zealanders who crewed *Black Magic*, the boat that failed to finish first in only one of 43 starts all year; the Kiwis swept all five races from Conner and the U.S. in the America's Cup final. The Virginia men and North Carolina women won NCAA soccer titles for the fourth straight year and the 12th in 13 years, respectively. At Stanford, "the Farm" to undergrads and alums, they seem to raise NCAA titles—the Cardinal won crowns in men's gymnastics, tennis and water polo and women's swimming and volleyball—like so many crops.

Sometimes the demarcation between winning and losing blurred so completely that one could pass for the other. NBA management won when labor won its fight against an effort by dissident players to decertify the union. The acclaimed documentary *Hoop Dreams*, an elegiac chronicle of inner-city life and basketball in Chicago, turned its snubbing for an Oscar into a windfall of sympathetic publicity—attention that allowed it to reach a much wider audience than it might have otherwise. Seles lost the U.S. Open final to Steffi Graf and showed the giddiness of a winner; Graf, the unwitting beneficiary of the unemployed lathe operator who had stabbed Seles 29 months earlier, won that event, and barricaded herself in a bathroom, crying her eyes out, distraught over the jailing of her father by German authorities for alleged tax evasion. The winners of two of the most prestigious events in their respective sports, Pete Sampras at Wimbledon and Ben Crenshaw at the Masters, took dewy-eyed inspiration from mentors ailing (Sampras's coach, Tim Gullikson, who suffered from brain cancer) or dead (Crenshaw's teacher, golf pedagogue and epigrammarian Harvey Penick). Thus the year's incongruous image: winners in tears.

Sampras had a brilliant season, but suffered with his ailing coach.

The NFL had to come to terms with the passing from existence of the Los Angeles Rams and the Los Angeles Raiders. Who could have envisioned the league with a team in the Carolinas and none on the West Coast south of Candlestick Park (which, in the spirit of disfigurement marking the year, will henceforth be known as 3Com Park)? The NFL *was* recognizable in that there was the usual Super Bowl blowout of the AFC champion, in this case the San Diego Chargers, by the NFC's best. With the Niners and the Cowboys meeting in the de facto title game two weeks earlier, a call went out for seeding the playoffs, as the NCAA does for its basketball tournament, in anticipation of a truly Super climax. Instead the NFC champs whupped the "junior circuit" for the 11th straight time—

BOB MARTIN

Boosted by Horry's superb play, the Rockets repeated as NBA champions.

as if the Super Bowl were nothing more than baseball's Midsummer Classic.

Speaking of baseball: Ringing up dingers in the thin mountain air, the expansion Colorado Rockies made the playoffs in only their third season, which was either (take your pick) an inspirationally meteoric rise or evidence of how watered-down the game had become. Seattle Mariner star Ken Griffey Jr., out from late May to mid-August with a broken wrist, may have assumed the title of Mr. October from Reggie Jackson. In the Mariners' thrilling five-game wild-card win over Jackson's former team, the Yankees, Griffey belted five round-trippers. Ironically it was the wild-card series, that much-maligned new round of play-offs, which turned out to be baseball's best case to woo the fans back.

Penn State's lot was that of the bridesmaid, several times over: The Nittany Lions were unbeaten but uncrowned, while their star tailback, Ki-Jana Carter, and quarterback Kerry Collins were left to congratulate Rashaan Salaam, the Colorado running back who won the Heisman Trophy. In this year of the nondescript, it was the faceless Huskers, known for the doughy, pasty mass of their offensive line, who scored the most satisfying of victories over Miami in the Orange Bowl.

Ed O'Bannon, the UCLA tri-captain with the warrior's knees, showed that a latter-day Bruin team won't always come up short on character in a big game; John Wooden looked talismanically on as the Bruins beat Arkansas for their first NCAA title since the old coach last unrolled his program. The Husky women of UConn did something with which Wooden is quite familiar, mushing their way from wire to wire without a loss; that they did so in the pale of Madison Avenue's tastemakers, and on the brink of an Olympics in Atlanta, touched off a whoopee over women's basketball that made a media star of their center, Wade Trophy–winner

JOHN W. McDONOUGH

Rebecca Lobo, and helped bring about a standing women's national team.

After 18 straight seasons in which no team successfully defended a title, the NBA has now crowned nothing but multiple-time wonders since 1986-87. The Houston Rockets seemed to take to heart all the bellyaching about the unsightliness with which they had beaten the New York Knicks in the Finals a year earlier; en route to defending their crown they looked sublime, particularly Robert Horry's feathery outside shooting and Hakeem Olajuwon's dreamy hipwork. Houston beat the San Antonio Spurs, the team with the league's best regular-season record and league MVP David Robinson, and then emphatically swept the Orlando Magic, a team of here-and-now flash and dash, of Shaq and Penny—but still only of the future. Meanwhile Jordan didn't have the most auspicious of comebacks. His shooting stroke came and went, he seemed occasionally out of sync with his teammates, and he famously frittered the ball away at a crucial moment of a playoff game against the Magic. But by laying 55 on the New York Knicks in Madison Square Garden only five games into his comeback, he left an impression of invulnerability.

The New Jersey Devils won the Stanley Cup in the most humdrum way possible—in a sweep and while employing an eye-glazing hockey tactic called the neutral-zone trap. Indeed, to summarize the difference between the sports year '94 and that of '95, one need only contrast the ado made over the New York Rangers' Cup victory with the palpable indifference when that cistern crossed the river. Even apart from the truncated 48-game regular season, things were slightly off form in the NHL. The "wrong" Lemieux set the tone for the playoffs: As Super Mario sat out the season to recover from Hodgkin's disease, Claude, the non-relative whose bruising style is found at the right extreme of the Devils' front line, saved his best hockey for the finals. Purists were alarmed at the ascendancy of brawn over skill, as Jersey's burlier line dominated the defter Detroit Red Wings in the finals, and

huge Philadelphia Flyer Eric Lindros supplanted Los Angeles King Wayne Gretzky as the league's totemic star.

Tyson's "return" was the year's singular sporting travesty. Peter McNeeley, a great white hopeless who had run up a 36–1 record by knocking over a row of opponents supplied by Contadina, promised to wrap the freed former heavyweight champ in "a cocoon of horror." Instead, 89 seconds into the first round, McNeeley's manager, Vinnie Vecchione, barged into the ring, putting a stop to the so-called fight. But there were sweet scientists whose efforts weren't shrouded in infamy. Lightweight Oscar De La Hoya—22 years old, already 19–0 and a self-described "young puppy in a game of big dogs"—proved to be so gifted and precocious that he invited comparisons to Sugar Ray Leonard. In winning the IBF super middleweight title with a pummeling of James Toney, who had been considered, pound-for-pound, the best fighter alive, Roy Jones Jr. appropriated that distinction. Meanwhile Pernell Whitaker distinguished himself as a fistic Renaissance man. By winning the WBA junior middleweight crown, he joined Leonard, Hearns and Duran as the only fighters to have won belts in four different divisions.

How could Thunder Gulch, a horse that had won the Fountain of Youth and the Florida Derby, go off at ridiculously long 25–1 odds when the Kentucky Derby rolled around? Well, it helped that the colt's trainer, D. Wayne Lukas, had also entered Timber Country and Serena's Song at Churchill Downs and talked them up so enthusiastically. By the end of Derby Day, Lukas looked like the guy who had gotten a bet down on every number on the wheel: Gulch, paying the highest price at the Derby in 28 years, outdistanced the field by more than two lengths. After Timber Country won the Preakness, and Gulch hoofed it to the winner's circle at the Belmont, Lukas became the first trainer to win the Triple Crown with different horses.

Like ducktailed greasers hot-rodding the strip, three drivers in their mid-20's auda-

Indurain took the Tour de France for an unprecedented fifth straight time.

ciously divvied up the auto racing universe among themselves. Jeff Gordon made NASCAR his own; Michael Schumacher assumed the mantle of the late Ayrton Senna, dominating the Formula One season; and Jacques Villeneuve, the son of racing great Gilles Villeneuve and the winner at Indy, lorded over the CART circuit.

Absent a World Cup, the U.S. national soccer team downed Chile, Argentina and Mexico in the Copa America, the team's most important competition outside the Mundial—and one from which two years earlier the Americans had made a prompt exit. (Alas, the Copa was available only regionally and on Spanish-language cable TV, so the benefit to the game's profile was minimal.) With no Olympics, there was no Kerriganza, no Tanyarama. In figure skating two workmanlike Americans, Todd Eldredge and Nicole Bobek, won the U.S. championships, and they were good citizens both. (What's that? Bobek had been named

in one burglary count of home invasion? Phooey; the charge was dropped.) At the worlds, the unindicted prevailed too: China's Chen Lu among the women, and Canada's Elvis Stojko among the men.

Track and field made do with a staging of the World Championships. "He's not doing anything for [fans of track and field]," grumbled Carl Lewis about Michael Johnson, the charisma-free sprinter with the tightly held emotions, who won three golds, including the 200 and 400 meters—a double never before accomplished at such a level. The reserve implied by the puritan name of British triple jumper Jonathan Edwards, who broke the 60-foot barrier in that event, got just about right the reception afforded track as a spectator sport on the Yank side of the pond.

There was nothing routine about the year to Corey Pavin, for a long time the best golfer never to win a major, who won the U.S. Open; or Mary Pierce, who won her first Grand Slam title, the Australian Open, without losing a set; or Boston Red Sox knuckleballer Tim Wakefield, who had the most losses in the American Association the season before and then fluttered his way to 16 wins in the majors. But much else about the year was routine, numbingly so. Nineteen-year-old Tiger Woods—yawn—won his second straight U.S. Amateur golf title, after bagging three Junior Amateur crowns in a row. Miguel Induráin—ho-hum—won the Tour de France, the 31-year-old Spaniard's fifth straight, a streak unmatched by Anquetil, Merckx, Hinault, LeMond or anyone else. Thomas Muster—so what else is new?—slugged out 35 straight victories on clay, including the final of the French. So it went, too, with Sergei Bubka (who at age 31 won yet another world pole-vault title) and Tony Gwynn (who once more slugged out hits more reliably than anyone in baseball).

The year marked the passing of NFL pioneer Woody Strode; sprinter Wilma Rudolph; boxer Jimmy Garcia, who died from injuries suffered in the ring; and two basketball big men who had somehow slipped into the crevices of obscurity, former Kentucky star Bill Spivey and Kresimir Cosic, the ex-BYU dervish from Croatia. The day after Fabio Casartelli was killed on a perilous descent during the Tour de France, the peloton saluted him by riding in a solemn processional. And the losses of the two most charismatic figures from their respective sports, Juan Manuel Fangio and Mickey Mantle, hit auto racing and baseball hard. Mantle seemed wryly conscious of the twisted world he would

soon be leaving; shortly after undergoing a liver transplant he wondered what his diseased organ might fetch on the memorabilia market.

So it went during this year of comings and goings, of activations and suspensions. With some things once part of the scene no longer there, and other things long gone suddenly restored, the 365 days could have been played out in the bustling ennui of a train station. In the end it really didn't matter so much who won or lost or even how they played the game. In the end, during 1995, what mattered most was that they played the game at all.

JONATHAN DANIEL/ALLSPORT

The great Gwynn rapped out 197 hits and batted .368.

The Year in Sport Calendar

compiled by John Bolster

Baseball

Nov 1, 1994—With major league baseball in the third month of its work stoppage, a group including former New York congressman Robert J. Mrazek and ex-Major League Players' Association lawyer Dick Moss calls a news conference in New York City to announce plans for the United Baseball League. The organizers plan to field 10 teams beginning in 1996. If successful, the UBL would be the first league to rival MLB since the Federal League in 1914-15.

Nov 4—Free agent pitcher Dwight Gooden, the former ace of the New York Met staff, is suspended for the entire 1995 season for violating his aftercare program and baseball's drug policy.

Nov 10—"I did not expect any breakthroughs, and there weren't any." Those are the comments of players' union chief Don Fehr after players and owners meet in Rye Brook, N.Y., with mediator Bill Usery. It is just the fifth meeting between the two sides, and the first with a mediator, since the players struck on Aug. 12.

Nov 17—Major league owners set aside their salary cap plan and propose in its stead a graduated luxury tax. The proposal would include taxes of up to 100% when teams exceed a predetermined payroll level. The meetings in Herndon, Va., are adjourned for a week to give the players' union time to study the 102-page proposal.

Nov 22—The Houston Astros re-sign first baseman Jeff Bagwell, the Most Valuable Player in the NL in 1994, for seven years and $27.5 million.

Nov 29—At the bargaining table in Leesburg, Va., major league players make no counterproposal to the owners luxury tax plan of Nov.17, prompting owners to state that they are prepared to open spring training with replacement players.

Nov 30—Mediator Bill Usery convinces the owners to delay the unilateral implementation of a salary cap. The move would have gone hand-in-hand with a declaration of an impasse in negotiations.

Nov 30—Reliever Mitch (Wild Thing) Williams signs a one-year, non-guaranteed deal with the California Angels.

Dec 5—The owners' chief negotiator Richard Ravitch announces he will resign when his contract expires on Dec. 31.

Dec 8—San Francisco Giant outfielder Darryl Strawberry and his agent Eric Goldschmidt are indicted on federal tax evasion charges.

Dec 9—The Texas Rangers trade Jose Canseco to the Red Sox for Otis Nixon and prospect Luis Ortiz.

Dec 14—After an exchange of counterproposals regarding the owners' graduated taxation plan, talks in Rye Brook, N.Y., between the owners and striking players break down without a settlement.

Dec 14—The Chicago White Sox trade 1993 Cy Young Award winner Jack McDowell to the New York Yankees for minor leaguers Keith Heberling, a pitcher, and Lyle Mouton, an outfielder.

Dec 15—Major league owners again vote to postpone implementation of the

TOM DIPACE

McDowell took the hill for New York.

RICHARD MACKSON

Nomo fanned 236 National League batters.

salary cap. They set the deadline for a settlement at Dec. 22.

Dec 15—The New York Yankees sign free agent shortstop Tony Fernandez.

Dec 19—Negotiations between players and owners resume in Washington, D.C., with the goal of ending the four-month-old work stoppage by the end of the week.

Dec 21—Former Chicago White Sox DH Julio Franco signs with the Chiba Lotte Marines of Japan for $7 million over two years. The deal is the most lucrative in Japanese baseball history.

Dec 22—Major league owners announce that they will declare an impasse and impose their final salary cap proposal as of midnight, thereby sending the bitter labor dispute to the courtroom.

Jan 1, 1995—With the two sides unable to agree on a suitable wage increase as they negotiate a new labor pact, major league owners lock out the umpires.

Jan 3—While major league owners begin the task of hiring replacements for striking players, the incoming Congress begins formulating legislation that will repeal baseball's antitrust exemption.

Jan 4—Free agent outfielder Shane Mack, who hit .333 for the Minnesota Twins in 1994, signs with the Yomiuri Giants of Japan.

Jan 9—Former Philadelphia Phillie third baseman Mike Schmidt is elected to the Hall of Fame. Schmidt, whose 548 home runs place him seventh on the alltime list, received the most votes (444 of 460) ever cast by the Baseball Writers Association of America.

Jan 18—Ron Luciano, the former American League umpire known for his flamboyant style, is found dead of self-inflicted carbon monoxide poisoning in his garage in Binghamton, N.Y.

Jan 26—President Clinton orders players and owners to resume negotiations and empowers mediator Bill Usery to recommend a solution if appreciable progress is not made by Feb. 6.

Feb 3—Fred Feinstein, general counsel of the National Labor Relations Board (NLRB), notifies baseball owners that he plans to issue a complaint of unfair labor practices against them.

Feb 7—Major league players firmly reject Bill Usery's six-year plan for labor peace in baseball, and President Clinton fails to bring the two sides any closer during a five-hour meeting at the White House. Clinton will go to Congress with legislation calling for binding arbitration to settle the dispute.

Feb 7—The Major League Players' Association files an unfair labor practices charge with the NLRB.

Feb 13—The Los Angeles Dodgers sign five-time Japanese All-Star pitcher Hideo Nomo. Nomo becomes the first player ever to move from the Japanese majors to a North American major league team.

Feb 16—Spring training camps open with replacement players.

Mar 1—With replacement teams squaring off down the road in Tempe, major league owners and players meet in Scottsdale, Ariz., working toward a March 5 deadline for settlement if the season is to begin on time with regular players.

Mar 5—Negotiations in Scottsdale, Ariz., break down without a settlement.

Mar 7—Richie Ashburn, who patrolled center field for the Philadelphia Phillies from 1948 to 1959, is selected by the Veterans Committee for induction into the Hall of Fame. Ashburn hit .308 for his 15-year career.

Mar 7—Leon Day, the 78-year-old former star pitcher in the Negro Leagues, is selected by the Veterans Committee for induction into the Hall of Fame. Day opened the 1946 season with the Newark Eagles by pitching an 18-strikeout no-hitter, fanning future Hall of Famer Roy Campanella three times. Six days after his selection, Day dies.

Mar 9—Major League Baseball welcomes, at a price of $130 million apiece, the expansion franchises the Tampa Bay Devil Rays and the

Arizona Diamondbacks. The teams will begin play in 1998.

Mar 14—The NLRB announces it will charge major league owners with two counts of unfair labor practices but does not seek an immediate injunction against the owners.

Mar 21—With opening day only 12 days away, mediator Bill Usery fails to achieve a settlement after two days of secret meetings in Washington, D.C., with player rep Don Fehr and interim Commissioner Bud Selig.

Mar 31—Major league players end their strike, begun Aug. 12, after U.S. District Judge Sonia Sotomayor issues an injunction forcing owners to to return to the rules of the old labor pact. Two days later the owners accept the players' offer to return without an agreement, and it is decided that the 1995 season will be played, beginning April 26, under the previous labor conditions.

Apr 3—Bo Jackson, who was a star in both the NFL and Major League Baseball until a hip injury ended his football career in 1991, announces his retirement from baseball.

Apr 7—Citing financial difficulty, the Kansas City Royals trade pitcher David Cone to the Toronto Blue Jays for three minor leaguers.

Apr 10—Major league umpires, locked out by the owners since Jan. 1, decide to picket selected spring training sites.

Apr 11—The New York Mets sign free agent centerfielder Brett Butler, 38, to a one-year, $2 million contract.

April 18—Pitcher Jack Morris, 39, announces his retirement. Morris was the MVP of the 1991 World Series.

April 19—After 22 seasons with nine different teams, Rich (Goose) Gossage, 43, announces his retirement. The following day reliever Jeff Reardon retires at the age of 39.

April 25—Darryl Strawberry is sentenced to three years probation and ordered to pay $350,000 for federal tax evasion.

April 25—Opening Night … Finally! Though the fans boo during pregame introductions, Miami's Joe Robbie Stadium is sold out for the league opener between the Florida Marlins and the Los Angeles Dodgers. The Dodgers' Raul Mondesi launches a 421-foot home run on the game's 11th pitch, and adds another in the seventh inning to pace Los Angeles's 8–7 victory. Labor problems persist, however, as the game is played with replacement umpires while the locked-out regular umps picket the stadium gates.

April 26—Opening days around the league, with exceptions in Colorado and Toronto, are significantly under-attended as the fans express their disillusionment after the offseason labor dispute.

May 1—Major League Baseball's 120-day lockout of the umpires ends as the two sides strike a five-year deal during nonstop weekend negotiations.

May 2—Hideo Nomo, the first Japanese-born major leaguer in 30 years, makes his debut with the Los Angeles Dodgers. He strikes out seven in five innings of work.

May 2—Rowdy fan protests break out at several major league stadiums during baseball's first week, with the most extreme case in Detroit during the Tigers-Indians game. Detroit fans hurl "ugly verbal abuse" as well as bottles, baseballs, beercans and a napkin dispenser at Cleveland players, nearly stopping the game.

May 7—The Minnesota Twins and Cleveland Indians play for six hours and 36 minutes, using a combined total of 47 players. Kenny Lofton puts an end to the marathon in the bottom of the 17th with an RBI single that gives the Indians a 10–9 victory.

May 8—Former Cincinnati Red Gus Bell, 66, dies after suffering a heart attack.

May 25—Oakland reliever Dennis Eckersley records the 300th save of his career.

May 26—Seattle centerfielder Ken Griffey Jr. breaks his left wrist after slamming into the wall while making a catch against the Orioles. The Mariner star will be out of action until August.

The Boss offered Strawberry a chance to get back on his feet.

DAVID LIAM KYLE

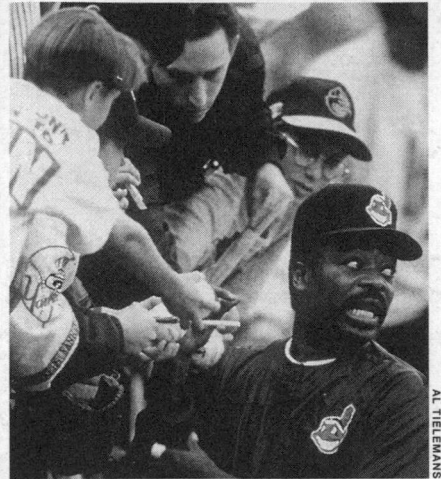

AL TIELEMANS

Murray wrote his own ticket to Cooperstown.

May 30—Glenn Burke, an outfielder for the Los Angeles Dodgers and the Oakland A's in the late '70s, dies of AIDS in San Leandro, Calif. Burke, 42, was the only major league ballplayer to go public about his homosexuality.

June 3—San Francisco Giant slugger Matt Williams fouls a ball off of his foot, breaking a bone and sidelining him for six weeks. At the time of his injury Williams is leading the league in hitting (.381), homers (13) and RBI (35).

June 3—Montreal pitcher Pedro Martinez takes a perfect game into the 10th inning before yielding a double to San Diego's Bip Roberts. The Expos win 1–0.

June 6—Don Zimmer, 64, retires after 47 years in the game as a player, coach and manager.

June 8—Hall of Famer Mickey Mantle undergoes liver transplant surgery in Dallas.

June 14—Hideo Nomo strikes out 16 Pirates in an 8–5 Dodger victory, and Giant infielder Mike Benjamin gets six hits against the Cubs to give him 14 over three games, a major league record.

June 19—The New York Yankees sign beleaguered outfielder Darryl Strawberry.

June 25—Colorado first baseman Andres Galarraga becomes the fourth player in history to homer in three consecutive innings during an 11–3 rout of the Padres.

June 30—Cleveland's Eddie Murray becomes the 20th major leaguer to amass 3,000 hits.

July 11—With three hits, all of them home runs, the National League wins the 66th All-Star Game, 3–2.

July 14—Ramon Martinez of the Dodgers

pitches the first and only no-hitter of the season against Florida.

July 20—Hall of Famers Duke Snider and Willie McCovey plead guilty to income tax evasion regarding income derived in autograph signings.

July 21—The Cincinnati Reds trade Deion Sanders to San Francisco in an eight-player deal.

July 23—Pitcher Dave Stewart, who starred for Oakland and Toronto, announces his retirement.

July 30—White Sox DH John Kruk singles in the first inning at Baltimore, then retires from baseball.

July 31—In a flurry of activity before the day's trading deadline, the New York Yankees acquire pitcher David Cone from Toronto and trade Danny Tartabull to Oakland for Ruben Sierra; the Colorado Rockies acquire pitcher Bret Saberhagen from the Mets for two minor leaguers; and the Mariners deal pitcher Ron Villone and outfielder Marc Newfield to San Diego for pitcher Andy Benes.

Aug 3—The Senate Judiciary Committee votes 9–8 to repeal baseball's antitrust exemption.

Aug 9—Doctors at Baylor University Medical Center in Dallas announce that Yankee legend Mickey Mantle has an aggressive form of cancer known as hepatoma. Mantle dies on Aug. 13.

Sept 4—Chicago White Sox third baseman Robin Ventura belts two grand slams in a 14–3 rout of the Texas Rangers. He is the eighth player in history to accomplish the feat.

Sept 5—Cal Ripken plays in his 2,130th consecutive game, tying Lou Gehrig's ironman record, set in 1939. Ripken homers in the sixth inning; the following day he hits another home run and eclipses Gehrig in an emotional celebration at Baltimore's Camden Yards.

Sept 8—The Cleveland Indians clinch the AL Central title, their first division crown since 1954.

Sept 13—The Atlanta Braves clinch the NL East, their fourth consecutive division title.

Sept 19—Colorado's Andres Galarraga hits his 30th home run, making the Rockies the second team in major league history to have four players hit 30 homers in a season.

Oct 2—Randy Johnson pitches a three-hitter with 12 strikeouts as Seattle beats California 9–1 in a one-game playoff to seal the AL West crown and their first trip to the playoffs in 19 years as a franchise.

Oct 6—The Indians beat the Red Sox 8–2 to sweep their first-round playoff series.

Oct 6—The Cincinnati Reds sweep the Dodgers out of the playoffs with a 10–1 rout in Game 3 of their division series.

Oct 7—The Atlanta Braves down Colorado 10–4 to take their first-round series in four games.

Oct 8—In the most exciting first-round playoff tilt

the Mariners beat New York 6–5 in 11 innings to take the series three games to two. The Yankees won Game 2 on a home run by Jim Leyritz in the 15th inning.

Oct 14—The Braves complete a four-game sweep of Cincinnati in the NLCS with a 6–0 win at Atlanta-Fulton County Stadium. Atlanta's pitching staff compiles a 1.15 ERA for the series, and Mike Devereaux, who has game-winning hits in Games 1 and 4, is named MVP.

Oct 17—The Indians defeat the Mariners 4–0 to win the ALCS in six games and advance to the World Series for the first time in 41 years. Orel Hershiser, who won Games 2 and 5 with a 1.29 ERA, is named MVP of the series.

Oct 28—The Braves win their first World Series title since 1957 with a 1–0 victory over Cleveland in Game 6 in Atlanta. David Justice hits a sixth-inning homer, and Tom Glavine, who throws eight innings of one-hit ball, is named World Series MVP.

Boxing

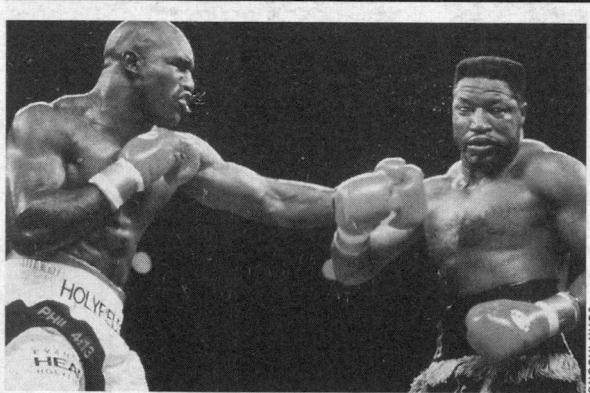

Holyfield (left) came back with a jarring win over Mercer.

Jan 9, 1995—Carlos Monzon, a former middleweight champion who was convicted in 1988 of murdering his estranged lover, is killed in a car accident outside Buenos Aires.

Feb 25—Gerald McClellan collapses and slips into a coma during the 10th round of his super middleweight title fight with Nigel Benn in London. Doctors say the immediate medical care he receives saves his life. He regains consciousness 11 days later.

Nov 5, 1994—George Foreman stuns Michael Moorer with a short right in the 10th round of their heavyweight title fight in Las Vegas. The blow knocks Moorer out and makes the 45-year-old Foreman, who last held the title in 1974, the oldest heavyweight champion in history.

Nov 12—Terry Norris loses his WBC junior middleweight title in Mexico City after being disqualified in the fourth round for hitting challenger Luis Santana in the neck. On the undercard, Humberto Gonzalez defends his WBC and IBF junior flyweight titles with a hard-fought majority decision over No. 1-contender Michael Carbajal; and Ricardo Lopez retains his WBC strawweight title with an eighth-round TKO of Javier Varguez.

Nov 16—Michael Moorer retires. He will un-retire the following spring.

Nov 18—Super middleweight Roy Jones Jr. runs his record to 27–0 and stakes his claim to the world "pound for pound" title with an impressive unanimous decision over James Toney in their IBF title bout.

Nov 23—Former heavyweight champion Evander Holyfield, who was diagnosed with a heart condition last April, receives medical clearance from the Mayo Clinic to resume his career.

Mar 25—Heavyweight Mike Tyson is released from the Indiana Youth Center in Plainfield where he served three years for rape. Five days later he confirms that Don King will be his promoter as he resumes his boxing career.

Apr 8—Two segments of the fractured, mediocre heavyweight division are settled in Las Vegas as Oliver McCall narrowly outpoints 45-year-old ex-champ Larry Holmes to retain the WBC title, and former Mike Tyson sparring partner Bruce Seldon stops Tony Tucker in the seventh round to win the WBA belt.

Apr 8—For the second time in five months junior middleweight Terry Norris is disqualified from a title fight with Luis Santana. This time he decks Santana seven seconds after the bell sounds to end the third round, and Santana, who had hit the canvas twice in Round 2, is carried out of the ring, still champion.

Apr 22—George Foreman narrowly retains his heavyweight title in Las Vegas with a disputed majority decision over little-known Axel Schulz of Germany.

May 19—Super featherweight Jimmy Garcia dies in a Las Vegas hospital from injuries he sustained in his May 6 title fight with Gabriel Ruelas.

May 20—Evander Holyfield is impressive in his return to the ring, outpointing a tough Ray Mercer over 10 rounds in Atlantic City.

June 17—Riddick Bowe floors Jorge Gonzalez in the sixth round of their WBO heavyweight title fight.

June 25—Undefeated IBF super middleweight champion Roy Jones Jr. stops Vinny Pazienza in the sixth round of their bout in Atlantic City.

July 9—Tracy Patterson, son of former heavyweight champ Floyd Patterson, scores a second-round TKO of Eddie Hopson in Reno for the IBF junior lightweight title.

Aug 19—Mike Tyson's much-anticipated return to the ring lends new dimension to the term *travesty*. With over a million pay-per-view customers tuning in at up to $50 a pop, and ringside seats going for $1,500, Tyson floors someone named Peter McNeeley, who sports a questionable 36–1 record, in six seconds. Less than 90 seconds later McNeeley's trainer, Vinnie Vecchione, jumps into the ring, causing the "fight" to end in a disqualification.

College Basketball

Nov 8, 1994—Southern Cal coach George Raveling walks with the help of a cane out of a Los Angeles hospital. He has spent six weeks recuperating from a Sept. 25 automobile accident in which he sustained lung and heart trauma, a broken collarbone and a broken pelvis. One week later he resigns as Southern Cal men's basketball coach in order to focus on his recovery. Former assistant Charlie Parker will take over as head coach.

Nov 20—In the women's Hall of Fame Tip-Off Classic in Jackson, Tenn., No. 1-ranked Tennessee downs No. 2 Louisiana Tech 69–62.

Nov 23—Washington wins the first preseason Women's National Invitation Tournament, defeating Texas Tech 79–75 in the final at Lubbock, Tex. The defeat ends Texas Tech's 25-game home winning streak.

Nov 26—Minnesota guard Voshon Lenard scores 24 points to lead the Gophers to a 79–74 victory over Brigham Young in the final of the men's Great Alaska Shootout.

Nov 25—Gary Trent of Ohio scores 33 points and grabs 20 rebounds during the 15th-ranked Bobcats' 84–80 overtime victory against New Mexico St. in the final of the preseason National Invitation Tournament.

Nov 28—For just the fourth time in NCAA basketball history a coaching matchup pitting father against son occurs as Hugh Durham leads Georgia to an 87–57 rout of his son Doug Durham's Georgia Southern team.

Dec 4—After a ten-year absence the dunk returns to women's basketball when six-foot Charlotte Smith of North Carolina steals a pass early in the Tar Heels 113–58 trouncing of North Carolina A&T, races the length of the court and throws it down one-handed.

Jan 16, 1995—Connecticut (13–0) grabs the No. 1 women's ranking by defeating previously unbeaten Tennessee, 77–66, at Storrs, Conn.

Jan 22—Duke athletic director Tom Butters announces that coach Mike Krzyzewski, recovering from back surgery and exhaustion, will be out for the rest of the season.

JOHN W. McDONOUGH

Floor general Edney specialized in the slash-and-dish.

Feb 7—Some 150 students take over the court at halftime of the Rutgers-UMass game to protest racially charged comments made by Rutgers University President Francis Lawrence.

Feb 13—After key weekend victories, both the Connecticut men's and women's teams are ranked No. 1 in the coaches' polls, an NCAA first.

Feb 21—Kansas loses to unranked Oklahoma, 76–73, to become the fourth team in four weeks to drop out of the top spot in the polls.

Mar 16—March Madness descends as No. 13-seed Manhattan, whose at-large bid was largely criticized, knocks off No. 4 Oklahoma in the Southeast Regional of the NCAA tournament. In the Midwest, No. 5 Arizona performs its seemingly annual swoon, falling to No. 12 Miami (OH), 71–62.

Mar 19—Top seed UCLA survives a scare from Missouri and wins, 75–74, thanks to guard Tyus Edney's coast-to-coast rush for a buzzer-beating layup. Georgetown joins the Bruins in the Sweet 16, and in similar fashion: Hoya forward Don Reid grabs a last-second air ball from guard Allen Iverson and stuffs it through for a 53–51 victory. Four ACC teams reach the Sweet 16, while the Big Ten, with six tourney bids, fails to place one team in the third round.

Mar 26—Fourth-seeded Oklahoma State surprises No. 2 Massachusetts, 68–54, to win the East Regional and advance to the Final Four where they join defending champ Arkansas, North Carolina and UCLA. In the women's tournament, unbeaten Connecticut reaches the semis with a 67–63 win over Virginia and will face Stanford (30–2). The other bracket pits Tennessee against Georgia.

Mar 29—Virginia Tech defeats Marquette 65–64 in overtime to win the National Invitation Tournament in New York City.

Apr 2—Connecticut defeats Tennessee 70–64 to win the women's national championship. The Huskies are the first team from the Northeast ever to win the tournament, and their 35–0 record is the best in Division I history.

Apr 3—UCLA defeats Arkansas 89–78 to win the school's first national title in 20 years. Ed O'Bannon scores 30 points and grabs 17 rebounds and is named the Outstanding Player of the Final Four. Bruin freshman Toby Bailey rises to the occasion with nine rebounds and 26 points.

May 8—Four days after teammate and fellow sophomore Rasheed Wallace does so, North Carolina's Jerry Stackhouse, a 6'6" forward, announces he will enter the NBA draft in June.

College Football

Oct 29, 1994—Third-ranked Nebraska (9–0) asserts itself as a national title contender with a convincing 24–7 win over No. 2 Colorado in Lincoln. In Eugene, Ore., the surprising Oregon Ducks upend eighth-ranked Arizona 10–9 to create a four-way tie for first in the Pac-10.

Nov 5—Despite a 35–29 victory over Indiana—which makes three late, meaningless scores—Penn State (8–0) drops out of the top spot in the polls it shared with Nebraska (10–0), a 45–17 winnner over Kansas.

Nov 5—Miami (7–1, No. 3) moves closer to the Big East title and an Orange Bowl bid with a 27–6 pasting of ninth-ranked Syracuse in the Carrier Dome. Sixth-ranked Florida State wins its 23rd consecutive game in the ACC, wrecking Georgia Tech 41–10.

Nov 8—Michigan State coach George Perles, who has been accused by a former player of violating NCAA rules and is feeling the pressure of several mediocre seasons, announces he will not return for the 1995-96 season.

Nov 10—Wisconsin running back Brent Moss, MVP of the 1994 Rose Bowl, is suspended from the Badger team in the wake of his arrest on a cocaine possession charge.

Nov 12—Trailing Illinois 31–21 in the fourth quarter in Champaign, Ill., No. 2 Penn State rallies to a 35–31 victory, preserving its 9–0 record. Third-ranked Alabama also rallies from a 10-point fourth-quarter deficit to remain undefeated, downing No. 20 Mississippi State 29–25 in Starkville, Miss. With the victory the Crimson Tide clinches its third straight trip to the SEC title game.

Nov 12—In Lawrence, Kan., Colorado's Heisman Trophy candidate Rashaan Salaam rushes for 232 yards and three TDs in the Buffaloes' 51–26 pounding of Kansas. Salaam regains the national lead in rushing yards with the performance, and his three scores give him 132 points on the year, breaking Byron (Whizzer) White's 57-year-old record for points in a season. Alcorn State's Steve McNair, another Heisman candidate, helps his case by passing for 476 yards and rushing for another 110 in a comeback win over Troy State.

Nov 17—Wisonsin running back Brent Moss pleads guilty to cocaine possession in Madison, Wisc., and is fined $250 and sentenced to two years' probation.

Nov 19—Oregon defeats Oregon State 17–13 to clinch the Pac-10 title and its first trip to the Rose Bowl since 1958. Many (including SI) had picked the Ducks to finish near the bottom of the conference, but after a 1–2 start the team wins eight of its last nine and heads to Pasadena.

Nov 19—In the annual war for bragging rights in the state of Alabama, Alabama (11–0) holds on to a 21–14 victory over Auburn (9-1-1) when the Tigers fall short on fourth-and-three in the closing seconds. Yale defeats Harvard 32–13 in the 111th game between the two schools. Ohio State beats Michigan for the first time in seven years, 22–6. Colorado State rallies to beat Fresno State 44–42 and win its first WAC title since joining the conference in 1968.

Nov 19—Rashaan Salaam of Colorado gains 259 yards rushing against Iowa State to raise his season total to 2,055 yards. Only three other backs—Marcus Allen (1981), Mike Rozier ('83) and Barry Sanders ('88)—have broken the 2,000-yard barrier in a season; all three won the Heisman. After the Buffs' 41–20 victory Colorado coach Bill McCartney announces he will resign following the season to spend more time with his family.

Nov 26—With quarterback Tommie Frazier back in the lineup for the first time since being sidelined Sept. 24 because of blood clots in his leg, top-ranked Nebraska flattens Oklahoma 13–3 to finish the regular season at 12–0. Penn State running back Ki-Jana Carter makes a strong closing statement for his Heisman Trophy candidacy with a 227-yard, five-TD performance in the Nittany Lions' 59–31 win over Michigan State. Rose Bowl-bound Penn State closes the regular season with a Big Ten title and an 11–0 record—but a No. 2 national ranking.

Nov 26—Florida State, down 31–3 in the fourth quarter, scores 28 unanswered points and ties Florida 31–31 before a record 80,210 in Tallahassee. Steve McNair ends his career at Alcorn State with a 63–20 first-round playoff loss to defending I-AA champ Youngstown State. Young's closing line: 52-for-82, 514 yards, 3 TD, 3 INT.

Nov 28—Bill Walsh, 63, resigns as head coach at Stanford. Rick Neuheisel is hired to replace Bill McCartney at Colorado.

Dec 3—Alabama sees its national title hopes dashed in a 24–23 loss to Florida in the SEC title game. The outcome puts Florida in the Sugar Bowl for a rematch with Florida State and relegates Alabama to the Citrus Bowl against Ohio State.

Dec 3—Army defeats Navy 22–20 thanks to Kurt Heiss's 52-yard field goal with six minutes remaining. Navy coach George Chaump, who is 1–4 against the Cadets, is fired the next day.

Dec 10—Colorado running back Rashaan Salaam wins the 1994 Heisman Trophy, outpointing Penn State's Ki-Jana Carter 1,743 to 901. In other awards presented during the week Nebraska's Zach Wiegert wins the Outland Trophy as the nation's top interior lineman, Kerry

DAVID LIAM KYLE

Air McNair meant instant 0 for Alcorn State.

Collins of Penn State wins the Davey O'Brien Memorial Award as the best quarterback in the country, and Illinois linebacker Dana Howard wins the Butkus Award.

Dec 10—North Alabama holds off Texas A&M-Kingsville to win the Division II national championship game in Florence, Ala., 16–10. In the Division III title tilt, also known as the Amos Alonzo Stagg Bowl, Albion routs Washington & Jefferson 38–15.

Dec 17—Youngstown State defeats Boise State 28–14 to win the Division I-AA national championship, the school's third title in four years.

Dec 19—Alcorn State quarterback Steve McNair wins the Walter Payton Award as the top player in Division I-AA. Jim Tressel of Youngstown State is named Division I-AA Coach of the Year.

Jan 1, 1995—Trailing Miami 17–9 entering the fourth quarter, Nebraska rallies behind fullback Corey Schlesinger's two fourth-quarter touchdown runs to win 24–17. It is Nebraska's first bowl victory in its past eight tries.

Jan 2—Penn State trounces Oregon 38–20 in the Rose Bowl to complete a perfect 12–0 season. Florida State (10-1-1) downs Florida 23–17 in the Sugar Bowl and Colorado (11–1) wins the Fiesta bowl 41–24 over Notre Dame.

College Football (Cont.)

Jan 3—Both the Associated Press and the *USA Today*/CNN polls rank 13–0 Nebraska No. 1, giving coach Tom Osborne his first national title in 22 years as a head coach. Penn State, which also finished undefeated, at 12–0, is ranked second in both polls, and Colorado is third.

Jan 3—Heisman Trophy winner Rashaan Salaam of Colorado decides to forego his final year of NCAA eligibility and enter the NFL draft. Also leaving for the NFL as juniors are Brigham Young quarterback John Walsh and Miami defensive end Warren Sapp.

Jan 4—The NCAA releases 1994-95 attendance figures and, for the 21st consecutive year, Michigan tops the list, averaging an alltime record 106,217 fans per game. Penn State is second with an average of 96,289. Attendance for all 568 NCAA teams tops 36 million.

Jan 11—Nebraska's Tom Osborne is named Division I-A Coach of the Year by the American Football Coaches Association.

May 1—Michigan coach Gary Moeller is suspended indefinitely with pay following a drunken altercation with police and customers in a Southfield, Mich., restaurant on April 28. Moeller was asked to leave the restaurant after he became abusive and disorderly. When he refused, police were called and the coach pushed and punched an officer in the chest. He spent the night in jail.

May 4—Gary Moeller resigns as Michigan football coach following his April 28 arrest on disorderly conduct and assault and battery charges. The school names former defensive coordinator Lloyd Carr as interim coach, and begins the search, with the season less than four months away, for a permanent successor. Moeller won three Big Ten titles and compiled a 44-13-3 record in five seasons at Michigan.

May 16—The NCAA announces the addition of the Haka Bowl, to be played in Auckland, New Zealand, as early as 1996. The bowl will be played in Auckland's 52,000-seat, Eden Park Stadium and most likely will involve Pac-10 or WAC teams.

July 18—The NCAA eligibility committee reduces the suspension of Maryland quarterback Scott Milanovich from eight to four games. Two days later Milanovich, who was suspended for

gambling on college football and college basketball from 1992 to '94, decides to remain at Maryland after considering a jump to the NFL.

Aug 2—After finding the Alabama football program guilty of several rules violations, including improper bank loans to a former player, the NCAA Committee on Infractions imposes a three-year probation, a one-year ban from postseason play and a reduction by four of the program's overall scholarship limit.

Aug 28—Ohio State and Boston College launch the 1995-96 season in the Kickoff Classic at Giants Stadium in East Rutherford, N.J. The tenth-ranked Buckeyes rout the No. 23 Eagles 38–6. In the Pigskin Classic in Ann Arbor, Mich., Michigan edges Virginia 18–17 with a touchdown on the game's final play.

Aug 31—Nebraska opens its defense of the national title in impressive fashion, overwhelming Oklahoma State 64–21 in Stillwater, Okla.

Sept 2—The season's first shocker occurs in South Bend, Ind., where unranked Northwestern upsets Notre Dame 17–15. The last time the Wildcats defeated the Irish was in 1962. In Pasadena, Calif., 15th-ranked UCLA trounces No. 9 Miami 31–8.

Sept 10—Running back Lawrence Phillips, a Heisman Trophy candidate for second-ranked Nebraska, is suspended from the Husker team following his arrest on misdemeanor assault of a female acquaintance.

Oct 7—Fourth-ranked Ohio State travels to State College, Pa., and nips defending Big Ten champ Penn State 28–25. The Buckeyes are 5–0.

Oct 14—Iowa gets off to its best start since 1986, going 5–0 with a 22–13 win against Indiana. Top-ranked Florida State, averaging 66 points per game in the ACC, torches Duke 72–13, and No. 2 Nebraska keeps pace, steamrolling Missouri 57–0. Others in the national title picture are Florida (6–0) and Ohio State (7–0).

Oct 21—Notre Dame rebounds from two early losses to hand USC its first loss of the season, 38–10 in South Bend. Northwestern improves to 6–1 with a 35–0 blanking of Wisconsin and assures its first winning season since 1971. Kansas streaks to 7–0—its best start since 1968—with a 38–17 win over Oklahoma.

Golf

Nov 27, 1994—Tom Watson sinks a 15-foot birdie putt on the first playoff hole to win The Skins Game Championship in Palm Desert, Calif. He earns $210,000 over the two-day event; Fred Couples finishes second, earning $170,000.

Dec 6—Ernie Els of South Africa, who earned a

rookie-record $684,000 in 1994, is named PGA Tour Rookie of the Year. Two days later Nick Price, who won five tournaments and $1,499,927, is named PGA Player of the Year.

Jan 22, 1995—Pat Bradley earns her first LPGA Tour victory since her Hall of Fame-clinching win

Daly showed his resilience by winning the British Open.

on Sept. 29, 1991, claiming the HealthSouth Inaugural title in Lake Buena Vista, Fla.

Feb 26—Corey Pavin becomes the first player since Arnold Palmer in 1966-67 to win back-to-back Nissan Open titles.

Mar 26—Nanci Bowen wins the Nabisco Dinah Shore in Rancho Mirage, Calif., shooting a final-round 70 to defeat Susie Redman by one stroke.

Apr 9—Tying Ben Hogan for the second-best score in Masters history, Ben Crenshaw shoots a 14-under-par 274 to win at Augusta for the second time in the past 12 years. It is an emotional victory for Crenshaw, who served as a pallbearer at his lifelong friend and mentor Harvey Penick's funeral on the eve of the tournament.

May 14—Trailing Britain's Laura Davies by three strokes with seven holes to play, Kelly Robbins rallies to win the LPGA Championship in Wilmington, Del.

June 18—Long known as one of the Tour's toughest competitors, Corey Pavin finally wins a major, taking the U.S. Open title at Shinnecock Hills in Southampton, New York. Pavin hits an instant classic of a shot on his approach to the 18th in the final round to secure the victory.

June 25—Betsy King shoots a final-round 67 to win the ShopRite Classic at Somers Point, N.J. It is the 30th victory of her career and makes her the 15th player to qualify for the LPGA Hall Of Fame.

July 2—Wearing a pink ribbon on his cap in honor of his wife, who is undergoing treatment for breast cancer, Tom Weiskopf shoots a 13-under-par 275 for a stirring victory at the U.S. Senior Open in Bethesda, Md.

July 16—Sweden's Annika Sorenstam shoots three consecutive birdies, beginning with the ninth hole, and then holds on for a one-stroke victory over Meg Mallon at the U.S. Open in Colorado Springs.

July 23—John Daly wins the British Open at St. Andrews, Scotland, following a four-hole playoff with Costantino Rocca.

Aug 13—Six strokes off the pace entering the final round of the PGA Championship in Pacific Palisades, Calif., Australia's Steve Elkington shoots a 64 to tie for the lead, then sinks a 25-foot putt to win on the first hole of a sudden-death playoff with Colin Montgomerie of Scotland.

Aug 27—Jenny Lidback gets her first career victory at the du Maurier Ltd. Classic in Pointe Claire, Quebec. Leading Sweden's Liselotte Neumann by one stroke throughout the tournament, Lidback shoots par in the final round to hold on for the win.

Aug 27—Tiger Woods wins his second consecutive U.S. Men's Amateur title in Newport, R.I., defeating Buddy Marucci, two-up. In Akron, Ohio, Greg Norman sinks a 66-foot chip shot on the first playoff hole to beat Nick Price and Billy Mayfair for the PGA Tour World Series of Golf title.

Sept 17—Shooting a course-record 61 in the final round, Hal Sutton wins for the first time in almost nine years, taking the B.C. Open by one stroke over Jim McGovern.

Sept 24—Europe wins seven of the last 10 singles matches to rally from a 10–7 deficit and defeat the U.S. at the Ryder Cup. It is Europe's second victory on U.S soil in the 62-year history of the event.

Oct 22—Duffy Waldorf shoots a final round 65 at the Texas Open for the first victory of his nine-year PGA career. The $198,000 he wins in prize money, however, is not enough to qualify him for the Tour Championship. Second place finisher Justin Leonard earns $118,000 to move from 33rd to 24th on the season money list. The top 30 earners qualify for the Tour Championship.

Oct 22—Scotland wins its first Dunhill Cup in 11 years, defeating Zimbabwe 2–1 at St. Andrews. Nick Price shoots a record 20-under-par to earn Zimbabwe's point. The U.S. finishes last in its group.

Nov 3, 1994—With the NHL lockout reaching its 33rd day the league announces it will cut 10 more games from the upcoming schedule, reducing it to 70 games.

Nov 15—Three men are inducted into the Hockey Hall of Fame in Toronto. Defenseman Lionel Conacher, who won Stanley Cup titles with Chicago and Montreal, and Harry Watson, a left wing who won four Stanley Cups with Toronto and one with Detroit, are inducted in the Veterans category, and administrator Brian O'Neill is inducted in the Builders category.

Nov 17—After an exchange of proposals between the players' union and NHL owners produces no settlement, the league cuts ten more games from the schedule, reducing the season to 60 games.

Nov 26—The players' union decides to take time out to study the proposals that have come out of six marathon negotiating sessions over the past 10 days.

Dec 6—With salary arbitration, free agency and a rookie salary cap among the major sticking points, talks in Chicago between players and NHL owners break down without a settlement. Commissioner Gary Bettman considers calling a deadline for canceling the season.

Dec 8—The NHL cancels the All-Star Game, scheduled for Jan. 21.

Dec 14—Bruce McNall resigns as owner of the Los Angeles Kings after pleading guilty to bank fraud. McNall pleads guilty to defrauding six banks of some $236 million and faces up to 45 years in prison and $1.75 million in fines.

Dec 29—NHL commissioner Gary Bettman sets a Jan. 16 deadline for settlement of the labor dispute. Without a settlement before that date, the season will be canceled.

Jan 11, 1995—With each side grumbling about concessions made to the other, the NHL owners and players' union sign a new six-year Collective Bargaining Agreement, thereby ending the 103-day lockout. The season, cut from 84 to 48 games, will begin Jan. 20.

Jan 20—The NHL season resumes, and if fans have resentment concerning the five-month labor dispute, they do not express it. With few exceptions, large crowds turn out around the league. In Tampa Bay the second-largest crowd in league history (26,387) attends the Lightning's opener against Pittsburgh.

Jan 26—Mark Messier signs a two-year deal with the New York Rangers that will pay him roughly $6 million a year, making him the second-highest paid player in the NHL, behind Wayne Gretzky.

Jan 26—Five-time All-Star Michel Goulet, a left wing who scored 548 goals during his 15-year career with Quebec and Chicago, announces his retirement.

Feb 2—Mike Keenan earns his 400th career coaching victory in the St Louis Blues' 5–4 defeat of Winnipeg. Keenan reaches the milestone in his 731st game, fourth fastest in NHL history.

Feb 7—Pittsburgh Penguin right wing Joe Mullen becomes the first U.S.-born player to score 1,000 career points. He reaches the 1,000-point plateau by assisting on John Cullen's second period goal during the Pens' 7–3 rout of Florida.

Feb 9—The Philadelphia Flyers deal right wing Mark Recchi to the Montreal Canadiens in exchange for center John LeClair, left wing Gilbert Dionne and defenseman Eric Desjardins.

Feb 18—The Pittsburgh Penguins lose to Hartford 4–2, ending their season-opening unbeaten streak at 13 games, third longest in NHL history.

Mar 13—Washington goalie Jim Carey is named NHL player of the week. Called up from the minors on

DAVID E. KLUTHO

Keith Primeau and the Red Wings had the NHL's best record, but no title.

Brodeur blanked Boston in three of five games.

Mar. 2, Carey goes 6-0-1, capping the run with a 3–0 shutout of Tampa Bay.

Mar 16—Pat LaFontaine returns to action for the first time since tearing his anterior cruciate ligament in Nov. 1993. The Buffalo center scores a goal and assists on another as the Sabres beat the Islanders 6–3.

Apr 1—Alexei Zhamnov of the Winnipeg Jets scores five goals in a 7–7 tie with Los Angeles.

Apr 2—For the first time in over 20 years the NHL returns to network television in the U.S. with six regional telecasts on the Fox Network.

Apr 2—Jim Carey becomes the first player ever to win both the player and rookie of the month awards. Starting every game since being called up from the minors March 2, the Washington goalie goes 12-2-2 with a 1.73 goals against average.

May 1—The Buffalo Sabres defeat Montreal 2–0, eliminating the Canadiens from playoff contention and snapping the Habs' streak of 24 straight playoff appearances, third longest in league history.

May 1—The defending Stanley Cup champion New York Rangers defeat the Philadelphia Flyers 2–0 to clinch a playoff berth on the last day of their regular season.

May 3—The Boston Bruins conclude the 28th straight season in which they have qualified for the playoffs, extending their NHL record.

May 12—New Jersey Devil Martin Brodeur becomes just the fifth goalie since 1939 to register three shutouts in a playoff series when he blanks the Bruins 1–0 in Game 3 of their first-round series.

May 15—The Vancouver Canucks score two shorthanded goals in an NHL-record 17 seconds during their 6–5 win over the St Louis Blues in Game 5 of the conference quarterfinals.

May 16—The New York Rangers, seeded eighth in the Eastern Conference playoffs, knock off top seed Quebec, four games to two. Nine days later the Nordiques are sold to a group in Denver, Colo., and announce they will relocate and play the 1995-96 season as the Colorado Avalanche.

May 19—Following a 19-25-4 regular season the San Jose Sharks eliminate the second-seeded Calgary Flames in the Western Conference quarterfinals. Ray Whitney scores the winner at 1:54 of the second overtime. Goalie Wade Flaherty makes 56 saves in the game.

June 11—The Detroit Red Wings defeat the Chicago Blackhawks 2–1 in double overtime to win the Western Conference final four games to one and advance to the Stanley Cup for the first time since 1966.

June 13—The New Jersey Devils down the

DAMIAN STROHMEYER

Philadelphia Flyers 4–2 to win the Eastern Conference final in six games and make their first trip to the Stanley Cup in the 14-year history of the franchise.

June 17—The Stanley Cup final begins, as the New Jersey Devils beat the Detroit Red Wings 2–1. Claude Lemieux scores the deciding goal, his third game-winner of the playoffs.

June 20—Trailing Detroit 2–1 in the third period, the Devils score three goals to win the game 4–2 and take a commanding 2–0 lead as the series heads to New Jersey. It is the 10th consecutive road win for the Devils, an NHL playoff record.

June 20—Pittsburgh superstar Mario Lemieux, who sat out the 1994-95 season for medical reasons, announces he will return for the 1995-96 season.

June 24—The New Jersey Devils beat Detroit 5–2 to complete a stunning four-game sweep to the Stanley Cup championship. New Jersey's Claude Lemieux, who led all playoff scorers with 13 goals, wins the Conn Smythe Trophy as the MVP of the playoffs.

Sept 11—Former Montreal Canadien Larry Robinson is elected to the Hockey Hall of Fame.

Sept 24—The San Jose Sharks release legendary right wing Sergei Makarov.

Sept 26—The Boston Bruins close Boston Garden with an exhibition game against the Montreal Canadiens, the same team they hosted in the Garden's first game in 1928.

Sept 27—Detroit defenseman Mark Howe announces his retirement after 22 NHL seasons.

Oct 17—After the team struggles to an 0–4 start the Montreal Canadiens announce the firings of General Manager Serge Savard, coach Jacques Demers and assistant GM Andre Boudrias.

Oct 18—A group from Minnesota headed by Richard Burke and Steven Gluckstern buys the Winnipeg Jets for $68 million.

Horse Racing

Nov 5, 1994—Trainer D. Wayne Lukas has a banner day at the Breeders' Cup, but his accomplishments—first place finishes by Timber Country and Flanders in the Juvenile and Juvenile Fillies, respectively, and the second place run of Tabasco Cat in the Classic—are tainted by the revelation that Flanders has fractured two small bones in her foreleg during her race.

Nov 5—Jockey Mike Smith rides Cherokee Run to victory in the Breeders' Cup Sprint and Tikannen to first place in the Turf for his 63rd and 64th stakes wins of the year, a national record; Ireland's Barathea, one of 27 European horses in the B.C., wins the mile; and One Dreamer, a 47–1 long shot, steals the Distaff.

Feb 12, 1995—Holy Bull, the 1994 Horse of the Year, pulls up lame during the Donn Handicap with a tendon injury in his left front leg. The injury ends the colt's racing career and he is shipped to

Cigar smoked the competition all year long.

stand stud at Jonabell Farm for the 1995 season. Cigar goes on to win the Donn.

Feb 26—Educated Risk closes out her career by winning the Rampart Handicap at Gulfstream Park. The 5-year-old mare has won 11 of 23 starts and earned $1,163,717; she will be bred to top stallion Danzig.

Mar 5—Erstwhile turf specialist Cigar wins the Gulfstream Park Handicap, his fifth consecutive victory since switching to the dirt.

Mar 11—Thunder Gulch establishes himself as an early Kentucky Derby favorite with a nose victory over Sauve Prospect in the $500,000 Florida Derby.

Apr 1—Serena's Song, another one of D. Wayne Lukas's Derby hopefuls, wins the Jim Beam Stakes. She is the first filly ever to win the race.

Apr 29—D. Wayne Lukas announces that the filly Serena's Song will skip the Kentucky Oaks and race in the Kentucky Derby, making her just

MANNY MILLAN

the 36th filly to enter the prestigious race. Three fillies have won the Derby.

May 6—Thunder Gulch, who went off at 25–1 odds because of lackluster recent performances, wins the 121st running of the Kentucky Derby in the sixth-fastest time ever.

May 20—In a reversal of the top three Kentucky Derby finishers, Timber Country overtakes stablemate Thunder Gulch and then Oliver's Twist to win the 120th running of the Preakness Stakes.

June 10—Kentucky Derby winner Thunder Gulch wins the Belmont Stakes by two lengths over Star Standard. The win gives trainer D. Wayne Lukas five straight Triple Crown victories and makes him the first trainer ever to sweep the Triple Crown in one year with different horses; the Lukas-trained Timber Country won the Preakness.

Sept 16—Cigar wins the Woodward Stakes at Belmont Park for his 10th consecutive victory.

Sept 21—Hall of Fame harness driver John Campbell win the third Little Brown Jug of his career.

Oct 1—Angel Cordero, 51, makes a triumphant return to the track from a Jan. 7, 1992 accident that left him with multiple injuries. He sets a track record and wins at El Commandante in Puerto Rico.

Oct 7—The year's biggest showdown is spoiled when Thunder Gulch fractures his leg in the Gold Cup at Belmont Park. The race was Gulch's first confrontation with his rival for Horse of the Year, Cigar, and would have set up a dramatic rematch at the Breeders' Cup on Oct. 28. Cigar wins the race for his 11th consecutive victory.

Motor Sports

Nov 7, 1994—Damon Hill wins the Japanese Grand Prix to pull within one point of Formula One standings leader Michael Schumacher with one race to go.

Nov 13—Michael Schumacher of Germany finishes 19th in the season-ending Australian Grand Prix, one place ahead of archrival Damon Hill with whom he collided during the race. The margin is enough to secure the first Formula One season title of Schumacher's career.

Nov 14—Despite finishing 31st in the season-ending Hampton 500 at the Atlanta Motor Speedway, Jeff Burton clinches the NASCAR Rookie of the Year award. The 27-year-old from South Boston, Va., had two top-five and three top-ten finishes during the season.

Jan 26, 1995—Former Indy Car driver Mario Andretti receives a shock when IMSA mandates rules changes that will ban his Porsche World Sports Car from competing in the 24 Hours of Daytona. Andretti had hoped to use the Daytona event to prepare for June's 24 Hours of LeMans.

Feb 5—Actor Paul Newman, 70, becomes the oldest driver ever to win a professionally sanctioned race when he co-drives—along with Mark Martin, Michael Brockman and Tommy Kendall—the Jack Roush-Ford Mustang to the GTS-1 class title at the 24 Hours of Daytona.

Feb 19—Sterling Marlin becomes the first driver to win consecutive Daytona 500s since Cale Yarborough in 1983-84. Dale Earnhardt makes a late charge but finishes second.

Feb 27—Jeff Gordon, 23, wins the pole and the race at the Rockingham 500 in North Carolina, taking home $167,600 for his efforts.

Mar 5—Jacques Villeneuve wins the first Indy Car event of the season, driving his Renault to victory at Miami.

Mar 19—Paul Tracy of Canada wins his second straight Indy Car Australian Grand Prix.

Mar 26—Defending Formula One champ Michael Schumacher wins the season-opening Brazilian Grand Prix.

Apr 9—Al Unser Jr. wins his sixth Long Beach Grand Prix with an average speed of 91.4 mph.

May 7—Dale Earnhardt, who has 64 career NASCAR victories, wins his first on a road course when he slips past Mark Martin with two laps remaining to win the Sonoma 300.

May 8—Arie Luyendyk zips off the fastest practice lap in Indy 500 history, rounding the 2.5 mile Brickyard course at an average speed of 234.107 mph.

May 23—The McLaren Formula One team fires driver Nigel Mansell less than four months after signing him.

May 28—Last year's second place finisher and Rookie of the Year Jacques Villeneuve wins the Indy 500. Villeneuve recovers from a two-lap penalty to regain the lead with four laps to go, then holds on for the win.

June 25—Three hours after winning the Portland 200, Indy Car driver Al Unser Jr. is stripped of the victory by the sport's sanctioning body for having less than the two inches of ground clearance beneath his Penske-Mercedes. The win is awarded to second place finisher Jimmy Vasser.

July 17—Grand Prix legend Juan Manuel Fangio, 84, dies of pneumonia in Buenos Aires.

Aug 5—Seventeen-year NASCAR veteran Dale Earnhardt holds Rusty Wallace to claim the Brickyard 400 title and $565,600.

Aug 16—In a day of multimillion-dollar signings by top racers, Formula One champion Michael

Schumacher announces he will leave Benetton-Renault for Ferrari, Indy 500 winner Jacques Villeneuve signs with Williams-Renault to make the jump to Formula One, and Damon Hill resigns with Williams, where he and Villeneuve will be teammates.

Sept 10—At the Italian Grand Prix in Monza, archrivals Michael Schumacher of Germany and Britain's Damon Hill nearly come to blows after colliding on the track. Hill is given a suspended one-race ban following the incident, the latest in a series of dust-ups between the two drivers.

Sep 10—Jacques Villeneuve finishes 11th at the season-ending Monterey Grand Prix, high enough to clinch his first Indy Car season title in just his second year on the circuit.

Oct 1—Wearing a patch over his left eye, Ernie Irvan returns to the track for the Wilkesboro 400 following a 13-month absence due to near-fatal injuries sustained in an August, 1994 crash. He finishes sixth in the race.

Oct 22—Michael Schumacher wins the Pacific Grand Prix to clinch his second straight Formula One season title. With two races remaining on the NASCAR circuit, Dale Earnhardt trails series leader Jeff Gordon by 162 points.

Olympics

Dec 4, 1994—The Olympic Council of Asia strips 11 Chinese athletes of medals they won in the Asian Games in Hiroshima, Japan, because they tested positive for a performance-enhancing testosterone derivative. The athletes had won medals in swimming, cycling and the decathlon.

Dec 14—In an effort to reclaim its status as a world power in women's basketball, USA Basketball announces that it will form a women's national team one year prior to the Olympics. The team will consist of 10 players, each compensated $50,000 for the year. Though top players can earn salaries of up to $150,000 competing in Europe, many say they will take a pay cut to remain in the U.S. Previously, the Olympic team was selected two or three months prior to the Games.

Feb 22, 1995—Four-time Olympic gold medalist Greg Louganis, who disclosed his homosexuality at the 1994 Gay Games, announces that he has AIDS.

Feb 27—Speed skater Dan Jansen, who competed in four Olympics and finally won a gold medal in the 1,000 meters at Lillehammer, is named the winner of the 65th annual James E. Sullivan Award as the country's top amateur athlete.

Mar 18—Bonnie Blair closes her legendary speed skating career with two gold medal performances in Calgary. She just misses the world record in winning the 500 meters, then wins the 1,000 meters in a U.S.-record 1:18.05.

June 16—In a stunning first-ballot victory (54 of 89 votes) in Budapest, Hungary, Salt Lake City is awarded the 2002 Winter Olympics by the International Olympic Committee.

June 16—In the fourth and final session of the IOC's Budapest meeting, IOC President Juan Antonio Samaranch, who is soon to turn 75, introduces a petition to raise the organization's mandatory retirement age from 75 to 80. There is some grumbling but after a swift show of hands, the motion passes.

June 25—Dick Schultz, 65, is elected as executive director of the United States Olympic Committee. He resigned as executive director of the NCAA in 1993.

July 19—Billy Payne, the president of the Atlanta Committee for the Olympic Games, announces that, with one year to go, 80% of the record $1.58 billion budgeted for the 1996 Atlanta Olympics has been raised.

July 31—At an international regatta in Savannah, Georgia, intended as a pre-Olympic

JOHN BIEVER

Blair closed her career—how else?—with a win.

st event, there are unanimous complaints from e 53 participating countries. The primary ievance concerns the two- to three-hour water w required to reach the racing courses in assaw Sound from the new Olympic marina ear Savannah.

ug 1—For the first time since the series began 1986 the U.S. national baseball team defeats uba in a four-game series. The U.S. wins the urth game 6–5 to complete a surprising sweep, nsettling the notion that Cuba is a lock for the old in Atlanta.

ug 4—NBC makes a blockbuster deal with the)C and Olympic organizers to broadcast both e 2000 Summer Games in Sydney, Australia, nd the 2002 Winter Games in Salt Lake City, aying $1.27 billion for the unprecedented rrangement.

ct 8—The U.S. women's gymnastic team wins e bronze medal at the World Championships in

Sabae, Japan. The U.S. men finish ninth. Both placings qualify the teams for the 1996 Summer Olympics.

Oct 8—At its board of directors meeting in Atlanta the United States Olympic Committee approves a budget that eliminates the U.S. Olympic festival and funding for the World University Games. The USOC festival, which cost $11 million dollars to stage in 1994, will be replaced by a smaller, possibly elite-level event beginning in 1999. U.S. Athletes will still be able to participate inthe World University Games, but will do so at the expense of their sport's national governing body.

Oct 24—Bruce Arena, 44, who coached the University of Virginia to an unprecedented four consecutive NCAA men's soccer championships, is hired to coach the U.S. Olympic men's soccer team.

Pro Basketball

Nov 1, 1994—The San Antonio Spurs suspend orward Dennis Rodman for the first three games f the season for "conduct detrimental to the lub." Rodman was ejected from the previous ight's preseason game against Charlotte after icking up his second technical foul. He then hrew a bag of ice toward the court.

Nov 3—Holdout rookie Glenn Robinson signs he most lucrative first-year contract in NBA nistory, getting a guaranteed $72 million over 10 years from the Milwaukee Bucks.

Nov 10—Los Angeles Laker forward James Worthy, 33, announces his retirement after 12 NBA seasons.

Nov 17—Former Michigan teammates Juwan Howard and Chris Webber are reunited as members of the Washington Bullets. Howard, an unsigned rookie, agrees to a 12-year, $41.3 million with the Bullets; and Webber, a holdout free agent unhappy with Golden State, agrees to terms with the Warriors, and they trade him to Washington for Tom Gugliotta and three future first-round draft picks.

Dec 7—The Los Angeles Clippers win their first game of the season after 16 straight losses, and avoid tying the NBA's worst-ever start, 0–17 by the 1988 Miami Heat.

Dec 7—Dennis Rodman fails to show up for practice following a month-long paid leave of absence, and is suspended again by the Spurs.

Dec 27—New York Knick Charles Oakley undergoes surgery for a dislocated toe and will be sidelined for six to eight weeks.

Jan 4, 1995—Gary Payton of the Seattle SuperSonics goes 14-for-14 from the field in a 116–84 win over the Cleveland Cavaliers.

Jan 6—Atlanta Hawk coach Lenny Wilkens earns career win No. 939 in a victory over the Washington Bullets. With the triumph Wilkens surpasses Red Auerbach as the NBA coach with the most wins.

Jan 14—Cleveland guard Mark Price breaks his right wrist in a game against Golden State. The injury will require surgery, shelving Price for six to eight weeks. He is the third Cav to be hit by significant injury this season.

Jan 26—Detroit's Grant Hill leads all vote-getters in fan balloting for the NBA All-Star Game. He is the first rookie ever to do so.

Feb 1—In a 129–88 rout of the Denver Nuggets Utah Jazz guard John Stockton becomes the NBA's alltime assist leader, surpassing Magic Johnson on his 11th assist of the game, the 9,922nd of his career.

Feb 2—Utah loses to the Houston Rockets 121–101, missing a chance to tie the NBA record of 16 consecutive road victories set by the Los Angeles Lakers in 1971-72.

Feb 6—The Phoenix Suns lose star forward Danny Manning for the season when he tears his anterior cruciate ligament in practice.

Feb 7—Kareem Abdul-Jabbar leads a class of two women and five men elected to the Basketball Hall of Fame. Former USC standout and current Trojan women's coach Cheryl Miller is also elected.

AL TIELEMANS

Kidd grew up fast in the NBA, sharing Rookie of the Year honors with Hill.

May 7—In Game 1 of the Eastern Conference semifinal, Indiana's Reggie Miller singlehandedly brings the Pacers back from a six-point deficit with 18 seconds left against the Knicks. Miller hits a three-pointer, makes a steal, sinks another trey, grabs a rebound and sinks two free-throws—all inside 1 seconds—to give the Pacers a stunning 107–105 victory. Indiana goes on to win the series in seven games.

May 10—Michael Jordan returns to his old No. 23 for Game 2 of the Eastern Conference semifinal against the Magic and scores 38 points as the Bulls even the series with a 104–94 victory.

May 11—Kevin Garnett, a 6'11" high school senior from Chicago, announces that he will forego college and enter the NBA draft.

May 17—Dallas guard Jason Kidd and Detroit forward Grant Hill are announced as co-Rookies of the Year. The only other such tie in NBA history was between Dave Cowens and Geoff Petrie in 1970-71.

May 18—The Orlando Magic defeat Chicago 108–102 at the United Center to clinch the Eastern Conference semifinal in six games. In Los Angeles, San Antonio knocks off the young Laker team 100–88 to take the Western semifinal four games to two.

May 20—For the second straight year Houston drops the first two games of the Western Conference semifinal to Phoenix, then comes back to eliminate the Suns in seven games. The Rockets win the tense seventh game at Phoenix, 115–114.

June 1—Houston's Hakeem Olajuwon caps a remarkable Western Conference final series with a 39-point, 17-rebound performance in Game 6 against San Antonio. With their 100–95 victory the Rockets eliminate the Spurs, the team with the NBA's best regular-season record, and win a return trip to the NBA Finals.

June 4—After losing Game 6 by 27 points, the Orlando Magic trounce the Indiana Pacers 105–81 in Game 7 to win an exciting, back-and-forth Eastern Conference final series.

June 15—The Houston Rockets dismiss the Orlando Magic in four games to win their second consecutive NBA title. After a 120–118 overtime victory in Game 1, the Rockets reel off three convincing wins. They take Game 4 113–101, and Hakeem Olajuwon, who averages 32.8 points and 11.5 rebounds for the series, wins the MVP award.

Feb 12—Mitch Richmond is named MVP of the All-Star game as he leads the West to a 139–112 win, sinking 10 of his 13 shots from the field.

Feb 13—Following a tumultuous stretch of poor play, injuries and feuds with players, Don Nelson resigns as coach and GM of the Warriors.

Feb 14—The Portland Trail Blazers trade Clyde Drexler to Houston for Otis Thorpe.

Mar 7—Boston's Dominique Wilkins becomes the ninth player in NBA history to score 25,000 career points. He reaches the milestone during a 115–110 loss to the Knicks.

Mar 19—Michael Jordan, wearing uniform No. 45 instead of his old 23, makes a dramatic return to the NBA after a 17-month retirement. He shows flashes of his old brilliance but shoots poorly; the Bulls lose 103–96 in overtime.

Mar 28—In his fifth game back in the NBA Michael Jordan scores 55 points as the Bulls defeat the Knicks 113–111 in Madison Square Garden.

Apr 5—The Hornets and the 76ers combine for 19 points in the second quarter of their game at Charlotte, registering the second-lowest scoring quarter in NBA history.

Apr 15—Miami's Glenn Rice scores 56 points in the Heat's 123–117 victory over Orlando.

May 4—For the second straight year, the Seattle SuperSonics follow an excellent regular season with a first-round exit from the playoffs, losing to the Lakers in four games.

June 15—Pat Riley resigns as coach of the New York Knicks following a dispute over his role in personnel decisions. He has one year remaining on his contract with New York, but after a deal is worked out between the Knicks and Miami, he signs to coach the Heat.

June 20—A group of players led by Michael Jordan and Patrick Ewing petitions for decertification of the players' union. They are displeased with the union's negotiations for a new collective bargaining agreement.

June 28—At the NBA draft in New York City, Golden State selects Maryland sophomore Joe Smith with the first pick. The LA Clippers take Alabama's Antonio McDyess with the second pick, then trade him to Denver for Rodney Rogers and 15th pick Brent Barry. North Carolina's Jerry Stackhouse goes third to Philadelphia.

July 1—With the two sides unable to reach a new collective bargaining agreement the NBA imposes a lockout on its players.

July 6—Don Nelson is hired to coach the New York Knicks.

Sept 12—The players vote 226–134 to retain the union. Two days later they vote 25–2 in favor of the new collective bargaining agreement.

Sept 18—The NBA lifts the 79-day player lockout, clearing the way for the 1995-96 season.

Sept 27—The Bullets sign top rookie Rasheed Wallace, and acquire Mark Price from Cleveland in exchange for a 1996 first-round draft pick.

Oct 2—The Bulls trade center Will Perdue to the Spurs for controversial rebound specialist Dennis Rodman.

Pro Football

Oct 23, 1994—The San Diego Chargers (6–1) are the last team to fall from the ranks of the unbeaten, losing to Denver 20–15.

Oct 24—Dallas Cowboy offensive lineman Erik Williams is injured in a 3 a.m. car accident in Dallas. Williams suffers two torn ligaments in his knee, a broken rib, torn ligaments in his left thumb and facial cuts. He later pleads no contest to a misdemeanor drunken driving charge.

Nov 2—The NFL announces that the expansion Jacksonville Jaguars and Carolina Panthers will play in the AFC Central and the NFC West, respectively.

Nov 6—With 261 yards in a 22–21 win over the Indianapolis Colts, Miami Dolphin quarterback Dan Marino passes Dan Fouts and moves into second place on the career passing yardage list. Marino has 43,151 career passing yards, second to Fran Tarkenton's 47,003.

Nov 12—In a showdown of the NFL's top two teams the San Francisco 49ers beat Dallas 21–14 in Candlestick Park.

Nov 12—Drew Bledsoe sets NFL records for completions (45) and attempts (70) while passing for 426 yards in New England's 26–20 overtime victory against Minnesota.

Nov 24—With Troy Aikman and Rodney Peete injured, Dallas Cowboy third-string quarterback Jason Garrett, a graduate of Princeton, completes 15 of 26 passes for 311 yards and two touchdowns to lead the Cowboys to 42–31 comeback win over Green Bay.

Dec 2—Seattle Seahawk defensive tackle Mike Frier is paralyzed in a car accident on a rain-slickened street near Seahawk headquarters. Frier's teammate running back Chris Warren is also in the car, and breaks two ribs.

PETER READ MILLER

Humphries passed the Chargers to a 6–0 start.

Dec 11—Jet wide receiver Art Monk breaks Steve Largent's record of 177 straight games with at least one reception when he catches a five-yard toss from Boomer Esiason on the first play of the Jets' 18–7 loss to the Detroit Lions.

Dec 18—The New England Patriots win their sixth straight game, downing Buffalo 41–17 and eliminating the Bills, the AFC champion for the past four years, from the playoffs.

DAMIAN STROHMEYER

Coates led the AFC in receptions with 96.

Dec 18—During their victory over the Bills the Patriots become the first team in NFL history to have five receivers with more than 51 catches in a season. Vincent Brisby becomes the fifth Patriot to reach 51 catches when he makes four against Buffalo. The others: AFC leader tight end Ben Coates (93), Michael Timpson (71), Le Roy Thompson (60) and Kevin Turner (52).

Dec 25—On the NFL's final weekend the Minnesota Vikings defeat the 49ers 21–14 to clinch the NFC Central title; the New England Patriots win their seventh consecutive game, 13–3 over Chicago, to finish 10–6 and clinch a wild-card berth; and the New York Giants, who will miss the playoffs, score a moral victory, defeating Dallas 15–10. Also, two records are safe as Detroit's Barry Sanders falls short of 2,000 rushing yards, needing 169 yards and gaining only 52 in a 27–20 loss to Miami; and Emmitt Smith (22 season touchdowns, two short of John Riggins's record) sits out with injuries against the Giants.

Dec 27—Miami defensive tackle Tim Bowens, considered by many a longshot for the NFL, is named Defensive Rookie of the Year.

Dec 28—Green Bay wide receiver Sterling Sharpe, who made 112 catches in 1993, announces he will have surgery to repair damaged vertebrae in his neck. He will require at least eight months to recover.

Dec 31—The playoffs begin with the Packers edging Detroit 16–12 in the NFC wild-card. In the AFC Miami knocks Joe Montana and the Chiefs

out with a 27–17 victory. The following day the Browns eliminate New England 30–13 and the Bears rout Minnesota 35–18.

Jan 5, 1995—The Jets fire first-year coach Pete Carroll after a 6–10 season and replace him with Rich Kotite, who was 7–9 this year with the Eagles.

Jan 7—The Pittsburgh Steelers flatten the Browns 29–9 in the AFC divisional playoffs. The following day the Chargers rally from a 21–6 first-half deficit to nip Miami 22–21.

Jan 8—The Dallas Cowboys overwhelm Green Bay 39–9 in the NFC divisional playoffs. The rout follows the 49ers' 44–15 shellacking of Chicago in the previous day's NFC divisional matchup.

Jan 11—The Seattle Seahawks sign former University of Miami coach Dennis Erickson to a five-year head coaching contract.

Jan 15—San Diego linebacker Dennis Gibson knocks down Steeler Neil O'Donnell's end zone pass to Barry Foster in the waning seconds of the AFC championship game to preserve a 17–13 Charger victory. The surprising Chargers, who again come from behind to win, advance to the Super Bowl for the first time in franchise history.

Jan 15—The San Francisco 49ers score three times in the first ten minutes of the NFC championship against Dallas, and go on to lead 31–14 at halftime. They withstand a second-half rally by Dallas and win 38–28 to advance to the Super Bowl.

Jan 16—Rams owner Georgia Frontiere announces she will move the team from Los Angeles to her hometown of St. Louis.

Jan 29—Former Seattle wide receiver Steve Largent is elected to the Pro Football Hall of Fame. Joining him are former GM Jim Finks, ex-Packer defensive great Henry Jordan, six-time Pro Bowler Lee Roy Selmon, who played for Tampa Bay, and ex-Charger tight end Kellen Winslow.

Jan 29—Scoring the fastest touchdown in Super Bowl history, a 44-yard pass from Steve Young to Jerry Rice at 1:24 of the first quarter, the 49ers set the tone for their 49–26 rout of San Diego in Super Bowl XXIX. San Francisco breaks or ties 16 records in the game, and Young, who completes 24 of 36 passes for 325 yards and six touchdowns, wins the MVP award.

Jan 31—The Denver Broncos hire former San Francisco offensive coordinator Mike Shanahan as head coach.

Feb 2—Ray Rhodes, who was the 49ers' defensive coordinator, signs to coach the Philadelphia Eagles. With Art Shell's firing by the Los Angeles Raiders on the same day, the number of African-American head coaches in the NFL remains two. Shell later signs with Kansas City as offensive line coach.

Feb 28—The Green Bay Packers release wide receiver Sterling Sharpe, who recently underwent surgery to repair damaged vertebrae in his neck.

Mar 8—Tampa Bay outbids the Jets for the services of free agent wide receiver Alvin Harper, formerly of Dallas. The next day the Buffalo Bills sign free agent linebacker Bryce Paup to a three-year, $7.6 million contract.

Mar 15—NFL owners vote down the Rams proposed move to St. Louis. Georgia Frontiere vows to continue her efforts to move the team.

Mar 27—Career backup Frank Reich, who

Drafted No. 5, Collins wears No. 12 for Carolina.

played 10 years with the Bills, signs a one-year contract with the expansion Carolina Panthers.

Apr 2—Herschel Walker, recently released from the Eagles for refusing a pay cut, signs with the Giants for three years and $4.8 million.

Apr 9—The World League of American Football (WLAF), shut down in 1992 for financial reasons, resumes play with six European franchises competing in a 10-week season. Rhein beats Scotland 19–17 in the league opener.

Apr 12—After paying roughly $30 million in relocation fees and another $17 million in licensing revenue, Rams owner Georgia Frontiere gets the 23 votes she needs from NFL owners to move her team St. Louis.

Apr 18—Joe Montana makes it official: After 16 NFL seasons, 40,551 passing yards and four Super Bowl titles, he is retiring.

Apr 23—At the NFL draft in New York City, the Cincinnati Bengals select Penn State running back Ki-Jana Carter with the No. 1 pick. Rounding out the top five are: USC offensive tackle Tony Boselli, to the Jacksonville Jaguars; Alcorn State quarterback Steve McNair to the Houston Oilers; Colorado receiver Michael Westbrook to Washington; and Penn State quarterback Kerry Collins to the Carolina Panthers.

June 18—The Frankfurt Galaxy wins World Bowl '95, the championship of the WLAF, defeating the Amsterdam Admirals 26–22 before 23,847 in Amsterdam's Olympic Stadium.

June 20—San Diego Charger linebacker David Griggs, 28, is killed in a one-car accident near Fort Lauderdale, Fla.

June 23—Al Davis signs a letter of intent to return the Raiders to Oakland. The move is later approved by the NFL and Oakland and Alameda County officials. The Raiders will resume occupancy of the Oakland Coliseum for the 1995 season.

July 19—Felicia Moon declines to press charges against her husband, Viking quarterback Warren Moon, after she flees the couple's home in Missouri City, Tex., following an argument in which Moon struck and choked her. The police responded to a 911 call, and term the investigation "still open."

July 20—New England quarterback Drew Bledsoe re-signs with the Patriots for seven years and $42 million. The New Orleans Saints cut kicker Morten Andersen with the hope of re-signing him at a lower salary, but the Falcons descend upon the six-time Pro Bowler and sign him to an undisclosed contract.

Sept 3—Opening day features nine new coaches, two relocated franchises and two new ones. Mike White leads the once-again Oakland

Raiders past the Chargers, 17–7; Rich Brooks guides the used-to-be LA Rams past the Packers 17–14. Tom Coughlin oversees the expansion Jaguars' tough 10–3 loss to Houston and Dom Capers' Carolina Panthers take Atlanta to overtime before succumbing 23–20.

Sept 4—Cowboy owner Jerry Jones announces a $2.5 million apparel-licensing deal with Nike that flouts NFL regulations.

Sept 6—Seattle Seahawk receiver Brian Blades is charged with manslaughter in the July 5 shooting death of his cousin Charles Blades. He insists the shooting was accidental.

Sept 10—The Dallas Cowboys sign free agent defensive back Deion Sanders to a seven-year, $25 million contract.

Sept 17—Former Saint kicker Morten Andersen boots four field goals, including the game-winner, in the Falcons 27–24 overtime win against his old team. In Denver, John Elway leads the 35th fourth-quarter comeback of his career, completing a 43-yard touchdown pass to Rod Smith on the game's final play to beat the Redskins 38–31.

Sept 18—NFL Properties files a $300 million suit against Dallas owner Jerry Jones alleging that the owner's outside marketing deals "undermine existing NFL Properties' sponsorships and contracts."

Oct 1—Quarterback Mark Brunell completes a 15-yard touchdown pass to Desmond Howard with 1:03 left to give the Jacksonville Jaguars their first victory in franchise history, 17–16 over Houston.

Oct 4—For the first time in modern league history the NFL fines two officials for blown calls in a game. Gordon Carter and Ben Montgomery are each fined one game's pay for incorrectly ruling that Pittsburgh had 12 men on the field while defending a field goal against Minnesota on Oct 1.

Oct 8—Dan Marino surpasses Fran Tarkenton to become the alltime completions leader, but the Dolphins lose to the Colts 27–24, and Marino hurts his right knee, requiring surgery which will shelve him for at least two weeks.

Oct 15—The Carolina Panthers get their first win, besting the Jets 26–15. The Colts knock off the 49ers 18–17 and knock Steve Young out of the lineup for four weeks with a shoulder injury. The following night the Denver Broncos defeat the Raiders for just the second time in 13 years, winning 27–0 at Mile High Stadium.

Nov 16, 1994—At a news conference in New York City the organizers of Major League Soccer (MLS) announce they will postpone the original start date for the league, moving the launch to April 1996, one year later than originally planned. They also disclose the charter team of financial backers for the league, which includes Kansas City Chief owner Lamar Hunt and Virginia billionaire John Kluge, among others. The league will have a single-entity ownership structure, meaning franchises will belong to MLS, and not to individual owners.

Nov 19—U.S. national team striker Eric Wynalda, who plays for VfL Bochum in the German Bundesliga, breaks his leg in a game against VfB Stuttgart and will be out for two months.

Dec 15—Tony Meola, who started in goal for the U.S. at the 1990 and '94 World Cups, signs with the Buffalo Blizzard of the indoor National Professional Soccer League.

Dec 19—Hristo Stoitchkov of Bulgaria, who co-led the 1994 World Cup in scoring, is named European Footballer of the Year.

Dec 19—Timo Liekoski is named director of coaching and player development for the U.S. Soccer Federation (USSF). He will coach the under-23 national team that will compete in the Pan Am Games and the Atlanta Olympics.

Jan 4, 1995—Midfielder Tab Ramos, who assisted on the U.S.'s game-winning goal against Colombia in the 1994 World Cup, becomes the first player to sign with Major League Soccer.

Jan 30—Brazil's Romario is named World Footballer of the Year.

Feb 24—The U.S. women's national team, pointing toward the World Championships in June, opens its 1995 season with a 7–0 thrashing of Denmark.

Apr 14—Bora Milutinovic, who coached the U.S national team to the second round of the 1994 World Cup, resigns when the USSF asks him to take on an expanded role that would include becoming the director of player development. Assistant coach Steve Sampson is named interim head coach.

May 15—In the search for a successor to Bora Milutinovic the USSF is turned down at the last minute by Carlos Queiroz, who enters negotiations then abruptly re-signs for three years to continue coaching Sporting Lisbon of the Portugese first division.

May 24—New England Patriots owner Robert Kraft joins the roster of MLS investors; he will oversee the franchise using Foxboro Stadium as its home field.

June 4—Goalkeeper Jorge Campos of Mexico signs a three-year contract to play with MLS. He will play for the Los Angeles franchise.

June 11—U.S. Cup '95 opens in Foxboro, Mass., with the U.S. defeating Nigeria 3–2 before a crowd of 22,578. Cobi Jones scores the game winner in the 67th minute.

June 15—At the second FIFA Women's World Championship in Sweden, the defending champion U.S. national team falls to Norway 1–0 in the semifinals.

June 18—Claudio Reyna scores a goal and assists on two others as the U.S. blanks Mexico 4–0 before 38,615 in Washington's RFK Stadium. Reyna, 21, was the youngest player on the '94 World Cup roster but didn't play because of an injury.

GEORGE TIEDEMANN

Foes tried everything to stop Harkes and Co. at U.S. Cup '95.

June 25—Defender Alexi Lalas, who is the first U.S. player ever to play in the top Italian league, signs a two-year contract with MLS. He will be on loan to MLS from Padova of Italy.

June 25—The U.S. ties Colombia 0–0 at Rutgers Stadium to clinch the 1995 U.S. Cup title.

July 2—The U.S. under-23 team defeats Chile 2–1 in a pre-Olympic tuneup at Hartwick College. UCLA star Ante Razov scores both goals.

July 9—With interim coach Steve Sampson still at the helm, the U.S. begins play in the Copa America, the world's oldest tournament, defeating Chile 2–1 in Paysandu, Uruguay. Eric Wynalda scores both goals.

July 11—Bolivia, which is outshot by a 2–1 margin, defeats the U.S. 1–0 in group play at the Copa America.

July 14—Needing at least a tie against heavily-favored Argentina to advance to the second round of the Copa America, the U.S. delivers a shocking 3–0 shutout of the world power. Frank Klopas, Alexi Lalas and Eric Wynalda are the goal scorers in the win that ranks with the best in U.S. soccer history.

July 17—The U.S. defeats Mexico on penalty kicks, 4–1, and advances to the semifinals of the Copa America.

July 20—World champion Brazil ends the U.S.'s stunning run through the Copa America with a 1–0 victory in the semifinals at Maldonado, Uruguay.

Aug 2—Steve Sampson is named permanent coach of the U.S. men's national team.

Aug 6—The U.S. women's national team wins U.S. Women's Cup '95, avenging their June loss to Norway with a 2–1 sudden death overtime victory in Washington, D.C. Tammy Pearlman scores the game-winner.

Aug 6—Frank Klopas and Roy Lassiter score for the U.S. in a 2–1 victory over Benfica (Portugal) in the consolation game of the Parmalat Cup at Giants Stadium.

Aug 13—Bora Milutinovic signs on—for the second time—to coach Mexico's national team. He guided Mexico to the quarterfinals of the 1986 World Cup.

Sept 26—Timo Liekoski is dismissed as Olympic (under-23) men's soccer coach.

Oct 1—Diego Maradona returns from a 15-month drug suspension to play for Boca Juniors as they defeat South Korea 2–1 in Seoul.

Oct 10—Cobi Jones, a midfielder on the U.S. national team, signs with Atletico Rentistas of the Brazilian first division, and is then loaned to Vasco da Gama of Rio de Janiero.

Oct 12—The Seattle Sounders win the 1995 A League Cup title with a 2–1 shootout victory over the Atlanta Ruckus at Memorial Stadium in Seattle.

Oct 16—MLS announces the signings of 1994 World Cup team members John Harkes, Mike Sorber and Tony Meola, bringing to five the number of World Cup starters committed to the new league.

Oct 17—At a news conference in New York City MLS unveils the nicknames and logos of the 10 franchises that will begin play on April 6.

Oct 19—Alexi Lalas is named Male Athlete of the Year by the USSF.

Oct 24—Bruce Arena, who led the University of Virginia to four consecutive NCAA men's soccer titles, is named to succeed Timo Liekoski as the U.S. Olympic coach.

Tennis

RON ANGLE

Pierce's Australian win was her first Slam title.

Nov 15, 1994—Martina Navratilova loses 6–4, 6–2 to Gabriela Sabatini in the first round of the Virginia Slims Championships and closes her career with the defeat.

Nov 20—Gabriela Sabatini and Pete Sampras close the season with victories as Sabatini takes the Virginia Slims title, defeating Lindsay Davenport 6–3, 6–2, 6–4, and Sampras wins the ATP Tour World Championship, beating Boris Becker in the final 4–6, 6–3, 7–5, 6–4.

Dec 20—Citing recurring back problems, Ivan Lendl retires.

Jan 24, 1995—Pete Sampras makes an emotional comeback in the quarterfinals of the Australian Open against Jim Courier. Unsuccessfully fighting back tears prompted by thoughts of his coach, Tim Gullikson, who has had two strokes in the past three months, Sampras battles back to beat Courier 6–7 (4-7), 6–7 (3-7), 6–3, 6–4, 6–3.

Jan 29—Andre Agassi wins his second straight Grand Slam title, defeating Pete Sampras 4–6, 6–1, 7–6 (8-6), 6–4 to win the Australian Open.

Jan 29—Mary Pierce wins the first Grand Slam title of her career, beating Arantxa Sanchez Vicario 6–3, 6–2 in the final of the Australian Open. She moves to No. 3 in the world with the victory.

Feb 20—Steffi Graf defeats Mary Pierce 6–2, 6–2 in the final of the Paris Open to reclaim the No. 1 ranking from Arantxa Sanchez Vicario.

Mar 26—In a showdown of the world No. 1 and 2 at the Lipton Championships final, Andre Agassi outduels Pete Sampras 3–6, 6–2, 7–6 (7-3). Steffi Graf wins the women's final for her fourth Lipton title.

Apr 10—Andre Agassi, who has beaten Pete Sampras in two of their three matches this year, replaces Sampras as the No. 1 player in the world. Sampras held the top spot for 82 weeks.

June 10—Though she has been plagued this season by a bad back, calf problems and the flu, Steffi Graf summons the strength to defeat Arantxa Sanchez Vicario 7–5, 4–6, 6–0 to claim her fourth French Open singles title.

June 11—Thomas Muster defeats Michael Chang 7–5, 6–2, 6-4 to take his 35th consecutive match on clay and win the French Open title.

July 1—Jeff Tarango, the 80th-ranked player on the tour, quits his third-round match at Wimbledon after accusing chair umpire Bruno Rebeuh of corruption.

July 3—Pancho Gonzales dies of cancer at the age of 67.

July 8—Steffi Graf wins her sixth Wimbledon singles title, defeating Arantxa Sanchez Vicario in the final, 4–6, 6–1, 7–5.

July 9—Pete Sampras defeats Boris Becker 6–7 (5-7), 6–2, 6–4, 6–2 to win his third consecutive Wimbledon title. He dedicates the victory to his coach Tim Gullikson, who is undergoing treatment for brain tumors.

July 17—Chris Evert is inducted into the International Tennis Hall of Fame.

July 23—Spain beats Germany 3–2 to advance to the finals of the Federation Cup, where they will meet the U.S., a 3–2 winner over France.

Aug 20—In her first tournament back since being stabbed by a demented fan in April 1993, Monica Seles blazes the field at the du Maurier Ltd. Open in Montreal. In the final she dispatches Amanda Coetzer 6–0, 6–1 for her 33rd career title.

Sept 9—The women's U.S. Open singles final is a storybook matchup of Monica Seles and Steffi Graf, the top two players in the world at the time of the attack on Seles. Graf, whose father is imprisoned in Germany on tax evasion charges, prevails 7–6 (7-5), 0–6, 6–3 for her third Grand Slam title of the year.

Sept 10—Pete Sampras becomes the fourth player with three Wimbledon and three U.S. Open titles when he defeats world No. 1 Andre Agassi 6–4, 6–3, 4–6, 7–5 in the final of the U.S. Open.

Sept 24—Todd Martin of the U.S. defeats Sweden's Thomas Enqvist 7–5, 7–5, 7–6 (6-2) to preserve a 4–1 team victory and send the U.S. into the Davis Cup finals, where they will meet Russia, a 3–2 winner over Germany.

Oct 17, 1994—Greg Welch defeats Dave Scott at the Ironman Triathlon World Championship in Kailua-Kona, Hawaii. Welch completes the 2.5-mile swim, 100-mile bike and 26-mile run in 8 hours, 20 minutes, 27 seconds, four minutes ahead of Scott. Paula Newby-Fraser wins her fourth straight women's title in 9:20:14.

Nov 6—German Silva wins the New York City Marathon in 2:11:21. Tecla Loroupe wins the women's race in 2:27:37.

Nov 6—Tony Rominger of Switzerland breaks his own world record for the one-hour bicycle ride, covering 34.357 miles, nine-tenths more than he did on his last attempt.

Nov 12—Wilma Rudolph, who won three gold medals at the 1960 Olympics in Rome, dies of cancer in Nashville.

Nov 20—The North Carolina women's soccer team wraps up its ninth consecutive NCAA title with a 5–0 blanking of Notre Dame. Senior midfielder Tisha Venturini, a three-time All-America, scores two goals as she and nine others in her class leave the school with a 97-1-1 record over four years. It is the Tar Heels 12th championship in the past 13 years.

Nov 21—The Iowa State men knock off four-time defending champion Arkansas to win the NCAA cross-country title, while the Villanova women, under new coach John Marshall and without star Carole Zajac, capture their sixth straight.

Dec 3—Three-time Tour de France winner Greg LeMond announces his retirement, citing mitochondrial myopathy, a rare muscular disease.

Dec 4—Ruben Reina wins the national men's cross-country championship in Portland, Ore. Olga Appell defeats Gwyn Coogan and eight-time champion Lynn Jennings to claim the women's title.

Dec 5—The Virginia Cavaliers win an unprecedented fourth consecutive NCAA men's soccer title. Forward A.J Wood scores in the 1–0 championship game victory over Indiana.

Dec 7—Chinese swimmer Lu Bin, who set a world record and won four gold medals at the Asian Games, is suspended for two years for failing a drug test.

Dec 9—Following the lead of teammate Hilary Lindh, who won at Vail on Dec. 2, U.S. skier

Street made fresh tracks for the U.S. in the downhill.

Picabo Street wins World Cup downhill at Lake Louise, Alberta.

Dec 11—Ty Murray wins his sixth consecutive and seventh career all-around title at the National Finals Rodeo. Other winners include Marvin Garrett in the bareback, Dan Mortensen in the saddle-bronc, Herbert Theriot in calf roping and Blaine Pederson in steer wrestling.

Jan 9, 1995—The NCAA announces it will wait one year before raising academic standards for incoming athletes. Revisions including higher grade point average requirements and higher standardized test scores will be enacted in August 1996.

Jan 21—U.S. skier Kyle Rasmussen wins his first World Cup downhill title at Wengen, Switzerland.

Jan 22—Picabo Street wins the downhill at Cortina d'Ampezzo, Italy for her second World Cup victory of the season.

Feb 8—USA Track and Field announces there will be legalized gambling on races at the Reno Air Games, the second of five indoor track events NBC will televise this year The move is designed to revive flagging interest in the sport in the U.S.

Feb 10—Though there is little gambling action at the Reno Air Games, the action on the track is spectacular enough, as Michael Johnson of the U.S. sets a world record (44.97) in the 400 meters and the following day Lance Deal breaks the world record in the 35-pound weight throw with a mark of 81 feet 8½ inches.

Feb 11—Todd Eldredge defeats Scott Davis to win the U.S. men's figure skating title in Providence, R.I. With the victory he completes his comeback from a career-threatening back injury he suffered after winning the title 1991. Nicole

CARL YARBROUGH

Bobek upends the favored Michelle Kwan for the women's title.

Feb 12—Moses Kiptanui of Kenya breaks his 3,000-meter world record by more than two seconds, running 7:35.15 in Ghent, Belgium. In Karlsruhe, Germany, China's Sun Caiyun vaults 13'6½" to set her fourth pole vault record in 15 days.

Feb 14—Allen Johnson sets a world record in the 110-meter hurdles at the Russian winter track and field championships, clocking 13.34 in Moscow.

Feb 18—Picabo Street wins her third World CUp downhill of the year, taking the race in Are, Sweden.

Feb 19—Alberto Tomba sees his seven-race winning streak in the slalom ended at Furano, Japan when he loses to Austria's Michael Tritscher. Tomba complains that the course is subpar.

Feb 19—Linford Christie of Great Britain breaks the world indoor 200-meter record, clocking 20.25. Second-place finisher Frankie Fredericks of Namibia also broke the record.

Feb 25—Scott Alexander wins the Pro Bowlers Association National Championship in Toledo, Ohio, defeating Wayne Webb 246–210 in the championship game.

Mar 4—Michael Johnson wins his 40th consecutive race at the USA/Mobil Indoor Championships in Atlanta. He runs 44.63 in the 400 meters to break his previous indoor world record of 44.97.

Mar 9—Todd Eldredge of the U.S. wins the silver medal at the World Figure Skating Championships in Birmingham, England, narrowly losing to Canada's Elvis Stojko.

Mar 11—U.S. skater Nicole Bobek, who has struggled recently with injuries, a weight problem and charges (later dropped) of breaking and entering, wins the bronze medal at the World Championships in Birmingham, England. China's Chen Lu is first and Surya Bonaly of France wins the silver. In the pairs, Todd Sand and Jenni Meno of the U.S. win the bronze.

Mar 11—Arkansas wins its 12th consecutive NCAA men's indoor track title, and the LSU women win their third straight. Another astonishing NCAA dynasty, that of the Kenyon women in Division III swimming, is extended to 12 straight national titles.

Mar 12—Picabo Street wins her fourth consecutive downhill in Lenzeheide, Switzerland, wrapping up the season title with the victory. She is the first U.S. skier in history to win a season downhill title.

Mar 14—Doug Swingley shatters Marin Buser's

1994 record by over 24 hours when he wins the Iditarod Trail Sled Dog Race in 9 days 2 hours 42 minutes and 19 seconds. He receives $52,500 and a pickup truck for winning the 1,100-mile race.

Mar 15—Picabo Street closes her astonishing downhill season with her fifth consecutive victory and her sixth of the year with a win in Bormio, Italy. Street and teammate Hilary Lindh have combined to win eight of the nine downhills this season.

Mar 18—Janet Evans wins her 45th national title at the indoor National Championships in Minneapolis, taking the 1,500-meter freestyle

Mar 18—Kenyon College wins an astonishing 16th consecutive NCAA Division III men's swimming title, with a meet-record 687 points. Second-place finisher Hope scores 259 points. Seven Kenyon swimmers win individual events.

Mar 18—The Iowa Hawkeyes clinch their fourth NCAA wrestling title in five years, outpointing second-place Oregon 134–77½. The Hawkeyes' Jeff McGinness wins the 126-pound title but Iowa's Lincoln McIlravy sees his 57-match winning streak stopped by Illinois' Steve Marianetti, who defeats him 13–10 in the 150-pound final.

Mar 19—Stanford, led by Jenny Thompson, wins its fourth consecutive NCAA Division I women's swimming title in Texas. The Cardinal rallies to defeat Michigan 497½ to 478½. Thompson wins three events and is a member of two winning relay teams.

Mar 25—Michigan wins the NCAA Division I men's swimming title in Indianapolis, with 561 points to Stanford's 475. Michigan's Tom Dolan is the star of the meet, winning the 400-yard IM and the 500- and 1,650-yard freestyles, setting U.S. records in each event.

Mar 25—Paul Tergat of Kenya wins the senior men's title at the world cross-country championships in Durham, England. Derartu Tulu of Ethiopia wins the women's title.

Mar 28—Olga Kalinovskaya leads Penn State to the NCAA men's and women's fencing title. She wins her third consecutive women's foil title and Penn State finishes with 440 points, 27 better than runner-up St. John's (N.Y.). Sean McClain of Stanford wins the men's foil title.

Apr 1—Boston University routs Maine 6–2 to win the NCAA men's hockey title, the school's first since 1978.

Apr 17—Uta Pippig wins her second consecutive Boston Marathon in 2:25:11. Cosmas N'Deti repeats as men's winner, finishing in 2:09:22.

Apr 17—Skier Vreny Schneider of Switzerland, who has 55 World Cup titles, announces her retirement. Schneider won gold medals in the

BOB MARTIN

championship game. With the victory, Aulby becomes the first bowler in history to win all four major titles—the PBA, the U.S. Open, the Tournament of Champions and the ABC Masters.

May 7—Lance Armstrong of the U.S. defeats defending champion Viatcheslav Ekimov of Russia by 2 minutes to win cycling's 1,130-mile, 12-day Tour DuPont.

May 18—Sandy Postma beats Carolyn Dorin 226–187 to win the WIBC Queens bowling tournament.

May 21—Maryland defeats Princeton 13–5 to win the NCAA women's Division I lacrosse championship.

May 29—Syracuse wins the men's NCAA Division I lacrosse title, defeating host Maryland 13–9 before a crowd of 26,229.

May 29—Tanya Harding (no, not the skater) pitches UCLA to a 4–2 victory over Arizona for the NCAA Division I softball title.

June 3—Arkansas captures its fourth consecutive team title at the men's NCAA Division I outdoor track and field championships. LSU women win their eighth straight title, the second-longest title reign in NCAA outdoor track and field history.

June 4—Cyclist Norm Alvis of the U.S. nips Italy's Maurizio De Pasquale by 55 seconds to win the CoorStates USPRO championships in Philadelphia.

June 5—Ethiopia's Haile Gebrselassie sets his third world record of the year, clocking 26:43.53 in the 10,000-meters at Hengelo, Netherlands.

June 10—Cal State-Fullerton overwhelms Southern California 11–5 to win its third NCAA Division I baseball title. Titan Mark Kotsay, an outfielder/relief pitcher who hit .563 with three home runs and ten RBIs for the tournament, wins the Most Outstanding Player award.

June 18—Michael Johnson wins the 200- and 400-meters at the USA/Mobil track and field championships in Sacramento, a feat unmatched in the 20th century.

June 20—Stanford wins the Sears Directors' Cup for all-around excellence in college athletics. The Cardinal won national titles in five sports—women's water polo, men's gymnastics, men's

slalom and giant slalom in the 1988 Olympics and the slalom in 1994 at Lillehammer.

Apr 22—Kentucky's Jenny Hansen becomes the most successful female gymnast in NCAA history when she wins four individual titles at the national championships at the University of Georgia, raising her career total to eight. The Utah women win their second consecutive team title, their ninth in the 14-year history of the event. Stanford edges Nebraska 232.4–231.525 for the men's team title. Richard Grace of Nebraska wins the all-around and parallel bar individual titles.

Apr 22—Mike Aulby captures bowling's General Tire Tournament of Champions, defeating Bob Spaulding 237–232 in Lake Zurich, Illinois.

May 6—At the U.S. National Wrestling Championships in Las Vegas, heavyweight Bruce Baumgartner wins his 16th national title, breaking a U.S. record.

May 6—UCLA beats Penn State in the NCAA men's volleyball championship to avenge its loss of the previous year.

May 6—Mike Aulby wins the American Bowling Congress Masters Tournament in Reno, Nev., defeating Mark Williams 200–187 in the

tennis, women's volleyball and women's swimming and diving—in 1994-95.

June 24—South Africa defeats New Zealand 15–12 in extra time at Johannesburg for the Rugby World Cup title.

July 12—Noureddine Morceli of Algeria breaks the world record in the 1,500-meters, clocking 3:27.37 in Nice.

July 18—Fabio Casartelli of Italy is killed in a mountain crash during the 15th stage of the Tour de France. He is the third cyclist to die during the race in the Tour's 92-year history.

July 23—Spain's Miguel Induráin becomes the only cyclist to win the Tour de France five consecutive times, defeating Alex Zulle of Switzerland by 4 minutes, 35 seconds.

Aug 4—Fifteen-year-old Brooke Bennett wins the 1,500-meter freestyle to complete a sweep of the distance free events at the U.S. outdoor championships in Pasadena. She defeats perennial champion Janet Evans in each event. In the men's competition, Tripp Schwenk sets an U.S. record in the 200-meter backstroke with a time of 1:58.33.

Aug 7—Mark Davis pulls a total of 47 pounds, 14 ounces of bass out of High Rock Lake in North Carolina to claim the $50,000 first prize at the BASS Masters Classic. Davis also becomes the first fisherman to win the Classic and angler of the year honors in the same season.

Aug 7—Triple jumper Jonathan Edwards of Great Britain becomes the first man to break 60' in the event, with a world record leap of 60'¼'' at the world championships in Göteborg, Sweden.

Aug 11—Michael Johnson of the U.S. completes an unprecedented double at the world championships in Göteborg, Sweden, when he wins the 200-meter in 19.79. He won the 400-meter on Aug. 9 in 43.39, the second-fastest time in history.

Aug 11—Ana Quirot of Cuba completes a miraculous recovery from a 1993 accident that left her with third-degree burns by winning the 800-meters at the world championships in Göteborg, Sweden.

Aug 12—The U.S. men's 4x100 freestyle relay team sets an American and world record at the Pan Pacific championships in Atlanta, clocking 3:15.11. The following day, Amy Van Dyken sets the only women's American record of the year in the 50-meter freestyle with a time of 25.03.

Aug 16—Moses Kiptanui of Kenya becomes the first man to break eight minutes in the 3,000-meter steeplechase when he runs 7:59.18 in Zurich. At the same meet, Kiptanui loses a record to Ethiopia's Haile Gebrselassie, who

shatters the 5,000-meter world mark by nearly 11 seconds with a time of 12:44.39.

Aug 18—Thirteen-year-old Dominique Moceanu becomes the youngest champion in U.S. history after winning the overall title at the U.S. Gymnastics Championships in New Orleans. Dominique Dawes wins the floor exercise and uneven bars.

Aug 23—Denis Pankratov of Russia sets his second world record of the year with a 52.32 win in the 100 butterfly at the European championships in Vienna. On June 14 in Canet, France, he set a record in the 200 butterfly, winning in 1:55.22.

Aug 26—Taiwan wins its 16th Little League World Series title with a 17–3 drubbing of Spring, Tex., at Williamsport, Pa. The game is called after four innings because of the 10-run mercy rule.

Sept 6—Yu Zhoucheng of China wins the men's one-meter springboard at the ninth Diving World Cup in Atlanta. Vera Ilyina of Russia takes the women's title.

Sept 20—The U.S. Swimming Board of Directors votes to award $50,000 to swimmers winning gold medals at the 1996 Olympics. Silver and bronze medalists will receive approximately $10,000 and $5,000 each. Relay teams will divide prize money.

Oct 7—Thirty-seven-year-old Mark Allen of Boulder, Colo., makes an astounding comeback to win his sixth Ironman Triathlon title in Kailua-Kona, Hawaii. Allen trails 24-year-old Thomas Hellriegel of Germany by 13 minutes entering the marathon stage and makes up the deficit at the 24-mile mark, moving by Hellriegel and never looking back. In the women's race, seven-time winner Paula Newby-Fraser of the U.S. suffers a physical and mental breakdown 500 feet from the finish line and is passed by Karen Smyers of Massachusetts, who wins her first Ironman title in 9:16:46. Newby-Fraser finishes fifth.

Oct 10—Cheryl Daniels wins the BPAA Women's U.S. Open at the National Sports Center in Blaine, Minn, defeating Tish Johnson 235–180 in the championship game.

Oct 10—Gary Kasparov of Russia retains his world chess championship, defeating India's Viswanathan Anand 10½ to 7½ in New York City's World Trade Center. Kasparov, making his fifth defense since he became the youngest world champion at 22 in 1985, takes home $900,000 to Anand's $450,000.

Oct 10—Dominique Moceanu wins the only individual medal for the U.S. in the World Gymnastics Championships in Sabae, Japan, taking the silver medal in the balance beam.

Baseball

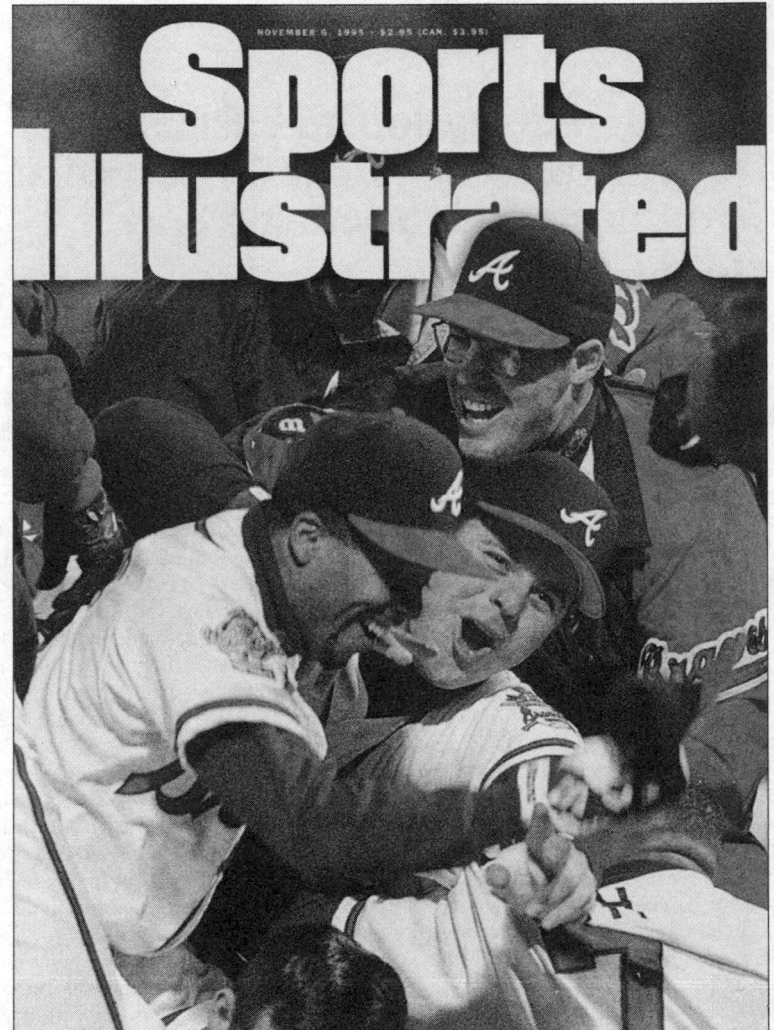

NOVEMBER 6, 1995 · $2.95 (CAN. $3.95)

Sports Illustrated

JOHN IACONO

Winners At Last

A season of redemption for baseball ended in a dramatic victory for perennial Series bridesmaids the Atlanta Braves

by Tim Kurkjian

WHEN ATLANTA centerfielder Marquis Grissom caught the final out of the 1995 World Series, the strike, the replacement players and the cancelled '94 Series seemed a lifetime away. Finally, after two crushing setbacks in the Series in this decade, the Braves were the world champions. And at least for one night, baseball was back.

It took a staunch union activist, pitcher Tom Glavine, to deliver the first major sports championship to Atlanta with a near-perfect performance in Game 6. Glavine stopped the mighty Cleveland Indians on one hit over eight innings and David Justice's home run in the sixth inning gave the Braves a 1–0 win. Reliever Mark Wohlers got the final three outs, sending a sellout crowd at Atlanta-Fulton County Stadium into a frenzy. "This was a great series for us and great for baseball," Wohlers said, dripping with champagne during the celebration. "I want to play this game until they plant me in the ground."

The '95 Series will be remembered for great pitching, mostly by the spectacular Atlanta staff. The Indians, making their first World Series appearance since 1954, batted only .179 and scored only 19 runs in the six games. In four of the six, they managed six or fewer hits. This was astonishing considering Cleveland had hit .291 with 207 homers in the regular season and their offense was being called the best baseball had seen since Cincinnati's Big Red Machine. But the Indians, who went 100–44 in the strike-shortened season, were no match for the crafty Atlanta hurlers, who made the Cleveland hitters look silly with a barrage of changeups and perfectly-located fastballs.

The game's best pitcher, Atlanta's Greg Maddux, was magnificent in Game 1, firing a two-hitter (both opposite-field singles), walking no one and allowing only four balls out of the infield in a 3–2 win. Both runs were unearned. Cleveland's Orel Hershiser was nearly Maddux's match for six innings, but he walked the first two hitters in the seventh, then took himself out of the game because he had lost the release point on his pitches. Another walk followed a run-scoring ground out and a squeeze bunt gave Maddux a 3–1 lead. It seemed like 30–1.

Glavine started Game 2, and he didn't make many mistakes, either. One came in

until Braves first baseman Fred McGriff homered in the sixth and Ryan Klesko homered in the seventh. The Braves scored three times in the eighth—twice off tiring starter Charles Nagy—to take a 6–5 lead. But the Indians tied it in the last of the eighth on a run-scoring double by Sandy Alomar off Wohlers, who proceeded to end the threat by striking out Omar Vizquel on three pitches and inducing Carlos Baerga to ground out.

That started an epic duel of closers, Wohlers against Cleveland's Jose Mesa. "When's the last time you saw two closers throwing 100 miles an hour each for three innings?" Hershiser asked. Mesa won the duel, but Wohlers didn't get the loss. He was replaced by Alejandro Pena to start the 11th. Baerga drilled a lead-off double. Following an intentional walk to Belle, Murray rifled Pena's first pitch to center field, scoring Baerga for a 7–6 win. "They were fighting for a championship," said Hershiser. "And we were fighting for our lives."

The Braves had more fight in them the next night. Steve Avery, chosen to start so Maddux could get another day's rest, quashed the critics by allowing three hits in six innings of a 5–2 win. The hitting star was Justice, whose two-run single in the seventh atoned for a mostly disappointing postseason at that point.

With Maddux pitching in Game 5, the Series was supposed to be all but over. But it was obvious early on that this wouldn't be the same kind of dominant performance

the second inning when Eddie Murray drilled a belt-high fastball over the left field fence for a 2–0 lead. It gave Murray a World Series homer in three decades; Yogi Berra and Joe DiMaggio are the only other players who can make that claim. But the Braves tied it off Dennis Martinez in the third, then took a 4–2 lead in the sixth on a two-run homer by catcher Javy Lopez. Glavine and three relievers, the last being Wohlers, held on for a 4–3 victory.

So it was on to Jacobs Field for Game 3. And the first Series game played in Cleveland since 1954 was a classic despite a wind chill temperature at game time of 29°. The Indians came out flying, rocking Atlanta starter John Smoltz for six hits and four runs in 2⅓ innings. The 4–1 lead seemed safe

RICHARD MACKSON

Maddux was unhittable in Series Game 1, but mortal in Game 5.

Maddux posted in Game 1. In the first, Cleveland's Albert Belle lined a two-run homer to right for a 2–0 lead. The Braves tied it in the fifth, but the Indians' Jim Thome and Manny Ramirez singled home runs with two out in the sixth for a 4–2 lead. Hershiser allowed one earned run in eight innings of a 5–4 victory, sending the Series back to Atlanta for Game 6 and Glavine's magnificent Series-clinching performance.

"From day one this year, we were on a mission," Glavine said. "We knew that the only thing that would make our season a success would be a World Series title."

Finally, they got it.

The long-suffering Indians fell two wins shy of the ring. They advanced to the World Series by eliminating the darlings of the playoffs, the Mariners, who were making their first postseason trip in their 19-year history. Seattle was 12½ games out of first place in the AL West on Aug. 15, came back to beat the Angels in a one-game playoff, lost the first two games to the Yankees in the Division Series, then swept the next three for the right to play for the pennant.

The Mariners won Game 1 in Seattle behind rookie Bob Wolcott, who was starting only because the rest of the staff was exhausted from overwork. Wolcott pitched seven strong innings in a 3–2 win—the fourth of his major league career. Hershiser threw a gem in Game 2—four hits in eight innings—to spark a 5–2 win for the Indians. The ALCS shifted to Cleveland where Mariner rightfielder Jay Buhner bashed a three-run homer off reliever Eric Plunk in the 11th for a 5–2 victory. Indians fans were worried. Seattle fans repeated their battle cry: Refuse to Lose.

But that was it for the Mariners. Ken Hill and relief help blanked Seattle in Game 4, 7–0, and the Indians took a 3–2 lead back to Seattle with a 3–2 win in Game 5. Even 50,000-plus fans screaming inside the Kingdome couldn't help the M's in Game 6. Randy Johnson, the AL's best pitcher, gave up an unearned run in the fifth, then three more in the eighth—two of them scoring on a passed ball as Cleveland's Kenny Lofton made a daring dash home from second on the play. Dennis Martinez, 40, outdueled Johnson in the 4–0 victory.

The Braves had a much easier time in the NLCS. Their World's Greatest Pitching Staff enjoyed its finest hour against the formidable Reds, holding them to five runs in the four-game sweep (an NLCS record for fewest runs scored in a four-game series). Atlanta's awesome starting pitching staff compiled a 1.29 ERA and the bullpen, a disappointment in previous postseasons, allowed just one run in 11 innings. "I'm numb, I'm dumbfounded," said Cincinnati shortstop Barry Larkin, wondering how a series that was supposed to go seven games could end so quickly. How could this happen? Well, Cincinnati's 3-4 hitters, Ron Gant and Reggie Sanders, went a combined 5 for 32 and Sanders struck out 10 times. In his seven postseason games this year, Sanders struck out 19 times—four more than Tony Gwynn did all year.

Yet the MVP of the NLCS wasn't a pitcher, it was Mike Devereaux, a reserve outfielder who was acquired in late August from the White Sox. In Game 1, Devereaux's

DAVID LIAM KYLE

At 37, Hershiser showed he can still get them out.

11th-inning single gave Atlanta a 2–1 win. The Braves also won Game 2 in extra innings, 6–2, on a run-scoring wild pitch by Mark Portugal followed by a three-run homer by catcher Javy Lopez. Another Atlanta catcher, Charlie O'Brien, nailed a three-run homer in Game 3 to give Maddux and the Braves a 5–2 win. They clinched the next night, 6–0, when Devereaux hit a three-run homer in the seventh to support Steve Avery's standout pitching.

The best series of the postseason came in the divisional playoffs, a system widely derided because it allowed a wild-card team into the playoffs for the first time. As it turned out, it was a great idea. The Mariners and the Yankees, the wild-card team, played one of the greatest series in baseball history.

The Bombers won the first two games in New York; the second, a 7–5, 15-inning marathon, was the longest postseason game (five hours and 12 minutes) ever. Only two teams had ever lost the first two games of a five-game series in a non-strike season and come back to win. But the Mariners were heading home to the Kingdome, where they had been invincible down the stretch. They won Game 3, 7–4, behind Johnson. The Mariners fell behind 5–0 after three innings of Game 4 but rallied to win 11–8. DH Edgar Martinez's second homer of the game—a grand slam off John Wetteland in the eighth—gave him seven RBIs, the most ever in a postseason game.

In Game 5, the Yankees took a 4–2 lead into the eighth behind David Cone. But Ken Griffey Jr. crushed his fifth homer of the series—making him the first player to hit that many in a five-game series—to bring the

Mariners within a run at 4–3. It was the 22nd homer in the series, another record in a series of any length. A tiring Cone walked in another run to tie the score. Johnson, working on one day's rest, made his first relief appearance since 1993 and bailed the Mariners out of a jam in the ninth. He struck out the side in the 10th, but Randy Velarde's RBI single gave the Yankees a 5–4 lead in the 11th. New York's Jack McDowell, also working on one day's rest, entered in the 10th inning for the first relief appearance of his major league career. Joey Cora beat out a bunt to start the 11th. Griffey singled. Martinez drilled a double down the leftfield line. Griffey scored from first to win it 6–5. The Kingdome exploded.

"The guys put their careers on the line. One pitch could have blown out their arms," Cone said. "You hear the rap people put on the modern-day player—I, I, I and me, me, me—well, this series was anything but that. If this doesn't do a lot to diminish the greedy ballplayer image, I don't know what will."

The Atlanta-Colorado series couldn't match its AL counterpart, but it was great theater nonetheless. Atlanta won in four games, but the first three games were decided in the final at bat—a first in postseason history. The Braves won the first two in Colorado as rookie third baseman Chipper Jones homered in the ninth to win Game 1, then doubled to start the ninth in Game 2, sparking a four-run rally that gave Atlanta a 7–4 win. The wild-card Rockies, who reached the postseason faster (in their third season) than any expansion team in history, fought back, winning Game 3 in 10 innings, 7–5, after blowing another lead in the ninth. But Brave first baseman Fred McGriff homered twice in Game 4, and Marquis Grissom went 5 for 5 to lead a 10–4 victory.

The other two series ended quickly. The Indians swept the Red Sox, who ran their postseason losing streak to a record 13 games. The series turned in Game 1 when Cleveland backup catcher Tony Pena homered in the 13th inning off Zane Smith for a 5–4 win. The Indians won the next two 4–0 and 8–2. The Reds had an even easier time with the underachieving Dodgers. They trailed for a total of three innings en route to a 7–2, 5–4 and 10–1 sweep.

The terrific play in the divisional series followed a fascinating regular season—especially if you're a fan of lots of hitting and Oriole shortstop Cal Ripken Jr.

On Sept. 6 Ripken became the greatest ironman in major league history when he played in his 2,131st consecutive game, passing the great Lou Gehrig. It was time for celebration not only in Baltimore but also all across baseball, when the banner on the warehouse beyond the rightfield wall at Camden Yards was changed to 2,131 before the bottom of the fifth inning. During a 22-minute stoppage in play—perhaps the most stirring, emotional 22 minutes in baseball history—Ripken made five curtain calls, took off his jersey and hat and presented them to his two young children, and then, after much prodding from his teammates, circled the warning track with a victory lap. He slapped hands with fans, and hugged opposing players and umpires.

"It was like an out-of-body experience," said Ripken. "It's like when your wife has a baby. You're standing there watching and thinking, This can't be happening to me.

This can't be my wife. This can't be my baby. I kept thinking this was happening to someone else. This couldn't be happening to me." For one night, all was right in baseball and America.

Ripken wasn't the only player to enter the record books in 1995. His former teammate from Baltimore, Eddie Murray of the Indians, became the 19th player in history to reach 3,000 hits—guaranteeing him a spot in Cooperstown. The Dodgers' Ramon Martinez pitched the only no-hitter of the season, dominating the Marlins on July 14, 7–0. But the best game of the season was pitched by his little brother. On June 3, Montreal's Pedro Martinez pitched nine perfect innings against the Padres, but the score was tied after nine innings. He gave up a hit to start the 10th and was taken out. Under the new rules of baseball, he won't be credited with a perfect game or a no-hitter.

There were a few other pitching highlights. Maddux, a lock for his fourth straight NL Cy Young Award, went 19–2 with a 1.63 ERA, and became the first pitcher since Walter Johnson (1918–19) to post consecutive seasons with an ERA under 1.80. Maddux struck out 181 and walked 23—the greatest strikeout-to-walk ratio of any pitcher in history with 200 or more innings. Seattle's Johnson was nearly as dominant, going 18–2 and leading the league in ERA (2.48) and strikeouts (294). Baltimore's Mike Mussina won 19 games, preventing Johnson from becoming the first AL pitcher since Hal Newhouser (1945) to finish first in the league in wins, ERA and strikeouts. Mussina was also part of an Oriole staff that tied the AL record (held by the '74 Orioles) with five straight shutouts to end the season. As for ending games, no one topped Cleveland's Jose Mesa, who saved 46.

For starters there was no one more intriguing than Dodger pitcher Hideo Nomo, the second Japanese player ever to play in the major leagues. Nomo, 26, dazzled NL hitters all season but was virtually unhittable in the first half, going 6–1 and starting the All-Star Game in Arlington, Texas, against Seattle's Johnson. Nomo, using a delivery called the Tornado, literally turned his back to the hitter

Wakefield and his baffling knuckleball produced 16 wins in 1995.

but his home run–per–at bat ratio wasn't the highest in the league. That belonged to Oakland's Mark McGwire, who hit 39 in 317 at bats—the greatest ratio ever. Belle also was the eighth player in history to amass 100 extra-base hits. San Diego's Tony Gwynn won his sixth batting title (.368) and became the first NL player to hit at least .350 for three consecutive seasons since St. Louis's Ducky Medwick had his third straight in 1937. Seattle's Edgar Martinez won the AL batting title (.356). Bichette led the league in homers (40) and RBIs (128) and was third in hitting (.340)— the last NL player to match those totals in a season was Duke Snider in 1954.

Another disappointing season in Detroit (60–84) forced the resignation of manager Sparky Anderson, who had guided the Tigers since 1979 but hadn't been to the playoffs since 1987. He wasn't the only manager on the move. The White Sox's Gene Lamont was canned on June 2. The Cardinals' Joe Torre was axed two weeks later, but neither team improved much with the changes.

The White Sox were supposed to be a major player in the AL Central race but lost seven of their first eight and were never a factor, finishing 32 games out. But even in a good year Chicago would have been no match for Cleveland. The Indians won 15 of their first 21 to open a four-game lead that wasn't challenged. They set a major league record for the largest lead—30 games.

There was only slightly more suspense in the AL East. Boston, picked by most to finish fourth, took the lead for good on May 13. A

during his windup, then exploded toward the plate with, among other pitches, a demonic forkball. Trailed all season by a huge media contingent from Japan, Nomo tailed off in the second half but finished 13–6 and led the NL in strikeouts (236).

The comeback story of the season was Boston knuckleballer Tim Wakefield. He was perhaps the worst pitcher in Triple A last season, but he appeared from nowhere in late May and carried the Red Sox staff for nearly three months. He was 14–1 and a leading candidate for the AL Cy Young in mid-August, but the magic finally wore off, and he faltered down the stretch to finish 16–8.

The rest of the season belonged to the hitters. Despite the 144-game schedule, 60 players hit 20 homers, 21 hit 30 homers, four hit 40, and Cleveland's Albert Belle hit 50—

12-game winning streak in early August opened a 10-game lead that made September almost irrelevant. The East's underachiever was Baltimore, which finished 15 games out.

The best race in the AL came in the West. The Angels, picked to finish last in the division, moved into a tie for the lead on July 2, scored 201 runs in that month and opened a 10½-game lead by Aug. 15. But 36 days later they had fallen into a first-place tie with the Mariners. It marked the quickest disappearance in this century of a lead that big. After dropping three games behind Seattle, the Angels won their last five games to force a one-game playoff. But Seattle's Johnson beat them 9–1 on a three-hitter with 12 strikeouts.

The Braves ran away with the NL East title, winning by 21 games. But it didn't come easily, at least not initially. The Phillies set a National League record by not losing two games in a row the first 34 games of the year. But as soon as their sizzling start (37–18) ended, they went nearly a month without winning two in a row. Atlanta took over first on July 5 and never looked back.

The Reds lost their first six games, and eight of their first nine, but won their next six and 22 of their next 27 to take over first place for good on June 5. They won by nine games over the Astros, who were derailed in late July when star first baseman Jeff Bagwell broke his left hand.

The Giants were in contention until star third baseman Matt Williams broke his right foot with a foul ball on June 3 and was lost for almost three months. Without

McGwire knocked out an amazing 39 home runs in just 317 at bats.

him the Giants weren't a serious factor, nor were the Padres, other than a brief surge in mid-August. That left the Rockies and the Dodgers to fight it out. L.A. won the division on the second-to-last day of the season. The Rockies came from six runs down against the Giants on the last day of the season to win 10–9 and secure the wild-card.

In the end, baseball was left with one burning question: Was this season exciting enough to bring the fans back? It's a tough question to answer, but if next season has as many home runs, as many postseason thrills and a hero as simply decent as Ripken, America's pastime might have a chance to be just that again.

JOHN IACONO

Final Standings

National League

EASTERN DIVISION

Team	Won	Lost	Pct	GB	Home	Away
Atlanta	90	54	.625	—	44-28	46-26
New York	69	75	.479	21	40-32	29-43
Philadelphia	69	75	.479	21	35-37	34-38
Florida	67	76	.469	22½	37-34	30-42
Montreal	66	78	.458	24	31-41	35-37

CENTRAL DIVISION

Team	Won	Lost	Pct	GB	Home	Away
Cincinnati	85	59	.590	—	44-28	41-31
Houston	76	68	.528	9	36-36	40-32
Chicago	73	71	.507	12	34-38	39-33
St. Louis	62	81	.434	22½	39-33	23-48
Pittsburgh	58	86	.403	27	31-41	27-45

WESTERN DIVISION

Team	Won	Lost	Pct	GB	Home	Away
Los Angeles	78	66	.542	—	39-33	39-33
Colorado	77	67	.535	1	44-28	33-39
San Diego	70	74	.486	8	40-32	30-38
San Francisco	67	77	.465	11	37-35	30-42

American League

EASTERN DIVISION

Team	Won	Lost	Pct	GB	Home	Away
Boston	86	58	.597	—	42-30	44-28
New York	79	65	.549	7	46-26	33-39
Baltimore	71	73	.493	15	36-36	35-37
Detroit	60	84	.417	26	35-37	25-47
Toronto	56	88	.389	30	29-43	27-45

CENTRAL DIVISION

Team	Won	Lost	Pct	GB	Home	Away
Cleveland	100	44	.694	—	54-18	46-26
Kansas City	70	74	.486	30	35-37	35-37
Chicago	68	76	.472	32	38-34	30-44
Milwaukee	65	79	.451	35	33-39	32-40
Minnesota	56	88	.389	44	29-43	27-45

WESTERN DIVISION

Team	Won	Lost	Pct	GB	Home	Away
California	78	66	.542	—	39-33	39-33
Seattle	78	66	.542	—	45-27	33-39
Texas	74	70	.514	4	41-31	33-39
Oakland	67	77	.465	11	38-34	29-43

1995 Playoffs

National League Divisional Playoffs

Oct 3 ....Atlanta 5 at Colorado 4
Oct 4 ....Atlanta 7 at Colorado 4
Oct 6 ....Colorado 7 at Atlanta 5 (10 innings)
Oct 7 ....Colorado 4 at Atlanta 10

(Atlanta won series 3–1.)

Oct 3 ....Cincinnati 7 at Los Angeles 2
Oct 4 ....Cincinnati 5 at Los Angeles 4
Oct 6 ....Los Angeles 1 at Cincinnati 10

(Cincinnati won series 3–0.)

National League Championship Series

Oct 10 ....Atlanta 2 at Cincinnati 1 (11 innings)
Oct 11 ....Atlanta 6 at Cincinnati 2 (10 innings)
Oct 13 ....Cincinnati 2 at Atlanta 5
Oct 14 ....Cincinnati 0 at Atlanta 6

(Atlanta won series 4–0.)

GAME 1

Atlanta	0 0 0	0 0 0	0 0 1	0 1	—2
Cincinnati	0 0 0	1 0 0	0 0 0	0 0	—1

WP—Wohlers. **LP**—Jackson. **Save**—McMichael.
LOB—Atlanta 9, Cincinnati 6. **2B**—Cincinnati: Larkin (1), Morris (1), Howard (1). **3B**—Cincinnati: Larkin (1). **CS**—Atlanta: Klesko. **Sac**—Atlanta: Polonia. **GIDP**—Cincinnati: Boone (2), Walton, Santiago, Sanders. **T**—3:18. **A**—40,382.
Recap: Tom Glavine and Pete Schourek pitched well, giving up one earned run apiece in 7 and 8⅓ innings, respectively. Trailing 2–1 in the ninth, Atlanta tied it up when Chipper Jones singled, went to third on Fred McGriff's single and scored on David Justice's grounder to second. Atlanta won in the 11th when McGriff walked, took second on Luis Polonia's sacrifice fly and then scored on Mike Devereaux's single.

GAME 2

Atlanta	1 0 0	1 0 0	0 0 0	4	—6
Cincinnati	0 0 0	0 2 0	0 0 0	0	—2

WP—McMichael. **LP**—Portugal.
E—Atlanta: Smoltz (1); Cincinnati: Sanders (1). **LOB**—Atlanta 8, Cincinnati 9. **2B**—Atlanta: McGriff (3), Devereaux (1); Cincinnati: Larkin (2). **HR**—Atlanta: Lopez (1). **SB**—Atlanta: Smoltz (1); Cincinnati: Branson (1), Harris (1), Larkin (1), Morris (1). **CS**—Cincinnati: Howard, Sanders. **Sac**—Cincinnati: Branson. **GIDP**—Atlanta: Devereaux. **T**—3:26. **A**—44,624.
Recap: After Jeff Branson stole home—a NLCS first—in the fifth inning, the game went into extra innings tied 2–2. In the top of the 10th, Mark Lemke singled off reliever Mark Portugal and eventually scored on a wild pitch. Fred McGriff and David Justice scored when Javy Lopez homered down the leftfield line.

National League Championship Series *(Cont.)*

GAME 3

Cincinnati	0	0	0	0	0	0	0	1	1	—2
Atlanta	0	0	0	0	0	3	2	0	x	—5

WP—Maddux. **LP**—Wells.
E—Atlanta: Grissom (1). **LOB**—Cincinnati 9, Atlanta 8. **2B**—Cincinnati: Branson (1); Atlanta: McGriff (4). **HR**—Atlanta: Jones (1), O'Brien (1). **SB**—Atlanta: Jones (1). **CS**—Cincinnati: Larkin. **Sac**—Cincinnati: Howard. **GIDP**—Atlanta: Lemke. **T**—2:42. **A**—51,424.
Recap: Greg Maddux went eight strong innings, giving up just one earned run. Chipper Jones had three hits for the Braves, including a two-run homer in the seventh.

GAME 4

Cincinnati	0	0	0	0	0	0	0	0	0	—0
Atlanta	0	0	1	0	0	0	5	0	x	—6

WP—Avery. **LP**—Schourek.
E—Cincinnati: Larkin (1); Atlanta: Belliard (1). **LOB**—Cincinnati 4, Atlanta 11. **2B**—Atlanta: Lopez (1). **3B**—Atlanta: Grissom (1). **HR**—Atlanta: Devereaux (1). **GIDP**—Cincinnati: Duncan, Sanders, Gant; Atlanta: Devereaux. **T**—2:54. **A**—52,067.
Recap: In a pitchers' duel, Steve Avery and Pete Schourek each went six innings, Avery giving up no earned runs and only two hits, Schourek just one earned run. In the seventh, Marquis Grissom's triple to left center opened the door for Atlanta to storm ahead. Grissom scored on a passed ball, then Mike Devereaux hit a three-run homer to bury the Reds.

American League Divisional Playoffs

American League Championship Series

GAME 1

Cleveland	0	0	1	0	0	0	1	0	0	—2
Seattle	0	2	0	0	0	0	1	0	x	—3

WP—Wolcott. **LP**—Martinez.
E—Cleveland: Thome (1). **LOB**—Cleveland 12, Seattle 7. **2B**—Cleveland: Sorrento (1); Seattle: Cora (1), Buhner (1), Sojo (1), Griffey (1). **3B**—Cleveland: Lofton (1). **HR**—Seattle: Belle (1); Seattle: Blowers (1). **CS**—Seattle: Griffey (1). **GIDP**—Cleveland: Sorrento; Seattle: E. Martinez. **T**—3:07. **A**—57,065.
Recap: Bob Wolcott, returned to the roster for the postseason, pitched seven strong innings, yielding just two earned runs. Mike Blowers's two-run homer in the second was the single big blow for the Mariners.

GAME 2

Cleveland	0	0	0	0	2	2	0	1	0	—5
Seattle	0	0	0	0	0	1	0	0	1	—2

WP—Hershiser. **LP**—Belcher.
E—Seattle: Sojo (1). **LOB**—Cleveland 10, Seattle 7. **3B**—Cleveland: Alomar (1). **HR**—Cleveland: Ramirez 2 (2); Seattle: Griffey (1), Buhner (1). **SB**—Cleveland: Vizquel (1); Seattle: Coleman (1). **GIDP**—Cleveland: Sorrento, Thome. **T**—3:14. **A**—58,144.
Recap: Orel Hershiser gave up just one earned run and Manny Ramirez went 4 for 4 with two homers to power the Indians.

GAME 3

Seattle	0	1	1	0	0	0	0	0	0	3	—5
Cleveland	0	0	0	1	0	0	0	1	0	0	—2

WP—Charlton. **LP**—Tavarez.
E—Seattle: Buhner (1); Cleveland: Alomar (1), Espinoza (1). **LOB**—Seattle 5, Cleveland 6. **3B**—Cleveland: Lofton (1). **HR**—Seattle: Buhner 2 (3). **SB**—Seattle: Griffey (1), Cora (1); Cleveland: Lofton (1). **CS**—Cleveland: Perry; Seattle: E. Martinez. **Sac**—Cleveland: Vizquel. **T**—3:18. **A**—43,643.
Recap: Cleveland suffered its first extra-inning loss of the year on a three-run homer by Jay Buhner in the top of the 11th. Randy Johnson struck out six in eight innings.

GAME 4

Seattle	0	0	0	0	0	0	0	0	0	—0
Cleveland	3	1	2	0	0	1	0	0	x	—7

WP—Hill. **LP**—Benes.
E—Seattle: Wilson (1). **LOB**—Seattle 9, Cleveland 7. **2B**—Seattle: Buhner (2); Cleveland: Vizquel (1). **HR**—Cleveland: Murray (1), Thome (1). **SB**—Seattle: Coleman (2), Griffey (2); Cleveland: Lofton (2), Kirby (1). **Sac**—Cleveland: Lofton. **GIDP**—Cleveland: Sorrento, Kirby. **T**—3:30. **A**—43,686.
Recap: Ken Hill was superlative, pitching seven scoreless innings while Andy Benes got shelled, giving up six earned runs in 2⅓ innings.

American League Championship Series *(Cont.)*

GAME 5

Seattle	0	0	1	0	1	0	0	0	0	—2
Cleveland	1	0	0	0	0	2	0	0	x	—3

WP—Hershiser (2). **LP**—Bosio. **Save**—Mesa. **E**—Seattle: T. Martinez (1), Griffey (1); Cleveland: Belle (2), Sorrento (2). **LOB**—Seattle 9, Cleveland 11. **2B**—Seattle: Griffey (2), Diaz (1); Cleveland: Murray (1), Alomar (1). **HR**—Cleveland: Thome (2). **SB**—Seattle: Cora (2), Coleman (3); Cleveland: Vizquel 2 (3), Lofton 2 (4). **Sac**—Seattle: Strange (1); Cleveland: Kirby (1). **GIDP**—Cleveland: Ramirez. **T**—3:37. **A**—43,607. **Recap:** Orel Hershiser struck out eight to continue his perfect record in the postseason. Eddie Murray doubled to right and scored on Thome's homer in the sixth.

GAME 6

Cleveland	0	0	0	0	1	0	0	3	0	—4
Seattle	0	0	0	0	0	0	0	0	0	—0

WP—D. Martinez. **LP**—Johnson. **E**—Seattle: Cora (1). **LOB**—Cleveland 4, Seattle 6. **2B**—Cleveland: Belle (1), Pena (1); Seattle: Sojo (1). **HR**—Cleveland: Baerga (1). **SB**—Cleveland: Lofton (5); Seattle: Coleman (4), E. Martinez (1). **GIDP**—Seattle: Sojo. **T**—2:54. **A**—58,489. **Recap:** 40-year-old Dennis Martinez got the first postseason victory of his long career, pitching seven shutout innings to become the oldest pitcher to win an LCS game. AL stolen-base king Kenny Lofton scored from second base on a passed ball in the eighth.

Composite Box Scores

National League Championship Series

ATLANTA

BATTING	AB	R	H	HR	RBI	Avg
Polonia	2	0	1	0	1	.500
Jones	16	3	7	1	3	.438
McGriff	16	5	7	0	0	.438
O'Brien	5	1	2	1	3	.400
Lopez	14	2	5	1	3	.357
Devereaux	13	2	4	1	5	.308
Belliard	11	1	3	0	0	.273
Justice	11	1	3	0	1	.273
Grissom	19	2	5	0	0	.263
Lemke	18	2	3	0	1	.167
8 others	24	0	2	0	0	.083
Totals	149	19	42	4	17	.282

PITCHING	G	IP	H	BB	SO	ERA
Avery	2	6	2	4	6	0.00
Pena	3	3	2	1	4	0.00
McMichael	3	2⅔	0	1	2	0.00
Clontz	1	⅓	1	0	0	0.00
Maddux	1	8	7	2	4	1.13
Glavine	1	7	7	2	5	1.29
Wohlers	4	5	2	0	8	1.80
Smoltz	1	7	7	2	2	2.57
Totals	4	39	28	12	31	1.15

CINCINNATI

BATTING	AB	R	H	HR	RBI	Avg
Harris	2	0	2	0	1	1.000
Taubensee	2	0	1	0	0	.500
Wells	2	0	1	0	0	.500
Larkin	18	1	7	0	0	.389
Howard	8	0	2	0	1	.250
Lewis	4	0	1	0	0	.250
Santiago	13	0	3	0	0	.231
Boone	14	1	3	0	0	.214
Gant	16	1	3	0	1	.188
Morris	12	0	2	0	1	.167
Sanders	16	0	2	0	0	.125
Branson	9	2	1	0	0	.111
6 others	18	0	0	0	0	.000
Totals	134	5	28	0	4	.209

PITCHING	G	IP	H	BB	SO	ERA
Burba	2	3⅓	4	0	0	0.00
Brantley	2	2⅔	0	2	1	0.00
Carrasco	1	1⅓	1	0	3	0.00
Schourek	2	14⅓	14	3	13	1.26
Smiley	1	5	5	0	1	3.60
Wells	1	6	8	2	3	4.50
Jackson	3	2⅓	5	4	1	23.14
Hernandez	1	⅔	3	0	0	27.00
Portugal	1	1	3	1	0	36.00
Totals	4	37	42	16	22	4.62

American League Championship Series

CLEVELAND

BATTING	AB	R	H	HR	RBI	Avg
Lofton	24	4	11	0	3	.458
Baerga	25	3	10	1	4	.400
Pena	6	1	2	0	0	.333
Ramirez	21	2	6	2	2	.286
Alomar	15	0	4	0	1	.267
Thome	15	2	4	2	5	.267
Murray	24	2	6	1	3	.250
Belle	18	1	4	1	1	.222
Kirby	5	2	1	0	0	.200
Sorrento	13	2	2	0	0	.154
Espinoza	8	1	1	0	0	.125
Vizquel	23	2	2	0	2	.087
2 others	9	1	0	0	0	.000
Totals	206	23	53	7	21	.257

PITCHING	G	IP	H	BB	SO	ERA
Hill	1	7	5	3	6	0.00
Assenmacher	3	1⅓	0	1	2	0.00
Poole	1	1	0	0	2	0.00
Nagy	1	8	5	0	6	1.12
Hershiser	2	14	9	3	15	1.29
D. Martinez	2	13⅓	10	3	7	2.03
Mesa	4	4	3	1	1	2.25
Tavarez	4	3⅓	3	1	2	2.70
Plunk	3	2	1	3	2	9.00
Totals	6	55	37	15	46	1.64

SEATTLE

BATTING	AB	R	H	HR	RBI	Avg
Diaz	7	0	3	0	0	.429
Griffey Jr.	21	2	7	1	2	.333
Buhner	23	5	7	3	5	.304
Sojo	20	2	5	0	1	.250
Cora	23	2	4	0	0	.174
Blowers	18	1	4	1	2	.222
T. Martinez	22	0	3	0	0	.136
Coleman	20	0	2	0	0	.100
E. Martinez	23	0	2	0	0	.087
Wilson	16	0	0	0	0	.000
Strange	4	0	0	0	0	.000
4 others	4	0	0	0	0	.000
Totals	201	12	37	5	10	.184

PITCHING	G	IP	H	BB	SO	ERA
Charlton	3	6	1	1	5	0.00
Nelson	3	3	3	5	3	0.00
Risley	3	2⅔	2	1	2	0.00
Johnson	2	15⅓	12	2	13	2.35
Ayala	2	3⅔	3	3	3	2.45
Wolcott	1	7	8	5	2	2.57
Wells	1	3	2	2	2	3.00
Bosio	1	5⅓	7	2	3	3.38
Belcher	1	5⅔	9	2	1	6.35
Benes	1	2⅓	6	2	3	23.14
Totals	6	54	53	25	37	3.33

1995 World Series

Oct 21 ....Cleveland 2 at Atlanta 3
Oct 22 ....Cleveland 3 at Atlanta 4
Oct 24 ....Atlanta 6 at Cleveland 7 (11 innings)

Oct 25 ....Atlanta 5 at Cleveland 2
Oct 26 ....Atlanta 4 at Cleveland 5
Oct 28 ....Cleveland 0 at Atlanta 1

(Atlanta won series 4–2.)

GAME 1

Cleveland	1 0 0	0 0 0	0 0 1	—2
Atlanta	0 1 0	0 0 0	2 0 x	—3

WP—Maddux. **LP**—Hershiser.
E—Atlanta: Belliard (1), McGriff (1). **LOB**—Cleveland 1, Atlanta 4. **HR**—Atlanta: McGriff (1). **SB**—Cleveland: Lofton (2). **Sac**—Atlanta: Belliard.
T—2:37. **A**—51,876.
Recap: Greg Maddux shut down Cleveland, holding them to their lowest hit total (2) this season. Orel Hershiser suffered his first postseason defeat after seven victories. Kenny Lofton tied a series record, stealing two bases in the first inning.

GAME 2

Cleveland	0 2 0	0 0 0	1 0 0	—3
Atlanta	0 0 2	0 0 2	0 0 x	—4

WP—Glavine. **LP**—Martinez. **Save**—Wohlers.
E—Cleveland: Martinez (1), Belle (1); Atlanta: Jones (1), Devereaux (1). **LOB**—Cleveland 9, Atlanta 7. **2B**—Atlanta: Jones (1). **HR**—Cleveland: Murray (1); Atlanta: Lopez (1). **SB**—Cleveland: Lofton 2 (4), Vizquel (1). **Sac**—Atlanta: Jones. **GIDP**—Atlanta: McGriff, Belliard. **T**—3:17. **A**—51,877.
Recap: Javy Lopez hit a two-run homer to center in the sixth inning to put the Braves ahead. Mark Wohlers got the save in 1¼ innings.

GAME 3

Atlanta	1 0 0	0 0 1	1 3 0	0 0	—6
Cleveland	2 0 2	0 0 0	1 1 0	0 1	—7

WP—Mesa. **LP**—A. Pena.
E—Atlanta: Belliard (2); Cleveland: Baerga (1), Sorrento (1). **LOB**—Atlanta 7, Cleveland 13. **2B**—Atlanta: Grissom (1), Jones (2); Cleveland: Lofton (1), Baerga (1), S. Alomar (1). **3B**—Cleveland: Vizquel (1). **HR**—Atlanta: McGriff (2), Klesko (1). **SB**—Atlanta: Polonia (1), McGriff (1); Cleveland: Lofton (5), M. Ramirez (1). **CS**—Atlanta: Grissom (1); Cleveland: Lofton (1). **Sac**—Atlanta: Mordecai. **GIDP**—Atlanta: Grissom, Lopez; Cleveland: M. Ramirez. **T**—4:09. **A**—43,584.
Recap: Eddie Murray drove in Jose Espinoza with an 11th-inning single to win the game for Cleveland. The Indians had tied the game in the bottom of the eighth when Manny Ramirez scored on Sandy Alomar's double to right. Some controversy followed Cleveland manager Mike Hargrove's decision to stick with starter Charles Nagy until early in the eighth. Kenny Lofton continued his postseason brilliance, going 3 for 3 with three runs scored and raising his series batting average to .417.

1995 World Series (Cont.)

GAME 4

Atlanta	0	0	0		0	0	1		3	0 1 —5
Cleveland	0	0	0		0	0	1		0	0 1 —2

WP—Avery. **LP**—Hill. **Save**—Borbon.
E—Lemke. **LOB**—Atlanta 12, Cleveland 8. **2B**—Atlanta: Lopez (2), Polonia (1), McGriff (1); Cleveland: Thome (1), Sorrento (1). **HR**—Atlanta: Klesko (2); Cleveland: Belle (1), Ramirez (1). **SB**—Atlanta: Grissom (2). **CS**—Cleveland: Espinoza.
GIDP—Cleveland: Baerga (1). **T**—3:14. **A**—43,578.
Recap: Steve Avery pitched six strong innings, again virtually shutting down the Cleveland hitters. With the game tied 1–1 in the top of the seventh, the Braves scored three when Marquis Grissom walked then scored on Luis Polonia's double to right center. David Justice's single brought in two runs.

GAME 5

Atlanta	0	0	0		1	1	0		0	0 2 —4
Cleveland	2	0	0		0	0	2		0	1 x —5

WP—Hershiser. **LP**—Maddux. **Save**—Mesa.
E—Cleveland: Hershiser (1). **LOB**—Atlanta 3, Cleveland 5. **2B**—Atlanta: Jones (3), McGriff (2); Cleveland: Alomar (2), Baerga (2). **HR**—Atlanta: Polonia (1), Klesko (3); Cleveland: Belle (2), Thome (1). **Sac**—Atlanta: O'Brien. **GIDP**—Atlanta: Polonia. **T**—2:33. **A**—43,595.
Recap: Greg Maddux lost his aura of invincibility in the first inning when Cleveland's Albert Belle broke out of his slump with a two-run homer to right. The Indians chased Maddux with two more runs in the sixth, and starter Orel Hershiser pitched eight brilliant innings, striking out six and giving up just one earned run.

GAME 6

Cleveland	0	0	0		0	0	0		0	0 0 —0
Atlanta	0	0	0		0	0	1		0	0 0 —1

WP—Glavine. **LP**—Poole. **Save**—Wohlers (2).
E—Cleveland: Thome (1). **LOB**—Cleveland 3, Atlanta 11. **2B**—Atlanta: Justice (1). **HR**—Atlanta: Justice (1). **SB**—Cleveland: Lofton (6); Atlanta: Grissom (3). **CS**—Cleveland: Belle (1); Atlanta: Lemke (1). **Sac**—Atlanta: Lemke (1). **GIDP**—Atlanta: Belliard. **T**—3:02. **A**—51,875.
Recap: Atlanta starter Tom Glavine pitched eight outstanding innings, striking out eight and giving up just one hit to earn MVP honors for the series. Atlanta's sole run came in the bottom of the sixth when David Justice, who had incurred the wrath of Atlanta fans by criticizing their lack of support early in the series, hit a homer to right off Jim Poole. Mark Wohlers earned his second save of the series to help make the Braves the first team to win titles in three cities—Boston, Milwaukee and their present home, Atlanta.

1995 World Series Composite Box Score

ATLANTA

BATTING	AB	R	H	HR	RBI	Avg
Smith	2	0	1	0	0	.500
Grissom	25	3	9	0	1	.360
Mordecai	3	0	1	0	0	.333
Klesko	16	4	5	3	4	.313
Jones	21	3	6	0	1	.286
Polonia	14	3	4	1	4	.286
Lemke	22	1	6	0	0	.273
McGriff	23	5	6	2	3	.261
Justice	20	3	5	1	5	.250
Devereaux	4	0	1	0	1	.250
Lopez	17	1	3	1	3	.176
Belliard	16	0	0	0	1	.000
3 others	10	0	0	0	0	.000
Totals	193	23	47	8	23	.244

PITCHING	G	IP	H	BB	SO	ERA
Borbon	1	1	0	0	2	0.00
Glavine	2	14	4	6	11	1.29
Avery	1	6	3	5	3	1.50
Wohlers	4	5	4	3	3	1.80
Maddux	2	16	9	3	8	2.25
Clontz	2	3⅓	2	0	2	2.70
McMichael	3	3⅓	3	2	2	2.70
Mercker	1	2	1	2	2	4.50
A. Pena	2	1	3	2	0	9.00
Smoltz	1	2⅓	6	2	4	15.43
Totals	6	54	35	25	37	2.67

CLEVELAND

BATTING	AB	R	H	HR	RBI	Avg
Espinoza	2	1	1	0	0	.500
Belle	17	4	4	2	4	.235
Ramirez	18	2	4	1	2	.222
Thome	19	1	4	1	2	.211
Lofton	25	6	5	0	0	.200
Alomar	15	0	3	0	1	.200
Baerga	26	1	5	0	4	.192
Sorrento	11	0	2	0	0	.182
Vizquel	23	3	4	0	1	.174
T. Pena	6	0	1	0	0	.167
Murray	19	1	2	1	3	.105
Perry	5	0	0	0	0	.000
Martinez	3	0	0	0	0	.000
4 others	6	0	0	0	0	.000
Totals	195	19	35	5	17	.179

PITCHING	G	IP	H	BB	SO	ERA
Tavarez	5	4⅓	3	2	1	0.00
Hershiser	2	14	8	4	13	2.57
Embree	2	3⅓	2	2	2	2.70
Martinez	2	10⅓	12	8	5	3.48
Poole	2	2⅓	1	0	1	3.86
Hill	2	6⅓	7	4	1	4.26
Mesa	2	4	5	1	4	4.50
Nagy	1	7	8	1	4	6.43
Assenmacher	4	1⅓	1	3	3	6.75
Totals	6	53	47	25	34	3.57

1995 Individual Leaders

National League Batting

BATTING AVERAGE

Gwynn, SD	.368
Piazza, LA	.346
Bichette, Col	.340
Bell, Hou	.334
Grace, Chi	.326
Larkin, Cin	.319
Segui, Mtl	.309
Castilla, Col	.309
Jefferies, Phil	.306
Walker, Col	.306
Sanders, Cin	.306

HITS

Bichette, Col	197
Gwynn, SD	197
Grace, Chi	180
Biggio, Hou	167
Finley, SD	167
McRae, Chi	167
Karros, LA	164
Castilla, Col	163
Caminiti, SD	159
Larkin, Cin	158

DOUBLES

Grace, Chi	51
Bichette, Col	38
McRae, Chi	38
Sanders, Cin	36

Three tied with 35.

TRIPLES

Butler, LA	9
Young, Col	9
Sanders, SF	8
Finley, SD	8
Gonzalez, Chi	8

HOME RUNS

Bichette, Col	40
Walker, Col	36
Sosa, Chi	36
Bonds, SF	33
Karros, LA	32
Piazza, LA	32
Castilla, Col	32
Galarraga, Col	31
Gant, Cin	29
Sanders, Cin	28

RUNS SCORED

Biggio, Hou	123
Bonds, SF	109
Finley, SD	104
Bichette, Col	103
Larkin, Cin	98
Grace, Chi	97
Walker, Col	96
McRae, Chi	92
Mondesi, LA	91
Sanders, Cin	91

TOTAL BASES

Bichette, Col	359
Walker, Col	300
Castilla, Col	297
Karros, LA	295
Bonds, SF	292

STOLEN BASES

Veras, Fla	56
Larkin, Cin	51
DeShields, LA	39
Sanders, Cin	36
Young, Col	35
Finley, SD	35

RUNS BATTED IN

Bichette, Col	128
Sosa, Chi	119
Galarraga, Col	106
Conine, Fla	105
Karros, LA	105
Bonds, SF	104
Walker, Col	101
Sanders, Cin	99
Caminiti, SD	94
Piazza, Cin	93

SLUGGING PERCENTAGE

Bichette, Col	.620
Walker, Col	.607
Piazza, LA	.606
Sanders, Cin	.579
Bonds, SF	.577

ON-BASE PERCENTAGE

Bonds, SF	.431
Biggio, Hou	.406
Gwynn, SD	.404
Weiss, Col	.403
Piazza, LA	.400

BASES ON BALLS

Bonds, SF	120
Weiss, Col	98
Biggio, Hou	80
Veras, Fla	80
Bagwell, Hou	79

National League Pitching

EARNED RUN AVERAGE

Maddux, Atl	1.63
Nomo, LA	2.54
Ashby, SD	2.94
Valdes, LA	3.05
Glavine, Atl	3.08
Hamilton, SD	3.08
Smoltz, Atl	3.18
Castillo, Chi	3.21
Schourek, Cin	3.22
Navarro, Chi	3.28

SAVES

Myers, Chi	38
Henke, StL	36
Beck, SF	33
Slocumb, Phil	32
Worrell, LA	32
Hoffman, SD	31
Rojas, Mtl	30
Franco, NY	29
Brantley, Cin	28
Wohlers, Atl	25

WINS

Maddux, Atl	19
Schourek, Cin	18
Martinez, LA	17
Glavine, Atl	16
Burkett, Fla	14
Navarro, Chi	14
Martinez, Mtl	14
Rapp, Fla	14

Four tied with 13.

GAMES PITCHED

Leskanic, Col	76
Veres, Hou	72
Reed, Col	71
Perez, Fla	69

Three tied with 68.

INNINGS PITCHED

Neagle, Pit	209⅔
Maddux, Atl	209⅔
Martinez, LA	206⅓
Hamilton, SD	204⅓
Navarro, Chi	200⅓

STRIKEOUTS

Nomo, LA	236
Smoltz, Atl	193
Maddux, Atl	181
Reynolds, Hou	175
Martinez, Mtl	174
Fassero, Mtl	164
Schourek, Cin	160
Valdes, LA	150
Neagle, Pit	150
Ashby, SD	149

COMPLETE GAMES

Maddux, Atl	10
Leiter, SF	7
Valdes, LA	6
Neagle, Pit	5
Nomo, LA	5

SHUTOUTS

Maddux, Atl	3
Nomo, LA	3

Ten tied with two.

American League Batting

BATTING AVERAGE

E. Martinez, Sea	.356
Knoblauch, Minn	.333
Salmon, Cal	.330
Boggs, NY	.324
Murray, Clev	.323
Surhoff, Mil	.320
Davis, Cal	.318
Belle, Clev	.317
Baerga, Clev	.314
Puckett, Minn	.314
Thome, Clev	.314

HITS

Johnson, Chi	186
E. Martinez, Sea	182
Knoblauch, Minn	179
Salmon, Cal	177
Baerga, Clev	175
Nixon, Tex	174
Williams, NY	173
Belle, Clev	173
Palmeiro, Balt	172
Puckett, Minn	169

DOUBLES

Belle, Clev	52
E. Martinez, Sea	52
Puckett, Minn	39
Valentin, Bos	37
T. Martinez, Sea	35

TRIPLES

Lofton, Clev	13
Johnson, Chi	12
Anderson, Balt	10
Williams, NY	9
Knoblauch, Minn	8

HOME RUNS

Belle, Clev	50
Buhner, Sea	40
Thomas, Chi	40
Vaughn, Bos	39
McGwire, Oak	39
Palmeiro, Balt	39
Gaetti, KC	35
Salmon, Cal	34
Edmonds, Cal	33
Tettleton, Tex	32

RUNS SCORED

Belle, Clev	121
E. Martinez, Sea	121
Phillips, Cal	120
Edmonds, Cal	119
Salmon, Cal	111
Anderson, Balt	108
Valentin, Bos	108
Knoblauch, Minn	107
Thomas, Chi	102
Johnson, Chi	98
Vaughn, Bos	98

TOTAL BASES

Belle, Clev	377
Palmeiro, Balt	323
E. Martinez, Sea	321
Salmon, Cal	319
Vaughn, Bos	316

STOLEN BASES

Lofton, Clev	54
Nixon, Tex	50
Goodwin, KC	50
Knoblauch, Minn	46
Coleman, Sea	41

RUNS BATTED IN

Belle, Clev	126
Vaughn, Bos	126
Buhner, Sea	121
E. Martinez, Sea	113
Thomas, Chi	111
T. Martinez, Sea	111
Edmonds, Cal	107
Ramirez, Clev	107
Salmon, Cal	105
Palmeiro, Bal	104

SLUGGING PERCENTAGE

Belle, Clev	.690
E. Martinez, Sea	.628
Thomas, Chi	.606
Salmon, Cal	.594
Palmeiro, Balt	.583

ON-BASE PERCENTAGE

E. Martinez, Sea	.479
Thomas, Chi	.454
Thome, Clev	.438
Davis, Cal	.429
Salmon, Cal	.429

BASES ON BALLS

Thomas, Chi	136
E. Martinez, Sea	116
Phillips, Cal	113
Tettleton, Tex	107
Thome, Clev	97

American League Pitching

EARNED RUN AVERAGE

Johnson, Sea	2.48
Wakefield, Bos	2.95
Martinez, Clev	3.08
Mussina, Balt	3.29
Rogers, Tex	3.38
Cone, NY	3.57
Brown, Balt	3.60
Abbott, Cal	3.70
Gubicza, KC	3.75
Leiter, Tor	3.79

SAVES

Mesa, Clev	46
Smith, Cal	37
Aguilera, Bos	32
Hernandez, Chi	32
Montgomery, KC	31
Wetteland, NY	31
Eckersley, Oak	29
Jones, Balt	22
Fetters, Mil	22
Russell, Tex	20

WINS

Mussina, Balt	19
Cone, NY	18
Johnson, Sea	18
Rogers, Tex	17
Hershiser, Clev	16
Nagy, Clev	16
Wakefield, Bos	16

Five tied with 15.

GAMES PITCHED

Orosco, Balt	65
McDowell, Tex	64
Ayala, Sea	63
Belinda, Bos	63
Wickman, NY	63

INNINGS PITCHED

Cone, NY	229⅓
Mussina, Balt	221⅔
McDowell, NY	217⅔
Johnson, Sea	214⅓
Gubicza, KC	213⅓

STRIKEOUTS

Johnson, Sea	294
Stottlemyre, Oak	205
Finley, Cal	195
Cone, NY	191
Appier, KC	185
Fernandez, Chi	159
Mussina, Balt	158
McDowell, NY	157
Leiter, Tor	153
Pavlik, Tex	149

COMPLETE GAMES

McDowell, NY	8
Erickson, Balt	7
Mussina, Balt	7
Cone, NY	6
Johnson, Sea	6
Wakefield, Bos	6

SHUTOUTS

Mussina, Balt	4
Johnson, Sea	3

Six tied with two.

1995 Team Statistics

National League

TEAM BATTING	BA	AB	R	H	TB	2B	3B	HR	RBI	SB	BB	SO
Colorado	.282	4994	785	1406	2351	259	43	200	749	125	483	942
Houston	.275	5096	747	1402	2032	259	22	109	695	176	568	990
San Diego	.272	4951	668	1345	1968	233	20	116	618	122	446	871
Cincinnati	.270	4899	746	1325	2155	277	35	161	695	190	518	946
New York	.267	4958	657	1323	1983	217	34	125	616	57	446	994
Chicago	.265	4964	693	1315	2134	267	39	158	648	104	440	953
Los Angeles	.264	4942	634	1303	1976	191	31	140	593	127	468	1026
Florida	.262	4884	673	1278	1982	214	29	144	638	131	516	915
Philadelphia	.262	4950	614	1295	1902	265	30	94	576	70	497	886
Pittsburgh	.260	4936	629	1281	1955	245	27	125	587	82	456	969
Montreal	.259	4905	621	1268	1935	265	24	118	572	120	400	900
San Francisco	.254	4975	653	1257	2008	229	33	152	611	138	472	1056
Atlanta	.250	4814	645	1202	1971	211	27	168	618	72	519	933
St Louis	.247	4779	563	1182	1788	237	24	107	533	80	436	916

TEAM PITCHING	ERA	W	L	Sho	CG	SV	Inn	H	R	ER	BB	SO
Atlanta	3.44	90	54	12	19	34	1291⅔	1184	540	494	436	1087
Los Angeles	3.68	78	66	11	17	37	1295	1188	609	529	462	1059
New York	3.88	69	75	9	9	36	1291	1296	618	556	401	901
Cincinnati	4.03	85	59	10	9	38	1289⅓	1270	623	578	423	901
Houston	4.06	76	68	8	6	32	1320⅓	1356	674	595	459	1055
Montreal	4.10	66	78	9	7	42	1282⅔	1286	638	584	416	950
St Louis	4.10	62	81	6	4	38	1265⅔	1289	658	576	445	843
Chicago	4.12	73	71	13	6	44	1301	1312	671	596	519	926
San Diego	4.15	70	74	10	6	35	1284⅔	1242	672	593	512	1044
Philadelphia	4.21	69	75	8	8	41	1290⅓	1240	658	603	538	980
Florida	4.27	67	76	7	12	29	1286	1299	673	610	562	994
Pittsburgh	4.71	58	86	7	1	29	1275⅓	1407	736	668	477	871
San Francisco	4.86	67	77	5	12	34	1293⅔	1368	776	699	505	801
Colorado	4.97	77	67	1	1	43	1288⅓	1443	783	711	512	891

American League

TEAM BATTING	BA	AB	R	H	TB	2B	3B	HR	RBI	SB	BB	SO
Cleveland	.291	5028	840	1461	2407	279	23	207	804	132	542	766
Boston	.280	4997	791	1399	2272	286	31	175	754	99	560	922
Chicago	.280	5060	755	1417	2181	252	37	146	712	110	576	767
Minnesota	.279	5005	703	1398	2096	270	34	120	662	105	471	916
California	.277	5020	801	1390	2250	252	25	186	761	58	563	890
New York	.276	4946	749	1365	2079	280	34	122	709	50	625	851
Seattle	.275	4991	794	1375	2237	276	20	182	767	110	549	872
Milwaukee	.266	5000	740	1329	2046	249	42	128	699	104	502	800
Texas	.265	4913	691	1304	2011	247	23	138	648	90	526	877
Oakland	.264	4915	730	1296	2067	228	18	169	696	112	565	911
Baltimore	.262	4837	704	1267	2070	230	27	173	669	91	576	805
Kansas City	.260	4908	631	1277	1944	240	35	119	579	121	475	849
Toronto	.260	5036	642	1309	2058	275	27	140	613	75	492	906
Detroit	.247	4865	654	1204	1966	227	29	159	619	72	549	985

TEAM PITCHING	ERA	W	L	Sho	CG	SV	Inn	H	R	ER	BB	SO
Cleveland	3.84	100	44	10	10	50	1301	1261	607	555	445	926
Baltimore	4.32	71	73	10	19	29	1267	1165	640	608	523	930
Boston	4.40	86	58	9	7	39	1292⅔	1339	698	632	476	888
Kansas City	4.49	70	74	10	11	37	1288	1322	691	642	503	763
California	4.42	78	67	9	8	41	1284⅓	1309	697	645	486	901
Seattle	4.52	79	66	8	10	39	1289⅓	1343	708	647	592	1068
New York	4.55	79	65	5	18	35	1284⅔	1284	688	649	535	908
Texas	4.67	74	70	4	14	34	1285	1385	720	667	514	839
Milwaukee	4.83	65	79	4	7	31	1286	1391	747	690	603	699
Chicago	4.85	68	76	4	12	36	1284⅔	1374	758	693	617	892
Toronto	4.90	56	88	8	16	22	1292⅔	1336	777	704	654	894
Oakland	4.97	67	77	4	8	34	1273	1320	761	703	556	890
Detroit	5.50	60	84	3	5	38	1275	1509	844	779	536	728
Minnesota	5.77	56	88	2	7	27	1272⅔	1452	889	816	533	791

Atlanta Braves

BATTING	BA	G	AB	R	H	TB	2B	3B	HR	RBI	SB	BB	SO
Lopez, Javy	.315	100	333	37	105	166	11	4	14	51	0	14	57
Klesko, Ryan	.310	107	329	48	102	200	25	2	23	70	5	47	72
McGriff, Fred	.280	144	528	85	148	258	27	1	27	93	3	65	99
Mordecai, Mike	.280	69	75	10	21	36	6	0	3	11	0	9	16
Jones, Chipper	.265	140	524	87	139	236	22	3	23	86	8	73	99
Polonia, Luis	.264	28	53	6	14	21	7	0	0	2	3	3	9
Grissom, Marquis	.258	139	551	80	142	207	23	3	12	42	29	47	61
Devereaux, Mike	.255	29	55	7	14	20	3	0	1	8	2	2	11
Lemke, Mark	.253	116	399	42	101	142	16	5	5	38	2	44	40
Justice, David	.253	120	411	73	104	197	17	2	24	78	4	73	68
Smith, Dwight	.252	103	131	16	33	54	8	2	3	21	0	13	35
O'Brien, Charlie	.227	67	198	18	45	79	7	0	9	23	0	29	40
Belliard, Rafael	.222	75	180	12	40	44	2	1	0	7	2	6	28
Blauser, Jeff	.211	115	431	60	91	147	16	2	12	31	8	57	107
Kelly, Mike	.190	97	137	26	26	43	6	1	3	17	7	11	49

PITCHING	ERA	W	L	G	GS	CG	SV	INN	H	R	ER	BB	SO
Maddux, Greg	1.63	19	2	28	28	10	0	209⅔	147	39	38	23	181
Wohlers, Mark	2.09	7	3	65	0	0	25	64⅔	51	16	15	24	90
Pena, Alejandro	2.61	2	0	27	0	0	0	31	22	9	9	7	39
McMichael, Greg	2.79	7	2	67	0	0	2	80⅔	64	27	25	32	74
Glavine, Tom	3.08	16	7	29	29	3	0	198⅔	182	76	68	66	127
Borbon, Pedro	3.09	2	2	41	0	0	2	32	29	12	11	17	33
Smoltz, John	3.18	12	7	29	29	2	0	192⅔	166	76	68	72	193
Clontz, Brad	3.65	8	1	59	0	0	4	69	71	29	28	22	55
Mercker, Kent	4.15	7	8	29	26	0	0	143	140	73	66	61	102
Avery, Steve	4.67	7	13	29	29	3	0	173⅓	165	92	90	52	141
Stanton, Mike	5.59	1	1	26	0	0	1	19½	31	14	12	6	13

Chicago Cubs

BATTING	BA	G	AB	R	H	TB	2B	3B	HR	RBI	SB	BB	SO
Haney, Todd	.411	25	73	11	30	44	8	0	2	6	0	7	11
Grace, Mark	.326	143	552	97	180	285	51	3	16	92	6	65	46
Dunston, Shawon	.296	127	477	58	141	225	30	6	14	69	10	10	75
McRae, Brian	.288	137	580	92	167	255	38	7	12	48	27	47	92
Sanchez, Rey	.278	114	428	57	119	154	22	2	3	27	6	14	48
Gonzalez, Luis	.276	133	471	69	130	214	29	8	13	69	6	57	63
Bullett, Scott	.273	104	150	19	41	69	5	7	3	22	8	12	30
Sosa, Sammy	.268	144	564	89	151	282	17	3	36	119	34	58	134
Servais, Scott	.265	80	264	38	70	131	22	0	13	47	2	32	52
Timmons, Ozzie	.263	77	171	30	45	81	10	1	8	28	3	13	32
Zeile, Todd	.246	113	426	50	105	169	22	0	14	52	1	34	76
Hernandez, Jose	.245	93	245	37	60	118	11	4	13	40	1	13	69
Parent, Mark	.234	81	265	30	62	127	11	0	18	38	0	26	69
Johnson, Howard	.195	87	169	26	33	60	4	1	7	22	1	34	46
Buechele, Steve	.189	32	106	10	20	25	2	0	1	9	0	11	19

PITCHING	ERA	W	L	G	GS	CG	SV	INN	H	R	ER	BB	SO
Swartzbaugh, Dave	0.00	0	0	7	0	0	0	7⅓	5	2	0	3	5
Casian, Larry	1.93	1	0	42	0	0	0	23⅓	23	6	5	15	11
Castillo, Frank	3.21	11	10	29	29	2	0	188	179	75	67	52	135
Walker, Mike	3.22	1	3	42	0	0	1	44⅔	45	22	16	24	20
Navarro, Jaime	3.28	14	6	29	29	1	0	200⅓	194	79	73	56	128
Perez, Mike	3.66	2	6	68	0	0	2	71⅓	72	30	29	27	49
Young, Anthony	3.70	3	4	32	1	0	2	41⅓	47	20	17	14	15
Myers, Randy	3.88	1	2	57	0	0	38	55⅔	49	25	24	28	59
Bullinger, Jim	4.14	12	8	24	24	1	0	150	152	80	69	65	93
Foster, Kevin	4.51	12	11	30	28	0	0	167⅔	149	90	84	65	146
Wendell, Turk	4.92	3	1	43	0	0	0	60⅓	71	35	33	24	50
Trachsel, Steve	5.15	7	13	30	29	2	0	160⅓	174	104	92	76	117
Nabholz, Chris	5.40	0	1	34	0	0	0	23⅓	22	15	14	14	21
Rivera, Roberto	5.40	0	0	7	0	0	0	5	8	3	3	2	2
Edens, Tom	6.00	1	0	5	0	0	0	3	6	3	2	3	2

Cincinnati Reds

BATTING	BA	G	AB	R	H	TB	2B	3B	HR	RBI	SB	BB	SO
Lewis, Mark	.339	81	171	25	58	82	13	1	3	30	0	21	33
Larkin, Barry	.319	131	496	98	158	244	29	6	15	66	51	61	49
Sanders, Reggie	.306	133	484	91	148	280	36	6	28	99	36	69	122
Howard, Thomas	.302	113	281	42	85	113	15	2	3	26	17	20	37
Walton, Jerome	.290	102	162	32	47	85	12	1	8	22	10	17	25
Duncan, Mariano	.287	81	265	36	76	112	14	2	6	36	1	5	62
Santiago, Benito	.286	81	266	40	76	129	20	0	11	44	2	24	48
Taubensee, Eddie	.284	80	218	32	62	107	14	2	9	44	2	22	52
Morris, Hal	.279	101	359	53	100	162	25	2	11	51	1	29	58
Gant, Ron	.276	119	410	79	113	227	19	4	29	88	23	74	108
Anthony, Eric	.269	47	134	19	36	57	6	0	5	23	2	13	30
Boone, Bret	.267	138	513	63	137	220	34	2	15	68	5	41	84
Branson, Jeff	.260	122	331	43	86	144	18	2	12	45	2	44	69
Lewis, Darren	.250	132	472	66	118	140	13	3	1	24	32	34	57
Hunter, Brian	.215	40	79	9	17	26	6	0	1	9	2	11	21
Harris, Lenny	.208	101	197	32	41	61	8	3	2	16	10	14	20

PITCHING	ERA	W	L	G	GS	CG	SV	INN	H	R	ER	BB	SO
Jackson, Mike	2.39	6	1	40	0	0	2	49	38	13	13	19	41
Brantley, Jeff	2.82	3	2	56	0	0	28	70⅓	53	22	22	20	62
Schourek, Pete	3.22	18	7	29	29	2	0	190⅓	158	72	68	45	160
Smiley, John	3.46	12	5	28	27	1	0	176⅔	173	72	68	39	124
Wells, David	3.59	6	5	11	11	3	0	72⅔	74	34	29	16	50
Pugh, Tim	3.84	6	5	28	12	0	0	98⅓	100	46	42	32	38
Burba, Dave	3.97	10	4	52	9	1	0	106⅔	90	50	47	51	96
Portugal, Mark	4.01	11	10	31	31	1	0	181⅓	185	91	81	56	96
Carrasco, Hector	4.12	2	7	64	0	0	5	87⅓	86	45	40	46	64
Rijo, Jose	4.17	5	4	14	14	0	0	69	76	33	32	22	62
Hernandez, Xavier	4.60	7	2	59	0	0	3	90	95	47	46	31	84
Jarvis, Kevin	5.70	3	4	19	11	1	0	79	91	56	50	32	33

Colorado Rockies

BATTING	BA	G	AB	R	H	TB	2B	3B	HR	RBI	SB	BB	SO
VanderWal, John	.347	105	101	15	35	60	8	1	5	21	1	16	23
Bichette, Dante	.340	139	579	102	197	359	38	2	40	128	13	22	96
Young, Eric	.317	120	366	68	116	173	21	9	6	36	35	49	29
Hubbard, Trenidad	.310	24	58	13	18	31	4	0	3	9	2	8	6
Castilla, Vinny	.309	139	527	82	163	297	34	2	32	90	2	30	87
Walker, Larry	.306	131	494	96	151	300	31	5	36	101	16	49	72
Galarraga, Andres	.280	143	554	89	155	283	29	3	31	106	12	32	146
Kingery, Mike	.269	119	350	66	94	144	18	4	8	37	13	45	40
Bates, Jason	.267	116	322	42	86	135	17	4	8	46	3	42	70
Burks, Ellis	.266	103	278	41	74	138	10	6	14	49	7	39	72
Girardi, Joe	.262	125	462	63	121	166	17	2	8	55	3	29	76
Weiss, Walt	.260	137	427	65	111	137	17	3	1	25	15	98	57
Owens, Jayhawk	.244	18	45	7	11	25	2	0	4	12	0	2	15
Tatum, Jim	.235	34	34	4	8	11	1	1	0	4	0	1	7

PITCHING	ERA	W	L	G	GS	CG	SV	INN	H	R	ER	BB	SO
Ruffin, Bruce	2.12	0	1	37	0	0	11	34	26	8	8	19	23
Reed, Steve	2.14	5	2	71	0	0	3	84	61	24	20	21	79
Holmes, Darren	3.24	6	1	68	0	0	14	66⅔	59	26	24	28	61
Leskanic, Curt	3.40	6	3	76	0	0	10	98	83	38	37	33	107
Saberhagen, Bret	4.18	7	6	25	25	3	0	153	165	78	71	33	100
Ritz, Kevin	4.21	11	11	31	28	0	2	173⅓	171	91	81	65	120
Painter, Lance	4.37	3	0	33	1	0	1	45⅓	55	23	22	10	36
Swift, Bill	4.94	9	3	19	19	0	0	105⅔	122	62	58	43	68
Rekar, Bryan	4.98	4	6	15	14	1	0	85	95	51	47	24	60
Bailey, Roger	4.98	7	6	39	6	0	0	81⅓	88	49	45	39	33
Grahe, Joe	5.08	4	3	17	9	0	0	56⅔	69	42	32	27	27
Reynoso, Armando	5.32	7	7	20	18	0	0	93	116	61	55	36	40
Freeman, Marvin	5.89	3	7	22	18	0	0	94⅔	122	64	62	41	61

Florida Marlins

BATTING

BATTING	BA	G	AB	R	H	TB	2B	3B	HR	RBI	SB	BB	SO
Sheffield, Gary	.324	63	213	46	69	125	8	0	16	46	19	55	45
Conine, Jeff	.302	133	483	72	146	251	26	2	25	105	2	66	94
Pendleton, Terry	.290	133	513	70	149	225	32	1	14	78	1	38	84
Tavarez, Jesus	.289	63	190	31	55	71	6	2	2	13	7	16	27
Morman, Russ	.278	34	72	9	20	33	2	1	3	7	0	3	12
Colbrunn, Greg	.277	138	528	70	146	239	22	1	23	89	11	22	69
Arias, Alex	.269	94	216	22	58	80	9	2	3	26	1	22	20
Veras, Quilvio	.261	124	440	86	115	164	20	7	5	32	56	80	68
Dawson, Andre	.257	79	226	30	58	98	10	3	8	37	0	9	45
Browne, Jerry	.255	77	184	21	47	54	4	0	1	17	1	25	20
Abbott, Kurt	.255	120	420	60	107	190	18	7	17	60	4	36	110
Johnson, Charles	.251	97	315	40	79	129	15	1	11	39	0	46	71
Gregg, Tommy	.237	72	156	20	37	60	5	0	6	20	3	16	33
Carr, Chuck	.227	105	308	54	70	96	20	0	2	20	25	46	49
Decker, Steve	.226	51	133	12	30	43	2	1	3	13	1	19	22

PITCHING

PITCHING	ERA	W	L	G	GS	CG	SV	INN	H	R	ER	BB	SO
Nen, Robb	3.29	0	7	62	0	0	23	65⅔	62	26	24	23	68
Mathews, Terry	3.38	4	4	57	0	0	3	82⅔	70	32	31	27	72
Rapp, Pat	3.44	14	7	28	28	3	0	167⅔	158	72	64	76	102
Lewis, Richie	3.75	0	1	21	1	0	0	36	30	15	15	15	32
Hammond, Chris	3.80	9	6	25	24	3	0	161	157	73	68	47	126
Veres, Randy	3.88	4	4	47	0	0	1	48⅔	46	25	21	22	31
Witt, Bobby	3.90	2	7	19	19	1	0	110⅔	104	52	48	47	95
Burkett, John	4.30	14	14	30	30	4	0	188⅓	208	95	90	57	126
Gardner, Mark	4.49	5	5	39	11	1	1	102⅓	109	60	51	43	87
Perez, Yorkis	5.21	2	6	69	0	0	1	46⅔	35	29	27	28	47
Banks, Willie	5.66	2	6	25	15	0	0	90⅔	106	71	57	58	62
Weathers, Dave	5.98	4	5	28	15	0	0	90⅓	104	68	60	52	60
Groom, Buddy	7.20	1	2	14	0	0	0	15	26	12	12	6	12
Murphy, Rob	10.95	1	2	14	0	0	0	12⅓	14	16	15	8	7
Garces, Rich	4.44	0	2	18	0	0	0	24⅓	25	15	12	11	22

Houston Astros

BATTING

BATTING	BA	G	AB	R	H	TB	2B	3B	HR	RBI	SB	BB	SO
Bell, Derek	.334	112	452	63	151	200	21	2	8	86	27	33	71
Cangelosi, John	.318	90	201	46	64	79	5	2	2	18	21	48	42
Magadan, Dave	.313	127	348	44	109	139	24	0	2	51	2	71	56
Hunter, Brian	.302	78	321	52	97	127	14	5	2	28	24	21	52
Biggio, Craig	.302	141	553	123	167	267	30	2	22	77	33	80	85
May, Derrick	.301	78	206	29	62	103	15	1	8	41	5	19	24
Donnels, Chris	.300	19	30	4	9	9	0	0	0	2	0	3	6
Eusebio, Tony	.299	113	368	46	110	151	21	1	6	58	0	31	59
Bagwell, Jeff	.290	114	448	88	130	222	29	0	21	87	12	79	102
Gutierrez, Ricky	.276	52	156	22	43	49	6	0	0	12	5	10	33
Shipley, Craig	.263	92	232	23	61	80	8	1	3	24	6	8	28
Miller, Orlando	.262	92	324	36	85	122	20	1	5	36	3	22	71
Mouton, James	.262	104	298	42	78	112	18	2	4	27	25	25	59
Simms, Mike	.256	50	121	14	31	62	4	0	9	24	1	13	28
Thompson, Milt	.220	92	132	14	29	44	9	0	2	19	4	14	37
Wilkins, Rick	.203	65	202	30	41	65	3	0	7	19	0	46	61

PITCHING

PITCHING	ERA	W	L	G	GS	CG	SV	INN	H	R	ER	BB	SO
Veres, Dave	2.26	5	1	72	0	0	1	103⅓	89	29	26	30	94
Jones, Todd	3.07	6	5	68	0	0	15	99⅔	89	38	34	52	96
Hartgraves, Dean	3.22	2	0	40	0	0	0	36⅓	30	14	13	16	24
Tabaka, Jeff	3.23	1	0	34	0	0	0	30⅔	27	11	11	17	25
Hampton, Mike	3.35	9	8	24	24	0	0	150⅔	141	73	56	49	115
Reynolds, Shane	3.47	10	11	30	30	3	0	189⅓	196	87	73	37	175
Brocail, Doug	4.19	6	4	36	7	0	1	77⅓	87	40	36	22	39
Swindell, Greg	4.47	10	9	33	26	1	0	153	180	86	76	39	96
Drabek, Doug	4.77	10	9	31	31	2	0	185	205	104	98	54	143
Dougherty, Jim	4.92	8	4	56	0	0	0	67⅔	76	37	37	25	49
Kile, Darryl	4.96	4	12	25	21	0	0	127	114	81	70	73	113

Los Angeles Dodgers

BATTING	BA	G	AB	R	H	TB	2B	3B	HR	RBI	SB	BB	SO
Piazza, Mike	.346	112	434	82	150	263	17	0	32	93	1	39	80
Butler, Brett	.300	129	513	78	154	193	18	9	1	38	32	67	51
Karros, Eric	.298	143	551	83	164	295	29	3	32	105	4	61	115
Hansen, Dave	.287	100	181	19	52	65	10	0	1	14	0	28	28
Offerman, Jose	.287	119	429	69	123	161	14	6	4	33	2	69	67
Mondesi, Raul	.285	139	536	91	153	266	23	6	26	88	27	33	96
Fonville, Chad	.278	102	320	43	89	97	6	1	0	16	20	23	42
Kelly, Roberto	.278	136	504	58	140	188	23	2	7	57	19	22	79
Parker, Rick	.276	27	29	3	8	8	0	0	0	4	1	2	4
Wallach, Tim	.266	97	327	24	87	140	22	2	9	38	0	27	69
DeShields, Delino	.256	127	425	66	109	157	18	3	8	37	39	63	83
Ashley, Billy	.237	81	215	17	51	80	5	0	8	27	0	25	88
Hollandsworth, Todd	.233	41	103	16	24	41	2	0	5	13	2	10	29
Gwynn, Chris	.214	67	84	8	18	28	3	2	1	10	0	6	23

PITCHING	ERA	W	L	G	GS	CG	SV	INN	H	R	ER	BB	SO
Worrell, Todd	2.02	4	1	59	0	0	32	62⅓	50	15	14	19	61
Nomo, Hideo	2.54	13	6	28	28	4	0	191⅓	124	63	54	78	236
Cummings, John	3.00	3	1	35	0	0	0	39	38	16	13	10	21
Valdes, Ismael	3.05	13	11	33	27	6	1	197⅔	168	76	67	51	150
Candiotti, Tom	3.50	7	14	30	30	1	0	190½	187	93	74	58	141
Martinez, Ramon	3.66	17	7	30	30	4	0	206½	176	95	84	81	138
Astacio, Pedro	4.24	7	8	48	11	1	0	104	103	53	49	29	80
Osuna, Antonio	4.43	2	4	39	0	0	0	44⅔	39	22	22	20	46
Tapani, Kevin	5.05	4	2	13	11	0	0	57	72	37	32	14	43
Seanez, Rudy	6.75	1	3	37	0	0	3	34⅔	39	27	26	18	29
Daal, Omar	7.20	4	0	28	0	0	0	20	29	19	16	15	11

Montreal Expos

BATTING	BA	G	AB	R	H	TB	2B	3B	HR	RBI	SB	BB	SO
Berry, Sean	.318	103	314	38	100	166	22	1	14	55	3	25	53
Segui, David	.309	130	456	68	141	210	25	4	12	68	2	40	47
Santangelo, F.P.	.296	35	98	11	29	39	5	1	1	9	1	12	9
White, Rondell	.295	130	474	87	140	220	33	4	13	57	25	41	87
Cordero, Wilfredo	.286	131	514	64	147	216	35	2	10	49	9	36	88
Fletcher, Scott	.286	110	350	42	100	156	21	1	11	45	0	32	23
Alou, Moises	.273	93	344	48	94	158	22	0	14	58	4	29	56
Silvestri, Dave	.264	39	72	12	19	31	6	0	2	7	2	9	27
Lansing, Mike	.255	127	467	47	119	183	30	2	10	62	27	28	65
Tarasco, Tony	.249	126	438	64	109	177	18	4	14	40	24	51	78
Grudzielanek, Mark	.245	78	269	27	66	85	12	2	1	20	8	14	47
Rodriguez, Henry	.239	45	138	13	33	45	4	1	2	15	0	11	28
Laker, Tim	.234	64	141	17	33	52	8	1	3	20	0	14	38
Andrews, Shane	.214	84	220	27	47	83	10	1	8	31	1	17	68
Treadway, Jeff	.209	58	67	6	14	18	2	1	0	13	0	5	4

PITCHING	ERA	W	L	G	GS	CG	SV	INN	H	R	ER	BB	SO
Harris, Greg	2.61	2	3	45	0	0	0	48⅓	45	18	14	16	47
Henry, Butch	2.84	7	9	21	21	1	0	126⅔	133	47	40	28	60
Rueter, Kirk	3.23	5	3	9	9	1	0	47⅓	38	17	17	9	28
Martinez, Pedro	3.51	14	10	30	30	2	0	194½	158	79	76	66	174
Perez, Carlos	3.69	10	8	28	23	2	0	141½	142	61	58	28	106
Scott, Tim	3.98	2	0	62	0	0	2	63½	52	30	28	23	57
Rojas, Mel	4.12	1	4	59	0	0	30	67⅓	69	32	31	29	61
Heredia, Gil	4.31	5	6	40	18	0	1	119	137	60	57	21	74
Fassero, Jeff	4.33	13	14	30	30	1	0	189	207	102	91	74	164
Shaw, Jeff	4.62	1	6	50	0	0	3	62½	58	35	32	26	45
Alvarez, Tavo	6.75	1	5	8	8	0	0	37⅓	46	30	28	14	17

National League Team-by-Team Statistical Leaders *(Cont.)*

New York Mets

BATTING	BA	G	AB	R	H	TB	2B	3B	HR	RBI	SB	BB	SO
Bonilla, Bobby	.325	80	317	49	103	190	25	4	18	53	0	31	48
Bogar, Timothy	.290	78	145	17	42	52	7	0	1	21	1	9	25
Brogna, Rico	.289	134	495	72	143	240	27	2	22	76	0	39	111
Vizcaino, Jose	.287	135	509	66	146	186	21	5	3	56	8	35	76
Orsulak, Joe	.283	108	290	41	82	108	19	2	1	37	1	19	35
Jones, Chris	.280	79	182	33	51	85	6	2	8	31	2	13	45
Hundley, Todd	.280	90	275	39	77	133	11	0	15	51	1	42	64
Alfonzo, Edgar	.278	101	335	26	93	128	13	5	4	41	1	12	37
Kent, Jeff	.278	125	472	65	131	219	22	3	20	65	3	29	89
Everett, Carl	.260	79	289	48	75	126	13	1	12	54	2	39	67
Thompson, Ryan	.251	75	267	39	67	101	13	0	7	31	3	19	77
Buford, Damon	.235	44	136	24	32	49	5	0	4	12	7	19	28
Stinnett, Kelly	.219	77	196	23	43	65	8	1	4	18	2	29	65
Huskey, Butch	.189	28	90	8	17	27	1	0	3	11	1	10	16

PITCHING	ERA	W	L	G	GS	CG	SV	INN	H	R	ER	BB	SO
Birkbeck, Mike	1.63	0	1	4	4	0	0	27⅔	22	5	5	2	14
Byrd, Paul	2.05	2	0	17	0	0	0	22	18	6	5	7	26
Franco, John	2.44	5	3	48	0	0	29	51⅔	48	17	14	17	41
Isringhausen, Jason	2.81	9	2	14	14	1	0	93	88	29	29	31	55
Henry, Doug	2.96	3	6	51	0	0	4	67	48	23	22	25	62
Minor, Blas	3.66	4	2	35	0	0	1	46⅔	44	21	19	13	43
Harnisch, Pete	3.68	2	8	18	18	0	0	110	11	55	45	24	82
DiPoto, Jerry	3.78	4	6	58	0	0	2	78⅔	77	41	33	29	49
Pulsipher, Bill	3.98	5	7	17	17	2	0	126⅔	122	58	56	45	81
Jones, Bobby	4.19	10	10	30	30	3	0	195⅔	209	107	91	53	127
Mlicki, Dave	4.26	9	7	29	25	0	0	160⅔	160	82	76	54	123
Cornelius, Reid	5.54	3	7	18	10	0	0	66⅔	75	44	41	30	39

Philadelphia Phillies

BATTING	BA	G	AB	R	H	TB	2B	3B	HR	RBI	SB	BB	SO
Longmire, Tony	.356	59	104	21	37	53	7	0	3	19	1	11	19
Gallagher, Dave	.318	62	157	12	50	65	12	0	1	12	0	16	20
Eisenreich, Jim	.316	129	377	46	119	175	22	2	10	55	10	38	44
Jefferies, Gregg	.306	114	480	69	147	215	31	2	11	56	9	35	26
Marsh, Tom	.294	43	109	13	32	46	3	1	3	15	0	4	25
Morandini, Mickey	.283	127	494	65	140	206	34	7	6	49	9	42	80
Hayes, Charlie	.276	141	529	58	146	215	30	3	11	85	5	50	88
Whiten, Mark	.269	60	212	38	57	102	10	1	11	37	7	31	63
Webster, Lenny	.267	49	150	18	40	61	9	0	4	14	0	16	27
Dykstra, Lenny	.264	62	254	37	67	90	15	1	2	18	10	33	28
Varsho, Gary	.252	72	103	7	26	29	1	1	0	11	2	7	17
Daulton, Darren	.249	98	342	44	85	137	19	3	9	55	3	55	52
Van Slyke, Andy	.243	63	214	26	52	75	10	2	3	16	7	28	41
Hollins, Dave	.229	65	205	46	47	84	12	2	7	25	1	53	38
Stocker, Kevin	.218	125	412	42	90	113	14	3	1	32	6	43	75

PITCHING	ERA	W	L	G	GS	CG	SV	INN	H	R	ER	BB	SO
Bottalico, Ricky	2.46	5	3	62	0	0	1	87⅔	50	25	24	42	87
Slocumb, Heathcliff	2.89	5	6	61	0	0	32	65⅓	64	26	21	35	63
Williams, Mike	3.29	3	3	33	8	0	0	87⅔	78	37	32	29	57
Fernandez, Sid	3.34	6	1	11	11	0	0	64⅔	48	25	24	21	79
Schilling, Curt	3.57	7	5	17	17	1	0	116	96	52	46	26	114
West, David	3.79	3	2	8	8	0	0	38	34	17	16	19	25
Juden, Jeff	4.02	2	4	13	10	1	0	62⅔	53	31	28	31	47
Mimbs, Mike	4.15	9	7	35	19	2	1	136⅔	127	70	63	75	93
Quantrill, Paul	4.67	11	12	33	29	0	0	179⅓	212	102	93	44	103
Green, Tyler	5.31	8	9	26	25	4	0	140⅔	157	86	83	66	55

Pittsburgh Pirates

BATTING

	BA	G	AB	R	H	TB	2B	3B	HR	RBI	SB	BB	SO
Wehner, John	.308	52	107	13	33	39	0	3	0	5	3	10	17
Slaught, Don	.304	35	112	13	34	40	6	0	0	13	0	9	8
Merced, Orlando	.300	132	487	75	146	228	29	4	15	83	7	52	74
Garcia, Carlos	.294	104	367	41	108	154	24	2	6	50	8	25	55
Liriano, Nelson	.286	107	259	29	74	103	12	1	5	38	2	24	34
Martin, Al	.282	124	439	70	124	194	25	3	13	41	20	44	92
Clark, Dave	.281	77	196	30	55	73	6	0	4	24	3	24	38
Brumfield, Jacob	.271	116	402	64	109	148	23	2	4	26	22	37	71
King, Jeff	.265	122	445	61	118	203	27	2	18	87	7	55	63
Bell, Jay	.262	138	530	79	139	214	28	4	13	55	2	55	110
Aude, Rich	.248	42	109	10	27	41	8	0	2	19	1	6	20
Pegues, Steve	.246	82	171	17	42	68	8	0	6	16	1	4	36
Cummings, Midre	.243	59	152	13	37	52	7	1	2	15	1	13	30
Young, Kevin	.232	56	181	13	42	69	9	0	6	22	1	8	53
Encarnacion, Angelo	.226	58	159	18	36	53	7	2	2	10	1	13	28
Johnson, Mark	.208	79	221	32	46	93	6	1	13	28	5	37	66

PITCHING

	ERA	W	L	G	GS	CG	SV	INN	H	R	ER	BB	SO
Neagle, Denny	3.43	13	8	31	31	5	0	209⅔	221	91	80	45	150
Plesac, Dan	3.58	4	4	58	0	0	3	60⅓	53	26	24	27	57
Christiansen, Jason	4.15	1	3	63	0	0	0	56⅓	49	28	26	34	53
Dyer, Mike	4.34	4	5	55	0	0	0	74⅔	81	40	36	30	53
Ericks, John	4.58	3	9	19	18	1	0	106	108	59	54	50	80
Miceli, Dan	4.66	4	4	58	0	0	21	58	61	30	30	28	56
White, Rick	4.75	2	3	15	9	0	0	55	66	33	29	18	29
Wagner, Paul	4.80	5	16	33	25	3	1	165	174	96	88	72	120
McCurry, Jeff	5.02	1	4	55	0	0	1	61	82	38	34	30	27
Loaiza, Esteban	5.16	8	9	32	31	1	0	172⅔	205	115	99	55	85
Parris, Steve	5.38	6	6	15	15	1	0	82	89	49	49	33	61
Lieber, Jon	6.32	4	7	21	12	0	0	72⅔	103	56	51	14	45

St. Louis Cardinals

BATTING

	BA	G	AB	R	H	TB	2B	3B	HR	RBI	SB	BB	SO
Mabry, John	.307	129	388	35	119	157	21	1	5	41	0	24	45
Gilkey, Bernard	.298	121	480	73	143	235	33	4	17	69	12	42	70
Jordan, Brian	.296	131	490	83	145	239	20	4	22	81	24	22	79
Lankford, Ray	.277	132	483	81	134	248	35	2	25	82	24	63	110
Battle, Allen	.271	61	118	13	32	37	5	0	0	2	3	15	26
Pena, Geronimo	.267	32	101	20	27	38	6	1	1	8	3	16	30
Bell, David	.250	39	144	13	36	53	7	2	2	19	1	4	25
Sheaffer, Danny	.231	76	208	24	48	75	10	1	5	30	0	23	38
Cooper, Scott	.230	118	374	29	86	117	18	2	3	40	0	49	85
Cromer, Tripp	.226	105	345	36	78	112	19	0	5	18	0	14	66
Coles, Darnell	.225	63	138	13	31	31	7	0	3	16	0	16	20
Pagnozzi, Tom	.215	62	219	17	47	69	14	1	2	15	0	11	31
Oquendo, Jose	.209	88	220	31	46	66	8	3	2	17	1	35	21
Smith, Ozzie	.199	44	156	16	31	38	5	1	0	11	4	17	12
Hemond, Scott	.144	57	118	11	17	27	1	0	3	9	0	12	31
Oliva, Jose	.142	70	183	15	26	52	5	0	7	20	0	12	46

PITCHING

	ERA	W	L	G	GS	CG	SV	INN	H	R	ER	BB	SO
Fossas, Tony	1.47	3	0	58	0	0	0	36⅔	28	6	6	10	40
Mathews, T.J.	1.52	1	1	23	0	0	2	29⅔	21	7	5	11	28
Henke, Tom	1.82	1	1	52	0	0	36	54⅓	42	11	11	18	48
Habyan, John	2.88	3	2	31	0	0	0	40⅔	32	18	13	15	35
DeLucia, Rich	3.39	8	7	56	1	0	0	82⅓	63	38	31	36	76
Morgan, Mike	3.56	7	7	21	21	1	0	131⅓	133	56	52	34	61
Parrett, Jeff	3.64	4	7	59	0	0	0	76⅔	71	33	31	28	71
Urbani, Tom	3.70	3	5	24	13	0	0	82⅓	99	40	34	21	52
Osborne, Donovan	3.81	4	6	19	19	0	0	113⅓	112	58	48	34	82
Arocha, Rene	3.99	3	5	41	0	0	0	49⅔	55	24	22	18	25
Petkovsek, Mark	4.00	6	6	26	21	1	0	137⅓	136	71	61	35	71
Watson, Allen	4.96	7	9	21	19	0	0	114⅓	126	68	63	41	49
Hill, Ken	5.06	6	7	18	18	0	0	110⅓	125	71	62	45	50
Jackson, Danny	5.90	2	12	19	19	2	0	100⅔	120	82	66	48	52

San Diego Padres

BATTING	BA	G	AB	R	H	TB	2B	3B	HR	RBI	SB	BB	SO
Gwynn, Tony	.368	135	535	82	197	259	33	1	9	90	17	35	15
Livingstone, Scott	.337	99	196	26	66	96	15	0	5	32	2	15	22
Roberts, Bip	.304	73	296	40	90	110	14	0	2	25	20	17	36
Caminiti, Ken	.302	143	526	74	159	270	33	0	26	94	12	69	94
Finley, Steve	.297	139	562	104	167	236	23	8	10	44	36	59	62
Ausmus, Brad	.293	103	328	44	96	135	16	4	5	34	16	31	56
Cianfrocco, Archi	.263	51	118	22	31	53	7	0	5	31	0	11	28
Williams, Eddie	.260	97	296	35	77	126	11	1	12	47	0	23	47
Reed, Jody	.256	131	445	58	114	146	18	1	4	40	6	59	38
Plantier, Phil	.255	76	216	33	55	88	6	0	9	34	1	28	48
Johnson, Brian	.251	68	207	20	52	70	9	0	3	29	0	11	39
Petagine, Roberto	.234	89	124	15	29	46	8	0	3	17	0	26	41
Clark, Phil	.216	75	97	12	21	30	3	0	2	7	0	8	18
Cedeno, Andujar	.210	120	390	42	82	120	16	2	6	31	5	28	92
Nieves, Melvin	.205	98	234	32	48	98	6	1	14	38	2	19	88

PITCHING	ERA	W	L	G	GS	CG	SV	INN	H	R	ER	BB	SO
Ashby, Andy	2.94	12	10	31	31	2	0	192⅔	180	79	63	62	150
Florie, Bryce	3.01	2	2	47	0	0	1	68⅔	49	30	23	38	68
Hamilton, Joey	3.08	6	9	31	30	2	0	204½	189	89	70	56	123
Bochtler, Doug	3.57	4	4	34	0	0	1	45½	38	18	18	19	45
Hoffman, Trevor	3.88	7	4	55	0	0	31	53⅓	48	25	23	14	52
Benes, Andy	4.17	4	7	19	19	1	0	118⅓	121	65	55	45	126
Sanders, Scott	4.30	5	5	17	15	1	0	90	79	46	43	31	88
Blair, Willie	4.34	7	5	40	12	0	0	114	112	60	55	45	83
Valenzuela, Fernando	4.98	8	3	29	15	0	0	90½	101	53	50	34	57
Dishman, Glenn	5.01	4	8	19	16	0	0	97	104	60	54	34	43
Williams, Brian	6.00	3	10	44	6	0	0	72	79	54	48	38	75

San Francisco Giants

BATTING	BA	G	AB	R	H	TB	2B	3B	HR	RBI	SB	BB	SO
Williams, Matt	.336	76	283	53	95	183	17	1	23	65	2	30	58
Carreon, Mark	.301	117	396	53	119	194	24	0	17	65	0	23	37
Bonds, Barry	.294	144	506	109	149	292	30	7	33	104	31	120	83
Sanders, Deion	.268	85	343	48	92	137	11	8	6	28	24	27	60
Scarsone, Steve	.266	80	233	33	62	111	10	3	11	29	3	18	82
Reed, Jeff	.265	66	113	12	30	32	2	0	0	9	0	20	17
Hill, Glenallen	.264	132	497	71	131	240	29	4	24	86	25	39	98
Manwaring, Kirt	.251	118	379	21	95	126	15	2	4	36	1	27	72
Clayton, Royce	.244	138	509	56	124	174	29	3	5	58	24	38	109
Thompson, Robby	.223	95	336	51	75	114	15	0	8	23	1	42	76
Benjamin, Mike	.220	68	186	19	41	56	6	0	3	12	11	8	51
Patterson, John	.205	95	205	27	42	56	5	3	1	14	4	14	41
Phillips, J.R.	.195	92	231	27	45	81	9	0	9	28	19	1	69

PITCHING	ERA	W	L	G	GS	CG	SV	INN	H	R	ER	BB	SO
Dewey, Mark	3.13	1	0	27	0	0	0	31⅔	30	12	11	17	32
Service, Scott	3.19	3	1	28	0	0	0	31	18	11	11	20	30
Van Landingham, W.	3.67	6	3	18	18	1	0	122⅔	124	58	50	40	95
Leiter, Mark	3.82	10	12	30	29	7	0	195⅔	185	91	83	55	129
Wilson, Trevor	3.92	3	4	17	17	0	0	82⅔	82	42	36	38	38
Barton, Shawn	4.26	4	1	52	0	0	1	44½	37	22	21	19	22
Beck, Rod	4.45	5	6	60	0	0	33	58⅔	60	31	29	21	42
Brewington, Jamie	4.54	6	4	13	13	0	0	75½	68	38	38	45	45
Valdez, Sergio	4.75	4	5	13	11	1	0	66½	78	43	35	17	29
Aquino, Luis	5.10	0	3	34	0	0	2	42½	57	34	24	13	26
Hook, Chris	5.50	5	1	45	0	0	0	52½	56	33	32	29	40
Mulholland, Terry	5.80	5	13	29	24	2	0	149	190	112	96	38	65
Bautista, Jose	6.44	3	8	52	6	0	0	100⅔	120	77	72	26	45

Baltimore Orioles

BATTING	BA	G	AB	R	H	TB	2B	3B	HR	RBI	SB	BB	SO
Bonilla, Bobby	.333	61	237	47	79	129	12	4	10	46	0	23	31
Palmeiro, Rafael	.310	143	554	89	172	323	30	2	39	104	3	62	65
Baines, Harold	.299	127	385	60	115	208	19	1	24	63	0	70	45
Goodwin, Curtis	.293	87	289	40	76	96	11	3	1	24	22	15	53
Ripken, Cal, Jr.	.262	144	550	71	144	232	33	2	17	88	0	52	59
Anderson, Brady	.262	143	554	108	145	246	33	10	16	64	26	87	111
Zaun, Greg	.260	40	104	18	27	41	5	0	3	14	1	16	14
Manto, Jeff	.256	89	254	31	65	125	9	0	17	38	0	24	69
Hoiles, Chris	.250	114	352	53	88	162	15	1	19	58	1	67	80
Huson, Jeff	.248	66	161	24	40	51	4	2	1	19	5	15	20
Bass, Kevin	.244	111	295	32	72	99	12	0	5	32	8	24	47
Hammonds, Jeffrey	.242	57	178	18	43	66	9	1	4	23	4	9	30
Barberie, Bret	.241	90	237	32	57	77	14	0	2	25	3	36	50
Gomez, Leo	.236	53	127	16	30	47	5	0	4	12	0	18	23
Alexander, Manny	.236	94	242	35	57	77	9	1	3	23	11	20	3
Smith, Mark	.231	37	104	11	24	38	5	0	3	15	3	12	22

PITCHING	ERA	W	L	G	GS	CG	SV	INN	H	R	ER	BB	SO
Haynes, Jimmy	2.25	2	1	4	3	0	0	24	11	6	6	12	22
Orosco, Jesse	3.26	2	4	65	0	0	3	49⅔	28	19	18	27	58
Mussina, Mike	3.29	19	9	32	32	7	0	221⅓	187	86	81	50	158
Clark, Terry	3.46	2	5	38	0	0	1	39	40	15	15	15	18
Brown, Kevin	3.60	10	9	26	26	3	0	172⅓	155	73	69	48	117
McDonald, Ben	4.16	3	6	14	13	1	0	80	67	40	37	38	62
Oquist, Mike	4.17	2	1	27	0	0	0	54	51	27	25	41	27
Krivda, Rick	4.54	2	7	13	13	1	0	75⅓	76	40	38	25	53
Erickson, Scott	4.81	13	10	32	31	7	0	196⅓	213	108	105	67	106
Jones, Doug	5.01	0	4	52	0	0	22	46⅔	55	30	26	16	42
Moyer, Jamie	5.21	8	6	27	18	0	0	115⅔	117	70	67	30	65
Rhodes, Arthur	6.21	2	5	19	9	0	0	75⅓	68	53	52	48	77

Boston Red Sox

BATTING	BA	G	AB	R	H	TB	2B	3B	HR	RBI	SB	BB	SO
O'Leary, Troy	.308	112	399	60	123	196	31	6	10	49	5	29	64
Naehring, Tim	.307	126	433	61	133	194	27	2	10	57	0	77	66
Canseco, Jose	.306	102	396	64	121	220	25	1	24	81	4	42	93
Vaughn, Mo.	.300	140	550	98	165	316	28	3	39	126	11	68	150
Valentin, John	.298	135	520	108	155	277	37	2	27	102	20	81	67
Greenwell, Mike	.297	120	481	67	143	221	25	4	15	76	9	38	35
Jefferson, Reggie	.289	46	121	21	35	58	8	0	5	26	0	9	24
McGee, Willie	.285	67	200	32	57	80	11	3	2	15	5	9	41
Tinsley, Lee	.284	100	341	61	97	137	17	1	7	41	18	39	74
Alicea, Luis	.270	132	419	64	113	157	20	3	6	44	13	63	61
James, Chris	.268	42	82	8	22	32	4	0	2	8	1	7	14
Stairs, Matt	.261	39	88	8	23	35	7	1	1	17	0	4	14
Donnels, Chris	.253	40	91	13	23	35	2	2	2	11	0	9	18
Haselman, Bill	.243	64	152	22	37	60	6	1	5	23	0	17	30
MacFarlane, Mike	.225	115	164	45	82	147	18	1	15	51	2	38	78
Whiten, Mark	.185	32	108	13	20	26	3	0	1	10	1	8	23

PITCHING	ERA	W	L	G	GS	CG	SV	INN	H	R	ER	BB	SO
Aguilera, Rick	2.60	3	3	52	0	0	32	55⅓	46	16	16	13	52
Wakefield, Tim	2.95	16	8	27	27	6	0	195⅓	163	76	64	68	119
Sele, Aaron	3.06	3	1	6	6	0	0	32⅓	32	14	11	14	21
Belinda, Stan	3.10	8	1	63	0	0	10	69⅔	51	25	24	28	57
Maddux, Mike	3.61	4	1	36	4	0	1	89⅔	86	40	36	15	65
Cormier, Rheal	4.07	7	5	48	12	0	0	115	131	60	52	31	69
Clemens, Roger	4.18	10	5	23	3	0	0	140	141	70	65	60	132
Hanson, Erik	4.24	15	5	29	29	1	0	186⅔	187	94	88	59	139
Eshelman, Vaughn	4.85	6	3	23	14	0	0	81⅔	86	47	44	36	41
Ryan, Ken	4.96	0	4	28	0	0	7	32⅔	34	20	18	24	34
Smith, Zane	5.61	8	8	24	21	0	0	110⅔	114	78	69	23	47

California Angels

BATTING	BA	G	AB	R	H	TB	2B	3B	HR	RBI	SB	BB	SO
Salmon, Tim	.330	143	537	111	177	319	34	3	34	105	5	91	111
Anderson, Garret	.321	106	374	50	120	189	19	1	16	69	6	19	65
Davis, Chili	.318	119	424	81	135	218	23	0	20	86	3	89	79
DiSarcina, Gary	.307	99	362	61	111	166	28	6	5	41	7	20	25
Edmonds, Jim	.290	141	558	120	162	299	30	4	33	107	1	51	130
Snow, J.T.	.289	143	544	80	157	253	22	1	24	102	2	52	91
Aldrete, Mike	.268	78	149	19	40	60	8	0	4	24	0	19	31
Hudler, Rex	.265	84	223	30	59	93	16	0	6	27	12	10	48
Phillips, Tony	.261	139	525	119	137	241	21	1	27	61	13	113	35
Myers, Greg	.260	85	273	35	71	114	12	2	9	38	0	17	49
Fabregas, Jorge	.247	73	227	24	56	69	10	0	1	22	0	17	28
Lind, Jose	.236	44	140	9	33	38	5	0	0	7	0	6	12
Owen, Spike	.229	82	218	17	50	68	9	3	1	28	3	18	22
Easley, Damion	.216	114	357	35	77	107	14	2	4	35	5	32	47

PITCHING	ERA	W	L	G	GS	CG	SV	INN	H	R	ER	BB	SO
Percival, Troy	1.95	3	2	62	0	0	3	74	37	19	16	26	94
Patterson, Bob	3.04	5	2	62	0	0	0	53⅓	48	18	18	13	41
Smith, Lee	3.47	0	5	52	0	0	37	49⅓	42	19	19	25	43
Abbott, Jim	3.70	11	8	30	30	4	0	197	209	93	81	64	86
James, Mike	3.88	3	0	46	0	0	1	55⅓	49	27	24	26	36
Finley, Chuck	4.21	15	12	32	32	2	0	203	192	106	95	93	195
Langston, Mark	4.63	15	7	31	31	2	0	200⅓	212	109	103	64	142
Butcher, Mike	4.73	6	1	40	0	0	0	51⅓	49	28	27	31	29
Harkey, Mike	5.44	8	9	26	20	1	0	127⅓	155	78	77	47	56
Boskie, Shawn	5.64	7	7	20	20	1	0	111⅓	127	73	70	25	51
Anderson, Brian	5.87	6	8	18	17	1	0	99⅓	110	66	65	30	45
Bielecki, Mike	5.97	4	6	22	11	0	0	75⅓	80	56	50	31	45

Chicago White Sox

BATTING	BA	G	AB	R	H	TB	2B	3B	HR	RBI	SB	BB	SO
Thomas, Frank	.308	145	493	102	152	299	27	0	40	111	3	136	74
Kruk, John	.308	45	159	13	49	62	7	0	2	23	0	26	33
Martinez, Dave	.307	119	303	49	93	132	16	4	5	37	8	32	41
Johnson, Lance	.306	142	607	98	186	258	18	12	10	57	40	32	31
Devereaux, Mike	.306	92	333	48	102	155	21	1	10	55	6	25	51
Mouton, Lyle	.302	58	179	23	54	85	16	0	5	27	1	19	46
Ventura, Robin	.295	135	492	79	145	245	22	0	26	93	4	75	98
Raines, Tim	.285	133	502	81	143	212	25	4	12	67	13	70	52
Martin, Norberto	.269	72	160	17	43	64	7	4	2	17	5	3	25
Grebeck, Craig	.260	53	154	19	40	55	12	0	1	18	0	21	23
Durham, Ray	.257	125	471	68	121	181	27	6	7	51	18	31	83
Sabo, Chris	.254	20	71	10	18	26	5	0	1	8	2	3	12
Guillen, Ozzie	.248	122	415	50	103	132	20	3	1	41	6	13	25
LaValliere, Mike	.245	46	98	7	24	33	6	0	1	19	0	9	15
Karkovice, Ron	.217	113	323	44	70	125	14	1	13	51	2	39	84

PITCHING	ERA	W	L	G	GS	CG	SV	INN	H	R	ER	BB	SO
Karchner, Matt	1.69	4	2	31	0	0	0	32	33	8	6	12	24
Fernandez, Alex	3.80	12	8	30	30	5	0	203⅔	200	98	86	65	159
Hernandez, Roberto	3.92	3	7	60	0	0	32	59⅔	63	30	26	28	84
Sirotka, Mike	4.19	1	2	6	6	0	0	34⅓	39	16	16	17	19
Righetti, Dave	4.20	3	2	10	9	0	0	49⅓	65	24	23	18	29
Alvarez, Wilson	4.32	8	11	29	29	3	0	175	171	96	84	93	118
McCaskill, Kirk	4.89	6	4	55	1	0	2	81	97	50	44	33	50
Keyser, Brian	4.97	5	6	23	10	0	0	92⅓	114	53	51	27	48
DeLeon, Jose	5.19	5	3	38	0	0	0	67⅔	60	41	39	28	53
Radinsky, Scott	5.45	2	1	46	0	0	1	38	46	23	23	17	14
Fortugno, Tim	5.59	1	3	37	0	0	0	38⅔	30	24	24	19	24
Bere, Jason	7.19	8	15	27	27	1	0	137⅔	151	120	110	106	110

Cleveland Indians

BATTING	BA	G	AB	R	H	TB	2B	3B	HR	RBI	SB	BB	SO
Murray, Eddie	.323	113	436	68	141	225	21	0	21	82	5	39	65
Belle, Albert	.317	143	546	121	173	377	52	1	50	126	5	73	80
Perry, Herb	.315	52	162	23	51	75	13	1	3	23	1	13	28
Baerga, Carlos	.314	135	557	87	175	252	28	2	15	90	11	35	31
Thome, Jim	.314	137	452	92	142	252	29	3	25	73	4	97	113
Lofton, Kenny	.310	118	481	93	149	218	22	13	7	53	54	40	49
Ramirez, Manny	.308	137	484	85	149	270	26	1	31	107	6	75	112
Alomar, Sandy, Jr.	.300	66	203	32	61	97	6	0	10	35	3	7	26
Vizquel, Omar	.266	136	542	87	144	190	28	0	6	56	29	59	59
Pena, Tony	.262	91	263	25	69	99	15	0	5	28	1	14	44
Espinoza, Alvaro	.252	66	143	15	36	46	4	0	2	17	0	2	16
Sorrento, Paul	.235	104	323	50	76	165	14	0	25	79	1	51	71
Kirby, Wayne	.207	101	188	29	39	56	10	2	1	14	10	13	32
Winfield, Dave	.191	46	115	11	22	33	5	0	2	4	1	14	26

PITCHING	ERA	W	L	G	GS	CG	SV	INN	H	R	ER	BB	SO
Mesa, Jose	1.13	3	0	62	0	0	46	64	49	9	8	17	58
Tavarez, Julian	2.44	10	2	57	0	0	0	85	76	36	23	21	68
Plunk, Eric	2.67	6	2	56	0	0	2	64	48	19	19	27	71
Assenmacher, Paul	2.82	6	2	47	0	0	0	38⅓	32	13	12	12	40
Ogea, Chad	3.05	8	3	20	14	1	0	106½	95	38	36	29	57
Martinez, Dennis	3.08	12	5	28	28	3	0	187	174	71	64	46	99
Poole, Jim	3.75	3	3	42	0	0	0	50⅓	40	22	21	17	41
Hershiser, Orel	3.87	16	6	26	26	1	0	167⅓	151	76	72	51	111
Hill, Ken	3.98	4	1	12	11	1	0	74⅔	77	36	33	32	48
Nagy, Charles	4.55	16	6	29	29	2	0	178	194	95	90	61	139
Clark, Mark	5.27	9	7	22	21	2	0	124⅔	143	77	73	42	68
Black, Bud	6.85	4	2	11	10	0	0	47⅓	63	42	36	16	34

Detroit Tigers

BATTING	BA	G	AB	R	H	TB	2B	3B	HR	RBI	SB	BB	SO
Whitaker, Lou	.293	84	249	36	73	129	14	0	14	44	4	31	41
Fryman, Travis	.275	144	567	79	156	232	21	5	15	81	4	63	100
Trammell, Alan	.269	74	223	28	60	78	12	0	2	23	3	27	19
Curtis, Chad	.268	144	586	96	157	255	29	3	21	67	27	70	93
Gibson, Kirk	.260	70	227	37	59	102	12	2	9	35	9	33	61
Stubbs, Franklin	.250	62	116	13	29	46	11	0	2	19	0	19	27
Flaherty, John	.243	112	354	39	86	143	22	1	11	40	0	18	47
Fielder, Cecil	.243	136	494	70	120	233	18	1	31	82	0	75	116
Clark, Tony	.238	27	101	10	24	40	5	1	3	11	0	8	30
Fletcher, Scott	.231	67	182	19	42	57	10	1	1	17	1	19	27
Tingley, Ron	.226	54	124	14	28	50	8	1	4	16	0	15	38
Higginson, Bob	.224	131	410	61	92	161	17	5	14	43	6	62	107
Gomez, Leo	.223	123	431	49	96	153	20	2	11	50	4	41	96
Nevin, Phil	.219	29	96	9	21	32	3	1	2	12	0	11	27
Cuyler, Milt	.205	41	88	15	18	27	1	4	0	5	2	8	16
Bautista, Danny	.203	89	271	28	55	85	9	0	7	27	4	12	68

PITCHING	ERA	W	L	G	GS	CG	SV	INN	H	R	ER	BB	SO
Henneman, Mike	1.53	0	1	29	0	0	18	29⅓	24	5	5	9	24
Wells, David	3.04	10	3	18	18	3	0	130½	120	54	44	37	83
Christopher, Mike	3.82	4	0	36	0	0	1	61⅓	71	28	26	14	34
Lira, Felipe	4.31	9	13	37	22	0	1	146⅓	151	74	70	56	89
Doherty, John	5.10	5	9	48	2	0	6	113	130	66	64	37	46
Bergman, Sean	5.12	7	10	28	28	1	0	135½	169	95	77	67	86
Bohanon, Brian	5.54	1	1	52	10	0	1	105⅔	121	68	65	41	63
Lima, Jose	6.11	3	9	15	15	0	0	73⅔	85	52	50	18	37
Boever, Joe	6.39	5	7	60	0	0	3	98⅔	128	74	70	44	71
Maxcy, Brian	6.88	4	5	41	0	0	0	52⅓	61	48	40	31	20
Nitkowski, C.J.	7.09	1	4	11	11	0	0	39⅓	53	32	31	20	13
Groom, Buddy	7.52	1	3	23	4	0	1	40⅔	55	35	34	26	23
Moore, Mike	7.53	5	15	25	25	1	0	132⅔	179	118	111	68	64

American League Team-by-Team Statistical Leaders *(Cont.)*

Kansas City Royals

BATTING	BA	G	AB	R	H	TB	2B	3B	HR	RBI	SB	BB	SO
Lockhart, Keith	.321	94	274	41	88	131	19	3	6	33	8	14	21
Joyner, Wally	.310	131	465	69	144	208	28	0	12	83	3	69	65
Goodwin, Tom	.288	133	480	72	138	172	16	3	4	28	50	38	72
Damon, Johnny	.282	47	188	32	53	83	11	5	3	23	7	12	22
Samuel, Juan	.263	91	205	31	54	102	10	1	12	39	6	29	49
Gaetti, Gary	.261	137	514	76	134	266	27	0	35	96	3	47	91
Tucker, Mike	.260	62	177	23	46	68	10	0	4	17	2	18	51
Gagne, Greg	.256	120	430	58	110	161	25	4	6	49	3	38	60
Vitello, Joe	.254	53	130	13	33	58	4	0	7	21	0	8	25
Mayne, Brent	.251	110	307	23	77	100	18	1	1	27	0	25	41
Nunnally, Jon	.244	119	303	51	74	143	15	6	14	42	6	51	86
Howard, David	.243	95	255	23	62	83	13	4	0	19	6	24	41
Caceres, Edgar	.239	55	117	13	28	41	6	2	1	17	2	8	15
Borders, Pat	.231	52	143	14	33	55	8	1	4	13	0	7	22

PITCHING	ERA	W	L	G	GS	CG	SV	INN	H	R	ER	BB	SO
Montgomery, Jeff	3.43	2	3	54	0	0	31	65⅔	60	27	25	25	49
Haney, Chris	3.56	3	4	16	13	1	0	81⅓	78	35	33	33	31
Gubicza, Mark	3.75	12	14	33	33	3	0	213⅓	222	97	89	62	81
Appier, Kevin	3.89	15	10	31	31	4	0	201⅓	163	90	87	80	185
Olson, Gregg	4.09	3	3	23	0	0	3	33	28	15	15	19	21
Magnante, Mike	4.23	1	1	28	0	0	0	44⅔	45	23	21	16	28
Pichardo, Hipolito	4.36	8	4	44	0	0	1	64	66	34	31	30	43
Gordon, Tom	4.43	12	12	31	31	2	0	189	204	110	93	89	119
Meacham, Rusty	4.98	4	3	49	0	0	2	59⅔	72	36	33	19	30
Jacome, Jason	5.36	4	6	15	14	1	0	84	101	52	50	21	39
Brewer, Billy	5.56	2	4	48	0	0	0	45⅓	54	28	28	20	31
Fleming, Dave	5.96	1	6	25	12	1	0	80	84	61	53	53	40

Milwaukee Brewers

BATTING	BA	G	AB	R	H	TB	2B	3B	HR	RBI	SB	BB	SO
Surhoff, B.J.	.320	117	415	72	133	204	26	3	13	73	7	37	43
Jaha, John	.313	88	316	59	99	183	20	2	20	65	2	36	66
Seitzer, Kevin	.311	132	492	56	153	207	33	3	5	69	2	64	57
Nilsson, Dave	.278	81	263	41	73	123	12	1	12	53	2	24	41
Cirillo, Jeff	.277	125	328	57	91	145	19	4	9	39	7	47	42
Oliver, Joe	.273	97	337	43	92	148	20	0	12	51	2	27	66
Hamilton, Darryl	.271	112	398	54	108	155	20	6	5	44	11	47	35
Ward, Turner	.264	44	129	19	34	51	3	1	4	16	6	14	21
Vina, Fernando	.257	113	288	46	74	104	7	7	3	29	6	22	28
Mieske, Matt	.251	117	267	42	67	118	13	1	12	48	2	27	45
Hulse, David	.251	119	339	46	85	117	11	6	3	47	15	18	60
May, Derrick	.248	32	113	15	28	36	3	1	1	9	0	5	18
Matheny, Mike	.247	80	166	13	41	52	9	1	0	21	2	12	28
Vaughn, Greg	.224	108	392	67	88	160	19	1	17	59	10	55	89
Valentin, Jose	.219	112	338	62	74	136	23	3	11	49	16	37	83
Listach, Pat	.219	101	334	35	73	85	8	2	0	25	13	25	61

PITCHING	ERA	W	L	G	GS	CG	SV	INN	H	R	ER	BB	SO
Reyes, Al	2.43	1	1	27	0	0	1	33⅓	19	9	9	18	29
Fetters, Mike	3.38	0	3	40	0	0	22	34⅔	40	16	13	20	33
Kiefer, Mark	3.44	4	1	24	0	0	0	49⅔	37	20	19	27	41
Karl, Scott	4.14	6	7	25	18	1	0	124	141	65	57	50	59
Lloyd, Graeme	4.50	0	5	33	0	0	4	32	28	16	16	8	13
Bones, Ricky	4.63	10	12	32	31	3	0	200⅓	218	108	103	83	77
Sparks, Steve	4.63	9	11	33	27	3	0	202	210	111	104	86	96
McAndrew, Jamie	4.71	2	3	10	4	0	0	36⅓	37	21	19	12	19
Givens, Brian	4.95	5	7	19	19	0	0	107⅓	116	71	59	54	73
Miranda, Angel	5.23	4	5	30	10	0	1	74	83	47	43	49	45
Wegman, Bill	5.35	5	7	37	4	0	2	70⅔	89	45	42	21	50
Rightnowar, Ron	5.40	2	1	34	0	0	1	36⅔	35	23	22	18	22
Roberson, Sid	5.76	6	4	26	13	0	0	84⅓	102	55	54	37	40
Ignasiak, Mike	5.90	4	1	25	0	0	0	39⅔	51	27	26	23	26
Scanlan, Bob	6.59	4	7	17	14	0	0	83⅓	101	66	61	44	29

American League Team-by-Team Statistical Leaders (Cont.)

Minnesota Twins

BATTING	BA	G	AB	R	H	TB	2B	3B	HR	RBI	SB	BB	SO
Cole, Alex	.342	28	79	10	27	37	3	2	1	14	1	8	15
Clark, Jerald	.339	36	109	17	37	60	8	3	3	15	3	2	11
Knoblauch, Chuck	.333	136	538	107	179	262	34	8	11	63	46	78	95
Puckett, Kirby	.314	137	538	83	169	277	39	0	23	99	3	56	89
Munoz, Pedro	.301	104	376	45	113	184	17	0	18	58	0	19	86
Reboulet, Jeff	.292	87	216	39	63	86	11	0	4	23	1	27	34
Merullo, Matt	.282	76	195	19	55	74	14	1	1	27	0	14	27
Cordova, Marty	.277	137	512	81	142	249	27	4	24	84	20	52	111
Meares, Pat	.269	116	390	57	105	168	19	4	12	49	10	15	68
Stahoviak, Scott	.266	94	263	28	70	98	19	0	3	23	5	30	61
Hale, Chip	.262	69	103	10	27	37	4	0	2	18	0	11	20
Coomer, Ron	.257	37	101	15	26	46	3	1	5	19	0	9	11
Walbeck, Matt	.257	115	393	40	101	124	18	1	1	44	3	25	71
Leius, Scott	.247	117	372	51	92	130	16	5	4	45	2	49	54
Masteller, Dan	.237	71	198	21	47	68	12	0	3	21	1	18	19
Becker, Rich	.237	106	392	45	93	116	15	1	2	33	8	34	95

PITCHING	ERA	W	L	G	GS	CG	SV	INN	H	R	ER	BB	SO
Robertson, Rich	3.83	2	0	25	4	1	0	51⅔	48	28	22	31	38
Guthrie, Mark	4.46	5	3	36	0	0	0	42⅓	47	22	21	16	48
Tapani, Kevin	4.92	6	11	20	20	3	0	133⅔	155	79	73	34	88
Stevens, Dave	5.07	5	4	56	0	0	10	65⅔	74	40	37	32	47
Guardado, Eddie	5.12	4	9	51	5	0	2	91⅓	99	54	52	45	71
Radke, Brad	5.32	11	14	29	28	2	0	181	195	112	107	47	75
Trombley, Mike	5.62	4	8	20	18	0	0	97⅔	107	68	61	42	68
Rodriguez, Frank	6.13	5	8	25	18	0	0	105⅔	114	83	72	57	59
Mahomes, Pat	6.37	4	10	47	7	0	3	94⅔	100	74	67	47	67
Klingenbeck, Scott	7.12	2	4	24	9	0	0	79⅔	101	65	63	42	42
Parra, Jose	7.59	1	5	12	12	0	0	61⅔	83	59	52	22	29

New York Yankees

BATTING	BA	G	AB	R	H	TB	2B	3B	HR	RBI	SB	BB	SO
Boggs, Wade	.324	126	460	76	149	194	22	4	5	63	1	74	50
Williams, Bernie	.307	144	563	93	173	274	29	9	18	82	8	75	98
O'Neill, Paul	.300	127	460	82	138	242	30	4	22	96	1	71	76
Mattingly, Don	.288	128	458	59	132	189	32	2	7	49	0	40	35
James, Dion	.287	85	209	22	60	74	6	1	2	26	4	20	16
Velarde, Randy	.278	111	367	60	102	144	19	1	7	46	5	55	64
Strawberry, Darryl	.276	32	87	15	24	39	4	1	3	13	0	10	22
Davis, Russ	.276	40	98	14	27	42	5	2	2	12	0	10	26
Leyritz, Jim	.269	77	264	37	71	104	12	0	7	37	1	37	73
Stanley, Mike	.268	118	399	63	107	192	29	1	18	83	1	57	106
Sierra, Ruben	.263	126	479	73	126	215	32	0	19	86	5	46	76
Polonia, Luis	.261	67	238	37	62	83	9	3	2	15	10	25	29
Williams, Gerald	.247	100	182	33	45	85	18	2	6	28	4	22	34
Fernandez, Tony	.245	108	384	57	94	133	20	2	5	45	6	42	40
Kelly, Pat	.237	89	270	32	64	90	12	1	4	29	8	23	65

PITCHING	ERA	W	L	G	GS	CG	SV	INN	H	R	ER	BB	SO
Wetteland, John	2.93	1	5	60	0	0	31	61⅓	40	22	20	14	66
Honeycutt, Rick	2.96	5	1	52	0	0	2	45⅔	39	16	15	10	21
Cone, David	3.57	18	8	30	30	6	0	229⅓	195	95	91	88	191
McDowell, Jack	3.93	15	10	30	30	8	0	217⅔	211	106	95	78	157
Kamieniecki, Scott	4.01	7	6	17	16	1	0	89⅔	83	43	40	49	43
Wickman, Bob	4.05	2	4	63	1	0	1	80	77	38	36	33	51
Pettitte, Andy	4.17	12	9	31	26	3	0	175	183	86	81	63	114
Hitchcock, Sterling	4.70	11	10	27	27	4	0	168⅓	155	91	88	68	121
MacDonald, Bob	4.86	1	1	33	0	0	0	46⅓	50	25	25	22	41
Howe, Steve	4.96	6	3	56	0	0	2	49	66	29	27	17	28
Rivera, Mariano	5.51	5	3	19	10	0	0	67	71	43	41	30	51
Perez, Melido	5.58	5	5	13	12	1	0	69⅓	70	46	40	31	44
Key, Jimmy	5.64	1	2	5	5	0	0	30⅓	40	20	19	6	14
Ausanio, Joe	5.73	2	0	28	0	0	1	37⅔	42	24	24	23	36
Bankhead, Scott	6.00	1	1	20	1	0	0	39	44	26	26	16	20

Oakland Athletics

BATTING	BA	G	AB	R	H	TB	2B	3B	HR	RBI	SB	BB	SO
Henderson, Rickey	.300	112	407	67	122	182	31	1	9	54	32	72	66
Williams, George	.291	29	79	13	23	39	5	1	3	14	0	11	21
Berroa, Geronimo	.278	141	546	87	152	246	22	3	22	88	7	63	98
Steinbach, Terry	.278	114	406	43	113	186	26	1	15	65	1	25	74
Javier, Stan	.278	130	442	81	123	171	20	2	8	56	36	49	63
McGwire, Mark	.274	104	317	75	87	217	13	0	39	90	1	88	77
Bordick, Mike	.264	126	428	46	113	150	13	0	8	44	11	35	48
Brosius, Scott	.263	123	388	69	102	176	19	2	17	46	4	41	67
Giambi, Jason	.256	54	176	27	45	70	7	0	6	25	2	28	31
Gates, Brent	.254	136	524	60	133	180	24	4	5	56	3	46	84
Herrera, Jose	.243	33	70	9	17	22	1	2	0	2	1	6	11
Tartabull, Danny	.236	83	280	34	66	106	16	0	8	35	0	43	82
Gallego, Mike	.233	43	120	11	28	28	0	0	0	8	0	9	24
Paquette, Craig	.226	105	283	42	64	118	13	1	13	49	5	12	88

PITCHING	ERA	W	L	G	GS	CG	SV	INN	H	R	ER	BB	SO
Corsi, Jim	2.20	2	4	38	0	0	2	45	31	14	11	26	26
Ontiveros, Steve	4.37	9	6	22	22	2	0	129⅔	144	75	63	38	77
Stottlemyre, Todd	4.55	14	7	31	31	2	0	209⅔	228	117	106	80	205
Johns, Doug	4.61	5	3	11	9	1	0	54⅓	44	32	28	26	25
Eckersley, Dennis	4.83	4	6	52	0	0	29	50⅓	53	29	27	11	40
Van Poppel, Todd	4.88	4	8	36	14	1	0	138⅓	125	77	75	56	122
Prieto, Ariel	4.97	2	6	14	9	1	0	58	57	35	32	32	37
Reyes, Carlos	5.09	4	6	40	1	0	0	69	71	43	39	28	48
Wojciechowski, Steve	5.18	2	3	14	7	0	0	48⅔	51	28	28	28	13
Acre, Mark	5.71	1	2	43	0	0	0	52	52	35	33	28	47
Darling, Ron	6.23	4	7	21	21	1	0	104	124	79	72	46	69
Stewart, Dave	6.89	3	7	16	16	0	0	81	101	65	62	39	58

Seattle Mariners

BATTING	BA	G	AB	R	H	TB	2B	3B	HR	RBI	SB	BB	SO
Martinez, Edgar	.356	145	511	121	182	321	52	0	29	113	4	116	87
Cora, Joey	.297	120	427	64	127	159	19	2	3	39	18	37	31
Martinez, Tino	.293	141	519	92	152	286	35	3	31	111	0	62	91
Sojo, Luis	.289	102	339	50	98	141	18	2	7	39	4	23	19
Coleman, Vince	.288	115	455	66	131	181	23	6	5	29	42	37	80
Amaral, Rich	.282	90	238	45	67	91	14	2	2	19	21	21	33
Wilson, Dan	.278	119	399	40	111	166	22	3	9	51	2	33	63
Strange, Doug	.271	74	155	19	42	61	9	2	2	21	0	10	25
Buhner, Jay	.262	126	470	86	123	266	23	0	40	121	0	60	120
Newson, Warren	.261	84	157	34	41	62	2	2	5	15	2	39	45
Griffey, Ken, Jr	.258	72	260	52	67	125	7	0	17	42	4	52	53
Blowers, Mike	.257	134	439	59	113	208	24	1	23	96	2	53	128
Diaz, Alex	.248	103	270	44	67	90	14	0	3	27	18	13	27
Bragg, Darren	.234	52	145	20	34	50	5	1	3	12	9	18	37
Rodriguez, Alex	.232	48	142	15	33	58	6	2	5	19	4	6	42
Fermin, Felix	.195	73	200	21	39	45	6	0	0	15	2	6	6

PITCHING	ERA	W	L	G	GS	CG	SV	INN	H	R	ER	BB	SO
Charlton, Norm	1.51	2	1	30	0	0	14	47⅔	23	12	8	16	58
Nelson, Jeff	2.17	7	3	62	0	0	2	78⅔	58	21	19	27	96
Johnson, Randy	2.48	18	2	30	30	6	0	214⅓	159	65	59	65	294
Risley, Bill	3.13	2	1	45	0	0	1	60⅓	55	21	21	18	65
Wolcott, Bob	4.42	3	2	7	6	0	0	36⅔	43	18	18	14	19
Ayala, Bobby	4.44	6	5	63	0	0	19	71	73	42	35	30	77
Belcher, Tim	4.52	10	12	28	28	1	0	179½	188	101	90	88	96
Bosio, Chris	4.92	10	8	31	31	0	0	170	211	98	93	69	85
Carmona, Rafael	5.66	2	4	15	3	0	1	47⅔	55	31	30	34	28
Wells, Bob	5.75	4	3	30	4	0	0	76⅔	88	51	49	39	38
Benes, Andy	5.86	7	2	12	12	0	0	63	72	42	41	33	45
Torres, Salomon	6.00	3	8	16	13	1	0	72	87	53	48	42	45

Texas Rangers

BATTING	BA	G	AB	R	H	TB	2B	3B	HR	RBI	SB	BB	SO
Palmer, Dean	.336	36	119	30	40	73	6	0	9	24	1	21	21
Rodriguez, Ivan	.303	130	492	56	149	221	32	2	12	67	0	16	48
Clark, Will	.302	123	454	85	137	218	27	3	16	92	0	68	50
Gonzalez, Juan	.295	90	352	57	104	209	20	2	27	82	0	17	66
Nixon, Otis	.295	139	589	87	174	199	21	2	0	45	50	58	85
Frye, Jeff	.278	90	313	38	87	118	15	2	4	29	3	24	45
Greer, Rusty	.271	131	417	58	113	177	21	2	13	61	3	55	66
Maldonado, Candy	.263	74	190	28	50	93	16	0	9	30	1	32	50
McLemore, Mark	.261	129	467	73	122	167	20	5	5	41	21	59	71
Valle, Dave	.240	36	75	7	18	21	3	0	0	5	1	6	18
Tettleton, Mickey	.238	134	429	76	102	219	19	1	32	78	0	107	110
Pagliarulo, Mike	.232	86	241	27	56	84	16	0	4	27	0	15	49
Ortiz, Luis	.231	41	108	10	25	37	5	2	1	18	0	6	18
Worthington, Craig	.221	26	68	4	15	25	4	0	2	6	0	7	8
Gil, Benji	.219	130	415	36	91	144	20	3	9	46	2	26	147

PITCHING	ERA	W	L	G	GS	CG	SV	INN	H	R	ER	BB	SO
Vosberg, Ed	3.00	5	5	44	0	0	4	36	32	15	12	16	36
Russell, Jeff	3.03	1	0	37	0	0	20	32⅔	36	12	11	9	21
Rogers, Kenny	3.38	17	7	31	31	3	0	208	192	87	78	76	140
McDowell, Roger	4.02	7	4	64	0	0	4	85	86	39	38	34	49
Whiteside, Matt	4.08	5	4	40	0	0	3	53	48	24	24	19	46
Oliver, Darren	4.22	4	2	17	7	0	0	47	47	25	23	32	39
Pavlik, Roger	4.37	10	10	31	31	2	0	191⅓	174	96	93	90	149
Cook, Dennis	4.53	0	2	46	1	0	2	57⅔	63	32	29	26	53
Witt, Bobby	4.55	3	4	10	10	1	0	61⅔	81	35	31	21	46
Tewksbury, Bob	4.58	8	7	21	21	4	0	129⅔	169	75	66	20	53
Gross, Kevin	5.54	9	15	31	30	4	0	183⅔	200	124	113	89	106
Burrows, Terry	6.45	2	2	28	3	0	1	44⅔	60	37	32	19	22
Darwin, Danny	7.45	3	10	20	15	1	0	99	131	87	82	31	58

Toronto Blue Jays

BATTING	BA	G	AB	R	H	TB	2B	3B	HR	RBI	SB	BB	SO
Alomar, Roberto	.300	130	517	71	155	232	24	7	13	66	30	47	45
Olerud, John	.291	135	492	72	143	199	32	0	8	54	0	84	54
Green, Shawn	.288	121	379	52	109	193	31	4	15	54	1	20	68
White, Devon	.283	101	427	61	121	184	23	5	10	53	11	29	97
Molitor, Paul	.270	130	525	63	142	222	31	2	15	60	12	61	57
Carter, Joe	.253	139	558	70	141	239	23	0	25	76	12	37	87
Perez, Tomas	.245	41	98	12	24	32	3	1	1	8	10	7	18
Sprague, Ed	.244	144	521	77	127	212	27	2	18	74	0	58	96
Gonzalez, Alex	.243	111	367	51	89	146	19	4	10	42	4	44	114
Martinez, Angel	.241	62	191	12	46	64	12	0	2	25	0	7	45
Cedeno, Domingo	.236	51	161	18	38	58	6	1	4	14	0	10	35
Huff, Mike	.232	61	138	14	32	46	9	1	1	9	1	22	21
Knorr, Randy	.212	45	132	18	28	45	8	0	3	16	0	11	28
Parrish, Lance	.202	70	178	15	36	57	9	0	4	22	0	15	52

PITCHING	ERA	W	L	G	GS	CG	SV	INN	H	R	ER	BB	SO
Timlin, Mike	2.14	4	3	31	0	0	5	42	38	13	10	17	36
Crabtree, Tim	3.09	0	2	31	0	0	0	32	30	16	11	13	21
Castillo, Tony	3.22	1	5	55	0	0	13	72⅔	64	27	26	24	38
Leiter, Al	3.64	11	11	28	28	2	0	183	162	80	74	108	153
Williams, Woody	3.69	1	2	23	3	0	0	53⅔	44	23	22	28	41
Robinson, Ken	3.69	1	2	21	0	0	0	39	25	21	16	22	31
Menhart, Paul	4.92	1	4	21	9	1	0	78⅔	72	49	43	47	50
Hentgen, Pat	5.11	10	14	30	30	2	0	200¾	236	129	114	90	135
Hurtado, Edwin	5.45	5	2	14	10	1	0	77¾	81	50	47	40	33
Guzman, Juan	6.32	4	14	24	24	3	0	135⅓	151	101	95	73	94
Carrara, Giovanni	7.21	2	4	12	7	1	0	48¾	64	46	49	25	27
Cox, Danny	7.40	1	3	24	0	0	0	45	57	40	37	33	38

The World Series

Results

1903 ....Boston (A) 5, Pittsburgh (N) 3	1950 ....New York (A) 4, Philadelphia (N) 0
1904 ....No series	1951 ....New York (A) 4, New York (N) 2
1905 ....New York (N) 4, Philadelphia (A) 1	1952 ....New York (A) 4, Brooklyn (N) 3
1906 ....Chicago (A) 4, Chicago (N) 2	1953 ....New York (A) 4, Brooklyn (N) 2
1907 ....Chicago (N) 4, Detroit (A) 0; 1 tie	1954 ....New York (N) 4, Cleveland (A) 0
1908 ....Chicago (N) 4, Detroit (A) 1	1955 ....Brooklyn (N) 4, New York (A) 3
1909 ....Pittsburgh (N) 4, Detroit (A) 3	1956 ....New York (A) 4, Brooklyn (N) 3
1910 ....Philadelphia (A) 4, Chicago (N) 1	1957 ....Milwaukee (N) 4, New York (A) 3
1911 ....Philadelphia (A) 4, New York (N) 2	1958 ....New York (A) 4, Milwaukee (N) 3
1912 ....Boston (A) 4, New York (N) 3; 1 tie	1959 ....Los Angeles (N) 4, Chicago (A) 2
1913 ....Philadelphia (A) 4, New York (N) 1	1960 ....Pittsburgh (N) 4, New York (A) 3
1914 ....Boston (N) 4, Philadelphia (A) 0	1961 ....New York (A) 4, Cincinnati (N) 1
1915 ....Boston (A) 4, Philadelphia (N) 1	1962 ....New York (A) 4, San Francisco (N) 3
1916 ....Boston (A) 4, Brooklyn (N) 1	1963 ....Los Angeles (N) 4, New York (A) 0
1917 ....Chicago (A) 4, New York (N) 2	1964 ....St Louis (N) 4, New York (A) 3
1918 ....Boston (A) 4, Chicago (N) 2	1965 ....Los Angeles (N) 4, Minnesota (A) 3
1919 ....Cincinnati (N) 5, Chicago (A) 3	1966 ....Baltimore (A) 4, Los Angeles (N) 0
1920 ....Cleveland (A) 5, Brooklyn (N) 2	1967 ....St Louis (N) 4, Boston (A) 3
1921 ....New York (N) 5, New York (A) 3	1968 ....Detroit (A) 4, St Louis (N) 3
1922 ....New York (N) 4, New York (A) 0; 1 tie	1969 ....New York (N) 4, Baltimore (A) 1
1923 ....New York (A) 4, New York (N) 2	1970 ....Baltimore (A) 4, Cincinnati (N) 1
1924 ....Washington (A) 4, New York (N) 3	1971 ....Pittsburgh (N) 4, Baltimore (A) 3
1925 ....Pittsburgh (N) 4, Washington (A) 3	1972 ....Oakland (A) 4, Cincinnati (N) 3
1926 ....St Louis (N) 4, New York (A) 3	1973 ....Oakland (A) 4, New York (N) 3
1927 ....New York (A) 4, Pittsburgh (N) 0	1974 ....Oakland (A) 4, Los Angeles (N) 1
1928 ....New York (A) 4, St Louis (N) 0	1975 ....Cincinnati (N) 4, Boston (A) 3
1929 ....Philadelphia (A) 4, Chicago (N) 1	1976 ....Cincinnati (N) 4, New York (A) 0
1930 ....Philadelphia (A) 4, St Louis (N) 2	1977 ....New York (A) 4, Los Angeles (N) 2
1931 ....St Louis (N) 4, Philadelphia (A) 3	1978 ....New York (A) 4, Los Angeles (N) 2
1932 ....New York (A) 4, Chicago (N) 0	1979 ....Pittsburgh (N) 4, Baltimore (A) 3
1933 ....New York (N) 4, Washington (A) 1	1980 ....Philadelphia (N) 4, Kansas City (A) 2
1934 ....St Louis (N) 4, Detroit (A) 3	1981 ....Los Angeles (N) 4, New York (A) 2
1935 ....Detroit (A) 4, Chicago (N) 2	1982 ....St Louis (N) 4, Milwaukee (A) 3
1936 ....New York (A) 4, New York (N) 2	1983 ....Baltimore (A) 4, Philadelphia (N) 1
1937 ....New York (A) 4, New York (N) 1	1984 ....Detroit (A) 4, San Diego (N) 1
1938 ....New York (A) 4, Chicago (N) 0	1985 ....Kansas City (A) 4, St Louis (N) 3
1939 ....New York (A) 4, Cincinnati (N) 0	1986 ....New York (N) 4, Boston (A) 3
1940 ....Cincinnati (N) 4, Detroit (A) 3	1987 ....Minnesota (A) 4, St Louis (N) 3
1941 ....New York (A) 4, Brooklyn (N) 1	1988 ....Los Angeles (N) 4, Oakland (A) 1
1942 ....St Louis (N) 4, New York (A) 1	1989 ....Oakland (A) 4, San Francisco (N) 0
1943 ....New York (A) 4, St Louis (N) 1	1990 ....Cincinnati (N) 4, Oakland (A) 0
1944 ....St Louis (N) 4, St Louis (A) 2	1991 ....Minnesota (A) 4, Atlanta (N) 3
1945 ....Detroit (A) 4, Chicago (N) 3	1992 ....Toronto (A) 4, Atlanta (N) 2
1946 ....St Louis (N) 4, Boston (A) 3	1993 ....Toronto (A) 4, Philadelphia (N) 2
1947 ....New York (A) 4, Brooklyn (N) 3	1994 ....Series canceled due to players' strike
1948 ....Cleveland (A) 4, Boston (N) 2	1995 ....Atlanta (N) 4, Cleveland (A) 2
1949 ....New York (A) 4, Brooklyn (N) 1	

Reverse Jordan

Perhaps you've heard of the Chicago athlete, accustomed to competition at the highest level of his game, who left the Windy City to try his hand at another sport, one he hadn't played in years. No, we're not referring to that smooth-pated former Bull—we're talking about Cub relief pitcher Randy Myers. Tired of cooling his heels during the baseball strike, Myers decided to kick them up on the basketball court at Clark College, a juco in Vancouver, Wash. Myers, 32, played baseball at Clark in 1981 and '82 but never went out for hoops. He hadn't even played in high school. After enrolling in business courses this winter, Myers showed up for a few workouts and won the 12th spot on the roster. It's a long way from Wrigley Field, but in one respect the 6'1" Myers, who in February was averaging 1.3 points per game for the 14–7 Penguins, should have felt at home. "Randy tends to get in toward the end of the game, when we have things sewn up," says Clark athletic director Roger Daniels.

Yes, but does he get the save?

Most Valuable Players

1955	Johnny Podres, Bklyn
1956	Don Larsen, NY (A)
1957	Lew Burdette, Mil
1958	Bob Turley, NY (A)
1959	Larry Sherry, LA
1960	Bobby Richardson, NY (A)
1961	Whitey Ford, NY (A)
1962	Ralph Terry, NY (A)
1963	Sandy Koufax, LA
1964	Bob Gibson, StL
1965	Sandy Koufax, LA
1966	Frank Robinson, Balt
1967	Bob Gibson, StL
1968	Mickey Lolich, Det
1969	Donn Clendenon, NY (N)
1970	Brooks Robinson, Balt
1971	Roberto Clemente, Pitt
1972	Gene Tenace, Oak
1973	Reggie Jackson, Oak
1974	Rollie Fingers, Oak
1975	Pete Rose, Cin
1976	Johnny Bench, Cin

1977	Reggie Jackson, NY (A)
1978	Bucky Dent, NY (A)
1979	Willie Stargell, Pitt
1980	Mike Schmidt, Phil
1981	Ron Cey, LA
	Pedro Guerrero, LA
	Steve Yeager, LA
1982	Darrell Porter, StL
1983	Rick Dempsey, Balt
1984	Alan Trammell, Det
1985	Bret Saberhagen, KC
1986	Ray Knight, NY (N)
1987	Frank Viola, Minn
1988	Orel Hershiser, LA
1989	Dave Stewart, Oak
1990	Jose Rijo, Cin
1991	Jack Morris, Minn
1992	Pat Borders, Tor
1993	Paul Molitor, Tor
1994	Series canceled due to strike
1995	Tom Glavine, Atl

Career Batting Leaders (Minimum 50 at bats)

GAMES

Yogi Berra	75
Mickey Mantle	65
Elston Howard	54
Hank Bauer	53
Gil McDougald	53
Phil Rizzuto	52
Joe DiMaggio	51
Frankie Frisch	50
Pee Wee Reese	44
Roger Maris	41
Babe Ruth	41

AT BATS

Yogi Berra	259
Mickey Mantle	230
Joe DiMaggio	199
Frankie Frisch	197
Gil McDougald	190
Hank Bauer	188
Phil Rizzuto	183
Elston Howard	171
Pee Wee Reese	169
Roger Maris	152

HITS

Yogi Berra	71
Mickey Mantle	59
Frankie Frisch	58
Joe DiMaggio	54
Pee Wee Reese	46
Hank Bauer	46
Phil Rizzuto	45
Gil McDougald	45
Lou Gehrig	43
Eddie Collins	42
Babe Ruth	42
Elston Howard	42

BATTING AVERAGE

Pepper Martin	.418
Paul Molitor	.418
Lou Brock	.391
Thurman Munson	.373
George Brett	.373
Hank Aaron	.364
Frank Baker	.363
Roberto Clemente	.362
Lou Gehrig	.361
Reggie Jackson	.357

HOME RUNS

Mickey Mantle	18
Babe Ruth	15
Yogi Berra	12
Duke Snider	11
Reggie Jackson	10
Lou Gehrig	10
Frank Robinson	8
Bill Skowron	8
Joe DiMaggio	8
Goose Goslin	7
Hank Bauer	7
Gil McDougald	7

RUNS BATTED IN

Mickey Mantle	40
Yogi Berra	39
Lou Gehrig	35
Babe Ruth	33
Joe DiMaggio	30
Bill Skowron	29
Duke Snider	26
Reggie Jackson	24
Bill Dickey	24
Hank Bauer	24
Gil McDougald	24

RUNS

Mickey Mantle	42
Yogi Berra	41
Babe Ruth	37
Lou Gehrig	30
Joe DiMaggio	27
Roger Maris	26
Elston Howard	25
Gil McDougald	23
Jackie Robinson	22
Gene Woodling	21
Reggie Jackson	21
Duke Snider	21
Phil Rizzuto	21
Hank Bauer	21

STOLEN BASES

Lou Brock	14
Eddie Collins	14
Frank Chance	10
Davey Lopes	10
Phil Rizzuto	10
Honus Wagner	9
Frankie Frisch	9
Johnny Evers	8
Pepper Martin	7
Joe Morgan	7
Rickey Henderson	7

TOTAL BASES

Mickey Mantle	123
Yogi Berra	117
Babe Ruth	96
Lou Gehrig	87
Joe DiMaggio	84
Duke Snider	79
Hank Bauer	75
Reggie Jackson	74
Frankie Frisch	74
Gil McDougald	72

Career Batting Leaders *(Cont.)*

SLUGGING AVERAGE		STRIKEOUTS	
Reggie Jackson	.755	Mickey Mantle	54
Paul Molitor	.636	Elston Howard	37
Babe Ruth	.744	Duke Snider	33
Lou Gehrig	.731	Babe Ruth	30
Al Simmons	.658	Gil McDougald	29
Lou Brock	.655	Bill Skowron	26
Pepper Martin	.636	Hank Bauer	25
Hank Greenberg	.624	Reggie Jackson	24
Charlie Keller	.611	Bob Meusel	24
Jimmie Foxx	.609	Frank Robinson	23
Dave Henderson	.606	George Kelly	23
		Tony Kubek	23
		Joe DiMaggio	23

Career Pitching Leaders (Minimum 25 innings pitched)

GAMES		LOSSES		COMPLETE GAMES	
Whitey Ford	22	Whitey Ford	8	Christy Mathewson	10
Rollie Fingers	16	Eddie Plank	5	Chief Bender	9
Allie Reynolds	15	Schoolboy Rowe	5	Bob Gibson	8
Bob Turley	15	Joe Bush	5	Red Ruffing	7
Clay Carroll	14	Rube Marquard	5	Whitey Ford	7
Clem Labine	13	Christy Mathewson	5	George Mullin	6
Waite Hoyt	12			Eddie Plank	6
Catfish Hunter	12	**SAVES**		Art Nehf	6
Art Nehf	12			Waite Hoyt	6
Paul Derringer	11	Rollie Fingers	6		
Carl Erskine	11	Allie Reynolds	4	**STRIKEOUTS**	
Rube Marquard	11	Johnny Murphy	4		
Christy Mathewson	11	Roy Face	3	Whitey Ford	94
Vic Raschi	11	Herb Pennock	3	Bob Gibson	92
		Kent Tekulve	3	Allie Reynolds	62
INNINGS PITCHED		Firpo Marberry	3	Sandy Koufax	61
		Will McEnaney	3	Red Ruffing	61
Whitey Ford	146	Todd Worrell	3	Chief Bender	59
Christy Mathewson	101⅔	Tug McGraw	3	George Earnshaw	56
Red Ruffing	85⅔			Waite Hoyt	49
Chief Bender	85	**EARNED RUN AVERAGE**		Christy Mathewson	48
Waite Hoyt	83⅔			Bob Turley	46
Bob Gibson	81	Jack Billingham	.36		
Art Nehf	79	Harry Brecheen	.83	**BASES ON BALLS**	
Allie Reynolds	77	Babe Ruth	.87		
Jim Palmer	65	Sherry Smith	.89	Whitey Ford	34
Catfish Hunter	63	Sandy Koufax	.95	Allie Reynolds	32
		Hippo Vaughn	1.00	Art Nehf	32
WINS		Monte Pearson	1.01	Jim Palmer	31
		Christy Mathewson	1.15	Bob Turley	29
Whitey Ford	10	Babe Adams	1.29	Paul Derringer	27
Bob Gibson	7	Eddie Plank	1.32	Red Ruffing	27
Red Ruffing	7			Don Gullett	26
Allie Reynolds	7	**SHUTOUTS**		Burleigh Grimes	26
Lefty Gomez	6			Vic Raschi	25
Chief Bender	6	Christy Mathewson	4		
Waite Hoyt	6	Three Finger Brown	3		
Jack Coombs	5	Whitey Ford	3		
Three Finger Brown	5	Bill Hallahan	2		
Herb Pennock	5	Lew Burdette	2		
Christy Mathewson	5	Bill Dinneen	2		
Vic Raschi	5	Sandy Koufax	2		
Catfish Hunter	5	Allie Reynolds	2		
		Art Nehf	2		
		Bob Gibson	2		

National League

1969	New York (E) 3, Atlanta (W) 0
1970	Cincinnati (W) 3, Pittsburgh (E) 0
1971	Pittsburgh (E) 3, San Francisco (W) 1
1972	Cincinnati (W) 3, Pittsburgh (E) 2
1973	New York (E) 3, Cincinnati (W) 2
1974	Los Angeles (W) 3, Pittsburgh (E) 1
1975	Cincinnati (W) 3, Pittsburgh (E) 0
1976	Cincinnati (W) 3, Philadelphia (E) 0
1977	Los Angeles (W) 3, Philadelphia (E) 1
1978	Los Angeles (W) 3, Philadelphia (E) 1
1979	Pittsburgh (E) 3, Cincinnati (W) 0
1980	Philadelphia (E) 3, Houston (W) 2
1981	Los Angeles (W) 3, Montreal (E) 2
1982	St Louis (E) 3, Atlanta (W) 0
1983	Philadelphia (E) 3, Los Angeles (W) 1
1984	San Diego (W) 3, Chicago (E) 2
1985	St Louis (E) 4, Los Angeles (W) 2
1986	New York (E) 4, Houston (W) 2
1987	St Louis (E) 4, San Francisco (W) 3
1988	Los Angeles (W) 4, New York (E) 3
1989	San Francisco (W) 4, Chicago (E) 1
1990	Cincinnati (W) 4, Pittsburgh (E) 2
1991	Atlanta (W) 4, Pittsburgh (E) 3
1992	Atlanta (W) 4, Pitsburgh (E) 3
1993	Philadelphia (E) 4, Atlanta (W) 2
1994	Playoffs canceled due to players' strike
1995	Atlanta (E) 4, Cincinnati (C) 0

American League

1969	Baltimore (E) 3, Minnesota (W) 0
1970	Baltimore (E) 3, Minnesota (W) 0
1971	Baltimore (E) 3, Oakland (W) 0
1972	Oakland (W) 3, Detroit (E) 2
1973	Oakland (W) 3, Baltimore (E) 2
1974	Oakland (W) 3, Baltimore (E) 1
1975	Boston (E) 3, Oakland (W) 0
1976	New York (E) 3, Kansas City (W) 2
1977	New York (E) 3, Kansas City (W) 2
1978	New York (E) 3, Kansas City (W) 1
1979	Baltimore (E) 3, California (W) 1
1980	Kansas City (W) 3, New York (E) 0
1981	New York (E) 3, Oakland (W) 0
1982	Milwaukee (E) 3, California (W) 2
1983	Baltimore (E) 3, Chicago (W) 1
1984	Detroit (E) 3, Kansas City (W) 0
1985	Kansas City (W) 4, Toronto (E) 3
1986	Boston (E) 4, California (W) 3
1987	Minnesota (W) 4, Detroit (E) 1
1988	Oakland (W) 4, Boston (E) 0
1989	Oakland (W) 4, Toronto (E) 1
1990	Oakland (W) 4, Boston (E) 0
1991	Minnesota (W) 4, Toronto (E) 1
1992	Toronto (E) 4, Oakland (W) 2
1993	Toronto (E) 4, Chicago (W) 2
1994	Playoffs canceled due to players' strike
1995	Cleveland (C) 4, Seattle (W) 2

NLCS Most Valuable Player

1977	Dusty Baker, LA	1984	Steve Garvey, SD	1990	Randy Myers, Cin
1978	Steve Garvey, LA	1985	Ozzie Smith, StL		Rob Dibble, Cin
1979	Willie Stargell, Pitt	1986	Mike Scott, Hou	1991	Steve Avery, Atl
1980	Manny Trillo, Phil	1987	Jeffrey Leonard, SF	1992	John Smoltz, Atl
1981	Burt Hooton, LA	1988	Orel Hershiser, LA	1993	Curt Schilling, Phil
1982	Darrell Porter, StL	1989	Will Clark, SF	1994	Playoffs canceled
1983	Gary Matthews, Phil			1995	Mike Devereaux, Atl

ALCS Most Valuable Player

1980	Frank White, KC	1986	Marty Barrett, Bos	1992	Roberto Alomar, Tor
1981	Graig Nettles, NY	1987	Gary Gaetti, Minn	1993	Dave Stewart, Tor
1982	Fred Lynn, Calif	1988	Dennis Eckersley, Oak	1994	Playoffs canceled
1983	Mike Boddicker, Balt	1989	Rickey Henderson, Oak	1995	Orel Hershiser, Clev
1984	Kirk Gibson, Det	1990	Dave Stewart, Oak		
1985	George Brett, KC	1991	Kirby Puckett, Minn		

The All Star Game

Results

Date	Winner	Score	Site
7-6-33	American	4-2	Comiskey Park, Chi
7-10-34	American	9-7	Polo Grounds, NY
7-8-35	American	4-1	Municipal Stadium, Clev
7-7-36	National	4-3	Braves Field, Bos
7-7-37	American	8-3	Griffith Stadium, Wash
7-6-38	National	4-1	Crosley Field, Cin
7-11-39	American	3-1	Yankee Stadium, NY
7-10-40	National	4-0	Sportsman's Park, StL
7-8-41	American	7-5	Briggs Stadium, Det
7-6-42	American	3-1	Polo Grounds, NY
7-13-43	American	5-3	Shibe Park, Phil
7-11-44	National	7-1	Forbes Field, Pitt
1945	No game due to wartime travel restrictions		
7-9-46	American	12-0	Fenway Park, Bos
7-8-47	American	2-1	Wrigley Field, Chi
7-13-48	American	5-2	Sportsman's Park, StL

Results *(Cont.)*

Date	Winner	Score	Site
7-12-49	American	11-7	Ebbets Field, Bklyn
7-11-50	National	4-3	Comiskey Park, Chi
7-10-51	National	8-3	Briggs Stadium, Det
7-8-52	National	3-2	Shibe Park, Phil
7-14-53	National	5-1	Crosley Field, Cin
7-13-54	American	11-9	Municipal Stadium, Clev
7-12-55	National	6-5	County Stadium, Mil
7-10-56	National	7-3	Griffith Stadium, Wash
7-9-57	American	6-5	Busch Stadium, StL
7-8-58	American	4-3	Memorial Stadium, Balt
7-7-59	National	5-4	Forbes Field, Pitt
8-3-59	American	5-3	Memorial Coliseum, LA
7-11-60	National	5-3	Municipal Stadium, KC
7-13-60	National	6-0	Yankee Stadium, NY
7-11-61	National	5-4	Candlestick Park, SF
7-31-61	Tie*	1-1	Fenway Park, Bos
7-10-62	National	3-1	D.C. Stadium, Wash
7-30-62	American	9-4	Wrigley Field, Chi
7-9-63	National	5-3	Municipal Stadium, Clev
7-7-64	National	7-4	Shea Stadium, NY
7-13-65	National	6-5	Metropolitan Stadium, Minn
7-12-66	National	2-1	Busch Stadium, StL
7-11-67	National	2-1	Anaheim Stadium, Anaheim
7-9-68	National	1-0	Astrodome, Hou
7-23-69	National	9-3	R.F.K. Memorial Stadium, Wash
7-14-70	National	5-4	Riverfront Stadium, Cin
7-13-71	American	6-4	Tiger Stadium, Det
7-25-72	National	4-3	Atlanta Stadium, Atl
7-24-73	National	7-1	Royals Stadium, KC
7-23-74	National	7-2	Three Rivers Stadium, Pitt
7-15-75	National	6-3	County Stadium, Mil
7-13-76	National	7-1	Veterans Stadium, Phil
7-19-77	National	7-5	Yankee Stadium, NY
7-11-78	National	7-3	Jack Murphy Stadium, SD
7-17-79	National	7-6	Kingdome, Sea
7-8-80	National	4-2	Dodger Stadium, LA
8-9-81	National	5-4	Municipal Stadium, Clev
7-13-82	National	4-1	Olympic Stadium, Mtl
7-6-83	American	13-3	Comiskey Park, Chi
7-10-84	National	3-1	Candlestick Park, SF
7-16-85	National	6-1	Metrodome, Minn
7-15-86	American	3-2	Astrodome, Hou
7-14-87	National	2-0	Oakland Coliseum, Oak
7-12-88	American	2-1	Riverfront Stadium, Cin
7-11-89	American	5-3	Anaheim Stadium, Anaheim
7-10-90	American	2-0	Wrigley Field, Chi
7-9-91	American	4-2	SkyDome, Toronto
7-14-92	American	13-6	Jack Murphy Stadium, SD
7-13-93	American	9-3	Camden Yards, Balt
7-12-94	National	8-7	Three Rivers Stadium, Pitt
7-11-95	National	3-2	The Ballpark in Arlington, TX

*Game called because of rain after 9 innings.

Most Valuable Players

1962	Maury Wills, LA	NL	1974	Steve Garvey, LA	NL
	Leon Wagner, LA	AL	1975	Bill Madlock, Chi	NL
1963	Willie Mays, SF	NL		Jon Matlack, NY	NL
1964	Johnny Callison, Phil	NL	1976	George Foster, Cin	NL
1965	Juan Marichal, SF	NL	1977	Don Sutton, LA	NL
1966	Brooks Robinson, Balt	AL	1978	Steve Garvey, LA	NL
1967	Tony Perez, Cin	NL	1979	Dave Parker, Pitt	NL
1968	Willie Mays, SF	NL	1980	Ken Griffey, Cin	NL
1969	Willie McCovey, SF	NL	1981	Gary Carter, Mtl	NL
1970	Carl Yastrzemski, Bos	AL	1982	Dave Concepcion, Cin	NL
1971	Frank Robinson, Balt	AL	1983	Fred Lynn, Calif	AL
1972	Joe Morgan, Cin	NL	1984	Gary Carter, Mtl	NL
1973	Bobby Bonds, SF	NL	1985	LaMarr Hoyt, SD	NL

Most Valuable Players *(Cont.)*

1986 ....Roger Clemens, Bos	AL	1991 ....Cal Ripken Jr, Balt	AL
1987 ....Tim Raines, Mtl	NL	1992 ....Ken Griffey Jr, Sea	AL
1988 ....Terry Steinbach, Oak	AL	1993 ....Kirby Puckett, Minn	AL
1989 ....Bo Jackson, KC	AL	1994 ....Fred McGriff, Atl	NL
1990 ....Julio Franco, Tex	AL	1995 ....Jeff Conine, Fla	NL

The Regular Season

Most Valuable Players

NATIONAL LEAGUE

Year	Name and Team	Position	Noteworthy
1911 ....Wildfire Schulte, Chi		Outfield	21 HR†, 121 RBI†, .300
1912 ....*Larry Doyle, NY		Second base	10 HR, 90 RBI, .330
1913 ....Jake Daubert, Bklyn		First base	52 RBI, .350†
1914 ....*Johnny Evers, Bos		Second base	F.A. .976†, .279
1915-23 ....No selection			
1924 ....Dazzy Vance, Bklyn		Pitcher	28†-6, 2.16 ERA†, 262 K†
1925 ....Rogers Hornsby, StL		Second base, Manager	39 HR†, 143 RBI†, .403†
1926 ....*Bob O'Farrell, StL		Catcher	7 HR, 68 RBI, .293
1927 ....*Paul Waner, Pitt		Outfield	237 hits†, 131 RBI†, .380†
1928 ....*Jim Bottomley, StL		First base	31 HR†, 136 RBI†, .325
1929 ....*Rogers Hornsby, Chi		Second base	39 HR, 149 RBI, 156 runs†, .380
1930 ....No selection			
1931 ....*Frankie Frisch, StL		Second base	4 HR, 82 RBI, 28 SB†, .311
1932 ....Chuck Klein, Phil		Outfield	38 HR†, 137 RBI, 226 hits†, .348
1933 ....*Carl Hubbell, NY		Pitcher	23†-12, 1.66 ERA†, 10 SO†
1934 ....*Dizzy Dean, StL		Pitcher	30†-7, 2.66 ERA, 195 K†
1935 ....*Gabby Hartnett, Chi		Catcher	13 HR, 91 RBI, .344
1936 ....*Carl Hubbell, NY		Pitcher	26†-6, 2.31 ERA†
1937 ....Joe Medwick, StL		Outfield	31 HR‡, 154 RBI†, 111 runs†, .374†
1938 ....Ernie Lombardi, Cin		Catcher	19 HR, 95 RBI, .342†
1939 ....*Bucky Walters, Cin		Pitcher	27†-11, 2.29 ERA†, 137 K‡
1940 ....*Frank McCormick, Cin		First base	19 HR, 127 RBI, 191 hits†, .309
1941 ....*Dolph Camilli, Bklyn		First base	34 HR†, 120 RBI†, .285
1942 ....*Mort Cooper, StL		Pitcher	22†-7, 1.78 ERA†, 10 SO†
1943 ....*Stan Musial, StL		Outfield	13 HR, 81 RBI, 220 hits†, .357†
1944 ....*Marty Marion, StL		Shortstop	F.A. .972†, 63 RBI
1945 ....*Phil Cavarretta, Chi		First base	6 HR, 97 RBI, .355†
1946 ....*Stan Musial, StL		First base, Outfield	103 RBI, 124 runs†, 228 hits†, .365†
1947 ....Bob Elliott, Bos		Third base	22 HR, 113 RBI, .317
1948 ....Stan Musial, StL		Outfield	39 HR, 131 RBI†, .376†
1949 ....*Jackie Robinson, Bklyn		Second base	16 HR, 124 RBI, 37 SB†, .342†
1950 ....*Jim Konstanty, Phil		Pitcher	16-7, 22 saves†, 2.66 ERA
1951 ....Roy Campanella, Bklyn		Catcher	33 HR, 108 RBI, .325
1952 ....Hank Sauer, Chi		Outfield	37 HR‡, 121 RBI†, .270
1953 ....*Roy Campanella, Bklyn		Catcher	41 HR, 142 RBI†, .312
1954 ....*Willie Mays, NY		Outfield	41 HR, 110 RBI, 13 3B†, .345†
1955 ....*Roy Campanella, Bklyn		Catcher	32 HR, 107 RBI, .318
1956 ....*Don Newcombe, Bklyn		Pitcher	27†-7, 3.06 ERA
1957 ....*Hank Aaron, Mil		Outfield	44 HR†, 132 RBI†, .322
1958 ....Ernie Banks, Chi		Shortstop	47 HR†, 129 RBI†, .313
1959 ....Ernie Banks, Chi		Shortstop	45 HR, 143 RBI†, .304
1960 ....*Dick Groat, Pitt		Shortstop	2 HR, 50 RBI, .325†
1961 ....*Frank Robinson, Cin		Outfield	37 HR, 124 RBI, .323
1962 ....Maury Wills, LA		Shortstop	104 SB†, 208 hits, .299, GG
1963 ....*Sandy Koufax, LA		Pitcher	25‡-5, 1.88 ERA†, 306 K†
1964 ....*Ken Boyer, StL		Third Base	24 HR, 119 RBI†, .295
1965 ....Willie Mays, SF		Outfield	52 HR†, 112 RBI, .317, GG
1966 ....Roberto Clemente, Pitt		Outfield	29 HR, 119 RBI, 202 hits, .317, GG
1967 ....*Orlando Cepeda, StL		First base	25 HR, 111 RBI†, .325
1968 ....*Bob Gibson, StL		Pitcher	22-9, 1.12 ERA†, 268 K†, 13 SO†, GG
1969 ....Willie McCovey, SF		First base	45 HR†, 126 RBI†, .320
1970 ....*Johnny Bench, Cin		Catcher	45 HR†, 148 RBI†, .293, GG
1971 ....Joe Torre, StL		Third base	24 HR, 137 RBI†, .363†

*Played for pennant or, after 1968, division winner. †Led league. ‡Tied for league lead.

Most Valuable Players *(Cont.)*

NATIONAL LEAGUE *(Cont.)*

Year	Name and Team	Position	Noteworthy
1972	*Johnny Bench, Cin	Catcher	40 HR†, 125 RBI†, .270, GG
1973	*Pete Rose, Cin	Outfield	5 HR, 64 RBI, .338†, 230 hits†
1974	*Steve Garvey, LA	First base	21 HR, 111 RBI, 200 hits, .312, GG
1975	*Joe Morgan, Cin	Second base	17 HR, 94 RBI, 67 SB, .327, GG
1976	*Joe Morgan, Cin	Second base	27 HR, 111 RBI, 60 SB, .320, GG
1977	George Foster, Cin	Outfield	52 HR†, 149 RBI†, .320
1978	Dave Parker, Pitt	Outfield	30 HR, 117 RBI, .334†, GG
1979	Keith Hernandez, StL	First base	11 HR, 105 RBI, 210 hits, .344†, GG
	*Willie Stargell, Pitt	First base	32 HR, 82 RBI, .281
1980	*Mike Schmidt, Phil	Third base	48 HR†, 121 RBI†, .286, GG
1981	Mike Schmidt, Phil	Third base	31 HR†, 91 RBI†, 78 runs†, .316, GG
1982	*Dale Murphy, Atl	Outfield	36 HR, 109 RBI‡, .281, GG
1983	Dale Murphy, Atl	Outfield	36 HR, 121 RBI†, .302, GG
1984	*Ryne Sandberg, Chi	Second base	19 HR, 84 RBI, 114 runs†, .314, GG
1985	*Willie McGee, StL	Outfield	10 HR, 82 RBI, 18 3B†, .353†, GG
1986	Mike Schmidt, Phil	Third base	37 HR†, 119 RBI†, .290, GG
1987	Andre Dawson, Chi	Outfield	49 HR†, 137 RBI†, .287, GG
1988	*Kirk Gibson, LA	Outfield	25 HR, 76 RBI, 106 runs, .290
1989	*Kevin Mitchell, SF	Outfield	47 HR†, 125 RBI†, .291
1990	*Barry Bonds, Pitt	Outfield	33 HR, 114 RBI, .301
1991	*Terry Pendleton, Atl	Third base	23 HR, 86 RBI, .319†
1992	Barry Bonds, SF	Outfield	34 HR, 103 RBI, .311
1993	Barry Bonds, SF	Outfield	46 HR†, 123 RBI†, .336
1994	Jeff Bagwell, Hou	First base	39 HR, 116 RBI†, .368

AMERICAN LEAGUE

Year	Name and Team	Position	Noteworthy
1911	Ty Cobb, Det	Outfield	8 HR, 144 RBI†, 24 3B†, .420†
1912	*Tris Speaker, Bos	Outfield	10 HR‡, 98 RBI, 53 2B†, .383
1913	Walter Johnson, Wash	Pitcher	36†-7, 1.09 ERA†, 11 SO†, 243 K†
1914	*Eddie Collins, Phil	Second base	2 HR, 85 RBI, 122 runs†, .344
1915-21	No selection		
1922	George Sisler, StL	First base	8 HR, 105 RBI, 246 hits†, .420†
1923	*Babe Ruth, NY	Outfield	41 HR†, 131 RBI†, .393
1924	*Walter Johnson, Wash	Pitcher	23†-7, 2.72 ERA†, 158 K†
1925	*Roger Peckinpaugh, Wash	Shortstop	4 HR, 64 RBI, .294
1926	George Burns, Clev	First base	114 RBI, 216 hits†, 64 2B†, .358
1927	*Lou Gehrig, NY	First base	47 HR, 175 RBI†, 52 2B†, .373
1928	Mickey Cochrane, Phil	Catcher	10 HR, 57 RBI, .293
1929	No selection		
1930	No selection		
1931	*Lefty Grove, Phil	Pitcher	31†-4, 2.06 ERA†, 175 K†
1932	Jimmie Foxx, Phil	First base	58 HR†, 169 RBI†, 151 runs†, .364
1933	Jimmie Foxx, Phil	First base	48 HR†, 163 RBI†, .356†
1934	*Mickey Cochrane, Det	Catcher	2 HR, 76 RBI, .320
1935	*Hank Greenberg, Det	First base	36 HR†, 170 RBI†, 203 hits, .328
1936	*Lou Gehrig, NY	First base	49 HR†, 152 RBI, 167 runs†, .354
1937	Charlie Gehringer, Det	Second base	14 HR, 96 RBI, 133 runs, .371†
1938	Jimmie Foxx, Bos	First base	50 HR, 175 RBI†, .349†
1939	*Joe DiMaggio, NY	Outfield	30 HR, 126 RBI, .381†
1940	*Hank Greenberg, Det	Outfield	41 HR†, 150 RBI†, 50 2B†, .340
1941	*Joe DiMaggio, NY	Outfield	30 HR, 125 RBI†, .357
1942	*Joe Gordon, NY	Second base	18 HR, 103 RBI, .322
1943	*Spud Chandler, NY	Pitcher	20†-4, 1.64 ERA†, 5 SO‡
1944	Hal Newhouser, Det	Pitcher	29†-9, 2.22 ERA†, 187 K†
1945	*Hal Newhouser, Det	Pitcher	25†-9, 1.81 ERA†, 8 SO†, 212 K†
1946	*Ted Williams, Bos	Outfield	38 HR, 123 RBI, 142 runs†, .342
1947	*Joe DiMaggio, NY	Outfield	20 HR, 97 RBI, .315
1948	*Lou Boudreau, Clev	Shortstop	18 HR, 106 RBI, .355
1949	Ted Williams, Bos	Outfield	43 HR†, 159 RBI†, 150 runs†, .343
1950	*Phil Rizzuto, NY	Shortstop	125 runs, 200 hits, .324
1951	*Yogi Berra, NY	Catcher	27 HR, 88 RBI, .294
1952	Bobby Shantz, Phil	Pitcher	24†-7, 2.48 ERA

*Played for pennant or, after 1968, division winner. †Led league. ‡Tied for league lead.

Most Valuable Players *(Cont.)*

AMERICAN LEAGUE *(Cont.)*

Year	Name and Team	Position	Noteworthy
1953	Al Rosen, Clev	Third base	43 HR†, 145 RBI†, 115 runs†, .336
1954	Yogi Berra, NY	Catcher	22 HR, 125 RBI, .307
1955	*Yogi Berra, NY	Catcher	27 HR, 108 RBI, .272
1956	*Mickey Mantle, NY	Outfield	52 HR†, 130 RBI†, 132 runs†, .353†
1957	*Mickey Mantle, NY	Outfield	34 HR, 94 RBI, 121 runs†, .365
1958	Jackie Jensen, Bos	Outfield	35 HR, 122 RBI†, .286
1959	*Nellie Fox, Chi	Second base	2 HR, 70 RBI, .306, GG
1960	*Roger Maris, NY	Outfield	39 HR, 112 RBI†, .283, GG
1961	*Roger Maris, NY	Outfield	61 HR†, 142 RBI†, .269
1962	*Mickey Mantle, NY	Outfield	30 HR, 89 RBI, .321, GG
1963	*Elston Howard, NY	Catcher	28 HR, 85 RBI, .287, GG
1964	Brooks Robinson, Balt	Third base	28 HR, 118 RBI†, .317, GG
1965	*Zoilo Versalles, Minn	Shortstop	126 runs†, 45 2B‡, 12 3B‡, GG
1966	*Frank Robinson, Balt	Outfield	49 HR†, 122 RBI†, 122 runs†, .316†
1967	*Carl Yastrzemski, Bos	Outfield	44 HR‡, 121 RBI†, 112 runs†, .326†, .326
1968	*Denny McLain, Det	Pitcher	31†-6, 1.96 ERA, 280 K
1969	*Harmon Killebrew, Minn	Third base, First base	49 HR†, 140 RBI†, .276
1970	*Boog Powell, Balt	First base	35 HR, 114 RBI, .297
1971	*Vida Blue, Oak	Pitcher	24-8, 1.82 ERA†, 8 SO†, 301 K
1972	Dick Allen, Chi	First base	37 HR†, 113 RBI†, .308
1973	*Reggie Jackson, Oak	Outfield	32 HR†, 117 RBI†, 99 runs†, .293
1974	Jeff Burroughs, Tex	Outfield	25 HR, 118 RBI†, .301
1975	*Fred Lynn, Bos	Outfield	21 HR, 105 RBI, 103 runs†, .331, GG
1976	*Thurman Munson, NY	Catcher	17 HR, 105 RBI, .302
1977	Rod Carew, Minn	First base	100 RBI, 128 runs†, 239 hits†, .388†
1978	Jim Rice, Bos	Outfield, designated hitter	46 HR†, 139 RBI†, 213 hits†, .315
1979	*Don Baylor, Calif	Outfield, designated hitter	36 HR, 139 RBI†, 120 runs†, .296
1980	*George Brett, KC	Third base	24 HR, 118 RBI, .390†
1981	*Rollie Fingers, Mil	Pitcher	6-3, 28 saves†, 1.04 ERA
1982	*Robin Yount, Mil	Shortstop	29 HR, 114 RBI, 210 hits†, .331, GG
1983	*Cal Ripken, Balt	Shortstop	27 HR, 102 RBI, 121 runs†, 211 hits†, .318
1984	*Willie Hernandez, Det	Pitcher	9-3, 32 saves, 1.92 ERA
1985	Don Mattingly, NY	First base	35 HR, 145 RBI†, 48 2B†, .324, GG
1986	*Roger Clemens, Bos	Pitcher	24†-4, 2.48 ERA†, 238 K
1987	George Bell, Tor	Outfield	47 HR, 134 RBI†, .308
1988	*Jose Canseco, Oak	Outfield	42 HR†, 124 RBI†, 40 SB, .307
1989	Robin Yount, Mil	Outfield	21 HR, 103 RBI, 101 runs, .318
1990	*Rickey Henderson, Oak	Outfield	28 HR, 119 runs†, 65 SB†, .325
1991	Cal Ripken, Jr, Balt	Shortstop	34 HR, 114 RBI, .323
1992	Dennis Eckersley, Oak	Pitcher	7-1, 1.91 ERA, 51 saves
1993	Frank Thomas, Chi	First base	41 HR, 128 RBI, .317
1994	Frank Thomas, Chi	First base	38 HR, 101 RBI, .353

*Played for pennant or, after 1968, division winner. †Led league. ‡Tied for league lead.

Notes: 2B=doubles; 3B=triples; F.A.=fielding average; GG=won Gold Glove, award begun in 1957; K=strikeouts; SO=shutouts; SB=stolen bases.

Rookies of the Year

NATIONAL LEAGUE		AMERICAN LEAGUE	
1947*	Jackie Robinson, Bklyn (1B)	1949	Roy Sievers, StL (OF)
1948*	Alvin Dark, Bos (SS)	1950	Walt Dropo, Bos (1B)
1949	Don Newcombe, Bklyn (P)	1951	Gil McDougald, NY (3B)
1950	Sam Jethroe, Bos (OF)	1952	Harry Byrd, Phil (P)
1951	Willie Mays, NY (OF)	1953	Harvey Kuenn, Det (SS)
1952	Joe Black, Bklyn (P)	1954	Bob Grim, NY (P)
1953	Junior Gilliam, Bklyn (2B)	1955	Herb Score, Clev (P)
1954	Wally Moon, StL (OF)	1956	Luis Aparicio, Chi (SS)
1955	Bill Virdon, StL (OF)	1957	Tony Kubek, NY (OF, SS)
1956	Frank Robinson, Cin (OF)	1958	Albie Pearson, Wash (OF)
1957	Jack Sanford, Phil (P)	1959	Bob Allison, Wash (OF)
1958	Orlando Cepeda, SF (1B)	1960	Ron Hansen, Balt (SS)

*Just one selection for both leagues.

Rookies of the Year (Cont.)

NATIONAL LEAGUE (Cont.)

1959	Willie McCovey, SF (1B)
1960	Frank Howard, LA (OF)
1961	Billy Williams, Chi (OF)
1962	Ken Hubbs, Chi (2B)
1963	Pete Rose, Cin (2B)
1964	Dick Allen, Phil (3B)
1965	Jim Lefebvre, LA (2B)
1966	Tommy Helms, Cin (2B)
1967	Tom Seaver, NY (P)
1968	Johnny Bench, Cin (C)
1969	Ted Sizemore, LA (2B)
1970	Carl Morton, Mont (P)
1971	Earl Williams, Atl (C)
1972	Jon Matlack, NY (P)
1973	Gary Matthews, SF (OF)
1974	Bake McBride, StL (OF)
1975	John Montefusco, SF (P)
1976	Pat Zachry, Cin (P)
	Butch Metzger, SD (P)
1977	Andre Dawson, Mont (OF)
1978	Bob Horner, Atl (3B)
1979	Rick Sutcliffe, LA (P)
1980	Steve Howe, LA (P)
1981	Fernando Valenzuela, LA (P)
1982	Steve Sax, LA (2B)
1983	Darryl Strawberry, NY (OF)
1984	Dwight Gooden, NY (P)
1985	Vince Coleman, StL (OF)
1986	Todd Worrell, StL (P)
1987	Benito Santiago, SD (C)
1988	Chris Sabo, Cin (3B)
1989	Jerome Walton, Chi (OF)
1990	Dave Justice, Atl (OF)
1991	Jeff Bagwell, Hou (3B)
1992	Eric Karros, LA (1B)
1993	Mike Piazza, LA (C)
1994	Raul Mondesi, LA (OF)

AMERICAN LEAGUE (Cont.)

1961	Don Schwall, Bos (P)
1962	Tom Tresh, NY (SS)
1963	Gary Peters, Chi (P)
1964	Tony Oliva, Minn (OF)
1965	Curt Blefary, Balt (OF)
1966	Tommie Agee, Chi (OF)
1967	Rod Carew, Minn (2B)
1968	Stan Bahnsen, NY (P)
1969	Lou Piniella, KC (OF)
1970	Thurman Munson, NY (C)
1971	Chris Chambliss, Clev (1B)
1972	Carlton Fisk, Bos (C)
1973	Al Bumbry, Balt (OF)
1974	Mike Hargrove, Tex (1B)
1975	Fred Lynn, Bos (OF)
1976	Mark Fidrych, Det (P)
1977	Eddie Murray, Balt (DH)
1978	Lou Whitaker, Det (2B)
1979	Alfredo Griffin, Tor (SS)
	John Castino, Minn (3B)
1980	Joe Charboneau, Clev (OF)
1981	Dave Righetti, NY (P)
1982	Cal Ripken, Balt (SS)
1983	Ron Kittle, Chi (OF)
1984	Alvin Davis, Sea (1B)
1985	Ozzie Guillen, Chi (SS)
1986	Jose Canseco, Oak (OF)
1987	Mark McGwire, Oak (1B)
1988	Walt Weiss, Oak (SS)
1989	Gregg Olson, Balt (P)
1990	Sandy Alomar Jr, Clev (C)
1991	Chuck Knoblauch, Minn (2B)
1992	Pat Listach, Mil (SS)
1993	Tim Salmon, Calif (OF)
1994	Bob Hamelin, Minn (DH)

Cy Young Award

Year	W-L	Sv	ERA	Year	W-L	Sv	ERA
1956....*Don Newcombe, Bklyn (NL)	27-7	0	3.06	1962....Don Drysdale, LA (NL)	25-9	1	2.83
1957....Warren Spahn, Mil (NL)	21-11	3	2.69	1963....*Sandy Koufax, LA (NL)	25-5	0	1.88
1958....Bob Turley, NY (AL)	21-7	1	2.97	1964....Dean Chance, LA (AL)	20-9	4	1.65
1959....Early Wynn, Chi (AL)	22-10	0	3.17	1965....Sandy Koufax, LA (NL)	26-8	2	2.04
1960....Vernon Law, Pitt (NL)	20-9	0	3.08	1966....Sandy Koufax, LA (NL)	27-9	0	1.73
1961....Whitey Ford, NY (AL)	25-4	0	3.21				

NATIONAL LEAGUE

Year	W-L	Sv	ERA
1967.....Mike McCormick, SF	22-10	0	2.85
1968.....*Bob Gibson, StL	22-9	0	1.12
1969.....Tom Seaver, NY	25-7	0	2.21
1970.....Bob Gibson, StL	23-7	0	3.12
1971.....Ferguson Jenkins, Chi	24-13	0	2.77
1972.....Steve Carlton, Phil	27-10	0	1.97
1973.....Tom Seaver, NY	19-10	0	2.08
1974.....Mike Marshall, LA	15-12	21	2.42
1975.....Tom Seaver, NY	22-9	0	2.38
1976.....Randy Jones, SD	22-14	0	2.74
1977.....Steve Carlton, Phil	23-10	0	2.64
1978.....Gaylord Perry, SD	21-6	0	2.72
1979.....Bruce Sutter, Chi	6-6	37	2.23
1980.....Steve Carlton, Phil	24-9	0	2.34

AMERICAN LEAGUE

Year	W-L	Sv	ERA
1967.....Jim Lonborg, Bos	22-9	0	3.16
1968.....*Denny McLain, Det	31-6	0	1.96
1969.....Denny McLain, Det	24-9	0	2.80
	Mike Cuellar, Balt	23-11	0	2.38
1970.....Jim Perry, Minn	24-12	0	3.03
1971.....*Vida Blue, Oak	24-8	0	1.82
1972.....Gaylord Perry, Clev	24-16	1	1.92
1973.....Jim Palmer, Balt	22-9	1	2.40
1974.....Catfish Hunter, Oak	25-12	0	2.49
1975.....Jim Palmer, Balt	23-11	1	2.09
1976.....Jim Palmer, Balt	22-13	0	2.51
1977.....Sparky Lyle, NY	13-5	26	2.17
1978.....Ron Guidry, NY	25-3	0	1.74
1979.....Mike Flanagan, Balt	23-9	0	3.08

Cy Young Award (Cont.)

NATIONAL LEAGUE				AMERICAN LEAGUE			
Year	W-L	Sv	ERA	Year	W-L	Sv	ERA
1981.....Fernando Valenzuela, LA	13-7	0	2.48	1980.....Steve Stone, Balt	25-7	0	3.23
1982.....Steve Carlton, Phil	23-11	0	3.10	1981.....*Rollie Fingers, Mil	6-3	28	1.04
1983.....John Denny, Phil	19-6	0	2.37	1982.....Pete Vuckovich, Mi	18-6	0	3.34
1984.....†Rick Sutcliffe, Chi	16-1	0	2.69	1983.....LaMarr Hoyt, Chi	24-10	0	3.66
1985.....Dwight Gooden, NY	24-4	0	1.53	1984.....*Willie Hernandez, Det	9-3	32	1.92
1986.....Mike Scott, Hou	18-10	0	2.22	1985.....Bret Saberhagen, KC	20-6	0	2.87
1987.....Steve Bedrosian, Phil	5-3	40	2.83	1986.....*Roger Clemens, Bos	24-4	0	2.48
1988.....Orel Hershiser, LA	23-8	1	2.26	1987.....Roger Clemens, Bos	20-9	0	2.97
1989.....Mark Davis, SD	4-3	44	1.85	1988.....Frank Viola, Minn	24-7	0	2.64
1990.....Doug Drabek, Pitt	22-6	0	2.76	1989.....Bret Saberhagen, KC	23-6	0	2.16
1991.....Tom Glavine, Atl	20-11	0	2.55	1990.....Bob Welch, Oak	27-6	0	2.95
1992.....Greg Maddux, Chi	20-11	0	2.18	1991.....Roger Clemens, Bos	18-10	0	2.62
1993.....Greg Maddux, Atl	20-10	0	2.36	1992.....*Dennis Eckersley, Oak	7-1	51	1.91
1994.....Greg Maddux, Atl	16-6	0	1.56	1993.....Jack McDowell, Chi	22-10	0	3.37
				1994.....David Cone, KC	16-4	0	2.94

*Pitchers who won the MVP and Cy Young awards in the same season.

†NL games only. Sutcliffe pitched 15 games with Cleveland before being traded to the Cubs.

Career Individual Batting

GAMES

Pete Rose	3562
Carl Yastrzemski	3308
Hank Aaron	3298
Ty Cobb	3035
Stan Musial	3026
Willie Mays	2992
Dave Winfield	2973
Rusty Staub	2951
Brooks Robinson	2896
Robin Yount	2856
Al Kaline	2834
Eddie Collins	2826
Reggie Jackson	2820
Eddie Murray	2819
Frank Robinson	2808
Honus Wagner	2792
Tris Speaker	2789
Tony Perez	2777
Mel Ott	2730
George Brett	2707

HOME RUNS

Hank Aaron	755
Babe Ruth	714
Willie Mays	660
Frank Robinson	586
Harmon Killebrew	573
Reggie Jackson	563
Mike Schmidt	548
Mickey Mantle	536
Jimmie Foxx	534
Ted Williams	521
Willie McCovey	521
Eddie Mathews	512
Ernie Banks	512
Mel Ott	511
Lou Gehrig	493
Eddie Murray	479
Willie Stargell	475
Stan Musial	475
Dave Winfield	465
Carl Yastrzemski	452

BATTING AVERAGE

Ty Cobb	.366
Rogers Hornsby	.358
Joe Jackson	.356
Ed Delahanty	.346
Tris Speaker	.345
Ted Williams	.344
Billy Hamilton	.344
Dan Brouthers	.342
Babe Ruth	.342
Harry Heilmann	.342
Pete Browning	.341
Willie Keeler	.341
Bill Terry	.341
George Sisler	.340
Lou Gehrig	.340
Jesse Burkett	.338
Nap Lajoie	.338
Tony Gwynn	.336
Riggs Stephenson	.336
Wade Boggs	.334
Al Simmons	.334

AT BATS

Pete Rose	14053
Hank Aaron	12364
Carl Yastrzemski	11988
Ty Cobb	11434
Robin Yount	11008
Dave Winfield	11003
Stan Musial	10972
Willie Mays	10881
Brooks Robinson	10654
Eddie Murray	10603
Honus Wagner	10430
George Brett	10349
Lou Brock	10332
Luis Aparicio	10230
Tris Speaker	10195
Al Kaline	10116
Rabbit Maranville	10078
Frank Robinson	10006
Eddie Collins	9949
Andre Dawson	9869

HITS

Pete Rose	4256
Ty Cobb	4189
Hank Aaron	3771
Stan Musial	3630
Tris Speaker	3514
Carl Yastrzemski	3419
Honus Wagner	3415
Eddie Collins	3312
Willie Mays	3283
Nap Lajoie	3242
George Brett	3154
Paul Waner	3152
Robin Yount	3142
Dave Winfield	3110
Eddie Murray	3071
Rod Carew	3053
Lou Brock	3023
Al Kaline	3007
Roberto Clemente	3000
Cap Anson	2995

RUNS

Ty Cobb	2246
Babe Ruth	2174
Hank Aaron	2174
Pete Rose	2165
Willie Mays	2062
Stan Musial	1949
Lou Gehrig	1888
Tris Speaker	1882
Mel Ott	1859
Frank Robinson	1829
Eddie Collins	1821
Carl Yastrzemski	1816
Ted Williams	1798
Charlie Gehringer	1774
Jimmie Foxx	1751
Honus Wagner	1736
Jesse Burkett	1720
Cap Anson	1719
Rickey Henderson	1719
Willie Keeler	1719

Career Individual Batting (Cont.)

DOUBLES

Tris Speaker	792
Pete Rose	746
Stan Musial	725
Ty Cobb	724
George Brett	665
Nap Lajoie	657
Carl Yastrzemski	646
Honus Wagner	640
Hank Aaron	624
Paul Waner	605
Robin Yount	583
Charlie Gehringer	574
Harry Heilmann	542
Rogers Hornsby	541
Joe Medwick	540
Dave Winfield	540
Al Simmons	539
Lou Gehrig	534
Eddie Murray	532
Al Oliver	529

TRIPLES

Sam Crawford	309
Ty Cobb	295
Honus Wagner	252
Jake Beckley	243
Roger Connor	233
Tris Speaker	222
Fred Clarke	220
Dan Brouthers	205
Joe Kelley	194
Paul Waner	191
Bid McPhee	188
Eddie Collins	186
Ed Delahanty	185
Sam Rice	184
Jesse Burkett	182
Edd Roush	182
Ed Konetchy	181
Buck Ewing	178
Rabbit Maranville	177
Stan Musial	177

BASES ON BALLS

Babe Ruth	2056
Ted Williams	2019
Joe Morgan	1865
Carl Yastrzemski	1845
Mickey Mantle	1733
Mel Ott	1708
Eddie Yost	1614
Darrell Evans	1605
Stan Musial	1599
Pete Rose	1566
Harmon Killebrew	1559
Rickey Henderson	1550
Lou Gehrig	1508
Mike Schmidt	1507
Eddie Collins	1499
Willie Mays	1464
Jimmie Foxx	1452
Eddie Mathews	1444
Frank Robinson	1420
Hank Aaron	1402

RUNS BATTED IN

Hank Aaron	2297
Babe Ruth	2213
Lou Gehrig	1995
Stan Musial	1951
Ty Cobb	1937
Jimmie Foxx	1922
Willie Mays	1903
Cap Anson	1879
Mel Ott	1860
Carl Yastrzemski	1844
Ted Williams	1839
Dave Winfield	1833
Al Simmons	1827
Eddie Murray	1820
Frank Robinson	1812
Honus Wagner	1732
Reggie Jackson	1702
Tony Perez	1652
Ernie Banks	1636
Goose Goslin	1609

SLUGGING AVERAGE

Babe Ruth	.690
Ted Williams	.634
Lou Gehrig	.632
Jimmie Foxx	.609
Hank Greenberg	.605
Joe DiMaggio	.579
Rogers Hornsby	.577
Johnny Mize	.562
Stan Musial	.559
Willie Mays	.557
Mickey Mantle	.557
Hank Aaron	.555
Ralph Kiner	.548
Hack Wilson	.545
Chuck Klein	.543
Barry Bonds	.541
Duke Snider	.540
Frank Robinson	.537
Al Simmons	.535
Fred McGriff	.535

STOLEN BASES

Rickey Henderson	1149
Lou Brock	938
Billy Hamilton	912
Ty Cobb	892
Tim Raines	777
Eddie Collins	744
Vince Coleman	740
Arlie Latham	739
Max Carey	738
Honus Wagner	722
Joe Morgan	689
Willie Wilson	668
Tom Brown	657
Bert Campaneris	649
George Davis	616
Dummy Hoy	594
Maury Wills	586
George Van Haltren	583
Hugh Duffy	574
Ozzie Smith	573

PINCH HITS

Manny Mota	150
Smoky Burgess	145
Greg Gross	143
Jose Morales	123
Jerry Lynch	116
Red Lucas	114
Steve Braun	113
Terry Crowley	108
Denny Walling	108
Gates Brown	107
Mike Lum	103
Jim Dwyer	102
Rusty Staub	100
Larry Biittner	95
Vic Davalillo	95
Jerry Hairston	94
Dave Philley	93
Joel Youngblood	93
Jay Johnstone	92
Ed Kranepool	90
Elmer Valo	90

TOTAL BASES

Hank Aaron	6856
Stan Musial	6134
Willie Mays	6066
Ty Cobb	5854
Babe Ruth	5793
Pete Rose	5752
Carl Yastrzemski	5539
Frank Robinson	5373
Dave Winfield	5221
Eddie Murray	5108
Tris Speaker	5101
Lou Gehrig	5060
George Brett	5044
Mel Ott	5041
Jimmie Foxx	4956
Ted Williams	4884
Honus Wagner	4862
Al Kaline	4852
Reggie Jackson	4834
Andre Dawson	4763

STRIKEOUTS

Reggie Jackson	2597
Willie Stargell	1936
Mike Schmidt	1883
Tony Perez	1867
Dave Kingman	1816
Bobby Bonds	1757
Dale Murphy	1748
Lou Brock	1730
Mickey Mantle	1710
Harmon Killebrew	1699
Dwight Evans	1697
Dave Winfield	1686
Lee May	1570
Dick Allen	1556
Willie McCovey	1550
Dave Parker	1537
Frank Robinson	1532
Lance Parrish	1527
Willie Mays	1526
Rick Monday	1513

Career Individual Pitching

GAMES

Hoyt Wilhelm	1070
Kent Tekulve	1050
Goose Gossage	1002
Lindy McDaniel	987
Rollie Fingers	944
Lee Smith	943
Gene Garber	931
Cy Young	906
Dennis Eckersley	901
Sparky Lyle	899
Jim Kaat	898
Jeff Reardon	880
Don McMahon	874
Phil Niekro	864
Charlie Hough	858
Roy Face	848
Tug McGraw	824
Jesse Orosco	819
Nolan Ryan	807
Walter Johnson	802

INNINGS PITCHED

Cy Young	7356.2
Pud Galvin	5941.1
Walter Johnson	5914.2
Phil Niekro	5404.1
Nolan Ryan	5386.0
Gaylord Perry	5350.1
Don Sutton	5282.1
Warren Spahn	5243.2
Steve Carlton	5217.1
Grover Alexander	5190.0
Kid Nichols	5056.1
Tim Keefe	5047.1
Bert Blyleven	4970.0
Mickey Welch	4802.0
Tom Seaver	4782.2
Christy Mathewson	4780.2
Tommy John	4710.1
Robin Roberts	4688.2
Early Wynn	4564.0
John Clarkson	4536.1

WINS

Cy Young	511
Walter Johnson	417
Grover Alexander	373
Christy Mathewson	373
Warren Spahn	363
Kid Nichols	361
Pud Galvin	360
Tim Keefe	342
Steve Carlton	329
John Clarkson	328
Eddie Plank	326
Nolan Ryan	324
Don Sutton	324
Phil Niekro	318
Gaylord Perry	314
Tom Seaver	311
Charley Radbourn	309
Mickey Welch	307
Lefty Grove	300
Early Wynn	300

LOSSES

Cy Young	316
Pud Galvin	308
Nolan Ryan	292
Walter Johnson	279
Phil Niekro	274
Gaylord Perry	265
Don Sutton	256
Jack Powell	254
Eppa Rixey	251
Bert Blyleven	250
Robin Roberts	245
Warren Spahn	245
Steve Carlton	244
Early Wynn	244
Jim Kaat	237
Frank Tanana	236
Gus Weyhing	232
Tommy John	231
Bob Friend	230
Ted Lyons	230

WINNING PERCENTAGE

Dave Foutz	.690
Whitey Ford	.690
Bob Caruthers	.688
Lefty Grove	.680
Vic Raschi	.667
Larry Corcoran	.665
Christy Mathewson	.665
Sam Leever	.660
Sal Maglie	.657
Sandy Koufax	.655
Johnny Allen	.654
Ron Guidry	.651
Roger Clemens	.650
Lefty Gomez	.649
Dwight Gooden	.649
John Clarkson	.648
Three Finger Brown	.648
Dizzy Dean	.644
Grover Alexander	.642
Jim Palmer	.638

SAVES

Lee Smith	471
Jeff Reardon	367
Rollie Fingers	341
Dennis Eckersley	323
Tom Henke	311
Goose Gossage	310
Bruce Sutter	300
John Franco	295
Dave Righetti	252
Dan Quisenberry	244
Randy Myers	243
Doug Jones	239
Sparky Lyle	238
Hoyt Wilhelm	227
Gene Garber	218
Jeff Montgomery	218
Dave Smith	216
Rick Aguilera	211
Bobby Thigpen	201
Roy Face	193

EARNED RUN AVERAGE

Ed Walsh	1.82
Addie Joss	1.89
Three Finger Brown	2.06
John Ward	2.10
Christy Mathewson	2.13
Rube Waddell	2.16
Walter Johnson	2.17
Orval Overall	2.23
Tommy Bond	2.25
Ed Reulbach	2.28
Will White	2.28
Jim Scott	2.30
Eddie Plank	2.35
Larry Corcoran	2.36
Eddie Cicotte	2.38
Ed Killian	2.38
George McQuillan	2.38
Doc White	2.39
Nap Rucker	2.42
Terry Larkin	2.43
Jim McCormick	2.43
Jeff Tesreau	2.43

SHUTOUTS

Walter Johnson	110
Grover Alexander	90
Christy Mathewson	79
Cy Young	76
Eddie Plank	69
Warren Spahn	63
Nolan Ryan	61
Tom Seaver	61
Bert Blyleven	60
Don Sutton	58
Pud Galvin	57
Ed Walsh	57
Bob Gibson	56
Three Finger Brown	55
Steve Carlton	55
Jim Palmer	53
Gaylord Perry	53
Juan Marichal	52
Rube Waddell	50
Vic Willis	50

COMPLETE GAMES

Cy Young	749
Pud Galvin	639
Tim Keefe	554
Walter Johnson	531
Kid Nichols	531
Mickey Welch	525
Charley Radbourn	489
John Clarkson	485
Tony Mullane	468
Jim McCormick	466
Gus Weyhing	448
Grover Alexander	437
Christy Mathewson	434
Jack Powell	422
Eddie Plank	410
Will White	394
Amos Rusie	392
Vic Willis	388
Warren Spahn	382
Jim Whitney	377

Career Individual Pitching *(Cont.)*

STRIKEOUTS		BASES ON BALLS	
Nolan Ryan	5714	Nolan Ryan	2795
Steve Carlton	4136	Steve Carlton	1833
Bert Blyleven	3701	Phil Niekro	1809
Tom Seaver	3640	Early Wynn	1775
Don Sutton	3574	Bob Feller	1764
Gaylord Perry	3534	Bobo Newsom	1732
Walter Johnson	3509	Amos Rusie	1704
Phil Niekro	3342	Charlie Hough	1665
Ferguson Jenkins	3192	Gus Weyhing	1566
Bob Gibson	3117	Red Ruffing	1541
Jim Bunning	2855	Bump Hadley	1442
Mickey Lolich	2832	Warren Spahn	1434
Cy Young	2803	Earl Whitehill	1431
Frank Tanana	2773	Tony Mullane	1408
Warren Spahn	2583	Sad Sam Jones	1396
Bob Feller	2581	Jack Morris	1390
Jerry Koosman	2556	Tom Seaver	1390
Tim Keefe	2543	Gaylord Perry	1379
Christy Mathewson	2502	Mike Torrez	1371
Don Drysdale	2486	Walter Johnson	1363

Individual Batting (Single Season)

HITS		TOTAL BASES		RUNS BATTED IN	
George Sisler, 1920	257	Babe Ruth, 1921	457	Hack Wilson, 1930	190
Lefty O'Doul, 1929	254	Rogers Hornsby, 1922	450	Lou Gehrig, 1931	184
Bill Terry, 1930	254	Lou Gehrig, 1927	447	Hank Greenberg, 1937	183
Al Simmons, 1925	253	Chuck Klein, 1930	445	Lou Gehrig, 1927	175
Rogers Hornsby, 1922	250	Jimmie Foxx, 1932	438	Jimmie Foxx, 1938	175
Chuck Klein, 1930	250	Stan Musial, 1948	429	Lou Gehrig, 1930	174
Ty Cobb, 1911	248	Hack Wilson, 1930	423	Babe Ruth, 1921	171
George Sisler, 1922	246	Chuck Klein, 1932	420	Chuck Klein, 1930	170
Heinie Manush, 1928	241	Lou Gehrig, 1930	419	Hank Greenberg, 1935	170
Babe Herman, 1930	241	Joe DiMaggio, 1937	418	Jimmie Foxx, 1932	169

BATTING AVERAGE		TRIPLES		STRIKEOUTS	
Hugh Duffy, 1894	.440	Chief Wilson, 1912	36	Bobby Bonds, 1970	189
Tip O'Neill, 1887	.435	Dave Orr, 1886	31	Bobby Bonds, 1969	187
Ross Barnes, 1876	.429	Heinie Reitz, 1894	31	Rob Deer, 1987	186
Nap Lajoie, 1901	.426	Perry Werden, 1893	29	Pete Incaviglia, 1986	185
Willie Keeler, 1897	.424	Harry Davis, 1897	28	Cecil Fielder, 1990	182
Rogers Hornsby, 1924	.424	George Davis, 1893	27	Mike Schmidt, 1975	180
George Sisler, 1922	.420	Sam Thompson, 1894	27	Rob Deer, 1986	179
Ty Cobb, 1911	.420	Jimmy Williams, 1899	27	Dave Nicholson, 1963	175
Fred Dunlap, 1884	.412	John Reilly, 1890	26	Gorman Thomas, 1979	175
Ed Delahanty, 1899	.410	George Treadway, 1894	26	Jose Canseco, 1986	175
		Joe Jackson, 1912	26	Rob Deer, 1991	175
		Sam Crawford, 1914	26		
DOUBLES		Kiki Cuyler, 1925	26		
Earl Webb, 1931	67			RUNS	
George Burns, 1926	64	HOME RUNS		Billy Hamilton, 1894	192
Joe Medwick, 1936	64			Tom Brown, 1891	177
Hank Greenberg, 1934	63	Roger Maris, 1961	61	Babe Ruth, 1921	177
Paul Waner, 1932	62	Babe Ruth, 1927	60	Tip O'Neill, 1887	167
Charlie Gehringer, 1936	60	Babe Ruth, 1921	59	Lou Gehrig, 1936	167
Tris Speaker, 1923	59	Jimmie Foxx, 1932	58	Billy Hamilton, 1895	166
Chuck Klein, 1930	59	Hank Greenberg, 1938	58	Willie Keeler, 1894	165
Billy Herman, 1936	57	Hack Wilson, 1930	56	Joe Kelley, 1894	165
Billy Herman, 1935	57	Babe Ruth, 1920	54	Arlie Latham, 1887	163
		Babe Ruth, 1928	54	Babe Ruth, 1928	163
		Ralph Kiner, 1949	54	Lou Gehrig, 1931	163
		Mickey Mantle, 1961	54		

Individual Batting (Single Season) (Cont.)

STOLEN BASES

Hugh Nicol, 1887	138
Rickey Henderson, 1982	130
Arlie Latham, 1887	129
Lou Brock, 1974	118
Charlie Comiskey, 1887	117
John Ward, 1887	111
Billy Hamilton, 1889	111
Billy Hamilton, 1891	111
Vince Coleman, 1985	110
Arlie Latham, 1888	109
Vince Coleman, 1987	109

BASES ON BALLS

Babe Ruth, 1923	170
Ted Williams, 1947	162
Ted Williams, 1949	162
Ted Williams, 1946	156
Eddie Yost, 1956	151
Eddie Joost, 1949	149
Babe Ruth, 1920	148
Eddie Stanky, 1945	148
Jimmy Wynn, 1969	148
Jimmy Sheckard, 1911	147

SLUGGING AVERAGE

Babe Ruth, 1920	.847
Babe Ruth, 1921	.846
Babe Ruth, 1927	.772
Lou Gehrig, 1927	.765
Babe Ruth, 1923	.764
Rogers Hornsby, 1925	.756
Jeff Bagwell, 1994	.750
Jimmie Foxx, 1932	.749
Babe Ruth, 1924	.739
Babe Ruth, 1926	.737

Individual Pitching (Single Season)

GAMES

Mike Marshall, 1974	106
Kent Tekulve, 1979	94
Mike Marshall, 1973	92
Kent Tekulve, 1978	91
Wayne Granger, 1969	90
Mike Marshall, 1979	90
Kent Tekulve, 1987	90
Mark Eichhorn, 1987	89
Wilbur Wood, 1968	88
Rob Murphy, 1987	87

WINS

Charley Radbourn, 1884	59
John Clarkson, 1885	53
Guy Hecker, 1884	52
John Clarkson, 1889	49
Charley Radbourn, 1883	48
Charlie Buffinton, 1884	48
Al Spalding, 1876	47
John Ward, 1879	47
Jim Galvin, 1883	46
Jim Galvin, 1884	46
Matt Kilroy, 1887	46

SAVES

Bobby Thigpen, 1990	57
Randy Myers, 1993	53
Dennis Eckersley, 1992	51
Dennis Eckersley, 1990	48
Rod Beck, 1993	48
Lee Smith, 1991	47
Lee Smith, 1993	46
Dave Righetti, 1986	46
Bryan Harvey, 1991	46
Jose Mesa, 1995	46
Six tied with 45.	

GAMES STARTED

Will White, 1879	75
Jim Galvin, 1883	75
Jim McCormick, 1880	74
Charley Radbourn, 1884	73
Guy Hecker, 1884	73
Jim Galvin, 1884	72
John Clarkson, 1889	72
Bill Hutchison, 1892	71
John Clarkson, 1885	70
Matt Kilroy, 1887	69

LOSSES

John Coleman, 1883	48
Will White, 1880	42
Larry McKeon, 1884	41
George Bradley, 1879	40
Jim McCormick, 1879	40
Henry Porter, 1888	37
Kid Carsey, 1891	37
George Cobb, 1892	37
Stump Weidman, 1886	36
Bill Hutchison, 1892	36

EARNED RUN AVERAGE

Tim Keefe, 1880	0.86
Dutch Leonard, 1914	0.96
Three Finger Brown, 1906	1.04
Bob Gibson, 1968	1.12
Christy Mathewson, 1909	1.14
Walter Johnson, 1913	1.14
Jack Pfiester, 1907	1.15
Addie Joss, 1908	1.16
Carl Lundgren, 1907	1.17
Denny Driscoll, 1882	1.21

INNINGS PITCHED

Will White, 1878	680.0
Charley Radbourn, 1884	678.2
Guy Hecker, 1884	670.2
Jim McCormick, 1880	657.2
Jim Galvin, 1883	656.1
Jim Galvin, 1884	636.1
Charley Radbourn, 1883	632.1
Bill Hutchison, 1892	627.0
John Clarkson, 1885	623.0
Jim Devlin, 1876	622.0

WINNING PERCENTAGE

Roy Face, 1959	.947
Johnny Allen, 1937	.938
Greg Maddux, 1995	.905
Randy Johnson, 1995	.900
Ron Guidry, 1978	.893
Freddie Fitzsimmons, 1940	.889
Lefty Grove, 1931	.886
Bob Stanley, 1978	.882
Preacher Roe, 1951	.880
Fred Goldsmith, 1880	.875
Tom Seaver, 1981	.875

SHUTOUTS

George Bradley, 1876	16
Grover Alexander, 1916	16
Jack Coombs, 1910	13
Bob Gibson, 1968	13
Jim Galvin, 1884	12
Ed Morris, 1886	12
Grover Alexander, 1915	12
Tommy Bond, 1879	11
Charley Radbourn, 1884	11
Dave Foutz, 1886	11
Christy Mathewson, 1908	11
Ed Walsh, 1908	11
Walter Johnson, 1913	11
Sandy Koufax, 1963	11
Dean Chance, 1964	11

Individual Pitching (Single Season) (*Cont.*)

COMPLETE GAMES		STRIKEOUTS		BASES ON BALLS	
Will White, 1879	75	Matt Kilroy, 1886	513	Amos Rusie, 1890	289
Charley Radbourn, 1884	73	Toad Ramsey, 1886	499	Mark Baldwin, 1889	274
Jim McCormick, 1880	72	Hugh Daily, 1884	483	Amos Rusie, 1892	267
Jim Galvin, 1883	72	Dupee Shaw, 1884	451	Amos Rusie, 1891	262
Guy Hecker, 1884	72	Charley Radbourn, 1884	441	Mark Baldwin, 1890	249
Jim Galvin, 1884	71	Charlie Buffinton, 1884	417	Jack Stivetts, 1891	232
Tim Keefe, 1883	68	Guy Hecker, 1884	385	Mark Baldwin, 1891	227
John Clarkson, 1885	68	Nolan Ryan, 1973	383	Phil Knell, 1891	226
John Clarkson, 1889	68	Sandy Koufax, 1965	382	Bob Barr, 1890	219
Bill Hutchison, 1892	67	Bill Sweeney, 1884	374	Amos Rusie 1893	218

Manager of the Year

NATIONAL LEAGUE		AMERICAN LEAGUE	
1983	Tommy Lasorda, LA	1983	Tony La Russa, Chi
1984	Jim Frey, Chi	1984	Sparky Anderson, Det
1985	Whitey Herzog, StL	1985	Bobby Cox, Tor
1986	Hal Lanier, Hou	1986	John McNamara, Bos
1987	Buck Rodgers, Mtl	1987	Sparky Anderson, Det
1988	Tommy Lasorda, LA	1988	Tony La Russa, Oak
1989	Don Zimmer, Chi	1989	Frank Robinson, Balt
1990	Jim Leyland, Pitt	1990	Jeff Torborg, Chi
1991	Bobby Cox, Atl	1991	Tom Kelly, Minn
1992	Jim Leyland, Pitt	1992	Tony La Russa, Oak
1993	Dusty Baker, SF	1993	Gene Lamont, Chi
1994	Felipe Alou, Mtl	1994	Buck Showalter, NY

Individual Batting (Single Game)

MOST RUNS

7 ....Guy Hecker, Lou   Aug 15, 1886

MOST HITS

7 ....Wilbert Robinson, Balt   June 10, 1892
Rennie Stennett, Pitt   Sept 16, 1975

MOST HOME RUNS

4	Bobby Lowe, Bos (N)	May 30, 1894
	Ed Delahanty, Phil	July 13, 1896
	Lou Gehrig, NY (A)	June 3, 1932
	Gil Hodges, Bklyn	Aug 31, 1950
	Joe Adcock, Mil (N)	July 31, 1954
	Rocky Colavito, Clev	June 10, 1959
	Willie Mays, SF	April 30, 1961
	Bob Horner, Atl	July 6, 1986
	Mark Whiten, StL	Sept 7, 1993

MOST GRAND SLAMS

2	Tony Lazzeri, NY (A)	May 24, 1936
	Jim Tabor, Bos (A)	July 4, 1939
	Rudy York, Bos (A)	July 27, 1946
	Jim Gentile, Balt	May 9, 1961
	Tony Cloninger, Atl	July 3, 1966
	Jim Northrup, Det	June 24, 1968
	Frank Robinson, Balt	June 26, 1970
	Robin Ventura, Chi (A)	Sept 4, 1995

MOST RBI

| 12 ..... | Jim Bottomley, StL | Sept 16, 1924 |
| | Mark Whiten, StL | Sept 7, 1993 |

Individual Batting (Single Inning)

MOST RUNS

3	Tommy Burns, Chi (N)	Sept 6, 1883, 7th inning
	Ned Williamson, Chi (N)	Sept 6, 1883, 7th inning
	Sammy White, Bos (A)	June 18, 1953, 7th inning

MOST HITS

3	Tommy Burns, Chi (N)	Sept 6, 1883, 7th inning
	Fred Pfeiffer, Chi (N)	Sept 6, 1883, 7th inning
	Ned Williamson, Chi (N)	Sept 6, 1883, 7th inning
	Gene Stephens, Bos (A)	June 18, 1953, 7th inning

MOST RBI

6	Fred Merkle, NY (N)	May 13, 1911 (RBIs not officially adopted until 1920)
	Bob Johnson, Phil (A)	Aug 29, 1937
	Tom McBride, Bos (A)	Aug 4, 1945
	Joe Astroth, Phil (A)	Sept 23, 1950
	Gil McDougald, NY (A)	May 3, 1951
	Sam Mele, Chi (A)	June 10, 1952
	Jim Lemon, Wash	Sept 5, 1959
	Jim Ray Hart, SF	July 8, 1970
	Andre Dawson, Mont	Sept 24, 1985
	Dale Murphy, Atl	July 27, 1989
	Carlos Quintana, Bos (A)	July 30, 1991

Note: All single game hitting records for nine-inning game.

Individual Pitching (Single Game)

MOST INNINGS PITCHED

26 .....Leon Cadore, Bklyn — May 1, 1920, tie 1-1
     Joe Oeschger, Bos (N) — May 1, 1920, tie 1-1

MOST RUNS ALLOWED

24 .....Al Travers, Det — May 18, 1912 (only major league game)

MOST HITS ALLOWED

36 .....Jack Wadsworth, Lou — Aug 17, 1894

MOST STRIKEOUTS

20 .....Roger Clemens, Bos (A) April 29, 1986

MOST WALKS ALLOWED

16 .....Bill George, NY (N) — May 30, 1887
     George Van Haltren, Chi (N) — June 27, 1887
     Henry Gruber, Clev — Apr 19, 1890
     Bruno Haas, Phil (A) — June 2, 1915

MOST WILD PITCHES

6 .......J.R. Richard, Hou — April 10, 1979
     Phil Niekro, Atl — Aug 14, 1979
     Bill Gullickson, Mtl — April 10, 1982

Individual Pitching (Single Inning)

MOST RUNS ALLOWED

13 .....Lefty O'Doul, Bos (A) — July 7, 1923

MOST WALKS ALLOWED

8 ....Dolly Gray, Wash — Aug 28, 1909

MOST WILD PITCHES

4 ....Walter Johnson, Wash — Sept 21, 1914
     Phil Niekro, Atl — Aug 14, 1979

Miscellaneous

LONGEST GAME, BY INNINGS

26 .....Brooklyn 1, Boston 1 — May 1, 1920

LONGEST NINE-INNING GAME, BY TIME

4:18...LA 8, SF 7 — Oct 2, 1962

Baseball Hall of Fame

Players

	Position	Career Dates	Year Selected		Position	Career Dates	Year Selected
Hank Aaron	OF	1954-76	1982	Jack Chesbro	P	1899-1909	1946
Grover Alexander	P	1911-30	1938	Fred Clarke	OF	1894-1915	1945
Cap Anson	1B	1876-97	1939	John Clarkson	P	1882-94	1963
Luis Aparicio	SS	1956-73	1984	Roberto Clemente	OF	1955-72	1973
Luke Appling	SS	1930-50	1964	Ty Cobb	OF	1905-28	1936
Richie Ashburn	OF	1948-62	1995	Mickey Cochrane	C	1925-37	1947
Earl Averill	OF	1929-41	1975	Eddie Collins	2B	1906-30	1939
Frank Baker	3B	1908-22	1955	Jimmy Collins	3B	1895-1908	1945
Dave Bancroft	SS	1915-30	1971	Earle Combs	OF	1924-35	1970
Ernie Banks	SS-1B	1953-71	1977	Roger Connor	1B	1880-97	1976
Jake Beckley	1B	1888-1907	1971	Stan Coveleski	P	1912-28	1969
Cool Papa Bell*	OF		1974	Sam Crawford	OF	1899-1917	1957
Johnny Bench	C	1967-83	1989	Joe Cronin	SS	1926-45	1956
Chief Bender	P	1903-25	1953	Candy Cummings	P	1872-77	1939
Yogi Berra	C	1946-65	1972	Kiki Cuyler	OF	1921-38	1968
Jim Bottomley	1B	1922-37	1974	Ray Dandridge*	3B		1987
Lou Boudreau	SS	1938-52	1970	Leon Day*	P		1995
Roger Bresnahan	C	1897-1915	1945	Dizzy Dean	P	1930-47	1953
Lou Brock	OF	1961-79	1985	Ed Delahanty	OF	1888-1903	1945
Dan Brouthers	1B	1879-1904	1945	Bill Dickey	C	1928-46	1954
Three Finger Brown	P	1903-16	1949	Martin Dihigo*	P-OF		1977
Jesse Burkett	OF	1890-1905	1946	Joe DiMaggio	OF	1936-51	1955
Roy Campanella	C	1948-57	1969	Bobby Doerr	2B	1937-51	1986
Rod Carew	1B-2B	1967-85	1991	Don Drysdale	P	1956-69	1984
Max Carey	OF	1910-29	1961	Hugh Duffy	OF	1888-1906	1945
Steve Carlton	P	1965-88	1994	Johnny Evers	2B	1902-29	1939
Frank Chance	1B	1898-1914	1946	Buck Ewing	C	1880-97	1946
Oscar Charleston*	OF		1976	Red Faber	P	1914-33	1964

Note: Career dates indicate first and last appearances in the majors.
*Elected on the basis of his career in the Negro leagues.

Players (Cont.)

	Position	Career Dates	Year Selected		Position	Career Dates	Year Selected
Bob Feller	P	1936-56	1962	Joe McGinnity	P	1899-1908	1946
Rick Ferrell	C	1929-47	1984	Joe Medwick	OF	1932-48	1968
Rollie Fingers	P	1968-85	1992	Johnny Mize	1B	1936-53	1981
Elmer Flick	OF	1898-1910	1963	Joe Morgan	2B	1963-84	1990
Whitey Ford	P	1950-67	1974	Stan Musial	OF-1B	1941-63	1969
Jimmie Foxx	1B	1925-45	1951	Hal Newhouser	P	1939-55	1992
Frankie Frisch	2B	1919-37	1947	Kid Nichols	P	1890-1906	1949
Pud Galvin	P	1879-92	1965	Jim O'Rourke	OF	1876-1904	1945
Lou Gehrig	1B	1923-39	1939	Mel Ott	OF	1926-47	1951
Charlie Gehringer	2B	1924-42	1949	Satchel Paige*	P	1948-65	1971
Bob Gibson	P	1959-75	1981	Jim Palmer	P	1965-84	1990
Josh Gibson*	C		1972	Herb Pennock	P	1912-34	1948
Lefty Gomez	P	1930-43	1972	Gaylord Perry	P	1962-83	1991
Goose Goslin	OF	1921-38	1968	Eddie Plank	P	1901-17	1946
Hank Greenberg	1B	1930-47	1956	Charley Radbourn	P	1880-91	1939
Burleigh Grimes	P	1916-34	1964	Pee Wee Reese	SS	1940-58	1984
Lefty Grove	P	1925-41	1947	Sam Rice	OF	1915-35	1963
Chick Hafey	OF	1924-37	1971	Eppa Rixey	P	1912-33	1963
Jesse Haines	P	1918-37	1970	Phil Rizzuto	SS	1941-56	1994
Billy Hamilton	OF	1888-1901	1961	Robin Roberts	P	1948-66	1976
Gabby Hartnett	C	1922-41	1955	Brooks Robinson	3B	1955-77	1983
Harry Heilmann	OF	1914-32	1952	Frank Robinson	OF	1956-76	1982
Billy Herman	2B	1931-47	1975	Jackie Robinson	2B	1947-56	1962
Harry Hooper	OF	1909-25	1971	Edd Roush	OF	1913-31	1962
Rogers Hornsby	2B	1915-37	1942	Red Ruffing	P	1924-47	1967
Waite Hoyt	P	1918-38	1969	Amos Rusie	P	1889-1901	1977
Carl Hubbell	P	1928-43	1947	Babe Ruth	OF	1914-35	1936
Catfish Hunter	P	1965-79	1987	Ray Schalk	C	1912-29	1955
Monte Irvin*	OF	1949-56	1973	Mike Schmidt	3B	1972-89	1995
Reggie Jackson	OF	1967-87	1993	Red Schoendienst	2B	1945-63	1989
Travis Jackson	SS	1922-36	1982	Tom Seaver	P	1967-86	1992
Ferguson Jenkins	P	1965-83	1991	Joe Sewell	SS	1920-33	1977
Hugh Jennings	SS	1891-1918	1945	Al Simmons	OF	1924-44	1953
Judy Johnson*	3B		1975	George Sisler	1B	1915-30	1939
Walter Johnson	P	1907-27	1936	Enos Slaughter	OF	1938-59	1985
Addie Joss	P	1902-10	1978	Duke Snider	OF	1947-64	1980
Al Kaline	OF	1953-74	1980	Warren Spahn	P	1942-65	1973
Tim Keefe	P	1880-93	1964	Al Spalding	P	1871-78	1939
Willie Keeler	OF	1892-1910	1939	Tris Speaker	OF	1907-28	1937
George Kell	3B	1943-57	1983	Willie Stargell	OF-1B	1962-82	1988
Joe Kelley	OF	1891-1908	1971	Bill Terry	1B	1923-36	1954
George Kelly	1B	1915-32	1973	Sam Thompson	OF	1885-1906	1974
King Kelly	C	1878-93	1945	Joe Tinker	SS	1902-16	1946
Harmon Killebrew	1B-3B	1954-75	1984	Pie Traynor	3B	1920-37	1948
Ralph Kiner	OF	1946-55	1975	Dazzy Vance	P	1915-35	1955
Chuck Klein	OF	1928-44	1980	Arky Vaughan	SS	1932-48	1985
Sandy Koufax	P	1955-66	1972	Rube Waddell	P	1897-1910	1946
Nap Lajoie	2B	1896-1916	1937	Honus Wagner	SS	1897-1917	1936
Tony Lazzeri	2B	1926-39	1991	Bobby Wallace	SS	1894-1918	1953
Bob Lemon	P	1941-58	1976	Ed Walsh	P	1904-17	1946
Buck Leonard*	1B		1977	Lloyd Waner	OF	1927-45	1967
Fred Lindstrom	3B	1924-36	1976	Paul Waner	OF	1926-45	1952
Pop Lloyd*	SS-1B		1977	John Ward	2B-P	1878-94	1964
Ernie Lombardi	C	1931-47	1986	Mickey Welch	P	1880-92	1973
Ted Lyons	P	1923-46	1955	Zach Wheat	OF	1909-27	1959
Mickey Mantle	OF	1951-68	1974	Hoyt Wilhelm	P	1952-72	1985
Heinie Manush	OF	1923-39	1964	Billy Williams	OF	1959-76	1987
Rabbit Maranville	SS-2B	1912-35	1954	Ted Williams	OF	1939-60	1966
Juan Marichal	P	1960-75	1983	Vic Willis	P	1898-1910	1995
Rube Marquard	P	1908-25	1971	Hack Wilson	OF	1923-34	1979
Eddie Mathews	3B	1952-68	1978	Early Wynn	P	1939-63	1972
Christy Mathewson	P	1900-16	1936	Carl Yastrzemski	OF	1961-83	1989
Willie Mays	OF	1951-73	1979	Cy Young	P	1890-1911	1937
Tommy McCarthy	OF	1884-96	1946	Ross Youngs	OF	1917-26	1972
Willie McCovey	1B	1959-80	1986				

Umpires

	Year Selected
Al Barlick	1989
Jocko Conlan	1974
Tom Connolly	1953
Billy Evans	1973
Cal Hubbard	1976
Bill Klem	1953
Bill McGowan	1992

Pioneers/Executives

	Year Selected
Ed Barrow (manager-executive)	1953
Morgan Bulkeley (executive)	1937
Alexander Cartwright (executive)	1938
Henry Chadwick (writer-executive)	1938
Happy Chandler (commissioner)	1982
Charles Comiskey (manager-executive)	1939
Rube Foster (player-manager-executive)	1981
Ford Frick (commissioner-executive)	1970
Warren Giles (executive)	1979
Will Harridge (executive)	1972
William Hulbert (executive)	1995
Ban Johnson (executive)	1937
Kenesaw M. Landis (commissioner)	1944
Larry MacPhail (executive)	1978
Branch Rickey (manager-executive)	1967
Al Spalding (player-executive)	1939
Bill Veeck (owner)	1991
George Weiss (executive)	1971
George Wright (player-manager)	1937
Harry Wright (player-manager-executive)	1953
Tom Yawkey (executive)	1980

Managers

	Years Managed	Year Selected
Walt Alston	1954-76	1983
Leo Durocher	1939-73	1994
Clark Griffith	1901-20	1946
Bucky Harris	1924-56	1975
Miller Huggins	1913-29	1964
Al Lopez	1951-69	1977
Connie Mack	1894-1950	1937
Joe McCarthy	1926-50	1957
John McGraw	1899-1932	1937
Bill McKechnie	1915-46	1962
Wilbert Robinson	1902-31	1945
Casey Stengel	1934-65	1966

THEY SAID IT

Ron Davis, former Minnesota Twin reliever who had a knack for giving up late-game homers, on the boos he still hears at appearances in the Twin Cities: "When it's 10 years later and they still hate you, that's what you call charisma."

Notable Achievements

No-Hit Games, 9 Innings or More

NATIONAL LEAGUE

Date		Pitcher and Game
1876	July 15	George Bradley, StL vs Hart 2-0
1880	June 12	John Richmond, Wor vs Clev 1-0 (perfect game)
	June 17	Monte Ward, Prov vs Buff 5-0 (perfect game)
	Aug 19	Larry Corcoran, Chi vs Bos 6-0
	Aug 20	Pud Galvin, Buff at Wor 1-0
1882	Sep 20	Larry Corcoran, Chi vs Wor 5-0
	Sep 22	Tim Lovett, Bklyn vs NY 4-0
1883	July 25	Hoss Radbourn, Prov at Clev 8-0
	Sep 13	Hugh Daily, Clev at Phil 1-0
1884	June 27	Larry Corcoran, Chi vs Prov 6-0
	Aug 4	Pud Galvin, Buff at Det 18-0
1885	July 27	John Clarkson, Chi at Prov 4-0
	Aug 29	Charles Ferguson, Phil vs Prov 1-0
1891	July 31	Amos Rusie, NY vs Bklyn 6-0
	June 22	Tom Lovett, Bklyn vs NY 4-0
1892	Aug 6	Jack Stivetts, Bos vs Bklyn 11-0
	Aug 22	Alex Sanders, Lou vs Balt 6-2
	Oct 15	Bumpus Jones, Cin vs Pitt 7-1 (first major league game)
1893	Aug 16	Bill Hawke, Balt vs Wash 5-0

Date		Pitcher and Game
1897	Sep 18	Cy Young, Clev vs Cin 6-0
1898	Apr 22	Ted Breitenstein, Cin vs Pitt 11-0
	Apr 22	Jim Hughes, Balt vs Bos 8-0
	July 8	Frank Donahue, Phil vs Bos 5-0
	Aug 21	Walter Thornton, Chi vs Bklyn 2-0
1899	May 25	Deacon Phillippe, Lou vs NY 7-0
	Aug 7	Vic Willis, Bos vs Wash 7-1
1900	July 12	Noodles Hahn, Cin vs Phil 4-0
1901	July 15	Christy Mathewson, NY at StL 5-0
1903	Sep 18	Chick Fraser, Phil at Chi 10-0
1904	June 11	Bob Wicker, Chi at NY 1-0 (hit in 10th; won in 12th)
1905	June 13	Christy Mathewson, NY at Chi 1-0
1906	May 1	John Lush, Phil at Bklyn 6-0
	July 20	Mal Eason, Bklyn at StL 2-0
	Aug 1	Harry McIntire, Bklyn vs Pitt 0-1 (hit in 11th; lost in 13th)
1907	May 8	Frank Pfeffer, Bos vs Cin 6-0
	Sep 20	Nick Maddox, Pitt vs Bklyn 2-1
1908	July 4	George Wiltse, NY vs Phil 1-0 (10 innings)
	Sep 5	Nap Rucker, Bklyn vs Bos 6-0

No-Hit Games, 9 Innings or More *(Cont.)*

NATIONAL LEAGUE *(Cont.)*

Date	Pitcher and Game
1909......Apr 15	Leon Ames, NY vs Bklyn 0-3
	(hit in 10th; lost in 13th)
1912......Sep 6	Jeff Tesreau, NY at Phil 3-0
1914......Sep 9	George Davis, Bos vs Phil 7-0
1915......Apr 15	Rube Marquard, NY vs Bklyn 2-0
Aug 31	Jimmy Lavender, Chi at NY 2-0
1916......June 16	Tom Hughes, Bos vs Pitt 2-0
1917......May 2	Jim Vaughn, Chi vs Cin 0-1
	(hit in 10th; lost in 10th)
May 2	Fred Toney, Cin at Chi 1-0
	(10 innings)
1919......May 11	Hod Eller, Cin vs StL 6-0
1922......May 7	Jesse Barnes, NY vs Phil 6-0
1924......July 17	Jesse Haines, StL vs Bos 5-0
1925......Sep 13	Dazzy Vance, Bklyn vs Phil 10-1
1929......May 8	Carl Hubbell, NY vs Pitt 11-0
1934......Sep 21	Paul Dean, StL vs Bklyn 3-0
1938......June 11	Johnny Vander Meer, Cin vs Bos 3-0
June 15	Johnny Vander Meer, Cin at Bklyn 6-0
1940......Apr 30	Tex Carleton, Bklyn at Cin, 3-0
1941......Aug 30	Lon Warneke, StL at Cin 2-0
1944......Apr 27	Jim Tobin, Bos vs Bklyn 2-0
May 15	Clyde Shoun, Cin vs Bos 1-0
1946......Apr 23	Ed Head, Bklyn vs Bos 5-0
1947......June 18	Ewell Blackwell, Cin vs Bos 6-0
1948......Sep 9	Rex Barney, Bklyn at NY 2-0
1950......Aug 11	Vern Bickford, Bos vs Bklyn 7-0
1951......May 6	Cliff Chambers, Pitt at Bos 3-0
1952......June 19	Carl Erskine, Bklyn vs Chi 5-0
1954......June 12	Jim Wilson, Mil vs Phil 2-0
1955......May 12	Sam Jones, Chi vs Pitt 4-0
1956......May 12	Carl Erskine, Bklyn vs NY 3-0
Sep 25	Sal Maglie, Bklyn vs Phil 5-0
1959......May 26	Harvey Haddix, Pitt at Mil 0-1
	(hit in 13th; lost in 13th)
1960......May 15	Don Cardwell, Chi vs StL 4-0
Aug 18	Lew Burdette, Mil vs Phil 1-0
Sep 16	Warren Spahn, Mil vs Phil 4-0
1961......Apr 28	Warren Spahn, Mil vs SF 1-0
1962......June 30	Sandy Koufax, LA vs NY 5-0
1963......May 11	Sandy Koufax, LA vs SF 8-0
May 17	Don Nottebart, Hou vs Phil 4-1
June 15	Juan Marichal, SF vs Hou 1-0
1964......Apr 23	Ken Johnson, Hou vs Cin 0-1
June 4	Sandy Koufax, LA at Phil 3-0
June 21	Jim Bunning, Phil at NY 6-0
	(perfect game)
1965......June 14	Jim Maloney, Cin vs NY 0-1
	(hit in 11th; lost in 11th)

Date	Pitcher and Game
1965......Aug 19	Jim Maloney, Cin at Chi 1-0
	(10 innings)
Sep 9	Sandy Koufax, LA vs Chi 1-0
	(perfect game)
1967......June 18	Don Wilson, Hou vs Atl 2-0
1968......July 29	George Culver, Cin at Phil 6-1
Sep 17	Gaylord Perry, SF vs StL 1-0
Sep 18	Ray Washburn, StL at SF 2-0
1969......Apr 17	Bill Stoneman, Mtl at Phil 7-0
Apr 30	Jim Maloney, Cin vs Hou 10-0
May 1	Don Wilson, Hou at Cin 4-0
Aug 19	Ken Holtzman, Chi vs Atl 3-0
Sep 20	Bob Moose, Pitt at NY 4-0
1970......June 12	Dock Ellis, Pitt at SD 2-0
July 20	Bill Singer, LA vs Phil 5-0
1971......June 3	Ken Holtzman, Chi at Cin 1-0
June 23	Rick Wise, Phil at Cin 4-0
Aug 14	Bob Gibson, StL at Pitt 11-0
1972......Apr 16	Burt Hooton, Chi vs Phil 4-0
Sep 2	Milt Pappas, Chi vs SD 8-0
Oct 2	Bill Stoneman, Mtl vs NY 7-0
1973......Aug 5	Phil Niekro, Atl vs SD 9-0
1975......Aug 24	Ed Halicki, SF vs NY 6-0
1976......July 9	Larry Dierker, Hou vs Mtl 6-0
Aug 9	John Candelaria, Pitt vs LA 2-0
Sep 29	John Mtlefusco, SF at Atl 9-0
1978......Apr 16	Bob Forsch, StL vs Phil 5-0
June 16	Tom Seaver, Cin vs StL 4-0
1979......Apr 7	Ken Forsch, Hou vs Atl 6-0
1980......June 27	Jerry Reuss, LA at SF 8-0
1981......May 10	Charlie Lea, Mtl vs SF 4-0
Sep 26	Nolan Ryan, Hou vs LA 5-0
1983......Sep 26	Bob Forsch, StL vs Mtl 3-0
1986......Sep 25	Mike Scott, Hou vs SF 2-0
1988......Sep 16	Tom Browning, Cin vs LA 1-0
	(perfect game)
1990......June 29	Fernando Valenzuela, LA vs StL 6-0
1990......Aug 15	Terry Mulholland, Phil vs SF 6-0
1991......May 23	Tommy Greene, Phil at Mtl 2-0
July 26	Mark Gardner, Mtl at LA 0-1
	(hit in 10th, lost in 10th)
July 28	Dennis Martinez, Mtl at LA 2-0
	(perfect game)
Sep 11	Kent Mercker (6), Mark Wohlers (2), and Alejandro Pena (1), Atl at SD 1-0
1992......Aug 17	Kevin Gross, LA vs SF 2-0
1993......Sep 8	Darryl Kile, Hou vs NY 7-1
1994......Apr 8	Kent Mercker, Atl vs LA 6-0
1995......June 3	Pedro Martinez, Mtl vs SD 1-0
	(perfect through 9, hit in 10th)
July 14	Ramon Martinez, LA vs Fla 7-0

Note: Includes the games struck from the record book on September 4, 1991, when baseball's committee on statistical accuracy voted to define no-hitters as games of 9 innings or more that end with a team getting no hits.

No-Hit Games, 9 Innings or More *(Cont.)*

AMERICAN LEAGUE

Date	Pitcher and Game	Date	Pitcher and Game
1901......May 9	Earl Moore, Clev vs Chi 2-4 (hit in 10th; lost in 10th)	1966......Oct 8	Don Larsen, NY (A) vs Bklyn (N) 2-0 (World Series) (perfect game)
1902......Sep 20	Jimmy Callahan, Chi vs Det 3-0	1957......Aug 20	Bob Keegan, Chi vs Wash 6-0
1904......May 5	Cy Young, Bos vs Phil 3-0 (perfect game)	1958......July 20	Jim Bunning, Det at Bos 3-0
Aug 17	Jesse Tannehill, Bos at Chi 6-0	Sep 20	Hoyt Wilhelm, Balt vs NY 1-0
1905......July 22	Weldon Henley, Phil at StL 6-0	1962......May 5	Bo Belinsky, LA vs Balt 2-0
Sep 6	Frank Smith, Chi at Det 15-0	June 26	Earl Wilson, Bos vs LA 2-0
Sep 27	Bill Dinneen, Bos vs Chi 2-0	Aug 1	Bill Monbouquette, Bos at Chi 1-0
1908......June 30	Cy Young, Bos at NY 8-0	Aug 26	Jack Kralick, Minn vs KC 1-0
Sep 18	Bob Rhoades, Clev vs Bos 2-1	1965......Sep 16	Dave Morehead, Bos vs Clev 2-0
Sep 20	Frank Smith, Chi vs Phil 1-0	1966......June 10	Sonny Siebert, Clev vs Wash 2-0
Oct 2	Addie Joss, Clev vs Chi 1-0 (perfect game)	1967......Apr 30	Steve Barber (8⅔) and Stu Miller (⅓), Balt vs Det 1-2
1910......Apr 20	Addie Joss, Clev at Chi 1-0	Aug 25	Dean Chance, Minn at Clev 2-1
May 12	Chief Bender, Phil vs Clev 4-0	Sep 10	Joel Horlen, Chi vs Det 6-0
Aug 30	Tom Hughes, NY vs Clev 0-5 (hit in 10th; lost in 11th)	1968......Apr 27	Tom Phoebus, Balt vs Bos 6-0
1911......July 29	Joe Wood, Bos vs StL 5-0	May 8	Catfish Hunter, Oak vs Minn 4-0 (perfect game)
Aug 27	Ed Walsh, Chi vs Bos 5-0	1969......Aug 13	Jim Palmer, Balt vs Oak 8-0
1912......July 4	George Mullin, Det vs StL 7-0	1970......July 3	Clyde Wright, Calif vs Oak 4-0
Aug 30	Earl Hamilton, StL at Det 5-1	Sep 21	Vida Blue, Oak vs Minn 6-0
1914......May 14	Jim Scott, Chi at Wash 0-1 (hit in 10th; lost in 10th)	1973......Apr 27	Steve Busby, KC at Det 3-0
May 31	Joe Benz, Chi vs Clev 6-1	May 15	Nolan Ryan, Calif at KC 3-0
1916......June 21	George Foster, Bos vs NY 2-0	July 15	Nolan Ryan, Calif at Det 6-0
Aug 26	Joe Bush, Phil vs Clev 5-0	July 30	Jim Bibby, Tex at Oak 6-0
Aug 30	Dutch Leonard, Bos vs StL 4-0	1974......June 19	Steve Busby, KC at Mil 2-0
1917......Apr 14	Ed Cicotte, Chi at StL 11-0	July 19	Dick Bosman, Clev vs Oak 4-0
Apr 24	George Mogridge, NY at Bos 2-1	Sep 28	Nolan Ryan, Calif vs Minn 4-0
May 5	Ernie Koob, StL vs Chi 1-0	1975......June 1	Nolan Ryan, Calif vs Balt 1-0
May 6	Bob Groom, StL vs Chi 3-0	Sep 28	Vida Blue (5), Glenn Abbott and Paul Lindblad (1), Rollie Fingers (2), Oak vs Calif 5-0
June 23	Ernie Shore, Bos vs Wash 4-0 (perfect game)	1976......July 28	John Odom (5) and Francisco Barrios (4), Chi at Oak 2-1
1918......June 3	Dutch Leonard, Bos at Det 5-0	1977......May 14	Jim Colborn, KC vs Tex 6-0
1919......Sep 10	Ray Caldwell, Clev at NY 3-0	May 30	Dennis Eckersley, Clev vs Calif 1-0
1920......July 1	Walter Johnson, Wash at Bos 1-0	Sep 22	Bert Blyleven, Tex at Calif 6-0
1922......Apr 30	Charlie Robertson, Chi at Det 2-0 (perfect game)	1981......May 15	Len Barker, Clev vs Tor 3-0 (perfect game)
1923......Sep 4	Sam Jones, NY at Phil 2-0	1983......July 4	Dave Righetti, NY vs Bos 4-0
Sep 7	Howard Ehmke, Bos at Phil 4-0	Sep 29	Mike Warren, Oak vs Chi 3-0
1926......Aug 21	Ted Lyons, Chi at Bos 6-0	1984......Apr 7	Jack Morris, Det at Chi 4-0
1931......Apr 29	Wes Ferrell, Clev vs StL 9-0	Sep 30	Mike Witt, Calif at Tex 1-0 (perfect game)
Aug 8	Bob Burke, Wash vs Bos 5-0	1986......Sep 19	Joe Cowley, Chi at Calif 7-1
1934......Sep 18	Bobo Newsom, StL vs Bos 1-2 (hit in 10th; lost in 10th)	1987......Apr 15	Juan Nieves, Mil at Balt 7-0
1935......Aug 31	Vern Kennedy, Chi vs Clev 5-0	1990......Apr 11	Mark Langston (7), Mike Witt (2), Calif vs Sea 1-0
1937......June 1	Bill Dietrich, Chi vs StL 8-0	June 2	Randy Johnson, Sea vs Det 2-0
1938......Aug 27	Mtle Pearson, NY vs Clev 13-0	June 11	Nolan Ryan, Tex at Oak 5-0
1940......Apr 16	Bob Feller, Clev at Chi 1-0 (opening day)	June 29	Dave Stewart, Oak at Tor 5-0
1945......Sep 9	Dick Fowler, Phil vs StL 1-0	1990......July 1	Andy Hawkins, NY at Chi 0-4 (pitched 8 innings of 9-inning game)
1946......Apr 30	Bob Feller, Clev at NY 1-0	Sep 2	Dave Stieb, Tor at Clev 3-0
1947......July 10	Don Black, Clev vs Phil 3-0	1991......May 1	Nolan Ryan, Tex vs Tor 3-0
Sep 3	Bill McCahan, Phil vs Wash 3-0	July 13	Bob Milacki (6), Mike Flanagan (1), Mark Williamson (1), and Gregg Olson (1), Balt at Oak 2-0
1948......June 30	Bob Lemon, Clev at Det 2-0	Aug 11	Wilson Alvarez, Chi at Balt 7-0
1951......July 1	Bob Feller, Clev vs Det 2-1	Aug 26	Bret Saberhagen, KC vs Chi 7-0
July 12	Allie Reynolds, NY at Clev 1-0	1993......Apr 22	Chris Bosio, Sea vs Bos 7-0
Sep 28	Allie Reynolds, NY vs Bos 8-0	Sep 4	Jim Abbott, NY vs Clev 4-0
1952......May 15	Virgil Trucks, Det vs Wash 1-0	1994......Apr 27	Scott Erickson, Minn vs Mil 6-0
Aug 25	Virgil Trucks, Det at NY 1-0	July 28	Kenny Rogers, Texas vs Calif. 4-0 (perfect game)
1953......May 6	Bobo Holloman, StL vs Phil 6-0 (first major league start)		
1956......July 14	Mel Parnell, Bos vs Chi 4-0		

Longest Hitting Streaks

NATIONAL LEAGUE				AMERICAN LEAGUE			
Player and Team	**Year**	**G**		**Player and Team**	**Year**	**G**	
Willie Keeler, Balt.	1897	44		Joe DiMaggio, NY	1941	56	
Pete Rose, Cin	1978	44		George Sisler, StL	1922	41	
Bill Dahlen, Chi	1894	42		Ty Cobb, Det	1911	40	
Tommy Holmes, Bos	1945	37		Paul Molitor, Mil	1987	39	
Billy Hamilton, Phil	1894	36		Ty Cobb, Det	1917	35	
Fred Clarke, Lou	1895	35		Ty Cobb, Det	1912	34	
Benito Santiago, SD	1987	34		George Sisler, StL	1925	34	
George Davis, NY	1893	33		John Stone, Det	1930	34	
Rogers Hornsby, StL	1922	32		George McQuinn, StL	1938	34	
Ed Delahanty, Phil	1899	31		Dom DiMaggio, Bos	1949	34	
Willie Davis, LA	1969	31		Hal Chase, NY	1907	33	
Rico Carty, Atl	1970	31		Heinie Manush, Wash	1933	33	
				Nap Lajoie, Clev	1906	31	
				Sam Rice, Wash	1924	31	
				Ken Landreaux, Minn	1980	31	

Triple Crown Hitters

NATIONAL LEAGUE					AMERICAN LEAGUE				
Player and Team	**Year**	**HR**	**RBI**	**BA**	**Player and Team**	**Year**	**HR**	**RBI**	**BA**
Paul Hines, Prov	1878	4	50	.358	Nap Lajoie, Phil	1901	14	125	.422
Hugh Duffy, Bos	1894	18	145	.438	Ty Cobb, Det	1909	9	115	.377
Heinie Zimmerman*, Chi	1912	14	103	.372	Jimmie Foxx, Phil	1933	48	163	.356
Rogers Hornsby, StL	1922	42	152	.401	Lou Gehrig, NY	1934	49	165	.363
	1925	39	143	.403	Ted Williams, Bos	1942	36	137	.356
Chuck Klein, Phil	1933	28	120	.368		1947	32	114	.343
Joe Medwick, StL	1937	31	154	.374	Mickey Mantle, NY	1956	52	130	.353
					Frank Robinson, Balt	1966	49	122	.316
					Carl Yastrzemski, Bos	1967	44	121	.326

*Zimmerman ranked first in RBIs as calculated by Ernie Lanigan, but only third as calculated by Information Concepts Inc.

Triple Crown Pitchers

NATIONAL LEAGUE						AMERICAN LEAGUE				
Player and Team	**Year**	**W**	**L**	**SO**	**ERA**	**Player and Team**	**Year**	**W**	**L**	**SO**	**ERA**
Tommy Bond, Bos	1877	40	17	170	2.11	Cy Young, Bos	1901	33	10	158	1.62
Hoss Radbourn, Prov	1884	60	12	441	1.38	Rube Waddell, Phil	1905	26	11	287	1.48
Tim Keefe, NY	1888	35	12	333	1.74	Walter Johnson, Wash	1913	36	7	303	1.09
John Clarkson, Bos	1889	49	19	284	2.73		1918	23	13	162	1.27
Amos Rusie, NY	1894	36	13	195	2.78		1924	23	7	158	2.72
Christy Mathewson, NY	1905	31	8	206	1.27	Lefty Grove, Phil	1930	28	5	209	2.54
	1908	37	11	259	1.43		1931	31	4	175	2.06
Grover Alexander, Phil	1915	31	10	241	1.22	Lefty Gomez, NY	1934	26	5	158	2.33
	1916	33	12	167	1.55		1937	21	11	194	2.33
	1917	30	13	201	1.86	Hal Newhouser, Det	1945	25	9	212	1.81
Hippo Vaughn, Chi	1918	22	10	148	1.74						
Grover Alexander, Chi	1920	27	14	173	1.91						
Dazzy Vance, Bklyn	1924	28	6	262	2.16						
Bucky Walters, Cin	1939	27	11	137	2.29						
Sandy Koufax, LA	1963	25	5	306	1.88						
	1965	26	8	382	2.04						
	1966	27	9	317	1.73						
Steve Carlton, Phil	1972	27	10	310	1.97						
Dwight Gooden, NY	1985	24	4	268	1.53						

Consecutive Games Played, 500 or More Games

Cal Ripken Jr	2153*	Frank McCormick	652
Lou Gehrig	2130	Sandy Alomar Sr	648
Everett Scott	1307	Eddie Brown	618
Steve Garvey	1207	Roy McMillan	585
Billy Williams	1117	George Pinckney	577
Joe Sewell	1103	Steve Brodie	574
Stan Musial	895	Aaron Ward	565
Eddie Yost	829	Candy LaChance	540
Gus Suhr :	822	Buck Freeman	535
Nellie Fox	798	Fred Luderus	533
Pete Rose	745	Clyde Milan	511
Dale Murphy	740	Charlie Gehringer	511
Richie Ashburn	730	Vada Pinson	508
Ernie Banks	717	Tony Cuccinello	504
Earl Averill	673	Charlie Gehringer	504
Pete Rose	678	Omar Moreno	503

*Streak in progress at the end of the 1995 season.

Unassisted Triple Plays

Player and Team	Date	Pos	Opp	Opp Batter
Neal Ball, Clev	7-19-09	SS	Bos	Amby McConnell
Bill Wambsganss, Clev	10-10-20	2B	Bklyn	Clarence Mitchell
George Burns, Bos	9-14-23	1B	Clev	Frank Brower
Ernie Padgett, Bos	10-6-23	SS	Phil	Walter Holke
Glenn Wright, Pitt	5-7-25	SS	StL	Jim Bottomley
Jimmy Cooney, Chi	5-30-27	SS	Pitt	Paul Waner
Johnny Neun, Det	5-31-27	1B	Clev	Homer Summa
Ron Hansen, Wash	7-30-68	SS	Clev	Joe Azcue
Mickey Morandini, Phil	9-20-92	2B	Pitt	Jeff King
John Valentin, Bos	7-15-94	SS	Minn	Marc Newfield

National League

Pennant Winners

Year	Team	Manager	W	L	Pct	GA
1900	Brooklyn	Ned Hanlon	82	54	.603	4½
1901	Pittsburgh	Fred Clarke	90	49	.647	7½
1902	Pittsburgh	Fred Clarke	103	36	.741	27½
1903	Pittsburgh	Fred Clarke	91	49	.650	6½
1904	New York	John McGraw	106	47	.693	13
1905	New York	John McGraw	105	48	.686	9
1906	Chicago	Frank Chance	116	36	.763	20
1907	Chicago	Frank Chance	107	45	.704	17
1908	Chicago	Frank Chance	99	55	.643	1
1909	Pittsburgh	Fred Clarke	110	42	.724	6½
1910	Chicago	Frank Chance	104	50	.675	13
1911	New York	John McGraw	99	54	.647	7½
1912	New York	John McGraw	103	48	.682	10
1913	New York	John McGraw	101	51	.664	12½
1914	Boston	George Stallings	94	59	.614	10½
1915	Philadelphia	Pat Moran	90	62	.592	7
1916	Brooklyn	Wilbert Robinson	94	60	.610	2½
1917	New York	John McGraw	98	56	.636	10
1918	Chicago	Fred Mitchell	84	45	.651	10½
1919	Cincinnati	Pat Moran	96	44	.686	9
1920	Brooklyn	Wilbert Robinson	93	61	.604	7
1921	New York	John McGraw	94	59	.614	4
1922	New York	John McGraw	93	61	.604	7
1923	New York	John McGraw	95	58	.621	4½
1924	New York	John McGraw	93	60	.608	1½

Pennant Winners *(Cont.)*

Year	Team	Manager	W	L	Pct	GA
1925	Pittsburgh	Bill McKechnie	95	58	.621	8½
1926	St Louis	Rogers Hornsby	89	65	.578	2
1927	Pittsburgh	Donie Bush	94	60	.610	1½
1928	St Louis	Bill McKechnie	95	59	.617	2
1929	Chicago	Joe McCarthy	98	54	.645	10½
1930	St Louis	Gabby Street	92	62	.597	2
1931	St Louis	Gabby Street	101	53	.656	13
1932	Chicago	Charlie Grimm	90	64	.584	4
1933	New York	Bill Terry	91	61	.599	5
1934	St Louis	Frankie Frisch	95	58	.621	2
1935	Chicago	Charlie Grimm	100	54	.649	4
1936	New York	Bill Terry	92	62	.597	5
1937	New York	Bill Terry	95	57	.625	3
1938	Chicago	Gabby Hartnett	89	63	.586	2
1939	Cincinnati	Bill McKechnie	97	57	.630	4½
1940	Cincinnati	Bill McKechnie	100	53	.654	12
1941	Brooklyn	Leo Durocher	100	54	.649	2½
1942	St Louis	Billy Southworth	106	48	.688	2
1943	St Louis	Billy Southworth	105	49	.682	18
1944	St Louis	Billy Southworth	105	49	.682	14½
1945	Chicago	Charlie Grimm	98	56	.636	3
1946	St Louis*	Eddie Dyer	98	58	.628	2
1947	Brooklyn	Burt Shotton	94	60	.610	5
1948	Boston	Billy Southworth	91	62	.595	6½
1949	Brooklyn	Burt Shotton	97	57	.630	1
1950	Philadelphia	Eddie Sawyer	91	63	.591	2
1951	New York†	Leo Durocher	98	59	.624	1
1952	Brooklyn	Chuck Dressen	96	57	.627	4½
1953	Brooklyn	Chuck Dressen	105	49	.682	13
1954	New York	Leo Durocher	97	57	.630	5
1955	Brooklyn	Walt Alston	98	55	.641	13½
1956	Brooklyn	Walt Alston	93	61	.604	1
1957	Milwaukee	Fred Haney	95	59	.617	8
1958	Milwaukee	Fred Haney	92	62	.597	8
1959	Los Angeles‡	Walt Alston	88	68	.564	2
1960	Pittsburgh	Danny Murtaugh	95	59	.617	7
1961	Cincinnati	Fred Hutchinson	93	61	.604	4
1962	San Francisco#	Al Dark	103	62	.624	1
1963	Los Angeles	Walt Alston	99	63	.611	6
1964	St Louis	Johnny Keane	93	69	.574	1
1965	Los Angeles	Walt Alston	97	65	.599	2
1966	Los Angeles	Walt Alston	95	67	.586	1½
1967	St Louis	Red Schoendienst	101	60	.627	10½
1968	St Louis	Red Schoendienst	97	65	.599	9
1969	New York (E)††	Gil Hodges	100	62	.617	8
1970	Cincinnati (W)††	Sparky Anderson	102	60	.630	14½
1971	Pittsburgh (E)††	Danny Murtaugh	97	65	.599	7
1972	Cincinnati (W)††	Sparky Anderson	95	59	.617	10½
1973	New York (E)††	Yogi Berra	82	79	.509	1½
1974	Los Angeles (W)††	Walt Alston	102	60	.630	4
1975	Cincinnati (W)††	Sparky Anderson	108	54	.667	20
1976	Cincinnati (W)††	Sparky Anderson	102	60	.630	10
1977	Los Angeles (W)††	Tommy Lasorda	98	64	.605	10
1978	Los Angeles (W)††	Tommy Lasorda	95	67	.586	2½
1979	Pittsburgh (E)††	Chuck Tanner	98	64	.605	2
1980	Philadelphia (E)††	Dallas Green	91	71	.562	1
1981	Los Angeles (W)††	Tommy Lasorda	63	47	.573	**
1982	St Louis (E)††	Whitey Herzog	92	70	.568	3
1983	Philadelphia (E)††	Pat Corrales/Paul Owens	90	72	.556	6
1984	San Diego (W)††	Dick Williams	92	70	.568	12

*Defeated Brooklyn, two games to none, in playoff for pennant. †Defeated Brooklyn, two games to one, in playoff for pennant. ‡Defeated Milwaukee, two games to none, in playoff for pennant. #Defeated Los Angeles, two games to one, in playoff for pennant. ††Won Championship Series **First half 36-21; second half 27-26, in season split by strike; defeated Houston in playoff for Western Division title.

Pennant Winners (Cont.)

Year	Team	Manager	W	L	Pct	GA
1985	St Louis (E)††	Whitey Herzog	101	61	.623	3
1986	New York (E)††	Dave Johnson	108	54	.667	21½
1987	St Louis (E)††	Whitey Herzog	95	67	.586	3
1988	Los Angeles (W)††	Tommy Lasorda	94	67	.584	7
1989	San Francisco (W)††	Roger Craig	92	70	.568	3
1990	Cincinnati (W)††	Lou Piniella	91	71	.562	5
1991	Atlanta (W)††	Bobby Cox	94	68	.580	1
1992	Atlanta (W)††	Bobby Cox	98	64	.605	8
1993	Philadelphia (E)††	Jim Fregosi	97	65	.599	3
1994	Season ended Aug. 11 due to players' strike					
1995	Atlanta (E)††	Bobby Cox	90	54	.625	21

††Won Championship Series

Leading Batsmen

Year	Player and Team	BA	Year	Player and Team	BA
1900	Honus Wagner, Pitt	.381	1930	Bill Terry, NY	.401
1901	Jesse Burkett, StL	.382	1931	Chick Hafey, StL	.349
1902	Ginger Beaumtl, Pitt	.357	1932	Lefty O'Doul, Bklyn	.368
1903	Honus Wagner, Pitt	.355	1933	Chuck Klein, Phil	.368
1904	Honus Wagner, Pitt	.349	1934	Paul Waner, Pitt	.362
1905	Cy Seymour, Cin	.377	1935	Arky Vaughan, Pitt	.385
1906	Honus Wagner, Pitt	.339	1936	Paul Waner, Pitt	.373
1907	Honus Wagner, Pitt	.350	1937	Joe Medwick, StL	.374
1908	Honus Wagner, Pitt	.354	1938	Ernie Lombardi, Cin	.342
1909	Honus Wagner, Pitt	.339	1939	Johnny Mize, StL	.349
1910	Sherry Magee, Phil	.331	1940	Debs Garms, Pitt	.355
1911	Honus Wagner, Pitt	.334	1941	Pete Reiser, Bklyn	.343
1912	Heinie Zimmerman, Chi	.372	1942	Ernie Lombardi, Bos	.330
1913	Jake Daubert, Bklyn	.350	1943	Stan Musial, StL	.357
1914	Jake Daubert, Bklyn	.329	1944	Dixie Walker, Bklyn	.357
1915	Larry Doyle, NY	.320	1945	Phil Cavarretta, Chi	.355
1916	Hal Chase, Cin	.339	1946	Stan Musial, StL	.365
1917	Edd Roush, Cin	.341	1947	Harry Walker, StL-Phil	.363
1918	Zach Wheat, Bklyn	.335	1948	Stan Musial, StL	.376
1919	Edd Roush, Cin	.321	1949	Jackie Robinson, Bklyn	.342
1920	Rogers Hornsby, StL	.370	1950	Stan Musial, StL	.346
1921	Rogers Hornsby, StL	.397	1951	Stan Musial, StL	.355
1922	Rogers Hornsby, StL	.401	1952	Stan Musial, StL	.336
1923	Rogers Hornsby, StL	.384	1953	Carl Furillo, Bklyn	.344
1924	Rogers Hornsby, StL	.424	1954	Willie Mays, NY	.345
1925	Rogers Hornsby, StL	.403	1955	Richie Ashburn, Phil	.338
1926	Bubbles Hargrave, Cin	.353	1956	Hank Aaron, Mil	.328
1927	Paul Waner, Pitt	.380	1957	Stan Musial, StL	.351
1928	Rogers Hornsby, Bos	.387	1958	Richie Ashburn, Phil	.350
1929	Lefty O'Doul, Phil	.398	1959	Hank Aaron, Mil	.355

THEY SAID IT

Kevin Malone, Montreal Expo general manager, on his team's needs during the players' strike: "For 25 years the Expos have been looking for a shortstop who could pick it. Now we're looking for a shortstop who won't picket."

Leading Batsmen (Cont.)

Year	Player and Team	BA	Year	Player and Team	BA
1960	Dick Groat, Pitt	.325	1978	Dave Parker, Pitt	.334
1961	Roberto Clemente, Pitt	.351	1979	Keith Hernandez, StL	.344
1962	Tommy Davis, LA	.346	1980	Bill Buckner, Chi	.324
1963	Tommy Davis, LA	.326	1981	Bill Madlock, Pitt	.341
1964	Roberto Clemente, Pitt	.339	1982	Al Oliver, Mtl	.331
1965	Roberto Clemente, Pitt	.329	1983	Bill Madlock, Pitt	.323
1966	Matty Alou, Pitt	.342	1984	Tony Gwynn, SD	.351
1967	Roberto Clemente, Pitt	.357	1985	Willie McGee, StL	.353
1968	Pete Rose, Cin	.335	1986	Tim Raines, Mtl	.334
1969	Pete Rose, Cin	.348	1987	Tony Gwynn, SD	.370
1970	Rico Carty, Atl	.366	1988	Tony Gwynn, SD	.313
1971	Joe Torre, StL	.363	1989	Tony Gwynn, SD	.336
1972	Billy Williams, Chi	.333	1990	Willie McGee, StL	.335
1973	Pete Rose, Cin	.338	1991	Terry Pendleton, Atl	.319
1974	Ralph Garr, Atl	.353	1992	Gary Sheffield, SD	.330
1975	Bill Madlock, Chi	.354	1993	Andres Galarraga, Col	.370
1976	Bill Madlock, Chi	.339	1994	Tony Gwynn, SD	.394
1977	Dave Parker, Pitt	.338	1995	Tony Gwynn, SD	.368

Leaders in Runs Scored

Year	Player and Team	Runs	Year	Player and Team	Runs
1900	Roy Thomas, Phil	131	1938	Mel Ott, NY	116
1901	Jesse Burkett, StL	139	1939	Billy Werber, Cin	115
1902	Honus Wagner, Pitt	105	1940	Arky Vaughan, Pitt	113
1903	Ginger Beaumont, Pitt	137	1941	Pete Reiser, Bklyn	117
1904	George Browne, NY	99	1942	Mel Ott, NY	118
1905	Mike Donlin, NY	124	1943	Arky Vaughan, Bklyn	112
1906	Honus Wagner, Pitt	103	1944	Bill Nicholson, Chi	116
	Frank Chance, Chi	103	1945	Eddie Stanky, Bklyn	128
1907	Spike Shannon, NY	104	1946	Stan Musial, StL	124
1908	Fred Tenney, NY	101	1947	Johnny Mize, NY	137
1909	Tommy Leach, Pitt	126	1948	Stan Musial, StL	135
1910	Sherry Magee, Phil	110	1949	Pee Wee Reese, Bklyn	132
1911	Jimmy Sheckard, Chi	121	1950	Earl Torgeson, Bos	120
1912	Bob Bescher, Cin	120	1951	Stan Musial, StL	124
1913	Tommy Leach, Chi	99		Ralph Kiner, Pitt	124
	Max Carey, Pitt	99	1952	Stan Musial, StL	105
1914	George Burns, NY	100		Solly Hemus, StL	105
1915	Gavvy Cravath, Phil	89	1953	Duke Snider, Bklyn	132
1916	George Burns, NY	105	1954	Stan Musial, StL	120
1917	George Burns, NY	103		Duke Snider, Bklyn	120
1918	Heinie Groh, Cin	88	1955	Duke Snider, Bklyn	126
1919	George Burns, NY	86	1956	Frank Robinson, Cin	122
1920	George Burns, NY	115	1957	Hank Aaron, Mil	118
1921	Rogers Hornsby, StL	131	1958	Willie Mays, SF	121
1922	Rogers Hornsby, StL	141	1959	Vada Pinson, Cin	131
1923	Ross Youngs, NY	121	1960	Bill Bruton, Mil	112
1924	Frankie Frisch, NY	121	1961	Willie Mays, SF	129
	Rogers Hornsby, StL	121	1962	Frank Robinson, Cin	134
1925	Kiki Cuyler, Pitt	144	1963	Hank Aaron, Mil	121
1926	Kiki Cuyler, Pitt	113	1964	Dick Allen, Phil	125
1927	Lloyd Waner, Pitt	133	1965	Tommy Harper, Cin	126
	Rogers Hornsby, NY	133	1966	Felipe Alou, Atl	122
1928	Paul Waner, Pitt	142	1967	Hank Aaron, Atl	113
1929	Rogers Hornsby, Chi	156		Lou Brock, StL	113
1930	Chuck Klein, Phil	158	1968	Glenn Beckert, Chi	98
1931	Bill Terry, NY	121	1969	Bobby Bonds, SF	120
	Chuck Klein, Phil	121		Pete Rose, Cin	120
1932	Chuck Klein, Phil	152	1970	Billy Williams, Chi	137
1933	Pepper Martin, StL	122	1971	Lou Brock, StL	126
1934	Paul Waner, Pitt	122	1972	Joe Morgan, Cin	122
1935	Augie Galan, Chi	133	1973	Bobby Bonds, SF	131
1936	Arky Vaughan, Pitt	122	1974	Pete Rose, Cin	110
1937	Joe Medwick, StL	111	1975	Pete Rose, Cin	112

Leader in Runs Scored (Cont.)

Year	Player and Team	Runs	Year	Player and Team	Runs
1976	Pete Rose, Cin	130	1987	Tim Raines, Mtl	123
1977	George Foster, Cin	124	1988	Brett Butler, SF	109
1978	Ivan DeJesus, Chi	104	1989	Howard Johnson, NY	104
1979	Keith Hernandez, StL	116		Will Clark, SF	104
1980	Keith Hernandez, StL	111		Ryne Sandberg, Chi	104
1981	Mike Schmidt, Phil	78	1990	Ryne Sandberg, Chi	116
1982	Lonnie Smith, StL	120	1991	Brett Butler, LA	112
1983	Tim Raines, Mtl	133	1992	Barry Bonds, Pitt	109
1984	Ryne Sandberg, Chi	114	1993	Lenny Dykstra, Phil	143
1985	Dale Murphy, Atl	118	1994	Jeff Bagwell, Hou	104
1986	Von Hayes, Phil	107	1995	Craig Biggio, Hou	123
	Tony Gwynn, SD	107			

Leaders in Hits

Year	Player and Team	Hits	Year	Player and Team	Hits
1900	Willie Keeler, Bklyn	208	1945	Tommy Holmes, Bos	224
1901	Jesse Burkett, StL	228	1946	Stan Musial, StL	228
1902	Ginger Beaumont, Pitt	194	1947	Tommy Holmes, Bos	191
1903	Ginger Beaumont, Pitt	209	1948	Stan Musial, StL	230
1904	Ginger Beaumont, Pitt	185	1949	Stan Musial, StL	207
1905	Cy Seymour, Cin	219	1950	Duke Snider, Bklyn	199
1906	Harry Steinfeldt, Chi	176	1951	Richie Ashburn, Phil	221
1907	Ginger Beaumont, Bos	187	1952	Stan Musial, StL	194
1908	Honus Wagner, Pitt	201	1953	Richie Ashburn, Phil	205
1909	Larry Doyle, NY	172	1954	Don Mueller, NY	212
1910	Honus Wagner, Pitt	178	1955	Ted Kluszewski, Cin	192
	Bobby Byrne, Pitt	178	1956	Hank Aaron, Mil	200
1911	Doc Miller, Bos	192	1957	Red Schoendienst, NY-Mil	200
1912	Heinie Zimmerman, Chi	207	1958	Richie Ashburn, Phil	215
1913	Gavvy Cravath, Phil	179	1959	Hank Aaron, Mil	223
1914	Sherry Magee, Phil	171	1960	Willie Mays, SF	190
1915	Larry Doyle, NY	189	1961	Vada Pinson, Cin	208
1916	Hal Chase, Cin	184	1962	Tommy Davis, LA	230
1917	Heinie Groh, Cin	182	1963	Vada Pinson, Cin	204
1918	Charlie Hollocher, Chi	161	1964	Roberto Clemente, Pitt	211
1919	Ivy Olson, Bklyn	164		Curt Flood, StL	211
1920	Rogers Hornsby, StL	218	1965	Pete Rose, Cin	209
1921	Rogers Hornsby, StL	235	1966	Felipe Alou, Atl	218
1922	Rogers Hornsby, StL	250	1967	Roberto Clemente, Pitt	209
1923	Frankie Frisch, NY	223	1968	Felipe Alou, Atl	210
1924	Rogers Hornsby, StL	227		Pete Rose, Cin	210
1925	Jim Bottomley, StL	227	1969	Matty Alou, Pitt	231
1926	Eddie Brown, Bos	201	1970	Pete Rose, Cin	205
1927	Paul Waner, Pitt	237		Billy Williams, Chi	205
1928	Freddy Lindstrom, NY	231	1971	Joe Torre, StL	230
1929	Lefty O'Doul, Phil	254	1972	Pete Rose, Cin	198
1930	Bill Terry, NY	254	1973	Pete Rose, Cin	230
1931	Lloyd Waner, Pitt	214	1974	Ralph Garr, Atl	214
1932	Chuck Klein, Phil	226	1975	Dave Cash, Phil	213
1933	Chuck Klein, Phil	223	1976	Pete Rose, Cin	215
1934	Paul Waner, Pitt	217	1977	Dave Parker, Pitt	215
1935	Billy Herman, Chi	227	1978	Steve Garvey, LA	202
1936	Joe Medwick, StL	223	1979	Garry Templeton, StL	211
1937	Joe Medwick, StL	237	1980	Steve Garvey, LA	200
1938	Frank McCormick, Cin	209	1981	Pete Rose, Phil	140
1939	Frank McCormick, Cin	209	1982	Al Oliver, Mtl	204
1940	Stan Hack, Chi	191	1983	Jose Cruz, Hou	189
	Frank McCormick, Cin	191		Andre Dawson, Mtl	189
1941	Stan Hack, Chi	186	1984	Tony Gwynn, SD	213
1942	Enos Slaughter, StL	188	1985	Willie McGee, StL	216
1943	Stan Musial, StL	220	1986	Tony Gwynn, SD	211
1944	Stan Musial, StL	197	1987	Tony Gwynn, SD	218
	Phil Cavarretta, Chi	197	1988	Andres Galarraga, Mtl	184

Leaders in Hits *(Cont.)*

Year	Player and Team	Hits	Year	Player and Team	Hits
1989	Tony Gwynn, SD	203	1993	Lenny Dykstra, Phil	194
1990	Brett Butler, SF	192	1994	Tony Gwynn, SD	165
	Lenny Dykstra, Phil	192	1995	Dante Bichette, Col	197
1991	Terry Pendleton, Atl	187		Tony Gwynn, SD	197
1992	Terry Pendleton, Atl	199			
	Andy Van Slyke, Pitt	199			

Home Run Leaders

Year	Player and Team	HR	Year	Player and Team	HR
1900	Herman Long, Bos	12	1947	Ralph Kiner, Pitt	51
1901	Sam Crawford, Cin	16		Johnny Mize, NY	51
1902	Tommy Leach, Pitt	6	1948	Ralph Kiner, Pitt	40
1903	Jimmy Sheckard, Bklyn	9		Johnny Mize, NY	40
1904	Harry Lumley, Bklyn	9	1949	Ralph Kiner, Pitt	54
1905	Fred Odwell, Cin	9	1950	Ralph Kiner, Pitt	47
1906	Tim Jordan, Bklyn	12	1951	Ralph Kiner, Pitt	42
1907	Dave Brain, Bos	10	1952	Ralph Kiner, Pitt	37
1908	Tim Jordan, Bklyn	12		Hank Sauer, Chi	37
1909	Red Murray, NY	7	1953	Eddie Mathews, Mil	47
1910	Fred Beck, Bos	10	1954	Ted Kluszewski, Cin	49
	Wildfire Schulte, Chi	10	1955	Willie Mays, NY	51
1911	Wildfire Schulte, Chi	21	1956	Duke Snider, Bklyn	43
1912	Heinie Zimmerman, Chi	14	1957	Hank Aaron, Mil	44
1913	Gavvy Cravath, Phil	19	1958	Ernie Banks, Chi	47
1914	Gavvy Cravath, Phil	19	1959	Eddie Mathews, Mil	46
1915	Gavvy Cravath, Phil	24	1960	Ernie Banks, Chi	41
1916	Dave Robertson, NY	12	1961	Orlando Cepeda, SF	46
	Cy Williams, Chi	12	1962	Willie Mays, SF	49
1917	Dave Robertson, NY	12	1963	Hank Aaron, Mil	44
	Gavvy Cravath, Phil	12		Willie McCovey, SF	44
1918	Gavvy Cravath, Phil	8	1964	Willie Mays, SF	47
1919	Gavvy Cravath, Phil	12	1965	Willie Mays, SF	52
1920	Cy Williams, Phil	15	1966	Hank Aaron, Atl	44
1921	George Kelly, NY	23	1967	Hank Aaron, Atl	39
1922	Rogers Hornsby, StL	42	1968	Willie McCovey, SF	36
1923	Cy Williams, Phil	41	1969	Willie McCovey, SF	45
1924	Jack Fournier, Bklyn	27	1970	Johnny Bench, Cin	45
1925	Rogers Hornsby, StL	39	1971	Willie Stargell, Pitt	48
1926	Hack Wilson, Chi	21	1972	Johnny Bench, Cin	40
1927	Hack Wilson, Chi	30	1973	Willie Stargell, Pitt	44
	Cy Williams, Phil	30	1974	Mike Schmidt, Phil	36
1928	Hack Wilson, Chi	31	1975	Mike Schmidt, Phil	38
	Jim Bottomley, StL	31	1976	Mike Schmidt, Phil	38
1929	Chuck Klein, Phil	43	1977	George Foster, Cin	52
1930	Hack Wilson, Chi	56	1978	George Foster, Cin	40
1931	Chuck Klein, Phil	31	1979	Dave Kingman, Chi	48
1932	Chuck Klein, Phil	38	1980	Mike Schmidt, Phil	48
	Mel Ott, NY	38	1981	Mike Schmidt, Phil	31
1933	Chuck Klein, Phil	28	1982	Dave Kingman, NY	37
1934	Ripper Collins, StL	35	1983	Mike Schmidt, Phil	40
	Mel Ott, NY	35	1984	Dale Murphy, Atl	36
1935	Wally Berger, Bos	34		Mike Schmidt, Phil	36
1936	Mel Ott, NY	33	1985	Dale Murphy, Atl	37
1937	Mel Ott, NY	31	1986	Mike Schmidt, Phil	37
	Joe Medwick, StL	31	1987	Andre Dawson, Chi	49
1938	Mel Ott, NY	36	1988	Darryl Strawberry, NY	39
1939	Johnny Mize, StL	28	1989	Kevin Mitchell, SF	47
1940	Johnny Mize, StL	43	1990	Ryne Sandberg, Chi	40
1941	Dolph Camilli, Bklyn	34	1991	Howard Johnson, NY	38
1942	Mel Ott, NY	30	1992	Fred McGriff, SD	35
1943	Bill Nicholson, Chi	29	1993	Barry Bonds, SF	46
1944	Bill Nicholson, Chi	33	1994	Matt Williams, SF	43
1945	Tommy Holmes, Bos	28	1995	Dante Bichette, Col	40
1946	Ralph Kiner, Pitt	23			

Runs Batted In Leaders

Year	Player and Team	RBI	Year	Player and Team	RBI
1900	Elmer Flick, Phil	110	1948	Stan Musial, StL	131
1901	Honus Wagner, Pitt	126	1949	Ralph Kiner, Pitt	127
1902	Honus Wagner, Pitt	91	1950	Del Ennis, Phil	126
1903	Sam Mertes, NY	104	1951	Monte Irvin, NY	121
1904	Bill Dahlen, NY	80	1952	Hank Sauer, Chi	121
1905	Cy Seymour, Cin	121	1953	Roy Campanella, Bklyn	142
1906	Jim Nealon, Pitt	83	1954	Ted Kluszewski, Cin	141
	Harry Steinfeldt, Chi	83	1955	Duke Snider, Bklyn	136
1907	Sherry Magee, Phil	85	1956	Stan Musial, StL	109
1908	Honus Wagner, Pitt	109	1957	Hank Aaron, Mil	132
1909	Honus Wagner, Pitt	100	1958	Ernie Banks, Chi	129
1910	Sherry Magee, Phil	123	1959	Ernie Banks, Chi	143
1911	Wildfire Schulte, Chi	121	1960	Hank Aaron, Mil	126
1912	Heinie Zimmerman, Chi	103	1961	Orlando Cepeda, SF	142
1913	Gavvy Cravath, Phil	128	1962	Tommy Davis, LA	153
1914	Sherry Magee, Phil	103	1963	Hank Aaron, Mil	130
1915	Gavvy Cravath, Phil	115	1964	Ken Boyer, StL	119
1916	Heinie Zimmerman, Chi-NY	83	1965	Deron Johnson, Cin	130
1917	Heinie Zimmerman, NY	102	1966	Hank Aaron, Atl	127
1918	Sherry Magee, Phil	76	1967	Orlando Cepeda, StL	111
1919	Hi Myers, Bklyn	73	1968	Willie McCovey, SF	105
1920	George Kelly, NY	94	1969	Willie McCovey, SF	126
	Rogers Hornsby, StL	94	1970	Johnny Bench, Cin	148
1921	Rogers Hornsby, StL	126	1971	Joe Torre, StL	137
1922	Rogers Hornsby, StL	152	1972	Johnny Bench, Cin	125
1923	Irish Meusel, NY	125	1973	Willie Stargell, Pitt	119
1924	George Kelly, NY	136	1974	Johnny Bench, Cin	129
1925	Rogers Hornsby, StL	143	1975	Greg Luzinski, Phil	120
1926	Jim Bottomley, StL	120	1976	George Foster, Cin	121
1927	Paul Waner, Pitt	131	1977	George Foster, Cin	149
1928	Jim Bottomley, StL	136	1978	George Foster, Cin	120
1929	Hack Wilson, Chi	159	1979	Dave Winfield, SD	118
1930	Hack Wilson, Chi	190	1980	Mike Schmidt, Phil	121
1931	Chuck Klein, Phil	121	1981	Mike Schmidt, Phil	91
1932	Don Hurst, Phil	143	1982	Dale Murphy, Atl	109
1933	Chuck Klein, Phil	120		Al Oliver, Mtl	109
1934	Mel Ott, NY	135	1983	Dale Murphy, Atl	121
1935	Wally Berger, Bos	130	1984	Gary Carter, Mtl	106
1936	Joe Medwick, StL	138		Mike Schmidt, Phil	106
1937	Joe Medwick, StL	154	1985	Dave Parker, Cin	125
1938	Joe Medwick, StL	122	1986	Mike Schmidt, Phil	119
1939	Frank McCormick, Cin	128	1987	Andre Dawson, Chi	137
1940	Johnny Mize, StL	137	1988	Will Clark, SF	109
1941	Dolph Camilli, Bklyn	120	1989	Kevin Mitchell, SF	125
1942	Johnny Mize, NY	110	1990	Matt Williams, SF	122
1943	Bill Nicholson, Chi	128	1991	Howard Johnson, NY	117
1944	Bill Nicholson, Chi	122	1992	Darren Daulton, Phil	109
1945	Dixie Walker, Bklyn	124	1993	Barry Bonds, SF	123
1946	Enos Slaughter, StL	130	1994	Jeff Bagwell, Hou	116
1947	Johnny Mize, NY	138	1995	Dante Bichette, Col	128

AWL (Acronym We Like)

Connoisseurs of the inspired acronym will remember CREEP, the Watergate-era Committee to Re-Elect the President; and COYOTE, the prostitutes' rights organization whose initials stand for Cast Off Your Old Tired Ethics. Well, the baseball strike created at least one by-product for which we are grateful: A group of disaffected fans mustered as the Newly Organized Society to Condemn Artificial Baseball, or NO-SCAB.

Leading Base Stealers

Year	Player and Team	SB	Year	Player and Team	SB
1900	George Van Haltren, NY	45	1953	Bill Bruton, Mil	26
	Patsy Donovan, StL	45	1954	Bill Bruton, Mil	34
1901	Honus Wagner, Pitt	48	1955	Bill Bruton, Mil	35
1902	Honus Wagner, Pitt	43	1956	Willie Mays, NY	40
1903	Jimmy Sheckard, Bklyn	67	1957	Willie Mays, NY	38
	Frank Chance, Chi	67	1958	Willie Mays, SF	31
1904	Honus Wagner, Pitt	53	1959	Willie Mays, SF	27
1905	Billy Maloney, Chi	59	1960	Maury Wills, LA	50
	Art Devlin, NY	59	1961	Maury Wills, LA	35
1906	Frank Chance, Chi	57	1962	Maury Wills, LA	104
1907	Honus Wagner, Pitt	61	1963	Maury Wills, LA	40
1908	Honus Wagner, Pitt	53	1964	Maury Wills, LA	53
1909	Bob Bescher, Cin	54	1965	Maury Wills, LA	94
1910	Bob Bescher, Cin	70	1966	Lou Brock, StL	74
1911	Bob Bescher, Cin	80	1967	Lou Brock, StL	52
1912	Bob Bescher, Cin	67	1968	Lou Brock, StL	62
1913	Max Carey, Pitt	61	1969	Lou Brock, StL	53
1914	George Burns, NY	62	1970	Bobby Tolan, Cin	57
1915	Max Carey, Pitt	36	1971	Lou Brock, StL	64
1916	Max Carey, Pitt	63	1972	Lou Brock, StL	63
1917	Max Carey, Pitt	46	1973	Lou Brock, StL	70
1918	Max Carey, Pitt	58	1974	Lou Brock, StL	118
1919	George Burns, NY	40	1975	Davey Lopes, LA	77
1920	Max Carey, Pitt	52	1976	Davey Lopes, LA	63
1921	Frankie Frisch, NY	49	1977	Frank Taveras, Pitt	70
1922	Max Carey, Pitt	51	1978	Omar Moreno, Pitt	71
1923	Max Carey, Pitt	51	1979	Omar Moreno, Pitt	77
1924	Max Carey, Pitt	49	1980	Ron LeFlore, Mtl	97
1925	Max Carey, Pitt	46	1981	Tim Raines, Mtl	71
1926	Kiki Cuyler, Pitt	35	1982	Tim Raines, Mtl	78
1927	Frankie Frisch, StL	48	1983	Tim Raines, Mtl	90
1928	Kiki Cuyler, Chi	37	1984	Tim Raines, Mtl	75
1929	Kiki Cuyler, Chi	43	1985	Vince Coleman, StL	110
1930	Kiki Cuyler, Chi	37	1986	Vince Coleman, StL	107
1931	Frankie Frisch, StL	28	1987	Vince Coleman, StL	109
1932	Chuck Klein, Phil	20	1988	Vince Coleman, StL	81
1933	Pepper Martin, StL	26	1989	Vince Coleman, StL	65
1934	Pepper Martin, StL	23	1990	Vince Coleman, StL	77
1935	Augie Galan, Chi	22	1991	Marquis Grissom, Mtl	76
1936	Pepper Martin, StL	23	1992	Marquis Grissom, Mtl	78
1937	Augie Galan, Chi	23	1993	Chuck Carr, Flor	58
1938	Stan Hack, Chi	16	1994	Craig Biggio, Hou	39
1939	Stan Hack, Chi	17	1995	Quilvio Veras, Fla	56
	Lee Handley, Pitt	17			
1940	Lonny Frey, Cin	22			
1941	Danny Murtaugh, Phil	18			
1942	Pete Reiser, Bklyn	20			
1943	Arky Vaughan, Bklyn	20			
1944	Johnny Barrett, Pitt	28			
1945	Red Schoendienst, StL	26			
1946	Pete Reiser, Bklyn	34			
1947	Jackie Robinson, Bklyn	29			
1948	Richie Ashburn, Phil	32			
1949	Jackie Robinson, Bklyn	37			
1950	Sam Jethroe, Bos	35			
1951	Sam Jethroe, Bos	35			
1952	Pee Wee Reese, Bklyn	30			

THEY SAID IT

Steve Blass, Pittsburgh Pirate broadcaster, on Buc replacement player Jimmy Boudreau, who last appeared professionally in 1986: "He should have been better, pitching on 3,195 days' rest."

Leading Pitchers—Winning Percentage

Year	Pitcher and Team	W	L	Pct	Year	Pitcher and Team	W	L	Pct
1900	Jesse Tannehill, Pitt	20	6	.769	1949	Preacher Roe, Bklyn	15	6	.714
1901	Jack Chesbro, Pitt	21	10	.677	1950	Sal Maglie, NY	18	4	.818
1902	Jack Chesbro, Pitt	28	6	.824	1951	Preacher Roe, Bklyn	22	3	.880
1903	Sam Leever, Pitt	25	7	.781	1952	Hoyt Wilhelm, NY	15	3	.833
1904	Joe McGinnity, NY	35	8	.814	1953	Carl Erskine, Bklyn	20	6	.769
1905	Sam Leever, Pitt	20	5	.800	1954	Johnny Antonelli, NY	21	7	.750
1906	Ed Reulbach, Chi	19	4	.826	1955	Don Newcombe, Bklyn	20	5	.800
1907	Ed Reulbach, Chi	17	4	.810	1956	Don Newcombe, Bklyn	27	7	.794
1908	Ed Reulbach, Chi	24	7	.774	1957	Bob Buhl, Mil	18	7	.720
1909	Christy Mathewson, NY	25	6	.806	1958	Warren Spahn, Mil	22	11	.667
	Howie Camnitz, Pitt	25	6	.806		Lew Burdette, Mil	20	10	.667
1910	King Cole, Chi	20	4	.833	1959	Roy Face, Pitt	18	1	.947
1911	Rube Marquard, NY	24	7	.774	1960	Ernie Broglio, StL	21	9	.700
1912	Claude Hendrix, Pitt	24	9	.727	1961	Johnny Podres, LA	18	5	.783
1913	Bert Humphries, Chi	16	4	.800	1962	Bob Purkey, Cin	23	5	.821
1914	Bill James, Bos	26	7	.788	1963	Ron Perranoski, LA	16	3	.842
1915	Grover Alexander, Phil	31	10	.756	1964	Sandy Koufax, LA	19	5	.792
1916	Tom Hughes, Bos	16	3	.842	1965	Sandy Koufax, LA	26	8	.765
1917	Ferdie Schupp, NY	21	7	.750	1966	Juan Marichal, SF	25	6	.806
1918	Claude Hendrix, Chi	19	7	.731	1967	Dick Hughes, StL	16	6	.727
1919	Dutch Ruether, Cin	19	6	.760	1968	Steve Blass, Pitt	18	6	.750
1920	Burleigh Grimes, Bklyn	23	11	.676	1969	Tom Seaver, NY	25	7	.781
1921	Bill Doak, StL	15	6	.714	1970	Bob Gibson, StL	23	7	.767
1922	Pete Donohue, Cin	18	9	.667	1971	Don Gullett, Cin	16	6	.727
1923	Dolf Luque, Cin	27	8	.771	1972	Gary Nolan, Cin	15	5	.750
1924	Emil Yde, Pitt	16	3	.842	1973	Tommy John, LA	16	7	.696
1925	Bill Sherdel, StL	15	6	.714	1974	Andy Messersmith, LA	20	6	.769
1926	Ray Kremer, Pitt	20	6	.769	1975	Don Gullett, Cin	15	4	.789
1927	Larry Benton, Bos-NY	17	7	.708	1976	Steve Carlton, Phil	20	7	.741
1928	Larry Benton, NY	25	9	.735	1977	John Candelaria, Pitt	20	5	.800
1929	Charlie Root, Chi	19	6	.760	1978	Gaylord Perry, SD	21	6	.778
1930	Freddie Fitzsimmons, NY	19	7	.731	1979	Tom Seaver, Cin	16	6	.727
1931	Paul Derringer, StL	18	8	.692	1980	Jim Bibby, Pitt	19	6	.760
1932	Lon Warneke, Chi	22	6	.786	1981*	Tom Seaver, Cin	14	2	.875
1933	Ben Cantwell, Bos	20	10	.667	1982	Phil Niekro, Atl	17	4	.810
1934	Dizzy Dean, StL	30	7	.811	1983	John Denny, Phil	19	6	.760
1935	Bill Lee, Chi	20	6	.769	1984	Rick Sutcliffe, Chi	16	1	.941
1936	Carl Hubbell, NY	26	6	.813	1985	Orel Hershiser, LA	19	3	.864
1937	Carl Hubbell, NY	22	8	.733	1986	Bob Ojeda, NY	18	5	.783
1938	Bill Lee, Chi	22	9	.710	1987	Dwight Gooden, NY	15	7	.682
1939	Paul Derringer, Cin	25	7	.781	1988	David Cone, NY	20	3	.870
1940	Freddie Fitzsimmons, Bklyn	16	2	.889	1989	Mike Bielecki, Chi	18	7	.720
1941	Elmer Riddle, Cin	19	4	.826	1990	Doug Drabeck, Pitt	22	6	.786
1942	Larry French, Bklyn	15	4	.789	1991	John Smiley, Pitt	20	8	.714
1943	Mort Cooper, StL	21	8	.724		Jose Rijo, Cin	15	6	.714
1944	Ted Wilks, StL	17	4	.810	1992	Bob Tewksbury, StL	16	5	.762
1945	Harry Brecheen, StL	15	4	.789	1993	Tom Glavine, Atl	22	6	.786
1946	Murray Dickson, StL	15	6	.714	1994	Ken Hill, Mtl	16	5	.762
1947	Larry Jansen, NY	21	5	.808	1995	Greg Maddux, Atl	19	2	.905
1948	Harry Brecheen, StL	20	7	.741					

*1981 percentages based on 10 or more victories.

Note: Based on 15 or more victories.

Stale Air Down There

With fresh angles to the story of Michael Jordan's leaving baseball to return to the NBA in short supply, the Chicago media have been hard-pressed to find new variations on old themes. A particularly desperate reporter asked Jordan last April, "Michael, a lot of people have said you don't have your height back. Is that true?" Replied Jordan, "No, I'm still 6'6"."

Leading Pitchers—Earned-Run Average

Year	Player and Team	ERA	Year	Player and Team	ERA
1900	Rube Waddell, Pitt	2.37	1948	Harry Brecheen, StL	2.24
1901	Jesse Tannehill, Pitt	2.18	1949	Dave Koslo, NY	2.50
1902	Jack Taylor, Chi	1.33	1950	Jim Hearn, StL-NY	2.49
1903	Sam Leever, Pitt	2.06	1951	Chet Nichols, Bos	2.88
1904	Joe McGinnity, NY	1.61	1952	Hoyt Wilhelm, NY	2.43
1905	Christy Mathewson, NY	1.27	1953	Warren Spahn, Mil	2.10
1906	Three Finger Brown, Chi	1.04	1954	Johnny Antonelli, NY	2.29
1907	Jack Pfiester, Chi	1.15	1955	Bob Friend, Pitt	2.84
1908	Christy Mathewson, NY	1.43	1956	Lew Burdette, Mil	2.71
1909	Christy Mathewson, NY	1.14	1957	Johnny Podres, Bklyn	2.66
1910	George McQuillan, Phil	1.60	1958	Stu Miller, SF	2.47
1911	Christy Mathewson, NY	1.99	1959	Sam Jones, SF	2.82
1912	Jeff Tesreau, NY	1.96	1960	Mike McCormick, SF	2.70
1913	Christy Mathewson, NY	2.06	1961	Warren Spahn, Mil	3.01
1914	Bill Doak, StL	1.72	1962	Sandy Koufax, LA	2.54
1915	Grover Alexander, Phil	1.22	1963	Sandy Koufax, LA	1.88
1916	Grover Alexander, Phil	1.55	1964	Sandy Koufax, LA	1.74
1917	Grover Alexander, Phil	1.83	1965	Sandy Koufax, LA	2.04
1918	Hippo Vaughn, Chi	1.74	1966	Sandy Koufax, LA	1.73
1919	Grover Alexander, Chi	1.72	1967	Phil Niekro, Atl	1.87
1920	Grover Alexander, Chi	1.91	1968	Bob Gibson, StL	1.12
1921	Bill Doak, StL	2.58	1969	Juan Marichal, SF	2.10
1922	Rosy Ryan, NY	3.00	1970	Tom Seaver, NY	2.81
1923	Dolf Luque, Cin	1.93	1971	Tom Seaver, NY	1.76
1924	Dazzy Vance, Bklyn	2.16	1972	Steve Carlton, Phil	1.98
1925	Dolf Luque, Cin	2.63	1973	Tom Seaver, NY	2.08
1926	Ray Kremer, Pitt	2.61	1974	Buzz Capra, Atl	2.28
1927	Ray Kremer, Pitt	2.47	1975	Randy Jones, SD	2.24
1928	Dazzy Vance, Bklyn	2.09	1976	John Denny, StL	2.52
1929	Bill Walker, NY	3.08	1977	John Candelaria, Pitt	2.34
1930	Dazzy Vance, Bklyn	2.61	1978	Craig Swan, NY	2.43
1931	Bill Walker, NY	2.26	1979	J.R. Richard, Hou	2.71
1932	Lon Warneke, Chi	2.37	1980	Don Sutton, LA	2.21
1933	Carl Hubbell, NY	1.66	1981	Nolan Ryan, Hou	1.69
1934	Carl Hubbell, NY	2.30	1982	Steve Rogers, Mtl	2.40
1935	Cy Blanton, Pitt	2.59	1983	Atlee Hammaker, SF	2.25
1936	Carl Hubbell, NY	2.31	1984	Alejandro Pena, LA	2.48
1937	Jim Turner, Bos	2.38	1985	Dwight Gooden, NY	1.53
1938	Bill Lee, Chi	2.66	1986	Mike Scott, Hou	2.22
1939	Bucky Walters, Cin	2.29	1987	Nolan Ryan, Hou	2.76
1940	Bucky Walters, Cin	2.48	1988	Joe Magrane, StL	2.18
1941	Elmer Riddle, Cin	2.24	1989	Scott Garrelts, SF	2.28
1942	Mort Cooper, StL	1.77	1990	Danny Darwin, Hou	2.21
1943	Howie Pollet, StL	1.75	1991	Dennis Martinez, Mtl	2.39
1944	Ed Heusser, Cin	2.38	1992	Bill Swift, SF	2.08
1945	Hank Borowy, Chi	2.14	1993	Greg Maddux, Atl	2.36
1946	Howie Pollet, StL	2.10	1994	Greg Maddux, Atl	1.56
1947	Warren Spahn, Bos	2.33	1995	Greg Maddux, Atl	1.63

Note: Based on 10 complete games through 1950, then 154 innings until National League expanded in 1962, when it became 162 innings. In strike-shortened 1981, one inning per game required.

Leading Pitchers—Strikeouts

Year	Player and Team	SO	Year	Player and Team	SO
1900	Rube Waddell, Pitt	133	1912	Grover Alexander, Phil	195
1901	Noodles Hahn, Cin	233	1913	Tom Seaton, Phil	168
1902	Vic Willis, Bos	226	1914	Grover Alexander, Phil	214
1903	Christy Mathewson, NY	267	1915	Grover Alexander, Phil	241
1904	Christy Mathewson, NY	212	1916	Grover Alexander, Phil	167
1905	Christy Mathewson, NY	206	1917	Grover Alexander, Phil	200
1906	Fred Beebe, Chi-StL	171	1918	Hippo Vaughn, Chi	148
1907	Christy Mathewson, NY	178	1919	Hippo Vaughn, Chi	141
1908	Christy Mathewson, NY	259	1920	Grover Alexander, Chi	173
1909	Orval Overall, Chi	205	1921	Burleigh Grimes, Bklyn	136
1910	Christy Mathewson, NY	190	1922	Dazzy Vance, Bklyn	134
1911	Rube Marquard, NY	237	1923	Dazzy Vance, Bklyn	197

Leading Pitchers—Strikeouts *(Cont.)*

Year	Player and Team	SO	Year	Player and Team	SO
1924	Dazzy Vance, Bklyn	262	1959	Don Drysdale, LA	242
1925	Dazzy Vance, Bklyn	221	1960	Don Drysdale, LA	246
1926	Dazzy Vance, Bklyn	140	1961	Sandy Koufax, LA	269
1927	Dazzy Vance, Bklyn	184	1962	Don Drysdale, LA	232
1928	Dazzy Vance, Bklyn	200	1963	Sandy Koufax, LA	306
1929	Pat Malone, Chi	166	1964	Bob Veale, Pitt	250
1930	Bill Hallahan, StL	177	1965	Sandy Koufax, LA	382
1931	Bill Hallahan, StL	159	1966	Sandy Koufax, LA	317
1932	Dizzy Dean, StL	191	1967	Jim Bunning, Phil	253
1933	Dizzy Dean, StL	199	1968	Bob Gibson, StL	268
1934	Dizzy Dean, StL	195	1969	Ferguson Jenkins, Chi	273
1935	Dizzy Dean, StL	182	1970	Tom Seaver, NY	283
1936	Van Lingle Mungo, Bklyn	238	1971	Tom Seaver, NY	289
1937	Carl Hubbell, NY	159	1972	Steve Carlton, Phil	310
1938	Clay Bryant, Chi	135	1973	Tom Seaver, NY	251
1939	Claude Passeau, Phil-Chi	137	1974	Steve Carlton, Phil	240
	Bucky Walters, Cin	137	1975	Tom Seaver, NY	243
1940	Kirby Higbe, Phil	137	1976	Tom Seaver, NY	235
1941	Johnny Vander Meer, Cin	202	1977	Phil Niekro, Atl	262
1942	Johnny Vander Meer, Cin	186	1978	J.R. Richard, Hou	303
1943	Johnny Vander Meer, Cin	174	1979	J.R. Richard, Hou	313
1944	Bill Voiselle, NY	161	1980	Steve Carlton, Phil	286
1945	Preacher Roe, Pitt	148	1981	Fernando Valenzuela, LA	180
1946	Johnny Schmitz, Chi	135	1982	Steve Carlton, Phil	286
1947	Ewell Blackwell, Cin	193	1983	Steve Carlton, Phil	275
1948	Harry Brecheen, StL	149	1984	Dwight Gooden, NY	276
1949	Warren Spahn, Bos	151	1985	Dwight Gooden, NY	268
1950	Warren Spahn, Bos	191	1986	Mike Scott, Hou	306
1951	Warren Spahn, Bos	164	1987	Nolan Ryan, Hou	270
	Don Newcombe, Bklyn	164	1988	Nolan Ryan, Hou	228
1952	Warren Spahn, Bos	183	1989	Jose DeLeon, StL	201
1953	Robin Roberts, Phil	198	1990	David Cone, NY	233
1954	Robin Roberts, Phil	185	1991	David Cone, NY	241
1955	Sam Jones, Chi	198	1992	John Smoltz, Atl	215
1956	Sam Jones, Chi	176	1993	Jose Rijo, Cin	227
1957	Jack Sanford, Phil	188	1994	Andy Benes, SD	189
1958	Sam Jones, StL	225	1995	Hideo Nomo, LA	236

Leading Pitchers—Saves

Year	Player and Team	SV	Year	Player and Team	SV
1947	Hugh Casey, Bklyn	18	1971	Dave Giusti, Pitt	30
1948	Harry Gumpert, Cin	17	1972	Clay Carroll, Cin	37
1949	Ted Wilks, StL	9	1973	Mike Marshall, Mtl	13
1950	Jim Konstanty, Phil	22	1974	Mike Marshall, LA	21
1951	Ted Wilks, StL, Pitt	13	1975	Al Hrabosky, StL	22
1952	Al Brazle, StL	16		Rawly Eastwick, Cin	22
1953	Al Brazle, StL	18	1976	Rawly Eastwick, Cin	26
1954	Jim Hughes, Bklyn	24	1977	Rollie Fingers, SD	35
1955	Jack Meyer, Phil	16	1978	Rollie Fingers, SD	37
1956	Clem Labine, Bklyn	19	1979	Bruce Sutter, Chi	37
1957	Clem Labine, Bklyn	17	1980	Bruce Sutter, Chi	28
1958	Roy Face, Pitt	20	1981	Bruce Sutter, StL	25
1959	Lindy McDaniel, StL	15	1982	Bruce Sutter, StL	36
	Don McMahon, Mil	15	1983	Lee Smith, Chi	29
1960	Lindy McDaniel, StL	26	1984	Bruce Sutter, StL	45
1961	Stu Miller, SF	17	1985	Jeff Reardon, Mtl	41
	Roy Face, Pitt	17	1986	Todd Worrell, StL	36
1962	Roy Face, Pitt	28	1987	Steve Bedrosian, Phil	40
1963	Lindy McDaniel, Chi	22	1988	John Franco, Cin	39
1964	Hal Woodeshick, Hou	23	1989	Mark Davis, SD	44
1965	Ted Abernathy, Chi	31	1990	John Franco, NY	33
1966	Phil Regan, LA	21	1991	Lee Smith, StL	47
1967	Ted Abernathy, Cin	28	1992	Lee Smith, StL	42
1968	Phil Regan, Chi, LA	25	1993	Randy Myers, Chi	53
1969	Fred Gladding, Hou	29	1994	John Franco, NY	30
1970	Wayne Granger, Cin	35	1995	Randy Myers, Chi	38

Pennant Winners

Year	Team	Manager	W	L	Pct	GA
1901	Chicago	Clark Griffith	83	53	.610	4
1902	Philadelphia	Connie Mack	83	53	.610	5
1903	Boston	Jimmy Collins	91	47	.659	14½
1904	Boston	Jimmy Collins	95	59	.617	1½
1905	Philadelphia	Connie Mack	92	56	.622	2
1906	Chicago	Fielder Jones	93	58	.616	3
1907	Detroit	Hughie Jennings	92	58	.613	1½
1908	Detroit	Hughie Jennings	90	63	.588	½
1909	Detroit	Hughie Jennings	98	54	.645	3½
1910	Philadelphia	Connie Mack	102	48	.680	14½
1911	Philadelphia	Connie Mack	101	50	.669	13½
1912	Boston	Jake Stahl	105	47	.691	14
1913	Philadelphia	Connie Mack	96	57	.627	6½
1914	Philadelphia	Connie Mack	99	53	.651	8½
1915	Boston	Bill Carrigan	101	50	.669	2½
1916	Boston	Bill Carrigan	91	63	.591	2
1917	Chicago	Pants Rowland	100	54	.649	9
1918	Boston	Ed Barrow	75	51	.595	2½
1919	Chicago	Kid Gleason	88	52	.629	3½
1920	Cleveland	Tris Speaker	98	56	.636	2
1921	New York	Miller Huggins	98	55	.641	4½
1922	New York	Miller Huggins	94	60	.610	1
1923	New York	Miller Huggins	98	54	.645	16
1924	Washington	Bucky Harris	92	62	.597	2
1925	Washington	Bucky Harris	96	55	.636	8½
1926	New York	Miller Huggins	91	63	.591	3
1927	New York	Miller Huggins	110	44	.714	19
1928	New York	Miller Huggins	101	53	.656	2½
1929	Philadelphia	Connie Mack	104	46	.693	18
1930	Philadelphia	Connie Mack	102	52	.662	8
1931	Philadelphia	Connie Mack	107	45	.704	13½
1932	New York	Joe McCarthy	107	47	.695	13
1933	Washington	Joe Cronin	99	53	.651	7
1934	Detroit	Mickey Cochrane	101	53	.656	7
1935	Detroit	Mickey Cochrane	93	58	.616	3
1936	New York	Joe McCarthy	102	51	.667	19½
1937	New York	Joe McCarthy	102	52	.662	13
1938	New York	Joe McCarthy	99	53	.651	9½
1939	New York	Joe McCarthy	106	45	.702	17
1940	Detroit	Del Baker	90	64	.584	1
1941	New York	Joe McCarthy	101	53	.656	17
1942	New York	Joe McCarthy	103	51	.669	9
1943	New York	Joe McCarthy	98	56	.636	13½
1944	St Louis	Luke Sewell	89	65	.578	1
1945	Detroit	Steve O'Neill	88	65	.575	1½
1946	Boston	Joe Cronin	104	50	.675	12
1947	New York	Bucky Harris	97	57	.630	12
1948	Cleveland†	Lou Boudreau	97	58	.626	1
1949	New York	Casey Stengel	97	57	.630	1
1950	New York	Casey Stengel	98	56	.636	3
1951	New York	Casey Stengel	98	56	.636	5
1952	New York	Casey Stengel	95	59	.617	2
1953	New York	Casey Stengel	99	52	.656	8½
1954	Cleveland	Al Lopez	111	43	.721	8
1955	New York	Casey Stengel	96	58	.623	3
1956	New York	Casey Stengel	97	57	.630	9
1957	New York	Casey Stengel	98	56	.636	8
1958	New York	Casey Stengel	92	62	.597	10
1959	Chicago	Al Lopez	94	60	.610	5
1960	New York	Casey Stengel	97	57	.630	8
1961	New York	Ralph Houk	109	53	.673	8
1962	New York	Ralph Houk	96	66	.593	5
1963	New York	Ralph Houk	104	57	.646	10½
1964	New York	Yogi Berra	99	63	.611	1

Pennant Winners (Cont.)

Year	Team	Manager	W	L	Pct	GA
1965	Minnesota	Sam Mele	102	60	.630	7
1966	Baltimore	Hank Bauer	97	63	.606	9
1967	Boston	Dick Williams	92	70	.568	1
1968	Detroit	Mayo Smith	103	59	.636	12
1969	Baltimore (E)‡	Earl Weaver	109	53	.673	19
1970	Baltimore (E)‡	Earl Weaver	108	54	.667	15
1971	Baltimore (E)‡	Earl Weaver	101	57	.639	12
1972	Oakland (W)‡	Dick Williams	93	62	.600	5½
1973	Oakland (W)‡	Dick Williams	94	68	.580	6
1974	Oakland (W)‡	Al Dark	90	72	.556	5
1975	Boston (E)‡	Darrell Johnson	95	65	.594	4½
1976	New York (E)‡	Billy Martin	97	62	.610	10½
1977	New York (E)‡	Billy Martin	100	62	.617	2½
1978	New York (E)†‡	Billy Martin, Bob Lemon	100	63	.613	1
1979	Baltimore (E)‡	Earl Weaver	102	57	.642	8
1980	Kansas City (W)‡	Jim Frey	97	65	.599	14
1981	New York (E)‡	Gene Michael, Bob Lemon	59	48	.551	#
1982	Milwaukee (E)‡	Buck Rodgers, Harvey Kuenn	95	67	.586	1
1983	Baltimore (E)‡	Joe Altobelli	98	64	.605	6
1984	Detroit (E)‡	Sparky Anderson	104	58	.642	15
1985	Kansas City (W)‡	Dick Howser	91	71	.562	1
1986	Boston (E)‡	John McNamara	95	66	.590	5½
1987	Minnesota (W)‡	Tom Kelly	85	77	.525	2
1988	Oakland (W)‡	Tony La Russa	104	58	.642	13
1989	Oakland (W)‡	Tony La Russa	99	63	.611	7
1990	Oakland (W)‡	Tony La Russa	103	59	.636	9
1991	Minnesota (W)‡	Tom Kelly	95	67	.586	8
1992	Toronto‡	Cito Gaston	96	66	.593	4
1993	Toronto‡	Cito Gaston	95	67	.586	7
1994	Season ended Aug. 11 due to players' strike					
1995	Cleveland (C)‡	Mike Hargrove	100	44	.694	30

†Defeated Boston in one-game playoff. ‡Won championship series.

#First half 34-22; second 25-26, in season split by strike; defeated Milwaukee in playoff for Eastern Divison title.

Leading Batsmen

Year	Player and Team	BA	Year	Player and Team	BA
1901	Nap Lajoie, Phil	.422	1925	Harry Heilmann, Det	.393
1902	Ed Delahanty, Wash	.376	1926	Heinie Manush, Det	.378
1903	Nap Lajoie, Clev	.355	1927	Harry Heilmann, Det	.398
1904	Nap Lajoie, Clev	.381	1928	Goose Goslin, Wash	.379
1905	Elmer Flick, Clev	.306	1929	Lew Fonseca, Clev	.369
1906	George Stone, StL	.358	1930	Al Simmons, Phil	.381
1907	Ty Cobb, Det	.350	1931	Al Simmons, Phil	.390
1908	Ty Cobb, Det	.324	1932	Dale Alexander, Det-Bos	.367
1909	Ty Cobb, Det	.377	1933	Jimmie Foxx, Phil	.356
1910	Nap Lajoie, Clev*	.383	1934	Lou Gehrig, NY	.363
1911	Ty Cobb, Det	.420	1935	Buddy Myer, Wash	.349
1912	Ty Cobb, Det	.410	1936	Luke Appling, Chi	.388
1913	Ty Cobb, Det	.390	1937	Charlie Gehringer, Det	.371
1914	Ty Cobb, Det	.368	1938	Jimmie Foxx, Bos	.349
1915	Ty Cobb, Det	.369	1939	Joe DiMaggio, NY	.381
1916	Tris Speaker, Clev	.386	1940	Joe DiMaggio, NY	.352
1917	Ty Cobb, Det	.383	1941	Ted Williams, Bos	.406
1918	Ty Cobb, Det	.382	1942	Ted Williams, Bos	.356
1919	Ty Cobb, Det	.384	1943	Luke Appling, Chi	.328
1920	George Sisler, StL	.407	1944	Lou Boudreau, Clev	.327
1921	Harry Heilmann, Det	.394	1945	Snuffy Stirnweiss, NY	.309
1922	George Sisler, StL	.420	1946	Mickey Vernon, Wash	.353
1923	Harry Heilmann, Det	.403	1947	Ted Williams, Bos	.343
1924	Babe Ruth, NY	.378	1948	Ted Williams, Bos	.369

Leading Batsmen *(Cont.)*

Year	Player and Team	BA	Year	Player and Team	BA
1949	George Kell, Det	.343	1973	Rod Carew, Minn	.350
1950	Billy Goodman, Bos	.354	1974	Rod Carew, Minn	.364
1951	Ferris Fain, Phil	.344	1975	Rod Carew, Minn	.359
1952	Ferris Fain, Phil	.327	1976	George Brett, KC	.333
1953	Mickey Vernon, Wash	.337	1977	Rod Carew, Minn	.388
1954	Bobby Avila, Clev	.341	1978	Rod Carew, Minn	.333
1955	Al Kaline, Det	.340	1979	Fred Lynn, Bos	.333
1956	Mickey Mantle, NY	.353	1980	George Brett, KC	.390
1957	Ted Williams, Bos	.388	1981	Carney Lansford, Bos	.336
1958	Ted Williams, Bos	.328	1982	Willie Wilson, KC	.332
1959	Harvey Kuenn, Det	.353	1983	Wade Boggs, Bos	.361
1960	Pete Runnels, Bos	.320	1984	Don Mattingly, NY	.343
1961	Norm Cash, Det	.361	1985	Wade Boggs, Bos	.368
1962	Pete Runnels, Bos	.326	1986	Wade Boggs, Bos	.357
1963	Carl Yastrzemski, Bos	.321	1987	Wade Boggs, Bos	.363
1964	Tony Oliva, Minn	.323	1988	Wade Boggs, Bos	.366
1965	Tony Oliva, Minn	.321	1989	Kirby Puckett, Minn	.339
1966	Frank Robinson, Balt	.316	1990	George Brett, KC	.329
1967	Carl Yastrzemski, Bos	.326	1991	Julio Franco, Tex	.341
1968	Carl Yastrzemski, Bos	.301	1992	Edgar Martinez, Sea	.343
1969	Rod Carew, Minn	.332	1993	John Olerud, Tor	.363
1970	Alex Johnson, Calif	.329	1994	Paul O'Neill, NY	.359
1971	Tony Oliva, Minn	.337	1995	Edgar Martinez, Sea	.356
1972	Rod Carew, Minn	.318			

*League president Ban Johnson declared Ty Cobb batting champion with a .385 average, beating Lajoie's .384. However, subsequent research has led to the revision of Lajoie's average to .383 and Cobb's to .382.

Leaders in Runs Scored

Year	Player and Team	Runs	Year	Player and Team	Runs
1901	Nap Lajoie, Phil	145	1936	Lou Gehrig, NY	167
1902	Dave Fultz, Phil	110	1937	Joe DiMaggio, NY	151
1903	Patsy Dougherty, Bos	108	1938	Hank Greenberg, Det	144
1904	Patsy Dougherty, Bos-NY	113	1939	Red Rolfe, NY	139
1905	Harry Davis, Phil	92	1940	Ted Williams, Bos	134
1906	Elmer Flick, Clev	98	1941	Ted Williams, Bos	135
1907	Sam Crawford, Det	102	1942	Ted Williams, Bos	141
1908	Matty McIntyre, Det	105	1943	George Case, Wash	102
1909	Ty Cobb, Det	116	1944	Snuffy Stirnweiss, NY	125
1910	Ty Cobb, Det	106	1945	Snuffy Stirnweiss, NY	107
1911	Ty Cobb, Det	147	1946	Ted Williams, Bos	142
1912	Eddie Collins, Phil	137	1947	Ted Williams, Bos	125
1913	Eddie Collins, Phil	125	1948	Tommy Henrich, NY	138
1914	Eddie Collins, Phil	122	1949	Ted Williams, Bos	150
1915	Ty Cobb, Det	144	1950	Dom DiMaggio, Bos	131
1916	Ty Cobb, Det	113	1951	Dom DiMaggio, Bos	113
1917	Donie Bush, Det	112	1952	Larry Doby, Clev	104
1918	Ray Chapman, Clev	84	1953	Al Rosen, Clev	115
1919	Babe Ruth, Bos	103	1954	Mickey Mantle, NY	129
1920	Babe Ruth, NY	158	1955	Al Smith, Clev	123
1921	Babe Ruth, NY	177	1956	Mickey Mantle, NY	132
1922	George Sisler, StL	134	1957	Mickey Mantle, NY	121
1923	Babe Ruth, NY	151	1958	Mickey Mantle, NY	127
1924	Babe Ruth, NY	143	1959	Eddie Yost, Det	115
1925	Johnny Mostil, Chi	135	1960	Mickey Mantle, NY	119
1926	Babe Ruth, NY	139	1961	Mickey Mantle, NY	132
1927	Babe Ruth, NY	158		Roger Maris, NY	132
1928	Babe Ruth, NY	163	1962	Albie Pearson, LA	115
1929	Charlie Gehringer, Det	131	1963	Bob Allison, Minn	99
1930	Al Simmons, Phil	152	1964	Tony Oliva, Minn	109
1931	Lou Gehrig, NY	163	1965	Zoilo Versalles, Minn	126
1932	Jimmie Foxx, Phil	151	1966	Frank Robinson, Balt	122
1933	Lou Gehrig, NY	138	1967	Carl Yastrzemski, Bos	112
1934	Charlie Gehringer, Det	134	1968	Dick McAuliffe, Det	95
1935	Lou Gehrig, NY	125	1969	Reggie Jackson, Oak	123

Leaders in Runs Scored *(Cont.)*

Year	Player and Team	Runs	Year	Player and Team	Runs
1970	Carl Yastrzemski, Bos	125	1984	Dwight Evans, Bos	121
1971	Don Buford, Balt	99	1985	Rickey Henderson, NY	146
1972	Bobby Murcer, NY	102	1986	Rickey Henderson, NY	130
1973	Reggie Jackson, Oak	99	1987	Paul Molitor, Mil	114
1974	Carl Yastrzemski, Bos	93	1988	Wade Boggs, Bos	128
1975	Fred Lynn, Bos	103	1989	Rickey Henderson, NY-Oak	113
1976	Roy White, NY	104		Wade Boggs, Bos	113
1977	Rod Carew, Minn	128	1990	Rickey Henderson, Oak	119
1978	Ron LeFlore, Det	126	1991	Paul Molitor, Mil	133
1979	Don Baylor, Calif	120	1992	Tony Phillips, Det	114
1980	Willie Wilson, KC	133	1993	Rafael Palmeiro, Tex	124
1981	Rickey Henderson, Oak	89	1994	Frank Thomas, Chi	106
1982	Paul Molitor, Mil	136	1995	Albert Belle, Clev	121
1983	Cal Ripken, Balt	121		Edgar Martinez, Sea	121

Leaders in Hits

Year	Player and Team	Hits	Year	Player and Team	Hits
1901	Nap Lajoie, Phil	229	1943	Dick Wakefield, Det	200
1902	Piano Legs Hickman, Bos-Clev	194	1944	Snuffy Stirnweiss, NY	205
1903	Patsy Dougherty, Bos	195	1945	Snuffy Stirnweiss, NY	195
1904	Nap Lajoie, Clev	211	1946	Johnny Pesky, Bos	208
1905	George Stone, StL	187	1947	Johnny Pesky, Bos	207
1906	Nap Lajoie, Clev	214	1948	Bob Dillinger, StL	207
1907	Ty Cobb, Det	212	1949	Dale Mitchell, Clev	203
1908	Ty Cobb, Det	188	1950	George Kell, Det	218
1909	Ty Cobb, Det	216	1951	George Kell, Det	191
1910	Nap Lajoie, Clev	227	1952	Nellie Fox, Chi	192
1911	Ty Cobb, Det	248	1953	Harvey Kuenn, Det	209
1912	Ty Cobb, Det	227	1954	Nellie Fox, Chi	201
1913	Joe Jackson, Clev	197		Harvey Kuenn, Det	201
1914	Tris Speaker, Bos	193	1955	Al Kaline, Det	200
1915	Ty Cobb, Det	208	1956	Harvey Kuenn, Det	196
1916	Tris Speaker, Clev	211	1957	Nellie Fox, Chi	196
1917	Ty Cobb, Det	225	1958	Nellie Fox, Chi	187
1918	George Burns, Phil	178	1959	Harvey Kuenn, Det	198
1919	Ty Cobb, Det	191	1960	Minnie Minoso, Chi	184
	Bobby Veach, Det	191	1961	Norm Cash, Det	193
1920	George Sisler, StL	257	1962	Bobby Richardson, NY	209
1921	Harry Heilmann, Det	237	1963	Carl Yastrzemski, Bos	183
1922	George Sisler, StL	246	1964	Tony Oliva, Minn	217
1923	Charlie Jamieson, Clev	222	1965	Tony Oliva, Minn	185
1924	Sam Rice, Wash	216	1966	Tony Oliva, Minn	191
1925	Al Simmons, Phil	253	1967	Carl Yastrzemski, Bos	189
1926	George Burns, Clev	216	1968	Bert Campaneris, Oak	177
	Sam Rice, Wash	216	1969	Tony Oliva, Minn	197
1927	Earle Combs, NY	231	1970	Tony Oliva, Minn	204
1928	Heinie Manush, StL	241	1971	Cesar Tovar, Minn	204
1929	Dale Alexander, Det	215	1972	Joe Rudi, Oak	181
	Charlie Gehringer, Det	215	1973	Rod Carew, Minn	203
1930	Johnny Hodapp, Clev	225	1974	Rod Carew, Minn	218
1931	Lou Gehrig, NY	211	1975	George Brett, KC	195
1932	Al Simmons, Phil	216	1976	George Brett, KC	215
1933	Heinie Manush, Wash	221	1977	Rod Carew, Minn	239
1934	Charlie Gehringer, Det	214	1978	Jim Rice, Bos	213
1935	Joe Vosmik, Clev	216	1979	George Brett, KC	212
1936	Earl Averill, Clev	232	1980	Willie Wilson, KC	230
1937	Beau Bell, StL	218	1981	Rickey Henderson, Oak	135
1938	Joe Vosmik, Bos	201	1982	Robin Yount, Mil	210
1939	Red Rolfe, NY	213	1983	Cal Ripken, Balt	211
1940	Rip Radcliff, StL	200	1984	Don Mattingly, NY	207
	Barney McCosky, Det	200	1985	Wade Boggs, Bos	240
	Doc Cramer, Bos	200	1986	Don Mattingly, NY	238
1941	Cecil Travis, Wash	218	1987	Kirby Puckett, Minn	207
1942	Johnny Pesky, Bos	205		Kevin Seitzer, KC	207

Leaders in Hits (Cont.)

Year	Player and Team	Hits	Year	Player and Team	Hits
1988	Kirby Puckett, Minn	234	1992	Kirby Puckett, Minn	210
1989	Kirby Puckett, Minn	215	1993	Paul Molitor, Tor	211
1990	Rafael Palmeiro, Tex	191	1994	Kenny Lofton, Clev	160
1991	Paul Molitor, Mil	216	1995	Lance Johnson, Chi	186

Home Run Leaders

Year	Player and Team	HR	Year	Player and Team	HR
1901	Nap Lajoie, Phil	13	1951	Gus Zernial, Chi-Phil	33
1902	Socks Seybold, Phil	16	1952	Larry Doby, Clev	32
1903	Buck Freeman, Bos	13	1953	Al Rosen, Clev	43
1904	Harry Davis, Phil	10	1954	Larry Doby, Clev	32
1905	Harry Davis, Phil	8	1955	Mickey Mantle, NY	37
1906	Harry Davis, Phil	12	1956	Mickey Mantle, NY	52
1907	Harry Davis, Phil	8	1957	Roy Sievers, Wash	42
1908	Sam Crawford, Det	7	1958	Mickey Mantle, NY	42
1909	Ty Cobb, Det	9	1959	Rocky Colavito, Clev	42
1910	Jake Stahl, Bos	10		Harmon Killebrew, Wash	42
1911	Frank Baker, Phil	9	1960	Mickey Mantle, NY	40
1912	Frank Baker, Phil	10	1961	Roger Maris, NY	61
	Tris Speaker, Bos	10	1962	Harmon Killebrew, Minn	48
1913	Frank Baker, Phil	13	1963	Harmon Killebrew, Minn	45
1914	Frank Baker, Phil	9	1964	Harmon Killebrew, Minn	49
1915	Braggo Roth, Chi-Clev	7	1965	Tony Conigliaro, Bos	32
1916	Wally Pipp, NY	12	1966	Frank Robinson, Balt	49
1917	Wally Pipp, NY	9	1967	Harmon Killebrew, Minn	44
1918	Babe Ruth, Bos	11		Carl Yastrzemski, Bos	44
	Tilly Walker, Phil	11	1968	Frank Howard, Wash	44
1919	Babe Ruth, Bos	29	1969	Harmon Killebrew, Minn	49
1920	Babe Ruth, NY	54	1970	Frank Howard, Wash	44
1921	Babe Ruth, NY	59	1971	Bill Melton, Chi	33
1922	Ken Williams, StL	39	1972	Dick Allen, Chi	37
1923	Babe Ruth, NY	41	1973	Reggie Jackson, Oak	32
1924	Babe Ruth, NY	46	1974	Dick Allen, Chi	32
1925	Bob Meusel, NY	33	1975	Reggie Jackson, Oak	36
1926	Babe Ruth, NY	47		George Scott, Mil	36
1927	Babe Ruth, NY	60	1976	Graig Nettles, NY	32
1928	Babe Ruth, NY	54	1977	Jim Rice, Bos	39
1929	Babe Ruth, NY	46	1978	Jim Rice, Bos	46
1930	Babe Ruth, NY	49	1979	Gorman Thomas, Mil	45
1931	Babe Ruth, NY	46	1980	Reggie Jackson, NY	41
	Lou Gehrig, NY	46		Ben Oglivie, Mil	41
1932	Jimmie Foxx, Phil	58	1981	Tony Armas, Oak	22
1933	Jimmie Foxx, Phil	48	1981	Dwight Evans, Bos	22
1934	Lou Gehrig, NY	49		Bobby Grich, Calif	22
1935	Jimmie Foxx, Phil	36		Eddie Murray, Balt	22
	Hank Greenberg, Det	36	1982	Reggie Jackson, Calif	39
1936	Lou Gehrig, NY	49		Gorman Thomas, Mil	39
1937	Joe DiMaggio, NY	46	1983	Jim Rice, Bos	39
1938	Hank Greenberg, Det	58	1984	Tony Armas, Bos	43
1939	Jimmie Foxx, Bos	35	1985	Darrell Evans, Det	40
1940	Hank Greenberg, Det	41	1986	Jesse Barfield, Tor	40
1941	Ted Williams, Bos	37	1987	Mark McGwire, Oak	49
1942	Ted Williams, Bos	36	1988	Jose Canseco, Oak	42
1943	Rudy York, Det	34	1989	Fred McGriff, Tor	36
1944	Nick Etten, NY	22	1990	Cecil Fielder, Det	51
1945	Vern Stephens, StL	24	1991	Jose Canseco, Oak	44
1946	Hank Greenberg, Det	44		Cecil Fielder, Det	44
1947	Ted Williams, Bos	32	1992	Juan Gonzalez, Tex	43
1948	Joe DiMaggio, NY	39	1993	Juan Gonzalez, Tex	46
1949	Ted Williams, Bos	43	1994	Ken Griffey Jr, Sea	40
1950	Al Rosen, Clev	37	1995	Albert Belle, Clev	50

Runs Batted In Leaders

Year	Player and Team	RBI	Year	Player and Team	RBI
1907	Ty Cobb, Det	116	1951	Gus Zernial, Chi-Phil	129
1908	Ty Cobb, Det	108	1952	Al Rosen, Clev	105
1909	Ty Cobb, Det	107	1953	Al Rosen, Clev	145
1910	Sam Crawford, Det	120	1954	Larry Doby, Clev	126
1911	Ty Cobb, Det	144	1955	Ray Boone, Det	116
1912	Frank Baker, Phil	133		Jackie Jensen, Bos	116
1913	Frank Baker, Phil	126	1956	Mickey Mantle, NY	130
1914	Sam Crawford, Det	104	1957	Roy Sievers, Wash	114
1915	Sam Crawford, Det	112	1958	Jackie Jensen, Bos	122
	Bobby Veach, Det	112	1959	Jackie Jensen, Bos	112
1916	Del Pratt, StL	103	1960	Roger Maris, NY	112
1917	Bobby Veach, Det	103	1961	Roger Maris, NY	142
1918	Bobby Veach, Det	78	1962	Harmon Killebrew, Minn	126
1919	Babe Ruth, Bos	114	1963	Dick Stuart, Bos	118
1920	Babe Ruth, NY	137	1964	Brooks Robinson, Balt	118
1921	Babe Ruth, NY	171	1965	Rocky Colavito, Clev	108
1922	Ken Williams, StL	155	1966	Frank Robinson, Balt	122
1923	Babe Ruth, NY	131	1967	Carl Yastrzemski, Bos	121
1924	Goose Goslin, Wash	129	1968	Ken Harrelson, Bos	109
1925	Bob Meusel, NY	138	1969	Harmon Killebrew, Minn	140
1926	Babe Ruth, NY	145	1970	Frank Howard, Wash	126
1927	Lou Gehrig, NY	175	1971	Harmon Killebrew, Minn	119
1928	Babe Ruth, NY	142	1972	Dick Allen, Chi	113
	Lou Gehrig, NY	142	1973	Reggie Jackson, Oak	117
1929	Al Simmons, Phil	157	1974	Jeff Burroughs, Tex	118
1930	Lou Gehrig, NY	174	1975	George Scott, Mil	109
1931	Lou Gehrig, NY	184	1976	Lee May, Balt	109
1932	Jimmie Foxx, Phil	169	1977	Larry Hisle, Minn	119
1933	Jimmie Foxx, Phil	163	1978	Jim Rice, Bos	139
1934	Lou Gehrig, NY	165	1979	Don Baylor, Calif	139
1935	Hank Greenberg, Det	170	1980	Cecil Cooper, Mil	122
1936	Hal Trosky, Clev	162	1981	Eddie Murray, Balt	78
1937	Hank Greenberg, Det	183	1982	Hal McRae, KC	133
1938	Jimmie Foxx, Bos	175	1983	Cecil Cooper, Mil	126
1939	Ted Williams, Bos	145		Jim Rice, Bos	126
1940	Hank Greenberg, Det	150	1984	Tony Armas, Bos	123
1941	Joe DiMaggio, NY	125	1985	Don Mattingly, NY	145
1942	Ted Williams, Bos	137	1986	Joe Carter, Clev	121
1943	Rudy York, Det	118	1987	George Bell, Tor	134
1944	Vern Stephens, StL	109	1988	Jose Canseco, Oak	124
1945	Nick Etten, NY	111	1989	Ruben Sierra, Tex	119
1946	Hank Greenberg, Det	127	1990	Cecil Fielder, Det	132
1947	Ted Williams, Bos	114	1991	Cecil Fielder, Det	133
1948	Joe DiMaggio, NY	155	1992	Cecil Fielder, Det	124
1949	Ted Williams, Bos	159	1993	Albert Belle, Clev	129
	Vern Stephens, Bos	159	1994	Kirby Puckett, Minn	112
1950	Walt Dropo, Bos	144	1995	Albert Belle, Clev	126
	Vern Stephens, Bos	144		Mo Vaughn, Bos	126

Note: Runs Batted In not compiled before 1907; officially adopted in 1920.

Leading Base Stealers

Year	Player and Team	SB	Year	Player and Team	SB
1901	Frank Isbell, Chi	48	1911	Ty Cobb, Det	83
1902	Topsy Hartsel, Phil	54	1912	Clyde Milan, Wash	88
1903	Harry Bay, Clev	46	1913	Clyde Milan, Wash	75
1904	Elmer Flick, Clev	42	1914	Fritz Maisel, NY	74
	Harry Bay, Clev	42	1915	Ty Cobb, Det	96
1905	Danny Hoffman, Phil	46	1916	Ty Cobb, Det	68
1906	Elmer Flick, Clev	39	1917	Ty Cobb, Det	55
	John Anderson, Wash	39	1918	George Sisler, StL	45
1907	Ty Cobb, Det	49	1919	Eddie Collins, Chi	33
1908	Patsy Dougherty, Chi	47	1920	Sam Rice, Wash	63
1909	Ty Cobb, Det	76	1921	George Sisler, StL	35
1910	Eddie Collins, Phil	81	1922	George Sisler, StL	51

Leading Base Stealers (Cont.)

Year	Player and Team	SB	Year	Player and Team	SB
1923	Eddie Collins, Chi	49	1959	Luis Aparicio, Chi	56
1924	Eddie Collins, Chi	42	1960	Luis Aparicio, Chi	51
1925	John Mostil, Chi	43	1961	Luis Aparicio, Chi	53
1926	John Mostil, Chi	35	1962	Luis Aparicio, Chi	31
1927	George Sisler, StL	27	1963	Luis Aparicio, Balt	40
1928	Buddy Myer, Bos	30	1964	Luis Aparicio, Balt	57
1929	Charlie Gehringer, Det	27	1965	Bert Campaneris, KC	51
1930	Marty McManus, Det	23	1966	Bert Campaneris, KC	52
1931	Ben Chapman, NY	61	1967	Bert Campaneris, KC	55
1932	Ben Chapman, NY	38	1968	Bert Campaneris, Oak	62
1933	Ben Chapman, NY	27	1969	Tommy Harper, Sea	73
1934	Bill Werber, Bos	40	1970	Bert Campaneris, Oak	42
1935	Bill Werber, Bos	29	1971	Amos Otis, KC	52
1936	Lyn Lary, StL	37	1972	Bert Campaneris, Oak	52
1937	Bill Werber, Phil	35	1973	Tommy Harper, Bos	54
	Ben Chapman, Wash-Bos	35	1974	Bill North, Oak	54
1938	Frank Crosetti, NY	27	1975	Mickey Rivers, Calif	70
1939	George Case, Wash	51	1976	Bill North, Oak	75
1940	George Case, Wash	35	1977	Freddie Patek, KC	53
1941	George Case, Wash	33	1978	Ron LeFlore, Det	68
1942	George Case, Wash	44	1979	Willie Wilson, KC	83
1943	George Case, Wash	61	1980	Rickey Henderson, Oak	100
1944	Snuffy Stirnweiss, NY	55	1981	Rickey Henderson, Oak	56
1945	Snuffy Stirnweiss, NY	33	1982	Rickey Henderson, Oak	130
1946	George Case, Clev	28	1983	Rickey Henderson, Oak	108
1947	Bob Dillinger, StL	34	1984	Rickey Henderson, Oak	66
1948	Bob Dillinger, StL	28	1985	Rickey Henderson, NY	80
1949	Bob Dillinger, StL	20	1986	Rickey Henderson, NY	87
1950	Dom DiMaggio, Bos	15	1987	Harold Reynolds, Sea	60
1951	Minnie Minoso, Clev-Chi	31	1988	Rickey Henderson, NY	93
1952	Minnie Minoso, Chi	22	1989	Rickey Henderson, NY-Oak	77
1953	Minnie Minoso, Chi	25	1990	Rickey Henderson, Oak	65
1954	Jackie Jensen, Bos	22	1991	Rickey Henderson, Oak	58
1955	Jim Rivera, Chi	25	1992	Kenny Lofton, Clev	66
1956	Luis Aparicio, Chi	21	1993	Kenny Lofton, Clev	70
1957	Luis Aparicio, Chi	28	1994	Kenny Lofton, Clev	60
1958	Luis Aparicio, Chi	29	1995	Kenny Lofton, Clev	54

Leading Pitchers—Winning Percentage

Year	Pitcher and Team	W	L	Pct	Year	Pitcher and Team	W	L	Pct
1901	Clark Griffith, Chi	24	7	.774	1926	George Uhle, Clev	27	11	.711
1902	Bill Bernhard, Phil-Clev	18	5	.783	1927	Waite Hoyt, NY	22	7	.759
1903	Earl Moore, Clev	22	7	.759	1928	General Crowder, StL	21	5	.808
1904	Jack Chesbro, NY	41	12	.774	1929	Lefty Grove, Phil	20	6	.769
1905	Jess Tannehill, Bos	22	9	.710	1930	Lefty Grove, Phil	28	5	.848
1906	Eddie Plank, Phil	19	6	.760	1931	Lefty Grove, Phil	31	4	.886
1907	Wild Bill Donovan, Det	25	4	.862	1932	Johnny Allen, NY	17	4	.810
1908	Ed Walsh, Chi	40	15	.727	1933	Lefty Grove, Phil	24	8	.750
1909	George Mullin, Det	29	8	.784	1934	Lefty Gomez, NY	26	5	.839
1910	Chief Bender, Phil	23	5	.821	1935	Eldon Auker, Det	18	7	.720
1911	Chief Bender, Phil	17	5	.773	1936	Monte Pearson, NY	19	7	.731
1912	Smoky Joe Wood, Bos	34	5	.872	1937	Johnny Allen, Clev	15	1	.938
1913	Walter Johnson, Wash	36	7	.837	1938	Red Ruffing, NY	21	7	.750
1914	Chief Bender, Phil	17	3	.850	1939	Lefty Grove, Bos	15	4	.789
1915	Smoky Joe Wood, Bos	15	5	.750	1940	Schoolboy Rowe, Det	16	3	.842
1916	Eddie Cicotte, Chi	15	7	.682	1941	Lefty Gomez, NY	15	5	.750
1917	Reb Russell, Chi	15	5	.750	1942	Ernie Bonham, NY	21	5	.808
1918	Sad Sam Jones, Bos	16	5	.762	1943	Spud Chandler, NY	20	4	.833
1919	Eddie Cicotte, Chi	29	7	.806	1944	Tex Hughson, Bos	18	5	.783
1920	Jim Bagby, Clev	31	12	.721	1945	Hal Newhouser, Det	25	9	.735
1921	Carl Mays, NY	27	9	.750	1946	Boo Ferriss, Bos	25	6	.806
1922	Joe Bush, NY	26	7	.788	1947	Allie Reynolds, NY	19	8	.704
1923	Herb Pennock, NY	19	6	.760	1948	Jack Kramer, Bos	18	5	.783
1924	Walter Johnson, Wash	23	7	.767	1949	Ellis Kinder, Bos	23	6	.793
1925	Stan Coveleski, Wash	20	5	.800	1950	Vic Raschi, NY	21	8	.724

Leading Pitchers—Winning Percentage (Cont.)

Year	Pitcher and Team	W	L	Pct	Year	Pitcher and Team	W	L	Pct
1951	Bob Feller, Clev	22	8	.733	1974	Mike Cuellar, Balt	22	10	.688
1952	Bobby Shantz, Phil	24	7	.774	1975	Mike Torrez, Balt	20	9	.690
1953	Ed Lopat, NY	16	4	.800	1976	Bill Campbell, Minn	17	5	.773
1954	Sandy Consuegra, Chi	16	3	.842	1977	Paul Splittorff, KC	16	6	.727
1955	Tommy Byrne, NY	16	5	.762	1978	Ron Guidry, NY	25	3	.893
1956	Whitey Ford, NY	19	6	.760	1979	Mike Caldwell, Mil	16	6	.727
1957	Dick Donovan, Chi	16	6	.727	1980	Steve Stone, Balt	25	7	.781
	Tom Sturdivant, NY	16	6	.727	1981*	Pete Vuckovich, Mil	14	4	.778
1958	Bob Turley, NY	21	7	.750	1982	Pete Vuckovich, Mil	18	6	.750
1959	Bob Shaw, Chi	18	6	.750		Jim Palmer, Balt	15	5	.750
1960	Jim Perry, Clev	18	10	.643	1983	Richard Dotson, Chi	22	7	.759
1961	Whitey Ford, NY	25	4	.862	1984	Doyle Alexander, Tor	17	6	.739
1962	Ray Herbert, Chi	20	9	.690	1985	Ron Guidry, NY	22	6	.786
1963	Whitey Ford, NY	24	7	.774	1986	Roger Clemens, Bos	24	4	.857
1964	Wally Bunker, Balt	19	5	.792	1987	Roger Clemens, Bos	20	9	.690
1965	Mudcat Grant, Minn	21	7	.750	1988	Frank Viola, Minn	24	7	.774
1966	Sonny Siebert, Clev	16	8	.667	1989	Bret Saberhagen, KC	23	6	.793
1967	Joel Horlen, Chi	19	7	.731	1990	Bob Welch, Oak	27	6	.818
1968	Denny McLain, Det	31	6	.838	1991	Scott Erickson, Minn	20	8	.714
1969	Jim Palmer, Balt	16	4	.800	1992	Mike Mussina, Balt	18	5	.783
1970	Mike Cuellar, Balt	24	8	.750	1993	Jimmy Key, NY	18	6	.750
1971	Dave McNally, Balt	21	5	.808	1994	Jimmy Key, NY	17	4	.810
1972	Catfish Hunter, Oak	21	7	.750	1995	Randy Johnson, Sea	18	2	.900
1973	Catfish Hunter, Oak	21	5	.808					

*1981 percentages based on 10 or more victories.

Note: Based on 15 or more victories.

Leading Pitchers—Earned-Run Average

Year	Player and Team	ERA	Year	Player and Team	ERA
1913	Walter Johnson, Wash	1.14	1949	Mel Parnell, Bos	2.78
1914	Dutch Leonard, Bos	1.01	1950	Early Wynn, Clev	3.20
1915	Smoky Joe Wood, Bos	1.49	1951	Saul Rogovin, Det-Chi	2.78
1916	Babe Ruth, Bos	1.75	1952	Allie Reynolds, NY	2.07
1917	Eddie Cicotte, Chi	1.53	1953	Ed Lopat, NY	2.43
1918	Walter Johnson, Wash	1.27	1954	Mike Garcia, Clev	2.64
1919	Walter Johnson, Wash	1.49	1955	Billy Pierce, Chi	1.97
1920	Bob Shawkey, NY	2.46	1956	Whitey Ford, NY	2.47
1921	Red Faber, Chi	2.47	1957	Bobby Shantz, NY	2.45
1922	Red Faber, Chi	2.80	1958	Whitey Ford, NY	2.01
1923	Stan Coveleski, Clev	2.76	1959	Hoyt Wilhelm, Balt	2.19
1924	Walter Johnson, Wash	2.72	1960	Frank Baumann, Chi	2.68
1925	Stan Coveleski, Wash	2.84	1961	Dick Donovan, Wash	2.40
1926	Lefty Grove, Phil	2.51	1962	Hank Aguirre, Det	2.21
1927	Wilcy Moore, NY#	2.28	1963	Gary Peters, Chi	2.33
1928	Garland Braxton, Wash	2.52	1964	Dean Chance, LA	1.65
1929	Lefty Grove, Phil	2.81	1965	Sam McDowell, Clev	2.18
1930	Lefty Grove, Phil	2.54	1966	Gary Peters, Chi	1.98
1931	Lefty Grove, Phil	2.06	1967	Joe Horlen, Chi	2.06
1932	Lefty Grove, Phil	2.84	1968	Luis Tiant, Clev	1.60
1933	Monte Pearson, Clev	2.33	1969	Dick Bosman, Wash	2.19
1934	Lefty Gomez, NY	2.33	1970	Diego Segui, Oak	2.56
1935	Lefty Grove, Bos	2.70	1971	Vida Blue, Oak	1.82
1936	Lefty Grove, Bos	2.81	1972	Luis Tiant, Bos	1.91
1937	Lefty Gomez, NY	2.33	1973	Jim Palmer, Balt	2.40
1938	Lefty Grove, Bos	3.07	1974	Catfish Hunter, Oak	2.49
1939	Lefty Grove, Bos	2.54	1975	Jim Palmer, Balt	2.09
1940	Bob Feller, Clev†	2.62	1976	Mark Fidrych, Det	2.34
1941	Thornton Lee, Chi	2.37	1977	Frank Tanana, Calif	2.54
1942	Ted Lyons, Chi	2.10	1978	Ron Guidry, NY	1.74
1943	Spud Chandler, NY	1.64	1979	Ron Guidry, NY	2.78
1944	Dizzy Trout, Det	2.12	1980	Rudy May, NY	2.47
1945	Hal Newhouser, Det	1.81	1981	Steve McCatty, Oak	2.32
1946	Hal Newhouser, Det	1.94	1982	Rick Sutcliffe, Clev	2.96
1947	Spud Chandler, NY	2.46	1983	Rick Honeycutt, Tex	2.42
1948	Gene Bearden, Clev	2.43	1984	Mike Boddicker, Balt	2.79

Leading Pitchers—Earned-Run Average (Cont.)

Year	Player and Team	ERA	Year	Player and Team	ERA
1985	Dave Stieb, Tor	2.48	1991	Roger Clemens, Bos	2.62
1986	Roger Clemens, Bos	2.48	1992	Roger Clemens, Bos	2.41
1987	Jimmy Key, Tor	2.76	1993	Kevin Appier, KC	2.56
1988	Allan Anderson, Minn	2.45	1994	Steve Ontiveros, Oak	2.65
1989	Bret Saberhagen, KC	2.16	1995	Randy Johnson, Sea	2.48
1990	Roger Clemens, Bos	1.93			

Note: Based on 10 complete games through 1950, then, 154 innings until the American League expanded in 1961, when it became 162 innings. In strike-shortened 1981, one inning per game required. Earned runs not tabulated in American League prior to 1913.

#Wilcy Moore pitched only six complete games——he started 12—in 1927, but was recognized as leader because of 213 innings pitched.

†Ernie Bonham, New York, had 1.91 ERA and 10 complete games in 1940, but appeared in only 12 games and 99 innings, and Bob Feller was recognized as leader.

Leading Pitchers—Strikeouts

Year	Player and Team	SO	Year	Player and Team	SO
1901	Cy Young, Bos	159	1948	Bob Feller, Clev	164
1902	Rube Waddell, Phil	210	1949	Virgil Trucks, Det	153
1903	Rube Waddell, Phil	301	1950	Bob Lemon, Clev	170
1904	Rube Waddell, Phil	349	1951	Vic Raschi, NY	164
1905	Rube Waddell, Phil	286	1952	Allie Reynolds, NY	160
1906	Rube Waddell, Phil	203	1953	Billy Pierce, Chi	186
1907	Rube Waddell, Phil	226	1954	Bob Turley, Balt	185
1908	Ed Walsh, Chi	269	1955	Herb Score, Clev	245
1909	Frank Smith, Chi	177	1956	Herb Score, Clev	263
1910	Walter Johnson, Wash	313	1957	Early Wynn, Clev	184
1911	Ed Walsh, Chi	255	1958	Early Wynn, Chi	179
1912	Walter Johnson, Wash	303	1959	Jim Bunning, Det	201
1913	Walter Johnson, Wash	243	1960	Jim Bunning, Det	201
1914	Walter Johnson, Wash	225	1961	Camilo Pascual, Minn	221
1915	Walter Johnson, Wash	203	1962	Camilo Pascual, Minn	206
1916	Walter Johnson, Wash	228	1963	Camilo Pascual, Minn	202
1917	Walter Johnson, Wash	188	1964	Al Downing, NY	217
1918	Walter Johnson, Wash	162	1965	Sam McDowell, Clev	325
1919	Walter Johnson, Wash	147	1966	Sam McDowell, Clev	225
1920	Stan Coveleski, Clev	133	1967	Jim Lonborg, Bos	246
1921	Walter Johnson, Wash	143	1968	Sam McDowell, Clev	283
1922	Urban Shocker, StL	149	1969	Sam McDowell, Clev	279
1923	Walter Johnson, Wash	130	1970	Sam McDowell, Clev	304
1924	Walter Johnson, Wash	158	1971	Mickey Lolich, Det	308
1925	Lefty Grove, Phil	116	1972	Nolan Ryan, Calif	329
1926	Lefty Grove, Phil	194	1973	Nolan Ryan, Calif	383
1927	Lefty Grove, Phil	174	1974	Nolan Ryan, Calif	367
1928	Lefty Grove, Phil	183	1975	Frank Tanana, Calif	269
1929	Lefty Grove, Phil	170	1976	Nolan Ryan, Calif	327
1930	Lefty Grove, Phil	209	1977	Nolan Ryan, Calif	341
1931	Lefty Grove, Phil	175	1978	Nolan Ryan, Calif	260
1932	Red Ruffing, NY	190	1979	Nolan Ryan, Calif	223
1933	Lefty Gomez, NY	163	1980	Len Barker, Clev	187
1934	Lefty Gomez, NY	158	1981	Len Barker, Clev	127
1935	Tommy Bridges, Det	163	1982	Floyd Bannister, Sea	209
1936	Tommy Bridges, Det	175	1983	Jack Morris, Det	232
1937	Lefty Gomez, NY	194	1984	Mark Langston, Sea	204
1938	Bob Feller, Clev	240	1985	Bert Blyleven, Clev-Minn	206
1939	Bob Feller, Clev	246	1986	Mark Langston, Sea	245
1940	Bob Feller, Clev	261	1987	Mark Langston, Sea	262
1941	Bob Feller, Clev	260	1988	Roger Clemens, Bos	291
1942	Bobo Newsom, Wash	113	1989	Nolan Ryan, Tex	301
	Tex Hughson, Bos	113	1990	Nolan Ryan, Tex	232
1943	Allie Reynolds, Clev	151	1991	Roger Clemens, Bos	241
1944	Hal Newhouser, Det	187	1992	Randy Johnson, Sea	241
1945	Hal Newhouser, Det	212	1993	Randy Johnson, Sea	308
1946	Bob Feller, Clev	348	1994	Randy Johnson, Sea	204
1947	Bob Feller, Clev	196	1995	Randy Johnson, Sea	294

Leading Pitchers—Saves

Year	Player and Team	SV	Year	Player and Team	SV
1947	Joe Page, NY	17	1972	Sparky Lyle, NY	35
1948	Russ Christopher, Clev	17	1973	John Hiller, Det	38
1949	Joe Page, NY	29	1974	Terry Forster, Chi	24
1950	Mickey Harris, Wash	15	1975	Goose Gossage, Chi	26
1951	Ellis Kinder, Bos	14	1976	Sparky Lyle, NY	23
1952	Harry Dorish, Chi	11	1977	Bill Campbell, Bos	31
1953	Ellis Kinder, Bos	27	1978	Goose Gossage, NY	27
1954	Johnny Sain, NY	22	1979	Mike Marshall, Minn	32
1955	Ray Narleski, Clev	19	1980	Dan Quisenberry, KC	33
1956	George Zuverink, Bal	16	1981	Goose Gossage, NY	33
1957	Bob Grim, NY	19	1982	Rollie Fingers, Mil	28
1958	Ryne Duren, NY	20	1983	Dan Quisenberry, KC	35
1959	Turk Lown, Chi	15	1984	Dan Quisenberry, KC	45
1960	Mike Fornieles, Bos	14	1985	Dan Quisenberry, KC	37
	Johnny Klippstein, Clev	14	1986	Dave Righetti, NY	46
1961	Luis Arroyo, NY	29	1987	Tom Henke, Tor	34
1962	Dick Radatz, Bos	24	1988	Dennis Eckersley, Oak	45
1963	Stu Miller, Bal	27	1989	Jeff Russell, Tex	38
1964	Dick Radatz, Bos	29	1990	Bobby Thigpen, Chi	57
1965	Ron Kline, Wash	29	1991	Bryan Harvey, Cal	46
1966	Jack Aker, KC	32	1992	Dennis Eckersley, Oak	51
1967	Minnie Rojas, Cal	27	1993	Jeff Montgomery, KC	45
1968	Al Worthington, Minn	18		Duane Ward, Tor	45
1969	Ron Perranoski, Minn	31	1994	Lee Smith, Bal	33
1970	Ron Perranoski, Minn	34	1995	Jose Mesa, Clev	46
1971	Ken Sanders, Mil	31			

The Commissioners of Baseball

Kenesaw Mountain Landis .... Elected November 12, 1920. Served until his death on November 25, 1944.

Happy Chandler .... Elected April 24, 1945. Served until July 15, 1951.

Ford Frick .... Elected September 20, 1951. Served until November 16, 1965.

William Eckert .... Elected November 17, 1965. Served until December 20, 1968.

Bowie Kuhn .... Elected February 8, 1969. Served until September 30, 1984.

Peter Ueberroth .... Elected March 3, 1984. Took office October 1, 1984. Served through March 31, 1989.

A. Bartlett Giamatti .... Elected September 8, 1988. Took office April 1, 1989. Served until his death on September 1, 1989.

Francis Vincent Jr .... Appointed Acting Commissioner September 2, 1989. Elected Commissioner September 13, 1989. Served through September 7, 1992.

Allan H. (Bud) Selig .... Elected chairman of the executive council and given the powers of interim commissioner on September 9, 1992.

THEY SAID IT

Marge Schott, Cincinnati Red owner, when asked if she had plans to do anything "special" for fans returning after the strike: "What do you mean?"

Pro Football

FEBRUARY 6, 1995 · $2.95 (CAN. $3.95)

Sports Illustrated

Victory!

Super Bowl MVP
Steve Young

PETER READ MILLER

Shedding the Weight

With his MVP performance in the Niners' Super Bowl rout of San Diego, Steve Young got a Montana-sized monkey off his back

by Peter King

WHEN SUPER Bowl XXIX Most Valuable Player Steve Young walked (levitated?) onto the victors' podium in the San Francisco 49er locker room after the Niners' 49–26 dismantling of San Diego in January 1995, the first thing he did was hug the trophy. And hug it. And hug it some more.

The nice guy finished first.

"Aaaaahhhhh," he said. He squeezed and caressed this Vince Lombardi Trophy like a father might hug a son just returned from kidnappers. He put his head down on the sterling-silver football on top of the trophy as though it were a pillow, rocking back and forth. And then, after a while, Young gave the team its postgame speech. Not George Seifert, the coach. Steve Young, the quarterback, gave the team its talking-to after the 49ers won their fifth Super Bowl title, a record.

"There were times this was hard!" he shouted, his voice hoarse from a day of signal-calling and touchdown-celebrating. "But this is the greatest feeling IN THE WORLD!" Then, with the veins sticking out of his neck, he almost blew his vocal cords with: "No one—NO ONE—can ever take this away from us! NO ONE! EVER! It's ours!"

Quite true. The fifth 49er Super Bowl title—the most any NFL franchise has won—established owner Eddie DeBartolo's team as one of the most enduring dynasties in NFL history. It also gave the weight-of-the-world-on-his-shoulders Young, the first man to win four consecutive NFL passing titles, the credit he deserves for being a great player, the credit that so often eluded him as the Man Who Succeeded Joe Montana.

But it gave the 49ers one more thing, as every recent champion in Salary Cap Ball has learned: a very heavy crown. Because after the 49ers begged, borrowed and deferred on the way to their January 1995 Super Bowl win, the rest of 1995 became a struggle akin to their annual Armageddon bowls against the Cowboys. The week after the win over San Diego, both coordinators (Mike Shanahan on offense, Ray Rhodes

Rice opened the scoring in Super Bowl XXIX with a 44-yard TD reception.

on defense) left to become head coaches—Shanahan to Denver and Rhodes to Philadelphia. This had nothing to do with the cap, only with the terrific pedigree of 49er coaches. But then free agency stripped the 49ers of one star and a big chunk of their depth. To Philadelphia went prize running back Ricky Watters and backup defensive tackle Rhett Hall. To Denver went backup quarterback Bill Musgrave and wideout Ed McCaffrey. The Jets stole return specialist Dexter Carter, and punter Klaus Wilmsmeyer went to New Orleans. Veteran elements like defensive end Rickey Jackson and cornerback Toi Cook were late re-signees, and defensive end Richard Dent left to test the waters of free agency. And some were predicting that the loss of cornerback Deion Sanders to arch-rival Dallas in September would do more damage to the Niners title chances than all of their off-season depletions combined.

This is the way football works now. It's just business, baby. Perfect example: The 49ers, still snug up against the salary cap, were pursuing one of the better two-way defensive ends in free agency last March, the Jets' Jeff Lageman. In the midst of said pursuit, Dent filed an injury grievance against the club, claiming it cut him while he was still injured, which would be a violation of NFL rules if true. Because the grievance required the 49ers to keep half of Dent's $1.7 million 1995 salary counting against the cap, the 49ers had to drop out of the Lageman stakes. He signed with Jacksonville. "Do you know how well Lageman would have fit in with our team?" a thoroughly disappointed 49er president Carmen Policy said. "We loved him. He'd have been perfect for us."

The cap and its various vagaries were helping the league keep San Francisco fairly close to the pack. Their only free agent of significance, cornerback Marquez Pope, made nary a Dent in their losses. Still, entering the 1995–96 season, the NFL bal-

WALTER IOOSS, JR.

San Diego and Humphries were the NFC's 11th straight Super Bowl victims.

ance of power had changed remarkably little from the previous year. The 49ers and Dallas were a clear one-two, and everyone else was fighting for number three. The 49er-Cowboy fight was the story of the year in the NFL, with only a few sidelights competing for attention on that level: the April move of the Rams to St. Louis, the June return of the Raiders to Oakland (*see sidebar*) and the September openings of expansionists Carolina and Jacksonville. It was so simple to see why the Cowboys and the 49ers dominated. They had great supporting casts, desperado front offices and starry youth. They also had franchise-foundation quarterbacks in Young and Troy Aikman.

Young and Aikman. Aikman and Young. Who's better? Depends on which Sunday you're talking about. It's no myth that a preeminent team needs a preeminent quarterback, and these two guys were the best the NFL had to offer after the 1994 season.

At 28—the age at which many quarterbacks are just beginning a starting career—Aikman has won more Super Bowls (two) than Dan Marino, John Elway, Warren Moon, Jim Kelly and Young combined have won (one) in 56 collective seasons. Aikman's 7–1 playoff record is the best record of any playoff quarterback ever. And he's piloting a team with the talent and the playoff savvy to be a contender for the rest of the century. "From the time he came into the league," says Dallas wide receiver Michael Irvin, "I've always thought, This is the man I want to play with for the rest of my career. He's that special, that great."

What sets Aikman apart is what set Montana apart for so many years. He plays his best when it matters the most. That's a rare trait in any sport and almost always leads to greatness. In his two Super Bowl victories, both against Buffalo, Aikman completed a combined 72% of his passes. That's 10% higher than the already fine completion percentage he has earned for his career. He almost led the Cowboys to a third

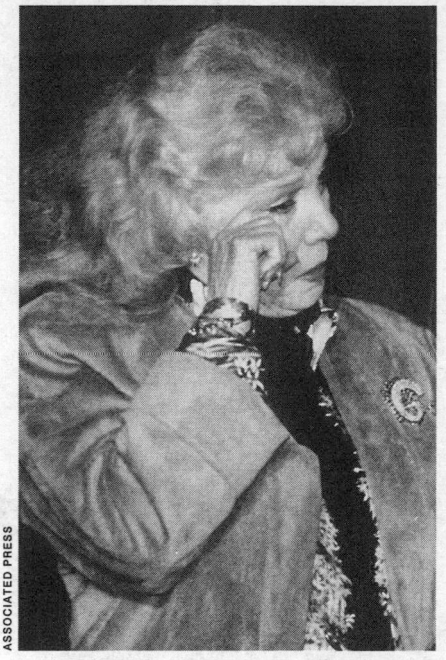

ASSOCIATED PRESS

straight Super Bowl after the 1994 season, rescuing the team from a late-year slump. When the Cowboys were stalled and misfiring entering the playoffs against Green Bay, Aikman took the brunt of the blame, and two nights before the game swore we would see the real Aikman on Sunday. "Troy Aikman ain't dead," he said pointedly. Against the Packers only two of his 30 passes were uncatchable, and the Cowboys hung on to 23 of the throws in a 35–9 rout. "You saw the real Troy Aikman out there today," said coach Barry Switzer. It *was* the real Troy Aikman out there: self-assured, determined, rifle-armed and filled with a quiet bravado.

Young's path to greatness wasn't quite as smooth. The 1994 season was his 11th as a pro. He'd bounced from the United States Football League's Los Angeles Express to the downtrodden Tampa Bay Yucs before landing as Montana's backup with the 49ers in 1987. He spent four years yo-yoing from bench to field, then won the job when Montana was hurt in 1991. And though he won passing championships in each of his four starting seasons, it was never enough … until that night in January, when he just embarrassed the Chargers. Twenty-four of his 36 passes were complete, for 325 yards, six touchdowns and one MVP trophy. "The weight of the entire world was on his shoulders," said tackle Harris Barton. "Everyone was waiting for Steve to fall apart." In the winners' locker room that night Young said, "It's great to play your best game in the biggest game of your life. I wasn't going to let all the expectations drag me down, even though it was frustrating at times. Harris Barton has come up to me before every game and rubbed my back and said, 'I'm taking the monkey off your back.' Today he said, 'I'm taking it off for the last time.' You know, for a long time I tried to pretend it wasn't there. But I guess it was." The Montana thing, he meant.

After the Super Bowl, in a Miami hotel suite provided by the club, 44 people (mostly Mormons, like Young) stayed until the wee hours. In this small two-room unit were his mom and dad, four siblings and three of their spouses, six relatives, nine BYU buddies led by Bengal punter Lee Johnson, girlfriend Stephanie Weston, 10 Mormon friends, three agents, one reporter, some other hangers-on … and soon, three members of the Metro Dade Fire Rescue 35 unit. They had to give a dehydrated Young a couple of pints of IV saline solution, right there on the bed. There he received visitors like a bedridden ambassador. "Is this great or what?" he said to no one in particular. "I mean, I haven't thrown six touchdown passes in any game in my life. Then I throw six today in the Super Bowl! Unbelievable." Someone in the crowd said, "Joe who?" "No, don't do that," Young said. "Don't worry about that. That's the past. Let's talk the future."

When Johnson walked into the room, he went to Young's side and kneeled. "Bro!" he said. "It happened! How great is that?"

Young, leaning over on one elbow, said, "I wish every player who ever played in the NFL could feel what I feel right now. It's so incredible after all I've gone through to finally be on the mountaintop looking down."

Alas, only one team and its players can be on that mountaintop. The NFL roadside was littered with news from other contenders and pretenders as 1995 went on. That news:

• Whither the Rams? In March the NFL blocked a move of the Rams from Anaheim to St. Louis, then took $40 million in a ransom-like transfer fee to allow the club to move in April. So the NFL was left with only the peripatetic Raiders in the number two market in the country. And that didn't last long. Owner Al Davis kept making noise about moving to Baltimore or to any other city that would have him, and then in June he hightailed it back to Oakland with his franchise. Just like that, the league's second-biggest market is laid to waste. For now, at least.

• Why Can't the AFC Win the Big One? San Francisco's rout of San Diego made the Super Bowl scoreboard NFC 11, AFC 0 since 1984, which is certainly one of sport's biggest continuing oddities. The NFC leads the interconference series only 290–275, with one tie, from 1984 through the 1994 season, and yet the Super Bowl has been ridiculously lopsided. Why? Try this one on for size: In the 10 Super Bowls previous to the Charger-49er game, the NFC offensive

Just Move, Baby

In the end, Al Davis took the easy way out. When the calculating Raider owner moved his team back up the California coast from Los Angeles to Oakland 10 weeks before the start of the 1995 season, it wasn't a bold, insightful or brilliant move. It was the only move that, given Davis's Quixotic nature, made sense to him.

The return to home gave Davis:

• A comfort zone. In July, when Davis held his first press conference after the move, *The Oakland Tribune* bannered this headline: WELCOME BACK, MR. DAVIS. Los Angeles was always a sort of show-me city for the Raiders—for any entity, really. The East Bay never seemed to hate the Raiders, even though the franchise had jilted one of the most supportive NFL cities in history by moving south before the 1982 season. In the month after it became apparent that Davis would move the Raiders back, 80,000 calls flooded the Coliseum switchboard looking for ticket applications. Davis and his minions can sit back now and concentrate on football, not football and marketing, which leads us to point number two.

• A reprieve from the realities of the football world. In Los Angeles, Davis would have had to go into business with the folks at Hollywood Park, where a fabulous new stadium with guarantees of hosting two future Super Bowls would have been built for him. He would have had to market his team, selling the Raiders to the business community, making big spenders spend big bucks on luxury boxes and seat-licensing fees. He would have had to win over a town that never bought into the blindly loyal, just-win-baby mentality—until playoff games or

Davis took his team back to the comfort zone of the Oakland Coliseum.

JOHN W. McDONOUGH

line outweighed the AFC defensive front seven by an average of 238 pounds. Not so coincidentally, in those 10 games the NFC teams outrushed the AFC teams by a 2-to-1 margin.

• Go, Joe, Go. After months of speculation, Joe Montana finally retired in April, hanging his Superman cape in a closet on 1,100 acres in the Napa Valley, where he hoped to become an amateur vintner. Hard to believe. Montana doesn't stay an amateur at anything for very long. The pro's pro left his mark on the game as, quite arguably, the greatest quarterback in history.

JOE TRAVER

the Cowboys came to town. Instead of spending all the time and energy to get L.A. hot for the Raiders, Davis and the Raiders went back into the womb.

• His best chance to win. "The roar of the Oakland crowd will live with me forever," Davis said. There is little doubt that the Oakland Coliseum will be worth points to the Raiders over the coming seasons. The mausoleum that is the Los Angeles Coliseum never gave the Raiders a true home field edge. In Oakland, Davis estimates the fan frenzy will mean a four- to six-point advantage per Sunday. That's almost impossible to quantify, but all the Raiders know is that they never had the fan edge in Los Angeles. "People in L.A. never understood the importance of the 12th man," said Raider defensive tackle Nolan Harrison. "You don't just show up for playoff games."

The loss of the Raiders left the league embarrassingly without a team in the second-largest TV market. On the day the city of Oakland announced that the Raiders were returning, 18 moving vans left Anaheim for St. Louis with all of the Rams' belongings. It's likely that the league will be without a team in the Los Angeles area.

through the 1996–97 season. But no one at 410 Park Avenue in Manhattan, where the league does business, was crying.

The NFL will probably help entice a struggling team (Tampa Bay, perhaps) to move to Los Angeles in the next year or two by giving a prospective owner a stadium deal he can't refuse. Then, in the next wave of expansion (probably around 1999), Los Angeles will get another team. So long, Raiders and Rams. Hello, Bucs and Llamas—or whatever the expansion team would be called.

The smart move, however, might be to make L.A. a one-team market. Harrison is right. The region doesn't deserve two teams. It barely has the spirit to support one. "What makes you think L.A.'s going to support some team that comes in from another city and isn't as good?" Harrison asked, with reason.

Those are other owners' problems. Davis, 66, did the best thing for his team and his adoptive city for now. For the first time in over a decade he has a region nutso over his team. And for the first time in years he has a legitimate home field advantage. He did take the easy way out, but for this time and this team, it was the only way out.

AL TIELEMANS

Eagle coach Rhodes (left): "the best available man for the job."

Favre of Green Bay, the NFL has no proven great quarterbacks of the future. So concerned is the league that it hired former 49er coach Bill Walsh, the quarterback guru, as its "director of quarterback development" in January 1995. Walsh worked with quarterbacks in the revitalized World League, retooled the delivery of No. 1 Carolina draft pick Kerry Collins and polished other quarterbacks before the draft. The problem is, it's a tougher position than ever, the pass rushers are faster than ever, and the schemes are more complicated than ever. The 1995 rookie crop—a pretty good one, led by Collins, Alcorn State's Steve McNair and USC's Rob Johnson—hopes to reverse the recent trend of mediocre young quarterbacks.

• Retire, Phil, Retire. One of the game's stranger stories was the saga of Phil Simms. In 1994, at 38, he spurned an offer from the Cardinals to come out of retirement in order to stay on the ESPN pro football set. In 1995, at 39, he ditched ESPN for the Cleveland Browns, agreeing to terms (but not signing) to be Vinny Testaverde's back-up for the 1995 season. Few people thought Testaverde would keep Simms on the bench for long, and with Cleveland signing receiving ace Andre Rison in free agency, the Browns looked to be a solid challenger for Super Bowl XXX. Oops. Simms decided to ditch Cleveland to return to TV—only not with ESPN but with NBC, to be a game analyst. ESPN cried foul, saying Simms owed them a second year on a verbal contract agreement. The Browns were stunned. NBC shuffled its announcing teams to find a comfy spot in big games for Simms. "I hate controversy," Simms said. Phil, in early 1995, you patented it.

• The Dearth of Young Quarterbacks. Annual story. Other than 25-and-under kids Drew Bledsoe of New England and Brett

• The Continuing Problem of Affirmative Action. Although about 60% of the league's players are African-Americans, among the league's 30 head coaches, only the Eagles' Ray Rhodes and the Vikings' Dennis Green are black, and none of the general managers or club presidents are. (Jacksonville does have a vice president of football operations, Michael Huygue, who is African-American.) And it's progressively becoming a bigger and bigger mark of shame for the league. Before Rhodes got the job, the 20 previous coaching hires in the NFL had been white. It seems ludicrous that Minnesota defensive coordinator Tony Dungy, who is black, could run the NFL's top-rated defense in 1993 and then go two straight off-seasons without getting a head coaching job. Asked about the pressure of being the only African-American hired as a coach this season, Rhodes said, "I was hired as the best available man for the job. That's what's important to me."

It should be important to the rest of the league too.

FOR THE RECORD·1994–1995

1994 NFL Final Standings

American Football Conference

EASTERN DIVISION

	W	L	T	Pct	Pts	OP
Miami	10	6	0	.625	389	327
†New England	10	6	0	.625	351	312
Indianapolis	8	8	0	.500	307	320
Buffalo	7	9	0	.438	340	356
NY Jets	6	10	0	.375	264	320

CENTRAL DIVISION

	W	L	T	Pct	Pts	OP
Pittsburgh	12	4	0	.750	316	234
†Cleveland	11	5	0	.688	340	204
Cincinnati	3	13	0	.188	276	406
Houston	2	14	0	.125	226	352

WESTERN DIVISION

	W	L	T	Pct	Pts	OP
San Diego	11	5	0	.688	381	306
†Kansas City	9	7	0	.563	319	298
LA Raiders	9	7	0	.563	303	327
Denver	7	9	0	.438	347	396
Seattle	6	10	0	.375	287	323

† Wild-card team.

National Football Conference

EASTERN DIVISION

	W	L	T	Pct	Pts	OP
Dallas	12	4	0	.750	414	248
NY Giants	9	7	0	.563	279	305
Arizona	8	8	0	.500	235	267
Philadelphia	7	9	0	.438	308	308
Washington	3	13	0	.188	320	412

CENTRAL DIVISION

	W	L	T	Pct	Pts	OP
Minnesota	10	6	0	.625	356	314
†Green Bay	9	7	0	.563	382	287
†Detroit	9	7	0	.563	357	342
†Chicago	9	7	0	.563	271	307
Tampa Bay	6	10	0	.375	251	351

WESTERN DIVISION

	W	L	T	Pct	Pts	OP
San Francisco	13	3	0	.813	505	296
New Orleans	7	9	0	.438	348	407
Atlanta	7	9	0	.438	313	389
LA Rams	4	12	0	.250	286	365

1995 NFL Playoffs

AFC FIRST ROUND — **AFC DIVISIONAL PLAYOFF** — **AFC CHAMPIONSHIP** — **NFC CHAMPIONSHIP** — **NFC DIVISIONAL PLAYOFF** — **NFC FIRST ROUND**

SUPER BOWL XXIX
January 29, 1995

Kansas City 17
Miami 27

Miami 21

San Diego 17

San Diego 22

SAN FRANCISCO 49
San Diego 26

Green Bay 9

Dallas 28

Dallas 35

Green Bay 16
Detroit 12

New England 13
Cleveland 20

Cleveland 9

Pittsburgh 13

Pittsburgh 29

Chicago 15

San Francisco 38

San Francisco 44

Chicago 35
Minnesota 18

NFL Playoff Box Scores

AFC Wild-card Games

New England..........0	10	0	3—13	
Cleveland...............3	7	7	3—20	

FIRST QUARTER

Cleveland: FG Stover 30, 7:20. Drive: 74 yards, 10 plays.

SECOND QUARTER

New England: Thompson 13 pass from Bledsoe (Bahr kick), 4:12. Drive: 60 yards, 9 plays.
Cleveland: Carrier 5 pass from Testaverde (Stover kick), 7:57. Drive: 51 yards, 7 plays.
New England: FG Bahr 23, 14:30. Drive: 71 yards, 16 plays.

THIRD QUARTER

Cleveland: Hoard 10 run (Stover kick), 12:39. Drive: 79 yards, 10 plays.

FOURTH QUARTER

Cleveland: FG Stover 21, 11:24. Drive: 33 yards, 7 plays.
New England: FG Bahr 33, 13:30. Drive: 63 yards, 14 plays.

A: 77,452; T: 2:57.

Kansas City..........14	3	0	0—17	
Miami 7	10	10	0—27	

FIRST QUARTER

Kansas City: Walker 1 pass from Montana (Elliott kick), 6:28. Drive: 80 yards, 11 plays.
Miami: Parmalee 1 run (Stoyanovich kick), 12:40. Drive: 72 yards, 10 plays.
Kansas City: Anders 57 pass from Montana (Elliott kick),14:20. Drive: 83 yards, 4 plays.

SECOND QUARTER

Miami: FG Stoyanovich 40, 2:45. Drive 35 yards, 7 plays.
Kansas City: FG Elliot 21, 8:48. Drive 69 yards, 12 plays.
Miami: R. Williams 1 pass from Marino (Stoyanovich kick), 14:38. Drive: 80 yards, 13 plays.

THIRD QUARTER

Miami: Fryar 7 pass from Marino (Stoyanovich kick), 3:02. Drive: 64 yards, 6 plays.
Miami: FG Stoyanovich 40, 13:14. Drive: 59 yards, 10 plays.

A: 67,487; T: 2:47.

NFC Wild-card Games

Detroit 0	0	3	9—12	
Green Bay 7	3	3	3—16	

FIRST QUARTER

Green Bay: Levens 3 run (Jacke kick), 7:24. Drive: 76 yards, 14 plays.

SECOND QUARTER

Green Bay: FG Jacke 51, 12:04. Drive: 37 yards, 8 plays.

THIRD QUARTER

Detroit: FG Hanson 38, 9:22. Drive: 41 yards, 5 plays.
Green Bay: FG Jacke 32, 14:49. Drive: 32 yards, 6 plays.

FOURTH QUARTER

Detroit: Perriman 3 pass from Krieg (Hanson kick), 1:25. Drive: 18 yards, 5 plays.
Green Bay: FG Jacke 28, 9:25. Drive: 40 yards, 8 plays.

A: 58,125; T: 3:07.

Chicago..................0	14	7	14—35	
Minnesota 3	6	3	6—18	

FIRST QUARTER

Minnesota: FG Reveiz 29, 6:59. Drive: minus 6 yards, 4 plays.

SECOND QUARTER

Chicago: Tillman 1 run (Butler kick), 3:14. Drive: 80 yards, 16 plays.
Chicago: Jennings 9 pass from S. Walsh (Butler kick), 6:57. Drive: 71 yards, 4 plays.
Minnesota: C. Carter 4 pass from Moon (pass failed), 14:41. Drive 47 yards, 6 plays.

THIRD QUARTER

Chicago: Ra. Harris 29 run (Butler kick), 2:03. Drive 75 yards, 4 plays
Minnesota: FG Reveiz 48, 14:55. Drive: 37 yards, 6 plays.

FOURTH QUARTER

Chicago: J. Graham 21 pass from S. Walsh (Butler kick), 2:18. Drive 60 yards, 6 plays.
Minnesota: Lee 11 pass from Moon (pass failed), 9:24. Drive: 76 yards, 16 plays.
Chicago: Miniefield 48 fumble return (Butler kick), 11:55.

A: 60,347; T: 3:14.

AFC Divisional Games

Cleveland	0	3	0	6— 9
Pittsburgh	3	21	3	2—29

Miami	7	14	0	0—21
San Diego	0	6	9	7—22

FIRST QUARTER

Pittsburgh: FG Anderson 39, 9:38. Drive: 65 yards, 13 plays.

SECOND QUARTER

Pittsburgh: Green 2 pass from O'Donnell (Anderson kick), :48. Drive 53 yards, 8 plays.
Pittsburgh: J. Williams 26 run (Anderson kick), 5:57. Drive: 74 yards, 6 plays.
Cleveland: FG Stover 22, 12:23. Drive: 25 yards, 6 plays.
Pittsburgh Thigpen 9 pass from O'Donnell (Anderson kick), 14:44. Drive: 6 yards, 3 plays.

THIRD QUARTER

Pittsburgh: FG Anderson 40, 12:25. Drive 72 yards, 14 plays.

FOURTH QUARTER

Cleveland: McCardell 20 pass from Testaverde (pass failed), 9:07. Drive: 73 yards, 3 plays.
Pittsburgh: Safety (Lake sacked Testaverde in end zone), 12:15.

A: 58, 185; T: 2:56.

FIRST QUARTER

Miami: K. Jackson 8 pass from Marino (Stoyanovich kick), 12:36. Drive 79 yards, 9 plays.

SECOND QUARTER

San Diego: FG Carney 20, 4:24. Drive 72 yards, 15 plays.
Miami: K. Jackson 9 pass from Marino (Stoyanovich kick), 7:39. Drive 52 yards, 6 plays.
San Diego: FG Carney 21, 12:13. Drive: 70 yards, 9 plays.
Miami: M. Williams 16 pass from Marino (Stoyanovich kick), 14:33. Drive: 70 yards, 9 plays.

THIRD QUARTER

San Diego: Safety (R. Davis tackled Parmalee in end zone), 8:06.
San Diego: Means 24 run (Carney kick), 12:18. Drive: 54 yards, 6 plays.

FOURTH QUARTER

San Diego: Seay 8 pass from Humphries (Carney kick), 14:25. Drive: 61 yards, 10 plays.

A: 63,381; T: 3:03.

NFC Divisional Games

Green Bay	3	6	0	0— 9
Dallas	14	14	0	7—35

Chicago	3	0	0	12—15
San Francisco	7	23	7	7—44

FIRST QUARTER

Dallas: E. Smith 5 run (Boniol kick), 3:53. Drive 51 yards, 7 plays.
Green Bay: FG Jacke 50, 7:28. Drive: 42 yards, 9 plays.
Dallas: Harper 94 pass from Aikman (Boniol kick), 11:20. Drive 94 yards, 1 play.

SECOND QUARTER

Dallas: B. Thomas 1 run (Boniol kick), 8:15. Drive 80 yards, 7 plays.
Green Bay: Bennett 1 run (pass failed), 10:29. Drive 74 yards, 6 plays.
Dallas: Galbraith 1 pass from Aikman (Boniol kick), 14:49. Drive 48 yards, 12 plays.

FOURTH QUARTER

Dallas: B. Thomas 2 run (Boniol kick), 3:32. Drive 60 yards, 9 plays.

A:64,745; T: 3:20.

FIRST QUARTER

Chicago: FG Butler 39, 3:58. Drive: 14 yards, 6 plays.
San Francisco: Floyd 2 run (Brien kick), 11:19. Drive 68 yards, 13 plays.

SECOND QUARTER

San Francisco: Jones 8 pass from S. Young (kick failed), :44. Drive: 54 yards, 6 plays.
San Francisco: Floyd 4 run (Brien kick), 8:56. Drive: 61 yards, 9 plays.
San Francisco: FG Brien 36, 12:15. Drive: 14 yards, 8 plays.
San Francisco: S. Young 6 run (Brien kick), 13:43. Drive: 32 yards, 5 plays.

THIRD QUARTER

San Francisco: Floyd 1 run (Brien kick), 8:01. Drive: 70 yards, 9 plays.

FOURTH QUARTER

Chicago: Flanigan 2 pass from Kramer (pass failed), :49. Drive: 71 yards, 10 plays.
San Francisco: Walker 1 run (Brien kick), 3:09. Drive: 37 yards, 4 plays.
Chicago: Tillman 1 run (pass failed), 9:16. Drive 70 yards, 16 plays.

A:64,644; T: 3:03.

AFC Championship

```
San Diego..............0   3   7   7—17
Pittsburgh............7   3   3   0—13
```

FIRST QUARTER

Pittsburgh: Williams 16 pass from O'Donnell (Anderson kick), 7:32. Drive 67 yards, 13 plays.

SECOND QUARTER

San Diego: FG Carney 20, 11:19. Drive 77 yards, 6 plays.
Pittsburgh: FG Anderson 39, 14:51. Drive 51 yards, 12 plays.

THIRD QUARTER

Pittsburgh: FG Anderson 23, 4:23. Drive 50 yards, 9 plays.
San Diego: Pupunu 43 pass from Humphries (Carney kick), 6:57. Drive 64 yards, 5 plays.

FOURTH QUARTER

San Diego: Martin 43 pass from Humphries (Carney kick), 9:47. Drive 80 yards, 8 plays.

A: 61,545; T: 2:54.

NFC Championship

```
Dallas....................7    7    7    7—28
San Francisco......21   10    7    0—38
```

FIRST QUARTER

San Francisco: Davis 44 int. return (Brien kick), 1:02.
San Francisco: Watters 29 pass from S. Young (Brien kick), 4:19. Drive: 39 yards, 5 plays.
San Francisco: Floyd 1 run (Brien kick), 7:27. Drive 35 yards, 7 plays.
Dallas: Irvin 44 pass from Aikman (Boniol kick), 12:46. Drive: 62 yards, 8 plays.

SECOND QUARTER

San Francisco: FG Brien 34, 9:06. Drive: 64 yards, 11 plays.
Dallas: E. Smith 4 run (Boniol kick), 3:12. Drive: 63 yards, 8 plays.
San Francisco: Rice 28 pass from S. Young (Brien kick), 14:52. Drive: 39 yards, 3 plays.

THIRD QUARTER

Dallas: E. Smith 1 run (Boniol kick), 3:12. Drive: 25 yards, 7 plays.
San Francisco: S. Young 3 run (Brien kick), 8:21. Drive 70 yards, 10 plays.

FOURTH QUARTER

Dallas: Irvin 10 pass from Aikman (Boniol kick), 6:31. Drive: 89 yards, 14 plays.

A: 69,125; T: 3:26.

Super Bowl Box Score

```
San Diego..............7    3    8    8—26
San Francisco......14   14   14   7—49
```

FIRST QUARTER

San Francisco: Rice 44 pass from Young (Brien kick), 1:24. Drive: 3 plays, 59 yards. Key play: SD Miller 15-yard face mask penalty on opening kickoff. San Francisco 7-0.
San Francisco: Watters 51 pass from Young (Brien kick), 4:55. Drive: 4 plays, 79 yards. Key play: Young 21-yard run on 3rd-and-3 to SF 49. San Francisco 14-0.
San Diego: Means 1 run (Carney kick), 12:16. Drive: 13 plays, 78 yards. Key plays: Humphries 17-yard pass to Harmon on 3rd-and-4 to SF 43; Harmon 10-yard run on 3rd-and-1 to SF 24; Pass interference on Sanders in end zone gives SD a 1st-and-goal at the 1. San Francisco 14-7.

SECOND QUARTER

San Francisco: Floyd 5 pass from Young (Brien kick), 1:58. Drive: 9 plays, 69 yards. Key plays: Young 19-yard pass to Rice to SF 49; Young 15-yard run to SD 15; San Francisco 21-7.
San Francisco: Watters 8 pass from Young (Brien kick), 1:58. Drive: 9 plays, 69 yards. Key plays: Young 19-yard pass to Rice to SF 49; Young 15-yard run to SD 15. San Francisco 21-7.
San Francisco: Watters 8 pass from Young (Brien kick), 10:16. Drive: 9 plays, 49 yards. Key plays: Young 11-yard pass to Rice to SD 27; Young 8-yard pass to Rice to SD 15. San Francisco 28-7.

San Diego: FG Carney 31, 13:16. Drive: 8 plays, 62 yards. Key plays: Humphries 17-yard pass to Seay to SD 44; Jefferson 10-yard run on reverse to SF 46; Humphries 33-yard pass to Bieniemy to SF 13. San Francisco 28-10.

THIRD QUARTER

San Francisco: Watters 9 run (Brien kick), 5:25. Drive: 7 plays, 62 yards. Key plays: Young 21-yard pass to Rice on 3rd-and-17 to SD 32; Young 16-yard pass to Taylor to San Diego 16. San Francisco 35-10.
San Francisco: Rice 15 pass from Young (Brien kick), 11:42. Drive 10 plays, 67 yards. Key plays: 22-yard pass interference on Gordon on 3rd-and-14 to SD 38; Young 13-yard run to SD 12. San Francisco 42-10.
San Diego: Coleman 98 kickoff return (Humphries pass to Seay), 11:59. San Francisco 42-18.

FOURTH QUARTER

San Francisco: Rice 7 pass from Young (Brien kick), 1:11. Drive: 6 plays, 32 yards. Key plays: Watters 13-yard run on 3rd-and-2 to San Diego 11. San Francisco 49-18.
San Diego: Martin 30 pass from Humphries (Humphries pass to Pupunu), 12:35. Drive: 8 plays, 67 yards. Key plays: Humphries 12-yard pass to Martin to SF 43; Humphries 22-yard pass to Seay to SF 30. San Francisco 49-26.

A: 74,107; T: 3:36.

Team Statistics

	S.D.	S.F.
FIRST DOWNS	20	28
Rushing	5	10
Passing	14	17
Penalty	1	1
THIRD DOWN EFF	6-16	7-13
FOURTH DOWN EFF	0-4	0-0
TOTAL NET YARDS	354	449
Total plays	76	73
Avg gain	4.7	6.2
NET YARDS RUSHING	67	133
Rushes	19	32
Avg per rush	3.5	4.2
NET YARDS PASSING	287	316
Completed-Att.	27-55	25-38
Yards per pass	5.0	7.7
Sacked-yards lost	2-18	3-15
Had intercepted	3	0
PUNTS-Avg	4-48.8	5-39.8
TOTAL RETURN YARDS	243	76
Punt returns	3-1	2-12
Kickoff returns	8-242	4-48
Interceptions	0-0	3-16
PENALTIES-Yds	6-63	3-18
FUMBLES-Lost	1-0	2-0
TIME OF POSSESSION	28:29	31:31

Passing

SAN DIEGO

	Comp	Att	Yds	Int	TD
Humphries	24	49	275	2	0
Gilbert	3	6	30	1	0

SAN FRANCISCO

	Comp	Att	Yds	Int	TD
S. Young	24	36	325	0	6

Rushing

SAN DIEGO

	No.	Yds	Lg	TD
Means	13	33	11	1
Harmon	2	10	10	0
Jefferson	1	10	10	0
Gilbert	1	8	8	0
Bieniemy	1	3	3	0
Humphries	1	3	3	0

SAN FRANCISCO

	No.	Yds	Lg	TD
S. Young	5	49	21	0
Watters	15	47	13	1
Floyd	9	32	6	0
Rice	1	10	10	0
Carter	2	-5	1	0

Receiving

SAN DIEGO

	No.	Yds	Lg	TD
Harmon	8	68	20	0
Seay	7	75	22	0
Pupunu	4	48	23	0
Martin	3	59	30	1
Jefferson	2	15	9	0
Bieniemy	1	33	33	0
Means	1	4	4	0
D. Young	1	3	3	0

SAN FRANCISCO

	No.	Yds	Lg	TD
Rice	10	149	44	3
J. Taylor	4	43	16	0
Floyd	4	26	9	1
Watters	3	61	51	2
Jones	2	41	33	0
Popson	1	6	6	0
McCaffrey	1	5	5	0

Defense

SAN DIEGO

	Tck	Ast	Int	Sack
Gibson	9	2	0	0
J. Seau	9	2	0	1
Gordon	5	0	0	0
Mims	5	0	0	0
Griggs	3	2	0	0
Carrington	4	0	0	0
D. Harper	3	0	0	0
Johnson	2	0	0	2
Lee	2	0	0	0
Richard	1	1	0	0
Clark	1	0	0	0
R. Davis	1	0	0	0
O'Neal	1	0	0	0
Vanhorse	1	0	0	0

SAN FRANCISCO

	Tck	Ast	Int	Sack
McDonald	8	1	0	0
Norton	5	2	0	0
Davis	6	0	1	0
Drakeford	4	0	0	0
D. Brown	3	1	0	.5
Plummer	2	2	0	0
Sanders	2	2	1	0
Young	3	0	0	0
Cook	2	1	1	0
Jackson	2	0	0	0
Stubblefield	2	0	0	1
D. Hall	1	1	0	0
Hanks	1	1	0	0
Harris	1	1	0	.5
Mann	1	0	0	0
Woodall	0	1	0	0

OFFENSE

Jerry Rice, San Francisco	Wide Receiver
Cris Carter, Minnesota	Wide Receiver
Ben Coates, New England	Tight End
William Roaf, New Orleans	Tackle
Richmond Webb, Miami	Tackle
Nate Newton, Dallas	Guard
Randall McDaniel, Minnesota	Guard
Dermontti Dawson, Pittsburgh	Center
Steve Young, San Francisco	Quarterback
Barry Sanders, Detroit	Running Back
Emmitt Smith, Dallas	Running Back

DEFENSE

Charles Haley, Dallas	Defensive End
Bruce Smith, Buffalo	Defensive End
Cortez Kennedy, Seattle	Defensive Tackle
John Randle, Minnesota	Nose Tackle
Greg Lloyd, Pittsburgh	Outside Linebacker
Kevin Greene, Pittsburgh	Outside Linebacker
Junior Seau, San Diego	Inside Linebacker
Rod Woodson, Pittsburgh	Cornerback
Deion Sanders, San Francisco	Cornerback
Eric Turner, Cleveland	Safety
Darren Woodson, Dallas	Safety

SPECIALISTS

John Carney, San Diego	Kicker
Reggie Roby, Washington	Punter
Mel Gray, Detroit	Kick Returner

1994 AFC Team-by-Team Results

BUFFALO BILLS (7-9)			CINCINNATI BENGALS (3-13)			CLEVELAND BROWNS (11-5)		
3	N.Y. JETS	23	20	CLEVELAND	28	28	at Cincinnati	20
38	at New England	35	10	at San Diego	27	10	PITTSBURGH	17
15	at Houston	7	28	NEW ENGLAND	31	32	ARIZONA	0
27	DENVER	20	13	at Houston	20	21	at Indianapolis	14
13	at Chicago	20	7	MIAMI	23	27	N.Y. JETS	7
21	MIAMI	11		OPEN DATE			OPEN DATE	
17	INDIANAPOLIS	27	10	at Pittsburgh	14	11	at Houston	8
	OPEN DATE		13	at Cleveland	37	37	CINCINNATI	13
44	KANSAS CITY	10	20	DALLAS	23	14	at Denver	26
17	at N.Y. Jets	22	20	at Seattle	17	13	NEW ENGLAND	6
10	at Pittsburgh	23	34	HOUSTON	31	26	at Philadelphia	7
29	GREEN BAY	20	13	INDIANAPOLIS	17	13	at Kansas City	20
21	at Detroit	35	13	at Denver	15	34	HOUSTON	10
42	at Miami	31	15	PITTSBURGH	38	13	N.Y. GIANTS	16
17	MINNESOTA	21	20	at N.Y. Giants	27	19	at Dallas	14
17	NEW ENGLAND	41	7	at Arizona	28	7	at Pittsburgh	17
9	at Indianapolis	10	33	PHILADELPHIA	30	35	SEATTLE	9
329		242	276		406	340		204

DENVER BRONCOS (7-9)

34	SAN DIEGO	37
22	at N.Y. Jets	25
16	L.A. RAIDERS	48
20	at Buffalo	27
	OPEN DATE	
16	at Seattle	9
28	KANSAS CITY	31
20	at San Diego	15
26	CLEVELAND	14
21	at L.A. Rams	27
17	SEATTLE	10
32	ATLANTA	28
15	CINCINNATI	13
20	at Kansas City	17(OT)
13	at L.A. Raiders	23
19	at San Francisco	42
28	NEW ORLEANS	30
347		396

HOUSTON OILERS (2-14)

21	at Indianapolis	45
17	at Dallas	20
7	BUFFALO	15
20	CINCINNATI	13
14	at Pittsburgh	30
	OPEN DATE	
8	CLEVELAND	11
6	at Philadelphia	21
14	at L.A. Raiders	17
9	PITTSBURGH	12
31	at Cincinnati	34
10	N.Y. GIANTS	13
10	at Cleveland	34
12	ARIZONA	30
14	SEATTLE	16
9	at Kansas City	31
24	N.Y. JETS	10
226		352

INDIANAPOLIS COLTS (8-8)

45	HOUSTON	21
10	at Tampa Bay	24
21	at Pittsburgh	31
14	CLEVELAND	21
17	SEATTLE	15
6	at N.Y. Jets	16
27	at Buffalo	17
27	WASHINGTON	41
28	N.Y. JETS	25
21	at Miami	22
	OPEN DATE	
17	at Cincinnati	13
10	NEW ENGLAND	12
31	at Seattle	19
13	at New England	28
10	MIAMI	6
10	BUFFALO	9
307		320

KANSAS CITY CHIEFS (9-7)

30	at New Orleans	17
24	SAN FRANCISCO	17
30	at Atlanta	10
0	L.A. RAMS	16
	OPEN DATE	
6	at San Diego	20
31	at Denver	28
38	SEATTLE	23
10	at Buffalo	44
13	L.A. RAIDERS	3
13	SAN DIEGO	14
20	CLEVELAND	13
9	at Seattle	10
17	DENVER	20(OT)
28	at Miami	45
31	HOUSTON	9
19	at L.A. Raiders	9
319		298

LOS ANGELES RAIDERS (9-7)

14	at San Francisco	44
9	SEATTLE	38
48	at Denver	16
24	SAN DIEGO	26
	OPEN DATE	
21	at New England	17
17	at Miami	20(OT)
30	ATLANTA	17
17	HOUSTON	14
3	at Kansas City	13
20	at L.A. Rams	17
24	NEW ORLEANS	19
3	PITTSBURGH	21
24	at San Diego	17
23	DENVER	13
17	at Seattle	16
9	KANSAS CITY	19
306		326

MIAMI DOLPHINS (10-6)

39	New England	35
24	vs. Green Bay	14
28	N.Y. JETS	14
35	at Minnesota	38
23	at Cincinnati	7
11	at Buffalo	21
20	L.A. RAIDERS	17(OT)
	OPEN DATE	
23	at New England	3
22	INDIANAPOLIS	21
14	CHICAGO	17
13	at Pittsburgh	16(OT)
28	at N.Y. Jets	24
31	BUFFALO	42
45	KANSAS CITY	28
6	at Indianapolis	10
27	DETROIT	20
389		327

NEW ENGLAND PATRIOTS (10-6)

35	at Miami	39
35	BUFFALO	38
31	at Cincinnati	28
23	at Detroit	17
17	GREEN BAY	16
17	L.A. RAIDERS	21
17	at N.Y. Jets	24
	OPEN DATE	
3	MIAMI	23
6	at Cleveland	13
26	MINNESOTA	20
23	SAN DIEGO	17
12	at Indianapolis	10
24	N.Y. JETS	13
28	INDIANAPOLIS	13
41	at Buffalo	17
13	at Chicago	3
351		312

NEW YORK JETS (6-10)

23	at Buffalo	3
25	DENVER	22
14	at Miami	28
7	CHICAGO	19
7	at Cleveland	27
16	INDIANAPOLIS	6
24	NEW ENGLAND	17
	OPEN DATE	
25	at Indianapolis	28
22	BUFFALO	17
10	at Green Bay	17
31	at Minnesota	21
24	MIAMI	28
24	at New England	24
7	DETROIT	18
6	SAN DIEGO	21
10	at Houston	24
264		320

PITTSBURGH STEELERS (12-4)

9	DALLAS	26
17	at Cleveland	10
31	INDIANAPOLIS	21
13	at Seattle	30
30	HOUSTON	14
	OPEN DATE	
14	CINCINNATI	10
10	at N.Y. Giants	6
17	at Arizona	20
12	at Houston	9
23	BUFFALO	10
16	MIAMI	13(OT)
21	at L.A. Raiders	3
38	at Cincinnati	15
14	PHILADELPHIA	3
17	CLEVELAND	7
34	at San Diego	37
316		234

SAN DIEGO CHARGERS (11-5)

37	at Denver	34
27	CINCINNATI	10
24	at Seattle	10
26	at L.A. Raiders	24
	OPEN DATE	
20	KANSAS CITY	6
36	at New Orleans	22
15	DENVER	20
35	SEATTLE	15
9	at Atlanta	10
14	at Kansas City	13
17	at New England	23
31	L.A. RAMS	17
17	L.A. RAIDERS	24
15	SAN FRANCISCO	38
21	at N.Y. Jets	6
37	PITTSBURGH	34
381		306

SEATTLE SEAHAWKS (6-10)

28	at Washington	7
38	at L.A. Raiders	9
10	SAN DIEGO	24
30	PITTSBURGH	13
15	at Indianapolis	17
9	DENVER	16
	OPEN DATE	
23	at Kansas City	38
15	at San Diego	35
17	CINCINNATI	20
10	at Denver	17
22	TAMPA BAY	21
10	KANSAS CITY	9
19	INDIANAPOLIS	31
16	at Houston	14
16	L.A. RAIDERS	17
9	at Cleveland	35
287		323

1994 NFC Team-by-Team Results

ARIZONA (8-8)

12	at L.A. Rams	14
17	N.Y. GIANTS	20
0	at Cleveland	32
	OPEN DATE	
17	MINNESOTA	7
3	at Dallas	38
19	at Washington	16(OT)
21	DALLAS	28
20	PITTSBURGH	17(OT)
7	at Philadelphia	17
10	at N.Y. Giants	9
12	PHILADELPHIA	6
16	CHICAGO	19(OT)
30	at Houston	12
17	WASHINGTON	15
28	CINCINNATI	7
6	at Atlanta	10
235		267

ATLANTA FALCONS (7-9)

28	at Detroit	31
31	L.A. RAMS	13
10	KANSAS CITY	30
27	at Washington	20
8	at L.A. Rams	5
34	TAMPA BAY	13
3	SAN FRANCISCO	42
17	at L.A. Raiders	30
	OPEN DATE	
10	SAN DIEGO	9
32	at New Orleans	33
28	at Denver	32
28	PHILADELPHIA	21
14	at San Francisco	50
20	NEW ORLEANS	29
17	vs. Green Bay	21
10	ARIZONA	6
313		389

CHICAGO BEARS (9-7)

21	TAMPA BAY	9
22	at Philadelphia	30
14	MINNESOTA	42
19	N.Y. JETS	7
20	BUFFALO	13
17	NEW ORLEANS	7
	OPEN DATE	
16	at Detroit	21
6	GREEN BAY	33
20	at Tampa Bay	6
17	at Miami	14
20	DETROIT	10
19	at Arizona	16(OT)
27	at Minnesota	33(OT)
3	at Green Bay	40
27	L.A. RAMS	13
3	NEW ENGLAND	13
271		307

DALLAS COWBOYS (12-4)

26	at Pittsburgh	9
20	HOUSTON	17
17	DETROIT	20
	OPEN DATE	
34	at Washington	7
38	ARIZONA	3
24	PHILADELPHIA	13
28	at Arizona	21
23	at Cincinnati	20
38	N.Y. GIANTS	10
14	at San Francisco	21
31	WASHINGTON	7
42	GREEN BAY	31
31	at Philadelphia	19
14	CLEVELAND	19
24	at New Orleans	16
10	at N.Y. Giants	15
414		248

DETROIT LIONS (9-7)

31	ATLANTA	28
3	at Minnesota	10
20	at Dallas	17
17	NEW ENGLAND	23
14	at Tampa Bay	24
21	SAN FRANCISCO	27
	OPEN DATE	
21	CHICAGO	16
28	at N.Y. Giants	25
30	vs. Green Bay	38
14	TAMPA BAY	9
10	at Chicago	20
35	BUFFALO	21
34	GREEN BAY	31
18	at N.Y. Jets	17
41	MINNESOTA	19
20	at Miami	27
357		342

GREEN BAY PACKERS (9-7)

16	MINNESOTA	10
14	MIAMI	24
7	at Philadelphia	13
30	TAMPA BAY	3
16	at New England	17
24	L.A. RAMS	17
	OPEN DATE	
10	at Minnesota	13(OT)
38	at Chicago	6
33	DETROIT	30
17	N.Y. JETS	10
20	at Buffalo	29
31	at Dallas	42
31	at Detroit	34
40	CHICAGO	3
21	ATLANTA	17
34	at Tampa Bay	19
382		287

LOS ANGELES RAMS (4-12)

14	ARIZONA	12
13	at Atlanta	31
19	SAN FRANCISCO	34
16	at Kansas City	0
5	ATLANTA	8
17	at Green Bay	24
17	N.Y. GIANTS	10
34	at New Orleans	37
	OPEN DATE	
27	DENVER	21
17	L.A. RAIDERS	20
27	at San Francisco	31
17	at San Diego	31
15	NEW ORLEANS	31
14	at Tampa Bay	24
13	at Chicago	27
21	WASHINGTON	24
286		**365**

MINNESOTA VIKINGS (10-6)

10	at Green Bay	16
10	DETROIT	3
42	at Chicago	14
38	MIAMI	35
7	at Arizona	17
27	at N.Y. Giants	10
	OPEN DATE	
13	GREEN BAY	10(OT)
36	at Tampa Bay	13
21	NEW ORLEANS	20
20	at New England	26
21	N.Y. JETS	31
17	TAMPA BAY	20
33	CHICAGO	27(OT)
21	at Buffalo	17
19	at Detroit	41
21	SAN FRANCISCO	14
356		**314**

NEW ORLEANS SAINTS (7-9)

17	KANSAS CITY	30
24	WASHINGTON	38
9	at Tampa Bay	7
13	at San Francisco	24
27	N.Y. GIANTS	22
7	at Chicago	17
22	SAN DIEGO	36
37	L.A. RAMS	34
	OPEN DATE	
20	at Minnesota	21
33	ATLANTA	32
19	at L.A. Raiders	24
14	SAN FRANCISCO	35
31	at L.A. Rams	15
29	at Atlanta	20
16	DALLAS	24
30	at Denver	28
348		**407**

NEW YORK GIANTS (9-7)

28	PHILADELPHIA	23
20	at Arizona	17
31	WASHINGTON	23
	OPEN DATE	
22	at New Orleans	27
10	MINNESOTA	27
10	at L.A. Rams	17
6	PITTSBURGH	10
25	DETROIT	28
10	at Dallas	38
9	ARIZONA	10
13	at Houston	10
21	at Washington	19
16	at Cleveland	13
27	CINCINNATI	20
16	at Philadelphia	13
15	DALLAS	10
279		**305**

PHILADELPHIA EAGLES (7-9)

23	at N.Y. Giants	28
30	CHICAGO	22
13	GREEN BAY	7
	OPEN DATE	
40	at San Francisco	8
21	WASHINGTON	17
13	at Dallas	24
21	HOUSTON	6
31	at Washington	29
17	ARIZONA	7
7	CLEVELAND	26
6	at Arizona	12
21	at Atlanta	28
19	DALLAS	31
3	at Pittsburgh	14
13	N.Y. GIANTS	16
30	at Cincinnati	33
308		**308**

SAN FRANCISCO 49ERS (13-3)

44	L.A. RAIDERS	14
17	at Kansas City	24
34	at L.A. Rams	19
24	NEW ORLEANS	13
8	PHILADELPHIA	40
27	at Detroit	21
42	at Atlanta	3
41	TAMPA BAY	16
	OPEN DATE	
37	at Washington	22
21	DALLAS	14
31	L.A. RAMS	27
35	at New Orleans	14
50	ATLANTA	14
3	at San Diego	15
42	DENVER	19
14	at Minnesota	21
505		**296**

TAMPA BAY BUCCANEERS (6-10)

9	at Chicago	21
24	INDIANAPOLIS	10
7	NEW ORLEANS	9
3	at Green Bay	30
24	DETROIT	14
13	at Atlanta	34
	OPEN DATE	
16	at San Francisco	41
13	MINNESOTA	36
6	CHICAGO	20
9	at Detroit	14
21	at Seattle	22
20	at Minnesota	17(OT)
26	WASHINGTON	21
24	L.A. RAMS	14
17	at Washington	14
19	GREEN BAY	34
382		**287**

WASHINGTON REDSKINS (3-13)

7	SEATTLE	28
38	at New Orleans	24
23	at N.Y. Giants	31
20	ATLANTA	27
7	DALLAS	34
17	at Philadelphia	21
16	ARIZONA	19(OT)
41	at Indianapolis	27
29	PHILADELPHIA	31
22	SAN FRANCISCO	37
	OPEN DATE	
7	at Dallas	31
19	N.Y. GIANTS	21
21	at Tampa Bay	26
15	at Arizona	17
14	TAMPA BAY	17
24	at L.A. Rams	21
320		**412**

American Football Conference
Scoring

TOUCHDOWNS	TD	Rush	Rec	Ret	Pts	KICKING	PAT	FG	Lg	Pts
Faulk, Ind	12	11	1	0	72	Carney, SD	33/33	34/38	50	135
Means, SD	12	12	0	0	72	Elam, Den	29/29	30/37	54	119
C. Warren, Sea	11	9	2	0	68	Bahr, NE	36/36	27/34	48	117
Pickens, Cin	11	0	11	0	66	Christie, Buf	38/38	24/28	52	110
Brown, Rai	9	0	9	0	54	Stover, Cle	32/32	26/28	45	110
Hoard, Cle	9	5	4	0	54	Pelfrey, Cin	24/25	28/33	54	108
L. Russell, Den	9	9	0	0	54	Stoyanovich, Mia	35/35	24/31	50	107
T. Thomas, Buf	9	7	2	0	54	Elliott, KC	30/30	25/30	49	105
Butts, NE	8	8	0	0	48	Anderson, Pitt	32/32	24/29	50	104
Reed, Buf	8	0	8	0	48	Jaeger, Rai	31/31	22/28	51	97

Passing

	Att	Comp	Pct Comp	Yds	Avg Gain	TD	Pct TD	Int	Pct Int	Lg	Rating Pts
Marino, Mia	615	385	62.6	4453	7.24	30	4.9	17	2.8	t64	89.2
Elway, Den	494	307	62.1	3490	7.06	16	3.2	10	2.0	63	85.7
Kelly, Buf	448	285	63.6	3114	6.95	22	4.9	17	3.8	t83	84.6
Montana, KC	493	299	60.6	3283	6.66	16	3.2	9	1.8	t57	83.6
Humphries, SD	453	264	58.3	3209	7.08	17	3.8	12	2.6	t99	81.6
Hostetler, Rai	454	263	57.9	3334	7.34	20	4.4	16	3.5	t77	81.0
O'Donnell, Pitt	370	212	57.3	2443	6.60	13	3.5	9	2.4	t60	78.9
Esiason, NYJ	440	255	58.0	2782	6.32	17	3.9	13	3.0	69	77.3
Blake, Cin	306	156	51.0	2154	7.04	14	4.6	9	2.9	76	76.9
Bledsoe, NE	691	400	57.9	4555	6.59	25	3.6	27	3.9	t62	73.6

Pass Receiving

RECEPTIONS	No.	Yds	Avg	Lg	TD	YARDS	Yds	No.	Avg	Lg	TD
Coates, NE	96	1174	12.2	t62	7	Brown, Rai	1309	89	14.7	t77	9
Reed, Buf	90	1303	14.5	t83	8	Reed, Buf	1303	90	14.5	t83	8
Brown, Rai	89	1309	14.7	t77	9	Fryar, Mia	1270	73	17.4	t54	7
Sharpe, Den	87	1010	11.6	44	4	Coates, NE	1174	96	12.2	t62	7
Blades, Sea	81	1086	13.4	45	4	Pickens, Cin	1127	71	15.9	t70	11
Moore, NYJ	78	1010	12.9	t41	6	Miller, Den	1107	60	18.5	76	5
Milburn, Den	77	549	7.1	33	3	Blades, Sea	1086	81	13.4	45	4
Timpson, NE	74	941	12.7	37	3	Moore, NYJ	1010	78	12.9	t41	6
Fryar, Mia	73	1270	17.4	t54	7	Sharpe, Den	1010	87	11.6	44	4
Pickens, Cin	71	1127	15.9	t70	11	Timpson, NE	941	74	12.7	37	3

Rushing

	Att	Yds	Avg	Lg	TD
C. Warren, Sea	333	1545	4.6	41	9
Means, SD	343	1350	3.9	25	12
Faulk, Ind	314	1282	4.1	52	11
T. Thomas, Buf	287	1093	3.8	29	7
H. Williams, Rai	282	983	3.5	28	4
J. Johnson, NYJ	240	931	3.9	90	3
Hoard, Cle	209	890	4.3	39	5
Parmalee, Mia	216	868	4.0	t47	6
Foster, Pitt	216	851	3.9	t29	5
Morris, Pitt	198	836	4.2	20	7

Total Yards from Scrimmage

	Total	Rush	Rec
C. Warren, Sea	1868	1545	323
Faulk, Ind	1804	1282	522
Means, SD	1585	1350	235
T. Thomas, Buf	1442	1093	349
Reed, Buf	1390	87	1303
H. Williams, Rai	1374	983	391
Hoard, Cle	1335	890	445
Brown, Rai	1309	0	1309
Fryar, Mia	1270	0	1270
J. Johnson, NYJ	1234	931	303

Interceptions

	No.	Yds	Lg	TD
Turner, Cle	9	199	t93	1
Buchanan, Ind	8	221	t90	3
McDaniel, Rai	7	103	35	2
Hurst, NE	7	68	24	0
Perry, Pitt	7	112	42	0

Four tied with 5

Sacks

Greene, Pitt	14.0
O'Neal, SD	12.5
N. Smith, KC	11.5
Mims, SD	11.0
Thomas, KC	11.0
B. Smith, Buf	10.0
Burnett, Cle	10.0
Lloyd, Pitt	10.0

American Football Conference (*Cont.*)

Punting

	No.	Yds	Avg	Net Avg	TB	In 20	Lg	Blk	Ret	Ret Yds
Gossett, Rai	77	3377	43.9	35.2	15	19	65	0	38	366
L. Johnson, Cin	79	3461	43.8	35.3	9	19	64	1	43	459
Rouen, Den	76	3258	42.9	37.1	8	23	59	0	39	275
Tuten, Sea	91	3905	42.9	36.7	7	23	64	0	43	426
Camarillo, Hou	96	4115	42.9	36.4	9	34	58	0	50	438

Punt Returns

	No.	Yds	Avg	Lg	TD
Gordon, SD	36	475	13.2	t90	2
Brown, Rai	40	487	12.2	48	0
Sawyer, Cin	26	307	11.8	t82	1
Burris, Buff	32	332	10.4	57	0
Metcalf, Cle	35	348	9.9	t92	2

Kickoff Returns

	No.	Yds	Avg	Lg	TD
Baldwin, Cle	28	753	26.9	t85	1
Coleman, SD	49	1293	26.4	t90	2
By'Not'e, Den	24	545	22.7	41	0
Dickerson, KC	21	472	22.5	62	0
Humphrey, Ind	35	783	22.4	t95	1

National Football Conference

Scoring

TOUCHDOWNS	TD	Rush	Rec	Ret	Pts
E. Smith, Dall	22	21	1	0	132
Sharpe, GB	18	0	18	0	108
Rice, SF	15	2	13	0	92
Mathis, Atl	11	0	11	0	70
H. Moore, Det	11	0	11	0	66
Watters, SF	11	6	5	0	66
Jones, SF	9	0	9	0	56
Bennett, GB	9	5	4	0	54
Allen, Minn	8	8	0	0	50
Rison, Atl	8	0	8	0	50

KICKING	PAT	FG	Lg	Pts
Reveiz, Minn	30/30	34/39	51	132
Andersen, NO	32/32	28/29	48	116
Boniol, Dall	48/48	22/29	47	114
Brien, SF	60/62	15/20	48	105
Jacke, GB	41/43	19/26	50	98
Murray, Phil	33/33	21/25	42	96
N. Johnson, Atl	32/32	21/25	50	95
Hanson, Det	39/40	18/27	49	93
Lohmiller, Wash	30/32	20/28	54	90
Husted, TB	20/20	23/35	53	89

Passing

	Att	Comp	Pct Comp	Yds	Avg Gain	TD	Pct TD	Int	Pct Int	Lg	Rating Pts
S. Young, SF	461	324	70.3	3969	8.61	35	7.6	10	2.2	t69	112.8
Favre, GB	582	363	62.4	3882	6.67	33	5.7	14	2.4	49	90.7
Everett, NO	540	346	64.1	3855	7.14	22	4.1	18	3.3	t78	84.9
Aikman, Dall	361	233	64.5	2676	7.41	13	3.6	12	3.3	90	84.9
J. George, Atl	524	322	61.5	3734	7.13	23	4.4	18	3.4	t85	83.3
Erickson, TB	399	225	56.4	2919	7.32	16	4.0	10	2.5	t71	82.5
Moon, Minn	601	371	61.7	4264	7.09	18	3.0	19	3.2	t65	79.9
Walsh, Chi	343	208	60.6	2078	6.06	10	2.9	8	2.3	50	77.9
Cunningham, Phil	490	265	54.1	3229	6.59	16	3.3	13	2.7	93	74.4
Miller, Rams	317	173	54.6	2104	6.64	16	5.0	14	4.4	54	73.6

Pass Receiving

RECEPTIONS	No.	Yds	Avg	Lg	TD
Carter, Minn	122	1256	10.3	t65	7
Rice, SF	112	1499	13.4	t69	13
Mathis, Atl	111	1342	12.1	81	11
Sharpe, GB	94	1119	11.9	49	18
Reed, Minn	85	1175	13.8	59	4
Early, NO	82	894	10.9	33	4
Rison, Atl	81	1088	13.4	t69	8
Irvin, Dall	79	1241	15.7	t65	6
Barnett, Phil	78	1127	14.4	54	5
Bennett, GB	78	546	7.0	40	4

YARDS	Yds	No.	Avg	Lg	TD
Rice, SF	1499	112	13.4	t69	13
Ellard, Wash	1397	74	18.9	t73	6
Mathis, Atl	1342	111	12.1	81	11
Carter, Minn	1256	122	10.3	t65	7
Irvin, Dall	1241	79	15.7	t65	6
Reed, Minn	1175	85	13.8	59	4
H. Moore, Det	1173	72	16.3	t51	11
Barnett, Phil	1127	78	14.4	54	5
Sharpe, GB	1119	94	11.9	49	18
Rison, Atl	1088	81	13.4	t69	8

National Football Conference *(Cont.)*

Rushing

	Att	Yds	Avg	Lg	TD
Sanders, Det	331	1883	5.7	85	7
E. Smith, Dall	368	1484	4.0	46	21
Hampton, NYG	327	1075	3.3	t27	6
Allen, Minn	255	1031	4.0	45	8
Bettis, Rams	319	1025	3.2	19	3
Rhett, TB	284	1011	3.6	27	7
Tillman, Chi	275	899	3.3	t25	7
Watters, SF	239	877	3.7	23	6
R. Moore, Ariz	232	780	3.4	24	4
Heyward, Atl	183	779	4.3	17	7

Total Yards from Scrimmage

	Total	Rush	Rec
Sanders, Det	2166	1883	283
E. Smith, Dall	1825	1484	341
Watters, SF	1596	877	719
Rice, SF	1592	93	1499
Ellard, Wash	1392	-5	1397
Mathis, Atl	1342	0	1342
Bettis, Rams	1318	1025	293
Carter, Minn	1256	0	1256
Irvin, Dall	1241	0	1241
Allen, Minn	1179	1031	148

Interceptions

	No.	Yds	Lg	TD
A. Williams, Ariz	9	89	43	0
Hanks, SF	7	93	38	0
Sanders, SF	6	303	t93	3
G. Jackson, Phil	6	86	t55	1

Six tied with 5

Sacks

Harvey, Wash	13.5
Randle, Minn	13.5
Haley, Dall	12.5
C. Smith, Atl	11.0
Conner, NO	10.5
Jones, GB	10.5
Fuller, Phil	10.5
Martin, NO	10.0

Punting

	No.	Yds	Avg	Net Avg	TB	In 20	Lg	Blk	Ret	Ret Yds
Landeta, Rams	78	3494	44.8	34.3	9	23	62	0	47	637
Roby, Wash	82	3639	44.4	36.1	12	21	65	0	45	441
Montgomery, Det	63	2782	44.2	34.2	8	19	64	1	36	431
Barnhardt, NO	67	2920	43.6	33.5	9	14	57	0	40	495
Saxon, Minn	77	3301	42.9	36.2	5	28	67	0	44	410

Punt Returns

	No.	Yds	Avg	Lg	TD
Mitchell, Wash	32	452	14.1	t78	2
Meggett, NYG	26	323	12.4	t68	2
Gray, Det	21	233	11.1	24	0
Turner, TB	21	218	10.4	t80	1
Sydner, Phil	40	381	9.5	49	0

Kickoff Returns

	No.	Yds	Avg	Lg	TD
Gray, Det	45	1276	28.4	t102	3
Walker, Phil	21	581	27.7	t94	1
K. Williams, Dall	43	1148	26.7	t87	1
Mitchell, Wash	58	1478	25.5	86	0
Lewis, Chi	35	874	25.0	55	0

Preseason Sack

The comments that Denver Bronco quarterback John Elway made before his team's final preseason game against the Arizona Cardinals last August—"I could care less.... This game means absolutely nothing, just like this whole preseason"—sting the ears of fans who shell out as much as 45 bucks to sit in the stands for these games. Still, Elway was voicing an opinion that was heard more and more around the league in past weeks.

The notion that four or five preseason games are necessary to prepare a team for the season is absurd. Further, it's a pity that fans pay top dollar for games that are often little more than controlled scrimmages. Before one preseason game the opposing coaches got together and decided they would blitz only four players in order to protect the quarterbacks. Says one coach, "That kind of thing happens in the preseason all the time."

When it comes to preseason football games, it's obviously caveat emptor.

1994 NFL Team Leaders

AFC Total Offense

	Total Yds	Yds Rush	Yds Pass	Time of Poss	Avg Pts/Game
Miami	6078	1658	4420	31:46	24.3
Kansas City	5962	1732	3960	30:55	19.9
New England	5776	1332	4444	32:08	21.9
Denver	5487	1470	4017	30:58	21.7
Buffalo	5244	1831	3413	29:21	21.3
San Diego	5220	1852	3368	30.19	23.8
Pittsburgh	5138	2180	2958	31:58	19.8
Cleveland	4832	1657	3175	28:44	21.3
Cincinnati	4792	1556	3236	27:11	17.2
L.A. Raiders	4779	1512	3267	29:30	19.1
N.Y. Jets	4703	1566	3137	29:54	16.5
Seattle	4652	2084	2568	28:35	17.9
Houston	4481	1682	2799	29:06	14.1
Indianapolis	4413	2060	2353	28:39	19.2

AFC Total Defense

	Opp Total Yds	Opp Yds Rush	Opp Yds Pass	Avg PA/Game
Pittsburgh	4326	1452	2874	14.6
Cleveland	4826	1669	3157	12.8
Houston	4915	2120	2795	22.0
L.A. Raiders	4943	1543	3400	20.4
Kansas City	5000	1734	3266	18.6
San Diego	5056	1404	3652	19.1
Cincinnati	5154	1906	3248	25.4
Buffalo	5175	1515	3660	15.1
New England	5207	1760	3447	19.5
Miami	5224	1430	3794	20.4
Indianapolis	5325	1646	3679	20.0
N.Y. Jets	5338	1809	3529	20.0
Seattle	5349	1952	3397	20.2
Denver	5907	1752	4155	14.8

NFC Total Offense

	Total Yds	Yds Rush	Yds Pass	Time of Poss	Avg Pts/Game
San Francisco	6060	1897	4163	31:38	31.6
Minnesota	5848	1524	4324	32:06	22.2
Atlanta	5361	1249	4112	29:10	19.6
Dallas	5321	1953	3368	31:35	25.9
Green Bay	5316	1543	3773	30:56	23.9
New Orleans	5182	1336	3846	29:04	21.8
Philadelphia	5125	1761	3364	30:47	19.3
Detroit	5002	2080	2922	26:06	22.3
Washington	4793	1415	3378	26:55	20.0
Tampa Bay	4754	1489	3265	29:55	23.9
L.A. Rams	4747	1389	3358	27:59	17.9
Chicago	4679	1588	3091	31:37	16.9
Arizona	4607	1560	3047	32:37	14.7
N.Y. Giants	4316	1754	2562	30:28	17.4

NFC Total Defense

	Opp Total Yds	Opp Yds Rush	Opp Yds Pass	Avg PA/Game
Dallas	4313	1561	2752	15.5
Arizona	4453	1370	3038	16.7
Philadelphia	4710	1616	3094	19.3
Minnesota	4742	1090	3652	19.6
Green Bay	4764	1363	3401	17.9
San Francisco	4839	1338	3501	18.5
N.Y. Giants	4950	1728	3222	19.1
Chicago	5009	1922	3087	19.2
L.A. Rams	5170	1781	3389	22.8
Tampa Bay	5336	1964	3372	17.9
Detroit	5405	1859	3546	21.4
New Orleans	5569	1758	3811	25.4
Washington	5609	1975	3634	25.8
Atlanta	5829	1693	4136	24.3

Takeaways/Giveaways

AFC

	Takeaways Int	Takeaways Fum	Takeaways Total	Giveaways Int	Giveaways Fum	Giveaways Total	Net Diff
Pittsburgh	17	14	31	9	8	17	14
Kansas City	12	26	38	14	12	26	12
N.Y. Jets	17	21	38	18	10	28	10
San Diego	17	15	32	14	9	23	9
New England	22	18	40	27	11	38	2
Seattle	19	11	30	9	19	28	2
Miami	23	9	32	18	14	32	0
Indianapolis	18	10	28	14	17	31	-3
Cleveland	18	13	31	21	14	35	-4
Denver	12	14	26	13	18	31	-5
L.A. Raiders	12	13	25	16	14	30	-5
Buffalo	16	12	28	21	13	34	-6
Houston	14	12	26	17	25	42	-16
Cincinnati	10	8	18	19	22	41	-23

NFC

	Takeaways Int	Takeaways Fum	Takeaways Total	Giveaways Int	Giveaways Fum	Giveaways Total	Net Diff
San Francisco	23	12	35	11	13	24	11
Green Bay	21	12	33	14	8	22	11
Philadelphia	21	14	35	14	12	26	9
N.Y. Giants	16	16	32	18	7	25	7
Arizona	23	13	36	19	10	29	7
Dallas	22	9	31	14	10	24	7
Minnesota	18	16	34	20	14	34	0
New Orleans	17	14	31	18	14	32	-1
Detroit	12	11	23	14	10	24	-1
Tampa Bay	9	12	21	16	7	23	-2
Atlanta	22	11	33	25	11	36	-3
Chicago	12	10	22	16	10	26	-4
L.A. Rams	14	6	20	18	13	31	-11
Washington	17	6	23	27	13	40	-17

THEY SAID IT

Bum Philllips, ex-NFL coach, on how he's spending his retirement: "I ain't doing a damn thing, and I don't start until noon."

Conference Rankings

American Football Conference

		Offense			Defense	
	Total	Rush	Pass	Total	Rush	Pass
Buffalo	5	5	5	8	4	11
Cincinnati	9	11	8	7	12	4
Cleveland	8	9	9	2	7	3
Denver	4	13	3	14	9	14
Houston	13	7	12	3	14	1
Indianapolis	14	3	14	11	6	12
Kansas City	3	6	4	5	8	5
L.A. Raiders	10	12	7	4	5	7
Miami	1	8	2	10	2	13
New England	2	14	1	9	10	8
N.Y. Jets	11	10	10	12	11	9
Pittsburgh	7	1	11	1	3	2
San Diego	6	4	6	6	1	10
Seattle	12	2	13	13	13	6

National Football Conference

		Offense			Defense	
	Total	Rush	Pass	Total	Rush	Pass
Arizona	13	7	12	2	4	2
Atlanta	3	14	3	14	7	14
Chicago	12	6	11	8	12	3
Dallas	4	2	7	1	5	1
Detroit	8	1	13	11	11	10
Green Bay	5	8	5	5	3	8
L.A. Rams	11	12	9	9	10	7
Minnesota	2	9	1	4	1	12
New Orleans	6	13	4	12	9	13
N.Y. Giants	14	5	14	7	8	5
Philadelphia	7	4	8	3	6	4
San Francisco	1	3	2	6	2	9
Tampa Bay	10	10	10	10	13	6
Washington	9	11	6	13	14	11

1994 AFC Team-by-Team Statistical Leaders

Buffalo Bills

SCORING	Rush	TD Rec	Ret	PAT	FG	S	Pts
Christie	0	0	0	38/38	24/28	0	110
T. Thomas	7	2	0	0/0	0/0	0	54
Reed	0	8	0	0/0	0/0	0	48
Metzelaars	0	5	0	0/0	0/0	0	30
Beebe	0	4	0	0/0	0/0	0	24

RUSHING	No.	Yds	Avg	Lg	TD
T. Thomas	287	1093	3.8	29	7
K. Davis	91	381	4.2	60	2
Gardner	41	135	3.3	13	4

PASSING	Att	Comp	Pct Comp	Yds	Avg Gain	TD	Int	Rating Pts
Kelly	448	285	63.6	3114	6.95	22	17	84.6
Reich	93	56	60.2	568	6.11	1	4	63.4

RECEIVING	No.	Yds	Avg	Lg	TD
Reed	90	1303	14.5	t83	8
T. Thomas	50	349	7.0	28	2
Metzelaars	49	428	8.7	t35	5
Bi. Brooks	42	482	11.5	32	2
Beebe	40	527	13.2	t72	4
Copeland	21	255	12.1	35	1
K. Davis	18	82	4.6	12	0

INTERCEPTIONS: Darby, 4

PUNTING	No.	Yds	Avg	Net Avg	TB	In 20	Lg	Blk
Mohr	67	2799	41.8	36.0	3	13	71	0

SACKS: Smith, 10

Cincinnati Bengals

SCORING	Rush	TD Rec	Ret	PAT	FG	S	Pts
Pelfrey	0	0	0	24/25	28/33	0	108
Pickens	0	11	0	0/0	0/0	0	66
Scott	0	5	0	0/0	0/0	0	30
Broussard	2	0	0	0/0	0/0	0	14

Two tied with 12 pts.

RUSHING	No.	Yds	Avg	Lg	TD
Fenner	141	468	3.3	21	1
Broussard	94	403	4.3	t37	2
Green	76	223	2.9	22	1
Blake	37	204	5.5	16	1

PASSING	Att	Comp	Pct Comp	Yds	Avg Gain	TD	Int	Rating Pts
Blake	306	156	51.0	2154	7.04	14	9	76.9
Klinger	231	131	56.7	1327	5.74	6	9	65.7

RECEIVING	No.	Yds	Avg	Lg	TD
Pickens	71	1127	15.9	t70	11
Scott	46	866	18.8	76	5
To. McGee	40	492	12.3	54	1
Fenner	36	276	7.7	29	1
Broussard	34	218	6.4	25	0

INTERCEPTIONS: Oliver, 3

PUNTING	No.	Yds	Avg	Net Avg	TB	In 20	Lg	Blk
L. Johnson	79	3461	43.8	35.3	9	19	64	1

SACKS: A. Williams, 9.5

Cleveland Browns

SCORING

	TD						
	Rush	Rec	Ret	PAT	FG	S	Pts
Stover	0	0	0	32/32	26/28	0	110
Hoard	5	4	0	0/0	0/0	0	54
Metcalf	2	3	0	0/0	0/0	0	42
Carrier	1	5	0	0/0	0/0	0	36
Alexander	0	2	0	0/0	0/0	0	14

Three tied with 12 pts.

RUSHING

	No.	Yds	Avg	Lg	TD
Hoard	209	890	4.3	39	5
Metcalf	93	329	3.5	t37	2
Byner	75	219	2.9	15	2

PASSING

	Att	Comp	Pct Comp	Yds	Avg Gain	TD	Int	Rating Pts
Testaverde	377	207	54.9	2575	6.83	16	18	70.6
Rypien	127	59	46.5	694	5.46	4	3	64.2

RECEIVING

	No.	Yds	Avg	Lg	TD
Alexander	48	828	17.3	t81	2
Metcalf	47	436	9.3	t57	3
Hoard	45	445	9.9	t65	4
Carrier	29	452	15.6	43	5

INTERCEPTIONS: Turner, 9

PUNTING

	No.	Yds	Avg	Net Avg	TB	In 20	Lg	Blk
Tupa	80	3211	65	35.4	8	27	65	0

SACKS: Burnett, 10

Houston Oilers

SCORING

	TD						
	Rush	Rec	Ret	PAT	FG	S	Pts
Del Greco	0	0	0	18/18	16/20	0	66
Jeffires	0	6	0	0/0	0/0	0	42
G. Brown	4	1	0	0/0	0/0	0	30
White	3	1	0	0/0	0/0	0	24

Three tied with 12.

RUSHING

	No.	Yds	Avg	Lg	TD
White	191	757	4.0	33	3
G. Brown	169	648	3.8	18	4
Richardson	30	217	7.2	18	1

PASSING

	Att	Comp	Pct Comp	Yds	Avg Gain	TD	Int	Rating Pts
Tolliver	240	121	50.4	1287	5.36	6	7	62.6
Richardson	181	94	51.9	1202	6.64	6	6	70.3
Carlson	132	59	44.7	727	5.51	1	4	52.2

RECEIVING

	No.	Yds	Avg	Lg	TD
Slaughter	68	846	12.4	57	2
Jeffires	68	783	11.5	50	6
Givins	36	521	14.5	t76	1
White	21	188	9.0	41	1
Coleman	20	298	14.9	81	1
G. Brown	18	194	10.8	24	1

INTERCEPTIONS: D. Lewis, 5

PUNTING

	No.	Yds	Avg	Net Avg	TB	In 20	Lg	Blk
Camarillo	96	4115	42.9	36.4	9	34	58	0

SACKS: Lathon, 8.5

Denver Broncos

SCORING

	TD						
	Rush	Rec	Ret	PAT	FG	S	Pts
Elam	0	0	0	29/29	30/37	0	119
L. Russell	9	0	0	0/0	0/0	0	54
Miller	0	5	0	0/0	0/0	0	32
Sharpe	0	4	0	0/0	0/0	0	28

Two tied with 24.

RUSHING

	No.	Yds	Avg	Lg	TD
L. Russell	190	620	3.3	t22	9
Elway	58	235	4.1	22	4
Milburn	58	201	3.5	20	1
Clark	56	168	3.0	12	3

PASSING

	Att	Comp	Pct Comp	Yds	Avg Gain	TD	Int	Rating Pts
Elway	494	307	62.1	3490	7.06	16	10	85.7
Millen	131	81	61.8	893	6.82	2	3	77.6

RECEIVING

	No.	Yds	Avg	Lg	TD
Sharpe	87	1010	11.6	44	4
Milburn	77	549	7.1	33	3
Miller	60	1107	18.5	76	5
L. Russell	38	227	6.0	19	0
Tillman	28	455	16.3	63	1

INTERCEPTIONS: Jones, Hillard and Crockett, 2

PUNTING

	No.	Yds	Avg	Net Avg	TB	In 20	Lg	Blk
Rouen	76	3258	42.9	37.1	8	23	59	0

SACKS: Fletcher, 7

Indianapolis Colts

SCORING

	TD						
	Rush	Rec	Ret	PAT	FG	S	Pts
Biasucci	0	0	0	37/37	16/24	0	85
Faulk	11	1	0	0/0	0/0	0	72
Turner	0	6	0	0/0	0/0	0	36

Two tied with 18.

RUSHING

	No.	Yds	Avg	Lg	TD
Faulk	314	1282	4.1	52	11
Potts	77	336	4.4	52	1

PASSING

	Att	Comp	Pct Comp	Yds	Avg Gain	TD	Int	Rating Pts
Harbaugh	202	125	61.9	1440	7.13	9	6	85.8
Majkowski	152	84	55.3	1010	6.64	6	7	69.8

RECEIVING

	No.	Yds	Avg	Lg	TD
Turner	52	593	11.4	28	6
Faulk	52	522	10.0	t85	1
Dawkins	51	742	14.5	49	5
Potts	26	251	9.7	30	1
Cash	16	190	11.9	24	1
Jackson	8	97	12.1	22	1
Warren	3	47	15.7	29	0

INTERCEPTIONS: Buchanan, 8

PUNTING

	No.	Yds	Avg	Net Avg	TB	In 20	Lg	Blk
Stark	73	3092	42.4	34.1	10	22	60	1

SACKS: Bennett, 9

Kansas City Chiefs

SCORING	Rush	TD Rec	Ret	PAT	FG	S	Pts
Elliot	0	0	0	30/30	25/30	0	105
Allen	7	0	0	0/0	0/0	0	44
W. Davis	0	5	0	0/0	0/0	0	32
Vaughn	1	1	2	0/0	0/0	0	26

RUSHING	No.	Yds	Avg	Lg	TD
Allen	189	709	3.8	t36	7
Hill	141	574	4.1	20	1
Anders	62	231	3.7	19	2

PASSING	Att	Comp	Pct Comp	Yds	Avg Gain	TD	Int	Rating Pts
Montana	493	299	60.6	3283	6.66	16	9	83.6
Bono	117	66	56.4	796	6.80	4	4	74.6

RECEIVING	No.	Yds	Avg	Lg	TD
Anders	67	525	7.8	30	1
W. Davis	51	822	16.1	t62	5
Birden	48	637	13.3	44	4
Allen	42	349	8.3	38	0
Dawson	37	537	14.5	50	2
D. Walker	36	382	10.6	t57	2

INTERCEPTIONS: Mincy, 3

PUNTING	No.	Yds	Avg	Net Avg	TB	In 20	Lg	Blk
Aguiar	85	3582	42.1	34.5	7	15	61	0

SACKS: Smith, 11.5

Miami Dolphins

SCORING	Rush	TD Rec	Ret	PAT	FG	S	Pts
Stoyanovich	0	0	0	35/35	24/31	0	107
Fryar	0	7	0	0/0	0/0	0	46
Parmalee	6	1	0	0/0	0/0	0	44
K. Jackson	0	7	0	0/0	0/0	0	44
Byars	2	5	0	0/0	0/0	0	42
Ingram	0	6	0	0/0	0/0	0	36

RUSHING	No.	Yds	Avg	Lg	TD
Parmalee	216	868	4.0	t47	6
Spikes	70	312	4.5	40	2
Kirby	60	233	3.9	30	2

PASSING	Att	Comp	Pct Comp	Yds	Avg Gain	TD	Int	Rating Pts
Marino	615	385	62.6	4453	7.24	30	17	89.2

RECEIVING	No.	Yds	Avg	Lg	TD
Fryar	73	1270	17.4	t54	7
K. Jackson	59	673	11.4	35	7
Byars	49	418	8.5	34	5
Ingram	44	506	11.5	t64	6
McDuffie	37	488	13.2	30	3
Parmalee	34	249	7.3	22	1

INTERCEPTIONS: Vincent, 5

PUNTING	No.	Yds	Avg	Net Avg	TB	In 20	Lg	Blk
Arnold	46	1810	39.3	33.5	4	14	53	0
Kidd	14	602	43.0	29.1	3	2	58	0

SACKS: Cross, 9.5

Los Angeles Raiders

SCORING	Rush	TD Rec	Ret	PAT	FG	S	Pts
Jaeger	0	0	0	31/31	22/28	0	97
Brown	0	9	0	0/0	0/0	0	54
H. Williams	4	3	0	0/0	0/0	0	44
Ismail	0	5	0	0/0	0/0	0	30
McDaniel	0	0	3	0/0	0/0	0	18

Three tied with 12 pts.

RUSHING	No.	Yds	Avg	Lg	TD
H. Williams	282	983	3.5	28	4
Hostetler	46	159	3.5	14	2
Rathman	28	118	4.2	14	0

PASSING	Att	Comp	Pct Comp	Yds	Avg Gain	TD	Int	Rating Pts
Hostetler	454	263	57.9	3334	7.34	20	16	81.0
Evans	33	18	54.5	222	6.73	2	0	95.8

RECEIVING	No.	Yds	Avg	Lg	TD
Brown	89	1309	14.7	t77	9
H. Williams	47	391	8.3	t27	3
Ismail	34	513	15.1	42	5
Glover	33	371	11.2	t27	2
Rathman	26	194	7.5	18	0

INTERCEPTIONS: McDaniel, 7

PUNTING	No.	Yds	Avg	Net Avg	TB	In 20	Lg	Blk
Gossett	77	3377	43.9	35.2	15	19	65	0

SACKS: McGlockton, 9.5

New England Patriots

SCORING	Rush	TD Rec	Ret	PAT	FG	S	Pts
Bahr	0	0	0	36/36	27/34	0	117
Butts	8	0	0	0/0	0/0	0	48
Coates	0	7	0	0/0	0/0	0	42
Thompson	2	5	0	0/0	0/0	0	42
Brisby	0	5	0	0/0	0/0	0	30

RUSHING	No.	Yds	Avg	Lg	TD
Butts	243	703	2.9	26	8
Thompson	102	312	3.1	13	2
Turner	36	111	3.1	13	1

PASSING	Att	Comp	Pct Comp	Yds	Avg Gain	TD	Int	Rating Pts
Bledsoe	691	400	57.9	4555	6.59	25	27	73.6

RECEIVING	No.	Yds	Avg	Lg	TD
Coates	96	1174	12.2	t62	7
Timpson	74	941	12.7	37	3
Thompson	65	465	7.2	t27	5
Brisby	58	904	15.6	43	5
Turner	52	471	9.1	32	2
Crittenden	28	379	13.5	32	3

INTERCEPTIONS: Hurst, 7

PUNTING	No.	Yds	Avg	Net Avg	TB	In 20	Lg	Blk
O'Neill	69	2841	41.2	35.7	6	25	67	0

SACKS: Slade, 9.5

New York Jets

SCORING	TD Rush	Rec	Ret	PAT	FG	S	Pts
Lowery	0	0	0	26/27	20/23	0	86
Moore	0	6	0	0/0	0/0	0	40
J. Johnson...........	3	2	0	0/0	0/0	0	30
B. Baxter	4	0	0	0/0	0/0	0	24
Mitchell................	0	4	0	0/0	0/0	0	24
Monk	0	3	0	0/0	0/0	0	18

RUSHING	No.	Yds	Avg	Lg	TD
J. Johnson	240	931	3.9	90	3
R. Anderson	43	207	4.8	55	1
B. Baxter....................	60	170	2.8	13	4

PASSING	Att	Comp	Pct Comp	Yds	Avg Gain	TD	Int	Rating Pts
Esiason....	440	255	58.0	2782	6.32	17	13	77.3
Trudeau.....	91	50	54.9	496	5.45	1	4	55.9

RECEIVING	No.	Yds	Avg	Lg	TD
Moore	78	1010	12.9	t41	6
Mitchell....................	58	7.49	12.9	55	4
Monk	46	581	12.6	69	3
J. Johnson................	42	303	7.2	24	2
R.Anderson	25	212	8.5	t27	1

INTERCEPTIONS: Turner and Hasty, 5

PUNTING	No.	Yds	Avg	Net Avg	TB	In 20	Lg	Blk
Hansen.....	84	3534	42.1	36.1	12	25	64	0

SACKS: Lageman, 6.5

San Diego Chargers

SCORING	TD Rush	Rec	Ret	PAT	FG	S	Pts
Carney	0	0	0	33/33	34/38	0	135
Means	12	0	0	0/0	0/0	0	72
Martin	0	7	0	0/0	0/0	0	42
Seay	0	6	0	0/0	0/0	0	36
Jefferson	0	3	0	0/0	0/0	0	18
Harmon	1	1	0	0/0	0/0	0	12

RUSHING	No.	Yds	Avg	Lg	TD
Means......................	343	1350	3.9	25	12
Bieniemy...................	73	295	4.0	36	0

PASSING	Att	Comp	Pct Comp	Yds	Avg Gain	TD	Int	Rating Pts
Humphries	453	264	58.3	3209	7.08	17	12	81.6
Gilbert	67	41	61.2	410	6.12	3	1	87.3

RECEIVING	No.	Yds	Avg	Lg	TD
Seay	58	645	11.1	t49	6
Harmon	58	615	10.6	35	1
Martin	50	885	17.7	t99	7
Jefferson	43	627	14.6	t52	3
Means	39	235	6.0	22	0
Pupunu.....................	21	214	10.2	25	2

INTERCEPTIONS: Richard and Gordon, 4

PUNTING	No.	Yds	Avg	Net Avg	TB	In 20	Lg	Blk
Wagner	65	2702	41.6	35.3	3	20	59	0

SACKS: O'Neal, 12.5

Pittsburgh Steelers

SCORING	TD Rush	Rec	Ret	PAT	FG	S	Pts
Anderson	0	0	0	32/32	24/29	0	104
Morris	7	0	0	0/0	0/0	0	42
Foster	5	0	0	0/0	0/0	0	30
Thigpen	0	4	0	0/0	0/0	0	24
Green	0	4	0	0/0	0/0	0	24

RUSHING	No.	Yds	Avg	Lg	TD
Foster	216	851	3.9	t29	5
Morris	198	836	4.2	20	7
J. Williams	68	317	4.7	23	1

PASSING	Att	Comp	Pct Comp	Yds	Avg Gain	TD	Int	Rating Pts
O'Donnell....	370	212	57.3	2443	6.60	13	9	78.9
Tomczak	93	54	58.1	804	8.65	4	0	100.8

RECEIVING	No.	Yds	Avg	Lg	TD
J. Williams	51	378	7.4	23	2
Green	46	618	13.4	46	4
Johnson....................	38	577	15.2	t84	3
Thigpen....................	36	546	15.2	t60	4
Morris	22	204	9.3	49	0
Hastings	20	281	14.1	46	2
Foster	20	124	6.2	27	0

INTERCEPTIONS: Perry, 7

PUNTING	No.	Yds	Avg	Net Avg	TB	In 20	Lg	Blk
Royals	97	3849	39.7	35.7	6	35	64	0

SACKS: Greene, 14

Seattle Seahawks

SCORING	TD Rush	Rec	Ret	PAT	FG	S	Pts
Kasay	0	0	0	25/26	20/24	0	85
C. Warren	9	2	0	0/0	0/0	0	68
Blades...................	0	4	0	0/0	0/0	0	26
S. Smith	2	1	0	0/0	0/0	0	18

RUSHING	No.	Yds	Avg	Lg	TD
C. Warren	333	1545	4.6	41	9
Mirer	34	153	4.5	14	0
Strong......................	27	114	4.2	14	2

PASSING	Att	Comp	Pct Comp	Yds	Avg Gain	TD	Int	Rating Pts
Mirer........	381	195	51.2	2151	5.65	11	7	70.2
McGwire..	105	51	48.6	578	5.50	1	2	60.7

RECEIVING	No.	Yds	Avg	Lg	TD
Blades......................	81	1086	13.4	45	4
Martin	56	681	12.2	32	1
C. Warren	41	323	7.9	51	2
Green	30	208	6.9	20	1
S. Smith	11	142	12.9	25	1
Johnson....................	10	91	9.1	17	0

INTERCEPTIONS: Four tied with 3.

PUNTING	No.	Yds	Avg	Net Avg	TB	In 20	Lg	Blk
Tuten	91	3905	42.9	36.7	7	33	64	0

SACKS: Sinclair, 4.5

Arizona Cardinals

SCORING

	TD Rush	Rec	Ret	PAT	FG	S	Pts
Davis	0	0	0	17/17	20/26	0	77
Centers	5	2	0	0/0	0/0	0	42
R. Moore	4	1	0	0/0	0/0	0	32
Proehl	0	5	0	0/0	0/0	0	30
Five tied with 6							

RUSHING

	No.	Yds	Avg	Lg	TD
R. Moore	232	780	3.4	24	4
Centers	115	336	2.9	17	5
Hearst	37	169	4.6	36	1

PASSING

	Att	Comp	Pct Comp	Yds	Avg Gain	TD	Int	Rating Pts
Beuerlein	255	130	51.0	1545	6.06	5	9	61.6
Schroeder	238	133	55.9	1510	6.34	4	7	68.4
McMahon	43	23	53.5	219	5.09	1	3	46.6

RECEIVING

	No.	Yds	Avg	Lg	TD
Centers	77	647	8.4	36	2
Proehl	51	651	12.8	63	5
Clark	50	771	15.4	45	1
R. Hill	38	544	14.3	51	0
Ware	17	171	10.1	33	1

INTERCEPTIONS: A. Williams, 9

PUNTING

	No.	Yds	Avg	Net Avg	TB	In 20	Lg	Blk
Feagles	98	3997	40.8	36.0	10	33	54	0

SACKS: Swann, 7.5

Atlanta Falcons

SCORING

	TD Rush	Rec	Ret	PAT	FG	S	Pts
N. Johnson	0	0	0	32/32	21/25	0	95
Mathis	0	11	0	0/0	0/0	0	70
Rison	0	8	0	0/0	0/0	0	50
Heyward	7	1	0	0/0	0/0	0	48
Emanuel	0	4	0	0/0	0/0	0	24

RUSHING

	No.	Yds	Avg	Lg	TD
Heyward	183	779	4.3	17	7
Pegram	103	358	3.5	25	1

PASSING

	Att	Comp	Pct Comp	Yds	Avg Gain	TD	Int	Rating Pts
J. George	524	322	61.5	3734	7.13	23	18	83.3
Hebert	103	52	50.5	610	5.92	2	6	51.0

RECEIVING

	No.	Yds	Avg	Lg	TD
Mathis	111	1342	12.1	81	11
Rison	81	1088	13.4	t69	8
Sanders	67	599	8.9	28	1
Emanuel	46	649	14.1	t85	4
Heyward	32	335	10.5	34	1
Pegram	16	99	6.2	28	0

INTERCEPTIONS: D. Johnson, 5

PUNTING

	No.	Yds	Avg	Net Avg	TB	In 20	Lg	Blk
Alexander	71	2836	39.9	34.8	6	12	61	0

SACKS: C. Smith, 11

Chicago Bears

SCORING

	TD Rush	Rec	Ret	PAT	FG	S	Pts
Butler	0	0	0	24/24	21/29	0	87
Tillman	7	0	0	0/0	0/0	0	42
Graham	0	4	1	0/0	0/0	0	32
Gedney	0	3	0	0/0	0/0	0	18
Jennings	0	3	0	0/0	0/0	0	18

RUSHING

	No.	Yds	Avg	Lg	TD
Tillman	275	899	3.3	t25	7
Harris	123	464	3.8	13	1
Green	25	122	4.9	14	0

PASSING

	Att	Comp	Pct Comp	Yds	Avg Gain	TD	Int	Rating Pts
Walsh	343	208	60.6	2078	6.06	10	8	77.9
Kramer	158	99	62.7	1129	7.15	8	8	79.9

RECEIVING

	No.	Yds	Avg	Lg	TD
Graham	68	944	13.9	t76	4
Conway	39	546	14.0	t85	2
Harris	39	236	6.1	18	0
Tillman	27	222	8.2	39	0
Waddle	25	244	9.8	22	1
Green	24	199	8.3	t39	2
Cook	21	212	10.1	34	1

INTERCEPTIONS: Woolford, 5

PUNTING

	No.	Yds	Avg	Net Avg	TB	In 20	Lg	Blk
Gardocki	76	2871	37.8	32.4	9	23	57	0

SACKS: Armstrong, 7.5

Dallas Cowboys

SCORING

	TD Rush	Rec	Ret	PAT	FG	S	Pts
E. Smith	21	1	0	0/0	0/0	0	132
Boniol	0	0	0	48/48	22/29	0	114
Harper	0	8	0	0/0	0/0	0	48
Irvin	0	6	0	0/0	0/0	0	36
Johnston	2	2	0	0/0	0/0	0	24

RUSHING

	No.	Yds	Avg	Lg	TD
E. Smith	368	1484	4.0	46	21
Coleman	64	180	2.8	13	1
Johnston	40	138	3.5	t9	2

PASSING

	Att	Comp	Pct Comp	Yds	Avg Gain	TD	Int	Rating Pts
Aikman	361	233	64.5	2676	7.41	13	12	84.9
Peete	56	33	58.9	470	8.39	4	1	102.5
Garrett	31	16	51.6	315	10.16	2	1	95.5

RECEIVING

	No.	Yds	Avg	Lg	TD
Irvin	79	1241	15.7	t65	6
E. Smith	50	341	6.8	68	1
Novacek	47	475	10.1	27	2
Johnston	44	325	7.4	24	2
Harper	33	821	24.9	90	8
K. Williams	13	181	13.9	29	0

INTERCEPTIONS: Woodson and Washington, 5

PUNTING

	No.	Yds	Avg	Net Avg	TB	In 20	Lg	Blk
Jett	70	2935	41.9	35.4	4	26	58	0

SACKS: Haley, 12.5

Detroit Lions

SCORING	Rush	TD Rec	Ret	PAT	FG	S	Pts
Hanson	0	0	0	39/40	18/27	0	93
H. Moore	0	11	0	0/0	0/0	0	66
Sanders	7	1	0	0/0	0/0	0	48
Perriman	0	4	0	0/0	0/0	0	28
D. Moore	4	0	0	0/0	0/0	0	24

RUSHING	No.	Yds	Avg	Lg	TD
Sanders	331	1883	5.7	85	7
Perriman	9	86	9.6	25	0

PASSING	Att	Comp	Pct Comp	Yds	Avg Gain	TD	Int	Rating Pts
Mitchell	246	119	48.4	1456	5.92	10	11	62.0
Krieg	212	131	61.8	1629	7.68	14	3	101.7

RECEIVING	No.	Yds	Avg	Lg	TD
H. Moore	72	1173	16.3	t51	11
Perriman	56	761	13.6	39	4
Sanders	44	283	6.4	22	1
Matthews	29	359	12.4	33	3
Holman	17	163	9.6	18	0
Hall	10	106	10.6	18	0

INTERCEPTIONS: Massey, 4

PUNTING	No.	Yds	Avg	Net Avg	TB	In 20	Lg	Blk
M'gomery	63	2782	44.2	34.2	8	19	64	1

SACKS: Thomas, 7

Los Angeles Rams

SCORING	Rush	TD Rec	Ret	PAT	FG	S	Pts
Zendejas	0	0	0	28/28	18/23	0	82
Drayton	0	6	0	0/0	0/0	0	36
Anderson	0	5	0	0/0	0/0	0	30
Bettis	3	1	0	0/0	0/0	0	28
Kinchen	1	3	0	0/0	0/0	0	24

RUSHING	No.	Yds	Avg	Lg	TD
Bettis	319	1025	3.2	19	3
Miller	20	100	5.0	16	0

PASSING	Att	Comp	Pct Comp	Yds	Avg Gain	TD	Int	Rating Pts
Miller	317	173	54.6	2104	6.64	16	14	73.6
Chandler	176	108	61.4	1352	7.68	7	2	93.8

RECEIVING	No.	Yds	Avg	Lg	TD
J. Bailey	58	516	8.9	28	0
Anderson	46	945	20.5	t72	5
Hester	45	644	14.3	41	3
Drayton	32	276	8.6	t22	6
Bettis	31	293	9.5	34	1
Kinchen	23	352	15.3	43	3
Bruce	21	272	13.0	t34	3

INTERCEPTIONS: Pope and Henley, 3

PUNTING	No.	Yds	Avg	Net Avg	TB	In 20	Lg	Blk
Landeta	78	3494	44.8	34.3	9	23	62	0

SACKS: Young, 6.5

Green Bay Packers

SCORING	Rush	TD Rec	Ret	PAT	FG	S	Pts
Jacke	0	0	0	41/43	19/26	0	98
Sharpe	0	18	0	0/0	0/0	0	108
Bennett	5	4	0	0/0	0/0	0	54
Brooks	0	4	2	0/0	0/0	0	36
Two tied with 24							

RUSHING	No.	Yds	Avg	Lg	TD
Bennett	178	623	3.5	t39	5
Cobb	153	579	3.8	30	3
Favre	42	202	4.8	t36	2

PASSING	Att	Comp	Pct Comp	Yds	Avg Gain	TD	Int	Rating Pts
Favre	582	363	62.4	3882	6.67	33	14	90.7
Brunell	27	12	44.4	95	3.52	0	0	53.8

RECEIVING	No.	Yds	Avg	Lg	TD
Sharpe	94	1119	11.9	49	18
Bennett	78	546	7.0	40	4
Brooks	58	648	11.2	35	4
Cobb	35	299	8.5	t37	1
West	31	377	12.2	26	2
Morgan	28	397	14.2	t47	4

INTERCEPTIONS: Buckley, 5

PUNTING	No.	Yds	Avg	Net Avg	TB	In 20	Lg	Blk
Hentrich	81	3351	41.4	35.5	10	24	70	0

SACKS: Jones, 10.5

Minnesota Vikings

SCORING	Rush	TD Rec	Ret	PAT	FG	S	Pts
Reveiz	0	0	0	30/30	34/39	0	132
Allen	8	0	0	0/0	0/0	0	50
Carter	0	7	0	0/0	0/0	0	46
Ismail	0	5	0	0/0	0/0	0	30
Reed	0	4	0	0/0	0/0	0	24

RUSHING	No.	Yds	Avg	Lg	TD
Allen	255	1031	4.0	45	8
Graham	64	207	3.2	11	2
R. Smith	31	106	3.4	t14	1

PASSING	Att	Comp	Pct Comp	Yds	Avg Gain	TD	Int	Rating Pts
Moon	601	371	61.7	4264	7.09	18	19	79.9
Johnson	37	22	59.5	150	4.05	0	0	68.5
Salisbury	34	16	47.1	156	4.59	0	1	48.2

RECEIVING	No.	Yds	Avg	Lg	TD
Carter	122	1256	10.3	t65	7
Reed	85	1175	13.8	59	4
Ismail	45	696	15.5	t65	5
Lee	45	368	8.2	35	2
A. Jordan	35	336	9.6	25	0
Cooper	32	363	11.3	34	0
Allen	17	148	8.7	31	0

INTERCEPTIONS: Parker and Glenn, 4

PUNTING	No.	Yds	Avg	Net Avg	TB	In 20	Lg	Blk
Saxon	77	3301	42.9	36.2	5	28	67	0

SACKS: Randle, 13.5

New Orleans Saints

SCORING

SCORING	Rush	Rec	Ret	PAT	FG	S	Pts
Andersen	0	0	0	32/32	28/39	0	116
Bates	6	0	0	0/0	0/0	0	36
Small	0	5	0	0/0	0/0	0	32
Haynes	0	5	0	0/0	0/0	0	30
Walls	0	4	0	0/0	0/0	0	26

RUSHING	No.	Yds	Avg	Lg	TD
Bates	151	579	3.8	40	6
Brown	146	489	3.3	16	3

PASSING	Att	Comp	Pct Comp	Yds	Avg Gain	TD	Int	Rating Pts
Everett	540	346	64.1	3855	7.14	22	18	84.9
W. Wilson	28	20	71.4	172	6.14	0	0	87.2

RECEIVING	No.	Yds	Avg	Lg	TD
Early	82	894	10.9	33	4
Haynes	77	985	12.8	t78	5
Small	49	719	14.7	t75	5
Brown	44	428	9.7	37	1
Smith	41	330	8.0	19	3
Walls	38	406	10.7	31	4
Ned	13	86	6.6	19	0

INTERCEPTIONS: Spencer, 5

PUNTING	No.	Yds	Avg	Net Avg	TB	In 20	Lg	Blk
Barnhardt	67	2920	43.6	33.5	9	14	57	0

SACKS: Conner, 10.5

Philadelphia Eagles

SCORING	Rush	Rec	Ret	PAT	FG	S	Pts
Murray	0	0	0	33/33	21/25	0	96
Walker	5	2	1	0/0	0/0	0	48
Barnett	0	5	0	0/0	0/0	0	30

Five tied with 18

RUSHING	No.	Yds	Avg	Lg	TD
Walker	113	528	4.7	t91	5
Garner	109	399	3.7	t28	3
Hebron	82	325	4.0	19	2
Cunningham	65	288	4.4	22	3

PASSING	Att	Comp	Pct Comp	Yds	Avg Gain	TD	Int	Rating Pts
Cunn'ham	490	265	54.1	3229	6.59	16	13	74.4
Brister	76	51	67.1	507	6.67	2	1	89.1

RECEIVING	No.	Yds	Avg	Lg	TD
Barnett	78	1127	14.4	54	5
C. Williams	58	813	14.0	53	3
Walker	50	500	10.0	93	2
Joseph	43	344	8.0	t35	2
M. Johnson	21	204	9.7	22	2
Bailey	20	311	15.6	61	1
Hebron	18	137	7.6	29	0
Bavaro	17	215	12.6	t27	3

INTERCEPTIONS: G. Jackson, 6

PUNTING	No.	Yds	Avg	Net Avg	TB	In 20	Lg	Blk
Barker	66	2696	40.8	36.3	7	20	67	0
Berger	25	951	38.0	31.3	2	8	57	0

SACKS: Fuller, 10.5

New York Giants

SCORING	Rush	Rec	Ret	PAT	FG	S	Pts
Treadwell	0	0	0	22/23	11/17	0	55
Hampton	6	0	0	0/0	0/0	0	38
Meggett	4	0	2	0/0	0/0	0	36
Sherrrard	0	6	0	0/0	0/0	0	36
Pierce	0	4	0	0/0	0/0	0	24
Cross	0	4	0	0/0	0/0	0	24

RUSHING	No.	Yds	Avg	Lg	TD
Hampton	327	1075	3.3	t27	6
Meggett	91	298	3.3	t26	4
Da. Brown	60	196	3.3	21	2

PASSING	Att	Comp	Pct Comp	Yds	Av Gain	TD	Int	Rating Pts
Da. Brown	350	201	57.4	2536	7.25	12	16	72.5
Graham	53	24	45.3	295	5.57	3	2	66.5

RECEIVING	No.	Yds	Avg	Lg	TD
Sherrard	53	825	15.6	55	6
Calloway	43	666	15.5	t51	2
Meggett	32	293	9.2	34	0
Cross	31	364	11.7	40	4
Pierce	20	214	10.7	29	4
Marshall	16	219	13.7	34	0
Hampton	14	103	7.4	17	0

INTERCEPTIONS: Booty and Sparks, 3

PUNTING	No.	Yds	Avg	Net Avg	TB	In 20	Lg	Blk
Horan	85	3521	41.4	35.3	7	25	63	2

SACKS: Hamilton, 6.5

San Francisco 49ers

SCORING	Rush	Rec	Ret	PAT	FG	S	Pts
Brien	0	0	0	60/62	15/20	0	105
Rice	2	13	0	0/0	0/0	0	92
Watters	6	5	0	0/0	0/0	0	66
Jones	0	9	0	0/0	0/0	0	56
S. Young	7	0	0	0/0	0/0	0	42
Floyd	6	0	0	0/0	0/0	0	36
Taylor	0	5	0	0/0	0/0	0	30
Sanders	0	0	3	0/0	0/0	0	18

RUSHING	No.	Yds	Avg	Lg	TD
Watters	239	877	3.7	23	6
Floyd	87	305	3.5	26	6
S. Young	58	293	5.1	27	7

PASSING	Att	Comp	Pct Comp	Yds	Avg Gain	TD	Int	Rating Pts
S.Young	461	324	70.3	3969	8.61	35	10	112.8
Grbac	50	35	70.0	393	7.86	2	1	98.2

RECEIVING	No.	Yds	Avg	Lg	TD
Rice	112	1499	13.4	t69	13
Watters	66	719	10.9	t65	5
Jones	49	670	13.7	t69	9
Taylor	41	531	13.0	35	5
Singleton	21	294	14.0	t43	2

INTERCEPTIONS: Hanks, 7

PUNTING	No.	Yds	Avg	Net Avg	TB	In 20	Lg	Blk
Wil'meyer	54	2235	41.4	35.8	3	18	60	0

SACKS: Stubblefield, 8.5

Tampa Bay Buccaneers

SCORING	Rush	TD Rec	Ret	PAT	FG	S	Pts
Husted	0	0	0	20/20	23/35	0	89
Rhett...................	7	0	0	0/0	0/0	0	44
C. Wilson.............	0	6	0	0/0	0/0	0	36
Hawkins	0	5	0	0/0	0/0	0	30
J. Harris...............	0	3	0	0/0	0/0	0	20

RUSHING	No.	Yds	Avg	Lg	TD
Rhett......................	284	1011	3.6	27	7
Workman	79	291	3.7	18	0

PASSING	Att	Comp	Pct Comp	Yds	Avg Gain	TD	Int	Rating Pts
Erickson	399	225	56.4	2919	7.32	16	10	82.5
Dilfer..............	82	38	46.3	433	5.28	1	6	36.3

RECEIVING	No.	Yds	Avg	Lg	TD
Dawsey	46	673	14.6	46	1
Hawkins....................	37	438	11.8	32	5
C. Wilson	31	652	21.0	t71	6
McDowell	29	193	6.7	19	1
J. Harris...................	26	337	13.0	t48	3
Armstrong	22	265	12.0	29	1
Rhett........................	22	119	5.4	12	0

INTERCEPTIONS: King, 3

PUNTING	No.	Yds	Avg	Net Avg	TB	In 20	Lg	Blk
Stryzinski..	72	2800	38.9	35.9	6	20	53	0

SACKS: Culpepper, 4

Washington Redskins

SCORING	Rush	TD Rec	Ret	PAT	FG	S	Pts
Lohmiller	0	0	0	30/32	20/28	0	90
Ellard....................	0	6	0	0/0	0/0	0	36
Howard	0	5	0	0/0	0/0	0	32
Jenkins.................	0	4	0	0/0	0/0	0	24
Ervins	3	1	0	0/0	0/0	0	24

RUSHING	No.	Yds	Avg	Lg	TD
Ervins.......................	185	650	3.5	49	3
Mitchell	78	311	4.0	33	0
Brooks	100	297	3.0	15	2

PASSING	Att	Comp	Pct Comp	Yds	Avg Gain	TD	Int	Rating Pts
Shuler	265	120	45.3	1658	6.26	10	12	59.6
Friesz.......	180	105	58.3	1266	7.03	10	9	77.7
Frerotte....	100	46	46.0	600	6.00	5	5	61.3

RECEIVING	No.	Yds	Avg	Lg	TD
Ellard	74	1397	18.9	t73	6
Ervins	51	293	5.7	21	1
Howard.....................	40	727	18.2	t81	5
Mitchell.....................	26	236	9.1	t46	1
Winans	19	344	18.1	51	2

INTERCEPTIONS: A. Collins, 4

PUNTING	No.	Yds	Avg	Net Avg	TB	In 20	Lg	Blk
Roby	82	3639	44.4	36.1	12	21	65	0

SACKS: Harvey, 13.5

Tipping the Cap

After being dumped by the New York Giants last summer, quarterback Phil Simms said, "I'd still be a Giant if the salary cap didn't exist." Who could argue? NFL commissioner Paul Tagliabue, for one. He said, "It wasn't only the effect of the cap on the Giants that produced the Phil Simms retirement."

It's true that New York couldn't be sure that the 38-year-old Simms would make it through another 16-game season. But it's just as certain he would be calling signals for the Giants if the owners and players' union had not agreed on the cap, which this season mandates that each team spend no more than $34.6 million on its player payroll. Last year Simms threw for 3,000 yards and led New York to 12 wins. Now two unproven quarterbacks have taken his place, and he's an ESPN commentator.

Having heard Tagliabue repeatedly say that, even with the cap, teams will be able to keep the players they want, Simms finally vented his feelings. "He should be tested for drugs," he told *The New York Times*. "I was not let go because of the salary cap? That's one of the stupidest things I've ever heard."

It's time for Tagliabue and the players' union to admit that the cap can cripple teams—the Giants, for example, have lost seven starters since last season because of caponomics—and to say it will take a couple of years for everyone to adjust to the new NFL. To deny the cap's impact in the waiving of players like Simms and 1993 AFC reception leader Reggie Langhorne (by the Indianapolis Colts) is, to quote Simms again, "absurd."

First two rounds of the 60th annual NFL Draft held April 22-23 in New York City.

First Round

Team	Selection	Position
1. ....Cincinnati	Ki-Jana Carter, Penn St	RB
2. ....Jacksonville	Tony Boselli, USC	OT
3. ....Houston	Steve McNair, Alcorn St	QB
4. ....Washington	Michael Westbrook, Col	WR
5. ....Carolina	Kerry Collins, Penn St	QB
6. ....St Louis	Kevin Carter, Florida	DE
7. ....Philadelphia	Mike Mamula, Boston College	DE
8. ....Seattle	Joey Galloway, Ohio St	WR
9. ....NY Jets	Kyle Brady, Penn St	TE
10. ......San Francisco	J.J. Stokes, UCLA	WR
11. ......Minnesota	Derrick Alexander, Florida St	DE
12. ......Tampa Bay	Warren Sapp, Miami (FL)	DT
13. ......New Orleans	Mark Fields, Wash St	LB
14. ......Buffalo	Reuben Brown, Pitt	G
15. ......Indianapolis	Ellis Johnson, Florida	DT
16. ......NY Jets	Hugh Douglas, Central State (OH)	DE
17. ......NY Giants	Tyrone Wheatley, Michigan	RB
18. ......Los Angeles	Napoleon Kaufman, Washington	RB
19. ......Jacksonville	James Stewart, Tenn	RB
20. ......Detroit	Luther Elliss, Utah	DE
21. ......Chicago	Rashaan Salaam, Col	RB
22. ......Carolina	Tyrone Poole, Fort Valley St	CB
23. ......New England	Ty Law, Michigan	CB
24. ......Minnesota	Korey Stringer, Ohio St	OT
25. ......Miami	Billy Milner, Houston	OT
26. ......Atlanta	Devin Bush, Florida St	SS
27. ......Pittsburgh	Mark Bruener, Washington	TE
28. ......Tampa Bay	Derrick Brooks, Florida St	LB
29. ......Carolina	Blake Brockermeyer, Texas	OT
30. ......Cleveland	Craig Powell, Ohio St	LB
31. ......Kansas City	Trezelle Jenkins, Mich	OT
32. ......Green Bay	Craig Newsome, Arizona St	CB

Second Round

Team	Selection	Position
33. ......NY Jets	Matt O'Dwyer, Northwestern	G
34. ......San Diego	Terrance Shaw, Stephen F. Austin	DB
35. ......Houston	Anthony Cook, S Carolina St	DT
36. ......Carolina	Shawn King, NE Louisiana	DE
37. ......Washington	Cory Raymer, Wisconsin	C
38. ......St. Louis	Zach Wiegert, Nebraska	OT
39. ......Seattle	Christian Fauria, Colorado	TE
40. ......Jacksonville	Brian DeMarco, Mich St	OT
41. ......Atlanta	Ronald Davis, Tennessee	DB
42. ......Minnesota	Orlando Thomas, SW Louisiana	DB
43. ......Tampa Bay	Melvin Johnson, Kentucky	DB
44. ......New Orleans	Ray Zellars, Notre Dame	RB
45. ......Buffalo	Todd Collins, Michigan	QB
46. ......Dallas	Sherman Williams, Alabama	RB
47. ......Arizona	Frank Sanders, Auburn	WR
48. ......Indianapolis	Ken Dilger, Illinois	TE
49. ......Los Angeles	Barret Robbins, TCU	C
50. ......Philadelphia	Bobby Taylor, Notre Dame	DB
51. ......San Diego	Terrell Fletcher, Wisconsin	RB
52. ......Chicago	Patrick Riley, Miami (FL)	DT
53. ......Miami	Andrew Greene, Indiana	G
54. ......NY Giants	Scott Gragg, Montana	OT
55. ......Minnesota	Corey Fuller, Florida St	DB
56. ......Chicago	Todd Sauerbrun, W Va	P
57. ......New England	Ted Johnson, Colorado	LB
58. ......Philadelphia	Barrett Brooks, Kansas St	OT
59. ......Dallas	Kendall Watkins, Mississippi St	TE
60. ......Pittsburgh	Kordell Stewart, Colorado	QB
61. ......San Diego	Jimmy Oliver, TCU	WR
62. ......St. Louis	Jesse James, Miss St	G
63. ......Dallas	Shane Hannah, Michigan St	G
64. ......Jacksonville	Bryan Schwartz, Augustana (SD)	LB

Keeping the Books

If you take his answering machine seriously, John Pease, who was hired on January 12 as defensive line coach of the expansion Jacksonville Jaguars of the NFL, took more than hard feelings with him when he left his former employers, the New Orleans Saints, who fired him late in December 1994. The recorded greeting on his home phone now offers callers copies of Saint playbooks.

1995 World League of American Football

Second Half Standings

	W	L	T	Pct	Pts/ Tm	Pts/ Opp
Amsterdam	4	1	0	.800	137	107
Frankfurt	4	1	0	.800	164	105
Barcelona	2	3	0	.400	123	145
London	2	3	0	.400	84	102
Rhein	2	3	0	.400	134	157
Scotland	1	4	0	.200	99	125

Final Standings

	W	L	T	Pct	Pts/ Tm	Pts/ Opp
Amsterdam*	9	1	0	.800	246	152
Frankfurt*	6	4	0	.600	279	202
Barcelona	5	5	0	.500	237	247
London	4	6	0	.400	174	220
Rhein	4	6	0	.400	221	279
Scotland	2	8	0	.200	153	210

*Clinched World Bowl '95 berth.

1995 World Bowl

June 17, 1995 in Amsterdam, Holland

Frankfurt	0	6	14	6—26
Amsterdam	0	7	0	15—22

SECOND QUARTER

Amsterdam: E. Jones 5 pass from Furrer (Belden kick), 13:44

Frankfurt: Olive 11 pass from Justin (Kleinman kick failed), 14:10

THIRD QUARTER

Frankfurt: Olive 4 pass from Justin (Kleinman kick), 7:26

Frankfurt: Bellamy 31 pass from Justin (Kleinmann kick), 11:08

FOURTH QUARTER

Frankfurt: Bolton 30 run (Kleinmann kick failed), 4:37

Amsterdam: Wright 1 run (Belden kick), 5:06

Amsterdam: Wright 9 pass from Furrer (Beach pass from Furrer), 14:28

A: 23,847.

WLAF Individual Leaders

PASSING

	Att	Comp	Pct Comp	Yds	Avg Gain	TD	Pct TD	Int	Pct Int	Lg	Rating Pts
P. Justin, Frankfurt	279	172	61.6	2394	8.58	17	6.1	12	4.3	64	91.6
J. Martin, Amsterdam	219	126	57.5	1433	6.54	11	5.0	6	2.7	t68	82.6
B. Johnson, London	328	194	59.1	2227	6.79	13	4.0	14	4.3	t58	75.1
G. Torretta, Rhein	144	81	56.3	940	6.53	5	3.5	6	4.2	t49	70.4
J. Walker, Barcelona	288	146	50.7	1874	6.51	7	2.4	7	2.4	t71	69.4

RECEIVING

RECEPTIONS	No.	Yds	Avg	Lg	TD	YARDS	Yds	No.	Avg	Lg	TD
B. Olive, Frankfurt	57	899	15.8	64	2	B. Olive, Frankfurt	899	57	15.8	64	2
T. Davis, Barcelona	56	855	15.3	t69	6	T. Davis, Barcelona	855	56	15.3	t69	6
M. Bailey, Frankfurt	46	654	14.2	t59	7	A. Allen, London	781	38	20.6	t58	4
M. Titley, London	45	457	10.2	45	3	M. Bailey, Frankfurt	654	46	14.2	t59	7
A. DeGraffenreid, Scot	44	624	14.2	t65	4	A. DeGraffenreid, Scot	624	44	14.2	t65	4

RUSHING

	Att	Yds	Avg	Lg	TD
S. Stacy, Scotland	214	785	3.7	48	5
T. Brooks, London	172	480	2.8	30	5
R. Dawkins, Amster	132	479	3.6	t38	3
N. Bolton, Frankfurt	106	420	4.0	42	3
R. Blake, Barcelona	98	398	4.1	t29	2

Other Statistical Leaders

Points (TDs)	M. Bellamy, Frankfurt	48
Points (Kicking)	S. Szeredy, Barcelona	85
Yards from Scrimmage	S. Stacy, Scotland	1109
Interceptions	C. Hall, Frankfurt	8
Sacks	M. Showell, Amsterdam	8.5
Punting Avg.	D. Alcorn, Frankfurt	40.6
Punt Return Avg.	T.C. Wright, Amsterdam	13.4
Kickoff Return Avg.	A. DeGraffenreid, Scot	23.3

EASTERN DIVISION

	W	L	T	Pts	Pct	PF	PA
Winnipeg	13	5	0	26	.722	651	572
Baltimore	12	6	0	24	.687	561	431
Toronto	7	11	0	14	.389	504	578
Ottawa	4	14	0	8	.222	480	647
Hamilton	4	14	0	8	.222	436	582
Shreveport	3	15	0	6	.167	330	661

WESTERN DIVISION

	W	L	T	Pts	Pct	PF	PA
Calgary	15	3	0	30	.833	686	356
Edmonton	13	5	0	26	.722	518	401
B.C.	11	6	1	23	.647	604	456
Saskatchewan	11	7	0	22	.611	512	454
Sacramento	9	8	1	19	.529	438	436
Las Vegas	5	13	0	10	.278	447	622

Regular Season Statistical Leaders

Points (TDs)	Pitts, Calgary	126
Points (Kicking)	Westwood, Winnipeg	213
Yards (Rushing)	Pringle, Baltimore	1972
Yards (Passing)	Flutie, Calgary	5728
Yards (Receiving)	Pitts, Calgary	2036
Receptions	Pitts, Calgary	126

1994 Playoff Results

DIVISION SEMIFINALS

Eastern:	Toronto 15, BALTIMORE 34
	Ottawa 16, WINNIPEG 26
Western:	British Columbia 24, EDMONTON 23
	Saskatchewan 3, CALGARY 36

DIVISION FINALS

Eastern:	Baltimore 14, WINNIPEG 12
Western:	British Columbia 37, CALGARY 36

1994 Grey Cup Championship

Nov. 27, 1994, at Vancouver

Baltimore CFL'ers	0	17	3	3—23
British Columbia Lions	3	7	10	6—26

A: 55,097

No Gain

Over the past three years the NFL, some 60% of whose players are black, ran its string of white head-coaching hires to 20. During the streak the Dallas Cowboys signed Barry Switzer, who had no pro experience and had not lifted a clipboard for nearly six years; the New York Jets chose Richie Kotite who was fresh from leading the Philadelphia Eagles to seven straight losses; and the Carolina Panthers preferred Don Capers, a soft-spoken, teaching-oriented, white defensive coordinator who turned the Pittsburgh Steeler defense into the second best in the league in 1994, to Tony Dungy, a soft-spoken, teaching-oriented black defensive coordinator who turned the Minnesota Vikings into the *best* in the league in 1993.

It was encouraging to see the Eagles hire an African-American, San Francisco 49er defensive coordinator Ray Rhodes, in early February.

But Rhodes's hiring came the same day that the Los Angeles Raiders fired Art Shell, which left the league with the same number of black head coaches—two—as 37 months ago. Rhodes was the only black interviewee for the current vacancy in St. Louis, even though Dungy, Washington Redskin receivers coach Terry Robiskie and Buffalo Bill assistant head coach Elijah Pitts are qualified candidates.

"We're concerned about this," says NFL commissioner Paul Tagliabue, who lobbied behind the scenes on Rhodes behalf. The pool of high-profile black assistants *is* small, but that's not an excuse, only another symptom of the problem. It may be time for Tagliabue to browbeat his owners into reserving more spots on all staffs for black assistants. Otherwise, the NFL risks not joining the 20th century until that century is over.

The Super Bowl

Results

Date	Winner (Share)	Loser (Share)	Score	Site (Attendance)
I 1-15-67	Green Bay ($15,000)	Kansas City ($7,500)	35-10	Los Angeles (61,946)
II 1-14-68	Green Bay ($15,000)	Oakland ($7,500)	33-14	Miami (75,546)
III 1-12-69	NY Jets ($15,000)	Baltimore ($7,500)	16-7	Miami (75,389)
IV 1-11-70	Kansas City ($15,000)	Minnesota ($7,500)	23-7	New Orleans (80,562)
V 1-17-71	Baltimore ($15,000)	Dallas ($7,500)	16-13	Miami (79,204)
VI 1-16-72	Dallas ($15,000)	Miami ($7,500)	24-3	New Orleans (81,023)
VII 1-14-73	Miami ($15,000)	Washington ($7,500)	14-7	Los Angeles (90,182)
VIII 1-13-74	Miami ($15,000)	Minnesota ($7,500)	24-7	Houston (71,882)
IX 1-12-75	Pittsburgh ($15,000)	Minnesota ($7,500)	16-6	New Orleans (80,997)
X 1-18-76	Pittsburgh ($15,000)	Dallas ($7,500)	21-17	Miami (80,187)
XI 1-9-77	Oakland ($15,000)	Minnesota ($7,500)	32-14	Pasadena (103,438)
XII 1-15-78	Dallas ($18,000)	Denver ($9,000)	27-10	New Orleans (75,583)
XIII 1-21-79	Pittsburgh ($18,000)	Dallas ($9,000)	35-31	Miami (79,484)
XIV 1-20-80	Pittsburgh ($18,000)	Los Angeles ($9,000)	31-19	Pasadena (103,985)
XV 1-25-81	Oakland ($18,000)	Philadelphia ($9,000)	27-10	New Orleans (76,135)
XVI 1-24-82	San Francisco ($18,000)	Cincinnati ($9,000)	26-21	Pontiac (81,270)
XVII 1-30-83	Washington ($36,000)	Miami ($18,000)	27-17	Pasadena (103,667)
XVIII 1-22-84	LA Raiders ($36,000)	Washington ($18,000)	38-9	Tampa (72,920)
XIX 1-20-85	San Francisco ($36,000)	Miami ($18,000)	38-16	Stanford (84,059)
XX 1-26-86	Chicago ($36,000)	New England ($18,000)	46-10	New Orleans (73,818)
XXI 1-25-87	NY Giants ($36,000)	Denver ($18,000)	39-20	Pasadena (101,063)
XXII 1-31-88	Washington ($36,000)	Denver ($18,000)	42-10	San Diego (73,302)
XXIII 1-22-89	San Francisco ($36,000)	Cincinnati ($18,000)	20-16	Miami (75,129)
XXIV 1-28-90	San Francisco ($36,000)	Denver ($18,000)	55-10	New Orleans (72,919)
XXV 1-27-91	NY Giants ($36,000)	Buffalo ($18,000)	20-19	Tampa (73,813)
XXVI 1-26-92	Washington ($36,000)	Buffalo ($18,000)	37-24	Minneapolis (63,130)
XXVII 1-31-93	Dallas ($36,000)	Buffalo ($18,000)	52-17	Pasadena (98,374)
XXVIII 1-30-94	Dallas ($38,000)	Buffalo ($23,500)	30-13	Atlanta (72,817)
XXIX 1-29-95	San Francisco ($42,000)	San Diego ($26,000)	49-26	Miami (74,107)

Most Valuable Players

		Position
I	Bart Starr, GB	QB
II	Bart Starr, GB	QB
III	Joe Namath, NY Jets	QB
IV	Len Dawson, KC	QB
V	Chuck Howley, Dall	LB
VI	Roger Staubach, Dall	QB
VII	Jake Scott, Mia	S
VIII	Larry Csonka, Mia	RB
IX	Franco Harris, Pitt	RB
X	Lynn Swann, Pitt	WR
XI	Fred Biletnikoff, Oak	WR
XII	Randy White, Dall	DT
	Harvey Martin, Dall	DE
XIII	Terry Bradshaw, Pitt	QB
XIV	Terry Bradshaw, Pitt	QB
XV	Jim Plunkett, Oak	QB
XVI	Joe Montana, SF	QB
XVII	John Riggins, Wash	RB
XVIII	Marcus Allen, LA Raiders	RB
XIX	Joe Montana, SF	QB
XX	Richard Dent, Chi	DE
XXI	Phil Simms, NY Giants	QB
XXII	Doug Williams, Wash	QB
XXIII	Jerry Rice, SF	WR
XXIV	Joe Montana, SF	QB
XXV	Ottis Anderson, NY Giants	RB
XXVI	Mark Rypien, Washington	QB
XXVII	Troy Aikman, Dallas	QB
XXVIII	Emmitt Smith, Dallas	RB
XXIX	Steve Young, SF	QB

Composite Standings

	W	L	Pct	Pts	Opp Pts
San Francisco 49ers	5	0	1.000	188	89
Pittsburgh Steelers	4	0	1.000	103	73
Green Bay Packers	2	0	1.000	68	24
N.Y. Giants	2	0	1.000	59	39
Chicago Bears	1	0	1.000	46	10
N.Y. Jets	1	0	1.000	16	7
Oakland/LA Raiders	3	1	.750	111	66
Washington Redskins	3	2	.600	122	103
Dallas Cowboys	4	3	.571	194	115
Baltimore Colts	1	1	.500	23	29
Kansas City Chiefs	1	1	.500	33	42
Miami Dolphins	2	3	.400	74	103
L.A. Rams	0	1	.000	19	31
New England Patriots	0	1	.000	10	46
Philadelphia Eagles	0	1	.000	10	27
San Diego Chargers	0	1	.000	26	49
Cincinnati Bengals	0	2	.000	37	46
Buffalo Bills	0	4	.000	73	139
Denver Broncos	0	4	.000	50	163
Minnesota Vikings	0	4	.000	34	95

Career Leaders
Passing

	GP	Att	Comp	Pct Comp	Yds	Avg Gain	TD	Pct TD	Int	Pct Int	Lg	Rating Pts
Joe Montana, SF	4	122	83	68.0	1142	9.36	11	9.0	0	0.0	44	127.8
Jim Plunkett, Raiders	2	46	29	63.0	433	9.41	4	8.7	0	0.0	t80	122.8
Troy Aikman, Dall	2	57	41	71.9	480	8.42	4	7.0	1	1.8	t56	113.2
Terry Bradshaw, Pitt	4	84	49	58.3	932	11.10	9	10.7	4	4.8	t75	112.8
Bart Starr, GB...	2	47	29	61.7	452	9.62	3	6.4	1	2.1	t62	106.0
Roger Staubach, Dall	4	98	61	62.2	734	7.49	8	8.2	4	4.1	t45	95.4
Len Dawson, KC	2	44	28	63.6	353	8.02	2	4.5	2	4.5	t46	84.8
Bob Griese, Mia	3	41	26	63.4	295	7.20	1	2.4	2	4.9	t28	72.7
Dan Marino, Mia	1	50	29	58.0	318	6.36	1	2.0	2	4.0	30	66.9
Jim Kelly, Buff	4	145	81	55.9	829	5.72	2	1.4	7	4.8	61	57.2
Joe Theismann, Wash	2	58	31	53.4	386	6.66	2	3.4	4	6.9	60	57.1

Note: Minimum 40 attempts.

Rushing

	GP	Yds	Att	Avg	Lg	TD
Franco Harris, Pitt	4	354	101	3.5	25	4
Larry Csonka, Mia	3	297	57	5.2	9	2
Emmitt Smith, Dall	2	240	52	4.6	38	3
John Riggins, Wash	2	230	64	3.6	43	2
Timmy Smith, Wash	1	204	22	9.3	58	2
Thurman Thomas, Buff	4	204	52	3.9	31	4
Roger Craig, SF	3	198	52	3.8	18	2
Marcus Allen, LA Raiders	1	191	20	9.6	t74	2
Tony Dorsett, Dall	2	162	31	5.2	29	1
Mark van Eeghen, Oak	2	148	36	4.1	11	0

Receiving

	GP	No.	Yds	Avg	Lg	TD
Jerry Rice, SF	3	28	512	18.3	t44	7
Andre Reed, Buff	4	27	323	11.9	40	0
Roger Craig, SF	3	20	212	10.6	40	2
Thurman Thomas, Buff	4	20	144	7.2	24	0
Lynn Swann, Pitt	4	16	364	22.8	t64	3
Chuck Foreman, Minn	3	15	139	9.3	26	0
Cliff Branch, Raiders	3	14	181	12.9	50	3
Preston Pearson, Balt-Pitt-Dall	5	12	105	8.8	14	0
Don Beebe, Buff	3	12	171	14.3	43	2
Tom Novacek, Dall	2	12	128	10.6	23	1
Kenneth Davis, Buff	4	12	72	6.0	19	0

Single-Game Leaders

Scoring

	Pts
Roger Craig: XIX, San Francisco vs Miami (1 R, 2 P)	18
Jerry Rice: XXIV, San Francisco vs Denver (3 P); XXIX SF vs San Diego (3 P)	18
Ricky Watters: XXIX, San Francisco vs San Diego (1 R, 2 P)	18

Touchdown Passes

	No.
Steve Young: XXIX, San Francisco vs San Diego	6
Joe Montana: XXIV, San Francisco vs Denver	5
Terry Bradshaw: XIII, Pittsburgh vs Dallas	4
Doug Williams: XXII, Washington vs Denver	4
Troy Aikman: XXVII, Dallas vs Buffalo	4

Four tied with 3

Rushing Yards

	Yds
Timmy Smith: XXII, Washington vs Denver	204
Marcus Allen: XVIII, LA Raiders vs Washington	191
John Riggins: XVII, Washington vs Miami	166
Franco Harris: IX, Pittsburgh vs Minnesota	158
Larry Csonka: VIII, Miami vs Minnesota	145
Clarence Davis: XI, Oakland vs Minnesota	137
Thurman Thomas: XXV, Buffalo vs NY Giants	135
Emmitt Smith: XXVIII, Dallas vs Buffalo	132

Receiving Yards

	Yds
Jerry Rice: XXIII, San Francisco vs Cincinnati	215
Ricky Sanders: XXII, Washington vs Denver	193
Lynn Swann: X, Pittsburgh vs Dallas	161
Andre Reed: XXVII, Buffalo vs Dallas	152
Jerry Rice: XXIX, San Francisco vs San Diego	149
Jerry Rice: XXIV, San Francisco vs Denver	148
Max McGee: I, Green Bay vs Kansas City	138
George Sauer: III, NY Jets vs Baltimore	133

Receptions

	No.
Dan Ross: XVI, Cincinnati vs San Francisco	11
Jerry Rice: XXIII, San Francisco vs Cincinnati	11
Tony Nathan: XIX, Miami vs San Francisco	10
Jerry Rice: XXIX, San Francisco vs San Diego	10
Ricky Sanders: XXII, Washington vs Denver	9

Five tied with 8

Passing Yards

	Yds
Joe Montana: XXIII, San Francisco vs Cincinnati	357
Doug Williams: XXII, Washington vs Denver	340
Joe Montana: XIX, San Francisco vs Miami	331
Steve Young: XXIX, San Francisco vs San Diego	325
Terry Bradshaw: XIII, Pittsburgh vs Dallas	318
Dan Marino: XIX, Miami vs San Francisco	318
Terry Bradshaw: XIV, Pittsburgh vs LA Rams	309
John Elway: XXI, Denver vs NY Giants	304

1933
NFL championship   Chicago Bears 23, NY Giants 21

1934
NFL championship   NY Giants 30, Chicago Bears 13

1935
NFL championship   Detroit 26, NY Giants 7

1936
NFL championship   Green Bay 21, Boston 6

1937
NFL championship   Washington 28,
Chicago Bears 21

1938
NFL championship   NY Giants 23, Green Bay 17

1939
NFL championship   Green Bay 27, NY Giants 0

1940
NFL championship   Chicago Bears 73, Washington 0

1941
W. div. playoff   Chicago Bears 33, Green Bay 14
NFL championship   Chicago Bears 37, NY Giants 9

1942
NFL championship   Washington 14, Chicago Bears 6

1943
E. div. playoff   Washington 28, NY Giants 0
NFL championship   Chicago Bears 41,
Washington 21

1944
NFL championship   Green Bay 14, NY Giants 7

1945
NFL championship   Cleveland 15, Washington 14

1946
NFL championship   Chicago Bears 24, NY Giants 14

1947
E. div. playoff   Philadelphia 21, Pittsburgh 0
NFL championship   Chicago Cardinals 28,
Philadelphia 21

1948
NFL championship   Philadelphia 7,
Chicago Cardinals 0

1949
NFL championship   Philadelphia 14, Los Angeles 0

1950
Am. Conf. playoff   Cleveland 8, NY Giants 3
Nat. Conf. playoff   Los Angeles 24,
Chicago Bears 14
NFL championship   Cleveland 30, Los Angeles 28

1951
NFL championship   Los Angeles 24, Cleveland 17

1952
Nat. Conf. playoff   Detroit 31, Los Angeles 21
NFL championship   Detroit 17, Cleveland 7

1953
NFL championship   Detroit 17, Cleveland 16

1954
NFL championship   Cleveland 56, Detroit 10

1955
NFL championship   Cleveland 38, Los Angeles 14

1956
NFL championship   NY Giants 47, Chicago Bears 7

1957
W. Conf. playoff   Detroit 31, San Francisco 27
NFL championship   Detroit 59, Cleveland 14

1958
E. Conf. playoff   NY Giants 10, Cleveland 0
NFL championship   Baltimore 23, NY Giants 17

1959
NFL championship   Baltimore 31, NY Giants 16

1960
NFL championship   Philadelphia 17, Green Bay 13
AFL championship   Houston 24, LA Chargers 16

1961
NFL championship   Green Bay 37, NY Giants 0
AFL championship   Houston 10, San Diego 3

1962
NFL championship   Green Bay 16, NY Giants 7
AFL championship   Dallas Texans 20, Houston 17

1963
NFL championship   Chicago 14, NY Giants 10
AFL E. div. playoff   Boston 26, Buffalo 8
AFL championship   San Diego 51, Boston 10

1964
NFL championship   Cleveland 27, Baltimore 0
AFL championship   Buffalo 20, San Diego 7

1965
NFL W. Conf.
playoff   Green Bay 13, Baltimore 10
NFL championship   Green Bay 23, Cleveland 12
AFL championship   Buffalo 23, San Diego 0

1966
NFL championship   Green Bay 34, Dallas 27
AFL championship   Kansas City 31, Buffalo 7

1967
NFL E. Conf.
championship   Dallas 52, Cleveland 14
NFL W. Conf.
championship   Green Bay 28, Los Angeles 7
NFL championship   Green Bay 21, Dallas 17
AFL championship   Oakland 40, Houston 7

1968

NFL E. Conf. championship	Cleveland 31, Dallas 20
NFL W. Conf. championship	Baltimore 24, Minnesota 14
NFL championship	Baltimore 34, Cleveland 0
AFL W. div. playoff	Oakland 41, Kansas City 6
AFL championship	NY Jets 27, Oakland 23

1969

NFL E. Conf. championship	Cleveland 38, Dallas 14
NFL W. Conf. championship	Minnesota 23, Los Angeles 20
NFL championship	Minnesota 27, Cleveland 7
AFL div. playoffs	Kansas City 13, NY Jets 6
	Oakland 56, Houston 7
AFL championship	Kansas City 17, Oakland 7

1970

AFC div. playoffs	Baltimore 17, Cincinnati 0
	Oakland 21, Miami 14
AFC championship	Baltimore 27, Oakland 17
NFC div. playoffs	Dallas 5, Detroit 0
	San Francisco 17, Minnesota 14
NFC championship	Dallas 17, San Francisco 10

1971

AFC div. playoffs	Miami 27, Kansas City 24
	Baltimore 20, Cleveland 3
AFC championship	Miami 21, Baltimore 0
NFC div. playoffs	Dallas 20, Minnesota 12
	San Francisco 24, Washington 20
NFC championship	Dallas 14, San Francisco 3

1972

AFC div. playoffs	Pittsburgh 13, Oakland 7
	Miami 20, Cleveland 14
AFC championship	Miami 21, Pittsburgh 17
NFC div. playoffs	Dallas 30, San Francisco 28
	Washington 16, Green Bay 3
NFC championship	Washington 26, Dallas 3

1973

AFC div. playoffs	Oakland 33, Pittsburgh 14
	Miami 34, Cincinnati 16
AFC championship	Miami 27, Oakland 10
NFC div. playoffs	Minnesota 27, Washington 20
	Dallas 27, Los Angeles 16
NFC championship	Minnesota 27, Dallas 10

1974

AFC div. playoffs	Oakland 28, Miami 26
	Pittsburgh 32, Buffalo 14
AFC championship	Pittsburgh 24, Oakland 13
NFC div. playoffs	Minnesota 30, St Louis 14
	Los Angeles 19, Washington 10
NFC championship	Minnesota 14, Los Angeles 10

1975

AFC div. playoffs	Pittsburgh 28, Baltimore 10
	Oakland 31, Cincinnati 28
AFC championship	Pittsburgh 16, Oakland 10
NFC div. playoffs	Los Angeles 35, St Louis 23
	Dallas 17, Minnesota 14
NFC championship	Dallas 37, Los Angeles 7

1976

AFC div. playoffs	Oakland 24, New England 21
	Pittsburgh 40, Baltimore 14
AFC championship	Oakland 24, Pittsburgh 7
NFC div. playoffs	Minnesota 35, Washington 20
	Los Angeles 14, Dallas 12
NFC championship	Minnesota 24, Los Angeles 13

1977

AFC div. playoffs	Denver 34, Pittsburgh 21
	Oakland 37, Baltimore 31
AFC championship	Denver 20, Oakland 17
NFC div. playoffs	Dallas 37, Chicago 7
	Minnesota 14, Los Angeles 7
NFC championship	Dallas 23, Minnesota 6

1978

AFC 1st-rd. playoff	Houston 17, Miami 9
AFC div. playoffs	Houston 31, New England 14
	Pittsburgh 33, Denver 10
AFC championship	Pittsburgh 34, Houston 5
NFC 1st-rd. playoff	Atlanta 14, Philadelphia 13
NFC div. playoffs	Dallas 27, Atlanta 20
	Los Angeles 34, Minnesota 10
NFC championship	Dallas 28, Los Angeles 0

1979

AFC 1st-rd. playoff	Houston 13, Denver 7
AFC div. playoffs	Houston 17, San Diego 14
	Pittsburgh 34, Miami 14
AFC championship	Pittsburgh 27, Houston 13
NFC 1st-rd. playoff	Philadelphia 27, Chicago 17
NFC div. playoffs	Tampa Bay 24, Philadelphia 17
	Los Angeles 21, Dallas 19
NFC championship	Los Angeles 9, Tampa Bay 0

1980

AFC 1st-rd. playoff	Oakland 27, Houston 7
AFC div. playoffs	San Diego 20, Buffalo 14
	Oakland 14, Cleveland 12
AFC championship	Oakland 34, San Diego 27
NFC 1st-rd. playoff	Dallas 34, Los Angeles 13
NFC div. playoffs	Philadelphia 31, Minnesota 16
	Dallas 30, Atlanta 27
NFC championship	Philadelphia 20, Dallas 7

1981

AFC 1st-rd. playoff	Buffalo 31, NY Jets 27
AFC div. playoffs	San Diego 41, Miami 38
	Cincinnati 28, Buffalo 21
AFC championship	Cincinnati 27, San Diego 7
NFC 1st-rd. playoff	NY Giants 27, Philadelphia 21
NFC div. playoffs	Dallas 38, Tampa Bay 0
	San Francisco 38, NY Giants 24
NFC championship	San Francisco 28, Dallas 27

1982

AFC 1st-rd. playoffs	Miami 28, New England 13
	LA Raiders 27, Cleveland 10
	NY Jets 44, Cincinnati 17
	San Diego 31, Pittsburgh 28
AFC div. playoffs	NY Jets 17, LA Raiders 14
	Miami 34, San Diego 13
AFC championship	Miami 14, NY Jets 0
NFC 1st-rd. playoffs	Washington 31, Detroit 7
	Green Bay 41, St Louis 16
	Minnesota 30, Atlanta 24

1982 (Cont.)

NFC 1st-rd. (*cont.*)	Dallas 30, Tampa Bay 17
NFCdiv. playoffs	Washington 21, Minnesota 7
	Dallas 37, Green Bay 26
NFC championship	Washington 31, Dallas 17

1983

AFC 1st-rd. playoff	Seattle 31, Denver 7
AFC div. playoffs	Seattle 27, Miami 20
	LA Raiders 38, Pittsburgh 10
AFC championship	LA Raiders 30, Seattle 14
NFC 1st-rd. playoff	LA Rams 24, Dallas 17
NFC div. playoffs	San Francisco 24, Detroit 23
	Washington 51, LA Rams 7
NFC championship	Washington 24, San Francisco 21

1984

AFC 1st-rd. playoff	Seattle 13, LA Raiders 7
AFC div. playoffs	Miami 31, Seattle 10
	Pittsburgh 24, Denver 17
AFC championship	Miami 45, Pittsburgh 28
NFC 1st-rd. playoff	NY Giants 16, LA Rams 13
NFC div. playoffs	San Francisco 21, NY Giants 10
	Chicago 23, Washington 19
NFC championship	San Francisco 23, Chicago 0

1985

AFC 1st-rd. playoff	New England 26, NY Jets 14
AFC div. playoffs	Miami 24, Cleveland 21
	New England 27, LA Raiders 20
AFC championship	New England 31, Miami 14
NFC 1st-rd. playoff	NY Giants 17, San Francisco 3
NFC div. playoffs	LA Rams 20, Dallas 0
	Chicago 21, NY Giants 0
NFC championship	Chicago 24, LA Rams 0

1986

AFC 1st-rd. playoff	NY Jets 35, Kansas City 15
AFC div. playoffs	Cleveland 23, NY Jets 20
	Denver 22, New England 17
AFC championship	Denver 23, Cleveland 20
NFC 1st-rd. playoff	Washington 19, LA Rams 7
NFC div playoffs	Washington 27, Chicago 13
	NY Giants 49, San Francisco 3
NFC championship	NY Giants 17, Washington 0

1987

AFC div. playoffs	Cleveland 38, Indianapolis 21
	Denver 34, Houston 10
AFC championship	Denver 38, Cleveland 33
NFC 1st-rd. playoff	Minnesota 44, New Orleans 10
NFC div playoffs	Minnesota 36, San Francisco 24
	Washington 21, Chicago 17
NFC championship	Washington 17, Minnesota 10

1988

AFC 1st-rd. playoff	Houston 24, Cleveland 23
AFC div. playoffs	Cincinnati 21, Seattle 13
	Buffalo 17, Houston 10
AFC championship	Cincinnati 21, Buffalo 10
NFC 1st-rd. playoff	Minnesota 28, LA Rams 17
NFC div. playoffs	Chicago 20, Philadelphia 12
	San Francisco 34, Minnesota 9
NFC championship	San Francisco 28, Chicago 3

1989

AFC 1st-rd. playoff	Pittsburgh 26, Houston 23
AFC div. playoffs	Cleveland 34, Buffalo 30

1989 (Cont.)

AFC div. playoffs (*cont.*)	Denver 24, Pittsburgh 23
AFC championship	Denver 37, Cleveland 21
NFC 1st-rd. playoff	LA Rams 21, Philadelphia 7
NFC div. playoffs	LA Rams 19, NY Giants 13
	San Francisco 41, Minnesota 13
NFC championship	San Francisco 30, LA Rams 3

1990

AFC 1st-rd. playoffs	Miami 17, Kansas City 16
	Cincinnati 41, Houston 14
AFC div. playoffs	Buffalo 44, Miami 34
	LA Raiders 20, Cincinnati 10
AFC championship	Buffalo 51, LA Raiders 3
NFC 1st-rd. playoffs	Chicago 16, New Orleans 6
	Washington 20, Philadelphia 6
NFC div. playoffs	NY Giants 31, Chicago 3
	San Francisco 28, Washington 10
NFC championship	NY Giants 15, San Francisco 13

1991

AFC 1st-rd. playoffs	Houston 17, NY Jets 10
	Kansas City 10, LA Raiders 6
AFC div. playoffs	Denver 26, Houston 24
	Buffalo 37, Kansas City 14
AFC championship	Buffalo 10, Denver 7
NFC 1st-rd. playoffs	Atlanta 27, New Orleans 20
	Dallas 17, Chicago 13
NFC div. playoffs	Washington 24, Atlanta 7
	Detroit 38, Dallas 6
NFC championship	Washington 41, Detroit 10

1992

AFC 1st-rd. playoffs	San Diego 17, Kansas City 0
	Buffalo 41, Houston 38 (OT)
AFC div. playoffs	Buffalo 24, Pittsburgh 3
	Miami 31, San Diego 0
AFC championship	Buffalo 29, Miami 10
NFC 1st-rd. playoffs	Washington 24, Minnesota 7
	Philadelphia 36, New Orleans 20
NFC div. playoffs	San Francisco 20, Washington 13
	Dallas 34, Philadelphia 10
NFC championship	Dallas 30, San Francisco 20

1993

AFC 1st-rd. playoffs	LA Raiders 42, Denver 24
	Kansas City 27. Pittsburgh 24 (OT)
AFC div. playoffs	Buffalo 29, LA Raiders 23
	Kansas City 28, Houston 20
AFC championship	Buffalo 30, Kansas City 13
NFC 1st-rd. playoffs	NY Giants 17, Minnesota 10
	Green Bay 28, Detroit 24
NFC div. playoffs	San Francisco 44, NY Giants 3
	Dallas 27, Green Bay 17
NFC championship	Dallas 38, San Francisco 21

1994

AFC 1st-rd. playoffs	Miami 27, Kansas City 17
	Cleveland 20, New England 13
AFC div. playoffs	San Diego 22, Miami 21
	Pittsburgh 29, Cleveland 9
AFC championship	San Diego 17, Pittsburgh 13
NFC 1st-rd. playoffs	Green Bay 16, Detroit 12
	Chicago 35, Minnesota 18
NFC div. playoffs	Dallas 35, Green Bay 9
	San Francisco 44, Chicago 15
NFC championship	San Francisco 38, Dallas 28

Career Leaders

Scoring

	Yrs	TD	FG	PAT	Pts
George Blanda	26	9	335	943	2002
Jan Stenerud	19	0	373	580	1699
†Nick Lowery	16	0	349	512	1559
Pat Leahy	18	0	304	558	1470
Jim Turner	16	1	304	521	1439
Mark Moseley	16	0	300	482	1382
Jim Bakken	17	0	282	534	1380
Fred Cox	15	0	282	519	1365
†Eddie Murray	17	0	298	465	1359
Lou Groza	17	1	234	641	1349
†Gary Anderson	13	0	309	416	1343
†Matt Bahr	17	0	277	495	1326
†Morten Andersen	13	0	302	412	1318
Jim Breech	14	0	243	517	1246
Chris Bahr	14	0	241	490	1213
†Norm Johnson	13	0	243	476	1205
Gino Cappelletti	11	42	176	350	1130
Ray Wersching	15	0	222	456	1122
Don Cockroft	13	0	216	432	1080
Garo Yepremian	14	0	210	444	1074

Cappelletti's total includes four two-point conversions.

Rushing

	Yrs	Att	Yds	Avg	Lg	TD
Walter Payton	13	3,838	16,726	4.4	76	110
Eric Dickerson	13	2,996	13,259	4.4	85	90
Tony Dorsett	12	2,936	12,739	4.3	99	77
Jim Brown	9	2,359	12,312	5.2	80	106
Franco Harris	13	2,949	12,120	4.1	75	91
John Riggins	14	2,916	11,352	3.9	66	104
O.J. Simpson	11	2,404	11,236	4.7	94	61
Ottis Anderson	16	2,562	10,273	4.0	76	81
†Marcus Allen	13	2,485	10,018	4.0	61	98
Earl Campbell	8	2,187	9,407	4.3	81	74
†Thurman Thomas	7	2,018	8,724	4.3	80	48
†Barry Sanders	6	1,763	8,672	4.9	85	62
Jim Taylor	10	1,941	8,597	4.4	84	83
Joe Perry	14	1,737	8,378	4.8	78	53
Roger Craig	11	1,991	8,189	4.1	71	56
Gerald Riggs	10	1,989	8,188	4.2	58	69
Larry Csonka	11	1,891	8,081	4.3	54	64
Freeman McNeil	12	1,798	8,074	4.5	69	38
†Herschel Walker	11	1,907	7,996	4.2	91	59
James Brooks	12	1,685	7,962	4.7	65	49

Touchdowns

	Yrs	Rush	Pass Rec	Ret	Total TD
†Jerry Rice	10	8	131	0	139
Jim Brown	9	106	20	0	126
Walter Payton	13	110	15	0	125
†Marcus Allen	13	98	21	1	120
John Riggins	14	104	12	0	116
Lenny Moore	12	63	48	2	113
Don Hutson	11	3	99	3	105
Steve Largent	14	1	100	0	101
Franco Harris	13	91	9	0	100
Eric Dickerson	13	90	6	0	96

	Yrs	Rush	Pass Rec	Ret	Total TD
Jim Taylor	10	83	10	0	93
Tony Dorsett	12	77	13	1	91
Bobby Mitchell	11	18	65	8	91
Leroy Kelly	10	74	13	3	90
Charley Taylor	13	11	79	0	90
Don Maynard	15	0	88	0	88
Lance Alworth	11	2	85	0	87
Paul Warfield	13	1	85	0	86
Ottis Anderson	13	81	5	0	86
Tommy McDonald	12	0	84	1	85
Mark Clayton	11	0	85	0	85

Longest Plays

RUSHING

	Opponent	Year	Yds
Tony Dorsett, Dall	Minn	1983	99
Andy Uram, GB	Chi Cards	1939	97
Bob Gage, Pitt	Chi	1949	97
Jim Spitival, Balt	GB	1950	96
Bob Hoernschemeyer, Det	NY Yanks	1950	96

PASSING

	Opponent	Year	Yds
Frank Filchock to Andy Farkas, Washington	Pitt	1939	99
George Izo to Bobby Mitchell, Washington	Cle	1963	99
Karl Sweetan to Pat Studstill, Detroit	Balt	1966	99
Sonny Jurgensen to Gerry Allen, Washington	Chi	1968	99
Jim Plunkett to Cliff Branch, LA Raiders	Wash	1983	99
Ron Jaworski to Mike Quick, Philadelphia	Atl	1985	99

FIELD GOALS

	Opponent	Year	Yds
Tom Dempsey, NO	Det	1970	63
Steve Cox, Cle	Cin	1984	60
Morten Andersen, NO	Chi	1991	60

PUNTS

	Opponent	Year	Yds
Steve O'Neal, NY Jets	Den	1969	98
Joe Lintzenich, Chi	NY Giants	1931	94
Shawn McCarthy, NE	Buff	1991	93
Randall Cunningham, Phi	NY Giants	1989	91

THEY SAID IT

Buddy Ryan, Arizona Cardinal coach, on the salary options he gave wide receiver Gary Clark: "It's either a 30% cut or a 100% cut."

† Active player

Career Leaders *(Cont.)*

Combined Yards Gained

	Yrs	Total	Rush	Rec	Int Ret	Punt Ret	Kickoff Ret	Fum Ret
Walter Payton	13	21,803	16,726	4,538	0	0	539	0
Tony Dorsett	12	16,326	12,739	3,554	0	0	0	33
Jim Brown	9	15,459	12,312	2,499	0	0	648	0
Eric Dickerson	13	15,396	13,259	2,137	0	0	0	15
†Marcus Allen	13	14,863	10,018	4,845	0	0	0	0
James Brooks	12	14,644	7,962	3,621	0	565	2,762	0
Franco Harris	13	14,622	12,120	2,287	0	0	233	−18
O.J. Simpson	11	14,368	11,236	2,142	0	0	990	0
James Lofton	16	14,234	246	13,988	0	0	0	27
Bobby Mitchell	11	14,078	2,735	7,954	0	699	2,690	0
†Jerry Rice	10	13,986	711	13,275	0	0	0	0
John Riggins	14	13,435	11,352	2,090	0	0	0	−7
Steve Largent	14	13,396	83	13,089	0	68	156	0
Ottis Anderson	14	13,364	10,273	3,062	0	0	0	29
Greg Pruitt	12	13,262	5,672	3,069	0	2,007	2,514	0
Roger Craig	11	13,100	8,189	4,911	0	0	0	0
†Art Monk	15	12,939	332	12,607	0	0	0	0
Ollie Matson	14	12,884	5,173	3,285	51	595	3,746	34
Tim Brown	10	12,684	3,862	3,399	0	639	4,781	3
Lenny Moore	12	12,451	5,174	6,039	0	56	1,180	2

*Passing

	Yrs	Att	Comp	Pct Comp	Yds	Avg Gain	TD	Pct TD	Int	Pct Int	Rating Pts
†Steve Young	10	2,429	1,546	63.7	19,869	8.18	140	5.8	68	2.8	96.9
Joe Montana	15	5,391	3,409	63.2	40,551	7.52	273	5.1	139	2.6	92.3
†Dan Marino	12	6,049	3,604	59.6	45,173	7.47	328	5.4	185	3.1	88.0
†Jim Kelly	9	3,942	2,397	60.8	29,527	7.49	201	5.1	143	3.6	86.0
Roger Staubach	11	2,958	1,685	57.0	22,700	7.67	153	5.2	109	3.7	83.4
†Dave Krieg	15	4,390	2,562	58.4	32,114	7.32	231	5.3	166	3.8	83.1
Neil Lomax	8	3,153	1,817	57.6	22,771	7.22	136	4.3	90	2.9	82.7
Sonny Jurgensen	18	4,262	2,433	57.1	32,224	7.56	255	6.0	189	4.4	82.6
Len Dawson	19	3,741	2,136	57.1	28,711	7.67	239	6.4	183	4.9	82.6
†Bernie Kosar	10	3,225	1,896	58.8	22,394	6.94	120	3.7	82	2.5	81.9
Ken Anderson	16	4,475	2,654	59.3	32,838	7.34	197	4.4	160	3.6	81.9
†Brett Favre	4	1,580	983	62.2	10,412	6.59	70	4.4	53	3.4	81.9
Danny White	13	2,950	1,761	59.7	21,959	7.44	155	5.3	132	4.5	81.7
†Troy Aikman	6	2,281	1,424	62.4	16,303	7.15	82	3.6	78	3.4	81.7
†Boomer Esiason	11	4,291	2,440	56.9	31,874	7.43	207	4.8	153	3.6	81.5
Ken O'Brien	10	3,602	2,110	58.6	25,094	6.97	128	3.6	98	2.7	80.7
†Warren Moon	11	5,147	3,003	58.4	37,949	7.37	214	4.2	185	3.6	80.5
Bart Starr	16	3,149	1,808	57.4	24,718	7.85	152	4.8	138	4.4	80.5
Fran Tarkenton	18	6,467	3,686	57.0	47,003	7.27	342	5.3	266	4.1	80.4
Dan Fouts	15	5,604	3,297	58.8	43,040	7.68	254	4.5	242	4.3	80.2

*1,500 or more attempts. The passing ratings are based on performance standards established for completion percentage, interception percentage, touchdown percentage, and average gain. Passers are allocated points according to how their marks compare with those standards.

Receiving

	Yrs	No.	Yds	Avg	Lg	TD		Yrs	No.	Yds	Avg	Lg	TD
†Art Monk	15	934	12,607	13.5	79	68	Drew Hill	14	634	9,831	15.5	81	60
†Jerry Rice	10	820	13,275	16.2	96	131	Don Maynard	15	633	11,834	18.7	87	88
Steve Largent	14	819	13,089	16.0	74	100	Raymond Berry	13	631	9,275	14.7	70	68
James Lofton	16	763	13,988	18.3	80	75	†Sterling Sharpe	7	595	8,134	13.7	76	65
Charlie Joiner	18	750	12,146	16.2	87	65	Harold Carmichael	14	590	8,985	15.2	79	79
†Andre Reed	10	676	9,536	14.1	83	66	Fred Biletnikoff	14	589	8,974	15.2	82	76
†Henry Ellard	12	667	11,158	16.7	81	54	Mark Clayton	11	582	8,974	15.4	78	85
†Gary Clark	10	662	10,331	15.6	84	63	Harold Jackson	16	579	10,372	17.9	79	76
Ozzie Newsome	13	662	7,980	12.1	74	47	Lionel Taylor	10	567	7,195	12.7	80	45
Charley Taylor	13	649	9,110	14.0	88	79	Roger Craig	11	566	4,911	8.7	73	17

† Active player

Career Leaders (Cont.)

Interceptions

	Yrs	No.	Yds	Avg	Lg	TD
Paul Krause	16	81	1185	14.6	81	3
Emlen Tunnell	14	79	1282	16.2	55	4
Dick (Night Train) Lane	14	68	1207	17.8	80	5
Ken Riley	15	65	596	9.2	66	5
†Ronnie Lott	14	63	730	11.3	83	5

Punt Returns

	Yrs	No.	Yds	Avg	Lg	TD
George McAfee	8	112	1431	12.8	74	2
Jack Christiansen	8	85	1084	12.8	89	8
Claude Gibson	5	110	1381	12.6	85	3
Bill Dudley	9	124	1515	12.2	96	3
Rick Upchurch	9	248	3008	12.1	92	8

Punting

	Yrs	No.	Yds	Avg	Lg	Blk
Sammy Baugh	16	338	15,245	45.1	85	9
Tommy Davis	11	511	22,833	44.7	82	2
Yale Lary	11	503	22,279	44.3	74	4
†Rohn Stark	13	985	43,152	43.8	72	7
Horace Gillom	7	385	16,872	43.8	80	5

†Active player

Kickoff Returns

	Yrs	No.	Yds	Avg	Lg	TD
Gale Sayers	7	91	2781	30.6	103	6
Lynn Chandnois	7	92	2720	29.6	93	3
Abe Woodson	9	193	5538	28.7	105	5
Claude (Buddy) Young	6	90	2514	27.9	104	2
Travis Williams	5	102	2801	27.5	105	6

Single-Season Leaders

Scoring

POINTS

	Year	TD	PAT	FG	Pts
Paul Hornung, GB	1960	15	41	15	176
Mark Moseley, Wash.	1983	0	62	33	161
Gino Cappelletti, Bos.	1964	7	38	25	155
Chip Lohmiller, Wash.	1991	0	56	31	149
Gino Cappelletti, Bos.	1961	8	48	17	147
Paul Hornung, GB	1961	10	41	15	146
Jim Turner, NY Jets	1968	0	43	34	145
John Riggins, Wash	1983	24	0	0	144
Kevin Butler, Chi	1985	0	51	31	144
Tony Franklin, NE	1986	0	44	32	140

Note: Cappelletti's 1964 total includes a two-point conversion.

TOUCHDOWNS

	Year	Rush	Rec	Ret	Total
John Riggins, Wash	1983	24	0	0	24
O.J. Simpson, Buff	1975	16	7	0	23
Jerry Rice, SF	1987	1	22	0	23
Gale Sayers, Chi	1965	14	6	2	22
Emmitt Smith, Dall	1994	21	1	0	22

FIELD GOALS

	Year	Att	No.
Jeff Jaeger, LA Raiders	1993	44	35
Ali Haji-Sheikh, NY Giants	1983	42	35
Jim Turner, NY Jets	1968	46	34
Jason Hanson, Det	1993	43	34
John Carney, SD	1994	38	34
Fuad Reveiz, Minn	1994	39	34

Rushing

YARDS GAINED

	Year	Att	Yds	Avg
Eric Dickerson, LA Rams	1984	379	2105	5.6
O.J. Simpson, Buff	1973	332	2003	6.0
Earl Campbell, Hou	1980	373	1934	5.2
Jim Brown, Clev	1963	291	1883	6.4
Barry Sanders, Det	1994	331	1883	5.7
Walter Payton, Chi	1977	339	1852	5.5
Eric Dickerson, LA Rams	1986	404	1821	4.5
O.J. Simpson, Buff	1975	329	1817	5.5
Eric Dickerson, LA Rams	1983	390	1808	4.6
Marcus Allen, LA Raiders	1985	390	1759	4.6
Gerald Riggs, Atl	1985	397	1719	4.3
Emmitt Smith, Dall	1992	373	1713	4.6

AVERAGE GAIN

	Year	Avg
Beattie Feathers, Chi	1934	8.44
Randall Cunningham, Phil	1990	7.98
Bobby Douglass, Chi	1972	6.87

TOUCHDOWNS

	Year	No.
John Riggins, Wash	1983	24
Emmitt Smith, Dall	1994	22
Joe Morris, NY Giants	1985	21
Jim Taylor, GB	1962	19
Earl Campbell, Hou	1979	19
Chuck Muncie, SD	1981	19
Emmitt Smith, Dall	1992	18

Single-Season Leaders *(Cont.)*
Passing

YARDS GAINED

	Year	Att	Comp	Pct	Yds
Dan Marino, Mia	1984	564	362	64.2	5084
Dan Fouts, SD	1981	609	360	59.1	4802
Dan Marino, Mia	1986	623	378	60.7	4746
Dan Fouts, SD	1980	589	348	59.1	4715
Warren Moon, Hou	1991	655	404	61.7	4690
Warren Moon, Hou	1990	584	362	62.0	4689
Neil Lomax, StL	1984	560	345	61.6	4614
Drew Bledsoe, NE	1994	691	400	57.9	4555
Lynn Dickey, GB	1983	484	289	59.7	4458
Dan Marino, Mia	1994	615	385	62.6	4453
Dan Marino, Mia	1988	606	354	58.4	4434
Bill Kenney, KC	1983	603	346	57.4	4348

PASS RATING

	Year	Rat.
Steve Young, SF	1994	112.8
Joe Montana, SF	1989	112.4
Milt Plum, Clev	1960	110.4
Sammy Baugh, Wash	1945	109.9
Dan Marino, Mia	1984	108.9

TOUCHDOWNS

	Year	No.
Dan Marino, Mia	1984	48
Dan Marino, Mia	1986	44
George Blanda, Hou	1961	36
Y. A. Tittle, NY Giants	1963	36
Steve Young, SF	1994	35

Receiving

RECEPTIONS

	Year	No.	Yds
Cris Carter, Minn	1994	122	1256
Sterling Sharpe, GB	1993	112	1274
Jerry Rice, SF	1994	112	1499
Terance Mathis, Atl	1994	111	1342
Sterling Sharpe, GB	1992	108	1461
Art Monk, Wash	1984	106	1372
Charley Hennigan, Hou	1964	101	1546
Lionel Taylor, Den	1961	100	1176
Jerry Rice, SF	1990	100	1502
Haywood Jeffires, Hou	1991	100	1181
Jerry Rice, SF	1993	98	1503
Ben Coates, NE	1994	96	1174
Todd Christensen, Rai	1986	95	1153

YARDS GAINED

	Year	Yds
Charley Hennigan, Hou	1961	1746
Lance Alworth, SD	1965	1602
Jerry Rice, SF	1986	1570
Roy Green, StL	1984	1555

TOUCHDOWNS

	Year	No.
Jerry Rice, SF	1987	22
Mark Clayton, Mia	1984	18
Sterling Sharpe, GB	1994	18
Don Hutson, GB	1942	17
Elroy (Crazylegs) Hirsch, LA Rams	1951	17
Bill Groman, Hou	1961	17
Jerry Rice, SF	1989	17

All-Purpose Yards

	Year	Run	Rec	Ret	Total
Lionel James, SD	1985	516	1027	992	2535
Terry Metcalf, StL	1975	816	378	1268	2462
Mack Herron, NE	1974	824	474	1146	2444
Gale Sayers, Chi	1966	1231	447	762	2440
Timmy Brown, Phil	1963	841	487	1100	2428
Tim Brown, Rai	1988	50	725	1542	2317
Marcus Allen, Rai	1985	1759	555	–6	2308
Timmy Brown, Phil	1962	545	849	912	2306
Gale Sayers, Chi	1965	867	507	898	2272
Eric Dickerson, LA Rams	1984	2105	139	15	2259
O.J. Simpson, Buff	1975	1817	426	0	2243

Punting

	Year	No.	Yds	Avg
Sammy Baugh, Wash	1940	35	1799	51.4
Yale Lary, Det	1963	35	1713	48.9
Sammy Baugh, Wash	1941	30	1462	48.7
Yale Lary, Det	1961	52	2516	48.4
Sammy Baugh, Wash	1942	37	1783	48.2

Sacks

	Year	No.
Mark Gastineau, NY Jets	1984	22
Reggie White, Phil	1987	21
Chris Doleman, Minn	1989	21
Lawrence Taylor, NY Giants	1986	20.5

Interceptions

	Year	No.
Dick (Night Train) Lane, LA Rams	1952	14
Dan Sandifer, Wash	1948	13
Spec Sanders, NY Yanks	1950	13
Lester Hayes, Oak	1980	13

Kickoff Returns

	Year	Avg
Travis Williams, GB	1967	41.1
Gale Sayers, Chi	1967	37.7
Ollie Matson, Chi Cardinals	1958	35.5
Jim Duncan, Balt	1970	35.4
Lynn Chandnois, Pitt	1952	35.2

Punt Returns

	Year	Avg
Herb Rich, Balt	1950	23.0
Jack Christiansen, Det	1952	21.5
Dick Christy, NY Titans	1961	21.3
Bob Hayes, Dall	1968	20.8

Single-Game Leaders
Scoring

POINTS

	Date	Pts
Ernie Nevers, Cards vs Bears	11-28-29	40
Dub Jones, Clev vs Chi Bears	11-25-51	36
Gale Sayers, Chi Bears vs SF	12-12-65	36
Paul Hornung, GB vs Balt	10-8-61	33

On Thanksgiving Day, 1929, Nevers scored all the Cardinals' points on six rushing TDs and four PATs. The Cards defeated Red Grange and the Bears, 40-6. Jones and Sayers each rushed for four touchdowns and scored two more on returns in their teams' victories. Hornung scored four touchdowns and kicked 6 PATs and a field goal in a 45-7 win over the Colts.

FIELD GOALS

	Date	No.
Jim Bakken, StL vs Pitt	9-24-67	7
Rich Karlis, Minn vs LA Rams	11-5-89	7
Eight players tied with 6 FGs each.		

Bakken was 7 for 9, Karlis 7 for 7.

TOUCHDOWNS

	Date	No.
Ernie Nevers, Cards vs Bears	11-28-29	6
Dub Jones, Clev vs Chi Bears	11-25-51	6
Gale Sayers, Chi vs SF	12-12-65	6
Bob Shaw, Chi Cards vs Balt	10-2-50	5
Jim Brown, Clev vs Balt	11-1-59	5
Abner Haynes, Dall Texans vs Oak	11-26-61	5
Billy Cannon, Hous vs NY Titans	12-10-61	5
Cookie Gilchrist, Buff vs NY Jets	12-8-63	5
Paul Hornung, GB vs Balt	12-12-65	5
Kellen Winslow, SD vs Oak	11-22-81	5
Jerry Rice, SF vs Atl	10-14-90	5

Rushing

YARDS GAINED

	Date	Yds
Walter Payton, Chi vs Minn	11-20-77	275
O.J. Simpson, Buff vs Det	11-25-76	273
O.J. Simpson, Buff vs NE	9-16-73	250
Willie Ellison, LA Rams vs NO	12-5-71	247
Cookie Gilchrist, Buff vs NY Jets	12-8-63	243

TOUCHDOWNS

	Date	No.
Ernie Nevers, Cards vs Bears	11-28-29	6
Jim Brown, Clev vs Balt	11-1-59	5
Cookie Gilchrist, Buff vs NY Jets	12-8-63	5

CARRIES

	Date	No.
Jamie Morris, Wash vs Cin	12-17-88	45
Butch Woolfolk, NY Giants vs Phil	11-20-83	43
James Wilder, TB vs GB	9-30-84	43
James Wilder, TB vs Pitt	10-30-83	42
Franco Harris, Pitt vs Cin	10-17-76	41
Gerald Riggs, Atl vs LA Rams	11-17-85	41

Passing

YARDS GAINED

	Date	Yds
Norm Van Brocklin, LA vs NY Yanks	9-28-51	554
Warren Moon, Hou vs KC	12-16-90	527
Dan Marino, Mia vs NY Jets	10-23-88	521
Phil Simms, NY Giants vs Cin	10-13-85	513
Vince Ferragamo, LA Rams vs Chi	12-26-82	509
Y. A. Tittle, NY Giants vs Wash	10-28-62	505

COMPLETIONS

	Date	No.
Drew Bledsoe, NE vs Minn	11-13-94	45
Richard Todd, NY Jets vs SF	9-21-80	42
Warren Moon, Hou vs Dall	11-10-91	41
Ken Anderson, Cin vs SD	12-20-82	40
Phil Simms, NY Giants vs Cin	10-13-85	40
Dan Marino, Mia vs Buff	11-16-86	39

Two tied with 38

TOUCHDOWNS

	Date	No.
Sid Luckman, Chi Bears vs NY Giants	11-14-43	7
Adrian Burk, Phil vs Wash	10-17-54	7
George Blanda, Hou vs NY Titans	11-19-61	7
Y. A. Tittle, NY Giants vs Wash	10-28-62	7
Joe Kapp, Minn vs Balt	9-28-69	7

THEY SAID IT

Buffalo Bill linebacker Cornelius Bennett, after a loss to New England ended the Bills' playoff hopes and their AFC dynasty: "It hurts ... looking across the field and seeing someone else celebrate the way we used to."

Single-Game Leaders (Cont.)
Receiving

RECEIVING

YARDS GAINED	Date	Yds	RECEPTIONS	Date	No.
Flipper Anderson, LA Rams vs NO	11-26-89	336	Tom Fears, LA Rams vs GB	12-3-50	18
Stephone Paige, KC vs SD	12-22-85	309	Clark Gaines, NY Jets vs SF	9-21-80	17
Jim Benton, Clev vs Det	11-22-45	303	Sonny Randle, StL vs NY Giants	11-4-62	16
Cloyce Box, Det vs Balt	12-3-50	302	Jerry Rice, SF vs LA Rams	11-20-94	16
John Taylor, SF vs LA Rams	12-11-89	286	Rickey Young, Minn vs NE	12-16-79	15
			William Andrews, Atl vs Pitt	11-15-81	15
			Andre Reed Buff vs GB	11-20-94	15

TOUCHDOWNS

	Date	No.
Bob Shaw, Chi Cards vs Balt	10-2-50	5
Kellen Winslow, SD vs Oak	11-22-81	5
Jerry Rice, SF vs Atl	10-14-90	5

All-Purpose Yards

	Date	Yds
Billy Cannon, Hou vs NY Titans	12-10-61	373
Lionel James, SD vs LA Raiders	11-10-85	345
Timmy Brown, Phil vs StL	12-16-62	341
Gale Sayers, Chi vs Minn	12-18-66	339
Gale Sayers, Chi vs SF	12-12-65	336

Annual NFL Individual Statistical Leaders

Rushing

Year	Player, Team	Att.	Yards	Avg.	TD	Year	Player, Team	Att.	Yards	Avg.	TD
1932	Cliff Battles, Bos	148	576	3.9	3	1961	Jim Brown, Clev, NFL	305	1408	4.6	8
1933	Jim Musick, Bos	173	809	4.7	5		Billy Cannon, Hou, AFL	200	948	4.7	6
1934	Beattie Feathers, Chicago Bears	101	1004	9.9	8	1962	Jim Taylor, GB, NFL	272	1474	5.4	19
1935	Doug Russell, Chicago Cards	140	499	3.6	0		Cookie Gilchrist, Buff, AFL	214	1096	5.1	13
1936	Alphonse Leemans, NY	206	830	4.0	2	1963	Jim Brown, Clev, NFL	291	1863	6.4	12
1937	Cliff Battles, Wash	216	874	4.0	5		Clem Daniels, Oak, AFL	215	1099	5.1	3
1938	Byron White, Pitt	152	567	3.7	4	1964	Jim Brown, Clev, NFL	280	1446	5.2	7
1939	Bill Osmanski, Chi	121	699	5.8	7		Cookie Gilchrist, Buff, AFL	230	981	4.3	6
1940	Byron White, Det	146	514	3.5	5	1965	Jim Brown, Clev, NFL	289	1544	5.3	17
1941	Clarence Manders, Bklyn	111	486	4.4	5		Paul Lowe, SD, AFL	222	1121	5.0	7
1942	Bill Dudley, Pitt	162	696	4.3	5	1966	Jim Nance, Bos, AFL	299	1458	4.9	11
1943	Bill Paschal, NY	147	572	3.9	10		Gale Sayers, Chi, NFL	229	1231	5.4	8
1944	Bill Paschal, NY	196	737	3.8	9	1967	Jim Nance, Bos, AFL	269	1216	4.5	7
1945	Steve Van Buren, Phil	143	832	5.8	15		Leroy Kelly, Clev, NFL	235	1205	5.1	11
1946	Bill Dudley, Pitt	146	604	4.1	3	1968	Leroy Kelly, Clev, NFL	248	1239	5.0	16
1947	Steve Van Buren, Phil	217	1008	4.6	13		Paul Robinson, Cinn, AFL	238	1023	4.3	8
1948	Steve Van Buren, Phil	201	945	4.7	10	1969	Gale Sayers, Chi, NFL	236	1032	4.4	8
1949	Steve Van Buren, Phil	263	1146	4.4	11		Dickie Post, SD, AFL	182	873	4.8	6
1950	Marion Motley, Clev	140	810	5.8	3	1970	Larry Brown, Wash, NFC	237	1125	4.7	5
1951	Eddie Price, NY	271	971	3.6	7		Floyd Little, Den, AFC	209	901	4.3	3
1952	Dan Towler, LA	156	894	5.7	10	1971	Floyd Little, Den, AFC	284	1133	4.0	6
1953	Joe Perry, SF	192	1018	5.3	10		John Brockington, GB, NFC	216	1105	5.1	4
1954	Joe Perry, SF	173	1049	6.1	8	1972	O.J. Simpson, Buff, AFC	292	1251	4.3	6
1955	Alan Ameche, Balt	213	961	4.5	9		Larry Brown, Wash, NFC	285	1216	4.3	8
1956	Rick Casares, Chicago Bears	234	1126	4.8	12	1973	O.J. Simpson, Buff, AFC	332	2003	6.0	12
1957	Jim Brown, Clev	202	942	4.7	9		John Brockington, GB, NFC	265	1144	4.3	3
1958	Jim Brown, Clev	257	1527	5.9	17						
1959	Jim Brown, Clev	290	1329	4.6	14						
1960	Jim Brown, Clev, NFL	215	1257	5.8	9						
	Abner Haynes, Dall Texans, AFL	156	875	5.6	9						

Rushing *(Cont.)*

Year	Player, Team	Att	Yards	Avg	TD
1974	Otis Armstrong, Den, AFC	263	1407	5.3	9
	Lawrence McCutcheon, LA Rams, NFC	236	1109	4.7	3
1975	O.J. Simpson, Buff, AFC	329	1817	5.5	16
	Jim Otis, StL, NFC	269	1076	4.0	5
1976	O.J. Simpson, Buff, AFC	290	1503	5.2	8
	Walter Payton, Chi, NFC	311	1390	4.5	13
1977	Walter Payton, Chi, NFC	339	1852	5.5	14
	Mark van Eeghen, Oak, AFC	324	1273	3.9	7
1978	Earl Campbell, Hou, AFC	302	1450	4.8	13
	Walter Payton, Chi, NFC	333	1395	4.2	11
1979	Earl Campbell, Hou, AFC	368	1697	4.6	19
	Walter Payton, Chi, NFC	369	1610	4.4	14
1980	Earl Campbell, Hou, AFC	373	1934	5.2	13
	Walter Payton, Chi, NFC	317	1460	4.6	6
1981	George Rogers, NO, NFC	378	1674	4.4	13
	Earl Campbell, Hou, AFC	361	1376	3.8	10
1982	Freeman McNeil, NY Jets, AFC	151	786	5.2	6
	Tony Dorsett, Dall, NFC	177	745	4.2	5
1983	Eric Dickerson, LA Rams, NFC	390	1808	4.6	18
	Curt Warner, Sea, AFC	335	1449	4.3	13
1984	Eric Dickerson, LA Rams, NFC	379	2105	5.6	14
	Earnest Jackson, SD, AFC	296	1179	4.0	8
1985	Marcus Allen, LA Raiders, AFC	380	1759	4.6	11
	Gerald Riggs, Atl, NFC	397	1719	4.3	10
1986	Eric Dickerson, LA Rams, NFC	404	1821	4.5	11
	Curt Warner, Sea, AFC	319	1481	4.6	13
1987	Charles White, LA Rams, NFC	324	1374	4.2	11
	Eric Dickerson, Ind, AFC	223	1011	4.5	5
1988	Eric Dickerson, Ind, AFC	388	1659	4.3	14
	Herschel Walker, Dall, NFC	361	1514	4.2	5
1989	Christian Okoye, KC, AFC	370	1480	4.0	12
	Barry Sanders, Det, NFC	280	1470	5.3	14
1990	Barry Sanders, Det, NFC	255	1304	5.1	13
	Thurman Thomas, Buff, AFC	271	1297	4.8	11
1991	Emmitt Smith, Dall, NFC	365	1563	4.3	12
	Thurman Thomas, Buff, AFC	288	1407	4.9	7
1992	Emmitt Smith, Dall, NFC	373	1713	4.6	18
	Barry Foster, Pitt, AFC	390	1690	4.3	11
1993	Emmitt Smith, Dall, NFC	283	1486	5.3	9
	Thurman Thomas, Buff, AFC	355	1315	3.7	6
1994	Barry Sanders, Det, NFC	331	1883	5.7	7
	Chris Warren, Sea, AFC	333	1545	4.6	9

Passing

Year	Player, Team	Att	Comp	Yards	TD	Int
1932	Arnie Herber, GB	101	37	639	9	9
1933	Harry Newman, NY	136	53	973	11	17
1934	Arnie Herber, GB	115	42	799	8	12
1935	Ed Danowski, NY	113	57	794	10	9
1936	Arnie Herber, GB	173	77	1239	11	13
1937	Sammy Baugh, Wash	171	81	1127	8	14
1938	Ed Danowski, NY	129	70	848	7	8
1939	Parker Hall, Clev	208	106	1227	9	13
1940	Sammy Baugh, Wash	177	111	1367	12	10
1941	Cecil Isbell, GB	206	117	1479	15	11
1942	Cecil Isbell, GB	268	146	2021	24	14
1943	Sammy Baugh, Wash	239	133	1754	23	19
1944	Frank Filchock, Wash	147	84	1139	13	9
1945	Sammy Baugh, Wash	182	128	1669	11	4
	Sid Luckman, Chi	217	117	1725	14	10
1946	Bob Waterfield, LA	251	127	1747	18	17
1947	Sammy Baugh, Wash	354	210	2938	25	15
1948	Tommy Thompson, Phi	246	141	1965	25	11
1949	Sammy Baugh, Wash	255	145	1903	18	14
1950	Norm Van Brocklin, LA	233	127	2061	18	14
1951	Bob Waterfield, LA	176	88	1566	13	10
1952	Norm Van Brocklin, LA	205	113	1736	14	17
1953	Otto Graham, Clev	258	167	2722	11	9
1954	Norm Van Brocklin, LA	260	139	2637	13	21
1955	Otto Graham, Clev	185	98	1721	15	8
1956	Ed Brown, Chi	168	96	1667	11	12
1957	Tommy O'Connell, Clev.	110	63	1229	9	8
1958	Eddie LeBaron, Wash	145	79	1365	11	10
1959	Charlie Conerly, NY	194	113	1706	14	4
1960	Milt Plum, Clev, NFL	250	151	2297	21	5
	Jack Kemp, LA, AFL	406	211	3018	20	25
1961	George Blanda, Hou, AFL	362	187	3330	36	22
	Milt Plum, Clev, NFL	302	177	2416	18	10
1962	Len Dawson, Dall, AFL	310	189	2759	29	17
	Bart Starr, GB, NFL	285	178	2438	12	9
1963	Y.A. Tittle, NY, NFL	367	221	3145	36	14
	Tobin Rote, SD, AFL	286	170	2510	20	17
1964	Len Dawson, KC, AFL	354	199	2879	30	18
	Bart Starr, GB, NFL	272	163	2144	15	4
1965	Rudy Bukich, Chi, NFL	312	176	2641	20	9
	John Hadl, SD, AFL	348	174	2798	20	21
1966	Bart Starr, GB, NFL	251	156	2257	14	3
	Len Dawson, KC, AFL	284	159	2527	26	10
1967	Sonny Jurgensen, Wash, NFL	508	288	3747	31	16
	Daryle Lamonica, Oakland, AFL	425	220	3228	30	20
1968	Len Dawson, KC, AFL	224	131	2109	17	9
	Earl Morrall, Balt, NFL	317	182	2909	26	17
1969	Sonny Jurgensen, Wash, NFL	442	274	3102	22	15
	Greg Cook, Cin, AFL	197	106	1854	15	11
1970	John Brodie, SF, NFC	378	223	2941	24	10
	Daryle Lamonica, Oak, AFC	356	179	2516	22	15

Passing (Cont.)

Year	Player, Team	Att.	Comp	Yards	TD	Int
1971	Roger Staubach, Dall, NFC	211	126	1882	15	4
	Bob Griese, Mia, AFC	263	145	2089	19	9
1972	Norm Snead, NY, NFC	325	196	2307	17	12
	Earl Morrall, Mia, AFC	150	83	1360	11	7
1973	Roger Staubach, Dall, NFC	286	179	2428	23	15
	Ken Stabler, Oak, AFC	260	163	1997	14	10
1974	Ken Anderson, Cin, AFC	328	213	2667	18	10
	Sonny Jurgensen, Wash, NFC	167	107	1185	11	5
1975	Ken Anderson, Cin, AFC	377	228	3169	21	11
	Fran Tarkenton, Minn, NFC	425	273	2994	25	13
1976	Ken Stabler, Oak, AFC	291	194	2737	27	17
	James Harris, LA, NFC	158	91	1460	8	6
1977	Bob Griese, Mia, AFC	307	180	2252	22	13
	Roger Staubach, Dall, NFC	361	210	2620	18	9
1978	Roger Staubach, Dall, NFC	413	231	3190	25	16
	Terry Bradshaw, Pitt, AFC	368	207	2915	28	20
1979	Roger Staubach, Dall, NFC	461	267	3586	27	11
	Dan Fouts, SD, AFC	530	332	4082	24	24
1980	Brian Sipe, Clev, AFC	554	337	4132	30	14
	Ron Jaworski, Phi, NFC	451	257	3529	27	12
1981	Ken Anderson, Cin, AFC	479	300	3754	29	10
	Joe Montana, SF, NFC	488	311	3565	19	12
1982	Ken Anderson, Cin, AFC	309	218	2495	12	9
	Joe Theismann, Wash, NFC	252	161	2033	13	9
1983	Steve Bartkowski, Atl, NFC	432	274	3167	22	5
	Dan Marino, Mia AFC	296	173	2210	20	6
1984	Dan Marino, Mia, AFC	564	362	5084	48	17
	Joe Montana, SF, NFC	432	279	3630	28	10
1985	Ken O'Brien, NY, AFC	488	297	3888	25	8
	Joe Montana, SF, NFC	494	303	3653	27	13
1986	Tommy Kramer, Minn, NFC	372	208	3000	24	10
	Dan Marino, Mia, AFC	623	378	4746	44	23
1987	Bernie Kosar, Clev, AFC	389	241	3033	22	9
1988	Boomer Esiason, Cin, AFC	388	223	3572	28	14
	Wade Wilson, Minn, NFC	332	204	2746	15	9
1989	Joe Montana, SF, NFC	386	271	3521	26	8
	Boomer Esiason, Cin, AFC	455	258	3525	28	11
1990	Jim Kelly, Buffalo, AFC	346	219	2829	24	9
	Phil Simms, NY, NFC	311	184	2284	15	4
1991	Steve Young, SF, NFC	279	180	2517	17	8
	Jim Kelly, Buff, AFC	474	304	3844	33	17
1992	Steve Young, SF, NFC	402	268	3465	25	7
	Warren Moon, Hou AFC	346	224	2521	18	12
1993	Steve Young, SF, NFC	462	314	4023	29	16
	John Elway, Den, AFC	551	348	4030	25	10
1994	Steve Young, SF, NFC	461	324	3969	35	10
	Dan Marino, Mia, AFC	615	385	4453	30	17

Pass Receiving

Year	Player, Team	No.	Yds	Avg	TD
1932	Ray Flaherty, NY	21	350	16.7	3
1933	John Kelly, Brooklyn	22	246	11.2	3
1934	Joe Carter, Phil	16	238	14.9	4
	Morris Badgro, NY	16	206	12.9	1
1935	Tod Goodwin, NY	26	432	16.6	4
1936	Don Hutson, GB	34	536	15.8	8
1937	Don Hutson, GB	41	552	13.5	7
1938	Gaynell Tinsley, Chi Cards	41	516	12.6	1
1939	Don Hutson, GB	34	846	24.9	6
1940	Don Looney, Phil	58	707	12.2	4
1941	Don Hutson, GB	58	738	12.7	10
1942	Don Hutson, GB	74	1211	16.4	17
1943	Don Hutson, GB	47	776	16.5	11
1944	Don Hutson, GB	58	866	14.9	9
1945	Don Hutson, GB	47	834	17.7	9
1946	Jim Benton, LA	63	981	15.6	6
1947	Jim Keane, Chi	64	910	14.2	10
1948	Tom Fears, LA	51	698	13.7	4
1949	Tom Fears, LA	77	1013	13.2	4
1950	Tom Fears, LA	84	1116	13.3	7
1951	Elroy Hirsch, LA	66	1495	22.7	17
1952	Mac Speedie, Clev	62	911	14.7	5
1953	Pete Pihos, Phil	63	1049	16.7	10
1954	Pete Pihos, Phil	60	872	14.5	10
	Billy Wilson, SF	60	830	13.8	5
1955	Pete Pihos, Phil	62	864	13.9	7
1956	Billy Wilson, SF	60	889	14.8	5
1957	Billy Wilson, SF	52	757	14.6	6
1958	Raymond Berry, Balt	56	794	14.2	9
	Pete Retzlaff, Phil	56	766	13.7	2
1959	Raymond Berry, Balt	66	959	14.5	14
1960	Lionel Taylor, Den, AFL	92	1235	13.4	12
	Raymond Berry, Baltimore, NFL	74	1298	17.5	10
1961	Lionel Taylor, Den, AFL	100	1176	11.8	4
	Jim Phillips, LA, NFL	78	1092	14.0	5
1962	Lionel Taylor, Den, AFL	77	908	11.8	4
	Bobby Mitchell, Wash, NFL	72	1384	19.2	11
1963	Lionel Taylor, Den, AFL	78	1101	14.1	10
	Bobby Joe Conrad, St. Louis, NFL	73	967	13.2	10
1964	Charley Hennigan, Houston, AFL	101	1546	15.3	8
	Johnny Morris, Chi, NFL	93	1200	12.9	10
1965	Lionel Taylor, Den, AFL	85	1131	13.3	6
	Dave Parks, SF, NFL	80	1344	16.8	12
1966	Lance Alworth, SD, AFL	73	1383	18.9	13
	Charley Taylor, Wash, NFL	72	1119	15.5	12
1967	George Sauer, NY, AFL	75	1189	15.9	6
	Charley Taylor, Wash, NFL	70	990	14.1	9

Pass Receiving *(Cont.)*

Year	Player, Team	No.	Yds	Avg	TD
1968	Clifton McNeil, SF, NFL	71	994	14.0	7
	Lance Alworth, SD, AFL	68	1312	19.3	10
1969	Dan Abramowicz, NO, NFL	73	1015	13.9	7
	Lance Alworth, SD, AFL	64	1003	15.7	4
1970	Dick Gordon, Chi, NFC	71	1026	14.5	13
	Marlin Briscoe, Buff, AFC	57	1036	18.2	8
1971	Fred Biletnikoff, Oak, AFC	61	929	15.2	9
	Bob Tucker, NY, NFC	59	791	13.4	4
1972	Harold Jackson, Phi, NFC	62	1048	16.9	4
	Fred Biletnikoff, Oak, AFC	58	802	13.8	7
1973	Harold Carmichael, Phi, NFC	67	1116	16.7	9
	Fred Willis, Hou, AFC	57	371	6.5	1
1974	Lydell Mitchell, Balt, AFC	72	544	7.6	2
	Charles Young, Phi, NFC	63	696	11.0	3
1975	Chuck Foreman, Minn, NFC	73	691	9.5	9
	Reggie Rucker, Clev, AFC	60	770	12.8	3
	Lydell Mitchell, Balt, AFC	60	544	9.1	4
1976	MacArthur Lane, KC, AFC	66	686	10.4	1
	Drew Pearson, Dall, NFC	58	806	13.9	6
1977	Lydell Mitchell, Balt, AFC	71	620	8.7	4
	Ahmad Rashad, Minn, NFC	51	681	13.4	2
1978	Rickey Young, Minn, NFC	88	704	8.0	5
	Steve Largent, Sea, AFC	71	1168	16.5	8
1979	Joe Washington, Balt, AFC	82	750	9.1	3
	Ahmad Rashad, Minn, NFC	80	1156	14.5	9
1980	Kellen Winslow, SD, AFC	89	1290	14.5	9
	Earl Cooper, SF, NFC	83	567	6.8	4
1981	Kellen Winslow, SD, AFC	88	1075	12.2	10
	Dwight Clark, SF, NFC	85	1105	13.0	4
1982	Dwight Clark, SF, NFC	60	913	15.2	5
	Kellen Winslow, SD, AFC	54	721	13.4	6
1983	Todd Christensen, Los Angeles, AFC	92	1247	13.6	12
	Roy Green, StL, NFC	78	1227	15.7	14
	Charlie Brown, Wash, NFC	78	1225	15.7	8
	Earnest Gray, NY, NFC	78	1139	14.6	5
1984	Art Monk, Wash, NFC	106	1372	12.9	7
	Ozzie Newsome, Clev, AFC	89	1001	11.2	5
1985	Roger Craig, SF, NFC	92	1016	11.0	6
	Lionel James, SD, AFC	86	1027	11.9	6
1986	Todd Christensen, Los Angeles, AFC	95	1153	12.1	8
	Jerry Rice, SF, NFC	86	1570	18.3	15
1987	J.T. Smith, StL, NFC	91	1117	12.3	8
	Al Toon, NY, AFC	68	976	14.4	5
1988	Al Toon, NY, AFC	93	1067	11.5	5
	Henry Ellard, LA Rams, NFC	86	1414	16.4	10
1989	Sterling Sharpe, GB, NFC	90	1423	15.8	12
	Andre Reed, Buff, AFC	88	1312	14.9	9
1990	Jerry Rice, SF, NFC	100	1502	15.0	13
	Haywood Jeffires, Houston, AFC	74	1048	14.2	8
	Drew Hill, Hou, AFC	74	1019	13.8	5
1991	Haywood Jeffires, Hou, AFC	100	1181	11.8	7
	Michael Irvin, Dall, NFC	93	1523	16.4	8
1992	Sterling Sharpe, GB, NFC	108	1461	13.5	13
	Haywood Jeffires, Hou, AFC	90	913	10.1	9
1993	Sterling Sharpe, GB, NFC	112	1274	11.4	11
	Reggie Langhorne, Ind, AFC	85	1038	12.2	3
1994	Cris Carter, Minn, NFC	122	1256	10.3	7
	Ben Coates, NE, AFC	96	1174	12.2	7

Scoring

Year	Player, Team	TD	FG	PAT	TP
1932	Earl Clark, Portsmouth	6	3	10	55
1933	Ken Strong, NY	6	5	13	64
	Glenn Presnell, Ports	6	6	10	64
1934	Jack Manders, Chi	3	10	31	79
1935	Earl Clark, Det	6	1	16	55
1936	Earl Clark, Det	7	4	19	73
1937	Jack Manders, Chi	5	18	15	69
1938	Clarke Hinkle, GB	7	3	7	58
1939	Andy Farkas, Wash	11	0	2	68
1940	Don Hutson, GB	7	0	15	57
1941	Don Hutson, GB	12	1	20	95
1942	Don Hutson, GB	17	1	33	138
1943	Don Hutson, GB	12	3	36	117
1944	Don Hutson, GB	9	0	31	85
1945	Steve Van Buren, Phil	18	0	2	110
1946	Ted Fritsch, GB	10	9	13	100
1947	Pat Harder, Chicago Cards	7	7	39	102
1948	Pat Harder, Chicago Cards	6	7	53	110
1949	Pat Harder, Chicago Cards	8	3	45	102
	Gene Roberts, NY	17	0	0	102
1950	Doak Walker, Det	11	8	38	128
1951	Elroy Hirsch, LA	17	0	0	102
1952	Gordy Soltau, SF	7	6	34	94
1953	Gordy Soltau, SF	6	10	48	114
1954	Bobby Walston, Phil	11	4	36	114
1955	Doak Walker, Det	7	9	27	96
1956	Bobby Layne, Det	5	12	33	99
1957	Sam Baker, Wash	1	14	29	77
	Lou Groza, Clev	0	15	32	77
1958	Jim Brown, Clev	18	0	0	108
1959	Paul Hornung, GB	7	7	31	94
1960	Paul Hornung, GB, NFL	15	15	41	176
	Gene Mingo, Den, AFL	6	18	33	123
1961	Gino Cappelletti, Bos, AFL	8	17	48	147
	Paul Hornung, GB, NFL	10	15	41	146
1962	Gene Mingo, Den, AFL	4	27	32	137
	Jim Taylor, GB, NFL	19	0	0	114
1963	Gino Cappelletti, Bos, AFL	2	22	35	113
	Don Chandler, NY, NFL	0	18	52	106
1964	Gino Cappelletti, Bos, AFL	7	25	36	155
	Lenny Moore, Balt, NFL	20	0	0	120
1965	Gale Sayers, Chi, NFL	22	0	0	132
	Gino Cappelletti, Bos, AFL	9	17	27	132
1966	Gino Cappelletti, Bos, AFL	6	16	35	119
	Bruce Gossett, LA, NFL	0	28	29	113
1967	Jim Bakken, StL, NFL	0	27	36	117
	George Blanda, Oak, AFL	0	20	56	116
1968	Jim Turner, NY, AFL	0	34	43	145
	Leroy Kelly, Clev, NFL	20	0	0	120

Scoring *(Cont.)*

Year	Player, Team	TD	FG	PAT	TP
1969	Jim Turner, NY, AFL 0		32	33	129
	Fred Cox, Minn, NFL 0		26	43	121
1970	Fred Cox, Minn, NFC 0		30	35	125
	Jan Stenerud, KC, AFC 0		30	26	116
1971	Garo Yepremian, Mia, AFC 0		28	33	117
	Curt Knight, Wash, NFC 0		29	27	114
1972	Chester Marcol, GB, NFC.......0		33	29	128
	Bobby Howfield, NY AFC 0		27	40	121
1973	David Ray, LA, NFC 0		30	40	130
	Roy Gerela, Pitt, AFC............0		29	36	123
1974	Chester Marcol, GB, NFC.......0		25	19	94
	Roy Gerela, Pitt, AFC............0		20	33	93
1975	O.J. Simpson, Buff, AFC.......23		0	0	138
	Chuck Foreman, Minn, NFC .22		0	0	132
1976	Toni Linhart, Balt, AFC..........0		20	49	109
	Mark Moseley, Wash, NFC 0		22	31	97
1977	Errol Mann, Oak, AFC............0		20	39	99
	Walter Payton, Chi, NFC.......16		0	0	96
1978	Frank Corral, LA, NFC 0		29	31	118
	Pat Leahy, NY, AFC 0		22	41	107
1979	John Smith, NE, AFC 0		23	46	115
	Mark Moseley, Wash, NFC 0		25	39	114
1980	John Smith, NE, AFC 0		26	51	129
	Ed Murray, Det, NFC 0		27	35	116
1981	Ed Murray, Det, NFC 0		25	46	121
	Rafael Septien, Dall, NFC......0		27	40	121
	Jim Breech, Cin, AFC 0		22	49	115
	Nick Lowery, KC, AFC............0		26	37	115

Year	Player, Team	TD	FG	PAT	TP
1982	Marcus Allen, LA, AFC 14		0	0	84
	Wendell Tyler, LA, NFC 13		0	0	78
1983	Mark Moseley, Wash, NFC 0		33	62	161
	Gary Anderson, Pitt, AFC 0		27	38	119
1984	Ray Wersching, SF, NFC........0		25	56	131
	Gary Anderson, Pitt, AFC 0		24	45	117
1985	Kevin Butler, Chi, NFC...........0		31	51	144
	Gary Anderson, Pitt, AFC 0		33	40	139
1986	Tony Franklin, NE, AFC 0		32	44	140
	Kevin Butler, Chi, NFC...........0		28	36	120
1987	Jerry Rice, SF, NFC 23		0	0	138
	Jim Breech, Cin, AFC 0		24	25	97
1988	Scott Norwood, Buff, AFC 0		32	33	129
	Mike Cofer, SF, NFC 0		27	40	121
1989	Mike Cofer, SF, NFC 0		29	49	136
	David Treadwell, Den, AFC 0		27	39	120
1990	Nick Lowery, KC, AFC 0		34	37	139
	Chip Lohmiller, Wash, NFC 0		30	41	131
1991	Chip Lohmiller, Wash, NFC 0		31	56	149
	Pete Stoyanovich, Mia, AFC ..0		31	28	121
1992	Pete Stoyanovich, Mia, AFC ..0		30	34	124
	Morten Anderson, NO, NFC ...0		29	33	120
	Chip Lohmiller, Wash, NFC 0		30	30	120
1993	Jeff Jaeger, Rai, AFC 0		35	27	132
	Jason Hanson, Det, NFC........0		34	28	130
1994	John Carney, SD, AFC 0		34	33	135
	Fuad Reveiz, Minn, NFC.........0		34	30	132
	Emmitt Smith, Dall, NFC 22		0	0	132

Pro Bowl Alltime Results

Date	Result
1-15-39 ......NY Giants 13, Pro All-Stars 10
1-14-40 ......Green Bay 16, NFL All-Stars 7
12-29-40 ......Chi Bears 28, NFL All-Stars 14
1-4-42 ....Chi Bears 35, NFL All-Stars 24
12-27-42 ......NFL All-Stars 17, Washington 14
1-14-51 ......A Conf 28, N Conf 27
1-12-52 ......N Conf 30, A Conf 13
1-10-53 ......N Conf 27, A Conf 7
1-17-54 ......East 20, West 9
1-16-55 ......West 26, East 19
1-15-56 ......East 31, West 30
1-13-57 ......West 19, East 10
1-12-58 ......West 26, East 7
1-11-59 ......East 28, West 21
1-17-60 ......West 38, East 21
1-15-61 ......West 35, East 31

Date	Result
1-7-62 ....AFL West 47, East 27
1-14-62 ......NFL West 31, East 30
1-13-63 ......AFL West 21, East 14
1-13-63 ......NFL East 30, West 20
1-12-64 ......NFL West 31, East 17
1-19-64 ......AFL West 27, East 24
1-10-65 ......NFL West 34, East 14
1-16-65 ......AFL West 38, East 14
1-15-66 ......AFL All-Stars 30, Buffalo 19
1-15-66 ......NFL East 36, West 7
1-21-67 ......AFL East 30, West 23
1-22-67 ......NFL East 20, West 10
1-21-68 ......AFL East 25, West 24
1-21-68 ......NFL West 38, East 20
1-19-69 ......AFL West 38, East 25
1-19-69 ......NFL West 10, East 7
1-17-70 ......AFL West 26, East 3
1-18-70 ......NFL West 16, East 13
1-24-71 ......NFC 27, AFC 6
1-23-72 ......AFC 26, NFC 13
1-21-73 ......AFC 33, NFC 28

Date	Result
1-20-74 ......AFC 15, NFC 13
1-20-75 ......NFC 17, AFC 10
1-26-76 ......NFC 23, AFC 20
1-17-77 ......AFC 24, NFC 14
1-23-78 ......NFC 14, AFC 13
1-29-79 ......NFC 13, AFC 7
1-27-80 ......NFC 37, AFC 27
2-1-81 ....NFC 21, AFC 7
1-31-82 ......AFC 16, NFC 13
2-6-83 ....NFC 20, AFC 19
1-29-84 ......NFC 45, AFC 3
1-27-85 ......AFC 22, NFC 14
2-2-86 ....NFC 28, AFC 24
2-1-87 ....AFC 10, NFC 6
2-7-88 ....AFC 15, NFC 6
1-29-89 ......NFC 34, AFC 3
2-4-90 ....NFC 27, AFC 21
2-3-91 ....AFC 23, NFC 21
2-2-92 ....NFC 21, AFC 15
2-7-93 ....AFC 23, NFC 20
2-6-94 ....NFC 17, AFC 3
2-5-95 ....AFC 41, NFC 13

Chicago All-Star Game Results

Date	Result (Attendance)
8-31-34	Chi Bears 0, All-Stars 0 (79,432)
8-29-35	Chi Bears 5, All-Stars 0 (77,450)
9-3-36	All-Stars 7, Detroit 7 (76,000)
9-1-37	All-Stars 6, Green Bay 0 (84,560)
8-31-38	All-Stars 28, Washington 16 (74,250)
8-30-39	NY Giants 9, All-Stars 0 (81,456)
8-29-40	Green Bay 45, All-Stars 28 (84,567)
8-28-41	Chi Bears 37, All-Stars 13 (98,203)
8-28-42	Chi Bears 21, All-Stars 0 (101,100)
8-25-43	All-Stars 27, Washington 7 (48,471)
8-30-44	Chi Bears 24, All-Stars 21 (48,769)
8-30-45	Green Bay 19, All-Stars 7 (92,753)
8-23-46	All-Stars 16, Los Angeles 0 (97,380)
8-22-47	All-Stars 16, Chi Bears 0 (105,840)
8-20-48	Chi Cardinals 28, All-Stars 0 (101,220)
8-12-49	Philadelphia 38, All-Stars 0 (93,780)
8-11-50	All-Stars 17, Philadelphia 7 (88,885)
8-17-51	Cleveland 33, All-Stars 0 (92,180)
8-15-52	Los Angeles 10, All-Stars 7 (88,316)
8-14-53	Detroit 24, All-Stars 10 (93,818)
8-13-54	Detroit 31, All-Stars 6 (93,470)
8-12-55	All-Stars 30, Cleveland 27 (75,000)

Date	Result (Attendance)
8-10-56	Cleveland 26, All-Stars 0 (75,000)
8-9-57	NY Giants 22, All-Stars 12 (75,000)
8-15-58	All-Stars 35, Detroit 19 (70,000)
8-14-59	Baltimore 29, All-Stars 0 (70,000)
8-12-60	Baltimore 32, All-Stars 7 (70,000)
8-4-61	Philadelphia 28, All-Stars 14 (66,000)
8-3-62	Green Bay 42, All-Stars 20 (65,000)
8-2-63	All-Stars 20, Green Bay 17 (65,000)
8-7-64	Chicago 28, All-Stars 17 (65,000)
8-6-65	Cleveland 24, All-Stars 16 (68,000)
8-5-66	Green Bay 38, All-Stars 0 (72,000)
8-4-67	Green Bay 27, All-Stars 0 (70,934)
8-2-68	Green Bay 34, All-Stars 17 (69,917)
8-1-69	NY Jets 26, All-Stars 24 (74,208)
7-31-70	Kansas City 24, All-Stars 3 (69,940)
7-30-71	Baltimore 24, All-Stars 17 (52,289)
7-28-72	Dallas 20, All-Stars 7 (54,162)
7-27-73	Miami 14, All-Stars 3 (54,103)
1974	No game
8-1-75	Pittsburgh 21, All-Stars 14 (54,103)
7-23-76	Pittsburgh 24, All-Stars 0 (52,895)

Alltime Winningest NFL Coaches

Most Career Wins

Coach	Yrs	Teams	Regular Season				Career			
			W	L	T	Pct	W	L	T	Pct
†Don Shula	32	Colts, Dolphins	319	149	6	.679	338	165	6	.670
George Halas	40	Bears	319	148	31	.672	324	151	31	.671
Tom Landry	29	Cowboys	250	162	6	.605	270	178	6	.601
Curly Lambeau	33	Packers, Cardinals, Redskins	226	132	22	.623	229	134	22	.623
Chuck Noll	23	Steelers	193	148	1	.566	209	156	1	.572
Chuck Knox	21	Rams, Bills, Seahawks	186	147	1	.558	193	158	1	.550
Paul Brown	21	Browns, Bengals	166	100	6	.621	170	108	6	.609
Bud Grant	18	Vikings	158	96	5	.620	168	108	5	.607
Steve Owen	23	Giants	151	100	17	.595	153	108	17	.582
Joe Gibbs	12	Redskins	124	60	0	.674	140	65	0	.683
†Dan Reeves	14	Broncos, Giants	130	85	1	.604	137	91	1	.600
Hank Stram	17	Chiefs, Saints	131	97	10	.571	136	100	10	.573
Weeb Ewbank	20	Colts, Jets	130	129	7	.502	134	130	7	.507
†Marv Levy	14	Chiefs, Bills	117	90	0	.565	127	96	0	.570
Sid Gillman	18	Rams, Chargers, Oilers	122	99	7	.550	123	104	7	.541
George Allen	12	Rams, Redskins	116	47	5	.705	118	54	5	.681
Don Coryell	14	Cardinals, Chargers	111	83	1	.572	114	89	1	.561
John Madden	10	Raiders	103	32	7	.750	112	39	7	.731
Mike Ditka	11	Bears	106	62	0	.631	112	68	0	.622
†M. Schottenheimer	11	Browns, Chiefs	103	63	1	.620	108	72	1	.600

Top Winning Percentages

	W	L	T	Pct		W	L	T	Pct
Vince Lombardi	105	35	6	.740	†Don Shula	338	165	6	.670
John Madden	112	39	7	.731	Curly Lambeau	229	134	22	.623
Joe Gibbs	140	65	0	.683	Mike Ditka	112	68	0	.622
George Allen	118	54	5	.681	Bill Walsh	102	63	1	.617
George Halas	324	151	31	.671	Paul Brown	170	108	6	.609

Note: Minimum 100 victories

†Active coach

Alltime Number-One Draft Choices

Year	Team	Selection	Position
1936	Philadelphia	Jay Berwanger, Chicago	HB
1937	Philadelphia	Sam Francis, Nebraska	FB
1938	Cleveland	Corbett Davis, Indiana	FB
1939	Chicago Cardinals	Ki Aldrich, Texas Christian	C
1940	Chicago Cardinals	George Cafego, Tennessee	HB
1941	Chicago Bears	Tom Harmon, Michigan	HB
1942	Pittsburgh	Bill Dudley, Virginia	HB
1943	Detroit	Frank Sinkwich, Georgia	HB
1944	Boston	Angelo Bertelli, Notre Dame	QB
1945	Chicago Cardinals	Charley Trippi, Georgia	HB
1946	Boston	Frank Dancewicz, Notre Dame	QB
1947	Chicago Bears	Bob Fenimore, Oklahoma A&M	HB
1948	Washington	Harry Gilmer, Alabama	QB
1949	Philadelphia	Chuck Bednarik, Pennsylvania	C
1950	Detroit	Leon Hart, Notre Dame	E
1951	New York Giants	Kyle Rote, Southern Methodist	HB
1952	Los Angeles	Bill Wade, Vanderbilt	QB
1953	San Francisco	Harry Babcock, Georgia	E
1954	Cleveland	Bobby Garrett, Stanford	QB
1955	Baltimore	George Shaw, Oregon	QB
1956	Pittsburgh	Gary Glick, Colorado A&M	DB
1957	Green Bay	Paul Hornung, Notre Dame	HB
1958	Chicago Cardinals	King Hill, Rice	QB
1959	Green Bay	Randy Duncan, Iowa	QB
1960	Los Angeles	Billy Cannon, Louisiana St	RB
1961	Minnesota	Tommy Mason, Tulane	RB
	Buffalo (AFL)	Ken Rice, Auburn	G
1968	Minnesota	Ron Yary, Southern California	T
1969	Buffalo (AFL)	O.J. Simpson, Southern California	RB
1970	Pittsburgh	Terry Bradshaw, Louisiana Tech	QB
1971	New England	Jim Plunkett, Stanford	QB
1972	Buffalo	Walt Patulski, Notre Dame	DE
1973	Houston	John Matuszak, Tampa	DE
1974	Dallas	Ed Jones, Tennessee St	DE
1975	Atlanta	Steve Bartkowski, California	QB
1976	Tampa Bay	Lee Roy Selmon, Oklahoma	DE
1977	Tampa Bay	Ricky Bell, Southern California	RB
1978	Houston	Earl Campbell, Texas	RB
1979	Buffalo	Tom Cousineau, Ohio St	LB
1980	Detroit	Billy Sims, Oklahoma	RB
1981	New Orleans	George Rogers, South Carolina	RB
1982	New England	Kenneth Sims, Texas	DT
1983	Baltimore	John Elway, Stanford	QB
1984	New England	Irving Fryar, Nebraska	WR
1985	Buffalo	Bruce Smith, Virginia Tech	DE
1986	Tampa Bay	Bo Jackson, Auburn	RB
1987	Tampa Bay	Vinny Testaverde, Miami (FL)	QB
1988	Atlanta	Aundray Bruce, Auburn	LB
1989	Dallas	Troy Aikman, UCLA	QB
1990	Indianapolis	Jeff George, Illinois	QB
1991	Dallas	Russell Maryland, Miami (FL)	DT
1992	Indianapolis	Steve Emtman, Washington	DT
1993	New England	Drew Bledsoe, Washington St	QB
1994	Cincinnati	Dan Wilkinson, Ohio St	DT
1995	Cincinnati	Ki-Jana Carter, Penn St	RB

From 1947 through 1958, the first selection in the draft was a bonus pick, awarded to the winner of a random draw. That club, in turn, forfeited its last-round draft choice. The winner of the bonus choice was eliminated from future draws. The system was abolished after 1958, by which time all clubs had received a bonus choice.

Members of the Pro Football Hall of Fame

Herb Adderley
Lance Alworth
Doug Atkins
Morris "Red" Badgro
Lem Barney
Cliff Battles
Sammy Baugh
Chuck Bednarik
Bert Bell
Bobby Bell
Raymond Berry
Charles W. Bidwill, Sr.
Fred Biletnikoff
George Blanda
Mel Blount
Terry Bradshaw
Jim Brown
Paul Brown
Roosevelt Brown
Willie Brown
Buck Buchanan
Dick Butkus
Earl Campbell
Tony Canadeo
Joe Carr
Guy Chamberlin
Jack Christiansen
Earl "Dutch" Clark
George Connor
Jimmy Conzelman
Larry Csonka
Al Davis
Willie Davis
Len Dawson
Mike Ditka
Art Donovan
Tony Dorsett
John "Paddy" Driscoll
Bill Dudley
Glen "Turk" Edwards
Weeb Ewbank
Tom Fears
Jim Finks
Ray Flaherty
Len Ford
Dan Fortmann
Dan Fouts
Frank Gatski
Bill George
Frank Gifford
Sid Gillman
Otto Graham
Harold "Red" Grange
Bud Grant
Joe Greene
Forrest Gregg
Bob Griese
Lou Groza
Joe Guyon
George Halas

Jack Ham
John Hannah
Franco Harris
Ed Healey
Mel Hein
Ted Hendricks
Wilbur "Pete" Henry
Arnie Herber
Bill Hewitt
Clarke Hinkle
Elroy "Crazylegs" Hirsch
Paul Hornung
Ken Houston
Cal Hubbard
Sam Huff
Lamar Hunt
Don Hutson
Jimmy Johnson
John Henry Johnson
David "Deacon" Jones
Stan Jones
Henry Jordan
Sonny Jurgensen
Leroy Kelly
Walt Kiesling
Frank "Bruiser" Kinard
Earl "Curly" Lambeau
Jack Lambert
Tom Landry
Dick "Night Train" Lane
Jim Langer
Willie Lanier
Steve Largent
Yale Lary
Dante Lavelli
Bobby Layne
Alphonse "Tuffy" Leemans
Bob Lilly
Larry Little
Vince Lombardi
Sid Luckman
Roy "Link" Lyman
John Mackey
Tim Mara
Gino Marchetti
George Preston Marshall
Ollie Matson
Don Maynard
George McAfee
Mike McCormack
Hugh McElhenny
Johnny "Blood" McNally
Mike Michalske
Wayne Millner
Bobby Mitchell
Ron Mix
Lenny Moore
Marion Motley
George Musso
Bronko Nagurski

Joe Namath
Earle "Greasy" Neale
Ernie Nevers
Ray Nitschke
Chuck Noll
Leo Nomellini
Merlin Olsen
Jim Otto
Steve Owen
Alan Page
Clarence "Ace" Parker
Jim Parker
Walter Payton
Joe Perry
Pete Pihos
Hugh "Shorty" Ray
Dan Reeves
John Riggins
Jim Ringo
Andy Robustelli
Art Rooney
Pete Rozelle
Bob St. Clair
Gale Sayers
Joe Schmidt
Tex Schramm
Lee Roy Selmon
Art Shell
O. J. Simpson
Jackie Smith
Bart Starr
Roger Staubach
Ernie Stautner
Jan Stenerud
Ken Strong
Joe Stydahar
Fran Tarkenton
Charley Taylor
Jim Taylor
Jim Thorpe
Y. A. Tittle
George Trafton
Charley Trippi
Emlen Tunnell
Clyde "Bulldog" Turner
Johnny Unitas
Gene Upshaw
Norm Van Brocklin
Steve Van Buren
Doak Walker
Bill Walsh
Paul Warfield
Bob Waterfield
Arnie Weinmeister
Randy White
Bill Willis
Larry Wilson
Kellen Winslow
Alex Wojciechowicz
Willie Wood

Canadian Football League Grey Cup

Year	Results	Site	Attendance
1909	U of Toronto 26, Parkdale 6	Toronto	3,807
1910	U of Toronto 16, Hamilton Tigers 7	Hamilton	12,000
1911	U of Toronto 14, Toronto 7	Toronto	13,687
1912	Hamilton Alerts 11, Toronto 4	Hamilton	5,337
1913	Hamilton Tigers 44, Parkdale 2	Hamilton	2,100
1914	Toronto 14, U of Toronto 2	Toronto	10,500
1915	Hamilton Tigers 13, Toronto RAA 7	Toronto	2,808
1916-19	No game		
1920	U of Toronto 16, Toronto 3	Toronto	10,088
1921	Toronto 23, Edmonton 0	Toronto	9,558
1922	Queen's U 13, Edmonton 1	Kingston	4,700
1923	Queen's U 54, Regina 0	Toronto	8,629
1924	Queen's U 11, Balmy Beach 3	Toronto	5,978
1925	Ottawa Senators 24, Winnipeg 1	Ottawa	6,900
1926	Ottawa Senators 10, Toronto U 7	Toronto	8,276
1927	Balmy Beach 9, Hamilton Tigers 6	Toronto	13,676
1928	Hamilton Tigers 30, Regina 0	Hamilton	4,767
1929	Hamilton Tigers 14, Regina 3	Hamilton	1,906
1930	Balmy Beach 11, Regina 6	Toronto	3,914
1931	Montreal AAA 22, Regina 0	Montreal	5,112
1932	Hamilton Tigers 25, Regina 6	Hamilton	4,806
1933	Toronto 4, Sarnia 3	Sarnia	2,751
1934	Sarnia 20, Regina 12	Toronto	8,900
1935	Winnipeg 18, Hamilton Tigers 12	Hamilton	6,405
1936	Sarnia 26, Ottawa RR 20	Toronto	5,883
1937	Toronto 4, Winnipeg 3	Toronto	11,522
1938	Toronto 30, Winnipeg 7	Toronto	18,778
1939	Winnipeg 8, Ottawa 7	Ottawa	11,738
1940	Ottawa 12, Balmy Beach 5	Ottawa	1,700
1940	Ottawa 8, Balmy Beach 2	Toronto	4,998
1941	Winnipeg 18, Ottawa 16	Toronto	19,065
1942	Toronto RCAF 8, Winnipeg RCAF 5	Toronto	12,455
1943	Hamilton F Wild 23, Winnipeg RCAF 14	Toronto	16,423
1944	Montreal St H-D Navy 7, Hamilton F Wild 6	Hamilton	3,871
1945	Toronto 35, Winnipeg 0	Toronto	18,660
1946	Toronto 28, Winnipeg 6	Toronto	18,960
1947	Toronto 10, Winnipeg 9	Toronto	18,885
1948	Calgary 12, Ottawa 7	Toronto	20,013
1949	Montreal Als 28, Calgary 15	Toronto	20,087
1950	Toronto 13, Winnipeg 0	Toronto	27,101
1951	Ottawa 21, Saskatchewan 14	Toronto	27,341
1952	Toronto 21, Edmonton 11	Toronto	27,391
1953	Hamilton Ticats 12, Winnipeg 6	Toronto	27,313
1954	Edmonton 26, Montreal 25	Toronto	27,321
1955	Edmonton 34, Montreal 19	Vancouver	39,417
1956	Edmonton 50, Montreal 27	Toronto	27,425
1957	Hamilton 32, Winnipeg 7	Toronto	27,051
1958	Winnipeg 35, Hamilton 28	Vancouver	36,567
1959	Winnipeg 21, Hamilton 7	Toronto	33,133
1960	Ottawa 16, Edmonton 6	Vancouver	38,102
1961	Winnipeg 21, Hamilton 14	Toronto	32,651
1962	Winnipeg 28, Hamilton 27	Toronto	32,655
1963	Hamilton 21, British Columbia 10	Vancouver	36,545
1964	British Columbia 34, Hamilton 24	Toronto	32,655
1965	Hamilton 22, Winnipeg 16	Toronto	32,655
1966	Saskatchewan 29, Ottawa 14	Vancouver	36,553
1967	Hamilton 24, Saskatchewan 1	Ottawa	31,358
1968	Ottawa 24, Calgary 21	Toronto	32,655
1969	Ottawa 29, Saskatchewan 11	Montreal	33,172
1970	Montreal 23, Calgary 10	Toronto	32,669
1971	Calgary 14, Toronto 11	Vancouver	34,484
1972	Hamilton 13, Saskatchewan 10	Hamilton	33,993
1973	Ottawa 22, Edmonton 18	Toronto	36,653
1974	Montreal 20, Edmonton 7	Vancouver	34,450
1975	Edmonton 9, Montreal 8	Calgary	32,454

Canadian Football League Grey Cup (Cont.)

Year	Results	Site	Attendance
1976	Ottawa 23, Saskatchewan 20	Toronto	53,467
1977	Montreal 41, Edmonton 6	Montreal	68,318
1978	Edmonton 20, Montreal 13	Toronto	54,695
1979	Edmonton 17, Montreal 9	Montreal	65,113
1980	Edmonton 48, Hamilton 10	Toronto	54,661
1981	Edmonton 26, Ottawa 23	Montreal	52,478
1982	Edmonton 32, Toronto 16	Toronto	54,741
1983	Toronto 18, British Columbia 17	Vancouver	59,345
1984	Winnipeg 47, Hamilton 17	Edmonton	60,081
1985	British Columbia 37, Hamilton 24	Montreal	56,723
1986	Hamilton 39, Edmonton 15	Vancouver	59,621
1987	Edmonton 38, Toronto 36	Vancouver	59,478
1988	Winnipeg 22, British Columbia 21	Ottawa	50,604
1989	Saskatchewan 43, Hamilton 40	Toronto	54,088
1990	Winnipeg 50, Edmonton 11	Vancouver	46,968
1991	Toronto 36, Calgary 21	Winnipeg	51,985
1992	Calgary 24, Winnipeg 10	Toronto	45,863
1993	Edmonton 33, Winnipeg 23	Calgary	50,035
1994	British Columbia 26, Baltimore 23	Vancouver	55,097

In 1909, Earl Grey, the Governor-General of Canada, donated a trophy for the Rugby Football Championship of Canada. The trophy, which subsequently became known as the Grey Cup, was originally open only to teams registered with the Canada Rugby Union. Since 1954, it has been awarded to the winner of the Canadian Football League's championship game.

AMERICAN FOOTBALL LEAGUE I

Year	Champion	Record
1926	Philadelphia Quakers	7-2

AMERICAN FOOTBALL LEAGUE II

Year	Champion	Record
1936	Boston Shamrocks	8-3
1937	LA Bulldogs	8-0

AMERICAN FOOTBALL LEAGUE III

Year	Champion	Record
1940	Columbus Bullies	8-1-1
1941	Columbus Bullies	5-1-2

WORLD LEAGUE OF AMERICAN FOOTBALL

Year	Champion	Record
1992	Sacramento	8-2-0
1995	Frankfurt	6-4-0

ALL-AMERICAN FOOTBALL CONFERENCE

Year	Championship Game
1946	Cleveland 14, NY Yankees 9
1947	Cleveland 14, NY Yankees 3
1948	Cleveland 49, Buffalo 7
1949	Cleveland 21, San Francisco 7

WORLD FOOTBALL LEAGUE

Year	World Bowl Championship
1974	Birmingham 22, Florida 21
1975	Disbanded midseason

UNITED STATES FOOTBALL LEAGUE

Year	Championship Game
1983	Michigan 24, Philadelphia 22, at Denver
1984	Philadelphia 23, Arizona 3, at Tampa
1985	Baltimore 28, Oakland 24, at East Rutherford

Taglia-Boo

The mahogany-walled auditorium of New York City's 92nd Street Y is usually a forum for poetry readings and cultural symposia. But last December the commissioners of the three major league sports that still *have* commissioners got together to adress the the state of their respective games. The NBA's David Stern, the NHL's Gary Bettman and the NFL's Paul Tagliabue took turns responding to questions from journalist David Halberstam, and their anwers were predictably guarded and equivocal on the subject of labor relations. More troubling—and less explicable—was Tagliabue's cavalier response to a query about head injuries in football. Calling the matter "a pack journalism issue," he waved away concern, saying that the NFL has "one concussion every three or four games." After a few more calculations, Tagliabue pronounced a figure of 2.5 concussions for every 22,000 players engaged." His response echoes for Halberstam, who won a Pulitzer Prize for his war coverage in Souteast Asia. "I feel like I'm back in Vietnam hearing McNamara give statistics," he said.

Tagliabue's numbers still mean about four concussions a week. The last player to become a statistic was Boomer Esiason, whom Junior Seau knocked senseless during the New York Jets' 21–6 loss to the San Diego Chargers in late '94. Tagliabue's head has been spared this season's spate of bruising hits; on this issue he ought to be making better use of it.

College Football

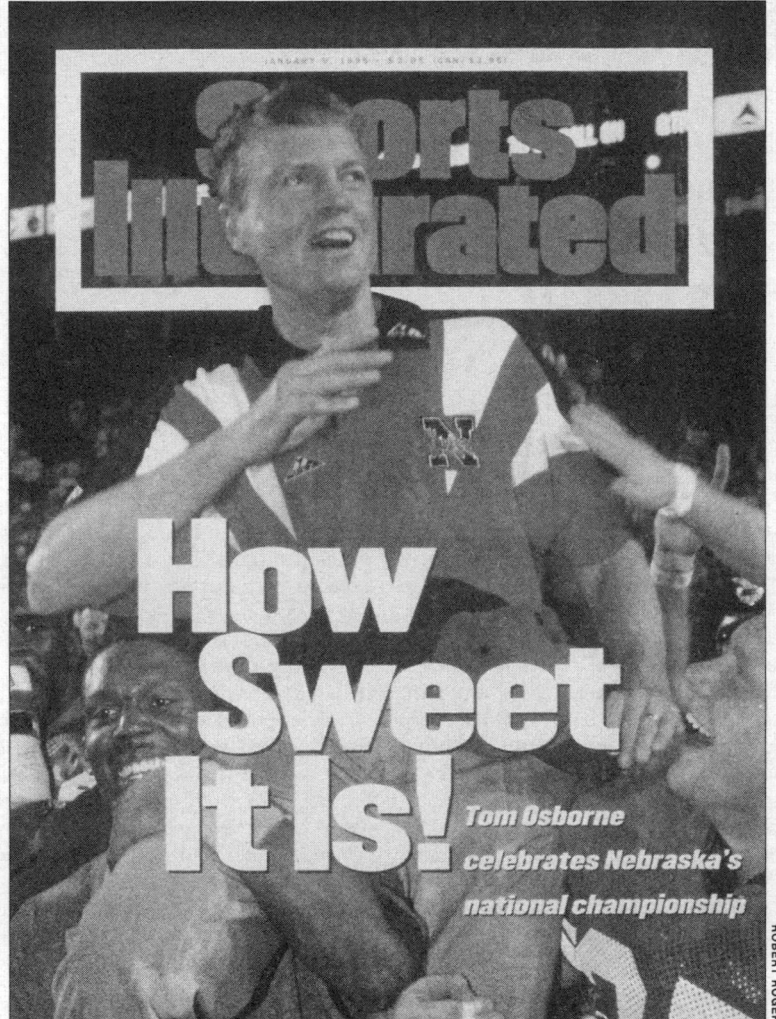

JANUARY 9, 1995 · $2.95 (CAN. $3.95)

Sports Illustrated

How Sweet It Is!

Tom Osborne celebrates Nebraska's national championship

Unfinished Business

The Nebraska Cornhuskers considered themselves the best team in the land in 1993; in '94 they proved it

by Tim Layden

NEBRASKA COACH Tom Osborne was carried from the floor of the Orange Bowl on the shoulders of his players on New Year's night. Surely it was a light load, as Osborne was unburdened of more than two decades of waiting. It was never intended that the national championship of college football become a Lifetime Achievement Award, although in recent years it has come to coaches and programs with long histories of success (Washington's Don James in 1991 and Florida State's Bobby Bowden in 1993), but without the imprimatur of a title. None have waited more patiently than Osborne or lingered as close to greatness as Nebraska.

Their chase ended with a 24–17 victory over Miami, the final step in a 13–0 season, in a stadium where some of the Cornhuskers' most exasperating scenes have been played. Junior quarterback Tommie Frazier, who hadn't played since a blood clot was found in his right leg more than three months earlier, led the Cornhuskers on two fourth-quarter touchdown drives

that overhauled the Hurricanes and made meaningless unbeaten No. 2 Penn State's Rose Bowl victory the following day.

In 1994, college football gave us a season of frozen images and of teams and players falling just short. The snapshot of Osborne, whisked from the field by his players, is the one exception—a finished product.

Beginning in the heat of summer, Nebraska promised to complete the job that it had started in 1993, when the Cornhuskers were beaten 18–16 in the Orange Bowl by Florida State. "Unfinished Business" was the theme of their season. They practiced every day with 1:16 on the scoreboard clock, because with that much time remaining, they had gone ahead of Florida State, only to lose on a field goal with 21 seconds left. "We played well enough to win that game last year," Osborne said.

Nebraska left nothing unfinished in '94. Other teams and players rose high and often came up agonizingly short:
• Penn State, which for the fourth time in coach Joe Paterno's sublime 28-year reign

Frazier engineered two fourth-quarter TD drives in the Orange Bowl.

as king of the Nittany Lions went undefeated and failed to win the national championship. The Lions featured an offense that crunched numbers like a CD-ROM drive (an average of 47.8 points a game in the regular season) and won the Big Ten in their second year of membership. Tailback Ki-Jana Carter and quarterback Kerry Collins both finished in the top five in voting for the Heisman Trophy, and wideout Bobby Engram and tight end Kyle Brady were both first team All-Americas. Southern California coach John Robinson's Trojans lost at Penn State 38-14 in September, and when Robinson considered the possibility of a Rose Bowl rematch with the Lions, he said, "If it's us, we're not going."

But after reaching No. 1 with a 31–24 victory over Michigan in Ann Arbor on Oct. 15, the Nittany Lions lost control of their destiny in a puzzling two-week drop. On Oct. 29, Penn State annihilated a decent Ohio State team 63–14, yet dropped out of first place in the Associated Press media poll. "We dropped?" said Penn State linebacker Willie Smith on the day the poll was announced. "What do they want us to do to these teams?" The reason for the fall? Nebraska's dominating 24–7 win over Colorado on the same day, moving the Cornhuskers into No. 1.

A week later Penn State beat Indiana by the artificially close score of 35–29. The Nittany Lions led 35–14 with 1:49 to play. The Hoosiers subsequently scored twice against Penn State reserves, including a Hail Mary pass on the last play of the game, and the result was that Penn State dropped to No. 2 in the *CNN/USA Today* coaches' poll. "That was ridiculous," said Paterno. "That game was never in doubt. Never. We had a bunch of kids in at the end who hadn't even *practiced*." (It also was ironic, since it was the coaches who in previous poll controversies had derided media for placing too much emphasis on margins of victory.)

In the end it didn't matter in the least that Penn State finished its regular season without a loss or that the Lions beat Oregon in the Rose Bowl 38–20. Their hopes of winning the national championship came to an end as they sat in their rooms at the Hotel Inter-Continental, watching the Orange Bowl. When Nebraska fullback Cory Schlesinger scored the winning touchdown, Penn State defensive back Brian

Carter was runner-up in the Heisman voting but No. 1 in the draft.

Miller said, "I heard a big crash next door. I guess some guys were throwing things around." They knew it was over.

• Colorado quarterback Kordell Stewart and receiver Michael Westbrook provided the single most electric moment of the season: the Catch on Oct. 24 at Michigan Stadium. On that splendid Midwestern afternoon Michigan rode the momentum of a victory over Notre Dame two weeks earlier and led Colorado 26–14 with 3:52 to play.

The Buffaloes drove 72 yards and made it 26–21 on Rashaan Salaam's one-yard run with 2:16 left. A Michigan punt pinned Colorado to its 15-yard line with 15 seconds left and no timeouts. Stewart threw 21 yards over the middle to Westbrook and then slammed the ball into the ground to stop the clock with six seconds left and 64 yards of grass in front of him. Stewart dropped back into a deep pocket, bought time against Michigan's inexplicable three-man

AL TIELEMANS

rush and then threw a tight spiral into the twilight. "I just heaved it out there," said Stewart. Six players—three from each team—converged as the ball reached the goal line. Colorado's Blake Anderson, the son of NFL Hall of Fame defensive back Dick Anderson, a Colorado alumnus, batted the ball with his right hand, keeping it alive. Westbrook, a senior who was raised on the west side of Detroit, not 20 miles from the Michigan campus, soared in from the sideline and plucked the ball off the back of Michigan defender Ty Law's jersey, cradling it against his chest as he fell to the ground. Two officials simultaneously signaled touchdown, making Colorado a 27–26 winner. Most in the crowd of more than 106,000 fell instantly silent. "That was some sound, all of a sudden," said Colorado safety Steve Rosga.

And some play. It was the most remarkable single moment in a college football game since Doug Flutie's bomb to Gerard Phelan gave Boston College a 47–45 victory over Miami, 10 years earlier.

It also might have forewarned that Colorado was destined to win its second national championship in five years (the first was in 1990). But on the last Saturday of October, five weeks after the Catch, came the Rout. Nebraska steamrollered the Buffaloes. Colorado went on to finish 11–1, but there was more to the Buffalo season.

On Nov. 19, just after his team had beaten Iowa State, Colorado coach Bill McCartney shocked the school by announcing his resignation. He was replaced nine days later by 33-year-old assistant coach Rick Neuheisel, who beat out three other more tenured staff members for the job. And finally, on Dec. 9, Salaam, who rushed for a school-record 2,000 yards, became the first Colorado player to win the Heisman Trophy.

• Steve McNair of Alcorn State was the most spectacular player in the nation throughout the season, yet could finish no better than third in the Heisman voting. McNair eclipsed Ty Detmer's career total offensive output and finished with 16,823

yards. He averaged more than 500 yards a game in his senior season; he was a smart, skilled passer and a dangerous scrambler. Yet his season-long excellence was tainted by incessant debate over his Heisman worthiness, focusing on the fact that he played only in Division I-AA. All of this became moot when McNair was selected in the first round of the NFL draft by the Houston Oilers and was projected to have a long and prosperous career.

• Michigan running back Tyrone Wheatley was projected after the 1993 season to be one of the top picks in the NFL draft—if he chose to skip his senior year. But Wheatley returned ... and injured his right shoulder on the first day of full-contact practice. He returned in the third game of the season and rushed for 1,144 yards but also became the poster child for athletes who choose to risk injury by staying in school an extra year. When Penn State's Carter was mulling his draft decision (he ultimately left early and was the No. 1 player picked), he said, "I don't know if Wheatley's stock dropped at all, but something like that makes you think hard." Sadly, Carter's words proved to be prophetic. He ended up tearing his anterior cruciate ligament in the preseason with the Cincinnati Bengals and missed what would have been his rookie year in the NFL.

• Florida State, in pursuit of a second consecutive national title, became only the latest major program tainted by scandal. A *Sports Illustrated* investigation showed that six members of the Seminoles' '93 championship team received cash payments and took part in an in-season buying binge at a Tallahassee sporting goods store, all sponsored by a sports agent. Playing under NCAA scrutiny, the Seminoles nonetheless went 10-1-1, losing only to Miami at the Orange Bowl and rallying from a 31–3 deficit to tie Florida 31–31 in the last game of the regular season.

• Oregon, which hadn't played in the Rose Bowl since 1958, was picked in some quarters (SI was one) to finish last in the Pac-10. But under veteran coach Rich Brooks (who has since left to coach the St. Louis Rams),

JOHN BIEVER

Alabama in Birmingham. In '95 they rejoin the bowl eligibles. The Crimson Tide threatened to repeat its silent national championship assault of 1992 but lost to Florida in the SEC title game. That loss only served to fortify what critics of the game have always suspected: An 11-game regular-season schedule is tough enough; forcing SEC teams to play a title game will make it nearly impossible for the conference to win a national title.

• Notre Dame had no such worries. Amid preseason predictions of greatness for the team and first-year quarterback Ron Powlus, the Fighting Irish stammered to a 6-5-1 record, including back-to-back midseason losses to Boston College and Brigham Young. "I can give you a million excuses, but no reasons," coach Lou Holtz said. "Some seasons things just don't fit."

In their own way, Nebraskans could sympathize with Holtz. The Cornhuskers' drought between national championships had lasted 23 years, broken down into small moments of agony, impatience and frustration. Nebraska won consecutive titles in 1970 and '71 under legendary coach Bob Devaney and in the process built itself into a national power of the highest magnitude. It seemed only reasonable to expect that more titles would be brought home to Lincoln and that someday Nebraska would fill trophy cases not just with the busts of famous offensive linemen and running backs but also with championship booty. When Devaney retired in 1973, Osborne replaced him. He won 81.1% of his games in 21 years but lost enough of the most important ones to leave

the Ducks emerged from a wild conference race with a 7–1 league record (9–3 overall) and earned the right to play Penn State in the Rose Bowl. Even there, the Ducks hung together, playing the mighty Lions to a 14–14 stalemate deep into the third quarter.

• In the Southeastern Conference, Auburn continued its remarkable, probation-strapped run under 38-year-old coach Terry Bowden, Bobby's son. The Tigers, who went 11–0 in '93, their first year of probation, won their first nine games before tying Georgia and losing the annual Iron Bowl to

Nebraska always somewhere beneath No. 1 on the second day in January.

In 1975 Nebraska was 10–0 and ranked No. 2 in the country when they lost 35–10 to Oklahoma. The Sooners went on to win the national championship. In '79 the Cornhuskers were 10–0 and ranked No. 3 before losing to Oklahoma and Houston to finish the season. In '81 they lost to national champion Clemson in the Orange Bowl. And from 1987 to '93 Nebraska lost seven consecutive bowl games, carving out a reputation as cornfed bullies who could annually drill Oklahoma State but never win a truly big game.

Their combination of excellence and futility reached comic proportions in the latter half of the '80s. In the 10 years from 1984 through 1993, Nebraska won 98 games, a ridiculous average of nearly 10 wins a season. But the Cornhuskers also lost eight of 10 bowl games, including those seven in a row, beginning with a 31–28 Fiesta Bowl loss to Florida State on Jan. 1, 1988.

The Orange Bowl held its own particular demons. It was there that Osborne's 1983 team—the Mike Rozier–Irving Fryar–Turner Gill outfit that some people called the best college team ever assembled—was expected to beat upstart Miami for its 13th win in an unbeaten season and win that first title. Instead Miami and quarterback Bernie Kosar beat the Cornhuskers 31–30 to win its first national championship. Nebraska scored with 48 seconds to play and could have kicked an extra point to tie the game, and still probably have been voted No. 1, but Osborne elected to play for the victory. Gill's pass was batted away in the end zone by Miami defensive back Ken Calhoun.

Nebraska returned to the Orange Bowl again after the 1988 season and again lost to Miami. It was after that loss that the Huskers vowed to expand their recruiting, to chase the type of speed that dominated sunbelt rosters. "But then we had to go out and get the personnel," said Nebraska defensive coordinator Charlie McBride, "which wasn't something that happened overnight." And while the Huskers retooled, they lost more bowl games, including the Orange after the '91 and '92 seasons. That they came so close to Florida State after '93 was a shock to some.

To the Cornhuskers it was a sign that they were ready. "We were the best team last year," said offensive tackle Zach Wiegert, the anchor of a brilliant and powerful offensive line. "We're back to win the national championship."

The season began as if it would be a waltz, with a 31–0 pasting of West Virginia in the Kickoff Classic in New Jersey. Texas Tech fell on a Thursday night in Lubbock, Texas, and in what was supposed to be Nebraska's first test of the season, the Huskers waxed UCLA 49–21 in Lincoln. But the following Saturday, in a laughable 70–21 victory over Pacific, Frazier played only sparingly, and the next day, Sept. 25, doctors discovered a blood clot behind and slightly above his right knee. It was expected that Frazier's absence would be brief, but tests on Oct. 4 showed that the clot had re-formed, and it was suddenly likely that Frazier—the catalyst, one of the players who set the Cornhuskers apart from previous Nebraska teams—would not play again in '94.

But somehow Nebraska rolled on. Brook Berringer, a tall junior from Goodland, Kans., replaced Frazier and suffered a collapsed lung in his first game and a recollapse in his second. Osborne put his faith in that offensive line and in sophomore running back Lawrence Phillips, who ran for 1,722 yards, a Big Eight sophomore class record. The offense was altered and sometimes improvised. Matt Turman, a 165-pound walk-on quarterback from Wahoo, Neb., played the entire second half of a 32–3 victory over Oklahoma State. Berringer and Turman were asked to throw only 11 passes in a 17–3 win over a good Kansas State team. "Coach thought they might be susceptible to smashmouth football," said Turman after that game. Nebraska football, in other words. It began to look as if Nebraska, not Colorado, was blessed by the Midwestern football gods.

CHRIS COVATTA

Florida State and finished at 10–1. And while Frazier started and wrestled with his timing, Miami took a 17–9 lead early in the fourth quarter. Berringer, back in the game, threw an interception in the end zone, and Miami players ran off the field in celebration. "We were pretty much saying, 'Ball game,'" said Hurricane defensive tackle Warren Sapp.

But before the lights were turned out on another Nebraska season, Frazier was re-inserted into the game. Twice he drove the Cornhuskers to touchdowns. Frazier led and created; the offensive line pounded weary and outweighed Miami. Frazier was named the MVP of the game; Osborne was freed from the weight of past failures. Yet he remained in character to the end. "I know everybody wants me to say, 'Gee, everything's different,'" Osborne said. "But I feel about the same as after any game we won."

Two mornings later the Cornhuskers were summarily voted into their title. And there was a bonus to consider. Beginning with the 1995 season, bowl matchups will be determined by a new alliance, with the No. 1 and No. 2 available teams (all those except the winners of the Big Ten and the Pac-10, who will continue to play in the Rose Bowl) playing in one of three bowls: the Fiesta, Sugar or Orange. After the '95 season it will be the Fiesta Bowl, after '96 the Sugar and after '97 the Orange. All conference tie-ins are eliminated, meaning that the Big Eight champion no longer goes to the Orange Bowl.

And the Orange Bowl game itself is moving north to Joe Robbie Stadium for the 1997 edition. So for Nebraska the exorcism is complete, the picture finished. Win the title, beat Miami, close the stadium. And ride off the field, as light as dust.

They rolled through the rest of the season, pounding Colorado to dash the Buffs' hopes. They beat back stubborn Oklahoma and its lame duck coach, Gary Gibbs, 13–3, and wrapped up a spot in the ... gulp ... Orange Bowl. "We're like the Buffalo Bills," said offensive guard Rob Zatechka. "We're back. Live with it."

A quarterback discussion dominated the week leading up to the game. Frazier was taken off anticoagulants in late December and would dress for the game. But would he start? The other principal topic was Nebraska's past Orange Bowl failures. Miami had struggled occasionally during the regular season, losing its 58-game Orange Bowl winning streak to Washington on Sept. 24., but still the Hurricanes beat

Final Polls

Associated Press

	Record	Pts	Head Coach	SI Preseason Rank
1.........................Nebraska (51½)	13-0-0	1539½	Tom Osborne	3
2.........................Penn State (10½)	12-0-0	1497½	Joe Paterno	6
3...........................Colorado	11-1-0	1410	Bill McCartney	2
4...........................Florida St	10-1-1	1320	Bobby Bowden	10
5...........................Alabama	12-1-0	1312	Gene Stallings	16
6...........................Miami (FL)	10-2-0	1249	Dennis Erickson	7
7...........................Florida	10-2-1	1153	Steve Spurrier	8
8...........................Texas A&M	10-0-1	1117	R.C. Slocum	22
9...........................Auburn	9-1-1	1110	Terry Bowden	18
10.........................Utah	10-2-0	955	Ron McBride	20
11.........................Oregon	9-4-0	810	Rich Brooks	74
12.........................Michigan	8-4-0	732	Gary Moeller	4
13.........................Southern Cal	8-3-1	691	John Robinson	14
14.........................Ohio St	9-4-0	672	John Cooper	29
15.........................Virginia	9-3-0	648	George Welsh	36
16.........................Colorado St	10-2-0	630	Sonny Lubick	32
17.........................N Carolina St	9-3-0	511	Mike O'Cain	40
18.........................Brigham Young	10-3-0	500	LaVell Edwards	26
19.........................Kansas St	9-3-0	496	Bill Snyder	30
20.........................Arizona	8-4-0	364	Dick Tomey	1
21.........................Washington St	8-4-0	344	Mike Price	63
22.........................Tennessee	8-4-0	303	Phillip Fulmer	9
23.........................Boston College	7-4-1	236	Dan Henning	19
24.........................Mississippi St	8-4-0	160	Jackie Sherrill	37
25.........................Texas	8-4-0	90	John Mackovic	24

Note: As voted by panel of 60 sportswriters and broadcasters following bowl games (1st-place votes in parentheses).

USA Today/CNN

	Pts	Prev Rank		Pts	Prev Rank
1 ....Nebraska (54)	1542	1	14 ....Colorado St	681	10
2 ....Penn St (8)	1496	2	15 ....Southern Cal	670	22
3 ....Colorado	1382	5	16 ....Kansas St	661	8
4 ....Alabama	1344	6	17 ....N Carolina St	626	20
5 ....Florida St	1329	7	18 ....Tennessee	520	24
6 ....Miami (FL)	1229	3	19 ....Washington St	449	23
7 ....Florida	1186	4	20 ....Arizona	405	13
8 ....Utah	1029	12	21 ....N Carolina	313	14
9 ....Ohio St	842	11	22 ....Boston College	304	25
10 ....Brigham Young	832	19	23 ....Texas	244	—
11 ....Oregon	831	9	24 ....Virginia Tech	189	15
12 ....Michigan	787	18	25 ....Mississippi St	158	17
13 ....Virginia	765	16			

Note: As voted by panel of 60 Division I-A head coaches; 25 points for 1st, 24 for 2nd, etc. (1st-place votes in parentheses).

Bowls and Playoffs

NCAA Division I-A Bowl Results

Date	Bowl	Result	Payout/Team ($)	Attendance
12-15-94 ....Las Vegas		UNLV 52, Central Michigan 24	247,688	17,562
12-25-94 ....Aloha		Boston College 12, Kansas St 7	750,000	44,862
12-28-94 ....Independence		Virginia 20, Texas Christian 10	750,000	27,242
12-29-94 ....Copper		Brigham Young 30, Oklahoma 6	750,000	45,122
12-29-94 ....Freedom		Utah 16, Arizona 13	750,000	27,477
12-30-94 ....Holiday		Michigan 24, Colorado St 14	1.7 million	59,453
12-30-94 ....Sun		Texas 35, N Carolina 31	1.1 million	50,612

NCAA Division I-A Bowl Results

Date	Bowl	Result	Payout/Team ($)	Attendance
12-30-94	Gator	Tennessee 45, Virginia Tech 23	3 million	62,200
12-31-94	Liberty	Illinois 30, East Carolina 0	776,000	33,280
12-31-94	Alamo	Washington State 10, Baylor 3	750,000	44,106
1-1-95	Orange	Nebraska 24, Miami (FL) 17	4.6 million	81,753
1-1-95	Peach	N Carolina State 28, Miss State 24	1.131 million	64,902
1-2-95	Cotton	Southern Cal 55, Texas Tech 14	3 million	70,218
1-2-95	Fiesta	Colorado 41, Notre Dame 24	3 million	73,968
1-2-95	Sugar	Florida State 23, Florida 17	4.45 million	76,224
1-2-95	Hall of Fame	Wisconsin 34, Duke 20	1 million	61,384
1-2-95	Florida Citrus	Alabama 24, Ohio State 17	2.5 million	71,195
1-2-95	Carquest	South Carolina 24, West Virginia 21	1 million	50,833
1-2-95	Rose	Penn St 38, Oregon 20	6.7 million	102,247

NCAA Division I-AA Championship Boxscore

Youngstown St	0	14	7	7—28
Boise St	7	0	0	7—14

FIRST QUARTER
BSU: Matyshock 5 pass from Hilde (Erickson kick), 2:46.

SECOND QUARTER
YSU: Brungard 2 run (Massaro kick), 9:43.
YSU: Brungard 38 run (Massaro kick), 0:35.

THIRD QUARTER
YSU: Zwisler 5 pass from Brungard (Massaro kick), 3:02

FOURTH QUARTER
YSU: Patton 55 run (Massaro kick), 7:15
BSU: Matyshock 6 pass from Hilde (Erickson kick), 4:19

	YSU	BSU
First downs	20	13
Rushing yardage	263	59
Passing yardage	159	166
Return yardage	18	58
Passes (comp-att-int)	9-19-2	17-31-2
Punts (no.-avg)	6-37.0	6-38.8
Fumbles (no.-lost)	1-0	3-0
Penalties (no.-yards)	3-40	4-40

Att: 27,674

Small College Championship Summaries

NCAA DIVISION II

First round: Ferris St 43, West Chester 40; Indiana (PA) 35, Grand Valley St 27; Texas A&M-Kingsville 43, Western 7; Portland St 29, Angelo St 0; N Dakota St 18, Pittsburg St 12 (3 OT); North Dakota 18, NE Missouri St 6; North Alabama 17, Carson-Newman 13; Valdosta St 14, Albany St (GA) 7
Quarterfinals: Indiana (PA) 21, Ferris St 17; Texas A&M-Kingsville 21, Portland St 16; North Dakota 14, N Dakota St 7; North Alabama 27, Valdosta St 24 (2 OT).
Semifinals: Texas A&M-Kingsville 46, Indiana (PA) 20; North Alabama 35, North Dakota 7.

Championship: 12-10-94 Florence, AL

Texas A&M-Kingsville	0	3	7	0—10
North Alabama	7	9	0	0—16

NCAA DIVISION III

First round: Mount Union 28, Allegheny 19; Albion 28, Augustana (IL) 21; Wartburg 22, Central (IA) 21; St John's (MN) 51, La Verne 12; Dickinson 0; Wash&Jeff. 28, Trinity (TX) 0; Plymouth St 19, Merchant Marine 18; Ithaca 10, Buffalo St 7 (2 OT).
Quarterfinals: Albion 34, Mt Union 33; St John's (MN) 42, Wartburg 14; Wash&Jeff. 37, Widener 21; Ithaca 22, Plymouth St 7.
Semifinals: Albion 19, St John's (MN) 16; Wash&Jeff 23, Ithaca 19.

Championship: 12-10-93 Salem, VA

Albion	7	17	7	7—38
Washington&Jefferson	7	0	0	8—15

NAIA DIVISION I PLAYOFFS

First Round: Arkansas-Pine Bluff 21, Central St (OH)14; Northeastern St (OK) 14, Moorhead St (MN) 7; Western Montana 48, Glenville St (WV) 38; Langston (OK) 56, Arkansas Tech 42.
Semifinals: Arkansas-Pine Bluff 60, Western Montana 53 (OT); Northeastern St (OK) 3, Langston (OK) 0.

Championship: 12-10-94 Pine Bluff, AR

Northeastern St (OK)	0	3	3	7—13
Arkansas-Pine Bluff	3	7	0	2—12

NAIA DIVISION II PLAYOFFS

First round: Western Washington 21, Linfield (OR) 2; Pacific Lutheran (WA) 34, Midland Lutheran (NE) 14; Westminster (PA) 41, Findlay (OH) 30; Tiffin (OH) 41, Eureka (IL) 14; Hardin-Simmons (TX) 49, Missouri Valley 21; Minot St (ND) 20, Sioux Falls (SD) 13; Lambuth (TN) 48, Evangel (MO) 19; Northwestern (IA) 38, Trinity (IL) 20.
Quarterfinals: Lambuth (TN) 57, Hardin-Simmons (TX) 54; Westminster (PA) 42, Tiffin (OH) 14; Northwestern (IA) 28, Minot St (ND) 26; Pacific Lutheran (WA) 25, Western Washington 20.
Semifinals: Pacific Lutheran (WA) 28, Northwestern (IA) 7; Westminster (PA) 46, Lambuth (TN) 6.

Championship: 12-17-94 Portland, OR

Westminster (PA)	7	7	7	6—27
Pacific Lutheran (WA)	0	7	0	0—7

Awards

Heisman Memorial Trophy

Player/School	Class	Pos	1st	2nd	3rd	Total
Rashaan Salaam, Colorado ....Jr		RB	400	229	85	1,743
Ki-Jana Carter, Penn St.................Jr		RB	115	205	146	901
Steve McNair, Alcorn St ....Sr		QB	111	85	152	655
Kerry Collins, Penn St.....................Sr		QB	101	117	102	639
Jay Barker, Alabama......................Sr		QB	36	58	71	295
Warren Sapp, Miami (FL) ....Jr		DT	17	37	67	192
Eric Zeier, Georgia ....Sr		QB	7	15	32	83
Lawrence Phillips, Nebraska..........So		RB	1	8	21	40
Napoleon Kaufman, Washington ...Sr		RB	3	3	12	27
Zach Wiegert, Nebraska ....Sr		OT	1	7	10	27

Note: Former Heisman winners and the media vote, with ballots allowing for 3 names (3 points for 1st, 2 for 2nd, 1 for 3rd).

Offensive Players of the Year

Maxwell Award (Player)...............................Kerry Collins, Penn St, QB
Walter Camp Player of the Year (Back) .....Rashaan Salaam, Colorado, RB
Davey O'Brien Award (QB) ....Kerry Collins, Penn St, QB
Doak Walker Award (RB) ....Rashaan Salaam, Colorado, RB

Other Awards

Vince Lombardi/Rotary Award (Lineman) ..Waren Sapp, Miami (FL), DT
Outland Trophy (Interior lineman) ....Zach Wiegert, Nebraska, OG
Butkus Award (Linebacker)........................Dana Howard, Illinois, LB
Jim Thorpe Award (Defensive back)..........Chris Hudson, Colorado, DB
Sporting News Player of the Year ....Rashaan Salaam, Colorado, RB
Walter Payton Award (Div I-AA Player) ......Steve McNair, Alcorn St, QB
Harlon Hill Trophy (Div II Player) ....Chris Hatcher, Valdosta St, QB

Coaches' Awards

Walter Camp Award ....Joe Paterno, Penn St
Eddie Robinson Award (Div I-AA)..............Jim Tressel, Youngstown St
Bobby Dodd Award ....Fred Goldsmith, Duke
Bear Bryant Award ....Rich Brooks, Oregon

AFCA COACHES OF THE YEAR

Division I-A ....Tom Osborne, Nebraska
Division I-AA ....Jim Tressel, Youngstown St
Division II and NAIA Division I....................Bobby Wallace, North Alabama
Division III and NAIA Division II..................Pete Schmidt, Albion

Football Writers Association of America All-America Team

OFFENSE

Jack Jackson, Florida, Jr ....Wide receiver
Frank Sanders, Auburn, Sr..................Wide receiver
Pete Mitchell, Boston College, Sr........Tight end
Clay Shiver, Florida St, Jr ....OL
Tony Boselli, Southern Caifornia, Sr....OL
Blake Brockermeyer, Texas, Jr ....OL
Brenden Stai, Nebraska, Sr..................OL
Zach Wiegert, Nebraska, Sr................OL
Kerry Collins, Penn St, Sr ....Quarterback
Ki-Jana Carter, Penn St, Jr..................Running back
Rashaan Salaam, Colorado, Jr ....Running back
Steve McLaughlin, Arizona, Sr ....PK
Leeland McElroy, Texas A&M, So.......Kick returner

DEFENSE

Luther Elliss, Utah, Sr..........................DL
Warren Sapp, Miami (FL), Jr ....DL
Derrick Alexander, Florida St, Jr ....DL
Tedy Bruschi, Arizona, Jr ....DL
Derrick Brooks, Florida St, Sr ....Linebacker
Dana Howard, Illinois, Sr.....................Linebacker
Ed Stewart, Nebraska, Sr ....Linebacker
Chris Hudson, Colorado, Sr ....Defensive back
Greg Myers, Colorado St, Jr ....Defensive back
Herman O'Berry, Oregon, Sr..............Defensive back
Chris Shelling, Auburn, Sr...................Defensive back
Todd Sauerbrun, West Virginia, Sr......Punter

Division I-A

ATLANTIC COAST CONFERENCE

	Conference				Full Season			
	W	L	T		W	L	T	Pct
Florida St	8	0	0		10	1	1	.875
N Carolina St	6	2	0		9	3	0	.750
Virginia	5	3	0		9	3	0	.750
Duke	5	3	0		8	4	0	.667
N Carolina	5	3	0		8	4	0	.667
Clemson	4	4	0		5	6	0	.455
Maryland	2	6	0		4	7	0	.364
Wake Forest	1	7	0		3	8	0	.273
Georgia Tech	0	8	0		1	10	0	.091

BIG EAST CONFERENCE

	Conference				Full Season			
	W	L	T		W	L	T	Pct
Miami (FL)	7	0	0		10	2	0	.833
Virginia Tech	5	2	0		8	4	0	.667
Syracuse	4	3	0		7	4	0	.636
W Virginia	4	3	0		7	6	0	.539
Boston College	3	3	1		7	4	1	.625
Rutgers	2	4	1		5	5	1	.500
Pittsburgh	2	5	0		3	8	0	.273
Temple	0	7	0		2	9	0	.182

BIG EIGHT CONFERENCE

	Conference				Full Season			
	W	L	T		W	L	T	Pct
Nebraska	7	0	0		13	0	0	1.000
Colorado	6	1	0		11	1	0	.917
Kansas St	5	2	0		9	3	0	.750
Oklahoma	4	3	0		6	6	0	.500
Kansas	3	4	0		6	5	0	.545
Missouri	2	5	0		3	8	1	.292
Oklahoma St	0	6	1		3	7	1	.318
Iowa St	0	6	1		0	10	1	.045

BIG TEN CONFERENCE

	Conference				Full Season			
	W	L	T		W	L	T	Pct
Penn St	8	0	0		12	0	0	1.000
Ohio St	6	2	0		9	4	0	.692
Michigan	5	3	0		8	4	0	.667
Wisconsin	4	3	1		7	4	1	.625
Illinois	4	4	0		7	5	0	.583
Michigan St	4	4	0		5	6	0	.455
Iowa	3	4	1		5	5	1	.500
Indiana	3	5	0		6	5	0	.545
Purdue	2	4	2		4	5	2	.455
Northwestern	2	6	0		3	7	0	.300
Minnesota	1	7	0		3	8	0	.273

BIG WEST CONFERENCE

	Conference				Full Season			
	W	L	T		W	L	T	Pct
Nevada	5	1	0		9	2	0	.818
UNLV	5	1	0		7	5	0	.583
SW Louisiana	5	1	0		6	5	0	.545
Pacific	4	2	0		6	5	0	.545
N Illinois	3	3	0		4	7	0	.364
San Jose St	3	3	0		3	8	0	.273
New Mexico St	2	4	0		3	8	0	.273
Utah St	2	4	0		3	8	0	.273
La Tech	1	5	0		3	8	0	.273
Arkansas St	0	6	0		1	10	0	.091

Division I-A *(Cont.)*

MID-AMERICAN CONFERENCE

	Conference			Full Season			
	W	L	T	W	L	T	Pct
Cent Michigan	8	1	0	9	3	0	.750
Bowling Green	7	1	0	9	2	0	.818
W Michigan	5	3	0	7	4	0	.636
Miami (OH)	5	3	0	5	5	1	.500
Ball St	5	3	1	5	5	1	.500
Toledo	4	3	1	6	4	1	.590
E Michigan	5	4	0	5	6	0	.455
Kent	2	7	0	2	9	0	.181
Akron	1	8	0	1	10	0	.091
Ohio U	0	9	0	0	11	0	.000

PACIFIC-10 CONFERENCE

	Conference			Full Season			
	W	L	T	W	L	T	Pct
Oregon	7	1	0	9	4	0	.692
Southern Cal	6	2	0	8	3	1	.708
Arizona	6	2	0	8	4	0	.667
Washington St	5	3	0	8	4	0	.667
Washington	4	4	0	7	4	0	.636
UCLA	3	5	0	5	6	0	.455
California	3	5	0	4	7	0	.364
Oregon St	2	6	0	4	7	0	.364
Stanford	2	6	0	3	7	1	.318
Arizona St	2	6	0	3	8	0	.273

SOUTHEASTERN CONFERENCE

	Conference			Full Season*			
EAST	W	L	T	W	L	T	Pct
Florida	8	1	0	10	2	1	.808
Tennessee	5	3	0	8	4	0	.667
S Carolina	4	4	0	7	5	0	.583
Georgia	3	4	1	6	4	1	.590
Vanderbilt	2	6	0	5	6	0	.455
Kentucky	0	8	0	1	10	0	.091
WEST							
Alabama	8	1	0	12	1	0	.923
Auburn	6	1	1	9	1	1	.818
Mississippi St	5	3	0	8	4	0	.667
Louisiana St	3	5	0	4	7	0	.364
Arkansas	2	6	0	4	7	0	.364
Mississippi	2	6	0	4	7	0	.364

*Full season record includes SEC Championship Game in which Florida defeated Alabama, 24–23, on Dec 3. Auburn was ineligible for postseason play in 1994 due to NCAA probation.

SOUTHWEST ATHLETIC CONFERENCE

	Conference			Full Season			
	W	L	T	W	L	T	Pct
Texas A&M	6	0	1	10	0	1	.955
Texas	4	3	0	8	4	0	.667
Baylor	4	3	0	7	5	0	.583
TCU	4	3	0	7	5	0	.583
Texas Tech	4	3	0	6	6	0	.500
Rice	4	3	0	5	6	0	.454
Houston	1	6	0	1	10	0	.091
SMU	0	6	1	1	9	1	.136

Division I-A (Cont.)

WESTERN ATHLETIC CONFERENCE

	Conference			Full Season			
	W	L	T	W	L	T	Pct
Colorado St	7	1	0	10	2	0	.833
Utah	6	2	0	10	2	0	.833
BYU	6	2	0	10	3	0	.769
Air Force	6	2	0	8	4	0	.667
Wyoming	4	4	0	6	6	0	.500
New Mexico	4	4	0	5	7	0	.417
Fresno St	3	4	1	5	7	1	.423
San Diego St	2	6	0	4	7	0	.364
UTEP	1	6	1	3	7	1	.318
Hawaii	0	8	0	3	8	1	.292

INDEPENDENTS

	Full Season			
	W	L	T	Pct
E Carolina	7	5	0	.583
Notre Dame	6	5	1	.542
Louisville	6	5	0	.545
Memphis	6	5	0	.545
S Mississippi	6	5	0	.545
Army	4	7	0	.364
Navy	3	8	0	.273
NE Louisiana	3	8	0	.273
Tulsa	3	8	0	.273
Cincinnati	2	8	1	.227
Tulane	1	10	0	.091

Division I-AA

BIG SKY CONFERENCE

	Conference			Full Season			
	W	L	T	W	L	T	Pct
Boise St	6	1	0	13	2	0	.867
Montana	5	2	0	11	3	0	.786
Idaho	5	2	0	9	3	0	.750
N Arizona	4	3	0	7	4	0	.636
Idaho St	4	3	0	6	5	0	.546
Weber St	2	5	0	5	6	0	.455
E Washington	2	5	0	4	7	0	.364
Montana St	0	7	0	3	8	0	.273

GATEWAY COLLEGIATE ATHLETIC CONFERENCE

	Conference			Full Season			
	W	L	T	W	L	T	Pct
N Iowa	6	0	0	8	4	0	.667
W Illinois	4	2	0	8	3	0	.727
E Illinois	4	2	0	6	5	0	.546
Illinois St	3	3	0	5	5	1	.500
Indiana St	2	4	0	5	6	0	.455
SW Missouri St	2	4	0	4	7	0	.364
S Illinois	0	6	0	1	10	0	.091

Division I-AA *(Cont.)*

IVY GROUP

	Conference			Full Season			
	W	L	T	W	L	T	Pct
Penn	7	0	0	9	0	0	1.000
Brown	4	3	0	7	3	0	.700
Princeton	4	3	0	7	3	0	.700
Cornell	3	4	0	6	4	0	.600
Columbia	3	4	0	5	4	1	.550
Yale	3	4	0	5	5	0	.500
Dartmouth	2	5	0	4	6	0	.400
Harvard	2	5	0	4	6	0	.400

MID-EASTERN ATHLETIC CONFERENCE

	Conference			Full Season			
	W	L	T	W	L	T	Pct
S Carolina St	6	0	0	10	2	0	.833
Delaware St	4	2	0	7	4	0	.636
N Carolina A&T	3	3	0	6	5	0	.545
Bethune-Cookman	3	3	0	5	6	0	.455
Florida A&M	2	4	0	6	5	0	.546
Morgan St	2	4	0	3	8	0	.273
Howard	1	5	0	4	7	0	.364

OHIO VALLEY CONFERENCE

	Conference			Full Season			
	W	L	T	W	L	T	Pct
Eastern Kentucky	8	0	0	10	3	0	.769
Middle Tennessee St	7	1	0	8	3	1	.708
SE Missouri	5	3	0	7	5	0	.583
Murray St	4	4	0	5	6	0	.455
Tennessee St	4	4	0	5	6	0	.455
Tenn-Martin	3	5	0	6	5	0	.545
Tennessee Tech	3	5	0	5	6	0	.455
Austin Peay	2	6	0	3	8	0	.273
Morehead	0	8	0	0	11	0	.000

PATRIOT LEAGUE

	Conference			Full Season			
	W	L	T	W	L	T	Pct
Lafayette	5	0	0	5	6	0	.455
Lehigh	3	2	0	5	5	1	.500
Holy Cross	3	2	0	3	8	0	.273
Bucknell	2	3	0	5	6	0	.455
Colgate	2	3	0	3	8	0	.273
Fordham	0	5	0	0	11	0	.000

SOUTHERN CONFERENCE

	Conference			Full Season			
	W	L	T	W	L	T	Pct
Marshall	7	1	0	12	2	0	.857
Appalachian St	6	2	0	9	4	0	.692
Georgia Southern	5	3	0	6	5	0	.545
W Carolina	5	3	0	6	5	0	.545
Citadel	4	4	0	6	5	0	.545
E Tennessee St	4	4	0	6	5	0	.545
Furman	2	6	0	3	8	0	.273
TN-Chattanooga	2	6	0	3	8	0	.273
Virginia Military	1	7	0	1	10	0	.091

Division I-AA *(Cont.)*

SOUTHLAND CONFERENCE

	Conference			Full Season			
	W	L	T	W	L	T	Pct
North Texas	5	0	1	7	4	1	.625
McNeese St	5	1	0	10	3	0	.769
SF Austin St	4	1	1	6	3	2	.636
Northwestern (LA)	3	3	0	5	6	0	.455
Sam Houston St	1	5	0	6	5	0	.545
Nicholls St	1	5	0	5	6	0	.455
SW Texas St	1	5	0	4	7	0	.364

SOUTHWESTERN ATHLETIC CONFERENCE

	Conference			Full Season			
	W	L	T	W	L	T	Pct
Grambling	6	1	0	9	3	0	.750
Alcorn St	6	1	0	8	3	1	.708
Southern	5	2	0	6	5	0	.545
Jackson St	4	3	0	7	4	0	.636
Alabama St	3	4	0	6	5	0	.545
Texas Southern	2	5	0	4	7	0	.364
Mississippi Valley	2	5	0	3	7	0	.300
Prairie View A&M	0	7	0	0	11	0	.000

YANKEE CONFERENCE

	Conference			Full Season			
	W	L	T	W	L	T	Pct
MID-ATLANTIC							
James Madison	6	2	0	10	3	0	.769
William & Mary	6	2	0	8	3	0	.727
Delaware	5	3	0	7	3	1	.682
Villanova	2	6	0	5	6	0	.455
Northeastern	2	6	0	2	9	0	.182
Richmond	1	7	0	3	8	0	.273
NEW ENGLAND							
New Hampshire	8	0	0	10	2	0	.833
Boston University	6	2	0	9	3	0	.750
Massachusetts	4	4	0	5	6	0	.455
Connecticut	4	4	0	4	7	0	.364
Maine	2	6	0	3	8	0	.273
Rhode Island	2	6	0	2	9	0	.182

INDEPENDENTS

	Full Season			
	W	L	T	Pct
Youngstown St	14	0	1	.967
Hofstra	8	1	1	.850
Robert Morris	7	1	1	.833
Towson St	8	2	0	.800
Monmouth (NJ)	7	2	0	.778
St. Mary's (CA)	7	3	0	.700
Troy St	8	4	0	.667
Alabama-Birmingham	7	4	0	.636
Central Florida	7	4	0	.636
Wagner	6	5	0	.545
Liberty	5	6	0	.455
W Kentucky	5	6	0	.455
Samford	4	6	1	.409
Central Connecticut	4	6	0	.400
Davidson	3	7	0	.300
Buffalo	3	8	0	.273
St. Francis (PA)	2	7	1	.250
Charleston Southern	0	11	0	.000

Division I-A

SCORING

	Class	GP	TD	XP	FG	Pts	Pts/Game
Rashaan Salaam, Colorado	Jr	11	24	0	0	144	13.09
Ki-Jana Carter, Penn St	Jr	11	23	0	0	138	12.55
Brian Pruitt, Central Michigan	Sr	11	22	0	0	132	12.00
Brian Leaver, Bowling Green	Sr	11	0	42	21	105	9.55
Judd Davis, Florida	Sr	12	0	65	14	107	8.92
Rodney Thomas, Texas A&M	Sr	11	16	0	0	96	8.73
Tyrone Wheatley, Michigan	Sr	9	13	0	0	78	8.67
Remy Hamilton, Michigan	So	11	0	23	24	95	8.64
Steve McLaughlin, Arizona	Sr	11	0	26	23	95	8.64
Brett Conway, Penn St	So	11	0	62	10	92	8.36

FIELD GOALS

	Class	GP	FGA	FG	Pct	FG/Game
Remy Hamilton, Michigan	So	11	29	24	.828	2.18
Steve McLaughlin, Arizona	Sr	11	29	23	.793	2.09
Brian Leaver, Bowling Green	Sr	11	24	21	.875	1.91
Nick Garritano, UNLV	Sr	11	26	21	.808	1.91
Ryan Williams, Virginia Tech	Sr	10	21	17	.810	1.70
Mike Chalberg, Minnesota	Jr	10	23	17	.739	1.70
John Wales, Washington	So	11	25	18	.720	1.64

TOTAL OFFENSE

			Rushing		Passing		Total Offense			
	Class	GP	Car	Net	Att	Yds	Yds	Yds/Play	TDR*	Yds/Game
Mike Maxwell, Nevada	Jr	11	30	-39	447	3537	3498	7.33	32	318.00
Eric Zeier, Georgia	Sr	11	21	61	433	3396	3457	7.61	25	314.27
Stoney Case, New Mexico	Sr	12	140	532	409	3117	3649	6.65	33	304.08
Steve Stenstrom, Stanford	Sr	9	65	-108	333	2822	2714	6.82	19	301.56
John Walsh, Brigham Young	Jr	12	77	-239	463	3712	3473	6.43	29	289.42
Mike McCoy, Utah	Sr	11	75	69	381	3035	3104	6.81	29	282.18
Craig Whelihan, Pacific (CA)	Sr	9	24	-12	326	2318	2306	6.59	18	256.22
Marcus Crandell, E Carolina	So	11	71	96	401	2687	2783	5.90	22	253.00
Anthony Hill, Colorado St	Sr	11	93	163	290	2552	2715	7.09	21	246.82
Kordell Stewart, Colorado	Sr	11	122	639	237	2071	2710	7.55	17	246.36

*Touchdowns responsible for.

RUSHING

	Class	GP	Car	Yds	Avg	TD	Yds/Game
Rashaan Salaam, Colorado	Jr	11	298	2055	6.9	24	186.82
Brian Pruitt, Central Michigan	Sr	11	292	1890	6.5	20	171.82
Lawrence Phillips, Nebraska	So	12	286	1722	6.0	16	143.50
Ki-Jana Carter, Penn St	Jr	11	198	1539	7.8	23	139.91
Andre Davis, Texas Christian	Jr	11	260	1494	5.7	7	135.82
Alex Smith, Indiana	Fr	11	265	1475	5.6	10	134.09
Chris Darkins, Minnesota	Jr	11	277	1443	5.2	11	131.18
Napoleon Kaufman, Washington	Sr	11	255	1390	5.5	9	126.36
Billy West, Pittsburgh	So	11	252	1358	5.4	6	123.45
Ryan Christopherson, Wyoming	Sr	12	300	1455	4.8	10	121.25

Signing Off?

Down South, when the February college football signing date rolls around, recruiting and rumors go together like grits and gravy. Recently word reached *The Atlanta Journal-Constitution* that Chauncey McGee, a six-foot, 180-pound defensive back at Atlanta's Westlake High, had committed suicide. The paper quickly dispatched a correspondent to check out the report. "Chauncey didn't commit suicide," word came back. "Chauncey committed to Mississippi State."

Division I-A (Cont.)

PASSING EFFICIENCY

	Class	GP	Att	Comp	Pct Comp	Yds	Yds/Att	TD	Int	Rating Pts
Kerry Collins, Penn St..................Sr		11	264	176	66.67	2679	10.15	21	7	172.9
Terry Dean, Florida......................Jr		10	180	109	60.56	1492	8.29	20	10	155.7
Jay Barker, Alabama...................Sr		12	226	139	61,50	1996	8.83	14	5	151.7
Danny Wuerffel, Florida ....So		12	212	132	62.26	1754	8.27	18	9	151.3
Rob Johnson, Southern Cal ....Sr		9	255	170	66.67	2210	8.67	12	6	150.3
Mike McCoy, Utah.......................Sr		11	381	247	64.83	3035	7.97	28	11	150.2
Max Knake, Texas Christian........Jr		11	316	184	58.23	2624	8.30	24	7	148.6
Steve Stenstrom, Stanford...........Sr		9	333	217	65.17	2822	8.47	16	6	148.6
Todd Collins, Michigan ....Sr		11	264	172	65.15	2356	8.92	11	7	148.6
Ryan Henry, Bowling Green ......So		11	293	174	59.39	2368	8.08	25	11	147.9
Kordell Stewart, Colorado ....Sr		11	237	147	62.03	2071	8.74	10	3	146.8
John Gustin, Wyoming ....Sr		12	306	181	59.15	2757	9.01	17	13	144.7

Note: Minimum 15 attempts per game.

RECEPTIONS PER GAME

	Class	GP	No.	Yds	TD	R/Game
Alex Van Dyke, Nevada.......................Jr		11	98	1246	10	8.91
Randy Gatewood, UNLV ....Sr		11	88	1203	6	8.00
Mick Rossley, Southern Methodist ....Sr		11	83	857	4	7.55
Geroy Simon, Maryland........................So		11	77	891	5	7.00
Wes Caswell, Tulsa ....So		11	74	893	3	6.73

RECEIVING YARDS PER GAME

	Class	GP	No.	Yds	TD	Yds/Game
Marcus Harris, Wyoming ....So		12	71	1431	11	119.25
Keyshawn Johnson, Southern Cal.....Jr		10	58	1140	6	114.00
Alex Van Dyke, Nevada....................Jr		11	98	1246	10	113.27
Kevin Jordan, UCLA..........................Jr		11	73	1228	7	111.64
Randy Gatewood, UNLV ....Sr		11	88	1203	6	109.36

ALL-PURPOSE RUNNERS

	Class	GP	Rush	Rec	PR	KOR	Yds	Yds/Game
Rashaan Salaam, Colorado ....Jr		11	2055	294	0	0	2349	213.55
Brian Pruitt, Central Michigan ....Sr		11	1890	69	0	330	2289	208.09
Andre Davis, Texas Christian............Jr		11	1494	522	0	0	2016	183.27
Napoleon Kaufman, Washington ....Sr		11	1390	199	8	229	1826	166.00
Ki-Jana Carter, Penn St.....................Jr		11	1539	123	0	81	1743	158.45

INTERCEPTIONS

	Class	GP	No.	Yds	TD	Int/Game
Aaron Beasley, West Virginia............Jr		12	10	133	2	.83
Brian Robinson, Auburn.....................Jr		11	8	140	1	.73
Ronde Barber, Virginia......................Fr		11	8	56	0	.73
Demetrice Martin, Michigan St..........Jr		11	7	41	0	.64

PUNTING

	Class	No.	Avg
Todd Sauerbrun, West Virginia.............Sr		72	48.42
Jason Bender, Georgia Tech ....Sr		55	45.51
Brad Maynard, Ball St..........................Jr		59	45.49

Note: Minimum of 3.6 per game.

PUNT RETURNS

	Class	No.	Yds	TD	Avg
Steve Clay, E Michigan ....Jr		14	278	1	19.86
Nilo Silvan, Tennessee.............Jr		15	272	0	18.13
Ray Peterson, San Diego St....Jr		12	190	2	15.83
Kevin Alexander, Utah St ....Jr		14	199	1	14.21
Eddie Kennison, LSU ....So		36	439	1	12.19

Note: Minimum 1.2 per game.

Division I-A (Cont.)

KICKOFF RETURNS

	Class	No.	Yds	TD	Avg
Eric Moulds, Mississippi St	Jr	13	426	0	32.77
David Dunn, Fresno St	Sr	35	1013	0	28.94
Marcus Wall, N Carolina	Jr	27	743	1	27.52
Parrish Foster, New Mexico St	Sr	14	385	0	27.50
Derrick Mason, Michigan St	So	36	966	1	26.83
Joey Galloway, Ohio St	Sr	15	401	1	26.73

Note: Minimum of 1.2 per game.

Division I-A Single-Game Highs

RUSHING AND PASSING

Rushing and passing plays: 77—Stoney Case, New Mexico, Sep 10 (vs Texas Christian).

Rushing and passing yards: 494—Eric Zeier, Georgia, Sep 3 (vs S Carolina).

Rushing plays: 44—Jason Cooper, Louisiana Tech, Oct 8 (vs UNLV).

Net rushing yards: 356—Brian Pruitt, Central Michigan, Nov 5 (vs Toledo).

Passes attempted: 62—Stoney Case, New Mexico, Sep 10 (vs Texas Christian).

Passes completed: 40—Danny Kanell, Florida St, Nov 26 (vs Florida).

Passing yards: 485—Eric Zeier, Georgia, Sep 3 (vs S Carolina).

RECEIVING AND RETURNS

Passes caught: 23—Randy Gatewood, UNLV, Sep 17 (vs Idaho).

Receiving yards: 363—Randy Gatewood, UNLV, Sep 17 (vs Idaho).

Punt return yards: 194—Ryan Roskelly, Memphis, Sep 10 (vs Tulsa).

Kickoff return yards: 186—Derrick Mason, Michigan St Nov 26 (vs Penn St).

Division I-AA

SCORING

	Class	GP	TD	XP	FG	Pts	Pts/Game
Michael Hicks, S Carolina St	Jr	11	22	0	0	132	12.00
Arnold Mickens, Butler	Jr	10	18	0	0	108	10.80
Brian McCarty, Towson St	Sr	10	17	0	0	102	10.20
Chris Parker, Marshall	Jr	11	18	2	0	110	10.00
Wayne Chrebet, Hofstra	Sr	10	16	2	0	98	9.80

FIELD GOALS

	Class	GP	FGA	FG	Pct	FG/Game
Andy Glockner, Pennsylvania	Sr	9	20	14	.700	1.56
Matt Waller, Northern Iowa	So	11	26	17	.654	1.55
Jim Richter, Furman	Jr	11	19	16	.842	1.45
Bob Warden, Brown	Sr	10	16	14	.875	1.40
John Coursey, James Madison	So	11	23	15	.652	1.36

Division I-AA (Cont.)

TOTAL OFFENSE

			Rushing				Passing		Total Offense			
	Class	GP	Car	Gain	Loss	Net	Att	Yds	Yds	Yds/Play	TDR*	Yds/Game
Steve McNair, Alcorn St	Sr	11	119	1128	192	936	530	4863	5799	8.94	53	527.18
Dave Dickenson, Montana	Jr	9	95	361	306	55	336	3053	3108	7.21	27	345.33
Jeff Lewis, N Arizona	Jr	11	108	338	306	32	450	3355	3387	6.07	32	307.91
Mitch Maher, North Texas	Sr	10	79	321	146	175	319	2840	3015	7.58	31	301.50
Robert Dougherty, BU	Sr	11	90	350	258	92	387	3173	3265	6.84	29	296.82

*Touchdowns responsible for.

RUSHING

	Class	GP	Car	Yds	Avg	TD	Yds/Game
Arnold Mickens, Butler	Jr	10	409	2255	5.5	18	225.50
Tim Hall, Robert Morris	Jr	9	154	1336	8.7	11	148.44
Don Wilkerson, SW Texas St	Sr	11	302	1569	5.2	9	142.64
Thomas Haskins, Virginia Military	So	11	258	1509	5.8	11	137.18
Rene Ingoglia, Massachusetts	Jr	11	258	1505	5.8	14	136.82

PASSING EFFICIENCY

	Class	GP	Att	Comp	Pct Comp	Yds	Yds/Att	TD	Int	Rating Pts
Dave Dickenson, Montana	Jr	9	336	229	68.15	3053	9.09	24	6	164.5
Todd Donnan, Marshall	Sr	11	288	182	63.19	2403	8.34	28	8	159.8
Brian Brennan, Idaho	Fr	10	200	116	58.00	1766	8.83	18	4	157.9
Mitch Maher, North Texas	Sr	10	319	202	63.32	2840	8.90	25	12	156.4
Steve McNair, Alcorn St	Sr	11	530	304	57.36	4863	9.18	44	17	155.4

Note: Minimum 15 attempts per game.

RECEPTIONS PER GAME

	Class	GP	No.	Yds	TD	R/Game
Jeff Johnson, E Tenn St	Sr	9	73	857	8	8.11
Ray Marshall, St. Peter's	Sr	9	69	797	4	7.67
Derrick Ingram, Alabama-Birmingham	Sr	11	83	1457	13	7.55
Heston Sutman, Central Conn St	Sr	10	70	1018	7	7.00
Tim McNair, Alcorn St	Sr	11	74	1230	13	6.73

RECEIVING YARDS PER GAME

	Class	GP	No.	Yds	TD	Yds/Game
Mark Orlando, Towson St	Sr	9	55	1223	12	135.89
Derrick Ingram, Alabama-Birmingham	Sr	11	83	1457	13	132.45
Wayne Chrebet, Hofstra	Sr	10	57	1200	16	120.00
Reggie Barlow, Alabama St	Jr	11	58	1267	12	115.18
Tim McNair, Alcorn St	Sr	11	74	1230	13	111.82

ALL-PURPOSE RUNNERS

	Class	GP	Rush	Rec	PR	KOR	Yds*	Yds/Game
Arnold Mickens, Butler	Jr	10	2250	7	0	0	2262	226.20
Anthony Jordan, Samford	Sr	11	924	400	169	767	2260	205.45
Tim Hall, Robert Morris	Jr	9	1336	460	0	0	1796	199.56
Don Wilkerson, SW Texas St	Sr	11	1569	131	21	327	2048	186.18
Ozzie Young, Valparaiso	Jr	9	606	426	96	533	1661	184.56

*Includes interceptions return yards

INTERCEPTIONS

	Class	GP	No.	Yds	TD	Int/Game
Joseph Vaughn, Cal St-Northridge	Sr	10	9	265	4	.90
Brian Clark, Hofstra	Jr	10	9	56	0	.90
Chris Hanson, Cornell	Sr	10	8	83	0	.80
Jason Wilson, St Francis (PA)	Sr	10	8	52	1	.80
Shayne Snider, Valparaiso	Sr	10	8	49	0	.80

Three tied at .70 Int/Game.

Division I-AA (Cont.)

PUNTING

	Class	No.	Avg
Scott Holmes, Samford	Jr	49	42.84
Brian Desselles, Nicholls St	Sr	54	42.76
Ross Schulte, W Illinois	Sr	43	42.26
Kevin O'Leary, N Arizona	Jr	44	42.02

Note: Minimum 3.6 per game.

Division II

SCORING

	Class	GP	TD	XP	FG	Pts	Pts/Game
Leonard Davis, Lenoir-Rhyne	Sr	9	19	0	0	114	12.7
LaMonte Coleman, Slippery Rock	Sr	10	21	0	0	126	12.6
Bobby Felix, W New Mexico	Jr	8	16	4	0	100	12.5
Dave Ludy, Winona St	Sr	11	22	4	0	136	12.4
Darick Holmes, Portland St	Sr	10	19	0	0	114	11.4

FIELD GOALS

	Class	GP	FGA	FG	Pct	FG/Game
Matt Seagraves, E Stroudsburg	So	10	26	15	57.7	1.50
Ryan Anderson, N Colorado	Jr	11	23	14	60.9	1.27
Scott Doyle, Chadron St	Jr	11	19	14	73.7	1.27
Matt Hemenway, St Cloud St	Fr	10	20	12	60.0	1.20
Eric Myers, W Virginia Wesleyan	So	10	17	12	70.6	1.20
Mike Foster, Mesa St	So	10	16	12	75.0	1.20

TOTAL OFFENSE

	Class	GP	Yds	Yds/Game
Grady Benton, W Texas A&M	Jr	9	3699	411.0
Alfred Montez, W New Mexico	Jr	6	2130	355.0
Kevin Vickers, Tarleton St	Sr	10	3232	323.2
Chris Hatcher, Valdosta St	Sr	11	3512	319.3
Aaron Sparrow, Norfolk St	Jr	10	3152	315.2

RUSHING

	Class	GP	Car	Yds	TD	Yds/Game
Leonard Davis, Lenoir-Rhyne	Sr	9	216	1559	19	173.2
Larry Jackson, Edinboro	Sr	10	274	1660	15	166.0
Richard Huntley, Winston-Salem	Jr	11	251	1815	18	165.0
Joe Aska, Central Oklahoma	Sr	10	278	1629	15	162.9
Fred Lane, Lane	Fr	11	280	1779	14	161.7

PASSING EFFICIENCY

	Class	GP	Att	Comp	Yds	Pct Comp	TD	Int	Rating Pts
Chris Hatcher, Valdosta St	Sr	11	430	321	3591	74.6	50	9	179.0
Robb Stamey, Lenoir-Rhyne	Sr	10	197	106	1986	53.8	18	3	165.6
Sultan Cooper, Albany St (GA)	Jr	11	190	114	1539	60.0	22	4	162.0
Alfred Montez, W New Mexico	Jr	6	231	133	2182	57.5	18	7	156.6
Aaron Sparrow, Norfolk St	Jr	10	361	216	3212	59.8	31	14	155.2

Note: Minimum 15 attempts per game.

RECEPTIONS PER GAME

	Class	GP	No.	Yds	TD	Rec/Game
Chris George, Glenville St	Sr	10	113	1339	15	11.3
Brad Bailey, W Texas A&M	Sr	11	119	1552	16	10.8
Keylie Martin, N Mex Highlands	Jr	10	87	911	10	8.7
Greg Hopkins, Slippery Rock	Sr	10	83	1283	12	8.3
Jerry Garrett, Wayne St (Neb.)	Sr	10	83	879	9	8.3
Byron Chamberlin, Wayne St (Neb.)	Sr	10	83	926	7	8.3

Division II *(Cont.)*

RECEIVING YARDS PER GAME

	Class	GP	No.	Yds	TD	Yds/Game
James Roe, Norfolk St	Jr	10	77	1454	17	145.4
Brad Bailey, W Texas A&M	Sr	11	119	1552	16	141.1
Chris George, Glenville St	Sr	10	113	1339	15	133.9
Greg Hopkins, Slippery Rock	Sr	10	83	1283	12	128.3
Brian Penecale, West Chester	Jr	11	77	1283	18	116.6

INTERCEPTIONS

	Class	GP	No.	Yds	Int/Game
Keith Hawkins, Humboldt St	Sr	10	11	159	1.1
Elton Rhoades, Central Okla	Sr	10	11	126	1.1
Scott Elwer, Hillsdale	Jr	11	10	136	.9
Tyrone Andrews, Miles	Jr	9	8	111	.9

Three tied with .8 Int/Game

PUNTING

	Class	No.	Avg
Pat Hogelin, CO-Mines	Sr	48	45.1
Adam Vinatieri, S Dakota St	Sr	57	43.5
Bob Koning, NM Highlands	Sr	54	43.0
Phil Schmitten, Fort Lewis	So	58	42.9
John McGhee, Indiana (PA)	Jr	42	42.1

Note: Minimum 3.6 per game.

Division III

SCORING

	Class	GP	TD	XP	FG	Pts	Pts/Game
Carey Bender, Coe	Sr	10	32	2	0	194	19.4
Rob Marchitello, Maine-Maritime	Jr	9	25	4	0	154	17.1
Steve Harris, Carroll (WI)	Sr	9	20	2	0	122	13.6
Matt Taylor, Catholic	So	10	22	2	0	134	13.4
Mark Kacmarynski, Central (IA)	Jr	10	21	2	0	128	12.8

FIELD GOALS

	Class	GP	FGA	FG	Pct	FG/Game
Chris Kondik, Baldwin-Wallace	Fr	10	17	13	76.5	1.30
Dennis Unger, Albright	Fr	9	19	11	57.9	1.22
Jason Goldberg, John Carroll	So	10	16	12	75.0	1.20
Mike LaCroix, Alfred	So	9	16	10	62.5	1.11
Evan Hjerpe, Center	Jr	10	13	11	84.6	1.10
Brian Anthony, Cortland St	So	10	16	11	68.8	1.10

TOTAL OFFENSE

	Class	GP	Yds	Yds/Game
Terry Peebles, Hanover	Jr	10	3441	344.1
Eric Noble, Wilmington (OH)	Jr	9	3072	341.3
John Shipp, Claremont-M-S	Sr	9	2871	319.0
Mark Novara, Lakeland	Fr	9	2576	286.2
Darrin Fox, Bluffton	So	9	2551	283.4

RUSHING

	Class	GP	Car	Yds	TD	Yds/Game
Carey Bender, Coe	Sr	10	295	2243	29	224.3
Kelvin Gladney, Millsaps	Sr	10	307	1882	19	188.2
Mark Kacmarynski, Central (IA)	Jr	10	236	1741	21	174.1
Spencer Johnson, WI-Whitewater	Sr	10	290	1697	18	169.7
Rob Marchitello, Maine-Maritime	Jr	9	298	1457	25	161.9

PASSING EFFICIENCY

	Class	GP	Att	Comp	Yds	Pct Comp	TD	Int	Rating Pts
Mike Simpson, Eureka	So	10	158	116	1988	73.4	25	5	225.0
Kurt Ramler, St John's (MN)	So	9	154	93	1560	60.3	22	4	187.4
Paul Bell, Allegheny	Sr	10	215	142	2137	66.0	17	2	173.8
Chris Adams, Gettysburg	Sr	10	211	139	1977	65.8	19	2	172.4
Kyle Klein, Albion	So	9	146	87	1488	59.5	13	4	169.0

Note: Minimum 15 attempts per game

Division III (Cont.)

RECEPTIONS PER GAME

	Class	GP	No.	Yds	TD	C/Game
Jason Tincher, Wilmington (OH)...Sr		9	85	1298	9	9.4
Steve Wilkerson, Catholic.............Sr		10	90	1457	13	9.0
Ryan Ditze, Albright......................Jr		10	82	1023	5	8.2
Mike Cook, Claremont-M-S..........So		9	70	1014	12	7.8
Ryan Davis, St Thomas (MN)........Jr		10	75	1164	9	7.5

RECEIVING YARDS PER GAME

	Class	GP	No.	Yds	TD	Yds/Game
Steve Wilkerson, Catholic.............Sr		10	90	1457	13	145.7
Jason Tincher, Wilmington (OH)...Sr		9	85	1298	9	144.2
D.R. Moreland, Menlo...................Sr		9	66	1179	6	131.0
Ryan Davis, St Thomas (MN)........Jr		10	75	1164	9	116.4
Mike Cook, Claremont-M-S...........So		9	70	1014	12	112.7

INTERCEPTIONS

	Class	GP	No.	Yds	Int/Game
Antonio Moore, Widener............So		10	13	116	1.3
Greg Schramm, Trinity (CT).......Sr		8	8	66	1.0
Ron Contreras, Salve Regina ....So		8	8	88	1.0
Brian Fitzpatrick, Wooster St ....Sr		10	9	223	.9
Adam Smith, Heidelberg ....Sr		10	9	194	.9
Chad Zollman, Kalamazoo ....Jr		9	8	137	.9
Heath Allard, Cornell College ....Jr		9	8	80	.9
Mike Benson, Redlands.............So		9	8	52	.9

PUNTING

	Class	No.	Avg
Ryan Haley, John Carroll ....Sr		54	42.8
Tomek Mikler, Redlands.....................Jr		45	41.6
Kevin Feighery, Merchant Marine......Sr		36	40.1
Bryan Weber, WI-Platteville ....Jr		39	39.8
Matt Carlson, North Central ....Jr		38	39.2

Note: Minimum 3.6 per game

1994 NCAA Division I-A Team Leaders

Offense

SCORING

	GP	Pts	Avg
Penn St....................................11	11	526	47.8
Florida 12	12	521	43.4
Nevada 11	11	414	37.6
Utah..11	11	410	37.3
Florida St 11	11	405	36.8
Nebraska.................................12	12	435	36.3
Colorado..................................11	11	398	36.2
Bowling Green.........................11	11	391	35.5
Colorado St.............................11	11	386	35.1
Central Michigan 11	11	376	34.2

RUSHING

	GP	Car	Yds	Avg	TD	Yds/Game
Nebraska.................12	12	687	4080	5.9	44	340.0
Air Force..................12	12	720	3657	5.1	36	304.8
Colorado 11	11	517	3206	6.2	40	291.5
Central Michigan.....11	11	571	3132	5.5	37	284.7
Oregon St................11	11	640	3072	4.8	24	279.3
Penn St...................11	11	450	2760	6.1	45	250.9
Army.......................11	11	619	2738	4.4	22	248.9
Kansas 11	11	558	2718	4.9	31	247.1
Toledo 11	11	509	2667	5.2	28	242.5
Wisconsin...............11	11	497	2649	5.3	23	240.8

TOTAL OFFENSE

	GP	Plays	Yds	Avg	TD*	Yds/Game
Penn St 11	11	749	5722	7.6	68	520.18
Nevada.....................................11	11	901	5581	6.2	55	507.36
Colorado...................................11	11	773	5448	7.0	52	495.27
Florida St 11	11	853	5314	6.2	52	483.09
Nebraska 12	12	897	5734	6.4	59	477.83
New Mexico 12	12	937	5664	6.0	51	472.00
Georgia.....................................11	11	754	5135	6.8	41	466.82
Florida.......................................12	12	851	5553	6.5	62	462.75
Brigham Young..........................12	12	955	5489	5.7	45	457.42
Wyoming...................................12	12	929	5468	5.9	38	455.67

*Defensive and special teams TDs not included.

PASSING

	G	Att	Comp	Yds	Pct Comp	Yds/Att	TD	Int	Yds/Game
Georgia	11	462	276	3721	59.7	8.1	25	14	338.3
Nevada	11	463	279	3625	60.3	7.8	29	16	329.5
Brigham Young	12	475	287	3755	60.4	7.9	29	14	312.9
Florida	12	435	267	3740	61.4	8.6	43	21	311.7
Stanford	11	422	255	3358	60.4	8.0	18	12	305.3
San Diego St	11	410	257	3244	62.7	7.9	27	16	294.9
Florida St	11	441	264	3234	59.9	7.3	21	18	294.0
Wyoming	12	409	225	3367	55.0	8.2	21	19	280.6
Utah	11	387	249	3061	64.3	7.9	28	11	278.3
Maryland	11	428	291	3037	68.0	7.1	23	13	276.1

Single-Game Highs

Points scored: 73—Florida, Sep 10 (vs Kentucky).
Net rushing yards: 564—Indiana, Sep 17 (vs Kentucky).
Passing yards: 635—UNLV, Sep 17 (vs Idaho).
Total yards: 731—Florida St, Sep 10 (vs Maryland).
Fewest total yards allowed: 46—Illinois, Sep 10 (vs Missouri).
Passes attempted: 62—New Mexico, Sep 10 (vs Texas Christian).
Passes completed: 40—Florida St, Nov 26 (vs Florida).

Defense

SCORING

	GP	Pts	Avg
Miami (FL)	11	119	10.8
Nebraska	12	145	12.1
Washington St	11	133	12.1
Texas A&M	11	147	13.4
Kansas St	11	156	14.2
Illinois	11	156	14.2
Alabama	12	173	14.4
Memphis	11	159	14.5
Boston College	11	162	14.7
Ohio St	12	187	15.6

TOTAL DEFENSE

	GP	Plays	Yds	Avg	Yds/Game
Miami (FL)	11	702	2430	3.5	220.9
Washington St	11	732	2519	3.4	229.0
Memphis	11	729	2774	3.8	252.2
Nebraska	12	765	3106	4.1	258.8
Texas A&M	11	758	2920	3.9	265.5
Boston College	11	697	2927	4.2	266.1
Florida St	11	754	2937	3.9	267.0
W Michigan	11	726	3047	4.2	277.0
Illinois	11	700	3138	4.5	285.3
Arizona	11	688	3140	4.6	285.5

RUSHING

	GP	Car	Yds	Avg	TD	Yds/Game
Virginia	11	323	700	2.2	9	63.6
Arizona	11	369	715	1.9	6	65.0
Washington St	11	418	812	1.9	4	73.8
Nebraska	12	401	951	2.4	8	79.3
Florida	12	387	1015	2.6	9	84.6
Texas A&M	11	440	1016	2.3	11	92.4
Miami (FL)	11	409	1065	2.6	4	96.8
Florida St	11	378	1077	2.8	6	97.9
Utah	11	410	1163	2.8	11	105.7
Memphis	11	419	1172	2.8	8	106.5

TURNOVER MARGIN

		Turnovers Gained			Turnovers Lost			Margin/
	GP	Fum	Int	Total	Fum	Int	Total	Game
Clemson	11	13	16	29	2	10	12	1.55
Duke	11	12	17	29	4	9	13	1.45
Auburn	11	11	22	33	11	7	18	1.36
Mississippi	11	13	19	32	13	6	19	1.18
SMU	11	20	9	29	6	10	16	1.18
Kansas St	11	12	12	24	5	6	11	1.18
Penn St	11	12	11	23	4	7	11	1.09

PASSING EFFICIENCY

	GP	Att	Comp	Yds	Pct Comp	Yds/Att	TD	Pct TD	Int	Pct Int	Rating Pts
Miami (FL)	11	293	143	1365	48.8	4.7	5	1.7	18	6.1	81.3
SW Louisiana	11	309	135	1626	43.7	5.3	10	3.2	19	6.2	86.3
Texas Tech	11	283	122	1623	43.1	5.7	8	2.8	17	6.0	88.6
Florida St	11	376	180	1860	47.9	5.0	13	3.5	15	4.0	92.9
Washington St	11	314	140	1707	44.6	5.4	9	2.9	10	3.2	93.3
Mississippi	11	300	134	1708	44.7	5.7	13	4.3	19	6.3	94.1
Kansas St	11	279	130	1596	46.6	5.7	7	2.5	12	4.3	94.3
Virginia Tech	11	354	168	1945	47.5	5.5	10	2.8	15	4.2	94.5
Memphis	11	310	162	1602	52.3	5.2	7	2.3	13	4.2	94.7
Nebraska	12	364	172	2155	47.3	5.9	10	2.8	17	4.7	96.7

National Champions

Year	Champion	Record	Bowl Game	Head Coach
1883	Yale	8-0-0	No bowl	Ray Tompkins (Captain)
1884	Yale	9-0-0	No bowl	Eugene L. Richards (Captain)
1885	Princeton	9-0-0	No bowl	Charles DeCamp (Captain)
1886	Yale	9-0-1	No bowl	Robert N. Corwin (Captain)
1887	Yale	9-0-0	No bowl	Harry W. Beecher (Captain)
1888	Yale	13-0-0	No bowl	Walter Camp
1889	Princeton	10-0-0	No bowl	Edgar Poe (Captain)
1890	Harvard	11-0-0	No bowl	George A. Stewart/George C. Adams
1891	Yale	13-0-0	No bowl	Walter Camp
1892	Yale	13-0-0	No bowl	Walter Camp
1893	Princeton	11-0-0	No bowl	Tom Trenchard (Captain)
1894	Yale	16-0-0	No bowl	William C. Rhodes
1895	Pennsylvania	14-0-0	No bowl	George Woodruff
1896	Princeton	10-0-1	No bowl	Garrett Cochran
1897	Pennsylvania	15-0-0	No bowl	George Woodruff
1898	Harvard	11-0-0	No bowl	W. Cameron Forbes
1899	Harvard	10-0-1	No bowl	Benjamin H. Dibblee
1900	Yale	12-0-0	No bowl	Malcolm McBride
1901	Michigan	11-0-0	Won Rose	Fielding Yost
1902	Michigan	11-0-0	No bowl	Fielding Yost
1903	Princeton	11-0-0	No bowl	Art Hillebrand
1904	Pennsylvania	12-0-0	No bowl	Carl Williams
1905	Chicago	11-0-0	No bowl	Amos Alonzo Stagg
1906	Princeton	9-0-1	No bowl	Bill Roper
1907	Yale	9-0-1	No bowl	Bill Knox
1908	Pennsylvania	11-0-1	No bowl	Sol Metzger
1909	Yale	10-0-0	No bowl	Howard Jones
1910	Harvard	8-0-1	No bowl	Percy Houghton
1911	Princeton	8-0-2	No bowl	Bill Roper
1912	Harvard	9-0-0	No bowl	Percy Houghton
1913	Harvard	9-0-0	No bowl	Percy Houghton
1914	Army	9-0-0	No bowl	Charley Daly
1915	Cornell	9-0-0	No bowl	Al Sharpe
1916	Pittsburgh	8-0-0	No bowl	Pop Warner
1917	Georgia Tech	9-0-0	No bowl	John Heisman
1918	Pittsburgh	4-1-0	No bowl	Pop Warner
1919	Harvard	9-0-1	Won Rose	Bob Fisher
1920	California	9-0-0	Won Rose	Andy Smith
1921	Cornell	8-0-0	No bowl	Gil Dobie
1922	Cornell	8-0-0	No bowl	Gil Dobie
1923	Illinois	8-0-0	No bowl	Bob Zuppke
1924	Notre Dame	10-0-0	Won Rose	Knute Rockne
1925	Alabama (H)	10-0-0	Won Rose	Wallace Wade
	Dartmouth (D)	8-0-0	No bowl	Jesse Hawley
1926	Alabama (H)	9-0-1	Tied Rose	Wallace Wade
	Stanford (D)(H)	10-0-1	Tied Rose	Pop Warner
1927	Illinois	7-0-1	No bowl	Bob Zuppke
1928	Georgia Tech (H)	10-0-0	Won Rose	Bill Alexander
	Southern Cal (D)	9-0-1	No bowl	Howard Jones
1929	Notre Dame	9-0-0	No bowl	Knute Rockne
1930	Notre Dame	10-0-0	No bowl	Knute Rockne
1931	Southern Cal	10-1-0	Won Rose	Howard Jones
1932	Southern Cal (H)	10-0-0	Won Rose	Howard Jones
	Michigan (D)	8-0-0	No bowl	Harry Kipke
1933	Michigan	7-0-1	No bowl	Harry Kipke
1934	Minnesota	8-0-0	No bowl	Bernie Bierman
1935	Minnesota (H)	8-0-0	No bowl	Bernie Bierman
	Southern Meth (D)	12-1-0	Lost Rose	Matty Bell
1936	Minnesota	7-1-0	No bowl	Bernie Bierman
1937	Pittsburgh	9-0-1	No bowl	Jock Sutherland
1938	Texas Christian (AP)	11-0-0	Won Sugar	Dutch Meyer
	Notre Dame (D)	8-1-0	No bowl	Elmer Layden
1939	Southern Cal (D)	8-0-2	Won Rose	Howard Jones
	Texas A&M (AP)	11-0-0	Won Sugar	Homer Norton

Year	Champion	Record	Bowl Game	Head Coach
1940	Minnesota	8-0-0	No bowl	Bernie Bierman
1941	Minnesota	8-0-0	No bowl	Bernie Bierman
1942	Ohio St	9-1-0	No bowl	Paul Brown
1943	Notre Dame	9-1-0	No bowl	Frank Leahy
1944	Army	9-0-0	No bowl	Red Blaik
1945	Army	9-0-0	No bowl	Red Blaik
1946	Notre Dame	8-0-1	No bowl	Frank Leahy
1947	Notre Dame	9-0-0	No bowl	Frank Leahy
	Michigan*	10-0-0	Won Rose	Fritz Crisler
1948	Michigan	9-0-0	No bowl	Bennie Oosterbaan
1949	Notre Dame	10-0-0	No bowl	Frank Leahy
1950	Oklahoma	10-1-0	Lost Sugar	Bud Wilkinson
1951	Tennessee	10-1-0	Lost Sugar	Bob Neyland
1952	Michigan St	9-0-0	No bowl	Biggie Munn
1953	Maryland	10-1-0	Lost Orange	Jim Tatum
1954	Ohio St	10-0-0	Won Rose	Woody Hayes
	UCLA (UP)	9-0-0	No bowl	Red Sanders
1955	Oklahoma	11-0-0	Won Orange	Bud Wilkinson
1956	Oklahoma	10-0-0	No bowl	Bud Wilkinson
1957	Auburn	10-0-0	No bowl	Shug Jordan
	Ohio St (UP)	9-1-0	Won Rose	Woody Hayes
1958	Louisiana St	11-0-0	Won Sugar	Paul Dietzel
1959	Syracuse	11-0-0	Won Cotton	Ben Schwartzwalder
1960	Minnesota	8-2-0	Lost Rose	Murray Warmath
1961	Alabama	11-0-0	Won Sugar	Bear Bryant
1962	Southern Cal	11-0-0	Won Rose	John McKay
1963	Texas	11-0-0	Won Cotton	Darrell Royal
1964	Alabama	10-1-0	Lost Orange	Bear Bryant
1965	Alabama	9-1-1	Won Orange	Bear Bryant
	Michigan St (UPI)	10-1-0	Lost Rose	Duffy Daugherty
1966	Notre Dame	9-0-1	No bowl	Ara Parseghian
1967	Southern Cal	10-1-0	Won Rose	John McKay
1968	Ohio St	10-0-0	Won Rose	Woody Hayes
1969	Texas	11-0-0	Won Cotton	Darrell Royal
1970	Nebraska	11-0-1	Won Orange	Bob Devaney
	Texas (UPI)	10-1-0	Lost Cotton	Darrell Royal
1971	Nebraska	13-0-0	Won Orange	Bob Devaney
1972	Southern Cal	12-0-0	Won Rose	John McKay
1973	Notre Dame	11-0-0	Won Sugar	Ara Parseghian
	Alabama (UPI)	11-1-0	Lost Sugar	Bear Bryant
1974	Oklahoma	11-0-0	No bowl	Barry Switzer
	Southern Cal (UPI)	10-1-1	Won Rose	John McKay
1975	Oklahoma	11-1-0	Won Orange	Barry Switzer
1976	Pittsburgh	12-0-0	Won Sugar	Johnny Majors
1977	Notre Dame	11-1-0	Won Cotton	Dan Devine
1978	Alabama	11-1-0	Won Sugar	Bear Bryant
	Southern Cal (UPI)	12-1-0	Won Rose	John Robinson
1979	Alabama	12-0-0	Won Sugar	Bear Bryant
1980	Georgia	12-0-0	Won Sugar	Vince Dooley
1981	Clemson	12-0-0	Won Orange	Danny Ford
1982	Penn St	11-1-0	Won Sugar	Joe Paterno
1983	Miami (FL)	11-1-0	Won Orange	Howard Schnellenberger
1984	Brigham Young	13-0-0	Won Holiday	LaVell Edwards
1985	Oklahoma	11-1-0	Won Orange	Barry Switzer
1986	Penn St	12-0-0	Won Fiesta	Joe Paterno
1987	Miami (FL)	12-0-0	Won Orange	Jimmy Johnson
1988	Notre Dame	12-0-0	Won Fiesta	Lou Holtz
1989	Miami (FL)	11-1-0	Won Sugar	Dennis Erickson
1990	Colorado	11-1-1	Won Orange	Bill McCartney
	Georgia Tech (UPI)	11-0-1	Won Citrus	Bobby Ross
1991	Miami (FL)	12-0-0	Won Orange	Dennis Erickson
	Washington (CNN)	12-0-0	Won Rose	Don James
1992	Alabama	13-0-0	Won Sugar	Gene Stallings
1993	Florida St	12-1-0	Won Orange	Bobby Bowden
1994	Nebraska	13-0-0	Won Orange	Tom Osborne

*The AP, which had voted Notre Dame No. 1, took a second vote, giving the national title to Michigan after its 49-0 win over Southern Cal in the Rose Bowl.

Note: Selectors: Helms Athletic Foundation (H) 1883-1935, The Dickinson System (D) 1924-40, The Associated Press (AP) 1936-present, United Press International (UPI) 1958-90, and USA Today/CNN (CNN) 1991-present.

Results of Major Bowl Games

Rose Bowl

1-1-2 ....Michigan 49, Stanford 0
1-1-16 ....Washington St 14, Brown 0
1-1-17 ....Oregon 14, Pennsylvania 0
1-1-18 ....Mare Island 19, Camp Lewis 7
1-1-19 ....Great Lakes 17, Mare Island 0
1-1-20 ....Harvard 7, Oregon 6
1-1-21 ....California 28, Ohio St 0
1-2-22 ....Washington & Jefferson 0, California 0
1-1-23 ....Southern Cal 14, Penn St 3
1-1-24 ....Navy 14, Washington 14
1-1-25 ....Notre Dame 27, Stanford 10
1-1-26 ....Alabama 20, Washington 19
1-1-27 ....Alabama 7, Stanford 7
1-2-28 ....Stanford 7, Pittsburgh 6
1-1-29 ....Georgia Tech 8, California 7
1-1-30 ....Southern Cal 47, Pittsburgh 14
1-1-31 ....Alabama 24, Washington St 0
1-1-32 ....Southern Cal 21, Tulane 12
1-2-33 ....Southern Cal 35, Pittsburgh 0
1-1-34 ....Columbia 7, Stanford 0
1-1-35 ....Alabama 29, Stanford 13
1-1-36 ....Stanford 7, Southern Meth 0
1-1-37 ....Pittsburgh 21, Washington 0
1-1-38 ....California 13, Alabama 0
1-2-39 ....Southern Cal 7, Duke 3
1-1-40 ....Southern Cal 14, Tennessee 0
1-1-41 ....Stanford 21, Nebraska 13
1-1-42 ....Oregon St 20, Duke 16
1-1-43 ....Georgia 9, UCLA 0
1-1-44 ....Southern Cal 29, Washington 0
1-1-45 ....Southern Cal 25, Tennessee 0
1-1-46 ....Alabama 34, Southern Cal 14
1-1-47 ....Illinois 45, UCLA 14
1-1-48 ....Michigan 49, Southern Cal 0
1-1-49 ....Northwestern 20, California 14
1-2-50 ....Ohio St 17, California 14
1-1-51 ....Michigan 14, California 6
1-1-52 ....Illinois 40, Stanford 7
1-1-53 ....Southern Cal 7, Wisconsin 0
1-1-54 ....Michigan St 28, UCLA 20
1-1-55 ....Ohio St 20, Southern Cal 7
1-2-56 ....Michigan St 17, UCLA 14
1-1-57 ....Iowa 35, Oregon St 19
1-1-58 ....Ohio St 10, Oregon 7
1-1-59 ....Iowa 38, California 12
1-1-60 ....Washington 44, Wisconsin 8
1-2-61 ....Washington 17, Minnesota 7
1-1-62 ....Minnesota 21, UCLA 3
1-1-63 ....Southern Cal 42, Wisconsin 37
1-1-64 ....Illinois 17, Washington 7
1-1-65 ....Michigan 34, Oregon St 7
1-1-66 ....UCLA 14, Michigan St 12
1-2-67 ....Purdue 14, Southern Cal 13
1-1-68 ....Southern Cal 14, Indiana 3
1-1-69 ....Ohio St 27, Southern Cal 16
1-1-70 ....Southern Cal 10, Michigan 3
1-1-71 ....Stanford 27, Ohio St 17
1-1-72 ....Stanford 13, Michigan 12
1-1-73 ....Southern Cal 42, Ohio St 17
1-1-74 ....Ohio St 42, Southern Cal 21
1-1-75 ....Southern Cal 18, Ohio St 17
1-1-76 ....UCLA 23, Ohio St 10
1-1-77 ....Southern Cal 14, Michigan 6
1-2-78 ....Washington 27, Michigan 20
1-1-79 ....Southern Cal 17, Michigan 10
1-1-80 ....Southern Cal 17, Ohio St 16
1-1-81 ....Michigan 23, Washington 6

1-1-82 ....Washington 28, Iowa 0
1-1-83 ....UCLA 24, Michigan 14
1-2-84 ....UCLA 45, Illinois 9
1-1-85 ....Southern Cal 20, Ohio St 17
1-1-86 ....UCLA 45, Iowa 28
1-1-87 ....Arizona St 22, Michigan 15
1-1-88 ....Michigan St 20, Southern Cal 17
1-2-89 ....Michigan 22, Southern Cal 14
1-1-90 ....Southern Cal 17, Michigan 10
1-1-91 ....Washington 46, Iowa 34
1-1-92 ....Washington 34, Michigan 14
1-1-93 ....Michigan 38, Washington 31
1-1-94 ....Wisconsin 21, UCLA 16
1-2-95 ....Penn St 38, Oregon 20

City: Pasadena.

Stadium: Rose Bowl.

Capacity: 104,091.

Automatic Berths: Pacific-10 champ vs Big 10 champ
(since 1947).

Playing Sites: Tournament Park (1902, 1916-22), Rose Bowl
(1923-41, since 1943), Duke Stadium, Durham, NC (1942).

Orange Bowl

1-1-35 ....Bucknell 26, Miami (FL) 0
1-1-36 ....Catholic 20, Mississippi 19
1-1-37 ....Duquesne 13, Mississippi St 12
1-1-38 ....Auburn 6, Michigan St 0
1-2-39 ....Tennessee 17, Oklahoma 0
1-1-40 ....Georgia Tech 21, Missouri 7
1-1-41 ....Mississippi St 14, Georgetown 7
1-1-42 ....Georgia 40, Texas Christian 26
1-1-43 ....Alabama 37, Boston College 21
1-1-44 ....Louisiana St 19, Texas A&M 14
1-1-45 ....Tulsa 26, Georgia Tech 12
1-1-46 ....Miami (FL) 13, Holy Cross 6
1-1-47 ....Rice 8, Tennessee 0
1-1-48 ....Georgia Tech 20, Kansas 14
1-1-49 ....Texas 41, Georgia 28
1-2-50 ....Santa Clara 21, Kentucky 13
1-1-51 ....Clemson 15, Miami (FL) 14
1-1-52 ....Georgia Tech 17, Baylor 14
1-1-53 ....Alabama 61, Syracuse 6
1-1-54 ....Oklahoma 7, Maryland 0
1-1-55 ....Duke 34, Nebraska 7
1-2-56 ....Oklahoma 20, Maryland 6
1-1-57 ....Colorado 27, Clemson 21
1-1-58 ....Oklahoma 48, Duke 21
1-1-59 ....Oklahoma 21, Syracuse 6
1-1-60 ....Georgia 14, Missouri 0
1-2-61 ....Missouri 21, Navy 14
1-1-62 ....Louisiana St 25, Colorado 7
1-1-63 ....Alabama 17, Oklahoma 0
1-1-64 ....Nebraska 13, Auburn 7
1-1-65 ....Texas 21, Alabama 17
1-1-66 ....Alabama 39, Nebraska 28
1-2-67 ....Florida 27, Georgia Tech 12
1-1-68 ....Oklahoma 26, Tennessee 24
1-1-69 ....Penn St 15, Kansas 14
1-1-70 ....Penn St 10, Missouri 3
1-1-71 ....Nebraska 17, Louisiana St 12
1-1-72 ....Nebraska 38, Alabama 6
1-1-73 ....Nebraska 40, Notre Dame 6
1-1-74 ....Penn St 16, Louisiana St 9
1-1-75 ....Notre Dame 13, Alabama 11
1-1-76 ....Oklahoma 14, Michigan 6
1-1-77 ....Ohio St 27, Colorado 10

Orange Bowl *(Cont.)*

1-2-78.............Arkansas 31, Oklahoma 6
1-1-79.............Oklahoma 31, Nebraska 24
1-1-80.............Oklahoma 24, Florida St 7
1-1-81.............Oklahoma 18, Florida St 17
1-1-82.............Clemson 22, Nebraska 15
1-1-83.............Nebraska 21, Louisiana St 20
1-2-84.............Miami (FL) 31, Nebraska 30
1-1-85.............Washington 28, Oklahoma 17
1-1-86.............Oklahoma 25, Penn St 10
1-1-87.............Oklahoma 42, Arkansas 8
1-1-88.............Miami (FL) 20, Oklahoma 14
1-2-89.............Miami (FL) 23, Nebraska 3
1-1-90.............Notre Dame 21, Colorado 6
1-1-91.............Colorado 10, Notre Dame 9
1-1-92.............Miami (FL) 22, Nebraska 0
1-1-93.............Florida State 27, Nebraska 14
1-1-94.............Florida State 18, Nebraska 16
1-1-95.............Nebraska 24, Miami (FL) 17

City: Miami.
Stadium: Orange Bowl.
Capacity: 75,500.
Automatic Berths: Big 8 champ (1954-64, since 1976).

Sugar Bowl

1-1-35.............Tulane 20, Temple 14
1-1-36.............Texas Christian 3, Louisiana St 2
1-1-37.............Santa Clara 21, Louisiana St 14
1-1-38.............Santa Clara 6, Louisiana St 0
1-2-39.............Texas Christian 15, Carnegie Tech 7
1-1-40.............Texas A&M 14, Tulane 13
1-1-41.............Boston Col 19, Tennessee 13
1-1-42.............Fordham 2, Missouri 0
1-1-43.............Tennessee 14, Tulsa 7
1-1-44.............Georgia Tech 20, Tulsa 18
1-1-45.............Duke 29, Alabama 26
1-1-46.............Oklahoma St 33, St Mary's (CA) 13
1-1-47.............Georgia 20, N Carolina 10
1-1-48.............Texas 27, Alabama 7
1-1-49.............Oklahoma 14, N Carolina 6
1-2-50.............Oklahoma 35, Louisiana St 0
1-1-51.............Kentucky 13, Oklahoma 7
1-1-52.............Maryland 28, Tennessee 13
1-1-53.............Georgia Tech 24, Mississippi 7
1-1-54.............Georgia Tech 42, W Virginia 19
1-1-55.............Navy 21, Mississippi 0
1-2-56.............Georgia Tech 7, Pittsburgh 0
1-1-57.............Baylor 13, Tennessee 7
1-1-58.............Mississippi 39, Texas 7
1-1-59.............Louisiana St 7, Clemson 0
1-1-60.............Mississippi 21, Louisiana St 0
1-2-61.............Mississippi 14, Rice 6
1-1-62.............Alabama 10, Arkansas 3
1-1-63.............Mississippi 17, Arkansas 13
1-1-64.............Alabama 12, Mississippi 7
1-1-65.............Louisiana St 13, Syracuse 10
1-1-66.............Missouri 20, Florida 18
1-2-67.............Alabama 34, Nebraska 7
1-1-68.............Louisiana St 20, Wyoming 13
1-1-69.............Arkansas 16, Georgia 2
1-1-70.............Mississippi 27, Arkansas 22
1-1-71.............Tennessee 34, Air Force 13
1-1-72.............Oklahoma 40, Auburn 22
12-31-72.........Oklahoma 14, Penn St 0
12-31-73.........Notre Dame 24, Alabama 23
12-31-74.........Nebraska 13, Florida 10
12-31-75.........Alabama 13, Penn St 6

Sugar Bowl *(Cont.)*

1-1-77.............Pittsburgh 27, Georgia 3
1-2-78.............Alabama 35, Ohio St 6
1-1-79.............Alabama 14, Penn St 7
1-1-80.............Alabama 24, Arkansas 9
1-1-81.............Georgia 17, Notre Dame 10
1-1-82.............Pittsburgh 24, Georgia 20
1-1-83.............Penn St 27, Georgia 23
1-2-84.............Auburn 9, Michigan 7
1-1-85.............Nebraska 28, Louisiana St 10
1-1-86.............Tennessee 35, Miami (FL) 7
1-1-87.............Nebraska 30, Louisiana St 15
1-1-88.............Syracuse 16, Auburn 16
1-2-89.............Florida St 13, Auburn 7
1-1-90.............Miami (FL) 33, Alabama 25
1-1-91.............Tennessee 23, Virginia 22
1-1-92.............Notre Dame 39, Florida 28
1-1-93.............Alabama 34, Miami (FL) 13
1-1-94.............Florida 41, West Virginia 7
1-2-95.............Florida St 23, Florida 17

City: New Orleans.
Stadium: Louisiana Superdome.
Capacity: 69,548.
Automatic Berths: Southeastern champ (since 1977).
Playing Sites: Tulane Stadium (1935-74), Superdome (1974)

Cotton Bowl

1-1-37.............Texas Christian 16, Marquette 6
1-1-38.............Rice 28, Colorado 14
1-2-39.............St. Mary's (CA) 20, Texas Tech 13
1-1-40.............Clemson 6, Boston Col 3
1-1-41.............Texas A&M 13, Fordham 12
1-1-42.............Alabama 29, Texas A&M 21
1-1-43.............Texas 14, Georgia Tech 7
1-1-44.............Texas 7, Randolph Field 7
1-1-45.............Oklahoma St 34, Texas Christian 0
1-1-46.............Texas 40, Missouri 27
1-1-47.............Arkansas 0, Louisiana St 0
1-1-48.............Southern Meth 13, Penn St 13
1-1-49.............Southern Meth 21, Oregon 13
1-2-50.............Rice 27, N Carolina 13
1-1-51.............Tennessee 20, Texas 14
1-1-52.............Kentucky 20, Texas Christian 7
1-1-53.............Texas 16, Tennessee 0
1-1-54.............Rice 28, Alabama 6
1-1-55.............Georgia Tech 14, Arkansas 6
1-2-56.............Mississippi 14, Texas Christian 13
1-1-57.............Texas Christian 28, Syracuse 27
1-1-58.............Navy 20, Rice 7
1-1-59.............Texas Christian 0, Air Force 0
1-1-60.............Syracuse 23, Texas 14
1-2-61.............Duke 7, Arkansas 6
1-1-62.............Texas 12, Mississippi 7
1-1-63.............Louisiana St 13, Texas 0
1-1-64.............Texas 28, Navy 6
1-1-65.............Arkansas 10, Nebraska 7
1-1-66.............Louisiana St 14, Arkansas 7
12-31-66.........Georgia 24, Southern Meth 9
1-1-68.............Texas A&M 20, Alabama 16
1-1-69.............Texas 36, Tennessee 13
1-1-70.............Texas 21, Notre Dame 17
1-1-71.............Notre Dame 24, Texas 11
1-1-72.............Penn St 30, Texas 6
1-1-73.............Texas 17, Alabama 13
1-1-74.............Nebraska 19, Texas 3
1-1-75.............Penn St 41, Baylor 20

Cotton Bowl *(Cont.)*

1-1-76 ....Arkansas 31, Georgia 10
1-1-77 ....Houston 30, Maryland 21
1-2-78 ....Notre Dame 38, Texas 10
1-1-79 ....Notre Dame 35, Houston 34
1-1-80 ....Houston 17, Nebraska 14
1-1-81 ....Alabama 30, Baylor 2
1-1-82 ....Texas 14, Alabama 12
1-1-83 ....Southern Meth 7, Pittsburgh 3
1-2-84 ....Georgia 10, Texas 9
1-1-85 ....Boston Col 45, Houston 28
1-1-86 ....Texas A&M 36, Auburn 16
1-1-87 ....Ohio St 28, Texas A&M 12
1-1-88 ....Texas A&M 35, Notre Dame 10
1-2-89 ....UCLA 17, Arkansas 3
1-1-90 ....Tennessee 31, Arkansas 27
1-1-91 ....Miami (FL) 46, Texas 3
1-1-92 ....Florida St 10, Texas A&M 2
1-1-93 ....Notre Dame 28, Texas A&M 3
1-1-94 ....Notre Dame 24, Texas A&M 21
1-2-95 ....Southern Cal 55, Texas Tech 14
City: Dallas.
Stadium: Cotton Bowl.
Capacity: 72,032.
Automatic Berths: Southwest champ (since 1942).
Playing Sites: Fair Park Stadium (1937), Cotton Bowl (since 1938).

Sun Bowl

1-1-36 ....Hardin-Simmons 14, New Mexico St 14
1-1-37 ....Hardin-Simmons 34, UTEP 6
1-1-38 ....W Virginia 7, Texas Tech 6
1-2-39 ....Utah 26, New Mexico 0
1-1-40 ....Catholic 0, Arizona St 0
1-1-41 ....Case Reserve 26, Arizona St 13
1-1-42 ....Tulsa 6, Texas Tech 0
1-1-43 ....2nd Air Force 13, Hardin-Simmons 7
1-1-44 ....Southwestern (TX) 7, New Mexico 0
1-1-45 ....Southwestern (TX) 35, New Mexico 0
1-1-46 ....New Mexico 34, Denver 24
1-1-47 ....Cincinnati 18, Virginia Tech 6
1-1-48 ....Miami (OH) 13, Texas Tech 12
1-1-49 ....W Virginia 21, UTEP 12
1-2-50 ....UTEP 33, Georgetown 20
1-1-51 ....West Texas St 14, Cincinnati 13
1-1-52 ....Texas Tech 25, Pacific 14
1-1-53 ....Pacific 26, Southern Miss 7
1-1-54 ....UTEP 37, Southern Miss 14
1-1-55 ....UTEP 47, Florida St 20
1-2-56 ....Wyoming 21, Texas Tech 14
1-1-57 ....George Washington 13, UTEP 0
1-1-58 ....Louisville 34, Drake 20
12-31-58 ....Wyoming 14, Hardin-Simmons 6
12-31-59 ....New Mexico St 28, N Texas 8
12-31-60 ....New Mexico St 20, Utah St 13
12-30-61 ....Villanova 17, Wichita St 9
12-31-62 ....W Texas St 15, Ohio 14
12-31-63 ....Oregon 21, Southern Meth 14
12-26-64 ....Georgia 7, Texas Tech 0
12-31-65 ....UTEP 13, Texas Christian 12
12-24-66 ....Wyoming 28, Florida St 20
12-30-67 ....UTEP 14, Mississippi 7
12-28-68 ....Auburn 34, Arizona 10
12-20-69 ....Nebraska 45, Georgia 6
12-19-70 ....Georgia Tech 17, Texas Tech 9
12-18-71 ....Louisiana St 33, Iowa St 15
12-30-72 ....N Carolina 32, Texas Tech 28

Sun Bowl *(Cont.)*

12-29-73 ....Missouri 34, Auburn 17
12-28-74 ....Mississippi St 26, N Carolina 24
12-26-75 ....Pittsburgh 33, Kansas 19
1-2-77 ....Texas A&M 37, Florida 14
12-31-77 ....Stanford 24, Louisiana St 14
12-23-78 ....Texas 42, Maryland 0
12-22-79 ....Washington 14, Texas 7
12-27-80 ....Nebraska 31, Mississippi St 17
12-26-81 ....Oklahoma 40, Houston 14
12-25-82 ....N Carolina 26, Texas 10
12-24-83 ....Alabama 28, Southern Meth 7
12-22-84 ....Maryland 28, Tennessee 27
12-28-85 ....Georgia 13, Arizona 13
12-25-86 ....Alabama 28, Washington 6
12-25-87 ....Oklahoma St 35, W Virginia 33
12-24-88 ....Alabama 29, Army 28
12-30-89 ....Pittsburgh 31, Texas A&M 28
12-31-90 ....Michigan St 17, Southern Cal 16
12-31-91 ....UCLA 6, Illinois 3
12-31-92 ....Baylor 20, Arizona 15
12-24-93 ....Oklahoma 41, Texas Tech 10
12-30-94 ....Texas 35, N Carolina 31
City: El Paso.
Stadium: Sun Bowl.
Capacity: 52,000.
Automatic Berths: None.
Name Changes: Sun Bowl (1936-86; 94-), John Hancock Sun Bowl (1987-88), John Hancock Bowl (1989-93).
Playing Sites: Kidd Field (1936-62), Sun Bowl (since 1963).

Gator Bowl

1-1-46 ....Wake Forest 26, S Carolina 14
1-1-47 ....Oklahoma 34, N Carolina St 13
1-1-48 ....Maryland 20, Georgia 20
1-1-49 ....Clemson 24, Missouri 23
1-2-50 ....Maryland 20, Missouri 7
1-1-51 ....Wyoming 20, Washington & Lee 7
1-1-52 ....Miami (FL) 14, Clemson 0
1-1-53 ....Florida 14, Tulsa 13
1-1-54 ....Texas Tech 35, Auburn 13
12-31-54 ....Auburn 33, Baylor 13
12-31-55 ....Vanderbilt 25, Auburn 13
12-29-56 ....Georgia Tech 21, Pittsburgh 14
12-28-57 ....Tennessee 3, Texas A&M 0
12-27-58 ....Mississippi 7, Florida 3
1-2-60 ....Arkansas 14, Georgia Tech 7
12-31-60 ....Florida 13, Baylor 12
12-30-61 ....Penn St 30, Georgia Tech 15
12-29-62 ....Florida 17, Penn St 7
12-28-63 ....N Carolina 35, Air Force 0
1-2-65 ....Florida St 36, Oklahoma 19
12-31-65 ....Georgia Tech 31, Texas Tech 21
12-31-66 ....Tennessee 18, Syracuse 12
12-30-67 ....Penn St 17, Florida St 17
12-28-68 ....Missouri 35, Alabama 10
12-27-69 ....Florida 14, Tennessee 13
1-2-71 ....Auburn 35, Mississippi 28
12-31-71 ....Georgia 7, N Carolina 3
12-30-72 ....Auburn 24, Colorado 3
12-29-73 ....Texas Tech 28, Tennessee 19
12-30-74 ....Auburn 27, Texas 3
12-29-75 ....Maryland 13, Florida 0
12-27-76 ....Notre Dame 20, Penn St 9
12-30-77 ....Pittsburgh 34, Clemson 3
12-29-78 ....Clemson 17, Ohio St 15
12-28-79 ....N Carolina 17, Michigan 15

Gator Bowl *(Cont.)*

12-29-80..........Pittsburgh 37, S Carolina 9
12-28-81..........N Carolina 31, Arkansas 27
12-30-82..........Florida St 31, W Virginia 12
12-30-83..........Florida 14, Iowa 6
12-28-84..........Oklahoma St 21, S Carolina 14
12-30-85..........Florida St 34, Oklahoma St 23
12-27-86..........Clemson 27, Stanford 21
12-31-87..........Louisiana St 30, S Carolina 13
1-1-89..............Georgia 34, Michigan St 27
12-30-89..........Clemson 27, W Virginia 7
1-1-91..............Michigan 35, Mississippi 3
12-29-91..........Oklahoma 48, Virginia 14
12-31-92..........Florida 27, N Carolina St 10
12-31-93..........Alabama 24, North Carolina 10
12-30-94..........Tennessee 45, Virginia Tech 23
City: Jacksonville, FL.
Stadium: Gator Bowl.
Capacity: 82,000. Automatic Berths: None.

Florida Citrus Bowl

1-1-47..............Catawba 31, Maryville (TN) 6
1-1-48..............Catawba 7, Marshall 0
1-1-49..............Murray St 21, Sul Ross St 21
1-2-50..............St Vincent 7, Emory & Henry 6
1-1-51..............Morris Harvey 35, Emory & Henry 14
1-1-52..............Stetson 35, Arkansas St 20
1-1-53..............E Texas St 33, Tennessee Tech 0
1-1-54..............E Texas St 7, Arkansas St 7
1-1-55..............NE-Omaha 7, Eastern Kentucky 6
1-2-56..............Juniata 6, Missouri Valley 6
1-1-57..............W Texas St 20, Southern Miss 13
1-1-58..............E Texas St 10, Southern Miss 9
12-27-58..........E Texas St 26, Missouri Valley 7
1-1-60..............Middle Tennessee St 21, Presbyterian 12
12-30-60..........Citadel 27, Tennessee Tech 0
12-29-61..........Lamar 21, Middle Tennessee St 14
12-22-62..........Houston 49, Miami (OH) 21
12-28-63..........Western Kentucky 27, Coast Guard 0
12-12-64..........E Carolina 14, Massachusetts 13
12-11-65..........E Carolina 31, Maine 0
12-10-66..........Morgan St 14, West Chester 6
12-16-67..........TN-Martin 25, West Chester 8
12-27-68..........Richmond 49, Ohio 42
12-26-69..........Toledo 56, Davidson 33
12-28-70..........Toledo 40, William & Mary 12
12-28-71..........Toledo 28, Richmond 3
12-29-72..........Tampa 21, Kent St 18
12-22-73..........Miami (OH) 16, Florida 7
12-21-74..........Miami (OH) 21, Georgia 10
12-20-75..........Miami (OH) 20, S Carolina 7
12-18-76..........Oklahoma St 49, Brigham Young 21
12-23-77..........Florida St 40, Texas 17
12-23-78..........N Carolina St 30, Pittsburgh 17
12-22-79..........Louisiana St 34, Wake Forest 10
12-20-80..........Florida 35, Maryland 20
12-19-81..........Missouri 19, Southern Miss 17
12-18-82..........Auburn 33, Boston Col 26
12-17-83..........Tennessee 30, Maryland 23
12-22-84..........Georgia 17, Florida St 17
12-28-85..........Ohio St 10, Brigham Young 7
1-1-87..............Auburn 16, Southern Cal 7
1-1-88..............Clemson 35, Penn St 10
1-2-89..............Clemson 13, Oklahoma 6
1-1-90..............Illinois 31, Virginia 21
1-1-91..............Georgia Tech 45, Nebraska 21
1-1-92..............California 37, Clemson 13

Florida Citrus Bowl *(Cont.)*

1-1-93..............Georgia 21, Ohio State 14
1-1-94..............Penn State 31, Tennessee 13
1-2-95..............Alabama 24, Ohio St 17
City: Orlando, FL.
Stadium: Florida Citrus Bowl-Orlando.
Capacity: 52,300. Automatic Berths: None.
Name Change: Tangerine Bowl (1947-82), Florida Citrus Bowl (since 1983).
Playing Sites: Tangerine Bowl (1947-72, 1974-82); Florida Field, Gainesville (1973); Orlando Stadium (1983-85); Florida Citrus Bowl- Orlando (since 1986). Tangerine Bowl, Orlando Stadium and Florida Citrus Bowl-Orlando are identical site.

Liberty Bowl

12-19-59..........Penn St 7, Alabama 0
12-17-60..........Penn St 41, Oregon 12
12-16-61..........Syracuse 15, Miami (FL) 14
12-15-62..........Oregon St 6, Villanova 0
12-21-63..........Mississippi St 16, N Carolina St
12-19-64..........Utah 32, W Virginia 6
12-18-65..........Mississippi 13, Auburn 7
12-10-66..........Miami (FL) 14, Virginia Tech 7
12-16-67..........N Carolina St 14, Georgia 7
12-14-68..........Mississippi 34, Virginia Tech 17
12-13-69..........Colorado 47, Alabama 33
12-12-70..........Tulane 17, Colorado 3
12-20-71..........Tennessee 14, Arkansas 13
12-18-72..........Georgia Tech 31, Iowa St 30
12-17-73..........N Carolina St 31, Kansas 18
12-16-74..........Tennessee 7, Maryland 3
12-22-75..........Southern Cal 20, Texas A&M 0
12-20-76..........Alabama 36, UCLA 6
12-19-77..........Nebraska 21, N Carolina 17
12-23-78..........Missouri 20, Louisiana St 15
12-22-79..........Penn St 9, Tulane 6
12-27-80..........Purdue 28, Missouri 25
12-30-81..........Ohio St 31, Navy 28
12-29-82..........Alabama 21, Illinois 15
12-29-83..........Notre Dame 19, Boston Col 18
12-27-84..........Auburn 21, Arkansas 15
12-27-85..........Baylor 21, Louisiana St 7
12-29-86..........Tennessee 21, Minnesota 14
12-29-87..........Georgia 20, Arkansas 17
12-28-88..........Indiana 34, S Carolina 10
12-28-89..........Mississippi 42, Air Force 29
12-27-90..........Air Force 23, Ohio St 11
12-29-91..........Air Force 38, Mississippi St 15
12-31-92..........Mississippi 13, Air Force 0
12-28-93..........Louisville 18, Michigan St 7
12-31-94..........Illinois 30, E Carolina 0
City: Memphis (since 1965).
Stadium: Liberty Bowl Memorial Stadium.
Capacity: 63,000.
Automatic Berths: 1989-92, winner of Commander-in-Chief's Trophy (Air Force, Army, Navy).
Playing Sites: Philadelphia (Municipal Stadium, 1959-63), Atlantic City (Convention Center, 1964), Memphis.

Peach Bowl

12-30-68..........Louisiana St 31, Florida St 27
12-30-69..........W Virginia 14, S Carolina 3
12-30-70..........Arizona St 48, N Carolina 26
12-30-71..........Mississippi 41, Georgia Tech 18
12-29-72..........N Carolina St 49, W Virginia 13

Peach Bowl *(Cont.)*

12-28-73 ....Georgia 17, Maryland 16
12-28-74 ....Vanderbilt 6, Texas Tech 6
12-31-75 ....W Virginia 13, N Carolina St 10
12-31-76 ....Kentucky 21, N Carolina 0
12-31-77 ....N Carolina St 24, Iowa St 14
12-25-78 ....Purdue 41, Georgia Tech 21
12-31-79 ....Baylor 24, Clemson 18
1-2-81 ....Miami (FL) 20, Virginia Tech 10
12-31-81 ....W Virginia 26, Florida 6
12-31-82 ....Iowa 28, Tennessee 22
12-30-83 ....Florida St 28, N Carolina 3
12-31-84 ....Virginia 27, Purdue 24
12-31-85 ....Army 31, Illinois 29
12-31-86 ....Virginia Tech 25, N Carolina St 24
1-2-88 ....Tennessee 27, Indiana 22
12-31-88 ....N Carolina St 28, Iowa 23
12-30-89 ....Syracuse 19, Georgia 18
12-29-90 ....Auburn 27, Indiana 23
1-1-92 ....E Carolina 37, N Carolina St 34
1-2-93 ....North Carolina 21, Miss. St 17
12-31-93 ....Clemson 14, Kentucky 13
1-1-95 ....N Carolina St 28, Mississippi St 24

City: Atlanta.
Stadium: Atlanta Fulton County Stadium.
Capacity: 59,800.
Automatic Berths: None.
Playing Sites: Grant Field (1968-70), Atlanta Stadium (since 1971).

Fiesta Bowl

12-27-71 ....Arizona St 45, Florida St 38
12-23-72 ....Arizona St 49, Missouri 35
12-21-73 ....Arizona St 28, Pittsburgh 7
12-28-74 ....Oklahoma St 16, Brigham Young 6
12-26-75 ....Arizona St 17, Nebraska 14
12-25-76 ....Oklahoma 41, Wyoming 7
12-25-77 ....Penn St 42, Arizona St 30
12-25-78 ....Arkansas 10, UCLA 10
12-25-79 ....Pittsburgh 16, Arizona 10
12-26-80 ....Penn St 31, Ohio St 19
1-1-82 ....Penn St 26, Southern Cal 10
1-1-83 ....Arizona St 32, Oklahoma 21
1-2-84 ....Ohio St 28, Pittsburgh 23
1-1-85 ....UCLA 39, Miami (FL) 37
1-1-86 ....Michigan 27, Nebraska 23
1-2-87 ....Penn St 14, Miami (FL) 10
1-1-88 ....Florida St 31, Nebraska 28
1-2-89 ....Notre Dame 34, W Virginia 21
1-1-90 ....Florida St 41, Nebraska 17
1-1-91 ....Louisville 34, Alabama 7
1-1-92 ....Penn St 42, Tennessee 17
1-1-93 ....Syracuse 26, Colorado 22
1-1-94 ....Arizona 29, Miami (FL) 0
1-2-95 ....Colorado 41, Notre Dame 24

City: Tempe, AZ.
Stadium: Sun Devil Stadium.
Capacity: 74,000.
Automatic Berths: None.

Independence Bowl

12-13-76 ....McNeese St 20, Tulsa 16
12-17-77 ....Louisiana Tech 24, Louisville 14
12-16-78 ....E Carolina 35, Louisiana Tech 13
12-15-79 ....Syracuse 31, McNeese St 7

Independence Bowl *(Cont.)*

12-13-80 ....Southern Miss 16, McNeese St 14
12-12-81 ....Texas A&M 33, Oklahoma St 16
12-11-82 ....Wisconsin 14, Kansas St 3
12-10-83 ....Air Force 9, Mississippi 3
12-15-84 ....Air Force 23, Virginia Tech 7
12-21-85 ....Minnesota 20, Clemson 13
12-20-86 ....Mississippi 20, Texas Tech 17
12-19-87 ....Washington 24, Tulane 12
12-23-88 ....Southern Miss 38, UTEP 18
12-16-89 ....Oregon 27, Tulsa 24
12-15-90 ....Louisiana Tech 34, Maryland 34
12-29-91 ....Georgia 24, Arkansas 15
12-31-92 ....Wake Forest 39, Oregon 35
12-31-93 ....Virginia Tech 45, Indiana 20
12-28-94 ....Virginia 20, Texas Christian 10

City: Shreveport, LA.
Stadium: Independence Stadium.
Capacity: 50,560.
Automatic Berths: None.

All-American Bowl (Discontinued)

12-22-77 ....Maryland 17, Minnesota 7
12-20-78 ....Texas A&M 28, Iowa St 12
12-29-79 ....Missouri 24, S Carolina 14
12-27-80 ....Arkansas 34, Tulane 15
12-31-81 ....Mississippi St 10, Kansas 0
12-31-82 ....Air Force 36, Vanderbilt 28
12-22-83 ....W Virginia 20, Kentucky 16
12-29-84 ....Kentucky 20, Wisconsin 19
12-31-85 ....Georgia Tech 17, Michigan St 14
12-31-86 ....Florida St 27, Indiana 13
12-22-87 ....Virginia 22, Brigham Young 16
12-29-88 ....Florida 14, Illinois 10
12-28-89 ....Texas Tech 49, Duke 21
12-28-90 ....N Carolina St 31, S Mississippi 27

City: Birmingham, AL.
Stadium: Legion Field.
Capacity: 75,808.
Automatic Berths: None.
Name Change: Hall of Fame Classic (1977-84), All-American Bowl (1985-90).

Holiday Bowl

12-22-78 ....Navy 23, Brigham Young 16
12-21-79 ....Indiana 38, Brigham Young 37
12-19-80 ....Brigham Young 46, SMU 45
12-18-81 ....Brigham Young 38, Washington St 36
12-17-82 ....Ohio St 47, Brigham Young 17
12-23-83 ....Brigham Young 21, Missouri 17
12-21-84 ....Brigham Young 24, Michigan 17
12-22-85 ....Arkansas 18, Arizona St 17
12-30-86 ....Iowa 39, San Diego St 38
12-30-87 ....Iowa 20, Wyoming 19
12-30-88 ....Oklahoma St 62, Wyoming 14
12-29-89 ....Penn St 50, Brigham Young 39
12-29-90 ....Texas A&M 65, Brigham Young 14
12-30-91 ....Iowa 13, Brigham Young 13
12-30-92 ....Hawaii 27, Illinois 17
12-30-93 ....Ohio St 28, Brigham Young 21
12-30-94 ....Michigan 24, Colorado St 14

City: San Diego.
Stadium: Jack Murphy Stadium.
Capacity: 60,750.
Automatic Berths: Western Athletic champ (except 1985).

Las Vegas Bowl

12-19-81 ....Toledo 27, San Jose St 25
12-18-82 ....Fresno St 29, Bowling Green 28
12-17-83 ....Northern Illinois 20, Cal St-Fullerton 13
12-15-84 ....NV-Las Vegas 30, Toledo 13*
12-14-85 ....Fresno St 51, Bowling Green 7
12-13-86 ....San Jose St 37, Miami (OH) 7
12-12-87 ....Eastern Michigan 30, San Jose St 27
12-10-88 ....Fresno St 35, Western Michigan 30
12-9-89 ....Fresno St 27, Ball St 6
12-8-90 ....San Jose St 48, Central Michigan 24
12-14-91 ....Bowling Green 28, Fresno St 21
12-18-92 ....Bowling Green 35, Nevada 34
12-17-93 ....Utah St 42, Ball St 33
12-15-94 ....UNLV 52, Central Michigan 24
* Toledo won later by forfeit.
City: Fresno, CA.
Stadium: Bulldog Stadium. Capacity: 30,000.
Automatic Berths: Mid-American and Big West champs.
Name change: California Bowl (1981-91).

Aloha Bowl

12-25-82 ....Washington 21, Maryland 20
12-26-83 ....Penn St 13, Washington 10
12-29-84 ....Southern Meth 27, Notre Dame 20
12-28-85 ....Alabama 24, Southern Cal 3
12-27-86 ....Arizona 30, N Carolina 21
12-25-87 ....UCLA 20, Florida 16
12-25-88 ....Washington St 24, Houston 22
12-25-89 ....Michigan St 33, Hawaii 13
12-25-90 ....Syracuse 28, Arizona 0
12-25-91 ....Georgia Tech 18, Stanford 17
12-25-92 ....Kansas 23, Brigham Young 20
12-25-93 ....Colorado 41, Fresno St 30
12-25-94 ....Boston College 12, Kansas St 7
City: Honolulu.
Stadium: Aloha Stadium.
Capacity: 50,000.
Automatic Berths: None.

Freedom Bowl

12-16-84 ....Iowa 55, Texas 17
12-30-85 ....Washington 20, Colorado 17
12-30-86 ....UCLA 31, Brigham Young 10
12-30-87 ....Arizona St 33, Air Force 28
12-29-88 ....Brigham Young 20, Colorado 17
12-30-89 ....Washington 34, Florida 7
12-29-90 ....Colorado St 32, Oregon 31
12-30-91 ....Tulsa 28, San Diego St 17
12-29-92 ....Fresno St 24, Southern Cal 7
12-30-93 ....Southern Cal 28, Utah 21
12-29-94 ....Utah 16, Arizona 13
City: Anaheim.
Stadium: Anaheim Stadium.
Capacity: 70,500.
Automatic Berths: None.

Hall of Fame Bowl

12-23-86 ....Boston College 27, Georgia 24
1-2-88 ....Michigan 28, Alabama 24
1-2-89 ....Syracuse 23, Louisiana St 10
1-1-90 ....Auburn 31, Ohio St 14
1-1-91 ....Clemson 30, Illinois 0
1-1-92 ....Syracuse 24, Ohio St 17

Hall of Fame Bowl *(Cont.)*

1-1-93 ....Tennessee 38, Boston College 23
1-1-94 ....Michigan 42, N Carolina St 7
1-2-95 ....Wisconsin 34, Duke 20
City: Tampa.
Stadium: Tampa Stadium.
Capacity: 74,315.
Automatic Berths: None.

Copper Bowl

12-31-89 ....Arizona 17, N Carolina St 10
12-31-90 ....California 17, Wyoming 15
12-31-91 ....Indiana 24, Baylor 0
12-29-92 ....Washington St 31, Utah 28
12-29-93 ....Kansas St 52, Wyoming 17
12-29-94 ....Brigham Young 31, Oklahoma 6
City: Tucson.
Stadium: Arizona Stadium.
Capacity: 57,000.
Automatic Berths: None.

Carquest Bowl

12-28-90 ....Florida St 24, Penn St 17
12-28-91 ....Alabama 30, Colorado 25
1-1-93 ....Stanford 24, Penn St 3
1-1-94 ....Boston College 31, Virginia 13
1-2-95 ....S Carolina 24, W Virginia 21
City: Miami.
Stadium: Joe Robbie.
Capacity: 75,000.   Automatic Berths: None
Name Change: Blockbuster Bowl (1990-93).

Bluebonnet Bowl (Discontinued)

12-19-59 ....Clemson 23, Texas Christian 7
12-17-60 ....Texas 3, Alabama 3
12-16-61 ....Kansas 33, Rice 7
12-22-62 ....Missouri 14, Georgia Tech 10
12-21-63 ....Baylor 14, LSU 7
12-19-64 ....Tulsa 14, Mississippi 7
12-18-65 ....Tennessee 27, Tulsa 6
12-17-66 ....Texas 19, Mississippi 0
12-23-67 ....Colorado 31, Miami (FL) 21
12-31-68 ....Southern Meth 28, Oklahoma 27
12-31-69 ....Houston 36, Auburn 7
12-31-70 ....Alabama 24, Oklahoma 24
12-31-71 ....Colorado 29, Houston 17
12-30-72 ....Tennessee 24, LSU 17
12-29-73 ....Houston 47, Tulane 7
12-23-74 ....N Carolina St 31, Houston 31
12-27-75 ....Texas 38, Colorado 21
12-31-76 ....Nebraska 27, Texas Tech 24
12-31-77 ....Southern Cal 47, Texas A&M 28
12-31-78 ....Stanford 25, Georgia 22
12-31-79 ....Purdue 27, Tennessee 22
12-31-80 ....N Carolina 16, Texas 7
12-31-81 ....Michigan 33, UCLA 14
12-31-82 ....Arkansas 28, Florida 24
12-31-83 ....Oklahoma St 24, Baylor 14
12-31-84 ....W Virginia 31, Texas Christian 14
12-31-85 ....Air Force 24, Texas 16
12-31-86 ....Baylor 21, Colorado 9
12-31-87 ....Texas 32, Pittsburgh 27
City: Houston. Name change: Astro-Bluebonnet Bowl ('68-'76).
Playing sites: Rice Stadium (1959-67; 1985-86),
Astrodome (1968-84, 1987).

NCAA Divisional Championships

Division I-AA

Year	Winner	Runner-Up	Score
1978	Florida A&M	Massachusetts	35-28
1979	Eastern Kentucky	Lehigh	30-7
1980	Boise St	Eastern Kentucky	31-29
1981	Idaho St	Eastern Kentucky	34-23
1982	Eastern Kentucky	Delaware	17-14
1983	Southern Illinois	Western Carolina	43-7
1984	Montana St	Louisiana Tech	19-6
1985	Georgia Southern	Furman	44-42
1986	Georgia Southern	Arkansas St	48-21
1987	NE Louisiana	Marshall	43-42
1988	Furman	Georgia Southern	17-12
1989	Georgia Southern	SF Austin St	37-34
1990	Georgia Southern	NV-Reno	36-13
1991	Youngstown St	Marshall	25-17
1992	Marshall	Youngstown St	31-28
1993	Youngstown St	Marshall	17-5
1994	Youngstown St	Boise St	28-14

Division II

Year	Winner	Runner-Up	Score
1973	Louisiana Tech	Western Kentucky	34-0
1974	Central Michigan	Delaware	54-14
1975	Northern Michigan	Western Kentucky	16-14
1976	Montana St	Akron	24-13
1977	Lehigh	Jacksonville St	33-0
1978	Eastern Illinois	Delaware	10-9
1979	Delaware	Youngstown St	38-21
1980	Cal Poly SLO	Eastern Illinois	21-13
1981	SW Texas St	N Dakota St	42-13
1982	SW Texas St	UC-Davis	34-9
1983	N Dakota St	Central St (OH)	41-21
1984	Troy St	N Dakota St	18-17
1985	N Dakota St	N Alabama	35-7
1986	N Dakota St	S Dakota	27-7
1987	Troy St	Portland St	31-17
1988	N Dakota St	Portland St	35-21
1989	Mississippi Col	Jacksonville St	3-0
1990	N Dakota St	Indiana (PA)	51-11
1991	Pittsburg St	Jacksonville St	23-6
1992	Jacksonville St	Pittsburg St	17-13
1993	N Alabama	Indiana (PA)	41-34
1994	N Alabama	Texas A&M-Kingsville	16-10

Division III

Year	Winner	Runner-Up	Score
1973	Wittenberg	Juniata	41-0
1974	Central (IA)	Ithaca	10-8
1975	Wittenberg	Ithaca	28-0
1976	St John's (MN)	Towson St	31-28
1977	Widener	Wabash	39-36
1978	Baldwin-Wallace	Wittenberg	24-10
1979	Ithaca	Wittenberg	14-10
1980	Dayton	Ithaca	63-0
1981	Widener	Dayton	17-10
1982	W Georgia	Augustana (IL)	14-0
1983	Augustana (IL)	Union (NY)	21-17
1984	Augustana (IL)	Central (IA)	21-12
1985	Augustana (IL)	Ithaca	20-7
1986	Augustana (IL)	Salisbury St	31-3
1987	Wagner	Dayton	19-3
1988	Ithaca	Central (IA)	39-24
1989	Dayton	Union (NY)	17-7
1990	Allegheny	Lycoming	21-14 (OT)
1991	Ithaca	Dayton	34-20
1992	Wisconsin-LaCrosse	Washington & Jefferson	16-12
1993	Mount Union	Rowan	34-24
1994	Albion	Washington & Jefferson	38-15

Division I

Year	Winner	Runner-Up	Score
1956	St Joseph's (IN) /Montana St		0-0
1957	Kansas St-Pittsburg	Hillsdale (MI)	27-26
1958	Northeastern Oklahoma	Northern Arizona	19-13
1959	Texas A&I	Lenoir-Rhyne (NC)	20-7
1960	Lenoir-Rhyne	Humboldt St (CA)	15-14
1961	Kansas St-Pittsburg	Linfield (OR)	12-7
1962	Central St (OK)	Lenoir-Rhyne (NC)	28-13
1963	St John's (MN)	Prairie View (TX)	33-27
1964	Concordia-Moorhead/Sam Houston		7-7
1965	St John's (MN)	Linfield (OR)	33-0
1966	Waynesburg (PA)	WI-Whitewater	42-21
1967	Fairmont St (WV)	Eastern Washington	28-21
1968	Troy St (MI)	Texas A&I	43-35
1969	Texas A&I	Concordia-Moorhead	32-7
1970	Texas A&I	Wofford (SC)	48-7
1971	Livingston (AL)	Arkansas Tech	14-12
1972	E Texas St	Carson-Newman	21-18
1973	Abilene Christian	Elon (NC)	42-14
1974	Texas A&I	Henderson St (AR)	34-23
1975	Texas A&I	Salem (WV)	37-0
1976	Texas A&I	Central Arkansas	26-0
1977	Abilene Christian	Southwestern Oklahoma	24-7
1978	Angelo St	Elon (NC)	34-14
1979	Texas A&I	Central St (OK)	20-14
1980	Elon (NC)	Northeastern Oklahoma	17-10
1981	Elon (NC)	Pittsburg St	3-0
1982	Central St (OK)	Mesa (CO)	14-11
1983	Carson-Newman (TN)	Mesa (CO)	36-28
1984	Carson-Newman (TN) Central Arkansas		19-19
1985	Central Arkansas/ Hillsdale (MI)		10-10
1986	Carson-Newman (TN)	Cameron (OK)	17-0
1987	Cameron (OK)	Carson-Newman (TN)	30-2
1988	Carson-Newman (TN)	Adams St (CO)	56-21
1989	Carson-Newman (TN)	Emporia St (KS)	34-20
1990	Central St (OH)	Mesa St (CO)	38-16
1991	Central Arkansas	Central St (OH)	19-16
1992	Central St (OH)	Gardner-Webb (NC)	19-16
1993	East Central (OK)	Glenville St (WV)	49-35
1994	Northeastern St (OK)	Arkansas-Pine Bluff	13-12

Division II

Year	Winner	Runner-Up	Score
1970	Westminster (PA)	Anderson (IN)	21-16
1971	California Lutheran	Westminster (PA)	30-14
1972	Missouri Southern	Northwestern (IA)	21-14
1973	Northwestern (IA)	Glenville St (WV)	10-3
1974	Texas Lutheran	Missouri Valley	42-0
1975	Texas Lutheran	California Lutheran	34-8
1976	Westminster (PA)	Redlands (CA)	20-13
1977	Westminster (PA)	California Lutheran	17-9
1978	Concordia-Moorhead	Findlay (OH)	7-0
1979	Findlay (OH)	Northwestern (IA)	51-6
1980	Pacific Lutheran	Wilmington	38-10
1981	Austin Coll./ Conc.-Moorhead		24-24
1982	Linfield (OR)	William Jewell (MO)	33-15
1983	Northwestern (IA)	Pacific Lutheran	25-21
1984	Linfield (OR)	Northwestern (IA)	33-22
1985	WI-La Crosse	Pacific Lutheran	24-7
1986	Linfield (OR)	Baker (KS)	17-0
1987	Pacific Lutheran	WI-Stevens Point*	16-16
1988	Westminster (PA)	WI-La Crosse	21-14
1989	Westminster (PA)	WI-La Crosse	51-30
1990	Peru St (NEB)	Westminster (PA)	17-7
1991	Georgetown (KY)	Pacific Lutheran	28-20
1992	Findlay (OH)	Linfield (OR)	26-13
1993	Pacific Lutheran (WA)	Westminster (PA)	50-20
1994	Westminster (PA)	Pacific Lutheran (WA)	27-7

*Forfeited 1987 season due to use of an ineligible player.

Awards

Heisman Memorial Trophy

Awarded to the best college player by the Downtown Athletic Club of New York City. The trophy is named after John W. Heisman, who coached Georgia Tech to the national championship in 1917 and later served as DAC athletic director.

Year	Winner, College, Position Winner's Season Statistics	Runner-up, College
1935	**Jay Berwanger, Chicago, HB** Rush: 119 Yds: 577 TD: 6	Monk Meyer, Army
1936	**Larry Kelley, Yale, E** Rec: 17 Yds: 372 TD: 6	Sam Francis, Nebraska
1937	**Clint Frank, Yale, HB** Rush: 157 Yds: 667 TD: 11	Byron White, Colorado
1938	**†Davey O'Brien, Texas Christian, QB** Att/Comp: 194/110 Yds: 1733 TD: 19	Marshall Goldberg, Pittsburgh
1939	**Nile Kinnick, Iowa, HB** Rush: 106 Yds: 374 TD: 5	Tom Harmon, Michigan
1940	**Tom Harmon, Michigan, HB** Rush: 191 Yds: 852 TD: 16	John Kimbrough, Texas A&M
1941	**†Bruce Smith, Minnesota, HB** Rush: 98 Yds: 480 TD: 6	Angelo Bertelli, Notre Dame
1942	**Frank Sinkwich, Georgia, HB** Att/Comp: 166/84 Yds: 1392 TD: 10	Paul Governali, Columbia
1943	**Angelo Bertelli, Notre Dame, QB** Att/Comp: 36/25 Yds: 511 TD: 10	Bob Odell, Pennsylvania
1944	**Les Horvath, Ohio State, QB** Rush: 163 Yds: 924 TD: 12	Glenn Davis, Army
1945	***†Doc Blanchard, Army, FB** Rush: 101 Yds: 718 TD: 13	Glenn Davis, Army
1946	**Glenn Davis, Army, HB** Rush: 123 Yds: 712 TD: 7	Charley Trippi, Georgia
1947	**†John Lujack, Notre Dame, QB** Att/Comp: 109/61 Yds: 777 TD: 9	Bob Chappius, Michigan
1948	***Doak Walker, Southern Methodist, HB** Rush: 108 Yds: 532 TD: 8	Charlie Justice, N Carolina
1949	**†Leon Hart, Notre Dame, E** Rec: 19 Yds: 257 TD: 5	Charlie Justice, N Carolina
1950	***Vic Janowicz, Ohio St, HB** Att/Comp: 77/32 Yds: 561 TD: 12	Kyle Rote, Southern Methodist
1951	**Dick Kazmaier, Princeton, HB** Rush: 149 Yds: 861 TD: 9	Hank Lauricella, Tennessee
1952	**Billy Vessels, Oklahoma, HB** Rush: 167 Yds: 1072 TD: 17	Jack Scarbath, Maryland
1953	**John Lattner, Notre Dame, HB** Rush: 134 Yds: 651 TD: 6	Paul Giel, Minnesota
1954	**Alan Ameche, Wisconsin, FB** Rush: 146 Yds: 641 TD: 9	Kurt Burris, Oklahoma
1955	**Howard Cassady, Ohio St, HB** Rush: 161 Yds: 958 TD: 15	Jim Swink, Texas Christian
1956	**Paul Hornung, Notre Dame, QB** Att/Comp: 111/59 Yds: 917 TD: 3	Johnny Majors, Tennessee
1957	**John David Crow, Texas A&M, HB** Rush: 129 Yds: 562 TD: 10	Alex Karras, Iowa
1958	**Pete Dawkins, Army, HB** Rush: 78 Yds: 428 TD: 6	Randy Duncan, Iowa
1959	**Billy Cannon, Louisiana St, HB** Rush: 139 Yds: 598 TD: 6	Rich Lucas, Penn St
1960	**Joe Bellino, Navy, HB** Rush: 168 Yds: 834 TD: 18	Tom Brown, Minnesota
1961	**Ernie Davis, Syracuse, HB** Rush: 150 Yds: 823 TD: 15	Bob Ferguson, Ohio St
1962	**Terry Baker, Oregon St, QB** Att/Comp: 203/112 Yds: 1738 TD: 15	Jerry Stovall, Louisiana St
1963	***Roger Staubach, Navy, QB** Att/Comp: 161/107 Yds: 1474 TD: 7	Billy Lothridge, Georgia Tech
1964	**John Huarte, Notre Dame, QB** Att/Comp: 205/114 Yds: 2062 TD: 16	Jerry Rhome, Tulsa

Heisman Memorial Trophy (Cont.)

Year	Winner, College, Position Winner's Season Statistics	Runner-up, College
1965	**Mike Garrett, Southern Cal, HB** Rush: 267 Yds: 1440 TD: 16	Howard Twilley, Tulsa
1966	**Steve Spurrier, Florida, QB** Att/Comp: 291/179 Yds: 2012 TD: 16	Bob Griese, Purdue
1967	**Gary Beban, UCLA, QB** Att/Comp: 156/87 Yds: 1359 TD: 8	O.J. Simpson, Southern Cal
1968	**O.J. Simpson, Southern Cal, HB** Rush: 383 Yds: 1880 TD: 23	Leroy Keyes, Purdue
1969	**Steve Owens, Oklahoma, FB** Rush: 358 Yds: 1523 TD: 23	Mike Phipps, Purdue
1970	**Jim Plunkett, Stanford, QB** Att/Comp: 358/191 Yds: 2715 TD: 18	Joe Theismann, Notre Dame
1971	**Pat Sullivan, Auburn, QB** Att/Comp: 281/162 Yds: 2012 TD: 20	Ed Marinaro, Cornell
1972	**Johnny Rodgers, Nebraska, FL** Rec: 55 Yds: 942 TD: 17	Greg Pruitt, Oklahoma
1973	**John Cappelletti, Penn St, HB** Rush: 286 Yds: 1522 TD: 17	John Hicks, Ohio St
1974	***Archie Griffin, Ohio St, HB** Rush: 256 Yds: 1695 TD: 12	Anthony Davis, Southern Cal
1975	**Archie Griffin, Ohio St, HB** Rush: 262 Yds: 1450 TD: 4	Chuck Muncie, California
1976	**†Tony Dorsett, Pittsburgh, HB** Rush: 370 Yds: 2150 TD: 23	Ricky Bell, Southern Cal
1977	**Earl Campbell, Texas, FB** Rush: 267 Yds: 1744 TD: 19	Terry Miller, Oklahoma St
1978	***Billy Sims, Oklahoma, HB** Rush: 231 Yds: 1762 TD: 20	Chuck Fusina, Penn St
1979	**Charles White, Southern Cal, HB** Rush: 332 Yds: 1803 TD: 19	Billy Sims, Oklahoma
1980	**George Rogers, S Carolina, HB** Rush: 324 Yds: 1894 TD: 14	Hugh Green, Pittsburgh
1981	**Marcus Allen, Southern Cal, HB** Rush: 433 Yds: 2427 TD: 23	Herschel Walker, Georgia
1982	***Herschel Walker, Georgia, HB** Rush: 335 Yds: 1752 TD: 17	John Elway, Stanford
1983	**Mike Rozier, Nebraska, HB** Rush: 275 Yds: 2148 TD: 29	Steve Young, Brigham Young
1984	**Doug Flutie, Boston College, QB** Att/Comp: 396/233 Yds: 3454 TD: 27	Keith Byars, Ohio St
1985	**Bo Jackson, Auburn, HB** Rush: 278 Yds: 1786 TD: 17	Chuck Long, Iowa
1986	**Vinny Testaverde, Miami (FL), QB** Att/Comp: 276/175 Yds: 2557 TD: 26	Paul Palmer, Temple
1987	**Tim Brown, Notre Dame, WR** Rec: 39 Yds: 846 TD: 7	Don McPherson, Syracuse
1988	***Barry Sanders, Oklahoma St, RB** Rush: 344 Yds: 2628 TD: 39	Rodney Peete, Southern Cal
1989	***Andre Ware, Houston, QB** Att/Comp: 578/365 Yds: 4699 TD: 46	Anthony Thompson, Indiana
1990	***Ty Detmer, Brigham Young, QB** Att/Comp: 562/361 Yds: 5188 TD: 41	Raghib Ismail, Notre Dame
1991	***Desmond Howard, Michigan, WR** Rec: 61 Yds: 950 TD: 23	Casey Weldon, Florida St
1992	**Gino Torretta, Miami (FL), QB** Att/Comp: 402/228 Yds: 3060 TD: 19	Marshall Faulk, San Diego St
1993	**†Charlie Ward, Florida St, QB** Att/Comp: 380/264 Yds: 3032 TD: 27	Heath Shuler, Tennessee
1994	**Rashaan Salaam, Colorado, RB** Rush: 298 Yds: 2055 TD: 24	Ki-Jana Carter, Penn St

*Juniors (all others seniors). †Winners who played for national championship teams the same year.

Note: Former Heisman winners and national media cast votes, with ballots allowing for three names (3 points for first, 2 for second and 1 for third).

Jim Thorpe Award

Given to the best defensive back of the year, the award is presented by the Jim Thorpe Athletic Club of Oklahoma City.

Year	Player, College	Year	Player, College
1986	Thomas Everett, Baylor	1990	Darryl Lewis, Arizona
1987	Bennie Blades, Miami (FL)	1991	Terrell Buckley, Florida St
	Rickey Dixon, Oklahoma	1992	Deon Figures, Colorado
1988	Deion Sanders, Florida St	1993	Antonio Langham, Alabama
1989	Mark Carrier, Southern Cal	1994	Chris Hudson, Colorado

Outland Trophy

Given to the outstanding interior lineman, selected by the Football Writers Association of America.

Year	Player, College, Position	Year	Player, College, Position
1946	George Connor, Notre Dame, T	1971	Larry Jacobson, Nebraska, DT
1947	Joe Steffy, Army, G	1972	Rich Glover, Nebraska, MG
1948	Bill Fischer, Notre Dame, G	1973	John Hicks, Ohio St, OT
1949	Ed Bagdon, Michigan St, G	1974	Randy White, Maryland, DE
1950	Bob Gain, Kentucky, T	1975	Lee Roy Selmon, Oklahoma, DT
1951	Jim Weatherall, Oklahoma, T	1976	*Ross Browner, Notre Dame, DE
1952	Dick Modzelewski, Maryland, T	1977	Brad Shearer, Texas, DT
1953	J. D. Roberts, Oklahoma, G	1978	Greg Roberts, Oklahoma, G
1954	Bill Brooks, Arkansas, G	1979	Jim Ritcher, N Carolina St, C
1955	Calvin Jones, Iowa, G	1980	Mark May, Pittsburgh, OT
1956	Jim Parker, Ohio St, G	1981	*Dave Rimington, Nebraska, C
1957	Alex Karras, Iowa, T	1982	Dave Rimington, Nebraska, C
1958	Zeke Smith, Auburn, G	1983	Dean Steinkuhler, Nebraska, G
1959	Mike McGee, Duke, T	1984	Bruce Smith, Virginia Tech, DT
1960	Tom Brown, Minnesota, G	1985	Mike Ruth, Boston Col, NG
1961	Merlin Olsen, Utah St, T	1986	Jason Buck, Brigham Young, DT
1962	Bobby Bell, Minnesota, T	1987	Chad Hennings, Air Force, DT
1963	Scott Appleton, Texas, T	1988	Tracy Rocker, Auburn, DT
1964	Steve DeLong, Tennessee, T	1989	Mohammed Elewonibi, Brigham Young, G
1965	Tommy Nobis, Texas, G	1990	Russell Maryland, Miami (FL), DT
1966	Loyd Phillips, Arkansas, T	1991	*Steve Emtman, Washington, DT
1967	Ron Yary, Southern Cal, T	1992	Will Shields, Nebraska, G
1968	Bill Stanfill, Georgia, T	1993	Rob Waldrop, Arizona, NG
1969	Mike Reid, Penn St, DT	1994	Zach Wiegert, Nebraska, G
1970	Jim Stillwagon, Ohio St, MG		

*Juniors (all others seniors).

Vince Lombardi/Rotary Award

Given to the outstanding college lineman of the year, the award is sponsored by the Rotary Club of Houston.

Year	Player, College, Position	Year	Player, College, Position
1970	Jim Stillwagon, Ohio St, MG	1982	Dave Rimington, Nebraska, C
1971	Walt Patulski, Notre Dame, DE	1983	Dean Steinkuhler, Nebraska, G
1972	Rich Glover, Nebraska, MG	1984	Tony Degrate, Texas, DT
1973	John Hicks, Ohio St, OT	1985	Tony Casillas, Oklahoma, NG
1974	Randy White, Maryland, DT	1986	Cornelius Bennett, Alabama, LB
1975	Lee Roy Selmon, Oklahoma, DT	1987	Chris Spielman, Ohio St, LB
1976	Wilson Whitley, Houston, DT	1988	Tracy Rocker, Auburn, DT
1977	Ross Browner, Notre Dame, DE	1989	Percy Snow, Michigan St, LB
1978	Bruce Clark, Penn St, DT	1990	Chris Zorich, Notre Dame, NG
1979	Brad Budde, Southern Cal, G	1991	Steve Emtman, Washington, DT
1980	Hugh Green, Pittsburgh, DE	1992	Marvin Jones, Florida St, LB
1981	Kenneth Sims, Texas, DT	1993	Aaron Taylor, Notre Dame, OT
		1994	Warren Sapp, Miami (FL), DT

Butkus Award

Given to the top collegiate linebacker, the award was established by the Downtown Athletic Club of Orlando and named for college hall of famer Dick Butkus of Illinois.

Year	Player, College	Year	Player, College
1985	Brian Bosworth, Oklahoma	1990	Alfred Williams, Colorado
1986	Brian Bosworth, Oklahoma	1991	Erick Anderson, Michigan
1987	Paul McGowan, Florida St	1992	Marvin Jones, Florida St
1988	Derrick Thomas, Alabama	1993	Trev Alberts, Nebraska
1989	Percy Snow, Michigan St	1994	Dana Howard, Illinois

Davey O'Brien National Quarterback Award

Given to the No. 1 quarterback in the nation by the Davey O'Brien Educational and Charitable Trust of Fort Worth. Named for Texas Christian Hall of Fame quarterback Davey O'Brien (1936-38).

Year	Player, College	Year	Player, College
1981	Jim McMahon, Brigham Young	1988	Troy Aikman, UCLA
1982	Todd Blackledge, Penn St	1989	Andre Ware, Houston
1983	Steve Young, Brigham Young	1990	Ty Detmer, Brigham Young
1984	Doug Flutie, Boston College	1991	Ty Detmer, Brigham Young
1985	Chuck Long, Iowa	1992	Gino Torretta, Miami (FL)
1986	Vinny Testaverde, Miami (FL)	1993	Charlie Ward, Florida St
1987	Don McPherson, Syracuse	1994	Kerry Collins, Penn St

Note: Originally known as the Davey O'Brien Memorial Trophy, honoring the outstanding football player in the Southwest as follows: 1977—Earl Campbell, Texas, RB; 1978—Billy Sims, Oklahoma, RB; 1979—Mike Singletary, Baylor, LB; 1980—Mike Singletary, Baylor, LB.

Maxwell Award

Given to the nation's outstanding college football player by the Maxwell Football Club of Philadelphia.

Year	Player, College, Position	Year	Player, College, Position
1937	Clint Frank, Yale, HB	1966	Jim Lynch, Notre Dame, LB
1938	Davey O'Brien, Texas Christian, QB	1967	Gary Beban, UCLA, QB
1939	Nile Kinnick, Iowa, HB	1968	O.J. Simpson, Southern Cal, RB
1940	Tom Harmon, Michigan, HB	1969	Mike Reid, Penn St, DT
1941	Bill Dudley, Virginia, HB	1970	Jim Plunkett, Stanford, QB
1942	Paul Governali, Columbia, QB	1971	Ed Marinaro, Cornell, RB
1943	Bob Odell, Pennsylvania, HB	1972	Brad Van Pelt, Michigan St, DB
1944	Glenn Davis, Army, HB	1973	John Cappelletti, Penn St, RB
1945	Doc Blanchard, Army, FB	1974	Steve Joachim, Temple, QB
1946	Charley Trippi, Georgia, HB	1975	Archie Griffin, Ohio St, RB
1947	Doak Walker, Southern Meth, HB	1976	Tony Dorsett, Pittsburgh, RB
1948	Chuck Bednarik, Pennsylvania, C	1977	Ross Browner, Notre Dame, DE
1949	Leon Hart, Notre Dame, E	1978	Chuck Fusina, Penn St, QB
1950	Reds Bagnell, Pennsylvania, HB	1979	Charles White, Southern Cal, RB
1951	Dick Kazmaier, Princeton, HB	1980	Hugh Green, Pittsburgh, DE
1952	John Lattner, Notre Dame, HB	1981	Marcus Allen, Southern Cal, RB
1953	John Lattner, Notre Dame, HB	1982	Herschel Walker, Georgia, RB
1954	Ron Beagle, Navy, E	1983	Mike Rozier, Nebraska, RB
1955	Howard Cassady, Ohio St, HB	1984	Doug Flutie, Boston College, QB
1956	Tommy McDonald, Oklahoma, HB	1985	Chuck Long, Iowa, QB
1957	Bob Reifsnyder, Navy, T	1986	Vinny Testaverde, Miami (FL), QB
1958	Pete Dawkins, Army, HB	1987	Don McPherson, Syracuse, QB
1959	Rich Lucas, Penn St, QB	1988	Barry Sanders, Oklahoma St, RB
1960	Joe Bellino, Navy, HB	1989	Anthony Thompson, Indiana, RB
1961	Bob Ferguson, Ohio St, FB	1990	Ty Detmer, Brigham Young, QB
1962	Terry Baker, Oregon St, QB	1991	Desmond Howard, Michigan, WR
1963	Roger Staubach, Navy, QB	1992	Gino Torretta, Miami (FL), QB
1964	Glenn Ressler, Penn St, C	1993	Charlie Ward, Florida St, QB
1965	Tommy Nobis, Texas, LB	1994	Kerry Collins, Penn St, QB

Walter Payton Player of the Year Award

Given to the top Division I-AA football player, the award is sponsored by Sports Network and voted on by Division I-AA sports information directors.

Year	Player, College, Position
1987	Kenny Gamble, Colgate, RB
1988	Dave Meggett, Towson St, RB
1989	John Friesz, Idaho, QB
1990	Walter Dean, Grambling, RB
1991	Jamie Martin, Weber St, QB
1992	Michael Payton, Marshall, QB
1993	Doug Nussmeier, Idaho, QB
1994	Steve McNair, Alcorn St, QB

The Harlon Hill Trophy

Given to the outstanding NCAA Division II college football player, the award is sponsored by the National Harlon Hill Awards Committee, Florence, AL.

Year	Player, College, Position
1986	Jeff Bentrim, N Dakota St, QB
1987	Johnny Bailey, Texas A&I, RB
1988	Johnny Bailey, Texas A&I, RB
1989	Johnny Bailey, Texas A&I, RB
1990	Chris Simdorn, N Dakota St, QB
1991	Ronnie West, Pittsburg St, WR
1992	Ronald Moore, Pittsburg St, RB
1993	Roger Graham, New Haven, RB
1994	Chris Hatcher, Valdosta St, QB

NCAA Division I-A Individual Records

Career

SCORING

Most Points Scored: 423 — Roman Anderson, Houston, 1988-91
Most Points Scored per Game: 12.1 — Marshall Faulk, San Diego St, 1991-93
Most Touchdowns Scored: 65 — Anthony Thompson, Indiana, 1986-89
Most Touchdowns Scored per Game: 2.0 — Marshall Faulk, San Diego St, 1991-93
Most Touchdowns Scored, Rushing: 64 — Anthony Thompson, Indiana, 1986-89
Most Touchdowns Scored, Passing: 121 — Ty Detmer, Brigham Young, 1988-91
Most Touchdowns Scored, Receiving: 43 — Aaron Turner, Pacific, 1989-92
Most Touchdowns Scored, Interception Returns: 5 — Ken Thomas, San Jose St, 1979-82; Jackie Walker, Tennessee, 1969-71
Most Touchdowns Scored, Punt Returns: 7 — Johnny Rodgers, Nebraska, 1970-72; Jack Mitchell, Oklahoma, 1946-48
Most Touchdowns Scored, Kickoff Returns: 6 — Anthony Davis, Southern Cal, 1972-74

TOTAL OFFENSE

Most Plays: 1795 — Ty Detmer, Brigham Young, 1988-91
Most Plays per Game: 48.5 — Doug Gaynor, Long Beach St, 1984-85
Most Yards Gained: 14,665 — Ty Detmer, Brigham Young, 1988-91 (15,031 passing, -366 rushing)
Most Yards Gained per Game: 320.9 — Chris Vargas, Nevada, 1992-93
Most 300+ Yard Games: 33 —Ty Detmer, Brigham Young, 1988-91

RUSHING

Most Rushes: 1215 — Steve Bartalo, Colorado St, 1983-86 (4813 yds)
Most Rushes per Game: 34.0 — Ed Marinaro, Cornell, 1969-71
Most Yards Gained: 6082 — Tony Dorsett, Pittsburgh, 1973-76
Most Yards Gained per Game: 174.6 — Ed Marinaro, Cornell, 1969-71
Most 100+ Yard Games: 33 — Tony Dorsett, Pittsburgh, 1973-76; Archie Griffin, Ohio St, 1972-75
Most 200+ Yard Games: 11 — Marcus Allen, Southern Cal, 1978-81

SPECIAL TEAMS

Highest Punt Return Average: 23.6 — Jack Mitchell, Oklahoma, 1946-48
Highest Kickoff Return Average: 36.2 — Forrest Hall, San Francisco, 1946-47
Highest Average Yards per Punt: 46.3 — Todd Sauerbrun, West Virginia, 1991-94

PASSING

Highest Passing Efficiency Rating: 162.7 — Ty Detmer, Brigham Young, 1988-91 (1530 attempts, 958 completions, 65 interceptions, 15,031 yards, 121 TD passes)
Most Passes Attempted: 1,530 — Ty Detmer, Brigham Young, 1988-91
Most Passes Attempted per Game: 39.6 — Mike Perez, San Jose St, 1986-87
Most Passes Completed: 958 — Ty Detmer, Brigham Young, 1988-91
Most Passes Completed per Game: 25.9 — Doug Gaynor, Long Beach St, 1984-85
Highest Completion Percentage: 65.2 — Steve Young, Brigham Young, 1981-83
Most Yards Gained: 15,031 — Ty Detmer, Brigham Young, 1988-91
Most Yards Gained per Game: 326.7 — Ty Detmer, Brigham Young, 1988-91

RECEIVING

Most Passes Caught: 266 — Aaron Turner, Pacific, 1989-92
Most Passes Caught per Game: 10.5 — Emmanuel Hazard, Houston, 1989-90
Most Yards Gained: 4,357— Ryan Yarborough, Wyoming, 1990-93
Most Yards Gained per Game: 128.6 — Howard Twilley, Tulsa, 1963-65
Highest Average Gain per Reception: 25.7 — Wesley Walker, California, 1973-75

ALL-PURPOSE RUNNING

Most Plays: 1347 — Steve Bartalo, Colorado St, 1983-86 (1215 rushes, 132 receptions)
Most Yards Gained: 7172 — Napoleon McCallum, Navy, 1981-85 (4179 rushing, 796 receiving, 858 punt returns, 1339 kickoff returns)
Most Yards Gained per Game: 237.8 — Ryan Benjamin, Pacific, 1990-92
Highest Average Gain per Play: 17.4 — Anthony Carter, Michigan, 1979-82.

INTERCEPTIONS

Most Passes Intercepted: 29 — Al Brosky, Illinois, 1950-52
Most Passes Intercepted per Game: 1.1 — Al Brosky, Illinois, 1950-52
Most Yards on Interception Returns: 501 — Terrell Buckley, Florida St, 1989-91
Highest Average Gain per Interception: 26.5 — Tom Pridemore, W Virginia, 1975-77

Single Season

SCORING

Most Points Scored: 234 — Barry Sanders, Oklahoma St, 1988
Most Points Scored per Game: 21.27 — Barry Sanders, Oklahoma St, 1988
Most Touchdowns Scored: 39 — Barry Sanders, Oklahoma St, 1988
Most Touchdowns Scored, Rushing: 37 — Barry Sanders, Oklahoma St, 1988
Most Touchdowns Scored, Passing: 54 — David Klingler, Houston, 1990
Most Touchdowns Scored, Receiving: 22 — Emmanuel Hazard, Houston, 1989
Most Touchdowns Scored, Interception Returns: 3 — by many players
Most Touchdowns Scored, Punt Returns: 4 — James Henry, Southern Miss, 1987; Golden Richards, Brigham Young, 1971; Cliff Branch , Colorado, 1971
Most Touchdowns Scored, Kickoff Returns: 3 — Leland McElroy, Texas A&M, 1993; Terance Mathis, New Mexico, 1989; Willie Gault, Tennessee, 1980; Anthony Davis, Southern Cal, 1974; Stan Brown, Purdue, 1970; Forrest Hall, San Francisco, 1946

TOTAL OFFENSE

Most Plays: 704 — David Klingler, Houston, 1990
Most Yards Gained: 5221 — David Klingler, Houston, 1990
Most Yards Gained per Game: 474.6 — David Klingler, Houston, 1990
Most 300+ Yard Games: 12 — Ty Detmer, Brigham Young, 1990

RUSHING

Most Rushes: 403 — Marcus Allen, Southern Cal, 1981
Most Rushes per Game: 39.6 — Ed Marinaro, Cornell, 1971
Most Yards Gained: 2628 — Barry Sanders, Oklahoma St, 1988
Most Yards Gained per Game: 238.9 — Barry Sanders, Oklahoma St, 1988
Most 100+ Yard Games: 11 — By nine players, most recently Barry Sanders, Oklahoma St, 1988

PASSING

Highest Passing Efficiency Rating: 176.9 — Jim McMahon, Brigham Young, 1980 (445 attempts, 284 completions, 18 interceptions, 4571 yards, 47 TD passes)
Most Passes Attempted: 643 — David Klingler, Houston, 1990
Most Passes Attempted per Game: 58.5 — David Klingler, Houston, 1990
Most Passes Completed: 374 — David Klingler, Houston, 1990
Most Passes Completed per Game: 34.0 — David Klingler, Houston, 1990
Highest Completion Percentage: 71.3 — Steve Young, Brigham Young, 1983
Most Yards Gained: (12 games) 5188 — Ty Detmer, Brigham Young, 1990; (11 games) 5140 — David Klingler, Houston, 1990
Most Yards Gained per Game: 467.3 — David Klingler, Houston, 1990

RECEIVING

Most Passes Caught: 142 — Emmanuel Hazard, Houston, 1989
Most Passes Caught per Game: 13.4 — Howard Twilley, Tulsa, 1965
Most Yards Gained: 1779 — Howard Twilley, Tulsa, 1965
Most Yards Gained per Game: 177.9 — Howard Twilley, Tulsa, 1965
Highest Average Gain per Reception: 27.9 — Elmo Wright, Houston, 1968 (min. 30 receptions)

ALL-PURPOSE RUNNING

Most Plays: 432 — Marcus Allen, Southern Cal, 1981
Most Yards Gained: 3250 — Barry Sanders, Oklahoma St, 1988
Most Yards Gained per Game: 295.5 — Barry Sanders, Oklahoma St, 1988
Highest Average Gain per Play: 18.5 — Henry Bailey, UNLV, 1992

INTERCEPTIONS

Most Passes Intercepted: 14 — Al Worley, Washington, 1968
Most Yards on Interception Returns: 302 — Charles Phillips, Southern Cal, 1974
Highest Average Gain per Interception: 50.6 — Norm Thompson, Utah, 1969

SPECIAL TEAMS

Highest Punt Return Average: 25.9 — Bill Blackstock, Tennessee, 1951
Highest Kickoff Return Average: 38.2 — Forrest Hall, San Francisco, 1946
Highest Average Yards per Punt: 49.8 — Reggie Roby, Iowa, 1981

Single Game

SCORING

Most Points Scored: 48 — Howard Griffith, Illinois, 1990 (vs Southern Illinois)

Most Field Goals: 7 — Dale Klein, Nebraska, 1985 (vs Missouri); Mike Prindle, Western Michigan, 1984 (vs Marshall)

Most Extra Points (Kick): 13 — Derek Mahoney, Fresno St, 1991 (vs New Mexico); 13 — Terry Leiweke, Houston, 1968 (vs Tulsa)

Most Extra Points (2-Pts): 6 — Jim Pilot, New Mexico St, 1961 (vs Hardin-Simmons)

TOTAL OFFENSE

Most Yards Gained: 732 — David Klingler, Houston, 1990 (vs Arizona St)

RUSHING

Most Yards Gained: 396 — Tony Sands, Kansas, 1991 (vs Missouri)

RUSHING (Cont.)

Most Touchdowns Rushed: 8 — Howard Griffith, Illinois, 1990 (vs Southern Illinois)

PASSING

Most Passes Completed: 48 — David Klingler, Houston, 1990 (vs Southern Methodist)

Most Yards Gained: 716 — David Klingler, Houston, 1990 (vs Arizona St)

Most Touchdowns Passed: 11 — David Klingler, Houston, 1990 [vs Eastern Washington (I-AA)]

RECEIVING

Most Passes Caught: 23 — Randy Gatewood, UNLV, 1994 (vs Idaho)

Most Yards Gained: 363 — Randy Gatewood, UNLV, 1994 (vs Idaho)

Most Touchdown Catches: 6 — Tim Delaney, San Diego St, 1969 (vs New Mexico St)

NCAA Division I-AA Individual Records

Career

SCORING

Most Points Scored: 385 — Marty Zendejas, NV-Reno, 1984-87

Most Touchdowns Scored: 61 — Sherriden May, Idaho, 1992-94

Most Touchdowns Scored, Rushing: 55 — Kenny Gamble, Colgate, 1984-87

Most Touchdowns Scored, Passing: 139 — Willie Totten, Mississippi Valley, 1982-85

Most Touchdowns Scored, Receiving: 50 — Jerry Rice, Mississippi Valley, 1981-84

PASSING

Highest Passing Efficiency Rating: 170.8 — Shawn Knight, William & Mary, 1991-94

Most Passes Attempted: 1,680 — Steve McNair, Alcorn St, 1991-94

Most Passes Completed: 938 — Neil Lomax, Portland St, 1977-80

Most Passes Completed per Game: 23.8 — Stan Greene, Boston U, 1989-90

Highest Completion Percentage: 66.9 — Jason Garrett, Princeton, 1987-88

PASSING (CONT.)

Most Yards Gained: 14,496 — Steve McNair, Alcorn St, 1991-94

Most Yards Gained per Game: 345.1 — Steve McNair, Alcorn St, 1991-94

RUSHING

Most Rushes: 1,027 — Erik Marsh, Lafayette, 1991-94

Most Rushes per Game: 24.5 — Keith Elias, Princeton, 1991-93

Most Yards Gained: 5,333 — Frank Hawkins, NV-Reno, 1977-80

Most Yards Gained per Game: 124.3 — Kenny Gamble, Colgate, 1984-87

RECEIVING

Most Passes Caught: 301 — Jerry Rice, Mississippi Valley, 1981-84

Most Yards Gained: 4,693 — Jerry Rice, Mississippi Valley, 1981-84

Most Yards Gained per Game: 114.5 — Jerry Rice, Mississippi Valley, 1981-84

Highest Average Gain per Reception: 24.3 — John Taylor, Delaware St, 1982-85

Single Season

SCORING

Most Points Scored: 170 — Geoff Mitchell, Weber St, 1991

Most Touchdowns Scored: 28 — Geoff Mitchell, Weber St, 1991

Most Touchdowns Scored, Rushing: 24 — Geoff Mitchell, Weber St, 1991

Most Touchdowns Scored, Passing: 56 — Willie Totten, Mississippi Valley, 1984

Most Touchdowns Scored, Receiving: 27 — Jerry Rice, Mississippi Valley, 1984

PASSING

Highest Passing Efficiency Rating: 204.6 — Shawn Knight, William & Mary, 1993

PASSING (CONT.)

Most Passes Attempted: 530 — Steve McNair, Alcorn St, 1994

Most Passes Completed: 324 — Willie Totten, Mississippi Valley, 1984

Most Passes Completed per Game: 32.4 — Willie Totten, Mississippi Valley, 1984

Highest Completion Percentage: 68.2 — Jason Garrett, Princeton, 1988; Dave Dickenson, Montana, 1994

Most Yards Gained: 4,863 — Steve McNair, Alcorn St, 1994

Most Yards Gained per Game: 455.7 — Willie Totten, Mississippi Valley, 1984

Single Season (Cont.)

RUSHING
Most Rushes: 409 — Arnold Mickens, Butler, 1994
Most Rushes per Game: 40.9 — Arnold Mickens, Butler, 1994
Most Yards Gained: 2255 — Arnold Mickens, Butler, 1994
Most Yards Gained per Game: 225.5 — Arnold Mickens, Butler, 1994

RECEIVING
Most Passes Caught: 115 — Brian Forster, Rhode Island, 1985
Most Yards Gained: 1,682 — Jerry Rice, Mississippi Valley, 1984
Most Yards Gained per Game: 168.2 — Jerry Rice, Mississippi Valley, 1984
Highest Average Gain per Reception: 26.3 — Brian Allen, Idaho, 1983 (min. 30 receptions)

Single Game

SCORING
Most Points Scored: 36 — By five players. Most recently Erwin Matthews, Richmond, 1987 (vs Massachusetts)
Most Field Goals: 8 — Goran Lingmerth, Northern Arizona, 1986 (vs Idaho)

PASSING
Most Passes Completed: 47 — Jamie Martin, Weber St, 1991 (vs Idaho St)
Most Yards Gained: 649 — Steve McNair, Alcorn St, 1994 (vs Southern-BR)
Most Touchdowns Passed: 9 — Willie Totten, Mississippi Valley, 1984 (vs Kentucky St)

RUSHING
Most Yards Gained: 364 — Tony Vinson, Towson St, 1993 (vs Bucknell)
Most Touchdowns Rushed: 6 — Gene Lake, Delaware St, 1984 (vs. Howard); Gill Fenerty, Holy Cross, 1983 (vs Columbia); Henry Odom, S Carolina St, 1980 (vs Morgan St)

RECEIVING
Most Passes Caught: 24 — Jerry Rice, Mississippi Valley 1983 (vs Southern-BR)
Most Yards Gained: 370 — Michael Lerch, Princeton, 1991 (vs Brown)
Most Touchdown Catches: 5 — Rennie Benn, Lehigh, 1985 [vs Indiana (PA)]; Jerry Rice, Mississippi Valley, 1984 (vs Prairie View and vs Kentucky St)

NCAA Division II Individual Records

Career

SCORING
Most Points Scored: 464 — Walter Payton, Jackson St, 1971-74
Most Touchdowns Scored: 72 — Shawn Graves, Wofford, 1989-92
Most Touchdowns Scored, Rushing: 72 — Shawn Graves, Wofford, 1989-92
Most Touchdowns Scored, Passing: 93 — Doug Williams, Grambling, 1974-77
Most Touchdowns Scored, Receiving: 49 — Bruce Cerone, Yankton/Emporia St, 1966-69

PASSING
Highest Passing Efficiency Rating: 164.0 — Chris Petersen, UC-Davis, 1985-86
Most Passes Attempted: 1,442 — Earl Harvey, N Carolina Central, 1985-88
Most Passes Completed: 748 — Rob Tomlinson, Cal-St Chico, 1988-91
Most Passes Completed per Game: 25.0 — Tim Von Dulm, Portland St, 1969-70
Highest Completion Percentage: 69.6 — Chris Petersen, UC-Davis, 1985-86
Most Yards Gained: 10,621 — Earl Harvey, N Carolina Central, 1985-88
Most Yards Gained per Game: 298.4 — Tim Von Dulm, Portland St, 1969-70

RUSHING
Most Rushes: 1,072 — Bernie Peeters, Luther, 1968-71
Most Rushes per Game: 29.8 — Bernie Peeters, Luther, 1968-71
Most Yards Gained: 6,320 — Johnny Bailey, Texas A&I*, 1986-89
Most Yards Gained per Game: 162.1 — Johnny Bailey, Texas A&I*, 1986-89

RECEIVING
Most Passes Caught: 253 — Chris Myers, Kenyon, 1967-70
Most Yards Gained: 4,354 — Bruce Cerone, Yankton/Emporia St, 1966-69
Most Yards Gained per Game: 137.3 — Ed Bell, Idaho St, 1968-69
Highest Average Gain per Reception: 22.8 — Tyrone Johnson, Western St (CO), 1990-93

*Became Texas A&M-Kingsville in 1993

Single Season

SCORING

Most Points Scored: 178 — Terry Metcalf, Long Beach St, 1971
Most Touchdowns Scored: 29 — Terry Metcalf, Long Beach St, 1971
Most Touchdowns Scored, Rushing: 28 — Terry Metcalf, Long Beach St, 1971
Most Touchdowns Scored, Passing: 50 — Chris Hatcher, Valdosta St, 1994
Most Touchdowns Scored, Receiving: 20 — Ed Bell, Idaho St, 1969

PASSING

Highest Passing Efficiency Rating: 210.1 — Boyd Crawford, College of Idaho, 1953
Most Passes Attempted: 515 — Todd Mayfield, W Texas St, 1986
Most Passes Completed: 334 — Chris Hatcher, Valdosta St, 1993
Most Passes Completed per Game: 30.4 — Chris Hatcher, Valdosta St, 1993
Highest Completion Percentage: 74.6 — Chris Hatcher, Valdosta St, 1994
Most Yards Gained: 3,757 — Perry Klein, LIU-CW Post, 1993
Most Yards Gained per Game: 393.4 — Grady Benton, W Texas A&M, 1994

RUSHING

Most Rushes: 385 — Joe Gough, Wayne St (MI), 1994
Most Rushes per Game: 38.6 — Mark Perkins, Hobart, 1968
Most Yards Gained: 2,011 — Johnny Bailey, Texas A&I, 1986
Most Yards Gained per Game: 182.8 — Johnny Bailey, Texas A&I, 1986

RECEIVING

Most Passes Caught: 119 — Brad Bailey, W Texas A&M, 1994
Most Yards Gained: 1,876 — Chris George, Glenville St, 1993
Most Yards Gained per Game: 187.6 — Chris George, Glenville St, 1993
Highest Average Gain per Reception: 32.5 — Tyrone Johnson, Western St, 1991 (min. 30 receptions)

Single Game

SCORING

Most Points Scored: 48 — Paul Zaeske, N Park, 1968 (vs N Central); Junior Wolf, Panhandle St, 1958 [vs St Mary (KS)]
Most Field Goals: 6 — Steve Huff, Central Missouri St, 1985 (vs SE Missouri St)

PASSING

Most Passes Completed: 45 — Chris Hatcher, Valdosta St, 1993 (vs W Georgia; vs Miss. College)
Most Yards Gained: 614 — Alfred Montez, W New Mexico, 1994 (vs W Texas A&M); Perry Klein, LI-C.W. Post, 1993 (vs Salisbury St)
Most Touchdowns Passed: 10 — Bruce Swanson, N Park, 1968 (vs N Central)

RUSHING

Most Yards Gained: 382 — Kelly Ellis, Northern Iowa, 1979 (vs Western Illinois)
Most Touchdowns Rushed: 8 — Junior Wolf, Panhandle St, 1958 [vs St Mary (KS)]

RECEIVING

Most Passes Caught: 23 — Chris George, Glenville St, 1994 (vs W VA Wesleyan); Barry Wagner, Alabama A&M, 1989 (vs Clark Atlanta)
Most Yards Gained: 370 — Barry Wagner, Alabama A&M, 1989 (vs Clark Atlanta)
Most Touchdown Catches: 8 — Paul Zaeske, N Park, 1968 (vs N Central)

NCAA Division III Individual Records

Career

SCORING

Most Points Scored: 474 — Joe Dudek, Plymouth St, 1982-85
Most Touchdowns Scored: 79 — Joe Dudek, Plymouth St, 1982-85
Most Touchdowns Scored, Rushing: 76 — Joe Dudek, Plymouth St, 1982-85
Most Touchdowns Scored, Passing: 115 — Jim Ballard, Wilmington (OH)1990, Mt Union (OH) 91-93
Most Touchdowns Scored, Receiving: 55 — Chris Bisaillon, Illinois Wesleyan, 1989-92

RUSHING

Most Rushes: 1,152 — Anthony Russo, St John's (NY), 1990-93
Most Rushes per Game: 32.7 — Chris Sizemore, Bridgewater (VA), 1972-74
Most Yards Gained: 5,834 — Anthony Russo, St John's (NY), 1990-93
Most Yards Gained per Game: 154.8 — Kirk Matthieu, Maine-Maritime, 1989-93

Career *(Cont.)*

PASSING

Highest Passing Efficiency Rating: 159.5 — Jim Ballard, Wilmington (OH)1990, Mt Union (OH) 91-93
Most Passes Attempted: 1,696 — Kirk Baumgartner, WI-Stevens Point, 1986-89
Most Passes Completed: 883 — Kirk Baumgartner, WI-Stevens Point, 1986-89
Most Passes Completed per Game: 24.9 — Keith Bishop, Illinois Wesleyan, 1981; Wheaton (IL), 1983-85
Highest Completion Percentage: 62.2 — Brian Moore, Baldwin-Wallace, 1981-84
Most Yards Gained: 13,028 — Kirk Baumgartner, WI-Stevens Point, 1986-89
Most Yards Gained per Game: 317.8 — Kirk Baumgartner, WI-Stevens Point, 1986-89

RECEIVING

Most Passes Caught: 287 — Matt Newton, Principia (IL), 1990-93
Most Yards Gained: 3,846 — Dale Amos, Franklin & Marshall, 1986-89
Most Yards Gained per Game: 110.5 — Matt Newton, Principia (IL), 1990-93
Highest Average Gain per Reception: 20.0 — Marty Redlawsk, Concordia (IL), 1984-87

Single Season

SCORING

Most Points Scored: 194 — Carey Bender, Coe, 1994
Most Points Scored per Game: 19.4 — Carey Bender, Coe, 1994
Most Touchdowns Scored: 32 — Carey Bender, Coe, 1994
Most Touchdowns Scored, Rushing: 29 — Carey Bender, Coe, 1994
Most Touchdowns Scored, Passing: 39 — Kirk Baumgartner, WI-Stevens Point, 1989
Most Touchdowns Scored, Receiving: 20 — John Aromando, Trenton St, 1983

RUSHING

Most Rushes: 380 — Mike Birosak, Dickinson, 1989
Most Rushes per Game: 38.0 — Mike Birosak, Dickinson, 1989
Most Yards Gained: 2,243 — Carey Bender, Coe, 1994
Most Yards Gained per Game: 224.3 — Carey Bender, Coe, 1994

PASSING

Highest Passing Efficiency Rating: 225.0 — Mike Simpson, Eureka, 1994
Most Passes Attempted: 527 — Kirk Baumgartner, WI-Stevens Point, 1988
Most Passes Completed: 276 — Kirk Baumgartner, WI-Stevens Point, 1988
Most Passes Completed per Game: 29.1 — Keith Bishop, Illinois Wesleyan, 1985
Highest Completion Percentage: 73.4 — Mike Simpson, Eureka, 1994
Most Yards Gained: 3,828 — Kirk Baumgartner, WI-Stevens Point, 1988
Most Yards Gained per Game: 369.2 — Kirk Baumgartner, WI-Stevens Point, 1989

RECEIVING

Most Passes Caught: 106 — Theo Blanco, WI-Stevens Point, 1987
Most Yards Gained: 1,693 — Sean Munroe, Mass-Boston, 1992
Most Yards Gained per Game: 188.1 — Sean Munroe, Mass-Boston 1992
Highest Average Gain per Reception: 26.9 — Marty Redlawsk, Concordia (IL), 1985

Single Game

SCORING

Most Field Goals: 6 — Jim Hever, Rhodes, 1984 (vs Millsaps)

PASSING

Most Passes Completed: 50 — Tim Lynch, Hofstra, 1991 (vs Fordham)
Most Yards Gained: 602 — Tom Stallings, St Thomas (MN), 1993 (vs Bethel)
Most Touchdowns Passed: 8 — Steve Austin, Mass-Boston, 1992 (vs Framingham St); Kirk Baumgartner, WI-Stevens Point, 1989 (vs WI-Superior)

RUSHING

Most Yards Gained: 417 — Corey Bender, Coe, 1993 (vs Grinnell)
Most Touchdowns Rushed: 6 — Eric Leiser, Eureka, 1991, (vs Concordia); Rob Sinclair, Simpson, 1990 (vs Upper Iowa)

RECEIVING

Most Passes Caught: 23 — Sean Munroe, Mass-Boston, 1992 (vs Mass-Maritime)
Most Yards Gained: 332 — Sean Munroe, Mass-Boston, 1992 (vs Mass-Maritime)
Most Touchdown Catches: 5 — By 10 players. Most Recent: Sean Munroe, Mass-Boston, 1992 (vs Framingham St)

Career

Scoring

POINTS (KICKERS)

	Years	Pts
Roman Anderson, Houston	1988-91	423
Carlos Huerta, Miami (FL)	1988-91	397
Jason Elam, Hawaii	1988-92	395
Derek Schmidt, Florida St	1984-87	393
Luis Zendejas, Arizona St	1981-84	368

POINTS (NON-KICKERS)

	Years	Pts
Anthony Thompson, Indiana	1986-89	394
Marshall Faulk, San Diego St	1991-93	376
Tony Dorsett, Pittsburgh	1973-76	356
Glenn Davis, Army	1943-46	354
Art Luppino, Arizona	1953-56	337

POINTS PER GAME (NON-KICKERS)

	Years	Pts/Game
Marshall Faulk, San Diego St	1991-93	12.1
Bob Gaiters, New Mexico St	1959-60	11.9
Ed Marinaro, Cornell	1969-71	11.8
Bill Burnett, Arkansas	1968-70	11.3
Steve Owens, Oklahoma	1967-69	11.2

Total Offense

YARDS GAINED

	Years	Yds
Ty Detmer, Brigham Young	1988-91	14,665
Doug Flutie, Boston Col	1981-84	11,317
Alex Van Pelt, Pittsburgh	1989-92	10,814
Todd Santos, San Diego St	1984-87	10,513
Kevin Sweeney, Fresno St	1982-86	10,252

YARDS PER GAME

	Years	Yds/Game
Chris Vargas, Nevada	1992-93	320.9
Ty Detmer, Brigham Young	1988-91	318.8
Mike Perez, San Jose St	1986-87	309.1
Doug Gaynor, Long Beach St	1984-85	305.0
Tony Eason, Illinois	1981-82	299.5

Rushing

YARDS GAINED

	Years	Yds
Tony Dorsett, Pittsburgh	1973-76	6,082
Charles White, Southern Cal	1976-79	5,598
Herschel Walker, Georgia	1980-82	5,259
Archie Griffin, Ohio St	1972-75	5,177
Darren Lewis, Texas A&M	1987-90	5,012

YARDS PER GAME

	Years	Yds/Game
Ed Marinaro, Cornell	1969-71	174.6
O. J. Simpson, Southern Cal	1967-68	164.4
Herschel Walker, Georgia	1980-82	159.4
LeShon Johnson, N Illionis	1992-93	150.6
Marshall Faulk, San Diego St	1991-93	148.0

TOUCHDOWNS RUSHING

	Years	TD
Anthony Thompson, Indiana	1986-89	64
Marshall Faulk, San Diego St	1991-93	57
Steve Owens, Oklahoma	1967-69	56
Tony Dorsett, Pittsburgh	1973-76	55
Ed Marinaro, Cornell	1969-71	50

Passing

PASSING EFFICIENCY

	Years	Rating
Ty Detmer, Brigham Young	1988-91	162.7
Jim McMahon, Brigham Young	1977-78, 80-81	156.9
Steve Young, Brigham Young	1982, 84-86	149.8
Robbie Bosco, Brigham Young	1981-83	149.4
Chuck Long, Iowa	1981-85	148.9

Note: Minimum 500 completions.

YARDS GAINED

	Years	Yds
Ty Detmer, Brigham Young	1988-91	15,031
Todd Santos, San Diego St	1984-87	11,425
Alex Van Pelt, Pittsburgh	1989-92	10,913
Kevin Sweeney, Fresno St	1982-86	10,623
Doug Flutie, Boston Col	1981-84	10,579

Note: Minimum 500 completions.

COMPLETIONS

	Years	Comp
Ty Detmer, Brigham Young	1988-91	958
Todd Santos, San Diego St	1984-87	910
Brian McClure, Bowling Green	1982-85	900
Eric Wilhelm, Oregon St	1989-92	870
Alex Van Pelt, Pittsburgh	1989-92	845

Note: Minimum 500 completions.

TOUCHDOWNS PASSING

	Years	TD
Ty Detmer, Brigham Young	1988-91	121
David Klingler, Houston	1988-91	92
Troy Kopp, Pacific	1989-92	87
Jim McMahon, Brigham Young	1977-78,80-81	84
Joe Adams, Tennessee St	1977-80	81

Receiving

CATCHES

	Years	No.
Aaron Turner, Pacific	1989-92	266
Terance Mathis, New Mexico	1985-87, 89	263
Mark Templeton, Long Beach St	1983-86	262
Howard Twilley, Tulsa	1963-65	261
David Williams, Illinois	1983-85	245

CATCHES PER GAME

	Years	No./Game
Emmanuel Hazard, Houston	1989-90	10.5
Howard Twilley, Tulsa	1963-65	10.0
Jason Phillips, Houston	1987-88	9.4
Bryan Reeves Nevada	1991-93	7.6

Two tied with 7.4 rec. per game

YARDS GAINED

	Years	Yds
Ryan Yarborough	1990-93	4,357
Aaron Turner, Pacific	1989-92	4,345
Terance Mathis, New Mexico	1985-87,89	4,254
Marc Zeno, Tulane	1984-87	3,725
Ron Sellers, Florida St	1966-68	3,598

TOUCHDOWN CATCHES

	Years	TD
Aaron Turner, Pacific	1989-92	43
Ryan Yarborough, Wyoming	1990-93	42
Clarkston Hines, Duke	1986-89	38
Terance Mathis, New Mexico	1985-87,89	36
Elmo Wright, Houston	1968-70	34

Career *(Cont.)*

All-Purpose Running

YARDS GAINED	Years	Yds
Napoleon McCallum, Navy	1981-85	7172
Darrin Nelson, Stanford	1977-78,80-81	6885
Terance Mathis, New Mexico	1985-87,89	6691
Tony Dorsett, Pittsburgh	1973-76	6615
Paul Palmer, Temple	1983-86	6609

YARDS PER GAME	Years	Yds/Game
Ryan Benjamin, Pacific,	1990-92	237.8
Sheldon Canley, San Jose St	1988-90	205.8
Howard Stevens, Louisville	1971-72	193.7
O.J. Simpson, Southern Cal	1967-68	192.9
Ed Marinaro, Cornell	1969-71	183.0

Interceptions

PLAYER/SCHOOL	Years	Int
Al Brosky, Illinois	1950-52	29
John Provost, Holy Cross	1972-74	27
Martin Bayless, Bowling Green	1980-83	27
Tom Curtis, Michigan	1967-69	25
Tony Thurman, Boston Col	1981-84	25
Tracy Saul, Texas Tech	1989-92	25

Punting Average

PLAYER/SCHOOL	Years	Avg
Todd Sauerbrun, W Virginia	1991-94	46.3
Reggie Roby, Iowa	1979-82	45.6
Greg Montgomery, Michigan St	1985-87	45.4
Tom Tupa, Ohio St	1984-87	45.2
Barry Helton, Colorado	1984-87	44.9

Note: At least 150 punts kicked.

Punt Return Average

PLAYER/SCHOOL	Years	Avg
Jack Mitchell, Oklahoma	1946-48	23.6
Gene Gibson, Cincinnati	1949-50	20.5
Eddie Macon, Pacific	1949-51	18.9
Jackie Robinson, UCLA	1939-40	18.8
Mike Fuller, Auburn	1972-74	17.7
Bobby Dillon, Texas	1949-51	17.7

Note: At least 1.2 punt returns per game.

Kickoff Return Average

PLAYER/SCHOOL	Years	Avg
Forrest Hall, San Francisco	1946-47	36.2
Anthony Davis, Southern Cal	1972-74	35.1
Overton Curtis, Utah St	1957-58	31.0
Fred Montgomery, New Mexico St	1991-92	30.5
Altie Taylor, Utah St	1966-68	29.3

Note: At least 1.2 kickoff returns per game.

Mr. O'Leary's Cow

Rarely is heard a discouraging word these days from coaches about juniors who come out for the NFL draft. Rarely, but not never. "I'll be seeing you Sundays if I go to an NFL game," Georgia Tech assistant George O'Leary told Elliott Fortune, the Yellow Jacket defensive tackle who threw his name into the 1995 draft last spring. "Same as you, I'll be buying a ticket."

With his decision the 276-pound Fortune is severely testing his surname. Last season he started only four games. Still, he might have expected at least some moral support from his coach. Instead, O'Leary says, "I wish him well in his pursuit of impossibility. I told him. 'You've done some dumb things, but this is the dumbest.'"

Single Season

Scoring

POINTS	Year	Pts
Barry Sanders, Oklahoma St	1988	234
Mike Rozier, Nebraska	1983	174
Lydell Mitchell, Penn St	1971	174
Art Luppino, Arizona	1954	166
Bobby Reynolds, Nebraska	1950	157

FIELD GOALS	Year	FG
John Lee, UCLA	1984	29
Paul Woodside, W Virginia	1982	28
Luis Zendejas, Arizona St	1983	28
Fuad Reveiz, Tennessee	1982	27

Note: Three tied with 25 each.

All-Purpose Running

YARDS GAINED	Year	Yds
Barry Sanders, Oklahoma St	1988	3250
Ryan Benjamin, Pacific	1991	2995
Mike Pringle, Fullerton St	1989	2690
Paul Palmer, Temple	1986	2633
Ryan Benjamin, Pacific	1992	2597

All-Purpose Running *(Cont.)*

YARDS PER GAME	Years	Yds/Game
Barry Sanders, Oklahoma St	1988	295.5
Ryan Benjamin, Pacific	1991	249.6
Byron (Whizzer) White, Colorado	1937	246.3
Mike Pringle, Fullerton St	1989	244.6
Paul Palmer, Temple	1986	239.4

Total Offense

YARDS GAINED	Year	Yds
David Klingler, Houston	1990	5221
Ty Detmer, Brigham Young	1990	5022
Andre Ware, Houston	1989	4661
Jim McMahon, Brigham Young	1980	4627
Ty Detmer, Brigham Young	1989	4433

YARDS PER GAME	Year	Yds/Game
David Klingler, Houston	1990	474.6
Andre Ware, Houston	1989	423.7
Ty Detmer, Brigham Young	1990	418.5
Steve Young, Brigham Young	1983	395.1
Chris Vargas, Nevada	1993	393.8

Single Season (Cont.)

Rushing

YARDS GAINED

	Year	Yds
Barry Sanders, Oklahoma St	1988	2628
Marcus Allen, Southern Cal	1981	2342
Mike Rozier, Nebraska	1983	2148
Rashaan Salaam, Colorado	1994	2055
LeShon Johnson, N Illinois	1993	1976

YARDS PER GAME

	Year	Yds/Game
Barry Sanders, Oklahoma St	1988	238.9
Marcus Allen, Southern Cal	1981	212.9
Ed Marinaro, Cornell	1971	209.0
Rashaan Salaam, Colorado	1994	186.8
Charles White, Southern Cal	1979	180.3

TOUCHDOWNS RUSHING

	Year	TD
Barry Sanders, Oklahoma St	1988	37
Mike Rozier, Nebraska	1983	29
Ed Marinaro, Cornell	1971	24
Anthony Thompson, Indiana	1988	24
Anthony Thompson, Indiana	1989	24
Rashaan Salaam, Colorado	1994	24

Passing

PASSING EFFICIENCY

	Year	Rating
Jim McMahon, Brigham Young	1980	176.9
Ty Detmer, Brigham Young	1989	175.6
Trent Dilfer, Fresno St	1993	173.1
Kerry Collins, Penn St	1994	172.9
Jerry Rhome, Tulsa	1964	172.6

Passing (Cont.)

YARDS GAINED

	Year	Yds
Ty Detmer, Brigham Young	1990	5188
David Klingler, Houston	1990	5140
Andre Ware, Houston	1989	4699
Jim McMahon, Brigham Young	1980	4571
Ty Detmer, Brigham Young	1989	4560

COMPLETIONS

	Year	Att	Comp
David Klingler, Houston	1990	643	374
Andre Ware, Houston	1989	578	365
Ty Detmer, Brigham Young	1990	562	361
Robbie Bosco, Brigham Young	1985	511	338
Chris Vargas, Nevada	1993	490	331

TOUCHDOWNS PASSING

	Year	TD
David Klingler, Houston	1990	54
Jim McMahon, Brigham Young	1980	47
Andre Ware, Houston	1989	46
Ty Detmer, Brigham Young	1990	41
Dennis Shaw, San Diego St	1969	39

Receiving

CATCHES

	Year	GP	No.
Emmanuel Hazard, Houston	1989	11	142
Howard Twilley, Tulsa	1965	10	134
Jason Phillips, Houston	1988	11	108
Fred Gilbert, Houston	1991	11	106
Chris Penn, Tulsa	1993	11	105

CATCHES PER GAME

	Year	No.	No./Game
Howard Twilley, Tulsa	1965	134	13.4
Emmanuel Hazard, Houston	1989	142	12.9
Jason Phillips, Houston	1988	108	9.8
Chris Penn, Tulsa	1993	105	9.6
Fred Gilbert, Houston	1991	106	9.6
Jerry Hendren, Idaho	1969	95	9.5
Howard Twilley, Tulsa	1964	95	9.5

YARDS GAINED

	Year	Yds
Howard Twilley, Tulsa	1965	1779
Emmanuel Hazard, Houston	1989	1689
Aaron Turner, Pacific	1991	1604
Chris Penn, Tulsa	1993	1578
Chuck Hughes, UTEP*	1965	1519

*UTEP was Texas Western in 1965.

TOUCHDOWN CATCHES

	Year	TD
Emmanuel Hazard, Houston	1989	22
Desmond Howard, Michigan	1991	19
Aaron Turner, Pacific	1991	18
Dennis Smith, Utah	1989	18
Tom Reynolds, San Diego St	1969	18

Single Game

Scoring

POINTS

	Opponent	Year	Pts
Howard Griffith, Illinois	Southern Illinois	1990	48
Marshall Faulk, San Diego St	Pacific	1991	44
Jim Brown, Syracuse	Colgate	1956	43
Showboat Boykin, Mississippi	Mississippi St	1951	42
Fred Wendt, UTEP*	New Mexico St	1948	42
Dick Bass, Pacific	San Diego St	1958	38

*UTEP was Texas Mines in 1948.

FIELD GOALS

	Opponent	Year	FG
Dale Klein, Nebraska	Missouri	1985	7
Mike Prindle, Western Michigan	Marshall	1984	7

Note: Klein's distances were 32-22-43-44-29-43-43.
Prindle's distances were 32-44-42-23-48-41-27.

Single Game (Cont.)

Total Offense

YARDS GAINED	Opponent	Year	Yds
David Klingler, Houston ...Arizona St		1990	732
Matt Vogler, Texas Christian ....Houston		1990	696
David Klingler, Houston ...Texas Christian		1990	625
Scott Mitchell, Utah ....Air Force		1988	625
Jimmy Klingler, Houston ..Rice		1992	612

Passing

YARDS GAINED	Opponent	Year	Yds
David Klingler, Houston ...Arizona St		1990	716
Matt Vogler, Texas Christian ....Houston		1990	690
Scott Mitchell, Utah ....Air Force		1988	631
Jeremy Leach, New Mexico ....Utah		1989	622
Dave Wilson, Illinois ....Ohio St		1980	621

COMPLETIONS	Opponent	Year	Comp
David Klingler, Houston ....Southern Methodist		1990	48
Jimmy Klingler, Houston ....Rice		1992	46
Sandy Schwab, Northwestern............................Michigan		1982	45
Chuck Hartlieb, Iowa ....Indiana		1988	44
Jim McMahon, Brigham Young ....Colorado St		1981	44

TOUCHDOWNS PASSING	Opponent	Year	TD
David Klingler, Houston...........E. Wash		1990	11

Note: Klingler's TD passes were 5-48-29-7-3-7-40-10-7-8-51.

Rushing

YARDS GAINED	Opponent	Year	Yds
Tony Sands, Kansas.........Missouri		1991	396
Marshall Faulk, San Diego St.....................Pacific		1991	386
Anthony Thompson, Indiana.............................Wisconsin		1989	377
Mike Pringle, California St-Fullerton ....New Mexico St		1989	357
Rueben Mayes, Washington St ....Oregon		1984	357

TOUCHDOWNS RUSHING	Opponent	Year	TD
Howard Griffith, Illinois .....Southern Illinois		1990	8

Note: Griffith's TD runs were 5-51-7-41-5-18-5-3.

Receiving

CATCHES	Opponent	Year	No.
Randy Gatewood, UNLV.....Idaho		1994	23
Jay Miller, Brigham Young ..New Mexico		1973	22
Rick Eber, Tulsa...............Idaho St		1967	20
Emmanuel Hazard, Hou......Texas Christian		1989	19
Emmanuel Hazard, Hou......Texas		1989	19
Ron Fair, Arizona St ....Washington St		1989	19
Howard Twilley, Tulsa ....Colorado St		1965	19

YARDS GAINED	Opponent	Year	Yds
Randy Gatewood, UNLV ....Idaho		1994	363
Chuck Hughes, UTEP*...........N Texas St		1965	349
Rick Eber, Tulsa...................Idaho St		1967	322
Harry Wood, Tulsa...................Idaho St		1967	318
Jeff Evans, New Mexico St......Southern Illinois		1978	316

*UTEP was Texas Western in 1965.

TOUCHDOWN CATCHES	Opponent	Year	TD
Tim Delaney, San Diego St ...New Mexico St		1969	6

Note: Delaney's TD catches were 2-22-34-31-30-9.

Longest Plays (since 1941)

RUSHING	Opponent	Year	Yds
Gale Sayers, Kansas ....Nebraska		1963	99
Max Anderson, Arizona St......Wyoming		1967	99
Ralph Thompson, W Texas St..............................Wichita St		1970	99
Kelsey Finch, Tennessee ....Florida		1977	99

PASSING	Opponent	Year	Yds
Fred Owens to Jack Ford, Portland ....St Mary's (CA)		1947	99
Bo Burris to Warren McVea, Houston ....Washington St		1966	99
Colin Clapton to Eddie Jenkins, Holy Cross ....Boston U		1970	99
Terry Peel to Robert Ford, Houston ....Syracuse		1970	99
Terry Peel to Robert Ford, Houston ....San Diego St		1972	99
Cris Collinsworth to Derrick Gaffney, Florida ....Rice		1977	99
Scott Ankrom to James Maness, Texas Christian .....Rice		1984	99
Gino Toretta to Horace Copeland, Miami ....Arkansas		1991	99

FIELD GOALS	Opponent	Year	Yds
Steve Little, Arkansas ....Texas		1977	67
Russell Erxleben, Texas ....Rice		1977	67
Joe Williams, Wichita St.....Southern Illinois		1978	67
Tony Franklin, Texas A&M.Baylor		1976	65
Tony Franklin, Texas A&M.Baylor		1976	64
Russell Erxleben, Texas ....Oklahoma		1977	64

PUNTS	Opponent	Year	Yds
Pat Brady, Nevada* ....Loyola (CA)		1950	99
George O'Brien, Wisconsin....Iowa		1952	96
John Hadl, Kansas...............Oklahoma		1959	94
Carl Knox, Texas Christian.....Oklahoma St		1947	94
Preston Johnson, SMU...........Pittsburgh		1940	94

*Note: Nevada was Nevada-Reno in 1950.

Notable Achievements

DIVISION I-A WINNINGEST TEAMS
Alltime Winning Percentage

	Yrs	W	L	T	Pct	GP	Bowl Record
Notre Dame	106	729	216	42	.760	987	12-7-0
Michigan	115	747	246	36	.743	1,029	13-13-0
Alabama	100	703	238	44	.736	985	27-17-3
Oklahoma	100	665	246	52	.718	963	20-11-1
Texas	102	695	277	32	.708	1,004	17-16-2
Southern Cal	102	638	256	53	.702	947	24-13-0
Ohio St	105	668	269	53	.702	990	13-14-0
Nebraska	105	686	290	40	.695	1,016	15-18-0
Penn St	108	686	291	41	.694	1,018	19-10-2
Tennessee	98	644	280	53	.686	977	19-16-0
Central Michigan	94	489	258	36	.648	783	3-2-0
Florida St	48	325	177	17	.643	519	15-7-2
Washington	105	569	314	49	.637	932	12-8-1
Army	105	592	336	50	.632	976	2-1-0
Miami (OH)	106	551	313	43	.631	907	5-2-0
Georgia	101	595	337	54	.631	986	15-13-3
Louisiana St	101	577	332	46	.628	955	11-16-1
Arizona St	82	447	263	24	.625	734	9-5-1
Auburn	102	567	336	47	.622	950	12-9-2
Colorado	105	568	349	36	.615	953	7-12-0
Miami (FL)	68	421	262	19	.613	702	10-11-0
Bowling Green	76	398	245	52	.610	695	2-3-0
Michigan St	98	526	334	43	.606	903	5-6-0
UCLA	76	442	286	37	.602	765	10-8-1
Minnesota	111	558	367	43	.599	968	2-3-0

Note: Includes bowl games.

Alltime Victories

Michigan	747	Georgia	595	Minnesota	558
Notre Dame	729	Army	592	N Carolina	556
Alabama	703	Syracuse	590	Georgia Tech	556
Texas	695	Louisiana St	577	Arkansas	554
Penn St	686	Pittsburgh	569	Miami (OH)	551
Nebraska	686	Washington	569	Navy	549
Ohio St	668	Colorado	568	Rutgers	535
Oklahoma	665	Auburn	567	California	533
Tennessee	644	W Virginia	564	Clemson	530
Southern Cal	638	Texas A&M	559	Michigan St	526

NUMBER ONE VS NUMBER TWO

The number 1 and number 2 teams, according to the Associated Press Poll, have met 29 times, including 10 bowl games, since the poll's inception in 1936. The number 1 teams have a 17-10-2 record in these matchups. Notre Dame (4-3-2) has played in 9 of the games.

Date	Results	Stadium
10-9-43	No. 1 Notre Dame 35, No. 2 Michigan 12	Michigan (Ann Arbor)
11-20-43	No. 1 Notre Dame 14, No. 2 Iowa Pre-Flight 13	Notre Dame (South Bend)
12-2-44	No. 1 Army 23, No. 2 Navy 7	Municipal (Baltimore)
11-10-45	No. 1 Army 48, No. 2 Notre Dame 0	Yankee (New York)
12-1-45	No. 1 Army 32, No. 2 Navy 13	Municipal (Philadelphia)
11-9-46	No. 1 Army 0, No. 2 Notre Dame 0	Yankee (New York)
1-1-63	No. 1 Southern Cal 42, No. 2 Wisconsin 37 (Rose Bowl)	Rose Bowl (Pasadena)
10-12-63	No. 2 Texas 28, No. 1 Oklahoma 7	Cotton Bowl (Dallas)
1-1-64	No. 1 Texas 28, No. 2 Navy 6 (Cotton Bowl)	Cotton Bowl (Dallas)
11-19-66	No. 1 Notre Dame 10, No. 2 Michigan St 10	Spartan (East Lansing)
9-28-68	No. 1 Purdue 37, No. 2 Notre Dame 22	Notre Dame (South Bend)
1-1-69	No. 1 Ohio St 27, No. 2 Southern Cal 16 (Rose Bowl)	Rose Bowl (Pasadena)
12-6-69	No. 1 Texas 15, No. 2 Arkansas 14	Razorback (Fayetteville)
11-25-71	No. 1 Nebraska 35, No. 2 Oklahoma 31	Owen Field (Norman)
1-1-72	No. 1 Nebraska 38, No. 2 Alabama 6 (Orange Bowl)	Orange Bowl (Miami)

NUMBER ONE VS NUMBER TWO *(Cont.)*

Date	Results	Stadium
1-1-79	No. 2 Alabama 14, No. 1 Penn St 7 (Sugar Bowl)	Sugar Bowl (New Orleans)
9-26-81	No. 1 Southern Cal 28, No. 2 Oklahoma 24	Coliseum (Los Angeles)
1-1-83	No. 2 Penn St 27, No. 1 Georgia 23 (Sugar Bowl)	Sugar Bowl (New Orleans)
10-19-85	No. 1 Iowa 12, No. 2 Michigan 10	Kinnick (Iowa City)
9-27-86	No. 2 Miami (FL) 28, No. 1 Oklahoma 16	Orange Bowl (Miami)
1-2-87	No. 2 Penn St 14, No. 1 Miami (FL) 10 (Fiesta Bowl)	Fiesta Bowl (Tempe)
11-21-87	No. 2 Oklahoma 17, No. 1 Nebraska 7	Memorial (Lincoln)
1-1-88	No. 2 Miami (FL) 20, No. 1 Oklahoma 14 (Orange Bowl)	Orange Bowl (Miami)
11-26-88	No. 1 Notre Dame 27, No. 2 Southern Cal 10	Coliseum (Los Angeles)
9-16-89	No. 1 Notre Dame 24, No. 2 Michigan 19	Michigan (Ann Arbor)
11-16-91	No. 2 Miami (FL) 17, No. 1 Florida St 16	Campbell (Tallahassee)
1-1-93	No. 2 Alabama 34, No. 1 Miami (FL) 13	Superdome (New Orleans)
11-13-93	No. 2 Notre Dame 31, No. 1 Florida St 24	Notre Dame (South Bend)
1-1-94	No. 1 Florida St 18, No. 2 Nebraska 16 (Orange Bowl)	Orange Bowl (Miami)

Longest Winning Streaks

Wins	Team	Yrs	Ended by	Score
47	Oklahoma	1953-57	Notre Dame	7-0
39	Washington	1908-14	Oregon St	0-0
37	Yale	1890-93	Princeton	6-0
37	Yale	1887-89	Princeton	10-0
35	Toledo	1969-71	Tampa	21-0
34	Pennsylvania	1894-96	Lafayette	6-4
31	Oklahoma	1948-50	Kentucky	13-7
31	Pittsburgh	1914-18	Cleveland Naval Reserve	10-9
31	Pennsylvania	1896-98	Harvard	10-0
30	Texas	1968-70	Notre Dame	24-11
29	Michigan	1901-03	Minnesota	6-6
29	Miami (FL)	1990-93	Alabama	34-13

Longest Unbeaten Streaks

No.	W	T	Team	Yrs	Ended by	Score
63	59	4	Washington	1907-17	California	27-0
56	55	1	Michigan	1901-05	Chicago	2-0
50	46	4	California	1920-25	Olympic Club	15-0
48	47	1	Oklahoma	1953-57	Notre Dame	7-0
48	47	1	Yale	1885-89	Princeton	10-0
47	42	5	Yale	1879-85	Princeton	6-5
44	42	2	Yale	1894-96	Princeton	24-6
42	39	3	Yale	1904-08	Harvard	4-0
39	37	2	Notre Dame	1946-50	Purdue	28-14
37	36	1	Oklahoma	1972-75	Kansas	23-3
37	37	0	Yale	1890-93	Princeton	6-0
35	35	0	Toledo	1969-71	Tampa	21-0
35	34	1	Minnesota	1903-05	Wisconsin	16-12
34	33	1	Nebraska	1912-16	Kansas	7-3
34	34	0	Pennsylvania	1894-96	Lafayette	6-4
34	32	2	Princeton	1884-87	Harvard	12-0
34	29	5	Princeton	1877-82	Harvard	1-0
33	30	3	Tennessee	1926-30	Alabama	18-6
33	31	2	Georgia Tech	1914-18	Pittsburgh	32-0
33	30	3	Harvard	1911-15	Cornell	10-0
32	31	1	Nebraska	1969-71	UCLA	20-17
32	30	2	Army	1944-47	Columbia	21-20
32	31	1	Harvard	1898-1900	Yale	28-0
31	30	1	Penn St	1967-70	Colorado	41-13
31	30	1	San Diego St	1967-70	Long Beach St	27-11
31	29	2	Georgia Tech	1950-53	Notre Dame	27-14
31	30	1	Alabama	1991-93	Louisiana St	17-13
31	31	0	Oklahoma	1948-50	Kentucky	13-7
31	31	0	Pittsburgh	1919-22	Cleveland Naval	10-9
31	31	0	Pennsylvania	1896-98	Harvard	10-0

Note: Includes bowl games.

Longest Losing Streaks

L		Seasons	Ended Against	Score
44	Columbia	1983-88	Princeton	16-14
34	Northwestern	1979-82	Northern Illinois	31-6
28	Virginia	1958-61	William & Mary	21-6
28	Kansas St	1945-48	Arkansas St	37-6
27	Eastern Michigan	1980-82	Kent St	9-7

Longest Series

GP	Opponents (Series Leader Listed First)	Record	First Game	GP	Opponents (Series Leader Listed First)	Record	First Game
104	Minnesota-Wisconsin	57-39-8	1890	95	Navy-Army	44-44-7	1890
103	Missouri-Kansas	48-46-9	1891	92	Penn St-Pittsburgh†	47-41-4	1893
101	Nebraska-Kansas	77-21-3	1892	92	Louisiana St-Tulane*	63-22-7	1893
101	Texas Christian-Baylor	47-47-7	1899	92	Clemson-S Carolina	54-34-4	1896
101	Texas-Texas A&M	64-32-5	1894	92	Kansas-Kansas St	61-26-5	1902
99	N Carolina-Virginia	54-41-4	1892	92	Oklahoma-Kansas	62-24-6	1903
99	Miami (OH)-Cincinnati	53-39-7	1888	92	Utah-Utah St	61-27-4	1892
98	Auburn-Georgia	46-44-8	1892	91	Michigan-Ohio St	51-34-6	1897
98	Oregon-Oregon St	48-40-10	1894	91	Mississippi-Miss St	52-33-6	1901
97	Purdue-Indiana	58-33-6	1891	90	Auburn-Georgia Tech#	47-39-4	1892
97	Stanford-California	47-39-11	1892				

†Have not met since 1992; *Disputed series record.
Tulane claims 23-61-7 record. #Have not met since 1989

NCAA Coaches' Records

ALLTIME WINNINGEST DIVISION I-A COACHES
By Percentage

Coach (Alma mater)	Colleges Coached	Yrs	W	L	T	Pct
Knute Rockne (Notre Dame '14)†	Notre Dame 1918-30	13	105	12	5	.881
Frank W. Leahy (Notre Dame '31)†	Boston Col 1939-40; Notre Dame 1941-43, 1946-53	13	107	13	9	.864
George W. Woodruff (Yale '89)†	Pennsylvania 1892-01; Illinois 1903; Carlisle 1905	12	142	25	2	.846
Barry Switzer (Arkansas '60)	Oklahoma 1973-88	16	157	29	4	.837
Percy D. Haughton (Harvard '99)†	Cornell 1899-1900; Harvard 1908-16; Columbia 1923-24	13	96	17	6	.832
Bob Neyland (Army '16)†	Tennessee 1926-34, 1936-40, 1946-52	21	173	31	12	.829
Fielding (Hurry Up) Yost (Lafayette '97)†	Ohio Wesleyan 1897; Nebraska 1898; Kansas 1899; Stanford 1900; Michigan 1901-23, 1925-26	29	196	36	12	.828
Bud Wilkinson (Minnesota '37)†	Oklahoma 1947-63	17	145	29	4	.826
Tom Osborne (Hastings '59)*	Nebraska 1973-present	22	219	47	3	.820
Jock Sutherland (Pittsburgh '18)†	Lafayette 1919-23; Pittsburgh 1924-38	20	144	28	14	.812
Bob Devaney (Alma, MI '39)†	Wyoming 1957-61; Nebraska 1962-72	16	136	30	7	.806
Frank W. Thomas (Notre Dame '23)†	Chattanooga 1925-28; Alabama 1931-42, 1944-46	19	141	33	9	.795
Joe Paterno (Brown '50)*	Penn St 1966-present	29	269	69	3	.793
Henry L. Williams (Yale '91)†	Army 1891; Minnesota 1900-21	23	141	34	12	.786
Gil Dobie (Minnesota '02)†	N Dakota St 1906-07; Washington 1908-16; Navy 1917-19; Cornell 1920-35; Boston Col 1936-38	33	180	45	15	.781
Paul W. (Bear) Bryant (Alabama '36)†	Maryland 1945; Kentucky 1946-53; Texas A&M 1954-57; Alabama 1958-82	38	323	85	17	.780

*Active coach. †Hall of Fame member.
Note: Minimum 10 years as head coach at Division I institutions; record at 4-year colleges only; bowl games included; ties computed as half won, half lost.

ALLTIME WINNINGEST DIVISION I-A COACHES (Cont.)
By Victories

	Yrs	W	L	T	Pct		Yrs	W	L	T	Pct
Paul (Bear) Bryant	38	323	85	17	.780	Jess Neely	40	207	176	19	.539
Glenn (Pop) Warner	44	319	106	32	.733	*LaVell Edwards	23	207	76	3	.729
Amos Alonzo Stagg	57	314	199	35	.605	*Hayden Fry	33	205	157	10	.563
*Joe Paterno	29	269	69	3	.793	Warren Woodson	31	203	95	14	.673
*Bobby Bowden	29	249	79	4	.756	Vince Dooley	25	201	77	10	.715
Woody Hayes	33	238	72	10	.759	Eddie Anderson	39	201	128	15	.606
Bo Schembechler	27	234	65	8	.775	Lou Holtz	25	199	89	7	.686
*Tom Osborne	22	219	47	3	.820	Dana Bible	33	198	72	23	.715

Most Bowl Victories

	W	L	T		W	L	T
*Joe Paterno	16	8	1	*Terry Donahue	8	3	1
Paul (Bear) Bryant	15	12	2	Barry Switzer	8	5	0
*Bobby Bowden	14	3	1	Darrell Royal	8	7	1
Jim Wacker	13	2	0	Vince Dooley	8	10	2
Don James	10	5	0	Bob Devaney	7	3	0
*Lou Holtz	10	7	2	Dan Devine	7	3	0
John Vaught	10	8	0	Earle Bruce	7	5	0
Bobby Dodd	9	4	0	Charlie McClendon	7	6	0
*Johnny Majors	9	7	0	*Active coach.			
*Tom Osborne	9	13	0				

WINNINGEST ACTIVE DIVISION I-A COACHES
By Percentage

Coach, College	Yrs	W	L	T	Pct#	Bowls		
						W	L	T
R.C. Slocum, Texas A&M	6	59	12	2	.822	1	4	0
Tom Osborne, Nebraska	22	219	47	3	.820	9	13	0
Joe Paterno, Penn St	29	269	69	3	.793	16	8	1
John Robinson, Southern Cal	9	83	22	3	.782	6	1	0
Bobby Bowden, Florida St	29	249	79	4	.756	14	3	1
Steve Spurrier, Florida	8	69	25	2	.729	2	3	0
LaVell Edwards, Brigham Young	23	207	76	3	.729	6	12	1
Danny Ford, Arkansas	14	105	41	5	.712	6	2	0
Lou Holtz, Notre Dame	25	199	89	7	.686	10	7	2
Terry Donahue, UCLA	19	144	69	8	.670	8	3	1

#Bowl games included. Ties computed as half win, half loss.
Note: Minimum 5 years as Division I-A head coach; record at 4-year colleges only.

Happy Valley Trails

After 33 college underclassmen renounced their remaining eligibility in mid-January to enter April's NFL draft, we were struck by how a hide-bound attitude, long prevalent in college football, has diminished over the past decade. Remember when Bernie Kosar left Miami in 1985 with two years of eligibility remaining? Though Kosar had already earned his degree, doing so in 3.27 style, and delivered a national championship to Coral Gables, he was labled an ingrate by the Miami faithful, and the school declined to retire his number. A year and a half later the Hurricanes' Vinny Testaverde, who indentured himself for four seasons, had his jersey retired—even though he didn't graduate or win a national title.

Contrast those reactions with the way Penn State handled the news that Ki-Jana Carter, who intends to graduate with this year's class, will pass up his senior season. Fans, students, local sportswriters and coach Joe Paterno have all wished Carter the best. It has taken a while, but the college football world seems finally to have gotten the message: You go to college to get your degree. After that it's O.K. to get on with your life, whether or not that life includes the NFL.

WINNINGEST ACTIVE DIVISION I-A COACHES (Cont.)
By Victories

Joe Paterno, Penn St	269	Don Nehlen, W Virginia	163
Bobby Bowden, Florida St	249	Bill Mallory, Indiana	162
Tom Osborne, Nebraska	219	Al Molde, W Michigan	159
LaVell Edwards, Brigham Young	207	Jim Wacker, Minnesota	153
Hayden Fry, Iowa	205	Terry Donahue, UCLA	144
Lou Holtz, Notre Dame	199	George Welsh, Virginia	144
Jim Sweeney, Fresno St	191	John Cooper, Ohio St	135
Johnny Majors, Tennessee, Pitt	179		

WINNINGEST ACTIVE DIVISION I-AA COACHES
By Percentage

Coach, College	Yrs	W	L	T	Pct*
Terry Allen, N Iowa	6	55	19	0	.743
Jim Donnan, Marshall	5	52	18	0	.743
Roy Kidd, Eastern Kentucky	31	257	91	8	.733
Eddie Robinson, Grambling	52	397	143	15	.729
Jim Tressel, Youngstown St	9	84	33	2	.714
Tubby Raymond, Delaware	29	239	95	3	.714
Tim Stowers, Georgia Southern	5	42	19	0	.689
Steve Tosches, Princeton	8	53	26	1	.669
Bobby Keasler, McNeese St	5	40	20	2	.661
Bill Hayes, N Carolina A&T	19	137	71	2	.657

*Playoff games included.
Note: Minimum 5 years as a Division I-A and/or Division I-AA head coach; record at 4-year colleges only.

By Victories

Eddie Robinson, Grambling	397	Bill Bowes, New Hampshire	152
Roy Kidd, Eastern Kentucky	257	Willie Jeffries, S Carolina St	142
Tubby Raymond, Delaware	239	Don Read, Montana	141
Carmen Cozza, Yale	174	Bill Hayes, N Carolina A&T	137
Ron Randleman, Sam Houston St	161	James Donnelly, Middle Tennessee St	132

WINNINGEST ACTIVE DIVISION II COACHES
By Percentage

Coach, College	Yrs	W	L	T	Pct*
Chuck Broyles, Pittsburg St	5	57	7	1	.885
Rocky Hager, N Dakota St	8	75	18	1	.803
Ken Sparks, Carson-Newman	15	140	37	2	.788
Peter Yetten, Bentley	7	49	13	1	.786
Ron Taylor, Quincy	6	43	15	2	.733
Bob Cortese, Fort Hays St	15	119	43	4	.729
Danny Hale, Bloomsburg	7	53	22	0	.707
Frank Cignetti, Indiana (PA)	13	109	45	1	.706
Dick Lowry, Hillsdale	21	159	66	3	.704
Hal Mumme, Valdosta St	6	48	20	1	.703

*Ties computed as half win, half loss. Playoff games included.

Note: Minimum 5 years as a college head coach; record at 4-year colleges only.

By Victories

Jim Malosky, MN-Duluth	235	Bud Elliott, E New Mexico St	143
Gene Carpenter, Millersville	175	Ken Sparks, Carson-Newman	140
Ron Harms, Texas A&M-Kingsville*	175	Claire Boroff, Kearney St	140
Dick Lowry, Hillsdale	159	Dennis Douds, E Stroudsburg	129
Willard Bailey, Virginia Union	158	Bob Cortese, Fort Hays St	119
Douglas Porter, Fort Valley St	146	*Formerly Texas A&I	

WINNINGEST ACTIVE DIVISION III COACHES
By Percentage

Coach, College	Yrs	W	L	T	Pct*
Ken O'Keefe, Allegheny	5	51	6	1	.888
Bob Reade, Augustana (IL)	16	146	23	1	.862
Dick Farley, Williams	8	53	9	2	.844
Larry Kehres, Mt Union	9	84	15	3	.838
Ron Schipper, Central (IA)	34	270	63	3	.808
John Luckhardt, Wash&Jeff	13	108	27	2	.796
Bob Packard, Baldwin-Wallace	14	111	29	2	.789
Roger Harring, WI-LaCrosse	26	218	62	7	.772
Pete Schmidt, Albion	12	87	25	4	.767
John Gagliardi, St John's (MN)	46	317	98	10	.758

*Ties computed as half win, half loss. Playoff games included.

Note: Minimum 5 years as a college head coach; record at 4-year colleges only.

By Victories

John Gagliardi, St John's (MN)	317	Frank Girardi, Lycoming	161
Ron Schipper, Central (IA)	270	Don Miller, Trinity (CT)	154
Roger Harring, WI-LaCrosse	218	Joe McDaniel, Centre	150
Bill Manlove, Delaware Valley	189	Bob Reade, Augustana (IL)	146
Jim Christopherson, Concordia-M'head	181	Peter Mazzaferro, Bridgewater (MA)	145

NAIA Coaches' Records

WINNINGEST ACTIVE NAIA COACHES
By Percentage

Coach, College	Yrs	W	L	T	Pct*
Ted Kessinger, Bethany (KS)	19	154	36	1	.809
Frosty Westering, Pacific Lutheran (WA)	29	235	73	6	.758
Hank Biesiot, Dickinson State, (ND)	19	117	42	1	.734
Dick Strahm, Findlay (OH)	21	142	57	3	.710
Dick Lowry, Hillsdale (MI)	20	159	66	3	.704
Bob Petrino, Carroll (MT)	24	147	63	1	.699
Brian Byers, Friends (KS)	7	48	25	0	.658
Jimmie Keeling, Hardin-Simmons (TX)	5	36	19	0	.655
Rob Smith, Western Washington	6	36	20	1	.640
Morris Sloan, Southeastern Oklahoma	6	36	20	3	.636

*Playoff games included.

Note: Minimum five years as a collegiate head coach and includes record against four-year institutions only.

By Victories

Frosty Westering, Pacific Lutheran (WA)	235	Dick Strahm, Findlay (OH)	142
Buddy Benson, Ouachita Baptist (AR)	160	Bill Ramseyer, Clinch Valley (VA)	131
Dick Lowry, Hillsdale (MI)	159	Hank Biesiot, Dickinson State (ND)	117
Ted Kessinger, Bethany (KS)	154	Tom Dowling, Cumberland (KY)	104
Bob Petrino, Carroll (MT)	147	Bob Brush, Georgetown (KY)	104

Pro Basketball

JUNE 19, 1995 · $2.95 (CAN. $3.95)

Sports Illustrated

RED HOT

Clyde Drexler lifts the
Houston Rockets toward their
second straight NBA title

JOHN W. MCDONOUGH

Recurring Dream

Hakeem Olajuwon put together an awesome postseason and led the Rockets to an improbable second straight NBA title

by Phil Taylor

IT WAS a time machine of a season. One moment we were years into the future, watching tomorrow's team, the Orlando Magic, dominate the NBA as if its time had already come. The next second we had taken a step back into the league's recent, glorious past, as Michael Jordan laid down his bat and glove and made a thrilling return to the Chicago Bulls, at times soaring and slashing as if he had never left, a memory come back to life.

But in the end the Houston Rockets brought us back to the present and made us realize that they are the team of the moment. The Rockets meandered through the 1994–95 regular season largely unnoticed as flashier teams and players took turns grabbing the public's attention. But the spotlight finally came back to Houston, and when it did, it found the Rockets hugging the championship trophy for the second consecutive year after finishing a four-game sweep of Orlando.

Indeed, the season ended much as it had the year before, with Houston center Hakeem (The Dream) Olajuwon, the 7-foot

package of grace and class from Nigeria, carrying the Rockets to the title and earning another Finals MVP award. But this time Olajuwon surpassed even his own lofty standards. The Rockets, who entered the playoffs with only the sixth-best record in the Western Conference, became champions again largely because Olajuwon would not let them lose. The Dream produced a playoff performance for the ages, one of the greatest series of individual efforts any sport has seen in years.

Olajuwon averaged 33 points and 10.3 rebounds in the playoffs, including 16 games of more than 30 points and five of more than 40, but numbers cannot do him justice. With his feints and spins and pump fakes, he not only outplayed opponents, he embarrassed them. Even David Robinson, the San Antonio Spurs' All-Star center, was victimized by the Dream. The Spurs had finished with the best record in the regular season, Robinson had been named the league MVP, and San Antonio had won five of the six games against Houston in the regular season, but it quickly became clear that none of that mat-

Olajuwon's performance in the conference final was one for the ages.

tered because this was Olajuwon's series. He so thoroughly humiliated Robinson that the San Antonio center looked lost. "I've never felt this way before," Robinson said after the Rockets had won the series in six games. "The strange thing is, I actually thought I played him pretty well."

It wasn't that Robinson played poorly, it was that Olajuwon was magnificent. "The series he played against San Antonio is going to be legendary," Houston coach Rudy Tomjanovich said. "People will be talking about that series and how he played for many, many years to come."

But despite Olajuwon's brilliance, the Rockets' championship will be associated just as much with his close friend guard Clyde Drexler. College teammates at the University of Houston, Drexler and Olajuwon were members of the 1983 Phi Slama Jama squad that fell to North Carolina State in one of the greatest championship game upsets in history. Drexler, a Houston native, had gone on to a stellar pro career with the Portland Trail Blazers, but unlike Olajuwon, he had never been able to complete the climb to a championship. The two had often talked over the years about how wonderful it would be to play together again, but neither thought it would ever be anything more than a fantasy until the Rockets traded forward Otis Thorpe to Portland in February for Drexler and forward Tracy Murray.

championship, his desire for a title was evident with every length-of-the-court rush he took in the Finals, racing headlong for the basket as if the championship ring were waiting there. "It's as sweet as I thought it would be," he said when it was over. "I don't know if I can describe the feeling." He didn't have to.

Jordan is quite familiar with that championship feeling. He led the Bulls to three straight titles before retiring in 1993 and taking up baseball. But discouraged by the labor problems in baseball and by his .202 batting average with the Double A Birmingham Barons, Jordan abruptly decided to return to the NBA in March, in time for the Bulls' last 17 regular-season games and the playoffs. After weeks of speculation and rumors, Jordan made his return official by issuing a two-word statement, "I'm back."

His return—wearing number 45 instead of his old number 23—sent a buzz of excitement through the league. At 32, could he simply pick up where he left off, in midair? Could he transform the Bulls from a mediocre team to a championship contender almost overnight? Some nights, the answer to both questions seemed to be yes. Although his jump shot betrayed him in the early going, as in his 7-for-28 shooting performance in his first game back, against Indiana, Jordan was his old spectacular self amazingly often. He beat the Atlanta Hawks with a buzzer-beating jumper in his first week back, then "dropped a double-nickel on the Knicks," as film director Spike Lee put it, devastating New York with an incendiary 55-point performance that ended with a brilliant pass to teammate Bill

The Houston front office was heavily criticized for the trade, even by some of the Rocket players. By giving up Thorpe the Rockets had created a rebounding hole that they appeared unable to fill. "Nothing against Clyde, but this is a hard one to figure out," forward Mario Elie said the day after the trade was announced. "I don't know how we're going to replace O.T."

But Drexler eventually won his teammates over by providing badly needed offense, especially during a 15-day stretch in March and April when Olajuwon was sidelined by anemia. In addition to offense, Drexler brought hunger to Houston. If there was any complacency among the Rockets after their first championship, bringing in a 32-year-old star who had never won a title was the perfect antidote. Although Drexler is a master of the plain vanilla quote, even when talking about his passion for winning a

Shaq was a force, leading the Magic all the way to the Finals.

Wennington for a dunk that won the game for Chicago.

But it eventually became clear that not even the great Jordan could come back and dominate the league as if he had never left. Age, rust and lack of familiarity with his teammates combined to keep him from leading the Bulls back to the championship. In the eagerly anticipated and over-hyped Eastern Conference semifinals against Orlando—the battle of Air Jordan vs. Shaq—Jordan made misplays in Games 1 and 6 that cost the Bulls dearly, and the Magic dispatched Chicago in six games.

In retrospect it's clear that anyone who expected Jordan to turn back the clock to the Bulls' championship years was asking too much. Jordan was competing not so much against other NBA teams as against our memory of him, which had become distorted during his absence. We remembered only the hang time and the wagging tongue and the championships, and so the mistakes caught us by surprise. In the end even Jordan gave in to the temptation to try to step back in time. After Game 1 against Orlando, in which Magic guard Nick Anderson stole the ball from him in the final minutes to help Orlando to a come-from-behind win, Jordan came out for Game 2 in number 23, despite the fact that the Bulls had retired it in an emotional ceremony before the season. The switch came as a complete surprise to even Jordan's teammates and especially to the officials in the NBA office, who fined the Bulls for the unapproved switch.

Jordan wore 23 for the rest of the playoffs, but that couldn't stop the Magic. After Orlando eliminated the Bulls, Jordan sat at his locker for more than an hour, analyzing his return for reporters. "I probably expected too much of myself," he said. "I saw a league where only Houston had any real championship experience, and I thought there was a chance for me to come in and maybe help this team steal a title. But my teammates and I never really got to know each other as well as you have to if you're going to win a championship. It didn't work out as well as I planned, but I have no regrets about doing it this way. I'm glad I came back." Basketball fans around the world no doubt felt the same way.

Jordan's return made O'Neal the second-most-famous player in the league, but it didn't keep Shaq from winning his first scoring title, with 29.3 points per game. O'Neal and the Magic looked close to invincible for most of the season, maintaining the league's best record for much of the year before stumbling during the last month of the regular season. O'Neal was still busy with endorsements and other off-the-court

MANNY MILLAN

riors, which in turn led to Nelson's resignation three months later. Nelson, however, wasn't unemployed for long. In July he was named the new coach of the Knicks.

Other players missed practices and shootarounds without permission, including New Jersey Net forward Derrick Coleman, Golden State guard Latrell Sprewell, Minnesota Timberwolf guard Isaiah Rider, and the poster child for misbehavior, San Antonio Spur forward Dennis Rodman. Seattle forward Vincent Askew refused coach George Karl's order to enter a game (although he later acknowledged his mistake and apologized for it), but the single most ridiculous act of defiance was perpetrated by New Jersey's Chris Morris. The Nets' forward took the floor for a practice shootaround one morning in December with his shoelaces undone. Then he refused coach Butch Beard's order to tie them. His explanation: "I wasn't planning on doing much running."

Fortunately for the NBA, Grant Hill came along just in time to remind everyone that not all of the league's young players were immature and spoiled. Hill, the first-round draft choice of the Detroit Pistons, was a model of humility and grace as well as a smooth and explosive forward. Fans loved him as much for his off-the-court personality as for his on-the-court excellence, and they showed it by making him the leading vote-getter in the All-Star Game balloting. It was the first time a rookie had ever earned the most All-Star votes, but Hill had to share the Rookie of the Year award with Dallas Maverick guard Jason Kidd, a passing and defensive marvel whose suspect outside shot improved dramatically by season's end.

It was an excellent year for rookies. The Milwaukee Bucks' Glenn Robinson, the top overall pick of the draft, was such an offensive threat that teams quickly began double-teaming him on a regular basis, a rare kind of honor for a rookie. After an early-season holdout, Robinson led the

activities, but he silenced many of those who criticized him for not working hard enough to improve his basketball skills by unveiling a variety of new offensive moves.

In fact, the 23-year-old Shaq set an example for behavior both on and off the court that several of the other young players in the league would have done well to follow. Players rebelled against their coaches during the 1994–95 season as never before, and the lack of respect for authority was especially apparent in, but not limited to, some of the league's young stars. The confrontation between Golden State coach Don Nelson and his star forward, second-year player Chris Webber, set the tone for the season. Unhappy with what he considered overly harsh treatment by Nelson, Webber held out at the start of the year and basically forced the Warrior management to choose between him and Nelson. The Warriors ended up losing both men. Golden State traded Webber to the Washington Bullets in November, which led to a malaise among the other War-

Bucks in scoring, with 21.9 points per game. Washington's Juwan Howard progressed even faster than even the Bullets expected, and a pair of rookie forwards, Brian Grant and Michael Smith, helped transform the previously hapless Sacramento Kings into a competitive club that missed the playoffs by only one game.

But although the action on the floor was as exciting as ever, the league continued to suffer blemishes in other areas. *The Wall Street Journal* delivered a serious blow with a story in March that suggested that the death of Boston Celtic star Reggie Lewis two years earlier was not simply the tragic case of a player succumbing to a heart abnormality. *The Journal* alleged that Lewis was a cocaine user and that the drug might have been a contributing factor in his death. The story also raised several other issues, the most serious of which were that the Celtics may have allowed financial and public-relations concerns to take precedence over Lewis's medical care; that the supposedly enlightened NBA drug policy helped prevent an accurate assessment of Lewis's condition; and that his wife, Donna Harris Lewis, intimidated the state of Massachusetts into officially declaring a phony cause of death.

The Celtics and Harris Lewis angrily denied the article's allegations, and though some questions remained unanswered about Lewis's death, it didn't stop the Celtics from staging an emotional ceremony retiring his number a few weeks after the publication of the article. Whatever the circumstances surrounding his death, it was clear that a great many Celtic fans chose to remember his life and career fondly.

Again, the games came to the rescue. The allegations about Lewis arose at almost exactly the same time that word of Jordan's comeback plans became public. San Antonio fans went wild over the Spurs' brilliant 62–20 regular season, highlighted by Robinson's MVP award and the relentless rebounding—and rotating hair colors—of

Miller smoked the Knicks for eight points in 18 seconds in the semis.

JOHN W. MCDONOUGH

Rodman. But Rodman's individualism finally became a problem in the playoffs when he was benched for a game because he took his shoes off and blatantly ignored coach Bob Hill in a timeout during the Spurs' series against the Los Angeles Lakers. That was just the beginning, as Rodman made a spectacle of himself during the playoffs and proved a distraction to the Spurs, who finally fell to Houston in the conference finals.

But if the Spurs had a disappointing playoff performance, others, like Olajuwon and Indiana Pacer guard Reggie Miller, had superb ones. The highlight of Miller's post-season effort—and perhaps the single best individual performance of the playoffs—was his last-second devastation of the Knicks. With New York leading by six points with 18 seconds left, it appeared that the Knicks had the victory in Game 1 of their semifinal series wrapped up. But Miller hit a three-pointer, made a steal, hit another three-pointer, grabbed a rebound

and made two foul shots all in that 18 second span to give the Pacers a 107–105 victory. The stunned Knicks never really recovered from that game, losing the series in seven to the Pacers.

Miller's Game 1 heroics began the final chapter in New York coach Pat Riley's tenure with the Knicks. Three weeks after the Knicks' elimination, Riley resigned, unhappy with Knick management's refusal to give him greater front-office control of the club. Riley and Knick president Dave Checketts parted bitterly, and the Knicks filed tampering charges against the Miami Heat when it became clear that Riley was interested in taking over as the Heat's coach. Miami and New York finally reached a settlement, with the Heat giving the Knicks a first-round draft pick and $1 million in exchange for the Knicks dropping their tampering charge and releasing Riley from the final year of his contract. Several days later Riley signed a lucrative deal with the Heat that made him coach—at a reported $3 million per year—and part owner of the team.

Riley's move was one of the few transactions in the two months following the NBA Finals, because the league imposed a lockout of the players on July 1, having reached an impasse in negotiations with the NBA Players Association for a new collective bargaining agreement. The issue quickly became even more complicated than most labor disputes in sports, with a large segment of the players, led by Jordan and Knick center Patrick Ewing, pushing for decertification of the NBAPA.

However, as the summer came to a close and the opening of training camps loomed, the players voted by a landslide margin to both retain the union and ratify the new collective bargaining agreement, thereby ending the 79-day lockout.

No doubt the fans will have forgotten the entire dispute by the time they see Jordan soar to the hoop in November, and therein lies a lesson for all pro sports.

FOR THE RECORD·1994–1995

NBA Final Standings

Eastern Conference

ATLANTIC DIVISION					CENTRAL DIVISION				
Team	W	L	Pct	GB	Team	W	L	Pct	GB
Orlando	57	25	.695	—	Indiana	52	30	.634	—
New York	55	27	.671	2	Charlotte	50	32	.610	2
Boston	35	47	.427	22	Chicago	47	35	.573	5
Miami	32	50	.390	25	Cleveland	43	39	.524	9
New Jersey	30	52	.366	27	Atlanta	42	40	.512	10
Philadelphia	24	58	.293	33	Milwaukee	34	48	.415	17
Washington	21	61	.256	36	Detroit	28	54	.341	24

Western Conference

MIDWEST DIVISION					PACIFIC DIVISION				
Team	W	L	Pct	GB	Team	W	L	Pct	GB
San Antonio	62	20	.756	—	Phoenix	59	23	.720	—
Utah	60	22	.732	2	Seattle	57	25	.695	2
Houston	47	35	.573	15	LA Lakers	48	34	.585	11
Denver	41	41	.500	21	Portland	44	38	.537	15
Dallas	36	46	.439	26	Sacramento	39	43	.476	20
Minnesota	21	61	.256	41	Golden State	26	56	.317	33
					LA Clippers	17	65	.207	42

1995 NBA Playoffs

EASTERN CONFERENCE

1st ROUND · SEMIFINALS · FINALS

Orlando
Boston — Orlando (3-1)
Charlotte — Orlando (4-2)
Chicago — Chicago (3-1)
New York — Orlando (4-3)
Cleveland — New York (3-1)
Indiana — Indiana (4-3)
Atlanta — Indiana (3-0)

NBA FINALS

HOUSTON (4-0)

WESTERN CONFERENCE

FINALS · SEMIFINALS · 1st ROUND

San Antonio (3-0) — San Antonio
San Antonio (4-2) — Denver
Phoenix (3-0) — Phoenix
Houston (4-2) — Portland
Houston (3-2) — Utah
Houston (4-3) — Houston
LA Lakers (3-1) — Seattle
LA Lakers

Eastern Conference First Round

Apr 27	Atlanta	82	at Indiana	90	
Apr 29	Atlanta	97	at Indiana	105	
May 2	Indiana	105	at Atlanta	89	

Indiana won series 3–0.

Apr 27	Cleveland	79	at New York	103	
Apr 29	Cleveland	90	at New York	84	
May 1	New York	83	at Cleveland	81	
May 4	New York	93	at Cleveland	80	

New York won series 3–1.

Apr 28	Boston	77	at Orlando	124	
Apr 30	Boston	99	at Orlando	92	
May 3	Orlando	82	at Boston	77	
May 5	Orlando	95	at Boston	92	

Orlando won series 3–1.

Apr 28	Chicago	108	at Charlotte	100*	
Apr 30	Chicago	89	at Charlotte	106	
May 2	Charlotte	80	at Chicago	103	
May 4	Charlotte	84	at Chicago	85	

Chicago won series 3–1.

Western Conference First Round

Apr 28	Denver	88	at San Antonio	104	
Apr 30	Denver	96	at San Antonio	122	
May 2	San Antonio	99	at Denver	95	

San Antonio won series 3–0.

Apr 27	Houston	100	at Utah	102	
Apr 29	Houston	140	at Utah	126	
May 3	Utah	95	at Houston	82	
May 5	Utah	106	at Houston	123	
May 7	Houston	95	at Utah	91	

Houston won series 3–2.

Apr 28	Portland	102	at Phoenix	129	
Apr 30	Portland	94	at Phoenix	103	
May 2	Phoenix	117	at Portland	109	

Phoenix won series 3–0.

Apr 27	LA Lakers	71	at Seattle	96	
Apr 29	LA Lakers	84	at Seattle	82	
May 1	Seattle	101	at LA Lakers	105	
May 4	Seattle	110	at LA Lakers	114	

LA Lakers won series 3–1.

Eastern Conference Semifinals

May 7	Indiana	107	at New York	105	
May 9	Indiana	77	at New York	96	
May 11	New York	95	at Indiana	97*	
May 13	New York	84	at Indiana	98	
May 17	Indiana	95	at New York	96	
May 19	New York	92	at Indiana	82	
May 21	Indiana	97	at New York	95	

Indiana won series 4–3.

May 7	Chicago	91	at Orlando	94	
May 10	Chicago	104	at Orlando	94	
May 12	Orlando	110	at Chicago	101	
May 14	Orlando	95	at Chicago	106	
May 16	Chicago	95	at Orlando	103	
May 18	Orlando	108	at Chicago	102	

Orlando won series 4–2.

Western Conference Semifinals

May 6	LA Lakers	94	at San Antonio	110	
May 8	LA Lakers	90	at San Antonio	97*	
May 12	San Antonio	85	at LA Lakers	92	
May 14	San Antonio	80	at LA Lakers	71	
May 16	LA Lakers	98	at San Antonio	96*	
May 18	San Antonio	100	at LA Lakers	88	

San Antonio won series 4–2.

May 9	Houston	108	at Phoenix	130	
May 11	Houston	94	at Phoenix	118	
May 13	Phoenix	85	at Houston	118	
May 14	Phoenix	114	at Houston	110	
May 16	Houston	103	at Phoenix	97*	
May 18	Phoenix	103	at Houston	116	
May 20	Houston	115	at Phoenix	114	

Houston won series 4–3.

Eastern Conference Finals

May 23	Indiana	101	at Orlando	105	
May 25	Indiana	114	at Orlando	119	
May 27	Orlando	100	at Indiana	105	
May 29	Orlando	93	at Indiana	94	
May 31	Indiana	106	at Orlando	108	
June 2	Orlando	96	at Indiana	123	
June 4	Indiana	81	at Orlando	105	

Orlando won series 4–3.

Western Conference Finals

May 22	Houston	94	at San Antonio	93	
May 24	Houston	106	at San Antonio	96	
May 26	San Antonio	107	at Houston	102	
May 28	San Antonio	103	at Houston	81	
May 30	Houston	111	at San Antonio	90	
June 1	San Antonio	95	at Houston	100	

Houston won series 4–2.

Finals

June 7	Houston	120	at Orlando	118*	
June 9	Houston	117	at Orlando	106	
June 11	Orlando	103	at Houston	106	
June 15	Orlando	101	at Houston	113	

Houston won series 4–0.

* Overtime game.

NBA Finals Composite Box Score

HOUSTON ROCKETS

Player	GP	Field Goals		3-Pt FG		Free Throws		Rebounds		A	Stl	TO	BS	Avg	Hi
		FGM	Pct	FGM	FGA	FTM	Pct	Off	Total						
Olajuwon	4	56	48.3	1	1	18	69.2	11	46	22	8	11	8	32.8	35
Drexler	4	27	45.0	2	13	30	78.9	13	38	27	4	6	1	21.5	25
Horry	4	23	43.4	11	29	14	66.7	9	40	15	12	5	9	17.8	21
Elie	4	24	64.9	8	14	9	90.0	4	17	13	8	7	0	16.3	22
Cassell	4	15	42.9	7	15	20	83.3	1	7	12	7	6	0	12	31
Smith	4	11	37.9	8	19	0	—	2	7	16	1	2	0	7.5	23
Brown	4	5	45.4	0	1	2	100.0	3	11	0	0	1	2	3.0	8
Jones	4	1	50.0	0	0	2	100.0	1	7	0	0	1	0	1.0	2
Chilcutt	3	0	—	0	0	0	—	0	0	0	0	0	0	0.0	0
Total	4	162	47.2	37	92	95	77.2	44	173	105	40	39	20	114.0	120

ORLANDO MAGIC

Player	GP	Field Goals		3-Pt FG		Free Throws		Rebounds		A	Stl	TO	BS	Avg	Hi
		FGM	Pct	FGM	FGA	FTM	Pct	Off	Total						
O'Neal	4	44	59.5	0	0	24	57.1	11	50	25	1	21	10	28.0	33
Hardaway	4	35	50.0	11	24	21	91.3	6	19	32	5	14	3	25.5	32
Grant	4	25	53.2	0	0	4	80.0	19	48	6	2	6	2	13.5	18
Shaw	4	20	42.5	10	28	0	—	4	13	13	2	8	1	12.5	17
Anderson	4	18	36.0	10	31	3	30.0	6	34	17	7	5	2	12.3	26
Scott	4	13	30.9	7	27	9	100.0	2	14	9	4	7	1	10.5	14
Bowie	4	6	60.0	1	2	0	—	0	2	6	0	2	1	3.3	5
Turner	4	2	20.0	2	6	0	—	0	4	2	0	1	0	1.5	3
Royal	1	0	—	0	0	0	—	0	0	0	0	0	0	0.0	0
Total	4	163	46.6	41	118	61	68.5	48	184	110	21	64	20	107.0	118

NBA Finals Box Scores

Game 1

HOUSTON 120

HOUSTON	Min	FG M-A	FT M-A	Reb O-T	A	PF	S	TO	TP
Horry	47	7-18	1-2	0-8	3	4	3	0	19
Elie	39	7-11	3-4	2-5	4	2	3	4	18
Olajuwon	48	13-26	5-7	1-6	7	5	2	3	31
Drexler	48	7-19	8-8	4-11	7	3	1	1	23
Smith	42	8-13	0-0	0-3	9	3	0	1	23
Cassell	11	1-3	1-2	0-1	1	2	0	2	4
Brown	14	1-5	0-0	2-5	0	0	0	0	2
Jones	15	0-1	0-0	0-2	0	2	0	0	0
Chilcutt	1	0-0	0-0	0-0	0	0	0	0	0
Totals	265	44-96	18-23	9-41	31	21	9	11	120

Percentages: FG—.458, FT—.783. 3-pt goals: 14-32, .438 (Horry 4-10, Elie 1-2, Drexler 1-6, Smith 7-11, Cassell 1-2, C. Brown 0-1). Team rebounds: 10. Blocked shots: 10 (Horry 5, Olajuwon 4, Drexler).

ORLANDO 118

ORLANDO	Min	FG M-A	FT M-A	Reb O-T	A	PF	S	TO	TP
Scott	38	3-10	3-3	0-4	5	4	1	1	11
Grant	47	7-15	1-1	7-16	2	2	0	1	15
O'Neal	44	10-16	6-9	3-16	9	5	0	7	26
Anderson	45	11-25	3-3	2-4	5	3	2	3	26
Hardaway	50	9-18	0-4	3-11	5	0	3	2	22
Turner	14	1-4	0-0	0-1	1	1	0	1	3
Shaw	22	5-12	0-0	1-5	4	4	1	2	11
Bowie	4	2-3	0-0	0-0	1	3	0	1	4
Royal	1	0-0	0-0	0-0	0	0	0	0	0
Totals	265	48-103	13-20	16-57	32	22	7	18	118

Percentages: FG—.466, FT—.650. 3-pt goals: 9-30, .300 (Scott 2-7, Anderson 1-6, Hardaway 4-10, Turner 1-2, Shaw 1-5). Team rebounds: 11. Blocked shots: 6 (O'Neal 3, Grant, Hardaway, Anderson). A: 16,610. Officials: J. Crawford, Bavetta, Javie.

THEY SAID IT

Gary Payton, the Seattle SuperSonics' $2.7 million-a-year guard, on the most recent NBA collective bargaining proposal: "People would have to cut their lifestyle, and they'd live like penny-pinchers."

Game 2

HOUSTON 117

HOUSTON	Min	FG M-A	FT M-A	Reb O-T	A	PF	S	TO	TP
Elie	41	2-6	4-4	2-7	4	2	1	0	8
Horry	48	2-10	2-2	2-10	3	7	1	1	11
Olajuwon	42	14-30	6-9	3-11	2	5	1	3	34
Drexler	32	7-10	9-12	1-5	5	4	7	1	23
Smith	19	0-2	0-0	0-0	1	1	0	1	0
Brown	12	4-5	0-0	1-2	0	1	0	1	8
Jones	15	0-0	2-2	0-2	0	5	0	0	2
Cassell	30	8-12	11-12	0-1	3	4	3	2	34
Chilcutt	1	0-0	0-0	0-0	0	0	0	0	0
Totals	240	39-75	34-41	9-38	18	23	13	9	117

Percentages: FG—.520, FT—.829. 3-pt goals: 5-14, .357 (Elie 0-2, Horry 1-5, Smith 0-1, Cassell 4-6). Team rebounds: 6. Blocked shots: 7 (Olajuwon 4, Horry 2, Brown).

ORLANDO 106

ORLANDO	Min	FG M-A	FT M-A	Reb O-T	A	PF	S	TO	TP
Scott	35	3-10	1-1	1-3	1	2	0	1	9
Grant	40	4-7	2-2	5-10	1	5	0	0	10
O'Neal	45	12-22	9-14	3-12	7	5	0	4	33
Hardaway	44	12-21	4-5	2-5	8	3	0	5	32
Anderson	43	4-13	2-4	1-6	5	2	2	2	11
Shaw	19	3-8	0-0	2-3	2	3	1	2	8
Turner	11	1-4	0-0	0-1	0	4	0	0	3
Bowie	3	0-0	0-0	0-1	0	2	0	1	0
Totals	240	39-85	18-26	14-41	24	26	3	15	106

Percentages: FG—.459, FT—.692. 3-pt goals: 10-26, .385 (Scott 2-7, Hardaway 4-6, Anderson 1-5, Shaw 2-5, Turner 1-3). Team rebounds: 12. Blocked shots: 1 (Anderson).

A: 16,610. Officials: E. T. Rush, Hollins, D. Crawford.

Game 3

ORLANDO 103

ORLANDO	Min	FG M-A	FT M-A	Reb O-T	A	PF	S	TO	TP
Grant	40	9-13	0-0	3-10	1	3	1	3	18
Scott	39	2-11	3-3	1-6	0	5	1	1	8
O'Neal	45	11-17	6-11	2-10	6	3	1	4	28
Anderson	37	4-14	0-0	0-10	3	3	0	0	12
Hardaway	44	4-10	10-11	1-4	14	4	1	3	19
Shaw	20	6-12	0-0	0-1	3	3	0	1	14
Turner	11	0-1	0-0	0-0	1	1	0	0	0
Bowie	7	2-3	0-0	0-0	2	1	0	0	4
Totals	240	38-81	19-25	7-14	30	23	4	12	103

Percentages: FG—.469, FT—.760. 3-pt goals: 8-31, .258 (Scott 1-9, Anderson 4-12, Hardaway 1-4, Shaw 2-5, Turner 0-1). Team rebounds: 7. Blocked shots: 6 (O'Neal 3, Hardaway 2, Grant).

HOUSTON 106

HOUSTON	Min	FG M-A	FT M-A	Reb O-T	A	PF	S	TO	TP
Elie	38	6-9	2-2	0-2	3	2	0	1	17
Horry	46	6-11	6-8	2-9	4	2	0	2	10
Olajuwon	45	14-30	3-5	4-14	7	4	2	0	31
Drexler	41	9-18	6-10	5-13	7	4	0	2	25
Smith	22	1-7	0-0	0-2	3	2	1	0	2
Jones	12	0-0	0-0	0-0	0	4	0	1	0
Cassell	26	3-9	2-3	0-2	4	2	3	2	9
Chilcutt	1	0-0	0-0	0-0	0	0	0	0	0
Brown	9	0-0	2-2	0-4	0	1	0	0	2
Totals	240	39-84	21-30	11-46	28	21	7	10	106

Percentages: FG—.464, FT—.700. 3-pt goals: 7-19, .368 (Elie 3-4, Horry 2-5, Drexler 1-3, Smith 0-4, Cassell 1-3). Team rebounds: 9. Blocked shots: 2 (Horry 2).

A: 16,611. Officials: Evans, Mathis, Salvatore.

Game 4

ORLANDO 101

ORLANDO	Min	FG M-A	FT M-A	Reb O-T	A	PF	S	TO	TP
Grant	41	5-12	1-2	4-12	2	3	1	2	11
Scott	38	5-11	2-2	0-1	3	1	2	4	14
O'Neal	46	11-9	3-8	3-12	3	5	0	6	25
Anderson	31	1-5	1-2	2-7	4	4	3	0	4
Hardaway	42	8-14	4-4	1-6	5	5	1	4	25
Shaw	23	6-15	0-0	1-4	4	5	0	3	17
Turner	7	0-1	0-0	0-2	0	0	0	0	0
Bowie	12	2-4	0-0	0-1	3	3	0	0	5
Totals	240	38-81	11-18	11-45	24	26	7	19	101

Percentages: FG—.469, FT—.611. 3-pt goals: 4-31, .452 (Scott 2-6, Anderson 1-4, Hardaway 5-8, Shaw 5-11, Bowie 1-2). Team rebounds: 6. Blocked shots: 7 (O'Neal 4, Scott, Shaw, Bowie).

HOUSTON 113

HOUSTON	Min	FG M-A	FT M-A	Reb O-T	A	PF	S	TO	TP
Elie	43	9-11	0-0	0-3	2	3	4	2	22
Horry	46	6-14	5-9	5-13	5	2	1	2	21
Olajuwon	44	15-30	4-5	3-15	6	4	3	4	35
Drexler	41	4-13	7-8	3-9	8	3	2	4	15
Smith	22	2-7	0-0	2-2	3	1	0	0	5
Cassell	26	3-11	6-7	1-3	4	1	1	0	13
Brown	3	0-1	0-0	0-0	0	0	0	1	2
Jones	15	1-1	0-0	1-3	0	4	0	0	2
Totals	240	40-88	22-29	15-48	28	18	11	11	113

Percentages: FG—.455, FT—.759. 3-pt goals: 11-27, .407 (Elie 4-6, Horry 4-9, Olajuwon 1-1, Drexler 0-4, Smith 1-3, Cassell 1-4). Team rebounds: 6. Blocked shots: 1 (Brown).

A: 16,611. Officials: J. Crawford, Kersey, Oakes.

NBA Awards

All-NBA Teams

FIRST TEAM

G John Stockton, Utah
G Anfernee Hardaway, Orlando
C David Robinson, San Antonio
F Karl Malone, Utah
F Scottie Pippen, Chicago

SECOND TEAM

Mitch Richmond, Sacramento
Gary Payton, Seattle
Shaquille O'Neal, Orlando
Charles Barkley, Phoenix
Shawn Kemp, Seattle

THIRD TEAM

Clyde Drexler, Houston
Reggie Miller, Indiana
Hakeem Olajuwon, Houston
Dennis Rodman, San Antonio
Detlef Schrempf, Seattle

Master Lock NBA All-Defensive Teams

FIRST TEAM

G Gary Payton, Seattle
G Mookie Blaylock, Atlanta
C David Robinson, San Antonio
F Scottie Pippen, Chicago
F Dennis Rodman, San Antonio

SECOND TEAM

John Stockton, Utah
Nate McMillan, Seattle
Dikembe Mutombo, Denver
Horace Grant, Orlando
Derrick McKey, Indiana

All-Rookie Teams
(Chosen Without Regard to Position)

FIRST TEAM

Jason Kidd, Dallas
Grant Hill, Detroit
Glenn Robinson, Milwaukee
Eddie Jones, LA Lakers
Brian Grant, Sacramento

SECOND TEAM

Juwan Howard, Washington
Eric Montross, Boston
Wesley Person, Phoenix
Jalen Rose, Denver
Donyell Marshall, Golden State
Sharone Wright, Philadelphia

Dressing Down

At first glance Houston Rocket center Hakeem Olajuwon's signing of a new sneaker deal may not seem like big news. But in a significant break from the established practice of superstar athletes, Olajuwon's shoe contract isn't with Nike, Reebok or any of the other "top-end" manufacturers that produce the $100-and-up, bells-and-whistles models that young people hanker for. The NBA's reigning MVP has instead agreed to a deal with Spalding under which he will endorse a line of shoes retailing for no more than $60 a pair and available in discount stores like Wal-Mart, Payless and Target, where Americans buy close to half of the 400 million pairs of athletic shoes sold in the U.S. each year.

Olajuwon, who for the Rockets' seven games leading up to the All-Star break wore the prototype of a model scheduled to reach the stores in the fall, signed the contract in part because he's alarmed at the values he sometimes sees youngsters espouse. "A lot of kids just go with the name brand," he says. "They bother their parents for "$150 shoes." A cheaper shoe needn't impair performance, he believes—and he demonstrated that in those seven games, shooting 56.8% while in Spaldings, compared with his season average of 49.7%. Of course, Hakeem would still be the Dream even in Birkenstocks. It's nonetheless refreshing when a star athlete has the ability to see the big picture.

NBA Individual Leaders

Scoring

	GP	Pts	Avg
Shaquille O'Neal, Orl	79	2315	29.3
Hakeem Olajuwon, Hou	72	2005	27.9
David Robinson, SA	81	2238	27.6
Karl Malone, Utah	82	2187	26.7
Jimmy Jackson, Dal	51	1309	25.7
Jamal Mashburn, Dal	80	1926	24.1
Patrick Ewing, NY	79	1886	23.9
Charles Barkley, Phoe	68	1561	23.0
Mitch Richmond, Sac	82	1867	22.8
Glenn Rice, Mia	82	1831	22.3

Rebounds

	GP	Reb	Avg
Dennis Rodman, SA	49	823	16.8
Dikembe Mutombo, Den	82	1029	12.6
Shaquille O'Neal, Orl	79	901	11.4
Charles Barkley, Pho	68	756	11.1
Patrick Ewing, NY	79	867	11.0
Tyrone Hill, Cle	70	765	10.9
Kevin Willis, Mia	67	732	10.9
Shawn Kemp, Sea	82	893	10.9
David Robinson, SA	81	872	10.8
Hakeem Olajuwon, Hou	72	775	10.8

Assists

	GP	Assists	Avg
John Stockton, Utah	82	1011	12.3
Kenny Anderson, NJ	72	680	9.4
Tim Hardaway, GS	62	578	9.3
Rod Strickland, Por	64	562	8.8
Tyrone Bogues, Char	78	675	8.7
Nick Van Exel, LA Lakers	80	660	8.3
Avery Johnson, SA	82	670	8.2
Pooh Richardson, LA Clippers	80	632	7.9
Mookie Blaylock, Atl	80	616	7.7
Jason Kidd, Dal	79	607	7.7

Field-Goal Percentage

	FGA	FGM	Pct
Chris Gatling, GS	512	324	63.3
Shaquille O'Neal, Orl	1594	930	58.3
Horace Grant, Orl	707	401	56.7
Otis Thorpe, Por	681	385	56.5
Dale Davis, Ind	576	324	56.3
Gheorghe Muresan, Was	541	303	56.0
Dikembe Mutombo, Den	628	349	55.6
Danny Manning, Pho	622	340	54.7
Shawn Kemp, Sea	1000	545	54.5
Olden Polynice, Sea	691	376	54.4

Free-Throw Percentage

	FTA	FTM	Pct
Spud Webb, Sac	242	226	93.4
Mark Price, Clev	162	148	91.4
Dana Barros, Phi	386	347	89.9
Reggie Miller, Ind	427	383	89.7
Tyrone Bogues, Char	180	160	88.9
Scott Skiles, Was	202	179	88.6
Mahmoud Abdul-Rauf, Den	156	138	88.5
B.J. Armstrong, Chi	233	206	88.4
Jeff Hornacek, Utah	322	284	88.2
Keith Jennings, GS	153	134	87.6

Three-Point Field-Goal Percentage

	FGA	FGM	Pct
Steve Kerr, Chi	170	89	52.4
Detlef Schrempf, Sea	181	93	51.4
Dana Barros, Phi	426	197	46.2
Hubert Davis, NY	288	131	45.5
John Stockton, Utah	227	102	44.9
Hersey Hawkins, Char	298	131	44.0
Wesley Person, Pho	266	116	43.6
Kenny Smith, Hou	331	142	42.9
Dell Curry, Char	361	154	42.7
B.J. Armstrong, Chi	253	108	42.7

Steals

	GP	Steals	Avg
Scottie Pippen, Chi	79	232	2.94
Mookie Blaylock, Atl	80	200	2.50
Gary Payton, Sea	82	204	2.49
John Stockton, Utah	82	194	2.37
Nate McMillan, Sea	80	165	2.06
Eddie Jones, LA Lakers	64	131	2.05
Rod Strickland, Por	64	123	1.92
Jason Kidd, Dal	79	151	1.91
Elliot Perry, Pho	82	155	1.89
Hakeem Olajuwon, Hou	72	133	1.85

Blocked Shots

	GP	BS	Avg
Dikembe Mutombo, Den	82	321	3.91
Hakeem Olajuwon, Hou	72	242	3.36
Shawn Bradley, Phi	82	274	3.34
David Robinson, SA	81	262	3.23
Alonzo Mourning, Char	77	225	2.92
Shaquille O'Neal, Orl	79	192	2.43
Vlade Divac, LA Lakers	80	174	2.18
Patrick Ewing, NY	79	159	2.01
Bo Outlaw, LA Clippers	81	151	1.86
Oliver Miller, Det	64	116	1.81

NBA Team Statistics

Offense

Team	Field Goals FGM	Pct	3-Pt Field Goals 3FGM	Pct	Free Throws FTM	Pct	Rebounds Off	Total	A	Stl	Scoring Avg
Orlando	3460	50.2	523	37.0	1648	66.9	1149	3606	2281	672	110.9
Phoenix	3356	48.2	584	36.9	1777	75.6	1027	3430	2198	687	110.6
Seattle	3310	49.1	491	37.6	1944	75.8	1068	3405	2115	917	110.4
San Antonio	3236	48.4	434	37.5	1836	73.8	1029	3690	1919	656	106.6
Utah	3243	51.2	301	37.6	1939	78.1	874	3286	2256	758	106.4
Golden State	3217	46.8	546	34.1	1687	70.4	1101	3472	2017	649	105.7
LA Lakers	3284	46.3	525	35.2	1523	73.5	1126	3442	2078	750	105.1
Houston	3159	48.0	646	36.8	1527	74.9	880	3320	2060	721	103.5
Dallas	3227	44.0	386	32.2	1622	73.4	1514	3947	1941	579	103.2
Portland	3217	45.1	462	36.5	1555	69.7	1352	3795	1846	668	103.1
Boston	3179	46.4	362	36.8	1708	75.3	1156	3476	1783	612	102.8
Chicago	3191	47.6	443	37.3	1500	72.6	1106	3400	1970	797	101.5
Denver	3098	47.9	413	35.6	1700	73.8	1040	3442	1836	660	101.3
Miami	3144	46.7	436	36.9	1569	73.6	1092	3364	1779	662	101.1
Charlotte	3051	47.4	560	39.7	1587	77.7	832	3227	2072	620	100.6
Washington	3176	46.0	433	34.3	1457	72.4	1044	3263	1749	648	100.5
Milwaukee	3022	45.9	494	36.6	1608	71.2	1063	3250	1737	674	99.3
Indiana	2983	47.7	374	38.0	1796	75.1	1051	3341	1877	703	99.2
Sacramento	3025	46.8	359	34.6	1647	71.1	1073	3398	1824	650	98.2
New York	2985	46.7	532	36.8	1552	73.4	929	3402	2055	591	98.2
Detroit	3060	46.1	494	35.4	1439	74.1	958	3162	1872	705	98.2
New Jersey	2939	43.6	414	31.9	1750	75.9	1213	3782	1884	544	98.1
LA Clippers	3060	44.4	331	31.5	1476	71.0	1064	3140	1805	787	96.7
Atlanta	2986	44.7	539	34.1	1410	72.4	1104	3376	1757	738	96.6
Philadelphia	2949	44.8	355	37.9	1567	73.7	1105	3335	1556	643	95.4
Minnesota	2792	44.9	318	31.3	1824	77.5	883	2973	1780	609	94.2
Cleveland	2756	44.1	398	38.5	1507	76.0	1045	3282	1672	630	90.5

Defense (Opponent's Statistics)

Team	Field Goals FGM	Pct	3-Pt Field Goals 3FGM	Pct	Free Throws FTM	Pct	Rebounds Off	Total	Stl	Scoring Avg	Diff
Cleveland	2803	46.1	396	35.7	1364	75.7	851	3097	556	89.8	+0.6
New York	2800	43.7	397	34.1	1802	73.6	1021	3338	639	95.1	+3.1
Atlanta	3001	46.3	420	34.7	1394	72.6	1051	3442	608	95.3	+1.3
Indiana	2921	45.6	475	36.4	1516	72.6	1048	3204	691	95.5	+3.7
Chicago	2923	45.7	401	34.9	1682	73.8	1068	3320	687	96.7	+4.8
Charlotte	3088	45.4	429	33.3	1375	74.0	1102	3467	535	97.3	+3.3
Utah	2845	45.3	546	38.2	1835	74.1	917	3042	648	98.4	+8.0
Sacramento	2964	45.3	377	30.4	1833	74.1	1145	3413	756	99.2	-1.0
Portland	2951	45.6	442	37.2	1794	75.4	883	3178	638	99.2	+3.8
Philadelphia	3100	46.5	467	36.3	1569	76.3	1143	3460	712	100.4	-5.1
Denver	3050	45.6	419	34.7	1721	75.0	1021	3228	640	100.5	+0.8
San Antonio	3168	45.4	426	34.1	1491	71.4	1017	3320	633	100.6	+6.0
New Jersey	3182	46.1	440	37.4	1495	72.1	1056	3491	733	101.2	-3.1
Houston	3202	45.3	506	37.6	1407	75.1	1165	3551	744	101.4	+2.1
Seattle	3008	45.3	520	34.3	1848	73.5	1064	3271	652	102.2	+8.2
Miami	3092	47.1	511	36.1	1732	74.0	1039	3391	656	102.8	-1.6
Minnesota	3088	47.4	468	37.7	1820	73.1	1169	3474	703	103.2	-9.0
Milwaukee	3248	49.3	491	39.5	1517	72.9	1014	3351	770	103.7	-4.4
Orlando	3242	45.7	468	37.8	1560	74.1	1136	3362	700	103.8	+7.1
Boston	3303	48.4	375	35.8	1601	72.0	1064	3399	653	104.7	-1.9
LA Lakers	3299	46.8	456	35.2	1580	70.8	1283	3757	644	105.3	-0.2
Detroit	3120	47.6	448	36.0	1936	72.2	1147	3579	693	105.5	-7.3
LA Clippers	3207	49.6	388	37.0	1876	75.0	1083	3619	693	105.8	-9.2
Dallas	3407	48.8	432	36.6	1454	73.4	1053	3432	722	106.1	-2.9
Washington	3246	48.0	438	38.3	1771	76.5	1107	3628	701	106.1	-5.6
Phoenix	3320	47.7	525	34.0	1590	74.4	1038	3469	658	106.8	+3.9
Golden State	3527	48.8	492	35.5	1565	72.0	1196	3723	865	111.1	-5.4

NBA Team-by-Team Statistical Leaders

Atlanta Hawks

Player	GP	Min	Field Goals		3-Pt FG		Free Throws		Rebounds		A	Stl	TO	BS	Avg
			FGM	Pct	FGA	FGM	FTM	Pct	Off	Total					
Blaylock	80	3,069	509	42.5	555	199	156	72.9	117	393	616	200	242	26	17.2
Smith	80	2,665	428	42.6	416	137	312	84.1	104	276	274	62	155	33	16.3
Augmon	76	2,362	397	45.3	26	7	252	72.8	157	368	197	100	152	47	13.9
Norman	74	1,879	388	45.3	285	98	64	45.7	103	362	94	34	96	20	12.7
Long	81	2,641	342	47.8	31	11	244	75.1	191	606	131	109	155	34	11.6
Ehlo	49	1,166	191	45.3	134	51	44	62.0	55	147	113	46	73	6	9.7
Lang	82	2,340	320	47.3	3	2	152	80.9	154	456	72	45	108	144	9.7
Corbin	81	1,389	205	44.2	56	14	78	68.4	98	262	67	55	74	16	6.2
Anderson	51	622	57	54.8	0	0	34	47.9	62	188	17	23	32	32	2.9
Koncak	62	945	77	41.2	36	12	13	54.2	23	184	52	36	20	46	2.9
Whatley	27	292	24	45.3	8	2	20	62.5	9	30	54	19	19	0	2.6
Les	24	188	11	28.9	23	5	20	85.2	6	26	44	4	21	0	2.1
Edwards	38	212	22	45.8	1	0	23	71.9	19	48	13	5	22	4	1.8
Hawks	82	19,855	2,986	44.7	1,580	539	1,410	72.4	1,104	3,376	1,757	738	1,221	412	96.6
Opponents	82	19,855	3,001	46.3	1,212	420	1,394	72.6	1,051	3,442	1,733	608	1,359	320	95.3

Boston Celtics

Player	GP	Min	Field Goals		3-Pt FG		Free Throws		Rebounds		A	Stl	TO	BS	Avg
			FGM	Pct	FGA	FGM	FTM	Pct	Off	Total					
Wilkins	77	2,423	496	42.4	289	112	266	78.2	157	401	166	61	173	14	17.8
Radja	66	2,147	450	49.0	1	0	233	75.9	149	573	111	60	159	86	17.2
Brown	79	2,792	437	44.7	327	126	236	85.2	63	249	301	110	146	49	15.6
Douglas	65	2,048	365	47.5	82	20	204	68.9	48	170	446	80	162	2	14.7
Montross	78	2,315	307	53.4	1	0	167	63.5	196	566	36	29	112	61	10.0
Fox	53	1,039	169	48.1	75	31	95	77.2	61	155	139	52	78	19	8.8
McDaniel	68	1,430	246	45.1	21	6	89	71.2	94	300	108	30	89	20	8.6
Wesley	51	1,380	128	40.9	119	51	71	75.5	31	117	266	82	87	9	7.4
Ellison	55	1,083	152	50.7	2	0	71	71.7	124	309	34	22	76	54	6.8
Strong	70	1,344	149	45.3	7	2	141	82.0	136	375	44	24	79	13	6.3
Minor	63	945	155	51.5	12	2	65	83.3	49	137	66	32	44	16	6.0
Dawson	2	13	3	37.5	3	1	1	100.0	0	3	1	0	2	0	4.0
Earl	30	206	26	38.2	0	0	14	48.3	19	45	2	6	14	8	2.2
Humphries	18	201	8	23.5	4	2	2	50.0	4	13	19	9	17	0	1.1
Celtics	82	19,805	3,179	46.4	984	362	1,708	75.3	1,156	3,476	1,783	612	1,305	361	102.8
Opponents	82	19,805	3,303	48.4	1,047	375	1,601	72.0	1,064	3,399	1,999	653	1,232	454	104.7

Charlotte Hornets

Player	GP	Min	Field Goals		3-Pt FG		Free Throws		Rebounds		A	Stl	TO	BS	Avg
			FGM	Pct	FGA	FGM	FTM	Pct	Off	Total					
Mourning	77	2,941	571	51.9	34	11	490	76.1	200	761	111	49	241	225	21.3
Johnson	81	3,234	585	48.0	210	81	274	77.4	190	585	369	78	207	28	18.8
Hawkins	82	2,731	390	48.2	298	131	261	86.7	60	314	262	122	150	18	14.3
Curry	69	1,718	343	44.1	361	154	95	85.6	41	168	113	55	98	18	13.6
Burrell	65	2,014	277	46.7	235	96	100	69.4	96	368	161	75	85	40	11.5
Bogues	78	2,629	348	47.7	30	6	160	88.9	51	257	675	103	132	0	11.1
Adams	29	443	67	45.3	81	29	25	83.3	6	29	95	23	26	1	6.5
Gattison	21	409	47	47.0	1	0	31	60.8	21	75	17	7	22	15	6.0
Sutton	53	690	94	40.9	115	43	32	71.1	8	56	91	33	51	2	5.0
Parish	81	1,352	159	42.7	0	0	71	70.3	93	350	44	27	66	36	4.8
Bennett	3	46	6	46.2	9	2	0	—	0	2	4	0	3	0	4.7
Hancock	46	424	68	56.2	3	1	16	41.0	14	53	30	19	30	4	3.3
Wingate	52	515	50	41.0	22	4	18	75.0	11	60	56	19	27	6	2.3
Wolf	63	583	38	46.9	6	2	12	75.0	34	129	37	9	22	6	1.4
Hornets	82	19,805	3,051	47.4	1,409	560	1,587	77.7	832	3,227	2,072	620	1,224	399	100.6
Opponents	82	19,805	3,088	45.4	1,289	429	1,375	74.0	1,102	3,467	1,898	535	1,216	368	97.3

Chicago Bulls

Player	GP	Min	FGM	Pct	FGA	FGM	FTM	Pct	Off	Total	A	Stl	TO	BS	Avg
			Field Goals		3-Pt FG		Free Throws		Rebounds						
Jordan	17	668	166	41.1	32	16	109	80.1	25	117	90	30	35	13	26.9
Pippen	79	3,014	634	48.0	316	109	315	71.6	175	639	409	232	271	89	21.4
Kukoc	81	2,584	487	50.4	198	62	235	74.8	155	440	372	102	165	16	15.7
Armstrong	82	2,577	418	46.8	253	108	206	88.4	25	186	244	84	103	8	14.0
Kerr	82	1,839	261	52.7	170	89	63	77.8	20	119	151	44	48	3	8.2
Perdue	78	1,592	254	55.3	1	0	113	58.2	211	522	90	26	116	56	8.0
Harper	77	1,536	209	42.6	110	31	81	61.8	51	180	157	97	100	27	6.9
Longley	55	1,001	135	44.7	2	0	88	82.2	82	263	73	24	86	45	6.5
Wennington	73	956	156	49.2	4	0	51	81.0	64	190	40	22	39	17	5.0
Myers	71	1,270	119	41.5	39	10	70	61.4	57	139	148	58	88	15	4.5
Krystkowiak	19	287	28	38.9	0	0	27	90.0	19	59	26	9	25	2	4.4
Buechler	57	605	90	49.2	48	15	22	56.4	36	98	50	24	30	12	3.8
Blount	68	889	100	47.6	2	0	38	56.7	107	240	60	26	59	33	3.5
Simpkins	59	586	78	42.4	0	0	50	69.4	60	151	37	10	45	7	3.5
Bulls	**82**	**19,830**	**3,191**	**47.6**	**1,187**	**443**	**1,500**	**72.6**	**1,106**	**3,400**	**1,970**	**797**	**1,297**	**352**	**101.5**
Opponents	**82**	**19,830**	**2,923**	**45.7**	**1,150**	**401**	**1,682**	**73.8**	**1,068**	**3,320**	**1,713**	**687**	**1,485**	**369**	**96.7**

Cleveland Cavaliers

Player	GP	Min	FGM	Pct	FGA	FGM	FTM	Pct	Off	Total	A	Stl	TO	BS	Avg
			Field Goals		3-Pt FG		Free Throws		Rebounds						
Price	48	1,375	253	41.3	253	103	148	91.4	25	112	335	35	142	4	15.8
Hill	70	2,397	350	50.4	1	0	263	66.2	269	765	55	55	151	41	13.8
Brandon	67	1,961	341	44.8	121	48	159	85.5	35	186	363	107	144	14	13.3
Williams	74	2,641	366	45.2	5	1	196	68.5	173	507	192	83	149	101	12.6
Mills	80	2,814	359	42.0	240	94	174	81.7	99	366	154	59	120	35	12.3
Phillis	80	2,500	338	41.4	55	19	183	77.9	90	265	180	115	113	25	11.0
Ferry	82	1,290	223	44.6	233	94	74	88.1	30	143	96	27	59	22	7.5
Campbell	78	1,128	161	41.1	42	15	132	83.0	60	153	69	32	65	8	6.0
Cage	82	2,040	177	52.1	2	0	53	60.2	203	564	56	61	56	67	5.0
Battle	28	280	43	37.7	31	11	19	73.1	3	11	37	8	17	1	4.1
Roberts	21	223	28	38.9	11	4	20	76.9	13	34	8	6	7	3	3.8
Colter	57	752	67	39.6	35	8	54	76.1	13	59	101	30	36	6	3.4
Dreiling	58	483	42	41.2	0	0	26	63.4	32	116	22	6	25	22	1.9
Cavs	**82**	**19,930**	**2,756**	**44.1**	**1,033**	**398**	**1,507**	**76.0**	**1,045**	**3,282**	**1,672**	**630**	**1,176**	**349**	**90.5**
Opponents	**82**	**19,930**	**2,803**	**46.1**	**1,108**	**396**	**1,364**	**75.7**	**851**	**3,097**	**1,812**	**556**	**1,213**	**433**	**89.8**

Dallas Mavericks

Player	GP	Min	FGM	Pct	FGA	FGM	FTM	Pct	Off	Total	A	Stl	TO	BS	Avg
			Field Goals		3-Pt FG		Free Throws		Rebounds						
Jackson	51	1,962	484	47.2	110	35	306	80.5	120	260	191	28	160	12	25.7
Mashburn	80	2,980	683	43.6	344	113	447	73.9	116	331	298	82	235	8	24.1
Tarpley	55	1,354	292	47.9	18	5	102	83.6	142	449	58	45	109	55	12.6
Kidd	79	2,668	330	38.5	257	70	192	69.8	152	430	607	151	250	24	11.7
Jones	80	2,385	372	44.3	12	1	80	64.5	329	844	163	35	124	27	10.3
McCloud	42	802	144	43.9	89	34	80	83.3	82	147	53	23	40	9	9.6
Harris	79	1,695	280	45.9	142	55	136	80.0	85	220	132	58	77	14	9.5
Brooks	59	808	126	45.8	69	25	64	81.0	14	66	116	34	47	4	5.4
Smith	63	826	131	41.7	12	1	57	76.0	43	144	44	29	37	26	5.1
Durnas	58	613	96	38.4	73	22	50	64.9	32	62	57	13	50	4	4.6
Williams	82	2,383	145	47.7	0	0	38	37.6	291	690	124	52	105	148	4.0
Hodge	54	633	83	40.7	14	4	39	76.5	40	122	41	10	39	14	3.9
Davis	46	580	49	43.3	2	0	42	63.6	63	156	10	6	30	3	3.0
Mavericks	**82**	**19,930**	**3,227**	**44.0**	**1,200**	**386**	**1,622**	**73.4**	**1,514**	**3,947**	**1,941**	**579**	**1,345**	**348**	**103.2**
Opponents	**82**	**19,930**	**3,407**	**48.8**	**1,181**	**432**	**1,454**	**73.4**	**1,053**	**3,432**	**1,991**	**722**	**1,250**	**502**	**106.1**

Denver Nuggets

Player	GP	Min	Field Goals		3-Pt FG		Free Throws		Rebounds		A	Stl	TO	BS	Avg
			FGM	Pct	FGA	FGM	FTM	Pct	Off	Total					
Abdul-Rauf	73	2,082	472	47.0	215	83	138	88.5	32	137	263	77	119	9	16.0
R. Williams	74	2,198	388	45.9	266	85	132	75.9	94	329	231	114	124	67	13.4
Rogers	80	2,142	375	48.8	148	50	179	65.1	132	385	161	95	173	46	12.2
Pack	42	1,144	170	43.0	72	30	137	78.3	19	113	290	61	134	6	12.1
Mutombo	82	3,100	349	55.6	0	0	248	65.4	319	1029	113	40	192	321	11.5
D. Ellis	81	1,996	351	45.3	263	106	110	86.6	56	222	57	37	81	9	11.3
Stith	81	2,329	312	47.2	68	20	267	82.4	95	268	153	91	110	18	11.2
Rose	81	1,798	227	45.4	114	36	173	73.9	57	217	389	65	160	22	8.2
B. Williams	63	1,261	196	58.9	0	0	106	65.4	98	298	53	38	114	43	7.9
Hammonds	70	956	139	53.5	1	0	132	74.6	55	222	36	11	56	14	5.9
Slater	25	236	40	49.4	0	0	40	72.7	21	57	12	7	26	3	4.8
L. Ellis	6	58	9	36.0	0	0	6	100.0	7	17	4	1	5	5	4.0
Levingston	57	469	55	42.3	1	0	19	42.2	49	124	27	13	21	20	2.3
Grant	14	151	10	30.3	7	2	9	75.0	2	9	43	6	14	2	2.2
Randall	8	39	3	30.0	1	0	0	—	4	12	1	0	1	0	0.8
Nuggets	**82**	**19,980**	**3,098**	**47.9**	**1,160**	**413**	**1,700**	**73.8**	**1,040**	**3,442**	**1,836**	**660**	**1,381**	**585**	**101.3**
Opponents	**82**	**19,980**	**3,050**	**45.6**	**1,208**	**419**	**1,721**	**75.0**	**1,021**	**3,228**	**1,784**	**640**	**1,167**	**460**	**100.5**

Detroit Pistons

Player	GP	Min	Field Goals		3-Pt FG		Free Throws		Rebounds		A	Stl	TO	BS	Avg
			FGM	Pct	FGA	FGM	FTM	Pct	Off	Total					
Hill	70	2,678	508	47.7	27	4	374	73.2	125	445	353	124	202	62	19.9
Dumars	67	2,544	417	43.0	338	103	277	80.5	47	158	368	72	219	7	18.1
Mills	72	2,514	417	44.7	285	109	175	79.9	124	558	160	68	144	33	15.5
Houston	76	1,996	398	46.3	373	158	147	86.0	29	167	164	61	113	14	14.5
Miller	64	1,558	232	55.5	13	3	78	62.9	162	475	93	60	115	116	8.5
Addison	79	1,776	279	47.6	83	24	74	74.7	67	242	109	53	76	25	8.3
Hunter	42	944	119	37.4	108	36	40	72.7	24	75	159	51	79	7	7.5
West	67	1,543	217	55.6	0	0	66	47.8	160	408	18	27	85	102	7.5
Macon	55	721	101	38.1	62	20	54	79.4	29	76	63	67	41	1	5.0
Knight	47	708	85	39.7	28	11	18	72.0	21	61	127	21	49	5	4.2
Leckner	57	623	87	52.7	2	0	51	70.8	47	174	14	15	39	15	3.9
Curley	53	595	58	43.3	0	0	27	75.0	54	124	25	21	25	21	2.7
Newbill	34	331	16	35.6	0	0	8	36.4	40	81	17	11	12	11	1.2
Pistons	**82**	**19,730**	**3,060**	**46.1**	**1,396**	**494**	**1,439**	**74.1**	**958**	**3,162**	**1,872**	**705**	**1,318**	**420**	**98.2**
Opponents	**82**	**19,730**	**3,120**	**47.6**	**1,235**	**448**	**1,963**	**72.2**	**1,147**	**3,579**	**2,013**	**693**	**1,286**	**439**	**105.5**

Golden State Warriors

Player	GP	Min	Field Goals		3-Pt FG		Free Throws		Rebounds		A	Stl	TO	BS	Avg
			FGM	Pct	FGA	FGM	FTM	Pct	Off	Total					
Sprewell	69	2,771	490	41.8	326	90	350	78.1	58	256	279	112	230	46	20.6
Hardaway	62	2,321	430	42.7	444	168	219	76.0	46	190	578	88	214	12	20.1
Mullin	25	890	170	48.9	93	42	94	87.9	25	115	125	38	93	19	19.0
Gatling	58	1,470	324	63.3	1	0	148	59.2	144	443	51	39	117	52	13.7
Marshall	72	2,066	345	39.4	243	69	147	66.2	137	405	105	45	115	88	12.6
Pierce	27	673	111	43.7	70	23	93	87.7	12	64	40	22	24	2	12.5
Seikaly	36	1,035	162	51.6	0	0	111	69.4	77	266	45	20	104	37	12.1
Alexander	50	1,237	230	51.5	25	6	36	60.0	87	291	60	28	76	29	10.0
Rogers	49	1,017	180	52.9	14	2	76	52.1	108	278	37	22	84	52	8.9
Jennings	80	1,722	190	44.7	204	75	134	87.6	26	148	373	95	120	2	7.4
Lorthridge	37	672	106	47.5	14	3	57	64.8	24	71	101	28	57	1	7.4
Legler	24	371	60	52.2	50	26	30	88.2	12	40	27	12	20	1	7.3
Rozier	66	1,494	189	48.5	7	2	68	44.7	200	486	45	35	89	39	6.8
Wood	78	1,336	153	46.9	91	31	91	77.8	83	241	65	28	53	13	5.5
Morton	41	395	50	38.8	25	9	58	68.2	21	58	18	11	27	15	4.1
Warriors	**82**	**19,905**	**3,217**	**46.8**	**1,602**	**546**	**1,687**	**70.4**	**1,101**	**3,472**	**2,017**	**649**	**1,497**	**391**	**105.7**
Opponents	**82**	**19,905**	**3,527**	**48.8**	**1,384**	**492**	**1,565**	**72.0**	**1,196**	**3,723**	**2,345**	**865**	**1,326**	**412**	**111.1**

Houston Rockets

Player	GP	Min	Field Goals		3-Pt FG		Free Throws		Rebounds		A	Stl	TO	BS	Avg
			FGM	Pct	FGA	FGM	FTM	Pct	Off	Total					
Olajuwon	72	2,853	798	51.7	16	3	406	75.6	172	775	255	133	237	242	27.8
Drexler	76	2,728	571	46.1	480	147	364	82.4	152	480	362	136	186	45	21.8
Maxwell	64	2,038	306	39.4	441	143	99	68.8	18	164	274	75	137	13	13.3
Smith	81	2,030	287	48.4	331	142	126	85.1	27	155	323	71	123	10	10.4
Horry	64	2,074	240	44.7	227	86	86	76.1	81	324	216	94	122	76	10.2
Cassell	82	1,882	253	42.7	191	63	214	84.3	38	211	405	94	167	14	9.5
Elie	81	1,896	243	49.9	201	80	144	84.2	50	196	189	65	104	12	8.8
Herrera	61	1,331	171	52.3	2	0	73	62.4	98	278	44	40	71	38	6.8
Brown	41	814	105	60.3	3	1	38	61.3	64	189	30	11	29	14	6.1
Chilcutt	68	1,347	146	44.5	86	35	31	73.8	106	317	66	25	61	43	5.3
Murray	54	516	95	40.8	86	35	32	73.0	20	59	19	14	35	4	4.8
Breaux	42	340	45	37.2	25	6	32	65.3	16	34	15	11	16	4	3.0
Tabak	37	182	24	45.3	1	0	27	61.4	23	57	4	2	18	7	2.0
Rockets	**82**	**19,730**	**3,159**	**48.0**	**1,757**	**646**	**1,527**	**74.9**	**880**	**3,320**	**2,060**	**721**	**1,322**	**514**	**103.5**
Opponents	**82**	**19,730**	**3,202**	**45.3**	**1,345**	**506**	**1,407**	**75.1**	**1,165**	**3,551**	**1,940**	**744**	**1,274**	**365**	**101.4**

Indiana Pacers

Player	GP	Min	Field Goals		3-Pt FG		Free Throws		Rebounds		A	Stl	TO	BS	Avg
			FGM	Pct	FGA	FGM	FTM	Pct	Off	Total					
Miller	81	2,665	505	46.2	470	195	383	89.7	30	210	242	98	151	16	19.6
Smits	78	2,381	558	52.6	2	0	284	75.3	192	601	111	40	189	79	17.9
McKey	81	2,805	411	49.3	89	32	221	74.4	125	394	276	125	168	49	13.3
D. Davis	74	2,346	324	56.3	1	0	138	53.3	259	696	58	72	124	116	10.6
Scott	80	1,528	265	45.5	203	79	193	85.0	18	151	108	61	119	13	10.0
A. Davis	44	1,030	109	44.5	0	0	117	67.2	105	280	25	19	64	29	7.6
Jackson	82	2,402	239	42.2	87	27	119	77.8	73	306	616	105	210	16	7.6
Mitchell	81	1,377	201	48.7	10	1	126	72.4	95	243	61	43	54	20	6.5
Fleming	55	686	93	49.5	7	0	65	72.2	20	88	109	27	43	1	4.6
Workman	69	1,028	101	37.5	98	35	55	74.3	21	111	194	59	73	5	4.2
Ferrell	56	607	83	48.0	6	1	64	75.3	50	88	31	26	43	6	4.1
Thompson	38	453	49	41.5	0	0	14	87.5	28	89	18	18	33	10	2.9
Kite	11	77	3	17.6	0	0	2	20.0	12	22	1	0	6	0	0.7
Pacers	**82**	**19,780**	**2,983**	**47.7**	**985**	**374**	**1,796**	**75.1**	**1,051**	**3,341**	**1,877**	**703**	**1,340**	**363**	**99.2**
Opponents	**82**	**19,780**	**2,921**	**45.6**	**1,304**	**475**	**1,516**	**72.6**	**1,048**	**3,204**	**1,804**	**691**	**1,370**	**416**	**95.5**

Los Angeles Clippers

Player	GP	Min	Field Goals		3-Pt FG		Free Throws		Rebounds		A	Stl	TO	BS	Avg
			FGM	Pct	FGA	FGM	FTM	Pct	Off	Total					
Vaught	80	2,966	609	51.4	33	7	176	71.0	261	772	139	104	166	29	17.5
Murray	81	2,556	439	40.2	218	65	199	75.4	132	354	133	72	163	55	14.1
Sealy	60	1,604	291	43.5	73	22	174	78.0	77	214	107	72	83	25	13.0
Richardson	80	2,664	353	39.4	244	87	81	64.8	38	261	632	129	171	12	10.9
Dehere	80	1,774	279	40.7	163	48	229	78.4	35	152	225	45	157	7	10.4
Massenburg	80	2,127	282	46.9	3	0	177	75.3	160	455	67	48	118	58	9.3
Piatkowski	81	1,208	201	44.1	198	74	90	78.3	63	133	77	37	63	15	7.0
Spencer	19	368	52	44.1	1	0	28	56.0	11	65	25	14	48	23	6.9
Grant	33	470	78	47.0	16	4	45	81.8	8	35	93	29	44	3	6.2
Smith	29	319	63	47.0	8	1	26	86.7	13	56	20	6	18	2	5.3
Outlaw	81	1,655	170	52.3	5	0	82	44.1	121	313	84	90	78	151	5.2
Riley	40	434	65	44.8	1	0	47	73.4	45	112	11	17	31	35	4.4
Ellis	69	656	91	48.1	13	1	69	59.0	56	88	40	67	49	12	3.7
Woods	62	495	37	31.6	74	22	28	73.7	10	44	134	41	55	0	2.0
Clippers	**82**	**19,880**	**3,060**	**44.4**	**1,051**	**331**	**1,476**	**71.0**	**1,064**	**3,140**	**1,805**	**787**	**1,334**	**435**	**96.7**
Opponents	**82**	**19,880**	**3,207**	**49.6**	**1,049**	**388**	**1,876**	**75.0**	**1,083**	**3,619**	**1,917**	**693**	**1,506**	**459**	**105.8**

Los Angeles Lakers

Player	GP	Min	FGM	Pct	FGA	FGM	FTM	Pct	Off	Total	A	Stl	TO	BS	Avg
			Field Goals		3-Pt FG		Free Throws		Rebounds						
Ceballos	58	2,029	497	50.9	146	58	209	71.6	169	464	105	60	143	19	21.7
Van Exel	80	2,944	465	42.0	511	183	235	78.3	27	223	660	97	220	6	16.9
Divac	80	2,807	485	50.7	53	10	297	77.7	261	829	329	109	205	174	16.0
Jones	64	1,981	342	46.0	246	91	122	72.2	79	249	128	131	75	41	14.0
Campell	73	2,076	360	45.9	1	0	193	66.6	168	445	92	69	98	132	12.5
Peeler	73	1,559	285	43.2	216	84	102	79.7	62	168	122	52	82	13	10.4
Threatt	59	1,384	217	49.7	95	36	88	79.3	21	124	248	54	70	12	9.5
Lynch	56	953	138	46.8	21	3	62	72.1	75	184	62	51	73	10	6.1
Smith	61	1,024	132	42.7	91	32	44	69.8	43	107	102	46	50	7	5.6
Bowie	67	1,225	118	44.2	11	2	68	76.4	72	288	118	21	91	80	4.6
Miller	46	527	70	53.0	5	2	47	61.8	67	152	35	20	38	7	4.1
Keys	6	83	9	34.6	9	0	2	100.0	6	17	2	1	2	2	3.3
Harvey	59	572	77	43.8	1	1	24	53.3	39	102	23	15	25	41	3.0
Rambis	26	195	18	51.4	0	0	8	66.7	10	34	16	3	8	9	1.7
Lakers	**82**	**19,905**	**3,284**	**46.3**	**1,492**	**525**	**1,523**	**73.5**	**1,126**	**3,442**	**2,078**	**750**	**1,243**	**563**	**105.1**
Opponents	**82**	**19,905**	**3,299**	**46.8**	**1,294**	**456**	**1,580**	**70.8**	**1,283**	**3,757**	**2,203**	**644**	**1,390**	**489**	**105.3**

Miami Heat

Player	GP	Min	FGM	Pct	FGA	FGM	FTM	Pct	Off	Total	A	Stl	TO	BS	Avg
			Field Goals		3-Pt FG		Free Throws		Rebounds						
Rice	82	3,014	667	47.5	451	185	312	85.5	99	378	192	112	153	14	22.3
Willis	67	2,390	473	46.6	15	3	205	69.0	227	732	86	60	162	36	17.2
Owens	70	2,296	403	49.1	22	2	194	62.0	203	502	246	80	204	30	14.3
Coles	68	2,207	261	43.0	76	16	141	81.0	46	191	416	99	156	13	10.0
Reeves	67	1,462	206	44.3	171	67	140	71.4	52	186	288	77	132	10	9.2
Geiger	74	1,712	260	53.6	10	4	93	65.0	146	413	55	41	113	51	8.3
Gamble	77	1,223	220	48.9	98	39	87	78.4	29	122	119	52	49	10	7.4
Eackles	54	898	143	43.9	41	18	91	72.2	33	95	72	19	53	2	7.3
Miner	45	871	123	40.3	49	14	69	72.6	38	117	69	15	77	6	7.3
Salley	75	1,955	197	49.9	0	0	153	73.9	110	336	123	47	97	85	7.3
Askins	50	854	81	39.1	78	21	46	80.7	86	198	39	35	25	17	4.6
Lohaus	61	730	97	42.0	155	63	10	66.7	28	102	43	20	29	25	4.4
Pritchard	19	194	18	40.6	8	2	16	76.2	0	12	34	2	12	1	2.3
Heat	**82**	**19,805**	**3,144**	**46.7**	**1,182**	**436**	**1,569**	**73.6**	**1,092**	**3,364**	**1,779**	**662**	**1,291**	**298**	**101.1**
Opponents	**82**	**19,805**	**3,092**	**47.1**	**1,417**	**511**	**1,732**	**74.0**	**1,036**	**3,391**	**1,860**	**656**	**1,332**	**385**	**102.8**

Milwaukee Bucks

Player	GP	Min	FGM	Pct	FGA	FGM	FTM	Pct	Off	Total	A	Stl	TO	BS	Avg
			Field Goals		3-Pt FG		Free Throws		Rebounds						
Robinson	80	2,958	636	45.1	268	86	397	79.6	169	513	197	115	313	22	21.9
Baker	82	3,361	594	48.3	24	7	256	59.3	289	846	296	86	221	116	17.7
Day	82	2,717	445	42.4	418	163	257	75.4	95	322	134	104	157	63	16.0
Murdock	75	2,158	338	41.5	240	90	211	79.0	48	214	482	113	194	12	13.0
Conlon	82	2,064	344	53.2	29	8	119	61.3	160	426	110	42	123	18	9.9
Newman	82	1,896	226	46.3	128	45	137	80.1	72	173	91	69	86	13	7.7
Mayberry	82	1,744	172	42.2	177	72	58	69.9	21	82	276	51	106	4	5.8
Mobley	46	587	78	59.1	2	2	22	48.9	55	153	21	8	24	27	3.9
Barry	52	602	57	42.5	48	16	61	76.3	15	49	85	30	41	4	3.7
Lister	60	776	66	49.3	1	0	35	50.0	67	236	12	16	38	57	2.8
Pinckney	62	835	48	49.5	0	0	44	71.0	65	211	21	34	26	17	2.3
George	3	8	1	33.3	1	0	2	100	1	1	0	0	2	0	1.3
Bucks	**82**	**19,855**	**3,022**	**45.9**	**1,349**	**494**	**1,608**	**71.2**	**1,063**	**3,250**	**1,737**	**674**	**1,393**	**359**	**99.3**
Opponents	**82**	**19,855**	**3,248**	**49.3**	**1,242**	**491**	**1,517**	**72.9**	**1,014**	**3,351**	**2,103**	**770**	**1,359**	**407**	**103.7**

Minnesota Timberwolves

Player	GP	Min	FGM	Pct	FGA	FGM	FTM	Pct	Off	Total	A	Stl	TO	BS	Avg
			Field Goals		3-Pt FG		Free Throws		Rebounds						
Rider	75	2,645	558	44.7	396	139	277	81.7	90	249	245	69	232	23	20.4
Laettner	81	2,770	450	48.9	40	13	409	81.8	164	613	234	101	225	87	16.3
West	71	2,328	351	46.1	61	11	206	83.7	60	227	185	65	126	24	12.9
Gugliotta	77	2,568	371	44.3	186	60	174	69.0	165	572	279	132	189	62	12.7
Rooks	80	2,405	289	47.0	5	0	290	76.1	165	486	97	29	142	71	10.9
Martin	34	803	95	40.8	38	7	57	87.7	14	64	133	34	62	0	7.5
Garland	73	1,931	170	41.5	75	19	89	79.5	48	168	318	71	105	13	6.1
Williams	1	28	1	25.0	0	0	4	80.0	0	1	3	2	3	0	6.0
King	50	792	99	46.7	1	0	68	66.7	54	165	26	24	64	20	5.3
Durham	59	852	117	49.4	26	5	63	65.6	37	94	53	36	45	32	5.1
Smith	64	1,073	116	43.9	108	47	41	65.1	14	73	146	32	50	22	5.0
Foster	78	1,144	150	47.2	23	7	78	70.3	85	259	39	15	71	28	4.9
Shackleford	21	239	39	60.0	0	0	16	80.0	16	67	8	8	8	6	4.5
Guibert	17	167	16	34.0	4	0	13	68.4	16	45	10	8	12	1	2.6
T'wolves	82	19,780	2,792	44.9	1,016	318	1,824	77.5	883	2,973	1,780	609	1,400	402	94.2
Opponents	82	19,780	3,088	47.4	1,243	468	1,820	73.1	1,169	3,474	2,069	703	1,323	512	103.2

New Jersey Nets

Player	GP	Min	FGM	Pct	FGA	FGM	FTM	Pct	Off	Total	A	Stl	TO	BS	Avg
			Field Goals		3-Pt FG		Free Throws		Rebounds						
Coleman	56	2,103	371	42.4	120	28	376	76.7	167	591	187	35	172	94	20.5
Anderson	72	2,689	411	39.9	294	97	348	84.1	73	250	680	103	225	14	17.6
Gilliam	82	2,472	455	50.3	2	0	302	77.0	192	613	99	67	152	89	14.8
Edwards	14	466	69	44.8	45	18	40	95.2	10	37	27	19	35	5	14.0
Morris	71	2,131	351	41.0	317	106	142	72.8	181	402	147	86	117	51	13.4
Benjamin	61	1,598	271	51.0	0	0	133	76.0	94	440	38	23	125	64	11.1
Brown	80	2,466	254	44.6	24	4	139	67.1	178	487	135	69	80	135	8.1
Walters	80	1,435	206	43.9	196	71	40	76.9	18	93	121	37	71	16	6.5
Childs	53	1,021	106	38.0	125	41	55	75.3	14	69	219	42	76	3	5.8
Williams	75	982	149	46.1	5	0	65	53.3	179	425	35	26	59	33	4.8
Higgins	57	735	105	38.5	78	23	35	87.5	25	77	29	10	35	9	4.7
Floyd	48	831	71	33.5	88	25	30	69.8	8	54	126	13	51	6	4.1
Mahorn	58	630	79	52.3	3	1	39	79.6	45	162	26	11	34	12	3.4
Schintzius	43	318	41	38.0	0	0	6	54.5	29	81	15	3	17	17	2.0
Dare	1	3	0	00.0	0	0	0	—	0	1	0	0	1	0	0.0
Nets	82	19,880	2,939	43.6	1,297	414	1,750	75.9	1,213	3,782	1,884	544	1,300	548	98.1
Opponents	82	19,880	3,182	46.1	1,176	440	1,495	72.1	1,056	3,491	1,826	733	1,104	440	101.2

New York Knickerbockers

Player	GP	Min	FGM	Pct	FGA	FGM	FTM	Pct	Off	Total	A	Stl	TO	BS	Avg
			Field Goals		3-Pt FG		Free Throws		Rebounds						
Ewing	79	2,920	730	50.3	21	6	420	75.0	157	867	212	68	256	159	23.9
Starks	80	2,725	419	39.5	611	217	168	73.7	34	219	411	92	160	4	15.3
Smith	76	2,150	352	47.1	31	7	255	79.2	144	324	120	49	147	95	12.7
Harper	80	2,716	337	44.6	292	106	139	72.4	31	194	458	79	151	10	11.5
Oakley	50	1,567	192	48.9	12	3	119	79.3	155	445	126	60	103	7	10.1
Davis	82	1,697	296	48.0	288	131	97	80.8	30	110	150	35	87	11	10.0
Mason	77	2,496	287	56.6	1	0	191	64.1	182	650	240	69	123	21	9.9
Anthony	61	943	128	43.7	155	56	60	78.9	7	64	160	50	57	7	6.1
Bonner	58	1,126	88	45.6	5	1	44	65.7	113	262	80	48	79	23	3.8
M. Williams	41	503	60	45.1	8	0	17	44.7	42	98	49	20	41	4	3.3
H. Williams	56	743	82	45.6	0	0	23	62.2	23	132	27	13	40	45	3.3
Ward	10	44	4	21.1	10	1	7	70.0	1	6	4	2	8	0	1.6
Christie	12	79	5	22.7	7	1	4	80.0	3	13	8	2	13	1	1.3
Knicks	82	19,780	2,985	46.7	1,446	532	1,552	73.4	929	3,402	2,055	591	1,305	387	98.2
Opponents	82	19,780	2,800	43.7	1,165	397	1,802	73.6	1,021	3,338	1,584	639	1,264	324	95.1

Orlando Magic

Player	GP	Min	Field Goals		3-Pt FG		Free Throws		Rebounds		A	Stl	TO	BS	Avg
			FGM	Pct	FGA	FGM	FTM	Pct	Off	Total					
O'Neal	79	2,923	930	58.3	5	0	455	53.3	328	901	214	73	204	192	29.3
Hardaway	77	2,901	585	51.2	249	87	356	76.9	139	336	551	130	258	26	20.9
Anderson	76	2,588	439	47.6	431	179	143	70.4	85	335	314	125	141	22	15.8
Scott	62	1,499	283	43.9	352	150	86	75.4	25	146	131	45	57	14	12.9
Grant	74	2,693	401	56.7	8	0	146	69.2	223	715	173	76	85	88	12.8
Royal	70	1,841	206	47.5	4	0	223	74.6	83	279	198	45	125	16	9.1
Shaw	78	1,836	192	38.9	184	48	70	73.7	52	241	406	73	184	18	6.4
Bowie	77	1,261	177	48.0	40	12	61	83.6	54	139	159	47	86	21	5.5
Turner	49	576	73	41.0	75	27	26	89.7	23	97	38	12	22	3	4.1
Hammink	1	7	1	33.3	0	0	2	100.0	0	2	1	0	0	0	4.0
Avent	71	1066	105	43.0	0	0	48	64.0	97	293	41	28	53	50	3.6
Armstrong	3	8	3	37.5	6	2	2	100.0	1	1	3	1	1	0	3.3
Thompson	38	246	45	39.5	58	18	8	66.7	7	23	43	10	27	2	3.1
Rollins	51	478	20	47.6	0	0	21	67.7	31	95	9	7	23	36	1.2
Magic	**82**	**19,930**	**3,460**	**50.2**	**1,412**	**523**	**1,648**	**66.9**	**1,149**	**3,606**	**2,281**	**672**	**1,297**	**488**	**110.9**
Opponents	**82**	**19,930**	**3,242**	**45.7**	**1,239**	**468**	**1,560**	**74.1**	**1,136**	**3,362**	**1,986**	**700**	**1,234**	**367**	**103.8**

Philadelphia 76ers

Player	GP	Min	Field Goals		3-Pt FG		Free Throws		Rebounds		A	Stl	TO	BS	Avg
			FGM	Pct	FGA	FGM	FTM	Pct	Off	Total					
Barros	82	3,318	571	49.0	425	197	347	89.9	27	242	619	149	242	4	20.6
Malone	19	660	144	50.7	28	11	51	86.4	11	29	29	15	29	0	18.4
Weatherspoon	76	2,991	543	43.9	21	4	283	75.1	144	191	215	115	191	67	18.1
Burton	53	1,564	243	40.1	275	106	220	82.4	49	122	96	32	122	19	15.3
Wright	79	2,044	361	46.5	8	0	182	64.5	191	151	48	37	151	104	11.4
Bradley	82	2,365	315	45.5	3	0	148	63.8	243	142	53	54	142	274	9.5
Grayer	47	1,098	163	42.8	15	5	58	69.9	58	56	74	27	56	4	8.3
Williams	77	1,781	206	47.5	7	0	79	73.8	173	84	59	71	84	40	6.4
Graham	50	775	95	42.6	28	6	55	75.3	19	48	66	29	48	6	5.0
Gaines	11	280	24	47.1	15	2	5	45.5	1	14	33	8	14	1	5.0
Alston	64	1,032	120	46.5	4	0	59	49.2	98	53	33	39	53	35	4.7
Harmon	10	158	21	39.6	1	1	3	50.0	9	7	12	9	7	0	4.6
Tyler	55	809	72	38.1	51	16	35	70.0	13	97	174	36	97	2	3.5
Perry	42	446	27	34.6	14	0	22	55.0	38	21	12	10	21	15	1.8
76ers	**82**	**19,805**	**2,949**	**44.8**	**936**	**355**	**1,567**	**73.7**	**1,105**	**3,335**	**1,566**	**643**	**1,355**	**576**	**95.4**
Opponents	**82**	**19,805**	**3,100**	**46.5**	**1,287**	**467**	**1,569**	**76.3**	**1,143**	**3,406**	**1,992**	**712**	**1,299**	**422**	**100.4**

Phoenix Suns

Player	GP	Min	Field Goals		3-Pt FG		Free Throws		Rebounds		A	Stl	TO	BS	Avg
			FGM	Pct	FGA	FGM	FTM	Pct	Off	Total					
Barkley	68	2,382	554	48.6	219	74	379	74.8	203	756	276	110	150	45	23.0
Manning	46	1,510	340	54.7	21	6	136	67.3	97	276	154	41	121	57	17.9
Majerle	82	3,091	438	42.5	548	199	206	73.0	104	375	340	96	105	38	15.6
Johnson	47	1,352	246	47.0	26	4	234	81.0	32	115	360	47	105	18	15.5
Green	82	2,687	311	50.4	127	43	251	73.2	194	669	127	55	114	31	11.2
Person	78	1,800	309	48.4	266	116	80	79.2	67	201	105	48	79	24	10.4
Tisdale	65	1,276	278	48.4	0	0	94	77.0	83	247	45	29	64	27	10.0
Perry	82	1,977	306	52.0	60	25	158	81.0	51	151	394	156	163	4	9.7
Ainge	74	1,374	194	46.0	214	78	105	80.8	25	109	210	46	79	7	7.7
Dumas	15	167	37	50.7	1	0	8	50.0	18	29	7	10	9	2	5.5
Ruffin	49	319	84	42.6	99	38	27	71.1	8	23	48	14	47	2	4.8
Schayes	69	823	126	50.8	1	1	50	72.5	57	208	89	20	64	37	4.4
Kleine	75	968	119	44.9	2	0	42	85.7	82	259	39	14	35	18	3.7
Lang	12	53	4	40.0	0	0	3	75.0	3	4	1	0	5	2	0.9
Suns	**82**	**19,830**	**3,356**	**48.2**	**1,584**	**584**	**1,777**	**75.6**	**1,027**	**3,430**	**2,198**	**687**	**1,167**	**312**	**110.6**
Opponents	**82**	**19,830**	**3,320**	**47.7**	**1,544**	**525**	**1,590**	**74.4**	**1,038**	**3,469**	**2,149**	**658**	**1,285**	**391**	**106.8**

Portland Trail Blazers

Player	GP	Min	Field Goals		3-Pt FG		Free Throws		Rebounds		A	Stl	TO	BS	Avg
			FGM	Pct	FGA	FGM	FTM	Pct	Off	Total					
C. Robinson......	75	2,725	597	45.2	383	142	265	69.4	152	423	198	79	158	82	21.3
Strickland......	64	2,267	441	46.6	123	46	283	74.5	73	317	562	123	209	9	18.9
Thorpe.............	70	2,096	385	56.5	7	0	167	59.4	202	558	112	41	132	28	13.4
Williams...........	82	2,422	309	51.2	2	1	138	67.3	251	669	78	67	119	69	9.2
J. Robinson...	71	1,539	255	40.9	223	76	65	59.1	42	132	180	48	127	13	9.2
Grant	75	1,771	286	46.1	26	8	103	70.5	103	284	82	56	62	53	9.1
Porter...............	35	770	105	39.3	114	44	58	70.7	18	81	133	30	58	2	8.9
Kersey	63	1,143	203	41.5	27	7	95	76.6	93	256	82	52	64	35	8.1
McKie	45	827	116	44.4	28	11	50	68.5	35	129	89	36	39	16	6.5
Dudley	82	2,245	181	40.6	1	0	85	46.4	325	764	34	43	81	126	5.5
Bryant	49	658	101	52.6	2	1	41	65.1	55	161	28	19	39	16	5.0
Henson	37	380	37	43.0	52	23	22	88.0	3	26	85	9	30	0	3.2
Edwards	28	266	32	38.6	0	0	11	64.7	10	43	8	5	14	8	2.7
Trail Blazers...	82	19,705	3,217	45.1	1,266	462	1,555	69.7	1,352	3,795	1,846	668	1,212	467	103.1
Opponents......	82	19,705	2,951	45.6	1,189	442	1,794	75.4	883	3,178	1,789	638	1,302	405	99.2

Sacramento Kings

Player	GP	Min	Field Goals		3-Pt FG		Free Throws		Rebounds		A	Stl	TO	BS	Avg
			FGM	Pct	FGA	FTM	FTM	Pct	Off	Total					
Richmond........	82	3,172	668	44.6	424	156	375	84.3	69	234	311	91	234	29	22.8
Williams	77	2,739	445	44.6	296	103	266	73.1	100	243	316	123	243	63	16.4
Grant	80	2,289	413	51.1	4	1	231	63.6	207	163	99	49	163	116	13.2
Webb...............	76	2,458	302	43.8	145	48	266	93.4	29	185	468	75	185	8	11.6
Polynice...........	81	2,534	376	54.4	1	1	231	63.9	277	113	62	48	113	52	10.8
M. Smith	82	1,736	220	54.2	2	0	226	48.5	174	106	67	61	106	49	6.9
Simmons...........	58	1,064	131	42.0	16	6	124	70.2	61	70	89	28	70	23	5.6
Brown...............	67	1,086	124	43.2	47	14	127	67.1	24	78	133	99	78	19	4.7
Hurley	68	1,105	103	36.3	76	21	59	76.3	14	110	226	29	110	0	4.2
Causwell...........	58	820	76	51.7	1	0	55	58.2	57	33	15	14	33	80	3.6
Turner	30	149	23	40.4	5	2	58	57.1	17	12	7	8	12	1	2.3
Lee	22	75	9	36.0	18	7	57	85.7	0	5	5	6	5	3	2.0
Phelps..............	3	5	0	00.0	0	0	20	00.0	0	0	1	0	0	0	0.0
Kings	82	19,855	3,025	46.8	1,037	359	1,647	71.1	1,073	3,398	1,824	650	1,449	457	98.2
Opponents......	82	19,855	2,964	45.3	1,240	377	1,833	74.1	1,145	3,413	1,820	756	1,348	515	99.2

San Antonio Spurs

Player	GP	Min	Field Goals		3-Pt FG		Free Throws		Rebounds		A	Stl	TO	BS	Avg
			FGM	Pct	FGA	FGM	FTM	Pct	Off	Total					
Robinson	81	3,074	788	53.0	20	6	656	77.4	234	877	236	134	233	262	27.6
Elliott................	81	2,858	502	46.8	333	136	326	80.7	63	287	206	78	151	38	18.1
Johnson............	82	3,011	448	51.9	22	3	202	68.5	49	208	670	114	207	13	13.4
Del Negro........	75	2,360	372	48.6	162	66	128	79.0	28	192	226	61	56	14	12.5
Person	81	2,033	317	42.3	445	172	66	64.7	49	258	106	45	102	12	10.8
Rodman............	49	1,568	137	57.1	2	0	75	67.6	274	823	97	31	98	23	7.1
Reid	81	1,566	201	50.8	2	1	160	68.7	120	393	55	60	113	32	7.0
Cummings........	76	1,273	224	48.3	0	0	72	58.5	138	378	59	36	95	19	6.8
Rivers	63	989	108	35.8	127	45	60	73.2	15	109	162	65	60	21	5.1
Anderson..........	38	556	76	46.9	19	3	30	73.2	15	55	52	26	38	10	4.9
Malone.............	17	149	13	37.1	2	1	22	68.8	20	46	6	2	11	3	2.9
Haley	31	117	26	42.6	1	0	21	65.5	8	27	2	3	13	5	2.4
Nwosu	23	84	9	32.1	0	0	13	76.5	11	24	3	0	9	3	1.3
Spurs	82	19,855	3,236	48.4	1,158	434	1,836	73.8	1,029	3,690	1,919	656	1,246	456	106.6
Opponents......	82	19,855	3,168	45.4	1,251	426	1,491	71.4	1,017	3,320	1,878	633	1,182	408	100.6

Seattle SuperSonics

Player	GP	Min	FGM	Pct	FGA	FGM	FTM	Pct	Off	Total	A	Stl	TO	BS	Avg
			Field Goals		3-Pt FG		Free Throws		Rebounds						
Payton	82	3,015	685	50.9	232	70	249	71.6	108	281	583	204	201	13	20.6
Schrempf	82	2,886	521	52.3	181	93	437	83.9	135	508	310	93	176	35	19.2
Kemp	82	2,679	545	54.7	7	2	438	74.9	318	893	149	102	259	122	18.7
Gill	73	2,125	392	45.7	171	63	155	74.2	99	290	192	117	138	28	13.7
Perkins	82	2,356	346	46.6	343	136	215	79.9	96	398	135	72	77	45	12.7
Askew	71	1,721	248	49.2	94	31	176	73.9	65	181	176	49	85	13	9.9
Marciulionis	66	1,194	216	47.3	87	35	145	73.2	17	68	110	72	98	3	9.3
McMillan	80	2,070	166	41.8	155	53	34	58.6	65	302	421	165	126	53	5.2
Houston	39	258	49	45.8	22	6	28	73.7	20	55	6	13	20	5	3.4
Johnson	64	907	85	44.3	1	0	29	63.0	101	289	16	17	54	67	3.1
Cartwright	29	430	27	39.1	0	0	15	62.5	25	87	10	6	18	3	2.4
Wingfield	20	81	18	35.3	12	2	8	80.0	11	30	3	5	8	3	2.3
Scheffler	18	102	12	52.2	0	0	15	83.3	8	23	4	2	3	2	2.2
King	2	6	0	00.0	0	0	0	00.0	0	0	0	0	0	0	0.0
SuperSonics	82	19,830	3,310	49.1	1,305	491	1,944	75.8	1,068	3,405	2,115	917	1,295	392	110.4
Opponents	82	19,830	3,008	45.3	1,514	520	1,848	73.5	1,064	3,271	1,849	652	1,485	493	102.2

Utah Jazz

Player	GP	Min	FGM	Pct	FGA	FGM	FTM	Pct	Off	Total	A	Stl	TO	BS	Avg
			Field Goals		3-Pt FG		Free Throws		Rebounds						
Malone	82	3,126	830	53.6	41	11	516	74.2	156	871	285	129	236	85	26.7
Hornacek	81	2,696	482	51.4	219	89	284	82.2	53	210	347	129	145	17	16.5
Stockton	82	2,867	429	54.2	227	102	246	80.4	57	251	1011	194	267	22	14.7
Benoit	71	1,841	285	48.6	115	38	132	84.1	96	368	58	45	75	47	10.4
Carr	78	1,677	290	53.1	4	1	165	82.1	81	265	67	24	87	68	9.6
Spenser	34	905	105	48.8	0	0	107	79.3	90	260	17	12	68	32	9.3
Edwards	67	1,112	181	46.1	75	22	75	83.3	50	130	77	43	81	16	6.9
Chambers	81	1,240	195	45.7	24	4	109	80.7	66	213	73	25	52	30	6.2
Keefe	75	1,270	172	57.7	0	0	117	67.6	135	327	30	36	62	25	6.1
Russell	63	860	104	43.7	44	13	62	66.7	44	141	34	48	42	11	4.5
Crotty	80	1,019	93	40.3	36	11	98	81.0	27	97	205	39	70	6	3.7
Watson	60	673	76	50.0	19	5	38	67.9	16	74	59	35	51	11	3.3
Donaldson	43	613	44	59.5	0	0	22	71.0	19	107	14	6	22	28	2.6
Jazz	82	19,780	3,243	51.2	801	301	1,939	78.1	874	3,286	2,256	758	1,289	392	106.4
Opponents	82	19,780	2,845	45.3	1,431	546	1,835	74.1	917	3,042	1,713	648	1,353	429	98.4

Washington Bullets

Player	GP	Min	FGM	Pct	FGA	FGM	FTM	Pct	Off	Total	A	Stl	TO	BS	Avg
			Field Goals		3-Pt FG		Free Throws		Rebounds						
Webber	54	2,067	464	49.5	145	40	117	50.2	200	518	256	83	167	85	20.1
Howard	65	2,348	455	48.9	7	0	194	66.4	184	545	165	52	166	15	17.0
Cheaney	78	2,651	512	45.3	283	96	173	81.2	105	321	177	80	151	21	16.6
Chapman	45	1,468	254	39.7	274	86	137	86.2	23	113	128	67	62	15	16.2
Skiles	62	2,077	265	45.5	228	96	179	88.6	26	159	452	70	172	6	13.0
MacLean	39	1,052	158	43.8	40	10	104	76.5	46	165	51	15	44	3	11.0
Muresan	73	1,720	303	56.0	0	0	124	70.9	179	488	38	48	115	127	10.0
Butler	76	1,554	214	42.1	141	46	123	66.5	43	170	91	61	106	10	7.9
Duckworth	40	818	118	44.2	10	2	45	64.3	65	195	20	21	59	24	7.1
Overton	82	1,704	207	41.6	125	53	109	87.2	26	143	246	53	104	2	7.0
Tucker	62	982	96	45.7	1	0	51	61.4	44	170	68	46	56	11	3.9
Stewart	40	346	41	46.1	2	0	20	66.7	28	67	18	16	16	9	2.6
Walker	24	266	18	42.9	0	0	21	75.0	19	47	7	5	15	5	2.4
McIlvaine	55	534	34	47.9	0	0	28	68.3	40	105	10	10	19	60	1.7
Bullets	82	19,855	3,176	46.0	1,264	433	1,457	72.4	1,044	3,263	1,749	648	1,301	404	100.5
Opponents	82	19,855	3,246	48.0	1,145	438	1,771	76.5	1,107	3,628	1,959	701	1,359	446	106.1

1995 NBA Draft

First Round

1. Joe Smith, Golden State
2. Antonio McDyess, LA Clippers (to Den)
3. Jerry Stackhouse, Philadelphia
4. Rasheed Wallace, Washington
5. Kevin Garnett, Minnesota
6. Bryant Reeves, Vancouver
7. Damon Stoudamire, Toronto
8. Shawn Respert, Portland (to Milwaukee)
9. Ed O'Bannon, New Jersey
10. Kurt Thomas, Miami
11. Gary Trent, Milwaukee (to Portland)
12. Cherokee Parks, Dallas
13. Corliss Williamson, Sacramento
14. Eric Williams, Boston
15. Brent Barry, Denver (to LA Clippers)
16. Alan Henderson, Atlanta
17. Bob Sura, Cleveland
18. Theo Ratliff, Detroit
19. Randolph Childress, Detroit
20. Jason Caffey, Chicago
21. Michael Finley, Phoenix
22. George Zidek, Charlotte
23. Travis Best, Indiana
24. Loren Meyer, Dallas
25. David Vaughn, Orlando
26. Sherell Ford, Seattle
27. Mario Bennett, Phoenix
28. Greg Ostertag, Utah
29. Cory Alexander, San Antonio

Second Round

30. Lou Roe, Detroit
31. Dragan Tarlac, Chicago
32. Terrence Rencher, Washington
33. Junior Burrough, Boston
34. Andrew DeClercq, Golden State
35. Jimmy King, Toronto
36. Lawrence Moten, Vancouver
37. Frankie King, LA Lakers
38. Rashard Griffith, Milwaukee
39. Donny Marshall, Cleveland
40. Dwayne Whitfield, Golden State
41. Erik Meek, Houston
42. Donnie Boyce, Atlanta
43. Eric Snow, Milwukee
44. Anthony Pelle, Denver
45. Troy Brown, Atlanta
46. George Banks, Miami
47. Tyus Edney, Sacramento
48. Mark Davis, Minnesota
49. Jerome Allen, Minnesota
50. Martin Lewis, Golden State
51. Dejan Bodiroga, Sacramento
52. Fred Holberg, Indiana
53. Constantin Popa, LA Clippers
54. Zydrunas Ilgauskas, Seattle
55. Michael McDonald, Golden State
56. Chris Carr, Phoenix
57. Cuonzo Martin, Atlanta
58. Don Reid, Detroit

THEY SAID IT

Bryant Reeves, senior Oklahoma State center, when asked if his strong performance during the NCAAs might have bolstered his status in the NBA draft: "What happens to me next year will happen to me no matter what happens."

Clothes Call

The usual protocol for players on NBA injured lists is simple: You show up in mufti for home games and sit on the bench. But what happens if two disabled players wear almost exactly the same thing—as Derrick Coleman and Sean Higgins did for the New Jersey Nets' game against the Charlotte Hornets at the Meadowlands Arena last week? Each came in black courduroy slacks and a $400 Coogi multicolored sweater that appeared to have been designed at a state fair spin-art booth. "They looked like twins," said New Jersey coach Butch Beard.

Did either say to the other, "Well, one of us is going to have to go home and change"? Uh, no. Coleman and Higgins holed up in the locker room and watched the game on TV—vanity particularly surprising from Coleman, who earlier this season offered Beard a blank check for the fines he would incur for his flouting of the Nets' dress code on road trips.

NBA Champions

Season	Winner	Series	Runner-Up	Winning Coach
1946-47	Philadelphia	4–1	Chicago	Eddie Gottlieb
1947-48	Baltimore	4–2	Philadelphia	Buddy Jeannette
1948-49	Minneapolis	4–2	Washington	John Kundla
1949-50	Minneapolis	4–2	Syracuse	John Kundla
1950-51	Rochester	4–3	New York	Les Harrison
1951-52	Minneapolis	4–3	New York	John Kundla
1952-53	Minneapolis	4–1	New York	John Kundla
1953-54	Minneapolis	4–3	Syracuse	John Kundla
1954-55	Syracuse	4–3	Ft Wayne	Al Cervi
1955-56	Philadelphia	4–1	Ft Wayne	George Senesky
1956-57	Boston	4–3	St Louis	Red Auerbach
1957-58	St Louis	4–2	Boston	Alex Hannum
1958-59	Boston	4–0	Minneapolis	Red Auerbach
1959-60	Boston	1–3	St Louis	Red Auerbach
1960-61	Boston	4–1	St Louis	Red Auerbach
1961-62	Boston	4–3	LA Lakers	Red Auerbach
1962-63	Boston	4–2	LA Lakers	Red Auerbach
1963-64	Boston	4–1	San Francisco	Red Auerbach
1964-65	Boston	4–1	LA Lakers	Red Auerbach
1965-66	Boston	4–3	LA Lakers	Red Auerbach
1966-67	Philadelphia	4–2	San Francisco	Alex Hannum
1967-68	Boston	4–2	LA Lakers	Bill Russell
1968-69	Boston	4–3	LA Lakers	Bill Russell
1969-70	New York	4–3	LA Lakers	Red Holzman
1970-71	Milwaukee	4–0	Baltimore	Larry Costello
1971-72	LA Lakers	4–1	New York	Bill Sharman
1972-73	New York	4–1	LA Lakers	Red Holzman
1973-74	Boston	4–3	Milwaukee	Tommy Heinsohn
1974-75	Golden State	4–0	Washington	Al Attles
1975-76	Boston	4–2	Phoenix	Tommy Heinsohn
1976-77	Portland	4–2	Philadelphia	Jack Ramsay
1977-78	Washington	4–3	Seattle	Dick Motta
1978-79	Seattle	4–1	Washington	Lenny Wilkens
1979-80	LA Lakers	4–2	Philadelphia	Paul Westhead
1980-81	Boston	4–2	Houston	Bill Fitch
1981-82	LA Lakers	4–2	Philadelphia	Pat Riley
1982-83	Philadelphia	4–0	LA Lakers	Billy Cunningham
1983-84	Boston	4–3	LA Lakers	K.C. Jones
1984-85	LA Lakers	4–2	Boston	Pat Riley
1985-86	Boston	4–2	Houston	K.C. Jones
1986-87	LA Lakers	4–2	Boston	Pat Riley
1987-88	LA Lakers	4–3	Detroit	Pat Riley
1988-89	Detroit	4–0	LA Lakers	Chuck Daly
1989-90	Detroit	4–1	Portland	Chuck Daly
1990-91	Chicago	4–1	LA Lakers	Phil Jackson
1991-92	Chicago	4–2	Portland	Phil Jackson
1992-93	Chicago	4–2	Phoenix	Phil Jackson
1993-94	Houston	4–3	New York	Rudy Tomjanovich
1994-95	Houston	4–0	Orlando	Rudy Tomjanovich

NBA Finals Most Valuable Player

1969	Jerry West, LA	1983	Moses Malone, Phil
1970	Willis Reed, NY	1984	Larry Bird, Bos
1971	Kareem Abdul-Jabbar, Mil	1985	Kareem Abdul-Jabbar, LA Lakers
1972	Wilt Chamberlain, LA	1986	Larry Bird, Bos
1973	Willis Reed, NY	1987	Magic Johnson, LA Lakers
1974	John Havlicek, Bos	1988	James Worthy, LA Lakers
1975	Rick Barry, GS	1989	Joe Dumars, Det
1976	JoJo White, Bos	1990	Isiah Thomas, Det
1977	Bill Walton, Port	1991	Michael Jordan, Chi
1978	Wes Unseld, Wash	1992	Michael Jordan, Chi
1979	Dennis Johnson, Sea	1993	Michael Jordan, Chi
1980	Magic Johnson, LA	1994	Hakeem Olajuwon, Hou
1981	Cedric Maxwell, Bos	1995	Hakeem Olajuwon, Hou
1982	Magic Johnson, LA		

NBA Most Valuable Player: Maurice Podoloff Trophy

Season	Player, Team	GP	Field Goals FGM	Pct	3-Pt FG FGM	Pct	Free Throws FTM	Pct	Rebounds Off	Total	A	Stl	BS	Avg
1955-56	Bob Pettit, StL	72	646	42.9	–	–	557	73.6	–	1,164	189	–	–	25.7
1956-57	Bob Cousy, Bos	64	478	37.8	–	–	363	82.1	–	309	478	–	–	20.6
1957-58	Bill Russell, Bos	69	456	44.2	–	–	230	51.9	–	1,564	202	–	–	16.6
1958-59	Bob Pettit, StL	72	719	43.8	–	–	667	75.9	–	1,182	221	–	–	29.2
1959-60	Wilt Chamberlain, Phil	72	1,065	46.1	–	–	577	58.2	–	1,941	168	–	–	37.6
1960-61	Bill Russell, Bos	78	532	42.6	–	–	258	55.0	–	1,868	264	–	–	16.9
1961-62	Bill Russell, Bos	76	575	45.7	–	–	286	59.5	–	1,891	341	–	–	18.9
1962-63	Bill Russell, Bos	78	511	43.2	–	–	287	55.5	–	1,843	348	–	–	16.8
1963-64	Oscar Robertson, Cin	79	840	48.3	–	–	800	85.3	–	783	868	–	–	31.4
1964-65	Bill Russell, Bos	78	429	43.8	–	–	244	57.3	–	1,878	410	–	–	14.1
1965-66	Wilt Chamberlain, Phil	79	1,074	54.0	–	–	501	51.3	–	1,943	414	–	–	33.5
1966-67	Wilt Chamberlain, Phil	81	785	68.3	–	–	386	44.1	–	1,957	630	–	–	24.1
1967-68	Wilt Chamberlain, Phil	82	819	59.5	–	–	354	38.0	–	1,952	702	–	–	24.3
1968-69	Wes Unseld, Balt	82	427	47.6	–	–	277	60.5	–	1,491	213	–	–	13.8
1969-70	Willis Reed, NY	81	702	50.7	–	–	351	75.6	–	1,126	161	–	–	21.7
1970-71	Kareem Abdul-Jabbar, Mil	82	1,063	57.7	–	–	470	69.0	–	1,311	272	–	–	31.7
1971-72	Kareem Abdul-Jabbar, Mil	81	1,159	57.4	–	–	504	68.9	–	1,346	370	–	–	34.8
1972-73	Dave Cowens, Bos	82	740	45.2	–	–	204	77.9	–	1,329	333	–	–	20.5
1973-74	Kareem Abdul-Jabbar, Mil	81	948	53.9	–	–	295	70.2	287	1,178	386	112	283	27.0
1974-75	Bob McAdoo, Buff	82	1,095	51.2	–	–	641	80.5	307	1,155	179	92	174	34.5
1975-76	Kareem Abdul-Jabbar, LA	82	914	52.9	–	–	447	70.3	272	1,383	413	119	338	27.7
1976-77	Kareem Abdul-Jabbar, LA	82	888	57.9	–	–	376	70.1	266	1,090	319	101	261	26.2
1977-78	Bill Walton, Port	58	460	52.2	–	–	177	72.0	118	766	291	60	146	18.9
1978-79	Moses Malone, Hou	82	716	54.0	–	–	599	73.9	587	1,444	147	79	119	24.8
1979-80	Kareem Abdul-Jabbar, LA	82	835	60.4	0	00.0	364	76.5	190	886	371	81	280	24.8
1980-81	Julius Erving, Phil	82	794	52.1	4	22.2	422	78.7	244	657	364	173	147	24.6
1981-82	Moses Malone, Hou	81	945	51.9	0	00.0	630	76.2	558	1,188	142	76	125	31.1
1982-83	Moses Malone, Phil	78	654	50.1	0	00.0	600	76.1	445	1,194	101	89	157	24.5
1983-84	Larry Bird, Bos	79	758	49.2	18	24.7	374	88.8	181	796	520	144	69	24.2
1984-85	Larry Bird, Bos	80	918	52.2	56	42.7	403	88.2	164	842	531	129	98	28.7
1985-86	Larry Bird, Bos	82	796	49.6	82	42.3	441	89.6	190	805	557	166	51	25.8
1986-87	Magic Johnson, LA Lakers	80	683	52.2	8	20.5	535	84.8	122	504	977	138	36	23.9
1987-88	Michael Jordan, Chi	82	1,069	53.5	7	13.2	723	84.1	139	449	485	259	131	35.0
1988-89	Magic Johnson, LA Lakers	77	579	50.9	59	31.4	513	91.1	111	607	988	138	22	22.5
1989-90	Magic Johnson, LA Lakers	79	546	48.0	106	38.4	567	89.0	128	522	907	132	34	22.3
1990-91	Michael Jordan, Chi	82	990	53.9	29	31.2	571	85.1	118	492	453	223	83	31.5
1991-92	Michael Jordan, Chi	80	943	51.9	27	27.0	491	83.2	91	511	489	182	75	30.1
1992-93	Charles Barkley, Phoe	76	716	52.0	67	30.5	445	76.5	237	928	385	119	74	25.6
1993-94	Hakeem Olajuwon, Hou	80	894	52.8	8	42.1	388	71.6	229	955	287	128	297	27.3
1994-95	David Robinson, SA	81	788	53.0	6	30.0	656	77.4	234	877	236	134	262	27.6

Coach of the Year: Arnold "Red" Auerbach Trophy

1962-63	Harry Gallatin, StL
1963-64	Alex Hannum, SF
1964-65	Red Auerbach, Bos
1965-66	Dolph Schayes, Phil
1966-67	Johnny Kerr, Chi
1967-68	Richie Guerin, StL
1968-69	Gene Shue, Balt
1969-70	Red Holzman, NY
1970-71	Dick Motta, Chi
1971-72	Bill Sharman, LA
1972-73	Tom Heinsohn, Bos
1973-74	Ray Scott, Det
1974-75	Phil Johnson, KC-Oma
1975-76	Bill Fitch, Clev
1976-77	Tom Nissalke, Hou
1977-78	Hubie Brown, Atl
1978-79	Cotton Fitzsimmons, KC
1979-80	Bill Fitch, Bos
1980-81	Jack McKinney, Ind
1981-82	Gene Shue, Wash
1982-83	Don Nelson, Mil
1983-84	Frank Layden, Utah
1984-85	Don Nelson, Mil
1985-86	Mike Fratello, Atl
1986-87	Mike Schuler, Port
1987-88	Doug Moe, Den
1988-89	Cotton Fitzsimmons, Phoe
1989-90	Pat Riley, LA Lakers
1990-91	Don Chaney, Hou
1991-92	Don Nelson, GS
1992-93	Pat Riley, NY
1993-94	Lenny Wilkens, Atl
1994-95	Del Harris, LA Lakers

Note: Award named after Auerbach in 1986.

NBA Rookie of the Year: Eddie Gottlieb Trophy

1952-53...Don Meineke, FW
1953-54...Ray Felix, Balt
1954-55...Bob Pettit, Mil
1955-56...Maurice Stokes, Roch
1956-57...Tom Heinsohn, Bos
1957-58...Woody Sauldsberry, Phil
1958-59...Elgin Baylor, Minn
1959-60...Wilt Chamberlain, Phil
1960-61...Oscar Robertson, Cin
1961-62...Walt Bellamy, Chi
1962-63...Terry Dischinger, Chi
1963-64...Jerry Lucas, Cin
1964-65...Willis Reed, NY
1965-66...Rick Barry, SF
1966-67...Dave Bing, Det

1967-68...Earl Monroe, Balt
1968-69...Wes Unseld, Balt
1969-70...K. Abdul-Jabbar, Mil
1970-71...Dave Cowens, Bos
        Geoff Petrie, Port
1971-72...Sidney Wicks, Port
1972-73...Bob McAdoo, Buff
1973-74...Ernie DiGregorio, Buff
1974-75...Keith Wilkes, GS
1975-76...Alvan Adams, Phoe
1976-77...Adrian Dantley, Buff
1977-78...Walter Davis, Phoe
1978-79...Phil Ford, KC
1979-80...Larry Bird, Bos
1980-81...Darrell Griffith, Utah

1981-82...Buck Williams, NJ
1982-83...Terry Cummings, SD
1983-84...Ralph Sampson, Hou
1984-85...Michael Jordan, Chi
1985-86...Patrick Ewing, NY
1986-87...Chuck Person, Ind
1987-88...Mark Jackson, NY
1988-89...Mitch Richmond, GS
1989-90...David Robinson, SA
1990-91...Derrick Coleman, NJ
1991-92...Larry Johnson, Char
1992-93...Shaquille O'Neal, Orl
1993-94...Chris Webber, GS
1994-95...Jason Kidd, Dal
        Grant Hill, Det

NBA Defensive Player of the Year

1982-83.............................Sidney Moncrief, Mil
1983-84.............................Sidney Moncrief, Mil
1984-85.............................Mark Eaton, Utah
1985-86.............................Alvin Robertson, SA
1986-87.............................Michael Cooper, LA Lakers
1987-88.............................Michael Jordan, Chi
1988-89.............................Mark Eaton, Utah
1989-90.............................Dennis Rodman, Det
1990-91.............................Dennis Rodman, Det
1991-92.............................David Robinson, SA
1992-93.............................Hakeem Olajuwon, Hou
1993-94.............................Hakeem Olajuwon, Hou
1994-95.............................Dikembe Mutombo, Den

NBA Sixth Man Award

1982-83.............................Bobby Jones, Phil
1983-84.............................Kevin McHale, Bos
1984-85.............................Kevin McHale, Bos
1985-86.............................Bill Walton, Bos
1986-87.............................Ricky Pierce, Mil
1987-88.............................Roy Tarpley, Dall
1988-89.............................Eddie Johnson, Phoe
1989-90.............................Ricky Pierce, Mil
1990-91.............................Detlef Schrempf, Ind
1991-92.............................Detlef Schrempf, Ind
1992-93.............................Cliff Robinson, Port
1993-94.............................Dell Curry, Char
1994-95.............................Anthony Mason, NY

J. Walter Kennedy Citizenship Award

1974-75.............................Wes Unseld, Wash
1975-76.............................Slick Watts, Sea
1976-77.............................Dave Bing, Wash
1977-78.............................Bob Lanier, Det
1978-79.............................Calvin Murphy, Hou
1979-80.............................Austin Carr, Clev
1980-81.............................Mike Glenn, NY
1981-82.............................Kent Benson, Det
1982-83.............................Julius Erving, Phil
1983-84.............................Frank Layden, Utah
1984-85.............................Dan Issel, Den
1985-86.............................Michael Cooper, LA Lakers
        Rory Sparrow, NY
1986-87.............................Isiah Thomas, Det
1987-88.............................Alex English, Den
1988-89.............................Thurl Bailey, Utah

Kennedy Citizenship Award (Cont.)

1989-90.............................Glenn Rivers, Atl
1990-91.............................Kevin Johnson, Phoe
1991-92.............................Magic Johnson, LA Lakers
1992-93.............................Terry Porter, Port
1993-94.............................Joe Dumars, Det
1994-95.............................Joe O'Toole, Atl

NBA Most Improved Player

1985-86.............................Alvin Robertson, SA
1986-87.............................Dale Ellis, Sea
1987-88.............................Kevin Duckworth, Port
1988-89.............................Kevin Johnson, Phoe
1989-90.............................Rony Seikaly, Mia
1990-91.............................Scott Skiles, Orl
1991-92.............................Pervis Ellison, Wash
1992-93.............................Chris Jackson, Den
1993-94.............................Don MacLean, Wash
1994-95.............................Dana Barros, Phil

NBA Executive of the Year

1972-73.............................Joe Axelson, KC-Oma
1973-74.............................Eddie Donovan, Buff
1974-75.............................Dick Vertlieb, GS
1975-76.............................Jerry Colangelo, Phoe
1976-77.............................Ray Patterson, Hou
1977-78.............................Angelo Drossos, SA
1978-79.............................Bob Ferry, Wash
1979-80.............................Red Auerbach, Bos
1980-81.............................Jerry Colangelo, Phoe
1981-82.............................Bob Ferry, Wash
1982-83.............................Zollie Volchok, Sea
1983-84.............................Frank Layden, Utah
1984-85.............................Vince Boryla, Den
1985-86.............................Stan Kasten, Atl
1986-87.............................Stan Kasten, Atl
1987-88.............................Jerry Krause, Chi
1988-89.............................Jerry Colangelo, Phoe
1989-90.............................Bob Bass, SA
1990-91.............................Bucky Buckwalter, Port
1991-92.............................Wayne Embry, Cle
1992-93.............................Jerry Colangelo, Phoe
1993-94.............................Bob Whitsitt, Seattle
1994-95.............................Jerry West, LA Lakers

Selected by *The Sporting News*.

Scoring

MOST POINTS, LIFETIME

Kareem Abdul-Jabbar	38,387
Wilt Chamberlain	31,419
Moses Malone	27,409
Elvin Hayes	27,313
Oscar Robertson	26,710
John Havlicek	26,395
Alex English	25,613
Dominique Wilkins	25,389
Jerry West	25,192
Adrian Dantley	23,177

MOST POINTS, SEASON

Wilt Chamberlain, Phil	4,029	1961-62
Wilt Chamberlain, SF	3,586	1962-63
Michael Jordan, Chi	3,041	1986-87
Wilt Chamberlain, Phil	3,033	1960-61
Wilt Chamberlain, SF	2,948	1963-64
Michael Jordan, Chi	2,868	1986-87
Bob McAdoo, Buff	2,831	1974-75
Rick Barry, SF	2,775	1966-67
Michael Jordan, Chi	2,753	1989-90
Elgin Baylor, LA	2,719	1962-63

HIGHEST SCORING AVERAGE, CAREER

Michael Jordan	32.2	684 games
Wilt Chamberlain	30.1	1,045 games
Elgin Baylor	27.4	846 games
Jerry West	27.0	932 games
Bob Pettit	26.4	792 games
George Gervin	26.2	791 games
Karl Malone	26.0	816 games
Dominique Wilkins	25.8	984 games
David Robinson	25.7	475 games
Oscar Robertson	25.7	1,040 games

HIGHEST SCORING AVERAGE, SEASON

Wilt Chamberlain, Phil	50.4	1961-62
Wilt Chamberlain, SF	44.8	1962-63
Wilt Chamberlain, Phil	38.4	1960-61
Wilt Chamberlain, Phil	37.6	1959-60
Michael Jordan, Chi	37.1	1986-87
Wilt Chamberlain, SF	36.9	1963-64
Rick Barry, SF	35.6	1966-67
Michael Jordan, Chi	35.0	1987-88
Elgin Baylor, LA	34.8	1960-61

Note: Minimum 70 games.

MOST POINTS, GAME

	Player, Team	Opp	Date
100	Wilt Chamberlain, Phi	NY	3/2/62
78	Wilt Chamberlain, Phi	LA	12/8/61
73	Wilt Chamberlain, Phi	Chi	1/13/62
73	Wilt Chamberlain, SF	NY	11/16/62
73	David Thompson, Den	Det	4/9/78
72	Wilt Chamberlain, SF	LA	11/3/62
71	David Robinson, SA	LAC	4/24/94
71	Elgin Baylor, LA	NY	11/15/60
70	Wilt Chamberlain, SF	Syr	3/10/63
69	Michael Jordan, Chi	Cle	3/28/90

THEY SAID IT

Brian Williams, Denver Nugget forward, on how the fractious atmosphere surrounding his team could be improved: "We all need to join hands and sing 'Kumbaya.'"

Field Goal Percentage

Highest Field Goal Percentage, Career: .599—Artis Gilmore
Highest Field Goal Percentage, Season: .727—Wilt Chamberlain, LA Lakers, 1972-73 (426/586)

Free Throw Percentage

HIGHEST FREE THROW PERCENTAGE, CAREER

Mark Price	.906
Rick Barry	.900
Calvin Murphy	.892
Scott Skiles	.890
Larry Bird	.886

Note: Minimum 1200 free throws made.

HIGHEST FREE THROW PERCENTAGE, SEASON

Calvin Murphy, Hou	.958	1980-81
Mahmoud Abdul-Rauf	.956	1993-94
Mark Price, Clev	.948	1992-93
Mark Price, Clev	.947	1991-92
Rick Barry, Hou	.946	1978-79

Three-Point Field Goal Percentage*

Most Three-Point Field Goals, Career: Dale Ellis—1,119
Highest Three-Point Field Goal Percentage, Career: Steve Kerr—.467
Most Three-Point Field Goals, Season: John Starks, NY—217, 1994-95
Highest Three-Point Field Goal Percentage, Season: Steve Kerr, Chi—.524, 1994-95
Most Three-Point Field Goals, Game: 10—Brian Shaw, Miami vs Milwaukee, 4/8/93; Joe Dumars, Detroit vs Minnesota, 11/8/94

*First Year of Shot: 1979-80.

Steals

Most Steals, Career: 2,310—Maurice Cheeks
Most Steals, Season: 301—Alvin Robertson, San Antonio, 1985-86
Most Steals, Game: 11—Larry Kenon, San Antonio vs Kansas City, 12/26/76

Rebounds

MOST REBOUNDS, CAREER

Wilt Chamberlain	23,924
Bill Russell	21,620
Kareem Abdul-Jabbar	17,440
Elvin Hayes	16,279
Moses Malone	16,212
Nate Thurmond	14,464
Robert Parish	14,323
Walt Bellamy	14,241
Wes Unseld	13,769
Jerry Lucas	12,942

MOST REBOUNDS, SEASON

Wilt Chamberlain, Phil	2,149	1960-61
Wilt Chamberlain, Phil	2,052	1961-62
Wilt Chamberlain, Phil	1,957	1966-67
Wilt Chamberlain, Phil	1,952	1967-68
Wilt Chamberlain, SF	1,946	1962-63
Wilt Chamberlain, Phil	1,943	1965-66
Wilt Chamberlain, Phil	1,941	1959-60
Bill Russell, Bos	1,930	1963-64
Bill Russell, Bos	1,878	1964-65
Bill Russell, Bos	1,868	1960-61

MOST REBOUNDS, GAME

	Player, Team	Opp	Date
55	Wilt Chamberlain, Phi	Bos	11/24/60
51	Bill Russell, Bos	Syr	2/5/60
49	Bill Russell, Bos	Phi	11/16/57
49	Bill Russell, Bos	Det	3/11/65
45	Wilt Chamberlain, Phil	Syr	2/6/60
45	Wilt Chamberlain, Phil	LA	1/21/61

Assists

MOST ASSISTS, CAREER

John Stockton	10,394
Magic Johnson	9,921
Oscar Robertson	9,887
Isiah Thomas	9,061
Maurice Cheeks	7,392

MOST ASSISTS, SEASON

John Stockton, Utah	1,164	1990-91
John Stockton, Utah	1,134	1989-90
John Stockton, Utah	1,128	1987-88
John Stockton, Utah	1,126	1991-92
Isiah Thomas, Det	1,123	1984-85

MOST ASSISTS, GAME: 30—Scott Skiles, Orlando vs Denver, 12/30/90

Blocked Shots

MOST BLOCKED SHOTS, CAREER

Kareem Abdul-Jabbar	3,189
Mark Eaton	3,064
Hakeem Olajuwon	2,983
Wayne (Tree) Rollins	2,542

MOST BLOCKED SHOTS, SEASON

Mark Eaton, Utah	456	1984-85
Manute Bol, Wash	397	1985-86
Elmore Smith, LA	393	1973-74

MOST BLOCKED SHOTS, GAME: 17—Elmore Smith, LA Lakers vs Portland, 10/28/73

NBA Season Leaders

Scoring

1946-47	Joe Fulks, Phil	1389		
1947-48	Max Zaslofsky, Chi	1007		
1948-49	George Mikan, Minn	1698		
1949-50	George Mikan, Minn	1865		
1950-51	George Mikan, Minn	1932		
1951-52	Paul Arizin, Phil	1674		
1952-53	Neil Johnston, Phil	1564		
1953-54	Neil Johnston, Phil	1759		
1954-55	Neil Johnston, Phil	1631		
1955-56	Bob Pettit, StL	1849		
1956-57	Paul Arizin, Phil	1817		
1957-58	George Yardley, Det	2001		
1958-59	Bob Pettit, StL	2105		
1959-60	Wilt Chamberlain, Phil	2707		
1960-61	Wilt Chamberlain, Phil	3033		
1961-62	Wilt Chamberlain, Phil	4029		
1962-63	Wilt Chamberlain, SF	3586		
1963-64	Wilt Chamberlain, SF	2948		
1964-65	Wilt Chamberlain, SF-Phil	2534		
1965-66	Wilt Chamberlain, Phil	2649		
1966-67	Rick Barry, SF	2775		
1967-68	Dave Bing, Det	2142		
1968-69	Elvin Hayes, SD	2327		
1969-70	Jerry West, LA	*31.2		
1970-71	Kareem Abdul-Jabbar, Mil	31.7		
1971-72	Kareem Abdul-Jabbar, Mil	34.8		
1972-73	Nate Archibald, KC-Oma	34.0		
1973-74	Bob McAdoo, Buff	30.6		
1974-75	Bob McAdoo, Buff	34.5		
1975-76	Bob McAdoo, Buff	31.1		
1976-77	Pete Maravich, NO	31.1		
1977-78	George Gervin, SA	27.2		
1978-79	George Gervin, SA	29.6		
1979-80	George Gervin, SA	33.1		
1980-81	Adrian Dantley, Utah	30.7		
1981-82	George Gervin, SA	32.3		
1982-83	Alex English, Den	28.4		
1983-84	Adrian Dantley, Utah	30.6		
1984-85	Bernard King, NY	32.9		
1985-86	Dominique Wilkins, Atl	30.3		
1986-87	Michael Jordan, Chi	37.1		
1987-88	Michael Jordan, Chi	35.0		
1988-89	Michael Jordan, Chi	32.5		
1989-90	Michael Jordan, Chi	33.6		
1990-91	Michael Jordan, Chi	31.5		
1991-92	Michael Jordan, Chi	30.1		
1992-93	Michael Jordan, Chi	32.6		
1993-94	David Robinson, SA	29.8		
1994-95	Shaquille O'Neal, Orl	29.3		

*Based on per game average since 1969-70.

Rebounding

1950-51..............Dolph Schayes, Syr	1080	
1951-52..............Larry Foust, FW	880	
Mel Hutchins, Mil	880	
1952-53..............George Mikan, Minn	1007	
1953-54..............Harry Gallatin, NY	1098	
1954-55..............Neil Johnston, Phil	1085	
1955-56..............Bob Pettit, StL	1164	
1956-57..............Maurice Stokes, Roch	1256	
1957-58..............Bill Russell, Bos	1564	
1958-59..............Bill Russell, Bos	1612	
1959-60..............Wilt Chamberlain, Phil	1941	
1960-61..............Wilt Chamberlain, Phil	2149	
1961-62..............Wilt Chamberlain, Phil	2052	
1962-63..............Wilt Chamberlain, SF	1946	
1963-64..............Bill Russell, Bos	1930	
1964-65..............Bill Russell, Bos	1878	
1965-66..............Wilt Chamberlain, Phil	1943	
1966-67..............Wilt Chamberlain, Phil	1957	
1967-68..............Wilt Chamberlain, Phil	1952	
1968-69..............Wilt Chamberlain, LA	1712	
1969-70..............Elvin Hayes, SD	*16.9	
1970-71..............Wilt Chamberlain, LA	18.2	
1971-72..............Wilt Chamberlain, LA	19.2	

1972-73..............Wilt Chamberlain, LA	18.6
1973-74..............Elvin Hayes, Capital	18.1
1974-75..............Wes Unseld, Wash	14.8
1975-76..............Kareem Abdul-Jabbar, LA	16.9
1976-77..............Bill Walton, Port	14.4
1977-78..............Len Robinson, NO	15.7
1978-79..............Moses Malone, Hou	17.6
1979-80..............Swen Nater, SD	15.0
1980-81..............Moses Malone, Hou	14.8
1981-82..............Moses Malone, Hou	14.7
1982-83..............Moses Malone, Phil	15.3
1983-84..............Moses Malone, Phil	13.4
1984-85..............Moses Malone, Phil	13.1
1985-86..............Bill Laimbeer, Det	13.1
1986-87..............Charles Barkley, Phil	14.6
1987-88..............Michael Cage, LA Clippers	13.0
1988-89..............Hakeem Olajuwon, Hou	13.5
1989-90..............Hakeem Olajuwon, Hou	14.0
1990-91..............David Robinson, SA	13.0
1991-92..............Dennis Rodman, Detroit	18.7
1992-93..............Dennis Rodman, Detroit	18.3
1993-94..............Dennis Rodman, San Antonio	17.3
1994-95..............Dennis Rodman, San Antonio	16.8

*Based on per game average since 1969-70.

Assists

1946-47..............Ernie Calverly, Prov	202
1947-48..............Howie Dallmar, Phil	120
1948-49..............Bob Davies, Roch	321
1949-50..............Dick McGuire, NY	386
1950-51..............Andy Phillip, Phil	414
1951-52..............Andy Phillip, Phil	539
1952-53..............Bob Cousy, Bos	547
1953-54..............Bob Cousy, Bos	578
1954-55..............Bob Cousy, Bos	557
1955-56..............Bob Cousy, Bos	642
1956-57..............Bob Cousy, Bos	478
1957-58..............Bob Cousy, Bos	463
1958-59..............Bob Cousy, Bos	557
1959-60..............Bob Cousy, Bos	715
1960-61..............Oscar Robertson, Cin	690
1961-62..............Oscar Robertson, Cin	899
1962-63..............Guy Rodgers, SF	825
1963-64..............Oscar Robertson, Cin	868
1964-65..............Oscar Robertson, Cin	861
1965-66..............Oscar Robertson, Cin	847
1966-67..............Guy Rodgers, Chi	908
1967-68..............Wilt Chamberlain, Phil	702
1968-69..............Oscar Robertson, Cin	772
1969-70..............Len Wilkens, Sea	*9.1
1970-71..............Norm Van Lier, Cin	10.1

1971-72..............Jerry West, LA	9.7
1972-73..............Nate Archibald, KC-Oma	11.4
1973-74..............Ernie DiGregorio, Buff	8.2
1974-75..............Kevin Porter, Wash	8.0
1975-76..............Don Watts, Sea	8.1
1976-77..............Don Buse, Ind	8.5
1977-78..............Kevin Porter, NJ-Det	10.2
1978-79..............Kevin Porter, Det	13.4
1979-80..............Micheal Richardson, NY	10.1
1980-81..............Kevin Porter, LA	9.1
1981-82..............Johnny Moore, SA	9.6
1982-83..............Magic Johnson, LA	10.5
1983-84..............Magic Johnson, LA	13.1
1984-85..............Isiah Thomas, Det	13.9
1985-86..............Magic Johnson, LA Lakers	12.6
1986-87..............Magic Johnson, LA Lakers	12.2
1987-88..............John Stockton, Utah	13.8
1988-89..............John Stockton, Utah	13.6
1989-90..............John Stockton, Utah	14.5
1990-91..............John Stockton, Utah	14.2
1991-92..............John Stockton, Utah	13.7
1992-93..............John Stockton, Utah	12.0
1993-94..............John Stockton, Utah	12.6
1994-95..............John Stockton, Utah	12.3

*Based on per game average since 1969-70.

Field Goal Percentage

1946-47..............Bob Feerick, Wash	40.1
1947-48..............Bob Feerick, Wash	34.0
1948-49..............Arnie Risen, Roch	42.3
1949-50..............Alex Groza, Ind	47.8
1950-51..............Alex Groza, Ind	47.0
1951-52..............Paul Arizin, Phil	44.8
1952-53..............Neil Johnston, Phil	45.2
1953-54..............Ed Macauley, Bos	48.6
1954-55..............Larry Foust, FW	48.7
1955-56..............Neil Johnston, Phil	45.7
1956-57..............Neil Johnston, Phil	44.7

1957-58..............Jack Twyman, Cin	45.2
1958-59..............Ken Sears, NY	49.0
1959-60..............Ken Sears, NY	47.7
1960-61..............Wilt Chamberlain, Phil	50.9
1961-62..............Walt Bellamy, Chi	51.9
1962-63..............Wilt Chamberlain, SF	52.8
1963-64..............Jerry Lucas, Cin	52.7
1964-65..............Wilt Chamberlain, SF-Phil	51.0
1965-66..............Wilt Chamberlain, Phil	54.0
1966-67..............Wilt Chamberlain, Phil	68.3
1967-68..............Wilt Chamberlain, Phil	59.5

Field Goal Percentage *(Cont.)*

1968-69	Wilt Chamberlain, LA	58.3	1982-83..............Artis Gilmore, SA	62.6
1969-70	Johnny Green, Cin	55.9	1983-84..............Artis Gilmore, SA	63.1
1970-71	Johnny Green, Cin	58.7	1984-85..............James Donaldson, LA Clippers	63.7
1971-72	Wilt Chamberlain, LA	64.9	1985-86..............Steve Johnson, SA	63.2
1972-73	Wilt Chamberlain, LA	72.7	1986-87..............Kevin McHale, Bos	60.4
1973-74	Bob McAdoo, Buff	54.7	1987-88..............Kevin McHale, Bos	60.4
1974-75	Don Nelson, Bos	53.9	1988-89..............Dennis Rodman, Det	59.5
1975-76	Wes Unseld, Wash	56.1	1989-90..............Mark West, Phoe	62.5
1976-77	Kareem Abdul-Jabbar, LA	57.9	1990-91..............Buck Williams, Port	60.2
1977-78	Bobby Jones, Den	57.8	1991-92..............Buck Williams, Port	60.4
1978-79	Cedric Maxwell, Bos	58.4	1992-93..............Cedric Ceballos, Phoe	57.6
1979-80	Cedric Maxwell, Bos	60.9	1993-94..............Shaquille O'Neal, Orl	59.9
1980-81	Artis Gilmore, Chi	67.0	1994-95..............Chris Gatling, GS	63.3
1981-82	Artis Gilmore, Chi	65.2		

Free Throw Percentage

1946-47	Fred Scolari, Wash	81.1	1971-72..............Jack Marin, Balt	89.4
1947-48	Bob Feerick, Wash	78.8	1972-73..............Rick Barry, GS	90.2
1948-49	Bob Feerick, Wash	85.9	1973-74..............Ernie DiGregorio, Buff	90.2
1949-50	Max Zaslofsky, Chi	84.3	1974-75..............Rick Barry, GS	90.4
1950-51	Joe Fulks, Phil	85.5	1975-76..............Rick Barry, GS	92.3
1951-52	Bob Wanzer, Roch	90.4	1976-77..............Ernie DiGregorio, Buff	94.5
1952-53	Bill Sharman, Bos	85.0	1977-78..............Rick Barry, GS	92.4
1953-54	Bill Sharman, Bos	84.4	1978-79..............Rick Barry, Hou	94.7
1954-55	Bill Sharman, Bos	89.7	1979-80..............Rick Barry, Hou	93.5
1955-56	Bill Sharman, Bos	86.7	1980-81..............Calvin Murphy, Hou	95.8
1956-57	Bill Sharman, Bos	90.5	1981-82..............Kyle Macy, Phoe	89.9
1957-58	Dolph Schayes, Syr	90.4	1982-83..............Calvin Murphy, Hou	92.0
1958-59	Bill Sharman, Bos	93.2	1983-84..............Larry Bird, Bos	88.8
1959-60	Dolph Schayes, Syr	89.2	1984-85..............Kyle Macy, Phoe	90.7
1960-61	Bill Sharman, Bos	92.1	1985-86..............Larry Bird, Bos	89.6
1961-62	Dolph Schayes, Syr	89.6	1986-87..............Larry Bird, Bos	91.0
1962-63	Larry Costello, Syr	88.1	1987-88..............Jack Sikma, Mil	92.2
1963-64	Oscar Robertson, Cin	85.3	1988-89..............Magic Johnson, LA Lakers	91.1
1964-65	Larry Costello, Phil	87.7	1989-90..............Larry Bird, Bos	93.0
1965-66	Larry Siegfried, Bos	88.1	1990-91..............Reggie Miller, Ind	91.8
1966-67	Adrian Smith, Cin	90.3	1991-92..............Mark Price, Clev	94.7
1967-68	Oscar Robertson, Cin	87.3	1992-93..............Mark Price, Clev	94.8
1968-69	Larry Siegfried, Bos	86.4	1993-94..............Mahmoud Abdul-Rauf, Den	95.6
1969-70	Flynn Robinson, Mil	89.8	1994-95..............Spud Webb, Sac	93.4
1970-71	Chet Walker, Chi	85.9		

Three-Point Field Goal Percentage

1979-80	Fred Brown, Sea	44.3	1987-88..............Craig Hodges, Mil-Phoe	49.1
1980-81	Brian Taylor, SD	38.3	1988-89..............Jon Sundvold, Mia	52.2
1981-82	Campy Russell, NY	43.9	1989-90..............Steve Kerr, Clev	50.7
1982-83	Mike Dunleavy, SA	34.5	1990-91..............Jim Les, Sac	46.1
1983-84	Darrell Griffith, Utah	36.1	1991-92..............Dana Barros, Sea	44.6
1984-85	Byron Scott, LA Lakers	43.3	1992-93..............B.J. Armstrong, Chi	45.3
1985-86	Craig Hodges, Mil	45.1	1993-94..............Tracy Murray, Por	45.9
1986-87	Kiki Vandeweghe, Por	48.1	1994-95..............Steve Kerr, Chi	52.4

Steals

1973-74	Larry Steele, Por	2.68	1984-85..............Micheal Richardson, NJ	2.96
1974-75	Rick Barry, GS	2.85	1985-86..............Alvin Robertson, SA	3.67
1975-76	Don Watts, Sea	3.18	1986-87..............Alvin Robertson, SA	3.21
1976-77	Don Buse, Ind	3.47	1987-88..............Michael Jordan, Chi	3.16
1977-78	Ron Lee, Phoe	2.74	1988-89..............John Stockton, Utah	3.21
1978-79	M. L. Carr, Det	2.46	1989-90..............Michael Jordan, Chi	2.77
1979-80	Micheal Richardson, NY	3.23	1990-91..............Alvin Robertson, Mil	3.04
1980-81	Magic Johnson, LA	3.43	1991-92..............John Stockton, Utah	2.98
1981-82	Magic Johnson, LA	2.67	1992-93..............Michael Jordan, Chi	2.83
1982-83	Micheal Richardson, GS-NJ	2.84	1993-94..............Nate McMillan, Sea	2.96
1983-84	Rickey Green, Utah	2.65	1994-95..............Scottie Pippen, Chi	2.94

Blocked Shots

1973-74	Elmore Smith, LA	4.85	1984-85	Mark Eaton, Utah	5.56
1974-75	Kareem Abdul-Jabbar, Mil	3.26	1985-86	Manute Bol, Wash	4.96
1975-76	Kareem Abdul-Jabbar, LA	4.12	1986-87	Mark Eaton, Utah	4.06
1976-77	Bill Walton, Port	3.25	1987-88	Mark Eaton, Utah	3.71
1977-78	George Johnson, NJ	3.38	1988-89	Manute Bol, GS	4.31
1978-79	Kareem Abdul-Jabbar, LA	3.95	1989-90	Hakeem Olajuwon, Hou	4.59
1979-80	Kareem Abdul-Jabbar, LA	3.41	1990-91	Hakeem Olajuwon, Hou	3.95
1980-81	George Johnson, SA	3.39	1991-92	David Robinson, SA	4.49
1981-82	George Johnson, SA	3.12	1992-93	Hakeem Olajuwon, Hou	4.17
1982-83	Wayne Rollins, Atl	4.29	1993-94	Dikembe Mutombo, Den	4.10
1983-84	Mark Eaton, Utah	4.28	1994-95	Dikembe Mutombo, Den	3.91

NBA All-Star Game Results

Year	Result	Site	Winning Coach	Most Valuable Player
1951	East 111, West 94	Boston	Joe Lapchick	Ed Macauley, Bos
1952	East 108, West 91	Boston	Al Cervi	Paul Arizin, Phil
1953	West 79, East 75	Ft Wayne	John Kundla	George Mikan, Minn
1954	East 98, West 93 (OT)	New York	Joe Lapchick	Bob Cousy, Bos
1955	East 100, West 91	New York	Al Cervi	Bill Sharman, Bos
1956	West 108, East 94	Rochester	Charley Eckman	Bob Pettit, StL
1957	East 109, West 97	Boston	Red Auerbach	Bob Cousy, Bos
1958	East 130, West 118	St Louis	Red Auerbach	Bob Pettit, StL
1959	West 124, East 108	Detroit	Ed Macauley	Bob Pettit, StL
				Elgin Baylor, Minn
1960	East 125, West 115	Philadelphia	Red Auerbach	Wilt Chamberlain, Phil
1961	West 153, East 131	Syracuse	Paul Seymour	Oscar Robertson, Cin
1962	West 150, East 130	St Louis	Fred Schaus	Bob Pettit, StL
1963	East 115, West 108	Los Angeles	Red Auerbach	Bill Russell, Bos
1964	East 111, West 107	Boston	Red Auerbach	Oscar Robertson, Cin
1965	East 124, West 123	St Louis	Red Auerbach	Jerry Lucas, Cin
1966	East 137, West 94	Cincinnati	Red Auerbach	Adrian Smith, Cin
1967	West 135, East 120	San Francisco	Fred Schaus	Rick Barry, SF
1968	East 144, West 124	New York	Alex Hannum	Hal Greer, Phil
1969	East 123, West 112	Baltimore	Gene Shue	Oscar Robertson, Cin
1970	East 142, West 135	Philadelphia	Red Holzman	Willis Reed, NY
1971	West 108, East 107	San Diego	Larry Costello	Lenny Wilkens, Sea
1972	West 112, East 110	Los Angeles	Bill Sharman	Jerry West, LA
1973	East 104, West 84	Chicago	Tom Heinsohn	Dave Cowens, Bos
1974	West 134, East 123	Seattle	Larry Costello	Bob Lanier, Det
1975	East 108, West 102	Phoenix	K. C. Jones	Walt Frazier, NY
1976	East 123, West 109	Philadelphia	Tom Heinsohn	Dave Bing, Wash
1977	West 125, East 124	Milwaukee	Larry Brown	Julius Erving, Phil
1978	East 133, West 125	Atlanta	Billy Cunningham	Randy Smith, Buff
1979	West 134, East 129	Detroit	Lenny Wilkens	David Thompson, Den
1980	East 144, West 135 (OT)	Washington	Billy Cunningham	George Gervin, SA
1981	East 123, West 120	Cleveland	Billy Cunningham	Nate Archibald, Bos
1982	East 120, West 118	New Jersey	Bill Fitch	Larry Bird, Bos
1983	East 132, West 123	Los Angeles	Billy Cunningham	Julius Erving, Phil
1984	East 154, West 145 (OT)	Denver	K. C. Jones	Isiah Thomas, Det
1985	West 140, East 129	Indiana	Pat Riley	Ralph Sampson, Hou
1986	East 139, West 132	Dallas	K. C. Jones	Isiah Thomas, Det
1987	West 154, East 149 (OT)	Seattle	Pat Riley	Tom Chambers, Sea
1988	East 138, West 133	Chicago	Mike Fratello	Michael Jordan, Chi
1989	West 143, East 134	Houston	Pat Riley	Karl Malone, Utah
1990	East 130, West 113	Miami	Chuck Daly	Magic Johnson, LA Lakers
1991	East 116, West 114	Charlotte	Chris Ford	Charles Barkley, Phil
1992	West 153, East 113	Orlando	Don Nelson	Magic Johnson, LA Lakers
1993	West 135, East 132	Salt Lake City	Paul Westphal	Karl Malone, Utah
				John Stockton, Utah
1994	East 127, West 118	Minneapolis	Lenny Wilkens	Scottie Pippen, Chi
1995	West 139, East 112	Phoenix	Paul Westphal	Mitch Richmond, Sac

Members of the Basketball Hall of Fame

Contributors

Senda Abbott (1984)
Forest C. "Phog" Allen (1959)
Clair F. Bee (1967)
Walter A. Brown (1965)
John W. Bunn (1964)
Bob Douglas (1971)
Al Duer (1981)
Clifford Fagan (1983)
Harry A. Fisher (1973)
Larry Fleisher (1991)
Edward Gottlieb (1971)
Luther H. Gulick (1959)
Lester Harrison (1979)
Ferenc Hepp (1980)
Edward J. Hickox (1959)

Paul D. "Tony" Hinkle (1965)
Ned Irish (1964)
R. William Jones (1964)
J. Walter Kennedy (1980)
Emil S. Liston (1974)
John B. McLendon (1978)
Bill Mokray (1965)
Ralph Morgan (1959)
Frank Morgenweck (1962)
James Naismith (1959)
Peter F. Newell (1978)
John J. O'Brien (1961)
Larry O'Brien (1991)
Harold G. Olsen (1959)
Maurice Podoloff (1973)

H.V. Porter (1960)
William A. Reid (1963)
Elmer Ripley (1972)
Lynn W. St. John (1962)
Abe Saperstein (1970)
Arthur A. Schabinger (1961)
Amos Alonzo Stagg (1959)
Boris Stankovic (1991)
Edward Steitz (1983)
Chuck Taylor (1968)
Oswald Tower (1959)
Arthur L. Trester (1961)
Clifford Wells (1971)
Lou Wilke (1982)

Players

Kareem Abdul-Jabbar (1995)
Nate "Tiny" Archibald (1991)
Paul J. Arizin (1977)
Thomas B. Barlow (1980)
Rick Barry (1986)
Elgin Baylor (1976)
John Beckman (1972)
Walt Bellamy (1993)
Sergei Belov (1992)
Dave Bing (1989)
Carol Blazejowski (1994)
Bennie Borgmann (1961)
Bill Bradley (1982)
Joseph Brennan (1974)
Al Cervi (1984)
Wilt Chamberlain (1978)
Charles "Tarzan" Cooper (1976)
Bob Cousy (1970)
Dave Cowens (1991)
Billy Cunningham (1985)
Bob Davies (1969)
Forrest S. DeBernardi (1961)
Dave DeBusschere (1982)
H. G. "Dutch" Dehnert (1968)
Anne Donovan (1995)
Paul Endacott (1971)
Julius Erving (1993)
Harold "Bud" Foster (1964)
Walter "Clyde" Frazier (1986)
Max "Marty" Friedman (1971)
Joe Fulks (1977)
Lauren "Laddie" Gale (1976)
Harry "the Horse" Gallatin (1991)
William Gates (1988)

Tom Gola (1975)
Hal Greer (1981)
Robert "Ace" Gruenig (1963)
Clifford O. Hagan (1977)
Victor Hanson (1960)
John Havlicek (1983)
Connie Hawkins (1992)
Elvin Hayes (1989)
Tom Heinsohn (1985)
Nat Holman (1964)
Robert J. Houbregs (1986)
Chuck Hyatt (1959)
Dan Issel (1993)
Harry (Buddy) Jeannette (1994)
William C. Johnson (1976)
D. Neil Johnston (1989)
K. C. Jones (1988)
Sam Jones (1983)
Edward "Moose" Krause (1975)
Bob Kurland (1961)
Joe Lapchick (1966)
Clyde Lovellette (1987)
Jerry Lucas (1979)
Angelo "Hank" Luisetti (1959)
C. Edward Macauley (1960)
Peter P. Maravich (1986)
Slater Martin (1981)
Branch McCracken (1960)
Jack McCracken (1962)
Bobby McDermott (1987)
Dick McGuire (1993)
Ann Meyers (1993)
George L. Mikan (1959)
Vern Mikkelsen (1995)

Cheryl Miller (1995)
Earl Monroe (1989)
Calvin Murphy (1993)
Charles "Stretch" Murphy (1960)
H. O. "Pat" Page (1962)
Bob Pettit (1970)
Andy Phillip (1961)
Jim Pollard (1977)
Frank Ramsey (1981)
Willis Reed (1981)
Oscar Robertson (1979)
John S. Roosma (1961)
Bill Russell (1974)
John "Honey" Russell (1964)
Adolph Schayes (1972)
Ernest J. Schmidt (1973)
John J. Schommer (1959)
Barney Sedran (1962)
Uljana Semjonova (1993)
Bill Sharman (1975)
Christian Steinmetz (1961)
Lusia Harris Stewart (1992)
John A. "Cat" Thompson (1962)
Nate Thurmond (1984)
Jack Twyman (1982)
Wes Unseld (1987)
Robert "Fuzzy" Vandivier (1974)
Edward A. Wachter (1961)
Bill Walton (1993)
Robert F. Wanzer (1986)
Jerry West (1979)
Nera White (1992)
Lenny Wilkens (1988)
John R. Wooden (1960)

Coaches

Harold Anderson (1984)
Red Auerbach (1968)
Sam Barry (1978)
Ernest A. Blood (1960)
Howard G. Cann (1967)
H. Clifford Carlson (1959)
Lou Carnesecca (1992)
Ben Carnevale (1969)
Everett Case (1981)
Denny Crum (1994)
Chuck Daly (1994)
Everett S. Dean (1966)

Edgar A. Diddle (1971)
Bruce Drake (1972)
Clarence Gaines (1981)
Jack Gardner (1983)
Amory T. "Slats" Gill (1967)
Aleksandr Gomelsky (1995)
Marv Harshman (1984)
Edgar S. Hickey (1978)
Howard A. Hobson (1965)
Red Holzman (1985)
Hank Iba (1968)
Alvin F. "Doggie" Julian (1967)

Frank W. Keaney (1960)
George E. Keogan (1961)
Bob Knight (1991)
John Kundla (1995)
Ward L. Lambert (1960)
Harry Litwack (1975)
Kenneth D. Loeffler (1964)
A. C. "Dutch" Lonborg (1972)
Arad A. McCutchan (1980)
Al McGuire (1992)
Frank McGuire (1976)
Walter E. Meanwell (1959)

Note: Year of election in parentheses.

Coaches *(Cont.)*

Raymond J. Meyer (1978)
Ralph Miller (1987)
Jack Ramsay (1992)
Cesare Rubini (1994)
Adolph F. Rupp (1968)

Leonard D. Sachs (1961)
Everett F. Shelton (1979)
Dean Smith (1982)
Fred R. Taylor (1985)

Bertha Teague (1984)
Margaret Wade (1984)
Stanley H. Watts (1985)
John R. Wooden (1972)

Referees

James E. Enright (1978)
George T. Hepbron (1960)
George Hoyt (1961)
Matthew P. Kennedy (1959)
Lloyd Leith (1982)
Zigmund J. Mihalik (1985)
John P. Nucatola (1977)
Ernest C. Quigley (1961)
J. Dallas Shirley (1979)
Earl Strom (1995)
David Tobey (1961)
David H. Walsh (1961)

Teams

Buffalo Germans (1961)
First Team (1959)
Original Celtics (1959)
Renaissance (1963)

Note: Year of election in parentheses.

ABA Champions

Year	Champion	Series	Loser	Winning Coach
1968	Pittsburgh Pipers	4–2	New Orleans Bucs	Vince Cazetta
1969	Oakland Oaks	4–1	Indiana Pacers	Alex Hannum
1970	Indiana Pacers	4–2	Los Angeles Stars	Bob Leonard
1971	Utah Stars	4–3	Kentucky Colonels	Bill Sharman
1972	Indiana Pacers	4–2	New York Nets	Bob Leonard
1973	Indiana Pacers	4–3	Kentucky Colonels	Bob Leonard
1974	New York Nets	4–1	Utah Stars	Kevin Loughery
1975	Kentucky Colonels	4–1	Indiana Pacers	Hubie Brown
1976	New York Nets	4–2	Denver Nuggets	Kevin Loughery

ABA Postseason Awards

Most Valuable Player

1967-68	Connie Hawkins, Pitt
1968-69	Mel Daniels, Ind
1969-70	Spencer Haywood, Den
1970-71	Mel Daniels, Ind
1971-72	Artis Gilmore, Ken
1972-73	Billy Cunningham, Car
1973-74	Julius Erving, NY
1974-75	Julius Erving, NY
	George McGinnis, Ind
1975-76	Julius Erving, NY

Rookie of the Year

1967-68	Mel Daniels, Minn
1968-69	Warren Armstrong, Oak
1969-70	Spencer Haywood, Den
1970-71	Charlie Scott, Vir
	Dan Issel, Ken
1071-72	Artis Gilmore, Ken
1972-73	Brian Taylor, NY
1973-74	Swen Nater, SA
1974-75	Marvin Barnes, SL
1975-76	David Thompson, Den

Coach of the Year

1967-68	Vince Cazetta, Pitt
1968-69	Alex Hannum, Oak
1969-70	Bill Sharman, LA
	Joe Belmont, Den
1970-71	Al Bianchi, Vir
1971-72	Tom Nissalke, Dall
1972-73	Larry Brown, Car
1973-74	Babe McCarthy, Ken
	Joe Mullaney, Utah
1974-75	Larry Brown, Den
1975-76	Larry Brown, Den

THEY SAID IT

Craig Kilborn, ESPN anchor, on notoriously porous Washington Bullet forward Don MacLean, who got into a brawl while defending a girlfriend: "That's the first person he's defended this year."

ABA Season Leaders

Scoring

		GP	Pts	Avg
1967-68	Connie Hawkins, Pitt	70	1875	26.8
1968-69	Rick Barry, Oak	35	1190	34.0
1969-70	Spencer Haywood, Den	84	2519	30.0
1970-71	Dan Issel, Ken	83	2480	29.4
1971-72	Charlie Scott, Vir	73	2524	34.6
1972-73	Julius Erving, Vir	71	2268	31.9
1973-74	Julius Erving, NY	84	2299	27.4
1974-75	George McGinnis, Ind	79	2353	29.8
1975-76	Julius Erving, NY	84	2462	29.3

Rebounds

1967-68	Mel Daniels, Minn	15.6
1968-69	Mel Daniels, Ind	16.5
1969-70	Spencer Haywood, Den	19.5
1970-71	Mel Daniels, Ind	18.0
1971-72	Artis Gilmore, Ken	17.8
1972-73	Artis Gilmore, Ken	17.5
1973-74	Artis Gilmore, Ken	18.3
1974-75	Swen Nater, SA	16.4
1975-76	Artis Gilmore, Ken	15.5

Assists

1967-68	Larry Brown, NO	6.5
1968-69	Larry Brown, Oak	7.1
1969-70	Larry Brown, Wash	7.1
1970-71	Bill Melchionni, NY	8.3
1971-72	Bill Melchionni, NY	8.4
1972-73	Bill Melchionni, NY	7.5
1973-74	Al Smith, Den	8.2
1974-75	Mack Calvin, Den	7.7
1975-76	Don Buse, Ind	8.2

Steals

1973-74	Ted McClain, Car	2.98
1974-75	Brian Taylor, NY	2.80
1975-76	Don Buse, Ind	4.12

Blocked Shots

1973-74	Caldwell Jones, SD	4.00
1974-75	Caldwell Jones, SD	3.24
1975-76	Billy Paultz, SA	3.05

World Championship of Basketball

Year	Winner	Runner-Up	Score	Site
1950	Argentina	United States	†	Rio de Janeiro
1954	United States	Brazil	†	Rio de Janeiro
1959	Brazil	United States	†	Santiago, Chile
1963	Brazil	Yugoslavia	†	Rio de Janeiro
1967	Soviet Union	Yugoslavia	†	Montevideo, Uruguay
1970	Yugoslavia	Brazil	†	Ljubljana, Yugoslavia
1974	Soviet Union	Yugoslavia	†	San Juan
1978	Yugoslavia	Soviet Union	82-81 OT	Manila
1982	Soviet Union	United States	95-94	Cali, Colombia
1986	United States	Soviet Union	87-85	Madrid
1990	Yugoslavia	Soviet Union	92-75	Buenos Aires
1994*	United States	Russia	137-91	Toronto

*U.S. professionals began competing in 1994.
†Result determined by overall record in final round of competition.

THEY SAID IT

Brother Ray Page, teacher at St. Anthony High School in Jersey City, on alumnus and Sacramento King guard Bobby Hurley: "He once asked me if Beirut was named after that famous baseball player who hit home runs."

College Basketball

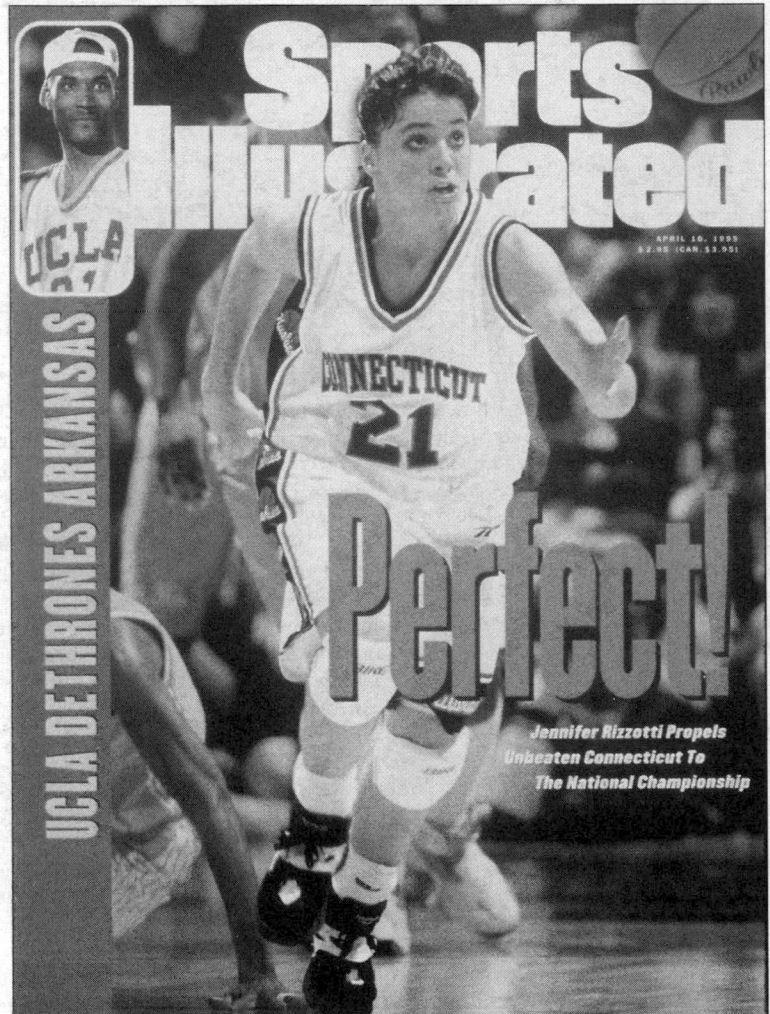

Sports Illustrated

APRIL 10, 1995
$2.95 (CAN. $3.95)

UCLA DETHRONES ARKANSAS

CONNECTICUT 21

Perfect!

Jennifer Rizzotti Propels
Unbeaten Connecticut To
The National Championship

JOHN BIEVER (INSET), DAVID E. KLUTHO

History Made, and Repeated

An unpredictable season ended with the first NCAA title for the women of UConn and a record 11th for the men of UCLA

by Jack McCallum

WHY PLAY? Why test the stress level of all those excitable coaches, spend all that money on cross-country travel and expose all those helpless eardrums to relentless attacks of Vitale-ism? Just hand the NCAA championship trophy to defending champion Arkansas and schedule Nolan Richardson and the boys for another Rose Garden summit with the Chief Hog on Pennsylvania Avenue.

That is only a slight exaggeration of the preseason prognoses centering around the near certainty that Arkansas, a talented and tenacious squad that wore the presidential stamp of approval on its big snout, would repeat as the 1995 college basketball king.

Oh, when will the experts learn? Chalk picks in this sport went out with Johnny Wooden and hightop Converse, and, aside from Duke's back-to-backer in 1991 and '92, so did repeat champions. Yet almost everyone looked at the Hogs' roster, intact from the 1994 championship season, and wondered how they could lose. That in-

cluded the Hogs themselves. "Bring that pressure on," said Richardson in the preseason. "We love it. We want it."

But something was, if not exactly rotten, then a little out of kilter in Fayetteville. Corliss Williamson came back slightly overweight and still not fully healed from a broken wrist suffered in the 1994 championship game against Duke. Shooting guard and title-game hero Scotty Thurman had lost some of the consistency on his shot and, perhaps, a little of his competitive edge. Ditto for point guard and spiritual leader Corey Beck, who had preseason arthroscopic knee surgery. With Williamson, Thurman and off-the-bench flinger Alex Dillard all looking to the hoop, it was sometimes hard for big men Dwight Stewart, Darnell Robinson and Lee Wilson to find their shots in the offense. Richardson's work with the Black Coaches Association and other organizations admittedly distracted him sometimes from the task at hand.

But most of all, there were simply too

With Camby (21) ruling the paint, UMass dominated the early going.

many great teams in the land to guarantee Arkansas a smooth road to No. 1. And the Razorbacks ran into one of them right away. On the day after Thanksgiving, at the Tipoff Classic in Springfield, Mass., the Hogs were thoroughly humiliated by the University of Massachusetts 104–80. Williamson, in particular, seemed to shrink in stature right before our eyes as Minutemen power forward Lou Roe went over, around and through him for 34 points and 13 rebounds. Yes, the college season that promised to be a second Hog toast began as a Hog roast.

But UMass was no fluke ... and no one was more eager to tell you that than UMass. On Oct. 19, four days after preseason practice began, *The Boston Globe* had reported that seven of UMass's 13 scholarship players were either on academic probation or "academic warning." The Minutemen felt violated by the report and others that followed. Armed with righteous indignation, a formidable frontcourt of Roe and center Marcus Camby and plenty of depth, UMass set out to *make a statement*, a slight variation on the we-don't-get-no-respect theme that had been played to perfection last year by Richardson and Arkansas. And no one was better at righteous indignation than Minutemen coach John Calipari. Hardly a sentence could be written about the 36-year-old Calipari without conjuring up the name of the young genius from whom he seemed cloned—Kentucky's Rick Pitino. See, there was one right there.

Inevitably UMass's high profile went

down when its Atlantic-10 season began. The Minutemen did lose three games in the conference (one to Temple and two to George Washington), but even hard core fans had trouble *naming* the league's 10 teams much less caring about them. Still, the college season's biggest off-the-court story occurred in the Atlantic-10. A statement made by Rutgers president Francis Lawrence was construed as racist by a segment of the student body, which protested by taking over the court at halftime of the Rutgers-UMass game on Feb. 7. It was, then, an off-the-court story that became an on-the-court story. The suspended game was replayed on March 3 with UMass winning 77–62.

UMass also shared early-season

Lobo lifted the Huskies to an undefeated season and the national title.

DAVID E. KLUTHO

attention, as well as a turn at No. 1, with not-so-friendly neighbor Connecticut, which is located in Storrs, just 50 miles from UMass's Amherst campus. Husky coach Jim Calhoun may have ducked a nonconference showdown with the Minutemen over the years, but on the court UConn wasn't afraid of anyone. Their tone of toughness was set by point guard Kevin Ollie, who hails from inner-city Los Angeles, and smooth swingman Ray Allen, who for the first two months of the season played as well as anyone in the college game.

But UConn didn't only feel tweaked by the attention given UMass. Right on its own campus another phenomenon was building—Lobo Fever. Game after game, week after week, the UConn women's team, led by All-America Rebecca Lobo, dismantled everyone in its path. Sure, the Big East was not a strong women's conference, but when it came time for the Husky women to step up and play then-No. 1 Tennessee from the powerful Southeast Conference, Lobo & Co. responded with a 77–66 victory. The win on Jan. 16 at Storrs was as big a regular-season game as the women's sport had ever seen, and there were few doubts that a UConn-Tennessee rematch in the NCAA final on April 2 would, if it happened, be a major moment for the women's game.

Despite its success in recent years, the UConn men were not the consensus favorite to win the Big East title—Syracuse and Georgetown were mentioned as frequently. And the most watched players in the conference were not Ollie and Allen but newcomers Allen Iverson of Georgetown and Felipe Lopez of St. John's. Iverson was so good so fast that conservative Hoya coach John Thompson all but turned his offense over to the gifted young point guard, sometimes with spectacular results, sometimes with disastrous ones. As for Lopez, the burden of carrying a team on his back seemed overwhelming at times, and the question of whether or not he will live up to his advance billing has not yet been answered.

The ACC certainly lived up to its advance billing as the deepest and best conference in the country. On the first night of intraconference play, in fact, one of the league's worst, North Carolina State, beat one of the ACC's best, North Carolina. That did not indicate a trend, however. While State struggled after that initial upset, the Tar Heels, led by super sophs Jerry Stackhouse and Rasheed Wallace, quickly played their way into the nation's elite. Moreover, they did it with a brand of up-and-down basketball that seemed to go against the nature of coach Dean Smith. Observers wondered, though, how far the run-and-gun Heels would go with only a six-deep rotation. They got their answer in the NCAA tournament—pretty far.

The most refreshing story in the ACC was the continued renaissance of Maryland. The sad days of recruiting violations and NCAA probation that followed the cocaine-induced death of Len Bias were all but erased by the firebrand coaching of Gary Williams and the graceful, no-nonsense play of center Joe Smith. Other perennials that made the ACC tough were Virginia, which flourished in surprising fashion after star guard Cory Alexander went down with a broken ankle, Wake Forest (with a one-two punch of guard Randolph Childress and center Tim Duncan), Georgia Tech and Florida State.

Wait a minute—an ACC roundup without Duke? That's right. Blue Devil coach Mike Krzyzewski, by any standard the most successful college coach of the last decade, began the season with a protective brace and instructions to take it easy following off-season back surgery. He didn't do it. By Jan. 4 Krzyzewski was off the bench and at home, and the Blue Devils were en route to their worst season ever—a 13–18 record that didn't get them within sniffing distance of even the NIT. But Coach K will be back for the 1995–96 season, and, armed with a lot of young talent, so will the Devils.

The SEC was the only other conference that could rightfully challenge the ACC for No. 1, not just because of Arkansas and archrival Kentucky, but also because of Mississippi State, Alabama and Florida. Two of the nation's better unknown players emerged from the SEC, too—State's Erick

Dampier and Alabama's Antonio McDyess, a pair of quiet, no-frills inside bangers. Arguably the best regular-season game of the year was Arkansas's nationally televised 94–92 win over visiting Kentucky on Jan. 29, achieved when Mr. Clutch, Thurman, hit a three-pointer with 11 seconds left.

As the season wore on, the Big Eight had something to say about toughness, too. The Kansas Jayhawks were the No. 1 team in the country in late February, yet they had to struggle to stay ahead of: Oklahoma, which was led by two-sport star Ryan Minor, a pro pitching prospect; Iowa State, which was led by homegrown jump shooter Fred Hoiberg, a player so popular in Ames that he is known as the Mayor; Oklahoma State, which was led by one of the most successful "projects" in NCAA history, Bryant (Big Country) Reeves; and Missouri, whose tenacious playing style raised ire around the league. And out in the West, even the much criticized Pac-10 made some noise. Arizona State flexed unexpected muscle early by winning the Maui Invitational, and, at times, Stanford, Cal, Washington State and Oregon all made a run at perennial powers Arizona and UCLA.

But, really, could the pack in the Pac-10 be taken seriously? All right, maybe Arizona. The Wildcats boasted both a superstar (point guard extraordinaire and player of the year candidate Damon Stoudamire) and a track record, having been the only Pac-10 team to make the Final Four in the past 15 years. (They did it twice—last year and in 1988.) The best talent in the conference belonged to UCLA but so did the best chance for failure. "We know what people think about us," senior leader Ed O'Bannon said during the season. What people thought about the Bruins was that they were an underachieving band of choke artists, as they had been the year before when, after a 21–7 regular season, they were rudely nudged from the NCAA tournament field by Tulsa, 112–102.

But there was something different about this UCLA team, something, to borrow an

DAMIAN STROHMEYER

Richardson exhorted Arkansas all the way back to the championship game.

expression from La-La Land, a little gnarly. Yes, Ed and his brother Charles could play above the rim, and point guard Tyus Edney was a blur with the ball, probably only a step slower than the Bruins' alltime burner, "Rocket" Rod Foster, a member of the last Bruin team (1980) to play for the NCAA title. But they did the tough things, too, the blue-collar battling that had never been associated with either the Pac-10 or the Bruins.

In seasons past, perhaps, the Bruins might've been battling UNLV for supremacy in the West. But Jerry Tarkanian is gone and so, it seems, is the Runnin' Rebels' good fortune. They had little of it during the 1994–95 season. Head coach Tim Grgurich, a former Tark assistant who was widely considered the only man who could restore the past magic, ended up being hospitalized for exhaustion and left the job after seven games. UNLV finished in the middle of the Big West Conference with no sign that its winning number would be coming up anytime soon.

A more subtle, yet more widespread flameout, occurred in the Big Ten, a conference in which only two teams played up to their potential—Michigan State and

Purdue. Yes, Indiana flexed its muscle from time to time, particularly in an 80–61 dismantling of Kansas on Dec. 17, and Minnesota, Illinois and underachieving Michigan weren't bad. But the conference simply did not deserve the six NCAA bids received on Selection Sunday, not when teams like Georgia Tech from the ACC and George Washington from the Atlantic-10 (conquerors of both Syracuse and UMass) were left out.

Otherwise, though, the selection committee did a reasonable job. The No. 1 seeds were Wake Forest in the East, Kentucky in the Southeast, Kansas in the Midwest and UCLA in the West. All were considered legitimate title contenders, as were all four No. 2's—Arkansas (Midwest), North Carolina (Southeast), UConn (West) and UMass (East). None of that, of course, would prevent at least one "nonfavorite" from coming out of nowhere to make the Final Four. It turned out to be the team with the big, country-boy center and the collective twang—Oklahoma State.

But much went on before the Cowboys bulled their way to Seattle along with UCLA, Arkansas and North Carolina. Arizona's Stoudamire was held to six of 18 shooting from the field in a shocking 71–62 first-round loss to Miami of Ohio in the Midwest. Indiana coach Bobby Knight went ballistic on an unassuming NCAA official after a 65–60 loss to Missouri in the West. The college game said goodbye to its most congenial curmudgeon, Jud Heathcote, when his Michigan State Spartans lost to Weber State 79–72 in the Southeast. And in that regional's final, North Carolina's Smith bested Kentucky's Pitino in a battle of superstar coaches and superstar programs.

If there was an unfortunate loser in the tournament it had to be Syracuse. With its Midwest second-rounder all but won, Lawrence Moten's call of a fourth timeout with 4.3 seconds left resulted in a technical foul and an eventual 96–94 loss in overtime. And if there was a lucky winner it had to be Arkansas, which was the beneficiary not only of Moten's timeout gaffe but also of a one-point first-round victory over Texas Southern and an overtime edging of Memphis in the Sweet 16. Did all those great escapes mean they were primed to fall or destined to prevail?

"Winning an NCAA championship is all about knowing how to win the close ones," Richardson said before the Hogs packed their bags for Seattle. "And no one knows about that more than us."

If Oklahoma State felt intimidated by its role as Final Four underdog, then Reeves didn't show it. On Friday afternoon, 24 hours before the semifinal against UCLA, Country unleashed a powerful dunk during shootaround that tore down a basket at the Kingdome. "I guess he's trying to send a message to all of us," said North Carolina's Wallace. But the real messenger was UCLA's Edney, nicknamed (ironically) Scary Boy, who scored 21 points, collected

JOHN BIEVER

Making Jordanesque moves to the hoop, Bruin freshman Bailey scored 26 points in the title game.

Big Country couldn't stop Charles O'Bannon (13) or UCLA.

his wrist, Williamson and Thurman played video games with family and friends at their hotel, and a record number of TV viewers for a women's game tuned into the Connecticut-Tennessee final in Minneapolis to see if storybook unbeaten seasons still happen. "The other teams here are playing for a national championship," UConn coach Geno Auriemma said before the title game. "We're playing for a piece of history." And they got it. The Huskies beat the Lady Vols 70–64 to finish with a 35–0 record and the school's first NCAA hoops title.

History was a big part of the men's final, too. Legendary Bruin coach John Wooden, who won 10 titles in 12 years in Westwood, slipped into the Kingdome minutes before the game to silently cheer on the Bruins and particularly Harrick, to whom he was extremely close. UCLA's play against Arkansas, however, was distinctly contemporary. Edney's wrist kept him out for all but the first few minutes, but his replacement, sophomore Cameron Dollar, slipped and slithered through seams in the Arkansas defense to create plays. Freshman Toby Bailey was a West Coast miniversion of—don't laugh—Michael Jordan, making countless athletic plays for which Arkansas had no counter. And the high-wire act of the O'Bannons, combined with the old-fashioned power of pivotman George Zidek, contained Williamson, who was held to 12 points. All this produced a decisive 89–78 victory and the Bruins' first title since 1975, when Wooden last patrolled the sidelines with his rolled-up program.

UCLA's final season record was 31–2, which put the combined mark of the two national champions at a remarkable 66–2. But, listen, just don't expect repeat performances next year—it won't happen.

five assists and turned in most of the big plays in a 74–61 victory over the Cowboys that was much closer than it sounds. Unbeknownst to most Bruin fans, however, Edney had severely sprained his right wrist during a first-half fall and spent part of Saturday night getting it wrapped in a temporary cast. Had Carolina been able to keep a wrap on its patience, it just might have prevailed in the other semifinal against Arkansas. But the cumulative effects of Hog pressure unnerved the Tar Heels down the stretch, and Arkansas stormed into its second straight NCAA final, a remarkable achievement itself, with a 75–68 victory.

On the off day between the semis and the Monday night final, UCLA coach Jim Harrick accompanied Ed O'Bannon to the Kingdome while the UCLA senior received a player of the year award, Edney nursed

NCAA Championship Game Box Score

Arkansas 78

ARKANSAS	Min	FG M-A	FT M-A	Reb O-T	A	PF	TP
Thurman	32	2-9	0-0	0-3	1	2	5
Williamson	33	3-16	6-10	2-4	6	1	12
Martin	6	1-2	0-0	1-3	1	2	3
McDaniel	35	5-10	3-4	1-3	1	5	16
Beck	25	4-6	1-2	2-3	2	3	11
Stewart	22	5-10	1-2	2-5	0	4	12
Dillard	15	2-4	0-0	1-2	1	1	6
Robinson	10	2-3	0-0	0-2	0	3	4
Rimac	12	1-1	0-0	1-2	3	0	2
Wilson	7	3-4	1-2	0-0	0	1	7
Williams	1	0-0	0-0	0-0	0	0	0
Totals	200	28-65	12-20	10-27	15	22	78

Percentages: FG—.431, FT—.600. 3-pt goals: 10-28, .357 (Thurman 1-7, Martin 1-2, McDaniel 3-7, Beck 2-3, Stewart 1-5, Dillard 2-3, Robinson 0-1). Team rebounds: 4. Blocked shots: 4 (Robinson 2, Beck, Wilson). Turnovers: 18 (Williamson 3, Beck 2, Dillard 2, Martin 2, Rimac 2, Robinson 2, Stewart 2, Thurman 2, McDaniel). Steals: 15 (Williamson 4, McDaniel 4, Beck 3, Rimac 2, Martin, Thurman).

UCLA 89

UCLA	Min	FG M-A	FT M-A	Reb O-T	A	PF	TP
E. O'Bannon	40	10-21	9-11	6-17	3	2	30
C. O'Bannon	36	4-10	3-4	4-9	6	1	11
Zidek	29	5-8	4-7	4-6	0	4	14
Bailey	39	12-20	1-2	4-9	3	3	26
Edney	3	0-0	0-0	0-0	0	0	0
Dollar	36	1-4	4-5	0-3	8	4	6
Henderson	17	1-5	0-0	1-2	1	1	2
Totals	200	33-68	21-29	19-46	21	15	89

Percentages: FG—.485, FT—.724. 3-pt goals: 2-7, .286 (E. O'Bannon 1-4, Bailey 1-2, Dollar 0-1). Team rebounds: 4. Blocked shots: 4 (C. O'Bannon 2, Dollar, Henderson). Turnovers: 20 (E. O'Bannon 5, Bailey 3, C. O'Bannon 3, Dollar 3, Henderson 3, Zidek 2, Edney). Steals: 11 (Dollar 4, E. O'Bannon 3, Bailey 2, C. O'Bannon 2).
Halftime: UCLA 40, Arkansas 39. A: 38,540. Officials: Valentine, Cahill, Burr.

Final AP Top 25

Poll taken before NCAA Tournament.

1. UCLA 25–2	14. Oklahoma St 23–9
2. Kentucky 25–4	15. Arizona.......................23–7
3. Wake Forest 24–5	16. Arizona St..................22–8
4. North Carolina 24–5	17. Oklahoma 23–8
5. Kansas 23–5	18. Mississippi St 20–7
6. Arkansas 27–6	19. Utah 27–5
7. Massachusetts 26–4	20. Alabama.....................22–9
8. Connecticut............25–4	21. Western Kentucky.......26–3
9. Villanova................25–7	22. Georgetown 19–9
10. Maryland................24–7	23. Missouri.....................19–8
11. Michigan St 22–5	24. Iowa St 22–10
12. Purdue 24–6	25. Syracuse 19–9
13. Virginia 22–8	

National Invitation Tournament Scores

First round: Penn St 62, Miami (FL) 56; Nebraska 69, Georgia 61; Iowa 96, DePaul 87; Ohio 83, George Washington 71; Marquette 68, Auburn 61; St Bonaventure 75, Southern Miss 70; Coppin St 75, St Joseph 68 (OT); South Florida 74, St John's (NY) 67; Providence 72, Charleston 67; Virginia Tech 62, Clemson 54; New Mexico St 97, Colorado 83; UTEP 90, Montana 60; Bradley 86, Eastern Michigan 85 (2OT); Canisius 83, Seton Hall 71; Illinois St 93, Utah St 87; Washington St 94, Texas Tech 82.
Second round: Penn St 65, Nebraska 59; Iowa 66, Ohio 62; Marquette 70, St Bonaventure 61; South Florida 75, Coppin St 50; Virginia Tech 91, Providence 78; New Mexico St 92, UTEP 89; Canisius 55, Bradley 53; Washington St 83, Illinois St 80 (OT).
Third round: Penn St 67, Iowa 64; Marquette 57, South Florida 50 (OT); Virginia Tech 64, New Mexico St 61; Canisius 89, Washington St 80.
Semifinals: Marquette 87, Penn St 79; Virginia Tech 71, Canisius 59.
Championship: Virginia Tech 65, Marquette 64 (OT).
Consolation game: Penn St 66, Canisius 62.

1995 NCAA Basketball Men's Division I Tournament

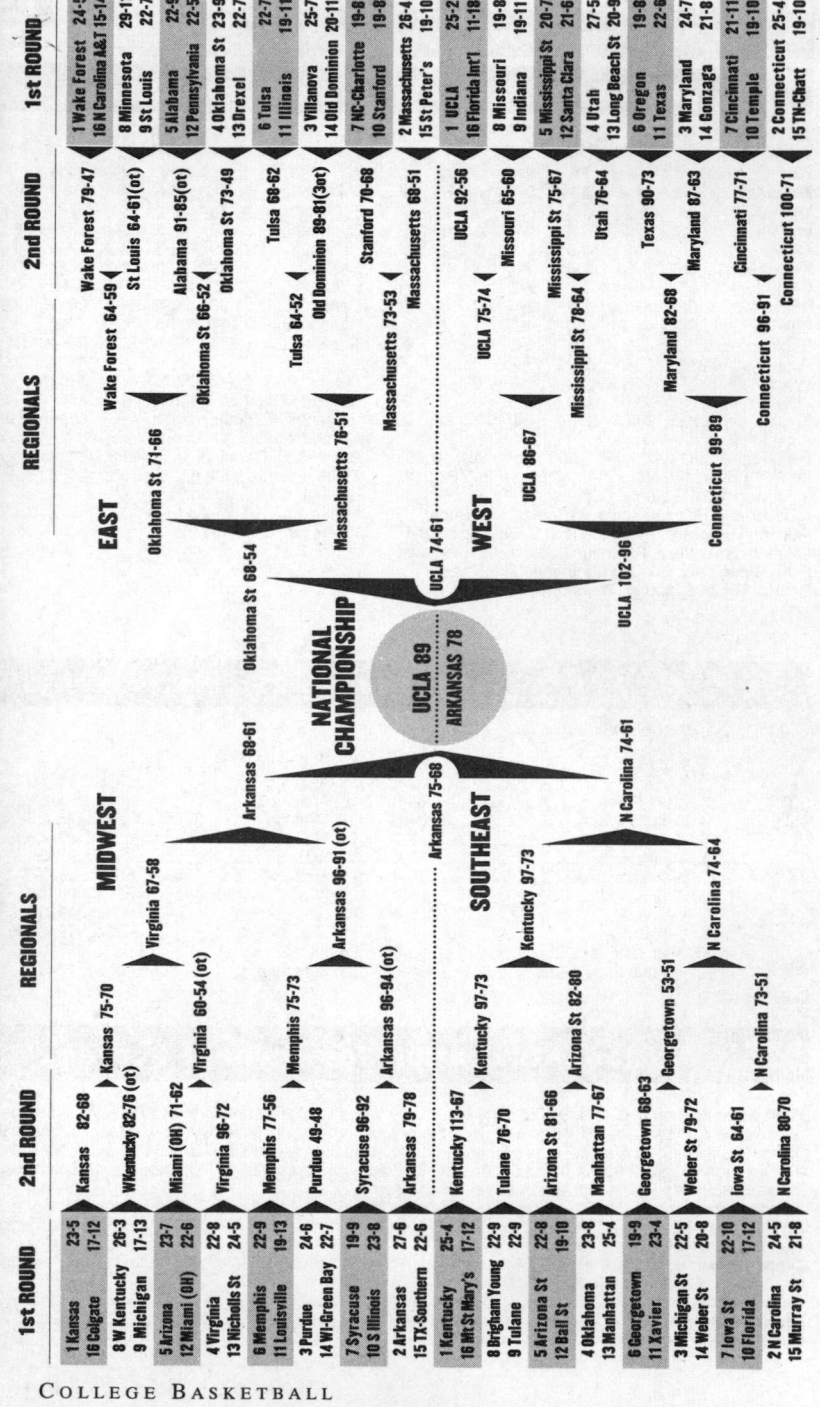

1st ROUND — 2nd ROUND — REGIONALS — 2nd ROUND — 1st ROUND

EAST

1st ROUND
- 1 Wake Forest 24-5
- 16 N Carolina A&T 15-14
- 8 Minnesota 29-11
- 9 St Louis 22-7
- 5 Alabama 22-9
- 12 Pennsylvania 22-5
- 4 Oklahoma St 23-9
- 13 Drexel 22-7
- 6 Tulsa 22-7
- 11 Illinois 19-11
- 3 Villanova 25-7
- 14 Old Dominion 20-11
- 7 NC-Charlotte 19-8
- 10 Stanford 19-8
- 2 Massachusetts 26-4
- 15 St Peter's 19-10

2nd ROUND
- Wake Forest 79-47
- St Louis 64-59
- Alabama 91-85(ot)
- Oklahoma St 73-49
- Tulsa 68-62
- Old Dominion 89-81(3ot)
- Stanford 70-68
- Massachusetts 68-51

REGIONALS
- Wake Forest 64-59
- Oklahoma St 66-52
- Oklahoma St 71-66
- Tulsa 64-52
- Massachusetts 76-51
- Massachusetts 73-53
- Oklahoma St 68-54

UCLA 74-61

WEST

1st ROUND
- 1 UCLA 25-2
- 16 Florida Int'l 11-18
- 8 Missouri 19-8
- 9 Indiana 19-11
- 5 Mississippi St 20-7
- 12 Santa Clara 21-6
- 4 Utah 27-5
- 13 Long Beach St 20-9
- 6 Oregon 19-8
- 11 Texas 22-6
- 3 Maryland 24-7
- 14 Gonzaga 21-8
- 7 Cincinnati 21-11
- 10 Temple 19-10
- 2 Connecticut 25-4
- 15 TN-Chatt 19-10

2nd ROUND
- UCLA 82-56
- Missouri 65-60
- Mississippi St 75-67
- Utah 76-64
- Texas 90-73
- Maryland 87-63
- Cincinnati 77-71
- Connecticut 100-71

REGIONALS
- UCLA 75-74
- Mississippi St 78-64
- UCLA 86-67
- Maryland 82-68
- Connecticut 96-89
- Connecticut 99-89
- UCLA 102-96

NATIONAL CHAMPIONSHIP

UCLA 89 — ARKANSAS 78

MIDWEST

1st ROUND
- 1 Kansas 23-5
- 16 Colgate 17-12
- 8 W Kentucky 26-3
- 9 Michigan 17-13
- 5 Arizona 23-7
- 12 Miami (OH) 22-6
- 4 Virginia 22-8
- 13 Nicholls St 24-5
- 6 Memphis 22-9
- 11 Louisville 19-13
- 3 Purdue 24-6
- 14 Wi-Green Bay 22-7
- 7 Syracuse 19-9
- 10 S Illinois 23-8
- 2 Arkansas 27-6
- 15 TX-Southern 22-6

2nd ROUND
- Kansas 82-68
- W Kentucky 82-76 (ot)
- Miami (OH) 71-62
- Virginia 96-72
- Memphis 77-56
- Purdue 49-48
- Syracuse 96-92
- Arkansas 79-78

REGIONALS
- Kansas 75-70
- Virginia 60-54 (ot)
- Virginia 67-58
- Memphis 75-73
- Arkansas 96-91 (ot)
- Arkansas 96-94 (ot)
- Arkansas 68-61

Arkansas 75-68

SOUTHEAST

1st ROUND
- 1 Kentucky 25-4
- 16 Mt St Mary's 17-12
- 8 Brigham Young 22-9
- 9 Tulane 22-9
- 5 Arizona St 22-8
- 12 Ball St 19-10
- 4 Oklahoma 23-8
- 13 Manhattan 25-4
- 6 Georgetown 19-9
- 11 Xavier 23-4
- 3 Michigan St 22-5
- 14 Weber St 20-8
- 7 Iowa St 22-10
- 10 Florida 17-12
- 2 N Carolina 24-5
- 15 Murray St 21-8

2nd ROUND
- Kentucky 113-67
- Tulane 76-70
- Arizona St 81-66
- Manhattan 77-67
- Georgetown 68-63
- Weber St 79-72
- Iowa St 64-61
- N Carolina 80-70

REGIONALS
- Kentucky 97-73
- Arizona St 82-80
- Kentucky 97-73
- Georgetown 53-51
- N Carolina 73-51
- N Carolina 74-64
- N Carolina 74-61

Assoc. of Mid-Continent

	Conference			All Games		
	W	L	Pct	W	L	Pct
Valparaiso*†	14	4	.778	20	8	.714
Western Illinois	13	5	.722	20	8	.714
Buffalo	12	6	.667	18	10	.643
Youngstown St	10	8	.556	18	10	.643
Eastern Illinois	10	8	.556	16	3	.842
Troy St	10	8	.556	11	16	.407
MO-Kansas City	7	11	.389	7	19	.269
Central Conn	6	12	.333	8	18	.308
Chicago St	6	12	.333	6	20	.231
NE Illinois	2	16	.111	4	22	.154

Atlantic Coast

	Conference			All Games		
	W	L	Pct	W	L	Pct
Wake Forest*†	12	4	.750	26	6	.813
North Carolina	12	4	.750	27	6	.818
Maryland	12	4	.750	26	8	.765
Virginia	12	4	.750	25	9	.735
Georgia Tech	8	8	.500	18	12	.600
Clemson	5	11	.313	15	13	.535
Florida St	5	11	.313	12	15	.444
N Carolina St	4	12	.250	12	15	.444
Duke	2	14	.125	13	18	.419

Atlantic 10

	Conference			All Games		
	W	L	Pct	W	L	Pct
Massachusetts*†	13	3	.813	29	5	.853
Temple	10	6	.625	19	11	.633
Geo Washington	10	6	.625	18	14	.563
St Joseph's	9	7	.563	17	12	.586
St Bonaventure	9	7	.563	18	13	.581
West Virginia	7	9	.438	13	13	.500
Rutgers	7	9	.438	13	15	.464
Dusquesne	5	11	.313	10	18	.357
Rhode Island	2	14	.125	7	20	.259

Big East

	Conference			All Games		
	W	L	Pct	W	L	Pct
Connecticut*	16	2	.889	28	5	.848
Villlanova†	14	4	.777	25	8	.758
Syracuse	12	6	.667	20	10	.667
Georgetown	11	7	.611	21	10	.677
Miami (FL)	9	9	.500	15	13	.536
Providence	7	11	.389	17	13	.566
Seton Hall	7	11	.389	16	14	.533
St John's	7	11	.389	14	14	.500
Pittsburgh	5	13	.277	10	18	.357
Boston College	2	16	.111	9	19	.321

Big Eight

	Conference			All Games		
	W	L	Pct	W	L	Pct
Kansas*	11	3	.786	25	6	.806
Oklahoma St†	10	4	.714	27	10	.729
Oklahoma	9	5	.642	23	9	.718
Missouri	8	6	.571	20	9	.689
Iowa St	6	8	.428	23	11	.676
Colorado	5	9	.357	15	13	.535
Nebraska	4	10	.285	18	14	.562
Kansas St	3	11	.214	12	15	.444

Big Sky

	Conference			All Games		
	W	L	Pct	W	L	Pct
Weber St*†	11	3	.785	21	9	.700
Montana	11	3	.785	21	9	.700
Montana St	8	6	.571	21	8	.724
Idaho St	7	7	.500	18	10	.642
Boise St	7	7	.500	17	10	.629
Idaho	6	8	.428	12	15	.444
Northern Arizona	4	10	.285	8	18	.307
Eastern Washington	2	12	.142	6	20	.230

Big South

	Conference			All Games		
	W	L	Pct	W	L	Pct
NC-Greensboro*	14	2	.875	23	6	.793
Charleston So†	12	4	.750	19	10	.655
MD-Balt. County	10	6	.625	13	14	.481
Radford	9	7	.562	16	12	.571
Liberty	7	9	.437	12	16	.428
NC-Asheville	7	9	.437	11	16	.407
Towson St	6	10	.375	12	15	.444
Winthrop	4	12	.250	7	20	.259
Coastal Carolina	3	13	.187	6	20	.230

Big Ten

	Conference			All Games		
	W	L	Pct	W	L	Pct
Purdue	15	3	.833	25	7	.781
Michigan St	14	4	.777	22	6	.785
Michigan	11	7	.611	17	14	.548
Indiana	11	7	.611	19	12	.612
Illinois	10	8	.556	19	12	.612
Minnesota	10	8	.556	19	12	.612
Iowa	9	9	.500	21	11	.656
Penn St	9	9	.500	20	11	.645
Wisconsin	7	11	.388	13	14	.481
Ohio St	2	16	.111	6	22	.214
Northwestern	1	17	.055	5	22	.185

*Conf. champ; †Conf. tourney winner.

Big West

	Conference			All Games		
	W	L	Pct	W	L	Pct
Utah St*	14	4	.777	21	8	.724
New Mexico St	13	5	.722	25	10	.714
Long Beach St†	13	5	.722	20	10	.667
Nevada	12	6	.667	18	10	.642
Pacific	9	9	.500	14	13	.518
UC-Santa Barbara	8	10	.444	13	14	.928
UNLV	7	11	.388	12	16	.428
UC-Irvine	6	12	.333	13	16	.448
Cal St Fullerton	5	13	.277	7	20	.259
San Jose St	3	15	.166	4	23	.148

Colonial Athletic Association

	Conference			All Games		
	W	L	Pct	W	L	Pct
Old Dominion*†	12	2	.857	21	12	.636
NC-Wilmington	10	4	.714	16	11	.592
James Madison	9	5	.642	16	13	.551
E Carolina	7	7	.500	18	11	.620
American	7	7	.500	9	19	.321
William & Mary	6	8	.428	8	19	.296
Richmond	3	11	.214	8	20	.285
George Mason	2	12	.142	7	20	.259

Great Midwest

	Conference			All Games		
	W	L	Pct	W	L	Pct
Memphis*	9	3	.750	25	10	.714
St Louis	8	4	.667	23	8	.741
Cincinnati†	7	5	.583	22	12	.647
Marquette	7	5	.583	20	12	.625
DePaul	6	6	.500	18	11	.642
AL-Birmingham	5	7	.416	14	16	.466
Dayton	0	12	.000	7	20	.259

Ivy League

	Conference			All Games		
	W	L	Pct	W	L	Pct
Pennsylvania*	14	0	1.000	22	6	.785
Princeton	10	4	.714	16	10	.615
Dartmouth	10	4	.714	13	13	.500
Brown	8	6	.571	13	13	.500
Yale	5	9	.357	9	17	.346
Cornell	4	10	.285	9	17	.346
Harvard	4	10	.285	6	20	.230
Columbia	1	13	.071	4	22	.153

Metro

	Conference			All Games		
	W	L	Pct	W	L	Pct
NC-Charlotte*	8	4	.667	19	9	.678
Tulane	7	5	.583	23	10	.696
Louisville†	7	5	.583	19	14	.575
Virginia Tech	6	6	.500	24	10	.705
S Mississippi	6	6	.500	17	12	.586
S Florida	5	7	.416	18	12	.600
VCU	3	9	.250	16	14	.533

Metro Atlantic

	Conference			All Games		
	W	L	Pct	W	L	Pct
Manhattan*	12	2	.857	26	5	.838
St Peter's†	10	4	.714	19	11	.633
Canisius	10	4	.714	21	13	.617
Fairfield	6	8	.428	13	15	.464
Iona	6	8	.428	10	17	.370
Loyola (MD)	5	9	.357	9	18	.333
Siena	5	9	.357	8	19	.296
Niagara	2	12	.142	5	25	.166

Mid-American

	Conference			All Games		
	W	L	Pct	W	L	Pct
Miami (OH)*	16	2	.888	23	7	.766
Ohio University	13	5	.722	24	10	.705
E Michigan	12	6	.667	20	10	.667
Ball St†	11	7	.611	19	11	.633
Bowling Green	10	8	.556	16	11	.593
Toledo	10	8	.556	16	11	.593
W Michigan	9	9	.500	14	13	.518
Kent	5	13	.277	8	19	.296
Akron	4	14	.222	8	18	.307
Central Michigan	0	18	.000	3	23	.130

Mid-Eastern Athletic

	Conference			All Games		
	W	L	Pct	W	L	Pct
Coppin St*	15	1	.937	21	10	.677
S Carolina St	11	5	.687	15	13	.535
N Carolina A&T†	10	6	.625	15	15	.500
MD-Eastern Shore	9	7	.562	13	14	.481
Bethune-Cookman	9	7	.562	12	16	.428
Howard	8	8	.500	9	18	.333
Morgan St	5	11	.312	5	22	.185
Delaware St	3	13	.187	7	21	.250
Florida A&M	2	14	.125	5	22	.185

Midwestern Collegiate

	Conference			All Games		
	W	L	Pct	W	L	Pct
Xavier (OH)*	14	0	1.000	23	5	.821
WI-Green Bay†	11	4	.733	22	8	.733
Illinois-Chicago	11	4	.733	18	9	.666
Detroit	9	5	.642	13	15	.464
Butler	8	7	.533	15	12	.555
La Salle	7	7	.500	13	14	.481
N Illinois	7	8	.466	19	10	.655
Wright St	6	8	.428	13	17	.433
Cleveland St	3	11	.214	10	17	.370
Loyola (IL)	2	13	.133	5	22	.074
WI-Milwaukee	2	13	.133	3	24	.111

*Conf. champ; †Conf. tourney winner.

Missouri Valley

	Conference			All Games		
	W	L	Pct	W	L	Pct
Tulsa*	15	3	.833	24	8	.750
S Illinois†	13	5	.722	23	9	.719
Illinois St	13	5	.722	20	13	.606
Bradley	12	6	.667	20	10	.667
Evansville	11	7	.611	18	9	.667
SW Missouri St	9	9	.500	16	11	.593
Drake	9	9	.500	12	15	.444
Wichita St	6	12	.333	13	14	.482
N Iowa	4	14	.222	8	20	.400
Creighton	4	14	.222	7	19	.269
Indiana St	3	15	.167	7	19	.269

North Atlantic

	Conference			All Games		
	W	L	Pct	W	L	Pct
Drexel*†	12	4	.750	22	8	.733
New Hampshire	11	5	.688	19	9	.678
Northeastern	10	6	.625	18	11	.620
Vermont	7	9	.438	14	13	.518
Boston U	7	9	.438	15	16	.483
Delaware	7	9	.438	12	15	.444
Hartford	7	9	.438	11	16	.407
Maine	6	10	.375	11	16	.407
Hofstra	5	11	.313	10	18	.357

Northeast

	Conference			All Games		
	W	L	Pct	W	L	Pct
Rider*	13	5	.722	18	11	.620
Marist	12	6	.667	17	11	.607
Mt St Mary's†	12	6	.667	17	13	.566
FDU-Teaneck	11	7	.611	16	12	.571
Monmouth (NJ)	11	7	.611	13	14	.481
Wagner	9	9	.500	10	17	.370
LIU-Brooklyn	8	10	.444	11	17	.392
St Francis (PA)	7	11	.388	12	16	.428
St Francis (NY)	5	13	.277	9	18	.333
Robert Morris	2	16	.111	4	23	.148

Ohio Valley

	Conference			All Games		
	W	L	Pct	W	L	Pct
Tennessee St*	11	5	.687	17	10	.629
Murray St†	11	5	.687	21	9	.700
Morehead St	10	6	.625	15	12	.555
Tennessee Tech	9	7	.562	13	14	.481
Austin Peay	8	8	.500	13	16	.448
SE Missouri	7	9	.438	13	14	.481
E Kentucky	6	10	.375	9	19	.321
Middle Tenn St	5	11	.312	12	15	.444
TN-Martin	5	11	.312	7	20	.259

Pacific-10

	Conference			All Games		
	W	L	Pct	W	L	Pct
UCLA*	16	2	.888	31	2	.939
Arizona	13	5	.722	23	8	.741
Arizona St	12	6	.667	24	9	.727
Oregon	11	7	.611	19	9	.678
Stanford	10	8	.556	20	9	.689
Washington St	10	8	.556	18	12	.600
Oregon St	6	12	.333	9	18	.333
California	5	13	.277	13	14	.481
Washington	5	13	.277	9	18	.333
Southern Cal	2	16	.111	7	21	.250

Patriot

	Conference			All Games		
	W	L	Pct	W	L	Pct
Colgate*†	11	3	.785	17	13	.566
Bucknell	11	3	.785	13	14	.481
Navy	10	4	.714	20	9	.689
Holy Cross	9	5	.643	15	12	.555
Fordham	6	8	.428	11	17	.392
Lehigh	5	9	.357	11	16	.407
Army	4	10	.286	12	16	.428
Lafayette	0	14	.000	2	25	.074

Southeastern

EAST

	Conference			All Games		
	W	L	Pct	W	L	Pct
Kentucky*†	14	2	.875	28	5	.875
Georgia	9	7	.562	18	10	.642
Florida	8	8	.500	17	13	.566
Vanderbilt	6	10	.375	13	15	.464
S Carolina	5	11	.454	10	17	.370
Tennessee	4	12	.250	11	16	.407

WEST

	Conference			All Games		
	W	L	Pct	W	L	Pct
Arkansas	12	4	.750	32	7	.820
Mississippi St	12	4	.750	22	8	.733
Alabama	10	6	.625	23	10	.696
Auburn	7	9	.437	16	13	.551
LSU	6	10	.375	12	15	.444
Mississippi	3	13	.187	8	19	.296

*Conf. champ; †Conf. tourney winner.

Southern

NORTH

	Conference			All Games		
	W	L	Pct	W	L	Pct
Marshall	10	4	.714	18	9	.666
E Tennessee St	9	5	.642	14	14	.500
Davidson	7	7	.500	14	13	.518
VMI	6	8	.428	10	17	.370
Appalachian St	4	10	.285	9	20	.333

SOUTH

	Conference			All Games		
	W	L	Pct	W	L	Pct
TN-Chattanooga*†	11	3	.785	19	11	.633
W Carolina	8	6	.571	14	14	.500
The Citadel	6	8	.428	11	16	.407
Furman	6	8	.428	10	17	.370
Georgia Southern	3	11	.214	8	20	.285

Southland

	Conference			All Games		
	W	L	Pct	W	L	Pct
Nicholls St*†	17	1	.944	24	6	.800
TX-San Antonio	11	7	.611	15	13	.535
NE Louisiana	11	7	.611	14	18	.437
N Texas St	9	9	.500	14	13	.518
Stephen Austin	9	9	.500	14	13	.518
NW Louisana	8	10	.444	13	14	.481
SW Texas St	7	11	.388	12	14	.461
McNeese St	7	11	.388	11	16	.407
TX-Arlington	7	11	.388	10	17	.370
Sam Houston St	4	14	.222	7	19	.269

Southwest

	Conference			All Games		
	W	L	Pct	W	L	Pct
Texas*†	11	3	.785	23	7	.766
Texas Tech	11	3	.785	20	10	.666
TCU	8	6	.571	16	11	.592
Rice	8	6	.571	15	13	.535
Texas A&M	7	7	.500	14	16	.466
Houston	5	9	.357	9	19	.321
Baylor	3	11	.214	9	19	.321
SMU	3	11	.214	7	20	.259

Southwestern Athletic

	Conference			All Games		
	W	L	Pct	W	L	Pct
Texas Southern*†	12	2	.857	22	7	.758
Miss Valley St	10	4	.714	17	10	.629
Alabama St	8	6	.571	10	15	.400
Southern-BR	7	7	.500	13	13	.500
Jackson St	7	7	.500	12	19	.444
Grambling St	5	9	.357	11	17	.392
Alcorn St	4	10	.285	7	19	.250
Prairie View	3	11	.214	5	21	.192

*Conf. champ; †Conf. tourney winner.

Sun Belt

	Conference			All Games		
	W	L	Pct	W	L	Pct
W Kentucky*†	17	1	.944	27	4	.870
New Orleans	13	5	.722	20	11	.645
Jacksonville	12	6	.667	18	9	.667
TX-Pan American	10	8	.555	14	14	.500
AR-Little Rock	9	9	.500	17	12	.586
Louisiana Tech	9	9	.500	14	13	.518
South Alabama	7	11	.388	9	18	.333
Lamar	6	12	.333	11	16	.407
SW Louisiana	4	14	.222	7	22	.241
Arkansas St	3	15	.166	8	20	.285

Trans-America

	Conference			All Games		
	W	L	Pct	W	L	Pct
Coll of Charleston*	15	1	.937	23	6	.793
Samford	11	5	.687	16	11	.592
Stetson	11	5	.687	16	11	.592
Mercer	8	8	.500	15	14	.517
SE Louisiana	7	9	.437	12	16	.428
Central Florida	7	9	.437	11	16	.407
Centenary	7	9	.437	10	17	.370
Georgia St	6	10	.375	11	17	.392
Florida Int'l†	4	12	.250	11	19	.366
Campbell	4	12	.250	8	18	.307
Florida Atlantic	0	0	.000	9	18	.333

West Coast

	Conference			All Games		
	W	L	Pct	W	L	Pct
Santa Clara*	12	2	.857	21	7	.750
Portland	10	4	.714	21	8	.724
St Mary's	10	4	.714	18	10	.642
Gonzaga†	7	7	.500	21	9	.700
San Diego	5	9	.357	11	16	.407
Loyola Marymount	4	10	.285	13	15	.464
San Francisco	4	10	.285	10	19	.344
Pepperdine	4	10	.285	8	19	.296

Western Athletic

	Conference			All Games		
	W	L	Pct	W	L	Pct
Utah*†	15	3	.833	28	6	.823
BYU	13	5	.722	22	10	.687
UTEP	13	5	.722	20	10	.666
New Mexico	9	9	.500	15	15	.500
Wyoming	9	9	.500	13	15	.464
Hawaii	8	10	.444	16	13	.551
Colorado St	7	11	.388	17	14	.548
Fresno St	7	11	.388	13	15	.464
San Diego St	5	13	.277	11	17	.392
Air Force	4	14	.222	8	20	.285

Independents

	W	L	Pct
Notre Dame	15	12	.555
Oral Roberts	10	17	.370

Scoring

	Class	GP	Field Goals			3-Pt FG		Free Throws			Reb	Pts	Avg
			FGA	FG	Pct	FGA	FG	FTA	FT	Pct			
Kurt Thomas, Texas Christian	Sr	27	526	288	54.8	12	3	283	202	71.4	393	781	28.9
Frankie King, Western Carolina	Sr	28	520	249	47.9	134	52	232	193	83.2	204	743	26.5
Kenny Sykes, Grambling	Sr	26	571	245	42.9	220	82	146	112	76.7	107	684	26.3
Sherell Ford, IL-Chicago	Sr	27	562	265	47.2	113	47	170	130	76.5	283	707	26.2
Tim Roberts, Southern-BR	Jr	26	570	233	40.9	313	108	145	106	73.1	123	680	26.2
Kareem Townes, La Salle	Sr	27	553	242	43.8	284	103	139	112	80.6	88	699	25.9
Joe Griffin, LIU-Brooklyn	Sr	28	548	271	49.5	31	11	256	170	66.4	229	723	25.8
Shawn Respert, Michigan St	Sr	28	484	229	47.3	251	119	160	139	86.9	111	716	25.6
Rob Feaster, Holy Cross	Sr	27	503	225	44.7	168	55	226	167	73.9	186	672	24.9
Shannon Smith, WI-Milwaukee	Jr	27	505	199	39.4	157	51	268	212	79.1	148	661	24.5
Mark Lueking, Army	Jr	28	498	204	41.0	243	98	202	176	87.1	65	682	24.4
Otis Jones, Air Force	Sr	28	495	213	43.0	210	71	228	173	75.9	130	670	23.9
Ryan Minor, Oklahoma	Jr	32	535	260	48.6	176	69	203	167	82.3	269	756	23.6
Alan Henderson, Indiana	Sr	31	476	284	59.7	10	2	251	159	63.3	302	729	23.5
Ronnie Henderson, LSU	So	27	511	219	42.9	212	68	169	124	73.4	142	630	23.3
Scott Drapeau, New Hampshire	Sr	28	456	241	52.9	65	21	205	145	70.7	273	648	23.1
Tucker Neale, Colgate	Sr	30	509	229	45.0	224	84	195	150	76.9	138	692	23.1
Gary Trent, Ohio	Jr	33	556	293	52.7	35	8	254	163	64.2	423	757	22.9
Joe Wilbert, Texas A&M	Sr	30	473	253	53.5	14	4	245	177	72.2	226	687	22.9
Damon Stoudamire, Arizona	Sr	30	466	222	47.6	241	112	155	128	82.6	128	684	22.8
Marcus Brown, Murray St	Jr	30	429	219	51.0	119	44	211	189	89.6	147	671	22.4
Matt Alosa, New Hampshire	Jr	28	476	197	41.4	234	87	168	142	84.5	106	623	22.3
Danya Abrams, Boston College	So	28	418	215	51.4	8	0	264	190	72.0	254	620	22.1
Petey Sessoms, Old Dominion	Sr	33	495	213	43.0	242	89	259	215	83.0	276	730	22.1
Chris Carr, Southern Illinois	Jr	32	521	250	46.0	101	40	214	165	77.1	232	705	22.0
Aundre Branch, Baylor	Sr	28	506	213	42.1	278	104	104	78	75.0	127	608	21.7
Louis Rowe, James Madison	Sr	29	453	241	53.2	92	33	148	114	77.0	164	629	21.7
Reggie Jackson, Nicholls St	Sr	30	433	251	58.0	4	0	228	147	64.5	325	649	21.6
Gerard King, Nicholls St	Sr	28	423	238	56.3	1	1	182	128	70.3	218	605	21.6
Bryant Reeves, Oklahoma St	Sr	37	493	289	58.6	5	0	310	219	70.6	350	797	21.5

REBOUNDS

	Class	GP	Reb	Avg
Kurt Thomas, Texas Christian	Sr	27	393	14.6
Malik Rose, Drexel	Jr	30	404	13.5
Gary Trent, Ohio	Jr	33	423	12.8
Dan Callahan, Northeastern	Sr	29	364	12.6
Tim Duncan, Wake Forest	So	32	401	12.5
Adonal Foyle, Colgate	Fr	30	371	12.4
Tunji Awojobi, Boston University	So	31	378	12.2
Kareem Carpenter, E Michigan	Sr	29	343	11.8
Marcus Mann, Mississippi Valley	Jr	27	317	11.7
Chris Ensminger, Valparaiso	Jr	28	315	11.3

ASSISTS

	Class	GP	A	Avg
Nelson Haggerty, Baylor	Sr	28	284	10.1
Curtis McCants, George Mason	So	27	251	9.3
Raimonds Miglinieks, UC-Irvine	Jr	29	245	8.4
Eric Snow, Michigan St	Sr	28	217	7.8
Jacque Vaughn, Kansas	So	31	238	7.7
Anthony Foster, South Alabama	Sr	27	203	7.5
Tony Miller, Marquette	Sr	33	248	7.5
Hassan Sanders, Southern-BR	Jr	24	179	7.5
Ray Washington, Nicholls St	Sr	29	213	7.3
Damon Stoudamire, Arizona	Sr	30	220	7.3
Eathan O'Bryant, Nevada	Sr	29	211	7.3
Marcell Capers, Arizona St	Sr	33	233	7.1

3-POINT FIELD GOALS MADE PER GAME

	Class	GP	FG	Avg
Mitch Taylor, Southern-BR	Jr	25	109	4.4
Shawn Respert, Michigan St	Sr	28	119	4.3
Tim Roberts, Southern-BR	Jr	26	108	4.2
Randy Rutherford, Oklahoma St	Sr	37	146	3.9
Kareem Townes, La Salle	Sr	27	103	3.8
Lazelle Durden, Cincinnati	Sr	34	127	3.7
Damon Stoudamire, Arizona	Sr	30	112	3.7
Aundre Branch, Baylor	Sr	28	104	3.7
Noy Castillo, Citadel	So	27	96	3.6
Chris Kingsbury, Iowa	So	33	117	3.5
Adam Jacobsen, Pacific (CA)	So	27	95	3.5

3-POINT FIELD GOAL PERCENTAGE

	Class	GP	FGA	FG	Pct
Brian Jackson, Evansville	Jr	27	95	53	55.8
Scott Kegler, Pennsylvania	Sr	28	114	58	50.9
Chris Westlake, WI-Green Bay	Sr	30	174	87	50.0
Dante Calabria, N Carolina	Jr	33	133	66	49.6
Malik Hightower, Marshall	Jr	27	95	46	48.4
Jeremy Lake, Montana	Sr	30	157	76	48.4
Dion Cross, Stanford	Jr	29	171	82	48.0
Shawn Respert, Michigan St	Sr	28	251	119	47.4
Daryl Christopher, Southern Utah	Jr	27	112	53	47.3
Rob Wooster, St. Francis (PA)	Jr	28	174	82	47.1

Note: Minimum 1.5 made per game.

STEALS

	Class	GP	S	Avg
Roderick Anderson, Texas	Sr	30	101	3.4
Greg Black, TX-Pan American	Sr	28	94	3.4
Nate Langley, George Mason	So	26	87	3.3
Ray Washington, Nicholls St	Sr	29	88	3.0
Clarence Ceasar, LSU	Sr	22	66	3.0
Allen Iverson, Georgetown	Fr	30	89	3.0
Shandue McNeill, St Bonaventure	So	31	90	2.9
Dominick Young, Fresno St	So	28	81	2.9
Erick Strickland, Nebraska	Jr	31	89	2.9
Gerald Walker, San Francisco	Jr	28	80	2.9

BLOCKED SHOTS

	Class	GP	BS	Avg
Keith Closs, Central Conn St	Fr	26	139	5.3
Theo Ratcliff, Wyoming	Sr	28	144	5.1
Adonal Foyle, Colgate	Fr	30	147	4.9
Pascal Fleury, MD-Baltimore County	Sr	27	124	4.6
Lorenzo Coleman, Tennessee Tech	So	27	122	4.5
Tim Duncan, Wake Forest	So	32	145	4.2
Brian Gilpin, Dartmouth	So	26	92	3.5
Mario Bennett, Arizona St	Jr	33	115	3.5
Peter Aluma, Liberty	So	28	97	3.5

Four tied with 3.4.

FIELD GOAL PERCENTAGE

	Class	GP	FGA	FG	Pct
Shane Kline-Ruminski, Bowl Gr	Sr	26	265	181	68.3
George Spain, Davidson	Sr	27	210	141	67.1
Rasheed Wallace, N Carolina	So	34	364	238	65.4
Erick Dampier, Mississippi St	So	30	239	153	64.0
Alexander Koul, Geo Wash	Fr	32	253	160	63.2
Joe McNaull, Long Beach St	Sr	30	248	156	62.9
Mark Hendrickson, Wash St	Jr	30	292	183	62.7
Darnell McCulloch, Fresno St	So	28	244	152	62.3
Lorenzo Coleman, Tenn Tech	So	27	270	168	62.2
Chuckie Robinson, E Carolina	Sr	29	293	181	61.8

Note: Minimum 5 made per game.

FREE-THROW PERCENTAGE

	Class	GP	FTA	FT	Pct
Greg Bibb, Tennessee Tech	Jr	27	117	106	90.6
Scott Hartzell, NC-Greensboro	Jr	29	108	97	89.8
Marcus Brown, Murray St	Jr	30	211	189	89.6
Keith Cornett, TX-Arlington	Jr	27	79	70	88.6
Arlando Johnson, E Kentucky	Sr	28	139	123	88.5
Danny Basile, Marist	Jr	28	84	74	88.1
Steve Nash, Santa Clara	Jr	27	174	153	87.9
John Rillie, Gonzaga	Sr	30	99	87	87.9
Lance Barker, Valparaiso	Sr	28	82	72	87.8
Michael Heary, Navy	Fr	28	105	120	87.5

Note: Minimum 2.5 made per game.

Single-Game Highs

POINTS

56 ....Tim Roberts, Southern-BR, Dec 12 (vs Faith Baptist)
52 ....Jareem Townes, La Salle, Feb 4 (vs Loyola [IL])
50 ....Kenny Sykes, Grambling, Jan 8 (vs Southern BR)

REBOUNDS

27 ....Kareem Carpenter, Eastern Mich, Feb 8 (vs Western Michigan)
26 ....Kareem Carpenter, Eastern Mich, Jan 14 (vs Central Michigan)

ASSISTS

20 ....Ray Washington, Nicholls St, Jan 28 (vs McNeese St)

3-POINT FIELD GOALS

12 ....Mitch Taylor, Southern-BR, Dec 1 (vs LA Christian)
11 ....Randy Rutherford, Oklahoma St, Mar 5 (vs Kansas)

FREE THROWS

21 ....Steve Nash, Santa Clara, Jan 7 (vs St Mary's [CA])
19 ....Malik Rose, Drexel, Feb 5 (vs Hofstra)
19 ....Sidney Goodman, Coppin St, Feb 18 (vs N Carolina A&T)

Single-Game Highs *(Cont.)*

STEALS

11 ....Tyus Edney, UCLA, Dec 22 (vs George Mason)
10 ....Brandon Born, TN-Chatt, Nov 26 (vs SC-Aiken)
10 ....Mario Miller, Bethune-Cookman, Dec 3 (vs Warner Southern)
10 ....Tick Rogers, Louisville, Dec 5 (vs Western Carolina)

BLOCKED SHOTS

13 ....Keith Closs, Central Conn St, Dec 21 (vs St Francis [PA])
12 ....Kurt Thomas, Texas Christian, Feb 25 (vs Texas A&M)
Three tied with 11.

NCAA Men's Division I Team Leaders

SCORING OFFENSE

	GP	W	L	Pts	Avg		GP	W	L	Pts	Avg
Texas Christian	27	16	11	2529	93.7	Nicholls St	30	24	6	2709	90.3
Southern-BR	26	13	13	2425	93.3	Texas Tech	30	20	10	2664	88.8
Texas	30	23	7	2787	92.9	Stephen F. Austin	28	14	14	2461	87.9
George Mason	27	7	20	2499	92.6	Arkansas	39	32	7	3416	87.6
Troy St	27	11	16	2468	91.4	UCLA	33	31	2	2889	87.5

SCORING DEFENSE

	GP	W	L	Pts	Avg		GP	W	L	Pts	Avg
Princeton	26	16	10	1501	57.7	Clemson	28	15	13	1749	62.5
WI-Green Bay	30	22	8	1767	58.9	St Louis	31	23	8	1940	62.6
Temple	30	19	11	1792	59.7	Charleston (SC)	29	23	6	1819	62.7
Miami (OH)	30	23	7	1827	60.9	Wake Forest	32	26	6	2011	62.8
Manhattan	31	26	5	1929	62.2	TX-Pan American	28	14	14	1769	63.2

SCORING MARGIN

	Off	Def	Mar		Off	Def	Mar
Kentucky	87.4	69.0	18.4	Evansville	77.0	63.7	13.3
Massachusetts	80.9	65.7	15.1	St Louis	75.8	62.6	13.2
Pennsylvania	82.2	67.5	15.1	Manhattan	75.3	62.2	13.0
UCLA	87.5	73.9	13.7	Kansas	83.0	70.0	13.0
Montana St	84.2	70.8	13.4	Oklahoma St	77.3	64.3	12.9

FIELD GOAL PERCENTAGE

	FGA	FG	Pct		FGA	FG	Pct
Washington St	1743	902	51.7	Utah St	1650	831	50.4
UCLA	2102	1079	51.3	Oklahoma St	2025	1016	50.2
North Carolina	2055	1044	50.8	Michigan St	1664	829	49.8
Montana St	1832	930	50.8	Maryland	2080	1035	49.8
Bowling Green	1427	721	50.5	Evansville	1457	723	49.6

FIELD GOAL PERCENTAGE DEFENSE

	FGA	FG	Pct		FGA	FG	Pct
Alabama	2048	771	37.6	Massachusetts	2072	799	38.6
Kansas	2032	768	37.8	Temple	1623	628	38.7
Marquette	1957	747	38.2	Wake Forest	1898	736	38.8
Mississippi St	1821	698	38.3	Virginia	2058	803	39.0
Manhattan	1747	670	38.4	Charleston (SC)	1634	639	39.1

FREE-THROW PERCENTAGE

	FTA	FT	Pct		FTA	FT	Pct
Brigham Young	798	617	77.3	Coppin St	633	476	75.2
Murray St	719	553	76.9	Towson St	503	377	75.0
Wake Forest	622	475	76.4	Oklahoma	755	564	74.7
Samford	622	472	75.9	Morehead St	572	427	74.7
Iowa St	610	806	75.7	Connecticut	746	556	74.5
				NC-Charlotte	626	466	74.4

3-POINT FIELD GOALS MADE PER GAME

	GP	FG	Avg		GP	FG	Avg
Troy St	27	287	10.6	Southern-BR	26	361	9.3
Samford	27	279	10.3	St Louis	31	284	9.2
Vermont	27	268	9.9	VMI	27	247	9.1
Baylor	28	265	9.5	Stephen F. Austin	28	248	8.9
Marshall	27	253	9.4	Pennsylvania	28	247	8.8
Arkansas	39	361	9.3				

3-POINT FIELD GOAL PERCENTAGE

	GP	FGA	FG	Pct		GP	FGA	FG	Pct
Southern Utah	28	571	244	42.7	Michigan St	28	387	158	40.8
Evansville	27	424	181	42.7	Pennsylvania	28	387	158	40.8
WI-Green Bay	30	451	188	41.7	Gonzaga	30	573	232	40.5
Arizona	31	593	245	41.3	Southern Illinois	32	645	257	39.8
N Carolina	34	648	266	41.0	Ohio St	28	404	160	39.6
					Valparaiso	28	528	209	39.6
					Samford	27	705	279	39.6

Note: Minimum 3.0 made per game.

NCAA Women's Championship Game Box Score

Connecticut 70

Connecticut	Min	FG M-A	FT M-A	Reb O-T	A	PF	TP
Elliot	39	5-7	3-4	2-7	3	3	13
Lobo	28	5-10	7-8	2-8	2	4	17
Wolters	31	4-9	2-4	1-3	0	4	10
Rizzotti	32	6-8	2-2	0-3	3	3	15
Webber	17	0-1	0-0	1-1	2	1	0
Sales	33	4-12	1-4	2-6	3	3	10
Berube	20	1-6	3-5	2-3	2	0	5
Totals	200	25-53	18-27	10-31	15	18	70

Percentages: FG—.472, FT—.667. 3-pt goals: 2-10, .200 (Lobo 0-2, Rizzotti 1-2, Webber 0-1, Sales 1-4, Berube 0-1). Team rebounds: 12. Blocked shots: 4 (Lobo 2, Wolters 2). Turnovers: 16 (Elliot 5, Rizzotti 4, Berube 3, Lobo 2, Sales, Wolters). Steals: 7 (Rizzotti 3, Sales 3, Elliot).

Tennessee 64

Tennessee	Min	FG M-A	FT M-A	Reb O-T	A	PF	TP
McCray	31	3-12	1-2	3-5	4	2	7
Thompson	10	1-1	2-2	3-3	1	2	4
D. Johnson	33	3-11	3-3	3-10	0	2	9
Marciniak	30	3-11	1-3	0-0	5	3	8
Davis	31	5-12	0-1	3-5	1	4	11
Ward	16	2-5	2-2	1-2	1	3	6
T. Johnson	21	3-7	1-1	2-5	1	3	7
M. Johnson	13	2-3	0-0	0-3	1	2	5
Milligan	10	1-3	2-2	0-0	2	0	4
Conklin	5	1-1	0-0	1-1	0	1	3
Totals	200	24-66	12-16	16-34	16	22	64

Percentages: FG—.364, FT—.750. 3-pt goals: 4-14, .286 (McCray 0-1, Marciniak 1-6, Davis 1-4, M. Johnson 1-2, Conklin 1-1). Team rebounds: 3. Blocked shots: 1 (T. Johnson). Turnovers: 14 (Marciniak 3, McCray 3, Conklin 2, T. Johnson 2, D. Johnson, Davis, Milligan, Thompson). Steals: 6 (D. Johnson 2, Marciniak 2, Davis, McCray).

Halftime: Tennessee 38, Connecticut 32.
A: 18,038. Officials: Kantner, Shepherd.

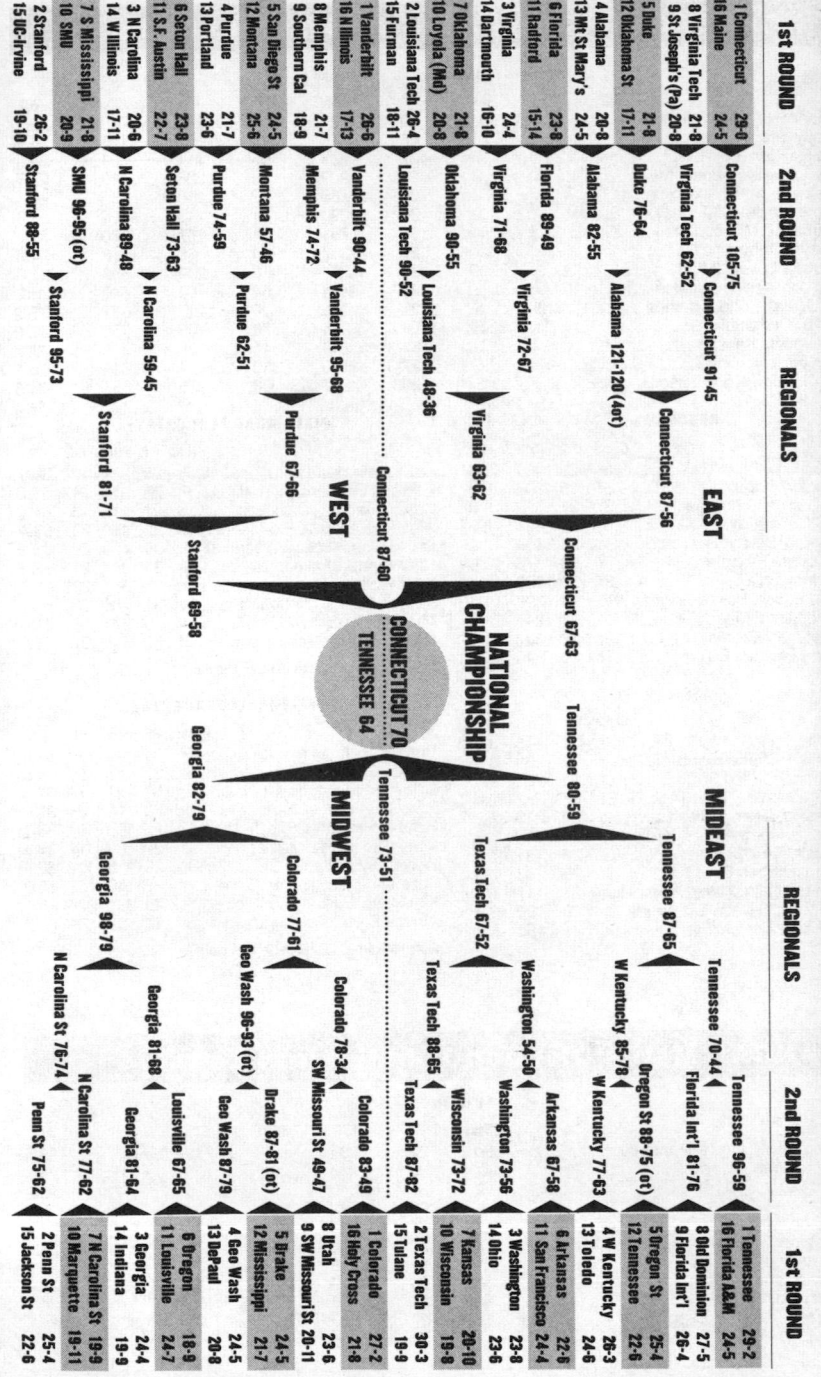

1995 NCAA Basketball Women's Division I Tournament

EAST

1st ROUND	2nd ROUND	REGIONALS
1 Connecticut 29-0	Connecticut 105-75	Connecticut 91-45
16 Maine 24-5		
8 Virginia Tech 21-8	Virginia Tech 62-52	
9 St.Joseph's (Pa) 20-8		
5 Duke 21-8	Duke 76-64	Alabama 121-120 (4ot)
12 Oklahoma St. 17-11		
4 Alabama 20-8	Alabama 82-55	
13 Mt St Mary's 24-5		
3 Virginia 24-4	Virginia 71-68	Virginia 72-67
14 Dartmouth 16-10		
6 Florida 23-8	Florida 89-49	
11 Radford 15-14		
7 Oklahoma 21-8	Oklahoma 90-55	Virginia 63-62
10 Loyola (Md) 20-8		
2 Louisiana Tech 26-4	Louisiana Tech 96-52	Louisiana Tech 48-36
15 Furman 18-11		

Connecticut 87-56

WEST

1st ROUND	2nd ROUND	REGIONALS
1 Vanderbilt 25-6	Vanderbilt 90-44	Vanderbilt 95-68
16 Illinois 17-13		
8 Memphis 21-7	Memphis 74-72	
9 Southern Cal 18-9		
5 San Diego St 24-5	Montana 57-46	Purdue 67-66
12 Montana 25-6		
4 Purdue 21-7	Purdue 74-59	
13 Portland 23-6		
6 Seton Hall 23-8	Seton Hall 73-63	N Carolina 59-45
11 S.F. Austin 22-7		
3 N Carolina 20-6	N Carolina 89-48	
14 W Illinois 17-11		
7 S Mississippi 21-8	SMU 96-95 (ot)	Stanford 81-71
10 SMU 20-9		
2 Stanford 26-2	Stanford 88-55	Stanford 95-73
15 UC-Irvine 19-10		

Stanford 69-58

Connecticut 87-60

NATIONAL CHAMPIONSHIP

CONNECTICUT 70
TENNESSEE 64

Connecticut 67-63

Tennessee 73-51

MIDEAST

1st ROUND	2nd ROUND	REGIONALS
1 Tennessee 29-2	Tennessee 96-59	Tennessee 70-44
16 Florida A&M 24-5		
8 Old Dominion 27-5	Florida Int'l 81-76	
9 Florida Int'l 26-4		
5 Oregon St 25-4	Oregon St 88-75 (ot)	W Kentucky 95-78
12 Tennessee 22-6		
4 W Kentucky 26-3	W Kentucky 77-63	
13 Toledo 24-6		
6 Arkansas 22-6	Arkansas 67-58	Washington 54-50
11 San Francisco 24-4		
3 Washington 23-8	Washington 73-56	
14 Ohio 23-6		
7 Kansas 20-10	Wisconsin 73-72	Texas Tech 88-65
10 Wisconsin 19-8		
2 Texas Tech 30-3	Texas Tech 87-82	Texas Tech 67-52
15 Tulane 19-9		

Tennessee 87-65

Tennessee 80-59

MIDWEST

1st ROUND	2nd ROUND	REGIONALS
1 Colorado 27-2	Colorado 78-34	Colorado 77-61
16 Holy Cross 21-8		
8 Utah 23-6	SW Missouri St 49-47	
9 SW Missouri St 20-11		
5 Drake 24-5	Drake 87-81 (ot)	Geo Wash 96-93 (ot)
12 Mississippi 21-7		
4 Geo Wash 24-5	Geo Wash 87-79	
13 DePaul 20-8		
6 Oregon 18-9	Louisville 67-65	Georgia 81-68
11 Louisville 24-7		
3 Georgia 24-4	Georgia 81-64	
14 Indiana 19-9		
7 N Carolina St 19-9	N Carolina St 77-62	N Carolina St 76-74
10 Marquette 19-11		
2 Penn St 25-4	Penn St 75-62	Georgia 98-79
15 Jackson St 22-6		

Colorado 83-49

Georgia 82-79

NCAA Women's Division I Individual Leaders

SCORING

	Class	GP	TFG	3FG	FT	Pts	Avg
Koko Lahanas, Cal St-Fullerton	Jr	29	329	0	120	778	26.8
Latasha Byears, DePaul	Jr	28	316	11	97	740	26.4
Cornelia Gayden, LSU	Sr	27	239	105	114	697	25.8
Kim Mays, Eastern Kentucky	Sr	28	229	35	226	719	25.7
Anita Maxwell, New Mexico St	Jr	29	288	2	160	738	25.4
DeShawne Blocker, E Tennessee St	Sr	30	290	1	149	730	24.3
Gray Harris, SE Missouri St	Jr	26	231	1	167	630	24.2
Korie Hlede, Duquesne	Fr	26	257	34	80	628	24.2
Patty Stoffey, Loyola (MD)	Sr	29	244	0	209	697	24.0
Shannon Johnson, S Carolina	Jr	27	214	64	154	646	23.9
Melissa Gower, Long Beach St	Sr	27	235	0	167	637	23.6
Sha Hopson, Grambling	Sr	28	238	73	106	655	23.4
Angela Aycock, Kansas	Sr	31	240	41	195	716	23.1
Amy Burnett, Wyoming	Sr	27	195	30	194	614	22.7
Carolyn Aldridge, Tennessee St	Sr	29	217	98	125	657	22.7

REBOUNDS

	Class	GP	Reb	Avg
Tera Sheriff, Jackson St	Sr	29	401	13.8
Rene Doctor, Coppin St	Sr	25	344	13.8
Melissa Gower, Long Beach St	Sr	27	352	13.0
Oberon Pitterson, W Illinois	Sr	28	354	12.6
Dana Wynne, Seton Hall	So	33	415	12.6
Joskeen Garner, Northwestern St	Jr	30	376	12.6
Niamh Darcy, VCU	Sr	30	363	12.1
Scherrie Jackson, Beth.-Cookman	So	25	298	11.9
Stephanie Minor, Murray St	So	21	245	11.7
Carrie Coffman, Bradley	Sr	26	302	11.6
DeShawne Blocker, E Tenn St	Sr	30	345	11.5

ASSISTS

	Class	GP	A	Avg
Andrea Nagy, Florida Int'l	Sr	32	315	9.8
Dayna Smith, Rhode Island	Jr	27	239	8.9
Tina Nicholson, Penn St	Jr	31	250	8.1
Tabitha Truesdale, Texas Tech	Sr	37	281	7.6
Tiffany Martin, Georgia Tech	So	30	220	7.3
Lori Goerlitz, Marquette	Jr	31	222	7.2
Dani Maziur, New Orleans	Jr	27	191	7.1
Boky Vidic, Oregon St	Jr	29	203	7.0
Gretchen Hollifield, Wake Forest	Jr	21	147	7.0
Gwynn Hobbs, Nevada-Las Vegas	Sr	26	180	6.9
Heather Fiore, Canisius	So	27	185	6.9

FIELD GOAL PERCENTAGE

	Class	GP	FGA	FG	Pct
Alisha Hill, Howard	Fr	28	281	194	69.0
LeFreda Deckard, N Texas	Fr	27	217	147	67.7
Kristen Ferrucci, Davidson	Jr	27	216	139	64.4
Albena Branzova, Florida Int'l	Sr	32	459	291	63.4
DeShawne Blocker, E Tenn St	Sr	30	459	290	63.2
Kristi Kinne, Drake	Sr	31	344	217	63.1
Kara Wolters, Connecticut	So	33	354	222	62.7
Katryna Gaither, Notre Dame	So	31	406	252	62.1
Myndee Larsen, S Utah	Jr	26	271	167	61.6
Dana Johnson, Tennessee	Sr	37	349	215	61.6

Note: Minimum 5 made per game.

FREE-THROW PERCENTAGE

	Class	GP	FTA	FT	Pct
Christy Smith, Arkansas	Fr	30	149	134	89.9
Shelley Sheetz, Colorado	Sr	33	115	103	89.6
Julie Krommenhoek, Utah	Fr	30	89	78	87.6
Lisa Gerton, NC-Charlotte	Jr	20	96	84	87.5
Heather Prater, Middle Tenn St	Jr	28	105	91	86.7
Kerry Giroux, Rhode Island	Jr	27	89	77	86.5
Sally Crowe, Oregon	So	26	118	102	86.4
Suzanne Ressa, Santa Clara	Jr	28	146	126	86.3
Kim Mays, Eastern Kentucky	Sr	28	264	226	85.6
Albena Branzova, Florida Int'l	Sr	32	95	81	85.3

Note: Minimum 2.5 made per game.

NCAA Men's Division II Individual Leaders

SCORING

	Class	GP	TFG	3FG	FT	Pts	Avg
Carlos Knox, IU/PU-Indianapolis	So	29	284	39	218	825	28.4
Eric Bovaird, West Liberty St	Sr	26	215	92	193	715	27.5
Dennis Edwards, Fort Hayes St	Sr	30	340	0	126	806	26.9
Tyrone Mason, Edinboro	Jr	26	242	83	124	691	26.6
Brett Beeson, Moorhead St	Jr	27	246	34	189	715	26.5
Tyrone Latimer, Central Missouri St	Sr	32	300	55	177	832	26.0
Shawn Hadley, W Georgia	Sr	19	158	64	98	478	25.2
Hassan Robinson, Springfield	Sr	26	239	67	105	650	25.0
Joel McDonald, St Cloud St	Sr	27	195	100	180	670	24.8
Jason Kaiser, AK-Anchorage	Sr	27	259	59	91	668	24.7

NCAA Men's Division II Individual Leaders *(Cont.)*

REBOUNDS

	Class	GP	Reb	Avg
Lorenzo Poole, Albany St (GA)	Sr	26	417	16.0
Garth Joseph, St Rose	Fr	31	396	12.8
Rob Layton, Emporia St	Jr	25	300	12.0
Kevin Lee, Shippensburg	So	26	307	11.8
Larry Steimer, Molloy	Fr	24	278	11.6
Joe Banks, NM Highlands	Sr	27	309	11.4
Jonathan Maddox, Tuskegee	Sr	27	299	11.1
Dalon Bynum, AK-Fairbanks	Jr	27	296	11.0
J.D. Asselta, Bentley	Jr	27	296	11.0
Steve Ryan, Northwood	Sr	26	284	10.9

ASSISTS

	Class	GP	A	Avg
Ernest Jenkins, NM Highlands	Sr	27	291	10.8
Brent Schremp, Slippery Rock	Sr	25	259	10.4
Rob Paternostro, New Hamp Coll	Sr	33	309	9.4
Craig Lottie, Alabama A&M	Jr	32	287	9.0
Marcus Talbert, CO Christian	Sr	27	230	8.5
Cal Butler, Morris Brown	Jr	26	216	8.3
Jordan Canfield, Washburn	Jr	30	242	8.1
Candice Pickens, California (PA)	Jr	29	228	7.9
Trent McHenry, Tuskegee	Jr	27	209	7.7
Deon Moyd, AK-Fairbanks	Sr	27	208	7.7
Willis Cheaney, Kentucky Wesleyan	Sr	29	214	7.4

FIELD GOAL PERCENTAGE

	Class	GP	FGA	FG	Pct
John Pruett, SIU-Edwardsville	Fr	26	193	138	71.5
Chris Morris, Alderson-Broaddus	Jr	28	326	231	70.9
Garth Joseph, St Rose	Fr	31	271	184	67.9
Al Lindsey, Henderson St	Jr	23	198	133	67.2
DeWayne Ansley, Queens (NC)	Jr	26	228	153	67.1
DeRon Rutledge, TX A&M-King	Jr	28	377	252	66.8
Anthony Russell, W Florida	Fr	28	226	150	66.4
Yogi Leo, Queens (NC)	Jr	27	217	144	66.4
Jason Burkholder, Oakland	Jr	29	266	176	66.2
Dennis Edwards, Fort Hays St	Sr	30	514	340	66.1

Note: Minimum 5 made per game.

FREE-THROW PERCENTAGE

	Class	GP	FTA	FT	Pct
Jim Borodawka, Mass-Lowell	So	27	80	74	92.5
Marcus Albert, MO-St Louis	Sr	27	93	101	92.1
Travis Tuttle, North Dakota	So	28	99	108	91.7
Mike Lake, Hillsdale	Sr	29	143	129	90.2
Lance Luitjens, Northern St	Jr	33	172	155	90.1
Jake Biddle, Francis Marion	Fr	26	97	87	89.7
Thaddeus Breckenridge, Concord	Jr	31	199	178	89.4
Michael Shue, Lock Haven	So	26	136	121	89.0
Mike Ellzy, Bloomsburg	So	27	118	104	88.1
Jason Holmes, SIU-Edwardsville	So	26	132	116	87.9

Note: Minimum 2.5 made per game.

NCAA Women's Division II Individual Leaders

SCORING

	Class	GP	TFG	3FG	FT	Pts	Avg
Shander Gary, Lynn	Sr	20	235	0	149	619	31.0
Nicole Collins, Angelo St	Sr	25	231	80	98	640	25.6
Jennifer Clarkson, Abilene Christian	Jr	28	255	2	182	694	24.8
Rachel Matakas, Central Missouri St	Jr	27	264	12	124	664	24.6
LeAnn Freeland, Southern Indiana	So	27	265	2	126	658	24.4
Attala Young, Erskine	Sr	27	236	1	163	636	23.6
Debra Williams, Lincoln (MO)	Jr	26	249	0	104	602	23.2
Michelle Doonan, Stonehill	Sr	33	265	68	160	758	23.0
Libby Corry, Wofford	Sr	24	205	20	119	549	22.9
Marqueetta Randolph, Virginia Union	So	26	240	2	105	587	22.6

REBOUNDS

	Class	GP	Reb	Avg
Robin Scott, Lees-McRae	Sr	19	309	16.3
Kisha Conway, Francis Marion	Jr	26	366	14.1
Rachel Matakas, Central Missouri St	Jr	27	374	13.9
Sharon Yarbrough, W Georgia	Sr	27	367	13.6
Carrolyn Burke, Queens (NY)	Jr	23	312	13.6
Krista Barnett, St Rose	Fr	31	412	13.3
Monique Pierce, St Augustine's	So	28	356	12.7
Christine DeSaine, West Va Tech	Sr	24	301	12.5
Christine Hollins, Fayetteville St	Jr	29	359	12.4
Marchelle Bonner, Henderson St	Jr	26	321	12.3

ASSISTS

	Class	GP	A	Avg
Lorraine Lynch, District of Columbia	Jr	26	246	9.5
Cynthia Thomas, Wingate	Sr	31	289	9.3
Joanna Bernabei, West Liberty St	So	30	278	9.3
Carla Bronson, Mankato St	Jr	27	248	9.2
Ursula Jackson, Alderson-Broaddus	Jr	22	195	8.9
Lisa Rice, Norfolk St	Sr	30	264	8.8
Stephanie Hall, Charleston (WV)	Jr	26	226	8.7
Hayley Lystlund, Augusta	Jr	28	229	8.2
Barbara Hester, Columbus	Jr	28	228	8.1
Theresa Perry, Delta St	Sr	30	234	7.8

NCAA Women's Division II Individual Leaders (Cont.)

FIELD GOAL PERCENTAGE

	Class	GP	FGA	FG	Pct
Tarra Blackwell, Fla Southern ...Fr		32	361	239	66.2
Angela Watson, Central Arkansas ..Jr		26	297	195	65.7
Jennifer Clarson,					
Abilene Christian ....Jr		28	392	255	65.1
Danielle Box, SW Baptist.............Jr		25	220	142	64.5
Kim Davis, Mississippi College...Fr		27	308	197	64.0
LeAnn Freeland, S Indiana........So		27	420	265	63.1
Elizabeth Davies, Bryant ....Jr		27	301	186	61.8
Kim Trudel, Stonehill ....So		33	223	361	61.8
Paulita Murrell, W Texas A&M...Jr		30	269	166	61.7
Krista Kandere, St Rose............Fr		31	342	207	60.5

Two tied with 60.1.

Note: Minimum 5 made per game.

FREE-THROW PERCENTAGE

	Class	GP	FTA	FT	Pct
Darlene Hildebrand,					
Philadelphia Textile..................Sr		31	230	210	91.3
Janelle Needham, Kutztown ....So		20	58	51	87.9
Melissa Graham, Indianapolis ..Sr		28	132	115	87.1
Elizabeth Davies, Bryant ....Jr		27	204	172	84.3
Julie Plahn, MN-Morris ....So		28	127	107	84.3
Julie Jensen, Northern St..........Sr		28	151	127	84.1
Trina Pinner, Texas Woman's....Fr		21	75	63	84.0
Melissa Swain, E Stroudsburg ..Jr		30	91	76	83.5
Kathleen Shippee, St Anselm ...Sr		31	115	96	83.5
Heather Lopes, Bryant ....Jr		27	94	78	83.0

Note: Minimum 2.5 made per game.

NCAA Men's Division III Individual Leaders

SCORING

	Class	GP	TFG	3FG	FT	Pts	Avg
Steve Diekman, Grinnell..............................Sr		20	223	137	162	745	37.3
David Otte, Simpson ....Sr		26	284	0	229	797	30.7
Ed Brands, Grinnell ....Jr		20	196	129	88	609	30.5
Lance Castle, Monmouth (IL)......................Sr		23	230	71	127	658	28.6
Rick Hughes, Thomas More.........................Jr		24	257	1	143	658	27.4
Billy Collins, Nichols..................................Sr		21	189	87	104	569	27.1
Phil Dixon, Shenandoah ....Jr		25	230	90	127	677	27.1
Kyle Jefferson, Salisbury St........................Sr		25	231	20	194	676	27.0
Will Flowers, Aurora ....Sr		25	228	43	166	665	26.6
Alex Marsh, Gwynedd-Mercy......................Sr		24	255	13	104	627	26.1

REBOUNDS

	Class	GP	Reb	Avg
Scott Suhr, Milwaukee Engr...........Sr		25	349	14.0
Sean McGee, Baruch.....................So		23	318	13.8
Kevin Braaten, Baldwin-Wallace....So		28	373	13.3
Antoine Harden, Eastern ....Jr		23	298	13.0
Andrew South, New Jersey Tech....Sr		27	335	12.4
Jason Hayes, Marietta ....So		24	295	12.3
Mark Harris, Coast Guard ....Jr		27	326	12.1
Joe Mrozienski, Hamilton ....Jr		27	320	11.9
Eric Fisher, Delaware Valley ....Sr		25	293	11.7
Larry Jones, Lehman ....So		27	302	11.2

ASSISTS

	Class	GP	A	Avg
Joe Marcotte, New Jersey Tech .....Sr		30	292	9.7
Phil Dixon, Shenandoah ....Jr		25	226	9.0
Andre Bolton, Christopher Newport ..Jr		28	243	8.7
David Genovese, Mt St Vincent......Sr		27	234	8.7
Troy McKelvin, Trinity (CT).............Jr		29	226	7.8
Greg Small, Gwynedd-Mercy ....Sr		24	186	7.8
Adam Dzierzynski, Chapman ....So		25	188	7.5
Kevin Alexander, Emory & Henry....Jr		26	192	7.4
Sammy Briggs, Catholic ....So		26	189	7.3
Chad Hutson, Illinois Wesleyan ......Sr		28	198	7.1

FIELD GOAL PERCENTAGE

	Class	GP	FGA	FG	Pct
Justin Wilkins, Neb Wesleyan ....Sr		28	237	163	68.8
David Otte, Simpson.................Sr		26	416	284	68.3
Alida Ellerbee, New Jersey Tech..So		30	280	185	66.1
Dan Rush, Bridgewater (VA).....Sr		25	379	250	66.0
Jamie Yount, Bluffton ....Sr		26	298	195	65.4
Brad Keenan, Concordia-M'head.Sr		25	225	146	64.9
Brent Nerat, WI-Oshkosh ....Jr		23	217	138	63.6
Scott Launiger, Gust. Adolphus ..Jr		24	314	199	63.4
Neal Richards, Mount Union ....So		26	242	153	63.2
Rick Hughes, Thomas More......Jr		24	407	257	63.1

Note: Minimum 5 made per game.

FREE-THROW PERCENTAGE

	Class	GP	FTA	FT	Pct
Matt Freesemann, Wartburg .....Sr		24	138	128	92.8
Ryan Billet, Elizabethtown ....So		24	79	71	89.9
Mike Guth, Franklin ....Sr		24	116	104	89.7
Jordan Barnhorst, Macalester.....Fr		22	65	58	89.2
Travis Crozier, Elizabethtown ...Sr		24	74	66	89.2
Darin Pint, Coe.........................Sr		23	109	97	89.0
Kurt Axe, Randolph-Macon.......Jr		24	99	88	88.9
Bernie Rogers, Ursinus ....Jr		24	99	88	88.9
Mark Specht, Neb Wesleyan.....Jr		27	128	113	88.3
Matt George, Colby-Sawyer.......Fr		28	140	123	87.9

Note: Minimum 2.5 made per game.

NCAA Women's Division III Individual Leaders

SCORING

	Class	GP	TFG	3FG	FT	Pts	Avg
Emilie Hanson, Central (IA)	Sr	25	277	11	128	693	27.7
Leslee Rogers, La Verne	Jr	25	224	88	98	634	25.4
Peggie Sweeney, Pine Manor	Jr	25	203	20	208	634	25.4
Rita Hurtgen, WI-River Falls	So	26	225	0	199	649	25.0
Katie Smith, Geneseo St	Sr	29	294	11	110	709	24.4
Denise Murray, Gwynedd-Mercy	Jr	23	199	0	144	542	23.6
Ellen Cosgrove, Ursinus	Sr	26	229	57	87	602	23.2
Danielle Potter, Rockford	Sr	25	203	28	140	574	23.0
Rebecca Morris, Wentworth Inst	So	20	148	10	153	459	23.0
Jennifer Nish, Scranton	So	26	238	3	117	596	22.9

REBOUNDS

	Class	GP	Reb	Avg
Sybil Smith, Baruch	Sr	22	523	*23.8
Jennifer White, Neumann	Jr	24	421	17.5
Denise Murray, Gwynedd-Mercy	Jr	23	354	15.4
Leslie Ferguson, Redlands	Sr	25	362	14.5
Glossary Smith, Ferrum	So	27	374	13.9
Carolyn McGuire, Manchester	Sr	24	328	13.7
Sue Burtoft, Bridgewater (MA)	Sr	23	313	13.6
Allison Palmer, Wesleyan (CT)	Sr	23	310	13.5
Koren Miller, Haverford	Sr	24	321	13.4
Erin Preseau, Utica	Jr	21	276	13.1

ASSISTS

	Class	GP	A	Avg
Chris Webb, NC Wesleyan	Jr	26	204	7.8
Stephanie Teter, Mary Washington	Jr	24	180	7.5
Shelly Anderson, Oglethorpe	Sr	23	168	7.3
Megan Dillon, Cabrini	So	26	184	7.1
Cathy Finney, Marymount (VA)	Sr	28	194	6.9
Ivette Correa, Salem St	Jr	32	219	6.8
Colleen Mewes, Carthage	So	25	171	6.8
Kim Wilson, York (NY)	Sr	19	119	6.3
Emili McCluer, Defiance	So	27	169	6.3
Stephanie Rom, Binghamton	Fr	27	168	6.2

*Division III record.

FIELD GOAL PERCENTAGE

	Class	GP	FGA	FG	Pct
Kari Tufte, Luther	Jr	26	320	210	65.6
Tina Kampa, St Benedict	Sr	29	254	165	65.0
Steph Sprenger, Lakeland	Jr	25	233	145	62.2
Rita Hurtgen, WI-River Falls	So	26	362	225	62.2
Natalie DeMichei, WI-Oshkosh	Sr	31	293	181	61.8
Lanett Stephan, Franklin	Jr	26	272	164	60.3
Arlene Meinholz, WI-Eau Claire	Sr	29	370	221	59.7
Alisa Haase, Lawrence	Jr	21	203	120	59.1
Mindy Bagatelos, Claremont-M-S	So	27	248	146	58.9
Jody Prete, Upper Iowa	Sr	24	220	129	58.6

Note: Minimum 5 made per game.

FREE-THROW PERCENTAGE

	Class	GP	FTA	FT	Pct
Kari Tufte, Luther	Jr	26	127	112	88.2
Jasmine Obhrai, Bowdoin	Fr	25	86	75	87.2
Tina Sharp, Eureka	Jr	24	91	79	86.8
Felicia Lofton, Millsaps	Sr	26	98	85	86.7
Angie Sapp, Illinois College	So	24	87	75	86.2
Sarah Bay, Wellesley	Jr	23	99	84	84.8
Stephanie Duncan, Methodist	Sr	23	77	65	84.4
Shelly Brown, Trenton St	Jr	24	120	101	84.2
Cindy Pearson, Bridgewater (VA)	Jr	25	93	78	83.9
Kim Coia, W New England	Sr	25	85	71	83.5

Note: Minimum 2.5 made per game.

One-Armed Guard

During an AAU game in Washington, D.C. last summer, 18-year-old Doug Dormu knocked down five straight three-pointers against a bunch of guys two years his senior. As Doug peeled back on defense following his fifth trey, he could hear the opposing coach melting down: That boy has one arm. What's wrong with you guys?

That was one of the few times in recent years that Doug, a senior guard at Washington's Theodore Roosevelt High, has been conscious of his handicap on the court. Born with nerve damage in his left shoulder that kept his left arm from fully developing, he still has feeling in his left hand. So when as an eight-year-old he first taught himself to play basketball, he cradled the ball between his left elbow and right hand and shot from that position.

At the end of last week Doug was averaging 17 points in D.C.'s rarefied public league.

Earlier this season he scored 40 points against Eastern High. Doug, who also played fullback on the Roosevelt football team this season, believes he can do anything any other guard can do—and some things others can't, like dunk. "When Doug first came here, of course, I had some reservations about what his limitations might be," says Roosevelt coach Maurice Butler. "But we have a lot of guys on this team that can't use their left hand. And they have two hands."

Though he'll likely enroll at a junior college next fall, Doug's dream is to play at a Division I school. "I like to surprise people," he says. "Most people know me now, but there was a time I'd warm up before a game and be messing around, dribbling the ball off my feet, throwing up bricks, and guys were dying to take me. Pretty soon the same guys were saying, 'Let's stay away from the guy with the arm. He's got game!'"

NCAA Division I Men's Championship Results

NCAA Final Four Results

Year	Winner	Score	Runner-up	Third Place	Fourth Place	Winning Coach
1939	Oregon	46-33	Ohio St	*Oklahoma	*Villanova	Howard Hobson
1940	Indiana	60-42	Kansas	*Duquesne	*Southern Cal	Branch McCracken
1941	Wisconsin	39-34	Washington St	*Pittsburgh	*Arkansas	Harold Foster
1942	Stanford	53-38	Dartmouth	*Colorado	*Kentucky	Everett Dean
1943	Wyoming	46-34	Georgetown	*Texas	*DePaul	Everett Shelton
1944	Utah	42-40 (OT)	Dartmouth	*Iowa St	*Ohio St	Vadal Peterson
1945	Oklahoma St	49-45	NYU	*Arkansas	*Ohio St	Hank Iba
1946	Oklahoma St	43-40	N Carolina	Ohio St	California	Hank Iba
1947	Holy Cross	58-47	Oklahoma	Texas	CCNY	Alvin Julian
1948	Kentucky	58-42	Baylor	Holy Cross	Kansas St	Adolph Rupp
1949	Kentucky	46-36	Oklahoma St	Illinois	Oregon St	Adolph Rupp
1950	CCNY	71-68	Bradley	N Carolina St	Baylor	Nat Holman
1951	Kentucky	68-58	Kansas St	Illinois	Oklahoma St	Adolph Rupp
1952	Kansas	80-63	St John's (NY)	Illinois	Santa Clara	Forrest Allen
1953	Indiana	69-68	Kansas	Washington	Louisiana St	Branch McCracken
1954	La Salle	92-76	Bradley	Penn St	Southern Cal	Kenneth Loeffler
1955	San Francisco	77-63	La Salle	Colorado	Iowa	Phil Woolpert
1956	San Francisco	83-71	Iowa	Temple	Southern Meth	Phil Woolpert
1957	N Carolina	54-53†	Kansas	San Francisco	Michigan St	Frank McGuire
1958	Kentucky	84-72	Seattle	Temple	Kansas St	Adolph Rupp
1959	California	71-70	W Virginia	Cincinnati	Louisville	Pete Newell
1960	Ohio St	75-55	California	Cincinnati	NYU	Fred Taylor
1961	Cincinnati	70-65 (OT)	Ohio St	Vacated‡	Utah	Edwin Jucker
1962	Cincinnati	71-59	Ohio St	Wake Forest	UCLA	Edwin Jucker
1963	Loyola (IL)	60-58 (OT)	Cincinnati	Duke	Oregon St	George Ireland
1964	UCLA	98-83	Duke	Michigan	Kansas St	John Wooden
1965	UCLA	91-80	Michigan	Princeton	Wichita St	John Wooden
1966	UTEP	72-65	Kentucky	Duke	Utah	Don Haskins
1967	UCLA	79-64	Dayton	Houston	N Carolina	John Wooden
1968	UCLA	78-55	N Carolina	Ohio St	Houston	John Wooden
1969	UCLA	92-72	Purdue	Drake	N Carolina	John Wooden
1970	UCLA	80-69	Jacksonville	New Mexico St	St Bonaventure	John Wooden
1971	UCLA	68-62	Vacated‡	Vacated‡	Kansas	John Wooden
1972	UCLA	81-76	Florida St	N Carolina	Louisville	John Wooden
1973	UCLA	87-66	Memphis St	Indiana	Providence	John Wooden
1974	N Carolina St	76-64	Marquette	UCLA	Kansas	Norm Sloan
1975	UCLA	92-85	Kentucky	Louisville	Syracuse	John Wooden
1976	Indiana	86-68	Michigan	UCLA	Rutgers	Bob Knight
1977	Marquette	67-59	N Carolina	NV-Las Vegas	NC-Charlotte	Al McGuire
1978	Kentucky	94-88	Duke	Arkansas	Notre Dame	Joe Hall
1979	Michigan St	75-64	Indiana St	DePaul	Penn	Jud Heathcote
1980	Louisville	59-54	Vacated‡	Purdue	Iowa	Denny Crum
1981	Indiana	63-50	N Carolina	Virginia	Louisiana St	Bob Knight
1982	N Carolina	63-62	Georgetown	*Houston	*Louisville	Dean Smith
1983	N Carolina St	54-52	Houston	*Georgia	*Louisville	Jim Valvano
1984	Georgetown	84-75	Houston	*Kentucky	*Virginia	John Thompson
1985	Villanova	66-64	Georgetown	*St John's (NY)	Vacated‡	Rollie Massimino
1986	Louisville	72-69	Duke	*Kansas	*Louisiana St	Denny Crum
1987	Indiana	74-73	Syracuse	*NV-Las Vegas	*Providence	Bob Knight
1988	Kansas	83-79	Oklahoma	*Arizona	*Duke	Larry Brown
1989	Michigan	80-79 (OT)	Seton Hall	*Duke	*Illinois	Steve Fisher
1990	UNLV	103-73	Duke	*Arkansas	*Georgia Tech	Jerry Tarkanian
1991	Duke	72-65	Kansas	*UNLV	*N Carolina	Mike Krzyzewski
1992	Duke	71-51	Michigan	*Cincinnati	*Indiana	Mike Krzyzewski
1993	N Carolina	77-71	Michigan	*Kansas	*Kentucky	Dean Smith
1994	Arkansas	76-72	Duke	*Arizona	*Florida	Nolan Richardson
1995	UCLA	89-78	Arkansas	*N Carolina	*Oklahoma St	Jim Harrick

*Tied for third place.

†Three overtimes.

‡Student-athletes representing St Joseph's (PA) in 1961, Villanova in 1971 (runner-up), Western Kentucky in 1971 (third), UCLA (1980) and Memphis State (1985) were declared ineligible subsequent to the tournament. Under NCAA rules, the teams' and ineligible student-athletes' records were deleted, and the teams' places in the standings were vacated.

NCAA Final Four MVPs

Year	Winner, School	GP	Field Goals FGM	Pct	3-Pt FG FGA	FGM	Free Throws FTM	Pct	Reb	A	Stl	BS	Avg
1939	....None selected												
1940	....Marv Huffman, Indiana	2	7	—	—	—	4	—	—	—	—	—	9.0
1941	....John Kotz, Wisconsin	2	8	—	—	—	6	—	—	—	—	—	11.0
1942	....Howard Dallmar, Stanford	2	8	—	—	—	4	66.7	—	—	—	—	10.0
1943	....Ken Sailors, Wyoming	2	10	—	—	—	8	72.7	—	—	—	—	14.0
1944	....Arnie Ferrin, Utah	2	11	—	—	—	6	—	—	—	—	—	14.0
1945	....Bob Kurland, Oklahoma St	2	16	—	—	—	5	—	—	—	—	—	18.5
1946	....Bob Kurland, Oklahoma St	2	21	—	—	—	10	66.7	—	—	—	—	26.0
1947	....George Kaftan, Holy Cross	2	18	—	—	—	12	70.6	—	—	—	—	24.0
1948	....Alex Groza, Kentucky	2	16	—	—	—	5	—	—	—	—	—	18.5
1949	....Alex Groza, Kentucky	2	19	—	—	—	14	—	—	—	—	—	26.0
1950	....Irwin Dambrot, CCNY	2	12	42.9	—	—	4	50.0	—	—	—	—	14.0
1951	....None selected												
1952	....Clyde Lovellette, Kansas	2	24	—	—	—	18	—	—	—	—	—	33.0
1953	....*B.H. Horn, Kansas	2	17	—	—	—	17	—	—	—	—	—	25.5
1954	....Tom Gola, La Salle	2	12	—	—	—	14	—	—	—	—	—	19.0
1955	....Bill Russell, San Francisco	2	19	—	—	—	9	—	—	—	—	—	23.5
1956	....*Hal Lear, Temple	2	32	—	—	—	16	—	—	—	—	—	40.0
1957	....*Wilt Chamberlain, Kansas	2	18	51.4	—	—	19	70.4	25	—	—	—	32.5
1958	....*Elgin Baylor, Seattle	2	18	34.0	—	—	12	75.0	41	—	—	—	24.0
1959	....*Jerry West, West Virginia	2	22	66.7	—	—	22	68.8	25	—	—	—	33.0
1960	....Jerry Lucas, Ohio State	2	16	66.7	—	—	3	100.0	23	—	—	—	17.5
1961	....*Jerry Lucas, Ohio State	2	20	71.4	—	—	16	94.1	25	—	—	—	28.0
1962	....Paul Hogue, Cincinnati	2	23	63.9	—	—	12	63.2	38	—	—	—	29.0
1963	....Art Heyman, Duke	2	18	41.0	—	—	15	68.2	19	—	—	—	25.5
1964	....Walt Hazzard, UCLA	2	11	55.0	—	—	8	66.7	10	—	—	—	15.0
1965	....*Bill Bradley, Princeton	2	34	63.0	—	—	19	95.0	24	—	—	—	43.5
1966	....*Jerry Chambers, Utah	2	25	53.2	—	—	20	83.3	35	—	—	—	35.0
1967	....Lew Alcindor, UCLA	2	14	60.9	—	—	11	45.8	38	—	—	—	19.5
1968	....Lew Alcindor, UCLA	2	22	62.9	—	—	9	90.0	34	—	—	—	26.5
1969	....Lew Alcindor, UCLA	2	23	67.7	—	—	16	64.0	41	—	—	—	31.0
1970	....Sidney Wicks, UCLA	2	15	71.4	—	—	9	60.0	34	—	—	—	19.5
1971	....*Howard Porter, Villanova	2	20	48.8	—	—	7	77.8	24	—	—	—	23.5
1972	....Bill Walton, UCLA	2	20	69.0	—	—	17	73.9	41	—	—	—	28.5
1973	....Bill Walton, UCLA	2	28	82.4	—	—	2	40.0	30	—	—	—	29.0
1974	....David Thompson, NC State	2	19	51.4	—	—	11	78.6	17	—	—	—	24.5
1975	....Richard Washington, UCLA	2	23	54.8	—	—	8	72.7	20	—	—	—	27.0
1976	....Kent Benson, Indiana	2	17	50.0	—	—	7	63.6	18	—	—	—	20.5
1977	....Butch Lee, Marquette	2	11	34.4	—	—	8	100.0	6	2	1	1	15.0
1978	....Jack Givens, Kentucky	2	28	65.1	—	—	8	66.7	17	4	1	3	32.0
1979	....Earvin Johnson, Michigan St	2	17	68.0	—	—	19	86.4	17	3	0	2	26.5
1980	....Darrell Griffith, Louisville	2	23	62.2	—	—	11	68.8	7	15	0	2	28.5
1981	....Isiah Thomas, Indiana	2	14	56.0	—	—	9	81.8	4	9	3	4	18.5
1982	....James Worthy, N Carolina	2	20	74.1	—	—	2	28.6	8	9	0	4	21.0
1983	....*Akeem Olajuwon, Houston	2	16	55.2	—	—	9	64.3	40	3	2	5	20.5
1984	....Patrick Ewing, Georgetown	2	8	57.1	—	—	2	100.0	18	1	15	1	9.0
1985	....Ed Pinckney, Villanova	2	8	57.1	—	—	12	75.0	15	6	3	0	14.0
1986	....Pervis Ellison, Louisville	2	15	60.0	—	—	6	75.0	24	2	3	1	18.0
1987	....Keith Smart, Indiana	2	14	63.6	1	0	7	77.8	7	7	0	2	17.5
1988	...Danny Manning, Kansas	2	25	55.6	1	0	6	66.7	17	4	8	9	28.0
1989	....Glenn Rice, Michigan	2	24	49.0	16	7	4	100.0	16	1	0	3	29.5
1990	....Anderson Hunt, UNLV	2	19	61.3	16	9	2	50.0	4	9	1	1	24.5
1991	....Christian Laettner, Duke	2	12	54.5	1	1	21	91.3	17	2	1	2	23.0
1992	....Bobby Hurley, Duke	2	10	41.7	12	7	8	80.0	3	11	0	3	17.5
1993	....Donald Williams, N Carolina	2	15	65.2	14	10	10	100.0	4	2	2	0	25.0
1994	....Corliss Williamson, Arkansas	2	21	50.0	0	0	10	71.4	21	8	4	3	26.0
1995	....Ed O'Bannon, UCLA	2	16	45.7	8	3	10	76.9	25	3	7	1	22.5

*Not a member of the championship-winning team.

NCAA Division I Men's Championship Results (Cont.)

Best NCAA Tournament Single-Game Scoring Performances

Player and Team	Year	Round	FG	3FG	FT	TP
Austin Carr, Notre Dame vs Ohio	1970	1st	25	—	11	61
Bill Bradley, Princeton vs Wichita St.	1965	C*	22	—	14	58
Oscar Robertson, Cincinnati vs Arkansas	1958	C	21	—	14	56
Austin Carr, Notre Dame vs Kentucky	1970	2nd	22	—	8	52
Austin Carr, Notre Dame vs Texas Christian	1971	1st	20	—	12	52
David Robinson, Navy vs Michigan	1987	1st	22	0	6	50
Elvin Hayes, Houston vs Loyola (IL)	1968	1st	20	—	9	49
Hal Lear, Temple vs Southern Meth	1956	C*	17	—	14	48
Austin Carr, Notre Dame vs Houston	1971	C	17	—	13	47
Dave Corzine, DePaul vs Louisville	1978	2nd	18	—	10	46
Bob Houbregs, Washington vs Seattle	1953	2nd	20	—	5	45
Austin Carr, Notre Dame vs Iowa	1970	C	21	—	3	45
Bo Kimble, Loyola Marymount vs New Mexico St	1990	1st	17	5	6	45

C regional third place; C* third-place game.

NIT Championship Results

Year	Winner	Score	Runner-up	Year	Winner	Score	Runner-up
1938	Temple	60-36	Colorado	1967	Southern Illinois	71-56	Marquette
1939	Long Island U	44-32	Loyola (IL)	1968	Dayton	61-48	Kansas
1940	Colorado	51-40	Duquesne	1969	Temple	89-76	Boston College
1941	Long Island U	56-42	Ohio U	1970	Marquette	65-53	St John's (NY)
1942	W Virginia	47-45	W Kentucky	1971	N Carolina	84-66	Georgia Tech
1943	St John's (NY)	48-27	Toledo	1972	Maryland	100-69	Niagara
1944	St John's (NY)	47-39	DePaul	1973	Virginia Tech	92-91 (OT)	Notre Dame
1945	DePaul	71-54	Bowling Green	1974	Purdue	97-81	Utah
1946	Kentucky	46-45	Rhode Island	1975	Princeton	80-69	Providence
1947	Utah	49-45	Kentucky	1976	Kentucky	71-67	NC-Charlotte
1948	St Louis	65-52	NYU	1977	St Bonaventure	94-91	Houston
1949	San Francisco	48-47	Loyola (IL)	1978	Texas	101-93	N Carolina St
1950	CCNY	69-61	Bradley	1979	Indiana	53-52	Purdue
1951	BYU	62-43	Dayton	1980	Virginia	58-55	Minnesota
1952	La Salle	75-64	Dayton	1981	Tulsa	86-84 (OT)	Syracuse
1953	Seton Hall	58-46	St John's (NY)	1982	Bradley	67-58	Purdue
1954	Holy Cross	71-62	Duquesne	1983	Fresno St	69-60	DePaul
1955	Duquesne	70-58	Dayton	1984	Michigan	83-63	Notre Dame
1956	Louisville	93-80	Dayton	1985	UCLA	65-62	Indiana
1957	Bradley	84-83	Memphis St	1986	Ohio St	73-63	Wyoming
1958	Xavier (OH)	78-74 (OT)	Dayton	1987	Southern Miss	84-80	La Salle
1959	St John's (NY)	76-71 (OT)	Bradley	1988	Connecticut	72-67	Ohio St
1960	Bradley	88-72	Providence	1989	St John's (NY)	73-65	St Louis
1961	Providence	62-59	St Louis	1990	Vanderbilt	74-72	St Louis
1962	Dayton	73-67	St John's (NY)	1991	Stanford	78-72	Oklahoma
1963	Providence	81-66	Canisius	1992	Virginia	81-76	Notre Dame
1964	Bradley	86-54	New Mexico	1993	Minnesota	62-61	Georgetown
1965	St John's (NY)	55-51	Villanova	1994	Villanova	80-73	Vanderbilt
1966	BYU	97-84	NYU	1995	Virginia Tech	65-64 (OT)	Marquette

NCAA Division I Men's Season Leaders

Scoring Average

Year	Player and Team	Ht	Class	GP	FG	3FG	FT	Pts	Avg
1948	Murray Wier, Iowa	5-9	Sr	19	152	—	95	399	21.0
1949	Tony Lavelli, Yale	6-3	Sr	30	228	—	215	671	22.4
1950	Paul Arizin, Villanova	6-3	Sr	29	260	—	215	735	25.3
1951	Bill Mlkvy, Temple	6-4	Sr	25	303	—	125	731	29.2
1952	Clyde Lovellette, Kansas	6-9	Sr	28	315	—	165	795	28.4
1953	Frank Selvy, Furman	6-3	Jr	25	272	—	194	738	29.5
1954	Frank Selvy, Furman	6-3	Sr	29	427	—	355	1209	41.7
1955	Darrell Floyd, Furman	6-1	Jr	25	344	—	209	897	35.9
1956	Darrell Floyd, Furman	6-1	Sr	28	339	—	268	946	33.8
1957	Grady Wallace, S Carolina	6-4	Sr	29	336	—	234	906	31.2
1958	Oscar Robertson, Cincinnati	6-5	So	28	352	—	280	984	35.1

Scoring Average (Cont.)

Year	Player and Team	Ht	Class	GP	FG	3FG	FT	Pts	Avg
1959	Oscar Robertson, Cincinnati	6-5	Jr	30	331	—	316	978	32.6
1960	Oscar Robertson, Cincinnati	6-5	Sr	30	369	—	273	1011	33.7
1961	Frank Burgess, Gonzaga	6-1	Sr	26	304	—	234	842	32.4
1962	Billy McGill, Utah	6-9	Sr	26	394	—	221	1009	38.8
1963	Nick Werkman, Seton Hall	6-3	Jr	22	221	—	208	650	29.5
1964	Howard Komives, Bowling Green	6-1	Sr	23	292	—	260	844	36.7
1965	Rick Barry, Miama (FL)	6-7	Sr	26	340	—	293	973	37.4
1966	Dave Schellhase, Purdue	6-4	Sr	24	284	—	213	781	32.5
1967	Jim Walker, Providence	6-3	Sr	28	323	—	205	851	30.4
1968	Pete Maravich, Louisiana St	6-5	So	26	432	—	274	1138	43.8
1969	Pete Maravich, Louisiana St	6-5	Jr	26	433	—	282	1148	44.2
1970	Pete Maravich, Louisiana St	6-5	Sr	31	522	—	337	1381	44.5
1971	Johnny Neumann, Mississippi	6-6	So	23	366	—	191	923	40.1
1972	Dwight Lamar, Southwestern Louisiana	6-1	Jr	29	429	—	196	1054	36.3
1973	William Averitt, Pepperdine	6-1	Sr	25	352	—	144	848	33.9
1974	Larry Fogle, Canisius	6-5	So	25	326	—	183	835	33.4
1975	Bob McCurdy, Richmond	6-7	Sr	26	321	—	213	855	32.9
1976	Marshall Rodgers, TX-Pan American	6-2	Sr	25	361	—	197	919	36.8
1977	Freeman Williams, Portland St	6-4	Jr	26	417	—	176	1010	38.8
1978	Freeman Williams, Portland St	6-4	Sr	27	410	—	149	969	35.9
1979	Lawrence Butler, Idaho St	6-3	Sr	27	310	—	192	812	30.1
1980	Tony Murphy, Southern-BR	6-3	Sr	29	377	—	178	932	32.1
1981	Zam Fredrick, S Carolina	6-2	Sr	27	300	—	181	781	28.9
1982	Harry Kelly, Texas Southern	6-7	Jr	29	336	—	190	862	29.7
1983	Harry Kelly, Texas Southern	6-7	Sr	29	333	—	169	835	28.8
1984	Joe Jakubick, Akron	6-5	Sr	27	304	—	206	814	30.1
1985	Xavier McDaniel, Wichita St	6-8	Sr	31	351	—	142	844	27.2
1986	Terrance Bailey, Wagner	6-2	Jr	29	321	—	212	854	29.4
1987	Kevin Houston, Army	5-11	Sr	29	311	63	268	953	32.9
1988	Hersey Hawkins, Bradley	6-3	Sr	31	377	87	284	1125	36.3
1989	Hank Gathers, Loyola Marymount	6-7	Jr	31	419	0	177	1015	32.7
1990	Bo Kimble, Loyola Marymount	6-5	Sr	32	404	92	231	1131	35.3
1991	Kevin Bradshaw, U.S. Int'l	6-6	Sr	28	358	60	278	1054	37.6
1992	Brett Roberts, Morehead St	6-8	Sr	29	278	66	193	815	28.1
1993	Greg Guy, TX-Pan American	6-1	Jr	19	189	67	111	556	29.3
1994	Glenn Robinson, Purdue	6-8	Jr	34	368	79	215	1030	30.3
1995	Kurt Thomas, Texas Christian	6-9	Sr	27	288	3	202	781	28.9

Rebounds

Year	Player and Team	Ht	Class	GP	Reb	Avg
1951	Ernie Beck, Pennsylvania	6-4	So	27	556	20.6
1952	Bill Hannon, Army	6-3	So	17	355	20.9
1953	Ed Conlin, Fordham	6-5	So	26	612	23.5
1954	Art Quimby, Connecticut	6-5	Jr	26	588	22.6
1955	Charlie Slack, Marshall	6-5	Jr	21	538	25.6
1956	Joe Holup, George Washington	6-6	Sr	26	604	†.256
1957	Elgin Baylor, Seattle	6-6	Jr	25	508	†.235
1958	Alex Ellis, Niagara	6-5	Sr	25	536	†.262
1959	Leroy Wright, Pacific	6-8	Jr	26	652	†.238
1960	Leroy Wright, Pacific	6-8	Sr	17	380	†.234
1961	Jerry Lucas, Ohio St	6-8	Jr	27	470	†.198
1962	Jerry Lucas, Ohio St	6-8	Sr	28	499	†.211
1963	Paul Silas, Creighton	6-7	Sr	27	557	20.6
1964	Bob Pelkington, Xavier (OH)	6-7	Sr	26	567	21.8
1965	Toby Kimball, Connecticut	6-8	Sr	23	483	21.0
1966	Jim Ware, Oklahoma City	6-8	Sr	29	607	20.9
1967	Dick Cunningham, Murray St	6-10	Jr	22	479	21.8
1968	Neal Walk, Florida	6-10	Jr	25	494	19.8
1969	Spencer Haywood, Detroit	6-8	So	22	472	21.5
1970	Artis Gilmore, Jacksonville	7-2	Jr	28	621	22.2
1971	Artis Gilmore, Jacksonville	7-2	Sr	26	603	23.2
1972	Kermit Washington, American	6-8	Jr	23	455	19.8
1973	Kermit Washington, American	6-8	Sr	22	439	20.0
1974	Marvin Barnes, Providence	6-9	Sr	32	597	18.7
1975	John Irving, Hofstra	6-9	So	21	323	15.4

Rebounds (Cont.)

Year	Player and Team	Ht	Class	GP	Reb	Avg
1976	Sam Pellom, Buffalo	6-8	So	26	420	16.2
1977	Glenn Mosley, Seton Hall	6-8	Sr	29	473	16.3
1978	Ken Williams, N Texas St	6-7	Sr	28	411	14.7
1979	Monti Davis, Tennessee St	6-7	Jr	26	421	16.2
1980	Larry Smith, Alcorn St	6-8	Sr	26	392	15.1
1981	Darryl Watson, Miss Valley	6-7	Sr	27	379	14.0
1982	LaSalle Thompson, Texas	6-10	Jr	27	365	13.5
1983	Xavier McDaniel, Wichita St	6-7	So	28	403	14.4
1984	Akeem Olajuwon, Houston	7-0	Jr	37	500	13.5
1985	Xavier McDaniel, Wichita St	6-8	Sr	31	460	14.8
1986	David Robinson, Navy	6-11	Jr	35	455	13.0
1987	Jerome Lane, Pittsburgh	6-6	So	33	444	13.5
1988	Kenny Miller, Loyola (IL)	6-9	Fr	29	395	13.6
1989	Hank Gathers, Loyola (CA)	6-7	Jr	31	426	13.7
1990	Anthony Bonner, St Louis	6-8	Sr	33	456	13.8
1991	Shaquille O'Neal, Louisiana St	7-1	So	28	411	14.7
1992	Popeye Jones, Murray St	6-8	Sr	30	431	14.4
1993	Warren Kidd, Middle Tenn St	6-9	Sr	26	386	14.8
1994	Jerome Lambert, Baylor	6-8	Jr	24	355	14.8
1995	Kurt Thomas, Texas Christian	6-9	Sr	27	393	14.6

†From 1956-1962, title was based on highest individual recoveries out of total by both teams in all games.

Assists

Year	Player and Team	Class	GP	A	Avg
1984	Craig Lathen, IL-Chicago	Jr	29	274	9.45
1985	Rob Weingard, Hofstra	Sr	24	228	9.50
1986	Mark Jackson, St John's (NY)	Jr	36	328	9.11
1987	Avery Johnson, Southern-BR	Jr	31	333	10.74
1988	Avery Johnson, Southern-BR	Sr	30	399	13.30
1989	Glenn Williams, Holy Cross	Sr	28	278	9.93
1990	Todd Lehmann, Drexel	Sr	28	260	9.29
1991	Chris Corchiani, N Carolina St	Sr	31	299	9.65
1992	Van Usher, Tennessee Tech	Sr	29	254	8.76
1993	Sam Crawford, New Mex St	Sr	34	310	9.12
1994	Jason Kidd, California	So	30	272	9.06
1995	Nelson Haggerty, Baylor	Sr	28	284	10.1

Blocked Shots

Year	Player and Team	Class	GP	BS	Avg
1986	David Robinson, Navy	Jr	35	207	5.91
1987	David Robinson, Navy	Sr	32	144	4.50
1988	Rodney Blake, St Joseph's (PA)	Sr	29	116	4.00
1989	Alonzo Mourning, Georgetown	Fr	34	169	4.97
1990	Kenny Green, Rhode Island	Sr	26	124	4.77
1991	Shawn Bradley, Brigham Young	Fr	34	177	5.21
1992	Shaquille O'Neal, Louisiana St	Jr	30	157	5.23
1993	Theo Ratliff, Wyoming	Jr	28	124	4.43
1994	Grady Livingston, Howard	Jr	26	115	4.42
1995	Keith Closs, Central Conn St	Fr	26	139	5.35

Steals

Year	Player and Team	Class	GP	S	Avg
1986	Darron Brittman, Chicago St	Sr	28	139	4.96
1987	Tony Fairley, Charleston Sou	Sr	28	114	4.07
1988	Aldwin Ware, Florida A&M	Sr	29	142	4.90
1989	Kenny Robertson, Cleveland St	Jr	28	111	3.96
1990	Ronn McMahon, E Washington	Sr	29	130	4.48
1991	Van Usher, Tennessee Tech	Jr	28	104	3.71
1992	Victor Snipes, NE Illinois	So	25	86	3.44
1993	Jason Kidd, California	Fr	29	110	3.80
1994	Shawn Griggs, SW Louisiana	Sr	30	120	4.00
1995	Roderick Anderson, Texas	Sr	30	101	3.37

Single-Game Records

SCORING HIGHS VS DIVISION I OPPONENT

Pts	Player and Team vs Opponent	Date
72	Kevin Bradshaw, U.S. Int'l vs Loyola Marymount	1-5-91
69	Pete Maravich, Louisiana St vs Alabama	2-7-70
68	Calvin Murphy, Niagara vs Syracuse	12-7-68
66	Jay Handlan, Washington & Lee vs Furman	2-17-51
66	Pete Maravich, Louisiana St vs Tulane	2-10-69
66	Anthony Roberts, Oral Roberts vs N Carolina A&T	2-19-77
65	Anthony Roberts, Oral Roberts vs Oregon	3-9-77
65	Scott Haffner, Evansville vs Dayton	2-18-89
64	Pete Maravich, Louisiana St vs Kentucky	2-21-70
63	Johnny Neumann, Mississippi vs Louisiana St	1-30-71
63	Hersey Hawkins, Bradley vs Detroit	2-22-88

SCORING HIGHS VS NON-DIVISION I OPPONENT

Pts	Player and Team vs Opponent	Date
100	Frank Selvy, Furman vs Newberry	2-13-54
85	Paul Arizin, Villanova vs Philadelphia NAMC	2-12-49
81	Freeman Williams, Portland St vs Rocky Mountain	2-3-78
73	Bill Mlkvy, Temple vs Wilkes	3-3-51
71	Freeman Williams, Portland St vs Southern Oregon	2-9-77

REBOUNDING HIGHS BEFORE 1973

Reb	Player and Team vs Opponent	Date
51	Bill Chambers, William & Mary vs Virginia	2-14-53
43	Charlie Slack, Marshall vs Morris Harvey	1-12-54
42	Tom Heinsohn, Holy Cross vs Boston College	3-1-55
40	Art Quimby, Connecticut vs Boston U	1-11-55
39	Maurice Stokes, St Francis (PA) vs John Carroll	1-28-55
39	Dave DeBusschere, Detroit vs Central Michigan	1-30-60
39	Keith Swagerty, Pacific vs UC-Santa Barbara	3-5-65

REBOUNDING HIGHS SINCE 1973

Reb	Player and Team vs Opponent	Date
34	David Vaughn, Oral Roberts vs Brandeis	1-8-73
33	Robert Parish, Centenary vs Southern Miss	1-22-73
32	Jervaughn Scales, Southern-BR vs Grambling	2-7-94
32	Durand Macklin, Louisiana St vs Tulane	11-26-76
31	Jim Bradley, Northern Illinois vs WI-Milwaukee	2-19-73
31	Calvin Natt, Northeast Louisiana vs Georgia Southern	12-29-76

ASSISTS

A	Player and Team vs Opponent	Date
22	Tony Fairley, Baptist vs Armstrong St	2-9-87
22	Avery Johnson, Southern-BR vs Texas Southern	1-25-88
22	Sherman Douglas, Syracuse vs Providence	1-28-89
21	Mark Wade, NV-Las Vegas vs Navy	12-29-86
21	Kelvin Scarborough, New Mexico vs Hawaii	2-13-87
21	Anthony Manuel, Bradley vs UC-Irvine	12-19-87
21	Avery Johnson, Southern-BR vs Alabama St	1-16-88

STEALS

S	Player and Team vs Opponent	Date
13	Mookie Blaylock, Oklahoma vs Centenary	12-12-87
13	Mookie Blaylock, Oklahoma vs Loyola Marymount	12-17-88
12	Kenny Robertson, Cleveland St vs Wagner	12-3-88
12	Terry Evans, Oklahoma vs Florida A&M	1-27-93
11	Darron Brittman, Chicago St vs McKendree	2-24-86
11	Darron Brittman, Chicago St vs St Xavier	2-8-86
11	Marty Johnson, Towson St vs Bucknell	2-17-88
11	Aldwin Ware, Florida A&M vs Tuskegee	2-24-88
11	Mark Macon, Temple vs Notre Dame	1-29-89
11	Carl Thomas, E Michigan vs Chicago St	2-20-91
11	Ron Arnold, St Francis (NY) vs Mt St Mary's (MD)	2-4-93
11	Tyus Edney, UCLA vs George Mason	12-22-94

Single-Game Records (Cont.)
BLOCKED SHOTS

BS	Player and Team vs Opponent	Date
14	David Robinson, Navy vs NC-Wilmington	1-4-86
14	Shawn Bradley, Brigham Young vs E Kentucky	12-7-90
13	Kevin Roberson, Vermont vs New Hampshire	1-9-92
13	Jim McIlvaine, Marquette vs Northeastern (IL)	12-9-92
13	Keith Closs, Central Conn St vs St. Francis (PA)	12-21-94
12	David Robinson, Navy vs James Madison	1-9-86
12	Derrick Lewis, Maryland vs James Madison	1-28-87
12	Rodney Blake, St Joseph's (PA) vs Cleveland St	12-2-87
12	Walter Palmer, Dartmouth vs Harvard	1-9-88
12	Alan Ogg, AL-Birmingham vs Florida A&M	12-16-88
12	Dikembe Mutombo, Georgetown vs St John's (NY)	1-23-89
12	Shaquille O'Neal, Louisiana St vs Loyola Marymount	2-3-90
12	Cedric Lewis, Maryland vs S Florida	1-19-91
12	Ervin Johnson, New Orleans vs Texas A&M	12-29-92
12	Kurt Thomas, Texas Christian vs Texas A&M	2-25-95

Season Records
POINTS

Player and Team	Year	GP	FG	3FG	FT	Pts
Pete Maravich, Louisiana St	1970	31	522	—	337	1381
Elvin Hayes, Houston	1968	33	519	—	176	1214
Frank Selvy, Furman	1954	29	427	—	355	1209
Pete Maravich, Louisiana St	1969	26	433	—	282	1148
Pete Maravich, Louisiana St	1968	26	432	—	274	1138
Bo Kimble, Loyola Marymount	1990	32	404	92	231	1131
Hersey Hawkins, Bradley	1988	31	377	87	284	1125
Austin Carr, Notre Dame	1970	29	444	—	218	1106
Austin Carr, Notre Dame	1971	29	430	—	241	1101
Otis Birdsong, Houston	1977	36	452	—	186	1090

SCORING AVERAGE

Player and Team	Year	GP	FG	FT	Pts	Avg
Pete Maravich, Louisiana St	1970	31	522	337	1381	44.5
Pete Maravich, Louisiana St	1969	26	433	282	1148	44.2
Pete Maravich, Louisiana St	1968	26	432	274	1138	43.8
Frank Selvy, Furman	1954	29	427	355	1209	41.7
Johnny Neumann, Mississippi	1971	23	366	191	923	40.1
Freeman Williams, Portland St	1977	26	417	176	1010	38.8
Billy McGill, Utah	1962	26	394	221	1009	38.8
Calvin Murphy, Niagara	1968	24	337	242	916	38.2
Austin Carr, Notre Dame	1970	29	444	218	1106	38.1
Austin Carr, Notre Dame	1971	29	430	241	1101	38.0
Kevin Bradshaw, U.S. Int'l	1991	28	358	278	1054	37.6

REBOUNDS

Player and Team	Year	GP	Reb	Player and Team	Year	GP	Reb
Walt Dukes, Seton Hall	1953	33	734	Artis Gilmore, Jacksonville	1970	28	621
Leroy Wright, Pacific	1959	26	652	Tom Gola, La Salle	1955	31	618
Tom Gola, La Salle	1954	30	652	Ed Conlin, Fordham	1953	26	612
Charlie Tyra, Louisville	1956	29	645	Art Quimby, Connecticut	1955	25	611
Paul Silas, Creighton	1964	29	631	Bill Russell, San Francisco	1956	29	609
Elvin Hayes, Houston	1968	33	624	Jim Ware, Oklahoma City	1966	29	607

REBOUND AVERAGE BEFORE 1973

Player and Team	Year	GP	Reb	Avg
Charlie Slack, Marshall	1955	21	538	25.6
Leroy Wright, Pacific	1959	26	652	25.1
Art Quimby, Connecticut	1955	25	611	24.4
Charlie Slack, Marshall	1956	22	520	23.6
Ed Conlin, Fordham	1953	26	612	23.5

Season Records *(Cont.)*

REBOUND AVERAGE SINCE 1973

Player and Team	Year	GP	Reb	Avg
Kermit Washington, American	1973	22	439	20.0
Marvin Barnes, Providence	1973	30	571	19.0
Marvin Barnes, Providence	1974	32	597	18.7
Pete Padgett, NV-Reno	1973	26	462	17.8
Jim Bradley, Northern Illinois	1973	24	426	17.8

ASSISTS

Player and Team	Year	GP	A	Player and Team	Year	GP	A
Mark Wade, UNLV	1987	38	406	Sherman Douglas, Syracuse	1989	38	326
Avery Johnson, Southern-BR	1988	30	399	Sam Crawford, N Mex St	1993	34	310
Anthony Manuel, Bradley	1988	31	373	Greg Anthony, UNLV	1991	35	310
Avery Johnson, Southern-BR	1987	31	333	Reid Gettys, Houston	1984	37	309
Mark Jackson, St John's (NY)	1986	32	328	Carl Golston, Loyola (IL)	1985	33	305

ASSIST AVERAGE

Player and Team	Year	GP	A	Avg	Player and Team	Year	GP	A	Avg
Avery Johnson, Southern-BR	1988	30	399	13.3	Chris Corchiani, N Carolina St	1991	31	299	9.6
Anthony Manuel, Bradley	1988	31	373	12.0	Tony Fairley, Baptist	1987	28	270	9.6
Avery Johnson, Southern-BR	1987	31	333	10.7	Tyrone Bogues, Wake Forest	1987	29	276	9.5
Mark Wade, NV-Las Vegas	1987	38	406	10.7	Craig Neal, Georgia Tech	1988	32	303	9.5
Nelson Haggerty, Baylor	1995	28	284	10.1	Ron Weingard, Hofstra	1985	24	228	9.5
Glenn Williams, Holy Cross	1989	28	278	9.9					

FIELD-GOAL PERCENTAGE

Player and Team	Year	GP	FG	FGA	Pct
Steve Johnson, Oregon St	1981	28	235	315	74.6
Dwayne Davis, Florida	1989	33	179	248	72.2
Keith Walker, Utica	1985	27	154	216	71.3
Steve Johnson, Oregon St	1980	30	211	297	71.0
Oliver Miller, Arkansas	1991	38	254	361	70.4
Alan Williams, Princeton	1987	25	163	232	70.3
Mark McNamara, California	1982	27	231	329	70.2
Warren Kidd, Middle Tennessee St	1991	30	173	247	70.0
Pete Freeman, Akron	1991	28	175	250	70.0
Joe Senser, West Chester	1977	25	130	186	69.9
Lee Campbell, SW Missouri St	1990	29	192	275	69.8
Stephen Scheffler, Purdue	1990	30	173	248	69.8

Based on qualifiers for annual championship.

FREE-THROW PERCENTAGE

Player and Team	Year	GP	FT	FTA	Pct
Craig Collins, Penn St	1985	27	94	98	95.9
Rod Foster, UCLA	1982	27	95	100	95.0
Danny Basile, Marist	1994	27	84	89	94.4
Carlos Gibson, Marshall	1978	28	84	89	94.4
Jim Barton, Dartmouth	1986	26	65	69	94.2
Jack Moore, Nebraska	1982	27	123	131	93.9
Dandrea Evans, Troy St	1994	27	72	77	93.5
Rob Robbins, New Mexico	1990	34	101	108	93.5
Tommy Boyer, Arkansas	1962	23	125	134	93.3
Damon Goodwin, Dayton	1986	30	95	102	93.1
Brian Magid, George Washington	1980	26	79	85	92.9
Mike Joseph, Bucknell	1990	29	144	155	92.9

Based on qualifiers for annual championship.

Season Records *(Cont.)*

THREE-POINT FIELD-GOAL PERCENTAGE

Player and Team	Year	GP	3FG	3FGA	Pct
Glenn Tropf, Holy Cross	1988	29	52	82	63.4
Sean Wightman, Western Michigan	1992	30	48	76	63.2
Keith Jennings, E Tennessee St	1991	33	84	142	59.2
Dave Calloway, Monmouth (NJ)	1989	28	48	82	58.5
Steve Kerr, Arizona	1988	38	114	199	57.3
Reginald Jones, Prairie View	1987	28	64	112	57.1
Joel Tribelhorn, Colorado St	1989	33	76	135	56.3
Mike Joseph, Bucknell	1988	28	65	116	56.0
Brian Jackson, Evansville	1995	27	53	95	55.8
Christian Laettner, Duke	1992	35	54	97	55.7
Reginald Jones, Prairie View	1988	27	85	155	54.8

Based on qualifiers for annual championship.

STEALS

Player and Team	Year	GP	S
Mookie Blaylock, Oklahoma	1988	39	150
Aldwin Ware, Florida A&M	1988	29	142
Darron Brittman, Chicago St	1986	28	139
Nadav Henefeld, Connecticut	1990	37	138
Mookie Blaylock, Oklahoma	1989	35	131

BLOCKED SHOTS

Player and Team	Year	GP	BS
David Robinson, Navy	1986	35	207
Shawn Bradley, BYU	1991	34	177
Alonzo Mourning, Georgetown	1989	34	169
Alonzo Mourning, Georgetown	1992	32	160
Shaquille O'Neal, Louisiana St	1992	30	157

STEAL AVERAGE

Player and Team	Year	GP	S	Avg
Darron Brittman, Chicago St	1986	28	139	4.96
Aldwin Ware, Florida A&M	1988	29	142	4.90
Ronn McMahon, E Washington	1990	29	130	4.48
Jim Paguaga, St Francis (NY)	1986	28	120	4.29
Marty Johnson, Towson St	1988	30	124	4.13

BLOCKED SHOT AVERAGE

Player and Team	Year	GP	BS	Avg
David Robinson, Navy	1986	35	207	5.91
Keith Closs, Central Conn St	1995	26	139	5.34
Shaquille O'Neal, Louisiana St	1992	30	157	5.23
Shawn Bradley, BYU	1991	34	177	5.21
Theo Ratliff, Wyoming	1995	28	144	5.14

Career Records

POINTS

Player and Team	Ht	Final Year	GP	FG	3FG*	FT	Pts
Pete Maravich, Louisiana St	6-5	1970	83	1387	—	893	3667
Freeman Williams, Portland St	6-4	1978	106	1369	—	511	3249
Lionel Simmons, La Salle	6-7	1990	131	1244	56	673	3217
Alphonso Ford, Mississippi Valley	6-2	1993	109	1121	333	590	3165
Harry Kelly, Texas Southern	6-7	1983	110	1234	—	598	3066
Hersey Hawkins, Bradley	6-3	1988	125	1100	118	690	3008
Oscar Robertson, Cincinnati	6-5	1960	88	1052	—	869	2973
Danny Manning, Kansas	6-10	1988	147	1216	10	509	2951
Alfredrick Hughes, Loyola (IL)	6-5	1985	120	1226	—	462	2914
Elvin Hayes, Houston	6-8	1968	93	1215	—	454	2884
Larry Bird, Indiana St	6-9	1979	94	1154	—	542	2850
Otis Birdsong, Houston	6-4	1977	116	1176	—	480	2832
Kevin Bradshaw, Bethune-Cookman, U.S. Int'l	6-6	1991	111	1027	132	618	2804
Allan Houston, Tennessee	6-6	1993	128	902	346	651	2801
Hank Gathers, Southern Cal, Loyola Marymount	6-7	1990	117	1127	0	469	2723
Reggie Lewis, Northeastern	6-7	1987	122	1043	30 (1)	592	2708
Daren Queenan, Lehigh	6-5	1988	118	1024	29	626	2703
Byron Larkin, Xavier (OH)	6-3	1988	121	1022	51	601	2696
David Robinson, Navy	7-1	1987	127	1032	1	604	2669
Wayman Tisdale, Oklahoma	6-9	1985	104	1077	—	507	2661

*Listed is the number of three-pointers scored since it became the national rule in 1987; the number in the parentheses is number scored prior to 1987—these counted as three points in the game but counted as two-pointers in the national rankings. The three-pointers in the parentheses are not included in total points.

Career Records *(Cont.)*

SCORING AVERAGE

Player and Team	Final Year	GP	FG	FT	Pts	Avg
Pete Maravich, Louisiana St	1968	83	1387	893	3667	44.2
Austin Carr, Notre Dame	1971	74	1017	526	2560	34.6
Oscar Robertson, Cincinnati	1960	88	1052	869	2973	33.8
Calvin Murphy, Niagara	1970	77	947	654	2548	33.1
Dwight Lamar, Southwestern Louisiana	1973	57	768	326	1862	32.7
Frank Selvy, Furman	1954	78	922	694	2538	32.5
Rick Mount, Purdue	1970	72	910	503	2323	32.3
Darrell Floyd, Furman	1956	71	868	545	2281	32.1
Nick Werkman, Seton Hall	1964	71	812	649	2273	32.0
Willie Humes, Idaho St	1971	48	565	380	1510	31.5
William Averitt, Pepperdine	1973	49	615	311	1541	31.4
Elgin Baylor, Coll of Idaho, Seattle	1958	80	956	588	2500	31.3
Elvin Hayes, Houston	1968	93	1215	454	2884	31.0
Freeman Williams, Portland St	1978	106	1369	511	3249	30.7
Larry Bird, Indiana St	1979	94	1154	542	2850	30.3

REBOUNDS BEFORE 1973

Player and Team	Final Year	GP	Reb
Tom Gola, La Salle	1955	118	2201
Joe Holup, George Washington	1956	104	2030
Charlie Slack, Marshall	1956	88	1916
Ed Conlin, Fordham	1955	102	1884
Dickie Hemric, Wake Forest	1955	104	1802

REBOUNDS FOR CAREERS BEGINNING IN 1973 OR AFTER*

Player and Team	Final Year	GP	Reb
Derrick Coleman, Syracuse	1990	143	1537
Ralph Sampson, Virginia	1983	132	1511
Pete Padgett, NV-Reno	1976	104	1464
Lionel Simmons, La Salle	1990	131	1429
Anthony Bonner, St Louis	1990	133	1424

ASSISTS

Player and Team	Final Year	GP	A
Bobby Hurley, Duke	1993	140	1076
Chris Corchiani, N Carolina St	1991	124	1038
Keith Jennings, E Tennessee St	1991	127	983
Sherman Douglas, Syracuse	1989	138	960
Tony Miller, Marquette	1995	123	956

FIELD-GOAL PERCENTAGE

Player and Team	Final Year	FG	FGA	Pct
Ricky Nedd, Appalachian St	1994	412	597	69.0
Stephen Scheffler, Purdue	1990	408	596	68.5
Steve Johnson, Oregon St	1981	828	1222	67.8
Murray Brown, Florida St	1980	566	847	66.8
Lee Campbell, SW Missouri St	1990	411	618	66.6

Note: Minimum 400 field goals.

FREE-THROW PERCENTAGE

Player and Team	Final Year	FT	FTA	Pct
Greg Starrick, Kentucky, Southern Illinois	1972	341	375	90.9
Jack Moore, Nebraska	1982	446	495	90.1
Steve Henson, Kansas St	1990	361	401	90.0
Steve Alford, Indiana	1987	535	596	89.8
Bob Lloyd, Rutgers	1967	543	605	89.8

Note: Minimum 300 free throws.
*Freshmen became eligible for varsity play in 1973

Career Records (Cont.)

THREE-POINT FIELD GOALS MADE

Player and Team	Final Year	GP	3FG
Doug Day, Radford	1993	117	401
Ronnie Schmitz, MO-Kansas City	1993	112	378
Mark Alberts, Akron	1993	103	375
Jeff Fryer, Loyola Marymount	1990	112	363
Dennis Scott, Georgia Tech	1990	99	351

THREE-POINT FIELD-GOAL PERCENTAGE

Player and Team	Final Year	3FG	3FGA	Pct
Tony Bennett, WI-Green Bay	1992	290	584	49.7
Keith Jennings, E Tennessee St	1991	223	452	49.3
Kirk Manns, Michigan St	1990	212	446	47.5
Tim Locum, Wisconsin	1991	227	481	47.2
David Olson, Eastern Illinois	1992	262	562	46.6

Note: Minimum 200 3-point field goals.

STEALS

Player and Team	Final Year	GP	S
Eric Murdock, Providence	1991	117	376
Michael Anderson, Drexel	1988	115	341
Kenny Robertson, New Mexico, Clev St	1990	119	341
Keith Jennings, E Tennessee St	1991	127	334
Greg Anthony, Portland, UNLV	1991	138	329

BLOCKED SHOTS

Player and Team	Final Year	GP	BS
Alonzo Mourning, Georgetown	1992	120	453
Theo Ratliff, Wyoming	1995	111	425
Rodney Blake, St Joseph's (PA)	1988	116	419
Shaquille O'Neal, Louisiana St	1992	90	412
Kevin Roberson, Vermont	1992	112	409

NCAA Division I Team Leaders

Division I Team Alltime Wins

Team	First Year	Yrs	W	L	T
N Carolina	1911	85	1626	577	0
Kentucky	1903	92	1615	518	1
Kansas	1899	97	1567	703	0
St John's (NY)	1908	88	1508	666	0
Duke	1906	90	1474	727	0
Temple	1895	99	1435	780	0
Oregon St	1902	94	1430	927	0
Pennsylvania	1902	94	1408	796	0
Syracuse	1901	94	1403	661	0
Notre Dame	1898	90	1389	730	1
Indiana	1901	95	1369	732	0
UCLA	1920	76	1351	588	0
Washington	1896	93	1332	861	0
Western Kentucky	1915	76	1331	621	0
Princeton	1901	95	1313	830	0

Note: Years in Division I only.

Division I Alltime Winning Percentage

Team	First Year	Yrs	W	L	T	Pct
Kentucky	1903	92	1616	518	1	.757
NV-Las Vegas	1959	37	779	268	0	.744
N Carolina	1911	85	1626	577	0	.738
UCLA	1920	76	1351	588	0	.697
St John's (NY)	1908	88	1508	666	0	.694
Kansas	1899	97	1567	703	0	.690
Western Kentucky	1915	76	1331	621	0	.682
Syracuse	1901	94	1403	661	0	.680
Duke	1906	90	1474	727	0	.670
DePaul	1924	72	1166	582	0	.667

Note: Minimum of 20 years in Division I.

NCAA Division I Men's Winning Streaks

Longest—Full Season

Team	Games	Years	Ended by
UCLA	88	1971-74	Notre Dame (71-70)
San Francisco	60	1955-57	Illinois (62-33)
UCLA	47	1966-68	Houston (71-69)
UNLV	45	1990-91	Duke (79-77)
Texas	44	1913-17	Rice (24-18)
Seton Hall	43	1939-41	LIU-Brooklyn (49-26)
LIU-Brooklyn	43	1935-37	Stanford (45-31)
UCLA	41	1968-69	Southern Cal (46-44)
Marquette	39	1970-71	Ohio St (60-59)
Cincinnati	37	1962-63	Wichita St (65-64)
N Carolina	37	1957-58	W Virginia (75-64)

Longest—Home Court

Team	Games	Years
Kentucky	129	1943-55
St Bonaventure	99	1948-61
UCLA	98	1970-76
Cincinnati	86	1957-64
Marquette	81	1967-73
Arizona	81	1945-51
Lamar	80	1978-84
Long Beach St	75	1968-74
NV-Las Vegas	72	1974-78
Arizona	71	1987-92
Cincinnati	68	1972-78

Longest—Regular Season

Team	Games	Years	Ended by
UCLA	76	1971-74	Notre Dame (71-70)
Indiana	57	1975-77	Toledo (59-57)
Marquette	56	1970-72	Detroit (70-49)
Kentucky	54	1952-55	George Tech (59-58)
San Francisco	51	1955-57	Illinois (62-33)
Pennsylvania	48	1970-72	Temple (57-52)
Ohio St	47	1960-62	Wisconsin (86-67)
Texas	44	1913-17	Rice (24-18)
UCLA	43	1966-68	Houston (71-69)
LIU-Brooklyn	43	1935-37	Stanford (45-31)
Seton Hall	42	1939-41	LIU-Brooklyn (49-26)

NCAA Division I Winningest Men's Coaches

Active Coaches

WINS

Coach and Team	W
Dean Smith, N Carolina	830
James Phelan, Mt St Mary's (MD)	737
Don Haskins, UTEP	665
Norm Stewart, Missouri	660
Bob Knight, Indiana	659
Lefty Driesell, James Madison	657
Lou Henson, Illinois	645
Gene Bartow, AL-Birmingham	631
Jerry Tarkanian, Fresno St	625
Denny Crum, Louisville	565

Note: Minimum 5 years as a Division I head coach; includes record at 4-year colleges only.

WINNING PERCENTAGE

Coach and Team	Yrs	W	L	Pct
Jerry Tarkanian, Fresno St	24	625	122	.837
Roy Williams, Kansas	7	184	51	.783
Dean Smith, N Carolina	34	830	236	.779
Nolan Richardson, Arkansas	15	371	119	.757
Jim Boeheim, Syracuse	19	454	150	.752
John Chaney, Temple	23	520	175	.748
Larry Hunter, Ohio	19	414	145	.741
Bob Knight, Indiana	30	659	235	.737
Denny Crum, Louisville	24	565	212	.727
Eddie Sutton, Oklahoma St	25	553	209	.726

Note: Minimum 5 years as a Division I head coach; includes record at 4-year colleges only.

Alltime Winningest Division I Men's Coaches

WINS

Coach (Team)	W
Adolph Rupp (Kentucky)	876
Dean Smith (N Carolina)	830
Hank Iba (NW Missouri St, Colorado, Oklahoma St)	767
Ed Diddle (Western Kentucky)	759
Phog Allen (Baker, Kansas, Haskell, Central Missouri St, Kansas)	746
Ray Meyer (DePaul)	724
Don Haskins (UTEP)	665
John Wooden (Indiana St, UCLA)	664
Norm Stewart (Missouri)	660
Bob Knight (Army, Indiana)	659
Lefty Driesell (Davidson, Maryland, James Madison)	657
Ralph Miller (Wichita St, Iowa, Oregon St)	657
Marv Harshman (Pacific Lutheran, Washington St, Washington)	654
Lou Henson (Hardin-Simmons, New Mexico St, Illinois)	645
Gene Bartow (C MO St, Valparaiso, Memphis St, Illinois, UCLA, UAB)	631

Note: Minimum 10 head coaching seasons in Division I.

WINNING PERCENTAGE

Coach (Team)	Yrs	W	L	Pct
Jerry Tarkanian (Long Beach St 69-73, UNLV 74-92, Fresno St 95-)	24	625	122	.837
Clair Bee (Rider 29-31, LIU-Brooklyn 32-45, 46-51)	21	412	87	.826
Adolph Rupp (Kentucky 31-72)	41	876	190	.822
John Wooden (Indiana St 47-48, UCLA 49-75)	29	664	162	.804
Dean Smith (N Carolina 62-)	34	830	236	.779
Harry Fisher (Columbia 07-16, Army 22-23, 25)	13	147	44	.770
Frank Keaney (Rhode Island 21-48)	27	387	117	.768
George Keogan (St Louis 16, Allegheny 19, Valparaiso 20-21, Notre Dame 24-43)	24	385	117	.767
Jack Ramsay (St Joseph's [PA] 56-66)	11	231	71	.765
Vic Bubas (Duke 60-69)	10	213	67	.761
Nolan Richardson (Tulsa 81-85, Arkansas 86-)	15	371	119	.757
Jim Boeheim (Syracuse 77-)	19	454	150	.752
John Chaney (Cheyney 73-82, Temple 83-)	23	520	175	.748
Charles "Chick" Davies (Duquesne 25-43, 47-48)	21	314	106	.748
Ray Mears (Wittenberg 57-62, Tennessee 63-77)	21	399	135	.747
Phog Allen (Baker 06-08, Kansas 08-09, Haskell 09, Cent MO St 13-19, Kansas 20-56)	48	746	264	.739
Al McGuire (Belmont Abbey 58-64, Marquette 65-77)	20	405	143	.739
Everett Chase (N Carolina St 47-64)	18	376	133	.739
Bob Knight (Army 66-71, Indiana 72-)	30	659	235	.737
Walter Meanwell (Wisconsin 12-17, 21-34; Missouri 18, 20)	22	280	101	.735

Note: Minimum 10 head coaching seasons in Division I.

NCAA Division I Women's Championship Results

Year	Winner	Score	Runner-up	Winning Coach
1982	Louisiana Tech	76–62	Cheyney	Sonja Hogg
1983	Southern Cal	69–67	Louisiana Tech	Linda Sharp
1984	Southern Cal	72–61	Tennessee	Linda Sharp
1985	Old Dominion	70–65	Georgia	Marianne Stanley
1986	Texas	97–81	Southern Cal	Jody Conradt
1987	Tennessee	67–44	Louisiana Tech	Pat Summitt
1988	Louisiana Tech	56–54	Auburn	Leon Barmore
1989	Tennessee	76–60	Auburn	Pat Summitt
1990	Stanford	88–81	Auburn	Tara VanDerveer
1991	Tennessee	70–67 (OT)	Virginia	Pat Summitt
1992	Stanford	78–62	Western Kentucky	Tara VanDerveer
1993	Texas Tech	84–82	Ohio State	Marsha Sharp
1994	N Carolina	60–59	Louisiana Tech	Sylvia Hatchell
1995	Connecticut	70–64	Tennessee	Geno Auriemma

NCAA Division I Women's Alltime Individual Leaders

Single-Game Records

SCORING HIGHS

Pts	Player and Team vs Opponent	Year
60	Cindy Brown, Long Beach St vs San Jose St	1987
58	Kim Perrot, SW Louisiana vs SE Louisiana	1990
58	Lorri Bauman, Drake vs SW Missouri St	1984
55	Patricia Hoskins, Mississippi Valley vs Southern-BR	1989
55	Patricia Hoskins, Mississippi Valley vs Alabama St	1989
54	Anjinea Hopson, Grambling vs Jackson St	1994
54	Mary Lowry, Baylor vs Texas	1994
54	Wanda Ford, Drake vs SW Missouri St	1986
53	Felisha Edwards, NE Louisiana vs Southern Mississippi	1991
53	Chris Starr, NV-Reno vs Cal St-Sacramento	1983
53	Sheryl Swoopes, Texas Tech vs Texas	1993

REBOUNDING HIGHS

Reb	Player and Team vs Opponent	Year
40	Deborah Temple, Delta St vs AL-Birmingham	1983
37	Rosina Pearson, Bethune-Cookman vs Florida Memorial	1985
33	Maureen Formico, Pepperdine vs Loyola (CA)	1985

REBOUNDING HIGHS *(Cont.)*

Reb	Player and Team vs Opponent	Year
31	Darlene Beale, Howard vs S Carolina St	1987
30	Cindy Bonforte, Wagner vs Queens (NY)	1983
30	Kayone Hankins, New Orleans vs. Nicholls St	1994
29	Gail Norris, Alabama St vs Texas Southern	1992
29	Joy Kellogg, Oklahoma City vs Oklahoma Christian	1984
29	Joy Kellogg, Oklahoma City vs UTEP	1984

Six tied with 28.

ASSISTS

A	Player and Team vs Opponent	Year
23	Michelle Burden, Kent St vs Ball St	1991
22	Shawn Monday, Tennessee Tech vs Morehead St	1988
22	Veronica Pettry, Loyola (IL) vs Detroit	1989
22	Tine Freil, Pacific vs Wichita St	1991
21	Tine Freil, Pacific vs Fresno St	1992
21	Amy Bauer, Wisconsin vs Detroit	1989
21	Neacole Hall, Alabama St vs Southern-BR	1989
20	Anja Bordt, St Mary's (CA) vs Loyola (CA)	1991
20	Gaynor O'Donnell, E Carolina vs NC-Asheville	1992
20	Ira Fuquay, Alcorn St vs Grambling	1993

Season Records

POINTS

Player and Team	Year	GP	FG	3FG	FT	Pts
Cindy Brown, Long Beach St	1987	35	362	—	250	974
Genia Miller, Cal St-Fullerton	1991	33	376	0	217	969
Sheryl Swoopes, Texas Tech	1993	34	356	32	211	955
Andrea Congreaves, Mercer	1992	28	353	77	142	925
Wanda Ford, Drake	1986	30	390	—	139	919
Barbara Kennedy, Clemson	1982	31	392	—	124	908
Patricia Hoskins, Mississippi Valley	1989	27	345	13	205	908
LaTaunya Pollard, Long Beach St	1983	31	376	—	155	907
Tina Hutchinson, San Diego St	1984	30	383	—	132	898
Jan Jensen, Drake	1991	30	358	6	166	888

SEASON SCORING AVERAGE

Player and Team	Year	GP	FG	3FG	FT	Pts	Avg
Patricia Hoskins, Mississippi Valley	1989	27	345	13	205	908	33.6
Andrea Congreaves, Mercer	1992	28	353	77	142	925	33.0
Deborah Temple, Delta St	1984	28	373	—	127	873	31.2
Andrea Congreaves, Mercer	1993	26	302	51	150	805	31.0
Wanda Ford, Drake	1986	30	390	—	139	919	30.6
Anucha Browne, Northwestern	1985	28	341	—	173	855	30.5
LeChandra LeDay, Grambling	1988	28	334	36	146	850	30.4
Kim Perrot, Southwestern Louisiana	1990	28	308	95	128	839	30.0
Tina Hutchinson, San Diego St	1984	30	383	—	132	898	29.9
Jan Jensen, Drake	1991	30	358	6	166	888	29.6
Genia Miller, Cal St-Fullerton	1991	33	376	0	217	969	29.4
Barbara Kennedy, Clemson	1982	31	392	—	124	908	29.3
LaTaunya Pollard, Long Beach St	1983	31	376	—	155	907	29.3
Lisa McMullen, Alabama St	1991	28	285	126	119	815	29.1
Tresa Spaulding, BYU	1987	28	347	—	116	810	28.9
Hope Linthicum, Central Conn St	1987	23	282	—	101	665	28.9

Season Records (Cont.)

REBOUNDS

Player and Team	Year	GP	Reb	Player and Team	Year	GP	Reb
Wanda Ford, Drake	1985	30	534	Rosina Pearson, Beth-Cookman	1985	26	480
Wanda Ford, Drake	1986	30	506	Patricia Hoskins, Miss Valley	1987	28	476
Anne Donovan, Old Dominion	1983	35	504	Cheryl Miller, Southern Cal	1985	30	474
Darlene Jones, Miss Valley	1983	31	487	Darlene Beale, Howard	1987	29	459
Melanie Simpson, Okla City	1982	37	481	Olivia Bradley, W Virginia	1985	30	458

REBOUND AVERAGE

Player and Team	Year	GP	Reb	Avg
Rosina Pearson, Bethune-Cookman	1985	26	480	18.5
Wanda Ford, Drake	1985	30	534	17.8
Katie Beck, E Tennessee St	1988	25	441	17.6
DeShawne Blocker, E Tenn St	1994	26	450	17.3
Patricia Hoskins, Mississippi Valley	1987	28	476	17.0
Wanda Ford, Drake	1986	30	506	16.9
Patricia Hoskins, Mississippi Valley	1989	27	440	16.3
Joy Kellogg, Oklahoma City	1984	23	373	16.2
Deborah Mitchell, Mississippi Coll	1983	28	447	16.0

FIELD-GOAL PERCENTAGE

Player and Team	Year	GP	FG	FGA	Pct
Renay Adams, Tennessee Tech	1991	30	185	258	71.7
Regina Days, Georgia Southern	1986	27	234	332	70.5
Kim Wood, WI-Green Bay	1994	27	188	271	69.4
Kelly Lyons, Old Dominion	1990	31	308	444	69.4
Alisha Hill, Howard	1995	28	194	281	69.0
Trina Roberts, Georgia Southern	1982	31	189	277	68.2
Lidiya Varbanova, Boise St	1991	22	128	188	68.1
LaFreda Deckard, North Texas	1995	27	147	217	67.7
Sharon McDowell, NC-Wilmington	1987	28	170	251	67.7
Lidiya Varbanova, Boise St	1992	29	228	338	67.5
Mary Raese, Idaho	1986	31	254	380	66.8
Lydia Sawney, Tennessee Tech	1983	27	167	250	66.8

Based on qualifiers for annual championship.

FREE-THROW PERCENTAGE

Player and Team	Year	GP	FT	FTA	Pct
Ginny Doyle, Richmond	1992	29	96	101	95.0
Linda Cyborski, Delaware	1991	29	74	79	93.7
Jennifer Howard, N Carolina St	1994	27	118	127	92.9
Keely Feeman, Cincinnati	1986	30	76	82	92.7
Amy Slowikowski, Kent St	1989	27	112	121	92.6
Lea Ann Parsley, Marshall	1990	28	96	104	92.3
Chris Starr, NV-Reno	1986	25	119	129	92.2
DeAnn Craft, Central Florida	1987	24	94	102	92.2
Tracey Sneed, La Salle	1988	30	151	165	91.5

Based on qualifiers for annual championship.

THEY SAID IT

Geno Auriemma, Connecticut women's basketball coach, to his 33–0 Huskies prior to the Final Four: "The other teams here are playing for a national championship. We're playing for a piece of history."

Career Records

POINTS

Player and Team	Yrs	GP	Pts
Patricia Hoskins, Mississippi Valley	1985-89	110	3122
Lorri Bauman, Drake	1981-84	120	3115
Cheryl Miller, Southern Cal	1983-86	128	3018
Valorie Whiteside, Appalachian St	1984-88	116	2944
Joyce Walker, Louisiana St	1981-84	117	2906
Sandra Hodge, New Orleans	1981-84	107	2860
Andrea Congreaves, Mercer	1989-93	108	2796
Karen Pelphrey, Marshall	1983-86	114	2746
Cindy Brown, Long Beach St	1983-87	128	2696
Carolyn Thompson, Texas Tech	1981-84	121	2655
Sue Wicks, Rutgers	1984-88	125	2655

SCORING AVERAGE

Player and Team	Yrs	GP	FG	3FG	FT	Pts	Avg
Patricia Hoskins, Mississippi Valley	1985-89	110	1196	24	706	3122	28.4
Sandra Hodge, New Orleans	1981-84	107	1194	—	472	2860	26.7
Lorri Bauman, Drake	1981-84	120	1104	—	907	3115	26.0
Andrea Congreaves, Mercer	1989-93	108	1107	153	429	2796	25.9
Valorie Whiteside, Appalachian St	1984-88	116	1153	0	638	2944	25.4
Joyce Walker, Louisiana St	1981-84	117	1259	—	388	2906	24.8
Tarcha Hollis, Grambling	1988-91	85	904	3	247	2058	24.2
Karen Pelphrey, Marshall	1983-86	114	1175	—	396	2746	24.1
Erma Jones, Bethune-Cookman	1982-84	87	961	—	173	2095	24.1
Cheryl Miller, Southern Cal	1983-86	128	1159	—	700	3018	23.6
Chris Starr, Nevada-Reno	1983-86	101	881	—	594	2356	23.3

NCAA Division II Men's Championship Results

Year	Winner	Score	Runner-up	Third Place	Fourth Place
1957	Wheaton (IL)	89-65	Kentucky Wesleyan	Mount St Mary's (MD)	Cal St-Los Angeles
1958	S Dakota	75-53	St Michael's	Evansville	Wheaton (IL)
1959	Evansville	83-67	SW Missouri St	N Carolina A&T	Cal St-Los Angeles
1960	Evansville	90-69	Chapman	Kentucky Wesleyan	Cornell College
1961	Wittenberg	42-38	SE Missouri St	S Dakota St	Mount St Mary's (MD)
1962	Mount St Mary's (MD)	58-57 (OT)	Cal St-Sacramento	Southern Illinois	Nebraska Wesleyan
1963	S Dakota St	44-42	Wittenberg	Oglethorpe	Southern Illinois
1964	Evansville	72-59	Akron	N Carolina A&T	Northern Iowa
1965	Evansville	85-82 (OT)	Southern Illinois	N Dakota	St Michael's
1966	Kentucky Wesleyan	54-51	Southern Illinois	Akron	N Dakota
1967	Winston-Salem	77-74	SW Missouri St	Kentucky Wesleyan	Illinois St
1968	Kentucky Wesleyan	63-52	Indiana St	Trinity (TX)	Ashland
1969	Kentucky Wesleyan	75-71	SW Missouri St	†Vacated	Ashland
1970	Philadelphia Textile	76-65	Tennessee St	UC-Riverside	Buffalo St
1971	Evansville	97-82	Old Dominion	†Vacated	Kentucky Wesleyan
1972	Roanoke	84-72	Akron	Tennessee St	Eastern Mich
1973	Kentucky Wesleyan	78-76 (OT)	Tennessee St	Assumption	Brockport St
1974	Morgan St	67-52	SW Missouri St	Assumption	New Orleans
1975	Old Dominion	76-74	New Orleans	Assumption	TN-Chattanooga
1976	Puget Sound	83-74	TN-Chattanooga	Eastern Illinois	Old Dominion
1977	TN-Chattanooga	71-62	Randolph-Macon	N Alabama	Sacred Heart
1978	Cheyney	47-40	WI-Green Bay	Eastern Illinois	Central Florida
1979	N Alabama	64-50	WI-Green Bay	Cheyney	Bridgeport
1980	Virginia Union	80-74	New York Tech	Florida Southern	N Alabama
1981	Florida Southern	73-68	Mount St Mary's (MD)	Cal Poly-SLO	WI-Green Bay
1982	District of Columbia	73-63	Florida Southern	Kentucky Wesleyan	Cal St-Bakersfield
1983	Wright St	92-73	District of Columbia	*Cal St-Bakersfield	*Morningside
1984	Central Missouri St	81-77	St Augustine's	*Kentucky Wesleyan	*N Alabama
1985	Jacksonville St	74-73	S Dakota St	*Kentucky Wesleyan	*Mount St Mary's (MD)
1986	Sacred Heart	93-87	SE Missouri St	*Cheyney	*Florida Southern
1987	Kentucky Wesleyan	92-74	Gannon	*Delta St	*Eastern Montana

Year	Winner	Score	Runner-up	Third Place	Fourth Place
1988	........Lowell	75-72	AK-Anchorage	Florida Southern	Troy St
1989	........N Carolina Central	73-46	SE Missouri St	UC-Riverside	Jacksonville St
1990	........Kentucky Wesleyan	93-79	Cal St-Bakersfield	N Dakota	Morehouse
1991	........N Alabama	79-72	Bridgeport (CT)	*Cal St-Bakersfield	*Virginia Union
1992	........Virginia Union	100-75	Bridgeport (CT)	*Cal St-Bakersfield	*California (PA)
1993	........Cal St-Bakersfield	85-72	Troy St (AL)	*New Hampshire Coll	*Wayne St (MI)
1994	........Cal St-Bakersfield	92-86	Southern Indiana	*New Hampshire Coll	*Washburn
1995	........Southern Indiana	71-63	UC-Riverside	*Norfolk St	*Indiana (PA)

*Indicates tied for third. †Student-athletes representing American International in 1969 and Southwestern Louisiana in 1971 were declared ineligible subsequent to the tournament. Under NCAA rules, the teams' and ineligible student-athletes' records were deleted, and the teams' places in the final standings were vacated.

NCAA Division II Men's Alltime Individual Leaders

SINGLE-GAME SCORING HIGHS

Pts	Player and Team vs Opponent	Date
113	............................Bevo Francis, Rio Grande vs Hillsdale	1954
84	..............................Bevo Francis, Rio Grande vs Alliance	1954
82	..............................Bevo Francis, Rio Grande vs Bluffton	1954
80	............................Paul Crissman, Southern Cal Col vs Pacific Christian	1966
77	............................William English, Winston-Salem vs Fayetteville St	1968

Season Records

SCORING AVERAGE

Player and Team	Year	GP	FG	FT	Pts	Avg
Bevo Francis, Rio Grande...1954		27	444	367	1255	46.5
Earl Glass, Mississippi Industrial.............................1963		19	322	171	815	42.9
Earl Monroe, Winston-Salem...................................1967		32	509	311	1329	41.5
John Rinka, Kenyon..1970		23	354	234	942	41.0
Willie Shaw, Lane...1964		18	303	121	727	40.4

REBOUND AVERAGE

Player and Team	Year	GP	Reb	Avg
Tom Hart, Middlebury 1956		21	620	29.5
Tom Hart, Middlebury 1955		22	649	29.5
Frank Stronczek, American Int'l 1966		26	717	27.6
R.C. Owens, College of Idaho 1954		25	677	27.1
Maurice Stokes, St Francis (PA) 1954		26	689	26.5

ASSISTS

Player and Team	Year	GP	A
Steve Ray, Bridgeport 1989		32	400
Steve Ray, Bridgeport 1990		33	385
Tony Smith, Pfeiffer........................1992		35	349
Jim Ferrer, Bentley 1989		31	309
Brian Gregory, Oakland 1989		28	300

ASSIST AVERAGE

Player and Team	Year	GP	A	Avg
Steve Ray, Bridgeport................1989		32	400	12.5
Steve Ray, Bridgeport................1990		33	385	11.7
Demetri Beekman, Assumption...1993		23	264	11.5
Ernest Jenkins, NM Highlands 1995		27	291	10.8
Brian Gregory, Oakland 1989		28	300	10.7

FIELD-GOAL PERCENTAGE

Player and Team	Year	Pct
Todd Linder, Tampa......................1987		75.2
Maurice Stafford, N Alabama.........1984		75.0
Matthew Cornegay, Tuskegee 1982		74.8
Brian Moten, W Georgia.................1992		73.4
Ed Phillips, Alabama A&M..............1968		73.3

FREE-THROW PERCENTAGE

Player and Team	Year	Pct
Billy Newton, Morgan St 1976		94.4
Kent Andrews, McNeese St 1968		94.4
Mike Sanders, Northern Colorado..1987		94.3
Jay Harrie, E Montana....................1994		93.5
Joe Cullen, Hartwick......................1969		93.2

Career Records

POINTS

Player and Team	Yrs	Pts
Travis Grant, Kentucky St	1969-72	4045
Bob Hopkins, Grambling	1953-56	3759
Tony Smith, Pfeiffer	1989-92	3350
Earnest Lee, Clark Atlanta	1984-87	3298
Joe Miller, Alderson-Broaddus	1954-57	3294

CAREER SCORING AVERAGE

Player and Team	Yrs	GP	Pts	Avg
Travis Grant, Kentucky St	1969-72	121	4045	33.4
John Rinka, Kenyon	1967-70	99	3251	32.8
Florindo Vieira, Quinnipiac	1954-57	69	2263	32.8
Willie Shaw, Lane	1961-64	76	2379	31.3
Mike Davis, Virginia Union	1966-69	89	2758	31.0

REBOUND AVERAGE

Player and Team	Yrs	GP	Reb	Avg
Tom Hart, Middlebury	1953, 55-56	63	1738	27.6
Maurice Stokes, St Francis (PA)	1953-55	72	1812	25.2
Frank Stronczek, American Int'l	1965-67	62	1549	25.0
Bill Thieben, Hofstra	1954-56	76	1837	24.2
Hank Brown, Lowell Tech	1965-67	49	1129	23.0

ASSISTS

Player and Team	Yrs	A
Demetri Beekman, Assumption	1990-93	1044
Rob Paternostro, New Hamp Coll	1992-95	919
Gallagher Driscoll, St Rose	1989-92	878
Tony Smith, Pfeiffer	1989-92	828
Steve Ray, Bridgeport	1989-90	785

ASSIST AVERAGE

Player and Team	Yrs	GP	A	Avg
Steve Ray, Bridgeport	1989-90	65	785	12.1
Demetri Beekman, Assumption	1990-93	119	1044	8.8
Ernest Jenkins, NM Highlands	1992-95	84	699	8.3
Mark Benson, Texas A&I	1989-91	86	674	7.8
Pat Madden, Jacksonville St	1989-91	88	688	7.8

Note: Minimum 550 Assists.

FIELD-GOAL PERCENTAGE

Player and Team	Yrs	Pct
Todd Linder, Tampa	1984-87	70.8
Tom Schurfranz, Bellarmine	1989-92	70.2
Chad Scott, California (PA)	1991-94	70.0
Ed Phillips, Alabama, A&M	1968-71	68.9
Ulysses Hackett, SC-Spartanburg	1990-92	67.9

Note: Minimum 400 FGM.

FREE-THROW PERCENTAGE

Player and Team	Yrs	Pct
Kent Andrews, McNeese St	1967-69	91.6
Jon Hagen, Mankato St	1963-65	90.0
Dave Reynolds, Davis & Elkins	1986-89	89.3
Terry Gill, New Orleans	1972-74	88.2
Tony Budzik, Mansfield	1989-92	88.2

Note: Minimum 250 FTM.

NCAA Division III Men's Championship Results

Year	Winner	Score	Runner-up	Third Place	Fourth Place
1975	LeMoyne-Owen	57-54	Glassboro St	Augustana (IL)	Brockport St
1976	Scranton	60-57	Wittenberg	Augustana (IL)	Plattsburgh St
1977	Wittenberg	79-66	Oneonta St	Scranton	Hamline
1978	North Park	69-57	Widener	Albion	Stony Brook
1979	North Park	66-62	Potsdam St	Franklin & Marshall	Centre
1980	North Park	83-76	Upsala	Wittenberg	Longwood
1981	Potsdam St	67-65 (OT)	Augustana (IL)	Ursinus	Otterbein
1982	Wabash	83-62	Potsdam St	Brooklyn	Cal St-Stanislaus
1983	Scranton	64-63	Wittenberg	Roanoke	WI-Whitewater
1984	WI-Whitewater	103-86	Clark (MA)	DePauw	Upsala
1985	North Park	72-71	Potsdam St	Nebraska Wesleyan	Widener
1986	Potsdam St	76-73	LeMoyne-Owen	Nebraska Wesleyan	Jersey City St
1987	North Park	106-100	Clark (MA)	Wittenberg	Stockton St
1988	Ohio Wesleyan	92-70	Scranton	Nebraska Wesleyan	Hartwick
1989	WI-Whitewater	94-86	Trenton St	Southern Maine	Centre
1990	Rochester	43-42	DePauw	Washington (MD)	Calvin
1991	WI-Platteville	81-74	Franklin & Marshall	Otterbein	Ramapo (NJ)
1992	Calvin	62-49	Rochester	WI-Platteville	Jersey City St
1993	Ohio Northern	71-68	Augustana	Mass-Dartmouth	Rowan
1994	Lebanon Valley Coll	66-59 (OT)	New York University	Wittenberg	St Thomas (MN)
1995	WI-Platteville	69-55	Manchester	Rowan	Trinity (CT)

NCAA Division III Men's Alltime Individual Leaders

SINGLE-GAME SCORING HIGHS

Pts	Player and Team vs Opponent	Year
69	Steve Diekmann, Grinnell vs Simpson	1995
63	Joe DeRoche, Thomas vs St Joseph's (ME)	1988
62	Shannon Lilly, Bishop vs Southwest Assembly of God	1983
61	Steve Honderd, Calvin vs Kalamazoo	1993
61	Dana Wilson, Husson vs Ricker	1974

Season Records

SCORING AVERAGE

Player and Team	Year	GP	FG	FT	Pts	Avg
Steve Diekmann, Grinnell	1995	20	223	162	745	37.3
Rickey Sutton, Lyndon St	1976	14	207	93	507	36.2
Shannon Lilly, Bishop	1983	26	345	218	908	34.9
Dana Wilson, Husson	1974	20	288	122	698	34.9
Rickey Sutton, Lyndon St	1977	16	223	112	558	34.9

REBOUND AVERAGE

Player and Team	Year	GP	Reb	Avg
Joe Manley, Bowie St	1976	29	579	20.0
Fred Petty, New Hampshire College	1974	22	436	19.8
Larry Williams, Pratt	1977	24	457	19.0
Charles Greer, Thomas	1977	17	318	18.7
Larry Parker, Plattsburgh St	1975	23	430	18.7

ASSISTS

Player and Team	Year	GP	A
Robert James, Kean	1989	29	391
Ricky Spicer, WI-Whitewater	1989	31	295
Joe Marcotte, New Jersey Tech	1995	30	292
Ron Torgalski, Hamilton	1989	26	275
Albert Kirchner, Mt St Vincent	1990	24	267

ASSIST AVERAGE

Player and Team	Year	GP	A	Avg
Robert James, Kean	1989	29	391	13.5
Albert Kirchner, Mt St Vincent	1990	24	267	11.1
Ron Torgalski, Hamilton	1989	26	275	10.6
Louis Adams, Rust	1989	22	227	10.3
Eric Johnson, Coe	1991	24	238	9.9

FIELD-GOAL PERCENTAGE

Player and Team	Year	Pct
Travis Weiss, St John's (MN)	1994	76.6
Pete Metzelaars, Wabash	1982	75.3
Tony Rychlec, Mass Maritime	1981	74.9
Tony Rychlec, Mass Maritime	1982	73.1
Russ Newnan, Menlo	1991	73.0

FREE-THROW PERCENTAGE

Player and Team	Year	Pct
Andy Enfield, Johns Hopkins	1991	95.3
Yudi Teichman, Yeshiva	1989	95.2
Chris Carideo, Widener	1992	95.2
Mike Scheib, Susquehanna	1977	94.1
Jason Prevenost, Middlebury	1994	93.8

Career Records

POINTS

Player and Team	Yrs	Pts
Andre Foreman, Salisbury St	1989-92	2940
Lamont Strothers, Chris Newport	1988-91	2709
Matt Hancock, Colby	1987-90	2678
Scott Fitch, Geneseo St	1990-94	2634
Greg Grant, Trenton St	1987-89	2611

CAREER SCORING AVERAGE

Player and Team	Yrs	GP	Avg
Dwain Govan, Bishop	1974-75	55	32.8
Dave Russell, Shepherd	1974-75	60	30.6
Rickey Sutton, Lyndon St	1976-79	80	29.7
John Atkins, Knoxville	1976-78	70	28.7
Jeff deLaveaga, Cal Lutheran	1989-92	80	28.1

REBOUND AVERAGE

Player and Team	Yrs	GP	Reb	Avg
Larry Parker, Plattsburgh St	1975-78	85	1482	17.4
Charles Greer, Thomas	1975-77	58	926	16.0
Willie Parr, LeMoyne-Owen	1974-76	76	1182	15.6
Michael Smith, Hamilton	1989-92	107	1632	15.2
Dave Kufeld, Yeshiva	1977-80	81	1222	15.1

ASSIST AVERAGE

Player and Team	Yrs	Avg
Steve Artis, Chris. Newport	1990-93	8.1
David Genovese, Mt St Vincent	1992-95	7.5
Kevin Root, Eureka	1989-91	7.1
Dennis Jacobi, Bowdoin	1989-92	7.1
Eric Johnson, Coe	1989-92	7.1
Pat Skerry, Tufts	1989-92	6.6

Hockey

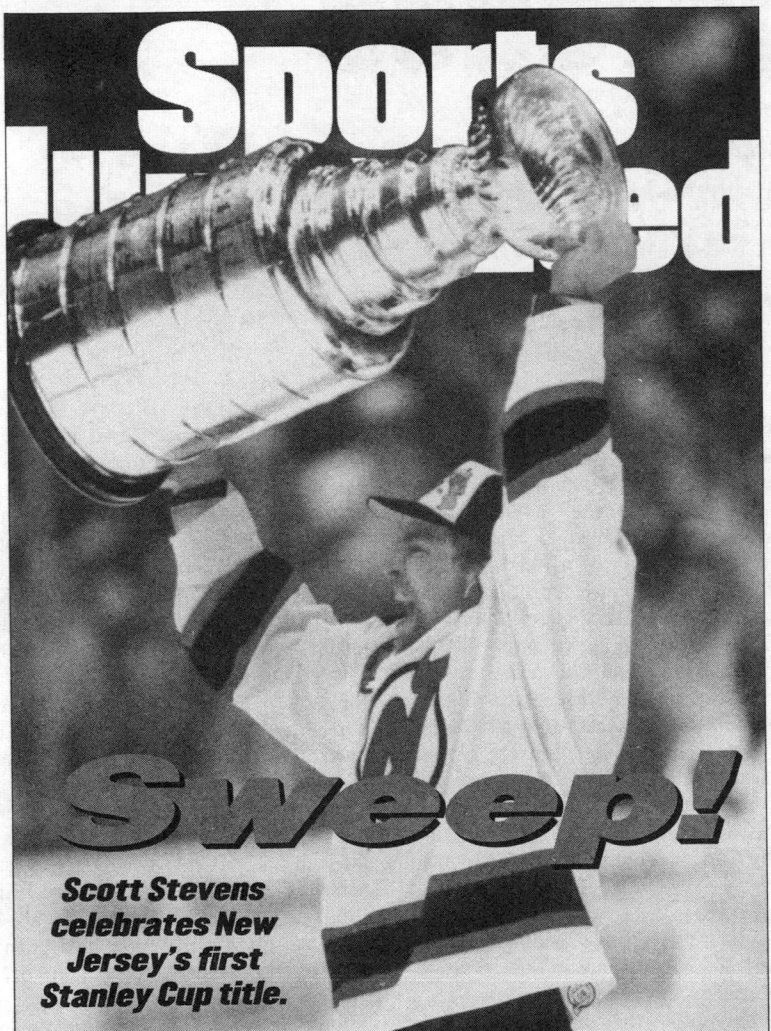

Sweep!

Scott Stevens celebrates New Jersey's first Stanley Cup title.

LOU CAPOZZOLA

A Devilish Defense

Employing the confounding—some say boring—neutral-zone trap, the New Jersey Devils won their first Stanley Cup

by Michael Farber

THE MOST aggravating of National Hockey League seasons belonged to the swamp-dwellin', trap-playin', low-payin' New Jersey Devils, the best, and most aggravating, team in hockey.

The season began with a 103-day lockout and featured more interference than Bill Clinton gets from the Republican Congress. High-flying action was choked by the neutral-zone trap, and the game's top line was the Maginot Line. The playoff picture threatened to degenerate into a full-scale game of franchise roulette and the playoffs themselves failed to offer a single seven-game series after the first round. In view of all this, there was no more appropriate Stanley Cup champion than the little-loved Devils.

The Devils, the third franchise in the New York area in terms of history and, until recently, fan support, are an iron-on patch on the fabric of New Jersey life—a team that seems to be from the state but not of the state. These Rand-McNallys of the rink began life in 1974 as the Kansas City

Scouts, transmogrified two seasons later into the Colorado Rockies (a team so egregiously pathetic it gave an entire mountain range a bad name), skedaddled to the Meadowlands in 1982 and, as they neared their crowning moment, seemed headed to the hockey hotbed of Nashville. (A new lease agreed upon after the playoffs by owner John McMullen and the New Jersey Sports and Exposition Authority averted the move.) As rumors about an imminent departure swirled during the final against Detroit, the nonplussed Devils rallied behind brilliant sophomore goaltender Martin Brodeur, defenseman Scott Stevens and rightwinger Claude Lemieux to sweep the Red Wings.

If the NHL was going to have an anti-season, there was no worthier playoff MVP than the game's ultimate anti-hero, Lemieux. The playoffs always have brought out the overachiever in Lemieux, once named the most hated player in hockey. He scored two overtime winners in his rookie season with the 1986 Montreal Canadiens,

and the player who personifies chalk squealing on a blackboard has been as much Mr. May as Mr. Mayhem ever since. Lemieux, who ranks 30th in career playoff goals with 52, wound up putting the con back in Conn Smythe by scoring 13 playoff goals in 20 games (including three winners) and checking mercilessly after a somnambulant regular season in which he scored six goals in 45 games, had a protracted contract dispute and was nearly traded.

Just two of Lemieux's goals came in the finals, but it hardly mattered because 17 different Devils contributed points in the four games. Their depth was as overwhelming as their selflessness. While the Devils lack the copious talent that might brand them as a dynasty, they do have a blueprint for success—size and speed—in a league where hooking, holding and interference are commonplace. The Devils, whose forwards were a half inch taller and nine pounds heavier than the preternaturally skilled Red Wings, dominated a team that had lost just twice in three playoff rounds. Because they did not

The scrappy Lemieux (22) elevated his game for the playoffs, scoring 13 goals, including three game-winners.

see Detroit during the season—the truncated 48-game schedule had no interconference play—the Devils were apprehensive about facing Team Octopus. At least for the first 10 minutes of Game 1. "We heard how good they were," said Devil center Bob Carpenter, one of 11 U.S.-born players on the team, a strikingly high number in a league which takes just 18% of its players from the lower 48. "But in those 10 minutes, we found out we could play with them, we could check them."

"I thought our guys deserved a little more [respect] from their opponents," New Jersey coach Jacques Lemaire said. "That's the one reason our guys were aggressive on the ice. They showed up every game mad. They wanted to win because they got no credit. It's great to see a bunch of guys play together and score more than the guys with talent."

Lemaire is a hockey purist, a coach who

lives for the 60 minutes but none of the other, if you will pardon the expression, trappings of big-time hockey. If it were up to him, Lemaire probably would coach in a hermetically sealed laboratory, which, until recently, was an apt description of the Meadowlands. Lemaire installed the trap, hockey's latest four-letter word. Of course Lemaire didn't invent this forechecking system, which forces the opposing puck carrier to the boards and then floods center ice with defenders who cut off passing lanes. "Montreal trapped for 23 Cups," Calgary Flame coach Pierre Pagé said. But unlike the 17 other teams that employed the trap in 1995, the Devils played it with an uncommon verve, using their defense to create offense. If the Devil trap seemed dull, at its best it was no more boring than the Chicago Bear 46 defense of the mid-1980s. Still

styles make hockey matches as surely as they make fights, and some officials were concerned that games between trapping teams would take the NHL to the yawn of a new era, death for a league in which 65% of revenues are generated at the gate. Pagé predicted the proliferation of the trap would follow a Devil victory, but early indications are the trap has reached a plateau. Trapmeister Roger Neilson, whose upstart Florida Panthers missed the playoffs by one point their first two years by utilizing the most cautious, stultifying forecheck in the NHL, was fired after the season.

The Red Wings, who have not won the Cup since 1955, were the Devils' antithesis, the rare team capable of playing firewagon hockey in the year when swamp hockey was the rage. But even Detroit tightened up considerably from its old devil-may-care

Game On, for Now

In the year of labor pains for North American sports, the game that once had the coziest relationship between owners and players was not immune to a work stoppage.

The kid gloves were dropped early in the 103-day National Hockey League lockout when Chicago Blackhawk defenseman Chris Chelios said he wouldn't be surprised if someone tried to hurt Commissioner Gary Bettman, a suggestion that usually comes from those serving a few years in medium-security facilities rather than two minutes in penalty boxes. Bettman brushed off the implied threat, and, of course, hockey survived the craziness, too. The season, which finally began on Jan. 20, was pared to 48 games, and the playoffs ran until June 24—Game 7 of the Stanley Cup final was scheduled for June 30— but hockey's natural rhythms returned for the 1995–96 season. Although either side can reopen it after the 1997–98 season, the six-year contract proved that a) players don't necessarily have to win a

labor dispute, and b) the gestation period for a collective bargaining agreement in hockey is shorter than in baseball.

The battlegrounds of the baseball strike and the hockey lockout were similar: the salary cap and its more subtle sibling, the luxury tax. As they wrestled with their own profligacy and mushrooming salaries—the St. Louis Blues' payroll shot up from $3.5 million in 1989–90 to $23 million in 1995—owners viewed a salary cap or luxury tax as a fail safe system that would control labor costs. But the National Hockey League Players Association carved a line in the ice, insisting it would abide neither. The association stood steadfast on the cap/tax, except in the case of rookies, but it yielded so much in the areas of free agency and arbitration that its victory was Pyrrhic.

The toll:
•Elimination of restricted free agency for players with less than three years experience;

style with a system known as the left wing lock. A forward, usually a leftwinger, would hang back near the attacking blue line, playing almost like a third defenseman, to prevent the odd-man breaks that had made the Wings first-round playoff victims the previous two springs. Coach Scott Bowman did an extraordinary job selling a new style to a veteran team, getting the Wings to rein in some of their offensive instincts and prodding roving defenseman Paul Coffey to take care of his own end first. Detroit had the best regular-season record with 70 points, and Coffey, who last won the Norris Trophy in 1986, was voted the league's best defenseman; the stretch of nine years between major awards is the third longest in NHL history.

Detroit disposed of Dallas in five games in the first round

and then whipped San Jose 6–0, 6–2, 6–2, 6–2 in what reads in agate type like a bad tennis match. The Red Wings eliminated Chicago in the Western Conference final in a Hobbesian series: nasty, brutish and short (five games). Despite the efficiency with which the Red Wings barged into the final, they were banged up against New Jersey, especially at center. Steve Yzerman needed arthroscopic surgery on his knee after the San Jose series. Sergei Fedorov suffered a separated shoulder in Game 3 against Chicago and returned for Game 5 only after prodding by teammate Slava Fetisov. But the biggest Wing loss might have been Keith Primeau, who injured his oblique muscles in his side in the opener against

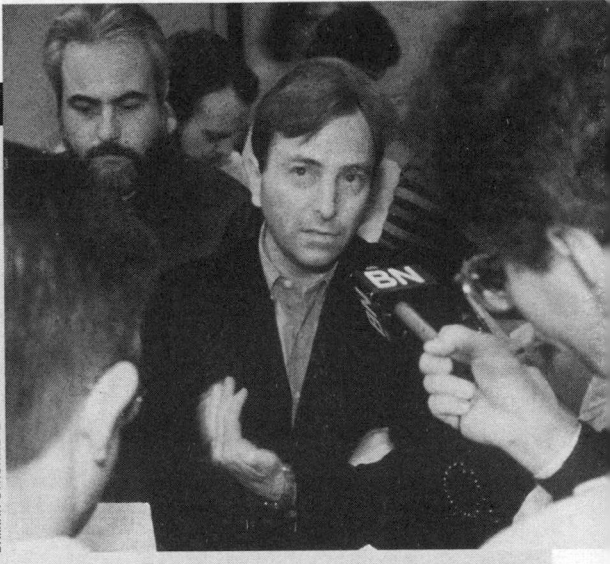

DAMIAN STROHMEYER

In his second year at the helm Bettman negotiated some very rough waters.

• A rookie salary cap of $850,000, the death knell for mind-boggling inflationary deals like the five-year, $12.25 million contract No. 1 draft pick Alexandre Daigle signed with Ottawa in 1993;
• No salary arbitration for the first five years; owners can walk away from three arbitration awards in a two-year period;
• Mandatory two-way contracts (a player takes a salary cut if he is sent to the minors);
• Players now can become unrestricted free agents at 32, but with lower entry-level pay and reduced possibilities for arbitration, veterans' salaries are expected to rise more slowly. Since 1989 the average salary has exploded from $232,000 to $733,000 last season.

The players ratified the deal on Jan. 13—Friday the 13th, naturally. At a press conference Bettman and Bob Goodenow, the players' association executive director, donned black hats emblazoned with GAME ON, a slogan borrowed from the movie *Wayne's World.* "Sure," Goodenow said, "concessions were made, but the game's in a position to go forward." Party on, Bob. Party on, Gary.

New Jersey. The 6'5½", 215-pounder had been the dominant player in the grinding series against Chicago, a breakout five games for Primeau that established him as a player to watch.

As size assumes a premium place in the pantheon of NHL attributes for the first time since the Broad Street Bullies era, it is fitting that the biggest of the big boys is in Philadelphia. Eric Lindros is maybe an inch shorter than Primeau, but he is as thick as a sequoia and as artful a passer as any behemoth ever to play the game. After two injury-marred seasons—greatness postponed—Lindros became the NHL's poster

Talented, tenacious and telegenic: Lindros emerged as the superstar to carry the NHL into the 21st century.

boy in 1995, a star capable of carrying the league on his hopelessly broad shoulders for the next decade. He is the package: mean, tough, smart, telegenic, well-spoken. And English is his first language, a fact not lost on a league that has had to count on Europeans for its flair the past few seasons. The NHL remains a league of teams and not of players, but in terms of its marketing for the rest of the decade, NHL might as well stand for Now Here's Lindros. "The best player in the world," Buffalo general manager John Muckler raved. Flyer teammate Shawn Antoski said, "There's no one else out there capable of scoring 50 goals and using you as a speed bump." Lindros, who tied Pittsburgh's Jaromir Jagr with 70 points but lost the scoring title because Jagr had 32 goals to his 29, won the first of what figures to be a string of Hart Trophies. Lindros was flanked on the Legion of Doom by Mikael Renberg (6'1", 218) and John Leclair (6'2", 219). Leclair came in February from Montreal with Eric Desjardins, who was the Flyers' best defenseman, as part of a package for rightwinger Mark Recchi, a no-brainer as Most Lopsided Trade of the Year. Managing director Serge Savard now must rebuild the Canadiens, who failed to make the playoffs for the first time in a quarter of a century. Savard has practice; with one trade he rebuilt the Flyers.

The Flyers breezed into the Stanley Cup semifinals by brushing aside the New York Rangers in four games. The Rangers' Stanley Cup jinx now stands at one year. After ending a 54-year Cup drought the previous spring, the Rangers were a shadow of their dynamic and committed championship team. Indeed, New York was fortunate to even make the playoffs, slipping into the final spot in the Eastern Conference with 47 points. Goalie Mike Richter and defenseman Brian Leetch slipped, and many of New York's gritty players, including Esa Tikkanen, were exiled and replaced by able but inconsistent will-o'-the-wisps such as Petr Nedved. Only Mark Messier seemed to soldier on under Colin Campbell, who did not have the presence of former coach Mike Keenan.

Of course, few do. After winning the Cup Keenan lammed it to St. Louis, where, as coach and general manager, he began stockpiling veterans with Stanley Cup rings. Keenan and the Blues' deep pockets—the payroll reached $23 million last season—were supposed to produce immediate fireworks if not a Stanley Cup. Alas, the Blues were a dud. Not only did St. Louis lose to Vancouver in the first round, but there were also only a few of the contretemps surrounding a Keenan team that always provide dubious entertainment value. Keenan got along famously with his best scorer, Brett Hull, but clashed with Brendan Shanahan, a star power forward, and Curtis Joseph, a past playoff hero. They were traded during a wild summer in St. Louis as the Blues signed free agents Grant Fuhr, Dale Hawerchuk and Geoff Courtnall and acquired, among others, Shayne Corson and Chris Pronger. Keenan was on the prowl for "Mike kind of guys." The Blues finished with a creditable 61 points in 1995 and should be better in 1996, although the pregame introductions will be for the players' benefit as much as the fans'. This franchise takes some getting used to.

Hockey fans also will have to get used to the idea that Wayne Gretzky is mortal. Considering that the Great One owns every NHL career scoring record, this might be difficult. But Gretzky, who turned 34 last January, averaged (just!) one point per game in 1995, an estimable figure for almost anyone except a legend who entered the season averaging 2.185 points per game. Stuck on a mediocre Los Angeles King team with muddled ownership, Gretzky's genius came in flashes instead of in the floodlights. Perhaps the return of scoring rival Mario Lemieux to Pittsburgh in 1996—Lemieux skipped 1995 because of a bad back—and new coach Larry Robinson will lift Gretzky.

One team on the rise in 1995 was the Quebec Nordiques. They went from 300 feet above sea level to a mile high, moving to Denver when Marcel Aubut's ownership group sold them to COMSAT for $75 million after the season. The inevitable dividends of the Nordiques' ineptitude—since 1986 they drafted lower than 10th just once—finally paid off under rookie coach Marc Crawford, the Coach of the Year. The quicksilver Nordiques won the Eastern Conference with 65 points before losing to the Rangers in the first round. As the Denver Avalanche, the artists formerly known

DAVID E. KLUTHO

Quebec fans will miss Rookie of the Year Forsberg and the rest of the Nordiques, who are bound for Denver.

as the Nordiques have a nucleus that should make it the most exciting team of the late 1990s. Peter Forsberg, who had been called the best player not in the league, had a brilliant first NHL season, beating out Washington goalie Jim Carey, a March call-up, and Anaheim left wing Paul Kariya as Rookie of the Year.

The defection of the Nordiques and a last-minute and perhaps temporary reprieve for the seemingly Minneapolis-bound Winnipeg Jets sent a chill through the Great White North. Canada, victimized by its weak dollar (relative to the U.S. buck) and the smaller economy of scale, sensed that it was losing its game to the Americans. Attendance problems in many Canadian cities were attributed to lingering resentment over the lockout. Commissioner Gary Bettman said Canada will always be an important part of the NHL, and the league has vowed to tackle the discrepancies between currencies and a growing gap between haves and have-nots. But pessimists, including Hall of Famer Guy Lafleur, have predicted that of the seven remaining Canadian franchises, only Toronto and Montreal will still be in the NHL in 10 years. Woe, Canada.

FOR THE RECORD·1994–1995

NHL Final Team Standings

Western Conference

CENTRAL DIVISION

	GP	W	L	T	GF	GA	Pts
Detroit	48	33	11	4	180	117	70
St Louis	48	28	15	5	178	135	61
Chicago	48	24	19	5	156	115	53
Toronto	48	21	19	8	135	146	50
Dallas	48	17	23	8	136	135	42
Winnipeg	48	16	25	7	157	177	39

PACIFIC DIVISION

	GP	W	L	T	GF	GA	Pts
Calgary	48	24	17	7	163	135	55
Vancouver	48	18	18	12	153	148	48
San Jose	48	19	25	4	129	161	42
Los Angeles	48	16	23	9	142	174	41
Edmonton	48	17	27	4	136	183	38
Anaheim	48	16	27	5	125	164	37

Eastern Conference

NORTHEAST DIVISION

	GP	W	L	T	GF	GA	Pts
Quebec	48	30	13	5	185	134	65
Pittsburgh	48	29	16	3	181	158	61
Boston	48	27	18	3	150	127	57
Buffalo	48	22	19	7	130	119	51
Hartford	48	19	24	5	127	141	43
Montreal	48	18	23	7	125	148	43
Ottawa	48	9	34	5	117	174	23

ATLANTIC DIVISION

	GP	W	L	T	GF	GA	Pts
Philadelphia	48	28	16	4	150	132	60
New Jersey	48	22	18	8	136	121	52
Washington	48	22	18	8	136	120	52
NY Rangers	48	22	23	3	139	134	47
Florida	48	20	22	6	115	127	46
Tampa Bay	48	17	28	3	120	144	37
NY Islanders	48	15	28	5	126	158	35

1995 Stanley Cup Playoffs

Stanley Cup Playoff Results

Conference Quarterfinals

EASTERN CONFERENCE

May 6	NY Rangers	4	at Quebec	5	
May 8	NY Rangers	8	at Quebec	3	
May 10	Quebec	3	at NY Rangers	4	
May 12	Quebec	2	at NY Rangers	3*	
May 14	NY Rangers	2	at Quebec	4	
May 16	Quebec	2	at NY Rangers	4	
	NY Rangers won series 4-2.				

May 7	Buffalo	3	at Philadelphia	4*
May 8	Buffalo	1	at Philadelphia	3
May 10	Philadelphia	1	at Buffalo	3
May 12	Philadelphia	4	at Buffalo	2
May 14	Buffalo	4	at Philadelphia	6
	Philadelphia won series 4-1.			

Conference Quarterfinals (Cont.)

EASTERN CONFERENCE (Cont.)

May 6	Washington	5	at Pittsburgh	4	May 7	New Jersey	5	at Boston	0
May 8	Washington	3	at Pittsburgh	5	May 8	New Jersey	3	at Boston	0
May 10	Pittsburgh	2	at Washington	6	May 10	Boston	3	at New Jersey	2
May 12	Pittsburgh	2	at Washington	6	May 12	Boston	0	at New Jersey	1*
May 14	Washington	5	at Pittsburgh	6*	May 14	New Jersey	3	at Boston	2
May 16	Pittsburgh	7	at Washington	1		New Jersey won series 4-1.			
May 18	Washington	0	at Pittsburgh	3					

Pittsburgh won series 4-3.

WESTERN CONFERENCE

May 7	Dallas	3	at Detroit	4	May 7	San Jose	5	at Calgary	4
May 9	Dallas	1	at Detroit	4	May 9	San Jose	5	at Calgary	4*
May 11	Detroit	5	at Dallas	1	May 11	Calgary	9	at San Jose	2
May 14	Detroit	1	at Dallas	4	May 13	Calgary	6	at San Jose	4
May 15	Dallas	1	at Detroit	3	May 15	San Jose	0	at Calgary	5
	Detroit won series 4-1.				May 17	Calgary	3	at San Jose	5
					May 19	San Jose	5	at Calgary	4†

San Jose won series 4-3.

May 7	Vancouver	1	at St Louis	2	May 7	Toronto	5	at Chicago	3
May 9	Vancouver	5	at St Louis	3	May 9	Toronto	3	at Chicago	0
May 11	St Louis	1	at Vancouver	6	May 11	Chicago	3	at Toronto	2
May 13	St Louis	5	at Vancouver	2	May 13	Chicago	3	at Toronto	1
May 15	Vancouver	6	at St Louis	5*	May 15	Toronto	2	at Chicago	4
May 17	St Louis	8	at Vancouver	2	May 17	Chicago	4	at Toronto	5*
May 19	Vancouver	5	at St Louis	3	May 19	Toronto	2	at Chicago	5

Vancouver won series 4-3.   Chicago won series 4-3.

Conference Semifinals

WESTERN CONFERENCE

May 21	San Jose	0	at Detroit	6
May 23	San Jose	2	at Detroit	6
May 25	Detroit	6	at San Jose	2
May 27	Detroit	6	at San Jose	2

Detroit won series 4-0.

EASTERN CONFERENCE

May 21	NY Rangers	4	at Philadelphia	5*
May 22	NY Rangers	3	at Philadelphia	4*
May 24	Philadelphia	5	at NY Rangers	2
May 26	Philadelphia	4	at NY Rangers	1

Philadelphia won series 4-0.

May 21	Vancouver	1	at Chicago	2*
May 23	Vancouver	0	at Chicago	2
May 25	Chicago	3	at Vancouver	2*
May 27	Chicago	4	at Vancouver	3*

Chicago won series 4-0.

May 20	New Jersey	2	at Pittsburgh	3
May 22	New Jersey	4	at Pittsburgh	2
May 24	Pittsburgh	1	at New Jersey	5
May 26	Pittsburgh	1	at New Jersey	2*
May 28	New Jersey	4	at Pittsburgh	1

New Jersey won series 4-1.

Western Final

June 1	Chicago	1	at Detroit	2*
June 4	Chicago	2	at Detroit	3
June 6	Detroit	4	at Chicago	3†
June 8	Detroit	2	at Chicago	5
June 11	Chicago	1	at Detroit	2†

Detroit won series 4-1.

Eastern Final

June 3	New Jersey	4	at Philadelphia	1
June 5	New Jersey	5	at Philadelphia	2
June 7	Philadelphia	3	at New Jersey	2*
June 10	Philadelphia	4	at New Jersey	2
June 11	New Jersey	3	at Philadelphia	2
June 13	Philadelphia	2	at New Jersey	4

New Jersey won series 4-2.

Stanley Cup Championship

June 17	New Jersey	2	at Detroit	1
June 20	New Jersey	4	at Detroit	2
June 22	Detroit	2	at New Jersey	5
June 24	Detroit	2	at New Jersey	5

New Jersey won series 4-0.

*Overtime game. †Double overtime game.

Stanley Cup Championship Box Scores

Game 1

New Jersey 0   1   1—2
Detroit 0   1   0—1

FIRST PERIOD

Scoring: None. Penalties: Guerin, NJ (holding), 6:47; Konstantinov, Det (holding stick), 11:05.

SECOND PERIOD

Scoring: 1, NJ, Richer 5 (power play) (Albelin, Broten), 9:41. 2, Det, Ciccarelli 9 (power play) (Lidstrom, Coffey), 13:03. Penalties: Draper, Det (roughing), 9:35; Holik, NJ (high-sticking), 11:37; Lemieux, NJ (hooking),

13:41; Daneyko, NJ (roughing), 15:44; Ciccarelli, Det (roughing), 15:44

THIRD PERIOD

Scoring: 3, NJ, Lemieux 12 (MacLean, Chorske), 3:17. Penalty: Brown, Det (tripping), 4:48.

Shots on goal: NJ—9-10-9—28. Det—7-5-5—17.
Power-play opportunities: NJ 1-of-3; Det 1-of-3.
Goalies: NJ, Brodeur (17 shots, 16 saves). Det, Vernon (28 shots, 26 saves). A: 19,875.
Referee: McCreary. Linesmen: Murphy, Collins.

Game 2

New Jersey 0   1   3—4
Detroit 0   1   1—2

FIRST PERIOD

Scoring: None. Penalties: Stevens, NJ (roughing), :37; Ciccarelli, Det (slashing), 5:57; McCarty, Det (roughing), 8:49; Broten, NJ (high-sticking), 9:27.

SECOND PERIOD

Scoring: 1, Det, Kozlov 9 (power play) (Ciccarelli, Fedorov), 7:17. 2, NJ, MacLean 5 (Niedermayer, Broten), 9:40. Penalties: Brodeur, NJ, served by Rolston (delay of game), 6:56; Guerin, NJ (slashing), 8:58; McCarty, Det (slashing), 8:58; Errey, Det (charging), 16:01; Dowd, NJ (interference), 18:30.

THIRD PERIOD

Scoring: 3, Det, Fedorov 5 (Brown, Fetisov), 1:36. 4, NJ Niedermayer 4 (Dowd), 9:47. 5, NJ, Dowd 2 (Chambers, Albelin), 18:36. 6, NJ, Richer 6 (empty net) (Niedermayer), 19:39. Penalties: Holik, NJ (boarding), 4:58.

Shots on goal: NJ—3-9-11—23. Det—7-6-5—18.
Power-play opportunities: NJ 0-of 3; Det 1-of-5.
Goalies: NJ, Brodeur (18 shots, 16 saves). Det, Vernon (22 shots, 19 saves). A: 19,875.
Referee: Gregson. Linesmen: Scapinello, Bonney.

Game 3

Detroit 0   0   2—2
New Jersey 2   2   1—5

FIRST PERIOD

Scoring: 1, NJ, Driver 1 (power play) (Broten, MacLean), 10:30. 2, NJ, Lemieux 13 (Carpenter, Stevens), 16:52. Penalties: Lemieux, NJ (roughing), 1:09; Primeau, Det (slashing), 1:09; Konstantinov, Det (holding stick), 8:56; Holik, NJ (tripping), 10:58; Guerin, NJ (unsportsmanlike conduct), 16:38; Lapointe, Det (unsportsmanlike conduct), 16:38.

SECOND PERIOD

Scoring: 3, NJ, Broten 5 (Stevens, MacLean), 6:59. 4, NJ, McKay 8 (Holik, Driver), 8:20. Penalties: Broten, NJ (holding stick), 11:01; Primeau, Det (tripping), 16:03; Carpenter, NJ (cross checking), 19:47.

THIRD PERIOD

Scoring: 5, NJ, Holik 4 (power play) (Guerin, Richer), 8:14. 6, Det, Fedorov 6 (power play) (Fetisov, Brown),

16:57. 7, Det, Yzerman 4 (power play) (Sheppard, Lidstrom), 18:27. Penalties: Albelin, NJ (high sticking), 2:30; Konstantinov, Det (high sticking), 4:25; Draper, Det (high sticking), 5:17; Primeau, Det (cross checking), 6:31; Holik, NJ (cross checking), 8:44; Richer, NJ (hooking), 12:28; Taylor, Det (roughing), 15:37; Lapointe, Det (double roughing minor), 15:37; Ciccarelli, Det (roughing), 15:37; Guerin, NJ (boarding, roughing), 15:37; Brylin, NJ (high sticking, roughing), 15:37; Zelepukin, NJ (double roughing minor), 15:37.

Shots on goal: Det—7-5-12—24. NJ—15-8-8—31.
Power-play opportunities: Det 2-of-8; NJ 2-of-5.
Goalies: Det, Vernon (20 shots, 16 saves), Osgood (8:20 of 2nd period; 11 shots, 10 saves). NJ, Brodeur (24 shots, 22 saves). A: 19,040.
Referee: Fraser. Linesmen: Collins, Murphy.

Game 4

Detroit 2   0   0—2
New Jersey 2   1   2—5

FIRST PERIOD

Scoring: 1, NJ, Broten 6 (Richer, Chorske), 1:08. 2, Det, Fedorov 7 (Lapointe, Fetisov), 2:03. 3, Det, Coffey 6 (shorthanded) (Brown, Fedorov), 13:01. 4, NJ, Chambers 3 (Driver, MacLean), 17:45. Penalties: Errey, Det (hooking), 11:03; Daneyko, NJ (roughing), 13:36; Primeau, Det (goalie interference), 15:36.

SECOND PERIOD

Scoring: 5, NJ, Broten 7 (Niedermayer, Guerin), 7:56. Penalties: Daneyko, NJ (slashing), :30; Lapointe, Det (roughing), 10:09; Stevens, NJ (roughing), 10:09; Guerin, NJ (interference), 12:40; Konstantinov, Det (hooking), 19:12.

THIRD PERIOD

Scoring: 6, NJ, Brylin 1 (Rolston, Guerin), 7:46. 7, NJ, Chambers 4 (Brylin, Guerin), 12:32. Penalty: Grimson, Det (roughing), 10:24.

Shots on goal: Det—8-7-1—16. NJ—8-8-10—26.
Power-play opportunities: Det 0-of-3; NJ 0-of-4.
Goalies: Det, Vernon (26 shots, 21 saves). NJ, Brodeur (16 shots, 14 saves). A: 19,040.
Referee: McCreary. Linesmen: Bonney, Scapinello.

Individual Playoff Leaders

Scoring

POINTS

Player and Team	GP	G	A	Pts	+/–	PM	Player and Team	GP	G	A	Pts	+/–	PM
Sergei Fedorov, Det	17	7	17	24	13	6	Vyacheslav Kozlov, Det	18	9	7	16	12	10
Stephane Richer, NJ	19	6	15	21	9	2	Nicklas Lidstrom, Det	18	4	12	16	4	8
Neal Broten, NJ	20	7	12	19	13	6	Jaromir Jagr, Pitt	12	10	5	15	3	6
Ron Francis, Pitt	12	6	13	19	3	4	Rod Brind'amour, Phil	15	6	9	15	5	8
Denis Savard, Chi	16	7	11	18	12	10	Eric Lindros, Phil	12	4	11	15	7	18
Paul Coffey, Det	18	6	12	18	4	10	Larry Murphy, Pitt	12	2	13	15	3	0
John MacLean, NJ	20	5	13	18	8	14	Theoren Fleury, Cgy	7	7	7	14	8	2
Claude Lemieux, NJ	20	13	3	16	12	20	Brian Leetch, NYR	10	6	8	14	-1	8

GOALS

Player and Team	GP	G
Claude Lemieux, NJ	20	13
Jaromir Jagr, Pitt	12	10
Dino Ciccarelli, Det	16	9
Joe Murphy, Chi	16	9
Vyacheslav Koslov, Det	18	9

GAME WINNING GOALS

Player and Team	GP	GW
Vyacheslav Koslov, Det	18	4
Neal Broten, NJ	20	4
Chris Chelios, Chi	16	3
Joe Murphy, Chi	16	3
Claude Lemieux, NJ	20	3

ASSISTS

Player and Team	GP	A
Sergei Fedorov, Det	17	17
Stephane Richer, NJ	19	15
Ron Francis, Pitt	12	13
Larry Murphy, Pitt	12	13
John MacLean, NJ	20	13

POWER PLAY GOALS

Player and Team	GP	PP
Dino Ciccarelli, Det	16	6
Mike Rathje, SJ	11	5

10 tied with 3.

SHORT HANDED GOALS

Player and Team	GP	SH
Russ Courtnall, Van	11	2
Pavel Bure, Van	11	2

25 tied with one.

PLUS/MINUS

Player and Team	GP	+/–
Doug Brown, Det	18	14
Eric Desjardins, Phil	15	13
Bruce Driver, NJ	17	13
Sergei Fedorov, Det	17	13
Neal Broten, NJ	20	13

Goaltending (Minimum 420 minutes)

GOALS AGAINST AVERAGE

Player and Team	GP	Mins	GA	Avg
Martin Brodeur, NJ	20	1222	34	1.67
Ed Belfour, Chi	16	1014	37	2.19
Mike Vernon, Det	18	1063	41	2.31
Ron Hextall, Phil	15	897	42	2.81
Felix Potvin, Tor	7	424	20	2.83

SAVE PERCENTAGE

Player and Team	GP	Mins	GA	SA	Pct	W	L
Martin Brodeur, NJ	20	1222	34	463	.927	16	4
Ed Belfour, Chi	16	1014	37	479	.923	9	7
Felix Potvin, Tor	7	424	20	253	.920	3	4
Ken Wregget, Pitt	11	661	33	349	.905	5	6
Ron Hextall, Phil	15	897	42	437	.904	10	5

Expunsion Teams

There's a late-night parlor game that sports fans play in which one fan names a place and another comes up with the punniest possible nickname for a franchise based there. A team in Norman, Okla., for instance, would be called the Conquest; one in Augusta, Maine, would be the Wind. If you were a commissioner of a loopy sports league, you would want to expand to Alaska, so you could add the Nome Chomskys and the Juneau Whats, while an International Division would include the Havana Good Times, the Kenya Believeits, the Crimea Rivers and the Nice Guys, who would always finish last.

One perennial favorite in this fanciful league—the Macon Whoopees—actually existed in the old Southern Hockey League for a few months before folding during the 1973-1974 season. Last spring came word that those icemen of euphemism will be back. On May 2,1995, the Macon City Council approved the request of two businessmen, who are reviving the Whoopees, to play in that Georgia city's coliseum as part of a reconsituted SHL. Look for the Whoopees to begin play in the '96–'97 season. No word yet on whether Bob Eubanks wil do play-by-play.

Award	Player and Team	Award	Player and Team
Hart Trophy (MVP)	Eric Lindros, Phil	Selke Trophy (top defensive forward)	Ron Francis, Pitt
Calder Trophy (top rookie)	Peter Forsberg, Que	Adams Award (top coach)	Marc Crawford, Que
Vezina Trophy (top goaltender)	Dominik Hasek, Buff	Jennings Trophy (goaltender on	
Norris Trophy (top defenseman)	Paul Coffey, Det	club allowing fewest goals)	Ed Belfour, Chi
Lady Byng Trophy		Conn Smythe Trophy	
(for gentlemanly play)	Ron Francis, Pitt	(playoff MVP)	Claude Lemieux, NJ

NHL Individual Leaders

Scoring

POINTS

Player and Team	GP	G	A	Pts	+/−	PM	Player and Team	GP	G	A	Pts	+/−	PM
Jaromir Jagr, Pitt	48	32	38	70	23	37	Mikael Renberg, Phil	47	26	31	57	20	20
Eric Lindros, Phil	46	29	41	70	27	60	John Leclair, Mtl-Phil	46	26	28	54	20	30
Alexei Zhamnov, Winn	48	30	35	65	5	20	Mark Messier, NYR	46	14	39	53	8	40
Joe Sakic, Que	47	19	43	62	7	30	Adam Oates, Bos	48	12	41	53	-11	8
Ron Francis, Pitt	44	11	48	59	30	18	Bernie Nicholls, Chi	48	22	29	51	4	32
Theoren Fleury, Cgy	47	29	29	58	6	112	Keith Tkachuk, Winn	48	22	29	51	-4	152
Paul Coffey, Det	45	14	44	58	18	72	Four tied with 50.						

GOALS

Player and Team	GP	G
Peter Bondra, Wash	47	34
Jaromir Jagr, Pitt	48	32
Ray Sheppard, Det	43	30
Owen Nolan, Que	46	30
Alexei Zhamnov, Win	48	30

GAME WINNING GOALS

Player and Team	GP	GW
Owen Nolan, Que	46	8
Donald Audette, Buff	46	7
John Leclair, Mtl-Phil	46	7
Jaromir Jagr, Pitt	48	7
Brendan Shanahan, StL	45	6
Brett Hull, StL	48	6

ASSISTS

Player and Team	GP	A
Ron Francis, Pitt	44	48
Paul Coffey, Det	45	44
Joe Sakic, Que	47	43
Eric Lindros, Phil	46	41
Adam Oates, Bos	48	41

POWER PLAY GOALS

Player and Team	GP	PP
Cam Neely, Bos	42	16
Donald Audette, Buff	46	13
Owen Nolan, Que	46	13
Alex Mogilny, Buff	44	12
Peter Bondra, Wash	47	12

SHORT HANDED GOALS

Player and Team	GP	SHG
Peter Bondra, Wash	47	6
Wayne Presley, Buff	46	5
Eight tied with three.		

PLUS/MINUS

Player and Team	GP	+/−
Ron Francis, Pitt	44	30
Curtis Leschyshyn, Que	44	29
Steve Duchesne, StL	47	29
Eric Lindros, Phil	46	27
Jaromir Jagr, Pitt	48	23

Goaltending
(Minimum 13 games)

GOALS AGAINST AVERAGE

Player and Team	GP	Mins	GA	Avg
Dominik Hasek, Buff	41	2416	85	2.11
Rick Tabaracci, Wsh-Cgy	13	596	21	2.11
*Jim Carey, Wash	28	1604	57	2.13
Chris Osgood, Det	19	1087	41	2.26
Ed Belfour, Chi	42	2450	93	2.28

WINS

Player and Team	GP	Mins	W	L	T
Ken Wregget, Pitt	38	2208	25	9	2
Ed Belfour, Chi	42	2450	22	15	3
Trevor Kidd, Cgy	43	2463	22	14	6
Curtis Joseph, StL	36	1914	20	10	1
Four tied with 19.					

SAVE PERCENTAGE

Player and Team	GP	GA	SA	Pct	W	L	T
Dominik Hasek, Buff	41	85	1221	.930	19	14	7
Chris Osgood, Det	19	41	496	.917	14	5	0
Jocelyn Thibault, Que	18	35	423	.917	12	2	2
Andy Moog, Dall	31	72	846	.915	10	12	7
*Damian Rhodes, Tor	13	34	404	.915	6	6	1
J. Vanbiesbrouck, Fla	37	86	1000	.914	14	15	4

Three tied at .913.

SHUTOUTS

Player and Team	GP	Mins	SO	W	L	T
Dominik Hasek, Buff	41	2416	5	19	14	7
Ed Belfour, Chi	42	2450	5	22	15	3
*Jim Carey, Wash	28	1604	4	18	6	3
*Blaine Lacher, Bos	35	1965	4	19	11	2
Arturs Irbe, SJ	38	2043	4	14	19	3
J. Vanbiesbrouck, Fla	37	2087	4	14	15	4

* Rookie.

Anaheim Mighty Ducks

SCORING

Player	GP	G	A	Pts	+/–	PM
*Paul Kariya, L	47	18	21	39	-17	4
Shaun Van Allen, C	45	8	21	29	-4	32
Stephan Lebeau, C	38	8	16	24	6	12
Todd Krygier, L	35	11	11	22	1	10
Peter Douris, R	46	10	11	21	4	12
Patrik Carnback, R	41	6	15	21	-8	32
Bobby Dollas, D	45	7	13	20	-3	12
Bob Corkum, C	44	10	9	19	-7	25
Joe Sacco, R	41	10	8	18	-8	23
*Steve Rucchin, C	43	6	11	17	7	23
Mike Sillinger, R	28	4	11	15	4	8
*Oleg Tverdovsky, D	36	3	9	12	-6	14
*Valeri Karpov, L	30	4	7	11	-4	6
*Jason York, D	25	1	10	11	4	14
*Milos Holan, D	25	2	8	10	4	14
Garry Valk, L	36	3	6	9	-4	34
Tom Kurvers, D	22	4	3	7	-13	6
Randy Ladouceur, D	44	2	4	6	2	36
Dave Karpa, D	28	1	5	6	-1	91
*John Lilley, C	9	2	2	4	2	5
David Williams, D	21	2	2	4	-5	26
*Denny Lambert, L	13	1	3	4	3	4
Robert Dirk, D	38	1	3	4	-3	56

GOALTENDING

Player	GP	Mins	Avg	W	L	T	SO
Guy Hebert	39	2092	3.13	12	20	4	2
Mikhail Shtalenkov	18	810	3.63	4	7	1	0
Team total	48	2913	3.38	16	27	5	2

*Rookie.

Boston Bruins

SCORING

Player	GP	G	A	Pts	+/–	PM
Adam Oates, C	48	12	41	53	-11	8
Ray Bourque, D	46	12	31	43	3	20
Cam Neely, R	42	27	14	41	7	72
Bryan Smolinski, C	44	18	13	31	-3	31
*Mariusz Czerkawski, R	47	12	14	26	4	31
Mats Naslund, L	34	8	14	22	-4	4
Don Sweeney, D	47	3	19	22	6	24
Ted Donato, C	47	10	10	20	3	10
Jozef Stumpel, R	44	5	13	18	4	8
Steve Heinze, R	36	7	9	16	0	23
Alexei Kasatonov, D	44	2	14	16	-2	33
Brent Hughes, L	44	6	6	12	6	139
Stephen Leach, R	35	5	6	11	-3	68
*Jon Rohloff, D	34	3	8	11	1	39
Dave Reid, L	38	5	5	10	8	10
*Sandy Moger, R	18	2	6	8	-1	6
Glen Murray, R	35	5	2	7	-11	46
David Shaw, D	44	3	4	7	-9	36
Jamie Huscroft, D	34	0	6	6	-3	103
*John Gruden, D	38	0	6	6	3	22
*Fred Knipscheer, L	16	3	1	4	1	2
Mikko Makela, R	11	1	2	3	0	0

GOALTENDING

Player	GP	Mins	Avg	W	L	T	SO
*Blaine Lacher	35	1965	2.41	19	11	2	4
Vincent Riendeau	11	565	2.87	3	6	1	0
†Craig Billington	8	373	3.06	5	1	0	0
Team total	48	2911	2.62	27	18	3	4

†Played 9 games with Ottawa.

Child of Kings

When she was two years old and had been attending Los Angeles King games for less than a year, Jenna Belcher admonished her mother: "Sit down. I can't see the power play." Now, four years later, Jenna is an experienced television analyst. Filling in on Prime Sports network's pre-game show on April 12, Jenna, 6, appeared at ease, flashing made-for-TV dimples that disappeared only when she assessed the Kings' grim playoff prospects. Later that day Jenna joined the L.A. media in its ritual of tormenting coach Barry Melrose. "He's traded all the good players," she said of Melrose, who was fired nine days later.

Jenna's angelic blue eyes and drape of blonde hair belie an uncommon fearlessness. While attending one game, she rose to her full stature (4' 4") to challenge a fan who had been heckling goalie Kelly Hrudey. "Leave Kelly alone," she said. "He hurt his knee, and he can't get low."

Buffalo Sabres

SCORING

Player	GP	G	A	Pts	+/-	PM
Alexander Mogilny, R	44	19	28	47	0	36
Donald Audette, R	46	24	13	37	-3	27
Garry Galley, D	47	3	29	32	4	30
Pat LaFontaine, C	22	12	15	27	2	4
Yuri Khmylev, L	48	8	17	25	8	14
Derek Plante, C	47	3	19	22	-4	12
Doug Bodger, D	44	3	17	20	-3	47
Wayne Presley, R	46	14	5	19	5	41
Dale Hawerchuk, C	23	5	11	16	-2	2
Dave Hannan, C	42	4	12	16	3	32
Alexei Zhitnik, D	32	4	10	14	-6	61
Jason Dawe, L	42	7	4	11	-6	19
Craig Simpson, L	24	4	7	11	-5	26
Richard Smehlik, D	39	4	7	11	5	46
Bob Sweeney, C	45	5	4	9	-6	18
Scott Pearson, L	42	3	5	8	-14	74
Charlie Huddy, D	41	2	5	7	-7	42
Brad May, L	33	3	3	6	5	87
Craig Muni, D	40	0	6	6	-4	36
*Mark Astley, D	14	2	1	3	-2	12
Doug Houda, D	28	1	2	3	1	68
*Brian Holzinger, C	4	0	3	3	2	0
Rob Ray, L	46	0	3	3	-4	173

GOALTENDING

Player	GP	Mins	Avg	W	L	T	SO
Dominik Hasek	41	2416	2.11	19	14	7	5
†Robb Stauber	6	317	3.79	2	3	0	0
Grant Fuhr	3	180	4.00	1	2	0	0
Team total	48	2920	2.45	22	19	7	5

†Played 1 game with Los Angeles.

Calgary Flames

SCORING

Player	GP	G	A	Pts	+/-	PM
Theoren Fleury, R	47	29	29	58	6	112
Joe Nieuwendyk, C	46	21	29	50	11	33
Phil Housley, D	43	8	35	43	17	18
Robert Reichel, C	48	18	17	35	-2	28
Zarley Zalapski, D	48	4	24	28	9	46
Steve Chiasson, D	45	2	23	25	10	39
German Titov, C	40	12	12	24	6	16
Joel Otto, C	47	8	13	21	8	130
Wes Walz, C	39	6	12	18	7	11
Paul Kruse, L	45	11	5	16	13	141
Sheldon Kennedy, R	30	7	8	15	5	45
Ronnie Stern, R	39	9	4	13	4	163
Kevin Dahl, D	34	4	8	12	8	38
Kelly Kisio, C	12	7	4	11	2	6
Mike Sullivan, C	38	4	7	11	-2	14
Nikolai Borschevsky, R	27	0	10	10	10	0
James Patrick, D	43	0	10	10	-3	14
Sandy McCarthy, R	37	5	3	8	1	101
Leonard Esau, D	15	0	6	6	-10	15
Dan Keczmer, D	28	2	3	5	7	10
Alan May, L	34	2	3	5	3	119
Frank Musil, D	35	0	5	5	6	61
Gary Roberts, L	8	2	2	4	1	43
*Vesa Viitakoski, L	10	1	2	3	-1	6

GOALTENDING

Player	GP	Mins	Avg	W	L	T	SO
*Jason Muzzatti	1	10	.00	0	0	0	0
†Rick Tabaracci	5	202	1.49	2	0	1	0
Trevor Kidd	43	2463	2.61	22	14	6	3
*Andrei Trefilov	6	236	4.07	0	3	0	0
Team total	48	2922	2.77	24	17	7	3

†Played 8 games with Washington.

Chicago Blackhawks

SCORING

Player	GP	G	A	Pts	+/-	PM
Bernie Nicholls, C	48	22	29	51	4	32
Joe Murphy, R	40	23	18	41	7	89
Chris Chelios, D	48	5	33	38	17	72
Gary Suter, D	48	10	27	37	14	42
Tony Amonte, R	48	15	20	35	7	41
Jeremy Roenick, C	33	10	24	34	5	14
Patrick Poulin, L	45	15	15	39	13	53
Denis Savard, C	43	10	15	25	-3	18
*Sergei Krivokrasov, R	41	12	7	19	9	33
Jeff Shantz, C	45	6	12	18	11	33
Brent Sutter, C	47	7	8	15	6	51
Dirk Graham, R	40	4	9	13	2	42
Eric Weinrich, D	48	3	10	13	1	33
Steve Smith, D	48	1	12	13	6	128
Murray Craven, L	16	4	3	7	2	2
Brent Grieve, L	24	1	5	6	2	23
Jim Cummins, R	37	4	1	5	-6	158
Gerald Diduck, D	35	2	3	5	-5	63
Cam Russell, D	33	1	3	4	4	88
Greg Smyth, D	22	0	3	3	2	33
Ed Belfour, G	42	0	3	3	0	11

GOALTENDING

Player	GP	Mins	Avg	W	L	T	SO
Ed Belfour	42	2450	2.28	22	15	3	5
Jeff Hackett	7	328	2.38	1	3	2	0
Jim Waite	2	119	2.52	1	1	0	0
Team total	48	2909	2.37	24	19	5	5

*Rookie.

Dallas Stars

SCORING

Player	GP	G	A	Pts	+/–	PM
Dave Gagner, C	48	14	28	42	2	42
Mike Modano, C	30	12	17	29	7	8
Kevin Hatcher, D	47	10	19	29	-4	66
Mike Donnelly, L	44	12	15	27	-4	33
Corey Millen, C	45	5	18	23	6	36
Trent Klatt, R	47	12	10	22	-2	26
Greg Adams, L	43	8	13	21	-3	16
*Todd Harvey, C	40	11	9	20	-3	67
*Mike Kennedy, L	44	6	12	18	4	33
Grant Ledyard, D	38	5	13	18	6	20
Paul Broten, R	47	7	9	16	-7	36
Derian Hatcher, D	43	5	11	16	3	105
Dean Evason, C	47	8	7	15	3	48
Brent Gilchrist, C	32	9	4	13	-3	16
Paul Cavallini, D	44	1	11	12	8	28
Peter Zezel, C	30	6	5	11	-6	19
Craig Ludwig, D	47	2	7	9	-6	61
Doug Zmolek, D	42	0	5	5	-6	67
Shane Churla, R	27	1	3	4	0	186
*Jarkko Varvio, R	5	1	1	2	1	0
Richard Matvichuk, D	14	0	2	2	-7	14

GOALTENDING

Player	GP	Mins	Avg	W	L	T	SO
Andy Moog	31	1770	2.44	10	12	7	2
*E. Fernandez	1	59	3.05	0	1	0	0
Darcy Wakaluk	15	754	3.18	4	8	0	2
*Mike Torchia	6	327	3.30	3	2	1	0
Team	48	2925	2.77	17	23	8	4

Detroit Red Wings

SCORING

Player	GP	G	A	Pts	+/–	PM
Paul Coffey, D	45	14	44	58	18	72
Sergei Fedorov, C	42	20	30	50	6	24
Dino Ciccarelli, R	42	16	27	43	12	39
Keith Primeau, L	45	15	27	42	17	99
Ray Sheppard, R	43	30	10	40	11	17
Steve Yzerman, C	47	12	26	38	6	40
Vyacheslav Kozlov, C	46	13	20	33	12	45
Nicklas Lidstrom, D	43	10	16	26	15	6
Doug Brown, R	45	9	12	21	14	16
Bob Errey, L	43	8	13	21	13	58
Viacheslav Fetisov, D	18	3	12	15	1	2
Shawn Burr, L	42	6	8	14	13	60
Vlad. Konstantinov, D	47	3	11	14	10	101
Darren McCarty, R	31	5	8	13	5	88
Martin Lapointe, R	39	4	6	10	1	73
Greg Johnson, C	22	3	5	8	1	-14
Kris Draper, C	36	2	6	8	1	22
Bob Rouse, D	48	1	7	8	14	36
Mark Howe, D	18	1	5	6	-3	10
Mike Krushelnyski, C	20	2	3	5	3	6
*Tim Taylor, C	22	0	4	4	3	16
Terry Carkner, D	20	1	2	3	7	21
Mike Ramsey, D	33	1	2	3	11	23

GOALTENDING

Player	GP	Mins	Avg	W	L	T	S
Chris Osgood	19	1087	2.26	14	5	0	1
Mike Vernon	30	1807	2.52	19	6	4	1
Team total	48	2900	2.42	33	11	4	2

Edmonton Oilers

SCORING

Player	GP	G	A	Pts	+/–	PM
Doug Weight, C	48	7	33	40	-17	69
Jason Arnott, C	42	15	22	37	-14	128
Shayne Corson, L	48	12	24	36	-17	86
*David Oliver, R	44	16	14	30	-11	20
*Todd Marchant, C	45	13	14	28	-3	32
Kelly Buchberger, L	48	7	17	24	0	82
Scott Thornton, C	47	10	12	22	-4	89
Igor Kravchuk, D	36	7	11	18	-15	29
Mike Stapleton, C	46	6	11	17	-12	21
Luke Richardson, D	46	3	10	13	-6	40
Jiri Slegr, D	31	2	10	12	-5	46
Kirk Maltby, R	47	8	3	11	-11	49
Dean Kennedy, D	40	2	8	10	2	25
Fredrik Olausson, D	33	0	10	10	-4	20
Boris Mironov, D	29	1	7	8	-9	40
Ken Sutton, D	24	4	3	7	-3	42
*Peter White, C	9	2	4	6	1	0
Bryan Marchment, D	40	1	5	6	-11	184
Zdeno Ciger, L	5	2	2	4	-1	0
Iain Fraser, C	13	3	0	3	0	0
Louie Debrusk, L	34	2	0	2	-4	93
Gordon Mark, D	18	0	2	2	-9	35
Bill Ranford, G	40	0	2	2	0	2

GOALTENDING

Player	GP	Mins	Avg	W	L	T	SO
Bill Ranford	40	2203	3.62	15	20	3	2
*Fred Brathwaite	14	601	3.99	2	5	1	0
*Joaquin Gage	2	99	4.24	0	2	0	0
Team total	48	2912	3.77	17	27	4	2

* Rookie.

Florida Panthers

SCORING

Player	GP	G	A	Pts	+/-	PM
Jesse Belanger, C	47	15	14	29	-5	18
Stu Barnes, C	41	10	19	29	7	8
Scott Mellanby, R	48	13	12	25	-16	90
Gord Murphy, D	46	6	16	22	-14	24
Dave Lowry, L	45	10	10	20	-3	25
Jody Hull, R	46	11	8	19	-1	8
Bill Lindsay, L	48	10	9	19	1	46
Tom Fitzgerald, R	48	3	13	16	-3	31
Brian Skrudland, C	48	5	9	14	0	88
Johan Garpenlov, L	40	4	10	14	1	2
Mike Hough, L	48	6	7	13	1	38
Jason Woolley, D	34	4	9	13	-1	18
Gaetan Duchesne, L	46	3	9	12	-3	16
Rob Niedermayer, C	48	4	6	10	-13	36
Bob Kudelski, R	26	6	3	9	2	2
Brian Benning, D	24	1	7	8	-6	18
Magnus Svensson, D	19	2	5	7	5	10
Andrei Lomakin, L	31	1	6	7	-5	6
Paul Laus, D	37	0	7	7	12	138

GOALTENDING

Player	GP	Mins	Avg	W	L	T	SO
J. Vanbiesbrouck	37	2087	2.47	14	15	4	4
Mark Fitzpatrick	15	819	2.64	6	7	2	2
Team total	48	2916	2.61	20	22	6	6

Hartford Whalers

SCORING

Player	GP	G	A	Pts	+/-	PM
Andrew Cassels, C	46	7	30	37	-3	18
Darren Turcotte, C	47	17	18	35	1	22
Geoff Sanderson, C	46	18	14	32	-10	24
Steven Rice, R	40	11	10	21	2	61
Paul Ranheim, L	47	6	14	20	-3	10
Frantisek Kucera, D	48	3	17	20	3	30
Jimmy Carson, C	38	9	10	19	5	29
Robert Kron, C	38	10	8	18	-3	10
*Andrei Nikolishin, R	39	8	10	18	7	10
Adam Burt, D	46	7	11	18	0	65
Glen Wesley, D	48	2	14	16	-6	50
Chris Pronger, D	43	5	9	14	-12	54
Jocelyn Lemieux, L	41	6	5	11	-7	32
Ted Drury, C	34	3	6	9	-3	21
Mark Janssens, C	46	2	5	7	-8	93
Brian Glynn, D	43	1	6	7	-2	32
*Kevin Smyth, R	16	1	5	6	-3	13
Igor Chibirev, C	8	3	1	4	1	0
Kelly Chase, R	28	0	4	4	0	141
Glen Featherstone, D	19	2	1	3	-7	50
Jim Storm, L	6	0	3	3	2	0
*Scott Daniels, L	12	0	2	2	1	55

GOALTENDING

Player	GP	Mins	Avg	W	L	T	SO
Sean Burke	42	2418	2.68	17	19	4	0
Jeff Reese	11	477	3.27	2	5	1	0
Team total	48	2914	2.90	19	24	5	0

*Rookie.

Los Angeles Kings

SCORING

Player	GP	G	A	Pts	+/-	PM
Wayne Gretzky, C	48	11	37	48	-20	6
Rick Tocchet, R	36	18	17	35	-8	70
Dan Quinn, C	44	14	17	31	-3	32
Jari Kurri, L	38	10	19	29	-17	24
Tony Granato, L	33	13	11	24	9	68
Darryl Sydor, D	48	4	19	23	-2	36
Marty McSorley, D	41	3	18	21	-14	83
John Druce, R	43	15	5	20	-3	20
Randy Burridge, L	40	4	15	19	-4	10
Michel Petit, D	40	5	12	18	4	84
*Eric Lacroix, L	45	9	7	16	2	54
Pat Conacher, L	48	7	9	16	-9	12
Robert Lang, C	36	4	8	12	-7	4
Rob Blake, D	24	4	7	11	-16	38
Kevin Todd, C	33	3	8	11	-5	12
Gary Shuchuk, C	22	3	6	9	-2	6
*Chris Snell, D	32	2	7	9	-7	22
Rob Cowie, D	32	2	7	9	-6	20
*Yanic Perreault, C	26	2	5	7	3	20
Philippe Boucher, D	15	2	4	6	3	4
*Kevin Brown, R	23	2	3	5	-7	18
Troy Crowder, R	29	1	2	3	0	99

GOALTENDING

Player	GP	Mins	Avg	W	L	T	SO
*Pauli Jaks	1	40	3.00	0	0	0	0
Kelly Hrudey	35	1894	3.14	14	13	5	0
*Jamie Storr	5	263	3.88	1	3	1	0
†Grant Fuhr	14	698	4.04	1	7	3	0
Robb Stauber	1	16	7.50	0	0	0	0
Team total	48	2925	3.57	16	23	9	0

†Played 3 games with Buffalo.

Montreal Canadiens

SCORING

Player	GP	G	A	Pts	+/-	PM
Mark Recchi, R	49	16	32	48	-9	28
Pierre Turgeon, C	49	24	23	47	0	14
Vincent Damphousse, L	48	10	30	40	15	42
Benoit Brunet, L	45	7	18	25	7	16
Vladimir Malakhov, D	40	4	17	21	-3	46
Mike Keane, R	48	10	10	20	5	15
*Brian Savage, C	37	12	7	19	5	27
Brian Bellows, L	41	8	8	16	-7	8
Patrice Brisebois, D	35	4	8	12	-2	26
Yves Racine, D	47	4	7	11	-1	42
Lyle Odelein, D	48	3	7	10	-13	152
J. J. Daigneault, D	45	3	5	8	2	40
*Turner Stevenson, R	41	6	1	7	0	86
Bryan Fogarty, D	21	5	2	7	-3	34
Oleg Petrov, R	12	2	3	5	-7	4
Ed Ronan, R	30	1	4	5	-7	12
Peter Popovic, D	33	0	5	5	-10	8
*Valeri Bure, R	24	3	1	4	-1	6
Mark Lamb, C	47	1	2	3	-12	20
*Donald Brashear, L	20	1	1	2	-5	63

GOALTENDING

Player	GP	Mins	Avg	W	L	T	SO
Patrick Roy	43	2566	2.97	17	20	6	1
Ron Tugnutt	7	346	3.12	1	3	1	0
Team total	48	2921	3.04	18	23	7	1

New Jersey Devils

SCORING

Player	GP	G	A	Pts	+/–	PM
Stephane Richer, R	45	23	16	39	8	10
Neal Broten, C	47	8	24	32	1	24
John MacLean, R	46	17	12	29	13	32
Bill Guerin, R	48	12	13	25	6	72
Scott Stevens, D	48	2	20	22	4	56
Shawn Chambers, D	45	4	17	21	2	12
Bobby Holik, L	48	10	10	20	9	18
Claude Lemieux, R	45	6	13	19	2	86
Scott Niedermayer, D	48	4	15	19	19	18
Tom Chorske, L	42	10	8	18	-4	16
*Brian Rolston, C	40	7	11	18	5	17
Bob Carpenter, L	41	5	11	16	-1	19
Bruce Driver, D	41	4	12	16	-1	18
Tommy Albelin, D	48	5	10	15	9	20
*Sergei Brylin, C	26	6	8	14	12	8
Randy McKay, R	33	5	7	12	10	44
Mike Peluso, L	46	2	9	11	5	167
Danton Cole, R	38	4	5	9	-1	14
Jim Dowd, C	10	1	4	5	-5	0
Valeri Zelepukin, L	4	1	2	3	3	6
Ken Daneyko, D	25	1	2	3	4	54
*Chris McAlpine, D	24	0	3	3	4	17

GOALTENDING

Player	GP	Mins	Avg	W	L	T	SO
Martin Brodeur	40	2184	2.45	19	11	6	3
Chris Terreri	15	734	2.53	3	7	2	0
Team total	48	2926	2.48	22	18	8	3

New York Islanders

SCORING

Player	GP	G	A	Pts	+/–	PM
Ray Ferraro, C	47	22	21	43	1	30
Mathieu Schneider, D	43	8	21	29	-8	79
Kirk Muller, L	45	11	16	27	-18	47
Patrick Flatley, R	45	7	20	27	9	12
Steve Thomas, L	47	11	15	26	-14	60
Derek King, L	43	10	16	26	-5	41
*Zigmund Palffy, L	33	10	7	17	3	6
Marty McInnis, C	41	9	7	16	-1	8
Scott Lachance, D	26	6	7	13	2	26
Travis Green, C	42	5	7	12	-10	25
Dennis Vaske, D	41	1	11	12	3	53
Bob Beers, D	22	2	7	9	-8	6
Brent Severyn, D	28	2	4	6	-2	71
Brad Dalgarno, R	22	3	2	5	-8	14
*Chris Marinucci, C	12	1	4	5	-1	2
Ron Sutter, C	27	1	4	5	-8	21
*Brett Lindros, R	33	1	3	4	-8	100
Chris Luongo, D	47	1	3	4	-2	36
Paul Stanton, D	18	0	4	4	-6	9
*Chris Taylor, C	10	0	3	3	1	2

GOALTENDING

Player	GP	Mins	Avg	W	L	T	SO
*Tommy Salo	6	358	3.02	1	5	0	0
T. Soderstrom	26	1350	3.11	8	12	3	1
*Jamie McLennan	21	1185	3.39	6	11	2	0
Team total	48	2909	3.26	15	28	5	1

* Rookie.

New York Rangers

SCORING

Player	GP	G	A	Pts	+/–	PM
Mark Messier, C	46	14	39	53	8	40
Brian Leetch, D	48	9	32	41	0	18
Sergei Zubov, D	38	10	26	36	-2	18
Pat Verbeek, R	48	17	16	33	-2	71
Adam Graves, C	47	17	14	31	9	51
Steve Larmer, R	47	14	15	29	8	16
Alexei Kovalev, R	48	13	15	28	-6	30
Brian Noonan, R	45	14	13	27	-3	26
Petr Nedved, C	46	11	12	23	-1	26
Sergei Nemchinov, C	47	7	6	13	-6	16
A. Karpovtsev, D	47	4	8	12	-4	30
Troy Loney, L	30	5	4	9	-2	23
Jay Wells, D	43	2	7	9	0	36
Nathan Lafayette, C	39	4	4	8	3	2
Stephane Matteau, L	41	3	5	8	-8	25
Kevin Lowe, D	44	1	7	8	-2	58
Mark Osborne, L	37	1	3	4	-2	19
Nick Kypreos, L	40	1	3	4	0	93
Jeff Beukeboom, D	44	11	3	4	3	70
Joey Kocur, R	48	1	2	3	-4	71
*Mattias Norstrom, D	9	0	3	3	2	2

GOALTENDING

Player	GP	Mins	Avg	W	L	T	SO
Glenn Healy	17	888	2.36	8	6	1	1
Mike Richter	35	1993	2.92	14	17	2	2
Team total	48	2895	2.78	22	23	3	3

Ottawa Senators

SCORING

Player	GP	G	A	Pts	+/–	PM
Alexei Yashin, C	47	21	23	44	-20	20
Alexandre Daigle, C	47	16	21	37	-22	14
Sylvain Turgeon, L	33	11	8	19	-1	29
Martin Straka, R	37	5	13	18	-1	16
*Steve Larouche, C	18	8	7	15	-5	6
Sean Hill, D	45	1	14	15	-11	30
Rob Gaudreau, C	36	5	9	14	-16	8
Michel Picard, L	24	5	8	13	-1	14
Scott Levins, C	24	5	6	11	4	51
Dave McLlwain, C	43	5	6	11	-26	22
*Radek Bonk, C	42	3	8	11	-5	28
Randy Cunneyworth, L	48	5	5	10	-19	68
Pat Elynuik, R	41	3	7	10	-11	51
Troy Mallette, L	23	3	5	8	6	35
Chris Dahlquist, D	46	1	7	8	-30	36
*Pavol Demitra, R	16	4	3	7	-4	0
Phil Bourque, L	38	4	37	7	-17	20
Kerry Huffman, D	37	2	4	6	-17	46
David Archibald, C	14	2	2	4	-7	19
*Stanislav Neckar, D	48	1	3	4	-20	37
Dennis Vial, D	27	0	4	4	0	65
Evgeny Davydov, R	3	1	2	3	2	0

GOALTENDING

Player	GP	Mins	Avg	W	L	T	SO
*Mike Bales	1	3	.00	0	0	0	0
Don Beaupre	38	2161	3.36	8	25	3	1
Darrin Madeley	5	255	3.53	1	3	0	0
Craig Billington	9	472	4.07	0	6	2	0
Team total	48	2913	3.58	9	34	5	1

Philadelphia Flyers

SCORING

Player	GP	G	A	Pts	+/–	PM
Eric Lindros, C	46	29	41	70	27	60
Mikael Renburg, L	47	26	31	57	20	20
John Leclair, C	46	26	28	54	20	30
Rod Brind'amour, C	48	12	27	39	-4	33
Eric Desjardins, D	43	5	24	29	12	14
Dimitri Yushkevich, D	40	5	9	14	-4	47
Kevin Dineen, R	40	8	5	13	-1	39
*Chris Therien, D	48	3	10	13	8	38
Brent Fedyk, R	30	8	4	12	-2	14
Craig MacTavish, C	45	3	9	12	2	23
Anatoli Semenov, C	41	4	6	10	-12	10
Shjon Podein, C	44	3	7	10	-2	33
Kevin Haller, D	36	2	7	9	16	48
Gilbert Dionne, L	26	0	9	9	-4	4
Karl Dykhuis, D	33	2	6	8	7	37
Petr Svoboda, D	37	0	8	8	-5	70
*Patrick Juhlin, L	42	4	3	7	-13	6
Rob Dimaio, C	36	3	1	4	8	53
Dave Brown, R	28	1	2	3	-1	53
Jim Montgomery, C	13	1	1	2	-4	8

GOALTENDING

Player	GP	Mins	Avg	W	L	T	SO
Dominic Roussel	19	1075	2.34	11	7	0	1
Ron Hextall	31	1824	2.89	17	9	4	1
Team total	48	2906	2.73	28	16	4	2

Pittsburgh Penguins

SCORING

Player	GP	G	A	Pts	+/–	PM
Jaromir Jagr, R	48	32	38	70	23	37
Ron Francis, C	44	11	48	59	30	18
Tomas Sandstrom, R	47	21	23	44	1	42
Luc Robitaille, L	46	23	19	42	10	37
Larry Murphy, D	48	13	25	38	12	18
Joe Mullen, R	45	16	21	37	15	6
John Cullen, C	46	13	24	37	-4	66
Kevin Stevens, L	27	15	12	27	0	51
Shawn McEachern, C	44	13	13	26	4	22
Norm Maciver, D	41	4	16	20	-2	16
Troy Murray, C	46	4	12	16	-2	39
Ulf Samuelsson, D	44	1	15	16	11	113
Chris Joseph, D	33	5	10	15	3	46
*Len Barrie, C	48	3	11	14	-4	66
Mike Hudson, C	40	2	9	11	-1	34
Kjell Samuelsson, D	41	1	6	7	8	54
Greg Hawgood, D	21	1	4	5	2	25
Markus Naslund, R	14	2	2	4	0	2
*Greg Andrusak, D	7	0	4	4	-1	6
Jim McKenzie, L	39	2	1	3	-7	63

GOALTENDING

Player	GP	Mins	Avg	W	L	T	SO
*P. De Rouville	1	60	3.00	1	0	0	0
Ken Wregget	38	2208	3.21	25	9	2	0
Wendell Young	10	497	3.26	3	6	0	0
Tom Barrasso	2	125	3.84	0	1	1	0
Team total	48	2901	3.27	29	16	3	0

Quebec Nordiques

SCORING

Player	GP	G	A	Pts	+/–	PM
Joe Sakic, C	47	19	43	62	7	30
*Peter Forsberg, C	47	15	35	50	17	16
Owen Nolan, R	46	30	19	49	21	46
Scott Young, R	48	18	21	39	9	14
Mike Ricci, C	48	15	21	36	5	40
Wendel Clark, L	37	12	18	30	-1	45
Valeri Kamensky, L	40	10	20	30	3	22
Bob Bassen, C	47	12	15	27	14	33
Andrei Kovalenko, R	45	14	10	24	-4	31
Uwe Krupp, D	44	6	17	23	14	20
*Adam Deadmarsh, R	48	9	8	17	16	56
Curtis Leschyshyn, D	44	2	13	15	29	20
Sylvain Lefebvre, D	48	2	11	13	13	17
Claude Lapointe, C	29	4	8	12	5	41
Chris Simon, L	29	3	9	12	14	106
Martin Rucinsky, L	20	3	6	9	5	14
Craig Wolanin, D	40	3	6	9	12	40
Adam Foote, D	35	0	7	7	17	52
Bill Huard, L	33	3	3	6	0	77
Paul MacDermid, R	14	3	1	4	3	22
*Dwayne Norris, R	13	1	2	3	1	2
Alexei Gusarov, D	14	1	2	3	-1	6
*Rene Corbet, L	8	0	3	3	3	2
*Aaron Miller, D	9	0	3	3	2	6
*Janne Laukkanen, D	11	0	3	3	3	4
Stephane Fiset, G	32	0	3	3	0	2
Steven Finn, D	40	0	3	3	1	64

GOALTENDING

Player	GP	Mins	Avg	W	L	T	SO
Jocelyn Thibault	18	898	2.34	12	2	2	1
Stephane Fiset	32	1879	2.78	17	10	3	2
*Garth Snow	2	119	5.55	1	1	0	0
Team total	48	2908	2.76	30	13	5	3

* Rookie.

St Louis Blues
SCORING

Player	GP	G	A	Pts	+/–	PM
Brett Hull, R	48	29	21	50	13	10
Brendan Shanahan, L	45	20	21	40	7	136
Steve Duchesne, D	47	12	26	38	29	36
Esa Tikkanen, L	43	12	23	35	13	22
Adam Creighton, C	48	14	20	34	17	74
Jeff Norton, D	48	3	27	30	22	72
Al MacInnis, D	32	8	20	28	19	43
*Ian Laperriere, C	37	13	14	27	12	85
Glenn Anderson, R	36	12	14	26	9	37
Greg Gilbert, L	46	11	14	25	22	11
Todd Elik, C	35	9	14	23	8	22
Bill Houlder, D	41	5	13	18	16	20
*Denis Chasse, R	47	7	9	16	12	133
Guy Carbonneau, C	42	5	11	16	11	16
*Patrice Tardif, C	27	3	10	13	4	29
*David Roberts, L	19	6	5	11	2	10
Vitali Karamnov, L	26	3	7	10	7	14
Doug Lidster, D	37	2	7	9	9	12
*Craig Johnson, L	15	3	3	6	4	6
Rick Zombo, D	23	1	4	5	7	24
Basil McRae, L	21	0	5	5	4	72
Murray Baron, D	39	0	5	5	9	93
Tony Twist, L	28	3	0	3	0	89
Donald Dufresne, D	22	0	3	3	2	10
Peter Stastny, C	6	1	1	2	1	0

GOALTENDING

Player	GP	Mins	Avg	W	L	T	SO
Jon Casey	19	872	2.75	7	5	4	0
Curtis Joseph	36	1914	2.79	20	10	1	1
*Geoff Sarjeant	4	120	3.00	1	0	0	0
Team total	48	2912	2.78	28	15	5	1

San Jose Sharks
SCORING

Player	GP	G	A	Pts	+/–	PM
Ulf Dahlen, R	46	11	23	34	-2	11
Craig Janney, C	35	7	20	27	-1	10
*Jeff Friesen, L	48	15	10	25	-8	14
Ray Whitney, C	39	13	12	25	-7	14
Sandis Ozolinsh, D	48	9	16	25	-6	30
Sergei Makarov, R	43	10	14	24	-4	40
Igor Larionov, C	33	4	20	24	-3	14
Kevin Miller, R	36	8	12	20	4	13
Pat Falloon, R	46	12	7	19	-4	25
Tom Pederson, D	47	5	11	16	-14	31
Chris Tancill, C	26	3	11	14	1	10
Jamie Baker, C	43	7	4	11	-7	22
Mike Rathje, D	42	2	7	9	-1	29
*Andrei Nazarov, R	26	3	5	8	-1	94
Jeff Odgers, R	48	4	3	7	-8	117
Jim Kyte, D	18	2	5	7	-7	33
Jay More, D	45	0	6	6	7	71
Ilya Byakin, D	13	0	5	5	-9	14
*Michal Sykora, D	16	0	4	4	6	10

GOALTENDING

Player	GP	Mins	Avg	W	L	T	SO
Wade Flaherty	18	852	3.10	5	6	1	1
Arturs Irbe	38	2043	3.26	14	19	3	4
Team total	48	2904	3.33	19	25	4	5

Tampa Bay Lightning
SCORING

Player	GP	G	A	Pts	+/–	PM
Brian Bradley, C	46	13	27	40	-6	42
Paul Ysebaert, L	44	12	16	28	3	18
Chris Gratton, C	46	7	20	27	-2	89
Petr Klima, R	47	13	13	26	-13	26
John Tucker, R	46	12	13	25	-10	14
Roman Hamrlik, D	48	12	11	23	-18	86
Alexander Semak, C	41	7	11	18	-7	25
*Alexander Selivanov, R	43	10	6	16	-2	14
Rob Zamuner, L	43	9	6	15	-3	24
Marc Bureau, C	48	2	12	14	-8	30
Mikael Andersson, L	36	4	7	11	-3	4
Enrico Ciccone, D	41	2	4	6	3	225
Mark Bergevin, D	44	2	4	6	-6	51
*Cory Cross, D	43	1	5	6	-6	41

Player	GP	G	A	Pts	+/–	PM
Bob Halkidis, D	31	1	4	5	-10	46
*Jason Wiemer, L	36	1	4	5	-2	44
*Eric Charron, D	45	1	4	5	1	26
Adrien Plavsic, D	18	2	2	4	8	8
*Brantt Myhres, R	15	2	0	2	-2	81
Rudy Poeschek, D	25	1	1	2	0	92
*Ben Hankinson, R	26	0	2	2	-5	13

GOALTENDING

Player	GP	Mins	Avg	W	L	T	SO
Daren Puppa	36	2013	2.68	14	19	2	1
J.C. Bergeron	17	883	3.33	3	9	1	1
Team total	48	2906	2.97	17	28	3	2

* Rookie.

Toronto Maple Leafs

SCORING

Player	GP	G	A	Pts	+/–	PM
Mats Sundin, C	47	23	24	47	-5	14
Dave Andreychuk, L	48	22	16	38	-7	34
Mike Ridley, C	48	10	27	37	1	14
Doug Gilmour, C	44	10	23	33	-5	26
Todd Gill, D	47	7	25	32	-8	64
Randy Wood, L	48	13	11	24	7	34
Mike Gartner, R	38	12	8	20	0	6
Dmitri Mironov, D	33	5	12	17	6	28
Benoit Hogue, C	45	9	7	16	0	34
Dave Ellett, D	33	5	10	15	-6	26
Paul Dipietro, C	34	5	6	11	-9	10
Mike Craig, R	37	5	5	10	-21	12
Jamie Macoun, D	46	2	8	10	-6	75
Tie Domi, R	40	4	5	9	-5	159
*Kenny Jonsson, D	39	2	7	9	-8	16
Garth Butcher, D	45	1	7	8	-5	59
Warren Rychel, L	33	1	6	7	-4	120
Bill Berg, L	32	5	1	6	-11	26
Grant Jennings, D	35	0	6	6	-4	43
Terry Yake, R	19	3	2	5	1	2
Dixon Ward, R	22	0	3	3	-4	31
Rich Sutter, R	37	0	3	3	-6	38

GOALTENDING

Player	GP	Mins	Avg	W	L	T	SO
*Damian Rhodes	13	760	2.68	6	6	1	0
Felix Potvin	36	2144	2.91	15	13	7	0
Team total	48	2920	3.00	21	19	8	0

Vancouver Canucks

SCORING

Player	GP	G	A	Pts	+/–	PM
Pavel Bure, L	44	20	23	43	-8	47
Trevor Linden, C	48	18	22	40	-5	40
Russ Courtnall, R	45	11	24	35	2	17
Geoff Courtnall, L	45	16	18	34	2	81
Josef Beranek, C	51	13	18	31	-7	30
Jeff Brown, D	33	8	23	31	-2	16
Sergio Momesso, L	48	10	15	25	-2	65
Cliff Ronning, C	41	6	19	25	-4	27
Martin Gelinas, L	46	13	10	23	8	36
*Roman Oksiuta, R	38	16	4	20	-12	10
Christian Ruuttu, C	45	7	11	18	14	29
Jyrki Lumme, D	36	5	12	17	4	26
Dave Babych, D	40	3	11	14	-13	18
Bret Hedican, D	45	2	11	13	-3	34
*Mike Peca, C	33	6	6	12	-6	30
Gino Odjick, L	23	4	5	9	-3	109
Dana Murzyn, D	40	0	8	8	14	129
Tim Hunter, R	34	3	2	5	1	120
John McIntyre, C	28	0	4	4	-3	37
*Jassen Cullimore, D	34	1	2	3	-2	39
*Y. Namestnikov, D	16	0	3	3	2	4

GOALTENDING

Player	GP	Mins	Avg	W	L	T	SO
Kirk McLean	40	2374	2.75	18	12	10	1
Kay Whitmore	11	558	3.98	0	6	2	0
Team total	48	2942	3.02	18	18	12	1

Washington Capitals

SCORING

Player	GP	G	A	Pts	+/–	PM
Peter Bondra, R	47	34	9	43	9	24
Joe Juneau, C	44	5	38	43	-1	8
Michal Pivonka, C	46	10	23	33	3	50
Calle Johansson, D	46	5	26	31	-6	35
Dimitri Khristich, L	48	12	14	26	0	41
Steve Konowalchuk, C	46	11	14	25	7	44
Kelly Miller, L	48	10	13	23	5	6
Dale Hunter, C	45	8	15	23	-4	101
Keith Jones, R	40	14	6	20	-2	65
Sylvain Cote, D	47	5	14	19	2	53
Jim Johnson, D	47	0	13	13	6	43
Mark Tinordi, D	42	3	9	12	-5	71
Dave Poulin, C	29	4	5	9	2	10
Mike Eagles, C	40	3	4	7	-11	48
*Sergei Gonchar, D	31	2	5	7	4	22
Joe Reekie, D	48	1	6	7	10	97
Craig Berube, L	43	2	4	6	-5	173
Rob Pearson, R	32	0	6	6	-6	96
Igor Ulanov, D	22	1	4	5	1	29
*Ken Klee, D	23	3	1	4	2	41
Pat Peake, C	18	0	4	4	-6	12
*Martin Gendron, R	8	2	1	3	3	2
*Jason Allison, C	12	2	1	3	-3	6
John Slaney, D	16	0	3	3	-3	6

GOALTENDING

Player	GP	Mins	Avg	W	L	T	SO
*Jim Carey	28	1604	2.13	18	6	3	4
Rick Tabaracci	8	394	2.44	1	3	2	0
*Olaf Kolzig	14	724	2.49	2	8	2	0
*Bryan Dafoe	4	187	3.53	1	1	1	0
Team total	48	2922	2.46	22	18	8	4

* Rookie.

Winnipeg Jets

SCORING

Player	GP	G	A	Pts	+/−	PM	Player	GP	G	A	Pts	+/−	PM
Alexei Zhamnov, C	48	30	35	65	5	20	Darrin Shannon, L	19	5	3	8	-6	14
Keith Tkachuk, L	48	22	29	51	-4	152	Kris King, L	48	4	2	6	0	85
Teemu Selanne, R	45	22	26	48	1	2	Neil Wilkinson, D	40	1	4	5	-26	75
Nelson Emerson, R	48	14	23	37	-12	26	*Michal Grosek, L	24	2	2	4	-3	21
Igor Korolev, R	45	8	22	30	1	10	Greg Brown, D	9	0	3	3	1	17
Dallas Drake, C	43	8	18	26	-6	30	Rob Murray, C	10	0	2	2	1	2
Stephane Quintal, D	43	6	17	23	0	78	Oleg Mikulchik, D	25	0	2	2	10	12
Teppo Numminen, D	42	5	16	21	12	16							
Mike Eastwood, C	49	8	11	19	-9	36							
Dave Manson, D	44	3	15	18	-20	139							
Thomas Steen, C	31	5	10	15	-13	14							
Darryl Shannon, D	40	5	9	14	1	48							
Ed Olczyk, C	33	4	9	13	-1	12							
Randy Gilhen, C	44	5	6	11	-17	52							

GOALTENDING

Player	GP	Mins	Avg	W	L	T	SO
*N. Khabibulin	26	1339	3.41	8	9	4	0
Tim Cheveldae	30	1571	3.70	8	16	3	0
Team total	48	2923	3.63	16	25	7	0

* Rookie.

1995 NHL Draft

First Round

The opening round of the 1995 NHL draft was held in Edmonton on July 8.

Team	Selection	Position	Team	Selection	Position
1.....Ottawa	Bryan Berard, Detroit	D	14...Hartford	J. S. Giguere, Halifax	G
2.....NY Islanders	Wade Redden, Brandon	D	15...Toronto	Jeff Ware, Oshawa	D
3.....Los Angeles	Aki-Petteri Berg, Kiekko	D	16...Buffalo	Martin Biron, Beauport	G
4.....Anaheim	Chad Kilger, Kingston	C	17...Washington	Brad Church, Prince Albert	L
5.....Tampa Bay	Daymond Langkow, Tri-City	C	18...New Jersey	Petr Sykora, Detroit	L
6.....Edmonton	Steve Kelly, Prince Albert	C	19...Chicago	Dimitri Nabokov, Krylja Sovetov	C
7.....Winnipeg	Shane Doan, Kamloops	R	20...Calgary	Denis Gauthier, Drummondville	D
8.....Montreal	Terry Ryan, Tri-City	L	21...Boston	Sean Brown, Belleville	D
9.....Boston	Kyle McLaren, Tacoma	D	22...Philadelphia	Brian Boucher, Tri-City	G
10...Florida	Radek Dvorak, Budjovice	C	23...Washington	Mikka Elomo, Kiekko Jr.	L
11...Dallas	Jarome Iginla, Kamloops	R	24...Pittsburgh	Alexei Morozov, Krylja Sovetov	R
12...San Jose	Teemu Riihijarvi, Espoo Jr.	L	25...Colorado	Marc Denis, Chicoutimi	G
13...Buffalo	Jay McKee, Niagara Falls	D	26...Detroit	M. Kuznetsov, Dynamo Moscow	D

Spamdemonium

The folks in the front office of the Minnesota Moose of the International Hockey League have fashioned a new recipe: Spam on ice. Between periods at the Saint Paul Civic Center, the Spamboni, a Zamboni painted like a giant can of Spam, resurfaces the rink. Hormel Foods, the Minnesota-based company that produces the hamlike food product, bought the ad rights to the Zamboni for the season, and the success of its advertising vehicle has spawned everything from Spamburger giveaways to the frightening notion of Spam as training-table fare. "Our players are required to eat at least 100 pounds of Spam per season," says Moose vice president of business operations Ron Minegar. "It's why we have the best-conditioned team in the league. I'm joking, of course."

The Stanley Cup

Awarded annually to the team that wins the NHL's best-of-seven final-round playoffs. The Stanley Cup is the oldest trophy competed for by professional athletes in North America. It was donated in 1893 by Frederick Arthur, Lord Stanley of Preston.

Results

WINNERS PRIOR TO FORMATION OF NHL IN 1917

1892-93	Montreal A.A.A.	1904-05	Ottawa Silver Seven
1893-94	Montreal A.A.A.	1905-06	Ottawa Silver Seven (Feb)
1894-95	Montreal Victorias	1905-06	Montreal Wanderers (Mar)
1895-96	Winnipeg Victorias (Feb)	1906-07	Kenora Thistles (Jan)
1895-96	Montreal Victorias (Dec)	1906-07	Montreal Wanderers (Mar)
1896-97	Montreal Victorias	1907-08	Montreal Wanderers
1897-98	Montreal Victorias	1908-09	Ottawa Senators
1898-99	Montreal Victorias (Feb)	1909-10	Montreal Wanderers
1898-99	Montreal Shamrocks (Mar)	1910-11	Ottawa Senators
1899-1900	Montreal Shamrocks	1911-12	Quebec Bulldogs
1900-01	Winnipeg Victorias	1912-13	Quebec Bulldogs
1901-02	Winnipeg Victorias (Jan)	1913-14	Toronto Blueshirts
1901-02	Montreal A.A.A. (Mar)	1914-15	Vancouver Millionaires
1902-03	Montreal A.A.A. (Feb)	1915-16	Montreal Canadiens
1902-03	Ottawa Silver Seven (Mar)	1916-17	Seattle Metropolitans
1903-04	Ottawa Silver Seven		

NHL WINNERS AND FINALISTS

Season	Champion	Finalist	GP in Final
1917-18	Toronto Arenas	Vancouver Millionaires	5
1918-19	No decision*	No decision*	5
1919-20	Ottawa Senators	Seattle Metropolitans	5
1920-21	Ottawa Senators	Vancouver Millionaires	5
1921-22	Toronto St Pats	Vancouver Millionaires	5
1922-23	Ottawa Senators	Vancouver Millionaires, Edmonton	3, 2
1923-24	Montreal Canadiens	Vancouver Millionaires, Calgary	2, 2
1924-25	Victoria Cougars	Montreal Canadiens	4
1925-26	Montreal Maroons	Victoria Cougars	4
1926-27	Ottawa Senators	Boston Bruins	4
1927-28	New York Rangers	Montreal Maroons	5
1928-29	Boston Bruins	New York Rangers	2
1929-30	Montreal Canadiens	Boston Bruins	2
1930-31	Montreal Canadiens	Chicago Blackhawks	5
1931-32	Toronto Maple Leafs	New York Rangers	3
1932-33	New York Rangers	Toronto Maple Leafs	4
1933-34	Chicago Blackhawks	Detroit Red Wings	4
1934-35	Montreal Maroons	Toronto Maple Leafs	3
1935-36	Detroit Red Wings	Toronto Maple Leafs	4
1936-37	Detroit Red Wings	New York Rangers	5
1937-38	Chicago Blackhawks	Toronto Maple Leafs	4
1938-39	Boston Bruins	Toronto Maple Leafs	5
1939-40	New York Rangers	Toronto Maple Leafs	6
1940-41	Boston Bruins	Detroit Red Wings	4
1941-42	Toronto Maple Leafs	Detroit Red Wings	7
1942-43	Detroit Red Wings	Boston Bruins	4
1943-44	Montreal Canadiens	Chicago Blackhawks	4
1944-45	Toronto Maple Leafs	Detroit Red Wings	7
1945-46	Montreal Canadiens	Boston Bruins	5
1946-47	Toronto Maple Leafs	Montreal Canadiens	6
1947-48	Toronto Maple Leafs	Detroit Red Wings	4
1948-49	Toronto Maple Leafs	Detroit Red Wings	4
1949-50	Detroit Red Wings	New York Rangers	7
1950-51	Toronto Maple Leafs	Montreal Canadiens	5
1951-52	Detroit Red Wings	Montreal Canadiens	4
1952-53	Montreal Canadiens	Boston Bruins	5
1953-54	Detroit Red Wings	Montreal Canadiens	7

NHL WINNERS AND FINALISTS (Cont.)

1954-55	Detroit Red Wings	Montreal Canadiens	7
1955-56	Montreal Canadiens	Detroit Red Wings	5
1956-57	Montreal Canadiens	Boston Bruins	5
1957-58	Montreal Canadiens	Boston Bruins	6
1958-59	Montreal Canadiens	Toronto Maple Leafs	5
1959-60	Montreal Canadiens	Toronto Maple Leafs	4
1960-61	Chicago Blackhawks	Detroit Red Wings	6
1961-62	Toronto Maple Leafs	Chicago Blackhawks	6
1962-63	Toronto Maple Leafs	Detroit Red Wings	5
1963-64	Toronto Maple Leafs	Detroit Red Wings	7
1964-65	Montreal Canadiens	Chicago Blackhawks	7
1965-66	Montreal Canadiens	Detroit Red Wings	6
1966-67	Toronto Maple Leafs	Montreal Canadiens	6
1967-68	Montreal Canadiens	St Louis Blues	4
1968-69	Montreal Canadiens	St Louis Blues	4
1969-70	Boston Bruins	St Louis Blues	4
1970-71	Montreal Canadiens	Chicago Blackhawks	7
1971-72	Boston Bruins	New York Rangers	6
1972-73	Montreal Canadiens	Chicago Blackhawks	6
1973-74	Philadelphia Flyers	Boston Bruins	6
1974-75	Philadelphia Flyers	Buffalo Sabres	6
1975-76	Montreal Canadiens	Philadelphia Flyers	4
1976-77	Montreal Canadiens	Boston Bruins	4
1977-78	Montreal Canadiens	Boston Bruins	6
1978-79	Montreal Canadiens	New York Rangers	5
1979-80	New York Islanders	Philadelphia Flyers	6
1980-81	New York Islanders	Minnesota North Stars	5
1981-82	New York Islanders	Vancouver Canucks	4
1982-83	New York Islanders	Edmonton Oilers	4
1983-84	Edmonton Oilers	New York Islanders	5
1984-85	Edmonton Oilers	Philadelphia Flyers	5
1985-86	Montreal Canadiens	Calgary Flames	6
1986-87	Edmonton Oilers	Philadelphia Flyers	7
1987-88	Edmonton Oilers	Boston Bruins	4
1988-89	Calgary Flames	Montreal Canadiens	6
1989-90	Edmonton Oilers	Boston Bruins	5
1990-91	Pittsburgh Penguins	Minnesota North Stars	6
1991-92	Pittsburgh Penguins	Chicago Blackhawks	4
1992-93	Montreal Canadiens	Los Angeles Kings	5
1993-94	New York Rangers	Vancouver Canucks	7
1994-95	New Jersey Devils	Detroit Red Wings	4

*In 1919 the Montreal Canadiens traveled to meet Seattle, the PCHL champions. After 5 games had been played—the teams were tied at 2 wins and 1 tie—the series was called off by the local Department of Health because of the influenza epidemic and the death of Canadian defenseman Joe Hall from influenza.

Conn Smythe Trophy

Awarded to the Most Valuable Player of the Stanley Cup playoffs, as selected by the Professional Hockey Writers Association. The trophy is named after the former coach, general manager, president and owner of the Toronto Maple Leafs.

1965	Jean Beliveau, Mtl	1981	Butch Goring, NYI
1966	Roger Crozier, Det	1982	Mike Bossy, NYI
1967	Dave Keon, Tor	1983	Bill Smith, NYI
1968	Glenn Hall, StL	1984	Mark Messier, Edm
1969	Serge Savard, Mtl	1985	Wayne Gretzky, Edm
1970	Bobby Orr, Bos	1986	Patrick Roy, Mtl
1971	Ken Dryden, Mtl	1987	Ron Hextall, Phil
1972	Bobby Orr, Bos	1988	Wayne Gretzky, Edm
1973	Yvan Cournoyer, Mtl	1989	Al MacInnis, Cgy
1974	Bernie Parent, Phil	1990	Bill Ranford, Edm
1975	Bernie Parent, Phil	1991	Mario Lemieux, Pitt
1976	Reggie Leach, Phil	1992	Mario Lemieux, Pitt
1977	Guy Lafleur, Mtl	1993	Patrick Roy, Mtl
1978	Larry Robinson, Mtl	1994	Brian Leetch, NYR
1979	Bob Gainey, Mtl	1995	Claude Lemieux, NJ
1980	Bryan Trottier, NYI		

Alltime Stanley Cup Playoff Leaders

Points

	Yrs	GP	G	A	Pts		Yrs	GP	G	A	Pts
*Wayne Gretzky, Edm, LA	14	180	110	236	346	*Doug Gilmour, StL, Cgy, Tor	11	132	48	104	152
*Mark Messier, Edm, NYR	15	210	102	170	272	Stan Mikita, Chi	18	155	59	91	150
*Jari Kurri, Edm, LA	12	174	102	120	222	Brian Propp, Phil, Bos, Minn	13	160	64	84	148
*Glenn Anderson, four teams	14	214	92	117	209	Larry Robinson, Mtl, LA	20	227	28	116	144
Bryan Trottier, NYI, Pitt	17	221	71	113	184	Jacques Lemaire, Mtl	11	145	61	78	139
Jean Beliveau, Mtl	17	162	79	97	176	*Ray Bourque, Bos	16	157	33	106	139
*Paul Coffey,Edm,Pitt,LA,Det	13	155	53	119	172	Phil Esposito, Chi, Bos, NYR	15	130	61	76	137
*Denis Savard, Chi, Mtl	14	153	65	105	170	Guy Lafleur, Mtl, NYR	14	128	58	76	134
Denis Potvin, NYI	14	185	56	108	164	Steve Larmer, Chi, NYR	13	140	56	75	131
Mike Bossy, NYI	10	129	85	75	160	Bobby Hull, Chi, Hart	14	119	62	67	129
Gordie Howe, Det, Hart	20	157	68	92	160	Henri Richard, Mtl	18	180	49	80	129
Bobby Smith, Minn, Mtl	13	184	64	96	160	*Active player.					

Goals

	Yrs	GP	G
*Wayne Gretzky, Edm, LA	14	180	110
*Jari Kurri, Edm, LA	12	174	102
*Mark Messier, Edm, NYR	15	210	102
*Glenn Anderson, four teams	14	214	92
Mike Bossy, NYI	10	129	85
Maurice Richard, Mtl	15	133	82
Jean Beliveau, Mtl	17	162	79
Bryan Trottier, NYI, Pitt	17	221	71
Gordie Howe, Det, Hart	20	157	68
Yvan Cournoyer, Mtl	12	147	64
Brian Propp, Phil, Bos, Minn	13	160	64
Bobby Smith, Minn, Mtl	13	184	64
*Active player.			

Assists

	Yrs	GP	A
*Wayne Gretzky, Edm, LA	15	180	236
*Mark Messier, Edm, NYR	15	210	170
*Jari Kurri, Edm, LA	12	174	120
*Paul Coffey, Edm, Pitt, LA, Det	13	155	119
*Glenn Anderson, four teams	14	214	117
Larry Robinson, Mtl, LA	20	227	116
Bryan Trottier, NYI, Pitt	17	221	113
Denis Potvin, NYI	14	185	108
*Ray Bourque, Bos	16	157	106
*Denis Savard, Chi, Mtl	14	153	105
*Doug Gilmour, StL, Cgy, Tor	11	132	104
*Active player.			

Goaltending

WINS	W	L	Pct
Billy Smith, LA, NYI	88	36	.710
Ken Dryden, Mtl	80	32	.714
*Grant Fuhr, Edm, Tor, Buff, LA	77	36	.681
Jacques Plante, five teams	71	37	.657
*Patrick Roy, Mtl	70	42	.625
*Andy Moog, Edm, Bos, Dall	61	48	.560
Turk Broda, Tor	58	42	.580
*Mike Vernon, Cgy, Det	55	39	.585
Terry Sawchuk, five teams	54	48	.529
Glenn Hall, Det, Chi, StL	49	65	.429
*Active player.			

SHUTOUTS	GP	W	SO
Clint Benedict, Ott, Mtl M	48	25	15
Jacques Plante, five teams	112	71	14
Turk Broda, Tor	101	58	13
Terry Sawchuk, five teams	106	54	12
Ken Dryden, Mtl	112	80	10

GOALS AGAINST AVG	Avg
George Hainsworth, Mtl, Tor	1.93
Turk Broda, Tor	1.98
Jacques Plante, five teams	2.17
Ken Dryden, Mtl	2.40
Bernie Parent, Bos, Tor, Phil	2.43

Note: At least 50 games played.

Alltime Stanley Cup Standings

TEAM	W	L	Pct	TEAM	W	L	Pct
Montreal	374	235	.614	Pittsburgh	74	63	.540
Boston	227	238	.488	Calgary	69	83	.454
Toronto	200	217	.480	Buffalo	62	81	.434
Detroit	180	188	.489	Los Angeles	55	87	.387
Chicago	179	206	.465	Vancouver	52	66	.441
NY Rangers	169	183	.480	Washington	50	60	.454
NY Islanders	128	90	.587	New Jersey	47	40	.540
Philadelphia	126	112	.529	Quebec	35	45	.437
Edmonton	120	60	.667	Hartford	18	31	.367
St Louis	96	121	.442	Winnipeg	17	39	.304
Dallas*	86	94	.478	San Jose	11	18	.379

*Minnesota North Stars 1967-93. Note: Teams ranked by playoff victories.

Stanley Cup Coaching Records

Coach	Team	Yrs	Series	Series W	Series L	Games G	Games W	L	T	Cups	Pct
Toe Blake....................Mtl		13	23	18	5	119	82	37	0	8	.689
Glen Sather.................Edm		11	30	23	7	*142	97	45	0	4	.683
†Jacques Lemaire.......Mtl, NJ		4	13	10	3	67	42	25	0	1	.627
†Scott Bowman ....Five teams		21	44	29	15	244	152	92	0	6	.622
Hap Day ....Tor		9	14	10	4	80	49	31	0	5	.613
Al Arbour ....StL, NYI		16	42	30	12	209	123	86	0	4	.589
†Mike Keenan..............Phil, Chi, NYR, StL		10	26	17	9	147	84	63	0	1	.571
Fred Shero...................Phil, NYR		8	21	15	6	108	61	47	0	2	.565
Jacques Demers ....Que, StL, Det, Mtl		8	19	12	7	98	55	43	0	1	.561
Lester Patrick.............NYR		12	24	14	10	65	31	26	8	2	.538

*Does not include suspended game, May 24, 1988.
Note: Coaches ranked by winning percentage. Minimum: 65 games. †Active coach.

The 10 Longest Overtime Games

Date	Scorer	OT	Results	Series	Series Winner
3-24-36 ....Mud Bruneteau		116:30	Det 1 vs Mtl M 0	SF	Det
4-3-33 ....Ken Doraty		104:46	Tor 1 vs Bos 0	SF	Tor
3-23-43 ....Jack McLean		70:18	Tor 3 vs Det 2	SF	Det
3-28-30 ....Gus Rivers		68:52	Mtl 2 vs NYR 1	SF	Mtl
4-18-87 ....Pat LaFontaine		68:47	NYI 3 vs Wash 2	DSF	NYI
4-27-94 ....Dave Hannan		65:43	Buff 1 vs NJ 0	CQF	NJ
3-27-51 ....Maurice Richard		61:09	Mtl 3 vs Det 2	SF	Mtl
3-27-38 ....Lorne Carr		60:40	NYA 3 vs NYR 2	QF	NYA
3-26-32 ....Fred Cook		59:32	NYR 4 vs Mtl 3	SF	NYR
3-21-39 ....Mel Hill		59:25	Bos 2 vs NYR 1	SF	Bos

NHL Awards

Hart Memorial Trophy

Awarded annually "to the player adjudged to be the most valuable to his team." The original trophy was donated by Dr. David A. Hart, father of Cecil Hart, former manager-coach of the Montreal Canadiens. In the decade of the 1980s Wayne Gretzky won the award nine of 10 times.

	Winner	Key Statistics	Runner-Up
1924	Frank Nighbor, Ott	10 goals, 3 assists in 20 games	Sprague Cleghorn, Mtl
1925	Billy Burch, Ham	20 goals, 4 assists in 27 games	Howie Morenz, Mtl
1926	Nels Stewart, Mtl M	42 points in 36 games	Sprague Cleghorn, Mtl
1927	Herb Gardiner, Mtl	12 points in 44 games as defenseman	Bill Cook, NYR
1928	Howie Morenz, Mtl	33 goals, 18 assists	Roy Worters, Pitt
1929	Roy Worters, NYA	1.21 goals against, 13 shutouts	Ace Bailey, Tor
1930	Nels Stewart, Mtl M	39 goals, 16 assists	Lionel Hitchman, Bos
1931	Howie Morenz, Mtl	28 goals, 23 assists	Eddie Shore, Bos
1932	Howie Morenz, Mtl	24 goals, 25 assists	Ching Johnson, NYR
1933	Eddie Shore, Bos	27 assists in 48 games as defenseman	Bill Cook, NYR
1934	Aurel Joliat, Mtl	27 points	Lionel Conacher, Chi
1935	Eddie Shore, Bos	26 assists in 48 games as defenseman	Charlie Conacher, Tor
1936	Eddie Shore, Bos	16 assists in 46 games as defenseman	Hooley Smith, Mtl M
1937	Babe Siebert, Mtl	28 points	Lionel Conacher, Mtl M
1938	Eddie Shore, Bos	17 points in 47 games as defenseman	Paul Thompson, Chi
1939	Toe Blake, Mtl	led NHL in points (47)	Syl Apps, Tor
1940	Ebbie Goodfellow, Det	28 points	Syl Apps, Tor
1941	Bill Cowley, Bos	led NHL in assists (45) and points (62)	Dit Clapper, Bos
1942	Tom Anderson, Bos	41 points	Syl Apps, Tor
1943	Bill Cowley, Bos	led NHL in assists (45)	Doug Bentley, Chi
1944	Babe Pratt, Tor	57 points in 50 games	Bill Cowley, Bos
1945	Elmer Lach, Mtl	led NHL in assists (54) and points (80)	Maurice Richard, Mtl
1946	Max Bentley, Chi	61 points in 47 games	Gaye Stewart, Tor
1947	Maurice Richard, Mtl	led NHL in goals (45); 26 assists	Milt Schmidt, Bos
1948	Buddy O'Connor, NYR	60 points in 60 games	Frank Brimsek, Bos
1949	Sid Abel, Det	28 goals, 26 assists	Bill Durnan, Mtl

Hart Memorial Trophy (Cont.)

Winner	Key Statistics	Runner-Up
1950.............Charlie Rayner, NYR	6 shutouts	Ted Kennedy, Tor
1951.............Milt Schmidt, Bos	61 points in 62 games	Maurice Richard, Mtl
1952.............Gordie Howe, Det	led NHL in goals (47) and points (86)	Elmer Lach, Mtl
1953.............Gordie Howe, Det	led NHL in goals (49) and points (95)	Al Rollins, Chi
1954.............Al Rollins, Chi	5 shutouts	Red Kelly, Det
1955.............Ted Kennedy, Tor	52 points	Harry Lumley, Tor
1956.............Jean Beliveau, Mtl	led NHL in goals (47) and points (88)	Tod Sloan, Tor
1957.............Gordie Howe, Det	led NHL in goals (44) and points (89)	Jean Beliveau, Mtl
1959.............Andy Bathgate, NYR	74 points in 70 games	Gordie Howe, Det
1960.............Gordie Howe, Det	45 assists, 73 points	Bobby Hull, Chi
1961.............Bernie Geoffrion, Mtl	50 goals, 95 points	Johnny Bower, Tor
1962.............Jacques Plante, Mtl	42 wins, 2.37 goals against	Doug Harvey, NYR
1963.............Gordie Howe, Det	47 assists, 73 points	Stan Mikita, Chi
1964.............Jean Beliveau, Mtl	50 assists, 78 points	Bobby Hull, Chi
1965.............Bobby Hull, Chi	39 goals, 32 assists	Norm Ullman, Det
1966.............Bobby Hull, Chi	led NHL in goals (54) and points (97)	Jean Beliveau, Mtl
1967.............Stan Mikita, Chi	led NHL in assists (62) and points (97)	Ed Giacomin, NYR
1968.............Stan Mikita, Chi	40 goals, 47 assists	Jean Beliveau, Mtl
1969.............Phil Esposito, Bos	led NHL in assists (77) and points (126)	Jean Beliveau, Mtl
1970.............Bobby Orr, Bos	led NHL in assists (87) and points (120)	Tony Esposito, Chi
1971.............Bobby Orr, Bos	102 assists, 139 points	Tony Esposito, Chi
1972.............Bobby Orr, Bos	80 assists, 117 points	Ken Dryden, Mtl
1973.............Bobby Clarke, Phil	67 assists, 104 points	Phil Esposito, Bos
1974.............Phil Esposito, Bos	led NHL in goals (68) and points (145)	Bernie Parent, Phil
1975.............Bobby Clarke, Phil	89 assists, 116 points	Rogatien Vachon, LA
1976.............Bobby Clarke, Phil	89 assists, 119 points	Denis Potvin, NYI
1977.............Guy Lafleur, Mtl	led NHL in assists (80) and points (136)	Bobby Clarke, Phil
1978.............Guy Lafleur, Mtl	led NHL in goals (60) and points (132)	Bryan Trottier, NYI
1979.............Bryan Trottier, NYI	led NHL in assists (87) and points (134)	Guy Lafleur, Mtl
1980.............Wayne Gretzky, Edm	51 goals, 86 assists	Marcel Dionne, LA
1981.............Wayne Gretzky, Edm	led NHL in assists (109) and points (164)	Mike Liut, StL
1982.............Wayne Gretzky, Edm	NHL-record 92 goals and 212 points	Bryan Trottier, NYI
1983.............Wayne Gretzky, Edm	led NHL in goals (71) and points (196)	Pete Peeters, Bos
1984.............Wayne Gretzky, Edm	led NHL in goals (87) and points (205)	Rod Langway, Wash
1985.............Wayne Gretzky, Edm	led NHL in goals (73) and points (208)	Dale Hawerchuk, Winn
1986.............Wayne Gretzky, Edm	NHL-record 163 assists and 215 points	Mario Lemieux, Pitt
1987.............Wayne Gretzky, Edm	led NHL in assists (121) and points (183)	Ray Bourque, Bos
1988.............Mario Lemieux, Pitt	led NHL in goals (70) and points (168)	Grant Fuhr, Edm
1989.............Wayne Gretzky, LA	114 assists, 168 points	Mario Lemieux, Pitt
1990.............Mark Messier, Edm	84 assists, 129 points	Ray Bourque, Bos
1991.............Brett Hull, StL	led NHL in goals (86); 131 points	Wayne Gretzky, LA
1992.............Mark Messier, NYR	72 assists, 107 points	Patrick Roy, Mtl
1993.............Mario Lemieux, Pitt	69 goals, 91 assists in 60 games	Doug Gilmour, Tor
1994.............Sergei Fedorov, Det	56 goals, 64 assists	Dominik Hasek, Buff
1995.............Eric Lindros, Phil	29 goals, 41 assists in 46 games	Jaromir Jagr, Pitt

Art Ross Trophy

Awarded annually "to the player who leads the league in scoring points at the end of the regular season." The trophy was presented to the NHL in 1947 by Arthur Howie Ross, former manager-coach of the Boston Bruins. The tie-breakers, in order, are as follows: (1) player with most goals, (2) player with fewer games played, (3) player scoring first goal of the season. Bobby Orr is the only defenseman in NHL history to win this trophy, and he won it twice (1970 and 1975).

Winner	Pts	Winner	Pts
1919.............Newsy Lalonde, Mtl	44	1927 ....Bill Cook, NYR	42
1920.............Joe Malone, Que	30	1928 ....Howie Morenz, Mtl	37
1921.............Newsy Lalonde, Mtl	48	1929 ....Ace Bailey, Tor	51
1922.............Punch Broadbent, Ott	41	1930 ....Cooney Weiland, Bos	32
1923.............Babe Dye, Tor	46	1931 ....Howie Morenz, Mtl	73
1924.............Cy Denneny, Ott	37	1932 ....Harvey Jackson, Tor	51
1925.............Babe Dye, Tor	23	1933 ....Bill Cook, NYR	53
1926.............Nels Stewart, Mtl M	44	1934 ....Charlie Conacher, Tor	50

Art Ross Trophy (Cont.)

	Winner	Pts		Winner	Pts
1935	Charlie Conacher, Tor	57	1966	Bobby Hull, Chi	97
1936	Sweeney Schriner, NYA	45	1967	Stan Mikita, Chi	97
1937	Sweeney Schriner, NYA	46	1968	Stan Mikita, Chi	87
1938	Gordie Drillon, Tor	52	1969	Phil Esposito, Bos	126
1939	Toe Blake, Mtl	47	1970	Bobby Orr, Bos	120
1940	Milt Schmidt, Bos	52	1971	Phil Esposito, Bos	152
1941	Bill Cowley, Bos	62	1972	Phil Esposito, Bos	133
1942	Bryan Hextall, NYR	56	1973	Phil Esposito, Bos	130
1943	Doug Bentley, Chi	73	1974	Phil Esposito, Bos	145
1944	Herb Cain, Bos	82	1975	Bobby Orr, Bos	135
1945	Elmer Lach, Mtl	80	1976	Guy Lafleur, Mtl	125
1946	Max Bentley, Chi	61	1977	Guy Lafleur, Mtl	136
1947	*Max Bentley, Chi	72	1978	Guy Lafleur, Mtl	132
1948	Elmer Lach, Mtl	61	1979	Bryan Trottier, NYI	134
1949	Roy Conacher, Chi	68	1980	Marcel Dionne, LA	137
1950	Ted Lindsay, Det	78	1981	Wayne Gretzky, Edm	164
1951	Gordie Howe, Det	86	1982	Wayne Gretzky, Edm	212
1952	Gordie Howe, Det	86	1983	Wayne Gretzky, Edm	196
1953	Gordie Howe, Det	95	1984	Wayne Gretzky, Edm	205
1954	Gordie Howe, Det	81	1985	Wayne Gretzky, Edm	208
1955	Bernie Geoffrion, Mtl	75	1986	Wayne Gretzky, Edm	215
1956	Jean Beliveau, Mtl	88	1987	Wayne Gretzky, Edm	183
1957	Gordie Howe, Det	89	1988	Mario Lemieux, Pitt	168
1958	Dickie Moore, Mtl	84	1989	Mario Lemieux, Pitt	199
1959	Dickie Moore, Mtl	96	1990	Wayne Gretzky, LA	142
1960	Bobby Hull, Chi	81	1991	Wayne Gretzky, LA	163
1961	Bernie Geoffrion, Mtl	95	1992	Mario Lemieux, Pitt	131
1962	Bobby Hull, Chi	84	1993	Mario Lemieux, Pitt	160
1963	Gordie Howe, Det	86	1994	Wayne Gretzky, LA	130
1964	Stan Mikita, Chi	89	1995	Jaromir Jagr, Pitt	70
1965	Stan Mikita, Chi	87			

Note: Listing includes scoring leaders prior to inception of Art Ross Trophy in 1947-48.

Lady Byng Memorial Trophy

Awarded annually "to the player adjudged to have exhibited the best type of sportsmanship and gentlemanly conduct combined with a high standard of playing ability." Lady Byng, who first presented the trophy in 1925, was the wife of Canada's Governor-General. She donated a second trophy in 1936 after the first was given permanently to Frank Boucher of the New York Rangers, who won it seven times in eight seasons. Stan Mikita, one of the league's most penalized players during his early years in the NHL, won the trophy twice late in his career (1967 and 1968).

1925	Frank Nighbor, Ott	1949	Bill Quackenbush, Det	1973	Gilbert Perreault, Buff
1926	Frank Nighbor, Ott	1950	Edgar Laprade, NYR	1974	John Bucyk, Bos
1927	Billy Burch, NYA	1951	Red Kelly, Det	1975	Marcel Dionne, Det
1928	Frank Boucher, NYR	1952	Sid Smith, Tor	1976	Jean Ratelle, NYR-Bos
1929	Frank Boucher, NYR	1953	Red Kelly, Det	1977	Marcel Dionne, LA
1930	Frank Boucher, NYR	1954	Red Kelly, Det	1978	Butch Goring, LA
1931	Frank Boucher, NYR	1955	Sid Smith, Tor	1979	Bob MacMillan, Atl
1932	Joe Primeau, Tor	1956	Earl Reibel, Det	1980	Wayne Gretzky, Edm
1933	Frank Boucher, NYR	1957	Andy Hebenton, NYR	1981	Rick Kehoe, Pitt
1934	Frank Boucher, NYR	1958	Camille Henry, NYR	1982	Rick Middleton, Bos
1935	Frank Boucher, NYR	1959	Alex Delvecchio, Det	1983	Mike Bossy, NYI
1936	Doc Romnes, Chi	1960	Don McKenney, Bos	1984	Mike Bossy, NYI
1937	Marty Barry, Det	1961	Red Kelly, Tor	1985	Jari Kurri, Edm
1938	Gordie Drillon, Tor	1962	Dave Keon, Tor	1986	Mike Bossy, NYI
1939	Clint Smith, NYR	1963	Dave Keon, Tor	1987	Joe Mullen, Cgy
1940	Bobby Bauer, Bos	1964	Ken Wharram, Chi	1988	Mats Naslund, Mtl
1941	Bobby Bauer, Bos	1965	Bobby Hull, Chi	1989	Joe Mullen, Cgy
1942	Syl Apps, Tor	1966	Alex Delvecchio, Det	1990	Brett Hull, StL
1943	Max Bentley, Chi	1967	Stan Mikita, Chi	1991	Wayne Gretzky, LA
1944	Clint Smith, Chi	1968	Stan Mikita, Chi	1992	Wayne Gretzky, LA
1945	Billy Mosienko, Chi	1969	Alex Delvecchio, Det	1993	Pierre Turgeon, NYI
1946	Toe Blake, Mtl	1970	Phil Goyette, StL	1994	Wayne Gretzky, LA
1947	Bobby Bauer, Bos	1971	John Bucyk, Bos	1995	Ron Francis, Pitt
1948	Buddy O'Connor, NYR	1972	Jean Ratelle, NYR		

James Norris Memorial Trophy

Awarded annually "to the defense player who demonstrates throughout the season the greatest all-around ability in the position." James Norris was the former owner-president of the Detroit Red Wings. Bobby Orr holds the record for most consecutive times winning the award (eight, 1968-1975).

1954 ......Red Kelly, Det	1968 ......Bobby Orr, Bos	1982 ......Doug Wilson, Chi
1955 ......Doug Harvey, Mtl	1969 ......Bobby Orr, Bos	1983 ......Rod Langway, Wash
1956 ......Doug Harvey, Mtl	1970 ......Bobby Orr, Bos	1984 ......Rod Langway, Wash
1957 ......Doug Harvey, Mtl	1971 ......Bobby Orr, Bos	1985 ......Paul Coffey, Edm
1958 ......Doug Harvey, Mtl	1972 ......Bobby Orr, Bos	1986 ......Paul Coffey, Edm
1959 ......Tom Johnson, Mtl	1973 ......Bobby Orr, Bos	1987 ......Ray Bourque, Bos
1960 ......Doug Harvey, Mtl	1974 ......Bobby Orr, Bos	1988 ......Ray Bourque, Bos
1961 ......Doug Harvey, Mtl	1975 ......Bobby Orr, Bos	1989 ......Chris Chelios, Mtl
1962 ......Doug Harvey, NYR	1976 ......Denis Potvin, NYI	1990 ......Ray Bourque, Bos
1963 ......Pierre Pilote, Chi	1977 ......Larry Robinson, Mtl	1991 ......Ray Bourque, Bos
1964 ......Pierre Pilote, Chi	1978 ......Denis Potvin, NYI	1992 ......Brian Leetch, NYR
1965 ......Pierre Pilote, Chi	1979 ......Denis Potvin, NYI	1993 ......Chris Chelios, Chi
1966 ......Jacques Laperriere, Mtl	1980 ......Larry Robinson, Mtl	1994 ......Ray Bourque, Bos
1967 ......Harry Howell, NYR	1981 ......Randy Carlyle, Pitt	1995 ......Paul Coffey, Det

Calder Memorial Trophy

Awarded annually "to the player selected as the most proficient in his first year of competition in the National Hockey League." Frank Calder was a former NHL president. Sergei Makarov, who won the award in 1989-1990, was the oldest recipient of the trophy, at 31. Players are no longer eligible for the award if they are 26 or older as of September 15th of the season in question.

1933 ......Carl Voss, Det	1954 ......Camille Henry, NYR	1975 ......Eric Vail, Atl
1934 ......Russ Blinko, Mtl M	1955 ......Ed Litzenberger, Chi	1976 ......Bryan Trottier, NYI
1935 ......Dave Schriner, NYA	1956 ......Glenn Hall, Det	1977 ......Willi Plett, Atl
1936 ......Mike Karakas, Chi	1957 ......Larry Regan, Bos	1978 ......Mike Bossy, NYI
1937 ......Syl Apps, Tor	1958 ......Frank Mahovlich, Tor	1979 ......Bobby Smith, Minn
1938 ......Cully Dahlstrom, Chi	1959 ......Ralph Backstrom, Mtl	1980 ......Ray Bourque, Bos
1939 ......Frank Brimsek, Bos	1960 ......Bill Hay, Chi	1981 ......Peter Stastny, Que
1940 ......Kilby MacDonald, NYR	1961 ......Dave Keon, Tor	1982 ......Dale Hawerchuk, Winn
1941 ......Johnny Quilty, Mtl	1962 ......Bobby Rousseau, Mtl	1983 ......Steve Larmer, Chi
1942 ......Grant Warwick, NYR	1963 ......Kent Douglas, Tor	1984 ......Tom Barrasso, Buff
1943 ......Gaye Stewart, Tor	1964 ......Jacques Laperriere, Mtl	1985 ......Mario Lemieux, Pitt
1944 ......Gus Bodnar, Tor	1965 ......Roger Crozier, Det	1986 ......Gary Suter, Cgy
1945 ......Frank McCool, Tor	1966 ......Brit Selby, Tor	1987 ......Luc Robitaille, LA
1946 ......Edgar Laprade, NYR	1967 ......Bobby Orr, Bos	1988 ......Joe Nieuwendyk, Cgy
1947 ......Howie Meeker, Tor	1968 ......Derek Sanderson, Bos	1989 ......Brian Leetch, NYR
1948 ......Jim McFadden, Det	1969 ......Danny Grant, Minn	1990 ......Sergei Makarov, Cgy
1949 ......Pentti Lund, NYR	1970 ......Tony Esposito, Chi	1991 ......Ed Belfour, Chi
1950 ......Jack Gelineau, Bos	1971 ......Gilbert Perreault, Buff	1992 ......Pavel Bure, Van
1951 ......Terry Sawchuk, Det	1972 ......Ken Dryden, Mtl	1993 ......Teemu Selanne, Winn
1952 ......Bernie Geoffrion, Mtl	1973 ......Steve Vickers, NYR	1994 ......Martin Brodeur, NJ
1953 ......Gump Worsley, NYR	1974 ......Denis Potvin, NYI	1995 ......Peter Forsberg, Que

Vezina Trophy

Awarded annually "to the goalkeeper adjudged to be the best at his position." The trophy is named after Georges Vezina, an outstanding goalie for the Montreal Canadiens who collapsed during a game on November 28, 1925, and died a few months later of tuberculosis. The general managers of the 21 NHL teams vote on the award.

1927 ......George Hainsworth, Mtl	1940 ......Dave Kerr, NYR	1953 ......Terry Sawchuk, Det
1928 ......George Hainsworth, Mtl	1941 ......Turk Broda, Tor	1954 ......Harry Lumley, Tor
1929 ......George Hainsworth, Mtl	1942 ......Frank Brimsek, Bos	1955 ......Terry Sawchuk, Det
1930 ......Tiny Thompson, Bos	1943 ......Johnny Mowers, Det	1956 ......Jacques Plante, Mtl
1931 ......Roy Worters, NYA	1944 ......Bill Durnan, Mtl	1957 ......Jacques Plante, Mtl
1932 ......Charlie Gardiner, Chi	1945 ......Bill Durnan, Mtl	1958 ......Jacques Plante, Mtl
1933 ......Tiny Thompson, Bos	1946 ......Bill Durnan, Mtl	1959 ......Jacques Plante, Mtl
1934 ......Charlie Gardiner, Chi	1947 ......Bill Durnan, Mtl	1960 ......Jacques Plante, Mtl
1935 ......Lorne Chabot, Chi	1948 ......Turk Broda, Tor	1961 ......Johnny Bower, Tor
1936 ......Tiny Thompson, Bos	1949 ......Bill Durnan, Mtl	1962 ......Jacques Plante, Mtl
1937 ......Normie Smith, Det	1950 ......Bill Durnan, Mtl	1963 ......Glenn Hall, Chi
1938 ......Tiny Thompson, Bos	1951 ......Al Rollins, Tor	1964 ......Charlie Hodge, Mtl
1939 ......Frank Brimsek, Bos	1952 ......Terry Sawchuk, Det	

Vezina Trophy (Cont.)

1965	Terry Sawchuk, Tor Johnny Bower, Tor	1975	Bernie Parent, Phil	1985	Pelle Lindbergh, Phil
1966	Gump Worsley, Mtl Charlie Hodge, Mtl	1976	Ken Dryden, Mtl	1986	John Vanbiesbrouck, NYR
1967	Glenn Hall, Chi Rogie Vachon, Mtl	1977	Ken Dryden, Mtl Michel Larocque, Mtl	1987	Ron Hextall, Phil
1969	Jacques Plante, StL Glenn Hall, StL	1978	Ken Dryden, Mtl Michel Larocque, Mtl	1988	Grant Fuhr, Edm
1970	Tony Esposito, Chi	1979	Ken Dryden, Mtl Michel Larocque, Mtl	1989	Patrick Roy, Mtl
1971	Ed Giacomin, NYR Gilles Villemure, NYR	1980	Bob Sauve, Buff Don Edwards, Buff	1990	Patrick Roy, Mtl
1972	Tony Esposito, Chi Gary Smith, Chi	1981	Richard Sevigny, Mtl Denis Herron, Mtl Michel Larocque, Mtl	1991	Ed Belfour, Chi
1973	Ken Dryden, Mtl	1982	Bill Smith, NYI	1992	Patrick Roy, Mtl
1974	Bernie Parent, Phil Tony Esposito, Chi	1983	Pete Peeters, Bos	1993	Ed Belfour, Chi
		1984	Tom Barrasso, Buff	1994	Dominik Hasek, Buff
				1995	Dominik Hasek, Buff

Selke Trophy

Awarded annually "to the forward who best excels in the defensive aspects of the game." The trophy is named after Frank J. Selke, the architect of the Montreal Canadiens dynasty that won five consecutive Stanley Cups in the late '50s. The winner is selected by a vote of the Professional Hockey Writers Association.

1978	Bob Gainey, Mtl	1984	Doug Jarvis, Wash	1990	Rick Meagher, StL
1979	Bob Gainey, Mtl	1985	Craig Ramsay, Buff	1991	Dirk Graham, Chi
1980	Bob Gainey, Mtl	1986	Troy Murray, Chi	1992	Guy Carbonneau, Mtl
1981	Bob Gainey, Mtl	1987	Dave Poulin, Phil	1993	Doug Gilmour, Tor
1982	Steve Kasper, Bos	1988	Guy Carbonneau, Mtl	1994	Sergei Fedorov, Det
1983	Bobby Clarke, Phil	1989	Guy Carbonneau, Mtl	1995	Ron Francis, Pitt

Adams Award

Awarded annually "to the NHL coach adjudged to have contributed the most to his team's success." The trophy is named in honor of Jack Adams, longtime coach and general manager of the Detroit Red Wings. The winner is selected by a vote of the National Hockey League Broadcasters' Association.

1974	Fred Shero, Phil	1982	Tom Watt, Winn	1990	Bob Murdoch, Winn
1975	Bob Pulford, LA	1983	Orval Tessier, Chi	1991	Brian Sutter, StL
1976	Don Cherry, Bos	1984	Bryan Murray, Wash	1992	Pat Quinn, Van
1977	Scott Bowman, Mtl	1985	Mike Keenan, Phil	1993	Pat Burns, Tor
1978	Bobby Kromm, Det	1986	Glen Sather, Edm	1994	Jacques Lemaire, NJ
1979	Al Arbour, NYI	1987	Jacques Demers, Det	1995	Marc Crawford, Que
1980	Pat Quinn, Phil	1988	Jacques Demers, Det		
1981	Red Berenson, StL	1989	Pat Burns, Mtl		

Help, Can't Stop

It looks as if we've opened a Texarkana Worms with our item about the soon-to-be real-life Macon (Ga.) Whoopees of the Southern Hockey League and other groan-inducing expunsion teams (see page 312). Reader Michael McConnell of Fort Worth writes to nominate the Worms—along with the Altoona Fish, the Schenectady Dots, the Tucumcari Okies, the Olympia Zadoras, the Helena Handbaskets and a pair of potential farm clubs for the Minnesota Twins, the Bemidji Whiz and the Mankato Kaelins. Another correspondent, James P. Finnegan of Chappaqua, N.Y., evinces a more international bent. He suggests the Ankara Ways, the Sofia Lorens, the Bonn Vivants, the Riga Mortis, the Manila Folders, the Taiwan Ons and the New Delhi Catessans.

Dangerously, McConnell's flights of fancy extend beyond sports franchises. He suggests that someone open a racetrack in Alabama and call it Eufaula Downs.

Alltime Point Leaders

	Player	Yrs	GP	G	A	Pts	Pts/game
1.	*Wayne Gretzky, Edm, LA	16	1173	814	1692	2506	2.136
2.	Gordie Howe, Det, Hart	26	1767	801	1049	1850	1.047
3.	Marcel Dionne, Det, LA, NYR	18	1348	731	1040	1771	1.314
4.	Phil Esposito, Chi, Bos, NYR	18	1282	717	873	1590	1.240
5.	Stan Mikita, Chi	22	1394	541	926	1467	1.052
6.	Bryan Trottier, NYI, Pitt	18	1279	524	901	1425	1.114
7.	John Bucyk, Det, Bos	23	1540	556	813	1369	.889
8.	*Mark Messier, Edm, NYR	16	1127	492	877	1369	1.215
9.	Guy Lafleur, Mtl, NYR, Que	17	1126	560	793	1353	1.201
10.	*Paul Coffey, Edm, Pitt, LA, Det	15	1078	358	978	1336	1.240
11.	Gilbert Perreault, Buff	17	1191	512	814	1326	1.113
12.	*Dale Hawerchuk, Winn, Buff	14	1055	489	825	1314	1.246
13.	*Jari Kurri, Edm, LA	14	1028	565	731	1296	1.261
14.	Alex Delvecchio, Det	24	1549	456	825	1281	.827
15.	Jean Ratelle, NYR, Bos	21	1281	491	776	1267	.989

*Active player.

Alltime Goal-Scoring Leaders

	Player	Yrs	GP	G	G/game
1.	*Wayne Gretzky, Edm, LA	16	1173	814	.693
2.	Gordie Howe, Det, Hart	26	1767	801	.453
3.	Marcel Dionne, Det, LA, NYR	18	1348	731	.542
4.	Phil Esposito, Chi, Bos, NYR	18	1282	717	.559
5.	*Mike Gartner, Wash, Minn, NYR, Tor	16	1208	629	.521
6.	Bobby Hull, Chi, Winn, Hart	16	1063	610	.574
7.	Mike Bossy, NYI	10	752	573	.762
8.	*Jari Kurri, Edm, LA	14	1028	565	.550
9.	Guy Lafleur, Mtl, NYR, Que	17	1126	560	.497
10.	John Bucyk, Det, Bos	23	1540	556	.361

*Active player.

Alltime Assist Leaders

	Player	Yrs	GP	A	A/game
1.	*Wayne Gretzky, Edm, LA	16	1173	1692	1.443
2.	Gordie Howe, Det, Hart	26	1767	1049	.594
3.	Marcel Dionne, Det, LA, NYR	18	1348	1040	.772
4.	*Paul Coffey, Edm, Pitt, LA, Det	15	1078	978	.907
5.	Stan Mikita, Chi	22	1394	926	.664
6.	*Ray Bourque, Bos	16	1146	908	.792
7.	Bryan Trottier, NYI, Pitt	18	1279	901	.705
8.	*Mark Messier, Edm, NYR	16	1127	877	.778
9.	Phil Esposito, Chi, Bos, NYR	18	1282	873	.681
10.	Bobby Clarke, Phil	15	1144	852	.745

*Active player.

Alltime Penalty Minutes Leaders

	Player	Yrs	GP	PIM	Min/game
1.	Dave Williams, Tor, Van, Det, LA, Hart	13	962	3966	4.12
2.	*Dale Hunter, Que, Wash	15	1099	3104	2.82
3.	Chris Nilan, Mtl, NYR, Bos	13	688	3043	4.42
4.	*Tim Hunter, Cgy, Que, Van	14	709	2889	4.08
5.	*Marty McSorley, Edm, LA	12	707	2723	3.85
6.	Willi Plett, Atl, Cgy, Minn, Bos	12	834	2572	3.08
7.	*Basil McRae, Que, Tor, Det, Minn, StL	14	550	2405	4.37
8.	Dave Schultz, Phil, LA, Pitt, Buff	9	535	2294	4.29
9.	*Jay Wells, LA, Phil, Buff, NYR	16	1001	2279	2.28
10.	Laurie Boschman, Tor, Edm, Winn, NJ, Ott	14	1009	2265	2.24

*Active player.

Goaltending Records

ALLTIME WIN LEADERS

Goaltender	W	L	T	Pct
Terry Sawchuk, five teams	435	337	188	.551
Jacques Plante, five teams	434	246	137	.615
Tony Esposito, Mtl, Chi	423	307	151	.566
Glenn Hall, Det, Chi, StL	407	327	165	.544
Rogie Vachon, Mtl, LA, Det, Bos	355	291	115	.542
Gump Worsley, NYR, Mtl, Minn	335	353	150	.489
Harry Lumley, five teams	332	324	143	.505
*Andy Moog, Edm, Bos, Dall	313	160	71	.641
Billy Smith, LA, NYI	305	233	105	.556
Turk Broda, Tor	302	224	101	.562

*Active player.

ACTIVE GOALTENDING LEADERS

Goaltender	W	L	T	Pct
Andy Moog, Edm, Bos	313	160	71	.641
Mike Vernon, Cgy, Det	267	161	55	.610
Patrick Roy, Mtl	277	166	65	.609
Ed Belfour, Chi	168	106	40	.599
Grant Fuhr, Edm, Tor, Buff, LA	290	195	71	.585
Tom Barrasso, Buff, Pitt	266	197	61	.566
Ron Hextall, Phil, Que, NYI	203	161	46	.551
Tim Cheveldae, Det, Winn	141	117	34	.541
Kelly Hrudey, NYI, LA	244	210	71	.532
Daren Puppa, Buff, Tor, TB	138	122	36	.527

Note: Ranked by winning percentage; minimum 250 games played.

ALLTIME SHUTOUT LEADERS

Goaltender	Team	Yrs	GP	SO
Terry Sawchuk	Det, Bos, Tor, LA, NYR	21	971	103
George Hainsworth	Mtl, Tor	11	464	94
Glenn Hall	Det, Chi, StL	18	906	84
Jacques Plante	Mtl, NYR, StL, Tor, Bos	18	837	82
Tiny Thompson	Bos, Det	12	553	81
Alex Connell	Ott, Det, NYA, Mtl M	12	417	81
Tony Esposito	Mtl, Chi	16	886	76
Lorne Chabot	NYR, Tor, Mtl, Chi, Mtl M, NYA	11	411	73
Harry Lumley	Det, NYR, Chi, Tor, Bos	16	804	71
Roy Worters	Pitt Pir, NYA, *Mtl	12	484	66

*Played 1 game for Canadiens in 1929-30, not a shutout.

Coaching Records

Coach	Team	Seasons	W	L	T	Pct*
Scott Bowman	five teams	1967–	913	421	234	.657
Toe Blake	Mtl	1955-68	500	255	159	.634
Glen Sather	Edm	1979-89, 93-94	464	268	110	.616
Fred Shero	Phil, NYR	1971-81	390	225	119	.612
Tommy Ivan	Det, Chi	1947-54, 56-58	302	196	112	.587
Emile Francis	NYR, StL	1965-77, 81-83	393	273	112	.577
Bryan Murray	Wash, Det	1981-93	467	337	112	.571
Billy Reay	Tor, Chi	1957-59, 63-77	542	385	175	.571
Al Arbour	StL, NYI	1970-86, 88-94	781	577	248	.564
Dick Irvin	Chi, Tor, Mtl	1930-56	690	521	226	.559

*Percentage arrived at by dividing possible points into actual points.
Note: Minimum 600 regular-season games. Ranked by percentage.

Single-Season Records

Points per Game

Player	Season	GP	Pts	Avg	Player	Season	GP	Pts	Avg
Wayne Gretzky, Edm	1985-86	80	215	2.69	Wayne Gretzky, LA	1990-91	78	163	2.08
Mario Lemieux, Pitt	1992-93	60	160	2.66	Mario Lemieux, Pitt	1989-90	59	123	2.08
Wayne Gretzky, Edm	1981-82	80	212	2.65	Wayne Gretzky, Edm	1980-81	80	164	2.05
Mario Lemieux, Pitt	1988-89	76	199	2.62	Bill Cowley, Bos	1943-44	36	71	1.97
Wayne Gretzky, Edm	1984-85	80	208	2.60	Phil Esposito, Bos	1970-71	78	152	1.95
Wayne Gretzky, Edm	1982-83	80	196	2.45	Wayne Gretzky, LA	1989-90	73	142	1.95
Wayne Gretzky, Edm	1987-88	64	149	2.33	Steve Yzerman, Det	1988-89	80	155	1.94
Wayne Gretzky, Edm	1986-87	79	183	2.32	Bernie Nicholls, LA	1988-89	79	150	1.90
Mario Lemieux, Pitt	1987-88	77	168	2.18	Phil Esposito, Bos	1973-74	78	145	1.86
Wayne Gretzky, LA	1988-89	78	168	2.15					

Goals per Game

Player	Season	GP	G	Avg
Joe Malone, Mtl	1917-18	20	44	2.20
Cy Denneny, Ott	1917-18	22	36	1.64
Newsy Lalonde, Mtl	1917-18	14	23	1.64
Joe Malone, Que	1919-20	24	39	1.63
Newsy Lalonde, Mtl	1919-20	23	36	1.57
Joe Malone, Ham	1920-21	20	30	1.50
Babe Dye, Ham-Tor	1920-21	24	35	1.46
Cy Denneny, Ott	1920-21	24	34	1.42
Reg Noble, Tor	1917-18	20	28	1.40
Newsy Lalonde, Mtl	1920-21	24	33	1.38

Note: Minimum 20 goals in one season.

Assists per Game

Player	Season	GP	A	Avg
Wayne Gretzky, Edm	1985-86	80	163	2.04
Wayne Gretzky, Edm	1987-88	64	109	1.70
Wayne Gretzky, Edm	1984-85	80	135	1.69
Wayne Gretzky, Edm	1983-84	74	118	1.59
Wayne Gretzky, Edm	1982-83	80	125	1.56
Wayne Gretzky, LA	1990-91	78	122	1.56
Wayne Gretzky, Edm	1986-87	79	121	1.53
Mario Lemieux, Pitt	1992-93	60	91	1.52
Wayne Gretzky, Edm	1981-82	80	120	1.50
Mario Lemieux, Pitt	1988-89	76	114	1.50
Adam Oates, StL	1990-91	60	90	1.50

Shutout Leaders

	Season	SO	Length of Schedule		Season	SO	Length of Schedule
George Hainsworth, Mtl	1928-29	22	44	Bernie Parent, Phil	1973-74	12	78
Alex Connell, Ott	1925-26	15	36	Bernie Parent, Phil	1974-75	12	80
Alex Connell, Ott	1927-28	15	44	Lorne Chabot, NYR	1927-28	11	44
Hal Winkler, Bos	1927-28	15	44	Harry Holmes, Det	1927-28	11	44
Tony Esposito, Chi	1969-70	15	76	Clint Benedict, Mtl M	1928-29	11	44
George Hainsworth, Mtl	1926-27	14	44	Joe Miller, Pitt Pirates	1928-29	11	44
Clint Benedict, Mtl M	1926-27	13	44	Tiny Thompson, Bos	1932-33	11	48
Alex Connell, Ott	1926-27	13	44	Terry Sawchuk, Det	1950-51	11	70
George Hainsworth, Mtl	1927-28	13	44	Lorne Chabot, NYR	1926-27	10	44
Roy Worters, NYA	1927-28	13	44	Roy Worters, Pitt Pirates	1927-28	10	44
John Roach, NYR	1928-29	13	44	Clarence Dolson, Det	1928-29	10	44
Roy Worters, NYA	1928-29	13	44	John Roach, Det	1932-33	10	48
Harry Lumley, Tor	1953-54	13	70	Chuck Gardiner, Chi	1933-34	10	48
Tiny Thompson, Bos	1928-29	12	44	Tiny Thompson, Bos	1935-36	10	48
Lorne Chabot, Tor	1928-29	12	44	Frank Brimsek, Bos	1938-39	10	48
Chuck Gardiner, Chi	1930-31	12	44	Bill Durnan, Mtl	1948-49	10	60
Terry Sawchuk, Det	1951-52	12	70	Gerry McNeil, Mtl	1952-53	10	70
Terry Sawchuk, Det	1953-54	12	70	Harry Lumley, Tor	1952-53	10	70
Terry Sawchuk, Det	1954-55	12	70	Tony Esposito, Chi	1973-74	10	78
Glenn Hall, Det	1955-56	12	70	Ken Dryden, Mtl	1976-77	10	80

Single-Game Records

Goals

	Date	G
Joe Malone, Que vs Tor	1-31-20	7
Newsy Lalonde, Mtl vs Tor	1-10-20	6
Joe Malone, Que vs Ott	3-10-20	6
Corb Denneny, Tor vs Ham	1-26-21	6
Cy Denneny, Ott vs Ham	3-7-21	6
Syd Howe, Det vs NYR	2-3-44	6
Red Berenson, StL vs Phil	11-7-68	6
Darryl Sittler, Tor vs Bos	2-7-76	6

Assists

	Date	A
Billy Taylor, Det vs Chi	3-16-47	7
Wayne Gretzky, Edm vs Wash	2-15-80	7
Wayne Gretzky, Edm vs Chi	12-11-85	7
Wayne Gretzky, Edm vs Que	2-14-86	7

Note: 19 tied with 6.

Points

	Date	G	A	Pts
Darryl Sittler, Tor vs Bos	2-7-76	6	4	10
Maurice Richard, Mtl vs Det	12-28-44	5	3	8
Bert Olmstead, Mtl vs Chi	1-9-54	4	4	8
Tom Bladon, Phil vs Clev	12-11-77	4	4	8
Bryan Trottier, NYI vs NYR	12-23-78	5	3	8
Peter Stastny, Que vs Wash	2-22-81	4	4	8
Anton Stastny, Que vs Wash	2-22-81	3	5	8
Wayne Gretzky, Edm vs NJ	11-19-83	3	5	8
Wayne Gretzky, Edm vs Minn	1-4-84	4	4	8
Paul Coffey, Edm vs Det	3-14-86	2	6	8
Mario Lemieux, Pitt vs StL	10-15-88	2	6	8
Bernie Nicholls, LA vs Tor	12-1-88	2	6	8
Mario Lemieux, Pitt vs NJ	12-31-88	5	3	8

Points

Season	Player and Club	Pts	Season	Player and Club	Pts
1917-18	Joe Malone, Mtl	44*	1957-58	Dickie Moore, Mtl	84
1918-19	Newsy Lalonde, Mtl	30	1958-59	Dickie Moore, Mtl	96
1919-20	Joe Malone, Que	48	1959-60	Bobby Hull, Chi	81
1920-21	Newsy Lalonde, Mtl	41	1960-61	Bernie Geoffrion, Mtl	95
1921-22	Punch Broadbent, Ott	46	1961-62	Andy Bathgate, NY	84
1922-23	Babe Dye, Tor	37		Bobby Hull, Chi	84
1923-24	Cy Denneny, Ott	23	1962-63	Gordie Howe, Det	86
1924-25	Babe Dye, Tor	44	1963-64	Stan Mikita, Chi	89
1925-26	Nels Stewart, Mtl M	42	1964-65	Stan Mikita, Chi	87
1926-27	Bill Cook, NY	37	1965-66	Bobby Hull, Chi	97
1927-28	Howie Morenz, Mtl	51	1966-67	Stan Mikita, Chi	97
1928-29	Ace Bailey, Tor	32	1967-68	Stan Mikita, Chi	87
1929-30	Cooney Weiland, Bos	73	1968-69	Phil Esposito, Bos	126
1930-31	Howie Morenz, Mtl	51	1969-70	Bobby Orr, Bos	120
1931-32	Harvey Jackson, Tor	53	1970-71	Phil Esposito, Bos	152
1932-33	Bill Cook, NY	50	1971-72	Phil Esposito, Bos	133
1933-34	Charlie Conacher, Tor	52	1972-73	Phil Esposito, Bos	130
1934-35	Charlie Conacher, Tor	57	1973-74	Phil Esposito, Bos	145
1935-36	Sweeney Schriner, NYA	45	1974-75	Bobby Orr, Bos	135
1936-37	Sweeney Schriner, NYA	46	1975-76	Guy Lafleur, Mtl	125
1937-38	Gord Drillon, Tor	52	1976-77	Guy Lafleur, Mtl	136
1938-39	Hector Blake, Mtl	47	1977-78	Guy Lafleur, Mtl	132
1939-40	Milt Schmidt, Bos	52	1978-79	Bryan Trottier, NYI	134
1940-41	Bill Cowley, Bos	62	1979-80	Marcel Dionne, LA	137
1941-42	Bryan Hextall, NY	54		Wayne Gretzky, Edm	137
1942-43	Doug Bentley, Chi	73	1980-81	Wayne Gretzky, Edm	164
1943-44	Herb Cain, Bos	82	1981-82	Wayne Gretzky, Edm	212
1944-45	Elmer Lach, Mtl	80	1982-83	Wayne Gretzky, Edm	196
1945-46	Max Bentley, Chi	61	1983-84	Wayne Gretzky, Edm	205
1946-47	Max Bentley, Chi	72	1984-85	Wayne Gretzky, Edm	208
1947-48	Elmer Lach, Mtl	61	1985-86	Wayne Gretzky, Edm	215
1948-49	Roy Conacher, Chi	68	1986-87	Wayne Gretzky, Edm	183
1949-50	Ted Lindsay, Det	78	1987-88	Mario Lemieux, Pitt	168
1950-51	Gordie Howe, Det	86	1988-89	Mario Lemieux, Pitt	199
1951-52	Gordie Howe, Det	86	1989-90	Wayne Gretzky, LA	142
1952-53	Gordie Howe, Det	95	1990-91	Wayne Gretzky, LA	163
1953-54	Gordie Howe, Det	81	1991-92	Mario Lemieux, Pitt	131
1954-55	Bernie Geoffrion, Mtl	75	1992-93	Mario Lemieux, Pitt	160
1955-56	Jean Beliveau, Mtl	88	1993-94	Wayne Gretzky, LA	130
1956-57	Gordie Howe, Det	89	1994-95	Jaromir Jagr, Pitt	70

Goals

Season	Player and Club	Pts	Season	Player and Club	Pts
1917-18	Joe Malone, Mtl	44	1936-37	Larry Aurie, Det	23
1918-19	Odie Cleghorn, Mtl	23		Nels Stewart, Bos-NYA	23
1919-20	Joe Malone, Que	39	1937-38	Gord Drill, Tor	26
1920-21	Babe Dye, Ham-Tor	35	1938-39	Roy Conacher, Bos	26
1921-22	Punch Broadbent, Ott	32	1939-40	Bryan Hextall, NY	24
1922-23	Babe Dye, Tor	26	1940-41	Bryan Hextall, NY	26
1923-24	Cy Denneny, Ott	22	1941-42	Lynn Patrick, NY	32
1924-25	Babe Dye, Tor	38	1942-43	Doug Bentley, Chi	43
1925-26	Nels Stewart, Mtl	34	1943-44	Doug Bentley, Chi	38
1926-27	Bill Cook, NY	33	1944-45	Maurice Richard, Mtl	50
1927-28	Howie Morenz, Mtl	33	1945-46	Gaye Stewart, Tor	37
1928-29	Ace Bailey, Tor	22	1946-47	Maurice Richard, Mtl	50
1929-30	Cooney Weiland, Bos	43	1947-48	Ted Lindsay, Det	33
1930-31	Bill Cook, NY	30	1948-49	Sid Abel, Det	28
1931-32	Charlie Conacher, Tor	34	1949-50	Maurice Richard, Mtl	43
	Bill Cook, NY	34	1950-51	Gordie Howe, Det	43
1932-33	Bill Cook, NY	28	1951-52	Gordie Howe, Det	47
1933-34	Charlie Conacher, Tor	32	1952-53	Gordie Howe, Det	49
1934-35	Charlie Conacher, Tor	36	1953-54	Maurice Richard, Mtl	37
1935-36	Charlie Conacher, Tor	23	1954-55	Bernie Geoffrion, Mtl	38
	Bill Thoms, Tor	23		Maurice Richard, Mtl	38
			1955-56	Jean Beliveau, Mtl	47
			1956-57	Gordie Howe, Det	44

Goals (Cont.)

Season	Player and Club	G	Season	Player and Club	G
1957-58	Dickie Moore, Mtl	36	1977-78	Guy Lafleur, Mtl	60
1958-59	Jean Beliveau, Mtl	45	1978-79	Mike Bossy, NYI	69
1959-60	Bobby Hull, Chi	39	1979-80	Charlie Simmer, LA	56
	Bronco Horvath, Bos	39		Blaine Stoughton, Hart	56
1960-61	Bernie Geoffrion, Mtl	50	1980-81	Mike Bossy, NYI	68
1961-62	Bobby Hull, Chi	50	1981-82	Wayne Gretzky, Edm	92
1962-63	Gordie Howe, Det	38	1982-83	Wayne Gretzky, Edm	71
1963-64	Bobby Hull, Chi	43	1983-84	Wayne Gretzky, Edm	87
1964-65	Norm Ullman, Det	42	1984-85	Wayne Gretzky, Edm	73
1965-66	Bobby Hull, Chi	54	1985-86	Jari Kurri, Edm	68
1966-67	Bobby Hull, Chi	52	1986-87	Wayne Gretzky, Edm	62
1967-68	Bobby Hull, Chi	44	1987-88	Mario Lemieux, Pitt	70
1968-69	Bobby Hull, Chi	58	1988-89	Mario Lemieux, Pitt	85
1969-70	Phil Esposito, Bos	43	1989-90	Brett Hull, StL	72
1970-71	Phil Esposito, Bos	76	1990-91	Brett Hull, StL	78
1971-72	Phil Esposito, Bos	66	1991-92	Brett Hull, StL	70
1972-73	Phil Esposito, Bos	55	1992-93	Alexander Mogilny, Buff	76
1973-74	Phil Esposito, Bos	68		Teemu Selanne, Winn	76
1974-75	Phil Esposito, Bos	61	1993-94	Pavel Bure, Van	60
1975-76	Guy Lafleur, Mtl	56	1994-95	Peter Bondra, Wash	34
1976-77	Steve Shutt, Mtl	60			

Assists

Season	Player and Club	A	Season	Player and Club	A
1917-18	statistic not kept		1958-59	Dickie Moore, Mtl	55
1918-19	Newsy Lalonde, Mtl	9	1959-60	Bobby Hull, Chi	42
1919-20	Corbett Denneny, Tor	12	1960-61	Jean Beliveau, Mtl	58
1920-21	Louis Berlinquette, Mtl	9	1961-62	Andy Bathgate, NY	56
1921-22	Punch Broadbench, Ott	14	1962-63	Henri Richard, Mtl	50
1922-23	Babe Dye, Tor	11	1963-64	Andy Bathgate, NY-Tor	58
1923-24	Billy Boucher, Mtl	6	1964-65	Stan Mikita, Chi	59
1924-25	Cy Denneny, Ott	15	1965-66	Stan Mikita, Chi	48
1925-26	Cy Denneny, Ott	12		Bobby Rousseau, Mtl	48
1926-27	Dick Irvin, Chi	18		Jean Beliveau, Mtl	48
1927-28	Howie Morenz, Mtl	18	1966-67	Stan Mikita, Chi	62
1928-29	Frank Boucher, NY	16	1967-68	Phil Esposito, Bos	49
1929-30	Frank Boucher, NY	36	1968-69	Phil Esposito, Bos	77
1930-31	Joe Primeau, Tor	36	1969-70	Bobby Orr, Bos	87
1931-32	Joe Primeau, Tor	37	1970-71	Bobby Orr, Bos	102
1932-33	Frank Boucher, NY	28	1971-72	Bobby Orr, Bos	80
1933-34	Joe Primeau, Tor	32	1972-73	Phil Esposito, Bos	75
1934-35	Art Chapman, NYA	28	1973-74	Bobby Orr, Bos	89
1935-36	Art Chapman, NYA	28	1974-75	Bobby Clarke, Phil	89
1936-37	Syl Apps, Tor	29		Bobby Orr, Bos	89
1937-38	Syl Apps, Tor	29	1975-76	Bobby Clarke, Phil	89
1938-39	Bill Cowley, Bos	34	1976-77	Guy Lafleur, Mtl	80
1939-40	Milt Schmidt, Bos	30	1977-78	Bryan Trottier, NYI	77
1940-41	Bill Cowley, Bos	45	1978-79	Bryan Trottier, NYI	87
1941-42	Phil Watson, NY	37	1979-80	Wayne Gretzky, Edm	86
1942-43	Bill Cowley, Bos	45	1980-81	Wayne Gretzky, Edm	109
1943-44	Clint Smith, Chi	49	1981-82	Wayne Gretzky, Edm	120
1944-45	Elmer Lach, Mtl	54	1982-83	Wayne Gretzky, Edm	125
1945-46	Elmer Lach, Mtl	34	1983-84	Wayne Gretzky, Edm	118
1946-47	Billy Taylor, Det	46	1984-85	Wayne Gretzky, Edm	135
1947-48	Doug Bentley, Chi	37	1985-86	Wayne Gretzky, Edm	163
1948-49	Doug Bentley, Chi	43	1986-87	Wayne Gretzky, Edm	121
1949-50	Ted Lindsay, Det	55	1987-88	Wayne Gretzky, Edm	109
1950-51	Gordie Howe, Det	43	1988-89	Wayne Gretzky, LA	114
	Ted Kennedy, Tor	43		Mario Lemieux, Pitt	114
1951-52	Elmer Lach, Mtl	50	1989-90	Wayne Gretzky, LA	102
1952-53	Gordie Howe, Det	46	1990-91	Wayne Gretzky, LA	122
1953-54	Gordie Howe, Det	48	1991-92	Wayne Gretzky, LA	90
1954-55	Bert Olmstead, Mtl	48	1992-93	Adam Oates, Bos	97
1955-56	Bert Olmstead, Mtl	56	1993-94	Wayne Gretzky, LA	92
1956-57	Ted Lindsay, Det	55	1994-95	Ron Francis, Pitt	48
1957-58	Henri Richard, Mtl	52			

Goals Against Average

Season	Goaltender and Club	GP	Min	GA	SO	Avg
1917-18	Georges Vezina, Mtl	21	1282	84	1	3.93
1918-19	Clint Benedict, Ott	18	1113	53	2	2.86
1919-20	Clint Benedict, Ott	24	1444	64	5	2.66
1920-21	Clint Benedict, Ott	24	1457	75	2	3.09
1921-22	Clint Benedict, Ott	24	1508	84	2	3.34
1922-23	Clint Benedict, Ott	24	1478	54	4	2.19
1923-24	Georges Vezina, Mtl	24	1459	48	3	1.97
1924-25	Georges Vezina, Mtl	30	1860	56	5	1.81
1925-26	Alex Connell, Ott	36	2251	42	15	1.12
1926-27	Clint Benedict, Mtl M	43	2748	65	13	1.42
1927-28	George Hainsworth, Mtl	44	2730	48	13	1.05
1928-29	George Hainsworth, Mtl	44	2800	43	22	0.92
1929-30	Tiny Thompson, Bos	44	2680	98	3	2.19
1930-31	Roy Worters, NYA	44	2760	74	8	1.61
1931-32	Chuck Gardiner, Chi	48	2989	92	4	1.85
1932-33	Tiny Thompson, Bos	48	3000	88	11	1.76
1933-34	Wilf Cude, Det-Mtl	30	1920	47	5	1.47
1934-35	Lorne Chabot, Chi	48	2940	88	8	1.80
1935-36	Tiny Thompson, Bos	48	2930	82	10	1.68
1936-37	Normie Smith, Det	48	2980	102	6	2.05
1937-38	Tiny Thompson, Bos	48	2970	89	7	1.80
1938-39	Frank Brimsek, Bos	43	2610	68	10	1.56
1939-40	Dave Kerr, NYR	48	3000	77	8	1.54
1940-41	Turk Broda, Tor	48	2970	99	5	2.00
1941-42	Frank Brimsek, Bos	47	2930	115	3	2.35
1942-43	Johnny Mowers, Det	50	3010	124	6	2.47
1943-44	Bill Durnan, Mtl	50	3000	109	2	2.18
1944-45	Bill Durnan, Mtl	50	3000	121	1	2.42
1945-46	Bill Durnan, Mtl	40	2400	104	4	2.60
1946-47	Bill Durnan, Mtl	60	3600	138	4	2.30
1947-48	Turk Broda, Tor	60	3600	143	5	2.38
1948-49	Bill Durnan, Mtl	60	3600	126	10	2.10
1949-50	Bill Durnan, Mtl	64	3840	141	8	2.20
1950-51	Al Rollins, Tor	40	2367	70	5	1.77
1951-52	Terry Sawchuk, Det	70	4200	133	12	1.90
1952-53	Terry Sawchuk, Det	63	3780	120	9	1.90
1953-54	Harry Lumley, Tor	69	4140	128	13	1.86
1954-55	Harry Lumley, Tor	69	4140	134	8	1.94
	Terry Sawchuk, Det	68	4060	132	12	1.94
1955-56	Jacques Plante, Mtl	64	3840	119	7	1.86
1956-57	Jacques Plante, Mtl	61	3660	123	9	2.02
1957-58	Jacques Plante, Mtl	57	3386	119	9	2.11
1958-59	Jacques Plante, Mtl	67	4000	144	9	2.16
1959-60	Jacques Plante, Mtl	69	4140	175	3	2.54
1960-61	Johnny Bower, Tor	58	3480	145	2	2.50
1961-62	Jacques Plante, Mtl	70	4200	166	4	2.37
1962-63	Jacques Plante, Mtl	56	3320	138	5	2.49
1963-64	Johnny Bower, Tor	51	3009	106	5	2.11
1964-65	Johnny Bower, Tor	34	2040	81	3	2.38
1965-66	Johnny Bower, Tor	35	1998	75	3	2.25
1966-67	Glenn Hall, Chi	32	1664	66	2	2.38
1967-68	Gump Worsley, Mtl	40	2213	73	6	1.98
1968-69	Jacques Plante, StL	37	2139	70	5	1.96
1969-70	Ernie Wakely, StL	30	1651	58	4	2.11
1970-71	Jacques Plante, Tor	40	2329	73	4	1.88
1971-72	Tony Esposito, Chi	48	2780	82	9	1.77
1972-73	Ken Dryden, Mtl	54	3165	119	6	2.26
1973-74	Bernie Parent, Phil	73	4314	136	12	1.89
1974-75	Bernie Parent, Phil	68	4041	137	12	2.03
1975-76	Ken Dryden, Mtl	62	3580	121	8	2.03
1976-77	Michael Larocque, Mtl	26	1525	53	4	2.09
1977-78	Ken Dryden, Mtl	52	3071	105	5	2.05
1978-79	Ken Dryden, Mtl	47	2814	108	5	2.30
1979-80	Bob Sauve, Buff	32	1880	74	4	2.36
1980-81	Richard Sevigny, Mtl	33	1777	71	2	2.40
1981-82	Denis Herron, Mtl	27	1547	68	3	2.64

Goals Against Average *(Cont.)*

Season	Goaltender and Club	GP	Min	GA	SO	Avg
1982-83	Pete Peeters, Bos	62	3611	142	8	2.36
1983-84	Pat Riggin, Wash	41	2299	102	4	2.66
1984-85	Tom Barrasso, Buff	54	3248	144	5	2.66
1985-86	Bob Froese, Phil	51	2728	116	5	2.55
1986-87	Brian Hayward, Mtl	37	2178	102	1	2.81
1987-88	Pete Peeters, Wash	35	1896	88	2	2.78
1988-89	Patrick Roy, Mtl	48	2744	113	4	2.47
1989-90	Patrick Roy, Mtl	54	3173	134	3	2.53
	Mike Liut, Hart-Wash	37	2161	91	4	2.53
1990-91	Ed Belfour, Chi	74	4127	170	4	2.47
1991-92	Patrick Roy, Mtl	67	3935	155	5	2.36
1992-93	*Felix Potvin, Tor	48	2781	116	2	2.50
1993-94	Dominik Hasek, Buff	58	3358	109	7	1.95
1994-95	Dominik Hasek, Buff	41	2416	85	5	2.11

*Rookie.

Penalty Minutes

Season	Player and Club	GP	PIM	Season	Player and Club	GP	PIM
1918-19	Joe Hall, Mtl	17	85	1957-58	Lou Fontinato, NYR	70	152
1919-20	Cully Wilson, Tor	23	79	1958-59	Ted Lindsay, Chi	70	184
1920-21	Bert Corbeau, Mtl	24	86	1959-60	Carl Brewer, Tor	67	150
1921-22	S Cleghorn, Mtl	24	63	1960-61	Pierre Pilote, Chi	70	165
1922-23	Billy Boucher, Mtl	24	52	1961-62	Lou Fontinato, Mtl	54	167
1923-24	Bert Corbeau, Tor	24	55	1962-63	Howie Young, Det	64	273
1924-25	Billy Boucher, Mtl	30	92	1963-64	Vic Hadfield, NYR	69	151
1925-26	Bert Corbeau, Tor	36	121	1964-65	Carl Brewer, Tor	70	177
1926-27	Nels Stewart, Mtl M	44	133	1965-66	R Fleming, Bos-NYR	69	166
1927-28	Eddie Shore, Bos	44	165	1966-67	John Ferguson, Mtl	67	177
1928-29	Red Dutton, Mtl M	44	139	1967-68	Barclay Plager, StL	49	153
1929-30	Joe Lamb, Ott	44	119	1968-69	F Kennedy, Phil-Tor	77	219
1930-31	Harvey Rockburn, Det	42	118	1969-70	Keith Magnuson, Chi	76	213
1931-32	Red Dutton, NYA	47	107	1970-71	Keith Magnuson, Chi	76	291
1932-33	Red Horner, Tor	48	144	1971-72	Brian Watson, Pitt	75	212
1933-34	Red Horner, Tor	42	126	1972-73	Dave Schultz, Phil	76	259
1934-35	Red Horner, Tor	46	125	1973-74	Dave Schultz, Phil	73	348
1935-36	Red Horner, Tor	43	167	1974-75	Dave Schultz, Phil	76	472
1936-37	Red Horner, Tor	48	124	1975-76	S Durbano, Pitt-KC	69	370
1937-38	Red Horner, Tor	47	82	1976-77	Dave Williams, Tor	77	338
1938-39	Red Horner, Tor	48	85	1977-78	Dave Schultz, LA-Pitt	74	405
1939-40	Red Horner, Tor	30	87	1978-79	Dave Williams, Tor	77	298
1940-41	Jimmy Orlando, Det	48	99	1979-80	Jimmy Mann, Winn	72	287
1941-42	Jimmy Orlando, Det	48	81	1980-81	Dave Williams, Van	77	343
1942-43	Jimmy Orlando, Det	40	89	1981-82	Paul Baxter, Pitt	76	409
1943-44	Mike McMahon, Mtl	42	98	1982-83	Randy Holt, Wash	70	275
1944-45	Pat Egan, Bos	48	86	1983-84	Chris Nilan, Mtl	76	338
1945-46	Jack Stewart, Det	47	73	1984-85	Chris Nilan, Mtl	77	358
1946-47	Gus Mortson, Tor	60	133	1985-86	Joey Kocur, Det	59	377
1947-48	Bill Barilko, Tor	57	147	1986-87	Tim Hunter, Cgy	73	361
1948-49	Bill Ezinicki, Tor	52	145	1987-88	Bob Probert, Det	74	398
1949-50	Bill Ezinicki, Tor	67	144	1988-89	Tim Hunter, Cgy	75	375
1950-51	Gus Mortson, Tor	60	142	1989-90	Basil McRae, Minn	66	351
1951-52	Gus Kyle, Bos	69	127	1990-91	Bob Ray, Buff	66	350
1952-53	Maurice Richard, Mtl	70	112	1991-92	Mike Peluso, Chi	63	408
1953-54	Gus Mortson, Chi	68	132	1992-93	Marty McSorley, LA	81	399
1954-55	Fern Flaman, Bos	70	150	1993-94	Tie Domi, Winn	81	347
1955-56	Lou Fontinato, NYR	70	202	1994-95	Enrico Ciccone, TB	41	225
1956-57	Gus Mortson, Chi	70	147				

NHL All-Star Game

First played in 1947, this game was scheduled before the start of the regular season and used to match the defending Stanley Cup champions against a squad made up of league All-Stars from other teams. In 1966 the games were moved to mid-season, although there was no game that year. The format changed to a conference versus conference showdown in 1969.

Results

Year	Site	Score	MVP	Attendance
1947	Toronto	All-Stars 4, Toronto 3	None named	14,169
1948	Chicago	All-Stars 3, Toronto 1	None named	12,794
1949	Toronto	All-Stars 3, Toronto 1	None named	13,541
1950	Detroit	Detroit 7, All-Stars 1	None named	9,166
1951	Toronto	1st team 2, 2nd team 2	None named	11,469
1952	Detroit	1st team 1, 2nd team 1	None named	10,680
1953	Montreal	All-Stars 3, Montreal 1	None named	14,153
1954	Detroit	All-Stars 2, Detroit 2	None named	10,689
1955	Detroit	Detroit 3, All-Stars 1	None named	10,111
1956	Montreal	All-Stars 1, Montreal 1	None named	13,095
1957	Montreal	All-Stars 5, Montreal 3	None named	13,003
1958	Montreal	Montreal 6, All-Stars 3	None named	13,989
1959	Montreal	Montreal 6, All-Stars 1	None named	13,818
1960	Montreal	All-Stars 2, Montreal 1	None named	13,949
1961	Chicago	All-Stars 3, Chicago 1	None named	14,534
1962	Toronto	Toronto 4, All-Stars 1	Eddie Shack, Tor	14,236
1963	Toronto	All-Stars 3, Toronto 3	Frank Mahovlich, Tor	14,034
1964	Toronto	All-Stars 3, Toronto 2	Jean Beliveau, Mtl	14,232
1965	Montreal	All-Stars 5, Montreal 2	Gordie Howe, Det	13,529
1967	Montreal	Montreal 3, All-Stars 0	Henri Richard, Mtl	14,284
1968	Toronto	Toronto 4, All-Stars 3	Bruce Gamble, Tor	15,753
1969	Montreal	East 3, West 3	Frank Mahovlich, Det	16,260
1970	St Louis	East 4, West 1	Bobby Hull, Chi	16,587
1971	Boston	West 2, East 1	Bobby Hull, Chi	14,790
1972	Minnesota	East 3, West 2	Bobby Orr, Bos	15,423
1973	NY Rangers	East 5, West 4	Greg Polis, Pitt	16,986
1974	Chicago	West 6, East 4	Garry Unger, StL	16,426
1975	Montreal	Wales 7, Campbell 1	Syl Apps Jr, Pitt	16,080
1976	Philadelphia	Wales 7, Campbell 5	Pete Mahovlich, Mtl	16,436
1977	Vancouver	Wales 4, Campbell 3	Rick Martin, Buff	15,607
1978	Buffalo	Wales 3, Campbell 2 (OT)	Billy Smith, NYI	16,433
1980	Detroit	Wales 6, Campbell 3	Reg Leach, Phil	21,002
1981	Los Angeles	Campbell 4, Wales 1	Mike Liut, StL	15,761
1982	Washington	Wales 4, Campbell 2	Mike Bossy, NYI	18,130
1983	NY Islanders	Campbell 9, Wales 3	Wayne Gretzky, Edm	15,230
1984	NJ Devils	Wales 7, Campbell 6	Don Maloney, NYR	18,939
1985	Calgary	Wales 6, Campbell 4	Mario Lemieux, Pitt	16,825
1986	Hartford	Wales 4, Campbell 3 (OT)	Grant Fuhr, Edm	15,100
1988	St Louis	Wales 6, Campbell 5 (OT)	Mario Lemieux, Pitt	17,878
1989	Edmonton	Campbell 9, Wales 5	Wayne Gretzky, LA	17,503
1990	Pittsburgh	Wales 12, Campbell 7	Mario Lemieux, Pitt	16,236
1991	Chicago	Campbell 11, Wales 5	Vince Damphousse, Tor	18,472
1992	Philadelphia	Campbell 10, Wales 6	Brett Hull, StL	17,380
1993	Montreal	Wales 16, Campbell 6	Mike Gartner, NYR	17,137
1994	NY Rangers	East 9, West 8	Mike Richter, NYR	18,200

Note: The Challenge Cup, a series between the NHL All-Stars and the Soviet Union, was played instead of the All-Star Game in 1979. Eight years later, Rendez-Vous '87, a two-game series matching the Soviet Union and the NHL All-Stars, replaced the All-Star Game. The 1995 NHL All-Star game was cancelled due to a labor dispute.

Hockey Hall of Fame

Located in Toronto, the Hockey Hall of Fame was officially opened on August 26, 1961. The current president is Ian "Scotty" Morrison, a former NHL referee. There are, at present, 281 members of the Hockey Hall of Fame—192 players, 77 "Builders," and 12 on-ice officials. To be eligible, player and referee/linesman candidates should have been out of the game for three years, but the Hall's Board of Directors can make exceptions.

Players

Sid Abel (1969)
Jack Adams (1959)
Charles "Syl" Apps (1961)
George Armstrong (1975)
Irvine "Ace" Bailey (1975)
Donald H. "Dan" Bain (1945)
Hobey Baker (1945)
Bill Barber (1990)
Marty Barry (1965)
Andy Bathgate (1978)
Jean Beliveau (1972)
Clint Benedict (1965)
Douglas Bentley (1964)
Max Bentley (1966)
Hector "Toe" Blake (1966)
Leo Boivin (1986)
Dickie Boon (1952)
Mike Bossy (1991)
Emile "Butch" Bouchard (1966)
Frank Boucher (1958)
George "Buck" Boucher (1960)
Johnny Bower (1976)
Russell Bowie (1945)
Frank Brimsek (1966)
Harry L. "Punch" Broadbent (1962)
Walter "Turk" Broda (1967)
John Bucyk (1981)
Billy Burch (1974)
Harry Cameron (1962)
Gerry Cheevers (1985)
Francis "King" Clancy (1958)
Aubrey "Dit" Clapper (1947)
Bobby Clarke (1987)
Sprague Cleghorn (1958)
Neil Colville (1967)
Charlie Conacher (1961)
Lionel Conacher (1994)
Alex Connell (1958)
Bill Cook (1952)
Arthur Coulter (1974)
Yvan Cournoyer (1982)
Bill Cowley (1968)
Samuel "Rusty" Crawford (1962)
Jack Darragh (1962)
Allan M. "Scotty" Davidson (1950)
Clarence "Hap" Day (1961)
Alex Delvecchio (1977)
Cy Denneny (1959)
Marcel Dionne (1992)
Gordie Drillon (1975)
Charles Drinkwater (1950)
Ken Dryden (1983)
Woody Dumart (1992)

Thomas Dunderdale (1974)
Bill Durnan (1964)
Mervyn A. "Red" Dutton (1958)
Cecil "Babe" Dye (1970)
Phil Esposito (1984)
Tony Esposito (1988)
Arthur F. Farrell (1965)
Ferdinand "Fern" Flaman (1990)
Frank Foyston (1958)
Frank Frederickson (1958)
Bill Gadsby (1970)
Bob Gainey (1992)
Chuck Gardiner (1945)
Herb Gardiner (1958)
Jimmy Gardner (1962)
Bernie "Boom Boom" Geoffrion (1972)
Eddie Gerard (1945)
Ed Giacomin (1987)
Rod Gilbert (1982)
Hamilton "Billy" Gilmour (1962)
Frank "Moose" Goheen (1952)
Ebenezer R. "Ebbie" Goodfellow (1963)
Mike Grant (1950)
Wilfred "Shorty" Green (1962)
Si Griffis (1950)
George Hainsworth (1961)
Glenn Hall (1975)
Joe Hall (1961)
Doug Harvey (1973)
George Hay (1958)
William "Riley" Hern (1962)
Bryan Hextall (1969)
Harry "Hap" Holmes (1972)
Tom Hooper (1962)
George "Red" Horner (1965)
Miles "Tim" Horton (1977)
Gordie Howe (1972)
Syd Howe (1965)
Harry Howell (1979)
Bobby Hull (1983)
John "Bouse" Hutton (1962)
Harry M. Hyland (1962)
James "Dick" Irvin (1958)
Harvey "Busher" Jackson (1971)
Ernest "Moose" Johnson (1952)
Ivan "Ching" Johnson (1958)
Tom Johnson (1970)
Aurel Joliat (1947)
Gordon "Duke" Keats (1958)
Leonard "Red" Kelly (1969)
Ted "Teeder" Kennedy (1966)
Dave Keon (1986)

Elmer Lach (1966)
Guy Lafleur (1988)
Edouard "Newsy" Lalonde (1950)
Jacques Laperriere (1987)
Guy LaPointe (1993)
Edgar Laprade (1993)
Jean "Jack" Laviolette (1962)
Hugh Lehman (1958)
Jacques Lemaire (1984)
Percy LeSueur (1961)
Herbert A. Lewis (1989)
Ted Lindsay (1966)
Harry Lumley (1980)
Lanny McDonald (1992)
Frank McGee (1945)
Billy McGimsie (1962)
George McNamara (1958)
Duncan "Mickey" MacKay (1952)
Frank Mahovlich (1981)
Joe Malone (1950)
Sylvio Mantha (1960)
Jack Marshall (1965)
Fred G. "Steamer" Maxwell (1962)
Stan Mikita (1983)
Dicky Moore (1974)
Patrick "Paddy" Moran (1958)
Howie Morenz (1945)
Billy Mosienko (1965)
Frank Nighbor (1947)
Reg Noble (1962)
Herbert "Buddy" O'Connor (1988)
Harry Oliver (1967)
Bert Olmstead (1985)
Bobby Orr (1979)
Bernie Parent (1984)
Brad Park (1988)
Lester Patrick (1947)
Lynn Patrick (1980)
Gilbert Perreault (1990)
Tommy Phillips (1945)
Pierre Pilote (1975)
Didier "Pit" Pitre (1962)
Jacques Plante (1978)
Denis Potvin (1991)
Walter "Babe" Pratt (1966)
Joe Primeau (1963)
Marcel Pronovost (1978)
Bob Pulford (1991)
Harvey Pulford (1945)
Hubert "Bill" Quackenbush (1976)

Players *(Cont.)*

Frank Rankin (1961)
Jean Ratelle (1985)
Claude "Chuck" Rayner (1973)
Kenneth Reardon (1966)
Henri Richard (1979)
Maurice "Rocket" Richard
 (1961)
George Richardson (1950)
Gordon Roberts (1971)
Art Ross (1945)
Blair Russel (1965)
Ernest Russell (1965)
Jack Ruttan (1962)
Serge Savard (1986)
Terry Sawchuk (1971)
Fred Scanlan (1965)
Milt Schmidt (1961)
Dave "Sweeney" Schriner
 (1962)
Earl Seibert (1963)
Oliver Seibert (1961)
Eddie Shore (1947)
Steve Shutt (1993)
Albert C. "Babe" Siebert (1964)
Harold "Bullet Joe" Simpson
 (1962)
Daryl Sittler (1989)
Alfred E. Smith (1962)
Billy Smith (1993)
Clint Smith (1991)
Reginald "Hooley" Smith (1972)
Thomas Smith (1973)
Allan Stanley (1981)
Russell "Barney" Stanley
 (1962)
John "Black Jack" Stewart
 (1964)
Nels Stewart (1962)
Bruce Stuart (1961)
Hod Stuart (1945)
Frederic "Cyclone" (O.B.E.)
 Taylor (1947)
Cecil R. "Tiny" Thompson
 (1959)
Vladislav Tretiak (1989)
Harry J. Trihey (1950)
Norm Ullman (1982)
Georges Vezina (1945)
Jack Walker (1960)
Marty Walsh (1962)
Harry Watson (1994)
Harry E. Watson (1962)
Ralph "Cooney" Weiland (1971)
Harry Westwick (1962)
Fred Whitcroft (1962)
Gordon "Phat" Wilson (1962)
Lorne "Gump" Worsley (1980)
Roy Worters (1969)

Builders

Charles Adams (1960)
Weston W. Adams (1972)
Thomas "Frank" Ahearn (1962)
John "Bunny" Ahearne (1977)
Montagu Allan (C.V.O.) (1945)
Keith Allen (1992)
Harold Ballard (1977)
David Bauer (1989)
John Bickell (1978)
Scott Bowman (1991)
George V. Brown (1961)
Walter A. Brown (1962)
Frank Buckland (1975)
Jack Butterfield (1980)
Frank Calder (1947)
Angus D. Campbell (1964)
Clarence Campbell (1966)
Joe Cattarinich (1977)
Joseph "Leo" Dandurand
 (1963)
Francis Dilio (1964)
George S. Dudley (1958)
James A. Dunn (1968)
Alan Eagleson (1989)
Emile Francis (1982)
Jack Gibson (1976)
Tommy Gorman (1963)
Frank Griffiths (1993)
William Hanley (1986)
Charles Hay (1974)
James C. Hendy (1968)
Foster Hewitt (1965)
William Hewitt (1947)
Fred J. Hume (1962)
George "Punch" Imlach (1984)
Tommy Ivan (1974)
William M. Jennings (1975)
Bob Johnson (1992)
Gordon W. Juckes (1979)
John Kilpatrick (1960)
Seymour Knox III (1993)
George Leader (1969)
Robert LeBel (1970)
Thomas F. Lockhart (1965)
Paul Loicq (1961)
Frederic McLaughlin (1963)
John Mariucci (1985)
Frank Mathers (1992)
John "Jake" Milford (1984)
Hartland Molson (1973)
Francis Nelson (1947)
Bruce A. Norris (1969)
James Norris, Sr. (1958)
James D. Norris (1962)
William M. Northey (1947)
John O'Brien (1962)
Brian O'Neill (1994)
Fred Page (1993)
Frank Patrick (1958)
Allan W. Pickard (1958)
Rudy Pilous (1985)
Norman "Bud" Poile (1990)

Builders *(Cont.)*

Samuel Pollock (1978)
Donat Raymond (1958)
John Robertson (1947)
Claude C. Robinson (1947)
Philip D. Ross (1976)
Frank J. Selke (1960)
Harry Sinden (1983)
Frank D. Smith (1962)
Conn Smythe (1958)
Edward M. Snider (1988)
Lord Stanley of Preston
 (G.C.B.) (1945)
James T. Sutherland (1947)
Anatoli V. Tarasov (1974)
Lloyd Turner (1958)
William Tutt (1978)
Carl Potter Voss (1974)
Fred C. Waghorn (1961)
Arthur Wirtz (1971)
Bill Wirtz (1976)
John A. Ziegler, Jr. (1987)

Referees/Linesmen

Neil Armstrong (1991)
John Ashley (1981)
William L. Chadwick (1964)
John D'Amico (1993)
Chaucer Elliott (1961)
George Hayes (1988)
Robert W. Hewitson (1963)
Fred J. "Mickey" Ion (1961)
Matt Pavelich (1987)
Mike Rodden (1962)
J. Cooper Smeaton (1961)
Roy "Red" Storey (1967)
Frank Udvari (1973)

Note: Year of election to the Hall
of Fame is in parentheses after
the member's name.

Tennis

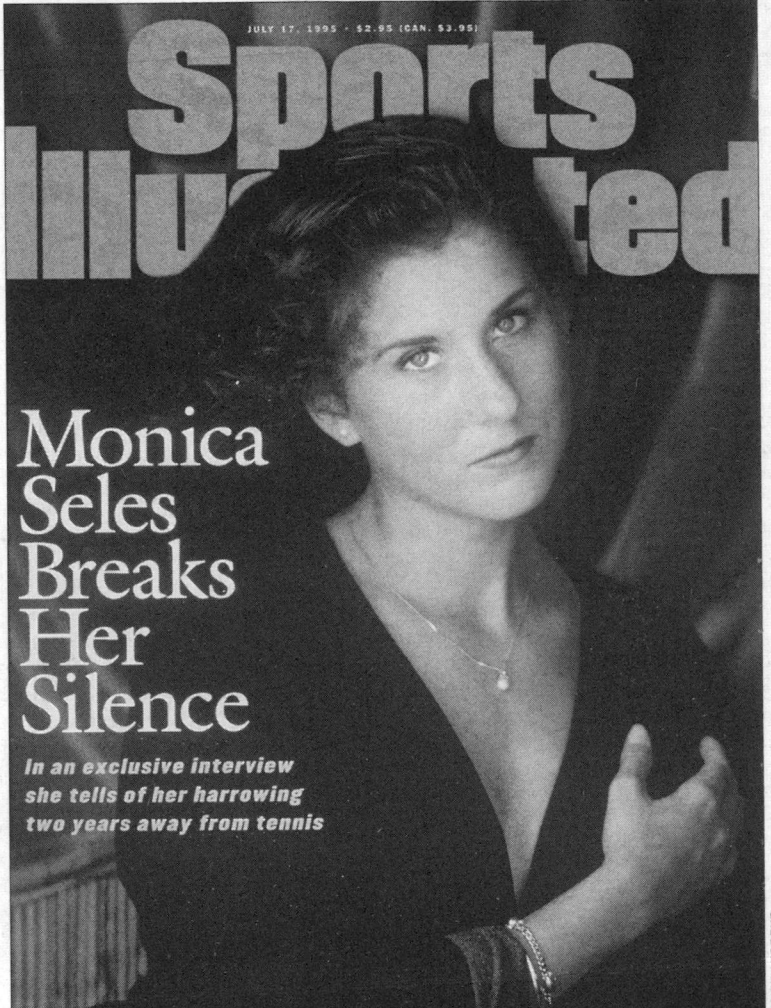

JULY 17, 1995 · $2.95 (CAN. $3.95)

Sports Illustrated

Monica Seles Breaks Her Silence

In an exclusive interview she tells of her harrowing two years away from tennis

GREGORY HEISLER

Eyes On The Prize

The game's top players had outstanding seasons despite a plethora of off-court distractions

by Sally Jenkins

IT WAS a year of comebacks and heartaches. Everyone won, and everyone cried. Twenty-eight months after she was stabbed by a German fanatic, Monica Seles made an emotional and triumphant return to the game she once dominated. Pained by a chronic back ailment and beset by family scandal, Steffi Graf tearfully clung to the No. 1 ranking through it all. Silencing critics who said he would never be a true champion, Andre Agassi became the top-ranked men's player. And Pete Sampras endured personal tragedy to stake a claim as the most accomplished player of his generation.

It all began with Agassi's haircut. He appeared at the Australian Open for the first Grand Slam event of the season shorn of the flowing peroxided mane that had been his signature. Judging by his cropped head and scaled-down entourage, Agassi meant business. (He had gotten the new do from a fashionable hairdresser while lounging in the kitchen of girlfriend Brooke Shields's New York City apartment over the Christmas break, after fortifying

himself with champagne.) Australians labeled him the Pirate King and the Black Prince, for the bandana he sported. However, not all of Agassi's fans were charmed by the new image. While his older constituency wholeheartedly approved, the teenybopper set was furious. "An oldy, baldy codger" is how one Australian adolescent described him.

Agassi didn't care. The reason for the redesign of his head was twofold: First, it was time to admit that his hairline was receding. Second, he wanted a tough new image emblematic of his newfound professional commitment. "To be honest, I think it was long overdue," he said. Agassi thus served notice that he would finally blend consistency and dedication with his talent. The time that he used to put into his hair now went into his tennis. "It used to take about 27 minutes a day, now it takes six and half," he said.

Agassi was determined to make the Australian a convincing follow-up to the U.S. Open title with which he had closed out 1994. With a chance to win two Grand

**Unveiling a new attitude
as well as a new look, Agassi
pirated the Australian title.**

RUSS ADAMS

Slam events in a row for the first time in his career, he kept an uncharacteristically low profile, cooking banana pancakes for himself in his rented home and getting his game face on by watching slasher and action movies: Freddy Krueger films, *Die Harder* and *The Exorcist*. "I've come to terms with myself and with my tennis," he said. "It used to be I thought I had to live up to something, to validate what I did on the TV commercials. Now everything has its rightful place." The result of his focus: He swept into the final at Flinders Park without losing so much as a set. He then defeated 4–6, 6–1, 7–6 (8–6), 6–4 an emotionally spent Sampras, who had a far more dramatic path to the final.

On the women's side, Graf sat out the Australian in an effort to rest her aching back. Suffering from a painful bone spur in her spine, Graf wondered if she would be able to play again at all. Such thoughts also went through the mind of Seles, who struggled with depression and was only beginning to contemplate a return. The Australian thus belonged to Mary Pierce, the expressive 20-year-old with blinding hair and roundhouse strokes. Pierce claimed the first Grand Slam title of her career, finally arriving as a champion, without the loss of a set or more than six games in any match, including the final. She overwhelmed second-ranked Arantxa Sanchez Vicario 6–3, 6–2. "Everybody said, 'Mary can play, but can she play well all the time?'" Pierce said. "This was important for me."

But ultimately the Australian would be remembered less for its victors than for a tragic event off the court. Sampras's coach and good friend, Tim Gullikson, was hospi-

talized in midtournament after collapsing with what was later diagnosed as brain cancer. Sampras spent much of his time at Gullikson's side. When Sampras asked a local specialist for a worst-case scenario, he was told Gullikson might have only six months to live. Devastated, Sampras carried on. Twice he rallied from two sets down to win matches, including a quarterfinal meeting with Jim Courier that ranked among the most stirring on-court confrontations ever. Fatigued and agonizing over Gullikson, Sampras stood in the middle of the court during the fifth set and sobbed openly. "I started thinking about Tim, and it just broke my heart," he said.

Sampras will never again be mistaken for a casual or passionless player, two labels with which he had been stuck in his exceedingly shy youth. In fact he is a deeply feeling young man. Sampras tried to compose himself on a changeover but had to bury his head in a towel, shoulders heaving. When he took the court again, Sampras leaned on his racket, still crying uncontrollably. Courier, on the far side of the net, could not tell what was going on. "You O.K., Pete?" he asked. "We can come back and finish this tomorrow." Sampras straightened up and stopped weeping. And served an ace. He went on to one of the defining victories of his career: 6–7 (4–7), 6–7 (3–7), 6–3, 6–4, 6–3.

Sampras was clearly exhausted physically and emotionally against Agassi as he surrendered the title. Disappointment would be the hallmark of Sampras's first half of the year. He played without complaint through a sprained ankle, a first-round loss at the French Open and the loss of his No. 1 ranking to Agassi.

The French Open was a tale of persistence and renewal for Thomas Muster of Austria. Muster was 21 and a rising star in 1989 when he was hit by a car in the parking lot at a tournament in Miami, severing the ligaments in his left knee. It was not certain that Muster would ever walk normally again, much less play. But Muster was practicing again within six months, albeit from a specially designed wheelchair. When he left Paris this year he was a career-high No. 3 and on a remarkable winning streak, although he still could not completely extend his left leg. By defeating Michael Chang in the final in straight sets, he ran his clay court record for '95 to 35–0.

The French also marked the return of Graf, whose fitness was a moment-to-moment affair, but who dispatched Sanchez Vicario 7–5, 4–6, 6–0, for one of the most surprising titles of her career. Two weeks prior to the tournament, Graf wasn't even sure she could play—because of the bone spur. "I didn't expect to be in the finals, or win it," Graf said. She was so taken aback that when she accepted a microphone to speak to the stadium crowd she said, "The only thing I can say is, *Mon chapeau est bien*," drawing a burst of laughter from spectators.

The profiles in courage continued at Wimbledon, where Sampras resurfaced to win his first Grand Slam title in a year and accomplish his historical "ThreePete"; he's only the third man since World War I to win three consecutive titles at the All England Club. Sampras's victory lent some decorum to an otherwise weird and controversial tournament, which seemed to go sun silly in the 100° temperatures: Three players were defaulted, including Jeff Tarango, who was fined and suspended for accusing an umpire of corruption.

Sampras's unexpected opponent in the final was the renewed Boris Becker. On the 10th anniversary of his first Wimbledon title, won at the age of 17, the now 27-year-old Becker celebrated by reaching his first Grand Slam final since 1991. He was the oldest finalist since 31-year-old Jimmy Connors in 1984. The age factor was barely perceptible but told in the end.

Becker played a semifinal against Agassi that was reminiscent of his old bullying style, when it seemed that he could turn a match around by simply imposing his will. Trailing a set and two service breaks to Agassi, Becker, making thunderous shots, turned the match around and won 2–6, 7–6, 6–4, 7–6. Agassi was reduced to a little chap in funny clothes as he was able to take only a single point in each of the tiebreakers.

But Becker could not follow that upset with another. Heavy-legged against Sampras the following day, he was unable to cope with the defending champion's 125 mph serve, while committing 15 double faults of his own. Sampras struck 68 winners to just seven unforced errors, and when Becker tried to match that marvelous level of play, he seemed to be reaching for something no longer there. In defeat (6–7, 6–2, 6–4, 6–2) Becker was forced to concede that Sampras had displaced him once and for all as the

Muster's French Open victory marked the end of his long road back.

RUSS ADAMS

preeminent grass court player in the world. "This used to be my court; now it's his," said Becker.

The normally reticent Sampras tore off his shirt and flung it into the crowd, following that with a cup of water. Sampras then dedicated the victory to Gullikson. The ankle injury, the loss of his ranking, the loss at the French, all paled in comparison to the illness of his best friend. "This is the most emotional one, just because of the way the year has been," Sampras said later, lounging in the basement of the stadium court. "There is no better feeling than waking up after one of these. If I ever get to sleep."

For Graf, too, Wimbledon represented yet another long hard pull. Her sixth title at the All England Club may have been her hardest won. Yet another injury, this one to her wrist, caused her to fly home to Germany for treatment four days before the tournament began. She played pumped full of anti-inflammatories to quell the constant ache in her back. However, she went on to defeat the most durable player around, and her ever-present foil, Sanchez Vicario. In what was arguably one of the best women's matches ever played on Centre Court, Graf prevailed 4–6, 6–1, 7–5. The turning point was the 11th game of the final set, a 32-point, 13-deuce affair that broke the Spaniard's serve and spirit.

There was one last crescendo: the U.S. Open. A dramatic buildup began long before the field arrived in New York. Seles finally stepped on the court again, in an exhibition against Martina Navratilova at Caesars Palace in Atlantic City, her first public match since the horrific stabbing that sidelined her. (Seles was knifed in the back by an unemployed German lathe operator, Günther Parche, during a tournament in Hamburg in 1993. Parche said his aim was to return the No. 1 ranking to his heroine, Graf.)

In a hilariously campy but convincing exhibition complete with Caesars, Cleopatras and centurions, Seles defeated Navratilova with blockbuster strokes. She then entered the Canadian Open in Toronto, her first official event in 2½ years. Seles devoured the field there like mere appetizers, tearing through the draw without the loss of a set. She was back, make no mis-

No one welcomed the return of Seles (right) more than Graf, her biggest rival.

take about it. Seles had won seven of eight Grand Slam titles before the knifing, and it is clear she intends to compile more.

Meanwhile, off-court events once again marred the game. Graf's father, Peter, who served as her financial manager, was jailed in Germany on tax-evasion charges. Graf herself was also the target of investigators, who claimed Peter had failed to pay taxes on millions of dollars of unreported income. Peter was denied bond, and Steffi was prohibited from communicating with him.

In New York, Graf and Seles admitted to roiling nerves and emotions throughout. Nevertheless they each got to the final without losing a set. Their pairing made for the most intriguing story of the year: Each was saddled with emotional baggage concerning Seles's long absence, and Graf carried the additional burden of her father's legal troubles. Both said that they never expected to reach the final. Under the circumstances, Graf's 7–6, 0–6, 6–4 victory was surely the crowning achievement of her career. It was also her 18th career Grand Slam singles title, tying her with

Chris Evert and Navratilova for third on the alltime list. "This has been the biggest win I have ever achieved," said Graf. "There is nothing that even comes close to this one." But Seles could take a moral victory from it as well: Though she was perhaps not yet match-tough, her long battle to recuperate mentally and physically was over. She was back.

The men's side was resolved in equally fitting and satisfying fashion. Agassi and Sampras met in the final with a private gentleman's agreement that whoever won should be considered the player of the year. The victor was Sampras in four sets, 6–4, 6–3, 4–6, 7–5. Agassi would continue to hold the No. 1 ranking mathematically, but the look on his face told the real story. Afterward he remarked that he would give back all of his smaller victories for that one trophy. Sampras had collected his third Open and seventh Grand Slam title at the tender age of 24. That tied him with John McEnroe and left him one shy of Connors.

As Sampras sat in his chair at courtside, he wept one last time. Then he looked into a TV camera and dedicated another trophy to Gullikson. "This is for you, Timmy," he said. "Thanks for your help, buddy. Wish you were here."

1995 Grand Slam Champions

Australian Open

Men's Singles

	Winner	Finalist	Score
Quarterfinals	Pete Sampras (1) ....Jim Courier (9)		6-7, 6-7, 6-3, 6-4, 6-3
	Michael Chang (5) ....Andrei Medvedev (13)		7-6 (9-7), 7-5, 6-3
	Aaron Krickstein......................Jacco Eltingh		7-6 (7-3), 6-4, 5-7, 6-4
	Andre Agassi (2) ....Yevgeny Kafelnikov (10)		6-2, 7-5, 6-0
Semifinals	Pete Sampras.........................Michael Chang		6-7 (6-8), 6-3, 6-4, 6-4
	Andre Agassi ....Aaron Krickstein		6-4, 6-4, 3-0 ret.
Final	Andre Agassi ....Pete Sampras		4-6, 6-1,7-6 (8-6), 6-4

Women's Singles

	Winner	Finalist	Score
Quarterfinals	Mary Pierce (4).........................Natasha Zvereva (8)		6-1, 6-4
	Conchita Martinez (2)..............Lindsay Davenport (6)		6-3, 4-6, 6-3
	Arantxa Sanchez Vicario (1) ...Naoka Sawamatsu		6-1, 6-3
	Marianne Werdel Witmeyer.....Angelica Gavaldon		6-1, 6-2
Semifinals	Mary Pierce ....Conchita Martinez		6-3, 6-1
	Arantxa Sanchez Vicario.........Marianne Werdel Witmeyer		6-4, 6-1
Final	Mary Pierce ....Arantxa Sanchez Vicario		6-3, 6-2

Doubles

	Winner	Finalist	Score
Men's Final	Jared Palmer/.........................Mark Knowles/		6-3, 3-6, 6-3, 6-2
	Richey Reneberg (13)	Daniel Nestor	
Women's Final	Jana Novtona/ ....Gigi Fernandez/		6-3, 6-7 (3-7), 6-4
	Arantxa Sanchez Vicario (2)	Natalia Zvereva (1)	
Mixed Final	Rick Leach/...............................Cyril Suk/		7-6 (7-4), 6-7 (3-7), 6-4
	Natasha Zvereva	Gigi Fernandez (5)	

French Open

Men's Singles

	Winner	Finalist	Score
Quarterfinals	Yevgeny Kafelnikov (9) ....Andre Agassi (1)		6-4, 6-3, 7-5
	Thomas Muster (5) ....Alberto Costa		6-2, 3-6, 6-7 (6-8), 7-5, 6-2
	Michael Chang (6) ....Adrian Voinea		7-5, 6-0, 6-1
	Sergi Bruguera (7) ....Renzo Furlan		6-2, 7-5, 6-2
Semifinals	Thomas Muster ....Yevgeny Kafelnikov		6-4, 6-0, 6-4
	Michael Chang ....Sergi Bruguera		6-4, 7-6 (7-5), 7-6 (7-0)
Final	Thomas Muster ....Michael Chang		7-5, 6-2, 6-4

Women's Singles

	Winner	Finalist	Score
Quarterfinals	Steffi Graf (2)...........................Gabriela Sabatini (8)		6-1, 6-0
	Conchita Martinez (4)..............Virginia Ruano-Pascual		6-0, 6-4
	Arantxa Sanchez-Vicario (1) ...Chanda Rubin		6-3, 6-1
	Kimiko Date (9) ....Iva Majoli (12)		7-5, 6-1
Semifinals	Steffi Graf ....Conchita Martinez		6-3, 6-7(5-7), 6-3
	Arantxa Sanchez Vicario.........Kimiko Date		7-5, 6-3
Final	Steffi Graf ....Arantxa Sanchez Vicario		7-5, 4-6, 6-0

Note: Seedings in parentheses.

French Open (Cont.)

Doubles

	Winner	Finalist	Score
Men's Final	Jacco Eltingh/ ....Paul Haarhuis (2)	Nicklas Kulti/ Magnus Larsson	6-7 (3-7), 6-4, 6-1
Women's Final	Gigi Fernandez/ ....Natasha Zvereva (2)	Arantxa Sanchez Vicario/ Jana Novotna (1)	6-7 (8-6), 6-4, 7-5
Mixed Final	Larisa Neiland/ ....Mark Woodforde (1)	Jill Hetherington/ John-Laffnie de Jager	7-6 (12-10), 7-6 (7-4)

Wimbledon

Men's Singles

	Winner	Finalist	Score
Quarterfinals	Pete Sampras (2) ....Goran Ivanisevic (4)................Boris Becker (3)	Shuzo Matsuoka Yevgeny Kafelnikov (6) Cedric Pioline	6-7 (5-7), 6-3, 6-4, 6-2 7-5, 7-6 (13-11), 6-3 6-3, 6-1, 6-7 (6-8), 6-7 (10-12), 9-7
Semifinals	Andre Agassi (1).....................Boris Becker.............................	Jacco Eltingh Andre Agassi	6-2, 6-3, 6-4 2-6, 7-6 (7-1), 6-4, 7-6 (7-1)
	Pete Sampras..........................	Goran Ivanisevic	7-6 (9-7), 4-6, 6-3, 4-6, 6-3
Final	Pete Sampras..........................	Boris Becker	6-7 (5-7), 6-2, 6-4, 6-2

Women's Singles

	Winner	Finalist	Score
Quarterfinals	Steffi Graf (1)...........................Jana Novotna (4)......................Arantxa Sanchez Vicario (2) ...Conchita Martinez (3).............	Mary Joe Fernandez (13) Kimiko Date (6) Brenda Schultz-McCarthy (15) Gabriela Sabatini (8)	6-3, 6-0 6-2, 6-3 6-4, 7-6 (7-4) 7-5, 7-6 (7-5)
Semifinals	Steffi Graf ....Arantxa Sanchez Vicario.........	Jana Novotna Conchita Martinez	5-7, 6-4, 6-2 6-3, 6-7 (5-7), 6-1
Final	Steffi Graf	Arantxa Sanchez Vicario	4-6, 6-1, 7-5

Doubles

	Winner	Finalist	Score
Men's Final	Todd Woodbridge/.................Mark Woodforde (1)	Rickey Leach/ Scott Melville	7-5, 7-6 (10-8), 7-6 (7-5)
Women's Final	Arantxa Sanchez Vicario/........Jana Novotna (2)	Gigi Fernandez/ Natasha Zvereva (1)	5-7, 7-5, 6-4
Mixed Final	Jonathan Stark/ ....Martina Navratilova (3)	Cyril Suk/ Gigi Fernandez (4)	6-4, 6-4

U.S. Open

Men's Singles

	Winner	Finalist	Score
Quarterfinals	Andre Agassi (1).....................Boris Becker (4)	Petr Korda Patrick McEnroe	6-4, 6-2, 1-6, 7-5 6-4, 7-6 (7-2), 6-7 (3-7), 7-6 (8-6)
Semifinals	Jim Courier (14).......................Pete Sampras (2) ....Andre Agassi	Michael Chang (5) Byron Black Boris Becker	7-6 (7-5), 7-6 (7-3), 7-5 7-6 (7-3), 6-4, 6-0 7-6 (7-4), 7-6 (7-2), 4-6, 6-4
Final	Pete Sampras..........................Pete Sampras..........................	Jim Courier Andre Agassi	7-4, 4-6, 6-4, 7-5 6-4, 6-3, 4-6, 7-5

Note: Seedings in parentheses.

Grand Slam Champions (Cont.)

U.S. Open (Cont.)

Women's Singles

	Winner	Finalist	Score
Quarterfinals	Steffi Graf (1)	Amy Frazier	6-2, 6-3
	Gabriela Sabatini (9)	Mary Joe Fernandez (14)	6-1, 6-3
	Monica Seles (2)	Jana Novotna (5)	7-6 (7-5), 6-2
	Conchita Martinez (4)	Brenda Schultz-McCarthy (16)	3-6, 7-6 (7-3), 6-2
Semifinals	Steffi Graf	Gabriela Sabatini	6-4, 7-6 (7-5)
	Monica Seles	Conchita Martinez	6-2, 6-2
Final	Steffi Graf	Monica Seles	7-6 (8-6), 0-6, 6-3

Doubles

	Winner	Finalist	Score
Men's Final	Todd Woodbridge/ Mark Woodforde (2)	Alex O'Brien/ Sandon Stolle (15)	6-3, 6-3
Women's Final	Gigi Fernandez/ Natasha Zvereva (2)	Brenda Schultz-McCarthy/ Rennae Stubbs (6)	7-5, 6-3
Mixed Final	Meredith McGrath/ Matt Lucena	Gigi Fernandez/ Cyril Suk (3)	6-4, 6-4

Note: Seedings in parentheses.

Major Tournament Results

Men's Tour (Late 1994)

Date	Tournament	Site	Winner	Finalist	Score
Sept 26-Oct 2	Swiss Indoors	Basel	Wayne Ferreira	Patrick McEnroe	6-6, 6-2, 7-6 (9-7), 6-3
Oct 3-9	Australian Indoor	Sydney	Richard Krajicek	Boris Becker	7-6 (7-5), 7-6 (9-7), 2-6, 6-3
Oct 10-16	Seiko Super Tennis	Tokyo	Goran Ivanisevic	Michael Chang	6-4, 6-4
Oct 17-23	Grand Prix de Tennis	Lyon	Marc Rosset	Jim Courier	6-4, 7-6 (7-2)
Oct 24-30	Stockholm Open	Stockholm	Boris Becker	Goran Ivanisevic	4-6, 6-4, 6-3, 7-6 (7-4)
Oct 31- Nov 6	Open de Paris	Paris	Andre Agassi	Marc Rosset	6-3, 6-3, 4-6, 7-5
Nov 7-13	European Comm Champ	Antwerp	Pete Sampras	Magnus Larsson	7-6 (7-5), 6-4
Nov 15-22	ATP Tour World Champ	Frankfurt	Pete Sampras	Boris Becker	4-6, 6-3, 7-5, 6-4

Men's Tour (through September 17, 1995)

Date	Tournament	Site	Winner	Finalist	Score
Jan 16-29	Australian Open	Melbourne	Andre Agassi	Pete Sampras	4-6, 6-1, 7-6 (8-6), 6-4
Feb 6-12	Dubai Tennis Open	Dubai, United Arab Emirates	Wayne Ferreira	Andrea Gaudenzi	3-6, 7-6 (7-3), 6-4
Feb 13-19	Milan Open	Milan	Yevgeny Kafelnikov	Boris Becker	7-5, 5-7, 7-6 (8-6)
Feb 20-26	Eurocard Open	Stuttgart	Richard Krajicek	Michael Stich	7-6 (7-4), 6-3 6-7 (6-8), 1-6, 6-3
Feb 27-Mar 5	Newsweek Champions Cup	Indian Wells, CA	Pete Sampras	Andre Agassi	7-5, 6-3, 7-5
Mar 16-26	Lipton Intl Players Championships	Key Biscayne	Andre Agassi	Pete Sampras	3-6, 6-2, 7-6 (7-3)
Apr 10-16	Japan Open Tennis Championship	Tokyo	Jim Courier	Andre Agassi	6-3, 6-4
Apr 24-30	Volvo Monte Carlo Open	Monte Carlo	Thomas Muster	Boris Becker	4-6, 5-7, 6-1, 7-6 (8-6), 6-0
May 8-14	Panasonic German Open	Hamburg	Andrei Medvedev	Goran Ivanisevic	6-3, 6-2, 6-1
May15-21	Mercedes Italian Open	Rome	Thomas Muster	Sergi Bruguera	3-6, 7-6 (7-5), 6-2, 6-3
May 29-Jun 11	French Open	Paris	Thomas Muster	Michael Chang	7-5, 6-2, 6-4

Men's Tour (through September 17) (Cont.)

Date	Tournament	Site	Winner	Finalist	Score
Jun 26-July 9	Wimbledon Championships	Wimbledon	Pete Sampras	Boris Becker	6-7 (5-7), 6-2, 6-4, 6-2
July 17-23	Mercedes Cup	Stuttgart	Thomas Muster	Jan Apell	6-2, 6-2
July 24-30	The du Maurier Ltd. Open	Montreal	Andre Agassi	Pete Sampras	3-6, 6-2, 6-3
Aug 7-13	Thriftway ATP Championship	Cincinnati	Andre Agassi	Michael Chang	7-5, 6-2
Aug 14-20	RCA/US Men's Hardcourt Championships	Indianapolis	Thomas Enqvist	Bernd Carbacher	6-4, 6-3
Aug 14-20	Volvo Intl Tennis Tournament	New Haven	Andre Agassi	Richard Krajicek	3-6, 7-6 (7-2), 6-3
Aug 28-Sept 10	US Open	New York	Pete Sampras	Andre Agassi	6-4, 6-3, 6-4, 7-5
Sept 11-17	Romanian Open	Bucharest	Thomas Muster	Gilbert Schaller	6-3, 6-4

Women's Tour (Late 1994)

Date	Tournament	Site	Winner	Finalist	Score
Sept 20-25	Nichirei International Ladies Championships	Tokyo	Arantxa Sanchez Vicario	Amy Frazier	6-1, 6-2
Sept 26-Oct 2	International Damen Grand Prix	Leipzig	Jana Novotna	Mary Pierce	7-5, 6-1
Oct 3-9	European Indoors	Zurich	Magdalena Maleeva	Natasha Zvereva	7-5, 3-6, 6-4
Oct 10-16	Porsche Tennis Grand Prix	Filderstadt, Germany	Anke Huber	Mary Pierce	6-4, 6-2
Oct 18-23	Brighton International	Brighton, England	Jana Novotna	Helena Sukova	6-7 (4-7), 6-3, 6-4
Oct 24-30	Nokia Grand Prix	Essen, Germany	Jana Novotna	Iva Majoli	6-2, 6-4
Oct 31-Nov 6	Bank of the West Classic	Oakland, CA	Arantxa Sanchez Vicario	Martina Navratilova	1-6, 7-6 (7-5), 7-6 (7-5)
Nov 7-13	Virginia Slims of Philadelphia	Philadelphia	Anke Huber	Mary Pierce	6-0, 6-7 (4-7), 7-5
Nov 14-20	Virginia Slims Championships	New York	Gabriela Sabatini	Lindsay Davenport	6-3, 6-2, 6-4

Women's Tour (through September 10, 1995)

Date	Tournament	Site	Winner	Finalist	Score
Jan 9-15	Peters International	Sydney	Gabriela Sabatini	Lindsay Davenport	6-3, 6-4
Jan 16-29	Australian Open	Melbourne	Mary Pierce	Arantxa Sanchez Vicario	6-3, 6-2
Jan 31-Feb 5	Toray Pan Pacific Open	Tokyo	Kimiko Date	Lindsay Davenport	6-1, 6-2
Feb 6-12	Ameritech Cup	Chicago	Magdalena Maleeva	Lisa Raymond	7-5, 7-6 (7-2)
Feb 14-19	Open Gaz de France	Paris	Steffi Graf	Mary Pierce	6-2, 6-2
Feb 27-Mar 5	State Farm Evert Cup	Indian Wells, CA	Mary Joe Fernandez	Natasha Zvereva	6-4, 6-3
Mar 6-12	Delray Beach Winter Championships	Delray Beach, FL	Steffi Graf	Conchita Martinez	6-2, 6-4
Mar 17-26	The Lipton Championships	Key Biscayne, FL	Steffi Graf	Kimiko Date	6-1, 6-4
Mar 27-Apr 2	Family Circle Magazine Cup	Hilton Head Island, SC	Conchita Martinez	Magdalena Maleeva	6-1, 6-1
Apr 3-9	Bausch & Lomb Championships	Amelia Island, FL	Conchita Martinez	Gabriela Sabatini	6-1, 6-4
Apr 10-18	Houston Women's Tennis Championships	Houston	Steffi Graf	Asa Carlsson	6-1, 6-1
Apr 24-30	International Championships of Spain	Barcelona	Arantxa Sanchez Vicario	Iva Majoli	5-7, 6-0, 6-2
May 1-7	Citizen Cup	Hamburg	Conchita Martinez	Martina Hingis	6-1, 6-0

Women's Tour *(Cont.)*

Date	Tournament	Site	Winner	Finalist	Score
May 8-14	Italian Open	Rome	Conchita Martinez	Arantxa Sanchez Vicario	6-3, 6-1
May 15-21	German Open	Berlin	Arantxa Sanchez Vicario	Magdalena Maleeva	6-4, 6-1
May 29-Jun 11	French Open	Paris	Steffi Graf	Arantxa Sanchez Vicario	7-5, 4-6, 6-0
June 19-25	Direct Line International Tennis Championships	Eastbourne, England	Nathalie Tauziat	Chanda Rubin	3-6, 6-0, 7-5
Jun 26-Jul 9	Wimbledon Championships	Wimbledon	Steffi Graf	Arantxa Sanchez Vicario	4-6, 6-1, 7-5
July 31-Aug 6	Toshiba Tennis Classic	San Diego	Conchita Martinez	Lisa Raymond	6-2, 6-0
Aug 7-13	Acura Classic	Manhattan Beach	Conchita Martinez	Chanda Rubin	4-6, 6-1, 6-3
Aug 14-21	Du Maurier Ltd. Open	Montreal	Monica Seles	Amanda Coetzer	6-0, 6-1
Aug 28-Sept 10	US Open	New York	Steffi Graf	Monica Seles	7-6 (8-6), 0-6, 6-3

1994 Singles Leaders

Men

Rank	Player	Tournament Wins	Match Record	Earnings ($)
1	Pete Sampras	10	74-11	3,607,812
2	Andre Agassi	5	51-13	1,941,667
3	Boris Becker	4	48-16	2,029,756
4	Sergi Bruguera	3	65-24	3,031,874
5	Goran Ivanisevic	2	63-26	2,060,278
6	Michael Chang	6	65-20	1,789,495
7	Stefan Edberg	3	60-25	2,489,161
8	Alberto Berasategui	7	65-25	939,651
9	Michael Stich	3	60-24	2,033,623
10	Todd Martin	2	51-19	888,324
11	Yevgeny Kafelnikov	3	67-28	1,011,563
12	Wayne Ferreira	5	69-25	1,063,341
13	Jim Courier	0	47-19	1,921,584
14	Marc Rosset	2	49-26	768,004
15	Andre Medvedev	2	34-17	1,211,134
16	Thomas Muster	3	58-24	654,829
17	Richard Krajicek	3	33-14	555,116
18	Petr Korda	0	38-22	612,012
19	Magnus Larsson	2	35-22	639,105
20	Jason Stoltenberg	1	38-25	498,842

Note: Compiled by the Association of Tennis Professionals (ATP).

Women

Rank	Player	Tournament Wins	Match Record	Earnings ($)
1	Steffi Graf	7	58-6	1,481,670
2	Arantxa Sanchez Vicario	8	74-9	2,563,675
3	Conchita Martinez	4	55-15	1,503,540
4	Jana Novotna	3	43-11	576,049
5	Mary Pierce	1	45-18	741,761
6	Lindsay Davenport	2	48-15	476,032
7	Gabriela Sabatini	1	42-17	807,612
8	Martina Navratilova	1	33-14	746,468
9	Kimiko Date	2	33-14	369,404
10	Natasha Zvereva	1	30-12	399,372
11	Magdalena Maleeva	2	33-12	311,723
12	Anke Huber	3	41-17	436,321
13	Iva Majoli	0	39-19	297,098
14	Mary Joe Fernandez	1	25-10	147,998
15	Brenda Schultz	1	49-23	290,337
16	Amy Frazier	1	28-15	219,381
17	Lori McNeil	1	26-15	233,701
18	Amanda Coetzer	1	38-19	292,404
19	Sabine Hack	1	35-18	279,396
20	Ines Gorrochategui	0	23-10	125,429

Note: Compiled by the Women's Tennis Association (WTA).

1994 Davis Cup
FINALS

Sweden d. Russia 4-1 at Moscow
Stefan Edberg (Swe) d. Alexander Volkov (Rus) 6-4, 6-2, 6-7, 0-6, 8-6
Magnus Larsson (Swe) d. Yevgeny Kafelnikov (Rus) 6-0, 6-2, 3-6, 2-6, 6-3
Jan Apell/Jonas Bjorkman (Swe) d. Yevgeny Kafelnikov/Andrei Olhovskiy (Rus) 6-7, 6-2, 6-3, 1-6, 8-6
Yevgeny Kafelnikov (Rus) d. Stefan Edberg (Swe) 4-6, 6-4, 6-0
Magnus Larsson (Swe) d. Alexander Volkov (Rus) 7-6, 6-4

1995 Davis Cup World Group

FIRST ROUND

United States d. France 4-1
Italy d. Czech Republic 4-1
Sweden d. Denmark 3-2
Austria d. Spain 4-1
South Africa d. Australia 3-2
Russia d. Belgium 4-1
Netherlands d. Switzerland 4-1
Germany d. Croatia 4-1

QUARTER FINAL ROUND

United States d. Italy 5-0
Sweden d. Austria 5-0
Russia d. South Africa 4-1
Germany d. Netherlands 4-1

SEMIFINALS

United States d. Sweden 4-1
Pete Sampras (U.S.) d. Thomas Enqvist (Swe) 6-3, 6-4, 3-6, 6-3
Andre Agassi (U.S.) d. Mats Wilander (Swe) 7-6 (7-5), 6-2, 6-2
Jonas Bjorkman/Stefan Edberg (Swe) d. Todd Martin/Jonathan Stark (U.S.) 6-3, 6-4, 6-4
Todd Martin (U.S.) d. Thomas Enqvist (Swe) 7-5, 7-5, 7-6 (7-2)
Pete Sampras (U.S.) d. Mats Wilander (Swe) 2-6, 7-6 (7-4), 6-3

Russia d. Germany 3-2
Boris Becker (Ger) d. Andrei Chesnokov (Rus) 6-7 (7-4), 6-3, 7-6 (7-3), 7-5
Michael Stich (Ger) d. Yevgeny Kafelnikov (Rus) 6-1, 4-6, 6-3, 6-4
Yevgeny Kafelnikov/Andrei Olhovskiy (Rus) d. Boris Becker/Michael Stich (Ger) 7-6 (7-3), 6-4, 2-6, 6-7 (5-7), 7-5
Yevgeny Kafelnikov (Rus) d. Bernd Karbacher (Ger) 6-1, 7-6 (7-5), 6-2
Andrei Chesnokov (Rus) d. Michael Stich (Ger) 6-4, 1-6, 1-6, 6-3, 14-12

FINAL: Russia versus United States to be held Dec 1-3 in Moscow.

1995 Federation Cup

FIRST ROUND

Spain d. Bulgaria 3-2
Germany d. Japan 4-1
France d. South Africa 3-2
United States d. Austria 5-0

SEMIFINALS

Spain d. Germany 3-2
Conchita Martinez (Spain) d. Anke Huber (Ger) 6-2, 2-6, 6-0
Sabine Hack (Ger) d. Arantxa Sanchez Vicario (Spain) 6-4, 6-2
Arantxa Sanchez Vicario (Spain) d. Anke Huber (Ger) 6-3, 1-6, 6-2
Conchita Martines (Spain) d. Sabine Hack (Ger) 6-0, 6-0
Anke Huber/Claudia Porwick (Ger) d. Virginia Ruano Pascual/ Maria Antonia Sanchez Lorenzo (Spain) 6-2, 6-2

United States d. France 3-2
Mary Pierce (Fra) d. Mary Joe Fernandez (U.S.) 7-6 (7-1), 6-3
Lindsay Davenport (U.S.) d. Julie Halard (Fra) 7-6 (7-0), 7-5
Lindsay Davenport (U.S.) d. Mary Pierce (Fra) 6-3, 4-6, 6-0
Julie Halard (Fra) d. Mary Joe Fernandez (U.S.) 1-6, 7-5, 6-1
Lindsay Davenport/Gigi Fernandez (U.S.) d. Julie Halard/Nathalie Tauziat (Fra) 6-1, 7-6 (7-2)

FINAL: Spain versus United States to be held Nov 25-26 in Spain.

Grand Slam Tournaments

MEN
Australian Championships

Year	Winner	Finalist	Score
1905	Rodney Heath	A. H. Curtis	4-6, 6-3, 6-4, 6-4
1906	Tony Wilding	H. A. Parker	6-0, 6-4, 6-4
1907	Horace M. Rice	H. A. Parker	6-3, 6-4, 6-4
1908	Fred Alexander	A. W. Dunlop	3-6, 3-6, 6-0, 6-2, 6-3
1909	Tony Wilding	E. F. Parker	6-1, 7-5, 6-2
1910	Rodney Heath	Horace M. Rice	6-4, 6-3, 6-2
1911	Norman Brookes	Horace M. Rice	6-1, 6-2, 6-3
1912	J. Cecil Parke	A. E. Beamish	3-6, 6-3, 1-6, 6-1, 7-5
1913	E. F. Parker	H. A. Parker	2-6, 6-1, 6-2, 6-3
1914	Pat O'Hara Wood	G. L. Patterson	6-4, 6-3, 5-7, 6-1
1915	Francis G. Lowe	Horace M. Rice	4-6, 6-1, 6-1, 6-4
1916-18	No tournament		
1919	A. R. F. Kingscote	E. O. Pockley	6-4, 6-0, 6-3
1920	Pat O'Hara Wood	Ron Thomas	6-3, 4-6, 6-8, 6-1, 6-3
1921	Rhys H. Gemmell	A. Hedeman	7-5, 6-1, 6-4
1922	Pat O'Hara Wood	Gerald Patterson	6-0, 3-6, 3-6, 6-3, 6-2
1923	Pat O'Hara Wood	C. B. St John	6-1, 6-1, 6-3
1924	James Anderson	R. E. Schlesinger	6-3, 6-4, 3-6, 5-7, 6-3
1925	James Anderson	Gerald Patterson	11-9, 2-6, 6-2, 6-3
1926	John Hawkes	J. Willard	6-1, 6-3, 6-1
1927	Gerald Patterson	John Hawkes	3-6, 6-4, 3-6, 18-16, 6-3
1928	Jean Borotra	R. O. Cummings	6-4, 6-1, 4-6, 5-7, 6-3
1929	John C. Gregory	R. E. Schlesinger	6-2, 6-2, 5-7, 7-5
1930	Gar Moon	Harry C. Hopman	6-3, 6-1, 6-3
1931	Jack Crawford	Harry C. Hopman	6-4, 6-2, 2-6, 6-1
1932	Jack Crawford	Harry C. Hopman	4-6, 6-3, 3-6, 6-3, 6-1
1933	Jack Crawford	Keith Gledhill	2-6, 7-5, 6-3, 6-2
1934	Fred Perry	Jack Crawford	6-3, 7-5, 6-1
1935	Jack Crawford	Fred Perry	2-6, 6-4, 6-4, 6-4
1936	Adrian Quist	Jack Crawford	6-2, 6-3, 4-6, 3-6, 9-7
1937	Vivian B. McGrath	John Bromwich	6-3, 1-6, 6-0, 2-6, 6-1
1938	Don Budge	John Bromwich	6-4, 6-2, 6-1
1939	John Bromwich	Adrian Quist	6-4, 6-1, 6-3
1940	Adrian Quist	Jack Crawford	6-3, 6-1, 6-2
1941-45	No tournament		
1946	John Bromwich	Dinny Pails	5-7, 6-3, 7-5, 3-6, 6-2
1947	Dinny Pails	John Bromwich	4-6, 6-4, 3-6, 7-5, 8-6
1948	Adrian Quist	John Bromwich	6-4, 3-6, 6-3, 2-6, 6-3
1949	Frank Sedgman	Ken McGregor	6-3, 6-3, 6-2
1950	Frank Sedgman	Ken McGregor	6-3, 6-4, 4-6, 6-1
1951	Richard Savitt	Ken McGregor	6-3, 2-6, 6-3, 6-1
1952	Ken McGregor	Frank Sedgman	7-5, 12-10, 2-6, 6-2
1953	Ken Rosewall	Mervyn Rose	6-0, 6-3, 6-4
1954	Mervyn Rose	Rex Hartwig	6-2, 0-6, 6-4, 6-2
1955	Ken Rosewall	Lew Hoad	9-7, 6-4, 6-4
1956	Lew Hoad	Ken Rosewall	6-4, 3-6, 6-4, 7-5
1957	Ashley Cooper	Neale Fraser	6-3, 9-11, 6-4, 6-2
1958	Ashley Cooper	Mal Anderson	7-5, 6-3, 6-4
1959	Alex Olmedo	Neale Fraser	6-1, 6-2, 3-6, 6-3
1960	Rod Laver	Neale Fraser	5-7, 3-6, 6-3, 8-6, 8-6
1961	Roy Emerson	Rod Laver	1-6, 6-3, 7-5, 6-4
1962	Rod Laver	Roy Emerson	8-6, 0-6, 6-4, 6-4
1963	Roy Emerson	Ken Fletcher	6-3, 6-3, 6-1
1964	Roy Emerson	Fred Stolle	6-3, 6-4, 6-2
1965	Roy Emerson	Fred Stolle	7-9, 2-6, 6-4, 7-5, 6-1
1966	Roy Emerson	Arthur Ashe	6-4, 6-8, 6-2, 6-3
1967	Roy Emerson	Arthur Ashe	6-4, 6-1, 6-1
1968	Bill Bowrey	Juan Gisbert	7-5, 2-6, 9-7, 6-4
1969*	Rod Laver	Andres Gimeno	6-3, 6-4, 7-5
1970	Arthur Ashe	Dick Crealy	6-4, 9-7, 6-2
1971	Ken Rosewall	Arthur Ashe	6-1, 7-5, 6-3

Australian Championships *(Cont.)*

Year	Winner	Finalist	Score
1972	Ken Rosewall	Mal Anderson	7-6, 6-3, 7-5
1973	John Newcombe	Onny Parun	6-3, 6-7, 7-5, 6-1
1974	Jimmy Connors	Phil Dent	7-6, 6-4, 4-6, 6-3
1975	John Newcombe	Jimmy Connors	7-5, 3-6, 6-4, 7-5
1976	Mark Edmondson	John Newcombe	6-7, 6-3, 7-6, 6-1
1977 (Jan)	Roscoe Tanner	Guillermo Vilas	6-3, 6-3, 6-3
1977 (Dec)	Vitas Gerulaitis	John Lloyd	6-3, 7-6, 5-7, 3-6, 6-2
1978	Guillermo Vilas	John Marks	6-4, 6-4, 3-6, 6-3
1979	Guillermo Vilas	John Sadri	7-6, 6-3, 6-2
1980	Brian Teacher	Kim Warwick	7-5, 7-6, 6-3
1981	Johan Kriek	Steve Denton	6-2, 7-6, 6-7, 6-4
1982	Johan Kriek	Steve Denton	6-3, 6-3, 6-2
1983	Mats Wilander	Ivan Lendl	6-1, 6-4, 6-4
1984	Mats Wilander	Kevin Curren	6-7, 6-4, 7-6, 6-2
1985 (Dec)	Stefan Edberg	Mats Wilander	6-4, 6-3, 6-3
1987 (Jan)	Stefan Edberg	Pat Cash	6-3, 6-4, 3-6, 5-7, 6-3
1988	Mats Wilander	Pat Cash	6-3, 6-7, 3-6, 6-1, 8-6
1989	Ivan Lendl	Miloslav Mecir	6-2, 6-2, 6-2
1990	Ivan Lendl	Stefan Edberg	4-6, 7-6, 5-2 ret
1991	Boris Becker	Ivan Lendl	1-6, 6-4, 6-4, 6-4
1992	Jim Courier	Stefan Edberg	6-3, 3-6, 6-4, 6-2
1993	Jim Courier	Stefan Edberg	6-2, 6-1, 2-6, 7-5
1994	Pete Sampras	Todd Martin	7-6 (7-4), 6-4, 6-4
1995	Andre Agassi	Pete Sampras	4-6, 6-1, 7-6 (8-6), 6-4

*Became Open (amateur and professional) in 1969.

French Championships

Year	Winner	Finalist	Score
1925†	Rene Lacoste	Jean Borotra	7-5, 6-1, 6-4
1926	Henri Cochet	Rene Lacoste	6-2, 6-4, 6-3
1927	Rene Lacoste	Bill Tilden	6-4, 4-6, 5-7, 6-3, 11-9
1928	Henri Cochet	Rene Lacoste	5-7, 6-3, 6-1, 6-3
1929	Rene Lacoste	Jean Borotra	6-3, 2-6, 6-0, 2-6, 8-6
1930	Henri Cochet	Bill Tilden	3-6, 8-6, 6-3, 6-1
1931	Jean Borotra	Claude Boussus	2-6, 6-4, 7-5, 6-4
1932	Henri Cochet	Giorgio de Stefani	6-0, 6-4, 4-6, 6-3
1933	Jack Crawford	Henri Cochet	8-6, 6-1, 6-3
1934	Gottfried von Cramm	Jack Crawford	6-4, 7-9, 3-6, 7-5, 6-3
1935	Fred Perry	Gottfried von Cramm	6-3, 3-6, 6-1, 6-3
1936	Gottfried von Cramm	Fred Perry	6-0, 2-6, 6-2, 2-6, 6-0
1937	Henner Henkel	Henry Austin	6-1, 6-4, 6-3
1938	Don Budge	Roderick Menzel	6-3, 6-2, 6-4
1939	Don McNeill	Bobby Riggs	7-5, 6-0, 6-3
1940	No tournament		
1941‡	Bernard Destremau	n/a	n/a
1942‡	Bernard Destremau	n/a	n/a
1943‡	Yvon Petra	n/a	n/a
1944‡	Yvon Petra	n/a	n/a
1945‡	Yvon Petra	Bernard Destremau	7-5, 6-4, 6-2
1946	Marcel Bernard	Jaroslav Drobny	3-6, 2-6, 6-1, 6-4, 6-3
1947	Joseph Asboth	Eric Sturgess	8-6, 7-5, 6-4
1948	Frank Parker	Jaroslav Drobny	6-4, 7-5, 5-7, 8-6
1949	Frank Parker	Budge Patty	6-3, 1-6, 6-1, 6-4
1950	Budge Patty	Jaroslav Drobny	6-1, 6-2, 3-6, 5-7, 7-5
1951	Jaroslav Drobny	Eric Sturgess	6-3, 6-3, 6-3
1952	Jaroslav Drobny	Frank Sedgman	6-2, 6-0, 3-6, 6-4
1953	Ken Rosewall	Vic Seixas	6-3, 6-4, 1-6, 6-2
1954	Tony Trabert	Arthur Larsen	6-4, 7-5, 6-1
1955	Tony Trabert	Sven Davidson	2-6, 6-1, 6-4, 6-2
1956	Lew Hoad	Sven Davidson	6-4, 8-6, 6-3
1957	Sven Davidson	Herbie Flam	6-3, 6-4, 6-4
1958	Mervyn Rose	Luis Ayala	6-3, 6-4, 6-4
1959	Nicola Pietrangeli	Ian Vermaak	3-6, 6-3, 6-4, 6-1
1960	Nicola Pietrangeli	Luis Ayala	3-6, 6-3, 6-4, 4-6, 6-3
1961	Manuel Santana	Nicola Pietrangeli	4-6, 6-1, 3-6, 6-0, 6-2

French Championships (Cont.)

Year	Winner	Finalist	Score
1962	Rod Laver	Roy Emerson	3-6, 2-6, 6-3, 9-7, 6-2
1963	Roy Emerson	Pierre Darmon	3-6, 6-1, 6-4, 6-4
1964	Manuel Santana	Nicola Pietrangeli	6-3, 6-1, 4-6, 7-5
1965	Fred Stolle	Tony Roche	3-6, 6-0, 6-2, 6-3
1966	Tony Roche	Istvan Gulyas	6-1, 6-4, 7-5
1967	Roy Emerson	Tony Roche	6-1, 6-4, 2-6, 6-2
1968*	Ken Rosewall	Rod Laver	6-3, 6-1, 2-6, 6-2
1969	Rod Laver	Ken Rosewall	6-4, 6-3, 6-4
1970	Jan Kodes	Zeljko Franulovic	6-2, 6-4, 6-0
1971	Jan Kodes	Ilie Nastase	8-6, 6-2, 2-6, 7-5
1972	Andres Gimeno	Patrick Proisy	4-6, 6-3, 6-1, 6-1
1973	Ilie Nastase	Nikki Pilic	6-3, 6-3, 6-0
1974	Bjorn Borg	Manuel Orantes	6-7, 6-0, 6-1, 6-1
1975	Bjorn Borg	Guillermo Vilas	6-2, 6-3, 6-4
1976	Adriano Panatta	Harold Solomon	6-1, 6-4, 4-6, 7-6
1977	Guillermo Vilas	Brian Gottfried	6-0, 6-3, 6-0
1978	Bjorn Borg	Guillermo Vilas	6-1, 6-1, 6-3
1979	Bjorn Borg	Victor Pecci	6-3, 6-1, 6-7, 6-4
1980	Bjorn Borg	Vitas Gerulaitis	6-4, 6-1, 6-2
1981	Bjorn Borg	Ivan Lendl	6-1, 4-6, 6-2, 3-6, 6-1
1982	Mats Wilander	Guillermo Vilas	1-6, 7-6, 6-0, 6-4
1983	Yannick Noah	Mats Wilander	6-2, 7-5, 7-6
1984	Ivan Lendl	John McEnroe	3-6, 2-6, 6-4, 7-5, 7-5
1985	Mats Wilander	Ivan Lendl	3-6, 6-4, 6-2, 6-2
1986	Ivan Lendl	Mikael Pernfors	6-3, 6-2, 6-4
1987	Ivan Lendl	Mats Wilander	7-5, 6-2, 3-6, 7-6
1988	Mats Wilander	Henri Leconte	7-5, 6-2, 6-1
1989	Michael Chang	Stefan Edberg	6-1, 3-6, 4-6, 6-4, 6-2
1990	Andres Gomez	Andre Agassi	6-3, 2-6, 6-4, 6-4
1991	Jim Courier	Andre Agassi	3-6, 6-4, 2-6, 6-1, 6-4
1992	Jim Courier	Petr Korda	7-5, 6-2, 6-1
1993	Sergi Bruguera	Jim Courier	6-4, 2-6, 6-2, 3-6, 6-3
1994	Sergi Bruguera	Alberto Berasategui	6-3, 7-5, 2-6, 6-1
1995	Thomas Muster	Michael Chang	7-5, 6-2, 6-4

†1925 was the first year that entries were accepted from all countries.
‡From 1941 to 1945 the event was called Tournoi de France and was closed to all foreigners.
*Became Open (amateur and professional) in 1968 but closed to contract professionals in 1972.

Wimbledon Championships

Year	Winner	Finalist	Score
1877	Spencer W. Gore	William C. Marshall	6-1, 6-2, 6-4
1878	P. Frank Hadow	Spencer W. Gore	7-5, 6-1, 9-7
1879	John T. Hartley	V. St Leger Gould	6-2, 6-4, 6-2
1880	John T. Hartley	Herbert F. Lawford	6-0, 6-2, 2-6, 6-3
1881	William Renshaw	John T. Hartley	6-0, 6-2, 6-1
1882	William Renshaw	Ernest Renshaw	6-1, 2-6, 4-6, 6-2, 6-2
1883	William Renshaw	Ernest Renshaw	2-6, 6-3, 6-3, 4-6, 6-3
1884	William Renshaw	Herbert F. Lawford	6-0, 6-4, 9-7
1885	William Renshaw	Herbert F. Lawford	7-5, 6-2, 4-6, 7-5
1886	William Renshaw	Herbert F. Lawford	6-0, 5-7, 6-3, 6-4
1887	Herbert F. Lawford	Ernest Renshaw	1-6, 6-3, 3-6, 6-4, 6-4
1888	Ernest Renshaw	Herbert F. Lawford	6-3, 7-5, 6-0
1889	William Renshaw	Ernest Renshaw	6-4, 6-1, 3-6, 6-0
1890	William J. Hamilton	William Renshaw	6-8, 6-2, 3-6, 6-1, 6-1
1891	Wilfred Baddeley	Joshua Pim	6-4, 1-6, 7-5, 6-0
1892	Wilfred Baddeley	Joshua Pim	4-6, 6-3, 6-3, 6-2
1893	Joshua Pim	Wilfred Baddeley	3-6, 6-1, 6-3, 6-2
1894	Joshua Pim	Wilfred Baddeley	10-8, 6-2, 8-6
1895	Wilfred Baddeley	Wilberforce V. Eaves	4-6, 2-6, 8-6, 6-2, 6-3
1896	Harold S. Mahoney	Wilfred Baddeley	6-2, 6-8, 5-7, 8-6, 6-3
1897	Reggie F. Doherty	Harold S. Mahoney	6-4, 6-4, 6-3
1898	Reggie F. Doherty	H. Laurie Doherty	6-3, 6-3, 2-6, 5-7, 6-1
1899	Reggie F. Doherty	Arthur W. Gore	1-6, 4-6, 6-2, 6-3, 6-3
1900	Reggie F. Doherty	Sidney H. Smith	6-8, 6-3, 6-1, 6-2

Wimbledon Championship (Cont.)

Year	Winner	Finalist	Score
1901	Arthur W. Gore	Reggie F. Doherty	4-6, 7-5, 6-4, 6-4
1902	H. Laurie Doherty	Arthur W. Gore	6-4, 6-3, 3-6, 6-0
1903	H. Laurie Doherty	Frank L. Riseley	7-5, 6-3, 6-0
1904	H. Laurie Doherty	Frank L. Riseley	6-1, 7-5, 8-6
1905	H. Laurie Doherty	Norman E. Brookes	8-6, 6-2, 6-4
1906	H. Laurie Doherty	Frank L. Riseley	6-4, 4-6, 6-2, 6-3
1907	Norman E. Brookes	Arthur W. Gore	6-4, 6-2, 6-2
1908	Arthur W. Gore	H. Roper Barrett	6-3, 6-2, 4-6, 3-6, 6-4
1909	Arthur W. Gore	M. J. G. Ritchie	6-8, 1-6, 6-2, 6-2, 6-2
1910	Anthony F. Wilding	Arthur W. Gore	6-4, 7-5, 4-6, 6-2
1911	Anthony F. Wilding	H. Roper Barrett	6-4, 4-6, 2-6, 6-2 ret
1912	Anthony F. Wilding	Arthur W. Gore	6-4, 6-4, 4-6, 6-4
1913	Anthony F. Wilding	Maurice E. McLoughlin	8-6, 6-3, 10-8
1914	Norman E. Brookes	Anthony F. Wilding	6-4, 6-4, 7-5
1915-18	No tournament		
1919	Gerald L. Patterson	Norman E. Brookes	6-3, 7-5, 6-2
1920	Bill Tilden	Gerald L. Patterson	2-6, 6-3, 6-2, 6-4
1921	Bill Tilden	Brian I. C. Norton	4-6, 2-6, 6-1, 6-0, 7-5
1922	Gerald L. Patterson	Randolph Lycett	6-3, 6-4, 6-2
1923	Bill Johnston	Francis T. Hunter	6-0, 6-3, 6-1
1924	Jean Borotra	Rene Lacoste	6-1, 3-6, 6-1, 3-6, 6-4
1925	Rene Lacoste	Jean Borotra	6-3, 6-3, 4-6, 8-6
1926	Jean Borotra	Howard Kinsey	8-6, 6-1, 6-3
1927	Henri Cochet	Jean Borotra	4-6, 4-6, 6-3, 6-4, 7-5
1928	Rene Lacoste	Henri Cochet	6-1, 4-6, 6-4, 6-2
1929	Henri Cochet	Jean Borotra	6-4, 6-3, 6-4
1930	Bill Tilden	Wilmer Allison	6-3, 9-7, 6-4
1931	Sidney B. Wood Jr	Francis X. Shields	walkover
1932	Ellsworth Vines	Henry Austin	6-4, 6-2, 6-0
1933	Jack Crawford	Ellsworth Vines	4-6, 11-9, 6-2, 2-6, 6-4
1934	Fred Perry	Jack Crawford	6-3, 6-0, 7-5
1935	Fred Perry	Gottfried von Cramm	6-2, 6-4, 6-4
1936	Fred Perry	Gottfried von Cramm	6-1, 6-1, 6-0
1937	Don Budge	Gottfried von Cramm	6-3, 6-4, 6-2
1938	Don Budge	Henry Austin	6-1, 6-0, 6-3
1939	Bobby Riggs	Elwood Cooke	2-6, 8-6, 3-6, 6-3, 6-2
1940-45	No tournament		
1946	Yvon Petra	Geoff E. Brown	6-2, 6-4, 7-9, 5-7, 6-4
1947	Jack Kramer	Tom P. Brown	6-1, 6-3, 6-2
1948	Bob Falkenburg	John Bromwich	7-5, 0-6, 6-2, 3-6, 7-5
1949	Ted Schroeder	Jaroslav Drobny	3-6, 6-0, 6-3, 4-6, 6-4
1950	Budge Patty	Frank Sedgman	6-1, 8-10, 6-2, 6-3
1951	Dick Savitt	Ken McGregor	6-4, 6-4, 6-4
1952	Frank Sedgman	Jaroslav Drobny	4-6, 6-3, 6-2, 6-3
1953	Vic Seixas	Kurt Nielsen	9-7, 6-3, 6-4
1954	Jaroslav Drobny	Ken Rosewall	13-11, 4-6, 6-2, 9-7
1955	Tony Trabert	Kurt Nielsen	6-3, 7-5, 6-1
1956	Lew Hoad	Ken Rosewall	6-2, 4-6, 7-5, 6-4
1957	Lew Hoad	Ashley Cooper	6-2, 6-1, 6-2
1958	Ashley Cooper	Neale Fraser	3-6, 6-3, 6-4, 13-11
1959	Alex Olmedo	Rod Laver	6-4, 6-3, 6-4
1960	Neale Fraser	Rod Laver	6-4, 3-6, 9-7, 7-5
1961	Rod Laver	Chuck McKinley	6-3, 6-1, 6-4
1962	Rod Laver	Martin Mulligan	6-2, 6-2, 6-1
1963	Chuck McKinley	Fred Stolle	9-7, 6-1, 6-4
1964	Roy Emerson	Fred Stolle	6-4, 12-10, 4-6, 6-3
1965	Roy Emerson	Fred Stolle	6-2, 6-4, 6-4
1966	Manuel Santana	Dennis Ralston	6-4, 11-9, 6-4
1967	John Newcombe	Wilhelm Bungert	6-3, 6-1, 6-1
1968*	Rod Laver	Tony Roche	6-3, 6-4, 6-2
1969	Rod Laver	John Newcombe	6-4, 5-7, 6-4, 6-4
1970	John Newcombe	Ken Rosewall	5-7, 6-3, 6-2, 3-6, 6-1
1971	John Newcombe	Stan Smith	6-3, 5-7, 2-6, 6-4, 6-4
1972	Stan Smith	Ilie Nastase	4-6, 6-3, 6-3, 4-6, 7-5
1973	Jan Kodes	Alex Metreveli	6-1, 9-8, 6-3
1974	Jimmy Connors	Ken Rosewall	6-1, 6-1, 6-4

Wimbledon Championships (Cont.)

Year	Winner	Finalist	Score
1975	Arthur Ashe	Jimmy Connors	6-1, 6-1, 5-7, 6-4
1976	Bjorn Borg	Ilie Nastase	6-4, 6-2, 9-7
1977	Bjorn Borg	Jimmy Connors	3-6, 6-2, 6-1, 5-7, 6-4
1978	Bjorn Borg	Jimmy Connors	6-2, 6-2, 6-3
1979	Bjorn Borg	Roscoe Tanner	6-7, 6-1, 3-6, 6-3, 6-4
1980	Bjorn Borg	John McEnroe	1-6, 7-5, 6-3, 6-7, 8-6
1981	John McEnroe	Bjorn Borg	4-6, 7-6, 7-6, 6-4
1982	Jimmy Connors	John McEnroe	3-6, 6-3, 6-7, 7-6, 6-4
1983	John McEnroe	Chris Lewis	6-2, 6-2, 6-2
1984	John McEnroe	Jimmy Connors	6-1, 6-1, 6-2
1985	Boris Becker	Kevin Curren	6-3, 6-7, 7-6, 6-4
1986	Boris Becker	Ivan Lendl	6-4, 6-3, 7-5
1987	Pat Cash	Ivan Lendl	7-6, 6-2, 7-5
1988	Stefan Edberg	Boris Becker	4-6, 7-6, 6-4, 6-2
1989	Boris Becker	Stefan Edberg	6-0, 7-6, 6-4
1990	Stefan Edberg	Boris Becker	6-2, 6-2, 3-6, 3-6, 6-4
1991	Michael Stich	Boris Becker	6-4, 7-6, 6-4
1992	Andre Agassi	Goran Ivanisevic	6-7, 6-4, 6-4, 1-6, 6-4
1993	Pete Sampras	Jim Courier	7-6 (7-3), 7-6 (8-6), 3-6, 6-3
1994	Pete Sampras	Goran Ivanisevic	7-6 (7-2), 7-6 (7-5), 6-0
1995	Pete Sampras	Boris Becker	6-7 (5-7), 6-2, 6-4, 6-2

*Became Open (amateur and professional) in 1968 but closed to contract professionals in 1972.
Note: Prior to 1922 the tournament was run on a challenge-round system. The previous year's winner "stood out" of an All Comers event, which produced a challenger to play him for the title.

United States Championships

Year	Winner	Finalist	Score
1881	Richard D. Sears	W. E. Glyn	6-0, 6-3, 6-2
1882	Richard D. Sears	C. M. Clark	6-1, 6-4, 6-0
1883	Richard D. Sears	James Dwight	6-2, 6-0, 9-7
1884	Richard D. Sears	H. A. Taylor	6-0, 1-6, 6-0, 6-2
1885	Richard D. Sears	G. M. Brinley	6-3, 4-6, 6-0, 6-3
1886	Richard D. Sears	R. L. Beeckman	4-6, 6-1, 6-3, 6-4
1887	Richard D. Sears	H. W. Slocum Jr	6-1, 6-3, 6-2
1888‡	H. W. Slocum Jr	H. A. Taylor	6-4, 6-1, 6-0
1889	H. W. Slocum Jr	Q. A. Shaw	6-3, 6-1, 4-6, 6-2
1890	Oliver S. Campbell	H. W. Slocum Jr	6-2, 4-6, 6-3, 6-1
1891	Oliver S. Campbell	Clarence Hobart	2-6, 7-5, 7-9, 6-1, 6-2
1892	Oliver S. Campbell	Frederick H. Hovey	7-5, 3-6, 6-3, 7-5
1893‡	Robert D. Wrenn	Frederick H. Hovey	6-4, 3-6, 6-4, 6-4
1894	Robert D. Wrenn	M. F. Goodbody	6-8, 6-1, 6-4, 6-4
1895	Frederick H. Hovey	Robert D. Wrenn	6-3, 6-2, 6-4
1896	Robert D. Wrenn	Frederick H. Hovey	7-5, 3-6, 6-0, 1-6, 6-1
1897	Robert D. Wrenn	Wilberforce V. Eaves	4-6, 8-6, 6-3, 2-6, 6-2
1898‡	Malcolm D. Whitman	Dwight F. Davis	3-6, 6-2, 6-2, 6-1
1899	Malcolm D. Whitman	J. Parmly Paret	6-1, 6-2, 3-6, 7-5
1900	Malcolm D. Whitman	William A. Larned	6-4, 1-6, 6-2, 6-2
1901‡	William A. Larned	Beals C. Wright	6-2, 6-8, 6-4, 6-4
1902	William A. Larned	Reggie F. Doherty	4-6, 6-2, 6-4, 8-6
1903	H. Laurie Doherty	William A. Larned	6-0, 6-3, 10-8
1904‡	Holcombe Ward	William J. Clothier	10-8, 6-4, 9-7
1905	Beals C. Wright	Holcombe Ward	6-2, 6-1, 11-9
1906	William J. Clothier	Beals C. Wright	6-3, 6-0, 6-4
1907‡	William A. Larned	Robert LeRoy	6-2, 6-2, 6-4
1908	William A. Larned	Beals C. Wright	6-1, 6-2, 8-6
1909	William A. Larned	William J. Clothier	6-1, 6-2, 5-7, 1-6, 6-1
1910	William A. Larned	Thomas C. Bundy	6-1, 5-7, 6-0, 6-8, 6-1
1911	William A. Larned	Maurice E. McLoughlin	6-4, 6-4, 6-2
1912†	Maurice E. McLoughlin	Bill Johnson	3-6, 2-6, 6-2, 6-4, 6-2
1913	Maurice E. McLoughlin	Richard N. Williams	6-4, 5-7, 6-3, 6-1
1914	Richard N. Williams	Maurice E. McLoughlin	6-3, 8-6, 10-8
1915	Bill Johnston	Maurice E. McLoughlin	1-6, 6-0, 7-5, 10-8
1916	Richard N. Williams	Bill Johnston	4-6, 6-4, 0-6, 6-2, 6-4
1917#	R. L. Murray	N. W. Niles	5-7, 8-6, 6-3, 6-3

United States Championships (Cont.)

Year	Winner	Finalist	Score
1918	R. L. Murray	Bill Tilden	6-3, 6-1, 7-5
1919	Bill Johnston	Bill Tilden	6-4, 6-4, 6-3
1920	Bill Tilden	Bill Johnston	6-1, 1-6, 7-5, 5-7, 6-3
1921	Bill Tilden	Wallace F. Johnson	6-1, 6-3, 6-1
1922	Bill Tilden	Bill Johnston	4-6, 3-6, 6-2, 6-3, 6-4
1923	Bill Tilden	Bill Johnston	6-4, 6-1, 6-4
1924	Bill Tilden	Bill Johnston	6-1, 9-7, 6-2
1925	Bill Tilden	Bill Johnston	4-6, 11-9, 6-3, 4-6, 6-3
1926	Rene Lacoste	Jean Borotra	6-4, 6-0, 6-4
1927	Rene Lacoste	Bill Tilden	11-9, 6-3, 11-9
1928	Henri Cochet	Francis T. Hunter	4-6, 6-4, 3-6, 7-5, 6-3
1929	Bill Tilden	Francis T. Hunter	3-6, 6-3, 4-6, 6-2, 6-4
1930	John H. Doeg	Francis X. Shields	10-8, 1-6, 6-4, 16-14
1931	Ellsworth Vines	George M. Lott Jr	7-9, 6-3, 9-7, 7-5
1932	Ellsworth Vines	Henri Cochet	6-4, 6-4, 6-4
1933	Fred Perry	Jack Crawford	6-3, 11-13, 4-6, 6-0, 6-1
1934	Fred Perry	Wilmer L. Allison	6-4, 6-3, 1-6, 8-6
1935	Wilmer L. Allison	Sidney B. Wood Jr	6-2, 6-2, 6-3
1936	Fred Perry	Don Budge	2-6, 6-2, 8-6, 1-6, 10-8
1937	Don Budge	Gottfried von Cramm	6-1, 7-9, 6-1, 3-6, 6-1
1938	Don Budge	Gene Mako	6-3, 6-8, 6-2, 6-1
1939	Bobby Riggs	Welby van Horn	6-4, 6-2, 6-4
1940	Don McNeill	Bobby Riggs	4-6, 6-8, 6-3, 6-3, 7-5
1941	Bobby Riggs	Francis Kovacs II	5-7, 6-1, 6-3, 6-3
1942	Ted Schroeder	Frank Parker	8-6, 7-5, 3-6, 4-6, 6-2
1943	Joseph R. Hunt	Jack Kramer	6-3, 6-8, 10-8, 6-0
1944	Frank Parker	William F. Talbert	6-4, 3-6, 6-3, 6-3
1945	Frank Parker	William F. Talbert	14-12, 6-1, 6-2
1946	Jack Kramer	Tom P. Brown	9-7, 6-3, 6-0
1947	Jack Kramer	Frank Parker	4-6, 2-6, 6-1, 6-0, 6-3
1948	Pancho Gonzales	Eric W. Sturgess	6-2, 6-3, 14-12
1949	Pancho Gonzales	Ted Schroeder	16-18, 2-6, 6-1, 6-2, 6-4
1950	Arthur Larsen	Herbie Flam	6-3, 4-6, 5-7, 6-4, 6-3
1951	Frank Sedgman	Vic Seixas	6-4, 6-1, 6-1
1952	Frank Sedgman	Gardnar Mulloy	6-1, 6-2, 6-3
1953	Tony Trabert	Vic Seixas	6-3, 6-2, 6-3
1954	Vic Seixas	Rex Hartwig	3-6, 6-2, 6-4, 6-4
1955	Tony Trabert	Ken Rosewall	9-7, 6-3, 6-3
1956	Ken Rosewall	Lew Hoad	4-6, 6-2, 6-3, 6-3
1957	Mal Anderson	Ashley J. Cooper	10-8, 7-5, 6-4
1958	Ashley J. Cooper	Mal Anderson	6-2, 3-6, 4-6, 10-8, 8-6
1959	Neale Fraser	Alex Olmedo	6-3, 5-7, 6-2, 6-4
1960	Neale Fraser	Rod Laver	6-4, 6-4, 9-7
1961	Roy Emerson	Rod Laver	7-5, 6-3, 6-2
1962	Rod Laver	Roy Emerson	6-2, 6-4, 5-7, 6-4
1963	Rafael Osuna	Frank Froehling III	7-5, 6-4, 6-2
1964	Roy Emerson	Fred Stolle	6-4, 6-2, 6-4
1965	Manuel Santana	Cliff Drysdale	6-2, 7-9, 7-5, 6-1
1966	Fred Stolle	John Newcombe	4-6, 12-10, 6-3, 6-4
1967	John Newcombe	Clark Graebner	6-4, 6-4, 8-6
1968**	Arthur Ashe	Bob Lutz	4-6, 6-3, 8-10, 6-0, 6-4
1968*	Arthur Ashe	Tom Okker	14-12, 5-7, 6-3, 3-6, 6-3
1969**	Stan Smith	Bob Lutz	9-7, 6-3, 6-1
1969*	Rod Laver	Tony Roche	7-9, 6-1, 6-3, 6-2
1970	Ken Rosewall	Tony Roche	2-6, 6-4, 7-6, 6-3
1971	Stan Smith	Jan Kodes	3-6, 6-3, 6-2, 7-6
1972	Ilie Nastase	Arthur Ashe	3-6, 6-3, 6-7, 6-4, 6-3
1973	John Newcombe	Jan Kodes	6-4, 1-6, 4-6, 6-2, 6-3
1974	Jimmy Connors	Ken Rosewall	6-1, 6-0, 6-1
1975	Manuel Orantes	Jimmy Connors	6-4, 6-3, 6-3
1976	Jimmy Connors	Bjorn Borg	6-4, 3-6, 7-6, 6-4
1977	Guillermo Vilas	Jimmy Connors	2-6, 6-3, 7-6, 6-0
1978	Jimmy Connors	Bjorn Borg	6-4, 6-2, 6-2
1979	John McEnroe	Vitas Gerulaitis	7-5, 6-3, 6-3
1980	John McEnroe	Bjorn Borg	7-6, 6-1, 6-7, 5-7, 6-4
1981	John McEnroe	Bjorn Borg	4-6, 6-2, 6-4, 6-3

United States Championships *(Cont.)*

Year	Winner	Finalist	Score
1982	Jimmy Connors	Ivan Lendl	6-3, 6-2, 4-6, 6-4
1983	Jimmy Connors	Ivan Lendl	6-3, 6-7, 7-5, 6-0
1984	John McEnroe	Ivan Lendl	6-3, 6-4, 6-1
1985	Ivan Lendl	John McEnroe	7-6, 6-3, 6-4
1986	Ivan Lendl	Miloslav Mecir	6-4, 6-2, 6-0
1987	Ivan Lendl	Mats Wilander	6-7, 6-0, 7-6, 6-4
1988	Mats Wilander	Ivan Lendl	6-4, 4-6, 6-3, 5-7, 6-4
1989	Boris Becker	Ivan Lendl	7-6, 1-6, 6-3, 7-6
1990	Pete Sampras	Andre Agassi	6-4, 6-3, 6-2
1991	Stefan Edberg	Jim Courier	6-2, 6-4, 6-0
1992	Stefan Edberg	Pete Sampras	3-6, 6-4, 7-6, 6-2
1993	Pete Sampras	Cédric Pioline	6-4, 6-4, 6-3
1994	Andre Agassi	Michael Stich	6-1, 7-6 (7-5), 7-5
1995	Pete Sampras	Andre Agassi	6-4, 6-3, 4-6, 7-5

*Became Open (amateur and professional) in 1968; †Challenge round abolished; ‡No challenge round played.
#National Patriotic Tournament; **Amateur event held.

WOMEN
Australian Championships

Year	Winner	Finalist	Score
1922	Margaret Molesworth	Esna Boyd	6-3, 10-8
1923	Margaret Molesworth	Esna Boyd	6-1, 7-5
1924	Sylvia Lance	Esna Boyd	6-3, 3-6, 6-4
1925	Daphne Akhurst	Esna Boyd	1-6, 8-6, 6-4
1926	Daphne Akhurst	Esna Boyd	6-1, 6-3
1927	Esna Boyd	Sylvia Harper	5-7, 6-1, 6-2
1928	Daphne Akhurst	Esna Boyd	7-5, 6-2
1929	Daphne Akhurst	Louise Bickerton	6-1, 5-7, 6-2
1930	Daphne Akhurst	Sylvia Harper	10-8, 2-6, 7-5
1931	Coral Buttsworth	Margorie Crawford	1-6, 6-3, 6-4
1932	Coral Buttsworth	Kathrine Le Messurier	9-7, 6-4
1933	Joan Hartigan	Coral Buttsworth	6-4, 6-3
1934	Joan Hartigan	Margaret Molesworth	6-1, 6-4
1935	Dorothy Round	Nancye Wynne Bolton	1-6, 6-1, 6-3
1936	Joan Hartigan	Nancye Wynne Bolton	6-4, 6-4
1937	Nancye Wynne Bolton	Emily Westacott	6-3, 5-7, 6-4
1938	Dorothy Bundy	D. Stevenson	6-3, 6-2
1939	Emily Westacott	Nell Hopman	6-1, 6-2
1940	Nancye Wynne Bolton	Thelma Coyne	5-7, 6-4, 6-0
1941-45	No tournament		
1946	Nancye Wynne Bolton	Joyce Fitch	6-4, 6-4
1947	Nancye Wynne Bolton	Nell Hopman	6-3, 6-2
1948	Nancye Wynne Bolton	Marie Toomey	6-3, 6-1
1949	Doris Hart	Nancye Wynne Bolton	6-3, 6-4
1950	Louise Brough	Doris Hart	6-4, 3-6, 6-4
1951	Nancye Wynne Bolton	Thelma Long	6-1, 7-5
1952	Thelma Long	H. Angwin	6-2, 6-3
1953	Maureen Connolly	Julia Sampson	6-3, 6-2
1954	Thelma Long	J. Staley	6-3, 6-4
1955	Beryl Penrose	Thelma Long	6-4, 6-3
1956	Mary Carter	Thelma Long	3-6, 6-2, 9-7
1957	Shirley Fry	Althea Gibson	6-3, 6-4
1958	Angela Mortimer	Lorraine Coghlan	6-3, 6-4
1959	Mary Carter-Reitano	Renee Schuurman	6-2, 6-3
1960	Margaret Smith	Jan Lehane	7-5, 6-2
1961	Margaret Smith	Jan Lehane	6-1, 6-4
1962	Margaret Smith	Jan Lehane	6-0, 6-2
1963	Margaret Smith	Jan Lehane	6-2, 6-2
1964	Margaret Smith	Lesley Turner	6-3, 6-2
1965	Margaret Smith	Maria Bueno	5-7, 6-4, 5-2 ret
1966	Margaret Smith	Nancy Richey	Default
1967	Nancy Richey	Lesley Turner	6-1, 6-4
1968	Billie Jean King	Margaret Smith	6-1, 6-2

Australian Championships (Cont.)

Year	Winner	Finalist	Score
1969*	Margaret Smith Court	Billie Jean King	6-4, 6-1
1970	Margaret Smith Court	Kerry Melville Reid	6-3, 6-1
1971	Margaret Smith Court	Evonne Goolagong	2-6, 7-6, 7-5
1972	Virginia Wade	Evonne Goolagong	6-4, 6-4
1973	Margaret Smith Court	Evonne Goolagong	6-4, 7-5
1974	Evonne Goolagong	Chris Evert	7-6, 4-6, 6-0
1975	Evonne Goolagong	Martina Navratilova	6-3, 6-2
1976	Evonne Goolagong Cawley	Renata Tomanova	6-2, 6-2
1977 (Jan)	Kerry Melville Reid	Dianne Balestrat	7-5, 6-2
1977 (Dec)	Evonne Goolagong Cawley	Helen Gourlay	6-3, 6-0
1978	Chris O'Neil	Betsy Nagelsen	6-3, 7-6
1979	Barbara Jordan	Sharon Walsh	6-3, 6-3
1980	Hana Mandlikova	Wendy Turnbull	6-0, 7-5
1981	Martina Navratilova	Chris Evert Lloyd	6-7, 6-4, 7-5
1982	Chris Evert Lloyd	Martina Navratilova	6-3, 2-6, 6-3
1983	Martina Navratilova	Kathy Jordan	6-2, 7-6
1984	Chris Evert Lloyd	Helena Sukova	6-7, 6-1, 6-3
1985 (Dec)	Martina Navratilova	Chris Evert Lloyd	6-2, 4-6, 6-2
1987 (Jan)	Hana Mandlikova	Martina Navratilova	7-5, 7-6
1988	Steffi Graf	Chris Evert	6-1, 7-6
1989	Steffi Graf	Helena Sukova	6-4, 6-4
1990	Steffi Graf	Mary Joe Fernandez	6-3, 6-4
1991	Monica Seles	Jana Novotna	5-7, 6-3, 6-1
1992	Monica Seles	Mary Joe Fernandez	6-2, 6-3
1993	Monica Seles	Steffi Graf	4-6, 6-3, 6-2
1994	Steffi Graf	Arantxa Sanchez Vicario	6-0, 6-2
1995	Mary Pierce	Arantxa Sanchez Vicario	6-3, 6-2

*Became Open (amateur and professional) in 1969.

French Championships

Year	Winner	Finalist	Score
1925†	Suzanne Lenglen	Kathleen McKane	6-1, 6-2
1926	Suzanne Lenglen	Mary K. Browne	6-1, 6-0
1927	Kea Bouman	Irene Peacock	6-2, 6-4
1928	Helen Wills	Eileen Bennett	6-1, 6-2
1929	Helen Wills	Simone Mathieu	6-3, 6-4
1930	Helen Wills Moody	Helen Jacobs	6-2, 6-1
1931	Cilly Aussem	Betty Nuthall	8-6, 6-1
1932	Helen Wills Moody	Simone Mathieu	7-5, 6-1
1933	Margaret Scriven	Simone Mathieu	6-2, 4-6, 6-4
1934	Margaret Scriven	Helen Jacobs	7-5, 4-6, 6-1
1935	Hilde Sperling	Simone Mathieu	6-2, 6-1
1936	Hilde Sperling	Simone Mathieu	6-3, 6-4
1937	Hilde Sperling	Simone Mathieu	6-2, 6-4
1938	Simone Mathieu	Nelly Landry	6-0, 6-3
1939	Simone Mathieu	Jadwiga Jedrzejowska	6-3, 8-6
1940-45	No tournament		
1946	Margaret Osborne	Pauline Betz	1-6, 8-6, 7-5
1947	Patricia Todd	Doris Hart	6-3, 3-6, 6-4
1948	Nelly Landry	Shirley Fry	6-2, 0-6, 6-0
1949	Margaret Osborne duPont	Nelly Adamson	7-5, 6-2
1950	Doris Hart	Patricia Todd	6-4, 4-6, 6-2
1951	Shirley Fry	Doris Hart	6-3, 3-6, 6-3
1952	Doris Hart	Shirley Fry	6-4, 6-4
1953	Maureen Connolly	Doris Hart	6-2, 6-4
1954	Maureen Connolly	Ginette Bucaille	6-4, 6-1
1955	Angela Mortimer	Dorothy Knode	2-6, 7-5, 10-8
1956	Althea Gibson	Angela Mortimer	6-0, 12-10
1957	Shirley Bloomer	Dorothy Knode	6-1, 6-3
1958	Zsuzsi Kormoczi	Shirley Bloomer	6-4, 1-6, 6-2
1959	Christine Truman	Zsuzsi Kormoczi	6-4, 7-5
1960	Darlene Hard	Yola Ramirez	6-3, 6-4
1961	Ann Haydon	Yola Ramirez	6-2, 6-1
1962	Margaret Smith	Lesley Turner	6-3, 3-6, 7-5

French Championships *(Cont.)*

Year	Winner	Finalist	Score
1963	Lesley Turner	Ann Haydon Jones	2-6, 6-3, 7-5
1964	Margaret Smith	Maria Bueno	5-7, 6-1, 6-2
1965	Lesley Turner	Margaret Smith	6-3, 6-4
1966	Ann Jones	Nancy Richey	6-3, 6-1
1967	Francoise Durr	Lesley Turner	4-6, 6-3, 6-4
1968*	Nancy Richey	Ann Jones	5-7, 6-4, 6-1
1969	Margaret Smith Court	Ann Jones	6-1, 4-6, 6-3
1970	Margaret Smith Court	Helga Niessen	6-2, 6-4
1971	Evonne Goolagong	Helen Gourlay	6-3, 7-5
1972	Billie Jean King	Evonne Goolagong	6-3, 6-3
1973	Margaret Smith Court	Chris Evert	6-7, 7-6, 6-4
1974	Chris Evert	Olga Morozova	6-1, 6-2
1975	Chris Evert	Martina Navratilova	2-6, 6-2, 6-1
1976	Sue Barker	Renata Tomanova	6-2, 0-6, 6-2
1977	Mima Jausovec	Florenza Mihai	6-2, 6-7, 6-1
1978	Virginia Ruzici	Mima Jausovec	6-2, 6-2
1979	Chris Evert Lloyd	Wendy Turnbull	6-2, 6-0
1980	Chris Evert Lloyd	Virginia Ruzici	6-0, 6-3
1981	Hana Mandlikova	Sylvia Hanika	6-2, 6-4
1982	Martina Navratilova	Andrea Jaeger	7-6, 6-1
1983	Chris Evert Lloyd	Mima Jausovec	6-1, 6-2
1984	Martina Navratilova	Chris Evert Lloyd	6-3, 6-1
1985	Chris Evert Lloyd	Martina Navratilova	6-3, 6-7, 7-5
1986	Chris Evert Lloyd	Martina Navratilova	2-6, 6-3, 6-3
1987	Steffi Graf	Martina Navratilova	6-4, 4-6, 8-6
1988	Steffi Graf	Natalia Zvereva	6-0, 6-0
1989	Arantxa Sanchez Vicario	Steffi Graf	7-6, 3-6, 7-5
1990	Monica Seles	Steffi Graf	7-6, 6-4
1991	Monica Seles	Arantxa Sanchez Vicario	6-3, 6-4
1992	Monica Seles	Steffi Graf	6-2, 3-6, 10-8
1993	Steffi Graf	Mary Joe Fernandez	4-6, 6-2, 6-4
1994	Arantxa Sanchez Vicario	Mary Pierce	6-4, 6-4
1995	Steffi Graf	Arantxa Sanchez Vicario	7-5, 4-6, 6-0

*Became Open (amateur and professional) in 1968 but closed to contract professionals in 1972.

†1925 was the first year that entries were accepted from all countries.

Wimbledon Championships

Year	Winner	Finalist	Score
1884	Maud Watson	Lilian Watson	6-8, 6-3, 6-3
1885	Maud Watson	Blanche Bingley	6-1, 7-5
1886	Blanche Bingley	Maud Watson	6-3, 6-3
1887	Charlotte Dod	Blanche Bingley	6-2, 6-0
1888	Charlotte Dod	Blanche Bingley Hillyard	6-3, 6-3
1889	Blanche Bingley Hillyard		
1890	Lena Rice		
1891	Charlotte Dod		
1892	Charlotte Dod	Blanche Bingley Hillyard	6-1, 6-1
1893	Charlotte Dod	Blanche Bingley Hillyard	6-8, 6-1, 6-4
1894	Blanche Bingley Hillyard		
1895	Charlotte Cooper		
1896	Charlotte Cooper	Mrs. W. H. Pickering	6-2, 6-3
1897	Blanche Bingley Hillyard	Charlotte Cooper	5-7, 7-5, 6-2
1898	Charlotte Cooper		
1899	Blanche Bingley Hillyard	Charlotte Cooper	6-2, 6-3
1900	Blanche Bingley Hillyard	Charlotte Cooper	4-6, 6-4, 6-4
1901	Charlotte Cooper Sterry	Blanche Bingley Hillyard	6-2, 6-2
1902	Muriel Robb	Charlotte Cooper Sterry	7-5, 6-1
1903	Dorothea Douglass		
1904	Dorothea Douglass	Charlotte Cooper Sterry	6-0, 6-3
1905	May Sutton	Dorothea Douglass	6-3, 6-4
1906	Dorothea Douglass	May Sutton	6-3, 9-7
1907	May Sutton	Dorothea Douglass Lambert Chambers	6-1, 6-4
1908	Charlotte Cooper Sterry		

Wimbledon Championships (Cont.)

Year	Winner	Finalist	Score
1909	Dora Boothby		
1910	Dorothea Douglass Lambert Chambers	Dora Boothby	6-2, 6-2
1911	Dorothea Douglass Lambert Chambers	Dora Boothby	6-0, 6-0
1912	Ethel Larcombe		
1913	Dorothea Douglass Lambert Chambers		
1914	Dorothea Douglass Lambert Chambers	Ethel Larcombe	7-5, 6-4
1915-18	No tournament		
1919	Suzanne Lenglen	Dorothea Douglass Lambert Chambers	10-8, 4-6, 9-7
1920	Suzanne Lenglen	Dorothea Douglass Lambert Chambers	6-3, 6-0
1921	Suzanne Lenglen	Elizabeth Ryan	6-2, 6-0
1922	Suzanne Lenglen	Molla Mallory	6-2, 6-0
1923	Suzanne Lenglen	Kathleen McKane	6-2, 6-2
1924	Kathleen McKane	Helen Wills	4-6, 6-4, 6-2
1925	Suzanne Lenglen	Joan Fry	6-2, 6-0
1926	Kathleen McKane Godfree	Lili de Alvarez	6-2, 4-6, 6-3
1927	Helen Wills	Lili de Alvarez	6-2, 6-4
1928	Helen Wills	Lili de Alvarez	6-2, 6-3
1929	Helen Wills	Helen Jacobs	6-1, 6-2
1930	Helen Wills Moody	Elizabeth Ryan	6-2, 6-2
1931	Cilly Aussem	Hilde Kranwinkel	7-5, 7-5
1932	Helen Wills Moody	Helen Jacobs	6-3, 6-1
1933	Helen Wills Moody	Dorothy Round	6-4, 6-8, 6-3
1934	Dorothy Round	Helen Jacobs	6-2, 5-7, 6-3
1935	Helen Wills Moody	Helen Jacobs	6-3, 3-6, 7-5
1936	Helen Jacobs	Hilde Kranwinkel Sperling	6-2, 4-6, 7-5
1937	Dorothy Round	Jadwiga Jedrzejowska	6-2, 2-6, 7-5
1938	Helen Wills Moody	Helen Jacobs	6-4, 6-0
1939	Alice Marble	Kay Stammers	6-2, 6-0
1940-45	No tournament		
1946	Pauline Betz	Louise Brough	6-2, 6-4
1947	Margaret Osborne	Doris Hart	6-2, 6-4
1948	Louise Brough	Doris Hart	6-3, 8-6
1949	Louise Brough	Margaret Osborne duPont	10-8, 1-6, 10-8
1950	Louise Brough	Margaret Osborne duPont	6-1, 3-6, 6-1
1951	Doris Hart	Shirley Fry	6-1, 6-0
1952	Maureen Connolly	Louise Brough	6-4, 6-3
1953	Maureen Connolly	Doris Hart	8-6, 7-5
1954	Maureen Connolly	Louise Brough	6-2, 7-5
1955	Louise Brough	Beverly Fleitz	7-5, 8-6
1956	Shirley Fry	Angela Buxton	6-3, 6-1
1957	Althea Gibson	Darlene Hard	6-3, 6-2
1958	Althea Gibson	Angela Mortimer	8-6, 6-2
1959	Maria Bueno	Darlene Hard	6-4, 6-3
1960	Maria Bueno	Sandra Reynolds	8-6, 6-0
1961	Angela Mortimer	Christine Truman	4-6, 6-4, 7-5
1962	Karen Hantze Susman	Vera Sukova	6-4, 6-4
1963	Margaret Smith	Billie Jean Moffitt	6-3, 6-4
1964	Maria Bueno	Margaret Smith	6-4, 7-9, 6-3
1965	Margaret Smith	Maria Bueno	6-4, 7-5
1966	Billie Jean King	Maria Bueno	6-3, 3-6, 6-1
1967	Billie Jean King	Ann Haydon Jones	6-3, 6-4
1968*	Billie Jean King	Judy Tegart	9-7, 7-5
1969	Ann Haydon Jones	Billie Jean King	3-6, 6-3, 6-2
1970	Margaret Smith Court	Billie Jean King	14-12, 11-9
1971	Evonne Goolagong	Margaret Smith Court	6-4, 6-1
1972	Billie Jean King	Evonne Goolagong	6-3, 6-3
1973	Billie Jean King	Chris Evert	6-0, 7-5
1974	Chris Evert	Olga Morozova	6-0, 6-4
1975	Billie Jean King	Evonne Goolagong Cawley	6-0, 6-1
1976	Chris Evert	Evonne Goolagong Cawley	6-3, 4-6, 8-6

Wimbledon Championships (Cont.)

Year	Winner	Finalist	Score
1977	Virginia Wade	Betty Stove	4-6, 6-3, 6-1
1978	Martina Navratilova	Chris Evert	2-6, 6-4, 7-5
1979	Martina Navratilova	Chris Evert Lloyd	6-4, 6-4
1980	Evonne Goolagong Cawley	Chris Evert Lloyd	6-1, 7-6
1981	Chris Evert Lloyd	Hana Mandlikova	6-2, 6-2
1982	Martina Navratilova	Chris Evert Lloyd	6-1, 3-6, 6-2
1983	Martina Navratilova	Andrea Jaeger	6-0, 6-3
1984	Martina Navratilova	Chris Evert Lloyd	7-6, 6-2
1985	Martina Navratilova	Chris Evert Lloyd	4-6, 6-3, 6-2
1986	Martina Navratilova	Hana Mandlikova	7-6, 6-3
1987	Martina Navratilova	Steffi Graf	7-5, 6-3
1988	Steffi Graf	Martina Navratilova	5-7, 6-2, 6-1
1989	Steffi Graf	Martina Navratilova	6-2, 6-7, 6-1
1990	Martina Navratilova	Zina Garrison	6-4, 6-1
1991	Steffi Graf	Gabriela Sabatini	6-4, 3-6, 8-6
1992	Steffi Graf	Monica Seles	6-2, 6-1
1993	Steffi Graf	Jana Novotna	7-6 (8-6), 1-6, 6-4
1994	Conchita Martinez	Martina Navratilova	6-4, 3-6, 6-3
1995	Steffi Graf	Arantxa Sanchez Vicario	4-6, 6-1, 7-5

*Became Open (amateur and professional) in 1968 but closed to contract professionals in 1972.

Note: Prior to 1922 the tournament was run on a challenge round system. The previous year's winner "stood out" of an All Comers event, which produced a challenger to play her for the title.

United States Championships

Year	Winner	Finalist	Score
1887	Ellen Hansell	Laura Knight	6-1, 6-0
1888	Bertha L. Townsend	Ellen Hansell	6-3, 6-5
1889	Bertha L. Townsend	Louise Voorhes	7-5, 6-2
1890	Ellen C. Roosevelt	Bertha L. Townsend	6-2, 6-2
1891	Mabel Cahill	Ellen C. Roosevelt	6-4, 6-1, 4-6, 6-3
1892	Mabel Cahill	Elisabeth Moore	5-7, 6-3, 6-4, 4-6, 6-2
1893	Aline Terry	Alice Schultze	6-1, 6-3
1894	Helen Hellwig	Aline Terry	7-5, 3-6, 6-0, 3-6, 6-3
1895	Juliette Atkinson	Helen Hellwig	6-4, 6-2, 6-1
1896	Elisabeth Moore	Juliette Atkinson	6-4, 4-6, 6-2, 6-2
1897	Juliette Atkinson	Elisabeth Moore	6-3, 6-3, 4-6, 3-6, 6-3
1898	Juliette Atkinson	Marion Jones	6-3, 5-7, 6-4, 2-6, 7-5
1899	Marion Jones	Maud Banks	6-1, 6-1, 7-5
1900	Myrtle McAteer	Edith Parker	6-2, 6-2, 6-0
1901	Elisabeth Moore	Myrtle McAteer	6-4, 3-6, 7-5, 2-6, 6-2
1902**	Marion Jones	Elisabeth Moore	6-1, 1-0 retired
1903	Elisabeth Moore	Marion Jones	7-5, 8-6
1904	May Sutton	Elisabeth Moore	6-1, 6-2
1905	Elisabeth Moore	Helen Homans	6-4, 5-7, 6-1
1906	Helen Homans	Maud Barger-Wallach	6-4, 6-3
1907	Evelyn Sears	Carrie Neely	6-3, 6-2
1908	Maud Barger-Wallach	Evelyn Sears	6-3, 1-6, 6-3
1909	Hazel Hotchkiss	Maud Barger-Wallach	6-0, 6-1
1910	Hazel Hotchkiss	Louise Hammond	6-4, 6-2
1911	Hazel Hotchkiss	Florence Sutton	8-10, 6-1, 9-7
1912†	Mary K. Browne	Eleanora Sears	6-4, 6-2
1913	Mary K. Browne	Dorothy Green	6-2, 7-5
1914	Mary K. Browne	Marie Wagner	6-2, 1-6, 6-1
1915	Molla Bjurstedt	Hazel Hotchkiss Wightman	4-6, 6-2, 6-0
1916	Molla Bjurstedt	Louise Hammond Raymond	6-0, 6-1
1917‡	Molla Bjurstedt	Marion Vanderhoef	4-6, 6-0, 6-2
1918	Molla Bjurstedt	Eleanor Goss	6-4, 6-3
1919	Hazel Hotchkiss Wightman	Marion Zinderstein	6-1, 6-2
1920	Molla Bjurstedt Mallory	Marion Zinderstein	6-3, 6-1
1921	Molla Bjurstedt Mallory	Mary K. Browne	4-6, 6-4, 6-2
1922	Molla Bjurstedt Mallory	Helen Wills	6-3, 6-1
1923	Helen Wills	Molla Bjurstedt Mallory	6-2, 6-1
1924	Helen Wills	Molla Bjurstedt Mallory	6-1, 6-3
1925	Helen Wills	Kathleen McKane	3-6, 6-0, 6-2

United States Championship *(Cont.)*

Year	Winner	Finalist	Score
1926	Molla Bjurstedt Mallory	Elizabeth Ryan	4-6, 6-4, 9-7
1927	Helen Wills	Betty Nuthall	6-1, 6-4
1928	Helen Wills	Helen Jacobs	6-2, 6-1
1929	Helen Wills	Phoebe Holcroft Watson	6-4, 6-2
1930	Betty Nuthall	Anna McCune Harper	6-1, 6-4
1931	Helen Wills Moody	Eileen Whitingstall	6-4, 6-1
1932	Helen Jacobs	Carolin Babcock	6-2, 6-2
1933	Helen Jacobs	Helen Wills Moody	8-6, 3-6, 3-0 retired
1934	Helen Jacobs	Sarah Palfrey	6-1, 6-4
1935	Helen Jacobs	Sarah Palfrey Fabyan	6-2, 6-4
1936	Alice Marble	Helen Jacobs	4-6, 6-3, 6-2
1937	Anita Lizane	Jadwiga Jedrzejowska	6-4, 6-2
1938	Alice Marble	Nancye Wynne	6-0, 6-3
1939	Alice Marble	Helen Jacobs	6-0, 8-10, 6-4
1940	Alice Marble	Helen Jacobs	6-2, 6-3
1941	Sarah Palfrey Cooke	Pauline Betz	7-5, 6-2
1942	Pauline Betz	Louise Brough	4-6, 6-1, 6-4
1943	Pauline Betz	Louise Brough	6-3, 5-7, 6-3
1944	Pauline Betz	Margaret Osborne	6-3, 8-6
1945	Sarah Palfrey Cooke	Pauline Betz	3-6, 8-6, 6-4
1946	Pauline Betz	Patricia Canning	11-9, 6-3
1947	Louise Brough	Margaret Osborne	8-6, 4-6, 6-1
1948	Margaret Osborne duPont	Louise Brough	4-6, 6-4, 15-13
1949	Margaret Osborne duPont	Doris Hart	6-4, 6-1
1950	Margaret Osborne duPont	Doris Hart	6-4, 6-3
1951	Maureen Connolly	Shirley Fry	6-3, 1-6, 6-4
1952	Maureen Connolly	Doris Hart	6-3, 7-5
1953	Maureen Connolly	Doris Hart	6-2, 6-4
1954	Doris Hart	Louise Brough	6-8, 6-1, 8-6
1955	Doris Hart	Patricia Ward	6-4, 6-2
1956	Shirley Fry	Althea Gibson	6-3, 6-4
1957	Althea Gibson	Louise Brough	6-3, 6-2
1958	Althea Gibson	Darlene Hard	3-6, 6-1, 6-2
1959	Maria Bueno	Christine Truman	6-1, 6-4
1960	Darlene Hard	Maria Bueno	6-4, 10-12, 6-4
1961	Darlene Hard	Ann Haydon	6-3, 6-4
1962	Margaret Smith	Darlene Hard	9-7, 6-4
1963	Maria Bueno	Margaret Smith	7-5, 6-4
1964	Maria Bueno	Carole Graebner	6-1, 6-0
1965	Margaret Smith	Billie Jean Moffitt	8-6, 7-5
1966	Maria Bueno	Nancy Richey	6-3, 6-1
1967	Billie Jean King	Ann Haydon Jones	11-9, 6-4
1968*	Virginia Wade	Billie Jean King	6-4, 6-4
1968#	Margaret Smith Court	Maria Bueno	6-2, 6-2
1969*	Margaret Smith Court	Nancy Richey	6-2, 6-2
1969#	Margaret Smith Court	Virginia Wade	4-6, 6-3, 6-0
1970	Margaret Smith Court	Rosie Casals	6-2, 2-6, 6-1
1971	Billie Jean King	Rosie Casals	6-4, 7-6
1972	Billie Jean King	Kerry Melville	6-3, 7-5
1973	Margaret Smith Court	Evonne Goolagong	7-6, 5-7, 6-2
1974	Billie Jean King	Evonne Goolagong	3-6, 6-3, 7-5
1975	Chris Evert	Evonne Goolagong Cawley	5-7, 6-4, 6-2
1976	Chris Evert	Evonne Goolagong Cawley	6-3, 6-0
1977	Chris Evert	Wendy Turnbull	7-6, 6-2
1978	Chris Evert	Pam Shriver	7-6, 6-4
1979	Tracy Austin	Chris Evert Lloyd	6-4, 6-3
1980	Chris Evert Lloyd	Hana Mandlikova	5-7, 6-1, 6-1
1981	Tracy Austin	Martina Navratilova	1-6, 7-6, 7-6
1982	Chris Evert Lloyd	Hana Mandlikova	6-3, 6-1
1983	Martina Navratilova	Chris Evert Lloyd	6-1, 6-3
1984	Martina Navratilova	Chris Evert Lloyd	4-6, 6-4, 6-4
1985	Hana Mandlikova	Martina Navratilova	7-6, 1-6, 7-6
1986	Martina Navratilova	Helena Sukova	6-3, 6-2
1987	Martina Navratilova	Steffi Graf	7-6, 6-1
1988	Steffi Graf	Gabriela Sabatini	6-3, 3-6, 6-1
1989	Steffi Graf	Martina Navratilova	3-6, 6-4, 6-2

United States Championship (Cont.)

Year	Winner	Finalist	Score
1990	Gabriela Sabatini	Steffi Graf	6-2, 7-6
1991	Monica Seles	Martina Narvatilova	7-6, 6-1
1992	Monica Seles	Arantxa Sanchez Vicario	6-3, 6-2
1993	Steffi Graf	Helena Sukova	6-3, 6-3
1994	Arantxa Sanchez Vicario	Steffi Graf	1-6, 7-6 (7-3), 6-4
1995	Steffi Graf	Monica Seles	7-6 (8-6), 0-6, 6-3

*Became Open (amateur and professional) in 1968; †Challenge round abolished.
‡National Patriotic Tournament; #Amateur event held; **Five-set final abolished.

Grand Slams

Singles

Don Budge, 1938
Maureen Connolly, 1953
Rod Laver, 1962, 1969
Margaret Smith Court, 1970
Steffi Graf, 1988

Doubles

Frank Sedgman and Ken McGregor, 1951
Martina Navratilova and Pam Shriver, 1984
Maria Bueno and two partners: Christine Truman
    (Australian), Darlene Hard (French, Wimbledon
    and U.S. Championships), 1960

Mixed Doubles

Margaret Smith and Ken Fletcher, 1963
Owen Davidson and two partners: Lesley Turner
    (Australian), Billie Jean King (French, Wimbledon
    and U.S. Championships), 1967

The Alltime Grand Slam Champions

MEN

Player	Aus. S-D-M	French S-D-M	Wim. S-D-M	U.S. S-D-M	Total
Roy Emerson	6-3-0	2-6-0	2-3-0	2-4-0	28
John Newcombe	2-5-0	0-3-0	3-6-0	2-3-1	25
Frank Sedgman	2-2-2	0-2-2	1-3-2	2-2-2	22
Bill Tilden	*	0-0-1	3-1-0	7-5-4	21
Rod Laver	3-4-0	2-1-1	4-1-2	2-0-0	20
John Bromwich	2-8-1	0-0-0	0-2-2	0-3-1	19
Jean Borotra	1-1-1	1-5-2	2-3-1	0-0-1	18
Fred Stolle	0-3-1	1-2-0	0-2-3	1-3-2	18
Ken Rosewall	4-3-0	2-2-0	0-2-0	2-2-1	18
Neale Fraser	0-3-1	0-3-0	1-2-0	2-3-3	18
Adrian Quist	3-10-0	0-1-0	0-2-0	0-1-0	17
John McEnroe	0-0-0	0-0-1	3-4-0	4-5-0	17
Jack Crawford	4-4-3	1-1-1	1-1-1	0-0-0	17

WOMEN

Player	Aus. S-D-M	French S-D-M	Wim. S-D-M	U.S. S-D-M	Total
Margaret Court	11-8-2	5-4-4	3-2-5	7-7-8	66
Martina Navratilova	3-8-0	2-7-2	9-7-3	4-9-2	56
Billie Jean King	1-0-1	1-1-2	6-10-4	4-5-4	39
Margaret duPont	*	2-3-0	1-5-1	3-13-9	37
Louise Brough	1-1-0	0-3-0	4-5-4	1-12-4	35
Doris Hart	1-1-2	2-5-3	1-4-5	2-4-5	35
Helen Wills Moody	*	4-2-0	8-3-1	7-4-2	31
Elizabeth Ryan	*	0-4-0	0-12-7	0-1-2	26
Suzanne Lenglen	*	6-2-2	6-6-3	0-0-0	25
Pam Shriver	0-7-0	0-4-1	0-5-0	0-5-0	22
Chris Evert	2-0-0	7-2-0	3-1-0	6-0-0	21
Darlene Hard	*	1-3-2	0-4-3	2-6-0	21
Steffi Graf	4-0-0	4-0-0	6-1-0	4-0-0	19
Maria Bueno	0-1-0	0-1-1	3-5-0	4-4-0	19
Thelma Coyne Long	2-12-4	0-0-1	0-0-0	0-0-0	19

*Did not compete.

Davis Cup

Started in 1900 as the International Lawn Tennis Challenge Trophy by America's Dwight Davis, the runner-up in the 1898 U.S. Championships. A Davis Cup meeting between two countries is known as a tie and is a three-day event consisting of two singles matches, followed by one doubles match and then two more singles matches. The United States boasts the greatest number of wins (30), followed by Australia (20).

Year	Winner	Finalist	Site	Score
1900	United States	Great Britain	Boston	3-0
1901	No tournament			
1902	United States	Great Britain	New York	3-2
1903	Great Britain	United States	Boston	4-1
1904	Great Britain	Belgium	Wimbledon	5-0
1905	Great Britain	United States	Wimbledon	5-0
1906	Great Britain	United States	Wimbledon	5-0
1907	Australasia	Great Britain	Wimbledon	3-2
1908	Australasia	United States	Melbourne	3-2
1909	Australasia	United States	Sydney	5-0
1910	No tournament			
1911	Australasia	United States	Christchurch, NZ	5-0
1912	Great Britain	Australasia	Melbourne	3-2
1913	United States	Great Britain	Wimbledon	3-2
1914	Australasia	United States	New York	3-2
1915-18	No tournament			
1919	Australasia	Great Britain	Sydney	4-1
1920	United States	Australasia	Auckland, NZ	5-0
1921	United States	Japan	New York	5-0
1922	United States	Australasia	New York	4-1
1923	United States	Australasia	New York	4-1
1924	United States	Australia	Philadelphia	5-0
1925	United States	France	Philadelphia	5-0
1926	United States	France	Philadelphia	4-1
1927	France	United States	Philadelphia	3-2
1928	France	United States	Paris	4-1
1929	France	United States	Paris	3-2
1930	France	United States	Paris	4-1
1931	France	Great Britain	Paris	3-2
1932	France	United States	Paris	3-2
1933	Great Britain	France	Paris	3-2
1934	Great Britain	United States	Wimbledon	4-1
1935	Great Britain	United States	Wimbledon	5-0
1936	Great Britain	Australia	Wimbledon	3-2
1937	United States	Great Britain	Wimbledon	4-1
1938	United States	Australia	Philadelphia	3-2
1939	Australia	United States	Philadelphia	3-2
1940-45	No tournament			
1946	United States	Australia	Melbourne	5-0
1947	United States	Australia	New York	4-1
1948	United States	Australia	New York	5-0
1949	United States	Australia	New York	4-1
1950	Australia	United States	New York	4-1
1951	Australia	United States	Sydney	3-2
1952	Australia	United States	Adelaide	4-1
1953	Australia	United States	Melbourne	3-2
1954	United States	Australia	Sydney	3-2
1955	Australia	United States	New York	5-0
1956	Australia	United States	Adelaide	5-0
1957	Australia	United States	Melbourne	3-2
1958	United States	Australia	Brisbane	3-2
1959	Australia	United States	New York	3-2
1960	Australia	Italy	Sydney	4-1
1961	Australia	Italy	Melbourne	5-0
1962	Australia	Mexico	Brisbane	5-0
1963	United States	Australia	Adelaide	3-2
1964	Australia	United States	Cleveland	3-2
1965	Australia	Spain	Sydney	4-1
1966	Australia	India	Melbourne	4-1
1967	Australia	Spain	Brisbane	4-1
1968	United States	Australia	Adelaide	4-1
1969	United States	Romania	Cleveland	5-0

Davis Cup *(Cont.)*

Year	Winner	Finalist	Site	Score
1970	United States	West Germany	Cleveland	5-0
1971	United States	Romania	Charlotte, NC	3-2
1972	United States	Romania	Bucharest	3-2
1973	Australia	United States	Cleveland	5-0
1974	South Africa	India	*	walkover
1975	Sweden	Czechoslovakia	Stockholm	3-2
1976	Italy	Chile	Santiago	4-1
1977	Australia	Italy	Sydney	3-1
1978	United States	Great Britain	Palm Springs	4-1
1979	United States	Italy	San Francisco	5-0
1980	Czechoslovakia	Italy	Prague	4-1
1981	United States	Argentina	Cincinnati	3-1
1982	United States	France	Grenoble	4-1
1983	Australia	Sweden	Melbourne	3-2
1984	Sweden	United States	Gothenburg	4-1
1985	Sweden	West Germany	Munich	3-2
1986	Australia	Sweden	Melbourne	3-2
1987	Sweden	India	Gothenburg	5-0
1988	West Germany	Sweden	Gothenburg	4-1
1989	West Germany	Sweden	Stuttgart	3-2
1990	United States	Australia	St Petersburg	3-2
1991	France	United States	Lyon	3-1
1992	United States	Switzerland	Fort Worth, TX	3-1
1993	Germany	Australia	Dusseldorf	4-1
1994	Sweden	Russia	Moscow	4-1

*India refused to play the final in protest over South Africa's governmental policy of apartheid.

Note: Prior to 1972 the challenge-round system was in effect, with the previous year's winner "standing out" of the competition until the finals. A straight 16-nation tournament has been held since 1981.

Federation Cup

The women's equivalent of the Davis Cup, this competition was started in 1963 by the International Lawn Tennis Federation (now the ITF). Unlike the Davis Cup, though, all entrants gather at one site at one time for a tournament that is concluded within one week. Matches consist of two singles and one doubles. The United States boasts the greatest number of wins (14), followed by Australia (7).

Year	Winner	Finalist	Site	Score
1963	United States	Australia	London	2-1
1964	Australia	United States	Philadelphia	2-1
1965	Australia	United States	Melbourne	2-1
1966	United States	West Germany	Turin	3-0
1967	United States	Great Britain	West Berlin	2-0
1968	Australia	Netherlands	Paris	3-0
1969	United States	Australia	Athens	2-1
1970	Australia	Great Britain	Freiburg	3-0
1971	Australia	Great Britain	Perth	3-0
1972	South Africa	Great Britain	Johannesburg	2-1
1973	Australia	South Africa	Bad Homburg	3-0
1974	Australia	United States	Naples	2-1
1975	Czechoslovakia	Australia	Aix-en-Provence	3-0
1976	United States	Australia	Philadelphia	2-1
1977	United States	Australia	Eastbourne	2-1
1978	United States	Australia	Melbourne	2-1
1979	United States	Australia	Madrid	3-0
1980	United States	Australia	West Berlin	3-0
1981	United States	Great Britain	Nagoya	3-0
1982	United States	West Germany	Santa Clara	3-0
1983	Czechoslovakia	West Germany	Zurich	2-1
1984	Czechoslovakia	Australia	Sao Paulo	2-1
1985	Czechoslovakia	United States	Tokyo	2-1
1986	United States	Czechoslovakia	Prague	3-0
1987	West Germany	United States	Vancouver	2-1
1988	Czechoslovakia	USSR	Melbourne	2-1
1989	United States	Spain	Tokyo	3-0
1990	United States	USSR	Atlanta	2-1
1991	Spain	United States	Nottingham	2-1

Federation Cup (Cont.)

Year	Winner	Finalist	Site	Score
1992	Germany	Spain	Frankfurt	2-1
1993	Spain	Australia	Frankfurt	3-0
1994	Spain	United States	Frankfurt	3-0

Rankings

ATP Computer Year-End Top 10

1973

Ilie Nastase
John Newcombe
Jimmy Connors
Tom Okker
Stan Smith
Ken Rosewall
Manuel Orantes
Rod Laver
Jan Kodes
Arthur Ashe

1974

Jimmy Connors
John Newcombe
Bjorn Borg
Rod Laver
Guillermo Vilas
Tom Okker
Arthur Ashe
Ken Rosewall
Stan Smith
Ilie Nastase

1975

Jimmy Connors
Guillermo Vilas
Bjorn Borg
Arthur Ashe
Manuel Orantes
Ken Rosewall
Ilie Nastase
John Alexander
Roscoe Tanner
Rod Laver

1976

Jimmy Connors
Bjorn Borg
Ilie Nastase
Manuel Orantes
Raul Ramirez
Guillermo Vilas
Adriano Panatta
Harold Solomon
Eddie Dibbs
Brian Gottfried

1977

Jimmy Connors
Guillermo Vilas
Bjorn Borg
Vitas Gerulaitis
Brian Gottfried
Eddie Dibbs
Manuel Orantes
Raul Ramirez
Ilie Nastase
Dick Stockton

1978

Jimmy Connors
Bjorn Borg
Guillermo Vilas
John McEnroe
Vitas Gerulaitis
Eddie Dibbs
Brian Gottfried
Raul Ramirez
Harold Solomon
Corrado Barazzutti

1979

Bjorn Borg
Jimmy Connors
John McEnroe
Vitas Gerulaitis
Roscoe Tanner
Guillermo Vilas
Arthur Ashe
Harold Solomon
Jose Higueras
Eddie Dibbs

1980

Bjorn Borg
John McEnroe
Jimmy Connors
Gene Mayer
Guillermo Vilas
Ivan Lendl
Harold Solomon
Jose-Luis Clerc
Vitas Gerulaitis
Eliot Teltscher

1981

John McEnroe
Ivan Lendl
Jimmy Connors
Bjorn Borg
Jose-Luis Clerc
Guillermo Vilas
Gene Mayer
Eliot Teltscher
Vitas Gerulaitis
Peter McNamara

1982

John McEnroe
Jimmy Connors
Ivan Lendl
Guillermo Vilas
Vitas Gerulaitis
Jose-Luis Clerc
Mats Wilander
Gene Mayer
Yannick Noah
Peter McNamara

1983

John McEnroe
Ivan Lendl
Jimmy Connors
Mats Wilander
Yannick Noah
Jimmy Arias
Jose Higueras
Jose-Luis Clerc
Kevin Curren
Gene Mayer

1984

John McEnroe
Jimmy Connors
Ivan Lendl
Mats Wilander
Andres Gomez
Anders Jarryd
Henrik Sundstrom
Pat Cash
Eliot Teltscher
Yannick Noah

ATP Computer Year-End Top 10 *(Cont.)*

1985

Ivan Lendl
John McEnroe
Mats Wilander
Jimmy Connors
Stefan Edberg
Boris Becker
Yannick Noah
Anders Jarryd
Miloslav Mecir
Kevin Curren

1986

Ivan Lendl
Boris Becker
Mats Wilander
Yannick Noah
Stefan Edberg
Henri Leconte
Joakim Nystrom
Jimmy Connors
Miloslav Mecir
Andres Gomez

1987

Ivan Lendl
Stefan Edberg
Mats Wilander
Jimmy Connors
Boris Becker
Miloslav Mecir
Pat Cash
Yannick Noah
Tim Mayotte
John McEnroe

1988

Mats Wilander
Ivan Lendl
Andre Agassi
Boris Becker
Stefan Edberg
Kent Carlsson
Jimmy Connors
Jakob Hlasek
Henri Leconte
Tim Mayotte

1989

Ivan Lendl
Boris Becker
Stefan Edberg
John McEnroe
Michael Chang
Brad Gilbert
Andre Agassi
Aaron Krickstein
Alberto Mancini
Jay Berger

1990

Stefan Edberg
Boris Becker
Ivan Lendl
Andre Agassi
Pete Sampras
Andres Gomez
Thomas Muster
Emilio Sanchez
Goran Ivanisevic
Brad Gilbert

1991

Stefan Edberg
Jim Courier
Boris Becker
Michael Stich
Ivan Lendl
Pete Sampras
Guy Forget
Karel Novacek
Petr Korda
Andre Agassi

1992

Jim Courier
Stefan Edberg
Pete Sampras
Goran Ivanisevic
Boris Becker
Michael Chang
Petr Korda
Ivan Lendl
Andre Agassi
Richard Krajicek

1993

Pete Sampras
Michael Stich
Jim Courier
Sergi Bruguera
Stefan Edberg
Andrei Medvedev
Goran Ivanisevic
Michael Chang
Thomas Muster
Cedric Pioline

1994

Pete Sampras
Andre Agassi
Boris Becker
Sergi Bruguera
Goran Ivanisevic
Michael Chang
Stefan Edberg
Alberto Berasategui
Michael Stich
Todd Martin

WTA Computer Year-End Top 10

1973

Margaret Smith Court
Billie Jean King
Evonne Goolagong
Chris Evert
Rosie Casals
Virginia Wade
Kerry Reid
Nancy Gunter
Julie Heldman
Helga Masthoff

1974

Billie Jean King
Evonne Goolagong
Chris Evert
Virginia Wade
Julie Heldman
Rosie Casals
Kerry Reid
Olga Morozova
Lesley Hunt
Francoise Durr

1975

Chris Evert
Billie Jean King
Evonne Goolagong Cawley
Martina Navratilova
Virginia Wade
Margaret Smith Court
Olga Morozova
Nancy Gunter
Francoise Durr
Rosie Casals

WTA Computer Year-End Top 10 (Cont.)

1976

Chris Evert
Evonne Goolagong Cawley
Virginia Wade
Martina Navratilova
Sue Barker
Betty Stove
Dianne Balestrat
Mima Jausovec
Rosie Casals
Francoise Durr

1977

Chris Evert
Billie Jean King
Martina Navratilova
Virginia Wade
Sue Barker
Rosie Casals
Betty Stove
Dianne Balestrat
Wendy Turnbull
Kerry Reid

1978

Martina Navratilova
Chris Evert
Evonne Goolagong Cawley
Virginia Wade
Billie Jean King
Tracy Austin
Wendy Turnbull
Kerry Reid
Betty Stove
Dianne Balestrat

1979

Martina Navratilova
Chris Evert Lloyd
Tracy Austin
Evonne Goolagong Cawley
Billie Jean King
Dianne Balestrat
Wendy Turnbull
Virginia Wade
Kerry Reid
Sue Barker

1980

Chris Evert Lloyd
Tracy Austin
Martina Navratilova
Hana Mandlikova
Evonne Goolagong Cawley
Billie Jean King
Andrea Jaeger
Wendy Turnbull
Pam Shriver
Greer Stevens

1981

Chris Evert Lloyd
Tracy Austin
Martina Navratilova
Andrea Jaeger
Hana Mandlikova
Sylvia Hanika
Pam Shriver
Wendy Turnbull
Bettina Bunge
Barbara Potter

1982

Martina Navratilova
Chris Evert Lloyd
Andrea Jaeger
Tracy Austin
Wendy Turnbull
Pam Shriver
Hana Mandlikova
Barbara Potter
Bettina Bunge
Sylvia Hanika

1983

Martina Navratilova
Chris Evert Lloyd
Andrea Jaeger
Pam Shriver
Sylvia Hanika
Jo Durie
Bettina Bunge
Wendy Turnbull
Tracy Austin
Zina Garrison

1984

Martina Navratilova
Chris Evert Lloyd
Hana Mandlikova
Pam Shriver
Wendy Turnbull
Manuela Maleeva
Helena Sukova
Claudia Kohde-Kilsch
Zina Garrison
Kathy Jordan

1985

Martina Navratilova
Chris Evert Lloyd
Hana Mandlikova
Pam Shriver
Claudia Kohde-Kilsch
Steffi Graf
Manuela Maleeva
Zina Garrison
Helena Sukova
Bonnie Gadusek

1986

Martina Navratilova
Chris Evert Lloyd
Steffi Graf
Hana Mandlikova
Helena Sukova
Pam Shriver
Claudia Kohde-Kilsch
Manuela Maleeva
Kathy Rinaldi
Gabriela Sabatini

1987

Steffi Graf
Martina Navratilova
Chris Evert
Pam Shriver
Hana Mandlikova
Gabriela Sabatini
Helena Sukova
Manuela Maleeva
Zina Garrison
Claudia Kohde-Kilsch

1988

Steffi Graf
Martina Navratilova
Chris Evert
Gabriela Sabatini
Pam Shriver
Manuela Maleeva-Fragniere
Natalia Zvereva
Helena Sukova
Zina Garrison
Barbara Potter

1989

Steffi Graf
Martina Navratilova
Gabriela Sabatini
Zina Garrison
Arantxa Sanchez Vicario
Monica Seles
Conchita Martinez
Helena Sukova
Manuela Maleeva-Fragniere
*Chris Evert

1990

Steffi Graf
Monica Seles
Martina Navratilova
Mary Joe Fernandez
Gabriela Sabatini
Katerina Maleeva
Arantxa Sanchez Vicario
Jennifer Capriati
Manuela Maleeva-Fragniere
Zina Garrison

*When Chris Evert announced her retirement at the 1989 United States Open, she was ranked 4 in the world. That was her last official series tournament.

WTA Computer Year-End Top 10 *(Cont.)*

1991

Monica Seles
Steffi Graf
Gabriela Sabatini
Martina Navratilova
Arantxa Sanchez Vicario
Jennifer Capriati
Jana Novotna
Mary Joe Fernandez
Conchita Martinez
Manuela Maleeva-Fragniere

1992

Monica Seles
Steffi Graf
Gabriela Sabatini
Arantxa Sanchez Vicario
Martina Navratilova

1992 *(Cont.)*

Mary Joe Fernandez
Jennifer Capriati
Conchita Martinez
Manuela Maleeva-Fragniere
Jana Novotna

1993

Steffi Graf
Arantxa Sanchez Vicario
Martina Navratilova
Conchita Martinez
Gabriela Sabatini
Jana Novotna
Mary Joe Fernandez
Monica Seles
Jennifer Capriati
Anke Huber

1994

Steffi Graf
Arantxa Sanchez Vicario
Conchita Martinez
Jana Novotna
Mary Pierce
Lindsay Davenport
Gabriela Sabatini
Martina Navratilova
Kimiko Date
Natasha Zvereva

Prize Money

Top 25 Men's Career Prize Money Leaders

	Earnings ($)
Ivan Lendl	21,262,417
Stefan Edberg	19,454,364
Pete Sampras	18,165,028
Boris Becker	16,908,195
John McEnroe	12,539,622
Michael Stich	11,396,054
Jim Courier	11,259,456
Andre Agassi	10,580,446
Michael Chang	10,144,480
Goran Ivanisevic	8,905,815
Jimmy Connors	8,637,490
Mats Wilander	7,882,555
Sergi Bruguera	7,813,785
Petr Korda	6,666,315
Thomas Muster	5,797,718
Brad Gilbert	5,507,195
Anders Jarryd	5,294,669
Emilio Sanchez	5,112,671
Guy Forget	4,956,640
Guillermo Vilas	4,923,882
David Wheaton	4,693,789
Jakob Hlasek	4,544,512
Andres Gomez	4,384,725
Mark Woodforde	3,999,722
Wayne Ferreira	3,991,873

Note: From arrival of Open tennis in 1968 through October 9, 1995.

Top 25 Women's Career Prize Money Leaders

	Earnings ($)
Martina Navratilova	20,337,902
Steffi Graf	16,530,040
Arantxa Sanchez Vicario	9,644,272
Chris Evert	8,896,195
Gabriela Sabatini	8,462,930
Monica Seles	7,805,991
Helena Sukova	5,447,678
Pam Shriver	5,363,285
Conchita Martinez	5,142,625
Jana Novotna	5,085,938
Natasha Zvereva	4,754,158
Zina Garrison Jackson	4,453,976
Gigi Fernandez	3,781,075
Mary Joe Fernandez	3,410,655
Hana Mandlikova	3,340,959
Manuela Maleeva-Fragniere	3,244,811
Lori McNeil	2,876,281
Wendy Turnbull	2,769,024
Larisa Neiland	2,768,276
Claudia Kohde-Kilsch	2,226,664
Katerina Maleeva	2,194,260
Nathalie Tauziat	2,108,099
Mary Pierce	2,096,510
Tracy Austin	1,992,380
Billie Jean King	1,966,487

Note: From arrival of Open tennis in 1968 through October 9, 1995.

Dutch Treat

After an ATP tour event in Stuttgart in July, 19-year-old Marcelo Rios of Chile wanted nothing more than to board an airliner back to his homeland. But Rios, a lefty who climbed 55 places in the rankings in 1995, missed his flight to Santiago. Stuck on the Continent, he did his ponytail and earring proud by schlepping to Amsterdam. There he took a qualifier's berth in the $500,000 Netherlands International, played his way into the tournament's main draw with two victories and then won five straight matches, including the final over Jan Siemerink of Holland, 6-4, 7-5, 6-4. All of which made Rios, the first qualifier to win any event on the circuit since 1993, king of the ATP detour.

Open Era Overall Wins

Men's Career Leaders—Tournaments Won

The top tournament-winning men from the institution of Open tennis in 1968 through October 9, 1995.

	W		W
Jimmy Connors	109	Pete Sampras	35
Ivan Lendl	94	Thomas Muster	34
John McEnroe	77	Arthur Ashe	33
Bjorn Borg	62	Mats Wilander	33
Guillermo Vilas	62	John Newcombe	32
Ilie Nastase	57	Manuel Orantes	32
Rod Laver	47	Ken Rosewall	32
Boris Becker	43	Andre Agassi	31
Stefan Edberg	41	Tom Okker	31
Stan Smith	39	Vitas Gerulaitis	27

Women's Career Leaders—Tournaments Won

The top tournament-winning women from the institution of Open tennis in 1968 through October 9, 1995.

	W		W
Martina Navratilova	167	Conchita Martinez	29
Chris Evert	157	Tracy Austin	29
Steffi Graf	93	Hana Mandlikova	27
Evonne Goolagong Cawley	88	Gabriela Sabatini	27
Margaret Court	79	Nancy Richey	25
Billie Jean King	67	Arantxa Sanchez Vicario	22
Virginia Wade	55	Kerry Melville Reid	22
Helga Masthoff	37	Sue Barker	21
Monica Seles	33	Pam Shriver	21
Olga Morozova	31	Julie Heldman	20

Annual ATP/WTA Champions

Men's ATP Tour—World Championship

Year	Player	Year	Player
1970	Stan Smith	1982	Ivan Lendl
1971	Ilie Nastase	1983	Ivan Lendl
1972	Ilie Nastase	1984	John McEnroe
1973	Ilie Nastase	1985	John McEnroe
1974	Guillermo Vilas	1986	Ivan Lendl
1975	Ilie Nastase	1986	Ivan Lendl
1976	Manuel Orantes	1987	Ivan Lendl
1977	Not held	1988	Boris Becker
1978	Jimmy Connors	1989	Stefan Edberg
1979	John McEnroe	1990	Andre Agassi
1980	Bjorn Borg	1991	Pete Sampras
1981	Bjorn Borg	1992	Boris Becker
		1993	Michael Stich
		1994	Pete Sampras

Note: Event held twice in 1986.

THEY SAID IT

Goran Ivanisevic, the screwy, seventh-ranked tennis player from Croatia, on why he would never see a sports psychologist: "You lie on a couch, they take your money, and you walk out more bananas than when you walk in."

Women—Virginia Slims Championship

Year	Player	Year	Player
1972	Chris Evert	1984	Martina Navratilova
1973	Chris Evert	1985	Martina Navratilova
1974	Evonne Goolagong	1986	Martina Navratilova
1975	Chris Evert	1986	Martina Navratilova
1976	Evonne Goolagong	1987	Steffi Graf
1977	Chris Evert	1988	Gabriela Sabatini
1978	Martina Navratilova	1989	Steffi Graf
1979	Martina Navratilova	1990	Monica Seles
1980	Tracy Austin	1991	Monica Seles
1981	Martina Navratilova	1992	Monica Seles
1982	Sylvia Hanika	1993	Steffi Graf
1983	Martina Navratilova	1994	Gabriela Sabatini

Note: Virginia Slims Championship held twice in 1986.

The Tarango Fandango

Senior writer Sally Jenkins reported from Wimbledon on tennis's new fun couple:

It was the ugliest display in the history of ugly Americans at Wimbledon. What was Jeff Tarango's point when he walked off during his third-round match at the All-England Club? Either Tarango had uncovered a nasty bit of corruption in tennis (extremely unlikely) or he was pitching a Grand Slam tantrum (much more likely). A third possibility was that Tarango is "absolutely barking," as one Wimbledon official described him.

Whether Tarango acted out of conviction, meanness or lunacy doesn't really matter. And his penalty—some $15,000 in fines—was not stiff enough. There was no justification for the behavior of Tarango and his wife, Benedicte Carriere, who verbally (he) and physically (she) attacked chair umpire Bruno Rebeuh after Tarango defaulted his match against Alex Mronz over a disputed call.

The rantings of the couple recalled the worst excesses of Jim Pierce, the belligerent father of Mary Pierce, who was banned from the women's tour for erratic behavior that included attacking a spectator at the French Open. If it's good enough for Jim, it's good enough for Benedicte, who slapped Rebeuh after the match, an outrage for which Tarango refused to apologize. "Women are emotional," he said.

So, it seems, are men. In his post-tantrum press conference, Tarango, who is 26 and ranked 80th on the tour, accused Rebeuh of throwing matches to his favorite players. It was not the first time Tarango had made that serious charge, even though Rebeuh is, in fact, one of the most respected chair umpires. Anyway, claiming that a chair umpire, whose role during a match is more peacekeeper and scorekeeper than anything else, can determine the outcome of a match is rather like claiming that a third base ump can throw a baseball game.

There is much to suggest that Tarango is either spoiled, attention-hungry or a few sandwiches shy of a picnic basket. As an undergraduate at Stanford, he once dumped doubles partner David Wheaton out of a golf cart by careening wildly down a steep hill. In Tokyo in 1994 he dropped his shorts on the court during a match with Michael Chang. At the Lipton Championships in Key Biscayne, Fla., in March 1995, he slugged a ball in frustration, striking a ball girl.

It was telling that no players came to Tarango's defense after the incident at Wimbledon. Andre Agassi seemed to express the prevailing mood among his peers when he said Tarango deserves whatever he gets. Tarango has achieved the attention he apparently craves—so has his wife—but could never earn with his tennis. He still has not moved beyond the third round of a Grand Slam event. He has had his 15 minutes of fame. Now give him the hook.

Pauline Betz Addie (1965)
George T. Adee (1964)
Fred B. Alexander (1961)
Wilmer L. Allison (1963)
Manuel Alonso (1977)
Arthur Ashe (1985)
Juliette Atkinson (1974)
Tracy Austin (1992)
Lawrence A. Baker (1975)
Maud Barger-Wallach (1958)
Angela Mortimer Barrett (1993)
Karl Behr (1969)
Mallory Molla Bjurstedt (1958)
Bjorn Borg (1987)
Jean Borotra (1976)
Maureen Connolly Brinker(1968)
John Bromwich (1984)
Norman Everard Brookes (1977)
Mary K. Browne (1957)
Jacques Brugnon (1976)
J. Donald Budge (1964)
Maria E. Bueno (1978)
May Sutton Bundy (1956)
Mabel E. Cahill (1976)
Oliver S. Campbell (1955)
Malcom Chace (1961)
Dorothea Douglass Lambert
Chambers (1981)
Philippe Chatrier (1992)
Louise Brough Clapp (1967)
Clarence Clark (1983)
Joseph S. Clark (1955)
William J. Clothier (1956)
Henri Cochet (1976)
Bud Collins (1994)
Ashley Cooper (1991)
Margaret Smith Court (1979)
Gottfried von Cramm (1977)
John H. Crawford (1979)
Joseph F. Cullman III (1990)
Allison Danzig (1968)
Sarah Palfrey Danzig (1963)
Dwight F. Davis (1956)
Charlotte Dod (1983)
John H. Doeg (1962)
Laurie Doherty (1980)
Reggie Doherty (1980)
Jaroslav Drobny (1983)
Margaret Osborne duPont
(1967)
James Dwight (1955)
Roy Emerson (1982)
Pierre Etchebaster (1978)
Chris Evert (1995)
Robert Falkenburg (1974)
Neale Fraser (1984)
Charles S. Garland (1969)
Althea Gibson (1971)

Kathleen McKane Godfree
(1978)
Richard A. Gonzales (1968)
Evonne Goolagong Cawley
(1988)
Bryan M. Grant Jr (1972)
David Gray (1985)
Clarence Griffin (1970)
King Gustaf V of Sweden
(1980)
Harold H. Hackett (1961)
Ellen Forde Hansell (1965)
Darlene R. Hard (1973)
Doris J. Hart (1969)
Gladys M. Heldman (1979)
W. E. "Slew" Hester Jr (1981)
Bob Hewitt (1992)
Lew Hoad (1980)
Harry Hopman (1978)
Fred Hovey (1974)
Joseph R. Hunt (1966)
Lamar Hunt (1993)
Francis T. Hunter (1961)
Shirley Fry Irvin (1970)
Helen Hull Jacobs (1962)
William Johnston (1958)
Ann Haydon Jones (1985)
Perry Jones (1970)
Billie Jean King (1987)
Jan Kodes (1990)
John A. Kramer (1968)
Rene Lacoste (1976)
Al Laney (1979)
William A. Larned (1956)
Arthur D. Larsen (1969)
Rod G. Laver (1981)
Suzanne Lenglen (1978)
Dorothy Round Little (1986)
George M. Lott Jr (1964)
Gene Mako (1973)
Hana Mandlikova (1994)
Alice Marble (1964)
Alastair B. Martin (1973)
William McChesney Martin (1982)
Chuck McKinley (1986)
Maurice McLoughlin (1957)
Frew McMillan (1992)
W. Donald McNeill (1965)
Elisabeth H. Moore (1971)
Gardnar Mulloy (1972)
R. Lindley Murray (1958)
Julian S. Myrick (1963)
Ilie Nastase (1991)
John D. Newcombe (1986)
Arthur C. Nielsen Sr (1971)
Betty Nuthall (1977)
Alex Olmedo (1987)
Rafael Osuna (1979)

Mary Ewing Outerbridge (1981)
Frank A. Parker (1966)
Gerald Patterson (1989)
Budge Patty (1977)
Theodore R. Pell (1967)
Fred Perry (1975)
Tom Pettitt (1982)
Nicola Pietrangeli (1986)
Adrian Quist (1984)
Dennis Ralston (1987)
Ernest Renshaw (1983)
Willie Renshaw (1983)
Vincent Richards (1961)
Robert L. Riggs (1967)
Helen Wills Moody Roark
(1959)
Anthony D. Roche (1986)
Ellen C. Roosevelt (1975)
Ken Rosewall (1980)
Elizabeth Ryan (1972)
Manuel Santana (1984)
Richard Savitt (1976)
Frederick R. Schroeder (1966)
Eleonora Sears (1968)
Richard D. Sears (1955)
Frank Sedgman (1979)
Pancho Segura (1984)
Vic Seixas Jr (1971)
Francis X. Shields (1964)
Henry W. Slocum Jr (1955)
Stan Smith (1987)
Fred Stolle (1985)
William F. Talbert (1967)
Bill Tilden (1959)
Lance Tingay (1982)
Ted Tinling (1986)
Bertha Townsend Toulmin
(1974)
Tony Trabert (1970)
James H. Van Alen (1965)
John Van Ryn (1963)
Guillermo Vilas (1991)
Ellsworth Vines (1962)
Virginia Wade (1989)
Marie Wagner (1969)
Holcombe Ward (1956)
Watson Washburn (1965)
Malcolm D. Whitman (1955)
Hazel Hotchkiss Wightman
(1957)
Anthony Wilding (1978)
Richard Norris Williams II
(1957)
Sidney B. Wood (1964)
Robert D. Wrenn (1955)
Beals C. Wright (1956)

Note: Years in parentheses are dates of induction.

Golf

JULY 31, 1995 • $2.95 (CAN. $3.95)

Sports Illustrated

LONG SHOT

Against all odds, John Daly powers his way to a dramatic British Open victory

JACQUELINE DUVOISIN

Pleasant Surprises

Expect the unexpected was the motto in a storybook season that produced a host of happy endings
by Jaime Diaz

GOLF BEING as unpredictable as a California jury, there were plenty of surprises in 1995. The U.S. lost the Ryder Cup on home turf, Nick Price didn't win a single tournament after two years in which he won ten, and Greg Norman started beating people with the kind of you've-got-to-be-kidding shots that used to beat him.

But it was the particularly nice surprises at the biggest moments that made 1995 special. More than anything else it was a year of beautiful, improbable, perfect marriages of people and places.

Specifically the couplings of Ben Crenshaw and Augusta, Corey Pavin and Shinnecock Hills, John Daly and St. Andrews and Tiger Woods and Newport all possessed a lasting poetry. Respectively they gave us the most sentimental Masters ever, a centennial U.S. Open in which the game's most inventive shotmaker was given the perfect canvas to paint a masterpiece, a British Open in which the game's longest hitter was validated as much more in the cradle of golf, and a U.S. Amateur on a historic site that proved another giant step toward stardom for the greatest teenager ever to play.

All four of the winners were Americans, which represented the best collective performance by U.S. players in the major championships in this decade. Only Steve Elkington of Australia prevented a clean sweep when he won the PGA Championship at Riviera.

Outside the majors, however, 1995 was a great year for golfers from the rest of the world. That other Australian, Norman, was the dominating force on the PGA Tour, winning three times and leading the money list despite playing in only 15 official events. In each of his victories—Memorial, Hartford and the World Series of Golf—Norman holed a shot from off the green either late in the final nine or in sudden death to ice the win. Annika Sorenstam of Sweden won the U.S. Women's Open at the Broadmoor in Colorado Springs. Meanwhile, in team events, it was the U.S. that got swept. Besides the upset at the Ryder Cup, Americans were also beaten in the Walker and Curtis Cups, marking the first time teams from this country have ever lost all three of the biennial matches in one year.

The most romantic episode belonged to Crenshaw at the 59th Masters. At the age of 43, Crenshaw came to Augusta a much beloved but waning force. Of his 18 official career victories, it seemed a given that his crowning glory would always be his triumph in the 1984 Masters, where he had overcome his own emotional attachment to golf history to win on the course of his idol, Bobby Jones. Crenshaw is one of the most mercurial of golfers; his four victories in the 1990s proved that he could be formidable when on his game. But he has rarely been on, particularly in the major championships. More and more the abiding passion in Crenshaw's life seemed to be building golf courses rather than playing them.

But the magic Crenshaw caught at the Masters will take a place in the annals he loves. The Sunday before the first round, his lifelong teacher, Harvey Penick, died at the age of 90 after a long illness. Since giving a six-year-old Crenshaw his first lesson at the Austin Country Club, Penick had remained his counselor and touchstone, and Crenshaw was grief stricken at the loss.

Somehow the occasion also filled him with the resolve and control. He had seen Penick for the last time a week before his death, when the old teacher had a look at his putting grip and sent him on his way with a gentle admonition: "Just trust yourself." By the time Crenshaw returned to

Norman won three of the 15 events he entered and topped the earnings list.

Augusta after he and Tom Kite served as pallbearers at Penick's funeral on Wednesday, Crenshaw said, "It was kind of like I felt this hand on my shoulder, guiding me along." Said Crenshaw's wife, Julie, "There was a calmness to him all week that I have never seen before."

The final piece was put in place by Crenshaw's Augusta caddie, Carl Jackson, who on the practice tee on Tuesday quietly said, "Put the ball a little bit back in your stance, Ben." Instantly Crenshaw started hitting the ball solid and straight. "I've never had a confidence transformation like that in my life," he would say later.

Crenshaw played steadily for three rounds, tying Brian Henninger for the 54-hole lead at 10-under-par 206. On Sunday he was tied with Norman and Davis Love III, who were several groups ahead. But when Love bogeyed the 16th and Norman the 17th Crenshaw's putting, perhaps the best the game has ever seen, took over. He sank a 15-footer for birdie on the 13th, a five-footer for another on the 16th after a spectacular six-iron, and finally "an absolute perfect putt" on a left-to-right 13-footer at the 17th to take a two-stroke lead.

Crenshaw needed the cushion, because his composure started to crumble under

BOB MARTIN

Major, and it was starting to bug him. After surviving some scratchy play to salvage an opening two-over-par 72, he dug in and took what Shinnecock offered, which was precious few birdies. But after starting the final round three strokes behind Norman (that name again) and Tom Lehman, Pavin vaulted into contention with a birdie on the hellacious par-4 9th, got into a four-way tie with another at the 12th and took the lead for the first time by holing a eight-footer for a birdie on the 15th. Behind him Lehman, Norman and Bob Tway were limping home, but Pavin only led by one when he stepped up to the 450-yard 18th. He got his drive into the fairway and then came through with his epic approach.

the gathering emotion. In the end he had an 18-inch for a bogey to win, and when it went in, Crenshaw "let it all go" and collapsed into the most enduring pose of 1995. As Crenshaw wept, with his hands on his knees, unable to right himself, Jackson solemnly patted his charge on the back while repeating the words, "It's all right."

A profoundly moved Crenshaw was still in a daze an hour later. "I believe in fate," he said in his characteristically slow cadence. "I don't know how it happened. I don't." Pressed to hazard a guess, Crenshaw put a bow on the fairy tale. "I had the 15th club in my bag," he said, "and it was Harvey."

At the U.S. Open, Pavin only carried 14 clubs, but one of them was a four-wood. And with it he hit the shot of the year, a low draw from 228 yards on the 72nd hole, against a strong left-to-right wind, that stopped five feet from the cup.

As it turned out, Pavin didn't need the putt, which he missed, but his approach was a symbol of the grit and skill with which he tamed Shinnecock.

Coming into the Open, Pavin was carrying the label Best Player Never to Have Won a

"The ball was blocking out the flagstick, and I thought, Oh, man, that thing might go in," said Pavin, who along with joining the major-championship club at the age of 35 cemented his position as golf's toughest competitor. "It was probably the best shot I've hit under pressure."

Pavin's closing 68 gave him a total of even par 280, two better than Norman, who finished with a 73 that included, once again, a bogey on the 71st hole. It was Norman's seventh second-place finish in a major, six of which came after he led after three rounds.

"No, it never haunts me," he said. "I put myself in there with a chance to win more times than anybody else."

Perhaps, but what then of John Daly, a player who is almost never in there, and has now won the same number of majors—two—as Norman? Daly went to St. Andrews, and in perhaps the most surprising result in a major championship since, well, since Daly won the 1991 PGA, took home the claret jug in the 124th British Open.

The incongruity was this. The world's oldest championship, particularly when it is at St. Andrews, stands for subtlety, shotmaking, keeping the ball close to the ground, patience, discipline, judgment and character. Coming into the championship, Daly stood for Grip It and Rip It, impossibly high iron shots, rehabilitation clinics, parking lot fights, unsigned scorecards, fast food and bad hair. British bookmakers made him 66–1 to win.

"It's unbelievable," said Daly after defeating Costantino Rocca of Italy in a four-hole playoff. It is a standard answer to many questions, but this time he was right.

Actually Daly came to St. Andrews with both a preference for the Old Course and a plan. "I can't explain it, but there is just something about this course that I love," said Daly, who had fond memories of St. Andrews from the 1993 Dunhill Cup. It was a week in which Daly felt free from the mood swings and withdrawal symptoms he said had committed him to sobriety in late 1992. His mantra for the week was "Stay patient, and stay out of bunkers." His caddie, Greg Rita, also saw something special after Daly's opening 67 tied him for the first-round lead. "John can lose interest, but when he is focused, he is tough. In the hunt, he is focused."

Daly stayed in the hunt throughout, although howling winds sent him to a 73 on Saturday that put him four strokes off the 54-hole pace. But on Sunday, Daly showed that he is talented enough to adapt to any conditions and that while he may have a troubled head, he is driven by a stout heart.

That was never more true than after Daly lost a three-stroke lead with three holes to go by bogeying the 16th and 17th holes. He finished with a par on the 18th, and seemed to be the winner after Rocca chunked his short pitch to the home hole and saw his ball roll sickeningly into the Valley of Sin. Simply trying to two-putt the remaining 60 feet, Rocca made the most improbable shot of the year by holing out for a tying birdie. As the Auld Grey Toon went nuts, Rocca fell facedown on the ground, and Daly's mouth nearly dropped the same distance.

To his everlasting credit Daly regrouped and overwhelmed Rocca in the playoff, smashing his drives down the center and on the second playoff hole making a 30-footer for a birdie that put him up by two. When Rocca took three to get out of the Road Bunker on the next hole, while Daly parred, the final hole became a formality.

"I've come through an awful lot the past few years," said Daly. "I know one thing. There's no way I would be here today, holding this trophy, if I was still drinking."

The 19-year-old Woods may not have Daly's baggage, but he also impressed with his maturity and mastery at the Newport Country Club, a classic, links-style course that was the site of the first U.S. Amateur, in 1895. Woods, who had won three straight U.S. Junior Amateur crowns, took his second consecutive Amateur by defeating 43-year-old George (Buddy) Marucci of Berwyn, Pa., 2 up in the final. Once again, Woods demonstrated his flair for the dramatic. On the final hole, with Marucci within 20 feet for a birdie putt that could have sent the match into extra holes, Woods hit a controlled eight-iron from 140 yards to within two feet of the hole. It was just the kind of geared-down shot Woods has been working on with his teacher, Butch Harmon, and the fact that he had the confidence to try it and the skill to pull it off in the pressure-packed situation is just more evidence that the young man is the real deal.

The U.S. team could have used a tiger in its tank on the final day of the Ryder Cup at Oak Hill in Rochester, N.Y. This was the year that looked like a walkover for America, with the Europeans missing José María Olazábal, and the games of stalwarts like Seve Ballesteros, Ian Woosnam and even Nick Faldo in various stages of disrepair. Moreover, captain Lanny Wadkins had ordered that Oak Hill be set up like a U.S. Open, all the better to thwart the Europeans. The projected blowout seemed on target when, punctuated by Pavin's winning chip-in for birdie on the 18th hole of Saturday's final best-ball match, the U.S. took a 9–7 lead into the singles.

Only twice since 1957 had an American team been outscored in the Ryder Cup sin-

JACQUELINE DUVOISIN

gles, so Sunday figured to be a pleasant formality for Wadkins's team. Instead, it turned into the most dramatic comeback—and most bitter defeat—in Ryder Cup history.

After going up 10–7 and needing only four more points in the remaining 11 matches to retain the cup, the Americans stalled. Five of the remaining matches went to the 18th hole, and the best the U.S. could do was get a half point in one of them. In the others, Peter Jacobsen, Brad Faxon, Curtis Strange and Jay Haas all lost one up.

Strange's match against Faldo was pivotal. The 40-year-old Virginian, who had been the most controversial of Wadkins's two wild-card picks because he is winless since the 1989 U.S. Open, stood one up on the 16th hole. He ended up losing when he missed a seven-foot putt on the final hole and Faldo holed from four feet.

The U.S. had a final chance to retain the Cup if Haas could salvage a tie with Philip Walton of Ireland, but after winning the 16th and 17th holes to get to one down on the 18th hole, Haas pulled his drive into the trees. When both men bogeyed, the cup that the U.S. had regained in 1991 was back in European hands by a score of 14½ to 13½. Just when it appeared that the golden days of the Ryder Cup might be over, the 1997 edition, to be played in Spain, promises to have more buildup than any since the 1991 War by the Shore at Kiawah Island.

Woods established himself as among the greatest amateurs ever.

The main dramas should not obscure some notable achievements. On the Senior tour, some of the game's greatest names added to their vitae. Lee Trevino, coming back from a serious neck injury at 55, recorded his 25th career Senior victory, passing Miller Barber as the alltime leader in wins. Jack Nicklaus, also 55, won another Senior major, the Tradition, and was second in two events. Gary Player won at Lexington two months before his 60th birthday, and Arnold Palmer, who played in his final British Open, shot his age for the first time, during the third round of the Northwest Classic on Sept. 10, the day he turned 66.

It was an eventful year for women's golf, with LPGA commissioner Charlie Mechem stepping down after five years at the helm to make way for Jim Ritts. On the golf course, Betsy King finally made the LPGA Hall of Fame with her 30th win at the ShopRite LPGA Classic, leaving Amy Alcott and Beth Daniel on the bubble. Along with Open winner Sorenstam, the other bona fide young star on the tour, Kelly Robbins, won the McDonald's LPGA Championship, while the other two women's majors, the Nabisco Dinah Shore and the du Maurier Classic, were taken by surprise winners Nanci Bowen and Jenny Lidback.

On the amateur scene, 18-year-old Kelli Kuehne followed her victory in last year's U.S. Girls' Junior Amateur by winning the U.S. Women's Amateur at the Country Club in Brookline, Mass.

As the year came to a close, the Golf Channel, the first 24-hour network devoted solely to golf, was gaining a foothold in the cable universe. Meanwhile, the PGA Tour breathed a sigh when the Federal Trade Commission abruptly dropped its five-year investigation of the Tour for possible unreasonable restraint of competition. Considering that Tour commissioner Tim Finchem saw the investigation as a threat to the existence of the Tour, it was one more nice surprise in a year of particularly nice surprises.

Men's Majors

The Masters

**Augusta National GC; Augusta, GA
(par 72; 6,925 yds) April 6-9**

Player	Score	Earnings ($)
Ben Crenshaw	70-67-69-68—274	396,000
Davis Love III	69-69-71-66—275	237,600
Greg Norman	73-68-68-68—277	127,600
Jay Haas	71-64-72-70—277	127,600
David Frost	66-71-71-71—279	83,600
Steve Elkington	73-67-67-72—279	83,600
Phil Mickelson	66-71-70-73—280	70,950
Scott Hoch	69-67-71-73—280	70,950
Curtis Strange	72-71-65-73—281	63,800
Fred Couples	71-69-67-75—282	57,200
Brian Henninger	70-68-68-76—282	57,200
Kenny Perry	73-70-71-69—283	48,400
Lee Janzen	69-69-74-71—283	48,400
José María Olazábal	66-74-72-72—284	39,600
Tom Watson	73-70-69-72—284	39,600
Hale Irwin	69-72-71-72—284	39,600
Ian Woosnam	69-72-71-73—285	28,786
Raymond Floyd	71-70-70-74—285	28,786
Brad Faxon	76-69-69-71—285	28,786
Paul Azinger	70-72-73-70—285	28,786
Colin Montgomerie	71-69-76-69—285	28,786
Corey Pavin	67-71-72-75—285	28,786
John Huston	70-66-72-77—285	28,786

U.S. Open

**Shinnecock Hills GC; Southampton, N.Y.
(par 70; 6,944 yds) June 15-18**

Player	Score	Earnings ($)
Corey Pavin	72-69-71-68—280	350,000
Greg Norman	68-67-74-73—282	207,000
Tom Lehman	70-72-67-74—283	131,974
Davis Love III	72-68-73-71—284	66,634
Phil Mickelson	68-70-72-74—284	66,634
Bill Glasson	69-70-76-69—284	66,634
Jay Haas	70-73-72-69—284	66,634
Neal Lancaster	70-72-77-65—284	66,634
Jeff Maggert	69-72-77-66—284	66,634
Frank Nobilo	72-72-70-71—285	44,184
Vijay Singh	70-71-72-72—285	44,184
Bob Tway	69-69-72-75—285	44,184
Nick Price	66-73-73-74—286	30,934
Steve Stricker	71-70-71-74—286	30,934
Mark McCumber	70-71-77-68—286	30,934
Duffy Waldorf	72-70-75-69—286	30,934
Brad Bryant	71-75-70-70—286	30,934
Jeff Sluman	72-69-74-71—286	30,934
Lee Janzen	70-72-72-72—286	30,934
Mark Roe	71-69-74-72—286	30,934

British Open

**Royal & Ancient; St Andrews, Scotland
(par 72; 6,933 yds) July 20-23**

Player	Score	Earnings ($)
John Daly*	67-71-73-71—282	200,000
Costantino Rocca	69-70-70-73—282	160,000
Michael Campbell	71-71-65-76—283	105,065
Steven Bottomley	70-72-72-69—283	105,065
Mark Brooks	70-69-73-71—283	105,065
Vijay Singh	68-72-73-71—284	64,800
Steve Elkington	72-69-69-74—284	64,800
Corey Pavin	69-70-72-74—285	53,333
Bob Estes	72-70-71-72—285	53,333
Mark James	72-75-68-70—285	53,333
Payne Stewart	72-68-75-71—286	41,600
Ernie Els	71-68-72-75—286	41,600
Sam Torrance	71-70-71-74—286	41,600
Brett Ogle	73-69-71-73—286	41,600
Greg Norman	71-74-72-70—287	29,120
Ben Crenshaw	67-72-76-72—287	29,120
Brad Faxon	71-67-75-74—287	29,120
Robert Allenby	71-74-71-71—287	29,120
Per-Ulrick Johansson	69-78-68-72—287	29,120
David Duval	71-75-70-72—288	21,600
Peter Mitchell	73-74-71-70—288	21,600
Andrew Coltart	70-74-71-73—288	21,600
Barry Lane	72-73-68-75—288	21,600

* won four-hole playoff

PGA Championship

**Riviera CC; Pacific Palisades, CA
(par 71; 6,956 yds) August 10-13**

Player	Score	Earnings ($)
Steve Elkington*	68-67-68-64—267	360,000
Colin Montgomerie	68-67-67-65—267	216,000
Ernie Els	66-65-66-72—269	116,000
Jeff Maggert	66-69-65-69—269	116,000
Brad Faxon	70-67-71-63—271	80,000
Mark O'Meara	64-67-69-73—273	68,500
Bob Estes	69-68-68-68—273	68,500
Craig Stadler	71-66-66-71—274	50,000
Steve Lowery	69-68-68-69—274	50,000
Justin Leonard	68-66-70-70—274	50,000
Jay Haas	69-71-64-70—274	50,000
Jeff Sluman	69-67-68-70—274	50,000
Payne Stewart	69-70-69-67—275	33,750
Kirk Triplett	71-69-68-67—275	33,750
Jim Furyk	68-70-69-68—275	33,750
Miguel Jimenez	69-69-67-70—275	33,750
Curtis Strange	72-68-68-68—276	26,000
Michael Campbell	71-65-71-69—276	26,000
Costantino Rocca	70-69-68-69—276	26,000
Jesper Parnevik	69-69-70-69—277	21,000
Greg Norman	66-69-70-72—277	21,000
Duffy Waldorf	69-69-67-72—277	21,000

* won on first playoff hole

Men's Tour Results

Late 1994 PGA Tour Events

Tournament	Final Round	Winner	Score/ Under Par	Earnings ($)
Kapalua International	Nov 6	Fred Couples	279/–13	180,000
World Cup of Golf	Nov 13	Fred Couples/Davis Love III	536/–40	150,000 each
JC Penney Classic	Dec 4	M. Figueras-Dotti/Brad Bryant****	262/–22	150,000 each

1995 PGA Tour Events

Tournament	Final Round	Winner	Score/ Under Par	Earnings ($)
Mercedes Championships	Jan 8	Steve Elkington**	278/–10	180,000
Hawaiian Open	Jan 15	John Morse	269/–19	216,000
Northern Telecom Open	Jan 23	Phil Mickelson	269/–18	225,000
Phoenix Open	Jan 29	Vijay Singh	269/–15	234,000
AT&T Pebble Beach National Pro-Am	Feb 5	Peter Jacobsen	271/–17	252,000
Buick Invitational	Feb 12	Peter Jacobsen	269/–19	216,000
Bob Hope Classic	Feb 19	Kenny Perry	335/–25	216,000
Los Angeles Open	Feb 26	Corey Pavin	268/–16	216,000
Doral Open	Mar 5	Nick Faldo	273/–15	270,000
Honda Classic	Mar 12	Mark O'Meara	275/–9	216,000
Nestle Invitational	Mar 19	Loren Roberts	272/–16	216,000
The Players Championship	Mar 26	Lee Janzen	283/–5	540,000
Freeport-McMoran Classic	Apr 2	Davis Love III**	274/–14	216,000
The Masters	Apr 9	Ben Crenshaw	274/–14	396,000
MCI Classic	Apr 16	Bob Tway **	275/–9	234,000
Greater Greensboro Open	Apr 23	Jim Gallagher Jr	274/–14	270,000
Houston Open	Apr 30	Payne Stewart*	276/–12	252,000
BellSouth Classic	May 7	Mark Calcavecchia	271/–17	234,000
Byron Nelson Classic	May 14	Ernie Els	263/–17	234,000
Buick Classic	May 21	Vijay Singh*****	278/–6	216,000
Colonial Invitation	May 28	Tom Lehman	271/–9	252,000
The Memorial	June 4	Greg Norman	269/–19	306,000
Kemper Open	June 11	Lee Janzen *	272/–12	252,000
U.S. Open	June 18	Corey Pavin	280/even	350,000
Greater Hartford Open	June 25	Greg Norman	267/–13	216,000
St. Jude Classic	July 2	Jim Gallagher Jr	267/–17	225,000
Western Open	July 9	Billy Mayfair	279/–9	360,000
Anheuser-Busch Classic	July 16	Ted Tryba	272/–12	198,200
British Open	July 23	John Daly@	282/–6	200,000
Deposit Guaranty Classic	July 23	Ed Dougherty	282/–16	126,000
Ideon Classic	July 30	Fred Funk	268/–16	180,000
Buick Open	Aug 6	Woody Austin**	270/–18	216,000
PGA Championship	Aug 13	Steve Elkington*	267/–17	360,000
The International	Aug 20	Lee Janzen	+34 ‡	270,000
World Series of Golf	Aug 27	Greg Norman*	278/–2	360,000
Greater Milwaukee Open	Sept 3	Scott Hoch	269/–15	180,000
Canadian Open	Sept 10	Mark O'Meara	274/–14	234,000
B.C. Open	Sept 17	Hal Sutton	269/–15	180,000
Quad City Open #	Sept 24	D.A. Weibring	197/–13	180,000
Buick Challenge	Oct 1	Fred Funk	272/–16	180,000
Disney World Classic #	Oct 8	Brad Bryant	198/–18	216,000
Las Vegas Invitational	Oct 15	Jim Furyk	331/–28	270,000
Texas Open	Oct 22	Duffy Waldorf	268/–20	198,000
TOUR Championship	Oct 28	Billy Mayfair	280/even	540,000

*Won on 1st playoff hole. **Won on 2nd playoff hole. ****Won on 4th playoff hole. *****Won on 5th playoff hole. @ Won four-hole playoff. ‡Revised Stableford scoring.

#Tournament shortened by rain.

Women's Majors

Nabisco Dinah Shore

Mission Hills CC; Rancho Mirage, CA
(par 72; 6,460 yds) March 23-26

Player	Score	Earnings ($)
Nanci Bowen	69-75-71-70—285	127,500
Susie Redman	75-70-70-71—286	79,129
Brandie Burton	76-71-71-69—287	42,237
Sherri Turner	72-74-71-70—287	42,237
Laura Davies	75-69-70-73—287	42,237
Nancy Lopez	74-71-68-74—287	42,237
Colleen Walker	74-73-69-72—288	23,738
Tammie Green	71-70-70-77—288	23,738
Dawn Coe-Jones	71-75-71-72—289	20,103
Caroline Pierce	77-71-73-69—290	17,964
Betsy King	77-75-71-68—291	14,200
Dottie Mochrie	78-73-70-70—291	14,200
Barb Mucha	74-74-72-71—291	14,200
Sandra Palmer	72-73-74-72—291	14,200
Debbie Massey	71-75-72-73—291	14,200
Alicia Dibos	77-74-75-66—292	10,056
Sherri Steinhauer	78-74-72-68—292	10,056
Alison Nicholas	75-74-73-70—292	10,056
Pat Bradley	74-75-71-72—292	10,056
Juli Inkster	76-70-73-73—292	10,056
Terry-Jo Myers	77-68-73-74—292	10,056
Michelle Estill	72-72-74-74—292	10,056
Meg Mallon	74-72-71-75—292	10,056

LPGA Championship

DuPont Country Club; Wilmington, DE
(par 71; 6,386 yds) May 11-14

Player	Score	Earnings ($)
Kelly Robbins	66-68-72-68—274	180,000
Laura Davies	68-68-69-70—275	111,711
Julie Larsen	71-68-69-71—280	65,416
Marianne Morris	67-71-70-72—280	65,416
Patty Sheehan	67-68-72-73—280	65,416
Barb Thomas	70-66-73-72—281	38,947
Dottie Mochrie	67-70-71-73—281	38,947
Pat Bradley	71-70-70-71—282	29,890
Tammie Green	69-72-70-71—282	29,890
Annika Sorenstam	71-71-72-69—283	25,362
Kristi Albers	71-71-72-70—284	20,681
Dale Eggeling	72-72-68-72—284	20,681
Joan Pitcock	75-66-71-72—284	20,681
Betsy King	69-71-72-72—284	20,681
Lisa Kiggens	70-70-75-70—285	16,504
Meg Mallon	70-72-71-72—285	16,504
Barb Mucha	71-69-71-74—285	16,504
Beth Daniel	71-73-72-70—286	13,080
Nancy Scranton	71-75-69-71—286	13,080
Susie Redman	73-71-71-71—286	13,080
Lori Garbacz	71-71-72-72—286	13,080
Kris Tschetter	73-69-71-73—286	13,080
Nancy Lopez	73-71-68-74—286	13,080
Colleen Walker	70-70-72-74—286	13,080
Alison Finney	71-68-70-77—286	13,080

U.S. Women's Open

Broadmoor GC, Colorado Springs, CO
(par 70; 6,398 yds) July 13-16

Player	Score	Earnings ($)
Annika Sorenstam	67-71-72-68—278	175,000
Meg Mallon	70-70-66-74—279	103,500
Betsy King	72-69-72-67—280	56,238
Pat Bradley	67-71-72-70—280	56,238
Leta Lindley	70-68-74-69—281	35,285
Rosie Jones	69-70-70-72—281	35,285
Tammie Green	68-70-75-69—282	28,009
Dawn Coe-Jones	68-70-74-70—282	28,009
Julie Larsen	68-71-68-75—282	28,009
Marianne Morris	73-73-70-67—283	22,190
Patty Sheehan	70-73-71-69—283	22,190
Val Skinner	68-72-72-71—283	22,190
Dottie Mochrie	73-70-69-72—284	18,007
Kris Tschetter	68-74-69-73—284	18,007
Kelly Robbins	74-68-74-69—284	18,007
Chris Johnson	71-70-74-70—285	14,454
Jill Briles-Hinton	66-72-74-73—285	14,454
Tania Abitol	67-72-72-74—285	14,454
Dale Eggeling	70-68-73-74—285	14,454
Michele Redman	70-75-71-70—286	12,449
Liselotte Neumann	70-71-75-71—287	11,154
Ayako Okamoto	70-73-71-73—287	11,154
Alice Ritzman	75-69-69-74—287	11,154

du Maurier Ltd. Classic

Beaconsfield GC; Pointe-Claire, Quebec
(par 72; 6,261 yds) August 24-27

Player	Score	Earnings ($)
Jenny Lidback	71-69-68-72—280	150,000
Liselotte Neumann	71-66-72-72—281	93,093
Juli Inkster	72-71-70-70—283	67,933
Tammie Green	75-71-68-70—284	52,837
Betsy King	76-70-67-72—285	38,998
Jane Geddes	71-73-69-72—285	38,998
Michelle Estill	73-77-69-67—286	27,928
L. Rinker-Graham	71-71-70-74—286	27,928
Helen Alfredsson	76-70-70-71—287	21,314
D. Ammaccapane	76-71-68-72—287	21,314
Hollis Stacy	73-73-69-72—287	21,314
Dottie Mochrie	74-73-72-69—288	16,136
Meg Mallon	73-72-73-70—288	16,136
Val Skinner	74-72-71-71—288	16,136
Kris Tschetter	75-70-71-72—288	16,136
Rosie Jones	79-70-73-67—289	13,369
Joan Pitcock	76-70-69-74—289	13,369
Emilee Klein	79-71-69-71—290	11,859
Cindy Schreyer	73-74-72-71—290	11,859
H. Kobayashi	76-70-72-72—290	11,859
Dana Dormann	74-72-72-72—290	11,859
Cindy Rarick	73-72-75-71—291	10,180
Tracy Kerdyk	76-72-71-72—291	10,180
Patty Jordan	72-72-74-73—291	10,180

Women's Tour Results

Late 1994 LPGA Tour Events

Tournament	Final Round	Winner	Score/ Under Par	Earnings ($)
JC Penney Classic	Dec 4	M. Figueras-Dotti/Brad Bryant****	262/–22	150,000 each

1995 LPGA Tour Events

Tournament	Final Round	Winner	Score/ Under Par	Earnings ($)
Tournament of Champions	Jan 15	Dawn Coe-Jones	281/–7	115,000
HEALTHSOUTH Inaugural	Jan 22	Pat Bradley	211/–5	67,500
Hawaiian Ladies Open	Feb 18	Barb Thomas	204/–12	82,500
Ping/Welch's Championship	Mar 12	Dottie Mochrie	278/–10	67,500
Standard Register/Ping	Mar 19	Laura Davies	280/–12	105,000
Nabisco Dinah Shore	Mar 26	Nanci Bowen	285/–3	127,500
Pinewild Women's Championship	Apr 16	Rosie Jones *	211/–5	97,500
Chick-fil-A Charity Championship	Apr 23	Laura Davies	201/–15	75,000
Spring Championship	Apr 30	Val Skinner	273/–15	180,000
Sara Lee Classic	May 7	Michelle McGann	202/–14	78,750
McDonald's LPGA Championship	May 14	Kelly Robbins	274/–10	180,000
The Star Bank LPGA Classic	May 21	Chris Johnson	210/–6	75,000
LPGA Corning Classic	May 28	Alison Nicholas	275/–13	82,500
Oldsmobile Classic	June 4	Dale Eggeling	274/–14	90,000
Edina Realty Classic	June 11	Julie Larsen	205/–11	75,000
Rochester International	June 18	Patty Sheehan	278/–10	82,500
ShopRite LPGA Classic	June 25	Betsy King	204/–9	97,500
Youngstown-Warren LPGA Classic	July 2	Michelle McGann ***	205/–11	82,500
Jamie Farr Toledo Classic	July 9	Kathryn Marshall	205/–8	75,000
U.S. Women's Open	July 16	Annika Sorenstam	278/–2	175,000
JAL Big Apple Classic	July 23	Tracy Kerdyk	273/–11	105,000
Friendly's Classic	July 30	Becky Iverson	276/–12	75,000
McCall's LPGA Classic	Aug 6	Dottie Mochrie	204/–12	75,000
PING Welch's Championship	Aug 14	Beth Daniel	271/–17	67,500
Weetabix Women's British Open	Aug 20	Karrie Webb	278/–10	92,400
du Maurier Ltd. Classic	Aug 27	Jenny Lidback	280/–8	150,000
LPGA Rail Classic	Sept 4	Mary Beth Zimmerman **	206/–10	82,500
Ping-AT&T LPGA Golf Championship	Sept 10	Alison Nicholas	207/–9	75,000
Safeco Classic	Sept 17	Patty Sheehan	274/–14	75,000
Heartland Classic	Sept 24	Annika Sorenstam	278/–10	78,750
Fieldcrest Cannon Classic	Oct 1	Gail Graham	273/–15	75,000
World Championship of Women's Golf	Oct 15	Annika Sorenstam*	282/–6	117,500

* Won on first hole of playoff. ** Won on second playoff hole. *** Won on third playoff hole.

Senior Men's Tour Results

Late 1994 Senior Tour Events

Tournament	Final Round	Winner	Score/ Under Par	Earnings ($)
Maui Kaanapali Classic	Oct 30	Bob Murphy	197/–16	82,500
Senior TOUR Championship	Nov 13	Ray Floyd*****	273/–15	240,000

1995 Senior Tour Events

Tournament	Final Round	Winner	Score/ Under Par	Earnings ($)
Senior Tournament of Champions	Jan 15	Jim Colbert***	209/–7	148,000
Royal Caribbean Classic	Feb 5	J.C. Snead*	209/–4	127,500
IntelliNet Challenge #	Feb 12	Bob Murphy	137/–7	90,000
GTE Suncoast Classic	Feb 19	Dave Stockton	204/–9	112,500
FHP Healthcare Classic	Mar 5	Bruce Devlin	130/–10	112,500
The Dominion Seniors	Mar 12	Jim Albus	205/–11	97,500

1995 Senior Tour Events (Cont.)

Tournament	Final Round	Winner	Score/ Under Par	Earnings ($)
Toshiba Senior Classic	Mar 19	George Archer	199/–11	120,000
The Tradition	Apr 2	Jack Nicklaus***	276/–12	150,000
PGA Seniors' Championship	Apr 16	Ray Floyd	277/–11	180,000
Las Vegas Senior Classic	Apr 30	Jim Colbert	205/–11	150,000
Paine Webber Invitational	May 7	Bob Murphy	203/–13	120,000
Cadillac NFL Classic	May 14	George Archer	205/–11	142,500
Bell Atlantic Classic	May 21	Jim Colbert	207/–3	135,000
Quicksilver Classic	May 28	Dave Stockton	208/–8	165,000
Bruno's Memorial Classic	June 4	Graham Marsh	201/–15	157,500
BellSouth Senior Classic	June 11	Jim Dent	203/–13	165,000
Dallas Reunion Pro Am	June 18	Tom Wargo	197/–13	82,500
Nationwide Championship	June 25	Bob Murphy	203/–13	180,000
U.S. Senior Open	July 2	Tom Weiskopf	275/–13	175,000
Kroger Classic	July 9	Mike Hill	196/–17	135,000
Ford Senior Players Championship	July 16	J.C. Snead	272/–16	225,000
First of America Classic	July 23	Jimmy Powell	201/–15	105,000
Ameritech Senior Open	July 30	Hale Irwin	195/–21	127,500
VFW Senior Championship	Aug 6	Bob Murphy	195/–15	135,000
Burnet Senior Classic	Aug 13	Raymond Floyd	201/–15	165,000
Northville Long Island	Aug 20	Lee Trevino	202/–14	120,000
Bank of Boston Senior Golf Classic	Aug 27	Isao Aoki	204/–12	120,000
Franklin Quest Championship	Sept 3	Tony Jacklin	206/–10	90,000
GTE Northwest Classic	Sept 10	Walt Morgan	203/–13	90,000
Brickyard Crossing Championship	Sept 17	Simon Hobday	204/–12	112,500
Bank One Classic	Sept 24	Gary Player	211/–5	90,000
Vantage Championship	Oct 1	Hale Irwin	199/–17	225,000
The Transamerica	Oct 8	Lee Trevino	201/–15	97,500
Raley's Senior Gold Rush	Oct 15	Don Bies	205/–11	105,000
Ralph's Senior Classic	Oct 22	John Bland	201/–12	120,000
Kaanapali Classic	Oct 29	Bob Charles***	204/–9	90,000

*Won on 1st playoff hole. *** Won on 3rd playoff hole. ***** Won on fifth playoff hole. # Tournament shortened by rain.

Amateur Results

Tournament	Final Round	Winner	Score	Runner-Up
Women's Amateur Public Links	June 25	Jo Jo Robertson	2 & 1	Betsy Dramboar
Men's Amateur Public Links	July 22	Chris Wollman	4 & 3	Bill Camping
Junior Amateur	July 29	D. Scott Hailes	1-up	James Driscoll
Girls' Junior	Aug 5	Marcy Newton	4 & 3	Andrea Cordova
Women's Amateur	Aug 12	Kelli Kuehne	4 & 3	Anne-Marie Knight
Men's Amateur	Aug 27	Tiger Woods	2 up	Buddy Marucci
Women's Mid-Amateur	Sept 23	Ellen Port	3 & 1	Brenda Corrie-Kuehn
Men's Mid-Amateur	Sept 21	Jerry Courville	1-up	Warren Sye
Senior Women	Sept 15	Jean Smith	228 (+9)	Marlene Streit
Senior Men	Oct 2	James Stahl Jr	2 & 1	Rennie Law

International Results

Tournament	Final Round	Winner	Score	Runner-Up
Walker Cup	Sept 10	GB/Ireland	14–10	United States
Ryder Cup	Sept 24	Europe	14½–13½	United States

PGA Tour Final 1995 Money Leaders

Name	Events	Best Finish	Scoring Average	Money ($)
Greg Norman	16	1 (3)	69.06	1,654,959
Billy Mayfair	28	1 (2)	70.29	1,543,192
Lee Janzen	28	1 (3)	70.58	1,378,966
Corey Pavin	22	1 (2)	70.04	1,340,079
Steve Elkington	21	1 (2)	69.59	1,254,352
Davis Love III	24	1	70.09	1,111,999
Peter Jacobsen	25	1 (2)	70.03	1,075,057
Jim Gallagher Jr	27	1 (2)	70.37	1,057,241
Vijay Singh	22	1 (2)	69.92	1,018,713
Mark O'Meara	27	1 (2)	70.25	914,129

LPGA Tour Final 1994 Money Leaders

Name	Events	Best Finish	Scoring Average	Money ($)
Laura Davies	22	1 (3)	70.91	687,201
Beth Daniel	25	1 (4)	71.90	659,426
Liselotte Neumann	21	1 (3)	71.46	505,701
Dottie Mochrie	27	1	70.98	472,728
Donna Andrews	23	1 (3)	71.18	429,015
Tammie Green	24	1	72.09	418,969
Sherri Steinhauer	27	1	71.60	413,398
Kelly Robbins	25	1	71.74	396,778
Betsy King	27	2 (2)	71.52	390,239
Meg Mallon	27	2	71.43	353,385

Senior Tour Final 1994 Money Leaders

Name	Events	Best Finish	Scoring Average	Money ($)
Dave Stockton	32	1 (3)	69.41	1,402,519
Ray Floyd	20	1 (4)	69.08	1,382,762
Jim Albus	35	1 (2)	69.85	1,237,128
Lee Trevino	23	1 (6)	69.55	1,202,369
Jim Colbert	33	1 (2)	70.15	1,012,115
Tom Wargo	36	1	69.88	1,005,344
Jim Dent	30	1	70.12	950,891
Bob Murphy	30	1 (2)	70.15	855,862
Larry Gilbert	31	1 (2)	70.44	848,544
George Archer	30	1	69.96	717,578

Messing Links

At age 100 the Van Cortlandt Park golf course in the Bronx is the oldest public course in the country, but its most challenging feature has only recently been added. The 203-yard par-3 17th hole now confronts Gotham's golfers with a 20,000-cubic-yard stretch of garbage alongside the fairway. The junk hazard, made up mostly of construction debris illegally dumped by contractors over the past year, has altered the soil chemistry around the hole, killing off 96 trees. American Golf Corp., which runs Van Cortlandt, called the dumping "an error on the part of one of our middle managers" and has promised to restore the "integrity" of the hole. Then again, American Golf also runs the Pelham/Split Rock Golf Course elsewhere in the Bronx. That's where detectives from the city's auto crimes division recently unearthed a 1988 Honda buried near Pelham's 14th hole.

Who says you can't find a parking place in New York?

FOR THE RECORD·Year by Year

Men's Golf

THE MAJOR TOURNAMENTS
The Masters

Year	Winner	Score	Runner-Up
1934	Horton Smith	284	Craig Wood
1935	Gene Sarazen* (144)	282	Craig Wood (149) (only 36-hole playoff)
1936	Horton Smith	285	Harry Cooper
1937	Byron Nelson	283	Ralph Guldahl
1938	Henry Picard	285	Ralph Guldahi, Harry Cooper
1939	Ralph Guldahl	279	Sam Snead
1940	Jimmy Demaret	280	Lloyd Mangrum
1941	Craig Wood	280	Byron Nelson
1942	Byron Nelson* (69)	280	Ben Hogan (70)
1943-45	No tournament		
1946	Herman Keiser	282	Ben Hogan
1947	Jimmy Demaret	281	Byron Nelson, Frank Stranahan
1948	Claude Harmon	279	Cary Middlecoff
1949	Sam Snead	282	Johnny Bulla, Lloyd Mangrum
1950	Jimmy Demaret	283	Jim Ferrier
1951	Ben Hogan	280	Skee Riegel
1952	Sam Snead	286	Jack Burke, Jr
1953	Ben Hogan	274	Ed Oliver, Jr
1954	Sam Snead* (70)	289	Ben Hogan (71)
1955	Cary Middlecoff	279	Ben Hogan
1956	Jack Burke, Jr	289	Ken Venturi
1957	Doug Ford	282	Sam Snead
1958	Arnold Palmer	284	Doug Ford, Fred Hawkins
1959	Art Wall, Jr	284	Cary Middlecoff
1960	Arnold Palmer	282	Ken Venturi
1961	Gary Player	280	Charles R. Coe, Arnold Palmer
1962	Arnold Palmer* (68)	280	Gary Player (71), Dow Finsterwald (77)
1963	Jack Nicklaus	286	Tony Lema
1964	Arnold Palmer	276	Dave Marr, Jack Nicklaus
1965	Jack Nicklaus	271	Arnold Palmer, Gary Player
1966	Jack Nicklaus* (70)	288	Tommy Jacobs (72), Gay Brewer, Jr (78)
1967	Gay Brewer, Jr	280	Bobby Nichols
1968	Bob Goalby	277	Roberto DeVicenzo
1969	George Archer	281	Billy Casper, George Knudson, Tom Weiskopf
1970	Billy Casper* (69)	279	Gene Littler (74)
1971	Charles Coody	279	Johnny Miller, Jack Nicklaus
1972	Jack Nicklaus	286	Bruce Crampton, Bobby Mitchell, Tom Weiskopf
1973	Tommy Aaron	283	J. C. Snead
1974	Gary Player	278	Tom Weiskopf, Dave Stockton
1975	Jack Nicklaus	276	Johnny Miller, Tom Weiskopf
1976	Ray Floyd	271	Ben Crenshaw
1977	Tom Watson	276	Jack Nicklaus
1978	Gary Player	277	Hubert Green, Rod Funseth, Tom Watson
1979†	Fuzzy Zoeller* (4-3)	280	Ed Sneed (4-4), Tom Watson (4-4)
1980	Seve Ballesteros	275	Gibby Gilbert, Jack Newton
1981	Tom Watson	280	Johnny Miller, Jack Nicklaus
1982	Craig Stadler* (4)	284	Dan Pohl (5)
1983	Seve Ballesteros	280	Ben Crenshaw, Tom Kite
1984	Ben Crenshaw	277	Tom Watson
1985	Bernhard Langer	282	Curtis Strange, Seve Ballesteros, Ray Floyd
1986	Jack Nicklaus	279	Greg Norman, Tom Kite
1987	Larry Mize* (4-3)	285	Seve Ballesteros (5), Greg Norman (4-4)
1988	Sandy Lyle	281	Mark Calcavecchia
1989	Nick Faldo* (5-3)	283	Scott Hoch (5-4)
1990	Nick Faldo* (4-4)	278	Ray Floyd (4-x)
1991	Ian Woosnam	277	José María Olázabal
1992	Fred Couples	275	Ray Floyd
1993	Bernhard Langer	277	Chip Beck
1994	José María Olazábal	279	Tom Lehman
1995	Ben Crenshaw	274	Davis Love III

*Winner in playoff. Playoff scores are in parentheses. †Playoff cut from 18 holes to sudden death.
Note: Played at Augusta National Golf Club, Augusta, GA.

United States Open Championship

Year	Winner	Score	Runner-Up	Site
1895	Horace Rawlins	†173	Willie Dunn	Newport GC, Newport, RI
1896	James Foulis	†152	Horace Rawlins	Shinnecock Hills GC, Southampton, NY
1897	Joe Lloyd	†162	Willie Anderson	Chicago GC, Wheaton, IL
1898	Fred Herd	328	Alex Smith	Myopia Hunt Club, Hamilton, MA
1899	Willie Smith	315	George Low	Baltimore CC, Baltimore
			Val Fitzjohn	
			W. H. Way	
1900	Harry Vardon	313	John H. Taylor	Chicago GC, Wheaton, IL
1901	Willie Anderson* (85)	331	Alex Smith (86)	Myopia Hunt Club, Hamilton, MA
1902	Laurie Auchterlonie	307	Stewart Gardner	Garden City GC, Garden City, NY
1903	Willie Anderson* (82)	307	David Brown (84)	Baltusrol GC, Springfield, NJ
1904	Willie Anderson	303	Gil Nicholls	Glen View Club, Golf, IL
1905	Willie Anderson	314	Alex Smith	Myopia Hunt Club, Hamilton, MA
1906	Alex Smith	295	Willie Smith	Onwentsia Club, Lake Forest, IL
1907	Alex Ross	302	Gil Nicholls	Philadelphia Cricket Club, Chestnut Hill, PA
1908	Fred McLeod* (77)	322	Willie Smith (83)	Myopia Hunt Club, Hamilton, MA
1909	George Sargent	290	Tom McNamara	Englewood GC, Englewood, NJ
1910	Alex Smith* (71)	298	John McDermott (75)	Philadelphia Cricket Club, Chestnut Hill, PA
			Macdonald Smith (77)	
1911	John McDermott* (80)	307	Mike Brady (82)	Chicago GC, Wheaton, IL
			George Simpson (85)	
1912	John McDermott	294	Tom McNamara	CC of Buffalo, Buffalo
1913	Francis Ouimet* (72)	304	Harry Vardon (77)	The Country Club, Brookline, MA
			Edward Ray (78)	
1914	Walter Hagen	290	Chick Evans	Midlothian CC, Blue Island, IL
1915	Jerry Travers	297	Tom McNamara	Baltusrol GC, Springfield, NJ
1916	Chick Evans	286	Jock Hutchison	Minikahda Club, Minneapolis
1917-18	No tournament			
1919	Walter Hagen* (77)	301	Mike Brady (78)	Brae Burn CC, West Newton, MA
1920	Edward Ray	295	Harry Vardon	Inverness CC, Toledo
			Jack Burke	
			Leo Diegel	
			Jock Hutchison	
1921	Jim Barnes	289	Walter Hagen	Columbia CC, Chevy Chase, MD
			Fred McLeod	
1922	Gene Sarazen	288	John L. Black	Skokie CC, Glencoe, IL
			Bobby Jones	
1923	Bobby Jones* (76)	296	Bobby Cruickshank (78)	Inwood CC, Inwood, NY
1924	Cyril Walker	297	Bobby Jones	Oakland Hills CC, Birmingham, MI
1925	W. MacFarlane* (75-72)	291	Bobby Jones (75-73)	Worcester CC, Worcester, MA
1926	Bobby Jones	293	Joe Turnesa	Scioto CC, Columbus, OH
1927	Tommy Armour* (76)	301	Harry Cooper (79)	Oakmont CC, Oakmont, PA
1928	Johnny Farrell* (143)	294	Bobby Jones (144)	Olympia Fields CC, Matteson, IL
1929	Bobby Jones* (141)	294	Al Espinosa (164)	Winged Foot GC, Mamaroneck, NY
1930	Bobby Jones	287	Macdonald Smith	Interlachen CC, Hopkins, MN
1931	Billy Burke* (149-148)	292	George Von Elm	Inverness Club, Toledo
			(149-149)	
1932	Gene Sarazen	286	Phil Perkins	Fresh Meadows CC, Flushing, NY
			Bobby Cruickshank	
1933	Johnny Goodman	287	Ralph Guldahl	North Shore CC, Glenview, IL
1934	Olin Dutra	293	Gene Srazen	Merion Cricket Club, Ardmore, PA
1935	Sam Parks, Jr	299	Jimmy Thompson	Oakmont CC, Oakmont, PA
1936	Tony Manero	282	Harry Cooper	Baltusrol GC (Upper Course), Springfield, NJ
1937	Ralph Guldahl	281	Sam Snead	Oakland Hills CC, Birmingham, MI
1938	Ralph Guldahl	284	Dick Metz	Cherry Hills CC, Denver, CO
1939	Byron Nelson* (68-70)	284	Craig Wood (68-73)	Philadelphia CC, Philadelphia
			Denny Shute (76)	
1940	Lawson Little* (70)	287	Gene Sarazen (73)	Canterbury GC, Cleveland
1941	Craig Wood	284	Denny Shute	Colonial Club, Fort Worth
1942-45	No tournament			
1946	Lloyd Mangrum* (72-72)	284	Vic Ghezzi (72-73)	Canterbury GC, Cleveland
			Byron Nelson (72-73)	
1947	Lew Worsham* (69)	282	Sam Snead (70)	St Louis CC, Clayton, MO
1948	Ben Hogan	276	Jimmy Demaret	Riviera CC, Los Angeles
1949	Cary Middlecoff	286	Sam Snead	Medinah CC, Medinah, IL
			Clayton Heafner	

United States Open Championship *(Cont.)*

Year	Winner	Score	Runner-Up	Site
1950	Ben Hogan* (69)	287	Lloyd Mangrum (73)	Merion GC, Ardmore, PA
			George Fazio (75)	
1951	Ben Hogan	287	Clayton Heafner	Oakland Hills CC, Birmingham, MI
1952	Julius Boros	281	Ed Oliver	Northwood CC, Dallas
1953	Ben Hogan	283	Sam Snead	Oakmont CC, Oakmont, PA
1954	Ed Furgol	284	Gene Littler	Baltusrol GC (Lower Course), Springfield, NJ
1955	Jack Fleck* (69)	287	Ben Hogan (72)	Olympic Club (Lake Course), San Francisco
1956	Cary Middlecoff	281	Ben Hogan	Oak Hill CC, Rochester, NY
			Julius Boros	
1957	Dick Mayer* (72)	282	Cary Middlecoff (79)	Inverness Club, Toledo
1958	Tommy Bolt	283	Gary Player	Southern Hills CC, Tulsa
1959	Billy Casper	282	Bob Rosburg	Winged Foot GC, Mamaroneck, NY
1960	Arnold Palmer	280	Jack Nicklaus	Cherry Hills CC, Denver
1961	Gene Littler	281	Bob Goalby	Oakland Hills CC, Birmingham, MI
			Doug Sanders	
1962	Jack Nicklaus* (71)	283	Arnold Palmer (74)	Oakmont CC, Oakmont, PA
1963	Julius Boros* (70)	293	Jacky Cupit (73)	The Country Club, Brookline, MA
			Arnold Palmer (76)	
1964	Ken Venturi	278	Tommy Jacobs	Congressional CC, Washington, DC
1965	Gary Player* (71)	282	Kel Nagle (74)	Bellerive CC, St Louis
1966	Billy Casper* (69)	278	Arnold Palmer (73)	Olympic Club (Lake Course), San Francisco
1967	Jack Nicklaus	275	Arnold Palmer	Baltusrol GC (Lower Course), Springfield, NJ
1968	Lee Trevino	275	Jack Nicklaus	Oak Hill CC, Rochester, NY
1969	Orville Moody	281	Deane Beman	Champions GC (Cypress Creek Course),
			Al Geiberger	Houston
			Bob Rosburg	
1970	Tony Jacklin	281	Dave Hill	Hazeltine GC, Chaska, MN
1971	Lee Trevino* (68)	280	Jack Nicklaus (71)	Merion GC (East Course), Ardmore, PA
1972	Jack Nicklaus	290	Bruce Crampton	Pebble Beach GL, Pebble Beach, CA
1973	Johnny Miller	279	John Schlee	Oakmont CC, Oakmont, PA
1974	Hale Irwin	287	Forrest Fezler	Winged Foot GC, Mamaroneck, NY
1975	Lou Graham* (71)	287	John Mahaffey (73)	Medinah CC, Medinah, IL
1976	Jerry Pate	277	Tom Weiskopf	Atlanta Athletic Club, Duluth, GA
			Al Geiberger	
1977	Hubert Green	278	Lou Graham	Southern Hills CC, Tulsa
1978	Andy North	285	Dave Stockton	Cherry Hills CC, Denver
			J. C. Snead	
1979	Hale Irwin	284	Gary Player	Inverness Club, Toledo
			Jerry Pate	
1980	Jack Nicklaus	272	Isao Aoki	Baltusrol GC (Lower Course), Springfield, NJ
1981	David Graham	273	George Burns	Merion GC, Ardmore, PA
			Bill Rogers	
1982	Tom Watson	282	Jack Nicklaus	Pebble Beach GL, Pebble Beach, CA
1983	Larry Nelson	280	Tom Watson	Oakmont CC, Oakmont, PA
1984	Fuzzy Zoeller* (67)	276	Greg Norman (75)	Winged Foot GC, Mamaroneck, NY
1985	Andy North	279	Dave Barr	Oakland Hills CC, Birmingham, MI
			T. C. Chen	
			Denis Watson	
1986	Ray Floyd	279	Lanny Wadkins	Shinnecock Hills GC, Southampton, NY
			Chip Beck	
1987	Scott Simpson	277	Tom Watson	Olympic Club (Lake Course), San Francisco
1988	Curtis Strange* (71)	278	Nick Faldo (75)	The Country Club, Brookline, MA
1989	Curtis Strange	278	Chip Beck	Oak Hill CC, Rochester, NY
			Mark McCumber	
			Ian Woosnam	
1990	Hale Irwin* (74) (3)	280	Mike Donald (74) (4)	Medinah CC, Medinah, IL
1991	Payne Stewart (75)	282	Scott Simpson (77)	Hazeltine GC, Chaska, MN
1992	Tom Kite	285	Jeff Sluman	Pebble Beach GL, Pebble Beach, CA
1993	Lee Janzen	272	Payne Stewart	Baltusrol GC, Springfield, NJ
1994	Ernie Els*	279	Loren Roberts	Oakmont CC, Oakmont, PA
			Colin Montgomerie	
1995	Corey Pavin	280	Greg Norman	Shinnecock Hills GC, Southampton, NY

*Winner in playoff. Playoff scores are in parentheses. The 1990 playoff went to one hole of sudden death after an 18-hole playoff. In the 1994 playoff, Montgomerie was eliminated after 18 playoff holes, and Els beat Roberts on the 20th.
†Before 1898, 36 holes. From 1898 on, 72 holes.

British Open

Year	Winner	Score	Runner-Up	Site
1860†	Willie Park	174	Tom Morris, Sr	Prestwick, Scotland
1861‡	Tom Morris, Sr	163	Willie Park	Prestwick, Scotland
1862	Tom Morris, Sr	163	Willie Park	Prestwick, Scotland
1863	Willie Park	168	Tom Morris, Sr	Prestwick, Scotland
1864	Tom Morris, Sr	160	Andrew Strath	Prestwick, Scotland
1865	Andrew Strath	162	Willie Park	Prestwick, Scotland
1866	Willie Park	169	David Park	Prestwick, Scotland
1867	Tom Morris, Sr	170	Willie Park	Prestwick, Scotland
1868	Tom Morris, Jr	154	Tom Morris, Sr	Prestwick, Scotland
1869	Tom Morris, Jr	157	Tom Morris, Sr	Prestwick, Scotland
1870	Tom Morris, Jr	149	David Strath	Prestwick, Scotland
			Bob Kirk	
1871	No tournament			
1872	Tom Morris, Jr	166	David Strath	Prestwick, Scotland
1873	Tom Kidd	179	Jamie Anderson	St Andrews, Scotland
1874	Mungo Park	159	No record	Musselburgh, Scotland
1875	Willie Park	166	Bob Martin	Prestwick, Scotland
1876	Bob Martin#	176	David Strath	St Andrews, Scotland
1877	Jamie Anderson	160	Bob Pringle	Musselburgh, Scotland
1878	Jamie Anderson	157	Robert Kirk	Prestwick, Scotland
1879	Jamie Anderson	169	Andrew Kirkaldy	St Andrews, Scotland
			James Allan	
1880	Robert Ferguson	162	No record	Musselburgh, Scotland
1881	Robert Ferguson	170	Jamie Anderson	Prestwick, Scotland
1882	Robert Ferguson	171	Willie Fernie	St Andrews, Scotland
1883	Willie Fernie*	159	Robert Ferguson	Musselburgh, Scotland
1884	Jack Simpson	160	Douglas Rolland	Prestwick, Scotland
			Willie Fernie	
1885	Bob Martin	171	Archie Simpson	St Andrews, Scotland
1886	David Brown	157	Willie Campbell	Musselburgh, Scotland
1887	Willie Park, Jr	161	Bob Martin	Prestwick, Scotland
1888	Jack Burns	171	Bernard Sayers	St Andrews, Scotland
			David Anderson	
1889	Willie Park, Jr* (158)	155	Andrew Kirkaldy (163)	Musselburgh, Scotland
1890	John Ball	164	Willie Fernie	Prestwick, Scotland
1891	Hugh Kirkaldy	166	Andrew Kirkaldy	St Andrews, Scotland
			Willie Fernie	
1892	Harold Hilton	**305	John Ball	Muirfield, Scotland
			Hugh Kirkaldy	
1893	William Auchterlonie	322	John E. Laidlay	Prestwick, Scotland
1894	John H. Taylor	326	Douglas Rolland	Royal St George's, England
1895	John H. Taylor	322	Alexander Herd	St Andrews, Scotland
1896	Harry Vardon* (157)	316	John H. Taylor (161)	Muirfield, Scotland
1897	Harold Hilton	314	James Braid	Hoylake, England
1898	Harry Vardon	307	Willie Park, Jr	Prestwick, Scotland
1899	Harry Vardon	310	Jack White	Royal St George's, England
1900	John H. Taylor	309	Harry Vardon	St Andrews, Scotland
1901	James Braid	309	Harry Vardon	Muirfield, Scotland
1902	Alexander Herd	307	Harry Vardon	Hoylake, England
1903	Harry Vardon	300	Tom Vardon	Prestwick, Scotland
1904	Jack White	296	John H. Taylor	Royal St George's, England
1905	James Braid	318	John H. Taylor	St Andrews, Scotland
			Rolland Jones	
1906	James Braid	300	John H. Taylor	Muirfield, Scotland
1907	Arnaud Massy	312	John H. Taylor	Hoylake, England
1908	James Braid	291	Tom Ball	Prestwick, Scotland
1909	John H. Taylor	295	James Braid	Deal, England
			Tom Ball	
1910	James Braid	299	Alexander Herd	St Andrews, Scotland
1911	Harry Vardon	303	Arnaud Massy	Royal St George's, England
1912	Ted Ray	295	Harry Vardon	Muirfield, Scotland
1913	John H. Taylor	304	Ted Ray	Hoylake, England
1914	Harry Vardon	306	John H. Taylor	Prestwick, Scotland
1915-19	No tournament			
1920	George Duncan	303	Alexander Herd	Deal, England
1921	Jock Hutchison* (150)	296	Roger Wethered (159)	St Andrews, Scotland

British Open (Cont.)

Year	Winner	Score	Runner-Up	Site
1922	Walter Hagen	300	George Duncan	Royal St George's, England
			Jim Barnes	
1923	Arthur G. Havers	295	Walter Hagen	Troon, Scotland
1924	Walter Hagen	301	Ernest Whitcombe	Hoylake, England
1925	Jim Barnes	300	Archie Compston	Prestwick, Scotland
			Ted Ray	
1926	Bobby Jones	291	Al Watrous	Royal Lytham and St Annes GC, St Anne's-on-the-Sea, England
1927	Bobby Jones	285	Aubrey Boomer	St Andrews, Scotland
1928	Walter Hagen	292	Gene Sarazen	Royal St George's, England
1929	Walter Hagen	292	Johnny Farrell	Muirfield, Scotland
1930	Bobby Jones	291	Macdonald Smith	Hoylake, England
			Leo Diegel	
1931	Tommy Armour	296	Jose Jurado	Carnoustie, Scotland
1932	Gene Sarazen	283	Macdonald Smith	Prince's, England
1933	Denny Shute* (149)	292	Craig Wood (154)	St Andrews, Scotland
1934	Henry Cotton	283	Sidney F. Brews	Royal St George's, England
1935	Alfred Perry	283	Alfred Padgham	Muirfield, Scotland
1936	Alfred Padgham	287	James Adams	Hoylake, England
1937	Henry Cotton	290	Reginald A. Whitcombe	Carnoustie, Scotland
1938	Reginald A. Whitcombe	295	James Adams	Royal St George's, England
1939	Richard Burton	290	Johnny Bulla	St Andrews, Scotland
1940-45	No tournament			
1946	Sam Snead	290	Bobby Locke	St Andrews, Scotland
			Johnny Bulla	
1947	Fred Daly	293	Reginald W. Horne	Hoylake, England
			Frank Stranahan	
1948	Henry Cotton	294	Fred Daly	Muirfield, Scotland
1949	Bobby Locke* (135)	283	Harry Bradshaw (147)	Royal St George's, England
1950	Bobby Locke	279	Roberto DeVicenzo	Troon, Scotland
1951	Max Faulkner	285	Tony Cerda	Portrush, Ireland
1952	Bobby Locke	287	Peter Thomson	Royal Lytham, England
1953	Ben Hogan	282	Frank Stranahan	Carnoustie, Scotland
			Dai Rees	
			Peter Thomson	
			Tony Cerda	
1954	Peter Thomson	283	Sidney S. Scott	Royal Birkdale, England
			Dai Rees	
			Bobby Locke	
1955	Peter Thomson	281	John Fallon	St Andrews, Scotland
1956	Peter Thomson	286	Flory Van Donck	Hoylake, England
1957	Bobby Locke	279	Peter Thomson	St Andrews, Scotland
1958	Peter Thomson* (139)	278	Dave Thomas (143)	Royal Lytham, England
1959	Gary Player	284	Fred Bullock	Muirfield, Scotland
			Flory Van Donck	
1960	Kel Nagle	278	Arnold Palmer	St Andrews, Scotland
1961	Arnold Palmer	284	Dai Rees	Royal Birkdale, England
1962	Arnold Palmer	276	Kel Nagle	Troon, Scotland
1963	Bob Charles* (140)	277	Phil Rodgers (148)	Royal Lytham, England
1964	Tony Lema	279	Jack Nicklaus	St Andrews, Scotland
1965	Peter Thomson	285	Brian Huggett	Southport, England
			Christy O'Connor	
1966	Jack Nicklaus	282	Doug Sanders	Muirfield, Scotland
			Dave Thomas	
1967	Robert DeVicenzo	278	Jack Nicklaus	Hoylake, England
1968	Gary Player	289	Jack Nicklaus	Carnoustie, Scotland
			Bob Charles	
1969	Tony Jacklin	280	Bob Charles	Royal Lytham, England
1970	Jack Nicklaus* (72)	283	Doug Sanders (73)	St Andrews, Scotland
1971	Lee Trevino	278	Lu Liang Huan	Royal Birkdale, England
1972	Lee Trevino	278	Jack Nicklaus	Muirfield, Scotland
1973	Tom Weiskopf	276	Johnny Miller	Troon, Scotland
1974	Gary Player	282	Peter Oosterhuis	Royal Lytham, England
1975	Tom Watson* (71)	279	Jack Newton (72)	Carnoustie, Scotland
1976	Johnny Miller	279	Jack Nicklaus	Royal Birkdale, England
			Seve Ballesteros	

British Open (Cont.)

Year	Winner	Score	Runner-Up	Site
1977	Tom Watson	268	Jack Nicklaus	Turnberry, Scotland
1978	Jack Nicklaus	281	Ben Crenshaw	St Andrews, Scotland
			Tom Kite	
			Ray Floyd	
			Simon Owen	
1979	Seve Ballesteros	283	Ben Crenshaw	Royal Lytham, England
			Jack Nicklaus	
1980	Tom Watson	271	Lee Trevino	Muirfield, Scotland
1981	Bill Rogers	276	Bernhard Langer	Royal St George's, England
1982	Tom Watson	284	Nick Price	Royal Troon, Scotland
			Peter Oosterhuis	
1983	Tom Watson	275	Andy Bean	Royal Birkdale, England
1984	Seve Ballesteros	276	Tom Watson	St Andrews, Scotland
			Bernhard Langer	
1985	Sandy Lyle	282	Payne Stewart	Royal St George's, England
1986	Greg Norman	280	Gordon Brand	Turnberry, Scotland
1987	Nick Faldo	279	Paul Azinger	Muirfield, Scotland
			Rodger Davis	
1988	Seve Ballesteros	273	Nick Price	Royal Lytham, England
1989††	Mark Calcavecchia* (4-3-3-3)	275	Wayne Grady (4-4-4-4) Greg Norman (3-3-4-x)	Royal Troon, Scotland
1990	Nick Faldo	270	Payne Stewart	St Andrews, Scotland
			Mark McNulty	
1991	Ian Baker-Finch	272	Mike Harwood	Royal Birkdale, England
1992	Nick Faldo	272	John Cook	Muirfield, Scotland
1993	Greg Norman	267	Nick Faldo	Royal St George's, England
1994	Nick Price	268	Jesper Parnevik	Turnberry, Scotland
1995	John Daly* (4-3-4-4)	282	C. Rocca (5-4-7-3)	St Andrews, Scotland

*Winner in playoff. Playoff scores are in parentheses. †The first event was open only to professional golfers.
‡The second annual open was open to amateurs and pros. #Tied, but refused playoff.
**Championship extended from 36 to 72 holes. ††Playoff cut from 18 holes to 4 holes.

PGA Championship

Year	Winner	Score	Runner-Up	Site
1916	Jim Barnes	1 up	Jock Hutchison	Siwanoy CC, Bronxville, NY
1917-18	No tournament			
1919	Jim Barnes	6 & 5	Fred McLeod	Engineers CC, Roslyn, NY
1920	Jock Hutchison	1 up	J. Douglas Edgar	Flossmoor CC, Flossmoor, IL
1921	Walter Hagen	3 & 2	Jim Barnes	Inwood CC, Far Rockaway, NY
1922	Gene Sarazen	4 & 3	Emmet French	Oakmont CC, Oakmont, PA
1923	Gene Sarazen	1 up 38 holes	Walter Hagen	Pelham CC, Pelham, NY
1924	Walter Hagen	2 up	Jim Barnes	French Lick CC, French Lick, IN
1925	Walter Hagen	6 & 5	William Mehlhorn	Olympia Fields CC, Olympia Fields, IL
1926	Walter Hagen	5 & 3	Leo Diegel	Salisbury GC, Westbury, NY
1927	Walter Hagen	1 up	Joe Turnesa	Cedar Crest CC, Dallas
1928	Leo Diegel	6 & 5	Al Espinosa	Five Farms CC, Baltimore
1929	Leo Diegel	6 & 4	Johnny Farrell	Hillcrest CC, Los Angeles
1930	Tommy Armour	1 up	Gene Sarazen	Fresh Meadow CC, Flushing, NY
1931	Tom Creavy	2 & 1	Denny Shute	Wannamoisett CC, Rumford, RI
1932	Olin Dutra	4 & 3	Frank Walsh	Keller GC, St Paul
1933	Gene Sarazen	5 & 4	Willie Goggin	Blue Mound CC, Milwaukee
1934	Paul Runyan	1 up	Craig Wood	Park CC, Williamsville, NY
1935	Johnny Revolta	5 & 4 38 holes	Tommy Armour	Twin Hills CC, Oklahoma City
1936	Denny Shute	3 & 2	Jimmy Thomson	Pinehurst CC, Pinehurst, NC
1937	Denny Shute	1 up 37 holes	Harold McSpaden	Pittsburgh FC, Aspinwall, PA
1938	Paul Runyan	8 & 7	Sam Snead	Shawnee CC, Shawnee-on-Delaware, PA
1939	Henry Picard	1 up 37 holes	Byron Nelson	Pomonok CC, Flushing, NY
1940	Byron Nelson	1 up	Sam Snead	Hershey CC, Hershey, PA
1941	Vic Ghezzi	1 up 38 holes	Byron Nelson	Cherry Hills CC, Denver
1942	Sam Snead	2 & 1	Jim Turnesa	Seaview CC, Atlantic City

PGA Championship (Cont.)

Year	Winner	Score	Runner-Up	Site
1943	No tournament			
1944	Bob Hamilton	1 up	Byron Nelson	Manito G & CC, Spokane, WA
1945	Byron Nelson	4 & 3	Sam Byrd	Morraine CC, Dayton
1946	Ben Hogan	6 & 4	Ed Oliver	Portland GC, Portland, OR
1947	Jim Ferrier	2 & 1	Chick Harbert	Plum Hollow CC, Detroit
1948	Ben Hogan	7 & 6	Mike Turnesa	Norwood Hills CC, St Louis
1949	Sam Snead	3 & 2	Johnny Palmer	Hermitage CC, Richmond
1950	Chandler Harper	4 & 3	Henry Williams, Jr	Scioto CC, Columbus, OH
1951	Sam Snead	7 & 6	Walter Burkemo	Oakmont CC, Oakmont, PA
1952	Jim Turnesa	1 up	Chick Harbert	Big Spring CC, Louisville
1953	Walter Burkemo	2 & 1	Felice Torza	Birmingham CC, Birmingham, MI
1954	Chick Harbert	4 & 3	Walter Burkemo	Keller GC, St Paul
1955	Doug Ford	4 & 3	Cary Middlecoff	Meadowbrook CC, Detroit
1956	Jack Burke	3 & 2	Ted Kroll	Blue Hill CC, Boston
1957	Lionel Hebert	2 & 1	Dow Finsterwald	Miami Valley CC, Dayton
1958	Dow Finsterwald	276	Billy Casper	Llanerch CC, Havertown, PA
1959	Bob Rosburg	277	Jerry Barber	Minneapolis GC, St Louis Park, MN
			Doug Sanders	
1960	Jay Hebert	281	Jim Ferrier	Firestone CC, Akron
1961	Jerry Barber* (67)	277	Don January (68)	Olympia Fields CC, Olympia Fields, IL
1962	Gary Player	278	Bob Goalby	Aronimink GC, Newton Square, PA
1963	Jack Nicklaus	279	Dave Ragan, Jr	Dallas Athletic Club, Dallas
1964	Bobby Nichols	271	Jack Nicklaus	Columbus CC, Columbus, OH
			Arnold Palmer	
1965	Dave Marr	280	Billy Casper	Laurel Valley CC, Ligonier, PA
			Jack Nicklaus	
1966	Al Geiberger	280	Dudley Wysong	Firestone CC, Akron
1967	Don January* (69)	281	Don Massengale (71)	Columbine CC, Littleton, CO
1968	Julius Boros	281	Bob Charles	Pecan Valley CC, San Antonio
			Arnold Palmer	
1969	Ray Floyd	276	Gary Player	NCR CC, Dayton
1970	Dave Stockton	279	Arnold Palmer	Southern Hills CC, Tulsa
			Bob Murphy	
1971	Jack Nicklaus	281	Billy Casper	PGA Natl GC, Palm Beach Gardens, FL
1972	Gary Player	281	Tommy Aaron	Oakland Hills CC, Birmingham, MI
			Jim Jamieson	
1973	Jack Nicklaus	277	Bruce Crampton	Canterbury GC, Cleveland
1974	Lee Trevino	276	Jack Nicklaus	Tanglewood GC, Winston-Salem, NC
1975	Jack Nicklaus	276	Bruce Crampton	Firestone CC, Akron
1976	Dave Stockton	281	Ray Floyd	Congressional CC, Bethesda, MD
			Don January	
1977†	Lanny Wadkins* (4-4-4)	282	Gene Littler (4-4-5)	Pebble Beach GL, Pebble Beach, CA
1978	John Mahaffey* (4-3)	276	Jerry Pate (4-4)	Oakmont CC, Oakmont, PA
			Tom Watson (4-5)	
1979	David Graham* (4-4-2)	272	Ben Crenshaw (4-4-4)	Oakland Hills CC, Birmingham, MI
1980	Jack Nicklaus	274	Andy Bean	Oak Hill CC, Rochester, NY
1981	Larry Nelson	273	Fuzzy Zoeller	Atlanta Athletic Club, Duluth, GA
1982	Raymond Floyd	272	Lanny Wadkins	Southern Hills CC, Tulsa
1983	Hal Sutton	274	Jack Nicklaus	Riviera CC, Pacific Palisades, CA
1984	Lee Trevino	273	Gary Player	Shoal Creek, Birmingham, AL
			Lanny Wadkins	
1985	Hubert Green	278	Lee Trevino	Cherry Hills CC, Denver
1986	Bob Tway	276	Greg Norman	Inverness CC, Toledo
1987	Larry Nelson* (4)	287	Lanny Wadkins (5)	PGA Natl GC, Palm Beach Gardens, FL
1988	Jeff Sluman	272	Paul Azinger	Oak Tree GC, Edmond, OK
1989	Payne Stewart	276	Mike Reid	Kemper Lakes GC, Hawthorn Woods, IL
1990	Wayne Grady	282	Fred Couples	Shoal Creek, Birmingham, AL
1991	John Daly	276	Bruce Lietzke	Crooked Stick GC, Carmel, IN
1992	Nick Price	278	Jim Gallagher Jr	Bellerive CC, St. Louis
1993	Paul Azinger* (4-4)	272	Greg Norman (4-5)	Inverness CC, Toldeo, OH
1994	Nick Price	269	Corey Pavin	Southern Hills CC, Tulsa, OK
1995	Steve Elkington*(3)	267	Colin Montgomerie (4)	Riviera CC, Pacific Palisades, CA

*Winner in playoff. Playoff scores are in parentheses.

†Playoff changed from 18 holes to sudden death.

THE PGA TOUR
Season Money Leaders

		Earnings ($)
1934	Paul Runyan	6,767.00
1935	Johnny Revolta	9,543.00
1936	Horton Smith	7,682.00
1937	Harry Cooper	14,138.69
1938	Sam Snead	19,534.49
1939	Henry Picard	10,303.00
1940	Ben Hogan	10,655.00
1941	Ben Hogan	18,358.00
1942	Ben Hogan	13,143.00
1943	No statistics compiled	
1944	Byron Nelson (war bonds)	37,967.69
1945	Byron Nelson (war bonds)	63,335.66
1946	Ben Hogan	42,556.16
1947	Jimmy Demaret	27,936.83
1948	Ben Hogan	32,112.00
1949	Sam Snead	31,593.83
1950	Sam Snead	35,758.83
1951	Lloyd Mangrum	26,088.83
1952	Julius Boros	37,032.97
1953	Lew Worsham	34,002.00
1954	Bob Toski	65,819.81
1955	Julius Boros	63,121.55
1956	Ted Kroll	72,835.83
1957	Dick Mayer	65,835.00
1958	Arnold Palmer	42,607.50
1959	Art Wall	53,167.60
1960	Arnold Palmer	75,262.85
1961	Gary Player	64,540.45
1962	Arnold Palmer	81,448.33
1963	Arnold Palmer	128,230.00
1964	Jack Nicklaus	113,284.50
1965	Jack Nicklaus	140,752.14

		Earnings ($)
1966	Billy Casper	121,944.92
1967	Jack Nicklaus	188,998.08
1968	Billy Casper	205,168.67
1969	Frank Beard	164,707.11
1970	Lee Trevino	157,037.63
1971	Jack Nicklaus	244,490.50
1972	Jack Nicklaus	320,542.26
1973	Jack Nicklaus	308,362.10
1974	Johnny Miller	353,021.59
1975	Jack Nicklaus	298,149.17
1976	Jack Nicklaus	266,438.57
1977	Tom Watson	310,653.16
1978	Tom Watson	362,428.93
1979	Tom Watson	462,636.00
1980	Tom Watson	530,808.33
1981	Tom Kite	375,698.84
1982	Craig Stadler	446,462.00
1983	Hal Sutton	426,668.00
1984	Tom Watson	476,260.00
1985	Curtis Strange	542,321.00
1986	Greg Norman	653,296.00
1987	Curtis Strange	925,941.00
1988	Curtis Strange	1,147,644.00
1989	Tom Kite	1,395,278.00
1990	Greg Norman	1,165,477.00
1991	Corey Pavin	979,430.00
1992	Fred Couples	1,344,188.00
1993	Nick Price	1,478,557.00
1994	Nick Price	1,499,927.00
1995	Greg Norman	1,654,959.00

Note: Total money listed from 1968 through 1974. Official money listed from 1975 on.

Career Money Leaders‡

		Earnings ($)
1.	Greg Norman	9,592,829
2.	Tom Kite	9,337,998
3.	Payne Stewart	7,389,479
4.	Nick Price	7,338,119
5.	Fred Couples	7,188,408
6.	Corey Pavin	7,175,523
7.	Tom Watson	7,072,113
8.	Paul Azinger	6,957,324
9.	Ben Crenshaw	6,845,235
10.	Curtis Strange	6,791,618
11.	Mark O'Meara	6,126,466
12.	Lanny Wadkins	6,028,855
13.	Craig Stadler	6,008,753
14.	Mark Calcavecchia	5,866,716
15.	Hale Irwin	5,845,024
16.	Chip Beck	5,755,844
17.	Bruce Lietzke	5,710,262

		Earnings ($)
18.	Davis Love III	5,623,890
19.	Scott Hoch	5,465,898
20.	David Frost	5,458,172
21.	Jack Nicklaus	5,440,357
22.	Jay Haas	5,426,821
23.	Ray Floyd	5,194,044
24.	Gil Morgan	4,991,433
25.	Fuzzy Zoeller	4,918,771
26.	Mark McCumber	4,799,702
27.	Scott Simpson	4,768,955
28.	Larry Mize	4,584,287
29.	Jim Gallagher, Jr	4,583,940
30.	Peter Jacobsen	4,547,564
31.	Steve Elkington	4,525,487
32.	Hal Sutton	4,486,587
33.	John Cook	4,461,954
34.	Wayne Levi	4,237,387

		Earnings ($)
35.	Lee Janzen	3,910,397
36.	Jeff Sluman	3,860,431
37.	John Mahaffey	3,828,008
38.	Bob Tway	3,815,540
39.	Loren Roberts	3,809,733
40.	Steve Pate	3,661,591
41.	David Edwards	3,646,2??
42.	D.A. Weibring	3,6??
43.	Joey Sindelar	3,5??
44.	Brad Faxon	3,537,5??
45.	Lee Trevino	3,478,45?
46.	John Huston	3,408,0??
47.	Billy Mayfair	3,397,6..
48.	Tim Simpson	3,351,47?
49.	Ken Green	3,347,802
50.	Larry Nelson	3,313,938

Top Single-Season Earnings‡

	Earnings ($)	Year
Greg Norman	1,654,959	1995
Billy Mayfair	1,543,192	1995
Nick Price	1,499,927	1994
Nick Price	1,478,557	1993
Paul Azinger	1,458,456	1993
Tom Kite	1,395,278	1989

	Earnings ($)	Year
Lee Janzen	1,378,966	1995
Greg Norman	1,359,653	1993
Fred Couples	1,344,188	1992
Corey Pavin	1,340,079	1995
Greg Norman	1,330,307	1994
Steve Elkington	1,254,352	1995

‡Through 10/31/95.

Ken Daneyko (top) and the New Jersey Devils upended the Detroit Red Wings in the Stanley Cup.

Steffi Graf won three majors in '95, including a dramatic win over Monica Seles in the U.S. Open.

Eric Alford and Nebraska were indeed No. 1 after trouncing Colorado 24–7 in October

Justice Smith ran for 147 yards as Boston College easily defeated Notre Dame 30–11.

Jerry Rice snared this TD pass from Steve Young to put the Niners up 31–14 in the NFC title game.

Natrone Means ran for 1,350 yards to power the San Diego Chargers to their first Super Bowl.

Clyde Drexler's arrival ignited the Rockets in their quest for a second straight NBA title.

Orlando's Shaquille O'Neal (top) and Houston's Hakeem Olajuwon clashed in the NBA Finals.

The midair artistry of Jerry Stackhouse was critical to North Carolina's success all season long.

UCLA's Toby Bailey helped the Bruins leap over UConn and into their first Final Four in 19 years.

Talkin Man charged to victory in the Wood in April, but faded to 12th in the Derby in May.

BOB MARTIN

Ben Crenshaw's victory in the Masters was one of the year's most emotional moments.

Dashing Double: Michael Johnson won the 200 (above) and the 400 at the world championships.

Eric Wynalda's sterling play produced three goals for the United States in the Copa America.

In a season of fan disillusionment, Dodger rookie Hideo Nomo was a breath of fresh air.

Cal Ripken took an unforgettable victory lap after breaking Lou Gehrig's iron-man record.

Most Career Wins‡

	Wins		Wins		Wins
Sam Snead	81	Billy Casper	51	Horton Smith	32
Jack Nicklaus	70	Walter Hagen	40	Tom Watson	32
Ben Hogan	63	Cary Middlecoff	40	Harry Cooper	31
Arnold Palmer	60	Gene Sarazen	38	Jimmy Demaret	31
Byron Nelson	52	Lloyd Mangrum	36	Leo Diegel	30

‡Statistics through 10/31/95.

Year by Year Statistical Leaders

SCORING AVERAGE

1980	Lee Trevino	69.73
1981	Tom Kite	69.80
1982	Tom Kite	70.21
1983	Raymond Floyd	70.61
1984	Calvin Peete	70.56
1985	Don Pooley	70.36
1986	Scott Hoch	70.08
1987	David Frost	70.09
1988	Greg Norman	69.38
1989	Payne Stewart	69.485†
1990	Greg Norman	69.10
1991	Fred Couples	69.59
1992	Fred Couples	69.38
1993	Greg Norman	68.90
1994	Greg Norman	68.81
1995	Greg Norman	69.06

Note: Scoring average per round, with adjustments made at each round for the field's course scoring average.

DRIVING DISTANCE

		Yds
1980	Dan Pohl	274.3
1981	Dan Pohl	280.1
1982	Bill Calfee	275.3
1983	John McComish	277.4
1984	Bill Glasson	276.5
1985	Andy Bean	278.2
1986	Davis Love III	285.7
1987	John McComish	283.9
1988	Steve Thomas	284.6
1989	Ed Humenik	280.9
1990	Tom Purtzer	279.6
1991	John Daly	288.9
1992	John Daly	283.4
1993	John Daly	288.9
1994	Davis Love III	283.8
1995	John Daly	289.0

Note: Average computed by charting distance of two tee shots on a predetermined par-four or par-five hole (one on front nine, one on back nine).

DRIVING ACCURACY

1980	Mike Reid	79.5
1981	Calvin Peete	81.9
1982	Calvin Peete	84.6
1983	Calvin Peete	81.3
1984	Calvin Peete	77.5
1985	Calvin Peete	80.6
1986	Calvin Peete	81.7
1987	Calvin Peete	83.0
1988	Calvin Peete	82.5
1989	Calvin Peete	82.6
1990	Calvin Peete	83.7

DRIVING ACCURACY (Cont.)

1991	Hale Irwin	78.3
1992	Doug Tewell	82.3
1993	Doug Tewell	82.5
1994	David Edwards	81.6
1995	Fred Funk	81.3

Note: Percentage of fairways hit on number of par-four and par-five holes played; par-three holes excluded.

GREENS IN REGULATION

1980	Jack Nicklaus	72.1
1981	Calvin Peete	73.1
1982	Calvin Peete	72.4
1983	Calvin Peete	71.4
1984	Andy Bean	72.1
1985	John Mahaffey	71.9
1986	John Mahaffey	72.0
1987	Gil Morgan	73.3
1988	John Adams	73.9
1989	Bruce Lietzke	72.6
1990	Doug Tewell	70.9
1991	Bruce Lietzke	73.3
1992	Tim Simpson	74.0
1993	Fuzzy Zoeller	73.6
1994	Bill Glasson	73.0
1995	Lenny Clements	72.3

Note: Average of greens reached in regulation out of total holes played; hole is considered hit in regulation if any part of the ball rests on the putting surface in two shots less than the hole's-five hit in two shots is one green in regulation.

PUTTING

1980	Jerry Pate	28.81
1981	Alan Tapie	28.70
1982	Ben Crenshaw	28.65
1983	Morris Hatalsky	27.96
1984	Gary McCord	28.57
1985	Craig Stadler	28.627†
1986	Greg Norman	1.736
1987	Ben Crenshaw	1.743
1988	Don Pooley	1.729
1989	Steve Jones	1.734
1990	Larry Rinker	1.7467†
1991	Jay Don Blake	1.7326†
1992	Mark O'Meara	1.731
1993	David Frost	1.739
1994	Loren Roberts	1.737
1995	Jim Furyk	1.708

Note: Average number of putts taken on greens reached in regulation; prior to 1986, based on average number of putts per 18 holes.

ALL-AROUND

1987	Dan Pohl	170
1988	Payne Stewart	170
1989	Paul Azinger	250
1990	Paul Azinger	162
1991	Scott Hoch	283
1992	Fred Couples	256
1993	Gil Morgan	252
1994	Bob Estes	227
1995	Justin Leonard	323

Note: Addition of the places of standing from the other nine statistical categories; the player with the number closest to zero leads.

SAND SAVES

1980	Bob Eastwood	65.4
1981	Tom Watson	60.1
1982	Isao Aoki	60.2
1983	Isao Aoki	62.3
1984	Peter Oosterhuis	64.7
1985	Tom Purtzer	60.8
1986	Paul Azinger	63.8
1987	Paul Azinger	63.2
1988	Greg Powers	63.5
1989	Mike Sullivan	66.0
1990	Paul Azinger	67.2
1991	Ben Crenshaw	64.9
1992	Mitch Adcock	66.9
1993	Ken Green	64.4
1994	Corey Pavin	65.4
1995	Billy Mayfair	68.6

Note: Percentage of up-and-down efforts from greenside sand traps only; fairway bunkers excluded.

PAR BREAKERS

1980	Tom Watson	.213
1981	Bruce Lietzke	.225
1982	Tom Kite	.2154†
1983	Tom Watson	.211
1984	Craig Stadler	.220
1985	Craig Stadler	.218
1986	Greg Norman	.248
1987	Mark Calcavecchia	.221
1988	Ken Green	.236
1989	Greg Norman	.224
1990	Greg Norman	.219

Note: Average based on total birdies and eagles scored out of total holes played. Discontinued as an official category after 1990.

† Number had to be carried to extra decimal place to determine winner.

Year by Year Statistical Leaders (Cont.)

EAGLES

1980	Dave Eichelberger	16
1981	Bruce Lietzke	12
1982	Tom Weiskopf	10
	J. C. Snead	10
	Andy Bean	10
1983	Chip Beck	15
1984	Gary Hallberg	15
1985	Larry Rinker	14
1986	Joey Sindelar	16
1987	Phil Blackmar	20
1988	Ken Green	21
1989	Lon Hinkle	14
	Duffy Waldorf	14
1990	Paul Azinger	14
1991	Andy Bean	15
1992	Dan Forsman	18
1993	Davis Love III	15
1994	Davis Love III	18
1995	Kelly Gibson	16

Note: Total of eagles scored.

BIRDIES

1980	Andy Bean	388
1981	Vance Heafner	388
1982	Andy Bean	392
1983	Hal Sutton	399
1984	Mark O'Meara	419
1985	Joey Sindelar	411
1986	Joey Sindelar	415
1987	Dan Forsman	409
1988	Dan Forsman	465
1989	Ted Schulz	415
1990	Mike Donald	401
1991	Scott Hoch	446
1992	Jeff Sluman	417
1993	John Huston	426
1994	Brad Bryant	397
1995	Steve Lowery	410

Note: Total of birdies scored.

PGA Player of the Year Award

1948	Ben Hogan		1964	Ken Venturi		1980	Tom Watson
1949	Sam Snead		1965	Dave Marr		1981	Bill Rogers
1950	Ben Hogan		1966	Billy Casper		1982	Tom Watson
1951	Ben Hogan		1967	Jack Nicklaus		1983	Hal Sutton
1952	Julius Boros		1968	Not awarded		1984	Tom Watson
1953	Ben Hogan		1969	Orville Moody		1985	Lanny Wadkins
1954	Ed Furgol		1970	Billy Casper		1986	Bob Tway
1955	Doug Ford		1971	Lee Trevino		1987	Paul Azinger
1956	Jack Burke		1972	Jack Nicklaus		1988	Curtis Strange
1957	Dick Mayer		1973	Jack Nicklaus		1989	Tom Kite
1958	Dow Finsterwald		1974	Johnny Miller		1990	Wayne Levi
1959	Art Wall		1975	Jack Nicklaus		1991	Fred Couples
1960	Arnold Palmer		1976	Jack Nicklaus		1992	Fred Couples
1961	Jerry Barber		1977	Tom Watson		1993	Nick Price
1962	Arnold Palmer		1978	Tom Watson		1994	Nick Price
1963	Julius Boros		1979	Tom Watson		1995	Greg Norman

Vardon Trophy: Scoring Average

Year	Winner	Avg	Year	Winner	Avg	Year	Winner	Avg
1937	Harry Cooper	*500	1960	Billy Casper	69.95	1979	Tom Watson	70.27
1938	Sam Snead	520	1961	Arnold Palmer	69.85	1980	Lee Trevino	69.73
1939	Byron Nelson	473	1962	Arnold Palmer	70.27	1981	Tom Kite	69.80
1940	Ben Hogan	423	1963	Billy Casper	70.58	1982	Tom Kite	70.21
1941	Ben Hogan	494	1964	Arnold Palmer	70.01	1983	Raymond Floyd	70.61
1942-46	No award		1965	Billy Casper	70.85	1984	Calvin Peete	70.56
1947	Jimmy Demaret	69.90	1966	Billy Casper	70.27	1985	Don Pooley	70.36
1948	Ben Hogan	69.30	1967	Arnold Palmer	70.18	1986	Scott Hoch	70.08
1949	Sam Snead	69.37	1968	Billy Casper	69.82	1987	Don Pohl	70.25
1950	Sam Snead	69.23	1969	Dave Hill	70.34	1988	Chip Beck	69.46
1951	Lloyd Mangrum	70.05	1970	Lee Trevino	70.64	1989	Greg Norman	69.49
1952	Jack Burke	70.54	1971	Lee Trevino	70.27	1990	Greg Norman	69.10
1953	Lloyd Mangrum	70.22	1972	Lee Trevino	70.89	1991	Fred Couples	69.59
1954	E. J. Harrison	70.41	1973	Bruce Crampton	70.57	1992	Fred Couples	69.38
1955	Sam Snead	69.86	1974	Lee Trevino	70.53	1993	Nick Price	69.11
1956	Cary Middlecoff	70.35	1975	Bruce Crampton	70.51	1994	Greg Norman	68.81
1957	Dow Finsterwald	70.30	1976	Don January	70.56	1995	Steve Elkington	69.62
1958	Bob Rosburg	70.11	1977	Tom Watson	70.32			
1959	Art Wall	70.35	1978	Tom Watson	70.16			

*Point system used, 1937-41.

Note: As of 1988, based on minimum of 60 rounds per year.

Alltime PGA Tour Records*

Scoring

90 HOLES

325—(67-67-64-65-62) by Tom Kite, at four courses, La Quinta, CA, in winning the 1993 Bob Hope Classic (35 under par).

72 HOLES

257—(60-68-64-65) by Mike Souchak, at Bracken-ridge Park GC, San Antonio, to win 1955 Texas Open (27 under par).

54 HOLES

Opening rounds

191—(66-64-61) by Gay Brewer, at Pensacola CC, Pensacola, FL, in winning the 1967 Pensacola Open.

Consecutive rounds

189—(63-63-63) by Chandler Harper in the last three rounds to win the 1954 Texas Open at Brackenridge Park GC, San Antonio.

36 HOLES

Opening rounds

126—(64-62) by Tommy Bolt, at Cavalier Yacht & CC, Virginia Beach, VA, in 1954 Virginia Beach Open.

126—(64-62) by Paul Azinger, at Oak Hills CC, San Antonio, in 1989 Texas Open.

Consecutive rounds

125—(64-61) by Gay Brewer in the middle rounds of the 1967 Pensacola Open, which he won, at Pensacola CC, Pensacola, FL.

125—(63-62) by Ron Streck in the last two rounds to win the 1978 Texas Open at Oak Hills CC, San Antonio.

125—(62-63) by Blaine McCallister in the middle two rounds in winning the 1988 Hardee's Golf Classic at Oakwood CC, Coal Valley, IL.

18 HOLES

59—by Al Geiberger, at Colonial Country Club, Memphis, in second round in winning 1977 Memphis Classic.

59—by Chip Beck, at Sunrise Golf Club, Las Vegas, in third round of the 1991 Las Vegas Invitational.

9 HOLES

27—by Mike Souchak, at Brackenridge Park GC, San Antonio, on par-35 second nine of first round in 1955 Texas Open.

27—by Andy North at En-Joie GC, Endicott, NY, on par-34 second nine of first round in 1975 BC Open.

MOST CONSECUTIVE ROUNDS UNDER 70

19—Byron Nelson in 1945.

MOST BIRDIES IN A ROW

8—Bob Goalby at Pasadena GC, St Petersburg, FL, during fourth round in winning the 1961 St Petersburg Open.

8—Fuzzy Zoeller, at Oakwood CC, Coal Valley, IL, during first round of 1976 Quad Cities Open.

8—Dewey Arnette, Warwick Hills GC, Grand Blanc, MI, during first round of the 1987 Buick Open.

Scoring (Cont.)

MOST BIRDIES IN A ROW TO WIN

5—Jack Nicklaus to win 1978 Jackie Gleason Inverrary Classic (last 5 holes).

Wins

MOST CONSECUTIVE YEARS WINNING AT LEAST ONE TOURNAMENT

17—Jack Nicklaus, 1962-78.
17—Arnold Palmer, 1955-71.
16—Billy Casper, 1956-71.

MOST CONSECUTIVE WINS

11—Byron Nelson, from Miami Four Ball, March 8-11, 1945, through Canadian Open, August 2-4, 1945.

MOST WINS IN A SINGLE EVENT

8—Sam Snead, Greater Greensboro Open, 1938, 1946, 1949, 1950, 1955, 1956, 1960, and 1965.

MOST CONSECUTIVE WINS IN A SINGLE EVENT

4—Walter Hagen, PGA Championships, 1924-27.

MOST WINS IN A CALENDAR YEAR

18—Byron Nelson, 1945

MOST YEARS BETWEEN WINS

12—Howard Twitty, 1980–93.

MOST YEARS FROM FIRST WIN TO LAST

29—Sam Snead, 1936-65.
29—Ray Floyd, 1963-92.

YOUNGEST WINNERS

John McDermott, 19 years and 10 months, 1911 US Open.

OLDEST WINNER

Sam Snead, 52 years and 10 months, 1965 Greater Greensboro Open.

WIDEST WINNING MARGIN: STROKES

16—Bobby Locke, 1948 Chicago Victory National Championship.

Putting

FEWEST PUTTS, ONE ROUND

18—Andy North, at Kingsmill GC, in second round of 1990 Anheuser Busch Golf Classic.

18—Kenny Knox, at Harbour Town GL, in first round of 1989 MCI Heritage Classic.

18—Mike McGee, at Colonial CC, in first round of 1987 Federal Express St Jude Classic.

18—Sam Trahan, at Whitemarsh Valley CC, in final round of 1979 IVB Philadelphia Golf Classic.

18—Jim McGovern, at TPC at Southwind, in second round of 1992 Federal Express St. Jude Classic.

FEWEST PUTTS, FOUR ROUNDS

93—Kenny Knox, in 1989 MCI Heritage Classic at Harbour Town GL.

*Through 10/31/95.

THE MAJOR TOURNAMENTS

LPGA Championship

Year	Winner	Score	Runner-Up	Site
1955	Beverly Hanson† (4 and 3)	220	Louise Suggs	Orchard Ridge CC, Ft Wayne, IN
1956	Marlene Hagge* (5)	291	Patty Berg (6)	Forest Lake CC, Detroit
1957	Louise Suggs	285	Wiffi Smith	Churchill Valley CC, Pittsburgh
1958	Mickey Wright	288	Fay Crocker	Churchill Valley CC, Pittsburgh
1959	Betsy Rawls	288	Patty Berg	Sheraton Hotel CC, French Lick, IN
1960	Mickey Wright	292	Louise Suggs	Sheraton Hotel CC, French Lick, IN
1961	Mickey Wright	287	Louise Suggs	Stardust CC, Las Vegas
1962	Judy Kimball	282	Shirley Spork	Stardust CC, Las Vegas
1963	Mickey Wright	294	Mary Lena Faulk Mary Mills Louise Suggs	Stardust CC, Las Vegas
1964	Mary Mills	278	Mickey Wright	Stardust CC, Las Vegas
1965	Sandra Haynie	279	Clifford A. Creed	Stardust CC, Las Vegas
1966	Gloria Ehret	282	Mickey Wright	Stardust CC, Las Vegas
1967	Kathy Whitworth	284	Shirley Englehorn	Pleasant Valley CC, Sutton, MA
1968	Sandra Post* (68)	294	Kathy Whitworth (75)	Pleasant Valley CC, Sutton, MA
1969	Betsy Rawls	293	Susie Berning Carol Mann	Concord GC, Kiameshia Lake, NY
1970	Shirley Englehorn* (74)	285	Kathy Whitworth (78)	Pleasant Valley CC, Sutton, MA
1971	Kathy Whitworth	288	Kathy Ahern	Pleasant Valley CC, Sutton, MA
1972	Kathy Ahern	293	Jane Blalock	Pleasant Valley CC, Sutton, MA
1973	Mary Mills	288	Betty Burfeindt	Pleasant Valley CC, Sutton, MA
1974	Sandra Haynie	288	JoAnne Carner	Pleasant Valley CC, Sutton, MA
1975	Kathy Whitworth	288	Sandra Haynie	Pine Ridge GC, Baltimore
1976	Betty Burfeindt	287	Judy Rankin	Pine Ridge GC, Baltimore
1977	Chako Higuchi	279	Pat Bradley Sandra Post Judy Rankin	Bay Tree Golf Plantation, N. Myrtle Beach, SC
1978	Nancy Lopez	275	Amy Alcott	Jack Nicklaus GC, Kings Island, OH
1979	Donna Caponi	279	Jerilyn Britz	Jack Nicklaus GC, Kings Island, OH
1980	Sally Little	285	Jane Blalock	Jack Nicklaus GC, Kings Island, OH
1981	Donna Caponi	280	Jerilyn Britz Pat Meyers	Jack Nicklaus GC, Kings Island, OH
1982	Jan Stephenson	279	JoAnne Carner	Jack Nicklaus GC, Kings Island, OH
1983	Patty Sheehan	279	Sandra Haynie	Jack Nicklaus GC, Kings Island, OH
1984	Patty Sheehan	272	Beth Daniel Pat Bradley	Jack Nicklaus GC, Kings Island, OH
1985	Nancy Lopez	273	Alice Miller	Jack Nicklaus GC, Kings Island, OH
1986	Pat Bradley	277	Patty Sheehan	Jack Nicklaus GC, Kings Island, OH
1987	Jane Geddes	275	Betsy King	Jack Nicklaus GC, Kings Island, OH
1988	Sherri Turner	281	Amy Alcott	Jack Nicklaus GC, Kings Island, OH
1989	Nancy Lopez	274	Ayako Okamoto	Jack Nicklaus GC, Kings Island, OH
1990	Beth Daniel	280	Rosie Jones	Bethesda CC, Bethesda, MD
1991	Meg Mallon	274	Pat Bradley Ayako Okamoto	Bethesda CC, Bethesda, MD
1992	Betsy King	267	Karen Noble	Bethesda CC, Bethesda, MD
1993	Patty Sheehan	275	Lauri Merten	Bethesda CC, Bethesda, MD
1994	Laura Davies	279	Alice Ritzman	DuPont CC, Wilmington, DE
1995	Kelly Robbins	274	Laura Davies	DuPont CC, Wilmington, DE

*Won in playoff. Playoff scores are in parentheses. 1956 was sudden death; 1968 and 1970 were 18-hole playoffs.
†Won match play final.

U.S. Women's Open

Year	Winner	Score	Runner-Up	Site
1946	Patty Berg	5 & 4	Betty Jameson	Spokane CC, Spokane, WA
1947	Betty Jameson	295	Sally Sessions Polly Riley	Starmount Forest CC, Greensboro, NC
1948	Babe Zaharias	300	Betty Hicks	Atlantic City CC, Northfield, NJ
1949	Louise Suggs	291	Babe Zaharias	Prince George's G & CC, Landover, MD
1950	Babe Zaharias	291	Betsy Rawls	Rolling Hills CC, Wichita, KS
1951	Betsy Rawls	293	Louise Suggs	Druid Hills GC, Atlanta

U.S. Women's Open (Cont.)

Year	Winner	Score	Runner-Up	Site
1952	Louise Suggs	284	Marlene Bauer Betty Jameson	Bala GC, Philadelphia
1953	Betsy Rawls* (71)	302	Jackie Pung (77)	CC of Rochester, Rochester, NY
1954	Babe Zaharias	291	Betty Hicks	Salem CC, Peabody, MA
1955	Fay Crocker	299	Mary Lena Faulk Louise Suggs	Wichita CC, Wichita, KS
1956	Kathy Cornelius* (75)	302	Barbara McIntire (82)	Northland CC, Duluth, MN
1957	Betsy Rawls	299	Patty Berg	Winged Foot GC, Mamaroneck, NY
1958	Mickey Wright	290	Louise Suggs	Forest Lake CC, Detroit
1959	Mickey Wright	287	Louise Suggs	Churchill Valley CC, Pittsburgh
1960	Betsy Rawls	292	Joyce Ziske	Worcester CC, Worcester, MA
1961	Mickey Wright	293	Betsy Rawls	Baltusrol GC (Lower Course), Springfield, NJ
1962	Murle Breer	301	Jo Ann Prentice Ruth Jessen	Dunes GC, Myrtle Beach, SC
1963	Mary Mills	289	Sandra Haynie Louise Suggs	Kenwood CC, Cincinnati
1964	Mickey Wright* (70)	290	Ruth Jessen (72)	San Diego CC, Chula Vista, CA
1965	Carol Mann	290	Kathy Cornelius	Atlantic City CC, Northfield, NJ
1966	Sandra Spuzich	297	Carol Mann	Hazeltine Natl GC, Chaska, MN
1967	Catherine LaCoste	294	Susie Berning Beth Stone	Hot Springs GC (Cascades Course), Hot Springs, VA
1968	Susie Berning	289	Mickey Wright	Moslem Springs GC, Fleetwood, PA
1969	Donna Caponi	294	Peggy Wilson	Scenic Hills CC, Pensacola, FL
1970	Donna Caponi	287	Sandra Haynie Sandra Spuzich	Muskogee CC, Muskogee, OK
1971	JoAnne Carner	288	Kathy Whitworth	Kahkwa CC, Erie, PA
1972	Susie Berning	299	Kathy Ahern Pam Barnett Judy Rankin	Winged Foot GC, Mamaroneck, NY
1973	Susie Berning	290	Gloria Ehret Shelley Hamlin	CC of Rochester, Rochester, NY
1974	Sandra Haynie	295	Carol Mann Beth Stone	La Grange CC, La Grange, IL
1975	Sandra Palmer	295	JoAnne Carner Sandra Post Nancy Lopez	Atlantic City CC, Northfield, NJ
1976	JoAnne Carner* (76)	292	Sandra Palmer (78)	Rolling Green CC, Springfield, PA
1977	Hollis Stacy	292	Nancy Lopez	Hazeltine Natl GC, Chaska, MN
1978	Hollis Stacy	289	JoAnne Carner Sally Little	CC of Indianapolis, Indianapolis
1979	Jerilyn Britz	284	Debbie Massey Sandra Palmer	Brooklawn CC, Fairfield, CT
1980	Amy Alcott	280	Hollis Stacy	Richland CC, Nashville
1981	Pat Bradley	279	Beth Daniel	La Grange CC, La Grange, IL
1982	Janet Anderson	283	Beth Daniel Sandra Haynie Donna White JoAnne Carner	Del Paso CC, Sacramento
1983	Jan Stephenson	290	JoAnne Carner Patty Sheehan	Cedar Ridge CC, Tulsa
1984	Hollis Stacy	290	Rosie Jones	Salem CC, Peabody, MA
1985	Kathy Baker	280	Judy Dickinson	Baltusrol GC (Upper Course), Springfield, NJ
1986	Jane Geddes* (71)	287	Sally Little (73)	NCR GC, Dayton
1987	Laura Davies* (71)	285	Ayako Okamoto (73) JoAnne Carner (74)	Plainfield CC, Plainfield, NJ
1988	Liselotte Neumann	277	Patty Sheehan	Baltimore CC, Baltimore
1989	Betsy King	278	Nancy Lopez	Indianwood G & CC, Lake Orion, MI
1990	Betsy King	284	Patty Sheehan	Atlanta Athletic Club, Duluth, GA
1991	Meg Mallon	283	Pat Bradley	Colonial Club, Fort Worth
1992	Patty Sheehan* (72)	280	Juli Inkster	Oakmont CC, Oakmont, PA
1993	Lauri Merten	280	Donna Andrew Helen Alfredsson	Crooked Stick, Carmel, IN
1994	Patty Sheehan	277	Tammie Green	Indianwood G & CC, Lake Orion, MI
1995	Annika Sorenstam	278	Meg Mallon	The Broadmoor GC, Colorado Springs, CO

*Winner in playoff. 18-hole playoff scores are in parentheses.

Dinah Shore

Year	Winner	Score	Runner-Up
1972	Jane Blalock	213	Carol Mann, Judy Rankin
1973	Mickey Wright	284	Joyce Kazmierski
1974	Jo Ann Prentice*	289	Jane Blalock, Sandra Haynie
1975	Sandra Palmer	283	Kathy McMullen
1976	Judy Rankin	285	Betty Burfeindt
1977	Kathy Whitworth	289	JoAnne Carner, Sally Little
1978	Sandra Post*	283	Penny Pulz
1979	Sandra Post	276	Nancy Lopez
1980	Donna Caponi	275	Amy Alcott
1981	Nancy Lopez	277	Carolyn Hill
1982	Sally Little	278	Hollis Stacy, Sandra Haynie
1983	Amy Alcott	282	Beth Daniel, Kathy Whitworth
1984	Juli Inkster*	280	Pat Bradley
1985	Alice Miller	275	Jan Stephenson
1986	Pat Bradley	280	Val Skinner
1987	Betsy King*	283	Patty Sheehan
1988	Amy Alcott	274	Colleen Walker
1989	Juli Inkster	279	Tammie Green, JoAnne Carner
1990	Betsy King	283	Kathy Postlewait, Shirley Furlong
1991	Amy Alcott	273	Dottie Mochrie
1992	Dottie Mochrie*	279	Juli Inkster
1993	Helen Alfredsson	284	Amy Benz, Tina Barrett, Betsy King
1994	Donna Andrews	276	Laura Davies
1995	Nanci Bowen	285	Susie Redman

*Winner in sudden-death playoff.

Note: Designated fourth major in 1983.

Played at Mission Hills CC, Rancho Mirage, CA.

du Maurier Classic

Year	Winner	Score	Runner-Up	Site
1973	Jocelyne Bourassa*	214	Sandra Haynie Judy Rankin	Montreal GC, Montreal
1974	Carole Jo Callison	208	JoAnne Carner	Candiac GC, Montreal
1975	JoAnne Carner*	214	Carol Mann	St George's CC, Toronto
1976	Donna Caponi*	212	Judy Rankin	Cedar Brae G & CC, Toronto
1977	Judy Rankin	214	Pat Meyers Sandra Palmer	Lachute G & CC, Montreal
1978	JoAnne Carner	278	Hollis Stacy	St George's CC, Toronto
1979	Amy Alcott	285	Nancy Lopez	Richelieu Valley CC, Montreal
1980	Pat Bradley	277	JoAnne Carner	St George's CC, Toronto
1981	Jan Stephenson	278	Nancy Lopez Pat Bradley	Summerlea CC, Dorion, Quebec
1982	Sandra Haynie	280	Beth Daniel	St George's CC, Toronto
1983	Hollis Stacy	277	JoAnne Carner Alice Miller	Beaconsfield GC, Montreal
1984	Juli Inkster	279	Ayako Okamoto	St George's G & CC, Toronto
1985	Pat Bradley	278	Jane Geddes	Beaconsfield CC, Montreal
1986	Pat Bradley*	276	Ayako Okamoto	Board of Trade CC, Toronto
1987	Jody Rosenthal	272	Ayako Okamoto	Islesmere GC, Laval, Quebec
1988	Sally Little	279	Laura Davies	Vancouver GC, Coquitlam, British Columbia
1989	Tammie Green	279	Pat Bradley Betsy King	Beaconsfield GC, Montreal
1990	Cathy Johnston	276	Patty Sheehan	Westmount G & CC, Kitchener, Ontario
1991	Nancy Scranton	279	Debbie Massey	Vancouver GC, Coquitlam, British Columbia
1992	Sherri Steinhauer	277	Judy Dickinson	St. Charles CC, Winnipeg, Manitoba
1993	Brandie Burton	277	Betsy King	London Hunt and CC, London, Ontario
1994	Martha Nause	279	Michelle McGann	Ottawa Hunt and GC, Ottawa, Ont.
1995	Jenny Lidback	280	Liselotte Neumann	Beaconsfield GC, Pointe-Claire, Quebec

*Winner in sudden-death playoff.

Note: Designated third major in 1979.

THE LPGA TOUR

Season Money Leaders

		Earnings ($)			Earnings ($)
1950	Babe Zaharias	14,800	1973	Kathy Whitworth	82,864
1951	Babe Zaharias	15,087	1974	JoAnne Carner	87,094
1952	Betsy Rawls	14,505	1975	Sandra Palmer	76,374
1953	Louise Suggs	19,816	1976	Judy Rankin	150,734
1954	Patty Berg	16,011	1977	Judy Rankin	122,890
1955	Patty Berg	16,492	1978	Nancy Lopez	189,814
1956	Marlene Hagge	20,235	1979	Nancy Lopez	197,489
1957	Patty Berg	16,272	1980	Beth Daniel	231,000
1958	Beverly Hanson	12,639	1981	Beth Daniel	206,998
1959	Betsy Rawls	26,774	1982	JoAnne Carner	310,400
1960	Louise Suggs	16,892	1983	JoAnne Carner	291,404
1961	Mickey Wright	22,236	1984	Betsy King	266,771
1962	Mickey Wright	21,641	1985	Nancy Lopez	416,472
1963	Mickey Wright	31,269	1986	Pat Bradley	492,021
1964	Mickey Wright	29,800	1987	Ayako Okamoto	466,034
1965	Kathy Whitworth	28,658	1988	Sherri Turner	350,851
1966	Kathy Whitworth	33,517	1989	Betsy King	654,132
1967	Kathy Whitworth	32,937	1990	Beth Daniel	863,578
1968	Kathy Whitworth	48,379	1991	Pat Bradley	763,118
1969	Carol Mann	49,152	1992	Dottie Mochrie	693,335
1970	Kathy Whitworth	30,235	1993	Betsy King	595,992
1971	Kathy Whitworth	41,181	1994	Laura Davies	687,201
1972	Kathy Whitworth	65,063			

Career Money Leaders*

	Earnings ($)		Earnings ($)		Earnings ($)
1. Betsy King	4,892,873.50	11. Jane Geddes	2,269,254.30	21. Deb Richard	1,674,690.00
2. Pat Bradley	4,772,115.03	12. Rosie Jones	2,193,048.97	22. Sally Little	1,648,210.80
3. Beth Daniel	4,492,091.80	13. Juli Inkster	2,070,418.23	23. D. Ammaccapane	1,631,836.00
4. Patty Sheehan	4,455,399.01	14. Hollis Stacy	2,005,087.99	24. Chris Johnson	1,553,666.50
5. Nancy Lopez	4,064,802.83	15. Colleen Walker	1,991,323.71	25. Dawn Coe-Jones	1,529,175.57
6. Amy Aloctt	3,064,889.14	16. Judy Dickinson	1,990,807.92	26. Sherri Steinhauer	1,468,046.00
7. JoAnne Carner	2,840,071.63	17. Meg Mallon	1,862,059.00	27. Donna Caponi	1,387,919.73
8. Ayako Okamoto	2,715,678.85	18. Kathy Whitworth	1,726,597.01	28. Kathy Postlewait	1,381,510.27
9. Dottie Mochrie	2,574,716.00	19. Tammie Green	1,715,863.00	29. L. Neumann	1,364,478.00
10. Jan Stephenson	2,275,075.00	20. Laura Davies	1,685,657.00	30. Alice Ritzman	1,362,909.32

*Through 12/31/94.

LPGA Player of the Year

1966	Kathy Whitworth		1981	JoAnne Carner
1967	Kathy Whitworth		1982	JoAnne Carner
1968	Kathy Whitworth		1983	Patty Sheehan
1969	Kathy Whitworth		1984	Betsy King
1970	Sandra Haynie		1985	Nancy Lopez
1971	Kathy Whitworth		1986	Pat Bradley
1972	Kathy Whitworth		1987	Ayako Okamoto
1973	Kathy Whitworth		1988	Nancy Lopez
1974	JoAnne Carner		1989	Betsy King
1975	Sandra Palmer		1990	Beth Daniel
1976	Judy Rankin		1991	Pat Bradley
1977	Judy Rankin		1992	Dottie Mochrie
1978	Nancy Lopez		1993	Betsy King
1979	Nancy Lopez		1994	Beth Daniel
1980	Beth Daniel			

Vare Trophy: Best Scoring Average

		Avg			Avg			Avg
1953	Patty Berg	75.00	1967	Kathy Whitworth	72.74	1981	JoAnne Carner	71.75
1954	Babe Zaharias	75.48	1968	Carol Mann	72.04	1982	JoAnne Carner	71.49
1955	Patty Berg	74.47	1969	Kathy Whitworth	72.38	1983	JoAnne Carner	71.41
1956	Patty Berg	74.57	1970	Kathy Whitworth	72.26	1984	Patty Sheehan	71.40
1957	Louise Suggs	74.64	1971	Kathy Whitworth	72.88	1985	Nancy Lopez	70.73
1958	Beverly Hanson	74.92	1972	Kathy Whitworth	72.38	1986	Pat Bradley	71.10
1959	Betsy Rawls	74.03	1973	Judy Rankin	73.08	1987	Betsy King	71.14
1960	Mickey Wright	73.25	1974	JoAnne Carner	72.87	1988	Colleen Walker	71.26
1961	Mickey Wright	73.55	1975	JoAnne Carner	72.40	1989	Beth Daniel	70.38
1962	Mickey Wright	73.67	1976	Judy Rankin	72.25	1990	Beth Daniel	70.54
1963	Mickey Wright	72.81	1977	Judy Rankin	72.16	1991	Pat Bradley	70.76
1964	Mickey Wright	72.46	1978	Nancy Lopez	71.76	1992	Dottie Mochrie	70.80
1965	Kathy Whitworth	72.61	1979	Nancy Lopez	71.20	1993	Nancy Lopez	70.83
1966	Kathy Whitworth	72.60	1980	Amy Alcott	71.51	1994	Beth Daniel	70.90

Most Career Wins*

	Wins		Wins		Wins
Kathy Whitworth	88	JoAnne Carner	42	Pat Bradley	30
Mickey Wright	82	Sandra Haynie	42	Amy Alcott	29
Patty Berg	57	Carol Mann	38	Jane Blalock	29
Betsy Rawls	55	Patty Sheehan	32	Betsy King	29
Louise Suggs	50	Babe Zaharias	31	Judy Rankin	26
Nancy Lopez	47	Beth Daniel	31		

*Through 12/31/94.

Alltime LPGA Tour Records*

Scoring

72 HOLES

268—(66-67-69-66) by Nancy Lopez to win at the Willow Creek GC, High Point, NC, in the 1985 Henredon Classic (20 under par).

268—(67-63-70-68) by Beth Daniel to win at the Walnut Hills CC, E. Lansing, MI, in the 1994 Oldsmobile Classic (20 under par).

54 HOLES

197—(67-65-65) by Pat Bradley to win at the Rail GC, Springfield, Ill., in the 1991 Rail Charity Golf Classic (19 under par).

36 HOLES

129—(64-65) by Judy Dickinson at Pasadena Yacht & CC, St Petersburg, in the 1985 S&H Golf Classic (15 under par).

18 HOLES

62—by Mickey Wright at Hogan Park GC, Midland, TX, in the first round in winning the 1964 Tall City Open (9 under par).

62—by Vicki Fergon at Almaden G & CC, San Jose, CA, in the second round of the 1984 San Jose Classic (11 under par).

62—by Laura Davies at the Rail Golf Club, Springfield, Ill., in the first round of the 1991 Rail Charity Golf Classic (10 under par).

62—by Hollis Stacy at Meridian Valley Country Club, Seattle, WA, in the second round of the 1992 Safeco Classic (10 under par).

9 HOLES

28—by Mary Beth Zimmerman at Rail GC, 1984 Rail Charity Golf Classic, Springfield, IL (par 36). Zimmerman shot 64.

28—by Pat Bradley at Green Gables CC, Denver,

Scoring *(Cont.)*

9 HOLES *(Cont.)*

1984 Columbia Savings Classic (par 35). Bradley shot 65.

28—by Muffin Spencer-Devlin at Knollwood CC, Elmsford, NY, in winning the 1985 MasterCard International Pro-Am (par 35). Spencer-Devlin shot 64.

28—by Peggy Kirsch at Squaw Creek CC, Vienna, OH, in the 1991 Phar-Mor (par 35).

MOST CONSECUTIVE ROUNDS UNDER 70

9—Beth Daniel, in 1990.

MOST BIRDIES IN A ROW

8—Mary Beth Zimmerman at Rail GC in Springfield, IL, in the second round of the 1984 Rail Charity Classic. Zimmerman shot 64 (8 under par).

Wins

MOST CONSECUTIVE WINS IN SCHEDULED EVENTS

4—Mickey Wright, in 1962.
4—Mickey Wright, in 1963.
4—Kathy Whitworth, in 1969.

MOST CONSECUTIVE WINS IN ENTERED TOURNAMENTS

5—Nancy Lopez, in 1987.

MOST WINS IN A CALENDAR YEAR

13—Mickey Wright, in 1963.

WIDEST WINNING MARGIN, STROKES

14—Louise Suggs, 1949 US Women's Open.
14—Cindy Mackey, 1986 MasterCard Int'l Pro-Am.

*Through 12/31/94.

U.S. Senior Open

Year	Winner	Score	Runner-Up	Site
1980	Roberto DeVicenzo	285	William C. Campbell	Winged Foot GC, Mamaroneck, NY
1981	Arnold Palmer* (70)	289	Bob Stone (74)	Oakland Hills CC, Birmingham, MI
			Billy Casper (77)	
1982	Miller Barber	282	Gene Littler	Portland GC, Portland, OR
			Dan Sikes, Jr	
1983	Billy Casper* (75) (3)	288	Rod Funseth (75) (4)	Hazeltine GC, Chaska, MN
1984	Miller Barber	286	Arnold Palmer	Oak Hill CC, Rochester, NY
1985	Miller Barber	285	Roberto DeVicenzo	Edgewood Tahoe GC, Stateline, NV
1986	Dale Douglass	279	Gary Player	Scioto CC, Columbus, OH
1987	Gary Player	270	Doug Sanders	Brooklawn CC, Fairfield, CT
1988	Gary Player* (68)	288	Bob Charles (70)	Medinah CC, Medinah, IL
1989	Orville Moody	279	Frank Beard	Laurel Valley GC, Ligonier, PA
1990	Lee Trevino	275	Jack Nicklaus	Ridgewood CC, Paramus, NJ
1991	Jack Nicklaus (65)	282	Chi Chi Rodriguez (69)	Oakland Hills CC, Birmingham, MI
1992	Larry Laoretti	275	Jim Colbert	Saucon Valley CC, Bethlehem, PA
1993	Jack Nicklaus	278	Tom Weiskopf	Cherry Hills CC, Englewood, CO
1994	Simon Hobday	274	Jim Albus	Pinehurst Resort & CC, Pinehurst, NC
1995	Tom Weiskopf	275	Jack Nicklaus	Congressional CC, Bethesda, MD

*Winner in playoff. Playoff scores are in parentheses. The 1983 playoff went to one hole of sudden death after an 18-hole playoff.

SENIOR TOUR

Season Money Leaders*

Year	Leader	Earnings ($)	Year	Leader	Earnings ($)
1980	Don January	44,100	1988	Bob Charles	533,929
1981	Miller Barber	83,136	1989	Bob Charles	725,887
1982	Miller Barber	106,890	1990	Lee Trevino	1,190,518
1983	Don January	237,571	1991	Mike Hill	1,065,657
1984	Don January	328,597	1992	Lee Trevino	1,027,002
1985	Peter Thomson	386,724	1993	Dave Stockton	1,175,944
1986	Bruce Crampton	454,299	1994	Dave Stockton	1,402,519
1987	Chi Chi Rodriguez	509,145			

Career Money Leaders*

	Player	Earnings ($)		Player	Earnings ($)
1.	Bob Charles	5,201,105	17.	Charles Coody	2,692,028
2.	Chi Chi Rodriguez	5,110,722	18.	Jim Albus	2,585,543
3.	Lee Trevino	5,108,902	19.	Ray Floyd	2,532,920
4.	Mike Hill	4,554,599	20.	Walter Zembriski	2,374,070
5.	George Archer	4,352,085	21.	Rocky Thompson	2,295,704
6	Dale Douglass	4,113,377	22.	Jim Ferree	2,126,146
7.	Jim Dent	3,618,605	23.	Dave Hill	2,067,259
8.	Bruce Crampton	3,604,534	24.	Simon Hobday	2,056,175
9.	Jim Colbert	3,498,521	25.	Gene Littler	2,044,991
10.	Gary Player	3,466,026	26.	Gibby Gilbert	2,009,702
11.	Miller Barber	3,393,652	27.	Don Bies	1,901,353
12.	Dave Stockton	3,247,885	28.	Jimmy Powell	1,822,473
13.	Al Geiberger	3,101,060	29.	J.C. Snead	1,805,843
14.	Orville Moody	3,057,323	30.	Bobby Nichols	1,637,662
15.	Harold Henning	2,942,073			
16.	Don January	2,827,192		*Through 12/31/94.	

Most Career Wins*

Player	Wins	Player	Wins
Miller Barber	24	Gary Player	17
Lee Trevino	24	Mike Hill	15
Chi Chi Rodriguez	22	Mike Hill	16
Don January	22	George Archer	15
Bob Charles	21	Orville Moody	11
Bruce Crampton	19	Peter Thompson	11

* Through 12/31/94.

MAJOR MEN'S AMATEUR CHAMPIONSHIPS

U.S. Amateur

Year	Winner	Score	Runner-Up	Site
1895	Charles B. Macdonald	12 & 11	Charles E. Sands	Newport GC, Newport, RI
1896	H. J. Whigham	8 & 7	J.G Thorp	Shinnecock Hills GC, Southampton, NY
1897	H. J. Whigham	8 & 6	W. Rossiter Betts	Chicago GC, Wheaton, IL
1898	Findlay S. Douglas	5 & 3	Walter B. Smith	Morris County GC, Morristown, NJ
1899	H. M. Harriman	3 & 2	Findlay S. Douglas	Onwentsia Club, Lake Forest, IL
1900	Walter Travis	2 up	Findlay S. Douglas	Garden City GC, Garden City, NY
1901	Walter Travis	5 & 4	Walter E. Egan	CC of Atlantic City, NJ
1902	Louis N. James	4 & 2	Eben M. Byers	Glen View Club, Golf, Ill.
1903	Walter Travis	5 & 4	Eben M. Byers	Nassau CC, Glen Cove, NY
1904	H. Chandler Egan	8 & 6	Fred Herreshoff	Baltusrol GC, Springfield, NJ
1905	H. Chandler Egan	6 & 5	D.E. Sawyer	Chicago GC, Wheaton, IL
1906	Eben M. Byers	2 up	George S. Lyon	Englewood GC, Englewood, NJ
1907	Jerry Travers	6 & 5	Archibald Graham	Euclid Club, Cleveland, OH
1908	Jerry Travers	8 & 7	Max H. Behr	Garden City GC, Garden City, NY
1909	Robert A. Gardner	4 & 3	H. Chandler Egan	Chicago GC, Wheaton, IL
1910	William C. Fownes, Jr	4 & 3	Warren K. Wood	The Country Club, Brookline, MA
1911	Harold Hilton	1 up	Fred Herreshoff	The Apawamis Club, Rye, NY
1912	Jerry Travers	7 & 6	Charles Evans, Jr.	Chicago GC, Wheaton, IL
1913	Jerry Travers	5 & 4	John G. Anderson	Garden City GC, Garden City, NY
1914	Francis Ouimet	6 & 5	Jerry Travers	Ekwanok CC, Manchester, VT
1915	Robert A. Gardner	5 & 4	John G. Anderson	CC of Detroit, Grosse Pt. Farms, MI
1916	Chick Evans	4 & 3	Robert A. Gardner	Merion Cricket Club, Haverford, PA
1917-18	No tournament			
1919	S. Davidson Herron	5 & 4	Bobby Jones	Oakmont CC, Oakmont, PA
1920	Chick Evans	7 & 6	Francis Ouimet	Engineers' CC, Roslyn, NY
1921	Jesse P. Guilford	7 & 6	Robert A. Gardner	St. Louis CC, Clayton, MO
1922	Jess W. Sweetser	3 & 2	Chick Evans	The Country Club, Brookline, MA
1923	Max R. Marston	1 up	Jess W. Sweetser	Flossmoor CC, Flossmoor, IL
1924	Bobby Jones	9 & 8	George Von Elm	Merion Cricket Club, Ardmore, PA
1925	Bobby Jones	8 & 7	Watts Gunn	Oakmont CC, Oakmont, PA
1926	George Von Elm	2 & 1	Bobby Jones	Baltusrol GC, Springfield, NJ
1927	Bobby Jones	8 & 7	Chick Evans	Minikahda Club, Minneapolis
1928	Bobby Jones	10 & 9	T. Phillip Perkins	Brae Burn CC, West Newton, MA
1929	Harrison R. Johnston	4 & 3	Dr. O.F. Willing	Del Monte G & CC, Pebble Beach, CA
1930	Bobby Jones	8 & 7	Eugene V. Homans	Merion Cricket Club, Ardmore, PA
1931	Francis Ouimet	6 & 5	Jack Westland	Beverly CC, Chicago, IL
1932	C. Ross Somerville	2 & 1	John Goodman	Baltimore CC, Timonium, MD
1933	George T. Dunlap, Jr	6 & 5	Max R. Marston	Kenwood CC, Cincinnati, OH
1934	Lawson Little	8 & 7	David Goldman	The Country Club, Brookline, MA
1935	Lawson Little	4 & 2	Walter Emery	The Country Club, Cleveland, OH
1936	John W. Fischer	1 up	Jack McLean	Garden City GC, Garden City, NY
1937	John Goodman	2 up	Raymond E. Billows	Alderwood CC, Portland, OR
1938	William P. Turnesa	8 & 7	B. Patrick Abbott	Oakmont CC, Oakmont, PA
1939	Marvin H. Ward	7 & 5	Raymond E. Billows	North Shore CC, Glenview, IL
1940	Richard D. Chapman	11 & 9	W. McCullough, Jr	Winged Foot GC, Mamaroneck, NY
1941	Marvin H. Ward	4 & 3	B. Patrick Abbott	Omaha Field Club, Omaha, NE
1942-45	No tournament			
1946	Ted Bishop	1 up	Smiley L. Quick	Baltusrol GC, Springfield, NJ
1947	Skee Riegel	2 & 1	John W. Dawson	Del Monte G & CC, Pebble Beach, CA
1948	William P. Turnesa	2 & 1	Raymond E. Billows	Memphis CC, Memphis, TN
1949	Charles R. Coe	11 & 10	Rufus King	Oak Hill CC, Rochester, NY
1950	Sam Urzetta	1 up	Frank Stranahan	Minneapolis GC, Minneapolis, MN
1951	Billy Maxwell	4 & 3	Joseph F. Gagliardi	Saucon Valley CC, Bethlehem, PA
1952	Jack Westland	3 & 2	Al Mengert	Seattle GC, Seattle, WA
1953	Gene Littler	1 up	Dale Morey	Oklahoma City G & CC, Oklahoma City
1954	Arnold Palmer	1 up	Robert Sweeny	CC of Detroit, Grosse Pt. Farms, MI
1955	E. Harvie Ward, Jr	9 & 8	Wm. Hyndman III	CC of Virginia, Richmond, VA
1956	E. Harvie Ward, Jr	5 & 4	Charles Kocsis	Knollwood Club, Lake Forest, IL
1957	Hillman Robbins, Jr	5 & 4	Dr. Frank M. Taylor	The Country Club, Brookline, MA
1958	Charles R. Coe	5 & 4	Tommy Aaron	Olympic Club, San Francisco, CA
1959	Jack Nicklaus	1 up	Charles R. Coe	Broadmoor GC, Colorado Springs, CO
1960	Deane Beman	6 & 4	Robert W. Gardner	St. Louis CC, Clayton, MO
1961	Jack Nicklaus	8 & 6	H. Dudley Wysong	Pebble Beach GL, Pebble Beach, CA

U.S. Amateur (Cont.)

Year	Winner	Score	Runner-Up	Site
1962	Labron E. Harris, Jr	1 up	Downing Gray	Pinehurst CC, Pinehurst, NC
1963	Deane Beman	2 & 1	Richard H. Sikes	Wakonda Club, Des Moines, IA
1964	William C. Campbell	1 up	Edgar M. Tutwiler	Canterbury GC, Cleveland, OH
1965	Robert J. Murphy, Jr	291	Robert B. Dickson	Southern Hills, CC, Tulsa, OK
1966	Gary Cowan	285-75	Deane Beman	Merion GC, Ardmore, PA
1967	Robert B. Dickson	285	Marvin Giles III	Broadmoor GC, Colorado Springs, CO
1968	Bruce Fleisher	284	Marvin Giles III	Scioto CC, Columbus, OH
1969	Steven N. Melnyk	286	Marvin Giles III	Oakmont CC, Oakmont, PA
1970	Lanny Wadkins	279	Tom Kite	Waverley CC, Portland, OR
1971	Gary Cowan	280	Eddie Pearce	Wilmington CC, Wilmington DE
1972	Marvin Giles, III	285	two tied	Charlotte CC, Charlotte, NC
1973	Craig Stadler	6 & 5	David Strawn	Inverness Club, Toledo, OH
1974	Jerry Pate	2 & 1	John P. Grace	Ridgewood CC, Ridgewood, NJ
1975	Fred Ridley	2 up	Keith Fergus	CC of Virginia, Richmond, VA
1976	Bill Sander	8 & 6	C. Parker Moore, Jr	Bel Air CC, Los Angeles, CA
1977	John Fought	9 & 8	Doug Fischesser	Aronimink GC, Newton Square, PA
1978	John Cook	5 & 4	Scott Hoch	Plainfield CC, Plainfield, NJ
1979	Mark O'Meara	8 & 7	John Cook	Canterbury GC, Cleveland, OH
1980	Hal Sutton	9 & 8	Bob Lewis	CC of North Carolina, Pinehurst, NC
1981	Nathaniel Crosby	1 up	Brian Lindley	Olympic Club, San Francisco, CA
1982	Jay Sigel	8 & 7	David Tolley	The Country Club, Brookline, MA
1983	Jay Sigel	8 & 7	Chris Perry	North Shore CC, Glenviedw IL
1984	Scott Verplank	4 & 3	Sam Randolph	Oak Tree GC, Edmond, OK
1985	Sam Randolph	1 up	Peter Persons	Montclair GC, West Orange, NJ
1986	Buddy Alexander	5 & 3	Chris Kite	Shoal Creek, Shoal Creek AL
1987	Bill Mayfair	4 & 3	Eric Rebmann	Jupiter Hills Club, Jupiter, FL
1988	Eric Meeks	7 & 6	Danny Yates	Va. Hot Springs G & CC, VA
1989	Chris Patton	3 & 1	Danny Green	Merion GC, Ardmore, PA
1990	Phil Mickelson	5 & 4	Manny Zerman	Cherry Hills CC, Englewood, CO
1991	Mitch Voges	7 & 6	Manny Zerman	The Honors Course, Ooltewah, TN
1992	Justin Leonard	8 & 7	Tom Scherrer	Muirfield Village GC, Dublin, OH
1993	John Harris	5 & 3	Danny Ellis	Champions GC, Houston, TX
1994	Tiger Woods	2 up	Trip Kuehne	TPC-Sawgrass, Ponte Vedre, FL
1995	Tiger Woods	2 up	Buddy Marucci	Newport Country Club, Newport, RI

Note: All stroke play from 1965 to 1972.

U.S. Junior Amateur

1948	Dean Lind	1964	Johnny Miller	1980	Eric Johnson
1949	Gay Brewer	1965	James Masserio	1981	Scott Erickson
1950	Mason Rudolph	1966	Gary Sanders	1982	Rich Marik
1951	Tommy Jacobs	1967	John Crooks	1983	Tim Straub
1952	Don Bisplinghoff	1968	Eddie Pearce	1984	Doug Martin
1953	Rex Baxter	1969	Aly Trompas	1985	Charles Rymer
1954	Foster Bradley	1970	Gary Koch	1986	Brian Montgomery
1955	William Dunn	1971	Mike Brannan	1987	Brett Quigley
1956	Harlan Stevenson	1972	Bob Byman	1988	Jason Widener
1957	Larry Beck	1973	Jack Renner	1989	David Duval
1958	Buddy Baker	1974	David Nevatt	1990	Mathew Todd
1959	Larry Lee	1975	Brett Mullin	1991	Tiger Woods
1960	Bill Tindall	1976	Madden Hatcher, III	1992	Tiger Woods
1961	Charles McDowell	1977	Willie Wood, Jr	1993	Tiger Woods
1962	Jim Wiechers	1978	Don Hurter	1994	Terry Noe
1963	Gregg McHatton	1979	Jack Larkin	1995	D. Scott Hailes

Note: Event is for amateur golfers younger than 18 years of age.

Mid-Amateur Championship

1981	Jim Holtgrieve	1986	Bill Loeffler	1991	Jim Stuart
1982	William Hoffer	1987	Jay Sigel	1992	Danny Yates
1983	Jay Sigel	1988	David Eger	1993	Jeff Thomas
1984	Mike Podolak	1989	James Taylor	1994	Tim Jackson
1985	Jay Sigel	1990	Jim Stuart	1995	Jerry Courville Jr

Note: Event is for amateur golfers at least 25 years of age.

British Amateur

1887 ....H. G. Hutchinson	1925 ....R. Harris	1964 ....C. Clark
1888 ....John Ball	1926 ....Jess Sweetser	1965 ....M. Bonallack
1889 .............J.E. Laidlay	1927 ....Dr. W. Tweddell	1966 .............C.R. Cole
1890 ....John Ball	1928 .............T.P. Perkins	1967 ....R. Dickson
1891 .............J.E. Laidlay	1929 .............C.J.H. Tolley	1968 ....M. Bonallack
1892 ....John Ball	1930 ....Robert T. Jones, Jr.	1969 ....M. Bonallack
1893 ....Peter Anderson	1931 ....E. Martin Smith	1970 ....M. Bonallack
1894 ....John Ball	1932 ....J. DeForest	1971 ....Steve Melnyk
1895 .............L.M.B. Melville	1933 ....M. Scott	1972 ....Trevor Homer
1896 .............F.G. Tait	1934 ....W. Lawson Little	1973 ....R. Siderowf
1897 .............A.J.T. Allan	1935 ....W. Lawson Little	1974 ....Trevor Homer
1898 .............F.G. Tait	1936 ....H. Thomson	1975 ....M. Giles
1899 ....John Ball	1937 ....R. Sweeney, Jr.	1976 ....R. Siderowf
1900 .............H.H. Hilton	1938 .............C.R. Yates	1977 ....P. McEvoy
1901 .............H.H. Hilton	1939 .............A.T. Kyle	1978 ....P. McEvoy
1902 ....C. Hutchings	1940-45 .... not held	1979 ....J. Sigel
1903 ....R. Maxwell	1946 ....J. Bruen	1980 ....D. Evans
1904 .............W.J. Travis	1947 ....Willie D. Turnesa	1981 ....P. Ploujoux
1905 .............A.G. Barry	1948 ....Frank R. Stranahan	1982 ....M. Thompson
1906 ....James Robb	1949 .............S.M. McReady	1983 ....A. Parkin
1907 ....John Ball	1950 ....Frank R. Stranahan	1984 .............J.M. Olazabal
1908 .............E.A. Lassen	1951 ....Richard D. Chapman	1985 ....G. McGimpsey
1909 ....R. Maxwell	1952 .............E.H. Ward	1986 ....D. Curry
1910 ....John Ball	1953 .............J.B. Carr	1987 ....P. Mayo
1911 .............H.H. Hilton	1954 .............D.W. Bachli	1988 ....C. Hardin
1912 ....John Ball	1955 .............J.W. Conrad	1989 ....S. Dodd
1913 .............H.H. Hilton	1956 .............J.C. Beharrel	1990 ....R. Muntz
1914 .............J.L.C. Jenkins	1957 ....R. Reid Jack	1991 ....G. Wolstenholme
1915-19 ....not held	1958 .............J.B. Carr	1992 ....S. Dundas
1920 .............C.J.H. Tolley	1959 ....Deane Beman	1993 ....I. Pyman
1921 .............W.I. Hunter	1960 .............J.B. Carr	1994 ....L. James
1922 .............E.W.E. Holderness	1961 ....M. Bonallack	1995 ....G. Sherry
1923 .............R.H. Wethered	1962 ....R. Davies	
1924 .............E.W.E. Holderness	1963 ....M. Lunt	

Amateur Public Links

1922 ....Edmund R. Held	1948 ....Michael R. Ferentz	1972 ....Bob Allard
1923 ....Richard J. Walsh	1949 ....Kenneth J. Towns	1973 ....Stan Stopa
1924 ....Joseph Coble	1950 ....Stanley Bielat	1974 ....Charles Barenaba
1925 ....Raymond J.	1951 ....Dave Stanley	1975 ....Randy Barenaba
..............McAuliffe	1952 ....Omer L. Bogan	1976 ....Eddie Mudd
1926 ....Lester Bolstad	1953 ....Ted Richards, Jr.	1977 ....Jerry Vidovic
1927 ....Carl F. Kauffmann	1954 ....Gene Andrews	1978 ....Dean Prince
1928 ....Carl F. Kauffmann	1955 ....Sam D. Kocsis	1979 ....Dennis Walsh
1929 ....Carl F. Kauffmann	1956 ....James H. Buxbaum	1980 ....Jodie Mudd
1930 ....Robert E. Wingate	1957 ....Don Essig III	1981 ....Jodie Mudd
1931 ....Charles Ferrera	1958 ....Daniel D. Sikes, Jr.	1982 ....Billy Tuten
1932 .............R.L. Miller	1959 ....William A. Wright	1983 ....Billy Tuten
1933 ....Charles Ferrera	1960 ....Verne Callison	1984 ....Bill Malley
1934 ....David A. Mitchell	1961 ....Richard H. Sikes	1985 ....Jim Sorenson
1935 ....Frank Strafaci	1962 ....Richard H. Sikes	1986 ....Bill Mayfair
1936 ....B. Patrick Abbott	1963 ....Robert Lunn	1987 ....Kevin Johnson
1937 ....Bruce N. McCormick	1964 ....William McDonald	1988 ....Ralph Howe, III
1938 ....Al Leach	1965 ....Arne Dokka	1989 ....Tim Hobby
1939 ....Andrew Szwedko	1966 ....Lamont Kaser	1990 ....Michael Combs
1940 ....Robert C. Clark	1967 ....Verne Callison	1991 ....David Berganio, Jr.
1941 ....William M. Welch, Jr.	1968 ....Gene Towry	1992 ....Warren Schulte
1942-45 ....not held	1969 ....John M. Jackson, Jr.	1993 ....David Berganio, Jr.
1946 ....Smiley L. Quick	1970 ....Robert Risch	1994 ....Guy Yamamoto
1947 ....Wilfred Crossley	1971 ....Fred Haney	1995 ....Chris Wollmann

U.S. Senior Golf

1955 ....J. Wood Platt	1969 ....Curtis Person, Sr	1983 ....William Hyndman, III
1956 ....Frederick J. Wright	1970 ....Gene Andrews	1984 ....Bob Rawlins
1957 ....J. Clark Espie	1971 ....Tom Draper	1985 ....Lewis W. Oehmig
1958 ....Thomas C. Robbins	1972 ....Lewis W. Oehmig	1986 ....Bo Williams
1959 ....J. Clark Espie	1973 ....William Hyndman, III	1987 ....John Richardson
1960 ....Michael Cestone	1974 ....Dale Morey	1988 ....Clarence Moore
1961 ....Dexter H. Daniels	1975 ....William F. Colm	1989 ....Bo Williams
1962 ....Merrill L. Carlsmith	1976 ....Lewis W. Oehmig	1990 ....Jackie Cummings
1963 ....Merrill L. Carlsmith	1977 ....Dale Morey	1991 ....Bill Bosshard
1964 ....William D. Higgins	1978 ....K. K. Compton	1992 ....Clarence Moore
1965 ....Robert B. Kiersky	1979 ....William C. Campbell	1993 ....Joe Ungvary
1966 ....Dexter H. Daniels	1980 ....William C. Campbell	1994 ....O. Gordon Brewer
1967 ....Ray Palmer	1981 ....Ed Updegraff	1995 ....James Stahl Jr
1968 ....Curtis Person, Sr	1982 ....Alton Duhon	

Event is for golfers at least 55 years of age.

MAJOR WOMEN'S AMATEUR CHAMPIONSHIPS

U.S. Women's Amateur

Year	Winner	Score	Runner-Up	Site
1895 ....Mrs. Charles S. Brown		132	Nellie Sargent	Meadow Brook Club, Hempstead, NY
1896 ....Beatrix Hoyt		2 & 1	Mrs. Arthur Turnure	Morris Couty GC, Morristown, NJ
1897 ....Beatrix Hoyt		5 & 4	Nellie Sargent	Essex County Club, Manchester, MA
1898 ....Beatrix Hoyt		5 &3	Maude Wetmore	Ardsley Club, Ardsley-on-Hudson, NY
1899 ....Ruth Underhill		2 & 1	Margaret Fox	Philadelphia CC, Philadelphia, PA
1900 ....Frances C. Griscom		6 & 5	Margaret Curtis	Shinnecock Hills GC, Shinnecock Hills, NY
1901 ....Genevieve Hecker		5 & 3	Lucy Herron	Baltusrol GC, Springfield, NJ
1902 ....Genevieve Hecker		4 & 3	Louisa A. Wells	The Country Club, Brookline, MA
1903 ....Bessie Anthony		7 & 6	J. Anna Carpenter	Chicago GC, Wheaton, IL
1904 ....Georgianna M. Bishop		5 & 3	Mrs. E.F. Sanford	Merion Cricket Club, Haverford, PA
1905 ....Pauline Mackay		1 up	Margaret Curtis	Morris County GC, Convent, NJ
1906 ....Harriot S. Curtis		2 & 1	Mary B. Adams	Brae Burn CC, West Newton, MA
1907 ....Margaret Curtis		7 & 6	Harriot S. Curtis	Midlothian CC, Blue Island, IL
1908 ....Katherine C. Harley		6 & 5	Mrs. T.H. Polhemus	Chevy Chase Club, Chevy Chase, MD
1909 ....Dorothy I. Campbell		3 & 2	Nonna Barlow	Merion Cricket Club, Haverford, PA
1910 ....Dorothy I. Campbell		2 & 1	Mrs. G.M. Martin	Homewood CC, Flossmoor, IL
1911 ....Margaret Curtis		5 & 3	Lillian B. Hyde	Baltusrol GC, Springfield, NJ
1912 ....Margaret Curtis		3 & 2	Nonna Barlow	Essex County Club, Manchester, MA
1913 ....Gladys Ravenscroft		2 up	Marion Hollins	Wilmington CC, Wilmington, DE
1914 ....Katherine Harley		1 up	Elaine V. Rosenthal	Nassau CC, Glen Cove, NY
1915 ....Florence Vanderbeck		3 & 2	Margaret Gavin	Onwentsia Club, Lake Forest, IL
1916 ....Alexa Stirling		2 & 1	Mildred Caverly	Belmont Springs CC, Waverley, MA
1917-18 ......No tournament				
1919 ....Alexa Stirling		6 & 5	Margaret Gavin	Shawnee CC, Shawnee-on Delaware, PA
1920 ....Alexa Stirling		5 & 4	Dorothy Campbell	Mayfield CC, Cleveland, OH
1921 ....Marion Hollins		5 & 4	Alexa Stirling	Hollywood GC, Deal, NJ.
1922 ....Glenna Collett		5 & 4	Margaret Gavin	Greenbrier GC, White Sulphur Springs, WV
1923 ....Edith Cummings		3 & 2	Alexa Stirling	Westchester-Biltmore CC, Rye, NY
1924 ....Dorothy Campbell		7 & 6	Mary K. Browne	Rhode Island CC, Nyatt, RI
1925 ....Glenna Collett		9 & 8	Alexa Stirling	St. Louis CC, Clayton, MO
1926 ....Helen Stetson		3 & 1	Elizabeth Goss	Merion Cricket Club, Ardmore, PA
1927 ....Miiriam Burns Horn		5 & 4	Maureen Orcutt	Cherry Valley Club, Garden City, NY
1928 ....Glenna Collett		13 & 12	Virginia Van Wie	Va. Hot Springs G & TC, Hot Springs, VA
1929 ....Glenna Collett		4 & 3	Leona Pressler	Oakland Hills CC, Birmingham, MI
1930 ....Glenna Collett		6 & 5	Virginia Van Wie	Los Angeles CC, Beverly Hills, CA
1931 ....Helen Hicks		2 & 1	Glenna Collet Vare	CC of Buffalo, Williamsville, NY
1932 ....Virginia Van Wie		10 & 8	Glenna Collet Vare	Salem CC, Peabody, MA
1933 ....Virginia Van Wie		4 & 3	Helen Hicks	Exmoor CC, Highland Park, IL
1934 ....Virginia Van Wie		2 & 1	Dorothy Traung	Whitemarsh Valley CC, Chestnut Hill, PA
1935 ....Glenna Collett Vare		3 & 2	Patty Berg	Interlachen CC, Hopkins, MN
1936 ....Pamela Barton		4 & 3	Maureen Orcutt	Canoe Brook CC, Summit, NJ
1937 ....Estelle Lawson		7 & 6	Patty Berg	Memphis CC, Memphis, TN
1938 ....Patty Berg		6 & 5	Estelle Lawson	Westmoreland CC, Wilmette, IL
1939 ....Betty Jameson		3 & 2	Dorothy Kirby	Wee Burn Club, Darien, CT

U.S. Women's Amateur (Cont.)

Year	Winner	Score	Runner-Up	Site
1940	Betty Jameson	6 & 5	Jane S. Cothran	Del Monte G & CC, Pebble Beach, CA
1941	Elizabeth Hicks	5 & 3	Helen Sigel	The Country Club, Brookline, MA
1942-45	No tournament			
1946	Babe Zaharias	11 & 9	Clara Sherman	Southern Hills CC, Tulsa, OK
1947	Louise Suggs	2 up	Dorothy Kirby	Franklin Hills CC, Franklin, MI
1948	Grace S. Lenczyk	4 & 3	Helen Sigel	Del Monte G & CC, Pebble Beach, CA
1949	Dorothy Porter	3 & 2	Dorothy Kielty	Merion GC, Ardmore, PA
1950	Beverly Hanson	6 & 4	Mae Murray	Atlanta AC, Atlanta, GA
1951	Dorothy Kirby	2 & 1	Claire Doran	Town & CC, St. Paul, MN
1952	Jacqueline Pung	2 & 1	Shirley McFedters	Waverley CC, Portland, OR
1953	Mary Lena Faulk	3 & 2	Polly Riley	Rhode Island CC, West Barrington, RI
1954	Barbara Romack	4 & 2	Mickey Wright	Allegheny CC, Sewickley, PA
1955	Patricia A. Lesser	7 & 6	Jane Nelson	Myers Park CC, Charlotte, NC
1956	Marlene Stewart	2 & 1	JoAnne Gunderson	Meridian Hills CC, Indianapolis, IN
1957	JoAnne Gunderson	8 & 6	Ann Casey Johnstone	Del Paso CC, Sacramento, CA
1958	Anne Quast	3 & 2	Barbara Romack	Wee Burn CC, Darien, CT
1959	Barbara McIntire	4 & 3	Joanne Goodwin	Congressional CC, Washington, D.C.
1960	JoAnne Gunderson	6 & 5	Jean Ashley	Tulsa CC, Tulsa, OK
1961	Anne Quast Sander	14 & 13	Phyllis Preuss	Tacoma G & CC, Tacoma, WA
1962	JoAnne Gunderson	9 & 8	Anne Baker	CC of Rochester, Rochester, NY
1963	Anne Quast Sander	2 & 1	Peggy Conley	Taconic GC, Williamstown, MA
1964	Barbara McIntire	3 & 2	JoAnne Gunderson	Prairie Dunes CC, Hutchinson, KS
1965	Jean Ashley	5 & 4	Anne Quast Sander	Lakewood CC, Denver, CO
1966	JoAnne Gunderson	1 up	Marlene Stewart Streit	Sewickley Heights GC, Sewickley, PA
1967	Mary Lou Dill	5 & 4	Jean Ashley	Annandale GC, Pasadena, CA
1968	JoAnne Gunderson Carner	5 & 4	Anne Quast Sander	Birmingham CC, Birmingham, MI
1969	Catherine Lacoste	3 & 2	Shelley Hamling	Las Colinas CC, Irving, TX
1970	Martha Wilkinson	3 & 2	Cynthia Hall	Wee Burn CC, Darien, CT
1971	Laura Baugh	1 up	Beth Barry	Atlanta CC, Atlanta, GA
1972	Mary Budke	5 & 4	Cynthia Hill	St. Louis CC, St. Louis, MO
1973	Carol Semple	1 up	Anne Quast Sander	Montclair GC, Montclair, NJ
1974	Cynthia Hill	5 & 4	Carol Semple	Broadmoor, Seattle, WA
1975	Beth Daniel	3 & 2	Donna Horton	Brae Burn CC, West Newton, MA
1976	Donna Horton	2 & 1	Marianne Bretton	Del Paso CC, Sacramento, CA
1977	Beth Daniel	3 & 1	Cathy Sherk	Cincinnati CC, Cincinnati, OH
1978	Cathy Sherk	4 & 3	Judith Oliver	Sunnybrook GC, Plymouth Meeting, PA
1979	Carolyn Hill	7 & 6	Patty Sheehan	Memphis CC, Memphis, TN
1980	Juli Inkster	2 up	Patti Rizzo	Prairie Dunes CC, Hutchinson, KS
1981	Juli Inkster	1 up	Lindy Goggin	Waverley CC, Portland, OR
1982	Juli Inkster	4 & 3	Cathy Hanlon	Broadmoor GC, Colorado Springs, CO
1983	Joanne Pacillo	2 & 1	Sally Quinlan	Canoe Brook CC, Summit, NJ
1984	Deb Richard	1 up	Kimberly Williams	Broadmoor GC, Seattle, WA
1985	Michiko Hattori	5 & 4	Cheryl Stacy	Fox Chapel CC, Pittsburgh, PA
1986	Kay Cockerill	9 & 7	Kathleen McCarthy	Pasatiempo GC, Santa Cruz, CA
1987	Kay Cockerill	3 & 2	Tracy Kerdyk	Rhode Island CC, Barrington, RI
1988	Pearl Sinn	6 & 5	Karen Noble	Minikahda Club, Miinneapolis, MN
1989	Vicki Goetze	4 & 3	Brandie Burton	Pinehurst CC (No. 2), Pinehurst, NC
1990	Pat Hurst	37 holes	Stephanie Davis	Canoe Brook CC, Summit, NJ
1991	Amy Fruhwirth	5 & 4	Heidi Voorhees	Prairie Dunes CC, Hutchinson, KN
1992	Vicki Goetz	1-up	Annika Sorensteam	Kemper Lakes GC, Hawthorne Hills, IL
1993	Jill McGill	1-up	Sarah Ingram	San Diego CC, Chula Vista, CA
1994	Wendy Ward	2 & 1	Jill McGill	The Homestead, Hot Springs, WV
1995	Kelli Kuehne	4 & 3	Anne-Marie Knight	The Country Club, Brookline, MA

Girls' Junior Championship

1949 ....Marlene Bauer	1966 ....Claudia Mayhew	1983 ....Kim Saiki
1950 ....Patricia Lesser	1967 ....Elizabeth Story	1984 ....Cathy Mockett
1951 ....Arlene Brooks	1968 ....Peggy Harmon	1985 ....Dana Lofland
1952 ....Mickey Wright	1969 ....Hollis Stacy	1986 ....Pat Hurst
1953 ....Millie Meyerson	1970 ....Hollis Stacy	1987 ....Michelle McGann
1954 ....Margaret Smith	1971 ....Hollis Stacy	1988 ....Jamille Jose
1955 ....Carole Jo Kabler	1972 ....Nancy Lopez	1989 ....Brandie Burton
1956 ....JoAnne Gunderson	1973 ....Amy Alcott	1990 ....Sandrine Mendiburu
1957 ....Judy Eller	1974 ....Nancy Lopez	1991 ....Emilee Klein
1958 ....Judy Eller	1975 ....Dayna Benson	1992 ....Jamie Koizumi
1959 ....Judy Rand	1976 ....Pilar Dorado	1993 ....Kellee Booth
1960 ....Carol Sorenson	1977 ....Althea Tome	1962 ....Maureen Orcutt
1961 ....Mary Lowell	1978 ....Lori Castillo	1963 ....Sis Choate
1962 ....Mary Lou Daniel	1979 ....Penny Hammel	1994 ....Kelli Kuehne
1963 ....Janis Ferraris	1980 ....Laurie Rinker	1995 ....Marcy Newton
1964 ....Peggy Conley	1981 ....Kay Cornelius	
1965 ....Gail Sykes	1982 ....Heather Farr	

Women's British Amateur

1893 ....Lady Margaret Scott	1927 ....Miss Thion de la	1961 ....M. Spearman
1894 ....Lady Margaret Scott	Chaume	1962 ....M. Spearman
1895 ....Lady Margaret Scott	1928 ....Miss N. Le Blan	1963 ....B. Varangot
1896 ....Miss Pascoe	1929 ....Miss J. Wethered	1964 ....C. Sorenson
1897 ....Miss E.C. Orr	1930 ....Miss D. Fishwick	1965 ....B. Varangot
1898 ....Miss L. Thomson	1931 ....Miss E. Wilson	1966 ....E. Chadwick
1899 ....Miss M. Hezlet	1932 ....Miss E. Wilson	1967 ....E. Chadwick
1900 ....Miss Adair	1933 ....Miss E. Wilson	1968 ....B. Varangot
1901 ....Miss Graham	1934 ....Mrs. A.M. Holm	1975 ....C. Lacoste
1902 ....Miss M. Hezlet	1935 ....Miss W. Morgan	1976 ....D. Oxley
1903 ....Miss Adair	1936 ....Miss P. Barton	1977 ....A. Uzielli
1904 ....Miss L. Dod	1937 ....Miss J. Anderson	1978 ....E. Kennedy
1905 ....Miss B. Thompson	1938 ....Mrs. A.M. Holm	1979 ....M. Madill
1906 ....Mrs. Kennon	1939 ....Miss P. Barton	1980 ....A. Quast
1907 ....Miss M. Hezlet	1940–45 ....not held	1981 ..............I.C. Robertson
1908 ....Miss M. Titterton	1946 ..............G.W. Hetherington	1982 ....K. Douglas
1909 ....Miss D. Campbell	1947 ....B. Zaharias	1983 ....J. Thornhill
1910 ....Miss Grant Suttie	1948 ....L. Suggs	1984 ....J. Rosenthal
1911 ....Miss D. Campbell	1949 ....F. Stephens	1985 ....L. Beman
1912 ....Miss G. Ravenscroft	1950 ....Vicomtesse de Saint	1986 ....M. McGuire
1913 ....Miss M. Dodd	Sauveur	1987 ....J. Collingham
1914 ....Miss C. Leitch	1951 ..............P.J. MacCann	1988 ....J. Furby
1915–19 ....not held	1952 ....M. Paterson	1989 ....H. Dobson
1920 ....Miss C. Leitch	1953 ....M. Stewart	1990 ....J. Hall
1921 ....Miss C. Leitch	1954 ....F. Stephens	1991 ....V. Michaud
1922 ....Miss J. Wethered	1955 ....J. Valentine	1992 ....P. Pedersen
1923 ....Miss D. Chambers	1956 ....M. Smith	1993 ....Catriona Lambert
1924 ....Miss J. Wethered	1957 ....P. Garvey	1994 ....Emma Duggleby
1925 ....Miss J. Wethered	1958 ....J. Valentine	1995 ....Julie Hall
1926 ....Miss C. Leitch	1959 ....E. Price	
	1960 ....B. McIntyre	

Women's Amateur Public Links

1977 ....Kelly Fuiks	1984 ....Heather Farr	1990 ....Cathy Mockett
1978 ....Kelly Fuiks	1985 ....Danielle	1991 ....Tracy Hanson
1979 ....Lori Castillo	Ammaccapane	1992 ....Amy Fruhwirth
1980 ....Lori Castillo	1986 ....Cindy Schreyer	1993 ....Connie Masterson
1981 ....Mary Enright	1987 ....Tracy Kerdyk	1994 ....Jill McGill
1982 ....Nancy Taylor	1988 ....Pearl Sinn	1995 ....Jo Jo Robertson
1983 ....Kelli Antolock	1989 ....Pearl Sinn	

U.S. Senior Women's Amateur

1964 ....Loma Smith	1975 ....Alberta Bower	1986 ....Connie Guthrie
1965 ....Loma Smith	1976 ....Cecile H. Maclaurin	1987 ....Anne Sander
1966 ....Maureen Orcutt	1977 ....Dorothy Porter	1988 ....Lois Hodge
1967 ....Marge Mason	1978 ....Alice Dye	1989 ....Anne Sander
1968 ....Carolyn Cudone	1979 ....Alice Dye	1990 ....Anne Sander
1969 ....Carolyn Cudone	1980 ....Dorothy Porter	1991 ....Phyllis Preuss
1970 ....Carolyn Cudone	1981 ....Dorothy Porter	1992 ....Rosemary Thompson
1971 ....Carolyn Cudone	1982 ....Edean Ihlanfeldt	1993 ....Anne Sander
1972 ....Carolyn Cudone	1983 ....Dorothy Porter	1994 ....Marlene Streit
1973 ....Gwen Hibbs	1984 ....Constance Guthrie	1995 ....Jean Smith
1974 ....Justine Cushing	1985 ....Marlene Streit	

Women's Mid-Amateur Championship

1987	Cindy Scholefield
1988	Martha Lang
1989	Robin Weiss
1990	Carol Semple Thompson
1991	Sarah LeBrun Ingram
1992	Marion Mamey-McInerney
1993	Sarah Ingram
1994	Sarah Ingram
1995	Ellen Port

International Golf

Ryder Cup Matches

Year	Results	Site
1927	United States 9½, Great Britain 2½	Worcester CC, Worcester, MA
1929	Great Britain 7, United States 5	Moortown GC, Leeds, England
1931	United States 9, Great Britain 3	Scioto CC, Columbus, OH
1933	Great Britain 6½, United States 5½	Southport and Ainsdale Courses, Southport, England
1935	United States 9, Great Britain 3	Ridgewood CC, Ridgewood, NJ
1937	United States 8, Great Britain 4	Southport and Ainsdale Courses, Southport, England
1939-1945	No tournament	
1947	United States 11, Great Britain 1	Portland GC, Portland, OR
1949	United States 7, Great Britain 5	Ganton GC, Scarborough, England
1951	United States 9½, Great Britain 2½	Pinehurst CC, Pinehurst, NC
1953	United States 6½, Great Britain 5½	Wentworth Club, Surrey, England
1955	United States 8, Great Britain 4	Thunderbird Ranch & CC, Palm Springs, CA
1957	Great Britain 7½, United States 4½	Lindrick GC, Yorkshire, England
1959	United States 8½, Great Britain 3½	Eldorado CC, Palm Desert, CA
1961	United States 14½, Great Britain 9½	Royal Lytham & St Anne's GC, St Anne's-on-the-Sea, England
1963	United States 23, Great Britain 9	East Lake CC, Atlanta
1965	United States 19½, Great Britain 12½	Royal Birkdale GC, Southport, England
1967	United States 23½, Great Britain 8½	Champions GC, Houston
1969	United States 16, Great Britain 16	Royal Birkdale GC, Southport, England
1971	United States 18½, Great Britain 13½	Old Warson CC, St Louis
1973	United States 19, Great Britain 13	Hon Co of Edinburgh Golfers, Muirfield, Scotland
1975	United States 21, Great Britain 11	Laurel Valley GC, Ligonier, PA
1977	United States 12½, Great Britain 7½	Royal Lytham & St Anne's GC, St Anne's-on-the-Sea, England
1979	United States 17, Europe 11	Greenbrier, White Sulphur Springs, WV
1981	United States 18½, Europe 9½	Walton Heath GC, Surrey, England
1983	United States 14½, Europe 13½	PGA National GC, Palm Beach Gardens, FL
1985	Europe 16½, United States 11½	Belfry GC, Sutton Coldfield, England
1987	Europe 15, United States 13	Muirfield GC, Dublin, OH
1989	Europe 14, United States 14	Belfry GC, Sutton Coldfield, England
1991	United States 14½, Europe 13½	Ocean Course, Kiawah Island, SC
1993	United States 15, Europe 13	Belfry GC, Sutton Coldfield, England
1995	Europe 14½, United States 13½	Oak Hill CC, Rochester, NY

Team matches held every odd year between US professionals and those of Great Britain/Europe (since 1979, prior to which was US vs GB). Team members selected on basis of finishes in PGA and European tour events.

Walker Cup Matches

Year	Results	Site
1922	United States 8, Great Britain 4	Nat. Golf Links of America, Southampton, NY
1923	United States 6, Great Britain 5	St. Andrews, Scotland
1924	United States 9, Great Britain 3	Garden City GC, Garden City, NY
1926	United States 6, Great Britain 5	St. Andrews, Scotland
1928	United States 11, Great Britain 1	Chicago GC, Wheaton, IL
1930	United States 10, Great Britain 2	Royal St. George GC, Sandwich, England
1932	United States 8, Great Britain 1	The Country Club, Brookline, MA
1934	United States 9, Great Britain 2	St. Andrews, Scotland
1936	United States 9, Great Britain 0	Pine Valley GC, Clementon, NJ
1938	Great Britain 7, United States 4	St. Andrews, Scotland
1940-46	No tournament	
1947	United States 8, Great Britain 4	St. Andrews, Scotland
1949	United States 10, Great Britain 2	Winged Foot GC, Mamaroneck, NY
1951	United States 6, Great Britain 3	Birkdale GC, Southport, England
1953	United States 9, Great Britain 3	The Kittansett Club, Marion, MA
1955	United States 10, Great Britain 2	St. Andrews, Scotland
1957	United States 8, Great Britain 3	Minikahda Club, Minneapolis, MN
1959	United States 9, Great Britain 3	Muirfield, Scotland
1961	United States 11, Great Britain 1	Seattle GC, Seattle, WA
1963	United States 12, Great Britain 8	Ailsa Course, Turnberry, Scotland
1965	Great Britain 11, United States 11	Baltimore CC, Five Farms, Baltimore, MD
1967	United States 13, Great Britain 7	Royal St. George's GC, Sandwich, England
1969	United States 10, Great Britain 8	Milwaukee CC, Milwaukee, WI
1971	Great Britain 13, United States 11	St. Andrews, Scotland
1973	United States 14, Great Britain 10	The Country Club, Brookline, MA
1975	United States 15½, Great Britain 8½	St. Andrews, Scotland
1977	United States 16, Great Britain 8	Shinnecock Hills GC, Southampton, NY
1979	United States 15½, Great Britain 8½	Muirfield, Scotland
1981	United States 15, Great Britain 9	Cypress Point Club, Pebble Beach, CA
1983	United States 13½, Great Britain 10½	Royal Liverpool GC, Hoylake, England
1985	United States 13, Great Britain 11	Pine Valley GC, Pine Valley, NJ
1987	United States 16½, Great Britain 7½	Sunningdale GC, Berkshire, England
1989	Great Britain 12½, United States 11½	Peachtree Golf Club, Atlanta, GA
1991	United States 14, Great Britain 10	Portmarnock, Dublin, Ireland
1993	United States 19, Great Britain 5	Interlachen CC, Edina, MN
1995	Great Britain/Ireland 14, United States 10	Royal Porthcawl, Porthcawl, Wales

Men's amateur team competition every other year between United States and Great Britain. US team members selected by USGA.

Curtis Cup Matches

Year	Results	Site
1932	United States 5½, British Isles 3½	Wentworth GC, Wentworth, England
1934	United States 6½, British Isles 2½	Chevy Chase Club, Chevy Chase, MD
1936	United States 4½, British Isles 4½	King's Course, Gleneagles, Scotland
1938	United States 5½, British Isles 3½	Essex CC, Manchester, MA
1940-46	No tournament	
1948	United States 6½, British Isles 2½	Birkdale GC, Southport, England
1950	United States 7½, British Isles 1½	CC of Buffalo, Williamsville, NY
1952	British Isles 5, United States 4	Muirfield, Scotland
1954	United States 6, British Isles 3	Merion GC, Ardmore, PA
1956	British Isles 5, United States 4	Prince's GC, Sandwich Bay, England
1958	British Isles 4½, United States 4½	Brae Burn CC, West Newton, Mass.
1960	United States 6½, British Isles 2½	Lindrick GC, Worksop, England
1962	United States 8, British Isles 1	Broadmoor CG, Colorado Springs,CO
1964	United States 10½, British Isles 7½	Royal Porthcawl GC, Porthcawl, South Wales
1966	United States 13, British Isles 5	Va. Hot Springs G & TC, Hot Springs, VA
1968	United States 10½, British Isles 7½	Royal County Down GC, Newcastle, N. Ire.
1970	United States 11½, British Isles 6½	Brae Burn CC, West Newton, MA
1972	United States 10, British Isles 8	Western Gailes, Ayrshire, Scotland
1974	United States 13, British Isles 5	San Francisco GC, San Francisco, CA
1976	United States 11½, British Isles 6½	Royal Lytham & St. Annes GC, England

Curtis Cup Matches (Cont.)

Year	Results	Site
1978	United States 12, British Isles 6	Apawamis Club, Rye, NY
1980	United States 13, British Isles 5	St. Pierre G & CC, Chepstow, Wales
1982	United States 14½, British Isles 3½	Denver CC, Denver, CO
1984	United States 9½, British Isles 8½	Muirfield, Scotland
1986	British Isles 13, United States 5	Prairie Dunes CC, Hutchinson, KS
1988	British Isles 11, United States 7	Royal St. George's GC, Sandwich, England
1990	United States 14, British Isles 4	Somerset Hills CC, Bernardsville, NJ
1992	Great Britain/Ireland 10, United States 8	Royal Liverpool GC, Hoylake, England
1994	Great Britain/Ireland 9, United States 9	The Honors Course, Ooltewah, TN

Women's amateur team competition every other year between the United States and Great Britain. US team members selected by USGA.

Fin de Siècle Shot

More than 38,000 holes in one are recorded annually in the U.S. Many of them are sunk by such worm burners as Brad Hockmeyer, a 44-year-old broadcasting executive who registered his first-ever hole in one last month at the Taos (N. Mex.) Country Club. What made Hockmeyer's ace notable was that it occurred on the 100th anniversary of what was, according to at least one account, the first hole in one in American history. The duffer who drained that shot? The late Otto Hockmeyer, Brad's great-grandfather.

While the significance of his feat was not lost on him, Brad had a more pressing concern. "I talked to somebody who once got a hole in one and had to spend $800 buying the club drinks," says Hockmeyer, referring to the traditional post-ace ritual. Otto's great-grandson was lucky: Taos C.C. has yet to construct a 19th hole.

Boxing

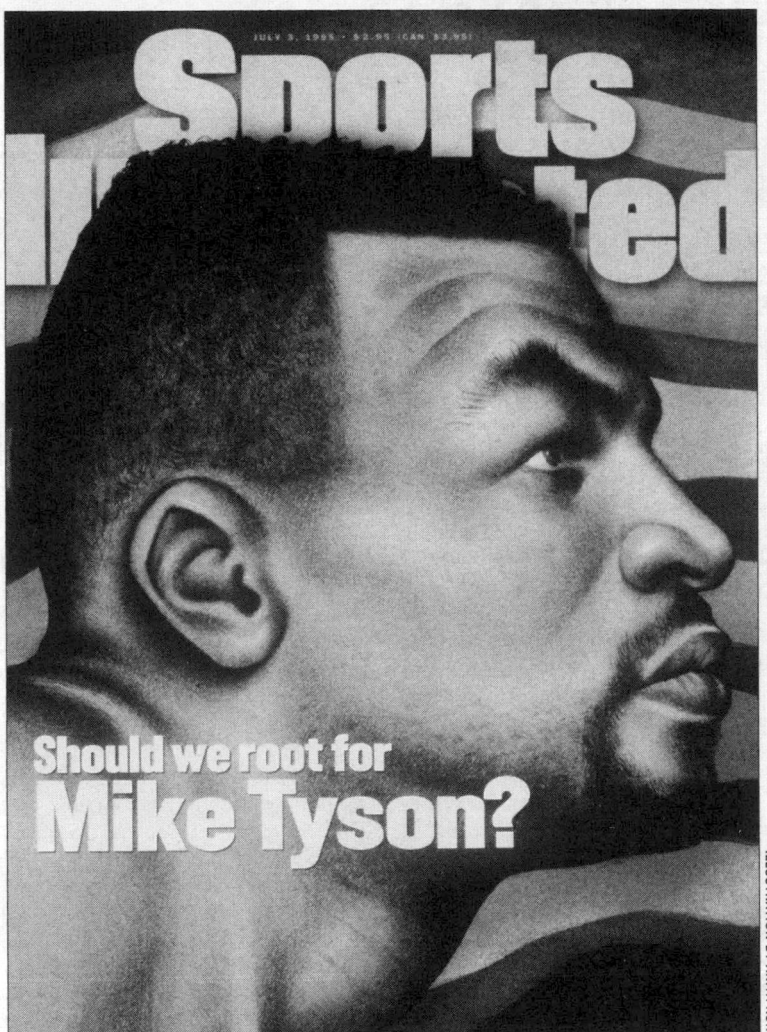

JULY 3, 1995 • $2.95 (CAN $3.95)

Sports Illustrated

Should we root for Mike Tyson?

Return of a Heavy

When Mike Tyson walked out of an Indiana prison in March, no one knew precisely how to handicap his boxing future

by Richard Hoffer

A MAN walked out of prison in the Indiana dawn last March, ducked into a black limousine and led a covey of helicopters, a fleet of rental cars, an armada of mini-cammed minivans down a two-lane road to a ... mosque. It was one of the most improbable left turns in all of sports history. Mike Tyson, boxing's most electrifying performer until his rape conviction and three-year prison term, had made prayer the first order of business upon freedom. And nobody could know what it signified. Wearing a white *kufi* cap, he knelt quietly on the soft carpet, met with religious leaders, took counsel from a similarly converted Muhammad Ali and then disappeared. Into retirement? Training? A life of good works? It was impossible to say.

But it was important to know. The game had been in a deepening state of confusion ever since he left. To be sure, he precipitated some of that confusion, losing the heavyweight titles he had so spectacularly unified to Buster Douglas in 1990. But the turnover of titles after that became almost comical (not to mention—talk about comedy—the

invention of three more governing bodies, bringing the number of potential champions to six). In the hapless parade of pretenders, some had not the skill to retain a title and some had not the sense. The period is memorable for big George Foreman, at 45, winning one of the titles from Michael Moorer (with one punch) and for young Riddick Bowe actually discarding one of his in a garbage can (from which it was more or less retrieved by Lennox Lewis, who immediately lost it to Oliver McCall, who handed off to Frank Bruno—you get the idea).

So here was Mike Tyson, only 29 at his release, able but perhaps not willing to resuscitate boxing. His longtime promoter Don King had gotten control of two extremely mediocre heavyweight champions by the time Tyson was sprung (the third mediocre champion would come into his fold a little later), thus preparing the stage for the fighter's return to title-unifying glory. All Tyson had to do was give a nod.

Well, he finally nodded. After a monumental spending spree—new cars for friends, fabulous threads for himself, and a

ANDY UZZLE

new compound in Las Vegas—he re-upped with King, aligned himself with two boyhood friends as managers and signed a six-fight deal with the MGM Grand and Showtime's pay-per-view arm for a minimum of $35 million. Then he got down to training. Although he worked secretly and allowed no more than passing glimpses of his growing bulk, boxing was nevertheless relieved. Tyson had made his intentions plain. He was back.

He returned just in time. Not only had the heavyweight division grown ridiculous, with 45-year-old Larry Holmes nearly outpointing McCall in a title fight and Foreman abandoning all his titles rather than suffer a rematch with the redoubtable Axel Schulz, but the rest of boxing suffered as well. Although there were memorable performances—super middleweight champion Roy Jones Jr. solidified his "pound-for-pound" title (won in 1994's methodical destruction of James Toney) with an impressive dismantling of Vinny Pazienza in June—there was far more despair than delight in 1995.

Shortly before Tyson's release from

His look was tough, but Tyson's first fight revealed little about his skills.

prison, former middleweight champion Gerald McClellan traveled to London in grim pursuit of Nigel Benn's WBC super middleweight title. McClellan, who often compared himself to his three pit bulls, was a vicious fighter accustomed to quick knockouts. He'd had eight first-round knockouts in his last 10 fights, including his last three title defenses. He was a violent caricature of a boxer, the kind of character much celebrated in the ring. And indeed McClellan knocked Benn clean out of the ring in the first round of their fight. Getting the better of Benn for much of the fight, he floored him again in the eighth round. Benn came back each time, in a fight that observers recalled as ragged yet memorable. By the time the 10th round began, McClellan was ahead on two of the three judges' cards.

Then as the 10th progressed, McClellan seemed strangely weak. He took a solid right from Benn, went down on a knee for a seven count, then resumed action. But 20 seconds later, after a no-account uppercut from Benn, he again took a knee. The announcers wondered at this strange surrender. McClellan rose, stepped back to his corner and, sliding into a coma before everyone's eyes, slumped to the canvas.

Nothing could arrest his descent. Ringside medical care was immediate, and it was agreed that there was nothing more that could have been done. This, of course, rallied boxing's critics all the more. They pointed out that there was no further reform to be made. There was nothing that could have saved McClellan except the sport's abolition. Boxing had done this.

McClellan came out of his coma and, though badly damaged, is undergoing rehabilitation at home in Detroit. Not so fortunate was Jimmy Garcia, a light hitter of slim credentials who traveled from Colombia to take an undercard payday in Las Vegas last May. Although Garcia was challenging Gabriel Ruelas for the WBC super-featherweight title, the night's attraction was Oscar De La Hoya, the Golden Boy from Los Angeles, the country's only gold medal winner from the 1992 Olympics, all teeth and charisma and flashing left hooks.

De La Hoya, 22, was becoming a promotional engine. Although he is cheeky and given to arrogant dismissals of his opponents ("an ordinary fighter" is how he handicapped rival Rafael Ruelas, Gabe's brother), he has the looks, the wit and the enormous skills to be a superstar. Sports agent Leigh Steinberg, who ordinarily represents NFL quarterbacks, was trailing De La Hoya the week of the fight, putting together endorsement deals for him. That's how big he was becoming.

Love him or hate him, the fighter delivers. He stopped Ruelas in the second round to add the IBF lightweight belt to the WBO belt he already owned. The ease with which he did so, in only his 18th fight, promised many more belts to come.

Unfortunately De La Hoya's little stop on the way to greatness will be better remembered as the night that Jimmy Garcia absorbed a fatal beating. Gabriel Ruelas, in the undercard, battered his challenger relentlessly, until Garcia, attended in his corner by family, slumped unconscious to the canvas after the fight was stopped in the 11th round. Garcia may not have ever belonged in the same ring with Ruelas, but he certainly didn't belong there in the later rounds, when it became obvious he couldn't possibly win. Now, he couldn't possibly live. He died from his injuries two weeks later.

This was disheartening stuff, and there wasn't much going on elsewhere to balance it. The heavyweights awaiting Tyson's return were a largely dispiriting bunch, their only redeeming quality being their guaranteed safety in the ring. It was unlikely that one of these heavyweights would ever hurt another.

It might have been enough to know that the middle-aged Foreman had knocked out Moorer to win the WBA and IBF titles in late 1994. Foreman was a popular performer, but he did not shape up as the future of boxing. That was evident when he engaged little-known Schulz last April in Las Vegas. It was supposed to be a walkthrough, a warmup for a mega-payday down the road with Tyson. But Schulz, confounding Foreman by actually moving in the ring (about which Foreman would complain bitterly, as if opponents were contractually obligated to remain as still as the heavy bag), nearly outpointed the champion. In fact, the decision given to Foreman was so unpopular that the IBF immediately called for a rematch, preferably in Schulz's homeland of Germany. Foreman, who came out of the fight with a welt on his brow the size of a bratwurst, politely declined and let his titles lapse. Schulz and Frans Botha were later paired for the vacant IBF championship, a fight to be promoted by King. The world did not hold its breath.

King's other heavyweights were similarly uninspiring. In April, McCall, a former Tyson sparring partner, had all he could handle in the aged Holmes, a fighter the Las Vegas commission had been shocked to learn had made his last fight there

The brash De La Hoya, an easy winner over Ruelas, has looks and skills to match.

wearing contact lenses. By normal athletic standards, Holmes ought to require a cane as well. Even so, the closeness of that match did not augur well for McCall's continued reign. At year's end he lost his title in London to perennial also-ran Bruno.

The WBA title, which King also controlled and which was decided on the McCall-Holmes undercard, did not look much more permanent. Contender Bruce Seldon, despite his marvelous physique, was more famous for a jail term, a fondness for nightlife and back-to-back KO losses to McCall and Bowe. Going into his fight with veteran Tony Tucker for the other title vacated by Foreman, Seldon presented himself as newly dedicated, reformed and eager. Any one of those qualities was refreshing in this division. As it happened, Seldon was a bit luckier than Tucker, stopping him on cuts to win the title.

Now that King controlled the three major titles, all the other heavyweights were on the outside looking in. Bowe, by consensus the most talented of them, had been made WBO champion, but nobody took that very seriously. He has been on-again off-again since Evander Holyfield decisioned him in their 1993 rematch, but he was truly impressive in his summer bout with MGM house fighter Jorge Gonzalez, the Cuban madman. Bowe destroyed him. This set up a third meeting with Holyfield, scheduled for November. Holyfield, who has come back from what he says was an incorrectly diagnosed heart condition, set up that match by beating a tough Ray Mercer.

Nonetheless, everything seemed a kind of orchestrated prelude to Tyson's return, as if only he could restore excitement to boxing. Largely forgotten was the fact that it had been four years since Tyson had fought at all, in a lackluster bout with Razor Ruddock, and perhaps 10 since he had fought with the brilliance he is celebrated for. Veteran trainer Emmanuel Steward would not abide comparisons to Muhammad Ali, who came back from his three-year political exile to become a greater fighter than he had ever been. "Ali's style permitted longevity," Steward said. "Tyson, his kind don't have long careers." Indeed, the history has been that fast, furious, aggressive fighters like Tyson flame out, a la Joe Frazier. Indeed, Tyson may have flamed out before he ever went in.

Still, the reality was that Tyson didn't have to be as good as he had been. Or very good at all. His undeniable charisma—the shocking ring violence complicated by his recklessness outside it—would be riveting enough to satisfy this crowd. The reality, for the moment,

WILL HART

Forget about his 36–1 record: McNeeley went down fast in his fight with Tyson.

was that Tyson didn't even need an opponent.

For Tyson's first fight back, King scrounged up a fellow named Peter McNeeley, whose ring record of 36–1 with 30 KOs promised Tyson some danger. But closer inspection of McNeeley's record, which included fights with a large number of winless stiffs, seemed to promise him and the promoter scorn instead. The MGM was pricing ringside seats at $1,500, and Showtime was pricing the pay-per-view show as high as $50. To be sure, this wasn't being promoted as a McNeeley fight, but wasn't this a bit rich just to watch a Tyson workout, one that might not even require a sweat? "First punch knocks this guy out," said rival promoter Bob Arum.

Tyson's handlers limited his prefight media exposure and generally encouraged an atmosphere of mystery about their fighter. This was shrewd as it turned out. The curiosity factor, really, was all this fight had going for it. Could Tyson still hit? Could he take a punch? Would he return to the style, the peek-a-boo defense, that made him so frightening in the 1980s?

The MGM was full for the August fight, and more than one million viewers coughed up the pay-per-view dough, making it a bonanza for Team Tyson (the fighter got at least $25 million, perhaps $40 million). But the fight itself was so terrible—it answered none of the important questions about his comeback—that Team Tyson had to scramble to fend off a backlash. Tyson, in the so-called fight, was hardly sharp, though he floored McNeeley twice in the first round. But whatever fireworks display he planned was shelved when McNeeley's manager, Vinnie Vecchione, jumped into the ring 89 seconds into the first round to save his fighter and disqualify him. Everybody agreed that McNeeley was not going to last, but they also agreed that Vecchione's stoppage was premature. The fans were robbed of the only thing the promoters dared promise, a Tyson knockout.

So what began in mystery—Tyson leaving prison for morning prayer—ended in mystery. Tyson was back, that much was obvious, but it couldn't be known for how long. Apparently King was going to nurse him along—one more setup, against Buster Mathis Jr., was scheduled for November—until he could grab the titles, one by one, from Seldon, Bruno and the Botha-Schulz winner. It would be difficult, under these circumstances, for Tyson to fail to unify the division. Given that, it still remained for him to restore some excitement to boxing, and who knows if and when he can do that? One wonders, after this extended drought, if it's even possible.

FOR THE RECORD·1994–1995

Current Champions

Division	Weight Limit	WBC Champion	WBA Champion	IBF Champion
Heavyweight	None	Frank Bruno	Bruce Seldon	vacant
Cruiserweight	190	Marcelo Dominguez	Nate Miller	Alfred Cole
Light heavyweight	175	Fabrice Tiozzo	Virgil Hill	Henry Maske
Super middleweight	168	Nigel Benn	Frank Liles	Roy Jones
Middleweight	160	Quincy Taylor	Jorge Castro	Bernard Hopkins
Junior middleweight	154	Terry Norris	Carl Daniels	Paul Vaden
Welterweight	147	Pernell Whitaker	Ike Quartey	Felix Trinidad
Junior welterweight	140	Julio César Chávez	Frankie Randall	Konstantin Tszyu
Lightweight	135	Miguel Gonzalez	Orzubek Nazarov	Phillip Holiday
Junior lightweight	130	Gabriel Ruelas	vacant	Tracy Patterson
Featherweight	126	Manuel Medina	Eloy Rojas	Tom Johnson
Junior featherweight	122	Hector Acero Sanchez	Antonio Cermeno	Vuyani Bungu
Bantamweight	118	Wayne McCullough	Veeraphol Sahaprom	Mbulelo Botile
Junior bantamweight	115	Hiroshi Kawashima	Alimi Goitia	Carlos Salazar
Flyweight	112	Yuri Arbachakov	Saen Sow Ploenchit	Danny Romero
Junior flyweight	108	Saman Sorjaturong	Choi Hi-Yong	Saman Sorjaturong
Strawweight	105	Ricardo Lopez	Chana Porpaoin	Ratanaapol Sow Voraphin

Note: WBC = World Boxing Council; WBA = World Boxing Association; IBF = International Boxing Federation

Championship and Major Fights of 1994 and 1995

Abbreviations: WBC=World Boxing Council; WBA= World Boxing Association; IBF=International Boxing Federation; KO=knockout; TKO=technical knockout; Dec=decision; Split=split decision; Disq=disqualification.

Heavyweight

Date	Winner	Loser	Result	Title	Site
Nov 4	George Foreman	Michael Moorer	KO 10	IBF, WBA	Las Vegas
Mar 11	Riddick Bowe	Herbie Hide	KO 6	WBO	Las Vegas
Apr 22	George Foreman	Axel Schulz	Dec 12	IBF	Las Vegas
Aug 19	Bruce Seldon	Joe Hipp	TKO 10	WBA	Las Vegas
Sept 2	Frank Bruno	Oliver McCall	Dec 12	WBC	London

Cruiserweight

Date	Winner	Loser	Result	Title	Site
Nov 12	Orlin Norris	James Heath	KO 2	WBA	Mexico City
Dec 3	Anaclet Wamba	Marcelo Dominguez	Dec 12	WBC	Salta, Argentina
Mar 18	Orlin Norris	Adolpho Washington	Dec 12	WBA	Worcester, MA
June 24	Alfred Cole	Uriah Grant	Dec 12	IBF	Atlantic City, NJ
July 23	Nate Miller	Orlin Morris	KO 8	WBA	London
Sept 2	Marcelo Dominguez	Reynaldo Gimenez	TKO 12	WBC	Gualeguaychu, Arg.

Light Heavyweight

Date	Winner	Loser	Result	Title	Site
Oct 8	Henry Maske	Iran Barkley	TKO 9	IBF	Halle, Germany
Feb 25	Mike McCallum	Carl Jones	TKO 7	WBC	London
Apr 1	Virgil Hill	Crawford Ashley	Dec 12	WBA	Stateline, NV
May 27	Henry Maske	Graciano Rocchigiani	Dec 12	IBF	Dortmund, Germany
June 16	Fabrice Tiozzo	Mike McCallum	Dec 12	WBC	Lyon, France
Sept 2	Virgil Hill	Drake Thadzi	Dec 12	WBA	London

Super Middleweight

Date	Winner	Loser	Result	Title	Site
Dec 17	Frank Liles	Michael Nunn	Dec 12	WBA	Quito, Ecuador
Feb 25	Nigel Benn	Gerald McClellan	KO 10	WDC	London
Mar 18	Roy Jones	Antoine Byrd	TKO 1	IBF	Pensacola, FL
May 27	Frank Liles	Frederic Seillier	TKO 6	WBA	Fort Lauderdale, FL
June 24	Roy Jones	Vinny Pazienza	TKO 6	IBF	Atlantic City, NJ
Sept 2	Nigel Benn	Danny Perez	KO 7	WBC	London
Sept 30	Roy Jones	Tony Thornton	TKO 3	IBF	Pensacola, FL

Middleweight

Date	Winner	Loser	Result	Title	Site
Nov 5	Jorge Castro	Alex Ramos	KO 2	WBA	Caleta Olivia, Argentina
Dec 10	Jorge Castro	John David Jackson	TKO 9	WBA	Monterrey, Mexico
Mar 17	Julian Jackson	Agostino Cardamone	TKO 2	WBC	Worcester, MA
Apr 29	Bernard Hopkins	Segundo Mercado	TKO 7	IBF	Landover, MD
May 27	Jorge Castro	Anthony Andrews	TKO 12	WBA	Fort Lauderdale, FL
Aug 19	Quincy Taylor	Julian Jackson	TKO 6	WBC	Las Vegas

Junior Middleweight (Super Welterweight)

Date	Winner	Loser	Result	Title	Site
Nov 11	Julio César Vasquez	Tony Marshall	Dec 12	WBA	Tucuman, Argentina
Nov 12	Luis Santana	Terry Norris	Disq 5	WBC	Mexico City
Mar 4	Pernell Whitaker	Julio César Vasquez	Dec 12	WBA	Atlantic City, NJ
Apr 8	Luis Santana	Terry Norris	Disq 3	WBC	Las Vegas
Apr 29	Vincent Pettway	Simon Brown	KO 6	IBF	Landover, MD
June 16	Carl Daniels	Julio César Vasquez	Dec 12	WBA	Lyon, France
Aug 12	Paul Vaden	Vincent Pettway	TKO 12	IBF	Las Vegas
Aug 19	Terry Norris	Luis Santana	TKO 2	WBC	Las Vegas

Welterweight

Date	Winner	Loser	Result	Title	Site
Oct 1	Pernell Whitaker	Buddy McGirt	Dec 12	WBC	Norfolk, VA
Dec 10	Felix Trinidad	Oba Carr	TKO 8	IBF	Monterrey, Mexico
Mar 4	Ike Quartey	Park Jung-Oh	TKO 4	WBA	Atlantic City, NJ
Apr 8	Felix Trinidad	Roger Turner	TKO 2	IBF	Las Vegas
Aug 23	Ike Quartey	Andrew Murray	TKO 4	WBA	Rocheville, France
Aug 26	Pernell Whitaker	Gary Jacobs	Dec 12	WBC	Atlantic City

Junior Welterweight (Super Lightweight)

Date	Winner	Loser	Result	Title	Site
Dec 10	Julio César Chávez	Tony Lopez	TKO 10	WBC	Monterrey, Mexico
Dec 10	Frankie Randall	Rodney Moore	TKO 7	WBA	Monterrey, Mexico
Jan 28	Konstantin Tszyu	Jake Rodriguez	TKO 6	IBF	Las Vegas
Apr 8	Julio César Chávez	Giovanni Parisi	Dec 12	WBC	Las Vegas
June 16	Frankie Randall	Jose Barboza	Split 12	WBA	Lyon, France
June 25	Kostya Tszyu	Roger Mayweather	Dec 12	IBF	Newcastle, Australia
Sept 16	Julio César Chávez	David Kamau	Dec 12	WBC	Las Vegas

Lightweight

Date	Winner	Loser	Result	Title	Site
Nov 18	Oscar De La Hoya	Carl Griffith	TKO 3	WBO	Las Vegas
Dec 10	Orzubek Nazarov	Joey Gamache	TKO 2	WBA	Portland, ME
Dec 10	Oscar De La Hoya	John Avila	TKO 9	WBO	Los Angeles
Dec 13	Miguel Angel Gonzalez	Calvin Grove	TKO 5	WBC	Albuquerque, NM
Jan 28	Rafael Ruelas	Billy Schwer	TKO 8	IBF	Las Vegas
Feb 18	Oscar De La Hoya	Juan Molina	Dec 12	WBO	Las Vegas
Apr 25	Miguel Angel Gonzalez	Ricardo Silva	Dec 12	WBC	South Padre Island, TX
May 6	Oscar De La Hoya	Rafael Ruelas	TKO 2	WBO/IBF	Las Vegas
May 15	Orzubek Nazarov	Won Park	KO 2	WBA	Tokyo
June 2	Miguel Angel Gonzalez	Marty Jakubowski	Dec 12	WBC	Mashantucket, CT
Aug 19	Miguel Angel Gonzalez	Lamar Murphy	Dec 12	WBC	Las Vegas
Aug 19	Phillip Holiday	Miguel Julio	TKO 10	IBF	Sun City, South Africa
Sept 9	Oscar De La Hoya	Genaro Hernandez	TKO 6	WBO	Las Vegas

Junior Lightweight (Super Featherweight)

Date	Winner	Loser	Result	Title	Site
Nov 12	Genaro Hernandez	Jimmy Garcia	Dec 12	WBA	Mexico City
Nov 26	Juan Molina	Wilson Rodriguez	KO 10	IBF	Bayamon, Puerto Rico
Jan 28	Gabriel Ruelas	Fred Libertore	TKO 2	WBC	Las Vegas
Apr 22	Eddie Hopson	Moises Pedroza	KO 7	IBF	Atlantic City, NJ
May 6	Gabriel Ruelas	Jimmy Garcia	TKO 11	WBC	Las Vegas
July 9	Tracy Patterson	Eddie Hopson	TKO 2	IBF	Reno, Nevada

Featherweight

Date	Winner	Loser	Result	Title	Site
Oct 22	Tom Johnson	Francisco Segura	Dec 12	IBF	Atlantic City, NJ
Dec 3	Eloy Rojas	Luis Mendoza	Dec 12	WBA	Bogota, Columbia
Jan 7	Alejandro Gonzalez	Kevin Kelley	TKO 10	WBC	San Antonio, TX
Jan 28	Tom Johnson	Manuel Medina	Dec 12	IBF	Atlantic City, NJ
Mar 31	Alejandro Gonzalez	Louie Espinoza	Dec 12	WBC	Anaheim, CA
May 27	Eloy Rojas	Park Yong-Kyun	Split 12	WBA	Kwangju, South Korea
June 2	Alejandro Gonzalez	Tony Green	TKO 9	WBC	Mashantucket, CT
May 28	Tom Johnson	Eddie Croft	Dec 12	IBF	South Padre Island, TX
Aug 13	Eloy Rojas	Nobutoshi Hiranaka	Dec 12	WBA	Tagawa City, Japan
Sept 23	Manuel Medina	Alejandro Gonzalez	Split 12	WBC	Sacramento, CA

Junior Featherweight (Super Bantamweight)

Date	Winner	Loser	Result	Title	Site
Oct 13	Wilfredo Vasquez	Juan Polo Perez	Dec 12	WBA	Levallois-Perret, France
Nov 19	Vuyani Bungu	Felix Camacho	Dec 12	IBF	Hammanskraal, S.A.
Jan 7	Wilfredo Vasquez	Orlando Canizales	Split 12	WBA	San Antonio, TX
Mar 4	Vuyani Bungu	Mohammed Nurhuda	Dec 12	IBF	Hammanskraal, S.A.
Mar 11	Hector Acero-Sanchez	Julio Gervacio	Dec 12	WBC	Atlantic City, NJ
Apr 29	Vuyani Bungu	Victor Llerena	Dec 12	IBF	Johannesburg, S.A.
May 13	Antonio Cermeno	Wilfredo Vasquez	Dec 12	WBA	Bayamon, Puerto Rico
Jun 2	Hector Acero-Sanchez	Daniel Zaragoza	Maj draw	WBC	Mashantucket, CT
Sept 26	Vuyani Bungu	Laureano Ramirez	Dec 12	IBF	Hammanskraal, S.A.

Bantamweight

Date	Winner	Loser	Result	Title	Site
Oct 15	Orlando Canizales	Sergio Reyes	Dec 12	IBF	Laredo, TX
Nov 20	Daorung Chuvatana	Koh In-Sik	TKO 5	WBA	Chiang Rai, Thailand
Dec 4	Yasuei Yakushiji	Joichiro Tatsuyoshi	Dec 12	WBC	Nagoya, Japan
Jan 21	Harold Mestre	Juvenal Berrio	TKO 8	IBF	Cartagena, Columbia
Apr 29	Mbulelo Botile	Harold Mestre	TKO 2	IBF	Johannesburg, S.A.
May 27	Daorung Chuvatana	Lakhin CP Gym	Split draw	WBA	Nakhon Si Thammarat, Thailand
July 4	Mbulelo Botile	Sammy Stewart	Dec 12	IBF	Hammanskraal, S.A.
July 30	Wayne McCullough	Yasuei Yakusiji	Split 12	WBC	Nagoya, Japan
Sept 17	Veerapol Sahaprom	Daorung MP-Petroleum	Split 12	WBA	Bangkok, Thailand

Junior Bantamweight (Super Flyweight)

Date	Winner	Loser	Result	Title	Site
Dec 17	Harold Grey	Vincenzo Belcastro	Split 12	IBF	Cagliari, Italy
Jan 18	Hiroshi Kawashima	Jose Luis Bueno	Dec 12	WBC	Yokohama, Japan
Feb 25	Lee Hyung-Chul	Tomonori Tamura	TKO 12	WBA	Pusan, South Korea
Mar 18	Harold Grey	Orlando Tobon	Dec 12	IBF	Cartagena, Columbia
May 24	Hiroshi Kawashima	Lee Seung-Koo	Dec 12	WBC	Yokohama, Japan
June 24	Harold Grey	Julio Cesar Borboa	Split 12	IBF	Cartagena, Columbia
July 22	Alimi Goitia	Lee Hyung-Chul	KO 4	WBA	Seoul, South Korea
Oct 6	Carlos Salazar	Harold Grey	Split 12	WBC	Mar del Plata, Arg.

Flyweight

Date	Winner	Loser	Result	Title	Site
Sep 25	Saen Sow Ploenchit	Kim Yong-Kang	Dec 12	WBA	Kanchanaburi, Thailand
Dec 25	Saen Sow Ploenchit	Danny Nunez	TKO 11	WBA	Rayong, Thailand
Jan 30	Yuri Arbachakov	Oscar Arciniega	Dec 12	WBC	Sapporo, Japan
Feb 18	Francisco Tejedor	Jose Luis Zepeda	TKO 6	IBF	Cartagena, Colombia
Apr 22	Danny Romero	Francisco Tejedor	Dec 12	IBF	Las Vegas
May 7	Saen Sow Ploenchit	Evangelio Perez	Dec 12	WBA	Hat Yai, Thailand
July 29	Danny Romero	Miguel Martinez	KO 6	IBF	San Antonio, TX
Sept 25	Yuri Arbachakov	Chatchai Elite-Gym	Dec 12	WBC	Tokyo

Junior Flyweight

Date	Winner	Loser	Result	Title	Site
Oct 9	Leo Gamez	P. Sithbangprachan	TKO 6	WBA	Bangkok, Thailand
Nov 12	Humberto Gonzalez	Michael Carbajal	Dec 12	WBC/IBF	Mexico City
Feb 4	Choi Hi-Yong	Leo Gamez	Dec 12	WBA	Ulsan, South Korea
Mar 31	Humberto Gonzalez	Jesus Zuniga	KO 5	WBC/IBF	Anaheim, CA
July 15	Saman Sor Jaturong	Humberto Gonzalez	KO 7	WBC/IBF	Inglewood, CA
Sept 5	Choi Hi-Yong	Keiji Yamaguchi	Split 12	WBA	Osaka, Japan

Strawweight (Mini Flyweight)

Date	Winner	Loser	Result	Title	Site
Nov 5	Chana Porpaoin	Manuel Herrera	Split 12	WBA	Hat Yai, Thailand
Nov 12	Ratanapal Sow Voraphin	Carlos Rodriguez	TKO 3	IBF	Khon Kaen, Thailand
Nov 12	Ricardo Lopez	Javier Varguez	TKO 8	WBC	Mexico City
Dec 10	Ricardo Lopez	Yamil Caraballo	TKO 1	WBC	Monterrey, Mexico
Jan 28	Chana Porpaoin	Kim Jin-Ho	Dec 12	WBA	Bangkok, Thailand
Feb 25	Ratanapal Sow Voraphin	Jerry Pahayahay	TKO 3	IBF	Bangkok, Thailand
Apr 1	Ricardo Lopez	Andy Tabanas	TKO 12	WBC	Stateline, NV
May 20	Ratanapal Sow Voraphin	Oscar Flores	TKO 2	IBF	Chiang Mai, Thailand
Aug 6	Chana Popaoin	Ernesto Rubillar Jr	KO 6	WBA	Bangkok, Thailand

Harlem Shuffle

Reaction to the announced homecoming celebration for New York City native Mike Tyson has sent the former heavyweight champ's supporters reeling as if they'd been hit by a Buster Douglas left. The local *Amsterdam News* reported in June that a "gala festival" for Tyson, feauring a parade and a musical tribute, had been planned for June 20 in Harlem. Event organizer Sylvester Leaks boasted that the celebration would "surpass anything ever accorded any sports figure in New York or the entire nation."

The counterpunching began almost immediately. The idea of feting a recently released rapist was condemned by columnists, Mayor Rudolph Giuliani and a civic group that billed itself as the Committee for Rational African Americans Against the Parade (CRAAAP). Even the usually staid *New York Times* ran the tabloidlike headline on its op-ed page: WELCOME HOME, CONVICTED MOLESTER.

Gala backers, most notably New York congressman Charles Rangel, backed off. Even the normally mouthy Al Sharpton, another of the event's organizers, found himself against the ropes. In the end the occasion was scaled back to a couple of press conferences. That such a celebration was even proposed reflects Tyson's enduring appeal. But it's one thing to allow him to put his past behind him, quite another to extend a hero's welcome suggesting the civic credo Be Like Mike.

FOR THE RECORD·Year by Year

World Champions

Sanctioning bodies include the National Boxing Association (NBA), the New York State Athletic Commission (NY), the World Boxing Association (WBA), the World Boxing Council (WBC), and the International Boxing Federation (IBF).

Heavyweights
(Weight: Unlimited)

Champion	Reign	Champion	Reign	Champion	Reign
John L. Sullivan	1885-92	Ingemar Johansson	1959-60	Pinklon Thomas* WBC	1984-86
James J. Corbett	1892-97	Floyd Patterson	1960-62	Greg Page* WBA	1984-85
Bob Fitzsimmons	1897-99	Sonny Liston	1962-64	Michael Spinks	1985-87
James J. Jeffries	1899-1905†	Muhammad Ali	1964-70	Tim Witherspoon* WBA	1986
Marvin Hart	1905-06	Ernie Terrell* WBA	1965-67	Trevor Berbick* WBC	1986
Tommy Burns	1906-08	Joe Frazier* NY	1968-70	Mike Tyson* WBC	1986-87
Jack Johnson	1908-15	Jimmy Ellis* WBA	1968-70	James Bonecrusher	
Jess Willard	1915-19	Joe Frazier	1970-73	Smith* WBA	1986-87
Jack Dempsey	1919-26	George Foreman	1973-74	Tony Tucker* IBF	1987
Gene Tunney	1926-28	Muhammad Ali	1974-78	Mike Tyson	1987-90
Max Schmeling	1930-32	Leon Spinks	1978	Buster Douglas	1990
Jack Sharkey	1932-33	Ken Norton* WBC	1978	Evander Holyfield	1990-92
Primo Carnera	1933-34	Larry Holmes* WBC	1978-80	Lennox Lewis* WBC	1993-95
Max Baer	1934-35	Muhammad Ali	1978-79†	Riddick Bowe	1992-93
James J. Braddock	1935-37	John Tate* WBA	1979-80	Evander Holyfield	1993-94
Joe Louis	1937-49†	Mike Weaver* WBA	1980-82	Michael Moorer	1994
Ezzard Charles	1949-51	Larry Holmes	1980-85	George Foreman	1994-95
Jersey Joe Walcott	1951-52	Michael Dokes* WBA	1982-83	Frank Bruno* WBC	1995-
Rocky Marciano	1952-56†	Gerrie Coetzee* WBA	1983-84	Bruce Seldon* WBA	1995-
Floyd Patterson	1956-59	Tim Witherspoon* WBC	1984		

Cruiserweights
(Weight Limit: 190 pounds)

Champion	Reign	Champion	Reign	Champion	Reign
Marvin Camel* WBC	1980	Evander Holyfield * WBA	1986-88	Massimiliano	
Carlos De Leon* WBC	1980-82	Ricky Parkey* IBF	1986-87	Duran* WBC	1990-91
Ossie Ocasio* WBA	1982-84	Evander Holyfield		Bobby Czyz*† WBA	1991-92
S.T. Gordon* WBC	1982-83	* WBA/IBF	1987-88	Anaclet Wamba* WBC	1991-95
Carlos De Leon* WBC	1983-85	Evander Holyfield		James Pritchard* IBF	1991
Marvin Camel* IBF	1983-84	WBA/IBF/WBC	1988†	James Warring* IBF	1991-92
Lee Roy Murphy* IBF	1984-86	Toufik Belbouli* WBA	1989	Alfred Cole* IBF	1992-
Piet Crous* WBA	1984-85	Robert Daniels* WBA	1989-91	Orlin Norris* WBA	1993-95
Alfonso Ratliff* WBC	1985	Carlos De Leon* WBC	1989-90	Nate Miller* WBA	1995-
Dwight Braxton* WBA	1985-86	Glenn McCrory* IBF	1989-90	Marcello	
Bernard Benton* WBC	1985-86	Jeff Lampkin* IBF	1990	Dominguez* WBC	1995-
Carlos De Leon* WBC	1986-88				

Note: Division called Junior Heavyweights by the WBA.

Light Heavyweights
(Weight Limit: 175 pounds)

Champion	Reign	Champion	Reign	Champion	Reign
Jack Root	1903	George Nichols* NBA	1932	Dick Tiger	1966-68
George Gardner	1903	Bob Godwin* NBA	1933	Bob Foster	1968-74†
Bob Fitzsimmons	1903-05	Bob Olin	1934-35	Vicente Rondon* WBA	1971-72
Philadelphia Jack		John Henry Lewis	1935-38	John Conteh* WBC	1974-77
O'Brien	1905-12†	Melio Bettina	1939	Victor Galindez* WBA	1974-78
Jack Dillon	1914-16	Billy Conn	1939-40†	Miguel A. Cuello* WBC	1977-78
Battling Levinsky	1916-20	Anton Christoforidis	1941	Mate Parlov* WBC	1978
Georges Carpentier	1920-22	Gus Lesnevich	1941-48	Mike Rossman* WBA	1978-79
Battling Siki	1922-23	Freddie Mills	1948-50	Marvin Johnson* WBC	1978-79
Mike McTigue	1923-25	Joey Maxim	1950-52	Matthew Saad	
Paul Berlenbach	1925-26	Archie Moore	1952-62†	Muhammad* WBC	1979-81
Jack Delaney	1926-27†	Harold Johnson* NBA	1961	Marvin Johnson* WBA	1979-80
Jimmy Slattery* NBA	1927	Harold Johnson	1962-63	Eddie Mustapha	
Tommy Loughran	1927-29	Willie Pastrano	1963-65	Muhammad* WBA	1980-81
Maxie Rosenbloom	1930-34	Jose Torres	1965-66	Michael Spinks* WBA	1981-83

*Champion not generally recognized. †Champion retired or relinquished title.

Light Heavyweights *(Cont.)*

Champion	Reign
Dwight Muhammad Qawi* WBC	1981-83
Michael Spinks	1983-85†
J. B. Williamson* WBC	1985-86
Slobodan Kacar* IBF	1985-86
Marvin Johnson* WBA	1986-87
Dennis Andries* WBC	1986-87
Bobby Czyz* IBF	1986-87
Leslie Stewart* WBA	1987

Champion	Reign
Virgil Hill* WBA	1987
Prince Charles Williams* IBF	1987-
Thomas Hearns* WBC	1987†
Donny Lalonde* WBC	1987-88
Sugar Ray Leonard* WBC	1988
Dennis Andries* WBC	1989
Jeff Harding* WBC	1989-90
Dennis Andries* WBC	1990-91

Champion	Reign
Thomas Hearns* WBA	1991-92
Jeff Harding* WBC	1991-94
Iran Barkley* WBA	1992
Virgil Hill* WBA	1992-
Henry Maske* IBF	1993-
Mike McCallum* WBC	1994-95
Fabrice Tiozzo* WBC	1995-

Super Middleweights
(Weight Limit: 168 pounds)

Champion	Reign
Murray Sutherland* IBF	1984
Chong-Pal Park* IBF	1984-87
Chong-Pal Park* WBA	1987-88
G. Rocchigiani* IBF	1988-89
F. Obelmejias* WBA	1988-89
Sugar Ray Leonard* WBC	1988-90†

Champion	Reign
In-Chul Baek* WBA	1989-90
Lindell Holmes* IBF	1990-91
C. Tiozzo* WBA	1990-91
Mauro Galvano* WBC	1990-
Victor Cordova* WBA	1991
Darrin Van Horn* IBF	1991-92
Iran Barkley *WBA	1992

Champion	Reign
Nigel Benn* WBC	1992-
James Toney* IBF	1992-94
Michael Nunn* WBA	1992-94
Steve Little* WBA	1994
Frank Liles* WBA	1994-
Roy Jones* IBF	1994-

Middleweights
(Weight Limit: 160 pounds)

Champion	Reign
Jack Dempsey	1884-91
Bob Fitzsimmons	1891-97
Kid McCoy	1897-98
Tommy Ryan	1898-1907
Stanley Ketchel	1908
Billy Papke	1908
Stanley Ketchel	1908-10
Frank Klaus	1913
George Chip	1913-14
Al McCoy	1914-17
Mike O'Dowd	1917-20
Johnny Wilson	1920-23
Harry Greb	1923-26
Tiger Flowers	1926
Mickey Walker	1926-31†
Gorilla Jones	1931-32
Marcel Thil	1932-37
Fred Apostoli	1937-39
Al Hostak* NBA	1938
Solly Krieger* NBA	1938-39
Al Hostak* NBA	1939-40
Ceferino Garcia	1939-40
Ken Overlin	1940-41
Tony Zale* NBA	1940-41
Billy Soose	1941

Champion	Reign
Tony Zale	1941-47
Rocky Graziano	1947-48
Tony Zale	1948
Marcel Cerdan	1948-49
Jake La Motta	1949-51
Sugar Ray Robinson	1951
Randy Turpin	1951
Sugar Ray Robinson	1951-52
Bobo Olson	1953-55
Sugar Ray Robinson	1955-57
Gene Fullmer	1957
Sugar Ray Robinson	1957
Carmen Basilio	1957-58
Sugar Ray Robinson	1958-60
Gene Fullmer* NBA	1959-62
Paul Pender	1960-61
Terry Downes	1961-62
Paul Pender	1962-63
Dick Tiger* WBA	1962-63
Dick Tiger	1963
Joey Giardello	1963-65
Dick Tiger	1965-66
Emile Griffith	1966-67
Nino Benvenuti	1967
Emile Griffith	1967-68

Champion	Reign
Nino Benvenuti	1968-70
Carlos Monzon	1970-77†
Rodrigo Valdez* WBC	1974-76
Rodrigo Valdez	1977-78
Hugo Corro	1978-79
Vito Antuofermo	1979-80
Alan Minter	1980
Marvin Hagler	1980-87
Sugar Ray Leonard	1987
Frank Tate* IBF	1987-88
Sumbu Kalambay* WBA	1987-89
Thomas Hearns* WBC	1987-88
Iran Barkley* WBC	1988-89
Michael Nunn* IBF	1988-91
Roberto Duran* WBC	1989-90
Mike McCallum* WBA	1989-91
Julian Jackson* WBC	1990-
James Toney* IBF	1991-
Reggie Johnson* WBA	1992-94
Roy Jones*† IBF	1993-95
G. McClellan*† WBC	1993-95
Jorge Castro* WBA	1994-
Jullian Jackson* WBC	1995
Quincy Taylor* WBC	1995-
Bernard Hopkins* IBF	1995-

Junior Middleweights
(Weight Limit: 154 pounds)

Champion	Reign
Emile Griffith (EBU)	1962-63
Dennis Moyer	1962-63
Ralph Dupas	1963
Sandro Mazzinghi	1963-65
Nino Benvenuti	1965-66
Ki-Soo Kim	1966-68
Sandro Mazzinghi	1968
Freddie Little	1969-70
Carmelo Bossi	1970-71
Koichi Wajima	1971-74
Oscar Albarado	1974-75

Champion	Reign
Koichi Wajima	1975
Miguel de Oliveira* WBC	1975-76
Jae-Do Yuh	1975-76
Elisha Obed* WBC	1975-76
Koichi Wajima	1976
Jose Duran	1976
Eckhard Dagge* WBC	1976-77
Miguel Angel Castellini	1976-77
Eddie Gazo	1977-78
Rocky Mattioli* WBC	1977-79
Masashi Kudo	1978-79

Champion	Reign
Maurice Hope* WBC	1979-81
Ayub Kalule	1979-81
Wilfred Benitez* WBC	1981-82
Sugar Ray Leonard	1981-82
Tadashi Mihara* WBA	1981-82
Davey Moore* WBA	1982-83
Thomas Hearns* WBC	1982-84
Roberto Duran* WBA	1983-84
Mark Medal* IBF	1984
Thomas Hearns	1984-86
Mike McCallum* WBA	1984-87

*Champion not generally recognized. †Champion retired or relinquished title.

Junior Middleweights (Cont.)

Champion	Reign	Champion	Reign	Champion	Reign
Carlos Santos* IBF	1984-86	Robert Hines* IBF	1988-89	Julio C. Vasquez* WBA	1992-95
Buster Drayton* IBF	1986-87	Darrin Van Horn* IBF	1989	Simon Brown* WBC	1994
Duane Thomas* WBC	1986-87	Rene Jacquot* WBC	1989	Terry Norris *WBC	1994-
Matthew Hilton* IBF	1987-88	John Mugabi* WBC	1989-90	Vincent Pettway* IBF	1994-95
Lupe Aquino* WBC	1987	Gianfranco Rosi* IBF	1989-94	Paul Vaden* IBF	1995-
Gianfranco Rosi* WBC	1987-88	Terry Norris* WBC	1990-94	Carl Daniels* WBA	1995-
Julian Jackson* WBA	1987-90	Gilbert Dele* WBA	1991		
Donald Curry* WBC	1988-89	Vinny Pazienza* WBA	1991-92		

Note: Division called Super Welterweight by the WBC.

Welterweights
(Weight Limit: 147 pounds)

Champion	Reign	Champion	Reign	Champion	Reign
Paddy Duffy	1888-90	Young Corbett III	1933	John H. Stracey	1975-76
Mysterious Billy Smith	1892-94	Jimmy McLarnin	1933-34	Carlos Palomino	1976-79
Tommy Ryan	1894-98	Barney Ross	1934	Pipino Cuevas* WBA	1976-80
Mysterious Billy Smith	1898-1900	Jimmy McLarnin	1934-35	Wilfredo Benitez	1979
Rube Ferns	1900	Barney Ross	1935-38	Sugar Ray Leonard	1979-80
Matty Matthews	1900-01	Henry Armstrong	1938-40	Roberto Duran	1980
Rube Ferns	1901	Fritzie Zivic	1940-41	Thomas Hearns* WBA	1980-81
Joe Walcott	1901-04	Red Cochrane	1941-46	Sugar Ray Leonard	1980-82
The Dixie Kid	1904-05	Marty Servo	1946	Donald Curry* WBA	1983-85
Honey Mellody	1906-07	Sugar Ray Robinson	1946-51†	Milton McCrory* WBC	1983-85
Twin Sullivan	1907-08	Johnny Bratton	1951	Donald Curry	1985-86
Jimmy Gardner	1908	Kid Gavilan	1951-54	Lloyd Honeyghan	1986-87
Jimmy Clabby	1910-11	Johnny Saxton	1954-55	Jorge Vaca WBC	1987-88
Waldemar Holberg	1914	Tony DeMarco	1955	Lloyd Honeyghan WBC	1988-89
Tom McCormick	1914	Carmen Basilio	1955-56	Mark Breland* WBA	1987
Matt Wells	1914-15	Johnny Saxton	1956	Marlon Starling* WBA	1987-88
Mike Glover	1915	Carmen Basilio	1956-57	Tomas Molinares* WBA	1988-89
Jack Britton	1915	Virgil Akins	1958	Simon Brown* IBF	1988-91
Ted "Kid" Lewis	1915-16	Don Jordan	1958-60	Mark Breland* WBA	1989-90
Jack Britton	1916-17	Kid Paret	1960-61	Marlon Starling* WBC	1989-90
Ted "Kid" Lewis	1917-19	Emile Griffith	1961	Aaron Davis* WBA	1990-91
Jack Britton	1919-22	Kid Paret	1961-62	Maurice Blocker* WBC	1990-91
Mickey Walker	1922-26	Emile Griffith	1962-63	Meldrick Taylor* WBA	1991-1992
Pete Latzo	1926-27	Luis Rodriguez	1963	Simon Brown* WBC	1991
Joe Dundee	1927-29	Emile Griffith	1963-66	Buddy McGirt* WBC	1991-1993
Jackie Fields	1929-30	Curtis Cokes	1966-69	Felix Trinidad* IBF	1992-
Young Jack Thompson	1930	Jose Napoles	1969-70	Pernell Whitaker WBC	1993-
Tommy Freeman	1930-31	Billy Backus	1970-71	Crisanto Espana* WBA	1992-94
Young Jack Thompson	1931	Jose Napoles	1971-75	Ike Quartey* WBA	1994-
Lou Brouillard	1931-32	Hedgemon Lewis* NY	1972-73		
Jackie Fields	1932-33	Angel Espada* WBA	1975-76		

Junior Welterweight
(Weight Limit: 140 pounds)

Champion	Reign	Champion	Reign	Champion	Reign
Pinkey Mitchell	1922-25	Eddie Perkins	1963-65	Saoul Mamby* WBC	1980-82
Red Herring	1925	Carlos Hernandez	1965-66	Aaron Pryor* WBA	1980-83
Mushy Callahan	1926-30	Sandro Lopopolo	1966-67	Leroy Haley* WBC	1982-83
Jack (Kid) Berg	1930-31	Paul Fujii	1967-68	Aaron Pryor* IBF	1983-85
Tony Canzoneri	1931-32	Nicolino Loche	1968-72	Bruce Curry* WBC	1983-84
Johnny Jadick	1932-33	Pedro Adigue* WBC	1968-70	Johnny Bumphus* WBA	1984
Sammy Fuller*	1932-33	Bruno Arcari* WBC	1970-74	Bill Costello* WBC	1984-
Battling Shaw	1933	Alfonso Frazer	1972	Gene Hatcher* WBA	1984-85
Tony Canzoneri	1933	Antonio Cervantes	1972-76	Ubaldo Sacco* WBA	1985-86
Barney Ross	1933-35	Perico Fernandez* WBC	1974-75	Lonnie Smith* WBC	1985-86
Tippy Larkin	1946	S. Muangsurin* WBC	1975-76	Patrizio Oliva* WBA	1986-87
Carlos Ortiz	1959-60	Wilfred Benitez	1976-79	Gary Hinton* IBF	1986
Duilio Loi	1960-62	M. Velasquez* WBC	1976	Rene Arredondo* WBC	1986
Eddie Perkins	1962	S. Muangsurin* WBC	1976-78	Tsuyoshi Hamada* WBC	1986-87
Duilio Loi	1962-63	A. Cervantes* WBA	1977-80	Joe Louis Manley* IBF	1986-87
Roberto Cruz* WBA	1963	Sang-Hyun Kim* WBC	1978-80	Terry Marsh* IBF	1987

*Champion not generally recognized. †Champion retired or relinquished title.

Junior Welterweights *(Cont.)*

Champion	Reign	Champion	Reign	Champion	Reign
J. M. Coggi* WBA	1987-90	Loreto Garza* WBA	1990-91	Jake Rodriguez* IBF	1994-95
Rene Arredondo* WBC	1987	Juan Coggi* WBA	1991	Juan Coggi* WBA	1993-94
R. Mayweather* WBC	1987-89	Edwin Rosario* WBA	1991-92	Frankie Randall* IBF	1994
James McGirt* IBF	1988	Rafael Pineda* IBF	1991-92	Frankie Randall* WBA	1994-
Meldrick Taylor* IBF	1988-90	Akinobu Hiranaka* WBA	1992	Julio César Chávez WBC	1994-
Julio César Chávez* WBC	1989-94	Pernell Whitaker*† IBF	1992-93	Kostantin Tszyu* IBF	1995-
Julio César Chávez* IBF	1990-91	Charles Murray* IBF	1993-94		

Lightweights
(Weight Limit: 135 pounds)

Champion	Reign	Champion	Reign	Champion	Reign
Jack McAuliffe	1886-94	Juan Zurita* NBA	1944-45	Edwin Rosario* WBC	1983-84
Kid Lavigne	1896-99	Ike Williams	1947-51	Choo Choo Brown* IBF	1984
Frank Erne	1899-1902	James Carter	1951-52	L. Bramble* WBA	1984-86
Joe Gans	1902-04	Lauro Salas	1952	Jose Luis Ramirez* WBC	1984-85
Jimmy Britt	1904-05	James Carter	1952-54	Harry Arroyo* IBF	1984-85
Battling Nelson	1905-06	Paddy DeMarco	1954	Jimmy Paul* IBF	1985-86
Joe Gans	1906-08	James Carter	1954-55	Hector Camacho* WBC	1985-86
Battling Nelson	1908-10	Wallace Smith	1955-56	Greg Haugen* IBF	1986-87
Ad Wolgast	1910-12	Joe Brown	1956-62	Edwin Rosario* WBA	1986-87
Willie Ritchie	1912-14	Carlos Ortiz	1962-65	Julio César Chávez* WBA	1987-88
Freddie Welsh	1915-17	Ismael Laguna	1965	Jose Luis Ramirez* WBC	1987-88
Benny Leonard	1917-25†	Carlos Ortiz	1965-68	Julio César Chávez	1988-89
Jimmy Goodrich	1925	Carlos Teo Cruz	1968-69	Vinny Pazienza* IBF	1987-88
Rocky Kansas	1925-26	Mando Ramos	1969-70	Greg Haugen* IBF	1988-89
Sammy Mandell	1926-30	Ismael Laguna	1970	P. Whitaker* WBC, IBF	1989-90
Al Singer	1930	Ken Buchanan	1970-72	Edwin Rosario* WBA	1989-90
Tony Canzoneri	1930-33	Roberto Duran	1972-79†		1991-92
Barney Ross	1933-35†	Chango Carmona* WBC	1972	Juan Nazario* WBA	1990
Tony Canzoneri	1935-36	Rodolfo Gonzalez* WBC	1972-74	P. Whitaker* WBA, WBC	1990-92
Lou Ambers	1936-38	Ishimatsu Suzuki* WBC	1974-76	Pernell Whitaker* IBF	1991-92
Henry Armstrong	1938-39	Estaban DeJesus* WBC	1976-78	Julio César Chávez* IBF	1990-91
Lou Ambers	1939-40	Jim Watt* WBC	1979-81	Julio César Chávez* WBC	1990-92
Sammy Angott* NBA	1940-41	Ernesto Espana* WBA	1979-80	Miguel Gonzalez* WBC	1992-
Lew Jenkins	1940-41	Hilmer Kenty* WBA	1980-81	Joey Gamache* WBA	1992-93
Sammy Angott*	1941-42†	Sean O'Grady* WBA	1981	Dingaan Thobela* WBA	1993
Beau Jack* NY	1942-43	Claude Noel* WBA	1981	Fred Pendleton* IBF	1993-94
Bob Montgomery* NY	1943	Alexis Arguello* WBC	1981-82	Orzubek Nazarov* WBA	1994-
Sammy Angott* NBA	1943-44	Arturo Frias* WBA	1981-82	Rafael Ruelas* IBF	1994-95
Beau Jack* NY	1943-44	Ray Mancini* WBA	1982-84	Phillip Holiday* IBF	1995-
Bob Montgomery* NY	1944-47	Alexis Arguello	1982-83		

Junior Lightweights
(Weight Limit: 130 pounds)

Champion	Reign	Champion	Reign	Champion	Reign
Johnny Dundee	1921-23	Kuniaki Shibata	1973	Wilfredo Gomez	1985-86
Jack Bernstein	1923	Ben Villaflor	1973-76	Barry Michael* IBF	1985-87
Johnny Dundee	1923-24	Kuniaki Shibata* WBC	1974-75	Alfredo Layne* WBA	1986
Steve (Kid) Sullivan	1924-25	Alfredo Escalera* WBC	1975-78	Brian Mitchell* WBA	1986-91
Mike Ballerino	1925	Samuel Serrano	1976-80	Rocky Lockridge* IBF	1987-88
Tod Morgan	1925-29	Alexis Arguello* WBC	1978-80	Azumah Nelson* WBC	1988-94
Benny Bass	1929-31	Yasutsune Uehara	1980-81	Tony Lopez* IBF	1988-89
Kid Chocolate	1931-33	Rafael Limon* WBC	1980-81	Juan Molina* IBF	1989-90
Frankie Klick	1933-34	C. Boza-Edwards* WBC	1981	Tony Lopez* IBF	1990-91
Sandy Saddler	1949-50	Samuel Serrano	1981-83	Joey Gamache, WBA	1991
Harold Gomes	1959-60	R. Navarrete* WBC	1981-82	Brian Mitchell* IBF	1991
Gabriel (Flash) Elorde	1960-67	Rafael Limon* WBC	1982	Genaro Hernandez* WBA	1991-95
Yoshiaki Numata	1967	Bobby Chacon* WBC	1982-83	James Leija* WBC	1994
Hiroshi Kobayashi	1967-71	Roger Mayweather* WBC	1983-84	Juan Molina* IBF	1991-95
Rene Barrientos* WBC	1969-70	Hector Camacho* WBC	1983-84	Gabriel Ruelas* WBC	1994-
Yoshiaki Numata* WBC	1970-71	Rocky Lockridge	1984-85	Eddie Hopson* IBF	1995
Alfredo Marcano	1971-72	Hwan-Kil Yuh* IBF	1984-85	Tracy Patterson* IBF	1995-
R. Arredondo* WBC	1971-74	Julio César Chávez* WBC	1984-87		
Ben Villaflor	1972-73	Lester Ellis* IBF	1985-		

*Champion not generally recognized. †Champion retired or relinquished title.

Featherweights
(Weight Limit: 126 pounds)

Champion	Reign
Torpedo Billy Murphy	1890
Young Griffo	1890-92
George Dixon	1892-97
Solly Smith	1897-98
Dave Sullivan	1898
George Dixon	1898-1900
Terry McGovern	1900-01
Young Corbett II	1901-04
Jimmy Britt	1904
Tommy Sullivan	1904-05
Abe Attell	1906-12
Johnny Kilbane	1912-23
Eugene Criqui	1923
Johnny Dundee	1923-24
"Kid" Kaplan	1925-26
Benny Bass	1927-28
Tony Canzoneri	1928
Andre Routis	1928-29
Battling Battalino	1929-32
Tommy Paul* NBA	1932-33
Kid Chocolate* NY	1932-33
Freddie Miller* NBA	1933-36
Mike Beloise* NY	1936-37
Petey Sarron* NBA	1936-37
Maurice Holtzer	1937-38
Henry Armstrong	1937-38
Joey Archibald* NY	1938-39
Leo Rodak* NBA	1938-39
Joey Archibald	1939-40
Petey Scalzo* NBA	1940-41

Champion	Reign
Harry Jeffra	1940-41
Joey Archibald	1941
Richie Lamos* NBA	1941
Chalky Wright	1941-42
Jackie Wilson* NBA	1941-43
Willie Pep	1942-48
Jackie Callura* NBA	1943
Phil Terranova* NBA	1943-44
Sal Bartolo* NBA	1944-46
Sandy Saddler	1948-49
Willie Pep	1949-50
Sandy Saddler	1950-57†
Kid Bassey	1957-59
Davey Moore	1959-63
Sugar Ramos	1963-64
Vicente Saldivar	1964-67†
Paul Rojas* WBA	1968
Jose Legra* WBC	1968-69
Shozo Saijyo* WBA	1968-71
J. Famechon* WBC	1969-70
Vicente Saldivar WBC	1970
Kuniaki Shibata WBC	1970-72
Antonio Gomez* WBA	1971-72
C. Sanchez WBC	1972
Ernesto Marcel* WBA	1972-74
Jose Legra WBC	1972-73
Eder Jofre WBC	1973-74
Ruben Olivares* WBA	1974
Bobby Chacon* WBC	1974-75
Alexis Arguello WBA	1974-76

Champion	Reign
Ruben Olivares* WBC	1975
Poison Kotey* WBC	1975-76
Danny Lopez WBC	1976-80
Rafael Ortega* WBA	1977
Cecilio Lastra* WBA	1977-78
Eusebio Pedroza* WBA	1978-85
S. Sanchez WBC	1980-82
Juan LaPorte* WBC	1982-84
Wilfredo Gomez* WBC	1984
Min-Keun Oh* IBF	1984-85
Azumah Nelson* WBC	1984-88
Barry McGuigan* WBA	1985-86
Ki Young Chung* IBF	1985-86
Steve Cruz* WBA	1986-87
Antonio Rivera* IBF	1986-88
A. Esparragoza* WBA	1987-91
Calvin Grove* IBF	1988
Jorge Paez* IBF	1988-91
Jeff Fenech* WBC	1988-90†
Marcos Villasana* WBC	1990-91
Paul Hodkinson* WBC	1991-
Troy Dorsey* IBF	1991
Manuel Medina* IBF	1991-
Yung Kyun Park* WBA	1991-93
Gregorio Vargas* WBC	1993
Tom Johnson* IBF	1993-
Eloy Rojas* WBA	1993-
Kevin Kelley* WBC	1993-95
A. Gonzalez* WBC	1995
Manuel Medina* WBC	1995-

Junior Featherweights
(Weight Limit: 122 pounds)

Champion	Reign
Jack (Kid) Wolfe*	1922-23
Carl Duane*	1923-24
Rigoberto Riasco* WBC	1976
Royal Kobayashi* WBC	1976
Dong-Kyun Yum* WBC	1976-77
Wilfredo Gomez* WBC	1977-83
Soo-Hwan Hong* WBA	1977-78
Ricardo Cardona* WBA	1978-80
Leo Randolph* WBA	1980
Sergio Palma* WBA	1980-82
Leonardo Cruz* WBA	1982-84
Jaime Garza* WBC	1983
Bobby Berna* IBF	1983-84
Loris Stecca* WBA	1984
Seung-Il Suh* IBF	1984-85

Champion	Reign
Victor Callejas* WBA	1984-86
Juan (Kid) Meza* WBC	1984-85
Ji-Won Kim* IBF	1985-86
Lupe Pintor* WBC	1985-86
Samart Payakaroon* WBC	1986-87
Seung-Hoon Lee* IBF	1987-88
Louie Espinoza* WBA	1987
Jeff Fenech* WBC	1987
Julio Gervacio* WBA	1987-88
Daniel Zaragoza* WBC	1988-90
Jose Sanabria* IBF	1988-89
Bernardo Pinango* WBA	1988
Juan Jose Estrada* WBA	1988-89

Champion	Reign
Fabrice Benichou* IBF	1989-90
Jesus Salud* WBA	1989-90
Welcome Ncita* IBF	1990-
Paul Banke* WBC	1990
Luis Mendoza* WBA	1990-91
Rual Perez* WBA	1992-
Pedro Decima* WBC	1990-91
Kiyoshi Hatanaka* WBC	1991
Daniel Zaragoza* WBC	1991-92
Tracy Patterson* WBC	1992-94
Kennedy McKinney* IBF	1993-94
Wilfredo Vasquez* WBA	1992-95
Vuyani Bungu* IBF	1994-
H. Acero Sanchez* WBC	1994-
Antonio Cermeno* WBA	1995-

Note: Division called Super Bantamweight by the WBC.

Bantamweights
(Weight Limit: 118 pounds)

Champion	Reign
Spider Kelly	1887
Hughey Boyle	1887-88
Spider Kelly	1889
Chappie Moran	1889-90
George Dixon	1890-91
Pedlar Palmer*	1895-99
Terry McGovern	1899-1900
Harry Harris	1901-2

Harry Forbes	1902-3
Frankie Neil	1903-4
Joe Bowker	1904-5
Jimmy Walsh	1905-6
Owen Moran	1907-8
Monte Attell*	1909-10
Frankie Conley	1910-11
Johnny Coulon	1911-14
Kid Williams	1914-17

Kewpie Ertle*	1915
Pete Herman	1917-20
Joe Lynch	1920-21
Pete Herman	1921
Johnny Buff	1921-22
Joe Lynch	1922-24
Abe Goldstein	1924
Cannonball Martin	1924-25
Phil Rosenberg	1925-27

*Champion not generally recognized. †Champion retired or relinquished title.

Bantamweights (Cont.)

Champion	Reign
Bud Taylor NBA	1927-28
Bushy Graham* NY	1928-29
Panama Al Brown	1929-35
Sixto Escobar* NBA	1934-35
Baltazar Sangchilli	1935-36
Lou Salica* NBA	1935
Sixto Escobar* NBA	1935-36
Tony Marino	1936
Sixto Escobar	1936-37
Harry Jeffra	1937-38†
Sixto Escobar	1938-39
Georgie Pace NBA	1939-40
Lou Salica	1940-42
Manuel Ortiz	1942-47
Harold Dade	1947
Manuel Ortiz	1947-50
Vic Toweel	1950-52
Jimmy Carruthers	1952-54†
Robert Cohen	1954-56
Paul Macias* NBA	1955-57
Mario D'Agata	1956-57
Alphonse Halimi	1957-59
Joe Becerra	1959-60†
Eder Jofre	1961-65

Champion	Reign
Fighting Harada	1965-68
Lionel Rose	1968-69
Ruben Olivares	1969-70
Chucho Castillo	1970-71
Ruben Olivares	1971-72
Rafael Herrera	1972
Enrique Pinder	1972-73
Romeo Anaya	1973
Rafael Herrera* WBC	1973-74
Soo-Hwan Hong	1974-75
Rodolfo Martinez* WBC	1974-76
Alfonso Zamora	1975-77
Carlos Zarate* WBC	1976-79
Jorge Lujan	1977-80
Lupe Pintor* WBC	1979-83
Julian Solis	1980
Jeff Chandler	1980-84
Albert Davila* WBC	1983-85
Richard Sandoval	1984-86
Satoshi Shingaki* IBF	1984-85
Jeff Fenech* IBF	1985
Daniel Zaragoza* WBC	1985
Miguel Lora* WBC	1985-88
Gaby Canizales	1986

Champion	Reign
Bernardo Pinango	1986-87
W. Vasquez* WBA	1987-88
Kevin Seabrooks* IBF	1987-88
Kaokor Galaxy* WBA	1988
Moon Sung-Kil* WBA	1988-89
Kaokor Galaxy* WBA	1989
Raul Perez* WBC	1988-91
O. Canizales* IBF	1988-95
Luisito Espinosa* WBA	1989-91
Israel Contreras* WBA	1991-92
Eddie Cook* WBA	1992-93
Greg Richardson* WBC	1991
J. Tatsuyoshi, WBC	1991-92
Victor Rabanales* WBC	1992-93
Jung-Il Byun* WBC	1993
Jorge Julio WBA	1993
Yasuei Yakushiji* WBC	1993-95
Junior Jones WBA*	1994
John M. Johnson* WBA	1994
D. Chuvatana*WBA	1994-95
V. Sahaprom* WBA	1995-
W. McCullough* WBC	1995-
Harold Mestre* IBF	1995
Mbulelo Botile* IBF	1995-

Junior Bantamweights
(Weight Limit: 115 pounds)

Champion	Reign
Rafael Orono* WBC	1980-81
Chul-Ho Kim* WBC	1981-82
Gustavo Ballas* WBA	1981
Rafael Pedroza* WBA	1981-82
Rafael Orono* WBC	1982-83
Jiro Watanabe* WBA	1982-84
Payao Poontarat* WBC	1983-84
Joo-Do Chun* IBF	1983-85
Jiro Watanabe	1984-86
Kaosai Galaxy* WBA	1984
Ellyas Pical* IBF	1985-86

Champion	Reign
Cesar Polanco* IBF	1986
Gilberto Roman* WBC	1986-87
Ellyas Pical* IBF	1986
Santos Laciar* WBC	1987
Tae-Il Chang* IBF	1987
Sugar Rojas* WBC	1987-88
Ellyas Pical* IBF	1987-89
Giberto Roman* WBC	1988-89
Juan Polo Perez* IBF	1989-90
Nana Konadu* WBC	1989-90
Sung-Kil Moon* WBC	1990-93

Champion	Reign
Robert Quiroga* IBF	1990-93
Julio Borboa* IBF	1993-94
Katsuya Onizuka* WBA	1993-94
Lee Hyung-Chul* WBA	1994-95
Jose Luis Bueno* WBC	1993-94
Hiroshi Kawashima*WBC	1994-
Harold Grey* IBF	1994-95
Alimi Goitia* WBA	1995-
Carlos Salazar* IBF	1995-

Note: Division called Super Flyweight by the WBC.

Flyweights
(Weight Limit: 112 pounds)

Champion	Reign
Sid Smith	1913
Bill Ladbury	1913-14
Percy Jones	1914
Joe Symonds	1914-16
Jimmy Wilde	1916-23
Pancho Villa	1923-25
Fidel LaBarba	1925-27†
Frenchy Belanger NBA	1927-28
Izzy Schwartz NY	1927-29
Frankie Genaro NBA	1928-29
Spider Pladner NBA	1929
Frankie Genaro NBA	1929-31
Midget Wolgast* NY	1930-35
Young Perez NBA	1931-32
Jackie Brown NBA	1932-35
Benny Lynch	1935-38
Small Montana* NY	1935-37
Peter Kane	1938-43
Little Dado* NY	1938-40
Jackie Paterson	1943-48

Champion	Reign
Rinty Monaghan	1948-50
Terry Allen	1950
Dado Marino	1950-52
Yoshio Shirai	1953-54
Pascual Perez	1954-60
Pone Kingpetch	1960-62
Masahiko Harada	1962-63
Pone Kingpetch	1963
Hiroyuki Ebihara	1963-64
Pone Kingpetch	1964-65
Salvatore Burrini	1965-66
H. Accavallo* WBA	1966-68
Walter McGowan	1966
Chartchai Chionoi	1966-69
Efren Torres	1969-70
Hiroyuki Ebihara* WBA	1969
B. Villacampo* WBA	1969-70
Chartchai Chionoi	1970
B. Chartvanchai* WBA	1970
Masao Ohba* WBA	1970-73

Champion	Reign
Erbito Salavarria	1970-73
B. Gonzalez* WBA	1972
V. Borkorsor* WBC	1972-73
Venice Borkorsor	1973
Chartchai Chionoi* WBA	1973-74
B. Gonzalez* WBA	1973-74
Shoji Oguma* WBC	1974-75
S. Hanagata* WBA	1974-75
Miguel Canto* WBC	1975-79
Erbito Salavarria* WBA	1975-76
Alfonso Lopez* WBA	1976
G. Espadas* WBA	1976-78
B. Gonzalez* WBA	1978-79
Chan-Hee Park* WBC	1979-80
Luis Ibarra* WBA	1979-80
Tae-Shik Kim* WBA	1980
Shoji Oguma* WBC	1980-81
Peter Mathebula* WBA	1980-81
Santos Laciar* WBA	1981
Antonio Avelar* WBC	1981-82

*Champion not generally recognized. †Champion retired or relinquished title.

Flyweights (Cont.)

Champion	Reign	Champion	Reign	Champion	Reign
Luis Ibarra* WBA	1981	Chong-Kwan		Yul-Woo Lee* WBA	1990
Juan Herrera* WBA	1981-82	Chung* IBF	1985-86	L. Tamakuma* WBA	1990-91
P. Cardona* WBC	1982	Bi-Won Chung* IBF	1986	M. Kittikasem* WBC	1991-92
Santos Laciar* WBA	1982-85	Hi-Sup Shin* IBF	1986-87	Yuri Arbachakov* WBC	1992-
Freddie Castillo* WBC	1982	Dodie Penalosa* IBF	1987	Yong Kang Kim* WBA	1991-92
E. Mercedes* WBA	1982-83	Fidel Bassa* WBA	1987-89	Rodolfo Blanco* IBF	1992-93
Charlie Magri* WBC	1983	Choi-Chang Ho* IBF	1987-88	P. Sithbangprachan* IBF	1993-95
Frank Cedeno* WBC	1983-84	Rolando Bohol* IBF	1988	David Griman* WBA	1992-94
Soon-Chun Kwon* IBF	1983-85	Yong-Kang Kim* WBC	1988-89	S. S. Ploenchit* WBA	1994-
Koji Kobayashi* WBC	1984	Duke McKenzie* IBF	1988-89	Francisco Tejedor* IBF	1995
Gabriel Bernal* WBC	1984	Sot Chitalada* WBC	1989-91	Danny Romero* IBF	1995-
Sot Chitalada* WBC	1984-88	Dave McAuley* IBF	1989-92		
Hilario Zapate* WBA	1985-87	Jesus Rojas* WBA	1989-90		

Junior Flyweights
(Weight Limit: 108 pounds)

Champion	Reign	Champion	Reign	Champion	Reign
Franco Udella* WBC	1975	Tadashi Tomori* WBC	1982	Humberto	
Jaime Rios* WBA	1975-76	Hilario Zapata* WBC	1982-83	Gonzalez* WBC	1989-90
Luis Estaba* WBC	1975-78	Jung-Koo Chang* WBC	1983-88	Michael Carbajal* IBF	1990-94
Juan Guzman* WBA	1976	Lupe Madera* WBA	1983-84	R. Pascua* WBC	1990
Yoko Gushiken* WBA	1976-81	Dodie Penalosa* IBF	1983-86	M. C. Castro* WBC	1991
Freddy Castillo* WBC	1978	Francisco Quiroz* WBA	1984-85	H. Gonzalez* WBC	1991-93
Netrnoi Vorasingh* WBC	1978	Joey Olivo* WBA	1985	Hirokia Ioka* WBA	1991-92
Sung-Jun Kim* WBC	1978-80	Myung-Woo Yuh* WBA	1985-91	Michael Carbajal, WBC	1993-94
Shigeo Nakajima* WBC	1980	Jum-Hwan Choi* IBF	1986-88	Myung-Woo Yuh* WBA	1993
Hilario Zapata* WBC	1980-82	Tacy Macalos* IBF	1988-89	Leo Gamez* WBA	1993-95
Pedro Flores* WBA	1981	German Torres* WBC	1988-89	H. Gonzalez* WBC, IBF	1994-95
Hwan-Jin Kim* WBA	1981	Yul-Woo Lee* WBC	1989	Choi Hi-Yong* WBA	1995-
Katsuo Tokashiki* WBA	1981-83	Muangchai		S. Sorjaturong* WBC, IBF	1995-
Amado Urzua* WBC	1982	Kittikasem* IBF	1989-90		

Note: Division called Light Flyweight by the WBC.

Strawweights
(Weight Limit: 105 pounds)

Champion	Reign	Champion	Reign	Champion	Reign
Franco Udella* WBC	1975	Katsuo Tokashiki* WBA	1981-83	German Torres* WBC	1988-89
Jaime Rios* WBA	1975-76	Amado Urzua* WBC	1982	Yul-Woo Lee* WBC	1989
Luis Estaba* WBC	1975-78	Tadashi Tomori* WBC	1982	M. Kittikasem* IBF	1989-90
Juan Guzman* WBA	1976	Hilario Zapata* WBC	1982-83	H. Gonzalez* WBC	1989-90
Yoko Gushiken* WBA	1976-81	Jung-Koo Chang* WBC	1983-88	Michael Carbajal* IBF	1990
Freddy Castillo* WBC	1978	Lupe Madera* WBA	1983-84	Rolando Pascua* WBC	1990
Netrnoi Vorasingh* WBC	1978	Dodie Penalosa* IBF	1983-86	M. C. Castro* WBC	1991
Sung-Jun Kim* WBC	1978-80	Francisco Quiroz* WBA	1984-85	Ricardo Lopez* WBC	1990-
Shigeo Nakajima* WBC	1980	Joey Olivo* WBA	1985	R. Voraphin* IBF	1992-
Hilario Zapata* WBC	1980-82	Myung-Woo Yuh* WBA	1985-93	Chana Porpaoin* WBA	1993-
Pedro Flores* WBA	1981	Jum-Hwan Choi* IBF	1986-88		
Hwan-Jin Kim* WBA	1981	Tacy Macalos* IBF	1988-89		

*Champion not generally recognized.

Total Bouts

Name	Years Active	Bouts	Name	Years Active	Bouts
Len Wickwar	1928-47	463	Maxie Rosenbloom	1923-39	299
Jack Britton	1905-30	350	Harry Greb	1913-26	298
Johnny Dundee	1910-32	333	Young Stribling	1921-33	286
Billy Bird	1920-48	318	Battling Levinsky	1910-29	282
George Marsden	1928-46	311	Ted (Kid) Lewis	1909-29	279

Note: Based on records in *The Ring Record Book* and *Boxing Encyclopedia*.

Most Knockouts

Name	Years Active	KOs	Name	Years Active	KOs
Archie Moore	1936-63	130	Sandy Saddler	1944-56	103
Young Stribling	1921-33	126	Sam Langford	1902-26	102
Billy Bird	1920-48	125	Henry Armstrong	1931-45	100
George Odwell	1930-45	114	Jimmy Wilde	1911-23	98
Sugar Ray Robinson	1940-65	110	Len Wickwar	1928-47	93

Note: Based on records in *The Ring Record Book* and *Boxing Encyclopedia*.

World Heavyweight Championship Fights

Date	Winner	Wgt	Loser	Wgt	Result	Site
Sept 7, 1892	James J. Corbett*	178	John L. Sullivan	212	KO 21	New Orleans
Jan 25, 1894	James J. Corbett	184	Charley Mitchell	158	KO 3	Jacksonville, FL
Mar 17, 1897	Bob Fitzsimmons*	167	James J. Corbett	183	KO 14	Carson City, NV
June 9, 1899	James J. Jeffries*	206	Bob Fitzsimmons	167	KO 11	Coney Island, NY
Nov 3, 1899	James J. Jeffries	215	Tom Sharkey	183	Ref 25	Coney Island, NY
Apr 6, 1900	James J. Jeffries	n/a	Jack Finnegan	n/a	KO 1	Detroit
May 11, 1900	James J. Jeffries	218	James J. Corbett	188	KO 23	Coney Island, NY
Nov 15, 1901	James J. Jeffries	211	Gus Ruhlin	194	TKO 6	San Francisco
July 25, 1902	James J. Jeffries	219	Bob Fitzsimmons	172	KO 8	San Francisco
Aug 14, 1903	James J. Jeffries	220	James J. Corbett	190	KO 10	San Francisco
Aug 25, 1904	James J. Jeffries	219	Jack Munroe	186	TKO 2	San Francisco
July 3, 1905	Marvin Hart*	190	Jack Root	171	KO 12	Reno
Feb 23, 1906	Tommy Burns*	180	Marvin Hart	188	Ref 20	Los Angeles
Oct 2, 1906	Tommy Burns	n/a	Jim Flynn	n/a	KO 15	Los Angeles
Nov 28, 1906	Tommy Burns	172	Jack O'Brien	163½	Draw 20	Los Angeles
May 8, 1907	Tommy Burns	180	Jack O'Brien	167	Ref 20	Los Angeles
Jul 4, 1907	Tommy Burns	181	Bill Squires	180	KO 1	Colma, CA
Dec 2, 1907	Tommy Burns	177	Gunner Moir	204	KO 10	London
Feb 10, 1908	Tommy Burns	n/a	Jack Palmer	n/a	KO 4	London
Mar 17, 1908	Tommy Burns	n/a	Jem Roche	n/a	KO 1	Dublin
Apr 18, 1908	Tommy Burns	n/a	Jewey Smith	n/a	KO 5	Paris
June 13, 1908	Tommy Burns	184	Bill Squires	183	KO 8	Paris
Aug 24, 1908	Tommy Burns	181	Bill Squires	184	KO 13	Sydney
Sept 2, 1908	Tommy Burns	183	Bill Lang	187	KO 6	Melbourne
Dec 26, 1908	Jack Johnson*	192	Tommy Burns	168	TKO 14	Sydney
Mar 10, 1909	Jack Johnson	n/a	Victor McLaglen	n/a	ND 6	Vancouver
May 19, 1909	Jack Johnson	205	Jack O'Brien	161	ND 6	Philadelphia
June 30, 1909	Jack Johnson	207	Tony Ross	214	ND 6	Pittsburgh
Sept 9, 1909	Jack Johnson	209	Al Kaufman	191	ND 10	San Francisco
Oct 16, 1909	Jack Johnson	205½	Stanley Ketchel	170¼	KO 12	Colma, CA
July 4, 1910	Jack Johnson	208	James J. Jeffries	227	KO 15	Reno
July 4, 1912	Jack Johnson	195½	Jim Flynn	175	TKO 9	Las Vegas
Dec 19, 1913	Jack Johnson	n/a	Jim Johnson	n/a	Draw 10	Paris
June 27, 1914	Jack Johnson	221	Frank Moran	203	Ref 20	Paris
Apr 5, 1915	Jess Willard*	230	Jack Johnson	205½	KO 26	Havana
Mar 25, 1916	Jess Willard	225	Frank Moran	203	ND 10	New York City
July 4, 1919	Jack Dempsey*	187	Jess Willard	245	TKO 4	Toledo, OH
Sept 6, 1920	Jack Dempsey	185	Billy Miske	187	KO 3	Benton Harbor, MI
Dec 14, 1920	Jack Dempsey	188¼	Bill Brennan	197	KO 12	New York City
July 2, 1921	Jack Dempsey	188	Georges Carpentier	172	KO 4	Jersey City
July 4, 1923	Jack Dempsey	188	Tommy Givvons	175½	Ref 15	Shelby, MT
Sept 14, 1923	Jack Dempsey	192½	Luis Firpo	216½	KO 2	New York City
Sept 23, 1926	Gene Tunney*	189½	Jack Dempsey	190	UD 10	Philadelphia
Sept 22, 1927	Gene Tunney	189½	Jack Dempsey	192½	UD 10	Chicago
July 26, 1928	Gene Tunney	192	Tom Heeney	203½	TKO 11	New York City
June 12, 1930	Max Schmeling*	188	Jack Sharkey	197	Foul 4	New York City
July 3, 1931	Max Schmeling	189	Young Stribling	186½	TKO 15	Cleveland
June 21, 1932	Jack Sharkey*	205	Max Schmeling	188	Split 15	Long Island City
June 29, 1933	Primo Carnera*	260½	Jack Sharkey	201	KO 6	Long Island City
Oct 22, 1933	Primo Carnera	259½	Paulino Uzcudun	229¼	UD 15	Rome
Mar 1, 1934	Primo Carnera	270	Tommy Loughran	184	UD 15	Miami
June 14, 1934	Max Baer*	209½	Primo Carnera	263¼	TKO 11	Long Island City
June 13, 1935	James J. Braddock*	193¾	Max Baer	209½	UD 15	Long Island City
June 22, 1937	Joe Louis	197¼	James J. Braddock	197	KO 8	Chicago
Aug 30, 1937	Joe Louis	197	Tommy Farr	204¼	UD 15	New York City
Feb 23, 1938	Joe Louis	200	Nathan Mann	193½	KO 3	New York City

Date	Winner	Wgt	Loser	Wgt	Result	Site
Apr 1, 1938........Joe Louis		202½	Harry Thomas	196	KO 5	Chicago
June 22, 1938....Joe Louis		198¼	Max Schmeling	193	KO 1	New York City
Jan 25, 1939....Joe Louis		200¼	John Henry Lewis	180¾	KO 1	New York City
Apr 17, 1939....Joe Louis		201¼	Jack Roper	204¾	KO 1	Los Angeles
June 28, 1939....Joe Louis		200¾	Tony Galento	233¾	TKO 4	New York City
Sept 20, 1939....Joe Louis		200	Bob Pastor	183	KO 11	Detroit
Feb 9, 1940......Joe Louis		203	Arturo Godoy	202	Split 15	New York City
Mar 29, 1940.....Joe Louis		201½	Johnny Paychek	187½	KO 2	New York City
June 20, 1940....Joe Louis		199	Arturo Godoy	201¼	TKO 8	New York City
Dec 16, 1940....Joe Louis		202¼	Al McCoy	180¾	TKO 6	Boston
Jan 31, 1941......Joe Louis		202½	Red Burman	188	KO 5	New York City
Feb 17, 1941....Joe Louis		203½	Gus Dorazio	193½	KO 2	Philadelphia
Mar 21, 1941....Joe Louis		202	Abe Simon	254½	TKO 13	Detroit
Apr 8, 1941........Joe Louis		203½	Tony Musto	199½	TKO 9	St Louis
May 23, 1941....Joe Louis		201½	Buddy Baer	237½	Disq 7	Washington, DC
June 18, 1941....Joe Louis		199½	Billy Conn	174	KO 13	New York City
Sept 29, 1941....Joe Louis		202¼	Lou Nova	202½	TKO 6	New York City
Jan 9, 1942....Joe Louis		206¾	Buddy Baer	250	KO 1	New York City
Mar 27, 1942....Joe Louis		207½	Abe Simon	255½	KO 6	New York City
June 9, 1946......Joe Louis		207	Billy Conn	187	KO 8	New York City
Sept 18, 1946....Joe Louis		211	Tami Mauriello	198½	KO 1	New York City
Dec 5, 1947....Joe Louis		211½	Jersey Joe Walcott	194½	Split 15	New York City
June 25, 1948....Joe Louis		213½	Jersey Joe Walcott	194¾	KO 11	New York City
June 22, 1949...Ezzard Charles*		181¾	Jersey Joe Walcott	195½	UD 15	Chicago
Aug 10, 1949......Ezzard Charles		180	Gus Lesnevich	182	TKO 8	New York City
Oct 14, 1949......Ezzard Charles		182	Pat Valentino	188½	KO 8	San Francisco
Aug 15, 1950......Ezzard Charles		183¼	Freddie Beshore	184½	TKO 14	Buffalo
Sept 27, 1950......Ezzard Charles		184½	Joe Louis	218	UD 15	New York City
Dec 5, 1950.......Ezzard Charles		185	Nick Barone	178½	KO 11	Cincinnati
Jan 12, 1951......Ezzard Charles		185	Lee Oma	193	TKO 10	New York City
Mar 7, 1951......Ezzard Charles		186	Jersey Joe Walcott	193	UD 15	Detroit
May 30, 1951.....Ezzard Charles		182	Joey Maxim	181½	UD 15	Chicago
July 18, 1951.....Jersey Joe Walcott*		194	Ezzard Charles	182	KO 7	Pittsburgh
June 5, 1952....Jersey Joe Walcott		196	Ezzard Charles	191½	UD 15	Philadelphia
Sept 23, 1952....Rocky Marciano*		184	Jersey Joe Walcott	196	KO 13	Philadelphia
May 15, 1953....Rocky Marciano		184½	Jersey Joe Walcott	197¾	KO 1	Chicago
Sept 24, 1953....Rocky Marciano		185	Roland LaStarza	184¾	TKO 11	New York City
June 17, 1954....Rocky Marciano		187½	Ezzard Charles	185½	UD 15	New York City
Sept 17, 1954....Rocky Marciano		187	Ezzard Charles	192½	KO 8	New York City
May 16, 1955....Rocky Marciano		189	Don Cockell	205	TKO 9	San Francisco
Sept 21, 1955....Rocky Marciano		188¼	Archie Moore	188	KO 9	New York City
Nov 30, 1956....Floyd Patterson*		182¼	Archie Moore	187¾	KO 5	Chicago
July 29, 1957.....Floyd Patterson		184	Tommy Jackson	192½	TKO 10	New York City
Aug 22, 1957.....Floyd Patterson		187¼	Pete Rademacher	202	KO 6	Seattle
Aug 18, 1958.....Floyd Patterson		184½	Roy Harris	194	TKO 13	Los Angeles
May 1, 1959.....Floyd Patterson		182½	Brian London	206	KO 11	Indianapolis
June 26, 1959....Ingemar Johansson*		196	Floyd Patterson	182	TKO 3	New York City
June 20, 1960....Floyd Patterson*		190	Ingemar Johansson	194¾	KO 5	New York City
Mar 13, 1961....Floyd Patterson		194¾	Ingemar Johansson	206½	KO 6	Miami Beach
Dec 4, 1961.......Floyd Patterson		188½	Tom McNeeley	197	KO 4	Toronto
Sept 25, 1962....Sonny Liston*		214	Floyd Patterson	189	KO 1	Chicago
July 22, 1963....Sonny Liston		215	Floyd Patterson	194½	KO 1	Las Vegas
Feb 25, 1964.....Cassius Clay		210½	Sonny Liston	218	TKO 7	Miami Beach
Mar 5, 1965....Ernie Terrell WBA*		199	Eddie Machen	192	UD 15	Chicago
May 25, 1965....Muhammad Ali		206	Sonny Liston	215¼	KO 1	Lewiston, ME
Nov 1, 1965.......Ernie Terrell WBA*		206	George Chuvalo	209	UD 15	Toronto
Nov 22, 1965....Muhammad Ali		210	Floyd Patterson	196¾	TKO 12	Las Vegas
Mar 29, 1966....Muhammad Ali		214½	George Chuvalo	216	UD 15	Toronto
May 21, 1966....Muhammad Ali		201½	Henry Cooper	188	TKO 6	London
June 28, 1966....Ernie Terrell WBA*		209½	Doug Jones	187½	UD 15	Houston
Aug 6, 1966........Muhammad Ali		209½	Brian London	201½	KO 3	London
Sept 10, 1966....Muhammad Ali		203½	Karl Mildenberger	194¼	TKO 12	Frankfurt
Nov 14, 1966....Muhammad Ali		212¾	Cleveland Williams	210½	TKO 3	Houston
Feb 6, 1967....Muhammad Ali		212¼	Ernie Terrell WBA	212½	UD 15	Houston
Mar 22, 1967.....Muhammad Ali		211½	Zora Folley	202½	KO 7	New York City
Mar 4, 1968.......Joe Frazier*		204½	Buster Mathis	243½	TKO 11	New York City
Apr 27, 1968.....Jimmy Ellis*		197	Jerry Quarry	195	Maj 15	Oakland
June 24, 1968....Joe Frazier NY*		203½	Manuel Ramos	208	TKO 2	New York City

Date	Winner	Wgt	Loser	Wgt	Result	Site
Aug 14, 1968	Jimmy Ellis WBA*	198	Floyd Patterson	188	Ref 15	Stockholm
Dec 10, 1968	Joe Frazier NY*	203	Oscar Bonavena	207	UD 15	Philadelphia
Apr 22, 1969	Joe Frazier NY*	204½	Dave Zyglewicz	190½	KO 1	Houston
June 23, 1969	Joe Frazier NY*	203½	Jerry Quarry	198½	TKO 8	New York City
Feb 16, 1970	Joe Frazier NY*	205	Jimmy Ellis WBA	201	TKO 5	New York City
Nov 18, 1970	Joe Frazier*	209	Bob Foster	188	KO 2	Detroit
Mar 8, 1971	Joe Frazier*	205½	Muhammad Ali	215	UD 15	New York City
Jan 15, 1972	Joe Frazier*	215½	Terry Daniels	195	TKO 4	New Orleans
May 26, 1972	Joe Frazier	217½	Ron Stander	218	TKO 5	Omaha
Jan 22, 1973	George Foreman*	217½	Joe Frazier	214	TKO 2	Kingston, Jam.
Sept 1, 1973	George Foreman	219½	Jose Roman	196½	KO 1	Tokyo
Mar 26, 1974	George Foreman	224¼	Ken Norton	212¼	TKO 2	Caracas
Oct 30, 1974	Muhammad Ali*	216-½	George Foreman	220	KO 8	Kinshasa, Zaire
Mar 24, 1975	Muhammad Ali	223½	Chuck Wepner	225	TKO 15	Cleveland
May 16, 1975	Muhammad Ali	224½	Ron Lyle	219	TKO 11	Las Vegas
July 1, 1975	Muhammad Ali	224½	Joe Bugner	230	UD 15	Kuala Lumpur, Malaysia
Oct 1, 1975	Muhammad Ali	224½	Joe Frazier	215	TKO 15	Manila
Feb 20, 1976	Muhammad Ali	226	Jean Pierre Coopman	206	KO 5	San Juan
Apr 30, 1976	Muhammad Ali	230	Jimmy Young	209	UD 15	Landover, MD
May 24, 1976	Muhammad Ali	230	Richard Dunn	206½	TKO 5	Munich
Sept 28, 1976	Muhammad Ali	221	Ken Norton	217½	UD 15	New York City
May 16, 1977	Muhammad Ali	221¼	Alfredo Evangelista	209¼	UD 15	Landover, MD
Sept 29, 1977	Muhammad Ali	225	Earnie Shavers	211¼	UD 15	New York City
Feb 15, 1978	Leon Spinks*	197¼	Muhammad Ali	224¼	Split 15	Las Vegas
June 9, 1978	Larry Holmes*	209	Ken Norton WBC	220	Split 15	Las Vegas
Sept 15, 1978	Muhammad Ali*	221	Leon Spinks	201	UD 15	New Orleans
Nov 10, 1978	Larry Holmes WBC*	214	Alfredo Evangelista	208¼	KO 7	Las Vegas
Mar 23, 1979	Larry Holmes WBC*	214	Osvaldo Ocasio	207	TKO 7	Las Vegas
June 22, 1979	Larry Holmes WBC*	215	Mike Weaver	202	TKO 12	New York City
Sept 28, 1979	Larry Holmes WBC*	210	Earnie Shavers	211	TKO 11	Las Vegas
Oct 20, 1979	John Tate*	240	Gerrie Coetzee	222	UD 15	Pretoria
Feb 3, 1980	Larry Holmes WBC*	213½	Lorenzo Zanon	215	TKO 6	Las Vegas
Mar 31, 1980	Mike Weaver*	232	John Tate WBA	232	KO 15	Knoxville
Mar 31, 1980	Larry Holmes WBC*	211	Leroy Jones	254½	TKO 8	Las Vegas
July 7, 1980	Larry Holmes WBC*	214¼	Scott LeDoux	226	TKO 7	Minneapolis
Oct 2, 1980	Larry Holmes WBC*	211¼	Muhammad Ali	217½	TKO 11	Las Vegas
Oct 25, 1980	Mike Weaver WBA*	210	Gerrie Coetzee	226½	KO 13	Sun City
Apr 11, 1981	Larry Holmes	215	Trevor Berbick	215½	UD 15	Las Vegas
June 12, 1981	Larry Holmes	212¼	Leon Spinks	200¼	TKO 3	Detroit
Oct 3, 1981	Mike Weaver WBA*	215	James Quick Tillis	209	UD 15	Rosemont, IL
Nov 6, 1981	Larry Holmes	213¼	Renaldo Snipes	215¾	TKO 11	Pittsburgh
June 11, 1982	Larry Holmes	212½	Gerry Cooney	225½	TKO 13	Las Vegas
Nov 26, 1982	Larry Holmes	217½	Tex Cobb	234¼	UD 15	Houston
Dec 10, 1982	Michael Dokes*	216	Mike Weaver WBA	209¾	TKO 1	Las Vegas
Mar 27, 1983	Larry Holmes	221	Lucien Rodriguez	209	UD 12	Scranton
May 20, 1983	Michael Dokes WBA*	223	Mike Weaver	218½	Draw 15	Las Vegas
May 20, 1983	Larry Holmes	213	Tim Witherspoon	219½	Split 12	Las Vegas
Sept 10, 1983	Larry Holmes	223	Scott Frank	211¼	TKO 5	Atlantic City
Sept 23, 1983	Gerrie Coetzee*	215	Michael Dokes WBA	217	KO 10	Richfield, OH
Nov 25, 1983	Larry Holmes	219	Marvis Frazier	200	TKO 1	Las Vegas
Mar 9, 1984	Tim Witherspoon	220¼	Greg Page	239½	Maj 12	Las Vegas
Aug 31, 1984	Pinklon Thomas*	216	Tim Witherspoon WBC	217	Maj 12	Las Vegas
Nov 9, 1984	Larry Holmes IBF	221½	James Smith	227	TKO 12	Las Vegas
Dec 1, 1984	Greg Page*	236½	Gerrie Coetzee WBA	218	KO 8	Sun City
Mar 15, 1985	Larry Holmes	223½	David Bey	233¼	TKO 10	Las Vegas
Apr 29, 1985	Tony Tubbs*	229	Greg Page WBA	239½	UD 15	Buffalo
May 20, 1985	Larry Holmes	224¼	Carl Williams	215	UD 15	Las Vegas
June 15, 1985	Pinklon Thomas*	220¼	Mike Weaver	221¼	KO 8	Las Vegas
Sept 21, 1985	Michael Spinks*	200	Larry Holmes IBF	221½	UD 15	Las Vegas
Jan 17, 1986	Tim Witherspoon	227	Tony Tubbs WBA	229	Maj 15	Atlanta
Mar 22, 1986	Trevor Berbick*	218½	Pinklon Thomas WBC	222¾	UD 15	Las Vegas
Apr 19, 1986	Michael Spinks	205	Larry Holmes	223	Split 15	Las Vegas
July 19, 1986	Tim Witherspoon*	234¾	Frank Bruno	228	TKO 11	Wembley, Eng.
Sept 6, 1986	Michael Spinks	201	Steffen Tangstad	214¾	TKO 4	Las Vegas
Nov 22, 1986	Mike Tyson*	221¼	Trevor Berbick WBC	218½	TKO 2	Las Vegas
Dec 12, 1986	James Smith*	228½	Tim Witherspoon WBA	233½	TKO 1	New York City
Mar 7, 1987	Mike Tyson WBC*	219	James Smith WBA	233	UD 12	Las Vegas

Date	Winner	Wgt	Loser	Wgt	Result	Site
May 30, 1987.....Mike Tyson*		218¾	Pinklon Thomas	217¾	TKO 6	Las Vegas
May 30, 1987....Tony Tucker		222¼	Buster Douglas	227¼	TKO 10	Las Vegas
June 15, 1987...Michael Spinks		208¾	Gerry Cooney	238	TKO 5	Atlantic City
Aug 1, 1987.......Mike Tyson*		221	Tony Tucker IBF	221	UD 12	Las Vegas
Oct 16, 1987.....Mike Tyson*		216	Tyrell Biggs	228¾	TKO 7	Atlantic City
Jan 22, 1988.....Mike Tyson*		215¾	Larry Holmes	225¾	TKO 4	Atlantic City
Mar 20, 1988 .....Mike Tyson*		216¼	Tony Tubbs	238¼	KO 2	Tokyo
June 27, 1988...Mike Tyson*		218¼	Michael Spinks	212¼	KO 1	Atlantic City
Feb 25, 1989 .....Mike Tyson		218	Frank Bruno	228	TKO 5	Las Vegas
July 21, 1989 .....Mike Tyson		219¼	Carl Williams	218	TKO 1	Atlantic City
Feb 10, 1990 .....Buster Douglas*		231½	Mike Tyson	220½	KO 10	Tokyo
Oct 25, 1990......Evander Holyfield		208	Buster Douglas	246	KO 3	Las Vegas
Apr 19, 1991......Evander Holyfield		212	George Foreman	257	UD 12	Atlantic City
Nov 23, 1991....Evander Holyfield		210	Bert Cooper	215	TKO 7	Atlanta
June 19, 1992....Evander Holyfield		210	Larry Holmes	233	UD 12	Las Vegas
Nov 13, 1992 ....Riddick Bowe		235	Evander Holyfield	205	UD 12	Las Vegas
Feb 6, 1993 ......Riddick Bowe		243	Michael Dokes	244	KO 1	New York City
May 8, 1993......Lennox Lewis		235	Tony Tucker	235	UD 12	Las Vegas
May 22, 1993....Riddick Bowe		244	Jesse Ferguson	224	KO 2	Washington, DC
Oct 2, 1993.......Lennox Lewis		229	Frank Bruno	233	KO 7	London
Nov 6, 1993 ....Evander Holyfield		217	Riddick Bowe	246	Split 12	Las Vegas
Apr 22, 1994.....Michael Moorer		214	Evander Holyfield	214	Split 12	Las Vegas
May 6, 1994......Lennox Lewis		235	Phil Jackson	218	TKO 8	Atlantic City
Nov 6, 1994......George Foreman		250	Michael Moorer	222	KO 10	Las Vegas
Mar 11, 1995....Riddick Bowe		241	Herbie Hide	214	KO 6	Las Vegas
Apr 8, 1995........Oliver McCall		231	Larry Holmes	236	UD 12	Las Vegas
Apr 8, 1995........Bruce Seldon		236	Tony Tucker	243	TKO 7	Las Vegas
Apr 22, 1995.....George Foreman		256	Axel Schulz	221	Split 12	Las Vegas
Jun 17, 1995.....Riddick Bowe		243	Jorge Luis Gonzalez	237	KO 6	Las Vegas
Aug 19, 1995....Bruce Seldon		234	Joe Hipp	233	TKO 10	Las Vegas
Sept 2, 1995 .....Frank Bruno		247¾	Oliver McCall	234¾	UD 12	London

*Champion not generally recognized.

KO=knockout; TKO=technical knockout; UD=unanimous decision; Split=split decision; Ref=referee's decision; Disq=disqualification; ND=no decision.

Ring Magazine Fighter and Fight of the Year

Year	Fighter	Year	Fighter	Year	Fighter
1928	Gene Tunney	1935	Barney Ross	1941	Joe Louis
1929	Tommy Loughran	1936	Joe Louis	1942	Ray Robinson
1930	Max Schmeling	1937	Henry Armstrong	1943	Fred Apostoli
1932	Jack Sharkey	1938	Joe Louis	1944	Beau Jack
1933	No award	1939	Joe Louis		
1934	T. Canzoneri/B. Ross	1940	Billy Conn		

Note: No fight of the year named until 1945

Year	Fighter	Fight	Winner	Site
1945	Willie Pep	Rocky Graziano-Cochrane	Rocky Graziano	New York City
1946	Tony Zale	Tony Zale-Rocky Graziano	Tony Zale	New York City
1947	Gus Lesnevich	Rocky Graziano-Tony Zale	Rocky Graziano	Chicago
1948	Ike Williams	Marcel Cerdan-Tony Zale	Marcel Cerdan	Jersey City
1949	Ezzard Charles	Willie Pep-Sandy Saddler	Willie Pep	New York City
1950	Ezzard Charles	Jake LaMotta-Laurent Dauthuille	Jake LaMotta	Detroit
1951	Ray Robinson	Jersey Joe Walcott-Ezzard Charles	Jersey Joe Walcott	Pittsburgh
1952	Rocky Marciano	Rocky Marciano-Jersey Joe Walcott	Rocky Marciano	Philadelphia
1953	Carl Olson	Rocky Marciano-Roland LaStarza	Rocky Marciano	New York City
1954	Rocky Marciano	Rocky Marciano-Ezzard Charles	Rocky Marciano	New York City
1955	Rocky Marciano	Carmen Basilio-Tony DeMarco	Carmen Basilio	Boston
1956	Floyd Patterson	Carmen Basilio-Johnny Saxton	Carmen Basilio	Syracuse
1957	Carmen Basilio	Carmen Basilio-Ray Robinson	Carmen Basilio	New York City
1958	Ingemar Johansson	Ray Robinson-Carmen Basilio	Ray Robinson	Chicago
1959	Ingemar Johansson	Gene Fullmer-Carmen Basilio	Gene Fullmer	San Francisco
1960	Floyd Patterson	Floyd Patterson-Ingemar Johansson	Floyd Patterson	New York City
1961	Joe Brown	Joe Brown-Dave Charnley	Joe Brown	London
1962	Dick Tiger	Joey Giardello-Henry Hank	Joey Giardello	Philadelphia
1963	Cassius Clay	Cassius Clay-Doug Jones	Cassius Clay	New York City
1964	Emile Griffith	Cassius Clay-Sonny Liston	Cassius Clay	Miami Beach

Year	Fighter	Fight	Winner	Site
1965	Dick Tiger	Floyd Patterson-George Chuvalo	Floyd Patterson	New York City
1966	No award	Jose Torres-Eddie Cotton	Jose Torres	Las Vegas
1967	Joe Frazier	Nino Benvenuti-Emile Griffith	Nino Benvenuti	New York City
1968	Nino Benvenuti	Dick Tiger-Frank DePaula	Dick Tiger	New York City
1969	Jose Napoles	Joe Frazier-Jerry Quarry	Joe Frazier	New York City
1970	Joe Frazier	Carlos Monzon-Nino Benvenuti	Carlos Monzon	Rome
1971	Joe Frazier	Joe Frazier-Muhammed Ali	Joe Frazier	New York City
1972	Muhammed Ali Carlos Monzon	Bob Foster-Chris Finnegan	Bob Foster	London
1973	George Foreman	George Foreman-Joe Frazier	George Foreman	Kingston, Jam.
1974	Muhammed Ali	Muhammed Ali-George Foreman	Muhammed Ali	Kinshasa
1975	Muhammed Ali	Muhammed Ali-Joe Frazier	Muhammed Ali	Manila
1976	George Foreman	George Foreman-Ron Lyle	George Foreman	Las Vegas
1977	Carlos Zarate	Joe Young-George Foreman	Joe Young	San Juan
1978	Muhammed Ali	Leon Spinks-Muhammed Ali	Leon Spinks	La Vegas
1979	Ray Leonard	Danny Lopez-Tony Ayala	Danny Lopez	San Antonio
1980	Thomas Hearns	Saad Muhammed-Danny Lopez	Saad Muhammed	McAfee, NJ
1981	Ray Leonard Salvador Sanchez	Ray Leonard-Tonny Hearns	Ray Leonard	Las Vegas
1982	Larry Holmes	Bobby Chacon-Rafael Limon	Bobby Chacon	Sacramento
1983	Marvin Hagler	Bobby Chacon-Cornelius Boza-Edwards	Bobby Chacon	Las Vegas
1984	Thomas Hearns	Jose Luis Ramirez-Edwin Rosario	Jose Luis Ramirez	San Juan
1985	Donald Curry Marvin Hagler	Marvin Hagler-Tommy Hearns	Marvin Hagler	Las Vegas
1986	Mike Tyson	Stevie Cruz-Barry McGuigan	Stevie Cruz	Las Vegas
1987	Evander Holyfield	Ray Leonard-Marvin Hagler	Ray Leonard	Las Vegas
1988	Mike Tyson	Tony Lopez-Rocky Lockridge	Tony Lopez	Inglewood, CA
1989	Pernell Whitaker	Roberto Duran-Iran Barkley	Roberto Duran	Atlantic City
1990	Julio César Chávez	Julio César Chávez-Meldrick Taylor	Julio César Chávez	Las Vegas
1991	James Toney	Robert Quiroga-Kid Akeem Anifowoshe	Robert Quiroga	San Antonio
1992	Riddick Bowe	Riddick Bowe-Evander Holyfield	Riddick Bowe	Las Vegas
1993	Michael Carbajal	Michael Carbajal-Humberto Gonzalez	Michael Carbajal	Las Vegas
1994	Roy Jones	Jorge Castro-John David Jackson	Jorge Castro	Monterrey, Mex.

U.S. Olympic Gold Medalists

LIGHT FLYWEIGHT

| 1984 | Paul Gonzales |

FLYWEIGHT

1904	George Finnegan
1920	Frank Di Gennara
1024	Fidel LaBarba
1952	Nathan Brooks
1976	Leo Randolph
1984	Steve McCrory

BANTAMWEIGHT

| 1904 | Oliver Kirk |
| 1988 | Kennedy McKinney |

FEATHERWEIGHT

1904	Oliver Kirk
1924	John Fields
1984	Meldrick Taylor

LIGHTWEIGHT

1904	Harry Spanger
1920	Samuel Mosberg
1968	Ronald W. Harris

LIGHTWEIGHT *(Cont.)*

1976	Howard Davis
1984	Pernell Whitaker
1992	Oscar De La Hoya

LIGHT WELTERWEIGHT

1952	Charles Adkins
1972	Ray Seales
1976	Ray Leonard
1984	Jerry Page

WELTERWEIGHT

1904	Albert Young
1932	Edward Flynn
1960	Wilbert McClure
1984	Mark Breland
1984	Frank Tate

MIDDLEWEIGHT

1904	Charles Mayer
1932	Carmen Bath
1952	Floyd Patterson
1960	Edward Crook
1976	Michael Spinks

LIGHT HEAVYWEIGHT

1920	Eddie Eagan
1952	Norvel Lee
1956	James Boyd
1960	Cassius Clay
1976	Leon Spinks
1988	Andrew Maynard

HEAVYWEIGHT

| 1984 | Henry Tillman |
| 1988 | Ray Mercer |

SUPER HEAVYWEIGHT

1904	Samuel Berger
1952	H. Edward Sanders
1956	T. Peter Rademacher
1964	Joe Frazier
1968	George Foreman
1984	Tyrell Biggs

Horse Racing

Sports Illustrated

Victory Cigar

Cigar gallops to a big payday at the Massachusetts Handicap

JOHN IACONO

D. Wayne's Delights

D. Wayne Lukas had a number of fine horses in his stable, but Thunder Gulch and Timber Country brought him the Triple Crown

by William F. Reed

AT YEAR'S end it was as if everyone in thoroughbred racing had been packed into a drawing room for after-dinner drinks and conversation. As usual, a large crowd was gathered around trainer D. Wayne Lukas, hearing about how he had become the first trainer to win the Triple Crown with different horses. Or about how he had brought along Serena's Song, the marvelous filly. But it was impossible to concentrate completely on the garrulous Lukas because of all that Cigar smoke coming from the corner where trainer Bill Mott and owner Allen Paulson were toasting the remarkable 5-year-old who had inspired the year's most popular headline: CIGAR SMOKES FIELD.

The wonderful thing about the final tableau was the number of surprises it contained. At the beginning, the year was supposed to be dominated by Holy Bull, the 1994 Horse of the Year as a 3-year-old. Sadly, the Bull pulled up in the Don Handicap on Feb. 11 with what turned out to be a career-ending leg injury, opening the way for Cigar, an erstwhile turf specialist, to win his fourth consecutive race since being switched to the dirt. Nevertheless, Cigar hardly seemed dominating enough to make anyone think he could win the $500,000 bonus offered by Boston's Suffolk Downs to any horse that swept the Gulfstream Park Handicap, Oaklawn Handicap, Pimlico Special and Massachusetts Handicap.

"After the race in Florida," said Suffolk executive vice president Louis J. Raffeto Jr., "I didn't think Cigar would go to Hot Springs [for the Oaklawn Handicap], and even if he did, I didn't think he was a legitimate route horse." But owner Paulson and trainer Mott surprised Raffeto by sending Cigar to Arkansas for the April 15 race. The classy field included Concern, winner of the 1994 Breeders Cup Classic; Best Pal, then the richest horse in training; and Silver Goblin, who had won eight consecutive races. Despite being banged around in the first turn and inadvertently hit on the nose by a rival jockey's whip while turning for home, Cigar came from off the pace to win by 2½ lengths in what Oaklawn president Charles Cella called "the most impressive race ever put together at Oaklawn Park."

BILL FRAKES

While these developments were unfolding in the handicap division, the Kentucky Derby field was being shaped by the major prep races in New York, Florida, Arkansas, California and Kentucky. Many experts were excited about the likes of Afternoon Deelites, a reputed supercolt owned by songwriter Burt Bacharach, and Talkin Man, an impressive winner of the Wood Memorial in New York. But the trainer who seemed to be holding the strongest hand was Lukas, who had ended a long slump in 1994 by winning the Preakness and the Belmont Stakes with Tabasco Cat.

As the Kentucky Derby approached, Lukas daily issued rave reviews about Timber Country, the 2-year-old champion of 1994, and Serena's Song, an easy winner in the Jim Beam Stakes. He also had a third contender, Thunder Gulch, who had nipped Suave Prospect at the wire in both the Fountain of Youth and the Florida Derby but then had dropped out of sight after finishing a poor fourth in the Blue Grass Stakes.

In the Derby, however, Thunder Gulch and jockey Gary Stevens charged out of the

Thunder Gulch was just an also-ran until he ran away with the Derby.

19-horse pack to take the lead in the stretch, then withstood the late charges of Tejano Run, who finished second, and Timber Country, who was flying at the end after finally breaking free of the pack. Incredibly, Thunder Gulch had gone off at odds of almost 25–1, meaning that he paid $51 for a $2 win bet, the highest price since Proud Clarion paid $62.20 in 1967.

Thunder Gulch's owner, Michael Tabor, a resident of Monte Carlo who owns a string of betting shops in Great Britain, had paid $450,000 for the colt the previous fall. The same man who had found the colt for Tabor, Irish veterinarian Demi O'Byrne, also hooked him up with Lukas. Yet the media, instead of giving Lukas credit for developing Thunder Gulch, mainly chastized him for not giving the colt equal billing with Timber Country and Serena's Song. Unfazed, Lukas said he had never slighted Thunder Gulch, then greeted the media the morning after the Derby wearing

Timber Country (far left) made a late charge to win the Preakness.

a Timber Country cap—a statement more pointed than anything he said.

The week after the Derby the spotlight swung to Pimlico in Baltimore and back to Cigar. Ted Dipple, a Boston-area insurance executive who had underwritten a policy against the $500,000 bonus through Lloyd's of London, realized going into the Pimlico Special that Cigar might indeed be good enough to sweep the four races. So on May 13, the day Cigar went after the third leg of the bonus, Dipple attempted to recoup some of his potential loss by plunging $5,000 on Cigar at Pimlico and another £2,500 (about $4,000) with the William Hill bookmaking establishment in London. "I wanted to bet £25,000, but they [Hill] would only take 2,500," said Dipple. The problem was, Cigar went off at odds of only 2–5. Cigar again lit up the field, this time going wire-to-wire.

Shortly after Cigar moved out of Pimlico, the 3-year-olds moved in. Asked about Timber Country's Derby finish, Lukas blamed jockey Pat Day's inability to extricate the colt from traffic in time to make a serious run. But Lukas refused to dump Day after the Derby when some members of the Timber Country camp argued that Day's laid-back riding style didn't fit the colt's laid-back personality.

On the Monday before the Preakness, Day worked Timber Country at Churchill Downs with strict orders from Lukas to "startle him if you can." The idea was to sharpen the colt, get him to run more aggressively—something to snap his 0-for-4 record in 1995. When the workout was over, the :59⅗ clocking didn't impress Lukas and Day nearly as much as the way the colt came off the track. "He went jiggedy-jog, just tugging on the bridle," Day said. "He hadn't done that all spring."

That same day Lukas made an announcement about Serena's Song that caused almost as much of a stir in the racing world as his decision three weeks earlier to run her against colts in the Derby: He was shipping her to Baltimore along with Timber Country and Thunder Gulch so she could run against fillies in the Black-Eyed Susan the day before the Preakness.

By the time the Lukas horses were checked into the Pimlico stakes barn on Wednesday afternoon, Serena was the subject of another debate, again inspired by Lukas's decision. In the Derby she had been pressured into setting a suicidal pace that cost her any chance of victory. Mercifully, when it had become obvious that Serena's Song was out of gas, jockey Corey Nakatani had wrapped up on her. So, observers wondered, didn't she need a long rest? Wasn't running her back in the Black-Eyed Susan putting her at risk of a career-ending injury? As he waited for the Black-Eyed Susan to begin, Lukas knew the vultures were circling. "You don't think my head's on the chopping block, do you?" he said. To his relief, Serena's Song responded with a nine-length victory.

But there was still the main business of the week, the second leg of racing's Triple Crown. After the fifth race on Saturday, Lukas visited the Pimlico jockeys' quarters to see Day and Stevens. The trainer devoted most of his attention to Day, reminding him to "be a pilot, not a passenger." And Day, long one of the nation's top riders, understood what was at stake. "My contract lasts only as long as the end of the race," he said.

Moments before the race Day tapped Timber Country with his whip in the post parade "to let him know it was time for business," and he whacked him on the left side as soon as the starting gate sprang open. The result was as desired: Timber Country was never worse than sixth in the 11-horse field and made a powerful move in the stretch to take the lead inside the 16th pole. Timber Country and Day vindicated Lukas's faith by taking a half-length victory over Oliver's Twist. Thunder Gulch, whose game run proved his Derby win was no fluke, was third by a neck. So now the Belmont Stakes shaped up as the rubber match between the two Lukas-trained colts. "We'll get them ready," Lukas said, "then let the horses decide it."

While racing fans were awaiting the Belmont, officials at Suffolk Downs were sweating out whether Cigar would go for the bonus in the Mass 'Cap on Saturday, June 3. Even $500,000 is virtually inconsequential to Paulson, who had made a fortune in the aerospace business, and if Suffolk racing secretary John H. Morrissey assigned too much weight to Cigar—he had carried 120 at Oaklawn and 122 at Pimlico—Paulson wouldn't have hesitated to skip Boston en route to preparing a fresh Cigar for the world's richest race, the $3 million Breeders' Cup Classic on Oct. 28 at Belmont Park. But when Morrissey assigned Cigar 124 pounds—the track wasn't going to smoke Cigar out—Paulson and Mott decided to bring their star to New England.

The trainers of the other top handicap horses felt that 124 was too light for Cigar, and they expressed their displeasure by keeping their runners elsewhere, leaving the Mass 'Cap with a weak field that grew even weaker when three horses, all based in New York, were scratched on race day. Naturally, insurance man Dipple had mixed feelings. On the one hand, he wished that Cigar had drawn tougher competition and more weight. On the other, however, the bonus had achieved the desired goal. "We wanted to bring the best handicap horses to Boston," Dipple said, "but we sort of over-cooked the stew."

On the Friday before the race Paulson and his entourage were the guests of honor on a Boston harbor cruise sponsored by the track. Sitting on the top deck with Mott, Paulson talked about his unlikely star. A nonsmoker, Paulson named Cigar after a pilot's checkpoint in the Gulf of Mexico between Miami and New Orleans. The only time he had ever tried a cigar, Paulson said, was when he was in the Air Force during World War II. "It made me sort of dizzy, as I recall," Paulson said. Which, of course, is how he had come to feel about Cigar in the wake of the amazing transformation that began on Oct. 28, 1994, when Cigar won his debut on the dirt by eight lengths at Aqueduct. "We did it as sort of an experiment," Mott said. "We were desperate, because he hadn't run well on the grass."

On Mass 'Cap day, Suffolk passed out expensive Macanudo cigars to the first 2,000 customers who wanted them. But Dipple and his associates declined the free stogies,

Lukas followed a banner season in 1994 with a historic one in '95.

PETER READ MILLER

having brought their own Cuban-made cigars obtained through Great Britain. "We're hoping the horse doesn't like cigar smoke," Dipple quipped, "because all our employees will be along the rail, blowing cigar smoke as he comes down the stretch."

This time Dipple, resigned to the inevitable, didn't bet in England because of Cigar's unenticing 1–5 odds, the lowest price ever on a Mass 'Cap favorite. The crowd of 12,238 was rewarded with a superstar performance. Down the stretch, jockey Jerry Bailey gathered in his reins, showed Cigar his whip, and hit him twice righthanded, just to make sure his mount kept his wire on his business. At the wire the coasting Cigar was an easy winner. "I wouldn't even say that he's at the top of his game right now," Mott said. "Maybe we reached that a race or two ago, and he's just holding his own now." Added Paulson, "This guy's different."

So, as it turned out, was Thunder Gulch.

At about 5 p.m. on June 9, less than an hour after he had won the prestigious Mother Goose Stakes with Serena's Song, Lukas called the Belmont press box to announce that Timber Country would be scratched from the Belmont Stakes because of fever. Although he might have gambled that the colt's temperature would go down by Saturday morning, Lukas opted to treat him immediately with an anti-inflammatory drug. That meant he had to scratch the colt from the Belmont, because horses taking such medication were not then allowed to race in New York. "There's no sense in crying about it," Lukas said. "We've got to start thinking about getting the other one ready to run."

The other one. That had been Thunder Gulch's plight all spring. But in the Belmont, he became the One. At the top of the stretch, Thunder Gulch hooked the pace-setting Star Standard, ridden by Julie Krone. As Krone kept pushing her colt with a furious lefthanded whip, Thunder Gulch drew clear at the 16th pole and hung on for the victory that made Lukas the first trainer to sweep the Triple Crown in the same year with different horses. He also became the first to win five consecutive Triple Crown races. Said Nick Zito, the trainer of Star Standard, "What he's done is tremendous, unbelievable. I guess I'll have to go get Pegasus to beat him."

Unfortunately for the sophisticated crowds who always patronize the prestigious late-summer meeting at Saratoga Springs, N.Y., both Cigar and Serena's Song stayed in the barn, resting up for the fall campaign. But Lukas brought in Thunder Gulch for the Travers Stakes on Aug. 19. Two days before that race, when Thunder Gulch should have been getting the attention that escaped him during the Triple Crown, Lukas announced that Timber Country had been retired to stud because of a torn tendon suffered in a workout. Poor Thunder Gulch. Even at that late date, Timber Country stole his thunder.

But then Thunder Gulch won the Travers so easily that even his detractors had to admit that they had been underrating him. "He's a pretty good horse," said Lukas, tongue in cheek. A couple of unlikely heroes, Thunder Gulch and Cigar, along with Serena's Song, saved 1995 and made it special. It was too bad that Holy Bull wasn't represented in the drawing room, but who knows? Maybe he would have found all that Lukas chatter as suffocating as the Cigar smoke.

FOR THE RECORD·1994–1995

THOROUGHBRED RACING

The Triple Crown

121st Kentucky Derby

May 6, 1995. Grade I, 3-year-olds; 8th race, Churchill Downs, Louisville. All 126 lbs.* Distance: 1¼ miles. Stakes value: $957,400; Winner: $707,400; Second: $145,000; Third: $70,000; Fourth: $35,000. Track: Fast. Off: 5:33 p.m. Winner: Thunder Gulch (Ch c by Gulch-Line of Thunder by Storm Bird); Times: 0:22⅗, 0:45⅘, 1:10⅕, 1:35⅗, 2:01⅕. Won: Driving. Breeder: Peter M. Brant.

Horse	Finish-PP	Margin	Jockey/Owner
Thunder Gulch	1-16	2¼	Gary Stevens/ Michael Tabor
Tejano Run	2-14	head	Jerry Bailey/ Roy Monroe
Timber Country	3-15	¾	Pat Day/ Overbrook Farm, Gainesway Stable and Robert and Beverly Lewis
Jumron	4-10	head	Goncalino Almeida/ Charles Dunn
Mecke	5-18	½	Robbie Davis/ James Lewis Jr
Eltish	6-7	3	Eddie Delahoussaye/ Juddmonte Farms
Knockadoon	7-2	neck	Chris McCarron/ William Warren Jr
Afternoon Deelites	8-12	neck	Kent Desormeaux/ Burt Bacharach
Citadeed	9-19	¾	Eddie Maple/ Ivan Allen
In Character	10-9	½	Chris Antley/ Vince Baker, Dave Farr & Bruce Jackson
Suave Prospect	11-6	½	Julie Krone/ William Condren and Michael Sherman
Talkin Man	12-11	½	Mike Smith/ Kinghaven Farms, Helen Stollery and Peter Wall
Dazzling Falls	13-1	neck	Garrett Gomez/ Chateau Ridge Farm
Ski Captain	14-17	1½	Yutake Take/ Shadai Racehorse Company Ltd.
Jambalaya Jazz	15-5	neck	Craig Perret/ John Oxley
Serena's Song	16-13	1½	Corey Nakatani/ Robert and Beverly Lewis
Pyramid Peak	17-3	6	Herb McCauley/ John Oxley
Lake George	18-8	21	Shane Sellers/ Bedford Stable and Stonehenge Stable
Wild Syn	19-4	—	Randy Romero/ Jurgen Arnemann

*Except for Serena's Song, a filly, 121 lbs.

120th Preakness Stakes

May 20, 1995. Grade I, 3-year-olds; 10th race, Pimlico Race Course, Baltimore. All 126 lbs. Distance: 1³⁄₁₆ miles; Stakes value: $687,400; Winner: $446,810; Second: $137,480; Third: $68,740; Fourth: $34,370. Track: Fast. Off: 5:33 p.m. Winner: Timber Country (Ch C Woodman-Fall Aspen by Pretense); Times: 0:23⅕, 0:47⅕, 1:10⅘, 1:35⅘, 1:54⅗. Won: Driving. Breeder: Lowquest Ltd.

Horse	Finish-PP	Margin	Jockey/Owner
Timber Country	1-7	½	Pat Day/ Overbrook Farm, Gainesway Stable and R.& B. Lewis
Oliver's Twist	2-10	neck	Alberto Delgado/ Charles Oliver
Thunder Gulch	3-11	4	Gary Stevens/ Michael Tabor
Star Standard	4-8	½	Chris McCarron/ William Condren and Joseph Cornacchia
Mecke	5-9	neck	Robbie Davis/ James Lewis Jr
Talkin Man	6-4	5¾	Mike Smith/ Kinghaven Farms, Helen Stollery and Peter Wall
Our Gatsby	7-2	neck	Kent Desormeaux/ Charles Heider
Mystery Storm	8-3	9	Craig Perret/ David Beard
Tejano Run	9-5	2¾	Jerry Bailey/ Roy Monroe
Pana Brass	10-6	17	Eddie Maple/ Robert Perez
Itron	11-1	—	Ricky Frazier/ David Albert

127th Belmont Stakes

June 10, 1995. Grade I, 3-year-olds; 9th race, Belmont Park, Elmont, NY. All 126 lbs. Distance: 1½ miles. Stakes purse: $692,400; Winner: $415,440; Second: $138,480; Third: $76,164; Fourth: $41,544. Track: Fast. Off: 5:33 p.m. Winner: Thunder Gulch (Ch c, 3, by Gulch-Line of Thunder by Storm Bird); Times: 0:24⅗, 0:50⅕, 1:15⅕, 1:40, 2:05⅘, 2:32. Won: Driving. Breeder: Peter M. Brant.

Horse	Finish-PP	Margin	Jockey/Owner
Thunder Gulch	1-10	2	Gary Stevens/ Michael Tabor
Star Standard	2-11	3½	Julie Krone/ William Condren and Joseph Cornacchia
Citadeed	3-1	1½	Eddie Maple/ Ivan Allen
Knockadoon	4-9	4½	Chris McCarron/ William Warren Jr
Pana Brass	5-3	5	Wigberto Ramos/ Robert Perez
Off'n'Away	6-2	1	Mike Smith/ Moyglare Stud
Ave's Flag	7-5	4	John Velazquez/ David McNulty and Josef Omland
Composer	8-6	7½	Jerry Bailey/ Henryk de Kwiatkowski
Colonial Secretary	9-8	3	Jose Santos/ Buckland Farm
Is Sveikatas	10-4	6½	Jorge Chavez/ Clarke Whitaker and Alfred Duncan
Wild Syn	11-7	—	Randy Romero/ Jurgen Arnemann

Major Stakes Races

Late 1994

Date	Race	Track	Distance	Winner	Jockey/Trainer	Purse ($)
Sep 17	The Woodward	Belmont Park	1⅛ miles	Holy Bull	Mike Smith/ Jimmy Croll	500,000
Sep 17	Man O'War	Belmont Park	1⅜ miles	Royal Mountain Inn	Julie Krone/ B. Tagg	400,000
Sep 18	Molson Export Million	Woodbine	1⅛ miles	Dramatic Gold	Corey Nakatani/ D. Hofmans	1,000,000
Oct 1	Super Derby XV	Louisiana Downs	1¼ miles	Soul of the Matter	Kent Desormeaux/ Richard Mandella	750,000
Oct 2	Prix De L'Arc De Triomphe	Longchamp	1½ miles	Carnegie	T. Jarnet/ Andre Fabre	1,146,208
Oct 8	Jockey Club Gold Cup	Belmont Park	1¼ miles	Colonial Affair	Jose Santos/ F. Schulfofer	750,000
Oct 8	Turf Classic Invitational	Belmont Park	1½ miles	Tikkanen	Cash Asmussen/ J. Pease	500,000
Oct 8	Moet Champagne	Belmont Park	1¹⁄₁₆ miles	Timber Country	Pat Day/ D. Wayne Lukas	500,000
Oct 8	Frizette Stakes	Belmont Park	1¹⁄₁₆ miles	Flanders	Pat Day/ D. Wayne Lukas	250,000
Oct 8	Beldame Stakes	Belmont Park	1⅛ miles	Heavenly Prize	Pat Day/ Claude McGaughey	250,000
Oct 15	Washington D.C. Int'l.	Laurel	1¼ miles	Paradise Creek	Pat Day/ William Mott	600,000
Nov 5	Breeders' Cup Sprint	Churchill Downs	6 furlongs	Cherokee Run	Mike Smith/ F. Alexander	1,000,000
Nov 5	Breeders' Cup Juvenile Fillies	Churchill Downs	1¹⁄₁₆ miles	Flanders	Pat Day/ D. Wayne Lukas	1,000,000
Nov 5	Breeders' Cup Distaff	Churchill Downs	1⅛ miles	One Dreamer	Gary Stevens/ T. Proctor	1,000,000
Nov 5	Breeders' Cup Mile	Churchill Downs	1 mile	Barathea	Frankie Dettori/ L. Cumani	1,000,000
Nov 5	Breeders' Cup Juvenile	Churchill Downs	1¹⁄₁₆ miles	Timber Country	Pat Day/ D. Wayne Lukas	1,000,000
Nov 5	Breeders' Cup Turf	Churchill Downs	1½ miles	Tikkanen	Mike Smith/ J. Pease	2,000,000
Nov 5	Breeders' Cup Classic	Churchill Downs	1¼ miles	Concern	Jerry Bailey/ Richard Small	3,000,000
Nov 6	Yellow Ribbon Invitational	Oak Tree	1¼ miles	Aube Indienne	Kent Desormeaux/ C. Whittingham	400,000
Nov 26	NYRA Mile	Aqueduct	1 mile	Cigar	Jerry Bailey/ William Mott	250,000
Nov 27	Japan Cup	Tokyo	1½ miles	Marvelous Crown	Katsumi Minai/ Osawa	3,475,345
Nov 27	Matriarch Stakes	Hollywood Park	1⅛ miles	Exchange	Laffit Pincay, Jr/ B. Spawr	400,000

1995 (Through September 30)

Date	Race	Track	Distance	Winner	Jockey/Trainer	Purse ($)
Feb 5	Charles H. Strub Stakes	Santa Anita	1¼ miles	Dare and Go	Alex Solis/ Richard Mandella	500,000
Feb 11	Don Handicap	Gulfstream Park	1⅛ miles	Cigar	Jerry Bailey/ William Mott	300,000
Feb 12	San Antonio Handicap	Santa Anita	1⅛ miles	Best Pal	Chris McCarron/ Richard Mandella	250,000
Feb 18	Fountain of Youth Stakes	Gulfstream Park	1¹⁄₁₆ miles	Thunder Gulch	Mike Smith/ D. Wayne Lukas	200,000
Feb 20	San Luis Obispo Handicap	Santa Anita	1½ miles	Square Cut	Chris Antley/ J. Devereux	220,000
Feb 26	Santa Margarita Handicap	Santa Anita	1⅛ miles	Queens Court Queen	Corey Nakatani/ Ron McAnally	300,000
Mar 5	Gulfstream Park Handicap	Gulfstream Park	1¼ miles	Cigar	Jerry Bailey/ William Mott	500,000
Mar 11	Santa Anita Handicap	Santa Anita	1¼ miles	Urgent Request	Gary Stevens/ S. Aitken	1,000,000
Mar 11	Florida Derby	Gulfstream Park	1⅛ miles	Thunder Gulch	Jerry Bailey/ D. Wayne Lukas	500,000

1995 (Through September 30) (Cont.)

Date	Race	Track	Distance	Winner	Jockey/Trainer	Purse ($)
Mar 12 ....Santa Anita Oaks		Santa Anita	1¹⁄₁₆ miles	Serena's Song	Corey Nakatani/ D. Wayne Lukas	200,000
Mar 16 ....Pan American Handicap		Gulfstream Park	1½ miles	Awad	Eddie Maple/ D. Donk	300,000
Mar 19 ....Louisiana Derby		Fair Grounds	1¹⁄₁₆ miles	Petionville	Chris Antley/ R. Bradshaw	350,000
Mar 25 ....Gotham Stakes		Aqueduct	1 mile	Talkin Man	Mike Smith/ Roger Attfield	250,000
Mar 26 ....San Luis Rey Stakes		Santa Anita	1½ miles	Sandpit	Cory Nakatani/ Richard Mandella	250,000
Apr 1 ....Jim Beam Stakes		Turfway Park	1⅛ miles	Serena's Song	Corey Nakatani/ D. Wayne Lukas	600,000
Apr 8 ....Santa Anita Derby		Santa Anita	1⅛ miles	Larry the Legend	Gary Stevens/ C. Lewis	700,000
Apr 8 ....Remington Park Derby		Remington Park	1⅛ miles	Dazzling Falls	Garrett Gomez/ C.Turco	300,000
Apr 15 .....The Wood Memorial		Aqueduct	1⅛ miles	Talkin Man	Shane Sellers/ Roger Attfield	500,000
Apr 15 .....The Oaklawn Handicap		Oaklawn Park	1⅛ miles	Cigar	Jerry Bailey/ William Mott	750,000
Apr 15 .....The Blue Grass		Keeneland	1⅛ miles	Wild Syn	Randy Romero/ T. Arnemann	500,000
Apr 21 .....Apple Blossom Handicap		Oaklawn Park	1¹⁄₁₆ miles	Heavenly Prize	Pat Day/ Claude McGaughey	500,000
Apr 22 .....Arkansas Derby		Oaklawn Park	1⅛ miles	Dazzling Falls	Garrett Gomez/ D. Turco	500,000
Apr 23 .....San Juan Capistrano		Santa Anita	1¾ miles	Red Bishop	Mike Smith/ Saeed Bin Suroor	400,000
Apr 23 .....Ashland Stakes		Keeneland	1¹⁄₁₆ miles	Urbane	Eddie Delahous-saye/B. Mayberry	334,650
May 5 ......Kentucky Oaks		Churchill Downs	1⅛ miles	Gal in a Ruckus	Herb McCauley/ J. Ward, Jr	300,000
May 6 ......Kentucky Derby		Churchill Downs	1¼ miles	Thunder Gulch	Gary Stevens/ D. Wayne Lukas	957,400
May 13 ....Illinois Derby		Sportsman's Park	1⅛ miles	Peaks and Valley	Julie Krone/ J. Day	500,000
May 13 ....Pimlico Special		Pimlico	1³⁄₁₆ miles	Cigar	Jerry Bailey/ William Mott	600,000
May 20 ....The Preakness Stakes		Pimlico	1³⁄₁₆ miles	Timber Country	Pat Day/ D. Wayne Lukas	687,400
May 29 ....Hollywood Turf Handicap		Hollywood Park	1¼ miles	Earl of Barking	G. Almeida/ R. Cross	500,000
May 29 ....Metropolitan Handicap		Belmont Park	1 mile	You and I	Jorge Chavez/ R. Frankel	500,000
June 3 .....Massachusetts Handicap		Suffolk Downs	1⅛ miles	Cigar	Jerry Bailey/ William Mott	750,000
June 10...Belmont Stakes		Belmont Park	1½ miles	Thunder Gulch	Gary Stevens/ D. Wayne Lukas	692,400
June 11...Californian Stakes		Hollywood Park	1⅛ miles	Concern	Mike Smith/ Richard Small	273,400
June 25...Caesars International Handicap		Atlantic City	1³⁄₁₆ miles	Sandpit	Corey Nakatani/ Richard Mandella	500,000
July 2 ......Budweiser Irish Derby		The Curragh	1½ miles	Winged Love	O. Peslier/ Andre Fabre	925,683
July 2 ......Hollywood Gold Cup Handicap		Hollywood Park	1¼ miles	Cigar	Jerry Bailey/ William Mott	1,000,000
July 4 ......Suburban Handicap		Belmont Park	1¼ miles	Key Contender	Jerry Bailey/ J. Martin	350,000
July 8 ......Coaching Club American Oaks		Belmont Park	1¼ miles	Golden Bri	Jose Santos/ J. Kimmel	250,000
July 9 ......Queen's Plate		Woodbine	1¼ miles	Regal Discovery	T. Kabel/ Roger Attfield	400,000
July 15 ....Frank J. DeFranics Memorial Dash Stakes		Laurel	6 furlongs	Lite the Fuse	Julie Krone/ R. Dutrow	300,000
July 22 ....Caesars Palace Turf Handicap		Hollywood Park	1½ miles	Sandpit	Corey Nakatani/ Richard Mandella	250,000

1995 (Through September 30) (Cont.)

Date	Race	Track	Distance	Winner	Jockey/Trainer	Purse ($)
July 23	American Derby	Arlington Park	1³⁄₁₆ miles	Gold and Steel	A. T. Gryder/ J. Rouget	300,000
July 23	Swaps Stakes	Hollywood Park	1⅛ miles	Thunder Gulch	Gary Stevens/ D. Wayne Lukas	300,000
July 23	Vanity Handicap	Hollywood Park	1⅛ miles	Private Persuasion	Gary Stevens/ D. Hendricks	300,000
July 29	Sword Dancer Invitational Handicap	Saratoga	1½ miles	Kiri's Clown	Mike Luzzi/ P. Johnson	250,000
July 30	Haskell Invitational Handicap	Monmouth Park	1⅛ miles	Serena's Song	Gary Stevens/ D. Wayne Lukas	500,000
Aug 5	Whitney Handicap	Saratoga	1⅛ miles	Unaccounted For	Pat Day/ F. Schulhofer	350,000
Aug 5	Ramona Handicap	Del Mar	1⅛ miles	Possibly Perfect	Corey Nakatani/ Robert Frankel	300,000
Aug 6	Eddie Rad Handicap	Del Mar	1⅛ miles	Fastness	Gary Stevens/ J. Sahadi	300,000
Aug 13	Pacific Classic Stakes	Del Mar	1¼ miles	Tinners Way	Eddie Delahoussaye/Robert Frankel	1,000,000
Aug 19	Travers Stakes	Saratoga	1¼ miles	Thunder Gulch	Gary Stevens/ D. Wayne Lukas	750,000
Aug 26	Beverly D. Stakes	Arlington Park	1³⁄₁₆ miles	Possible Perfect	Cory Nakatani/ Robert Frankel	500,000
Aug 27	Arlington Million	Arlington Park	1¼ miles	Awad	Eddie Maple/ D. Donk	1,000,000
Sep 3	Gazelle Handicap	Belmont Park	1⅛ miles	Serena's Song	Gary Stevens/ D. Wayne Lukas	150,000
Sep 16	Man O'War	Belmont Park	1⅜ miles	Millkom	Gary Stevens/ J. C. Rouget	400,000
Sep 16	Woodward Stakes	Belmont Park	1⅛ miles	Cigar	Jerry Bailey/ William Mott	500,000
Sep 17	Molson Export Million	Woodbine	1⅛ miles	Peaks and Valleys	Julie Krone/ J. Day	1,000,000
Sep 23	Kentucky Cup Classic	Turfway Park	1⅛ miles	Thunder Gulch	Gary Stevens/ D. Wayne Lukas	400,000
Sep 30	Isle of Capri Super Derby	Louisiana Downs	1¼ miles	Mecke	Jerry Bailey/ E. Tortora	750,000

1994 Statistical Leaders

Horses

Horse	Starts	1st	2nd	3rd	Purses ($)	Horse	Starts	1st	2nd	3rd	Purses ($)
Paradise Creek	11	8	2	1	2,610,187	Dramatic Gold	10	4	2	2	1,294,850
Concern	14	3	5	6	2,541,670	Go for Gin	11	2	4	1	1,178,596
Tabasco Cat	12	5	3	1	2,164,334	Devil His Due	12	3	6	1	1,142,000
Holy Bull	10	8	0	0	2,095,000	Cherokee Run	9	3	3	3	943,690
Tikkanen	9	3	1	2	1,508,344	Timber Country	7	4	0	2	927,025

Jockeys

Jockey	Mounts	1st	2nd	3rd	Purses ($)	Win Pct	$ Pct*
Mike Smith	1,484	317	250	196	15,979,820	.21	.51
Pat Day	1,147	316	194	168	14,543,715	.27	.59
Gary Stevens	1,402	258	221	236	12,651,291	.18	.51
Jerry Bailey	1,221	255	189	167	11,515,912	.21	.50
Kent Desormeaux	1,163	251	188	176	11,275,077	.22	.53
Chris McCarron	870	156	142	117	10,921,495	.18	.48
Corey Nakatani	1,015	194	165	152	9,676,658	.19	.50
Eddie Delahoussaye	1,012	184	156	166	8,609,179	.18	.50
Jose Santos	1,249	208	176	189	8,329,940	.17	.46
Alex Solis	1,372	222	197	188	7,685,647	.16	.44

*Percentage in the Money (1st, 2nd, and 3rd).

Trainers

Trainer	Starts	1st	2nd	3rd	Purses ($)	Win Pct	$ Pct*
D. Wayne Lukas	693	147	88	103	9,247,457	.21	.49
William Mott	575	137	89	91	7,043,317	.24	.55
Richard Mandella	350	68	53	67	4,984,977	.19	.54
H. Allen Jerkens	454	111	69	75	4,940,476	.24	.56
Ron McAnally	461	80	71	59	4,736,496	.17	.45
Robert Frankel	280	52	42	41	4,692,793	.19	.48
Shug McGaughey	258	80	46	41	4,453,376	.31	.65
Richard Small	268	49	42	51	4,273,199	.18	.53
Gary Jones	301	66	47	41	4,160,037	.22	.51
Scotty Schulhofer	411	74	61	59	3,753,869	.18	.47

*Percentage in the Money (1st, 2nd, and 3rd).

Owners

Owner	Starts	1st	2nd	3rd	Purses ($)
John Franks	1,080	193	156	132	4,518,088
Juddmonte Farms	170	34	26	24	4,323,395
Golden Eagle Farm	513	94	74	78	4,087,680
Robert E. Meyerhoff	192	41	33	41	3,978,752
Frank H. Stronach	417	88	70	46	3,745,412
Allen E. Paulson	445	79	63	44	3,195,070
Augustin Stables	287	67	40	45	2,822,196
Overbrook/Reynolds	30	11	6	3	2,257,035
Warren A. Croll, Jr	38	11	3	4	2,135,445
Dogwood Stable	377	45	69	49	2,110,005

Note: 1994 statistical leaders courtesy of *Daily Racing Form*.

HARNESS RACING

Major Stakes Races (late 1994)

Date	Race	Location	Winner	Driver/Trainer	Purse ($)
Oct 7	Kentucky Futurity	The Red Mile	Bullville Victory	John Campbell/ Per Eriksson	162,700
Oct 15	BC Three and up Mare Trot	Freehold Raceway	Armbro Keepsake	Stig Johansson/ Stig Johansson	250,000
Oct 15	BC Three and up Horse/Gelding Trot	Freehold Raceway	Pine Chip	John Campbell/ Charles Sylvester	300,000
Oct 15	BC Three and up Mare Pace	Freehold Raceway	Shady Daisy	Michel Lachance/ Louis Bauslaugh	250,000
Oct 15	BC Three and up Horse/Gelding Pace	Freehold Raceway	Village Jiffy	Paul MacDonell/ William Wellwood	334,000
Oct 21	BC Three-year-old Filly Trot	Garden State Park	Imageofa Clear Day	Bill O'Donnell/ Doug McIntosh	325,000
Oct 21	BC Three-year-old Filly Pace	Garden State Park	Hardie Hanover	Tim Twaddle/ John Burns	325,000
Oct 21	BC Three-year-old Colt/Gelding Pace	Garden State Park	Incredible Abe	Italo Tamborrino/ Chuck Sylvester	400,000
Oct 21	BC Three-year-old Colt/Gelding Pace	Garden State Park	Magical Mike	Michel Lachance/ Tom Haughton	400,000
Oct 28	BC Two-year-old Filly Trot	Woodbine	Lookout Victory	John Patterson, Jr/ Per Eriksson	334,000
Oct 28	BC Two-year-old Colt/Gelding Trot	Woodbine	Eager Seelster	Teddy Jacobs/ Teddy Jacobs	384,500
Oct 28	BC Two-year-old Filly Pace	Woodbine	Yankee Cashmere	Peter Wrenn/ Brett Bittle	501,400
Oct 28	BC Two-year-old Colt/Gelding Pace	Woodbine	Jenna's Beach Boy	Bill Fahy/Joe Holloway	670,000
Nov 19	Governor's Cup	Garden State Park	CA Connection	Joe Anderson/ Kevin Thomas	616,400

1995 (Through September 22)

Date	Race	Location	Winner	Driver/Trainer	Purse ($)
June 24	North America Cup	Woodbine	David's Pass	John Campbell/ Brett Pelling	1,000,000
July 1	Messenger Stakes	Ladbroke at The Meadows	David's Pass	John Campbell/ Brett Pelling	328,825
July 8	Yonkers Trot	Yonkers	CR Kay Suzie	Rod Allen/Carl Allen	276,564
July 15	Meadowlands Pace	Meadowlands	David's Pass	John Campbell/ Brett Pelling	1,000,000
Aug 1	Peter Haughton Memorial	Meadowlands	Dancer's Victory	John Campbell/ Stanley Dancer	400,000
Aug 2	Merrie Annabelle Final	Meadowlands	Missie Will Do It	Bill O'Donnell/ John Brennan	300,500
Aug 5	Hambletonian	Meadowlands	Tagliabue	John Campbell/ Jim Campbell	1,200,000
Aug 5	Hambletonian Oaks	Meadowlands	Lookout Victory	John Patterson, Jr/ Per Eriksson	375,500
Aug 12	Sweetheart	Meadowlands	On Her Way	Cat Manzi/Jim Brittingham	571,100
Aug 12	Woodrow Wilson	Meadowlands	A Stud Named Sue	George Brennan, Jr/Liz Quesnal	585,500
Aug 12	Adios Final	Ladbroke at The Meadows	David's Pass	John Campbell/ Brett Pelling	441,282
Aug 26	Cane Pace	Yonkers	Mattgilla Gorilla	David Ingraham/ William Andrews	384,375
Sep 2	World Trotting Derby	Du Quoin	CR Kay Suzie	Rod Allen/Carl Allen	585,000
Sep 20	BC Three and up Mare Trot	Delaware	CR Kay Suzie	Rod Allen/Carl Allen	300,000
Sep 21	BC Three and up Horse/Gelding Trot	Delaware	Panifesto	Luc Ouellette/Bill Robinson	300,000
Sep 21	Little Brown Jug	Delaware	Nick's Fantasy	John Campbell/ Caroline Lyon	543,670
Sep 22	BC Three and up Mare Pace	Northfield Park	Ellamony	Mike Saftic/ Stephen Doyle	250,000
Sep 22	BC Three and up Horse/Gelding Pace	Northfield Park	Thatll Be Me	Roger Mayotte/ Robert Young	300,000

Major Races

The Hambletonian

Horse	Driver	PP	¼	½	¾	Stretch	Finish
Tagliabue	John Campbell	1	3	1	1	1-5	1-2¼
Abundance	William Fahy	2	4	5	5	3-6½	2-2¼
Giant Hit	John Patterson, Jr	3	1	2	2	2-5	3-2¼
Earthquake	Berndt Lindstedt	4	5	8	7	4-9¼	4-4
Climbing Bud	Malvern Burroughs	10	8	7	8	5-10¾	5-5¾
Deliberate Speed	Per Henriksen	8	2	3	3	6-14¾	6-15¾
Super Star Ranger	Jack Moiseyev	9	6	4	6	7-19¾	7-23
Trustworthy	William O'Donnell	7	9	9	9	8-dis	8-dis
Uma	Cat Manzi	5	7	6	4	9-dis	9-dis
King Pine	Michel Lachance	6	10	10	10	10-dis	10-dis

Time: :28, :56.1, 1:24.4, 1:54.4; Fast

The Little Brown Jug

Horse	Driver	PP	¼	½	¾	Stretch	Finish
Nick's Fantasy ....John Campbell		1	3	3	2	1-4	1-4
Village Connection ....Paul MacDonell		3	2	2	3	2-4	2-4
Lisryan......................Luc Oulette		9	4	4	5	4-5¼	3-4¼
Hensell Hanover........Mike Saftic		6	7	5	4	5-6¼	4-8
Powerful Structure ....David Miller		2	1	1	1	3-4¼	5-8½
Pan It's Cold ....B. D. Allen		5	6	8	8	7-7¾	6-9¼
Fun Time Go Getter...Ken Holliday		4	5	7	6	6-6¾	7-11
Viking Commander....G. M. Haston		8	9	6	7	8-10¼	8-13
Wild Dancer...............S. O. Noble III		7	8	9	9	9-10¾	9-14

Time: :26.4, :55.4, 1:23.3, 1:51.2; Fast

1994 Statistical Leaders

1994 Leading Moneywinners by Age, Sex and Gait

Division	Horse	Starts	1st	2nd	3rd	Earnings ($)
2-Year-Old Pacing Colts ....Dontgetinmyway		16	6	6	1	610,018
2-Year-Old Pacing Fillies ....Efishnc		16	7	4	1	503,789
3-Year-Old Pacing Colts ....Cam's Card Shark		18	15	2	0	2,264,714
3-Year-Old Pacing Fillies ....Electric Slide		21	13	2	2	659,007
Aged Pacing Horses....................................Village Jiffy		28	8	6	5	578,585
Aged Pacing Mares.....................................Shady Daisy		32	7	9	5	288,235
2-Year-Old Trotting Colts ....Donerail		15	13	0	1	636,925
2-Year-Old Trotting Fillies ....CR Kay Suzie		9	7	0	0	450,596
3-Year-Old Trotting Colts ....Victory Dream		17	9	4	1	992,662
3-Year-Old Trotting Fillies ....Imageofa Clear Day		22	11	7	1	383,578
Aged Trotting Horses..................................SJ's Photo		23	9	5	3	379,659
Aged Trotting Mares....................................Lifetime Dream		18	5	2	4	140,791

Drivers

Driver	Earnings ($)	Driver	Earnings ($)
John Campbell 9,834,139		Cat Manzi...4,569,712	
Jack Moiseyev 7,108,020		Dave Magee...4,358,819	
Michel Lachance 6,255,284		Steve Condren.......................................3,460,635	
Ron Waples 4,913,926		Luc Oulette...3,301,289	
Doug Brown...4,701,237		Bill Faby...3,141,330	

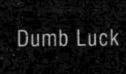

Dumb Luck

Just seconds before post time for the sixth race at Laurel Park on Feb. 20, a track patron placed a $72 bet with a pari-mutuel clerk—only to have it canceled when the clerk inadvertently punched out a ticket worth $738 that the bettor didn't want to pay for. Unable to correct his error in time, the clerk, under track rules, had to assume the obligation for the ticket, a triple box combination that included a 40-1 nag named Nun Bee Wiser.

Nun Bee Luckier is more like it. When Nun Bee Wiser won the race, and the other horses in the triple finished second and third, the once beleaguered clerk found himself with a ticket worth $22,238.40. "After winning he quietly went back to his window and worked through the rest of his shift," says Mary Zambreny, an assistant pari-mutuel manager at Laurel. "I guess he figured he could afford any future mistakes."

FOR THE RECORD · Year by Year

THOROUGHBRED RACING

Kentucky Derby

Run at Churchill Downs, Louisville, KY, on the first Saturday in May.

Year	Winner (Margin)	Jockey	Second	Third	Time
1875	Aristides (1)	Oliver Lewis	Volcano	Verdigris	2:37¾
1876	Vagrant (2)	Bobby Swim	Creedmoor	Harry Hill	2:38¼
1877	Baden-Baden (2)	William Walker	Leonard	King William	2:38
1878	Day Star (2)	Jimmie Carter	Himyar	Leveler	2:37¼
1879	Lord Murphy (1)	Charlie Shauer	Falsetto	Strathmore	2:37
1880	Fonso (1)	George Lewis	Kimball	Bancroft	2:37½
1881	Hindoo (4)	Jimmy McLaughin	Lelex	Alfambra	2:40
1882	Apollo (½)	Babe Hurd	Runnymede	Bengal	2:40¼
1883	Leonatus (3)	Billy Donohue	Drake Carter	Lord Raglan	2:43
1884	Buchanan (2)	Isaac Murphy	Loftin	Audrain	2:40¼
1885	Joe Cotton (Neck)	Erskine Henderson	Bersan	Ten Booker	2:37¼
1886	Ben Ali (½)	Paul Duffy	Blue Wing	Free Knight	2:36½
1887	Montrose (2)	Isaac Lewis	Jim Gore	Jacobin	2:39¼
1888	MacBeth II (1)	George Covington	Gallifet	White	2:38¼
1889	Spokane (Nose)	Thomas Kiley	Proctor Knott	Once Again	2:34½
1890	Riley (2)	Isaac Murphy	Bill Letcher	Robespierre	2:45
1891	Kingman (1)	Isaac Murphy	Balgowan	High Tariff	2:52¼
1892	Azra (Nose)	Alonzo Clayton	Huron	Phil Dwyer	2:41½
1893	Lookout (5)	Eddie Kunze	Plutus	Boundless	2:39¼
1894	Chant (2)	Frank Goodale	Pearl Song	Sigurd	2:41
1895	Halma (3)	Soup Perkins	Basso	Laureate	2:37½
1896	Ben Brush (Nose)	Willie Simms	Ben Eder	Semper Ego	2:07¼
1897	Typhoon II (Head)	Buttons Garner	Ornament	Dr. Catlett	2:12½
1898	Plaudit (Neck)	Willie Simms	Lieber Karl	Isabey	2:09
1899	Manuel (2)	Fred Taral	Corsini	Mazo	2:12
1900	Lieut. Gibson (4)	Jimmy Boland	Florizar	Thrive	2:06¼
1901	His Eminence (2)	Jimmy Winkfield	Sannazarro	Driscoll	2:07¾
1902	Alan-a-Dale (Nose)	Jimmy Winkfield	Inventor	The Rival	2:08¾
1903	Judge Himes (¾)	Hal Booker	Early	Bourbon	2:09
1904	Elwood (½)	Frankie Prior	Ed Tierney	Brancas	2:08½
1905	Agile (3)	Jack Martin	Ram's Horn	Layson	2:10¾
1906	Sir Huon (2)	Roscoe Troxler	Lady Navarre	James Reddick	2:08⅕
1907	Pink Star (2)	Andy Minder	Zal	Ovelando	2:12⅗
1908	Stone Street (1)	Arthur Pickens	Sir Cleges	Dunvegan	2:15⅕
1909	Wintergreen (4)	Vincent Powers	Miami	Dr. Barkley	2:08⅕
1910	Donau (½)	Fred Herbert	Joe Morris	Fighting Bob	2:06⅖
1911	Meridian (¾)	George Archibald	Governor Gray	Colston	2:05
1912	Worth (Neck)	Carroll H. Schilling	Duval	Flamma	2:09⅖
1913	Donerail (½)	Roscoe Goose	Ten Point	Gowell	2:04⅘
1914	Old Rosebud (8)	John McCabe	Hodge	Bronzewing	2:03⅖
1915	Regret (2)	Joe Notter	Pebbles	Sharpshooter	2:05⅖
1916	George Smith (Neck)	Johnny Loftus	Star Hawk	Franklin	2:04
1917	Omar Khayyam (2)	Charles Borel	Ticket	Midway	2:04⅗
1918	Exterminator (1)	William Knapp	Escoba	Viva America	2:10⅘
1919	Sir Barton (5)	Johnny Loftus	Billy Kelly	Under Fire	2:09⅘
1920	Paul Jones (Head)	Ted Rice	Upset	On Watch	2:09
1921	Behave Yourself (Head)	Charles Thompson	Black Servant	Prudery	2:04⅕
1922	Morvich (½)	Albert Johnson	Bet Mosie	John Finn	2:04⅗
1923	Zev (1½)	Earl Sande	Martingale	Vigil	2:05⅖
1924	Black Gold (½)	John Mooney	Chilhowee	Beau Butler	2:05⅕
1925	Flying Ebony (1½)	Earl Sande	Captain Hal	Son of John	2:07⅗
1926	Bubbling Over (5)	Albert Johnson	Bagenbaggage	Rock Man	2:03⅘
1927	Whiskery (Head)	Linus McAtee	Osmond	Jock	2:06
1928	Reigh Count (3)	Chick Lang	Misstep	Toro	2:10⅖
1929	Clyde Van Dusen (2)	Linus McAtee	Naishapur	Panchio	2:10⅘
1930	Gallant Fox (2)	Earl Sande	Gallant Knight	Ned O.	2:07⅗
1931	Twenty Grand (4)	Charles Kurtsinger	Sweep All	Mate	2:01⅘
1932	Burgoo King (5)	Eugene James	Economic	Stepenfetchit	2:05⅕
1933	Brokers Tip (Nose)	Don Meade	Head Play	Charley O.	2:06⅘

Kentucky Derby *(Cont.)*

Year	Winner (Margin)	Jockey	Second	Third	Time
1934	Cavalcade (2½)	Mack Garner	Discovery	Agrarian	2:04
1935	Omaha (1½)	Willie Saunders	Roman Soldier	Whiskolo	2:05
1936	Bold Venture (Head)	Ira Hanford	Brevity	Indian Broom	2:03⅗
1937	War Admiral (1¾)	Charles Kurtsinger	Pompoon	Reaping Reward	2:03⅕
1938	Lawrin (1)	Eddie Arcaro	Dauber	Can't Wait	2:04⅘
1939	Johnstown (8)	James Stout	Challedon	Heather Broom	2:03⅗
1940	Gallahadion (1½)	Carroll Bierman	Bimelech	Dit	2:05
1941	Whirlaway (8)	Eddie Arcaro	Staretor	Market Wise	2:01⅖
1942	Shut Out (2½)	Wayne Wright	Alsab	Valdina Orphan	2:04⅖
1943	Count Fleet (3)	John Longden	Blue Swords	Slide Rule	2:04
1944	Pensive (4½)	Conn McCreary	Broadcloth	Stir Up	2:04⅕
1945	Hoop Jr. (6)	Eddie Arcaro	Pot o' Luck	Darby Dieppe	2:07
1946	Assault (8)	Warren Mehrtens	Spy Song	Hampden	2:06⅗
1947	Jet Pilot (Head)	Eric Guerin	Phalanx	Faultless	2:06⅘
1948	Citation (3½)	Eddie Arcaro	Coaltown	My Request	2:05⅖
1949	Ponder (3)	Steve Brooks	Capot	Palestinian	2:04⅕
1950	Middleground (1¼)	William Boland	Hill Prince	Mr. Trouble	2:01⅗
1951	Count Turf (4)	Conn McCreary	Royal Mustang	Ruhe	2:02⅗
1952	Hill Gail (2)	Eddie Arcaro	Sub Fleet	Blue Man	2:01⅗
1953	Dark Star (Head)	Hank Moreno	Native Dancer	Invigorator	2:02
1954	Determine (1½)	Ray York	Hasty Road	Hasseyampa	2:03
1955	Swaps (1½)	Bill Shoemaker	Nashua	Summer Tan	2:01⅘
1956	Needles (¾)	Dave Erb	Fabius	Come On Red	2:03⅖
1957	Iron Liege (Nose)	Bill Hartack	Gallant Man	Round Table	2:02⅕
1958	Tim Tam (½)	Ismael Valenzuela	Lincoln Road	Noureddin	2:05
1959	Tomy Lee (Nose)	Bill Shoemaker	Sword Dancer	First Landing	2:02⅕
1960	Venetian Way (3½)	Bill Hartack	Bally Ache	Victoria Park	2:02⅖
1961	Carry Back (¾)	John Sellers	Crozier	Bass Clef	2:04
1962	Decidedly (2¼)	Bill Hartack	Roman Line	Ridan	2:00⅖
1963	Chateaugay (1¼)	Braulio Baeza	Never Bend	Candy Spots	2:01⅘
1964	Northern Dancer (Neck)	Bill Hartack	Hill Rise	The Scoundrel	2:00
1965	Lucky Debonair (Neck)	Bill Shoemaker	Dapper Dan	Tom Rolfe	2:01⅕
1966	Kauai King (½)	Don Brumfield	Advocator	Blue Skyer	2:02
1967	Proud Clarion (1)	Bobby Ussery	Barbs Delight	Damascus	2:00⅗
1968	Forward Pass (Disq.)	Ismael Valenzuela	Francie's Hat	T.V. Commercial	2:02⅕
1969	Majestic Prince (Neck)	Bill Hartack	Arts and Letters	Dike	2:01⅘
1970	Dust Commander (5)	Mike Manganello	My Dad George	High Echelon	2:03⅖
1971	Canonero II (3¾)	Gustavo Avila	Jim French	Bold Reason	2:03⅕
1972	Riva Ridge (3¼)	Ron Turcotte	No Le Hace	Hold Your Peace	2:01⅘
1973	Secretariat (2½)	Ron Turcotte	Sham	Our Native	1:59⅖
1974	Cannonade (2¼)	Angel Cordero Jr	Hudson County	Agitate	2:04
1975	Foolish Pleasure (1¾)	Jacinto Vasquez	Avatar	Diabolo	2:02
1976	Bold Forbes (1)	Angel Cordero Jr	Honest Pleasure	Elocutionist	2:01⅗
1977	Seattle Slew (1¾)	Jean Cruguet	Run Dusty Run	Sanhedrin	2:02⅕
1978	Affirmed (1½)	Steve Cauthen	Alydar	Believe It	2:01⅕
1979	Spectacular Bid (2¾)	Ronald J. Franklin	General Assembly	Golden Act	2:02⅖
1980	Genuine Risk (1)	Jacinto Vasquez	Rumbo	Jaklin Klugman	2:02
1981	Pleasant Colony (¾)	Jorge Velasquez	Woodchopper	Partez	2:02
1982	Gato Del Sol (2½)	Eddie Delahoussaye	Laser Light	Reinvested	2:02⅕
1983	Sunny's Halo (2)	Eddie Delahoussaye	Desert Wine	Caveat	2:02⅕
1984	Swale (3¼)	Laffit Pincay Jr	Coax Me Chad	At the Threshold	2:02⅖
1985	Spend A Buck (5)	Angel Cordero Jr	Stephan's Odyssey	Chief's Crown	2:00⅕
1986	Ferdinand (2¼)	Bill Shoemaker	Bold Arrangement	Broad Brush	2:02⅘
1987	Alysheba (¾)	Chris McCarron	Bet Twice	Avies Copy	2:03⅖
1988	Winning Colors (Neck)	Gary Stevens	Forty Niner	Risen Star	2:02⅕
1989	Sunday Silence (2½)	Pat Valenzuela	Easy Goer	Awe Inspiring	2:05
1990	Unbridled (3½)	Craig Perret	Summer Squall	Pleasant Tap	2:02
1991	Strike the Gold (1¾)	Chris Antley	Best Pal	Mane Minister	2:03
1992	Lil E. Tee (1)	Pat Day	Casual Lies	Dance Floor	2:03
1993	Sea Hero (2½)	Jerry Bailey	Prairie Bayou	Wild Gale	2:02⅖
1994	Go for Gin (2½)	Chris McCarron	Strodes Creek	Blumin Affair	2:03⅗
1995	Thunder Gulch (2¼)	Gary Stevens	Tejano Run	Timber Country	2:01⅕

Note: Distance: 1½ miles (1875-95), 1¼ miles (1896-present).

Preakness

Run at Pimlico Race Course, Baltimore, Md., two weeks after the Kentucky Derby.

Year	Winner (Margin)	Jockey	Second	Third	Time
1873	Survivor (10)	G. Barbee	John Boulger	Artist	2:43
1874	Culpepper (¾)	W. Donohue	King Amadeus	Scratch	2:56½
1875	Tom Ochiltree (2)	L. Hughes	Viator	Bay Final	2:43½
1876	Shirley (4)	G. Barbee	Rappahannock	Algerine	2:44¾
1877	Cloverbrook (4)	C. Holloway	Bombast	Lucifer	2:45½
1878	Duke of Magenta (6)	C. Holloway	Bayard	Albert	2:41¾
1879	Harold (3)	L. Hughes	Jericho	Rochester	2:40½
1880	Grenada (¾)	L. Hughes	Oden	Emily F.	2:40½
1881	Saunterer (½)	T. Costello	Compensation	Baltic	2:40½
1882	Vanguard (Neck)	T. Costello	Heck	Col Watson	2:44½
1883	Jacobus (4)	G. Barbee	Parnell		2:42½
1884	Knight of Ellerslie (2)	S. Fisher	Welcher		2:39½
1885	Tecumseh (2)	Jim McLaughlin	Wickham	John C.	2:49
1886	The Bard (3)	S. Fisher	Eurus	Elkwood	2:45
1887	Dunboyne (1)	W. Donohue	Mahoney	Raymond	2:39½
1888	Refund (3)	F. Littlefield	Judge Murray	Glendale	2:49
1889	Buddhist (8)	W. Anderson	Japhet		2:17½
1890*	Montague (3)	W. Martin	Philosophy	Barrister	2:36¾
1894	Assignee (3)	Fred Taral	Potentate	Ed Kearney	1:49¼
1895	Belmar (1)	Fred Taral	April Fool	Sue Kittie	1:50½
1896	Margrave (1)	H. Griffin	Hamilton II	Intermission	1:51
1897	Paul Kauvar (1½)	C. Thorpe	Elkins	On Deck	1:51¼
1898	Sly Fox (2)	C. W. Simms	The Huguenot	Nuto	1:49⅗
1899	Half Time (1)	R. Clawson	Filigrane	Lackland	1:47
1900	Hindus (Head)	H. Spencer	Sarmation	Ten Candles	1:48⅖
1901	The Parader (2)	F. Landry	Sadie S.	Dr. Barlow	1:47⅕
1902	Old England (Nose)	L. Jackson	Major Daingerfield	Namtor	1:45⅘
1903	Flocarline (½)	W. Gannon	Mackey Dwyer	Rightful	1:44⅘
1904	Bryn Mawr (1)	E. Hildebrand	Wotan	Dolly Spanker	1:44⅕
1905	Cairngorm (Head)	W. Davis	Kiamesha	Coy Maid	1:45⅘
1906	Whimsical (4)	Walter Miller	Content	Larabie	1:45
1907	Don Enrique (1)	G. Mountain	Ethon	Zambesi	1:45⅖
1908	Royal Tourist (4)	E. Dugan	Live Wire	Robert Cooper	1:46⅖
1909	Effendi (1)	Willie Doyle	Fashion Plate	Hilltop	1:39⅘
1910	Layminster (½)	R. Estep	Dalhousie	Sager	1:40⅗
1911	Watervale (1)	E. Dugan	Zeus	The Nigger	1:51
1912	Colonel Holloway (5)	C. Turner	Bwana Tumbo	Tipsand	1:56⅗
1913	Buskin (Neck)	J. Butwell	Kleburne	Barnegat	1:53⅖
1914	Holiday (¾)	A. Schuttinger	Brave Cunarder	Defendum	1:53⅘
1915	Rhine Maiden (1½)	Douglas Hoffman	Half Rock	Runes	1:58
1916	Damrosch (1½)	Linus McAtee	Greenwood	Achievement	1:54⅘
1917	Kalitan (2)	E. Haynes	Al M. Dick	Kentucky Boy	1:54⅖
1918	War Cloud (¾)	Johnny Loftus	Sunny Slope	Lanius	1:53⅗
1918	Jack Hare, Jr (2)	C. Peak	The Porter	Kate Bright	1:53⅖
1919	Sir Barton (4)	Johnny Loftus	Eternal	Sweep On	1:53
1920	Man o' War (1½)	Clarence Kummer	Upset	Wildair	1:51⅗
1921	Broomspun (¾)	F. Coltiletti	Polly Ann	Jeg	1:54⅕
1922	Pillory (Head)	L. Morris	Hea	June Grass	1:51⅗
1923	Vigil (1¼)	B. Marinelli	General Thatcher	Rialto	1:53⅗
1924	Nellie Morse (1½)	J. Merimee	Transmute	Mad Play	1:57⅕
1925	Coventry (4)	Clarence Kummer	Backbone	Almadel	1:59
1926	Display (Head)	J. Maiben	Blondin	Mars	1:59⅘
1927	Bostonian (½)	A. Abel	Sir Harry	Whiskery	2:01⅗
1928	Victorian (Nose)	Sonny Workman	Toro	Solace	2:00⅕
1929	Dr. Freeland (1)	Louis Schaefer	Minotaur	African	2:01⅗
1930	Gallant Fox (¾)	Earl Sande	Crack Brigade	Snowflake	2:00⅗
1931	Mate (1½)	G. Ellis	Twenty Grand	Ladder	1:59
1932	Burgoo King (Head)	E. James	Tick On	Boatswain	1:59⅘
1933	Head Play (4)	Charles Kurtsinger	Ladysman	Utopian	2:02
1934	High Quest (Nose)	R. Jones	Cavalcade	Discovery	1:58⅕
1935	Omaha (6)	Willie Saunders	Firethorn	Psychic Bid	1:58⅖
1936	Bold Venture (Nose)	George Woolf	Granville	Jean Bart	1:59
1937	War Admiral (Head)	Charles Kurtsinger	Pompoon	Flying Scot	1:58⅖
1938	Dauber (7)	M. Peters	Cravat	Menow	1:59⅘

Preakness (Cont.)

Year	Winner (Margin)	Jockey	Second	Third	Time
1939	Challedon (1¼)	George Seabo	Gilded Knight	Volitant	1:59⅘
1940	Bimelech (3)	F. A. Smith	Mioland	Gallahadion	1:58⅗
1941	Whirlaway (5½)	Eddie Arcaro	King Cole	Our Boots	1:58⅘
1942	Alsab (1)	B. James	Requested Sun Again	(dead heat for second)	1:57
1943	Count Fleet (8)	Johnny Longden	Blue Swords	Vincentive	1:57⅖
1944	Pensive (¾)	Conn McCreary	Platter	Stir Up	1:59⅕
1945	Polynesian (2½)	W. D. Wright	Hoop Jr	Darby Dieppe	1:58⅘
1946	Assault (Neck)	Warren Mehrtens	Lord Boswell	Hampden	2:01⅖
1947	Faultless (1¼)	Doug Dodson	On Trust	Phalanx	1:59
1948	Citation (5½)	Eddie Arcaro	Vulcan's Forge	Boyard	2:02⅖
1949	Capot (Head)	Ted Atkinson	Palestinian	Noble Impulse	1:56
1950	Hill Prince (5)	Eddie Arcaro	Middleground	Dooley	1:59⅕
1951	Bold (7)	Eddie Arcaro	Counterpoint	Alerted	1:56⅖
1952	Blue Man (3½)	Conn McCreary	Jampol	One Count	1:57⅖
1953	Native Dancer (Neck)	Eric Guerin	Jamie K.	Royal Bay Gem	1:57⅘
1954	Hasty Road (Neck)	Johnny Adams	Correlation	Hasseyampa	1:57⅖
1955	Nashua (1)	Eddie Arcaro	Saratoga	Traffic Judge	1:54⅗
1956	Fabius (¾)	Bill Hartack	Needles	No Regrets	1:58⅖
1957	Bold Ruler (2)	Eddie Arcaro	Iron Liege	Inside Tract	1:56⅕
1958	Tim Tam (1½)	I. Valenzuela	Lincoln Road	Gone Fishin'	1:57⅕
1959	Royal Orbit (4)	William Harmatz	Sword Dancer	Dunce	1:57
1960	Bally Ache (4)	Bobby Ussery	Victoria Park	Celtic Ash	1:57⅗
1961	Carry Back (¾)	Johnny Sellers	Globemaster	Crozier	1:57⅗
1962	Greek Money (Nose)	John Rotz	Ridan	Roman Line	1:56⅕
1963	Candy Spots (3½)	Bill Shoemaker	Chateaugay	Never Bend	1:56⅕
1964	Northern Dancer (2¼)	Bill Hartack	The Scoundrel	Hill Rise	1:56⅘
1965	Tom Rolfe (Neck)	Ron Turcotte	Dapper Dan	Hail to All	1:56⅕
1966	Kauai King (1¾)	Don Brumfield	Stupendous	Amberoid	1:55⅖
1967	Damascus (2¼)	Bill Shoemaker	In Reality	Proud Clarion	1:55⅕
1968	Forward Pass (6)	I. Valenzuela	Out of the Way	Nodouble	1:56⅘
1969	Majestic Prince (Head)	Bill Hartack	Arts and Letters	Jay Ray	1:55⅗
1970	Personality (Neck)	Eddie Belmonte	My Dad George	Silent Screen	1:56⅕
1971	Canonero II (1½)	Gustavo Avila	Eastern Fleet	Jim French	1:54
1972	Bee Bee Bee (1¼)	Eldon Nelson	No Le Hace	Key to the Mint	1:55⅗
1973	Secretariat (2½)	Ron Turcotte	Sham	Our Native	1:54⅖
1974	Little Current (7)	Miguel Rivera	Neapolitan Way	Cannonade	1:54⅗
1975	Master Derby (1)	Darrel McHargue	Foolish Pleasure	Diabolo	1:56⅖
1976	Elocutionist (3)	John Lively	Play the Red	Bold Forbes	1:55
1977	Seattle Slew (1½)	Jean Cruguet	Iron Constitution	Run Dusty Run	1:54⅖
1978	Affirmed (Neck)	Steve Cauthen	Alydar	Believe It	1:54⅖
1979	Spectacular Bid (5½)	Ron Franklin	Golden Act	Screen King	1:54⅕
1980	Codex (4¾)	Angel Cordero Jr	Genuine Risk	Colonel Moran	1:54⅕
1981	Pleasant Colony (1)	Jorge Velasquez	Bold Ego	Paristo	1:54⅗
1982	Aloma's Ruler (½)	Jack Kaenel	Linkage	Cut Away	1:55⅖
1983	Deputed Testamony (2¾)	Donald Miller Jr	Desert Wine	High Honors	1:55⅖
1984	Gate Dancer (1½)	Angel Cordero Jr	Play On	Fight Over	1:53⅗
1985	Tank's Prospect (Head)	Pat Day	Chief's Crown	Eternal Prince	1:53⅖
1986	Snow Chief (4)	Alex Solis	Ferdinand	Broad Brush	1:54⅘
1987	Alysheba (½)	Chris McCarron	Bet Twice	Cryptoclearance	1:55⅘
1988	Risen Star (1¼)	E. Delahoussaye	Brian's Time	Winning Colors	1:56⅕
1989	Sunday Silence (Nose)	Pat Valenzuela	Easy Goer	Rock Point	1:53⅘
1990	Summer Squall (2¼)	Pat Day	Unbridled	Mister Frisky	1:53⅗
1991	Hansel (Head)	Jerry Bailey	Corporate Report	Mane Minister	1:54
1992	Pine Bluff (¾)	Chris McCarron	Alydeed	Casual Lies	1:55⅗
1993	Prairie Bayou (½)	Mike Smith	Cherokee Run	El Bakan	1:56⅗
1994	Tabasco Cat (¾)	Pat Day	Go For Gin	Concern	1:56⅖
1995	Timber Country (½)	Pat Day	Oliver's Twist	Thunder Gulch	1:54⅖

*Preakness was not run 1891-1893. In 1918, it was run in two divisions.

Note: Distance: 1½ miles (1873-88), 1¼ miles (1889), 1½ miles (1890), 1 1/16 miles (1894-1900), 1 mile and 70 yards (1901-1907), 1 1/16 miles (1908), 1 mile (1909-10), 1⅛ miles (1911-24), 1 3/16 miles (1925-present).

Belmont

Run at Belmont Park, Elmont, NY, three weeks after the Preakness Stakes. Held previously at two locations in the Bronx, NY: Jerome Park (1867—1889) and Morris Park (1890—1904).

Year	Winner (Margin)	Jockey	Second	Third	Time
1867	Ruthless (Head)	J. Gilpatrick	De Courcy	Rivoli	3:05
1868	General Duke (2)	R. Swim	Northumberland	Fannie Ludlow	3:02
1869	Fenian (Unknown)	C. Miller	Glenelg	Invercauld	3:04¼
1870	Kingfisher (½)	E. Brown	Foster	Midday	2:59½
1871	Harry Bassett (3)	W. Miller	Stockwood	By-the-Sea	2:56
1872	Joe Daniels (¾)	James Rowe	Meteor	Shylock	2:58¼
1873	Springbok (4)	James Rowe	Count d'Orsay	Strachino	3:01¾
1874	Saxon (Neck)	G. Barbee	Grinstead	Aaron Pennington	2:39½
1875	Calvin (2)	R. Swim	Aristides	Milner	2:40¼
1876	Algerine (Head)	W. Donahue	Fiddlestick	Barricade	2:40½
1877	Cloverbrook (1)	C. Holloway	Loiterer	Baden-Baden	2:46
1878	Duke of Magenta (2)	L. Hughes	Bramble	Sparta	2:43½
1879	Spendthrift (5)	S. Evans	Monitor	Jericho	2:42¾
1880	Grenada (½)	L. Hughes	Ferncliffe	Turenne	2:47
1881	Saunterer (Neck)	T. Costello	Eole	Baltic	2:47
1882	Forester (5)	James McLaughlin	Babcock	Wyoming	2:43
1883	George Kinney (2)	James McLaughlin	Trombone	Renegade	2:42½
1884	Panique (½)	James McLaughlin	Knight of Ellerslie	Himalaya	2:42
1885	Tyrant (3½)	Paul Duffy	St Augustine	Tecumseh	2:43
1886	Inspector B (1)	James McLaughlin	The Bard	Linden	2:41
1887	Hanover (28-32)	James McLaughlin	Oneko		2:43½
1888	Sir Dixon (12)	James McLaughlin	Prince Royal		2:40¼
1889	Eric (Head)	W. Hayward	Diable	Zephyrus	2:47
1890	Burlington (1)	S. Barnes	Devotee	Padishah	2:07¾
1891	Foxford (Neck)	E. Garrison	Montana	Laurestan	2:08¾
1892	Patron (Unknown)	W. Hayward	Shellbark		2:17
1893	Comanche (Head)(21)	Willie Simms	Dr. Rice	Rainbow	1:53¼
1894	Henry of Navarre (2-4)	Willie Simms	Prig	Assignee	1:56½
1895	Belmar (Head)	Fred Taral	Counter Tenor	Nanki Pooh	2:11½
1896	Hastings (Neck)	H. Griffin	Handspring	Hamilton II	2:24½
1897	Scottish Chieftain (1)	J. Scherrer	On Deck	Octagon	2:23¼
1898	Bowling Brook (8)	P. Littlefield	Previous	Hamburg	2:32
1899	Jean Bereaud (Head)	R. R. Clawson	Half Time	Glengar	2:23
1900	Ildrim (Head)	N. Turner	Petrucio	Missionary	2:21½
1901	Commando (½)	H. Spencer	The Parader	All Green	2:21
1902	Masterman (2)	John Bullmann	Ranald	King Hanover	2:22½
1903	Africander (2)	John Bullmann	Whorler	Red Knight	2:23⅕
1904	Delhi (3½)	George Odom	Graziallo	Rapid Water	2:06⅗
1905	Tanya (1/2)	E. Hildebrand	Blandy	Hot Shot	2:08
1906	Burgomaster (4)	L. Lyne	The Quail	Accountant	2:20
1907	Peter Pan (1)	G. Mountain	Superman	Frank Gill	Unknown
1908	Colin (Head)	Joe Notter	Fair Play	King James	Unknown
1909	Joe Madden (8)	E. Dugan	Wise Mason	Donald MacDonald	2:21⅗
1910*	Sweep (6)	J. Butwell	Duke of Ormonde		2:22
1913	Prince Eugene (½)	Roscoe Troxler	Rock View	Flying Fairy	2:18
1914	Luke McLuke (8)	M. Buxton	Gainer	Charlestonian	2:20
1915	The Finn (4)	G. Byrne	Half Rock	Pebbles	2:18⅖
1916	Friar Rock (3)	E. Haynes	Spur	Churchill	2:22
1917	Hourless (10)	J. Butwell	Skeptic	Wonderful	2:17⅘
1918	Johren (2)	Frank Robinson	War Cloud	Cum Sah	2:20⅖
1919	Sir Barton (5)	Johnny Loftus	Sweep On	Natural Bridge	2:17⅖
1920	Man o' War (20)	Clarence Kummer	Donnacona		2:14⅕
1921	Grey Lag (3)	Earl Sande	Sporting Blood	Leonardo II	2:16⅘
1922	Pillory (2)	C. H. Miller	Snob II	Hea	2:18⅘
1923	Zev (1½)	Earl Sande	Chickvale	Rialto	2:19
1924	Mad Play (2)	Earl Sande	Mr. Mutt	Modest	2:18⅘
1925	American Flag (8)	Albert Johnson	Dangerous	Swope	2:16⅘
1926	Crusader (1)	Albert Johnson	Espino	Haste	2:32⅕
1927	Chance Shot (1½)	Earl Sande	Bois de Rose	Flambino	2:32⅖
1928	Vito (3)	Clarence Kummer	Genie	Diavolo	2:33⅕

Belmont (Cont.)

Year	Winner (Margin)	Jockey	Second	Third	Time
1929	Blue Larkspur (¾)	Mack Garner	African	Jack High	2:32⅘
1930	Gallant Fox (3)	Earl Sande	Whichone	Questionnaire	2:31⅗
1931	Twenty Grand (10)	Charles Kurtsinger	Sun Meadow	Jamestown	2:29⅗
1932	Faireno (1½)	T. Malley	Osculator	Flag Pole	2:32⅘
1933	Hurryoff (1½)	Mack Garner	Nimbus	Union	2:32⅗
1934	Peace Chance (6)	W. D. Wright	High Quest	Good Goods	2:29⅕
1935	Omaha (1½)	Willie Saunders	Firethorn	Rosemont	2:30⅗
1936	Granville (Nose)	James Stout	Mr. Bones	Hollyrood	2:30
1937	War Admiral (3)	Charles Kurtsinger	Sceneshifter	Vamoose	2:28⅗
1938	Pasteurized (Neck)	James Stout	Dauber	Cravat	2:29⅖
1939	Johnstown (5)	James Stout	Belay	Gilded Knight	2:29⅗
1940	Bimelech (¾)	F. A. Smith	Your Chance	Andy K	2:29⅗
1941	Whirlaway (2½)	Eddie Arcaro	Robert Morris	Yankee Chance	2:31
1942	Shut Out (2)	Eddie Arcaro	Alsab	Lochinvar	2:29⅕
1943	Count Fleet (25)	Johnny Longden	Fairy Manhurst	Deseronto	2:28⅕
1944	Bounding Home (½)	G. L. Smith	Pensive	Bull Dandy	2:32⅕
1945	Pavot (5)	Eddie Arcaro	Wildlife	Jeep	2:30⅕
1946	Assault (3)	Warren Mehrtens	Natchez	Cable	2:30⅘
1947	Phalanx (5)	R. Donoso	Tide Rips	Tailspin	2:29⅖
1948	Citation (8)	Eddie Arcaro	Better Self	Escadru	2:28⅕
1949	Capot (½)	Ted Atkinson	Ponder	Palestinian	2:30⅕
1950	Middleground (1)	William Boland	Lights Up	Mr. Trouble	2:28⅗
1951	Counterpoint (4)	D. Gorman	Battlefield	Battle Morn	2:29
1952	One Count (2½)	Eddie Arcaro	Blue Man	Armageddon	2:30⅕
1953	Native Dancer (Neck)	Eric Guerin	Jamie K.	Royal Bay Gem	2:38⅗
1954	High Gun (Neck)	Eric Guerin	Fisherman	Limelight	2:30⅘
1955	Nashua (9)	Eddie Arcaro	Blazing Count	Portersville	2:29
1956	Needles (Neck)	David Erb	Career Boy	Fabius	2:29⅘
1957	Gallant Man (8)	Bill Shoemaker	Inside Tract	Bold Ruler	2:26⅗
1958	Cavan (6)	Pete Anderson	Tim Tam	Flamingo	2:30⅕
1959	Sword Dancer (¾)	Bill Shoemaker	Bagdad	Royal Orbit	2:28⅖
1960	Celtic Ash (5½)	Bill Hartack	Venetian Way	Disperse	2:29⅗
1961	Sherluck (2¼)	Braulio Baeza	Globemaster	Guadalcanal	2:29⅕
1962	Jaipur (Nose)	Bill Shoemaker	Admiral's Voyage	Crimson Satan	2:28⅘
1963	Chateaugay (2½)	Braulio Baeza	Candy Spots	Choker	2:30⅕
1964	Quadrangle (2)	Manuel Ycaza	Roman Brother	Northern Dancer	2:28⅖
1965	Hail to All (Neck)	John Sellers	Tom Rolfe	First Family	2:28⅖
1966	Amberold (2½)	William Boland	Buffle	Advocator	2:29⅗
1967	Damascus (2½)	Bill Shoemaker	Cool Reception	Gentleman James	2:28⅘
1968	Stage Door Johnny (1¼)	Hellodoro Gustines	Forward Pass	Call Me Prince	2:27⅕
1969	Arts and Letters (5½)	Braulio Baeza	Majestic Prince	Dike	2:28⅘
1970	High Echelon (¾)	John L. Rotz	Needles N Pins	Naskra	2:34
1971	Pass Catcher (¾)	Walter Blum	Jim French	Bold Reason	2:30⅖
1972	Riva Ridge (7)	Ron Turcotte	Ruritania	Cloudy Dawn	2:28
1973	Secretariat (31)	Ron Turcotte	Twice a Prince	My Gallant	2:24
1974	Little Current (7)	Miguel A. Rivera	Jolly Johu	Cannonade	2:29⅕
1975	Avatar (Neck)	Bill Shoemaker	Foolish Pleasure	Master Derby	2:28⅕
1976	Bold Forbes (Neck)	Angel Cordero Jr	McKenzie Bridge	Great Contractor	2:29
1977	Seattle Slew (4)	Jean Cruguet	Run Dusty Run	Sanhedrin	2:29⅗
1978	Affirmed (Head)	Steve Cauthen	Alydar	Darby Creek Road	2:26⅘
1979	Coastal (3¼)	Ruben Hernandez	Golden Act	Spectacular Bid	2:28⅗
1980	Temperence Hill (2)	Eddie Maple	Genuine Risk	Rockhill Native	2:29⅘
1981	Summing (Neck)	George Martens	Highland Blade	Pleasant Colony	2:29
1982	Conquistador Cielo (14½)	Laffit Pincay, Jr	Gato Del Sol	Illuminate	2:28⅕
1983	Caveat (3½)	Laffit Pincay Jr	Slew o'Gold	Barberstown	2:27⅘
1984	Swale (4)	Laffit Pincay Jr	Pine Circle	Morning Bob	2:27⅕
1985	Creme Fraiche (½)	Eddie Maple	Stephan's Odyssey	Chief's Crown	2:27
1986	Danzig Connection (1¼)	Chris McCarron	Johns Treasure	Ferdinand	2:29⅘

Belmont (Cont.)

Year	Winner (Margin)	Jockey	Second	Third	Time
1987	Bet Twice (14)	Craig Perret	Cryptoclearance	Gulch	2:28⅕
1988	Risen Star (14¾)	Eddie Delahoussaye	Kingpost	Brian's Time	2:26⅖
1989	Easy Goer (8)	Pat Day	Sunday Silence	Le Voyageur	2:26
1990	Go and Go (8¼)	Michael Kinane	Thirty Six Red	Baron de Vaux	2:27⅕
1991	Hansel (Head)	Jerry Bailey	Strike the Gold	Mane Minister	2:28
1992	A.P. Indy (¾)	Eddie Delahoussaye	My Memoirs	Pine Bluff	2:26
1993	Colonial Affair (2¼)	Julie Krone	Kissin Kris	Wild Gale	2:29⅘
1994	Tabasco Cat (2)	Pat Day	Go For Gin	Strodes Creek	2:26⅘
1995	Thunder Gulch (2)	Gary Stevens	Star Standard	Citadeed	2:32

*Race not held in 1911-1912.

Note: Distance: 1 mile 5 furlongs (1867-89), 1¼ miles (1890-1905), 1⅜ miles (1906-25), 1½ miles (1926-present).

Triple Crown Winners

Year	Horse	Jockey	Owner	Trainer
1919	Sir Barton	John Loftus	J. K. L. Ross	H. G. Bedwell
1930	Gallant Fox	Earle Sande	Belair Stud	James Fitzsimmons
1935	Omaha	William Saunders	Belair Stud	James Fitzsimmons
1937	War Admiral	Charles Kurtsinger	Samuel D. Riddle	George Conway
1941	Whirlaway	Eddie Arcaro	Calumet Farm	Ben Jones
1943	Count Fleet	John Longden	Mrs J. D. Hertz	Don Cameron
1946	Assault	Warren Mehrtens	King Ranch	Max Hirsch
1948	Citation	Eddie Arcaro	Calumet Farm	Jimmy Jones
1973	Secretariat	Ron Turcotte	Meadow Stable	Lucien Laurin
1977	Seattle Slew	Jean Cruguet	Karen L. Taylor	William H. Turner Jr
1978	Affirmed	Steve Cauthen	Harbor View Farm	Laz Barrera

Goodbye to the Bull

When Holy Bull suffered a career-ending leg injury during last February's $300,000 Donn Handicap at Gulfstream Park, thoroughbred racing lost more than just another good horse. With the sport battling for survival among the growing sprawl of casinos, lotteries and other forms of legalized gambling, Holy Bull, one of those rare horses who, like Secretariat, stir the public's imagination, was the hero that racing needed.

Why was there such acclaim and affection for a horse who finished 12th in the 1994 Kentucky Derby and didn't even compete in the other two Triple Crown races or the Breeders' Cup? To begin with, the Bull *was* good. In 1994, as a 3-year-old, he won eight of his 10 starts, twice beating the country's best older horses, which was enough to earn him Horse of the Year honors. Beyond that, fans loved his catchy name, his gray color and his front-running style. Whenever the Bull was running, everyone knew the script: Catch him if you can.

Something bad caught Holy Bull in the Donn. Dueling with eventual winner Cigar for the lead at the ⅝ pole, Holy Bull seemed to be running easily. But at that point a tendon in his left foreleg gave way. Said Jerry Bailey, who was riding Cigar a length ahead, "I heard a pop, and then I heard [the Bull's jockey] Mike Smith yell, 'Oh, no.'" Then I lost him as he pulled up his horse." Holy Bull came to a halt near the half-mile pole, where Smith dismounted and soothed him until the equine ambulance arrived.

For the racing world, sadness over the injury was tempered by the knowledge that Holy Bull is expected to recover enough to stand stud at Jonabell Farm in Lexington. Despite the Bull's lackluster pedigree, Jim Bell of Jonabell reports that there has already been keen interest in him as a stallion. Still, whatever his success at stud, the Bull is unlikely to sire a horse with his panache.

Awards

Horse of the Year

Year	Horse	Owner	Trainer	Breeder
1936	Granville	Belair Stud	James Fitzsimmons	Belair Stud
1937	War Admiral	Samuel D. Riddle	George Conway	Mrs. Samuel D. Riddle
1938	Seabiscuit	Charles S. Howard	Tom Smith	Wheatley Stable
1939	Challedon	William L. Brann	Louis J. Schaefer	Branncastle Farm
1940	Challedon	William L. Brann	Louis J. Schaefer	Branncastle Farm
1941	Whirlaway	Calumet Farm	Ben Jones	Calumet Farm
1942	Whirlaway	Calumet Farm	Ben Jones	Calumet Farm
1943	Count Fleet	Mrs. John D. Hertz	Don Cameron	Mrs. John D. Hertz
1944	Twilight Tear	Calumet Farm	Ben Jones	Calumet Farm
1945	Busher	Louis B. Mayer	George Odom	Idle Hour Stock Farm
1946	Assault	King Ranch	Max Hirsch	King Ranch
1947	Armed	Calumet Farm	Jimmy Jones	Calumet Farm
1948	Citation	Calumet Farm	Jimmy Jones	Calumet Farm
1949	Capot	Greentree Stable	John M. Gaver Sr	Greentree Stable
1950	Hill Prince	C. T. Chenery	Casey Hayes	C. T. Chenery
1951	Counterpoint	C. V. Whitney	Syl Veitch	C. V. Whitney
1952	One Count	Mrs. W. M. Jeffords	O. White	W. M. Jeffords
1953	Tom Fool	Greentree Stable	John M. Gaver Sr	D. A. Headley
1954	Native Dancer	A. G. Vanderbilt	Bill Winfrey	A. G. Vanderbilt
1955	Nashua	Belair Stud	James Fitzsimmons	Belair Stud
1956	Swaps	Ellsworth-Galbreath	Mesh Tenney	R. Ellsworth
1957	Bold Ruler	Wheatley Stable	James Fitzsimmons	Wheatley Stable
1958	Round Table	Kerr Stables	Willy Molter	Claiborne Farm
1959	Sword Dancer	Brookmeade Stable	Elliott Burch	Brookmeade Stable
1960	Kelso	Bohemia Stable	C. Hanford	Mrs. R. C. duPont
1961	Kelso	Bohemia Stable	C. Hanford	Mrs. R. C. duPont
1962	Kelso	Bohemia Stable	C. Hanford	Mrs. R. C. duPont
1963	Kelso	Bohemia Stable	C. Hanford	Mrs. R. C. duPont
1964	Kelso	Bohemia Stable	C. Hanford	Mrs. R. C. duPont
1965	Roman Brother	Harbor View Stable	Burley Parke	Ocala Stud
1966	Buckpasser	Ogden Phipps	Eddie Neloy	Ogden Phipps
1967	Damascus	Mrs. E. W. Bancroft	Frank Y. Whiteley Jr	Mrs. E. W. Bancroft
1968	Dr. Fager	Tartan Stable	John A. Nerud	Tartan Farms
1969	Arts and Letters	Rokeby Stable	Elliott Burch	Paul Mellon
1970	Fort Marcy	Rokeby Stable	Elliott Burch	Paul Mellon
1971	Ack Ack	E. E. Fogelson	Charlie Whittingham	H. F. Guggenheim
1972	Secretariat	Meadow Stable	Lucien Laurin	Meadow Stud
1973	Secretariat	Meadow Stable	Lucien Laurin	Meadow Stud
1974	Forego	Lazy F Ranch	Sherrill W. Ward	Lazy F Ranch
1975	Forego	Lazy F Ranch	Sherrill W. Ward	Lazy F Ranch
1976	Forego	Lazy F Ranch	Frank Y. Whiteley Jr	Lazy F Ranch
1977	Seattle Slew	Karen L. Taylor	Billy Turner Jr	B. S. Castleman
1978	Affirmed	Harbor View Farm	Laz Barrera	Harbor View Farm
1979	Affirmed	Harbor View Farm	Laz Barrera	Harbor View Farm
1980	Spectacular Bid	Hawksworth Farm	Bud Delp	Mmes. Gilmore and Jason
1981	John Henry	Dotsam Stable	Ron McAnally and Lefty Nickerson	Golden Chance Farm
1982	Conquistador Cielo	H. de Kwiatkowski	Woody Stephens	L. E. Landoli
1983	All Along	Daniel Wildenstein	P. L. Biancone	Dayton
1984	John Henry	Dotsam Stable	Ron McAnally	Golden Chance Farm
1985	Spend a Buck	Hunter Farm	Cam Gambolati	Irish Hill Farm & R. W. Harper
1986	Lady's Secret	Mr. & Mrs. Eugene Klein	D. Wayne Lukas	R. H. Spreen
1987	Ferdinand	Mrs. H. B. Keck	Charlie Whittingham	H. B. Keck
1988	Alysheba	D. & P. Scharbauer	Jack Van Berg	Preston Madden
1989	Sunday Silence	Gaillard, Hancock, & Whittingham	Charlie Whittingham	Oak Cliff Thoroughbreds

Horse of the Year (Cont.)

Year	Horse	Owner	Trainer	Breeder
1990	Criminal Type	Calumet Farm	D. Wayne Lukas	Calumet Farm
1991	Black Tie Affair	Jeffrey Sullivan	Ernie Poulos	Stephen D. Peskoff
1992	A.P. Indy	Tomonori Tsurumaki	Neil Drysdale	W.S. Farish & W.S. Kilroy
1993	Kotashaan	La Presle Farm	Richard Mandella	La Presle Farm
1994	Holy Bull	Jimmy Croll	Jimmy Croll	Pelican Stable

Note: From 1936 to 1970, the *Daily Racing Form* annually selected a "Horse of the Year." In 1971 the *Daily Racing Form*, with the Thoroughbred Racing Association and the National Turf Writers Association, jointly created the Eclipse Awards.

Eclipse Award Winners

2-YEAR-OLD COLT

1971	Riva Ridge
1972	Secretariat
1973	Protagonist
1974	Foolish Pleasure
1975	Honest Pleasure
1976	Seattle Slew
1977	Affirmed
1978	Spectacular Bid
1979	Rockhill Native
1980	Lord Avie
1981	Deputy Minister
1982	Roving Boy
1983	Devil's Bag
1984	Chief's Crown
1985	Tasso
1986	Capote
1987	Forty Niner
1988	Easy Goer
1989	Rhythm
1990	Fly So Free
1991	Arazi
1992	Gilded Time
1993	Dehere
1994	Timber Country

2-YEAR-OLD FILLY

1971	Numbered Account
1972	La Prevoyante
1973	Talking Picture
1974	Ruffian
1975	Dearly Precious
1976	Sensational
1977	Lakeville Miss
1978	Candy Eclair / It's in the Air
1979	Smart Angle
1980	Heavenly Cause
1981	Before Dawn
1982	Landaluce
1983	Althea
1984	Outstandingly
1985	Family Style
1986	Brave Raj
1987	Epitome
1988	Open Mind
1989	Go for Wand
1990	Meadow Star
1991	Pleasant Stage
1992	Eliza
1993	Phone Chatter
1994	Flanders

3-YEAR-OLD COLT

1971	Canonero II
1972	Key to the Mint
1973	Secretariat
1974	Little Current
1975	Wajima
1976	Bold Forbes
1977	Seattle Slew
1978	Affirmed
1979	Spectacular Bid
1980	Temperence Hill
1981	Pleasant Colony
1982	Conquistador Cielo
1983	Slew o' Gold
1984	Swale
1985	Spend A Buck
1986	Snow Chief
1987	Alysheba
1988	Risen Star
1989	Sunday Silence
1990	Unbridled
1991	Hansel
1992	A.P. Indy
1993	Prairie Bayou
1994	Holy Bull

3-YEAR-OLD FILLY

1971	Turkish Trousers
1972	Susan's Girl
1973	Desert Vixen
1974	Chris Evert
1975	Ruffian
1976	Revidere
1977	Our Mims
1978	Tempest Queen
1979	Davona Dale
1980	Genuine Risk
1981	Wayward Lass
1982	Christmas Past
1983	Heartlight No. One
1984	Life's Magic
1985	Mom's Command
1986	Tiffany Lass
1987	Sacahuista
1988	Winning Colors
1989	Open Mind
1990	Go for Wand
1991	Dance Smartly
1992	Saratoga Dew
1993	Hollywood Wildcat
1994	Heavenly Prize

OLDER COLT, HORSE OR GELDING

1971	Ack Ack (5)
1972	Autobiography (4)
1973	Riva Ridge (4)
1974	Forego (4)
1975	Forego (5)
1976	Forego (6)
1977	Forego (7)
1978	Seattle Slew (4)
1979	Affirmed (4)
1980	Spectacular Bid (4)
1981	John Henry (6)
1982	Lemhi Gold (4)
1983	Bates Motel (4)
1984	Slew o'Gold (4)
1985	Vanlandingham (4)
1986	Turkoman (4)
1987	Ferdinand (4)
1988	Alysheba (4)
1989	Blushing John (4)
1990	Criminal Type (5)
1991	Black Tie Affair (5)
1992	Pleasant Tap (5)
1993	Bertrando (4)
1994	The Wicked North (5)

OLDER FILLY OR MARE

1971	Shuvee (5)
1972	Typecast (6)
1973	Susan's Girl (4)
1974	Desert Vixen (4)
1975	Susan's Girl (6)
1976	Proud Delta (4)
1977	Cascapedia (4)
1978	Late Bloomer (4)
1979	Waya (5)
1980	Glorious Song (4)
1981	Relaxing (5)
1982	Track Robbery (6)
1983	Ambassador of Luck (4)
1984	Princess Rooney (4)
1985	Life's Magic (4)
1986	Lady's Secret (4)
1987	North Sider (5)
1988	Personal Ensign (4)
1989	Bayakoa (5)
1990	Bayakoa (6)
1991	Queena (5)
1992	Paseana (5)
1993	Paseana (6)
1994	Sky Beauty (4)

Eclipse Awards (Cont.)

CHAMPION TURF HORSE

1971.....Run the Gantlet (3)
1972.....Cougar II (6)
1973.....Secretariat (3)
1974.....Dahlia (4)
1975.....Snow Knight (4)
1976.....Youth (3)
1977.....Johnny D (3)
1978.....Mac Diarmida (3)

CHAMPION MALE TURF HORSE

1979.....Bowl Game (5)
1980.....John Henry (5)
1981.....John Henry (6)
1982.....Perrault (5)
1983.....John Henry (8)
1984.....John Henry (9)
1985.....Cozzene (4)
1986.....Manila (3)
1987.....Theatrical (5)
1988.....Sunshine Forever (3)
1989.....Steinlen (6)
1990.....Itsallgreektome (3)
1991.....Tight Spot (4)
1992.....Sky Classic (5)
1993.....Kotashaan (5)
1994.....Paradise Creek (5)

CHAMPION FEMALE TURF HORSE

1979.....Trillion (5)
1980.....Just a Game II (4)
1981.....De La Rose (3)
1982.....April Run (4)
1983.....All Along (4)
1984.....Royal Heroine (4)
1985.....Pebbles (4)
1986.....Estrapade (6)
1987.....Miesque (3)
1988.....Miesque (4)
1989.....Brown Bess (7)
1990.....Laugh and Be Merry (5)
1991.....Miss Alleged (4)
1992.....Flawlessly (4)
1993.....Flawlessly (5)
1994.....Hatoof (5)

STEEPLECHASE OR HURDLE HORSE

1971.....Shadow Brook (7)
1972.....Soothsayer (5)
1973.....Athenian Idol (5)
1974.....Gran Kan (8)
1975.....Life's Illusion (4)
1976.....Straight & True (6)
1977.....Cafe Prince (7)
1978.....Cafe Prince (8)
1979.....Martie's Anger (4)
1080.....Zaooio (4)
1981.....Zaccio (5)
1982.....Zaccio (6)
1983.....Flatterer (4)
1984.....Flatterer (5)
1985.....Flatterer (6)

STEEPLECHASE OR HURDLE HORSE (Cont.)

1986.....Flatterer (7)
1987.....Inlander (6)
1988.....Jimmy Lorenzo (6)
1989.....Highland Bud (4)
1990.....Morley Street (7)
1991.....Morley Street (8)
1992.....Lonesome Glory (4)
1993.....Lonesome Glory (5)
1994.....Warm Spell (6)

SPRINTER

1971.....Ack Ack (5)
1972.....Chou Croute (4)
1973.....Shecky Greene (3)
1974.....Forego (4)
1975.....Gallant Bob (3)
1976.....My Juliet (4)
1977.....What a Summer (4)
1978.....Dr. Patches (4)
　　　　　J. O. Tobin (4)
1979.....Star de Naskra (4)
1980.....Plugged Nickel (3)
1981.....Guilty Conscience (5)
1982.....Gold Beauty (3)
1983.....Chinook Pass (4)
1984.....Eillo (4)
1985.....Precisionist (4)
1986.....Smile (4)
1987.....Groovy (4)
1988.....Gulch (4)
1989.....Safely Kept (3)
1990.....Housebuster (3)
1991.....Housebuster (4)
1992.....Rubiano (5)
1993.....Cardmania (7)
1994.....Cherokee Run (4)

OUTSTANDING OWNER

1971.....Mr. & Mrs. E. E. Fogleson
1974.....Dan Lasater
1975.....Dan Lasater
1976.....Dan Lasater
1977.....Maxwell Gluck
1978.....Harbor View Farm
1979.....Harbor View Farm
1980.....Mr. & Mrs. Bertram
　　　　　Firestone
1981.....Dotsam Stable
1982.....Viola Sommer
1983.....John Franks
1984.....John Franks
1985.....Mr. & Mrs. Eugene Klein
1986.....Mr. & Mrs. Eugene Klein
1987.....Mr. & Mrs. Eugene Klein
1988.....Ogden Phipps
1080.....Ogdon Phippo
1990.....Frances Genter
1991.....Sam-Son Farm
1992.....Juddmonte Farms
1993.....John Franks
1994.....John Franks

OUTSTANDING TRAINER

1971.....Charlie Whittingham
1972.....Lucien Laurin
1973.....H. Allen Jerkens
1974.....Sherrill Ward
1975.....Steve DiMauro
1976.....Lazaro Barrera
1977.....Lazaro Barrera
1978.....Lazaro Barrera
1979.....Lazaro Barrera
1980.....Bud Delp
1981.....Ron McAnally
1982.....Charlie Whittingham
1983.....Woody Stephens
1984.....Jack Van Berg
1985.....D. Wayne Lukas
1986.....D. Wayne Lukas
1987.....D. Wayne Lukas
1988.....Claude R. McGaughey III
1989.....Charlie Whittingham
1990.....Carl Nafzger
1991.....Ron McAnally
1992.....Ron McAnally
1993.....Bobby Frankel
1994.....D. Wayne Lukas

OUTSTANDING JOCKEY

1971.....Laffit Pincay Jr
1972.....Braulio Baeza
1973.....Laffit Pincay Jr
1974.....Laffit Pincay Jr
1975.....Braulio Baeza
1976.....Sandy Hawley
1977.....Steve Cauthen
1978.....Darrel McHargue
1979.....Laffit Pincay Jr
1980.....Chris McCarron
1981.....Bill Shoemaker
1982.....Angel Cordero Jr
1983.....Angel Cordero Jr
1984.....Pat Day
1985.....Laffit Pincay Jr
1986.....Pat Day
1987.....Pat Day
1988.....Jose Santos
1989.....Kent Desormeaux
1990.....Craig Perret
1991.....Pat Day
1992.....Kent Desormeaux
1993.....Mike Smith
1994.....Mike Smith

OUTSTANDING APPRENTICE JOCKEY

1971.....Gene St. Leon
1972.....Thomas Wallis
1973.....Steve Valdez
1974.....Chris McCarron
1975.....Jimmy Edwards
1976.....George Martens
1977.....Steve Cauthen
1978.....Ron Franklin
1979.....Cash Asmussen

Note: Number in parentheses is horse's age.

Awards (Cont.)

Eclipse Awards (Cont.)

OUTSTANDING APPRENTICE JOCKEY *(Cont.)*

1980.....Frank Lovato Jr
1981.....Richard Migliore
1982.....Alberto Delgado
1983.....Declan Murphy
1984.....Wesley Ward
1985.....Art Madrid Jr
1986.....Allen Stacy
1987.....Kent Desormeaux
1988.....Steve Capanas
1989.....Michael Luzzi
1990.....Mark Johnston
1991.....Mickey Walls
1992.....Jesus A. Bracho
1993.....Juan Umana
1994.....Dale Beckner

OUTSTANDING BREEDER

1974.....John W. Galbreath
1975.....Fred W. Hooper
1976.....Nelson Bunker Hunt
1977.....Edward Plunket Taylor
1978.....Harbor View Farm

OUTSTANDING BREEDER *(Cont.)*

1979.....Claiborne Farm
1980.....Mrs. Henry D. Paxson
1981.....Golden Chance Farm
1982.....Fred W. Hooper
1983.....Edward Plunket Taylor
1984.....Claiborne Farm
1985.....Nelson Bunker Hunt
1986.....Paul Mellon
1987.....Nelson Bunker Hunt
1988.....Ogden Phipps
1989.....North Ridge Farm
1990.....Calumet Farm
1991.....John and Betty Mabee
1992.....William S. Farish III
1993.....Allen Paulson
1994.....William T. Young

AWARD OF MERIT

1976.....Jack J. Dreyfus
1977.....Steve Cauthen
1978.....Ogden Phipps
1979.....Frank E. Kilroe
1980.....John D. Schapiro

AWARD OF MERIT *(Cont.)*

1981.....Bill Shoemaker
1984.....John Gaines
1985.....Keene Daingerfield
1986.....Herman Cohen
1987.....J. B. Faulconer
1988.....John Forsythe
1989.....Michael P. Sandler
1991.....Fred W. Hooper
1994.....Alfred G. Vanderbilt

SPECIAL AWARD

1971.....Robert J. Kleberg
1974.....Charles Hatton
1976.....Bill Shoemaker
1980.....John T. Landry
Pierre E. Bellocq (Peb)
1984.....C. V. Whitney
1985.....Arlington Park
1987.....Anheuser-Busch
1988.....Edward J. DeBartolo Sr
1989.....Richard Duchossois
1994.....John Longden
Edward Arcaro

Note: Special Award and Award of Merit not presented annually. For long-term and/or outstanding service to the industry.

Breeders' Cup

Location: Hollywood Park (CA) 1984, 1987; Aqueduct Racetrack (NY) 1985; Santa Anita Park (CA) 1986, 1993; Churchill Downs (KY) 1988, 1991, 1995; Gulfstream Park (FL) 1989, 1992; Belmont Park (NY) 1990.

Juveniles

Year	Winner (Margin)	Jockey	Second	Third	Time
1984	Chief's Crown (¾)	Don MacBeth	Tank's Prospect	Spend a Buck	1:36⅕
1985	Tasso (Nose)	Laffit Pincay Jr	Storm Cat	Scat Dancer	1:36⅕
1986	Capote (1¼)	Laffit Pincay Jr	Qualify	Alysheba	1:43⅘
1987	Success Express (1¾)	Jose Santos	Regal Classic	Tejano	1:35⅕
1988	Is It True (1¼)	Laffit Pincay Jr	Easy Goer	Tagel	1:46⅗
1989	Rhythm (2)	Craig Perret	Grand Canyon	Slavic	1:43⅗
1990	Fly So Free (3)	Jose Santos	Take Me Out	Lost Mountain	1:43⅖
1991	Arazi (4¾)	Pat Valenzuela	Bertrando	Snappy Landing	1:44⅗
1992	Gilded Time (¾)	Chris McCarron	It'sali'lknownfact	River Special	1:43⅖
1993	Brocco (5)	Gary Stevens	Blumin Affair	Tabasco Cat	1:42⅘
1994	Timber Country (½)	Pat Day	Eltish	Tejano Run	1:44⅖

Note: One mile (1984–85, 87); 1¹⁄₁₆ miles (1986 and since 1988).

Juvenile Fillies

Year	Winner (Margin)	Jockey	Second	Third	Time
1984	Outstandingly*	Walter Guerra	Dusty Heart	Fine Spirit	1:37⅘
1985	Twilight Ridge (1)	Jorge Velasquez	Family Style	Steal a Kiss	1:35⅘
1986	Brave Raj (5½)	Pat Valenzuela	Tappiano	Saros Brig	1:43⅕
1987	Epitome (Nose)	Pat Day	Jeanne Jones	Dream Team	1:36⅖
1988	Open Mind (1¾)	Angel Cordero Jr	Darby Shuffle	Lea Lucinda	1:46⅗
1989	Go for Wand (2¾)	Randy Romero	Sweet Roberta	Stella Madrid	1:44⅕
1990	Meadow Star (5)	Jose Santos	Private Treasure	Dance Smartly	1:44
1991	Pleasant Stage (Neck)	Eddie Delahoussaye	La Spia	Cadillac Women	1:46⅖
1992	Eliza (1½)	Pat Valenzuela	Educated Risk	Boots 'n Jackie	1:42⅘
1993	Phone Chatter (Head)	Laffit Pincay	Sardula	Heavenly Prize	1:43
1994	Flanders (Head)	Pat Day	Serena's Song	Stormy Blues	1:45⅕

*In 1984, winner Fran's Valentine was disqualified for interference in the stretch and placed 10th.
Note: One mile (1984–85, 87); 1¹⁄₁₆ miles (1986 and since 1988).

Breeders' Cup (*Cont.*)

Sprint

Year	Winner (Margin)	Jockey	Second	Third	Time
1984	Eillo (Nose)	Craig Perret	Commemorate	Fighting Fit	1:10⅕
1985	Precisionist (¾)	Chris McCarron	Smile	Mt. Livermore	1:08⅖
1986	Smile (1¼)	Jacinto Vasquez	Pine Tree Lane	Bedside Promise	1:08⅖
1987	Very Subtle (4)	Pat Valenzuela	Groovy	Exclusive Enough	1:08⅘
1988	Gulch (¾)	Angel Cordero Jr	Play the King	Afleet	1:10⅖
1989	Dancing Spree (Neck)	Angel Cordero Jr	Safely Kept	Dispersal	1:09
1990	Safely Kept (Neck)	Craig Perret	Dayjur	Black Tie Affair	1:09⅗
1991	Sheikh Albadou (Neck)	Pat Eddery	Pleasant Tap	Robyn Dancer	1:09⅕
1992	Thirty Slews (Neck)	Eddie Delahoussaye	Meafara	Rubiano	1:08⅕
1993	Cardmania (Neck)	Eddie Delahoussaye	Meafara	Gilded Time	1:08⅗
1994	Cherokee Run (Head)	Mike Smith	Soviet Problem	Cardmania	1:09⅖

Note: Six furlongs (since 1984).

Mile

Year	Winner (Margin)	Jockey	Second	Third	Time
1984	Royal Heroine (1½)	Fernando Toro	Star Choice	Cozzene	1:32⅗
1985	Cozzene (2¼)	Walter Guerra	Al Mamoon*	Shadeed	1:35
1986	Last Tycoon (Head)	Yves St-Martin	Palace Music	Fred Astaire	1:35⅕
1987	Miesque (3½)	Freddie Head	Show Dancer	Sonic Lady	1:32⅘
1988	Miesque (4)	Freddie Head	Steinlen	Simply Majestic	1:38⅗
1989	Steinlen (¾)	Jose Santos	Sabona	Most Welcome	1:37⅕
1990	Royal Academy (Neck)	Lester Piggott	Itsallgreektome	Priolo	1:35⅕
1991	Opening Verse (2¼)	Pat Valenzuela	Val de Bois	Star of Cozzene	1:37⅖
1992	Lure (3)	Mike Smith	Paradise Creek	Brief Truce	1:32⅘
1993	Lure (2¼)	Mike Smith	Ski Paradise	Fourstars Allstar	1:33⅖
1994	Barathea (Head)	Frankie Dettori	Johann Quatz	Unfinished Symph	1:34⅖

*2nd place finisher Palace Music was disqualified for interference and placed 9th.

Distaff

Year	Winner (Margin)	Jockey	Second	Third	Time
1984	Princess Rooney (7)	Eddie Delahoussaye	Life's Magic	Adored	2:02⅖
1985	Life's Magic (6¼)	Angel Cordero Jr	Lady's Secret	Dontstop Themusic	2:02
1986	Lady's Secret (2½)	Pat Day	Fran's Valentine	Outstandingly	2:01⅕
1987	Sacahuista (2¼)	Randy Romero	Clabber Girl	Oueee Bebe	2:02⅘
1988	Personal Ensign (Nose)	Randy Romero	Winning Colors	Goodbye Halo	1:52
1989	Bayakoa (1½)	Laffit Pincay Jr	Gorgeous	Open Mind	1:47⅖
1990	Bayakoa (6¾)	Laffit Pincay Jr	Colonial Waters	Valay Maid	1:49⅕
1991	Dance Smarty (½)	Pat Day	Versailles Treaty	Brought to Mind	1:50⅘
1992	Paseana (4)	Chris McCarron	Versailles Treaty	Magical Maiden	1:48
1993	Hollywood Wildcat (Nose)	Eddie Delahoussaye	Paseana	Re Toss	1:48⅕
1994	One Dreamer (Neck)	Gary Stevens	Heavenly Prize	Miss Dominique	1:50⅗

Note: 1¼ miles (1984-87); 1⅛ miles (since 1988).

Turf

Year	Winner (Margin)	Jockey	Second	Third	Time
1984	Lashkari (Neck)	Yves St-Martin	All Along	Raami	2:25⅕
1985	Pebbles (Neck)	Pat Eddery	Strawberry Rd II	Mourjane	2:27
1986	Manila (Neck)	Jose Santos	Theatrical	Estrapade	2:25⅖
1987	Theatrical (½)	Pat Day	Trempolino	Village Star II	2:24⅖
1988	Great Communicator (½)	Ray Sibille	Sunshine Forever	Indian Skimmer	2:35⅕
1989	Prized (Head)	Eddie Delahoussaye	Sierra Roberta	Star Lift	2:28
1990	In the Wings (½)	Gary Stevens	With Approval	El Senor	2:29⅗
1991	Miss Alleged (2)	Eric Legrix	Itsallgreektome	Quest for Fame	2:30⅘
1992	Fraise (Nose)	Pat Valenzuela	Sky Classic	Quest For Fame	2:24
1993	Kotashaan (½)	Kent Desormeaux	Bien Bien	Luazar	2:25
1994	Tikkanen (1½)	Mike Smith	Hatoof	Paradise Creek	2:26⅖

Note: 1½ miles.

Classic

Year	Winner (Margin)	Jockey	Second	Third	Time
1984	Wild Again (Head)	Pat Day	Slew o' Gold*	Gate Dancer	2:03⅖
1985	Proud Truth (Head)	Jorge Velasquez	Gate Dancer	Turkoman	2:00⅘
1986	Skywalker (1¼)	Laffit Pincay Jr	Turkoman	Precisionist	2:00⅖

Breeders' Cup *(Cont.)*

Classic *(Cont.)*

Year	Winner (Margin)	Jockey	Second	Third	Time
1987	Ferdinand (Nose)	Bill Shoemaker	Alysheba	Judge Angelucci	2:01⅖
1988	Alysheba (Nose)	Chris McCarron	Seeking the Gold	Waquoit	2:04⅘
1989	Sunday Silence (½)	Chris McCarron	Easy Goer	Blushing John	2:00⅕
1990	Unbridled (1)	Pat Day	Ibn Bey	Thirty Six Red	2:02⅕
1991	Black Tie Affair (1¼)	Jerry Bailey	Twilight Agenda	Unbridled	2:02⅘
1992	A.P. Indy (2)	Eddie Delahoussaye	Pleasant Tap	Jolypha	2:00⅕
1993	Arcangues (2)	Jerry Bailey	Bertrando	Kissin Kris	2:00⅘
1994	Concern (Neck)	Jerry Bailey	Tabasco Cat	Dramatic Gold	2:02⅖

*2nd place finisher Gate Dancer was disqualified for interference and placed 3rd.
Note: 1¼ miles.

England's Triple Crown Winners

England's Triple Crown consists of the Two Thousand Guineas, held at Newmarket; the Epsom Derby, held at Epsom Downs; and the St. Leger Stakes, held at Doncaster.

Year	Horse	Owner	Year	Horse	Owner
1853	West Australian	Mr. Bowes	1900	Diamond Jubilee	Prince of Wales
1865	Gladiateur	F. DeLagrange	1903	*Rock Sand	J. Miller
1866	Lord Lyon	R. Sutton	1915	Pommern	S. Joel
1886	*Ormonde	Duke of Westminster	1917	Gay Crusader	Mr. Fairie
1891	Common	†F. Johnstone	1918	Gainsborough	Lady James Douglas
1893	Isinglass	H. McCalmont	1935	*Bahram	Aga Khan
1897	Galtee More	J. Gubbins	1970	‡Nijinsky II	C. W. Engelhard
1899	Flying Fox	Duke of Westminster			

*Imported into United States. †Raced in name of Lord Alington in Two Thousand Guineas. ‡Canadian-bred.

Annual Leaders

Horse—Money Won

Year	Horse	Age	Starts	1st	2nd	3rd	Winnings ($)
1919	Sir Barton	3	13	8	3	2	88,250
1920	Man o'War	3	11	11	0	0	166,140
1921	Morvich	2	11	11	0	0	115,234
1922	Pillory	3	7	4	1	1	95,654
1923	Zev	3	14	12	1	0	272,008
1924	Sarzen	3	12	8	1	1	95,640
1925	Pompey	2	10	7	2	0	121,630
1926	Crusader	3	15	9	4	0	166,033
1927	Anita Peabody	2	7	6	0	1	111,905
1928	High Strung	2	6	5	0	0	153,590
1929	Blue Larkspur	3	6	4	1	0	153,450
1930	Gallant Fox	3	10	9	1	0	308,275
1931	Gallant Flight	2	7	7	0	0	219,000
1932	Gusto	3	16	4	3	2	145,940
1933	Singing Wood	2	9	3	2	2	88,050
1934	Cavalcade	3	7	6	1	0	111,235
1935	Omaha	3	9	6	1	2	142,255
1936	Granville	3	11	7	3	0	110,295
1937	Seabiscuit	4	15	11	2	2	168,580
1938	Stagehand	3	15	8	2	3	189,710
1939	Challedon	3	15	9	2	3	184,535
1940	Bimelech	3	7	4	2	1	110,005
1941	Whirlaway	3	20	13	5	2	272,386
1942	Shut Out	3	12	8	2	0	238,872
1943	Count Fleet	3	6	6	0	0	174,055
1944	Pavot	2	8	8	0	0	179,040
1945	Busher	3	13	10	2	1	273,735
1946	Assault	3	15	8	2	3	424,195
1947	Armed	6	17	11	4	1	376,325
1948	Citation	3	20	19	1	0	709,470

Note: Annual leaders on pages 460-465 courtesy of *The American Racing Manual*, a publication of Daily Racing Form, Inc.

Horse—Money Won (Cont.)

Year	Horse	Age	Starts	1st	2nd	3rd	Winnings ($)
1949	Ponder	3	21	9	5	2	321,825
1950	Noor	5	12	7	4	1	346,940
1951	Counterpoint	3	15	7	2	1	250,525
1952	Crafty Admiral	4	16	9	4	1	277,225
1953	Native Dancer	3	10	9	1	0	513,425
1954	Determine	3	15	10	3	2	328,700
1955	Nashua	3	12	10	1	1	752,550
1956	Needles	3	8	4	2	0	440,850
1957	Round Table	3	22	15	1	3	600,383
1958	Round Table	4	20	14	4	0	662,780
1959	Sword Dancer	3	13	8	4	0	537,004
1960	Bally Ache	3	15	10	3	1	445,045
1961	Carry Back	3	16	9	1	3	565,349
1962	Never Bend	2	10	7	1	2	402,969
1963	Candy Spots	3	12	7	2	1	604,481
1964	Gun Bow	4	16	8	4	2	580,100
1965	Buckpasser	2	11	9	1	0	568,096
1966	Buckpasser	3	14	13	1	0	669,078
1967	Damascus	3	16	12	3	1	817,941
1968	Forward Pass	3	13	7	2	0	546,674
1969	Arts and Letters	3	14	8	5	1	555,604
1970	Personality	3	18	8	2	1	444,049
1971	Riva Ridge	2	9	7	0	0	503,263
1972	Droll Role	4	19	7	3	4	471,633
1973	Secretariat	3	12	9	2	1	860,404
1974	Chris Evert	3	8	5	1	2	551,063
1975	Foolish Pleasure	3	11	5	4	1	716,278
1976	Forego	6	8	6	1	1	401,701
1977	Seattle Slew	3	7	6	0	1	641,370
1978	Affirmed	3	11	8	2	0	901,541
1979	Spectacular Bid	3	12	10	1	1	1,279,334
1980	Temperence Hill	3	17	8	3	1	1,130,452
1981	John Henry	6	10	8	0	0	1,798,030
1982	Perrault	5	8	4	1	2	1,197,400
1983	All Along	4	7	4	1	1	2,138,963
1984	Slew o'Gold	4	6	5	1	0	2,627,944
1985	Spend A Buck	3	7	5	1	1	3,552,704
1986	Snow Chief	3	9	6	1	1	1,875,200
1987	Alysheba	3	10	3	3	1	2,511,156
1988	Alysheba	4	9	7	1	0	3,808,600
1989	Sunday Silence	3	9	7	2	0	4,578,454
1990	Unbridled	3	11	4	3	2	3,718,149
1991	Dance Smartly	3	8	8	0	0	2,876,821
1992	A.P. Indy	3	7	5	0	1	2,622,560
1993	Kotashaan	3	10	6	3	0	2,619,014
1994	Paradise Creek	5	11	8	2	1	2,610,187

Trainer—Money Won

Year	Trainer	Wins	Winnings ($)	Year	Trainer	Wins	Winnings ($)
1908	James Rowe, Sr	50	284,335	1925	G. R. Tompkins	30	199,245
1909	Sam Hildreth	73	123,942	1926	Scott P. Harlan	21	205,681
1910	Sam Hildreth	84	148,010	1927	W. H. Bringloe	63	216,563
1911	Sam Hildreth	67	49,418	1928	John F. Schorr	65	258,425
1912	John F. Schorr	63	58,110	1929	James Rowe, Jr	25	314,881
1913	James Rowe, Sr	18	45,936	1930	Sunny Jim Fitzsimmons	47	397,355
1914	R. C. Benson	45	59,315	1931	Big Jim Healey	33	297,300
1915	James Rowe, Sr	19	75,596	1932	Sunny Jim Fitzsimmons	68	266,650
1916	Sam Hildreth	39	70,950	1933	Humming Bob Smith	53	135,720
1917	Sam Hildreth	23	61,698	1934	Humming Bob Smith	43	249,938
1918	H. Guy Bedwell	53	80,296	1935	Bud Stotler	87	303,005
1919	H. Guy Bedwell	63	208,728	1936	Sunny Jim Fitzsimmons	42	193,415
1920	L. Feustal	22	186,087	1937	Robert McGarvey	46	209,925
1921	Sam Hildreth	85	262,768	1938	Earl Sande	15	226,495
1922	Sam Hildreth	74	247,014	1939	Sunny Jim Fitzsimmons	45	266,205
1923	Sam Hildreth	75	392,124	1940	Silent Tom Smith	14	269,200
1924	Sam Hildreth	77	255,608	1941	Plain Ben Jones	70	475,318

Trainer—Money Won (Cont.)

Year	Trainer	Wins	Winnings ($)	Year	Trainer	Wins	Winnings ($)
1942	....John M. Gaver Sr	48	406,547	1969	....Elliott Burch	26	1,067,936
1943	....Plain Ben Jones	73	267,915	1970	....Charlie Whittingham	82	1,302,354
1944	....Plain Ben Jones	60	601,660	1971	....Charlie Whittingham	77	1,737,115
1945	....Silent Tom Smith	52	510,655	1972	....Charlie Whittingham	79	1,734,020
1946	....Hirsch Jacobs	99	560,077	1973	....Charlie Whittingham	85	1,865,385
1947	...Jimmy Jones	85	1,334,805	1974	....Pancho Martin	166	2,408,419
1948	...Jimmy Jones	81	1,118,670	1975	....Charlie Whittingham	93	2,437,244
1949	...Jimmy Jones	76	978,587	1976	....Jack Van Berg	496	2,976,196
1950	....Preston Burch	96	637,754	1977	...Laz Barrera	127	2,715,848
1951	....John M. Gaver Sr	42	616,392	1978	...Laz Barrera	100	3,307,164
1952	....Plain Ben Jones	29	662,137	1979	...Laz Barrera	98	3,608,517
1953	...Harry Trotsek	54	1,028,873	1980	...Laz Barrera	99	2,969,151
1954	...Willie Molter	136	1,107,860	1981	....Charlie Whittingham	74	3,993,302
1955	...Sunny Jim Fitzsimmons	66	1,270,055	1982	....Charlie Whittingham	63	4,587,457
1956	...Willie Molter	142	1,227,402	1983	...D. Wayne Lukas	78	4,267,261
1957	...Jimmy Jones	70	1,150,910	1984	....D. Wayne Lukas	131	5,835,921
1958	...Willie Molter	69	1,116,544	1985	....D. Wayne Lukas	218	11,155,188
1959	...Willie Molter	71	847,290	1986	....D. Wayne Lukas	259	12,345,180
1960	...Hirsch Jacobs	97	748,349	1987	....D. Wayne Lukas	343	17,502,110
1961	...Jimmy Jones	62	759,856	1988	....D. Wayne Lukas	318	17,842,358
1962	...Mesh Tenney	58	1,099,474	1989	....D. Wayne Lukas	305	16,103,998
1963	...Mesh Tenney	40	860,703	1990	....D. Wayne Lukas	267	14,508,871
1964	...Bill Winfrey	61	1,350,534	1991	....D. Wayne Lukas	289	15,942,223
1965	...Hirsch Jacobs	91	1,331,628	1992	....D. Wayne Lukas	230	9,806,436
1966	....Eddie Neloy	93	2,456,250	1993	....Robert Frankel	79	8,883,252
1967	....Eddie Neloy	72	1,776,089	1994	....D. Wayne Lukas	147	9,247,457
1968	....Eddie Neloy	52	1,233,101				

Jockey—Money Won

Year	Jockey	Mts	1st	2nd	3rd	Pct	Winnings ($)
1919	..........John Loftus	177	65	36	24	.37	252,707
1920	..........Clarence Kummer	353	87	79	48	.25	292,376
1921	..........Earl Sande	340	112	69	59	.33	263,043
1922	..........Albert Johnson	297	43	57	40	.14	345,054
1923	..........Earl Sande	430	122	89	79	.28	569,394
1924	..........Ivan Parke	844	205	175	121	.24	290,395
1925	..........Laverne Fator	315	81	54	44	.26	305,775
1926	..........Laverne Fator	511	143	90	86	.28	361,435
1927	..........Earl Sande	179	49	33	19	.27	277,877
1928	..........Pony McAtee	235	55	43	25	.23	301,295
1929	..........Mack Garner	274	57	39	33	.21	314,975
1930	..........Sonny Workman	571	152	88	79	.27	420,438
1931	..........Charles Kurtsinger	519	93	82	79	.18	392,095
1932	..........Sonny Workman	378	87	48	55	.23	385,070
1933	..........Robert Jones	471	63	57	70	.13	226,285
1934	..........Wayne D. Wright	919	174	154	114	.19	287,185
1935	..........Silvio Coucci	749	141	125	103	.19	319,760
1936	..........Wayne D. Wright	670	100	102	73	.15	264,000
1937	..........Charles Kurtsinger	765	120	94	106	.16	384,202
1938	..........Nick Wall	658	97	94	82	.15	385,161
1939	..........Basil James	904	191	165	105	.21	353,333
1940	..........Eddie Arcaro	783	132	143	112	.17	343,661
1941	..........Don Meade	1164	210	185	158	.18	398,627
1942	..........Eddie Arcaro	687	123	97	89	.18	481,949
1943	..........John Longden	871	173	140	121	.20	573,276
1944	..........Ted Atkinson	1539	287	231	213	.19	899,101
1945	..........John Longden	778	180	112	100	.23	981,977
1946	..........Ted Atkinson	1377	233	213	173	.17	1,036,825
1947	..........Douglas Dodson	646	141	100	75	.22	1,429,949
1948	..........Eddie Arcaro	726	188	108	98	.26	1,686,230
1949	..........Steve Brooks	906	209	172	110	.23	1,316,817
1950	..........Eddie Arcaro	888	195	153	144	.22	1,410,160
1951	..........Bill Shoemaker	1161	257	197	161	.22	1,329,890
1952	..........Eddie Arcaro	807	188	122	109	.23	1,859,591
1953	..........Bill Shoemaker	1683	485	302	210	.29	1,784,187
1954	..........Bill Shoemaker	1251	380	221	142	.30	1,876,760

Jockey—Money Won (Cont.)

Year	Jockey	Mts	1st	2nd	3rd	Pct	Winnings ($)
1955	Eddie Arcaro	820	158	126	108	.19	1,864,796
1956	Bill Hartack	1387	347	252	184	.25	2,343,955
1957	Bill Hartack	1238	341	208	178	.28	3,060,501
1958	Bill Shoemaker	1133	300	185	137	.26	2,961,693
1959	Bill Shoemaker	1285	347	230	159	.27	2,843,133
1960	Bill Shoemaker	1227	274	196	158	.22	2,123,961
1961	Bill Shoemaker	1256	304	186	175	.24	2,690,819
1962	Bill Shoemaker	1126	311	156	128	.28	2,916,844
1963	Bill Shoemaker	1203	271	193	137	.22	2,526,925
1964	Bill Shoemaker	1056	246	147	133	.23	2,649,553
1965	Braulio Baeza	1245	270	200	201	.22	2,582,702
1966	Braulio Baeza	1341	298	222	190	.22	2,951,022
1967	Braulio Baeza	1064	256	184	127	.24	3,088,888
1968	Braulio Baeza	1089	201	184	145	.18	2,835,108
1969	Jorge Velasquez	1442	258	230	204	.18	2,542,315
1970	Laffit Pincay Jr	1328	269	208	187	.20	2,626,526
1971	Laffit Pincay Jr	1627	380	288	214	.23	3,784,377
1972	Laffit Pincay Jr	1388	289	215	205	.21	3,225,827
1973	Laffit Pincay Jr	1444	350	254	209	.24	4,093,492
1974	Laffit Pincay Jr	1278	341	227	180	.27	4,251,060
1975	Braulio Baeza	1190	196	208	180	.16	3,674,398
1976	Angel Cordero Jr	1534	274	273	235	.18	4,709,500
1977	Steve Cauthen	2075	487	345	304	.23	6,151,750
1978	Darrel McHargue	1762	375	294	263	.21	6,188,353
1979	Laffit Pincay Jr	1708	420	302	261	.25	8,183,535
1980	Chris McCarron	1964	405	318	282	.20	7,666,100
1981	Chris McCarron	1494	326	251	207	.22	8,397,604
1982	Angel Cordero Jr	1838	397	338	227	.22	9,702,520
1983	Angel Cordero Jr	1792	362	296	237	.20	10,116,807
1984	Chris McCarron	1565	356	276	218	.23	12,038,213
1985	Laffit Pincay Jr	1409	289	246	183	.21	13,415,049
1986	Jose Santos	1636	329	237	222	.20	11,329,297
1987	Jose Santos	1639	305	268	208	.19	12,407,355
1988	Jose Santos	1867	370	287	265	.20	14,877,298
1989	Jose Santos	1459	285	238	220	.20	13,847,003
1990	Gary Stevens	1504	283	245	202	.19	13,881,198
1991	Chris McCarron	1440	265	228	206	.18	14,441,083
1992	Kent Desormeaux	1568	361	260	208	.23	14,193,006
1993	Mike Smith	1,510	343	235	214	.23	14,008,148
1994	Mike Smith	1,484	317	250	196	.21	15,979,820

Jockey—Races Won

Year	Jockey	Mts	1st	2nd	3rd	Pct
1895	J. Perkins	762	192	177	129	.25
1896	J. Scherrer	1093	271	227	172	.24
1897	H. Martin	803	173	152	116	.21
1898	T. Burns	973	277	213	149	.28
1899	T. Burns	1064	273	173	266	.26
1900	C. Mitchell	874	195	140	139	.23
1901	W. O'Connor	1047	253	221	192	.24
1902	J. Ranch	1069	276	205	181	.26
1903	G.C. Fuller	918	229	152	122	.25
1904	E. Hildebrand	1169	297	230	171	.25
1905	D. Nicol	861	221	143	136	.26
1906	W. Miller	1384	388	300	199	.28
1907	W. Miller	1194	334	226	170	.28
1908	V. Powers	1260	324	204	185	.26
1909	V. Powers	704	173	121	114	.25
1910	G. Garner	947	200	188	153	.20
1911	T. Koerner	813	162	133	112	.20
1912	P. Hill	967	168	141	129	.17
1913	M. Buxton	887	146	131	136	.16
1914	J. McTaggart	787	157	132	106	.20
1915	M. Garner	775	151	118	90	.19
1916	F. Robinson	791	178	131	124	.23

Jockey—Races Won (Cont.)

Year	Jockey	Mts	1st	2nd	3rd	Pct
1917	W. Crump	803	151	140	101	.19
1918	F. Robinson	864	185	140	108	.21
1919	C. Robinson	896	190	140	126	.21
1920	J. Butwell	721	152	129	139	.21
1921	C. Lang	696	135	110	105	.19
1922	M. Fator	859	188	153	116	.22
1923	I. Parke	718	173	105	95	.24
1924	I. Parke	844	205	175	121	.24
1925	A. Mortensen	987	187	145	138	.19
1926	R. Jones	1172	190	163	152	.16
1927	L. Hardy	1130	207	192	151	.18
1928	J. Inzelone	1052	155	152	135	.15
1929	M. Knight	871	149	132	133	.17
1930	H.R. Riley	861	177	145	123	.21
1931	H. Roble	1174	173	173	155	.15
1932	J. Gilbert	1050	212	144	160	.20
1933	J. Westrope	1224	301	235	166	.25
1934	M. Peters	1045	221	179	147	.21
1935	C. Stevenson	1099	206	169	146	.19
1936	B. James	1106	245	195	161	.22
1937	J. Adams	1265	260	186	177	.21
1938	J. Longden	1150	236	168	171	.21
1939	D. Meade	1284	255	221	180	.20
1940	E. Dew	1377	287	201	180	.21
1941	D. Meade	1164	210	185	158	.18
1942	J. Adams	1120	245	185	150	.22
1943	J. Adams	1069	228	159	171	.21
1944	T. Atkinson	1539	287	231	213	.19
1945	J.D. Jessop	1085	290	182	168	.27
1946	T. Atkinson	1377	233	213	173	.17
1947	J. Longden	1327	316	250	195	.24
1948	J. Longden	1197	319	233	161	.27
1949	G. Glisson	1347	270	217	181	.20
1950	W. Shoemaker	1640	388	266	230	.24
1951	C. Burr	1319	310	232	192	.24
1952	A. DeSpirito	1482	390	247	212	.26
1953	W. Shoemaker	1683	485	302	210	.29
1954	W. Shoemaker	1251	380	221	142	.30
1955	W. Hartack	1702	417	298	215	.25
1956	W. Hartack	1387	347	252	184	.25
1957	W. Hartack	1238	341	208	178	.28
1958	W. Shoemaker	1133	300	185	137	.26
1959	W. Shoemaker	1285	347	230	159	.27
1960	W. Hartack	1402	307	247	190	.22
1961	J. Sellers	1394	328	212	227	.24
1962	R. Ferraro	1755	352	252	226	.20
1963	W. Blum	1704	360	286	215	.21
1964	W. Blum	1577	324	274	170	.21
1965	J. Davidson	1582	319	228	190	.20
1966	A. Gomez	996	318	173	142	.32
1967	J. Velasquez	1939	438	315	270	.23
1968	A. Cordero Jr.	1662	345	278	219	.21
1969	L. Snyder	1645	352	290	243	.21
1970	S. Hawley	1908	452	313	265	.24
1971	L Pincay Jr.	1627	380	288	214	.23
1972	S. Hawley	1381	367	269	200	.27
1973	S. Hawley	1925	515	336	292	.27
1974	C.J. McCarron	2199	546	392	297	.25
1975	C.J. McCarron	2194	458	389	305	.21
1976	S. Hawley	1637	413	245	201	.25
1977	S. Cauthen	2075	487	345	304	.23
1978	E. Delahoussaye	1666	384	285	238	.23
1979	D. Gall	2146	479	396	326	.22
1980	C.J. McCarron	1964	405	318	282	.20
1981	D. Gall	1917	376	305	297	.20
1982	P. Day	1870	399	326	255	.21

Jockey—Races Won (Cont.)

Year	Jockey	Mts	1st	2nd	3rd	Pct
1983..........P. Day		1725	454	321	251	.26
1984..........P. Day		1694	399	296	259	.24
1985..........C.W. Antley		2335	469	371	288	.20
1986..........P. Day		1417	429	246	202	.30
1987..........K. Desormeaux		2207	450	370	294	.28
1988..........K. Desormeaux		1897	474	295	276	.25
1989..........K. Desormeaux		2312	598	385	309	.25
1990..........P. Day		1421	364	265	222	.26
1991..........P. Day		1405	430	256	213	.31
1992..........R.A. Baze		1691	433	296	237	.25
1993..........R.A. Baze		1579	410	297	225	.26
1994..........Mike Smith		1484	317	250	196	.21

Leading Jockeys—Career Records Through 1994

Jockey	Years Riding	Mts	1st	2nd	3rd	Win Pct	Winnings ($)
Shoemaker, W. (1990) 42		40,350	8,833	6,136	4,987	.219	123,375,524
Pincay, L. Jr. 29		39,902	8,213	6,550	5,514	.206	183,910,301
Cordero, A. Jr. 31		38,646	7,057	6,136	5,359	.183	164,526,217
Velasquez, J. 32		39,557	6,682	6,030	5,613	169	123,252,413
Gall, D. 38		37,859	6,611	5,794	5,457	.176	20,837,406
Snyder, L. 35		35,681	6,388	5,030	3,440	.179	47,207,289
Gambardella, C. 39		39,018	6,349	5,953	5,353	.163	29,389,041
Day, P. 22		28,591	6,308	4,833	3,975	.221	149,339,825
Hawley, S. 28		29,972	6,205	4,607	3,941	.207	81,883,408
McCarron, C. J. 20		28,967	6,074	4,794	3,964	.210	177,686,550
Longden, J. (1966) 40		32,413	6,032	4,914	4,273	.186	24,665,800
E. Fires 30		38,421	5,678	4,804	4,593	.148	86,450,725
Delahoussaye, E. J. 25		32,656	5,375	4,710	4,523	.165	138,120,927
Vasquez, J. 35		36,436	5,153	4,630	4,421	.141	78,464,935
Arcaro E. (1961) 31		24,092	4,779	3,807	3,302	.198	30,039,543
Baze, R. A. 21		25,774	4,749	3,994	3,564	.184	63,733,355
Brumfield, D. (1989) 37		33,223	4,573	4,076	3,758	.138	43,567,861
Brooks, S. (1975) 34		30,330	4,451	4,219	3,658	.147	18,239,817
Blum, W. (1975) 22		28,673	4,382	3,913	3,350	.153	26,497,189
Hartack, W. (1974) 22		21,535	4,272	3,370	2,871	.198	26,466,758
Maple, E. 27		32,063	4,227	4,278	4,103	.132	97,382,914
Gomez, A. (1980) 34		17,028	4,081	2,947	2,405	.240	11,777,297
Dittfach, H. (1989) 33		33,905	4,000	4,092	6,113	.118	13,506,052
Perret, C. 28		23,847	3,946	3,450	3,165	.165	84,805,894
Grove, P. 22		26,278	3,907	3,664	3,491	.149	15,720,989

Note: Records include available statistics for races ridden in foreign countries. Figures in parentheses after jockey's name indicate last year in which he rode.

Leading jockeys courtesy of *The American Racing Manual*, a publication of Daily Racing Form, Inc.

National Museum of Racing Hall of Fame

HORSES

Ack Ack (1986, 1966)
Affectionately (1989, 1960)
Affirmed (1980, 1975)
All Along (1990, 1979)
Alsab (1976, 1939)
Alydar (1989, 1975)
American Eclipse (1970, 1814)
Armed (1963, 1941)
Artful (1956, 1902)
Arts and Letters (1993, 1966)
Assault (1964, 1943)
Battleship (1969, 1927)
Bed o'Roses (1976, 1947)
Beldame (1956, 1901)

Ben Brush (1955, 1893)
Bewitch (1977, 1945)
Bimelech (1990, 1937)
Black Gold (1989, 1921)
Black Helen (1991, 1932)
Blue Larkspur (1957, 1926)
Bold Ruler (1973, 1954)
Bon Nouvel (1976, 1960)
Boston (1955, 1833)
Broomstick (1956, 1901)
Buckpasser (1970, 1963)
Busher (1964, 1942)
Bushranger (1967, 1930)
Cafe Prince (1985, 1970)

Carry Back (1975, 1958)
Challedon (1977, 1936)
Chris Evert (1988, 1971)
Cicada (1967, 1959)
Citation (1959, 1945)
Coaltown (1983, 1945)
Colin (1956, 1905)
Commando (1956, 1898)
Count Fleet (1961, 1940)
Crusader (1994, 1923)
Dahlia (1981, 1970)
Damascus (1974, 1964)
Dark Mirage (1974, 1965)
Davona Dale (1985, 1976)

HORSES *(Cont.)*

Desert Vixen (1979, 1970)
Devil Diver (1980, 1939)
Discovery (1969, 1931)
Domino (1955, 1891)
Dr. Fager (1971, 1964)
Eight Thirty (1993, 1936)
Elkridge (1966, 1938)
Emperor of Norfolk (1988, 1885)
Equipoise (1957, 1928)
Exterminator (1957, 1915)
Fairmount (1985, 1921)
Fair Play (1956, 1905)
Fashion (1980, 1837)
Firenze (1981, 1884)
Flatterer (1993, 1979)
Foolish Pleasure (1994, 1972)
Forego (1979, 1970)
Gallant Bloom (1977, 1966)
Gallant Fox (1957, 1927)
Gallant Man (1987, 1954)
Gallorette (1962, 1942)
Gamely (1980, 1964)
Genuine Risk (1986, 1977)
Good and Plenty (1956, 1900)
Grey Lag (1957, 1918)
Hamburg (1986, 1895)
Hanover (1955, 1884)
Henry of Navarre (1985, 1891)
Hill Prince (1991, 1947)
Hindoo (1955, 1878)
Imp (1965, 1894)
Jay Trump (1971, 1957)
John Henry (1990, 1975)

Johnstown (1992, 1982)
Jolly Roger (1965, 1922)
Kelso (1967, 1957)
Kentucky (1983, 1861)
Kingston (1955, 1884)
Lady's Secret (1992, 1982)
La Prevoyante (1994, 1970)
L'Escargot (1977, 1963)
Lexington (1955, 1850)
Longfellow (1971, 1867)
Luke Blackburn (1956, 1877)
Majestic Prince (1988, 1966)
Man o'War (1957, 1917)
Miss Woodford (1967, 1880)
Myrtlewood (1979, 1932)
Nashua (1965, 1952)
Native Dancer (1963, 1950)
Native Diver (1978, 1959)
Neji (1966, 1950)
Northern Dancer (1976, 1961)
Oedipus (1978, 1946)
Old Rosebud (1968, 1911)
Omaha (1965, 1932)
Pan Zareta (1972, 1910)
Parole (1984, 1879)
Peter Pan (1956, 1904)
Princess Doreen (1982, 1921)
Princess Rooney (1991, 1980)
Real Delight (1987, 1949)
Regret (1957, 1912)
Reigh Count (1978, 1925)
Roamer (1981, 1911)
Roseben (1956, 1901)

Round Table (1972, 1954)
Ruffian (1976, 1972)
Ruthless (1975, 1864)
Salvator (1955, 1886)
Sarazen (1957, 1921)
Seabiscuit (1958, 1933)
Searching (1978, 1952)
Seattle Slew (1981, 1974)
Secretariat (1974, 1970)
Shuvee (1975, 1966)
Silver Spoon (1978, 1956)
Sir Archy (1955, 1805)
Sir Barton (1957, 1916)
Slew o' Gold (1992, 1980)
Spectacular Bid (1982, 1976)
Stymie (1975, 1941)
Susan's Girl (1976, 1969)
Swaps (1966, 1952)
Sword Dancer (1977, 1956)
Sysonby (1956, 1902)
Ta Wee (1993, 1967)
Ten Broeck (1982, 1872)
Tim Tam (1985, 1955)
Tom Fool (1960, 1949)
Top Flight (1966, 1929)
Tosmah (1984, 1961)
Twenty Grand (1957, 1928)
Twilight Tear (1963, 1941)
Two Lea (1982, 1946)
War Admiral (1958, 1934)
Whirlaway (1959, 1938)
Whisk Broom II (1979, 1907)
Zev (1983, 1920)

Note: Years of election and foaling in parentheses.

HARNESS RACING

Major Races

Hambletonian

Year	Winner	Driver	Year	Winner	Driver
1926	Guy McKinney	Nat Ray	1949	Miss Tilly	Fred Egan
1927	Iosola's Worthy	Marvin Childs	1950	Lusty Song	Del Miller
1928	Spenser	W. H. Leese	1951	Mainliner	Guy Crippen
1929	Walter Dear	Walter Cox	1952	Sharp Note	Bion Shively
1930	Hanover's Bertha	Tom Berry	1953	Helicopter	Harry Harvey
1931	Calumet Butler	R. D. McMahon	1954	Newport Dream	Del Cameron
1932	The Marchioness	William Caton	1955	Scott Frost	Joe O'Brien
1933	Mary Reynolds	Ben White	1956	The Intruder	Ned Bower
1934	Lord Jim	Doc Parshall	1957	Hickory Smoke	J. Simpson Sr
1935	Greyhound	Sep Palin	1958	Emily's Pride	Flave Nipe
1936	Rosalind	Ben White	1959	Diller Hanover	Frank Ervin
1937	Shirley Hanover	Henry Thomas	1960	Blaze Hanover	Joe O'Brien
1938	McLin Hanover	Henry Thomas	1961	Harlan Dean	James Arthur
1939	Peter Astra	Doc Parshall	1962	A. C.'s Viking	Sanders Russell
1940	Spencer Scott	Fred Egan	1963	Speedy Scot	Ralph Baldwin
1941	Bill Gallon	Lee Smith	1964	Ayres	J. Simpson, Sr
1942	The Ambassador	Ben White	1965	Egyptian Candor	Del Cameron
1943	Volo Song	Ben White	1966	Kerry Way	Frank Ervin
1944	Yankee Maid	Henry Thomas	1967	Speedy Streak	Del Cameron
1945	Titan Hanover	H. Pownall Sr	1968	Nevele Pride	Stanley Dancer
1946	Chestertown	Thomas Berry	1969	Lindy's Pride	H. Beissinger
1947	Hoot Mon	Sep Palin	1970	Timothy T.	J. Simpson, Jr
1948	Demon Hanover	Harrison Hoyt	1971	Speedy Crown	H. Beissinger

Hambletonian *(Cont.)*

Year	Winner	Driver	Year	Winner	Driver
1972	Super Bowl	Stanley Dancer	1985	Prakas	Bill O'Donnell
1973	Flirth	Ralph Baldwin	1986	Nuclear Kosmos	Ulf Thoresen
1974	Christopher T.	Bill Haughton	1987	Mack Lobell	John Campbell
1975	Bonefish	Stanley Dancer	1988	Armbro Goal	John Campbell
1976	Steve Lobell	Bill Haughton	1989	Park Avenue Joe*	Ron Waples
1977	Green Speed	Bill Haughton		Probe*	Bill Fahy
1978	Speedy Somolli	H. Beissinger	1990	Harmonious	John Campbell
1979	Legend Hanover	George Sholty	1991	Giant Victory	Jack Moiseyev
1980	Burgomeister	Bill Haughton	1992	Alf Palema	Mickey McNichol
1981	Shiaway St. Pat	Ray Remmen	1993	American Winner	Ron Pierce
1982	Speed Bowl	Tom Haughton	1994	Victory Dream	Michel Lachance
1983	Duenna	Stanley Dancer	1995	Tagliabue	John Campbell
1984	Historic Freight	Ben Webster			

*Park Avenue Joe and Probe dead-heated for win. Park Avenue Joe finished first in the summary 2-1-1 to Probe's 1-9-1 finish.
Note: Run at 1 mile since 1947.

Little Brown Jug

Year	Winner	Driver	Year	Winner	Driver
1946	Ensign Hanover	Wayne Smart	1971	Nansemond	Herve Filion
1947	Forbes Chief	Del Cameron	1972	Strike Out	Keith Waples
1948	Knight Dream	Frank Safford	1973	Melvin's Woe	Joe O'Brien
1949	Good Time	Frank Ervin	1974	Armbro Omaha	Bill Haughton
1950	Dudley Hanover	Del Miller	1975	Seatrain	Ben Webster
1951	Tar Heel	Del Cameron	1976	Keystone Ore	Stanley Dancer
1952	Meadow Rice	Wayne Smart	1977	Governor Skipper	John Chapman
1953	Keystoner	Frank Ervin	1978	Happy Escort	William Popfinger
1954	Adios Harry	Morris MacDonald	1979	Hot Hitter	Herve Filion
1955	Quick Chief	Bill Haughton	1980	Niatross	Clint Galbraith
1956	Noble Adios	John Simpson Sr	1981	Fan Hanover	Glen Garnsey
1957	Torpid	John Simpso Sr	1982	Merger	John Campbell
1958	Shadow Wave	Joe O'Brien	1983	Ralph Hanover	Ron Waples
1959	Adios Butler	Clint Hodgins	1984	Colt Fortysix	Chris Boring
1960	Bullet Hanover	John Simpson Sr	1985	Nihilator	Bill O'Donnell
1961	Henry T. Adios	Stanley Dancer	1986	Barberry Spur	Bill O'Donnell
1962	Lehigh Hanover	Stanley Dancer	1987	Jaguar Spur	Dick Stillings
1963	Overtrick	John Patterson	1988	B. J. Scoot	Michel Lachance
1964	Vicar Hanover	Bill Haughton	1989	Goalie Jeff	Michel Lachance
1965	Bret Hanover	Frank Ervin	1990	Beach Towel	Ray Remmen
1966	Romeo Hanover	George Sholty	1991	Precious Bunny	Jack Moiseye
1967	Best of All	James Hackett	1992	Fake Left	Ron Waples
1968	Rum Customer	Bill Haughton	1993	Life Sign	John Campbell
1969	Laverne Hanover	Bill Haughton	1994	Magical Mike	Michel Lachance
1970	Most Happy Fella	Stanley Dancer	1995	Nick's Fantasy	John Campbell

Breeders' Crown

	1984			**1985**	
Div	Winner	Driver	Div	Winner	Driver
2PC	Dragon's Lair	Jeff Mallet	2PC	Robust Hanover	John Campbell
2PF	Amneris	John Campbell	2PF	Caressable	Herve Filion
3PC	Troublemaker	Bill O'Donnell	3PC	Nihilator	Bill O'Donnell
3PF	Naughty But Nice	Tommy Haughton	3PF	Stienam	Buddy Gilmour
2TC	Workaholic	Berndt Lindstedt	2TC	Express Ride	John Campbell
2TF	Conifer	George Sholty	2TF	JEF's Spice	Mickey McNichol
3TC	Baltic Speed	Jan Nordin	3TC	Prakas	John Campbell
3TF	Fancy Crown	Bill O'Donnell	3TF	Armbro Devona	Bill O'Donnell
			AP	Division Street	Michel Lachance
			AT	Sandy Bowl	John Campbell

Note: 2=Two-year-old; T=Trotter; C=Colt; 3=Three-year-old; P=Pacer; F=Filly; A=Aged; H=Horse; M=Mare.

Breeders' Crown (Cont.)

1986

Div	Winner	Driver
2PC	Sunset Warrior	Bill Gale
2PF	Halcyon	Ray Remmen
3PC	Masquerade	Richard Silverman
3PF	Glow Softly	Ron Waples
2TC	Mack Lobell	John Campbell
2TF	Super Flora	Ron Waples
3TC	Sugarcane Hanover	Ron Waples
3TF	JEF's Spice	Bill O'Donnell
APM	Samshu Bluegrass	Michel Lachance
ATM	Grades Singing	Herve Filion
APH	Forrest Skipper	Lucien Fontaine
ATH	Nearly Perfect	Mickey McNichol

1987

Div	Winner	Driver
2PC	Camtastic	Bill O'Donnell
2PF	Leah Almahurst	Bill Fahy
3PC	Call For Rain	Clint Galbraith
3PF	Pacific	Tom Harmer
2TC	Defiant One	Howard Beissinger
2TF	Nan's Catch	Berndt Lindstedt
3TC	Mack Lobell	John Campbell
3TF	Armbro Fling	George Sholty
APM	Follow My Star	John Campbell
ATM	Grades Singing	Olle Goop
APH	Armbro Emerson	Walter Whelan
ATH	Sugarcane Hanover	Ron Waples

1988

Div	Winner	Driver
2PC	Kentucky Spur	Dick Stillings
2PF	Central Park West	John Campbell
3PC	Camtastic	Bill O'Donnell
3PF	Sweet Reflection	Bill O'Donnell
2TC	Valley Victory	Bill O'Donnell
2TF	Peace Corps	John Campbell
3TC	Firm Tribute	Mark O'Mara
3TF	Nalda Hanover	Mickey McNichol
APM	Anniecrombie	Dave Magee
ATM	Armbro Flori	Larry Walker
APH	Call For Rain	Clint Galbraith
ATH	Mack Lobell	John Campbell

1989

Div	Winner	Driver
2PC	Till We Meet Again	Mickey McNichol
2PF	Town Pro	Doug Brown
3PC	Goalie Jeff	Michel Lachance
3PF	Cheery Hello	John Campbell
2TC	Royal Troubador	Carl Allen
2TF	Delphi's Lobell	Ron Waples
3TC	Esquire Spur	Dick Stillings
3TF	Pace Corps	John Campbell
APM	Armbro Feather	John Kopas
ATM	Grades Singing	Olle Goop
APH	Matt's Scooter	Michel Lachance
ATH	Delray Lobell	John Campbell

1990

Div	Winner	Driver
2PC	Artsplace	John Campbell
2PF	Miss Easy	John Campbell
3PC	Beach Towel	Ray Remmen
3PF	Town Pro	Doug Brown
2TC	Crysta's Best	Dick Richardson Jr
2TF	Jean Bi	Jan Nordin
3TC	Embassy Lobell	Michel Lachance
3TF	Me Maggie	Berndt Lindstedt
APM	Caesar's Jackpot	Bill Fahy
ATM	Peace Corps	Stig Johansson
APH	Bay's Fella	Paul MacDonell
ATH	No Sex Please	Ron Waples

1991

Div	Winner	Driver
2PC	Digger Almahurst	Doug Brown
2PF	Hazleton Kay	John Campbell
3PC	Three Wizzards	Bill Gale
3PF	Miss Easy	John Campbell
2TC	King Conch	Bill Gale
2TF	Armbro Keepsake	John Campbell
3TC	Giant Victory	Ron Pierce
3TF	Twelve Speed	Ron Waples
APM	Delinquent Account	Bill O'Donnell
ATM	Me Maggie	Berndt Lindstedt
APH	Camluck	Michel Lachance
ATH	Billyjojimbob	Paul MacDonell

1992

Div	Winner	Driver
2PC	Village Jiffy	Ron Waples
2PF	Immortality	John Campbell
3PC	Kingsbridge	Roger Mayotte
3PF	So Fresh	John Campbell
2TC	Giant Chill	John Patterson, Jr
2TF	Winky's Goal	Cat Manzi
3TC	Baltic Striker	Michel Lachance
3TF	Imperfection	Michel Lachance
APM	Shady Daisy	Ron Pierce
ATM	Peace Corps	Torbjorn Jansson
APH	Artsplace	John Campbell
ATH	No Sex Please	Ron Waples

1993

Div	Winner	Driver
2PC	Expensive Scooter	Jack Moiseyev
2PF	Electric Scooter	Mike LaChance
3PC	Life Sign	John Campbell
3PF	Immortality	John Campbell
2TC	Westgate Crown	John Campbell
2TF	Gleam	Jimmy Takter
3TC	Pine Chip	John Campbell
3TF	Expressway Hanover	Per Henriksen
APM	Swing Back	Kelly Sheppard
ATM	Lifetime Dream	Paul MacDonnell
APH	Staying Together	Bill O'Donnell
ATH	Earl	Chris Christoforou Jr

Note: 2=Two-year-old; T=Trotter; C=Colt; 3=Three-year-old; P=Pacer; F=Filly; A=Aged; H=Horse; M=Mare.

Major Races (Cont.)

Breeders' Crown (Cont.)

1994

Div	Winner	Driver
2PC	Jenna's Beach Boy	Bill Fahy
2PF	Yankee Cashmere	Peter Wrenn
3PC	Magical Mike	Michel Lachance
3PF	Hardie Hanover	Tim Twaddle
2TC	Eager Seelster	Teddy Jacobs
2TF	Lookout Victory	John Patterson

1994 (Cont.)

Div	Winner	Driver
3TC	Incredible Abe	Italo Tamborrino
3TF	Imageofa Clear Day	Bill O'Donnell
APM	Shady Daisy	Michel Lachance
ATM	Armbro Keepsake	Stig Johansson
APH	Village Jiffy	Paul MacDonell
ATH	Pine Chip	John Campbell

Note: 2=Two-year-old; T=Trotter; C=Colt; 3=Three-year-old; P=Pacer; F=Filly; A=Aged; H=Horse; M=Mare.

Triple Crown Winners

Trotting

Trotting's Triple Crown consists of the Hambletonian (first run in 1926), the Kentucky Futurity (first run in 1893), and the Yonkers Trot (known as the Yonkers Futurity when it began in 1955).

Year	Horse	Owner	Breeder	Trainer & Driver
1955	Scott Frost	S.A. Camp Farms	Est of W. N. Reynolds	Joe O'Brien
1963	Speedy Scot	Castleton Farms	Castleton Farms	Ralph Baldwin
1964	Ayres	Charlotte Sheppard	Charlotte Sheppard	John Simpson Sr
1968	Nevele Pride	Nevele Acres & Lou Resnick	Mr & Mrs E. C. Quin	Stanley Dancer
1969	Lindy's Pride	Lindy Farm	Hanover Shoe Farms	Howard Beissinger
1972	Super Bowl	Rachel Dancer & Rose Hild Breeding Farm	Stoner Creek Stud	Stanley Dancer

Pacing

Pacing's Triple Crown consists of the Cane Pace (called the Cane Futurity when it began in 1955), the Little Brown Jug (first run in 1946), and the Messenger Stake (first run in 1956).

Year	Horse	Owner	Breeder	Trainer/Driver
1959	Adios Butler	Paige West & Angelo Pellillo	R. C. Carpenter	Paige West/Clint Hodgins
1965	Bret Hanover	Richard Downing	Hanover Shoe Farms	Frank Ervin
1966	Romeo Hanover	Lucky Star Stables & Morton Finder	Hanover Shoe Farms	Jerry Silverman/ William Meyer (Cane) & George Sholty (Jug & Messenger)
1968	Rum Customer	Kennilworth Farms & L. C. Mancuso	Mr. & Mrs. R. C. Larkin	Bill Haughton
1970	Most Happy Fella	Egyptian Acres Stable	Stoner Creek Stud	Stanley Dancer
1980	Niatross	Niagara Acres, C. Galbraith & Niatross Stables	Niagara Acres	Clint Galbraith
1983	Ralph Hanover	Waples Stable, Pointsetta Stable, Grant's Direct Stable & P. J. Baugh	Hanover Shoe Farms	Stew Firlotte/Ron Waples

Awards

Horse of the Year

Year	Horse	Gait	Owner	Year	Horse	Gait	Owner
1947	Victory Song	T	Castleton Farm	1956	Scott Frost	T	S. A. Camp Farms
1948	Rodney	T	R. H. Johnston	1957	Torpid	P	Sherwood Farm
1949	Good Time	P	William Cane	1958	Emily's Pride	T	Walnut Hall and Castleton Farms
1950	Proximity	T	Ralph and Gordon Verhurst	1959	Bye Bye Byrd	P	Mr. and Mrs. Rex Larkin
1951	Pronto Don	T	Hayes Fair Acres Stable	1960	Adios Butler	P	Adios Butler Syndicate
1952	Good Time	P	William Cane	1961	Adios Butler	P	Adios Butler Syndicate
1953	Hi Lo's Forbes	P	Mr. and Mrs. Earl Wagner	1962	Su Mac Lad	T	I. W. Berkemeyer
1954	Stenographer	T	Max Hempt	1963	Speedy Scot	T	Castleton Farm
1955	Scott Frost	T	S. A. Camp Farms	1964	Bret Hanover	P	Richard Downing

Horse of the Year *(Cont.)*

Year	Horse	Gait	Owner
1965	Bret Hanover	P	Richard Downing
1966	Bret Hanover	P	Richard Downing
1967	Nevele Pride	T	Nevele Acres
1968	Nevele Pride	T	Nevele Acres, Louis Resnick
1969	Nevele Pride	T	Nevele Acres, Louis Resnick
1970	Fresh Yankee	T	Duncan MacDonald
1971	Albatross	P	Albatross Stable
1972	Albatross	P	Amicable Stable
1973	Sir Dalrae	P	A La Carte Racing Stable
1974	Delmonica Hanover	T	Delvin Miller, W. Arnold Hanger
1975	Savoir	T	Allwood Stable
1976	Keystone Ore	P	Mr. and Mrs. Stanley Dancer, Rose Hild Farms, Robert Jones
1977	Green Speed	T	Beverly Lloyds
1978	Abercrombie	P	Shirley Mitchell, L. Keith Bulen
1979	Niatross	P	Niagara Acres, Clint Galbraith
1980	Niatross	P	Niatross Syndicate, Niagara Acres, Clint Galbraith
1981	Fan Hanover	P	Dr. J. Glen Brown
1982	Cam Fella	P	Norm Clements, Norm Faulkner
1983	Cam Fella	P	JEF's Standardbred, Norm Clements, Norm Faulkner
1984	Fancy Crown	T	Fancy Crown Stable
1985	Nihilator	P	Wall Street-Nihilator Syndicate
1986	Forrest Skipper	P	Forrest L. Bartlett
1987	Mack Lobell	T	One More Time Stable and Fair Wind Farm
1988	Mack Lobell	T	John Erik Magnusson
1989	Matt's Scooter	P	Gordon and Illa Rumpel, Charles Jurasvinski
1990	Beach Towel	P	Uptown Stables
1991	Precious Bunny	P	R. Peter Heffering
1992	Artsplace	P	George Segal
1993	Staying Together	P	Robert Hamather
1994	Cam's Card Shark	P	Jeffrey S. Snyder

Note: Balloting is conducted by the U.S Trotting Association and U.S. Harness Writers Association.

Leading Drivers—Money Won

Year	Driver	Winnings ($)	Year	Driver	Winnings ($)
1946	Thomas Berry	121,933	1971	Herve Filion	1,915,945
1947	H. C. Fitzpatrick	133,675	1972	Herve Filion	2,473,265
1948	Ralph Baldwin	153,222	1973	Herve Filion	2,233,303
1949	Clint Hodgins	184,108	1974	Herve Filion	3,474,315
1950	Del Miller	306,813	1975	Carmine Abbatiello	2,275,093
1951	John Simpson Sr	333,316	1976	Herve Filion	2,278,634
1952	Bill Haughton	311,728	1977	Herve Filion	2,551,058
1953	Bill Haughton	374,527	1978	Carmine Abbatiello	3,344,457
1954	Bill Haughton	415,577	1979	John Campbell	3,308,984
1955	Bill Haughton	599,455	1980	John Campbell	3,732,306
1956	Bill Haughton	572,945	1981	Bill O'Donnell	4,065,608
1957	Bill Haughton	586,950	1982	Bill O'Donnell	5,755,067
1958	Bill Haughton	816,659	1983	John Campbell	6,104,082
1959	Bill Haughton	771,435	1984	Bill O'Donnell	9,059,184
1960	Del Miller	567,282	1985	Bill O'Donnell	10,207,372
1961	Stanley Dancer	674,723	1986	John Campbell	9,515,055
1962	Stanley Dancer	760,343	1987	John Campbell	10,186,495
1963	Bill Haughton	790,086	1988	John Campbell	11,148,565
1964	Stanley Dancer	1,051,538	1989	John Campbell	9,738,450
1965	Bill Haughton	889,943	1990	John Campbell	11,620,878
1966	Stanley Dancer	1,218,403	1991	Jack Moiseyev	9,568,468
1967	Bill Haughton	1,305,773	1992	John Campbell	8,202,108
1968	Bill Haughton	1,654,463	1993	John Campbell	9,926,482
1969	Del Insko	1,635,463	1994	John Campbell	9,834,139
1970	Herve Filion	1,647,837			

Motor Sports

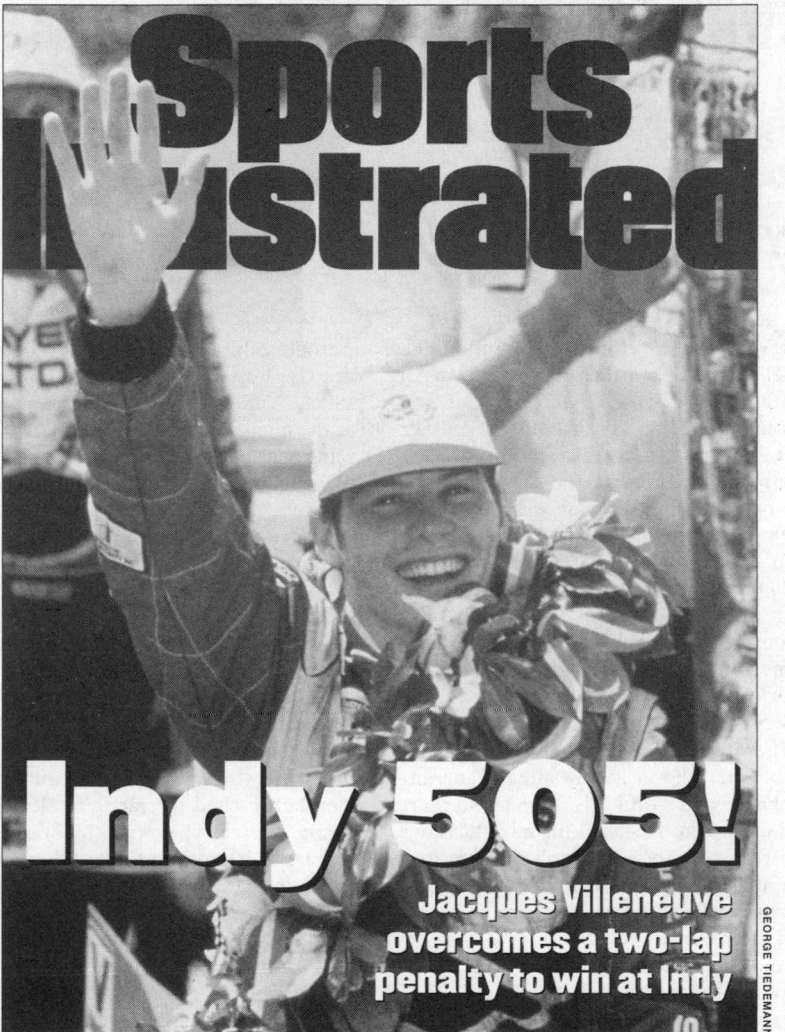

Sports Illustrated

Indy 505!

Jacques Villeneuve overcomes a two-lap penalty to win at Indy

GEORGE TIEDEMANN

Youth Movement

Showing no respect for their elders, three young stars drove into the spotlight in '95
by Ed Hinton

NEVER HAD youth commanded the limelights of the world's big three forms of motor racing—NASCAR, Indy Car and Formula One—as consistently as in 1995. With veteran stars obscured across the board, and the prodigies so savvy and sure, the only remaining debate was over which of three youngsters was the hottest property in all of auto racing.

There was Jeff Gordon of NASCAR, who didn't even turn 24 until halfway through the season in which he emerged as something stock car racing fans hadn't known before—a bona fide darling in an otherwise rough-cut, hard-bitten realm.

There was Michael Schumacher of Formula One, who at 26 was already gunning for his second world driving championship, and in midseason signed the most lucrative contract ever for one man's services at a steering wheel for a single season—at least $24 million, and perhaps as high as $30 million, from Ferrari, for 1996.

And then there was Jacques Villeneuve, who at 24 won the Indianapolis 500, then breezed to the CART Indy Car season championship, then signed to jump to Formula One in 1996—not for the customary apprenticeship with a marginal team, but with the best racing organization on the planet, Williams Grand Prix Engineering, for the highest rookie-season salary in auto racing history, $6 million.

Depending on the criteria for "hotness," as sports agents call lucrative charisma nowadays, a case could be made for each of the three as the hottest driver in the world.

But it was Villeneuve who soared farthest, fastest. He is the son of the late Gilles Villeneuve, the Quebecois Formula One star who was killed in a crash in 1982, when Jacques was 11. Jacques was born in Quebec, raised in Monaco and schooled in Switzerland—and therefore wasn't even sure what the Indy 500 was until 1992, when he watched the race on television in Japan. Yet in his rookie season he appeared virtually out of nowhere at the end of the 1994 Indy 500 to finish second and hint powerfully at what was to come.

Suddenly, during the week leading up to the 1995 running of the 500, Villeneuve found himself the consensus favorite among most observers. During time trials the 1993 and '94 winners of the race, Penske teammates Emerson Fittipaldi and

Fox survived his terrifying wreck in the opening seconds at Indy.

Al Unser Jr., had been bewildered to find their 1995 Penske-Mercedes cars unaccountably, and incurably, ill-engineered for the old 2.5-mile Indianapolis Motor Speedway oval and had failed to make the field at all. With a dark horse, Scott Brayton, on the pole with a suspect stock-block engine in his car, young Villeneuve, with his reputation for smooth, patient driving, was elevated to prerace favorite.

Villeneuve delivered, despite the severest penalty any Indy winner has ever had to overcome, two laps, a judgment levied against him by United States Auto Club officials on the 39th of the race's 200 laps, for failing to fall in behind the pace car during a caution period. By running conservatively to get better fuel mileage, Villeneuve was able to stay out on the track while leaders pitted during ensuing caution periods and made up his two laps. Then, near the end of the race, retributive justice set up Villeneuve for the win. With 10 laps to go, another Canadian driver, Scott Goodyear of Toronto, who appeared to be

in command of the race at that point, passed the pace car a split-second before the final caution period ended and was himself penalized, leaving Villeneuve in the lead for keeps.

Goodyear and his car owner, Steve Horne, protested vehemently but to no avail. The official ruling stood, and public sentiment for them was hard to muster, especially after they'd lost to Villeneuve, who himself had been victim of a penalty whose harshness was suspect. After all, as Villeneuve's team owner, Barry Green, pointed out jubilantly in the moments after the checkered flag, "We've just won the first Indianapolis 505!"

The race had been marred from the opening seconds by an incident darker by far than the driver penalties. Just after the green flag signaled the start of the race, the car of Stan Fox, a veteran of midget and sprint car racing whose custom was to move up to Indy Cars annually just for the 500, veered suddenly and inexplicably to the right, making contact with Eddie Cheever's car before slamming horrifically into the retaining wall between Turns 1 and 2 of the track. Fox suffered severe head

GEORGE TIEDEMANN

Gordon and his wife Brooke shared the winner's circle at the Bristol 500.

injuries, and lay in critical condition at Indianapolis's Methodist Hospital as the race concluded. But in the ensuing weeks, Fox began an amazing recovery, and in July left the hospital able to walk and talk, though months of rehabilitation remained ahead for him.

The Indy 500 win, coupled with a victory in the CART Indy Car season-opening Miami Grand Prix, put Villeneuve firmly in the points lead for the season championship, and he never faltered from first place. While veterans such as Unser, Fittipaldi and Michael Andretti struggled through sporadic seasons, Villeneuve's only real challenge for the championship came from another young driver, 26-year-old Robby Gordon (no relation to Jeff Gordon), and even that challenge was snuffed in July. During practice for the Marlboro 500 at Michigan International Speedway, Gordon crashed due to a suspension failure and was knocked unconscious. Though he wasn't seriously injured, Indy Car rules require any driver who has suffered unconsciousness to wait seven days before racing again. Gordon missed the Michigan race and therefore scored no points that week-

end, leaving Villeneuve in clear command of the championship standings.

Dominant as Villeneuve was, there were rumblings even as he won the Indy 500 that he might not return to defend that victory—that his heart lay in his father's old realm, Formula One, and that the youngster had the superb skills to match his ambitions. But not since Mario Andretti in the 1970s had a driver with an Indy Car background landed a truly competitive ride in Formula One (Michael Andretti had failed miserably in F/1 in 1993, with a McLaren team that wasn't nearly up to its usual competitiveness). During the summer of '95, two major F/1 team bosses, Flavio Briatore of Benetton and Ron Dennis of McLaren, said publicly that they weren't interested in young Villeneuve. So it was expected that if Villeneuve went to F/1 in '96, he would have to settle for at least one "learning year" with a lesser team, a nonwinner.

Surprisingly, it was the two hardest taskmasters for a driver to please in all of Formula One, team owner Frank Williams and his chief engineer, Patrick Head, who gave Villeneuve a chance with their Didcot, England–based operation. Villeneuve tested a Williams car for them and wowed them, and they signed him to replace David Coulthard of Scotland and pair with Damon Hill, son of the late two-time world champion Graham Hill, on the Williams team.

And so in 1996, a North American–born driver will have a realistic chance to win Formula One races for the first time since, well, Gilles Villeneuve in the early '80s.

Jeff Gordon was the youngest of the young stars, and was clearly up against the oldest, savviest, toughest competition of the three. Headed down the stretch of the 31-race NASCAR Winston Cup schedule— the most grueling in major motor sports— Gordon, in his third year of competition in stock car racing's top series, led the season point standings, with three vastly more experienced drivers on his tail: Sterling Marlin (age 38, in his 20th year of Winston

GEROGE TIEDEMANN

Earnhardt (3) couldn't keep Marlin at bay in the Daytona 500.

Cup competition), Mark Martin (36, in his 15th year) and seven-time Winston Cup champion Dale Earnhardt (44, in his 21st year). And three more older drivers, brothers Bobby and Terry Labonte, 31 and 38, respectively, and Dale Jarrett, 38, though not factors in the points race, combined to dominate late summer in outright wins and slow Gordon's bid to run away in the season standings.

The NASCAR season began as a premature celebration of what was expected to be an Earnhardt cakewalk to a third straight championship and a record eighth career Winston Cup, breaking his tie with the legendary Richard Petty for career season titles.

Even Earnhardt's traditional heartbreak in the season-opener seemed to be a good omen for him. Marlin won his second straight Daytona 500 and Earnhardt finished second, failing for the 17th straight year to win NASCAR's most-prestigious race. That seemed to project a repetition of Earnhardt's usual course of recent years: Lose the Daytona 500 by a nose, win the Winston Cup by a mile.

But Gordon began a post-Daytona blitz, winning three of the season's first six races. Though Gordon didn't get his fourth win until the season's midway point, the Pepsi 400 at Daytona in July, he was by then bearing down on the lead in the point standings by virtue of consistently high finishes in races he didn't win outright. Meanwhile Earnhardt, through the shank of the season, finished out of the top 20 a whopping seven times, his most inconsistent stretch in three years.

And so nearly all season, the polite, darkly handsome Gordon, widespread favorite of new-breed NASCAR fans, overshadowed the hard-nosed Earnhardt as the leading figure of America's most popular racing series. Winston Cup attendance, after several years in the three-million-plus per season range, had jumped to 4.9 million in 1994 and was expected to top five million in '95, by the season finale on Nov. 12 at Atlanta Motor Speedway. Though there were several factors behind the big increases the past two seasons—including the addition of the Brickyard 400 at Indianapolis Motor Speedway, with its more than 300,000 seats, to the '94 and '95 Winston Cup schedules—Gordon clearly appealed to an influx of younger, female NASCAR fans. But Gordon lacked one basic measure of the hottest driver, a bid-

PASCAL RONDEAU/ALLSPORT

ding war for his services, because he was in the third year of a five-year contract with his team owner, Rick Hendrick.

Schumacher, peerless in the global fishbowl of Formula One since the death of three-time world champion Ayrton Senna in May 1994, overcame more vulnerability to distraction than his NASCAR and Indy Car counterparts in '95. In the final year of his contract with Benetton, the young German kept his focus on driving despite the monumental auction swirling around him—his manager, Willi Weber, had stipulated that the bidding for '96 *open* at $20 million a year, which in itself would have been a near-record salary—and despite recurring controversy between the Benetton team and the Federation Internationale de l'Automobile, F/1's governing body.

The FIA initially stripped Schumacher of 10 world championship points earned for winning the season-opening Grand Prix of Brazil on March 26, because the gasoline in his Benetton didn't match the chromatographic "fingerprint" of the fuel designated by the team to the FIA before the season. At first Schumacher appeared headed for a season exasperatingly similar to 1994, in which he'd become the youngest driver ever to win the world championship despite FIA sanctions that banned him from two races and stripped him of points earned in two others that year. But the '95 season set-

tled down to a level playing field for him on April 13, when an FIA appeals tribunal restored his points from Brazil after finding that the fuel mix-up was not advantageous and was simply the result of a shipping mistake by Benetton's fuel supplier, Elf.

Perhaps Schumacher's greatest distraction of '95 was personal. In what quickly turned into a two-man contest for the world championship, Schumacher missed midseason opportunities to put away his increasingly bitter rival, 32-year-old Damon Hill. The rivalry reached a crescendo in July at the British Grand Prix, when Schumacher, leading, was aggressively trying to block Hill, and Hill was struggling to pass in a corner, and they wrecked each other. Next, at the German Grand Prix, Hill fell out early and Schumacher won, increasing his points lead to a borderline-insurmountable 21. Still, he couldn't break the championship chase open. At the next Grand Prix, in Hungary, it was Hill who won and Schumacher who fell out early, and Hill was back to within 11 points. Then in Belgium, Schumacher and Hill finished one-two in the rain, leaving Schumacher 15 points ahead but still not cakewalking to the championship of a season that would end Nov. 12 with the Grand Prix of Australia in Adelaide.

Hot as Schumacher was in sheer money terms, and cool as Gordon remained through a sizzling summer against the best quality and quantity of competition in all the world's motor racing, it was Villeneuve who won the world's biggest race, then dominated his series more relentlessly and took the largest leap to a bigger challenge at season's end. And so, of the three, Jacques Villeneuve emerged as the hottest of the hot.

CART Racing

Indianapolis 500

Results of the 79th running of the Indianapolis 500 and 6th round of the 1995 Indy Car season. Held Sunday, May 28, at the 2.5-mile Indianapolis Motor Speedway in Speedway, IN.

Distance, 500 miles; starters, 33; time of race, 3:15:18; average speed, 153.616 mph; margin of victory, 2.5 seconds; caution flags, 9 for 58 laps; lead changes, 23 among 10 drivers.

TOP 10 FINISHERS

Pos	Driver (start pos.)	Car	Qual. Speed	Laps	Status
1	Jacques Villeneuve (5)	Reynard-Ford	228.397	200	running
2	*Christian Fittipaldi (27)	Reynard-Ford	226.387	200	running
3	Bobby Rahal (21)	Lola-Mercedes	227.086	200	running
4	*Eliseo Salazar (24)	Lola-Ford	225.028	200	running
5	Robby Gordon (7)	Reynard-Ford	227.531	200	running
6	Mauricio Gugelmin (6)	Reynard-Ford	227.935	200	running
7	Arie Luyendyk (2)	Lola-Menard	231.036	200	running
8	Teo Fabi (15)	Reynard-Ford	225.918	199	running
9	Danny Sullivan (18)	Reynard-Ford	225.507	199	running
10	Hiro Matsushita (10)	Reynard-Ford	226.872	199	running

1995 Indy Car Results

Date	Track/Distance	Winner (start pos.)	Car	Avg Speed
Mar 5	Miami Grand Prix	Jacques Villeneuve (8)	Reynard-Ford	82.801
Mar 19	IndyCar Australia	Paul Tracy (9)	Lola-Ford	92.335
Apr 2	Phoenix 200	Robby Gordon (9)	Reynard-Ford	133.980
Apr 9	Long Beach Grand Prix	Al Unser Jr (4)	Penske-Mercedes	91.442
Apr 23	Nazareth Grand Prix	Emerson Fittipaldi (4)	Penske-Mercedes	131.305
May 28	Indianapolis 500	Jacques Villeneuve (5)	Reynard-Ford	153.616
June 4	Milwaukee 200	Paul Tracy (7)	Lola-Ford	137.304
June 11	Detroit Grand Prix	Robby Gordon (1)	Reynard-Ford	83.499
June 25	Portland 200	Al Unser Jr (3)	Penske-Mercedes	103.933
July 9	Elkhart Lake 200	Jacques Villeneuve (1)	Reynard-Ford	103.901
July 16	Indy Toronto	Michael Andretti (6)	Lola-Ford	94.787
July 23	Cleveland Grand Prix	Jacques Villeneuve (2)	Reynard-Ford	130.113
July 30	Michigan 500	Scott Pruett (12)	Lola-Ford	159.676
Aug 13	Mid-Ohio 200	Al Unser Jr (8)	Penske-Mercedes	107.110
Aug 20	New England 200	*Andre Ribeiro (1)	Reynard-Honda	134.203
Sep 3	Indy Vancouver	Al Unser Jr (9)	Penske-Mercedes	95.571
Sep 10	Monterey Grand Prix	*Gil de Ferran (3)	Reynard-Mercedes	98.493

*Rookie. Note: Distances are in miles.

Championship Standings

Driver	Starts	Wins	Pts
Jacques Villeneuve	17	4	172
Al Unser Jr	16	4	161
Bobby Rahal	17	0	128
Michael Andretti	17	1	123
Robby Gordon	16	2	121
Paul Tracy	17	2	115
Scott Pruett	17	1	112
Jimmy Vasser	17	0	92
Teo Fabi	17	0	83
Mauricio Gugelmin	17	0	80

NASCAR Racing

Daytona 500

Results of the opening round of the 1995 Winston Cup series. Held Sunday, February 19, at the 2.5-mile high-banked Daytona International Speedway.

Distance, 500 miles; starters, 42; time of race, 3:31:42; average speed, 141.710 mph; margin of victory, .61 second; caution flags, 10 for 41 laps; lead changes, 12 among 7 drivers.

TOP 10 FINISHERS

Pos	Driver (start pos.)	Car	Laps	Winnings ($)
1	Sterling Marlin (3)	Chevrolet	200	300,460
2	Dale Earnhardt (2)	Chevrolet	200	212,250
3	Mark Martin (6)	Ford	200	153,700
4	Ted Musgrave (12)	Ford	200	111,200
5	Dale Jarrett (1)	Ford	200	119,855
6	Michael Waltrip (15)	Pontiac	200	86,205
7	Steve Grissom (35)	Chevrolet	200	72,065
8	Terry Labonte (11)	Chevrolet	200	78,940
9	Ken Schrader (9)	Chevrolet	200	70,140
10	Morgan Shepherd (30)	Ford	200	66,690

Late 1994 NASCAR Results

Date	Track/Distance	Winner (start pos.)	Car	Avg Speed	Winnings ($)
Oct 23	Rockingham 500	Dale Earnhardt (20)	Chevrolet	126.408	60,600
Oct 30	Phoenix 500K	Terry Labonte (19)	Chevrolet	107.463	67,885
Nov 13	Atlanta 500	Mark Martin (5)	Ford	148.982	104,200

Note: Distances are in miles unless followed by * (laps) or K (kilometers).

1995 NASCAR Results (through October 1)

Date	Track/Distance	Winner (start pos.)	Car	Avg Speed	Winnings ($)
Feb 19	Daytona 500	Sterling Marlin (3)	Chevrolet	141.710	300,460
Feb 26	Rockingham 500	Jeff Gordon (1)	Chevrolet	125.305	167,600
Mar 5	Richmond 400*	Terry Labonte (24)	Chevrolet	106.425	82,950
Mar 12	Atlanta 500	Jeff Gordon (3)	Chevrolet	150.115	104,950
Mar 26	Darlington 400	Sterling Marlin (5)	Chevrolet	111.392	86,185
Apr 2	Bristol 500*	Jeff Gordon (2)	Chevrolet	92.011	67,645
Apr 9	N Wilkesboro 400*	Dale Earnhardt (5)	Chevrolet	102.424	77,400
Apr 23	Martinsville 500*	Rusty Wallace (15)	Ford	72.145	61,945
Apr 30	Talladega 500	Mark Martin (3)	Ford	178.902	98,565
May 7	Sonoma 300K	Dale Earnhardt (4)	Chevrolet	70.681	74,860
May 28	World 600	Bobby Labonte (2)	Chevrolet	151.952	163,850
June 4	Dover Downs 500	Kyle Petty (37)	Pontiac	119.880	77,655
June 11	Pocono 500	Terry Labonte (27)	Chevrolet	137.720	71,175
June 18	Michigan 400	Bobby Labonte (19)	Chevrolet	134.141	84,080
July 1	Daytona 400	Jeff Gordon (3)	Chevrolet	166.976	96,580
July 9	New Hampshire 300*	Jeff Gordon (21)	Chevrolet	107.029	160,300
July 16	Pocono 500	Dale Jarrett (15)	Ford	134.038	72,970
July 23	Talladega 500	Sterling Martin (1)	Chevrolet	173.188	219,425
Aug 5	Indianapolis 400	Dale Earnhardt (13)	Chevrolet	155.206	565,600
Aug 13	Watkins Glen 90*	Mark Martin (1)	Ford	103.030	95,290
Aug 20	Michigan 400	Bobby Labonte (1)	Chevrolet	157.739	97,445
Aug 26	Bristol 500*	Terry Labonte (2)	Chevrolet	81.979	66,940
Sept 3	Southern 500	Jeff Gordon (5)	Chevrolet	121.231	70,630
Sept 9	Richmond 400	Rusty Wallace (7)	Ford	104.459	64,515
Sept 17	Dover 500	Jeff Gordon (2)	Chevrolet	124.740	74,655
Sept 24	Martinsville 500*	Dale Earnhardt (2)	Chevrolet	73.963	78,150
Oct 1	N Wilkesboro 400*	Mark Martin (2)	Ford	102.998	71,590

Note: Distances are in miles unless followed by * (laps) or K (kilometers).

NASCAR Racing *(Cont.)*

1994 Winston Cup Standings

Driver	Car	Starts	Wins	Pts
Dale Earnhardt	Chevy	31	4	4694
Mark Martin	Ford	31	2	4250
Rusty Wallace	Ford	31	8	4207
Ken Schrader	Chevy	31	—	4060
Ricky Rudd	Ford	31	1	4050
Morgan Shepherd	Ford	31	—	4029
Terry Labonte	Chevy	31	3	3876
Jeff Gordon	Chevy	31	2	3776
Darrell Waltrip	Chevy	31	—	3688
Bill Elliott	Ford	31	1	3617

1994 Winston Cup Driver Winnings

Driver	Winnings ($)
Dale Earnhardt	3,400,733
Rusty Wallace	1,959,072
Jeff Gordon	1,799,523
Mark Martin	1,678,906
Ernie Irvan	1,311,522
Geoff Bodine	1,287,626
Ken Schrader	1,211,062
Terry Labonte	1,150,921
Sterling Marlin	1,140,683
Morgan Shepherd	1,119,038

Formula One/Grand Prix Racing

1995 Formula One Results (through October 1)

Date	Grand Prix	Winner	Car	Avg Speed
Mar 26	Brazil	Michael Schumacher	Benetton-Renault	114.06
Apr 9	Argentina	Damon Hill	Williams-Renault	115.672
April 30	San Marino	Damon Hill	Williams-Renault	113.701
May 14	Spain	Michael Schumacher	Benetton-Renault	121.392
May 28	Monaco	Michael Schumacher	Benetton-Renault	85.52
June 11	Canada	Jean Alesi	Ferrari	106.747
July 2	France	Michael Schumacher	Benetton-Renault	115.806
July 16	Great Britain	Johnny Herbert	Benetton-Renault	121.595
July 30	Germany	Michael Schumacher	Benetton-Renault	133.272
Aug 13	Hungary	Damon Hill	Williams-Renault	107.047
Aug 27	Belgium	Michael Schumacher	Benetton-Renault	118.878
Sept 10	Italy	Johnny Herbert	Benetton-Renault	146.134
Sept 24	Portugal	David Coulthard	Williams-Renault	113.949
Oct 1	Europe	Michael Schumacher	Benetton-Renault	109.908

1994 World Championship Standings

Drivers compete in Grand Prix races for the title of World Driving Champion. Below are the top 10 results from the 1994 season. Points are awarded for places 1-6 as follows: 10-6-4-3-2-1.

Driver, Country	Starts	Wins	Car	Pts
Michael Schumacher, Germany	16	8	Benetton-Ford	92
Damon Hill, Great Britain	16	6	Williams-Renault	91
Gerhard Berger, Austria	16	1	Ferrari	41
Mika Hakkinen, Finland	16	0	McLaren-Mercedes	26
Jean Alesi, France	16	0	Ferrari	24
Ruebens Barrichello, Brazil	16	0	Jordan-Peugeot	19
Martin Brundle, Great Britain	16	0	Ligier-Mugen Honda	16
David Coulthard, Great Britain	16	0	Williams-Renault	14
Nigel Mansell, Great Britain	16	1	Williams-Renault	13
Jos Verstappen, Netherlands	16	0	Lotus-Ford	10

IMSA Racing

The 24 Hours of Daytona

Held at the Daytona International Speedway on February 4-5, 1995, the 24 Hours of Daytona annually serves as the opening round for the International Motor Sports Association sports car season.

Place	Drivers	Car	Distance
1	Jeremy Dale, Fredrik Ekblom, Jay Cochran	Olds Spice BDG02	685 laps (101.342 mph)
2	Massimo Sigala, Fabrizio Barbazza, Gianfranco Brancatelli, Elton Julian	Ferrari 333SP	645 laps
3	Jim Downing, Butch Hamlet, Tim McAdam, Jim Pace	Mazda Kudzu	637 laps
4	Lee Payne, Brian Williams, David Loring, John Mirro	Olds Denau	512 (Engine)
5	Chuck Cottrell, Chuck Goldsborough, Ted Anderson Mike Holt, Elias Chocron, Leigh Miller	Buick Kudzu	480 laps

Note: World Sports Cars.

1995 World Sports Car Championship Results (through October 1)

Date	Race	Winner(s)	Car (Class)
Feb 4-5	24 Hours of Daytona	Jeremy Dale/Fredrik Ekblom/Jay Cochran	Oldsmobile BDG02
Mar 18	12 Hours of Sebring	Andy Evans/Fermin Velez/Eric Van De Poele	Ferrari 333SP
Apr 30	Atlanta GP	James Weaver	Ford R&S MK-3
May 21	Halifax GP	Mauro Baldi/Fermin Velez	Ferrari 333SP
May 29	Lime Rock GP	Wayne Taylor	Ferrari 333SP
June 24	Glen Continental	James Weaver/Butch Leitzinger	Ford R&S MK-3
July 16	California GP	James Weaver	Ford R&S MK-3
Aug 13	Mosport 500	James Weaver/Andy Wallace	Ford R&S MK-3
Sept 10	Texas World GP	Wayne Taylor	Ferrari 333SP
Sept 30	WSC Championships*	Fermin Velez	Ferrari 333SP

*The World Sports Car Championships are for World Sports Cars and GTS-1 Cars.

1995 Supreme GT Series Results (through October 1)

Date	Race	Winner(s)	Car (Class)
Feb 4-5	24 Hours of Daytona	Paul Newman/Michael Brockman/Tommy Kendall/Mark Martin	Ford Mustang
Mar 18	12 Hours of Sebring	Steve Millen/Johnny O'Connell/John Morton	Nissan 300ZX
Apr 30	Atlanta GP	Irv Hoerr	Oldsmobile
May 21	Halifax	Johnny O'Connell	Nissan 300ZX
May 29	Lime Rock GP	Darin Brassfield	Oldsmobile
June 24	Glen Continental	Irv Hoerr	Oldsmobile
July 16	California GP	Johnny O'Connell	Nissan 300ZX
Aug 13	Mosport 500	Charles Morgan/Rob Morgan	Oldsmobile
Sept 10	Texas World GP	Irv Hoerr	Oldsmobile

Note: GTS-1 cars.

1995 World Sports Car Championship Standings (through October 1)

Driver	Pts
Fermin Velez	235
James Weaver	224
Mauro Baldi	220
Jim Pace	208
Wayne Taylor	203
Butch Leitzinger	157
Roger Mandeville	137
Henry Camferdam	137
Gianpiero Moretti	118
Leigh Miller	111

FIA World Sports Car Racing

The 24 Hours of LeMans

Held at LeMans, France, on June 17-18, 1995, the 24 Hours of LeMans is the most prestigious event in the FIA World Sports Car Championship.

Place	Drivers	Car	Distance
1	Yannick Dalmas, J.J. Lehto, Masanori Sekiya	McLaren F1 GTR	2518.652
2	B. Wollek, M. Andretti, E. Helary	Courage C34	2512.776

The 24 Hours of LeMans *(Cont.)*

Place	Drivers	Car	Distance
3............A.Wallace, J. Bell, D. Bell		McLaren F1 GTR	2502.897
4............R. Bellm, M. Sala, M. Blundell		McLaren F1 GTR	2463.403
5............F. Giroix, O. Grouillard, J. Deletraz		McLaren F1 GTR	2456.877
6............R. Stuck, T. Boutsen, C. Bouchut		Kremer K8	2446.368
7............Y. Yerada, JJ Downing, F. Freon		Mazda DG-3	2388.680
8............K. Takahashi, K. Tsuchiya, A. Iida		Honda NSX GT	2326.861
9............J. Unser, F. Jelinsky, E. Bertaggia		Callaway GT2	2305.956
10..........H. Fukuyama, M. Kondo, S. Kasuya		Nismo GT-R LM	2295.141

Drag Racing

National Hot Rod Association
1995 Results (through September 17)

TOP FUEL

Date	Race, Site	Winner	Time	Speed
Feb 5 ....Winternationals, Pomona, CA	Eddie Hill	4.859	299.50
Feb 19 ....ATSCO Nationals, Phoenix	Larry Dixon	4.821	300.00
Mar 5 ....Slick 50 Nationals, Houston	Mike Dunn	4.857	296.34
Mar 19 ....Gatornationals, Gainesville, FL	Larry Dixon	4.734	302.72
Apr 9 ....Winston Invitational, Rockingham, NC	Scott Kalitta	4.886	288.46
Apr 23 ....Fram Nationals, Atlanta	Cory McClenathan	4.806	298.90
May 7 ....Mid-South Nationals, Memphis	Cory McClenathan	4.810	307.48
May 23 ....Mopar Nationals, Englishtown, NJ	Larry Dixon	4.991	281.77
June 4 ....Virginia Nationals, Richmond	Cory McClenathan	4.962	293.82
June 11 ....Springnationals, Columbus, OH	Scott Kalitta	4.772	305.18
July 2...............Western Auto Nationals, Topeka, KS	Scott Kalitta	4.820	295.27
July 23.............Mile-High Nationals, Denver	Scott Kalitta	4.813	298.30
July 30.............Autolite Nationals, Sonoma, CA	Mike Dunn	5.107	276.83
Aug 6...............Northwest Nationals, Seattle	Ron Capps	4.930	295.76
Aug 20.............Champion Auto Nationals, Brainerd, MN	Mike Dunn	4.952	291.63
Sept 4..............U.S. Nationals, Indianapolis	Larry Dixon	4.931	293.25
Sept 17............Keystone Nationals, Reading, PA	Scott Kalitta	4.801	298.90

FUNNY CAR

Date	Race, Site	Winner	Time	Speed
Feb 5 ....Winternationals, Pomona, CA	Cruz Pedregon	5.304	278.72
Feb 19 ....ATSCO Nationals, Phoenix	John Force	5.057	298.30
Mar 5 ....Slick 50 Nationals, Houston	Al Hofmann	5.207	293.15
Mar 19 ....Gatornationals, Gainesville, FL	John Force	5.347	263.00
Apr 9 ....Winston Invitational, Rockingham, NC	John Force	5.235	283.64
Apr 23 ....Fram Nationals, Atlanta	John Force	5.174	297.22
May 7 ....Mid-South Nationals, Memphis	Gary Clapshaw	5.339	286.89
May 23 ....Mopar Nationals, Englishtown, NJ	Cruz Pedregon	5.246	294.31
June 4 ....Virginia Nationals, Richmond	John Force	5.193	270.59
June 11 ....Springnationals, Columbus, OH	Al Hofmann	5.125	299.90
July 2...............Western Auto Nationals, Topeka, KS	Cruz Pedregon	5.912	273.39
July 23.............Mile-High Nationals, Denver	John Force	5.258	291.16
July 30.............Autolite Nationals, Sonoma, CA	Al Hofmann	5.107	276.83
Aug 6...............Northwest Nationals, Seattle	Al Hofmann	5.200	285.80
Aug 20.............Champion Auto Nationals, Brainerd, MN	John Force	5.284	291.92
Sept 4..............U.S. Nationals, Indianapolis	Cruz Pedregon	5.075	304.67
Sept 17............Keystone Nationals, Reading, PA	Chuck Etchells	6.121	264.31

National Hot Rod Association *(Cont.)*

PRO STOCK

Date	Race, Site	Winner	Time	Speed
Feb 5	Winternationals, Pomona, CA	Darrell Alderman	7.054	196.03
Feb 19	ATSCO Nationals, Phoenix	Darrell Alderman	7.073	194.46
Mar 5	Slick 50 Nationals, Houston	Scott Geoffrion	7.062	196.03
Mar 19	Gatornationals, Gainesville, FL	Darrell Alderman	7.031	196.29
Apr 9	Winston Invitational, Rockingham, NC	Darrell Alderman	7.037	196.93
Apr 23	Fram Nationals, Atlanta	Mark Osborne	7.141	194.17
May 7	Mid-South Nationals, Memphis	Mark Pawuk	7.195	192.80
May 23	Mopar Nationals, Englishtown, NJ	Bob Glidden	7.117	194.42
June 4	Virginia Nationals, Richmond	Warren Johnson	7.062	196.03
June 11	Springnationals, Columbus, OH	Steve Schmidt	7.125	193.21
July 2	Western Auto Nationals, Topeka, KS	Warren Johnson	7.069	194.46
July 23	Mile-High Nationals, Denver	Kurt Johnson	7.491	183.29
July 30	Autolite Nationals, Sonoma, CA	Jim Yates	7.143	193.79
Aug 6	Northwest Nationals, Seattle	Warren Johnson	7.022	197.23
Aug 20	Champion Auto Nationals, Brainerd, MN	Warren Johnson	7.202	193.05
Sept 4	U.S. Nationals, Indianapolis	Warren Johnson	7.059	197.02
Sept 17	Keystone Nationals, Reading, PA	Warren Johnson	7.060	195.43

1994 Standings

TOP FUEL

Driver	Wins	Pts
Scott Kalitta	5	13,600
Don Prudhomme	3	12,090
Cory McClenathan	2	10,924
Connie Kalitta	3	10,582
Joe Amato	1	10,244
Kenny Bernstein	1	9,646
Mike Dunn	—	8,638
Pat Austin	1	8,588
Tommy Johnson Jr	1	8,414
Shelly Anderson	1	7,936

FUNNY CAR

Driver	Wins	Pts
John Force	10	16,776
Cruz Pedregon	3	12,512
Al Hofmann	1	11,496
Chuck Etchells	—	10,852
K. C. Spurlock	1	9,388

FUNNY CAR *(Cont.)*

Driver	Wins	Pts
Gordie Bonin	2	8,302
Jim Epler	—	7,922
Dean Skuza	—	7,832
Gary Bolger	—	7,824
Kenji Okazaki	—	7,570

PRO STOCK

Driver	Wins	Pts
Darrell Alderman	5	16,034
Scott Geoffrion	6	15,252
Warren Johnson	4	13,918
Jim Yates	1	11,382
Kurt Johnson	—	10,450
Larry Morgan	1	8,866
Steve Schmidt	1	8,340
Mark Pawuk	—	7,908
Mark Osborne	—	7,450
Bob Glidden	—	6,600

CART Racing

Indianapolis 500

First held in 1911, the Indy 500—200 laps of the 2.5-mile Indianapolis Motor Speedway Track (called the Brickyard in honor of its original pavement)—has grown to become the most famous auto race in the world. Held on Memorial Day weekend, it annually draws the largest crowd of any sporting event in the world.

Year	Winner (Start Position)	Car	Avg MPH	Pole Winner	MPH
1911	Ray Harroun (28)	Marmon Wasp	74.590	Lewis Strang	Awarded pole
1912	Joe Dawson (7)	National	78.720	Gil Anderson	Drew pole
1913	Jules Goux (7)	Peugeot	75.930	Caleb Bragg	Drew pole
1914	Rene Thomas (15)	Delage	82.470	Jean Chassagne	Drew pole
1915	Ralph DePalma (2)	Mercedes	89.840	Howard Wilcox	98.90
1916	Dario Resta (4)	Peugeot	84.000	John Aitken	96.69
1917-18	No race				
1919	Howard Wilcox (2)	Peugeot	88.050	Rene Thomas	104.78
1920	Gaston Chevrolet (6)	Monroe	88.620	Ralph DePalma	99.15
1921	Tommy Milton (20)	Frontenac	89.620	Ralph DePalma	100.75
1922	Jimmy Murphy (1)	Murphy Special	94.480	Jimmy Murphy	100.50
1923	Tommy Milton (1)	H.C.S. Special	90.950	Tommy Milton	108.17
1924	L. L. Corum Joe Boyer (21)	Duesenberg Special	98.230	Jimmy Murphy	108.037
1925	Peter DePaolo (2)	Duesenberg Special	101.130	Leon Duray	113.196
1926	Frank Lockhart (20)	Miller Special	95.904	Earl Cooper	111.735
1927	George Souders (22)	Duesenberg	97.545	Frank Lockhart	120.100
1928	Louis Meyer (13)	Miller Special	99.482	Leon Duray	122.391
1929	Ray Keech (6)	Simplex Piston Ring Special	97.585	Cliff Woodbury	120.599
1930	Billy Arnold (1)	Miller Hartz Special	100.448	Billy Arnold	113.268
1931	Louis Schneider (13)	Bowes Seal-Fast Special	96.629	Russ Snowberger	112.796
1932	Fred Frame (27)	Miller Hartz Special	104.144	Lou Moore	117.363
1933	Louis Meyer (6)	Tydol Special	104.162	Bill Cummings	118.524
1934	Bill Cummings (10)	Boyle Products Special	104.863	Kelly Petillo	119.329
1935	Kelly Petillo (22)	Gilmore Speedway Special	106.240	Rex Mays	120.736
1936	Louis Meyer (28)	Ring-Free Special	109.069	Rex Mays	119.664
1937	Wilbur Shaw (2)	Shaw-Gilmore Special	113.580	Bill Cummings	123.343
1938	Floyd Roberts (1)	Burd Piston Ring Special	117.200	Floyd Roberts	125.681
1939	Wilbur Shaw (3)	Boyle Special	115.035	Jimmy Snyder	130.138
1940	Wilbur Shaw (2)	Boyle Special	114.277	Rex Mays	127.850
1941	Floyd Davis Mauri Rose (17)	Noc-Out Hose Clamp Special	115.117	Mauri Rose	128.691
1942-45	No race				
1946	George Robson (15)	Thorne Engineering Special	114.820	Cliff Bergere	126.471
1947	Mauri Rose (3)	Blue Crown Spark Plug Special	116.338	Ted Horn	126.564
1948	Mauri Rose (3)	Blue Crown Spark Plug Special	119.814	Rex Mays	130.577
1949	Bill Holland (4)	Blue Crown Spark Plug Special	121.327	Duke Nalon	132.939
1950	Johnnie Parsons (5)	Wynn's Friction Proofing	124.002	Walt Faulkner	134.343
1951	Lee Wallard (2)	Belanger Special	126.244	Duke Nalon	136.498
1952	Troy Ruttman (7)	Agajanian Special	128.922	Fred Agabashian	138.010
1953	Bill Vukovich (1)	Fuel Injection Special	128.740	Bill Vukovich	138.392
1954	Bill Vukovich (19)	Fuel Injection Special	130.840	Jack McGrath	141.033
1955	Bob Sweikert (14)	John Zink Special	128.209	Jerry Hoyt	140.045
1956	Pat Flaherty (1)	John Zink Special	128.490	Pat Flaherty	145.596
1957	Sam Hanks (13)	Belond Exhaust Special	135.601	Pat O'Connor	143.948
1958	Jim Bryan (7)	Belond AP Parts Special	133.791	Dick Rathmann	145.974
1959	Rodger Ward (6)	Leader Card 500 Roadster	135.857	Johnny Thomson	145.908
1960	Jim Rathmann (2)	Ken-Paul Special	138.767	Eddie Sachs	146.592
1961	A. J. Foyt (7)	Bowes Seal-Fast Special	139.130	Eddie Sachs	147.481
1962	Rodger Ward (2)	Leader Card 500 Roadster	140.293	Parnelli Jones	150.370
1963	Parnelli Jones (1)	Agajanian-Willard Special	143.137	Parnelli Jones	151.153
1964	A. J. Foyt (5)	Sheraton-Thompson Special	147.350	Jim Clark	158.828
1965	Jim Clark (2)	Lotus Ford	150.686	A. J. Foyt	161.233
1966	Graham Hill (15)	American Red Ball Special	144.317	Mario Andretti	165.899
1967	A. J. Foyt (4)	Sheraton-Thompson Special	151.207	Mario Andretti	168.982
1968	Bobby Unser (3)	Rislone Special	152.882	Joe Leonard	171.559
1969	Mario Andretti (2)	STP Oil Treatment Special	156.867	A. J. Foyt	170.568
1970	Al Unser (1)	Johnny Lightning 500 Special	155.749	Al Unser	170.221

Indianapolis 500 *(Cont.)*

Year	Winner (Start Position)	Car	Avg MPH	Pole Winner	MPH
1971	Al Unser (5)	Johnny Lightning Special	157.735	Peter Revson	178.696
1972	Mark Donohue (3)	Sunoco McLaren	162.962	Bobby Unser	195.940
1973	Gordon Johncock (11)	STP Double Oil Filters	159.036	Johnny Rutherford	198.413
1974	Johnny Rutherford (25)	McLaren	158.589	A. J. Foyt	191.632
1975	Bobby Unser (3)	Jorgensen Eagle	149.213	A. J. Foyt	193.976
1976	Johnny Rutherford (1)	Hy-Gain McLaren/Goodyear	148.725	Johnny Rutherford	188.957
1977	A. J. Foyt (4)	Gilmore Racing Team	161.331	Tom Sneva	198.884
1978	Al Unser (5)	FNCTC Chaparral Lola	161.361	Tom Sneva	202.156
1979	Rick Mears (1)	The Gould Charge	158.899	Rick Mears	193.736
1980	Johnny Rutherford (1)	Pennzoil Chaparral	142.862	Johnny Rutherford	192.256
1981	Bobby Unser (1)	Norton Spirit Penske PC-9B	139.084	Bobby Unser	200.546
1982	Gordon Johncock (5)	STP Oil Treatment	162.026	Rick Mears	207.004
1983	Tom Sneva (4)	Texaco Star	162.117	Teo Fabi	207.395
1984	Rick Mears (3)	Pennzoil Z-7	163.612	Tom Sneva	210.029
1985	Danny Sullivan (8)	Miller American Special	152.982	Pancho Carter	212.583
1986	Bobby Rahal (4)	Budweiser/Truesports/March	170.722	Rick Mears	216.828
1987	Al Unser (20)	Cummins Holset Turbo	162.175	Mario Andretti	215.390
1988	Rick Mears (1)	Penske-Chevrolet	144.809	Rick Mears	219.198
1989	Emerson Fittipaldi (3)	Penske-Chevrolet	167.581	Rick Mears	223.885
1990	Arie Luyendyk (3)	Domino's Pizza Chevrolet	185.981*	Emerson Fittipaldi	225.301†
1991	Rick Mears (1)	Penske-Chevrolet	176.457	Rick Mears	224.113
1992	Al Unser Jr (12)	G92-Chevrolet	134.477	Roberto Guerrero	232.482
1993	Emerson Fittipaldi (9)	Penske-Chevrolet	157.207	Arie Luyendyk	223.967
1994	Al Unser Jr. (1)	Penske-Mercedes	160.872	Al Unser Jr.	228.011
1995	Jacques Villeneuve (5)	Reynard-Ford	153.616	Scott Brayton	231.616

*Track record, winning time. †Track record, qualifying time.

Indianapolis 500 Rookie of the Year Award

1952 ... Art Cross	1968 ... Billy Vukovich	1984 ... Michael Andretti
1953 ... Jimmy Daywalt	1969 ... Mark Donohue*	Roberto Guerrero
1954 ... Larry Crockett	1970 ... Donnie Allison	1985 ... Arie Luyendyk
1955 ... Al Herman	1971 ... Denny Zimmerman	1986 ... Randy Lanier
1956 ... Bob Veith	1972 ... Mike Hiss	1987 ... Fabrizio Barbazza
1957 ... Don Edmunds	1973 ... Graham McRae	1988 ... Billy Vukovich III
1958 ... George Amick	1974 ... Pancho Carter	1989 ... Bernard Jourdain
1959 ... Bobby Grim	1975 ... Bill Puterbaugh	Scott Pruett
1960 ... Jim Hurtubise	1976 ... Vern Schuppan	1990 ... Eddie Cheever
1961 ... Parnelli Jones*	1977 ... Jerry Sneva	1991 ... Jeff Andretti
Bobby Marshman	1978 ... Rick Mears*	1992 ... Lyn St. James
1962 ... Jimmy McElreath	Larry Rice	1993 ... Nigel Mansell
1963 ... Jim Clark*	1979 ... Howdy Holmes	1994 ... Jacques Villeneuve*
1964 ... Johnny White	1980 ... Tim Richmond	1995 ... Gil de Ferran
1965 ... Mario Andretti*	1981 ... Josele Garza	
1966 ... Jackie Stewart	1982 ... Jim Hickman	
1967 ... Denis Hulme	1983 ... Teo Fabi	*Future winner of Indy 500.

Indy Car Champions

From 1909 to 1955, this championship was awarded by the American Automobile Association (AAA), and from 1956 to 1979 by United States Auto Club (USAC). Since 1979, Championship Auto Racing Teams (CART) has conducted the championship.

1909 ... George Robertson	1925 ... Peter DePaolo	1941 ... Rex Mays
1910 ... Ray Harroun	1926 ... Harry Hartz	1942-45 ... No racing
1911 ... Ralph Mulford	1927 ... Peter DePaolo	1946 ... Ted Horn
1912 ... Ralph DePalma	1928 ... Louis Meyer	1947 ... Ted Horn
1913 ... Earl Cooper	1929 ... Louis Meyer	1948 ... Ted Horn
1914 ... Ralph DePalma	1930 ... Billy Arnold	1949 ... Johnnie Parsons
1915 ... Earl Cooper	1931 ... Louis Schneider	1950 ... Henry Banks
1916 ... Dario Resta	1932 ... Bob Carey	1951 ... Tony Bettenhausen
1917 ... Earl Cooper	1933 ... Louis Meyer	1952 ... Chuck Stevenson
1918 ... Ralph Mulford	1934 ... Bill Cummings	1953 ... Sam Hanks
1919 ... Howard Wilcox	1935 ... Kelly Petillo	1954 ... Jimmy Bryan
1920 ... Tommy Milton	1936 ... Mauri Rose	1955 ... Bob Sweikert
1921 ... Tommy Milton	1937 ... Wilbur Shaw	1956 ... Jimmy Bryan
1922 ... Jimmy Murphy	1938 ... Floyd Roberts	1957 ... Jimmy Bryan
1923 ... Eddie Hearne	1939 ... Wilbur Shaw	1958 ... Tony Bettenhausen
1924 ... Jimmy Murphy	1940 ... Rex Mays	1959 ... Rodger Ward

Indy Car Champions (Cont.)

1960 ....A. J. Foyt	1973 ....Roger McCluskey	1985 ....Al Unser
1961 ....A. J. Foyt	1974 ....Bobby Unser	1986 ....Bobby Rahal
1962 ....Rodger Ward	1975 ....A. J. Foyt	1987 ....Bobby Rahal
1963 ....A. J. Foyt	1976 ....Gordon Johncock	1988 ....Danny Sullivan
1964 ....A. J. Foyt	1977 ....Tom Sneva	1989 ....Emerson Fittipaldi
1965 ....Mario Andretti	1978 ....Tom Sneva	1990 ....Al Unser Jr
1966 ....Mario Andretti	1979 ....A. J. Foyt	1991 ....Michael Andretti
1967 ....A. J. Foyt	1979 ....Rick Mears	1992 ....Bobby Rahal
1968 ....Bobby Unser	1980 ....Johnny Rutherford	1993 ....Nigel Mansell
1969 ....Mario Andretti	1981 ....Rick Mears	1994 ....Al Unser Jr.
1970 ....Al Unser	1982 ....Rick Mears	1995 ....Jacques Villeneuve
1971 ....Joe Leonard	1983 ....Al Unser	
1972 ....Joe Leonard	1984 ....Mario Andretti	

Alltime Indy Car Leaders

WINS		WINNINGS ($)		POLE POSITIONS	
A. J. Foyt	67	*Al Unser Jr	15,240,093	Mario Andretti	67
Mario Andretti	52	*Bobby Rahal	14,044,508	A. J. Foyt	53
Al Unser	39	*Emerson Fittipaldi	12,937,375	Bobby Unser	49
Bobby Unser	35	*Michael Andretti	11,917,869	Rick Mears	38
*Al Unser Jr.	31	Mario Andretti	11,279,654	*Michael Andretti	30
*Michael Andretti	30	Rick Mears	11,050,807	Al Unser	27
Rick Mears	29	Danny Sullivan	8,254,673	Johnny Rutherford	23
Johnny Rutherford	27	*Arie Luyendyk	7,092,188	Gordon Johncock	20
Rodger Ward	26	Al Unser	6,740,843	Rex Mays	19
*Bobby Rahal	24	*Raul Boesel	5,544,137	*Danny Sullivan	19
Ralph DePalma	24	A. J. Foyt	5,357,589	*Bobby Rahal	18
Tommy Milton	23	*Scott Brayton	4,807,214	*Emerson Fittipaldi	17
Tony Bettenhausen	22	*Teo Fabi	4,573,131	Tony Bettenhausen	14
*Emerson Fittipaldi	22	Tom Sneva	4,392,993	Don Branson	14
Earl Cooper	20	*Roberto Guerrero	4,275,163	Tom Sneva	14
Jimmy Murphy	19	Johnny Rutherford	4,209,232	Parnelli Jones	12
Jimmy Bryan	19	*Scott Goodyear	4,133,201	Danny Ongais	11
Ralph Mulford	17	*Jaques Villeneuve	3,748,982	Rodger Ward	11
*Danny Sullivan	17	*Paul Tracy	3,584,020		
		Gordon Johncock	3,431,414	Four tied with 10.	

*Active driver.

Note: Leaders through September 11, 1995.

NASCAR Racing

Stock Car Racing's Major Events

Winston offers a $1 million bonus to any driver to win 3 of NASCAR's top 4 events in the same season. These races are the richest (Daytona 500), the fastest (Talladega 500), the longest (World 600 at Charlotte) and the oldest (Southern 500 at Darlington). These events form the backbone of NASCAR racing. Only 3 drivers, LeeRoy Yarbrough (1969), David Pearson (1976) and Bill Elliott (1985), have scored the 3-track hat trick.

Daytona 500

Year	Winner	Car	Avg MPH	Pole Winner	MPH
1959	Lee Petty	Oldsmobile	135.520	Cotton Owens	143.198
1960	Junior Johnson	Chevrolet	124.740	Fireball Roberts	151.556
1961	Marvin Panch	Pontiac	149.601	Fireball Roberts	155.709
1962	Fireball Roberts	Pontiac	152.529	Fireball Roberts	156.995
1963	Tiny Lund	Ford	151.566	Johnny Rutherford	165.183
1964	Richard Petty	Plymouth	154.345	Paul Goldsmith	174.910
1965	Fred Lorenzen	Ford	141.539	Darel Dieringer	171.151
1966	Richard Petty	Plymouth	160.627	Richard Petty	175.165
1967	Mario Andretti	Ford	149.926	Curtis Turner	180.831
1968	Cale Yarborough	Mercury	143.251	Cale Yarborough	189.222
1969	LeeRoy Yarbrough	Ford	157.950	David Pearson	190.029
1970	Pete Hamilton	Plymouth	149.601	Cale Yarborough	194.015
1971	Richard Petty	Plymouth	144.462	A. J. Foyt	182.744
1972	A. J. Foyt	Mercury	161.550	Bobby Isaac	186.632

Daytona 500 *(Cont.)*

Year	Winner	Car	Avg MPH	Pole Winner	MPH
1973	Richard Petty	Dodge	157.205	Buddy Baker	185.662
1974	Richard Petty	Dodge	140.894	David Pearson	185.017
1975	Benny Parsons	Chevrolet	153.649	Donnie Allison	185.827
1976	David Pearson	Mercury	152.181	A. J. Foyt	185.943
1977	Cale Yarborough	Chevrolet	153.218	Donnie Allison	188.048
1978	Bobby Allison	Ford	159.730	Cale Yarborough	187.536
1979	Richard Petty	Oldsmobile	143.977	Buddy Baker	196.049
1980	Buddy Baker	Oldsmobile	177.602*	A. J. Foyt	195.020
1981	Richard Petty	Buick	169.651	Bobby Allison	194.624
1982	Bobby Allison	Buick	153.991	Benny Parsons	196.317
1983	Cale Yarborough	Pontiac	155.979	Ricky Rudd	198.864
1984	Cale Yarborough	Chevrolet	150.994	Cale Yarborough	201.848
1985	Bill Elliott	Ford	172.265	Bill Elliott	205.114
1986	Geoff Bodine	Chevrolet	148.124	Bill Elliott	205.039
1987	Bill Elliott	Ford	176.263	Bill Elliott	210.364†
1988	Bobby Allison	Buick	137.531	Ken Schrader	193.823
1989	Darrell Waltrip	Chevrolet	148.466	Ken Schrader	196.996
1990	Derrike Cope	Chevrolet	165.761	Ken Schrader	196.515
1991	Earnie Irvan	Chevrolet	148.148	Davey Allison	195.955
1992	Davey Allison	Ford	160.256	Sterling Marlin	192.213
1993	Dale Jarrett	Chevrolet	154.972	Kyle Petty	189.426
1994	Sterling Marlin	Chevrolet	156.931	Loy Allen Jr.	190.158
1995	Sterling Marlin	Chevrolet	141.710	Dale Jarrett	193.498

*Track record, winning time. †Track record, qualifying time. Note: The Daytona 500, held annually in February, now opens the NASCAR season with 200 laps around the high-banked Daytona, FL, superspeedway.

World 600

Year	Winner	Car	Avg MPH	Pole Winner
1960	Joe Lee Johnson	Chevrolet	107.752	J.L. Johnson
1961	David Pearson	Pontiac	111.634	Richard Petty
1962	Nelson Stacy	Ford	125.552	Fireball Roberts
1963	Fred Lorenzen	Ford	132.418	Junior Johnson
1964	Jim Paschal	Plymouth	125.772	Junior Johnson
1965	Fred Lorenzen	Ford	121.772	Fred Lorenzon
1966	Marvin Panch	Plymouth	135.042	Paul Goldsmith
1967	Jim Paschal	Plymouth	135.832	Cale Yarborough
1968	Buddy Baker	Dodge	104.207	Donnie Allison
1969	Lee Yarbrough	Mercury	134.631	Donnie Allison
1970	Donnie Allison	Ford	129.680	Bobby Isaac
1971	Bobby Allison	Mercury	140.442	Charlie Glotzbach
1972	Buddy Baker	Dodge	142.255	Bobby Allison
1973	Buddy Baker	Dodge	134.890	Buddy Baker
1974	David Pearson	Mercury	135.720	David Pearson
1975	Richard Petty	Dodge	145.327	David Pearson
1976	David Pearson	Mercury	137.352	David Pearson
1977	Richard Petty	Dodge	137.636	David Pearson
1978	Darrell Waltrip	Chevrolet	138.355	David Pearson
1979	Darrell Waltrip	Chevrolet	136.674	Neil Bonnet
1980	Benny Parsons	Chevrolet	119.265	Cale Yarborough
1981	Bobby Allison	Buick	129.326	Neil Bonnet
1982	Neil Bonnett	Ford	130.508	David Pearson
1983	Neil Bonnett	Chevrolet	140.406	Buddy Baker
1984	Bobby Allison	Buick	129.233	Harry Gant
1985	Darrell Waltrip	Chevrolet	141.807	Bill Elliott
1986	Dale Earnhardt	Chevrolet	140.406	Geoff Bodine
1987	Kyle Petty	Ford	131.483	Bill Elliott
1988	Darrell Waltrip	Chevrolet	124.460	Davey Allison
1989	Darrell Waltrip	Chevrolet	144.077	Alan Kulwicki
1990	Rusty Wallace	Pontiac	137.650	Ken Schrader
1991	Davey Allison	Ford	138.951	Mark Martin
1992	Dale Earnhardt	Chevrolet	132.980	Bill Elliott
1993	Dale Earnhardt	Chevrolet	145.504	Ken Schrader
1994	Jeff Gordon	Chevrolet	139.445	Jeff Gordon
1995	Bobby Labonte	Chevrolet	151.952	Jeff Gordon

Note: Held at the 1.5-mile Charlotte, NC, Motor Speedway on Memorial Day weekend.

Talladega 500

Year	Winner	Car	Avg MPH	Pole Winner	MPH
1969	Richard Brickhouse	Dodge	153.778	Charlie Glotzbach	199.466
1970	Pete Hamilton	Plymouth	158.517	Bobby Isaac	186.834
1971	Bobby Allison	Mercury	145.945	Davey Allison	187.323
1972	James Hylton	Mercury	148.728	Bobby Isaac	190.677
1973	Dick Brooks	Plymouth	145.454	Bobby Allison	187.064
1974	Richard Petty	Dodge	148.637	David Pearson	184.926
1975	Buddy Baker	Ford	130.892	Dave Marcis	191.340
1976	Dave Marcis	Dodge	157.547	Dave Marcis	190.651
1977	Davey Allison	Chevrolet	162.524	Benny Parsons	192.682
1978	Lennie Pond	Olds	174.700	Cale Yarborough	192.917
1979	Darrell Waltrip	Olds	161.229	Neil Bonnet	193.600
1980	Neil Bonnet	Mercury	166.894	Buddy Baker	198.545
1981	Ron Bouchard	Buick	156.737	Harry Gant	195.897
1982	Darrell Waltrip	Buick	168.157	Geoff Bodine	199.400
1983	Dale Earnhardt	Ford	170.611	Cale Yarborough	201.744
1984	Dale Earnhardt	Chevrolet	155.485	Cale Yarborough	202.474
1985	Cale Yarborough	Ford	148.772	Bill Elliott	207.578
1986	Bobby Hillin	Buick	151.552	Bill Elliott	209.005
1987	Bill Elliott	Ford	171.293	Bill Elliott	203.827
1988	Ken Schrader	Chevrolet	154.505	Darrell Waltrip	196.274
1989	Terry Labonte	Ford	157.354	Mark Martin	194.800
1990	Dale Earnhardt	Chevrolet	174.430	Dale Earnhardt	192.513
1991	Harry Gant	Olds	165.620	Sterling Marlin	192.085
1992	Ernie Irvan	Chevrolet	176.309	Sterling Marlin	190.586
1993	Dale Earnhardt	Chevrolet	153.858	Bill Elliott	192.397
1994	Jimmy Spencer	Ford	163.217	Dale Earnhardt	193.470
1995	Sterling Marlin	Chevrolet	173.188	Sterling Marlin	194.212

Note: Held at the 2.66-mile high-banked Talladega, AL, Superspeedway on the last weekend in July.

Southern 500

Year	Winner	Car	Avg MPH	Pole Winner
1950	Johnny Mantz	Plymouth	76.260	Wally Campbell
1951	Herb Thomas	Hudson	76.900	Marshall Teague
1952	Fonty Flock	Olds	74.510	Dick Rathman
1953	Buck Baker	Olds	92.780	Fonty Flock
1954	Herb Thomas	Hudson	94.930	Buck Baker
1955	Herb Thomas	Chevrolet	92.281	Tim Flock
1956	Curtis Turner	Ford	95.067	Buck Baker
1957	Speedy Thompson	Chevrolet	100.100	Paul Goldsmith
1958	Fireball Roberts	Chevrolet	102.590	Fireball Roberts
1959	Jim Reed	Chevrolet	111.836	Fireball Roberts
1960	Buck Baker	Pontiac	105.901	Cotton Owens
1961	Nelson Stacy	Ford	117.880	Fireball Roberts
1962	Larry Frank	Ford	117.965	Fireball Roberts
1963	Fireball Roberts	Ford	129.784	Fireball Roberts
1964	Buck Baker	Dodge	117.757	Richard Petty
1965	Ned Jarrett	Ford	115.924	Junior Johnson
1966	Darel Dieringer	Mercury	114.830	Lee Yarborough
1967	Richard Petty	Plymouth	131.933	David Pearson
1968	Cale Yarborough	Mercury	126.132	Charlie Glotzbach
1969	Lee Yarbrough	Ford	105.612	Cale Yarborough
1970	Buddy Baker	Dodge	128.817	David Pearson
1971	Bobby Allison	Mercury	131.398	Bobby Allison
1972	Bobby Allison	Chevrolet	128.124	David Pearson
1973	Cale Yarborough	Chevrolet	134.033	David Pearson
1974	Cale Yarborough	Chevrolet	111.075	Richard Petty
1975	Bobby Allison	Matador	116.825	David Pearson
1976	David Pearson	Mercury	120.534	David Pearson
1977	David Pearson	Mercury	106.797	Darrell Waltrip
1978	Cale Yarborough	Olds	116.828	David Pearson
1979	David Pearson	Chevrolet	126.259	Bobby Allison
1980	Terry Labonte	Chevrolet	115.210	Darrell Waltrip
1981	Neil Bonnett	Ford	126.410	Harry Gant
1982	Cale Yarborough	Buick	126.703	David Pearson
1983	Bobby Allison	Buick	123.343	Neil Bonnett

Southern 500 *(Cont.)*

Year	Winner	Car	Avg MPH	Pole Winner
1984	Harry Gant	Chevrolet	128.270	Harry Gant
1985	Bill Elliott	Ford	121.254	Bill Elliott
1986	Tim Richmond	Chevrolet	121.068	Tim Richmond
1987	Dale Earnhardt	Chevrolet	115.520	Davey Allison
1988	Bill Elliott	Ford	128.297	Bill Elliott
1989	Dale Earnhardt	Chevrolet	135.462	Alan Kulwicki
1990	Dale Earnhardt	Chevrolet	123.141	Dale Earnhardt
1991	Harry Gant	Olds	133.508	Davey Allison
1992	Darrell Waltrip	Chevrolet	129.114	Sterling Marlin
1993	Mark Martin	Ford	137.932	Ken Schrader
1994	Bill Elliott	Ford	127.915	Geoff Bodine
1995	Jeff Gordon	Chevrolet	121.231	John Andretti

Note: Held at the 1.366-mile Darlington, SC, International Raceway on Labor Day weekend.

Winston Cup NASCAR Champions

Year	Driver	Car	Wins	Poles	Winnings ($)
1949	Red Byron	Oldsmobile	2	0	5,800
1950	Bill Rexford	Oldsmobile	1	0	6,175
1951	Herb Thomas	Hudson	7	4	18,200
1952	Tim Flock	Hudson	8	4	20,210
1953	Herb Thomas	Hudson	11	10	27,300
1954	Lee Petty	Dodge	7	3	26,706
1955	Tim Flock	Chrysler	18	19	33,750
1956	Buck Baker	Chrysler	14	12	29,790
1957	Buck Baker	Chevrolet	10	5	24,712
1958	Lee Petty	Olds	7	4	20,600
1959	Lee Petty	Plymouth	10	2	45,570
1960	Rex White	Chevrolet	6	3	45,260
1961	Ned Jarrett	Chevrolet	1	4	27,285
1962	Joe Weatherly	Pontiac	9	6	56,110
1963	Joe Weatherly	Mercury	3	6	58,110
1964	Richard Petty	Plymouth	9	8	98,810
1965	Ned Jarrett	Ford	13	9	77,966
1966	David Pearson	Dodge	14	7	59,205
1967	Richard Petty	Plymouth	27	18	130,275
1968	David Pearson	Ford	16	12	118,824
1969	David Pearson	Ford	11	14	183,700
1970	Bobby Isaac	Dodge	11	13	121,470
1971	Richard Petty	Plymouth	21	9	309,225
1972	Richard Petty	Plymouth	8	3	227,015
1973	Benny Parsons	Chevrolet	1	0	114,345
1974	Richard Petty	Dodge	10	7	299,175
1975	Richard Petty	Dodge	13	3	378,865
1976	Cale Yarborough	Chevrolet	9	2	387,173
1977	Cale Yarborough	Chevrolet	9	3	477,499
1978	Cale Yarborough	Oldsmobile	10	8	530,751
1979	Richard Petty	Chevrolet	5	1	531,292
1980	Dale Earnhardt	Chevrolet	5	0	588,926
1981	Darrell Waltrip	Buick	12	11	693,342
1982	Darrell Waltrip	Buick	12	7	873,118
1983	Bobby Allison	Buick	6	0	828,355
1984	Terry Labonte	Chevrolet	2	2	713,010
1985	Darrell Waltrip	Chevrolet	3	4	1,318,735
1986	Dale Earnhardt	Chevrolet	5	1	1,783,880
1987	Dale Earnhardt	Chevrolet	11	1	2,099,243
1988	Bill Elliott	Ford	6	6	1,574,639
1989	Rusty Wallace	Pontiac	6	4	2,247,950
1990	Dale Earnhardt	Chevrolet	9	4	3,083,056
1991	Dale Earnhardt	Chevrolet	4	0	2,396,685
1992	Alan Kulwicki	Ford	2	6	2,322,561
1993	Dale Earnhardt	Chevrolet	6	2	3,353,789
1994	Dale Earnhardt	Chevrolet	4	2	3,400,733

Alltime NASCAR Leaders

WINS		WINNINGS ($)		POLE POSITIONS	
Richard Petty	200	Dale Earnhardt*	24,754,799	Richard Petty	127
David Pearson	105	Bill Elliott*	15,229,173	David Pearson	113
Bobby Allison	84	Darrell Waltrip*	14,258,959	Cale Yarborough	70
Darrell Waltrip*	84	Rusty Wallace*	12,245,778	Darrell Waltrip*	58
Cale Yarborough	83	Terry Labonte*	9,990,201	Bobby Allison	57
Dale Earnhardt*	66	Ricky Rudd*	9,567,960	Bobby Isaac	51
Lee Petty	54	Mark Martin*	9,375,069	Bill Elliott*	48
Ned Jarrett	50	Geoff Bodine*	9,178,233	Junior Johnson	47
Junior Johnson	50	Harry Gant	8,438,094	Buck Baker	44
Herb Thomas	49	Richard Petty	7,757,964	Buddy Baker	40
Buck Baker	46	Ken Schrader*	7,533,412	Geoff Bodine*	40
Rusty Wallace*	41	Bobby Allison	7,102,233	Herb Thomas	38
Tim Flock	40	Kyle Petty*	7,085,574	Tim Flock	37
Bill Elliott*	40	Sterling Marlin*	6,607,840	Fireball Roberts	37
Bobby Isaac	37	Morgan Shepherd*	6,466,832	Ned Jarrett	36
Fireball Roberts	32	Davey Allison	6,210,589	Rex White	36

*Active drivers.

Note: NASCAR Leaders through September 17,1995.

Formula One/Grand Prix Racing

World Driving Champions

Year	Winner	Car	Year	Winner	Car
1950	Guiseppe Farina, Italy	Alfa Romeo	1969	Jackie Stewart, Scotland	Matra-Ford
1951	Juan-Manuel Fangio, Argentina	Alfa Romeo	1970	Jochen Rindt, Austria*	Lotus-Ford
1952	Alberto Ascari, Italy	Ferrari	1971	Jackie Stewart, Scotland	Tyrell-Ford
1953	Alberto Ascari, Italy	Ferrari	1972	Emerson Fittipaldi, Brazil	Lotus-Ford
1954	Juan-Manuel Fangio, Argentina	Maserati/ Mercedes	1973	Jackie Stewart, Scotland	Tyrell-Ford
			1974	Emerson Fittipaldi, Brazil	McLaren-Ford
1955	Juan-Manuel Fangio, Argentina	Mercedes	1975	Niki Lauda, Austria	Ferrari
			1976	James Hunt, England	McLaren-Ford
1956	Juan-Manuel Fangio, Argentina	Ferrari	1977	Niki Lauda, Austria	Ferrari
			1978	Mario Andretti, U.S.	Lotus-Ford
1957	Juan-Manuel Fangio, Argentina	Maserati	1979	Jody Scheckter, S Africa	Ferrari
			1980	Alan Jones, Australia	Williams-Ford
1958	Mike Hawthorne, England	Ferrari	1981	Nelson Piquet, Brazil	Brabham-Ford
1959	Jack Brabham, Australia	Cooper-Climax	1982	Keke Rosberg, Finland	Williams-Ford
1960	Jack Brabham, Australia	Cooper-Climax	1983	Nelson Piquet, Brazil	Brabham-BMW
1961	Phil Hill, United States	Ferrari	1984	Niki Lauda, Austria	McLaren-Porsche
1962	Graham Hill, England	BRM	1985	Alain Prost, France	McLaren-Porsche
1963	Jim Clark, Scotland	Lotus-Climax	1986	Alain Prost, France	McLaren-Porsche
1964	John Surtees, England	Ferrari	1987	Nelson Piquet, Brazil	Williams-Honda
1965	Jim Clark, Scotland	Lotus-Climax	1988	Ayrton Senna, Brazil	McLaren-Honda
1966	Jack Brabham, Australia	Brabham-Climax	1989	Alain Prost, France	McLaren-Honda
1967	Denis Hulme, New Zealand	Brabham-Repco	1990	Ayrton Senna, Brazil	McLaren-Honda
			1991	Ayrton Senna, Brazil	McLaren-Honda
1968	Graham Hill, England	Lotus-Ford	1992	Nigel Mansell, Britain	Williams-Renault
			1993	Alain Prost, France	Williams-Renault
			1994	Michael Schumacher, Germ	Benetton-Ford

*The championship was awarded after Rindt was killed in practice for the Italian Grand Prix.

Alltime Grand Prix Winners

Driver	Wins	Driver	Wins
Alain Prost, France	51	Juan-Manuel Fangio, Argentina	24
Ayrton Senna, Brazil	41	Nelson Piquet, Brazil	20
Jackie Stewart, Scotland	27	Stirling Moss, England	16
Nigel Mansell, England*	29	Michael Schumacher, Germany*	17
Jim Clark, Scotland	25	Jack Brabham, Australia	14
Niki Lauda, Austria	25	Graham Hill, England	14
		Emerson Fittipaldi, Brazil*	14

*Active driver. Note: Grand Prix Winners through October 1, 1995.

Alltime Grand Prix Pole Winners

Driver	Poles	Driver	Poles
Ayrton Senna, Brazil	65	Mario Andretti, United States	18
Alain Prost, France	41	Jackie Stewart, Scotland	17
Jim Clark, Scotland	33	Stirling Moss, England	16
Juan-Manuel Fangio, Argentina	28	Alberto Ascari, Italy	14
Niki Lauda, Austria	24	Ronnie Peterson, Sweden	14
Nelson Piquet, Brazil	24	James Hunt, England	14

Note: Pole Winners through 1994 season.

IMSA Racing

The 24 Hours of Daytona

Year	Winner	Car	Avg Speed	Distance
1962	Dan Gurney	Lotus 19-Class SP11	104.101 mph	3 hrs (312.42 mi)
1963	Pedro Rodriguez	Ferrari-Class 12	102.074 mph	3 hrs (308.61 mi)
1964	Pedro Rodriguez/Phil Hill	Ferrari 250 LM	98.230 mph	2,000 km
1965	Ken Miles/Lloyd Ruby	Ford	99.944 mph	2,000 km
1966	Ken Miles/Lloyd Ruby	Ford Mark II	108.020 mph	24 hrs (2,570.63 mi)
1967	Lorenzo Bandini/Chris Amon	Ferrari 330 P4	105.688 mph	24 hrs (2,537.46 mi)
1968	Vic Elford/Jochen Neerpasch	Porsche 907	106.697 mph	24 hrs (2,565.69 mi)
1969	Mark Donohue/Chuck Parsons	Chevy Lola	99.268 mph	24 hrs (2,383.75 mi)
1970	Pedro Rodriguez/Leo Kinnunen	Porsche 917	114.866 mph	24 hrs (2,758.44 mi)
1971	Pedro Rodriguez/Jackie Oliver	Porsche 917K	109.203 mph	24 hrs (2,621.28 mi)
1972*	Mario Andretti/Jacky Ickx	Ferrari 312/P	122.573 mph	6 hrs (738.24 mi)
1973	Peter Gregg/Hurley Haywood	Porsche Carrera	106.225 mph	24 hrs (2,552.7 mi)
1974	(No race)			
1975	Peter Gregg/Hurley Haywood	Porsche Carrera	108.531 mph	24 hrs (2,606.04 mi)
1976†	Peter Gregg/Brian Redman/ John Fitzpatrick	BMW CSL	104.040 mph	24 hrs (2,092.8 mi)
1977	John Graves/Hurley Haywood/ Dave Helmick	Porsche Carrera	108.801 mph	24 hrs (2,615 mi)
1978	Rolf Stommelen/ Antoine Hezemans/Peter Gregg	Porsche Turbo	108.743 mph	24 hrs (2,611.2 mi)
1979	Ted Field/Danny Ongais/ Hurley Haywood	Porsche Turbo	109.249 mph	24 hrs (2,626.56 mi)
1980	Volkert Meri/Rolf Stommelen/ Reinhold Joest	Porsche Turbo	114.303 mph	24 hrs
1981	Bob Garretson/Bobby Rahal/ Brian Redman	Porsche Turbo	113.153 mph	24 hrs
1982	John Paul, Jr/John Paul, Sr/ Rolf Stommelen	Porsche Turbo	114.794 mph	24 hrs
1983	Preston Henn/Bob Wollek/ Claude Ballot-Lena/A. J. Foyt	Porsche Turbo	98.781 mph	24 hrs
1984	Sarel van der Merwe/ Graham Duxbury/Tony Martin	Porsche March	103.119 mph	24 hrs (2,476.8 mi)
1985	A. J. Foyt/Bob Wollek/ Al Unser, Sr/Thierry Boutsen	Porsche 962	104.162 mph	24 hrs (2,502.68 mi)
1986	Al Holbert/Derek Bell/Al Unser Jr	Porsche 962	105.484 mph	24 hrs (2,534.72 mi)
1987	Chip Robinson/Derek Bell/ Al Holbert/Al Unser Jr	Porsche 962	111.599 mph	24 hrs (2,680.68 mi)
1988	Martin Brundle/John Nielsen/ Raul Boesel	Jaguar XJR-9	107.943 mph	24 hrs (2,591.68 mi)
1989	John Andretti/Derek Bell/ Bob Wollek	Porsche 962	92.009 mph	24 hrs (2,210.76 mi)
1990	Davy Jones/Jan Lammers/ Andy Wallace	Jaguar XJR-12	112.857 mph	24 hrs (2,709.16 mi)
1991	Hurley Haywood/John Winter/ Frank Jelinski/Henri Pescarolo/ Bob Wollek	Porsche 962C	106.633 mph	24 hrs (2,559.64 mi)
1992	Massahiro Hasemi/ Kazuoyshi Hoshino/Toshio Suzuki/Anders Olofsson	Nissan R91CP	112.987	24 hrs (2,712.72 mi)
1993	P.J. Jones/Mark Dismore/ Rocky Moran	Toyota Eagle MK III	103.537	24 hrs (2,484.88 mi)
1994	Paul Gentilozzi/ Scott Pruett/ Butch Leitzinger/ Steve Millen	Nissan 300 ZX	104.80	24 hrs (2693.67)

The 24 Hours of Daytona *(Cont.)*

Year	Winner	Car	Avg Speed	Distance
1995	Jeremy Dale/ Fredrik Ekblom/ Jay Cochran	Oldsmoblie BDG02	101.342 mph	685 laps

*Race shortened due to fuel crisis.

†Course lengthened from 3.81 miles to 3.84 miles.

World Champions

Year	Winner	Car	Year	Winner	Car
1971	Peter Gregg/ Hurley Haywood	Porsche 914	1982	John Paul Jr	Chevy Lola
			1983	Al Holbert	Chevy March
1972	Hurley Haywood	Porsche 911	1984	Randy Lanier	Chevy March
1973	Peter Gregg	Porsche Carrera	1985	Al Holbert	Porsche 962
1974	Peter Gregg	Porsche Carrera	1986	Al Holbert	Porsche 962
1975	Peter Gregg	Porsche Carrera	1987	Chip Robinson	Porsche 962
1976	Al Holbert	Chevy Monza	1988	Geoff Brabham	Nissan GTP
1977	Al Holbert	Chevy Monza	1989	Geoff Brabham	Nissan GTP
1978	Peter Gregg	Porsche 935	1990	Geoff Brabham	Nissan GTP
1979	Peter Gregg	Porsche 935	1991	Geoff Brabham	Nissan NPT
1980	John Fitzpatrick	Porsche 935	1992	Juan Fangio II	Toyota EGL MKIII
1981	Brian Redman	Chevy Lola	1993	Juan Fangio II	Toyota EGL MKIII
			1994	Wayne Taylor	Mazda Kudzu

Alltime IMSA Leaders

WINS		FASTEST QUALIFIERS	
Al Holbert	49	Peter Gregg	37
Peter Gregg	41	Al Holbert	27
Hurley Haywood	28	Geoff Brabham	26
Irv Hoerr	28	John Paul Jr	19
Geoff Brabham	26	John Fitzpatrick	12
Gene Felton	25	Sarel Van der Merwe	11
Parker Johnstone	25	Chip Robinson	11
Jim Downing	23	Davy Jones	10
Don Devendorf	22	Danny Ongais	10
Tommy Riggins	22	David Hobbs	9
Jack Baldwin	21	Klaus Ludwig	9
Bob Earl	21	John Greenwood	8
Juan Fangio II	21	Hans Stuck	8
		Bill Whittington	7

Note: Leaders through 1994 season.

FIA World Sports Car Racing

The 24 Hours of LeMans

Year	Winning Drivers	Car
1923	André Lagache/René Léonard	Chenard & Walker
1924	John Duff/Francis Clement	Bentley 3-litre
1925	Gérard de Courcelles/André Rossignol	La Lorraine
1926	Robert Bloch/André Rossignol	La Lorraine
1927	J. Dudley Benjafield/Sammy Davis	Bentley 3-litre
1928	Woolf Barnato/Bernard Rubin	Bentley 4½
1929	Woolf Barnato/Sir Henry Birkin	Bentley Speed Six
1930	Woolf Barnato/Glen Kidston	Bentley Speed Six
1931	Earl Howe/Sir Henry Birkin	Alfa Romeo 8C-2300 sc
1932	Raymond Sommer/Luigi Chinetti	Alfa Romeo 8C-2300 sc
1933	Raymond Sommer/Tazio Nuvolari	Alfa Romeo 8C-2300 sc
1934	Luigi Chinetti/Philippe Etancelin	Alfa Romeo 8C-2300 sc

The 24 Hours of LeMans (Cont.)

Year	Winning Drivers	Car
1935	John Hindmarsh/Louis Fontés	Lagonda M45R
1936	Race cancelled	
1937	Jean-Pierre Wimille/Robert Benoist	Bugatti 57G sc
1938	Eugene Chaboud/Jean Tremoulet	Delahaye 135M
1939	Jean-Pierre Wimille/Pierre Veyron	Bugatti 57G sc
1940-48	Races cancelled	
1949	Luigi Chinetti/Lord Selsdon	Ferrari 166MM
1950	Louis Rosier/Jean-Louis Rosier	Talbot-Lago
1951	Peter Walker/Peter Whitehead	Jaguar C
1952	Hermann Lang/Fritz Reiss	Mercedes-Benz 300 SL
1953	Tony Rolt/Duncan Hamilton	Jaguar C
1954	Froilan Gonzales/Maurice Trintignant	Ferrari 375
1955	Mike Hawthorn/Ivor Bueb	Jaguar D
1956	Ron Flockhart/Ninian Sanderson	Jaguar D
1957	Ron Flockhart/Ivor Buab	Jaguar D
1958	Olivier Gendebien/Phil Hill	Ferrari 250 TR58
1959	Carroll Shelby/Roy Salvadori	Aston Martin DBR1
1960	Olivier Gendebien/Paul Fräre	Ferrari 250 TR59/60
1961	Olivier Gendebien/Phil Hill	Ferrari 250 TR61
1962	Olivier Gendebien/Phil Hill	Ferrari 250P
1963	Lodovico Scarfiotti/Lorenzo Bandini	Ferrari 250P
1964	Jean Guichel/Nino Vaccarella	Ferrari 275P
1965	Jochen Rindt/Masten Gregory	Ferrari 250LM
1966	Chris Amon/Bruce McLaren	Ford Mk2
1967	Dan Gurney/A. J. Foyt	Ford Mk4
1968	Pedro Rodriguez/Lucien Bianchi	Ford GT40
1969	Jacky Ickx/Jackie Oliver	Ford GT40
1970	Hans Herrmann/Richard Attwood	Porsche 917
1971	Helmut Marko/Gijs van Lennep	Porsche 917
1972	Henri Pescarolo/Graham Hill	Matra-Simca MS670
1973	Henri Pescarolo/Gérard Larrousse	Matra-Simca MS670B
1974	Henri Pescarolo/Gérard Larrousse	Matra-Simca MS670B
1975	Jacky Ickx/Derek Bell	Mirage-Ford MB
1976	Jacky Ickx/Gijs van Lennep	Porsche 936
1977	Jacky Ickx/Jurgen Barth/Hurley Haywood	Porsche 936
1978	Jean-Pierre Jaussaud/Didier Pironi	Renault-Alpine A442
1979	Klaus Ludwig/Bill Whttington/Don Whittington	Porsche 935
1980	Jean-Pierre Jaussaud/Jean Rondeau	Rondeau-Ford M379B
1981	Jacky Ickx/Derek Bell	Porsche 936-81
1982	Jacky Ickx/Derek Bell	Porsche 956
1983	Vern Schuppan/Hurley Haywood/Al Holbert	Porsche 956-83
1984	Klaus Ludwig/Henri Pescarolo	Porsche 956B
1985	Klaus Ludwig/Paolo Barilla/John Winter	Porsche 956B
1986	Derek Bell/Hans-Joachim Stuck/Al Holbert	Porsche 962C
1987	Derek Bell/Hans-Joachim Stuck/Al Holbert	Porsche 962C
1988	Jan Lammers/Johnny Dumfries/Andy Wallace	Jaguar XJR9LM
1989	Jochen Mass/Manuel Reuter/Stanley Dickens	Sauber-Mercedes C9-88
1990	John Nielsen/Price Cobb/Martin Brundle	TWR Jaguar XJR-12
1991	Volker Weidler/Johnny Herbert/Bertrand Gachof	Mazda 787B
1992	Derek Warwick/Yannick Dalmas/Mark Blundell	Peugeot 905B
1993	Geoff Brabham/Christophe Bouchut/Eric Helary	Peugeot 905
1994	Yannick Dalmas/Hurley Haywood/Mauro Baldi	Porsche 962
1995	Yannick Dalmas/J.J. Lehto/Masanori Sekiya	McLaren F1 GTR

Drag Racing: Milestone Performances

Top Fuel

ELAPSED TIME

9.00	Jack Chrisman	Feb 18, 1961	Pomona, CA
8.97	Jack Chrisman	May 20, 1961	Empona, VA
7.96	Bobby Vodnick	May 16, 1964	Bayview, MD
6.97	Don Johnson	May 7, 1967	Carlsbad, CA
5.97	Mike Snively	Nov 17, 1972	Ontario, CA
5.78	Don Garlits	Nov 18, 1973	Ontario, CA
5.698	Gary Beck	Oct 10, 1975	Ontario, CA
5.573	Gary Beck	Oct 18, 1981	Irvine, CA
5.484	Gary Beck	Sept 6, 1982	Clermont, IN
5.391	Gary Beck	Oct 1, 1983	Fremont, CA
5.280	Darrell Gwynn	Sept 25, 1986	Ennis, TX
5.176	Darrell Gwynn	April 4, 1987	Ennis, TX
5.090	Joe Amato	Oct 1, 1987	Ennis, TX
4.990	Eddie Hill	April 9, 1988	Ennis, TX
4.881	Gary Ormsby	Sept 28, 1990	Topeka, KS
4.799	Cory McClenathan	Sept 19, 1992	Mohnton, PA
4.762	Cory McClenathan	Oct 3, 1993	Topeka, KS
4.690	Michael Brotherton	May 20, 1994	Englishtown, NJ

SPEED

180.36	Connie Kalitta	Sept 3, 1962	Indianapolis
190.26	Don Garlits	Sept 21, 1963	East Haddam, CT
201.34	Don Garlits	Aug 1, 1964	Great Meadows, NJ
211.26	Donny Milani	May 15, 1965	Sacramento, CA
223.32	Don Cook	Apr 24, 1965	Fremont, CA
230.17	James Warren	Apr 10, 1967	Fresno, CA
243.24	Don Garlits	March 18, 1973	Gainesville, FL
250.69	Don Garlits	Oct 11, 1975	Ontario, CA
260.11	Joe Amato	March 18, 1984	Gainesville, FL
272.56	Don Garlits	March 23, 1986	Gainesville, FL
282.13	Joe Amato	Sept 5, 1987	Clermont, IN
291.54	Connie Kalitta	Feb 11, 1989	Pomona, CA
301.70	Kenny Bernstein	March 20, 1992	Gainesville, FL
311.86	Kenny Bernstein	Oct 30, 1994	Pomona, CA

Funny Car

ELAPSED TIME

6.92	Leroy Goldstein	Sept 3, 1970	Clermont, IN
5.987	Don Prudhomme	Oct 12, 1975	Ontario, CA
5.868	Raymond Beadle	July 16, 1981	Englishtown, NJ
5.799	Tom Anderson	Sept 3, 1982	Clermont, IN
5.637	Don Prudhomme	Sept 4, 1982	Clermont, IN
5.588	Rick Johnson	Feb 3, 1985	Pomona, CA
5.425	Kenny Bernstein	Sept 26, 1986	Ennis, TX
5.397	Kenny Bernstein	April 5, 1987	Ennis, TX
5.255	Ed McCulloch	April 17, 1988	Ennis, TX
5.193	Don Prudhomme	March 2, 1989	Baytown, TX
5.077	Cruz Pedregon	Sept 20, 1992	Mohnton, PA
4.987	Chuck Etcholis	Oct 2, 1993	Topeka, KA

SPEED

200.44	Gene Snow	August, 1968	Houston, TX
250.00	Don Prudhomme	May 23, 1982	Baton Rouge, LA
260.11	Kenny Bernstein	March 18, 1984	Gainesville, FL
271.41	Kenny Bernstein	Aug 30, 1986	Indianapolis
280.72	Mike Dunn	Oct 2, 1987	Ennis, TX
290.13	Jim White	Oct 11, 1991	Ennis TX
291.82	Jim White	Oct 25, 1991	Pomona, CA
300.40	Jim Epler	Oct 3, 1993	Topeka, KS

Pro Stock

ELAPSED TIME

7.778	Lee Shepherd	March 12, 1982	Gainesville, FL
7.655	Lee Shepherd	Oct 1, 1982	Fremont, CA
7.557	Bob Glidden	Feb 2, 1985	Pomona, CA
7.497	Bob Glidden	Sep 13, 1985	Maple Grove, PA
7.377	Bob Glidden	Aug 28, 1986	Clermont, IN
7.294	Frank Sanchez	Oct 7, 1988	Baytown, TX
7.184	Darrell Alderman	Oct 12, 1990	Ennis, TX
7.099	Scott Geoffrion	Sep 19, 1992	Mohnton, PA
6.988	Kurt Johnson	May 20, 1994	Englishtown, NJ

SPEED

181.08	Warren Johnson	Oct 1, 1982	Fremont, CA
190.07	Warren Johnson	Aug 29, 1986	Clermont, IN
191.32	Bob Glidden	Sep 4, 1987	Clermont, IN
192.18	Warren Johnson	Oct 13, 1990	Ennis, TX
193.21	Bob Glidden	July 28, 1991	Sonoma, CA
194.51	Warren Johnson	July 31, 1992	Sonoma, CA
195.99	Warren Johnson	May 21, 1993	Englishtown, NJ
196.24	Warren Johnson	Mar 19, 1993	Gainesville, FL
197.15	Warren Johnson	Apr 23, 1994	Commerce, GA

Alltime Drag Racing Leaders

NATIONAL EVENT WINS

Bob Glidden	84
Don Prudhomme	49
Warren Johnson	47
Kenny Bernstein	42
John Force	42
Don Garlits	35
Joe Amato	34
David Schultz	34
Lee Shepherd	26
Terry Vance	24

BEST WON-LOST RECORD (WINNING PCT)

David Schultz	205-44 (.823)
John Myers	158-37 (.810)
Bob Glidden	768-187 (.804)
Darrell Alderman	171-56 (.753)
John Force	370-156 (70.3)
Warren Johnson	416-180 (.698)
James Bernard	68-30 (.694)
Joe Amato	356-160 (.690)
Cruz Pedregon	109-53 (.673)
Kenny Bernstein	366-181 (.669)

Note: Drag Racing Leaders through 1994 season.

THEY SAID IT

*Scott Pruett, Indy Car driver, who
counts among his sponsors Firestone
tires: "It's been a very good year.
Excuse me, it's been a
very fine year."*

Bowling

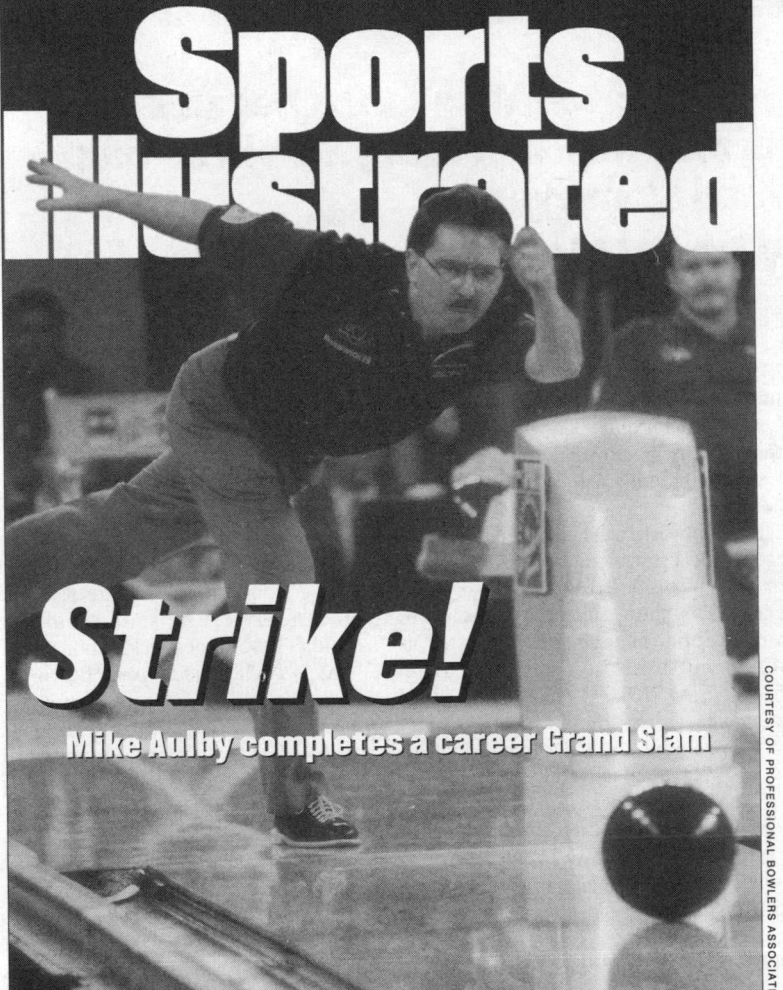

Sports Illustrated

Strike!

Mike Aulby completes a career Grand Slam

Aulby Darned

A rejuvenated Mike Aulby became the only man in history to win all four Grand Slam events

by Franz Lidz

LATE LAST summer the Agriculture Department ruled that if you can bowl with a grocery store chicken, it's not fresh. Henceforth, chickens frozen solid enough to double as bowling balls will be labeled "hard chilled."

Lack of network cash had a similar chilling effect on the Professional Bowlers Association. The tour, the PBA's showcase and a weekend TV fixture since the Eisenhower administration, headed for the gutter as ABC-TV cut back its rights fees from $3.52 million to $700,000, and the number of tournaments it aired from 24 to 14. "Ratings aren't a problem," said Dennis Lewin of ABC, which has televised the tour for the last 33 years. "Revenues are." Unable to find title sponsors for two of its 15 winter events, the PBA had to scale back events and offer smaller purses. And since entry fees kept getting higher, many bowlers reduced their schedules or retired.

In Bowling's Year of the Frozen Chicken, it was turkeys that resurrected Mike Aulby's career. In the 1980s Aulby was voted Bowler of the Decade. In the early '90s he was remembered mostly for having mowed down rows of beer mugs, family-sized bottles of ketchup and pitchers of strawberry Kool-Aid on David Letterman's show.

Aulby entered 1995 on the heels of a disheartening '94—a year in which his father died, he won a meager $32,303, and he failed to win a single tournament. "I gladly kissed 1994 goodbye at one minute past midnight on January 1," he said. "And that day couldn't have come quickly enough."

At 16 Aulby made *Ripley's Believe It or Not* for racking up six 300's in six months. At 34 the most lethal lefthander since Earl Anthony achieved an even more astounding feat by becoming the first kegler ever to complete bowling's Grand Slam.

The Aulby or Nothing Show hit the road in February at the Peoria Open, where he set a PBA record by averaging 251.3 for 42 games of qualifying and match play, only to fizzle in the final. The next week in Toledo he finished third behind Wayne Webb and the victorious Scott Alexander at the PBA National Championship, an event Aulby had won in 1979 and '85. In early April he barely missed the

COURTESY OF WOMEN'S INTERNATIONAL BOWLING CONGRESS

edge of elimination. Needing 28 points on his final three shots, Aulby got a turkey. The rest was just giblets: easy wins over Larry Laub, Pat Healey, Kelly Coffman and Ryan Shafer put him in the winner's bracket finals against Mark Williams, the only other unbeaten player. Though Williams triumphed 697-609, Aulby creamed Shafer 711-598 in the stepladder finals to become the No. 2 qualifier. That was all Aulby needed. Williams didn't survive a fourth-frame washout and chalked up a 187. Aulby's 200 made him the first bowler in history to have all four major titles—the PBA, the U.S. Open, the Tournament of Champions and the ABC Masters—on his resumé.

Bowling historians take note: Linda Wallace became the first ABC female member to compete at the Masters since its inception in 1951. Not everyone was bowled over by Wallace's participation, however. When she tried to enter the squad room, a male official snapped, "You can't come in here. Only bowlers are allowed."

"I am bowling," said Wallace, who had qualified by winning the 1994 Arizona Masters.

"There are no women bowling in this."

"I am," said Wallace and handed him a sheet that listed her starting time. She finished 540th in a field of 608. "It's a once in a lifetime thing," Wallace said. "I can't be unhappy no matter how I bowled."

One winner who was the tiniest bit unhappy was Sandy Postma, the 48-year-old grandmother who came out of nowhere to win the Women's International Bowling Congress Queens title in Tucson. A part-timer who took up the sport at 29 to keep busy while her two kids were in school, she had been winless in an 11-year pro career. Postma lost track of the score in the 10th frame and quietly asked Queens officials if she had won. Missing at the victory party was Postma's husband, Richard, who couldn't get off work. Asked to name the worst part of being alone, she said, "I had no one to hug."

championship round of the U.S. Open, finishing a respectable sixth. The Open crown, which Aulby last wore in 1989, was snared by Dave Husted, the '82 champion.

Two weeks later Aulby stormed into the title game of the Brunswick Tournament of Champions in Palatin, Ill. The event's top qualifier, Bob Spaulding, led most of the contest. But he left a 7–10 split in his ninth frame before striking out in the 10th. "How did I feel after I struck out?" sputtered Spaulding. "I felt like I'd lost." Aulby needed a double and four pins to win. He got a double and eight to become only the fourth triple crown winner in the PBA's 36-year history. "There are great bowlers in this game and greater bowlers," observed tour veteran Parker Bohn III. "If you don't consider Mike Aulby one of the greatest bowlers who ever lived after this victory, you don't know much about the sport."

Aulby showed why some think he is the Greatest two weeks later in Reno at the American Bowling Congress Masters, a tournament he won in 1989. In his opening match with Sam Ventura, he tottered on the

The Majors

MEN

Chevrolet PBA National Championship

CHAMPIONSHIP ROUND

Bowler	Games	Total	Earnings ($)
Scott Alexander	1	246	35,000
Wayne Webb	4	948	18,000
Mike Aulby	1	215	10,000
Don Genalo	1	215	8,000
Jason Couch	1	225	6,500

Playoff Results: Webb def. Couch, 235-225; Webb def. Genalo, 248-215; Webb def. Aulby, 255-215; Alexander def. Webb, 246-210.

Held at Ducat's Imperial Lanes, Toledo, OH, Feb 19-25, 1995.

BPAA United States Open

CHAMPIONSHIP ROUND

Bowler	Games	Total	Earnings ($)
Dave Husted	1	266	46,000
Paul Koehler	2	523	24,000
Steve Hoskins	3	743	14,000
Parker Bohn III	1	216	10,500
Dave D'Entremont	1	212	8,500

Playoff Results: Hoskins def. D'Entremont, 231-212; Hoskins def. Bohn, 256-216; Koehler def. Hoskins, 278-256; Husted def. Koehler, 266-245.

Held at Bowl One, Troy, MI, April 2-8, 1995.

Brunswick World Tournament of Champions

CHAMPIONSHIP ROUND

Bowler	Games	Total	Earnings ($)
Mike Aulby	2	502	60,000
Bob Spaulding	1	232	33,000
Pat Healey	2	408	24,000
Dennis Horan	2	490	18,000
Parker Bohn III	1	243	12,000

Playoff Results: Horan def. Bohn, 265-243; Healey def. Horan, 231-225; Aulby def. Healey, 265-177; Aulby def. Spaulding, 237-232.

Held at Brunswick Deer Park Lanes, Lake Zurich, IL, April 18-22, 1995.

ABC Masters Tournament

CHAMPIONSHIP ROUND

Bowler	Games	Total	Earnings ($)
Mike Aulby	2	422	50,600
Mark Williams	1	187	26,600
Ryan Shafer	2	360	20,600
Bob Benoit	2	352	15,600
Larry Laub	1	186	10,800

Playoff Results: Benoit def. Laub, 195–186; Shafer def. Benoit, 190–157; Aulby def. Shafer, 222–170; Aulby def. Williams, 200–187.

Held at National Bowling Stadium, Reno, NV, May 2–6, 1995.

WOMEN

Sam's Town Invitational

CHAMPIONSHIP ROUND

Bowler	Games	Total	Earnings ($)
Tish Johnson..............................1		178	18,000
Carol Gianotti............................2		388	9,000
Tammy Turner............................3		681	4,700
Dede Davidson.........................1		177	4,300
Jackie Sellers.............................1		188	3,800

Playoff Results: Turner def. Sellers, 214-188; Turner def. Davidson, 277-177; Gianotti def. Turner, 216-290; Johnson def. Gianotti, 178-172.

Held at Sam's Town Bowling Center, Las Vegas, NV, Nov 12-19, 1994.

WIBC Queens

CHAMPIONSHIP ROUND

Bowler	Games	Total	Earnings ($)
Sandra Postma 2		467	12,525
Carolyn Dorin.............................1		187	7,450
Kim Canady 2		469	4,650
Cathy Dorin................................2		424	3,450
Tish Johnson.............................1		192	2,600

Playoff Results: Cathy Dorin def. Johnson, 244-192; Canady def. Cathy Dorin, 239-180; Postma def. Canady, 241-230; Postma def. Carolyn Dorin, 226-187.

Held at Golden Pins Lanes, Tucson, AZ, May 14-18, 1995.

BPAA United States Open

CHAMPIONSHIP ROUND

Bowler	Games	Total	Earnings ($)
Cheryl Daniels 2		458	18,000
Tish Johnson..,..........................1		180	9,000
Diana Teeters 3		694	7,000
Wendy Macpherson-Papanos ...1		183	5,000
Sandra Jo Shiery 1		212	4,000

Playoff Results: Teeters def. Shiery 247-212; Teeters def. Macpherson-Papanos 225-183; Daniels def. Teeters 223-222; Daniels def. Johnson 235-180.

Championship round held at National Sports Center, Blaine, MN, Oct 6, 1995.

In a Dark Alley

It was a kegler ritual not seen since the dark ages of Fred Flinstone. On the evening of April 12, 1995, 150 men crouched around lane 17 of Marcel's Pinarama Bowl in Oswego, N.Y., many of them holding lighters and flashlights. In the middle of this muddle stood Matt Berlin, a 30-year-old sanitation worker and Wednesday-night bowler in the local Elks league. An hour earlier he had been one strike shy of a perfect game. Then the power went out. "Not only was it pitch black, but there were no sounds," says Berlin. "Normally you hear the hum of the machines and the smack of pins being knocked down, but there was nothing."

With his friends showing the way, Berlin stared into the half-light and threw a strike. The next minute he found himself at the bottom of a jubilant pile; the next morning, at the bottom of the front page of *The Palladium Times*. "From now on," he says, "I'm just going to look down at the fourth dot and pretend it's dark around me."

PBA Tour Results

1994 Fall Tour

Date	Event	Winner	Earnings ($)	Runner-Up
Sep 30-Oct 5	AMF Dick Weber Classic	John Mazza	60,000	Parker Bohn III
Oct 8-12	Touring Players Championship	Walter Ray Williams Jr	16,000	Butch Soper
Oct 15-19	Greater Detroit Open	Bryan Goebel	14,000	Eric Forkel
Oct 22-26	Rochester Open	Norm Duke	16,000	Doug Kent
Oct 29-Nov 2	Great Lakes PBA Classic	Dave Ferraro	16,000	Norm Duke
Nov 3-9	Brunswick Memorial World Open	Erik Forkel	45,492	David Ozio

1995 Winter Tour

Date	Event	Winner	Earnings ($)	Runner-Up
Jan 10-14	AC-Delco Classic	Jess Stayrook	45,000	Bob Learn Jr
Jan 17-21	Hilton Hotels Classic	Justin Hromek	35,000	Mike Scroggins
Jan 22-28	Showboat Invitational	Dave Husted	37,000	Ricky Ward
Jan 31-Feb 4	Quaker State 250	Bob Spaulding	48,000	Kelly Coffman
Feb 7-11	Choice Hotels Classic	Dave D'Entremont	45,000	Tommy Evans
Feb 14-18	Greater Peoria Open	Dave D'Entremont	20,000	Mike Aulby
Feb 19-25	Chevrolet PBA National Championship	Scott Alexander	35,000	Wayne Webb
Feb 28-Mar 4	Greater Baltimore Open	David Traber	18,000	Eric Forkel
Mar 7-11	Brunswick Johnny Petraglia Open	John Gant	34,000	Ken McNeely
Mar 14-18	Bud Light Championship	Jess Stayrook	37,000	Philip Ringener
Mar 21-25	Tums Classic	Jack Jurek	25,000	David Traber
Mar 28-Apr 1	Splitfire Spark Plug Open	Danny Wiseman	39,000	Steve Jaros
Apr 2-8	BPAA U.S. Open	Dave Husted	46,000	Paul Koehler
Apr 11-15	IOF Foresters Open	Mike Roth	45,000	Walter Ray Williams, Jr
Apr 18-22	Brunswick World Tournament of Champions	Mike Aulby	60,000	Bob Spaulding

1995 Summer Tour

Date	Event	Winner	Earnings ($)	Runner-Up
July 7-11	Northwest Classic	John Handegard	18,000	Mark Williams
July 14-18	Oregon Open	Norm Duke	18,000	Justin Hromek
July 21-25	Tucson Open	Bryan Goebel	16,000	Bob Belmont
July 28-Aug 1	Columbia 300 Open	Parker Bohn III	19,000	Jason Couch
Aug 4-8	Ebonite Kentucky Classic	Randy Pedersen	19,000	Mark Williams
Aug 11-15	Cleveland Open	Norm Duke	16,000	Bob Learn Jr
Aug 18-22	Bowlers Journal Classic	Jason Couch	18,500	Dave D'Entremont

1994 Senior Fall Tour

Date	Event	Winner	Earnings ($)	Runner-Up
Sep 15-20	Naples Senior Open	Barry Gurney	10,000	Richard Beattie
Sep 22-27	St Petersburg/Clearwater Senior Open	Gary Dickinson	15,000	Bobby Knipple
Oct 1-5	Palm Beach Senior Classic	Larry Laub	8,000	Barry Gurney

1995 Senior Tour (through Aug 29)

Date	Event	Winner	Earnings ($)	Runner-Up
Jan 7-11	Tri-Cities PBA Senior Classic	Tommy Evans	7,500	Dave Soutar
Jan 14-18	Northwest PBA Senior Classic	Tommy Evans	7,500	John Handegard
June 3-8	Greater Providence Senior Open	Gary Dickinson	8,000	Allie Clarke
June 25-30	ABC Senior Masters	Dave Davis	38,000	John Handegard
July 2-6	Twin Falls PBA Senior Open	Hobo Boothe	6,500	Bobby Knipple
July 30-Aug 3	Rocky Mountain Senior Open	Barry Gurney	10,000	Avery LeBlanc
Aug 7-12	Showboat Senior Invitational	Denny Torgerson	20,000	Gene Stus
Aug 17-21	Hoosier PBA Senior Classic	Dan Roche	8,000	Les Zikes
Aug 23-29	Jackson PBA Senior Championship	John Handegard	16,000	Avery LeBlanc

LPBT Tour Results

1994 Fall Tour

Date	Event	Winner	Earnings ($)	Runner-Up
Sep 29-Oct 6	BPAA US Open	Aleta Sill	18,000	Anne Marie Duggan
Oct 8-13	Hammer Midwest Open	Kim Canady	13,500	Marianne DiRupo
Oct 16-20	Brunswick Three Rivers Open	Kim Straub	13,500	Nikki Gianulas
Oct 22-27	Columbia 300 Delaware Open	Aleta Sill	13,500	Tish Johnson
Oct 29-Nov 3	Hammer Eastern Open	Carol Gianotti	13,500	Anne Marie Duggan
Nov 6-10	South Bend Open	Sandra Jo Shiery	9,000	Carol Gianotti
Nov 12-19	Sam's Town Invitational	Tish Johnson	18,000	Carol Gianotti

1995 Winter Tour

Date	Event	Winner	Earnings ($)	Runner-Up
Feb 5-9	Texas Border Shoot-Out	Aleta Sill	10,800	Tish Johnson
Feb 12-16	South Texas Open	Sandra Jo Shiery	10,800	Rachel Perez
Feb 19-23	Claremore Classic	Kim Canady	10,800	Michelle Mullen
Feb 26-Mar 2	Alexandria Louisiana Open	Tish Johnson	10,800	Anne Marie Duggan
Mar 5-9	New Orleans Classic	Robin Romeo	10,800	Carolyn Dorin
Mar 12-16	AMF XS Challenge	Anne Marie Duggan	12,600	Carolyn Dorin

1995 Spring Tour

Date	Event	Winner	Earnings ($)	Runner-Up
May 6-10	California Classic	Robin Romeo	10,800	Cheryl Daniels
May 14-18	WIBC Queens Tournament	Sandra Postma	12,525	Carolyn Dorin
May 21-25	Omaha Lancers Open	Wendy Macpherson	13,500	Kim Straub

1995 Summer Tour

Date	Event	Winner	Earnings ($)	Runner-Up
July 9-13	Quantum Technologies Old Dominion Open	Lisa Wagner	13,500	Carol Norman
July 16-20	Rocket City Challenge	Tammy Turner	10,800	Michelle Mullen
July 24-28	Sam's Town Tunica Classic	Tish Johnson	10,800	Sandra Jo Shiery

PBA

MONEY LEADERS

Name	Titles	Tournaments	Earnings ($)
Norm Duke	5	21	273,753
Walter Ray Williams Jr	2	28	189,745
Bryan Goebel	4	30	173,922
Eric Forkel	1	23	138,639
John Mazza	2	23	129,500

AVERAGE

Name	Games	Pinfall	Average
Norm Duke	808	180,050	222.83
Walter Ray Williams Jr	1062	236,397	222.59
Amleto Monacelli	760	167,669	220.61
Parker Bohn III	896	196,414	219.21
Bryan Goebel	988	216,474	219.10

Seniors

MONEY LEADERS

Name	Titles	Tournaments	Earnings ($)
Gary Dickinson	1	13	54,095
Delano Boothe	1	13	48,048
John Handegard	2	12	46,980
Tommy Evans	1	13	42,033
Rich Moores	0	12	38,567

AVERAGE

Name	Games	Pinfall	Average
John Handegard	459	101,956	222.12
Dave Davis	376	83,172	221.20
Gene Stus	511	112,985	221.10
Larry Laub	344	75,866	220.54
Gary Dickinson	451	99,325	220.23

LPBT

MONEY LEADERS

Name	Titles	Tournaments	Earnings ($)
Aleta Sill	4	21	126,325
Anne Marie Duggan	3	22	124,722
Tish Johnson	1	21	82,756
Marianne DiRupo	1	21	72,369
Carol Gianotti	1	20	68,039

AVERAGE

Name	Games	Pinfall	Average
Anne Marie Duggan	762	162,667	213.47
Dana Miller-Mackie	480	101,132	210.69
Tish Johnson	806	169,736	210.59
Marianne DiRupo	661	139,046	210.36
Kim Couture	716	150,415	210.08

Men's Majors

BPAA United States Open

Year	Winner	Score	Runner-Up	Site
1942	John Crimmins	265.09-262.33	Joe Norris	Chicago
1943	Connie Schwoegler	not available	Frank Benkovic	Chicago
1944	Ned Day	315.21-298.21	Paul Krumske	Chicago
1945	Buddy Bomar	304.46-296.16	Joe Wilman	Chicago
1946	Joe Wilman	310.27-305.37	Therman Gibson	Chicago
1947	Andy Varipapa	314.16-308.04	Allie Brandt	Chicago
1948	Andy Varipapa	309.23-309.06	Joe Wilman	Chicago
1949	Connie Schwoegler	312.31-307.27	Andy Varipapa	Chicago
1950	Junie McMahon	318.37-307.17	Ralph Smith	Chicago
1951	Dick Hoover	305.29-304.07	Lee Jouglard	Chicago
1952	Junie McMahon	309.29-305.41	Bill Lillard	Chicago
1953	Don Carter	304.17-297.36	Ed Lubanski	Chicago
1954	Don Carter	308.02-307.25	Bill Lillard	Chicago
1955	Steve Nagy	307.17-303.34	Ed Lubanski	Chicago
1956	Bill Lillard	304.30-304.22	Joe Wilman	Chicago
1957	Don Carter	308.49-305.45	Dick Weber	Chicago
1958	Don Carter	311.03-308.09	Buzz Fazio	Minneapolis
1959	Billy Welu	311.48-310.26	Ray Bluth	Buffalo
1960	Harry Smith	312.24-308.12	Bob Chase	Omaha
1961	Bill Tucker	318.49-309.11	Dick Weber	San Bernardino, CA
1962	Dick Weber	299.34-297.38	Roy Lown	Miami Beach
1963	Dick Weber	642-591	Billy Welu	Kansas City, MO
1964	Bob Strampe	714-616	Tommy Tuttle	Dallas
1965	Dick Weber	608-586	Jim St. John	Philadelphia
1966	Dick Weber	684-681	Nelson Burton Jr	Lansing, MI
1967	Les Schissler	613-610	Pete Tountas	St. Ann, MO
1968	Jim Stefanich	12,401-12,104	Billy Hardwick	Garden City, NY
1969	Billy Hardwick	12,585-11,463	Dick Weber	Miami
1970	Bobby Cooper	12,936-12,307	Billy Hardwick	Northbrook, IL
1971	Mike Limongello	397 (2 games)	Teata Semiz	St. Paul, MN
1972	Don Johnson	233 (1 game)	George Pappas	New York City
1973	Mike McGrath	712 (3 games)	Earl Anthony	New York City
1974	Larry Laub	749 (3 games)	Dave Davis	New York City
1975	Steve Neff	279 (1 game)	Paul Colwell	Grand Prairie, TX
1976	Paul Moser	226 (1 game)	Jim Frazier	Grand Prairie, TX
1977	Johnny Petraglia	279 (1 game)	Bill Spigner	Greensboro, NC
1978	Nelson Burton Jr	873 (4 games)	Jeff Mattingly	Greensboro, NC
1979	Joe Berardi	445 (2 games)	Earl Anthony	Windsor Locks, CT
1980	Steve Martin	930 (4 games)	Earl Anthony	Windsor Locks, CT
1981	Marshall Holman	684 (3 games)	Mark Roth	Houston
1982	Dave Husted	1011 (4 games)	Gil Sliker	Houston
1983	Gary Dickinson	214 (1 game)	Steve Neff	Oak Lawn, IL
1984	Mark Roth	244 (1 game)	Guppy Troup	Oak Hill, IL
1985	Marshall Holman	233 (1 game)	Wayne Webb	Venice, FL
1986	Steve Cook	467 (2 games)	Frank Ellenburg	Venice, FL
1987	Del Ballard Jr	525 (2 games)	Pete Weber	Tacoma, WA
1988	Pete Weber	929 (4 games)	Marshall Holman	Atlantic City, NJ
1989	Mike Aulby	429 (2 games)	Jim Pencak	Edmond, OK
1990	Ron Palombi Jr	269 (1 game)	Amleto Monacelli	Indianapolis
1991	Pete Weber	956 (4 games)	Mark Thayer	Indianapolis
1992	Robert Lawrence	667 (3 games)	Scott Devers	Canandaigua, NY
1993	Del Ballard Jr	505 (2 games)	Walter Ray Williams Jr	Canandaigua, NY
1994	Justin Hromek	267 (1 game)	Parker Bohn III	Troy, MI
1995	Dave Husted	266 (1 game)	Paul Koehler	Troy, MI

Note: From 1942 to 1970, the tournament was called the BPAA All-Star. Peterson scoring was used from 1942 through 1962. Under this system, the winner of an individual match game gets one point, plus one point for each 50 pins knocked down. From 1963 through 1967, a three-game championship was held between the two top qualifiers. From 1968 through 1970 total pinfall determined the winner. From 1971 to the present, five qualifiers compete for the championship.

PBA National Championship

Year	Winner	Score	Runner-Up	Site
1960	Don Carter	6512 (30 games)	Ronnie Gaudern	Memphis
1961	Dave Soutar	5792 (27 games)	Morrie Oppenheim	Cleveland
1962	Carmen Salvino	5369 (25 games)	Don Carter	Philadelphia
1963	Billy Hardwick	13,541 (61 games)	Ray Bluth	Long Island, NY
1964	Bob Strampe	13,979 (61 games)	Ray Bluth	Long Island, NY
1965	Dave Davis	13,895 (61 games)	Jerry McCoy	Detroit
1966	Wayne Zahn	14,006 (61 games)	Nelson Burton Jr	Long Island, NY
1967	Dave Davis	421 (2 games)	Pete Tountas	New York City
1968	Wayne Zahn	14,182 (60 games)	Nelson Burton Jr	New York City
1969	Mike McGrath	13,670 (60 games)	Bill Allen	Garden City, NY
1970	Mike McGrath	660 (3 games)	Dave Davis	Garden City, NY
1971	Mike Limongello	911 (4 games)	Dave Davis	Paramus, NJ
1972	Johnny Guenther	12,986 (56 games)	Dick Ritger	Rochester, NY
1973	Earl Anthony	212 (1 game)	Sam Flanagan	Oklahoma City
1974	Earl Anthony	218 (1 game)	Mark Roth	Downey, CA
1975	Earl Anthony	245 (1 game)	Jim Frazier	Downey, CA
1976	Paul Colwell	191 (1 game)	Dave Davis	Seattle
1977	Tommy Hudson	206 (1 game)	Jay Robinson	Seattle
1978	Warren Nelson	453 (2 games)	Joseph Groskind	Reno
1979	Mike Aulby	727 (3 games)	Earl Anthony	Las Vegas
1980	Johnny Petraglia	235 (1 game)	Gary Dickinson	Sterling Heights, MI
1981	Earl Anthony	242 (1 game)	Ernie Schlegel	Toledo, OH
1982	Earl Anthony	233 (1 game)	Charlie Tapp	Toledo, OH
1983	Earl Anthony	210 (1 game)	Mike Durbin	Toledo, OH
1984	Bob Chamberlain	961 (4 games)	Dan Eberl	Toledo, OH
1985	Mike Aulby	476 (2 games)	Steve Cook	Toledo, OH
1986	Tom Crites	190 (1 game)	Mike Aulby	Toledo, OH
1987	Randy Pedersen	759 (3 games)	Amleto Monacelli	Toledo, OH
1988	Brian Voss	246 (1 game)	Todd Thompson	Toledo, OH
1989	Pete Weber	221 (1 game)	Dave Ferraro	Toledo, OH
1990	Jim Pencak	900 (4 games)	Chris Warren	Toledo, OH
1991	Mike Miller	450 (2 games)	Norm Duke	Toledo, OH
1992	Eric Forkel	833 (4 games)	Bob Vespi	Toledo, OH
1993	Ron Palombi Jr	237 (1 game)	Eugene McCune	Toledo, OH
1994	David Traber	196 (1 game)	Dale Traber	Toledo, OH
1995	Scott Alexander	246 (1 game)	Wayne Webb	Toledo, OH

Note: Totals from 1963-66, 1968-69 and 1972 include bonus pins.

Tournament of Champions

Year	Winner	Score	Runner-Up	Site
1965	Billy Hardwick	484 (2 games)	Dick Weber	Akron, OH
1966	Wayne Zahn	595 (3 games)	Dick Weber	Akron, OH
1967	Jim Stefanich	227 (1 game)	Don Johnson	Akron, OH
1968	Dave Davis	213 (1 game)	Don Johnson	Akron, OH
1969	Jim Godman	266 (1 game)	Jim Stefanich	Akron, OH
1970	Don Johnson	299 (1 game)	Dick Ritger	Akron, OH
1971	Johnny Petraglia	245 (1 game)	Don Johnson	Akron, OH
1972	Mike Durbin	775 (3 games)	Tim Harahan	Akron, OH
1973	Jim Godman	451 (2 games)	Barry Asher	Akron, OH
1974	Earl Anthony	679 (3 games)	Johnny Petraglia	Akron, OH
1975	Dave Davis	448 (2 games)	Barry Asher	Akron, OH
1976	Marshall Holman	441 (2 games)	Billy Hardwick	Akron, OH
1977	Mike Berlin	434 (2 games)	Mike Durbin	Akron, OH
1978	Earl Anthony	237 (1 game)	Teata Semiz	Akron, OH
1979	George Pappas	224 (1 game)	Dick Ritger	Akron, OH
1980	Wayne Webb	750 (3 games)	Gary Dickinson	Akron, OH
1981	Steve Cook	287 (1 game)	Pete Couture	Akron, OH
1982	Mike Durbin	448 (2 games)	Steve Cook	Akron, OH
1983	Joe Berardi	865 (4 games)	Henry Gonzalez	Akron, OH
1984	Mike Durbin	950 (4 games)	Mike Aulby	Akron, OH
1985	Mark Williams	616 (3 games)	Bob Handley	Akron, OH
1986	Marshall Holman	233 (1 game)	Mark Baker	Akron, OH
1987	Pete Weber	928 (4 games)	Jim Murtishaw	Akron, OH
1988	Mark Williams	237 (1 game)	Tony Westlake	Fairlawn, OH

Tournament of Champions (Cont.)

Year	Winner	Score	Runner-Up	Site
1989	Del Ballard Jr	490 (2 games)	Walter Ray Williams Jr	Fairlawn, OH
1990	Dave Ferraro	226 (1 game)	Tony Westlake	Fairlawn, OH
1991	David Ozio	476 (2 games)	Amleto Monacelli	Fairlawn, OH
1992	Marc McDowell	471 (2 games)	Don Genalo	Fairlawn, OH
1993	George Branham III	227 (1 game)	Parker Bohn III	Fairlawn, OH
1994	Norm Duke	422 (2 games)	Eric Forkel	Fairlawn, OH
1995	Mike Aulby	502 (2 games)	Bob Spaulding	Lake Zurich, IL

ABC Masters Tournament

Year	Winner	Scoring Avg	Runner-Up	Site
1951	Lee Jouglard	201.8	Joe Wilman	St. Paul, MN
1952	Willard Taylor	200.32	Andy Varipapa	Milwaukee
1953	Rudy Habetler	200.13	Ed Brosius	Chicago
1954	Eugene Elkins	205.19	W. Taylor	Seattle
1955	Buzz Fazio	204.13	Joe Kristof	Ft. Wayne, IN
1956	Dick Hoover	209.9	Ray Bluth	Rochester, NY
1957	Dick Hoover	216.39	Bill Lillard	Ft. Worth, TX
1958	Tom Hennessy	209.15	Lou Frantz	Syracuse, NY
1959	Ray Bluth	214.26	Billy Golembiewski	St. Louis, MO
1960	Billy Golembiewski	206.13	Steve Nagy	Toledo, OH
1961	Don Carter	211.18	Dick Hoover	Detroit
1962	Billy Golembiewski	223.12	Ron Winger	Des Moines, IA
1963	Harry Smith	219.3	Bobby Meadows	Buffalo
1964	Billy Welu	227	Harry Smith	Oakland, CA
1965	Billy Welu	202.12	Don Ellis	St. Paul, MN
1966	Bob Strampe	219.80	Al Thompson	Rochester, NY
1967	Lou Scalia	216.9	Bill Johnson	Miami Beach
1968	Pete Tountas	220.15	Buzz Fazio	Cincinnati
1969	Jim Chestney	223.2	Barry Asher	Madison, WI
1970	Don Glover	215.10	Bob Strampe	Knoxville, TN
1971	Jim Godman	229.8	Don Johnson	Detroit
1972	Bill Beach	220.27	Jim Godman	Long Beach, CA
1973	Dave Soutar	218.61	Dick Ritger	Syracuse, NY
1974	Paul Colwell	234.17	Steve Neff	Indianapolis
1975	Eddie Ressler	213.51	Sam Flanagan	Dayton, OH
1976	Nelson Burton Jr	220.79	Steve Carson	Oklahoma City
1977	Earl Anthony	218.21	Jim Godman	Reno
1978	Frank Ellenburg	200.61	Earl Anthony	St. Louis
1979	Doug Myers	202.9	Bill Spigner	Tampa, FL
1980	Neil Burton	206.69	Mark Roth	Louisville
1981	Randy Lightfoot	218.3	Skip Tucker	Memphis
1982	Joe Berardi	207.12	Ted Hannahs	Baltimore
1983	Mike Lastowski	212.65	Pete Weber	Niagara Falls, NY
1984	Earl Anthony	212.5	Gil Sliker	Reno
1985	Steve Wunderlich	210.4	Tommy Kress	Tulsa, OK
1986	Mark Fahy	206.5	Del Ballard Jr	Las Vegas
1987	Rick Steelsmith	210.7	Brad Snell	Niagara Falls, NY
1988	Del Ballard Jr	219.1	Keith Smith	Jacksonville, FL
1989	Mike Aulby	218.5	Mike Edwards	Wichita
1990	Chris Warren	231.6	David Ozio	Reno
1991	Doug Kent	226.8	George Branham III	Toledo, OH
1992	Ken Johnson	230.0	Dave D'Entremont	Corpus Christi, TX
1993	Norm Duke	245.68	Patrick Allen	Tulsa, OK
1994	Steve Fehr	213.09	Steve Anderson	Greenacres, FL
1995	Mike Aulby	230.7	Mark Williams	Reno

Women's Majors

BPAA United States Open

Year	Winner	Score	Runner-Up	Site
1949	Marion Ladewig	113.26-104.26	Catherine Burling	Chicago
1950	Marion Ladewig	151.46-146.06	Stephanie Balogh	Chicago
1951	Marion Ladewig	159.17-148.03	Sylvia Wene	Chicago
1952	Marion Ladewig	154.39-142.05	Shirley Garms	Chicago
1953	Not held			
1954	Marion Ladewig	148.29-143.01	Sylvia Wene	Chicago
1955	Sylvia Wene	142.30-141.11	Sylvia Fanta	Chicago
1955	Anita Cantaline	144.40-144.13	Doris Porter	Chicago
1956	Marion Ladewig	150.16-145.41	Marge Merrick	Chicago
1957	Not held			
1958	Merle Matthews	145.09-143.14	Marion Ladewig	Minneapolis
1959	Marion Ladewig	149.33-143.00	Donna Zimmerman	Buffalo
1960	Sylvia Wene	144.14-143.26	Marion Ladewig	Omaha
1961	Phyllis Notaro	144.13-143.12	Hope Riccilli	San Bernardino, CA
1962	Shirley Garms	138.44-135.49	Joy Abel	Miami Beach
1963	Marion Ladewig	586-578	Bobbie Shaler	Kansas City, MO
1964	LaVerne Carter	683-609	Evelyn Teal	Dallas
1965	Ann Slattery	597-550	Sandy Hooper	Philadelphia
1966	Joy Abel	593-538	Bette Rockwell	Lansing, MI
1967	Gloria Bouvia	578-516	Shirley Garms	St. Ann, MO
1968	Dotty Fothergill	9,000-8,187	Doris Coburn	Garden City, NY
1969	Dotty Fothergill	8,284-8,258	Kayoka Suda	Miami
1970	Mary Baker	8,730-8,465	Judy Cook	Northbrook, IL
1971	Paula Carter	5,660-5,650	June Llewellyn	Kansas City, MO
1972	Lorrie Nichols	5,272-5,189	Mary Baker	Denver
1973	Millie Martorella	5,553-5,294	Patty Costello	Garden City, NY
1974	Patty Costello	219-216	Betty Morris	Irving, TX
1975	Paula Carter	6,500-6,352	Lorrie Nichols	Toledo, OH
1976	Patty Costello	11,341-11,281	Betty Morris	Tulsa, OK
1977	Betty Morris	10,511-10,358	Virginia Norton	Milwaukee
1978	Donna Adamek	236-202	Vesma Grinfelds	Miami
1979	Diana Silva	11,775-11,718	Bev Ortner	Phoenix
1980	Pat Costello	223-199	Shinobu Saitoh	Rockford, IL
1981	Donna Adamek	201-190	Nikki Gianulias	Rockford, IL
1982	Shinobu Saitoh	12,184-12,028	Robin Romeo	Hendersonville, TN
1983	Dana Miller-Mackie	247-200	Aleta Sill	St. Louis
1984	Karen Ellingsworth	236-217	Lorrie Nichols	St. Louis
1985	Pat Mercatani	214-178	Nikki Gianulias	Topeka, KS
1986	Wendy Macpherson	265-179	Lisa Wagner	Topeka, KS
1987	Carol Norman	206-179	Cindy Coburn	Mentor, OH
1988	Lisa Wagner	226-218	Lorrie Nichols	Winston-Salem, NC
1989	Robin Romeo	187-163	Michelle Mullen	Addison, IL
1990	Dana Miller-Mackie	190-189	Tish Johnson	Dearborn Heights, MI
1991	Anne Marie Duggan	196-185	Leanne Barrette	Fountain Valley, CA
1992	Tish Johnson	216-213	Aleta Sill	Fountain Valley, CA
1993	Dede Davidson	213-194	Dana Miller-Mackie	Garland, TX
1994	Aleta Sill	229-170	Anne Marie Duggan	Wichita
1995	Cheryl Daniels	235-180	Tish Johnson	Blaine, MN

Note: From 1942 to 1970, the tournament was called the BPAA All-Star. Peterson scoring was used from 1949 through 1962. Under this system, the winner of an individual match game gets one point, plus one point for each 50 pins knocked down. From 1963 through 1967, a three-game championship was held between the two top qualifiers. From 1968 through 1973, 1975-77, 1979 and 1982, total pinfall determined the winner. In the other years, five qualifiers competed in a playoff for the championship, with the final match listed above.

WIBC Queens

Year	Winner	Score	Runner-Up	Site
1961	Janet Harman	794-776	Eula Touchette	Fort Wayne, IN
1962	Dorothy Wilkinson	799-794	Marion Ladewig	Phoenix, AZ
1963	Irene Monterosso	852-803	Georgette DeRosa	Memphis, TN
1964	D. D. Jacobson	740-682	Shirley Garms	Minneapolis, MN
1965	Betty Kuczynski	772-739	LaVerne Carter	Portland, OR
1966	Judy Lee	771-742	Nancy Peterson	New Orleans, LA
1967	Millie Ignizio	840-809	Phyllis Massey	Rochester, NY
1968	Phyllis Massey	884-853	Marian Spencer	San Antonio, TX
1969	Ann Feigel	832-765	Millie Ignizio	San Diego, CA
1970	Millie Ignizio	807-797	Joan Holm	Tulsa, OK
1971	Millie Ignizio	809-778	Katherine Brown	Atlanta, GA
1972	Dotty Fothergill	890-841	Maureen Harris	Kansas City, MO
1973	Dotty Fothergill	804-791	Judy Soutar	Las Vegas, NV
1974	Judy Soutar	939-705	Betty Morris	Houston, TX
1975	Cindy Powell	758-674	Patty Costello	Indianapolis, IN
1976	Pam Buckner	214-178	Shirley Sjostrom	Denver, CO
1977	Dana Stewart	175-167	Vesma Grinfelds	Milwaukee, WI
1978	Loa Boxberger	197-176	Cora Fiebig	Miami, FL
1979	Donna Adamek	216-181	Shinobu Saitoh	Tucson, AZ
1980	Donna Adamek	213-165	Cheryl Robinson	Seattle, WA
1981	Katsuko Sugimoto	166-158	Virginia Norton	Baltimore, MD
1982	Katsuko Sugimoto	160-137	Nikki Gianulias	St. Louis, MO
1983	Aleta Sill	214-188	Dana Miller-Mackie	Las Vegas, NV
1984	Kazue Inahashi	248-222	Aleta Sill	Niagara Falls, NY
1985	Aleta Sill	279-192	Linda Graham	Toledo, OH
1986	Cora Fiebig	223-177	Barbara Thorberg	Orange County, CA
1987	Cathy Almeida	850-817	Lorrie Nichols	Hartford, CT
1988	Wendy Macpherson	213-199	Leanne Barrette	Reno/Carson City, NV
1989	Carol Gianotti	207-177	Sandra Jo Shiery	Bismarck-Mandan, ND
1990	Patty Ann	207-173	Vesma Grinfelds	Tampa, FL
1991	Dede Davidson	231-159	Jeanne Maiden	Cedar Rapids, IA
1992	Cindy Coburn-Carroll	184-170	Dana Miller-Mackie	Lansing, MI
1993	Jan Schmidt	201-163	Pat Costello	Baton Rouge, LA
1994	Anne Marie Duggan	224-177	Wendy Macpherson-Papanos	Salt Lake City, UT
1995	Sandra Postma	226-187	Carolyn Dorin	Tucson, AZ

Sam's Town Invitational

Year	Winner	Score	Runner-Up	Site
1984	Aleta Sill	238 (1 game)	Cheryl Daniels	Las Vegas, NV
1985	Patty Costello	236 (1 game)	Robin Romeo	Las Vegas, NV
1986	Aleta Sill	238 (1 game)	Dina Wheeler	Las Vegas, NV
1987	Debbie Bennett	880 (4 games)	Lorrie Nichols	Las Vegas, NV
1988	Donna Adamek	634 (3 games)	Robin Romeo	Las Vegas, NV
1989	Tish Johnson	210 (1 game)	Dede Davidson	Las Vegas, NV
1990	Wendy Macpherson	900 (4 games)	Jeanne Maiden	Las Vegas, NV
1991	Lorrie Nichols	469 (2 games)	Dana Miller-Mackie	Las Vegas, NV
1992	Tish Johnson	279 (1 game)	Robin Romeo	Las Vegas, NV
1993	Robin Romeo	194 (1 game)	Tammy Turner	Las Vegas, NV
1994	Tish Johnson	178 (1 game)	Carol Gianotti	Las Vegas, NV

PWBA Championships

Year	Winner	Year	Winner
1960	Marion Ladewig	1971	Patty Costello
1961	Shirley Garms	1972	Patty Costello
1962	Stephanie Balogh	1973	Betty Morris
1963	Janet Harman	1974	Pat Costello
1964	Betty Kuczynski	1975	Pam Buckner
1965	Helen Duval	1976	Patty Costello
1966	Joy Abel	1977	Vesma Grinfelds
1967	Betty Mivalez	1978	Toni Gillard
1968	Dotty Fothergill	1979	Cindy Coburn
1969	Dotty Fothergill	1980	Donna Adamek
1970	Bobbe North		

BWAA Bowler of the Year

1942 ....Johnny Crimmins	1961 ....Dick Weber	1978 ....Mark Roth
1943 ....Ned Day	1962 ....Don Carter	1979 ....Mark Roth
1944 ....Ned Day	1963 ....Dick Weber,	1980 ....Wayne Webb
1945 ....Buddy Bomar	Billy Hardwick (PBA)*	1981 ....Earl Anthony
1946 ....Joe Wilman	1964 ....Billy Hardwick,	1982 ....Earl Anthony
1947 ....Buddy Bomar	Bob Strampe (PBA)*	1983 ....Earl Anthony
1948 ....Andy Varipapa	1965 ....Dick Weber	1984 ....Mark Roth
1949 ....Connie Schwoegler	1966 ....Wayne Zahn	1985 ....Mike Aulby
1950 ....Junie McMahon	1967 ....Dave Davis	1986 ....Walter Ray Williams Jr
1951 ....Lee Jouglard	1968 ....Jim Stefanich	1987 ....Marshall Holman
1952 ....Steve Nagy	1969 ....Billy Hardwick	1988 ....Brian Voss
1953 ....Don Carter	1970 ....Nelson Burton Jr	1989 ....Mike Aulby,
1954 ....Don Carter	1971 ....Don Johnson	Amleto Monacelli (PBA)*
1955 ....Steve Nagy	1972 ....Don Johnson	1990 ....Amleto Monacelli
1956 ....Bill Lillard	1973 ....Don McCune	1991 ....David Ozio
1957 ....Don Carter	1974 ....Earl Anthony	1992 ....Dave Ferraro
1958 ....Don Carter	1975 ....Earl Anthony	1993 ....Walter Ray Williams Jr
1959 ....Ed Lubanski	1976 ....Earl Anthony	1994 ....Norm Duke
1960 ....Don Carter	1977 ....Mark Roth	

*The PBA began selecting a player of the year in 1963. Its selection has been the same as the BWAA's in all but three years.

Women's Awards

BWAA Bowler of the Year

1948 ....Val Mikiel	1965 ....Betty Kuczynski	1982 ....Nikki Gianulias
1949 ....Val Mikiel	1966 ....Joy Abel	1983 ....Lisa Wagner
1950 ....Marion Ladewig	1967 ....Millie Martorella	1984 ....Aleta Sill
1951 ....Marion Ladewig	1968 ....Dotty Fothergill	1985 ....Aleta Sill,
1952 ....Marion Ladewig	1969 ....Dotty Fothergill	Patty Costello (LPBT)*
1953 ....Marion Ladewig	1970 ....Mary Baker	1986 ....Lisa Wagner,
1954 ....Marion Ladewig	1971 ....Paula Sperber Carter	Jeanne Madden (LPBT)*
1955 ....Marion Ladewig	1972 ....Patty Costello	1987 ....Betty Morris
1956 ....Sylvia Martin	1973 ....Judy Soutar	1988 ....Lisa Wagner
1957 ....Anita Cantaline	1974 ....Betty Morris	1989 ....Robin Romeo
1958 ....Marion Ladewig	1975 ....Judy Soutar	1990 ....Tish Johnson,
1959 ....Marion Ladewig	1976 ....Patty Costello	Leanne Barrette (LPBT)*
1960 ....Sylvia Martin	1977 ....Betty Morris	1991 ....Leanne Barrette
1961 ....Shirley Garms	1978 ....Donna Adamek	1992 ....Tish Johnson
1962 ....Shirley Garms	1979 ....Donna Adamek	1993 ....Lisa Wagner
1963 ....Marion Ladewig	1980 ....Donna Adamek	1994 ....Anne Marie Duggan
1964 ....LaVerne Carter	1981 ....Donna Adamek	

*The LPBT began selecting a player of the year in 1983. Its selection has been the same as the BWAA's in all but three years.

Career Leaders

Earnings

MEN		WOMEN	
Pete Weber	$1,734,330	Aleta Sill	$656,931
Marshall Holman	$1,652,924	Tish Johnson	$585,605
Mike Aulby	$1,625,022	Lisa Wagner	$575,442
Walter Ray Williams Jr	$1,510,504	Robin Romeo	$512,539
Mark Roth	$1,484,948	Nikki Gianulias	$477,557

Titles

MEN		WOMEN	
Earl Anthony	41	Lisa Wagner	28
Mark Roth	34	Patty Costello	25
Don Johnson	26	Aleta Sill	23
Dick Weber	26	Donna Adamek	19
Mike Aulby	23	Tish Johnson	19

Soccer

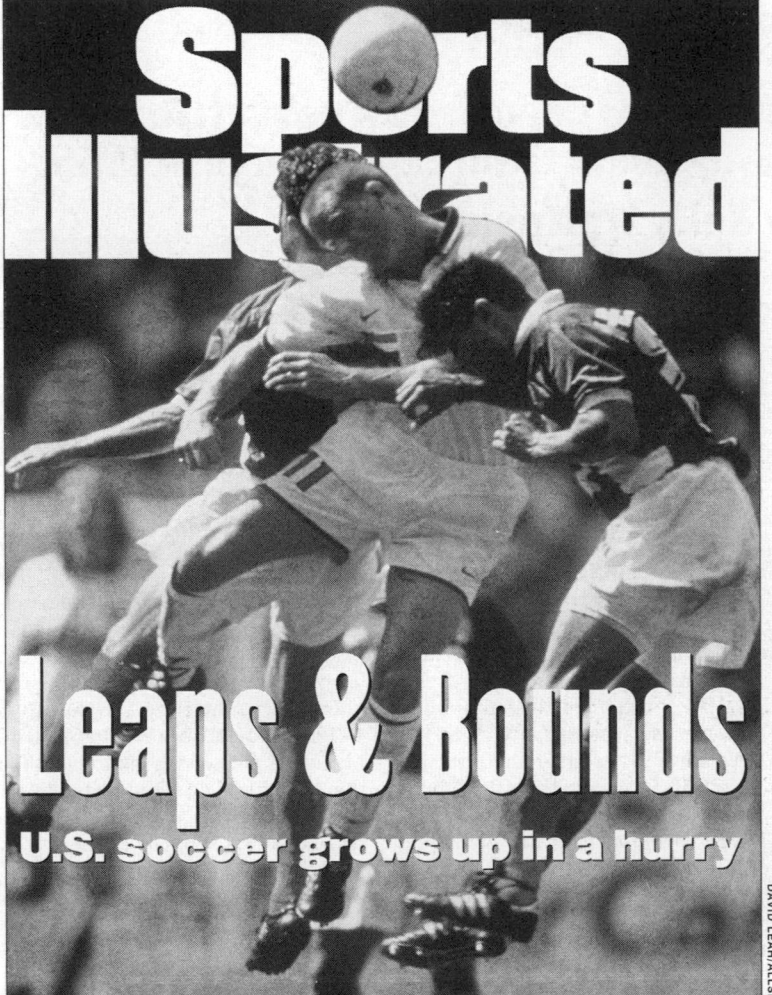

Sports Illustrated

Leaps & Bounds

U.S. soccer grows up in a hurry

DAVID LEAH/ALLSPORT

Breaking New Ground

With a new coach and a new attitude, the U.S. national team came of age in 1995

by Kelly Whiteside

TO STATE it simply and without hyperbole, July 1995 was the most magical month in U.S. soccer history. In Uruguay, from July 5 to July 23, 10 teams from South America, as well as guests Mexico and the U.S., competed in the oldest international tournament in soccer, the biennial Copa America. Though it was winter in the Southern Hemisphere, and the temperature was frigid at times, the U.S. men's national soccer team was hot. To South Americans, La Copa is as important as the World Cup. And for the North Americans in red, white and blue, La Copa runneth over in the summer of 1995.

Before the tournament began nobody expected very much from the U.S. as the team's record versus its first-round foes was a desultory 0-10-5. At such events the Americans have always been polite, yet dull guests, usually long-gone from the party before the fun really starts. At the previous tournament in 1993, the U.S. did not make it beyond the first round, blowing a three-goal lead in its last match against Venezuela.

"This Copa America is an opportunity for us to get more respect in the world," proclaimed U.S. forward Eric Wynalda before La Copa kicked off.

Respect? In Uruguay, U.S. interim coach Steve Sampson was called "Simpson" by local reporters. It was an unintentional slip, but a telling one: Even Homer Simpson was better known in South America than Sampson and his team.

However, the U.S.'s stunning run in Paysandu, Uruguay, soon changed all that. In the U.S.'s opening game, Wynalda scored two first-half goals, and the U.S. defeated Chile 2-1. The win marked the first time the American squad had beaten Chile and the first time it had defeated a South American team on South American soil in 65 years.

Three days later the U.S. lost to Bolivia 1-0 but played so well that even Diego Maradona, still serving the 15-month suspension he received after testing positive for five banned substances at the '94 World Cup, remarked, "It's very emotional to me to see the U.S. playing soccer at a very high level. The country we thought had only baseball, basketball and American football, now has very good soccer. They play clean, classy soccer. And, let's be honest, they didn't deserve to lose." (It should be noted that the Argentine star, who isn't known for always being clean or classy, was on his best behavior in

Wynalda got the U.S. off on the right foot at the Copa America.

DAVID LEAH/ALLSPORT

1995. He did not fire any pellet guns at reporters, though he still faces a possible four-year-prison term for the 1994 incident. His worst transgression was merely pelting a linesman with a water bottle while coaching a game. But don't expect 1996 to be as tame: Maradona's suspension expired Sept. 30, and he rejoined his old club, the Boca Juniors of Buenos Aires.)

Three days after the Bolivia game, the upstart Yanks beat one of the best teams in the world, Argentina, 3–0, for the first time in the 65-year head-to-head series. Since Paysandu is near the Argentine border, the U.S. defeated the gauchos practically on their home *tierra*, in front of a crowd of 18,000. "This has to rate as one of the biggest wins in U.S. soccer history," said the coach who hereafter should be called Homeric Sampson.

Indeed, the victory belongs on the U.S.'s short list of equally earth-shattering soccer events, joining the 1950 World Cup upset of England, the 1993 U.S. Cup win against England and the 1994 World Cup shocker over Colombia.

For Argentina—a two-time World Cup winner and the two-time defending Copa America champion—the game was to be a warmup for the quarterfinals, as they had already clinched a berth in the next round. Clearly Argentina coach Daniel Passarella had underestimated the Americans: Passarella rested nine of his 11 regulars at the start, then, with the game slipping away, brought on several of his top players for the second half. One local Uruguayan newspaper called the U.S.'s win over Argentina a triumph of humility over arrogance, a win by the *yanquis simpaticos* that marked the beginning of the end of "our brothers of the River Plate."

The apocalypse began in the 21st minute

when U.S. midfielder Frank Klopas buried an 18-yard shot low into the right corner for the first goal. In the 32nd minute U.S. midfielder Cobi Jones beat a defender down the right wing and crossed a ball to teammate Alexi Lalas at the near post. Lalas flicked the ball under keeper Carlos Bossio for the second score. In the 59th minute forward Joe-Max Moore fed Wynalda, who scored his third goal of the tournament, a sliding effort into an open net.

With the victory the U.S. won its group and the right to meet Mexico in the quarterfinals. After the teams played 90 minutes without a goal, the U.S. beat Mexico on penalty kicks, 4–1, and advanced to the semifinals of the Copa America. "The world respects us now," said Lalas following the game. Lalas, he of the flaming red hair, flowing goatee and flamboyant personality, quickly became a fan favorite. "For a kid from Detroit who never dreamed of playing professional soccer, it means a lot that people know who I am in a place called Paysandu," he said.

The day before the semifinals, the Copa

Kids from America were the big story in the local newspapers. A poll indicated that 16% of Uruguayans thought the U.S. could win the title, and a demographic survey revealed that the Yanks were particularly popular among the 14-to-34-year-old age group.

Meanwhile, back in the States, Prime Deportiva, a Spanish-language cable service available only regionally, was the sole station to carry the games. The quarterfinal package could be ordered for $19.95, interpreter not included. Somehow the U.S. Soccer Federation missed a historic opportunity to capitalize on its team's success yet again (see MLS further down) and failed to make the national-team games from Uruguay widely available on TV.

Playing in the semifinals of a major international tournament for the first time since the 1930 World Cup, the Americans faced the world's best team, Brazil, in Maldonado, and lost a hard-fought game 1–0. "We have closed the gap between the United States and Brazil," Sampson said. "We went forward and played attacking soccer where a year ago [in the second round of the World Cup, also a 1–0 loss for the U.S.] we were defending most of the game, hoping to get to penalty kicks."

The Americans had come far: Not so long ago the team kept close company with weaklings like Iceland and Moldova; now the U.S. was samba dancing with the likes of Brazil. And so it really didn't matter that the U.S. lost its third-place game against Colombia 4–1. (Uruguay beat Brazil 5–3 on penalty kicks after a 1–1 tie in regulation for the championship title.) Though there is no gold, silver or bronze medal for fourth place, the U.S. gained something even more valuable than championship hardware: respect. In terms of prestige, only the World Cup and the European Championships are bigger than the Copa America.

"Getting to the semifinals this time after not doing anything two years ago was a major success for U.S. soccer. We can walk away from this with our heads up very high," said U.S. midfielder John Harkes.

So how to explain the U.S. team's magical

AL TIELEMANS

Sampson won his way into the job as head coach of the national team.

run? Experience. Last season 18 of the team's 22 players were on professional clubs, mostly Latin American or European first- or second-division teams. As a point of comparison, consider that only two players on the 1990 World Cup roster had played abroad professionally.

The players also say that Sampson—and the attacking style of play he has implemented—deserves a double dose of credit. Not only was Sampson under pressure to win games, but the interim coach was also under pressure to win his job.

On April 14 the U.S. Soccer Federation announced that head coach Bora Milutinovic had "stepped down." Instead of giving Milutinovic a new contract as national team coach, the federation offered him a position that added several layers of responsibility, including overseeing the development of U.S. coaches and national team players in all age groups.

"I told them, to do this job I don't have time," the 51-year-old Milutinovic said. "There are so many [international] competitions. It's impossible." Unable to reach an agreement, the federation fired Milutinovic, and by default, 38-year-old assistant Sampson was named interim coach.

The handling of the whole affair was as

sloppy as Milutinovic's caught-in-a-typhoon hairdo. When Sampson took over, he was told to keep the seat warm until a coach with international experience was hired. The federation offered the position to two big-name coaches, Carlos Queiroz, a longtime manager in Portugal, and ex-Brazilian national coach Carlos Alberto Parreira. Both turned the job down.

Before the team's dazzling play in the Copa America, Sampson began proving that he was the right person for the job. In June the national team won the U.S. Cup title, beating 1994 African champion Nigeria, trouncing Mexico by four goals and holding Colombia to a scoreless tie in the finale.

But after the U.S. Cup, federation president Alan Rothenberg could only offer this feeble endorsement: "[Sampson's hiring] is probably inevitable, but I don't know if it's imminent," he said. On Aug. 2, following the team's stirring play in Uruguay, the word *interim* was officially removed from Sampson's title.

Meanwhile, in August, the U.S. women's national team hosted its own party, the four-team U.S. Women's Cup. In a match held at RFK Stadium in Washington, D.C., between the two best teams in the world, the U.S. beat Norway 2–1 in sudden-death overtime for the championship title.

Just two minutes into overtime, two substitutes connected for the game-winner. Jen Grubb, a high school senior who also kicks for her football team in Hoffmann Estates, Ill., sent a long ball near the top of the Norway box to U.S. forward Tammy Pearman, who was making her first national team appearance. Pearman, who has incomparable speed, nodded the ball past charging keeper Bente Nordby and scored into an open net. The win was watched by a record crowd of 7,083, including First Soccer Fan Chelsea Clinton, who mugged with several of her heroes on the field after the game.

The victory avenged a tough loss to Norway at the Women's World Cup in June. The U.S. had won the inaugural Women's World Cup in 1991 in China and entered the 1995 tournament, hosted by Sweden, as favorites. But they ran into 1991 world runner-up Norway in the semifinal game, were outplayed and lost 1–0. Norway went on to beat Germany 2–0 in the championship game in Stockholm.

Said U.S. coach Tony DiCicco after beating Norway in August, "They dethroned us. They took something away that we can never regain fully. But it worked to motivate us for this game, and I'm hoping it motivates us through the Olympics." (Women's soccer will debut at the 1996 Olympics.)

In addition to the men's wonderful Copa America performance and the women's climb back to the top of international soccer, 1995 should also be remembered for what did not happen.

Major League Soccer, a first-rank pro soccer league, was supposed to kick off in the spring of 1995. The extra time it took MLS chairman Rothenberg to collect roughly $75 million in start-up capital pushed the league's debut to April 1996.

Through the end of August, MLS had signed top U.S. national team players like Lalas and midfielder Tab Ramos, as well as international stars like Jorge Campos and Hugo Sanchez, both of Mexico, but six months away from the start of the season, the league's 10 teams did not have nicknames or logos or head coaches, and few fans knew anything about the league, causing some wags to call MLS the "Mythical Soccer League."

And because the start of the league was postponed for a year, MLS missed its chance to take advantage of the wave of excitement created by the 1994 World Cup. When Ramos returned in June from Mexico, where he plays for the first-division club Tigres, he remarked, "Being at home these last couple of weeks, it seems like soccer has disappeared again."

Indeed, from the World Cup until June, U.S. soccer did manage to perform a nifty disappearing act. But little did Ramos know what was to come later that summer. Who could have imagined that the men's national team would pull such victories out of thin air during the magical month of July?

FOR THE RECORD · 1994 – 1995

World Cup 1994

Group Standings

GROUP A

Country	GP	W	L	T	G	GA	Pts
†Romania 3		2	1	0	5	5	6
†Switzerland ..3		1	1	1	5	4	4
†United States .3		1	1	1	3	3	4
Colombia 3		1	2	0	4	5	3

GROUP B

Country	GP	W	L	T	G	GA	Pts
†Brazil 3		2	0	1	6	1	7
†Sweden ...3		1	0	2	6	4	5
Russia 3		1	2	0	7	6	3
Cameroon..3		0	2	1	3	11	1

GROUP C

Country	GP	W	L	T	G	GA	Pts
†Germany ..3		2	0	1	5	3	7
†Spain 3		1	0	2	6	4	5
S Korea 3		0	1	2	4	5	2
Bolivia........3		0	2	1	1	4	1

GROUP D

Country	GP	W	L	T	G	GA	Pts
†Nigeria.....3		2	1	0	6	2	6
†Bulgaria..3		2	1	0	6	3	6
†Argentina..3		2	1	0	6	3	6
Greece 3		0	3	0	0	8	0

GROUP E

Country	GP	W	L	T	G	GA	Pts
†Mexico....3		1	1	1	3	3	4
†Ireland 3		1	1	1	2	2	4
†Italy.........3		1	1	1	2	2	4
Norway 3		1	1	1	1	1	4

GROUP F

Country	GP	W	L	T	G	GA	Pts
†N'lands.....3		2	1	0	4	3	6
†S. Arabia ..3		2	1	0	4	3	6
†Belgium ...3		2	1	0	2	1	6
Morocco 3		0	3	0	2	5	0

†Advanced to second round.

Note: In the first round, teams are awarded three points for a victory, one for a tie. The top two in each group, plus the four third place teams with the best records, advance to the round of 16.

First Round Group Scores

GROUP A
U.S. 2, Colombia 1
U.S. 1, Switzerland 1
Romania 1, U.S. 0
Romania 3, Colombia 1
Switzerland 4, Romania 1
Colombia 2, Switzerland 0

GROUP B
Cameroon 2, Sweden 2
Brazil 2, Russia 0
Brazil 3, Cameroon 0

GROUP B *(Cont.)*
Sweden 3, Russia 1
Russia 6, Cameroon 1
Brazil 1, Sweden 1

GROUP C
Germany 1, Bolivia 0
Spain 2, South Korea 2
Germany 1, Spain 1
South Korea 0, Bolivia 0
Germany 3, South Korea 2
Spain 3, Bolivia 1

GROUP D
Argentina 4, Greece 0
Nigeria 3, Bulgaria 0
Argentina 2, Nigeria 1
Bulgaria 4, Greece 0
Nigeria 2, Greece 0
Bulgaria 2, Argentina 0

GROUP E
Ireland 1, Italy 0
Norway 1 Mexico 0
Italy 1, Norway 0

GROUP E *(Cont.)*
Mexico 2, Ireland 1
Ireland 0, Norway 0
Italy 1, Mexico 1

GROUP F
Belgium 1, Morocco 0
Netherlands 2, S. Arabia 1
Belgium 1, Netherlands 0
Saudi Arabia 2, Morocco 1
Netherlands 2, Morocco 1
Saudi Arabia 1, Belgium 0

World Cup Tournament

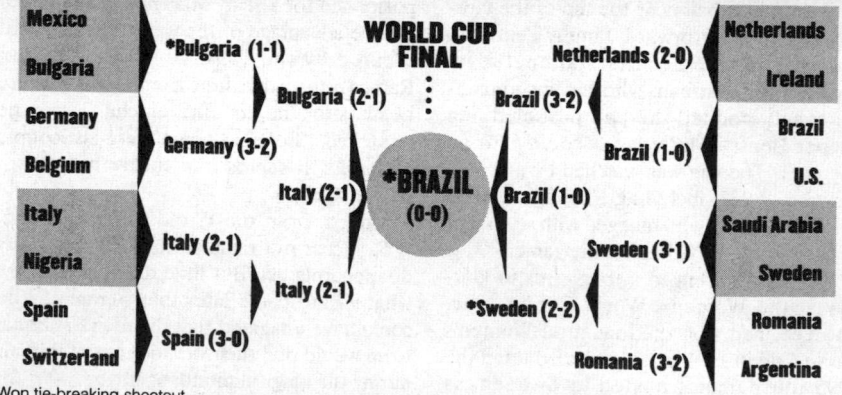

*Won tie-breaking shootout.

U.S. Men's National Team 1995 Results

Date	Opponent	Site	Result	U.S. Goals
March 25 ....Uruguay		Dallas	2-2 T#	Kerr, Stewart
April 22 ....Belgium		Brussels, Belgium	0-1 L	none
May 28..................Costa Rica		Tampa	1-2 L	Caligiuri
June 11.................Nigeria*		Boston	3-2 W	Harkes, Balboa, Jones
June 18.................Mexico*		Washington, D.C.	4-0 W	Wegerle, Dooley, Harkes, Reyna
June 25.................Colombia*		Piscataway, NJ	0-0 T	none
July 8 ....Chile†		Paysandu, Uruguay	2-1 W	Wynalda (2)
July 11 ....Bolivia†		Paysandu, Uruguay	0-1 L	none
July 14 ....Argentina†		Paysandu, Uruguay	3-0 W	Klopas, Lalas, Wynalda
July 17 ....Mexico†		Paysandu, Uruguay	0-0(4-1) W	none
July 20 ....Brazil†		Maldonado, Uruguay	0-1 L	none
July 22 ....Colombia†		Maldonado, Uruguay	1-4 L	Moore
Aug 4 ....Parma (Italy)		East Rutherford, NJ	1-2 L	Lapper
Aug 6...................Benfica (Portugal)		East Rutherford, NJ	2-1 W	Klopas, Lassiter
Aug 16.................Sweden		Norrkoping, Sweden	0-1 L	none

#Game suspended due to storm; 83 minutes played.

*U.S. Cup '95   †Copa America

U.S. Women's National Team 1995 Results

Date	Opponent	Site	Result	U.S. Goals
Feb 24...................Denmark		Winter Park, FL	7-0 W	Akers (3), Hamm (2), Lilly, Roberts
Mar 14..................Finland		Faro, Portugal	2-0 W	Lilly, Hamm
Mar 16..................Portugal		Portimao, Portugal	3-0 W	Milbrett, Gabarra, Lilly
Mar 17..................Denmark		Lagos, Portugal	0-2 L	none
Mar 19..................Norway		Quarteira, Portugal	3-3 (2-4) L	Akers, Gabarra, Lilly
April 11..................Italy		Poissy, France	3-0 W	Akers, Venturini, Gabarra
April 12..................Canada		St Maur, France	5-0 W	Hamm (3), Akers, Milbrett
April 15..................France		Strasbourg, France	3-0 W	Gabarra, Lilly, Hamm
April 28..................Finland		Decatur, Georgia	2-0 W	Akers, Venturini
April 30..................Finland		Davidson, NC	6-0 W	Lilly, Akers, own goal, Neaton, Foudy, Hamm
May 12 ....Brazil		Tacoma, WA	3-0 W	Hamm (2), Venturini
May 14 ....Brazil		Portland, OR	4-1 W	Akers (2), Gabarra, Milbrett
May 19 ....Canada		Dallas, TX	9-1 W	Akers, (2), Hamm (2), Gabarra (2), Lilly (2), Milbrett
May 22 ....Canada		Edmonton, Canada	2-1 W	Milbrett, Neaton
June 6 ....China*		Gavle, Sweden	3-3 T	Venturini, Milbrett, Hamm
June 8..................Denmark*		Gavle, Sweden	2-0 W	Lilly, Milbrett
June 10 ....Australia*		Helsingborg, Sweden	4-1 W	Foudy, Fawcett, Overbeck, Keller
June 13 ....Japan*		Gavle, Sweden	4-0 W	Lilly (2), Milbrett, Venturini
June 15 ....Norway*		Vasteras, Sweden	0-1 L	none
June 17 ....China*		Gavle, Sweden	2-0 W	Venturini, Hamm
July 30..................Taipei†		New Britain, CT	9-0 W	Venturini (3), Hamm (2), Akers (2) Overbeck (2)
Aug 3 ....Australia†		New Brunswick, NJ	4-2 W	Hamm (2), Akers, Lilly
Aug 6...................Norway†		Washington, D.C.	2-1 W	Hamm, Pearman

*FIFA Women's World Championship. †U.S. Women's Cup '95.

Time on their side

In 1995 the Ontario Lottery Corporation added British soccer to its Pro-Line lottery. Some might frown on what would appear to be government-sponsored gambling, but as the old saying goes, it ain't gambling if you know the outcome.

The scene: Feathers Pub in Toronto. The date: Jan. 2, 1995. A British soccer fan, seeking help in doping out his picks, places a call from the pub to his brother in Manchester, England. The brother proceeds to tick off not only the winners of the matches but the scores as well. Why, asks the Toronto brother, was he so sure? "Because," replies the Manchester brother, "those games ended 40 minutes ago." It seems that the day after New Year's was a holiday in Great Britain, and several matches were played in the afternoon rather than the evening, a wrinkle lottery officials failed to account for in setting the cutoff time for submitting picks. Anyone who caught on had 90 minutes to get in it and win it.

The Toronto brother tipped six of his pals to the scam, and they reportedly took home $12,000 apiece.

Looking for another sure thing? Bet that before its next lottery someone at Pro-Line checks a schedule.

Club Competition

1994 Toyota Cup Final

Competition between winners of European Cup and Libertadores Cup.

TOKYO: DEC 1, 1994

Velez Sarsfield (Arg.) 0   2 —2
A.C. Milan (Italy) 0   0 —0

Goals: Trotta, PK, (50), Asad (57).

Att: 55,860

Velez Sarsfield: Chilavert, Trotta, Cardozo, Almandoz, Gomez, Sotomayor, Bassedas, Basualdo, Asad, Pompei, Flores
A.C. Milan: Rossi, Tassotti, Maldini, Albertini, Costacurta, Baresi, Donadoni, Desailly, Boban, Savicevic (Simone, 60), Massaro (Panucci, 86).

European Cup

League champions of the countries belonging to UEFA (Union of European Football Associations).

VIENNA: MAY 24, 1995

Ajax (Netherlands) 0   1 —1
A.C. Milan (Italy) 0   0 —0

Goal: Kluivert (85).

Att: 49,730.

Ajax: Van Der Sar, Reiziger, Blind, Rijkaard, F. De Boer, Seedorf (Kanu, 53), Finidi, Davids, R. De Boer, Litmanen (Kluivert, 69), Overmars.
A.C. Milan: Rossi, Panucci, Maldini, Costacurta, Baresi, Donadoni, Desailly, Massaro (Eranio, 90), Boban (Lentini, 86), Simone.

European Cup-Winners' Cup

Cup winners of countries belonging to UEFA.

PARIS: MAY 10, 1995

Real Zaragoza(Spain) 0   1   1—2
Arsenal (England) 0   1   0—1
Goals: Esnaider (68), Nayim (120), Hartson (75).
Att: 42,424

Real Zaragoza: Cedrun, Belsue, Aguado, Caceres, Solana, Poyet, Aragon, Nayim, Pardeza, Esnaider, Higuera (Garcia Sanjuan, 67, Gelli, 114).
Arsenal: Seaman, Dixon, Linighan, Adams, Winterburn (Morrow, 47), Keown (Hillier, 46), Schwarz, Parlour, Merson, Wright, Hartson.

UEFA Cup

Competition between teams other than league champions and cup-winners from UEFA.

(SECOND LEG) MILAN: MAY 17, 1995

Parma (Italy) 0   1 —1
Juventus (Italy) 1   0 —1

Goals: Vialli (33), D. Baggio (53) (aggregate: Parma, 2–1).

Att: 80,750

Parma: Bucci, Benarrivo (Mussi 46), Di Chiara (Castellini, 80), Minotti, Susic, Cuoto, Fiore, D. Baggio, Crippa, Zola, Asprilla.
Juventus: Peruzzi, Ferrara, Jarni, Torricelli, Porrini Paulo Sousa, Di Livio (Carrera, 81), Marocchi (Del Piero, 74), Vialli, R. Baggio, Ravanelli.

Libertadores Cup

Competition between champion clubs and runners-up of 10 South American National Associations.

(SECOND LEG) MEDELLIN: AUG. 30, 1995

Gremio (Brazil) 0   1 —1
Atl. Nacional (Colombia) ...1   0 —1

Goals: Aristizabal (12), Dinho, PK (86) (aggregate: Gremio, 4–2).

Att: 52,000

Gremio: Danrlei, Arce, Rivarola, Adilson, Roger, Dinho, Carlos Miguel, Goiano, Arildson, Nunes (Alexandre, 64), Jardel (Nildo, 83).
Atl. Nacional: Higulta, Santa (Herrera, 57), Marulanda, Foranda, Mosquera (Pabon , 83), Serna, Arango, Gutierrez, Garcia, Aristizabal, Angel.

El Boss

Jesús Gil is the Steinbrennerian chairman of Atletico Madrid, one of Spain's biggest soccer clubs, but that's only one of the hats he wears. Gil is also mayor of Marbella, a city on the Costa del Sol, in which capacity he has begun performing marriages. Some 1,500 couples have applied to get hitched at Marbella's town hall, apparently untroubled that Gil has put asunder 17 coaches during the eight years he has run the club.

National Club Champions—Europe

Country	League Champion	Cup Winner
Albania	Tirana	Teuta
Armenia	Shirak Gyumri	Ararat Yerevan
Austria	Casino Salzburg	Rapid Vienna
Azerbaijan	TBC	TBC
Belarus	Minsk Dynamo	TBC
Belgium	Anderlecht	Club Brugge
Bulgaria	Levski	Lok. Sofia
Croatia	Hajduk Split	Croatia Zagreb
Cyprus	Anorthosis	Apoel
Czech Republic	Sparta Prague	Spartak Hradec Kralove
Denmark	Aab Aalborg	FC Copenhagen
England	Blackburn Rovers	Everton
Estonia	Lantana	Trans Narva
Faroe Isles	GI	KI
Finland	TVP Tampere	HJK Helsinki
France	Nantes	Paris St Germain

National Club Champions—Europe (Cont.)

Country	League Champion	Cup Winner
Georgia	Tibilisi Dynamo	Batumi
Germany	Borussia Dortmund	Borussia Monchengladbach
Greece	Panathinaikos	AEK Athens
Holland	Ajax	Feyenoord
Hungary	Ferencvaros	VAC Samsung
Iceland	IA Akranes	KR Reykjavik
Ireland	Dundalk	Derry City
Israel	Maccabi Tel Aviv	Maccabi Haifa
Italy	Juventus	Parma
Latvia	Skonto Riga	TBC
Liechtenstein	FC Vaduz	FC Vaduz
Lithuania	Inkaras	Zhalgiris Vilnius
Luxembourg	Jeunesse Esch	Grevenmacher
Macedonia	Vardar Skopje	Sileks
Malta	Hibernian	Valletta
Moldova	Zimbru	Tiligul
Northern Ireland	Crusaders	Linfield
Norway	Rosenborg	Molde
Poland	Legia Warsaw	GKS Katowice
Portugal	FC Porto	Sporting Lisbon
Romania	Steaua Bucharest	Petrolul Ploiesti
Russia	Moscow Spartak	Moscow Dynamo
Scotland	Rangers	Celtic
Slovakia	Slovan Bratislava	Inter Bratislava
Slovenia	Olympia	Mura Sobota
Spain	Real Madrid	Real Zaragoza
Sweden	IFK Gothenburg	Halmstad
Switzerland	Grasshopper	Sion
Turkey	Besiktas	Trabzonspor
Ukraine	Kiev Dynamo	Shakhtyor Donetsk
Wales	Bangor City	Wrexham
Yugoslavia	Red Star Belgrade	Obilic

National Professional Soccer League

1994–95 Final Standings

American	W	L	Pct	GB	PF	PA	National	W	L	Pct	GB	PF	PA
Cleveland	30	10	.750	—	742	524	St Louis	30	10	.750	—	711	465
Harrisburg	23	17	.575	7.0	594	526	Kansas City	29	11	.725	1.0	641	460
Baltimore	23	17	.575	7.0	615	572	Milwaukee	23	17	.575	7.0	535	459
Buffalo	20	20	.500	10.0	579	552	Detroit	18	22	.450	12.0	508	546
Dayton	15	25	.375	15.0	548	671	Wichita	17	23	.425	13.0	480	583
Canton	6	34	.150	24.0	443	752	Chicago	6	34	.150	24.0	420	706

1995 Playoff Results

HARRISBURG VS CLEVELAND

Date	Results	Attendance
Apr 7	Harrisburg 17 vs Cleveland 7	4,206
Apr 10	Cleveland 18 vs Harrisburg 24	5,050
Apr 12	Cleveland 12 vs Harrisburg 16	6,511

(Harrisburg wins series 3–0)

ST LOUIS VS KANSAS CITY

Date	Results	Attendance
Apr 6	St Louis 40 vs Kansas City 22	5,166
Apr 7	Kansas City 22 vs St Louis 18	4,391
Apr 9	Kansas City 6 vs St Louis 21	3,803
Apr 14	St Louis 11 vs Kansas City 12	9,269
Apr 15	St Louis 25 vs Kansas City 14	6,376

(St Louis wins series 3–2)

CHAMPIONSHIP SERIES

Date	Results	Attendance
Apr 20	St Louis 19 vs Harrisburg 9	5,878
Apr 22	St Louis 18 vs Harrisburg 8	12,206
Apr 23	Harrisburg 7 vs St Louis 12	6,578
Apr 25	Harrisburg 11 vs St Louis 14	4,013

(St Louis wins series 4–0)

Statistical Leaders

SCORING

Rank	Player	3PG	2PG	1PG	Assists	Points
1	Hector Marinaro, Clev	11	81	7	53	255
2	Zoran Karic, Clev	8	51	19	96	241
3	Mark Moser, StL	6	68	15	26	195
4	Dennis Brose, Day	8	62	16	27	191
5	Goran Kunjak, KC	3	54	12	52	181

THREE-POINT GOALS

	Player	Team	Games	3PG
1	Michael King	Mil	40	12
2	Hector Marinaro	Clev	32	11
2	Sean Bowers	Det	40	11
3	Joe Reiniger	StL	34	10
4	Zoran Karic	Clev	31	8

Three tied with 6.

ASSISTS

	Player	Team	Games	Assists
1	Zoran Karic	Clev	31	96
2	Wes Wade	KC	40	71
3	Pato Margetic	Det	37	62
4	Franklin McIntosh	Balt	27	59
5	Hector Marinaro	Clev	32	53

GOALKEEPING LEADERS (Minimum 1410 minutes)

	Player	Team	GP	Min	Shots	Svs	GA	PAA	W	L
1	Victor Nogueira	Mil	35	1917:21	586	422	164	10.30	20	14
2	Warren Westcoat	KC	29	1619:48	574	425	149	10.45	19	7
3	Jamie Swanner	StL	35	1961:11	825	626	199	11.63	25	8
4	Scoop Stanisic	Harr	25	1487:45	525	367	158	12.62	15	8
5	Bryan Finnerty	Det	36	2029:32	730	500	230	12.86	17	18

American Professional Soccer League*

1994 Final Standings

	W	L	GF	GA	Pts	Home	Road
Seattle Sounders	14	6	38	16	121	9-1	5-5
Los Angeles Salsa	12	8	36	22	106	7-3	5-5
Montreal Impact	12	8	27	18	93	7-3	5-5
Colorado Foxes	12	8	26	26	92	8-2	4-6
Fort Lauderdale Strikers	8	12	23	33	72	4-6	4-6
Vancouver Eighty-Sixers	7	13	25	41	65	5-5	2-8
Toronto Rockets	5	15	14	33	44	4-6	1-9

Point system—six points for each victory in regulation or overtime; four points for a Shootout win; two points for a Shootout loss; one bonus point for each goal in regulation up to a maximun of three (regardless of whether team wins or loses).

Playoff Results: Four teams—Seattle, Los Angeles, Montreal, and Colorado—qualified for the playoffs. Colorado defeated Seattle 2–1, Montreal defeated Los Angeles 2–1, in the Semis; Montreal defeated Colorado 1–0 in the finals for the APSL championship.

SCORING LEADERS

Player	Pts
Paul Wright, Los Angeles	27
Paulinho, Los Angeles	27
Chance Fry, Seattle	26
Jason Dunn, Seattle	23
Jean Harbor, Montreal	20

GOALS LEADERS

Player	
Paul Wright, Los Angeles	12
Paulinho, Los Angeles	11
Chance Fry, Seattle	11
Jason Dunn, Seattle	10
Jean Harbor, Montreal	8

ASSISTS LEADERS

Player	
Shawn Medved, Seattle	11
Dale Mitchell, Vancouver	9
Jason Farrell, Seattle	7
Paulinho, Los Angeles	5

Ten tied with 4.

GOALS-AGAINST-AVERAGE LEADERS

Player	
Marcus Hahnemann, Seattle	0.57
Mike Littman, Los Angeles	0.76
Pat Harrington, Montreal	0.95
Mario Jimenez, Los Angeles	1.05
Mark Dodd, Colorado	1.10

*Known as the A-League since 1995.

FOR THE RECORD·Year by Year

The World Cup

Results

Year	Champion	Score	Runner-Up	Winning Coach
1930	Uruguay	4-2	Argentina	Alberto Supicci
1934	Italy	2-1	Czechoslovakia	Vittorio Pozzo
1938	Italy	4-2	Hungary	Vittorio Pozzo
1950	Uruguay	2-1	Brazil	Juan Lopez
1954	West Germany	3-2	Hungary	Sepp Herberger
1958	Brazil	5-2	Sweden	Vicente Feola
1962	Brazil	3-1	Czechoslovakia	Aymore Moreira
1966	England	4-2	West Germany	Alf Ramsey
1970	Brazil	4-1	Italy	Mario Zagalo
1974	West Germany	2-1	Netherlands	Helmut Schoen
1978	Argentina	3-1	Netherlands	César Menotti
1982	Italy	3-1	West Germany	Enzo Bearzot
1986	Argentina	3-2	West Germany	Carlos Bilardo
1990	West Germany	1-0	Argentina	Franz Beckenbauer
1994	Brazil	0-0 (3-2)	Italy	Carlos Alberto Parreira

Alltime World Cup Participation

Of the 58 nations which have taken part in the World Cup, only Brazil has competed in each of the 15 tournaments held to date. West Germany or an undivided Germany (1934, '38 and '94) have played in 14 World Cups.

	Matches	W	T	L	Goals For	Goals Against
Brazil	73	49	13	11	159	68
*Germany	73	42	16	15	154	97
Italy	61	35	14	12	97	59
Argentina	52	26	9	17	90	65
England	41	18	12	11	55	38
†Russia	34	16	6	12	60	40
Uruguay	37	15	8	14	61	52
France	34	15	5	14	71	56
Yugoslavia	33	15	5	13	55	42
Hungary	32	15	3	14	87	57
Spain	37	15	9	13	53	44
Poland	25	13	5	7	39	29
Sweden	37	13	7	17	62	60
Austria	26	12	2	12	40	43
Czechoslovakia	30	11	5	14	44	45
Netherlands	25	11	6	8	43	29
Belgium	29	9	4	16	37	53
Mexico	33	7	8	18	31	68
Chile	21	7	3	11	26	32
Portugal	9	6	0	3	19	12
Romania	17	6	4	7	26	29
Switzerland	22	6	3	13	33	51
United States	14	4	1	9	17	33
Scotland	20	4	6	10	23	35
Peru	15	4	3	8	19	31
Bulgaria	22	3	7	12	21	42
Northern Ireland	13	3	5	5	13	23
Paraguay	11	3	4	4	16	25
Cameroon	11	3	4	4	11	21
Denmark	4	3	0	1	10	6
Nigeria	4	2	0	2	7	4
East Germany	6	2	2	2	5	5
Costa Rica	4	2	0	2	4	6
Saudi Arabia	4	2	0	2	5	6
Colombia	10	2	2	6	13	20
Algeria	6	2	1	3	6	10
Wales	5	1	3	1	4	4
Morocco	7	1	3	3	5	8
Republic of Ireland	9	1	5	3	4	7
Tunisia	3	1	1	1	3	2
North Korea	4	1	1	2	5	9
Cuba	3	1	1	1	5	12
Turkey	3	1	0	2	10	11
Norway	4	1	1	2	2	3
Israel	3	1	0	2	1	3
Honduras	3	0	2	1	2	3
Egypt	4	0	2	2	3	6
Kuwait	3	0	1	2	2	6
Australia	3	0	1	2	0	5
Iran	3	0	1	2	2	8
South Korea	11	0	3	8	9	34
Dutch East Indies	1	0	0	1	0	6
Iraq	3	0	0	3	1	4
Canada	3	0	0	3	0	5
United Arab Emirates	3	0	0	3	2	11
New Zealand	3	0	0	3	2	12
Haiti	3	0	0	3	2	14
Zaire	3	0	0	3	0	14
Bolivia	6	0	1	5	1	20
El Salvador	6	0	0	6	1	22
Greece	3	0	0	3	0	8

*Includes West Germany 1950-90. †Includes USSR 1930-1990.
Note: Matches decided by penalty kicks are shown as drawn games.

World Cup Final Box Scores

URUGUAY 1930

Uruguay 1	3	—4
Argentina........2	0	—2

FIRST HALF

Scoring: 1, Uruguay, Dorado (12); 2, Argentina, Peucelle (20); 3, Argentina, Stabile (37).

SECOND HALF

Scoring: 4, Uruguay, Cea (57); 5, Uruguay, Iriarte (68); 6, Uruguay, Castro (89).

Argentina: Botosso, Della Toree, Paternoster, Evaristo, J., Monti, Suarez, Peucelle, Varallo, Stabile, Ferreira, Evaristo, M.

Uruguay: Ballesteros, Nasazzi, Mascheroni, Andrade, Fernandez, Gestido, Dorado, Scarone, Castro, Cea, Iriarte.

Referee: Langenus (Belgium).

ITALY 1934

Italy..................0	1	1—2	
Czechoslovakia ..0	1	0—1	

SECOND HALF

Scoring: 1, Czech., Puc (70); 2, Italy, Orsi (80).

OVERTIME

Scoring: 3, Italy, Schiavio (95).

Italy: Combi, Monzeglio, Allemandi, Ferraris Monti, Monti, Bertolini, Guaita, Meazza, Schiavio, Ferrari, Orsi.

Czechoslovakia: Planicka, Zenisek, Ctyroky, Kostalek, Cambal, Cambal, Krcil, Junek, Svoboda, Sobotka, Nejedly, Puc.

Referee: Eklind (Sweden).

FRANCE 1938

Italy..................3	1	—4
Hungary 1	1	—2

FIRST HALF

Scoring: 1, Italy, Colaussi (5); 2, Hungary, Titkos (7); 3, Italy, Piola (16); 4, Italy, Piola (35).

SECOND HALF

Scoring: 5, Hungary, Sarosi (70); 6, Italy, Colaussi (82).

Italy: Olivieri, Foni, Rava, Serantoni, Andreolo, Locatelli, Biavati, Meazza, Piola, Ferrari, Colaussi.

Hungary: Szabo; Polger, Biro, Szalay, Szucs, Lazar, Sas, Vincze, Sarosi, Zsengeller, Titkos.

Referee: Capdeville (France).

BRAZIL 1950

Uruguay 0	2	—2
Brazil................0	1	—1

SECOND HALF

Scoring: 1, Brazil, Friaca (47); 2, Uruguay, Schiaffino (66); 3, Uruguay, Ghiggia (79).

Uruguay: Maspoli, Gonzales, Tejera, Gambretta, Varela, Andrade, Ghiggia, Perez, Miguez, Schiffiano, Moran

Brazil: Barbosa, Augusto, Juvenal, Bauer, Banilo, Bigode, Friaca, Zizinho, Ademir, Jair, Chico.

Referee: Reader (England).

SWITZERLAND 1954

W Germany 2	1	—3
Hungary 2	0	—2

FIRST HALF

Scoring: 1, Hungary, Puskas (6); 2, Hungary, Czibor (8); 3, W Germ, Morlock (10); 4, W Germ, Rahn (18).

SECOND HALF

Scoring: 5, W Germ, Rahn (84).

West Germany: Turek; Posipal, Kohlmeyer, Eckel, Liebrich, Mai, Rahn, Morlock, Walter, O., Walter, F., Schaefer.

Hungary: Grosics; Buzansky, Lantos, Bozsik, Lorant, Zakarias, Czibor, Kocsis, Hidegkuti, Puskas, Toth.

Referee: Ling (England).

SWEDEN 1958

Brazil.................2	3	—5
Sweden 1	1	—2

FIRST HALF

Scoring:1, Sweden, Liedholm (3); 2, Brazil, Vava (9); 3, Brazil, Vava (32).

SECOND HALF

Scoring: 4, Brazil, Pelé (55); 5, Brazil, Zagalo (68); 6, Sweden Simonsson (80); 7, Brazil, Pelé (90).

Brazil: Glymar, Santos, D., Santos, N., Zito, Bellini, Orlando, Garrincha, Didi, Vava, Pelé, Zagalo.

Sweden: Svensson, Bergmark, Axbom, Boerjesson, Gustavsson, Parling, Hamrin, Gren, Simonsson, Liedholm, Skoglund.

Referee: Guigue (France).

CHILE 1962

Brazil............................1	2	—3
Czechoslovakia 1	0	—1

FIRST HALF

Scoring: 1, Czech, Masopust (15); 2, Brazil, Amarildo (17).

SECOND HALF

Scoring: 3, Brazil, Zito (68); 4, Brazil, Vava (77).

Brazil: Glymar; Santos, D., Santos, N., Zito, Mauro, Zozimo, Garrincha, Didi, Vava, Amarildo, Zagalo.

Czechoslovakia: Schroiff, Tichy, Novak, Pluskal, Popluhar, Masopust, Pospichal, Scherer, Kvasnak, Kadraba, Jelinek.

Referee: Latychev (USSR).

World Cup Final Box Scores *(Cont.)*

ENGLAND 1966

England..............1	1	2——4
W. Germany..........1	1	0——2

FIRST HALF

Scoring: 1, Germany, Haller (12); 2, England, Hurst, (18).

SECOND HALF

Scoring: 3, England, Peters (78); 4, Germany, Weber (90).

OVERTIME

Scoring: 5, England, Hurst (101); 6, England, Hurst (120).

England: Banks, Cohen, Wilson, Stiles, Charlton, J., Moore, Ball, Hurst, Hunt, Charlton, R., Peters.

W. Germany: Tilkowski, Hottges, Schmellinger, Beckenbauer, Schulz, Weber, Held, Haller, Seeler, Overath, Emmerich.

Referee: Dienst (Switzerland).

W. GERMANY 1974

W. Germany 2	0 ——2
Netherlands.....1	0 ——1

FIRST HALF

Scoring: 1, The Netherlands, Neeskens, PK, (1); 2, W. Germany, Breitner, PK, (26); 3, W. Germany, Muller, (44).

W. Germany: Maier, Vogts, Beckenbauer, Schwarzenbeck, Breitner, Hoeness, Bonhof, Overath, Grabowski, Muller, Holzenbein.

The Netherlands: Jongbloed, Suurbier, Rijsbergen (de Jong), Haan, Krol, Jansen, Neeskens, van Hanagem, Cruyff, Rensenbrink (van der Kerkhof).

Referee: Taylor (England).

ITALY 1982

Italy...................0	3 ——3
W. Germany 0	1 ——1

SECOND HALF

Scoring: 1, Italy, Rossi (57); 2, Italy, Tardelli (68); 3, Italy, Altobelli (81); 4, Germany, Breitner (83).

Italy: Zoff, Bergomi, Scirea, Collovati, Cabrini, Oriali, Gentile, Tardelli, Conti, Rossi, Graziani (Altobelli, Causio).

W. Germany: Schumacher, Kaltz, Stielike, Foerster, K., Foerster, B., Dremmler (Hrubesch), Breitner, Briegel, Rummenigge (Mueller), Fishcher (Littbrarski).

Referee: Coelho (Brazil).

MEXICO 1970

Brazil.................1	3 ——4
Italy..................1	0 ——1

FIRST HALF

Scoring: 1, Brazil, Pelé (18); 2, Italy, Boninsegna (32).

SECOND HALF

Scoring: 3, Brazil, Gerson (65); 4, Brazil, Jairzinho (70); 5, Brazil, Alberto (86).

Brazil: Feliz, Alberto, Brito, Wilson, Piazza, Everaldo, Clodoaldo, Gerson, Jairzinho, Tostao, Pelé, Rivelino.

Italy: Albertosi, Burgnich, Cera, Rosato, Facchetti, Bertini (Juliano), Mazzola, De Sisti, Domenghini, Boninsegna (Rivera), Riva.

Referee: Glockner (E. Germany).

ARGENTINA 1978

Argentina 1	0	2——3
Netherlands 0	1	0——1

FIRST HALF

Scoring: 1, Argentina, Kempes (38).

SECOND HALF

Scoring: 2, The Netherlands, Nanninga (81).

OVERTIME

Scoring: 3, Arg., Kempes (104); 4, Arg., Bertoni (114).

Argentina: Fillol, Olguin, Galvan, Passarella, Tarantini, Ardiles (Larrosa), Gallego, Kempes, Bertoni, Luque, Ortiz (Houseman).

The Netherlands: Jongbloed, Jansen (Suurbier), Krol, Brandts, Poortvliet, Neeskens, Haan, van der Kerkhoff, W., van der Kerkhoff, R., Rep (Nanninga), Rensenbrink.

Referee: Gonella (Italy).

MEXICO 1986

Argentina 1	2 ——3
W. Germany 0	2 ——2

FIRST HALF

Scoring: 1, Argentina, Brown (22).

SECOND HALF

Scoring: 2, Arg., Valdano (55); 3, W. Germ., Rummenigge (73); 4, W. Germ., Voller (81); 5, Arg., Burruchaga (83).

Argentina: Pumpido, Brown, Cuciuffo, Ruggeri, Olarticoecha, Bastista, Giusti, Burruchaga (90, Trobbiani), Enrique, Maradona, Valdona.

W. Germany: Schumacher, Jakobs, Forster, Eder, Brehme, Matthaus, Berthold, Magath (62 Hoeness), Briegel, Rummenigge, Allofs (46 Voller).

Referee: Filho (Brazil).

World Cup Final Box Scores *(Cont.)*

ITALY 1990

| W Germany.........0 | 1——1 |
| Argentina...............0 | 0——0 |

SECOND HALF

Scoring: 1, W. Germany, Brehme, PK, (84).

W. Germany: Illgner, Brehme, Kohler, Augenthaler, Buchwald, Berthold (Reuter), Littbarski, Haessler, Mattaeus, Voeller, Klinsmann.

Argentina: Goychoechea, Lorenzo, Serrizuela, Sensini, Ruggeri (Monzon), Simon, Basualdo, Burruchag (Calderon), Maradona, Troglio, Dezottir.

Referee: Coelho (Brazil).

UNITED STATES 1994

| Italy.....................0 | 0 | 0——0 |
| Brazil.....................0 | 0 | 0——0 |

Scoring: None. Shootout goals: Italy—2: Albertini, Evani; Brazil—3: Romario, Branco, Dunga.

Italy: Pagliuca, Benarrivo, Maldini, Baresi, Mussi (Apolloni 35), Albertini, D. Baggio (Evani 95), Berti, Donadoni, Baggio, Massaro,

Brazil: Taffarel, Jorginho (Cafu 21), Branco, Aldair, Santos, Silva, Dunga, Zinho (Viola 106), Mazinho, Bebeto, Romario

Referee: Sandor Puhl (Hungary).

Alltime Leaders

GOALS

Player, Nation	Tournaments	Goals	Player, Nation	Tournaments	Goals
Gerd Muller, West Germany	1970, '74	14	Ademir, Brazil	1950	9
Just Fontaine, France	1958	13	Eusebio, Portugal	1966	9
Pelé, Brazil	1958, '62, '66, '70	12	Jairzinho, Brazil	1970, '74	9
Sandor Kocsis, Hungary	1954	11	Paolo Rossi, Italy	1982, '86	9
Teofilo Cubillas, Peru	1970, '78	10	Karl-Heinz Rummenigge,		
Gregorz Lato, Poland	1974, '78, '82	10	W. Germany	1978, '82, '86	9
Helmut Rahn, West Germany	1954, '58	10	Uwe Seeler, West Germany	1958, '62, '66, '70	9
Gary Lineker, England	1986, '90	10	Vava, Brazil	1958, '62	9

LEADING SCORER, CUP BY CUP

Year	Player/Nation	Goals	Year	Player/Nation	Goals
1930	Guillermo Stabile, Argentina	8	1962	Leonel Sanchez, Chile	4
1934	Oldrich Nejedly, Czechoslovakia	5		Vava, Brazil	
1938	Leonidas da Silva, Brazil	8	1966	Eusebio Ferreira, Portugal	9
1950	Ademir de Menenzes, Brazil	9	1970	Gerd Mueller, West Germany	10
1954	Sandor Kocsis, Hungary	11	1974	Gregorz Lato, Poland	7
1958	Just Fontaine, France	13	1978	Mario Kempes, Argentina	6
1962	Florian Albert, Hungary	4	1982	Paolo Rossi, Italy	6
	Valentin Ivanov, USSR		1986	Gary Lineker, England	6
	Garrincha, Brazil		1990	Salvatore Schillaci, Italy	6
	Drazan Jerkovic, Yugoslavia		1994	Hristo Stoitchkov, Bulgaria	6
				Oleg Salenko, Russia	

Most Goals, Individual, One Game

Goals	Player, Nation	Score	Date
5	Oleg Salenko, Russia	Russia-Cameroon, 6-1	6-28-94
4	Leonidas, Brazil	Brazil-Poland, 6-5	6-5-38
4	Ernest Willimowski, Poland	Brazil-Poland, 6-5	6-5-38
4	Gustav Wetterstrim, Sweden	Sweden-Cuba, 8-0	6-12-38
4	Juan Alberto Schiaffino, Uruguay	Uruguay-Bolivia, 8-0	7-2-50
4	Ademir, Brazil	Brazil-Sweden, 7-1	7-9-50
4	Sandor Kocsis, Hungary	Hungary-West Germany, 8-3	6-20-54
4	Just Fontaine, France	France-West Germany, 6-3	6-28-58
4	Eusebio, Portugal	Portugal-No. Korea, 5-3	7-23-66
4	Emilio Butragueño, Spain	Spain-Denmark, 5-1	6-18-86

Note: 30 players have scored 31 World Cup hat tricks. Gerd Muller of West Germany is the only man to have two World Cup hat tricks, both in 1970. The last hat tricks were 6-23-90, Tomas Skuhravy (Czech) vs. Costa Rica and Michel (Spain) vs. So. Korea, 6-17-90.

Attendance and Goal Scoring, Year by Year

Year	Site	No. of Games	Goals	Goals/Game	Attendance	Avg Att
1930	Uruguay	18	70	3.89	434,500	24,139
1934	Italy	17	70	4.12	395,000	23,235
1938	France	18	84	4.67	483,000	26,833
1950	Brazil	22	88	4.00	1,337,000	60,773
1954	Switzerland	26	140	5.38	943,000	36,269
1958	Sweden	35	126	3.60	868,000	24,800
1962	Chile	32	89	2.78	776,000	24,250
1966	England	32	89	2.78	1,614,677	50,459
1970	Mexico	32	95	2.97	1,673,975	52,312
1974	West Germany	38	97	2.55	1,774,022	46,685
1978	Argentina	38	102	2.68	1,610,215	42,374
1982	Spain	52	146	2.80	1,856,277	35,698
1986	Mexico	52	132	2.54	2,441,731	46,956
1990	Italy	52	115	2.21	2,514,443	48,354
1994	United States	52	140	2.69	3,567,415	68,604
Totals		516	1583	3.07	22,289,255	43,196

The United States in the World Cup

URUGUAY 1930: FINAL COMPETITION

Date	Opponent	Result	Scoring
7-13-30	Belgium	3-0 W	US: McGhee 2, Patenaude
7-17-30	Paraguay	3-0 W	US: Patenaude 2, Florie
7-26-30	Argentina	1-6 L	ARG: Monti 2, Scopelli 2, Stabile 2 US: Brown.

ITALY 1934: FINAL COMPETITION

Date	Opponent	Result	Scoring
5-27-34	Italy	1-7 L	US: Donelli ITA: Schiavio 3, Orsi 2, Meazza, Ferrari

BRAZIL 1950: FINAL COMPETITION

Date	Opponent	Result	Scoring
6-25-50	Spain	1-3 L	US: Pariani SPN: Igoa, Basora, Zarra
6-29-50	England	1-0 W	US: Gaetjens.
7-2-50	Chile	2-5 L	US: Wallace, Maca CHL: Robledo, Cremaschi 3, Prieto

ITALY 1990: FINAL COMPETITION

Date	Opponent	Result	Scoring
6-10-90	Czechoslovakia	1-5 L	US: Caligiuri Czech: Skuhravy 2, Hasek, Bilek, Luhovy
6-14-90	Italy	0-1 L	Italy: Giannini
6-19-90	Austria	1-2 L	US: Murray Austria: Rodax, Ogris

UNITED STATES 1994: FINAL COMPETITION

Date	Opponent	Result	Scoring
6-18-94	Switzerland	1-1 T	US: Wynalda Sui: Bregy
6-22-94	Colombia	2-1 W	US: Escobar (own goal), Stewart Colombia: Valencia
6-26-94	Romania	1-0 L	Romania: Petrescu
7-4-94	Brazil	1-0 L	Brazil: Bebeto

International Competition

European Championship

Official name: the European Football Championship. Held every four years since 1960.

Year	Champion	Score	Runner-up	Year	Champion	Score	Runner-up
1960	USSR	2-1	Yugoslavia	1980	West Germany	2-1	Belgium
1964	Spain	2-1	USSR	1984	France	2-0	Spain
1968	Italy	2-0	Yugoslavia	1988	Holland	2-0	USSR
1972	West Germany	3-0	USSR	1992	Denmark	2-0	Germany
1976	Czechoslovakia*	2-2	West Germany				

*Won on penalty kicks.

Under-20 World Championship

Year	Host	Champion	Runner-Up
1977	Tunisia	USSR	Mexico
1979	Japan	Argentina	USSR
1981	Australia	W. Germany	Qatar
1983	Mexico	Brazil	Argentina
1985	USSR	Brazil	Spain
1987	Chile	Yugoslavia	W. Germany
1989	Saudi Arabia	Portugal	Nigeria
1991	Portugal	Portugal	Brazil
1993	Australia	Brazil	Ghana
1995	Qatar	Argentina	Brazil

Under-17 World Championship

Year	
1985	Nigeria
1987	USSR
1989	Saudi Arabia
1991	Ghana

Under-17 (Cont.)

Year	
1993	Nigeria
1995	Ghana

Pan American Games

Year	
1951	Argentina
1955	Argentina
1959	Argentina
1963	Brazil
1967	Mexico
1971	Argentina
1975	Brazil-Mexico (tie)
1979	Brazil
1983	Uruguay
1987	Brazil
1991	United States
1995	Argentina

South American Championship (Copa America)

Year	Champion	Host	Year	Champion	Host
1916	Uruguay	Argentina	1947	Argentina	Ecuador
1917	Uruguay	Uruguay	1949	Brazil	Brazil
1919	Brazil	Brazil	1953	Paraguay	Peru
1920	Uruguay	Chile	1955	Argentina	Chile
1921	Argentina	Argentina	1956	Uruguay	Uruguay
1922	Brazil	Brazil	1957	Argentina	Peru
1923	Uruguay	Uruguay	1958	Argentina	Argentina
1924	Uruguay	Uruguay	1959	Uruguay	Ecuador
1925	Argentina	Argentina	1963	Bolivia	Bolivia
1926	Uruguay	Chile	1967	Uruguay	Uruguay
1927	Argentina	Peru	1975	Peru	Various sites
1929	Argentina	Argentina	1979	Paraguay	Various sites
1935	Uruguay	Peru	1983	Uruguay	Various sites
1937	Argentina	Argentina	1987	Uruguay	Argentina
1939	Peru	Peru	1989	Brazil	Brazil
1941	Argentina	Chile	1990	Brazil	Argentina
1942	Uruguay	Uruguay	1991	Argentina	Chile
1945	Argentina	Chile	1993	Argentina	Ecuador
1946	Argentina	Argentina	1995	Uruguay	Uruguay

Awards

European Footballer of the Year

Year	Player	Team	Year	Player	Team
1956	Stanley Matthews	Blackpool	1973	Johan Cruyff	Barcelona
1957	Alfredo Di Stefano	Real Madrid	1974	Johan Cruyff	Barcelona
1958	Raymond Kopa	Real Madrid	1975	Oleg Blokhin	Dynamo Kiev
1959	Alfredo Di Stefano	Real Madrid	1976	Franz Beckenbauer	Bayern Munich
1960	Luis Suarez	Barcelona	1977	Allan Simonsen	Borussia Moenchengladbach
1961	Omar Sivori	Juventus			
1962	Josef Masopust	Dukla Prague	1978	Kevin Keegan	SV Hamburg
1963	Lev Yashin	Moscow Dynamo	1979	Kevin Keegan	SV Hamburg
1964	Denis Law	Manchester United	1980	Karl-Heinz Rummenigge	Bayern Munich
1965	Eusebio	Benfica			
1966	Bobby Charlton	Manchester United	1981	Karl-Heinz Rummenigge	Bayern Munich
1967	Florian Albert	Ferencvaros			
1968	George Best	Manchester United	1982	Paolo Rossi	Juventus
1969	Gianni Rivera	AC Milan	1983	Michel Platini	Juventus
1970	Gerd Mueller	Bayern Munich	1984	Michel Platini	Juventus
1971	Johan Cruyff	Ajax	1985	Michel Platini	Juventus
1972	Franz Beckenbauer	Bayern Munich	1986	Igor Belanov	Dynamo Kiev
			1987	Ruud Gullit	AC Milan

European Footballer of the Year (Cont.)

1988	Marco Van Basten	AC Milan	1992	Marco Van Basten	AC Milan
1989	Marco Van Basten	AC Milan	1993	Roberto Baggio	Juventus
1990	Lothar Matthaeus	Inter Milan	1994	Hristo Stoichkov	Barcelona
1991	Jean-Pierre Papin	Olympique Marseille			

African Footballer of the Year

Year	Player	Team	Year	Player	Team
1970	Salif Keita	Mali	1983	Mahmoud Al-Khatib	Egypt
1971	Ibrahim Sunday	Ghana	1984	ThÇophile Abega	Cameroon
1972	Chérif Souleyman	Guinea	1985	Mohamed Timoumi	Morocco
1973	Tshimimu Bwanga	Zaire	1986	Badou Zaki	Morocco
1974	Paul Moukila	Congo	1987	Rabah Madjer	Algeria
1975	Ahmed Faras	Morocco	1988	Kalusha Bwalya	Zambia
1976	Roger Milla	Cameroon	1989	George Weah	Liberia
1977	Dhiab Tarak	Tunisia	1990	Roger Milla	Cameroon
1978	Abdul Razak	Ghana	1991	Abedi Pele	Ghana
1979	Thomas Nkono	Cameroon	1992	Abedi Pele	Ghana
1980	Jean Manga Onguene	Cameroon	1993	Rashidi Yekini	Nigeria
1981	Lakhdar Belloumi	Algeria	1994	George Weah	Liberia
1982	Thomas Nkono	Cameroon			

Selected by *France Football*.

South American Player of the Year

Year	Player	Team	Year	Player	Team
1971	Tostao	Cruzeiro	1983	Socrates	Corinthians
1972	Teofilo Cubillas	Alianza Lima	1984	Enzo Francescoli	River Plate
1973	Pelé	Santos	1985	Julio Cesar Romero	Fluminense
1974	Elias Figueroa	Internacional	1986	Antonio Alzamendi	River Plate
1975	Elias Figueroa	Internacional	1987	Carlos Valderrama	Deportivo Cali
1976	Elias Figueroa	Internacional	1988	Ruben Paz	Racing Buenos Aires
1977	Zico	Flamengo	1989	Bebeto	Vasco da Gama
1978	Mario Kempes	Valencia	1990	Raul Amarilla	Olimpia
1979	Diego Maradona	Argentinos Juniors	1991	Oscar Ruggeri	Velez Sarsfield
1980	Diego Maradona	Boca Juniors	1992	Rai	Sao Paulo
1981	Zico	Flamengo	1993	Carlos Valderrama	Junior Barranquilla
1982	Zico	Flamengo	1994	Cafu	Sao Paulo

Selected by Uruguayan magazine *El Pais*.

Club Competition

Toyota Cup

Competition between winners of European Champion Clubs' Cup and Libertadores Cup.

1960	Real Madrid, Spain	1972	Ajax, Holland	1984	Independiente, Argentina
1961	Penarol, Uruguay	1973	Independiente, Argentina	1985	Juventus, Italy
1962	Santos, Brazil	1974	Atletico de Madrid, Spain	1986	River Plate, Argentina
1963	Santos, Brazil	1975	No tournament	1987	Porto, Portugal
1964	Inter, Italy	1976	Bayern Munich	1988	Nacional, Uruguay
1965	Inter, Italy	1977	Boca Juniors, Argentina	1989	Milan, Italy
1966	Penarol, Uruguay	1978	No tournament	1990	Milan, Italy
1967	Racing Club, Argentina	1979	Olimpia, Paraguay	1991	Red Star Belgrade, Yugoslavia
1968	Estudiantes, Argentina	1980	Nacional, Uruguay	1992	Sao Paulo, Brazil
1969	Milan, Italy	1981	Flamengo, Brazil	1993	Sao Paulo, Brazil
1970	Feyenoord, Netherlands	1982	Penarol, Uruguay	1994	Velez Sarsfield, Argentina
1971	Nacional, Uruguay	1983	Gremio, Brazil		

Note: Until 1968 a best-of-three-games format decided the winner. After that a two-game/total-goal format was used until Toyota became the sponsor in 1980, moved the game to Tokyo, and switched the format to a one game championship. The European Cup runner-up substituted for the winner in 1971, 1973, 1974, and 1979.

European Cup

1956	Real Madrid, Spain	1961	Benfica, Portugal	1966	Real Madrid, Spain
1957	Real Madrid, Spain	1962	Benfica, Portugal	1967	Celtic, Scotland
1958	Real Madrid, Spain	1963	A.C. Milan, Italy	1968	Manchester United, England
1959	Real Madrid, Spain	1964	Inter-Milan, Italy	1969	A.C. Milan, Italy
1960	Real Madrid, Spain	1965	Inter-Milan, Italy		

European Cup *(Cont.)*

1970...Feyenoord, Netherlands
1971...Ajax Amsterdam, Netherlands
1972...Ajax Amsterdam, Netherlands
1973...Ajax Amsterdam, Netherlands
1974...Bayern Munich, West Germany
1975...Bayern Munich, West Germany
1976...Bayern Munich, West Germany

1977...Liverpool, England
1978...Liverpool, England
1979...Nottingham Forest, England
1980...Nottingham Forest, England
1981...Liverpool, England
1982...Aston Villa, England
1983...SV Hamburg, West Germany
1984...Liverpool, England
1985...Juventus, Italy

1986...Steaua Bucharest, Romania
1987...Porto, Portugal
1988...P.S.V. Eindhoven, Netherlands
1989...A.C. Milan, Italy
1990...A.C. Milan, Italy
1991....Red Star Belgrade, Yugoslav.
1992...Barcelona, Spain
1993...Olympique Marseille, France
1994...A.C. Milan, Italy
1995...Ajax Amsterdam, Netherlands

Note: On four occasions the European Cup winner has refused to play in the Intercontinental Cup (now Toyota Cup) and has been replaced by the runner-up: Panathinaikos (Greece) in 1971, Juventus (Italy) in 1973, Atletico Madrid (Spain) in 1974, and Malmo (Sweden) in 1979.

Libertadores Cup

Competition between champion clubs and runners-up of 10 South American National Associations.

1960...Penarol, Uruguay
1961...Penarol, Uruguay
1962...Santos, Brazil
1963...Santos, Brazil
1964...Independiente, Argentina
1965...Independiente, Argentina
1966...Penarol, Uruguay
1967...Racing Club, Argentina
1968...Estudiantes, Argentina
1969...Estudiantes, Argentina
1970...Estudiantes, Argentina
1971...Nacional, Uruguay
1972...Independiente, Argentina

1973...Independiente, Argentina
1974...Independiente, Argentina
1975...Independiente, Argentina
1976...Cruzeiro, Brazil
1977...Boca Juniors, Argentina
1978...Boca Juniors, Argentina
1979...Olimpia, Paraguay
1980...Nacional, Uruguay
1981...Flamengo, Brazil
1982...Penarol, Uruguay
1983...Gremio, Brazil
1984...Independiente, Argentina

1985...Argentinos Juniors, Argentina
1986...River Plate, Argentina
1987...Penarol, Uruguay
1988...Nacional, Uruguay
1989...Atletico Nacional, Colombia
1990...Olimpia, Paraguay
1991...Colo Colo, Chile
1992...Sao Paulo, Brazil
1993...Sao Paulo, Brazil
1994...Velez Sarsfield, Argentina
1995...Gremio, Brazil

UEFA Cup

Competition between teams other than league champions and cup winners from the Union of European Football Associations.

1958...Barcelona, Spain
1959...No tournament
1960...Barcelona, Spain
1961...AS Roma, Italy
1962...Valencia, Spain
1963...Valencia, Spain
1964...Real Zaragoza, Spain
1965...Ferencvaros, Hungary
1966...Barcelona, Spain
1967...Dynamo Zagreb, Yugoslavia
1968...Leeds United, England
1969...Newcastle United, England
1970...Arsenal, England
1971...Leeds United, England

1972...Tottenham Hotspur, England
1973...Liverpool, England
1974...Feyenoord, Netherlands
1975...Borussia Monchengladbach, West Germany
1976...Liverpool, England
1977...Juventus, Italy
1978...P.S.V. Eindhoven, Netherlands
1979...Borussia Monchengladbach, West Germany
1980...Eintracht Frankfurt, West Germany
1981...Ipswich Town, England
1982...I.F.K. Gothenburg, Sweden

1983...Anderlecht, Belgium
1984...Tottenham Hotspur, England
1985...Real Madrid, Spain
1986...Real Madrid, Spain
1987...I.F.K. Gothenburg, Sweden
1988...Bayer Leverkusen, West Germany
1989...Naples, Italy
1990...Juventus, Italy
1991...Inter-Milan, Italy
1992...Torino, Italy
1993...Juventus, Italy
1994...Internazionale, Italy
1995...Parma, Italy

European Cup-Winners' Cup

Competition between cup winners of countries belonging to UEFA.

1961...A.C. Fiorentina, Italy
1962...Atletico Madrid, Spain
1963...Tottenham Hotspur, England
1964...Sporting Lisbon, Portugal
1965...West Ham United, England
1966...Borussia Dortmund, West Germany
1967...Bayern Munich, West Germany

1968...A.C. Milan, Italy
1969...Slovan Bratislava, Czechoslovakia
1970...Manchester City, England
1971...Chelsea, England
1972...Glasgow Rangers, Scotland
1973...A.C. Milan, Italy
1974...Magdeburg, East Germany
1975...Dynamo Kiev, USSR

1976...Anderlecht, Belgium
1977...S.V. Hamburg, West Germany
1978...Anderlecht, Belgium
1979...Barcelona, Spain
1980...Valencia, Spain
1981...Dynamo Tbilisi, USSR
1982...Barcelona, Spain
1983...Aberdeen, Scotland
1984...Juventus, Italy

European Cup-Winners' Cup *(Cont.)*

1985...Everton, England
1986...Dynamo Kiev, USSR
1987...Ajax Amsterdam,
    Netherlands

1988...Mechelen, Belgium
1989...Barcelona, Spain
1990...Sampdoria, Italy
1991...Manchester United, England

1992...Werder Bremen, Germany
1993...Parma, Italy
1994...Arsenal, England
1995...Real Zaragoza, Spain

Major Soccer League

Results

Called the Major Indoor Soccer League from 1979–90. Folded in 1992.

	Champion	Series	Runner-Up	Championship Series Most Valuable Player
1979	NY Arrows	2-0	Philadelphia	Shep Messing, NY
1980	NY Arrows	7-4	Houston	Steve Zungul, NY
1981	NY Arrows	6-5	St Louis	Steve Zungul, NY
1982	NY Arrows	3-2	St Louis	Steve Zungul, NY
1983	San Diego	3-2	Baltimore	Juli Veee, SD
1984	Baltimore	4-1	St Louis	Scott Manning, Balt
1985	San Diego	4-1	Baltimore	Steve Zungul, SD
1986	San Diego	4-3	Minnesota	Brian Quinn, SD
1987	Dallas	4-3	Tacoma	Tatu, Dall
1988	San Diego	4-0	Cleveland	Hugo Perez, SD
1989	San Diego	4-3	Baltimore	Victor Nogueira, SD
1990	San Diego	4-2	Baltimore	Brian Quinn, SD
1991	San Diego	4-2	Cleveland	Ben Collins, SD
1992	San Diego	4-2	Dallas	Thomas Usiyan, SD

Championship format: 1979, best-of-three-games series; 1980-81, one-game championship; 1982-83, best-of-five-games series; 1984 to present, best-of-seven-games series.

Statistical Leaders

SCORING

Year	Player/Team	Points
1978-79	Fred Grgurev, Phil	74
1979-80	Steve Zungul, NY	136
1980-81	Steve Zungul, NY	152
1981-82	Steve Zungul, NY	163
1982-83	Steve Zungul, NY	122
1983-84	Stan Stamenkovic, Balt	97
1984-85	Steve Zungul, SD	136
1985-86	Steve Zungul, Tac	115
1986-87	Tatu, Dall	111
1987-88	Erik Rasmussen, Wich	112
1988-89	Preci, Tac	104
1989-90	Tatu, Dall	113
1990-91	Tatu, Dall	144
1991-92	Zoran Karic, Clev	102

GOALS

Year	Player/Team	Goals
1978-79	Fred Grgurev, Phil	46
1979-80	Steve Zungul, NY	90
1980-81	Steve Zungul, NY	108
1981-82	Steve Zungul, NY/GB	103
1982-83	Steve Zungul, NY/GB	75
1983-84	Mark Liveric, NY	58
1984-85	Steve Zungul, SD	68
1985-86	Erik Rasmussen, Wich	67
1986-87	Tatu, Dall	73
1987-88	Hector Marinaro, Minn	58
1988-89	Preki, Tac	51
1989-90	Tatu, Dall	64
1990-91	Tatu, Dall	78
1991-92	Hector Marinaro, Clev	53

ASSISTS

Year	Player/Team	Assists
1978-79	Fred Grgurev, Phil	28
1979-80	Steve Zungul, NY	46
1980-81	Jorgen Kristensen, Wich	52
1981-82	Steve Zungul, NY	60
1982-83	Stan Stamenkovic, Mem	65
1983-84	Stan Stamenkovic, Balt	63
1984-85	Steve Zungul, SD	68
1985-86	Steve Zungul, Tac	60
1986-87	Kai Haaskivi, Clev	55
1987-88	Preki, Tac	58
1988-89	Preki, Tac	53
1989-90	Jan Goossens, KC	55
1990-91	Tatu, Dall	66
1991-92	Zoran Karic, Clev	63

TOP GOALKEEPERS

Year	Player/Team	Goals Agst Avg
1978-79	Paul Hammond, Hous	4.16
1979-80	Sepp Gantenhammer, Hous	4.42
1980-81	Enzo DiPede, Chi	4.06
1981-82	Slobo Liijevski, StL	3.85*
1982-83	Zoltan Toth, NY	4.01
1983-84	Slobo Liijevski, StL	3.67
1984-85	Scott Manning, Balt	3.89
1985-86	Keith Van Eron, Balt	3.66
1986-87	Tino Lettieri, Minn	3.38
1987-88	Zoltan Toth, SD	2.94
1988-89	Victor Nogueira, SD	2.86
1989-90	Joe Papaleo, Dall	3.34
1990-91	Victor Nogueira, SD	4.37
1991-92	Victor Nogueira, SD	4.60

North American Soccer League

Formed in 1968 by the merger of the National Professional Soccer League and the USA League, both of which had begun operations a year earlier. The NPSL's lone champion was the Oakland Clippers. The USA League, which brought entire teams in from Europe, was won in 1967 by the LA Wolves, who were the English League's Wolverhampton Wanderers.

Year	Champion	Score	Runner-Up	Regular Season MVP
1968	Atlanta	0-0, 3-0	San Diego	John Kowalik, Chi
1969	Kansas City	No game	Atlanta	Cirilio Fernandez, KC
1970	Rochester	3-0,1-3	Washington	Carlos Metidieri, Roch
1971	Dallas	1-2, 4-1, 2-0	Atlanta	Carlos Metidieri, Roch
1972	NY	2-1	St Louis	Randy Horton, NY
1973	Philadelphia	2-0	Dallas	Warren Archibald, Mia
1974	Los Angeles	4-3*	Miami	Peter Silvester, Balt
1975	Tampa Bay	2-0	Portland	Steve David, Miami
1976	Toronto	3-0	Minnesota	Pelé, NY
1977	NY	2-1	Seattle	Franz Beckenbauer, NY
1978	NY	3-1	Tampa Bay	Mike Flanagan, NE
1979	Vancouver	2-1	Tampa Bay	Johan Cruyff, LA
1980	NY	3-0	Ft Lauderdale	Roger Davies, Sea
1981	Chicago	1-0*	NY	Giorgio Chinaglia, NY
1982	NY	1-0	Seattle	Peter Ward, Sea
1983	Tulsa	2-0	Toronto	Roberto Cabanas, NY
1984	Chicago	2-1, 3-2	Toronto	Steve Zungul, SJ

*Shootout.

Championship Format: 1968 & 1970: Two games/total goals. 1971 & 1984: Best-of-three game series. 1972-1983: One game championship. Title in 1969 went to the regular season champion.

Statistical Leaders

SCORING

Year	Player/Team	Pts	Year	Player/Team	Pts
1968	John Kowalik, Chi	69	1977	Steven David, LA	58
1969	Kaiser Motaung, Atl	36	1978	Giorgio Chinaglia, NY	79
1970	Kirk Apostolidis, Dall	35	1979	Oscar Fabbiani, Tampa Bay	58
1971	Carlos Metidieri, Roch	46	1980	Giorgio Chinaglia, NY	77
1972	Randy Horton, NY	22	1981	Giorgio Chinaglia, NY	74
1973	Kyle Rote, Dall	30	1982	Giorgio Chinaglia, NY	55
1974	Paul Child, San Jose	36	1983	Roberto Cabanas, NY	66
1975	Steven David, Miami	52	1984	Slavisa Zungul, Golden Bay	50
1976	Giorgio Chinaglia, NY	49			

American Professional Soccer League

Year	Champion	Score	Runner-Up	Regular Season MVP
1991	San Francisco	1-3, 2-0 (1-0 on penalty kicks)	Albany	Jean Harbor, MD
1992	Colorado	1-0	Tampa Bay	Taifour Diane, CO
1993	Colorado	3-1 (OT)	Los Angeles	Taifour Diane, CO
1994	Montreal	1-0	Colorado	Paulinho, LA

NCAA Sports

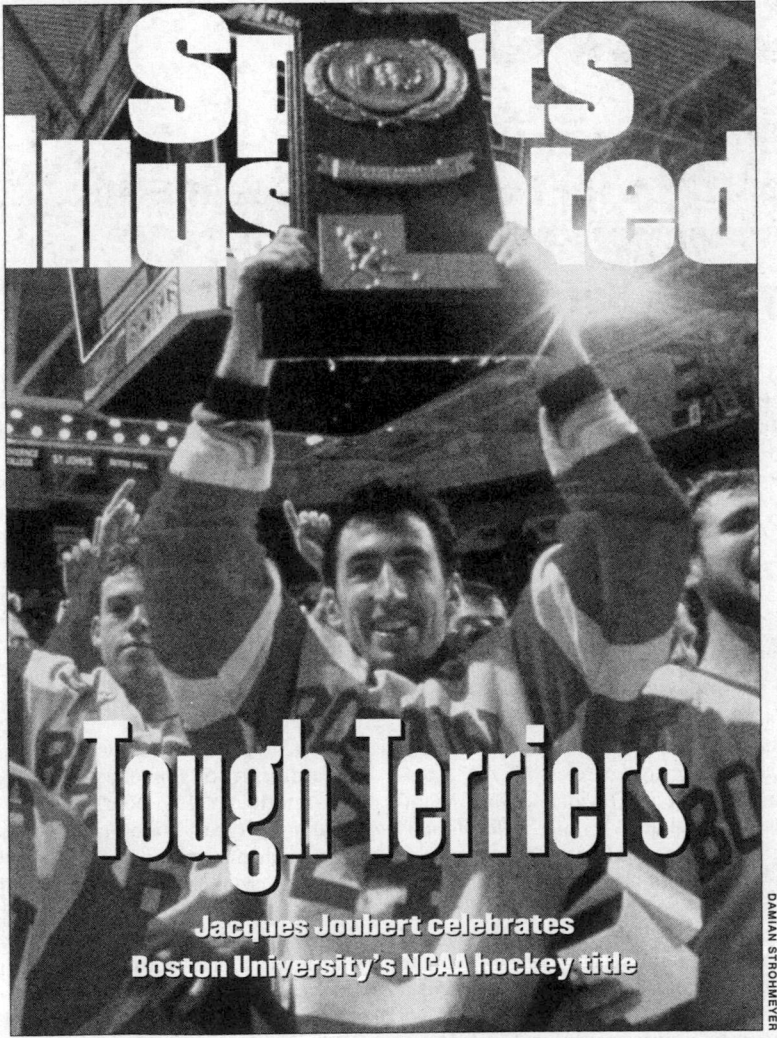

Tough Terriers

Jacques Joubert celebrates Boston University's NCAA hockey title

DAMIAN STROHMEYER

Shining Stars

The leading men seized the spotlight for the NCAA champions in soccer, hockey, and baseball

by Hank Hersch

YOU GOTTA dance with the gal you brung. That bit of wisdom—along with the need to both smell the roses and wait for the fat lady to sing—is cited regularly during NCAA tournaments, when contenders are urged to continue relying on their best players. All too often, however, those stalwarts cede the limelight to unlikelier heroes. In 1994–95, they didn't.

MEN'S SOCCER
The cross came into the penalty box low and hot from Virginia defender Brandon Pollard, striking senior forward A.J. Wood in the right shoulder and the neck. In the 21st minute of the scoreless NCAA championship game in Davidson, N.C., Wood settled the ball quickly onto his left foot as Indiana goalkeeper Scott Coufal charged out of the net to challenge. This was what the tireless Wood lived for, these glimmering moments when all his running and bumping and acting a "nuisance" to the opposition created an eyeblink of opportunity to score. An opportunity to finish.

Indeed, an opportunity to finish in his final match what Wood had spoken about before even starting his first. Shortly after he had arrived in Charlottesville from Rockville, Md., in September 1991, Wood let some of his fellow freshmen on the Virginia soccer team know exactly what their mission was. While walking to dinner he rattled on about their winning four national titles in the next four years. And as the seasons passed, Wood's pie-in-the-sky fantasy seemed increasingly prophetic. Entering their Dec. 11 showdown with Indiana, the Cavaliers under coach Bruce Arena had won an unprecedented three straight NCAA tournaments.

Wood and the three other seniors remaining from that freshman class of '91—midfielder Tain Nix, defender Clint Peay and forward Nate Friends—had left their 12 championship rings back in Charlottesville, symbolically demonstrating that these Cavs could not rely on their past glory to fulfill their four-ordained fate. But a far more integral talisman of their previous conquests was missing, too, in onetime classmate Claudio Reyna, a magical midfielder who had skipped his senior season to play for the U.S. World Cup team and

Wood hit net, delivering the Cavaliers their fourth straight title.

professionally in Germany. Deftly dictating the tempo, Reyna had been named the MVP of the two previous tournaments.

What's more, after defeating Rutgers 2–1 in the semis, Virginia found itself in an unusual position in the '94 finals: underdog. The Hoosiers entered with the top ranking in the country and the top midfielder, Todd Yeagley, whose father, Jerry, was the Indiana coach. Nonetheless, the Cavs' No. 4 ranking, their lack of jewelry and Reyna's absence couldn't convince Yeagley père that Virginia's depth and experience made them anything but the favorites. "I call this tournament the Bruce Arena Classic," he said. "He's here so much, the team should rent a condo."

"We're like locals here," Wood said of Davidson, host of the Final Four since 1992. "We've outlasted some restaurants. The place we always go to eat is a steakhouse now. Last year it was an Italian place. The year before, a sandwich shop."

Besides a fourth ring, only one achieve-

ment was missing from the 6'2" 180-pound Wood's college career: to score in a final match. *Soccer America*'s 1994 Player of the Year, Wood would finish as the second-leading scorer in Virginia history, with 56 goals, and his record-setting 23 goals and 56 points in 1994 paced the school's most prolific attack ever. But in his first three title games, Wood had failed to finish with any of his shots on goal. In the '92 final alone, Wood worked his way for eight chances—some of them almost point-blank—and whiffed on them all.

But when Pollard's cross arrived early in the game last December, Wood didn't rush. When Coufal committed, Wood used the outside of his foot to slip the ball into the left side of the net. Thanks to the Cavs' aggressive tackling in the midfield and to midfielder Billy Walsh's deflection of an eight-yard blast steaming straight for the net late in the first half—"Lucky, I guess," Walsh said—Arena and Co. made Wood's score stand up in a tense and hard-fought 1–0 victory.

The goal gave Wood a record 13 over his NCAA tournament career, and clinched an

O'Sullivan forged a brilliant effort from the fires of adversity.

unshatterable record for titles in a career by Virginia's fab four seniors. "That's the first goal I've scored in four finals, so I was very happy," Wood said afterward. "I just wanted to produce today in the clutch."

MEN'S HOCKEY

His first goal gave Boston University a 2–0 cushion in the NCAA final, a chip-in of linemate Steve Thornton's missile from the left side. His second came on the power play, a rebound after Maine goalie Blair Allison had blocked defenseman Rich Brennan's slap shot from the left point. That put the Terriers up 5–2 late in the third. Sophomore left wing Chris O'Sullivan punctuated both his goals by skating into the corner, dropping to his knees and, cradling the blade of his stick under his

armpit, pumping imaginary bullets into Allison and the rest of the Black Bears. "That's been going on all year," O'Sullivan would say after BU's 6–2 victory on April 1. "It's just emotion after I score."

While the stick shtick was on the tacky side, if anyone was entitled to a little latitude for passion's sake, it was the 19-year-old O'Sullivan. The eighth of 11 children, Chris suffered through the death of both his parents before he could lace up his skates at BU. John O'Sullivan, a Boston Edison employee, died of lymphatic cancer in May 1990, 17 months before Ann's brain cancer was diagnosed. She watched from a wheelchair as Chris helped Catholic Memorial to the state title in April 1992; three months later she was dead.

Eight O'Sullivan siblings ranging in age from 14 to 30 were at Providence Civic Center to see their brother score three times in dispatching first Minnesota in the semis, then archrival Maine in the title game. Peter, 25, was attending junior college in California, while Stephanie, 23, had gone West as well. The Eastern College Athletic Conference hockey player of the year and a forward on four Providence College NCAA championship teams, she was in San Jose to practice with the U.S. women's national team.

Along with his brothers and sisters, John and Ann were there for Chris in spirit. "Not a game goes by, whether in the locker room or on the ice, that I don't think about them," Chris said. "That gets me going. I'd love to look up and see them in the stands, but they were taken away from us, and we have to live with that and deal with it."

O'Sullivan has been tested by more than the deaths in his family, as the seven-inch scar down the back of his neck attests. As a freshman at BU, he slid headfirst into the boards in a game at Providence and broke a vertebra in his neck. During a six-hour operation, doctors used a bone from his hip to fuse two vertebrae together. After sitting out 1992–93 as a medical redshirt, he came back the following season to play 32 games as a defenseman, the position he had played almost exclusively in high school.

But a shortage of wingers forced Terrier coach Jack Parker to move O'Sullivan to the Red Line with sophomore right wing Mike Grier and Thornton, a senior center. "He had no choice," Parker said. "He has great hands, and he's a terrific puckhandler. Unbelievable. He hangs onto the puck as well as anybody. And he's pretty poised. He doesn't rush anything."

Firepower had been at a premium in BU's Final Four appearances the previous two seasons; they were eliminated in a pair of games by an aggregate score of 15–2. But against the Black Bears, the Terriers were especially effective when it mattered most, killing seven of eight power plays against them while converting on three man–advantages of their own. Maine could muster a mere 23 shots. And for the first time since 1972, BU accomplished a cham-

pionship hat trick, winning the Beanpot, the Hockey East and the NCAA titles.

With his two goals, Nos. 22 and 23 of the season, O'Sullivan wound up as the Terriers' leading scorer, with 56 points. He was also named the tournament's Most Valuable Player. It was an award he shared with John and Ann. "They were great parents," he said. "They instilled values in us. I know they're proud of me."

BASEBALL

After his club had pounded its way to the championship of the College World Series in Omaha, Cal State–Fullerton coach Augie Garrido noted that sophomore centerfielder Mark Kotsay had regularly imperiled the denizens of Henry Doorly Zoo, located down Rosenblatt Stadium's rightfield line. "We decided to protect one of the treasures here," Garrido said. "We put hard hats on the monkeys and the gorillas."

Not even an animal act could have upstaged Kotsay, who did a star turn last June worthy of Fullerton alum Kevin Costner. The climax to his record-breaking, week long run came before a record crowd of 22,027 in the CWS finale, when No. 1 Fullerton drilled USC 11–5. On his first swing, the 6-foot, 180-pound Kotsay smacked a three-run shot that cleared a revolving sign 400 feet away in right centerfield. On his next one he cleared the rightfield fence with a man on to cap a four-run second and put the Titans up to stay, 7–3.

His 5 RBIs set a record for the championship game, but Kotsay didn't stop there. He made a lunging, backhanded catch in right-center and then pitched the final 1⅔ innings without surrendering a run. Not that USC hadn't seen previews of Kotsay's heroics. On Feb. 21, he had driven in four runs, made a sliding grab in right-center and gotten the final out for a save in a 10–9 victory. "About Kotsay, what can you say?" Trojan coach Mike Gillespie asked in Omaha. "He's the messiah. He's unbelievable."

The son of an L.A. motorcycle cop, Kotsay went undrafted out of Santa Fe High in

Cal St.–Fullerton knocked off USC then mobbed all-around hero Kotsay.

Santa Fe Springs, Calif., and received only a partial scholarship to Fullerton. "All my life, it's either been my size or my speed," says Kotsay, who runs the 60 in 6.9 seconds. "When I'm in a game and the adrenaline's flowing, I can move pretty fast. When I run a 60, the stopwatches should be able to motivate me, but they don't."

Pride is another matter. "He's our hardest-working player in practice," Garrido says. "No matter how much he does, he still has an overachiever's mentality."

As a freshman Kotsay paid immediate dividends for Garrido, batting .372 for the season and .462 with 8 RBIs in the CWS. In 1995 he became the Titans' stopper as well, warming up his arm in the outfield before trotting in to the mound. In 29 innings he gave up one run while racking up 11 saves and a 2–1 record. At the plate he hit .422, belted 21 homers, drove in 90 runs and struck out only 15 times as Fullerton finished with its best mark ever, 57–9.

While Kotsay received some player of the year honors, he lost on a few ballots to Tennessee pitcher-first baseman Todd Helton. In their two head-to-head meetings at the CWS, Kotsay led the Titans to 11–0 and an 11–1 victories over Helton and the Volunteers. After one win Garrido was asked if there was anything Kotsay hadn't done for his team lately. "Well, he didn't drive the bus over here," Garrido said. "And he didn't pick up the dugout after the game."

By tournament's end Kotsay had hit .563 and slugged 1.250 to raise his career averages to .517 and 1.103, both CWS records.

"I knew the national championship was on the line," Kotsay said. "I just wanted to come in here and be a leader."

NCAA Team Champions

Fall 1994

Cross-Country

MEN

	Champion	Runner-Up
Division I:	Iowa St	Colorado
Division II:	Adams St	Western St
Division III:	Williams	N Central

WOMEN

	Champion	Runner-Up
Division I:	Villanova	Michigan
Division II:	Adams St	Western St
Division III:	Cortland St	Calvin

Field Hockey

WOMEN

	Champion	Runner-Up
Division I:	James Madison	N Carolina
Division II	Lock Haven	Bloomsburg
Division III:	Cortland St	Trenton St

Football

MEN

	Champion	Runner-Up
Division I-A:	Nebraska	Penn St
Division I-AA:	Youngstown St	Boise St
Division II:	N Alabama	Texas A&M Kingsville
Division III:	Albion	Washington & Jefferson

Soccer

MEN

	Champion	Runner-Up
Division I:	Virginia	Indiana
Division II:	Tampa	Oakland (MI)
Division III:	Bethany (W Va)	Johns Hopkins

WOMEN

	Champion	Runner-Up
Division I:	N Carolina	Notre Dame
Division II:	Franklin Pierce	Regis (CO)
Division III:	Trenton St	UC-San Diego

Volleyball

WOMEN

	Champion	Runner-Up
Division I:	Stanford	UCLA
Division II:	Northern Michigan	Cal St-Bakersfield
Division III:	Washington (MO)	WI-Oshkosh

Water Polo

MEN

Champion	Runner-Up
Stanford	Southern Cal

Winter 1994-1995

Basketball

MEN

	Champion	Runner-Up
Division I:	UCLA	Arkansas
Division II:	Southern Indiana	UC-Riverside
Division III:	WI-Platteville	Manchester

WOMEN

	Champion	Runner-Up
Division I:	Connecticut	Tennessee
Division II:	N Dakota St	Portland St
Division III:	Capital (OH)	WI-Oshkosh

Fencing

Champion	Runner-Up
Penn St	St John's (NY)

Gymnastics

MEN

Champion	Runner-Up
Stanford	Nebraska

WOMEN

	Runner-Up
Utah	Alabama/ Michigan

Ice Hockey

MEN

	Champion	Runner-Up
Division I:	Boston University	Maine
Division II:	Bemidji St	Mercyhurst
Division III:	Middlebury	Fredonia St

Rifle

Champion	Runner-Up
West Virginia	Air Force

Skiing

Champion	Runner-Up
Colorado	Utah

Swimming and Diving

MEN

	Champion	Runner-Up
Division I:	Michigan	Stanford
Division II:	Oakland (MI)	Cal St-Bakersfield
Division III:	Kenyon	Hope

WOMEN

	Champion	Runner-Up
Division I:	Stanford	Michigan
Division II:	Air Force	Oakland (MI)
Division III:	Kenyon	Williams

Wrestling

MEN

	Champion	Runner-Up
Division I:	Iowa	Oregon
Division II:	Central Oklahoma	NE-Omaha
Division III:	Augsburg	Trenton St

Winter 1994-1995 *(Cont.)*

Indoor Track

MEN

	Champion	Runner-Up
Division I:	Arkansas	George Mason
		Tennessee
Division II:	St Augustine's	Abilene Christian
Division III:	Lincoln (PA)	Albany (NY)

WOMEN

	Champion	Runner-Up
Division I:	Louisiana St	UCLA
Division II:	Abilene Christian	Adams St
Division III:	WI-Oshkosh	Cortland St

Spring 1995

Baseball

	Champion	Runner-Up
Division I:	Cal St-Fullerton	Southern Cal
Division II:	Florida Southern	Georgia College
Division III:	La Verne	Methodist

Golf

MEN

	Champion	Runner-Up
Division I:	Oklahoma St	Stanford
Division II:	Florida Southern	SC-Aiken
Division III:	Methodist	Otterbein

WOMEN

Champion	Runner-Up
Arizona St	San Jose St

Lacrosse

MEN

	Champion	Runner-Up
Division I:	Syracuse	Maryland
Division II:	Adelphi	Springfield
Division III:	Salisbury St	Nazareth

WOMEN

	Champion	Runner-Up
Division I:	Maryland	Princeton
Division III:	Trenton St	William Smith

Softball

	Champion	Runner-Up
Division I:	UCLA	Arizona
Division II:	Kennesaw St	Bloomsburg
Division III:	Chapman	Trenton St

Tennis

MEN

	Champion	Runner-Up
Division I:	Stanford	Mississippi
Division II:	Lander (SC)	N Florida
Division III:	UC-Santa Cruz	Washington (MD)

WOMEN

	Champion	Runner-Up
Division I:	Texas	Florida
Division II:	Armstrong St	Grand Canyon
Division III:	Kenyon	UC-San Diego

NCAA Team Champions (Cont.)

Spring 1995 (Cont.)
Outdoor Track
MEN

	Champion	Runner-Up
Division I:	Arkansas	UCLA
Division II:	St Augustine's	Abilene Christian
Division III:	Lincoln (PA)	Williams

WOMEN

	Champion	Runner-Up
Division I:	Louisiana St	UCLA
Division II:	Abilene Christian	Cal St-Los Angeles
Division III:	WI-Oshkosh	St Thomas (MN)

Volleyball
MEN

Champion	Runner-Up
UCLA	Penn St

NCAA Division I Individual Champions

Fall 1994
Cross-Country
MEN

Champion	Runner-Up
Martin Keino, Arizona	Adam Goucher, Colorado

WOMEN

Champion	Runner-Up
Jennifer Rhines, Villanova	Amy Rudolph, Providence

Winter 1994-1995
Fencing
MEN

	Champion	Runner-Up
Sabre	Paul Palesti, NYU	Bill Lester, Notre Dame
Foil	Sean McClain, Stanford	Brian Moroney, St John's (NY)
Épée	Mike Gattner, Lawrence	Keith Lichten, MIT

WOMEN

	Champion	Runner-Up
Foil	Olga Kalinovskaya, Penn St	Maria Panyi, Notre Dame
Épée	Tina Loven, St John's (NY)	Heidi Chang, Wellesley

Gymnastics
MEN

	Champion	Runner-Up
All-around	Richard Grace, Nebraska	Darren Elg, Brigham Young
Vault	Ian Bachrach, Stanford	Sebronzik Wright, William & Mary
Parallel bars	Richard Grace, Nebraska	Blaz Puljic, New Mexico
Horizontal bar	Rick Kieffer, Nebraska	Blaz Puljic, New Mexico
Floor exercise	Jay Thornton, Iowa	Josh Stein, Stanford
Pommel horse	Drew Durbin, Ohio St	Jeremiah Landry, Illinois
Rings	Dave Frank, Temple	Brian Fox, California
		Blaine Wilson, Ohio St

WOMEN

	Champion	Runner-Up
All-around	Jenny Hansen, Kentucky	Agina Simpkins, Georgia
Balance beam	Jenny Hansen, Kentucky	Kristen Guise, Florida
		Stella Umeh, UCLA

Gymnastics (Cont.)

WOMEN (Cont.)

	Champion	Runner-Up
Uneven bars	Beth Wymer, Michigan	Lori Strong, Georgia
Floor exercise	Jenny Hansen, Kentucky	Leah Brown, Georgia
	Stella Umeh, UCLA	Aimee Trepanier, Utah
	Leslie Angeles, Georgia	
Vault	Jenny Hansen, Kentucky	Leah Brown, Georgia

Skiing

MEN

	Champion	Runner-Up
Slalom	Scott Wither, Colorado	Hayden Barile, New Hampshire
Giant slalom	Bryan Sax, Colorado	Erik Roland, Denver
Freestyle cross country	Havard Solbaken, Utah	Alse Slettemoen, Utah
Classical cross country	Thomas Weman, Utah	Aki Partanen, Vermont

WOMEN

	Champion	Runner-Up
Slalom	Narcisa Sehovic, Denver	Christl Hager, Utah
Giant slalom	Christl Hager, Utah	Suzie Easterly, New Hampshire
Freestyle cross country	Heidi Selenes, Utah	Amy Crawford, Western St
Classical cross country	Heidi Selenes, Utah	Gina Marie Legueri, Western St

Wrestling

	Champion	Runner-Up
118 lb	Kelvin Jackson, Michigan St	Eric Ivins, Oklahoma
126 lb	Jeff McGinness, Iowa	Sanshiro Abe, Penn St
134 lb	T.J. Jaworsky, N Carolina	Babak Mohammadi, Oregon St
142 lb	John Hughes, Penn St	Gerry Abas, Fresno St
150 lb	Steve Marianetti, Illinois	Lincoln McIlravy, Iowa
158 lb	Ernest Benion, Illinois	Dan Wirnsberger, Michigan St
167 lb	Markus Mollica, Arizona St	Mark Branch, Oklahoma St
177 lb	Les Gutches, Oregon St	Mitch Clark, Ohio St
190 lb	J.J. McGrew, Oklahoma St	Joel Sharratt, Iowa
Heavyweight	Tolly Thompson, Nebraska	Justin Greenlee, Northern Iowa

Swimming and Diving

MEN

	Champion	Time	Runner-Up	Time
50-yard freestyle	Gustavo Borges, Michigan	19.68	Scott Claypool, Stanford	19.78
100-yard freestyle	Gustavo Borges, Michigan	42.85	Lars Frolander, SMU	43.16
200-yard freestyle	Gustavo Borges, Michigan	1:34.61	Ugur Taner, California	1:35.02
500-yard freestyle	Tom Dolan, Michigan	4:08.75*	Chad Carvin, Arizona	4:12.36
1650-yard freestyle	Tom Dolan, Michigan	14:29.31*	Chad Carvin, Arizona	14:38.32
100-yard backstroke	Brian Retterer, Stanford	45.43*	Kurt Jachimowski, Auburn	47.35
200-yard backstroke	Brian Retterer, Stanford	1:40.61	Royce Sharp, Michigan	1:43.03
100-yard breaststroke	Kurt Grote, Stanford	53.21	Jeremy Linn, Tennessee	53.25
200-yard breaststroke	Kurt Grote, Stanford	1:55.02	Nate Thomson, Louisiana St	1:56.45
100-yard butterfly	Lars Frolander, SMU	46.18*	Matt Beck, Texas	47.20
200-yard butterfly	Ugur Taner, California	1:44.39	Mike Merrell, Southern Cal	1:44.58
200-yard IM	Kurt Jachimowski, Auburn	1:45.11	Jason Lancaster, Michigan	1:45.63
400-yard IM	Tom Dolan, Michigan	3:38.18*	Chad Carvin, Arizona	3:43.55

	Champion	Pts	Runner-Up	Pts
1-meter diving†	Pat Bogart, Minnesota	593.60	Kevin McMahon, Louisiana St	581.20
3-meter diving†	Evan Stewart, Tennessee	655.40	Pat Bogart, Minnesota	649.45
Platform†	Tyce Routson, Miami (FL)	785.70	Bryan Gillooly, Miami (FL)	771.75

*Meet record. †Scoring based on 22 dives.

WOMEN

	Champion	Time	Runner-Up	Time
50-yard freestyle	Ashley Tappin, Arizona	22.34	Claudia Franco, Stanford	22.72
100-yard freestyle	Jenny Thompson, Stanford	48.38	Ashley Tappin, Arizona	48.81
200-yard freestyle	Ashley Tappin, Arizona	1:45.23	Kari Haag, N Carolina	1:46.28

NCAA Division I Individual Champions *(Cont.)*

Swimming and Diving *(Cont.)*

WOMEN *(Cont.)*

	Champion	Time	Runner-Up	Time
500-yard freestyle	Mimosa McNerney, Florida	4:41.86	Nikki Dryden, Florida	4:42.10
1650-yard freestyle	Mimosa McNerney, Florida	15:59.71	Sandra Cam, SMU	16:09.19
100-yard backstroke	Alecia Humphrey, Michigan	54.10	Jessica Tong, Stanford	54.83
200-yard backstroke	Alecia Humphrey, Michigan	1:54.68	Anna Simcic, California	1:56.24
100-yard breaststroke	Beata Kaszuba, Arizona St	59.71*	Penelope Heyns, Nebraska	1:00.41
200-yard breaststroke	Beata Kaszuba, Arizona St	2:09.71*	Rachel Gustin, Michigan	2:10.37
100-yard butterfly	Jenny Thompson, Stanford	52.77	Stacy Potter, Alabama	53.08
200-yard butterfly	Berit Puggaard, SMU	1:57.86	Barbara Franco, Florida	1:58.06
200-yard IM	Jenny Thompson, Stanford	1:57.63	Allison Wagner, Florida	1:57.71
400-yard IM	Allison Wagner, Florida	4:09.04	Kristine Quance, Southern Cal	4:10.53

	Champion	Pts	Runner-Up	Pts
1-meter diving#	Cheril Santini, SMU	454.00	Karen Dalton, Ohio St	453.75
3-meter diving†	Tracy Bonner, Tennessee	580.20	Cheril Santini, SMU	566.55
Platform†	Eileen Richetelli, Stanford	630.10	Tina Johnson, Kentucky	615.10

*Meet record. #Scoring based on 20 dives. †Scoring based on 22 dives.

Indoor Track

MEN

	Champion	Mark	Runner-Up	Mark
55-meter dash	Tim Harden, Kentucky	6.12	Donovan Powell, Texas Christian	6.19
55-meter hurdles	Philip Riley, Florida St	7.10	Reggie Torian, Wisconsin	7.13
200-meter dash	Dave Dopek, DePaul	20.78	Derrick Thompson, Arkansas	20.86
400-meter dash	Deon Minor, Baylor	46.00	Greg Haughton, George Mason	46.01
800-meter run	Michael Williams, Manhattan	1:48.12	Bryan Woodward, Georgetown	1:49.22
Mile run	Kevin Sullivan, Michigan	3:55.33*	Graham Hood, Arkansas	3:55.72
3000-meter run	Jason Bunston, Arkansas	8:06.81	Richie Boulet, California	8:06.92
5000-meter run	Mark Carroll, Providence	13:55.15	Godfrey Siamusiye, Arkansas	13:58.99
High jump	Petar Malesev, Nebraska	7 ft 4¼ in	Ray Doakes, Arkansas	7 ft 4¼ in
Long jump	Kareem Streete-Thompson, Rice	26 ft 4¼ in	Darius Pemberton, Tennessee	25 ft 5¼ in
Triple jump	Hrvoje Verzi, Georgia	54 ft 4½ in	Lenards Ozolinish, California	54 ft 2½ in
Shot put	John Godina, UCLA	66 ft 11¼ in	Mark Parlin, UCLA	62 ft 3¾ in
Pole vault	Tim Mack, Tennessee	18 ft 4½ in	Daren McDonough, Illinois	18 ft ½ in
35-pound wt throw	Alex Papadimitriou, UTEP	71 ft 5¼ in	Brian Murer, SMU	69 ft 10¾ in

WOMEN

	Champion	Mark	Runner-Up	Mark
55-meter dash	Melinda Sergent, UTEP	6.73	Sevatheda Fynes, Eastern Mich	6.72
55-meter hurdles	Gillian Russell, Miami (FL)	7.49	Latasha Colander, N Carolina	7.57
200-meter dash	Merlene Frazer, Texas	23.14	Sue Walton, Tennessee	23.23
400-meter dash	Youlanda Warren, Louisiana St	52.39	Ebony Robinson, Florida	52.71
800-meter run	Amy Wickus, Wisconsin	2:04.86	Jennifer Buckley, Kent	2:05.02
Mile run	Trine Pilskog, Arkansas	4:39.19	Becki Wells, Alabama	4:40.07
3000-meter run	Sarah Schwald, Arkansas	9:19.90	Christine Stief, Boston U	9:20.69
5000-meter run	Jennifer Rhines, Villanova	15:41.12*	Margie McMahon, Providence	16:50.55
High jump	Amy Acuff, UCLA	6 ft 5½ in*	Gwen Wentland, Kansas St	6 ft 3¼ in
Long jump	Diane Guthrie-Gresham, GMU	21 ft 8¼ in	Nicole Devonish, Texas	21 ft ¾ in
Triple jump	Najuma Fletcher, Pittsburgh	44 ft 2¾ in	Icolyn Kelly, Georgia	43 ft 9 in
Shot put	Dawn Dumble, UCLA	57 ft 8½ in	Paulette Mitchell, Nebraska	55 ft 5in

*Meet record.

Rifle

	Champion	Pts	Runner-Up	Pts
Smallbore	Oleg Seleznev, AK-Fairbanks	1177	Trevor Gathman, West Virginia	1170
Air rifle	Benji Belden, Murray St	390	Erik Anderson, Kentucky	390

Spring 1995

Golf

MEN

Champion	Score	Runner-Up	Score
Chip Spratlin, Auburn	283	Ted Purdy, Arizona	284
		Chris Tidland, Oklahoma St	284

WOMEN

Champion	Score	Runner-Up	Score
Kristel Mourgue d'Algue, Arizona St	283	Vibeke Stensrud, San Jose St	285
		Wendy Ward, Arizona St	285

Outdoor Track

MEN

	Champion	Mark	Runner-Up	Mark
100-meter dash	Tim Harden, Kentucky	10.05	Donovan Powell, Texas Christian	10.07
200-meter dash	Ato Bolden, UCLA	20.24	Dave Dopeck, DePaul	20.31
400-meter dash	Greg Haughton, George Mason	44.62	Marlon Ramsey, Baylor	44.74
800-meter run	Brandon Rock, Arkansas	1:46.37	Shaun Benefield, Georgia	1:47.13
1,500-meter run	Kevin Sullivan, Michigan	3:37.57	Paul McMullen, Eastern Mich	3:38.74
3,000-met. steeplech.	Jim Svenoy, UTEP	8:21.48	Dmitry Drozdov, Iowa St	8:35.51
5,000-meter run	Martin Keino, Arizona	14:36.78	Mark Carroll, Providence	14:37.08
10,000-meter run	Godfrey Siamusiye, Arkansas	28:59.60	Kamiel Maase, Texas	29:08.52
110-meter hurdles	Duane Ross, Clemson	13.32	Larry Wade, Texas A&M	13.41
400-meter hurdles	Ken Harnden, N Carolina	48.72	Octavius Terry, Georgia Tech	49.25
High jump	Ray Doakes, Arkansas	7 ft 4½ in	Ed Broxterman, Kansas St	7 ft 4½ in
Pole vault	Lawrence Johnson, Tennessee	18 ft 8¼ in	Chris Pallakis, Washington St	18 ft ½ in
Long jump	Kareem Streete-Thompson, Rice	27 ft 2in	Andrew Owusu, Alabama	26 ft 3¾ in
Triple jump	Ndabe Mdhlongwa, SW LA	55 ft 4¾ in	Jerome Romain, Arkansas	55 ft 2 in
Shot put	John Godina, UCLA	72 ft 2¼ in*	Brent Noon, Georgia	68 ft 9¾ in
Discus throw	John Godina, UCLA	202 ft 4 in	Andy Bloom, Wake Forest	191 ft 8 in
Hammer throw	Balazs Kiss, Southern Cal	261 ft 3 in*	Alex Papadimitriou, UTEP	241 ft 9 in
Javelin throw	Greg Johnson, UCLA	244 ft 3in	Nils Fearnley, Southern Cal	238 ft 8 in
Decathlon	Mario Sategna, Louisiana St	8172	Chad Smith, Tennessee	7992

WOMEN

	Champion	Mark	Runner-Up	Mark
100-meter dash	D'Andre Hill, Louisiana St	11.11	Sevatheda Fynes, Eastern Mich	11.12
200-meter dash	Sevatheda Fynes, Eastern Mich	22.63	Merlene Frazer, Texas	22.77
400-meter dash	Nicole Green, Kansas St	52.01	Charlene Maulseed, Louisiana St	52.03
800-meter run	Inez Turner, SW Texas St	2:00.27	Tosha Woodward, Villanova	2:02.51
1,500-meter run	Amy Wickus, Wisconsin	4:14.53	Amy Rudolph, Providence	4:15.73
3,000-meter run	Kathy Butler, Wisconsin	9:09.02	Joline Staeheli, Georgetown	9:11.62
5,000-meter run	Jen Rhines, Villanova	15:56.18	Marie McMahon, Providence	16:15.06
10,000-meter run	Katie Swords, SMU	34:28.46	Rachel Sauder, Auburn	34:53.91
100-meter hurdles	Gillian Russell, Miami (FL)	12.99	Anjanette Kirkland, Texas A&M	13.09
400-meter hurdles	Tonya Williams, Illinois	55.17	Lade Akinremi, Arizona St	55.44
High jump	Amy Acuff, UCLA	6 ft 5 in*	Najuma Fletcher, Pittsburgh	6 ft 2¾ in
			Gwen Wentland, Kansas St	6 ft 2¾ in
Long jump	Pat Itanyi, W Virginia	22 ft 1 in	Diane Guthrie-Gresham, GMU	22 ft ¼ in
Triple jump	Nicola Martial, Nebraska	45 ft 1 in	Icolyn Kelly, Georgia	44 ft 8¼ in
Shot put	Valeyta Althouse, UCLA	59 ft 11 ¾ in*	Dawn Dumble, UCLA	56 ft 5¾ in
Discus throw	Dawn Dumble, UCLA	187 ft 2 in	Melinda Wirtz, Kent	186 ft 1 in
Javelin throw	Valerie Tulloch, Rice	192 ft 1 in	Heather Berlin, Minnesota	183 ft 2 in
Heptathlon	Diane Guthrie-Gresham, GMU	6527*	Ali McKnight, Nevada	5832

*Meet record. w=wind-aided.

Tennis

MEN

	Champion	Score	Runner-Up
Singles	Sargis Sargsian, Arizona St	(3-6, 6-3, 6-4)	Brett Hansen, Southern Cal
Doubles	Mahesh Bhupathi & Ali Hamadeh, Mississippi	(7-6 (2), 6-2)	Chad Clark & Trey Phillips, Texas

WOMEN

	Champion	Score	Runner-Up
Singles	Keri Phebus, UCLA	(6-2, 6-3)	Kelly Pace, Texas
Doubles	Keri Phebus & Susie Starrett, UCLA	(6-3, 6-3)	Cristina Moros & Kelly Pace, Texas

CHAMPIONSHIP RESULTS

Baseball

DIVISION I

Year	Champion	Coach	Score	Runner-Up	Most Outstanding Player
1947	California*	Clint Evans	8-7	Yale	No award
1948	Southern Cal	Sam Barry	9-2	Yale	No award
1949	Texas*	Bibb Falk	10-3	Wake Forest	Charles Teague, Wake Forest, 2B
1950	Texas	Bibb Falk	3-0	Washington St	Ray VanCleef, Rutgers, CF
1951	Oklahoma*	Jack Baer	3-2	Tennnessee	Sidney Hatfield, Tennessee, P-1B
1952	Holy Cross	Jack Barry	8-4	Missouri	James O'Neill, Holy Cross, P
1953	Michigan	Ray Fisher	7-5	Texas	J. L. Smith, Texas, P
1954	Missouri	John "Hi" Simmons	4-1	Rollins	Tom Yewcic, Michigan St, C
1955	Wake Forest	Taylor Sanford	7-6	Western Michigan	Tom Borland, Oklahoma St, P
1956	Minnesota	Dick Siebert	12-1	Arizona	Jerry Thomas, Minnesota, P
1957	California*	George Wolfman	1-0	Penn St	Cal Emery, Penn St, P-1B
1958	Southern Cal	Rod Dedeaux	8-7†	Missouri	Bill Thom, Southern Cal, P
1959	Oklahoma St	Toby Greene	5-3	Arizona	Jim Dobson, Oklahoma St, 3B
1960	Minnesota	Dick Siebert	2-1‡	Southern Cal	John Erickson, Minnesota, 2B
1961	Southern Cal*	Rod Dedeaux	1-0	Oklahoma St	Littleton Fowler, Oklahoma St, P
1962	Michigan	Don Lund	5-4	Santa Clara	Bob Garibaldi, Santa Clara, P
1963	Southern Cal	Rod Dedeaux	5-2	Arizona	Bud Hollowell, Southern Cal, C
1964	Minnesota	Dick Siebert	5-1	Missouri	Joe Ferris, Maine, P
1965	Arizona St	Bobby Winkles	2-1#	Ohio St	Sal Bando, Arizona St, 3B
1966	Ohio St	Marty Karow	8-2	Oklahoma St	Steve Arlin, Ohio St, P
1967	Arizona St	Bobby Winkles	11-2	Houston	Ron Davini, Arizona St, C
1968	Southern Cal*	Rod Dedeaux	4-3	Southern Illinois	Bill Seinsoth, Southern Cal, 1B
1969	Arizona St	Bobby Winkles	10-1	Tulsa	John Dolinsek, Arizona St, LF
1970	Southern Cal	Rod Dedeaux	2-1	Florida St	Gene Ammann, Florida St, P
1971	Southern Cal	Rod Dedeaux	7-2	Southern Illinois	Jerry Tabb, Tulsa, 1B
1972	Southern Cal	Rod Dedeaux	1-0	Arizona St	Russ McQueen, Southern Cal, P
1973	Southern Cal*	Rod Dedeaux	4-3	Arizona St	Dave Winfield, Minnesota, P-OF
1974	Southern Cal	Rod Dedeaux	7-3	Miami (FL)	George Milke, Southern Cal, P
1975	Texas	Cliff Gustafson	5-1	S Carolina	Mickey Reichenbach, Texas, 1B
1976	Arizona	Jerry Kindall	7-1	Eastern Michigan	Steve Powers, Arizona, P-DH
1977	Arizona St	Jim Brock	2-1	S Carolina	Bob Horner, Arizona St, 3B
1978	Southern Cal*	Rod Dedeaux	10-3	Arizona St	Rod Boxberger, Southern Cal, P
1979	Cal St-Fullerton	Augie Garrido	2-1	Arkansas	Tony Hudson, Cal St-Fullerton, P
1980	Arizona	Jerry Kindall	5-3	Hawaii	Terry Francona, Arizona, LF
1981	Arizona St	Jim Brock	7-4	Oklahoma St	Stan Holmes, Arizona St, LF
1982	Miami (FL)*	Ron Fraser	9-3	Wichita St	Dan Smith, Miami (FL), P
1983	Texas*	Cliff Gustafson	4-3	Alabama	Calvin Schiraldi, Texas, P
1984	Cal St-Fullerton	Augie Garrido	3-1	Texas	John Fishel, Cal St-Fullerton, LF
1985	Miami (FL)	Ron Fraser	10-6	Texas	Greg Ellena, Miami (FL), DH
1986	Arizona	Jerry Kindall	10-2	Florida St	Mike Senne, Arizona, LF
1987	Stanford	Mark Marquess	9-5	Oklahoma St	Paul Carey, Stanford, RF
1988	Stanford	Mark Marquess	9-4	Arizona St	Lee Plemel, Stanford, P
1989	Wichita St	Gene Stephenson	5-3	Texas	Greg Brummett, Wichita St, P
1990	Georgia	Steve Webber	2-1	Oklahoma St	Mike Rebhan, Georgia, P
1991	Louisiana St	Skip Bertman	6-3	Wichita St	Gary Hymel, Louisiana St, C
1992	Pepperdine	Andy Lopez	3-2	Cal St-Fullerton	Phil Nevin, Cal St-Fullerton, 3B
1993	Louisiana St	Skip Bertman	8-0	Wichita St	Todd Walker, Louisiana St, 2B
1994	Oklahoma	Larry Cochell	13-5	Georgia Tech	Chip Glass, Oklahoma, CF
1995	Cal St-Fullerton*	Augie Garrido	11-5	Southern Cal	Mark Kotsay, Cal St-Fullerton, CF-P

*Undefeated teams in College World Series play. †12 innings. ‡10 innings. #15 innings.

DIVISION II

Year	Champion	Year	Champion	Year	Champion	Year	Champion
1968	Chapman*	1975	Florida Southern	1982	UC-Riverside*	1989	Cal Poly-SLO
1969	Illinois St*	1976	Cal Poly-Pomona	1983	Cal Poly-Pomona	1990	Jacksonville St
1970	Cal St-Northridge	1977	UC-Riverside	1984	Cal St-Northridge	1991	Jacksonville St
1971	Florida Southern	1978	Florida Southern	1985	Florida Southern*	1992	Tampa*
1972	Florida Southern	1979	Valdosta St	1986	Troy St	1993	Tampa
1973	UC-Irvine*	1980	Cal Poly-Pomona*	1987	Troy St*	1994	Central Missouri St
1974	UC-Irvine	1981	Florida Southern*	1988	Florida Southern*	1995	Florida Southern*

*Undefeated teams.

DIVISION III

Year	Champion	Year	Champion	Year	Champion
1976	Cal St-Stanislaus	1983	Marietta	1990	Eastern Connecticut St
1977	Cal St-Stanislaus	1984	Ramapo	1991	Southern Maine
1978	Glassboro St	1985	WI-Oshkosh	1992	William Patterson
1979	Glassboro St	1986	Marietta	1993	Montclair St
1980	Ithaca	1987	Montclair St	1994	WI-Oshkosh
1981	Marietta	1988	Ithaca	1995	La Verne
1982	Eastern Connecticut St	1989	NC Wesleyan		

Cross-Country

Men

DIVISION I

Year	Champion	Coach	Pts	Runner-Up	Pts	Individual Champion	Time
1938	Indiana	Earle Hayes	51	Notre Dame	61	Greg Rice, Notre Dame	20:12.9
1939	Michigan St	Lauren Brown	54	Wisconsin	57	Walter Mehl, Wisconsin	20:30.9
1940	Indiana	Earle Hayes	65	Eastern Michigan	68	Gilbert Dodds, Ashland	20:30.2
1941	Rhode Island	Fred Tootell	83	Penn St	110	Fred Wilt, Indiana	20:30.1
1942	Indiana	Earle Hayes	57			Oliver Hunter, Notre Dame	20:18.0
	Penn St	Charles Werner	57				
1943	No meet						
1944	Drake	Bill Easton	25	Notre Dame	64	Fred Feiler, Drake	21:04.2
1945	Drake	Bill Easton	50	Notre Dame	65	Fred Feiler, Drake	21:14.2
1946	Drake	Bill Easton	42	NYU	98	Quentin Brelsford, Ohio Wesleyan	20:22.9
1947	Penn St	Charles Werner	60	Syracuse	72	Jack Milne, N Carolina	20:41.1
1948	Michigan St	Karl Schlademan	41	Wisconsin	69	Robert Black, Rhode Island	19:52.3
1949	Michigan St	Karl Schlademan	59	Syracuse	81	Robert Black, Rhode Island	20:25.7
1950	Penn St	Charles Werner	53	Michigan St	55	Herb Semper Jr, Kansas	20:31.7
1951	Syracuse	Robert Grieve	80	Kansas	118	Herb Semper Jr, Kansas	20:09.5
1952	Michigan St	Karl Schlademan	65	Indiana	68	Charles Capozzoli, Georgetown	19:36.7
1953	Kansas	Bill Easton	70	Indiana	82	Wes Santee, Kansas	19:43.5
1954	Oklahoma St	Ralph Higgins	61	Syracuse	118	Allen Frame, Kansas	19:54.2
1955	Michigan St	Karl Schlademan	46	Kansas	68	Charles Jones, Iowa	19:57.4
1956	Michigan St	Karl Schlademan	28	Kansas	88	Walter McNew, Texas	19:55.7
1957	Notre Dame	Alex Wilson	121	Michigan St	127	Max Truex, Southern Cal	19:12.3
1958	Michigan St	Francis Dittrich	79	Western Michigan	104	Crawford Kennedy, Michigan State	20:07.1
1959	Michigan St	Francis Dittrich	44	Houston	120	Al Lawrence, Houston	20:35.7
1960	Houston	John Morriss	54	Michigan St	80	Al Lawrence, Houston	19:28.2
1961	Oregon St	Sam Bell	68	San Jose St	82	Dale Story, Oregon St	19:46.6
1962	San Jose St	Dean Miller	58	Villanova	69	Tom O'Hara, Loyola (IL)	19:20.3
1963	San Jose St	Dean Miller	53	Oregon	68	Victor Zwolak, Villanova	19:35.0
1964	Western Michigan	George Dales	86	Oregon	116	Elmore Banton, Ohio	20:07.5
1965	Western Michigan	George Dales	81	Northwestern	114	John Lawson, Kansas	29:24.0
1966	Villanova	James Elliott	79	Kansas St	155	Gerry Lindgren, Washington St	29:01.4
1967	Villanova	James Elliott	91	Air Force	96	Gerry Lindgren, Washington St	30:45.6
1968	Villanova	James Elliott	78	Stanford	100	Michael Ryan, Air Force	29:16.8
1969	UTEP	Wayne Vandenburg	74	Villanova	88	Gerry Lindgren, Washington St	28:59.2
1970	Villanova	James Elliott	85	Oregon	86	Steve Prefontaine, Oregon	28:00.2
1971	Oregon	Bill Dellinger	83	Washington St	122	Steve Prefontaine, Oregon	29:14.0
1972	Tennessee	Stan Huntsman	134	E Tennessee St	148	Neil Cusack, E Tennessee St	28:23.0
1973	Oregon	Bill Dellinger	89	UTEP	157	Steve Prefontaine, Oregon	28:14.0
1974	Oregon	Bill Dellinger	77	Western Kentucky	110	Nick Rose, Western Kentucky	29:22.0
1975	UTEP	Ted Banks	88	Washington St	92	Craig Virgin, Illinois	28:23.3
1976	UTEP	Ted Banks	62	Oregon	117	Henry Rono, Washington St	28:06.6

Men (Cont.)

DIVISION I (Cont.)

Year	Champion	Coach	Pts	Runner-Up	Pts	Individual Champion	Time
1977	Oregon	Bill Dellinger	100	UTEP	105	Henry Rono, Washington St	28:33.5
1978	UTEP	Ted Banks	56	Oregon	72	Alberto Salazar, Oregon	29:29.7
1979	UTEP	Ted Banks	86	Oregon	93	Henry Rono, Washington St	28:19.6
1980	UTEP	Ted Banks	58	Arkansas	152	Suleiman Nyambui, UTEP	29:04.0
1981	UTEP	Ted Banks	17	Providence	109	Mathews Motshwarateu, UTEP	28:45.6
1982	Wisconsin	Dan McClimon	59	Providence	138	Mark Scrutton, Colorado	30:12.6
1983	Vacated			Wisconsin	164	Zakarie Barie, UTEP	29:20.0
1984	Arkansas	John McDonnell	101	Arizona	111	Ed Eyestone, Brigham Young	29:28.8
1985	Wisconsin	Martin Smith	67	Arkansas	104	Timothy Hacker, Wisconsin	29:17.88
1986	Arkansas	John McDonnell	69	Dartmouth	141	Aaron Ramirez, Arizona	30:27.53
1987	Arkansas	John McDonnell	87	Dartmouth	119	Joe Falcon, Arkansas	29:14.97
1988	Wisconsin	Martin Smith	105	Northern Arizona	160	Robert Kennedy, Indiana	29:20.0
1989	Iowa St	Bill Bergan	54	Oregon	72	John Nuttall, Iowa St	29:30.55
1990	Arkansas	John McDonnell	68	Iowa St	96	Jonah Koech, Iowa St	29:05.0
1991	Arkansas	John McDonnell	52	Iowa St	114	Sean Dollman, Western Ky	30:17.1
1992	Arkansas	John McDonnell	46	Wisconsin	87	Bob Kennedy, Indiana	30:15.3
1993	Arkansas	John McDonnell	31	Brigham Young	153	Josephat Kapkory, Wash St	29:32.4
1994	Iowa St	Bill Bergan	65	Colorado	88	Martin Keino, Arizona	30:08.7

DIVISION II

Year	Champion	Year	Champion	Year	Champion
1958	Northern Illinois	1971	Cal St-Fullerton	1984	SE Missouri St
1959	S Dakota St	1972	N Dakota St	1985	S Dakota St
1960	Central St (OH)	1973	S Dakota St	1986	Edinboro
1961	Southern Illinois	1974	SW Missouri St	1987	Edinboro
1962	Central St (OH)	1975	UC-Irvine	1988	Edinboro/ Mankato St
1963	Emporia St	1976	UC-Irvine	1989	S Dakota St
1964	Kentucky St	1977	Eastern Illinois	1990	Edinboro
1965	San Diego St	1978	Cal Poly-SLO	1991	MA-Lowell
1966	San Diego St	1979	Cal Poly-SLO	1992	Adams St
1967	San Diego St	1980	Humboldt St	1993	Adams St
1968	Eastern Illinois	1981	Millersville	1994	Adams St
1969	Eastern Illinois	1982	Eastern Washington		
1970	Eastern Michigan	1983	Cal Poly-Pomona		

DIVISION III

Year	Champion	Year	Champion	Year	Champion
1973	Ashland	1981	North Central	1989	WI-Oshkosh
1974	Mount Union	1982	North Central	1990	WI-Oshkosh
1975	North Central	1983	Brandeis	1991	Rochester
1976	North Central	1984	St Thomas (MN)	1992	North Central
1977	Occidental	1985	Luther	1993	North Central
1978	North Central	1986	St Thomas (MN)	1994	Williams
1979	North Central	1987	North Central		
1980	Carleton	1988	WI-Oshkosh		

Women

DIVISION I

Year	Champion	Coach	Pts	Runner-Up	Pts	Individual Champion	Time
1981	Virginia	John Vasvary	36	Oregon	83	Betty Springs, N Carolina St	16:19.0
1982	Virginia	Martin Smith	48	Stanford	91	Lesley Welch, Virginia	16:39.7
1983	Oregon	Tom Heinonen	95	Stanford	98	Betty Springs, N Carolina St	16:30.7
1984	Wisconsin	Peter Tegen	63	Stanford	89	Cathy Branta, Wisconsin	16:15.6
1985	Wisconsin	Peter Tegen	58	Iowa St	98	Suzie Tuffey, N Carolina St	16:22.5
1986	Texas	Terry Crawford	62	Wisconsin	64	Angela Chalmers, N Arizona	16:55.49
1987	Oregon	Tom Heinonen	97	N Carolina St	99	Kimberly Betz, Indiana	16:10.85
1988	Kentucky	Don Weber	75	Oregon	128	Michelle Dekkers, Indiana	16:30.0
1989	Villanova	Marty Stern	99	Kentucky	168	Vicki Huber, Villanova	15:59.86
1990	Villanova	Marty Stern	82	Providence	172	Sonia O'Sullivan, Villanova	16:06.0
1991	Villanova	Marty Stern	85	Arkansas	168	Sonia O'Sullivan, Villanova	16:30.3
1992	Villanova	Marty Stern	123	Arkansas	130	Carole Zajac, Villanova	17:01.9
1993	Villanova	Marty Stern	66	Arkansas	71	Carole Zajac, Villanova	16:40.3
1994	Villanova	John Marshall	75	Michigan	108	Jennifer Rhines, Villanova	16:31.2

Women (Cont.)

DIVISION II

Year	Champion	Year	Champion	Year	Champion
1981	S Dakota St	1986	Cal Poly-SLO	1991	Cal Poly-SLO
1982	Cal Poly-SLO	1987	Cal Poly-SLO	1992	Adams St
1983	Cal Poly-SLO	1988	Cal Poly-SLO	1993	Adams St
1984	Cal Poly-SLO	1989	Cal Poly-SLO	1994	Adams St
1985	Cal Poly-SLO	1990	Cal Poly-SLO		

DIVISION III

Year	Champion	Year	Champion	Year	Champion
1981	Central (IA)	1986	St Thomas (MN)	1990	Cortland St
1982	St Thomas (MN)	1987	St Thomas (MN)	1991	WI-Oshkosh
1983	WI-La Crosse		WI-Oshkosh	1992	Cortland St
1984	St Thomas (MN)	1988	WI-Oshkosh	1993	Cortland St
1985	Franklin & Marshall	1989	Cortland St	1994	Cortland St

Fencing

Men

TEAM CHAMPIONS

Year	Champion	Coach	Pts	Runner-Up	Pts
1941	Northwestern	Henry Zettleman	28½	Illinois	27
1942	Ohio St	Frank Riebel	34	St John's (NY)	33½
1943-1946	No tournament				
1947	NYU	Martinez Castello	72	Chicago	50½
1948	CCNY	James Montague	30	Navy	28
1949	Army	Servando Velarde	63		
	Rutgers	Donald Cetrulo	63		
1950	Navy	Joseph Fiems	67½	NYU	66½
				Rutgers	66½
1951	Columbia	Servando Velarde	69	Pennsylvania	64
1952	Columbia	Servando Velarde	71	NYU	69
1953	Pennsylvania	Lajos Csiszar	94	Navy	86
1954	Columbia	Irving DeKoff	61		
	NYU	Hugo Castello	61		
1955	Columbia	Irving DeKoff	62	Cornell	57
1956	Illinois	Maxwell Garret	90	Columbia	88
1957	NYU	Hugo Castello	65	Columbia	64
1958	Illinois	Maxwell Garret	47	Columbia	43
1959	Navy	Andre Deladrier	72	NYU	65
1960	NYU	Hugo Castello	65	Navy	57
1961	NYU	Hugo Castello	79	Princeton	68
1962	Navy	Andre Deladrier	76	NYU	74
1963	Columbia	Irving DeKoff	55	Navy	50
1964	Princeton	Stan Sieja	81	NYU	79
1965	Columbia	Irving DeKoff	76	NYU	74
1966	NYU	Hugo Castello	5-0	Army	5-2
1967	NYU	Hugo Castello	72	Pennsylvania	64
1968	Columbia	Louis Bankuti	92	NYU	87
1969	Pennsylvania	Lajos Csiszar	54	Harvard	43
1970	NYU	Hugo Castello	71	Columbia	63
1971	NYU	Hugo Castello	68		
	Columbia	Louis Bankuti	68		
1972	Detroit	Richard Perry	73	NYU	70
1973	NYU	Hugo Castello	76	Pennsylvania	71
1974	NYU	Hugo Castello	92	Wayne St (MI)	87
1975	Wayne St (MI)	Istvan Danosi	89	Cornell	83
1976	NYU	Herbert Cohen	79	Wayne St (MI)	77
1977	Notre Dame	Michael DeCicco	114*	NYU	114
1978	Notre Dame	Michael DeCicco	121	Pennsylvania	110
1979	Wayne St (MI)	Istvan Danosi	119	Notre Dame	108
1980	Wayne St (MI)	Istvan Danosi	111	Pennsylvania	106
				MIT	106
1981	Pennsylvania	Dave Micahnik	113	Wayne St (MI)	111

Men *(Cont.)*

TEAM CHAMPIONS *(Cont.)*

Year	Champion	Coach	Pts	Runner-Up	Pts
1982	Wayne St (MI)	Istvan Danosi	85	Clemson	77
1983	Wayne St (MI)	Aladar Kogler	86	Notre Dame	80
1984	Wayne St (MI)	Gil Pezza	69	Penn St	50
1985	Wayne St (MI)	Gil Pezza	141	Notre Dame	140
1986	Notre Dame	Michael DeCicco	151	Columbia	141
1987	Columbia	George Kolombatovich	86	Pennsylvania	78
1988	Columbia	George Kolombatovich Aladar Kogler	90	Notre Dame	83
1989	Columbia	George Kolombatovich Aladar Kogler	88	Penn St	85
1990	Penn St	Emmanuil Kaidanov	36	Columbia-Barnard	35
1991	Penn St	Emmanuil Kaidanov	4700	Columbia-Barnard	4200
1992	Columbia-Barnard	George Kolombatovich Aladar Kogler	4150	Penn St	3646
1993	Columbia-Barnard	George Kolumbatovich Aladar Kogler	4525	Penn St	4500
1994	Notre Dame	Michael DeCicco	4350	Penn St	4075
1995	Penn St	Emmanuil Kaidanov	440	St John's (NY)	413

*Tie broken by a fence-off. Note: Beginning in 1990, men's and women's combined teams competed for the national championship.

INDIVIDUAL CHAMPIONS

	Foil	Sabre	Épée
1941	Edward McNamara, Northwestern	William Meyer, Dartmouth	G. H. Boland, Illinois
1942	Byron Kreiger, Wayne St (MI)	Andre Deladrier, St John's (NY)	Ben Burtt, Ohio St
1947	Abraham Balk, NYU	Oscar Parsons, Temple	Abraham Balk, NYU
1948	Albert Axelrod, CCNY	James Day, Navy	William Bryan, Navy
1949	Ralph Tedeschi, Rutgers	Alex Treves, Rutgers	Richard C. Bowman, Army
1950	Robert Nielsen, Columbia	Alex Treves, Rutgers	Thomas Stuart, Navy
1951	Robert Nielsen, Columbia	Chamberless Johnston, Princeton	Daniel Chafetz, Columbia
1952	Harold Goldsmith, CCNY	Frank Zimolzak, Navy	James Wallner, NYU
1953	Ed Nober, Brooklyn	Robert Parmacek, Pennsylvania	Jack Tori, Pennsylvania
1954	Robert Goldman, Pennsylvania	Steve Sobel, Columbia	Henry Kolowrat, Princeton
1955	Herman Velasco, Illinois	Barry Pariser, Columbia	Donald Tadrawski, Notre Dame
1956	Ralph DeMarco, Columbia	Gerald Kaufman, Columbia	Kinmont Hoitsma, Princeton
1957	Bruce Davis, Wayne St (MI)	Bernie Balaban, NYU	James Margolis, Columbia
1958	Bruce Davis, Wayne St (MI)	Art Schankin, Illinois	Roland Wommack, Navy
1959	Joe Paletta, Navy	Al Morales, Navy	Roland Wommack, Navy
1960	Gene Glazer, NYU	Mike Desaro, NYU	Gil Eisner, NYU
1961	Herbert Cohen, NYU	Israel Colon, NYU	Jerry Halpern, NYU
1962	Herbert Cohen, NYU	Barton Nisonson, Columbia	Thane Hawkins, Navy
1963	Jay Lustig, Columbia	Bela Szentivanyi, Wayne St (MI)	Larry Crum, Navy
1964	Bill Hicks, Princeton	Craig Bell, Illinois	Paul Pesthy, Rutgers
1965	Joe Nalven, Columbia	Howard Goodman, NYU	Paul Pesthy, Rutgers
1966	Al Davis, NYU	Paul Apostol, NYU	Bernhardt Hermann, Iowa
1967	Mike Gaylor, NYU	Todd Makler, Pennsylvania	George Masin, NYU
1968	Gerard Esponda, San Francisco	Todd Makler, Pennsylvania	Don Sieja, Cornell
1969	Anthony Kestler, Columbia	Norman Braslow, Pennsylvania	James Wetzler, Pennsylvania
1970	Walter Krause, NYU	Bruce Soriano, Columbia	John Nadas, Case Reserve
1971	Tyrone Simmons, Detroit	Bruce Soriano, Columbia	George Szunyogh, NYU
1972	Tyrone Simmons, Detroit	Bruce Soriano, Columbia	Ernesto Fernandez, Pennsylvania
1973	Brooke Makler, Pennsylvania	Peter Westbrock, NYU	Risto Hurme, NYU
1974	Greg Benko, Wayne St (MI)	Steve Danosi, Wayne St (MI)	Risto Hurme, NYU
1975	Greg Benko, Wayne St (MI)	Yuri Rabinovich, Wayne St (MI)	Risto Hurme, NYU
1976	Greg Benko, Wayne St (MI)	Brian Smith, Columbia	Randy Eggleton, Pennsylvania
1977	Pat Gerard, Notre Dame	Mike Sullivan, Notre Dame	Hans Wieselgren, NYU
1978	Ernest Simon, Wayne St (MI)	Mike Sullivan, Notre Dame	Bjorne Vaggo, Notre Dame
1979	Andrew Bonk, Notre Dame	Yuri Rabinovich, Wayne St (MI)	Carlos Songini, Cleveland St
1980	Ernest Simon, Wayne St (MI)	Paul Friedberg, Pennsylvania	Gil Pezza, Wayne St (MI)

Men (Cont.)

INDIVIDUAL CHAMPIONS (Cont.)

	Foil	Sabre	Épée
1981	Ernest Simon, Wayne St (MI)	Paul Friedberg, Pennsylvania	Gil Pezza, Wayne St (MI)
1982	Alexander Flom, George Mason	Neil Hick, Wayne St (MI)	Peter Schifrin, San Jose St
1983	Demetrios Valsamis, NYU	John Friedberg, North Carolina	Ola Harstrom, Notre Dame
1984	Charles Higgs-Coulthard, Notre Dame	Michael Lofton, NYU	Ettore Bianchi, Wayne St (MI)
1985	Stephan Chauvel, Wayne St (MI)	Michael Lofton, NYU	Ettore Bianchi, Wayne St (MI)
1986	Adam Feldman, Penn St	Michael Lofton, NYU	Chris O'Loughlin, Pennsylvania
1987	William Mindel, Columbia	Michael Lofton, NYU	James O'Neill, Harvard
1988	Marc Kent, Columbia	Robert Cottingham, Columbia	Jon Normile, Columbia
1989	Edward Mufel, Penn St	Peter Cox, Penn St	Jon Normile, Columbia
1990	Nick Bravin, Stanford	David Mandell, Columbia	Jubba Beshin, Notre Dame
1991	Ben Atkins, Columbia	Vitali Nazlimov, Penn St	Marc Oshima, Columbia
1992	Nick Bravin, Stanford	Tom Strzalkowski, Penn St	Harald Bauder, Wayne St
1993	Nick Bravin, Stanford	Tom Strzalkowski, Penn St	Ben Atkins, Columbia
1994	Kwame van Leeuwen, Harvard	Tom Strzalkowski, Penn St	Harald Winkman, Princeton
1995	Sean McClain, Stanford	Paul Palestis, NYU	Mike Gattner, Lawrence

Women

TEAM CHAMPIONS

Year	Champion	Coach	Rec	Runner-Up	Rec
1982	Wayne St (MI)	Istvan Danosi	7-0	San Jose St	6-1
1983	Penn St	Beth Alphin	5-0	Wayne St (MI)	3-2
1984	Yale	Henry Harutunian	3-0	Penn St	2-1
1985	Yale	Henry Harutunian	3-0	Pennsylvania	2-1
1986	Pennsylvania	David Micahnik	3-0	Notre Dame	2-1
1987	Notre Dame	Yves Auriol	3-0	Temple	2-1
1988	Wayne St (MI)	Gil Pezza	3-0	Notre Dame	2-1
1989	Wayne St (MI)	Gil Pezza	3-0	Columbia-Barnard	2-1

Note: Beginning in 1990, men's and women's combined teams competed for the national championship.

INDIVIDUAL CHAMPIONS

	Foil		Épée
1982	Joy Ellingson, San Jose St	1995	Tina Loven, St John's (NY)
1983	Jana Angelakis, Penn St		
1984	Mary Jane O'Neill, Pennsylvania	Note: The women's epée competition was added in 1995.	
1985	Caitlin Bilodeaux, Columbia-Barnard		
1986	Molly Sullivan, Notre Dame		
1987	Caitlin Bilodeaux, Columbia-Barnard		
1988	Molly Sullivan, Notre Dame		
1989	Yasemin Topcu, Wayne St (MI)		
1990	Tzu Moy, Columbia-Barnard		
1991	Heidi Piper, Notre Dame		
1992	Olga Cheryak, Penn St		
1993	Olga Kalinovskaya, Penn St		
1994	Olga Kalinovskaya, Penn St		
1995	Olga Kalinovskaya, Penn St		

Field Hockey

DIVISION I

Year	Champion	Coach	Score	Runner-Up
1981	Connecticut	Diane Wright	4-1	Massachusetts
1982	Old Dominion	Beth Anders	3-2	Connecticut
1983	Old Dominion	Beth Anders	3-1 (3 OT)	Connecticut
1984	Old Dominion	Beth Anders	5-1	Iowa
1985	Connecticut	Diane Wright	3-2	Old Dominion
1986	Iowa	Judith Davidson	2-1 (2 OT)	New Hampshire
1987	Maryland	Sue Tyler	2-1 (OT)	N Carolina
1988	Old Dominion	Beth Anders	2-1	Iowa
1989	N Carolina	Karen Shelton	2-1 (3 OT)*	Old Dominion
1990	Old Dominion	Beth Anders	5-0	N Carolina
1991	Old Dominion	Beth Anders	2-0	N Carolina

Field Hockey (Cont.)

DIVISION I (Cont.)

Year	Champion	Coach	Score	Runner-Up
1992 ....Old Dominion	Beth Anders	4-0	Iowa
1993 ....Maryland	Missy Meharg	2-1 (3 OT)*	N Carolina
1994 ....James Madison	Christy Morgan	2-1 (3 OT)*	N Carolina

*Penalty strokes.

DIVISION II (DISCONTINUED, THEN RENEWED)

Year	Champion	Coach	Score	Runner-Up
1981 ....Pfeiffer	Ellen Briggs	5-3	Bentley
1982 ....Lock Haven	Sharon E. Taylor	4-1	Bloomsburg
1983 ....Bloomsburg	Jan Hutchinson	1-0	Lock Haven
1992 ....Lock Haven	Sharon E. Taylor	3-1	Bloomsburg
1993 ....Bloomsburg	Jan Hutchison	2-1 (2 OT)	Lock Haven
1994 ....Lock Haven	Sharon E. Taylor	2-1	Bloomsburg

DIVISION III

Year	Champion	Year	Champion	Year	Champion
1981 ....Trenton St	1986 ....Salisbury St	1991 ....Trenton St
1982 ....Ithaca	1987 ....Bloomsburg	1992 ....William Smith
1983 ....Trenton St	1988 ....Trenton St	1993 ....Cortland St
1984 ....Bloomsburg	1989 ....Lock Haven	1994 ....Cortland St
1985 ....Trenton St	1990 ....Trenton St		

Golf

Men
DIVISION I
Results, 1897-1938

Year	Champion	Site	Individual Champion
1897 ....Yale	Ardsley Casino	Louis Bayard Jr, Princeton
1898 ....Harvard (spring)		John Reid Jr, Yale
1898 ....Yale (fall)		James Curtis, Harvard
1899 ....Harvard		Percy Pyne, Princeton
1900 ....No tournament		
1901 ....Harvard	Atlantic City	H. Lindsley, Harvard
1902 ....Yale (spring)	Garden City	Charles Hitchcock Jr, Yale
1902 ....Harvard (fall)	Morris County	Chandler Egan, Harvard
1903 ....Harvard	Garden City	F. O. Reinhart, Princeton
1904 ....Harvard	Myopia	A. L. White, Harvard
1905 ....Yale	Garden City	Robert Abbott, Yale
1906 ....Yale	Garden City	W. E. Clow Jr, Yale
1907 ....Yale	Nassau	Ellis Knowles, Yale
1908 ....Yale	Brae Burn	H. H. Wilder, Harvard
1909 ....Yale	Apawamis	Albert Seckel, Princeton
1910 ....Yale	Essex County	Robert Hunter, Yale
1911 ....Yale	Baltusrol	George Stanley, Yale
1912 ....Yale	Ekwanok	F. C. Davison, Harvard
1913 ....Yale	Huntingdon Valley	Nathaniel Wheeler, Yale
1914 ....Princeton	Garden City	Edward Allis, Harvard
1915 ....Yale	Greenwich	Francis Blossom, Yale
1916 ....Princeton	Oakmont	J. W. Hubbell, Harvard
1917-18.............No tournament		
1919 ....Princeton	Merion	A. L. Walker Jr, Columbia
1920 ....Princeton	Nassau	Jess Sweetster, Yale
1921 ....Dartmouth	Greenwich	Simpson Dean, Princeton
1922 ....Princeton	Garden City	Pollack Boyd, Dartmouth
1923 ....Princeton	Siwanoy	Dexter Cummings, Yale
1924 ....Yale	Greenwich	Dexter Cummings, Yale
1925 ....Yale	Montclair	Fred Lamprecht, Tulane
1926 ....Yale	Merion	Fred Lamprecht, Tulane
1927 ....Princeton	Garden City	Watts Gunn, Georgia Tech
1928 ....Princeton	Apawamis	Maurice McCarthy, Georgetown
1929 ....Princeton	Hollywood	Tom Aycock, Yale
1930 ....Princeton	Oakmont	G. T. Dunlap Jr, Princeton

Men (Cont.)
DIVISION I (Cont.)
Results, 1897-1938 (Cont.)

Year	Champion	Site	Individual Champion
1931	Yale	Olympia Fields	G. T. Dunlap Jr, Princeton
1932	Yale	Hot Springs	J. W. Fischer, Michigan
1933	Yale	Buffalo	Walter Emery, Oklahoma
1934	Michigan	Cleveland	Charles Yates, Georgia Tech
1935	Michigan	Congressional	Ed White, Texas
1936	Yale	North Shore	Charles Kocsis, Michigan
1937	Princeton	Oakmont	Fred Haas Jr, Louisiana St
1938	Stanford	Louisville	John Burke, Georgetown

Results, 1939-1995

Year	Champion	Coach	Score	Runner-Up	Score	Host or Site	Individual Champion
1939	Stanford	Eddie Twiggs	612	Northwestern	614	Wakonda	Vincent D'Antoni, Tulane
				Princeton	614		
1940	Princeton	Walter Bourne	601			Ekwanok	Dixon Brooke, Virginia
	Louisiana St	Mike Donahue	601				
1941	Stanford	Eddie Twiggs	580	Louisiana St	599	Ohio St	Earl Stewart, Louisiana St
1942	Louisiana St	Mike Donahue	590			Notre Dame	Frank Tatum Jr
	Stanford	Eddie Twiggs	590				
1943	Yale	William Neale Jr	614	Michigan	618	Olympia Fields	Wallace Ulrich, Carleton
1944	Notre Dame	George Holderith	311	Minnesota	312	Inverness	Louis Lick, Minnesota
1945	Ohio St	Robert Kepler	602	Northwestern	621	Ohio St	John Lorms, Ohio St
1946	Stanford	Eddie Twiggs	619	Michigan	624	Princeton	George Hamer, Georgia
1947	Louisiana St	T. P. Heard	606	Duke	614	Michigan	Dave Barclay, Michigan
1948	San Jose St	Wilbur Hubbard	579	Louisiana St	588	Stanford	Bob Harris, San Jose St
1949	N Texas	Fred Cobb	590	Purdue	600	Iowa St	Harvie Ward, N Carolina
				Texas	600		
1950	N Texas	Fred Cobb	573	Purdue	577	New Mexico	Fred Wampler, Purdue
1951	N Texas	Fred Cobb	588	Ohio St	589	Ohio St	Tom Nieporte, Ohio St
1952	N Texas	Fred Cobb	587	Michigan	593	Purdue	Jim Vickers, Oklahoma
1953	Stanford	Charles Finger	578	N Carolina	580	Broadmoor	Earl Moeller, Oklahoma St
1954	Southern Meth	Graham Ross	572	N Texas	573	Houston, Rice	Hillman Robbins, Memphis St
1955	Louisiana St	Mike Barbato	574	N Texas	583	Tennessee	Joe Campbell, Purdue
1956	Houston	Dave Williams	601	N Texas	602	Ohio St	Rick Jones, Ohio St
				Purdue	602		
1957	Houston	Dave Williams	602	Stanford	603	Broadmoor	Rex Baxter Jr, Houston
1958	Houston	Dave Williams	570	Oklahoma St	582	Williams	Phil Rodgers, Houston
1959	Houston	Dave Williams	561	Purdue	571	Oregon	Dick Crawford, Houston
1960	Houston	Dave Williams	603	Purdue	607	Broadmoor	Dick Crawford, Houston
				Oklahoma St	607		
1961	Purdue	Sam Voinoff	584	Arizona St	595	Lafayette	Jack Nicklaus, Ohio St
1962	Houston	Dave Williams	588	Oklahoma St	598	Duke	Kermit Zarley, Houston
1963	Oklahoma St	Labron Harris	581	Houston	582	Wichita St	R. H. Sikes, Ark.
1964	Houston	Dave Williams	580	Oklahoma St	587	Broadmoor	Terry Small, San Jose St
1965	Houston	Dave Williams	577	Cal St-LA	587	Tennessee	Marty Fleckman, Houston

Men (Cont.)
DIVISION I (Cont.)
Results, 1939-1995 (Cont.)

Year	Champion	Coach	Score	Runner-Up	Score	Host or Site	Individual Champion
1966 ....Houston	Dave Williams	582	San Jose St	586	Stanford	Bob Murphy, Florida
1967 ....Houston	Dave Williams	585	Florida	588	Shawnee, PA	Hale Irwin, Colorado
1968 ....Florida	Buster Bishop	1154	Houston	1156	New Mexico St	Grler Jones, Oklahoma St
1969 ....Houston	Dave Williams	1223	Wake Forest	1232	Broadmoor	Bob Clark, Cal St-LA
1970 Houston	Dave Williams	1172	Wake Forest	1182	Ohio St	John Mahaffey, Houston
1971 ....Texas	George Hannon	1144	Houston	1151	Arizona	Ben Crenshaw, Texas
1972 ....Texas	George Hannon	1146	Houston	1159	Cape Coral	Ben Crenshaw, Texas Tom Kite, Texas
1973 ....Florida	Buster Bishop	1149	Oklahoma St	1159	Oklahoma St	Ben Crenshaw, Texas
1974 ....Wake Forest	Jess Haddock	1158	Florida	1160	San Diego St	Curtis Strange, Wake Forest
1975 ....Wake Forest	Jess Haddock	1156	Oklahoma St	1189	Ohio St	Jay Haas, Wake Forest
1976 ....Oklahoma St	Mike Holder	1166	Brigham Young	1173	New Mexico	Scott Simpson, Southern Cal
1977 ....Houston	Dave Williams	1197	Oklahoma St	1205	Colgate	Scott Simpson, Southern Cal
1978 ....Oklahoma St	Mike Holder	1140	Georgia	1157	Oregon	David Edwards, Oklahoma St
1979 ....Ohio St	James Brown	1189	Oklahoma St	1191	Wake Forest	Gary Hallberg, Wake Forest
1980 ....Oklahoma St	Mike Holder	1173	Brigham Young	1177	Ohio St	Jay Don Blake, Utah St
1981 ....Brigham Young	Karl Tucker	1161	Oral Roberts	1163	Stanford	Ron Commans, Southern Cal
1982 ....Houston	Dave Williams	1141	Oklahoma St	1151	Pinehurst	Billy Ray Brown, Houston
1983 ....Oklahoma St	Mike Holder	1161	Texas	1168	Fresno St	Jim Carter, Arizona St
1984 ....Houston	Dave Williams	1145	Oklahoma St	1146	Houston	John Inman, N Carolina
1985 ....Houston	Dave Williams	1172	Oklahoma St	1175	Florida	Clark Burroughs, Ohio St
1986 ....Wake Forest	Jess Haddock	1156	Oklahoma St	1160	Wake Forest	Scott Verplank, Oklahoma St
1987 ....Oklahoma St	Mike Holder	1160	Wake Forest	1176	Ohio St	Brian Watts, Oklahoma St
1988 ....UCLA	Eddie Merrins	1176	UTEP Oklahoma Oklahoma St	1179 1179 1179	Southern Cal	E. J. Pfister, Oklahoma St
1989 ....Oklahoma	Gregg Grost	1139	Texas	1158	Oklahoma Oklahoma St	Phil Mickelson, Arizona St
1990 ....Arizona St	Steve Loy	1155	Florida	1157	Florida	Phil Mickelson, Arizona St
1991 ....Oklahoma St	Mike Holder	1161	N Carolina	1168	San Jose St	Warren Schutte, UNLV
1992 ....Arizona	Rick LaRose	1129	Arizona St	1136	New Mexico	Phil Mickelson, Arizona St
1993 ....Florida	Buddy Alexander	1145	Georgia Tech	1146	Kentucky	Todd Demsey, Arizona St

Golf (Cont.)

Men (Cont.)

DIVISION I (Cont.)

Results, 1939-1995 (Cont.)

Year	Champion	Coach	Score	Runner-Up	Score	Host or Site	Individual Champion
1994	....Stanford	Wally Goodwin	1129	Texas	1133	McKinney, TX	Justin Leonard, Texas
1995	....Oklahoma St*	Mike Holder	1156	Stanford	1156	Ohio St	Chip Spratlin, Auburn

*Won sudden death playoff. Notes: Match play, 1897-1964; par-70 tournaments held in 1969, 1973 and 1989; par-71 tournaments held in 1968, 1981 and 1988; all other championships par-72 tournaments. Scores are based on 4 rounds instead of 2 after 1967.

DIVISION II

Year	Champion	Year	Champion	Year	Champion
1963	........SW Missouri St	1974	.........Cal St-Northridge	1985	........Florida Southern
1964	........Southern Illinois	1975	.........UC-Irvine	1986	........Florida Southern
1965	........Middle Tennessee St	1976	.........Troy St	1987	........Tampa
1966	........Cal St-Chico	1977	.........Troy St	1988	........Tampa
1967	........Lamar	1978	.........Columbus	1989	........Columbus
1968	........Lamar	1979	.........UC-Davis	1990	........Florida Southern
1969	........Cal St-Northridge	1980	.........Columbus	1991	........Florida Southern
1970	........Rollins	1981	.........Florida Southern	1992	........Columbus
1971	........New Orleans	1982	.........Florida Southern	1993	........Abilene Christian
1972	........New Orleans	1983	.........SW Texas St	1994	........Columbus
1973	........Cal St-Northridge	1984	.........Troy St	1995	........Florida Southern

DIVISION III

Year	Champion	Year	Champion	Year	Champion
1975	........Wooster	1982	.........Rampano	1989	.........Cal St-Stanislaus
1976	........Cal St-Stanislaus	1983	.........Allegheny	1990	.........Methodist (NC)
1977	........Cal St-Stanislaus	1984	........Cal St-Stanislaus	1991	.........Methodist (NC)
1978	........Cal St-Stanislaus	1985	.........Cal St-Stanislaus	1992	.........Methodist (NC)
1979	........Cal St-Stanislaus	1986	.........Cal St-Stanislaus	1993	.........UC-San Diego
1980	........Cal St-Stanislaus	1987	.........Cal St-Stanislaus	1994	.........UC-San Diego
1981	........Cal St-Stanislaus	1988	.........Cal St-Stanislaus	1995	.........Methodist

Note: All championships par-72 except for 1986 and 1988, which were par-71; fourth round of 1975 championships canceled as a result of bad weather, first round of 1988 championships canceled as a result of rain.

Women

Year	Champion	Coach	Score	Runner-Up	Score	Individual Champion
1982	....Tulsa	Dale McNamara	1191	Texas Christian	1227	Kathy Baker, Tulsa
1983	....Texas Christian	Fred Warren	1193	Tulsa	1196	Penny Hammel, Miami (FL)
1984	....Miami (FL)	Lela Cannon	1214	Arizona St	1221	Cindy Schreyer, Georgia
1985	.....Florida	Mimi Ryan	1218	Tulsa	1233	Danielle Ammaccapane, Arizona St
1986	.....Florida	Mimi Ryan	1180	Miami (FL)	1188	Page Dunlap, Florida
1987	.....San Jose St	Mark Gale	1187	Furman	1188	Caroline Keggi, New Mexico
1988	.....Tulsa	Dale McNamara	1175	Georgia Arizona	1182 1182	Melissa McNamara, Tulsa
1989	.....San Jose St	Mark Gale	1208	Tulsa	1209	Pat Hurst, San Jose St
1990	.....Arizona St	Linda Vollstedt	1206	UCLA	1222	Susan Slaughter, Arizona
1991	.....UCLA*	Jackie Steinmann	1197	San Jose St	1197	Annika Sorenstam, Arizona
1992	.....San Jose St	Mark Gale	1171	Arizona	1175	Vicki Goetze, Georgia
1993	.....Arizona St	Linda Vollstedt	1187	Texas	1189	Charlotta Sorenstam, Texas
1994	.....Arizona St	Linda Vollstedt	1189	Southern Cal	1205	Emilee Klein, Arizona St
1995	.....Arizona St	Linda Vollstedt	1155	San Jose St	1181	Kristel Mourgue d'Algue, Arizona St

*Won sudden death playoff. Note: Par-74 tournaments held in 1983 and 1988; par-72 tournament held in 1990; all other championships par-73 tournaments.

Gymnastics

Men
Team Champions

Year	Champion	Coach	Pts	Runner-Up	Pts
1938	Chicago	Dan Hoffer	22	Illinois	18
1939	Illinois	Hartley Price	21	Army	17
1940	Illinois	Hartley Price	20	Navy	17
1941	Illinois	Hartley Price	68.5	Minnesota	52.5
1942	Illinois	Hartley Price	39	Penn St	30
1943-47	No tournament				
1948	Penn St	Gene Wettstone	55	Temple	34.5
1949	Temple	Max Younger	28	Minnesota	18
1950	Illinois	Charley Pond	26	Temple	25
1951	Florida St	Hartley Price	26	Illinois	23.5
				Southern Cal	23.5
1952	Florida St	Hartley Price	89.5	Southern Cal	75
1953	Penn St	Gene Wettstone	91.5	Illinois	68
1954	Penn St	Gene Wettstone	137	Illinois	68
1955	Illinois	Charley Pond	82	Penn St	69
1956	Illinois	Charley Pond	123.5	Penn St	67.5
1957	Penn St	Gene Wettstone	88.5	Illinois	80
1958	Michigan St	George Szypula	79		
	Illinois	Charley Pond	79		
1959	Penn St	Gene Wettstone	152	Illinois	87.5
1960	Penn St	Gene Wettstone	112.5	Southern Cal	65.5
1961	Penn St	Gene Wettstone	88.5	Southern Illinois	80.5
1962	Southern Cal	Jack Beckner	95.5	Southern Illinois	75
1963	Michigan	Newton Loken	129	Southern Illinois	73
1964	Southern Illinois	Bill Meade	84.5	Southern Cal	69.5
1965	Penn St	Gene Wettstone	68.5	Washington	51.5
1966	Southern Illinois	Bill Meade	187.200	California	185.100
1967	Southern Illinois	Bill Meade	189.550	Michigan	187.400
1968	California	Hal Frey	188.250	Southern Illinois	188.150
1969	Iowa	Mike Jacobson	161.175	Penn St	160.450
	Michigan*	Newton Loken		Colorado St	
1970	Michigan	Newton Loken	164.150	Iowa St	164.050
				New Mexico St	
1971	Iowa St	Ed Gagnier	319.075	Southern Illinois	316.650
1972	Southern Illinois	Bill Meade	315.925	Iowa St	312.325
1973	Iowa St	Ed Gagnier	325.150	Penn St	323.025
1974	Iowa St	Ed Gagnier	326.100	Arizona St	322.050
1975	California	Hal Frey	437.325	Louisiana St	433.700
1976	Penn St	Gene Wettstone	432.075	Louisiana St	425.125
1977	Indiana St	Roger Counsil	434.475		
	Oklahoma	Paul Ziert	434.475		
1978	Oklahoma	Paul Ziert	439.350	Arizona St	437.075
1979	Nebraska	Francis Allen	448.275	Oklahoma	446.625
1980	Nebraska	Francis Allen	563.300	Iowa St	557.650
1981	Nebraska	Francis Allen	284.600	Oklahoma	281.950
1982	Nebraska	Francis Allen	285.500	UCLA	281.050
1983	Nebraska	Francis Allen	287.800	UCLA	283.900
1984	UCLA	Art Shurlock	287.300	Penn St	281.250
1985	Ohio St	Michael Willson	285.350	Nebraska	284.550
1986	Arizona St	Don Robinson	283.900	Nebraska	283.600
1987	UCLA	Art Shurlock	285.300	Nebraska	284.750
1988	Nebraska	Francis Allen	288.150	Illinois	287.150
1989	Illinois	Yoshi Hayasaki	283.400	Nebraska	282.300
1990	Nebraska	Francis Allen	287.400	Minnesota	287.300
1991	Oklahoma	Greg Buwick	288.025	Penn St	285.500
1992	Stanford	Sadao Hamada	289.575	Nebraska	288.950
1993	Stanford	Sadao Hamada	276.500	Nebraska	275.500
1994	Nebraska	Francis Allen	288.250	Stanford	285.925
1995	Stanford	Sadao Hamada	232.400	Nebraska	231.525

*Trampoline.

Men (Cont.)
Individual Champions

ALL-AROUND

1938.....Joe Giallombardo, Illinois
1939.....Joe Giallombardo, Illinois
1940.....Joe Giallombardo, Illinois
        Paul Fina, Illinois
1941.....Courtney Shanken, Chicago
1942.....Newt Loken, Minnesota
1948.....Ray Sorenson, Penn St
1949.....Joe Kotys, Kent
1950.....Joe Kotys, Kent
1951.....Bill Roetzheim, Florida St
1952.....Jack Beckner, Southern Cal
1953.....Jean Cronstedt, Penn St
1954.....Jean Cronstedt, Penn St
1955.....Karl Schwenzfeier, Penn St
1956.....Don Tonry, Illlinois
1957.....Armando Vega, Penn St
1958.....Abie Grossfeld, Illinois
1959.....Armando Vega, Penn St
1960.....Jay Werner, Penn St
1961.....Gregor Weiss, Penn St
1962.....Robert Lynn, Southern Cal
1963.....Gil Larose, Michigan
1964.....Ron Barak, Southern Cal
1965.....Mike Jacobson, Penn St
1966.....Steve Cohen, Penn St
1967.....Steve Cohen, Penn St
1968.....Makoto Sakamoto, USC
1969.....Mauno Nissinen, Wash
1970.....Yoshi Hayasaki, Wash
1971.....Yoshi Hayasaki, Wash
1972.....Steve Hug, Stanford
1973.....Steve Hug, Stanford
        Marshall Avener, Penn St.
1974.....Steve Hug, Stanford
1975.....Wayne Young, BYU
1976   Peter Kormann, Southern
        Conn St
1977.....Kurt Thomas, Indiana St
1978.....Bart Conner, Oklahoma
1979.....Kurt Thomas, Indiana St
1980.....Jim Hartung, Nebraska
1981.....Jim Hartung, Nebraska
1982.....Peter Vidmar, UCLA
1983.....Peter Vidmar, UCLA
1984.....Mitch Gaylord, UCLA
1985.....Wes Suter, Nebraska
1986.....Jon Louis, Stanford
1987.....Tom Schlesinger, Nebraska
1988.....Vacated†
1989.....Patrick Kirsey, Nebraska
1990.....Mike Racanelli, Ohio St
1991.....John Roethlisberger, Minn
1992.....John Roethlisberger, Minn
1993.....John Roethlisberger, Minn
1994.....Dennis Harrison, Nebraska
1995.....Richard Grace, Nebraska

HORIZONTAL BAR

1938.....Bob Sears, Army
1939.....Adam Walters, Temple
1940.....Norm Boardman, Temple
1941.....Newt Loken, Minnesota
1942.....Norm Boardman, Temple
1948.....Joe Calvetti, Illinois

1949.....Bob Stout, Temple
1950.....Joe Kotys, Kent
1951.....Bill Roetzheim, Florida St
1952.....Charles Simms, USC
1953.....Hal Lewis, Navy
1954.....Jean Cronstedt, Penn St
1955.....Carlton Rintz, Michigan St
1956.....Ronnie Amster, Florida St
1957.....Abie Grossfeld, Illinois
1958.....Abie Grossfeld, Illinois
1959.....Stanley Tarshis, Mich St
1960.....Stanley Tarshis, Mich St
1961.....Bruno Klaus, Southern Ill
1962.....Robert Lynn, USC
1963.....Gil Larose, Michigan
1964.....Ron Barak, USC
1965.....Jim Curzi, Michigan St
        Mike Jacobsen, Penn St
1966.....Rusty Rock, Cal St-
        Northridge
1967.....Rich Grigsby, Cal St-
        Northridge
1968.....Makoto Sakamoto, USC
1969.....Bob Manna, New Mexico
1970.....Yoshi Hayasaki, Wash
1971.....Brent Simmons, Iowa St
1972.....Tom Lindner, Souhern Ill
1973.....Jon Aitken, New Mexico
1974.....Rick Banley, Indiana St
1975.....Rich Larsen, Iowa St
1976.....Tom Beach, California
1977.....John Hart, UCLA
1978.....Mel Cooley, Washington
1979.....Kurt Thomas, Indiana St
1980.....Philip Cahoy, Nebraska
1981.....Philip Cahoy, Nebraska
1982.....Peter Vidmar, UCLA
1983.....Scott Johnson, Nebraska
1984.....Charles Lakes, Illinois
1985.....Dan Hayden, Arizona St
        Wes Suter, Nebraska
1986.....Dan Hayden, Arizona St
1987.....David Moriel, UCLA
1988.....Vacated†
1989.....Vacated†
1990.....Chris Waller, UCLA
1991.....Luis Lopez, New Mexico
1992.....Jair Lynch, Stanford
1993.....Steve McCain, UCLA
1994.....Jim Foody, UCLA
1995.....Rick Kieffer, Nebraska

PARALLEL BARS

1938.....Erwin Beyer, Chicago
1939.....Bob Sears, Army
1940.....Bob Hanning, Minnesota
1941.....Caton Cobb, Illinois
1942.....Hal Zimmerman, Penn St
1948.....Ray Sorenson, Penn St
1949.....Joe Kotys, Kent
        Mel Stout, Michigan St
1950.....Joe Kotys, Kent
1951.....Jack Beckner, USC
1952.....Jack Beckner, USC
1953.....Jean Cronstedt, Penn St
1954.....Jean Cronstedt, Penn St

1955.....Carlton Rintz, Michigan St
1956.....Armando Vega, Penn St
1957.....Armando Vega, Penn St
1958.....Tad Muzyczko, Mich St
1959.....Armando Vega, Penn St
1960.....Robert Lynn, Southern Cal
1961.....Fred Tijerina, Southern Ill
        Jeff Cardinalli, Springfield
1962.....Robert Lynn, Southern Cal
1963.....Arno Lascari, Michigan
1964.....Ron Barak, Southern Cal
1965.....Jim Curzi, Michigan St
1966.....Jim Curzi, Michigan St
1967.....Makoto Sakamoto, USC
1968.....Makoto Sakamoto, USC
1969.....Ron Rapper, Michigan
1970.....Ron Rapper, Michigan
1971.....Brent Simmons, Iowa St
        Tom Dunn, Penn St
1972.....Dennis Mazur, Iowa St
1973.....Steve Hug, Stanford
1974.....Steve Hug, Stanford
1975.....Yoichi Tomita, Long
        Beach St
1976.....Gene Whelan, Penn St
1977.....Kurt Thomas, Indiana St
1978.....John Corritore, Michigan
1979.....Kurt Thomas, Indiana St
1980.....Philip Cahoy, Nebraska
1981.....Philip Cahoy, Nebraska
        Peter Vidmar, UCLA
        Jim Hartung, Nebraska
1982.....Jim Hartung, Nebraska
1983.....Scott Johnson, Nebraska
1984.....Tim Daggett, UCLA
1985.....Dan Hayden, Arizona St
        Noah Riskin, Ohio St
        Seth Riskin, Ohio St
1986.....Dan Hayden, Arizona St
1987.....Kevin Davis, Nebraska
        Tom Schlesinger, Nebraska
1988.....Kevin Davis, Nebraska
1989.....Vacated†
1990.....Patrick Kirksey, Nebraska
1991.....Scott Keswick, UCLA
        John Roethlisberger, Minn
1992.....Dom Minicucci, Temple
1993.....Jair Lynch, Stanford
1994.....Richard Grace, Nebraska
1995.....Richard Grace, Nebraska

VAULT

1938.....Erwin Beyer, Chicago
1939.....Marv Forman, Illinois
1940.....Earl Shanken, Chicago
1941.....Earl Shanken, Chicago
1942.....Earl Shanken, Chicago
1948.....Jim Peterson, Minnesota
1962.....Bruno Klaus, Southern Ill
1963.....Gil Larose, Michigan
1964.....Sidney Oglesby, Syracuse
1965.....Dan Millman, California
1966.....Frank Schmitz, S Illinois
1967.....Paul Mayer, S Illinois
1968.....Bruce Colter, Cal St-Los
        Angeles

Men *(Cont.)*
Individual Champions *(Cont.)*

1969.....Dan Bowles, California	1969.....Keith McCanless, Iowa	1978.....Curt Austin, Iowa St
Jack McCarthy, Illinois	1970.....Russ Hoffman, Iowa St	1979.....Mike Wilson, Oklahoma
1970.....Doug Boger, Arizona	John Russo, Wisconsin	Bart Conner, Oklahoma
1971.....Pat Mahoney, Cal St-	1971.....Russ Hoffman, Iowa St	1980.....Steve Elliott, Nebraska
Northridge	1972.....Russ Hoffman, Iowa St	1981.....James Yuhashi, Oregon
1972.....Gary Morava, Southern Ill	1973.....Ed Slezak, Indiana St	1982.....Steve Elliott, Nebraska
1973.....John Crosby, S Conn St	1974.....Ted Marcy, Stanford	1983.....Scott Johnson, Nebraska
1974.....Greg Goodhue, Oklahoma	1975.....Ted Marcy, Stanford	David Branch, Arizona St
1975.....Tom Beach, California	1976.....Ted Marcy, Stanford	Donnie Hinton, Arizona St
1976.....Sam Shaw, Cal St-	1977.....Chuck Walter, New Mexico	1984.....Kevin Ekburg, Northern Ill
Fullerton	1978.....Mike Burke, Northern Ill	1985.....Wes Suter, Nebraska
1977.....Steve Wejmar, Wash	1979.....Mike Burke, Northern Ill	1986.....Jerry Burrell, Arizona St
1978.....Ron Galimore, Louisiana St	1980.....David Stoldt, Illinois	Brian Ginsberg, UCLA
1979.....Leslie Moore, Oklahoma	1981.....Mark Bergman, California	1987.....Chad Fox, New Mexico
1980.....Ron Galimore, Iowa St	Steve Jennings, New Mexico	1988.....Chris Wyatt, Temple
1981.....Ron Galimore, Iowa St	1982.....Peter Vidmar, UCLA	1989.....Jody Newman, Arizona St
1982.....Randall Wickstrom, Cal	Steve Jennings, New Mexico	1990.....Mike Racanelli, Ohio St
Steve Elliott, Nebraska	1983.....Doug Kieso, Northern Ill	1991.....Brad Hayashi, UCLA
1983.....Chris Riegel, Nebraska	1984.....Tim Daggett, UCLA	1992.....Brian Winkler, Michigan
Mark Oates, Oklahoma	1985.....Tony Pineda, UCLA	1993.....Richard Grace, Nebraska
1984.....Chris Riegel, Nebraska	1986.....Curtis Holdsworth, UCLA	1994.....Mark Booth, Stanford
1985.....Derrick Cornelius,	1987.....Li Xiao Ping, Cal St-	1995.....Jay Thornton, Iowa
Cortland St	Fullerton	
1986.....Chad Fox, New Mexico	1988.....Vacated†	**RINGS**
1987.....Chad Fox, New Mexico	Mark Sohn, Penn St	1959.....Armando Vega, Penn St
1988.....Chad Fox, New Mexico	1989.....Mark Sohn, Penn St	1960.....Sam Garcia, Southern Cal
1989.....Chad Fox, New Mexico	Chris Waller, UCLA	1961.....Fred Orlofsky, Southern Ill
1990.....Brad Hayashi, UCLA	1990.....Mark Sohn, Penn St	1962.....Dale Cooper, Michigan St
1991.....Adam Carton, Penn St	1991.....Mark Sohn, Penn St	1963.....Dale Cooper, Michigan St
1992.....Jason Hebert, Syracuse	1992.....Che Bowers, Nebraska	1964.....Chris Evans, Arizona St
1993.....Steve Wiegel, N Mexico	1993.....John Roethlisberger, Minn	1965.....Glenn Gailis, Iowa
1994.....Steve McCain, UCLA	1994.....Jason Bertram, California	1966.....Ed Gunny, Michigan St
1995.....Ian Bachrach, Stanford	1995.....Drew Durbin, Ohio St	1967.....Josh Robison, California
		1968.....Pat Arnold, Arizona
POMMEL HORSE	**FLOOR EXERCISE**	1969.....Paul Vexler, Penn St
1938.....Erwin Beyer, Chicago	1941.....Lou Fina, Illinois	Ward Maythaler, Iowa St
1939.....Erwin Beyer, Chicago	1953.....Bob Sullivan, Illinois	1970.....Dave Seal, Indiana St
1940.....Harry Koehnemann, Illinois	1954.....Jean Cronstedt, Penn St	1971.....Charles Ropiequet, S Illinois
1941.....Caton Cobb, Illinois	1955.....Don Faber, UCLA	1972.....Dave Seal, Indiana St
1942.....Caton Cobb, Illinois	1956.....Jamile Ashmore, Florida St	1973.....Bob Mahorney, Indiana St
1948.....Steve Greene, Penn St	1957.....Norman Marks, Cal St-	1974.....Keith Heaver, Iowa St
1949.....Joe Berenato, Temple	Los Angeles	1975.....Keith Heaver, Iowa St
1950.....Gene Rabbitt, Syracuse	1958.....Abie Grossfeld, Illinois	1976.....Doug Wood, Iowa St
1951.....Joe Kotys, Kent	1959.....Don Tonry, Illinois	1977.....Doug Wood, Iowa St
1952.....Frank Bare, Illinois	1960.....Ray Hadley, Illinois	1978.....Scott McEldowney, Oregon
1953.....Carlton Rintz, Michigan St	1961.....Robert Lynn, Southern Cal	1979.....Kirk Mango, Northern Ill
1954.....Robert Lawrence, Penn St	1962.....Robert Lynn, Southern Cal	1980.....Jim Hartung, Nebraska
1955.....Carlton Rintz, Michigan St	1963.....Tom Seward, Penn St	1981.....Jim Hartung, Nebraska
1956.....James Brown, Cal St-	Mike Henderson, Michigan	1982.....Jim Hartung, Nebraska
Los Angeles	1964.....Rusty Mitchell, S Illinois	1983.....Alex Schwartz, UCLA
1957.....John Davis, Illinois	1965.....Frank Schmitz, S Illinois	1984.....Tim Daggett, UCLA
1958.....Bill Buck, Iowa	1966.....Frank Schmitz, S Illinois	1985.....Mark Diab, Iowa St
1959.....Art Shurlock, California	1967.....Dave Jacobs, Michigan	1986.....Mark Diab, Iowa St
1960.....James Fairchild, California	1968.....Toby Towson, Michigan St	1987.....Paul O'Neill, Houst Baptist
1961.....James Fairchild, California	1969.....Toby Towson, Michigan St	1988.....Paul O'Neill, New Mexico
1962.....Mike Aufrecht, Illinois	1970.....Tom Proulx, Colorado St	1989.....Vacated†
1963.....Russ Mills, Yale	1971.....Stormy Eaton, New Mexico	Paul O'Neill, New Mexico
1964.....Russ Mills, Yale	1972.....Odessa Lovin, Oklahoma	1990.....Wayne Cowden, Penn St
1965.....Bob Elsinger, Springfield	1973.....Odessa Lovin, Oklahoma	1991.....Adam Carton, Penn St
1966.....Gary Hoskins, Cal St-	1974.....Doug Fitzjarrell, Iowa St	1992.....Scott Keswick, UCLA
Los Angeles	1975.....Kent Brown, Arizona St	1993.....Chris LaMorte, N Mexico
1967.....Keith McCanless, Iowa	1976.....Bob Robbins, Colorado St	1994.....Chris LaMorte, N Mexico
1968.....Jack Ryan, Colorado	1977.....Ron Galimore, Louisiana St	1995.....Dave Frank, Temple

† Championships won by Miguel Rubio (All Around, 1988; Horizontal Bar, 1988-89) and Alfonso Rodriguez (Pommel Horse, 1988; Rings, 1989; Parallel Bars, 1989) were vacated by action of the NCAA Committee on Infractions.

Gymnastics *(Cont.)*

Men *(Cont.)*

DIVISION II (DISCONTINUED)

Year	Champion	Coach	Pts	Runner-Up	Pts
1968	Cal St-Northridge	Bill Vincent	179.400	Springfield	178.050
1969	Cal St-Northridge	Bill Vincent	151.800	Southern Connecticut St	145.075
1970	Northwestern Louisiana	Armando Vega	160.250	Southern Connecticut St	159.300
1971	Cal St-Fullerton	Dick Wolfe	158.150	Springfield	156.987
1972	Cal St-Fullerton	Dick Wolfe	160.550	Southern Connecticut St	153.050
1973	Southern Connecticut St	Abe Grossfeld	160.750	Cal St-Northridge	158.700
1974	Cal St-Fullerton	Dick Wolfe	309.800	Southern Connecticut St	309.400
1975	Southern Connecticut St	Abe Grossfeld	411.650	IL-Chicago	398.800
1976	Southern Connecticut St	Abe Grossfeld	419.200	IL-Chicago	388.850
1977	Springfield	Frank Wolcott	395.950	Cal St-Northridge	381.250
1978	IL-Chicago	C. Johnson/A. Gentile	406.850	Cal St-Northridge	400.400
1979	IL-Chicago	Clarence Johnson	418.550	WI-Oshkosh	385.650
1980	WI-Oshkosh	Ken Allen	260.550	Cal St-Chico	256.050
1981	WI-Oshkosh	Ken Allen	209.500	Springfield	201.550
1982	WI-Oshkosh	Ken Allen	216.050	East Stroudsburg	211.200
1983	East Stroudsburg	Bruno Klaus	258.650	WI-Oshkosh	257.850
1984	East Stroudsburg	Bruno Klaus	270.800	Cortland St	246.350

Women
Team Champions

Year	Champion	Coach	Pts	Runner-Up	Pts
1982	Utah	Greg Marsden	148.60	Cal St-Fullerton	144.10
1983	Utah	Greg Marsden	184.65	Arizona St	183.30
1984	Utah	Greg Marsden	186.05	UCLA	185.55
1985	Utah	Greg Marsden	188.35	Arizona St	186.60
1986	Utah	Greg Marsden	186.95	Arizona St	186.70
1987	Georgia	Suzanne Yoculan	187.90	Utah	187.55
1988	Alabama	Sarah Patterson	190.05	Utah	189.50
1989	Georgia	Suzanne Yoculan	192.65	UCLA	192.60
1990	Utah	Greg Marsden	194.900	Alabama	194.575
1991	Alabama	Sarah Patterson	195.125	Utah	194.375
1992	Utah	Greg Marsden	195.650	Georgia	194.600
1993	Georgia	Suzanne Yoculan	198.000	Alabama	196.825
1994	Utah	Greg Marsden	196.400	Alabama	196.350
1995	Utah	Greg Marsden	196.650	Alabama	196.425
				Michigan	196.425

Individual Champions

ALL-AROUND

1982 ..... Sue Stednitz, Utah
1983 ..... Megan McCunniff, Utah
1984 ..... Megan McCunniff-Marsden, Utah
1985 ..... Penney Hauschild, Alabama
1986 ..... Penney Hauschild, Alabama
Jackie Brummer, Arizona St
1987 ..... Kelly Garrison-Steves, Oklahoma
1988 ..... Kelly Garrison-Steves, Oklahoma
1989 ..... Corrinne Wright, Georgia
1990 ..... Dee Dee Foster, Alabama
1991 ..... Hope Spivey, Georgia
1992 ..... Missy Marlowe, Utah
1993 ..... Jenny Hansen, Kentucky
1994 ..... Jenny Hansen, Kentucky
1995 ..... Jenny Hansen, Kentucky

VAULT

1982 ..... Elaine Alfano, Utah
1983 ..... Elaine Alfano, Utah
1984 ..... Megan Marsden, Utah
1985 ..... Elaine Alfano, Utah
1986 ..... Kim Neal, Arizona St
Pam Loree, Penn St

1987 ..... Yumi Mordre, Washington
1988 ..... Jill Andrews, UCLA
1989 ..... Kim Hamilton, UCLA
1990 ..... Michele Bryant, Nebraska
1991 ..... Anna Basaldva, Arizona
1992 ..... Tammy Marshall, Massachusetts
Heather Stepp, Georgia
Kristein Kenoyer, Utah
1993 ..... Heather Stepp, Georgia
1994 ..... Jenny Hansen, Kentucky
1995 ..... Jenny Hansen, Kentucky

BALANCE BEAM

1982 ..... Sue Stednitz, Utah
1983 ..... Julie Goewey, Cal St-Fullerton
1984 ..... Heidi Anderson, Oregon St
1985 ..... Lisa Zeis, Arizona St
1986 ..... Jackie Brummer, Arizona St
1987 ..... Yumi Mordre, Washington
1988 ..... Kelly Garrison-Steves, Oklahoma
1989 ..... Jill Andrews, UCLA
Joy Selig, Oregon St

1990 ..... Joy Selig, Oregon St
1991 ..... Missy Marlowe, Utah
1992 ..... Missy Marlowe, Utah
Dana Dobransky, Alabama
1993 ..... Dana Dobransky, Alabama
1994 ..... Jenny Hansen, Kentucky
1995 ..... Jenny Hansen, Kentucky

FLOOR EXERCISE

1982 ..... Mary Ayotte-Law, Oregon St
1983 ..... Kim Neal, Arizona St
1984 ..... Maria Anz, Florida
1985 ..... Lisa Mitzel, Utah
1986 ..... Lisa Zeis, Arizona St
Penney Hauschild, Alabama
1987 ..... Kim Hamilton, UCLA
1988 ..... Kim Hamilton, UCLA
1989 ..... Corrinne Wright, Georgia
Kim Hamilton, UCLA
1990 ..... Joy Selig, Oregon St
1991 ..... Hope Spivey, Georgia
1992 ..... Missy Marlowe, Utah
1993 ..... Heather Stepp, Georgia
Tammy Marshall, UMass
Amy Durham, Oregon St

Gymnastics (Cont.)

Women (Cont.)
Individual Champions (Cont.)

1994 .....Hope Spivey-Sheeley, Georgia
1995 .....Jenny Hansen, Kentucky
Stella Umeh, UCLA
Leslie Angeles, Georgia

UNEVEN BARS

1982 .....Lisa Shirk, Pittsburgh
1983 .....Jeri Cameron, Arizona St
1984 .....Jackie Brummer, Arizona St

1985 .....Penney Hauschild, Alabama
1986 .....Lucy Wener, Georgia
1987 .....Lucy Wener, Georgia
1988 .....Kelly Garrison-Steves, Oklahoma
1989 .....Lucy Wener, Georgia
1990 .....Marie Roethlisberger, Minnesota
1991 .....Kelly Macy, Georgia

1992 .....Missy Marlowe, Utah
1993 .....Agina Simpkins, Georgia
Beth Wymer, Michigan
1994 .....Sandy Woolsey, Utah
Beth Wymer, Michigan
Lori Strong, Georgia
1995 .....Beth Wymer, Michigan

DIVISION II (DISCONTINUED)

Year	Champion	Coach	Pts	Runner-Up	Pts
1982	Cal St-Northridge	Donna Stuart	138.10	Jacksonville St	134.05
1983	Denver	Dan Garcia	174.80	Cal St-Northridge	174.35
1984	Jacksonville St	Robert Dillard	173.40	SE Missouri St	171.45
1985	Jacksonville St	Robert Dillard	176.85	SE Missouri St	173.95
1986	Seattle Pacific	Laurel Tindall	175.80	Jacksonville St	175.15

Ice Hockey

DIVISION I

Year	Champion	Coach	Score	Runner-Up	Most Outstanding Player
1948	Michigan	Vic Heyliger	8-4	Dartmouth	Joe Riley, Dartmouth, F
1949	Boston Col	John Kelley	4-3	Dartmouth	Dick Desmond, Dartmouth, G
1950	Colorado Col	Cheddy Thompson	13-4	Boston U	Ralph Bevins, Boston U, G
1951	Michigan	Vic Heyliger	7-1	Brown	Ed Whiston, Brown, G
1952	Michigan	Vic Heyliger	4-1	Colorado Col	Kenneth Kinsley, Colorado Col, G
1953	Michigan	Vic Heyliger	7-3	Minnesota	John Matchefts, Michigan, F
1954	Rensselaer	Ned Harkness	5-4 (OT)	Minnesota	Abbie Moore, Rensselaer, F
1955	Michigan	Vic Heyliger	5-3	Colorado Col	Philip Hilton, Colorado Col, D
1956	Michigan	Vic Heyliger	7-5	Michigan Tech	Lorne Howes, Michigan, G
1957	Colorado Col	Thomas Bedecki	13-6	Michigan	Bob McCusker, Colorado Col, F
1958	Denver	Murray Armstrong	6-2	N Dakota	Murray Massier, Denver, F
1959	N Dakota	Bob May	4-3 (OT)	Michigan St	Reg Morelli, N Dakota, F
1960	Denver	Murray Armstrong	5-3	Michigan Tech	Bob Marquis, Boston U, F
1961	Denver	Murray Armstrong	12-2	St Lawrence	Barry Urbanski, Boston U, G
1962	Michigan Tech	John MacInnes	7-1	Clarkson	Louis Angotti, Michigan Tech, F
1963	N Dakota	Barney Thorndycraft	6-5	Denver	Al McLean, N Dakota, F
1964	Michigan	Allen Renfrew	6-3	Denver	Bob Gray, Michigan, G
1965	Michigan Tech	John MacInnes	8-2	Boston Col	Gary Milroy, Michigan Tech, F
1966	Michigan St	Amo Bessone	6-1	Clarkson	Gaye Cooley, Michigan St, G
1967	Cornell	Ned Harkness	4-1	Boston U	Walt Stanowski, Cornell, D
1968	Denver	Murray Armstrong	4-0	N Dakota	Gerry Powers, Denver, G
1969	Denver	Murray Armstrong	4-3	Cornell	Keith Magnuson, Denver, D
1970	Cornell	Ned Harkness	6-4	Clarkson	Daniel Lodboa, Cornell, D
1971	Boston U	Jack Kelley	4-2	Minnesota	Dan Brady, Boston U, G
1972	Boston U	Jack Kelley	4-0	Cornell	Tim Regan, Boston U, G
1973	Wisconsin	Bob Johnson	4-2	Vacated	Dean Talafous, Wisconsin, F
1974	Minnesota	Herb Brooks	4-2	Michigan Tech	Brad Shelstad, Minnesota, G
1975	Michigan Tech	John MacInnes	6-1	Minnesota	Jim Warden, Michigan Tech, G
1976	Minnesota	Herb Brooks	6-4	Michigan Tech	Tom Vanelli, Minnesota, F
1977	Wisconsin	Bob Johnson	6-5 (OT)	Michigan	Julian Baretta, Wisconsin, G
1978	Boston U	Jack Parker	5-3	Boston Col	Jack O'Callahan, Boston U, D
1979	Minnesota	Herb Brooks	4-3	N Dakota	Steve Janaszak, Minnesota, G
1980	N Dakota	John Gasparini	5-2	Northern Michigan	Doug Smail, N Dakota, F
1981	Wisconsin	Bob Johnson	6-3	Minnesota	Marc Behrend, Wisconsin, G
1982	N Dakota	John Gasparini	5-2	Wisconsin	Phil Sykes, N Dakota, F
1983	Wisconsin	Jeff Sauer	6-2	Harvard	Marc Behrend, Wisconsin, G
1984	Bowling Green	Jerry York	5-4 (OT)	MN-Duluth	Gary Kruzich, Bowling Green, G
1985	Rensselaer	Mike Addesa	2-1	Providence	Chris Terreri, Providence, G
1986	Michigan St	Ron Mason	6-5	Harvard	Mike Donnelly, Michigan St, F
1987	N Dakota	John Gasparini	5-3	Michigan St	Tony Hrkac, N Dakota, F

DIVISION I (Cont.)

Year	Champion	Coach	Score	Runner-Up	Most Outstanding Player
1988	Lake Superior St	Frank Anzalone	4-3 (OT)	St Lawrence	Bruce Hoffort, Lake Superior St, G
1989	Harvard	Bill Cleary	4-3 (OT)	Minnesota	Ted Donato, Harvard, F
1990	Wisconsin	Jeff Sauer	7-3	Colgate	Chris Tancill, Wisconsin, F
1991	N Michigan	Rick Comley	8-7 (3OT)	Boston U	Scott Beattie, N Michigan, F
1992	Lake Superior St	Jeff Jackson	4-2	Wisconsin	Paul Constantin, Lake Superior St, F
1993	Maine	Shawn Walsh	5-4	Lake Superior St	Jim Montgomery, Maine, F
1994	Lake Superior St	Jeff Jackson	9-1	Boston U	Sean Tallaire, Lake Superior St, F
1995	Boston U	Jack Parker	6-2	Maine	Chris O'Sullivan, Boston U, F

DIVISION II (DISCONTINUED, THEN RENEWED)

Year	Champion	Coach	Score	Runner-Up
1978	Merrimack	Thom Lawler	12-2	Lake Forest
1979	Lowell	Bill Riley Jr	6-4	Mankato St
1980	Mankato St	Don Brose	5-2	Elmira
1981	Lowell	Bill Riley Jr	5-4	Plattsburgh St
1982	Lowell	Bill Riley Jr	6-1	Plattsburgh St
1983	Rochester Inst	Brian Mason	4-2	Bemidji St
1984	Bemidji St	R.H. (Bob) Peters	14-4*	Merrimack
1993	Bemidji St	R.H. (Bob) Peters	15-6*	Mercyhurst
1994	Bemidji St	R.H. (Bob) Peters	7-6*	AL-Huntsville
1995	Bemidji St	R.H. (Bob) Peters	11-6*	Mercyhurst

*Two-game, total-goal series.

DIVISION III

Year	Champion	Coach	Score	Runner-Up
1984	Babson	Bob Riley	8-0	Union (NY)
1985	Rochester Inst	Bruce Delventhal	5-1	Bemidji St
1986	Bemidji St	R.H. (Bob) Peters	8-5	Vacated
1987	Vacated			Oswego St
1988	WI-River Falls	Rick Kozuback	7-1, 3-5, 3-0	Elmira
1989	WI-Stevens Point	Mark Mazzoleni	3-3, 3-2	Rochester Inst
1990	WI-Stevens Point	Mark Mazzoleni	10-1, 3-6, 1-0	Plattsburgh St
1991	WI-Stevens Point	Mark Mazzoleni	6-2	Mankato St
1992	Plattsburgh St	Bob Emery	7-3	WI-Stevens Point
1993	WI-Stevens Point	Joe Baldarotta	4-3	WI-River Falls
1994	WI-River Falls	Dean Talafous	6-4	WI-Superior
1995	Middlebury	Bill Beany	1-0	Fredonia St

Lacrosse

Men

DIVISION I

Year	Champion	Coach	Score	Runner-Up
1971	Cornell	Richie Moran	12-6	Maryland
1972	Virginia	Glenn Thiel	13-12	Johns Hopkins
1973	Maryland	Bud Beardmore	10-9 (2 OT)	Johns Hopkins
1974	Johns Hopkins	Bob Scott	17-12	Maryland
1975	Maryland	Bud Beardmore	20-13	Navy
1976	Cornell	Richie Moran	16-13 (OT)	Maryland
1977	Cornell	Richie Moran	16-8	Johns Hopkins
1978	Johns Hopkins	Henry Ciccarone	13-8	Cornell
1979	Johns Hopkins	Henry Ciccarone	15-9	Maryland
1980	Johns Hopkins	Henry Ciccarone	9-8 (2 OT)	Virginia
1981	N Carolina	Willie Scroggs	14-13	Johns Hopkins
1982	N Carolina	Willie Scroggs	7-5	Johns Hopkins
1983	Syracuse	Roy Simmons Jr	17-16	Johns Hopkins
1984	Johns Hopkins	Don Zimmerman	13-10	Syracuse
1985	Johns Hopkins	Don Zimmerman	11-4	Syracuse
1986	N Carolina	Willie Scroggs	10-9 (OT)	Virginia
1987	Johns Hopkins	Don Zimmerman	11-10	Cornell
1988	Syracuse	Roy Simmons Jr	13-8	Cornell
1989	Syracuse	Roy Simmons Jr	13-12	Johns Hopkins
1990	Syracuse	Roy Simmons Jr	21-9	Loyola (MD)
1991	N Carolina	Dave Klarmann	18-13	Towson St

Men (Cont.)

DIVISION I (Cont.)

Year	Champion	Coach	Score	Runner-Up
1992	Princeton	Bill Tierney	10-9	Syracuse
1993	Syracuse	Roy Simmons Jr	13-12	N Carolina
1994	Princeton	Bill Tierney	9-8 (OT)	Virginia
1995	Syracuse	Roy Simmons Jr	13-9	Maryland

DIVISION II (DISCONTINUED, THEN RENEWED)

Year	Champion	Coach	Score	Runner-Up
1974	Towson St	Carl Runk	18-17 (OT)	Hobart
1975	Cortland St	Chuck Winters	12-11	Hobart
1976	Hobart	Jerry Schmidt	18-9	Adelphi
1977	Hobart	Jerry Schmidt	23-13	Washington (MD)
1978	Roanoke	Paul Griffin	14-13	Hobart
1979	Adelphi	Paul Doherty	17-12	MD-Baltimore County
1980	MD-Baltimore County	Dick Watts	23-14	Adelphi
1981	Adelphi	Paul Doherty	17-14	Loyola (MD)
1993	Adelphi	Kevin Sheehan	11-7	LIU-C.W. Post
1994	Springfield	Keith Bugbee	15-12	New York Tech
1995	Adelphi	Sandy Kapatos	12-10	Springfield

DIVISION III

Year	Champion	Coach	Score	Runner-Up
1980	Hobart	Dave Urick	11-8	Cortland St
1981	Hobart	Dave Urick	10-8	Cortland St
1982	Hobart	Dave Urick	9-8 (OT)	Washington (MD)
1983	Hobart	Dave Urick	13-9	Roanoke
1984	Hobart	Dave Urick	12-5	Washington (MD)
1985	Hobart	Dave Urick	15-8	Washington (MD)
1986	Hobart	Dave Urick	13-10	Washington (MD)
1987	Hobart	Dave Urick	9-5	Ohio Wesleyan
1988	Hobart	Dave Urick	18-9	Ohio Wesleyan
1989	Hobart	Dave Urick	11-8	Ohio Wesleyan
1990	Hobart	B.J. O'Hara	18-6	Washington (MD)
1991	Hobart	B.J. O'Hara	12-11	Salisbury St
1992	Nazareth (NY)	Scott Nelson	13-12	Hobart
1993	Hobart	B.J. O'Hara	16-10	Ohio Wesleyan
1994	Salisbury St	Jim Berkman	15-9	Hobart
1995	Salisbury St	Jim Berkman	22-13	Nazareth

Women

DIVISION I

Year	Champion	Coach	Score	Runner-Up
1982	Massachusetts	Pamela Hixon	9-6	Trenton St
1983	Delaware	Janet Smith	10-7	Temple
1984	Temple	Tina Sloan Green	6-4	Maryland
1985	New Hampshire	Marisa Didio	6-5	Maryland
1986	Maryland	Sue Tyler	11-10	Penn St
1987	Penn St	Susan Scheetz	7-6	Temple
1988	Temple	Tina Sloan Green	15-7	Penn St
1989	Penn St	Susan Scheetz	7-6	Harvard
1990	Harvard	Carole Kleinfelder	8-7	Maryland
1991	Virginia	Jane Miller	8-6	Maryland
1992	Maryland	Cindy Timchal	11-10	Harvard
1993	Virginia	Jane Miller	8-6 (OT)	Princeton
1994	Princeton	Chris Sailer	10-7	Virginia
1995	Maryland	Cindy Timchal	13-5	Princeton

DIVISION III

Year	Champion	Score	Runner-Up	Year	Champion	Score	Runner-Up
1985	Trenton St	7-4	Ursinus	1991	Trenton St	7-6	Ursinus
1986	Ursinus	12-10	Trenton St	1992	Trenton St	5-3	William Smith
1987	Trenton St	8-7 (OT)	Ursinus	1993	Trenton St	10-9	William Smith
1988	Trenton St	14-11	William Smith	1994	Trenton St	29-11	William Smith
1989	Ursinus	8-6	Trenton St	1995	Trenton St	14-13	William Smith
1990	Ursinus	7-6	St Lawrence				

Rifle

Men's and Women's Combined

						Individual Champions	
Year	Champion	Coach	Score	Runner-Up	Score	Air Rifle	Smallbore
1980	Tennessee Tech	James Newkirk	6201	W Virginia	6150	Rod Fitz-Randolph, Tennessee Tech	Rod Fitz-Randolph, Tennessee Tech
1981	Tennessee Tech	James Newkirk	6139	W Virginia	6136	John Rost, W Virginia	Kurt Fitz-Randolph, Tennessee Tech
1982	Tennessee Tech	James Newkirk	6138	W Virginia	6136	John Rost, W Virginia	Kurt Fitz-Randolph, Tennessee Tech
1983	W Virginia	Edward Etzel	6166	Tennessee Tech	6148	Ray Slonena, Tennessee Tech	David Johnson, W Virginia
1984	W Virginia	Edward Etzel	6206	East Tennessee St	6142	Pat Spurgin, Murray St	Bob Broughton, W Virginia
1985	Murray St	Elvis Green	6150	W Virginia	6149	Christian Heller, W Virginia	Pat Spurgin, Murray St
1986	W Virginia	Edward Etzel	6229	Murray St	6163	Marianne Wallace, Murray St	Mike Anti, W Virginia
1987	Murray St	Elvis Green	6205	W Virginia	6203	Rob Harbison, TN-Martin	Web Wright, W Virginia
1988	W Virginia	Greg Perrine	6192	Murray St	6183	Deena Wigger, Murray St	Web Wright, W Virginia
1989	W Virginia	Edward Etzel	6234	S Florida	6180	Michelle Scarborough S Florida	Deb Sinclair, AK-Fairbanks
1990	W Virginia	Marsha Beasley	6205	Navy	6101	Gary Hardy, W Virginia	Michelle Scarborough S Florida
1991	W Virginia	Marsha Beasley	6171	Alaska-Fairbanks	6110	Ann Pfiffner, W Virginia	Soma Dutta, UTEP
1991	W Virginia	Marsha Beasley	6171	Alaska-Fairbanks	6110	Ann Pfiffner, W Virginia	Soma Dutta, UTEP
1992	W Virginia	Marsha Beasley	6214	Alaska-Fairbanks	6166	Ann Pfiffner, W Virginia	Tim Manges, W Virginia
1993	W Virginia	Marsha Beasley	6179	Alaska-Fairbanks	6169	Trevor Gathman, W Virginia	Eric Uptagrafft, W Virginia
1994	AK-Fairbanks	Randy Pitney	6194	W Virginia	6187	Nancy Napolski, Kentucky	Cory Brunetti, AK-Fairbanks
1995	W Virginia	Marsha Beasley	6241	Air Force	6187	Benji Belden, Murray St	Oleg Selezner, AK-Fairbanks

Skiing

Men's and Women's Combined

Year	Champion	Coach	Pts	Runner-Up	Pts	Host or Site
1954	Denver	Willy Schaeffler	384.0	Seattle	349.6	NV-Reno
1955	Denver	Willy Schaeffler	567.05	Dartmouth	558.935	Norwich
1956	Denver	Willy Schaeffler	582.01	Dartmouth	541.77	Winter Park
1957	Denver	Willy Schaeffler	577.95	Colorado	545.29	Ogden Snow Basin
1958	Dartmouth	Al Merrill	561.2	Denver	550.6	Dartmouth
1959	Colorado	Bob Beattie	549.4	Denver	543.6	Winter Park
1960	Colorado	Bob Beattie	571.4	Denver	568.6	Bridger Bowl
1961	Denver	Willy Schaeffler	376.19	Middlebury	366.94	Middlebury
1962	Denver	Willy Schaeffler	390.08	Colorado	374.30	Squaw Valley
1963	Denver	Willy Schaeffler	384.6	Colorado	381.6	Solitude
1964	Denver	Willy Schaeffler	370.2	Dartmouth	368.8	Franconia Notch
1965	Denver	Willy Schaeffler	380.5	Utah	378.4	Crystal Mountain
1966	Denver	Willy Schaeffler	381.02	Western Colorado	365.92	Crested Butte
1967	Denver	Willy Schaeffler	376.7	Wyoming	375.9	Sugarloaf Mountain
1968	Wyoming	John Cress	383.9	Denver	376.2	Mount Werner
1969	Denver	Willy Schaeffler	388.6	Dartmouth	372.0	Mount Werner
1970	Denver	Willy Schaeffler	386.6	Dartmouth	378.8	Cannon Mountain
1971	Denver	Peder Pytte	394.7	Colorado	373.1	Terry Peak
1972	Colorado	Bill Marolt	385.3	Denver	380.1	Winter Park
1973	Colorado	Bill Marolt	381.89	Wyoming	377.83	Middlebury
1974	Colorado	Bill Marolt	176	Wyoming	162	Jackson Hole
1975	Colorado	Bill Marolt	183	Vermont	115	Fort Lewis
1976	Colorado	Bill Marolt	112			Bates
	Dartmouth	Jim Page	112			

Skiing (Cont.)

Year	Champion	Coach	Pts	Runner-Up	Pts	Host or Site
1977	Colorado	Bill Marolt	179	Wyoming	154.5	Winter Park
1978	Colorado	Bill Marolt	152.5	Wyoming	121.5	Cannon Mountain
1979	Colorado	Tim Hinderman	153	Utah	130	Steamboat Springs
1980	Vermont	Chip LaCasse	171	Utah	151	Lake Placid and Stowe
1981	Utah	Pat Miller	183	Vermont	172	Park City
1982	Colorado	Tim Hinderman	461	Vermont	436.5	Lake Placid
1983	Utah	Pat Miller	696	Vermont	650	Bozeman
1984	Utah	Pat Miller	750.5	Vermont	684	New Hampshire
1985	Wyoming	Tim Ameel	764	Utah	744	Bozeman
1986	Utah	Pat Miller	612	Vermont	602	Vermont
1987	Utah	Pat Miller	710	Vermont	627	Anchorage
1988	Utah	Pat Miller	651	Vermont	614	Middlebury
1989	Vermont	Chip LaCasse	672	Utah	668	Jackson Hole
1990	Vermont	Chip LaCasse	671	Utah	571	Vermont
1991	Colorado	Richard Rokos	713	Vermont	682	Park City
1992	Vermont	Chip LaCasse	693.5	New Mexico	642.5	New Hampshire
1993	Utah	Pat Miller	783	Vermont	700.5	Steamboat Springs
1994	Vermont	Chip LaCasse	688	Utah	667	Sugarloaf, ME
1995	Colorado	Richard Rokos	720.5	Utah	711	New Hampshire

Soccer

Men

DIVISION I

Year	Champion	Coach	Score	Runner-Up
1959	St Louis	Bob Guelker	5-2	Bridgeport
1960	St Louis	Bob Guelker	3-2	Maryland
1961	West Chester	Mel Lorback	2-0	St Louis
1962	St Louis	Bob Guelker	4-3	Maryland
1963	St Louis	Bob Guelker	3-0	Navy
1964	Navy	F. H. Warner	1-0	Michigan St
1965	St Louis	Bob Guelker	1-0	Michigan St
1966	San Francisco	Steve Negoesco	5-2	LIU-Brooklyn
1967	Michigan St	Gene Kenney	0-0	Game called
	St Louis	Harry Keough		due to inclement weather
1968	Maryland	Doyle Royal	2-2 (2 OT)	
	Michigan St	Gene Kenney		
1969	St Louis	Harry Keough	4-0	San Francisco
1970	St Louis	Harry Keough	1-0	UCLA
1971	Vacated		3-2	St Louis
1972	St Louis	Harry Keough	4-2	UCLA
1973	St Louis	Harry Keough	2-1 (OT)	UCLA
1974	Howard	Lincoln Phillips	2-1 (4 OT)	St Louis
1975	San Francisco	Steve Negoesco	4-0	SIU-Edwardsville
1976	San Francisco	Steve Negoesco	1-0	Indiana
1977	Hartwick	Jim Lennox	2-1	San Francisco
1978	Vacated		2-0	Indiana
1979	SIU-Edwardsville	Bob Guelker	3-2	Clemson
1980	San Francisco	Steve Negoesco	4-3 (OT)	Indiana
1981	Connecticut	Joe Morrone	2-1 (OT)	Alabama A&M
1982	Indiana	Jerry Yeagley	2-1 (8 OT)	Duke
1983	Indiana	Jerry Yeagley	1-0 (2 OT)	Columbia
1984	Clemson	I. M. Ibrahim	2-1	Indiana
1985	UCLA	Sigi Schmid	1-0 (8 OT)	American
1986	Duke	John Rennie	1-0	Akron
1987	Clemson	I. M. Ibrahim	2-0	San Diego St
1988	Indiana	Jerry Yeagley	1-0	Howard
1989	Santa Clara	Steve Sampson	1-1 (2 OT)	
	Virginia	Bruce Arena		
1990	UCLA	Sigi Schmid	1-0 (OT)	Rutgers
1991	Virginia	Bruce Arena	0-0*	Santa Clara
1992	Virginia	Bruce Arena	2-0	San Diego

*Under a rule passed in 1991, the NCAA determined that when a score is tied after regulation and overtime, and the championship is determined by penalty kicks, the official score will be 0-0.

Men (Cont.)
DIVISION I (Cont.)

Year	Champion	Coach	Score	Runner-Up
1993	Virginia	Bruce Arena	2-0	S Carolina
1994	Virginia	Bruce Arena	1-0	Indiana

DIVISION II

Year	Champion	Year	Champion	Year	Champion
1972	SIU-Edwardsville	1980	Lock Haven	1988	Florida Tech
1973	MO-St Louis	1981	Tampa	1989	New Hampshire Col
1974	Adelphi	1982	Florida Intl	1990	Southern Connecticut St
1975	Baltimore	1983	Seattle Pacific	1991	Florida Tech
1976	Loyola (MD)	1984	Florida Intl	1992	Southern Connecticut St
1977	Alabama A&M	1985	Seattle Pacific	1993	Seattle Pacific
1978	Seattle Pacific	1986	Seattle Pacific	1994	Tampa
1979	Alabama A&M	1987	Southern Connecticut St		

DIVISION III

Year	Champion	Year	Champion	Year	Champion
1974	Brockport St	1981	Glassboro St	1988	UC-San Diego
1975	Babson	1982	NC-Greensboro	1989	Elizabethtown
1976	Brandeis	1983	NC-Greensboro	1990	Glassboro St
1977	Lock Haven	1984	Wheaton (IL)	1991	UC-San Diego
1978	Lock Haven	1985	NC-Greensboro	1992	Kean
1979	Babson	1986	NC-Greensboro	1993	UC-San Diego
1980	Babson	1987	NC-Greensboro	1994	Bethany (WV)

Women
DIVISION I

Year	Champion	Coach	Score	Runner-Up
1982	N Carolina	Anson Dorrance	2-0	Central Florida
1983	N Carolina	Anson Dorrance	4-0	George Mason
1984	N Carolina	Anson Dorrance	2-0	Connecticut
1985	George Mason	Hank Leung	2-0	N Carolina
1986	N Carolina	Anson Dorrance	2-0	Colorado Col
1987	N Carolina	Anson Dorrance	1-0	Massachusetts
1988	N Carolina	Anson Dorrance	4-1	N Carolina St
1989	N Carolina	Anson Dorrance	2-0	Colorado Col
1990	N Carolina	Anson Dorrance	6-0	Connecticut
1991	N Carolina	Anson Dorrance	3-1	Wisconsin
1992	N Carolina	Anson Dorrance	9-1	Duke
1993	N Carolina	Anson Dorrance	6-0	George Mason
1994	N Carolina	Anson Dorrance	5-0	Notre Dame

DIVISION II

Year	Champion
1988	Cal St-Hayward
1989	Barry
1990	Sonoma St
1991	Cal St-Dominguez Hills
1992	Barry
1993	Barry
1994	Franklin Pierce

DIVISION III

Year	Champion
1986	Rochester
1987	Rochester
1988	William Smith
1989	UC-San Diego
1990	Ithaca
1991	Ithaca
1992	Cortland St
1993	Trenton St
1994	Trenton St

Softball

DIVISION I

Year	Champion	Coach	Score	Runner-Up
1982	UCLA*	Sharron Backus	2-0†	Fresno St
1983	Texas A&M	Bob Brock	2-0‡	Cal St-Fullerton
1984	UCLA	Sharron Backus	1-0#	Texas A&M
1985	UCLA	Sharron Backus	2-1**	Nebraska
1986	Cal St-Fullerton*	Judi Garman	3-0	Texas A&M

Softball (Cont.)

DIVISION I (Cont.)

Year	Champion	Coach	Score	Runner-Up
1987	Texas A&M	Bob Brock	4-1	UCLA
1988	UCLA	Sharron Backus	3-0	Fresno St
1989	UCLA*	Sharron Backus	1-0	Fresno St
1990	UCLA	Sharron Backus	2-0	Fresno St
1991	Arizona	Mike Candrea	5-1	UCLA
1992	UCLA*	Sharron Backus	2-0	Arizona
1993	Arizona	Mike Candrea	1-0	UCLA
1994	Arizona	Mike Candrea	4-0	Cal St-Northridge
1995	UCLA*	Sharron Backus/ Sue Enquist	4-2	Arizona

*Undefeated teams in final series. †8 innings. ‡12 innings. #13 innings. **9 innings.

DIVISION II

Year	Champion	Year	Champion	Year	Champion
1982	Sam Houston St	1987	Cal St-Northridge	1992	Missouri Southern
1983	Cal St-Northridge	1988	Cal St-Bakersfield	1993	Florida Southern
1984	Cal St-Northridge	1989	Cal St-Bakersfield	1994	Merrimack
1985	Cal St-Northridge	1990	Cal St-Bakersfield	1995	Kennesaw St
1986	SF Austin St	1991	Augustana (SD)		

DIVISION III

Year	Champion	Year	Champion	Year	Champion
1982	Sam Houston St	1986	Eastern Connecticut St	1991	Central (IA)
1982	Eastern Connecticut St*	1987	Trenton St*	1992	Trenton St
1983	Trenton St	1988	Central (IA)	1993	Central (IA)
1984	Buena Vista*	1989	Trenton St*	1994	Trenton St
1985	Eastern Connecticut St	1990	Eastern Connecticut St	1995	Chapman

*Undefeated teams in final series.

Swimming and Diving

Men

DIVISION I

Year	Champion	Coach	Pts	Runner-Up	Pts
1937	Michigan	Matt Mann	75	Ohio St	39
1938	Michigan	Matt Mann	46	Ohio St	45
1939	Michigan	Matt Mann	65	Ohio St	58
1940	Michigan	Matt Mann	45	Yale	42
1941	Michigan	Matt Mann	61	Yale	58
1942	Yale	Robert J. H. Kiphuth	71	Michigan	39
1943	Ohio St	Mike Peppe	81	Michigan	47
1944	Yale	Robert J. H. Kiphuth	39	Michigan	38
1945	Ohio St	Mike Peppe	56	Michigan	48
1946	Ohio St	Mike Peppe	61	Michigan	37
1947	Ohio St	Mike Peppe	66	Michigan	39
1948	Michigan	Matt Mann	44	Ohio St	41
1949	Ohio St	Mike Peppe	49	Iowa	35
1950	Ohio St	Mike Peppe	64	Yale	43
1951	Yale	Robert J. H. Kiphuth	81	Michigan St	60
1952	Ohio St	Mike Peppe	94	Yale	81
1953	Yale	Robert J. H. Kiphuth	96½	Ohio St	73½
1954	Ohio St	Mike Peppe	94	Michigan	67
1955	Ohio St	Mike Peppe	90	Yale	51
				Michigan	51
1956	Ohio St	Mike Peppe	68	Yale	54
1957	Michigan	Gus Stager	69	Yale	61
1958	Michigan	Gus Stager	72	Yale	63
1959	Michigan	Gus Stager	137½	Ohio St	44
1960	Southern Cal	Peter Daland	87	Michigan	73
1961	Michigan	Gus Stager	85	Southern Cal	62
1962	Ohio St	Mike Peppe	92	Southern Cal	46
1963	Southern Cal	Peter Daland	81	Yale	77
1964	Southern Cal	Peter Daland	96	Indiana	91
1965	Southern Cal	Peter Daland	285	Indiana	278½
1966	Southern Cal	Peter Daland	302	Indiana	286

Men (Cont.)
DIVISION I (Cont.)

Year	Champion	Coach	Pts	Runner-Up	Pts
1967	Stanford	Jim Gaughran	275	Southern Cal	260
1968	Indiana	James Counsilman	346	Yale	253
1969	Indiana	James Counsilman	427	Southern Cal	306
1970	Indiana	James Counsilman	332	Southern Cal	235
1971	Indiana	James Counsilman	351	Southern Cal	260
1972	Indiana	James Counsilman	390	Southern Cal	371
1973	Indiana	James Counsilman	358	Tennessee	294
1974	Southern Cal	Peter Daland	339	Indiana	338
1975	Southern Cal	Peter Daland	344	Indiana	274
1976	Southern Cal	Peter Daland	398	Tennessee	237
1977	Southern Cal	Peter Daland	385	Alabama	204
1978	Tennessee	Ray Bussard	307	Auburn	185
1979	California	Nort Thornton	287	Southern Cal	227
1980	California	Nort Thornton	234	Texas	220
1981	Texas	Eddie Reese	259	UCLA	189
1982	UCLA	Ron Ballatore	219	Texas	210
1983	Florida	Randy Reese	238	Southern Meth	227
1984	Florida	Randy Reese	287½	Texas	277
1985	Stanford	Skip Kenney	403½	Florida	302
1986	Stanford	Skip Kenney	404	California	335
1987	Stanford	Skip Kenney	374	Southern Cal	296
1988	Texas	Eddie Reese	424	Southern Cal	369½
1989	Texas	Eddie Reese	475	Stanford	396
1990	Texas	Eddie Reese	506	Southern Cal	423
1991	Texas	Eddie Reese	476	Stanford	420
1992	Stanford	Skip Kenney	632	Texas	356
1993	Stanford	Skip Kenney	520½	Michigan	396
1994	Stanford	Skip Kenney	566½	Texas	445
1995	Michigan	Jon Urbanchek	561	Stanford	475

DIVISION II

Year	Champion	Year	Champion	Year	Champion
1963	SW Missouri St	1974	Cal St-Chico	1985	Cal St-Northridge
1964	Bucknell	1975	Cal St-Northridge	1986	Cal St-Bakersfield
1965	San Diego St	1976	Cal St-Chico	1987	Cal St-Bakersfield
1966	San Diego St	1977	Cal St-Northridge	1988	Cal St-Bakersfield
1967	UC-Santa Barbara	1978	Cal St-Northridge	1989	Cal St-Bakersfield
1968	Long Beach St	1979	Cal St-Northridge	1990	Cal St-Bakersfield
1969	UC-Irvine	1980	Oakland (MI)	1991	Cal St-Bakersfield
1970	UC-Irvine	1981	Cal St-Northridge	1992	Cal St-Bakersfield
1971	UC-Irvine	1982	Cal St-Northridge	1993	Cal St-Bakersfield
1972	Eastern Michigan	1983	Cal St-Northridge	1994	Oakland (MI)
1973	Cal St-Chico	1984	Cal St-Northridge	1995	Oakland (MI)

DIVISION III

Year	Champion	Year	Champion	Year	Champion
1975	Cal St-Chico	1982	Kenyon	1989	Kenyon
1976	St Lawrence	1983	Kenyon	1990	Kenyon
1977	Johns Hopkins	1984	Kenyon	1991	Kenyon
1978	Johns Hopkins	1985	Kenyon	1992	Kenyon
1979	Johns Hopkins	1986	Kenyon	1993	Kenyon
1980	Kenyon	1987	Kenyon	1994	Kenyon
1981	Kenyon	1988	Kenyon	1995	Kenyon

Women
DIVISION I

Year	Champion	Coach	Pts	Runner-Up	Pts
1982	Florida	Randy Reese	505	Stanford	383
1983	Stanford	George Haines	418½	Florida	389½
1984	Texas	Richard Quick	392	Stanford	324
1985	Texas	Richard Quick	643	Florida	400
1986	Texas	Richard Quick	633	Florida	586
1987	Texas	Richard Quick	648½	Stanford	631½
1988	Texas	Richard Quick	661	Florida	542½

Women *(Cont.)*

DIVISION I *(Cont.)*

Year	Champion	Coach	Pts	Runner-Up	Pts
1989	Stanford	Richard Quick	610½	Texas	547
1990	Texas	Mark Schubert	632	Stanford	622½
1991	Texas	Mark Schubert	746	Stanford	653
1992	Stanford	Richard Quick	735½	Texas	651
1993	Stanford	Richard Quick	649½	Florida	421
1994	Stanford	Richard Quick	512	Texas	421
1995	Stanford	Richard Quick	497½	Michigan	478½

DIVISION II

Year	Champion	Year	Champion	Year	Champion
1982	Cal St-Northridge	1987	Cal St-Northridge	1992	Oakland (MI)
1983	Clarion	1988	Cal St-Northridge	1993	Oakland (MI)
1984	Clarion	1989	Cal St-Northridge	1994	Oakland (MI)
1985	S Florida	1990	Oakland (MI)	1995	Air Force
1986	Clarion	1991	Oakland (MI)		

DIVISION III

Year	Champion	Year	Champion	Year	Champion
1982	Williams	1987	Kenyon	1992	Kenyon
1983	Williams	1988	Kenyon	1993	Kenyon
1984	Kenyon	1989	Kenyon	1994	Kenyon
1985	Kenyon	1990	Kenyon	1995	Kenyon
1986	Kenyon	1991	Kenyon		

Tennis

Men

INDIVIDUAL CHAMPIONS 1883-1945

Year	Champion	Year	Champion
1883	Joseph Clark, Harvard (spring)	1914	George Church, Princeton
1883	Howard Taylor, Harvard (fall)	1915	Richard Williams II, Harvard
1884	W. P. Knapp, Yale	1916	G. Colket Caner, Harvard
1885	W. P. Knapp, Yale	1917-18	No tournament
1886	G. M. Brinley, Trinity (CT)	1919	Charles Garland, Yale
1887	P. S. Sears, Harvard	1920	Lascelles Banks, Yale
1888	P. S. Sears, Harvard	1921	Philip Neer, Stanford
1889	R. P. Huntington, Jr, Yale	1922	Lucien Williams, Yale
1890	Fred Hovey, Harvard	1923	Carl Fischer, Philadelphia Osteo
1891	Fred Hovey, Harvard	1924	Wallace Scott, Washington
1892	William Larned, Cornell	1925	Edward Chandler, California
1893	Malcolm Chace, Brown	1926	Edward Chandler, California
1894	Malcolm Chace, Yale	1927	Wilmer Allison, Texas
1895	Malcolm Chace, Yale	1928	Julius Seligson, Lehigh
1896	Malcolm Whitman, Harvard	1929	Berkeley Bell, Texas
1897	S. G. Thompson, Princeton	1930	Clifford Sutter, Tulane
1898	Leo Ware, Harvard	1931	Keith Gledhill, Stanford
1899	Dwight Davis, Harvard	1932	Clifford Sutter, Tulane
1900	Raymond Little, Princeton	1933	Jack Tidball, UCLA
1901	Fred Alexander, Princeton	1934	Gene Mako, Southern Cal
1902	William Clothier, Harvard	1935	Wilbur Hess, Rice
1903	E. B. Dewhurst, Pennsylvania	1936	Ernest Sutter, Tulane
1904	Robert LeRoy, Columbia	1937	Ernest Sutter, Tulane
1905	E. B. Dewhurst, Pennsylvania	1938	Frank Guernsey, Rice
1906	Robert LeRoy, Columbia	1939	Frank Guernsey, Rice
1907	G. Peabody Gardner, Jr, Harvard	1940	Donald McNeil, Kenyon
1908	Nat Niles, Harvard	1941	Joseph Hunt, Navy
1909	Wallace Johnson, Pennsylvania	1942	Frederick Schroeder, Jr, Stanford
1910	R. A. Holden, Jr, Yale	1943	Pancho Segura, Miami (FL)
1911	E. H. Whitney, Harvard	1944	Pancho Segura, Miami (FL)
1912	George Church, Princeton	1945	Pancho Segura, Miami (FL)
1913	Richard Williams II, Harvard		

Men (Cont.)

DIVISION I

Year	Champion	Coach	Pts	Runner-Up	Pts	Individual Champion
1946	Southern Cal	William Moyle	9	William & Mary	6	Robert Falkenburg, Southern Cal
1947	William & Mary	Sharvey G. Umbeck	10	Rice	4	Gardner Larned, William & Mary
1948	William & Mary	Sharvey G. Umbeck	6	San Francisco	5	Harry Likas, San Francisco
1949	San Francisco	Norman Brooks	7	Rollins/Tulane/ Washington	4	Jack Tuero, Tulane
1950	UCLA	William Ackerman	11	California	5	Herbert Flam, UCLA
				Southern Cal	5	
1951	Southern Cal	Louis Wheeler	9	Cincinnati	7	Tony Trabert, Cincinnati
1952	UCLA	J. D. Morgan	11	California	5	Hugh Stewart, Southern Cal
				Southern Cal	5	
1953	UCLA	J. D. Morgan	11	California	6	Hamilton Richardson, Tulane
1954	UCLA	J. D. Morgan	15	Southern Cal	10	Hamilton Richardson, Tulane
1955	Southern Cal	George Toley	12	Texas	7	Jose Aguero, Tulane
1956	UCLA	J. D. Morgan	15	Southern Cal	14	Alejandro Olmedo, Southern Cal
1957	Michigan	William Murphy	10	Tulane	9	Barry MacKay, Michigan
1958	Southern Cal	George Toley	13	Stanford	9	Alejandro Olmedo, Southern Cal
1959	Notre Dame	Thomas Fallon	8			Whitney Reed, San Jose St
	Tulane	Emmet Pare	8			
1960	UCLA	J. D. Morgan	18	Southern Cal	8	Larry Nagler, UCLA
1961	UCLA	J. D. Morgan	17	Southern Cal	16	Allen Fox, UCLA
1962	Southern Cal	George Toley	22	UCLA	12	Rafael Osuna, Southern Cal
1963	Southern Cal	George Toley	27	UCLA	19	Dennis Ralston, Southern Cal
1964	Southern Cal	George Toley	26	UCLA	25	Dennis Ralston, Southern Cal
1965	UCLA	J. D. Morgan	31	Miami (FL)	13	Arthur Ashe, UCLA
1966	Southern Cal	George Toley	27	UCLA	23	Charles Pasarell, UCLA
1967	Southern Cal	George Toley	28	UCLA	23	Bob Lutz, Southern Cal
1968	Southern Cal	George Toley	31	Rice	23	Stan Smith, Southern Cal
1969	Southern Cal	George Toley	35	UCLA	23	Joaquin Loyo-Mayo, Southern Cal
1970	UCLA	Glenn Bassett	26	Trinity (TX)	22	Jeff Borowiak, UCLA
				Rice	22	
1971	UCLA	Glenn Bassett	35	Trinity (TX)	27	Jimmy Connors, UCLA
1972	Trinity (TX)	Clarence Mabry	36	Stanford	30	Dick Stockton, Trinity (TX)
1973	Stanford	Dick Gould	33	Southern Cal	28	Alex Mayer, Stanford
1974	Stanford	Dick Gould	30	Southern Cal	25	John Whitlinger, Stanford
1975	UCLA	Glenn Bassett	27	Miami (FL)	20	Bill Martin, UCLA
1976	Southern Cal	George Toley	21			Bill Scanlon, Trinity (TX)
	UCLA	Glenn Bassett	21			
1977	Stanford	Dick Gould		Trinity (TX)		Matt Mitchell, Stanford
1978	Stanford	Dick Gould		UCLA		John McEnroe, Stanford
1979	UCLA	Glenn Bassett		Trinity (TX)		Kevin Curren, Texas
1980	Stanford	Dick Gould		California		Robert Van't Hof, Southern Cal
1981	Stanford	Dick Gould		UCLA		Tim Mayotte, Stanford
1982	UCLA	Glenn Bassett		Pepperdine		Mike Leach, Michigan
1983	Stanford	Dick Gould		Southern Meth		Greg Holmes, Utah
1984	UCLA	Glenn Bassett		Stanford		Mikael Pernfors, Georgia
1985	Georgia	Dan Magill		UCLA		Mikael Pernfors, Georgia
1986	Stanford	Dick Gould		Pepperdine		Dan Goldie, Stanford
1987	Georgia	Dan Magill		UCLA		Andrew Burrow, Miami (FL)
1988	Stanford	Dick Gould		Louisiana St		Robby Weiss, Pepperdine
1989	Stanford	Dick Gould		Georgia		Donni Leaycraft, Louisiana St
1990	Stanford	Dick Gould		Tennessee		Steve Bryan, Texas
1991	Southern Cal	Dick Leach		Georgia		Jared Palmer, Stanford
1992	Stanford	Dick Gould		Notre Dame		Alex O'Brien, Stanford
1993	Southern Cal	Dick Leach		Georgia		Chris Woodruff, Tennessee
1994	Southern Cal	Dick Leach		Stanford		Mark Merklein, Florida
1995	Stanford	Dick Gould		Mississippi		Sargis Sargsian, Arizona St

Note: Prior to 1977, individual wins counted in the team's total points. In 1977, a dual-match single-elimination team championship was initiated, eliminating the point system.

DIVISION II

Year	Champion	Year	Champion	Year	Champion
1963	Cal St-LA	1967	Long Beach St	1971	UC-Irvine
1964	Cal St-LA/ S Illinois	1968	Fresno St	1972	UC-Irvine/ Rollins
1965	Cal St-LA	1969	Cal St-Northridge	1973	UC-Irvine
1966	Rollins	1970	UC-Irvine	1974	San Diego

Men (Cont.)

DIVISION II (Cont.)

Year	Champion	Year	Champion	Year	Champion
1975	UC-Irvine/ San Diego	1982	SIU-Edwardsville	1989	Hampton
1976	Hampton	1983	SIU-Edwardsville	1990	Cal Poly-SLO
1977	UC-Irvine	1984	SIU-Edwardsville	1991	Rollins
1978	SIU-Edwardsville	1985	Chapman	1992	UC-Davis
1979	SIU-Edwardsville	1986	Cal Poly-SLO	1993	Lander (SC)
1980	SIU-Edwardsville	1987	Chapman	1994	Lander (SC)
1981	SIU-Edwardsville	1988	Chapman	1995	Lander (SC)

DIVISION III

Year	Champion	Year	Champion	Year	Champion
1976	Kalamazoo	1982	Gustavus Adolphus	1989	UC-Santa Cruz
1977	Swarthmore	1983	Redlands	1990	Swarthmore
1978	Kalamazoo	1984	Redlands	1991	Kalamazoo
1979	Redlands	1985	Swarthmore	1992	Kalamazoo
1980	Gustavus Adolphus	1986	Kalamazoo	1993	Kalamazoo
1981	Claremont-M-S	1987	Kalamazoo	1994	Washington (MD)
	Swarthmore	1988	Washington & Lee	1995	UC-Santa Cruz

Women

DIVISION I

Year	Champion	Coach	Runner-Up	Individual Champion
1982	Stanford	Frank Brennan	UCLA	Alycia Moulton, Stanford
1983	Southern Cal	Dave Borelli	Trinity (TX)	Beth Herr, Southern Cal
1984	Stanford	Frank Brennan	Southern Cal	Lisa Spain, Georgia
1985	Southern Cal	Dave Borelli	Miami (FL)	Linda Gates, Stanford
1986	Stanford	Frank Brennan	Southern Cal	Patty Fendick, Stanford
1987	Stanford	Frank Brennan	Georgia	Patty Fendick, Stanford
1988	Stanford	Frank Brennan	Florida	Shaun Stafford, Florida
1989	Stanford	Frank Brennan	UCLA	Sandra Birch, Stanford
1990	Stanford	Frank Brennan	Florida	Debbie Graham, Stanford
1991	Stanford	Frank Brennan	UCLA	Sandra Birch, Stanford
1992	Florida	Andy Brandi	Texas	Lisa Raymond, Florida
1993	Texas	Jeff Moore	Stanford	Lisa Raymond, Florida
1994	Georgia	Jeff Wallace	Stanford	Angela Lettiere, Georgia
1995	Texas	Jeff Moore	Florida	Keri Phebus, UCLA

DIVISION II

Year	Champion	Year	Champion	Year	Champion
1982	Cal St-Northridge	1987	SIU-Edwardsville	1992	Cal Poly-Pomona
1983	TN-Chattanooga	1988	SIU-Edwardsville	1993	UC-Davis
1984	TN-Chattanooga	1989	SIU-Edwardsville	1994	N Florida
1985	TN-Chattanooga	1990	UC-Davis	1995	Armstrong St
1986	SIU-Edwardsville	1991	Cal Poly-Pomona		

DIVISION III

Year	Champion	Year	Champion	Year	Champion
1982	Occidental	1987	UC-San Diego	1992	Pomona-Pitzer
1983	Principia	1988	Mary Washington	1993	Kenyon
1984	Davidson	1989	UC-San Diego	1994	UC San Diego
1985	UC-San Diego	1990	Gustavus Adolphus	1995	Kenyon
1986	Trenton St	1991	Mary Washington		

Indoor Track and Field

Men

DIVISION I

Year	Champion	Coach	Pts	Runner-Up	Pts
1965	Missouri	Tom Botts	14	Oklahoma St	12
1966	Kansas	Bob Timmons	14	Southern Cal	13
1967	Southern Cal	Vern Wolfe	26	Oklahoma	17
1968	Villanova	Jim Elliott	35	Southern Cal	25
1969	Kansas	Bob Timmons	41½	Villanova	33
1970	Kansas	Bob Timmons	27½	Villanova	26

Men *(Cont.)*

DIVISION I *(Cont.)*

Year	Champion	Coach	Pts	Runner-Up	Pts
1971	Villanova	Jim Elliott	22	UTEP	19¼
1972	Southern Cal	Vern Wolfe	19	Bowling Green/ Mich St	18
1973	Manhattan	Fred Dwyer	18	Kansas/Kent St/UTEP	12
1974	UTEP	Ted Banks	19	Colorado	18
1975	UTEP	Ted Banks	36	Kansas	17½
1976	UTEP	Ted Banks	23	Villanova	15
1977	Washington St	John Chaplin	25½	UTEP	25
1978	UTEP	Ted Banks	44	Auburn	38
1979	Villanova	Jim Elliott	52	UTEP	51
1980	UTEP	Ted Banks	76	Villanova	42
1981	UTEP	Ted Banks	76	Southern Meth	51
1982	UTEP	John Wedel	67	Arkansas	30
1983	Southern Meth	Ted McLaughlin	43	Villanova	32
1984	Arkansas	John McDonnell	38	Washington St	28
1985	Arkansas	John McDonnell	70	Tennessee	29
1986	Arkansas	John McDonnell	49	Villanova	22
1987	Arkansas	John McDonnell	39	Southern Meth	31
1988	Arkansas	John McDonnell	34	Illinois	29
1989	Arkansas	John McDonnell	34	Florida	31
1990	Arkansas	John McDonnell	44	Texas A&M	36
1991	Arkansas	John McDonnell	34	Georgetown	27
1992	Arkansas	John McDonnell	53	Clemson	46
1993	Arkansas	John McDonnell	66	Clemson	30
1994	Arkansas	John McDonnell	83	UTEP	45
1995	Arkansas	John McDonnell	59	GMU/Tennessee	26

DIVISION II

Year	Champion	Year	Champion	Year	Champion
1985	SE Missouri St	1989	St Augustine's	1993	Abilene Christian
1987	St Augustine's	1990	St Augustine's	1994	Abilene Christian
1988	Abilene Christian	1991	St Augustine's	1995	St Augustine's
	St Augustine's	1992	St Augustine's		

DIVISION III

Year	Champion	Year	Champion	Year	Champion
1985	St Thomas (MN)	1989	North Central	1993	WI-La Crosse
1986	Frostburg St	1990	Lincoln (PA)	1994	WI-La Crosse
1987	WI-La Crosse	1991	WI-La Crosse	1995	Lincoln (PA)
1988	WI-La Crosse	1992	WI-La Crosse		

Women

DIVISION I

Year	Champion	Coach	Pts	Runner-Up	Pts
1983	Nebraska	Gary Pepin	47	Tennessee	44
1984	Nebraska	Gary Pepin	59	Tennessee	48
1985	Florida St	Gary Winckler	34	Texas	32
1986	Texas	Terry Crawford	31	Southern Cal	26
1987	Louisiana St	Loren Seagrave	49	Tennessee	30
1988	Texas	Terry Crawford	71	Villanova	52
1989	Louisiana St	Pat Henry	61	Villanova	34
1990	Texas	Terry Crawford	50	Wisconsin	26
1991	Louisiana St	Pat Henry	48	Texas	39
1992	Florida	Bev Kearney	50	Stanford	26
1993	Louisiana St	Pat Henry	49	Wisconsin	44
1994	Louisiana St	Pat Henry	48	Alabama	29
1995	Louisiana St	Pat Henry	40	UCLA	37

DIVISION II

Year	Champion	Year	Champion	Year	Champion
1985	St Augustine's	1989	Abilene Christian	1993	Abilene Christian
1986	not held	1990	Abilene Christian	1994	Abilene Christian
1987	St Augustine's	1991	Abilene Christian	1995	Abilene Christian
1988	Abilene Christian	1992	Alabama A&M		

Women *(Cont.)*

DIVISION III

Year	Champion	Year	Champion	Year	Champion
1985	MA-Boston	1989	Christopher Newport	1993	Lincoln (PA)
1986	MA-Boston	1990	Christopher Newport	1994	WI-Oshkosh
1987	MA-Boston	1991	Cortland St	1995	WI-Oshkosh
1988	Christopher Newport	1992	Christopher Newport		

Outdoor Track and Field

Men

DIVISION I

Year	Champion	Coach	Pts	Runner-Up	Pts
1921	Illinois	Harry Gill	20†	Notre Dame	16†
1922	California	Walter Christie	28†	Penn St	19†
1923	Michigan	Stephen Farrell	29†	Mississippi St	16
1924	No meet				
1925	Stanford*	R. L. Templeton	31†		
1926	Southern Cal*	Dean Cromwell	27†		
1927	Illinois*	Harry Gill	35†		
1928	Stanford	R. L. Templeton	72	Ohio St	31
1929	Ohio St	Frank Castleman	50	Washington	42
1930	Southern Cal	Dean Cromwell	55†	Washington	40
1931	Southern Cal	Dean Cromwell	77†	Ohio St	31†
1932	Indiana	Billy Hayes	56	Ohio St	49†
1933	Louisiana St	Bernie Moore	58	Southern Cal	54
1934	Stanford	R. L. Templeton	63	Southern Cal	54†
1935	Southern Cal	Dean Cromwell	74†	Ohio St	40†
1936	Southern Cal	Dean Cromwell	103†	Ohio St	73
1937	Southern Cal	Dean Cromwell	62	Stanford	50
1938	Southern Cal	Dean Cromwell	67†	Stanford	38
1939	Southern Cal	Dean Cromwell	86	Stanford	44†
1940	Southern Cal	Dean Cromwell	47	Stanford	28†
1941	Southern Cal	Dean Cromwell	81†	Indiana	50
1942	Southern Cal	Dean Cromwell	85†	Ohio St	44†
1943	Southern Cal	Dean Cromwell	46	California	39
1944	Illinois	Leo Johnson	79	Notre Dame	43
1945	Navy	E. J. Thomson	62	Illinois	48†
1946	Illinois	Leo Johnson	78	Southern Cal	42†
1947	Illinois	Leo Johnson	59†	Southern Cal	34†
1948	Minnesota	James Kelly	46	Southern Cal	41†
1949	Southern Cal	Jess Hill	55†	UCLA	31
1950	Southern Cal	Jess Hill	49†	Stanford	28
1951	Southern Cal	Jess Mortenson	56	Cornell	40
1952	Southern Cal	Jess Mortenson	66†	San Jose St	24†
1953	Southern Cal	Jess Mortenson	80	Illinois	41
1954	Southern Cal	Jess Mortenson	66†	Illinois	31†
1955	Southern Cal	Jess Mortenson	42	UCLA	34
1956	UCLA	Elvin Drake	55†	Kansas	51
1957	Villanova	James Elliott	47	California	32
1958	Southern Cal	Jess Mortenson	48†	Kansas	40†
1959	Kansas	Bill Easton	73	San Jose St	48
1960	Kansas	Bill Easton	50	Southern Cal	37
1961	Southern Cal	Jess Mortenson	65	Oregon	47
1962	Oregon	William Bowerman	85	Villanova	40†
1963	Southern Cal	Vern Wolfe	61	Stanford	42
1964	Oregon	William Bowerman	70	San Jose St	40
1965	Oregon	William Bowerman	32		
	Southern Cal	Vern Wolfe	32		
1966	UCLA	Jim Bush	81	Brigham Young	33
1967	Southern Cal	Vern Wolfe	86	Oregon	40
1968	Southern Cal	Vern Wolfe	58	Washington St	57
1969	San Jose St	Bud Winter	48	Kansas	45
1970	Brigham Young	Clarence Robison	35		
	Kansas	Bob Timmons	35		
	Oregon	William Bowerman	35		

Men (Cont.)
DIVISION I (Cont.)

Year	Champion	Coach	Pts	Runner-Up	Pts
1971	UCLA	Jim Bush	52	Southern Cal	41
1972	UCLA	Jim Bush	82	Southern Cal	49
1973	UCLA	Jim Bush	56	Oregon	31
1974	Tennessee	Stan Huntsman	60	UCLA	56
1975	UTEP	Ted Banks	55	UCLA	42
1976	Southern Cal	Vern Wolfe	64	UTEP	44
1977	Arizona St	Senon Castillo	64	UTEP	50
1978	UCLA/UTEP	Jim Bush/Ted Banks	50		
1979	UTEP	Ted Banks	64	Villanova	48
1980	UTEP	Ted Banks	69	UCLA	46
1981	UTEP	Ted Banks	70	Southern Meth	57
1982	UTEP	John Wedel	105	Tennessee	94
1983	SMU	Ted McLaughlin	104	Tennessee	102
1984	Oregon	Bill Dellinger	113	Washington St	94½
1985	Arkansas	John McDonnell	61	Washington St	46
1986	Southern Meth	Ted McLaughlin	53	Washington St	52
1987	UCLA	Bob Larsen	81	Texas	28
1988	UCLA	Bob Larsen	82	Texas	41
1989	Louisiana St	Pat Henry	53	Texas A&M	51
1990	Louisiana St	Pat Henry	44	Arkansas	36
1991	Tennessee	Doug Brown	51	Washington St	42
1992	Arkansas	John McDonnell	60	Tennessee	46½
1993	Arkansas	John McDonnell	69	LSU/Ohio St	45
1994	Arkansas	John McDonnell	83	UTEP	45
1995	Arkansas	John McDonnell	61½	UCLA	55

*Unofficial championship. †Fraction of a point.

DIVISION II

Year	Champion	Year	Champion	Year	Champion
1963	MD-Eastern Shore	1974	Eastern Illinois	1984	Abilene Christian
1964	Fresno St		Norfolk St	1985	Abilene Christian
1965	San Diego St	1975	Cal St-Northridge	1986	Abilene Christian
1966	San Diego St	1976	UC-Irvine	1987	Abilene Christian
1967	Long Beach St	1977	Cal St-Hayward	1988	Abilene Christian
1968	Cal Poly-SLO	1978	Cal St-LA	1989	St Augustine's
1969	Cal Poly-SLO	1979	Cal Poly-SLO	1990	St Augustine's
1970	Cal Poly-SLO	1980	Cal Poly-SLO	1991	St Augustine's
1971	Kentucky St	1981	Cal Poly-SLO	1992	St Augustine's
1972	Eastern Michigan	1982	Abilene Christian	1994	St Augustine's
1973	Norfolk St	1983	Abilene Christian	1995	St Augustine's

DIVISION III

Year	Champion	Year	Champion	Year	Champion
1974	Ashland	1982	Glassboro St	1990	Lincoln (PA)
1975	Southern-N Orleans	1983	Glassboro St	1991	WI-La Crosse
1976	Southern-N Orleans	1984	Glassboro St	1992	WI-La Crosse
1977	Southern-N Orleans	1985	Lincoln (PA)	1993	WI-La Crosse
1978	Occidental	1986	Frostburg St	1994	North Central
1979	Slippery Rock	1987	Frostburg St	1995	Lincoln (PA)
1980	Glassboro St	1988	WI-La Crosse		
1981	Glassboro St	1989	North Central		

Women
DIVISION I

Year	Champion	Coach	Pts	Runner-Up	Pts
1982	UCLA	Scott Chisam	153	Tennessee	126
1983	UCLA	Scott Chisam	116½	Florida St	108
1984	Florida St	Gary Winckler	145	Tennessee	124
1985	Oregon	Tom Heinonen	52	Florida St/LSU	46
1986	Texas	Terry Crawford	65	Alabama	55
1987	Louisiana St	Loren Seagrave	62	Alabama	53
1988	Louisiana St	Loren Seagrave	61	UCLA	58
1989	Louisiana St	Pat Henry	86	UCLA	47
1990	Louisiana St	Pat Henry	53	UCLA	46
1991	Louisiana St	Pat Henry	78	Texas	67
1992	Louisiana St	Pat Henry	87	Florida	81
1993	Louisiana St	Pat Henry	93	Wisconsin	44
1994	Louisiana St	Pat Henry	86	Texas	43
1995	Louisiana St	Pat Henry	69	UCLA	58

Women (Cont.)

DIVISION II

Year	Champion	Year	Champion	Year	Champion
1982	Cal Poly-SLO	1987	Abilene Christian	1992	Alabama A&M
1983	Cal Poly-SLO	1988	Abilene Christian	1993	Alabama A&M
1984	Cal Poly-SLO	1989	Cal Poly-SLO	1994	Alabama A&M
1985	Abilene Christian	1990	Cal Poly-SLO	1995	Abilene Christian
1986	Abilene Christian	1991	Cal Poly-SLO		

DIVISION III

Year	Champion	Year	Champion	Year	Champion
1982	Central (IA)	1987	Chris. Newport	1992	Chris. Newport
1983	WI-La Crosse	1988	Chris. Newport	1993	Lincoln (PA)
1984	WI-La Crosse	1989	Chris. Newport	1994	Chris. Newport
1985	Cortland St	1990	WI-Oshkosh	1995	WI-Oshkosh
1986	MA-Boston	1991	WI-Oshkosh		

Volleyball

Men

Year	Champion	Coach	Score	Runner-Up	Most Outstanding Player
1970	UCLA	Al Scates	3-0	Long Beach St	Dane Holtzman, UCLA
1971	UCLA	Al Scates	3-0	UC-Santa Barbara	Kirk Kilgore, UCLA
					Tim Bonynge, UC-Santa Barbara
1972	UCLA	Al Scates	3-2	San Diego St	Dick Irvin, UCLA
1973	San Diego St	Jack Henn	3-1	Long Beach St	Duncan McFarland, San Diego St
1974	UCLA	Al Scates	3-2	UC-Santa Barbara	Bob Leonard, UCLA
1975	UCLA	Al Scates	3-1	UC-Santa Barbara	John Bekins, UCLA
1976	UCLA	Al Scates	3-0	Pepperdine	Joe Mika, UCLA
1977	Southern Cal	Ernie Hix	3-1	Ohio St	Celso Kalache, Southern Cal
1978	Pepperdine	Marv Dunphy	3-2	UCLA	Mike Blanchard, Pepperdine
1979	UCLA	Al Scates	3-1	Southern Cal	Sinjin Smith, UCLA
1980	Southern Cal	Ernie Hix	3-1	UCLA	Dusty Dvorak, Southern Cal
1981	UCLA	Al Scates	3-2	Southern Cal	Karch Kiraly, UCLA
1982	UCLA	Al Scates	3-0	Penn St	Karch Kiraly, UCLA
1983	UCLA	Al Scates	3-0	Pepperdine	Ricci Luyties, UCLA
1984	UCLA	Al Scates	3-1	Pepperdine	Ricci Luyties, UCLA
1985	Pepperdine	Marv Dunphy	3-1	Southern Cal	Bob Ctvrtlik, Pepperdine
1986	Pepperdine	Rod Wilde	3-2	Southern Cal	Steve Friedman, Pepperdine
1987	UCLA	Al Scates	3-0	Southern Cal	Ozzie Volstad, UCLA
1988	Southern Cal	Bob Yoder	3-2	UC-Santa Barbara	Jen-Kai Liu, Southern Cal
1989	UCLA	Al Scates	3-1	Stanford	Matt Sonnichsen, UCLA
1990	Southern Cal	Jim McLaughlin	3-1	Long Beach St	Bryan Ivie, Southern Cal
1991	Long Beach St	Ray Ratelle	3-1	Southern Cal	Brent Hilliard, Long Beach St
1992	Pepperdine	Marv Dunphy	3-0	Stanford	Alon Grinberg, Pepperdine
1993	UCLA	Al Scates	3-0	Cal St-Northridge	Mike Sealy/Jeff Nygaard, UCLA
1994	Penn St	Tom Peterson	3-2	UCLA	Ramon Hernandez, Penn St
1995	UCLA	Al Scates	3-0	Penn St	Jeff Nygaard, UCLA

Women

DIVISION I

Year	Champion	Coach	Score	Runner-Up
1981	Southern Cal	Chuck Erbe	3-2	UCLA
1982	Hawaii	Dave Shoji	3-2	Southern Cal
1983	Hawaii	Dave Shoji	3-0	UCLA
1984	UCLA	Andy Banachowski	3-2	Stanford
1985	Pacific	John Dunning	3-1	Stanford
1986	Pacific	John Dunning	3-0	Nebraska
1987	Hawaii	Dave Shoji	3-1	Stanford
1988	Texas	Mick Haley	3-0	Hawaii
1989	Long Beach St	Brian Gimmillaro	3-0	Nebraska
1990	UCLA	Andy Banachowski	3-0	Pacific
1991	UCLA	Andy Banachowski	3-2	Long Beach St
1992	Stanford	Don Shaw	3-1	UCLA
1993	Long Beach St	Brian Gimmillaro	3-1	Penn St
1994	Stanford	Don Shaw	3-1	UCLA

Women (Cont.)

DIVISION II

Year	Champion	Year	Champion	Year	Champion
1981	Cal St-Sacramento	1986	UC-Riverside	1991	West Texas St
1982	UC-Riverside	1987	Cal St-Northridge	1992	Portland St
1983	Cal St-Northridge	1988	Portland St	1993	Northern Michigan
1984	Portland St	1989	Cal St-Bakersfield	1994	Northern Michigan
1985	Portland St	1990	West Texas St		

DIVISION III

Year	Champion	Year	Champion	Year	Champion
1981	UC-San Diego	1986	UC-San Diego	1991	Washington (MO)
1982	La Verne	1987	UC-San Diego	1992	Washington (MO)
1983	Elmhurst	1988	UC-San Diego	1993	Washington (MO)
1984	UC-San Diego	1989	Washington (MO)	1994	Washington (MO)
1985	Elmhurst	1990	UC-San Diego		

Water Polo

Year	Champion	Coach	Score	Runner-Up
1969	UCLA	Bob Horn	5-2	California
1970	UC-Irvine	Ed Newland	7-6 (3 OT)	UCLA
1971	UCLA	Bob Horn	5-3	San Jose St
1972	UCLA	Bob Horn	10-5	UC-Irvine
1973	California	Pete Cutino	8-4	UC-Irvine
1974	California	Pete Cutino	7-6	UC-Irvine
1975	California	Pete Cutino	9-8	UC-Irvine
1976	Stanford	Art Lambert	13-12	UCLA
1977	California	Pete Cutino	8-6	UC-Irvine
1978	Stanford	Dante Dettamanti	7-6 (3 OT)	California
1979	UC-Santa Barbara	Pete Snyder	11-3	UCLA
1980	Stanford	Dante Dettamanti	8-6	California
1981	Stanford	Dante Dettamanti	17-6	Long Beach St
1982	UC-Irvine	Ed Newland	7-4	Stanford
1983	California	Pete Cutino	10-7	Southern Cal
1984	California	Pete Cutino	9-8	Stanford
1985	Stanford	Dante Dettamanti	12-11 (2 OT)	UC-Irvine
1986	Stanford	Dante Dettamanti	9-6	California
1987	California	Pete Cutino	9-8 (OT)	Southern Cal
1988	California	Pete Cutino	14-11	UCLA
1989	UC-Irvine	Ed Newland	9-8	California
1990	California	Steve Heaston	8-7	Stanford
1991	California	Steve Heaston	7-6	UCLA
1992	California	Steve Heaston	12-11	Stanford
1993	Stanford	Dante Dettamanti	11-9	Southern Cal
1994	Stanford	Dante Dettamanti	14-10	Southern Cal

Wrestling

DIVISION I

Year	Champion	Coach	Pts	Runner-Up	Pts	Most Outstanding Wrestler
1928	Oklahoma St*	E. C. Gallagher				
1929	Oklahoma St*	E. C. Gallagher	26	Michigan	18	
1930	Oklahoma St*	E. C. Gallagher	27	Illinois	14	
1931	Oklahoma St*	E. C. Gallagher		Michigan		
1932	Indiana*	W. H. Thom		Oklahoma St		Edwin Belshaw, Indiana
1933	Oklahoma St*	E. C. Gallagher				Allan Kelley, Oklahoma St
	Iowa St*	Hugo Otopalik				Pat Johnson, Harvard
1934	Oklahoma St	E. C. Gallagher	29	Indiana	19	Ben Bishop, Lehigh
1935	Oklahoma St	E. C. Gallagher	36	Oklahoma	18	Ross Flood, Oklahoma St
1936	Oklahoma	Paul Keen	14	Central St (OK)	10	Wayne Martin, Oklahoma
				Oklahoma St	10	
1937	Oklahoma St	E. C. Gallagher	31	Oklahoma	13	Stanley Henson, Oklahoma St
1938	Oklahoma St	E. C. Gallagher	19	Illinois	15	Joe McDaniels, Oklahoma St

Wrestling (Cont.)

DIVISION I (Cont.)

Year	Champion	Coach	Pts	Runner-Up	Pts	Most Outstanding Wrestler
1939	Oklahoma St	E. C. Gallagher	33	Lehigh	12	Dale Hanson, Minnesota
1940	Oklahoma St	E. C. Gallagher	24	Indiana	14	Don Nichols, Michigan
1941	Oklahoma St	Art Griffith	37	Michigan St	26	Al Whitehurst, Oklahoma St
1942	Oklahoma St	Art Griffith	31	Michigan St	26	David Arndt, Oklahoma St
1943-45	No tournament					
1946	Oklahoma St	Art Griffith	25	Northern Iowa	24	Gerald Leeman, Northern Iowa
1947	Cornell	Paul Scott	32	Northern Iowa	19	William Koll, Northern Iowa
1948	Oklahoma St	Art Griffith	33	Michigan St	28	William Koll, Northern Iowa
1949	Oklahoma St	Art Griffith	32	Northern Iowa	27	Charles Hetrick, Oklahoma St
1950	Northern Iowa	David McCuskey	30	Purdue	16	Anthony Gizoni, Waynesburg
1951	Oklahoma	Port Robertson	24	Oklahoma St	23	Walter Romanowski, Cornell
1952	Oklahoma	Port Robertson	22	Northern Iowa	21	Tommy Evans, Oklahoma
1953	Penn St	Charles Speidel	21	Oklahoma	15	Frank Bettucci, Cornell
1954	Oklahoma St	Art Griffith	32	Pittsburgh	17	Tommy Evans, Oklahoma
1955	Oklahoma St	Art Griffith	40	Penn St	31	Edward Eichelberger, Lehigh
1956	Oklahoma St	Art Griffith	65	Oklahoma	62	Dan Hodge, Oklahoma
1957	Oklahoma	Port Robertson	73	Pittsburgh	66	Dan Hodge, Oklahoma
1958	Oklahoma St	Myron Roderick	77	Iowa St	62	Dick Delgado, Oklahoma
1959	Oklahoma St	Myron Roderick	73	Iowa St	51	Ron Gray, Iowa St
1960	Oklahoma	Thomas Evans	59	Iowa St	40	Dave Auble, Cornell
1961	Oklahoma St	Myron Roderick	82	Oklahoma	63	E. Gray Simons, Lock Haven
1962	Oklahoma St	Myron Roderick	82	Oklahoma	45	E. Gray Simons, Lock Haven
1963	Oklahoma	Thomas Evans	48	Iowa St	45	Mickey Martin, Oklahoma
1964	Oklahoma St	Myron Roderick	87	Oklahoma	58	Dean Lahr, Colorado
1965	Iowa St	Harold Nichols	87	Oklahoma St	86	Yojiro Uetake, Oklahoma St
1966	Oklahoma St	Myron Roderick	79	Iowa St	70	Yojiro Uetake, Oklahoma St
1967	Michigan St	Grady Peninger	74	Michigan	63	Rich Sanders, Portland St
1968	Oklahoma St	Myron Roderick	81	Iowa St	78	Dwayne Keller, Oklahoma St
1969	Iowa St	Harold Nichols	104	Oklahoma	69	Dan Gable, Iowa St
1970	Iowa St	Harold Nichols	99	Michigan St	84	Larry Owings, Washington
1971	Oklahoma St	Tommy Chesbro	94	Iowa St	66	Darrell Keller, Oklahoma St
1972	Iowa St	Harold Nichols	103	Michigan St	72½	Wade Schalles, Clarion
1973	Iowa St	Harold Nichols	85	Oregon St	72½	Greg Strobel, Oregon St
1974	Oklahoma	Stan Abel	69½	Michigan	67	Floyd Hitchcock, Bloomsburg
1975	Iowa	Gary Kurdelmeier	102	Oklahoma	77	Mike Frick, Lehigh
1976	Iowa	Gary Kurdelmeier	123½	Iowa St	85¾	Chuch Yagla, Iowa
1977	Iowa St	Harold Nichols	95½	Oklahoma St	88¾	Nick Gallo, Hofstra
1978	Iowa	Dan Gable	94½	Iowa St	94	Mark Churella, Michigan
1979	Iowa	Dan Gable	122½	Iowa St	88	Bruce Kinseth, Iowa
1980	Iowa	Dan Gable	110¾	Oklahoma St	87	Howard Harris, Oregon St
1981	Iowa	Dan Gable	129¾	Oklahoma	100¼	Gene Mills, Syracuse
1982	Iowa	Dan Gable	131¾	Iowa St	111	Mark Schultz, Oklahoma
1983	Iowa	Dan Gable	155	Oklahoma St	102	Mike Sheets, Oklahoma St
1984	Iowa	Dan Gable	123¾	Oklahoma St	98	Jim Zalesky, Iowa
1985	Iowa	Dan Gable	145¼	Oklahoma	98½	Barry Davis, Iowa
1986	Iowa	Dan Gable	158	Oklahoma	84¼	Marty Kistler, Iowa
1987	Iowa St	Jim Gibbons	133	Iowa	108	John Smith, Oklahoma St
1988	Arizona St	Bobby Douglas	93	Iowa	85½	Scott Turner, N Carolina St
1989	Oklahoma St	Joe Seay	91¼	Arizona St	70½	Tim Krieger, Iowa St
1990	Oklahoma St	Joe Seay	117¾	Arizona St	104¾	Chris Barnes, Oklahoma St
1991	Iowa	Dan Gable	157	Oklahoma St	108¾	Jeff Prescott, Penn St
1992	Iowa	Dan Gable	149	Oklahoma St	100½	Tom Brands, Iowa
1993	Iowa	Dan Gable	123¾	Penn St	87½	Terry Steiner, Iowa
1994	Oklahoma St	John Smith	94¾	Iowa	76½	Pat Smith, Oklahoma St
1995	Iowa	Dan Gable	134	Oregon St	77½	T.J. Jaworsky, N Carolina

*Unofficial champions.

DIVISION II

Year	Champion	Year	Champion	Year	Champion
1963	Western St (CO)	1974	Cal Poly-SLO	1985	SIU-Edwardsville
1964	Western St (CO)	1975	Northern Iowa	1986	SIU-Edwardsville
1965	Mankato St	1976	Cal St-Bakersfield	1987	Cal St-Bakersfield
1966	Cal Poly-SLO	1977	Cal St-Bakersfield	1988	N Dakota St
1967	Portland St	1978	Northern Iowa	1989	Portland St
1968	Cal Poly-SLO	1979	Cal St-Bakersfield	1990	Portland St
1969	Cal Poly-SLO	1980	Cal St-Bakersfield	1991	NE-Omaha
1970	Cal Poly-SLO	1981	Cal St-Bakersfield	1992	Central Oklahoma
1971	Cal Poly-SLO	1982	Cal St-Bakersfield	1993	Central Oklahoma
1972	Cal Poly-SLO	1983	Cal St-Bakersfield	1994	Central Oklahoma
1973	Cal Poly-SLO	1984	SIU-Edwardsville	1995	Central Oklahoma

DIVISION III

Year	Champion	Year	Champion	Year	Champion
1974	Wilkes	1982	Brockport St	1990	Ithaca
1975	John Carroll	1983	Brockport St	1991	Augsburg
1976	Montclair St	1984	Trenton St	1992	Brockport
1977	Brockport St	1985	Trenton St	1993	Augsburg
1978	Buffalo	1986	Montclair St	1994	Ithaca
1979	Trenton St	1987	Trenton St	1995	Augsburg
1980	Brockport St	1988	St Lawrence		
1981	Trenton St	1989	Ithaca		

INDIVIDUAL CHAMPIONSHIP
RECORDS

Swimming and Diving

Men

Event	Time	Record Holder	Date
50-yard freestyle	19.14	David Fox, N Carolina St	3-25-93
100-yard freestyle	41.80	Matt Biondi, California	4-4-87
200-yard freestyle	1:33.03	Matt Biondi, California	4-3-87
500-yard freestyle	4:08.75	Tom Dolan, Michigan	3-23-95
1650-yard freestyle	14:29.31	Tom Dolan, Michigan	3-25-95
100-yard backstroke	45.43	Brian Retterer, Stanford	3-24-95
200-yard backstroke	1:40.64	Jeff Rouse, Stanford	3-28-92
100-yard breaststroke	52.48	Steve Lundquist, Southern Meth	3-25-83
200-yard breaststroke	1:53.77	Mike Barrowman, Michigan	3-24-90
100-yard butterfly	46.18	Lars Frolander, SMU	3-24-95
200-yard butterfly	1:41.78	Melvin Stewart, Tennessee	3-30-91
200-yard individual medley	1:43.52	Greg Burgess, Florida	3-25-93
400-yard individual medley	3:38.18	Tom Dolan, Michigan	3-24-95

Women

Event	Time	Record Holder	Date
50-yard freestyle	21.77	Amy Van Dyken, Colorado St	3-18-94
100-yard freestyle	47.61	Jenny Thompson, Stanford	3-21-92
200-yard freestyle	1:43.28	Nicole Haislett, Florida	3-20-92
500-yard freestyle	4:34.39	Janet Evans, Stanford	3-15-90
1650-yard freestyle	15:39.14	Janet Evans, Stanford	3-17-90
100-yard backstroke	53.98	Betsy Mitchell, Texas	3-21-92
200-yard backstroke	1:52.98	Whitney Hedgepeth, Texas	3-21-87
100-yard breaststroke	59.71	Beata Kaszuba, Arizona St	3-17-95
200-yard breaststroke	2:09.71	Beata Kaszuba, Arizona St	3-18-95
100-yard butterfly	51.75	Crissy Ahmann-Leighton, Arizona	3-20-92
200-yard butterfly	1:53.42	Summer Sanders, Stanford	3-21-92
200-yard individual medley	1:55.54	Summer Sanders, Stanford	3-20-92
400-yard individual medley	4:02.28	Summer Sanders, Stanford	3-20-92

Indoor Track and Field

Men

Event	Mark	Record Holder	Date
55-meter dash	6.00	Lee McRae, Pittsburgh	3-14-86
55-meter hurdles	7.07	Allen Johnson, N Carolina	3-13-92
200-meter dash	20.59	Michael Johnson, Baylor	3-10-89
400-meter dash	45.79	Gabriel Luke, Rice	3-10-90
800-meter run	1:46.19	George Kersh, Mississippi	3-9-91
Mile run	3:55.33	Kevin Sullivan, Michigan	3-11-95
3000-meter run	7:50.90	Josephat Kapkory, Wash St	3-11-94
5000-meter run	13:37.94	Jonah Koech, Iowa St	3-9-90
High jump	7 ft 9¼ in	Hollis Conway, Southwestern Louisiana	3-11-89
Pole vault	19 ft 1½ in	Lawrence Johnson, Tennessee	3-12-94
Long jump	27 ft 10 in	Carl Lewis, Houston	3-13-81
Triple jump	56 ft 9½ in	Keith Connor, Southern Meth	3-13-81

Men (Cont.)

Event	Mark	Record Holder	Date
Shot put	69 ft 8½ in	Michael Carter, SMU	3-13-81
		Soren Tallhem, Brigham Young	3-9-85
35-pound weight throw	76 ft 5½ in	Robert Weir, SMU	3-11-83

Women

Event	Mark	Record Holder	Date
55-meter dash	6.56	Gwen Torrence, Georgia	3-14-87
55-meter hurdles	7.44	Lynda Tolbert, Arizona St	3-9-90
200-meter dash	22.90	Holly Hyche, Indiana St	3-11-94
400-meter dash	51.05	Maicel Malone, Arizona St	3-9-91
800-meter run	2:02.05	Amy Wickus, Wisconsin	3-11-94
Mile run	4:30.63	Suzy Favor, Wisconsin	3-11-89
3000-meter run	8:54.98	Stephanie Herbst, Wisconsin	3-15-86
5000-meter run	15:41.12	Jennifer Rhines, Villanova	3-10-95
High jump	6 ft 5½ in	Amy Acuff, UCLA	3-11-95
Long jump	22 ft 1 in	Daphne Saunders, Louisiana St	3-12-94
Triple jump	45 ft 9 in	Sheila Hudson, California	3-10-90
Shot put	57 ft 11¾ in	Regina Cavanaugh, Rice	3-14-86

Outdoor Track and Field

Men

Event	Mark	Record Holder	Date
100-meter dash	10.03	Stanley Floyd, Houston	6-5-82
		Joe DeLoach, Houston	6-4-88
200-meter dash	19.87	Lorenzo Daniel, Mississippi St	6-3-88
400-meter dash	44.00	Quincy Watts, Southern Cal	6-6-92
800-meter run	1:44.70	Mark Everett, Florida	6-1-90
1500-meter run	3:35.30	Sydney Maree, Villanova	6-6-81
3000-meter steeplechase	8:12.39	Henry Rono, Washington St	6-1-78
5000-meter run	13:20.63	Sydney Maree, Villanova	6-2-79
10000-meter run	28:01.30	Suleiman Nyambui, UTEP	6-1-79
110-meter high hurdles	13.22	Greg Foster, UCLA	6-2-78
400-meter intermediate hurdles	47.85	Kevin Young, UCLA	6-3-88
High jump	7 ft 9¾ in	Hollis Conway, Southwestern Louisiana	6-3-89
Pole vault	19 ft ¼ in	Istvan Bagyula, George Mason	5-31-91
Long jump	28 ft	Erick Walder, Arkansas	6-3-93
Triple jump	57 ft 7¾ in	Keith Connor, Southern Meth	6-5-82
Shot put	72 ft 2¼ in	John Godina, UCLA	6-3-95
Discus throw	220 ft	Kamy Keshmiri, Nevada	6-5-92
Hammer throw	261 ft 3 in	Balazs Kiss, Southern Cal	5-31-95
Javelin throw	266 ft 9 in	Todd Riech, Fresno St	6-3-94
Decathlon	8279 pts	Tito Steiner, Brigham Young	6-2/3-81

Women

Event	Mark	Record Holder	Date
100-meter dash	10.78	Dawn Sowell, Louisiana St	6-3-89
200-meter dash	22.04	Dawn Sowell, Louisiana St	6-2-89
400-meter dash	50.18	Pauline Davis, Alabama	6-3-89
800-meter run	1:59.11	Suzy Favor, Wisconsin	6-1-90
1500-meter run	4:08.26	Suzy Favor, Wisconsin	6-2-90
3000-meter run	8:47.35	Vicki Huber, Villanova	6-3-88
5000-meter run	15:38.47	Annette Hand, Oregon	6-4-88
10000-meter run	32:28.57	Sylvia Mosqueda, Cal St-LA	6-1-88
100-meter hurdles	12.70	Tananjalyn Stanley, Louisiana St	6-3-89
400-meter hurdles	54.64	Latanya Sheffield, San Diego St	5-31-85
High jump	6 ft 5 in	Amy Acuff, UCLA	6-3-95
Long jump	22 ft 9¼ in	Sheila Echols, Louisiana St	6-5-87
Triple jump	46 ft ¾ in	Sheila Hudson, California	6-2-90
Shot put	59 ft 11¾ in	Valeyta Althouse, UCLA	6-1-95
Discus throw	209 ft 10 in	Leslie Deniz, Arizona St	6-4-83
Javelin throw	206 ft 9 in	Karin Smith, Cal Poly-SLO	6-4-82
Heptathlon	6527 pts	Diane Guthrie-Gresham, George Mason	6-2/3-95

Olympics

Sports Illustrated

The Big Splash

Atlanta gets set to host the
'96 Summer Olympics

SIMON BRUTY/ALLSPORT

Let the Games Begin

There was no Olympic competition in 1995 but there *was* plenty of action, and more than a few games being played

by William Oscar Johnson

NINETEEN-NINETY-five was an off year for the Olympics, and no Games with a capital *G* were played. That, however, is not to say that the Olympic movement was left without a goodly share of lowercase games, gamesmen and gamesmanship.

The biggest little *g* game of the year was the competition to choose a city to host the Winter Olympic Games in 2002. In the beginning no fewer than nine municipalities entered the contest. Some players were better equipped to compete than others.

Sochi on the Black Sea in Russia, a venerable old summer spa, hoped to transform itself into a year-round resort by constructing new Olympic ski runs, ski jumps and a bobsled/luge track in a roadless virgin forest outside town. The International Olympic Committee sent an evaluation commission to inspect Sochi, as it did all the bidding cities, and appalled commission members reported that "a lack of maps" made it all but impossible to locate competition sites in the trackless woods.

Worse, IOC inspectors ruled that the Sochi plan to finance an Olympics would be "burdened with an unbearable amount of risk" due to the wild and crazy state of the Russian economy. Another farfetched—and far-flung—bidder was Jaca, Spain, which called for Games spread over three widely separate venues in the Pyrenees, including one in the tiny land of Andorra, 3½ hours from Jaca. Graz, Austria, included in its Olympic dream a bobsled run that IOC inspectors found to be dangerously "exposed to rockfall." In Tarvisio, Italy, organizers hatched an idealistic blue-sky Olympian political vision that saw the governments of Italy, Slovenia and Austria cooperating as Olympic cohosts—"three countries which historically have not always lived peacefully together," the disbelieving IOC inspectors wisely noted. And in Poprad-Tatry in Slovakia inspectors were shocked to discover that organizers planned to build the media village in a nature reserve, the cross-country and

Alpine race courses in a national park and the Olympic Village in a protected wetlands area.

These five cities were mercifully scrubbed from the list of wannabes in January '95, and that left four in the running—the winner to be chosen at the annual IOC meeting in Budapest in mid-June. The candidates were Sion, Switzerland; Quebec City, Canada; Ostersund, Sweden; and Salt Lake City of the United States. All except one had flaws.

Sion had designed an ungainly, hugely spread-out Olympics with three separate Olympic Villages and the bobsled and luge runs located in St. Moritz—a six-hour train ride from Sion.

Quebec offered a nicely compact Games plan with no venue more than an hour from the city by car. However, the downhill ski course was to start at the top of a mountain whose natural summit stands 100 meters below official height for a world-class course. To bring it up to stan-

Samaranch may have extended his reign with some crafty politicking.

dard required an unwieldy height-enhancing pile of landfill, ramps and platforms. A potentially more serious problem: The province of Quebec is run by a secessionist government, which plans to declare independence from Canada someday—preferably soon. What havoc this might wreak on an Olympic bid is hard to predict, although IOC inspectors noted warily that they had been told that "secession is a very remote possibility before 2002."

Ostersund put forth a polished, professional bid, which was not surprising since it was the city's third attempt in nine years to win a Winter Olympics and Sweden's sixth straight. The overall plan was judged "very good" by IOC inspectors, but a major drawback was the IOC's resistance to holding another Olympics in Scandinavia so soon after Lillehammer's masterpiece in 1994.

And then there was long-suffering Salt Lake City. The city had been competing to get a Winter Olympics off and on since 1965, and in 1991 it had lost a perfectly beautiful bid for the 1998 Games to unknown and untested Nagano, Japan. This had happened because Atlanta already owned the '96 Summer Olympics, and the rules of the geopolitical games as played by the IOC didn't allow for two U.S.-based Olympics so close together. This time the outlook looked completely positive. IOC inspectors had given Salt Lake high marks, and European journalists, usually the meanest of nitpickers when it comes to things American, also raved. The Swiss newspaper *Sport* said, "The bid has no weaknesses." And Karl-Heinz Huba, publisher of an Olympic insiders' newsletter out of Musich, said, "Salt Lake

has everything in place, the competition sites, the infrastructure, the logistics, the hotels. The setting is beautiful besides."

Still, there was skepticism. Dick Pound, a Montreal lawyer who is also an IOC executive board member warned, "With the IOC you really never know what's going on." Tom Welch, president of the Salt Lake bid committee for 10 years, said worriedly, "I think the winners tend to be everyone's second choice." A loyal Swede agreed: "Being a front-runner is like chewing a wad of gum: After a while you want a new one."

But, no. The IOC stuck with the gum it was chewing, and Salt Lake won on the first secret ballot, taking 54 of the 89 votes cast, while plucky Ostersund tied Sion with 14, and Quebec finished last with seven. Never had there been such a landslide in

With one year to go, Payne predicted Atlanta would win over the world.

picking an Olympic city. Welch & Co. estimated the Games would cost $798 million but predicted they would bring Utah some $170 million in tourist dollars and that Olympic-related jobs would generate half a billion dollars. "This is only a beginning," crowed Welch, "but what a beginning."

Picking the site for 2002 was not the only little *g* game underway in Budapest, however. Early in the proceedings the craftiest gamesman of them all, IOC president Juan Antonio Samaranch, entertained a motion to get rid of the IOC's mandatory retirement age of 75, which had been set in 1985. Why? Interestingly enough, the old wizard was to turn 75 soon after the Budapest meeting. He was serving his fourth four-year term as president, and it would expire in 1997. Although he would be allowed to serve to the end of this term, he could not run a fifth time unless the age limit was raised or removed. At the first session Samaranch confidently called for a vote on the age limit. He needed a two-thirds majority, and to his disappointment and surprise, the motion ultimately failed passage by two slim votes. It was judged a stunning defeat for Samaranch, and people began to talk about who might replace him after 1997.

Ah, but the game wasn't over: In the fourth and final session of the meeting, a petition was suddenly introduced bearing the signatures of 70 members. It called for a rule change that would allow IOC delegates to retire at 75 if they wished but to stay on until 80 if they liked. Some members asked for a secret ballot, but Samaranch said that was "nonsense." He quickly called for a show of hands of those opposed to the motion. No more than 10 were counted, the gavel fell, and the new age limit in the IOC was suddenly 80. Did this mean that an octogenarian Juan Antonio would continue to be IOC president on into the 21st century? He was noncommittal at a press conference: "I know my age, and I will take the final decision only at the end of next year, close to the election, some seven months before, I think." Dick Pound, who voted against the age change and is considered a leading contender to replace Samaranch someday, sighed resignedly: "It comes as no surprise when he says he likes the job, and he does a terrific job. If it ain't broke, don't fix it."

There was also in this Olympic off-year a worldwide guessing game about what was going to be broke and what wasn't when the 1996 Summer Games opened in Atlanta next summer. Billy Payne, 48, the former University of Georgia football star who has been the evangelistic leader of the Atlanta Committee for the Olympic Games (ACOG) ever since he had a dream about an Atlanta Olympics eight years ago, has tried to offset any onrushing anxiety by fanning feverish optimism among his followers. He habitually refers to the coming spectacle as "the greatest peacetime gathering of nations in world history," and he promises that July 19, 1996, the first of the 17 days of the Games, "will be the greatest day in my life and in the life of Georgians everywhere. We'll be saying to ourselves at the opening ceremonies: Hey, it's pretty good isn't it? Hey, better than you thought, isn't it? Hey, we couldn't have done it better if we had a thousand years, could we?"

With about one year left to opening day, Payne declared that ACOG had raised 80% of the record-breaking $1.58 billion budgeted for the Games. He said the committee had completed 75% of the $500,000,000 worth of construction on Olympic sites, most of which would be available for local use after the Games were over—including transforming the $170 million, 85,000-seat Olympic Stadium (the first ever with luxury suites) into a new city-owned baseball stadium for the Atlanta Braves, giving five new Olympic Village dormitories to Georgia State University and establishing a permanent $50 million, 21-acre Centennial Olympic Park in downtown Atlanta.

Ebersol and top Sydney organizer Gary Pemberton (left) celebrate NBC's coup.

All of this, as Payne & Co. had long promised, was to come to pass without spending any taxpayers' money since all of it was pouring in from corporate sponsors, broadcasters, ticket buyers and merchandise sales. Indeed, if ACOG does reel in all the commercial sponsors it has on the line, it will shatter Olympic corporate funding records, with $500 million contributed by 45 wildly diverse corporations ranging from Coca-Cola to United Parcel to Xerox to Blue Cross and Blue Shield insurance. Individual company fees range as high as $50 million, and sponsors will not be bashful about displaying their wares and their logos. A 92-foot Swatch watch will adorn a downtown building. Coca-Cola will sponsor the Olympic Torch Relay. McDonald's will have six outlets in the athletes' Olympic Village. Daimler-Benz, the German automaker, is going to restore the crum-

bling house where Margaret Mitchell, author of *Gone with the Wind*, was born. Purists (of whom there are not so many these days) complain that such a massive dependence on—and display of—commercial products will make the formerly hallowed ground of the Olympics resemble nothing so much as a gargantuan trade show.

ACOG remains undaunted. "We're proud of what we've done," said Payne. "Even to the cynics it appears we're going to bring this thing in on time and on budget."

Not all cynics were buying the rosy predictions. As a late-summer headline in an Atlanta newspaper declared: DIRE POSSIBILITIES LURK UNDER UPBEAT REPORTS.

Dire indeed: Atlanta traffic is notorious for being a gridlock nightmare—and the city nearly stopped dead during the 1994 Super Bowl. Of course, Atlanta summers are famously scorching and even though ACOG insists that average temperatures over the last 100 years have been about 75° in July, no one can forget the killer heat wave that covered the U.S. in the summer of '95 and sent the mercury above 90° no fewer than 27 times in Atlanta in July alone. Atlanta hotel rooms are none too abundant and with the best ones reserved for the IOC elite, the press and thousands of corporation fat cats, many of the two million Olympic visitors will be forced to commute from far-off places like Chattanooga and Birmingham. Price-gouging has been rampant in the cradle of Southern hospitality: Owners of private homes closed wildly greedy deals with corporate renters, and apartment house owners threatened to bodily evict tenants who refused to pay Olympic-inflated rents of as much as $3,000.

There was also doubt among critics that some of ACOG's more ambitious construction projects will be completed on schedule—including Olympic Stadium itself and the much-ballyhooed Centennial Park, which lay fallow late last summer partly because an ambitious ACOG plan to finance the park by selling two million personalized park-path bricks for $35 each had faltered with a mere 160,000 bricks bought.

There was even bad news at sea for ACOG. The first of the facilities to be tested in a world-class pre-Olympic competition were the yachting venues in Savannah. Some 700 sailors from 53 nations arrived in July to participate in the NationsBank International Regatta. They were, to a man, enraged over the facilities they found. A chief complaint concerned the seemingly endless two- to three-hour motor tow required to bring racing vessels from the Olympic marina to the racing courses in the ocean. And once they had arrived at offshore launching locations, sailors were met with a desperate shortage of toilets, shade and fresh water. Indeed, as the regatta proceeded, the snafus multiplied and, finally, the president of the International Yacht Racing Union suggested the whole Olympic sailing competition be shifted to Miami.

Payne shrugged off all the many complaints with the same game grin: "This is just preliminary criticism, folks. Don't worry. Our friendliness will steal the show when we finally get to '96."

He might be right. For '95, however, the greatest Olympic show stealer of them all proved to be the NBC network. In the wiliest, gutsiest play of Olympic TV gamesmanship seen in years, the sharpies at NBC, led by network president Robert Wright and sports president Dick Ebersol, persuaded Samaranch and Pound, the IOC's lead TV negotiator, to secretly accept an unprecedented take-it-or-leave-it, preemptive bid of $1.27 billion to buy the rights to not one but *two* Olympics in the same package. The price was $715 million for the 2000 Summer Games in Sydney (where organizers expected only $500 million from TV) and $555 million for the 2002 Winter Games in Salt Lake City (where just $400 million was budgeted).

No other network was notified, and none was allowed to bring in a competing bid. Ethical or not, it was a monumental achievement for both NBC and the IOC. "It was a helluva deal," said Pound. "We could not let this go." Even the losers had to admire NBC's coup. A spokesman at the Fox network, which happens to be owned by Australian-born Rupert Murdoch, who had wanted the Sydney Games so badly that he had sneaked in his own secret preemptive bid of $701 million, declared coldly, "The Olympics are a great event. We wish NBC well." Later, off the record, he added, "There are many unhappy people here."

And so ended the year of lowercase Olympic games. Next come the big *G*'s of '96 which stand for Games, Georgia and God have mercy on ACOG.

1992 Summer Games

TRACK AND FIELD

Men

100 METERS

1. ..Linford Christie, Great Britain   9.96
2. ..Frank Fredericks, Namibia   10.02
3. ..Dennis Mitchell, United States   10.04

200 METERS

1. ..Mike Marsh, United States   20.01
2. ..Frank Fredericks, Namibia   20.13
3. ..Michael Bates, United States   20.38

400 METERS

1. ..Quincy Watts, United States   43.50OR
2. ..Steve Lewis, United States   44.21
3. ..Samson Kitur, Kenya   44.24

800 METERS

1. ..William Tanui, Kenya   1:43.66
2. ..Nixon Kiprotich, Kenya   1:43.70
3. ..Johnny Gray, United States   1:43.97

1500 METERS

1. ..Fermin Cacho, Spain   3:40.12
2. ..Rachid El-Basir, Morocco   3:40.62
3. ..Mohamed Ahmed Sulaiman, Qatar   3:40.69

5000 METERS

1. ..Dieter Baumann, Germany   13:12.52
2. ..Paul Bitok, Kenya   13:12.71
3. ..Fita Bayisa, Ethiopia   13:13.03

10,000 METERS

1. ..Khalid Skah, Morocco   27:46.70
2. ..Richard Chelimo, Kenya   27:47.72
3. ..Addis Abebe, Ethiopia   28.00.07

MARATHON

1. ..Hwang Young-Cho, South Korea   2:13:23
2. ..Koichi Morishita, Japan   2:13:45
3. ..Stephan Freigang, Germany   2:14:00

110-METER HURDLES

1. ..Mark McKoy, Canada   13.12
2. ..Tony Dees, United States   13.24
3. ..Jack Pierce, United States   13.26

400-METER HURDLES

1. ..Kevin Young, United States   46.78WR
2. ..Winthrop Graham, Jamaica   47.66
3. ..Kriss Akabusi, Great Britain   47.82

3000-METER STEEPLECHASE

1. ..Mathew Birir, Kenya   8:08.84
2. ..Patrick Sang, Kenya   8:09.55
3. ..William Mutwol, Kenya   8:10.74

4 X 100 METER RELAY

1. ..United States: Mike Marsh,   37.40WR
Leroy Burrell, Dennis Mitchell,
Carl Lewis
2. ..Nigeria   37.98
3. ..Cuba   38.00

4 X 400 METER RELAY

1. ..United States: Andrew Valmon,   2:55.74 WR
Quincy Watts, Michael Johnson,
Steve Lewis
2. ..Cuba   2:59.51
3. ..Great Britain   2:59.73

20-KILOMETER WALK

1. ..Daniel Plaza, Spain   1:21:45
2. ..Guillaume Leblanc, France   1:22:25
3. ..Giovanni De Benedictis, Italy   1:23:11

50-KILOMETER WALK

1. ..Andrey Perlov, Unified Team   3:50:13
2. ..Carlos Mercenario, Mexico   3:52:09
3. ..Ronald Weigel, Germany   3:53:45

HIGH JUMP

1. ..Javier Sotomayor, Cuba   7 ft 8 in
2. ..Patrik Sjoberg, Sweden   7 ft 8 in
3. ..Artur Partyka, Poland   7 ft 8 in
3. ..Timothy Forsythe, Australia   7 ft 8 in
3. ..Hollis Conway, United States   7 ft 8 in

POLE VAULT

1. ..Maksim Tarasov, Unified Team   19 ft ¼ in
2. ..Igor Trandenkov, Unified Team   19 ft ¼ in
3. ..Javier Garcia, Spain   18 ft 10¼ in

LONG JUMP

1. ..Carl Lewis, United States   28 ft 5½ in
2. ..Mike Powell, United States   28 ft 4¼ in
3. ..Joe Greene, United States   27 ft 4½in

TRIPLE JUMP

1. ..Mike Conley, United States   59 ft 7½ in
2. ..Charles Simpkins, United States   57 ft 9 in
3. ..Frank Rutherford, Bahamas   56 ft 11½in

SHOT PUT

1. ..Mike Stulce, United States   71 ft 2½in
2. ..Jim Doehring, United States   68 ft 9¼ in
3. ..Vyacheslav Lykho, Unified Team   68 ft 8½in

DISCUS THROW

1. ..Romas Ubartas, Lithuania   213 ft 8 in.
2. ..Jürgen Schult, Germany   213 ft 1 in
3. ..Roberto Moya, Cuba   210 ft 4 in

HAMMER THROW

1. ..Andrey Abduvaliyev, Unified Team   270 ft 9 in
2. ..Igor Astapkovich, Unified Team   268 ft 11 in
3. ..Igor Nikulin, Unified Team   267 ft

JAVELIN

1. ..Jan Zelezny, Czechoslovakia   294 ft 2 in OR
2. ..Seppo Räty, Finland   284 ft 1 in
3. ..Steve Backley, Great Britain   273 ft 7 in

DECATHLON

	Pts
1. ..Robert Zmelik, Czechoslovakia	8611
2. ..Antonio Peñalver, Spain	8412
3. ..Dave Johnson, United States	8309

Note: OR=Olympic record. WR=world record. EOR=equals Olympic record. EWR=equals world record

TRACK AND FIELD (Cont.)

Women

100 METERS

1. ..Gail Devers, United States — 10.82
2. ..Juliet Cuthbert, Jamaica — 10.83
3. ..Irina Privalova, Unified Team — 10.84

200 METERS

1. ..Gwen Torrence, United States — 21.81
2. ..Juliet Cuthbert, Jamaica — 22.02
3. ..Merlene Ottey, Jamaica — 22.09

400 METERS

1. ..Marie-Jose Péréc, France — 48.83
2. ..Olga Bryzgina, Unified Team — 49.05
3. ..Ximena Restrepo, Colombia — 49.64

800 METERS

1. ..Ellen Van Langen, The Netherlands — 1:55.54
2. ..Lilia Nurutdinova, Unified Team — 1:55.99
3. ..Ana Fidelia Quirot, Cuba — 1:56.80

1500 METERS

1. ..Hassiba Boulmerka, Algeria — 3:55.30
2. ..Lyudmila Rogacheva, Unified Team — 3:56.91
3. ..Qu Yunxia, China — 3:57.08

3000 METERS

1. ..Elena Romanova, Unified Team — 8:46.04
2. ..Tatiana Dorovskikh, Unified Team — 8:46.85
3. ..Angela Chalmers, Canada — 8:47.22

10,000 METERS

1. ..Derartu Tulu, Ethiopia — 31:06.02
2. ..Elana Meyer, South Africa — 31:11.75
3. ..Lynn Jennings, United States — 31:19.89

MARATHON

1. ..Valentina Yegorova, Unified Team — 2:32:41
2. ..Yuko Arimori, Japan — 2:32:49
3. ..Lorraine Moller, New Zealand — 2:33:59

100-METER HURDLES

1. ..Paraskevi Patoulidou, Greece — 12.64
2. ..LaVonna Martin, United States — 12.69
3. ..Yordanka Donkova, Bulgaria — 12.70

400-METER HURDLES

1. ..Sally Gunnell, Great Britain — 53.23
2. ..Sandra Farmer-Patrick, United States — 53.69
3. ..Janeene Vickers, United States — 54.31

4 X 100 METER RELAY

1. ..United States: Evelyn Ashford, Esther Jones, Carlette Guidry, Gwen Torrence — 42.11
2. ..Unified Team — 42.16
3. ..Nigeria — 42.81

4 X 400 METER RELAY

1. ..Unified Team: Yelena Ruzina, Lioudmila Dzhigalova, Olga Nazarova, Olga Bryzgina — 3:20.20
2. ..United States: Natasha Kaiser, Gwen Torrence, Jearl Miles, Rochelle Stevens — 3:20.92
3. ..Great Britain — 3:24.23

HIGH JUMP

1. ..Heike Henkel, Germany — 6 ft 7½ in
2. ..Galina Astafei, Romania — 6 ft 6¾ in
3. ..Joanet Quintero, Cuba — 6 ft 5½ in

LONG JUMP

1. ..Heike Drechsler, Germany — 23 ft 5¼ in
2. ..Inessa Kravets, Unified Team — 23 ft 4½ in
3. ..Jackie Joyner-Kersee, United States — 23 ft 2½ in

SHOT PUT

1. ..Svetlana Kriveleva, Unified Team — 69 ft 1¼ in
2. ..Huang Zhihong, China — 67 ft 2 in
3. ..Kathrin Neimke, Germany — 64 ft 10¾ in

DISCUS THROW

1. ..Maritza Martén, Cuba — 229 ft 10 in
2. ..Tzvetanka Mintcheva Khristova, Unified Team — 222 ft 4 in
3. ..Daniela Costian, Australia — 217 ft 4 in

JAVELIN

1. ..Silke Renk, Germany — 224 ft 2 in
2. ..Natalia Shikolenka, Unified Team — 223 ft 11 in
3. ..Karen Forkel, Germany — 219 ft 4 in

HEPTATHLON

	Pts
1. ..Jackie Joyner-Kersee, United States	7044
2. ..Irina Belova, Unified Team	6845
3. ..Sabine Braun, Germany	6649

BADMINTON

Men

SINGLES

1. ..Allan Budikusuma, Indonesia
2. ..Ardy B. Wiranata, Indonesia
3. ..Hermawan Susanto, Indonesia
3. ..Thomas Stuer-Lauridsen, Denmark

DOUBLES

1. ..Park Joo-Bong & Kim Moon Soo, South Korea
2. ..Rudy Gunawan & Eddy Hrtona, Indonesia
3. ..Razif Sidek & Jalani Sidek, Malaysia
3. ..Li Yongbo & Tian Bingyi, China

Women

SINGLES

1. ..Susi Susanti, Indonesia
2. ..Bang Soo Hyun, South Korea
3. ..Huang Hua, China
3. ..Tang Jiuhong, China

DOUBLES

1. ....Hwang Hye Young & Chung So Young, South Korea
2. ..Guan Weizhen & Nong Qunhua, China
3. ..Lin Yanfen & Yao Fen, China
3. ..Young Ah Gil & Eun Jung Shim, South Korea

BASEBALL

1. ....Cuba
2. ....Taiwan
3. ....Japan

CANOE/KAYAK

Men

C-1 FLATWATER 500 METERS

1. ....Nikolai Boukhalov, Bulgaria   1:51.14
2. ....Mikhail Slivinski, Unfied Team   1:51.40
3. ....Olaf Heukrodt, Germany   1:53.00

C-1 FLATWATER 1000 METERS

1. ....Nikolai Boukhalov, Bulgaria   4:05.92
2. ....Ivana Klementzjeve, Latvia   4:06.60
3. ....Gyorgy Zala, Hungary   4:07.35

C-2 FLATWATER 500 METERS

1. ....A. Maccekov & D. Dovgalenok,   1:41.54
    Unified Team
2. ....U. Papke & I. Spelly, Germany   1:41.68
3. ....M. Marinov & B. Stoyanov, Bulgaria   1:41.94

C-2 FLATWATER 1000 METERS

1. ....U. Papke & I. Spelly, Germany   3:37.42
2. ....A. Nielsson & C. Frederiksen, Denmark   3:39.26
3. ....D. Hoyer & O. Bolvin, France   3:39.51

C-1 WHITEWATER SLALOM

	Pts
1. ....Lukos Pollerr, Czechoslovakia	113.69
2. ....Gareth John Marriott, Great Britain	116.48
3. ....Jacky Avril, France	117.18

C-2 WHITEWATER SLALOM

	Pts
1. ....S. Strausbaugh & J, Jacobi, U.S.	122.41
2. ....M. Simek & J. Rohan, Czechosolvakia	124.25
3. ....F. Adisson & W. Forgues, France	124.38

K-1 FLATWATER 500 METERS

1. ....Mikko Kolehmainen, Finland   1:40.34
2. ....Zaolt Gyulay, Hungary   1:40.64
3. ....Knut Hofmann, Norway   1:40.71

K-1 FLATWATER 1000 METERS

1. ....Clint Robinson, Australia   3:37.26
2. ....Knut Hofmann, Norway   3:37.50
3. ....Greg Barton, United States   3:37.93

Men (Cont.)

K-2 FLATWATER 500 METERS

1. ....K. Bluhm & T. Gutsche, Germany   1:28.27
2. ....M. Freimut & W. Kurpiewski, Poland   1:29.84
3. ....A. Rossi & B. Dreossi, Italy   1:30.00

K-2 FLATWATER 1000 METERS

1. ....K. Bluhm & T. Gutsche, Germany   3:16.10
2. ....G. Olsson & K. Sundqvist, Sweden   3:17.70
3. ....G. Kotowicz & D. Bielkowski, Poland   3:18.86

K-4 FLATWATER 1000 METERS

1. ....Germany   2:54.18
2. ....Hungary   2:54.82
3. ....Australia   2:56.97

Women

K-1 WHITEWATER SLALOM

	Pts
1. ....Pierpaolo Ferrazzi, Italy	106.89
2. ....Sylvain Curiruer, France	107.06
3. ....Jochen Lettmann, Germany	108.52

K-1 FLATWATER 500 METERS

1. ....Birgit Schmidt, Germany   1:51.60
2. ....Rita Koban, Hungary   1:51.96
3. ....Izabella Dylewska, Poland   1:52.36

K-2 FLATWATER 500 METERS

1. ....R. Portwich & A. Von Seck, Germany   1:40.29
2. ....S. Gunnarsson & A. Andersson, Sweden   1:40.41
3. ....R. Koban & E. Donusz, Hungary   1:40.81

K-4 FLATWATER 500 METERS

1. ....Hungary   1:38.32
2. ....Germany   1:38.47
3. ....Sweden   1:39.79

K-1 WHITEWATER SLALOM

	Pts
1. ....Elizabeth Micheler, Germany	126.41
2. ....Danielle Woodward, Australia	128.27
3. ....Dana Chladek, United States	131.75

BASKETBALL

Men

Final: United States 117, Croatia 85
Lithuania (3rd)
United States: Christian Laettner, David Robinson, Patrick Ewing, Larry Bird, Scottie Pippen, Michael Jordan, Clyde Drexler, Karl Malone, John Stockton, Chris Mullin, Charles Barkley, Earvin Johnson

Women

Final: Unified Team 76, China 66
United States (3rd):
Teresa Edwards, Daedra Charles, Clarissa Davis, Tammy Jackson, Teresa Weatherspoon, Vickie Orr, Victoria Bullett, Carolyn Jones, Katrina McClain, Medina Dixon, Cynthia Cooper, Suzanne McConnell

BOXING

LIGHT FLYWEIGHT (106 LB)
1. ....Rogelio Marcelo, Cuba
2. ....Daniel Bojinov, Bulgaria
3. ....Jan Quast, Germany
3. ....Roel Velasco, Philippines

FLYWEIGHT (112 LB)
1. ....Su Choi Choi, North Korea
2. ....Raul Gonzalez, Cuba
3. ....Timothy Austin, United States
3. ....Istvan Kovacs, Hungary

BANTAMWEIGHT (119 LB)
1. ....Joel Casamayor, Cuba
2. ....Wayne McCullough, Ireland
3. ....Li Gwang Sik, North Korea
3. ....Mohamed Achik, Morocco

FEATHERWEIGHT (125 LB)
1. ....Andreas Tews, Germany
2. ....Faustino Reyes, Spain
3. ....Hocine Soltani, Algeria
3. ....Ramazi Paliani, Unified Team

LIGHTWEIGHT (132 LB)
1. ....Oscar De La Hoya, United States
2. ....Marco Rudolph, Germany
3. ....Hong Sung Sik, North Korea
3. ....Namjil Bayarsaikhan, Mongolia

LIGHT WELTERWEIGHT (139 LB)
1. ....Hector Vinent, Cuba
2. ....Mark Leduc, Canada
3. ....Jyri Kjall, Finland
3. ....Leonard Doroftei, Romania

WELTERWEIGHT (147 LB)
1. ....Michael Carruth, Ireland
2. ....Juan Hernandez, Cuba
3. ....Aniibal Acevedo Santiago, Puerto Rico
3. ....Arkom Chenglai, Thailand

LIGHT MIDDLEWEIGHT (156 LB)
1. ....Juan Lemus, Cuba
2. ....Orhan Delibas, Netherlands
3. ....Gyorgy Mizsei, Hungary
3. ....Robin Reid, Great Britain

MIDDLEWEIGHT (165 LB)
1. ....Ariel Hernandez, Cuba
2. ....Chris Byrd, United States
3. ....Chris Johnson, Canada
3. ....Lee Seung Bae, South Korea

LIGHT HEAVYWEIGHT (178 LB)
1. ....Torsten May, Germany
2. ....Rostislav Zaoulitchnyi, Unified Team
3. ....Zoltan Beres, Hungary
3. ....Wojciech Bartnik, Poland

HEAVYWEIGHT (201 LB)
1. ....Felix Savon, Cuba
2. ....David Izonritei, Nigeria
3. ....Arnold Van Der Lijde, The Netherlands
3. ....David Tua, New Zealand

SUPERHEAVYWEIGHT (201+ LB)
1. ....Roberto Balado, Cuba
2. ....Richard Igbineghu, Nigeria
3. ....Brian Nielsen, Denmark
3. ....Svilen Roussinov, Bulgaria

GYMNASTICS

Men

ALL-AROUND

		Pts
1.	Vitaly Scherbo, Unified Team	59.025
2.	Grigory Misiutin, Unified Team	58.925
3.	Valery Belenki, Unified Team	58.625

HORIZONTAL BAR

		Pts
1.	Trent Dimas, United States	9.875
1.	Grigory Misiutin, Unified Team	9.837
3.	Andreas Wecker, Germany	9.837

PARALLEL BARS

		Pts
1.	Vitaly Scherbo, Unified Team	9.900
2.	Li Jing, China	9.812
3.	Guo Linyao, China	9.800
3.	Igor Korobchinski, Unified Team	9.800
3.	Masayuki Matsunaga, Japan	9.800

VAULT

		Pts
1.	Vitaly Scherbo, Unified Team	9.856
2.	Grigory Misiutin, Unified Team	9.781
3.	Yoo Ok Ryul, South Korea	9.762

Women

ALL-AROUND

		Pts
1.	Tatiana Gutsu, Unified Team	39.737
2.	Shannon Miller, United States	39.725
3.	Lavinia Milosovici, Romania	39.687

VAULT

		Pts
1.	Henrietta Onodi, Hungary	9.925
1.	Lavinia Milosovici, Romania	9.925
3.	Tatiana Lisenko, Unified Team	9.912

UNEVEN BARS

		Pts
1.	Lu Li, China	10.000
2.	Tatiana Gutsu, Unified Team	9.975
3.	Shannon Miller, United States	9.962

BALANCE BEAM

		Pts
1.	Tatiana Lisenko, Unified Team	9.975
2.	Lu Li, China	9.912
2.	Shannon Miller, United States	9.912

GYMNASTICS (Cont.)

Men

POMMEL HORSE

	Pts
1. ....Vitaly Scherbo, Unified Team	9.925
1. ....Pae Gil Su, North Korea	9.925
3. ....Andreas Wecker, Germany	9.887

RINGS

	Pts
1. ....Vitaly Scherbo, Unified Team	9.937
1. ....Li Jing, China	9.875
3. ....Li Xiaosahuang, China	9.862
3. ....Andreas Wecker, Germany	9.862

FLOOR EXERCISE

	Pts
1. ....Li Xizosahuang, China	9.925
2. ....Grigory Misiutin, Unified Team	9.787
2. ....Yukio Iketani, Japan	9.787

TEAM COMBINED EXERCISES

	Pts
1. ....Unified Team	585.450
2. ....China	580.375
3. ....Japan	578.250

Women

FLOOR EXERCISE

	Pts
1. ....Lavinia Milosovici, Romania	10.000
2. ....Henrietta Onodi, Hungary	9.950
3. ....Shannon Miller, United States	9.912
3. ....Cristina Bontas, Romania	9.912
3. ....Tatiana Gutsu, Unified Team	9.912

TEAM COMBINED EXERCISES

	Pts
1. ....Unified Team	395.666
2. ....Romania	395.079
3. ....United States	394.704

RHYTHMIC ALL-AROUND

	Pts
1. ....Aleksandra Timoshenko, Unified Team	59.037
2. ....Carolina Pascual Gracia, Spain	58.100
3. ....Oksana Skaldina, Unified Team	57.912

SWIMMING

Men

50-METER FREESTYLE

1. ..Aleksandr Popov, Unified Team	21.91 OR
2. ..Matt Biondi, United States	22.09
3. ..Tom Jager, Unifed States	22.30

100-METER FREESTYLE

1. ..Aleksandr Popov, Unified Team	49.02
2. ..Gustavo Borges, Brazil	49.43
3. ..Stephan Caron, France	49.50

200-METER FREESTYLE

1. ..Evgueni Sadovyi, Unified Team	1:46.70 OR
2. ..Anders Holmertz, Sweden	1:46.86
3. ..Antti Kasvio, Finland	1:47.63

400-METER FREESTYLE

1. ..Evgueni Sadovyi, Unified Team	3:45.00 WR
2. ..Kieren Perkins, Australia	3:45.16
3. ..Anders Holmertz, Sweden	3:46.77

1500-METER FREESTYLE

1. ..Kieren Perkins, Australia	14:43.48 WR
2. ..Glen Housman, Australia	14:55.29
3. ..Jörg Hoffmann, Germany	15:02.29

100-METER BACKSTROKE

1. ..Mark Tewksbury, Canada	53.98 WR
2. ..Jeff Rouse, United States	54.04
3. ..David Berkoff, United States	54.78

100-METER BACKSTROKE

1. ..Martin Zubero-Lopez, Spain	1:58.47 OR
2. ..Vladimir Selkov, Unified Team	1:58.87
3. ..Stefano Battistelli, Italy	1:59.40

100-METER BREASTSTROKE

1. ..Nelson Diebel, United States	1:01.50 OR
2. ..Norbert Rozsa, Hungary	1:01.68
3. ..Philip Rogers, Australia	1:01.76

200-METER BREASTSTROKE

1. ..Mike Barrowman, United States	2:10.16 WR
2. ..Norbert Rozsa, Hungary	2:11.23
3. ..Nick Gillingham, Great Britain	2:11.29

100-METER BUTTERFLY

1. ..Pablo Morales, United States	53.32
2. ..Rafal Szukala, Poland	53.35
3. ..Anthony Nesty, Surinam	53.41

200-METER BUTTERFLY

1. ..Melvin Stewart, United States	1:56.26
2. ..Danyon Loader, New Zealand	1:57.93
3. ..Franck Esposito, France	1:58.51

200-METER INDIVIDUAL MEDLEY

1. ..Tamas Darnyi, Hungary	2:00.76
2. ..Greg Burgess, United States	2:00.97
3. ..Attila Czene, Hungary	2:01.00

400-METER INDIVIDUAL MEDLEY

1. ..Tamas Darnyi, Hungary	4:14.23 OR
2. ..Eric Namesnik, United States	4:15.57
3. ..Luca Sacchi, Italy	4:16.34

4 X 100 METER MEDLEY RELAY

1. ..United States: Jeff Rouse, Nelson Diebel, Pablo Morales, Jon Olsen	3:36.93 WR
2. ..Unified Team	3:38.56
3. ..Canada	3:39.66

Note: OR=Olympic record. WR=world record. EOR=equals Olympic record. EWR=equals world record

SWIMMING (Cont.)

Men (Cont.)

4 X 100 METER FREESTYLE RELAY

1. ..United States: Joe Hudepohl, Matt Biondi, Tom Jager, Jon Olsen	3:16.74
2. ..Unified Team	3:17.56
3. ..Germany	3:17.90

4 X 200 METER FREESTYLE RELAY

1. ..Unified Team: Dimitri Lepikov, Vladimir Pychenko, Veniamin Taianovitch, Evgueni Sadovyi	7:11.95 WR
2. ..Sweden	7:15.51
3. ..United States	7:16.23

Women

50-METER FREESTYLE

1. ..Yang Wenyi, China	24.79 WR
2. ..Zhuang Yong, China	25.08
3. ..Angel Martino, United States	25.23

100-METER FREESTYLE

1. ..Zhuang Yong, China	54.64 OR
2. ..Jenny Thompson, United States	54.84
3. ..Franziska Van Almsick, Germany	54.94

200-METER FREESTYLE

1. ..Nicole Haislett, United States	1:57.90
2. ..Franziska Van Almsick, Germany	1:58.00
3. ..Kerstin Kielgass, Germany	1:59.67

400-METER FREESTYLYE

1. ..Dagmar Hase, Germany	4:07.18
2. ..Janet Evans, United States	4:07.37
3. ..Hayley Lewis, Australia	4:11.22

800-METER FREESTYLE

1. ..Janet Evans, United States	8:25.52
2. ..Hayley Lewis, Australia	8:30.34
3. ..Jana Henke, Germany	8:30.99

100-METER BACKSTROKE

1. ..Krisztina Egerszegi, Hungary	1:00.68 OR
2. ..Tunde Szabo, Hungary	1:01.14
3. ..Lea Loveless, United States	1:01.43

200-METER BACKSTROKE

1. ..Krisztina Egerszegi, Hungary	2:07.06
2. ..Dagmar Hase, Germany	2:09.46
3. ..Nicole Stevenson, Australia	2:10.20

100-METER BREASTSTROKE

1. ..Elena Roudkovskaia, Unified Team	1:08.00
2. ..Anita Nall, United States	1:08.17
3. ..Samantha Riley, Australia	1:09.25

200-METER BREASTSTROKE

1. ..Kyoko Iwasaki, Japan	2:26.65 OR
2. ..Lin Li, China	2:26.85
3. ..Anita Nall, United States	2:26.88

100-METER BUTTERFLY

1. ..Qian Hong, China	58.62 OR
2. ..Crissy Ahmann-Leighton, United States	58.74
3. ..Catherine Plewinski, France	59.01

200-METER BUTTERFLY

1. ..Summer Sanders, United States	2:08.67
2. ..Wang Ziaohong, China	2:09.01
3. ..Susan O'Neill, Australia	2:09.03

200-METER INDIVIDUAL MEDLEY

1. ..Lin Li, China	2:11.65 WR
2. ..Summer Sanders, United States	2:11.91
3. ..Daniela Hunger, Germany	2:13.92

400-METER INDIVIDUAL MEDLEY

1. ..Krisztina Egerszegi, Hungary	4:36.54
2. ..Lin Li, China	4:36.73
3. ..Summer Sanders, United States	4:37.58

4 X 100 METER MEDLEY RELAY

1. ..United States: Lea Loveless, Anita Nall, Crissy Ahmann-Leighton, Jenny Thompson	4:02.54 WR
2. ..Germany	4:05.19
3. ..Unified Team	4:06.44

4 X 100 METER FREESTYLE RELAY

1. ..United States: Nicole Haislett, Dara Torres, Angel Martino, Jenny Thompson	3:39.46 WR
2. ..China	3:40.12
3. ..Germany	3:41.60

DIVING

Men

SPRINGBOARD

		Pts
1. ....Mark Lenzi, United States		676.53
2. ....Tan Liangde, China		645.57
3. ....Dmitri Saoutine, Unified Team		627.78

PLATFORM

		Pts
1. ....Sun Shuwei, China		677.31
2. ....Scott Donie, United States		633.63
3. ....Xiong Ni, China		600.15

Women

SPRINGBOARD

		Pts
1. ....Gao Min, China		572.40
2. ....Irina Lachko, Unified Team		514.14
3. ....Brita Pia Baldus, Germany		503.07

PLATFORM

		Pts
1. ....Fu Mingxia, China		461.43
2. ....Yelena Mirochina, Unified Team		411.63
3. ....Mary Ellen Clark, United States		401.91

Note: OR=Olympic record. WR=world record. EOR=equals Olympic record. EWR=equals world record

INDIVIDUAL ARCHERY

Men

1. ....Sebastien Flute, France
2. ....Chung Jae Hun, South Korea
3. ....Simon Terry, Great Britain

Women

1. ....Cho Youn Jeong, South Korea
2. ....Kim Soo Nyung, South Korea
3. ....Natalia Valeeva, Unified Team

CYCLING

Men

100 KM TEAM TIME TRIAL

1. ..Germany: Bernd Dittert,   2:01:39
   Christian Meyer, Uwe Peschel,
   Michael Rich
2. ..Italy   2:02:39
3. ..France   2:05:25

1 KM TIME TRIAL

1. ..Jose Moreno, Spain   1:03.342 OR
2. ..Shane Kelly, Australia   1:04.288
3. ..Erin Hartwell, United States   1:04.753

4000 METER INDIVIDUAL PURSUIT

1. ..Chris Boardman, Great Britain
2. ..Jens Lehmann, Germany
3. ..Gary Anderson, New Zealand

4000 METER TEAM PURSUIT

1. ..Germany: M. Gloeckner,   4:08.791
   Jens Lehmann, Stefan Steinweg,
   Guido Fulst
2. ..Australia   4:10.218
3. ..Denmark   4:15.860

POINTS RACE

1. ..Giovanni Lombardi, Italy   44
2. ..Leon Van Bon, The Netherlands   43
3. ..Cedric Mathy, Belgium   41

INDIVIDUAL ROAD RACE

1. ..Fabio Casartelli, Italy   4:35.21
2. ..Erik Dekker, The Netherlands   4:35.22
3. ..Dainis Ozols, Latvia   4:35.24

Women

SPRINT

1. ......Erika Saloumiae, Estonia
2. ......Annett Neumann, Germany
3. ......Ingrid Haringa, The Netherlands

ROAD RACE

1. ..Kathryn Watt, Australia   2:04.42
2. ..Jeannie Longo-Ciprelli, France   2:05.02
3. ..Monique Knol, The Netherlands   2:05.03

EQUESTRIAN

3-DAY TEAM

1. ......Australia: David Green,   288.60
   Gillian Rolton, Andrew Hoy
   Matthew Ryan
2. ......New Zealand   290.80
3. ......Germany   300.30

3-DAY INDIVIDUAL

1. ......Matthew Ryan, Australia   70.00
2. ......Herbert Blocker, Germany   81.30
3. ......Blyth Tait, New Zealand   87.60

TEAM DRESSAGE

1. ......Germany: Isabelle Werth,   5224
   Klaus Balkenhol,
   Monica Theodorescu, Nicole Uphoff
2. ......The Netherlands   4742
3. ......United States   4643

INDIVIDUAL DRESSAGE

1. ......Nicole Uphoff, Germany   1768
2. ......Isabelle Werth, Germany   1762
3. ......Klaus Balkenhol, Germany   1694

TEAM JUMPING

1. ......The Netherlands: Piet Raymakers,   12.00
   Bert Romp, Jan Tops, Jos Lansink
2. ......Austria   16.75
3. ......France   24.75

INDIVIDUAL JUMPING

1. ......Ludger Beerbaum, Germany   0.00
2. ......Piet Raymakers, The Netherlands   .25
3. ......Norman Dello Joio, United States   4.75

Note: OR=Olympic record. WR=world record. EOR=equals Olympic record. EWR=equals world record

INDIVIDUAL FENCING

Men

FOIL

1. ....Philippe Omnes, France
2. ....Sergei Goloubitski, Unified Team
3. ....Elvis Gregory Gil, Cuba

SABRE

1. ....Bence Szabo, Hungary
2. ....Marco Marin, Italy
3. ....Jean-Francois Lamour, France

Men *(Cont.)*

EPEE

1. ....Eric Srecki, France
2. ....Pavel Kolobkov, Unified Team
3. ....Jean-Michel Henry, France

Women

FOIL

1. ....Giovanna Trillini, Italy
2. ....Wang Huifeng, China
3. ....Tatiana Sadovskaia, Unified Team

FIELD HOCKEY

Men

1. ....Germany
2. ....Australia
3. ....Pakistan

Women

1. ....Spain
2. ....Germany
3. ....Great Britain

TEAM HANDBALL

Men

1. ....Unified Team
2. ....Sweden
3. ....France

Women

1. ....South Korea
2. ....Norway
3. ....Unified Team

JUDO

EXTRA-LIGHTWEIGHT

1. ....Nazim Guseinov, Unified Team
2. ....Yoon Hyun, South Korea
3. ....Tadanori Koshino, Japan
3. ....Richard Trautmann, Germany

HALF-LIGHTWEIGHT

1. ....Rogerio Sampaio Cardoso, Brazil
2. ....Josef Czak, Hungary
3. ....Udo Quellmalz, Germany
3. ....Israel Hernandez Planas, Cuba

LIGHTWEIGHT

1. ....Toshihiko Koga, Japan
2. ....Bertalan Hajtos, Hungary
3. ....Chung Hoon, South Korea
3. ....Shay Oren Smadga, Israel

HALF-MIDDLEWEIGHT

1. ....Hidehiko Yoshida, Japan
2. ....Jason Morris, United States
3. ....Bertrand Domaisin, France
3. ....Kim Byung Joo, South Korea

MIDDLEWEIGHT

1. ....Waldemar Legien, Poland
2. ....Pascal Tayot, France
3. ....Hirotaka Okada, Japan
3. ....Nicolas Gill, Canada

HALF-HEAVYWEIGHT

1. ....Antal Kovacs, Hungary
2. ....Raymond Stevens, Great Britain
3. ....Dmitri Sergeev, Unified Team
3. ....Theo Meijer, The Netherlands

HEAVYWEIGHT

1. ....David Khakaleshvili, Unified Team
2. ....Naoya Ogowa, Japan
3. ....David Douillet, France
3. ....Imre Csosz, Hungary

MODERN PENTATHLON

TEAM

1. ....Poland
2. ....Unified Team
3. ....Italy

INDIVIDUAL

1. ....Arkadiusz Skrzypaszek, Poland
2. ....Attila Mizser, Hungary
3. ....Eduard Zenovka, Unified Team

ROWING

Men

SINGLE SCULLS

1. ..Thomas Lange, Germany	6:51.40
2. ..Vaclav Chalupa, Czechoslovakia	6:52.93
3. ..Kajetan Broniewski, Poland	6:56.82

DOUBLE SCULLS

1. ..Australia	6:17.32
2. ..Austria	6:18.42
3. ..The Netherlands	6:22.82

COXLESS PAIR

1. ..Great Britain	. 6:27.72
2. ..Germany	6:32.68
3. ..Slovenia	6:33.43

COXED FOUR

1. ..Romania	5:59.37
2. ..Germany	6:00.34
3. ..Poland	6:03.27

COXED PAIR

1. ..Great Britain	6:49.83
2. ..Italy	6:50.98
3. ..Romania	6:51.58

QUADRUPLE SCULLS

1. ..Germany	5:45.17
2. ..Norway	5:47.09
3. ..Italy	5:47.33

COXLESS FOUR

1. ..Australia	5:55.04
2. ..United States	5:56.68
3. ..Slovenia	5:58.24

EIGHT-OARS

1. ..Canada	5:29.53
2. ..Romania	5:29.67
3. ..Germany	5:31.00

Women

SINGLE SCULLS

1. ..Elisabeta Lipa, Romania	7:25.54
2. ..Annelies Bredael, Belgium	7:26.64
3. ..Silken Suzette Laumann, Canada	7:28.85

DOUBLE SCULLS

1. ..Germany	6:49.00
2. ..Romania	6:51.47
3. ..China	6:55.16

COXLESS PAIR

1. ..Canada	7:06.22
2. ..Germany	7:07.96
3. ..United States	7:08.12

COXLESS FOUR

1. ..Canada	6:30.85
2. ..United States	6:31.86
3. ..Germany	6:32.34

QUADRUPLE SCULLS

1. ..Germany	6:20.18
2. ..Romania	6:24.34
3. ..Unified Team	6:25.07

EIGHT-OARS

1. ..Canada	6:02.62
2. ..Romania	6:06.26
3. ..Germany	6:07.80

SOCCER

1.	Spain
2.	Poland
3.	Ghana

SYNCHRONIZED SWIMMING

SOLO

	Pts
1. ....Kristen Babb-Sprague, United States	191.848
2. ....Sylvie Frechette, Canada	191.717
3. ....Fumiko Okuno, Japan	187.056

DUET

	Pts
1. ....Karen & Sarah Josephson, United States	192.175
2. ....Penny & Vicky Vilagos, Canada	189.394
3. ....Fumiko Okuno & Aki Takayama, Japan	186.868

SHOOTING

Men

THREE-POSITION RIFLE

	Pts
1......Gracha Petikian, Unified Team	1267.4
2......Bob Foth, United States	1266.6
3......Ryohei Koba, Japan	1265.9

AIR RIFLE

	Pts
1......Jury Fedkin, Unified Team	695.3
2......Franck Badiou, France	691.9
3......Johann Riederer, Germany	691.7

FREE RIFLE PRONE

	Pts
1......Eun-Chul Lee, South Korea	702.5
2......Harald Stenvaag, Norway	701.4
3......Stevan Pletikosic, Independent Team	701.1

FREE PISTOL

	Pts
1......Konstantine Loukachik, Unified Team	658
2......Yifu Wang, China	657
3......Ragnar Skanaker, Sweden	657

SHOOTING

Men

RAPID-FIRE PISTOL

	Pts
1......Ralf Schumann, Germany	885
2......Afanasij Kusmin, Latvia	882
3......Vladimir Vokhmianin, Unified Team	882

AIR PISTOL

	Pts
1......Yifu Wang, China	684.8
2......Sergei Pyzhianov, Unified Team	684.1
3......Sorin Babii, Romania	684.1

RUNNING TARGET

	Pts
1......Michael Jakosits, Germany	673
2......Anatolij Asrabaev, Unified Team	672
3......Lubos Racansky, Czechoslovakia	670

TRAP

	Pts
1......Petr Hrdlicka, Czechoslovakia	219
2......Kazumi Watanabe, Japan	219
3......Marco Venturini, Italy	218

SKEET

	Pts
1......Shan Zhang, China	223
2......Juan Giah, Peru	222
3......Bruno Rossetti, Italy	222

Women

THREE-POSITION RIFLE

	Pts
1......Launi Meili, United States	684.3
2......Nonca Matova, Bulgaria	682.7
3......Malgorzata Ksiazkiewicz, Poland	681.5

AIR RIFLE

	Pts
1......Kab-Soon Yeo, South Korea	498.2
2......Vessela Letcheva, Bulgaria	495.3
3......Aranka Binder, Independent Team	495.1

AIR PISTOL

	Pts
1......Marina Logvinenko, Unified Team	486.4
2......Jasna Sekaric, Independent Team	486.4
3......Maria Grousdeva, Bulgaria	481.6

SPORT PISTOL

	Pts
1......Marina Logvinenko, Unified Team	684
2......Duihong Li, China	680
3......Dorisuren Monchbajar, Mongolia	679

TABLE TENNIS

Men

SINGLES

1. ....Jan-Ove Waldner, Sweden
2. ....Jean Gatien, France
3. ....Kim Taek Soo, South Korea
3. ....Ma Wenge, China

DOUBLES

1. ....Lu Lin & Wang Tao, China
2. ....Steffan Fetzner & Jorg Rosskopf, Germany
3. ....Kang Hee Chan & Lee Chul Seung, South Korea
3. ....Kim Taek Soo & Yoo Nam Kyu, South Korea

Women

SINGLES

1. ....Deng Yaping, China
2. ....Qiao Hong, China
3. ....Hyun Jung Hwa, South Korea
3. ....Li Bun Hui, North Korea

DOUBLES

1. ....Deng Yaping & Qiao Hong, China
2. ....Chen Zihe & Gao Jun, China
3. ....Li Bun Hui & Yu Sun Bok, North Korea
3. ....Hong Cha Ok & Hyun Jung Hwa, South Korea

TENNIS

Men

SINGLES

1. ....Marc Rosset, Switzerland
2. ....Jordi Arrese, Spain
3. ....Goran Ivanisevic, Croatia
3. ....Andrei Cherkasov, Unified Team

DOUBLES

1. ....Boris Becker & Michael Stich, Germany
2. ....Wayne Ferreira & Piet Norval, South Africa
3. ....Goran Ivanisevic & Goran Prpic, Croatia
3. ....Javier Frana & Christian Carlos Miniussi, Argentina

Women

SINGLES

1. ....Jennifer Capriati, United States
2. ....Steffi Graf, Germany
3. ....Aranxta Sanchez Vicario, Spain
3. ....Mary Joe Fernandez, United States

DOUBLES

1. ....Gigi Fernandez & Mary Joe Fernandez, United States
2. ....Conchita Martinez & Aranxta Sanchez Vicario, Spain
3. ....Natalya Zvereva & Leila Meskhi, Unified Team
3. ....Rachel McQuillan & Nicole Provis, Australia

VOLLEYBALL

Men

1. ....Brazil
2. ....The Netherlands
3. ....United States: Bob Ctvrtlik, Doug Partie, Steve Timmons, Scott Fortune, Jeff Stork, Eric Sato, Dan Hanan, Dan Greenbaum, Uvaldo Acosta, Bryan Ivie, Bob Samuelson, Javier Gaspar, Trevor Schirman, Carlos Briceno, Nick Becker, Brent Hilliard, Mark Arnold, Allen Allen

Women

1. ....Cuba
2. ....Unified Team
3. ....United States: Tee Sanders, Yoko Zetterlund, Ann Schirman, Kim Oden, Lori Endicott, Paula Weishoff, Caren Kemner, Tammy Liley, Elaina Oden, Daiva Tomkus, Deitre Collins, Janet Cobbs, Tara Battle, Liane Sato, Ruth Lawanson, Bev Oden

WATER POLO

1. ....Italy
2. ....Spain
3. ....Unified Team

WEIGHTLIFTING

114 POUNDS

1. ....Ivan Ivanov, Bulgaria	584 lb
2. ....Lin Qisheng, China	579 lb
3. ....Traian Ciharean, Romania	557 lb

123 POUNDS

1. ....Chun Byun Kwan, South Korea	634 lb
2. ....Liu Shoubin, China	612 lb
3. ....Luo Jianming, China	612 lb

132 POUNDS

1. ....Naim Suleymanoglu, Turkey	705 lb
2. ....Nikolai Peshalov, Unified Team	672 lb
3. ....He Yingqiang, China	650 lb

148.5 POUNDS

1. ....Israel Militossian, Unified Team	744 lb
2. ....Yoto Yotov, Bulgaria	722 lb
3. ....Andreas Behm, Germany	706 lb

165 POUNDS

1. ....Fedor Kassapu, Unified Team	788 lb
2. ....Pablo Lara Rodriguez, Cuba	788 lb
3. ....Kim Myong Nam, North Korea	777 lb

181.5 POUNDS

1. ....Pyrros Dimas, Greece	816 lb
2. ....Krzysztof Siemion, Poland	816 lb
3. ....Ibragim Samadov, Unified Team	816 lb

198 POUNDS

1. ....Kakhi Kakhiachveili, Unified Team	910 lb OR
2. ....Sergei Sirtsov, Unified Team	910 lb OR
3. ....Sergivsz Wolczanjecki, Poland	865 lb

220 POUNDS

1. ....Victor Tregoubov, Unified Team	904 lb
2. ....Timour Taimazov, Unified Team	887 lb
3. ....Waldemar Malak, Poland	882 lb

243 POUNDS

1. ....Ronny Weller, Germany	953 lb
2. ....Artur Akoev, Unified Team	948 lb
3. ....Stefan Botev, Bulgaria	920 lb

243+ POUNDS

1. ....Aleksandr Kurlovich, Unified Team	992 lb
2. ....Leonid Taranenko, Unified Team	937 lb
3. ....Manfred Nerlinger, Germany	909 lb

FREESTYLE WRESTLING

106 POUNDS

1. ....Kim Il, North Korea
2. ....Kim Jong, South Korea
3. ....Vougar Oroudjov, Unified Team

115 POUNDS

1. ....Li Hak Son, North Korea
2. ....Zeke Jones, United States
3. ....Valentin Jordanov, Bulgaria

126 POUNDS

1. ....Alejandro Puerto Diaz, Cuba
2. ....Serguei Smal, Unified Team
3. ....Kim Yong Sik, North Korea

137 POUNDS

1. ....John Smith, United States
2. ....Asgari Mohammadian, Iran
3. ....Lazaro Reinoso, Cuba

150 POUNDS

1. ....Arsen Fadzaev, Unified Team
2. ....Valentin Getzov, Bulgaria
3. ....Kosei Akaishi, Japan

163 POUNDS

1. ....Park Jang-Soon, South Korea
2. ....Kenny Monday, United States
3. ....Amir Khadem, Iran

181 POUNDS

1. ....Kevin Jackson, United States
2. ....Elmadi Jabraijlov, Unified Team
3. ....Rasul Khadem, Iran

198 POUNDS

1. ....Makharbek Khadartsev, Unified Team
2. ....Kenan Simsek, Turkey
3. ....Chris Campbell, United States

220 POUNDS

1. ....Leri Khabelov, Unified Team
2. ....Heiko Balz, Germany
3. ....Ali Kayali, Turkey

286 POUNDS

1. ....Bruce Baumgartner, United States
2. ....Jeffrey Thue, Canada
3. ....David Gobedjichvili, Unified Team

Note: OR=Olympic record. WR=world record. EOR=equals Olympic record. EWR=equals world record

GRECO-ROMAN WRESTLING

106 POUNDS
1. ....Oleg Koutcherenko, Unified Team
2. ....Vincenzo Maenza, Italy
3. ....Wilber Sanchez, Cuba

115 POUNDS
1. ....Jon Ronningen, Norway
2. ....Alfred Ter-Mkrtychan, Unified Team
3. ....Min Kyung, South Korea

126 POUNDS
1. ....An Han-Bong, South Korea
2. ....Rifat Yildiz, Germany
3. ....Sheng Zetian, China

137 POUNDS
1. ....Akif Pirim, Turkey
2. ....Sergei Martynov, Unified Team
3. ....Juan Maren, Cuba

150 POUNDS
1. ....Attila Repka, Hungary
2. ....Islam Duguchiev, Unified Team
3. ....Rodney Smith, United States

163 POUNDS
1. ....Mnatsakan Iskandarian, Unified Team
2. ....Josef Tracz, Poland
3. ....Torbjoern Korbakk, Sweden

181 POUNDS
1. ....Peter Farkas, Hungary
2. ....Piotr Stepien, Poland
3. ....Daulet Tourlykhanov, Unified Team

198 POUNDS
1. ....Maik Bullmann, Germany
2. ....Hakki Basar, Turkey
3. ....Gogi Kogouachvili, Unified Team

220 POUNDS
1. ....Hector Millian, Cuba
2. ....Dennis Koslowski, United States
3. ....Sergei Demyashkevich, Unified Team

286 POUNDS
1. ....Aleksandr Karelin, Unified Team
2. ....Tomas Johansson, Sweden
3. ....Ioan Grigoras, Romania

YACHTING

SOLING CLASS
1. ....Denmark
2. ....United States
3. ....Great Britain

STAR CLASS
1. ....United States
2. ....New Zealand
3. ....Canada

FLYING DUTCHMAN CLASS
1. ....Spain
2. ....United States
3. ....Denmark

FINN CLASS
1. ....Jose Van Der Ploeg, Spain
2. ....Brian Ledbetter, United States
3. ....Craig Monk, New Zealand

TORNADO CLASS
1. ....France
2. ....United States
3. ....Australia

EUROPE CLASS
1. ....Linda Andersen, Norway
2. ....Natalia Via Dufresne, Spain
3. ....Julia Trotman, United States

MEN'S 470 CLASS
1. ....Spain
2. ....United States
3. ....Estonia

WOMEN'S 470 CLASS
1. ....Spain
2. ....New Zealand
3. ....United States

1994 Winter Games

BIATHLON

Men

10 KILOMETERS
1. ..Sergei Tchepikov, Russia	28:07.0
2. ..Ricco Gross, Germany	28:13.0
3. ..Sergei Tarasov, Russia	28:27.4

20 KILOMETERS
1. ..Sergei Tarasov, Russia	57:25.3
2. ..Frank Luck, Germany	57:28.7
3. ..Sven Fischer, Germany	57:41.9

4 X 7.5 KILOMETER RELAY
1. ....Germany	1:30:22.1
2. ....Russia	1:31:23.6
3. ....France	1:32:31.3

Women

7.5 KILOMETERS
1. ..Myriam Bedard, Canada	26:08.8
2. ..Svetlana Paramygina, Belarus	26:09.9
3. ..Valentyna Tserbe, Ukraine	26:10.0

15 KILOMETERS
1. ..Myriam Bedard, Canada	52:06.6
2. ..Anne Briand, France	52:53.3
3. ..Ursula Disl, Germany	53:15.3

3 X 7.5 KILOMETER RELAY
1. ....Russia	1:47:19.5
2. ....Germany	1:51:16.5
3. ....France	1:52:28.3

BOBSLED

4-MAN BOB		2-MAN BOB	
1. ....Germany II	3:27.78	1. ....Switzerland	3:30.81
2. ....Switzerland	3:27.84	2. ....Switzerland II	3:30.86
3. ....Germany	3:28.01	3. ....Italy	3:31.01

ICE HOCKEY

1. ....Sweden
2. ....Canada
3. ....Finland

LUGE

Men

SINGLES

1. ....Georg Hackl, Germany	3:21.571
2. ....Markus Prock, Austria	3:21.584
3. ....Armin Zoggeler, Italy	3:21.833

DOUBLES

1. ....K. Brugger and W. Huber, Italy	1:36.720
2. ....H. Raffl and N. Huber, Italy	1:36.769
3. ....S. Krausse and J. Behrendt, Ger.	1:36.945

Women

SINGLES

1. ....Gerda Weissensteiner, Italy	3:15.517
2. ....Susi Erdmann, Germany	3:16.276
3. ....Andrea Tagwerker, Austria	3:16.652

FIGURE SKATING

Men

1. ....Alexei Urmanov, Russia
2. ....Elvis Stojko, Canada
3. ....Philippe Candeloro, France

Women

1. ....Oksana Baiul, Ukraine
2. ....Nancy Kerrigan, United States
3. ....Chen Lu, China

Pairs

1. ..Ekaterina Gordeeva and Sergei Grinkov, Russia
2. ..Natalia Mishkutienok and Artur Dmitriev, Russia
3. ..Isabella Brasseur and Lloyd Eisler, Canada

Ice Dancing

1. ..Oksana Gritschuk and Evgeni Platov, Russia
2. ..Maia Usova and Alexander Zhulin, Russia
3. ..Jayne Torvill and Christopher Dean, Great Britain

SPEED SKATING

Men

500 METERS

1. ..Aleksandr Golubev, Russia	36.33 OR
2. ..Sergei Klevchenya, Russia	36.39
3. ..Manabu Horii, Japan	36.53

1000 METERS

1. ....Dan Jansen, United States	1:12.43 WR
2. ..Igor Zhelezovsky, Belarus	1:12.72
3. ..Sergei Klevchenya, Russia	1:12.85

1500 METERS

1. ..Johann Olav Koss, Norway	1:51.29 WR
2. ..Rintje Ritsma, The Netherlands	1:54.85
3. ..Falko Zandstra, The Netherlands	1:54.90

Women

500 METERS

1. ..Bonnie Blair, United States	39.25
2. ..Susan Auch, Canada	39.61
3. ..Franziska Schenk, Germany	39.70

1000 METERS

1. ..Bonnie Blair, United States	1:18.74
2. ..Anke Baier, Germany	1:20.12
3. ..Qiaobo Ye, China	1:20.22

1500 METERS

1. ..Emese Hunyady, Austria	2:02.19
2. ..Svetlana Fedotkina, Russia	2:02.69
3. ..Seiko Hashimoto, Japan	2:06.88

Note: OR=Olympic Record; WR=World Record; EOR=Equals Olympic Record; EWR=Equals World Record; WB=World Best.

SPEED SKATING *(Cont.)*

Men *(Cont.)*

5000 METERS

1. ..Johann Olav Koss, Norway	6:34.96 WR
2. ..Kjell Storelid, Norway	6:42.68
3. ..Rintje Ritsma, Netherlands	6:43.94

10,000 METERS

1. ..Johann Olav Koss, Norway	13:30.55 WR
2. ..Kjell Storelid, Norway	13:49.25
3. ..Bart Veldkamp, The Netherlands	13:56.73

Women *(Cont.)*

3000 METERS

1. ..Gunda Niemann, Germany	4:19.90
2. ..Heike Warnicke, Germany	4:22.88
3. ..Emese Hunyady, Austria	4:24.64

5000 METERS

1. ..Gunda Niemann, Germany	7:31.57
2. ..Heike Warnicke, Germany	7:37.59
3. ..Claudia Pechstein, Germany	7:39.80

SHORT TRACK SPEED SKATING

Men

500 METERS

1. ..Chae Ji-Hoon, South Korea	43.45
2. ..Mirko Vuillermin, Italy	43.47
3. ..Nicholas Gooch, Great Britain	43.68

1000 METERS

1. ...Ki-Hoon Kim, South Korea	1:34.57
2. ..Ji-Hoon Chae, South Korea	1:34.92
3. ..Marc Gagnon, Canada	DNF

5000-METER RELAY

1. ...Italy	7:11.74 OR
2. ..United States	7:13.37
3. ..Australia	7:13.68

Women

500 METERS

1. ..Cathy Turner, United States	45.98 OR
2. ..Yanmei Zhang, China	46.44
3. ..Amy Peterson, United States	46.76

1000 METERS

1. ..Chun Lee-Kyung, South Korea	1:36.87
2. ..Nathalie Lambert, Canada	1:36.97
3. ..Kim So-Hee, South Korea	1:37.09

3000-METER RELAY

1. ...South Korea	4:26.64 OR
2. ..Canada	4:32.04
3. ..United States	4:39.34

ALPINE SKIING

Men

DOWNHILL

1. ..Tommy Moe, United States	1:45.75
2. ..Kjetil Andre Aamodt, Norway	1:45.79
3. ..Edward Podivinsky, Canada	1:45.87

SUPER GIANT SLALOM

1. ..Markus Wasmeier, Germany	1:32.53
2. ..Tommy Moe, United States	1:32.61
3. ..Kjetil Andre Aamodt, Norway	1:32.93

GIANT SLALOM

1. ..Markus Wasmeier, Germany	2:52.46
2. ..Urs Kaelin, Switzerland	2:52.48
3. ..Christian Mayer, Austria	2:52.58

SLALOM

1. ..Thomas Stangassinger, Austria	2:02.02
2. ..Alberto Tomba, Italy	2:02.17
3. ..Jure Kosir, Slovenia	2:02.53

COMBINED

	Pts
1. ..Lasse Kjus, Norway	3:17.53
2. ..Kjell Andre Aamodt, Norway	3:18.55
3. ..Harald Strand Nilsen, Norway	3:19.14

Women

DOWNHILL

1. ..Katja Seizinger, Germany	1:35.93
2. ..Picabo Street, United States	1:36.59
3. ..Isolde Kostner, Italy	1:36.85

SUPER GIANT SLALOM

1. ..Diann Roffe-Steinrotter, U.S.	1:22.15
2. ..Svetlana Gladischeva, Russia	1:22.44
3. ..Isolde Kostner, Italy	1:22.45

GIANT SLALOM

1. ..Deborah Compagnoni, Italy	2:30.97
2. ..Martina Ertl, Germany	2:32.19
2. ..Vreni Schneider, Switzerland	2:32.97

SLALOM

1. ..Vreni Schneider, Switzerland	1:56.01
2. ..Elfriede Eder, Austria	1:56.35
3. ..Katja Koren, Slovenia	1:56.61

COMBINED

1. ..Pernilla Wiberg, Sweden	3:05.16
2. ..Vreni Schneider, Switzerland	3:05.29
3. ..Alenka Dovzan, Slovenia	3:06.64

Note: OR=Olympic Record; WR=World Record; EOR=Equals Olympic Record; EWR=Equals World Record; WB=World Best; DNF=Did Not Finish.

ALPINE SKIING *(Cont.)*

FREESTYLE SKIING

Men
MOGUL

		Pts
1.	..Jean-Luc Brassard, Canada	27.24
2.	..Sergei Shoupletsov, Russia	26.90
3.	..Edgar Grospiron, France	26.64

AERIAL

		Pts
1.	..Andreas Schoenbaechler, Switz.	234.67
2.	..Philippe Laroche, Canada	228.63
3.	..Lloyd Langlois, Canada	222.44

Women
MOGUL

		Pts
1.	..Stine Lise Hattestad, Norway	25.97
2.	..Liz McIntyre, United States	25.89
3.	..Elizaveta Kojevnikova, Russia	25.81

AERIAL

		Pts
1.	..Lina Cherjazova, Uzbekistan	166.84
2.	..Marie Lindgren, Sweden	165.88
3.	..Hilde Synnove Lid, Norway	164.13

NORDIC SKIING

Men

10 KILOMETERS (CLASSICAL)

1.	..Bjorn Daehlie, Norway	24:20.1
2.	..Vladimir Smirnov, Russia	24:38.3
3.	..Marco Albarello, Italy	24:42.3

30 KILOMETERS (CLASSICAL)

1.	..Thomas Alsgaard, Norway	1:12:26.4
2.	..Bjorn Daehlie, Norway	1:13:13.6
3.	..Myka Myllyla, Finland	1:14:14.5

50 KILOMETERS (FREESTYLE)

1.	..Vladimir Smirnov, Kazakhstan	2:07:20.3
2.	..Myka Myllyla, Finland	2:08:41.9
3.	..Sture Sivertsen, Norway	2:08:49.0

15 KILOMETERS (FREESTYLE)

1.	..Bjorn Daehlie, Norway	1:00:08.8
2.	..Vladimir Smirnov, Kazakhstan	1:00:38.0
3.	..Silvio Fauner, Italy	1:01:48.6

4 X 10 KILOMETER RELAY (MIXED)

1.	................Italy	1:41:15.0
2.	................Norway	1:41:15.4
3.	................Finland	1:42:15.6

SKI JUMPING (NORMAL HILL)

		Pts
1.	..Espen Bredesen, Norway	282.0
2.	..Lasse Ottesen, Norway	268.0
3.	..Dieter Thoma, Germany	260.5

SKI JUMPING (LARGE HILL)

		Pts
1.	..Jens Weisflogg, Germany	274.5
2.	..Espen Bredesen, Norway	266.5
3.	..Andreas Goldberger, Austria	255.0

TEAM SKI JUMPING

		Pts
1.	................Germany	970.1
2.	................Japan	956.9
3.	................Austria	918.9

NORDIC COMBINED

1.	................Fred B. Lundberg, Norway	457.970
2.	................Takanori Kono, Japan	446.345
3.	................Bjarte Engen Vik, Norway	446.175

TEAM COMBINED

1.	................Japan	1368.860
2.	................Norway	1310.940
3.	................Switzerland	1275.240

Women

5 KILOMETERS (CLASSICAL)

1.	..Lyubov Egorova, Russia	14:08.8
2.	..Manuela Di Centa, Italy	14:28.3
3.	..Marja-Liisa Kirvesniemi, Finland	14:36.0

15 KILOMETERS (FREESTYLE)

1.	..Manuela Di Centa, Italy	39:44.5
2.	..Lyubov Egorova, Russia	41:03.0
3.	..Nina Gavriluk, Russia	41:10.4

10 KILOMETERS (FREESTYLE)

1.	..Lyubov Egorova, Russia	41:38.1
2.	..Maunela Di Centa, Italy	41:46.4
3.	..Stefania Belmondo, Italy	42:21.1

30 KILOMETERS (CLASSICAL)

1.	..Manuela Di Centa, Italy	1:25:41.6
2.	..Marit Wold, Norway	1:25:57.8
3.	..Marja-Liisa Kirvesniemi, Finland	1:26:13.6

4 X 5 KILOMETER RELAY (MIXED)

1.	...................Russia	57:12.5
2.	...................Norway	57:42.6
3.	...................Italy	58:42.6

Olympic Games Locations and Dates

Summer

	Year	Site	Dates	Men	Women	Nations	Most Medals	US Medals
I	1896	Athens, Greece	Apr 6-15	311	0	13	Greece (10-19-18—47)	11-6-2—19 (2nd)
II	1900	Paris, France	May 20-Oct 28	1319	11	22	France (29-41-32—102)	20-14-19—53 (2nd)
III	1904	St Louis, United States	July 1-Nov 23	681	6	12	United States (80-86-72—238)	
—	1906	Athens, Greece	Apr 22-May 28	77	7	20	France (15-9-16—40)	12-6-5—23 (4th)
IV	1908	London, Great Britain	Apr 27-Oct 31	1999	36	23	Britain (56-50-39—145)	23-12-12—47 (2nd)
V	1912	Stockholm, Sweden	May 5-July 22	2490	57	28	Sweden (24-24-17—65)	23-19-19—61 (2nd)
VI	1916	Berlin, Germany	Cancelled because of war					
VII	1920	Antwerp, Belgium	Apr 20-Sep 12	2543	64	29	United States (41-27-28—96)	
VIII	1924	Paris, France	May 4-July 27	2956	136	44	United States (45-27-27—99)	
IX	1928	Amsterdam, Netherlands	May 17-Aug 12	2724	290	46	United States (22-18-16—56)	
X	1932	Los Angeles, United States	July 30-Aug 14	1281	127	37	United States (41-32-31—104)	
XI	1936	Berlin, Germany	Aug 1-16	3738	328	49	Germany (33-26-30—89)	24-20-12—56 (2nd)
XII	1940	Tokyo, Japan	Cancelled because of war					
XIII	1944	London, Great Britain	Cancelled because of war					
XIV	1948	London, Great Britain	July 29-Aug 14	3714	385	59	United States (38-27-19—84)	
XV	1952	Helsinki, Finland	July 19-Aug 3	4407	518	69	United States (40-19-17—76)	
XVI	1956	Melbourne, Australia*	Nov 22-Dec 8	2958	384	67	USSR (37-29-32—98)	32-25-17—74 (2nd)
XVII	1960	Rome, Italy	Aug 25-Sep 11	4738	610	83	USSR (43-29-31—103)	34-21-16—71 (2nd)
XVIII	1964	Tokyo, Japan	Oct 10-24	4457	683	93	United States (36-26-28—90)	
XIX	1968	Mexico City, Mexico	Oct 12-27	4750	781	112	United States (45-28-34—107)	
XX	1972	Munich, West Germany	Aug 26-Sep 10	5848	1299	122	USSR (50-27-22—99)	33-31-30—94 (2nd)
XXI	1976	Montreal, Canada	July 17-Aug 1	4834	1251	92†	USSR (49-41-35—125)	34-35-25—94 (2nd)
XXII	1980	Moscow, USSR	July 19-Aug 3	4265	1088	81‡	USSR (80-69-46—195)	Did not compete
XXIII	1984	Los Angeles, United States	July 28-Aug 12	5458	1620	141#	United States (83-61-30—174)	
XXIV	1988	Seoul, South Korea	Sep 17-Oct 2	7105	2476	160	USSR (55-31-46—132)	36-31-27—94 (3rd)
XXV	1992	Barcelona, Spain	July 25-Aug. 9	7555	3008	172	Unified Team (45-38-29—112)	37-34-37—108 (2nd)

*The equestrian events were held in Stockholm, Sweden, June 10-17, 1956.

†This figure includes Cameroon, Egypt, Morocco, and Tunisia, countries that boycotted the 1976 Olympics after some of their athletes had already competed.

‡The US was among 65 countries that refused to participate in the 1980 Summer Games in Moscow.

#The USSR, East Germany, and 14 other countries skipped the Summer Games in Los Angeles.

Winter

	Year	Site	Dates	Men	Women	Nations	Most Medals	US Medals
					Competitors			
I	1924	Chamonix, France	Jan 25-Feb 4	281	13	16	Norway (4-7-6—17)	1-2-1—4 (3rd)
II	1928	St Moritz, Switzerland	Feb 11-19	468	27	25	Norway (6-4-5—15)	2-2-2—6 (2nd)
III	1932	Lake Placid, United States	Feb 4-15	274	32	17	United States (6-4-2—12)	
IV	1936	Garmisch-Partenkirchen, Germany	Feb 6-16	675	80	28	Norway (7-5-3—15)	1-0-3—4 (T-5th)
—	1940	Garmisch-Partenkirchen, Germany	Cancelled because of war					
—	1944	Cortina d'Ampezzo, Italy	Cancelled because of war					
V	1948	St Moritz, Switzerland	Jan 30-Feb 8	636	77	28	Norway (4-3-3—10) Sweden (4-3-3—10) Switzerland (3-4-3—10)	3-4-2—9 (4th)
VI	1952	Oslo, Norway	Feb 14-25	623	109	30	Norway (7-3-6—16)	4-6-1—11 (2nd)
VII	1956	Cortina d'Ampezzo, Italy	Jan 26-Feb 5	686	132	32	USSR (7-3-6—16)	2-3-2—7 (T-4th)
VIII	1960	Squaw Valley, United States	Feb 18-28	521	144	30	USSR (7-5-9—21)	3-4-3—10 (2nd)
IX	1964	Innsbruck, Austria	Jan 29-Feb 9	986	200	36	USSR (11-8-6—25)	1-2-3—6 (7th)
X	1968	Grenoble, France	Feb 6-18	1081	212	37	Norway (6-6-2—14)	1-5-1—7 (T-7th)
XI	1972	Sapporo, Japan	Feb 3-13	1015	217	35	USSR (8-5-3—16)	3-2-3—8 (6th)
XII	1976	Innsbruck, Austria	Feb 4-15	900	228	37	USSR (13-6-8—27)	3-3-4—10 (T-3rd)
XIII	1980	Lake Placid, United States	Feb 14-23	833	234	37	USSR (10-6-6—22)	6-4-2—12 (3rd)
XIV	1984	Sarajevo, Yugoslavia	Feb 7-19	1002	276	49	USSR (6-10-9—25)	4-4-0—8 (T-5th)
XV	1988	Calgary, Canada	Feb 13-28	1128	317	57	USSR (11-9-9—29)	2-1-3—6 (T-8th)
XVI	1992	Albertville, France	Feb 8-23	1318	490	65	Germany (10-10-6—26)	5-4-2—11 (6th)
XVII	1994	Lillehammer, Norway	Feb 11-27	1302	542		Norway (10-11-5—26)	6-5-2—13 (T-5th)

Summer Games Champions

TRACK AND FIELD

Men

100 METERS

1896....Thomas Burke, United States	12.0	
1900....Frank Jarvis, United States	11.0	
1904....Archie Hahn, United States	11.0	
1906....Archie Hahn, United States	11.2	
1908....Reginald Walker, South Africa	10.8 OR	
1912....Ralph Craig, United States	10.8	
1920....Charles Paddock, United States	10.8	
1924....Harold Abrahams, Great Britain	10.6 OR	
1928....Percy Williams, Canada	10.8	
1932....Eddie Tolan, United States	10.3 OR	
1936....Jesse Owens, United States	10.3	
1948....Harrison Dillard, United States	10.3	
1952....Lindy Remigino, United States	10.4	
1956....Bobby Morrow, United States	10.5	
1960....Armin Hary, West Germany	10.2 OR	
1964....Bob Hayes, United States	10.0 EWR	
1968....Jim Hines, United States	9.95 WR	
1972....Valery Borzov, USSR	10.14	
1976....Hasely Crawford, Trinidad	10.06	
1980....Allan Wells, Great Britain	10.25	
1984....Carl Lewis, United States	9.99	
1988....Carl Lewis, United States*	9.92 WR	
1992....Linford Christie, Great Britain	9.96	

*Ben Johnson, Canada, disqualified.

TRACK AND FIELD *(Cont.)*

Men *(Cont.)*

200 METERS

Year	Champion	Time
1900	John Walter Tewksbury, United States	22.2
1904	Archie Hahn, United States	21.6 OR
1906	Not held	
1908	Robert Kerr, Canada	22.6
1912	Ralph Craig, United States	21.7
1920	Allen Woodring, United States	22.0
1924	Jackson Scholz, United States	21.6
1928	Percy Williams, Canada	21.8
1932	Eddie Tolan, United States	21.2 OR
1936	Jesse Owens, United States	20.7 OR
1948	Mel Patton, United States	21.1
1952	Andrew Stanfield, United States	20.7
1956	Bobby Morrow, United States	20.6 OR
1960	Livio Berruti, Italy	20.5 EWR
1964	Henry Carr, United States	20.3 OR
1968	Tommie Smith, United States	19.83 WR
1972	Valery Borzov, USSR	20.00
1976	Donald Quarrie, Jamaica	20.23
1980	Pietro Mennea, Italy	20.19
1984	Carl Lewis, United States	19.80 OR
1988	Joe DeLoach, United States	19.75 OR
1992	Mike Marsh, United States	20.01

400 METERS

Year	Champion	Time
1896	Thomas Burke, United States	54.2
1900	Maxey Long, United States	49.4 OR
1904	Harry Hillman, United States	49.2 OR
1906	Paul Pilgrim, United States	53.2
1908	Wyndham Halswelle, Great Britain	50.0
1912	Charles Reidpath, United States	48.2 OR
1920	Bevil Rudd, South Africa	49.6
1924	Eric Liddell, Great Britain	47.6 OR
1928	Ray Barbuti, United States	47.8
1932	William Carr, United States	46.2 WR
1936	Archie Williams, United States	46.5
1948	Arthur Wint, Jamaica	46.2
1952	George Rhoden, Jamaica	45.9
1956	Charles Jenkins, United States	46.7
1960	Otis Davis, United States	44.9 WR
1964	Michael Larrabee, United States	45.1
1968	Lee Evans, United States	43.86 WR
1972	Vincent Matthews, United States	44.66
1976	Alberto Juantorena, Cuba	44.26
1980	Viktor Markin, USSR	44.60
1984	Alonzo Babers, United States	44.27
1988	Steve Lewis, United States	43.87
1992	Quincy Watts, United States	43.50 OR

800 METERS

Year	Champion	Time
1896	Edwin Flack, Australia	2:11
1900	Alfred Tysoe, Great Britain	2:01.2
1904	James Lightbody, United States	1:56 OR
1906	Paul Pilgrim, United States	2:01.5
1908	Mel Sheppard, United States	1:52.8 WR
1912	James Meredith, United States	1:51.9 WR
1920	Albert Hill, Great Britain	1:53.4
1924	Douglas Lowe, Great Britain	1:52.4
1928	Douglas Lowe, Great Britain	1:51.8 OR

800 METERS *(Cont.)*

Year	Champion	Time
1932	Thomas Hampson, Great Britain	1:49.8 WR
1936	John Woodruff, United States	1:52.9
1948	Mal Whitfield, United States	1:49.2 OR
1952	Mal Whitfield, United States	1:49.2 EOR
1956	Thomas Courtney, United States	1:47.7 OR
1960	Peter Snell, New Zealand	1:46.3 OR
1964	Peter Snell, New Zealand	1:45.1 OR
1968	Ralph Doubell, Australia	1:44.3 EWR
1972	Dave Wottle, United States	1:45.9
1976	Alberto Juantorena, Cuba	1:43.50 WR
1980	Steve Ovett, Great Britain	1:45.40
1984	Joaquim Cruz, Brazil	1:43.00 OR
1988	Paul Ereng, Kenya	1:43.45
1992	William Tanui, Kenya	1:43.66

1500 METERS

Year	Champion	Time
1896	Edwin Flack, Australia	4:33.2
1900	Charles Bennett, Great Britain	4:06.2 WR
1904	James Lightbody, United States	4:05.4 WR
1906	James Lightbody, United States	4:12.0
1908	Mel Sheppard, United States	4:03.4 OR
1912	Arnold Jackson, Great Britain	3:56.8 OR
1920	Albert Hill, Great Britain	4:01.8
1924	Paavo Nurmi, Finland	3:53.6 OR
1928	Harry Larva, Finland	3:53.2 OR
1932	Luigi Beccali, Italy	3:51.2 OR
1936	Jack Lovelock, New Zealand	3:47.8 WR
1948	Henri Eriksson, Sweden	3:49.8
1952	Josef Barthel, Luxemburg	3:45.1 OR
1956	Ron Delany, Ireland	3:41.2 OR
1960	Herb Elliott, Australia	3:35.6 WR
1964	Peter Snell, New Zealand	3:38.1
1968	Kipchoge Keino, Kenya	3:34.9 OR
1972	Pekkha Vasala, Finland	3:36.3
1976	John Walker, New Zealand	3:39.17
1980	Sebastian Coe, Great Britain	3:38.4
1984	Sebastian Coe, Great Britain	3:32.53 OR
1988	Peter Rono, Kenya	3:35.96
1992	Fermin Cacho, Spain	3:40.12

5000 METERS

Year	Champion	Time
1912	Hannes Kolehmainen, Finland	14:36.6 WR
1920	Joseph Guillemot, France	14:55.6
1924	Paavo Nurmi, Finland	14:31.2 OR
1928	Villie Ritola, Finland	14:38
1932	Lauri Lehtinen, Finland	14:30 OR
1936	Gunnar Höckert, Finland	14:22.2 OR
1948	Gaston Reiff, Belgium	14:17.6 OR
1952	Emil Zatopek, Czechoslovakia	14:06.6 OR
1956	Vladimir Kuts, USSR	13:39.6 OR
1960	Murray Halberg, New Zealand	13:43.4
1964	Bob Schul, United States	13:48.8
1968	Mohamed Gammoudi, Tunisia	14:05.0
1972	Lasse Viren, Finland	13:26.4 OR
1976	Lasse Viren, Finland	13:24.76
1980	Miruts Yifter, Ethiopia	13:21.0
1984	Said Aouita, Morocco	13:05.59 OR
1988	John Ngugi, Kenya	13:11.70
1992	Dieter Baumann, Germany	13:12.52

Note: OR=Olympic Record; WR=World Record; EOR=Equals Olympic Record; EWR=Equals World Record; WB=World Best.

TRACK AND FIELD *(Cont.)*

Men *(Cont.)*

10,000 METERS

1912	Hannes Kolehmainen, Finland	31:20.8
1920	Paavo Nurmi, Finland	31:45.8
1924	Vilho (Ville) Ritola, Finland	30:23.2 WR
1928	Paavo Nurmi, Finland	30:18.8 OR
1932	Janusz Kusocinski, Poland	30:11.4 OR
1936	Ilmari Salminen, Finland	30:15.4
1948	Emil Zatopek, Czechoslovakia	29:59.6 OR
1952	Emil Zatopek, Czechoslovakia	29:17.0 OR
1956	Vladimir Kuts, USSR	28:45.6 OR
1960	Pyotr Bolotnikov, USSR	28:32.2 OR
1964	Billy Mills, United States	28:24.4 OR
1968	Naftali Temu, Kenya	29:27.4
1972	Lasse Viren, Finland	27:38.4 WR
1976	Lasse Viren, Finland	27:40.38
1980	Miruts Yifter, Ethiopia	27:42.7
1984	Alberto Cova, Italy	27:47.54
1988	Brahim Boutaib, Morocco	27:21.46 OR
1992	Khalid Skah, Morocco	27:46.70

MARATHON

1896	Spiridon Louis, Greece	2:58:50
1900	Michel Theato, France	2:59:45
1904	Thomas Hicks, United States	3:28:53
1906	William Sherring, Canada	2:51:23.6
1908	John Hayes, United States	2:55:18.4 OR
1912	Kenneth McArthur, South Africa	2:36:54.8
1920	Hannes Kolehmainen, Finland	2:32:35.8 WB
1924	Albin Stenroos, Finland	2:41:22.6
1928	Boughera El Ouafi, France	2:32:57
1932	Juan Zabala, Argentina	2:31:36 OR
1936	Kijung Son, Japan (Korea)	2:29:19.2 OR
1948	Delfo Cabrera, Argentina	2:34:51.6
1952	Emil Zatopek, Czechoslovakia	2:23:03.2 OR
1956	Alain Mimoun O'Kacha, France	2:25:00.0
1960	Abebe Bikila, Ethiopia	2:15:16.2 WB
1964	Abebe Bikila, Ethiopia	2:12:11.2 WB
1968	Mamo Wolde, Ethiopia	2:20:26.4
1972	Frank Shorter, United States	2:12:19.8
1976	Waldemar Cierpinski, East Germany	2:09:55 OR
1980	Waldemar Cierpinski, East Germany	2:11:03.0
1984	Carlos Lopes, Portugal	2:09:21.0 OR
1988	Gelindo Bordin, Italy	2:10:32
1992	Hwang Young-Cho, S Korea	2:13:23

Note: Marathon distances: 1896, 1904—40,000 meters; 1900—40,260 meters; 1906—41,860 meters; 1912—40,200 meters; 1920—42,750 meters; 1908 and since 1924—42,195 meters (26 miles, 385 yards).

110-METER HURDLES

1896	Thomas Curtis, United States	17.6
1900	Alvin Kraenzlein, United States	15.4 OR
1904	Frederick Schule, United States	16.0
1906	Robert Leavitt, United States	16.2
1908	Forrest Smithson, United States	15.0 WR
1912	Frederick Kelly, United States	15.1
1920	Earl Thomson, Canada	14.8 WR
1924	Daniel Kinsey, United States	15.0
1928	Sydney Atkinson, South Africa	14.8
1932	George Saling, United States	14.6
1936	Forrest Towns, United States	14.2
1948	William Porter, United States	13.9 OR
1952	Harrison Dillard, United States	13.7 OR
1956	Lee Calhoun, United States	13.5 OR
1960	Lee Calhoun, United States	13.8
1964	Hayes Jones, United States	13.6
1968	Willie Davenport, United States	13.3 OR
1972	Rod Milburn, United States	13.24 EWR
1976	Guy Drut, France	13.30
1980	Thomas Munkelt, East Germany	13.39
1984	Roger Kingdom, United States	13.20 OR
1988	Roger Kingdom, United States	12.98 OR
1992	Mark McKoy, Canada	13.12

400-METER HURDLES

1900	John Walter Tewksbury, United States	57.6
1904	Harry Hillman, United States	53.0
1906	Not held	
1908	Charles Bacon, United States	55.0 WR
1912	Not held	
1920	Frank Loomis, United States	54.0 WR
1924	F. Morgan Taylor, United States	52.6
1928	David Burghley, Great Britain	53.4 OR
1932	Robert Tisdall, Ireland	51.7
1936	Glenn Hardin, United States	52.4
1948	Roy Cochran, United States	51.1 OR
1952	Charles Moore, United States	50.8 OR
1956	Glenn Davis, United States	50.1 EOR
1960	Glenn Davis, United States	49.3 EOR
1964	Rex Cawley, United States	49.6
1968	Dave Hemery, Great Britain	48.12 WR
1972	John Akii-Bua, Uganda	47.82 WR
1976	Edwin Moses, United States	47.64 WR
1980	Volker Beck, East Germany	48.70
1984	Edwin Moses, United States	47.75
1988	Andre Phillips, United States	47.19 OR
1992	Kevin Young, United States	46.78 WR

THEY SAID IT

Rick Gentile, the senior vice president of CBS Sports, on host Greg Gumbel's Olympic performance at the Lillehammer Winter Games: "He filled the Greg Gumbel role very well."

TRACK AND FIELD (Cont.)

Men (Cont.)

3000-METER STEEPLECHASE

1920	Percy Hodge, Great Britain	10:00.4 OR
1924	Vilho (Ville) Ritola, Finland	9:33.6 OR
1928	Toivo Loukola, Finland	9:21.8 WR
1932	Volmari Iso-Hollo, Finland	10:33.4*
1936	Volmari Iso-Hollo, Finland	9:03.8 WR
1948	Thore Sjöstrand, Sweden	9:04.6
1952	Horace Ashenfelter, United States	8:45.4 WR
1956	Chris Brasher, Great Britain	8:41.2 OR
1960	Zdzislaw Krzyszkowiak, Poland	8:34.2 OR
1964	Gaston Roelants, Belgium	8:30.8 OR
1968	Amos Biwott, Kenya	8:51
1972	Kipchoge Keino, Kenya	8:23.6 OR
1976	Anders Gärderud, Sweden	8:08.2 WR
1980	Bronislaw Malinowski, Poland	8:09.7
1984	Julius Korir, Kenya	8:11.8
1988	Julius Kariuki, Kenya	8:05.51 OR
1992	Matthew Birir, Kenya	8:08.84

*About 3450 meters; extra lap by error.

4 X 100-METER RELAY

1912	Great Britain	42.4 OR
1920	United States	42.2 WR
1924	United States	41.0 EWR
1928	United States	41.0 EWR
1932	United States	40.0 EWR
1936	United States	39.8 WR
1948	United States	40.6
1952	United States	40.1
1956	United States	39.5 WR
1960	West Germany	39.5 EWR
1964	United States	39.0 WR
1968	United States	38.2 WR
1972	United States	38.19 EWR
1976	United States	38.33
1980	USSR	38.26
1984	United States	37.83 WR
1988	USSR	38.19
1992	United States	37.40 WR

4 X 400-METER RELAY

1908	United States	3:29.4
1912	United States	3:16.6 WR
1920	Great Britain	3:22.2
1924	United States	3:16.0 WR
1928	United States	3:14.2 WR
1932	United States	3:08.2 WR
1936	Great Britain	3:09.0
1948	United States	3:10.4 WR
1952	Jamaica	3:03.9 WR
1956	United States	3:04.8
1960	United States	3:02.2 WR
1964	United States	3:00.7 WR
1968	United States	2:56.16 WR
1972	Kenya	2:59.8
1976	United States	2:58.65
1980	USSR	3:01.1
1984	United States	2:57.91
1988	United States	2:56.16 EWR
1992	United States	2:55.74 WR

20-KILOMETER WALK

1956	Leonid Spirin, USSR	1:31:27.4
1960	Vladimir Golubnichiy, USSR	1:33:07.2
1964	Kenneth Mathews, Great Britain	1:29:34.0 OR
1968	Vladimir Golubnichiy, USSR	1:33:58.4
1972	Peter Frenkel, East Germany	1:26:42.4 OR
1976	Daniel Bautista, Mexico	1:24:40.6 OR
1980	Maurizio Damilano, Italy	1:23:35.5 OR
1984	Ernesto Canto, Mexico	1:23:13.0 OR
1988	Jozef Pribilinec, Czechoslovakia	1:19:57.0 OR
1992	Daniel Plaza, Spain	1:21:45.0

50-KILOMETER WALK

1932	Thomas Green, Great Britain	4:50:10
1936	Harold Whitlock, Great Britain	4:30:41.4 OR
1948	John Ljunggren, Sweden	4:41:52
1952	Giuseppe Dordoni, Italy	4:28:07.8 OR
1956	Norman Read, New Zealand	4:30:42.8
1960	Donald Thompson, Great Britain	4:25:30 OR
1964	Abdon Parnich, Italy	4:11:12.4 OR
1968	Christoph Höhne, East Germany	4:20:13.6
1972	Bernd Kannenberg, West Germany	3:56:11.6 OR
1980	Hartwig Gauder, East Germany	3:49:24.0 OR
1984	Raul Gonzalez, Mexico	3:47:26.0 OR
1988	Viacheslav Ivanenko, USSR	3:38:29.0 OR
1992	Andrey Perlov, Unified Team	3:50:13

HIGH JUMP

1896	Ellery Clark, United States	5 ft 11¼ in
1900	Irving Baxter, United States	6 ft 2¾ in OR
1904	Samuel Jones, United States	5 ft 11 in
1906	Cornelius Leahy, Great Britain/Ireland	5 ft 10 in
1908	Harry Porter, United States	6 ft 3 in OR
1912	Alma Richards, United States	6 ft 4 in OR
1920	Richmond Landon, United States	6 ft 4 in OR
1924	Harold Osborn, United States	6 ft 6 in OR
1928	Robert W. King, United States	6 ft 4½ in
1932	Duncan McNaughton, Canada	6 ft 5½ in
1936	Cornelius Johnson, United States	6 ft 8 in OR
1948	John L. Winter, Australia	6 ft 6 in
1952	Walter Davis, United States	6 ft 8½ in OR
1956	Charles Dumas, United States	6 ft 11½ in OR
1960	Robert Shavlakadze, USSR	7 ft 1 in OR
1964	Valery Brumel, USSR	7 ft 1¾ in OR
1968	Dick Fosbury, United States	7 ft 4¼ in OR
1972	Yuri Tarmak, USSR	7 ft 3¾ in
1976	Jacek Wszola, Poland	7 ft 4½ in OR
1980	Gerd Wessig, East Germany	7 ft 8¾ in WR
1984	Dietmar Mögenburg, West Germany	7 ft 8½ in
1988	Gennadiy Avdeyenko, USSR	7 ft 9¾ in OR
1992	Javier Sotomayor, Cuba	7 ft 8 in.

Note: OR=Olympic Record; WR=World Record;
EOR=Equals Olympic Record; EWR=Equals World Record;
WB=World Best.

TRACK AND FIELD (Cont.)

Men (Cont.)

POLE VAULT

1896	...William Hoyt, United States	10 ft 10 in
1900	...Irving Baxter, United States	10 ft 10 in
1904	...Charles Dvorak, United States	11 ft 5¾ in
1906	...Fernand Gonder, France	11 ft 5¾ in
1908	...Alfred Gilbert, United States Edward Cooke, Jr, United States	12 ft 2 in OR
1912	...Harry Babcock, United States	12 ft 11½ in OR
1920	...Frank Foss, United States	13 ft 5 in WR
1924	...Lee Barnes, United States	12 ft 11½ in
1928	...Sabin Carr, United States	13 ft 9¼ in OR
1932	...William Miller, United States	14 ft 1¾ in OR
1936	...Earle Meadows, United States	14 ft 3¼ in OR
1948	...Guinn Smith, United States	14 ft 1¼ in
1952	...Robert Richards, United States	14 ft 11 in OR
1956	...Robert Richards, United States	14 ft 11½ in OR
1960	...Don Bragg, United States	15 ft 5 in OR
1964	...Fred Hansen, United States	16 ft 8¾ in OR
1968	...Bob Seagren, United States	17 ft 8½ in OR
1972	...Wolfgang Nordwig, East Germany	18 ft ½ in OR
1976	...Tadeusz Slusarski, Poland	18 ft ½ in EOR
1980	...Wladyslaw Kozakiewicz, Poland	18 ft 11½ in WR
1984	...Pierre Quinon, France	18 ft 10¼ in
1988	...Sergei Bubka, USSR	19 ft 9¼ in OR
1992	...Maksim Tarasov, Unified Team	19 ft ¼ in

LONG JUMP

1896	...Ellery Clark, United States	20 ft 10 in
1900	...Alvin Kraenzlein, United States	23 ft 6¾ in OR
1904	...Meyer Prinstein, United States	24 ft 1 in OR
1906	...Meyer Prinstein, United States	23 ft 7½ in
1908	...Frank Irons, United States	24 ft 6½ in OR
1912	Albert Gutterson, United States	24 ft 11¼ in OR
1920	...William Petersson, Sweden	23 ft 5½ in
1924	...DeHart Hubbard, United States	24 ft 5 in
1928	...Edward B. Hamm, United States	25 ft 4½ in OR
1932	...Edward Gordon, United States	25 ft ¾ in
1936	...Jesse Owens, United States	26 ft 5½ in OR
1948	...William Steele, United States	25 ft 8 in
1952	...Jerome Biffle, United States	24 ft 10 in
1956	...Gregory Bell, United States	25 ft 8¼ in
1960	Ralph Boston, United States	26 ft 7¾ in OR
1964	...Lynn Davies, Great Britain	26 ft 5¾ in
1968	...Bob Beamon, United States	29 ft 2½ in WR

LONG JUMP (Cont.)

1972	...Randy Williams, United States	27 ft ½ in
1976	...Arnie Robinson, United States	27 ft 4¾ in
1980	...Lutz Dombrowski, East Germany	28 ft ¼ in
1984	...Carl Lewis, United States	28 ft ¼ in
1988	...Carl Lewis, United States	28 ft 7½ in
1992	...Carl Lewis, United States	28 ft 5½ in

TRIPLE JUMP

1896	...James Connolly, United States	44 ft 11¾ in
1900	...Meyer Prinstein, United States	47 ft 5¾ in OR
1904	...Meyer Prinstein, United States	47 ft 1 in
1906	...Peter O'Connor, Great Britain/Ireland	46 ft 2¼ in
1908	...Timothy Ahearne, Great Britain/Ireland	48 ft 11¼ in OR
1912	...Gustaf Lindblom, Sweden	48 ft 5¼ in
1920	...Vilho Tuulos, Finland	47 ft 7 in
1924	...Anthony Winter, Australia	50 ft 11¼ in WR
1928	...Mikio Oda, Japan	49 ft 11 in
1932	...Chuhei Nambu, Japan	51 ft 7 in WR
1936	...Naoto Tajima, Japan	52 ft 6 in WR
1948	...Arne Ahman, Sweden	50 ft 6¼ in
1952	...Adhemar da Silva, Brazil	53 ft 2¾ in WR
1956	...Adhemar da Silva, Brazil	53 ft 7¾ in OR
1960	...Jozef Schmidt, Poland	55 ft 2 in
1964	...Jozef Schmidt, Poland	55 ft 3½ in OR
1968	...Viktor Saneyev, USSR	57 ft ¾ in WR
1972	...Viktor Saneyev, USSR	56 ft 11¾ in
1976	...Viktor Saneyev, USSR	56 ft 8¾ in
1980	...Jaak Uudmae, USSR	56 ft 11¼ in
1984	...Al Joyner, United States	56 ft 7½ in
1988	...Khristo Markov, Bulgaria	57 ft 9½ in OR
1992	...Mike Conley, United States	59 ft 7½ in

SHOT PUT

1896	...Robert Garrett, United States	36 ft 9¾ in
1900	...Richard Sheldon, United States	46 ft 3¼ in OR
1904	...Ralph Rose, United States	48 ft 7 in WR
1906	...Martin Sheridan, United States	40 ft 5¼ in
1908	...Ralph Rose, United States	46 ft 7½ in
1912	...Pat McDonald, United States	50 ft 4 in OR
1920	...Ville Porhola, Finland	48 ft 7¼ in
1924	...Clarence Houser, United States	49 ft 2¼ in
1928	...John Kuck, United States	52 ft ¾ in WR
1932	...Leo Sexton, United States	52 ft 6 in OR
1936	...Hans Woellke, Germany	53 ft 1¾ in OR
1948	...Wilbur Thompson, United States	56 ft 2 in OR
1952	...Parry O'Brien, United States	57 ft ½ in OR
1956	...Parry O'Brien, United States	60 ft 11¼ in OR
1960	...William Nieder, United States	64 ft 6¾ in OR

TRACK AND FIELD (Cont.)

Men (Cont.)

SHOT PUT (Cont.)

1964	Dallas Long, United States	66 ft 8½ in OR
1968	Randy Matson, United States	67 ft 4¾ in
1972	Wladyslaw Komar, Poland	69 ft 6 in OR
1976	Udo Beyer, East Germany	69 ft ¾ in
1980	Vladimir Kiselyov, USSR	70 ft ½ in OR
1984	Alessandro Andrei, Italy	69 ft 9 in
1988	Ulf Timmermann, East Germany	73 ft 8¾ in OR
1992	Mike Stulce, United States	71 ft 2½ in

DISCUS THROW

1896	Robert Garrett, United States	95 ft 7½ in
1900	Rudolf Bauer, Hungary	118 ft 3 in OR
1904	Martin Sheridan, United States	128 ft 10½ in OR
1906	Martin Sheridan, United States	136 ft
1908	Martin Sheridan, United States	134 ft 2 in OR
1912	Armas Taipele, Finland	148 ft 3 in OR
1920	Elmer Niklander, Finland	146 ft 7 in
1924	Clarence Houser, United States	151 ft 4 in OR
1928	Clarence Houser, United States	155 ft 3 in OR
1932	John Anderson, United States	162 ft 4 in OR
1936	Ken Carpenter, United States	165 ft 7 in OR
1948	Adolfo Consolini, Italy	173 ft 2 in OR
1952	Sim Iness, United States	180 ft 6 in OR
1956	Al Oerter, United States	184 ft 11 in OR
1960	Al Oerter, United States	194 ft 2 in OR
1964	Al Oerter, United States	200 ft 1 in OR
1968	Al Oerter, United States	212 ft 6 in OR
1972	Ludvik Danek, Czechoslovakia	211 ft 3 in
1976	Mac Wilkins, United States	221 ft 5 in OR
1980	Viktor Rashchupkin, USSR	218 ft 8 in
1984	Rolf Dannenberg, West Germany	218 ft 6 in
1988	Jürgen Schult, East Germany	225 ft 9 in OR
1992	Romas Ubartas, Lithuania	213 ft 8 in

HAMMER THROW

1900	John Flanagan, United States	163 ft 1 in
1904	John Flanagan, United States	168 ft 1 in OR
1906	Not held	
1908	John Flanagan, United States	170 ft 4 in OR
1912	Matt McGrath, United States	179 ft 7 in OR
1920	Pat Ryan, United States	173 ft 5 in
1924	Fred Tootell, United States	174 ft 10 in
1928	Patrick O'Callaghan, Ireland	168 ft 7 in
1932	Patrick O'Callaghan, Ireland	176 ft 11 in
1936	Karl Hein, Germany	185 ft 4 in OR
1948	Imre Nemeth, Hungary	183 ft 11 in
1952	Jozsef Csermak, Hungary	197 ft 11 in WR
1956	Harold Connolly, United States	207 ft 3 in OR
1960	Vasily Rudenkov, USSR	220 ft 2 in OR

HAMMER THROW (Cont.)

1964	Romuald Klim, USSR	228 ft 10 in OR
1968	Gyula Zsivotsky, Hungary	240 ft 8 in OR
1972	Anatoli Bondarchuk, USSR	247 ft 8 in OR
1976	Yuri Sedykh, USSR	254 ft 4 in OR
1980	Yuri Sedykh, USSR	268 ft 4 in WR
1984	Juha Tiainen, Finland	256 ft 2 in
1988	Sergei Litvinov, USSR	278 ft 2 in OR
1992	Andrey Abduvaliyev, Unified Team	270 ft 9 in

JAVELIN

1908	Erik Lemming, Sweden	179 ft 10 in
1912	Erik Lemming, Sweden	198 ft 11 in WR
1920	Jonni Myyrä, Finland	215 ft 10 in OR
1924	Jonni Myyrä, Finland	206 ft 6 in
1928	Eric Lundkvist, Sweden	218 ft 6 in OR
1932	Matti Jarvinen, Finland	238 ft 6 in OR
1936	Gerhard Stöck, Germany	235 ft 8 in
1948	Kai Rautavaara, Finland	228 ft 10½ in
1952	Cy Young, United States	242 ft 1 in OR
1956	Egil Danielson, Norway	281 ft 2¼ in WR
1960	Viktor Tsibulenko, USSR	277 ft 8 in
1964	Pauli Nevala, Finland	271 ft 2 in
1968	Janis Lusis, USSR	295 ft 7 in OR
1972	Klaus Wolfermann, West Germany	296 ft 10 in OR
1976	Miklos Nemeth, Hungary	310 ft 4 in WR
1980	Dainis Kuta, USSR	299 ft 2⅜ in
1984	Arto Härkönen, Finland	284 ft 8 in
1988	Tapio Korjus, Finland	276 ft 6 in
1992	Jan Zelezny, Czechoslovakia	294 ft 2 in OR

DECATHLON

		Pts
1904	Thomas Kiely, Ireland	6036
1912	Jim Thorpe, United States*	8412 WR
1920	Helge Lövland, Norway	6803
1924	Harold Osborn, United States	7711 WR
1928	Paavo Yrjölä, Finland	8053.29 WR
1932	James Bausch, United States	8462 WR
1936	Glenn Morris, United States	7900 WR
1948	Robert Mathias, United States	7139
1952	Robert Mathias, United States	7887 WR
1956	Milton Campbell, United States	7937 OR
1960	Rafer Johnson, United States	8392 OR
1964	Willi Holdorf, West Germany	7887
1968	Bill Toomey, United States	8193 OR
1972	Nikolai Avilov, USSR	8454 WR
1976	Bruce Jenner, United States	8617 WR
1980	Daley Thompson, Great Britain	8495
1984	Daley Thompson, Great Britain	8798 EWR
1988	Christian Schenk, East Germany	8488
1992	Robert Zmelik, Czechoslovakia	8611

*In 1913, Thorpe was disqualified for having played professional baseball in 1910. His record was restored in 1982.

Note: OR=Olympic Record; WR=World Record;

EOR=Equals Olympic Record; EWR=Equals World Record; WB=World Best.

TRACK AND FIELD *(Cont.)*

Women

100 METERS

1928	...Elizabeth Robinson, United States	12.2 EWR
1932	...Stella Walsh, Poland	11.9 EWR
1936	...Helen Stephens, United States	11.5
1948	....Francina Blankers-Koen, Netherlands	11.9
1952	...Marjorie Jackson, Australia	11.5 EWR
1956	...Betty Cuthbert, Australia	11.5 EWR
1960	...Wilma Rudolph, United States	11.0
1964	...Wyomia Tyus, United States	11.4
1968	...Wyomia Tyus, United States	11.0 WR
1972	...Renate Stecher, East Germany	11.07
1976	...Annegret Richter, West Germany	11.08
1980	..Lyudmila Kondratyeva, USSR	11.06
1984	...Evelyn Ashford, United States	10.97 OR
1988	...Florence Griffith Joyner, United States	10.54
1992	...Gail Devers, United States	10.82

200 METERS

1948	...Francina Blankers-Koen, Netherlands	24.4
1952	..Marjorie Jackson, Australia	23.7
1956	..Betty Cuthbert, Australia	23.4 EOR
1960	..Wilma Rudolph, United States	24.0
1964	..Edith McGuire, United States	23.0 OR
1968	..Irena Szewinska, Poland	22.5 WR
1972	..Renate Stecher, East Germany	22.40 EWR
1976	..Bärbel Eckert, East Germany	22.37 OR
1980	..Bärbel Wöckel (Eckert), East Germany	22.03 OR
1984	...Valerie Brisco-Hooks, United States	21.81 OR
1988	..Florence Griffith Joyner, United States	21.34 WR
1992	..Gwen Torrence, United States	21.81

400 METERS

1964	...Betty Cuthbert, Australia	52.0 OR
1968	...Colette Besson, France	52.0 EOR
1972	...Monika Zehrt, East Germany	51.08 OR
1976	...Irena Szewinska, Poland	49.29 WR
1980	...Marita Koch, East Germany	48.88 OR
1984	...Valerie Brisco-Hooks, United States	48.83 OR
1988	...Olga Bryzgina, USSR	48.65 OR
1992	...Marie-José Pérec, France	48.83

800 METERS

1928	....Lina Radke, Germany	2:16.8 WR
1932	....Not held 1932-1956	
1960	....Lyudmila Shevtsova, USSR	2:04.3 EWR
1964	....Ann Packer, Great Britain	2:01.1 OR
1968	....Madeline Manning, United States	2:00.9 OR
1972	....Hildegard Falck, West Germany	1:58.55 OR
1976	....Tatyana Kazankina, USSR	1:54.94 WR
1980	....Nadezhda Olizarenko, USSR	1:53.42 WR
1984	....Doina Melinte, Romania	1:57.6
1988	....Sigrun Wodars, East Germany	1:56.10
1992	....Ellen Van Langen, the Netherlands	1:55.54

1500 METERS

1972	....Lyudmila Bragina, USSR	4:01.4 WR
1976	....Tatyana Kazankina, USSR	4:05.48
1980	....Tatyana Kazankina, USSR	3:56.6 OR
1984	....Gabriella Dorio, Italy	4:03.25

1500 METERS *(Cont.)*

1988	....Paula Ivan, Romania	3:53.96 OR
1992	....Hassiba Boulmerka, Algeria	3:55.30

3000 METERS

1984	....Maricica Puica, Romania	8:35.96 OR
1988	....Tatyana Samolenko, USSR	8:26.53 OR
1992	....Elena Romanova, Unified Team	8:46.04

10,000 METERS

1988	....Olga Bondarenko, USSR	31:05.21 OR
1992	....Derartu Tulu, Ethiopia	31:06.02

MARATHON

1984	....Joan Benoit, United States	2:24:52
1988	....Rosa Mota, Portugal	2:25:40
1992	....Valentin Yegorova, Unified Team	2:32:41

80-METER HURDLES

1932	..Babe Didrikson, United States	11.7 WR
1936	..Trebisonda Valla, Italy	11.7
1948	..Francina Blankers-Koen, Netherlands	11.2 OR
1952	..Shirley Strickland, Australia	10.9 WR
1956	..Shirley Strickland, Australia	10.7 OR
1960	..Irina Press, USSR	10.8
1964	..Karin Balzer, East Germany	10.5
1968	..Maureen Caird, Australia	10.3 OR

100-METER HURDLES

1972	....Annelie Ehrhardt, East Germany	12.59 WR
1976	....Johanna Schaller, East Germany	12.77
1980	....Vera Komisova, USSR	12.56 OR
1984	....Benita Fitzgerald-Brown, United States	12.84
1988	....Yordanka Donkova, Bulgaria	12.38 OR
1992	....Paraskevi Patoulidou, Greece	12.64

400-METER HURDLES

1984	....Nawal el Moutawakel, Morocco	54.61 OR
1988	....Debra Flintoff-King, Australia	53.17 OR
1992	....Sally Gunnell, Great Britain	53.23

4 X 100-METER RELAY

1928	...............Canada	48.4 WR
1932	...............United States	46.9 WR
1936	...............United States	46.9
1948	...............Netherlands	47.5
1952	...............United States	45.9 WR
1956	...............Australia	44.5 WR
1960	...............United States	44.5
1964	...............Poland	43.6
1968	...............United States	42.8 WR
1972	...............West Germany	42.81 EWR
1976	...............East Germany	42.55 OR
1980	...............East Germany	41.60 WR
1984	...............United States	41.65
1988	...............United States	41.98
1992	...............United States	42.11

Note: OR=Olympic Record; WR=World Record; EOR=Equals Olympic Record; EWR=Equals World Record; WB=World Best.

TRACK AND FIELD (Cont.)

Women (Cont.)

4 X 400-METER RELAY

1972	East Germany	3:23 WR
1976	East Germany	3:19.23 WR
1980	USSR	3:20.02
1984	United States	3:18.29 OR
1988	USSR	3:15.18 WR
1992	Unified Team	3:20.20

HIGH JUMP

1928	Ethel Catherwood, Canada	5 ft 2½ in
1932	Jean Shiley, United States	5 ft 5¼ in WR
1936	Ibolya Csak, Hungary	5 ft 3 in
1948	Alice Coachman, United States	5 ft 6 in OR
1952	Esther Brand, South Africa	5 ft 5¾ in
1956	Mildred L. McDaniel, United States	5 ft 9¼ in WR
1960	Iolanda Balas, Romania	6 ft ¾ in OR
1964	Iolanda Balas, Romania	6 ft 2¾ in OR
1968	Miloslava Reskova, Czechoslovakia	5 ft 11½ in
1972	Ulrike Meyfarth, West Germany	6 ft 3½ in EWR
1976	Rosemarie Ackermann, East Germany	6 ft 4 in OR
1980	Sara Simeoni, Italy	6 ft 5½ in OR
1984	Ulrike Meyfarth, West Germany	6 ft 7½ in OR
1988	Louise Ritter, United States	6 ft 8 in OR
1992	Heike Henkel, Germany	6 ft 7½ in

LONG JUMP

1948	Olga Gyarmati, Hungary	18 ft 8¼ in
1952	Yvette Williams, New Zealand	20 ft 5¾ in OR
1956	Elzbieta Krzeskinska, Poland	20 ft 10 in EWR
1960	Vyera Krepkina, USSR	20 ft 10¾ in OR
1964	Mary Rand, Great Britain	22 ft 2¼ in WR
1968	Viorica Viscopoleanu, Romania	22 ft 4½ in WR
1972	Heidemarie Rosendahl, West Germany	22 ft 3 in
1976	Angela Voigt, East Germany	22 ft ¾ in
1980	Tatyana Kolpakova, USSR	23 ft 2 in OR
1984	Anisoara Stanciu, Romania	22 ft 10 in
1988	Jackie Joyner-Kersee, United States	24 ft 3½ in OR
1992	Heike Drechsler, Germany	23 ft 5¼ in

SHOT PUT

1948	Micheline Ostermeyer, France	45 ft 1½ in
1952	Galina Zybina, USSR	50 ft 1¾ in WR
1956	Tamara Tyshkevich, USSR	54 ft 5 in OR
1960	Tamara Press, USSR	56 ft 10 in OR
1964	Tamara Press, USSR	59 ft 6¼ in OR
1968	Margitta Gummel, East Germany	64 ft 4 in WR
1972	Nadezhda Chizhova, USSR	69 ft WR
1976	Ivanka Hristova, Bulgaria	69 ft 5¼ in OR
1980	Ilona Slupianek, East Germany	73 ft 6¼ in
1984	Claudia Losch, West Germany	67 ft 2¼ in

SHOT PUT (Cont.)

1988	Natalya Lisovskaya, USSR	72 ft 11¾ in
1992	Svetlana Kriveleva, Unified Team	69 ft 1¼ in

DISCUS THROW

1928	Helena Konopacka, Poland	129 ft 11¾ in WR
1932	Lillian Copeland, United States	133 ft 2 in OR
1936	Gisela Mauermayer, Germany	156 ft 3 in OR
1948	Micheline Ostermeyer, France	137 ft 6 in
1952	Nina Romaschkova, USSR	168 ft 8 in OR
1956	Olga Fikotova, Czechoslovakia	176 ft 1 in OR
1960	Nina Ponomaryeva, USSR	180 ft 9 in OR
1964	Tamara Press, USSR	187 ft 10 in OR
1968	Lia Manoliu, Romania	191 ft 2 in OR
1972	Faina Melnik, USSR	218 ft 7 in OR
1976	Evelin Schlaak, East Germany	226 ft 4 in OR
1980	Evelin Jahl (Schlaak), East Germany	229 ft 6 in OR
1984	Ria Stalman, Netherlands	214 ft 5 in
1988	Martina Hellmann, East Germany	237 ft 2 in OR
1992	Maritza Martén, Cuba	229 ft 10 in

JAVELIN THROW

1932	Babe Didrikson, United States	143 ft 4 in OR
1936	Tilly Fleischer, Germany	148 ft 3 in OR
1948	Herma Bauma, Austria	149 ft 6 in
1952	Dana Zatopkova, Czechoslovakia	165 ft 7 in
1956	Inese Jaunzeme, USSR	176 ft 8 in
1960	Elvira Ozolina, USSR	183 ft 8 in OR
1964	Mihaela Penes, Romania	198 ft 7 in
1968	Angela Nemeth, Hungary	198 ft
1972	Ruth Fuchs, East Germany	209 ft 7 in OR
1976	Ruth Fuchs, East Germany	216 ft 4 in OR
1980	Maria Colon, Cuba	224 ft 5 in OR
1984	Tessa Sanderson, Great Britain	228 ft 2 in OR
1988	Petra Felke, East Germany	245 ft OR
1992	Silke Renk, Germany	224 ft 2 in

PENTATHLON

		Pts
1964	Irina Press, USSR	5246 WR
1968	Ingrid Becker, West Germany	5098
1972	Mary Peters, Great Britain	4801 WR*
1976	Siegrun Siegl, East Germany	4745
1980	Nadezhda Tkachenko, USSR	5083 WR

*In 1971, 100-meter hurdles replaced 80-meter hurdles, necessitating a change in scoring tables.

HEPTATHLON

		Pts
1984	Glynis Nunn, Australia	6390 OR
1988	Jackie Joyner-Kersee, United States	7291 WR
1992	Jackie Joyner-Kersee, United States	7044

BASKETBALL

Men

1936

Final: United States 19, Canada 8
United States: Ralph Bishop, Joe Fortenberry, Carl Knowles, Jack Ragland, Carl Shy, William Wheatley, Francis Johnson, Samuel Balter, John Gibbons, Frank Lubin, Arthur Mollner, Donald Piper, Duane Swanson, Willard Schmidt

1948

Final: United States 65, France 21
United States: Cliff Barker, Don Barksdale, Ralph Beard, Lewis Beck, Vince Boryla, Gordon Carpenter, Alex Groza, Wallace Jones, Bob Kurland, Ray Lumpp, Robert Pitts, Jesse Renick, Bob Robinson, Ken Rollins

1952

Final: United States 36, USSR 25
United States: Charles Hoag, Bill Hougland, Melvin Dean Kelley, Bob Kenney, Clyde Lovellette, Marcus Freiberger, Victor Wayne Glasgow, Frank McCabe, Daniel Pippen, Howard Williams, Ronald Bontemps, Bob Kurland, William Lienhard, John Keller

1956

Final: United States 89, USSR 55
United States: Carl Cain, Bill Hougland, K. C. Jones, Bill Russell, James Walsh, William Evans, Burdette Haldorson, Ron Tomsic, Dick Boushka, Gilbert Ford, Bob Jeangerard, Charles Darling

1960

Final: United States 90, Brazil 63
United States: Jay Arnette, Walt Bellamy, Bob Boozer, Terry Dischinger, Jerry Lucas, Oscar Robertson, Adrian Smith, Burdette Haldorson, Darrall Imhoff, Allen Kelley, Lester Lane, Jerry West

1964

Final: United States 73, USSR 59
United States: Jim Barnes, Bill Bradley, Larry Brown, Joe Caldwell, Mel Counts, Richard Davies, Walt Hazzard, Lucius Jackson, John McCaffrey, Jeff Mullins, Jerry Shipp, George Wilson

1968

Final: United States 65, Yugoslavia 50
United States: John Clawson, Ken Spain, Jo-Jo White, Michael Barrett, Spencer Haywood, Charles Scott, William Hosket, Calvin Fowler, Michael Silliman, Glynn Saulters, James King, Donald Dee

1972

Final: USSR 51, United States 50
United States: Kenneth Davis, Doug Collins, Thomas Henderson, Mike Bantom, Bobby Jones, Dwight Jones, James Forbes, James Brewer, Tom Burleson, Tom McMillen, Kevin Joyce, Ed Ratleff

1976

Final: United States 95, Yugoslavia 74
United States: Phil Ford, Steve Sheppard, Adrian Dantley, Walter Davis, Quinn Buckner, Ernie Grunfeld, Kenny Carr, Scott May, Michel Armstrong, Tom La Garde, Phil Hubbard, Mitch Kupchak

1980

Final: Yugoslavia 86, Italy 77
U.S. participated in boycott.

1984

Final: United States 96, Spain 65
United States: Steve Alford, Leon Wood, Patrick Ewing, Vern Fleming, Alvin Robertson, Michael Jordan, Joe Kleine, Jon Koncak, Wayman Tisdale, Chris Mullin, Sam Perkins, Jeff Turner

1988

Final: USSR 76, Yugoslavia 63
United States (3rd): Mitch Richmond, Charles E. Smith, IV, Vernell Coles, Hersey Hawkins, Jeff Grayer, Charles D. Smith, Willie Anderson, Stacey Augmon, Dan Majerle, Danny Manning, J. R. Reid, David Robinson

1992

Final: United States 117, Croatia 85
United States: David Robinson, Christian Laettner, Patrick Ewing, Larry Bird, Scottie Pippen, Michael Jordan, Clyde Drexler, Karl Malone, John Stockton, Chris Mullin, Charles Barkley, Earvin Johnson

Women

1976

Gold USSR; Silver, United States*
United States: Cindy Brogdon, Susan Rojcewicz, Ann Meyers, Lusia Harris, Nancy Dunkle, Charlotte Lewis, Nancy Lieberman, Gail Marquis, Patricia Roberts, Mary Anne O'Connor, Patricia Head, Julienne Simpson

*In 1976 the women played a round-robin tournament, with the gold medal going to the team with the best record. The USSR won with a 5-0 record, and the USA, with a 3-2 record, was given the silver by virtue of a 95-79 victory over Bulgaria, which was also 3-2.

1980

Final: USSR 104, Bulgaria 73
U.S. participated in boycott.

1984

Final: United States 85, Korea 55
United States: Teresa Edwards, Lea Henry, Lynette Woodard, Anne Donovan, Cathy Boswell, Cheryl Miller, Janice Lawrence, Cindy Noble, Kim Mulkey, Denise Curry, Pamela McGee, Carol Menken-Schaudt

BASKETBALL *(Cont.)*

Women *(Cont.)*

1988

Final: United States 77, Yugoslavia 70
United States: Teresa Edwards, Mary Ethridge, Cynthia Brown, Anne Donovan, Teresa Weatherspoon, Bridgette Gordon, Victoria Bullett, Andrea Lloyd, Katrina McClain, Jennifer Gillom, Cynthia Cooper, Suzanne McConnell

1992

Final: Unified Team 76, China 66
United States (3rd): Teresa Edwards, Teresa Weatherspoon, Victoria Bullett, Katrina McClain, Cynthia Cooper, Suzanne McConnell, Daedra Charles, Clarissa Davis, Tammy Jackson, Vickie Orr, Carolyn Jones, Medina Dixon

BOXING

LIGHT FLYWEIGHT (106 LB)

1968	Francisco Rodriguez, Venezuela
1972	Gyorgy Gedo, Hungary
1976	Jorge Hernandez, Cuba
1980	Shamil Sabyrov, USSR
1984	Paul Gonzalez, United States
1988	Ivailo Hristov, Bulgaria
1992	Rogelio Marcelo, Cuba

FLYWEIGHT (112 LB)

1904	George Finnegan, United States
1906-1912	Not held
1920	Frank Di Gennara, United States
1924	Fidel LaBarba, United States
1928	Antal Kocsis, Hungary
1932	Istvan Enekes, Hungary
1936	Willi Kaiser, Germany
1948	Pascual Perez, Argentina
1952	Nathan Brooks, United States
1956	Terence Spinks, Great Britain
1960	Gyula Torok, Hungary
1964	Fernando Atzori, Italy
1968	Ricardo Delgado, Mexico
1972	Georgi Kostadinov, Bulgaria
1976	Leo Randolph, United States
1980	Peter Lessov, Bulgaria
1984	Steve McCrory, United States
1988	Kim Kwang Sun, South Korea
1992	Su Choi Chol, North Korea

BANTAMWEIGHT (119 LB)

1904	Oliver Kirk, United States
1906	Not held
1908	A. Henry Thomas, Great Britain
1912	Not held
1920	Clarence Walker, South Africa
1924	William Smith, South Africa
1928	Vittorio Tamagnini, Italy
1932	Horace Gwynne, Canada
1936	Ulderico Sergo, Italy
1948	Tibor Csik, Hungary
1952	Pentti Hamalainen, Finland
1956	Wolfgang Behrendt, East Germany
1960	Oleg Grigoryev, USSR
1964	Takao Sakurai, Japan
1968	Valery Sokolov, USSR
1972	Orlando Martinez, Cuba
1976	Yong Jo Gu, North Korea
1980	Juan Hernandez, Cuba
1984	Maurizio Stecca, Italy
1988	Kennedy McKinney, United States
1992	Joel Casamayor, Cuba

FEATHERWEIGHT (125 LB)

1904	Oliver Kirk, United States
1906	Not held
1908	Richard Gunn, Great Britain
1912	Not held
1920	Paul Fritsch, France
1924	John Fields, United States
1928	Lambertus van Klaveren, Netherlands
1932	Carmelo Robledo, Argentina
1936	Oscar Casanovas, Argentina
1948	Ernesto Formenti, Italy
1952	Jan Zachara, Czechoslovakia
1956	Vladimir Safronov, USSR
1960	Francesco Musso, Italy
1964	Stanislav Stephashkin, USSR
1968	Antonio Roldan, Mexico
1972	Boris Kousnetsov, USSR
1976	Angel Herrera, Cuba
1980	Rudi Fink, East Germany
1984	Meldrick Taylor, United States
1988	Giovanni Parisi, Italy
1992	Andreas Tews, Germany

LIGHTWEIGHT (132 LB)

1904	Harry Spanger, United States
1906	Not held
1908	Frederick Grace, Great Britain
1912	Not held
1920	Samuel Mosberg, United States
1924	Hans Nielsen, Denmark
1928	Carlo Orlandi, Italy
1932	Lawrence Stevens, South Africa
1936	Imre Harangi, Hungary
1948	Gerald Dreyer, South Africa
1952	Aureliano Bolognesi, Italy
1956	Richard McTaggart, Great Britain
1960	Kazimierz Pazdzior, Poland
1964	Jozef Grudzien, Poland
1968	Ronald Harris, United States
1972	Jan Szczepanski, Poland
1976	Howard Davis, United States
1980	Angel Herrera, Cuba
1984	Pernell Whitaker, United States
1988	Andreas Zuelow, East Germany
1992	Oscar De La Hoya, United States

LIGHT WELTERWEIGHT (139 LB)

1952	Charles Adkins, United States
1956	Vladimir Yengibaryan, USSR
1960	Bohumil Nemecek, Czechoslovakia
1964	Jerzy Kulej, Poland
1968	Jerzy Kulej, Poland
1972	Ray Seales, United States
1976	Ray Leonard, United States

BOXING (Cont.)

LIGHT WELTERWEIGHT (Cont.)

1980 ....Patrizio Oliva, Italy
1984 ....Jerry Page, United States
1988 ....Viatcheslav Janovski, USSR
1992 ....Hector Vinent, Cuba

WELTERWEIGHT (147 LB)

1904 ....Albert Young, United States
1906-1912 ......Not held
1920 ....Albert Schneider, Canada
1924 ....Jean Delarge, Belgium
1928 ....Edward Morgan, New Zealand
1932 ....Edward Flynn, United States
1936 ....Sten Suvio, Finland
1948 ....Julius Torma, Czechoslovakia
1952 ....Zygmunt Chychla, Poland
1956 ....Nicolae Linca, Romania
1960 ....Giovanni Benvenuti, Italy
1964 ....Marian Kasprzyk, Poland
1968 ....Manfred Wolke, East Germany
1972 ....Emilio Correa, Cuba
1976 ....Jochen Bachfeld, East Germany
1980 ....Andres Aldama, Cuba
1984 ....Mark Breland, United States
1988 ....Robert Wangila, Kenya
1992 ....Michael Carruth, Ireland

LIGHT MIDDLEWEIGHT (156 LB)

1952 ....Laszlo Papp, Hungary
1956 ....Laszlo Papp, Hungary
1960 ....Wilbert McClure, United States
1964 ....Boris Lagutin, USSR
1968 ....Boris Lagutin, USSR
1972 ....Dieter Kottysch, West Germany
1976 ....Jerzy Rybicki, Poland
1980 ....Armando Martinez, Cuba
1984 ....Frank Tate, United States
1988 ....Park Si-Hun, South Korea
1992 ....Juan Lemus, Cuba

MIDDLEWEIGHT (165 LB)

1904 ....Charles Mayer, United States
1908 ....John Douglas, Great Britain
1912 ....Not held
1920 ....Harry Mallin, Great Britain
1924 ....Harry Mallin, Great Britain
1928 ....Piero Toscani, Italy
1932 ....Carmen Barth, United States
1936 ....Jean Despeaux, France
1948 ....Laszlo Papp, Hungary
1952 ....Floyd Patterson, United States
1956 ....Gennady Schatkov, USSR
1960 ....Edward Crook, United States
1964 ....Valery Popenchenko, USSR
1968 ....Christopher Finnegan, Great Britain
1972 ....Vyacheslav Lemechev, USSR
1976 ....Michael Spinks, United States

MIDDLEWEIGHT (Cont.)

1980 ....Jose Gomez, Cuba
1984 ....Shin Joon Sup, South Korea
1988 ....Henry Maske, East Germany
1992 ....Ariel Hernandez, Cuba

LIGHT HEAVYWEIGHT (178 LB)

1920 ....Edward Eagan, United States
1924 ....Harry Mitchell, Great Britain
1928 ....Victor Avendano, Argentina
1932 ....David Carstens, South Africa
1936 ....Roger Michelot, France
1948 ....George Hunter, South Africa
1952 ....Norvel Lee, United States
1956 ....James Boyd, United States
1960 ....Cassius Clay, United States
1964 ....Cosimo Pinto, Italy
1968 ....Dan Poznyak, USSR
1972 ....Mate Parlov, Yugoslavia
1976 ....Leon Spinks, United States
1980 ....Slobodan Kacer, Yugoslavia
1984 ....Anton Josipovic, Yugoslavia
1988 ....Andrew Maynard, United States
1992 ....Torsten May, Germany

HEAVYWEIGHT (OVER 201 LB)

1904 ....Samuel Berger, United States
1906 ....Not held
1908 ....Albert Oldham, Great Britain
1912 ....Not held
1920 ....Ronald Rawson, Great Britain
1924 ....Otto von Porat, Norway
1928 ....Arturo Rodriguez Jurado, Argentina
1932 ....Santiago Lovell, Argentina
1936 ....Herbert Runge, Germany
1948 ....Rafael Inglesias, Argentina
1952 ....H. Edward Sanders, United States
1956 ....T. Peter Rademacher, United States
1960 ....Franco De Piccoli, Italy
1964 ....Joe Frazier, United States
1968 ....George Foreman, United States
1972 ....Teofilo Stevenson, Cuba
1976 ....Teofilo Stevenson, Cuba
1980 ....Teofilo Stevenson, Cuba

HEAVYWEIGHT (201* LB)

1984 ....Henry Tillman, United States
1988 ....Ray Mercer, United States
1992 ....Felix Savon, Cuba

SUPER HEAVYWEIGHT (UNLIMITED)

1984 ....Tyrell Biggs, United States
1988 ....Lennox Lewis, Canada
1992 ....Roberto Balado, Cuba

*Until 1984 the heavyweight division was unlimited. With the addition of the super heavyweight division, a limit of 201 pounds was imposed.

SWIMMING

Men

50-METER FREESTYLE

1904	Zoltan Halmay, Hungary (50 yds)	28.0
1988	Matt Biondi, United States	22.14 WR
1992	Aleksandr Popov, Unified Team	22.30

100-METER FREESTLYE

1896	Alfred Hajos, Hungary	1:22.2 OR
1904	Zoltan Halmay, Hungary (100 yds)	1:02.8
1906	Charles Daniels, United States	1:13.4
1908	Charles Daniels, United States	1:05.6 WR
1912	Duke Kahanamoku, United States	1:03.4
1920	Duke Kahanamoku, United States	1:00.4 WR
1924	John Weissmuller, United States	59.0 OR
1928	John Weissmuller, United States	58.6 OR
1932	Yasuji Miyazaki, Japan	58.2
1936	Ferenc Csik, Hungary	57.6
1948	Wally Ris, United States	57.3 OR
1952	Clarke Scholes, United States	57.4
1956	Jon Henricks, Australia	55.4 OR
1960	John Devitt, Australia	55.2 OR
1964	Don Schollander, United States	53.4 OR
1968	Mike Wenden, Australia	52.2 WR
1972	Mark Spitz, United States	51.22 WR
1976	Jim Montgomery, United States	49.99 WR
1980	Jörg Woithe, East Germany	50.40
1984	Rowdy Gaines, United States	49.80 OR
1988	Matt Biondi, United States	48.63 OR
1992	Aleksandr Popov, Unified Team	49.02

200-METER FREESTYLE

1900	Frederick Lane, Australia	2:25.2 OR
1904	Charles Daniels, United States	2:44.2
1906	Not held 1906-1964	
1968	Michael Wenden, Australia	1:55.2 OR
1972	Mark Spitz, United States	1:52.78 WR
1976	Bruce Furniss, United States	1:50.29 WR
1980	Sergei Kopliakov, USSR	1:49.81 OR
1984	Michael Gross, West Germany	1:47.44 WR
1988	Duncan Armstrong, Australia	1:47.25 WR
1992	Evgueni Sadovyi, Unified Team	1:46.70

400-METER FREESTYLE

1896	Paul Neumann, Austria (500 yds)	8:12.6
1904	Charles Daniels, U.S. (440 yds)	6:16.2
1906	Otto Scheff (440 yds)	6:23.8
1908	Henry Taylor, Great Britain	5:36.8
1912	George Hodgson, Canada	5:24.4
1920	Norman Ross, United States	5:26.8
1924	John Weissmuller, United States	5:04.2 OR
1928	Albert Zorilla, Argentina	5:01.6 OR
1932	Buster Crabbe, United States	4:48.4 OR
1936	Jack Medica, United States	4:44.5 OR
1948	William Smith, United States	4:41.0 OR
1952	Jean Boiteux, France	4:30.7 OR
1956	Murray Rose, Australia	4:27.3 OR
1960	Murray Rose, Australia	4:18.3 OR
1964	Don Schollander, United States	4:12.2 WR
1968	Mike Burton, United States	4:09.0 OR
1972	Brad Cooper, Australia	4:00.27 OR
1976	Brian Goodell, United States	3:51.93 WR
1980	Vladimir Salnikov, USSR	3:51.31 OR
1984	George DiCarlo, United States	3:51.23 OR
1988	Uwe Dassler, East Germany	3:46.95 WR
1992	Evgueni Sadovyi, Unified Team	3:45.00 WR

1500-METER FREESTYLE

1908	Henry Taylor, Great Britain	22:48.4 WR
1912	George Hodgson, Canada	22:00.0 WR
1920	Norman Ross, United States	22:23.2
1924	Andrew Charlton, Australia	20:06.6 WR
1928	Arne Borg, Sweden	19:51.8 OR
1932	Kusuo Kitamura, Japan	19:12.4 OR
1936	Noboru Terada, Japan	19:13.7
1948	James McLane, United States	19:18.5
1952	Ford Konno, United States	18:30.3 OR
1956	Murray Rose, Australia	17:58.9
1960	John Konrads, Australia	17:19.6 OR
1964	Robert Windle, Australia	17:01.7 OR
1968	Mike Burton, United States	16:38.9 OR
1972	Mike Burton, United States	15:52.58 OR
1976	Brian Goodell, United States	15:02.40 WR
1980	Vladimir Salnikov, USSR	14:58.27 WR
1984	Michael O'Brien, United States	15:05.20
1988	Vladimir Salnikov, USSR	15:00.40
1992	Kieren Perkins, Australia	14:43.48 WR

100-METER BACKSTROKE

1904	Walter Brack, Germany (100 yds)	1:16.8
1908	Arno Bieberstein, Germany	1:24.6 WR
1912	Harry Hebner, United States	1:21.2
1920	Warren Kealoha, United States	1:15.2
1924	Warren Kealoha, United States	1:13.2 OR
1928	George Kojac, United States	1:08.2 WR
1932	Masaji Kiyokawa, Japan	1:08.6
1936	Adolph Kiefer, United States	1:05.9 OR
1948	Allen Stack, United States	1:06.4
1952	Yoshi Oyakawa, United States	1:05.4 OR
1956	David Thiele, Australia	1:02.2 OR
1960	David Thiele, Australia	1:01.9 OR
1964	Not held	
1968	Roland Matthes, East Germany	58.7 OR
1972	Roland Matthes, East Germany	56.58 OR
1976	John Naber, United States	55.49 WR
1980	Bengt Baron, Sweden	56.33
1984	Rick Carey, United States	55.79
1988	Daichi Suzuki, Japan	55.05
1992	Mark Tewksbury, Canada	53.98 WR

200-METER BACKSTROKE

1900	Ernst Hoppenberg, Germany	2:47.0
1904	Not held 1904-1960	
1964	Jed Graef, United States	2:10.3 WR
1968	Roland Matthes, East Germany	2:09.6 OR
1972	Roland Matthes, East Germany	2:02.82 EWR
1976	John Naber, United States	1:59.19 WR
1980	Sandor Wladar, Hungary	2:01.93
1984	Rick Carey, United States	2:00.23
1988	Igor Polianski, USSR	1:59.37
1992	Martin Lopez-Zubero, Spain	1:58.47 OR

100-METER BREASTSTROKE

1968	Don McKenzie, United States	1:07.7 OR
1972	Nobutaka Taguchi, Japan	1:04.94 WR
1976	John Hencken, United States	1:03.11 WR
1980	Duncan Goodhew, Great Britain	1:03.44
1984	Steve Lundquist, United States	1:01.65 WR
1988	Adrian Moorhouse, Great Britain	1:02.04
1992	Nelson Diebel, United States	1:01.50 OR

SWIMMING *(Cont.)*

Men *(Cont.)*

200-METER BREASTSTROKE

1908	Frederick Holman, Great Britain	3:09.2 WR
1912	Walter Bathe, Germany	3:01.8 OR
1920	Haken Malmroth, Sweden	3:04.4
1924	Robert Skelton, United States	2:56.6
1928	Yoshiyuki Tsuruta, Japan	2:48.8 OR
1932	Yoshiyuki Tsuruta, Japan	2:45.4
1936	Tetsuo Hamuro, Japan	2:41.5 OR
1948	Joseph Verdeur, United States	2:39.3 OR
1952	John Davies, Australia	2:34.4 OR
1956	Masura Furukawa, Japan	2:34.7 OR
1960	William Mulliken, United States	2:37.4
1964	Ian O'Brien, Australia	2:27.8 WR
1968	Felipe Munoz, Mexico	2:28.7
1972	John Hencken, United States	2:21.55 WR
1976	David Wilkie, Great Britain	2:15.11 WR
1980	Robertas Zhulpa, USSR	2:15.85
1984	Victor Davis, Canada	2:13.34 WR
1988	Jozsef Szabo, Hungary	2:13.52
1992	Mike Barrowman, United States	2:10.16 WR

100-METER BUTTERFLY

1968	Doug Russell, United States	55.9 OR
1972	Mark Spitz, United States	54.27 WR
1976	Matt Vogel, United States	54.35
1980	Pär Arvidsson, Sweden	54.92
1984	Michael Gross, West Germany	53.08 WR
1988	Anthony Nesty, Suriname	53.00 OR
1992	Pablo Morales, United States	53.32

200-METER BUTTERFLY

1956	William Yorzyk, United States	2:19.3 OR
1960	Michael Troy, United States	2:12.8 WR
1964	Kevin Berry, Australia	2:06.6 WR
1968	Carl Robie, United States	2:08.7
1972	Mark Spitz, United States	2:00.70 WR
1976	Mike Bruner, United States	1:59.23 WR
1980	Sergei Fesenko, USSR	1:59.76
1984	Jon Sieben, Australia	1:57.04 WR
1988	Michael Gross, West Germany	1:56.94 OR
1992	Melvin Stewart, United States	1:56.26 OR

200-METER INDIVIDUAL MEDLEY

1968	Charles Hickcox, United States	2:12.0 OR
1972	Gunnar Larsson, Sweden	2:07.17 WR
1984	Alex Baumann, Canada	2:01.42 WR
1988	Tamas Darnyi, Hungary	2:00.17 WR
1992	Tamas Darnyi, Hungary	2:00.76

400-METER INDIVIDUAL MEDLEY

1964	Richard Roth, United States	4:45.4 WR
1968	Charles Hickcox, United States	4:48.4
1972	Gunnar Larsson, Sweden	4:31.98 OR
1976	Rod Strachan, United States	4:23.68 WR
1980	Aleksandr Sidorenko, USSR	4:22.89 OR
1984	Alex Baumann, Canada	4:17.41 WR
1988	Tamas Darnyi, Hungary	4:14.75 WR
1992	Tamas Darnyi, Hungary	4:14.23 OR

4 X 100-METER MEDLEY RELAY

1960	United States	4:05.4 WR
1964	United States	3:58.4 WR
1968	United States	3:54.9 WR
1972	United States	3:48.16 WR
1976	United States	3:42.22 WR
1980	Australia	3:45.70
1984	United States	3:39.30 WR
1988	United States	3:36.93 WR
1992	United States	3:36.93 EWR

4 X 100-METER FREESTYLE RELAY

1964	United States	3:32.2 WR
1968	United States	3:31.7 WR
1972	United States	3:26.42 WR
1976-1980	Not held	
1984	United States	3:19.03 WR
1988	United States	3:16.53 WR
1992	United States	3:16.74

4 X 200-METER FREESTYLE RELAY

1906	Hungary (1000 m)	16:52.4
1908	Great Britain	10:55.6
1912	Australia/New Zealand	10:11.6 WR
1920	United States	10:04.4 WR
1924	United States	9:53.4 WR
1928	United States	9:36.2 WR
1932	Japan	8:58.4 WR
1936	Japan	8:51.5 WR
1948	United States	8:46.0 WR
1952	United States	8:31.1 OR
1956	Australia	8:23.6 WR
1960	United States	8:10.2 WR
1964	United States	7:52.1 WR
1968	United States	7:52.33
1972	United States	7:35.78 WR
1976	United States	7:23.22 WR
1980	USSR	7:23.50
1984	United States	7:15.69 WR
1988	United States	7:12.51 WR
1992	Unified Team	7:11.95 WR

Women

50-METER FREESTYLE

1988	Kristin Otto, East Germany	25.49 OR
1992	Yang Wenyi, China	24.79 WR

100-METER FREESTYLE

1912	Fanny Durack, Australia	1:22.2
1920	Ethelda Bleibtrey, United States	1:13.6 WR
1924	Ethel Lackie, United States	1:12.4
1928	Albina Osipowich, United States	1:11.0 OR

100-METER FREESTYLE *(Cont.)*

1932	Helene Madison, United States	1:06.8 OR
1936	Hendrika Mastenbroek, Netherlands	1:05.9 OR
1948	Greta Andersen, Denmark	1:06.3
1952	Katalin Szöke, Hungary	1:06.8
1956	Dawn Fraser, Australia	1:02.0 WR
1960	Dawn Fraser, Australia	1:01.2 OR
1964	Dawn Fraser, Australia	59.5 OR
1968	Jan Henne, United States	1:00.0

SWIMMING (Cont.)

Women (Cont.)

100-METER FREESTYLE (Cont.)

1972	Sandra Neilson, United States	58.59 OR
1976	Kornelia Ender, East Germany	55.65 WR
1980	Barbara Krause, East Germany	54.79 WR
1984	Carrie Steinseifer, United States	55.92
	Nancy Hogshead, United States	55.92
1988	Kristin Otto, East Germany	54.93
1992	Zhuang Yong, China	54.64 OR

200-METER FREESTYLE

1968	Debbie Meyer, United States	2:10.5 OR
1972	Shane Gould, Australia	2:03.56 WR
1976	Kornelia Ender, East Germany	1:59.26 WR
1980	Barbara Krause, East Germany	1:58.33 OR
1984	Mary Wayte, United States	1:59.23
1988	Heike Friedrich, East Germany	1:57.65 OR
1992	Nicole Haislett, United States	1:57.90

400-METER FREESTYLE

1924	Martha Norelius, United States	6:02.2 OR
1928	Martha Norelius, United States	5:42.8 WR
1932	Helene Madison, United States	5:28.5 WR
1936	Hendrika Mastenbroek, Netherlands	5:26.4 OR
1948	Ann Curtis, United States	5:17.8 OR
1952	Valeria Gyenge, Hungary	5:12.1 OR
1956	Lorraine Crapp, Australia	4:54.6 OR
1960	Chris von Saltza, United States	4:50.6 OR
1964	Virginia Duenkel, United States	4:43.3 OR
1968	Debbie Meyer, United States	4:31.8 OR
1972	Shane Gould, Australia	4:19.44 WR
1976	Petra Thümer, East Germany	4:09.89 WR
1980	Ines Diers, East Germany	4:08.76 WR
1984	Tiffany Cohen, United States	4:07.10 OR
1988	Janet Evans, United States	4:03.85 WR
1992	Dagmar Hase, Germany	4:07.18

800-METER FREESTYLE

1968	Debbie Meyer, United States	9:24.0 OR
1972	Keena Rothhammer, United States	8:53.68 WR
1976	Petra Thümer, East Germany	8:37.14 WR
1980	Michelle Ford, Australia	8:28.90 OR
1984	Tiffany Cohen, United States	8:24.95 OR
1988	Janet Evans, United States	8:20.20 OR
1992	Janet Evans, United States	8:25.52

100-METER BACKSTROKE

1924	Sybil Bauer, United States	1:23.2 OR
1928	Marie Braun, Netherlands	1:22.0
1932	Eleanor Holm, United States	1:19.4
1936	Dina Senff, Netherlands	1:18.9
1948	Karen Harup, Denmark	1:14.4 OR
1952	Joan Harrison, South Africa	1:14.3
1956	Judy Grinham, Great Britain	1:12.9 OR
1960	Lynn Burke, United States	1:09.3 OR
1964	Cathy Ferguson, United States	1:07.7 WR
1968	Kaye Hall, United States	1:06.2 WR
1972	Melissa Belote, United States	1:05.78 OR
1976	Ulrike Richter, East Germany	1:01.83 OR
1980	Rica Reinisch, East Germany	1:00.86 WR
1984	Theresa Andrews, United States	1:02.55
1988	Kristin Otto, East Germany	1:00.89
1992	Krisztina Egerszegi, Hungary	1:00.68 OR

200-METER BACKSTROKE

1968	Pokey Watson, United States	2:24.8 OR
1972	Melissa Belote, United States	2:19.19 WR
1976	Ulrike Richter, East Germany	2:13.43 OR
1980	Rica Reinisch, East Germany	2:11.77 WR
1984	Jolanda De Rover, Netherlands	2:12.38
1988	Krisztina Egerszegi, Hungary	2:09.29 OR
1992	Krisztina Egerszegi, Hungary	2:07.06

100-METER BREASTSTROKE

1968	Djurdjica Bjedov, Yugoslavia	1:15.8 OR
1972	Catherine Carr, United States	1:13.58 WR
1976	Hannelore Anke, East Germany	1:11.16
1980	Ute Geweniger, East Germany	1:10.22
1984	Petra Van Staveren, Netherlands	1:09.88 OR
1988	Tania Dangalakova, Bulgaria	1:07.95 OR
1992	Elena Roudkovskaia, Unified Team	1:08.00

200-METER BREASTSTROKE

1924	Lucy Morton, Great Britain	3:33.2 OR
1928	Hilde Schrader, Germany	3:12.6
1932	Clare Dennis, Australia	3:06.3 OR
1936	Hideko Maehata, Japan	3:03.6
1948	Petronella Van Vliet, Netherlands	2:57.2
1952	Eva Szekely, Hungary	2:51.7 OR
1956	Ursula Happe, West Germany	2:53.1 OR
1960	Anita Lonsbrough, Great Britain	2:49.5 WR
1964	Galina Prozumenshikova, USSR	2:46.4 OR
1968	Sharon Wichman, United States	2:44.4 OR
1972	Beverly Whitfield, Australia	2:41.71 OR
1976	Marina Koshevaia, USSR	2:33.35 WR
1980	Lina Kaciusyte, USSR	2:29.54 OR
1984	Anne Ottenbrite, Canada	2:30.38
1988	Silke Hoerner, East Germany	2:26.71 WR
1992	Kyoko Iwasaki, Japan	2:26.65 OR

100-METER BUTTERFLY

1956	Shelley Mann, United States	1:11.0 OR
1960	Carolyn Schuler, United States	1:09.5 OR
1964	Sharon Stouder, United States	1:04.7 WR
1968	Lynn McClements, Australia	1:05.5
1972	Mayumi Aoki, Japan	1:03.34 WR
1976	Kornelia Ender, East Germany	1:00.13 EWR
1980	Caren Metschuck, East Germany	1:00.42
1984	Mary T. Meagher, United States	59.26
1988	Kristin Otto, East Germany	59.00 OR
1992	Qian Hong, China	58.62 OR

200-METER BUTTERFLY

1968	Ada Kok, Netherlands	2:24.7 OR
1972	Karen Moe, United States	2:15.57 WR
1976	Andrea Pollack, East Germany	2:11.41 OR
1980	Ines Geissler, East Germany	2:10.44 OR
1984	Mary T. Meagher, United States	2:06.90 OR
1988	Kathleen Nord, East Germany	2:09.51
1992	Summer Sanders, United States	2:08.67

200-METER INDIVIDUAL MEDLEY

1968	Claudia Kolb, United States	2:24.7 OR
1972	Shane Gould, Australia	2:23.07 WR
1976	Not held 1976-1980	
1984	Tracy Caulkins, United States	2:12.64 OR

SWIMMING *(Cont.)*

Women *(Cont.)*

200-METER INDIVIDUAL MEDLEY *(Cont.)*

1988	....Daniela Hunger, East Germany	2:12.59 OR
1992	....Lin Li, China	2:11.65 WR

400-METER INDIVIDUAL MEDLEY

1964	....Donna de Varona, United States	5:18.7 OR
1968	....Claudia Kolb, United States	5:08.5 OR
1972	....Gail Neall, Australia	5:02.97 WR
1976	....Ulrike Tauber, East Germany	4:42.77 WR
1980	....Petra Schneider, East Germany	4:36.29 WR
1984	....Tracy Caulkins, United States	4:39.24
1988	....Janet Evans, United States	4:37.76
1992	....Krisztina Egerszegi, Hungary	4:36.54

4 X 100-METER MEDLEY RELAY

1960	...............United States	4:41.1 WR
1964	...............United States	4:33.9 WR
1968	...............United States	4:28.3 OR
1972	...............United States	4:20.75 WR
1976	...............East Germany	4:07.95 WR
1980	...............East Germany	4:06.67 WR
1984	...............United States	4:08.34
1988	...............East Germany	4:03.74 OR
1992	...............United States	4:02.54 WR

4 X 100-METER FREESTYLE RELAY

1912	..............Great Britain	5:52.8 WR
1920	..............United States	5:11.6 WR
1924	..............United States	4:58.8 WR
1928	..............United States	4:47.6 WR
1932	..............United States	4:38.0 WR
1936	..............Netherlands	4:36.0 OR
1948	..............United States	4:29.2 OR
1952	..............Hungary	4:24.4 WR
1956	..............Australia	4:17.1 WR
1960	..............United States	4:08.9 WR
1964	..............United States	4:03.8 WR
1968	..............United States	4:02.5 OR
1972	..............United States	3:55.19 WR
1976	..............United States	3:44.82 WR
1980	..............East Germany	3:42.71 WR
1984	..............United States	3:43.43
1988	..............East Germany	3:40.63 OR
1992	..............United States	3:39.46 WR

Note: OR=Olympic Record; WR=World Record; EOR=Equals Olympic Record; EWR=Equals World Record; WB=World Best.

DIVING

Men

SPRINGBOARD

		Pts
1908	.....Albert Zürner, Germany	85.5
1912	....Paul Günther, Germany	79.23
1920	.....Louis Kuehn, United States	675.40
1924	.....Albert White, United States	97.46
1928	.....Pete DesJardins, United States	185.04
1932	.....Michael Galitzen, United States	161.38
1936	.....Richard Degener, United States	163.57
1948	.....Bruce Harlan, United States	163.64
1952	.....David Browning, United States	205.29
1956	.....Robert Clotworthy, United States	159.56
1960	.....Gary Tobian, United States	170.00
1964	.....Kenneth Sitzberger, United States	159.90
1968	.....Bernie Wrightson, United States	170.15
1972	.....Vladimir Vasin, USSR	594.09
1976	.....Phil Boggs, United States	619.05
1980	.....Aleksandr Portnov, USSR	905.02
1984	.....Greg Louganis, United States	754.41
1988	.....Greg Louganis, United States	730.80
1992	.....Mark Lenzi, United States	676.53

PLATFORM

		Pts
1904	.....George Sheldon, United States	12.66
1906	.....Gottlob Walz, Germany	156.0
1908	.....Hjalmar Johansson, Sweden	83.75
1912	.....Erik Adlerz, Sweden	73.94
1920	.....Clarence Pinkston, United States	100.67
1924	.....Albert White, United States	97.46
1928	.....Pete DesJardins, United States	98.74
1932	.....Harold Smith, United States	124.80
1936	.....Marshall Wayne, United States	113.58
1948	.....Sammy Lee, United States	130.05
1952	.....Sammy Lee, United States	156.28
1956	.....Joaquin Capilla, Mexico	152.44
1960	.....Robert Webster, United States	165.56
1964	.....Robert Webster, United States	148.58
1968	.....Klaus Dibiasi, Italy	164.18
1972	.....Klaus Dibiasi, Italy	504.12
1976	.....Klaus Dibiasi, Italy	600.51
1980	.....Falk Hoffmann, East Germany	835.65
1984	.....Greg Louganis, United States	710.91
1988	.....Greg Louganis, United States	638.61
1992	.....Sun Shuwei, China	677.31

Women

SPRINGBOARD

		Pts
1920	.....Aileen Riggin, United States	539.90
1924	....Elizabeth Becker, United States	474.50
1928	....Helen Meany, United States	78.62
1932	....Georgia Coleman, United States	87.52
1936	....Marjorie Gestring, United States	89.27
1948	.....Victoria Draves, United States	108.74

SPRINGBOARD *(Cont.)*

		Pts
1952	....Patricia McCormick, United States	147.30
1956	....Patricia McCormick, United States	142.36
1960	.....Ingrid Krämer, East Germany	155.81
1964	.....Ingrid Engel Krämer, East Germany	145.00
1968	.....Sue Gossick, United States	150.77

DIVING (Cont.)

Women (Cont.)

SPRINGBOARD (Cont.)

		Pts
1972	Micki King, United States	450.03
1976	Jennifer Chandler, United States	506.19
1980	Irina Kalinina, USSR	725.91
1984	Sylvie Bernier, Canada	530.70
1988	Gao Min, China	580.23
1992	Gao Min, China	572.40

PLATFORM

		Pts
1912	Greta Johansson, Sweden	39.90
1920	Stefani Fryland-Clausen, Denmark	34.60
1924	Caroline Smith, United States	33.20
1928	Elizabeth B. Pinkston, United States	31.60

PLATFORM (Cont.)

		Pts
1932	Dorothy Poynton, United States	40.26
1936	Dorothy Poynton Hill, United States	33.93
1948	Victoria Draves, United States	68.87
1952	Patricia McCormick, United States	79.37
1956	Patricia McCormick, United States	84.85
1960	Ingrid Krämer, East Germany	91.28
1964	Lesley Bush, United States	99.80
1968	Milena Duchkova, Czechoslovakia	109.59
1972	Ulrika Knape, Sweden	390.00
1976	Elena Vaytsekhovskaya, USSR	406.59
1980	Martina Jäschke, East Germany	596.25
1984	Zhou Jihong, China	435.51
1988	Xu Yanmei, China	445.20
1992	Fu Mingxia, China	461.43

GYMNASTICS

Men

ALL-AROUND

		Pts
1900	Gustave Sandras, France	302
1904	Julius Lenhart, Austria	69.80
1906	Pierre Paysse, France	97
1908	Alberto Braglia, Italy	317.0
1912	Alberto Braglia, Italy	135.0
1920	Giorgio Zampori, Italy	88.35
1924	Leon Stukelj, Yugoslavia	110.340
1928	Georges Miez, Switzerland	247.500
1932	Romeo Neri, Italy	140.625
1936	Alfred Schwarzmann, Germany	113.100
1948	Veikko Huhtanen, Finland	229.70
1952	Viktor Chukarin, USSR	115.70
1956	Viktor Chukarin, USSR	114.25
1960	Boris Shakhlin, USSR	115.95
1964	Yukio Endo, Japan	115.95
1968	Sawao Kato, Japan	115.90
1972	Sawao Kato, Japan	114.65
1976	Nikolai Andrianov, USSR	116.65
1980	Aleksandr Dityatin, USSR	118.65
1984	Koji Gushiken, Japan	118.70
1988	Vladimir Artemov, USSR	119.125
1992	Vitaly Scherbo, Unified Team	59.025

HORIZONTAL BAR

		Pts
1896	Hermann Weingärtner, Germany	—
1900	Not held	
1904	Anton Heida, United States	40
1908-20	Not held	
1924	Leon Stukelj, Yugoslavia	19.73
1928	Georges Miez, Switzerland	19.17
1932	Dallas Bixler, United States	18.33
1936	Aleksanteri Saarvala, Finland	19.367
1948	Josef Stalder, Switzerland	19.85
1952	Jack Günthard, Switzerland	19.55
1956	Takashi Ono, Japan	19.60
1960	Takashi Ono, Japan	19.60
1964	Boris Shakhlin, USSR	19.625
1968	Akinori Nakayama, Japan	19.55
1972	Mitsuo Tsukahara, Japan	19.725

HORIZONTAL BAR (Cont.)

		Pts
1976	Mitsuo Tsukahara, Japan	19.675
1980	Stoyan Deltchev, Bulgaria	19.825
1984	Shinji Morisue, Japan	20.00
1988	Vladimir Artemov, USSR	19.90
1992	Trent Dimas, United States	9.875

PARALLEL BARS

		Pts
1896	Alfred Flatow, Germany	—
1900	Not held	
1904	George Eyser, United States	44
1908-20	Not held	
1924	August Güttinger, Switzerland	21.63
1928	Ladislav Vacha, Czechoslovakia	18.83
1932	Romeo Neri, Italy	18.97
1936	Konrad Frey, Germany	19.067
1948	Michael Reusch, Switzerland	19.75
1952	Hans Eugster, Switzerland	19.65
1956	Viktor Chukarin, USSR	19.20
1960	Boris Shakhlin, USSR	19.40
1964	Yukio Endo, Japan	19.675
1968	Akinori Nakayama, Japan	19.475
1972	Sawao Kato, Japan	19.475
1976	Sawao Kato, Japan	19.675
1980	Aleksandr Tkachyov, USSR	19.775
1984	Bart Conner, United States	19.95
1988	Vladimir Artemov, USSR	19.925
1992	Vitaly Scherbo, Unified Team	9.900

LONG HORSE VAULT

		Pts
1896	Karl Schumann, Germany	—
1900	Not held	
1904	George Eyser, United States	36
1908-20	Not held	
1924	Frank Kriz, United States	9.98
1928	Eugen Mack, Switzerland	9.58
1932	Savino Guglielmetti, Italy	18.03
1936	Alfred Schwarzmann, Germany	19.20
1948	Paavo Aaltonen, Finland	19.55

GYMNASTICS (Cont.)

Men (Cont.)

LONG HORSE VAULT (Cont.)

	Pts
1952 .....Viktor Chukarin, USSR	19.20
1956 .....Helmut Bantz, Germany	18.85
1960 .....Takashi Ono, Japan	19.35
1964 .....Haruhiro Yamashita, Japan	19.60
1968 .....Mikhail Voronin, USSR	19.00
1972 .....Klaus Köste, East Germany	18.85
1976 .....Nikolai Andrianov, USSR	19.45
1980 .....Nikolai Andrianov, USSR	19.825
1984 .....Lou Yun, China	19.95
1988 .....Lou Yun, China	19.875
1992 .....Vitaly Scherbo, Unified Team	9.856

SIDE HORSE

	Pts
1896 .....Louis Zutter, Switzerland	—
1900 .....Not held	
1904 .....Anton Heida, United States	42
1908-20.Not held	
1924 .....Josef Wilhelm, Switzerland	21.23
1928 .....Hermann Hänggi, Switzerland	19.75
1932 .....Istvan Pelle, Hungary	19.07
1936 .....Konrad Frey, Germany	19.333
1948 .....Paavo Aaltonen, Finland	19.35
1952 .....Viktor Chukarin, USSR	19.50
1956 .....Boris Shakhlin, USSR	19.25
1960 .....Eugen Ekman, Finland	19.375
1964 .....Miroslav Cerar, Yugoslavia	19.525
1968 .....Miroslav Cerar, Yugoslavia	19.325
1972 .....Viktor Klimenko, USSR	19.125
1976 .....Zoltan Magyar, Hungary	19.70
1980 .....Zoltan Magyar, Hungary	19.925
1984 .....Li Ning, China	19.95
1988 .....Dmitri Bilozerchev, USSR	19.95
1992 .....Vitaly Scherbo, Unified Team	9.925

RINGS

	Pts
1896 .....Ioannis Mitropoulos, Greece	—
1900 .....Not held	
1904 .....Hermann Glass, United States	45
1908-20.Not held	
1924 .....Francesco Martino, Italy	21.553
1928 .....Leon Stukelj, Yugoslavia	19.25
1932 .....George Gulack, United States	18.97
1936 .....Alois Hudec, Czechoslovakia	19.433
1948 .....Karl Frei, Switzerland	19.80
1952 .....Grant Shaginyan, USSR	19.75
1956 .....Albert Azaryan, USSR	19.35
1960 .....Albert Azaryan, USSR	19.725
1964 .....Takuji Haytta, Japan	19.475
1968 .....Akinori Nakayama, Japan	19.45

RINGS (Cont.)

	Pts
1972 .....Akinori Nakayama, Japan	19.35
1976 .....Nikolai Andrianov, USSR	19.65
1980 .....Aleksandr Dityatin, USSR	19.875
1984 .....Koji Gushiken, Japan	19.85
1988 .....Holger Behrendt, East Germany	19.925
1992 .....Vitaly Scherbo, Unified Team	9.937

FLOOR EXERCISES

	Pts
1896-28.Not held	
1932 .....Istvan Pelle, Hungary	9.60
1936 .....Georges Miez, Switzerland	18.666
1948 .....Ferenc Pataki, Hungary	19.35
1952 .....K. William Thoresson, Sweden	19.25
1956 .....Valentin Muratov, USSR	19.20
1960 .....Nobuyuki Aihara, Japan	19.45
1964 .....Franco Menichelli, Italy	19.45
1968 .....Sawao Kato, Japan	19.475
1972 .....Nikolai Andrianov, USSR	19.175
1976 .....Nikolai Andrianov, USSR	19.45
1980 .....Roland Brückner, East Germany	19.75
1984 .....Li Ning, China	19.925
1988 .....Sergei Kharkov, USSR	19.925
1992 .....Li Xiaosahuang, China	9.925

TEAM COMBINED EXERCISES

	Pts
1896-00...Not held	
1904 .....Turngemeinde Philadelphia	374.43
1906 .....Norway	19.00
1908 .....Sweden	438
1912 .....Italy	265.75
1920 .....Italy	359.855
1924 .....Italy	839.058
1928 .....Switzerland	1718.625
1932 .....Italy	541.850
1936 .....Germany	657.430
1948 .....Finland	1358.30
1952 .....USSR	574.40
1956 .....USSR	568.25
1960 .....Japan	575.20
1964 .....Japan	577.95
1968 .....Japan	575.90
1972 .....Japan	571.25
1976 .....Japan	576.85
1980 .....USSR	598.60
1984 .....United States	591.40
1988 .....USSR	593.35
1992 .....Unified Team	585.45

GYMNASTICS *(Cont.)*

Women

ALL-AROUND

	Pts
1952 .....Maria Gorokhovskaya, USSR	76.78
1956 .....Larissa Latynina, USSR	74.933
1960 .....Larissa Latynina, USSR	77.031
1964 .....Vera Caslavska, Czechoslovakia	77.564
1968 .....Vera Caslavska, Czechoslovakia	78.25
1972 .....Lyudmila Tousischeva, USSR	77.025
1976 .....Nadia Comaneci, Romania	79.275
1980 .....Yelena Davydova, USSR	79.15
1984 .....Mary Lou Retton, United States	79.175
1988 .....Yelena Shushunova, USSR	79.662
1992 .....Tatiana Gutsu, Unified Team	39.737

SIDE HORSE VAULT

	Pts
1952 .....Yekaterina Kalinchuk, USSR	19.20
1956 .....Larissa Latynina, USSR	18.833
1960 .....Margarita Nikolayeva, USSR	19.316
1964 .....Vera Caslavska, Czechoslovakia	19.483
1968 .....Vera Caslavska, Czechoslovakia	19.775
1972 .....Karin Janz, East Germany	19.525
1976 .....Nelli Kim, USSR	19.80
1980 .....Natalya Shaposhnikova, USSR	19.725
1984 .....Ecaterina Szabo, Romania	19.875
1988 .....Svetlana Boginskaya, USSR	19.905
1992 .....Henrietta Onodi, Hungary	9.925
Lavinia Milosovici, Romania	9.925

UNEVEN BARS

	Pts
1952 .....Margit Korondi, Hungary	19.40
1956 .....Agnes Keleti, Hungary	18.966
1960 .....Polina Astakhova, USSR	19.616
1964 .....Polina Astakhova, USSR	19.332
1968 .....Vera Caslavska, Czechoslovakia	19.65
1972 .....Karin Janz, East Germany	19.675
1976 .....Nadia Comaneci, Romania	20.00
1980 .....Maxi Gnauck, East Germany	19.875
1984 .....Ma Yanhong, China	19.95
1988 .....Daniela Silivas, Romania	20.00
1992 .....Lu Li, China	10.00

BALANCE BEAM

	Pts
1952 .....Nina Bocharova, USSR	19.22
1956 .....Agnes Keleti, Hungary	18.80
1960 .....Eva Bosakova, Czechoslovakia	19.283

BALANCE BEAM *(Cont.)*

	Pts
1964 .....Vera Caslavska, Czechoslovakia	19.449
1968 .....Natalya Kuchinskaya, USSR	19.65
1972 .....Olga Korbut, USSR	19.40
1976 .....Nadia Comaneci, Romania	19.95
1980 .....Nadia Comaneci, Romania	19.80
1984 .....Simona Pauca, Romania	19.80
1988 .....Daniela Silivas, Romania	19.924
1992 .....Tatiana Lisenko, Unified Team	9.975

FLOOR EXERCISES

	Pts
1952 .....Agnes Keleti, Hungary	19.36
1956 .....Agnes Keleti, Hungary	18.733
1960 .....Larissa Latynina, USSR	19.583
1964 .....Larissa Latynina, USSR	19.599
1968 .....Vera Caslavska, Czechoslovakia	19.675
1972 .....Olga Korbut, USSR	19.575
1976 .....Nelli Kim, USSR	19.85
1980 .....Nadia Comaneci, Romania	19.875
1984 .....Ecaterina Szabo, Romania	19.975
1988 .....Daniela Silivas, Romania	19.937
1992 .....Lavinia Milosovici, Romania	10.00

TEAM COMBINED EXERCISES

	Pts
1928 ....Holland	316.75
1932 ....Not held	
1936 ....Germany	506.50
1948 ....Czechoslovakia	445.45
1952 ....USSR	527.03
1956 ....USSR	444.800
1960 ....USSR	382.320
1964 ....USSR	280.890
1968 ....USSR	382.85
1972 ....USSR	380.50
1976 ....USSR	466.00
1980 ....USSR	394.90
1984 ....Romania	392.02
1988 ....USSR	395.475
1992 ....Unified Team	395.666

RHYTHMIC ALL-AROUND

	Pts
1984 .....Lori Fung, Canada	57.95
1988 .....Marina Lobach, USSR	60.00
1992 .....Aleksandra Timoshenko, UTeam	59.037

Sic Transit Gloria

The sad story of luge champion Gerda Weissensteiner only went from bad to worse. Within days of her gold-medal performance in the women's singles event at Lillehammer, the newly celebrated Italian star learned that her brother had been killed in a motorcycle accident. Then, while she was attending his funeral, her house was burglarized and her gold medal stolen.

BIATHLON

Men

10 KILOMETERS

1980	Frank Ullrich, East Germany	32:10.69
1984	Eirik Kvalfoss, Norway	30:53.8
1988	Frank-Peter Rötsch, W Germany	25:08.1
1992	Mark Kirchner, Germany	26:02.3
1994	Sergei Tchepikov, Russia	28:07.0

20 KILOMETERS

1960	Klas Lestander, Sweden	1:33:21.6
1964	Vladimir Melyanin, Soviet Union	1:20:26.8
1968	Magnar Solberg, Norway	1:13:45.9
1972	Magnar Solberg, Norway	1:15:55.5
1976	Nikolay Kruglov, Soviet Union	1:14:12.26
1980	Anatoliy Alyabiev, Soviet Union	1:08:16.31
1984	Peter Angerer, W Germany	1:11:52.7

20 KILOMETERS *(Cont.)*

1988	Frank-Peter Rötsch, W Germany	56:33.3
1992	Evgueni Redkine, Unified Team	57:34.4
1994	Sergei Tarasov, Russia	57:25.3

4 X 7.5-KILOMETER RELAY

1968	Soviet Union	2:13:02.4
1972	Soviet Union	1:51:44.92
1976	Soviet Union	1:57:55.64
1980	Soviet Union	1:34:03.27
1984	Soviet Union	1:38:51.7
1988	Soviet Union	1:22:30.0
1992	Germany	1:24:43.5
1994	Germany	1:30:22.1

Women

7.5 KILOMETERS

1992	Antissa Restzova, Unified Team	24:29.2
1994	Myriam Bedard, Canada	26:08.8

15 KILOMETERS

1992	Antje Misersky, Germany	51:47.2
1994	Myriam Bedard, Canada	52:06.6

3 X 7.5-KILOMETER RELAY

1992	France	1:15:55.6
1994	Russia	1:47:19.5

BOBSLED

4-MAN BOB

1924	Switzerland (Eduard Scherrer)	5:45.54
1928	United States (William Fiske) (5-man)	3:20.50
1932	United States (William Fiske)	7:53.68
1936	Switzerland (Pierre Musy)	5:19.85
1948	United States (Francis Tyler)	5:20.10
1952	Germany (Andreas Ostler)	5:07.84
1956	Switzerland (Franz Kapus)	5:10.44
1960	Not held	
1964	Canada (Victor Emery)	4:14.46
1968	Italy (Eugenio Monti) (2 runs)	2:17.39
1972	Switzerland (Jean Wicki)	4:43.07
1976	East Germany (Meinhard Nehmer)	3:40.43
1980	East Germany (Meinhard Nehmer)	3:59.92
1984	East Germany (Wolfgang Hoppe)	3:20.22
1988	Switzerland (Ekkehard Fasser)	3:47.51
1992	Austria (Ingo Appelt)	3:53.90
1994	Germany (Harold Czudaj)	3:27.78

Note: Driver in parentheses.

2-MAN BOB

1932	United States (Hubert Stevens)	8:14.74
1936	United States (Ivan Brown)	5:29.29
1948	Switzerland (Felix Endrich)	5:29.20
1952	Germany (Andreas Ostler)	5:24.54
1956	Italy (Lamberto Dalla Costa)	5:30.14
1960	Not held	
1964	Great Britain (Anthony Nash)	4:21.90
1968	Italy (Eugenio Monti)	4:41.54
1972	West Germany (Wolfgang Zimmerer)	4:57.07
1976	East Germany (Meinhard Nehmer)	3:44.42
1980	Switzerland (Erich Schärer)	4:09.36
1984	East Germany (Wolfgang Hoppe)	3:25.56
1988	USSR (Janis Kipours)	3:53.48
1992	Switzerland (Gustav Weder)	4:03.26
1994	Switzerland (Gustav Weder)	3:30.81

Note: Driver in parentheses.

ICE HOCKEY

1920*	Canada, United States, Czechoslovakia
1924	Canada, United States, Great Britain
1928	Canada, Sweden, Switzerland
1932	Canada, United States, Germany
1936	Great Britain, Canada, United States
1948	Canada, Czechoslovakia, Switzerland
1952	Canada, United States, Sweden
1956	USSR, United States, Canada
1960	United States, Canada, USSR
1964	USSR, Sweden, Czechoslovakia
1968	USSR, Czechoslovakia, Canada
1972	USSR, United States, Czechoslovakia
1976	USSR, Czechoslovakia, West Germany
1980	United States, USSR, Sweden
1984	USSR, Czechoslovakia, Sweden
1988	USSR, Finland, Sweden
1992	Unified Team, Canada, Czechoslovakia
1994	Sweden, Canada, Finland

*Competition held at summer games in Antwerp.
Note: Gold, silver, and bronze medals.

LUGE

Men

SINGLES

1964	Thomas Köhler, East Germany	3:26.77
1968	Manfred Schmid, Austria	2:52.48
1972	Wolfgang Scheidel, W Germany	3:27.58
1976	Detlef Guenther, West Germany	3:27.688
1980	Bernhard Glass, West Germany	2:54.796
1984	Paul Hildgartner, Italy	3:04.258
1988	Jens Müller, West Germany	3:05.548
1992	Georg Hackl, Germany	3:02.363
1994	Georg Hackl, Germany	3:21.571

DOUBLES

1964	Austria	1:41.62
1968	East Germany	1:35.85
1972	East Germany	1:28.35
1976	East Germany	1:25.604
1980	East Germany	1:19.331
1984	West Germany	1:23.620
1988	East Germany	1:31.940
1992	Germany	1:32.053
1994	Italy	1:36.720

Women

SINGLES

1964	Ortrun Enderlein, Germany	3:24.67
1968	Erica Lechner, Italy	2:28.66
1972	Anna-Maria Müller, East Germany	2:59.18
1976	Margit Schumann, East Germany	2:50.621
1980	Vera Zozulya, USSR	2:36.537

SINGLES *(Cont.)*

1984	Steffi Martin, East Germany	2:46.570
1988	Steffi Walter (Martin) E Germany	3:03.973
1992	Doris Neuner, Austria	3:06.696
1994	Gerda Weissensteiner, Italy	3:15.517

FIGURE SKATING

Men

SINGLES

1908*	Ulrich Salchow, Sweden
1920†	Gillis Grafström, Sweden
1924	Gillis Grafström, Sweden
1928	Gillis Grafström, Sweden
1932	Karl Schäfer, Austria
1936	Karl Schäfer, Austria
1948	Dick Button, United States
1952	Dick Button, United States
1956	Hayes Alan Jenkins, United States
1960	David Jenkins, United States
1964	Manfred Schnelldorfer, West Germany

SINGLES *(Cont.)*

1968	Wolfgang Schwarz, Austria
1972	Ondrej Nepela, Czechoslovakia
1976	John Curry, Great Britain
1980	Robin Cousins, Great Britain
1984	Scott Hamilton, United States
1988	Brian Boitano, United States
1992	Victor Petrenko, Unified Team
1994	Alexei Urmanov, Russia

*Competition held at summer games in London
†Competition held at summer games in Antwerp

Women

SINGLES

1908*	Madge Syers, Great Britain
1920†	Magda Julin, Sweden
1924	Herma Szabo-Planck, Austria
1928	Sonja Henie, Norway
1932	Sonja Henie, Norway
1936	Sonja Henie, Norway
1948	Barbara Ann Scott, Canada
1952	Jeanette Altwegg, Great Britain
1956	Tenley Albright, United States
1960	Carol Heiss, United States
1964	Sjoukje Dijkstra, Netherlands

SINGLES *(Cont.)*

1968	Peggy Fleming, United States
1972	Beatrix Schuba, Austria
1976	Dorothy Hamill, United States
1980	Anett Pötzsch, East Germany
1984	Katarina Witt, East Germany
1988	Katarina Witt, East Germany
1992	Kristi Yamaguchi, United States
1994	Oksana Baiul, Ukraine

*Competition held at summer games in London
†Competition held at summer games in Antwerp

FIGURE SKATING (Cont.)

Mixed

PAIRS

1908* ..Anna Hübler & Heinrich Burger, Germany
1920# ..Ludovika & Walter Jakobsson, Finland
1924 ....Helene Engelmann & Alfred Berger, Austria
1928 ....Andree Joly & Pierre Brunet, France
1932 ....Andree Brunet (Joly) & Pierre Brunet, France
1936 ....Maxi Herber & Ernst Baier, Germany
1948 ....Micheline Lannoy & Pierre Baugniet, Belgium
1952 ....Ria Falk and Paul Falk, West Germany
1956 ....Elisabeth Schwartz & Kurt Oppelt, Austria
1960 ....Barbara Wagner & Robert Paul, Canada
1964 ....Lyudmila Beloussova & Oleg Protopopov, USSR
1968 ....Lyudmila Beloussova & Oleg Protopopov, USSR
1972 ....Irina Rodnina & Alexei Ulanov, USSR
1976 ....Irina Rodnina & Aleksandr Zaitsev, USSR
1980 ....Irina Rodnina & Aleksandr Zaitsev, USSR
1984 ....Elena Valova & Oleg Vasiliev, USSR
1988 ....Ekaterina Gordeeva & Sergei Grinkov, USSR

PAIRS (Cont.)

1992 ....Natalia Michkouteniok & Artour Dmitriev, Unified Team
1994 ....Ekaterina Gordeeva and Sergei Grinkov, Russia

ICE DANCING

1976 ....Lyudmila Pakhomova & Aleksandr Gorshkov, USSR
1980 ....Natalia Linichuk & Gennadi Karponosov, USSR
1984 ....Jayne Torvill & Christopher Dean, Great Britain
1988 ....Natalia Bestemianova & Andrei Bukin, USSR
1992 ....Marina Klimova & Sergei Ponomarenko, Unified Team
1994 ....Oksana Gritschuk and Evgeni Platov, Russia

*Competition held at summer games in London.
#Competition held at summer games in Antwerp.

SPEED SKATING

Men

500 METERS

1924 ....Charles Jewtraw, United States	44.0	
1928 ....Clas Thunberg, Finland	43.4 OR	
Bernt Evensen, Norway	43.4 OR	
1932 ....John Shea, United States	43.4 EOR	
1936 ....Ivar Ballangrud, Norway	43.4 EOR	
1948 ....Finn Helgesen, Norway	43.1 OR	
1952 ....Kenneth Henry, United States	43.2	
1956 ....Yevgeny Grishin, USSR	40.2 EWR	
1960 ....Yevgeny Grishin, USSR	40.2 EWR	
1964 ....Terry McDermott, United States	40.1 OR	
1968 ....Erhard Keller, West Germany	40.3	
1972 ....Erhard Keller, West Germany	39.44 OR	
1976 ....Yevgeny Kulikov, USSR	39.17 OR	
1980 ....Eric Heiden, United States	38.03 OR	
1984 ....Sergei Fokichev, USSR	38.19	
1988 ....Uwe-Jens Mey, East Germany	36.45 WR	
1992 ....Uwe-Jens Mey, East Germany	37.14	
1994 ....Aleksandr Golubev, Russia	36.33	

1000 METERS

1976 ....Peter Mueller, United States ... 1:19.32
1980 ....Eric Heiden, United States ... 1:15.18 OR
1984 ....Gaetan Boucher, Canada ... 1:15.80
1988 ...Nikolai Gulyaev, USSR ... 1:13.03 OR
1992 ....Olaf Zinke, Germany ... 1:14.85
1994 ....Dan Jansen, United States ... 1:12.43 WR

1500 METERS

1924 ....Clas Thunberg, Finland ... 2:20.8
1928 ....Clas Thunberg, Finland ... 2:21.1
1932 ...John Shea, United States ... 2:57.5
1936 ....Charles Mathisen, Norway ... 2:19.2 OR
1948 ....Sverre Farstad, Norway ... 2:17.6 OR

1500 METERS (Cont.)

1952 ....Hjalmar Andersen, Norway ... 2:20.4
1956 ....Yevgeny Grishin, USSR ... 2:08.6 WR
Yuri Mikhailov, USSR ... 2:08.6 WR
1960 ....Roald Aas, Norway ... 2:10.4
Yevgeny Grishin, USSR ... 2:10.4
1964 ....Ants Anston, USSR ... 2:10.3
1968 ....Cornelis Verkerk, Netherlands ... 2:03.4 OR
1972 ....Ard Schenk, Netherlands ... 2:02.96 OR
1976 ....Jan Egil Storholt, Norway ... 1:59.38 OR
1980 ....Eric Heiden, United States ... 1:55.44 OR
1984 ....Gaetan Boucher, Canada ... 1:58.36
1988 ....Andre Hoffmann, East Germany ... 1:52.06 WR
1992 ....Johann Olav Koss, Norway ... 1:54.81
1994 ....Johann Olav Koss, Norway ... 1:51.29 WR

5000 METERS

1924 ....Clas Thunberg, Finland ... 8:39.0
1928 ....Ivar Ballangrud, Norway ... 8:50.5
1932 ....Irving Jaffee, United States ... 9:40.8
1936 ....Ivar Ballangrud, Norway ... 8:19.6 OR
1948 ....Reidar Liaklev, Norway ... 8:29.4
1952 ....Hjalmar Andersen, Norway ... 8:10.6 OR
1956 ....Boris Shilkov, USSR ... 7:48.7 OR
1960 ....Viktor Kosichkin, USSR ... 7:51.3
1964 ....Knut Johannesen, Norway ... 7:38.4 OR
1968 ....Fred Anton Maier, Norway ... 7:22.4 WR
1972 ....Ard Schenk, Netherlands ... 7:23.61
1976 ....Sten Stensen, Norway ... 7:24.48
1980 ....Eric Heiden, United States ... 7:02.29 OR
1984 ....Sven Tomas Gustafson, Sweden ... 7:12.28
1988 ....Tomas Gustafson, Sweden ... 6:44.63 WR
1992 ....Geir Karlstad, Norway ... 6:59.97
1994 ....Johann Olav Koss, Norway ... 6:34.96 WR

Note: OR=Olympic Record; WR=World Record; EOR=Equals Olympic Record; EWR=Equals World Record; WB=World Best.

SPEED SKATING *(Cont.)*

Men *(Cont.)*

10,000 METERS

1924	Julius Skutnabb, Finland	18:04.8
1928	Not held, thawing of ice	
1932	Irving Jaffee, United States	19:13.6
1936	Ivar Ballangrud, Norway	17:24.3 OR
1948	Ake Seyffarth, Sweden	17:26.3
1952	Hjalmar Andersen, Norway	16:45.8 OR
1956	Sigvard Ericsson, Sweden	16:35.9 OR
1960	Knut Johannesen, Norway	15:46.6 WR
1964	Jonny Nilsson, Sweden	15:50.1

10,000 METERS *(Cont.)*

1968	Johnny Höglin, Sweden	15:23.6 OR
1972	Ard Schenk, Netherlands	15:01.35 OR
1976	Piet Kleine, Netherlands	14:50.59 OR
1980	Eric Heiden, United States	14:28.13 WR
1984	Igor Malkov, USSR	14:39.90
1988	Tomas Gustafson, Sweden	13:48.20 WR
1992	Bart Veldkamp, The Netherlands	14:12.12
1994	Johann Olav Koss, Norway	13:30.55 WR

Women

500 METERS

1960	Helga Haase, East Germany	45.9
1964	Lydia Skoblikova, USSR	45.0 OR
1968	Lyudmila Titova, USSR	46.1
1972	Anne Henning, United States	43.33 OR
1976	Sheila Young, United States	42.76 OR
1980	Karin Enke, East Germany	41.78 OR
1984	Christa Rothenburger, East Germany	41.02 OR
1988	Bonnie Blair, United States	39.10 WR
1992	Bonnie Blair, United States	40.33
1994	Bonnie Blair, United States	39.25

1000 METERS

1960	Klara Guseva, USSR	1:34.1
1964	Lydia Skoblikova, USSR	1:33.2 OR
1968	Carolina Geijssen, Netherlands	1:32.6 OR
1972	Monika Pflug, West Germany	1:31.40 OR
1976	Tatiana Averina, USSR	1:28.43 OR
1980	Natalya Petruseva, USSR	1:24.10 OR
1984	Karin Enke, East Germany	1:21.61 OR
1988	Christa Rothenburger, East Germany	1:17.65 WR
1992	Bonnie Blair, United States	1:21.90
1994	Bonnie Blair, United States	1:18.74

1500 METERS

1960	Lydia Skoblikova, USSR	2:25.2 WR
1964	Lydia Skoblikova, USSR	2:22.6 OR
1968	Kaija Mustonen, Finland	2:22.4 OR
1972	Dianne Holum, United States	2:20.85 OR
1976	Galina Stepanskaya, USSR	2:16.58 OR
1980	Anne Borckink, Netherlands	2:10.95 OR
1984	Karin Enke, East Germany	2:03.42 WR
1988	Yvonne van Gennip, Netherlands	2:00.68 OR
1992	Jacqueline Boerner, Germany	2:05.87
1994	Emese Hunyady, Austria	2:02.19

3000 METERS

1960	Lydia Skoblikova, USSR	5:14.3
1964	Lydia Skoblikova, USSR	5:14.9
1968	Johanna Schut, Netherlands	4:56.2 OR
1972	Christina Baas-Kaiser, Netherlands	4:52.14 OR
1976	Tatiana Averina, USSR	4:45.19 OR
1980	Bjorg Eva Jensen, Norway	4:32.13 OR
1984	Andrea Schöne, East Germany	4:24.79 OR
1988	Yvonne van Gennip, Netherlands	4:11.94 WR
1992	Gunda Niemann, Germany	4:19.90
1994	Svetlana Bazhanova, Russia	4:17.43

5000 METERS

1988	Yvonne van Gennip, Netherlands	7:14.13 WR
1992	Gunda Niemann, Germany	7:31.57
1994	Claudia Pechstein, Germany	7:14.37

SHORT TRACK SPEED SKATING

Men

500 METERS

1994	Chae Ji-Hoon, South Korea	43.54

1000 METERS

1992	Kim Ki-Hoon, South Korea	1:30.76 WR
1994	Kim Ki-Hoon, South Korea	1:34.57

5000-METER RELAY

1992	Korea	7:14.02 WR
1994	Italy	7:11.74 OR

Women

500 METERS

1992	Cathy Turner, United States	47.04
1994	Cathy Turner, United States	45.98 OR

1000 METERS

1994	Chun Lee-Kyung, South Korea	1:36.87

3000-METER RELAY

1992	Canada	4:36.62
1994	South Korea	4:26.64 OR

ALPINE SKIING

Men

DOWNHILL

1948	Henri Oreiller, France	2:55.0
1952	Zeno Colo, Italy	2:30.8
1956	Anton Sailer, Austria	2:52.2
1960	Jean Vuarnet, France	2:06.0
1964	Egon Zimmermann, Austria	2:18.16
1968	Jean-Claude Killy, France	1:59.85
1972	Bernhard Russi, Switzerland	1:51.43
1976	Franz Klammer, Austria	1:45.73
1980	Leonhard Stock, Austria	1:45.50
1984	Bill Johnson, United States	1:45.59
1988	Pirmin Zurbriggen, Switzerland	1:59.63
1992	Patrick Ortlieb, Austria	1:50.37
1994	Tommy Moe, United States	1:45.75

SUPER GIANT SLALOM

1988	Franck Piccard, France	1:39.66
1992	Kjetil Andre Aamodt, Norway	1:13.04
1994	Markus Wasmeier, Germany	1:32.53

GIANT SLALOM

1952	Stein Eriksen, Norway	2:25.0
1956	Anton Sailer, Austria	3:00.1
1960	Roger Staub, Switzerland	1:48.3
1964	Francois Bonlieu, France	1:46.71
1968	Jean-Claude Killy, France	3:29.28
1972	Gustav Thöni, Italy	3:09.62
1976	Heini Hemmi, Switzerland	3:26.97
1980	Ingemar Stenmark, Sweden	2:40.74
1984	Max Julen, Switzerland	2:41.18
1988	Alberto Tomba, Italy	2:06.37
1992	Alberto Tomba, Italy	2:06.98
1994	Markus Wasmeier, Germany	2:52.46

SLALOM

1948	Edi Reinalter, Switzerland	2:10.3
1952	Othmar Schneider, Austria	2:00.0
1956	Anton Sailer, Austria	3:14.7
1960	Ernst Hinterseer, Austria	2:08.9
1964	Josef Stiegler, Austria	2:11.13
1968	Jean-Claude Killy, France	1:39.73
1972	Francisco Fernandez Ochoa, Spain	1:49.27
1976	Piero Gros, Italy	2:03.29
1980	Ingemar Stenmark, Sweden	1:44.26
1984	Phil Mahre, United States	1:39.41
1988	Alberto Tomba, Italy	1:39.47
1992	Finn Christian Jagge, Norway	1:44.39
1994	Thomas Stangassinger, Austria	2:02.02

*COMBINED

		Pts
1936	Franz Pfnür, Germany	99.25
1948	Henri Oreiller, France	3.27
1988	Hubert Strolz, Austria	36.55
1992	Josef Polig, Italy	14.58
1994	Lasse Kjus, Norway	3:17.53

*Beginning in 1994, scoring was based on time.

Women

DOWNHILL

1948	Hedy Schlunegger, Switzerland	2:28.3
1952	Trude Jochum-Beiser, Austria	1:47.1
1956	Madeleine Berthod, Switzerland	1:40.7
1960	Heidi Biebl, West Germany	1:37.6
1964	Christl Haas, Austria	1:55.39
1968	Olga Pall, Austria	1:40.87
1972	Marie-Theres Nadig, Switzerland	1:36.68
1976	Rosi Mittermaier, West Germany	1:46.16
1980	Annemarie Moser-Pröll, Austria	1:37.52
1984	Michela Figini, Switzerland	1:13.36
1988	Marina Kiehl, West Germany	1:25.86
1992	Kerrin Lee-Gartner, Canada	1:52.55
1994	Katja Seizinger, Germany	1:35.93

SUPER GIANT SLALOM

1988	Sigrid Wolf, Austria	1:19.03
1992	Deborah Compagnoni, Italy	1:21.22
1994	Diann Rolfe-Steinrotter	1:22.15

GIANT SLALOM

1952	Andrea Mead Lawrence, United States	2:06.8
1956	Ossi Reichert, West Germany	1:56.5
1960	Yvonne Rüegg, Switzerland	1:39.9
1964	Marielle Goitschel, France	1:52.24
1968	Nancy Greene, Canada	1:51.97
1972	Marie-Theres Nadig, Switzerland	1:29.90
1976	Kathy Kreiner, Canada	1:29.13
1980	Hanni Wenzel, Liechtenstein (2 runs)	2:41.66
1984	Debbie Armstrong, United States	2:20.98
1988	Vreni Schneider, Switzerland	2:06.49
1992	Pernilla Wiberg, Sweden	2:12.74
1994	Deborah Compagnoni, Italy	2:30.97

SLALOM

1948	Gretchen Fraser, United States	1:57.2
1952	Andrea Mead Lawrence, United States	2:10.6
1956	Renee Colliard, Switzerland	1:52.3
1960	Anne Heggtveigt, Canada	1:49.6
1964	Christine Goitschel, France	1:29.86
1968	Marielle Goitschel, France	1:25.86
1972	Barbara Cochran, United States	1:31.24
1976	Rosi Mittermaier, West Germany	1:30.54
1980	Hanni Wenzel, Liechtenstein	1:25.09
1984	Paoletta Magoni, Italy	1:36.47
1988	Vreni Schneider, Switzerland	1:36.69
1992	Petra Kronberger, Austria	1:32.68
1994	Vreni Schneider, Switzerland	1:56.01

*COMBINED

		Pts
1988	Anita Wachter, Austria	29.25
1992	Petra Kronberger, Austria	2.55
1994	Pernilla Wiberg, Sweden	3:05.16

NORDIC SKIING

Men

15 KILOMETERS (CLASSICAL)

*1924	..Thorlief Haug, Norway	1:14:31.0
†1928	..Johan Gröttumsbraaten, Norway	1:37:01.0
‡1932	..Sven Utterström, Sweden	1:23:07.0
*1936	..Erik-August Larsson, Sweden	14:38.0
*1948	..Martin Lundström, Sweden	13:50.0
*1952	..Hallgeir Brenden, Norway	1:34.0
1956	....Hallgeir Brenden, Norway	49:39.0
1960	....Haakon Brusveen, Norway	51:55.5
1964	....Eero Mantyränta, Finland	50:54.1
1968	....Harald Grönningen, Norway	47:54.2
1972	....Sven-Ake Lundback, Sweden	45:28.24
1976	...Nikolay Bajukov, Unified Team	43:58.47
1980	....Thomas Wassberg, Sweden	41:57.63
1984	....Gunde Swan, Sweden	41:25.6
1988	....Michael Deviatyarov, USSR	41:18.9
**1992	.Vegard Ulvang, Norway	27:36.0
**1994	.Bjorn Daehlie, Norway	24:20.1

*distance was 18 km; †distance was 19.7 km.;
‡distance was 18.2 km; **distance was 10 km.

30 KILOMETERS (CLASSICAL)

1956	....Veikko Hakulinen, Finland	1:44:06.0
1960	....Sixten Jernberg, Sweden	1:51:03.9
1964	....Eero Mantyränta, Finland	1:30:50.7
1968	....Franco Nones, Italy	1:35:39.2
1972	....Viaceslav Vedenine, USSR	1:36:31.2
1976	....Sergei Savelyev, USSR	1:30:29.38
1980	....Nikolai Simyatov, USSR	1:27:02.80
1984	....Nikolai Simyatov, USSR	1:28:56.3
1988	....Alexey Prokororov, USSR	1:24:26.3
1992	....Vegard Ulvang, Norway	1:22:27.8
1994	....Thomas Alsgaard, Norway	1:12:26.4

50 KILOMETERS (FREESTYLE)

1924	....Thorleif Haug, Norway	3:44:32.0
1928	....Per Erik Hedlund, Sweden	4:52:03.0
1932	....Veli Saarinen, Finland	4:28:00.0
1936	....Elis Wiklund, Sweden	3:30:11.0
1948	....Nils Karlsson, Sweden	3:47:48.0
1952	....Veikko Hakulinen, Finland	3:33:33.0
1956	....Sixten Jernberg, Sweden	2:50:27.0
1960	....Kalevi Hämäläinen, Finland	2:59:06.3
1964	....Sixten Jernberg, Sweden	2:43:52.6
1968	....Olle Ellefsaeter, Norway	2:28:45.8
1972	....Paal Tyldrum, Norway	2:43:14.75
1976	....Ivar Formo, Norway	2:37:30.50
1980	....Nikolai Simyatov, USSR	2:27:24.60
1984	....Thomas Wassberg, Sweden	2:15:55.8
1988	....Gunde Swan, Sweden	2:04:30.9
1992	....Bjorn Dählie, Norway	2:03:41.5
1994	....Vladimir Smirnov, Kazakhstan	2:07:20.3

15 KILOMETERS (FREESTYLE)

1992	....Bjorn Daehlie, Norway	1:05:37.9
1994	....Bjorn Daehlie, Norway	1:00:08.8

4 X 10 KILOMETER RELAY

1936	....................Finland	2:41:33.0
1948	....................Sweden	2:32:80.0
1952	....................Finland	2:20:16.0
1956	....................USSR	2:15:30.0
1960	....................Finland	2:18:45.6
1964	....................Sweden	2:18:34.6
1968	....................Norway	2:08:33.5
1972	....................USSR	2:04:47.94
1976	....................Finland	2:07:59.72
1980	....................USSR	1:57:03.46
1984	....................Sweden	1:55:06.3
1988	....................Sweden	1:43:58.6
1992	....................Norway	1:39:26.0
1994	....................Italy	1:41:15.0

SKI JUMPING (NORMAL HILL)

		Pts
1964	....Veikko Kankkonen, Finland	229.90
1968	....Jiri Raska, Czechoslovakia	216.5
1972	....Yukio Kasaya, Japan	244.2
1976	....Hans-Georg Aschenbach, East Germany	252.0
1980	....Toni Innauer, Austria	266.3
1984	....Jens Weissflog, East Germany	215.2
1988	....Matti Nykänen, Finland	229.1
1992	....Ernst Vettori, Austria	222.8
1994	....Espen Bredesen, Norway	282.0

SKI JUMPING (LARGE HILL)

		Pts
1924	....Jacob Tullin Thams, Norway	18.960
1928	....Alf Andersen, Norway	19.208
1932	....Birger Ruud, Norway	228.1
1936	....Birger Ruud, Norway	232.0
1948	....Petter Hugsted, Norway	228.1
1952	....Arnfinn Bergmann, Norway	226.0
1956	....Antti Hyvärinen, Finland	227.0
1960	....Helmut Recknagel, East Germany	227.2
1964	....Toralf Engan, Norway	230.70
1968	....Vladimir Beloussov, USSR	231.3
1972	....Wojciech Fortuna, Poland	219.9
1976	....Karl Schnabl, Austria	234.8
1980	....Jouko Tormanen, Finland	271.0
1984	....Matti Nykänen, Finland	231.2
1988	....Matti Nykänen, Finland	224.0
1992	....Toni Nieminen, Finland	239.5
1994	....Jens Weissflog, Germany	274.5

TEAM SKI JUMPING

		Pts
1988	....Finland	634.4
1992	....Finland	644.4
1994	....Germany	970.1

NORDIC COMBINED

		Pts
*1924	..Thorleif Haug, Norway	18.906
*1928	..Johan Gröttumsbraaten, Norway	17.833
1932	....Johan Gröttumsbraaten, Norway	446.0
1936	....Oddbjörn Hagen, Norway	430.30

NORDIC SKIING (Cont.)

Men (Cont.)

NORDIC COMBINED (Cont.)

	Pts
1948....Heikki Hasu, Finland	448.80
1952....Simon Slattvik, Norway	451.621
1956....Sverre Stenersen, Norway	455.0
1960....Georg Thoma, West Germany	457.952
1964....Tormod Knutsen, Norway	469.28
1968....Frantz Keller, West Germany	449.04
1972....Ulrich Wehling, East Germany	413.34
1976....Ulrich Wehling, East Germany	423.39
1980....Ulrich Wehling, East Germany	432.20
1984....Tom Sandberg, Norway	422.595
1988....Hippolyt Kempf, Switzerland	432.230
1992....Fabrice Guy, France	426.47
1994....Fred B. Lundberg, Norway	457.970

TEAM NORDIC COMBINED

1988....West Germany
1992....Japan
1994....Japan

*Different scoring system; 1924-1952 distance was 18 km.; 1952-present, 15 km.

Women

5 KILOMETERS (CLASSICAL)

1964....Klaudia Boyarskikh, USSR	17:50.5
1968....Toini Gustafsson, Sweden	16:45.2
1972....Galina Kulakova, USSR	17:00.50
1976....Helena Takalo, Finland	15:48.69
1980....Raisa Smetanina, USSR	15:06.92
1984....Marja-Liisa Hamalainen, Finland	17:04.0
1988....Marjo Matikainen, Finland	15:04.0
1992....Marjut Lukkarinen, Finland	14:13.8
1994....Lyubova Egorova, Russia	14:08.8

10 KILOMETERS (CLASSICAL)

1952....Lydia Widemen, Finland	41:40.0
1956....Lyubov Kosyryeva, USSR	38:11.0
1960....Maria Gusakova, USSR	39:46.6
1964....Klaudia Boyarskikh, USSR	40:24.3
1968....Toini Gustafsson, Sweden	36:46.5
1972....Galina Kulakova, USSR	34:17.8
1976....Raisa Smetanina, USSR	30:13.41
1980....Barbara Petzold, East Germany	30:31.54
1984....Marja-Lissa Hamalainen, Finland	31:44.2
1988....Vida Ventsene, USSR	30:08.3

15 KILOMETERS (CLASSICAL)

1992....Lyubov Egorova, Unified Team	42:20.8
1994....Manuela Di Centa, Italy	39:44.5

20 KILOMETERS (FREESTYLE)

1984....Marja-Liisa Hamalainen, Finland	1:01:45.0
1988....Tamara Tikhonova, USSR	55:53.6

30 KILOMETERS (FREESTYLE)

1992....Stefania Belmondo, Italy	1:22:30.1
1994....Manuela Di Centa, Italy	1:25:41.6

10 KILOMETERS FREESTYLE PURSUIT

1992....Lyubov Egorova, Unified Team	40:07.7
1994....Lyubov Egorova, Russia	41:38.1

4 X 5-KILOMETER RELAY

1956....Finland	1:9:01.0
1960....Sweden	1:4:21.4
1964....USSR	59:20.0
1968....Norway	57:30.0
1972....USSR	48:46.15
1976....USSR	1:07:49.75
1980....East Germany	1:02:11.10
1984....Norway	1:06:49.7
1988....USSR	59:51.1
1992....Unified Team	59:34.8
1994....Russia	57:12.5

Note: 10 km. (classical) changed to 15 km. (classical) in 1992; 20 km. (freestyle) changed to 30 km. (freestyle).

FREESTYLE SKIING

Men

MOGUL

	Pts
1992....Edgar Grospiron, France	25.81
1994....Jean-Luc Brassard, Canada	27.24

AERIAL

	Pts
1994....Andreas Schoenbaechler, SWI	234.67

Women

MOGUL

	Pts
1992....Donna Weinbrecht, United States	23.69
1994....Stine Lise Hattestad, Norway	25.97

AERIAL

	Pts
1994....Lina Cherjazova, Uzbekistan	166.84

Track and Field

Sports Illustrated

Double Trouble
Michael Johnson strikes twice at the worlds

Great Leaps Forward

Records came in bushels in '95, with five men staking claims to athlete of the year honors

by Merrell Noden

STEVE OVETT, who twice set the world record for the mile in the early '80s, thought that as we inched closer to the limits of human performance, we'd simply carry times out to another decimal place and go bonkers over someone "smashing" a record by .006. Just when it was beginning to look as if Ovett might be right, along comes a startling year like 1995, in which a slew of world records were broken, major barriers fell in the triple jump and the 3,000 steeplechase, and one man lowered the 5,000 record by a truly Beamonesque margin.

The season reached its climax at the fifth I.A.A.F. World Championships, held August 5 through August 13 at Ullevi Stadium in Göteborg, Sweden, where transition, the succession of generations, was the obvious theme. Sergei Bubka alone resisted the youthful tide, winning his fifth world outdoor title in the pole vault. Who would have guessed that Carl Lewis, Jackie Joyner-Kersee and Heike Drechsler—perhaps the sport's three greatest stars over the last dozen years—would come away without a single medal? While Joyner-Kersee and Drechsler competed in Göteborg—finishing sixth and ninth, respectively, in the long jump—Lewis,

feeling a strained left hamstring suffered at the U.S. Olympic Festival in Colorado Springs, went home from Göteborg without making a single attempt in the long jump, which was won easily by 22-year-old Cuban Ivan Pedroso with a leap of 28' 6½".

Instead, Lewis chose to snipe at the meet. "It's boring," said Lewis. "There's no buzz, no passionate missions." Without Lewis, who had failed to qualify for the 100, and the injured pair of world record holder Leroy Burrell and Dennis Mitchell, the top U.S. finisher in the 100 was Mike Marsh, who was fifth, far behind Canada's Donovan Bailey.

Not that the U.S. lacked a sprint star in Göteborg. Michael Johnson has yet to set an outdoor world record but he made history just the same. No one had completed a 200/400 double successfully at the world championship or Olympic level, which is just the kind of incentive Johnson now requires, so thoroughly does he dominate the long sprints. In Göteborg he narrowly missed Butch Reynolds's world record in the 400, clocking 43.39 to win by seven meters; won the 200 by three meters, in 19.79; and anchored the victorious U.S. 4 x 400 team in 44.11.

In most years, Johnson would have been a

shoe-in for athlete of the year honors. But in the annus mirabilis of 1995 four other men had seasons to rival his.

One was Haile Gebrselassie, who for this writer was the track and field athlete of 1995. All year the 22-year-old Ethiopian seemed to be thumbing his nose at the notion of peaking, running fast and frequently from May through September. He set world records for two miles (8:07.46) in May; for 10,000 (26:43.54) in June and for the 5,000 (12:44.39) in August. In Göteborg he won the 10,000 in 27:12.95—a superb time in what was essentially a tactical race—then surprised some people by choosing not to double. That decision looked positively brilliant when, eight days later in Zurich, he ran the last four laps of his 5,000 record in 4:00.4 to leave an excellent field more than a straightaway adrift. The time, 12:44.39, hacked an astonishing 10.91 seconds off the old record.

It's hard to see how Gebrselassie's heroics left room for anyone else in the middle and long distances, but two other men also made history in those events. Moses Kiptanui may have inspired Gebrselassie when on June 8 he broke the Ethiopian's old 5,000 mark, running 12:55.30 in Rome. Like Gebrselassie, Kiptanui held back in Göteborg, winning the 3,000 steeple in 8:04.16. In Zurich he ran the first sub-eight-minute steeple, clocking 7:59.18. Noureddine Morceli broke two world records and would have established more had he not set the world records so high in the middle distances. As it was, the incomparable Algerian, still only 25, became the first man to break 4:50 for the 2,000, clocking 4:47.88 on July 3 in Paris. Nine days later in Nice he broke the 1500 mark by running 3:27.37.

Jonathan Edwards began the year as an unlikely man to revolutionize the triple jump. After winning the bronze medal at the 1993 worlds, the Englishman missed most of 1994 with mononucleosis and decided only last year, at the age of 28, to give up his job as a lab technician to concentrate on the triple jump. After losing three records to trailing winds earlier in the season, Edwards finally nailed Willie Banks's 10-year-old mark of 58' 11½" on July 18 in Salamanca, Spain, bound-

England's Edwards hopped, skipped and jumped through the 60' barrier.

ing out 59'. And that was a mere hint of what was to come in Göteborg, where Edwards eclipsed both the 18-meter barrier and 60', jumping 59' 7" (18.16 meters) on his first attempt and 60' ¼" on his second.

Women set world records in five events, four of them relatively minor: the pole vault, the triple jump, the 1,000 and the 5,000. But the best *race* of the year, the women's 400 hurdles in Göteborg, also yeilded a world record when Kim Batten's lunge at the tape beat her U.S. teammate Tonja Buford, 52.61 to 52.62. Both women broke Sally Gunnell's 1993 world record. Batten's performance was all the more remarkable since she had her appendix out on May 21 and had been reduced for a time to just hobbling painfully around the track.

Their rematch should be one of the highlights of next year's Olympic Games in Atlanta. One of many, if 1996 bears any resemblance to its astonishing predecessor.

U.S. Outdoor Track and Field Championships

Sacramento, Calif., June 14–18, 1995

Men

100 METERS

1. ....Mike Marsh, Santa Monica TC — 10.23
2. ....Maurice Greene, Powerade AC — 10.23
3. ....Dennis Mitchell, Mizuno TC — 10.23

200 METERS

1. ....Michael Johnson, Nike Intl — 19.83 w
2. ....Kevin Little, US West — 20.16
3. ....Jeff Williams, unat — 20.20

400 METERS

1. ....Michael Johnson, Nike I — 43.66
2. ....Butch Reynolds, Foot Locker AC — 44.42
3. ....Darnell Hall, Powerade AC — 44.55

800 METERS

1. ....Brandon Rock, U. of Arkansas — 1:46.50
2. ....Mark Everett, New Balance TC — 1:47.63
3. ....Jose Parilla, adidas — 1:48.14

1500 METERS

1. ....Paul McMullen, Asics — 3:43.90
2. ....Brian Hyde, William and Mary — 3:43.90
3. ....Terrance Herrington, Reebok RC — 3:44.03

STEEPLECHASE

1. ....Mark Croghan, adidas — 8:17.54
2. ....Tom Nohilly, Reebok E — 8:26.54
3. ....Karl Van Calcar, Nike — 8:27.38

5000 METERS

1. ....Bob Kennedy, Nike I — 13:19.99
2. ....Mark Coogan, New Balance — 13:23.72
3. ....Matt Giusto, Foot Locker AC — 13:27.87

10,000 METERS

1. ....Todd Williams, adidas — 28:01.84
2. ....Chris Fox, unat — 28:23.94
3. ....Tom Ansberry, Nike — 28:27.85

110-METER HURDLES

1. ....Roger Kingdom, Foot Locker AC — 13.09 w
2. ....Allen Johnson, Goldwin TC — 13.11
3. ....Jack Pierce, Mizuno TC — 13.26

400-METER HURDLES

1. ....Derrick Adkins, Reebok RC — 48.44
2. ....Ryan Hayden, St Augustine — 49.04
3. ....Octavius Terry, Georgia Tech — 49.20

20-KILOMETER WALK

1. ....Allen James, Athletes in Action — 1:24:46.0
2. ....Herm Nelson, Club NW — 1:27:14.8
3. ....Gary Morgan, NYAC — 1:28:41.0

HIGH JUMP

1. ....Charles Austin, unat — 7 ft 6½ in
2T. ....Tony Barton, adidas — 7 ft 5¼ in
2T. ....Rick Noji, SSTC — 7 ft 5¼ in

POLE VAULT

1. ....Scott Huffman, Foot Locker RC — 19 ft ¼ in
2. ....Dean Starkey, Reebok RC — 18 ft 10¼ in
3. ....Bill Payne, unat — 18 ft 10¼ in

LONG JUMP

1. ....Mike Powell, Foot Locker AC — 28 ft ¾ in w
2. ....Carl Lewis, Santa Monica TC — 27 ft 8¾ in w
3. ....Kareem Streete-Thompson, unat — 27 ft 5¼ in w

TRIPLE JUMP

1. ....Mike Conley, Foot Locker AC — 56 ft 4½ in
2. ....Ivory Angello, Rice — 56 ft 1¼ in w
3. ....LaMark Carter, MidA — 54 ft 7¹/₄ in w

SHOT PUT

1. ....Brent Noon, unat — 69 ft 2 in
2. ....John Godina, Reebok RC — 68 ft 7 in
3. ....Randy Barnes, Goldwin TC — 68 ft 5 in

DISCUS THROW

1. ....Mike Buncic, Nike — 212 ft 8 in
2. ....John Godina, Reebok RC — 211 ft 11 in
3. ....Randy Heisler, Nike Indiana — 208 ft 8 in

HAMMER THROW

1. ....Lance Deal, NYAC — 254 ft 10 in
2. ....David Popejoy, Stanford — 240 ft 10 in
3. ....Kevin McMahon, Georgetown — 233 ft 11 in

JAVELIN THROW

1. ....Tom Pukstys, adidas — 267 ft 4 in
2. ....Erik Smith, Bruin — 242 ft 11 in
3. ....Jim Connolly, GEO — 242 ft 4 in

DECATHLON

1. ....Dan O'Brien, Foot Locker AC — 8682 pts.
2. ....Chris Huffins, Mizuno — 8351 pts.
3. ....Brian Brophy, Reebok RC — 8257 pts.

*Meet record. w=wind aided. AR=American Record.

Women

100 METERS

1.	Gwen Torrence, Mazda TC	11.04
2.	Carlette Guidry, adidas	11.12
3.	Celena Mondie-Milner, MidA	11.22

200 METERS

1.	Gwen Torrence, Mazda TC	22.03 w
2.	Carlette Guidry, adidas	22.57
3.	Celena Mondie-Milner, MidA	22.76

400 METERS

1.	Jearl Miles, Reebok RC	50.90
2.	Kim Graham, Nike	51.48
3.	Maicel Malone, Asics	51.56

800 METERS

1.	Meredith Rainey, Foot Locker AC	2:00.07
2.	Joetta Clark, Foot Locker AC	2:01.02
3.	Amy Wickus, Univ. of Wisconsin	2:01.26

1500 METERS

1.	Regina Jacobs, Mizuno TC	4:05.18
2.	Suzy Hamilton, Reebok RC	4:07.07
3.	Sarah Thorsett, Powerade AC	4:07.49

5,000 METERS

1.	Gina Procaccio, New Balance	15:26.34
2.	Laura Mykytok, Nike	15:27.52
3.	Libbie Johnson, Mizuno TC	15:28.27

10,000 METERS

1.	Lynn Jennings, Nike I	31:57.19
2.	Laurie Henes, adidas	32:05.32
3.	Anne Marie Lauck, Nike	32:07.43

10,000 METER WALK

1.	Teresa Vaill, unattached	45:01.0
2.	Michelle Rohl, Brooks	45:16.2
3.	Debbi Lawrence, NS	45:46.0

100-METER HURDLES

1.	Gail Devers, Nike I	12.77
2.	Marsha Guialdo, unat	12.98
3.	Doris Williams, Goldwin TC	13.03

400-METER HURDLES

1.	Kim Batten, Reebok RC	54.74
2.	Tonja Buford, unat	54.82
3.	Trevaia Williams, Atoms	55.43

HIGH JUMP

1.	Amy Acuff, UCLA	6 ft 4¾ in
2.	Tisha Waller, Goldwin	6 ft 3½ in
3.	Connie Teabury, Goldwin	6 ft 3½ in

LONG JUMP

1.	Jackie Joyner-Kersee, Honda	22 ft 7 in w
2.	Marieke Veltman, WC	22 ft 1½ in w
3.	Sharon Couch, Olst	21 ft 11 in w

TRIPLE JUMP

1.	Sheila Hudson-Strudwick, Reebok RC	48 ft 1¼ in w
2.	Cynthea Rhondes, unat	46 ft 4 in w
3.	Diana Orrange, PT	45 ft 7 in w

SHOT PUT

1	Connie Price-Smith, Reebok RC	62 ft 6 in
2.	Ramona Pagel, Nike Coast	61 ft 2¾ in
3.	Eileen Vanisi, Reebok RC	57 ft 8¼ in

DISCUS THROW

1.	Edie Boyer, unat	205 ft 4 in
2.	Pam Dukes, Nike Coast	195 ft 0 in
3.	Danyel Mitchell, unat	194 ft 9 in

JAVELIN

1	Donna Mayhew, Nike Coast	194 ft 1 in
2.	Ashley Selman, Asics	191 ft 4 in
3.	Erica Wheeler, Mizuno	183 ft 9 in

HEPTATHLON

1	Jackie Joyner-Kersee, Honda	6375 pts. w
2.	Kym Carter, Nike	6354 pts.†
3.	Kelly Blair, Reebok RC	6354 pts.†

† Second place awarded to Carter on basis of four-to-three advantage in head-to-head competition.

*Meet record. w=wind aided. AR=American Record.

Still Got a Shot

Margaret White, who lives in the Oklahoma panhandle town of Turpin, would seem to be perfectly comfortable filling her larder with unripe fruit. She's 100 but in such fine fettle that she put the shot during the Sooner State Games in Oklahoma City last January, setting an age group record with a throw of 11' 4" as the only entrant in the 100–104 division.

Her son Wendell Palmer, 62, is a senior circuit athlete too—a shot-putter, discus thrower and sprinter. But, his mother says, "Wendell is getting of an age that I don't think he ought to do it much longer."

Göteborg, Sweden, August 5–13, 1995

Men

100 METERS

1. ....Donovan Bailey, Canada   9.97
2. ....Bruny Surin, Canada   10.03
3. ....Ato Bolden, Trinidad   10.03

200 METERS

1. ....Michael Johnson, United States   19.79
2. ....Frank Fredericks, Namibia   20.12
3. ....Jeff Williams, United States   20.18

400 METERS

1. ....Michael Johnson, United States   43.39*
2. ....Butch Reynolds, United States   44.22
3. ....Greg Haughton, Jamaica   44.56

800 METERS

1. ....Wilson Kipketer, Denmark   1:45.08
2. ....Arthémon Hatungimana, Burundi   1:45.64
3. ....Vebjørn Rodal, Norway   1:45.68

1,500 METERS

1. ....Noureddine Morceli, Algeria   3:33.73
2. ....Hicham El Guerrouj, Morocco   3:35.28
3. ....Vénuste Niyongabo, Burundi   3:35.56

STEEPLECHASE

1. ....Moses Kiptanui, Kenya   8:04.16*
2. ....Christopher Koskei, Kenya   8:09.30
3. ....S. Shaddad Al-Asmari, Saudi Arabia   8:12.95

5,000 METERS

1. ....Ismael Kirui, Kenya   13:16.77
2. ....Khalid Boulami, Morocco   13:17.15
3. ....Shem Kororia, Kenya   13:17.59

10,000 METERS

1. ....Haile Gebrselassie, Ethiopia   27:12.95*
2. ....Khalid Skah, Morocco   27:14.53
3. ....Paul Tergat, Kenya   27:14.70

MARATHON

1. ....Martin Fiz, Spain   2:11:41
2. ....Dionisio Ceron, Mexico   2:12:13
3. ....Luis dos Santos, Brazil   2:12:49

110-METER HURDLES

1. ....Allen Johnson, United States   13.00
2. ....Tony Jarrett, Great Britain   13.04
3. ....Roger Kingdom, United States   13.19

400-METER HURDLES

1. ....Derrick Adkins, United States   47.98
2. ....Samuel Matete, Zambia   48.03
3. ....Stéphane Diagana, France   48.14

20-KILOMETER WALK

1. ....Michele Didoni, Italy   1:19:59
2. ....Valentí Massana, Spain   1:20:23
3. ....Yevgeniy Misyulya, Belarus   1:20:48

50-KILOMETER WALK

1. ....Valentin Kononen, Finland   3:43:42
2. ....Giovanni Perricelli, Italy   3:45:11
3. ....Robert Korzeniowski, Poland   3:45:57

4 X 100 METER RELAY

1. ....Canada   38.31
2. ....Australia   38.50
3. ....Italy   39.07

4 X 400 METER RELAY

1. ....United States   2:57.32
2. ....Jamaica   2:59.88
3. ....Nigeria   3:03.18

HIGH JUMP

1. ....Troy Kemp, Bahamas   7 ft 9¼ in
2. ....Javier Sotomayor, Cuba   7 ft 9¼ in
3. ....Artur Partyka, Poland   7 ft 8½ in

POLE VAULT

1. ....Sergei Bubka, Ukraine   19 ft 5 in
2. ....Maksim Tarasov, Russia   19 ft 2¾ in
3. ....Jean Galfione, France   19 ft 2¾ in

LONG JUMP

1. ....Ivan Pedroso, Cuba   28 ft 6½ in
2. ....James Beckford, Jamaica   27 ft 2¾ in
3. ....Mike Powell, United States   27 ft 2½ in

TRIPLE JUMP

1. ....Jonathan Edwards, Gr Britain   60 ft ¼ in†
2. ....Brian Wellman, Bermuda   57 ft 9¾ in w
3. ....Jerome Romain, Dominican R   57 ft 8½ in w

SHOT PUT

1. ....John Godina, United States   70 ft 5¼ in
2. ....Mika Halvari, Finland   68 ft 8 in
3. ....Randy Barnes, United States   66 ft 11½ in

DISCUS

1. ....Lars Reidel, Germany   225 ft 7 in
2. ....Vladimir Dubrovshchik, Belarus   216 ft 6 in
3. ....Vasiliy Kaptyukh, Belarus   216 ft 2 in

HAMMER

1. ....Andrey Abduvaliyev, Tajikistan   267 ft 7 in
2. ....Igor Astapkovich, Belarus   266 ft 1 in
3. ....Tibor Gécsek, Hungary   265 ft 8 in

JAVELIN

1. ....Jan Zelezny, Czech Republic   293 ft 11 in
2. ....Steve Backley, Great Britain   283 ft 2 in
3. ....Boris Henry, Germany   282 ft 5 in

DECATHLON

1. ....Dan O'Brien, United States   8695 pts
2. ....Eduard Hämäläinen, Belarus   8489 pts
3. ....Mike Smith, Canada   8419 pts

*Meet record. †World record

Göteborg, Sweden, August 5–13, 1995

Women

100 METERS

1. ....Gwen Torrence, United States — 10.85
2. ....Merlene Ottey, Jamaica — 10.94
3. ....Irina Privalova, Russia — 10.96

200 METERS

1. ....Merlene Ottey, Jamaica — 22.12
2. ....Irina Privalova, Russia — 22.12
3. ....Galina Malchugina, Russia — 22.37

400 METERS

1. ....Marie-José Pérec, France — 49.28
2. ....Pauline Davis, Bahamas — 49.96
3. ....Jearl Miles, United States — 50.00

800 METERS

1. ....Ana Quirot, Cuba — 1:56.11
2. ....Letitia Vriesde, Suriname — 1:56.68
3. ....Kelly Holmes, Great Britain — 1:56.95

1,500 METERS

1. ....Hassiba Boulmerka, Algeria — 4:02.42
2. ....Kelly Holmes, Great Britain — 4:03.04
3. ....Carla Sacramento, Portugal — 4:03.79

5,000 METERS

1. ....Sonia O'Sullivan, Ireland — 14:46.47*
2. ....Fernanda Ribeiro, Portugal — 14:48.54
3. ....Zohra Ouaziz, Morocco — 14:53.77

10,000 METERS

1. ....Fernanda Ribeiro, Portugal — 31:04.99
2. ....Derartu Tulu, Ethiopia — 31:08.10
3. ....Tecla Lorupe, Kenya — 31:17.66

MARATHON††

1. ....Manuela Machado, Portugal — 2:25:39
2. ....Anuta Catuna, Romania — 2:26:25
3. ....Ornella Ferrara, Italy — 2:30:11

100-METER HURDLES

1. ....Gail Devers, United States — 12.68
2. ....Olga Shishigina, Kazakstan — 12.80
3. ....Yuliya Graudyn, Russia — 12.85

400-METER HURDLES

1. ....Kim Batten, United States — 52.61†
2. ....Tonja Buford, United States — 52.62
3. ....Deon Hemmings, Jamaica — 53.48

10-KILOMETER WALK

1. ....Irina Stankina, Russia — 42:13*
2. ....Elisabetta Perrone, Italy — 42:16
3. ....Yelena Nikolayeva, Russia — 42:20

4 X 100 METER RELAY

1. ....United States — 42.12
2. ....Jamaica — 42.25
3. ....Germany — 43.01

4 X 400 METER RELAY

1. ....United States — 3:22.39
2. ....Russia — 3:23.98
3. ....Australia — 3:25.88

HIGH JUMP

1. ....Stefka Kostadinova, Bulgaria — 6 ft 7 in
2. ....Alina Astafei, Germany — 6 ft 6¼ in
3. ....Inga Babakova, Ukraine — 6 ft 6¼ in

LONG JUMP

1. ....Fiona May, Italy — 22 ft 10¾ in w
2. ....Niurka Montalvo, Cuba — 22 ft 6¼ in
3. ....Irina Mushailova, Russia — 22 ft 5 in w

TRIPLE JUMP

1. ....Inessa Kravets, Ukraine — 50 ft 10¼ in†
2. ....Iva Prandzheva, Bulgaria — 49 ft 9¾ in
3. ....Ana Biryukova, Russia — 49 ft 5¾ in

SHOT PUT

1. ....Astrid Kumbernuss, Germany — 69 ft 7½ in
2. ....Zhihong Huang, China — 65 ft 9 in
3. ....Svetla Mitkova, Bulgaria — 64 ft 2¼ in

DISCUS

1. ....Ellina Zvereva, Belarus — 225 ft 2 in
2. ....Ilke Wyludda, Germany — 220 ft 6 in
3. ....Olga Chernyavskaya, Russia — 219 ft 4 in

JAVELIN

1. ....Natalya Shikolenko, Belarus — 221 ft 8 in
2. ....Felicia Tilea, Romania — 214 ft 0 in
3. ....Mikaela Ingberg, Finland — 213 ft 9 in

HEPTATHLON

1. ....Ghada Shouaa, Syria — 6651 pts
2. ....Svetlana Moskalets, Russia — 6575 pts
3. ....Rita Ináncsi, Hungary — 6522 pts

*Meet record. **American record. †World record. †† 400 meters short.

IAAF World Cross-Country Championships

Durham, England, March 25, 1995

MEN (12,020 METERS; 7.41 MILES)

1.	Paul Tergat, Kenya	34:05
2.	Ismael Kirui, Kenya	34:13
3.	Salah Hissou, Morocco	34:14

WOMEN (6,470 METERS; 4.00 MILES)

1.	Derartu Tulu, Ethiopia	20:21
2.	Catherina McKiernan, Ireland	20:29
3.	Sally Barsosio, Kenya	20:39

Major Marathons

New York City: November 8, 1994

MEN

1.	German Silva, Mexico	2:11:21
2.	Benjamin Paredes, Mexico	2:11:23
3.	Arturo Barrios, United States	2:12:21

WOMEN

1.	Tecla Lorupe, Kenya	2:27:37
2.	Madina Biktagirova, Belarus	2:30:00
3.	Anne Marie Letko, United States	2:30:19

Tokyo: November 20, 1994

WOMEN ONLY

1.	Valentina Yegorova, Russia	2:30:09
2.	Sachiyo Seiyama, Japan	2:30:30
3.	Lisa Ondieki, Australia	2:31:01

Fukuoka, Japan: December 4, 1994

MEN ONLY

1.	Boay Akonay, Tanzania	2:09:45
2.	Manuel Matias, Portugal	2:09:50
3.	Valdenor dos Santos, Brazil	2:10:15

Honolulu: December 11, 1994

MEN

1.	Benson Masya, Kenya	2:15:04
2.	Thabiso Mogali, Lesotho	2:16:52
3.	Andrew Green, England	2:16:55

WOMEN

1.	Carla Beurskens, Netherlands	2:37:06
2.	Eriko Asai, Japan	2:38:21
3.	Lisa Weidenbach, United States	2:42:44

Los Angeles: March 5, 1995

MEN

1.	Rolando Vera, Ecuador	2:11:39
2.	Bob Kempainen, United States	2:11:59
3.	Martin Pitayo, Mexico	2:12:49

WOMEN

1.	Nadia Prasad, France	2:29:48
2.	Anna Rybicka, Poland	2:32:59
3.	Lyobov Klochko, Ukraine	2:33:31

Rotterdam: April 23, 1995

MEN

1.	Martin Fiz, Spain	2:08:57
2.	Bert van Vlaanderen, Netherlands	2:10:36
3.	Isaac Garcia, Mexico	2:10:54

WOMEN

1.	Monica Pont, Spain	2:30:34
2.	Carmen de Fuentes, Spain	2:31:20
3.	Carla Beurskens, Netherlands	2:32:39

London: April 2, 1995

MEN

1.	Dionisio Ceron, Mexico	2:08:30
2.	Steve Moneghetti, Australia	2:08:33
3.	Antonio Pinto, Portugal	2:08:48

WOMEN

1.	Malgorzata Sobanska, Poland	2:27:43
2.	Manuela Machado, Portugal	2:27:53
3.	Ritva Lemettinen, Finland	2:28:00

Boston: April 17, 1995

MEN

1.	Cosmas N'Deti, Kenya	2:09:22
2.	Moses Tanui, Kenya	2:10:22
3.	Luis dos Santos, Brazil	2:11:02

WOMEN

1.	Uta Pippig, Germany	2:25:11
2.	Elana Meyer, South Africa	2:26:51
3.	Madina Biktagirova, Belarus	2:29:00

TRACK AND FIELD

World Records

As of September 25, 1995. World outdoor records are recognized by the International Amateur Athletics Federation (IAAF).

Men

Event	Mark	Record Holder	Date	Site
100 meters	9.85	Leroy Burrell, United States	7-6-94	Lausanne, Switzerland
200 meters	19.72	Pietro Mennea, Italy	9-12-79	Mexico City
400 meters	43.29	Butch Reynolds, United States	8-17-88	Zurich
800 meters	1:41.73	Sebastian Coe, Great Britain	6-10-81	Florence
1,000 meters	2:12.18	Sebastian Coe, Great Britain	7-11-81	Oslo
1,500 meters	3:27.37	Noureddine Morceli, Algeria	7-12-95	Nice, France
Mile	3:44.29	Noureddine Morceli, Algeria	9-5-93	Rieti, Italy
2,000 meters	4:47.88	Noureddine Morceli, Algeria	7-3-95	Paris
3,000 meters	7:25.11	Noureddine Morceli, Algeria	8-2-94	Monte Carlo
Steeplechase	7:59.18	Moses Kiptanui, Kenya	8-16-95	Zurich
5,000 meters	12:44.39	Haile Gebrselassie, Ethiopia	8-16-95	Zurich
10,000 meters	26:43.53	Haile Gebrselassie, Ethiopia	6-5-95	Oslo
20,000 meters	56:55.6	Arturo Barrios, Mexico	3-30-91	La Flâche, France
Hour	21,101 meters	Arturo Barrios, Mexico	3-30-91	La Flâche, France
25,000 meters	1:13:55.8	Toshihiko Seko, Japan	3-22-81	Christchurch, New Zealand
30,000 meters	1:29:18.8	Toshihiko Seko, Japan	3-22-81	Christchurch, New Zealand
Marathon	2:06:50	Belayneh Densimo, Ethiopia	4-17-88	Rotterdam
110-meter hurdles	12.91	Colin Jackson, Great Britain	8-20-93	Stuttgart, Germany
400-meter hurdles	46.78	Kevin Young, United States	8-6-92	Barcelona
20 kilometer walk	1:17:26	Bernardo Segura, Mexico	5-7-94	Softeland, Norway
30 kilometer walk	2:01:44.1	Maurizio Damilano, Italy	10-3-92	Cuneo, Italy
50 kilometer walk	3:41:38.4	Raul Gonzalez, Mexico	5-25-79	Bergen, Norway
4x100-meter relay	37.40	United States (Mike Marsh, Leroy Burrell, Dennis Mitchell, Carl Lewis)	8-8-92	Barcelona
		United States (Jon Drummond, Andre Cason, Dennis Mitchell, Leroy Burrell)	8-22-93	Stuttgart, Germany
4x200-meter relay	1:18.68	Santa Monica TC (Mike Marsh, Leroy Burrell, Floyd Heard, Carl Lewis)	4-17-94	Walnut, CA
4x400-meter relay	2:54.29	United States (Andrew Valmon, Quincy Watts, Butch Reynolds, Michael Johnson)	8-22-93	Barcelona
4x800-meter relay	7:03.89	Great Britain (Peter Elliott, Garry Cook, Steve Cram, Sebastian Coe)	8-30-82	London
4x1500-meter relay	14:38.8	West Germany (Thomas Wessinghage, Harald Hudak, Michael Lederer, Karl Fleschen)	8-17-77	Cologne
High jump	8 ft ½ in	Javier Sotomayor, Cuba	7-27-93	Salamanca, Spain
Pole vault	20 ft 1¾ in	Sergei Bubka, Ukraine	7-31-94	Sestriere, Italy
Long jump	29 ft 4½ in	Mike Powell, United States	8-30-91	Tokyo
Triple jump	60 ft ¼ in	Jonathan Edwards, Great Britain	8-7-95	Göteborg, Sweden
Shot put	75 ft 10¼ in	Randy Barnes, United States	5-20-90	Westwood, CA
Discus throw	243 ft 0 in	Jürgen Schult, East Germany	6-6-86	Neubrandenburg, Germany
Hammer throw	284 ft 7 in	Yuri Syedikh, USSR	8-30-86	Stuttgart, Germany
Javelin throw	313 ft 10 in	Jan Zelezny, Czech Republic	8-29-93	Sheffield, England
Decathlon	8891 pts	Dan O'Brien, United States	9-4/5-92	Talence, France

Note: The decathlon consists of 10 events—the 100 meters, long jump, shot put, high jump and 400 meters on the first day; the 110-meter hurdles, discus, pole vault, javelin and 1500 meters on the second.

Women

Event	Mark	Record Holder	Date	Site
100 meters	10.49	Florence Griffith Joyner, United States	7-16-88	Indianapolis
200 meters	21.34	Florence Griffith Joyner, United States	9-29-88	Seoul
400 meters	47.60	Marita Koch, East Germany	10-6-85	Canberra, Australia
800 meters	1:53.28	Jarmila Kratochvílová, Czechoslovakia	7-26-83	Munich
1,000 meters	2:29.34	Maria Mutola, Mozambique	8-25-95	Brussels
1,500 meters	3:50.46	Qu Yunxia, China	9-11-93	Beijing
Mile	4:15.61	Paula Ivan, Romania	7-10-89	Nice
2,000 meters	5:25.36	Sonia O'Sullivan, Ireland	7-8-94	Edinburgh
3,000 meters	8:06.11	Wang Junxia, China	9-13-93	Beijing
5,000 meters	14:36.45	Fernanda Ribeiro, Portugal	7-22-95	Hechtel, Belgium
10,000 meters	29:31.78	Wang Junxia, China	9-8-93	Beijing
25,000 meters	1:29:29.2	Karolina Szabó, Hungary	4-22-88	Budapest
30,000 meters	1:49:05.6	Karolina Szabó, Hungary	4-22-88	Budapest
Marathon	2:21:06	Ingrid Kristiansen, Norway	4-21-85	London
100-meter hurdles	12.21	Yordanka Donkova, Bulgaria	8-20-88	Stara Zagora, Bulgaria
400-meter hurdles	52.61	Kim Batten, United States	8-11-95	Göteborg, Sweden
5-kilometer walk	20:17.19	Kerry Junna-Saxby, Australia	1-14-90	Sydney, Australia
10-kilometer walk	41:56.23	Nadezhda Ryashkina, USSR	7-24-90	Seattle
4x100-meter relay	41.37	East Germany (Silke Gladisch, Sabine Reiger, Ingrid Auerswald, Marlies Göhr)	10-6-85	Canberra, Australia
4x200-meter relay	1:28.15	East Germany (Marlies Göhr, Romy Müller, Bärbel Wöckel, Marita Koch)	8-9-80	Jena, East Germany
4x400-meter relay	3:15.17	USSR (Tatyana Ledovskaya, Olga Nazarova, Maria Pinigina, Olga Bryzgina)	10-1-88	Seoul
4x800-meter relay	7:50.17	USSR (Nadezhda Olizarenko, Lyubov Gurina, Lyudmila Borisova, Irina Podyalovskaya)	8-5-84	Moscow
High jump	6 ft 10¼ in	Stefka Kostadinova, Bulgaria	8-30-87	Rome
Pole Vault	13 ft 9¾ in	Daniella Bartova, Czech Republic	8-22-95	Linz, Austria
Long jump	24 ft 8¼ in	Galina Chistyakova, USSR	6-11-88	Leningrad
Triple Jump	50 ft 10¼ in	Inessa Kravets, Ukraine	8-10-95	Göteborg, Sweden
Shot put	74 ft 3 in	Natalya Lisovskaya, USSR	6-7-87	Moscow
Discus throw	252 ft 0 in	Gabriele Reinsch, East Germany	7-9-88	Neubrandenburg, Germany
Hammer throw	223 ft 7 in	Olga Kuzenkova, Russia	6-18-95	Moscow
Javelin throw	262 ft 5 in	Petra Felke, East Germany	9-9-88	Berlin
Heptathlon	7291 pts	Jackie Joyner-Kersee, United States	9-23/24-88	Seoul

Note: The heptathlon consists of 7 events—the 100-meter hurdles, high jump, shot put and 200 meters on the first day; the long jump, javelin and 800 meters on the second.

On Track Betting

Competitively, the U.S. remains the most powerful track and field nation in the world. Yet when it comes to the interest of the American public, the sport is limping like a sprinter with two torn hamstrings. Attendance at meets is down, longstanding events have been canceled, and media coverage is dwindling. In an effort to turn things around, USA Track & Field (USATF), the sport's national governing body, secured sponsorship from Mobil, Nike and Visa for a series of five indoor meets to be held on consecutive weekends this winter and televised by NBC. Having thus taken a stride toward increasing the sport's exposure, USATF promptly long-jumped into the absurd, announcing just before the second event in the series, last February's Reno Air Games, that it had persuaded the Eldorado Race and Sports Book in Reno to take action on the meet.

"We had to introduce new elements to make track more entertaining to the casual fan," said meet director John Mansoor. After consulting with sports-gambling experts in Las Vegas, the folks at the Eldorado set a line on eight of the meet's 16 events. "To protect the meet's integrity," said Mansoor, the USATF required all athletes to sign a statement saying they would not place any bets, even on themselves.

Despite all the hoopla, gambling on the meet was light, though spectators got a couple of payoffs nonetheless. Michael Johnson, a 1-to-5 favorite, set a world indoor record of 44.97 seconds in the 400 meters, and Jackie Joyner-Kersee, who went off at even money, ran 6.67 to break the U.S. indoor mark for the 50-meter hurdles. Those are the sorts of numbers American track should be betting on.

American Records

As of September 25, 1995. American outdoor records are recognized by USA Track and Field (USATF). WR=world record.

Men

Event	Mark	Record Holder	Date	Site
100 meters	9.85 WR	Leroy Burrell	7-6-94	Lausanne
200 meters	19.73	Mike Marsh	8-5-92	Barcelona
400 meters	43.29 WR	Butch Reynolds	8-17-88	Zurich
800 meters	1:42.60	Johnny Gray	8-28-85	Koblenz, Germany
1,000 meters	2:13.9	Rick Wohlhuter	7-30-74	Oslo
1,500 meters	3:29.77	Sydney Maree	8-25-85	Cologne
Mile	3:47.69	Steve Scott	7-7-82	Oslo
2,000 meters	4:52.44	Jim Spivey	9-15-87	Lausanne
3,000 meters	7:35.33	Bob Kennedy	7-18-94	Nice, France
Steeplechase	8:09.17	Henry Marsh	8-28-85	Koblenz, Germany
5,000 meters	13:01.15	Sydney Maree	7-27-85	Oslo
10,000 meters	27:20.56	Mark Nenow	9-5-86	Brussels
20,000 meters	58:25.0	Bill Rodgers	8-9-77	Boston
Hour	20,547 meters	Bill Rodgers	8-9-77	Boston
25,000 meters	1:14:11.8	Bill Rodgers	2-21-79	Saratoga, CA
30,000 meters	1:31:49	Bill Rodgers	2-21-79	Saratoga, CA
Marathon	2:10:04	Pat Petersen	4-23-89	London
110-meter hurdles	12.92	Roger Kingdom	8-16-89	Zurich
400-meter hurdles	46.78 WR	Kevin Young	8-6-92	Barcelona
20-kilometer walk	1:24:50	Tim Lewis	5-7-88	Seattle
30-kilometer walk	2:21:40	Herm Nelson	9-7-91	Bellevue, WA
50-kilometer walk	4:04:23.8	Herm Nelson	10-29-89	Seattle
4x100-meter relay	37.40 WR	United States (Mike Marsh, Leroy Burrell, Dennis Mitchell, Carl Lewis)	8-8-92	Barcelona
		United States (Jon Drummond, Andre Cason, Dennis Mitchell, Leroy Burrell)	8-22-93	Stuttgart, Germany
4x200-meter relay	1:18.68 WR	Santa Monica Track Club (Mike Marsh, Leroy Burrell, Floyd Heard, Carl Lewis)	4-17-94	Walnut, CA
4x400-meter relay	2:54.29 WR	United States (Andrew Valmon, Quincy Watts, Butch Reynolds, Michael Johnson)	8-22-93	Stuttgart, Germany
4x800-meter relay	7:06.5	Santa Monica Track Club (James Robinson, David Mack, Earl Jones, Johnny Gray)	4-26-86	Walnut, CA
4x1500-meter relay	14:46.3	National Team (Dan Aldredge, Andy Clifford, Todd Harbour, Tom Duits)	6-24-79	Bourges, France
High jump	7 ft 10½ in	Charles Austin	8-15-91	Zurich
Pole vault	19 ft 7 in	Scott Huffman	6-18-94	Knoxville, TN
Long jump	29 ft 4½ in WR	Mike Powell	8-30-91	Tokyo
Triple jump	58 ft 11½ in	Willie Banks	6-16-85	Indianapolis
Shot put	75 ft 10¼ in WR	Randy Barnes	5-20-90	Westwood, CA
Discus throw	237 ft 4 in	Ben Plucknett	7-7-81	Stockholm
Hammer throw	270 ft 8 in	Lance Deal	6-17-94	Knoxville, TN
Javelin throw	281 ft 2 in	Tom Pukstys	6-26-93	Kuortane, Finland
Decathlon	8891 pts WR	Dan O'Brien	9-4/5-92	Talence, France

Women

Event	Mark	Record Holder	Date	Site
100 meters	10.49 WR	Florence Griffith Joyner	7-16-88	Indianapolis
200 meters	21.34 WR	Florence Griffith Joyner	9-29-88	Seoul
400 meters	48.83	Valerie Brisco-Hooks	8-6-84	Los Angeles
800 meters	1:56.90	Mary Slaney	8-16-85	Bern, Switzerland
1,500 meters	3:57.12	Mary Slaney	7-26-83	Stockholm
Mile	4:16.71	Mary Slaney	8-21-85	Zurich
2,000 meters	5:32.7	Mary Slaney	8-3-84	Eugene, OR
3,000 meters	8:25.83	Mary Slaney	9-7-85	Rome
5,000 meters	14:56.07	Annette Peters	8-27-93	Berlin
10,000 meters	31:19.89	Lynn Jennings	8-7-92	Barcelona
Marathon	2:21:21	Joan Samuelson	10-20-85	Chicago
100-meter hurdles	12.46	Gail Devers	8-20-93	Stuttgart, Germany
400-meter hurdles	52.61	Kim Batten	8-11-95	Göteborg, Sweden
5,000 meter walk	21:28.17	Teresa Vaill	4-24-93	Philadelphia
10,000 meter walk	44:41.9	Michelle Rohl	7-26-94	Moscow
10-kilometer walk road	44:42	Debbi Lawrence	5-16-92	Kenosha, Wisconsin
4x100-meter relay	41.49	National Team (Michelle Finn, Gwen Torrence, Wenda Vereen, Gail Devers)	8-22-93	Stuttgart, Germany
4x200-meter relay	1:32.57	Louisiana State (Tananjalyn Stanley, Sylvia Brydson, Esther Jones, Dawn Sowell)	4-28-89	Des Moines
4x400-meter relay	3:15.51	Olympic Team (Denean Howard, Diane Dixon, Valerie Brisco, Florence Griffith Joyner)	10-1-88	Seoul
4x800-meter relay	8:17.09	Athletics West (Sue Addison, Lee Arbogast, Mary Decker, Chris Mullen)	4-24-83	Walnut, CA
High jump	6 ft 8 in	Louise Ritter	7-8-88	Austin, TX
		Louise Ritter	9-30-88	Seoul
Pole Vault	13 ft 1¾ in	Melissa Price	6-24-95	Walnut, CA
Long jump	24 ft 7 in	Jackie Joyner-Kersee	5-22-94	New York City
			7-31-94	Sestriere, Italy
Triple jump	46 ft 9 in	Sheila Hudson	7-25-95	Monaco
Shot put	66 ft 2½ in	Ramona Pagel	6-25-88	San Diego
Discus throw	216 ft 10 in	Carol Cady	5-31-86	San Jose
Javelin throw	227 ft 5 in	Kate Schmidt	9-10-77	Fürth, West Germany
Heptathlon	7291 pts WR	Jackie Joyner-Kersee	9-23/24-88	Seoul

World and American Indoor Records

Men

As of September 25, 1995. American indoor records are recognized by USA Track and Field. World Indoor records are recognized by the International Amateur Athletics Federation (IAAF).

Event	Mark	Record Holder	Date	Site
50 meters	5.61	Manfred Kokot, East Germany (W)	2-4-73	Berlin
	5.61	James Sanford (W, A)	2-20-81	San Diego
55 meters*	6.00	Lee McRae (A)	3-14-86	Oklahoma City
60 meters	6.41	Andre Cason (W, A)	2-14-92	Madrid
200 meters	20.25	Linford Christie, Great Britain (W)	2-19-95	Liévin, France
	20.55	Michael Johnson (A)	1-26-91	Liévin, France
400 meters	44.63	Michael Johnson (W, A)	3-4-95	Atlanta
800 meters	1:44.84	Paul Ereng, Kenya (W)	3-4-89	Budapest
	1:45.00	Johnny Gray (A)	3-8-92	Sindelfingen, Germany
1,000 meters	2:15.26	Noureddine Morceli, Algeria (W)	2-22-92	Birmingham, England
	2:18.19	Ocky Clark (A)	2-12-89	Stuttgart
1,500 meters	3:34.16	Noureddine Morceli, Algeria (W)	2-28-91	Seville
	3:38.12	Jeff Atkinson (A)	3-5-89	Budapest
Mile	3:49.78	Eamonn Coughlan, Ireland (W)	2-27-83	East Rutherford, NJ
	3:51.8	Steve Scott (A)	2-20-81	San Diego

Men *(Cont.)*

Event	Mark	Record Holder	Date	Site
3,000 meters	7:35.15	Moses Kiptanui, Kenya (W)	2-12-95	Ghent, Belgium
	7:39.94	Steve Scott (A)	2-10-89	East Rutherford, NJ
5,000 meters	13:20.4	Suleiman Nyambui, Tanzania (W)	2-6-81	New York City
	13:20.55	Doug Padilla (A)	2-12-82	Rosemont, Illinois
50-meter hurdles	6.25	Mark McKoy, Canada (W)	3-3-86	Kobe, Japan
	6.35	Greg Foster (A)	1-27-85	Rosemont, Illinois
	6.35	Greg Foster (A)	1-31-87	Ottawa, Ontario
55-meter hurdles*	6.82	Renaldo Nehemiah (A)	1-30-82	Dallas
60-meter hurdles	7.30	Colin Jackson, Great Britain (W)	3-6-94	Sindelfingen, Germany
	7.36	Greg Foster (A)	1-16-87	Los Angeles
5,000-meter walk	18:07.08	Mikhail Shchennikov, Russia	2-14-95	Moscow
4x200-meter relay	1:22.11	Great Britain (W) (Linford Christie, Darren Braithwaite, Ade Mafe, John Regis)	3-3-91	Glasgow
	1:22.71	National Team (Thomas Jefferson, Raymond Pierre, Antonio McKay Kevin Little)	3-3-91	Glasgow
4x400-meter relay	3:03.05	Germany (W) (Rico Lieder, Jens Carlowitz, Klaus Just, Thomas Schönlebe)	3-10-91	Seville
	3:03.24	National Team (A) (Raymond Pierre, Chip Jenkins, Andrew Valmon, Antonio McKay)	3-10-91	Seville
4x800-meter relay	7:17.8	Soviet Union (W) (Valeriy Taratynov, Stanislav Meshcherskikh, Aleksey Taranov, Viktor Semyashkin)	3-14-71	Sofia
	7:18.23	University of Florida (A) (Dedric Jones, Lewis Lacy, Stephen Adderly, Scott Peters)	3-14-92	Sindelfingen, Germany
High jump	7 ft 11½ in	Javier Sotomayor, Cuba (W)	3-4-89	Budapest
	7 ft 10½ in	Hollis Conway (A)	3-10-91	Seville
Pole vault	20 ft 2 in	Sergei Bubka, Ukraine (W)	2-21-93	Donetsk, Ukraine
	19 ft 3¾ in	Billy Olsen (A)	1-25-86	Albuquerque
Long jump	28 ft 10¼ in	Carl Lewis (W, A)	1-27-84	New York City
Triple jump	58 ft 3¾ in	Leonid Voloshin (W)	2-6-94	Grenoble, France
Shot put	74 ft 4¼ in	Randy Barnes (W, A)	1-20-89	Los Angeles
Weight Throw	84 ft 10¼ in	Lance Deal (W, A)	3-4-95	Atlanta
Pentathlon	4478 pts	Steve Fritz, United States (W, A)	1-14-95	Lawrence, KS
Heptathlon	6476 pts	Dan O'Brien (W, A)	3-13/14-93	Toronto

*No recognized world record

The Long Race

In 1990 Art Pease, who had been competing in the Special Olympics for three years, decided to enter a five-mile race being run in conjunction with the Portland Marathon. In the confusion at the starting line, however, Pease inadvertently took off with the runners who were competing in the full 26-mile, 385-yarder. It was about an hour later when Pease realized that "it sure seemed like a long race."

Then again, life has always been a long race for Pease, 27, who is mentally retarded. He was born into an abusive household, misdiagnosed as autistic and shuffled through a foster-care system. Things turned around in 1975 when he was taken in by Charles and Virginia Pease of Milton-Freewater, a rural community in northeast Oregon, and adopted by them five years later. Charles is a retired junior high school coach, and his and Virginia's other four sons and their daughter were all active in athletics. Art, too, was expected to be active, so he began running. "I was always pretty good at it," he says. Good enough to earn a varsity letter as a 3,000-meter runner in his hometown. Good enough to run a personal-best of three hours and 14 minutes in a 1993 marathon. Good enough to be named America's Special Olympics Male Athlete of the Year in 1994.

Last July, Pease and 36 other runners ran the streets of New Haven, Conn., in the first full marathon held at the International Special Olympics. As the Special Olympics movement keeps growing—more than 7,000 athletes from 145 countries and every state in the union competed in New Haven—the barriers for mentally challenged athletes keep falling. Nothing demonstrates this as dramatically as the addition of a grueling event like the marathon.

At several points in that 1990 Portland Marathon, officials kept asking Pease if he wanted to pull out. They were concerned since he had set off on the wrong course. It was exactly the right one. "I've finished all 11 marathons I've been in," says Pease. "Once I start, I'm not going to stop."

Women

Event	Mark	Record Holder	Date	Site
50 meters	5.96	Irina Privolova, Russia (W)	2-9-95	Madrid
	6.10	Gail Devers (A)	2-20-93	Los Angeles
55 meters*	6.56	Gwen Torrence (A)	3-14-87	Oklahoma City
60 meters	6.92	Irina Privalova, Russia (W)	2-11-93	Madrid
	6.92	Irina Privalova, Russia (W)	2-9-95	Madrid
	6.95	Gail Devers (A)	3-12-93	Toronto
200 meters	21.87	Merlene Ottey, Jamaica (W)	2-13-93	Liévin, France
	22.73	Carlotto Guidry (A)	3-4-95	Atlanta
400 meters	49.59	Jarmila Kratochvilová, Czech.	3-7-82	Milan
	50.64	Diane Dixon (A)	3-10-91	Seville
800 meters	1:56.40	Christine Wachtel, E Germany (W)	2-14-88	Vienna
	1:58.9	Mary Slaney (A)	2-22-80	San Diego
1,000 meters	2:34.41	Lyubov Kremlyova, Russia (W)	2-15-95	Erfurt, Germany
	2:37.60	Mary Slaney (A)	1-21-89	Portland
1,500 meters	4:00.27	Doina Melinte, Romania (W)	2-9-90	East Rutherford, NJ
	4:00.80	Mary Slaney (A)	2-8-80	New York City
Mile	4:17.14	Doina Melinte, Romania (W)	2-9-90	East Rutherford, NJ
	4:20.5	Mary Slaney (A)	2-19-82	San Diego
3,000 meters	8:33.82	Elly van Hulst, Netherlands (W)	3-4-89	Budapest
	8:40.45	Lynn Jennings (A)	2-23-90	New York City
5,000 meters	15:03.17	Liz McColgan, Scotland (W)	2-22-92	Birmingham, England
	15:22.64	Lynn Jennings (A)	1-7-90	Hanover, NH
50-meter hurdles	6.58	Cornelia Oschkenat, E Germany (W)	2-20-88	Berlin
	6.67	Jackie Joyner-Kersee (A)	2-10-95	Reno, NV
55-meter hurdles*	7.37	Jackie Joyner-Kersee (A)	2-3-89	New York City
60-meter hurdles	7.69	Lyudmila Narozhilenko, Russia (W)	2-4-90	Chelyabinsk, Russia
	7.81	Jackie Joyner-Kersee (A)	2-5-89	Fairfax, VA
3,000 meter walk	11:44.00	Yelena Ivanova, CIS (W)	2-7-92	Moscow
	12:20.42	Debbi Lawrence (A)	3-12-93	Toronto
4x200-meter relay	1:32.55	SC Eintracht Hamm, W Gemany (W) (Helga Arendt, Silke-Beate Knoll, Mechthild Kluth, Gisela Kinzel)	2-20-88	Dortmund, W Germany
	1:33.24	National Team (A) (Flirtisha Harris, Chryste Gaines, Terri Dendy, Michele Collins)	2-12-94	Glasgow
4x400-meter relay	3:27.22	Germany (W) (Sandra Seuser, Annett Hesselbarth, Katrin Schreiter, Grit Breuer)	3-10-91	Seville
	3:29.00	National Team (A) (Terri Dendy, Lillie Leatherwood, Jearl Miles, Diane Dixon)	3-10-91	Seville
4x800-meter relay	8:18.71	Russia (Natalya Zaytseva, Olga Kuvnetsova, Yelena Afanasyeva, Yekaterina Podkopayeva)	2-4-94	Moscow
High jump	6 ft 9½ in	Heike Henkel, Germany (W)	2-8-92	Karlsruhe, Germany
	6 ft 6¾ in	Coleen Sommer (A)	2-13-82	Ottawa
Long jump	24 ft 2¼ in	Heike Drechsler, E Germany (W)	2-13-88	Vienna
	23 ft 4¾ in	Jackie Joyner-Kersee (A)	3-5-94	Atlanta
Triple jump	49 ft 3¾ in	Yolanda Chen, Russia (W)	3-11-95	Barcelona
	46 ft 8¼ in	Sheila Hudson-Strudwick (A)	3-4-95	Atlanta
Shot put	73 ft 10 in	Helena Fibingerová, Czech. (W)	2-19-77	Jablonec, Czech.
	65 ft ¾ in	Ramona Pagel (A)	2-20-87	Inglewood, California
Weight Throw*	62 ft 10 in	Sonja Fitts (unatt)	2-28-92	Princeton, N.J.
Pentathlon	4991 pts	Irina Byelova, CIS (W)	2-14/15-92	Berlin
	4632 pts	Kym Carter (A)	3-10-95	Barcelona

*No recognized world record

World Track and Field Championships

Historically, the Olympics have served as the outdoor world championships for track and field. In 1983 the International Amateur Athletic Federation (IAAF) instituted a separate World Championship meet, to be held every 4 years between the Olympics. The first was held in Helsinki in 1983, the second in Rome in 1987, the third in Tokyo in 1991, the fourth in Stuttgart, Germany, in 1993 and the fifth in Göteborg, Sweden in 1995. In 1993 the IAAF began to hold the meet on a biennial basis.

Men

100 METERS

1983	Carl Lewis, United States	10.07
1987*	Carl Lewis, United States	9.93 WR
1991	Carl Lewis, United States	9.86 WR
1993	Linford Christie, Great Britain	9.87
1995	Donovan Bailey, Canada	9.97

200 METERS

1983	Calvin Smith, United States	20.14
1987	Calvin Smith United States	20.16
1991	Michael Johnson, United States	20.01
1993	Frank Fredericks, Namibia	19.85
1995	Michael Johnson, United States	19.79

400 METERS

1983	Bert Cameron, Jamaica	45.05
1987	Thomas Schoenlebe, E Germany	44.33
1991	Antonio Pettigrew, United States	44.57
1993	Michael Johnson, United States	43.65
1995	Michael Johnson, United States	43.39

800 METERS

1983	Willi Wulbeck, W Germany	1:43.65
1987	Billy Konchellah, Kenya	1:43.06
1991	Billy Konchellah, Kenya	1:43.99
1993	Paul Ruto, Kenya	1:44.71
1995	Wilson Kipketer, Denmark	1:45.08

1500 METERS

1983	Steve Cram, Great Britain	3:41.59
1987	Abdi Bile, Somalia	3:36.80
1991	Noureddine Morceli, Algeria	3:32.84
1993	Noureddine Morceli, Algeria	3:34.24
1995	Noureddine Morceli, Algeria	3:33.73

STEEPLECHASE

1983	Patriz Ilg, W Germany	8:15.06
1987	Francesco Panetta, Italy	8:08.57
1991	Moses Kiptanui, Kenya	8:12.59
1993	Moses Kiptanui, Kenya	8:06.36
1995	Moses Kiptanui, Kenya	8:04.16

5000 METERS

1983	Eamonn Coghlan, Ireland	13:28.53
1987	Said Aouita, Morocco	13:26.44
1991	Yobes Ondieki, Kenya	13:14.45
1993	Ismael Kirui, Kenya	13:02.75
1995	Ismael Kirui, Kenya	13:16.77

10,000 METERS

1983	Alberto Cova, Italy	28:01.04
1987	Paul Kipkoech, Kenya	27:38.63
1991	Moses Tanui, Kenya	27:38.74
1993	Haile Gebrselassie, Ethiopia	27:46.02
1995	Haile Gebrselassie, Ethiopia	27:12.95

MARATHON

1983	Rob de Castella, Australia	2:10:03
1987	Douglas Wakiihuri, Kenya	2:11:48
1991	Hiromi Taniguchi, Japan	2:14:57
1993	Mark Plaatjes, United States	2:13:57
1995	Martin Fiz, Spain	2:11:41

110-METER HURDLES

1983	Greg Foster, United States	13.42
1987	Greg Foster, United States	13.21
1991	Greg Foster, United States	13.06
1993	Colin Jackson, Great Britain	12.91 WR
1995	Allen Johnson, United States	13.00

400-METER HURDLES

1983	Edwin Moses, United States	47.50
1987	Edwin Moses, United States	47.46
1991	Samuel Matete, Zambia	47.64
1993	Kevin Young, United States	47.18
1995	Derrick Adkins, United States	47.98

20-KILOMETER WALK

1983	Ernesto Canto, Mexico	1:20:49
1987	Maurizio Damilano, Italy	1:20:45
1991	Maurizio Damilano, Italy	1:19:37
1993	Valentin Massana, Spain	1:22:31
1995	Michele Didoni, Italy	1:19:59

50-KILOMETER WALK

1983	Ronald Weigel, E Germany	3:43:08
1987	Hartwig Gauder, E Germany	3:40:53
1991	Aleksandr Potashov, USSR	3:53:09
1993	Jesus Angel Garcia, Spain	3:41:41
1995	Valentin Kononen, Finland	3:43:42

4 X 100 METER RELAY

1983	United States (Emmit King, Willie Gault, Calvin Smith, Carl Lewis)	37.86
1987	United States (Lee McRae, Lee McNeil, Harvey Glance, Carl Lewis)	37.90
1991	United States (Andre Cason Leroy Burrell, Dennis Mitchell Carl Lewis)	37.50 WR
1993	United States (Jon Drummond, Andre Cason, Dennis Mitchell, Leroy Burrell)	37.48
1995	Canada (Robert Esmie, Glenroy Gilbert, Bruny Surin, Donovan Bailey)	38.31

WR=World record.

*Ben Johnson, Canada, disqualified

Men *(Cont.)*

4 X 400 METER RELAY

1983...............USSR (Sergei Lovachev,	3:00.79	
Alecksandr Troschilo,		
Nikolay Chernyetski, Viktor Markin)		
1987...............United States (Danny Everett	2:57.29	
Rod Haley, Antonio McKay,		
Butch Reynolds)		
1991...............Great Britain (Roger Black	2:57.53	
Derek Redmond, John Regis,		
Kriss Akabusi)		
1993...............United States (Andrew	2:54.29 WR	
Valmon, Quincy Watts, Butch		
Reynolds, Michael Johnson)		
1995...............United States (Marlon Ramsey,	2:57.32	
Derek Mills, Butch Reynolds,		
Michael Johnson)		

HIGH JUMP

1983...............Gennadi Avdeyenko, USSR	7 ft 7¼ in
1987...............Patrik Sjoberg, Sweden	7 ft 9¾ in
1991...............Charles Austin, United States	7 ft 9¾ in
1993...............Javier Sotomayor, Cuba	7 ft 10½ in
1995...............Troy Kemp, Bahamas	7 ft 9¼ in

POLE VAULT

1983...............Sergei Bubka, USSR	18 ft 8¼ in
1987...............Sergei Bubka, USSR	19 ft 2¼ in
1991...............Sergei Bubka, USSR	19 ft 6¼ in
1993...............Sergei Bubka, Ukraine	19 ft 8¼ in
1995...............Sergei Bubka, Ukraine	19 ft 5 in

LONG JUMP

1983...............Carl Lewis, United States	28 ft ¾ in
1987...............Carl Lewis, United States	28 ft 5¼ in
1991...............Mike Powell, U.S.	29 ft 4½ in WR
1993...............Mike Powell, United States	28 ft 2¼ in
1995...............Ivan Pedroso, Cuba	28 ft 6½ in

TRIPLE JUMP

1983...............Zdzislaw Hoffmann, Poland	57 ft 2 in
1987...............Khristo Markov, Bulgaria	58 ft 9 ½ in
1991...............Kenny Harrison, United States	58 ft 4 in
1993...............Mike Conley, United States	58 ft 7¼ in
1995...............Jonathan Edwards, G.B.	60 ft ¼ in WR

SHOT PUT

1983...............Edward Sarul, Poland	70 ft 2¼ in
1987 ....Werner Günthör, Switzerland	72 ft 11¼ in
1991...............Werner Günthör, Switzerland	71 ft 1¼ in
1993...............Werner Günthör, Switzerland	72 ft 1 in
1995 ....John Godina, United States	70 ft 5¼ in

DISCUS THROW

1983...............Imrich Bugar, Czech.	222 ft 2 in
1987...............Juergen Schult, E Germany	225 ft 6 in
1991...............Lars Riedel, Germany	217 ft 2 in
1993...............Lars Riedel, Germany	222 ft 2 in
1995...............Lars Riedel, Germany	225 ft 7 in

HAMMER THROW

1983...............Sergei Litvinov, USSR	271 ft 3 in
1987...............Sergei Litvinov, USSR	272 ft 6 in
1991...............Yuriy Sedykh, USSR	268 ft
1993...............Andrey Abduvaliyev, Tajikistan	267 ft 10 in
1995...............Andrey Abduvaliyev, Tajikistan	267 ft 7 in

JAVELIN THROW

1983...............Detlef Michel, E Germany	293 ft 7 in
1987...............Seppo Räty, Finland	274 ft 1 in
1991...............Kimmo Kinnunen, Finland	297 ft 11 in
1993...............Jan Zelezny, Czech Republic	282 ft 1 in
1995...............Jan Zelezny, Czech Republic	293 ft 11 in

DECATHLON

1983...............Daley Thompson, G Britain	8666 pts
1987...............Torsten Voss, E Germany	8680 pts
1991...............Dan O'Brien, United States	8812 pts
1993...............Dan O'Brien, United States	8817 pts
1995...............Dan O'Brien, United States	8695 pts

Women

100 METERS

1983...............Marlies Gohr, E Germany	10.97
1987...............Silke Gladisch, E Germany	10.90
1991...............Katrin Krabbe, Germany	10.99
1993...............Gail Devers, United States	10.82
1995...............Gwen Torrence, United States	10.85

200 METERS

1983...............Marita Koch, E Germany	22.13
1987...............Silke Gladisch, E Germany	21.74
1991...............Katrin Krabbe, Germany	22.09
1993...............Merlene Ottey, Jamaica	21.98
1995...............Merlene Ottey, Jamaica	22.12

400 METERS

1983...............Jarmila Kratochvilova, Czech	47.99
1987...............Olga Bryzgina, USSR	49.38
1991...............Marie-José Pérec, France	49.13
1993...............Jearl Miles, United States	49.82
1995...............Marie-José Pérec, France	49.28

800 METERS

1983...............Jarmila Kratochvilova, Czech	1:54.68
1987...............Sigrun Wodars, E Germany	1:55.26
1991...............Lilia Nurutdinova, USSR	1:57.50
1993...............Maria Mutola, Mozambique	1:55.43
1995...............Ana Quirot, Cuba	1:56.11

1500 METERS

1983...............Mary Slaney, United States	4:00.90
1987...............Tatyana Samolenko, USSR	3:58.56
1991...............Hassiba Boulmerka, Algeria	4:02.21
1993...............Dong Liu, China	4:00.50
1995...............Hassiba Boulmerka, Algeria	4:02.42

3000 METERS*

1983...............Mary Slaney, United States	8:34.62
1987...............Tatyana Samolenko, USSR	8:38.73
1991...............Tatyana Dorovskikh, USSR	8:35.82
1993...............Qu Yunxia, China	8:28.71
1995...............Sonia O'Sullivan, Ireland	14:46.47

WR=World record. * contested at 5,000 meters in 1995.

Women *(Cont.)*

10,000 METERS

1987	Ingrid Kristiansen, Norway	31:05.85
1991	Liz McColgan, Great Britain	31:14.31
1993	Wang Junxia, China	30:49:30
1995	Fernanda Ribeiro, Portugal	31:04.99

MARATHON

1983	Grete Waitz, Norway	2:28:09
1987	Rosa Mota, Portugal	2:25:17
1991	Wanda Panfil, Poland	2:29:53
1993	Junko Asari, Japan	2:30:03
1995	Manuela Machado, Portugal	2:25:39*

100-METER HURDLES

1983	Bettine Jahn, E Germany	12.35
1987	Ginka Zagorcheva, Bulgaria	12.34
1991	Lyudmila Narozhilenko, USSR	12.59
1993	Gail Devers, United States	12.46
1995	Gail Devers, United States	12.68

400-METER HURDLES

1983	Yekaterina Fesenko, USSR	54.14
1987	Sabine Busch, E Germany	53.62
1991	Tatyana Ledovskaya, USSR	53.11
1993	Sally Gunnell, Great Britain	52.74 WR
1995	Kim Batten, United States	52.61

10-KILOMETER WALK

1987	Irina Strakhova, USSR	44:12
1991	Alina Ivanova, USSR	42:57
1993	Sari Essayah, Finland	42:59
1995	Irina Stankina, Russia	42:13

4 X 100 METER RELAY

1983	East Germany (Silke Gladisch, Marita Koch, Ingrid Auerswald, Marlies Gohr)	41.76
1987	United States (Alice Brown, Diane Williams, Florence Griffith, Pam Marshall)	41.58
1991	Jamaica (Dalia Duhaney, Juliet Cuthbert, Beverley McDonald, Merlene Ottey)	41.94
1993	Russia (Olga Bogoslovskaya, Galina Malchugina, Natalya Voronova, Irina Privalova)	41.49
1995	United States (Celena Mondie-Milner, Carlette Guidry, Chryste Gaines, Gwen Torrence)	42.12

4 X 400 METER RELAY

1983	East Germany (Kerstin Walther Sabine Busch, Marita Koch, Dagmar Rubsam)	3:19.73
1987	E Germany (Dagmar Neubauer, Kirsten Emmelmann, Petra Müller, Sabine Busch)	3:18.63

4 X 400 METER RELAY *(Cont.)*

1991	USSR (Tatyana Ledovskaya, Lyudmila Dzhigalova, Olga Nazarova, Olga Bryzgina)	3:18.43
1993	United States (Gwen Torrence, Maicel Malone, Natasha Kaiser-Brown, Jearl Miles)	3:16.71
1995	United States (Kim Graham, Rochelle Stevens, Camara Jones, Jearl Miles)	3:22.39

HIGH JUMP

1983	Tamara Bykova, USSR	6 ft 7 in
1987	Stefka Kostadinova, Bulgaria	6 ft 10¼ in
1991	Heike Henkel, Germany	6 ft 8¾ in
1993	Ioamnet Quintero, Cuba	6 ft 6¼ in
1995	Stefka Kostadinova, Bulgaria	6 ft 7 in

LONG JUMP

1983	Heike Daute, E Germany	23 ft 10¼ in
1987	Jackie Joyner-Kersee, U.S.	24 ft 1¾ in
1991	Jackie Joyner-Kersee, U.S.	24 ft ¼ in
1993	Heike Drechsler, Germany	23 ft 4 in
1995	Fiona May, Italy	22 ft 10¾ in w

TRIPLE JUMP

1993	Ana Biryukova, Russia	49 ft 6 ¼ in WR
1995	Inessa Kravets, Ukraine	50 ft 10¼ in WR

SHOT PUT

1983	Helena Fibingerova, Czech.	69 ft ¾ in
1987	Natalya Lisovskaya, USSR	69 ft 8¼ in
1991	Zhihong Huang, China	68 ft 4¼ in
1993	Zhihong Huang, China	67 ft 6 in
1995	Astrid Kumbernuss, Germany	69 ft 7½ in

DISCUS THROW

1983	Martina Opitz, E Germany	226 ft 2 in
1987	Martina Hellmann, E Germany	235 ft
1991	Tsvetanka Khristova, Bulgaria	233 ft
1993	Olga Burova, Russia	221 ft 1 in
1995	Ellina Zvereva, Belarus	225 ft 2 in

JAVELIN THROW

1983	Tiina Lillak, Finland	232 ft 4 in
1987	Fatima Whitbread, G Britain	251 ft 5 in
1991	Demei Xu, China	225 ft 8 in
1993	Trine Hattestad, Finland	227 ft
1995	Natalya Shikolenko, Belarus	221 ft 8 in

HEPTATHLON

1983	Ramona Neubert, E Germany	6714 pts
1987	Jackie Joyner-Kersee, U.S.	7128 pts
1991	Sabine Braun, Germany	6672 pts
1993	Jackie Joyner-Kersee, U.S.	6837 pts
1995	Ghada Shouaa, Syria	6651 pts

WR=World record. *400 meters short

Track & Field News Athlete of the Year

Each year (since 1959 for men and since 1974 for women) Track & Field News has chosen the outstanding athlete in the sport.

Men

Year	Athlete	Event
1959	Martin Lauer, West Germany	110-meter hurdles/Decathlon
1960	Rafer Johnson, United States	Decathlon
1961	Ralph Boston, United States	Long jump
1962	Peter Snell, New Zealand	800/1500 meters
1963	C. K. Yang, Taiwan	Decathlon/Pole vault
1964	Peter Snell, New Zealand	800/1500 meters
1965	Ron Clarke, Australia	5,000/10,000 meters
1966	Jim Ryun, United States	800/1500 meters
1967	Jim Ryun, United States	1500 meters
1968	Bob Beamon, United States	Long jump
1969	Bill Toomey, United States	Decathlon
1970	Randy Matson, United States	Shot put
1971	Rod Milburn, United States	110-meter hurdles
1972	Lasse Viren, Finland	5,000/10,000 meters
1973	Ben Jipcho, Kenya	1500/5000 meters/Steeplechase
1974	Rick Wohlhuter, United States	800/1500 meters
1975	John Walker, New Zealand	800/1500 meters
1976	Alberto Juantorena, Cuba	400/800 meters
1977	Alberto Juantorena, Cuba	400/800 meters
1978	Henry Rono, Kenya	5,000/10,000 meters/Steeplechase
1979	Sebastian Coe, Great Britain	800/1500 meters
1980	Edwin Moses, United States	400-meter hurdles
1981	Sebastian Coe, Great Britain	800/1500 meters
1982	Carl Lewis, United States	100/200 meters/Long jump
1983	Carl Lewis, United States	100/200 meters/Long jump
1984	Carl Lewis, United States	100/200 meters/Long jump
1985	Said Aouita, Morocco	1500/5000 meters
1986	Yuri Syedikh, USSR	Hammer throw
1987	Ben Johnson, Canada	100 meters
1988	Sergei Bubka, USSR	Pole vault
1989	Roger Kingdom, United States	110-meter hurdles
1990	Michael Johnson, United States	200/400 meters
1991	Sergei Bubka, CIS	Pole vault
1992	Kevin Young, United States	400-meter hurdles
1993	Noureddine Morceli, Algeria	1500/mile/3000
1994	Noureddine Morceli, Algeria	1500/mile/3000/5000

Women

Year	Athlete	Event
1974	Irena Szewinska, Poland	100/200/400 meters
1975	Faina Melnik, USSR	Shot put/Discus
1976	Tatyana Kazankina, USSR	800/1500 meters
1977	Rosemarie Ackermann, East Germany	High jump
1978	Marita Koch, East Germany	100/200/400 meters
1979	Marita Koch, East Germany	100/200/400 meters
1980	Ilona Briesenick, East Germany	Shot put
1981	Evelyn Ashford, United States	100/200 meters
1982	Marita Koch, East Germany	100/200/400 meters
1983	Jarmila Kratochvilova, Czechoslovakia	200/400/800 meters
1984	Evelyn Ashford, United States	100 meters
1985	Marita Koch, East Germany	100/200/400 meters
1986	Jackie Joyner-Kersee, United States	Long jump/Heptathlon
1987	Jackie Joyner-Kersee, United States	100-meter hurdles/Long jump/Heptathlon
1988	Florence Griffith Joyner, United States	100/200 meters
1989	Ana Quirot, Cuba	400/800 meters
1990	Merlene Ottey, Jamaica	100/200 meters
1991	Heike Henkel, Germany	High jump
1992	Heike Drechsler, Germany	Long Jump
1993	Wang Junxia, China	1500/3000/10,000/marathon
1994	Jackie Joyner-Kersee, United States	100-meter hurdles/Long jump/Heptathlon

MARATHON

World Record Progression

Men

Record Holder	Time	Date	Site
John Hayes, United States	2:55:18.4	7-24-08	Shepherd's Bush, London
Robert Fowler, United States	2:52:45.4	1-1-09	Yonkers, NY
James Clark, United States	2:46:52.6	2-12-09	New York City
Albert Raines, United States	2:46:04.6	5-8-09	New York City
Frederick Barrett, Great Britain	2:42:31	5-26-09	Shepherd's Bush, London
Harry Green, Great Britain	2:38:16.2	5-12-13	Shepherd's Bush, London
Alexis Ahlgren, Sweden	2:36:06.6	5-31-13	Shepherd's Bush, London
Johannes Kolehmainen, Finland	2:32:35.8	8-22-20	Antwerp, Belgium
Albert Michelsen, United States	2:29:01.8	10-12-25	Port Chester, NY
Fusashige Suzuki, Japan	2:27:49	3-31-35	Tokyo
Yasuo Ikenaka, Japan	2:26:44	4-3-35	Tokyo
Kitei Son, Japan	2:26:42	11-3-35	Tokyo
Yun Bok Suh, Korea	2:25:39	4-19-47	Boston
James Peters, Great Britain	2:20:42.2	6-14-52	Chiswick, England
James Peters, Great Britain	2:18:40.2	6-13-53	Chiswick, England
James Peters, Great Britain	2:18:34.8	10-4-53	Turku, Finland
James Peters, Great Britain	2:17:39.4	6-26-54	Chiswick, England
Sergei Popov, USSR	2:15:17	8-24-58	Stockholm
Abebe Bikila, Ethiopia	2:15:16.2	9-10-60	Rome
Toru Terasawa, Japan	2:15:15.8	2-17-63	Beppu, Japan
Leonard Edelen, United States	2:14:28	6-15-63	Chiswick, England
Basil Heatley, Great Britain	2:13:55	6-13-64	Chiswick, England
Abebe Bikila, Ethiopia	2:12:11.2	6-21-64	Tokyo
Morio Shigematsu, Japan	2:12:00	6-12-65	Chiswick, England
Derek Clayton, Australia	2:09:36.4	12-3-67	Fukuoka, Japan
Derek Clayton, Australia	2:08:33.6	5-30-69	Antwerp, Belgium
Rob de Castella, Australia	2:08:18	12-6-81	Fukuoka, Japan
Steve Jones, Great Britain	2:08:05	10-21-84	Chicago
Carlos Lopes, Portugal	2:07:12	4-20-85	Rotterdam, Netherlands
Belayneh Densimo, Ethiopia	2:06:50	4-17-88	Rotterdam, Netherlands

Women

Record Holder	Time	Date	Site
Dale Greig, Great Britain	3:27:45	5-23-64	Ryde, England
Mildred Simpson, New Zealand	3:19:33	7-21-64	Auckland, New Zealand
Maureen Wilton, Canada	3:15:22	5-6-67	Toronto
Anni Pede-Erdkamp, West Germany	3:07:26	9-16-67	Waldniel, West Germany
Caroline Walker, United States	3:02:53	2-28-70	Seaside, OR
Elizabeth Bonner, United States	3:01:42	5-9-71	Philadelphia
Adrienne Beames, Australia	2:46:30	8-31-71	Werribee, Australia
Chantal Langlace, France	2:46:24	10-27-74	Neuf Brisach, France
Jacqueline Hansen, United States	2:43:54.5	12-1-74	Culver City, CA
Liane Winter, West Germany	2:42:24	4-21-75	Boston
Christa Vahlensieck, West Germany	2:40:15.8	5-3-75	Dülmen, West Germany
Jacqueline Hansen, United States	2:38:19	10-12-75	Eugene, OR
Chantal Langlace, France	2:35:15.4	5-1-77	Oyarzun, France
Christa Vahlensieck, West Germany	2:34:47.5	9-10-77	West Berlin, West Germany
Grete Waitz, Norway	2:32:29.9	10-22-78	New York City
Grete Waitz, Norway	2:27:32.6	10-21-79	New York City
Grete Waitz, Norway	2:25:41.3	10-26-80	New York City
Grete Waitz, Norway	2:25:29	4-17-83	London
Joan Benoit Samuelson, United States	2:22:43	4-18-83	Boston
Ingrid Kristiansen, Norway	2:21:06	4-21-85	London

The Boston Marathon began in 1897 as a local Patriot's Day event. Run every year but 1918 since then, it has grown into one of the world's premier marathons.

Men

Year	Winner	Time	Year	Winner	Time
1897	John J. McDermott, United States	2:55:10	1946	Stylianos Kyriakides, Greece	2:29:27
1898	Ronald J. McDonald, United States	2:42:00	1947	Yun Bok Suh, Korea	2:25:39
1899	Lawrence J. Brignolia, United States	2:54:38	1948	Gerard Cote, Canada	2:31:02
1900	James J. Caffrey, Canada	2:39:44	1949	Karl Gosta Leandersson, Sweden	2:31:50
1901	James J. Caffrey, Canada	2:29:23	1950	Kee Yong Ham, Korea	2:32:39
1902	Sammy Mellor, United States	2:43:12	1951	Shigeki Tanaka, Japan	2:27:45
1903	John C. Lorden, United States	2:41:29	1952	Doroteo Flores, Guatemala	2:31:53
1904	Michael Spring, United States	2:38:04	1953	Keizo Yamada, Japan	2:18:51
1905	Fred Lorz, United States	2:38:25	1954	Veikko Karvonen, Finland	2:20:39
1906	Timothy Ford, United States	2:45:45	1955	Hideo Hamamura, Japan	2:18:22
1907	Tom Longboat, Canada	2:24:24	1956	Antti Viskari, Finland	2:14:14
1908	Thomas Morrissey, United States	2:25:43	1957	John J. Kelley, United States	2:20:05
1909	Henri Renaud, United States	2:53:36	1958	Franjo Mihalic, Yugoslavia	2:25:54
1910	Fred Cameron, Canada	2:28:52	1959	Eino Oksanen, Finland	2:22:42
1911	Clarence H. DeMar, United States	2:21:39	1960	Paavo Kotila, Finland	2:20:54
1912	Mike Ryan, United States	2:21:18	1961	Eino Oksanen, Finland	2:23:39
1913	Fritz Carlson, United States	2:25:14	1962	Eino Oksanen, Finland	2:23:48
1914	James Duffy, Canada	2:25:01	1963	Aurele Vandendriessche, Belgium	2:18:58
1915	Edouard Fabre, Canada	2:31:41	1964	Aurele Vandendriessche, Belgium	2:19:59
1916	Arthur Roth, United States	2:27:16	1965	Morio Shigematsu, Japan	2:16:33
1917	Bill Kennedy, United States	2:28:37	1966	Kenji Kimihara, Japan	2:17:11
1918	No race		1967	David McKenzie, New Zealand	2:15:45
1919	Carl Linder, United States	2:29:13	1968	Amby Burfoot, United States	2:22:17
1920	Peter Trivoulidas, Greece	2:29:31	1969	Yoshiaki Unetani, Japan	2:13:49
1921	Frank Zuna, United States	2:18:57	1970	Ron Hill, England	2:10:30
1922	Clarence H. DeMar, United States	2:18:10	1971	Alvaro Mejia, Colombia	2:18:45
1923	Clarence H. DeMar, United States	2:23:37	1972	Olavi Suomalainen, Finland	2:15:39
1924	Clarence H. DeMar, United States	2:29:40	1973	Jon Anderson, United States	2:16:03
1925	Chuck Mellor, United States	2:33:00	1974	Neil Cusack, Ireland	2:13:39
1926	John C. Miles, Canada	2:25:40	1975	Bill Rodgers, United States	2:09:55
1927	Clarence H. DeMar, United States	2:40:22	1976	Jack Fultz, United States	2:20:19
1928	Clarence H. DeMar, United States	2:37:07	1977	Jerome Drayton, Canada	2:14:46
1929	John C. Miles, Canada	2:33:08	1978	Bill Rodgers, United States	2:10:13
1930	Clarence H. DeMar, United States	2:34:48	1979	Bill Rodgers, United States	2:09:27
1931	James (Hinky) Henigan, United States	2:46:45	1980	Bill Rodgers, United States	2:12:11
1932	Paul de Bruyn, Germany	2:33:36	1981	Toshihiko Seko, Japan	2:09:26
1933	Leslie Pawson, United States	2:31:01	1982	Alberto Salazar, United States	2:08:52
1934	Dave Komonen, Canada	2:32:53	1983	Gregory A. Meyer, United States	2:09:00
1935	John A. Kelley, United States	2:32:07	1984	Geoff Smith, England	2:10:34
1936	Ellison M. (Tarzan) Brown, United States	2:33:40	1985	Geoff Smith, England	2:14:05
1937	Walter Young, Canada	2:33:20	1986	Rob de Castella, Australia	2:07:51
1938	Leslie Pawson, United States	2:35:34	1987	Toshihiko Seko, Japan	2:11:50
1939	Ellison M. (Tarzan) Brown, United States	2:28:51	1988	Ibrahim Hussein, Kenya	2:08:43
1940	Gerard Cote, Canada	2:28:28	1989	Abebe Mekonnen, Ethiopia	2:09:06
1941	Leslie Pawson, United States	2:30:38	1990	Gelindo Bordin, Italy	2:08:19
1942	Bernard Joseph Smith, United States	2:26:51	1991	Ibrahim Hussein, Kenya	2:11:06
1943	Gerard Cote, Canada	2:28:25	1992	Ibrahim Hussein, Kenya	2:08:14
1944	Gerard Cote, Canada	2:31:50	1993	Cosmas N'Deti, Kenya	2:09:33
1945	John A. Kelley, United States	2:30:40	1994	Cosmas N'Deti, Kenya	2:07:15
			1995	Cosmas N'Deti, Kenya	2:09:22

Women

Year	Winner	Time	Year	Winner	Time
1966	Roberta Gibb, United States	3:21:40*	1976	Kim Merritt, United States	2:47:10
1967	Roberta Gibb, United States	3:27:17*	1977	Miki Gorman, United States	2:48:33
1968	Roberta Gibb, United States	3:30:00*	1978	Gayle Barron, United States	2:44:52
1969	Sara Mae Berman, United States	3:22:46*	1979	Joan Benoit, United States	2:35:15
1970	Sara Mae Berman, United States	3:05:07*	1980	Jacqueline Gareau, Canada	2:34:28
1971	Sara Mae Berman, United States	3:08:30*	1981	Allison Roe, New Zealand	2:26:46
1972	Nina Kuscsik, United States	3:10:36	1982	Charlotte Teske, West Germany	2:29:33
1973	Jacqueline A. Hansen, United States	3:05:59	1983	Joan Benoit, United States	2:22:43
1974	Miki Gorman, United States	2:47:11	1984	Lorraine Moller, New Zealand	2:29:28
1975	Liane Winter, West Germany	2:42:24	1985	Lisa Larsen Weidenbach, United States	2:34:06

Boston Marathon *(Cont.)*

Women *(Cont.)*

Year	Winner	Time	Year	Winner	Time
1986...Ingrid Kristiansen, Norway		2:24:55	1992...Olga Markova, Russia		2:23:43
1987...Rosa Mota, Portugal		2:25:21	1993...Olga Markova, Russia		2:25:27
1988...Rosa Mota, Portugal		2:24:30	1994...Uta Pippig, Germany		2:21:45
1989...Ingrid Kristiansen, Norway		2:24:33	1995...Uta Pippig, Germany		2:25:11*
1990...Rosa Mota, Portugal		2:25:24	*Unofficial.		
1991...Wanda Panfil, Poland		2:24:18			

Note: Over the years the Boston course has varied in length. The distances have been 24 miles, 1232 yards (1897-1923); 26 miles, 209 yards (1924-1926); 26 miles 385 yards (1927-1952); and 25 miles, 958 yards (1953-1956). Since 1957, the course has been certified to be the standard marathon distance of 26 miles, 385 yards.

New York City Marathon

From 1970 through 1975 the New York City Marathon was a small local race run in the city's Central Park. In 1976 it was moved to the streets of New York's five boroughs. It has since become one of the biggest and most prestigious marathons in the world.

Men

Year	Winner	Time	Year	Winner	Time
1970...Gary Muhrcke, United States		2:31:38	1983...Rod Dixon, New Zealand		2:08:59
1971...Norman Higgins, United States		2:22:54	1984...Orlando Pizzolato, Italy		2:14:53
1972...Sheldon Karlin, United States		2:27:52	1985...Orlando Pizzolato, Italy		2:11:34
1973...Tom Fleming, United States		2:21:54	1986...Gianni Poli, Italy		2:11:06
1974...Norbert Sander, United States		2:26:30	1987...Ibrahim Hussein, Kenya		2:11:01
1975...Tom Fleming, United States		2:19:27	1988...Steve Jones, Great Britain		2:08:20
1976...Bill Rodgers, United States		2:10:10	1989...Juma Ikangaa, Tanzania		2:08:01
1977...Bill Rodgers, United States		2:11:28	1990...Douglas Wakiihuri, Kenya		2:12:39
1978...Bill Rodgers, United States		2:12:12	1991...Salvador Garcia, Mexico		2:09:28
1979...Bill Rodgers, United States		2:11:42	1992...Willie Mtolo, South Africa		2:09:29
1980...Alberto Salazar, United States		2:09:41	1993...Andres Espinosa, Mexico		2:10:04
1981...Alberto Salazar, United States		2:08:13	1994...German Silva, Mexico		2:11:21
1982...Alberto Salazar, United States		2:09:29			

Women

Year	Winner	Time	Year	Winner	Time
1970...No finisher			1983...Grete Waitz, Norway		2:27:00
1971...Beth Bonner, United States		2:55:22	1984...Grete Waitz, Norway		2:29:30
1972...Nina Kuscsik, United States		3:08:41	1985...Grete Waitz, Norway		2:28:34
1973...Nina Kuscsik, United States		2:57:07	1986...Grete Waitz, Norway		2:28:06
1974...Katherine Switzer, United States		3:07:29	1987...Priscilla Welch, Great Britain		2:30:17
1975...Kim Merritt, United States		2:46:14	1988...Grete Waitz, Norway		2:28:07
1976...Miki Gorman, United States		2:39:11	1989...Ingrid Kristiansen, Norway		2:25:30
1977...Miki Gorman, United States		2:43:10	1990...Wanda Panfiil, Poland		2:30:45
1978...Grete Waitz, Norway		2:32:30	1991...Liz McColgan, Scotland		2:27:23
1979...Grete Waitz, Norway		2:27:33	1992...Lisa Ondieki, Australia		2:24:40
1980...Grete Waitz, Norway		2:25:41	1993...Uta Pippig, Germany		2:26:24
1981...Allison Roe, New Zealand		2:25:29	1994...Tecla Lorupe, Kenya		2:27:37
1982...Grete Waitz, Norway		2:27:14			

CROSS COUNTRY

World Cross-Country Championships

Conducted by the International Amateur Athletic Federation (IAAF), this meet annually brings together the best runners in the world at every distance from the mile to the marathon to compete in the same cross-country race.

Men

Year	Winner	Winning Team	Year	Winner	Winning Team
1973.....Pekka Paivarinta, Finland	Belgium		1978.....John Treacy, Ireland	France	
1974.....Eric DeBeck, Belgium	Belgium		1979.....John Treacy, Ireland	England	
1975.....Ian Stewart, Scotland	New Zealand		1980.....Craig Virgin, United States	England	
1976.....Carlos Lopes, Portugal	England		1981.....Craig Virgin, United States	Ethiopia	
1977.....Leon Schots, Belgium	Belgium		1982.....Mohammed Kedir, Ethiopia	Ethiopia	

Men (Cont.)

Year	Winner	Winning Team	Year	Winner	Winning Team
1983	Bekele Debele, Ethiopia	Ethiopia	1990	Khalid Skah, Morocco	Kenya
1984	Carlos Lopes, Portugal	Ethiopia	1991	Khalid Skah, Morocco	Kenya
1985	Carlos Lopes, Portugal	Ethiopia	1992	John Ngugi, Kenya	Kenya
1986	John Ngugi, Kenya	Kenya	1993	William Sigei, Kenya	Kenya
1987	John Ngugi, Kenya	Kenya	1994	William Sigei, Kenya	Kenya
1988	John Ngugi, Kenya	Kenya	1995	Paul Tergat, Kenya	Kenya
1989	John Ngugi, Kenya	Kenya			

Women

Year	Winner	Winning Team	Year	Winner	Winning Team
1973	Paola Cacchi, Italy	England	1985	Zola Budd, England	United States
1974	Paola Cacchi, Italy	England	1986	Zola Budd, England	England
1975	Julie Brown, United States	United States	1987	Annette Sergent, France	United States
1976	Carmen Valero, Spain	USSR	1988	Ingrid Kristiansen, Norway	USSR
1977	Carmen Valero, Spain	USSR	1989	Annette Sergent, France	USSR
1978	Grete Waitz, Norway	Romania	1990	Lynn Jennings, United States	USSR
1979	Grete Waitz, Norway	United States	1991	Lynn Jennings, United States	Kenya
1980	Grete Waitz, Norway	USSR	1992	Lynn Jennings, United States	Kenya
1981	Grete Waitz, Norway	USSR	1993	Albertina Dias, Portugal	Kenya
1982	Maricica Puica, Romania	USSR	1994	Helen Chepngeno, Kenya	Portugal
1983	Grete Waitz, Norway	United States	1995	Derartu Tulu, Ethiopia	Kenya
1984	Maricica Puica, Romania	United States			

Notable Achievements

Longest Winning Streaks

MEN

Event	Name and Nationality	Streak	Years
100-meter dash	Bob Hayes, United States	49	1962–64
200-meter dash	Manfred Gemar, Germany	41	1956–60
400-meter run	Michael Johnson, United States	33	1989–
800-meter run	Mal Whitfield, United States	40	1951–54
1500-meter run	Josy Barthel, Luxembourg	17	1952
1500-meter run/mile	Steve Ovett, Great Britain	45	1977–80
Mile	Herb Elliott, Australia	35	1957–60
Steeplechase	Gaston Roelants, Belgium	45	1961–66
5000-meter run	Emil Zátopek, Czechoslovakia	48	1949–52
10,000-meter run	Emil Zátopek, Czechoslovakia	38	1948–54
Marathon	Frank Shorter, United States	6	1971–73
110-meter hurdles	Jack Davis, United States	44	1952-55
400-meter hurdles	Edwin Moses, United States	107	1977–87
High Jump	Ernie Shelton, United States	46	1953–55
Pole Vault	Bob Richards, United States	50	1950–52
Long Jump	Carl Lewis, United States	65	1981–91
Triple Jump	Adhemar da Silva, Brazil	60	1950–56
Shot Put	Parry O'Brien, United States	116	1952–56
Discus Throw	Ricky Bruch, Sweden	54	1972–73
Hammer Throw	Imre Nemeth, Hungary	73	1946–50
Javelin Throw	Janis Lusis, USSR	41	1967–70
Decathlon	Bob Mathias, United States	11	1948–56

WOMEN

Event	Name and Nationality	Streak	Years
100-meter dash	Merlene Ottey, Jamaica	56	1987–91
200-meter dash	Irena Szewinska, Poland	38	1973–75
400-meter run	Irena Szewinska, Poland	36	1973–78
800-meter run	Ana Fidelia Quirot, Cuba	36	1987–90
1500-meter run	Paula Ivan, Romania	15	1988–91
1500-meter run/mile	Paula Ivan, Romania	19	1988–90
3000-meter run	Mary Slaney, United States	10	1982–84
10,000-meter run	Ingrid Kristiansen, Norway	5	1985–87

Longest Winning Streaks (Cont.)

WOMEN (Cont.)

Event	Name and Nationality	Streak	Years
Marathon	Katrin Dörre, East Germany	10	1982–86
100-meter hurdles	Annelie Ernhardt, East Germany	44	1972–75
400-meter hurdles	Ann-Louise Skoglund, Sweden	18	1981–83
High Jump	Iolanda Balas, Romania	140	1956–67
Long Jump	Tatyana Shchelkanova, USSR	19	1964–66
Shot Put	Nadezhda Chizhova, USSR	57	1969–73
Discus Throw	Gisela Mauermeyer, Germany	65	1935–42
Javelin Throw	Ruth Fuchs, East Germany	30	1972–73
Multi	Heide Rosendahl, West Germany	15	1969–72

Most Consecutive Years Ranked No. 1 in the World

MEN

No.	Name and Nationality	Event	Years
9	Victor Saneyev, USSR	Triple Jump	1968–76
8	Bob Richards, United States	Pole Vault	1949–56
8	Ralph Boston, United States	Long Jump	1960–67
7	Emil Zátopek (Czech)	10,000-meter run	1948–54

WOMEN

No.	Name and Nationality	Event	Years
9	Iolanda Balas, Romania	High Jump	1958–66
8	Ruth Fuchs, East Germany	Javelin Throw	1972–79
7	Faina Melnick, USSR	Discus Throw	1971–77

Major Barrier Breakers

MEN

Event	Mark	Name and Nationality	Date	Site
sub 10-second 100-meter dash	9.95	Jim Hines, United States	Oct. 14, 1968	Mexico City
sub 20-second 200-meter dash	19.83	Tommie Smith, United States	Oct. 16, 1968	Mexico City
sub 45-second 400-meter run	44.9	Otis Davis, United States	Sept. 6, 1960	Rome
sub 1:45 800-meter run	1:44.3	Peter Snell, New Zealand	Feb. 3, 1962	Christchurch, New Zealand
sub four minute mile	3:59.4	Roger Bannister, Great Britain	May 6, 1954	Oxford
sub 3:50 mile	3:49.4	John Walker, New Zealand	Aug. 12, 1975	Göteborg
sub 13-minute 5,000-meter run	12:58.39	Said Aouita, Morocco	July 22, 1986	Rome
sub 27:00 10,000-meter run	26:58.38	Yobes Ondieki, Kenya	July 10, 1993	Oslo
sub 13-second 110-meter hurdles	12.93	Renaldo Nehemiah, United States	Aug. 19, 1981	Zurich
sub 50-second 400-meter hurdles	49.5	Glenn Davis, United States	June 29, 1956	Los Angeles
7' high jump	7' ⅝"	Charles Dumas, United States	June 29, 1956	Los Angeles
8' high jump	8'	Javier Sotomayor, Cuba	July 29, 1989	San Juan
60' triple jump	60'¼"	Jonathan Edwards, Great Britain	Aug. 7, 1995	Göteborg
20' pole vault	20'	Sergei Bubka, USSR	March 15, 1991	San Sebastian, Spain
70' shot put	70' 7¼"	Randy Matson, United States	May 5, 1965	College Station, Texas
200' discus throw	200' 5"	Al Oerter, United States	May 18, 1962	Los Angeles
300' (new) javelin	300' 1"	Steve Backley, Great Britain	Jan. 25, 1992	Auckland, New Zealand

WOMEN

Event	Mark	Name and Nationality	Date	Site
sub 11-second 100-meter dash	10.88	Marlies Oelsner, East Germany	July 1, 1977	Dresden
sub 22-second 200-meter dash	21.71	Marita Koch, East Germany	June 10, 1979	Karl Marx Stadt
sub 50-second 400-meter run	49.9	Irena Szewinska, Poland	June 22, 1974	Warsaw
sub 2:00 800-meter run	1:59.1	Shin Geum Dan, North Korea	Nov. 12, 1963	Djakarta
sub 4:00 1500-meter run	3:56.0	Tatyana Kazankina, USSR	June 28, 1976	Podolsk, USSR

Major Barrier Breakers (Cont.)

WOMEN *(Cont.)*

Event	Mark	Name and Nationality	Date	Site
sub 4:20 mile	4:17.55	Mary Decker, United States	Feb. 16, 1980	Houston
sub 15:00 5,000-meter run	14:58.89	Ingrid Kristiansen, Norway	June 28, 1984	Oslo
sub 30:00 10,000-meter run	29:31.78	Wang Junxia, China	Sept. 8, 1993	Beijing
sub 2:30 marathon	2:27:33	Grete Waitz, Norway	Oct. 21, 1979	New York City
sub 13-second 100-meter hurdles	12.9	Karin Balzer, East Germany	Sept. 5, 1969	Berlin
6' high jump	6'	Iolanda Balas, Romania	Oct. 18, 1958	Budapest
70' shot put	70' 4½"	Nadyezhda Chizhova, USSR	Sept. 29, 1973	Varna, Bulgaria
200' discus throw	201'	Liesel Westermann, West Germany	Nov. 5, 1967	Sao Paulo
200' javelin throw	201' 4"	Elvira Ozolina, USSR	Aug. 27, 1964	Kiev
first 7,000-point heptathlon	7,148	Jackie Joyner-Kersee, United States	July 6–7, 1986	Moscow

Olympic Accomplishments

Oldest Olympic gold medalist—Patrick (Babe) McDonald, United States, 42 years, 26 days, 56-pound weight throw, 1920

Oldest Olympic medalist—Tebbs Lloyd Johnson, Great Britain, 48 years, 115 days, 1948 (bronze), 50K walk

Youngest Olympic gold medalist—Barbara Jones, United States, 15 years 123 days, 1952, 4 x 100 relay

Youngest gold medalist in individual event—Ulrike Meyfarth, West Germany, 16 years, 123 days, 1972, high jump

World Record Accomplishments*

Most world records equaled or set in a day—6, Jesse Owens, United States, 5/25/35, (9.4 100-yard dash; 26' 8¼" long jump; 20.3 200-meter dash and 220-yard dash; and 22.6 220-yard hurdles and 200-meter hurdles

Most records in a year—10, Gunder Hägg, Sweden, 1941-42, 1500 to 5,000 meters

Most records in a career—35, Sergei Bubka, 1983-94, pole vault indoors and out

Longest span of record setting—11 years, 20 days, Irena Szewinska, Poland, 1965-76, 200-meter dash

Youngest person to set a set world record—Carolina Gisolf, Holland, 15 years, 5 days, 1928, high jump , 5' 3⅜"

Youngest man to set a world record—John Thomas, United States, 17 years, 355 days, 1959, high jump, 7' 1¼"

Oldest person to set world record—Carlos Lopes, Portugal, 38 years, 59 days, marathon, 2:07:12

Greatest percentage improvement—6.59, Bob Beamon, United States, 1968, long jump

Longest lasting record—long jump, 26' 8¼", Jesse Owens, United States, 25 years (1935-60)

Highest clearance over head, men—23¼", Franklin Jacobs United States (5' 8"), 1978

Highest clearance over head, woman—12¾", Yolanda Henry, United States (5' 6"), 1990

*Marks sanctioned by the IAAF

Primo Donna

The 1995 World Indoor Track and Field Championships in Barcelona featured fewer stars than had any of the event's four previous stagings. Among the absent were virually all of the sport's royalty: Jackie Joyner-Kersee, Michael Johnson, Gwen Torrence, Mike Powell, Noureddine Morceli and Carl Lewis. This didn't please Primo Nebiolo, president of the International Amateur Athletic Federation (IAAF), the event's organizer, who reacted like a little boy furious that people wouldn't come to his birthday party.

In his 14 years as head of the IAAF, Nebiolo has never quite accepted that the world doesn't regard his wishes as commands. When Olympic 100-meter champ Linford Christie announced on March 6 that because of fatigue at the end of a long season, he, too, would not be competing in Barcelona, the 71-year-old Nebiolo swung into action. "I appeal to him as a great champion to reconsider," said Nebiolo, hinting that he might grant Christie an unprecedented at-large invitation when Christie insisted that wouldn't be willing to bump Michael Rosswess, who had been awarded his place on the British team. Christie demurred just the same.

One reason so few stars were in Barcelona is the current glut of championships being billed as "major," a situation Nebiolo himself created. In 1987, when the first world indoor meet was held, its outdoor counterpart was contested only quadrenially. Now that each is held every two years, it's hard to persuade athletes who normally command appearance fees of $25,000 or more that it's worth their while to participate for glory alone. Currently there's only one meet they'll attend without the lure of prize money: the Olympics.

In early March Nebiolo did announce that prize money will be awarded at all IAAF championships after the 1996 Olympics. Providing cash payouts is only fair, given the many lucrative sponsorships the IAAF has, plus the five-year, $92 million TV contract the body signed last year with the European Broadcasting Union. Track's athletes are willing to be led, but they can't be blamed for liking their carrots green.

Swimming

Sports Illustrated

Tom Terrific

Michigan star Tom Dolan shatters three U.S. records at the NCAAs

The Next Wave

Two legends of U.S. swimming saw their Gehrigesque winning streaks ended as new stars swam into the spotlight

by Gerry Callahan

THEY WERE the Iron Horses of the sport of swimming, and in the summer of 1995, they sank. Janet Evans hadn't lost the 800-meter freestyle in eight years while Melvin Stewart's reign in the 200-meter butterfly dated back even further. No one had out-raced Stewart since 1986, and his string of consecutive national titles in the event was up to 12. The last time either Evans or Stewart had suffered a defeat in their respective specialties, Ronald Reagan was running the country and Cal Ripken had a full head of hair and no realistic chance of breaking Lou Gehrig's record.

While baseball celebrated Ripken's 2,131st straight game last summer, the most notable streaks in the sport of swimming were struck down. In August, Evans lost at the national championships in Pasadena, Calif., to Brooke Bennett, a brash 15-year-old who, earlier in the year, had stirred up controversy with some less-than-respectful comments about the legendary Evans. Bennett had said that Evans "gets a little scared" when the two go head-to-head, and then the teen phenom backed up her words with a national champi-

onship in the 800 freestyle. Evans, meanwhile, was not exactly left to lament a split-second defeat—she finished fourth, behind Bennett, Trina Jackson and Christina Teuscher. She also was beaten at the nationals by Bennett in the 400 and 1,500 freestyles.

Stewart's summer wasn't much better. On June 14 the defending Olympic champion in the 200-meter butterfly saw his world record wiped out by Denis Pankratov of Russia, and a few days later his nine-year winning streak was snapped at the Charlotte Ultra Swim. Then things really went south for Stewart: In Pasadena in August, Ray Carey of Stanford knocked off Stewart in the 200 butterfly to snap his national-title streak at an even dozen. Stewart was experimenting with an extended underwater dolphin kick that he had hoped would make him a favorite at the Atlanta Olympics next year. Instead the once untouchable Tennessee native looked like just another swimmer struggling to make the U.S. team.

It was that kind of year in the sport of swimming. Maybe the mighty didn't fall, but they sure did slip a notch. Even the contro-

After nearly a decade on top, Evans had little to smile about in '95.

RICHARD MACKSON

versial Chinese team, which left the '94 world championships with a planeload of world records, seemed to swim off the face of the earth in 1995. The Chinese women, virtually all newcomers to international competition, won 12 of 16 events in Rome and set five world records, and they did it all with charges of drug use swirling above the pool. In '95 the Chinese kept to themselves, revealing little about their national meets to the rest of the world, and no one is quite sure what to expect of them in Atlanta.

For the U.S., the best story to come out of Rome in '94 seemed to get even better back home this year. Tom Dolan, the University of Michigan star who set a world record at the age of 18 in the 400-meter individual medley in '94, won just about everything he entered in '95. At the NCAA championships in Indianapolis in March, Dolan set three U.S. records in three days, and when he reached the end of the pool, no one ever asked for a recount.

Dolan shattered the old NCAA marks in the 500 freestyle (by 2.84 seconds), the 400 individual medley (2.46 seconds) and the 1,650 freestyle (by 5.7 seconds). Dolan also joined three Michigan teammates to capture the 800 freestyle relay as the Wolverines won their first national title in 34 years. For the season at Michigan, Dolan lost only once in his specialty events. At the Pan Pacific Games in Atlanta, he christened the Olympic pool with gold medals in the 200 and 400 individual medleys. USA Swimming named Dolan its Swimmer of the Year for 1995.

"He's the best," says Michigan coach Jon Urbanchek. "He's got the body, the desire, the competitive instinct. Put it all together, and you've got a champion."

You've also got an incredible story. Dolan stands 6'6", weighs 180 pounds and moves through the water like an eel. He appears to be a natural-born swimmer—except for one minor drawback: He can't breathe. At least not as easily as the swimmers in the other lanes. Dolan, 20, has exercise-induced asthma and an unusually narrow windpipe that allows him only 20% of the oxygen intake of the average person. These conditions mean that, for Dolan, swimming is not nearly as difficult as coming up for air. "It can really get bad in our workouts," says Dolan. "There will be some real tightness in my chest, and I won't be able to get a lot of air. But my coach says it actually helps me in meets because it increases my ability to withstand stress."

At the national championships, the Southern California smog caused major problems for Dolan, and he lost out in the 400-meter individual medley to Eric Namesnik, a silver medalist in Barcelona in '92. Depending on the air quality in Atlanta, Dolan could be the United States's best hope for a gold medal in swimming next year.

Another bright spot for the U.S. in an otherwise forgettable '95 was the men's 400-free relay team, which set a world record at the Pan Pac Games. The foursome included David Fox, Joe Huderpohl, Jon Olsen and Gary Hall Jr., whose father broke world records seven times in the late '60s and early '70s. Young Hall also won gold medals at the Pan Pac Games in the 50 freestyle and the 100 freestyle. It wasn't a good year for legends of swimming in the U.S., but it wasn't bad for a son of a legend.

1995 Major Competitions

Men

U.S. INDOOR CHAMPIONSHIPS
Minneapolis, Minnesota, March 14-18

50 free	David Fox, unattached, 20.23
100 free	David Fox, unattached, 49.43
200 free	David Fox, unattached, 1:51.88
400 free	Reeve Irvin, Charleston, 3:57.11
800 free	Andy Potts, Eastern Express, 8:10.00
1500 free	Reeve Irvin, Charleston, 15:33.49
100 back	Bart Kizierowski, Mission Viejo, 56.83
200 back	Tate Blahnik, NJ Wave, 2:01.18
100 breast	Lief Engstrom, Ft Lauderdale, 1:03.49
200 breast	Lief Engstrom, Ft Lauderdale, 2:18.11
100 fly	Mel Stewart, Tennessee, 53.90
200 fly	Mel Stewart, Tennessee, 1:58.24
200 IM	Sergey Mariniuk, Santa Clara, 2:02.80
400 IM	Sergey Mariniuk, Santa Clara, 4:18.84
400 m relay	Ft Lauderdale, 3:48.59
400 f relay	Ohio State, 3:27.17
800 f relay	Mission Viejo, 7:36.04
1-m spgbd	David Pichler, Ft Lauderdale, 390.42
3-m spgbd	Mark Bradshaw, Ohio State, 646.50
Platform	David Pichler, Ft Lauderdale, 593.13
3-m sync dv.	Brian Earley/Kevin McMahon, 329.43
10-m sync plt.	Mark Ruiz/Kongzheng Li, 315.99

Diving competitions held in Midland, TX, April 19-23.

U.S. OUTDOOR CHAMPIONSHIPS
Pasadena, California, July 31-August 4

Jon Olsen, Curl-Burke, 22.42
Jon Olsen, Curl-Burke, 49.44
Chad Carvin, Hilldenbrand Aquatics, 1:48.43
John Piersma, Club Wolverine, 3:49.72
Peter Wright, JW, 8:06.27
Carlton Bruner, Club Wolverine, 15:17.17
Jeff Rouse, Phoenix, 55.29
Tripp Schwenk, SYS, 1:58.33‡
Kurt Grote, Stanford Swimming, 1:01.91
Eric Wunderlich, Napa Valley, 2:15.14
Mark Henderson, Curl-Burke, 53.59
Ray Carey, Stanford Swimming, 1:59.17
Paul Nelsen, FLST, 2:02.11
Eric Namesnik, Club Wolverine, 4:15.57
Phoenix, 3:41.56
Curl-Burke, 3:20.29
Curl-Burke, 7:25.89
David Pichler, Ft Lauderdale Diving, 377.97
Kent Ferguson, Miami Diving, 651.51
Patrick Jeffrey, Team Orlando, 584.16
Brain Earley/Kevin McMahon, 323.34
Chuck Wade/David Pichler, 323.46

Diving competitions held in Bartlesville, OK, August 9-13.

EUROPEAN CHAMPIONSHIPS
Vienna, Austria, August 22-29

50 free	Alexander Popov, Russia, 22.25
100 free	Alexander Popov, Russia, 49.10
200 free	Jani Sievinen, Finland, 1:48.98
400 free	Steffen Zesner, Germany, 3:50.35
800 free	not held
1500 free	Jorg Hoffmann, Germany, 15:11.25
100 back	Vladimir Selkov, Russia, 55.48
200 back	Vladimir Selkov, Russia, 1:58.48
100 breast	Frederic deBurghgraeve, Belgium, 1:01.12
200 breast	Andrei Korneev, Russia, 2:12.62
100 fly	Denis Pankratov, Russia, 52.32#
200 fly	Denis Pankratov, Russia, 1:56.34
200 IM	Jani Sievinen, Finland, 1:58.61
400 IM	Jani Sievinen, Finland, 4:14.75
400 m relay	Russia, 3:38.11
400 f relay	Russia, 3:18.84
800 f relay	Germany, 7:18.22

PAN PACIFIC CHAMPIONSHIPS
Atlanta, Georgia, August 10-13

Gary Hall, United States, 22.30
Gary Hall, United States, 49.47
Danyon Loader, New Zealand, 1:48.72
Daniel Kowalski, Australia, 3:50.01
Daniel Kowalski, Australia, 7:50.28
Kieren Perkins, Australia, 14:58.92
Jeff Rouse, United States, 54.98
Tripp Schwenk, United States, 1:58.87
Eric Wunderlich, United States, 1:01.80
Akira Hayashi, Japan, 2:13.60
Scott Miller, Australia, 53.07
Scott Miller, Australia, 1:57.86
Tom Dolan, United States, 2:00.89
Tom Dolan, United States, 4:14.77
United States, 3:37.04
United States, 3:15.11#
Australia, 7:17.52

WORLD UNIVERSITY GAMES
Fukuoka, Japan, August 24-29

50 free	Fernando Scherer, Brazil, 22.48
100 free	Fernando Scherer, Brazil, 49.89
200 free	Yann deFabrique, France, 1:50.04
400 free	Josh Davis, United States, 3:51.95
800 free	Christian Piper, Germany, 8:04.89
1500 free	Hisato Yasui, Japan, 15:26.81
100 back	Kurt Jachimowski, United States, 56.30
200 back	Sang Joon Ji, Korea, 2:01.19
100 breast	Akira Hayashi, Japan, 1:02.71
200 breast	Alexander Tkatchev, Russia, 2:14.69*
100 fly	Jason Lancaster, United States, 53.15

PAN AMERICAN GAMES
Mar del Plata, Argentina, March 12-17

Fernando deQueiroz, Brazil, 22.65
Gustavo Borges, Brazil, 49.31
Gustavo Borges, Brazil, 1:48.49
Josh Davis, United States, 3:55.59
not held
Carlton Bruehner, United States, 15:13.90
Jeff Rouse, United States, 54.74
Brad Bridgewater, United States, 2:00.79
Seth van Nueerden, United States, 1:02.48
Seth van Neerden, United States, 2:16.08
Mark Henderson, United States, 54:11

#World record; ‡American record.

Men *(Cont.)*

WORLD UNIVERSITY GAMES *(Cont.)*

200 fly ....Tom Malchow, United States, 2:00.78
200 IM ....Tom Wilkins, United States, 2:02.96
400 IM ....Ian Mull, United States, 4:21.41
400 m relay ..United States, 3:42.02*
400 f relay ....United States, 3:19.44*
800 f relay ....United States, 7:17.83*
1-m spgbd ...Zaho Xin, China, 395.37
3-m spgbd ...Fernando Platas, Mexico, 619.20
Platform ....Cheng Wei, China, 628.74

PAN AMERICAN GAMES *(Cont.)*

Nelson Molina, Venezuela, 2:00.38
Curtis Myden, Canada, 2:01.70
Curtis Myden, Canada, 4:18.55
United States, 3:41.24
United States, 3:18.60*
United States, 7:21.61*
Dean Panaro, United States, 404.82
Fernando Platas, Mexico, 661.80
Fernando Platas, Mexico, 617.52

FINA/ALAMO DIVING GRAND PRIX
Fort Lauderdale, Florida, May 11-14

1-m spgbd ...David Pichler, United States, 386.61
3-m spgbd ...Xiong Ni, China, 666.99
Platform ....Jan Hempel, Germany, 663.30
3-m sync ......Pichler/Ferguson, United States, 284.49
10-m sync ...Xu/Tian, China, 313.89

WORLD DIVING CUP
Atlanta, Georgia, September 5-9

Yu Zhoucheng, China, 418.50
Dmitry Sautin, Russia, 684.21
Sun Shuwei, China, 681.48
not held
not held

Women

U.S. INDOOR CHAMPIONSHIPS
Minneapolis, Minnesota, March 14-18

50 free ....Ashley Chandler, SwimAtlanta, 25.64
100 free ....Lauren Thies, Multnomah, 56.48
200 free ....Lauren Thies, Multnomah, 2:01.15
400 free ....Janet Evans, Trojan, 4:14.34
800 free ....Janet Evans, Trojan, 8:40.66
1500 free .....Janet Evans, Trojan, 16:34.43
100 back .....Shelly Ripple, Bengal, 1:03.21
200 back .....Beth Botsford, North Baltimore, 2:13.53
100 breast ...A. McReynolds, Scenic, 1:10.93
200 breast ...A. McReynolds, Scenic, 2:29.83
100 fly..........Karen Campbell, SW Michigan, 1:00.89
200 fly..........Collin Sherman, Bolles Sharks, 2:14.69
200 IM ....J. Parmenter, Canyons, 2:27.10
400 IM ....J. Parmenter, Canyons, 4:46.36
1-m spgbd...Carrie Zarse, unattached, 264.48
3-m spgbd...Melisa Moses, unattached, 512.52
Platform ....Patty Armstrong, Woodlands, 451.74
3-m sync .....Janae Lautenschlager/Amy Sloan, 274.14
10-m sync ...Kristin Ling/Paige Weiskittel, 272.19
Diving competitions held in Midland, TX, April 19-23.

EUROPEAN CHAMPIONSHIPS
Vienna, Austria, August 22-29

50 free ....Linda Olofsson, Sweden, 25.76
100 free ....Franziska van Almsick, Germany, 55.34
200 free ....Kerstin Kielgass, Germany, 2:00.56
400 free ....Franziska van Almsick, Germany, 4:08.37
800 free ....Julia Jung, Germany, 8:36.08
1500 free .....not held
100 back .....Mett Jacobsen, Denmark, 1:02.46
200 back .....Krisztina Egerszegi, Hungary, 2:07.24

U.S. OUTDOOR CHAMPIONSHIPS
Pasadena, California, July 31-August 4

Amy Van Dyken, RNT, 25.13
Angel Martino, Americus, 55.91
Cristina Teuscher, Badger, 2:00.78
Brooke Bennett, BSTC Blue Wave, 4:10.72
Brooke Bennett, BSTC Blue Wave, 8:31.84
Brooke Bennett, BSTC Blue Wave, 16:17.84
Lea Loveless, Badger, 1:02.44
Beth Botsford, North Baltimore, 2:12.82
Amanda Beard, Irvine Novas, 1:10.37
A. McReynolds, Scenic City, 2:28.92
Jenny Thompson, Stanford, 1:00.19
Michelle Griglione, Curl-Burke, 2:11.56
Allison Wagner, Florida Aquatics, 2:15.99
Kristine Quance, Trojan-CA, 4:45.97
Doris Glenn Easterly, Ft Lauderdale, 242.79
Eileen Richetelli, STD, 494.43
Becky Ruehl, Cincinnati Stingrays, 478.47
Jenny Keim/Reyne Borup, 253.56
Patty Armstrong/Laura Wilkinson, 248.85
Diving competitions held in Bartlesville, OK, August 9-13.

PAN PACIFIC CHAMPIONSHIPS
Atlanta, Georgia, August 10-13

Amy Van Dyken, United States, 25.03‡
Jenny Thompson, United States, 55.31
Suzu Chiba, Japan, 2:00.00
Brooke Bennett, United States, 4:10.46
Haley Lewis, Australia, 8:28.78
Brooke Bennett, United States, 16:15.58
Noriko Inada, Japan, 1:02.02
Nicole Stevenson, Australia, 2:11.26

*Meet record; ‡American record.

Women (Cont.)

EUROPEAN CHAMPIONSHIPS (Cont.)

100 breast	Brigitte Becue, Belgium,	1:09.30
200 breast	Brigitte Becue, Belgium,	2:27.60
100 fly	Mett Jacobsen, Denmark,	1:00.64
200 fly	Michelle Smith, Ireland,	2:11.60
200 IM	Michelle Smith, Ireland,	2:15.27
400 IM	Krisztina Egerszegi, Hungary,	4:40.33
400 m relay	Germany,	4:09.97
400 f relay	Germany,	3:43.89
800 f relay	Germany,	8:06.11

PAN PACIFIC CHAMPIONSHIPS (Cont.)

Penelope Haynes, South Africa, 1:08.09
Samantha Riley, Australia, 2:24.81
Susan O'Neill, Australia, 59:58
Susan O'Neill, Australia, 2:07.29
Ellie Overton, Australia, 2:14.68
Kumie Kurotori, Japan, 4:44.22
Australia, 4:02.93
United States, 3:41.59
United States, 8:02.68

WORLD UNIVERSITY GAMES
Fukuoka, Japan, August 24-29

50 free	Jilin Sun, China,	26.19
100 free	Martina Moravcova, Slovakia,	56.70
200 free	Lisa Jacob, United States,	2:02.03
400 free	Emily Peters, United States,	4:13.89
800 free	Tamako Kihara, Japan,	8:40.68
1500 free	Toby Smith, United States,	16:20.58
100 back	Kristin Heydenek, United States,	1:02.86
200 back	Yoko Koikawa, Japan,	2:14.61
100 breast	Penelope Hines, South Africa,	1:08.47
200 breast	Penelope Hines, South Africa,	2:28.44
100 fly	Liu Limin, China,	59:74*
200 fly	Tomoko Kunimitsu, Japan,	2:10.29
200 IM	Fumie Kurotori, Japan,	2:17.00
400 IM	Fumie Kurotori, Japan,	4:45.66
400 m relay	United States,	4:10.49*
400 f relay	United States,	3:46.68
800 f relay	United States,	8:05.18*
1-m spgbd	Dorte Lindner, Germany,	264.54
3-m spgbd	Rao Lang, China,	493.08
Platform	Eileen Richetelli, United States,	479.76

PAN AMERICAN GAMES
Mar del Plata, Argentina, March 12-17

Angel Martino, United States, 25.40*
Angel Martino, United States, 55.62
Christina Teuscher, United States, 2:01.49
Brooke Bennett, United States, 4:11.78
Trina Jackson, United States, 8:35.42
not held
B.J. Bedford, United States, 1:01.71*
B.J. Bedford, United States, 2:12.98*
Lisa Flood, Canada, 1:10.36
Lisa Flood, Canada, 2:31.33
Amy Van Dyken, United States, 1:00.71
Trina Jackson, United States, 2:12.37
Joanne Malar, Canada, 2:15.66*
Joanne Malar, Canada, 4:43.64
United States, 4:08.17*
United States, 3:44.71*
United States, 8:07.30
Mayte Garbey, Cuba, 270.15
Annie Pelletier, Canada, 519.81
Anne Montminy, Canada, 492.39

FINA/ALAMO DIVING GRAND PRIX
Fort Lauderdale, Florida, May 11-14

1-m spgbd	Yuki Motobuchi, Japan,	268.41
3-m spgbd	Tan Shuping, China,	522.03
Platform	Svetlana Timoshinina, Russia,	475.20
3-m sync	Fu/Tan, China,	268.02
10-m sync	Guo/Xiong, China,	303.84

WORLD DIVING CUP
Atlanta, Georgia, September 5-9

Vera Ilyina, Russia, 287.49
Fu Mingxia, China, 540.63
Chi Bin, China, 512.82
not held
not held

*Meet record

Men

Event	Mark	Record Holder	Date	Site
200 backstroke	1:58.33	Tripp Schwenk (A)	8-1-95	Pasadena
100 butterfly	52.32	Denis Pankratov, Russia (W)	8-23-95	Vienna
200 butterfly	1:55.22	Denis Pankratov, Russia (W)	6-14-95	Canet, France
400 freestyle relay	3:43.80	United States (David Fox, Joe Hudepohl, Jon Olsen, Gary Hall) (W,A)	8-12-95	Atlanta

Women

50 freestyle	25.03	Amy Van Dyken (A)	8-13-95	Atlanta

FOR THE RECORD·Year by Year

MEN
Freestyle

Event	Time	Record Holder	Date	Site
50 meters	21.81	Tom Jager (W,A)	3-24-90	Nashville
100 meters	48.42	Alexander Popov, Russia (W)	6-18-94	Monte Carlo
		Matt Biondi (A)	8-10-88	Austin
200 meters	1:46.69	Giorgio Lamberti, Italy (W)	8-15-89	Bonn
	1:47.72	Matt Biondi (A)	8-8-88	Austin
400 meters	3:43.80	Kieran Perkins, Australia (W)	9-9-94	Rome
	3:48.06	Matt Cetlinski (A)	8-11-88	Austin
800 meters	7:46.00	Kieran Perkins, Australia (W)	8-24-94	Vancouver, B.C.
	7:52.45	Sean Killion (A)	7-27-87	Clovis, CA
1500 meters	14:41.66	Kieran Perkins, Australia (W)	8-24-94	Vancouver, B.C.
	15:01.51	George DiCarlo (A)	6-30-84	Indianapolis

Backstroke

Event	Time	Record Holder	Date	Site
100 meters	53.86*	Jeff Rouse (W,A)	7-31-92	Barcelona
200 meters	1:56.57	Martin Zubero, Spain (W)	11-23-91	Tuscaloosa, AL
	1:58.33	Tripp Schwenk (A)	8-1-95	Pasadena

*Set on first leg of relay.

Breaststroke

Event	Time	Record Holder	Date	Site
100 meters	1:00.95	Karoly Guttler, Hungary (W)	8-5-93	Sheffield, England
	1:01.40	Nelson Diebel (A)	3-1-92	Indianapolis
	1:01.40	Seth Van Neerden (A)	8-14-94	Indianapolis
200 meters	2:10.16	Mike Barrowman (W,A)	7-29-92	Barcelona

Butterfly

Event	Time	Record Holder	Date	Site
100 meters	52.32	Denis Pankratov, Russia (W)	8-23-95	Vienna
	52.84	Pablo Morales (A)	6-23-86	Orlando, FL
200 meters	1:55.22	Denis Pankratov, Russia (W)	6-14-95	Canet, France
	1:55.69	Melvin Stewart (A)	1-12-91	Perth, Australia

Individual Medley

Event	Time	Record Holder	Date	Site
200 meters	1:59.36	Jani Sievinen, Finland (W)	9-11-94	Rome
	2:00.11	Dave Wharton (A)	8-20-89	Tokyo
400 meters	4:12.30	Tom Dolan (W,A)	9-6-94	Rome

Relays

Event	Time	Record Holder	Date	Site
400-meter medley	3:36.93	United States (David Berkoff, Rich Schroeder, Matt Biondi, Chris Jacobs) (W,A)	9-23-88	Seoul
	3:36.93	United States (Jeff Rouse, Nelson Diebel, Pablo Morales, Jon Olsen), (W, A)	7-31-92	Barcelona
400-meter freestyle	3:15.11	United States (David Fox, Joe Hudepohl, Jon Olsen, Gary Hall) (W,A)	8-12-95	Atlanta
800-meter freestyle	7:11.95	EUN (Dmitri Lepikov, Vladimir Taianovitch Veniamin Taianovitch, Yevgeny Sadovyi) (W)	7-27-92	Barcelona
	7:12.51	United States (Troy Dalbey, Matt Cetlinski, Doug Gjertsen, Matt Biondi) (A)	9-21-88	Seoul

WOMEN

Freestyle

Event	Time	Record Holder	Date	Site
50 meters	24.51	Li Jingyi, China (W)	9-11-94	Rome
	25.03	Amy Van Dyken (A)	8-13-95	Atlanta
100 meters	54.01	Li Jingyi, China (W)	9-5-94	Rome
	54.48	Jenny Thompson (A)	3-1-92	Indianapolis
200 meters	1:57.55	Franziska van Almsick, Germany (W)	9-6-94	Rome
	1:57.90	Nicole Haislett (A)	7-27-92	Barcelona
400 meters	4:03.85	Janet Evans (W,A)	9-22-88	Seoul
800 meters	8:16.22	Janet Evans (W,A)	8-20-89	Tokyo
1500 meters	15:52.10	Janet Evans (W,A)	3-26-88	Orlando, FL

Backstroke

Event	Time	Record Holder	Date	Site
100 meters	1:00.16	He Cihong, China (W)	9-10-94	Rome
	1:00.82†	Lea Loveless (A)	7-30-92	Barcelona
200 meters	2:06.62	Krisztina Egerszegi, Hungary (W)	8-26-91	Athens, Greece
	2:08.60	Betsy Mitchell (A)	6-27-86	Orlando, FL

Breaststroke

Event	Time	Record Holder	Date	Site
100 meters	1:07.69	Samantha Riley, Australia (W)	9-9-94	Rome
	1:08.17	Anita Nall (A)	7-29-92	Barcelona
200 meters	2:24.76	Rebecca Brown (W)	3-16-94	Queensland, Aus.
	2:25.35	Anita Nall (A)	3-2-92	Indianapolis

Butterfly

Event	Time	Record Holder	Date	Site
100 meters	57.93	Mary T. Meagher (W,A)	8-16-81	Brown Deer, WI
200 meters	2:05.96	Mary T. Meagher (W,A)	8-13-81	Brown Deer, WI

Individual Medley

Event	Time	Record Holder	Date	Site
200 meters	2:11.65	Lin Li, China (W)	7-30-92	Barcelona
	2:11.91	Summer Sanders (A)	7-30-92	Barcelona
400 meters	4:36.10	Petra Schneider, East Germany (W)	8-1-82	Guayaquil, Ecuador
	4:37.58	Summer Sanders (A)	7-26-92	Barcelona

Relays

Event	Time	Record Holder	Date	Site
400-meter medley	4:01.67	China (He Cihong, Dai Guohong, Liu Limin, Lo Jingyi) (W)	9-10-94	Rome
	4:02.54	United States (Lea Loveless, Anita Nall, Crissy Ahmann-Leighton, Jenny Thompson) (A)	7-30-92	Barcelona
400-meter freestyle	3:37.91	China (Le Jingyi, Ying Shan, Le Ying, Lu Bin) (W)	9-7-94	Rome
	3:39.46	United States (Nicole Haislett, Dara Torres Angel Martino, Jenny Thompson) (A)	7-28-92	Barcelona
800-meter freestyle	7:55.47	East Germany (Manuela Stellmach, Astrid Strauss, Anke Mohring, Heike Friedrich) (W)	8-18-87	Strasbourg, France
	8:02.12	United States (Betsy Mitchell, Mary T. Meagher, Kim Brown, Mary Wayte) (A)	8-22-86	Madrid

†Time swum on leadoff leg of 400-meter medley relay.

Venues: Belgrade, Sep 4-9, 1973; Cali, Colombia, July 18-27, 1975; West Berlin, Aug 20-28, 1978; Guayaquil, Equador, Aug 1-7, 1982; Madrid, Aug 17-22, 1986; Perth, Australia, Jan 7-13, 1991; Rome, Sep 1-11, 1994.

MEN

50-meter Freestyle

1986	Tom Jager, United States	22.49‡
1991	Tom Jager, United States	22.16‡
1994	Alexander Popov, Russia	22.17

100-meter Freestyle

1973	Jim Montgomery, United States	51.70
1975	Andy Coan, United States	51.25
1978	David McCagg, United States	50.24
1982	Jorg Woithe, East Germany	50.18
1986	Matt Biondi, United States	48.94
1991	Matt Biondi, United States	49.18
1994	Alexander Popov, Russia	49.12

200-meter Freestyle

1973	Jim Montgomery, United States	1:53.02
1975	Tim Shaw, United States	1:52.04‡
1978	Billy Forrester, United States	1:51.02‡
1982	Michael Gross, West Germany	1:49.84
1986	Michael Gross, West Germany	1:47.92
1991	Giorgio Lamberti, Italy	1:47.27‡
1994	Antti Kasvio, Finland	1:47.32

400-meter Freestyle

1973	Rick DeMont, United States	3:58.18‡
1975	Tim Shaw, United States	3:54.88‡
1978	Vladimir Salnikov, USSR	3:51.94‡
1982	Vladimir Salnikov, USSR	3:51.30‡
1986	Rainer Henkel, West Germany	3:50.05
1991	Joerg Hoffman, Germany	3:48.04‡
1994	Kieran Perkins, Australia	3:43.80*

1500-meter Freestyle

1973	Stephen Holland, Australia	15:31.85
1975	Tim Shaw, United States	15:28.92‡
1978	Vladimir Salnikov, USSR	15:03.99‡
1982	Vladimir Salnikov, USSR	15:01.77‡
1986	Rainer Henkel, West Germany	15:05.31
1991	Joerg Hoffman, Germany	14:50.36*
1994	Kieran Perkins, Australia	14:50.52

100-meter Backstroke

1973	Roland Matthes, East Germany	57.47
1975	Roland Matthes, East Germany	58.15
1978	Bob Jackson, United States	56.36‡
1982	Dirk Richter, East Germany	55.95
1986	Igor Polianski, USSR	55.58‡
1991	Jeff Rouse, United States	55.23‡
1994	Martin Lopez Zubero, Spain	55.17‡

200-meter Backstroke

1973	Roland Matthes, East Germany	2:01.87†
1975	Zoltan Varraszto, Hungary	2:05.05
1978	Jesse Vassallo, United States	2:02.16
1982	Rick Carey, United States	2:00.82‡
1986	Igor Polianski, USSR	1:58.78‡
1991	Martin Zubero, Spain	1:59.52
1994	Vladimir Selkov, Russia	1:57.42‡

100-meter Breaststroke

1973	John Hencken, United States	1:04.02†
1975	David Wilkie, Great Britain	1:04.26‡
1978	Walter Kusch, West Germany	1:03.56‡
1982	Steve Lundquist, United States	1:02.75‡
1986	Victor Davis, Canada	1:02.71
1991	Norbert Rozsa, Hungary	1:01.45*
1994	Norbert Rozsa, Hungary	1:01.24‡

200-meter Breaststroke

1973	David Wilkie, Great Britain	2:19.28†
1975	David Wilkie, Great Britain	2:18.23‡
1978	Nick Nevid, United States	2:18.37
1982	Victor Davis, Canada	2:14.77*
1986	Jozsef Szabo, Hungary	2:14.27‡
1991	Mike Barrowman, United States	2:11.23*
1994	Norbert Rozsa, Hungary	2:12.81

100-meter Butterfly

1973	Bruce Robertson, Canada	55.69
1975	Greg Jagenburg, United States	55.63
1978	Joe Bottom, United States	54.30
1982	Matt Gribble, United States	53.88‡
1986	Pablo Morales, United States	53.54‡
1991	Anthony Nesty, Suriname	53.29‡
1994	Rafal Szukala, Poland	53.51

200-meter Butterfly

1973	Robin Backhaus, United States	2:03.32
1975	Bill Forrester, United States	2:01.95‡
1978	Mike Bruner, United States	1:59.38‡
1982	Michael Gross, East Germany	1:58.85‡
1986	Michael Gross, East Germany	1:56.53‡
1991	Melvin Stewart, United States	1:55.69*
1994	Denis Pankratov, Russia	1:56.54

200-meter Individual Medley

1973	Gunnar Larsson, Sweden	2:08.36
1975	Andras Hargitay, Hungary	2:07.72
1978	Graham Smith, Canada	2:03.65*
1982	Alexander Sidorenko, USSR	2:03.30‡
1986	Tamás Darnyi, Hungary	2:01.57‡
1991	Tamás Darnyi, Hungary	1:59.36*
1994	Jani Sievin, Finland	1:58.16*

400-meter Individual Medley

1973	Andras Hargitay, Hungary	4:31.11
1975	Andras Hargitay, Hungary	4:32.57
1978	Jesse Vassallo, United States	4:20.05*
1982	Ricardo Prado, Brazil	4:19.78*
1986	Tamás Darnyi, Hungary	4:18.98‡
1991	Tamás Darnyi, Hungary	4:12.36*
1994	Tom Dolan, United States	4:12.30*

* World record; ‡Meet record.

MEN *(Cont.)*

400-meter Medley Relay

1973.....United States (Mike Stamm, 3:49.49
John Hencken, Joe Bottom,
Jim Montgomery)
1975.....United States (John Murphy, 3:49.00
Rick Colella, Greg Jagenburg,
Andy Coan)
1978.....United States (Robert Jackson, 3:44.63
Nick Nevid, Joe Bottom,
David McCagg)
1982.....United States (Rick Carey, 3:40.84*
Steve Lundquist, Matt Gribble,
Rowdy Gaines)
1986.....United States (Dan Veatch, 3:41.25
David Lundberg, Pablo Morales,
Matt Biondi)
1991.....United States (Jeff Rouse, 3:39.66‡
Eric Wunderlich, Mark Henderson
Matt Biondi)
1994.....United States (Jeff Rouse, 3:37.74‡
Eric Wunderlich, Mark Henderson,
Gary Hall)

400-meter Freestyle Relay

1973.....United States (Mel Nash, 3:27.18
Joe Bottom, Jim Montgomery,
John Murphy)
1975.....United States (Bruce Furniss, 3:24.85
Jim Montgomery, Andy Coan,
John Murphy)
1978.....United States (Jack Babashoff, 3:19.74
Rowdy Gaines, Jim Montgomery,
David McCagg)
1982.....United States (Chris Cavanaugh, 3:19.26*
Robin Leamy, David McCagg,
Rowdy Gaines)
1986.....United States (Tom Jager, 3:19.89
Mike Heath, Paul Wallace,
Matt Biondi)
1991.....United States (Tom Jager, 3:17.15‡
Brent Lang, Doug Gjertsen,
Matt Biondi)
1994.....United States (Jon Olsen, 3:16.90‡
Josh Davis, Ugur Taner, Gary Hall)

800-meter Freestyle Relay

1973.....United States (Kurt Krumpholz, 7:33.22*
Robin Backhaus, Rick Klatt,
Jim Montgomery)
1975.....West Germany (Klaus Steinbach, 7:39.44
Werner Lampe,
Hans Joachim Geisler, Peter Nocke)
1978.....United States (Bruce Furniss, 7:20.82
Billy Forrester, Bobby Hackett,
Rowdy Gaines)
1982.....United States (Rich Saeger, 7:21.09
Jeff Float, Kyle Miller,
Rowdy Gaines)

1986.....East Germany (Lars Hinneburg, 7:15.91‡
Thomas Flemming, Dirk Richter,
Sven Lodziewski)
1991.....Germany (Peter Sitt, 7:13.50‡
Steffan Zesner, Stefan Pfeiffer,
Michael Gross)
1994.....Sweden (Christer Waller, 7:17.34
Tommy Werner, Lars Frolander,
Anders Holmertz)

WOMEN

50-meter Freestyle

1986....Tamara Costache, Romania 25.28*
1991....Zhuang Yong, China 25.47
1994....Le Jingyi, China 24.51*

100-meter Freestyle

1973....Kornelia Ender, East Germany 57.54
1975....Kornelia Ender, East Germany 56.50
1978....Barbara Krause, East Germany 55.68‡
1982....Birgit Meineke, East Germany 55.79
1986....Kristin Otto, East Germany 55.05‡
1991....Nicole Haislett, United States 55.17
1994....Le Jingyi, China 54.01*

200-meter Freestyle

1973....Keena Rothhammer, United States 2:04.99
1975....Shirley Babashoff, United States 2:02.50
1978....Cynthia Woodhead, United States 1:58.53*
1982....Annemarie Verstappen, 1:59.53†
Netherlands
1986....Heike Friedrich, East Germany 1:58.26‡
1991....Hayley Lewis, Australia 2:00.48
1994....Franziska Van Almsick, Germany 1:56.78*

400-meter Freestyle

1973.....Heather Greenwood, United States 4:20.28
1975.....Shirley Babashoff, United States 4:22.70
1978.....Tracey Wickham, Australia 4:06.28*
1982....Carmela Schmidt, East Germany 4:08.98
1986....Heike Friedrich, East Germany 4:07.45
1991....Janet Evans, United States 4:08.63
1994....Yang Aihua, China 4:09.64

800-meter Freestyle

1973....Novella Calligaris, Italy 8:52.97
1975....Jenny Turrall, Australia 8:44.75‡
1978....Tracey Wickham, Australia 8:24.94‡
1982....Kim Linehan, United States 8:27.48
1986....Astrid Strauss, East Germany 8:28.24
1991....Janet Evans, United States 8:24.05‡
1994....Janet Evans, United States 8:29.85

100-meter Backstroke

1973....Ulrike Richter, East Germany 1:05.42
1975....Ulrike Richter, East Germany 1:03.30‡
1978....Linda Jezek, United States 1:02.55‡

* World record; ‡Meet record.

WOMEN *(Cont.)*

100-meter Backstroke *(Cont.)*

1982	....Kristin Otto, East Germany	1:01.30‡
1986	....Betsy Mitchell, United States	1:01.74
1991	....Krisztina Egerszegi, Hungary	1:01.78
1994	....He Cihong, China	1:00.57

200-meter Backstroke

1973	....Melissa Belote, United States	2:20.52
1975	....Birgit Treiber, East Germany	2:15.46*
1978	....Linda Jezek, United States	2:11.93*
1982	....Cornelia Sirch, East Germany	2:09.91*
1986	....Cornelia Sirch, East Germany	2:11.37
1991	....Krisztina Egerszegi, Hungary	2:09.15‡
1994	....He Cihong, China	2:07.40

100-meter Breaststroke

1973	....Renate Vogel, East Germany	1:13.74
1975	....Hannalore Anke, East Germany	1:12.72
1978	....Julia Bogdanova, USSR	1:10.31*
1982	....Ute Geweniger, East Germany	1:09.14‡
1986	....Sylvia Gerasch, East Germany	1:08.11*
1991	....Linley Frame, Australia	1:08.81
1994	....Samantha Riley, Australia	1:07.96*

200-meter Breaststroke

1973	....Renate Vogel, East Germany	2:40.01
1975	....Hannalore Anke, East Germany	2:37.25‡
1978	....Lina Kachushite, USSR	2:31.42*
1982	....Svetlana Varganova, USSR	2:28.82‡
1986	....Silke Hoerner, East Germany	2:27.40*
1991	....Elena Volkova, USSR	2:29.53
1994	....Samantha Riley, Australia	2:26.87‡

100-meter Butterfly

1973	....Kornelia Ender, East Germany	1:02.53
1975	....Kornelia Ender, East Germany	1:01.24*
1978	....Joan Pennington, United States	1:00.20‡
1982	....Mary T. Meagher, United States	59.41‡
1986	....Kornelia Gressler, East Germany	59.51
1991	....Qian Hong, China	59.68
1994	....Liu Limin, China	58.98‡

200-meter Butterfly

1973	....Rosemarie Kother, East Germany	2:13.76†
1975	....Rosemarie Kother, East Germany	2:15.92
1978	....Tracy Caulkins, United States	2:09.87*
1982	....Ines Geissler, East Germany	2:08.66‡
1986	....Mary T. Meagher, United States	2:08.41‡
1991	....Summer Sanders, United States	2:09.24
1994	....Liu Limin, China	2:07.25‡

200-meter Individual Medley

1973	....Andrea Huebner, East Germany	2:20.51
1975	....Kathy Heddy, United States	2:19.80
1978	....Tracy Caulkins, United States	2:14.07*
1982	....Petra Schneider, East Germany	2:11.79
1986	....Kristin Otto, East Germany	2:15.56
1991	....Li Lin, China	2:13.40
1994	....Lu Bin, China	2:12.34‡

* World record; ‡Meet record

400-meter Individual Medley

1973	....Gudrun Wegner, East Germany	4:57.71
1975	....Ulrike Tauber, East Germany	4:52.76‡
1978	....Tracy Caulkins, United States	4:40.83*
1982	....Petra Schneider, East Germany	4:36.10*
1986	....Kathleen Nord, East Germany	4:43.75
1991	....Lin Li, China	4:41.45
1994	....Dai Guohong, China	4:39.14

400-meter Medley Relay

1973	....East Germany (Ulrike Richter, Renate Vogel, Rosemarie Kother, Kornelia Ender)	4:16.84
1975	....East Germany (Ulrike Richter, Hannelore Anke, Rosemarie Kother, Kornelia Ender)	4:14.74
1978	....United States (Linda Jezek, Tracy Caulkins, Joan Pennington, Cynthia Woodhead)	4:08.21‡
1982	....East Germany (Kristin Otto, Ute Geweniger, Ines Geissler, Birgit Meineke)	4:05.8*
1986	....East Germany (Kathrin Zimmermann, Sylvia Gerasch, Kornelia Gressler, Kristin Otto)	4:04.82
1991	....United States (Janie Wagstaff, Tracey McFarlane, Crissy Ahmann-Leighton, Nicole Haislett)	4:06.51
1994	....China (He Cihong, Dai Guohong, Liu Limin, Lu Bin)	4:01.67*

400-meter Freestyle Relay

1973	....East Germany (Kornelia Ender, Andrea Eife, Andrea Huebner, Sylvia Eichner)	3:52.45
1975	....East Germany (Kornelia Ender, Barbara Krause, Claudia Hempel, Ute Bruckner)	3:49.37
1978	....United States (Tracy Caulkins, Stephanie Elkins, Joan Pennington, Cynthia Woodhead)	3:43.43*
1982	....East Germany (Birgit Meineke, Susanne Link, Kristin Otto, Caren Metschuk)	3:43.97
1986	....East Germany (Kristin Otto, Manuela Stellmach, Sabine Schulze, Heike Friedrich)	3:40.57*
1991	....United States (Nicole Haislett, Julie Cooper, Whitney Hedgepeth, Jenny Thompson)	3:43.26
1994	....China (Le Jingyi, Ying Shan, Le Ying, Lu Bin)	3:37.91*

800-meter Freestyle Relay

1986	....East Germany (Manuela Stellmach, Astrid Strauss, Nadja Bergknecht, Heike Friedrich)	7:59.33*
1991	....Germany (Kerstin Kielgass, Manuela Stellmach, Dagmar Hase, Stephanie Ortwig)	8:02.56
1994	....China (Le Ying, Yang Alhua, Zhou Guabin, Lu Bin)	7:57.96

World Diving Championships

MEN

1-meter Springboard

		Pts
1991	Edwin Jongejans, Holland	588.51
1994	Evan Stewart, Zimbabwe	382.14

3-meter Springboard

		Pts
1973	Phil Boggs, United States	618.57
1975	Phil Boggs, United States	597.12
1978	Phil Boggs, United States	913.95
1982	Greg Louganis, United States	752.67
1986	Greg Louganis, United States	750.06
1991	Kent Ferguson, United States	650.25
1994	Wu Zhuocheng, China	655.44

Platform

		Pts
1973	Klaus Dibiasi, Italy	559.53
1975	Klaus Dibiasi, Italy	547.98
1978	Greg Louganis, United States	844.11
1982	Greg Louganis, United States	634.26
1986	Greg Louganis, United States	668.58
1991	Sun Shuwel, China	626.79
1994	Dmitry Sautin, Russia	634.71

WOMEN

1-meter Springboard

		Pts
1991	Gao Min, China	478.26
1994	Chen Lixia, China	279.30

3-meter Springboard

		Pts
1973	Christa Koehler, East Germany	442.17
1975	Irina Kalinina, USSR	489.81
1978	Irina Kalinina, USSR	691.43
1982	Megan Neyer, United States	501.03
1986	Gao Min, China	582.90
1991	Gao Min, China	539.01
1994	Tan Shuping, China	548.49

Platform

		Pts
1973	Ulrike Knape, Sweden	406.77
1975	Janet Ely, United States	403.89
1978	Irina Kalinina, USSR	412.71
1982	Wendy Wyland, United States	438.79
1986	Chen Lin, China	449.67
1991	Fu Mingxia, China	426.51
1994	Fu Mingxia, China	434.04

Bidding Beijing Adieu

Olympic watchers have assumed that Beijing, disappointed runner-up to Sydney for the right to host the Games in the year 2000, will bid for the 2004 Games. But Chinese Olympic Committee general secretary Wei Jizhong says that two other Chinese citites, Shanghai and Guangzhou, may also mount bid campaigns. What's more, several old China hands tell SI that they wouldn't be surprised to see the country pass on the Games altogether.

One reason is that South Africa was a stout ally of Beijing's unsuccessful bid, and Chinese officials may not want to go up against Cape Town, which is a likely candidate for 2004. The other reason: In Chinese numerology, four is viewed as an inauspicious number; a bid in 2008 would be considered more promising because of the smoothness of the number eight and its intimations of infinity.

Men

50-METER FREESTYLE

1988....Matt Biondi — 22.14*

100-METER FREESTLYE

1906....Charles Daniels — 1:13.4
1908....Charles Daniels — 1:05.6*
1912....Duke Kahanamoku — 1:03.4
1920....Duke Kahanamoku — 1:00.4
1924....John Weissmuller — 59.0‡
1928....John Weissmuller — 58.6‡
1948....Wally Ris — 57.3‡
1952....Clarke Scholes — 57.4
1964....Don Schollander — 53.4‡
1972....Mark Spitz — 51.22*
1976....Jim Montgomery — 49.99*
1984....Rowdy Gaines — 49.80‡
1988....Matt Biondi — 48.63‡

200-METER FREESTYLE

1904....Charles Daniels — 2:44.2
1906....Not held 1906-1964
1972....Mark Spitz — 1:52.78*
1976....Bruce Furniss — 1:50.29*

400-METER FREESTYLE

1904....Charles Daniels (440 yds) — 6:16.2
1920....Norman Ross — 5:26.8
1924....John Weissmuller — 5:04.2‡
1932....Buster Crabbe — 4:48.4‡
1936....Jack Medica — 4:44.5‡
1948....William Smith — 4:41.0‡
1964....Don Schollander — 4:12.2*
1968....Mike Burton — 4:09.0‡
1976....Brian Goodell — 3:51.93*
1984....George DiCarlo — 3:51.23‡

1500-METER FREESTYLE

1920....Norman Ross — 22:23.2
1948....James McLane — 19:18.5
1952....Ford Konno — 18:30.3‡
1968....Mike Burton — 16:38.9‡
1972....Mike Burton — 15:52.58‡
1976....Brian Goodell — 15:02.40*
1984....Michael O'Brien — 15:05.20

100-METER BACKSTROKE

1912....Harry Hebner — 1:21.2
1920....Warren Kealoha — 1:15.2
1924....Warren Kealoha — 1:13.2‡
1928....George Kojac — 1:08.2*
1936....Adolph Kiefer — 1:05.9‡
1948....Allen Stack — 1:06.4
1952....Yoshi Oyakawa — 1:05.4‡
1976....John Naber — 55.49*
1984....Rick Carey — 55.79

200-METER BACKSTROKE

1964....Jed Graef — 2:10.3*
1976....John Naber — 1:59.19*
1984.....Rick Carey — 2:00.23

100-METER BREASTSTROKE

1968....Donald McKenzie — 1:07.7‡
1976....John Hencken — 1:03.11*
1984....Steve Lundquist — 1:01.65 *
1992....Nelson Diebel — 1:01.50‡

200-METER BREASTSTROKE

1924....Robert Skelton — 2:56.6
1948....Joseph Verdeur — 2:39.3‡
1960....William Mulliken — 2:37.4
1972....John Hencken — 2:21.55
1992....Mike Barrowman — 2:10.16*

100-METER BUTTERFLY

1968....Douglas Russell — 55.9‡
1972....Mark Spitz — 54.27*
1976....Matt Vogel — 54.35
1992....Pablo Morales — 53.32

200-METER BUTTERFLY

1956....William Yorzyk — 2:19.3‡
1960....Michael Troy — 2:12.8*
1968....Carl Robie — 2:08.7
1972....Mark Spitz — 2:00.70*
1976....Mike Bruner — 1:59.23*
1992....Melvin Stewart — 1:56.26

200-METER INDIVIDUAL MEDLEY

1968....Charles Hickcox — 2:12.0‡

400-METER INDIVIDUAL MEDLEY

1964....Richard Roth — 4:45.4*
1968....Charles Hickcox — 4:48.4
1976....Rod Strachan — 4:23.68*

3-METER SPRINGBOARD DIVING

1920....Louis Kuehn — 675.4 points
1924....Albert White — 696.4
1928....Pete Desjardins — 185.04
1932....Michael Galitzen — 161.38
1936....Richard Degener — 163.57
1948....Bruce Harlan — 163.64
1952....David Browning — 205.29
1956....Robert Clotworthy — 159.56
1960....Gary Tobian — 170.00
1964....Kenneth Sitzberger — 159.90
1968....Bernard Wrightson — 170.15
1976....Philip Boggs — 619.05
1984....Greg Louganis — 754.41
1988....Greg Louganis — 730.80

PLATFORM DIVING

1904....George Sheldon — 12.66
1920....Clarence Pinkston — 100.67
1924....Albert White — 97.46
1928....Pete Desjardins — 98.74
1932....Harold Smith — 124.80
1936....Marshall Wayne — 113.58
1948....Sammy Lee — 130.05
1952....Sammy Lee — 156.28
1960....Robert Webster — 165.56
1964....Robert Webster — 148.58
1984....Greg Louganis — 576.99
1988....Greg Louganis — 638.61

* World record; ‡Meet (Olympic) record.

Women

100-METER FREESTLYE

1920	Ethelda Bleibtrey	1:13.6*
1924	Ethel Lackie	1:12.4
1928	Albina Osipowich	1:11.0‡
1932	Helene Madison	1:06.8‡
1968	Jan Henne	1:00.0
1972	Sandra Neilson	58.59‡
1984	Carrie Steinseifer	55.92
	Nancy Hogshead	55.92

200-METER FREESTYLE

1968	Debbie Meyer	2:10.5‡
1984	Mary Wayte	1:59.23
1992	Nicole Haislett	1:57.90

400-METER FREESTYLE

1924	Martha Norelius	6:02.2‡
1928	Martha Norelius	5:42.8*
1932	Helene Madison	5:28.5*
1948	Ann Curtis	5:17.8‡
1960	Chris von Saltza	4:50.6
1964	Virginia Duenkel	4:43.3‡
1968	Debbie Meyer	4:31.8‡
1984	Tiffany Cohen	4:07.10‡
1988	Janet Evans	4:03.85*

800-METER FREESTYLE

1968	Debbie Meyer	9:24.0‡
1972	Keena Rothhammer	8:53.86*
1984	Tiffany Cohen	8:24.95‡
1988	Janet Evans	8:20.20‡
1992	Janet Evans	8:25.52

100-METER BACKSTROKE

1924	Sybil Bauer	1:23.2‡
1932	Eleanor Holm	1:19.4
1960	Lynn Burke	1:09.3‡
1964	Cathy Ferguson	1:07.7*
1968	Kaye Hall	1:06.2*
1972	Melissa Belote	1:05.78‡
1984	Theresa Andrews	1:02.55

200-METER BACKSTROKE

1968	Pokey Watson	2:24.8‡
1972	Melissa Belote	2:19.19*

100-METER BREASTSTROKE

1972	Catherine Carr	1:13.58*

200-METER BREASTSTROKE

1968	Sharon Wichman	2:44.4‡

100-METER BUTTERFLY

1956	Shelley Mann	1:11.0‡
1960	Carolyn Schuler	1:09.5‡
1964	Sharon Stouder	1:04.7*
1984	Mary T. Meagher	59.26

200-METER BUTTERFLY

1972	Karen Moe	2:15.57*
1984	Mary T. Meagher	2:06.90‡
1992	Summer Sanders	2:08.67

200-METER INDIVIDUAL MEDLEY

1968	Sharon Wichman	2:44.4‡
1984	Tracy Caulkins	2:12.64‡

400-METER INDIVIDUAL MEDLEY

1964	Donna De Varona	5:18.7‡
1968	Claudia Kolb	5:08.5‡
1984	Tracy Caulkins	4:39.24
1988	Janet Evans	4:37.76

3-METER SPRINGBOARD DIVING

1920	Aileen Riggin	539.9 points
1924	Elizabeth Becker	474.5
1928	Helen Meany	78.62
1932	Georgia Coleman	87.52
1936	Marjorie Gestring	89.27
1948	Victoria Draves	108.74
1952	Patricia McCormick	147.30
1956	Patricia McCormick	142.36
1968	Sue Gossick	150.77
1972	Micki King	450.03
1976	Jennifer Chandler	506.19

PLATFORM DIVING

1924	Caroline Smith	33.2
1928	Elizabeth Becker Pinkston	31.6
1932	Dorothy Poynton	40.26
1936	Dorothy Poynton Hill	33.93
1948	Victoria Draves	68.87
1952	Patricia McCormick	79.37
1956	Patricia McCormick	84.85
1964	Lesley Bush	99.80

* World record; ‡Meet (Olympic) record.

Notable Achievements

Barrier Breakers

MEN

Event	Barrier	Athlete and Nation	Time	Date
100 Freestyle	1:00	Johnny Weissmuller, United States	58.6	7-9-22
100 Freestyle	:50	James Montgomery, United States	49.99	7-25-76
200 Freestyle	2:00	Don Schollander, United States	1:58.8	7-27-63
200 Freestyle	1:50	Sergei Kopliakov, USSR	1:49.83	4-7-79
400 Freestyle	4:00	Rick DeMont, United States	3:58.18	9-6-73
400 Freestyle	3:50	Vladimir Salnikov, USSR	3:49.57	3-12-82
800 Freestyle	8:00	Vladimir Salnikov, USSR	7:56.49	3-23-79
1500 Freestyle	15:00	Vladimir Salnikov, USSR	14:58.27	7-22-80
100 Backstroke	1:00	Thompson Mann, United States	59.6	10-16-64
200 Backstroke	2:00	John Naber, United States	1:59.19	7-24-76
200 Breaststroke	2:30	Chester Jastremski, United States	2:29.6	8-19-61
100 Butterfly	1:00	Lance Larson, United States	59.0	6-29-60
200 Butterfly	2:00	Roger Pyttel, East Germany	1:59.63	6-3-76

WOMEN

Event	Barrier	Athlete and Nation	Time	Date
100 Freestyle	1:00	Dawn Fraser, Australia	59.9	10-27-62
200 Freestyle	2:00	Kornelia Ender, East Germany	1:59.78	6-2-76
400 Freestyle	4:30	Debbie Meyer, United States	4:29.0	8-18-67
800 Freestyle	10:00	Jane Cederqvist, Sweden	9:55.6	8-17-60
800 Freestyle	9:00	Ann Simmons, United States	8:59.4	9-10-71
1500 Freestyle	20:00	Ilsa Konrads, Australia	19:25.7	1-14-60
	16:00	Janet Evans, United States	15:52.10	3-26-88
200 Backstroke	2:30	Satoko Tanaka, Japan	2:29.6	2-10-63
100 Butterfly	1:00	Christiane Knacke, East Germany	59.78	8-28-77
400 Individual Medley	5:00	Gudrun Wegner, East Germany	4:57.51	9-6-73

Olympic Achievements

MOST INDIVIDUAL GOLDS IN SINGLE OLYMPICS

MEN

No.	Athlete and Nation	Olympic Year	Events
4	Mark Spitz, United States	1972	100, 200 Free; 100, 200 Fly

WOMEN

No.	Athlete and Nation	Olympic Year	Events
4	Kristin Otto, East Germany	1988	50, 100 Free; 100 Back; 100 Fly
3	Debbie Meyer, United States	1968	200, 400, 800 Free
3	Shane Gould, Australia	1972	200, 400 Free; 200 IM
3	Kornelia Ender, East Germany	1976	100, 200 Free; 100 Fly
3	Janet Evans, United States	1988	400, 800 Free; 400 IM
3	Krisztina Egerszegi, Hungary	1992	100, 200 Back; 400 IM

Olympic Achievements *(Cont.)*

MOST INDIVIDUAL OLYMPIC GOLD MEDALS, CAREER

MEN

No.	Athlete and Nation	Olympic Years and Events
4	Charles Meldrum Daniels, United States	1904 (220, 440 Free); 1906 (100 Free,) 1908 (100 Free)
4	Roland Matthes, East Germany	1968 (100, 200 Back); 1972 (100, 200 Back)
4	Mark Spitz, United States	1972 (100, 200 Free; 100, 200 Fly)

WOMEN

4	Kristin Otto, East Germany	1988 (50 Free; 100 Free, Back and Fly)

Most Olympic Gold Medals in a Single Olympics, Men—7, Mark Spitz, United States, 1972, 100, 200 Free; 100, 200 Fly; 4 x 100, 4 x 200 Free Relays; 4 x 100 Medley
Most Olympic Gold Medals in a Single Olympics, Women—6, Kristin Otto, East Germany, 1988, 50, 100 Free; 100 Back; 100 Fly; 4 x 100 Free Relay; 4 x 100 Medley Relay
Most Olympic Medals in a Career, Men—
11, Matt Biondi, United States:1984 (one gold), '88 (five gold, one silver, one bronze), 92 (two gold, one silver)
11, Mark Spitz, United States: 1968 (two gold, one silver, one bronze), 1972 (seven gold)
Most Olympic Medals in Career, Women—
8, Dawn Fraser, Australia: 1956 (two gold, one silver), '60 (one gold, two silver), '64 (one gold, one silver)
8, Kornelia Ender, East Germany: 1972 (three silver), '76 (four gold, one silver)
8, Shirley Babashoff, United States: 1972 (one gold, two silver), '76 (one gold, four silver)
Winner, Same Event, Three Consecutive Olympics—Dawn Fraser, Australia, 100 Freestyle, 1956, '60, '64.
Youngest Person to Win an Olympic Diving Gold—Marjorie Gestring, United States, 1936, 13 years, 9 months, springboard diving
Youngest Person to Win Olympic Swimming Gold—Krisztina Egerszegi, Hungary, 1988, 14 years, one month, 200 backstroke

World Record Achievements

Most World Records, Career, Women—42, Ragnhild Hveger, Denmark, 1936-42
Most World Records, Career, Men—32, Arne Borg, Sweden, 1921-29
Most Freestyle Records Held Concurrently—
5, Helene Madison, United States, 1931-33.
5, Shane Gould, Australia, 1972.
Most Consecutive Lowerings of a Record—10, Kornelia Ender, East Germany, 100 Freestyle, 7-13-73 to 7-19-76.
Longest Duration of World Record—19 years, 359 days, 1:04.6 in 100 Free, Willy den Ouden , the Netherlands

Skiing

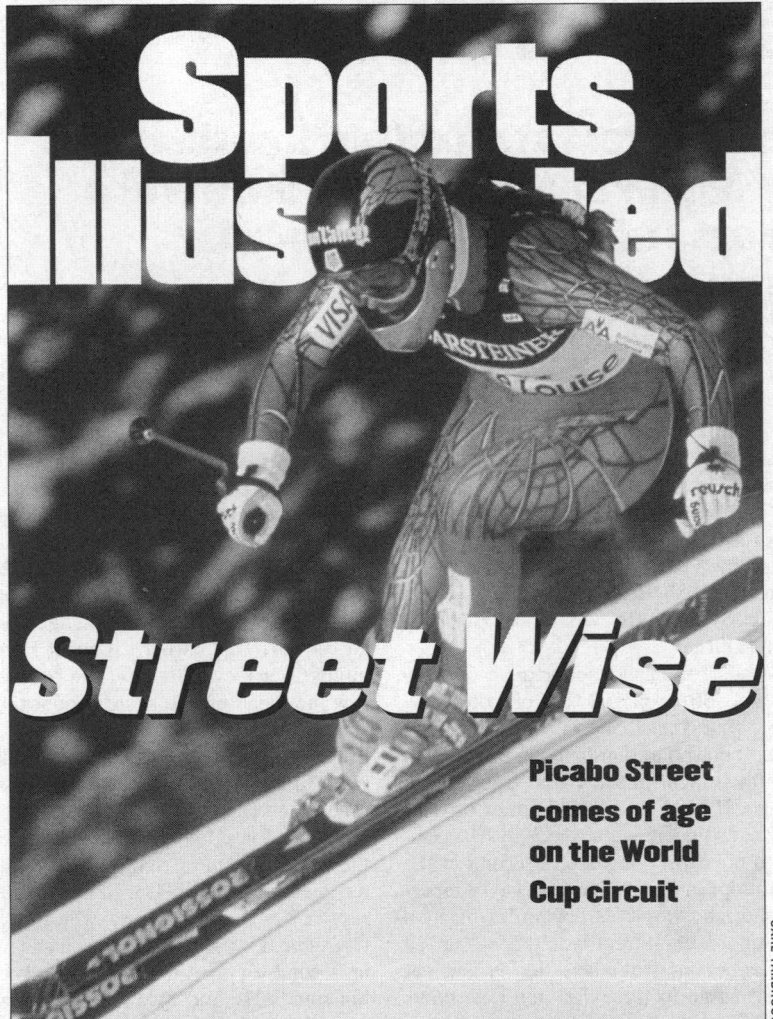

Sports Illustrated

Street Wise

Picabo Street comes of age on the World Cup circuit

CARL YARBROUGH

Picabo, We See You

Picabo Street stepped out from behind her bubbly image and gave the world a glimpse of a champion downhiller

by Michael Farber

PICABO STREET started the 1994–95 Alpine skiing season as a one-race wonder, a fast and frank flibbertigibbet who had squeezed a lot of mileage out of a bubbly personality, a fabulous name and an Olympic silver medal. She left it as a champion, the first U.S. skier to win a World Cup downhill title.

Instead of the childhood game evoked by her name, Street played "last one down the hill is a rotten egg." She won six of the nine women's downhills, finishing the season with her fifth straight at the World Cup final in Bormio. If Michaela Gerg-Leitner of Germany hadn't come out of the 30th start position to nip Street by .02 of a second in the first European downhill in Cortina d'Ampezzo—the only women's downhill won by a non-American—Street would have batted 1.000 on a continent where they usually eat white sausage for breakfast and U.S. skiers for lunch.

After her eye-catching silver medal in the Lillehammer Games, Street made the TV equivalent of the rubber-chicken circuit, showing up on *Sesame Street* and *American Gladiators*. But only the 1994–95 season made her a prime-time star. "This is about greatness, perseverance and consistency," said Street, who had begun the season without a World Cup victory. "That's what I strived for. That's what I thought I had the ability to achieve. Some of the people who saw me come up the skiing ladder thought that if anyone could do it, I could. Then other people looked at me and said, 'No way.' To those people, I say better guess next time."

And as for a 1994 SI story that described the U.S. ski team as "snow plows," well, better guess next time. Hilary Lindh, who is as reserved as Street is brassy, won two of the first three downhills of the season and wound up second to Street in the World Cup downhill standings. And Kyle Rasmussen, whose career was mired on the fringes of the circuit, broke through with a victory at the venerable Lauberhorn in Wengen. At first it seemed

Tombamania returned to the circuit as La Bomba won seven of nine slaloms.

like a journeyman shooting four rounds of 68s at Augusta, but Rasmussen proved it was no fluke when he later won at Kvitfjell. "We've dominated the downhill," said Paul Major, the U.S. Alpine program director. "The Europeans are in shock."

Of course the technical disciplines remained the domain of the Europeans, especially the indomitable Alberto Tomba. La Bomba was the only skier who could match results or, for that matter, personalities with Street in 1994–95. Tomba said it would be his last season—"Tomba says a lot of things," said his manager, Paolo Comellini—and then went on to become the first technical skier to win the men's overall World Cup title since Ingemar Stenmark in 1977–78, taking seven of nine slaloms and four giant slaloms. From December until mid February, he won seven straight races. "The most important thing is to be convinced of your chances," Tomba

said. He had been the World Cup runner-up three times, but 1994–95 put this over-the-top Italian truly over the top. Tombamania returned. Despite Street's stunning success, Tomba remains the only global skiing superstar, the eternal center ring in the Great White Circus.

Tomba once said his dream race included downing a glass of wine before the start and stopping midway down for a cigarette before crossing the line in first place. In a giant slalom in Alta Badia, the parallel lines of fact and fantasy seemed to cross. Tomba made a mistake midway down the course that forced him to a dead halt, his skis sideways to the gates. He straightened himself, pointed his skis south and still won the race. This was a quieter, more dedicated Tomba—an extra 25 days in his off-season training regimen helped him lose the suet that creeps on his frame between Olympics—but he had not lost his sense of playfulness. He celebrated the improbable Alta Badia victory by doing a somersault at the finish line, blowing kisses to

Schneider sails into retirement with 55 career World Cup wins.

his fans and kneeling to kiss his dog, Yukon.

The other constant of the 1994–95 World Cup season was the weather. "There's a four-letter word to describe the ski weather we've had," said Armin Assinger of Austria, who finished fourth behind men's downhill champion Luc Alphand of France. "Oops." That, too. The World Alpine Championships in Sierra Nevada were postponed until March 1996 because of lack of snow. Through the first week of March 1995, men downhillers had had only seven training runs and seven races.

There should have been an eighth. Thirty-one of the 68 racers were down Aspen Mountain in America's Downhill when a storm hit. AJ Kitt led by a ridiculous .58 of a second, and no one left at the start gate had a prayer of catching him, but he fretted as he waited for officials to declare it a valid race. "I don't want to be the most screwed ski racer in history," said Kitt, who had had two other seeming victories during his career wiped out by weather. Well, he is. On-site officials declared the results official, but a 17-member FIS panel overruled them three days later. Kitt, who now has four firsts but still only one World Cup victory, briefly considered retiring.

Vreni Schneider of Switzerland has 55 World Cup wins and did retire despite being close to the record of 62 victories held by Annemarie Moser-Pröll, the Austrian star of the 1970s. "I decided that now is the right moment to stop," said Schneider, 30. "I've already got enough records." Schneider won her third World Cup overall title—edging Katja Seizinger of Germany by six points with a brilliant slalom performance in Bormio—and the slalom and giant slalom titles, giving her a record 11 championships in individual disciplines. She has also won three world championships and three Olympic gold medals.

No one appreciates the magnitude of these accomplishments better than Schneider's peers, especially those coming up behind her. Of her first World Cup season title Street said, "This puts you in a special, elite category." If she can maintain the standard she set this season, Street will one day reach that next echelon—the one Schneider now exits.

FOR THE RECORD · 1994 – 1995

World Cup Season Race Results

Men

Date	Event	Site	Winner
12-3-94	Giant Slalom	Tignes, France	Achim Vogt, Liechtenstein
12-4-94	Slalom	Tignes, France	Alberto Tomba, Italy
12-11-94	Super G	Tignes, France	Patrick Ortlieb, Austria
12-12-94	Slalom	Sestriere, Italy	Alberto Tomba, Italy
12-16-94	Downhill	Val d'Isere, France	Josef Strobl, Austria
12-17-94	Downhill	Val d'Isere, France	Armin Assinger, Austria
12-18-94	Giant Slalom	Val d'Isere, France	Michael vonGruenigen, Switzerland
12-20-94	Slalom	Lech, Austria	Alberto Tomba, Italy
12-21-94	Slalom	Lech, Austria	Alberto Tomba, Italy
12-22-94	Giant Slalom	Alta Badia, Italy	Alberto Tomba, Italy
1-6-95	Giant Slalom	Kranjska Gora, Slovenia	Alberto Tomba, Italy
1-8-95	Slalom	Kranjska Gora, Slovenia	Alberto Tomba, Italy
1-14-95	Downhill	Kitzbuehel, Austria	Luc Alphand, France
1-14-95	Downhill	Kitzbuehel, Austria	Luc Alphand, France
1-15-95	Slalom	Kitzbuehel, Austria	Alberto Tomba, Italy
1-14/15-95	Combined	Kitzbuehel, Austria	Marc Girardelli, Luxembourg
1-16-95	Super G	Kitzbuehel, Austria	Guenther Mader, Austria
1-20-95	Downhill	Wengen, Switzerland	Kristian Ghedina, Italy
1-21-95	Downhill	Wengen, Switzerland	Kyle Rasmussen, United States
1-22-95	Slalom	Wengen, Switzerland	Alberto Tomba, Italy
1-22-95	Combined	Wengen, Switzerland	Marc Girardelli, Luxembourg
2-4-95	Giant Slalom	Adelboden, Switzerland	Alberto Tomba, Italy
2-19-95	Slalom	Furano, Japan	Michael Tritscher, Austria
2-20-95	Giant Slalom	Furano, Japan	Mario Reiter, Austria
2-25-95	Downhill	Whistler, British Columbia	Kristian Ghedina, Italy
2-26-95	Super G	Whistler, British Columbia	Peter Runggaldier, Italy
3-10-95	Super G	Kvitfjell, Norway	Werner Perathoner, Italy
3-11-95	Downhill	Kvitfjell, Norway	Pietro Vitalini, Italy
3-11-95	Downhill	Kvitfjell, Norway	Kyle Rasmussen, United States
3-15-95	Downhill	Bormio, Italy	Luc Alphand, France
3-16-95	Super G	Bormio, Italy	Richard Kroell, Austria
3-18-95	Giant Slalom	Bormio, Italy	Alberto Tomba, Italy
3-19-95	Slalom	Bormio, Italy	Ole Christian Furuseth, Norway

Women

Date	Event	Site	Winner
11-26-94	Giant Slalom	Park City, Utah	Heidi Zeller-Baehler, Switzerland
11-27-94	Slalom	Park City, Utah	Vreni Schneider, Switzerland
12-2-94	Downhill	Vail, Colorado	Hilary Lindh, United States
12-3-94	Super G	Vail, Colorado	Sylvia Eder, Austria
12-4-94	Giant Slalom	Vail, Colorado	Heidi Zeller-Baehler, Switzerland
12-9-94	Downhill	Lake Louise, Alberta	Picabo Street, United States
12-10-94	Downhill	Lake Louise, Alberta	Hilary Lindh, United States
12-11-94	Super G	Lake Louise, Alberta	Katja Seizinger, Germany
12-18-94	Slalom	Sestriere, Italy	Vreni Schneider, Switzerland
12-21-94	Giant Slalom	Alta Badia, Italy	Sabina Panzanini, Italy
12-30-94	Slalom	Meribel, France	Urska Hrovat, Slovenia
1-7-95	Super G	Haus, Austria	Anita Wachter, Austria
1-8-95	Giant Slalom	Haus, Austria	Deborah Compagnoni, Italy
1-10-95	Super G	Flachau, Austria	Renate Goetschl, Austria
1-14-95	Super G	Garmisch-Partenkirchen, Germany	Florence Masnada, France
1-15-95	Slalom	Garmisch-Partenkirchen, Germany	Martina Ertl, Germany
1-20-95	Downhill	Cortina d'Ampezzo, Italy	Michaela Gerg-Leitner, Germany
1-22-95	Downhill	Cortina d'Ampezzo, Italy	Picabo Street, United States
1-23-95	Giant Slalom	Cortina d'Ampezzo, Italy	Anita Wachter, Austria
2-17-95	Downhill	Are, Sweden	Picabo Street, United States
2-18-95	Giant Slalom	Are, Sweden	Anita Wachter, Austria
2-25-95	Giant Slalom	Maribor, Slovenia	Martina Ertl, Germany
2-26/27-95	Slalom	Maribor, Slovenia	Vreni Schneider, Switzerland
3-5-95	Downhill	Saalbach, Austria	Picabo Street, United States
3-5-95	Super G	Saalbach, Austria	Heidi Zeller-Baehler, Switzerland

Women *(Cont.)*

Date	Event	Site	Winner
3-11-95	Downhill	Lenzerheide, Switzerland	Picabo Street, United States
3-12-95	Slalom	Lenzerheide, Switzerland	Pernilla Wiberg, Sweden
3-11/12-95	Combined	Lenzerheide, Switzerland	Pernilla Wiberg, Sweden
3-15-95	Downhill	Bormio, Italy	Picabo Street, United States
3-16-95	Super G	Bormio, Italy	Katja Seizinger, Germany
3-18-95	Giant Slalom	Bormio, Italy	Spela Pretnar, Slovenia
3-19-95	Slalom	Bormio, Italy	Vreni Schneider, Switzerland

World Cup Standings

Men

OVERALL

	Pts
Alberto Tomba, Italy	1150
Günther Mader, Austria	775
Jure Kosir, Slovenia	760
Marc Girardelli, Luxembourg	744
Kjetil Andre Aamodt, Norway	710
Lasse Kjus, Norway	665
Kristian Ghedina, Italy	644
Luc Alphand, France	609

DOWNHILL

	Pts
Luc Aplhand, France	484
Kristian Ghedina, Italy	473
Patrick Ortlieb, Austria	426
Armin Assinger, Austria	419
Josef Strobl, Austria	307
Kyle Rasmussen, United States	288
Hannes Trinkl, Austria	273
Werner Perathoner, Italy	269

SLALOM

	Pts
Alberto Tomba, Italy	700
Michael Tritscher, Austria	477
Jure Kosir, Slovenia	405
Ole Christian Furuseth, Norway	401
Mario Reiter, Austria	341
Thomas Sykora, Austria	302
Michael VonGruenigen, Switz.	282
Sebastian Amiez, France	279

GIANT SLALOM

	Pts
Alberto Tomba, Italy	450
Jure Kosir, Slovenia	355
Harald Strand Nilsen, Norway	322
Kjetil Andre Aamodt, Norway	307
Michael Von Gruenigen, Switz.	296
Urs Kaelin, Switzerland	288
Achim Vogt, Liechtenstein	226
Mario Reiter, Austria	218

SUPER G

	Pts
Peter Runggaldier, Italy	332
Günther Mader, Austria	250
Werner Perathoner, Italy	237
Richard Kroell Austria	170
Kyle Rasmussen, United States	148
Atle Skaardal, Norway	142
Kristian Ghedina, Italy	126
Armin Assinger, Austria	123

Women

OVERALL

	Pts
Vreni Schneider, Switzerland	1248
Katja Seizinger, Germany	1242
Heidi Zeller-Baehler, Switz.	1044
Martina Ertl, Germany	985
Picabo Street, United States	905
Pernilla Wiberg, Sweden	816
Spela Pretnar, Slovenia	669
Anita Wachter, Austria	593

DOWNHILL

	Pts
Picabo Street, United States	709
Hilary Lindh, United States	493
Katja Seizinger, Germany	445
Warwara Zelenskaja, Russia	416
Isolde Kostner, Italy	310
Babara Merlin, Italy	304
Michaela Gerg-Leitner, Ger	262
Heidi Zurbriggen, Switzerland	252

SLALOM

	Pts
Vreni Schneider, Switzerland	560
Pernilla Wiberg, Sweden	355
Martina Ertl, Germany	278
Urska Hrovat, Slovenia	275
Kristina Andersson, Sweden	247
Leila Piccard, France	222
Patricia Chavet-Blanc, France	212
Marianne Kjoerstad, Norway	204

GIANT SLALOM

	Pts
Vreni Schneider, Switzerland	450
Heidi Zeller-Baehler, Switz	420
Spela Pretnar, Slovenia	352
Martina Ertl, Germany	333
Deborah Compagnoni, Italy	325
Sabina Panzanini, Italy	310
Anita Wachter, Austria	295
Urska Hrovat, Slovenia	260

SUPER G

	Pts
Katja Seizinger, Germany	446
Heidi Zeller-Baehler, Switz	366
Heidi Zurbriggen, Switzerland	251
Renate Goetschl, Austria	245
Martina Ertl, Germany	237
Sylvia Eder, Austria	230
Florance Masnada, France	198
Picabo Street, United States	196

FOR THE RECORD·Year by Year

Event Descriptions

Downhill: A speed event entailing a single run on a course with a minimum vertical drop of 500 meters (800 for Men's World Cup) and very few control gates.
Slalom: A technical event in which times for runs on 2 courses are totaled to determine the winner. Skiers must make many quick, short turns through a combination of gates (55-75 gates for men, 40-60 for women) over a short course (140-220-meter vertical drop for men, 120-180 for women).

Giant Slalom: A faster technical event with fewer, more broadly spaced gates than in the slalom. Times for runs on 2 courses with vertical drops of 250-400 meters (250-300 for women) are combined to determine the winner.
Super G: A speed event that is a cross between the downhill and the giant slalom.
Combined: An event in which scores from designated slalom and downhill races are combined to determine finish order.

FIS World Championships

Sites

1931	Mürren, Switzerland	1936	Innsbruck, Austria
1932	Cortina d'Ampezzo, Italy	1937	Chamonix, France
1933	Innsbruck, Austria	1938	Engelberg, Switzerland
1934	St Moritz, Switzerland	1939	Zakopane, Poland
1935	Mürren, Switzerland		

Men

DOWNHILL

1931	Walter Prager, Switzerland	1936	Rudolf Rominger, Switzerland
1932	Gustav Lantschner, Austria	1937	Émile Allais, France
1933	Walter Prager, Switzerland	1938	James Couttet, France
1934	David Zogg, Switzerland	1939	Hans Lantschner, Germany
1935	Franz Zingerle, Austria		

SLALOM

1931	David Zogg, Switzerland	1936	Rudi Matt, Austria
1932	Friedrich Dauber, Germany	1937	Émile Allais, France
1933	Anton Seelos, Austria	1938	Rudolf Rominger, Switzerland
1934	Franz Pfnür, Germany	1939	Rudolf Rominger, Switzerland
1935	Anton Seelos, Austria		

Women

DOWNHILL

1931	Esme Mackinnon, Great Britain	1936	Evie Pinching, Great Britain
1932	Paola Wiesinger, Italy	1937	Christel Cranz, Germany
1933	Inge Wersin-Lantschner, Austria	1938	Lisa Resch, Germany
1934	Anni Rüegg, Switzerland	1939	Christel Cranz, Germany
1935	Christel Cranz, Germany		

SLALOM

1931	Esme Mackinnon, Great Britain	1936	Gerda Paumgarten, Austria
1932	Rösli Streiff, Switzerland	1937	Christel Cranz, Germany
1933	Inge Wersin-Lantschner, Austria	1938	Christel Cranz, Germany
1934	Christel Cranz, Germany	1939	Christel Cranz, Germany
1935	Anni Rüegg, Switzerland		

FIS World Alpine Ski Championships

Sites

1950.............Aspen, Colorado	1978.............Garmisch-Partenkirchen, West Germany
1954.............Are, Sweden	1982.............Schladming, Austria
1958.............Badgastein, Austria	1985.............Bormio, Italy
1962.............Chamonix, France	1987.............Crans-Montana, Switzerland
1966.............Portillo, Chile	1989.............Vail, Colorado
1970.............Val Gardena, Italy	1991.............Saalbach-Hinterglemm, Austria
1974.............St Moritz, Switzerland	1993.............Morioka-Shizukuishi, Japan

Men
DOWNHILL

1950.............Zeno Colo, Italy	1978.............Josef Walcher, Austria
1954.............Christian Pravda, Austria	1982.............Harti Weirather, Austria
1958.............Toni Sailer, Austria	1985.............Pirmin Zurbriggen, Switzerland
1962.............Karl Schranz, Austria	1987.............Peter Müller, Switzerland
1966.............Jean-Claude Killy, France	1989.............Hansjörg Tauscher, West Germany
1970.............Bernard Russi, Switzerland	1991.............Franz Heinzer, Switzerland
1974.............David Zwilling, Austria	1993.............Urs Lehmann, Switzerland

SLALOM

1950.............Georges Schneider, Switzerland	1978.............Ingemar Stenmark, Sweden
1954.............Stein Eriksen, Norway	1982.............Ingemar Stenmark, Sweden
1958.............Josl Rieder, Austria	1985.............Jonas Nilsson, Sweden
1962.............Charles Bozon, France	1987.............Frank Wörndl, West Germany
1966.............Carlo Senoner, Italy	1989.............Rudolf Nierlich, Austria
1970.............Jean-Noël Augert, France	1991.............Marc Girardelli, Luxembourg
1974.............Gustavo Thoeni, Italy	1993.............Kjetil André Aamodt, Norway

GIANT SLALOM

1950.............Zeno Colo, Italy	1978.............Ingemar Stenmark, Sweden
1954.............Stein Eriksen, Norway	1982.............Steve Mahre, United States
1958.............Toni Sailer, Austria	1985.............Markus Wasmaier, West Germany
1962.............Egon Zimmermann, Austria	1987.............Pirmin Zurbriggen, Switzerland
1966.............Guy Périllat, France	1989.............Rudolf Nierlich, Austria
1970.............Karl Schranz, Austria	1991.............Rudolf Nierlich, Austria
1974.............Gustavo Thoeni, Italy	1993.............Kjetil André Aamodt, Norway

COMBINED

1982.............Michel Vion, France	1989.............Marc Girardelli, Luxembourg
1985.............Pirmin Zurbriggen, Switzerland	1991.............Stefan Eberharter, Austria
1987.............Marc Girardelli, Luxembourg	1993.............Lasse Kjus, Norway

SUPER G

1987.............Pirmin Zurbriggen, Switzerland	1991.............Stefan Eberharter, Austria
1989.............Martin Hangl, Switzerland	1993.............Cancelled due to weather

Women
DOWNHILL

1950.............Trude Beiser-Jochum, Austria	1978.............Annemarie Moser-Pröll, Austria
1954.............Ida Schopfer, Switzerland	1982.............Gerry Sorensen, Canada
1958.............Lucile Wheeler, Canada	1985.............Michela Figini, Switzerland
1962.............Christl Haas, Austria	1987.............Maria Walliser, Switzerland
1966.............Erika Schinegger, Austria	1989.............Maria Walliser, Switzerland
1970.............Annerösli Zryd, Switzerland	1991.............Petra Kronberger, Austria
1974.............Annemarie Moser-Pröll, Austria	1993.............Kate Pace, Canada

SLALOM

1950.............Dagmar Rom, Austria	1978.............Lea Sölkner, Austria
1954.............Trude Klecker, Austria	1982.............Erika Hess, Switzerland
1958.............Inger Bjornbakken, Norway	1985.............Perrine Pelen, France
1962.............Marianne Jahn, Austria	1987.............Erika Hess, Switzerland
1966.............Annie Famose, France	1989.............Mateja Svet, Yugoslavia
1970.............Ingrid Lafforgue, France	1991.............Vreni Schneider, Switzerland
1974.............Hanni Wenzel, Liechtenstein	1993.............Karin Buder, Austria

Women *(Cont.)*

GIANT SLALOM

1950 ....Dagmar Rom, Austria	1978 ....Maria Epple, West Germany
1954 ....Lucienne Schmith-Couttet, France	1982 ....Erika Hess, Switzerland
1958 ....Lucile Wheeler, Canada	1985 ....Diann Roffe, United States
1962 ....Marianne Jahn, Austria	1987 ....Vreni Schneider, Switzerland
1966 ....Marielle Goitschel, France	1989 ....Vreni Schneider, Switzerland
1970 ....Betsy Clifford, Canada	1991 ....Pernilla Wiberg, Sweden
1974 ....Fabienne Serrat, France	1993 ....Carole Merle, France

COMBINED

1982 ....Erika Hess, Switzerland	1989 ....Tamara McKinney, United States
1985 ....Erika Hess, Switzerland	1991 ....Chantal Bournissen, Switzerland
1987 ....Erika Hess, Switzerland	1993 ....Miriam Vogt, Germany

SUPER G

1987 ....Maria Walliser, Switzerland	1991 ....Ulrike Maier, Austria
1989 ....Ulrike Maier, Austria	1993 ....Katja Seizinger, Germany

Note: The 1995 FIS World Championships were cancelled due to the lack of snow.

World Cup Season Title Holders

Men

OVERALL

1967 ....Jean-Claude Killy, France	1982 ....Phil Mahre, United States
1968 ....Jean-Claude Killy, France	1983 ....Phil Mahre, United States
1969 ....Karl Schranz, Austria	1984 ....Pirmin Zurbriggen, Switzerland
1970 ....Karl Schranz, Austria	1985 ....Marc Girardelli, Luxembourg
1971 ....Gustavo Thoeni, Italy	1986 ....Marc Girardelli, Luxembourg
1972 ....Gustavo Thoeni, Italy	1987 ....Pirmin Zurbriggen, Switzerland
1973 ....Gustavo Thoeni, Italy	1988 ....Pirmin Zurbriggen, Switzerland
1974 ....Piero Gros, Italy	1989 ....Marc Girardelli, Luxembourg
1975 ....Gustavo Thoeni, Italy	1990 ....Pirmin Zurbriggen, Switzerland
1976 ....Ingemar Stenmark, Sweden	1991 ....Marc Girardelli, Luxembourg
1977 ....Ingemar Stenmark, Sweden	1992 ....Paul Accola, Switzerland
1978 ....Ingemar Stenmark, Sweden	1993 ....Marc Girardelli, Luxembourg
1979 ....Peter Lüscher, Switzerland	1994 ....Kjetil André Aamodt, Norway
1980 ....Andreas Wenzel, Liechtenstein	1995 ....Alberto Tomba, Italy
1981 ....Phil Mahre, United States	

DOWNHILL

1967 ....Jean-Claude Killy, France	1982 ....Steve Podborski, Canada
1968 ....Gerhard Nenning, Austria	Peter Müller, Switzerland
1969 ....Karl Schranz, Austria	1983 ....Franz Klammer, Austria
1970 ....Karl Schranz, Austria	1984 ....Urs Raber, Switzerland
Karl Cordin, Austria	1985 ....Helmut Höflehner, Austria
1971 ....Bernhard Russi, Switzerland	1986 ....Peter Wirnsberger, Austria
1972 ....Bernhard Russi, Switzerland	1987 ....Pirmin Zurbriggen, Switzerland
1973 ....Roland Collumbin, Switzerland	1988 ....Pirmin Zurbriggen, Switzerland
1974 ....Roland Collumbin, Switzerland	1989 ....Marc Girardelli, Luxembourg
1975 ....Franz Klammer, Austria	1990 ....Helmut Höflehner, Austria
1976 ....Franz Klammer, Austria	1991 ....Franz Heinzer, Switzerland
1977 ....Franz Klammer, Austria	1992 ....Franz Heinzer, Switzerland
1978 ....Franz Klammer, Austria	1993 ....Franz Heinzer, Switzerland
1979 ....Peter Müller, Switzerland	1994 ....Marc Girardelli, Luxembourg
1980 ....Peter Müller, Switzerland	1995 ....Luc Alphand, France
1981 ....Harti Weirather, Austria	

SLALOM

1967 ....Jean-Claude Killy, France	1973 ....Gustavo Thoeni, Italy
1968 ....Domeng Giovanoli, Switzerland	1974 ....Gustavo Thoeni, Italy
1969 ....Jean-Noël Augert, France	1975 ....Ingemar Stenmark, Sweden
1970 ....Patrick Russel, France	1976 ....Ingemar Stenmark, Sweden
Alain Penz, France	1977 ....Ingemar Stenmark, Sweden
1971 ....Jean-Noël Augert, France	1978 ....Ingemar Stenmark, Sweden
1972 ....Jean-Noël Augert, France	1979 ....Ingemar Stenmark, Sweden

Men *(Cont.)*

SLALOM *(Cont.)*

1980 ....Ingemar Stenmark, Sweden	1988 ....Alberto Tomba, Italy
1981 ....Ingemar Stenmark, Sweden	1989 ....Armin Bittner, West Germany
1982 ....Phil Mahre, United States	1990 ....Armin Bittner, West Germany
1983 ....Ingemar Stenmark, Sweden	1991 ....Marc Girardelli, Luxembourg
1984 ....Marc Girardelli, Luxembourg	1992 ....Alberto Tomba, Italy
1985 ....Marc Girardelli, Luxembourg	1993 ....Tomas Fogdof, Sweden
1986 ....Rok Petrovic, Yugoslavia	1994 ....Alberto Tomba, Italy
1987 ....Bojan Krizaj, Yugoslavia	1995 ....Alberto Tomba, Italy

GIANT SLALOM

1967 ....Jean-Claude Killy, France	1983 ....Phil Mahre, United States
1968 ....Jean-Claude Killy, France	1984 ....Ingemar Stenmark, Sweden
1969 ....Karl Schranz, Austria	...............Pirmin Zurbriggen, Switzerland
1970 ....Gustavo Thoeni, Italy	1985 ....Marc Girardelli, Luxembourg
1971 ....Patrick Russel, France	1986 ....Joël Gaspoz, Switzerland
1972 ....Gustavo Thoeni, Italy	1987 ....Joël Gaspoz, Switzerland
1973 ....Hans Hinterseer, Austria	...............Pirmin Zurbriggen, Switzerland
1974 ....Piero Gros, Italy	1988 ....Alberto Tomba, Italy
1975 ....Ingemar Stenmark, Sweden	1989 ....Pirmin Zurbriggen, Switzerland
1976 ....Ingemar Stenmark, Sweden	1990 ....Ole-Cristian Furuseth, Norway
1977 ....Heini Hemmi, Switzerland	...............Günther Mader, Austria
...............Ingemar Stenmark, Sweden	1991 ....Alberto Tomba, Italy
1978 ....Ingemar Stenmark, Sweden	1992 ....Alberto Tomba, Italy
1979 ....Ingemar Stenmark, Sweden	1993 ....Kjetil André Aamodt, Norway
1980 ....Ingemar Stenmark, Sweden	1994 ....Christian Mayer, Austria
1981 ....Ingemar Stenmark, Sweden	1995 ....Alberto Tomba, Italy
1982 ....Phil Mahre, United States	

SUPER G

1986 ....Markus Wasmeier, West Germany	1991 ....Franz Heinzer, Switzerland
1987 ....Pirmin Zurbriggen, Switzerland	1992 ....Paul Accola, Switzerland
1988 ....Pirmin Zurbriggen, Switzerland	1993 ....Kjetil André Aamodt, Norway
1989 ....Pirmin Zurbriggen, Switzerland	1994 ....Jan Einar Thorsen, Norway
1990 ....Pirmin Zurbriggen, Switzerland	1995 ....Peter Runggaldier, Italy

COMBINED

1979 ....Andreas Wenzel, Liechtenstein	1988 ....Hubert Strolz, Austria
1980 ....Andreas Wenzel, Liechtenstein	1989 ....Marc Girardelli, Luxembourg
1981 ....Phil Mahre, United States	1990 ....Pirmin Zurbriggen, Switzerland
1982 ....Phil Mahre, United States	1991 ....Marc Girardelli, Luxembourg
1983 ....Phil Mahre, United States	1992 ....Paul Accola, Switzerland
1984 ....Andreas Wenzel, Liechtenstein	1993 ....Marc Girardelli, Luxembourg
1985 ....Andreas Wenzel, Liechtenstein	1994 ....Kjetil-André Aamodt, Norway
1986 ....Markus Wasmeier, West Germany	1995 ....Marc Girardelli, Luxembourg
1987 ....Pirmin Zurbriggen, Switzerland	

Women

OVERALL

1967 ....Nancy Greene, Canada	1982 ....Erika Hess, Switzerland
1968 ....Nancy Greene, Canada	1983 ....Tamara McKinney, United States
1969 ....Gertrud Gabl, Austria	1984 ....Erika Hess, Switzerland
1970 ....Michèle Jacot, France	1985 ....Michela Figini, Switzerland
1971 ....Annemarie Pröll, Austria	1986 ....Maria Walliser, Switzerland
1972 ....Annemarie Pröll, Austria	1987 ....Maria Walliser, Switzerland
1973 ....Annemarie Pröll, Austria	1988 ....Michela Figini, Switzerland
1974 ....Annemarie Moser-Pröll, Austria	1989 ....Vreni Schneider, Switzerland
1975 ....Annemarie Moser-Pröll, Austria	1990 ....Petra Kronberger, Austria
1976 ....Rosi Mitermaier, West Germany	1991 ....Petra Kronberger, Austria
1977 ....Lise-Marie Morerod, Switzerland	1992 ....Petra Kronberger, Austria
1978 ....Hanni Wenzel, Liechtenstein	1993 ....Anita Wachter, Austria
1979 ....Annemarie Moser-Pröll, Austria	1994 ....Vreni Schneider, Switzerland
1980 ....Hanni Wenzel, Liechtenstein	1995 ....Vreni Schneider, Switzerland
1981 ....Marie-Thérèse Nadig, Switzerland	

Women *(Cont.)*

DOWNHILL

1967 ....Marielle Goitschel, France	1981 ....Marie-Thérèse Nadig, Switzerland
1968 ....Isabelle Mir, France	1982 ....Marie-Cecile Gros-Gaudenier, France
Olga Pall, Austria	1983 ....Doris De Agostini, Switzerland
1969 ....Wiltrud Drexel, Austria	1984 ....Maria Walliser, Switzerland
1970 ....Isabelle Mir, France	1985 ....Michela Figini, Switzerland
1971 ....Annemarie Pröll, Austria	1986 ....Maria Walliser, Switzerland
1972 ....Annemarie Pröll, Austria	1987 ....Michela Figini, Switzerland
1973 ....Annemarie Pröll, Austria	1988 ....Michela Figini, Switzerland
1974 ....Annemarie Moser-Pröll, Austria	1989 ....Michela Figini, Switzerland
1975 ....Annemarie Moser-Pröll, Austria	1990 ....Katrin Gutensohn-Knopf, Germany
1976 ....Brigitte Totschnig, Austria	1991 ....Chantal Bournissen, Switzerland
1977 ....Brigitte Totschnig-Habersatter, Austria	1992 ....Katja Seizinger, Germany
1978 ....Annemarie Moser-Pröll, Austria	1993 ....Katja Seizinger, Germany
1979 ....Annemarie Moser-Pröll, Austria	1994 ....Katja Seizinger, Germany
1980 ....Marie-Thérèse Nadig, Switzerland	1995 ....Picabo Street, United States

SLALOM

1967 ....Marielle Goitschel, France	1982 ....Erika Hess, Switzerland
1968 ....Marielle Goitschel, France	1983 ....Erika Hess, Switzerland
1969 ....Gertrud Gabl, Austria	1984 ....Tamara McKinney, United States
1970 ....Ingrid Lafforgue, France	1985 ....Erika Hess, Switzerland
1971 ....Britt Lafforgue, France	1986 ....Roswitha Steiner, Austria
1972 ....Britt Lafforgue, France	Erika Hess, Switzerland
1973 ....Patricia Emonet, France	1987 ....Corrine Schmidhauser, Switzerland
1974 ....Christa Zechmeister, West Germany	1988 ....Roswitha Steiner, Austria
1975 ....Lise-Marie Morerod, Switzerland	1989 ....Vreni Schneider, Switzerland
1976 ....Rosi Mittermaier, West Germany	1990 ....Vreni Schneider, Switzerland
1977 ....Lise-Marie Morerod, Switzerland	1991 ....Petra Kronberger, Austria
1978 ....Hanni Wenzel, Liechtenstein	1992 ....Vreni Schneider, Switzerland
1979 ....Regina Sackl, Austria	1993 ....Vreni Schneider, Switzerland
1980 ....Perrine Pelen, France	1994 ....Vreni Schneider, Switzerland
1981 ....Erika Hess, Switzerland	1995 ....Vreni Schneider, Switzerland

GIANT SLALOM

1967 ....Nancy Greene, Canada	1982 ....Irene Epple, West Germany
1968 ....Nancy Greene, Canada	1983 ....Tamara McKinney, United States
1969 ....Marilyn Cochran, United States	1984 ....Erika Hess, Switzerland
1970 ....Michèle Jacot, France	1985 ....Maria Keihl, West Germany
Françoise Macchi, France	Michela Figini, Switzerland
1971 ....Annemarie Pröll, Austria	1986 ....Vreni Schneider, Switzerland
1972 ....Annemarie Pröll, Austria	1987 ....Vreni Schneider, Switzerland
1973 ....Monika Kaserer, Austria	Maria Walliser, Switzerland
1974 ....Hanni Wenzel, Liechtenstein	1988 ....Mateja Svet, Yugoslavia
1975 ....Annemarie Moser-Pröll, Austria	1989 ....Vreni Schneider, Switzerland
1976 ....Lise-Marie Morerod, France	1990 ....Anita Wachter, Austria
1977 ....Lise-Marie Morerod, France	1991 ....Vreni Schneider, Switzerland
1978 ....Lise-Marie Morerod, France	1992 ....Carole Merle, France
1979 ....Christa Kinshofer, West Germany	1993 ....Carole Merle, France
1980 ....Hanni Wenzel, Liechtenstein	1994 ....Anita Wachter, Austria
1981 ....Marie-Thérèse Nadig, Switzerland	1995 ....Vreni Schneider, Switzerland

SUPER G

1986 ....Maria Keihl, West Germany	1991 ....Carole Merle, France
1987 ....Maria Walliser, Switzerland	1992 ....Carole Merle, France
1988 ....Michela Figini, Switzerland	1993 ....Katja Seizinger, Germany
1989 ....Carole Merle, France	1994 ....Katja Seizinger, Germany
1990 ....Carole Merle, France	1995 ....Katja Seizinger, Germany

COMBINED

1979 ....Annemarie Moser-Pröll, Austria	1983 ....Hanni Wenzel, Liechtenstein
Hanni Wenzel, Liechtenstein	1984 ....Erika Hess, Switzerland
1980 ....Hanni Wenzel, Liechtenstein	1985 ....Brigitte Oertli, Switzerland
1981 ....Marie-Thérèse Nadig, Switzerland	1986 ....Maria Walliser, Switzerland
1982 ....Irene Epple, West Germany	1987 ....Brigitte Oertli, Switzerland

World Cup Season Title Holders (Cont.)

Women (Cont.)

COMBINED (Cont.)

1988	Brigitte Oertli, Switzerland		1992	Sabine Ginther, Austria
1989	Brigitte Oertli, Switzerland		1993	Anita Wachter, Austria
1990	Anita Wachter, Austria		1994	Pernilla Wiberg, Sweden
1991	Sabine Ginther, Austria		1995	Pernilla Wiberg, Sweden

World Cup Career Victories

Men

DOWNHILL

25	Franz Klammer, Austria
19	Peter Müller, Switzerland
15	Franz Heinzer, Switzerland

SUPER G

10	Primin Zurbriggen, Switzerland
7	Marc Girardelli, Luxembourg*
6	Markus Wasmeier, Germany

SLALOM

40	Ingemar Stenmark, Sweden
29	Alberto Tomba, Italy*
16	Marc Girardelli, Luxembourg*

COMBINED

11	Phil Mahre, United States
	Pirmin Zurbriggen, Switzerland
10	Marc Girardelli, Luxembourg*

*still active

GIANT SLALOM

46	Ingemar Stenmark, Sweden
15	Alberto Tomba, Italy*
11	Gustavo Thoeni, Italy
	Pirmin Zurbriggen, Switzerland

Women

DOWNHILL

36	Annemarie Moser-Pröll, Austria
17	Michela Figini, Switzerland
14	Maria Walliser, Switzerland

SUPER G

12	Carole Merle, France
7	Katja Seizinger, Germany*
3	Maria Kiehl, Germany
	Maria Walliser, Switzerland
	Sigrid Wolf, Austria

SLALOM

33	Vreni Schneider, Switzerland*
21	Erika Hess, Switzerland
15	Perrine Pelen, France

COMBINED

8	Hanni Wenzel, Lichtenstein
7	Annemarie Moser-Pröll, Austria
7	Brigitte Oertli, Switzerland

*still active

GIANT SLALOM

21	Vreni Schneider, Switzerland*
16	Annemarie Moser-Pröll, Austria
14	Lise Marie Morerod, France

U.S. Olympic Gold Medalists

Men

Year	Winner	Event
1980	Phil Mahre	Combined
1984	Bill Johnson	Downhill
1984	Phil Mahre	Slalom
1994	Tommy Moe	Downhill

Women

Year	Winner	Event
1948	Gretchen Fraser	Slalom
1952	Andrea Mead Lawrence	Slalom
1952	Andrea Mead Lawrence	Giant Slalom
1972	Barbara Ann Cochran	Slalom
1984	Debbie Armstrong	Giant Slalom
1994	Diann Roffe-Steinrotter	Super G

Figure Skating

Ice Queen

China's Chen Lu wins the world figure skating title in Birmingham, England.

BOB MARTIN

Goodbye to All That

With the scandals of '94 forgotten, figure skating enjoyed a banner season

by Johnette Howard

THERE WAS no more thuggery. No more preoccupation with those four stooges who had ties to Tonya Harding. After the kneecapping of Nancy Kerrigan and Harding's venal sideshow at the 1994 Winter Olympics, the worry inside figure skating was how the dishonored sport would rebound in 1995. And the answer?

Better than anyone dared dream.

Perverse as it sounds, the saturated coverage of the Harding saga had an unexpected good result: The business of figure skating was booming by early 1995. In the U.S. alone, enrollment in basic skating courses jumped 200% to 300% over 1994 levels. TV ratings for figure skating events soared. An unprecedented glut of ersatz competitions, gauzy made-for-TV specials and show tours was spawned. When 1994 Olympic champion Oksana Baiul took the money and ran—forsaking her Olympic eligibility at age 16—some serious fretting began. Would amateur skating be eclipsed by the lucrative and unregulated pro events?

The International Skating Union swiftly announced that it would begin offering prize money at its major events. But in 1995 anyway, there was no need to worry. Olympic-style skating remained the place to go for authentic competition and unimpeachable judging. The major championships proved '95 to be the year of the resurrected star.

Todd Eldredge—a two-time U.S. champion by the age of 19, a feared washout by 21—stopped his three-year title drought with a giant-killing run that included his third national title, then an unforgettable duel with Canada's Elvis Stojko at the March world championships in Birmingham, England.

After seizing the first-day lead at the worlds, Eldredge missed two jumps in his final program that he absolutely had to have—a triple Axel and a triple-triple combination. Suddenly the 23-year-old American was left with a nerve-jangling choice: Should he play it safe in the dying moments of his routine or risk losing everything?

Eldredge went for the win. Improvising boldly now, he first made up the blown combination, then brazenly launched into an unscheduled triple Axel with 20 seconds left in his gutsy, scrambling, crescendoing

MANNY MILLAN (L), BOB MARTIN (R)

Eldredge (left) upped the ante but Stojko was more than equal to the challenge.

routine. "I just thought, the hell with it—this is the big time, this is the worlds," Eldredge said later, breaking into a grin.

By daring to be great, Eldredge knew he'd just forced Stojko to do the same. And Stojko, the defending world champion, was more than a match. A gruesome ankle injury kept him out of competition for seven weeks before the worlds. He still hadn't landed three of his five triple jumps until just 72 hours before he had to compete. But skating two spots after Eldredge, Stojko trumped Eldredge's effort with two triple-triple combinations to Eldredge's one, a triple Axel and an attempted quadruple which Stojko missed finishing—though he didn't need the quad to win.

Two nights later Chen Lu became China's first-ever world champion, staving off spirited challenges from Surya Bonaly of France and the U.S.'s Nicole Bobek and Michelle Kwan. Chen withdrew from the '94 worlds in Chiba, Japan, because of a foot stress fracture that didn't respond to the six daily shots of novocaine she took to try to compete. In Birmingham she had to rally to beat Bobek, the free-spirited, wholly unexpected U.S. champion.

Bobek has always been an arresting looking skater. But her halfhearted training habits and balky nerves often doomed her in big competitions. Kwan, just 14 but already a superior jumper, was heavily favored to win the '95 U.S. championships —until Bobek put together back-to-back programs that stopped the show.

In the four-week wait for worlds, Bobek's reputation was clouded again by published reports of a just-dismissed burglary charge against her in Michigan. But Bobek is nothing if not puckish. She shrugged off the uproar and comparisons to Harding by cracking jokes in her first press conference in England, then seizing the first-day lead, then announcing she was beefing up the difficulty in her long program. Like Eldredge, her training partner, Bobek was going for the win.

Though she hit her new move—the first triple-triple combination of her career—Bobek flubbed two subsequent jumps. Still, she left England with the bronze medal and some newfound respect. And Kwan, who finished fourth, gave her older rivals something to worry about in the future. Her closing performance featured seven triple jumps and pulled the Birmingham crowd to its feet with 10 seconds left—an accomplishment that left the 98-pound Kwan sobbing for joy at center ice as raucous cheers and a slanting rain of floral bouquets came down. The scene was among the sweetest moments in a good year—skating's boom year. And it was the sort of pure moment that figure skating craved, and gratefully received, after the embarrassments of '94.

FOR THE RECORD · 1994 - 1995

World Champions

Women

1........Chen Lu, China
2........Surya Bonaly, France
3........Nicole Bobek, United States

Men

1........Elvis Stojko, Canada
2........Todd Eldredge, United States
3........Phillippe Candeloro, France

Pairs

1........Radka Kovarikova and Rene Novotny, Czech
2........Evgenia Shishkova and Vadim Naumov, Russia
3........Jenni Meno and Todd Sand, United States

Dance

1........Oksana Gritschuk and Evgeny Platov, Russia
2........Susanna Rahkamo and Petri Kokko, Finland
3........Sophie Moniotte and Pascal Lavanchy, France

World Figure Skating Championships Medal Table

Birmingham, England, March 7–12

Country	Gold	Silver	Bronze	Total
United States	0	1	2	3
France	0	1	2	3
Russia	1	1	0	2
Canada	1	0	0	1
China	1	0	0	1
Czech Republic	1	0	0	1
Finland	0	1	0	1

Champions of the United States

Providence, Rhode Island, February 7–11

Women

1...........Nicole Bobek, Los Angeles FSC
2...........Michelle Kwan, Los Angeles FSC
3...........Tonia Kwiatkowski, Winterhurst FSC

Men

1...........Todd Elredge, Detroit SC
2...........Scott Davis, Broadmoor, SC
3...........Aren Nielsen, Winterhurst FSC

Pairs

1...........Jenni Meno and Todd Sand,
Winterhurst FSC/Los Angeles FSC
2...........Kyoko Ina and Jason Dungjen,
SC of New York/ SC of New York
3...........Stephanie Stiegler and Lance Travis
Los Angeles FSC/ Los Angeles FSC

Dance

1...........Renee Roca and Gorsha Sur
Broadmoor SC/Broadmoor SC
2...........Elizabeth Punsalan and Jerod Swallow
Detroit SC/Detroit SC
3...........Amy Webster and Ron Kravette
SC of Boston/SC of Boston

Special Achievements

Women successfully landing a triple Axel in competition:
Midori Ito, Japan, 1988 free-skating competition at Aichi, Japan.
Tonya Harding, United States, 1991 U.S. Figure Skating Championship.

Skating Terminology*

Basic Skating Terms

Edges: The two sides of the skating blade, on either side of the grooved center. There is an inside edge, on the inner side of the leg; and an outside edge, on the outer side of the leg.

Free Foot, Hip, Knee, Side, Etc.: The foot a skater is not skating on at any one time is the free foot; everything on that side of the body is then called "free." (See also "skating foot.")

Free Skating (Freestyle): A 4- or 5-minute competition program of free-skating components, choreographed to music, with no set elements. Skating moves include jumps, spins, steps and other linking movements.

Skating Foot, Hip, Knee, Side, Etc.: Opposite of the free foot, hip, knee, side, etc. The foot a skater is skating on at any one time is the skating foot; everything on that side of the body is then called "skating."

Toe Picks (Toe Rakes): The teeth at the front of the skate blade, used primarily for certain jumps and spins.

Trace, Tracing: The line left on the ice by the skater's blade.

Jumps

Waltz: A beginner's jump, involving half a revolution in the air, taken from a forward outside edge and landed on the back outside edge of the other foot.

Toe Loop: A one-revolution jump taken off from and landed on the same back outside edge. This jump is similar to the loop jump except that the skater kicks the toe pick of the free leg into the ice upon takeoff, providing added power.

Toe Walley: A jump similar to the toe loop, except that the takeoff is from the inside edge.

Flip: A jump taken off with the toe pick of the free leg from a back inside edge and landed on a back outside edge, with one in-air revolution.

Lutz: A toe jump similar to the flip, taken off with the toe pick of the free leg from a backwrd outside edge. The skater enters the jump skating in one direction, and concludes the jump skating in the opposite direction. Usually performed in the corners of the rink. Named after founder Alois Lutz, who first completed the jump in Vienna, 1918.

Salchow: A one-, two- or three-revolution jump. The skater takes off from the back inside edge of one foot and lands backwards on the outside edge of the right foot, the opposite foot from which the skater took off. Named for its originator and first Olympic champion (1908), Sweden's Ulrich Salchow.

Axel: A combination of the waltz and loop jumps, including one-and-a-half revolutions. The only jump begun from a forward outside edge, the axel is landed on the back outside edge of the opposite foot. Named for its inventor, Norway's Axel Paulsen.

Spins

Spin: The rotation of the body in one place on the ice. Various spins are the back, fast or scratch, sit, camel, butterfly and layback.

Camel Spin: A spin with the skater in an arabesque position (the free leg at right angles to the leg on the ice).

Flying Camel Spin: A jump spin ending in the camel-spin position.

Flying Sit Spin: A jump spin in which the skater leaps off the ice, assumes a sitting position at the peak of the jump, lands and spins in a similar sitting position.

Pair Movements/Techniques

Death Spiral: One of the most dramatic moves in figure skating. The man, acting as the center of a circle, holds tightly to the hand of his partner and pulls her around him. The woman, gliding on one foot, achieves a position almost horizontal to the ice.

Lifts: The most spectacular moves in pairs skating. They involve any maneuver in which the man lifts the woman off the ice. The man often holds his partner above his head with one hand.

Throws: The man lifts the woman into the air and throws her away from him. She spins in the air and lands on one foot.

Twist: The man throws the woman into the air. She spins in the air (either a double- or triple-twist), and he catches her at the landing.

*Compiled by the United States Figure Skating Assocation.

World Champions

Women

1906	Madge Sayers-Cave, Great Britain
1907	Madge Sayers-Cave, Great Britain
1908	Lily Kronberger, Hungary
1909	Lily Kronberger, Hungary
1910	Lily Kronberger, Hungary
1911	Lily Kronberger, Hungary
1912	Opika von Meray Horvath, Hungary
1913	Opika von Meray Horvath, Hungary
1914	Opika von Meray Horvath, Hungary
1915-21	No competition
1922	Herma Plank-Szabo, Austria
1923	Herma Plank-Szabo, Austria
1924	Herma Plank-Szabo, Austria
1925	Herma Jaross-Szabo, Austria
1926	Herma Jaross-Szabo, Austria
1927	Sonja Henie, Norway
1928	Sonja Henie, Norway
1929	Sonja Henie, Norway
1930	Sonja Henie, Norway
1931	Sonja Henie, Norway
1932	Sonja Henie, Norway
1933	Sonja Henie, Norway
1934	Sonja Henie, Norway
1935	Sonja Henie, Norway
1936	Sonja Henie, Norway
1937	Cecilia Colledge, Great Britain
1938	Megan Taylor, Great Britain
1939	Megan Taylor, Great Britain
1940-46	No competition
1947	Barbara Ann Scott, Canada
1948	Barbara Ann Scott, Canada
1949	Alena Vrzanova, Czechoslovakia
1950	Alena Vrzanova, Czechoslovakia
1951	Jeannette Altwegg, Great Britain
1952	Jacqueline duBief, France
1953	Tenley Albright, United States
1954	Gundi Busch, West Germany
1955	Tenley Albright, United States

Women *(Cont.)*

1956	Carol Heiss, United States
1957	Carol Heiss, United States
1958	Carol Heiss, United States
1959	Carol Heiss, United States
1960	Carol Heiss, United States
1961	No competition
1962	Sjoukje Dijkstra, Netherlands
1963	Sjoukje Dijkstra, Netherlands
1964	Sjoukje Dijkstra, Netherlands
1965	Petra Burka, Canada
1966	Peggy Fleming, United States
1967	Peggy Fleming, United States
1968	Peggy Fleming, United States
1969	Gabriele Seyfert, East Germany
1970	Gabriele Seyfert, East Germany
1971	Beatrix Schuba, Austria
1972	Beatrix Schuba, Austria
1973	Karen Magnussen, Canada
1974	Christine Errath, East Germany
1975	Dianne DeLeeuw, Netherlands
1976	Dorothy Hamill, United States
1977	Linda Fratianne, United States
1978	Annett Poetzsch, East Germany
1979	Linda Fratianne, United States
1980	Annett Poetzsch, East Germany
1981	Denise Biellmann, Switzerland
1982	Elaine Zayak, United States
1983	Rosalynn Sumners, United States
1984	Katarina Witt, East Germany
1985	Katarina Witt, East Germany
1986	Debi Thomas, United States
1987	Katarina Witt, East Germany
1988	Katarina Witt, East Germany
1989	Midori Ito, Japan
1990	Jill Trenary, United States
1991	Kristi Yamaguchi, United States
1992	Kristi Yamaguchi, United States
1993	Oksana Baiul, Ukraine
1994	Yuka Sato, Japan
1995	Chen Lu, China

Men

1896	Gilbert Fuchs, Germany
1897	Gustav Hugel, Austria
1898	Henning Grenander, Sweden
1899	Gustav Hugel, Austria
1900	Gustav Hugel, Austria
1901	Ulrich Salchow, Sweden
1902	Ulrich Salchow, Sweden
1903	Ulrich Salchow, Sweden
1904	Ulrich Salchow, Sweden
1905	Ulrich Salchow, Sweden
1906	Gilbert Fuchs, Germany
1907	Ulrich Salchow, Sweden
1908	Ulrich Salchow, Sweden
1909	Ulrich Salchow, Sweden
1910	Ulrich Salchow, Sweden
1911	Ulrich Salchow, Sweden
1912	Fritz Kachler, Austria
1913	Fritz Kachler, Austria
1914	Gosta Sandhal, Sweden
1915-21	No competition
1922	Gillis Grafstrom, Sweden
1923	Fritz Kachler, Austria
1924	Gillis Grafstrom, Sweden
1925	Willy Bockl, Austria
1926	Willy Bockl, Austria
1927	Willy Bockl, Austria
1928	Willy Bockl, Austria
1929	Gillis Grafstrom, Sweden
1930	Karl Schafer, Austria
1931	Karl Schafer, Austria
1932	Karl Schafer, Austria
1933	Karl Schafer, Austria
1934	Karl Schafer, Austria
1935	Karl Schafer, Austria
1936	Karl Schafer, Austria
1937	Felix Kaspar, Austria
1938	Felix Kaspar, Austria
1939	Graham Sharp, Great Britain
1940-46	No competition
1947	Hans Gerschwiler, Switzerland
1948	Dick Button, United States
1949	Dick Button, United States
1950	Dick Button, United States
1951	Dick Button, United States
1952	Dick Button, United States
1953	Hayes Alan Jenkins, United States
1954	Hayes Alan Jenkins, United States
1955	Hayes Alan Jenkins, United States
1956	Hayes Alan Jenkins, United States
1957	David W. Jenkins, United States
1958	David W. Jenkins, United States
1959	David W. Jenkins, United States
1960	Alan Giletti, France
1961	No competition
1962	Donald Jackson, Canada
1963	Donald McPherson, Canada
1964	Manfred Schneldorfer, W Germany
1965	Alain Calmat, France
1966	Emmerich Danzer, Austria
1967	Emmerich Danzer, Austria
1968	Emmerich Danzer, Austria
1969	Tim Wood, United States
1970	Tim Wood, United States
1971	Andrej Nepela, Czechoslovakia
1972	Andrej Nepela, Czechoslovakia
1973	Andrej Nepela, Czechoslovakia
1974	Jan Hoffmann, East Germany
1975	Sergei Volkov, USSR
1976	John Curry, Great Britain
1977	Vladimir Kovalev, USSR
1978	Charles Tickner, United States
1979	Vladimir Kovalev, USSR
1980	Jan Hoffmann, East Germany
1981	Scott Hamilton, United States
1982	Scott Hamilton, United States
1983	Scott Hamilton, United States
1984	Scott Hamilton, United States
1985	Aleksandr Fadeev, USSR
1986	Brian Boitano, United States
1987	Brian Orser, Canada
1988	Brian Boitano, United States
1989	Kurt Browning, Canada
1990	Kurt Browning, Canada
1991	Kurt Browning, Canada
1992	Viktor Petrenko, CIS
1993	Kurt Browning, Canada
1994	Elvis Stojko, Canada
1995	Elvis Stojko, Canada

Pairs

1908	Anna Hubler, Heinrich Burger, Germany	
1909	Phyllis Johnson, James H. Johnson, Great Britain	
1910	Anna Hubler, Heinrich Burger, Germany	
1911	Ludowika Eilers, Walter Jakobsson, Germany/Finland	
1912	Phyllis Johnson, James H. Johnson, Great Britain	
1913	Helene Engelmann, Karl Majstrik, Germany	
1914	Ludowika Jakobsson-Eilers, Walter Jakobsson-Eilers, Finland	
1915-21	No competition	
1922	Helene Engelmann, Alfred Berger, Germany	
1923	Ludowika Jakobsson-Eilers, Walter Jakobsson-Eilers, Finland	
1924	Helene Engelmann, Alfred Berger, Germany	
1925	Herma Jaross-Szabo, Ludwig Wrede, Austria	
1926	Andree Joly, Pierre Brunet, France	
1927	Herma Jaross-Szabo, Ludwig Wrede, Austria	
1928	Andree Joly, Pierre Brunet, France	
1929	Lilly Scholz, Otto Kaiser, Austria	
1930	Andree Brunet-Joly, Pierre Brunet-Joly, France	
1931	Emilie Rotter, Laszlo Szollas, Hungary	
1932	Andree Brunet-Joly, Pierre Brunet-Joly, France	
1933	Emilie Rotter, Laszlo Szollas, Hungary	
1934	Emilie Rotter, Laszlo Szollas, Hungary	
1935	Emilie Rotter, Laszlo Szollas, Hungary	
1936	Maxi Herber, Ernst Bajer, Germany	
1937	Maxi Herber, Ernst Bajer, Germany	
1938	Maxi Herber, Ernst Bajer, Germany	
1939	Maxi Herber, Ernst Bajer, Germany	
1940-46	No competition	
1947	Micheline Lannoy, Pierre Baugniet, Belgium	
1948	Micheline Lannoy, Pierre Baugniet, Belgium	
1949	Andrea Kekessy, Ede Kiraly, Hungary	
1950	Karol Kennedy, Peter Kennedy, United States	
1951	Ria Baran, Paul Falk, West Germany	
1952	Ria Baran Falk, Paul Falk, West Germany	
1953	Jennifer Nicks, John Nicks, Great Britain	
1954	Frances Dafoe, Norris Bowden, Canada	
1955	Frances Dafoe, Norris Bowden, Canada	
1956	Sissy Schwarz, Kurt Oppelt, Austria	
1957	Barbara Wagner, Robert Paul, Canada	
1958	Barbara Wagner, Robert Paul, Canada	
1959	Barbara Wagner, Robert Paul, Canada	
1960	Barbara Wagner, Robert Paul, Canada	
1961	No competition	
1962	Maria Jelinek, Otto Jelinek, Canada	
1963	Marika Kilius, Hans-Jurgen Baumler, West Germany	
1964	Marika Kilius, Hans-Jurgen Baumler, West Germany	
1965	Ljudmila Protopopov, Oleg Protopopov, USSR	
1966	Ljudmila Protopopov, Oleg Protopopov, USSR	
1967	Ljudmila Protopopov, Oleg Protopopov, USSR	
1968	Ljudmila Protopopov, Oleg Protopopov, USSR	
1969	Irina Rodnina, Alexsei Ulanov, USSR	
1970	Irina Rodnina, Alexsei Ulanov, USSR	
1971	Irina Rodnina, Sergei Ulanov, USSR	
1972	Irina Rodnina, Sergei Ulanov, USSR	
1973	Irina Rodnina, Aleksandr Zaitsev, USSR	
1974	Irina Rodnina, Aleksandr Zaitsev, USSR	
1975	Irina Rodnina, Aleksandr Zaitsev, USSR	
1976	Irina Rodnina, Aleksandr Zaitsev, USSR	
1977	Irina Rodnina, Aleksandr Zaitsev, USSR	
1978	Irina Rodnina, Aleksandr Zaitsev, USSR	
1979	Tai Babilonia, Randy Gardner, United States	
1980	Maria Cherkasova, Sergei Shakhrai, USSR	
1981	Irina Vorobieva, Igor Lisovsky, USSR	
1982	Sabine Baess, Tassilio Thierbach, East Germany	
1983	Elena Valova, Oleg Vasiliev, USSR	
1984	Barbara Underhill, Paul Martini, Canada	
1985	Elena Valova, Oleg Vasiliev, USSR	
1986	Yekaterina Gordeeva, Sergei Grinkov, USSR	
1987	Yekaterina Gordeeva, Sergei Grinkov, USSR	
1988	Elena Valova, Oleg Vasiliev, USSR	
1989	Yekaterina Gordeeva, Sergei Grinkov, USSR	
1990	Yekaterina Gordeeva, Sergei Grinkov, USSR	
1991	Natalia Mishkutienok, Artur Dmitriev, USSR	
1992	Natalia Mishkutienok, Artur Dmitriev, CIS	
1993	Isabelle Brasseur, Lloyd Eisler, Canada	
1994	Evgenia Shishkova, Vadim Naumov, Russia	
1995	Radka Kovarikova, Rene Novotny, Czech Republic	

Dance

1950..................Lois Waring, Michael McGean, U.S.	
1951..................Jean Westwood, Lawrence Demmy, Great Britain	
1952..................Jean Westwood, Lawrence Demmy, Great Britain	
1953..................Jean Westwood, Lawrence Demmy, Great Britain	
1954..................Jean Westwood, Lawrence Demmy, Great Britain	
1955..................Jean Westwood, Lawrence Demmy, Great Britain	
1956..................Pamela Wieght, Paul Thomas, Great Britain	
1957..................June Markham, Courtney Jones, Great Britain	
1958..................June Markham, Courtney Jones, Great Britain	
1959..................Doreen D. Denny, Courtney Jones, Great Britain	
1960..................Doreen D. Denny, Courtney Jones, Great Britain	
1961..................No competition	
1962..................Eva Romanova, Pavel Roman, Czechoslovakia	
1963..................Eva Romanova, Pavel Roman, Czechoslovakia	
1964..................Eva Romanova, Pavel Roman, Czechoslovakia	
1965..................Eva Romanova, Pavel Roman, Czechoslovakia	
1966..................Diane Towler, Bernard Ford, Great Britain	
1967..................Diane Towler, Bernard Ford, Great Britain	
1968..................Diane Towler, Bernard Ford, Great Britain	
1969..................Diane Towler, Bernard Ford, Great Britain	
1970..................Ljudmila Pakhomova, Aleksandr Gorshkov, USSR	
1971..................Ljudmila Pakhomova, Aleksandr Gorshkov, USSR	
1972..................Ljudmila Pakhomova, Aleksandr Gorshkov, USSR	
1973..................Ljudmila Pakhomova, Aleksandr Gorshkov, USSR	

1974..................Ljudmila Pakhomova, Aleksandr Gorshkov, USSR
1975..................Irina Moiseeva, Andreij Minenkov, USSR
1976..................Ljudmila Pakhomova, Aleksandr Gorshkov, USSR
1977..................Irina Moiseeva, Andreij Minenkov, USSR
1978..................Natalia Linichuk, Gennadi Karponosov, USSR
1979..................Natalia Linichuk, Gennadi Karponosov, USSR
1980..................Krisztina Regoeczy, Andras Sallai, Hungary
1981..................Jayne Torvill, Christopher Dean, Great Britain
1982..................Jayne Torvill, Christopher Dean, Great Britain
1983..................Jayne Torvill, Christopher Dean, Great Britain
1984..................Jayne Torvill, Christopher Dean, Great Britain
1985..................Natalia Bestemianova, Andrei Bukin, USSR
1986..................Natalia Bestemianova, Andrei Bukin, USSR
1987..................Natalia Bestemianova, Andrei Bukin, USSR
1988..................Natalia Bestemianova, Andrei Bukin, USSR
1989..................Marina Klimova, Sergei Ponomarenko, USSR
1990..................Marina Klimova, Sergei Ponomarenko, USSR
1991..................Isabelle Duchesnay, Paul Duchesnay, France
1992..................Marina Klimova, Sergei Ponomarenko , CIS
1993..................Renee Roca, Gorsha Sur, Broadmoor SC, United States
1994..................Oksana Gritschuk, Evgeny Platov, Russia
1995..................Oksana Gritschuk, Evgeny Platov, Russia

Champions of the United States

The championships held in 1914, 1918, 1920 and 1921 under the auspices of the International Skating Union of America were open to Canadians, although they were considered to be United States championships. Beginning in 1922, the championships have been held under the auspices of the United States Figure Skating Association.

Women

1914 ....Theresa Weld, SC of Boston	1928 ....Maribel Y. Vinson, SC of Boston
1915-17 ......No competition	1929 ....Maribel Y. Vinson, SC of Boston
1918............Rosemary S. Beresford, New York SC	1930 ....Maribel Y. Vinson, SC of Boston
1919 ....No competition	1931 ....Maribel Y. Vinson, SC of Boston
1920 ....Theresa Weld, SC of Boston	1932 ....Maribel Y. Vinson, SC of Boston
1921 ....Theresa Weld Blanchard, SC of Boston	1933 ....Maribel Y. Vinson, SC of Boston
1922 ....Theresa Weld Blanchard, SC of Boston	1934 ....Suzanne Davis, SC of Boston
1923 ....Theresa Weld Blanchard, SC of Boston	1935 ....Maribel Y. Vinson, SC of Boston
1924 ....Theresa Weld Blanchard, SC of Boston	1936 ....Maribel Y. Vinson, SC of Boston
1925 ....Beatrix Loughran, New York SC	1937 ....Maribel Y. Vinson, SC of Boston
1926 ....Beatrix Loughran, New York SC	1938 ....Joan Tozzer, SC of Boston
1927 ....Beatrix Loughran, New York SC	1939 ....Joan Tozzer, SC of Boston

Women *(Cont.)*

1940 ....Joan Tozzer, SC of Boston	1967 ....Peggy Fleming, Broadmoor SC
1941 ....Jane Vaughn, Philadelphia SC & HS	1968 ....Peggy Fleming, Broadmoor SC
1942 ....Jane Vaughn Sullivan,	1969 ....Janet Lynn, Wagon Wheel FSC
Philadelphia SC & HS	1970 ....Janet Lynn, Wagon Wheel FSC
1943...........Gretchen Van Zandt Merrill, SC of Boston	1971 ....Janet Lynn, Wagon Wheel FSC
1944...........Gretchen Van Zandt Merrill, SC of Boston	1972 ....Janet Lynn, Wagon Wheel FSC
1945...........Gretchen Van Zandt Merrill, SC of Boston	1973 ....Janet Lynn, Wagon Wheel FSC
1946...........Gretchen Van Zandt Merrill, SC of Boston	1974 ....Dorothy Hamill, SC of New York
1947...........Gretchen Van Zandt Merrill, SC of Boston	1975 ....Dorothy Hamill, SC of New York
1948...........Gretchen Van Zandt Merrill, SC of Boston	1976 ....Dorothy Hamill, SC of New York
1949 ....Yvonne Claire Sherman, SC of New York	1977 ....Linda Fratianne, Los Angeles FSC
1950 ....Yvonne Claire Sherman, SC of New York	1978 ....Linda Fratianne, Los Angeles FSC
1951 ....Sonya Klopfer, Junior SC of New York	1979 ....Linda Fratianne, Los Angeles FSC
1952 ....Tenley E. Albright, SC of Boston	1980 ....Linda Fratianne, Los Angeles FSC
1953 ....Tenley E. Albright, SC of Boston	1981 ....Elaine Zayak, SC of New York
1954 ....Tenley E. Albright, SC of Boston	1982 ....Rosalynn Sumners, Seattle SC
1955 ....Tenley E. Albright, SC of Boston	1983 ....Rosalynn Sumners, Seattle SC
1956 ....Tenley E. Albright, SC of Boston	1984 ....Rosalynn Sumners, Seattle SC
1957 ....Carol E. Heiss, SC of New York	1985 ....Tiffany Chin, San Diego FSC
1958 ....Carol E. Heiss, SC of New York	1986 ....Debi Thomas, Los Angeles FSC
1959 ....Carol E. Heiss, SC of New York	1987 ....Jill Trenary, Broadmoor SC
1960 ....Carol E. Heiss, SC of New York	1988 ....Debi Thomas, Los Angeles FSC
1961 ....Laurence R. Owen, SC of Boston	1989 ....Jill Trenary, Broadmoor SC
1962 ....Barbara Roles Pursley,	1990 ....Jill Trenary, Broadmoor SC
Arctic Blades FSC	1991 ....Tonya Harding, Carousel FSC
1963 ....Lorraine G. Hanlon, SC of Boston	1992 ....Kristi Yamaguchi, St Moritz ISC
1964 ....Peggy Fleming, Arctic Blades FSC	1993 ....Nancy Kerrigan, Colonial FSC
1965 ....Peggy Fleming, Arctic Blades FSC	1994 ....Tonya Harding, Portland FSC
1966 ....Peggy Fleming, City of Colorado Springs	1995 ....Nicole Bobek, Los Angeles FSC

Men

1914 ....Norman M. Scott, WC of Montreal	1951 ......Dick Button, SC of Boston
1915-17 ......No competition	1952 ......Dick Button, SC of Boston
1918 ....Nathaniel W. Niles, SC of Boston	1953 ......Hayes Alan Jenkins, Cleveland SC
1919 ....No competition	1954 ......Hayes Alan Jenkins, Broadmoor SC
1920 ....Sherwin C. Badger, SC of Boston	1955 ......Hayes Alan Jenkins, Broadmoor SC
1921 ....Sherwin C. Badger, SC of Boston	1956 ......Hayes Alan Jenkins, Broadmoor SC
1922 ....Sherwin C. Badger, SC of Boston	1957 ......David Jenkins, Broadmoor SC
1923 ....Sherwin C. Badger, SC of Boston	1958 ......David Jenkins, Broadmoor SC
1924 ....Sherwin C. Badger, SC of Boston	1959 ......David Jenkins, Broadmoor SC
1925 ....Nathaniel W. Niles, SC of Boston	1960 ......David Jenkins, Broadmoor SC
1926 ....Chris I. Christenson, Twin City FSC	1961 ......Bradley R. Lord, SC of Boston
1927 ....Nathaniel W. Niles, SC of Boston	1962 ......Monty Hoyt, Broadmoor SC
1928 ....Roger F. Turner, SC of Boston	1963 ......Thomas Litz, Hershey FSC
1929 ....Roger F. Turner, SC of Boston	1964 ......Scott Ethan Allen, SC of New York
1930 ....Roger F. Turner, SC of Boston	1965 ......Gary C. Visconti, Detroit SC
1931 ....Roger F. Turner, SC of Boston	1966 ......Scott Ethan Allen, SC of New York
1932 ....Roger F. Turner, SC of Boston	1967 ......Gary C. Visconti, Detroit SC
1933 ....Roger F. Turner, SC of Boston	1968 ......Tim Wood, Detroit SC
1934 ....Roger F. Turner, SC of Boston	1969 ......Tim Wood, Detroit SC
1935 ....Robin H. Lee, SC, New York	1970 ......Tim Wood, City of Colorado Springs
1936 ....Robin H. Lee, SC, New York	1971 ......John Misha Petkevich, Great Falls FSC
1937 ....Robin H. Lee, SC, New York	1972 ......Kenneth Shelley, Arctic Blades FSC
1938 ....Robin H. Lee, Chicago FSC	1973 ......Gordon McKellen, Jr, SC of Lake Placid
1939 ....Robin H. Lee, St Paul FSC	1974 ......Gordon McKellen, Jr, SC of Lake Placid
1940 ....Eugene Turner, Los Angeles FSC	1975 ......Gordon McKellen, Jr, SC of Lake Placid
1941 ....Eugene Turner, Los Angeles FSC	1976 ......Terry Kubicka, Arctic Blades FSC
1942 ....Robert Specht, Chicago FSC	1977 ......Charles Tickner, Denver FSC
1943 ....Arthur R. Vaughn, Jr,	1978 ......Charles Tickner, Denver FSC
Philadelphia SC & HS	1979 ......Charles Tickner, Denver FSC
1944-45 ......No competition	1980 ......Charles Tickner, Denver FSC
1946 ....Dick Button, Philadelphia SC & HS	1981 ......Scott Hamilton, Philadelphia SC & HS
1947 ....Dick Button, Philadelphia SC & HS	1982 ......Scott Hamilton, Philadelphia SC & HS
1948 ....Dick Button, Philadelphia SC & HS	1983 ......Scott Hamilton, Philadelphia SC & HS
1949 ....Dick Button, Philadelphia SC & HS	1984 ......Scott Hamilton, Philadelphia SC & HS
1950 ....Dick Button, SC of Boston	1985 ......Brian Boitano, Peninsula FSC

Men *(Cont.)*

1986 ......Brian Boitano, Peninsula FSC
1987 ......Brian Boitano, Peninsula FSC
1988 ......Brian Boitano, Peninsula FSC
1989 ......Christopher Bowman, Los Angeles FSC
1990 ......Todd Eldredge, Los Angeles FSC

1991 ......Todd Eldredge, Los Angeles FSC
1992 ......Christopher Bowman, Los Angeles FSC
1993 ......Scott Davis, Broadmoor SC
1994 ......Scott Davis, Broadmoor SC
1995 ......Todd Eldredge, Detroit SC

Pairs

1914 ......Jeanne Chevalier, Norman M. Scott, WC of Montreal
1915-17 .No competition
1918 ......Theresa Weld, Nathaniel W. Niles, SC of Boston
1919 ......No competition
1920 ......Theresa Weld, Nathaniel W. Niles, SC of Boston
1921 ......Theresa Weld Blanchard, Nathaniel W. Niles, SC of Boston
1922 ......Theresa Weld Blanchard, Nathaniel W. Niles, SC of Boston
1923 ......Theresa Weld Blanchard, Nathaniel W. Niles, SC of Boston
1924 ......Theresa Weld Blanchard, Nathaniel W. Niles, SC of Boston
1925 ......Theresa Weld Blanchard, Nathaniel W. Niles, SC of Boston
1926 ......Theresa Weld Blanchard, Nathaniel W. Niles SC of Boston
1927 ......Theresa Weld Blanchard, Nathaniel W. Niles, SC of Boston
1928 ......Maribel Y. Vinson, Thornton L. Coolidge, SC of Boston
1929 ......Maribel Y. Vinson, Thornton L. Coolidge, SC of Boston
1930 ......Beatrix Loughran, Sherwin C. Badger, SC of New York
1931 ......Beatrix Loughran, Sherwin C. Badger, SC of New York
1932 ......Beatrix Loughran, Sherwin C. Badger, SC of New York
1933 ......Maribel Y. Vinson, George E. B. Hill, SC of Boston
1934 ......Grace E. Madden, James L. Madden, SC of Boston
1935 ......Maribel Y. Vinson, George E. B. Hill, SC of Boston
1936 ......Maribel Y. Vinson, George E. B. Hill, SC of Boston
1937 ......Maribel Y. Vinson, George E. B. Hill, SC of Boston
1938 ......Joan Tozzer, M. Bernard Fox, SC of Boston
1939 ......Joan Tozzer, M. Bernard Fox, SC of Boston
1940 ......Joan Tozzer, M. Bernard Fox, SC of Boston
1941 ......Donna Atwood, Eugene Turner, Mercury FSC/Los Angeles FSC
1942 ......Doris Schubach, Walter Noffke, Springfield Ice Birds
1943 ......Doris Schubach, Walter Noffke, Springfield Ice Birds
1944 ......Doris Schubach, Walter Noffke, Springfield Ice Birds
1945 ......Donna Jeanne Pospisil, Jean-Pierre Brunet, SC of New York
1946 ......Donna Jeanne Pospisil, Jean-Pierre Brunet, SC of New York

1947 ......Yvonne Claire Sherman, Robert J. Swenning, SC of New York
1948 ......Karol Kennedy, Peter Kennedy, Seattle SC
1949 ......Karol Kennedy, Peter Kennedy, Seattle SC
1950 ......Karol Kennedy, Peter Kennedy, Broadmoor SC
1951 ......Karol Kennedy, Peter Kennedy, Broadmoor SC
1952 ......Karol Kennedy, Peter Kennedy, Broadmoor SC
1953 ......Carole Ann Ormaca, Robin Greiner, SC of Fresno
1954 ......Carole Ann Ormaca, Robin Greiner, SC of Fresno
1955 ......Carole Ann Ormaca, Robin Greiner, St Moritz ISC
1956 ......Carole Ann Ormaca, Robin Greiner, St Moritz ISC
1957 ......Nancy Rouillard Ludington, Ronald Ludington, Commonwealth FSC/ SC of Boston
1958 ......Nancy Rouillard Ludington, Ronald Ludington, Commonwealth FSC/ SC of Boston
1959 ......Nancy Rouillard Ludington, Ronald Ludington, Commonwealth FSC
1960 ......Nancy Rouillard Ludington, Ronald Ludington, Commonwealth FSC
1961 ......Maribel Y. Owen, Dudley S. Richards, SC of Boston
1962 ......Dorothyann Nelson, Pieter Kollen, Village of Lake Placid
1963 ......Judianne Fotheringill, Jerry J. Fotheringill, Broadmoor SC
1964 ......Judianne Fotheringill, Jerry J. Fotheringill, Broadmoor SC
1965 ......Vivian Joseph, Ronald Joseph, Chicago FSC
1966 ......Cynthia Kauffman, Ronald Kauffman, Seattle SC
1967 ......Cynthia Kauffman, Ronald Kauffman, Seattle SC
1968 ......Cynthia Kauffman, Ronald Kauffman, Seattle SC
1969 ......Cynthia Kauffman, Ronald Kauffman, Seattle SC
1970 ......Jo Jo Starbuck, Kenneth Shelley, Arctic Blades FSC
1971 ......Jo Jo Starbuck, Kenneth Shelley, Arctic Blades FSC
1972 ......Jo Jo Starbuck, Kenneth Shelley, Arctic Blades FSC
1973 ......Melissa Militano, Mark Militano, SC of New York
1974 ......Melissa Militano, Johnny Johns, SC of New York/Detroit SC
1975 ......Melissa Militano, Johnny Johns, SC of New York/Detroit SC

Pairs *(Cont.)*

1976 ......Tai Babilonia, Randy Gardner,
      Los Angeles FSC
1977 ......Tai Babilonia, Randy Gardner,
      Los Angeles FSC
1978 ......Tai Babilonia, Randy Gardner,
      Los Angeles FSC/Santa Monica FSC
1979 ......Tai Babilonia, Randy Gardner,
      Los Angeles FSC/Santa Monica FSC
1980 ......Tai Babilonia, Randy Gardner,
      Los Angeles FSC/Santa Monica FSC
1981 ......Caitlin Carruthers, Peter Carruthers,
      SC of Wilmington
1982 ......Caitlin Carruthers, Peter Carruthers,
      SC of Wilmington
1983 ......Caitlin Carruthers, Peter Carruthers,
      SC of Wilmington
1984 ......Caitlin Carruthers, Peter Carruthers,
      SC of Wilmington
1985 ......Jill Watson, Peter Oppegard,
      Los Angeles FSC

1986 ......Gillian Wachsman, Todd Waggoner,
      SC of Wilmington
1987 ......Jill Watson, Peter Oppegard,
      Los Angeles FSC
1988 ......Jill Watson, Peter Oppegard,
      Los Angeles FSC
1989 ......Kristi Yamaguchi, Rudi Galindo,
      St Moritz ISC
1990 ......Kristi Yamaguchi, Rudi Galindo,
      St Moritz ISC
1991 ......Natasha Kuchiki, Todd Sand,
      Los Angeles FSC
1992 ......Calla Urbanski, Rocky Marval,
      U of Delaware FSC/SC of New York
1993 ......Calla Urbanski, Rocky Marval,
      U of Delaware FSC/SC of New York
1994 ......Jenni Meno,Todd Sand,
      Winterhurst FSC/Los Angeles FSC
1995 ......Jenni Meno,Todd Sand,
      Winterhurst FSC/Los Angeles FSC

Dance

1914 ......Waltz
      Theresa Weld, Nathaniel W. Niles,
      SC of Boston
1915-19.No competition
1920 ......Waltz
      Theresa Weld, Nathaniel W. Niles, SC Boston
      Fourteenstep
      Gertrude Cheever Porter, Irving Brokaw,NYSC
1921 ......Waltz and Fourteenstep
      Theresa Weld Blanchard, Nathaniel W.
      Niles, SC of Boston
1922 ......Waltz
      Beatrix Loughran, Edward M. Howland,
      New York SC/SC of Boston
      Fourteenstep
      Theresa Weld Blanchard, Nathaniel W.
      Niles, SC of Boston
1923 ......Waltz
      Mr. & Mrs. Henry W. Howe, New York SC
      Fourteenstep
      Sydney Goode, James B. Greene, NYSC
1924 ......Waltz
      Rosaline Dunn, Frederick Gabel
      New York SC
      Fourteenstep
      Sydney Goode, James B. Greene,
      New York SC
1925 ......Waltz and Fourteenstep
      Virginia Slattery, Ferrier T. Martin,
      New York SC
1926 ......Waltz
      Rosaline Dunn, Joseph K. Savage,
      New York SC
      Fourteenstep
      Sydney Goode, James B. Greene,
      New York SC
1927 ......Waltz and Fourteenstep
      Rosaline Dunn, Joseph K. Savage,
      New York SC
1928 ......Waltz
      Rosaline Dunn, Joseph K. Savage,
      New York SC
      Fourteenstep
      Ada Bauman Kelly, George T. Braakman,
      New York SC

1929 ......Waltz and Original Dance combined
      Edith C. Secord, Joseph K. Savage,
      SC of New York
1930 ......Waltz
      Edith C. Secord, Joseph K. Savage,
      SC of New York
      Original
      Clara Rotch Frothingham, George E. B. Hill,
      SC of Boston
1931 ......Waltz
      Edith C. Secord, Ferrier T. Martin,
      SC of New York
      Original
      Theresa Weld Blanchard, Nathaniel W.
      Niles, SC of Boston
1932 ......Waltz
      Edith C. Secord, Joseph K. Savage,
      SC of New York
      Original
      Clara Rotch Frothingham, George E. B. Hill,
      SC of Boston
1933 ......Waltz
      Ilse Twaroschk, Frederick F. Fleishmann,
      Brooklyn FSC
      Original
      Suzanne Davis, Frederick Goodridge,
      SC of Boston
1934 ......Waltz
      Nettie C. Prantel, Roy Hunt, SC of New York
      Original
      Suzanne Davis, Frederick Goodridge,
      SC of Boston
1935 ......Waltz
      Nettie C. Prantel, Roy Hunt, SC of New York
1936 ......Marjorie Parker, Joseph K. Savage,
      SC of New York
1937 ......Nettie C. Prantel, Harold Hartshorne,
      SC of New York
1938 ......Nettie C. Prantel, Harold Hartshorne,
      SC, of New York
1939 ......Sandy Macdonald, Harold Hartshorne,
      SC of New York
1940 ......Sandy Macdonald, Harold Hartshorne,
      SC of New York
1941 ......Sandy Macdonald, Harold Hartshorne, SCNY

Dance *(Cont.)*

1942 ......Edith B. Whetstone, Alfred N. Richards, Jr,
Philadelphia SC & HS
1943 ......Marcella May, James Lochead, Jr,
Skate & Ski Club
1944 ......Marcella May, James Lochead, Jr,
Skate & Ski Club
1945 ......Kathe Mehl Williams, Robert J. Swenning,
SC of New York
1946 ......Anne Davies, Carleton C. Hoffner, Jr,
Washington FSC
1947 ......Lois Waring, Walter H. Bainbridge, Jr,
Baltimore FSC/Washigton FSC
1948 ......Lois Waring, Walter H. Bainbridge, Jr,
Baltimore FSC/Washington FSC
1949 ......Lois Waring, Walter H. Bainbridge, Jr,
Baltimore FSC/Washington FSC
1950 ......Lois Waring, Michael McGean, Baltimore FSC
1951 ......Carmel Bodel, Edward L. Bodel,
St Moritz ISC
1952 ......Lois Waring, Michael McGean,
Baltimore FSC
1953 ......Carol Ann Peters, Daniel C. Ryan,
Washington FSC
1954 ......Carmel Bodel, Edward L. Bodel, St Moritz ISC
1955 ......Carmel Bodel, Edward L. Bodel,
St Moritz ISC
1956 ......Joan Zamboni, Roland Junso,
Arctic Blades FSC
1957 ......Sharon McKenzie, Bert Wright,
Los Angeles FSC
1958 ......Andree Anderson, Donald Jacoby,
Buffalo SC
1959 ......Andree Anderson Jacoby, Donald Jacoby,
Buffalo SC
1960 ......Margie Ackles, Charles W. Phillips, Jr,
Los Angeles FSC/Arctic Blades FSC
1961 ......Diane C. Sherbloom, Larry Pierce,
Los Angeles FSC/WC of Indianapolis
1962 ......Yvonne N. Littlefield, Peter F. Betts,
Arctic Blades FSC/ Paramount, CA
1963 ......Sally Schantz, Stanley Urban,
SC of Boston/Buffalo SC
1964 ......Darlene Streich, Charles D. Fetter, Jr,
WC of Indianapolis
1965 ......Kristin Fortune, Dennis Sveum,
Los Angeles FSC
1966 ......Kristin Fortune, Dennis Sveum,
Los Angeles FSC
1967 ......Lorna Dyer, John Carrell, Broadmoor SC
1968 ......Judy Schwomeyer, James Sladky,
WC of Indianapolis/Genesee FSC
1969 ......Judy Schwomeyer, James Sladky,

WC of Indianapolis/Genesee FSC
1970 ......Judy Schwomeyer, James Sladky,
WC of Indianapolis/Genesee FSC
1971 ......Judy Schwomeyer, James Sladky,
WC of Indianapolis/Genesee FSC
1972 ......Judy Schwomeyer, James Sladky,
WC of Indianapolis/Genesee FSC
1973 ......Mary Karen Campbell, Johnny Johns,
Lansing SC/Detroit SC
1974 ......Colleen O'Connor, Jim Millns,
Broadmoor SC/City of Colorado Springs
1975 ......Colleen O'Connor, Jim Millns,
Broadmoor SC
1976 ......Colleen O'Connor, Jim Millns,
Broadmoor SC
1977 ......Judy Genovesi, Kent Weigle,
SC of Hartford/Charter Oak FSC
1978 ......Stacey Smith, John Summers,
SC of Wilmington
1979 ......Stacey Smith, John Summers,
SC of Wilmington
1980 ......Stacey Smith, John Summers,
SC of Wilmington
1981 ......Judy Blumberg, Michael Seibert,
Broadmoor SC/ISC of Indianapolis
1982 ......Judy Blumberg, Michael Seibert,
Broadmoor SC/ISC of Indianapolis
1983 ......Judy Blumberg, Michael Seibert,
Pittsburgh FSC
1984 ......Judy Blumberg, Michael Seibert,
Pittsburgh FSC
1985 ......Judy Blumberg, Michael Seibert,
Pittsburgh FSC
1986 ......Renee Roca, Donald Adair,
Genesee FSC/Academy FSC
1987 ......Suzanne Semanick, Scott Gregory,
U of Delaware SC
1988 ......Suzanne Semanick, Scott Gregory,
U of Delaware SC
1989 ......Susan Wynne, Joseph Druar,
Broadmoor SC/Seattle SC
1990 ......Susan Wynne, Joseph Druar,
Broadmoor SC/Seattle SC
1991 ......Elizabeth Punsalan, Jerod Swallow,
Broadmoor SC
1992 ......April Sargent, Russ Witherby,
Ogdensburg FSC/U of Delaware FSC
1993 ......Renee Roca, Gorsha Sur, Broadmoor SC
1994 ......Elizabeth Punsalan, Jerod Swallow,
Broadmoor SC/Detroit SC
1995 ......Renee Roca, Gorsha Sur,
Broadmoor SC/ Broadmoor SC

U.S. Olympic Gold Medalists

Women

1956	Tenley Albright	1976	Dorothy Hamill
1960	Carol Heiss	1992	Kristi Yamaguchi
1968	Peggy Fleming		

Men

1948	Richard Button	1960	David W. Jenkins
1952	Richard Button	1984	Scott Hamilton
1956	Hayes Alan Jenkins	1988	Brian Boitano

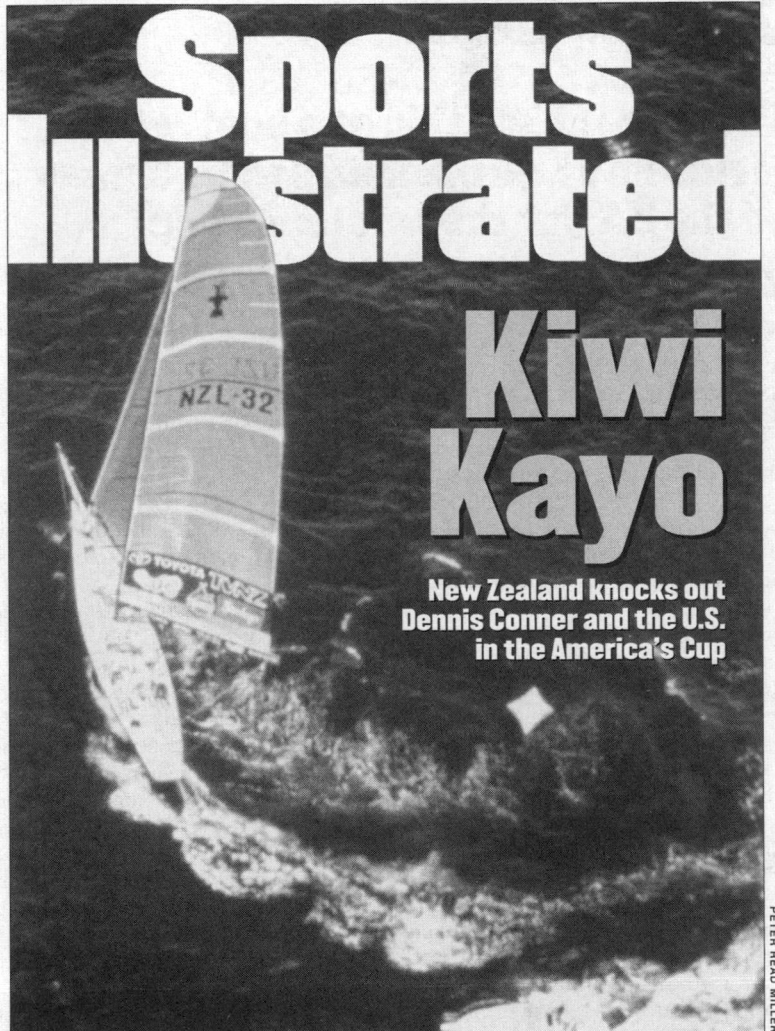

Sports Illustrated

Kiwi Kayo

New Zealand knocks out
Dennis Conner and the U.S.
in the America's Cup

PETER READ MILLER

A Clean Sweep

With their rocket ship of a boat, *Black Magic*, the Kiwis blanked Dennis Conner and the U.S. for the America's Cup

by E.M. Swift

THIS TIME. That was the motto of Team New Zealand. From the moment the Kiwis arrived in San Diego with a pair of sleek black-hulled International America's Cup Class (IACC) yachts, *Black Magic I* and *Black Magic II*, they were determined that after three previous failures, *this time* they would be carrying the most prestigious trophy in sailing back to Auckland, the city of sails.

The New Zealanders were led by Peter Blake, a rangy, shaggy-haired 47-year-old who in his sailing-mad homeland was already a national hero. In 1989–90 Blake had won the prestigious Whitbread round-the-world race, finishing first on every leg. In '94 he'd taken four days off the record for circumnavigation of the globe, accomplishing the feat in a catamaran in just under 75 days. Blake had logged over a half-million ocean racing miles, yet despite his impressive credentials, he assigned himself the role of the mainsheet traveler aboard *Black Magic*—a lowly grinder of winches. That set the tone for the entire Kiwi campaign: There were no superstars

among the New Zealanders. The team came first. And from January to May, in light, fluky breezes or heavy air, in big swells or flat seas, they *finished* first 42 times out of 43 starts. Team New Zealand and its extraordinary black beast skippered by Russell Coutts proved to be in a league of its own.

The event, as usual, was embroiled in nonstop controversy. A new rule, designed to hold down expenses, forbade individual syndicates from building more than two boats for the campaign. Yet both the Australians and the Japanese were accused of circumventing it—a charge that, in the case of the Australians, became moot when its newest and fastest hull, *oneAustralia 95*, sank in midrace on March 5. It was the most visually dramatic moment during the five months of racing: The mast disappeared beneath the waves less than 2½ minutes after a crack split the side of the hull, marking the first time in America's Cup history that a vessel had been lost at sea. No one was hurt, but the disaster was evidence of how far designers were pushing

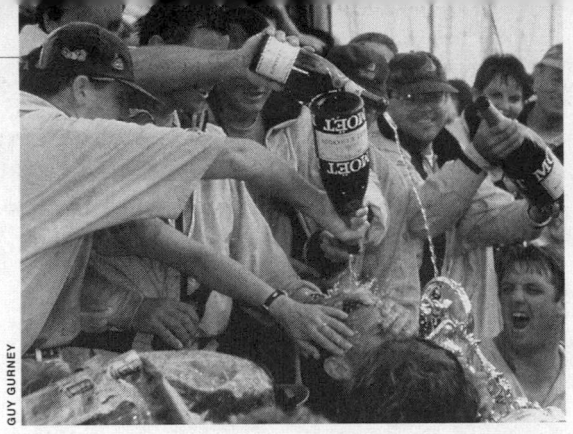

The Kiwis celebrated the way they won: as a team.

the envelope on the $3 million to $5 million carbon-fiber IACC yachts, trying to cut weight to optimize speed. The resilient Aussies, led by John Bertrand—who in 1983 became the first foreign skipper to win the America's Cup and hadn't competed in the event since—regrouped and advanced to the challenger finals sailing their older boat, *oneAustralia*. But they were easily eliminated there by their archrivals, the Kiwis, four races to one.

Over on the defender side, the hosts seemed to be doing everything in their power to kill interest in the event. Nineteen ninety-five will be remembered as the year Bill Koch sponsored an all-women's boat, then reneged on his commitment midway through the trials by putting red-whiskered Dave Dellenbaugh aboard as the starter and tactician. Koch's crew thus became known as 15 women and the bearded lady. The credibility of the event was further damaged when Koch, Dennis Conner and PACT 95 chief John Marshall struck an 11th-hour backroom deal that allowed all three boats to advance to the defender finals, rewriting the rules so that no syndicate would have to face the wrath of its corporate sponsors for going home before the races were shown live on ESPN. The 52-year-old Conner, who would have lost out if the original rules had been adhered to, subsequently pulled off one of the most improbable comebacks in Cup history, making up an astonishing five minutes over Koch's *Mighty Mary* in the final three-mile downwind leg, winning the right to defend.

The deal making and finagling wasn't finished. Convinced that his *Stars and Stripes* was the slowest of the three defender boats, Conner jettisoned it and rented PACT 95's *Young America* six days before the showdown with New Zealand. The switch enraged the plain-speaking Blake

and cemented Conner's reputation in New Zealand as "Dirty Den." "If we are fortunate enough to win this event," Blake said, "we're going to clean it up. We're not going to have rules that are different for one side than the other."

Blake will get his chance. *Young America* proved no match for the speedy *Black Magic*. In an anticlimactic best-of-nine series, the Kiwis won all five 18.5-mile races by an average margin of two minutes 51 seconds—roughly two fifths of a mile. They didn't trail at a single rounding mark. "I've never been in a race where I felt I had so little control over the outcome," said Paul Cayard, Team Dennis Conner's helmsman.

"We never guessed the entire defense effort was so far off the pace," said tactician Tom Whidden. "We can't even engage these guys in a race."

It was sweet revenge for the Kiwis, who'd been eliminated in 1987 and '88 by Conner and in '92 by Cayard, who then was sailing for Italy. *This time* was different. Fans of the America's Cup hope that next time the regatta will be different, too. San Diego and the America's Cup proved to be a bad marriage. In the seven years the San Diego Yacht Club held the Cup, it staged three turbulent defenses that were marred by court challenges, insolvency, light winds, boring races, unsportsmanlike conduct and an apathetic local populace. As the Auld Mug leaves San Diego for the bluer waters off Auckland, the chances are it will never return.

Archery

National Men's Champions

1879.......Will H. Thompson	1916 .....Dr. Robert Elmer	1959 .....Wilbert Vetrovsky
1880.....L. L. Pedinghaus	1919 .....Dr. Robert Elmer	1960 .....Robert Kadlec
1881 ......F. H. Walworth	1920 ......Dr. Robert Elmer	1961 .....Clayton Sherman
1882.....D. H. Nash	1921 .....James Jiles	1962 .....Charles Sandlin
1883.....Col. Robert Williams	1922 .....Dr. Robert Elmer	1963 .....Dave Keaggy, Jr.
1884 ......Col. Robert Williams	1923 .....Bill Palmer	1964 .....Dave Keaggy, Jr.
1885 ......Col. Robert Williams	1924 .....James Jiles	1965 .....George Slinzer
1886 ......W. A. Clark	1925 .....Dr. Paul Crouch	1966 .....Hardy Ward
1887 ......W. A. Clark	1926 .....Stanley Spencer	1967 .....Ray Rogers
1888 ......Lewis Maxson	1927 .....Dr. Paul Crouch	1968 .....Hardy Ward
1889 ......Lewis Maxson	1928 .....Bill Palmer	1969 .....Ray Rogers
1890 ......Lewis Maxson	1929 .....Dr. E. K. Roberts	1970 .....Joe Thornton
1891 ......Lewis Maxson	1930 .....Russ Hoogerhyde	1971 .....John Williams
1892 ......Lewis Maxson	1931 .....Russ Hoogerhyde	1972 .....Kevin Erlandson
1893 ......Lewis Maxson	1932 .....Russ Hoogerhyde	1973 .....Darrell Pace
1894 ......Lewis Maxson	1933 .....Ralph Miller	1974 .....Darrell Pace
1895 ......W. B. Robinson	1934 .....Russ Hoogerhyde	1975 .....Darrell Pace
1896 ......Lewis Maxson	1935 .....Gilman Keasey	1976 .....Darrell Pace
1897 ......W. A. Clark	1936 .....Gilman Keasey	1977 .....Rick McKinney
1898 ......Lewis Maxson	1937 .....Russ Hoogerhyde	1978 .....Darrell Pace
1899 ......M. C. Howell	1938 .....Pat Chambers	1979 .....Rick McKinney
1900 .....A. R. Clark	1939 .....Pat Chambers	1980 .....Rick McKinney
1901 ......Will H. Thompson	1940 .....Russ Hoogerhyde	1981 .....Rick McKinney
1902 ......Will H. Thompson	1941 ......Larry Hughes	1982 .....Rick McKinney
1903 ......Will H. Thompson	1946 .....Wayne Thompson	1983 .....Rick McKinney
1904 ......George Bryant	1947 ......Jack Wilson	1984 .....Darrell Pace
1905 ......George Bryant	1948 ......Larry Hughes	1985 .....Rick McKinney
1906 ......Henry Richardson	1949 ......Russ Reynolds	1986 .....Rick McKinney
1907 ......Henry Richardson	1950 ......Stan Overby	1987 .....Rick McKinney
1908 ......Will H. Thompson	1951 ......Russ Reynolds	1988 .....Jay Barrs
1909 ......George Bryant	1952 ......Robert Larson	1989 .....Ed Eliason
1910 ......Henry Richardson	1953 ......Bill Glackin	1990 .....Ed Eliason
1911 ......Dr. Robert Elmer	1954 ......Robert Rhode	1991 .....Ed Eliason
1912 ......George Bryant	1955 .....Joe Fries	1992 .....Alan Rasor
1913 ......George Bryant	1956 .....Joe Fries	1993 .....Jay Barrs
1914 ......Dr. Robert Elmer	1957 .....Joe Fries	1994 .....Jay Barrs
1915 ......Dr. Robert Elmer	1958 .....Robert Bitner	1995 ......Justin Huish

National Women's Champions

1879 ......Mrs. S. Brown	1903 ......Mrs. M. C. Howell	1929 ......Audrey Grubbs
1880 ......Mrs. T. Davies	1904 ......Mrs. M. C. Howell	1930 .....Audrey Grubbs
1881 ......Mrs. A. H. Gibbes	1905 ......Mrs. M. C. Howell	1931 ......Dorothy Cummings
1882 ......Mrs. A. H. Gibbes	1906 ......Mrs. E. C. Cook	1932 ......Ilda Hanchette
1883 ......Mrs. M. C. Howell	1907 ......Mrs. M. C. Howell	1933 ......Madelaine Taylor
1884 ......Mrs. H. Hall	1908 ......Harriet Case	1934 ......Desales Mudd
1885 ......Mrs. M. C. Howell	1909 ......Harriet Case	1935 ......Ruth Hodgert
1886 ......Mrs. M. C. Howell	1910 ......J. V. Sullivan	1936 ......Gladys Hammer
1887 ......Mrs. A. M. Phillips	1911 ......Mrs. J. S. Taylor	1937 ......Gladys Hammer
1888 ......Mrs. A. M. Phillips	1912 ......Mrs. Witwer Tayler	1938 ......Jean Tenney
1889 ......Mrs. A. M. Phillips	1913 ......Mrs. P. Fletcher	1939 ......Belvia Carter
1890 ......Mrs. M. C. Howell	1914 ......Mrs. B. P. Gray	1940 ......Ann Weber
1891 ......Mrs. M. C. Howell	1915 ......Cynthia Wesson	1941 ......Ree Dillinger
1892 ......Mrs. M. C. Howell	1916 ......Cynthia Wesson	1946 ......Ann Weber
1893 ......Mrs. M. C. Howell	1919 ......Dorothy Smith	1947 ......Ann Weber
1894 ......Mrs. Albert Kern	1920 ......Cynthia Wesson	1948 ......Jean Lee
1895 ......Mrs. M. C. Howell	1921 ......Mrs. L. C. Smith	1949 ......Jean Lee
1896 ......Mrs. M. C. Howell	1922 ......Dorothy Smith	1950 ......Jean Lee
1897 ......Mrs. J. S. Baker	1923 ......Norma Pierce	1951 ......Jean Lee
1898 ......Mrs. M. C. Howell	1924 ......Dorothy Smith	1952 ......Ann Weber
1899 ......Mrs. M. C. Howell	1925 ......Dorothy Smith	1953 ......Ann Weber
1900 ......Mrs. M. C. Howell	1926 ......Dorothy Smith	1954 ......Luarette Young
1901 ......Mrs. C. E. Woodruff	1927 ......Mrs. R. Johnson	1955 ......Ann Clark
1902 ......Mrs. M. C. Howell	1928 ......Beatrice Hodgson	1956 ......Carole Meinhart

National Women's Champions (Cont.)

1957 .....Carole Meinhart	1970 .....Nancy Myrick	1983 .....Nancy Myrick
1958 .....Carole Meinhart	1971 .....Doreen Wilber	1984 .....Ruth Rowe
1959 .....Carole Meinhart	1972 .....Ruth Rowe	1985 .....Terri Pesho
1960 .....Ann Clark	1973 .....Doreen Wilber	1986 .....Debra Ochs
1961 .....Victoria Cook	1974 .....Doreen Wilber	1987 .....Terry Quinn
1962 .....Nancy Vonderheide	1975 .....Irene Lorensen	1988 .....Debra Ochs
1963 .....Nancy Vonderheide	1976 .....Luann Ryon	1989 .....Debra Ochs
1964 .....Victoria Cook	1977 .....Luann Ryon	1990 .....Denise Parker
1965 .....Nancy Pfeiffer	1978 .....Luann Ryon	1991 .....Denise Parker
1966 .....Helen Thornton	1979 .....Lynette Johnson	1992 .....Sherry Block
1967 .....Ardelle Mills	1980 .....Judi Adams	1993 .....Denise Parker
1968 .....Victoria Cook	1981 .....Debra Metzger	1994 .....Judy Adams
1969 .....Doreen Wilber	1982 .....Luann Ryon	1995 .....Jessica Carlson

Chess

World Champions

FIDE	FIDE (Cont.)
1866-94....................Wilhelm Steinitz, Austria	1963-69....................Tigran Petrosian, USSR
1894-1921................Emanuel Lasker, Germany	1969-72....................Boris Spassky, USSR
1921-27....................Jose Capablanca, Cuba	1972-75....................Bobby Fischer, United States
1927-35....................Alexander Alekhine, France	1975-85....................Anatoly Karpov, USSR
1935-37....................Max Euwe, Holland	1985-93....................*Gary Kasparov, USSR
1937-47....................Alexander Alekhine, France	1993...........................vacant
1948-57....................Mikhail Botvinnik, USSR	1994-.........................Anatoly Karpov, Russia
1957-58....................Vassily Smyslov, USSR	*Kasparov stripped of title by FIDE in 1993.
1958-59....................Mikhail Botvinnik, USSR	**Professional Chess Association**
1960-61....................Mikhail Tal, USSR	1993-.........................Gary Kasparov
1961-63....................Mikhail Botvinnik, USSR	

United States Champions

1857-71 ....Paul Morphy	1951-54 ....Larry Evans	1983 ....Larry Christiansen
1871-76 ....George Mackenzie	1954-57 ....Arthur Bisguier	Walter Browne
1876-80 ....James Mason	1957-61 ....Bobby Fischer	1984-85 ....Lev Alburt
1880-89 ....George Mackenzie	1961-62 ....Larry Evans	1986 ....Yasser Seirawan
1889-90 ....Samuel Lipschutz	1962-68 ....Bobby Fischer	1987 ....Joel Benjamin
1890 ....Jackson Showalter	1968-69 ....Larry Evans	Nick DeFirmian
1890-91 ....Max Judd	1969-72 ....Samuel Reshevsky	1988 ....Michael Wilder
1891-92 ....Jackson Showalter	1972-73 ....Robert Byrne	1989 ....Roman
1892-94 ....Samuel Lipschutz	1973-74 ....Lubomir Kavale	Dzindzichashvili
1894 ....Jackson Showalter	John Grefe	Stuart Rachels
1894-95 ....Albert Hodges	1974-77 ....Walter Browne	Yasser Seirawan
1895-97 ....Jackson Showalter	1978-80 ....Lubomir Kavalek	1990 ....Lev Alburt
1897-1906 ....Harry Pillsbury	1980-81 ....Larry Evans	1991 ....Gata Kamski
1906-09 ....Vacant	Larry Christiansen	1992 ....Patrick Wolf
1909-36 ....Frank Marshall	Walter Browne	1993 ....A. Yermolinsky
1936-44 ....Samuel Reshevsky	1981-83 ....Walter Browne	A. Shabalov
1944-46 ....Arnold Denker	Yasser Seirawan	1994 ....Boris Gulko
1946-48 ....Samuel Reshevsky	1983 ....Roman	1995 ....Gary Kasparov
1948-51 ....Herman Steiner	Dzindzichashvili	

Curling

World Men's Champions

Year	Country, Skip	Year	Country, Skip	Year	Country, Skip
1972	Canada, Crest Melesnuk	1979	Norway, Kristian Soerum	1988	Norway, Eigil Ramsfjell
1973	Sweden, Kjell Oscarius	1980	Canada, Rich Folk	1989	Canada, Pat Ryan
1974	United States, Bud Somerville	1981	Switzerland, Jurg Tanner	1990	Canada, Ed Werenich
1975	Switzerland, Otto Danieli	1982	Canada, Al Hackner	1991	Scotland, David Smith
1976	United States, Bruce Roberts	1983	Canada, Ed Werenich	1992	Switzerland, Markus Eggler
1977	Sweden, Ragnar Kamp	1984	Norway, Eigil Ramsfjell	1993	Canada, Russ Howard
1978	United States, Bob Nichols	1985	Canada, Al Hackner	1994	Canada, Rick Folk
		1986	Canada, Ed Luckowich	1995	Canada, Kerry Burtnyk
		1987	Canada, Russ Howard		

Curling (Cont.)

World Women's Champions

Year	Country, Skip	Year	Country, Skip	Year	Country, Skip
1979	Switzerland, Gaby Casanova	1983	Switzerland, Erika Mueller	1990	Norway, Dordi Nordby
1980	Canada, Marj Mitchell	1984	Canada, Connie Lallberte	1991	Norway, Dordi Nordby
1981	Sweden, Elisabeth Hogstrom	1985	Canada, Linda Moore	1992	Sweden, Elisabet Johanssen
1982	Denmark, Marianne Jorgenson	1986	Canada, Marilyn Darte	1993	Canada, Sandra Peterson
		1987	Canada, Pat Sanders	1994	Canada, Sandra Peterson
		1988	Germany, Andrea Schopp	1995	Sweden, Elisabet Gustafson
		1989	Canada, Heather Houston		

U.S. Men's Champions

Year	Site	Winning Club	Skip
1957	Chicago, IL	Hibbing, MN	Harold Lauber
1958	Milwaukee, WI	Detroit, MI	Douglas Fisk
1959	Green Bay, WI	Hibbing, MN	Fran Kleffman
1960	Chicago, IL	Grafton, ND	Orvil Gilleshammer
1961	Grand Forks, ND	Seattle, WA	Frank Crealock
1962	Detroit, MI	Hibbing, MN	Fran Kleffman
1963	Duluth, MN	Detroit, MI	Mike Slyziuk
1964	Utica, NY	Duluth, MN	Robert Magle, Jr.
1965	Seattle, WA	Superior, WI	Bud Somerville
1966	Hibbing, MN	Fargo, ND	Joe Zbacnik
1967	Winchester, MA	Seattle, WA	Bruce Roberts
1968	Madison, WI	Superior, WI	Bud Somerville
1969	Grand Forks, ND	Superior, WI	Bud Somerville
1970	Ardsley, NY	Grafton, ND	Art Tallackson
1971	Duluth, MN	Edmore, ND	Dale Dalziel
1972	Wilmette, IL	Grafton, ND	Robert Labonte
1973	Colorado Springs, CO	Winchester, MA	Charles Reeves
1974	Schenectady, NY	Superior, WI	Bud Somerville
1975	Detroit, MI	Seattle, WA	Ed Risling
1976	Wausau, WI	Hibbing, MN	Bruce Roberts
1977	Northbrook, IL	Hibbing, MN	Bruce Roberts
1978	Utica, NY	Superior, WI	Bob Nichols
1979	Superior, WI	Bemidji, MN	Scott Baird
1980	Bemidji, MN	Hibbing, MN	Paul Pustovar
1981	Fairbanks, AK	Superior, WI	Bob Nichols
1982	Brookline, MA	Madison, WI	Steve Brown
1983	Colorado Springs, CO	Colorado Springs, CO	Don Cooper
1984	Hibbing, MN	Hibbing, MN	Bruce Roberts
1985	Mequon, WI	Wilmette, IL	Tim Wright
1986	Seattle, WA	Madison, WI	Steve Brown
1987	Lake Placid, NY	Seattle, WA	Jim Vukich
1988	St. Paul, MN	Seattle, WA	Doug Jones
1989	Detroit, MI	Seattle, WA	Jim Vukich
1990	Superior, WI	Seattle, WA	Doug Jones
1991	Utica, NY	Madison, WI	Steve Brown
1992	Grafton, ND	Seattle, WA	Doug Jones
1993	St Paul, MN	Bemidji, MN	Scott Baird
1994	Duluth, MN	Bemidji, MN	Scott Baird
1995	Appleton, WI	Superior, WI	Tim Somerville

U.S. Women's Champions

Year	Site	Winning Club	Skip
1977	Wilmette, IL	Hastings, NY	Margaret Smith
1978	Duluth, MN	Wausau, WI	Sandy Robarge
1979	Winchester, MA	Seattle, WA	Nancy Langley
1980	Seattle, WA	Seattle, WA	Sharon Kozal
1981	Kettle Moraine, WI	Seattle, WA	Nancy Langley
1982	Bowling Green, OH	Oak Park, IL	Ruth Schwenker
1983	Grafton, ND	Seattle, WA	Nancy Langley
1984	Wauwatosa, WI	Duluth, MN	Amy Hatten
1985	Hershey, PA	Fairbanks, AK	Bev Birklid
1986	Chicago, IL	St. Paul, MN	Gerri Tilden
1987	St. Paul, MN	Seattle, WA	Sharon Good
1988	Darien, CT	Seattle, WA	Nancy Langley
1989	Detroit, MI	Rolla, ND	Jan Lagasse
1990	Superior, WI	Denver, CO	Bev Behnke

U.S. Women's Champions *(Cont.)*

Year	Site	Winning Club	Skip
1991	Utica, NY	Houston, TX	Maymar Gemmell
1992	Grafton, ND	Madison, WI	Lisa Schoeneberg
1993	St Paul, MN	Denver, CO	Bev Behnke
1994	Duluth, MN	Denver, CO	Bev Behnke
1995	Appleton, WI	Madison, WI	Lisa Schoeneberg

Cycling

Professional Road Race World Champions

1927 ....Alfred Binda, Italy	1954 ....Louison Bobet, France	1975 ....Hennie Kuiper, Holland
1928 ....George Ronsse, Belgium	1955 ....Stan Ockers, Belgium	1976 ....Freddy Maertens, Belgium
1929 ....George Ronsse, Belgium	1956 ....Rik Van Steenbergen,	1977 ....Francesco Moser, Italy
1930 ....Alfred Binda, Italy	Belgium	1978 ....Gerri Knetemann, Holland
1931 ....Learco Guerra, Italy	1957 ....Rik Van Steenbergen,	1979 ....Jan Raas, Holland
1932 ....Alfred Binda, Italy	Belgium	1980 ....Bernard Hinault, France
1933 ....George Speicher, France	1958 ....Ercole Baldini, Italy	1981 ....Freddy Maertens, Belgium
1934 ....Karel Kaers, Belgium	1959 ....Andre Darrigade, France	1982 ....Giuseppe Saronni, Italy
1935 ....Jean Aerts, Belgium	1960 ....Rik van Looy, Belgium	1983 ....Greg LeMond,
1936 ....Antonio Magne, France	1961 ....Rik van Looy, Belgium	United States
1937 ....Elio Meulenberg, Belgium	1962 ....Jean Stablenski, France	1984 ....Claude Criquielion, Belgium
1938 ....Marcel Kint, Belgium	1963 ....Bennoni Beheyt, Belgium	1985 ....Joop Zoetemelk, Holland
1939-45.No competition	1964 ....Jan Janssen, Holland	1986 ....Moreno Argentin, Italy
1946 ....Hans Knecht, Switzerland	1965 ....Tommy Simpson, England	1987 ....Stephen Roche, Ireland
1947 ....Theo. Middelkamp, Holland	1966 ....Rudi Altig, West Germany	1988 ....Maurizio Fondriest, Italy
1948 ....Alberic Schotte, Belgium	1967 ....Eddy Merckx, Belgium	1989 ....Greg LeMond,
1949 ....Henri Van Steenbergen,	1968 ....Vittorio Adorni, Italy	United States
Belgium	1969 ....Harm Ottenbros,	1990 ....Rudy Dhaenene, Belgium
1950 ....Alberic Schotte, Belgium	Netherlands	1991 ....Gianni Bugno, Italy
	1970 ....J.P. Monseré, Belgium	1992 ....Gianni Bugno, Italy
1951 ....Ferdinand Kubler,	1971 ....Eddy Merckx, Belgium	1993 ....Lance Armstrong,
Switzerland	1972 ....Marino Basso, Italy	United States
1952 ....Heinz Mueller, Germany	1973 ....Felice Gimondi, Italy	1994 ....Luc LeBlanc, France
1953 ....Fausto Coppi, Italy	1974 ....Eddy Merckx, Belgium	1995 ....Abraham Olano, Spain

Tour DuPont Winners

Year	Winner	Time
1989	Dag Otto Lauritzen, Norway	33 hrs, 28 min, 48 sec
1990	Raul Alcala, Mexico	45 hrs, 20 min, 9 sec
1991	Erik Breukink, Holland	48 hrs, 56 min, 53 sec
1992	Greg LeMond, United States	44 hrs, 27 min, 43 sec
1993	Raul Alcala, Mexico	46 hrs, 42 min, 52 sec
1994	Viatcheslav Ekimov, Russia	47 hrs, 14 min, 29 sec
1995	Lance Armstrong, United States	46 hrs, 31 min, 16 sec

Tour de France Winners

Year	Winner	Time
1903	Maurice Garin, France	94 hrs, 33 min
1904	Henri Cornet, France	96 hrs, 5 min, 56 sec
1905	Louis Trousselier, France	110 hrs, 26 min, 58 sec
1906	Rene Pottier, France	Not available
1907	Lucien Petit-Breton, France	158 hrs, 54 min, 5 sec
1908	Lucien Petit-Breton, France	Not available
1909	Francois Faber, Luxembourg	157 hrs, 1 min, 22 sec
1910	Octave Lapize, France	162 hrs, 41 min, 30 sec
1911	Gustave Garrigou, France	195 hrs, 37 min
1912	Odile Defraye, Belgium	190 hrs, 30 min, 28 sec
1913	Philippe Thys, Belgium	197 hrs, 54 min
1914	Philippe Thys, Belgium	200 hrs, 28 min, 48 sec
1915-18	No race	
1919	Firmin Lambot, Belgium	231 hrs, 7 min, 15 sec
1920	Philippe Thys, Belgium	228 hrs, 36 min, 13 sec
1921	Leon Scieur, Belgium	221 hrs, 50 min, 26 sec
1922	Firmin Lambot, Belgium	222 hrs, 8 min, 6 sec

Tour de France Winners *(Cont.)*

Year	Winner	Time
1923	Henri Pelissier, France	222 hrs, 15 min, 30 sec
1924	Ottavio Bottechia, Italy	226 hrs, 18 min, 21 sec
1925	Ottavio Bottechia, Italy	219 hrs, 10 min, 18 sec
1926	Lucien Buysse, Belgium	238 hrs, 44 min, 25 sec
1927	Nicolas Frantz, Luxembourg	198 hrs, 16 min, 42 sec
1928	Nicolas Frantz, Luxembourg	192 hrs, 48 min, 58 sec
1929	Maurice Dewaele, Belgium	186 hrs, 39 min, 16 sec
1930	Andre Leducq, France	172 hrs, 12 min, 16 sec
1931	Antonin Magne, France	177 hrs, 10 min, 3 sec
1932	Andre Leducq, France	154 hrs, 12 min, 49 sec
1933	Georges Speicher, France	147 hrs, 51 min, 37 sec
1934	Antonin Magne, France	147 hrs, 13 min, 58 sec
1935	Romain Maes, Belgium	141 hrs, 32 min
1936	Sylvere Maes, Belgium	142 hrs, 47 min, 32 sec
1937	Roger Lapebie, France	138 hrs, 58 min, 31 sec
1938	Gino Bartali, Italy	148 hrs, 29 min, 12 sec
1939	Sylvere Maes, Belgium	132 hrs, 3 min, 17 sec
1940-46	No race	
1947	Jean Robic, France	148 hrs, 11 min, 25 sec
1948	Gino Bartali, Italy	147 hrs, 10 min, 36 sec
1949	Fausto Coppi, Italy	149 hrs, 40 min, 49 sec
1950	Ferdi Kubler, Switzerland	145 hrs, 36 min, 56 sec
1951	Hugo Koblet, Switzerland	142 hrs, 20 min, 14 sec
1952	Fausto Coppi, Italy	151 hrs, 57 min, 20 sec
1953	Louison Bobet, France	129 hrs, 23 min, 25 sec
1954	Louison Bobet, France	140 hrs, 6 min, 5 sec
1955	Louison Bobet, France	130 hrs, 29 min, 26 sec
1956	Roger Walkowiak, France	124 hrs, 1 min, 16 sec
1957	Jacques Anquetil, France	129 hrs, 46 min, 11 sec
1958	Charly Gaul, Luxembourg	116 hrs, 59 min, 5 sec
1959	Federico Bahamontes, Spain	123 hrs, 46 min, 45 sec
1960	Gastone Nencini, Italy	112 hrs, 8 min, 42 sec
1961	Jacques Anquetil, France	122 hrs, 1 min, 33 sec
1962	Jacques Anquetil, France	114 hrs, 31 min, 54 sec
1963	Jacques Anquetil, France	113 hrs, 30 min, 5 sec
1964	Jacques Anquetil, France	127 hrs, 9 min, 44 sec
1965	Felice Gimondi, Italy	116 hrs, 42 min, 6 sec
1966	Lucien Aimar, France	117 hrs, 34 min, 21 sec
1967	Roger Pingeon, France	136 hrs, 53 min, 50 sec
1968	Jan Janssen, Netherlands	133 hrs, 49 min, 32 sec
1969	Eddy Merckx, Belgium	116 hrs, 16 min, 2 sec
1970	Eddy Merckx, Belgium	119 hrs, 31 min, 49 sec
1971	Eddy Merckx, Belgium	96 hrs, 45 min, 14 sec
1972	Eddy Merckx, Belgium	108 hrs, 17 min, 18 sec
1973	Luis Ocana, Spain	122 hrs, 25 min, 34 sec
1974	Eddy Merckx, Belgium	116 hrs, 16 min, 58 sec
1975	Bernard Thevenet, France	114 hrs, 35 min, 31 sec
1976	Lucien Van Impe, Belgium	116 hrs, 22 min, 23 sec
1977	Bernard Thevenet, France	115 hrs, 38 min, 30 sec
1978	Bernard Hinault, France	108 hrs, 18 min
1979	Bernard Hinault, France	103 hrs, 6 min, 50 sec
1980	Joop Zoetemelk, Netherlands	109 hrs, 19 min, 14 sec
1981	Bernard Hinault, France	96 hrs, 19 min, 38 sec
1982	Bernard Hinault, France	92 hrs, 8 min, 46 sec
1983	Laurent Fignon, France	105 hrs, 7 min, 52 sec
1984	Laurent Fignon, France	112 hrs, 3 min, 40 sec
1985	Bernard Hinault, France	113 hrs, 24 min, 23 sec
1986	Greg LeMond, United States	110 hrs, 35 min, 19 sec
1987	Stephen Roche, Ireland	115 hrs, 27 min, 42 sec
1988	Pedro Delgado, Spain	84 hrs, 27 min, 53 sec
1989	Greg LeMond, United States	87 hrs, 38 min, 35 sec
1990	Greg LeMond, United States	90 hrs, 43 min, 20 sec
1991	Miguel Induráin, Spain	101 hrs, 1 min, 20 sec
1992	Miguel Induráin, Spain	100 hrs, 49 min, 30 sec
1993	Miguel Induráin, Spain	95 hrs, 57 min, 9 sec
1994	Miguel Induráin, Spain	103 hrs, 38 min, 38 sec
1995	Miguel Induráin, Spain	92 hrs, 44 min, 59 sec

Sled Dog Racing

Iditarod

Year	Winner	Time	Year	Winner	Time
1973	Dick Wilmarth	20 days, 00:49:41	1985	Libby Riddles	18 days, 00:20:17
1974	Carl Huntington	20 days, 15:02:07	1986	Susan Butcher	11 days, 15:06:00
1975	Emmitt Peters	14 days, 14:43:45	1987	Susan Butcher	11 days, 02:05:13
1976	Gerald Riley	18 days, 22:58:17	1988	Susan Butcher	11 days, 11:41:40
1977	Rick Swenson	16 days, 16:27:13	1989	Joe Runyan	11 days, 05:24:34
1978	Dick Mackey	14 days, 18:52:24	1990	Susan Butcher	11 days, 01:53:23
1979	Rick Swenson	15 days, 10:37:47	1991	Rick Swenson	12 days, 16:34:39
1980	Joe May	14 days, 07:11:51	1992	Martin Buser	10 days, 19:17:15
1981	Rick Swenson	12 days, 08:45:02	1993	Jeff King	10 days, 15:38:15
1982	Rick Swenson	16 days, 04:40:10	1994	Martin Buser	10 days, 13:02:39
1983	Dick Mackey	12 days, 14:10:44	1995	Doug Swingley	9 days, 02:42:19
1984	Dean Osmar	12 days, 15:07:33			

Fishing

Saltwater Fishing Records

Species	Weight	Where Caught	Date	Angler
Albacore	88 lb 2 oz	Gran Canaria, Canary Islands	Nov 19, 1977	Siegfried Dickemann
Amberjack, greater	155 lb 10 oz	Challenger Bank, Bermuda	June 24, 1981	Joseph Dawson
Amberjack, Pacific	104 lb	Baja California, Mexico	July 4, 1984	Richard Cresswell
Barracuda, great	85 lb	Christmas Island, Kiribati	April 11, 1992	John W. Helfrich
Barracuda, Mexican	21 lb	Phantom Isle, Costa Rica	Mar 27, 1987	E. Greg Kent
Barracuda, pickhandle	17 lb 4 oz	Sitra Channel, Arabian Gulf	Nov 21, 1995	Roger J. Cranswick
Bass, barred sand	13 lb 3 oz	Huntington Beach, CA	Aug 29, 1988	Robert Halal
Bass, black sea	9 lb 8 oz	Virginia Beach, VA	Jan 9, 1987	Joe Mizelle, Jr
Bass, European	20 lb 11 oz	Stes Maries de la Mer, France	May 6, 1986	Jean Baptiste Bayle
Bass, giant sea	563 lb 8 oz	Anacapa Island, CA	Aug 20, 1968	James D. McAdam, Jr
Bass, redeye	8 lb 12 oz	Apalatchicola River, FL	Jan 28, 1995	Carl W. Davis
Bass, striped	78 lb 8 oz	Atlantic City, NJ	Sep 21, 1982	Albert R. McReynolds
Bluefish	31 lb 12 oz	Hatteras Inlet, NC	Jan 30, 1972	James M. Hussey
Bonefish	19 lb	Zululand, South Africa	May 26, 1962	Brian W. Batchelor
Bonito, Atlantic	18 lb 4 oz	Faial Island, Azores	July 8, 1953	D. G. Higgs
Bonito, Pacific	14 lb 12 oz	Baja California, Mexico	Oct. 12, 1980	Jerome H. Rilling
Cabezon	23 lb	Juan De Fuca Strait, WA	Aug 4, 1990	Wesley Hunter
Cobia	135 lb 9 oz	Shark Bay, Australia	July 9, 1985	Peter W. Goulding
Cod, Atlantic	98 lb 12 oz	Isle of Shoals, NH	June 8, 1969	Alphonse Bielevich
Cod, Pacific	30 lb	Andrew Bay, AK	July 7, 1984	Donald R. Vaughn
Conger	133 lb 4 oz	South Devon, England	June 5, 1995	Vic Evans
Dolphin	87 lb	Papagallo Gulf, Costa Rica	Sep 25, 1976	Manuel Salazar
Drum, black	113 lb 1 oz	Lewes, DE	Sep 15, 1975	Gerald M. Townsend
Drum, red	94 lb 2 oz	Avon, NC	Nov 7, 1984	David Deuel
Eel, American	8 lb 8 oz	Brewster, MA	May 17, 1992	Gerald G. Lapierre, Sr
Eel, marbled	36 lb 1 oz	Durban, South Africa	June 10, 1984	Ferdie van Nooten
Flounder, southern	20 lb 9 oz	Nassau Sound, FL	Dec 23, 1983	Larenza W. Mungin
Flounder, summer	22 lb 7 oz	Montauk, NY	Sep 15, 1975	Charles Nappi
Grouper, warsaw	436 lb 12 oz	Destin, FL	Dec 22, 1985	Steve Haeusler
Halibut, Atlantic	255 lb 4 oz	Gloucester, MA	July 28, 1989	Sonny Manley
Halibut, California	53 lb 4 oz	Santa Rosa Island, CA	July 7, 1988	Russell J. Harmon
Halibut, Pacific	368 lb	Gustavus, AK	July 5, 1991	Celia H. Dueitt
Jack, crevalle	57 lb 5 oz	Barra do Kwanza, Angola	Oct 10, 1992	Cam Nicolson
Jack, horse-eye	24 lb 8 oz	Miami, FL	Dec 20, 1982	Tilo Schnau
Jack, Pacific crevalle	29 lb 8 oz	Playa Zancudo, Costa Rica	Jan 1, 1994	Ronald C. Snody
Jewfish	680 lb	Fernandina Beach, FL	May 20, 1961	Lynn Joyner
Kawakawa	29 lb	Isla Clarion, Mexico	Dec 17, 1986	Ronald Nakamura
Lingcod	69 lb	Langara Island, B.C.	June 16, 1992	Murray M. Romer
Mackerel, cero	17 lb 2 oz	Islamorada, FL	Apr 5, 1986	G. Michael Mills
Mackerel, king	90 lb	Key West, FL	Feb 16, 1976	Norton I. Thornton
Mackerel, narrowbarred	99 lb	Natal, South Africa	Mar 14, 1982	Michael J. Wilkinson
Mackerel, Spanish	13 lb	Ocracoke Inlet, NC	Nov 4, 1987	Robert Cranton
Marlin, Atlantic blue	1402 lb 2 oz	Vitoria, Brazil	Feb. 29, 1992	Paulo R. A. Amorim
Marlin, black	1560 lb	Cabo Blanco, Peru	Aug 4, 1953	A. C. Glassell, Jr
Marlin, Pacific blue	1376 lb	Kaaiwi Point, HI	May 31, 1982	J. W. deBeaubien
Marlin, striped	494 lb	Tutukaka, New Zealand	Jan 16, 1986	Bill Boniface
Marlin, white	181 lb 14 oz	Vitoria, Brazil	Dec 8, 1979	Evandro Luiz Caser

Saltwater Fishing Records (Cont.)

Species	Weight	Where Caught	Date	Angler
Permit	53 lb 4 oz	Lake Worth, FL	Mar 25, 1994	Roy Brooker
Pollock	46 lb 10 oz	Ogunquit, ME	Oct. 24, 1990	Linda M. Paul
Pompano, African	50 lb 8 oz	Daytona Beach, FL	Apr 21, 1990	Tom Sargent
Roosterfish	114 lb	La Paz, Mexico	June 1, 1960	Abe Sackheim
Runner, blue	8 lb 7 oz	Port Aransas, TX	Feb 13, 1995	Allen E. Windecker
Runner, rainbow	37 lb 9 oz	Isla Clarion, Mexico	Nov. 21, 1991	Tom Pfleger
Sailfish, Atlantic	135 lb 5 oz	Lagos, Nigeria	Nov. 10, 1991	Ron King
Sailfish, Pacific	221 lb	Santa Cruz Island, Ecuador	Feb 12, 1947	C. W. Stewart
Seabass, white	83 lb 12 oz	San Felipe, Mexico	Mar 31, 1953	L. C. Baumgardner
Seatrout, spotted	16 lb	Mason's Beach, VA	May 28, 1977	William Katko
Shark, bigeye thresher	802 lb	Tutukaka, New Zealand	Feb 8, 1981	Dianne North
Shark, blue	437 lb	Catherine Bay, NSW, Australia	Oct 2, 1976	Peter Hyde
Shark, grter hammrhd	991 lb	Sarasota, FL	May 30, 1982	Allen Ogle
Shark, Greenland	1708 lb 9 oz	Trondheimsfjord, Norway	Oct 18, 1987	Terje Nordtvedt
Shark, porbeagle	507 lb	Caithness, Scotland	Mar 9, 1993	Christopher Bennet
Shark, shortfin mako	1115 lb	Black River, Mauritius	Nov 16, 1988	Patrick Guillanton
Shark, tiger	1780 lb	Cherry Grove, SC	June 14, 1964	Walter Maxwell
Shark, tope	72 lb 12 oz	Parengarenga Harbor, New Zealand	Dec 19, 1986	Melanie Feldman
Shark, white	2664 lb	Ceduna, Australia	Apr 21, 1959	Alfred Dean
Skipjack, black	26 lb	Baja California, Mexico	Oct. 23, 1991	Clifford K. Hamaishi
Snapper, cubera	121 lb 8 oz	Cameron, LA	July 5, 1982	Mike Hebert
Snook	53 lb 10 oz	Parismina Ranch, Costa Rica	Oct 18, 1978	Gilbert Ponzi
Spearfish	90 lb 13 oz	Madeira Island, Portugal	June 2, 1980	Joseph Larkin
Swordfish	1182 lb	Iquique, Chile	May 7, 1953	L. Marron
Tarpon	283 lb 4 oz	Sherbro Island, Sierra Leone	April 16, 1991	Yvon Victor Sebag
Tautog	24 lb	Wachapreague, VA	Aug 25, 1987	Gregory Bell
Tilapia	6 lb 5 oz	Lake Arenal, Costa Rica	Feb 10, 1995	Marvin C. Smith
Trevally, bigeye	18 lb 1 oz	Clipperton Island, France	May 12,1990	Rebecca A. Mills
Trevally, giant	145 lb 8 oz	Maui, HI	Mar 28, 1991	Russell Mori
Tuna, Atlantic bigeye	375 lb 8 oz	Ocean City, MD	Aug 26, 1977	Cecil Browne
Tuna, blackfin	42 lb	Bermuda	June 2, 1978	Alan J. Card
		Challenger Bank, Bermuda	July 18, 1989	Gilbert C. Pearman
Tuna, bluefin	1496 lb	Aulds Cove, Nova Scotia	Oct 26, 1979	Ken Fraser
Tuna, longtail	79 lb 2 oz	Montague Island, NSW, Australia	Apr 12, 1982	Tim Simpson
Tuna, Pacific bigeye	435 lb	Cabo Blanco, Peru	Apr 17, 1957	Russel Lee
Tuna, skipjack	41 lb 14 oz	Pearl Beach, Mauritius	Nov 12, 1985	Edmund Heinzen
Tuna, southern bluefin	348 lb 5 oz	Whakatane, New Zealand	Jan 16, 1981	Rex Wood
Tuna, yellowfin	388 lb 12 oz	San Benedicto Is, Mexico	Apr 1, 1977	Curt Wiesenhutter
Tunny, little	35 lb 2 oz	Cape de Garde, Algeria	Dec 14, 1988	Jean Yves Chatard
Wahoo	155 lb 8 oz	San Salvador, Bahamas	Apr 3, 1990	William Bourne
Weakfish	19 lb 2 oz	Jones Beach Inlet, NY	Oct 11, 1984	Dennis Rooney
		Delaware Bay, Delaware	May 20, 1989	William E. Thomas
Yellowtail, California	79 lb 4 oz	Baja California, Mexico	July 2, 1991	Robert I. Welker
Yellowtail, southern	114 lb 10 oz	Tauranga, New Zealand	Feb 5, 1984	Mike Godfrey

Freshwater Fishing Records

Species	Weight	Where Caught	Date	Angler
Barramundi	63 lb 2 oz	Queensland, Australia	April 28, 1991	Scott Barnsley
Bass, largemouth	22 lb 4 oz	Montgomery Lake, GA	June 2, 1932	George W. Perry
Bass, peacock	27 lb	Rio Negro, Brazil	Dec 4,1994	Gerald "Doc" Lawson
Bass, rock	3 lb	York River, Ontario	Aug 1, 1974	Peter Gulgin
Bass, smallmouth	11 lb 15 oz	Dale Hollow Lake, KY	July 9, 1955	David L. Hayes
Bass, Suwannee	3 lb 14 oz	Suwannee River, FL	Mar 2, 1985	Ronnie Everett
Bass, white	6 lb 13 oz	Orange, VA	July 31, 1989	Ronald Sprouse
Bass, whiterock	24 lb 3 oz	Leesville Lake, VA	May 12, 1989	David Lambert
Bass, yellow	2 lb 4 oz	Lake Monroe, IN	Mar 27, 1977	Donald L. Stalker
Bluegill	4 lb 12 oz	Ketona Lake, AL	Apr 9, 1950	T. S. Hudson
Bowfin	21 lb 8 oz	Florence, SC	Jan 29, 1980	Robert Harmon
Buffalo, bigmouth	70 lb 5 oz	Bastrop, LA	Apr 21, 1980	Delbert Sisk
Buffalo, black	55 lb 8 oz	Cherokee Lake, TN	May 3, 1984	Edward McLain
Buffalo, smallmouth	68 lb 8 oz	Lake Hamilton, AR	May 16, 1984	Jerry Dolezal
Bullhead, brown	5 lb 11oz	Cedar Creek, FL	Mar 28, 1995	Robert Bengis
Bullhead, yellow	4 lb 4 oz	Mormon Lake, AZ	May 11, 1984	Emily Williams

Freshwater Fishing Records *(Cont.)*

Species	Weight	Where Caught	Date	Angler
Burbot	18 lb 4 oz	Pickford, MI	Jan 31, 1980	Thomas Courtemanche
Carp	75 lb 11 oz	Lac de St Cassien, France	May 21, 1987	Leo van der Gugten
Catfish, blue	109 lb 4 oz	Moncks Corner, SC	Mar 14, 1991	George A. Lijewski
Catfish, channel	58 lb	Santee-Cooper Reservoir, SC	July 7, 1964	W. B. Whaley
Catfish, flathead	91 lb 4 oz	Lake Lewisville, TX	Mar 28, 1982	Mike Rogers
Catfish, white	18 lb 14 oz	Inverness, FL	Sept. 21, 1991	Jim Miller
Char, Arctic	32 lb 9 oz	Tree River, Canada	July 30, 1981	Jeffrey Ward
Crappie, white	5 lb 3 oz	Enid Dam, MS	July 31, 1957	Fred L. Bright
Dolly Varden	18 lb 9 oz	Mashutuk River, AK	July 13, 1993	Richard B. Evans
Dorado	51 lb 5 oz	Corrientes, Argentina	Sep 27, 1984	Armando Giudice
Drum, freshwater	54 lb 8 oz	Nickajack Lake, TN	Apr 20, 1972	Benny E. Hull
Gar, alligator	279 lb	Rio Grande River, TX	Dec 2, 1951	Bill Valverde
Gar, Florida	21 lb 3 oz	Boca Raton, FL	June 3, 1981	Jeff Sabol
Gar, longnose	50 lb 5 oz	Trinity River, TX	July 30, 1954	Townsend Miller
Gar, shortnose	5 lb	Sally Jones Lake, OK	Apr 26, 1985	Buddy Croslin
Gar, spotted	9 lb 12 oz	Lake Mexia, TX	Apr 7, 1994	Rick Rivard
Grayling, Arctic	5 lb 15 oz	Katseyedie River, Northwest Territories	Aug 16, 1967	Jeanne P. Branson
Inconnu	53 lb	Pah River, AK	Aug 20, 1986	Lawrence Hudnall
Kokanee	9 lb 6 oz	Okanagan Lake, Vernon, BC	June 18, 1988	Norm Kuhn
Muskellunge	67 lb 8 oz	Hayward, WI	July 24,1949	Cal Johnson
Muskellunge, tiger	51 lb 3 oz	Lac Vieux-Desert, WI, MI	July 16, 1919	John Knobla
Perch, Nile	191 lb 8 oz	Lake Victoria, Kenya	Sept. 5, 1991	Andy Davison
Perch, white	4 lb 12 oz	Messalonskee Lake, ME	June 4, 1949	Mrs Earl Small
Perch, yellow	4 lb 3 oz	Bordentown, NJ	May 1865	C. C. Abbot
Pickerel, chain	9 lb 6 oz	Homerville, GA	Feb 17, 1961	Baxley McQuaig, Jr
Pike, northern	55 lb 1 oz	Lake of Grefeern, West Germany	Oct 16, 1986	Lothar Louis
Redhorse, greater	9 lb 3 oz	Salmon River, Pulaski, NY	May 11, 1985	Jason Wilson
Redhorse, silver	11 lb 7 oz	Plum Creek, WI	May 29, 1985	Neal Long
Salmon, Atlantic	79 lb 2 oz	Tana River, Norway	1928	Henrik Henriksen
Salmon, chinook	97 lb 4 oz	Kenai River, AK	May 17, 1985	Les Anderson
Salmon, chum	32 lb	Behm Canal, AK	June 7, 1985	Fredrick Thynes
Salmon, coho	33 lb 4 oz	Pulaski, NY	Sept 27, 1989	Jerry Lifton
Salmon, pink	13 lb 1 oz	Ontario, Canada	Sept. 23, 1992	Ray Higaki
Salmon, sockeye	15 lb 3 oz	Kenai River, AK	Aug 9, 1987	Stan Roach
Sauger	8 lb 12 oz	Lake Sakakawea, ND	Oct 6, 1971	Mike Fischer
Shad, American	11 lb 4 oz	Connecticut River, MA	May 19, 1986	Bob Thibodo
Sturgeon, white	468 lb	Benicia, CA	July 9, 1983	Joey Pallotta III
Sunfish, green	2 lb 2 oz	Stockton Lake, MO	June 18, 1971	Paul M. Dilley
Sunfish, redbreast	1 lb 12 oz	Suwannee River, FL	May 29, 1984	Alvin Buchanan
Sunfish, redear	5 lb 3 oz	Sacramento, CA	June 27, 1994	Anthony H. White, Sr
Tigerfish, giant	97 lb	Zaire River, Kinshasa, Zaire	July 9, 1988	Raymond Houtmans
Trout, Apache	5 lb 3 oz	Apache Reservation, AZ	May 29, 1991	John Baldwin
Trout, brook	14 lb 8 oz	Nipigon River, Ontario	July 1916	W. J. Cook
Trout, brown	40 lb 4 oz	Heber Springs, AR	May 9, 1992	Howard L. Collins
Trout, bull	32 lb	Lake Pond Oreille, ID	Oct 27, 1949	N. L. Higgins
Trout, cutthroat	41 lb	Pyramid Lake, NV	Dec 1925	J. Skimmerhorn
Trout, golden	11 lb	Cook's Lake, WY	Aug 5, 1948	Charles S. Reed
Trout, lake	66 lb 8 oz	Great Bear Lake, Northwest Territories	July 19, 1991	Rodney Harback
Trout, rainbow	42 lb 2 oz	Bell Island, AK	June 22, 1970	David Robert White
Trout, tiger	20 lb 13 oz	Lake Michigan, WI	Aug 12, 1978	Pete M. Friedland
Walleye	25 lb	Old Hickory Lake, TN	Aug 2, 1960	Mabry Harper
Warmouth	2 lb 7 oz	Yellow River, Holt, FL	Oct 19, 1985	Tony D. Dempsey
Whitefish, lake	14 lb 6 oz	Meaford, Ontario	May 21, 1984	Dennis Laycock
Whitefish, mountain	5 lb 6 oz	Rioh River, Saskatchewan, Canada	June 15, 1988	John Bell
Whitefish, broad	9 lb	Tozitna River, AK	July 17, 1989	Al Mathews
Whitefish, round	6 lb	Putahow River, Manitoba	June 14, 1984	Allan J. Ristori
Zander	25 lb 2 oz	Trosa, Sweden	June 12, 1986	Harry Lee Tennison

Greyhound Racing

Annual Greyhound Race of Champions Winners*

Year	Winner (Sex)	Affiliation/Owner	Year	Winner	Affiliation/Owner
1982	DD's Jackie (F)	Wonderland Park/R.H. Walters, Jr.	1988	BB's Old Yellow (M)	Supplemental (Southland)/ Margie Bonita Hyers
1983	Comin' Attraction (F)	Rocky Mt Greyhound Park/ Bob Riggin	1989	Osh Kosh Juliet (F)	Tampa Greyhound Track/ William F. Pollard
1984	Fallon (F)	Tampa Greyhound Track/ E.J. Alderson	1990	Daring Don (M)	Interstate Kennel Club/ Perry Padrta
1985	Lady Delight (F)	Lincoln Greyhound Park/ Julian A. Gay	1991	Mo Kick (M)	Flagler Greyhound Track/ Eric M. Kennon
1986	Ben G Speedboat (M)	Multnomah Kennel Club/ Louis Bennett	1992	Dicky Vallie (M)	Dairyland Greyhound Track/ George Benjamin
1987	ET's Pesky (F)	Supplemental (Flagler)/ Emil Tanis	1993	Mega Morris (M)	Jacksonville Kennel Club/ Ferrell's Kennel

* The Greyhound Race of Champions has not been held since 1993.

Gymnastics

World Champions
MEN
All-Around

Year	Champion and Nation	Year	Champion and Nation
1903	Joseph Martinez, France	1962	Yuri Titov, Soviet Union
1905	Marcel Lalue, France	1966	Mikhail Voronin, Soviet Union
1907	Joseph Czada, Czechoslovakia	1970	Eizo Kenmotsu, Japan
1909	Marcos Torres, France	1974	Shigeru Kasamatsu, Japan
1911	Ferdinand Steiner, Czechoslovakia	1978	Nikolai Andrianov, Soviet Union
1913	Marcos Torres, France	1979	Alexander Ditiatin, Soviet Union
1922	Peter Sumi, Yug./F. Pechacek, Czech.	1981	Yuri Korolev, Soviet Union
1926	Peter Sumi, Yugoslavia	1983	Dimitri Bilozertchev, Soviet Union
1930	Josip Primozic, Yugoslavia	1985	Yuri Korolev, Soviet Union
1934	Eugene Mack, Switzerland	1987	Dimitri Bilozertchev, Soviet Union
1938	Jan Gajdos, Czechoslovakia	1989	Igor Korobchinsky, Soviet Union
1950	Walter Lehmann, Switzerland	1991	Grigori Misutin, CIS
1954	Valentin Mouratov, Soviet Union	1993	Vitaly Scherbo, Belarus
	Victor Chukarin, Soviet Union	1994	Ivan Ivankov, Belarus
1958	Boris Shaklin, Soviet Union	1995	Li Xiaoshuang, China

Pommel Horse

Year	Champion and Nation	Year	Champion and Nation
1930	Josip Primozic, Yugoslavia	1981	Michael Mikolai, E Germ/Li Xiaoping, Chi
1934	Eugene Mack, Switzerland	1983	Dmitri Bilozertchev, Soviet Union
1938	Michael Reusch, Switzerland	1985	Valentin Moguilny, Soviet Union
1950	Josef Stalder, Switzerland	1987	Zsolt Borkai, Hungary
1954	Grant Chaguinjan, Soviet Union		Dmitri Bilozertchev, Soviet Union
1958	Boris Shaklin, Soviet Union	1989	Valentin Moguilny, Soviet Union
1962	Miroslav Cerar, Yugoslavia	1991	Valeri Belenki, Soviet Union
1966	Miroslav Cerar, Yugoslavia	1992	Pae Gil Su, North Korea/Vitaly Scherbo, CIS/ Li Jing, China
1970	Miroslav Cerar, Yugoslavia	1993	Pae Gil Su, North Korea
1974	Zoltan Magyar, Hungary	1994	Marius Urzica, Romania
1978	Zoltan Magyar, Hungary	1995	Li Donghua, Switzerland
1979	Zoltan Magyar, Hungary		

Floor Exercise

Year	Champion and Nation	Year	Champion and Nation
1930	Josip Primozic, Yugoslavia	1966	Akinori Nakayama, Japan
1934	Georges Miesz, Switzerland	1970	Akinori Nakayama, Japan
1938	Jan Gajdos, Czechoslovakia	1974	Shigeru Kasamatsu, Japan
1950	Josef Stalder, Switzerland	1978	Kurt Thomas, United States
1954	Valentin Mouratov, Soviet Union	1979	Kurt Thomas, United States
	Masao Takemoto, Japan		Roland Brucker, GDR
1958	Masao Takemoto, Japan	1981	Yuri Korolev, Sov. Union/Li Yuejui, Chi
1962	Nobuyuki Aihara, Japan	1983	Tong Fei, China
	Yukio Endo, Japan	1985	Tong Fei, China

World Champions *(Cont.)*

MEN *(Cont.)*

Floor Exercise *(Cont.)*

Year	Champion and Nation	Year	Champion and Nation
1987	Lou Yun, China	1993	Grigori Misutin, Ukraine
1989	Igor Korobchinsky, Soviet Union	1994	Vitaly Scherbo, Belarus
1991	Igor Korobchinsky, Soviet Union	1995	Vitaly Scherbo, Belarus

Rings

Year	Champion and Nation	Year	Champion and Nation
1930	Emanuel Loffler, Czechoslovakia	1979	Alexander Ditiatin, Soviet Union
1934	Alois Hudec, Czechoslovakia	1981	Alexander Ditiatin, Soviet Union
1938	Alois Hudec, Czechoslovakia	1983	Dimitri Bilozertchev, Soviet Union
1950	Walter Lehmann, Switzerland	1985	Li Ning, China/Yuri Korolev, Sov Union
1954	Albert Azarian, Soviet Union	1987	Yuri Korolev, Soviet Union
1958	Albert Azarian, Soviet Union	1989	Andreas Aguilar, West Germany
1962	Yuri Titov, Soviet Union	1991	Grigory Misutin, Soviet Union
1966	Mikhail Voronin, Soviet Union	1992	Vitaly Scherbo, CIS
1970	Akinori Nakayama, Japan	1993	Yuri Chechi, Italy
1974	N. Andrianov, Sov Union/D. Grecu, Rom	1994	Yuri Chechi, Italy
1978	Nikolai Andrianov, Soviet Union	1995	Yuri Chechi, Italy

Parallel Bars

Year	Champion and Nation	Year	Champion and Nation
1930	Josip Primozic, Yugoslavia	1983	Vladimir Artemov, Soviet Union
1934	Eugene Mack, Switzerland		Lou Yun, China
1938	Michael Reusch, Switzerland	1985	Sylvio Kroll, East Germany
1950	Hans Eugster, Switzerland		Valentin Moguilny, Soviet Union
1954	Victor Chukarin, Soviet Union	1987	Vladimir Artemov, Soviet Union
1958	Boris Shaklin, Soviet Union	1989	Li Jing, China
1962	Miroslav Cerar, Yugoslavia		Vladimir Artemov, Soviet Union
1966	Sergei Diamidov, Soviet Union	1991	Li Jing, China
1970	Akinori Nakayama, Japan	1992	Li Jin, China
1974	Eizo Kenmotsu, Japan		Alexei Voropaev, CIS
1978	Eizo Kenmotsu, Japan	1993	Vitaly Scherbo, Belarus
1979	Bart Conner, United States	1994	Huang Liping, China
1981	Koji Gushiken, Japan	1995	Vitaly Scherbo, Belarus
	Alexandr Ditiatin, Soviet Union		

High Bar

Year	Champion and Nation	Year	Champion and Nation
1930	Istvan Pelle, Hungary	1979	Kurt Thomas, United States
1934	Ernst Winter, Germany	1981	Alexander Takchev, Soviet Union
1938	Michael Reusch, Switzerland	1983	Dimitri Bilozertchev, Soviet Union
1950	Paavo Aaltonen, Finland	1985	Tong Fei, China
1954	Valentin Mouratov, Soviet Union	1987	Dimitri Bilozertchev, Soviet Union
1958	Boris Shaklin, Soviet Union	1989	Li Chunyang, China
1962	Takashi Ono, Japan	1991	Li Chunyang, China/R. Buechner, Germ
1966	Akinori Nakayama, Japan	1992	Grigori Misutin, CIS
1970	Eizo Kenmotsu, Japan	1993	Sergei Kharkov, Russia
1974	Eberhard Gienger, West Germany	1994	Vitaly Scherbo, Belarus
1978	Shigeru Kasamatsu, Japan	1995	Andreas Wecker, Germany

Vault

Year	Champion and Nation	Year	Champion and Nation
1934	Eugene Mack, Switzerland	1981	Ralf-Peter Hemmann, East Germany
1938	Eugene Mack, Switzerland	1983	Arthur Akopian, Soviet Union
1950	Ernst Gebendinger, Switzerland	1985	Yuri Korolev, Soviet Union
1954	Leo Sotornik, Czechoslovakia	1987	Lou Yun, China
1958	Yuri Titov, Soviet Union		Sylvio Kroll, East Germany
1962	Premysel Krbec, Czechoslovakia	1989	Joreg Behrend, East Germany
1966	Haruhiro Yamashita, Japan	1991	Yoo Ok Youl, South Korea
1970	Mitsuo Tsukahara, Japan	1992	Yoo Ok Youl, South Korea
1974	Shigeru Kasamatsu, Japan	1993	Vitaly Scherbo, Belarus
1978	Junichi Shimizu, Japan	1994	Vitaly Scherbo, Belarus
1979	Alexander Ditiatin, Soviet Union	1995	G. Misutin, Ukraine/A. Nemov Russia

World Champions (Cont.)
WOMEN
All-Around

Year	Champion and Nation	Year	Champion and Nation
1934	Vlasta Dekanova, Czechoslovakia	1981	Olga Bicherova, Soviet Union
1938	Vlasta Dekanova, Czechoslovakia	1983	Natalia Yurchenko, Soviet Union
1950	Helena Rakoczy, Poland	1985	Elena Shoushounova, Soviet Union
1954	Galina Roudiko, Soviet Union		Oksana Omeliantchik, Soviet Union
1958	Larissa Latynina, Soviet Union	1987	Aurelia Dobre, Romania
1962	Larissa Latynina, Soviet Union	1989	Svetlana Bouguinskaia, Soviet Union
1966	Vera Caslavska, Czechoslovakia	1991	Kim Zmeskal, United States
1970	Ludmilla Tourischeva, Soviet Union	1993	Shannon Miller, United States
1974	Ludmilla Tourischeva, Soviet Union	1994	Shannon Miller, United States
1978	Elena Mukhina, Soviet Union	1995	Lilia Podkopayeva, Ukraine
1979	Nelli Kim, Soviet Union		

Floor Exercise

Year	Champion and Nation	Year	Champion and Nation
1950	Helena Rakoczy, Poland	1985	Oksana Omeliantchik, Soviet Union
1954	Tamara Manina, Soviet Union	1987	Elena Shoushounova, Soviet Union
1958	Eva Bosakova, Czechoclovakia		Daniela Silivas, Romania
1962	Larissa Latynina, Soviet Union	1989	Svetlana Bouguinskaia, Soviet Union
1966	Natalia Kuchinskaya, Soviet Union		Daniela Silivas, Romania
1970	Ludmilla Tourischeva, Soviet Union	1991	Cristina Bontas, Romania
1974	Ludmilla Tourischeva, Soviet Union		Oksana Tchusovitina, Soviet Union
1978	Nelli Kim, Soviet Union	1992	Kim Zmeskal, United States
	Elena Mukhina, Soviet Union	1993	Shannon Miller, United States
1979	Emilia Eberle, Romania	1994	Dina Kochetkova, Russia
1981	Natalia Ilenko, Soviet Union	1995	Gina Gogean, Romania
1983	Ecaterina Szabo, Romania		

Uneven Bars

Year	Champion and Nation	Year	Champion and Nation
1950	Gertchen Kolar, Austria	1981	Maxi Gnauck, East Germany
	Anna Pettersson, Sweden	1983	Maxi Gnauck, East Germany
1954	Agnes Keleti, Hungary	1985	Gabriele Fahnrich, East Germany
1958	Larissa Latynina, Soviet Union	1987	Daniela Silivas, Romania
1962	Irina Pervuschina, Soviet Union		Doerte Thuemmler, East Germany
1966	Natalia Kuchinskaya, Soviet Union	1989	Fan Di, China/Daniela Silivas, Rom
1970	Karin Janz, East Germany	1991	Gwang Suk Kim, North Korea
1974	Annelore Zinke, East Germany	1992	Lavinia Milosivici, Romania
1978	Marcia Frederick, United States	1993	Shannon Miller, United States
1979	Ma Yanhong, China	1994	Luo Li, China
	Maxi Gnauck, East Germany	1995	Svetlana Chorkina, Russia

Balance Beam

Year	Champion and Nation	Year	Champion and Nation
1950	Helena Rakoczy, Poland	1983	Olga Mostepanova, Soviet Union
1954	Keiko Tanaka, Japan	1985	Daniela Silivas, Romania
1958	Larissa Latynina, Soviet Union	1987	Aurelia Dobre, Romania
1962	Eva Bosakova, Czechoslovakia	1989	Daniela Silivas, Romania
1966	Natalia Kuchinskaya, Soviet Union	1991	Svetlana Boguinskaia, Soviet Union
1970	Erika Zuchold, East Germany	1992	Kim Zmeskal, United States
1974	Ludmilla Tourischeva, Soviet Union	1993	Lavinia Milosovici, Romania
1978	Nadia Comaneci, Romania	1994	Shannon Miller, United States
1979	Vera Cerna, Czechoslovakia	1995	Mo Huilan, China
1981	Maxi Gnauck, East Germany		

Vault

Year	Champion and Nation	Year	Champion and Nation
1950	Helena Rakoczy, Poland	1983	Boriana Stoyanova, Bulgaria
1954	T Manina, Sov Union/A Pettersson, Swe	1985	Elena Shoushounova, Soviet Union
1958	Larissa Latynina, Soviet Union	1987	Elena Shoushounova, Soviet Union
1962	Vera Caslavska, Czechoslovakia	1989	Olesia Durnik, Soviet Union
1966	Vera Caslavska, Czechoslovakia	1991	Lavinia Milosovici, Romania
1970	Erika Zuchold, East Germany	1992	Henrietta Onodi, Hungary
1974	Olga Korbut, Soviet Union	1993	Elena Piskun, Belarus
1978	Nelli Kim, Soviet Union	1994	Gina Gogean, Romania
1979	Dumitrita Turner, Romania	1995	L. Podkopayeva, Ukr./S. Amanar, Rom.
1981	Maxi Gnauck, East Germany		

National Champions

MEN

All-Around

Year	Champion	Year	Champion	Year	Champion
1963	Art Shurlock	1974	John Crosby	1985	Brian Babcock
1964	Rusty Mitchell	1975	Tom Beach	1986	Tim Daggett
1965	Rusty Mitchell		Bart Conner	1987	Scott Johnson
1966	Rusty Mitchell	1976	Kurt Thomas	1988	Dan Hayden
1967	Katsuzoki Kanzaki	1977	Kurt Thomas	1989	Tim Ryan
1968	Yoshi Hayasaki	1978	Kurt Thomas	1990	John Roethlisberger
1969	Steve Hug	1979	Bart Conner	1991	Chris Waller
1970	Makoto Sakamoto	1980	Peter Vidmar	1992	John Roethlisberger
	Mas Watanabe	1981	Jim Hartung	1993	John Roethlisberger
1971	Yoshi Takei	1982	Peter Vidmar	1994	Scott Keswick
1972	Yoshi Takei	1983	Mitch Gaylord	1995	John Roethlisberger
1973	Marshall Avener	1984	Mitch Gaylord		

Floor Exercise

Year	Champion	Year	Champion	Year	Champion
1963	Tom Seward	1973	John Crosby	1986	Robert Sundstrom
1964	Rusty Mitchell	1974	John Crosby	1987	John Sweeney
1965	Rusty Mitchell	1975	Peter Korman	1988	Mark Oates
1966	Dan Millman	1977	Ron Galimore		Charles Lakes
1967	Katsuzoki Kanzaki	1978	Kurt Thomas	1989	Mike Racanelli
	Ron Aure	1979	Ron Galimore	1990	Bob Stelter
1968	Katsuzoki Kanzaki	1980	Ron Galimore	1991	Mike Racanelli
1969	Steve Hug	1981	Jim Hartung	1992	Gregg Curtis
	Dave Thor	1982	Jim Hartung	1993	Kerry Huston
1970	Makoto Sakamoto	1983	Mitch Gaylord	1994	Jeremy Killen
1971	John Crosby	1984	Peter Vidmar	1995	Daniel Stover
1972	Yoshi Takei	1985	Mark Oates		

Pommel Horse

Year	Champion	Year	Champion	Year	Champion
1963	Larry Spiegel	1973	Marshall Avener	1985	Phil Cahoy
1964	Sam Bailie	1974	Marshall Avener	1986	Phil Cahoy
1965	Jack Ryan	1975	Bart Conner	1987	Tim Daggett
1966	Jack Ryan	1977	Gene Whelan	1988	Kevin Davis
1967	Paul Mayer	1978	Jim Hartung	1989	Kevin Davis
	Dave Doty	1979	Bart Conner	1990	Patrick Kirksey
1968	Katsuoki Kanzaki	1980	Jim Hartung	1991	Chris Waller
1969	Dave Thor	1981	Jim Hartung	1992	Chris Waller
1970	Mas Watanabe	1982	Jim Hartung	1993	Chris Waller
1971	Leonard Caling	1983	Bart Conner	1994	Mihai Begiu
1972	Sadao Hamada	1984	Tim Daggett	1995	Mark Sohn

Rings

Year	Champion	Year	Champion	Year	Champion
1963	Art Shurlock	1973	Jim Ivicek	1985	Dan Hayden
1964	Glen Gailis	1974	Tom Weeden	1986	Dan Hayden
1965	Glen Gailis	1975	Tom Beach	1987	Scott Johnson
1966	Glen Gailis	1977	Kurt Thomas	1988	Dan Hayden
1967	Fred Dennis	1978	Mike Silverstein	1989	Scott Keswick
	Don Hatch	1979	Bart Conner	1990	Scott Keswick
1968	Yoshi Hayasaki	1980	Jim Hartung	1991	Scott Keswick
1969	Fred Dennis	1981	Jim Hartung	1992	Tim Ryan
	Bob Emery	1982	Jim Hartung	1993	John Roethlisberger
1970	Makoto Sakamoto		Peter Vidmar	1994	Scott Keswick
1971	Yoshi Takei	1983	Mitch Gaylord	1995	Paul O'Neill
1972	Yoshi Takei	1984	Jim Hartung		

National Champions (Cont.)
MEN (Cont.)

Vault

Year	Champion	Year	Champion	Year	Champion
1963	Art Shurlock	1974	John Crosby	1986	Scott Wilbanks
1964	Gary Hery	1975	Tom Beach	1987	John Sweeney
1965	Brent Williams	1977	Ron Galimore	1988	John Sweeney
1966	Dan Millman	1978	Jim Hartung		Bill Paul
1967	Jack Kenan	1979	Ron Galimore	1989	Bill Roth
	Sid Jensen	1980	Ron Galimore	1990	Lance Ringnald
1968	Rich Scorza	1981	Ron Galimore	1991	Scott Keswick
1969	Dave Butzman	1982	Jim Hartung	1992	Trent Dimas
1970	Makoto Sakamoto		Jim Mikus	1993	Bill Roth
1971	Gary Morava	1983	Chris Reigel	1994	Keith Wiley
1972	Mike Kelley	1984	Chris Reigel	1995	David St. Pierre
1973	Gary Morava	1985	Scott Johnson		
			Mark Oates		

Parallel Bars

Year	Champion	Year	Champion	Year	Champion
1963	Tom Seward	1975	Bart Conner	1985	Tim Daggett
1964	Rusty Mitchell	1977	Kurt Thomas	1986	Tim Daggett
1965	Glen Gailis	1978	Bart Conner	1987	Scott Johnson
1966	Ray Hadley	1979	Bart Conner	1988	Dan Hayden
1967	Katsuzoki Kanzaki	1980	Phil Cahoy		Kevin Davis
	Tom Goldsborough		Larry Gerard	1989	Conrad Voorsanger
1968	Yoshi Hayasaki	1981	Bart Conner	1990	Trent Dimas
1969	Steve Hug	1982	Peter Vidmar	1991	Scott Keswick
1970	Makoto Sakamoto	1983	Mitch Gaylord	1992	Jair Lynch
1971	Brent Simmons	1984	Peter Vidmar	1993	Chainey Umphrey
1972	Yoshi Takei		Mitch Gaylord	1994	Steve McCain
1973	Marshall Avener		Tim Daggett	1995	John Roethlisberger
1974	Jim Ivicek				

High Bars

Year	Champion	Year	Champion	Year	Champion
1963	Art Shurlock	1975	Tom Beach	1986	Dan Hayden
1964	Glen Gailis	1977	Kurt Thomas		David Moriel
1965	Rusty Mitchell	1978	Kurt Thomas	1987	David Moriel
1966	Katsuzoki Kanzaki	1979	Yoichi Tomita	1988	Dan Hayden
1967	Katsuzoki Kanzaki	1980	Jim Hartung	1989	Tim Ryan
	Jerry Fontana	1981	Bart Conner	1990	Trent Dimas
1968	Yoshi Hayasaki	1982	Mitch Gaylord		Lance Ringnald
1969	Rich Grisby	1983	Mario McCutcheon	1991	Lance Ringnald
1970	Makoto Sakamoto	1984	Peter Vidmar	1992	Jair Lynch
1971	Yoshi Takei		Tim Daggett	1993	Steve McCain
1972	Tom Lindner		Mitch Gaylord	1994	Scott Keswick
1973	John Crosby	1985	Dan Hayden	1995	John Roethlisberger
1974	Brent Simmons				

WOMEN

All-Around

Year	Champion	Year	Champion	Year	Champion
1963	Donna Schanezer	1973	Joan Moore Gnat	1985	Sabrina Mar
1965	Gail Daley	1974	Joan Moore Gnat	1986	Jennifer Sey
1966	Donna Schanezer	1975	Tammy Manville	1987	Kristie Phillips
1968	Linda Scott	1976	Denise Cheshire	1988	Phoebe Mills
1969	Joyce Tanac	1977	Donna Turnbow	1989	Brandy Johnson
	Schroeder	1978	Kathy Johnson	1990	Kim Zmeskal
1970	Cathy Rigby McCoy	1979	Leslie Pyfer	1991	Kim Zmeskal
1971	Joan Moore Gnat	1980	Julianne McNamara	1992	Kim Zmeskal
	Linda Metheny	1981	Tracee Talavera	1993	Shannon Miller
	Mulvihill	1982	Tracee Talavera	1994	Dominique Dawes
1972	Joan Moore Gnat	1983	Dianne Durham	1995	Dominique Moceanu
	Cathy Rigby McCoy	1984	Mary Lou Retton		

National Champions *(Cont.)*
WOMEN *(Cont.)*

Vault

Year	Champion	Year	Champion	Year	Champion
1963	Donna Schanezer	1974	Dianne Dunbar	1985	Yolanda Mavity
1965	Gail Daley	1975	Kolleen Casey	1986	Joyce Wilborn
1966	Donna Schanezer	1976	Debbie Wilcox	1987	Rhonda Faehn
1968	Terry Spencer	1977	Lisa Cawthron	1988	Rhonda Faehn
1969	Joyce Tanac	1978	Rhonda Schwandt	1989	Brandy Johnson
	Schroeder		Sharon Shapiro	1990	Brandy Johnson
	Cleo Carver	1979	Christa Canary	1991	Kerri Strug
1970	Cathy Rigby McCoy	1980	Julianne McNamara	1992	Kerri Strug
1971	Joan Moore Gnat		Beth Kline	1993	Dominique Dawes
	Adele Gleaves	1981	Kim Neal	1994	Dominique Dawes
1972	Cindy Eastwood	1982	Yumi Mordre	1995	Shannon Miller
1973	Roxanne Pierce	1983	Dianne Durham		
	Mancha	1984	Mary Lou Retton		

Uneven Bars

Year	Champion	Year	Champion	Year	Champion
1963	Donna Schanezer	1973	Roxanne Pierce	1984	Julianne McNamara
1965	Irene Haworth		Mancha	1985	Sabrina Mar
1966	Donna Schanezer	1974	Diane Dunbar	1986	Marie Roethlisberger
1968	Linda Scott	1975	Leslie Wolfsberger	1987	Melissa Marlowe
1969	Joyce Tanac	1976	Leslie Wolfsberger	1988	Chelle Stack
	Schroeder	1977	Donna Turnbow	1989	Chelle Stack
	Lisa Nelson	1978	Marcia Frederick	1990	Sandy Woolsey
1970	Roxanne Pierce	1979	Marcia Frederick	1991	Elisabeth Crandall
	Mancha	1980	Marcia Frederick	1992	Dominique Dawes
1971	Joan Moore Gnat	1981	Julianne McNamara	1993	Shannon Miller
1972	Cathy Rigby McCoy	1982	Marie Roethlisberger	1994	Dominique Dawes
		1983	Julianne McNamara	1995	Dominique Dawes

Balance Beam

Year	Champion	Year	Champion	Year	Champion
1963	Leissa Krol	1975	Kyle Gayner	1985	Kelly Garrison-Steves
1965	Gail Daley	1976	Carrie Englert	1988	Kelly Garrison-Steves
1966	Irene Haworth	1977	Donna Turnbow	1989	Brandy Johnson
	Linda Scott	1978	Christa Canary	1990	Betty Okino
1968	Linda Scott	1979	Heidi Anderson	1991	Shannon Miller
1969	Lonna Woodward	1980	Kelly Garrison-Steves	1992	Kerri Strug
1970	Joyce Tanac	1981	Tracee Talavera		Kim Zmeskal
	Schroeder	1982	Julianne McNamara	1993	Dominique Dawes
1971	Linda Metheny	1983	Dianne Durham	1994	Dominique Dawes
	Mulvihill	1984	Pam Bileck	1995	Doni Thompson
1972	Kim Chace		Tracee Talavera		Monica Flammer
1973	Nancy Thies Marshall	1986	Angie Denkins		
1974	Joan Moore Gnat	1987	Kristie Phillips		

Floor Exercise

Year	Champion	Year	Champion	Year	Champion
1963	Donna Schanezer	1975	Kathy Howard	1986	Yolanda Mavity
1965	Gail Daley	1976	Carrie Englert	1987	Kristie Phillips
1966	Donna Schanezer	1977	Kathy Johnson	1988	Phoebe Mills
1968	Linda Scott	1978	Kathy Johnson	1989	Brandy Johnson
1970	Cathy Rigby McCoy	1979	Heidi Anderson	1990	Brandy Johnson
1971	Joan Moore Gnat	1980	Beth Kline	1991	Kim Zmeskal
	Linda Metheny	1981	Michelle Goodwin		Dominique Dawes
	Mulvihill	1982	Amy Koopman	1992	Kim Zmeskal
1972	Joan Moore Gnat	1983	Dianne Durham	1993	Shannon Miller
1973	Joan Moore Gnat	1984	Mary Lou Retton	1994	Dominique Dawes
1974	Joan Moore Gnat	1985	Sabrina Mar	1995	Dominique Dawes

Handball

National Four-Wall Champions
MEN

1919 .....Bill Ranft	1939 .....Joe Platak	1959 .....John Sloan	1979 .....Naty Alvarado
1920 .....Max Gold	1940 .....Joe Platak	1960 .....Jimmy Jacobs	1980 .....Naty Alvarado
1921 .....Carl Haedge	1941 .....Joe Platak	1961 .....John Sloan	1981 .....Fred Lewis
1922 .....Art Shinners	1942 .....Jack Clemente	1962 .....Oscar Obert	1982 .....Naty Alvarado
1923 .....Joe Murray	1943 .....Joe Platak	1963 .....Oscar Obert	1983 .....Naty Alvarado
1924 .....Maynard Laswe	1944 .....Frank Coyle	1964 .....Jimmy Jacobs	1984 .....Naty Alvarado
1925 .....Maynard Laswe	1945 .....Joe Platak	1965 .....Jimmy Jacobs	1985 .....Naty Alvarado
1926 .....Maynard Laswe	1946 .....Angelo Trutio	1966 .....Paul Haber	1986 .....Naty Alvarado
1927 .....George Nelson	1947 .....Gus Lewis	1967 .....Paul Haber	1987 .....Naty Alvarado
1928 .....Joe Griffin	1948 .....Gus Lewis	1968 .....Stuffy Singer	1988 .....Naty Alvarado
1919 .....Al Banuet	1949 .....Vic Hershkowitz	1969 .....Paul Haber	1989 .....Poncho Monreal
1930 .....Al Banuet	1950 .....Ken Schneider	1970 .....Paul Haber	1990 .....Naty Alvarado
1931 .....Al Banuet	1951 .....Walter Plakan	1971 .....Paul Haber	1991 .....John Bike
1932 .....Angelo Trutio	1952 .....Vic Hershkowitz	1972 .....Fred Lewis	1992 .....Octavio Silveyra
1933 .....Sam Atcheson	1953 .....Bob Brady	1973 .....Terry Muck	1993 .....David Chapman
1934 .....Sam Atcheson	1954 .....Vic Hershkowitz	1974 .....Fred Lewis	1994 .....Octavio Silveyra
1935 .....Joe Platak	1955 .....Jimmy Jacobs	1975 .....Fred Lewis	1995 .....David Chapman
1936 .....Joe Platak	1956 .....Jimmy Jacobs	1976 .....Fred Lewis	
1937 .....Joe Platak	1957 .....Jimmy Jacobs	1977 .....Naty Alvarado	
1938 .....Joe Platak	1958 .....John Sloan	1978 .....Fred Lewis	

WOMEN

1980 .....Rosemary Bellini	1984 .....Rosemary Bellini	1988 .....Rosemary Bellini	1992 .....Lisa Fraser
1981 .....Rosemary Bellini	1985 .....Peanut Motal	1989 .....Anna Engele	1993 .....Anna Engele
1982 .....Rosemary Bellini	1986 .....Peanut Motal	1990 .....Anna Engele	1994 .....Anna Engele
1983 .....Diane Harmon	1987 .....Rosemary Bellini	1991 .....Anna Engele	1995 .....Anna Engele

National Three-Wall Champions
MEN

1950 .....Vic Hershkowitz	1962 .....Oscar Obert	1974 .....Fred Lewis	1986 .....Vern Roberts
1951 .....Vic Hershkowitz	1963 .....Marty Decatur	1975 .....Lou Russo	1987 .....Vern Roberts
1952 .....Vic Hershkowitz	1964 .....Marty Decatur	1976 .....Lou Russo	1988 .....Jon Kendler
1953 .....Vic Herskkowitz	1965 .....Carl Obert	1977 .....Fred Lewis	1989 .....John Bike
1954 .....Vic Hershkowitz	1966 .....Marty Decatur	1978 .....Fred Lewis	1990 .....Vince Munoz
1955 .....Vic Hershkowitz	1967 .....Carl Obert	1979 .....Naty Alvarado	1991 .....John Bike
1956 .....Vic Hershkowitz	1968 .....Marty Decatur	1980 .....Lou Russo	1992 .....John Bike
1957 .....Vic Hershkowitz	1969 .....Marty Decatur	1981 .....Naty Alvarado	1993 .....Eric Klarman
1958 .....Vic Hershkowitz	1970 .....Steve August	1982 .....Naty Alvarado	1994 .....David Chapman
1959 .....Jimmy Jacobs	1971 .....Lou Russo	1983 .....Naty Alvarado	1995 .....David Chapman
1960 .....Jimmy Jacobs	1972 .....Lou Russo	1984 .....Naty Alvarado	
1961 .....Jimmy Jacobs	1973 .....Paul Haber	1985 .....Vern Roberts	

WOMEN

1981 .....Allison Roberts	1985 .....Rosemary Bellini	1989 .....Rosemary Bellini	1993 .....Anna Engele
1982 .....Allison Roberts	1986 .....Rosemary Bellini	1990 .....Rosemary Bellini	1994 .....Anna Engele
1983 .....Allison Roberts	1987 .....Rosemary Bellini	1991 .....Rosemary Bellini	1995 .....Allison Roberts
1984 .....Rosemary Bellini	1988 .....Rosemary Bellini	1992 .....Anna Engele	

World Four-Wall Champions

1984 ....Merv Deckert, Canada	1991 ....Pancho Monreal, United States
1986 ....Vern Roberts, United States	1994 ....David Chapman, United States
1988 ....Naty Alvarado, United States	

Lacrosse

United States Club Lacrosse Association Champions

1960 ......Mt Washington Club	1972 ......Carling	1984 ......Maryland Lacrosse Club
1961 ......Baltimore Lacrosse Club	1973 ......Long Island Athletic Club	1985 ......LI-Hofstra Lacrosse Club
1962 ......Mt Washington Club	1974 ......Long Island Athletic Club	1986 ......LI-Hofstra Lacrosse Club
1963 ......University Club	1975 ......Mt Washington Club	1987 ......LI-Hofstra Lacrosse Club
1964 ......Mt Washington Club	1976 ......Mt Washington Club	1988 ......Maryland Lacrosse Club
1965 ......Mt Washington Club	1977 ......Mt Washington Club	1989 ......LI-Hofstra Lacrosse Club
1966 ......Mt Washington Club	1978 ......Long Island Athletic Club	1990 ......Mt Washington Club
1967 ......Mt Washington Club	1979 ......Maryland Lacrosse Club	1991 ......Mt Washington Club
1968 ......Long Island Athletic Club	1980 ......Long Island Athletic Club	1992 ......Maryland Lacrosse Club
1969 ......Long Island Athletic Club	1981 ......Long Island Athletic Club	1993 ......Mt Washington Club
1970 ......Long Island Athletic Club	1982 ......Maryland Lacrosse Club	1994 ......LI-Hofstra Lacrosse Club
1971 ......Long Island Athletic Club	1983 ......Maryland Lacrosse Club	1995 ......Mt Washington Club

Little League Baseball

Little League World Series Champions

Year	Champion	Runner-Up	Score	Year	Champion	Runner-Up	Score
1947	..Williamsport, PA	Lock Haven, PA	16-7	1972	..Taipei, Taiwan	Hammond, IN	6-0
1948	..Lock Haven, PA	St. Petersburg, FL	6-5	1973	..Tainan City, Taiwan	Tucson, AZ	12-0
1949	..Hammonton, NJ	Pensacola, FL	5-0	1974	..Kao Hsiung, Taiwan	El Cajun, CA	7-2
1950	..Houston, TX	Bridgeport, CT	2-1	1975	..Lakewood, NJ	Tampa, FL	4-3
1951	..Stamford, CT	Austin, TX	3-0	1976	..Tokyo, Japan	Campbell, CA	10-3
1952	..Norwalk, CT	Monongahela, PA	4-3	1977	..Kao Hsiung, Taiwan	El Cajun, CA	7-2
1953	..Birmingham, AL	Schenectady, NY	1-0	1978	..Pin-Tung, Taiwan	Danville, CA	11-1
1954	..Schenectady, NY	Colton, CA	7-5	1979	..Hsien, Taiwan	Campbell, CA	2-1
1955	..Morrisville, PA	Merchantville, NJ	4-3	1980	..Hua Lian, Taiwan	Tampa, FL	4-3
1956	..Roswell, NM	Merchantville, NJ	3-1	1981	..Tai-Chung, Taiwan	Tampa, FL	4-2
1957	..Monterrey, Mex.	LaMesa, CA	4-0	1982	..Kirkland, WA	Hsien, Taiwan	6-0
1958	..Monterrey, Mex.	Kankakee, IL	10-1	1983	..Marietta, GA	Barahona, D.Rep.	3-1
1959	..Hamtramck, MI	Auburn, CA	12-0	1984	..Seoul, S. Korea	Altamonte Sgs, FL	6-2
1960	..Levittown, PA	Ft. Worth, TX	5-0	1985	..Seoul, S. Korea	Mexicali, Mex.	7-1
1961	..El Cajon, CA	El Campo, TX	4-2	1986	..Tainan Park, Taiwan	Tucson, AZ	12-0
1962	..San Jose, CA	Kankakee, IL	3-0	1987	..Hua Lian, Taiwan	Irvine, CA	21-1
1963	..Granada Hills, CA	Stratford, CT	2-1	1988	..Tai-Chung, Taiwan	Pearl City, HI	10-0
1964	..Staten Island, NY	Monterrey, Mex.	4-0	1989	..Trumbull, CT	Kaohsiung, Taiwan	5-2
1965	..Windsor Locks, CT	Stoney Creek, Can.	3-1	1990	..Taipei, Taiwan	Shippensburg, PA	9-0
1966	..Houston, TX	W.New York, NJ	8-2	1991	..Tai-Chung, Taiwan	San Ramon Vly, CA	11-0
1967	..West Tokyo, Japan	Chicago, IL	4-1	1992*	.Long Beach, CA	Zamboanga, Phil.	6-0
1968	..Osaka, Japan	Richmond, VA	1-0	1993	..Long Beach, CA	David Chiriqui, Pan.	3-2
1969	..Taipei, Taiwan	Santa Clara, CA	5-0	1994	..Maracaibo, Venez	Northridge, CA	4-3
1970	..Wayne, NJ	Campbell, CA	2-0	1995	..Tainan, Taiwan	Sprint, TX	17-3
1971	..Tainan, Taiwan	Gary, IN	12-3				

*Long Beach declared a 6-0 winner after the international tournament committee determined that Zamboanga City had used players that were not within its city limits.

Motor Boat Racing

American Power Boat Association Gold Cup Champions

Year	Boat	Driver	Avg MPH	Year	Boat	Driver	Avg MPH
1904	....Standard (June)	Carl Riotte	23.160	1930	....Hotsy Totsy	Vic Kliesrath	52.673
1904	....Vingt-et-Un II (Sep)	W. Sharpe Kilmer	24.900	1931	....Hotsy Totsy	Vic Kliesrath	53.602
1905	....Chip I	J. Wainwright	15.000	1932	....Delphine IV	Bill Horn	57.775
1906	....Chip II	J. Wainwright	25.000	1933	....El Lagarto	George Reis	56.260
1907	....Chip II	J. Wainwright	23.903	1934	....El Lagarto	George Reis	55.000
1908	....Dixie II	E. J. Schroeder	29.938	1935	....El Lagarto	George Reis	55.056
1909	..Dixie II	E. J. Schroeder	29.590	1936	....Impshi	Kaye Don	45.735
1910	..Dixie III	F. K. Burnham	32.473	1937	....Notre Dame	Clell Perry	63.675
1911	..MIT II	J. H. Hayden	37.000	1938	....Alagi	Theo Rossi	64.340
1912	..P.D.Q. II	A. G. Miles	39.462	1939	....My Sin	Z. G. Simmons, Jr	66.133
1913	..Ankle Deep	Cas Mankowski	42.779	1940	....Hotsy Totsy III	Sidney Allen	48.295
1914	....Baby Speed Demon II	Jim Blackton & Bob Edgren	48.458	1941	....My Sin	Z. G. Simmons, Jr	52.509
				1942-45		No race	
1915	....Miss Detroit	Johnny Milot & Jack Beebe	37.656	1946	....Tempo VI	Guy Lombardo	68.132
				1947	....Miss Peps V	Danny Foster	57.000
1916	....Miss Minneapolis	Bernard Smith	48.860	1948	....Miss Great Lakes	Danny Foster	46.845
1917	....Miss Detroit II	Gar Wood	54.410	1949	....My Sweetie	Bill Cantrell	73.612
1918	....Miss Detroit II	Gar Wood	51.619	1950	....Slo-Mo-Shun IV	Ted Jones	78.216
1919	....Miss Detroit III	Gar Wood	42.748	1951	....Slo-Mo-Shun V	Lou Fageol	90.871
1920	....Miss America I	Gar Wood	62.022	1952	....Slo-Mo-Shun IV	Stan Dollar	79.923
1921	....Miss America I	Gar Wood	52.825	1953	....Slo-Mo-Shun IV	Joe Taggart & Lou Fageol	99.108
1922	....Packard Chriscraft	J. G. Vincent	40.253				
1923	....Packard Chriscraft	Caleb Bragg	43.867	1954	....Slo-Mo-Shun IV	Joe Taggart & Lou Fageol	92.613
1924	....Baby Bootlegger	Caleb Bragg	45.302				
1925	....Baby Bootlegger	Caleb Bragg	47.240	1955	....Gale V	Lee Schoenith	99.552
1926	....Greenwich Folly	George Townsend	47.984	1956	....Miss Thriftaway	Bill Muncey	96.552
				1957	....Miss Thriftaway	Bill Muncey	101.787
1927	....Greenwich Folly	George Townsend	47.662	1958	....Hawaii Kai III	Jack Regas	103.000
				1959	....Maverick	Bill Stead	104.481
1928	....No race			1960		No race	
1929	....Imp	Richard Hoyt	48.662	1961	....Miss Century 21	Bill Muncey	99.678

American Power Boat Association Gold Cup Champions (Cont.)

Year	Boat	Driver	Avg MPH
1962	Miss Century 21	Bill Muncey	100.710
1963	Miss Bardahl	Ron Musson	105.124
1964	Miss Bardahl	Ron Musson	103.433
1965	Miss Bardahl	Ron Musson	103.132
1966	Tahoe Miss	Mira Slovak	93.019
1967	Miss Bardahl	Bill Shumacher	101.484
1968	Miss Bardahl	Bill Shumacher	108.173
1969	Miss Budweiser	Bill Sterett	98.504
1970	Miss Budweiser	Dean Chenoweth	99.562
1971	Miss Madison	Jim McCormick	98.043
1972	Atlas Van Lines	Bill Muncey	104.277
1973	Miss U.S.	Dean Chenoweth	99.043
1974	Pay 'n Pak	George Henley	104.428
1975	Pay 'n Pak	George Henley	108.921
1976	Miss U.S.	Tom D'Eath	100.412
1977	Atlas Van Lines	Bill Muncey	111.822
1978	Atlas Van Lines	Bill Muncey	111.412
1979	Atlas Van Lines	Bill Muncey	100.765
1980	Miss Budweiser	Dean Chenoweth	106.932
1981	Miss Budweiser	Dean Chenoweth	116.932
1982	Atlas Van Lines	Chip Hanauer	120.050
1983	Atlas Van Lines	Chip Hanauer	118.507
1984	Atlas Van Lines	Chip Hanauer	130.175
1985	Miller American	Chip Hanauer	120.643
1986	Miller American	Chip Hanauer	116.523
1987	Miller American	Chip Hanauer	127.620
1988	Miss Circus Circus	Chip Hanauer & Jim Prevost	123.756
1989	Miss Budweiser	Tom D'Eath	131.209
1990	Miss Budweiser	Tom D'Eath	143.176
1991	Winston Eagle	Mark Tate	137.771
1992	Miss Budweiser	Chip Hanauer	136.282
1993	Miss Budweiser	Chip Hanauer	141.195
1994	Smokin' Joe Camel	Mark Tate	145.260
1995	Miss Budweiser	Chip Hanauer	149.160

American Power Boat Association Annual Champion Drivers

Year	Driver	Boats	Wins
1947	Danny Foster	Miss Peps V	6
1948	Dan Arena	Such Crust	2
1949	Bill Cantrell	My Sweetie	7
1950	Dan Foster	Such Crust/DaphneX	2
1951	Chuck Thompson	Miss Pepsi	5
1952	Chuck Thompson	Miss Pepsi	3
1953	Lee Schoenith	Gale II	1
1954	Lee Schoenith	Gale V	4
1955	Lee Schoenith	Gale V/Wha Hoppen	1
1956	Russ Schleeh	Shanty I	3
1957	Jack Regas	Hawaii Kai III	4
1958	Mira Slovak	Bardah/Miss Buren	3
1959	Bill Stead	Maverick	5
1960	Bill Muncey	Miss Thriftway	4
1961	Bill Muncey	Miss Century 21	4
1962	Bill Muncey	Miss Century 21	5
1963	Bill Cantrell	Gale V	0
1964	Ron Musson	Miss Bardahl	4
1965	Ron Musson	Miss Bardahl	4
1966	Mira Slovak	Tahoe Miss	4
1967	Bill Schumacher	Miss Bardahl	6
1968	Bill Schumacher	Miss Bardahl	4
1969	Bill Sterett, Sr.	Miss Budweiser	4
1970	Dean Chenoweth	Miss Budweiser	4
1971	Dean Chenoweth	Miss Budweiser	2
1972	Bill Muncey	Atlas Van Lines	6
1973	Mickey Remund	Pay 'n Pack	4
1974	George Henley	Pay 'n Pack	7
1975	Billy Schumacher	Weisfleld's	2
1976	Bill Muncey	Atlas Van Lines	5
1977	Mickey Remund	Miss Budweiser	3
1978	Bill Muncey	Atlas Van Lines	6
1979	Bill Muncey	Atlas Van Lines	7
1980	Dean Chenoweth	Miss Budweiser	5
1981	Dean Chenoweth	Miss Budweiser	6
1982	Chip Hanauer	Atlas Van Lines	5
1983	Chip Hanauer	Atlas Van Lines	3
1984	Jim Kropfeld	Miss Budweiser	6
1985	Chip Hanauer	Miller American	5
1986	Jim Kropfeld	Miss Budweiser	3
1987	Jim Kropfeld	Miss Budweiser	5
1988	Tom D'Eath	Miss Budweiser	4
1989	Chip Hanauer	Miss Circus Circus	3
1990	Chip Hanauer	Miss Circus Circus	6
1991	Mark Tate	Winston/Oberto	3
1992	Chip Hanauer	Miss Budweiser	7
1993	Chip Hanauer	Miss Budweiser	7
1994	Mark Tate	Smokin' Joe Camel	2

American Power Boat Association Annual Champion Boats

Year	Boat	Owner	Wins
1970	Miss Budweiser	Little-Friedkin	4
1971	Miss Budweiser	Little-Friedkin	2
1972	Atlas Van Lines	Joe Schoenith	6
1973	Pay 'n Pak	Dave Heerensperger	4
1974	Pay 'n Pak	Dave Heerensperger	7
1975	Pay 'n Pak	Dave Heerensperger	5
1976	Atlas Van Lines	Bill Muncey	5
1977	Miss Budweiser	Bernie Little	3
1978	Atlas Van Lines	Bill Muncey	6
1979	Atlas Van Lines	Bill Muncey	7
1980	Miss Budweiser	Bernie Little	5
1981	Miss Budweiser	Bernie Little	6
1982	Atlas Van Lines	Fran Muncey	5
1983	Atlas Van Lines	Muncey-Lucero	3
1984	Miss Budweiser	Bernie Little	6
1985	Miller American	Muncey-Lucero	5
1986	Miss Budweiser	Bernie Little	3
1987	Miss Budweiser	Bernie Little	5
1988	Miss Budweiser	Bernie Little	4
1989	Miss Budweiser	Bernie Little	4
1990	Circus Circus	Bill Bennett	6
1991	Miss Budweiser	Bernie Little	4
1992	Miss Budweiser	Bernie Little	7
1993	Miss Budweiser	Bernie Little	7
1994	Miss Budweiser	Bernie Little	4

Polo

United States Open Polo Champions

1904 ......Wanderers	1932 ......Templeton	1958 ......Dallas	1978 ......Abercrombie &
1905-09..Not contested	1933 .....Aurora	1959 .....Circle F	Kent
1910 ......Ranelagh	1934 .....Templeton	1960 ......Oak Brook—	1979 ......Retama
1911 .....Not contested	1935 .....Greentree	C.C.C.	1980 .....Southern Hills
1912 ......Cooperstown	1936 .....Greentree	1961 .....Milwaukee	1981 ......Rolex A & K
1913 ......Cooperstown	1937 ......Old Westbury	1962 .....Santa Barbara	1982 ......Retama
1914 ......Meadow Brook	1938 .....Old Westbury	1963 .....Tulsa	1983 ......Ft. Lauderdale
Magpies	1939 .....Bostwick Field	1964 .....Concar Oak	1984 ......Retama
1915 ......Not contested	1940 ......Aknusti	Brook	1985 .....Carter Ranch
1916 ......Meadow Brook	1941 .....Gulf Stream	1965 .....Oak Brook—	1986 ......Retama II
1917-18..Not contested	1942-45..Not contested	Santa Barbara	1987 ......Aloha
1919 ......Meadow Brook	1946 ......Mexico	1966 .....Tulsa	1988 .....Les Diables
1920 ......Meadow Brook	1947 ......Old Westbury	1967 .....Bunntyco—	Bleus
1921 ......Great Neck	1948 .....Hurricanes	Oak Brook	1989 .....Les Diables
1922 ......Argentine	1949 .....Hurricanes	1968 ......Midland	Bleus
1923 ......Meadow Brook	1950 .....Bostwick	1969 .....Tulsa Greenhill	1990 .....Les Diables
1924 ......Midwick	1951 .....Milwaukee	1970 .....Tulsa Greenhill	Bleus
1925 ......Orange County	1952 .....Beverly Hills	1971 ......Oak Brook	1991 ......Grant's Farm
1926 ......Hurricanes	1953 .....Meadow Brook	1972 .....Milwaukee	Manor
1927 ......Sands Point	1954 .....C.C.C.—	1973 .....Oak Brook	1992 ......Hanalei Bay
1928 ......Meadow Brook	Meadow Brook	1974 .....Milwaukee	1993 ......Gehache
1929 ......Hurricanes	1955 .....C.C.C.	1975 .....Milwaukee	1994 ......Aspen
1930 ......Hurricanes	1956 .....Brandywine	1976 .....Willow Bend	1995 ......Outback
1931 ......Santa Paula	1957 ......Detroit	1977 ......Retama	

Top-Ranked Players

The United States Polo Association ranks its registered players from minus 2 to plus 10 goals, with 10 Goal players being the game's best. At present, the USPA recognizes thirteen 10-Goal and nine 9-Goal players:

10-GOAL	9-GOAL
Mariano Aguerre (Greenwich)	A.D. Alberdi (Palm Beach)
Adolfo Cambiaso (Palm Beach)	Benjamin Araya (Palm Beach)
Carlos Gracida (San Antonio)	Michael Vincen Azzaro (San Antonio)
Guillermo Gracida, Jr (Palm Beach)	T. Fernandez-Llorente (Palm Beach)
Bautista Heguy (Palm Beach)	Ignacio Heguy (Palm Beach)
Eduardo Heguy (Palm Beach)	Esteban Panelo (Hidden Pond)
Gonzalo Heguy (Myopia)	Gonzalo Pieres (Palm Beach
Marcos Heguy (Palm Beach)	Owen R. Rinehart (Palm Beach)
Alberto Heguy, Jr (Palm Beach)	Martin Zubia (Palm Beach)
Christian LaPrida (Palm Beach)	
Juan Ignacio Merlos (Palm Beach)	
Sebastian Merlos (Aiken)	
Ernesto Trotz (Palm Beach)	

Rodeo

All-Around

1929....Earl Thode	1947....Todd Whatley	1963....Dean Oliver	1979....Tom Ferguson
1930...Clay Carr	1948....Gerald Roberts	1964...Dean Oliver	1980....Paul Tierney
1931...John Schneider	1949....Jim Shoulders	1965...Dean Oliver	1981....Jimmie Cooper
1932...Donald Nesbit	1950....Bill Linderman	1966...Larry Mahan	1982....Chris Lybbert
1933...Clay Carr	1951....Casey Tibbs	1967...Larry Mahan	1983....Roy Cooper
1934...Leonard Ward	1952....Harry Tompkins	1968...Larry Mahan	1984....Dee Picket
1935...Everett Bowman	1953....Bill Linderman	1969...Larry Mahan	1985....Lewis Feild
1936...John Bowman	1954....Buck Rutherford	1970...Larry Mahan	1986....Lewis Feild
1937...Everett Bowman	1955....Casey Tibbs	1971...Phil Lyne	1987....Lewis Feild
1938...Burel Mulkey	1956....Jim Shoulders	1972...Phil Lyne	1988....Dave Appleton
1939...Paul Carney	1957....Jim Shoulders	1973...Larry Mahan	1989....Ty Murray
1940...Fritz Truan	1958....Jim Shoulders	1974...Tom Ferguson	1990....Ty Murray
1941...Homer Pettigrew	1959....Jim Shoulders	1975...Tom Ferguson	1991....Ty Murray
1942...Gerald Roberts	1960....Harry Tompkins	1976...Tom Ferguson	1992....Ty Murray
1943...Louis Brooks	1961....Benny Reynolds	1977...Tom Ferguson	1993....Ty Murray
1944...Louis Brooks	1962....Tom Nesmith	1978....Tom Ferguson	1994....Ty Murray

Saddle Bronc Riding

1929....Earl Thode	1947....Carl Olson	1963....Guy Weeks	1979....Bobby Berger
1930....Clay Carr	1948....Gene Pruett	1964....Marty Wood	1980....Clint Johnson
1931....Earl Thode	1949....Casey Tibbs	1965....Shawn Davis	1981....B. Gjermundson
1932....Peter Knight	1950....Bill Linderman	1966....Marty Wood	1982....Monty Henson
1933....Peter Knight	1951....Casey Tibbs	1967....Shawn Davis	1983....B. Gjermundson
1934....Leonard Ward	1952....Casey Tibbs	1968....Shawn Davis	1984....B. Gjermundson
1935....Peter Knight	1953....Casey Tibbs	1969....Bill Smith	1985....B. Gjermundson
1936....Peter Knight	1954....Casey Tibbs	1970....Dennis Reiners	1986....Bud Munroe
1937....Burel Mulkey	1955....DebCopenhaver	1971....Bill Smith	1987....Clint Johnson
1938....Burel Mulkey	1956....DebCopenhaver	1972....Mel Hyland	1988....Clint Johnson
1939....Fritz Truan	1957....Alvin Nelson	1973....Bill Smith	1989....Clint Johnson
1940....Fritz Truan	1958....Marty Wood	1974....John McBeth	1990....Robert Etbauer
1941....Doff Aber	1959....Casey Tibbs	1975....Monty Henson	1991....Robert Etbauer
1942....Doff Aber	1960....Enoch Walker	1976....Monty Henson	1992....Billy Etbauer
1943....Louis Brooks	1961....Winston Bruce	1977....Bobby Berger	1993....Dan Mortensen
1944....Louis Brooks	1962....Kenny McLean	1978....Joe Marvel	1994....Dan Mortensen

Bareback Riding

1932....Smoky Snyder	1950....Jim Shoulders	1966....Paul Mayo	1982....Bruce Ford
1933....Nate Waldrum	1951....Casey Tibbs	1967....Clyde Vamvoras	1983....Bruce Ford
1934....Leonard Ward	1952....Harry Tompkins	1968....Clyde Vamvoras	1984....Larry Peabody
1935....Frank Schneider	1953....Eddy Akridge	1969....Gary Tucker	1985....Lewis Feild
1936....Smoky Snyder	1954....Eddy Akridge	1970....Paul Mayo	1986....Lewis Feild
1937....Paul Carney	1955....Eddy Adridge	1971....Joe Alexander	1987....Bruce Ford
1938....Pete Grubb	1956....Jim Shoulders	1972....Joe Alexander	1988....Marvin Garrett
1939....Paul Carney	1957....Jim Shoulders	1973....Joe Alexander	1989....Marvin Garrett
1940....Carl Dossey	1958....Jim Shoulders	1974....Joe Alexander	1990....Chuck Logue
1941....George Mills	1959....Jack Buschbom	1975....Joe Alexander	1991....Clint Corey
1942....Louis Brooks	1960....Jack Buschbom	1976....Joe Alexander	1992....Wayne Herman
1943....Bill Linderman	1961....Eddy Akridge	1977....Joe Alexander	1993....Deb Greenough
1944....Louis Brooks	1962....Ralph Buell	1978....Bruce Ford	1994....Marvin Garrett
1947....Larry Finley	1963....John Hawkins	1979....Bruce Ford	
1948....Sonny Tureman	1964....Jim Houston	1980....Bruce Ford	
1949....Jack Buschbom	1965....Jim Houston	1981....J.C. Trujillo	

Bull Riding

1929....John Schneider	1944....Ken Roberts	1963....Bill Kornell	1980....Don Gay
1930....John Schneider	1947....Wag Blessing	1964....Bob Wegner	1981....Don Gay
1931....Smokey Snyder	1948....Harry Tompkins	1965....Larry Mahan	1982....Charles Sampson
1932....John Schneider	1949....Harry Tompkins	1966....Ronnie Rossen	1983....Cody Snyder
1932....Smokey Snyder	1950....Harry Tompkins	1967....Larry Mahan	1984....Don Gay
John Schneider	1951....Jim Shoulders	1968....George Paul	1985....Ted Nuce
1933....Frank Schneider	1952....Harry Tompkins	1969....Doug Brown	1986....Tuff Hedeman
1934....Frank Schneider	1953....Todd Whatley	1970....Gary Leffew	1987....Lane Frost
1935....Smokey Snyder	1954....Jim Shoulders	1971....Bill Nelson	1988....Jim Sharp
1936....Smokey Snyder	1955....Jim Shoulders	1972....John Quintana	1989....Tuff Hedeman
1937....Smokey Snyder	1956....Jim Shoulders	1973....Bobby Steiner	1990....Jim Sharp
1938....Kid Fletcher	1957....Jim Shoulders	1974....Don Gay	1991....Tuff Hedeman
1939....Dick Griffith	1958....Jim Shoulders	1975....Don Gay	1992....Cody Custer
1940....Dick Griffith	1959....Jim Shoulders	1976....Don Gay	1993....Ty Murray
1941....Dick Griffith	1960....Harry Tompkins	1977....Don Gay	1994....Daryl Mills
1942....Dick Griffith	1961....Ronnie Rossen	1978....Don Gay	
1943....Ken Roberts	1962....Freckles Brown	1979....Don Gay	

Calf Roping

1929....Everett Bowman	1939....Toots Mansfield	1951....Don McLaughlin	1961....Dean Oliver
1930....Jake McClure	1940....Toots Mansfield	1952....Don McLaughlin	1962....Dean Oliver
1931....Herb Meyers	1941....Toots Mansfield	1953....Don McLaughlin	1963....Dean Oliver
1932.....Richard Merchant	1942....Clyde Burk	1954....Don McLaughlin	1964....Dean Oliver
1933....Bill McFarlane	1943....Toots Mansfield	1955....Dean Oliver	1965....Glen Franklin
1934....Irby Mundy	1944....Clyde Burk	1956....Ray Wharton	1966....Junior Garrison
1935....Everett Bowman	1947....Troy Fort	1957....Don McLaughlin	1967....Glen Franklin
1936....Clyde Burk	1948....Toots Mansfield	1958....Dean Oliver	1968....Glen Franklin
1937....Everett Bowman	1949....Troy Fort	1959....Jim Bob Altizer	1969....Dean Oliver
1938....Burel Mulkey	1950....Toots Mansfield	1960....Dean Oliver	

Calf Roping (Cont.)

1970....Junior Garrison	1977....Roy Cooper	1984....Roy Cooper	1991....Fred Whitfield
1971....Phil Lyne	1978....Roy Cooper	1985....Joe Beaver	1992....Joe Beaver
1972....Phil Lyne	1979....Paul Tierney	1986....Chris Lybbert	1993....Joe Beaver
1973....Ernie Taylor	1980....Roy Cooper	1987....Joe Beaver	1994....Herbert Theriot
1974....Tom Ferguson	1981....Roy Cooper	1988....Joe Beaver	
1975....Jeff copenhaver	1982....Roy Cooper	1989....Rabe Rabon	
1976....Roy Cooper	1983....Roy Cooper	1990....Troy Pruitt	

Steer Wrestling

1929....Gene Ross	1947....Todd Whatley	1963....Jim Bynum	1979....Stan Williamson
1930....Everett Bowman	1948....Homer Pettigrew	1964....C.R. Boucher	1980....Butch Myers
1931....Gene Ross	1949....Bill McGuire	1965....Harley May	1981....Byron Walker
1932....Hugh Bennett	1950....Bill Linderman	1966....Jack Roddy	1982....Stan Williamson
1933....Everett Bowman	1951....Dub Phillips	1967....Roy Duvall	1983....Joel Edmondson
1934....Shorty Ricker	1952....Harley May	1968....Jack Roddy	1984....John W. Jones
1935....Everett Bowman	1953....Ross Dollarhide	1969....Roy Duvall	1985....Ote Berry
1936....Jack Kerschner	1954....James Bynum	1970....John W. Jones	1986....Steve Duhon
1937....Gene Ross	1955....Benny Combs	1971....Billy Hale	1987....Steve Duhon
1938....Everett Bowman	1956....Harley May	1972....Roy Duvall	1988....John W. Jones
1939....Harry Hart	1957....Clark McEntire	1973....Bob Marshall	1989....John W. Jones
1940....Homer Pettigrew	1958....James Bynum	1974....Tommy Puryear	1990....Ote Berry
1941....Hub Whiteman	1959....Harry Charters	1975....F. Shepperson	1991....Ote Berry
1942....Homer Pettigrew	1960....Bob A. Robinson	1976....Tom Ferguson	1992....Mark Roy
1943....Homer Pettigrew	1961....Jim Bynum	1977....Larry Ferguson	1993....Steve Duhon
1944....Homer Pettigrew	1962....Tom Nesmith	1978....Byron Walker	1994....Blaine Pederson

Team Roping

1929....Charles Maggini	1944....Murphy Chaney	1963....Les Hirdes	1980....Tee Woolman
1930....Norman Cowan	1947....Jim Brister	1964....Bill Hamilton	1981....Walt Woodard
1931....Arthur Beloat	1948....Joe Glenn	1965....Jim Rodriguez Jr.	1982....Tee Woolman
1932....Ace Gardner	1949....Ed Yanez	1966....Ken Luman	1983....Leo Camarillo
1933....Roy Adams	1950....Buck Sorrels	1967....Joe Glenn	1984....Dee Pickett
1934....Andy Jauregui	1951....Olan Sims	1968....Art Arnold	1985....Jake Barnes
1935....Lawrence Conltk	1952....Asbury Schell	1969....Jerold Camarillo	1986....Clay O. Cooper
1936....John Rhodes	1953....Ben Johnson	1970....John Miller	1987....Clay O. Cooper
1937....Asbury Schell	1954....Eddie Schell	1971....John Miller	1988....Jake Barnes
1938....John Rhodes	1955....Vern Castro	1972....Leo Camarillo	1989....Jake Barnes
1939....Asbury Schell	1956....Dale Smith	1973....Leo Camarillo	1990....Allen Bach
1940....Pete Grubb	1957....Dale Smith	1974....H.P. Evetts	1991....Bob Harris
1941....Jim Hudson	1958....Ted Ashworth	1975....Leo Camarillo	1992....Clay O. Cooper
1942....Verne Castro	1959....Jim Rodriguez Jr.	1976....Leo Camarillo	1993....Bobby Hurley
........Vic Castro	1960....Jim Rodriguez Jr.	1977....Jerold Camarillo	1994....Jake Barnes
1943....Mark Hull	1961....Al Hooper	1978....Doyle Gellerman	........Clay O. Cooper
........Leonard Block	1962....Jim Rodriguez Jr.	1979....Allen Bach	

Steer Roping

1929....Charles Maggini	1946....Everett Shaw	1963....Don McLaughlin	1980....Guy Allen
1930....Clay Carr	1947....Ike Rude	1964....Sonny Davis	1981....Arnold Felts
1931....Andy Jauregui	1948....Everett Shaw	1965....Sonney Wright	1982....Guy Allen
1932....George Weir	1949....Shoat Webster	1966....Sonny Davis	1983....Roy Cooper
1933....John Bowman	1950....Shoat Webster	1967....Jim Bob Altizer	1984....Guy Allen
1934....John McEntire	1951....Everett Shaw	1968....Sonny Davis	1985....Jim Davis
1935.....Richard Merchant	1952....Buddy Neal	1969....Walter Arnold	1986....Jim Davis
1936....John Bowman	1953....Ike Rude	1970....Don McLaughlin	1987....Shaun Burchett
1937....Everett Bowman	1954....Shoat Webster	1971....Olin Young	1988....Shaun Burchett
1938....Hugh Bennett	1955....Shoat Webster	1972....Allen Keller	1989....Guy Allen
1939....Dick Truitt	1956....Jim Snively	1973....Roy Thompson	1990....Phil Lyne
1940....Clay Carr	1957....Clark McEntire	1974....Olin Young	1991....Guy Allen
1941....Ike Rude	1958....Clark McEntire	1975....Roy Thompson	1992....Guy Allen
1942....King Merritt	1959....Everett Shaw	1976....Marvin Cantrell	1993....Guy Allen
1943....Tom Rhodes	1960....Don McLaughlin	1977....Buddy Cockrell	1994....Guy Allen
1944....Tom Rhodes	1961....Clark McEntire	1978....Sonny Worrell	
1945....Everett Shaw	1962....Everett Shaw	1979....Gary Good	

Note: In 1945-46 champions were crowned only in Steer Roping.

Rowing

National Collegiate Rowing Champions
MEN'S EIGHT

1982 ....Yale	1987 ....Harvard	1992 ....Harvard
1983 ....Harvard	1988 ....Harvard	1993 ....Brown
1984 ....Washington	1989 ....Harvard	1994 ....Brown
1985 ....Harvard	1990 ....Wisconsin	1995 ....Brown
1986 ....Wisconsin	1991 ....Pennsylvania	

WOMEN'S EIGHT

1979 ....Yale	1985 ....Washington	1991 ....Boston University
1980 ....California	1986 ....Wisconsin	1992 ....Boston University
1981 ....Washington	1987 ....Washington	1993 ....Princeton
1982 ....Washington	1988 ....Washington	1994 ....Princeton
1983 ....Washington	1989 ....Cornell	1995 ....Princeton
1984 ....Washington	1990 ....Princeton	

Rugby

National Men's Club Championship

Year	Winner	Runner-Up	Year	Winner	Runner-Up
1979 ....Old Blues (Calif.)	St Louis Falcons		1988 ....Old Mission Beach AC	Milwaukee
1980 ....Old Blues (Calif.)	St. Louis Falcons		1989 ....Old Mission Beach AC	Philly/Whitemarsh
1981 ....Old Blues (Calif.)	Old Blue (NY)		1990 ....Denver Barbos	Old Blues (CA)
1982 ....Old Blues (Calif.)	Denver Barbos		1991 ....Old Mission Beach AC	Washington
1983 ....Old Blues (Calif.)	Dallas Harlequins		1992 ....Old Blues (Calif.)	Mystic River (MA)
1984 ....Dallas Harlequins	Los Angeles		1993 ....Old Mission Beach AC	Milwaukee
1985 ....Milwaukee	Denver Barbos		1994 ....Old Mission Beach AC	Life College (GA)
1986 ....Old Blues (Calif.)	Old Blue (NY)		1995 ....Potomac Athletic Club	Old Mission Beach
1987 ....Old Blues (Calif.)	Pittsburgh			

National Men's Collegiate Championship

Year	Winner	Runner-Up	Year	Winner	Runner-Up
1980 ....California	Air Force	1988 ....California	Dartmouth
1981 ....California	Harvard	1989 ....Air Force	Long Beach
1982 ....California	Life College	1990 ....Air Force	Army
1983 ....California	Air Force	1991 ....California	Army
1984 ....Harvard	Colorado	1992 ....California	Army
1985 ....California	Maryland	1993 ....California	Air Force
1986 ....California	Dartmouth	1994 ....California	Navy
1987 ....San Diego State	Air Force	1995 ....California	Air Force

World Cup Championship

Year	Winner	Runner-Up	Year	Winner	Runner-Up
1987 ....New Zealand	France	1995 ....South Africa	New Zealand
1991 ....Australia	England		

Sailing

America's Cup Champions
SCHOONERS AND J-CLASS BOATS

Year	Winner	Skipper	Series	Loser	Skipper
1851.......America	Richard Brown				
1870.......Magic	Andrew Comstock	1-0	Cambria, Great Britain	J. Tannock
1871.......Columbia (2-1)	Nelson Comstock	4-1	Livonia, Great Britain	J. R. Woods
Sappho (2-0)	Sam Greenwood			
1876.......Madeleine	Josephus Williams	2-0	Countess of Dufferin, Canada	J. E. Ellsworth
1881.......Mischief	Nathanael Clock	2-0	Atalanta, Canada	Alexander Cuthbert
1885.......Puritan	Aubrey Crocker	2-0	Genesta, Great Britain	John Carter
1886.......Mayflower	Martin Stone	2-0	Galatea, Great Britain	Dan Bradford
1887.......Volunteer	Henry Haff	2-0	Thistle, Great Britain	John Barr
1893.......Vigilant	William Hansen	3-0	Valkyrie II, Great Britain	William Granfield
1895.......Defender	Henry Haff	3-0	Valkyrie III, Great Britain	William Granfield
1899.......Columbia	Charles Barr	3-0	Shamrock I, Great Britain	Archie Hogarth
1901.......Columbia	Charles Barr	3-0	Shamrock II, Great Britain	E. A. Sycamore

America's Cup Champions (Cont.)

SCHOONERS AND J-CLASS BOATS (Cont.)

Year	Winner	Skipper	Series	Loser	Skipper
1903	Reliance	Charles Barr	3-0	Shamrock III, Great Britain	Bob Wringe
1920	Resolute	Charles F. Adams	3-2	Shamrock IV, Great Britain	William Burton
1930	Enterprise	Harold Vanderbilt	4-0	Shamrock V, Great Britain	Ned Heard
1934	Rainbow	Harold Vanderbilt	4-2	Endeavour, Great Britain	T. O. M. Sopwith
1937	Ranger	Harold Vanderbilt	4-0	Endeavour II, Great Britain	T. O. M. Sopwith

12-METER BOATS

Year	Winner	Skipper	Series	Loser	Skipper
1958	Columbia	Briggs Cunningham	4-0	Sceptre, Great Britain	Graham Mann
1962	Weatherly	Bus Mosbacher	4-1	Gretel, Australia	Jock Sturrock
1964	Constellation	Bob Bavier & Eric Ridder	4-0	Sovereign, Australia	Peter Scott
1967	Intrepid	Bus Mosbacher	4-0	Dame Pattie, Australia	Jock Sturrock
1970	Intrepid	Bill Ficker	4-1	Gretel II, Australia	Jim Hardy
1974	Courageous	Ted Hood	4-0	Southern Cross, Australia	John Cuneo
1977	Courageous	Ted Turner	4-0	Australia	Noel Robins
1980	Freedom	Dennis Conner	4-1	Australia	Jim Hardy
1983	Australia II	John Bertrand	4-3	Liberty, United States	Dennis Conner
1987	Stars & Stripes	Dennis Conner	4-0	Kookaburra III, Australia	Iain Murray

60-FOOT CATAMARAN VS 133-FOOT MONOHULL

Year	Winner	Skipper	Series	Loser	Skipper
1988	Stars & Stripes	Dennis Conner	2-0	New Zealand	David Barnes

75-FOOT MONOHULL (IACC)

Year	Winner	Skipper	Series	Loser	Skipper
1992	America[3]	Bill Koch	4-1	Il Moro di Vinezia, Italy	Paul Cayard
1995	Black Magic I	Russell Coutts	5-0	Young America, United States	Dennis Conner

Note: Winning entries have been from the United States every year but two; in 1983 an Australian vessel won, and in 1995 a vessel from New Zealand won.

Shooting World Champions

Men

50M FREE RIFLE PRONE

1947 .....O. Sannes, Norway
1949 .....A.C. Jackson, United States
1952 .....A.C. Jackson, United States
1954 .....G. Boa, Canada
1958 .....M. Nordquist
1962 .....K. Wenk, West Germany
1966 .....D. Boyd, United States
1970 .....M. Fiess, S. Africa
1974 .....K. Bulan, Czech.
1978 .....A. Allan, Great Britain
1982 .....V. Danilschenko, Soviet Union
1986 .....S. Bereczky, Hungary
1990 .....V. Bochkarev, Sov Union
1994 .....Venjie Li, China

AIR RIFLE

1966 .....G. Kümmet, W. Germany
1970 .....G. Kusterman, W. Germ.
1974 .....E. Pedzisz, Poland
1978 .....O. Schlipf, W. Germany
1979 .....K. Hillenbrand
1981 .....F. Bessy, France
1982 .....F. Rettkowski, E. Germ.
1983 .....P. Heberle, France
1985 .....P. Heberle, France
1986 .....H. Riederer, W. Germany
1987 .....K. Ivanov, Soviet Union

AIR RIFLE (Cont.)

1989 .....J. P. Amet, France
1990 .....H. Riederer, W. Germany
1994 .....Boris Polak, Israel

MEN'S TRAP

1929 .....De Lumniczer, Hungary
1930 .....M. Arie, United States
1931 .....Kiszkurno, Poland
1933 .....De Lumniczer, Hungary
1934 .....A. Montagh, Hungary
1935 .....R. Sack, W. Germany
1936 .....Kiszkurno, Poland
1937 .....K. Huber, Finland
1938 .....I. Strassburger, Hungary
1939 .....De Lumniczer, Hungary
1947 .....H. Liljedahl, Sweden
1949 .....F. Rocchi, Argentina
1950 .....C. Sala, Italy
1952 .....P.J. Grossi, Argentina
1954 .....C. Merlo, Italy
1958 .....F. Eisenlauer, United States
1959 .....H. Badravi, Egypt
1961 .....E. Mattarelli, Italy
1962 .....W. Zimenko, Soviet Union
1965 .....J.E. Lire, Chile
1966 .....K. Jones, United States
1967 .....G. Rennard, Belgium
1969 .....E. Mattarelli, Italy
1970 .....M. Carrega, France

MEN'S TRAP (Cont.)

1971 .....M. Carrega, France
1973 .....A. Andrushkin, Soviet Union
1974 .....M. Carrega, France
1975 .....J. Primrose, Canada
1977 .....E. Azkue, Spain
1978 .....E. Vallduvi, Spain
1979 .....M. Carrega, France
1981 .....A. Asanov, Soviet Union
1982 .....L. Giovonnetti, Italy
1983 .....J. Primrose, Canada
1985 .....M. Bednarik, Czech.
1986 .....M. Benarik, Czech.
1987 .....D. Monakov, Soviet Union
1989 .....M. Venturini, Italy
1990 .....J. Damne, E. Germany
1994 .....Dmitriy Monakov, Ukraine
1995 .....G. Pellielo, Italy

THREE POSITION RIFLE

1929 .....O. Ericsson, Sweden
1930 .....Petersen, Denmark
1931 .....Amundson, Norway
1933 .....De Lisle, France
1935 .....Leskinnen, Finland
1937 .....Mazoyer, France
1939 .....Steigelmann, Germany
1947 .....I. H. Erben, Sweden
1949 .....P. Janhonen, Finland
1952 .....Kongshaug, Norway

Men *(Cont.)*

THREE POSITION RIFLE *(Cont.)*
1954 .....A. Bugdanov,
     Soviet Union
1958 .....Itkis, Soviet Union
1962 .....G. Anderson,
     United States

THREE POSITION RIFLE *(Cont.)*
1966 .....G. Anderson,
     United States
1970 .....Parkhimovitch,
     Soviet Union
1974 .....L. Wigger, United States

THREE POSITION RIFLE *(Cont.)*
1978 .....E. Svensson, Sweden
1982 .....K. Ivanov, Soviet Union
1986 .....P. Heinz, W. Germany
1990 .....E. C. Lee, S. Korea
1994 .....Petr Kurka, Czech Republic

Women

THREE POSITION RIFLE
1966 .....M. Thompson,
     United States
1970 .....M. Thompson Murdock,
     United States
1974 .....A. Pelova, Bulgaria
1978 .....W. Oliver, United States
1982 .....M. Helbig, E. Germany
1986 .....V. Letcheva, Bulgaria
1990 .....V. Letcheva, Bulgaria
1994 .....A. Maloukhina, Russia

AIR RIFLE
1970 ....V. Cherkasque, Soviet Union
1974 .....T. Ratkinova, Soviet Union
1978 .....W. Oliver, United States
1979 .....K. Monez, United States
1981 .....S. Romaristova,
     Soviet Union

AIR RIFLE *(Cont.)*
1982 .....S. Lang, W. Germany
1983 .....M. Helbig, E. Germany
1985 .....E. Forian, Hungary
1986 .....V. Letcheva, Bulgaria
1987 .....V. Letcheva, Bulgaria
1989 .....V. Letcheva, Bulgaria
1990 .....E.Joc, Hungary
1994 .....S. Pfeilschifter, Germany

SPORT PISTOL
1966 .....N. Rasskazova,
     Soviet Union
1970 .....N. Stoljarova, Soviet Union
1974 .....N. Stoljarova, Soviet Union
1978 .....K. Dyer, United States
1982 .....P. Balogh, Hungary
1986 .....M. Dobrantcheva,
     Soviet Union

SPORT PISTOL *(Cont.)*
1990 .....M. Logvinenko, Sov Union
1994 .....Soon Hee Boo, S. Korea

AIR PISTOL
1970 .....S. Carroll, United States
1974 .....Z. Simonian, Soviet Union
1978 .....K. Hansson, Sweden
1979 .....R. Fox, United States
1981 .....N. Kalinina, Soviet Union
1982 .....M. Dobrantcheva,
     Soviet Union
1983 .....K. Bodin, Sweden
1985 .....M. Dobrantcheva, Sov Union
1986 .....A. Völker, E. Germany
1987 .....J. Brajkovic, Yugoslavia
1989 .....N. Salukvadse,
     Soviet Union
1990 .....Jasna Sekaric, Yugoslavia
1994 .....Jasna Sekaric, IOP

Softball

Men
MAJOR FAST PITCH

1933.................J. L. Gill Boosters, Chicago	1965.................Sealmasters, Aurora, IL
1934.................Ke-Nash-A, Kenosha, WI	1966.................Clearwater (FL) Bombers
1935.................Crimson Coaches, Toledo, OH	1967.................Sealmasters, Aurora, IL
1936.................Kodak Park, Rochester, NY	1968.................Clearwater (FL) Bombers
1937.................Briggs Body Team, Detroit	1969.................Raybestos Cardinals, Stratford, CT
1938.................The Pohlers, Cincinnati	1970.................Raybestos Cardinals, Stratford, CT
1939.................Carr's Boosters, Covington, KY	1971.................Welty Way, Cedar Rapids, IA
1940.................Kodak Park, Rochester, NY	1972.................Raybestos Cardinals, Stratford, CT
1941.................Bendix Brakes, South Bend, IN	1973.................Clearwater (FL) Bombers
1942.................Deep Rock Oilers, Midland	1974.................Gianella Bros, Santa Rosa, CA
1943.................Hammer Air Field, Fresno	1975.................Rising Sun Hotel, Reading, PA
1944.................Hammer Air Field, Fresno	1976.................Raybestos Cardinals, Stratford, CT
1945.................Zollner Pistons, Fort Wayne, IN	1977.................Billard Barbell, Reading, PA
1946.................Zollner Pistons, Fort Wayne, IN	1978.................Billard Barbell, Reading, PA
1947.................Zollner Pistons, Fort Wayne, IN	1979.................McArdle Pontiac/Cadillac, Midland, MI
1948.................Briggs Beautyware, Detroit	1980.................Peterbilt Western, Seattle
1949.................Tip Top Tailors, Toronto	1981.................Archer Daniels Midland, Decatur, IL
1950.................Clearwater (FL) Bombers	1982.................Peterbilt Western, Seattle
1951.................Dow Chemical, Midland, MI	1983.................Franklin Cardinals, Stratford, CT
1952.................Briggs Beautyware, Detroit	1984.................California Kings, Merced, CA
1953.................Briggs Beautyware, Detroit	1985.................Pay'n Pak, Seattle
1954.................Clearwater (FL) Bombers	1986.................Pay'n Pak, Seattle
1955.................Raybestos Cardinals, Stratford, CT	1987.................Pay'n Pak, Seattle
1956.................Clearwater (FL) Bombers	1988.................TransAire, Elkhart, IN
1957.................Clearwater (FL) Bombers	1989.................Penn Corp, Sioux City, IA
1958.................Raybestos Cardinals, Stratford, CT	1990.................Penn Corp, Sioux City, IA
1959.................Sealmasters, Aurora, IL	1991.................Guanella Brothers, Rohnert Park, CA
1960.................Clearwater (FL) Bombers	1992.................Natl Health Care Disc, Sioux City, IA
1961.................Sealmasters, Aurora, IL	1993.................Natl Health Care Disc, Sioux City, IA
1962.................Clearwater (FL) Bombers	1994.................Decatur Pride, Decatur, IL
1963.................Clearwater (FL) Bombers	1995.................Decatur Pride, Decatur, IL
1964.................Burch Tool, Detroit	

Men (Cont.)
SUPER SLOW PITCH

1981...............Howard's/Western Steer, Denver, NC	1989................Ritch's Salvage, Harrisburg, NC
1982...............Jerry's Catering, Miami, Fla.	1990................Steele's Silver Bullets, Grafton, OH
1983...............Howard's/Western Steer, Denver, NC	1991................Sunbelt/Worth, Centerville, GA
1984...............Howard's/Western Steer, Denver, NC	1992................Ritch's/Superior, Windsor Locks, CT
1985...............Steele's Sports, Grafton, OH	1993................Ritch's/Superior, Windsor Locks, CT
1986...............Steele's Sports, Grafton, OH	1994................Bell Corp, Tampa, Fla.
1987...............Steele's Sports, Grafton, OH	1995................Lighthouse Worth, Stone Mtn., GA
1988...............Starpath, Monticello, KY	

MAJOR SLOW PITCH

1953...............Shields Construction, Newport, KY	1975..........Pyramid Cafe, Lakewood, OH
1954...............Waldneck's Tavern, Cincinnati	1976..........Warren Motors, Jacksonville, FL
1955...............Lang Pet Shop, Covington, KY	1977..........Nelson Painting, Oklahoma City
1956...............Gatliff Auto Sales, Newport, KY	1978..........Campbell Carpets, Concord, CA
1957...............Gatliff Auto Sales, Newport, KY	1979..........Nelco Mfg Co, Oklahoma City
1958...............East Side Sports, Detroit	1980..........Campbell Carpets, Concord, CA
1959...............Yorkshire Restaurant, Newport, KY	1981..........Elite Coating, Gordon, CA
1960...............Hamilton Tailoring, Cincinnati	1982..........Triangle Sports, Minneapolis
1961...............Hamilton Tailoring, Cincinnati	1983..........No. 1 Electric & Heating, Gastonia, NC
1962...............Skip Hogan A.C., Pittsburgh	1984..........Lilly Air Systems, Chicago
1963...............Gatliff Auto Sales, Newport, KY	1985..........Blanton's, Fayetteville, NC
1964...............Skip Hogan A.C., Pittsburgh	1986..........Non-Ferrous Metals, Cleveland
1965...............Skip Hogan A.C., Pittsburgh	1987..........Starpath, Monticello, KY
1966...............Michael's Lounge, Detroit	1988..........Bell Corp/FAF, Tampa, FL
1967...............Jim's Sport Shop, Pittsburgh	1989..........Ritch's Salvage, Harrisburg, NC
1968...............County Sports, Levittown, NY	1990..........New Construction, Shelbyville, IN
1969...............Copper Hearth, Milwaukee	1991..........Riverside Paving, Louisville, KY
1970...............Little Caesar's, Southgate, MI	1992..........Vernon's, Jacksonville, FL
1971...............Pile Drivers, Virginia Beach, VA	1993..........Back Porch/Destin Roofing, Destin, FL
1972...............Jiffy Club, Louisville, KY	1994..........Riverside RAM/Taylor Bros., Louisville, KY
1973...............Howard's Furniture, Denver, NC	1995..........Riverside/RAM/Taylor/TPS, Louisville, KY
1974...............Howard's Furniture, Denver, NC	

Women
MAJOR FAST PITCH

1933..........Great Northerns, Chicago	1965..........Orange (CA) Lionettes
1934..........Hart Motors, Chicago	1966..........Raybestos Brakettes, Stratford, CT
1935..........Bloomer Girls, Cleveland	1967..........Raybestos Brakettes, Stratford, CT
1936..........Nat'l Screw & Mfg, Cleveland	1968..........Raybestos Brakettes, Stratford, CT
1937..........Nat'l Screw & Mfg, Cleveland	1969..........Orange (CA) Lionettes
1938..........J. J. Krieg's, Alameda, CA	1970..........Orange (CA) Lionettes
1939..........J. J. Krieg's, Alameda, CA	1971..........Raybestos Brakettes, Stratford, CT
1940..........Arizona Ramblers, Phoenix	1972..........Raybestos Brakettes, Stratford, CT
1941..........Higgins Midgets, Tulsa	1973..........Raybestos Brakettes, Stratford, CT
1942..........Jax Maids, New Orleans	1974..........Raybestos Brakettes, Stratford, CT
1943..........Jax Maids, New Orleans	1975..........Raybestos Brakettes, Stratford, CT
1944..........Lind & Pomeroy, Portland, OR	1976..........Raybestos Brakettes, Stratford, CT
1945..........Jax Maids, New Orleans	1977..........Raybestos Brakettes, Stratford, CT
1946..........Jax Maids, New Orleans	1978..........Raybestos Brakettes, Stratford, CT
1947..........Jax Maids, New Orleans	1979..........Sun City (AZ) Saints
1948..........Arizona Ramblers, Phoenix	1980..........Raybestos Brakettes, Stratford, CT
1949..........Arizona Ramblers, Phoenix	1981..........Orlando (FL) Rebels
1950..........Orange (CA) Lionettes	1982..........Raybestos Brakettes, Stratford, CT
1951..........Orange (CA) Lionettes	1983..........Raybestos Brakettes, Stratford, CT
1952..........Orange (CA) Lionettes	1984..........Los Angeles Diamonds
1953..........Betsy Ross Rockets, Fresno	1985..........Hi-Ho Brakettes, Stratford, CT
1954..........Leach Motor Rockets, Fresno	1986..........Southern California Invasion, Los Angeles
1955..........Orange (CA) Lionettes	1987..........Orange County Majestics, Anaheim, CA
1956..........Orange (CA) Lionettes	1988..........Hi-Ho Brakettes, Stratford, CT
1957..........Hacienda Rockets, Fresno	1989..........Whittier (CA) Raiders
1958..........Raybestos Brakettes, Stratford, CT	1990..........Raybestos Brakettes, Stratford, CT
1959..........Raybestos Brakettes, Stratford, CT	1991..........Raybestos Brakettes, Stratford, CT
1960..........Raybestos Brakettes, Stratford, CT	1992..........Raybestos Brakettes, Stratford, CT
1961..........Gold Sox, Whittier, CA	1993..........Redding Rebels, Redding, CA
1962..........Orange (CA) Lionettes	1994..........Redding Rebels, Redding, CA
1963..........Raybestos Brakettes, Stratford, CT	1995..........Redding Rebels, Redding, CA
1964..........Erv Lind Florists, Portland, OR	

Softball (Cont.)

Women (Cont.)
MAJOR SLOW PITCH

1959.........Pearl Laundry, Richmond, VA	1978.........Bob Hoffman's Dots, Miami
1960.........Carolina Rockets, High Pt, NC	1979.........Bob Hoffman's Dots, Miami
1961.........Dairy Cottage, Covington, KY	1980.........Howard's Rubi-Otts, Graham, NC
1962.........Dana Gardens, Cincinnati	1981.........Tifton (GA) Tomboys
1963.........Dana Gardens, Cincinnati	1982.........Richmond (VA) Stompers
1964.........Dana Gardens, Cincinnati	1983.........Spooks, Anoka, MN
1965.........Art's Acres, Omaha	1984.........Spooks, Anoka, MN
1966.........Dana Gardens, Cincinnati	1985.........Key Ford Mustangs, Pensacola, FL
1967.........Ridge Maintenance, Cleveland	1986.........Sur-Way Tomboys, Tifton, GA
1968.........Escue Pontiac, Cincinnati	1987.........Key Ford Mustangs, Pensacola, FL
1969.........Converse Dots, Hialeah, FL	1988.........Spooks, Anoka, MN
1970.........Rutenschruder Floral, Cincinnati	1989.........Canaan's Illusions, Houston
1971.........Gators, Ft Lauderdale, FL	1990.........Spooks, Anoka, MN
1972.........Riverside Ford, Cincinnati	1991.........Kannan's Illusions, San Antonio, TX
1973.........Sweeney Chevrolet, Cincinnati	1992.........Universal Plastics, Cookeville, TN
1974.........Marks Brothers Dots, Miami	1993.........Universal Plastics, Cookeville, TN
1975.........Marks Brothers Dots, Miami	1994.........Universal Plastics, Cookeville, TN
1976.........Sorrento's Pizza, Cincinnati	1995.........Armed Forces, Sacramento, CA
1977.........Fox Valley Lassies, St Charles, IL	

Speed Skating

All-Round World Champions
MEN

1891.....Joseph F. Donoghue, US	1933.....Hans Engnestangen, Nor	1969.....Dag Fornaes, Norway
1893.....Jaap Eden, Holland	1934.....Bernt Evensen, Norway	1970.....Ard Schenk, Holland
1895.....Jaap Eden, Holland	1935.....Michael Staksrud, Nor.	1971.....Ard Schenk, Holland
1896.....Jaap Eden, Holland	1936.....Ivar Ballangrud, Norway	1972.....Ard Schenk, Holland
1897.....Jack K. McCulloch, Can.	1937.....Michael Staksrud, Nor.	1973.....Göran Claeson, Sweden
1898.....Peder Ostlund, Norway	1938.....Ivar Ballangrud, Norway	1974.....Sten Stensen, Norway
1899.....Peder Ostlund, Norway	1939.....Birger Wasenius, Finland	1975.....Harm Kuipers, Holland
1900.....Edvard Engelsaas, Nor.	1947.....Lassi Parkkinen, Finland	1976.....Piet Kleine, Holland
1901.....Franz F. Wathan, Finland	1948.....Odd Lundberg, Norway	1977.....Eric Heiden, USA
1904.....Sigurd Mathisen, Norway	1949.....Kornel Pajor, Hungary	1978.....Eric Heiden, USA
1905.....C. Coen de Koning, Holl.	1950.....Hjalmar Andersen, Nor.	1979.....Eric Heiden, USA
1908.....Oscar Mathisen, Norway	1951.....Hjalmar Andersen, Nor.	1980.....Hilbert van der Duin, Holl.
1909.....Oscar Mathisen, Norway	1952.....Hjalmar Andersen, Nor.	1981.....Amund Sjobrand, Norway
1910.....Nikolai Strunnikov, Russia	1953.....Oleg Goncharenko, Sov U	1982.....Hilbert van der Duin, Holl
1911.....Nikolai Strunnikov, Russia	1954.....Boris Shilkov, Sov U	1983.....Rolf Falk-Larssen, Nor.
1912.....Oscar Mathisen, Norway	1955.....Sigvard Ericsson, Swe.	1984.....Oleg Bozhev, Sov U
1913.....Oscar Mathisen, Norway	1956.....Oleg Goncharenko, Sov U	1985.....Hein Vergeer, Holland
1914.....Oscar Mathisen, Norway	1957.....Knut Johannesen, Nor.	1986.....Hein Vergeer, Holland
1922.....Harald Strom, Norway	1958.....Oleg Goncharenko, Sov U	1987.....Nikolai Guliaev, Sov U
1923.....Klas Thunberg, Finland	1959.....Juhani Järvinen, Finland	1988.....Eric Flaim, USA
1924.....Roald Larsen, Norway	1960.....Boris Stenin, Sov U	1989.....Leo Visser, Holland
1925.....Klas Thunberg, Finland	1961.....Henk van der Grift, Holl.	1990.....Johann Olav Koss, Nor.
1926.....Ivar Ballangrud, Norway	1962.....Viktor Kosichkin, Sov U	1991.....Johann Olav Koss, Nor.
1927.....Bernt Evensen, Norway	1963.....Jonny Nilsson, Sweden	1992.....Roberto Sighel, Italy
1928.....Klas Thunberg, Finland	1964.....Knut Johannesen, Nor.	1993.....Falko Zandstra, Holland
1929.....Klas Thunberg, Finland	1965.....Per Ivar Moe, Norway	1994.....Johann Olav Koss, Nor.
1930.....Michael Staksrud, Nor.	1966.....Kees Verkerk, Holland	1995.....Rintje Ritsma, Holland
1931.....Klas Thunberg, Finland	1967.....Kees Verkerk, Holland	
1932.....Ivar Ballangrud, Norway	1968.....Fred Anton Maier, Nor.	

WOMEN

1936.....Kit Klein, USA	1951.....Eevi Huttunen, Finland	1958.....Inga Artamonova, Sov U
1937.....Laila Schou Nilsen, Nor.	1952.....Lidia Selikhova, Sov U	1959.....Tamara Rylova, Sov U
1938.....Laila Schou Nilsen, Nor.	1953.....Khalida Shchegoleeva,	1960.....Valentina Stenina, Sov U
1939.....Verné Lesche, Finland	Soviet Union	1961.....Valentina Stenina, Sov U
1947.....Verné Lesche, Finland	1954.....Lidia Selikhova, Sov U	1962.....Inga Artamonova, Sov U
1948.....Maria Isakova, Sov U	1955.....Rimma Zhukova, Sov U	1963.....Lidia Skoblikova, Sov U
1949.....Maria Isakova, Sov U	1956.....Sofia Kondakova, Sov U	1964.....Lidia Skoblikova, Sov U
1950.....Maria Isakova, Sov U	1957.....Inga Artamonova, Sov U	1965.....Inga Artamonova, Sov U

All-Round World Champions *(Cont.)*
WOMEN *(Cont.)*

1966 .....Valentina Stenina, Sov U	1977 .....Vera Bryndzej, Sov U	1988 .....Karin Kania, GDR
1967 .....Stien Kaiser, Holland	1978 .....Tatiana Averina, Sov U	1989 .....Constanze Moser, GDR
1968 .....Stien Kaiser, Holland	1979 .....Beth Heiden, USA	1990 .....Jacqueline Börner, GDR
1969 .....Lasma Kauniste, Sov U	1980 .....Natalia Petruseva, Sov U	1991 .....Gunda Kleemann, Ger.
1970 .....Atje Keulen-Deelstra, Holl.	1981 .....Natalia Petruseva, Sov U	1992 .....Gunda Niemann-
1971 .....Nina Statkevich, Sov U	1982 .....Karin Busch, GDR	Kleemann, Germany
1972 .....Atje Keulen-Deelstra, Holl.	1983 .....Andrea Schöne, GDR	1993 .....Gunda Niemann, Germany
1973 .....Atje Keulen-Deelstra, Holl.	1984 .....Karin Enke-Busch, GDR	1994 .....Emese Hunyady, Austria
1974 .....Atje Keulen-Deelstra, Holl.	1985 .....Andrea Schöne, GDR	1995 .....Gunda Niemann, Germany
1975 .....Karin Kessow, GDR	1986 .....Karin Kania-Enke, GDR	
1976 .....Sylvia Burka, Canada	1987 .....Karin Kania, GDR	

Squash

National Men's Champions

HARD BALL		HARD BALL *(Cont.)*		HARD BALL *(Cont.)*	
Year	**Champion**	**Year**	**Champion**	**Year**	**Champion**
1907 ....John A. Miskey		1943-45.....No tournament		1978 ....Michael Desaulniers	
1908 ....John A. Miskey		1946 ....Charles M. P. Britton		1979 ....Mario Sanchez	
1909 ....William L. Freeland		1947 ....Charles M. P. Britton		1980 ....Michael Desaulniers	
1910 ....John A. Miskey		1948 ....Stanley W. Pearson Jr.		1981 ....Mark Alger	
1911 ....Francis S. White		1949 ....H. Hunter Lott Jr.		1982 ....John Nimick	
1912 ....Constantine Hutchins		1950 ....Edward J. Hahn		1983 ....Kenton Jernigan	
1913 ....Morton L. Newhall		1951 ....Edward J. Hahn		1984 ....Kenton Jernigan	
1914 ....Constantine Hutchins		1952 ....Harry B. Conlon		1985 ....Kenton Jernigan	
1915 ....Stanley W. Pearson		1953 ....Ernest Howard		1986 ....Hugh LaBossier	
1916 ....Stanley W. Pearson		1954 ....G. Diehl Mateer Jr.		1987 ....Frank J. Stanley IV	
1917 ....Stanley W. Pearson		1955 ....Henri R. Salaun		1988 ....Scott Dulmage	
1918-19.....No tournament		1956 ....G. Diehl Mateer Jr.		1989 ....Rodolfo Rodriquez	
1920 ....Charles C. Peabody		1957 ....Henri R. Salaun		1990 ....Hector Barragan	
1921 ....Stanley W. Pearson		1958 ....Henri R. Salaun		1991 ....Hector Barragan	
1922 ....Stanley W. Pearson		1959 ....Benjamin H.		1992 ....Hector Barragan	
1923 ....Stanley W. Pearson		Heckscher		1993 ....Hector Barragan	
1924 ....Gerald Roberts		1960 ....G. Diehl Mateer Jr		1994 ....Hector Barragan	
1925 ....W. Palmer Dixon		1961 ....Henri R. Salaun		1995 ....W. Keen Butcher	
1926 ....W. Palmer Dixon		1962 ....Samuel P. Howe III			
1927 ....Myles Baker		1963 ....Benjamin H.		**SOFT BALL**	
1928 ....Herbert N. Rawlins Jr.		Heckscher		**Year**	**Champion**
1929 ....J. Lawrence Pool		1964 ....Ralph E. Howe		1983 ....Kenton Jernigan	
1930 ....Herbert N. Rawlins Jr.		1965 ....Stephen T. Vehslage		1984 ....Kenton Jernigan	
1931 ....J. Lawrence Pool		1966 ....Victor Niederhoffer		1985 ....Kenton Jernigan	
1932 ....Beckman H. Pool		1967 ....Samuel P. Howe III		1986 ....Darius Pandole	
1933 ....Beckman H. Pool		1968 ....Colin Adair		1987 ....Richard Hashim	
1934 ....Neil J. Sullivan II		1969 ....Anil Nayar		1988 ....John Phelan	
1935 ....Donald Strachan		1970 ....Anil Nayar		1989 ....Will Carlin	
1936 ....Germain G. Glidden		1971 ....Colin Adair		1990 ....Syed Jafry	
1937 ....Germain G. Glidden		1972 ....Victor Niederhoffer		1991 ....Hector Barragan	
1938 ....Germain G. Glidden		1973 ....Victor Niederhoffer		1992 ....Phil Yarrow	
1939 ....Donald Strachan		1974 ....Victor Niederhoffer		1993 ....Phil Yarrow	
1940 ....A. Willing Patterson		1975 ....Victor Niederhoffer		1994 ....Roberto Rosales	
1941 ....Charles M. P. Britton		1976 ....Peter Briggs		1995 ....A. Martin Clark	
1942 ....Charles M. P. Britton		1977 ....Thomas E. Page			

Squash *(Cont.)*

National Women's Champions

Year	Champion	Year	Champion	Year	Champion
HARD BALL		**HARD BALL** *(Cont.)*		**HARD BALL** *(Cont.)*	
1928	Eleanora Sears	1961	Margaret Varner	1990	Demer Holleran
1929	Margaret Howe	1962	Margaret Varner	1991	Demer Holleran
1930	Hazel Wightman	1963	Margaret Varner	1992	Demer Holleran
1931	Ruth Banks	1964	Ann Wetzel	1993	Demer Holleran
1932	Margaret Howe	1965	Joyce Davenport	1994	Demer Holleran
1933	Susan Noel	1966	Betty Meade	1995	Not held
1934	Margaret Howe	1967	Betty Meade	**SOFT BALL**	
1935	Margot Lumb	1968	Betty Meade	Year	Champion
1936	Anne Page	1969	Joyce Davenport	1983	Alicia McConnell
1937	Anne Page	1970	Nina Moyer	1984	Julie Harris
1938	Cecile Bowes	1971	Carol Thesieres	1985	Sue Clinch
1939	Anne Page	1972	Nina Moyer	1986	Julie Harris
1940	Cecile Bowes	1973	Gretchen Spruance	1987	Diana Staley
1941	Cecile Bowes	1974	Gretchen Spruance	1988	Sara Luther
1942-46	No tournament	1975	Ginny Akabane	1989	Nancy Gengler
1947	Anne Page Homer	1976	Gretchen Spruance	1990	Joyce Maycock
1948	Cecile Bowes	1977	Gretchen Spruance	1991	Ellie Pierce
1949	Janet Morgan	1978	Gretchen Spruance	1992	Demer Holleran
1950	Betty Howe	1979	Heather McKay	1993	Demer Holleran
1951	Jane Austin	1980	Barbara Maltby	1994	Demer Holleran
1952	Margaret Howe	1981	Barbara Maltby	1995	Ellie Pierce
1953	Margaret Howe	1982	Alicia McConnell		
1954	Lois Dilks	1983	Alicia McConnell		
1955	Janet Morgan	1984	Alicia McConnell		
1956	Betty Howe Constable	1985	Alicia McConnell		
1957	Betty Howe Constable	1986	Alicia McConnell		
1958	Betty Howe Constable	1987	Alicia McConnell		
1959	Betty Howe Constable	1988	Alicia McConnell		
1960	Margaret Varner	1989	Demer Holleran		

Triathlon

Ironman Championship

MEN

Date	Winner	Time	Site
1978	Gordon Haller	11:46	Waikiki Beach
1979	Tom Warren	11:15:56	Waikiki Beach
1980	Dave Scott	9:24:33	Ala Moana Park
1981	John Howard	9:38:29	Kailua-Kona
1982	Scott Tinley	9:19:41	Kailua-Kona
1982	Dave Scott	9:08:23	Kailua-Kona
1983	Dave Scott	9:05:57	Kailua-Kona
1984	Dave Scott	8:54:20	Kailua-Kona
1985	Scott Tinley	8:50:54	Kailua-Kona
1986	Dave Scott	8:28:37	Kailua-Kona
1987	Dave Scott	8:34:13	Kailua-Kona
1988	Scott Molina	8:31:00	Kailua-Kona
1989	Mark Allen	8:09:15	Kailua-Kona
1990	Mark Allen	8:28:17	Kailua-Kona
1991	Mark Allen	8:18:32	Kailua-Kona
1992	Mark Allen	8:09:09	Kailua-Kona
1993	Mark Allen	8:07:46	Kailua-Kona
1994	Greg Welch	8:20:27	Kailua-Kona
1995	Mark Allen	8:20:34	Kailua-Kona

WOMEN

Date	Winner	Time	Site
1978	No finishers		
1979	Lyn Lemaire	12:55	Waikiki Beach
1980	Robin Beck	11:21:24	Ala Moana Park
1981	Linda Sweeney	12:00:32	Kailua-Kona
1982	Kathleen McCartney	11:09:40	Kailua-Kona
1982	Julie Leach	10:54:08	Kailua-Kona
1983	Sylviane Puntous	10:43:36	Kailua-Kona

Ironman Championship *(Cont.)*
WOMEN *(Cont.)*

Date	Winner	Time	Site
1984	Sylviane Puntous	10:25:13	Kailua-Kona
1985	Joanne Ernst	10:25:22	Kailua-Kona
1986	Paula Newby-Fraser	9:49:14	Kailua-Kona
1987	Erin Baker	9:35:25	Kailua-Kona
1988	Paula Newby-Fraser	9:01:01	Kailua-Kona
1989	Paula Newby-Fraser	9:00:56	Kailua-Kona
1990	Erin Baker	9:13:42	Kailua-Kona
1991	Paula Newby-Fraser	9:07:52	Kailua-Kona
1992	Paula Newby-Fraser	8:55:29	Kailua-Kona
1993	Paula Newby-Fraser	8:58:23	Kailua-Kona
1994	Paula Newby-Fraser	9:20:14	Kailua-Kona
1995	Karen Smyers	9:16:46	Kailua-Kona

Note: The Ironman Championship was contested twice in 1982.

Volleyball

World Champions
MEN

Year	Winner	Runnerup	Site
1949	Soviet Union	Czechoslovakia	Prague, Czechoslovakia
1952	Soviet Union	Czechoslovakia	Moscow, Soviet Union
1956	Czechoslovakia	Soviet Union	Paris, France
1960	Soviet Union	Czechoslovakia	Rio de Janeiro, Brazil
1962	Soviet Union	Czechoslovakia	Moscow, Soviet Union
1966	Czechoslovakia	Romania	Prague, Czechoslovakia
1970	East Germany	Bulgaria	Sofia, Bulgaria
1974	Poland	Soviet Union	Mexico City
1978	Soviet Union	Italy	Rome, Italy
1982	Soviet Union	Brazil	Buenos Aires, Argentina
1986	United States	Soviet Union	Paris, France
1990	Italy	Cuba	Rio de Janeiro, Brazil
1994	Italy	Netherlands	Athens, Greece

WOMEN

Year	Winner	Runnerup	Site
1952	Soviet Union	Poland	Moscow, Soviet Union
1956	Soviet Union	Romania	Paris, France
1960	Soviet Union	Japan	Rio de Janeiro, Brazil
1962	Japan	Soviet Union	Moscow, Soviet Union
1966	Japan	United States	Prague, Czechoslovakia
1970	Soviet Union	Japan	Sofia, Bulgaria
1974	Japan	Soviet Union	Mexico City
1978	Cuba	Japan	Rome, Italy
1982	China	Peru	Lima, Peru
1986	China	Cuba	Prague, Czechoslovakia
1990	Soviet Union	China	Beijing, China
1994	Cuba	Brazil	Sao Paulo, Brazil

U.S. Men's Open Champions—Gold Division

1928	Germantown, PA YMCA	1945	North Ave. YMCA, IL
1929	Hyde Park YMCA, IL	1946	Pasadena, CA YMCA
1930	Hyde Park YMCA, IL	1947	North Ave. YMCA, IL
1931	San Antonio, TX YMCA	1948	Hollywood, CA YMCA
1932	San Antonio, TX YMCA	1949	Downtown YMCA, CA
1933	Houston, TX YMCA	1950	Long Beach, CA YMCA
1934	Houston, TX YMCA	1951	Hollywood, CA YMCA
1935	Houston, TX YMCA	1952	Hollywood, CA YMCA
1936	Houston, TX YMCA	1953	Hollywood, CA YMCA
1937	Duncan YMCA, IL	1954	Stockton, CA YMCA
1938	Houston, TX YMCA	1955	Stockton, CA YMCA
1939	Houston, TX YMCA	1956	Hollywood, CA YMCA Stars
1940	Los Angeles AC, CA	1957	Hollywood, CA YMCA Stars
1941	North Ave. YMCA, IL	1958	Hollywood, CA YMCA Stars
1942	North Ave. YMCA, IL	1959	Hollywood, CA YMCA Stars
1943-44	No championships	1960	Westside JCC, CA

U.S. Men's Open Champions—Gold Division (Cont.)

1961	Hollywood, CA YMCA	1979	Nautilus, Long Beach
1962	Hollywood, CA YMCA	1980	Olympic Club, San Francisco
1963	Hollywood, CA YMCA	1981	Nautilus, Long Beach
1964	Hollywood, CA YMCA Stars	1982	Chuck's, Los Angeles
1965	Westside JCC, CA	1983	Nautilus Pacifica, CA
1966	Sand & Sea Club, CA	1984	Nautilus Pacifica, CA
1967	Fresno, CA VBC	1985	Molten/SSI Torrance, CA
1968	Westside JCC, L.A., CA	1986	Molten, Torrance, CA
1969	Los Angeles, CA YMCA	1987	Molten, Torrance, CA
1970	Chart House, San Diego	1988	Molten, Torrance, CA
1971	Santa Monica, CA YMCA	1989	Not held
1972	Chart House, San Diego	1990	Nike, Carson, CA
1973	Chuck's Steak, L.A., CA	1991	Offshore, Woodland Hills, CA
1974	Un of CA Santa Barbara	1992	Creole Six Pack, Elmhurst, NY
1975	Chart House, San Diego	1993	Asics, Huntington Beach, CA
1976	Maliabu, L.A., CA	1994	Asics/Paul Mitchell, Hunt. Beach, CA
1977	Chuck's, Santa Barbara	1995	Shakter, Belagarad, Ukraine
1978	Chuck's, Los Angeles		

U.S. Women's Open Champions—Gold Division

1949	Eagles, Houston TX	1973	E Pluribus Unum, Houston
1950	Voit #1, Santa Monica, CA	1974	Renegades, Los Angeles, CA
1951	Eagles, Houston, TX	1975	Adidas, Norwalk, CA
1952	Voit #1, Santa Monica, CA	1976	Pasadena, TX
1953	Voit #1, Los Angeles, CA	1977	Spoilers, Hermosa, CA
1954	Houstonettes, Houston, TX	1978	Nick's, Los Angeles, CA
1955	Mariners, Santa Monica, CA	1979	Mavericks, Los Angeles, CA
1956	Mariners, Santa Monica, CA	1980	NAVA, Fountain Valley, CA
1957	Mariners, Santa Monica, CA	1981	Utah State, Logan, UT
1958	Mariners, Santa Monica, CA	1982	Monarchs, Hilo, HI
1959	Mariners, Santa Monica, CA	1983	Syntex, Stockton, CA
1960	Mariners, Santa Monica, CA	1984	Chrysler, Palo Alto, CA
1961	Breakers, Long Beach, CA	1985	Merrill Lynch, Arizona
1962	Shamrocks, Long Beach, CA	1986	Merrill Lynch, Arizona
1963	Shamrocks, Long Beach, CA	1987	Chrysler, Pleasanton, CA
1964	Shamrocks, Long Beach, CA	1988	Chrysler, Hayward, CA
1965	Shamrocks, Long Beach, CA	1989	Plymouth, Hayward, CA
1966	Renegades, Los Angeles, CA	1990	Plymouth, Hayward, CA
1967	Shamrocks, Long Beach, CA	1991	Fitness, Champaign, IL
1968	Shamrocks, Long Beach, CA	1992	Nick's Kronies, Chicago, IL
1969	Shamrocks, Long Beach, CA	1993	Nick's Fishmarket, Chicago, IL
1970	Shamrocks, Long Beach, CA	1994	Nick's Fishmarket, Chicago, IL
1971	Renegades, Los Angeles, CA	1995	Kittleman Assoc./Rudi's/Nick's,
1972	E Pluribus Unum, Houston		Chicago, Il

Wrestling

United States National Champions
1983

FREESTYLE		FREESTYLE (Cont.)		GRECO-ROMAN (Cont.)	
105.5	Rich Salamone	220	Greg Gibson	149.5	Jim Martinez
114.5	Joe Gonzales	Hvy	Bruce Baumgartner	163	James Andre
125.5	Joe Corso	Team	Sunkist Kids	180.5	Steve Goss
136.5	Rich Dellagatta*			198	Steve Fraser*
149.5	Bill Hugent	**GRECO-ROMAN**		220	Dennis Koslowski
163	Lee Kemp	105.5	T. J. Jones	Hvy	No champion
180.5	Chris Campbell	114.5	Mark Fuller	Team	Minnesota Wrestling
198	Pete Bush	125.5	Rob Hermann		Club
		136.5	Dan Mello		

1984

FREESTYLE		FREESTYLE (Cont.)		FREESTYLE (Cont.)	
105.5	Rich Salamone	163	Dave Schultz*	Team	Sunkist Kids
114.5	Charlie Heard	180.5	Mark Schultz	**GRECO-ROMAN**	
125.5	Joe Corso	198	Steve Fraser	105.5	T. J. Jones
136.5	Rich Dellagatta*	220	Harold Smith	114.5	Mark Fuller
149.5	Andre Metzger	Hvy	Bruce Baumgartner		

United States National Champions (Cont.)

1984 (Cont.)

GRECO-ROMAN (Cont.)
136.5 ......Dan Mello
149.5 ......Jim Martinez*
163 ....John Matthews

GRECO-ROMAN (Cont.)
180.5 ......Tom Press
198 ....Mike Houck
220 ....No champion

GRECO-ROMAN (Cont.)
Hvy ....No champion
Team............Adirondack Three-Style, WA

1985

FREESTYLE
105.5 ......Tim Vanni
114.5 ......Jim Martin
125.5 ......Charlie Heard
136.5 ......Darryl Burley
149.5 ......Bill Nugent*
163 ....Kenny Monday
180.5 ......Mike Sheets
198 ....Mark Schultz

FREESTYLE (Cont.)
220 ....Greg Gibson
286 ....Bruce Baumgartner
Team ....Sunkist Kids

GRECO-ROMAN
105.5 ......T. J. Jones
114.5 ......Mark Fuller
125.5 ......Eric Seward*

GRECO-ROMAN (Cont.)
136.5 ......Buddy Lee
149.5 ......Jim Martinez
163 ....David Butler
180.5 ......Chris Catallo
198 ....Mike Houck
220 ....Greg Gibson
286 ....Dennis Koslowski
Team .......U.S. Marine Corps

1986

FREESTYLE
105.5 ......Rich Salamone
114.5 ......Joe Gonzales
125.5 ......Kevin Darkus
136.5 ......John Smith
149.5 ......Andre Metzger*
163 ....Dave Schultz
180.5 ......Mark Schultz
198 ....Jim Scherr
220 ....Dan Severn

FREESTYLE (Cont.)
286 ....Bruce Baumgartner
Team ....Sunkist Kids (Div. I)
Hawkeye Wrestling
Club (Div. II)

GRECO-ROMAN
105.5 ......Eric Wetzel
114.5 ......Shawn Sheldon
125.5 ......Anthony Amado

GRECO-ROMAN (Cont.)
136.5 ......Frank Famiano
149.5 ......Jim Martinez
163 ....David Butler*
180.5 ......Darryl Gholar
198 ....Derrick Waldroup
220 ....Dennis Koslowski
286 ....Duane Koslowski
Team .......U.S. Marine Corps (Div. I)
U.S. Navy (Div. II)

1987

FREESTYLE
105.5 ......Takashi Irie
114.5 ......Mitsuru Sato
125.5 ......Barry Davis
136.5 ......Takumi Adachi
149.5 ......Andre Metzger
163 ....Dave Schultz*
180.5 ......Mark Schultz
198 ....Jim Scherr
220 ....Bill Scherr

FREESTYLE (Cont.)
286 ....Bruce Baumgartner
Team ....Sunkist Kids (Div. I)
Team Foxcatcher (Div. II)

GRECO-ROMAN
105.5 ......Eric Wetzel
114.5 ......Shawn Sheldon
125.5 ......Eric Seward
136.5 ......Frank Famiano

GRECO-ROMAN (Cont.)
149.5 ......Jim Martinez
163 ....David Butler
180.5 ......Chris Catallo
198 ....Derrick Waldroup*
220 ....Dennis Koslowski
286 ....Duane Koslowski
Team.......U.S. Marine Corp (Div. I)
U.S. Army (Div. II)

1988

FREESTYLE
105.5 ......Tim Vanni
114.5 ......Joe Gonzales
125.5 ......Kevin Darkus
136.5 ......John Smith*
149.5 ......Nate Carr
163 ....Kenny Monday
180.5 ......Dave Schultz
198 ....Melvin Douglas III
220 ....Bill Scherr

FREESTYLE (Cont.)
286 ....Bruce Baumgartner
Team ....Sunkist Kids (Div. I)
Team Foxcatcher (Div. II)

GRECO-ROMAN
105.5 ......T. J. Jones
114.5 ......Shawn Sheldon
125.5 ......Gogi Parseghian*
136.5 ......Dalen Wasmund

GRECO-ROMAN (Cont.)
149.5 ......Craig Pollard
163 ....Tony Thomas
180.5 ......Darryl Gholar
198 ....Mike Carolan
220 ....Dennis Koslowski
286 ....Duane Koslowski
Team .......U.S. Marine Corps (Div. I)
Sunkist Kids (Div. II)

1989

FREESTYLE
105.5 ......Tim Vanni
114.5 ......Zeke Jones
125.5 ......Brad Penrith
136.5 ......John Smith
149.5 ......Nate Carr
163 ....Rob Koll
180.5 ......Rico Chiapparelli
198 ....Jim Scherr*
220 ....Bill Scherr

FREESTYLE (Cont.)
286 ....Bruce Baumgartner
Team ....Sunkist Kids (Div. I)
Team Foxcatcher (Div. II)

GRECO-ROMAN
105.5 ......Lew Dorrance
114.5 ......Mark Fuller
125.5 ......Gogi Parseghian
136.5 ......Isaac Anderson

GRECO-ROMAN (Cont.)
149.5 ......Andy Seras*
163 ....David Butler
180.5 ......John Morgan
198 ....Michial Foy
220 ....Steve Lawson
286 ....Craig Pittman
Team .......U.S. Marine Corps (Div. I)
Jets USA (Div. II)

1990

FREESTYLE
105.5 ......Rob Eiter
114.5 ......Zeke Jones

FREESTYLE (Cont.)
125,5 ......Joe Melchiore
136.5 ......John Smith

FREESTYLE (Cont.)
149.5 ......Nate Carr
163 ....Rob Koll

United States National Champions (Cont.)
1990 (Cont.)

FREESTYLE (Cont.)
180.5 ......Royce Alger
198 ....Chris Campbell*
220 ....Bill Scherr
286 ....Bruce Baumgartner
Team ......Sunkist Kids (Div. I)
       Team Foxcatcher (Div. II)

GRECO-ROMAN
105.5 ......Lew Dorrance
114.5 ......Sam Henson
125.5 ......Mark Pustelnik
136.5 ......Isaac Anderson
149.5 ......Andy Seras
163 ....David Butler

GRECO-ROMAN (Cont.)
180.5 ......Derrick Waldroup
198 ....Randy Couture*
220 ....Chris Tironi
286 ....Matt Ghaffari
Team ....Jets USA (Div. I)
       California Jets (Div. II)

1991

FREESTYLE
105.5 ......Tim Vanni
114.5 ......Zeke Jones
125.5 ......Brad Penrith
136.5 ......John Smith*
149.5 ......Townsend Saunders
163 ....Kenny Monday
180.5 ......Kevin Jackson
198 ....Chris Campbell

FREESTYLE (Cont.)
220 ....Mark Coleman
286 ....Bruce Baumgartner
Team ......Sunkist Kids (Div. I)
       Jets USA (Div. II)

GRECO-ROMAN
105.5 ......Eric Wetzel
114.5 ......Shawn Sheldon
125.5 ......Frank Famiano

GRECO-ROMAN (Cont.)
136.5 ......Buddy Lee
149.5 ......Andy Seras
163 ....Gordy Morgan
180.5 ......John Morgan*
198 ....Michial Foy
220 ....Dennis Koslowski
286 ....Craig Pittman
Team ......Jets USA (Div. I)
       Sunkist Kids (Div. II)

1992

FREESTYLE
105.5 ......Rob Eiter
114.5 ......Jack Griffin
125.5 ......Kendall Cross*
136.5 ......John Fisher
149.5 ......Matt Demaray
163 ....Greg Elinsky
180.5 ......Royce Alger
198 ....Dan Chaid
220 ....Bill Scherr

FREESTYLE (Cont.)
286 ....Bruce Baumgartner
Team ......Sunkist Kids (Div. I)
       Team Foxcatcher (Div. II)

GRECO-ROMAN
105.5 ......Eric Wetzel
114.5 ......Mark Fuller
125.5 ......Dennis Hall
136.5 ......Buddy Lee*

GRECO-ROMAN (Cont.)
149.5 ......Rodney Smith
163 ....Travis West
180.5 ......John Morgan
198 ....Michial Foy
220 ....Dennis Koslowski
286 ....Matt Ghaffari
Team ......NY Athletic Club (Div. I)
       Sunkist Kids (Div. II)

1993

FREESTYLE
105.5 ......Rob Eiter
114.5 ......Zeke Jones
125.5 ......Brad Penrith
136.5 ......Tom Brands
149.5 ......Matt Demaray
163 ....Dave Schultz*
180.5 ......Kevin Jackson
198 ....Melvin Douglas
220 ....Kirk Trost

FREESTYLE (Cont.)
286 ....Bruce Baumgartner
Team ......Sunkist Kids (Div. I)
       Team Foxcatcher (Div. II)

GRECO-ROMAN
105.5 ......Eric Wetzel
114.5 ......Shawn Sheldon
125.5 ......Dennis Hall*
136.5 ......Shon Lewis

GRECO-ROMAN (Cont.)
149.5 ......Andy Seras
163 ....Gordy Morgan
180.5 ......Dan Henderson
198 ....Randy Couture
220 ....James Johnson
286 ....Matt Ghaffari
Team ......NY Athletic Club (Div. I)
       Sunkist Kids (Div. II)

1994

FREESTYLE
105.5 ......Tim Vanni
114.5 ......Zeke Jones
125.5 ......Terry Brands
136.5 ......Tom Brands
149.5 ......Matt Demaray
163 ....Dave Schultz
180.5 ......Royce Alger
198 ....Melvin Douglas
220 ....Mark Kerr

FREESTYLE (Cont.)
286 ....Bruce Baumgartner*
Team ......Sunkist Kids (Div. I)
       Team Foxcatcher (Div. II)

GRECO-ROMAN
105.5 ......Isaac Ramaswamy
114.5 ......Shawn Sheldon
125.5 ......Dennis Hall
136.5 ......Shon Lewis

GRECO-ROMAN (Cont.)
149.5 ......Andy Seras*
163 ....Gordy Morgan
180.5 ......Dan Henderson
198 ....Derrick Waldroup
220 ....James Johnson
286 ....Matt Ghaffari
Team ......Armed Forces (Div. I)
       NY Athletic Club (Div. II)

1995

FREESTYLE
105.5 ......Rob Eiter
114.5 ......Lou Rosselli
125.5 ......Kendall Cross*
136.5 ......Tom Brands
149.5 ......Matt Demaray
163 ....Dave Schultz
180.5 ......Kevin Jackson
198 ....Melvin Douglas
220 ....Kurt Angle

FREESTYLE (Cont.)
286 ....Bruce Baumgartner
Team ......Sunkist Kids (Div. I)
       Team Foxcatcher (Div. II)

GRECO-ROMAN
105.5 ......Isaac Ramaswamy
114.5 ......Shawn Sheldon
125.5 ......Dennis Hall*
136.5 ......Van Fronhofer

GRECO-ROMAN (Cont.)
149.5 ......Heath Sims
163 ....Matt Lindland
180.5 ......Marty Morgan
198 ....Michial Foy
220 ....James Johnson
286 ....Rulon Gardner
Team ......Armed Forces (Div. I)
       Sunkist Kids (Div. II)

*Outstanding wrestler

The Sports Market

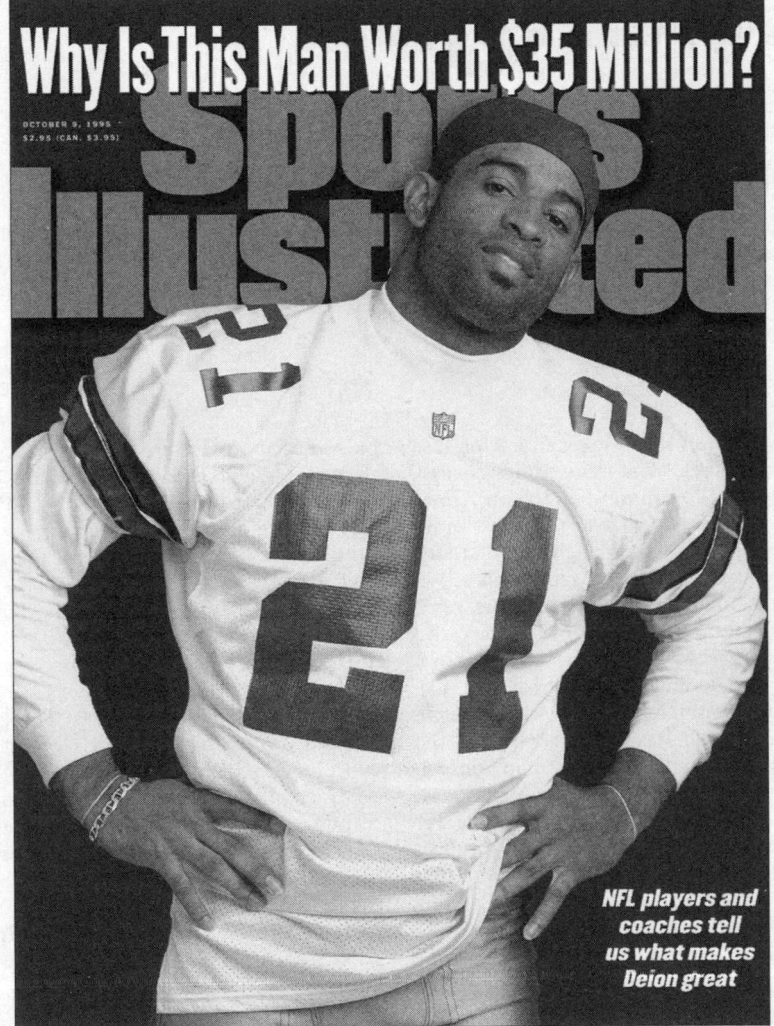

Why Is This Man Worth $35 Million?

OCTOBER 9, 1995
$2.95 (CAN. $3.95)

Sports Illustrated

NFL players and coaches tell us what makes Deion great

GEORGE LANGE

Same Changes

Despite a flurry of lockouts and lawsuits the business of sports was fundamentally unchanged

by John Steinbreder

IT WAS the French journalist Alphonse Karr who said, "The more things change, the more they remain the same," and though those words were uttered more than a century ago, they give a good idea of what went on in the sports market in 1995. A lot transpired during the year, but it seems that the core issues and headlines were not much different from those that dominated the scene in 1994.

Labor problems continued to plague Major League Baseball, and though the players and owners did get in an abbreviated season, they still weren't able to craft a new collective bargaining agreement and appeared as far apart on most issues as they were when the players first went on strike. The National Hockey League season resumed last January after a 103-day lockout, but five months later that bastion of tranquillity known as the National Basketball Association started having serious problems of its own. The owners locked out the players when they balked at approving a new labor pact, and then the players sued and threatened to decertify their union. The National Football League enjoyed a reasonably peaceful off-season, but at the end of the summer a fierce battle broke out among the owners when Jerry Jones of the Dallas Cowboys began to challenge the NFL's authority over licensing and marketing deals.

Baseball had a strange year. The players and owners bickered for most of the winter and still hadn't agreed on a new contract when it came time to start spring training. But instead of bringing in their regular players, who could have worked out while the two sides negotiated, the owners decided to field replacement squads and began playing exhibition games with ragtag units of beer league rejects, major league has-beens and minor league never-will-bes. The owners were ready to start the regular season with their replacement teams, but just

Inspired by Abbie Hoffman's sprinkling of money on the floor of the New York Stock Exchange in 1967, a trio of New Yorkers wearing T-shirts that spelled GREED across their chests dashed onto the field at Shea Stadium one night and tossed 150 $1 bills around the infield.

The stellar play of teams such as the Cleveland Indians and the Boston Red Sox made it a little easier for some fans to forgive and forget as the season progressed, but bad feelings toward the game lingered, and people stayed away from the ballparks in droves. As of mid-August, for example, average attendance for the

before the first pitch was to be thrown, U.S. District Court Judge Sonia Sotomayor granted a National Labor Relations Board request for a preliminary injunction against the owners for unilaterally rescinding several provisions from the old labor pact and ordered them restored until a new deal was cut. Rather than appealing the decision or running the legal risk of locking out players who had said they would report to camp if the judge ruled in their favor, the owners agreed to invite their regulars to a shortened spring training. And even though the two sides still didn't have a new collective bargaining agreement, the 1995 season was on.

The 144-game schedule began on April 26, and not surprisingly, neither the players nor the owners were welcomed back with open arms. A plane flew over Riverfront Stadium in Cincinnati during the first game pulling a a banner reading: OWNERS & PLAYERS: TO HELL WITH ALL OF YOU.

majors was down 19% from the previous year. Of baseball's 28 teams, only two recorded increases, while the rest posted drop-offs that in all but a couple of cases were greater than 10% and in some instances rose above 30%. Sales of licensed merchandise slumped, and the collectibles market fell off. In addition, ABC and NBC announced last July that due to financial losses and the generally sorry state of the game, they would abandon the Baseball Network partnership they had formed with team owners only two years before and forsake any involvement in the sport after the 1995 season.

Given baseball's rich heritage, it's sad to think of both the fans and the television networks turning their backs on what once truly was the national pastime. But until a new contract is signed and some semblance of trust restored, baseball will be a sport that evokes as much disdain among its fans as it does affection. And it will continue to suffer as a result.

KEVIN LARKIN/AP

Bob Goodenow led the players back to the ice, where they were warmly welcomed.

Hockey had a much easier time recovering from its labor problems. As soon as NHL players and owners ended the three-month lockout last winter and agreed to a new, six-year deal, fans began storming the ticket windows. More than 12,000 people crammed into the Spectrum in Philadelphia a few days after the settlement was announced to watch the Flyers scrimmage; and the New York Islanders, who have been struggling in the standings and at the box office the past several years, sold 15,000 tickets in one day, about five times what they expected to move. The Tampa Bay Lightning entertained crowds of more than 20,000 for their first two home games, and the Hartford Whalers reported more media and fan interest in their team than they have seen in five years.

Fortunately for the league, that enthusiasm continued throughout the year. Though total attendance numbers were down as a result of the shortened season, the average attendance per game was up. In addition, more people watched Games 1 and 4 of the Stanley Cup finals than had ever seen an NHL contest on TV before.

Why did hockey rebound so well? For one thing, labor disputes have not been a recurring problem for the sport, and its fans didn't feel nearly as betrayed or frustrated as their baseball brethren. Also, the league's labor problems happened to coincide with hockey's wild surge in popularity. Fueled in large part by a greater appreciation of the sport, better marketing by the league and a growing participation among weekend athletes not only in ice hockey but also in street versions of the game, the NHL has scarcely been more popular.

Largely as a result of those factors, the NHL has been able to attract the attention of corporate heavyweights who now see it as a terrific promotional vehicle for their products. Last year Anheuser-Busch decided to market its Bud Ice brand primarily through the league. And then Nike got into the game. In addition to signing a marketing agreement with the NHL, the Oregon-based footwear giant developed a street hockey shoe and cosponsored a national street hockey program that the league created in an effort to boost grass-roots interest in the game. Nike also demonstrated its faith in hockey's future by buying Canstar Sports, which makes Bauer skates and Cooper protective gear, and adding Red Wing star forward Sergei Federov to its stable of national spokesmen.

Basketball continues to prosper though it came perilously close this past year to suffering through the first work stoppage in its history. The problems began in June when NBA commissioner David Stern negotiated a new labor pact with Simon Gourdine, the head of the players' union. An agreement was announced just as the Houston Rockets were wrapping up their second NBA title, and it seemed that the NBA, which had played the previous season without a contract between its players and the owners, would once again avoid the sorts of labor troubles that have marred the other major sports leagues.

DAVID E. KLUTHO

would effectively limit what veterans could be paid when re-signing with their teams. A number of players, including Michael Jordan and Patrick Ewing, were so incensed at the deal that they called for decertification of the union. They quickly gathered more than the required number of signatures to force a vote on the matter and then began a vigorous campaign to take down the union. Faced with the threat of decertification, Gourdine and Stern, who had imposed a lockout on all NBA players when they chose not to ratify the first deal, went back to the table and worked out a new contract, this one without the luxury tax. That seemed to mollify many of the players, but the league and the union had to wait for the decertification vote before either side could act on the new deal.

But then the players got a look at what their union head had negotiated. Many thought that Gourdine, who had once worked for the NBA and served for a time as deputy commissioner, had sold out to the owners. Of particular concern was the inclusion of a luxury tax that

The vote was held on two separate days at the end of the summer, and in the end the union prevailed, with 226 players electing to keep it intact and 134 moving to decertify. With that out of the way, the player representatives from all NBA

Jones pushed the envelope of NFL regulations with his marketing deals.

teams got together and approved the revised contract by a vote of 25–2. Shortly afterward the owners approved the pact themselves, and Stern lifted the lockout.

Fortunately for the NBA, its 1995–96 season started on time. But while it narrowly averted a long and ugly labor battle, the league did not emerge completely unscathed. Divisions were sown among players, and the league's carefully nurtured image of order and prosperity has been tainted by the sight of extraordinarily wealthy athletes, owners and agents haggling over hundreds of millions of dollars in revenues.

A similar battle over money broke out in the NFL last summer, pitting Dallas

Cowboy owner Jerry Jones against the league. At issue was the concept of shared revenues. Traditionally the profits earned from the sale of NFL licensed merchandise are divided equally among all franchises. But that had begun to irk Jones, who took in the same $3 million that every other team got last year even though Cowboy-oriented apparel accounted for 24% of all sales. So in an effort to further capitalize on his team's logo, he began to do some marketing of his own. First he signed a 10-year, $25 million contract with Pepsi, making it the official soft drink of Texas Stadium. Then Jones signed a $2.5 million deal with Nike to make apparel for all Cowboy sideline personnel and help develop a theme park at the stadium. The problem was, many NFL officials and team

L: DAVID E. KLUTHO, R: KATHY WILLENS/AP

NBC's Dick Ebersol (right) and Sydney rep Gary Pemberton inked a record deal.

owners felt that those arrangements not only threatened a longstanding business philosophy that had brought great riches to all teams but also undermined lucrative marketing deals the NFL had already signed with Coca-Cola and Reebok, who just happen to be Pepsi's and Nike's biggest competitors. So when Jones was about to announce another marketing agreement, this time with American Express, the NFL filed a $300 million suit against the Cowboys' owner, seeking damages for his "ambush" contracts and demanding that he not sign any others.

A number of owners have spoken out against Jones's moves, saying that they will weaken the collective strength of the NFL. But some privately support his actions, believing it is only right that Jones, or any other owner, should be able to garner whatever outside revenues he can. What happens next is anybody's guess, but it seems likely that the suit will be settled out of court and a compromise reached, probably one that preserves the revenue-sharing ideals of the NFL but

also gives teams more of a right to make some extra money on the side.

Things on the Olympic front were much less contentious. As Atlanta continued to prepare itself for the 1996 Summer Games, the International Olympic Committee awarded the 2002 Winter Games to Salt Lake City. And shortly afterward NBC agreed to pay a record $1.27 billion for the right to televise the Summer Olympics from Sydney, Australia, in 2000 and the Salt Lake Games two years later.

That's just the way it seems to be with sports these days. Labor disputes shut down seasons, players complain about being underpaid, and owners cry poverty. But vast amounts of money keep flowing in, and in spite of all its perceived problems, the world of sports keeps getting stronger and stronger financially. Alphonse Karr would have appreciated the irony. The more things change, the more they remain the same.

Major League Baseball

Address: 350 Park Avenue
New York, NY 10022
Telephone: (212) 339-7800
Acting Commissioner and Chairman of the Executive
Council: Bud Selig
Executive Director: Richard Levin

Major League Baseball Players Association

Address: 12 East 49th Street 24th Floor
New York, NY 10017
Telephone: (212) 826-0808
Executive Director: Donald Fehr
Director of Marketing: Judy Heeter

American League

American League Office

Address: 350 Park Avenue
New York, NY 10022
Telephone: (212) 339-7600
President: Dr. Gene Budig
VP of Media Affairs and Administration: Phyllis
Merhige

Baltimore Orioles

Address: Oriole Park at Camden Yards
333 W Camden Street
Baltimore, MD 21201
Telephone: (410) 685-9800
Stadium (Capacity): Camden Yards (48,262)
Managing Partner/Owner: Peter G. Angelos
Vice Chairmen: Thomas Clancy and Joseph Foss
Manager: Phil Regan
Director of Public Relations: John Maroon

Boston Red Sox

Address: 4 Yawkey Way
Fenway Park
Boston, MA 02215
Telephone: (617) 267-9440
Stadium (Capacity): Fenway Park (33,871)
Majority Owner/Chairman of the Board: John Harrington
Executive VP of Baseball Operations: Lou Gorman
Executive VP and GM: Daniel F. Duquette
Manager: Kevin Kennedy
Vice President, Public Relations: Dick Bresciani

California Angels

Address: P.O. Box 2000
Anaheim Stadium
Anaheim, CA 92803
Telephone: (714) 937-7200 or (213) 625-1123
Stadium (Capacity): Anaheim Stadium (64,573)
Chairman of the Board: Gene Autry
General Manager: Bill Bavasi
Manager: Marcel Lachemann
Assistant VP of Media Relations: John Sevano

Chicago White Sox

Address: Comiskey Park
Chicago, IL 60616
Telephone: (312) 924-1000
Stadium (Capacity): Comiskey Park (44,321)
Chairman: Jerry Reinsdorf
General Manager: Ron Schueler
Manager: Terry Bevington
Director of Publc Relations: Doug Abel

Cleveland Indians

Address: Jacobs Field
2401 Ontario Street
Cleveland, OH 44115-4003
Telephone: (216) 861-1200
Stadium (Capacity): Jacobs Field (74,483)
Chairman of the Board and CEO: Richard Jacobs
Executive VP and General Manager: John Hart
Manager: Mike Hargrove
Vice President, Public Relations: Bob DiBiasio

Detroit Tigers

Address: 2121 Trumbull Ave.
Tiger Stadium
Detroit, MI 48216
Telephone: (313) 962-4000
Stadium (Capacity): Tiger Stadium (52,416)
Owner: Mike Ilitch
CEO and President: John McHale
Manager: Sparky Anderson
Vice President, Media and Public Relations: Dan
Ewald

Kansas City Royals

Address: P.O. Box 419969
Kansas City, MO 64141
Telephone: (816) 921-2200
Stadium (Capacity): Kauffman Stadium (40,625)
Chairman of the Board and CEO: David D. Glass
General Manager: Herk Robinson
Manager: Bob Boone
Vice President, Public Relations: Dean Vogelaar

Milwaukee Brewers

Address: P.O. Box 3099
Milwaukee, WI 53201-3099
Telephone: (414) 933-4114
Stadium (Capacity): Milwaukee County Stadium
(53,192)
President and Chief Executive Officer: Bud Selig
Senior VP, Baseball Operations: Sal Bando
Manager: Phil Garner
Media Relations: Jon Greenberg

Minnesota Twins

Address: 501 Chicago Avenue South
Hubert H. Humphrey Metrodome
Minneapolis, MN 55415
Telephone: (612) 375-1366
Stadium (Capacity): Hubert H. Humphrey Metrodome
(56,144)
Owner: Carl Pohlad
General Manager: Terry Ryan
Manager: Tom Kelly
Director of Media Relations: Rob Antony

New York Yankees

Address: Yankee Stadium
Bronx, NY 10451
Telephone: (718) 293-4300
Stadium (Capacity): Yankee Stadium (57,545)
Principal Owner: George Steinbrenner
VP and Executive Consul: David Sussman
General Manager: Gene Michael
Manager: Buck Showalter
Director of Media Relations and Publicity: Rob
Butcher

American League *(Cont.)*

Oakland Athletics
Address: Oakland-Alameda County Coliseum
                Oakland, CA 94621
Telephone: (510) 638-4900
Stadium (Capacity): Oakland-Alameda County
  Coliseum (46,990)
Owner/Managing General Partner: Walter Haas
President and General Manager: Sandy Alderson
Manager: Tony LaRussa
Director of Baseball Information: Jay Alves

Seattle Mariners
Address: P.O. Box 4100
                Seattle, WA 98104
Telephone: (206) 628-3555
Stadium (Capacity): The Kingdome (59,166)
Chairman: John Ellis
General Manager: Woody Woodward
Manager: Lou Piniella
Director of Public Relations: Dave Aust

Texas Rangers
Address: P.O. Box 90111
                Arlington, TX 76004
Telephone: (817) 273-5222
Stadium (Capacity): The Ballpark in Arlington (49,178)
General Partners: Rusty Rose and Thomas Schieffer
General Manager: Doug Melvin
Manager: Johnny Oates
Vice President, Public Relations: John Blake

Toronto Blue Jays
Address: SkyDome
                1 Blue Jays Way, Suite 3200
                Toronto, Ontario, Canada M5V 1J1
Telephone: (416) 341-1000
Stadium (Capacity): SkyDome (50,516)
Chairman of the Board: Peter N.T. Widdrington
President and CEO: Paul Beeston
Executive VP of Baseball Operations: Pat Gillick
Manager: Cito Gaston
Director of Public Relations: Howard Starkman

National League

National League Office
Address: 350 Park Avenue
                New York, NY 10022
Telephone: (212) 339-7700
President: Leonard Coleman
Director of Public Relations: Ricky Clemons

Atlanta Braves
Address: P.O. Box 4064
                Atlanta, GA 30302
Telephone: (404) 522-7630
Stadium (Capacity): Atlanta-Fulton County Stadium
  (52,007)
Owner: Ted Turner
General Manager: John Schuerholz
Manager: Bobby Cox
Director of Public Relations: Jim Schultz

Chicago Cubs
Address: Wrigley Field
                1060 West Addison
                Chicago, IL 60613
Telephone: (312) 404-2827
Stadium (Capacity): Wrigley Field (38,765)
President and CEO: Andrew B. MacPhail
Executive VP of Business Operations: Mark McGuire
General Manager: Ed Lynch
Manager: Jim Riggleman
Director of Media Relations: Sharon Panozzo

Cincinnati Reds
Address: 100 Riverfront Stadium
                Cincinnati, OH 45202
Telephone: (513) 421-4510
Stadium (Capacity): Riverfront Stadium (52,952)
General Partner: Marge Schott
General Manager: James G. Bowden
Manager: Davey Johnson
Publicity Director: Mike Ringering

Colorado Rockies
Address: 2001 Blake Street
                Denver, CO 00205
Telephone: (303) 292-0200
Stadium (Capacity): Coors Field (50,249)
President: Jerry McMorris
Executive VP of Baseball Operations: Keli McGregor
Manager: Don Baylor
Director of Public Relations: Mike Swanson

Florida Marlins
Address: 2267 N.W. 199th Street
                Miami, FL 33056
Telephone: (305) 626-7400
Stadium (Capacity): Joe Robbie Stadium (46,000)
Owner: H. Wayne Huizenga
Vice President and General Manager: David
  Dombrowski
Manager: Rene Lachemann
Director of Media Relations: Chuck Pool

Houston Astros
Address: P.O. Box 288
                Houston, TX 77001
Telephone: (713) 799-9500
Stadium (Capacity): Astrodome (54,313)
Chairman: Drayton McLane Jr.
General Manager: Bob Watson
Manager: Terry Collins
Director of Media Relations: Rob Matwick

Los Angeles Dodgers
Address: 1000 Elysian Park Avenue
                Los Angeles, CA 90012-1199
Telephone: (213) 224-1500
Stadium (Capacity): Dodger Stadium (56,000)
President: Peter O'Malley
Executive Vice President: Fred Claire
Manager: Tom Lasorda
Director of Publicity: Jay Lucas

Montreal Expos
Address: P.O. Box 500
                Station M
                Montreal
                Quebec, Canada H1V 3P2
Telephone: (514) 253-3434
Stadium (Capacity): Olympic Stadium (46,500)
President: Claude Brochu
Vice President and General Manager: Kevin Malone
Manager: Felipe Alou
Director, Media Relations: Pete Loyello

National League (Cont.)

New York Mets
Address: Shea Stadium
             Flushing, NY 11368
Telephone: (718) 507-6387
Stadium (Capacity): Shea Stadium (55,601)
Chairman: Nelson Doubleday
President and CEO: Fred Wilpon
Executive VP of Baseball Operations: Joe McIlvaine
Manager: Dallas Green
Director of Media Relations: Jay Horwitz

Philadelphia Phillies
Address: P.O. Box 7575
             Philadelphia, PA 19101-7575
Telephone: (215) 463-6000
Stadium (Capacity): Veterans Stadium (62,238)
President: Bill Giles
General Manager: Lee Thomas
Manager: Jim Fregosi
Vice President, Public Relations: Larry Shenk

Pittsburgh Pirates
Address: P.O. Box 7000
             Pittsburgh, PA 15212
Telephone: (412) 323-5000
Stadium (Capacity): Three Rivers Stadium (58,729)
President and CEO: Mark Sauer
General Manager: Cam Bonifay
Manager: Jim Leyland
Director of Media Relations: Jim Trdinich

St. Louis Cardinals
Address: 250 Stadium Plaza
             Busch Stadium
             St. Louis, MO 63102
Telephone: (314) 421-3060
Stadium (Capacity): Busch Stadium (57,001)
Chairman of the Board: August A. Busch III
General Manager: Walt Jocketty
Manager: Mike Jorgensen
Director of Public Relations: Brian Bartow

San Diego Padres
Address: P.O. Box 2000
             San Diego, CA 92112
Telephone: (619) 283-4494
Stadium (Capacity): San Diego/Jack Murphy Stadium
(60,000)
Chairman: John Moores
General Manager: TBA
Manager: Bruce Botchy
Director of Media Relations: Dennis Smythe

San Francisco Giants
Address: Candlestick Park
             San Francisco, CA 94124
Telephone: (415) 468-3700
Stadium (Capacity): Candlestick Park (63,000)
Chairman: Peter Magowan
General Manager: Bob Quinn
Manager: Dusty Baker
Director of Public Relations: Bob Rose

Pro Football Directory

National Football League
Address: 410 Park Avenue
             New York, New York 10022
Telephone: (212) 758-1500
Commissioner: Paul Tagliabue
Director of Communications: Greg Aiello

National Football League Players Association
Address: 2021 L Street, N.W.
             Washington, D.C. 20036
Telephone: (202) 463-2200
Executive Director: Gene Upshaw
Director, Public Relations: Frank Woschitz

National Conference

Arizona Cardinals
Address: P.O. Box 888
             Phoenix, AZ 85001
Telephone: (602) 379-0101
Stadium (Capacity): Sun Devil Stadium (73,377)
President and Owner: Bill Bidwill
Coach and General Manager: Buddy Ryan
Vice President: Larry Wilson
Director of Public Relations: Paul Jensen

Atlanta Falcons
Address: 1 Falcon Place
             Suwanee, GA 30174
Telephone: (404) 945-1111
Stadium (Capacity): Georgia Dome (71,228)
Chairman of the Board: Rankin M. Smith Sr.
President: Taylor W. Smith
Director of Player Personnel: Ken Herock
Coach: June Jones
Publicity Director: Charlie Taylor

Carolina Panthers
Address: 227 West Trade Street, Suite 1600
             Charlotte, NC 28202
Telephone: (803) 372-5116
Stadium (Capacity): Clemson Memorial Stadium
(76, 055)
Founder and Owner: Jerry Richardson
President: Mike McCormack
General Manager: Bill Polian
Coach: Dom Capers
Director of Communications: Charlie Dayton

Chicago Bears
Address: 250 N. Washington Road
             Lake Forest, IL 60045
Telephone: (708) 295-6600
Stadium (Capacity): Soldier Field (66,946)
President: Michael McCaskey
Coach: Dave Wannstedt
Director of Public Relations: Bryan Harlan

National Conference *(Cont.)*

Dallas Cowboys
Address: One Cowboys Parkway
              Irving, TX 75063
Telephone: (214) 556-9900
Stadium (Capacity): Texas Stadium (65,024)
Owner, President, and General Manager: Jerry Jones
Coach: Barry Switzer
Public Relations Director: Rich Dalrymple

Detroit Lions
Address: 1200 Featherstone Road
              Pontiac, MI 48342
Telephone: (810) 335-4131
Stadium (Capacity): Pontiac Silverdome (80,500)
President and Owner: William Clay Ford
Executive Vice President: Chuck Schmidt
Coach: Wayne Fontes
Media Relations Director: Mike Murray

Green Bay Packers
Address: 1265 Lombardi Avenue
              Green Bay, WI 54304
Telephone: (414) 496-5700
Stadium (Capacity): Lambeau Field (60,790)
President: Bob Harlan
General Manager: Ron Wolf
Coach: Mike Holmgren
Public Relations Director: Lee Remmel

Minnesota Vikings
Address: 9520 Viking Drive
              Eden Prairie, MN 55344
Telephone: (612) 828-6500
Stadium (Capacity): HHH Metrodome (63,000)
President: Roger L. Headrick
VP of Administrative and Team Operations: Jeff Diamond
Coach: Dennis Green
Public Relations Director: David Pelletier

New Orleans Saints
Address: 6928 Saints Drive
              Metairie, LA 70003
Telephone: (504) 733-0255
Stadium (Capacity): Louisiana Superdome (69,065)
Owner: Tom Benson
VP of Football Operations: Bill Kuharich
Executive VP of Administration: Jim Miller
VP/Head Coach: Jim Mora
Director of Media Relations: Rusty Kasmiersky

New York Giants
Address: Giants Stadium
              East Rutherford, NJ 07073
Telephone: (201) 935-8111
Stadium (Capacity): Giants Stadium (77,311)
President and co-CEO: Wellington T. Mara
Chairman and co-CEO: Preston Robert Tisch
General Manager: George Young
Coach: Dan Reeves
Director of Public Relations: Pat Hanlon

Philadelphia Eagles
Address: Veterans Stadium
              Broad Street and Pattison Avenue
              Philadelphia, PA 19148
Telephone: (215) 463-2500
Stadium (Capacity): Veterans Stadium (65,178)
Owner: Jeffrey Lurie
President and COO: TBA
Coach: Ray Rhodes
Director of Public Relations: Ron Howard

St. Louis Rams
Address: Matthews Dickey Building
              4245 North Kings Highway
              St. Louis, MO 63115
Telephone: (314) 877-3700
Stadium (Capacity): Busch Stadium (57,191);
   TWA Dome (65,000)
Owner and Chairman: Georgia Frontiere
President: John Shaw
Coach: Rich Brooks
Director of Public Relations: Rick Smith

San Francisco 49ers
Address: 4949 Centennial Boulevard
              Santa Clara, CA 95054
Telephone: (408) 562-4949
Stadium (Capacity): Candlestick Park (66,455)
Owner: Edward J. DeBartolo Jr.
General Manager: Dwight Clark
Coach: George Seifert
Public Relations Director: Rodney Knox

Tampa Bay Buccaneers
Address: One Buccaneer Place
              Tampa, FL 33607
Telephone: (813) 870-2700
Stadium (Capacity): Tampa Stadium (74,321)
Owner: Malcolm Glazer
Director of Football Operations and Coach: Sam
   Wyche
Director of Public Relations: Chip Namias

Washington Redskins
Address: 21300 Redskin Park Drive
              Ashburn, VA 22011
Telephone: (703) 478-8900
Stadium (Capacity): RFK Memorial Stadium (55,454)
Owner: Jack Kent Cooke
General Manager: Charley Casserly
Coach: Norv Turner
Director of Communications: Rick Vaughn

American Conference

Buffalo Bills
Address: One Bills Drive
              Orchard Park, NY 14127
Telephone: (716) 648-1800
Stadium (Capacity): Rich Stadium (80,024)
President: Ralph C. Wilson Jr.
Executive VP/General Manager: John Butler
Coach: Marv Levy
Director of Media Relations: Scott Berchtold

Cincinnati Bengals
Address: 200 Riverfront Stadium
              Cincinnati, OH 45202
Telephone: (513) 621-3550
Stadium (Capacity): Riverfront Stadium (60,389)
President and General Manager: Mike Brown
Vice President: John Sawyer
Coach: Dave Shula
Director of Public Relations: Jack Brennan

American Conference *(Cont.)*

Cleveland Browns
Address: 80 First Avenue
Berea, OH 44017
Telephone: (216) 891-5000
Stadium (Capacity): Cleveland Stadium (78,512)
President: Art Modell
Coach: Bill Belichick
VP and Director of Public Relations: Kevin Byrne

Denver Broncos
Address: 13655 Broncos Parkway
Englewood, CO 80112
Telephone: (303) 649-9000
Stadium (Capacity): Mile High Stadium (76,273)
President/CEO: Pat Bowlen
General Manager: John Beake
Coach: Mike Shanahan
Director of Media Relations: Jim Saccomano

Houston Oilers
Address: 6910 Fannin Street
Houston, TX 77030
Telephone: (713) 797-9111
Stadium (Capacity): Astrodome (59,969)
President: K. S. (Bud) Adams Jr.
General Manager: Floyd Reese
Coach: Jeff Fisher
Director of Media Relations: Dave Pearson

Indianapolis Colts
Address: P.O. Box 535000
Indianapolis, IN 46253
Telephone: (317) 297-2658
Stadium (Capacity): RCA Dome (60,129)
Owner: Robert Irsay
VP and General Manager: Jim Irsay
Coach: Ted Marchibroda
Public Relations Director: Craig Kelley

Jacksonville Jaguars
Address: One Stadium Place
Jacksonville, FL 32202
Telephone: (904) 633-6000
Stadium (Capacity): Jacksonville Municipal Stadium
(93,000)
Owner: J. Wayne Weaver
President and COO: David Seldin
Coach: Tom Coughlin
Executive Director of Communications: Dan Edwards

Kansas City Chiefs
Address: One Arrowhead Drive
Kansas City, MO 64129
Telephone: (816) 924-9300
Stadium (Capacity): Arrowhead Stadium (79,101)
Founder: Lamar Hunt
President and General Manager: Carl Peterson
Coach: Marty Schottenheimer
Public Relations Director: Bob Moore

Miami Dolphins
Address: Joe Robbie Stadium
7500 S.W. 30th Street
Davie, FL 33314
Telephone: (305) 452-7000
Stadium (Capacity): Joe Robbie Stadium (74,916)
Chairman of the Board/Owner: H. Wayne Huizenga
Executive VP/General Manager: Eddie J. Jones
Coach: Don Shula
Media Relations Director: Harvey Greene

New England Patriots
Address: Foxboro Stadium
60 Washington St.
Foxboro, MA 02035
Telephone: (508) 543-8200
Stadium (Capacity): Foxboro Stadium (60,292)
President and CEO: Robert K. Kraft
VP Owners Representative: Jonathan Kraft
VP Business Operations: Andy Wasynczuk
Coach: Bill Parcells
Dir. of Public and Community Relations: Donald Lowery

New York Jets
Address: 1000 Fulton Avenue
Hempstead, NY 11550
Telephone: (516) 538-6600
Stadium (Capacity): Giants Stadium (77,716)
Chairman of the Board: Leon Hess
Director of Player Personnel: Dick Haley
Coach: Rich Kotite
Director of Public Relations: Frank Ramos

Oakland Raiders
Address: 332 Center Street
El Segundo, CA 90245
Telephone: (310) 322-3451
Stadium (Capacity): Oakland-Alameda County
Coliseum (54,444)
President of the General Partner: Al Davis
Coach: Mike White
Executive Assistant: Al LoCasale

Pittsburgh Steelers
Address: Three Rivers Stadium
300 Stadium Circle
Pittsburgh, PA 15212
Telephone: (412) 323-1200
Stadium (Capacity): Three Rivers Stadium (59,600)
President: Dan Rooney
Director of Football Operations: Tom Donahoe
Coach: Bill Cowher
Media Relations Coordinator: Rob Boulware

San Diego Chargers
Address: San Diego Jack Murphy Stadium
P.O. Box 609609
San Diego, CA 92160
Telephone: (619) 280-2111
Stadium (Capacity): San Diego Jack Murphy Stadium
(61,863)
Chairman of the Board/President: Alex G. Spanos
General Manager: Bobby Beathard
Coach: Bobby Ross
Director of Public Relations: Bill Johnston

Seattle Seahawks
Address: 11220 N.E. 53rd Street
Kirkland, WA 98033
Telephone: (206) 827-9777
Stadium (Capacity): The Kingdome (66,400)
Owner: Ken Behring
President: David Behring
GM: Tom Flores
Coach: Dennis Erickson
VP of Administration and Communications: Gary Wright
Director of Public Relations: Dave Neubert

Pro Football Directory *(Cont.)*

Other Leagues

Canadian Football League
Address: 110 Eglinton Avenue West, 5th floor
             Toronto, Ontario M4R 1A3, Canada
Telephone: (416) 322-9650
Commissioner: Larry Smith
Communications Director: Michael Murray

World League of American Football
Address: 410 Park Avenue
             New York, NY 10022
Telephone: (212) 758-1500
President: Oliver Luck (London)
Chief Operating Officer: Dick Regan (London)
Director of Communications: Pete Abitante

Pro Basketball Directory

National Basketball Association
Address: 645 Fifth Avenue
             New York, NY 10022
Telephone: (212) 826-7000
Commissioner: David Stern
Deputy Commissioner: Russell Granik
Group VP and GM, Communications Group: Brian
  McIntyre

National Basketball Association Players Association
Address: 1775 Broadway
             Suite 2401
             New York, NY 10019
Telephone: (212) 333-7510
Executive Director: Simon Gourdine

Atlanta Hawks
Address: One CNN Center, South Tower
             Suite 405
             Atlanta, GA 30303
Telephone: (404) 827-3800
Arena (Capacity): The Omni (16,378)
Owner: Ted Turner
President: Stan Kasten
General Manager: Pete Babcock
Coach: Lenny Wilkens
Director of Media Relations: Arthur Triche

Boston Celtics
Address: 151 Merrimac Street
             Boston, MA 02114
Telephone: (617) 523-6050
Arena (Capacity): FleetCenter (18,600)
Owner and Chairman of the Board: Paul Gaston
President: Arnold (Red) Auerbach
Executive VP & General Manager: Jan Volk
Coach: M. L. Carr
Director of Public Relations: R. Jeffrey Twiss

Charlotte Hornets
Address: 100 Hive Drive
             Charlotte, NC 28217
Telephone: (704) 357-0252
Arena (Capacity): Charlotte Coliseum (24,042)
Owner: George Shinn
President: Spencer Stolpen
Coach: Allan Bristow
Director of Media Relations: Harold Kaufman

Chicago Bulls
Address: 1901 W. Madison
             Chicago, IL 60612
Telephone: (312) 455-4000
Arena (Capacity): United Center (21,711)
Chairman: Jerry Reinsdorf
General Manager: Jerry Krause
Coach: Phil Jackson
Director of Media Services: Tim Hallam

Cleveland Cavaliers
Address: One Center Court
             Cleveland, OH 44115
Telephone: (216) 420-2262
Arena (Capacity): Gund Arena (20,562)
Chairman of the Board: Gordon Gund
President/COO, Team Division: Wayne Embry
Coach: Mike Fratello
Director of Public Relations: Bob Zink

Dallas Mavericks
Address: Reunion Arena
             777 Sports Street
             Dallas, TX 75207
Telephone: (214) 748-1808
Arena (Capacity): Reunion Arena (17,502)
Owner and Chairman of the Board: Donald Carter
President and General Manager: Norm Sonju
Coach: Dick Motta
Director of Media Services: Kevin Sullivan

Denver Nuggets
Address: McNichols Sports Arena
             1635 Clay Street
             Denver, CO 80204
Telephone: (303) 893-6700
Arena (Capacity): McNichols Sports Arena (17,171)
Owners: Comsat Entertainment Group
General Manager and Coach: Bernie Bickerstaff
Media Relations Director: Tommy Sheppard

Detroit Pistons
Address: The Palace of Auburn Hills
             Two Championship Drive
             Auburn Hills, MI 48326
Telephone: (810) 377-0100
Arena (Capacity): The Palace of Auburn Hills
  (21,454)
Owner: William M. Davidson
VP of Player Personnel: Rick Sund
Coach: Doug Collins
VP, Public Relations: Matt Dobek

Golden State Warriors
Address: 7000 Coliseum Way
             Oakland Coliseum Arena
             Oakland, CA 94621
Telephone: (510) 638-6300
Arena (Capacity): Oakland Coliseum Arena (15,025)
Owner: Christopher Cohan
Chairman: James F. Fitzgerald
General Manager: Dave Twardzik
Coach: Rick Adelman
Director of Communications: Julie Marvel

Houston Rockets
Address: The Summit
Ten Greenway Plaza
Houston, TX 77046
Telephone: (713) 627-3865
Arena (Capacity): The Summit (16,611)
Owner: Leslie Alexander
Executive Vice-President: John Thomas
General Manager: Bob Weinhauer
Coach: Rudy Tomjanovich
Director of Media Information: Robert Falkoff

Indiana Pacers
Address: 300 E. Market Street
Indianapolis, IN 46204
Telephone: (317) 263-2100
Arena (Capacity): Market Square Arena (16,530)
Owners: Melvin Simon and Herbert Simon
President: Donnie Walsh
Coach: Larry Brown
Media Relations Director: David Benner

Los Angeles Clippers
Address: L.A. Memorial Sports Arena
3939 S. Figueroa Street
Los Angeles, CA 90037
Telephone: (213) 748-8000
Arena (Capacity): L.A. Memorial Sports Arena (16,021)
Owner: Donald T. Sterling
VP of Basketball Operations: Elgin Baylor
Coach: Bill Fitch
VP of Communications: Joe Safety

Los Angeles Lakers
Address: Great Western Forum
3900 West Manchester Boulevard
Inglewood, CA 90306
Telephone: (310) 419-3100
Arena (Capacity): The Great Western Forum (17,505)
Owner: Dr. Jerry Buss
General Manager: Jerry West
Coach: Del Harris
Director of Public Relations: John Black

Miami Heat
Address: Sun Trust International Center
One S.E. 3rd Ave., Suite 2300
Miami, FL 33131
Telephone: (305) 577-4328
Arena (Capacity): Miami Arena (15,200)
Managing Partner: Mickey Arison
Executive VP/Business Operations: Pauline Winick
Executive VP/Basketball Operations: Dave Wohl
President and Coach: Pat Riley
Director of Public Relations: Wayne Witt

Milwaukee Bucks
Address: The Bradley Center
1001 N. Fourth Street
Milwaukee, WI 53203
Telephone: (414) 227-0500
Arena (Capacity): The Bradley Center (18,633)
Owner: Herb Kohl
Coach and VP of Bask. Operations: Mike Dunleavy
Public Relations Director: Bill King II

Minnesota Timberwolves
Address: 600 First Avenue North
Minneapolis, MN 55403
Telephone: (612) 673-1602
Arena (Capacity): Target Center (19,006)
Owner: Glen Taylor
VP of Basketball Operations: Kevin McHale
Coach: Bill Blair
Manager of PR/Communications: Kent Wipf

New Jersey Nets
Address: 405 Murray Hill Parkway
East Rutherford, NJ 07073
Telephone: (201) 935-8888
Arena (Capacity): Meadowlands Arena (20,029)
Chairman/CEO: Alan L. Aufzien
Vice President of Basketball Operations: Willis Reed
Coach: Butch Beard
Director of Public Relations: John Mertz

New York Knickerbockers
Address: Madison Square Garden
Two Pennsylvania Plaza
New York, NY 10121
Telephone: (212) 465-6499
Arena (Capacity): Madison Square Garden (19,763)
Owner: ITT/Sheraton and Cablevision
President: David Checketts
General Manager: Ernie Grunfeld
Coach: Don Nelson
Director of Public Relations: Josh Rosenfeld

Orlando Magic
Address: P.O. Box 76
Orlando, FL 32802
Telephone: (407) 649-3200
Arena (Capacity): Orlando Arena (17,248)
Owner: Rich DeVos
General Manager: Pat Williams
Coach: Brian Hill
Director of Publicity/Media Relations: Alex Martins

Philadelphia 76ers
Address: Veterans Stadium
P.O. Box 25040
Broad Street and Pattison Avenue
Philadelphia, PA 19147
Telephone: (215) 339-7600
Arena (Capacity): CoreStates Spectrum (18,168)
Owner and President: Harold Katz
General Manager and Coach: John Lucas
Public Relations Director: Joe Favorito

Phoenix Suns
Address: P.O. Box 1369
Phoenix, AZ 85001
Telephone: (602) 379-7867
Arena (Capacity): America West Arena (19,023)
Owner: Jerry Colangelo
Coach: Paul Westphal
Media Relations Director: Julie Fie

Portland Trail Blazers
Address: One Center Court
Suite 200
Portland, OR 97227
Telephone: (503) 234-9291
Arena (Capacity): Rose Garden Arena (21,500)
Chairman of the Board: Paul Allen
President and GM of Blazers Basketball, Inc.: Bob Whitsitt
President of Trailblazers, Inc.: Marshall Glickman
Coach: P.J. Carlesimo
Director of Sports Communication: John Christiansen

Sacramento Kings

Address: One Sports Parkway
Sacramento, CA 95834
Telephone: (916) 928-0000
Arena (Capacity): ARCO Arena (17,317)
Managing General Partner: Jim Thomas
VP of Basketball Operations: Geoff Petrie
Coach: Garry St. Jean
Director of Media Relations: Travis Stanley

San Antonio Spurs

Address: AlamoDome
100 Montana
San Antonio, TX 78203
Telephone: (210) 554-7787
Arena (Capacity): AlamoDome (20,662)
Chairman: General Robert McDermott
President and CEO: John C. Diller
Coach: Bob Hill
Director of Media Services: Tom James

Seattle Supersonics

Address: 190 Queen Anne Avenue North
Suite 200
Seattle, WA 98109
Telephone: (206) 281-5800
Arena (Capacity): KeyArena (17,100)
Owner: Barry Ackerley
President and General Manager: Wally Walker
Coach: George Karl
Director of Public/Media Relations: Cheri White

Toronto Raptors

Address: 20 Bay Street, Suite 1702
Toronto, Ontario, Canada M5J 2N8
Telephone: (416) 214-2255
Arena (Capacity): SkyDome (22,911)
Owner: Bitove Investments, Inc., Slaight Investments
Inc., Bank of Nova Scotia, Phil Granovsky, David
Peterson, Isiah Thomas
VP, Basketball Operations: Isiah Thomas
Coach: Brendan Malone
Director of Media Relations: John Lashway

Utah Jazz

Address: 301 West So. Temple
Salt Lake City, UT 84101
Telephone: (801) 575-7800
Arena (Capacity): Delta Center (20,600)
Owner: Larry H. Miller
General Manager: R. Tim Howells
Coach: Jerry Sloan
Director of Media Services/Special Events: Kim Turner

Washington Bullets

Address: One Harry S. Truman Drive
Landover, MD 20785
Telephone: (301) 773-2255
Arena (Capacity): USAir Arena (18,756)
Owner: Abe Pollin
General Manager and Vice President: John Nash
Coach: Jim Lynam
Director of Public Relations: Maureen Lewis

Other League

Continental Basketball Association

Address: 701 Market Street, Suite 140
St. Louis, MO 63101
Telephone: (314) 621-7222
Commissioner: Tom Valdiserri
VP of Public Relations: Brett Meister

Hockey Directory

National Hockey League

Address: 1251 Avenue of Americas
47th floor
New York, NY 10020-1198
Telephone: (212) 789-2000
Commissioner: Gary Bettman
Senior VP and Chief Operating Officer: Steven Solomon
Vice President, Public Relations: Arthur Pincus

National Hockey League Players Association

Address: One Dundas Street West
Suite 2300
Toronto, Ontario
Canada M5G 1Z3
Telephone: (416) 408-4040
Executive Director: Bob Goodenow

Mighty Ducks of Anaheim

Address: P.O. Box 61077
Anaheim, CA 92803-6177
Telephone: (714) 704-2700
Arena (Capacity): Arrowhead Pond of Anaheim (17,174)
Owner: Disney Sports Enterprises
General Manager: Jack Ferreira
Coach: Ron Wilson
Director of Media Relations: Bill Robertson

Boston Bruins

Address: One FleetCenter
Suite 250
Boston, MA 02114
Telephone: (617) 624-1909
Arena (Capacity): FleetCenter (17,565)
Owner and Governor: Jeremy M. Jacobs
Alternative Governor, President and General
Manager: Harry Sinden
Coach: Steve Kasper
Director of Media Relations: Heidi Holland

Buffalo Sabres

Address: Memorial Auditorium
140 Main Street
Buffalo, NY 14202
Telephone: (716) 856-7300
Arena (Capacity): Memorial Auditorium (16,230)
Chairman of the Board: Seymour H. Knox III
President and CEO: Douglas G. Moss
General Manager: John Muckler
Coach: Ted Nolan
Director of Public Relations: Jeff Holbrook

Calgary Flames

Address: Canadian Airlines Saddledome
               P.O. Box 1540, Station M
               Calgary, Alberta T2P 3B9
Telephone: (403) 777-2177
Arena (Capacity): Canadian Airlines Saddledome (20,000)
Owners: Grant A. Bartlett, Harley N. Hotchkiss, N. Murray Edwards, Ronald V. Joyce, Alvin G. Libin, Allan P. Markin, J.R. McCaig, Byron J. Seaman, and Daryl K. Seaman
Executive VP and Alternate Governor: Al Coates
Director of Hockey Operations: Al MacNeil
VP/General Manager: Doug Risebrough
Coach: Pierre Page
Director of Public Relations: Rick Skaggs

Chicago Blackhawks

Address: United Center
               1901 W. Madison Street
               Chicago, IL 60612
Telephone: (312) 455-7000
Arena (Capacity): United Center (20,500)
President: William W. Wirtz
General Manager: Robert Pulford
Coach: Craig Hartsburg
Public Relations Director: Jim DeMaria

Colorado Avalanche

Address: McNichols Sports Arena
               1635 Clay Street
               Denver, CO 80204
Telephone: (303) 893-6700
Arena (Capacity): McNichols Sports Arena (16,061)
Owner: Comsat Entertainment Group
General Manager: Pierre Lacroix
Coach: Marc Crawford
Director of Press Relations: Jean Martineau

Dallas Stars

Address: 211 Cowboys Parkway
               Irving, TX 75063
Telephone: (214) 712-2890
Arena (Capacity): Reunion Arena (16,924)
Owner: Norman N. Green
General Manager and Coach: Bob Gainey
Director of Public Relations: Larry Kelly

Detroit Red Wings

Address: Joe Louis Sports Arena
               600 Civic Center Drive
               Detroit, MI 48226
Telephone: (313) 396-7544
Arena (Capacity): Joe Louis Sports Arena (19,275)
Senior Vice President: Jim Devellano
Director of Player Personnel and Head Coach: Scott Bowman
Assistant General Manager: Ken Holland
Director of Public Relations: Bill Jamieson

Edmonton Oilers

Address: Edmonton Coliseum
               Edmonton, Alberta T5B 4M9
Telephone: (403) 474-8561
Arena (Capacity): Edmonton Coliseum (17,103)
Owner and Governor: Peter Pocklington
General Manager: Glen Sather
Coach: Ron Low
Director of Public Relations: Bill Tuele

Florida Panthers

Address: 100 Northeast Third Avenue, 10th floor
               Fort Lauderdale, FL 33301
Telephone: (305) 768-1900
Arena (Capacity): Miami Arena (14,703)
Owner: H. Wayne Huizenga
General Manager: Bryan Murray
Coach: Doug MacLean
Director of Media Relations: Greg Bouris

Hartford Whalers

Address: 242 Trumbull Street, 8th floor
               Hartford, CT 06103
Telephone: (203) 728-3366
Arena (Capacity): Hartford Civic Center Coliseum (15,635)
Owner: KTR Hockey Ltd. Partnership
President and General Manager: Jim Rutherford
Assistant General Manager: Terry McDonnell
Coach: Paul Holmgren
Director of Public Relations: Chris Brown

Los Angeles Kings

Address: The Great Western Forum
               3900 West Manchester Boulevard
               P.O. Box 17013
               Inglewood, CA 90308
Telephone: (310) 419-3160
Arena (Capacity): The Great Western Forum (16,005)
President: Rogie Vachonl
General Manager: Sam McMaster
Coach: Larry Robinson
Media Relations: Rick Minch

Montreal Canadiens

Address: Montreal Forum
               2313 St. Catherine Street West
               Montreal, Quebec H3H 1N2
Telephone: (514) 932-2582
Arena (Capacity): Montreal Forum (16,259; standing: 1,700)
Chairman of the Board, President and Governor: Ronald Corey
General Manager: Serge A. Savard
Coach: Jacques Demers
Director of Communications: Donald Beauchamp

New Jersey Devils

Address: Byrne Meadowlands Arena
               P.O. Box 504
               East Rutherford, NJ 07073
Telephone: (201) 935-6050
Arena (Capacity): Byrne Meadowlands Arena (19,040)
Chairman: John J. McMullen
President and General Manager: Lou Lamoriello
Coach: Jacques Lemaire
Director of Information and Publications: Mike Levine

New York Islanders

Address: Nassau Veterans' Memorial Coliseum
               Uniondale, NY 11553
Telephone: (516) 794-4100
Arena (Capacity): Nassau Veterans' Memorial Coliseum (16,297)
Co-Chairmen: Robert Rosenthal, Stephen Walsh
General Manager: Don Maloney
Coach: Mike Milbury
Media Relations Director: Ginger Killian

New York Rangers
Address: Madison Square Garden
              2 Pennsylvania Plaza
              New York, NY 10121
Telephone: (212) 465-6000
Arena (Capacity): Madison Square Garden (18,200)
Owner: ITT Cablevision
President and General Manager: Neil Smith
Coach: Colin Campbell
Director of Communications: Brooks Thomas

Ottawa Senators
Address: 301 Moodie Drive
              Suite 200
              Nepean, Ontario K2H 9C4
Telephone: (613) 721-0115
Arena (Capacity): The Palladium (18,500)
Founder: Bruce M. Firestone
Chairman and Governor: Rod Bryden
President and General Manager: Randy Sexton
Coach: Rick Bowness
Director, Media Relations: Laurent Benoit

Philadelphia Flyers
Address: CoreStates Spectrum
              3601 S. Broad Street
              Philadelphia, PA 19148
Telephone: (215) 465-4500
Arena (Capacity): CoreStates Spectrum (17,380)
Majority Owners: Ed Snider and family
Limited Partners: Sylvan and Fran Tobin
President and General Manager: Bob Clarke
Coach: Terry Murray
Vice President of Public Relations: Mark Piazza

Pittsburgh Penguins
Address: Civic Arena
              300 Auditorium Place, Gate 9
              Pittsburgh, PA 15219
Telephone: (412) 642-1800
Arena (Capacity): Civic Arena (17,189)
Ownership: Howard Baldwin, Morris Belzberg,
   Thomas Ruta
General Manager: Craig Patrick
Coach: Eddie Johnston
Director of Media Relations: Harry Sanders

St. Louis Blues
Address: Kiel Center
              P.O. Box 66792
              St. Louis, MO 63166-6792
Telephone: (314) 622-2500
Arena (Capacity): Kiel Center (19,260)
President and CEO: Jack Quinn
General Manager and Coach: Mike Keenan
Director of Public Relations: Adam Fell

San Jose Sharks
Address: San Jose Arena
              525 West Santa Clara Street
              San Jose, CA 95113
Telephone: (408) 287-7070
Arena (Capacity): San Jose Arena (17,190)
Owners: George and Gordon Gund
Vice President and General Manager: Dean Lombardi
Coach: Kevin Constantine
Director of Media Relations: Ken Arnold

Tampa Bay Lightning
Address: 501 East Kennedy Boulvard
              Suite 175
              Tampa, FL 33602
Telephone: (813) 229-2658
Arena (Capacity): The Thunderdome (27,000)
President: Steve Oto
General Manager and President: Phil Esposito
Coach: Terry Crisp
Media Relations Manager: Gerry Helper

Toronto Maple Leafs
Address: Maple Leaf Gardens
              60 Carlton Street
              Toronto, Ontario M5B 1L1
Telephone: (416) 977-1641
Arena (Capacity): Maple Leaf Gardens (15,720)
CEO: Steve A. Stavro
General Manager: Cliff Fletcher
Coach: Pat Burns
Director of Business Operations and Communications:
   Bob Stellick

Vancouver Canucks
Address: General Motors Place
              800 Griffiths Way
              Vancouver, B.C. V6B 6G1
Telephone: (604) 899-4600
Arena (Capacity): General Motors Place (19,056)
Chairman and CEO: Arthur Griffiths
Vice Chairman: John E. McCaw Jr
President and C.O.O.: John Chaple
President, GM, and Alternate Governor: Pat Quinn
Coach: Rick Lee
Mgr. of Hockey Information: Devin Smith
Public and Community Relations Coordinator:
   Veronica Varhaug

Washington Capitals
Address: USAir Arena
              Landover, MD 20785
Telephone: (301) 386-7000
Arena (Capacity): USAir Arena (18,130)
Board of Directors: Abe Pollin, David P. Binderman,
   Stewart L. Binderman, James E. Cafritz, A. James
   Clark, Albert Cohen, J. Martin Irving, James T.
   Lewis, R. Robert Linowes, Arthur K. Mason, Dr.
   Jack Meshel, David M. Osnos, Richard M. Patrick
VP and General Manager: Dave Poile
Coach: Jim Schoenfeld
VP of Communications: Matt Williams

Winnipeg Jets
Address: 10th Floor
              1661 Portaze Avenue
              Winnipeg, Manitoba R3J 3T7
Telephone: (204) 982-5387
Arena (Capacity): Winnipeg Arena (15,393)
President and Governor: Barry L. Shenkarow
Alternate Governor: Bill Davis
Board of Directors: Barry L. Shenkarow, Dick Archer,
   Barry McQueen, Marvin Shenkarow, Steve
   Bannatyne, Harvey Secter, Bill Davis
General Manager: John Paddock
Coach: Terry Simpson
Director of Communications: Richard Nairn

College Sports Directory

NATIONAL COLLEGIATE ATHLETIC ASSOCIATION (NCAA)
Address: 6201 College Boulevard
             Overland Park, KS 66211
Telephone: (913) 339-1906
Executive Director: Cedric Dempsey
Director of Public Information: Kathryn Reith

ATLANTIC COAST CONFERENCE
Address: P.O. Drawer ACC
             Greensboro, NC 27419-6999
Telephone: (910) 854-8787
Commissioner: Eugene F. Corrigan
Director of Media Relations: Brian Morrison

Clemson University
Address: Clemson, SC 29633
Nickname: Tigers
Telephone: (803) 656-2114
Football Stadium (Capacity): Clemson Memorial
  Stadium (81,473)
Basketball Arena (Capacity): Littlejohn Coliseum (11,020)
President: Constantine Curris
Athletic Director: Bobby Robinson
Football Coach: Tommy West
Basketball Coach: Rick Barnes
Sports Information Director: Tim Bourret

Duke University
Address: Durham, NC 27708
Nickname: Blue Devils
Telephone: (919) 684-2633
Football Stadium (Capacity): Wallace Wade Stadium
  (33,941)
Basketball Arena (Capacity): Cameron Indoor
  Stadium (9,314)
President: Nan Keohane
Athletic Director: Tom Butters
Football Coach: Fred Goldsmith
Basketball Coach: Mike Krzyzewski
Sports Information Director: Mike Cragg

Florida State University
Address: P.O. Box 2195
             Tallahassee, FL 32316
Nickname: Seminoles
Telephone: (904) 644-1403
Football Stadium (Capacity): Doak S. Campbell
  Stadium (77,500)
Basketball Arena (Capacity): Leon County Civic
  Center (12,500)
President: Sandy D'Alemberte
Athletic Director: Dave Hart
Football Coach: Bobby Bowden
Basketball Coach: Pat Kennedy
Sports Information Director: Rob Wilson

Georgia Tech
Address: 150 Bobby Dodd Way
             Atlanta, GA 30332
Nickname: Yellow Jackets
Telephone: (404) 894-5445
Football Stadium (Capacity): Bobby Dodd
  Stadium/Grant Field (46,000)
Basketball Arena (Capacity): Alexander Memorial
  Coliseum at McDonald's Center (10,000)
President: G. Wayne Clough
Athletic Director: Dr. Homer Rice
Football Coach: George O'Leary
Basketball Coach: Bobby Cremins
Sports Information Director: Mike Finn

University of Maryland
Address: P.O. Box 295
             College Park, MD 20741
Nickname: Terrapins
Telephone: (301) 314-7064
Football Stadium (Capacity): Byrd Stadium (48,055)
Basketball Arena (Capacity): Cole Fieldhouse
  (14,500)
President: Dr. William E. Kirwin
Athletic Director: Deborah Yow
Football Coach: Mark Duffner
Basketball Coach: Gary Williams
Sports Information Director: Herb Hartnett

University of North Carolina
Address: P.O. Box 2126
             Chapel Hill, NC 27514
Nickname: Tar Heels
Telephone: (919) 962-2123
Football Stadium (Capacity): Kenan Memorial
  Stadium (52,000)
Basketball Arena (Capacity): Dean E. Smith Center
  (21,572)
Chancellor: Dr. Michael K. Hooker
Athletic Director: John Swofford
Football Coach: Mack Brown
Basketball Coach: Dean Smith
Sports Information Director: Rick Brewer

North Carolina State University
Address: Box 8501
             Raleigh, NC 27695
Nickname: Wolfpack
Telephone: (919) 515-2102
Football Stadium (Capacity): Carter-Finley Stadium
  (51,500)
Basketball Arena (Capacity): Reynolds Coliseum
  (12,400)
Chancellor: Dr. Larry K. Monteith
Athletic Director: Todd Turner
Football Coach: Mike O'Cain
Basketball Coach: Les Robinson
Sports Information Director: Mark Bockelman

University of Virginia
Address: P.O. Box 3785
             Charlottesville, VA 22903
Nickname: Cavaliers
Telephone: (804) 982-5151
Football Stadium (Capacity): Scott Stadium (42,000)
Basketball Arena (Capacity): University Hall (8,500)
President: John Casteen III
Athletic Director: Terry Holland
Football Coach: George Welsh
Basketball Coach: Jeff Jones
Sports Information Director: Rich Murray

Wake Forest University
Address: P.O. Box 7426
             Winston-Salem, NC 27109
Nickname: Demon Deacons
Telephone: (910) 759-5640
Football Stadium (Capacity): Groves Stadium
  (31,500)
Basketball Arena (Capacity): Lawrence Joel
  Memorial Coliseum (14,407)
President: Dr. Thomas K. Hearn Jr.
Athletic Director: Ron Wellman
Football Coach: Jim Caldwell
Basketball Coach: Dave Odom
Sports Information Director: John Justus

College Sports Directory (Cont.)

BIG EAST CONFERENCE
Address: 56 Exchange Terrace, 5th floor
Providence, RI 02903
Telephone: (401) 272-9108
Commissioner: Michael A. Tranghese
Ass't Commissioner for Public Relations: John Paquette

Boston College
Address: Chestnut Hill, MA 02167
Nickname: Eagles
Telephone: (617) 552-3004
Football Stadium (Capacity): Alumni Stadium (44,500)
Basketball Arena (Capacity): Silvio O. Conte Forum (8,604)
President: Rev. J. Donald Monan, S.J.
Athletic Director: Chet Gladchuk
Football Coach: Dan Henning
Basketball Coach: Jim O'Brien
Sports Information Director: Reid Oslin

University of Connecticut
Address: 2095 Hillside Road
Storrs, CT 06269-3078
Nickname: Huskies
Telephone: (203) 486-2725
Football Stadium (Capacity): Memorial Stadium (16,200)
Basketball Arena (Capacity): Gampel Pavilion (8,241)
President: Dr. Harry J. Hartley
Athletic Director: Lew Perkins
Football Coach: Skip Holtz
Basketball Coach: Jim Calhoun
Sports Information Director: Tim Tolokan
Note: Division I-AA football

Georgetown University
Address: McDonough Arena
Box 571124
Washington, DC 20057-1124
Nickname: Hoyas
Telephone: (202) 687-2435
Football Stadium (Capacity): Kehoe Field (2,000)
Basketball Arena (Capacity): USAir Arena (19,035)
President: Rev. Leo J. O'Donovan, S.J.
Senior Athletic Director: Francis X. Rienzo
Athletic Director: Joseph Lang
Football Coach: Robert Benson
Basketball Coach: John Thompson
Sports Information Director: Bill Shapland (basketball), Bill Hurd
Note: Division I-AA football

University of Miami
Address: One Hurricane Drive
Coral Gables, FL 33146
Nickname: Hurricanes
Telephone: (305) 284-3822
Football Stadium (Capacity): Orange Bowl (74,476)
Basketball Arena (Capacity): Miami Arena (15,388)
President: Edward Foote II
Athletic Director: Paul Dee
Football Coach: Butch Davis
Basketball Coach: Leonard Hamilton
Sports Information Director: John Hahn

University of Pittsburgh
Address: Dept. of Athletics, P.O. Box 7436
Pittsburgh, PA 15213
Nickname: Panthers
Telephone: (412) 648-8240
Football Stadium (Capacity): Pitt Stadium (56,500)
Basketball Arena (Capacity): Fitzgerald Field House (6,798), Pittsburgh Civic Arena (16,798)
Chancellor: J. Dennis O'Connor
Athletic Director: Oval Jaynes
Football Coach: Johnny Majors
Basketball Coach: Ralph Willard
Sports Information Director: Ron Wall

Providence College
Address: River Avenue
Providence, RI 02918
Nickname: Friars
Telephone: (401) 865-2265
Basketball Arena (Capacity): Providence Civic Center (13,410)
President: Rev. Philip A. Smith, O.P.
Athletic Director: John Marinatto
Basketball Coach: Pete Gillen
Sports Information Director: Tim Connor
Note: No football program

Rutgers University
Address: P.O. Box 1149
Piscataway, NJ 08855-1149
Nickname: Scarlet Knights
Telephone: (908) 445-4200
Football Stadium (Capacity): Rutgers Stadium (42,000), Giants Stadium (76,000)
Basketball Arena (Capacity): Louis Brown Athletic Center (9,000)
President: Dr. Francis L. Lawrence
Athletic Director: Frederick Gruninger
Football Coach: Doug Graber
Basketball Coach: Bob Wenzel
Sports Information Director: Peter Kowalski

St. John's University
Address: 8000 Utopia Parkway
Jamaica, NY 11439
Nickname: Red Storm
Telephone: (718) 990-6367
Football Stadium (Capacity): St. John's Stadium (3,000)
Basketball Arena (Capacity): Alumni Hall (6,008), Madison Square Garden (19,876)
President: Very Rev. Donald J. Harrington, C.M.
Athletic Director: Edward J. Manetta Jr.
Football Coach: Bob Ricca
Basketball Coach: Brian Mahoney
Sports Information Director: Frank Racaniello
Note: Division I-AA football

Seton Hall University
Address: 400 South Orange Avenue
South Orange, NJ 07079
Nickname: Pirates
Telephone: (201) 761-9497
Basketball Arena (Capacity): Walsh Auditorium (3,200), The Meadowlands (20,029)
President: Rev. Thomas R. Peterson
Athletic Director: Larry Keating
Basketball Coach: George Blaney
Sports Information Director: John Wooding
Note: No football program

Syracuse University
Address: Manley Field House
                Syracuse, NY 13244-5020
Nickname: Orangemen
Telephone: (315) 443-2608
Football Stadium (Capacity): Carrier Dome (50,000)
Basketball Arena (Capacity): Carrier Dome (33,000)
Chancellor: Dr. Kenneth Shaw
Athletic Director: Jake Crouthamel
Football Coach: Paul Pasqualoni
Basketball Coach: Jim Boeheim
Sports Information Director: Larry Kimball

Temple University
Address: McGonigle Hall
                Philadelphia, PA 19122
Nickname: Owls
Telephone: (215) 204-7445
Football Stadium (Capacity): Veterans Stadium
(66,592)
Basketball Arena (Capacity): McGonigle Hall (3,900)
President: Peter J. Liacouras
Athletic Director: R. C. Johnson
Football Coach: Ron Dickerson
Basketball Coach: John Chaney
Sports Information Director: Gerry Emig
Note: Plays football in Big East, basketball in Atlantic 10 Conference.

Villanova University
Address: 800 Lancaster Avenue
                Villanova, PA 19085
Nickname: Wildcats
Telephone: (610) 519-4110
Football Stadium (Capacity): Villanova Stadium (13,400)
Basketball Arena (Capacity): duPont Pavilion (6,500),
   CoreStates Spectrum (18,497)
President: Rev. Edmund Dobbin, O.S.A.
Athletic Director: Gene DeFilippo
Football Coach: Andy Talley
Basketball Coach: Steve Lappas
Sports Information Director: Karen Frascona
Note: Division I-AA football

Virginia Tech
Address: Jamerson Athletic Center
                Blacksburg, VA 24061
Nickname: Hokies
Telephone: (703) 231-6726
Football Stadium (Capacity): Lane Stadium/Worsham
   Field (51,000)
Basketball Arena (Capacity): Cassell Coliseum (9,971)
President: Dr. Paul Torgersen
Athletic Director: Dave Braine
Football Coach: Frank Beamer
Basketball Coach: Bill Foster
Sports Information Director: Dave Smith
Note: Plays football in Big East, basketball in Atlantic 10.

West Virginia University
Address: P.O. Box 0877
                Morgantown, WV 26507-0877
Nickname: Mountaineers
Telephone: (304) 293-2821
Football Stadium (Capacity): Mountaineer Field
(63,500)
Basketball Arena (Capacity): WVU Coliseum (14,000)
President: David Hardesty
Athletic Director: Ed Pastilong
Football Coach: Don Nehlen
Basketball Coach: Gale Catlett
Sports Information Director: Shelley Poe

BIG EIGHT CONFERENCE
Address: 104 West Ninth Street, Suite 408
                Kansas City, MO 64105
Telephone: (816) 471-5088
Commissioner: Carl C. James
Publicity Director: Jeff Bollig

University of Colorado
Address: Campus Box 357
                Boulder, CO 80309
Nickname: Buffaloes
Telephone: (303) 492-5626
Football Stadium (Capacity): Folsom Field (51,748)
Basketball Arena (Capacity): Coors Event Center
   (11,199)
President: Dr. Judith Albino
Athletic Director: Bill Marolt
Football Coach: Rick Neuheisel
Basketball Coach: Joe Harrington
Sports Information Director: David Plati

Iowa State University
Address: 1802 S. Fourth
                Olsen Annex
                Ames, IA 50011
Nickname: Cyclones
Telephone: (515) 294-3372
Football Stadium (Capacity): Cyclone Stadium-Jack
   Trice Field (43,000)
Basketball Arena (Capacity): Hilton Coliseum
   (14,020)
President: Dr. Martin C. Jischke
Athletic Director: Gene Smith
Football Coach: Dan McCarney
Basketball Coach: Tim Floyd
Sports Information Director: Tom Kroeschell

University of Kansas
Address: Allen Field House, Room 104
                Lawrence, KS 66045
Nickname: Jayhawks
Telephone: (913) 864-3417
Football Stadium (Capacity): Memorial Stadium
(50,250)
Basketball Arena (Capacity): Allen Field House
   (16,300)
Chancellor: Robert Hemenway
Athletic Director: Dr. Bob Fredrick
Football Coach: Glen Mason
Basketball Coach: Roy Williams
Sports Information Director: Doug Vance

Kansas State University

Address: Manhattan, KS 66502
Nickname: Wildcats
Telephone: (913) 532-6011
Football Stadium (Capacity): KSU Stadium (45,000)
Basketball Arena (Capacity): Bramlage Coliseum (13,500)
President: Dr. Jon Wefald
Athletic Director: Max Urick
Football Coach: Bill Snyder
Basketball Coach: Tom Asbury
Sports Information Director: Ben Boyle

University of Missouri

Address: P.O. Box 677
Columbia, MO 65205
Nickname: Tigers
Telephone: (314) 882-3241
Football Stadium (Capacity): Faurot Field/Memorial Stadium (62,000)
Basketball Arena (Capacity): Hearnes Center (13,349)
Chancellor: Dr. Charles Kiesler
Athletic Director: Joe Castiglione
Football Coach: Larry Smith
Basketball Coach: Norm Stewart
Sports Information Director: Bob Brendel

University of Nebraska

Address: 116 South Stadium
Lincoln, NE 68588
Nickname: Cornhuskers
Telephone: (402) 472-2263
Football Stadium (Capacity): Memorial Stadium (72,700)
Basketball Arena (Capacity): Bob Devaney Sports Center (14,302)
President: L. Dennis Smith
Athletic Director: Bill Byrne
Football Coach: Tom Osborne
Basketball Coach: Danny Nee
Sports Information Director: Chris Anderson

University of Oklahoma

Address: 180 W. Brooks, Room 235
Norman, OK 73019
Nickname: Sooners
Telephone: (405) 325-8231
Football Stadium (Capacity): Memorial Stadium/Owen Field (75,004)
Basketball Arena (Capacity): Lloyd Noble Center (11,100)
President: David Boren
Athletic Director: Donnie Duncan
Football Coach: Howard Schnellenberger
Basketball Coach: Kelvin Sampson
Sports Information Director: Mike Prusinski

Oklahoma State University

Address: 202 Gallagher-Iba Arena
Stillwater, OK 74078
Nickname: Cowboys
Telephone: (405) 744-5749
Football Stadium (Capacity): Lewis Field (50,614)
Basketball Arena (Capacity): Gallagher-Iba Arena (6,381)
President: Dr. James Halligan
Athletic Director: Terry Don Phillips
Football Coach: Bob Simmons
Basketball Coach: Eddie Sutton
Sports Information Director: Steve Buzzard

BIG TEN CONFERENCE

Address: 1500 West Higgins Road
Park Ridge, IL 60068
Telephone: (708) 696-1010
Commissioner: James E. Delany
Assistant Commissioner: Mark Rudner

University of Illinois

Address: 1817 S. Neil Street, Suite 201
Champaign, IL 61820
Nickname: Fighting Illini
Telephone: (217) 333-1390
Football Stadium (Capacity): Memorial Stadium (72,292)
Basketball Arena (Capacity): Assembly Hall (16,153)
President: James Stukel
Athletic Director: Ronald Guenther
Football Coach: Lou Tepper
Basketball Coach: Lou Henson
Sports Information Director: Mike Pearson

Indiana University

Address: 17th Street and Fee Lane/Assembly Hall
Bloomington, IN 47405
Nickname: Hoosiers
Telephone: (812) 855-2421
Football Stadium (Capacity): Memorial Stadium (52,354)
Basketball Arena (Capacity): Assembly Hall (17,357)
President: Myles Brand
Athletic Director: Clarence Doninger
Football Coach: Bill Mallory
Basketball Coach: Bob Knight
Sports Information Director: Kit Klingelhoffer

University of Iowa

Address: 205 Carver-Hawkeye Arena
Iowa City, IA 52242
Nickname: Hawkeyes
Telephone: (319) 335-9411
Football Stadium (Capacity): Kinnick Stadium (70,397)
Basketball Arena (Capacity): Carver-Hawkeye Arena (15,500)
President: Mary Sue Coleman
Athletic Director: Robert Bowlsby
Football Coach: Hayden Fry
Basketball Coach: Tom Davis
Sports Information Director: Phil Haddy

University of Michigan

Address: 1000 S. State Street
Ann Arbor, MI 48109
Nickname: Wolverines
Telephone: (313) 763-4423
Football Stadium (Capacity): Michigan Stadium (102,501)
Basketball Arena (Capacity): Crisler Arena (13,562)
President: James Duderstadt
Athletic Director: Dr. Joseph Roberson
Football Coach: Lloyd Carr
Basketball Coach: Steve Fisher
Sports Information Director: Bruce Madej

Michigan State University

Address: East Lansing, MI 48824
Nickname: Spartans
Telephone: (517) 355-2271
Football Stadium (Capacity): Spartan Stadium (72,027)
Basketball Arena (Capacity): Jack Breslin Student Events Center (15,138)
President: M. Peter McPherson
Athletic Director: Merritt J. Norvell Jr., Ph.D.
Football Coach: Nick Saban
Basketball Coach: Tom Izzo
Sports Information Director: Ken Hoffman

University of Minnesota

Address: 516 15th Avenue S.E.
Minneapolis, MN 55455
Nickname: Golden Gophers
Telephone: (612) 625-4090
Football Stadium (Capacity): Hubert H. Humphrey Metrodome (63,669)
Basketball Arena (Capacity): Williams Arena (14,300)
President: Nils Hasselmo
Athletic Director: McKinley Boston
Football Coach: Jim Wacker
Basketball Coach: Clem Haskins
Sports Information Director: Marc Ryan

Northwestern University

Address: 1501 Central Street
Evanston, IL 60208
Nickname: Wildcats
Telephone: (708) 491-3205
Football Stadium (Capacity): Dyche Stadium (49,256)
Basketball Arena (Capacity): Welsh-Ryan Arena (8,117)
President: Henry S. Bienen
Athletic Director: Rick Taylor
Football Coach: Gary Barnett
Basketball Coach: Ricky Byrdsong
Director of Media Services: Brad Hurlbut

Ohio State University

Address: 410 Woody Hayes Drive, Room 124
Columbus, OH 43210
Nickname: Buckeyes
Telephone: (614) 292-6861
Football Stadium (Capacity): Ohio Stadium (89,542)
Basketball Arena (Capacity): St. John Arena (13,276)
President: Dr. E. Gordon Gee
Athletic Director: Andy Geiger
Football Coach: John Cooper
Basketball Coach: Randy Ayers
Sports Information Director: Steve Snapp

Penn State University

Address: Recreation Building
University Park, PA 16802
Nickname: Nittany Lions
Telephone: (814) 865-1757
Football Stadium (Capacity): Beaver Stadium (93,967)
Basketball Arena (Capacity): Recreation Hall (6,846)
President: Dr. Graham Spanier
Athletic Director: Tim Curley
Football Coach: Joe Paterno
Basketball Coach: Jerry Dunn
Sports Information Director: Jeff Nelson

Purdue University

Address: Mackey Arena, Room 15
West Lafayette, IN 47907
Nickname: Boilermakers
Telephone: (317) 494-3200
Football Stadium (Capacity): Ross-Ade Stadium (67,861)
Basketball Arena (Capacity): Mackey Arena (14,123)
President: Dr. Steven C. Beering
Athletic Director: Morgan Burke
Football Coach: Jim Colletto
Basketball Coach: Gene Keady
Sports Information Director: Mark Adams

University of Wisconsin

Address: 1440 Monroe Street
Madison, WI 53711
Nickname: Badgers
Telephone: (608) 262-1811
Football Stadium (Capacity): Camp Randall Stadium (77,745)
Basketball Arena (Capacity): UW Fieldhouse (11,895)
Chancellor: David Ward
Athletic Director: Pat Richter
Football Coach: Barry Alvarez
Basketball Coach: Dick Bennett
Sports Information Director: Steve Malchow

BIG WEST CONFERENCE

Address: 2 Corporate Park
Suite 206
Irvine, CA 92714
Telephone: (714) 261-2525
Commissioner: Dennis Farrell
Publicity Director: Dennis Bickmeyer

California State University–Fullerton

Address: 800 North State College Boulevard
P.O. Box 34080
Fullerton, CA 92634-9480
Nickname: Titans
Telephone: (714) 773-2677
Basketball Arena (Capacity): Titan Gym (4,000)
President: Dr. Milton A. Gordon
Athletic Director: John Easterbrook
Basketball Coach: Bob Hawking
Sports Information Director: Mel Franks
Note: No football program in 1995.

Fresno State University

Address: 5305 N. Campus Drive, Room 153
Fresno, CA 93740-0027
Nickname: Bulldogs
Telephone: (209) 278-2643
Football Stadium (Capacity): Bulldog Stadium (41,031)
Basketball Arena (Capacity): Selland Arena (10,159)
President: Dr. John Welty
Interim Athletic Director: Dr. Benjamin Quillian
Football Coach: Jim Sweeney
Basketball Coach: Jerry Tarkanian
Sports Information Director: Scott Johnson

Long Beach State University

Address: 1250 Bellflower Boulevard
             Long Beach, CA 90840
Nickname: 49ers
Telephone: (310) 985-4655
Basketball Arena (Capacity): The Pyramid (5,000)
President: Dr. Robert C. Maxson
Athletic Director: David O'Brien
Basketball Coach: Seth Greenberg
Sports Information Director: Scott Cathcart

University of Nevada at Las Vegas

Address: 4505 Maryland Parkway
             Las Vegas, NV 89154
Nickname: Rebels
Telephone: (702) 895-3207
Football Stadium (Capacity): Sam Boyd Stadium
(32,000)
Basketball Arena (Capacity): Thomas and Mack
Center (18,500)
President: Carol C. Harter
Athletic Director: Charles Cavagnaro
Football Coach: Jeff Horton
Basketball Coach: Bill Bayno
Sports Information Director: Jim Gemma

New Mexico State University

Address: Box 30001, Dept. 3145
             Las Cruces, NM 88003
Nickname: Aggies
Telephone: (505) 646-4126
Football Stadium (Capacity): Aggie Memorial Stadium
(30,343)
Basketball Arena (Capacity): Pan American Center
(13,007)
President: Michael J. Orenduff
Athletic Director: Al Gonzales
Football Coach: Jim Hess
Basketball Coach: Neil McCarthy
Sports Information Director: Steve Shutt

University of the Pacific

Address: 3601 Pacific Avenue
             Stockton, CA 95211
Nickname: Tigers
Telephone: (209) 946-2479
Football Stadium (Capacity): Amos Alonzo Stagg
Memorial Stadium (30,000)
Basketball Arena (Capacity): A.G. Spanos Center
(6,150)
President: Dr. Donald DeRosa
Athletic Director: Bob Lee
Football Coach: Chuck Shelton
Basketball Coach: Bob Thomason
Sports Information Director: Mike Millerick

San Jose State University

Address: One Washington Square
             San Jose, CA 95192-0062
Nickname: Spartans
Telephone: (408) 924-1200
Football Stadium (Capacity): Spartan Stadium
(31,218)
Basketball Arena (Capacity): Event Center (4,600)
President: Dr. Robert L. Caret
Athletic Director: Dr. Tom Brennan
Football Coach: John Ralston
Basketball Coach: Stan Morrison
Sports Information Director: Lawrence Fan

Utah State University

Address: Logan, UT 84322-7400
Nickname: Aggies
Telephone: (801) 797-1850
Football Stadium (Capacity): Romney Stadium
(30,000)
Basketball Arena (Capacity): The Smith Spectrum
(10,270)
President: Dr. George H. Emert
Athletic Director: Chuck Bell
Football Coach: John L. Smith
Basketball Coach: Larry Eustachy
Sports Information Director: John Lewandowski

CONFERENCE USA

Address: 35 East Wacker Drive, Suite 650
             Chicago, IL 60601
Telephone: (312) 553-0483
Comissioner: Michael Slive
Media Relations Director: Brian Teter

University of Alabama-Birmingham

Address: UAB Arena
             617 13th Street South
             Birmingham, AL 35294
Nickname: Blazers
Telephone: (205) 934-7252
Football Stadium (Capacity): Legion Field (83,091)
Basketball Arena (Capacity): UAB Arena (8,500)
President: Dr. J. Claude Bennett
Athletic Director: Gene Bartow
Football Coach: Watson Brown
Basketball Coach: Gene Brown
Sports Information Director: Grant Shingleton
Note: Will begin conference play in football in 1996-97.

University of Cincinnati

Address: Cincinnati, OH 45221-0021
Nickname: Bearcats
Telephone: (513) 556-5601
Football Stadium (Capacity): Nippert Stadium (35,500)
Basketball Arena (Capacity): Myrl Shoemaker Center
(13,176)
President: Dr. Joseph A. Steger
Athletic Director: Gerald O'Dell
Football Coach: Rick Minter
Basketball Coach: Bob Huggins
Sports Information Director: Tom Hathaway
Note: Will begin conference play in football in 1996-97.

DePaul University

Address: 1011 West Belden Avenue
             Chicago, IL 60614
Nickname: Blue Demons
Telephone: (312) 325-7526
Basketball Arena (Capacity): Rosemont Horizon
(17,500)
President: Rev. John P. Minogue, C.M.
Athletic Director: Bill Bradshaw
Basketball Coach: Joey Meyer
Sports Information Director: John Lanctot
Note: No football program.

University of Houston
Address: 3100 Cullen Boulevard
                    Houston, TX 77004
Nickname: Cougars
Telephone: (713) 743-9370
Football Stadium (Capacity): Astrodome (65,000)
Basketball Arena (Capacity): Hofheinz Pavilion
  (10,060)
President: Dr. Glenn Goerke
Athletic Director: William C. Carr
Football Coach: Kim Helton
Basketball Coach: Alvin Brooks
Sports Information Director: Donna Turner
Note: Will begin conference play in 1996-97.

University of Louisville
Address: Louisville, KY 40292
Nickname: Cardinals
Telephone: (502) 852-5732
Football Stadium (Capacity): Cardinal Stadium
  (37,500)
Basketball Arena (Capacity): Freedom Hall (19,000)
President: Dr. John Schumaker
Athletic Director: William Olsen
Football Coach: Ron Cooper
Basketball Coach: Denny Crum
Sports Information Director: Kenny Klein
Note: Will begin conference play in football in 1996-97.

Marquette University
Address: P.O. Box 1881
                    Milwaukee, WI 53201-1881
Nickname: Golden Eagles
Telephone: (414) 288-7447
Basketball Arena (Capacity): Bradley Center (18,592)
President: Rev. Albert J. DiUlio, S.J.
Athletic Director: Bill Cords
Basketball Coach: Mike Deane
Sports Information Director: Kathleen Hohl
Note: No football program.

University of Memphis
Address: Memphis, TN 38152
Nickname: Tigers
Telephone: (901) 678-2337
Football Stadium (Capacity): Liberty Bowl Memorial
  Stadium/Rex Dockery Field (62,380)
Basketball Arena (Capacity): The Pyramid (20,142)
President: Dr. V. Lane Rawlins
Interim Athletic Director: Dr. Don Carson
Football Coach: Rip Scherer
Basketball Coach: Larry Finch
Sports Information Director: Bob Winn
Note: Will begin conference play in football in 1996-97.

University of North Carolina-Charlotte
Address: 9201 University City Boulevard
                    UNC-Charlotte
                    Belk Gymnasium
                    Charlotte, NC 28223-0001
Nickname: 49ers
Telephone: (704) 547-4937
Basketball Arena (Capacity): Independence Arena
  (9,575)
Chancellor: James H. Woodward
Athletic Director: Judy W. Rose
Basketball Coach: Jeff Mullins
Sports Information Director: Mark Colone
Note: No football program.

Saint Louis University
Address: 3672 West Pine Boulevard
                    St. Louis, MO 63108
Nickname: Billikens
Telephone: (314) 977-3177
Basketball Arena (Capacity): Kiel Center (20,000)
President: Rev. Lawrence Biondi, S.J.
Athletic Director: Doug Woolard
Basketball Coach: Charlie Spoonhour
Sports Information Director: Doug McIlhagga
Note: No football program.

University of South Florida
Address: 4202 East Fowler Ave., PED 214
                    Tampa, FL 33620
Nickname: Bulls
Telephone: (813) 974-2125
Basketball Arena (Capacity): Sun Dome (11,000)
President: Betty Castor
Athletic Director: Paul Griffin
Basketball Coach: Bobby Paschal
Sports Information Director: John Gerdes
Note: The football program will begin with the 1997 season.

University of Southern Mississippi
Address: P.O. Box 5161
                    Hattiesburg, MS 39406
Nickname: Golden Eagles
Telephone: (601) 266-5017
Football Stadium (Capacity): M. M. Roberts Stadium
  (33,000)
Basketball Arena (Capacity): Reed Green Coliseum
  (8,095)
President: Dr. Aubrey K. Lucas
Athletic Director: H. C. Bill McLellan
Football Coach: Jeff Bower
Basketball Coach: M. K. Turk
Sports Information Director: Regiel Napier
Note: Will begin conference play in football in 1996-97.

Tulane University
Address: James Wilson Jr. Center for
                    Intercollegiate Athletics
                    New Orleans, LA 70118
Nickname: Green Wave
Telephone: (504) 865-5501
Football Stadium (Capacity): Louisiana Superdome
  (71,000)
Basketball Arena (Capacity): Fogelman Arena (5,000)
President: Dr. Eamon Kelly
Athletic Director: Dr. Kevin White
Football Coach: Eugene (Buddy) Teevens
Basketball Coach: Perry Clark
Sports Information Director: Lenny Vangilder
Note: Will begin conference play in football in 1996-97.

IVY LEAGUE
Address: 120 Alexander Street, Princeton, NJ 08544
Telephone: (609) 258-6426
Executive Director: Jeff Orleans
Publicity Director: Chuck Yrigoyen

Brown University
Address: Hope Street, Providence, RI 02912
Nickname: Bears
Telephone: (401) 863-2211
Football Stadium (Capacity): Brown Stadium (20,000)
Basketball Arena (Capacity): Paul Bailey Pizzitola
  Memorial Sports Center (2,500)
President: Vartan Gregorian
Athletic Director: David Roach
Football Coach: Mark Whipple
Basketball Coach: Franklin Dobbs
Sports Information Director: Christopher Humm

Columbia University
Address: Dodge Physical Fitness Center,
             New York, NY 10027
Nickname: Lions
Telephone: (212) 854-2538
Football Stadium (Capacity): Lawrence A. Wien
  Stadium at Baker Field (17,000)
Basketball Arena (Capacity): Levien Gymnasium (3,400)
President: Dr. George Rupp
Athletic Director: Dr. John Reeves
Football Coach: Ray Tellier
Basketball Coach: Armond Hill
Sports Information Director: William C. Steinman

Cornell University
Address: Teagle Hall, Campus Road
             Ithaca, NY 14853
Nickname: Big Red
Telephone: (607) 255-5220
Football Stadium (Capacity): Schoellkopf Field (27,000)
Basketball Arena (Capacity): Newman Arena (4,750)
President: Hunter R. Rawlings III
Athletic Director: Charles Moore
Football Coach: Jim Hofher
Basketball Coach: Al Walker
Sports Information Director: Dave Wohlhueter

Dartmouth College
Address: 6083 Alumni Gym
             Hanover, NH 03755-3512
Nickname: Big Green
Telephone: (603) 646-2465
Football Stadium (Capacity): Memorial Field (20,416)
Basketball Arena (Capacity): Leede Arena (2,100)
President: James Freedman
Athletic Director: Richard G. Jaeger
Football Coach: John Lyons
Basketball Coach: Dave Faucher
Sports Information Director: Kathy Slattery

Harvard University
Address: 60 John F. Kennedy St.
             Cambridge, MA 02138
Nickname: Crimson
Telephone: (617) 495-2206
Football Stadium (Capacity): Harvard Stadium (37,967)
Basketball Arena (Capacity): Briggs Athletic Center
  (2,083)
President: Neil L. Rudentsine
Athletic Director: William J. Cleary Jr.
Football Coach: Tim Murphy
Basketball Coach: Frank Sullivan
Sports Information Director: John Veneziano

University of Pennsylvania
Address: Weightman Hall North
             235 South 33rd Street
             Philadelphia, PA 19104-6322
Nickname: Quakers
Telephone: (215)898-6121
Football Stadium (Capacity): Franklin Field (60,546)
Basketball Arena (Capacity): Palestra Arena (8,700)
President: Dr. Judith Rodin
Athletic Director: Steven Bilsky
Football Coach: Al Bagnoli
Basketball Coach: Fran Dunphy
Director, Media Relations: Gail Stasulli Zachary
Director, Athletic Communications: Shaun May

Princeton University
Address: P.O. Box 71
             Jadwin Gym
             Princeton, NJ 08544
Nickname: Tigers
Telephone: (609) 258-3568
Football Stadium (Capacity): Palmer Stadium (45,725)
Basketball Arena (Capacity): Jadwin Gym (7,550)
President: Harold Shapiro
Athletic Director: Gary D. Walters
Football Coach: Steve Tosches
Basketball Coach: Pete Carril
Sports Information Director: Kurt Kehl

Yale University
Address: Box 208216
             New Haven, CT 06520
Nickname: Bulldogs, Elis
Telephone: (203) 432-1456
Football Stadium (Capacity): Yale Bowl (64,269)
Basketball Arena (Capacity): Payne Whitney Gym
  (3,100)
President: Richard C. Levin
Athletic Director: Tom Beckett
Football Coach: Carmen Cozza
Basketball Coach: Dick Kuchen
Sports Information Director: Steve Conn

MID-AMERICAN CONFERENCE
Address: Four Seagate, Suite 102
             Toledo, OH 43604
Telephone: (419) 249-7177
Commissioner: Jerry Ippoliti
Publicity Director: Tom Lessig

Ball State University
Address: 2000 University Avenue
             Muncie, IN 47306
Nickname: Cardinals
Telephone: (317) 285-8225
Football Stadium (Capacity): Ball State University
  Stadium (16,319)
Basketball Arena (Capacity): University Arena
  (11,500)
President: Dr. John E. Worthen
Athletic Director: Andrea Seger
Football Coach: Bill Lynch
Basketball Coach: Ray McCallum
Sports Information Director: Joe Hernandez

Bowling Green University

Address: Bowling Green, OH 43403
Nickname: Falcons
Telephone: (419) 372-2401
Football Stadium (Capacity): Doyt L. Perry Stadium (30,599)
Basketball Arena (Capacity): Anderson Arena (5,000)
President: Dr. Sidney A. Ribeau
Athletic Director: Ron Zwierlein
Football Coach: Gary Blackney
Basketball Coach: Jim Larranga
Sports Information Director: Steve Barr

Central Michigan University

Address: Rose Center
             Mount Pleasant, MI 48859
Nickname: Chippewas
Telephone: (517) 774-3041
Football Stadium (Capacity): Kelly/Shorts Stadium (20,083)
Basketball Arena (Capacity): Rose Arena (6,000)
President: Leonard Plachta
Athletic Director: Herb Deromedi
Football Coach: Dick Flynn
Basketball Coach: Leonard Drake
Sports Information Director: Fred Stabley, Jr.

Eastern Michigan University

Address: Bowen Fieldhouse
             Ypsilanti, MI 48197
Nickname: Eagles
Telephone: (313) 487-0317
Football Stadium (Capacity): Rynearson Stadium (30,200)
Basketball Arena (Capacity): Bowen Arena (5,600)
President: Dr. William Shelton
Athletic Director: Tim Weiser
Football Coach: Rick Rasnick
Basketball Coach: Ben Braun
Sports Information Director: James Streeter

Kent State University

Address: Kent, OH 44242
Nickname: Golden Flashes
Telephone: (216) 672-3120
Football Stadium (Capacity): Dix Stadium (30,520)
Basketball Arena (Capacity): Memorial Athletic and Convocation Center (6,034)
President: Dr. Carol A. Cartwright
Athletic Director: Laing Kennedy
Football Coach: Jim Corrigall
Basketball Coach: Dave Grube
Sports Information Director: Dale Gallagher

Miami University

Address: Millett Hall
             Oxford, OH 45056
Nickname: Redskins
Telephone: (513) 529-3113
Football Stadium (Capacity): Yager Stadium (25,183)
Basketball Arena (Capacity): Millett Hall (9,200)
President: Dr. Paul G. Risser
Athletic Director: Eric Hyman
Football Coach: Randy Walker
Basketball Coach: Herb Sendek
Sports Information Director: John Estes

Ohio University

Address: P.O. Box 689
             Convocation Center
             Athens, OH 45701-2979
Nickname: Bobcats
Telephone: (614) 593-1174
Football Stadium (Capacity): Don Peden Stadium (20,000)
Basketball Arena (Capacity): Convocation Center (13,000)
President: Dr. Robert Glidden
Athletic Director: Thomas Boeh
Football Coach: Jim Grobe
Basketball Coach: Larry Hunter
Director of Media Services: George Mauzy

University of Toledo

Address: 2801 W. Bancroft St.
             Toledo, OH 43606
Nickname: Rockets
Telephone: (419) 537-4184
Football Stadium (Capacity): Glass Bowl (26,248)
Basketball Arena (Capacity): Savage Hall (9,000)
President: Dr. Frank E. Horton
Athletic Director: Dr. Allen R. Bohl
Football Coach: Gary Pinkel
Basketball Coach: Larry Gipson
Sports Information Director: Rod Brandt

Western Michigan University

Address: Kalamazoo, MI 49008
Nickname: Broncos
Telephone: (616) 387-4138
Football Stadium (Capacity): Waldo Stadium (30,062)
Basketball Arena (Capacity): University Arena (5,800)
President: Dr. D. H. Haenicke
Interim Athletic Director: Charles Elliott
Football Coach: Al Molde
Basketball Coach: Bob Donewald
Sports Information Director: John Beatty

PACIFIC-10 CONFERENCE

Address: 800 S. Broadway, Suite 400
             Walnut Creek, CA 94596
Telephone: (510) 932-4411
Commissioner: Thomas C. Hansen
Publicity Director: Jim Muldoon

University of Arizona

Address: 229 McHale Center
             Tuscon, AZ 85721
Nickname: Wildcats
Telephone: (602) 621-2211
Football Stadium (Capacity): Arizona Stadium (56,167)
Basketball Arena (Capacity): McHale Center (13,447)
President: Dr. Manuel Pacheco
Athletic Director: Jim Livengood
Football Coach: Dick Tomey
Basketball Coach: Lute Olson
Sports Information Director: Tom Duddleston

Arizona State University

Address: Tempe, AZ 85287
Nickname: Sun Devils
Telephone: (602) 965-6592
Football Stadium (Capacity): Sun Devil Stadium (73,656)
Basketball Arena (Capacity): University Activity Center (14,287)
President: Lattie Coor
Interim Athletic Director: Christine Wilkinson
Football Coach: Bruce Snyder
Basketball Coach: Bill Frieder
Sports Information Director: Mark Brand

University of California
Address: Berkeley, CA 94720
Nickname: Golden Bears
Telephone: (510) 642-5363
Football Stadium (Capacity): Memorial Stadium (75,662)
Basketball Arena (Capacity): Harmon Gym (6,578),
  Oakland-Alameda County Coliseum Arena (15,039)
Chancellor: Chang-Lin Tien
Athletic Director: John Kasser
Football Coach: Keith Gilbertson
Basketball Coach: Todd Bozeman
Sports Information Director: Kevin Reneau

University of California at Los Angeles
Address: P.O. Box 24044
             Los Angeles, CA 90024
Nickname: Bruins
Telephone: (310) 206-6831
Football Stadium (Capacity): Rose Bowl (102,083)
Basketball Arena (Capacity): Pauley Pavilion (12,819)
Chancellor: Dr. Charles Young
Athletic Director: Peter T. Dalis
Football Coach: Terry Donahue
Basketball Coach: Jim Harrick
Sports Information Director: Marc Dellins

University of Oregon
Address: Len Casanova Athletic Center
             2727 Leo Harris Parkway
             Eugene, OR 97401
Nickname: Ducks
Telephone: (503) 346-4481
Football Stadium (Capacity): Autzen Stadium (41,698)
Basketball Arena (Capacity): McArthur Court (10,063)
President: David Frohnmayer
Athletic Director: William Moos
Football Coach: Mike Bellotti
Basketball Coach: Jerry Green
Sports Information Director: Steve Hellyer

Oregon State University
Address: Gill Coliseum
             Corvallis, OR 97331
Nickname: Beavers
Telephone: (503) 737-3720
Football Stadium (Capacity): Parker Stadium (36,345)
Basketball Arena (Capacity): Gill Coliseum (10,400)
President: Dr. John V. Byrne
Athletic Director: Dutch Baughman
Football Coach: Jerry Pettibone
Basketball Coach: Eddie Payne
Sports Information Director: Hal Cowan

University of Southern California
Address: Los Angeles, CA 90089
Nickname: Trojans
Telephone: (213) 740-8480
Football Stadium (Capacity): Los Angeles Memorial
  Coliseum (94,159)
Basketball Arena (Capacity): Los Angeles Sports
  Arena (15,509)
President: Dr. Steven Sample
Athletic Director: Mike Garrett
Football Coach: John Robinson
Basketball Coach: Charlie Parker
Sports Information Director: Tim Tessalone

Stanford University
Address: Stanford, CA 94305
Nickname: Cardinal
Telephone: (415) 723-4418
Football Stadium (Capacity): Stanford Stadium (85,500)
Basketball Arena (Capacity): Maples Pavilion (7,500)
President: Gerhard Casper
Athletic Director: Dr. Ted Leland
Football Coach: Tyrone Willingham
Basketball Coach: Mike Montgomery
Sports Information Director: Gary Migdol

University of Washington
Address: UW Media Relations
             Graves Building, Box 354070
             Seattle, WA 98195-4070
Nickname: Huskies
Telephone: (206) 543-2230
Football Stadium (Capacity): Husky Stadium (72,500)
Basketball Arena (Capacity): Hec Edmundson
  Pavilion (8,000)
President: Richard L. McCormick
Athletic Director: Barbara Hedges
Football Coach: Jim Lambright
Basketball Coach: Bob Bender
Sports Information Director: Jim Daves

Washington State University
Address: 107 Bohler Gym
             Pullman, WA 99164-1610
Nickname: Cougars
Telephone: (509) 335-0270
Football Stadium (Capacity): Martin Stadium (40,000)
Basketball Arena (Capacity): Friel Court (12,058)
President: Dr. Samuel H. Smith
Athletic Director: Rick Dickson
Football Coach: Mike Price
Basketball Coach: Kevin Eastman
Sports Information Director: Rod Commons

SOUTHEASTERN CONFERENCE
Address: 2201 Civic Center Boulevard
             Birmingham, AL 35203
Telephone: (205) 458-3000
Commissioner: Roy Kramer
Publicity Director: Mark Whitworth

University of Alabama
Address: P.O. Box 870323
             Paul Bryant Drive
             Tuscaloosa, AL 35487
Nickname: Crimson Tide
Telephone: (205) 348-3600
Football Stadium (Capacity): Bryant-Denny Stadium
  (70,123)
Basketball Arena (Capacity): Coleman Coliseum
  (15,043)
President: Dr. Roger Sayers
Interim Athletic Director: Glen Tuckett
Football Coach: Gene Stallings
Basketball Coach: David Hobbs
Sports Information Director: Larry White

University of Arkansas

Address: Broyles Athletic Center
                 Fayetteville, AR 72701
Nickname: Razorbacks
Telephone: (501) 575-2751
Football Stadium (Capacity): Razorback Stadium
(51,000)
Basketball Arena (Capacity): Bud Walton Arena
(19,002)
Chancellor: Dr. Dan Ferritor
Athletic Director: Frank Broyles
Football Coach: Danny Ford
Basketball Coach: Nolan Richardson
Sports Information Director: Rick Schaeffer

Auburn University

Address: P.O. Box 351
                 Auburn, AL 36831-0351
Nickname: Tigers
Telephone: (334) 844-9800
Football Stadium (Capacity): Jordan Hare Stadium
(85,214)
Basketball Arena (Capacity): Beard-Eaves Memorial
Coliseum (13,500)
President: Dr. William V. Muse
Athletic Director: David Housel
Football Coach: Terry Bowden
Basketball Coach: Cliff Ellis
Sports Information Director: Kent Partridge

University of Florida

Address: P.O. Box 14485
                 Gainesville, FL 32604
Nickname: Gators
Telephone: (904) 375-4683
Football Stadium (Capacity): Ben Hill Griffin Stadium
at Florida Field (83,000)
Basketball Arena (Capacity): Stephen C. O'Connell
Center (12,000)
President: Dr. John Lombardi
Athletic Director: Jeremy Foley
Football Coach: Steve Spurrier
Basketball Coach: Lon Kruger
Sports Information Director: John Humenik

University of Georgia

Address: P.O. Box 1472
                 Athens, GA 30603-1472
Nickname: Bulldogs
Telephone: (706) 542-1621
Football Stadium (Capacity): Sanford Stadium (86,117)
Basketball Arena (Capacity): The Coliseum (10,512)
President: Dr. Charles Knapp
Athletic Director: Vince Dooley
Football Coach: Ray Goff
Basketball Coach: Tubby Smith
Sports Information Director: Claude Felton

University of Kentucky

Address: Memorial Coliseum
                 Lexington, KY 40506
Nickname: Wildcats
Telephone: (606) 257-3838
Football Stadium (Capacity): Commonwealth Stadium
(57,800)
Basketball Arena (Capacity): Rupp Arena (23,000)
President: Dr. Charles Wethington Jr.
Athletic Director: C. M. Newton
Football Coach: Bill Curry
Basketball Coach: Rick Pitino
Sports Information Director: Tony Neeley

Louisiana State University

Address: P.O. Box 25095
                 Baton Rouge, LA 70894
Nickname: Fighting Tigers
Telephone: (504) 388-8226
Football Stadium (Capacity): Tiger Stadium (79,940)
Basketball Arena (Capacity): Pete Maravich
Assembly Center (14,164)
Chancellor: Dr. William E. Davis
Athletic Director: Joe Dean
Football Coach: Gerry DiNardo
Basketball Coach: Dale Brown
Sports Information Director: Herb Vincent

University of Mississippi

Address: P.O. Box 217
                 University, MS 38677
Nickname: Rebels
Telephone: (601) 232-7522
Football Stadium (Capacity): Vaught-Hemingway
Stadium (42,577)
Basketball Arena (Capacity): C. M. (Tad) Smith
Coliseum (8,135)
Chancellor: Dr. Robert C. Khayat
Athletic Director: Pete Boone
Football Coach: Tommy Tuberville
Basketball Coach: Robert Evans
Sports Information Director: Langston Rogers

Mississippi State University

Address: P.O. Drawer 5308
                 Mississippi St., MS 39762
Nickname: Bulldogs
Telephone: (601) 325-2703
Football Stadium (Capacity): Scott Field (41,200)
Basketball Arena (Capacity): Humphrey Coliseum
(9,149)
President: Dr. Donald Zacharias
Athletic Director: Larry Templeton
Football Coach: Jackie Sherrill
Basketball Coach: Richard Williams
Sports Information Director: Mike Nemeth

University of South Carolina

Address: Rex Enright Athletic Center
                 1300 Rosewood Drive
                 Columbia, SC 29208
Nickname: Gamecocks
Telephone: (803) 777-5204
Football Stadium (Capacity): Williams-Brice Stadium
(72,400)
Basketball Arena (Capacity): Frank McGuire Arena
(12,401)
President: Dr. John Palms
Athletic Director: Dr. Mike McGee
Football Coach: Brad Scott
Basketball Coach: Eddie Fogler
Sports Information Director: Kerry Tharp

University of Tennessee

Address: P.O. Box 15016
                 Knoxville, TN 37901
Nickname: Volunteers
Telephone: (615) 974-1212
Football Stadium (Capacity): Neyland Stadium (91,902)
Basketball Arena (Capacity): Thompson Boling Arena
and Assembly Center (24,535)
President: Dr. Joseph E. Johnson
Athletic Director: Doug Dickey
Football Coach: Phillip Fulmer
Basketball Coach: Kevin O'Neill
Sports Information Director: Bud Ford

College Sports Directory *(Cont.)*

Vanderbilt University
Address: P.O. Box 120158
              Nashville, TN 37212
Nickname: Commodores
Telephone: (615) 322-4121
Football Stadium (Capacity): Vanderbilt Stadium
  (41,000)
Basketball Arena (Capacity): Memorial Gym (15,311)
Chancellor: Joe B. Wyatt
Athletic Director: Paul Hoolahan
Football Coach: Rod Dowhower
Basketball Coach: Jan Van Breda Kolff
Sports Information Director: Rod Williamson

SOUTHWEST ATHLETIC CONFERENCE
Address: P.O. Box 569420
              Dallas, TX 75356
Telephone: (214) 634-7353
Commissioner: Kyle Kallander
Director of Media Relations: Bo Carter

Baylor University
Address: 150 Bear Run
              Waco, TX 76711
Nickname: Bears
Telephone: (817) 755-1234
Football Stadium (Capacity): Floyd Casey Stadium
  (48,500)
Basketball Arena (Capacity): Ferrell Center (10,080)
President: Dr. Herbert H. Reynolds
Athletic Director: Dr. Dick Ellis
Football Coach: Chuck Reedy
Basketball Coach: Darrel Johnson
Sports Information Director: Maxey Parrish

Rice University
Address: 6100 Main, MS548
              Houston, TX 77005-1892
Nickname: Owls
Telephone: (713) 527-4034
Football Stadium (Capacity): Rice Stadium (70,000)
Basketball Arena (Capacity): Autry Court (5,000)
President: Malcolm Gillis
Athletic Director: Bobby May
Football Coach: Ken Hatfield
Basketball Coach: Willis Wilson
Sports Information Director: Bill Cousins

Southern Methodist University
Address: SMU Box 216
              Dallas, TX 75275
Nickname: Mustangs
Telephone: (214) 768-2883
Football Stadium (Capacity): Cotton Bowl (68,252)
Basketball Arena (Capacity): Moody Coliseum (9,007)
President: R. Gerald Turner
Athletic Director: Jim Copeland
Football Coach: Tom Rossley
Basketball Coach: Mike Dement
Sports Information Director: Jon Jackson

University of Texas
Address: P.O. Box 7399
              Austin, TX 78713
Nickname: Longhorns
Telephone: (512) 471-7437
Football Stadium (Capacity): Memorial Stadium
  (75,512)
Basketball Arena (Capacity): Erwin Special Events
  Center (16,231)
Chancellor: Dr. William Cunningham
Athletic Director: DeLoss Dodds
Football Coach: John Mackovic
Basketball Coach: Tom Penders
Sports Information Director: Dave Saba

Texas A&M University
Address: John Koldus Building
              College Station, TX 77843
Nickname: Aggies
Telephone: (409) 845-3218
Football Stadium (Capacity): Kyle Field (72,387)
Basketball Arena (Capacity): G. Rollie White
  Coliseum (7,800)
President: Dr. Ray Bowen
Athletic Director: Wally Groff
Football Coach: R. C. Slocum
Basketball Coach: Tony Barone
Sports Information Director: Alan Cannon

Texas Christian University
Address: P.O. Box 32924
              Fort Worth, TX 76129
Nickname: Horned Frogs
Telephone: (817) 921-7969
Football Stadium (Capacity): Amon G. Carter Stadium
  (46,000)
Basketball Arena (Capacity): Daniel-Meyer Coliseum
  (7,166)
Chancellor: Dr. William E. Tucker
Athletic Director: Frank Windegger
Football Coach: Pat Sullivan
Basketball Coach: Billy Tubbs
Sports Information Director: Glen Stone

Texas Tech University
Address: Box 43021
              Lubbock, TX 79409
Nickname: Red Raiders
Telephone: (806) 742-2770
Football Stadium (Capacity): Jones Stadium (50,500)
Basketball Arena (Capacity): Lubbock Municipal
  Coliseum (8,174)
President: Dr. Robert Lawless
Athletic Director: Bob Bockrath
Football Coach: Spike Dykes
Basketball Coach: James Dickey
Sports Information Director: Joe Hornaday

WESTERN ATHLETIC CONFERENCE

Address: 14 West Dry Creek Circle
             Littleton, CO 80120
Telephone: (303) 795-1962
Commissioner: Karl Benson
Publicity Director: Jeff Hurd

Air Force

Address: USAF Academy, CO 80840-9500
Nickname: Falcons
Telephone: (719) 472-4008
Football Stadium (Capacity): Falcon Stadium (50,126)
Basketball Arena (Capacity): Clune Arena (6,007)
President: Lt. Gen. Paul E. Stein
Athletic Director: Col. Kenneth L. Schweitzer
Football Coach: Fisher DeBerry
Basketball Coach: Reggie Minton
Sports Information Director: David Kellogg

Brigham Young University

Address: 30 Smith Field House
             Provo, UT 84602
Nickname: Cougars
Telephone: (801) 378-4911
Football Stadium (Capacity): Cougar Stadium (65,000)
Basketball Arena (Capacity): Marriott Center (23,000)
President: Robert B. Sloan
Athletic Director: Rondo Fehlberg
Football Coach: LaVell Edwards
Basketball Coach: Harry Miller
Sports Information Director: Ralph Zobell

Colorado State University

Address: Moby Arena
             Fort Collins, CO 80523
Nickname: Rams
Telephone: (303) 491-5300
Football Stadium (Capacity): Hughes Stadium (30,000)
Basketball Arena (Capacity): Moby Arena (9,001)
President: Dr. Albert C. Yates
Athletic Director: Tom Jurich
Football Coach: Sonny Lubick
Basketball Coach: Stew Morrill
Sports Information Director: Gary Ozello

University of Hawaii

Address: 1335 Lower Campus Road
             Honolulu, HI 96822-2370
Nickname: Rainbow Warriors
Telephone: (808) 956-8111
Football Stadium (Capacity): Aloha Stadium (50,000)
Basketball Arena (Capacity): Special Events Arena
  (10,225)
President: Dr. Kenneth Mortimer
Athletic Director: Hugh Yoshida
Football Coach: Bob Wagner
Basketball Coach: Riley Wallace
Interim Sports Information Director: Lois Manin

University of New Mexico

Address: 1414 University S.E.
             Albuquerque, NM 87131
Nickname: Lobos
Telephone: (505) 277-6375
Football Stadium (Capacity): University Stadium (30,646)
Basketball Arena (Capacity): University Arena—The
  Pit (18,100)
President: Dr. Richard Peck
Athletic Director: Rudy Davalos
Football Coach: Dennis Franchione
Basketball Coach: Dave Bliss
Sports Information Director: Greg Remington

San Diego State University

Address: San Diego, CA 92182
Nickname: Aztecs
Telephone: (619) 594-5163
Football Stadium (Capacity): San Diego Jack Murphy
  Stadium (61,104)
Basketball Arena (Capacity): San Diego Sports
  Arena (13,741)
President: Dr. Thomas B. Day
Athletic Director: Rick Bay
Football Coach: Ted Tollner
Basketball Coach: Fred Trenkle
Sports Information Director: John Rosenthal

University of Texas at El Paso

Address: 201 Baltimore
             El Paso, TX 79902
Nickname: Miners
Telephone: (915) 747-5347
Football Stadium (Capacity): Sun Bowl (53,000)
Basketball Arena (Capacity): Special Events Center
  (12,222)
President: Dr. Diana Natalicio
Athletic Director: John Thompson
Football Coach: Charlie Bailey
Basketball Coach: Don Haskins
Sports Information Director: Eddie Mullens

University of Utah

Address: Huntsman Center
             Salt Lake City, UT 84112
Nickname: Utes
Telephone: (801) 581-8171
Football Stadium (Capacity): Rice Stadium (35,000)
Basketball Arena (Capacity): Huntsman Center
  (15,000)
President: Dr. Arthur K. Smith
Athletic Director: Dr. Chris Hill
Football Coach: Ron McBride
Basketball Coach: Rick Majerus
Sports Information Director: Bruce Woodbury

University of Wyoming

Address: P.O. Box 3414
             Laramie, WY 82071-3414
Nickname: Cowboys
Telephone: (307) 766-2292
Football Stadium (Capacity): War Memorial Stadium
  (33,500)
Basketball Arena (Capacity): Arena-Auditorium (15,028)
President: Dr. Terry Roark
Athletic Director: Paul Roach
Football Coach: Joe Tiller
Basketball Coach: Joby Wright
Sports Information Director: Kevin McKinney

College Sports Directory (Cont.)

INDEPENDENTS

Army
Address: West Point, NY 10996
Nickname: Cadets/Black Knights
Telephone: (914) 938-3303
Football Stadium (Capacity): Michie Stadium (39,929)
Basketball Arena (Capacity): Cristl Arena (5,043)
Superintendent: Lt. Gen. Howard D. Graves
Athletic Director: Al Vanderbush
Football Coach: Bob Sutton
Basketball Coach: Dino Gaudio
Sports Information Director: Bob Peretta

Note: Plays football as indep,, basketball in Patriot League.

East Carolina University
Address: Greenville, NC 27858-4353
Nickname: Pirates
Telephone: (919) 328-4600
Football Stadium (Capacity): Dowdy-Ficklen Stadium (35,000)
Basketball Arena (Capacity): Williams Arena (7,500)
Chancellor: Dr. Richard R. Eakin
Athletic Director: Michael A. Hamrick
Football Coach: Steve Logan
Basketball Coach: Joe Dooley
Sports Information Director: Norm Reilly

Navy
Address: 566 Brownson Road, Ricketts Hall
             Annapolis, MD 21402
Nickname: Midshipmen
Telephone: (410) 268-6220
Football Stadium (Capacity): Navy-Marine Corps Memorial Stadium (30,000)
Basketball Arena (Capacity): Alumni Hall (5,710)
Superintendent: Adm. Charles A. Larson, USN
Athletic Director: Jack Lengyel
Football Coach: Charlie Weatherby
Basketball Coach: Don DeVoe
Sports Information Director: Thomas Bates

Note: Plays football as indep., basketball in Patriot League.

University of Notre Dame
Address: Notre Dame, IN 46556
Nickname: Fighting Irish
Telephone: (219) 631-6107
Football Stadium (Capacity): Notre Dame Stadium (59,075)
Basketball Arena (Capacity): Joyce Athletic and Convocation Center (11,418)
President: Rev. Edward A. Malloy, CSC
Athletic Director: Michael Wadsworth
Football Coach: Lou Holtz
Basketball Coach: John MacLeod
Sports Information Director: John Heisler

University of Tulsa
Address: 600 S. College
             Tulsa, OK 74104
Nickname: Golden Hurricane
Telephone: (918) 631-2395
Football Stadium (Capacity): Skelley Stadium (40,385)
Basketball Arena (Capacity): Tulsa Convention Center (8,659)
President: Dr. Robert H. Donaldson
Interim Athletic Director: Judy MacLeod
Football Coach: Dave Rader
Basketball Coach: Steve Robinson
Sports Information Director: Don Tomkalski

Olympic Sports Directory

United States Olympic Committee
Address: Olympic House
             1 Olympic Plaza
             Colorado Springs, CO 80909
Telephone: (719) 632-5551
Executive Director: Dick Schultz
Director of Media Relations: Mike Moran

U.S. Olympic Training Center
Address: 1 Olympic Plaza
             Colorado Springs, CO 80909
Telephone: (719) 578-4500
Director: John Smith

U.S. Olympic Training Center
Address: 421 Old Military Road
             Lake Placid, NY 12946
Telephone: (518) 523-2600
Associate Director: Jack Favro

International Olympic Committee
Address: Chateau de Vidy
             CH-1007 Lausanne
             Switzerland
Telephone: (41.21) 25 3271/3272
President: Juan Antonio Samaranch
Director General: Francois Carrard
Public Relations Officer: Michele Verdier

Atlanta Olympic Organizing Committee
Address: P.O. Box 1996
             Atlanta, GA 30301
Telephone: (404) 224-1996
Co-Chairman: Hon. Andrew Young
President: William Porter Payne
Executive Director: Doug Gatlin
(Games of the XXVIth Olympiad; Dates: July 19-August 4, 1996)

U.S. Olympic Organizations

Archery

National Archery Association (NAA)
Address: 1 Olympic Plaza
             Colorado Springs, CO 80909
Telephone: (719) 578-4576
President: Tom Stevenson, Jr.
Executive Director: Robert C. Balink

Athletics (Track & Field)

USA Track & Field (formerly TAC)
Address: P.O. Box 120
             Indianapolis, IN 46206
Telephone: (317) 261-0500
President: Larry Ellis
Executive Director: Ollan Cassell
Press Information Director: Pete Cava

Badminton

U.S. Badminton Association (USBA)
Address: 1 Olympic Plaza
             Colorado Springs, CO 80909
Telephone: (719) 578-4808
President: Diane Cornell
Executive Director: TBA

Baseball

U.S. Baseball Federation (USBF)
Address: 2160 Greenwood Avenue
             Trenton, NJ 08609
Telephone: (609) 586-2381
President: Mark Marquess
Executive Director: Richard Case
Communications Director: George Doig

Basketball

USA Basketball
Address: 5465 Mark Dabling Blvd.
             Colorado Springs, CO 80918
Telephone: (719) 590-4800
President: C.M. Newton
Executive Director: Warren Brown
Assistant Executive Director for Public Relations:
  Craig Miller

Biathlon

U.S. Biathlon Association (USBA)
Address: 421 Old Military Road
             Lake Placid, NY 12946
Telephone: (518) 523-3836
President: Don Edwards
Executive Director: Dusty Johnstone

Bobsled

U.S. Bobsled and Skeleton Federation
Address: P.O. Box 828
             Lake Placid, NY 12946
Telephone: (518) 523-1842
President: Jim Morris
Executive Director: Matt Roy
Marketing and Communications Director: Terry Kent

Bowling

U.S. Tenpin Bowling Federation
Address: 5301 South 76th Street
             Greendale, WI 53129
Telephone: (414) 421-9008
President: Max Skelton
Executive Director: Gerald Koenig
Communications Director: Christine Krebs

Boxing

USA Boxing
Address: 1 Olympic Plaza
             Colorado Springs, CO 80909
Telephone: (719) 578-4506
President: Jerry Dusenberry
Executive Director: Bruce Mathis
Director of Communications: Kurt Stenerson

Canoe/Kayak

U.S. Canoe and Kayak Team
Address: Pan American Plaza, Suite 610
             201 South Capitol Avenue
             Indianapolis, IN 46225
Telephone: (317) 237-5690
Chairman: Lamar Sims
Executive Director: Chuck Wielgus
Director of Comm. and Marketing: Craig Bohnert

Cycling

U.S. Cycling Federation (USCF)
Address: 1 Olympic Plaza
             Colorado Springs, CO 80909
Telephone: (719) 578-4581
President: Mike Fraysse
Executive Director: Lisa Voight
Media and Public Relations Director: Steve Penny

Diving

United States Diving, Inc. (USD)
Address: Pan American Plaza, Suite 430
             201 South Capitol Avenue
             Indianapolis, IN 46225
Telephone: (317) 237-5252
President: Steve McFarland
Executive Director: Todd Smith
Director of Communications: Dave Shatkowski

Equestrian

U.S. Equestrian Team (USET)
Address: Gladstone, NJ 07934
Telephone: (908) 234-0155
Executive Director: Robert C. Standish
Director of Public Relations: Marty Bauman

Olympic Sports Directory *(Cont.)*

Fencing

U.S. Fencing Association (USFA)
Address: 1 Olympic Plaza
                  Colorado Springs, CO 80909
Telephone: (719) 578-4511
President: Stephen Sobel
Executive Director: TBA
Media Relations Director: TBA

Field Hockey

U.S. Field Hockey Association (USFHA) (Women)
Address: 1 Olympic Plaza
                  Colorado Springs, CO 80909
Telephone: (719) 578-4567
President: Jenepher Shillingford
Executive Director: Carrie Haag
Director of Public Relations: Mark Whitney

Figure Skating

U.S. Figure Skating Association (USFSA)
Address: 20 First Street
                  Colorado Springs, CO 80906
Telephone: (719) 635-5200
President: Morry Stillwell
Executive Director: Jerry Lace
Communications Director: Kristin Matta

Gymnastics

U.S. Gymnastics Federation (USGF)
Address: Pan American Plaza, Suite 300
                  201 South Capitol Avenue
                  Indianapolis, IN 46225
Telephone: (317) 237-5050
Chairman of the Board: Sandy Knapp
President: Kathy Scanlan
Director of Public Relations: Luan Peszek

Hockey

USA Hockey
Address: 4965 North 30th Street
                  Colorado Springs, CO 80919
Telephone: (719) 599-5500
President: Walter Bush
Executive Director: Dave Ogrean
Public Relations Coordinator: Darryl Sibel

Judo

United States Judo, Inc. (USJ)
Address: P.O. Box 10013
                  El Paso, TX 79991
Telephone: (915) 565-8754
President and Media Contact: Frank Fullerton

Luge

U.S. Luge Association (USLA)
Address: P.O. Box 651
                  Lake Placid, NY 12946
Telephone: (518) 523-2071
President: Dwight Bell
Executive Director: Ron Rossi
Public Relations Coordinator: Sandy Caligiore

Modern Pentathlon

U.S. Modern Pentathlon Association (USMPA)
Address: 530 McCullough Avenue, Suite 619
                  San Antonio, TX 78215
Telephone: (210) 246-3000
President: Robert Marbut
Executive Director: W. Dean Billick

Racquetball

American Amateur Racquetball Association (AARA)
Address: 1685 West Uintah
                  Colorado Springs, CO 80904
Telephone: (719) 635-5396
President: Van Dubolsky
Executive Director: Luke St. Onge
Public Relations Director: Linda Mojer

Roller Skating

U.S. Amateur Confederation of Roller Skating (USAC/RS)
Address: 4730 South Street
                  P.O. Box 6579
                  Lincoln, NE 68506
Telephone: (402) 483-7551
President: Betty Ann Danna
Executive Director: George H. Pickard
Sports Information Director: Andy Seeley

Rowing

U.S. Rowing Association (USRA)
Address: Pan American Plaza, Suite 400
                  201 South Capitol Avenue
                  Indianapolis, IN 46225
Telephone: (317) 237-5656
President: Dave Vogel
Executive Director: Frank J. Coyle
Director of Communications: Maureen Merhoff

Shooting

USA Shooting Association
Address: 1 Olympic Plaza
                  Colorado Springs, CO 80909
Telephone: (719) 578-4670
President: Stevan B. Richards
Executive Director: Robert L. Jursnick
Director of Public Relations: Nancy Moore
Program Administrator: Stephen Ducoff

Skiing

U.S. Skiing
Address: P.O. Box 100
                  Park City, UT 84060
Telephone: (801) 649-9090
Chairman: Nick Badami
President and CEO: Tim Leiweki
Vice-Chairman: Suzette Cantin
President, U.S. Ski Team Foundation:
     Vinton Sommerville
Director of Communications: Tom Kelly
Media Services Coordinator: Deborah Engen

Soccer

U.S. Soccer Federation (USSF)
Address: 1801-1811 South Prairie Avenue
             Chicago, IL 60616
Telephone: (312) 808-1300
President: Alan Rothenberg
Executive Director: Hank Steinbrecher
Director of Communications: Tom Lang

Softball

Amateur Softball Association (ASA)
Address: 2801 N.E. 50th Street
             Oklahoma City, OK 73111
Telephone: (405) 424-5266
President: Wayne Myers
Executive Director: Don Porter
Director of Communications: Ron Babb

Speedskating

U.S. International Speedskating Association (USISA)
Address: P.O. Box 16157
             Rocky River, OH 44116
Telephone: (216) 899-0128
President: Bill Cushman
Executive Director: Katie Marquard
Media Contact: Susan Polakoff-Shaw

Swimming

U.S. Swimming, Inc. (USS)
Address: 1 Olympic Plaza
             Colorado Springs, CO 80909
Telephone: (719) 578-4578
President: Carol Zaleski
Executive Director: Ray Essick
Communications Director: Charlie Snyder

Synchronized Swimming

U.S. Synchronized Swimming, Inc. (USSS)
Address: Pan American Plaza, Suite 510
             201 South Capitol Avenue
             Indianapolis, IN 46225
Telephone: (317) 237-5700
President: Nancy Wichtman
Executive Director: Debbie Hesse
Membership and Communications: Laura LaMarca

Table Tennis

U.S. Table Tennis Association (USTTA)
Address: 1 Olympic Plaza
             Colorado Springs, CO 80909
Telephone: (719) 578-4583
Executive Director: Paul Montville
President: Terry Timmins
Deputy Executive Director: Linda Gleeson

Taekwondo

U.S. Taekwondo Union (USTU)
Address: 1 Olympic Plaza, Suite 405
             Colorado Springs, CO 80909
Telephone: (719) 578-4632
President: Hwa Chong
Executive Director: Robert Fujimura

Team Handball

U.S. Team Handball Federation (USTHF)
Address: 1 Olympic Plaza
             Colorado Springs, CO 80909
Telephone: (719) 578-4582
President: Dr. Thomas Rosandich
Executive Director: Michael D. Cavanaugh

Tennis

U.S. Tennis Association
Address: 70 West Red Oak Lane
             White Plains, NY 10604
Telephone: (914) 696-7000
President: Dr. Lester Snyder
Executive Director: TBA
Director of Communications: Page Crosland

Volleyball

U.S. Volleyball Association (USVBA)
Address: 3595 East Fountain Boulevard, Suite I-2
             Colorado Springs, CO 80910-1740
Telephone: (719) 637-8300
President: Jerry Sherman
Executive Director: John Carroll

Water Polo

United States Water Polo (USWP)
Address: Pan American Plaza, Suite 520
             201 South Capitol Avenue
             Indianapolis, IN 46225
Telephone: (317) 237-5599
President: Richard Foster
Executive Director: Bruce J. Wigo
Communications Director: Kevin Messenger

Weightlifting

U.S. Weightlifting Federation (USWF)
Address: 1 Olympic Plaza
             Colorado Springs, CO 80909
Telephone: (719) 578-4508
President: Jim Schmitz
Executive Director: George Greenway
Communications Director: John Halpin

Wrestling

USA Wrestling
Address: 6155 Lehman
             Colorado Springs, CO 80918
Telephone: (719) 598-8181
President: Larry Sciacchetano
Executive Director: Jim Scherr
Director of Communications: Gary Abbott

Yachting

U.S. Yacht Racing Union (USYRU)
Address: P.O. Box 1260
             Portsmouth, RI 02871
Telephone: (401) 683-0800
President: David Irish
Executive Director: Terry Hopper
Communications Director: Dana Marnane
Olympic Yachting Director: Jonathan R. Harley

Affiliated Sports Organizations

Amateur Athletic Union (AAU)
Address: 3400 West 86th Street
            P.O. Box 68207
            Indianapolis, IN 46268
Telephone: (317) 872-2900
President: Bobby Dodd
Associate Operations Directors: Bruce Hopp and
  Tom Leix

Curling

U.S. Curling Association (USCA)
Address: 1100 Center Point Drive
            Box 866
            Stevens Point, WI 54481
Telephone: (715) 344-1199
President: Warren Lowe
Executive Director: David Garber

Karate

USA Karate Federation
Address: 1300 Kenmore Boulevard
            Akron, OH 44314
Telephone: (216) 753-3114
President: George Anderson

Orienteering

U.S. Orienteering Federation
Address: P.O. Box 1444
            Forest Park, GA 30051
Telephone: (404) 363-2110
President: Rick Worner
Executive Director: Robin Shannonhouse
Media and Publicity Contact: John Nash
Publicity telephone: (207) 439-7096

Squash

U.S. Squash Racquets Association
Address: 23 Cynwyd Road
            P.O. Box 1216
            Bala Cynwyd, PA 19004
Telephone: (610) 667-4006
President: Andre Naniche
Executive Director: Craig Brand

Trampoline and Tumbling

American Trampoline and Tumbling Association
Address: 400 West Broadway, Suite 207
            or P.O. Box 306
            Brownfield, TX 79316-0306
Telephone: (806) 637-8670
President: Chris Sans
Executive Director: Ann Sims

Triathlon

Triathlon Federation USA
Address: 3595 East Fountain Boulevard, Suite F-1
            Colorado Springs, CO 80910
Telephone: (719) 597-9090
President: Rick Margiotta
Executive Director: Steve Locke
Deputy Director and Media Contact: Tim Yount

Underwater Swimming

Underwater Society of America
Address: 849 West Orange Avenue
            No. 1002
            South San Francisco, CA 94080
Telephone: (415) 583-8492
President: George Rose

Water Skiing

American Water Ski Association
Address: 799 Overlook Drive, S.E.
            Winter Haven, FL 33884
Telephone: (813) 324-4341
President: Andrea Plough
Executive Director: Duke Waldrop
Public Relations Manager: Don Cullimore

Miscellaneous Sports Directory

American Professional Soccer League
Address: 2 Village Road, Suite 5
            Horsham, PA 19044
Telephone: (215) 657-7440
Chairman of the Board: Scott Oki
Commissioner: Richard Groff
Director of Operations: Chris Branscome

Continental Indoor Soccer League
Address: 16027 Ventura Boulevard, Suite 605
            Encino, CA 91436
Telephone: (818) 906-7627
Commissioner: Ron Weinstein
Director of Public Relations: Dan Courtemanche

National Professional Soccer League
Address: 229 Third Street NW
            Canton, OH 44702
Telephone: (216) 455-4625
Commissioner: Steve Paxos
Director of Operations: Paul Luchowski

Ladies Professional Golf Association
Address: 2570 W International Speedway
            Boulevard, Suite B
            Daytona Beach, FL 32114
Telephone: (904) 254-8800
Commissioner: Charles S. Mechem Jr.
Commissioner/elect: Jim Ritts
Director of Communications: Elaine Scott

Professional Golfers Association
Address: 112 TPC Boulevard
Ponte Vedra, FL 32082
Telephone: (904) 285-3700
Commissioner: Ken Finchem
Director of Public Relations: John Morris

United States Golf Association
Address: P.O. Box 708, Golf House
Liberty Corner Road
Far Hills, NJ 07931-0708
Telephone: (908) 234-2300
President: Reg Murphy

Association of Tennis Professionals Tour
Address: 200 ATP Tour Boulevard
Ponte Vedra Beach, FL 32082
Telephone: (904) 285-8000
Chief Executive Officer: Mark Miles
Director of Communications: Pete Alfano

Women's Tennis Association
Address: 133 First Street N.E.
St. Petersburg, FL 33701
Telephone: (813) 895-5000
Chief Executive Officer: Anne Person-Worcester
Director of Public Relations: TBA

United States Tennis Association
Address: 70 West Red Oak Lane
White Plains, NY 10604
Telephone: (914) 696-7000
President: Dr. Lester Snyder
Executive Director: TBA
Director of Communications: Page Crosland

National Association for Stock Car Auto Racing (NASCAR)
Address: P.O. Box 2875, 1801 W International
Speedway Boulevard
Daytona Beach, FL 32120
Telephone: (904) 253-0611
President: Bill France Jr.
Director of Public Relations: Andy Hall

Championship Auto Racing Teams (CART)
Address: 755 West Big Beaver Road, Suite 800
Troy, MI 48084
Telephone: (810) 362-8800
President/CEO: Andrew Craig
Director of Publicity: Adam Sall

National Hot Rod Association
Address: 2035 East Financial Way
Glendora, CA 91741
Telephone: (818) 914-4761
President: Dallas Gardner
Director of Communications: Denny Darnell

International Motor Sports Association
Address: 3502 Henderson Boulevard
Tampa, FL 33609
Telephone: (813) 877-4672
President: George Silberman
Communications Director: Lynn Myfelt

Professional Rodeo Cowboys Association
Address: 101 Pro Rodeo Drive
Colorado Springs, CO 80919
Telephone: (719) 593-8840
Commissioner: Lewis Cryer
Director of Communications: Steve Fleming

Thoroughbred Racing Associations of America
Address: 420 Fair Hill Drive, Suite 1
Elkton, MD 21921
Telephone: (410) 392-9200
President: Clifford C. Goodrich
Director of Service Bureau: Conrad Sobkowiak

Thoroughbred Racing Communications, Inc.
Address: 40 East 52nd Street
New York, NY 10022
Telephone: (212) 371-5910
Executive Director: Tom Merritt
Director of Media Relations and Development:
Bob Curran

Breeders' Cup Limited
Address: 2525 Harrodsburg Road
Lexington, KY 40544-4230
Telephone: (606) 223-5444
President: James Bassett
Media Relations Directors: Ben Metzger and James
Gluckson

The Jockeys' Guild, Inc.
Address: 250 West Main Street, Suite 1820
Lexington, KY 40507
Telephone: (606) 259-3211
President: Jerry Bailey
National Manager/Secretary: John Giovanni

United States Trotting Association
Address: 750 Michigan Avenue
Columbus, OH 43215
Telephone: (614) 224-2291
President: Corwin Nixon
Publicity Department: John Pawlak

Professional Bowlers Association
Address: 1720 Merriman Road, P.O. Box 5118
Akron, OH 44334-0118
Telephone: (216) 836-5568
Commissioner: Michael Connor
Public Relations Director: Kevin Shippy

Ladies Pro Bowlers Tour
Address: 7171 Cherryvale Boulevard
Rockford, IL 61112
Telephone: (815) 332-5756
Executive Tournament Director: TBA
Media Director: Lennie Gessler

Women's International Bowling Congress
Address: 5301 South 76th Street
Greendale, WI 53129-1191
Telephone: (414) 421-9000
President: Joyce Deitch
Public Relations Manager: Dave DeLorenzo

American Bowling Congress
Address: 5301 South 76th Street
Greendale, WI 53129
Telephone: (414) 421-6400
President: Ben Palumbo
Communications Executive: Steve James

Association of Volleyball Professionals
Address: 15260 Ventura Blvd., Suite #2250
Sherman Oaks, CA 91403
Telephone: (818) 386-2486
President: Jon Stevenson
VP of Sales and Marketing: Alison Canfield

U.S. Chess Federation
Address: 186 Route 9W
            New Windsor, NY 12553
Telephone: (914) 562-8350
Executive Director: Al Lawrence
Director of Operations: George Filippone

Iditarod Trail Committee
Address: P.O. Box 870800
            Wasilla, AK 99687
Telephone: (907) 376-5155
Executive Director: Stan Hooley
Race Director: Joanne Potts

International Game Fish Association
Address: 1301 East Atlantic Boulevard
            Pompano Beach, FL 33060
Telephone: (305) 941-3474
President: Mike Leech

American Greyhound Track Operators Association
Address: 1065 Northeast 125th Street, Suite 219
            North Miami, FL 33161
Telephone: (305) 893-2101
President: Stanley S. Phillips
Secretary/Executive Director: Patrick E. Winters

U.S. Handball Association
Address: 2333 North Tucson Boulevard
            Tucson, AZ 85716
Telephone: (602) 795-0434
Executive Director: Vern Roberts
Director of Public Relations: Cheri Beltramo

U.S. Club Lacrosse Association
Address: c/o Lacrosse Foundation
            113 W University Parkway
            Baltimore, MD 21210
Telephone: (410) 235-6882
Executive Director: Steven B. Stenersen

Little League Baseball, Inc.
Address: P.O. Box 3485
            Williamsport, PA 17701
Telephone: (717) 326-1921
President: Stephen Keener
Communications Director: Dennis Sullivan

American Powerboating Association
Address: P.O. Box 377
            Eastpointe, MI 48021
Telephone: (810) 773-9700
Executive Administrator: Gloria Urbin

U.S. Polo Association
Address: 4059 Iron Works Pike
            Lexington, KY 40511
Telephone: (606) 255-0593
Executive Director: George Alexander, Jr.

U.S. Rubgy Football Union
Address: 3595 East Fountain Boulevard
            Colorado Springs, CO 80910
Telephone: (719) 637-1022
Executive Director: TBA

MINOR LEAGUES

Baseball (AAA)

American Association
Address: 6801 Miami Ave., Suite 3
            Cincinnati, OH 45243
Telephone: (513) 271-4800
President: Branch B. Rickey

International League
Address: 55 South High Street, Suite 202
            Dublin, OH 43017
Telephone: (614) 791-9300
President: Randy Mobley

Mexican League
Address: Angela Pola #16
            Col. Periodista, C.P. 11220
            Mexico D.F.
Telephone: 011-525-557-10-07
President: Pedro Cisneros

Pacific Coast League
Address: 2345 South Alma School Rd., Suite 110
            Mesa, AZ 85210
Telephone: (602) 838-2171
President: Bill Cutler

Hockey

American Hockey League
Address: 425 Union Street
            West Springfield, MA 01089
Telephone: (413) 781-2030
President: David Andrews
Senior VP of Hockey Operations: Gordon Anziano

International Hockey League
Address: 1577 North Woodward Ave., Suite 212
            Bloomfield Hills, MI 48304
Telephone: (810) 258-0580
Commissioner: Robert P. Ufer
VP of Public Relations: Tim Bryant

Hall of Fame Directory

National Baseball Hall of Fame and Museum
Address: P.O. Box 590
             Cooperstown, NY 13326
Telephone: (607) 547-9114
Vice President: Bill Guilfoile
Director of Public Relations: Jeff Idelson

Naismith Memorial Basketball Hall of Fame
Address: 1150 West Columbus Avenue
             Springfield, MA 01101
Telephone: (413) 781-6500
President: Joseph O'Brien
Director of Public Relations: Robin Deutsch

National Bowling Hall of Fame and Museum
Address: 111 Stadium Plaza
             St Louis, MO 63102
Telephone: (314) 231-6340
Executive Director: Gerald Baltz
Director of Marketing: Raleigh Ragan

National Boxing Hall of Fame
Address: 1 Hall of Fame Drive
             Canastota, NY 13032
Telephone: (315) 697-7095
President: Donald Ackerman
Executive Director: Edward Brophy

Professional Football Hall of Fame
Address: 2121 George Halas Drive NW
             Canton, OH 44708
Telephone: (216) 456-8207
Executive Director: Pete Elliott
Vice President, Public Relations: Don Smith

LPGA Hall of Fame
Address: 2570 West International Speedway
             Boulevard, Suite B
             Daytona Beach, FL 32114
Telephone: (904) 254-8800
Commissioner: Charles S. Mechem
Commissioner/elect: Jim Ritts
Communications Director: Elaine Scott

Professional Hockey Hall of Fame
Address: 30 Young Street BCE Place
             Toronto, Ontario Canada M5E 1X8
Telephone: (416) 360-7735
VP of Marketing and Communications: Bryan Blanc
VP of Finance: Jeff Denomme

National Museum of Racing and Hall of Fame
Address: 191 Union Avenue
             Saratoga Springs, NY 12866
Telephone: (518) 584-0400
Executive Director: Peter Hammell
Assistant Director: Catherine Maguire

National Soccer Hall of Fame
Address: 5-11 Ford Avenue
             Oneonta, NY 13820
Telephone: (607) 432-3351
Executive Director: Albert Colone
External Affairs: Will Lunn

International Swimming Hall of Fame
Address: 1 Hall of Fame Drive
             Fort Lauderdale, FL 33316
Telephone: (305) 462-6536
President: Dr. Samuel J. Freas
Director of Marketing: Michelle Mitchell-Rocha

International Tennis Hall of Fame
Address: 194 Bellevue Avenue
             Newport, RI 02840
Telephone: (401) 849-3990
Executive Director: Mark Stenning
Director of Public Relations: Linda Johnson

National Track & Field Hall of Fame
Address: 1 RCA Dome, Suite 140
             Indianapolis, IN 46225
Telephone: (317) 261-0500
Historian: Hal Bateman
Director of Media Relations: Pete Cava

Awards

sportswoman and sportsman of the year

Sports Illustrated

olympians
bonnie blair
and
johann olav koss

Athlete Awards

Sports Illustrated Sportsman of the Year

1954	Roger Bannister, Track
1955	Johnny Podres, Baseball
1956	Bobby Morrow, Track
1957	Stan Musial, Baseball
1958	Rafer Johnson, Track
1959	Ingemar Johansson, Boxing
1960	Arnold Palmer, Golf
1961	Jerry Lucas, Basketball
1962	Terry Baker, Football
1963	Pete Rozelle, Pro Football
1964	Ken Venturi, Golf
1965	Sandy Koufax, Baseball
1966	Jim Ryun, Track
1967	Carl Yastrzemski, Baseball
1968	Bill Russell, Pro Basketball
1969	Tom Seaver, Baseball
1970	Bobby Orr, Hockey
1971	Lee Trevino, Golf
1972	Billie Jean King, Tennis
	John Wooden, Basketball
1973	Jackie Stewart, Auto Racing
1974	Muhammad Ali, Boxing
1975	Pete Rose, Baseball
1976	Chris Evert, Tennis
1977	Steve Cauthen, Horse Racing
1978	Jack Nicklaus, Golf
1979	Terry Bradshaw, Pro Football

	Willie Stargell, Baseball
1980	US Olympic Hockey Team
1981	Sugar Ray Leonard, Boxing
1982	Wayne Gretzky, Hockey
1983	Mary Decker, Track
1984	Mary Lou Retton, Gymnastics
	Edwin Moses, Track
1985	Kareem Abdul-Jabbar, Pro Basketball
1986	Joe Paterno, Football
1987	Athletes Who Care
	Bob Bourne, Hockey
	Kip Keino, Track
	Judi Brown King, Track
	Dale Murphy, Baseball
	Chip Rives, Football
	Patty Sheehan, Golf
	Rory Sparrow, Pro Basketball
	Reggie Williams, Pro Football
1988	Orel Hershiser, Baseball
1989	Greg LeMond, Cycling
1990	Joe Montana, Pro Football
1991	Michael Jordan, Pro Basketball
1992	Arthur Ashe
1993	Don Shula, Pro Football
1994	Bonnie Blair, Speed Skating
	Johann Olav Koss, Speed Skating

Associated Press Athletes of the Year

	MEN	WOMEN
1931	Pepper Martin, Baseball	Helene Madison, Swimming
1932	Gene Sarazen, Golf	Babe Didrikson, Track
1933	Carl Hubbell, Baseball	Helen Jacobs, Tennis
1934	Dizzy Dean, Baseball	Virginia Van Wie, Golf
1935	Joe Louis, Boxing	Helen Wills Moody, Tennis
1936	Jesse Owens, Track	Helen Stephens, Track
1937	Don Budge, Tennis	Katherine Rawls, Swimming
1938	Don Budge, Tennis	Patty Berg, Golf
1939	Nile Kinnick, Football	Alice Marble, Tennis
1940	Tom Harmon, Football	Alice Marble, Tennis
1941	Joe DiMaggio, Baseball	Betty Hicks Newell, Golf
1942	Frank Sinkwich, Football	Gloria Callen, Swimming
1943	Gunder Haegg, Track	Patty Berg, Golf
1944	Byron Nelson, Golf	Ann Curtis, Swimming
1945	Bryon Nelson, Golf	Babe Didrikson Zaharias, Golf
1946	Glenn Davis, Football	Babe Didrikson Zaharias, Golf
1947	Johnny Lujack, Football	Babe Didrikson Zaharias, Golf
1948	Lou Boudreau, Baseball	Fanny Blankers-Koen, Track
1949	Leon Hart, Football	Marlene Bauer, Golf
1950	Jim Konstanty, Baseball	Babe Didrikson Zaharias, Golf
1951	Dick Kazmaier, Football	Maureen Connolly, Tennis
1952	Bob Mathias, Track	Maureen Connolly, Tennis
1953	Ben Hogan, Golf	Maureen Connolly, Tennis
1954	Willie Mays, Baseball	Babe Didrikson Zaharias, Golf
1955	Hopalong Cassidy, Football	Patty Berg, Golf
1956	Mickey Mantle, Baseball	Pat McCormick, Diving
1957	Ted Williams, Baseball	Althea Gibson, Tennis
1958	Herb Elliott, Track	Althea Gibson, Tennis
1959	Ingemar Johansson, Boxing	Maria Bueno, Tennis
1960	Rafer Johnson, Track	Wilma Rudolph, Track
1961	Roger Maris, Baseball	Wilma Rudolph, Track
1962	Maury Wills, Baseball	Dawn Fraser, Swimming
1963	Sandy Koufax, Baseball	Mickey Wright, Golf

Associated Press Athletes of the Year (Cont.)

	MEN	WOMEN
1964	Don Schollander, Swimming	Mickey Wright, Golf
1965	Sandy Koufax, Baseball	Kathy Whitworth, Golf
1966	Frank Robinson, Baseball	Kathy Whitworth, Golf
1967	Carl Yastrzemski, Baseball	Billie Jean King, Tennis
1968	Denny McLain, Baseball	Peggy Fleming, Skating
1969	Tom Seaver, Baseball	Debbie Meyer, Swimming
1970	George Blanda, Pro Football	Chi Cheng, Track
1971	Lee Trevino, Golf	Evonne Goolagong, Tennis
1972	Mark Spitz, Swimming	Olga Korbut, Gymnastics
1973	O. J. Simpson, Pro Football	Billie Jean King, Tennis
1974	Muhammad Ali, Boxing	Chris Evert, Tennis
1975	Fred Lynn, Baseball	Chris Evert, Tennis
1976	Bruce Jenner, Track	Nadia Comaneci, Gymnastics
1977	Steve Cauthen, Horse Racing	Chris Evert, Tennis
1978	Ron Guidry, Baseball	Nancy Lopez, Golf
1979	Willie Stargell, Baseball	Tracy Austin, Tennis
1980	US Olympic Hockey Team	Chris Evert Lloyd, Tennis
1981	John McEnroe, Tennis	Tracy Austin, Tennis
1982	Wayne Gretzky, Hockey	Mary Decker, Track
1983	Carl Lewis, Track	Martina Navratilova, Tennis
1984	Carl Lewis, Track	Mary Lou Retton, Gymnastics
1985	Dwight Gooden, Baseball	Nancy Lopez, Golf
1986	Larry Bird, Pro Basketball	Martina Navratilova, Tennis
1987	Ben Johnson, Track	Jackie Joyner-Kersee, Track
1988	Orel Hershiser, Baseball	Florence Griffith Joyner, Track
1989	Joe Montana, Pro Football	Steffi Graf, Tennis
1990	Joe Montana, Pro Football	Beth Daniel, Golf
1991	Michael Jordan, Pro Basketball	Monica Seles, Tennis
1992	Michael Jordan, Pro Basketball	Monica Seles, Tennis
1993	Michael Jordan, Pro Basketball	Sheryl Swoopes, College Basketball
1994	George Foreman, Boxing	Bonnie Blair, Speed Skating

James E. Sullivan Award

Presented annually by the Amateur Athletic Union to the athlete who "by his or her performance, example and influence as an amateur, has done the most during the year to advance the cause of sportsmanship."

1930	Bobby Jones, Golf	1960	Rafer Johnson, Track
1931	Barney Berlinger, Track	1961	Wilma Rudolph, Track
1932	Jim Bausch, Track	1962	Jim Beatty, Track
1933	Glenn Cunningham, Track	1963	John Pennel, Track
1934	Bill Bonthron, Track	1964	Don Schollander, Swimming
1935	Lawson Little, Golf	1965	Bill Bradley, Basketball
1936	Glenn Morris, Track	1966	Jim Ryun, Track
1937	Don Budge, Tennis	1967	Randy Matson, Track
1938	Don Lash, Track	1968	Debbie Meyer, Swimming
1939	Joe Burk, Rowing	1969	Bill Toomey, Track
1940	Greg Rice, Track	1970	John Kinsella, Swimming
1941	Leslie MacMitchell, Track	1971	Mark Spitz, Swimming
1942	Cornelius Warmerdam, Track	1972	Frank Shorter, Track
1943	Gilbert Dodds, Track	1973	Bill Walton, Basketball
1944	Ann Curtis, Swimming	1974	Rich Wohlhuter, Track
1945	Doc Blanchard, Football	1975	Tim Shaw, Swimming
1946	Arnold Tucker, Football	1976	Bruce Jenner, Track
1947	John B. Kelly, Jr, Rowing	1977	John Naber, Swimming
1948	Bob Mathias, Track	1978	Tracy Caulkins, Swimming
1949	Dick Button, Skating	1979	Kurt Thomas, Gymnastics
1950	Fred Wilt, Track	1980	Eric Heiden, Speed Skating
1951	Bob Richards, Track	1981	Carl Lewis, Track
1952	Horace Ashenfelter, Track	1982	Mary Decker, Track
1953	Sammy Lee, Diving	1983	Edwin Moses, Track
1954	Mal Whitfield, Track	1984	Greg Louganis, Diving
1955	Harrison Dillard, Track	1985	Joan B. Samuelson, Track
1956	Pat McCormick, Diving	1986	Jackie Joyner-Kersee, Track
1957	Bobby Morrow, Track	1987	Jim Abbott, Baseball
1958	Glenn Davis, Track	1988	Florence Griffith Joyner, Track
1959	Parry O'Brien, Track	1989	Janet Evans, Swimming

James E. Sullivan Award (Cont.)

1990 ....John Smith, Wrestling	1993 ....Charlie Ward, College Football, Basketball
1991 ....Mike Powell, Track	1994 ....Dan Jansen, Speed Skating
1992 ....Bonnie Blair, Speed Skating	

The Sporting News Man of the Year

1968 ....Denny McLain, Baseball	1983 ....Bowie Kuhn, Baseball
1969 ....Tom Seaver, Baseball	1984 ....Peter Ueberroth, LA Olympics
1970 ....John Wooden, Basketball	1985 ....Pete Rose, Baseball
1971 ....Lee Trevino, Golf	1986 ....Larry Bird, Pro Basketball
1972 ....Charles O. Finley, Baseball	1987 ....No award
1973 ....O. J. Simpson, Pro Football	1988 ....Jackie Joyner-Kersee, Track
1974 ....Lou Brock, Baseball	1989 ....Joe Montana, Pro Football
1975 ....Archie Griffin, Football	1990 ....Nolan Ryan, Baseball
1976 ....Larry O'Brien, Pro Basketball	1991 ....Michael Jordan, Pro Basketball
1977 ....Steve Cauthen, Horse Racing	1992 ....Mike Krzyzewski, College Basketball Coach
1978 ....Ron Guidry, Baseball	1993 ....Pat Gillick and Cito Gaston, Baseball
1979 ....Willie Stargell, Baseball	1994 ....Emmitt Smith, Pro Football
1980 ....George Brett, Baseball	
1981 ....Wayne Gretzky, Hockey	
1982 ....Whitey Herzog, Baseball	

United Press International Male and Female Athlete of the Year

	MEN	WOMEN
1974	Muhammad Ali, Boxing	Irena Szewinska, Track and Field
1975	Joao Oliveira, Track and Field	Nadia Comaneci, Gymnastics
1976	Alberto Juantorena, Track and Field	Nadia Comaneci, Gymnastics
1977	Alberto Juantorena, Track and Field	Rosie Ackermann, Track and Field
1978	Henry Rono, Track and Field	Tracy Caulkins, Swimming
1979	Sebastian Coe, Track and Field	Marita Koch, Track and Field
1980	Eric Heiden, Speed Skating	Hanni Wenzel, Alpine Skiing
1981	Sebastian Coe, Track and Field	Chris Evert Lloyd, Tennis
1982	Daley Thompson, Track and Field	Marita Koch, Track and Field
1983	Carl Lewis, Track and Field	Jarmila Kratochvilova, Track and Field
1984	Carl Lewis, Track and Field	Martina Navratilova, Tennis
1985	Steve Cram, Track and Field	Mary Decker Slaney, Track and Field
1986	Diego Maradona, Soccer	Heike Drechsler, Track and Field
1987	Ben Johnson, Track and Field	Steffi Graf, Tennis
1988	Matt Biondi, Swimming	Florence Griffith Joyner, Track and Field
1989	Boris Becker, Tennis	Steffi Graf, Tennis
1990	Stefan Edberg, Tennis	Merlene Ottey, Track and Field
1991	Michael Jordan, Pro Basketball	Monica Seles, Tennis
1992	Mario Lemieux, Hockey	Monica Seles, Tennis
1993	Michael Jordan, Pro Basketball	Steffi Graf, Tennis
1994	Nick Price, Golf	Bonnie Blair, Speed Skating

Dial Award

Presented annually by the Dial Corporation to the male and female national high school athlete/scholar of the year.

	MEN	WOMEN
1979	Herschel Walker, Football	No award
1980	Bill Fralic, Football	Carol Lewis, Track
1981	Kevin Willhite, Football	Cheryl Miller, Basketball
1982	Mike Smith, Basketball	Elaine Zayak, Skating
1983	Chris Spielman, Football	Melanie Buddemeyer, Swimming
1984	Hart Lee Dykes, Football	Nora Lewis, Basketball
1985	Jeff George, Football	Gea Johnson, Track
1986	Scott Schaffner, Football	Mya Johnson, Track
1987	Todd Marinovich, Football	Kristi Overton, Water Skiing
1988	Carlton Gray, Football	Courtney Cox, Basketball
1989	Robert Smith, Football	Lisa Leslie, Basketball
1990	Derrick Brooks, Football	Vicki Goetze, Golf
1991	Jeff Buckey, Football, Track	Katie Smith, Basketball, Volleyball, Track
1992	Jacque Vaughn, Basketball	Amanda White, Track, Swimming
1993	Tiger Woods, Golf	Kristin Folkl, Basketball
1994	Taymon Domzalski, Basketball	Shannon Miller, Gymnastics

Profiles

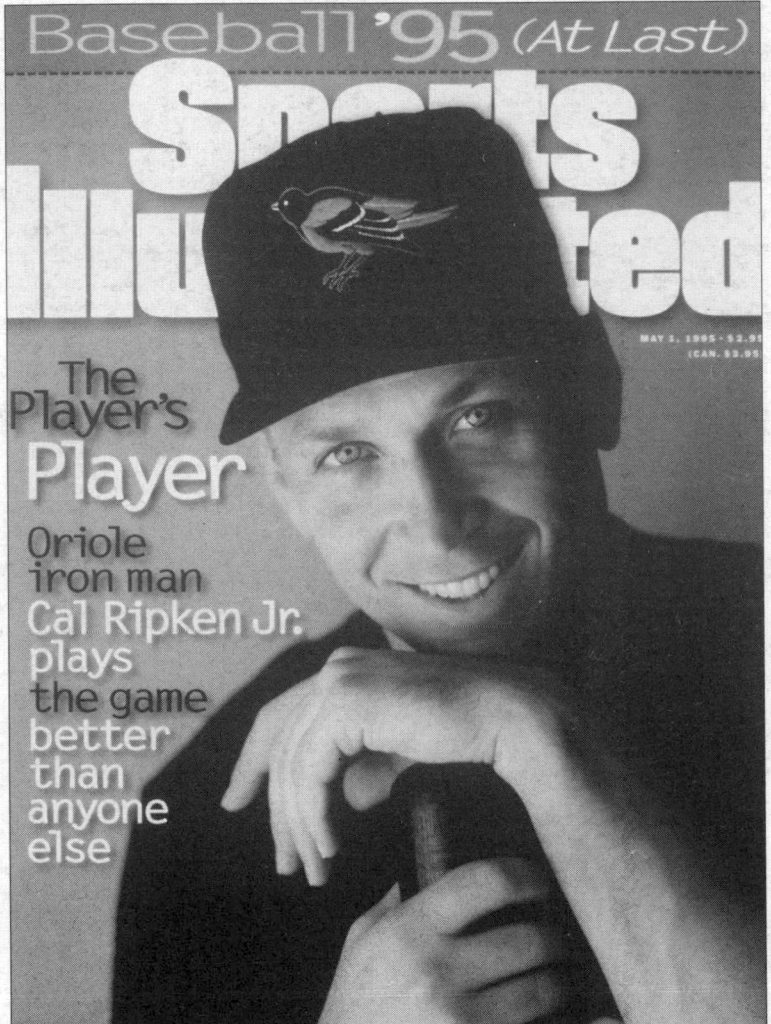

Baseball '95 *(At Last)*

Sports Illustrated

MAY 1, 1995 · $2.95
(CAN. $3.95)

The
Player's
Player

Oriole
iron man
Cal Ripken Jr.
plays
the game
better
than
anyone
else

WALTER IOOSS JR.

Profiles

Henry Aaron (b. 2-5-34): Baseball OF. "Hammerin' Hank." Alltime leader in HR (755) and RBI (2,297); third in hits (3,771). 1957 MVP. Led league in HR and RBI 4 times each, runs scored 3 times, hits and batting average 2 times. No. 44, he had 44 homers 4 times. Had 40+ HR 8 times; 100+ RBI 11 times; .300+ average 14 times. 24-time All-Star. Career span 1954–76; jersey number retired by Atlanta and Milwaukee.

Kareem Abdul-Jabbar (b. 4-16-47): Born Lew Alcindor. Basketball C. All-time leader points scored (38,387), field goals attempted (28,307), field goals made (15,837), blocked shots (3,189), games played (1,560), and years played (20); third all-time rebounds (17,440). Won 6 MVP awards (1971–72, 1974, 1976–77, 1980). Career scoring average was 24.6, rebounding average 11.2. 10-time All-Star, All-Defensive team 5 times. 1970 Rookie of the Year. Played on 6 championship teams; was playoff MVP in 1971, 1985. Career span 1969–88 with Milwaukee, Los Angeles. Also played on 3 NCAA championship teams with UCLA; tournament MVP 1967–69; Player of the Year 2 times.

Affirmed (b. 2-21-75): Thoroughbred race horse. Triple Crown winner in 1978 with jockey Steve Cauthen aboard. Trained by Laz Barrera.

Troy Aikman (b. 11-21-66): Football QB. MVP of Super Bowl XXVII, in which he completed 22 of 30 passes for 273 yards and four TDs with no interceptions. Led Cowboys to Super Bowl XXVIII victory. Career span since 1989 with Dallas Cowboys.

Tenley Albright (b. 7-18-35): Figure skater. Gold medalist at 1956 Olympics, silver medalist at 1952 Olympics. World champion 2 times (1953, 1955) and U.S. champion 5 consecutive years (1952–56).

Grover Cleveland Alexander (b. 2-26-1887, d. 11-4-50): Baseball RHP. Third alltime most wins (373), second most shutouts (90). Won 30+ games 3 times, 20+ games 6 other times. Set rookie record with 28 wins in 1911. Career span 1911–30 with Philadelphia (NL), Chicago (NL), St Louis (NL).

Vasili Alexeyev (b. 1942): Soviet weightlifter. Gold medalist at 2 consecutive Olympics in 1972, 1976. World champion 8 times.

Muhammad Ali (b. 1-17-42): Born Cassius Clay. Boxer. Heavyweight champion 3 times (1964–67, 1974–78, 1978–79). Stripped of title in 1967 because he refused to serve in the Vietnam War. Career record 56–5 with 37 KOs. Defended title 19 times. Also light heavyweight gold medalist at 1960 Olympics.

Phog Allen (b. 11-18-1885, d. 9-16-74): College baskeball coach. Fifth alltime most wins (746); .739 career winning percentage. Won 1952 NCAA championship. Most of career, 1920–56, with Kansas.

Bobby Allison (b. 12-3-37): Auto racer. Third all-time in NASCAR victories (84) at the time of his retirement. Won Daytona 500 3 times (1978, 1982, 1988). Also NASCAR champion in 1983.

Naty Alvarado (b. 7-25-55): Mexican-born handball player. "El Gato (The Cat)". Won a record 11 U.S. pro four-wall handball titles starting in 1977.

Lance Alworth (b. 8-3-40): Football WR. "Bambi" led NFL in receiving in 1966, '68 and '69. 200+ yards in a game 5 times in career, a record. Gained 100+ yards in game 41 times. In 1965 gained 1,602 yards, still second highest seasonal yardage ever. Career span 1962–70 with San Diego and 1971–72 with Dallas. Elected to Pro Football Hall of Fame 1978.

Sparky Anderson (b. 2-22-34): Baseball manager. Only manager to win World Series in both leagues (Detroit, 1984, Cincinnati, 1975–76); only manager to win 100 games in both leagues.

Willie Anderson (b. 1880, d. 1910): Scottish golfer. Won U.S. Open 4 times (1901 and an unmatched three straight, 1903–05). Also won 4 Western Opens between 1902 and 1909.

Mario Andretti (b. 2-28-40): Auto racer. The only driver in history to win Daytona 500 (1967), Indy 500 (1969) and Formula One world championship (1978). Second alltime in CART victories (52) as of retirement in Oct. 1994. Also 12 career Formula One victories. USAC/CART champion 4 times (consecutively 1965–66, 1969, 1984). Named Indy 500 Rookie of the Year in 1965.

Earl Anthony (b. 4-27-38): Bowler. Won PBA National Championship 6 times, more than any other bowler (consecutively 1973–75, 1981–83) and Tournament of Champions 2 times (1974, 1978). First bowler to top $1 million in career earnings. Bowler of the Year 6 times (consecutively 1974–76, 1981–83). Has won 45 career PBA titles since 1970.

Said Aouita (b. 11-2-60): Track and field. Moroccan set world records in 2,000 meters (4:50.81 in 1987), and 5,000 meters (12:58.39 in 1987). 1984 Olympic champion in 5,000; 1988 Olympic third place in 800.

Al Arbour (b. 11-1-32): Hockey D-coach. Led NY Islanders to 4 consecutive Stanley Cup championships (1980–83). Also played on 3 Stanley Cup champions: Detroit, Chicago and Toronto, from 1953 to 1971.

Eddie Arcaro (b. 2-19-16): Horse racing jockey. The only jockey to win the Triple Crown 2 times (aboard Whirlaway in 1941, Citation in 1948). Rode Preakness Stakes winner (1941, 1948, consecutively 1950–51, 1955, 1957) and Belmont Stakes winner (consecutively 1941–42, 1945, 1948, 1952, 1955) 6 times each and Kentucky Derby winner 5 times (1938, 1941, 1945, 1948, 1952). 4,779 career wins.

Nate Archibald (b. 9-2-48): Basketball player. "Tiny" only by NBA standards at 6' 1", 160 pounds. Drafted by Cincinnati in 1970. Averaged 34 points per game for K.C.-Omaha in 1972–73. Led NBA in scoring (34.0) and assists (910) in 1972–73. First team, all-NBA in 1973, '75 and '76. MVP of NBA All Star game in 1981. Retired in 1984.

Alexis Arguello (b. 4-19-52): Nicaraguan Boxer. Won world titles in three weight classes—featherweight, super featherweight and lightweight. Won first title, WBA featherweight, on 11-23-74 when he KO'd Ruben Olivares in 13. Won last title, vacant WBC lightweight, on 5-22-82 when he KO'd Andrew Ganigan in 5. Career record: 86 bouts; won 65 by KO, 15 by decision; lost 6, three by KO.

Henry Armstrong (b. 12-12-12): Boxer. Champion in 3 different weight classes: featherweight (1937—relinquished 1938), welterweight (1938–40) and lightweight (1938–39). Career record 145-20-9 with 98 KOs (27 consecutively, 1937–38) from 1931 to 1945.

Arthur Ashe (b. 7-10-43; d. 2-6-93): Tennis player. First black man to win U.S. Open (1968, as an amateur), Australian Open (1970) and Wimbledon singles titles (1975). 33 career tournament victories. Member of Davis Cup team 1963–78; captain 1980–85. Died of AIDS-related pneumonia.

Assault (b. 1943): Thoroughbred race horse. Horse of the Year for 1946; won Triple Crown that year. Won Kentucky Derby by 8 lengths; Preakness by a neck over Lord Boswell; and the Belmont by 3 lengths from Natchez. Trained by Max Hirsch.

Red Auerbach (b. 9-20-17): Basketball coach-executive.Second in wins (938). Coached Boston from 1946 to 1965, winning 9 championships, 8 consecutively. Had .662 career winning percentage, with 50+ wins 8 consecutive seasons. Also won 7 championships as general manager.

Hobey Baker (b. 1-15-1892, d. 12-21-18): Sportsman. Member of both college football and hockey Halls of Fame. College hockey and football star with Princeton, 1911–14. Fighter pilot in World War I, died in plane crash. College hockey Player of the Year award named in his honor.

Seve Ballesteros (b. 4-9-57): Spanish golfer. Notorious scrambler. Won British Opens in 1979, '84 and '88. Won Masters in 1980 and '83.

Ernie Banks (b. 1-31-31): Baseball SS-1B. "Mr. Cub." Won 2 consecutive MVP awards, in 1958–59. 512 career HR. League leader in HR, RBI 2 times each; career batting average of .274; 40+ HR 5 times; 100+ RBI 8 times. Most HR by a shortstop with 47 in 1958. Career span 1953–71 with Chicago.

Roger Bannister (b. 3-23-29): Track and field. British runner broke the 4-minute mile barrier, running 3:59.4 on May 6, 1954.

Red Barber (b. 2-17-08, d. 10-22-92): Sportscaster. TV-radio baseball announcer was the voice of Cincinnati, Brooklyn and NY Yankees. His expressions, such as "sitting in the catbird seat," "pea patch" and "rhubarb" captivated audiences from 1934 to 1966.

Charles Barkley (b. 2-20-63): Basketball F. Five-time first-team All-Star. All-Rookie team, 1985. Led NBA in rebounding, 1987. Averaged 20+ points in seven of 8 seasons with Philadelphia. 1992 Olympic team leading scorer. Traded to Phoenix before 1992-93 season. League MVP for 1992-93 season.

Rick Barry (b. 3-28-44): Basketball F. Only player in history to win scoring titles in NBA (San Francisco, 1967) and ABA (Oakland, 1969). Second alltime highest free throw percentage (.900). Career scoring average 23.2. Led league in free throw percentage 6 times, steals and scoring 1 time each. Averaged 30+ points 2 times, 20+ points 6 other times. 5-time All-Star. 1975 playoff MVP with Golden State. 1966 Rookie of the Year. Career span 1967–79.

Carmen Basilio (b. 4-2-27): Boxer. Won titles in two weight classes, welter and middle. Lost first welter title bid to Kid Gavilan on 9-18-53. Won world welter title by TKO of Tony DeMarco in 12 rounds on 6-10-55. Lost, regained and retained welter title in three fights with Johnny Saxton. Won and then lost middleweight title in two 15 round fights with Ray Robinson. Made three unsuccessful bids to regain middle title. *The Ring* Fighter of the Year for 1957. Career record: 78 bouts; won 26 by KO and 29 by decision; drew 7; lost 16, two by KO. Elected to Boxing Hall of Fame in 1969.

Sammy Baugh (b. 3-17-14): Football QB-P. Set records by leading league in passing 6 times and punting 4 times. Also holds record for highest career punting average (45.1) and highest season average (51.0 in 1940). Career span 1937–52 with Washington. Also All-America with Texas Christian 3 consecutive seasons.

Elgin Baylor (b. 9-16-34): Basketball F. Third alltime highest scoring average (27.4), scored 23,149 points. Averaged 30+ points 3 consecutive seasons, 20+ points 8 other times. 10-time All-Star. 1962 Rookie of the Year. Played in 8 finals without winning championship. Career span 1958–71 with Los Angeles. Also 1958 MVP in NCAA tournament with Seattle.

Bob Beamon (b. 8-29-46): Track and field. Gold medalist in long jump at 1968 Olympics with world record jump of 29' 2½" that stood until 1991.

Franz Beckenbauer (b. 1945): West German soccer player. Captain of 1974 World Cup champions and coach of 1990 champions. Also played for NY Cosmos from 1977 to 1980.

Boris Becker (b. 11-22-67): German tennis player. The youngest male player to win a Wimbledon singles title at age 17 in 1985. Has won 3 Wimbledon titles (consecutively 1985–86, 1989), 1 U.S. Open (1989) and 1 Australian Open title (1991). Led West Germany to 2 consecutive Davis Cup victories (1988–89).

Chuck Bednarik (b. 5-1-25): Football C-LB. Last of the great two-way players, was named All-Pro at both center and linebacker. Missed only 3 games in 14 seasons with Philadelphia from 1949–62. Also All-America 2 times at Pennsylvania.

Clair Bee (b. 3-2-1896, d. 5-20-83): Basketball coach. Originated 1-3-1 defense, helped develop three-second rule, 24-second clock. Won 82.7 percent of games as coach for Rider College and Long Island University. Coach Baltimore Bullets, 1952–54. Author, 23-volume Chip Hilton series for children, 21 nonfiction sports books.

Jean Beliveau (b. 8-31-31): Hockey C. Won MVP award 2 times (1956, 1964), playoff MVP in 1965. Led league in assists 3 times, goals 2 times and points 1 time. 507 career goals, 712 assists. All-Star 6 times. Played on 10 Stanley Cup champions with Montreal from 1950 to 1971.

Bert Bell (b. 2-25-1895, d. 10-11-59): Football executive. Second NFL commissioner (1946–59). Also owner of Philadelphia (1933–40) and Pittsburgh (1941–46). Proposed the first college draft in 1936.

James "Cool Papa" Bell (b. 5-17-03): Baseball OF. Legendary foot speed—according to Satchel Paige could flip light switch and be in bed before room was dark. Hit .392 in games against white major leaguers. Career span 1922–46 with many teams of the Negro Leagues, including the Pittsburgh Crawfords and the Homestead Grays. Inducted in the Hall of Fame in 1974.

Lyudmila Belousova/Oleg Protopov (no dates of birth available): Soviet figure skaters. Won Olympic gold medal in pairs competition in 1964 and 1968. Won four consecutive World and European championships (1965–68) and eight consecutive Soviet titles (1961–68).

Deane Beman (b. 4-22-38): Commissioner of the PGA Tour 1974–94. Won British Amateur title in 1959 and U.S. Amateur titles in 1960 and 1963.

Johnny Bench (b. 12-7-47): Baseball C. MVP in 1970, 1972; World Series MVP in 1976; Rookie of the Year in 1968. 389 career HR. League leader in HR 2 times, RBI 3 times. Career span 1967–83 with Cincinnati.

Patty Berg (b. 2-13-18): Golfer. Alltime women's leader in major championships (16), third alltime in career wins (57). Won Titleholders Championship (1937–39, 1948, 1953–54, 1957) and Western Open (1941, 1943, 1948, 1951, 1955, 1957–58) 7 times each, the most of any golfer. Also won U.S. Women's Amateur (1938) and U.S. Women's Open (1946).

Yogi Berra (b. 5-12-25): Baseball C. Played on 10 World Series winners. All-time Series leader in games, at bats, hits and doubles. MVP in 1951 and consecutively 1954–55. 358 career HR. Career span 1946–65. Also managed pennant-winning Yankees (1964) and NY Mets (1973).

Jay Berwanger (b. 3-19-14): College football RB. Won the first Heisman Trophy and named All-America with Chicago in 1935.

Raymond Berry (b. 2-27-33): Football E. Led NFL in receiving 1958–60. In 13-season career, caught 631 passes, 68 for TDs. Career span 1955–67, all with Baltimore Colts. Later coached New England Patriots from 1984–89 with 51–41 record.

George Best (b. 5-22-46): Irish soccer player. Led Manchester United to European Cup title in 1968. Named England's and Europe's Player of the Year in 1968. Played in North American Soccer League for Los Angeles (1976–78), Fort Lauderdale (1978–79) and San Jose (1980–81). Frequent troubles with alcohol and gambling overshadowed career.

Abebe Bikila (b. 8-7-32, d. 10-25-73): Track and field. Ethiopian barefoot runner won consecutive gold medals in the marathon at Olympics, in 1960 and 1964.

Fred Biletnikoff (b. 2-23-43): Football WR. In 14 pro seasons caught 589 passes for 8,974 yards and 76 TDs. In 1961 led NFL receivers with 61 catches; in '62 led AFC with 58. Career span 1965–78, all with Raiders. Elected to Pro Football Hall of Fame in 1988.

Dmitri Bilozerchev (b. 12-22-66): Soviet gymnast. Won 3 gold medals at 1988 Olympics. Made comeback after shattering his left leg into 44 pieces in 1985. Two-time world champion (1983, 1987). At 16, became youngest to win all-around world championship title in 1983.

Dave Bing (b. 11-24-43): Basketball G. Averaged 24.8 points a game in four years at Syracuse. NBA Rookie of Year in 1967. Led NBA in scoring (27.1) in 1968. MVP NBA All Star game in 1976. In 12 year career from 1967–78, most of it with Detroit Pistons, averaged 20.3 points.

Matt Biondi (b. 10-8-65): Swimmer. Winner of 5 gold medals, 1 silver medal and 1 bronze medal at 1988 Olympics. Won one gold and one silver at 1992 Olympics.

Larry Bird (b. 12-7-56): Basketball F. Won 3 consecutive MVP awards (1984–86) and 2 playoff MVP awards (1984, 1986). Also Rookie of the Year (1980) and All-Star 9 consecutive seasons. Has led league in free throw percentage 4 times. Averaged 20+ points 10 times. Career span 1979-1992 with Boston. Named College Player of the Year in 1979 with Indiana State.

Bonnie Blair (b. 3-18-64): Speed skater. Won gold medal in 500 meters and bronze medal in 1,000 meters

at 1988 Olympics and gold medals in both events in 1992 and '94. Also 1989 World Sprint champion. Winner of 1992 Sullivan Award.

Toe Blake (b. 8-21-12, d. 5-17-95): Hockey LW and coach. Second alltime highest winning percentage (.634) and fifth in wins (500). Led Montreal to 8 Stanley Cup championships from 1955 to 1968 (consecutively 1956–60, 1965–66, 1968). Also MVP and scoring leader in 1939. Played on 2 Stanley Cup champions with Montreal from 1932 to 1948.

Doc Blanchard (b. 12-11-24): College football FB. "Mr. Inside." Teamed with Glenn Davis to lead Army to 3 consecutive undefeated seasons (1944–46) and 2 consecutive national championships (1944–45). Won Heisman Trophy and Sullivan Award in 1945. Also All-America 3 times.

George Blanda (b. 9-17-27): Football QB-K. Alltime leader in seasons played (26), games played (340), points scored (2,002) and points after touchdown (943); third in field goals (335). Also passed for 26,920 career yards and 236 touchdowns. Tied record with 7 touchdown passes on Nov. 19, 1961. Player of the Year 2 times (1961, 1970). Retired at age 48, the oldest to ever play. Career span 1949–75 with Chicago, Houston, Oakland.

Fanny Blankers-Koen (b. 4-26-18): Track and field. Dutch athlete won four gold medals at 1948 Olympics, in 100-meters; 200 meters; 80-meter hurdles; and 400-meter relay. Versatile, she also set world records in high jump (5' 7-1/4" in 1943), long jump (20' 6" in 1943) and pentathlon (4,692 points in 1951).

Wade Boggs (b. 6-15-58): Baseball 3B. Won 5 batting titles (1983, consecutively 1985–88); has had .350+ average 5 times, 200+ hits 7 times. Career span 1982–92 with Boston, 1993- with New York Yankees.

Nick Bolletieri (b. 7-31-31): Tennis coach. Since 1976, has run Nick Bolletieri Tennis Academy in Bradenton, Fla. Former residents of the academy include Andre Agassi, Monica Seles and Jim Courier.

Barry Bonds (b. 7-24-64): Baseball OF. Three-time National League MVP (1990, '92, '93); Career span 1986 to '92, with Pirates; 1993- with Giants.

Bjorn Borg (b. 6-6-56): Swedish tennis player. Second alltime men's leader in Grand Slam singles titles (11—tied with Rod Laver). Set modern record by winning 5 consecutive Wimbledon titles (1976–80). Won 6 French Open titles (consecutively 1974–75, 1978–81). Reached U.S. Open final 4 times, but title eluded him. 65 career tournament victories. Led Sweden to Davis Cup win in 1975.

Julius Boros (b. 3-3-20): Golfer. Won US. Opens in 1952 at Northwood CC in Dallas and in 1963 at The Country Club in Brookline, Mass. Also won 1968 PGA Championship at Pecan Valley CC, San Antonio, when 48 years old, making him oldest winner of a major ever. Led PGA money list in 1952 and '55.

Mike Bossy (b. 1-22-57): Hockey RW. In 1978 set NHL rookie scoring record of 54 goals, broken in 1993. Scored 50 or more each of first nine seasons, totaling 573 goals and 1,126 points in 10 seasons (1977–78 through 1986–87) with New York Islanders. Elected to Hall of Fame in 1991.

Ralph Boston (b. 5-9-39): Track and field. Long jumper won medals at 3 consecutive Olympics; gold in 1960, silver in 1964, bronze in 1968.

Ray Bourque (b. 12-28-60): Hockey D. Won Norris Trophy as NHL's top defenseman five times. Career span since1979 with Boston Bruins.

Scotty Bowman (b. 9-18-33): Hockey coach. Entered 1995–96 season as alltime leader in regular season wins (913) and in regular season winning percentage (.657). Also alltime leader in playoff wins (152). Led Montreal to 5 Stanley Cups, and has also coached St Louis and Buffalo. Won Jack Adams Award, Coach of the Year, 1976–77.

Bill Bradley (b. 7-28-43): Basketball F. Played on 2 NBA championship teams with New York from 1967 to 1977. Player of the Year and NCAA tournament MVP in 1965 with Princeton; All-America 3 times; Sullivan Award winner in 1965. Rhodes scholar. U.S. Senator (D-NJ) since 1979.

Terry Bradshaw (b. 9-2-48): Football QB. Played on 4 Super Bowl champions (consecutively 1974–75, 1978–79); named Super Bowl MVP 2 consecutive seasons (1978–79). 212 career touchdown passes; 27,989 yards passing. Player of the Year in 1978. Career span 1970–83 with Pittsburgh.

George Brett (b. 5-15-53): Baseball 3B-1B. MVP in 1980 with .390 batting average; 3 batting titles, in 1976, 1980, 1990; and .300+ average 11 times. Led league in hits and triples 3 times. Reached 3,000-hit mark in 1992. Career span 1973–93, with Kansas City. Career totals: 3,153 hits; 317 HR; 1,595 RBIs; batting average .305.

Bret Hanover (b. 5-19-62): Horse. Son of Adios. Won 62 of 68 harness races and earned $922,616. Undefeated as two-year-old. From total of 1,694 foals, he sired winners of $61 million and 511 horses which have recorded sub-2:00 performances.

Lou Brock (b. 6-18-39): Baseball OF. Second alltime most stolen bases (938); second most season steals (118). Led league in steals 8 times, with 50+ steals 12 consecutive seasons. Alltime World Series leader in steals (14—tied with Eddie Collins); third in Series batting average (.391). 3,023 career hits. Career span 1961–79 with St Louis.

Jim Brown (b. 2-17-36): Football FB. Second alltime in touchdowns (126); and fourth in yards rushing (12,312). Led league in rushing a record 8 times. His 5.22-yards per carry average is also the best ever. Player of the Year 4 times (consecutively 1957–58, 1963, 1965) and Rookie of the Year in 1957. Rushed for 1,000+ yards in 7 seasons, 200+ yards in 4 games, 100+ yards in 54 other games. Career span 1957–65 with Cleveland; never missed a game. Also All-America with Syracuse.

Paul Brown (b. 9-7-08, d. 8-5-91): Football coach. Led Cleveland to 10 consecutive championship games. Won 4 consecutive AAFC titles (1946–49) and 3 NFL titles (1950, consecutively 1954–55). Coached Cleveland from 1946 to 1962; became first coach of Cincinnati, 1968–75, and then general manager. Career coaching record 222-113-9. Also won national championship with Ohio State in 1942.

Avery Brundage (b. 9-28-1887, d. 5-5-75): Amateur sports executive. President of International Olympic Committee 1952–72. Served as president of U.S. Olympic Committee 1929–53. Also president of Amateur Athletic Union 1928–35. Member of 1912 U.S. Olympic track and field team.

Paul "Bear" Bryant (b. 9-11-13, d. 1-26-83): College football coach. Alltime Division I-A leader in wins (323). Won 6 national championships (1961,

consecutively 1964–65, 1973, consecutively 1978–79) with Alabama. Career record 323–85–17, including 4 undefeated seasons. Also won 15 bowl games. Career span 1945–82 with Maryland, Kentucky, Texas A&M, Alabama.

Sergei Bubka (b. 12-4-63): Track and field. Ukrainian pole vaulter was gold medalist at 1988 Olympics. Only five-time world outdoor champion in any event (1983, 1987, 1991, 1993, 1995). First man to vault 20 feet, set world indoor record of 20' 2" on 2-21-93 and world outdoor record of 20' 1½", set on 9-20-92.

Buck Buchanan (b. 9-10-40): Football DT. Career span 1963–75 with Kansas City Chiefs. Elected to Pro Football Hall of Fame 1990.

Don Budge (b. 6-13-15): Tennis player. First player to achieve the Grand Slam, in 1938. Won 2 consecutive Wimbledon and U.S. singles titles (1937–38), 1 French and 1 Australian title (1938).

Dick Butkus (b. 12-9-42): Football LB. Recovered 25 opponents' fumbles, second most in history. Selected for Pro Bowl 8 times. Career span 1965–73 with Chicago. Also All-America 2 times with Illinois. Award recognizing the outstanding college linebacker named in his honor.

Dick Button (b. 7-18-29): Figure skater. Gold medalist at 2 consecutive Olympics in 1948, 1952. World champion 5 consecutive years (1948–52) and U.S. champion 7 consecutive years (1946–52). Sullivan Award winner in 1949.

Walter Byers (b. 3-13-22): Amateur sports executive. First executive director of NCAA, served from 1952 to 1987.

Frank Calder (b. 11-17-1877, d. 2-4-43): Hockey executive. First commissioner of NHL, served from 1917 to 1943. Rookie of the Year award named in his honor.

Walter Camp (b. 4-7-1859, d. 3-14-25): Football pioneer. Played for Yale in its first football game vs. Harvard on Nov. 17, 1876. Proposed rules such as 11 men per side, scrimmage line, center snap, yards and downs. Founded the All-America selections in 1889.

Roy Campanella (b. 11-19-21; d. 6-26-93): Baseball C. Career span 1948–57, ended when paralyzed in car crash. MVP in 1951, 1953, 1955. Played on 5 pennant winners; 1955 World Series winner with Brooklyn Dodgers.

Earl Campbell (b. 3-29-55): Football RB. Tenth alltime yards rushing (9,407); third alltime in season yards rushing (1,934 in 1980) and fourth in TDs rushing (19 in 1979). Led league in rushing 3 consecutive seasons. Rushed for 1,000+ yards in 5 seasons. Scored 74 career touchdowns. Player of the Year 2 consecutive seasons (1978–79). Rookie of the Year in 1978. Career span 1978–85 with Houston, New Orleans. Won Heisman Trophy with Texas in 1977.

John Campbell (b. 4-8-55): Canadian harness racing driver. Alltime leading money winner with over $100 million in earnings. Leading money winner 1986–90. Has more than 5,500 career wins.

Billy Cannon (b. 2-8-37): Football RB. Led Louisiana State to national championship in 1958 and won Heisman Trophy in 1959. Signed contract in both NFL (Los Angeles) and AFL (Houston). Houston won lawsuit for his services. Played in 6 AFL championship games with Houston, Oakland, Kansas City. Career span

1960–70. Served three-year jail term for 1983 conviction on counterfeiting charges.

Jose Canseco (b. 7-2-64): Baseball OF. Only player to top 40 homers (42) and 40 (40) steals in same season (1988). AL MVP in 1988, when he also batted .307 with 124 RBIs. Career span 1985–1992 with Oakland and since 1992 with Texas Rangers.

Harry Caray (b. 3-1-17): Sportscaster. TV-radio baseball announcer since 1945 with St Louis (NL), Oakland, Chicago (AL) and Chicago (NL). Achieved celebrity status on Cubs' superstation WGN by singing "Take Me Out to the Ballgame" with Wrigley Field fans.

Rod Carew (b. 10-1-45): Baseball 2B-1B. Won 7 batting titles (1969, consecutively 1972–75, 1977–78). Had .328 career average, 3,053 career hits, and .300+ average 15 times. 1977 MVP; 1967 Rookie of the Year. Career span 1967–85; jersey number (29) retired by Minnesota and California.

Steve Carlton (b. 12-22-44): Baseball LHP. Second alltime most strikeouts (4,136). 4 Cy Young awards (1972, 1977, 1980, 1982). 329 career wins; won 20+ games 6 times. League leader in wins 4 times, innings pitched and strikeouts 5 times each. Struck out 19 batters in 1 game in 1969. Career span 1965–88 with St. Louis, Philadelphia and four other teams in last two years.

JoAnne Carner (b. 4-21-39): Golfer. Won 42 titles, including US Women's Opens in 1971 and '76 and du Maurier Classic in 1975 and '78. LPGA top earner in 1974 and 1982–83. LPGA Player of the Year in 1974 and 1981–82. Won five Vare Trophies (1974–75 and 1981–83).

Joe Carr (b. 10-22-1880; d. 5-20-39): Football administrator. Instrumental in forming American Professional Football Association in 1920. President of AAFA from 1922 to '39.

Don Carter (b. 7-29-26): Bowler. Won All-Star Tournament 4 times (1952, 1954, 1956, 1958) and PBA National Championship in 1960. Voted Bowler of the Year 6 times (consecutively 1953–54, 1957–58, 1960, 1962).

Alexander Cartwright (b. 4-17-1820, d. 7-12-1892): Baseball pioneer. Organized the first baseball game on June 19, 1846, and set the basic rules of bases 90 feet apart, 9 men per side, 3 strikes per out and 3 outs per inning. In that first game his New York Knickerbockers lost to the New York Nine 23–1 at Elysian Fields in Hoboken, NJ.

Billy Casper (b. 6-24-31): Golfer. Famed putter. Won 51 PGA tournaments. PGA Player of Year in both 1966 and '70. Won Vardon Trophy in 1960, '63, '64, '65 and '68. Won the US Open twice, in 1959 at Winged Foot in Mamaronek, New York, and in 1966 in 18-hole playoff over Arnold Palmer at Olympic Club, San Francisco. Beat Gene Littler in 18 hole playoff to win 1970 Masters.

Tracy Caulkins (b. 1-11-63): Swimmer. Won 3 gold medals at 1984 Olympics. Won 48 U.S. national titles, more than any other swimmer, from 1978 to 1984. Also won Sullivan Award in 1978.

Steve Cauthen (b. 5-1-60): Jockey. In 1978 became youngest jockey to win Triple Crown, aboard Affirmed. First jockey to top $6 million in season earnings (1977). *Sports Illustrated* Sportsman of Year for 1977. Moved to England in 1979. Among the 1,389 winners he had ridden in England through end of 1990 were two

winners of Epsom Derby—Slip Anchor in 1985 and Reference Point in 1987.

Evonne Goolagong Cawley (b. 7-31-51): Tennis. Won 4 Australian Open titles from 1974 through '77; won '71 French Open; Wimbledon in 1971 and '80, Runnerup four straight years at U.S. Open (1973–76) which she never won.

Bill Chadwick (b. 10-10-15): Hockey referee. Spent 16 years as a referee despite vision in only one eye. Developed hand signals to signify penalties. Also former television announcer for the New York Rangers.

Wilt Chamberlain (b. 8-21-36): Basketball C. Alltime leader in rebounds (23,924) and rebounding average (22.9). Alltime season leader in points scored (4,029 in 1962), scoring average (50.4 in 1962), rebounding average (27.2 in 1961) and field goal percentage (.727 in 1973). Alltime single-game most points scored (100 in 1962) and most rebounds (55 in 1960). Second alltime most points scored (31,419) and most field goals made (12,681). 4 MVP awards (1960, consecutively 1966–68); playoff MVP in 1972 and 1960 Rookie of the Year. 7-time All-Star. 30.1 career scoring average. Career span 1959–72 with Philadelphia, Los Angeles. Also named College Player of the Year in 1957 at Kansas.

Colin Chapman (b. 1928, d. 12-16-83): Auto racing engineer. Founded Lotus race and street cars, designing the first Lotus racer in 1948. Introduced the monocoque design for Formula One cars in 1962 and ground effects in 1978. Four of his drivers, including Mario Andretti, won Formula One world championships.

Julio Cesar Chavez (b. 7-12-62): Boxer. Through 10-1-95 the current WBC junior welterweight champion. But many thought he lost fight against Pernell Whitaker on 9-10-93 in Alamodome which ended officially as a "majority draw". Also won titles as super featherweight (1984–87) and lightweight (1987–89).

Gerry Cheevers (b. 12-7-40): Hockey goalie. Goaltender for Stanley Cup-winning Boston Bruins teams of 1970 and '72. In 12 seasons with Boston had 230-94-74 record with a goals against average of 2.89. Also coached Bruins from 1980–84, with 204-126-46 record. Elected to Hall of Fame 1985.

Citation (b. 4-11-45, d. 8-8-70): Thoroughbred race horse. Triple Crown winner in 1948 with jockey Eddie Arcaro aboard. Trained by Ben A. Jones.

King Clancy (b. 2-25-03, d. 11-6-86): Hockey D. Four-time All-Star. Coach, Montreal Maroons, Toronto. Referee. Trophy named in his honor, recognizing leadership qualities and contribution to community.

Jim Clark (b. 3-4-36, d. 4-7-68): Scottish auto racer. Fifth alltime in Formula 1 victories (25—tied with Niki Lauda). Formula 1 champion 2 times (1963, 1965). Won Indy 500 1 time (1965). Named Indy 500 Rookie of the Year in 1963. Killed during competition in 1968 at age 32.

Bobby Clarke (b. 8-13-49): Hockey C. Won MVP award 3 times (1973, consecutively 1975–76). 358 career goals, 852 assists. Led league in assists 2 consecutive seasons and scored 100+ points 3 times. Played on 2 consecutive Stanley Cup champions (1974–75) with Philadelphia. Career span 1969 to 1984. Also general manager with Philadelphia from 1984 to 1990, Minnesota 1991-92, Florida 1993-94, and Philadelphia since 1994.

Roger Clemens (b. 8-4-62): Baseball RHP. Record 20 strikeouts in 1 game. Won 2 consecutive Cy Young Awards in 1986, 1987. Also 1986 MVP. League leader in ERA 4 times, wins and strikeouts 2 times each. Career span since 1984 with Boston.

Roberto Clemente (b. 8-18-34, d. 12-31-72): Baseball OF. Killed in plane crash while still an active player. Had 3,000 career hits and .317 career average. 4 batting titles; .300+ average 13 times. 1966 MVP; 1971 World Series MVP. 12 consecutive Gold Gloves; led league in assists 5 times. Career span 1955–72 with Pittsburgh.

Ty Cobb (b. 12-18-1886, d. 7-17-61): Baseball OF. Alltime leader in batting average (.367) and runs scored (2,245); second most hits (4,191); fourth most stolen bases (892). 1911 MVP and 1909 Triple Crown winner. 12 batting titles. Had .400+ average 3 times, .350+ average 13 other times; 200+ hits 9 times. Led league in hits 7 times, steals 6 times and runs scored 5 times. Career span 1905–28 with Detroit.

Mickey Cochrane (b. 4-6-03, d. 6-28-62): Baseball C. Alltime highest career batting average among catchers (.320). MVP in 1928, 1934. Had .300+ average 8 times. Career span 1925–37 with Philadelphia, Detroit.

Sebastian Coe (b. 9-29-56): Track and field. British runner was gold medalist in 1,500 meters and silver medalist in 800 meters at 2 consecutive Olympics in 1980, 1984. World record holder in 800 meters (1:41.73 set in 1981) and 1,000 meters (2:12.18 set in 1981). Now a member of parliament.

Eddie Collins (b. 5-2-1887, d. 3-25-51): Baseball 2B. Alltime leader among 2nd basemen in games, chances and assists; led league in fielding 9 times. 3,311 career hits; .333 career average; .330+ average 12 times. Fifth alltime most stolen bases (743—tied with Tim Raines); alltime most World Series steals (14—tied with Lou Brock); alltime leader in single-game steals (6, twice). 1914 MVP. Career span 1906–30 with Philadelphia, Chicago.

Nadia Comaneci (b. 11-12-61): Romanian gymnast. First ever to score a perfect 10 at Olympics (on uneven parallel bars in 1976). Won 3 gold, 2 silver and 1 bronze medal at 1976 Olympics. Also won 2 gold and 2 silver medals at 1980 Olympics.

Dennis Conner (b. 9-16-42): Sailing. Captain of America's Cup winner 3 times (1980, '87, '88).

Maureen Connolly (b. 9-17-34, d. 6-21-69): Tennis player. "Little Mo" first woman to achieve the Grand Slam, in 1953. Won the U.S. singles title in 1951 at age 16. Thereafter lost only 4 matches before retiring in 1954 because of a broken leg caused by a riding accident. Was never beaten in singles at Wimbledon, winning 3 consecutive titles (1952–54). Won 3 consecutive U.S. singles titles (1951–53) and 2 consecutive French titles (1953–54). Also won 1 Australian title (1953).

Jimmy Connors (b. 9-2-52): Tennis player. Alltime men's leader in tournament victories (109). Held men's #1 ranking a record 159 consecutive weeks, July 29, 1974 through Aug. 16, 1977. Won 5 U.S. Open singles titles on 3 different surfaces (grass 1974, clay 1976, hard 1978, consecutively 1982–83). Won 2 Wimbledon singles titles (1974, 1982) farther apart than anyone since Bill Tilden. Also won 1974 Australian Open title. Reached Grand Slam final 7 other times.

Jim Corbett (b. 9-1-1866; d. 2-18-33): Boxer. "Gentleman Jim". Invented jab. Fight with Australian Peter Jackson on 5-21-91 ruled no contest when neither could continue into 62nd round. Won heavyweight title on 9-7-92 with a KO of John Sullivan in 21 rounds; it was first heavyweight title fight using gloves. Retained title with KO of British champ Charley Mitchell. Lost title when KO'd by Bob Fitzsimmons in 14 on 3-17-1897, then lost two bids to regain it against Jim Jeffries. Career record: 19 fights; won 7 by KO and 4 by decision; drew 2; lost 4; 2 no decision. Elected to Boxing Hall of Fame in 1954.

Angel Cordero (b. 11-8-42): Jockey. At end of 1994 third alltime in wins (7,057) and earnings ($164,526,217). Led yearly earnings three times, in 1976 and 1982–83, winning Eclipse Awards in the last two years.

Howard Cosell (b. 3-25-18, d. 4-23-95): Sportscaster. Lawyer turned TV-radio sports commentator in 1953. Best known for his work on "Monday Night Football." His nasal voice and "tell it like it is" approach made him a controversial figure.

James "Doc" Counsilman (b. 12-28-20): Swimming coach. Coached Indiana from 1957 to 1990. Won 6 consecutive NCAA championships (1968–73). Career record 287–36–1. Coached U.S. men's team at Olympics in 1964, 1976. Also oldest person to swim English Channel (58 in 1979).

Count Fleet (b. 3-24-40, d. 12-3-73): Thoroughbred race horse. Triple Crown winner in 1943 with jockey Johnny Longden aboard. Trained by Don Cameron.

Yvan Cournoyer (b. 11-22-43): Hockey RW. "The Roadrunner" had 428 goals and 435 assists during his 15 season career with the Montreal Canadiens. Had 25 or more goals in 12 straight seasons. Played on 10 Stanley Cup championship teams. Elected to Hall of Fame in 1982.

Margaret Smith Court (b. 7-16-42): Australian tennis player. Alltime leader in Grand Slam singles titles (26) and total Grand Slam titles (66). Achieved Grand Slam in 1970 and mixed doubles Grand Slam in 1963 with Ken Fletcher. Won 11 Australian singles titles (consecutively 1960–66, 1969–71, 1973), 5 French titles (1962, 1964, consecutively 1969–70, 1973), 7 U.S. titles (1962, 1965, consecutively 1969–70, 1973) and 3 Wimbledon titles (1963, 1965, 1970). Also won 19 Grand Slam doubles titles and 19 mixed doubles titles.

Bob Cousy (b. 8-9-28): Basketball G. Finished career with 6,955 assists, second alltime most assists in a game (28 in 1958). League leader in assists 8 consecutive seasons. Averaged 18+ points and named to All-Star team 10 consecutive seasons. 1957 MVP. Played on 6 championship teams with Boston from 1950 to 1969. Also played on NCAA championship team in 1947 with Holy Cross.

Dave Cowens (b. 10-25-48): Basketball C. After college career at Florida State, NBA co-Rookie of Year in 1971. NBA MVP for 1973. All-Star game MVP in 1973. Career span 1970–71 through 1982–83, all but the last year with the Boston Celtics. Elected to Hall of Fame in 1991.

Ben Crenshaw (b. 1-11-52): Golfer. Legendary putter. Won 1984 Masters.

Larry Csonka (b. 12-25-46): Football RB. In 11 seasons rushed 1,891 times for 8,081 yards (4.3 per carry) and 64 TDs. MVP of Super Bowl VIII, when he rushed 33 times for a then Super Bowl record 145 yards in Miami's 24–7 defeat of Minnesota. Career span 1968–74, 1979 with Miami Dolphins; 1976–78 with New York Giants. Elected to Hall of Fame in 1987.

Billy Cunningham (b. 6-3-43): Basketball player and coach. Averaged 24.8 points a game at North Carolina. In nine seasons (1965–66 through 1975–76) with Philadelphia 76ers, averaged 20.8 points per game. All NBA first team 1969, '70 and '71. In 8 seasons as Sixer coach went 454–196 in season, 66–39 in playoffs and won NBA title in 1983. Elected to Hall of Fame in 1985.

Chuck Daly (b. 7-20-30): Basketball coach. Won 2 consecutive championships with Detroit (1989–90). Won 50+ games 4 consecutive seasons. Coach of 1992 Olympic team. Career span as pro coach 1983–92 with Pistons; 1992–94 with New Jersey Nets.

Damascus (b. 1964): Thoroughbred race horse. After finishing 3rd in 1967 Kentucky Derby, won the Preakness, the Belmont, the Dwyer, the American Derby, the Travers, the Woodward and others—12 of 16 starts. Unanimous Horse of the Year for 1967.

Stanley Dancer (b. 7-25-27): Harness racing driver. Only driver to win the Trotting Triple Crown 2 times (Nevele Pride in 1968, Super Bowl in 1972). Also won Pacing Triple Crown driving Most Happy Fella in 1970. Won The Hambletonian 4 times (1968, 1972, 1975, 1983). Driver of the Year in 1968.

Tamas Darnyi (b. 6-3-67): Hungarian swimmer. Gold medalist in 200-meter and 400-meter individual medleys at 1988 and 1992 Olympics. Also won both events at World Championships in 1986 and 1991. Set world records in these events at 1991 Championships (1:59.36 and 4:12.36).

Al Davis (b. 7-4-29): Football executive. Owner and general manager of Oakland-LA Raiders since 1963. Built winningest franchise in sports history (313-192-11—a .617 winning percentage entering the 1995 season). Team has won 3 Super Bowl championships (1976, 1980, 1983). Also served as AFL commissioner in 1966, helped negotiate AFL–NFL merger.

Ernie Davis (b. 12-14-39, d. 5-18-63): Football RB. Won Heisman Trophy in 1961, the first black man to win the award. All-America 3 times at Syracuse. First selection in 1962 NFL draft, but became fatally ill with leukemia and never played professionally.

Glenn Davis (b. 12-26-24): College football HB. "Mr. Outside." Teamed with Doc Blanchard to lead Army to 3 consecutive undefeated seasons (1944–46) and 2 consecutive national championships (1944–45). Won Heisman Trophy in 1946. Also named All-America 3 times.

John Davis (b. 1-12-21, d. 7-13-84): Weightlifter. Gold medalist at 2 consecutive Olympics in 1948, 1952. World champion 6 times.

Pete Dawkins (b. 3-8-38): Football RB. Starred at Army 1956–58. Won Heisman Trophy 1958. Was first captain of cadets, class president, top 5 percent of class academically, and football team captain; first man to do all four at West Point. Did not play pro football. Attended Oxford on Rhodes scholarship, won two Bronze Stars in Vietnam, rose to brigadier general before leaving Army to become investment banker. Made unsuccessful run for Senate from New Jersey in 1988.

Len Dawson (b. 6-20-35): Football QB. Completed 2,136 of 3,741 pass attempts with 239 TDs. In first

Super Bowl threw for one TD in 35–10 loss to Green Bay. MVP of Super Bowl IV, which Kansas City won 23–7 over Minnesota. Career span 1957–75, the last 13 seasons with Kansas City Chiefs. Elected to Hall of Fame in 1987.

Dizzy Dean (b. 1-16-11, d. 7-17-74): Baseball RHP. 1934 MVP with 30 wins. League leader in strikeouts, complete games 4 times each. 150 career wins. Arm trouble shortened career after 134 wins by age 26. Career span 1930–41 and 1947 with St Louis and Chicago Cubs.

Dave DeBusschere (b. 10-16-40): Basketball F. NBA First Team Defense six straight seasons, 1969–74. Member of NBA champion New York Knicks in 1970 and '73. Career span 1962–63 through middle of 1968–69 season with Detroit Pistons; through 1973–74 with Knicks. Youngest coach (24) in NBA history. Elected to NBA Hall of Fame in 1982.

Pierre de Coubertin (b. 1-1-1863, d. 9-2-37): Frenchman called the father of the Modern Olympics. President of International Olympic Committee from 1896 to 1925.

Jack Dempsey (b. 6-24-1895, d. 5-31-83): Boxer. Heavyweight champion (1919–26), lost title to Gene Tunney and rematch in the famous "long count" bout in 1927. Career record 62-6-10 with 49 KOs from 1914 to 1928.

Gail Devers (b. 11-19-66): Track and field sprinter/hurdler. Won 100 at 1992 Olympics; leading 100 hurdles when she tripped over final hurdle and finished fifth. Successfully completed same double at 1993 World Championships, winning 100 in 10.82 and 100 hurdles in American record 12.46. Also won world indoor title in 60 (6.95). Battled Graves Disease.

Klaus Dibiasi (b. 10-6-47): Italian diver. Gold medalist in platform at 3 consecutive Olympics (1968, 1972, 1976) and silver medalist at 1964 Olympics.

Eric Dickerson (b. 9-2-60): Football RB. Alltime season leader in yards rushing (2,105 in 1984), second alltime most career yards rushing (13,259). Rushed for 1,000+ yards a record 7 consecutive seasons; 100+ yards in 61 games, including 12 times in 1984. Led league in rushing 4 times. Rookie of the Year in 1983. Career span 1983–93 with Los Angeles Rams, Indianapolis, L.A. Raiders and Atlanta Falcons.

Bill Dickey (b. 6-6-07): Baseball C. Lifetime average .313. Hit 202 home runs. Played on 11 AL All-Star teams. In eight World Series, hit five homers and 24 RBIs. Career span 1928–43 and 1946, all with the New York Yankees. Inducted to Hall of Fame 1954.

Harrison Dillard (b. 7-8-23): Track and field. Only man to win Olympic gold medal in sprint (100 meters in 1948) and hurdles (110 meters in 1952). Sullivan Award winner in 1955.

Joe DiMaggio (b. 11-25-14): Baseball OF. Voted baseball's greatest living player. Record 56-game hitting streak in 1941. MVP in 1939, 1941, 1947. Had .325 career batting average; .300+ average 11 times; 100+ RBI 9 times. League leader in batting average, HR, and RBI 2 times each. Played on 10 World Series winners with NY Yankees. Career span 1936–51.

Mike Ditka (b. 10-18-39): Football TE-Coach. NFL Rookie of the Year in 1961. Named to Pro Bowl five times. Made 427 catches for 5,812 yards and 43 TDs.

Career span 1961 to '72 with Bears, Eagles and Cowboys. Coach of Bears from 1982–92 with 112–68 overall record. Coach of Bear team that won Super Bowl XX, 46–10 over New England. Elected to Hall of Fame 1988.

Tony Dorsett (b. 4-7-54): Football RB. Third alltime in yards rushing (12,739), fourth in attempts (2,936). Rushed for 1,000+ yards in 8 seasons. Set record for longest run from scrimmage with 99-yard touchdown run on January 3, 1983. Scored 91 career touchdowns. Named Rookie of the Year in 1977. Career span 1977–88 with Dallas, Denver. Also won Heisman Trophy in 1976, leading Pittsburgh to national championship. Alltime NCAA leader in yards rushing and only man to break 6,000-yard barrier (6,082).

Abner Doubleday (b. 6-26-1819, d. 1-26-1893): Civil War hero incorrectly credited as the inventor of baseball in Cooperstown, New York, in 1839. More recent research calls Alexander Cartwright the true father of the game.

Clyde Drexler (b. 6-22-62): Basketball G. Nicknamed "The Glide" for his smooth play. Member of U.S. "Dream Team" that won 1992 Olympic gold medal. Career span 1984–1994 with Portland Trail Blazers and 1995– with Houston Rockets, with whom he won his first NBA title in 1995.

Ken Dryden (b. 8-8-47): Hockey G. Goaltender of the Year 5 times (1973, consecutively 1976–79). Playoff MVP as a rookie in 1971, maintained rookie status and named Rookie of the Year in 1972. Led league in goals against average 5 times, wins and shutouts 4 times each. Career record 258-57-74, including 46 shutouts. Career 2.24 goals against average is the modern record. Second alltime in playoff wins (80). Tied record of 4 playoff shutouts in 1977. Played on 6 Stanley Cup champions with Montreal from 1970 to 1979.

Don Drysdale (b. 7-23-36, d. 7-3-93): Baseball RHP. Led NL three times in strikeouts (1959, '60, '62) and once in wins (1962). Won 1962 Cy Young Award with 25–9 mark. In 1968 pitched six straight shutouts en route to major league record—broken in 1988 by Orel Hershiser—of 58 consecutive scoreless innings. Career record of 209–166, with 2,484 K's and ERA of 2.95. Career span 1956–69, all with Dodgers. Inducted into Hall of Fame 1984.

Roberto Duran (b. 6-16-51): Panamanian boxer. Champion in 3 different weight classes: lightweight (1972–79), welterweight (1980, lost rematch to Sugar Ray Leonard in famous "no mas" bout) and junior middleweight (1983–84). Career record 90–9 with 62 KOs since 1967.

Leo Durocher (b. 7-27-05, d. 10-7-91): Baseball manager. "Leo the Lip." Said "Nice guys finish last." Managed 3 pennant winners and 1954 World Series winner. Won 2,008 games in 24 years. Led Brooklyn 1939–48; New York 1948–55; Chicago 1966–72; and Houston 1972–73.

Eddie Eagan (b. 4-26-1898, d. 6-14-67): Only American athlete to win gold medal at Summer and Winter Olympic Games (boxing 1920, bobsled 1932).

Alan Eagleson (b. 4-24-33): Hockey labor leader. Founder of NHL Players' Association and its executive director from 1967–92.

Dale Earnhardt (b. 4-29-52): Auto racer. NASCAR champion 7 times (1980, 1986–87, 1990–91, 1993-94). 66 career NASCAR victories through 9-17-95.

Stefan Edberg (b. 1-19-66): Swedish tennis player. Has won 2 Wimbledon singles titles (1988, 1990), 2 Australian Open titles (1985, 1987) and 2 U.S. Open titles (1991, 1992). Led Sweden to 3 Davis Cup victories (consecutively 1984–85, 1987).

Gertrude Ederle (b. 10-23-06): Swimmer. First woman to swim the English Channel, in 1926. Swam 21 miles from France to England in 14:39. Also won 3 medals at the 1924 Olympics.

Herb Elliott (b. 2-25-38): Track and field. Australian runner was gold medalist in 1960 Olympic 1,500 meters in world record 3:35.6. Also set world mile record of 3:54.5 in 1958. Undefeated at 1500 meters/mile in international competition. Retired at 21.

John Elway (b. 6-28-60): Football QB. First player taken in 1983 NFL draft. Topped 3,000 yards passing every season from 1985–91. Through '94 season had thrown for 37,736 yards, 199 TDs. Famous for last minute drives. Career span since 1983 with Denver Broncos.

Roy Emerson (b. 11-3-36): Australian tennis player. Alltime men's leader in Grand Slam singles titles (12). Won 6 Australian titles, 5 consecutively (1961, 1963–67), 2 consecutive Wimbledon titles (1964–65), 2 U.S. titles (1961, 1964) and 2 French titles (1963, 1967). Also won 13 Grand Slam doubles titles.

Kornelia Ender (b. 10-25-58): East German swimmer. Won 4 gold medals at 1976 Olympics and 3 silver medals at 1972 Olympics.

Julius Erving (b. 2-22-50): "Dr. J." Basketball F. Third alltime most points scored for combined ABA and NBA career (30,026). 24.2 scoring average. Averaged 20+ points 14 consecutive seasons. 4 MVP awards, consecutively 1974–76, 1981; playoff MVP 1974, 1976. All-Star 9 times. Led league in scoring 3 times. Played on 3 championship teams, with New York (ABA) and Philadelphia (NBA). Career span 1971 to 1986.

Phil Esposito (b. 2-20-42): Hockey C. "Espo." First to break the 100-point barrier (126 in 1969). Fourth alltime in points (1,590) and goals (717), ninth in assists (873). Led league in goals 6 consecutive seasons, points 5 times and assists 3 times. Won MVP award 2 times (1969, 1974). Scored 30+ goals 13 consecutive seasons and 100+ points 6 times. All-Star 6 times. Career span 1963–81 with Chicago, Boston, NY Rangers. Also general manager of NY Rangers from 1986 to 1989. Currently general manager of Tampa Bay.

Tony Esposito (b. 4-23-43): Hockey goalie. Brother of Phil. A five-time All Star during 16-season NHL career, almost all of it with the Chicago Blackhawks. In 886 games gave up 2,563 goals, an average of 2.92 per game. Won or shared Vezina Trophy three times. Elected to Hall of Fame in 1988.

Janet Evans (b. 8-28-71): Swimmer. Won 3 gold medals at 1988 Olympics and 1 at 1992 Olympics. Set world record in 400-meter freestyle (4:03.85 in 1988), 800-meter freestyle (8:16.22 in 1989) and 1,500-meter freestyle (15:52.10 in 1988). Sullivan Award winner in 1989.

Lee Evans (b. 2-25-47): Track and field. Gold medalist in 400 meters at 1968 Olympics with world record time of 43.86 that stood until 1988.

Chris Evert (b. 12-21-54): Also Chris Evert Lloyd. Tennis player. Second alltime in tournament victories

(157). Third alltime in women's Grand Slam singles titles (18—tied with Martina Navratilova). Won at least 1 Grand Slam singles title every year from 1974 to 1986. Won 7 French Open titles (1974–75, 1979–1980, 1983, 1985–86), 6 U.S. Open titles (1975–77, 1978, 1980, 1982), 3 Wimbledon titles (1974, 1976, 1981) and 2 Australian Open titles (1982, 1984). Reached Grand Slam finals 16 other times. Reached semifinals at 52 of her last 56 Grand Slam tournaments.

Weeb Ewbank (b. 5-6-07): Football coach. Only coach to win titles in both the NFL and AFL. Coached Baltimore Colts to classic overtime defeat of New York Giants in 1958 and New York Jets to their stunning 16–7 win over Baltimore in Super Bowl III. Career record of 134-130-7. Career span 1954–62 with Colts and 1963–73 with Jets. Elected to Hall of Fame in 1978.

Patrick Ewing (b. 8-5-62): Basketball C. 1986 Rookie of the Year with New York. 20+ points average in all 10 seasons with Knicks. All-NBA first team 1990. Played on 3 NCAA final teams with Georgetown (1982, 1984–85); tournament MVP in 1984. All-America 3 times.

Nick Faldo (b. 7-18-57): British golfer. Winner of the Masters 2 consecutive years (1989–90) and British Open 3 times (1987, 1990, 1992).

Juan Manuel Fangio (b. 6-24-11, d. 7-17-95): Argentinian auto racer. Seventh all-time in Formula 1 victories (24, but in just 51 starts). Formula 1 champion 5 times, the most of any driver (1951, consecutively 1954–57). Retired in 1958.

Bob Feller (b. 11-3-18): Baseball RHP. League leader in wins 6 times, strikeouts 7 times, innings pitched 5 times. Pitched 3 no-hitters and 12 one-hitters. 266 career wins; 2,581 career strikeouts. Won 20+ games 6 times. Served 4 years in military during career. Career span 1936–41, 1945–56 with Cleveland.

Tom Ferguson (b. 12-20-50): Rodeo. First to top $1 million in career earnings. All-Around champion 6 consecutive years (1974–79).

Enzo Ferrari (b. 2-8-1898, d. 8-14-88): Auto racing engineer. Team owner since 1929, he built first Ferrari race car in Italy in 1947 and continued to preside over Ferrari race and street cars until his death. In 61 years of competition, Ferrari's cars have won over 5,000 races.

Mark Fidrych (b. 8-14-54): Baseball RHP. "The Bird." Rookie of the Year in 1976 with Detroit. Had 19–9 record with league-best 2.39 ERA and 24 complete games. Habit of talking to the ball on the mound made him a cult hero. Arm injuries curtailed career.

Cecil Fielder (b. 9-21-63): Baseball 1B. The last man to hit 50+ HR (51 in 1990). Has led the major leagues in HR twice and RBI 3 consecutive seasons (1990–92) after spending 1989 season in Japanese league. Career span since 1985 with Toronto, Detroit.

Herve Filion (b. 2-1-40): Harness racing driver. Alltime leader in career wins (more than 13,000). Driver of the Year 10 times, more than any other driver (consecutively 1969–74, 1978, 1981, 1989).

Rollie Fingers (b. 8-25-46): Baseball RHP. Third alltime in saves (341); third in relief wins (107); fifth in appearances (944). 1981 Cy Young and MVP winner; 1974 World Series MVP. Alltime Series leader in saves (6). Career span 1968–85 with Oakland, San Diego, Milwaukee.

Bobby Fischer (b. 3-9-43): Chess. World champion from 1972 to 1975, the only American to hold title. Never played competitive chess during his reign. Forfeited title to Anatoly Karpov by refusing to play him.

Carlton Fisk (b. 12-26-47): Baseball C. Alltime HR leader among catchers (352) and second in games caught (2,226). 376 career HR, including a record 75 after age 40. Rookie of the Year in 1972 and All-Star 11 times. Hit dramatic 12th-inning HR to win Game 6 of 1975 World Series. Career span 1969-93 with Boston, Chicago (AL).

Emerson Fittipaldi (b. 12-12-46): Brazilian auto racer. Won Indy 500 in 1989 and '93. Won CART championship in 1989. Formula 1 champion 2 times (1972, 1974).

James Fitzsimmons (b. 7-23-1874, d. 3-11-66): Horse racing trainer. "Sunny Jim." Trained Triple Crown winner 2 times (Gallant Fox in 1930, Omaha in 1935). Trained Belmont Stakes winner 6 times (1930, 1932, consecutively 1935–36, 1939, 1955), Preakness Stakes winner 4 times (1930, 1935, 1955, 1957) and Kentucky Derby winner 3 times (1930, 1935, 1939).

Peggy Fleming (b. 7-27-48): Figure skater. Gold medalist at 1968 Olympics. World champion 3 consecutive years (1966–68) and U.S. champion 5 consecutive years (1964–68).

Curt Flood (b. 1-18-38): Baseball OF. Won 7 consecutive Gold Gloves from 1963 to 1969. Career batting average of .293. Refused to be traded after 1969 season, challenging baseball's reserve clause. Supreme Court rejected his plea, but baseball was eventually forced to adopt free agency system. Career span 1956–69 with St. Louis.

Whitey Ford (b. 10-21-26): Baseball LHP. All-time World Series leader in wins, losses, games started, innings pitched, hits allowed, walks and strikeouts. 236 career wins, 2.75 ERA. Third alltime best career winning percentage (.690). Led league in wins and winning percentage 3 times each; ERA, shutouts, innings pitched 2 times each. 1961 Cy Young winner and World Series MVP. Career span 1950, 1953–67 with New York Yankees.

Forego (b. 1970): Thoroughbred race horse. Horse of the Year in 1974 (won 8 of 13 starts); '75 (won 6 of 9); and '76 (won 6 of 8). Finished fourth in 1973 Kentucky Derby. Over six years won 34 of 57 starts and $1,938,957.

George Foreman (b. 1-22-48): Boxer. Heavyweight champion (1973–74). Retired in 1977, but returned to the ring in 1987. Lost 12–round decision to champion Evander Holyfield in 1991. Retired after losing to Tommy Morrison 6-7-93. Career record 72–4 with 67 KOs since 1969. Also heavyweight gold medalist at 1968 Olympics.

Dick Fosbury (b. 3-6-47): Track and field. Gold medalist in high jump at 1968 Olympics. Introduced back-to-the-bar style of high jumping, called the "Fosbury Flop."

Jimmie Foxx (b. 10-22-07, d. 7-21-67): Baseball 1B. Won 3 MVP awards, consecutively 1932–33, 1938. Fourth alltime highest slugging average (.609), with 534 career HR; hit 30+ HR 12 consecutive seasons, 100+ RBI 13 consecutive seasons. Won Triple Crown in 1933. Led league in HR 4 times, batting average 2 times. Career span 1925–45 with Philadelphia, Boston.

A. J. Foyt (b. 1-16-35): Auto racer. Alltime leader in Indy Car victories (67). Won Indy 500 4 times (1961, 1964, 1967, 1977), Daytona 500 1 time (1972), 24 Hours of Daytona 2 times (1983, 1985) and 24 Hours of LeMans 1 time (1967). USAC champion 7 times, more than any other driver (consecutively 1960–61, 1963–64, 1967, 1975, 1979).

William H. G. France (b. 9-26-09): Auto racing executive. Founder of NASCAR and president from 1948 to 1972, succeeded by his son Bill Jr. Builder of Daytona and Talladega speedways.

Dawn Fraser (b. 9-4-37): Australian swimmer. Only swimmer to win gold medal in same event at 3 consecutive Olympics (100-meter freestyle in 1956, 1960, 1964). First woman to break the 1-minute barrier at 100 meters (59.9 in 1962).

Joe Frazier (b. 1-12-44): Boxer. "Smokin' Joe." Heavyweight champion (1970–73). Best known for his 3 epic bouts with Muhammad Ali. Career record 32-4-1 with 27 KOs from 1965 to 1976. Also heavyweight gold medalist at 1964 Olympics.

Walt Frazier (b. 3-29-45): Basketball G. Point guard on championship Knick teams of 1970 and '73. First team All Star in 1970, '72, '74 and '75. First team All Defense every year from 1969–1975. Averaged 18.9 points per game in 13-season NBA career. Elected to Hall of Fame in 1986.

Frankie Frisch (b. 9-9-98, d. 3-12-73): Baseball IN. "The Fordham Flash." Led NL in hits in 1923 (223). Hit over .300 13 seasons. Scored 100+ runs 7 times. Drove in 100+ runs three times. Career .316 batting average. Career span 1919–26 with New York Giants and 1927–37 with St. Louis Cardinals "Gashouse Gang." NL MVP in 1931. Elected to Hall of Fame in 1947.

Dan Gable (b. 10-25-48): Wrestler. Gold medalist in 149–pound division at 1972 Olympics. Also NCAA champion 2 times (in 1968 at 130 pounds, in 1969 at 137 pounds). Coached Iowa to NCAA championship 13 years (consecutively 1978–86, 1991–93 and 1995).

Clarence Gaines (b. 5-21-23): College basketball coach. "Bighouse." Retired after 1992-93 season with 828 career wins in 46 seasons at Division II Winston-Salem State since 1947.

John Galbreath (b. 8-10-1897, d. 7-20-88): Horse racing owner. Owner of Darby Dan Farms from 1935 until his death and of baseball's Pittsburgh Pirates from 1946 to 1985. Only man to breed and own winners of both the Kentucky Derby (Chateaugay in 1963 and Proud Clarion in 1967) and the Epsom Derby (Roberto in 1972).

Gallant Fox (b. 3-23-27, d. 11-13-54): Thoroughbred race horse. Triple Crown winner in 1930 with jockey Earle Sande aboard. Trained by James Fitzsimmons. The only Triple Crown winner to sire another Triple Crown winner (Omaha in 1935).

Don Garlits (b. 1-14-32): Auto racer. "Big Daddy." Has won 35 National Hot Rod Association top fuel events. Won 3 NHRA top fuel points titles (1975, 1985–86). First top fuel driver to surpass 190 mph (1963), 200 mph (1964), 240 mph (1973), 250 mph (1975) and 270 mph (1986). Credited with developing rear engine dragster.

Lou Gehrig (b. 6-19-03, d. 6-2-41): Baseball 1B. "The Iron Horse." Second alltime in consecutive games played (2,130), leader in grand slam HR (23), third in RBI (1,990) and slugging average (.632). MVP in 1927, 1936; won Triple Crown in 1934. .340 career average; 493 career HR. 100+ RBI 13 consecutive seasons. Led league in RBI 5 times and HR 3 times. Played on 7 World Series winners with New York Yankees. Died of disease since named for him. Career span 1923–39.

Bernie Geoffrion (b. 2-16-31): Hockey RW. "Boom Boom" for his powerful slapshot. Won Hart Memorial Trophy for 1960–61. Scored 393 goals and 429 assists in 16 seasons (1950–51 through 1967–68), the first 14 with the Montreal Canadiens, the final two with the New York Rangers. Elected to Hall of Fame 1972.

Eddie Giacomin (b. 6-6-39): Hockey goalie. "Fast Eddie" led NHL goalies in games won for three straight seasons. Shared Vezina Trophy for 1970–71. In 610 games gave up 1,675 goals, a goals against average of 2.82. Career span 1965–75 with the New York Rangers and 1975–78 with Detroit Red Wings.

Althea Gibson (b. 8-25-27): Tennis player. Won 2 consecutive Wimbledon and U.S. singles titles (1957–58), the first black player to win these tournaments. Also won 1 French title (1956).

Bob Gibson (b. 11-9-35): Baseball RHP. 1968 Cy Young and MVP award winner with alltime National League best in ERA (1.12) and second most shutouts (13). Also 1970 Cy Young award winner. Record holder for most strikeouts in a World Series game (17); Series MVP in 1964, 1967. Won 20+ games 5 times. 251 career wins; 3,117 strikeouts. Pitched no-hitter in 1971. Career span 1959–75 with St. Louis.

Josh Gibson (b. 12-21-11, d. 1-20-47): Baseball C in Negro leagues. "The Black Babe Ruth." Couldn't play in major leagues because of color. Credited with 950 HR (75 in 1931, 69 in 1934) and .350 batting average. Had .400+ average 2 times. Career span 1930–46 with Homestead Grays, Pittsburgh Crawfords.

Kirk Gibson (b. 5-28-57): Baseball OF. Played on 2 World Series champions (Detroit in 1984 and Los Angeles in 1988). Hit dramatic pinch-hit HR in 9th inning to win Game 1 of 1988 series. MVP in 1988. Career span since 1979, currently with Detroit. Also starred in baseball and football at Michigan State.

Frank Gifford (b. 8-16-30): Football RB. NFL Player of Year in 1956 when he rushed for 819 yards and caught 51 passes. Played in seven Pro Bowls. Retired for one season after ferocious hit by Chuck Bednarik. Career span 1952–60 and 1962–64, all with New York Giants. Elected to Hall of Fame in 1977.

Rod Gilbert (b. 7-1-41): Hockey RW. Played 16 seasons, all with the New York Rangers (1960–61 through 1977–78), and had 406 goals and 615 assists. Elected to Hall of Fame 1982.

Sid Gillman (b. 10-26-11): Football coach. Developed wide-open, pass-oriented style of offense, introduced techniques for situational player substitutions and the study of game films. Won one division title with Los Angeles Rams and five division titles and one AFL championship (1963) with Los Angeles/San Diego Chargers. Career span 1955–59 Los Angeles Rams; 1960 Los Angeles Chargers; 1961–69 San Diego; 1973–74 Houston. Lifetime record 124-101-7. Also general manager in San Diego and Houston.

Pancho Gonzales (b. 5-9-28, d. 7-3-95): Tennis player. Won 2 consecutive U.S. singles titles (1948–49). In 1969, at age 41, beat Charlie Pasarell

22–24, 1–6, 16–14, 6–3, 11–9 in longest Wimbledon match ever (5:12).

Shane Gould (b. 11-23-56): Australian swimmer. Won 3 gold medals, 1 silver and 1 bronze at 1972 Olympics. Set 11 world records over 23-month period beginning in 1971. Held world record in 5 freestyle distances ranging from 100 meters to 1,500 meters in late 1971 and 1972. Retired at age 16.

Steffi Graf (b. 6-14-69): German tennis player. Achieved the Grand Slam in 1988. Has won 4 Australian Open singles titles (1988–90, '94), 6 Wimbledon titles (1988–89, 1991–93, '95), 4 French Open titles (1987–88, '93 and '95) and 4 U.S. Open titles (1988–89, '93 and '95). Held the #1 ranking a record 186 weeks; Aug. 17, 1987 through March 10, 1991. Gold medalist at 1988 Olympics.

Otto Graham (b. 12-6-21): Football QB. Led Cleveland to 10 championship games in his 10-year career. Played on 4 consecutive AAFC champions (1946–49) and 3 NFL champions (1950, consecutively 1954–55). Combined league totals: 23,584 yards passing, 174 touchdown passes. Player of the Year 2 times (1953, 1955). Led league in passing 6 times. Career span 1946–55.

Red Grange (b. 6-13-03, d. 1-28-91): Football HB. "The Galloping Ghost." All-America 3 consecutive seasons with Illinois (1923–25), scoring 31 touchdowns in 20–game collegiate career. Signed by George Halas of Chicago in 1925, attracted sellout crowds across the country. Established the first AFL with manager C. C. Pyle in 1926, but league folded after 1 year. Career span 1925–34 with Chicago, New York.

Rocky Graziano (b. 6-7-22, d. 5-22-90): Boxer. Middleweight champion from 1947 to 1948. Career record 67–13. Endured 3 brutal title fights against Tony Zale, with Zale winning by KO in 1946 and 1948, and Graziano winning by KO in 1947.

Hank Greenberg (b. 1-1-11, d. 9-4-86): Baseball 1B. 331 career HR (58 in 1938). MVP in 1935, 1940. League leader in HR and RBI 4 times each. Fifth alltime highest slugging average (.605). 100+ RBI 7 times. Career span 1933-41, 1945-47 with Detroit, Pittsburgh.

Joe Greene (b. 9-24-46): Football DT. "Mean Joe." Anchored Pittsburgh's famed "Steel Curtain" defense. Selected for Pro Bowl 10 times. Played on 4 Super Bowl champions (consecutively 1974-75, 1978-79). Career span 1969 to 1981.

Forrest Gregg (b. 10-18-33): Football OT/G. Played in then-record 188 straight games from 1956 through 1971. Named all-NFL eight straight years starting in 1960. Career span 1956–71, most of it with Green Bay Packers. Played on winning Packer team in first two Super Bowls. Inducted into Hall of Fame in 1977.

Wayne Gretzky (b. 1-26-61): Hockey C. "The Great One." Most dominant player in history. Alltime scoring leader in points (2,506), assists (1,692), and goals (814). Alltime single season scoring leader in points (215 in 1986), goals (92 in 1982) and assists (163 in 1986). Has won MVP award 9 times, more than any other player (consecutively 1980-87, 1989). Led league in assists 14 times, scoring 11 times, goals 5 times. Scored 200+ points 4 times, 100+ points 9 other times; 70+ goals 4 consecutive seasons, 50+ goals 5 other times; 100+ assists 11 consecutive seasons. Also alltime playoff scoring leader in points (346), goals (110) and assists (236). Playoff MVP 2 times (1985, 1988). All-Star 8 times. Played on 5

Stanley Cup champions with Edmonton from 1978 to 1988. Traded to Los Angeles on Aug. 9, 1988.

Bob Griese (b. 2-3-45): Football QB. Career span 1967–80 with Miami Dolphins. Played in three straight Super Bowls, 1971–73. Quarterback of 1972 Dolphin team that went 17–0. Won Super Bowl VII and VIII. In 14 seasons completed 1,926 passes for 25,092 yards and 192 TDs. Elected to Hall of Fame in 1990.

Archie Griffin (b. 8-21-54): College football RB. Only player to win the Heisman Trophy 2 times (consecutively 1974-75), with Ohio State. Fourth alltime NCAA most yards rushing (5,177), his 6.13 yards per carry is the collegiate record. Professional career span 1976-83 with Cincinnati; totaled 2,808 yards rushing and 192 receptions.

Lefty Grove (b. 3-6-00, d. 5-22-75): Baseball LHP. 300 career wins and fourth alltime highest winning percentage (.680). League leader in ERA 9 times, strikeouts 7 consecutive seasons. Won 20+ games 8 times. 1931 MVP. Career span 1925-41 with Philadelphia, Boston.

Tony Gwynn (b. 5-9-60): Baseball OF. 6 batting titles (1984, consecutively 1987-89, 1994-95). League leader in hits 6 times, with .300+ average 11 times, 200+ hits 4 times. Career span since 1982 with San Diego.

Walter Hagen (b. 12-21-1892, d. 10-5-69): Golfer. Third alltime leader in major championships (11). Won PGA Championship 5 times (1921, consecutively 1924-27), British Open 4 times (1922, 1924, consecutively 1928-29) and U.S. Open 2 times (1914, 1919). Won 40 career tournaments.

Marvin Hagler (b. 5-23-54): Boxer. "Marvelous." Middleweight champion (1980-87). Career record 62-3-2 with 52 KOs from 1973 to 1987. Defended title 13 times.

George Halas (b. 2-2-1895, d. 10-31-83): Football owner and coach. "Papa Bear." Alltime leader in seasons coaching (40) and second in wins (324). Career record 324-151-31 intermittently from 1920 to 1967. Remained as owner until his death. Chicago won a record 7 NFL championships during his tenure.

Glenn Hall (b. 10-3-31): Hockey goalie. "Mr. Goalie" was an All-Star goalie in 11 of his 18 seasons. Set record for consecutive games by a goaltender, with 502, and ended career with goals against average of 2.51. Won or shared Vezina Trophy three times. Career span 1952–53 through 1970–71.

Arthur B. "Bull" Hancock (b. 1-24-10, d. 9-14-72): Horse racing owner. Owner of Claiborne Farm and arguably the greatest breeder in history. For 15 straight years, from 1955 to 1969, a Claiborne stallion led the sire list. Foaled at Claiborne Farm were 4 Horses of the Year (Kelso, Round Table, Bold Ruler and Nashua).

Tom Harmon (b. 9-28-19, d. 3-17-90): Football RB. Won Heisman Trophy in 1940 with Michigan. Triple-threat back led nation in scoring and named All-America 2 consecutive seasons (1939-40). Awarded Silver Star and Purple Heart in World War II. Played in NFL with Los Angeles (1946-47).

Franco Harris (b. 3-7-50): Football RB. Fifth alltime most rushing yards (12,120) and fifth in rushing touchdowns (91). Rushed for 1,000+ yards in 8 seasons, 100+ yards in 47 games. Scored 100 career touchdowns. Selected for Pro Bowl 9 times. Rookie of the Year in 1972. Played on 4 Super Bowl champions (consecutively 1974-75, 1978-79) with Pittsburgh. Super Bowl MVP in 1974. Holds Super Bowl record for most rushing yards (354) and tied for most rushing touchdowns (4). Made the "Immaculate Reception" to win 1972 playoff game against Oakland. Career span 1972-83 with Pittsburgh.

Leon Hart (b. 11-2-28): Football DE. Won Heisman Trophy in 1949, the last lineman to win the award. Played on 3 national champions with Notre Dame (consecutively 1946–47, 1949) and the Irish went undefeated during his 4 years (36-0-2). Also played on 3 NFL champions with Detroit. Career span 1950-57.

Bill Hartack (b. 12-9-32): Horse racing jockey. Rode Kentucky Derby winner 5 times (1957, 1960, 1962, 1964, 1969), Preakness Stakes winner 3 times (1956, 1964, 1969) and Belmont Stakes winner 1 time (1960).

Doug Harvey (b. 12-19-24, d. 12-26-90): Hockey D. Defensive Player of the Year 7 times (consecutively 1954-57, 1959-61). Led league in assists in 1954. All-Star 10 times. Played on 6 Stanley Cup champions with Montreal from 1947 to 1968.

Billy Haughton (b. 11-2-23, d. 7-15-86): Harness racing driver. Won the Pacing Triple Crown driving Rum Customer in 1968. Won The Hambletonian 4 times (1974, consecutively 1976-77, 1980).

John Havlicek (b. 4-8-40): Basketball F/G. Member of Ohio State team that won 1960 NCAA title. "Hondo" averaged 20.8 points per game over 16-season NBA career, all with Boston. First team NBA All Star in 1971, '72, '73 and '74. Member of eight Celtic teams that won NBA title. Playoff MVP 1974. Elected to Hall of Fame in 1983.

Elvin Hayes (b. 11-17-45): Basketball C. 1968 *Sporting News* College Player of Year as Houston senior. Averaged 21.0 points per game over 16-season NBA career. Led NBA in scoring (28.4) in 1969 and in rebounding in 1970 (16.9 per game) and '74 (18.1). First team All NBA in 1975, '77 and '79. Elected to Hall of Fame in 1989.

Woody Hayes (b. 2-14-13, d. 3-12-87): College football coach. Sixth alltime in wins (238). Won national championship 3 times (1954, 1957, 1968) and Rose Bowl 4 times. Career record 238-72-10, including 4 undefeated seasons, with Ohio State from 1951 to 1978. Forced to resign after striking an opposing player during 1978 Gator Bowl.

Marques Haynes (b. 10-3-26): Basketball G. Known as "The World's Greatest Dribbler." Since 1946 has barnstormed more than 4 million miles throughout 97 countries for the Harlem Globetrotters, Harlem Magicians, Meadowlark Lemon's Bucketeers, Harlem Wizards.

Thomas Hearns (b. 10-18-58): Boxer. "Hit Man." Champion in 5 different weight classes: junior middleweight, light heavyweight, middleweight, super middleweight, and light heavyweight.

Eric Heiden (b. 6-14-58): Speed skater. Won 5 gold medals at 1980 Olympics. World champion 3 consecutive years (1977-79). Also won Sullivan Award in 1980.

Carol Heiss (b. 1-20-40): Figure skater. Gold medalist at 1960 Olympics, silver medalist at 1956 Olympics. World champion 5 consecutive years (1956-60) and U.S. champion 4 consecutive years (1957-60). Married 1956 gold medalist Hayes Jenkins.

Rickey Henderson (b. 12-25-57): Baseball OF. Alltime career stolen base leader (1117); alltime season

stolen base record holder (130) in 1982. Led league in steals 11 times. Scored 100+ runs 11 times. 1990 MVP. Alltime most HR leading off game. Career span since 1979 with Oakland, New York and Toronto.

Sonja Henie (b. 4-8-12, d. 10-12-69): Norwegian figure skater. Gold medalist at 3 consecutive Olympics (1928, 1932, 1936). World champion 10 consecutive years (1927-36).

Orel Hershiser (b. 9-16-58): Baseball RHP. Alltime leader most consecutive scoreless innings pitched (59 in 1988). Cy Young Award winner in 1988 and World Series MVP. Career span since 1983 with Los Angeles.

Foster Hewitt (b. 11-21-02, d. 4-22-85): Hockey sportscaster. In 1923, aired one of hockey's first radio broadcasts. Became the voice of hockey in Canada on radio and later television. Famous for the phrase, "He shoots ... he scores!"

Tommy Hitchcock (b. 2-11-00, d. 4-19-44): Polo. 10-goal rating 18 times in his 19-year career from 1922 to 1940. Killed in plane crash in World War II.

Lew Hoad (b. 11-23-34): Australian tennis player. Won 2 consecutive Wimbledon singles titles (1956-57). Also won French title and Australian title in 1956, but failed to achieve the Grand Slam when defeated at Forest Hills by countryman Ken Rosewall.

Ben Hogan (b. 8-13-12): Golfer. Third alltime in career wins (63). Won U.S. Open 4 times (1948, consecutively 1950-51, 1953), the Masters (1951, 1953) and PGA Championship (1946, 1948) 2 times each and British Open once (1953). PGA Player of the Year 4 times (1948, consecutively 1950-51, 1953).

Marshall Holman (b. 9-29-54): Bowler. Won 21 PBA titles between 1975 and 1988. Had leading average in 1987 (213.54) and was named PBA Bowler of the Year.

Nat Holman (b. 10-18-1896, d. 2-12-95): College basketball coach. Only coach in history to win NCAA and NIT championships in same season in 1950 with CCNY. 423 career wins, a .689 winning percentage.

Larry Holmes (b. 11-3-49): Boxer. Heavyweight champion (1978-85). Career record 53–3 with 37 KOs from 1973 to 1991. Defended title 21 times.

Lou Holtz (b. 1-6-37): Football coach. Coached Notre Dame to national championship in 1988 with 12–0 record and a 34–21 win over West Virginia in Fiesta Bowl. At start of '95 season had 199-89-7 career record. 10-7-2 career record in bowl games. Career span 1969–71 at William & Mary (13–20); 1972–75 at N.C. State (33-12-3); 1977–83 at Arkansas (60-21-2); 1984–85 at Minnesota 10–12); and since 1986 at Notre Dame (77-19-1).

Evander Holyfield (b. 10-19-62): Boxer. Won heavyweight crown Oct. 25, 1990 when he beat James "Buster" Douglas in Las Vegas. Lost title to Riddick Bowe in Las Vegas on 11-13-92, regained it from Bowe one year later, then lost to Michael Moorer on 4-22-94.

Red Holzman (b. 8-10-20): Basketball coach. Led New York Knicks to NBA title in 1970 and '73. NBA coach of the Year in 1970. Member of Rochester team that won NBA title in both 1946 (in NBL) and '51. After two-year coaching stints with Milwaukee and St. Louis, coached New York Knicks from 1968–82. Elected to Hall of Fame in 1985.

Harry Hopman (b. 8-12-06, d. 12-27-85): Australian tennis coach. As nonplaying captain, led Australia to 15 Davis Cup titles between 1950 and 1969. Mentor to Lew Hoad, Ken Rosewall, Rod Laver and John Newcombe.

Willie Hoppe (b. 10-11-1887, d. 2-1-59): Billiards. Won 51 world championship matches from 1904 to 1952.

Rogers Hornsby (b. 4-27-1896, d. 1-5-63): Baseball 2B. Second all-time highest career batting average (.358) and 7 batting titles, including .424 average in 1924. 200+ hits 7 times; .400+ average 3 times and .300+ average 12 other times. Led league in slugging average 9 times. Triple Crown winner in 1922, 1925; MVP award winner in 1925, 1929. Career span 1915-37 with St Louis (NL), New York (NL), Boston, Chicago (NL).

Paul Hornung (b. 12-23-35): Football RB-K. Led league in scoring 3 consecutive seasons, including a record 176 points in 1960 (15 touchdowns, 15 field goals, 41 extra points). Player of the Year in 1961. Career span 1957-66 with Green Bay. Suspended for 1963 season by Pete Rozelle for gambling. Also won Heisman Trophy in 1956 with Notre Dame.

Gordie Howe (b. 3-31-28): Hockey RW. Second alltime in goals (801), first in years played (26) and games (1,767). Second alltime in points (1,850) and assists (1,049). Won MVP award 6 times (consecutively 1952-53, 1957-58, 1960, 1963). Led league in scoring 6 times, goals 5 times and assists 3 times. Scored 40+ goals 5 times, 30+ goals 13 other times, 100+ points 3 times. All-Star 12 times. Played on 4 Stanley Cup champions with Detroit from 1946 to 1971. Teamed with sons Mark and Marty in the WHA with Houston and New England from 1973 to 1979, in NHL with Hartford in 1980.

Carl Hubbell (b. 6-22-03, d. 11-21-88): Baseball LHP. 253 career wins. MVP in 1933, 1936. League leader in wins and ERA 3 times each. Won 24 consecutive games from 1936 to 1937. Struck out Ruth, Gehrig, Foxx, Simmons and Cronin consecutively in 1934 All-Star game. Pitched no-hitter in 1929. Career span 1928-43 with New York.

Sam Huff (b. 10-4-34): Football LB. Made 30 interceptions. Career span 1956–69 with New York Giants and Washington Redskins. Elected to Hall of Fame in 1982.

Bobby Hull (b. 1-3-39): Hockey LW. "The Golden Jet." Sixth alltime in goals scored (610). Led league in goals 7 times and points 3 times. Scored 50+ goals 5 times, 30+ goals 8 other times. Won MVP award 2 consecutive seasons (1965-66). Son Brett won MVP award in 1991, the only father and son to be so honored. All-Star 10 times. Career span 1957-72 with Chicago, 1973-80 with Winnipeg of WHA.

Brett Hull (b. 8-9-64): Hockey RW. Son of Bobby Hull. Won Hart Memorial Trophy for 1990–91 season. Career span 1986–87 with Calgary Flames; since 1987 with St. Louis Blues.

Jim "Catfish" Hunter (b. 4-8-46): Baseball RHP. 1974 Cy Young award winner. Won 20+ games 5 consecutive seasons. Led league in wins and winning percentage 2 times each, ERA 1 time. 250+ innings pitched 8 times. Pitched perfect game in 1968. Member of 5 World Series champions for Oakland and New York Yankees. Career span 1965-79.

Don Hutson (b. 1-31-13): Football WR. Third alltime in touchdown receptions (99). Led league in pass receptions 8 times, receiving yards 7 times and scoring 5 consecutive seasons. Caught at least 1 pass in 95 consecutive games. Player of the Year 2 consecutive seasons (1941-42). Career span 1935-45 with Green Bay.

Hank Iba (b. 8-6-04; d. 1-15-93): College basketball coach. Coached Oklahoma A&M (which became Oklahoma State) from 1934 to 1970. Team won NCAA titles in 1945 and '46. 767 career wins is third alltime behind Adolph Rupp and Dean Smith.

Jackie Ickx (b. 1-1-45): Belgian auto racer. Won the 24 Hours of LeMans a record six times (1969, consecutively 1975-77, 1981-82) before retiring in 1985.

Punch Imlach (b. 3-15-18, d. 12-1-87): Hockey coach. 467 wins. With Toronto from 1958 to 1969. Won 4 Stanley Cup championships (consecutively 1962-64, 1967).

Bo Jackson (b. 11-30-62): Baseball OF and Football RB. Only person in history to be named to baseball All-Star game and football Pro Bowl game. 1985 Heisman Trophy winner at Auburn. First pick in 1986 NFL draft by Tampa Bay, but opted to play baseball at Kansas City. 1989 All-Star game MVP. Signed with football's LA Raiders in 1988. Sustained football injury in 1990, released from baseball contract by KC, signed by Chicago and returned from injury in early September 1991, but comeback failed at first. Had hip replacement surgery and hit homer in first at bat afterwards.

Joe Jackson (b. 7-16-1889, d. 12-5-51): Baseball OF. "Shoeless Joe." Third alltime highest career batting average (.356), with .300+ average 11 times. One of the "8 men out" banned from baseball for throwing 1919 World Series. Career span 1908-20 with Cleveland, Chicago.

Reggie Jackson (b. 5-18-46): Baseball OF. "Mr. October." Alltime leader in World Series slugging average (.755). 1977 Series MVP, hit 3 HR in final game on 3 consecutive pitches. 563 career HR total is sixth best alltime. Led league in HR 4 times. 1973 MVP. Alltime strikeout leader (2,597). In a 12-year period played on 10 first-place teams, 5 World Series winners. Career span 1967-87 with Oakland, New York, California. Inducted into baseball Hall of Fame in 1993.

Bruce Jenner (b. 10-28-49): Track and Field. Set world decathlon record (8,634) in winning gold medal at 1976 Olympics. Sullivan Award winner in 1976.

John Henry (b. 1975): Thoroughbred race horse. Sold as yearling for $1,100, the gelding was Horse of the Year in 1981 and in 1984 and retired with then-record $6,597,947 in winnings.

Ben Johnson (b. 12-30-61): Track and field. Canadian sprinter set world record in 100 meters (9.83 in 1987). Won event at 1988 Olympics in 9.79, but gold medal revoked for failing drug test. Both world records revoked for steroid usage. Suspended for life after testing positive for elevated testosterone level at an indoor meet in Montreal on 1-17-93.

Earvin "Magic" Johnson (b. 8-14-59): Basketball G. Retired Nov. 7, 1991 after being diagnosed with HIV, the virus that causes AIDS. Second alltime in assists (9,921); alltime playoff leader in assists (2,320) and steals (358). MVP award 3 times (1987, consecutively 1989-90) and playoff MVP 1980, 1982, 1987. Played on 5 championship teams with Los Angeles since 1979. All-Star 8 consecutive seasons.

League leader in assists 4 times, steals 2 times, free throw percentage 1 time. Also won NCAA championship and named tournament MVP in 1979 with Michigan State.

Jack Johnson (b. 3-31-1878, d. 6-10-46): Boxer. First black heavyweight champion (1908-15). Career record 78-8-12 with 45 KOs from 1897 to 1928.

Jimmy Johnson (b. 7-16-43): Football coach. Led the Cowboys from 1–15 in 1989, his first season in Dallas, to a 52–17 win over the Buffalo Bills in the Super Bowl XXVII just four seasons later. Also coached Super Bowl XXVIII champion Cowboys before resigning because of a dispute with owner Jerry Jones. Head coach at Oklahoma State from 1979–83 and Univ. of Miami 1984–88 with career collegiate record of 81-34-3. Johnson's Hurricanes won national championship in 1987.

Michael Johnson (b. 9-13-67): Track and field sprinter. Only person ever to break 44 seconds for 400 (best of 43.65) and 20 seconds for 200 (19.79). Won 200 at 1991 World Championships, 400 at '93 worlds and both events at the '95 worlds. Anchored US 4 x 400 team at 1993 World Championship to world record of 2:54.29 with fastest ever relay carry of 42.97.

Walter Johnson (b. 11-6-1887, d. 12-10-46): Baseball RHP. "Big Train." Alltime leader in shutouts (110), second in wins (416), fourth in losses (279) and third in innings pitched (5,923). His 2.17 career ERA and 3,508 career strikeouts are seventh best alltime. MVP in 1913, 1924. Won 20+ games 12 times. League leader in strikeouts 12 times, ERA 5 times, wins 6 times. Pitched no-hitter in 1920. Career span 1907-27 with Washington.

Ben A. Jones (b. 12-31-1882, d. 6-13-61): Horse racing trainer. Trained Triple Crown winner 2 times (Whirlaway in 1941, Citation in 1948). Trained Kentucky Derby winner 6 times, more than any other trainer (1938, 1941, 1944, consecutively 1948-49, 1952), Preakness Stakes winner 2 times (1941, 1944) and Belmont Stakes winner 1 time (1941).

Bobby Jones (b. 3-17-02, d. 12-18-71): Golfer. Achieved golf's only recognized Grand Slam in 1930. Second alltime in major championships (13). Won U.S. Amateur 5 times, more than any golfer (consecutively 1924-25, 1927-28, 1930), U.S. Open 4 times (1923, 1926, consecutively 1929-30), British Open 3 times (consecutively 1926-27, 1930) and British Amateur (1930). Also designed Augusta National course, site of the Masters, and founded the tournament. Winner of Sullivan Award in 1930.

K.C. Jones (b. 5-25-32): Basketball G-coach. Member of 8 straight NBA-championship Boston Celtic teams in his nine season career from 1958–59 through 1966–67. Averaged 7.4 points and 4.3 assists per game. Coached Celtics from 1983–84 through 1987–88, with 308–102 regular season record and 65–37 playoff record with NBA titles in 1984 and '86.

Robert Trent Jones (b. 6-20-06): English-born golf course architect designed or remodelled over 400 courses, including Baltusrol, Hazeltine, Oak Hill and Winged Foot. In the mid-60s five straight U.S. Opens were played on courses designed or remodelled by Jones.

Sam Jones (b. 6-24-33): Basketball G. Played 12 seasons with Boston Celtics (1958–69) and made the playoffs every year, winning NBA title every year from 1959–66 plus 1968 and '69. Averaged 17.7 points per game for career. Elected to Hall of Fame in 1983.

Michael Jordan (b. 2-17-63): Basketball G. "Air." After 1994-95 season, alltime highest regular season scoring average (32.2) and most points scored in a playoff game (63 in 1986). Led league in scoring 7 consecutive seasons, steals 3 times. MVP in 1988, 1991-92; playoff MVP in 1991-93; Rookie of the Year in 1985. All-Star team 6 consecutive seasons, All-Defensive team 5 consecutive seasons. Career span 1984–93, 1995- with Chicago. Announced retirement on 10-6-93, returned in March 1995. Also College Player of the Year in 1984. Played on NCAA championship team with North Carolina in 1982. Member of gold medal-winning 1984 and '92 Olympic teams.

Florence Griffith Joyner (b. 12-21-59): Track and field. Won 3 gold medals (100 meters, 200 meters, 4x100-meter relay) at 1988 Olympics; silver medalist at 1984 Olympics. Set world record in 100 (10.49) in 1988 and in 200 (21.34) at the 1988 Olympics. Sullivan Award winner in 1988.

Jackie Joyner-Kersee (b. 3-3-62): Track and field. Gold medalist in heptathlon and long jump at 1988 Olympics and in the former at the 1992 Olympics. Set heptathlon world record (7,291 points) at 1988 Olympics. Also won silver medal in heptathlon at 1984 Olympics and bronze in long jump at 1992 Olympics. Sullivan Award winner in 1986.

Alberto Juantorena (b. 3-12-51): Track and field. Cuban was gold medalist in 400 meters and 800 meters at 1976 Olympics.

Sonny Jurgensen (b. 8-23-34): Football QB. In 18 seasons completed 2,433 of 4,262 pass attempts for 32,224 yards and 255 TDs. Led NFL in passing both 1967 and '69. Career span 1957–1974 with Philadelphia Eagles and Washington Redskins. Elected to Hall of Fame in 1983.

Duke Kahanamoku (b. 8-24-1890, d. 1-22- 68): Swimmer. Won a total of 5 medals (3 gold and 2 silver) at 3 Olympics in 1912, 1920, 1924. Introduced the crawl stroke to America. Surfing pioneer and water polo player. Later sheriff of Honolulu.

Al Kaline (b. 12-19-34): Baseball OF. 3,007 career hits and 399 career HR. Youngest player to win batting title with .340 average as a 20-year-old in 1955. Had .300+ average 9 times. Played in 18 All-Star games. Career span 1953-74 with Detroit.

Anatoly Karpov (b. 5-23-61): Soviet chess player. First world champion to receive title by default, in 1975, when Bobby Fischer chose not to defend his crown. Champion until 1985 when beaten by Gary Kasparov. Recognized by FIDE as champion in 1994.

Gary Kasparov (b. 4-13-63): Born Harry Weinstein. Chess player. World champion from 1985 to 1993 when stripped of title by FIDE.

Kip Keino (b. 1-17-40): Track and field. Kenyan was gold medalist in 1,500 meters at 1968 Olympics and in steeplechase at 1972 Olympics.

Jim Kelly (b. 2-14-60): Football QB. Led NFL in passing in 1990 (219 of 346 for 2,829 yards and 24 TDs). Led AFC in passing in 1991. In nine seasons through '94 completed 2,397 of 3,942 attempts for 29,527 yards and 201 TDs. Career span 1983-85 with New Jersey Generals (USFL), since 1986 with

Buffalo Bills. Led Bills to four straight Super Bowls, all losses.

Kelso (b. 1957, d. 1983): Thoroughbred race horse. Gelding was Horse of the Year 5 straight years (1960-64). Finished in the money in 53 of 63 races. Career earnings $1,977,896.

Harmon Killebrew (b. 6-29-36): Baseball 3B-1B. 573 career HR total is fifth most alltime. 100+ RBI 9 times, 40+ HR 8 times. League leader in HR 6 times and RBI 4 times. 1969 MVP. 100+ walks and strikeouts 7 times each. Career span 1954-75 with Washington, Minnesota.

Jean Claude Killy (b. 8-30-43): French skier. Won 3 gold medals at 1968 Olympics. World Cup overall champion 2 consecutive years (1967-68).

Ralph Kiner (b. 10-27-22): Baseball OF. Second to Babe Ruth in alltime HR frequency (7.1 HR every 100 at bats). 369 career HR. Led league in HR 7 consecutive seasons, with 50+ HR 2 times; 100+ RBI and runs scored in same season 6 times; 100+ walks 6 times. Career span 1946-55 with Pittsburgh.

Billie Jean King (b. 11-22-43): Tennis player. Won a record 20 Wimbledon titles, including 6 singles titles (consecutively 1966-68, 1972-73, 1975). Won 4 U.S. singles titles (1967, consecutively 1971-72, 1974), and singles titles at Australian Open (1968) and French Open (1972). Won 27 Grand Slam doubles titles—total of 39 Grand Slam titles is third alltime. Helped found the women's pro tour in 1970, serving as president of the Women's Tennis Association 2 times. Helped form Team Tennis.

Nile Kinnick (b. 7-9-18, d. 6-2-43): College football RB. Won the Heisman Trophy in 1939 with Iowa. Premier runner, passer and punter was killed in plane crash during routine Navy training flight. Stadium in Iowa City named in his honor.

Tom Kite (b. 12-9-49): Golfer. PGA alltime money leader, with $9,159,418 through end of '94 season. Led PGA in scoring average in 1981 (69.80) and '82 (70.21). PGA Player of Year in 1989, when he won a then-record $1,395,278. Shook reputation for failing to win the big ones by winning 1992 US Open at windy Pebble Beach.

Franz Klammer (b. 12-3-54): Austrian alpine skier. Greatest downhiller ever. Gold medalist in downhill at 1976 Olympics. Also won four World Cup downhill titles (1975-78).

Bob Knight (b. 10-25-40): College basketball coach. Won 3 NCAA championships with Indiana in 1976, 1981, 1987. Coached U.S. Olympic team to gold medal in 1984. 659 career wins and .737 career winning percentage entering 1995-96 season. Career span since 1966.

Olga Korbut (b. 5-16-55): Soviet gymnast. First ever to complete backward somersault on balance beam. Won 3 gold medals at 1972 Olympics.

Sandy Koufax (b. 12-30-35): Baseball LHP. Cy Young Award winner 3 times (1963, consecutively 1965-66); and MVP in 1963; World Series MVP in 1963, 1965. Pitched 1 perfect game, 3 no-hitters. League leader in ERA 5 consecutive seasons, strikeouts 4 times. Won 25+ games 3 times. Career record 165-87, with 2.76 ERA. Career span 1955-66 with Brooklyn/Los Angeles.

Jack Kramer (b. 8-1-21): Tennis player. Won 2 consecutive U.S. singles titles (1946-47) and 1

Wimbledon title (1947). Also won 6 Grand Slam doubles titles. Served as executive director of Association of Tennis Professionals from 1972 to 1975.

Ingrid Kristiansen (b. 3-21-56): Track and field. Norwegian runner is only person—male or female—to hold world records in 5,000 meters (14:37.33 set in 1986), 10,000 meters (30:13.74 set in 1986) and marathon (2:21:06 set in 1985). Also won Boston Marathon 2 times (1986, 1989).

Bob Kurland (b. 12-23-24): College basketball player. 6' 10¼" center on Oklahoma A&M teams that won NCAA titles in 1945 and '46. Consensus All America and NCAA tournament MVP in both 1945 and '46. Led nation in scoring in '46. His habit of swatting shots off rim led to creation of goaltending rule in 1945. Won gold medals in both 1948 and '52 Olympics. Turned down lucrative pro offers, playing instead for Phillips 66 Oilers AAU team.

Rene Lacoste (b. 7-2-05): French tennis player. "The Crocodile." One of France's "Four Musketeers" of the 1920s. Won 3 French singles titles (1925, 1927, 1929), 2 consecutive U.S. titles (1926-27) and 2 Wimbledon titles (1925, 1928). Also designed casual shirt with embroidered crocodile that bears his name.

Marion Ladewig (b. 10-30-14): Bowler. Won All-Star Tournament 8 times (consecutively 1949-52, 1954, 1956, 1959, 1963) and WPBA National Championship once (1960). Also voted Bowler of the Year 9 times (consecutively 1950-54, 1957-59, 1963).

Guy Lafleur (b. 9-20-51): Hockey RW. Won MVP award 2 consecutive seasons (1977-78), playoff MVP in 1977. Scored 50+ goals and 100+ points 6 consecutive seasons. Led league in points scored 3 consecutive seasons, goals and assists 1 time each. 560 career goals, 793 assists. Played on 5 Stanley Cup champions with Montreal from 1971 to 1985.

Curly Lambeau (b. 4-9-1898; d. 6-1-65): Football QB and coach. Quarterback for Packer team in early 20's. Record of 212-106-21 in his 29 seasons (1921–49) as Packer coach, winning three NFL titles in 1929–31.

Jack Lambert (b. 7-8-52): Football LB. Anchored Pittsburgh's famed "Steel Curtain" defense. Selected for Pro Bowl 9 times. Played on 4 Super Bowl champions (consecutively 1974-75, 1978-79) with Pittsburgh from 1974 to 1984.

Jake LaMotta (b. 7-10-21): Boxer. "The Bronx Bull." Subject of *Raging Bull*, movie by Martin Scorcese, starring Robert DeNiro. Won middleweight title by knocking out Marcel Cerdan in 10 on 6-16-49. Lost title to Ray Robinson, who KO'd him in 13 on 2-13-51. Career record: 106 bouts; won 30 by KO and 53 by decision; drew 4; and lost 19, 4 by KO.

Kenesaw Mountain Landis (b. 11-20-1866, d. 11-25-44): Baseball's first and most powerful commissioner from 1920 to 1944. By banning the 8 "Black Sox" involved in the fixing of the 1919 World Series, he restored public confidence in the integrity of baseball.

Tom Landry (b. 9-11-24): Football coach. Third alltime in wins (270). The first coach in Dallas history, from 1960 to 1988. Led team to 13 division titles, 7 championship games and 5 Super Bowls. Won 2 Super Bowl championships (1971, 1977). Career record 270-178-6.

Dick "Night Train" Lane (b. 4-16-28): Football DB. Third alltime in interceptions (68) and second in interception yardage (1,207). Set record with 14 interceptions as a rookie in 1952. Career span 1952-65 with Los Angeles, Chicago Cardinals, Detroit.

Joe Lapchick (b. 4-12-00, d. 8-10-70): Basketball C-coach. One of the first big men in basketball, member of New York's Original Celtics. Coached St. John's (1936-47, 1956-65) winning four NIT Tournaments. Coached New York Knicks, 1947-56.

Steve Largent (b. 9-28-54): Football WR. Third alltime in pass receptions (819), second in TD receptions (100). 177 consecutive games with reception, 10 seasons with 50+ receptions and 8 seasons with 1,000+ yards receiving. Career span 1976-89 with Seattle.

Don Larsen (b. 8-7-29): Baseball RHP. Pitched only perfect game in World Series history for the NY Yankees on Oct. 8, 1956, beating the Dodgers 2-0; named World Series MVP. Career span 1953-67 for many teams.

Tommy Lasorda (b. 9-22-27): Baseball manager. Has spent nearly his entire minor and major league career in Dodgers organization as a player, coach and manager. Has managed Dodgers since 1977, winning 4 pennants and 2 World Series (1981, 1988).

Rod Laver (b. 8-9-38): Australian tennis player. "Rocket." Only player to achieve the Grand Slam twice (as an amateur in 1962 and as a pro in 1969). Second alltime in men's Grand Slam singles titles (11—tied with Bjorn Borg). Won 4 Wimbledon titles (consecutively 1961-62, 1968-69), 3 Australian titles (1960, 1962, 1969), 2 U.S. titles (1962, 69) and 2 French titles (1962, 1969). Also won 8 Grand Slam doubles titles. First player to earn $1 million in prize money. 47 career tournament victories. Member of undefeated Australian Davis Cup team from 1959 to 1962.

Andrea Mead Lawrence (b. 4-19-32): Skier. Gold medalist in slalom and giant slalom at 1952 Olympics.

Bobby Layne (b. 12-19-26; d. 12-1-86): Football QB. Led Detroit Lions to NFL championships in both 1952 and '53. In 1952 led NFL in every passing category. Career span 1948–62, most with the Detroit Lions. Elected to Hall of Fame in 1967.

Sammy Lee (b. 8-1-20): Diver. Gold medalist at 2 consecutive Olympics (highboard in 1948, 1952); bronze medalist in springboard at 1948 Olympics. Won the 1953 Sullivan Award. Also 1960 U.S. Olympic diving coach.

Jacques Lemaire (b. 9-7-45): Hockey C-Coach. As center for Montreal Canadiens from 1967–68 through 1978–79 was part of eight Stanley Cup winning teams. Over 12 seasons, all with Montreal, scored 366 goals and had 469 assists. Elected to Hall of Fame in 1984. Coached Canadiens 1983-85 and N.J. Devils since 1993.

Mario Lemieux (b. 10-5-65): Hockey C. Won MVP award in 1988, playoff MVP in 1991. Led league in most points 4 seasos and goals scored 2 consecutive seasons, assists 1 season. Scored 40+ goals and 100+ points 6 consecutive seasons, including 85 goals and 199 points in 1989. Rookie of the Year in 1985. Won 1992-93 scoring title despite sitting out six weeks to receive treatment for Hodgkin's disease, a form of cancer. Career span since 1984 with Pittsburgh.

Greg LeMond (b. 6-26-61): Cyclist. Only American to win Tour de France; won event 3 times (1986,

consecutively 1989-90). Recovered from hunting accident to win in 1989.

Ivan Lendl (b. 3-7-60): Tennis player. Second alltime men's most career tournament victories (94). Won 3 consecutive U.S. Open singles titles (1985-87) and 3 French Open titles (1984, consecutively 1985-86). Also won 2 consecutive Australian Open titles (1989-90). Reached Grand Slam final 9 other times. Alltime leader in prize money, with more than $20 million.

Suzanne Lenglen (b. 5-24-1899, d. 7-4-38): French tennis player. Lost only 1 match from 1919 to her retirement in 1926. Won 6 Wimbledon singles and doubles titles (consecutively 1919-23, 1925). Won 6 French singles and doubles titles (consecutively 1920-23, 1925-26).

Sugar Ray Leonard (b. 5-17-56): Boxer. Champion in 5 different weight classes: welterweight, junior middleweight, middleweight, light heavyweight and super middleweight. Career record 36-2-1 with 25 KOs from 1977 to 1991. Also light welterweight gold medalist at 1976 Olympics.

Carl Lewis (b. 7-1-61): Track and field. Held world record for 100 meters 9.86; set on 8-25-91 at World Championships in Tokyo. Duplicated Jesse Owens's feat by winning 4 gold medals at 1984 Olympics (100 and 200 meters, 4x100-meter relay and long jump). Also won 2 gold medals (100 meters, long jump) and 1 silver (200 meters) at 1988 Olympics and two gold medals (long jump, 4x100 relay) at 1992 Olympics. Sullivan Award winner in 1981.

Nancy Lieberman (b. 7-1-58): Basketball G. Three-time All-America at Old Dominion. Player of the Year (1979, 1980). Olympian, 1976, and selected for 1980 team, but quit because of Moscow boycott. Promoter of women's basketball, played in WPBL, WABA. First woman to play basketball in a men's professional league (USBL) in 1986.

Bob Lilly (b. 7-26-39): Football DT. Dallas Cowboys' first ever draft pick, first Pro Bowl player and first all-NFL choice. Made all-NFL eight times. Career span 1961–74, all with Cowboys. Elected to Hall of Fame in 1980.

Sonny Liston (b. 5-8-32, d. 12-30-70): Boxer. Heavyweight champion from 1962 to 1964. Won title by KO of Floyd Patterson on 9-25-62. Lost title when TKO'd by Cassius Clay (Muhammad Ali) on 2-25-64 and then lost rematch on 5-25-65 when KO'd in first round. Career record: 54 fights; won 39 by KO and 11 by decision; lost 4, three by KO.

Vince Lombardi (b. 6-11-13, d. 9-3-70): Football coach. Alltime highest winning percentage (.740). Career record 105-35-6. Won 5 NFL championships and 2 consecutive Super Bowl titles with Green Bay from 1959 to 1967. Coached Washington in 1969. Super Bowl trophy named in his honor.

Johnny Longden (b. 2-14-07): Horse racing jockey. Rode Triple Crown winner Count Fleet in 1943. 6,032 wins.

Nancy Lopez (b. 1-6-57): Golfer. LPGA Player of the Year 4 times (consecutively 1978-79, 1985, 1988). Winner of LPGA Championship 3 times (1978, 1985, 1989). Member of the LPGA Hall of Fame.

Greg Louganis (b. 1-29-60): Diver. Gold medalist in platform and springboard at 2 consecutive Olympics in 1984, 1988. World champion 5 times (platform in 1978, 1982, 1986; springboard in 1982, 1986). Also Sullivan Award winner in 1984.

Joe Louis (b. 5-13-14, d. 4-12-81): Boxer. "The Brown Bomber." Longest title reign of any heavyweight champion (11 years, 9 months) from June 1937 through March 1949. Career record 63-3 with 49 KOs from 1934 to 1951. Defended title 25 times.

Jerry Lucas (b. 3-30-40): Basketball F. Star at Ohio State. *Sporting News* College Player of Year in both 1961 and '62. In 1960 member of both NCAA championship team and gold-medal winning U.S. Olympic team. Averaged over 20 points and 20 rebounds a game for college career. NBA Rookie of Year in 1964. In 11 NBA seasons averaged 17 points a game. Elected to Hall of Fame in 1979.

Sid Luckman (b. 11-21-16): Football QB. Played on 4 NFL champions (consecutively 1940-41, 1943, 1946) with Chicago. Player of the Year in 1943. Tied record with 7 touchdown passes on Nov. 14, 1943. All-Pro 6 times. 137 career touchdown passes. Career span 1939-50. Also All-America with Columbia.

Jon Lugbill (b. 5-27-61): White water canoe racer. Won 5 world singles titles from 1979 to 1989.

Hank Luisetti (b. 6-16-16): Basketball F. The first player to use the one-handed shot. All-America at Stanford 3 consecutive years from 1936-38.

D. Wayne Lukas (b. 9-2-35): Horse racing trainer. Former college basketball coach and quarter horse trainer takes mass production approach with stables at most major tracks around country. Trained two Horses of the Year, Lady's Secret in 1986 and Criminal Type in 1990. Won 1988 Kentucky Derby with a filly, Winning Colors. Won 1994 Preakness and Belmont with Tabasco Cat. Won all three Triple Crown races in 1995, with Thunder Gulch (Kentucky Derby and Belmont) and Timber County (Preakness).

Connie Mack (b. 2-22-1862, d. 2-8-56): Born Cornelius McGillicuddy. Baseball manager. Managed Philadelphia for 50 years (1901-50) until age 87. All-time leader in games (7,755), wins (3,731) and losses (3,948). Won 9 pennants and 5 World Series (1910-11, 1913, 1929-30).

Larry Mahan (b. 11-21-43): Rodeo. All-Around champion 6 times (consecutively 1966-70, 1973).

Frank Mahovlich (b. 1-10-38): Hockey LW. Winner of Calder Trophy for top rookie for 1957–58 season. In 18 NHL seasons with Toronto Maple Leafs, Detroit Red Wings and Montreal Canadiens, had 533 goals and 570 assists. Played for six Stanley Cup winners. Elected to Hall of Fame 1981.

Phil Mahre (b. 5-10-57): Skier. Gold medalist in slalom at 1984 Olympics (twin brother Steve won silver medal). World Cup champion 3 consecutive years (1981-83).

Joe Malone (b. 2-28-1890, d. 5-15-69): Hockey F. "Phantom Joe." Led the NHL in its first season, 1917-18, with 44 goals in 20 games with Montreal. Led league in scoring 2 times (1918, 1920). Holds NHL record with most goals scored, single game (7) in 1920.

Karl Malone (b. 7-24-63): Basketball F. "The Mailman." Five-time first-team All-Star. All-Star MVP, 1989. All-Rookie team, 1986. Scored 20+ points per game in 10 of 11 seasons with Utah. Member of 1992 Olympic team. Career span since 1985 with Utah.

Moses Malone (b. 3-23-55): Basketball C. Entering 1995-96 season alltime leader free throws made (8,568), fifth in rebounds (16,212) and third in points

scored (27,409). 3 MVP awards in 1979, consecutively 1982-83; playoff MVP in 1983. 4-time All-Star. Led league in rebounding 6 times, 5 consecutively. Career span since 1976 with Houston, Philadelphia, Washington, Atlanta, Milwaukee.

Man o' War (b. 1917, d. 1947): Thoroughbred race horse. Won 20 of 21 races from 1919 to 1920. Only loss was in 1919 in Sanford Stakes to Upset. Passed up Derby but won both Preakness and Belmont. Winner of $249,465. Sire of War Admiral, 1937 Triple Crown winner.

Mickey Mantle (b. 10-20-31, d. 8-13-95): Baseball OF. Won 3 MVP awards, consecutively 1956-57 and 1962; won Triple Crown in 1956. 536 career HR. Greatest switch hitter in history. Played in 20 All-Star games. Alltime World Series leader in HR (18), RBI (40) and runs scored (42). No. 7 was a member of 7 World Series winners with NY Yankees. Career span 1951-68.

Diego Maradona (b. 10-30-60): Argentine soccer player. Led Argentina to 1986 World Cup victory and to 1990 World Cup finals. Led Naples to Italian League titles (1987, 1990), Italian Cup (1987) and to European Champion Clubs' Cup title (1989). Throughout 1980s often acknowledged as best player in the world. Tested positive for cocaine and suspended by FIFA and Italian Soccer Federation for 15 months in March 1991. Also failed drug test in 1994 World Cup and suspended before second round.

Pete Maravich (b. 6-22-47, d. 1-5-88): Basketball G. "Pistol Pete." Alltime NCAA leader in points scored (3,667), scoring average (44.2) and games scoring 50+ points (28, including then Division I record 69 points in 1970). Alltime season leader in points scored (1,381) and scoring average (44.5) in 1970. College Player of the Year in 1970. NCAA scoring leader and All-America 3 consecutive seasons from 1968 to 1970 with Louisiana State. Also led NBA in scoring in 1977. Averaged 20+ points 8 times. All-Star 2 times. Career span 1970-79 with Atlanta, New Orleans/Utah, Boston.

Gino Marchetti (b. 1-2-27): Football DE. Played in Pro Bowl every year from 1955 to '65, except 1958 when he broke right ankle tackling Frank Gifford in Colts' 23–17 win over the Giants. Career span 1952-66, almost all with Baltimore Colts. Inducted into Hall of Fame in 1972.

Rocky Marciano (b. 9-1-23, d. 8-31-69): Boxer. Heavyweight champion (1952-56). Career record 49-0 with 43 KOs from 1947 to 1956. Retired as undefeated champion.

Juan Marichal (b. 10-24-37): Baseball RHP. 243 career wins, 2.89 career ERA. Won 20+ games 6 times; 250+ innings pitched 8 times; 200+ strikeouts 6 times. Pitched no-hitter in 1963. Career span 1960-75, mostly with San Francisco.

Dan Marino (b. 9-15-61): Football QB. Set alltime season record for yards passing (5,084) and touchdown passes (48) in 1984. Prior to 1995-96 season had passed for 4,000+ yards 5 other seasons. Player of the Year in 1984. Career totals through 1994-95 season: 45,173 yards passing, 328 touchdown passes, second alltime in both categories. Career span since 1983 with Miami.

Roger Maris (b. 9-10-34, d. 12-14-85): Baseball OF. Broke Babe Ruth's alltime season HR record with 61 in

1961. Won consecutive MVP awards and led league in RBI 1960-61. Career span 1957-68 with Kansas City, New York (AL), St Louis.

Billy Martin (b. 5-16-28, d. 12-25-89): Baseball 2B-manager. Volatile manager was hired and fired by Minnesota, Detroit, Texas, New York Yankees (5 times!) and Oakland from 1969 to 1988. Won World Series with Yankees as manager in 1977 and as player 4 times.

Eddie Mathews (b. 10-13-31): Baseball 3B. 512 career HR and 30+ HR 9 consecutive seasons. League leader in HR 2 times, walks 4 times. Career span 1952-68 with Milwaukee.

Christy Mathewson (b. 8-12-1880, d. 10-7-25): Baseball RHP. Third alltime most wins (373) and shutouts (80); fifth alltime best ERA (2.13). Led league in wins 5 times; won 30+ games 4 times and 20+ games 9 other times. Led league in ERA and strikeouts 5 times each. 300+ innings pitched 11 times. Pitched 2 no-hitters. Pitched 3 shutouts in 1905 World Series. Career span 1900-16 with New York.

Bob Mathias (b. 11-17-30): Track and field. At age 17, youngest to win gold medal in decathlon at 1948 Olympics. First decathlete to win gold medal at consecutive Olympics (1948, 1952). Also won Sullivan Award in 1948.

Ollie Matson (b. 5-1-30): Football RB. Versatile runner totalled 12,884 combined yards rushing, receiving and kick returning. Scored 73 career touchdowns, including a 105-yard kickoff return on Oct. 14, 1956, the second longest ever. Career span 1952-66 with Chicago Cardinals, Los Angeles, Detroit, Philadelphia. Also won bronze medal in 400-meters at 1952 Olympics.

Roland Matthes (b. 11-17-50): German swimmer. Gold medalist in 100-meter and 200-meter backstroke at 2 consecutive Olympics (1968, 1972). Set 16 world records from 1967 to 1973.

Don Maynard (b. 1-25-37): Football WR. Retired in 1973 as the NFL's alltime leading receiver. In 15 seasons, 10 with the New York Jets, caught 633 passes for 11,834 yards and 88 TDs. Averaged 18.7 yards per catch for career. In 1967 and '68 led AFL with average of 20.2 and 22.8 yards per catch. Elected to Hall of Fame in 1987.

Willie Mays (b. 5-6-31): Baseball OF. "Say Hey Kid." MVP in 1954, 1965; Rookie of the Year in 1951. Third alltime most HR (660), with 50+ HR 2 times, 30+ HR 9 other times. Led league in HR 4 times. 100+ RBI 10 times; 100+ runs scored 12 consecutive seasons. 3,283 career hits. Led league in stolen bases 4 consecutive seasons. 30 HR and 30 steals in same season 2 times and first man in history to hit 300+ HR and steal 300+ bases. Won 11 consecutive Gold Gloves; set record for career putouts by an outfielder and league record for total chances. His catch in the 1954 World Series off the bat of Vic Wertz called the greatest ever. Career span 1951-73 with New York and San Francisco Giants, New York Mets.

Bill Mazeroski (b. 9-5-36): Baseball 2B. Hit dramatic 9th-inning home run in Game 7 to win 1960 World Series, first of only two Series' to end on a home run. Also a great fielder, won Gold Glove 8 times. Led league in assists 9 times, double plays 8 times and putouts 5 times.

Joe McCarthy (b. 4-21-1887, d. 1-3-78): Baseball manager. Alltime highest winning percentage among managers for regular season (.615) and World Series (.763). First manager to win pennants in both leagues (Chicago (NL), 1929, New York (AL), 1932). From 1926 to 1950 his teams won 7 World Series and 9 pennants.

Mark McCormack (b. 11-6-30): Sports marketing agent. Founded International Management Group in 1962. Also author of best-selling business advice books.

Pat McCormick (b. 5-12-30): Diver. Gold medalist in platform and springboard at 2 consecutive Olympics (1952, 1956). Also won Sullivan Award in 1956.

Willie McCovey (b. 1-10-38): Baseball 1B. Led NL in homers three times (1963, '68, '69) and in RBIs twice (1968-69). 521 career homers. .270 career batting average. Hit 18 grand slams. Rookie of Year 1959. NL MVP in 1969. Career span 1959-73 and 1977-80 with San Francisco Giants, 1974-76 with San Diego Padres and 1976 with Oakland A's. Elected to Hall of Fame in 1986.

John McEnroe (b. 2-26-59): Tennis player. Has won 4 U.S. Open singles titles (consecutively 1979-81, 1984) and 3 Wimbledon titles (1981, consecutively 1983-84). Also won 8 Grand Slam doubles titles. Third alltime men's most career tournament victories (77). Led U.S. to 5 Davis Cup victories (1978-79, 1981-82, 1992).

John McGraw (b. 4-7-1873, d. 2-25-34): Baseball manager. Second alltime most games (4,801) and wins (2,784). Guided New York Giants to 3 World Series titles and 10 pennants from 1902 to 1932.

Denny McLain (b. 3-29-44): Baseball RHP. Last pitcher to win 30+ games in a season (Detroit, 1968); won 20+ games 2 other times. Won 2 consecutive Cy Young Awards (1968-69). Led league in innings pitched 2 times. Served 2½-year jail term for 1985 conviction of extortion, racketeering and drug possession. Career span 1963-72.

Mary T. Meagher (b. 10-27-64): Swimmer. "Madame Butterfly." Won 3 gold medals at 1984 Olympics (100-meter butterfly, 200-meter butterfly and 400-medley relay). In 1981 set world records in 100-meter butterfly (57.93) and 200-meter butterfly (2:05.96).

Rick Mears (b. 12-3-51): Auto racer. Has won Indy 500 4 times (1979, 1984, 1988, 1991) and been CART champion 3 times (1979, consecutively 1981-82). Named Indy 500 Rookie of the Year in 1978.

Cary Middlecoff (b. 1-6-21): Golfer. Also a dentist. Won 40 PGA tournaments, including 1955 Masters and US Opens in 1949 and '56. Won 1956 Vardon Trophy.

George Mikan (b. 6-18-24): Basketball C. Averaged 20+ points per game and named to All-Star team 6 consecutive seasons. Led league in scoring 3 times, rebounding 1 time. Played on 5 championship teams in 6 years (1949-54) with Minneapolis. Also played on 1945 NIT championship team with DePaul. All-America 3 times. Served as ABA Commissioner from 1968 to 1969.

Stan Mikita (b. 5-20-40): Hockey C. Won MVP award 2 consecutive seasons (1967-68). Fifth alltime in assists (926); fifth alltime in points (1,467). Led league in assists 4 consecutive seasons and points 4 times. 541 career goals. All-Star 6 times. Career span 1958-80 with Chicago.

Del Miller (b. 7-5-13): Harness racing driver. Has raced in 8 decades since 1929, the longest career of any athlete. Won The Hambletonian in 1950.

Marvin Miller (b. 4-14-17): Labor negotiator. Union chief of Major League Baseball Players Association from 1966 to 1984. Led strikes in 1972 and 1981. Negotiated 5 labor contracts with owners that increased minimum salary and pension fund, allowed for agents and arbitration, and brought about the end of the reserve clause and the beginning of free agency.

Art Monk (b. 12-5-57): Football WR. Caught more passes than anyone in NFL history (934 for 12,607 and 68 TDs through end of 1994-95 season). 106 catches in 1984 was then NFL single season record. Twice caught 13 passes in single game. Career span 1980–93 with Redskins, since 1993 with New York Jets.

Earl Monroe (b. 11-21-44): Basketball G. "The Pearl" played 13 seasons (1968–80) with the Baltimore Bullets and New York Knicks. NBA Rookie of Year in 1968. Member of 1973 NBA championship Knicks team. Averaged 18.8 points a game. Elected to Hall of Fame 1989.

Joe Montana (b. 6-11-56): Football QB. Second alltime highest-rated passer (92.3), third in completions (3,409), fourth in passing yards (40,551) and fourth in touchdown passes (273). Won 4 Super Bowl championships (1981, 1984, consecutively 1988-89) with San Francisco since 1979. Named Super Bowl MVP 3 times (1981, 1984, 1989). Player of the Year in 1989. Also led Notre Dame to national championship in 1977.

Carlos Monzon (b. 8-7-42, d. 1-8-95): Argentine boxer. Longest title reign of any middleweight champion (6 years, 9 months) from Nov. 1970 through Aug. 1977. Career record 89-3-9 with 61 KOs from 1963 to 1977. Won 82 consecutive bouts from 1964 to 1977. Defended title 14 times. Retired as champion.

Helen Wills Moody (b. 10-6-05): Tennis player. Second alltime most women's Grand Slam singles titles (19). Her 8 Wimbledon titles are second most alltime (consecutively 1927-30, 1932-33, 1935, 1938). Won 7 U.S. titles (consecutively 1923-25, 1927-29, 1931) and 4 French titles (consecutively 1928-30, 1932). Also won 12 Grand Slam doubles titles.

Archie Moore (b. 12-13-16): Boxer. Longest title reign of any light heavyweight champion (9 years, 1 month) from Dec. 1952 through Feb. 1962. Career record 199-26-8 with an alltime record 145 KOs from 1935 to 1965. Retired at age 52.

Davey Moore (b. 11-1-33; d. 3-23-63): Boxer. Won featherweight title by KO of Kid Bassey in 13 on 3-18-59. Five successful defenses of title, before losing it on 3-21-63 to Sugar Ramos who KO'd him in 10. Died two days after fight of brain damage suffered during fight. Career record: 67 bouts; won 30 by KO, 28 by decision, 1 because of foul; drew 1; lost 7, two by KO.

Noureddine Morceli (b. 2-20-70). Algerian track and field middle distance runner. Set world record for mile (3:44.39) in Rieti, Italy, on 9-5-93. Set world record for 1,500 (3:28.86) on 9-5-92. World champion at 1,500 in both 1991 and '93. Finished a shocking seventh at 1992 Olympics. Only man ever to rank first in the world at 1,500/mile four straight years (1990–93).

Joe Morgan (b. 9-19-43): Baseball 2B. Won 2 consecutive MVP awards in 1975-76. Third alltime most walks (1,865). 689 stolen bases. Led league in walks 4 times. 100+ walks and runs scored 8 times each; 40+ stolen bases 9 times. Won 5 Gold Gloves. Second

alltime most games played by 2nd baseman (2,527). Career span 1963-84 with Houston, Cincinnati.

Willie Mosconi (b. 6-27-13; d. 9-16-93): Pocket billiards player. Won world title a record 15 straight times between 1941 and 1957. Once pocketed 526 balls without a miss.

Edwin Moses (b. 8-31-55): Track and field. Gold medalist in 400-meter hurdles at 2 Olympics, in 1976, 1984 (U.S. boycotted 1980 Games); bronze medalist at 1988 Olympics. Set four world records in 400-meter hurdles (best of 47.02 set on 8-31-83). Won 122 consecutive races from 1977 to 1987. Won Sullivan Award in 1983.

Marion Motley (b. 6-5-20): Football FB. All-time AAFC leader in yards rushing (3,024). Also led NFL in rushing 1 time. Combined league totals: 4,712 yards rushing, 39 touchdowns. Played on 4 consecutive AAFC champions (1946-49), 1 NFL champion (1950) with Cleveland from 1946 to 1953.

Shirley Muldowney (b. 6-19-40): Drag racer. First woman to win the Top Fuel championship, which she won 3 times (1977, 1980, 1982).

Anthony Munoz (b. 8-19-58): Football OT. Probably the greatest tackle ever. Made Pro Bowl a record-tying 11 times. Career span 1980–92 with the Cincinnati Bengals.

Isaac Murphy (b. 4-16-1861, d. 2-12-1896): Horse racing jockey. Top jockey of his era, Murphy, who was black, won 3 Kentucky Derbys (aboard Buchanan in 1884, Riley in 1890 and Kingman in 1891).

Eddie Murray (b. 2-24-56): Baseball 1B. 100+ RBIs 6 seasons and 30+ HRs five seasons. Through '94 season had 2,930 hits, 458 HRs and 1,738 RBI. Alltime leader in RBI by switch hitter. Career span 1977–88 with Baltimore Orioles; 1989–91 with LA Dodgers; 1992–93 with New York Mets, since 1994 with Cleveland Indians.

Jim Murray (b. 12-29-19): Sportswriter. Won Pulitzer Prize in 1990. Named Sportswriter of the Year 14 times. Columnist for *Los Angeles Times* since 1961.

Ty Murray (b. 10-11-69): Rodeo cowboy. All-Around world champion, 1989-93. Set single-season earnings record, 1990 ($213,771). Rookie of the Year, 1988. At 20 in 1989, became youngest man ever to win national all-around title.

Stan Musial (b. 11-21-20): Baseball OF-1B. "Stan the Man." Had .331 career batting average and 475 career HR. MVP award winner 1943, 1946, 1948. Fourth alltime in hits (3,630) and third in doubles (725). Won 7 batting titles. Led league in hits 6 times, slugging average 5 times, doubles 8 times. Had .300+ batting average 17 times, 200+ hits 6 times, 100+ RBI 10 times, and 100+ runs scored 11 times. 24-time All-Star. Career span 1941-63 with St. Louis.

John Naber (b. 1-20-56): Swimmer. Won 4 gold medals and 1 silver medal at 1976 Olympics. Sullivan Award winner in 1977.

Bronko Nagurski (b. 11-3-08, d. 1-7-90): Football FB. Punishing runner played on 3 NFL champions (consecutively 1932-33, 1943) with Bears. Rushed for 2,778 career yards, 1930-37 and 1943 with Chicago. Also All-America with Minnesota.

James Naismith (b. 11-6-1861, d. 11-28-39): Invented basketball in 1891 while an instructor at YMCA Training School in Springfield, Mass. Refined the game while a professor at Kansas from 1898 to 1937. Hall of Fame is named in his honor.

Joe Namath (b. 5-31-43): Football QB. "Broadway Joe." Super Bowl MVP in 1968 after he guaranteed victory for AFL. 173 career touchdown passes. Led league in yards passing 3 times, including 4,007 yards in 1967. Player of the Year in 1968, Rookie of the Year in 1965. Career span 1965-77 with NY Jets, LA Rams.

Ilie Nastase (b. 7-19-46): Romanian tennis player. "Nasty" for his unruly deportment on court. Beat Arthur Ashe to win 1972 US Open title. Won 1973 French Open. Twice Wimbledon runnerup (to Stan Smith in 1972 and Bjorn Borg in '76).

Martina Navratilova (b. 10-18-56): Tennis player. Third alltime most women's Grand Slam singles titles (18—tied with Chris Evert). Won a record 9 Wimbledon titles, including 6 consecutively (1978-79, 1982-87, 1990). Won 4 U.S. Open titles (consecutively 1983-84, 1986-87), 3 Australian Open titles (1981, 1983, 1985) and 2 French Open titles (1982, 1984). Reached Grand Slam final 13 other times. Also won 37 Grand Slam doubles titles. Her total of 55 Grand Slam titles is second alltime to Margaret Court's. Completed a non-calendar year Grand Slam in 1984-85. Set mark for longest winning streak with 74 matches in 1984. Also won the doubles Grand Slam in 1984 with Pam Shriver. Won 109 consecutive matches with Shriver from 1983 to 1985. Retired after 1994 season.

Byron Nelson (b. 2-14-12): Golfer. Won the Masters (1937, 1942) and PGA Championship (1940, 1945) 2 times each and U.S. Open once (1939). Won 52 career tournaments, including 11 consecutively in 1945.

Ernie Nevers (b. 6-11-03, d. 5-3-76): Football FB. Set alltime pro single game record for points scored (40) and touchdowns (6) on Nov. 28, 1929. Career span 1926-31 with Duluth, Chicago. Also a pitcher with St. Louis, surrendered 2 of Babe Ruth's 60 HR in 1927. All-America at Stanford, earned 11 letters in 4 sports.

John Newcombe (b. 5-23-44): Australian tennis player. Won 3 Wimbledon singles titles (1967, consecutively 1970-71), 2 U.S. titles (1967, 1973) and 2 Australian Open titles (1973, 1975). Also won 17 Grand Slam doubles titles.

Pete Newell (b. 8-31-15): College basketball coach. Despite coaching only 13 seasons, 1947 through 1960, was first coach to win NIT, NCAA and Olympic crowns. Led Univ. of San Francisco to 1949 NIT title, Cal to 1959 NCAA title, and the 1960 U.S. Olympic basketball team that included Jerry Lucas, Oscar Robertson and Jerry West to gold medal. Overall collegiate coaching record of 234–123.

Jack Nicklaus (b. 1-21-40): Golfer. "The Golden Bear." Alltime leader in major championships (20). Second alltime in career wins (70). Winner of the Masters 6 times, more than any golfer (1963, consecutively 1965-66, 1972, 1975, 1986—at age 46, the oldest player to win event), PGA Championship 5 times (1963, 1971, 1973, 1975, 1980), U.S. Open 4 times (1962, 1967, 1972, 1980), British Open 3 times (1966, 1970, 1978) and U.S. Amateur 2 times (1959, 1961). PGA Player of the Year 5 times (1967, consecutively 1972-73, 1975-76). Also NCAA champion with Ohio State in 1961.

Ray Nitschke (b. 12-29-36): Football LB. Defensive signal caller for the great Packer teams of the '60s.

Voted Packer MVP by teammates after 1967 season. MVP of the 1962 NFL title game. Career span 1958–72 with Green Bay Packers.

Greg Norman (b. 2-10-55): Golfer. "The Shark" led PGA in winnings in 1986 and '90. Won Vardon Trophy twice, 1989–90. Won two British Opens—in 1986 at Turnberry and in '93 at Royal St. George's—but is almost as famous for his heartbreaking misses. Beaten at the 1986 PGA when Bob Tway holed out a sand shot and at the 1987 Masters when Larry Mize chipped in from a tough downhill lie.

James D. Norris (b. 11-6-06, d. 2-25-66): Hockey executive. Owner of Detroit from 1933 to 1943 and Chicago from 1946 to 1966. Teams won 4 Stanley Cup championships (consecutively 1936-37, 1943, 1961). Defensive Player of the Year award named in his honor. Also a boxing promoter, operated International Boxing Club from 1949 to 1958.

Paavo Nurmi (b. 6-13-1897, d. 10-2-73): Track and field. Finnish middle- and long-distance runner won a total of 9 gold medals at 3 Olympics in 1920, 1924, 1928

Matti Nykänen (b. 7-17-63): Finnish ski jumper. Three-time Olympic gold medalist. Won 90-meter jump (1984, 1988) and 70-meter jump (1988). World champion on 90-meter jump in 1982. Won four World Cups (1983, 1985, 1986, 1988).

Dan O'Brien (b. 7-18-66): Track and field decathlete. Won world decathlon title in 1991, '93 and '95. Set world decathlon record of 8,891 in Talence, France, on 9-4/5-92. Heavily favored to win 1992 Olympic decathlon but missed making U.S. team when he no heighted in pole vault at U.S. Olympic Trials.

Parry O'Brien (b. 1-28-32): Track and field. Shot putter who revolutionized the event with his "glide" technique and won Olympic gold medals in 1952 and 1956, silver in 1960. Set 10 world records from 1953 to 1959, topped by a put of 63' 4" in 1959. Sullivan Award winner in 1959.

Al Oerter (b. 8-19-36): Track and field. Gold medalist in discus at 4 consecutive Olympics (1956, 1960, 1964, 1968), setting Olympic record each time. First to break the 200-foot barrier, throwing 200' 5" in 1962.

Sadaharu Oh (b. 5-20-40): Baseball 1B in Japanese league. 868 career HR in 22 seasons for the Tokyo Giants. Led league in HR 15 times, RBI 13 times, batting 5 times and runs 13 consecutive seasons. Awarded MVP 9 times; won 2 consecutive Triple Crowns and 9 Gold Gloves.

Hakeem Olajuwon (b. 1-21-63): Basketball C. From Nigeria. As part of the University of Houston's "Phi Slamma Jamma" his senior year led NCAA in field goal percentage, rebounding and blocked shots in 1984. All-NBA First Team 1987, '88, '89, '93, 94. Led NBA in rebounding in both 1989 (13.5 per game) and '90 (14.0). League MVP in 1994 as he led Houston to NBA title. Career span since1985 with the Rockets.

Merlin Olsen (b. 9-15-40): Fooball DT. Part of L.A. Rams "Fearsome Foursome" defensive line. Named to Pro Bowl 14 straight times. Career span 1962–76, all with L.A. Rams. Elected to Hall of Fame 1982.

Omaha (b. 1932): Thoroughbred race horse. In 1935 third horse to win Triple Crown. Won Kentucky Derby by 1½ lengths over Roman Soldier; Preakness by 6 over Firethorn; and the Belmont by 1½ from Firethorn. Trained by Sunny Jim Fitzsimmons.

Shaquille O'Neal (b. 3-6-72): Basketball C. As LSU junior led NCAA in blocked shots in 1992, with 5.23 a game, and averaged 4.58 over his 90-game, three-year career. Top pick of Orlando Magic in 1992 NBA draft. Almost unanimous NBA Rookie of the Year 1993. Averaged 23.4 points, 13.9 rebounds and 3.5 blocked shots in first NBA season. Led Magic to first ever playoff appearance in 1994. Led league in scoring with 29.3 average in 1994-95.

Bobby Orr (b. 3-20-48): Hockey D. Defensive Player of the Year more than any other player, 8 consecutive seasons (1968-75). Won MVP award 3 consecutive seasons (1970-72), playoff MVP 2 times (1970, 1972). Also Rookie of the Year in 1967. Led league in assists 5 times and scoring 2 times. Career span 1966-77 with Boston.

Mel Ott (b. 3-2-09, d. 11-21-58): Baseball OF. 511 career HR, 1,861 RBI, .304 batting average. League leader in HR and walks 6 times each. 100+ RBI 9 times and 100+ walks 10 times. Career span 1926-47 with New York.

Jim Otto (b. 1-5-38): Football C. Number 00 started every game (308) in his 15 year career (1960–74) with the Oakland Raiders. Inducted to Hall of Fame in 1980.

Kristin Otto (b. 1966): German swimmer. Won 6 gold medals for East Germany at 1988 Olympics.

Jesse Owens (b. 9-12-13, d. 3-31-80): Track and field. Gold medalist in 4 events (100 meters and 200 meters; 4x100-meter relay and long jump) at 1936 Olympics. At the 1935 Big 10 championship set or equaled 4 world record in 70 minutes, including 100 yards, long jump, 220-yard low hurdles and 220 dash.

Alan Page (b. 8-7-45): Football DT. First defensive player to be named NFL Player of the Year, in 1972. Career span 1967–78 with Minnesota Vikings and 1978–81 with Chicago Bears. Now sits on Minnesota Supreme Court.

Satchel Paige (b. 7-7-06, d. 6-8-82): Baseball RHP. Alltime greatest black pitcher, didn't pitch in major leagues until 1948 at age 42 with Cleveland. Oldest pitcher in major league history at age 59 with Kansas City in 1965. Pitched in the Negro leagues from 1926 to 1950 with Birmingham Black Barons, Pittsburgh Crawfords and Kansas City Monarchs. Estimated career record is 2,000 wins, 250 shutouts, 30,000 strikeouts, 45 no-hitters. Said "Don't look back. Something may be gaining on you."

Arnold Palmer (b. 9-10-29): Golfer. Fourth alltime in career wins (60). Won the Masters 4 times (1958, 1960, 1962, 1964), British Open 2 consecutive years (1961-62) and U.S. Open (1960) and U.S. Amateur (1954) once each. PGA Player of the Year 2 times (1960, 1962). The first golfer to surpass $1 million in career earnings. Also won Seniors Championship 2 times (1980, 1984) and U.S. Senior Open once (1981).

Jim Palmer (b. 10-15-45): Baseball RHP. 268 career wins, 2.86 ERA. Won 3 Cy Young Awards (1973, consecutively 1975-76). Won 20+ games 8 times. Led league in wins 3 times, innings pitched 4 times, ERA 2 times. Never allowed a grand slam HR. Pitched on 6 World Series teams with Baltimore, including shutout at 20 years old in 1966. Pitched no-hitter in 1969. Jockey underwear pitchman. Career span 1965-84.

Bernie Parent (b. 4-3-45): Hockey G. Alltime leader for wins in a season (47 in 1974). Goaltender of the Year, playoff MVP, league leader in wins, goals against average and shutouts 2 consecutive seasons

(1974-75). Career record 270-197-121, including 55 shutouts. Career 2.55 goals against average. Tied record of 4 playoff shutouts in 1975. Played on 2 consecutive Stanley Cup champions (1974-75). Career span 1965 to 1979 with Philadelphia. Also the first NHL player to sign with the WHA in 1972, with Philadelphia.

Brad Park (b. 7-6-48): Hockey D. Seven-time All Star. In 17 seasons with the New York Rangers, Boston Bruins and Detroit Red Wings (1968–69 through 1984–85) scored 213 goals and had 683 assists. Elected to Hall of Fame 1988.

Jim Parker (b. 4-3-34): Football T/G. Winner of 1956 Outland Trophy as Ohio State senior. Blocked for Johnny Unitas. All-NFL four times at guard, four times at tackle. Career span 1957–67, all with Baltimore Colts. Inducted to Hall of Fame in 1973.

Joe Paterno (b. 12-21-26): College football coach. Fourth alltime in wins in Division I-A (269—the most of any active coach at that level). Has won 2 national championships (1982, 1986) with Penn State since 1966. Career record 269-69-3, including 5 undefeated seasons. Has also won 16 bowl games.

Lester Patrick (b. 12-30-1883, d. 6-1-60): Hockey coach. Led NY Rangers to three Stanley Cup championships (1928, 1933, 1940). Originated the NHL's farm system and developed playoff format.

Floyd Patterson (b. 1-4-35): Boxer. Heavyweight champion 2 times (1956-59, 1960-62). First heavyweight to regain title, in rematch with Ingemar Johansson. Career record 55-8-1 with 40 KOs from 1952 to 1972. Also middleweight gold medalist at 1952 Olympics.

Walter Payton (b. 7-25-54): Football RB. Alltime leader in yards rushing (16,726), rushing attempts (3,838), seasons gaining 1,000+ yards rushing (10) and rushing touchdowns (110). His 125 total touchdowns rank third. Rushed for a career 275 yards on Nov. 20, 1977. Selected for Pro Bowl 9 times. Player of the Year 2 times (1977, 1985). Led league in rushing 5 consecutive seasons. Career span 1975-87 with Chicago.

Pele (b. 10-23-40): Born Edson Arantes do Nascimento. Brazilian soccer player. Soccer's great ambassador. Played on 3 World Cup winners with Brazil (1958, 1962, 1970). Helped promote soccer in U.S. by playing with NY Cosmos from 1975 to 1977. Scored 1,281 goals in 22 years.

Willie Pep (b. 9-19-22): Boxer. Featherweight champion 2 times (1942-48, 1949-50). Lost title to Sandy Saddler, won it back in rematch, then lost it to Saddler again. Career record 230-11-1 with 65 KOs from 1940 to 1966. Won 73 consecutive bouts from 1940 to 1943. Defended title 9 times.

Gil Perreault (b. 11-13-50): Hockey C. Won Calder Trophy as NHL's top rookie for 1970–71 season. Played 17 seasons (1970–71 through 1986–87), all with Buffalo Sabres. Scored 512 goals and had 814 assists in career. Elected to Hall of Fame in 1990.

Fred Perry (b. 5-18-09, d. 2-2-95): British tennis player. Won 3 consecutive Wimbledon singles titles (1934-36), the last British man to win the tournament. Also won 3 U.S. titles (consecutively 1933-34, 1936), 1 French title (1935) and 1 Australian title (1934).

Gaylord Perry (b. 9-15-38): Baseball RHP. Only pitcher to win Cy Young Award in both leagues (Cleveland 1972, San Diego 1978). 314 career wins,

3,534 strikeouts. 20+ wins 5 times; 200+ strikeouts 8 times; 250+ innings pitched 12 times. Pitched no-hitter in 1968. Admitted to throwing a spitter. Career span 1962-83 with San Francisco, Cleveland, San Diego.

Bob Pettit (b. 12-12-32): Basketball F. First player in history to break 20,000-point barrier (20,880 career points scored). Fifth alltime highest scoring average (26.4) and seventh most free throws made (6,182). Also grabbed 12,849 rebounds for 16.2 average. MVP in 1956, 1959; Rookie of the Year in 1955. All-Star 10 consecutive seasons. Led league in scoring 2 times, rebounding 1 time. Career span 1954-64 with St Louis.

Richard Petty (b. 7-2-37): Auto racer. Alltime leader in NASCAR victories (200). Daytona 500 winner (1964, 1966, 1971, consecutively 1973-74, 1979, 1981) and NASCAR champion (1964, 1967, consecutively 1971-72, 1974-75, 1979) 7 times each, the most of any driver. First stock car racer to reach $1 million in earnings. Son of Lee Petty, 3-time NASCAR champion (1954, consecutively 1958-59). Retired after 1992 season.

Laffit Pincay Jr. (b. 12-29-46): Jockey. Through 1994 had won more money than any other jockey ($183,910,301) and was second only to Bill Shoemaker in wins, with 8,213. Won 5 Eclipse Awards as outstanding jockey. Rode 3 Kentucky Derby winners; 2 Preakness winners; and 1 Belmont winner.

Jacques Plante (b. 1-17-29, d. 2-27-86): Hockey G. First goalie to wear a mask. Second alltime in wins (434) and second lowest modern goals against average (2.38). Goaltender of the Year 7 times, more than any other goalie (consecutively 1955-59, 1961, 1968). Won MVP award in 1961. Led league in goals against average 8 times, wins 6 times and shutouts 4 times. Was on 6 Stanley Cup champions with Montreal from 1952 to 1962 and played for 4 other teams until retirement in 1972.

Gary Player (b. 11-1-35): South African golfer. Won the Masters (1961, 1974, 1978) and British Open (1959, 1968, 1974) 3 times each, PGA Championship 2 times (1962, 1972) and U.S. Open (1965). Also won Seniors Championship 3 times (1986, 1988, 1990) and U.S. Senior Open 2 consecutive years (1987-88).

Sam Pollock (b. 12-15-25): Hockey executive. As general manager of Montreal from 1964 to 1978 won 9 Stanley Cup championships (1965-66, 1968-69, 1971, 1973, 1976-78).

Denis Potvin (b. 10-29-53): Hockey D. Seven time All Star during 15 season career (1973–74 through 1987–88), all with New York Islanders. Won Calder Trophy for 1973–74 season. Won Norris Trophy three times. Captained Islanders to four Stanley Cup championships. Elected to Hall of Fame in 1991.

Mike Powell (b. 11-10-63): Track and field. Long jumper broke Bob Beamon's 23-year-old world record at 1991 World Championships in Tokyo with a jump of 29' 4½".

Annemarie Moser-Pröll (b. 3-27-53): Austrian skier. Gold medalist in downhill at 1980 Olympics. World Cup overall champion 6 times, more than any other skier (consecutively 1971-75, 1979).

Alain Prost (b. 2-24-55): French auto racer. Alltime leader in Formula 1 victories. Formula 1 champion 4 times (consecutively 1985-86, 1989, 1993).

Jack Ramsay (b. 2-21-25): Basketball coach. Never played in NBA. Coached 11 seasons at St. Joseph's University, with 234–72 record. Overall record of

864–783 as NBA coach. Coach of NBA champion 1977 Portland Trail Blazers. Elected to Hall of Fame 1992.

Jean Ratelle (b. 10-3-40): Hockey C. In 21 season career (1960–61 through 1980–81) with the New York Rangers and Boston Bruins, scored 491 goals and had 776 assists. Twice won Lady Byng Trophy. Elected to Hall of Fame in 1985.

Willis Reed (b. 6-25-42): Basketball C. Played 10 seasons (1965–74), all with the New York Knicks. Career average of 18.7 points a game. NBA Rookie of Year in 1965. Playoff MVP of both Knick championship teams, in 1970 and '73. NBA MVP in 1970. Elected to Hall of Fame in 1970.

Harold Henry "Pee Wee" Reese (b. 7-23-18): Baseball SS. Played for 7 pennant-winning Dodger teams. Led NL in runs scored in 1949, with 132. Elected to Hall of Fame in 1984.

Mary Lou Retton (b. 1-24-68): Gymnast. Won 1 gold, 1 silver and 2 bronze medals at 1984 Olympics.

Grantland Rice (b. 11-1-1880, d. 7-13-54): Sportswriter. Legendary figure during sport's Golden Age of the 1920s. Wrote "When the Last Great Scorer comes / To mark against your name, / He'll write not 'won' or 'lost' / But how you played the game." Also named the 1924-25 Notre Dame backfield the "Four Horsemen."

Jerry Rice (b. 10-13-62): Football WR. Entering 1995 season, alltime leader in touchdowns (139), touchdown receptions (131) and in consecutive games with a TD reception (13 in 1988). Player of the Year in 1987 and led league in scoring (138 points on 23 touchdowns). Super Bowl MVP in 1989 with record 215 receiving yards on 11 catches. Also set Super Bowl record with 3 touchdown receptions in 1990. Career span since 1985 with San Francisco 49ers.

Henri Richard (b. 2-29-36): Hockey C. "The Pocket Rocket." Played on 11 Stanley Cup champions with Montreal. Four-time All-Star. Career span from 1955 to 1975.

Maurice Richard (b. 8-4-21): Hockey RW. "The Rocket." First player ever to score 50 goals in a season, in 1945. Led league in goals 5 times. 544 career goals. Won MVP award in 1947. All-Star 8 times. Tied playoff game record for most goals (5 on March 23, 1944). Played on 8 Stanley Cup champions with Montreal from 1942 to 1959.

Bob Richards (b. 2-2-26): Track and field. The only pole vaulter to win gold medal at 2 consecutive Olympics (1952, 1956). Also won Sullivan Award in 1951.

Branch Rickey (b. 12-20-1881, d. 12-9-65): Baseball executive. Integrated major league baseball in 1947 by signing Jackie Robinson to contract with Brooklyn Dodgers. Conceived minor league farm system in 1919 at St Louis; instituted batting cage and sliding pit.

Pat Riley (b. 3-20-45): Basketball coach. Going into 1995-96 season most playoff wins (137). Coached Los Angeles to 4 championships, 2 consecutively, from 1981 to 1989. 60+ wins 6 times (4 times consecutively), 50+ wins 4 other times. Led New York Knicks to NBA Finals in 1994.

Cal Ripken Jr (b. 8-24-60): Baseball SS. Enters 1996 season with longest consecutive game streak (2,153 since May 29, 1982). Set record for consecutive errorless games by a shortstop (95 in 1990). MVP in 1983 and Rookie of the Year in 1982. Hit 20+ HRs in

11 consecutive seasons and started in 11 consecutive All-Star games.

Glenn "Fireball" Roberts (b. 1-20-31, d. 7-2-64): Auto racer. Won 34 NASCAR races. Died as a result of fiery accident in World 600 at Charlotte Motor Speedway in May 1964. At time of his death had won more major races than any other driver in NASCAR history.

Oscar Robertson (b. 11-24-38): Basketball G. "The Big O." Third alltime in assists (9,887) second in free throws made (7,694) and fifth in points scored (26,710). 9,508 field goals made, 25.7 scoring average. MVP in 1964, All-Star 9 consecutive seasons and 1961 Rookie of the Year. Led league in assists 6 times, free throw percentage 2 times. Averaged 30+ points 6 times in 7 seasons, 20+ points 4 other times. Only player in history to average a season triple-double (1961). Career span 1960-72 with Cincinnati, Milwaukee. Also College Player of the Year, All-America and NCAA scoring leader 3 consecutive seasons from 1958 to 1960 with Cincinnati. Third all-time NCAA highest scoring average (33.8); seventh most points scored (2,973).

Brooks Robinson (b. 5-18-37): Baseball 3B. Alltime leader in assists, putouts, double plays and fielding average among 3rd baseman. Won 16 consecutive Gold Gloves. Led league in fielding average a record 11 times. MVP in 1964—led league in RBI—and MVP in 1970 World Series. Career span 1955-77 with Baltimore.

David Robinson (b. 8-6-65): Basketball C. *Sporting News* Player of the Year for 1987. Led college players in 1986 in both rebounding (13.0) and blocked shots (5.91, a record that still stands). NBA Rookie of Year in 1990. Led NBA in rebounding 1991 (13.0) and in blocked shots in 1992, when he was named Defensive Player of the Year. Named NBA MVP in 1995.

Eddie Robinson (b. 2-13-19): College football coach. Has had alltime college record 388 career wins at Division I-AA Grambling State since 1941.

Frank Robinson (b. 8-31-35): Baseball OF-manager. Only player to win MVP awards in both leagues (Cincinnati, 1961, Baltimore, 1966). Won Triple Crown and World Series MVP in 1966. Rookie of the Year in 1956. Fourth alltime most HR (586). 30+ HR 11 times; 100+ RBI 6 times; 100+ runs scored 8 times (led league 3 times). Had .300+ batting average 9 times. Became first black manager in major leagues, with Cleveland in 1975. Career span as player 1956-76. Career span as manager 1975-77 with Cleveland; 1981-84 with San Francisco; 1988-91 with Baltimore.

Jackie Robinson (b. 1-13-19, d. 10-24-72): Baseball 2B. Broke the color barrier as first black player in major leagues in 1947 with Brooklyn Dodgers. 1947 Rookie of the Year; 1949 MVP with .342 batting average to lead league. Had .311 career batting average. Led league in stolen bases 2 times; stole home 19 times. Played on 6 pennant winners in 10 years with Brooklyn.

Larry Robinson (b. 6-2-51): Hockey D. Twice won Norris Trophy as NHL's top defenseman. Career span 1972–73 through 1991–92, all but the last three with the Montreal Canadiens. Member of six Montreal teams that won Stanley Cup. Awarded Conn Smythe Trophy as MVP of 1978 Stanley Cup.

Sugar Ray Robinson (b. 5-3-21, d. 4-12-89): Born Walker Smith, Jr. Boxer. Called best pound-for-pound boxer in history. Welterweight champion (1946-51) and middleweight champion 5 times. Career record 174-19-6 with 109 KOs from 1940 to 1965. Won 91 consecutive bouts from 1943 to 1951. 15 of his 19 losses came after age 35. Retired at age 45.

Knute Rockne (b. 3-4-1888, d. 3-31-31): College football coach. Won national championship 3 times (1924, consecutively 1929-30). Alltime highest winning percentage (.881). Career record 105-12-5, including 5 undefeated seasons, with Notre Dame from 1918 to 1930.

Bill Rodgers (b. 12-23-47): Track and field. Won the Boston and New York City marathons 4 times each between 1975 and 1980.

Chi Chi Rodriguez (b. 10-23-35): Golfer. Led senior money list for 1987 ($509,145). Won 8 events during PGA career that began in 1960.

Art Rooney (b. 1-27-01; d. 8-25-88): Owner of Pittsburgh Steelers. Bought team in 1933 and ran it until his death in 1988. Elected to Hall of Fame in 1964.

Murray Rose (b. 1-6-39) Australian swimmer. Won 3 gold medals (including 400- and 1500-meter freestyle) at 1956 Olympics. Also won 1 gold, 1 silver and 1 bronze medal at 1960 Olympics.

Pete Rose (b. 4-14-41): Baseball OF-IF. "Charlie Hustle." Alltime leader in hits (4,256), games played (3,562) and at bats (14,053); second in doubles (746); fourth in runs scored (2,165). Had .303 career average and won 3 batting titles. Averaged .300+ 15 times, 200+ hits and 100+ runs scored each 10 times. Led league in hits 7 times, runs scored 4 times, doubles 5 times. 1963 Rookie of the Year; 1973 MVP; 1975 World Series MVP. Had 44-game hitting streak in 1978. Played in 17 All-Star games, starting at 5 different positions. Career span 1963-86 with Cincinnati, Philadelphia. Manager of Cincinnati from 1984 to 1989. Banned from baseball for life by Commissioner Bart Giamatti in 1989 for betting activities. Served 5-month jail term for tax evasion in 1990. Ineligible for Hall of Fame.

Ken Rosewall (b. 11-2-34): Australian tennis player. Won Grand Slam singles titles at ages 18 and 35. Won 4 Australian titles (1953, 1955, consecutively 1971-72), 2 French titles (1953, 1968) and 2 U.S. titles (1956, 1970). Reached 4 Wimbledon finals, but title eluded him.

Art Ross (b. 1-13-1886, d. 8-5-64): Hockey D-coach. Improved design of puck and goal net. Manager-coach of Boston, 1924-45, won Stanley Cup, 1938-39. The Art Ross Trophy is awarded to the NHL scoring champion.

Donald Ross (b. 1873, d. 4-26-48): Scottish-born golf course architect. Trained at St. Andrews under Old Tom Morris. Designed over 500 courses, including Pinehurst No. 2 course and Oakland Hills.

Patrick Roy (b. 10-5-65): Hockey G. Won Vezina Trophy as NHL's top goalie three times. Won Conn Smythe Trophy as MVP of 1993 Stanley Cup. Career span since 1984 with Montreal.

Pete Rozelle (b. 3-1-26): Football executive. Fourth NFL commissioner, served from 1960 to 1989. During his term, league expanded from 12 to 28 teams. Created Super Bowl in 1966 and negotiated merger with AFL. Devised plan for revenue sharing of lucrative TV monies among owners. Presided during players' strikes of 1982, 1987.

Wilma Rudolph (b. 6-23-40, d. 11-12-94): Track and field. Gold medalist in 3 events (100-, 200- and 4x100-meter relay) at 1960 Olympics. Also won Sullivan Award in 1961.

Adolph Rupp (b. 9-2-01, d. 12-10-77): College basketball coach. Alltime NCAA leader in wins (875) and third highest winning percentage (.822). Won 4 NCAA championships: consecutively 1948-49, 1951, 1958. Career span 1930-72 with Kentucky.

Amos Rusie (b. 5-3-1871, d. 12-6-42): Baseball RHP. Fastball was so intimidating that in 1893 the pitching mound was moved back 5' 6" to its present distance of 60' 6" Led league in strikeouts and walks 5 times each. Career record 246-174, 3.07 ERA with New York (NL) from 1889-1901.

Bill Russell (b. 2-12-34): Basketball C. Won MVP award 5 times (1958, consecutively 1961-63, 1965). Played on 11 championship teams, 8 consecutively, with Boston (1957, 1959-66, 1968-69). Player-coach 1968-69 (league's first black coach). Second alltime most rebounds (21,620) and second highest rebounding average (22.5); second most rebounds in a game (51 in 1960). Led league in rebounding 4 times. Also played on 2 consecutive NCAA championship teams with San Francisco in 1955-56; tournament MVP in 1955. Member of gold medal-winning 1956 Olympic team.

Babe Ruth (b. 2-6-1895, d. 8-16-48): Born George Herman Ruth. Baseball P-OF. Most dominant player in history. Alltime leader in slugging average (.690), HR frequency (8.5 HR every 100 at bats) and walks (2,056); second alltime most HR (714), RBI (2,211) and runs scored (2,174). Holds season record highest slugging average (.847 in 1920). 1923 MVP. Had .342 career batting average and 2,873 hits. 60 HR in 1927, 50+ HR 3 other times and 40+ HR 7 other times; 100+ RBI and 100+ walks 13 times each; 100+ runs scored 12 times. Second alltime most World Series HR (15), including his "called shot" off Charlie Root in 1932. Began career as a pitcher for Boston Red Sox: 94 career wins and 2.28 ERA. Won 20+ games 2 times; ERA leader in 1916. Played on 10 pennant winners, 7 World Series winners (3 with Boston, 4 with New York). Sold to Yankees in 1920 (Boston hasn't won World Series since). Career span 1914-35.

Nolan Ryan (b. 1-31-47): Baseball RHP. Pitched record 7th no hitter on May 1, 1991. Alltime leader in strikeouts (5,714), walks (2,795). League leader in strikeouts 11 times, walks 8 times, shutouts 3 times, ERA 2 times. 300+ strikeouts 6 times, including season record of 383 in 1973. 324 career wins. Career span 1966–93 with New York (NL), California, Houston, Texas.

Jim Ryun (b. 4-29-47): Track and field. Youngest ever to run under four minutes for the mile (3:59.0 at 17 years, 37 days). Set two world records in mile (3:51.3 in 1966 and 3:51.1 in 1967) and one in 1,500 (3:33.1 in 1967). Plagued by bad luck at Olympics; won silver medal in 1968 1,500 meters despite mononucleosis; was bumped and fell in 1972. Won Sullivan Award in 1967.

Toni Sailer (b. 11-17-35): Austrian skier. Won gold medals in 1956 Olympics in slalom, giant slalom and downhill, the first skier to accomplish the feat.

Juan Antonio Samaranch (b. 7-17-20): Amateur sports executive. Since 1980, Spaniard has served as president of International Olympic Committee.

Joan Benoit Samuelson (b. 5-16-57): Track and field. Gold medalist in first ever women's Olympic marathon (1984). Won Boston Marathon 2 times (1979, 1983). Sullivan Award winner in 1985.

Barry Sanders (b. 7-16-68): Football RB. Alltime NCAA season leader in yards rushing (2,628 in 1988).

Won Heisman Trophy in 1988 at Oklahoma State. Entered NFL in 1989 with Detroit and named Rookie of the Year. Gained 1,000+ yards rushing and named to Pro Bowl each of his first 6 seasons. Led league in rushing in 1990 and '94.

Gene Sarazen (b. 2-27-02): Golfer. Won PGA Championship 3 times (consecutively 1922-23, 1933), U.S. Open 2 times (1922, 1932), British Open once (1932) and the Masters once (1935). His win at the Masters included golf's most famous shot, a double eagle on the 15th hole of the final round to tie Craig Wood (Sarazen then won the playoff). Won 38 career tournaments. Also won Seniors Championship 2 times (1954, 1958). Pioneered the sand wedge in 1930.

Glen Sather (b. 9-2-43): Hockey coach and general manager. As coach, third alltime highest winning percentage (.616). 464 regular season wins. Led Edmonton to 4 Stanley Cup championships (consecutively 1984-85, 1987-88) from 1979 to 1989 and 1993-94. Also played for 6 teams from 1966 to 1976.

Terry Sawchuk (b. 12-28-29): Hockey G. All-time leader in wins (435) and shutouts (103). Career 2.52 goals against average. Goaltender of the Year 4 times (consecutively 1951-52, 1954, 1964). Led league in wins and shutouts 3 times and goals against average 2 times. Rookie of the Year in 1950. Tied record of 4 playoff shutouts in 1952. Played on 4 Stanley Cup champions with Detroit and Toronto from 1949 to 1969.

Gale Sayers (b. 5-30-43): Football RB. Alltime leader in kickoff return average (30.6). Scored 56 career touchdowns, including a rookie record 22 in 1965. Led league in rushing and gained 1,000+ yards rushing 2 times. Averaged 5 yards per carry. Rookie of the Year in 1965. Tied record with 6 rushing touchdowns on Dec. 12, 1965. Career span 1965-71 with Chicago cut short due to knee injury. Also All-America 2 times with Kansas.

Dolph Schayes (b. 5-19-28): Basketball player. College star at NYU. In 1960 became first NBA player to reach 15,000 career points. Also first NBA player to play in 1,000 games. Led NBA in free throw percentage three times, and averaged .843 for his career. Over stretch of 10 years played in 706 consecutive games. Elected to Hall of Fame 1972.

Bo Schembechler (b. 4-1-29): Football coach. In 21 seasons at Michigan from 1969–89, had a 194-48-5 record. Overall college coaching record 234-65-8.

Mike Schmidt (b. 9-27-49): Baseball 3B. Won 3 MVP awards (consecutively 1980-81, 1986). 548 career HR. Led league in HR 8 times, slugging average 5 times and RBI, walks and strikeouts 4 times each. 40+ HR 3 times, 30+ HR 10 other times; 100+ RBI 9 times, 100+ runs scored 7 times, 100+ strikeouts 12 times and third alltime most strikeouts (1,883). 100+ walks 7 times. Won 10 Gold Gloves. Career span 1972-89 with Philadelphia.

Don Schollander (b. 4-30-46): Swimmer. Won 4 gold medals (including 100- and 400-meter freestyle) at 1964 Olympics; won 1 gold and 1 silver medal in 1968 Olympics. Also won Sullivan Award in 1964.

Dick Schultz (b. 9-5-29): Amateur sports executive. Second executive director of the NCAA, served from 1987 to '93. Also served as athletic director at Cornell (1976-81) and Virginia (1981-87).

Seattle Slew (b. 1974): Thoroughbred race horse. Horse of the Year for 1977, when he won the Triple Crown, winning the Kentucky Derby by 1¾ lengths; the Preakness by 1½; and the Belmont by 4. In three year career from 1976–78, won 14 of 17 starts.

Tom Seaver (b. 11-17-44): Baseball RHP. "Tom Terrific." 311 career wins, 2.86 ERA. Cy Young Award winner 3 times (1969, 1973, 1975) and Rookie of the Year 1967. Fourth alltime most strikeouts (3,640). Led league in strikeouts 5 times, winning percentage 4 times and wins and ERA 3 times each. Won 20+ games 5 times; 200+ strikeouts 10 times. Struck out 19 batters in 1 game in 1970, including the final 10 in succession. Pitched no-hitter in 1978. Career span 1967-86 with New York (NL), Cincinnati, Chicago (AL), Boston.

Secretariat (b. 3-30-70, d. 10-4-89): Thoroughbred race horse. Triple Crown winner in 1973 with jockey Ron Turcotte aboard. Trained by Lucien Laurin.

Monica Seles (b. 12-2-73): Tennis player. Has won 3 consecutive French Open singles titles (1990-92), 3 Australian Open titles (1991-93) and 2 U.S. Open titles (1991-92). Seles' 1993 season ended on 4-30 when she was stabbed in the back by Gunther Parche while seated during a changeover in a tournament in Hamburg, Germany; also missed 1994 season.

Bill Sharman (b. 5-25-26): Basketball G. First team All Star four straight years 1956–59. Led NBA in free throw percentage every year from 1953–57, and in 1959 and '61. All Star Game MVP in 1955. NBA Coach of the Year in 1972, when his Lakers won NBA title. Elected to Hall of Fame in 1974.

Wilbur Shaw (b. 10-31-02, d. 10-30-54): Auto racer. Won Indy 500 3 times in 4 years (1937, consecutively 1939-40). AAA champion 2 times (1937, 1939). Also pioneered the use of the crash helmet after suffering skull fracture in 1923 crash.

Patty Sheehan (b. 10-27-57): Golfer. Won back-to-back LPGA championships, 1983–84. Won 1992 US Women's Open. 1983 LPGA Player of Year. Vare Trophy winner in 1984. Through '93 season, 31 career wins on LPGA tour; third alltime in earnings, with $4,131,837.01.

Fred Shero (b. 10-23-25, d. 11-24-90): Hockey coach. Fourth all-time highest winning percentage (.612, regular season). Led Philadelphia to 2 Stanley Cup championships (1974-75). Also coached NY Rangers. Played defense for NY Rangers, 1947-50.

Bill Shoemaker (b. 8-19-31): Horse racing jockey. Through 1994, alltime leader in wins (8,833). Rode Belmont Stakes winner 5 times (1957, 1959, 1962, 1967, 1975), Kentucky Derby winner 4 times (1955, 1959, 1965, 1986--at age 54, the oldest jockey to win Derby) and Preakness Stakes winner 2 times (1963, 1967). Also won Eclipse Award in 1981.

Eddie Shore (b. 11-25-02, d. 3-16-85): Hockey D. Won MVP award 4 times (1933, consecutively 1935-36, 1938). All-Star 7 times. Played on 2 Stanley Cup champions with Boston from 1926 to 1940.

Frank Shorter (b. 10-31-47): Track and field. Gold medalist in marathon at 1972 Olympics, the first American to win the event since 1908. Olympic silver medalist in 1976 marathon. Sullivan Award winner in 1972.

Jim Shoulders (b. 5-13-28): Rodeo. Alltime leader in career titles (16). All-Around champion 5 times (1949, consecutively 1956-59).

Don Shula (b. 1-4-30): Football coach. Alltime leader in wins (338 through 1994-95 season). Won 2 consecutive Super Bowl championships (1972-73) with Miami, including NFL's only undefeated season in 1972. Also reached Super Bowl 4 other times. Career span since 1963 with Baltimore and Miami.

Al Simmons (b. 5-22-02; d. 5-26-56): Baseball OF. "Bucketfoot Al" for hitting stance. Named AL MVP for 1929, when he led league 157 RBIs. Led league in batting average in 1930 (.381) and '31 (.390). Lifetime average of .334 with 307 homers. Career span 1924–44 with a variety of teams, but mostly Philadelphia A's. Elected to Hall of Fame in 1953.

O. J. Simpson (b. 7-9-47): Given name Orenthal James. Football RB. Seventh alltime in yards rushing (11,236). Gained 1,000+ yards rushing 5 consecutive seasons, including then-record 2,003 yards in 1973. Player of the Year 3 times (consecutively 1972-73, 1975). Led league in rushing 4 times. Gained 200+ yards rushing in a game a record 6 times, including 273 yards on Nov. 25, 1976. Scored 61 career touchdowns, including 23 in 1975. Also won Heisman Trophy with USC in 1968.

Sir Barton (b. 1916): Thoroughbred race horse. In 1919, before they were linked as the Triple Crown, became first horse to win the Kentucky Derby, the Preakness and the Belmont Stakes. Won 8 of 13 starts as 3-year-old.

George Sisler (b. 3-24-1893, d. 3-26-73): Baseball 1B. Alltime most hits in a season (257 in 1920). League leader in hits 2 times, with 200+ hits 6 times. Won 2 batting titles, including .420 average in 1922; averaged .400+ 2 times and .300+ 11 other times. Had 2,812 career hits and .340 average. Career span 1915-30 with St Louis.

Mary Decker Slaney (b. 8-4-58): Track and field. American record holder in 5 events ranging from 800 to 3,000 meters. Won 1,500 and 3,000 meters at World Championships in 1983. Lost chance for medal at 1984 Olympics when she tripped and fell after contact with Zola Budd. Won Sullivan Award in 1982.

Dean Smith (b. 2-28-31): College basketball coach. Entered 1995-96 season second alltime in wins (830), the most among active coaches; fifth alltime highest winning percentage (.779). Alltime most NCAA tournament appearances (25), reached Final Four 10 times. Won NCAA championship in 1982 and '93. Coached 1976 Olympic team to gold medal. Career span since 1962 with North Carolina.

Emmitt Smith (b. 5-15-69): Football RB. Led NFL in rushing in 1991 (1,563 yards) and '92 (1,713 and 18 TDs). Rushed for 108 yards in 52–17 Cowboy win over Bills in Super Bowl XXVII. Rushed for 132 yards and named MVP of Super Bowl XXVIII, a 30–13 Dallas victory over Buffalo. Career span since 1990 with Cowboys.

Ozzie Smith (b. 12-26-54): Baseball SS. "The Wizard of Oz." May be the best defensive shortstop in history. Holds alltime record for most assists in a season among shortstops (621 in 1980). 10 consecutive starts in All-Star game. Won 13 consecutive Gold Gloves. Career span since 1978 with San Diego, St Louis.

Red Smith (b. 9-25-05, d. 1-15-82): Sportswriter. Won Pulitzer Prize in 1976. After Grantland Rice, the most widely syndicated sports columnist. His literate essays appeared in the *NY Herald Tribune* from 1945 to 1971 and the *NY Times* from 1971 to 1982.

Stan Smith (b. 12-14-46): Tennis. Won 39 tournaments in career, including 1972 Wimbledon in 5 sets over Ilie Nastase. Won 1971 US Open over Jan Kodes and amateur version of U.S. Open in 1969. 1970 won inaugural Grand Prix Masters. Inducted to Tennis Hall of Fame in 1987.

Tommy Smith (b. 6-5-44): Track and field. Sprinter won 1968 Olympic 200 meters in record of 19.83, then was expelled from Olympic Village, along with bronze medalist John Carlos, for raising black-gloved fist and bowing head during playing of national anthem to protest racism in U.S.

Conn Smythe (b. 2-1-1895, d. 11-18-80): Hockey executive. As general manager with Toronto from 1929 to 1961 won 7 Stanley Cup championships (1932, 1942, 1945, consecutively 1947-49, 1951). Award for playoff MVP named in his honor.

Sam Snead (b. 5-27-12): Golfer. Alltime leader in career wins (81). Won the Masters (1949, 1952, 1954) and PGA Championship (1942, 1949, 1951) 3 times each and British Open (1946). Runner-up at U.S. Open 4 times, but title eluded him. PGA Player of the Year in 1949. Won Seniors Championship 6 times, more than any golfer (1964-65, 1967, 1970, 1972-73).

Peter Snell (b. 12-17-38): Track and field. New Zealand runner was gold medalist in 800 meters at 2 consecutive Olympics in 1960, 1964. Also gold medalist in 1,500 meters at 1964 Olympics. Twice broke world mile record; broke world 800 record once.

Duke Snider (b. 9-19-26): Baseball OF. Career .295 average, 407 HR and 1,333 RBIs. Hit 40+ HR 5 consecutive seasons and 100+ RBIs 6 times. Also led league in runs scored 3 consecutive seasons. Played on 6 pennant winners with the Brooklyn Dodgers. World Series total of 11 HR and 26 RBIs are NL best. Career span 1947-64.

Javier Sotomayor (b. 10-13-67): Track and field. Cuban high jumper broke the 8-foot barrier with world record jump of 8' 0" in 1989. Set current record of 8' ½" in 7-27-93 in Salamanca, Spain.

Warren Spahn (b. 4-23-21): Baseball LHP. Alltime leader in games won for a lefthander (363): 20+ wins 13 times. League leader in wins 8 times (5 seasons consecutively), complete games 9 times (7 seasons consecutively), strikeouts 4 consecutive seasons, innings pitched 4 times and ERA 3 times. 1957 Cy Young award. 63 career shutouts. Pitched 2 no-hitters after age 39. Career span 1942-65, all but last year with Boston (NL), Milwaukee.

Tris Speaker (b. 4-4-1888, d. 12-8-58): Baseball OF. Alltime leader in doubles (792), fifth in hits (3,514) and fifth in batting average (.345). 1 batting title (.386 in 1916), but .375+ average 6 times and .300+ average 12 other times. League leader in doubles 8 times, hits 2 times and HR and RBI 1 time each. 200+ hits 4 times, 40+ doubles 10 times and 100+ runs scored 7 times. MVP in 1912. Career span 1907-28 with Boston, Cleveland.

Michael Spinks (b. 7-13-56): Boxer. 1976 Olympic middleweight champion. Brother Leon was heavyweight champ. Won world light heavyweight title by decision over Mustafa Muhammad on 7-18-81. Defended it 5 times and then consolidated light heavy titles with decision over Dwight Braxton on 3-18-83. Defended four more times. Won heavyweight title on 9-22-85 in decision over Larry Holmes. Lost title to Mike Tyson in 91 seconds on 6-27-88.

Mark Spitz (b. 2-10-50): Swimmer. Won a record 7 gold medals (2 in freestyle, 2 in butterfly, 3 in relays) at 1972 Olympics, setting world record in each event. Also won 2 gold medals and 1 silver and 1 bronze medal at 1968 Olympics. Sullivan Award winner in 1971.

Amos Alonzo Stagg (b. 8-16-1862, d. 3-17-65): College football coach. Third alltime in wins (314). Won national championship with Chicago in 1905. Coach of the Year with Pacific in 1943 at age 81. Career record 314-199-35, including 5 undefeated seasons, from 1892 to 1946. Only person elected to both college football and basketball Halls of Fame. Played in the first basketball game in 1891.

Willie Stargell (b. 3-6-40): Baseball OF/1B. "Pops" achieved a 1979 MVP triple crown, winning NL regular season, playoff and World Series MVP awards. Led NL in homers in 1971 and '73. Hit 475 career homers. Drove in 1,540 runs. Had .282 career batting average. Played all 21 seasons with the Pirates. Elected to Hall of Fame in 1988.

Bart Starr (b. 1-9-34): Football QB. Played on 3 NFL champions (consecutively 1961-62, 1965) and first two Super Bowl champions (1966-67) with Green Bay. Also named MVP of first two Super Bowls. Player of the Year in 1966. Led league in passing 3 times. Also coached Green Bay to 53-77-3 record from 1975 to 1983.

Roger Staubach (b. 2-5-42): Football QB. Won Heisman Trophy with Navy as a junior in 1963. Served 4-year military obligation before turning pro. Led Dallas to 6 NFC Championships, 4 Super Bowls and 2 Super Bowl titles (1971, 1977). Player of the Year and Super Bowl MVP in 1971. Also led league in passing 4 times. Career span 1969-79.

Jan Stenerud (b. 11-26-42): Football K. Second to George Blanda on NFL scoring list, with 1,699 points. Converted an NFL record 373 field goals in 558 attempts. Career span 1967-79 with Kansas City Chiefs, 1980-83 with Green Bay Packers and 1984-85 with Minnesota Vikings. First pure kicker inducted to Hall of Fame 1991.

Casey Stengel (b. 7-30-1890, d. 9-29-75): Baseball manager. "The Ol' Perfesser." Managed New York Yankees to 10 pennants and 7 World Series titles (5 consecutively) in 12 years from 1949 to 1960. Alltime leader in World Series games (63), wins (37) and losses (26). Platoon system was his trademark strategy, Stengelese his trademark language ("You could look it up"). Managed New York Mets from 1962 to 1965. Jersey number (37) retired by Yankees and Mets.

Ingemar Stenmark (b. 3-18-56): Swedish skier. Gold medalist in slalom and giant slalom at 1980 Olympics. World Cup overall champion 3 consecutive years (1976-78).

Woody Stephens (b. 9-1-13): Horse racing trainer. Trained 2 Kentucky Derby winners (Cannonade, who won the 100th Derby in 1974 and Swale in 1984) and 5 straight Belmont winners from 1982-86, starting with 1982 Horse of the Year Conquistador Cielo.

David Stern (b. 9-22-42): Fourth NBA commissioner. Served since 1984. Average worth of a franchise has tripled from $20 million to $65 million. Owners rewarded him with 5-year, $27.5 million contract extension in 1990.

Jackie Stewart (b. 6-11-39): Scottish auto racer. Fourth alltime in Formula 1 victories (27); Formula 1 champion 3 times (1969, 1971, 1973). Also Indy 500 Rookie of the Year in 1966. Retired in 1973.

John L. Sullivan (b. 10-15-1858, d. 2-2-18): Boxer. Last bare knuckle champion. Heavyweight title holder (1882-92), lost to Jim Corbett. Career record 38-1-3 with 33 KOs from 1878 to 1892.

Paul Tagliabue (b. 11-24-40): Football executive. Fifth NFL commissioner, has served since 1989.

Anatoli Tarasov (b. 1918): Hockey coach. Orchestrated Soviet Union's emergence as a hockey power. Won 9 consecutive world amateur championships (1963-71) and 3 Olympic gold medals in 1964, 1968, 1972.

Fran Tarkenton (b. 2-3-40): Football QB. Through 1994-95 season, alltime leader in touchdown passes (342), yards passing (47,003), pass attempts (6,467) and pass completions (3,686). Player of the Year in 1975. Career span 1961-78 with Minnesota, NY Giants.

Lawrence Taylor (b. 2-4-59): Football LB. Revolutionized the linebacker position. Ended 1993 season as the alltime leader in sacks. Also named to Pro Bowl a record 10 consecutive seasons. Player of the Year in 1986. Has played on 2 Super Bowl champions with New York Giants (1986, 1990). Career span 1981-93 with Giants.

Isiah Thomas (b. 4-30-61): Basketball G. Member of Indiana University team that won 1981 NCAA title. Point guard for Detroit Pistons 1982-94. All-NBA First Team 1984, '85 and '86. NBA All Star Game MVP both 1984 and '86. Led NBA in assists (13.9) in 1984-85. Fourth alltime in assists (9,061). Member of Piston team that won NBA title in both 1989 and '90.

Thurman Thomas (b. 5-15-66): Football RB. Led AFC in rushing both 1990 (1,297 yards) and '91 (1,407). Career span since 1988 with Buffalo Bills.

Daley Thompson (b. 7-30-58): Track and field. British decathlete was gold medalist at 2 consecutive Olympics in 1980, 1984. At 1984 Olympics set world record (8,847 points) that lasted eight years.

John Thompson (b. 9-2-41): College basketball coach. From 1973 to present, head coach at Georgetown, where he taught Patrick Ewing, Alonzo Mourning and Dikembe Mutombo to play center. Won NCAA title in 1984, beating Houston 84-75. NCAA runnerup in 1982 and '85.

Bobby Thomson (b. 10-25-23): Baseball OF. Hit dramatic 9th-inning playoff home run to win NL pennant for New York Giants on Oct. 3, 1951. The Giants came from 13½ games behind the Brooklyn Dodgers on Aug. 11 to win the pennant on Thomson's 3-run homer off Ralph Branca in the final game of the 3-game playoff.

Jim Thorpe (b. 5-28-1888, d. 3-28-53): Sportsman. Gold medalist in decathlon and pentathlon at 1912 Olympics. Played pro baseball with New York (NL) and Cincinnati from 1913 to 1919, and pro football with several teams from 1919 to 1926. Also All-America 2 times with Carlisle.

Dick Tiger (b. 8-14-29; d. 12-14-71): Nigerian Boxer. Born Richard Ihetu. Won middleweight title by decision over Gene Fullmer on 10-23-62. Lost middle title to Joey Giardello on 12-7-63, then regained it from Giardello on 10-21-65. Won world light heavyweight title by decision over Jose Torres on 12-16-66, then lost it when KO'd by Bob Foster in 4 on 5-24-68. *The Ring* Fighter of the Year for 1962 and '65. Career record: 61-17-3. Elected to Boxing Hall of Fame 1974.

Bill Tilden (b. 2-10-1893, d. 6-5-53): Tennis player. "Big Bill." Won 7 U.S. singles titles, 6 consecutively (1920-25, 1929) and 3 Wimbledon titles (consecutively 1920-21, 1930). Also won 6 Grand Slam doubles titles. Led U.S. to 7 consecutive Davis Cup victories (1920-26).

Ted Tinling (b. 6-23-10, d. 5-23-90): British tennis couturier. The premier source on women's tennis from Suzanne Lenglen to Steffi Graf. Also designed tennis clothes, most notably the frilled lace panties worn by Gorgeous Gussy Moran at Wimbledon in 1949.

Y.A. Tittle (b. 10-24-26): Football QB. Threw 33 TD passes in 1962 and in '63 led league in passing, completing 221 of 367 attempts for 3,145 yards and 36 TDs. Career span 1948-64, mostly with San Francisco 49ers and New York Giants. Inducted into Hall of Fame 1971.

Jayne Torvill/Christopher Dean (b. 10-7-57/ b. 7-27-58): British figure skaters. Won 4 consecutive ice dancing world championships (1981-84) and Olympic ice dancing gold medal (1984). Won world professional championships in 1985. Won Olympic ice dancing bronze in 1994.

Vladislav Tretiak (b. 4-25-52): Hockey G. Led Soviet Union to 3 gold medals at Olympics in 1972, 1976, 1984. Played on 13 world amateur champions from 1970 to 1984.

Lee Trevino (b. 12-1-39): Golfer. Won U.S. Open (1968, 1971), British Open (consecutively 1971-72) and PGA Championship (1974, 1984) 2 times each. PGA Player of the Year in 1971. Also won U.S. Senior Open in 1990. First Senior $1 million season.

Emlen Tunnell (b. 3-29-25, d. 7-23-75): Football S. Alltime leader in interception yardage (1,282) and second in interceptions (79). All-Pro 9 times. Career span 1948-61 with New York Giants and Green Bay.

Gene Tunney (b. 5-25-1897, d. 11-7-78): Boxer. Heavyweight champion (1926-28). Defeated Jack Dempsey 2 times, including famous "long count" bout. Career record 65-2-1 with 43 KOs from 1915 to 1928. Retired as champion.

Ted Turner (b. 11-19-38): Sportsman. Skipper who successfully defended the America's Cup in 1977. Also owner of the Atlanta Braves since 1976 and Hawks since 1977. Founded the Goodwill Games in 1986.

Mike Tyson (b. 6-30-66): Boxer. Youngest heavyweight champion at 19 years old in 1986. Held title until knocked out by James "Buster" Douglas in Tokyo on Feb. 10, 1990. Career record as of 10-1-95 42-1 with 37 KOs since 1985. Convicted of rape in 1992, released from prison in 1995.

Johnny Unitas (b. 5-7-33): Football QB. 47 consecutive games throwing touchdown pass (1956-60), third alltime touchdown passes (290), fifth alltime yards passing (40,239). Led league in touchdown passes 4 consecutive seasons. Player of the Year 3 times (1959, 1964, 1967). Career span 1956-72 with Baltimore, San Diego.

Al Unser Sr. (b. 5-29-39): Auto racer. Won Indy 500 4 times (consecutively 1970-71, 1978, 1987). Third alltime in CART victories (39). USAC/CART champion 3 times (1970, 1983, 1985). Brother of Bobby.

Bobby Unser (b. 2-20-34): Auto racer. Won Indy 500 3 times (1968, 1975, 1981). Fourth alltime in CART victories (35). USAC champion 2 times (1968, 1974). Brother of Al, Sr.

Harold S. Vanderbilt (b. 7-6-1884, d. 7-4-70): Sailer. Owner and skipper who successfully defended the America's Cup 3 consecutive times (1930, 1934, 1937).

Glenna Collett Vare (b. 6-20-03, d. 2-2-89): Golfer. Won U.S. Women's Amateur 6 times, more than any golfer (1922, 1925, consecutively 1928-30, 1935).

Bill Veeck (b. 2-9-14, d. 1-2-86): Baseball owner. From 1946 to 1980, owned ballclubs in Cleveland, St Louis (AL), Chicago (AL). In 1948, Cleveland became baseball's first team to draw 2 million in attendance. That year Veeck integrated AL by signing Larry Doby and then Satchel Paige. A brilliant promoter, Veeck sent midget Eddie Gaedel up to bat for St Louis in 1951. Brought exploding scoreboard to stadiums and put players' names on uniforms.

Guillermo Vilas (b. 8-17-52): Tennis. Argentine won 50 straight matches in 1977. In '77 won French Open, where he beat Brian Gottfried, and the U.S. Open, where he beat Jimmy Connors. Also won Australian Open twice, 1978–79.

Lasse Viren (b. 7-22-49): Track and field. Finnish runner was gold medalist in 5,000 and 10,000 meters at 2 consecutive Olympics (1972, 1976).

Virginia Wade (b. 7-10-45): Tennis. Beloved in Britain, Wade won four major titles, most notably Wimbledon in 1977, its centenary year, where she triumphed over Betty Stove. Also won 1968 U.S. Open and '72 Australian Open.

Honus Wagner (b. 2-24-1874, d. 12-6-55): Baseball SS. Had .327 career batting average, 3,415 hits and 8 batting titles. Averaged .300+ 15 consecutive seasons. Led league in RBI 4 times, with 100+ RBI 9 times. Third alltime in triples (252) and league leader in doubles 8 times. 703 career stolen bases, league leader in steals 5 times. Career span 1897-1917 with Pittsburgh.

Grete Waitz (b. 10-1-53): Track and field. Norwegian runner has won New York City Marathon a record 9 times (consecutively 1978-80, 1982-86, 1988). Won the women's marathon at the 1983 World Championship.

Jersey Joe Walcott (b. 10-31-14): Boxer. Heavyweight champion from 1951 to 1952. Won title at age 37 on fifth attempt before surrendering it to Rocky Marciano. Later became sheriff of Camden, NJ.

Doak Walker (b. 1-1-27): Football HB. Led league in scoring 2 times, his first and final seasons. All-Pro 5 times. Played on 2 consecutive NFL champions (1952-53) with Detroit. Career span 1950 to 1955. Also won Heisman Trophy as a junior in 1948. All-America 3 consecutive seasons with SMU.

Herschel Walker (b. 3-3-62): Football RB. Won Heisman Trophy in 1982 with Georgia. Turned pro by entering USFL with New Jersey. Gained 7,000+ rushing yards and scored 61 touchdowns in 3 seasons before league folded. Entered NFL in 1986 with Dallas and led league in rushing yards (1,514 in 1988).

Bill Walsh (b. 11-30-31): Football coach. Led the San Francisco 49ers to four Super Bowl wins, after the 1981, '84, '88 and '89 seasons. Career record with 49ers 102-63-1. Developed short-passing game. Returned to Stanford University for 1992 season.

Bill Walton (b. 11-5-52): Basketball C. MVP in 1978, playoff MVP in 1977. Led league in rebounding and blocks in 1977. Career span 1974-86 with Portland, San Diego, Boston. Also College Player of the Year 3 consecutive seasons (1972-74). Played on 2

consecutive NCAA championship teams (1972-73) with UCLA; tournament MVP twice (1972-73). Sullivan Award winner in 1973.

Junxia Wang (b. 1963): Chinese distance runner. Broke four existing world records over six days in Sept. 1993. Broke 10,000 (29:31.78) on 9-8; ran 1500 in 3:51.92 in finishing second to countrywoman Qu Yunxia's world record of 3:50.46 on 9-11; ran 3,000 record of 8:12.19 in heats on 9-12 and lowered it to 8:06.11 on 9-13.

War Admiral (b. 1934): Thoroughbred race horse. A son of Man o' War, won Triple Crown and Horse of the Year honors in 1937.

Paul Warfield (b. 11-28-42): Football WR. Caught 427 passes for 8,565 yards and 85 TDs. Played on two Super Bowl-winning Miami Dolphin teams. Career span 1964–77, all with Cleveland Browns except for 1970–74 with Miami Dolphins. Inducted to Hall of Fame 1983.

Glenn "Pop" Warner (b. 4-5-1871, d. 9-7-54): College football coach. Second alltime in wins (319). Won 3 national championships with Pittsburgh (1916, 1918) and Stanford (1926). Career record 319-106-32 with 6 teams from 1896 to 1938.

Tom Watson (b. 9-4-49): Golfer. Winner of British Open 5 times (1975, 1977, 1980, consecutively 1982-83), the Masters 2 times (1977, 1981) and U.S. Open once (1982). PGA Player of the Year 6 times, more than any golfer (consecutively 1977-80, 1982, 1984).

Dick Weber (b. 12-23-29): Bowler. Won All-Star Tournament 4 times (consecutively 1962-63, 1965-66). Voted Bowler of the Year 3 times (1961, 1963, 1965). Won 31 career PBA titles.

Johnny Weismuller (b. 6-2-04, d. 1-21-84): Swimmer. Won 3 gold medals (including 100- and 400-meter freestyle) at 1924 Olympics and 2 gold medals at 1928 Olympics. Also played Tarzan in the movies.

Jerry West (b. 5-28-38): Basketball G. 10 time All-Star; All-Defensive Team 4 times; 1969 playoff MVP. Led league in assists and scoring 1 time each. Career span 1960-72 with Los Angeles. Currently general manager. Also NCAA tournament MVP in 1959. All-America 2 times with West Virginia. Played on 1960 gold medal-winning Olympic team.

Whirlaway (b. 4-2-38, d. 4-6-53): Thoroughbred race horse. Triple Crown winner in 1941 with jockey Eddie Arcaro aboard. Trained by Ben A. Jones.

Byron "Whizzer" White (b. 6-8-17): Football RB. Led NFL in rushing 2 times (Pittsburgh in 1938, Detroit in 1940). Led NCAA in scoring and rushing with Colorado in 1937; named All-America. Supreme Court justice from 1962 to '93.

Reggie White (b. 12-19-62): Football DE. Fearsome pass rusher. Winner in new era of free agency, signed with Green Bay Packers in 1993 for $17 million over four years. Career span: 1984 with Memphis Showboats, 1985–92 with Philadelphia Eagles and since 1993 with Green Bay.

Charles Whittingham (b. 4-13-13): Thoroughbred race horse trainer. "Bald Eagle" after losing hair to tropical disease in World War II. In 1986 became the oldest trainer to win Kentucky Derby, with Ferdinand. Led yearly earnings list for trainers from 1970-73 consecutively; in 1975; and in 1981–82 consecutively. Won three Eclipse Awards and trained two Horses of the Year (Ack Ack in 1971 and Ferdinand in 1987).

Kathy Whitworth (b. 9-27-39): Golfer. Alltime LPGA leader with 88 tour victories, including six majors. Won LPGA Championship in 1967, '71 and '75. Won 1977 Dinah Shore. Won Titleholders Championship (extinct major) in 1965 and '66. Won Western Open (extinct major) in 1967. Won Vare Trophy every year from 1965–72, except 1968. LPGA Player of Year from 1966–69 and 1971–73.

Hoyt Wilhelm (b. 7-26-23): Baseball RHP. Hall of Famer. Threw knuckleball until age 48. Alltime pitching leader in games (1,070). Career record: 143-122, 2.52 ERA, 227 saves. Hit home run in his first at bat (never hit another) and pitched no-hitter in 1958. Career span with 9 teams from 1952-72.

Bud Wilkinson (b. 4-23-15 d. 2-9-94): Football coach. Alltime NCAA leader in consecutive wins (47, 1953-57). Won 3 national championships (1950, consecutively 1955-56) with Oklahoma, where he coached from 1947 to 1963. Won Orange Bowl 4 times and Sugar Bowl 2 times. Career record 145-29-4, including 4 undefeated seasons. Also coached with St Louis of NFL in 1978-79.

Billy Williams (b. 6-15-38): Baseball OF. Nicknamed "Sweet Swinging". NL Rookie of the Year for 1961. Hit 426 career home runs. Drove in 1,475 runs. Lifetime averge of .290. Named to six NL All Star teams. Career span 1959–74 with Chicago Cubs, 1975–76 with Oakland A's. Elected to Hall of Fame in 1987.

Ted Williams (b. 8-30-18): Baseball OF. "The Splendid Splinter." Last player to hit .400 (.406 in 1941). MVP in 1946, 1949 and Triple Crown winner in 1942, 1947. Sixth alltime highest batting average (.344), second most walks (2,019) and second highest slugging average (.634). 521 career HR, 1,839 career RBIs. League leader in batting average and runs scored 6 times each, RBI and HR 4 times each, walks 8 times and doubles 2 times. Had .300+ average 15 consecutive seasons; 100+ RBI and runs scored 9 times each; 30+ HR 8 times; and 100+ walks 11 times. Lost nearly 5 seasons to military service. Career span 1939-42 and 1946-60 with Boston.

Hack Wilson (b. 4-26-00; d. 11-23-48): Baseball OF. Stood 5' 6" but weighed 210. Had five incredible seasons 1926–30. Best was 1930 when he hit .356, scored 146 runs, hit a NL record 56 homers and drove in 190, which is still the major league record. Declined through drinking. Career span 1923–34 with several teams. Elected to Hall of Fame in 1979.

Dave Winfield (b. 10-3-51): Baseball OF. Also drafted out of Univ. of Minnesota for both pro basketball and football. Led NL in RBIs in 1979 (118). In 1992, first 40-year-old to get 100+ RBIs, with 108. Had clutch double to win 1992 World Series. Got 3,000th hit, off Dennis Eckersley, on 9-16-93. Career span 1973–80 with San Diego; 1981–90 with Yankees; 1990–91 with California; 1992 with Toronto; 1993-94 with Minnesota; and 1995 with Cleveland.

Major W. C. Wingfield (b. 19-16-1833, d. 4-18-12): British tennis pioneer. Credited with inventing the game of tennis, which he called "Sphairistike" or "sticky" and patented in February 1874.

Colonel Matt Winn (b. 6-30-1861, d. 10-6-49): As general manager of Churchill Downs from 1904 until his death, promoted the Kentucky Derby into the premier race in the country.

Katarina Witt (b. 12-3-65): East German figure skater. Gold medalist at 2 consecutive Olympics in

1984, 1988. Also world champion 4 times (consecutively 1984-85, 1987-88).

John Wooden (b. 10-14-10): College basketball coach. Only member of basketball Hall of Fame as coach and player. Coached UCLA to 10 NCAA championships in 12 years (consecutively 1964-65, 1967-73, 1975). Alltime winning streak 88 games (1971-74). 664 career wins and fourth alltime highest winning percentage (.804). Career span 1949-75 with UCLA. Also 1932 College Player of the Year at Purdue.

Mickey Wright (b. 2-14-35): Golfer. Second alltime in career wins (82) and major championships (13— tied with Louise Suggs). Won U.S. Open 4 times (consecutively 1958-59, 1961, 1964), LPGA Championship 4 times (1958, consecutively 1960-61, 1963), Western Open 3 times (consecutively 1962-63, 1966) and Titleholders Championship twice (1961-62).

Cale Yarborough (b. 3-27-40): Auto racer. Won Daytona 500 4 times (1968, 1977, consecutively 1983-84). Fifth alltime in NASCAR victories (83). Also NASCAR champion 3 consecutive years (1976-78).

Carl Yastrzemski (b. 8-22-39): Baseball OF. "Yaz." 3,419 career hits, 452 HR. 1967 MVP and Triple Crown winner. 3 batting titles, including .301 in 1968, the lowest ever to win. Second alltime in games played (3,308) and fourth in walks (1,845). Career span 1961-83 with Boston.

Cy Young (b. 3-29-1867, d. 11-4-55): Baseball RHP. Alltime leader in wins (511), losses (315), innings pitched (7,354.2) and complete games (749); fourth in shutouts (76). Had 2.63 career ERA. Pitched 3 no-hitters, including a perfect game in 1904. Pitching award named in his honor. Career span 1890-1911 with Cleveland, Boston.

Robin Yount (b. 9-16-55): Baseball OF/SS. Became Brewer shortstop at 18. Landslide winner of 1982 AL MVP in 1982 when he hit .331 with 29 homers. Hit .414 in Brewers' 1982 Series loss to Cardinals. 3,142 hits. Shoulder injury made Yount move to outfield in 1984. Career span 1974–93, all with the Brewers.

Babe Didrikson Zaharias (b. 6-26-14, d. 9-27-56): Sportswoman. Gold medalist in 80-meter hurdles and javelin throw at 1932 Olympics; also won silver medal in high jump (her gold medal jump was disallowed for using the then-illegal western roll). Became a golfer in 1935 and won 12 major titles, including U.S. Open 3 times (1948, 1950, 1954—a year after cancer surgery). Also helped found the LPGA in 1949.

Tony Zale (b. 5-29-13): Boxer. Born Anthony Zaleski. "The Man of Steel." Won vacant middleweight title by decision over Georgie Abrams on 11-28-41. Lost title to Billy Conn on 2-13-42. Spent almost 4 years in Navy. In sensational 3 fight series with Rocky Graziano, retained title with KO in 6 on 9-27-46; lost it to Graziano by KO in 6 on 7-17-47; and then reclaimed it by KOing Graziano in 3 on 6-10-48. Lost title to Marcel Cerdan, who KO'd him in 12 on 9-21-48. Career record: 88 bouts; won 46 by KO and 24 by decision; drew 2; lost 16, 4 by KO. Elected to Boxing Hall of Fame 1958.

Emil Zatopek (b. 9-19-22): Track and field. Czechoslovakian runner became only athlete to win gold medal in 5,000 and 10,000 meters and marathon, at 1952 Olympics. Also gold medalist in 10,000 meters at 1948 Olympics.

Obituaries

AUGUST 21, 1995 · $2.95 (CAN. $3.95)

GEORGE SILK

793

Johnny Adams, 79, horse racing trainer. Adams's riding career began in the early 1930's. As a jockey, he rode 3,270 winners, which earned more than $9.7 million, and won the 1954 Preakness aboard Hasty Road. After retiring from riding in 1958, Adams became a trainer. One of the horses he trained, J.O. Tobin, beat the previously undefeated Seattle Slew, a Triple Crown winner, in the 1977 Swaps Stakes. In Arcadia, Calif., after a lengthy illness, August 19.

Bob Allison, 60, baseball player. The American League Rookie of the Year in 1959 with the Washington Senators, Allison was diagnosed five years ago with ataxia, a neurodegenerative disorder that affects nerve cells in the brain and impairs coordination. He and his family then founded the Bob Allison Ataxia Research Center at the University of Minnesota. He had been in a wheelchair for the last year and had difficulty reading, swallowing, and speaking. A two-time All-Star, Allison was one of the early stars of the Minnesota Twins and spent 13 years in the majors. His career batting average was .255, with 256 home runs and 769 RBIs. He twice topped 100 RBIs, and his 99 runs scored led the AL in 1963. In Rio Verde, Ariz., of aspiration in the lungs related to ataxia, April 9.

Francis "Reds" Bagnell, 66, football player. A fiery red-head, Bagnell anchored the powerful single-wing offense of the University of Pennsylvania football team from 1948 to 1950. He won the Maxwell Award and the Helms Athletic Award and finished third in the Heisman Trophy balloting in 1950, when he threw 88 passes without an interception. In a victory that fall over Dartmouth, Bagnell amassed 490 yards to establish the single-game collegiate record for total yardage. He earned nine varsity letters at Penn, three each in football, baseball and basketball. In 1990, he was elected president of the National Football Foundation and College Hall of Fame Board. In Philadelphia, of heart failure, July 10.

Sally Baile, 58, horse racing trainer. Baile was one of the first women to train thoroughbred race horses to victory in major U.S. stakes races. Her best-known horse was probably Win, whose victories included the 1985 Man o' War. In Mineola, Long Island, of cancer, August 21.

Gus Bell, 66, baseball player. The oldest member of a three-generation baseball family, Bell was an outfielder with the Cincinnati Reds for nine (1953-61) of his 15 seasons. His best years were 1953, when he batted .300 with 30 homers, and 1955, when he hit .308 with 27 home runs. Four times, the left-handed hitter knocked in more than 100 runs in a season. Bell was the Mets' right fielder in their first game on April 11, 1962, and got their first hit. His son Buddy and grandson David have also played in the major leagues. In Cincinnati, of a heart attack, May 7.

Hector "Toe" Blake, 83, hockey coach. During a 28-year NHL career, Blake won three Stanley Cups as a player and eight as a coach. During his playing years with the Montreal Maroons and Canadiens, the left wing appeared in 578 games and had 235 goals and 292 assists for 527 points. Blake won scoring and MVP honors in 1938-39, and was awarded the Lady Byng trophy for sportsmanship in 1945-46. As the Canadiens' coach for 13 seasons, he was 500-255-129. In Montreal, of Alzheimer's disease, May 17.

Glenn Burke, 42, baseball player. Burke was the first major league baseball player to publicly acknowledge his homosexuality. He played for the Los Angeles Dodgers and the Oakland Athletics for four and a half seasons, batting .237 and stealing 35 bases, but he left the game at the age of 27 in 1980. "Prejudice drove me out of baseball sooner than I should have," he said. "But I wasn't changing." In 1987, his right leg and foot were shattered when he was hit by a car in San Francisco. After the accident, his years-long drug use increased, and he served prison time for grand theft and possession of drugs. He was sometimes seen panhandling and wandering in the Castro district of San Francisco. In San Leandro, Calif., of complications from AIDS, May 30.

Fabio Casartelli, 24, cyclist. The third rider to die during the 92-year history of the Tour de France, Casartelli fractured his skull in a crash on a mountain bend. The Italian racer failed to negotiate a curve and appeared to hit a concrete block on the side of the road. Like most of the other riders, Casartelli rode without a helmet, and his death renewed debate about the cyclists' safety. Tour riders observed a minute of silence in Casartelli's memory at the start of the 16th stage, the day after his death. In Tarbes, France, of head injuries, July 18.

Howard Cosell, 77, broadcaster. The trailblazing journalist introduced sports journalism to television and brought entertainment to prime-time football. Cosell gave up a law career in the 1950s to go into broadcasting, where he stirred up controversy wherever he went. "Telling it like it is," Cosell once wrote, "I've had a remarkable life."

William Nack writes:

"On a winter night in 1983, in a dining room of the Ritz-Carlton Hotel in New York City, the face that had launched a thousand quips was up now and floating among the tables of network talking heads and sports celebrities.

"It was a dinner for the Special Olympics, and no one navigated such an occasion more noisily than Howard Cosell, particularly when he was fondling his ninth vodka martini. And suddenly there he was across the room, hovering over one table, scolding and sarcastic, loud and bombastic—the familiar cigar jabbing at the air, the voice growing louder as the Havana grew shorter. Howard was Coselling again, speaking of sports, of broadcasting, of anything that came to mind. Finally the rest of the room fell silent, and all to be heard was the voice of Howard, America's voice. During the lull, Howard's wife, Emmy, sitting across the room, summoned her husband back to earth with a voice that went boom in the night.

" 'Howard, shut up! Nobody cares.' "

"After it was announced on Sunday that Cosell had died of a heart embolism at 4 a.m. in a Manhattan hospital, the thought of that old rebuke came back again with a kind of eerie resonance. Of all the figures in modern American sport, none inspired a sense of ambivalence that ran quite as deep and powerful as did Howard Cosell, in life and in death, and this was nowhere more evident than in the eulogies served up on Sunday with a side of ice. Bob Costa's piece on NBC was delivered with a very dry eye, and even Cosell's former boss at ABC Sports, Roone Arledge, could summon nothing that could be properly described as emotion. 'Howard Cosell was one of the most original people ever to appear on American television,' Arledge said. 'He became a giant by telling the truth in an industry that was not used to hearing it and considered it revolutionary.'

"It all rang, in a rather unsettling way, as though nobody really gave a damn. It has been 10 years since Cosell left TV broadcasting, a dozen since he abandoned the book on *Monday Night Football*, and there is a whole new generation out there that has missed the gaudiest, smartest and most entertaining and unforgettable television broadcaster in the history of sports—a superb reporter who worked harder and asked better questions than anyone else who'd ever worn earphones. They also have missed a man who was, by turns, well.... Let him tell it like it was: 'Arrogant, pompous, obnoxious, vain, cruel, verbose, a showoff. I have been called all of these. Of course, I am.' All he forgot was irritating, generous, egomaniacal, funny, paranoid, charming, insecure and.... 'If Howard Cosell were a sport, he'd be roller derby,' said columnist Jimmy Cannon.

"Above all, he was sui generis, an unalloyed original who, as a homely Jewish lawyer from Brooklyn, brought to television what one writer called 'the grand slam of network liabilities.' Upon arriving on the national scene in the 1960s, Cosell got swept up in the political currents quickened by the civil rights movement and the Vietnam War. Unlike his buttoned-down peers, who ducked social issues and fled at the first whiff of controversy, Cosell waded into every major battle of his time, cutting his way against the grain. He allied himself with Curt Flood in the player's challenge to baseball's hoary reserve clause, and he championed Muhammad Ali in his fight against the draft, setting fire to the national shirt by insisting on calling Ali by his Muslim name. Many of his pen pals remained anonymous when they addressed him 'You nigger-loving Jew bastard....'

"If his alliance with Ali launched him as a social force—a regular in front of congressional committees and college classrooms—his 14 years on *Monday Night Football* made him an enduring celebrity, at once the most loved and the most reviled of broadcasters. On Monday nights bar owners all over America held contests in which the winner got to heave a brick at How-wud's visage on a television screen. One night in the 1970s, as he left the broadcast booth following a game in Baltimore, the crowd around him grew so menacing, pressing in and shouting obscenities, that policemen formed a wedge to shield him. Stepping onto the elevator, Cosell adjusted his tie and sniffed, 'Have you ever seen such *animals*?' By then, of course, the game had become the undercard to the main event. Cosell was the show.

"When his television career ended in the mid-1980s, he left as one of the most influential figures in sports, and very much in the Cosellian tradition, he did not leave quietly. He wrote two books attacking just about everything in sports, including a number of his former colleagues on *Monday Night Football*, leaving behind a bitter and angry history of his life and times in the world of games. Cosell was too much of an original to leave heirs, and the landscape of broadcast journalism that he left on Sunday looks much the way he found it 35 years ago. Once again the waves are filled with talking heads and apologists, with hometown cheerleaders and mindless drones. No one is asking the questions that he asked. And Emmy was right—nobody cares."

In New York City, of a heart embolism, April 23.

Leon Day, 78, baseball player. Day died just six days after he achieved his lifelong dream, being elected into baseball's Hall of Fame. He was considered one of the best pitchers in the Negro Leagues. Playing mainly for the Newark (N.J.) Eagles, Day pitched in a record seven All-Star games from 1934-50. In Baltimore, of a heart condition, March 13.

Edward J. DeBartolo, Sr., 85, team owner. DeBartolo, one of the country's richest businessmen, owned the San Francisco's 49ers and, for a time, the Pittsburgh Penguins (which he sold in 1991). He earned his fortune by parlaying a real estate business into one of the world's largest shopping center and development firms. DeBartolo also served as president of three horse tracks—Louisiana Downs, Thistledown in Cleveland and Remington Park in Oklahoma City. His son, Edward Jr., runs the 49ers. In Youngstown, Ohio, of complications from pneumonia, December 19, 1994.

Juan Manuel Fangio, 84, race car driver. Fangio dominated Grand Prix racing in the 1950s by winning 24 of the 51 world championship races he contested for the Mercedes-Benz, Alfa Romeo, Ferrari and Maserati teams. The world driving champion in 1951 and from 1954 through 1957, Fangio ranks seventh among alltime Grand Prix winners.

SI writes:

"During his brief, spectacular Formula One racing career, Argentina's Juan Manuel Fangio, who died last week of kidney failure at the age of 84, maintained a presence befitting so imperial a sport. The epitome of the old school driver, looking dashing in the cockpit of the elegant front-engined cars whose sleek bodywork was uncluttered by sponsor logos, Fangio was the standard by which all Grand Prix drivers measure themselves. Yet he somehow never lost the unassuming sensibilities of the common man.

"Even during the 1950s, one of the most volatile and divisive political decades in Latin American history, right-wing dictators and Marxist revolutionaries could agree on at least one thing: Fangio's greatness. Friends of the Maestro like to recall the time when, before a minor F/1 race in Havana in 1958, Fangio was captured by a group of pro-Castro insurgents hostile to the rightist Batista regime. The revolutionaries were so in awe of their hostage that they brought him breakfast in bed and watched the race with him before releasing him that night. When Fangio was buried last week in his birthplace of Balcarce, his open casket was surrounded by two enormous funeral wreaths, one from Fidel Castro and another from Arnold Rodriguez, the man who led the group that had kidnapped him from his Havana hotel.

"Although Fangio was already 37 when he began his Grand Prix career, he won an astounding 24 of 51 races in his 10 years on the F/1 circuit before retiring in 1958, citing his belief that champions, like actors and dictators, should go out while still on top. Yet in retirement the Maestro never failed to carry himself with the forbearance and humility that had defined him during his racing career. 'When one runs the risk of losing a sense of proportion,' he once said, 'it's time to go home, sleep in the same bed in which one dreamed while still a nobody and to eat the simple, healthy dishes of one's childhood.' "

In Buenos Aires, of pneumonia, July 17.

Richard "Pancho" Gonzales, 67, tennis player. A two-time national champion, the 6'3" Gonzales dominated the court with his powerful right-handed serve and precise, versatile ground strokes. He never won Wimbledon, although as a 41-year-old grandfather he won the longest match in Wimbledon history, a first-round bout that lasted 5 hours and 12 minutes and spanned two days. Gonzalez, who taught himself to play on the public courts in Los Angeles, turned pro in 1949 in the days before open (pro and amateur) tournaments, and spent his prime playing in Jack Kramer's "circus" tour. "He was a great competitor," said Kramer. "He would have won several Wimbledons if he hadn't turned professional. The records of Richard Gonzalez are obscured because of that. He never showed up at Wimbledon and Forest Hills until 1968...."

SI writes:

"A recurring theme in the obituaries of Richard (Pancho) Gonzales last week was that this great player was tennis's first enfant terrible, the progenitor of a generation of boors. Gonzales, in fact, did complain from time to time about questionable calls and even whacked an occasional ball into the seats in a fit of pique. He responded, often heatedly, to hecklers. He was not above teasing an opponent if he thought it might give him an edge. And once he even threw a courtside chair at a tournament referee whom he considered negligent.

"In his day such behavior was considered abhorrent. Now it is merely the norm. Or did you miss the farcical goings-on at Wimbledon, where not one player but three got the boot, and the wife of one of them took a poke at a chair umpire? If these churls are the inheritors of the Gonzales legacy, then poor Pancho ought to be committed immediately and without clemency to purgatory.

"Gonzales did have a chip on his shoulder. His court ferocity was fed in no small part by a sense of social inferiority that was accentuated in a sport then considered upper crust. No country-club kid, he learned his game on the public courts as an urban warrior. And if he behaved badly at times, it was not out of petulance, but out of a deep-seated dread of failure. Mostly, he was an imposing and even dignified presence on the court.

"Gonzales would certainly have resented suggestions that he had anything at all in common with the Visigoths who have succeeded him on the courts. And we agree. After all, in his lifetime he had five wives—including an older sister of Andre Agassi—and none of them ever slugged a chair umpire."

In Las Vegas, of stomach cancer, July 3.

David Griggs, 28, football player. Griggs was killed when he apparently lost control of his car on an expressway ramp. After five seasons with the Miami Dolphins, the linebacker had joined the San Diego Chargers as a free agent in 1994 and helped them win the AFC title. In Fort Lauderdale, of injuries sustained in a car accident, June 19.

Alex Groza, 68, basketball player. Groza, an all-America center for the championship Kentucky basketball teams of the late 1940's, played a prominent role in the game's biggest betting scandal. At 6'7", Groza parlayed size with quickness and finished with 1,744 points, which topped the Kentucky career list for 15 years after he left and still ranks seventh in school history. Groza went on to play for the NBA's Indianapolis Olympians, where he was second in scoring behind George Mikan in his two seasons. Before the start of the 1952 season, he and former teammates Ralph Beard and Dale Barnstable admitted to conspiring to shave points in return for bribes from gamblers while at Kentucky. They received suspended sentences and their professional careers were ended. Groza later became general manager and coach of the Kentucky Colonels and general manager of the San Diego Conquistadores of the ABA. He was the younger brother of Lou, a Hall of Fame tackle and place-kicker who starred for the Cleveland Browns. In San Diego, of cancer, January 21.

Pat Haggerty, 67, football referee. Haggerty's career as an NFL referee spanned 28 years and three Super Bowls. In Greeley, Colo., of prostate and bone cancer, December 9, 1994.

Nat Holman, 98, basketball coach. Holman, one of the greatest basketball players of the 1920's, coached the 1950 City College of New York team to victories in both the NCAA and the NIT championships, a feat that can no longer be duplicated because the tournaments are now held at the same time. A year later, several of his key players were arrested for point-shaving—trying to win a game by fewer points than the margin predicted by bookmakers. Holman knew nothing of the players' deceit, however. He was one of the few men who played both pro basketball and coached a college team at the same time. From 1921-27, he played with the Original Celtics, the famous barnstorming team that helped legitimize pro basketball, and was billed by the team as "the world's greatest basketball player." In Riverdale, Bronx, of natural causes, February 12.

Jim Lee Howell, 80, football coach. Howell, a stalwart on the Steve Owen Giants' teams that played in four NFL championship games from 1937 to 1948, is best remembered as Owen's successor as head coach. During that seven year span, from 1954 to 1960, Howell never had a losing season. His overall record of 55-29-4, for a winning percentage of .663, is the best of any Giant coach of comparable tenure. He coached some of the team's most acclaimed players, including Charley Conerly, Frank Gifford, Kyle Rote and San Huff. After leaving the head-coach position, he spent 19 years as the Giants' director of player personnel and seven as a special scout and consultant. During his playing days, the Arkansas native also served in his home state's Legislature. In Lonoke, Ark., of natural causes, January 4.

Jim Katcavage, 60, football player. A defensive end for the New York Giants, Katcavage began his career on the famous 1956 championship team, the first Giants team to win an NFL championship in 18 years (it would be another 30 years before the feat was duplicated). The title was won when the Giants, wearing basketball shoes on a frozen field, rolled to a 47-7 victory over the Chicago Bears. In his 13-year career, Katcavage was an All-Pro three times and scored a total of three safeties, tying for second on the league career list. In the 14-game 1963 season, 19 years before the league started keeping official sack records, he was credited with 25 sacks, three more than the official 16-game season record. In Maple Glen, Penn., of a heart attack, February 22.

Irving S. Kosloff, 82, team owner. Kosloff owned the Philadelphia 76ers teams that set NBA records for both the best (1966-67) and the worst (1972-73) seasons. During the period of his ownership, from 1963 to '76, the 76ers made the playoffs nine times, reached the Eastern Conference final three times and won the NBA championship in 1967 with Wilt Chamberlain at center. In Merion, Pa., of undisclosed causes, February 19.

Millicent Lang, 78, tennis player. Lang, a Bronx native, won her first public tournament at age 11. She captured three titles as a junior player in the 1930's and was a veteran player on the women's tennis circuit by the time she was 19. In the early 1940's, Lang was ranked 14th in the United States women's singles and No. 1 in the Eastern states. In Boca Raton, Fla., of a stroke, February 10.

Ron Luciano, 57, umpire. An American League umpire from 1968-79, Luciano was known for his wisecracks and arm-waving antics. After retiring from baseball, Luciano worked as a commentator for NBC, wrote four books about his umpiring exploits and became a hit on the talk-show circuit.

SI writes:

"It wasn't so much the things he did and said, but the way he did and said them. Ron Luciano, the umpire who struck back, made his calls with great histrionics and made his opinions known with similar flair. Anything refracted through his world view, an outlook that was equal parts Berra and Berle, came out so skewed that it somehow made perfect sense. 'When I started, baseball was played by nine tough competitors on grass in graceful ballparks,' he once said of the 11 years he spent wearing American League blue. 'By the time I finished, there were 10 men on a side, the game was played indoors on plastic, and I spent half my time watching out for a man dressed in a chicken suit who kept trying to kiss me.'

"Luciano said much more before last week when, at 57, perhaps out of loneliness, perhaps out of depression over his mother's Alzheimer's disease, he asphyxiated himself in his garage in Endicott, N.Y.

"*On himself:* 'I like to hunt, but I never hit anything. I don't see too well.'

" 'A double play takes 3.8 seconds. Even as dumb as I am, I can concentrate that long.'

" 'I never called a balk in my life. I didn't understand the rule.'

"*On his craft:* 'Umpiring is best described as the profession of standing between two seven-year-olds with one ice-cream cone.'

" 'There are a lot of salls and brikes that I have to call balls and strikes.'

" 'An indecisive umpire is as vulnerable as the rich sky diver who allows his only heir to pack his parachute.'

" 'When you're wrong, and you call something and they still believe you, that makes a great umpire.'

"*Upon being asked by Larry King if there are natural umpires:* 'Yeah, there really are, but nobody starts out that way.'

"*And:* 'Umpires never win.' "

In Endicott, N.Y., of carbon monoxide poisoning, January 18.

Mickey Mantle, 63, baseball player. His career with the New York Yankees spanned 18 seasons (1951-68); his hold on the nation's affections lasted even longer. Mantle, perhaps the most powerful switch-hitter ever, twice topped 50 homers, led the AL in home runs four times and finished with a total of 536. He achieved the Triple Crown in 1956, played in 20 All-Star games and earned three MVP Awards (in 1956, '57, and '62). Mantle's death two months after a much-publicized liver transplant prompted an effort to understand his place in American lore. Richard Hoffer offers this provocative essay on Mantle as man and myth:

"Mickey Mantle, with his death at 63, passes from these pages forever and becomes the property of anthropologists, people who can more properly put the calipers to celebrity, who can more accurately track the force of personality. We can't do it anymore, couldn't really do it to begin with. He batted this, hit that. You can look it up. Hell, we do all the time. But there's

nothing in our library, in all those numbers, that explains how Mantle moves so smoothly from baseball history into national legend, a country's touchstone, the lopsided grin on our society.

"He wasn't the greatest player who ever lived, not even of his time perhaps. He was a centerfielder of surprising swiftness, a switch-hitter of heart-stopping power, and he was given to spectacle: huge home runs (his team, the New York Yankees, invented the tape-measure home run for him); huge seasons (.353, 52 HRs, 130 RBIs to win the Triple Crown in 1956); one World Series after another (12 in his first 14 seasons). Yet, for one reason or another, he never became Babe Ruth or Joe DiMaggio—or, arguably, even Willie Mays, his exact contemporary.

"But for generations of men, he's the guy, has been the guy, will be the guy. And what does that mean exactly? A woman beseeches Mantle, who survived beyond his baseball career as a kind of corporate greeter, to make an appearance, to surprise her husband. Mantle materializes at some cocktail party, introductions are made, and the husband weeps in the presence of such fantasy made flesh. It means that, exactly.

"It's easy to account, at least partly, for the durability and depth of his fame: He played on baseball's most famous team during the game's final dominant era. From Mantle's rookie season in 1951—the lead miner's son signed out of Commerce, Oklahoma, for $1,100—to his injury-racked final year in 1968, baseball was still the preeminent game in the country. This was baseball B.C. (Before Cable), and a nation's attention was not scattered come World Series time. Year in, year out, men and boys in every corner of the country were given to understand during this autumnal rite that there really was only one baseball team and that there really was only one player: No. 7, talked with a twang, knocked the ball a country mile. But it was more than circumstance that fixed Mantle in the national psyche; he did hit 18 World Series home runs, a record, over the course of 65 of the most watched games of our lives.

"Even knowing that, acknowledging the pin-striped pedigree, the fascination still doesn't add up. If he was a pure talent, he was not, as we found out, a pure spirit. But to look upon his youthful mug today, three decades after he played, is to realize how uncluttered our memories of him are. Yes, he was a confessed drunk; yes, he shorted his potential—he himself said so. And still, looking at the slightly uplifted square jaw, all we see is America's romance with boldness, its celebration of muscle, a continent's comfort in power during a time when might did make right. Mantle was the last great player on the last great team in the last great country, a postwar civilization that was booming and confident, not a trouble in the world.

"Of course, even had he not reflected the times, Mantle would have been walking Americana. His career was storybook stuff, hewing more to our ideas of myth than any player's since Ruth. Spotted playing shortstop on the Baxter Springs Whiz Kids, he was delivered from a rural obscurity into America's distilled essence of glamour. One year Mantle is dropping 400 feet into the earth, very deep into Oklahoma, to mine lead on his father's crew, another he's spilling drinks with Whitey Ford and Billy Martin at the Copa.

"A lesson reaffirmed: Anything can happen to anybody in this country, so long as they're daring in their defeats and outsized in victory. Failure is forgiven of the big swingers, in whom even foolishness is flamboyant. Do you remember Mantle in Pittsburgh in the 1960 Series, twice whiffing in Game 1 and then, the next day, crushing two? Generations of men still do. The world will always belong to those who swing from the heels.

"Still, Mantle's grace was mostly between the lines; he developed no particular bonds beyond his teammates, and he established no popularity outside of baseball. As he was dying from liver cancer, none of the pre-tributes remarked much on his charm. And, as he was dying from a disease that many have presumed was drinking-related, there was a revisionist cast to the remembrances. Maybe he wasn't so much fun after all.

"But, back then, he most certainly was. Drunkenness had a kind of high-life cachet in the '50s: It was manly, inasmuch as you were a stand-up guy who could be counted on to perform the next afternoon, and it was glamorous. Down the road, as Mantle would later confess from the other side of rehabilitation, it was merely stupid. But palling around with Billy and Whitey—just boys, really, they all had little boys' names—it amounted to low grade mischief. Whatever harm was being done to families and friends, it was a small price to pay for the excitement conferred upon a workaday nation.

"In any event, we don't mind our heroes flawed, or even doomed. Actually, our interest in Mantle was probably piqued by his obvious destiny, the ruin he often foretold. As a Yankee he was never a whole person, having torn up his knee for the first first time in his first World Series in '51. Thereafter, increasingly, he played in gauze and pain, his prodigal blasts heroically backlit by chronic injury. But more: At the hospital after that '51 incident, Mantle learned that his father, Mutt, admitted to the same hospital that same day, was dying of Hodgkin's disease. It was a genetic devastation that claimed every Mantle male before the age of 40. The black knowledge of this looming end informed everything Mickey did; there was little time, and every event had to be performed on a grand scale, damn the consequences. Everything was excused.

"As we all know, having participated in this gloomy death watch, it didn't end with that kind of drama. It was Billy, the third of Mantle's four sons, who came down with Hodgkin's, and who later died of a heart attack at 36. Mickey lived much longer, prospering in an era of nostalgia, directionless in golf and drinking, coasting on a fame that confounded him (Why was this man, just introduced to him, weeping?).

"Then Mantle, who might forever have been embedded in a certain culture, square-jawed and unchanged, did a strange thing. Having failed to die in a way that might have satisfied mythmakers, he awoke with a start and checked himself into the Betty Ford Center. This was only a year and a half ago, and, of course, it was way too late almost any way you figure it. Still, his remorse seemed genuine. The waste seemed to gall him, and his anger shook the rest of us.

"The generation of men who watched him play baseball, flipped for his cards or examined every box score must now puzzle out the attraction he held. The day he died there was the usual rush for perspective and the expected sweep through the Yankee organization. They said the usual things. But former teammate Bobby Murcer reported that he had talked to the Mick before he had gone into the hospital the final time—neither a liver transplant nor chemotherapy could arrest the cancer or stop his cancer—and Mantle, first thing, asked how a fund-raiser for children affected by the Oklahoma City bombing was going, something he and Murcer, also from Oklahoma, were involved in. It was odd, like the sudden decision to enter rehab and

rescue his and his family's life, and it didn't really square with our idea of Mantle.

"But let's just say you were of this generation of men, that you once had been a kid growing up in the '50s, on some baseball team in Indiana, and you remember stitching a No. 7 on the back of your KIRCHNER'S PHARMACY T-shirt, using red thread and having no way of finishing off a stitch, meaning your hero's number would unravel indefinitely and you would have to do it over and over, stupid and unreformed in your idolatry. And today here's this distant demigod, in his death, taking human shape. What would you think now?"

In Dallas, of cancer, August 13, 1995.

Timothy J. Mara, 59, team owner. Mara, the grandson of the New York Giants' founder, was a co-owner of the team with his uncle Wellington Mara from 1965 until 1990. Tim Mara grew up on the Giants' sidelines, and was a close friend of Frank Gifford in his rookie days. Conflict with his uncle over personnel and coaching selections led to a long family feud. The two co-owners sat in separate owner's boxes at home games and communicated mostly through the general manager. After the 1990 season, Tim, representing his mother and his sister, sold their half-interest in the team to Preston Robert Tisch of the Loews Corporation. In Florida, of Hodgkins disease, May 1.

Carlos Monzon, 52, boxer. Monzon won the middleweight crown in 1970 on a 12th-round knockout of Nino Benvenutti. In 1988, he was convicted of killing his estranged lover, 32-year-old Alicia Muniz, when an autopsy revealed that she had been strangled to the point of unconsciousness before being hurled from a second-story balcony. The killing gripped Argentina, where Monzon was a hero. The boxer was sentenced to 11 years in prison but was free on a furlough program when he was killed in a car crash. In Santa Rosa de Calchines, Argentina, of injuries sustained in a car accident, January 8.

Lindsey Nelson, 76, broadcaster. Known for his collection of garish sports jackets and his erudition in the booth, Nelson was one of the New York Mets' three original announcers. He also covered the NFL, the Cotton Bowl, the San Francisco Giants and called 13 years of Notre Dame football. Nelson (who donated one of his jackets for display) was inducted into the broadcasters' wing of baseball's Hall of Fame in 1988. About 1962, his first year with the Mets, Nelson said in the book *Voices of the Game*: "Ralph [Kiner], Bob [Murphy] and I sat down and decided we were going to level and be straightforward; we had a bad club and we had to say so. And it seemed to work. The Yankees were winners, we were losers, and yet by July 1963, we passed them in radio and TV ratings." Nelson spent 17 years with the team and then called San Francisco Giants games for three seasons. In Atlanta, of complications of Parkinson's disease and pneumonia, June 10.

Ralph Neves, 78, jockey. Neves made headlines in 1936 when he walked out of a mortuary after being declared dead in a track accident. He was riding at Bay Meadows in San Mateo, Calif., when his horse threw him into a wooden rail. He was trampled by other horses and pronounced dead. At the mortuary, a doctor revived him with a shot of adrenaline in the heart. Neves awoke and, half-conscious, wandered to a cab stand where he got a ride back to the track. He was not allowed to race until the next day. Neves won 3,771 races, including 173 stakes, before retiring in 1964. In San Marcos, Calif., of lung cancer, July 7.